BARR AND
STROUD

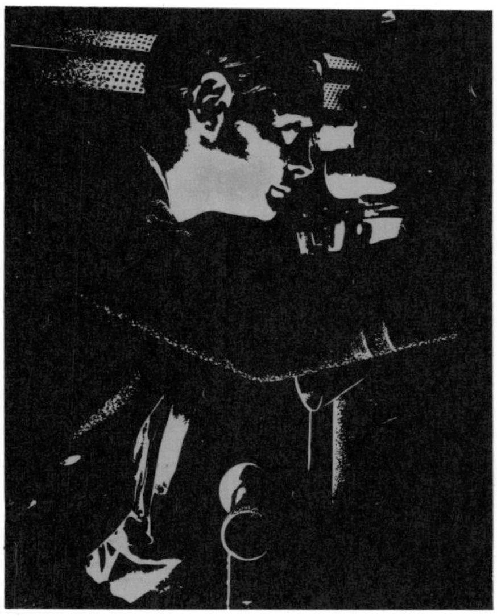

JANE'S FIGHTING SHIPS

Edited by **Captain John E. Moore**
RN, FRGS

Order of Contents

World Sales Distribution

Jane's Yearbooks,
Paulton House, 8 Shepherdess Walk,
London N1 7LW, England

All the World
except

United States of America and Canada:
Franklin Watts Inc.,
730 Fifth Avenue,
New York, NY 10019.

Editorial communication to:

The Editor, Jane's Fighting Ships
Jane's Yearbooks, Paulton House, 8 Shepherdess Walk
London N1 7LW, England
Telephone 01-251 1666

Advertisement communication to:

The Advertisment Manager
Jane's Yearbooks, Paulton House, 8 Shepherdess Walk
London N1 7LW, England
Telephone 01-251 1666

***Classified List of Advertisers**

The various products available from the advertisers in this edition are listed alphabetically in about 350 different headings.

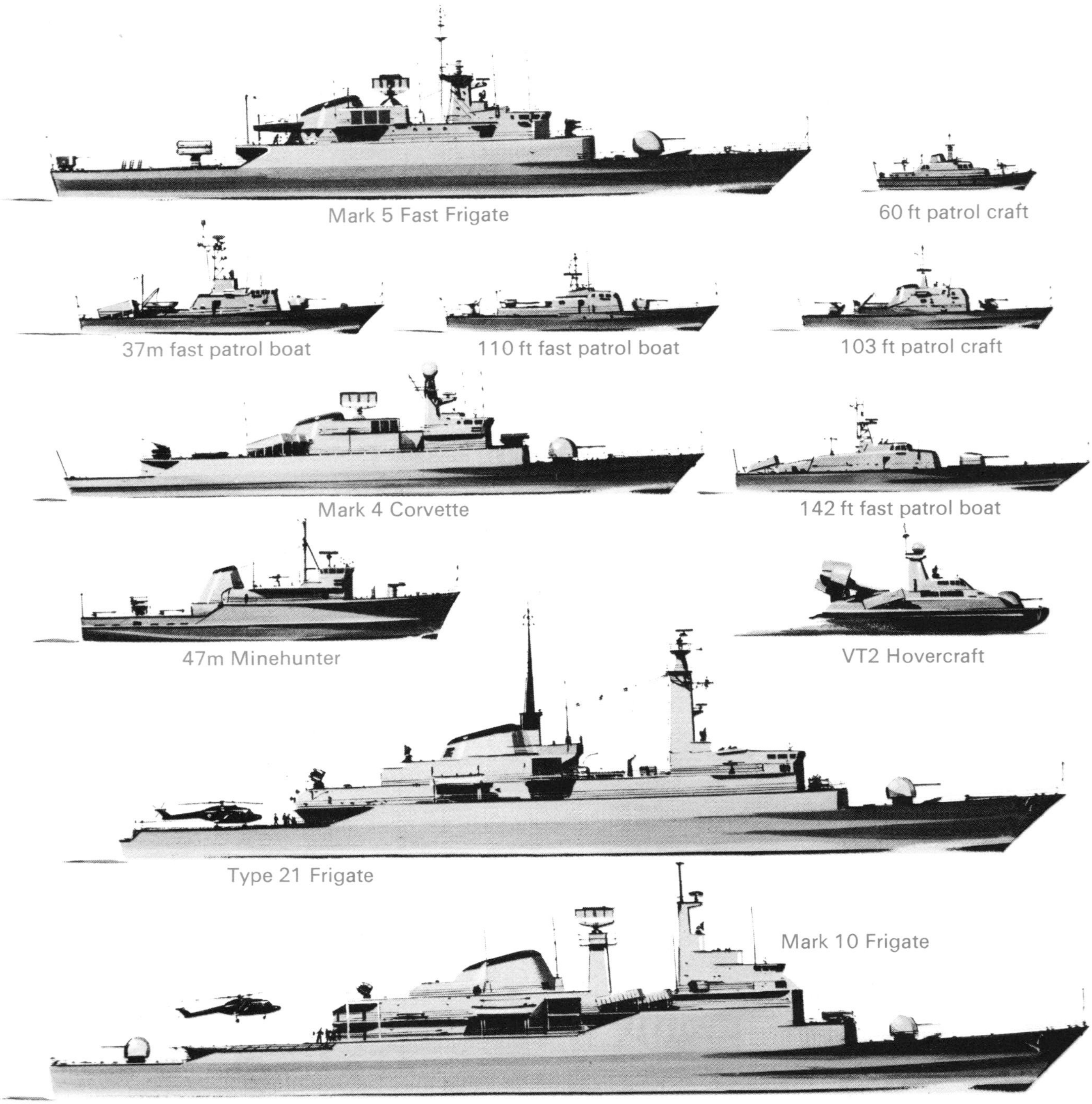

Alphabetical list of advertisers

1975/76 edition

Alphabetical list of advertisers

1975/76 edition—*continued*

I/32

CLASSIFIED LIST OF ADVERTISERS

ACTIVE INFORMATION SYSTEMS
D.T.C.N.
Ferranti Ltd.
Singer Librascope

ACTION INFORMATION TRAINERS
Ferranti Ltd.

AIR COMPRESSORS
C.I.T. Alcatel
Split Shipyard
D.T.C.N.

AIR CUSHION VEHICLES
Bell Aerospace Canada
British Hovercraft Corporation

AIRCRAFT ARRESTING GEAR
Aerospatiale
MacTaggart, Scott & Co. Ltd.
D.T.C.N.

AIRCRAFT CARRIERS
D.T.C.N.
Netherlands United Shipbuilding Bureaux Ltd.
Rhine-Schelde-Verolme

AIRCRAFT INSTRUMENTS
D.T.C.N.
Edo Corporation
Ferranti Ltd.
Thomson C.S.F.
Sperry Gyroscope

AIRFRAME MANUFACTURERS
Aerospatiale
British Hovercraft Corporation
Hawker Siddeley

ALIGNMENT EQUIPMENT
British Aircraft Corporation
D.T.C.N.

ALTERNATORS
Laurence Scott & Electromotors Ltd.

AMMUNITION
AB Bofors
Borletti Fratelli
D.T.C.N.
SOFREXAN

AMMUNITION HOISTS
Blohm & Voss AG
MacTaggart, Scott & Co. Ltd.
D.T.C.N.
OTO Melara S.p.A.

ANTI-SUBMARINE LAUNCHERS
Brooke Marine Ltd.
D.T.C.N.
F. R. Lurssen Werft
Netherlands United Shipbuilding Bureaux Ltd.
SOFREXAN
Vosper Thornycroft Group, The
Yarrow (Shipbuilders) Ltd.

ANTI-SUBMARINE ROCKET LAUNCHERS
AB Bofors
D.T.C.N.
SOFREXAN
Vosper Thornycroft Group, The

ANTI-SUBMARINE ROCKETS
AB Bofors
C.I.T. Alcatel
D.T.C.N.
SOFREXAN

ARMOUR PLATES
AB Bofors
D.T.C.N.

ASSAULT CRAFT
Bell Aerospace Canada
Blohm & Voss AG
British Hovercraft Corporation
Brooke Marine Ltd.
Cammenga Jachtbouw B.V.
D.T.C.N.
Netherlands United Shipbuilding Bureaux Ltd.
Vosper Thornycroft Group, The

ASSAULT SHIPS
Blohm & Voss AG
Brooke Marine Ltd.
Cantieri Baglietto
Cammenga Jachtbouw B.V.
D.T.C.N.
Netherlands United Shipbuilding Bureaux Ltd.
SOFREXAN
Vosper Thornycroft Group, The
Yarrow (Shipbuilders) Ltd.

AUTOMATIC CONTROL SYSTEMS
C.I.T. Alcatel
D.T.C.N.
Ferranti Ltd.
M.T.U.
Singer Librascope
Sperry Gyroscope
Thompson C.S.F.

AUTOMATIC STEERING
C.S.E.E.
Sperry Gyroscope

AUXILIARY MACHINERY
Blohm & Voss AG
D.T.C.N.
Korody-Colyer Corporation
M.T.U.
Termomeccanica

BINOCULARS
Barr & Stroud
British Aircraft Corporation

BOILERS
Blohm & Voss AG
Bremer Vulcan Schiffbau und Maschinenfabrik
Howaldtswerke-Deutsche Werft
Rhine-Schelde-Verolme
Ruston Paxman Diesels
Yarrow (Shipbuilders) Ltd.

BOOKS (NAVAL)
D.T.C.N.
Vosper Thornycroft Group, The

BULK CARRIER
Blohm & Voss AG
Bremer Vulcan Schiffbau und Maschinenfabrik
Dubigeon Normandie
Fr. Lürssen Werft
Howaldtswerke-Deutsche Werft
Rhine-Schelde-Verolme
Sippican Oceanographic Systems
Split Shipyards

CABLE LOOMS (WITH OR WITHOUT) CAISSONS
Brooke Marine Ltd.
D.T.C.N.

CAPSTANS AND WINDLASSES
MacTaggart, Scott & Co. Ltd.
Riva Calzoni

CAR FERRIES
Bell Aerospace Canada
Blohm & Voss AG
Bremer Vulcan Schiffbau und Maschinenfabrik
British Hovercraft Corporation
Brooke Marine Ltd.
D.T.C.N.
Dubigeon Normandie
Fr. Lürssen Werft
Rhine-Schelde-Verolme
Yarrow (Shipbuilders) Ltd.

CARGO HANDLING EQUIPMENT
Blohm & Voss AG
Bremer Vulcan Schiffbau und Maschinenfabrik
D.T.C.N.
MacTaggart, Scott & Co. Ltd.

CARGO SHIPS
Batservice Verft A/S
Bremer Vulcan Schiffbau und Maschinenfabrik
Blohm & Voss AG
D.T.C.N.
Dubigeon Normandie
Fr. Lürssen Werft
Howaldtswerke-Deutsche Werft
Rhine-Schelde-Verolme
Split Shipyards

CARGO SPACE MONITORS
D.T.C.N.

CASTINGS, ALUMINIUM-BRONZE
Rhine-Schelde-Verolme

CASTINGS, HIGH DUTY IRON
Bremer Vulcan Schiffbau und Maschinenfabrik

CASTINGS, SHELL, MOULDED
Bremer Vulcan Schiffbau und Maschinenfabrik

CASTINGS, S.G. IRON
Bremer Vulcan Schiffbau und Maschinenfabrik

CASTINGS, STEEL
AB Bofors
Bremer Vulcan Schiffbau und Maschinenfabrik
Rhine-Schelde-Verolme

CATHODIC PROTECTION EQUIPMENT
Marconi Radar Systems Ltd.
Thomson C.S.F.

CENTRALISED AND AUTOMATIC CONTROL
C.I.T. Alcatel
Thomson C.S.F.

COASTAL AND INSHORE MINESWEEPERS
Batservice Verft A/S
Bell Aerospace Canada
British Hovercraft Corporation
Brooke Marine Corp.
Cantieri Baglietto
Cantieri Navali Italcraft
D.T.C.N.
Netherlands United Shipbuilding Bureaux Ltd.
Rhine-Schelde-Verolme
Vosper Thornycroft Group, The
Sperry Gyroscope
Yarrow (Shipbuilders) Ltd.

COMPRESSED AIR STARTERS FOR GAS-TURBINES AND DIESEL ENGINES
D.T.C.N.
Hatch & Kirk
Korody-Colyer Corporation

COMPRESSORS
C.I.T. Alcatel
D.T.C.N.
Rhine-Schelde-Verolme
Split Shipyard

COMPUTER SERVICES
C.S.E.E.
Hollandse Signaalapparaten B.V.
Thomson C.S.F.
Yarrow (Shipbuilders) Ltd.

COMPUTERS
C.I.T. Alcatel
Ferranti Ltd.
Hollandse Signaalapparaten B.V.
Selenia
Singer Librascope
Sperry Gyroscope
Thomson C.S.F.

CONDENSER TUBES
Rhine-Schelde-Verolme

CONDENSERS
Blohm & Voss AG
Bremer Vulcan Schiffbau und Maschinenfabrik

CONTAINER SHIPS
Blohm & Voss AG
Bremer Vulcan Schiffbau und Maschinenfabrik
Brooke Marine Ltd.
D.T.C.N.
Dubigeon Normandie
Fr. Lürssen Werft
Howaldtswerke-Deutsche Werft
Netherlands United Shipbuilding Bureaux Ltd.
Rhine-Schelde-Verolme
Split Shipyard

CONTROL DESKS (ELECTRIC)
OTO Melara S.p.A.
Vosper Thornycroft Group, The
Whipp & Bourne Ltd.

CONTROL GEAR
Korody-Colyer Corporation
Rhine-Schelde-Verolme
Ruston Paxman Diesels
Vosper Thornycroft Group, The

CORVETTES
Blohm & Voss AG
Bremer Vulcan Schiffbau und Maschinenfabrik
D.T.C.N.
Dubigeon Normandie
Fr. Lürssen Werft
Netherlands United Shipbuilding Bureaux Ltd.
Rhine-Schelde-Verolme
SOFREXAN
Vosper Thornycroft Group, The
Yarrow (Shipbuilders) Ltd.

CRANES, SHIPS'
Dubigeon Normandie

CRUISERS
D.T.C.N.
Dubigeon Normandie
Netherlands United Shipbuilding Bureaux Ltd.
Rhine-Schelde-Verolme
SOFREXAN
Yarrow (Shipbuilders)Ltd.

DECK MACHINERY
D.T.C.N.
MacTaggart, Scott & Co. Ltd.

DESTROYERS
Blohm & Voss AG
D.T.C.N.
Dubigeon Normandie
Netherlands United Shipbuilding Bureaux Ltd.
Rhine-Schelde-Verolme
SOFREXAN
Split Shipyard
Vosper Thornycroft Group, The
Yarrow (Shipbuilders) Ltd.

DIESEL ENGINES, AUXILIARY
Blohm & Voss AG
Bremer Vulcan Schiffbau und Maschinenfabrik
D.T.C.N.
Hatch & Kirk, Inc.
Korody-Colyer Corporation
M.T.U.
Rhine-Schelde-Verolme
Ruston Paxman Diesels Ltd.
S.A.C.M.

DIESEL ENGINES, MAIN PROPULSION
Blohm & Voss AG
Bremer Vulcan Schiffbau und Maschinenfabrik
Chantiers de l'Atlantique
C.R.M. Fabbrica Motori Marini
D.T.C.N.
Grandi Motori Trieste
Hatch & Kirk, Inc.
Korody-Colyer Corporation
M.T.U.
Rhine-Schelde-Verolme
Ruston Paxman Diesels Ltd.
S.A.C.M.
SOFREXAN
Split Shipyard

DIESEL ENGINE SPARE PARTS
Blohm & Voss AG
Bremer Vulcan Schiffbau und Maschinenfabrik
Chantiers de l'Atlantique
C.R.M. Fabbrica Motori Marini
D.T.C.N.
Hatch & Kirk, Inc.
Korody-Colyer Corporation
M.T.U.
Rhine-Schelde-Verolme
Ruston Paxman Diesels Ltd.
Split Shipyard

DIESEL, FUEL INJECTION EQUIPMENT
D.T.C.N.
Hatch & Kirk, Inc.

DIVING EQUIPMENT
SOFREXAN

DOCK GATES
Bremer Vulcan Schiffbau und Maschinenfabrik
D.T.C.N.
Dubigeon Normandie
Rhine-Schelde-Verolme

DREDGERS
Brooke Marine Ltd.
Dubigeon Normandie
Rhine-Schelde-Verolme

DRY CARGO VESSELS
Batservice Verft A/S
Blohm & Voss AG
Bremer Vulcan Schiffbau und Maschinenfabrik
Dubigeon Normandie
Fr. Lürssen Werft
Howaldtswerke-Deutsche Werft
Rhine-Schelde-Verolme
Split Shipyard

DRY DOCK PROPRIETORS
Blohm & Voss AG
C.I.T. Alcatel
Rhine-Schelde-Verolme

DYNAMIC POSITIONING
D.T.C.N.
Thomson C.S.F.

ECHO SOUNDERS
D.T.C.N.
Thomson C.S.F.
Van Der Heem Electronics N.V.

ECONOMISERS
Netherlands United Shipbuilding Bureaux Ltd.

ELECTRIC CABLES
D.T.C.N.

ELECTRIC COUNTERMEASURES
British Aircraft Corporation
Decca Radar Ltd.
D.T.C.N.
Hollandse Signaalapparaten B.V.
Selenia
Singer Librascope
Sperry Gyroscope
Thomson C.S.F.

ELECTRICAL AUXILIARIES
D.T.C.N.
Rhine-Schelde-Verolme

ELECTRICAL EQUIPMENT

D.T.C.N.
Vosper Thornycroft Group, The

ELECTRICAL FITTINGS

D.T.C.N.
Vosper Thornycroft Group, The

ELECTRICAL INSTALLATIONS AND REPAIRS

Bremer Vulcan Schiffbau und Maschinenfabrik
Cossor Electronics Limited
D.T.C.N.
Fr. Lürssen Werft
Rhine-Schelde-Verolme
Vosper Thornycroft Group, The

ELECTRICAL SWITCHGEAR

D.T.C.N.
Fr. Lürssen Werft
Thomson C.S.F.
Whipp & Bourne Ltd.

ELECTRO-HYDRAULIC AUXILIARIES

D.T.C.N.
MacTaggart, Scott & Co. Ltd.
Vosper Thornycroft Group, The

ELECTRONIC EQUIPMENT

British Aircraft Corporation
C.I.T. Alcatel
Cossor Electronics Limited
Decca Radar Ltd.
D.T.C.N.
Edo Corporation
Ferranti Ltd.
M.T.U.
Plessey Company Ltd.
Rhine-Schelde-Verolme
Selenia
Singer Librascope
Sippican Oceanographic Systems
Sperry Gyroscope
Thomson C.S.F.
Van Der Heem Electronics N.V.
Vosper Thornycroft Group, The

ELECTRONIC EQUIPMENT REFITS

D.T.C.N.
Ferranti Ltd.
Plessey Company Ltd.
Singer Librascope
Sperry Gyroscope
Vosper Thornycroft Group, The

ENGINE MONITORS AND DATA LOGGERS

Decca Radar Ltd.

ENGINE PARTS DIESEL

Bremer Vulcan Schiffbau und Maschinenfabrik
C.R.M. Fabbrica Motori Marini
D.T.C.N.
Grandi Motori Trieste
Hatch & Kirk, Inc.
Korody-Colyer Corporation
Rhine-Schelde-Verolme

ENGINE SPEED CONTROLS

D.T.C.N.
Hatch & Kirk, Inc.
Vosper Thornycroft Group, The

ENGINE START AND SHUTDOWN CONTROLS

Hatch & Kirk, Inc.
Vosper Thornycroft Group, The

ENGINES, AIRCRAFT

D.T.C.N.
M.T.U. (Motoren-und-Turbinen-Union

ENGINES, DIESEL

Blohm & Voss, AG
Bremer Vulcan Schiffbau und Maschinenfabrik
Chantiers de l'Atlantique
C.R.M. Fabbrica Motori Marini
D.T.C.N.
Hatch & Kirk, Inc.
Korody-Colyer Corporation
M.T.U.
Ruston Paxman Diesels Ltd.
S.A.C.M.
SOFREXAN
Split Shipyard

ENGINES, GAS-TURBINE

C.I.T. Alcatel
D.T.C.N.
Fiat
M.T.U.
Rhine-Schelde-Verolme
Yarrow (Shipbuilders) Ltd.

ENGINES, STEAM TURBINE

Blohm & Voss AG
Bremer Vulcan Schiffbau und Maschinenfabrik
D.T.C.N.
SOFREXAN
Yarrow (Shipbuilders) Ltd.

EPICYCLIC GEARS

Vosper Thornycroft Group, The

ESCORT VESSELS

Blohm & Voss AG
Bremer Vulcan Schiffbau und Maschinenfabrik
Brooke Marine Ltd.
D.T.C.N.
Fr. Lürssen Werft
Netherlands United Shipbuilding Bureaux Ltd.
SOFREXAN
Vosper Thornycroft Group, The
Yarrow (Shipbuilders) Ltd.

FAST PATROL CRAFT

Batservice Verft A/S
Bell Aerospace Canada
British Hovercraft Corporation
Brooke Marine Ltd.
Cammenga Jachtbouw B.V.
Cantieri Baglietto
Cantieri Navali Italcraft
Cantiere Navaltecnica
D.T.C.N.
Fairey Marine Ltd.
Fr. Lürssen Werft
Netherland United Shipbuilding Bureaux Ltd.
SOFREXAN
Vosper Thornycroft Group, The
Yarrow (Shipbuilders) Ltd.

FAST WARSHIP DESIGN SERVICE

Cammenga Jachtbouw B.V.
D.T.C.N.
Fr. Lürssen Werft
Vosper Thornycroft Group, The
Yarrow (Shipbuilders) Ltd.

FEED WATER HEATERS

Blohm & Voss AG
Bremer Vulcan Schiffbau und Maschinenfabrik

FERRIES

Bell Aerospace Canada
Bremer Vulcan Schiffbau und Maschinenfabrik
British Hovercraft Corporation
Cantiere Navaltecnica
D.T.C.N.
Dubigeon Normandie
Rhine-Schelde-Verolme
Yarrow (Shipbuilders) Ltd.

FIBRE OPTICS

Barr & Stroud
D.T.C.N.

FIBREGLASS VESSELS AND OTHER PRODUCTS

Batservice Verft A/S
Cammenga Jachtbouw B.V.
Cantieri Navali Italcraft
D.T.C.N.
Fairey Marine Limited
SOFREXAN
Vosper Thornycroft Group, The

FILTERS

Alan Chobham Engineering

FILTERS/WATER SEPARATORS

Alan Chobham Engineering

FIRE AND SALVAGE VESSELS

Bell Aerospace Canada
Brooke Marine Ltd.
Cantieri Navali Italcraft
Vosper Thornycroft Group, The

FIRE CONTROL AND GUNNERY EQUIPMENT

AB Bofors
Ferranti Ltd.
Hollandse Signaalapparaten B.V.
Plessey Company Ltd.
Singer Librascope
SOFREXAN
Sperry Gyroscope
Thomson C.S.F.

FITTINGS, SHIPS

Rhine-Schelde-Verolme

FRIGATES

Blohm & Voss AG
Bremer Vulcan Schiffbau und Maschinenfabrik
D.T.C.N.
Dubigeon Normandie
Netherlands United Shipbuilding Bureaux Ltd.
Rhine-Schelde-Verolme
SOFREXAN
Vosper Thornycroft Group, The
Yarrow (Shipbuilders) Ltd.

FUEL FILTRATION EQUIPMENT

Alan Chobham Engineering

FUEL INJECTORS OIL

Hatch & Kirk, Inc.
Korody-Colyer Corporation

GAS-TURBINE BOATS
Bell Aerospace Canada
Blohm & Voss AG
Cantieri Baglietto
Cantieri Navali Italcraft
D.T.C.N.
Netherlands United Shipbuilding Bureaux Ltd.
Vosper Thornycroft Group, The
Yarrow (Shipbuilders) Ltd.

GAS-TURBINES
C.I.T. Alcatel
D.T.C.N.
M.T.U.
Rhine-Schelde-Verolme

GEAR CASINGS
Bremer Vulcan Schiffbau und Maschinenfabrik
Korody-Colyer Corporation
OTO Melara
Rhine-Schelde-Verolme

GEARS AND GEARING
Bremer Vulcan Schiffbau und Maschinenfabrik
C.R.M. Fabbrica Motori Marini
Korody-Colyer Corporation
OTO Melara
Rhine-Schelde-Verolme
Vosper Thornycroft Group, The

GEARS, HYPOID
Barr & Stroud
Korody-Colyer Corporation

GEARS, SPIRAL BEVEL
Barr & Stroud
Korody-Colyer Corporation

GEARS, REVERSE-REDUCTION
C.R.M. Fabbrica Motori Marini
Hatch & Kirk, Inc.
Korody-Colyer Corporation
M.T.U.
Vosper Thornycroft Group, The
Zahnradfabrik Friedrichshafen AG

GEARS, SPUR
Korody-Colyer Corporation

GEARS, VEE DRIVE
C.R.M. Fabbrica Motori Marini
Korody-Colyer Corporation
Vosper Thornycroft Group, The
Zahnradfabrik Friedrichshafen AG

GENERATORS, ELECTRIC
C.R.M. Fabbrica Motori Marini
D.T.C.N.
Ferranti Ltd.

GOVERNORS
D.T.C.N.
Hatch & Kirk, Inc.
Korody-Colyer Corporation

GOVERNORS, ENGINE SPEED
D.T.C.N.
Hatch & Kirk, Inc.
Korody-Colyer Corporation

GUIDED MISSILE SERVICING EQUIPMENT
Aerospatiale
British Aircraft Corporation
Cossor Electronics
D.T.C.N.
Korody-Colyer Corporation
SOFREXAN
Thomson C.S.F.

GUIDED MISSILE SHIPS
Blohm & Voss AG
Bremer Vulcan Schiffbau und Maschinenfabrik
Brooke Marine Ltd.
Cammenga Jachtbouw B.V.
D.T.C.N.
Fr. Lürssen Werft
Netherlands United Shipbuilding Bureaux Ltd.
Rhine-Schelde-Verolme
SOFREXAN
Vosper Thornycroft Group, The
Yarrow (Shipbuilders) Ltd.

GUIDED MISSILES
AB Bofors
Aerospatiale
British Aircraft Corporation
D.T.C.N.
SOFREXAN
Sperry Gyroscope

GUN BOATS
Batservice Verft A/S
Bell Aerospace Canada
Brooke Marine Ltd.
Cammenga Jachtbouw B.V.
Cantieri Baglietto
Cantieri Navali Italcraft
D.T.C.N.
Fairey Marine Ltd.
Fr. Lürssen Werft
Netherlands United Shipbuilding Bureaux Ltd.
SOFREXAN
Vosper Thornycroft Group, The
Yarrow (Shipbuilders) Ltd.

GUNS AND MOUNTINGS
AB Bofors
Breda Meccanica Bresciana
D.T.C.N.
Oerlikon Italiana S.I.P.A.
OTO Melara
SOFREXAN

GUN MOUNTS
AB Bofors
Breda Meccanica Bresciana
Brooke Marine Ltd.
D.T.C.N.
SOFREXAN

GUN-SIGHTING APARATUS AND HEIGHT FINDERS
Barr & Stroud
OTO Melara
Thomson C.S.F.

GYROSCOPIC COMPASSES
D.T.C.N.
Sperry Gyroscope
Thomson C.S.F.

HEAT EXCHANGERS
Blohm & Voss AG
Bremer Vulcan Schiffbau und Maschinenfabrik
Hatch & Kirk, Inc.
Howaldtswerke-Deutsche Werft
Korody-Colyer Corporation
Split Shipyard
Yarrow (Shipbuilders) Ltd.

HEATED WINDOWS
Barr & Stroud

HOVERCRAFT
Bell Aerospace Canada
British Hovercraft Corporation
Vosper Thornycroft Group, The

HYDRAULIC EQUIPMENT
D.T.C.N.
MacTaggart, Scott & Co. Ltd.
OTO Melara
Riva Calzoni
Vosper Thornycroft Group, The

HYDRAULIC MACHINERY
D.T.C.N.
MacTaggart, Scott & Co. Ltd.
Riva Calzoni
Vosper Thornycroft Group, The

HYDRAULIC PLANT
MacTaggart, Scott & Co. Ltd.
Riva Galzoni

HYDROFOILS
Aerospatiale
Blohm & Voss AG
Cantiere Navaltecnica
D.T.C.N.
Edo Corporation
Fr. Lürssen Werft
Vosper Thornycroft Group, The

HYDROGRAPHIC SURVEY EQUIPMENT
D.T.C.N.
Edo Corporation
SOFREXAN
Van der Heem Electronics N.V.

INDICATORS, ELECTRIC
D.T.C.N.
Korody-Colyer Corporation
Thomson C.S.F.
Van der Heem Electronics N.V.

I.F.F. RADAR
Bell Aerospace Canada
Cossor Electronics
D.T.C.N.
Hollandse Signaalapparaten B.V.
SOFREXAN
Thomson C.S.F.

I.F.F. Mk 10 SYSTEMS
Cossor Electronics Limited
Thomson C.S.F.

INFRA-RED MATERIALS
Barr & Stroud
D.T.C.N.
Thomson C.S.F.

INFRA-RED SYSTEMS
Barr & Stroud
D.T.C.N.
Selenia

INJECTORS
Hatch & Kirk, Inc.
Korody-Colyer Corporation

INERTIAL NAVIGATION SYSTEMS
Sperry Gyroscope

INSTRUMENT COMPONENTS (MECHANICAL)
Korody-Colyer Corporation
Thomson C.S.F.

INSTRUMENT PANELS

D.T.C.N.
Ferranti Ltd.
Korody-Colyer Corporation
OTO Melara
Thomson C.S.F.
Vosper Thornycroft Group, The

INSTRUMENTS, ELECTRONIC

AB Bofors
Cossor Electronics
D.T.C.N.
Ferranti Ltd.
Sippican Oceanographic Systems
Sperry Gyroscope
Thomson C.S.F.
Van Der Heem Electronics N.V.

INSTRUMENTS, NAUTICAL

D.T.C.N.
Sperry Gyroscope

INSTRUMENTS, PRECISION

Barr & Stroud
D.T.C.N.
Ferranti Ltd.
Korody-Colyer Corporation
Sperry Gyroscope

INSTRUMENTS, TEST EQUIPMENT

British Hovercraft Corporation
Cossor Electronics Limited
D.T.C.N.
Ferranti Ltd.
Korody-Colyer Corporation
Selenia
Singer Librascope
Sperry Gyroscope
Thomson C.S.F.

INTERIOR DESIGN AND FURNISHING FOR SHIPS

Blohm & Voss AG
Bremer Vulcan Schiffbau und Maschinenfabrik
Brooke Marine Ltd.
D.T.C.N.
Rhine-Schelde-Verolme
Vosper Thornycroft Group, The

INVERTERS AND BATTERY CHARGERS

Ferranti Ltd.
Vosper Thornycroft Group, The

LANDING CRAFT

Bell Aerospace Canada
Bremer Vulcan Schiffbau und Maschinenfabrik
British Hovercraft Corp.
Brooke Marine Ltd.
D.T.C.N.
Fr. Lürssen Werft
Netherlands United Shipbuilding Bureaux Ltd.
SOFREXAN
Yarrow (Shipbuilders) Ltd.

LASER RANGEFINDERS

AB Bofors
Barr & Stroud
Ferranti Ltd.
Selenia
Thomson C.S.F.

LASER SYSTEMS

Barr & Stroud
D.T.C.N.
Ferranti Ltd.
Selenia
Singer Librascope
Thomson C.S.F.

LIFTS, HYDRAULIC

MacTaggart, Scott & Co. Ltd.

LIGHTS AND LIGHTING

Rhine-Schelde-Verolme

LIQUID PETROLEUM GAS CARRIERS

Bremer Vulcan Schiffbau und Maschinenfabrik
D.T.C.N.
Dubigeon Normandie
Rhine-Schelde-Verolme

LOUDSPEAKER EQUIPMENT

Rhine-Schelde-Verolme
Thomson C.S.F.

MACHINED PARTS, FERROUS

Blohm & Voss AG
Bremer Vulcan Schiffbau und Maschinenfabrik

MACHINED PARTS NON-FERROUS

Blohm & Voss AG
OTO Melara

MAINTENANCE AND REPAIR SHIPS

Bremer Vulcan Schiffbau und Maschinenfabrik
Brooke Marine Ltd.
Cammenga Jachtbouw B.V.
Dubigeon Normandie
Fr. Lürssen Werft
Netherlands United Shipbuilders Bureaux Ltd.
Rhine-Schelde-Verolme
SOFREXAN
Vosper Thornycroft Group, The

MARINE ARCHITECTS

Bremer Vulcan Schiffbau und Maschinenfabrik
Cammenga Jachtbouw B.V.
D.T.C.N.
Fairey Marine Ltd.
Fr. Lürssen Werft
C.I.T. Alcatel
Ingenieurkontor Lübeck
Netherlands United Shipbuilding Bureaux Ltd.
Rhine-Schelde-Verolme
Vosper Thornycroft Group, The

MARINE ENGINE MONITORING AND DATA RECORDING SYSTEM

Decca Radar Ltd.
D.T.C.N.

MARINE RADAR

Decca Radar Ltd.
D.T.C.N.
Hollandse Signaalapparaten B.V.
Selenia
SOFREXAN
Thomson C.S.F.

MATERIALS HANDLING EQUIPMENT

D.T.C.N.
MacTaggart, Scott & Co. Ltd.

MERCHANT SHIPS

Blohm & Voss AG
Bremer Vulcan Schiffbau und Maschinenfabrik
Brooke Marine Ltd.
D.T.C.N.
Dubigeon Normandie
Fr. Lürssen Werft
Rhine-Schelde-Verolme
Split Shipyard

MICROPHONE EQUIPMENT

C.I.T. Alcatel
D.T.C.N.
Thomson C.S.F.

MINELAYERS

Blohm & Voss AG
Bremer Vulcan Schiffbau und Maschinenfabrik
Brooke Marine Ltd.
D.T.C.N.
Dubigeon Normandie
Netherlands United Shipbuilding Bureaux Ltd.
Rhine-Schelde-Verolme
SOFREXAN
Vosper Thornycroft Group, The
Yarrow (Shipbuilders) Ltd.

MINESWEEPERS

Batservice Verft A/S
Blohm & Voss AG
British Hovercraft Corporation
Brooke Marine Ltd.
Cantieri Navali Italcraft
Dubigeon Normandie
Edo Corporation
Netherlands United Shipbuilding Bureaux Ltd.
SOFREXAN
Sperry Gyroscope
Thomson C.S.F.
Vosper Thornycroft Group, The
Rhine-Schelde-Verolme
Yarrow (Shipbuilders) Ltd.

MISSILE CONTROL SYSTEMS

Aerospatiale
British Aircraft Corporation
C.I.T. Alcatel
D.T.C.N.
Ferranti Ltd.
Hollandse Signaalapparaten B.V.
Selenia
Singer Librascope
Sperry Gyroscope
Thomson C.S.F.

MISSILE INSTALLATIONS

Aerospatiale
British Aircraft Corporation
C.S.E.E.
D.T.C.N.
Fr. Lürssen Werft
OTO Melara
Selenia
Thomson C.S.F.

MISSILE LAUNCHING SYSTEMS

Aerospatiale
British Aircraft Corporation
C.I.T. Alcatel
D.T.C.N.
OTO Melara
Selenia
Singer Librascope
SOFREXAN

MISSILE SHIPS
Blohm & Voss AG
Bremer Vulcan Schiffbau und Maschinenfabrik
British Hovercraft Corporation
Cammenga Jachtbouw B.V.
Cantieri Navali Italcraft
D.T.C.N.
Fr. Lürssen Werft
Netherlands United Shipbuilding Bureaux Ltd.
Rhine-Schelde-Verolme
SOFREXAN
Vosper Thornycroft Group, The
Yarrow (Shipbuilders) Ltd.

MODEL MAKERS AND DESIGNERS
British Hovercraft Corporation
Ingenieurkontor Lübeck
Netherlands United Shipbuilding Bureaux Ltd.
Split Shipyard
Vosper Thornycroft Group, The
Yarrow (Shipbuilders) Ltd.

MODEL TEST TOWING TANK SERVICE
British Hovercraft Corporation

MOTOR CONTROL GEAR
Bremer Vulcan Schiffbau und Maschinenfabrik
Korody-Colyer Corporation
Thomson C.S.F.

MOTOR STARTERS
Hatch & Kirk, Inc.
Korody-Colyer Corporation
Thomson C.S.F.

MOTOR TORPEDO BOATS
Batservice Verft A/S
Brooke Marine Ltd.
Cammenga Jachtbouw B.V.
D.T.C.N.
Dubigeon Normandie
Fairey Marine Ltd.
Fr. Lürssen Werft
SOFREXAN
Thomson C.S.F.
Vosper Thornycroft Group, The
Yarrow (Shipbuilders) Ltd.

MOTORS, ELECTRIC
Thomson C.S.F.

MINE COUNTER MEASURES
British Hovercraft Corporation
D.T.C.N.
Plessey Company
Sperry Gyroscope
Vosper Thornycroft Group, The

NAVAL GUNS
AB Bofors
Breda Meccanica Bresciana
D.T.C.N.
OTO Melara
SOFREXAN

NAVAL RADAR
Cossor Electronics
Decca Radar Ltd.
D.T.C.N.
Hollandse Signaalapparaten B.V.
Selenia
SOFREXAN
Sperry Gyroscope
Thomson C.S.F.

NAVIGATION AIDS
British Aircraft Corporation
D.T.C.N.
Decca Radar
SOFREXAN
Sperry Gyroscope
Thomson C.S.F.

NIGHT VISION SYSTEM
Barr & Stroud
D.T.C.N.
Singer Librascope
SOFREXAN
Thomson C.S.F.

NON-MAGNETIC MINESWEEPERS
British Hovercraft Corporation
D.T.C.N.
Dubigeon Normandie
Netherlands United Shipbuilding Bureaux Ltd.
Rhine-Schelde-Verolme
SOFREXAN
Sperry Gyroscope
Vosper Thornycroft Group, The

OCEANOGRAPHIC ELECTRONIC SYSTEMS
D.T.C.N.
Sippican Oceanographic Systems
Van der Heem Electronics N.V.

OCEANOGRAPHIC SURVEY SHIPS
Bremer Vulcan Schiffbau und Maschinenfabrik
Brooke Marine Ltd.
D.T.C.N.
Fr. Lürssen Werft
Netherlands United Shipbuilding Bureaux Ltd.
Rhine-Schelde-Verolme
SOFREXAN
Van Der Heem Electronics N.V.
Yarrow (Shipbuilders)

OIL DRILLING RIGS
Bremer Vulcan Schiffbau und Maschinenfabrik
C.I.T. Alcatel
Howaldtswerke-Deutsche Werft

OIL FUEL HEATERS
Blohm & Voss AG

OIL RIG SUPPLY VESSELS AND WORK BOATS
Bell Aerospace Canada
Batservice Verft A/S
Brooke Marine Ltd.
Cantiere Navaltecnica
Dubigeon Normandie
Fr. Lürssen Werft
Vosper Thornycroft Group, The
Yarrow (Shipbuilders) Ltd.

OPTICAL EQUIPMENT
Barr & Stroud
D.T.C.N.
Singer Librascope

OPTICAL FILTERS
Barr & Stroud
D.T.C.N.

ORDNANCE
AB Bofors
Borletti Fratelli
OTO Melara
SOFREXAN

PARTS FOR DIESEL ENGINES
Blohm & Voss AG
C.R.M. Fabbrica Motori Marini
Grandi Motori Trieste
Hatch & Kirk, Inc.
Korody-Colyer Corporation
Rhine-Schelde-Verolme

PASSENGER SHIPS
Batservice Verft A/S
Blohm & Voss
Bremer Vulcan Schiffbau und Maschinenfabrik
Brooke Marine Ltd.
D.T.C.N.
Fr. Lürssen Werft
Howaldtswerke-Deutsche Werft
Rhine-Schelde-Verolme
Split Shipyard

PATROL BOATS, LAUNCHES, TENDERS AND PINNACLES
Bell Aerospace Canada
British Hovercraft Corporation
Brooke Marine Ltd.
Cantieri Baglietto
Cantieri Navali Italcraft
Cammenga Jachtbouw BV
D.T.C.N.
Dubigeon Normandie
Fairey Marine Ltd.
Fr. Lürssen Werft
Netherlands United Shipbuilding Bureaux Ltd.
SOFREXAN
Vosper Thornycroft Group, The

PERISCOPE FAIRINGS
D.T.C.N.
Edo Corporation
MacTaggart, Scott & Co. Ltd.

PERISCOPES
Barr & Stroud
D.T.C.N.
SOFREXAN

PIPES, COPPER AND BRASS
Rhine-Schelde-Verolme

PIPES, SEA WATER
D.T.C.N.
Rhine-Schelde-Verolme

PISTONS, PISTON RINGS AND GUDGEON PINS
Bremer Vulcan Schiffbau und Maschinenfabrik
D.T.C.N.
Hatch & Kirk, Inc.
Korody-Colyer Corporation
Rhine-Schelde-Verolme

PLOTTING TABLES
D.T.C.N.
Hollandse Signaalapparaten B.V.
SOFREXAN

PLUGS AND SOCKETS
D.T.C.N.
Plessey Company
Rhine-Schelde-Verolme
Thomson C.S.F.

BOATSERVICE SM45 Patrol
— designed, built and equipped for offshore patrols but equally suitable for up-river operation thanks to a shallow draft —
This is the 45-footer which does 30 knots plus with two standard 300 HP diesel engines.
Sea trials of the prototype began in the summer of 1972, and in 1974 series production to Lloyd's requirements was started at Båtservice Verft A/S -- highly experienced builders of fast naval craft for the Royal Norwegian Navy as well as foreign navies.
The patrol boat pictured here is one of the first in a series of 20 units ordered by the Customs Authorities in India.
Båtservice Verft a/s
Telephones: (042) 61 011
Telegrams: Westboat - Telex: 11862 yard n
P.O.Box 113
N-4501 Mandal - Norway

fast patrol boats...........
production range: 7 — 35 metres
maximum speeds: 18 — 55 knots
naval architects' shead design
for further information please contact the manager of the fast patrol boat division
amsterdam/holland
p.o.box 3040
tel. 020 - 362468
telex 15246
Cammenga

PONTOONS, SELF-PROPELLED
Bremer Vulcan Schiffbau und Maschinenfabrik
Brooke Marine Ltd.
Netherlands United Shipbuilding Bureaux Ltd.

PRESSURE VESSELS
Bremer Vulcan Schiffbau und Maschinenfabrik
D.T.C.N.
Netherlands United Shipbuilding Bureaux Ltd.
Yarrow (Shipbuilders) Ltd.

PROPELLENTS
AB Bofors

PROPELLERS, SHIPS'
AB Bofors
SOFREXAN
Split Shipyard

PROPELLERS, SHIPS' RESEARCH
D.T.C.N.
Vosper Thornycroft Group, The

PROPULSION MACHINERY
Blohm & Voss AG
Bremer Vulcan Schiffbau und Maschinenfabrik
Korody-Colyer Corporation
M.T.U. (Motoren-und-Turbinen-Union)
Netherlands United Shipbuilding Bureaux Ltd.
Rhine-Schelde-Verolme
Ruston Paxman Diesels Ltd.
SOFREXAN

PUBLISHERS
Macdonald and Jane's

PUMPS
C.I.T. Alcatel
Korody-Colyer Corporation
MacTaggart, Scott & Co. Ltd.
UNELEC

PUMPS, COMPONENT PARTS
Korody-Colyer Corporation

RADAR AERIALS
British Aircraft Corporation
Cossor Electronics
Decca Radar Ltd.
Hollandse Signaalapparaten B.V.
Thomson C.S.F.

RADAR FOR FIRE CONTROL
Cossor Electronics
Ferranti Ltd.
Hollandse Signaalapparaten B.V.
Marconi Radar Systems Ltd.
Selenia
SOFREXAN
Sperry Gyroscope
Thomson C.S.F.

RADAR FOR HARBOUR SUPER-VISION
Decca Radar Ltd.
D.T.C.N.
Hollandse Signaalapparaten B.V.
Selenia
Thomson C.S.F.

RADAR FOR NAVIGATION WARNING INTERCEPTION
Decca Radar
D.T.C.N.
Hollandse Signaalapparaten B.V.
Selenia
Thomson C.S.F.

RADIO, AIR
R.F. Communications
Thomson C.S.F.

RADIO EQUIPMENT
Marconi Communications Systems Ltd.
Thomson C.S.F.

RADIO TRANSMITTERS AND RECEIVERS
Ferranti Ltd.
Marconi Communications Systems Ltd.
SOFREXAN
Thomson C.S.F.

RADOMES
British Aircraft Corporation
British Hovercraft Corporation
D.T.C.N.
Thomson C.S.F.

RAMJETS
Aerospatiale

RANGEFINDERS
Barr & Stroud
SOFREXAN
Thomson C.S.F.

RELOCALISATION DEVICE
C.I.T. Alcatel

REMOTE CONTROLS
Howaldtswerke-Deutsche Werft
Thomson C.S.F.
Vosper Thornycroft Group, The

REPLACEMENT PARTS FOR DIESEL ENGINES
Blohm & Voss AG
Bremer Vulcan Schiffbau und Maschinenfabrik
Chantiers de l'Atlantique
C.R.M. Fabbrica Motori Marini
Hatch & Kirk, Inc.
Korody-Colyer Corporation
MacTaggart, Scott & Co. Ltd.
Rhine-Schelde-Verolme

RESEARCH SHIPS
Bell Aerospace Canada
Bremer Vulcan Schiffbau und Maschinenfabrik
Brooke Marine Ltd.
D.T.C.N.
Dubigeon Normandie
Fr. Lürssen Werft
Netherlands United Shipbuilding Bureaux Ltd.
Rhine-Schelde-Verolme
SOFREXAN
Yarrow (Shipbuilding) Ltd.

REVERSE REDUCTION GEARS, OIL OPERATED
Hatch & Kirk, Inc.
Korody-Colyer Corporation

REVERSING GEARS
C.R.M. Fabbrica Motori Marini
Korody-Colyer Corporation

ROCKET LAUNCHERS
Breda Meccanica Bresciana

ROLL DAMPING FINS
Blohm & Voss AG
Hatch & Kirk, Inc.
Vosper Thornycroft Group, The

RUDDERS
Bremer Vulcan Schiffbau und Maschinenfabrik
Fr. Lürssen Werft
Howaldtswerke-Deutsche Werft
Rhine-Schelde-Verolme
Yarrow (Shipbuilders) Ltd.

SALVAGE AND BOOM VESSELS
Bremer Vulcan Schiffbau und Maschinenfabrik
Brooke Marine Ltd.
Netherlands United Shipbuilding Bureaux Ltd.
SOFREXAN
Yarrow (Shipbuilders) Ltd.

SCIENTIFIC INSTRUMENTS
Barr & Stroud
Ferranti Ltd.
Sippican Oceanographic Systems
Thomson C.S.F.

SHIP BUILDERS AND SHIP REPAIRERS
Blohm & Voss AG
Bremer Vulcan Schiffbau und Maschinenfabrik
Brooke Marine Ltd.
Cammenga Jachtbouw B.V.
Cantiere Navali Del Tirreno e Riuniti
Cantiere Navaltecnica
D.T.C.N.
Dubigeon Normandie
Fr. Lürssen Werft
Howaldtswerke-Deutsche Werft
Rhine-Schelde-Verolme
Split Shipyard
Vosper Thornycroft Group, The
Yarrow (Shipbuilders) Ltd.

SHIP AND SUBMARINE DESIGN
Brooke Marine Ltd.
Cammenga Jachtbouw B.V.
Dubigeon Normandie
D.T.C.N.
Howaldtswerke-Deutsche Werft
Ingenieurkontor Lübeck
Netherlands United Shipbuilding Bureaux Ltd.
Rhine-Schelde-Verolme
Split Shipyard
Vosper Thornycroft Group, The
Yarrow (Shipbuilders) Ltd.

SHIP MACHINERY
Blohm & Voss AG
Bremer Vulcan Schiffbau und Maschinenfabrik
D.T.C.N.
M.T.U. (Motoren-und-Turbinen-Union)
Rhine-Schelde-Verolme
Yarrow (Shipbuilders) Ltd.

SHIP STABILISERS
Blohm & Voss AG
D.T.C.N.
Vosper Thornycroft Group, The

SHIP SYSTEMS ENGINEERING
D.T.C.N.
Netherlands United Shipbuilding Bureaux Ltd.
Rhine-Schelde-Verolme
Singer Librascope
Vosper Thornycroft Group, The

SHIPS BRASS FOUNDRY FOR SONAR AND RADAR
C.S.E.E.
D.T.C.N.
Van Der Heem Electronics B.V.

SHIPS' MAGNETIC COMPASS TEST TABLES
Barr & Stroud
D.T.C.N.

SIMULATORS
C.I.T. Alcatel
D.T.C.N.
Ferranti Ltd.
Laurence Scott & Electromotors Ltd.
SOFREXAN
Van Der Heem Electronics B.V.

SMOKE INDICATORS
Barr & Stroud
Plessey Company Ltd.
SOFREXAN

SOCKETS AND PLUGS, ELECTRIC WATERTIGHT
Thomson C.S.F.

SOCKETS AND PLUGS, MULTI-PIN PATTERNS
Thomson C.S.F.

SOCKET TERMINATIONS
Thomson C.S.F.

SONAR EQUIPMENT
British Aircraft Corporation
C.I.T. Alcatel
D.T.C.N.
Edo Corporation
Hollandse Signaalapparaten B.V.
Plessey Company Ltd.
Sippican Oceanographic Systems
SOFREXAN
Thomson C.S.F.
USEA
Van Der Heem Electronics N.V.

SONAR EQUIPMENT (PASSIVE ACTIVE-INTERCEPT)
C.I.T. Alcatel
D.T.C.N.
Edo Corporation
Hollandse Signaalapparaten B.V.
Plessey Company Ltd.
Selenia
SOFREXAN
Thomson C.S.F.
USEA
Van Der Heem Electronics N.V.

SONAR EQUIPMENT, HULL FITTINGS AND HYDRAULICS
C.I.T. Alcatel
D.T.C.N.
Plessey Company Ltd.

SPARE PARTS FOR DIESEL ENGINES
Blohm & Voss AG
Bremer Vulcan Schiffbau und Maschinenfabrik
C.R.M. Fabbrica Motori Marini
Fairey Marine
Grandi Motori Trieste
Hatch & Kirk, Inc.
Korody-Colyer Corporation
Rhine-Schelde-Verolme

SPEED BOATS
Batservice Verft A/S
Bell Aerospace Canada
Brooke Marine Ltd.
Cammenga Jachtbouw B.V.
Cantiere Navaltecnica
D.T.C.N.
Fairey Marine Ltd.
Fr. Lürssen Werft
SOFREXAN
Vosper Thornycroft Group, The

STABILISING EQUIPMENT
Blohm & Voss AG
Ferranti Ltd.
Vosper Thornycroft Group, The

STABILISING EQUIPMENT FOR FIRE CONTROL
Ferranti Ltd.
Hollandse Signaalapparaten B.V.

STEAM-RAISING PLANT, CONVENTIONAL
Blohm & Voss AG
Bremer Vulcan Schiffbau und Maschinenfabrik
Yarrow (Shipbuilders) Ltd.

STEAM-RAISING PLANT, NUCLEAR
D.T.C.N.
Yarrow (Shipbuilders) Ltd.

STEAM TURBINES
Blohm & Voss AG
Bremer Vulcan Schiffbau und Maschinenfabrik
D.T.C.N.
Howaldtswerke-Deutsche Werft

STEEL, ALLOY AND SPECIAL
AB Bofors

STEEL FORGINGS, PLATES AND SECTIONS, STAMPINGS
AB Bofors
Rhine-Schelde-Verolme

STEEL, MANGANESE, WEAR RESISTING
AB Bofors

STEERING GEAR
Rhine-Schelde-Verolme
Vosper Thornycroft Group, The

STRESS RELIEVING
Bremer Vulcan Schiffbau und Maschinenfabrik
Yarrow (Shipbuilders) Ltd.

SUBMARINE DISTRESS BUOY
Barr & Stroud
D.T.C.N.
SOFREXAN
Thomson C.S.F.

SUBMARINE FIRE CONTROL
C.I.T. Alcatel
Hollandse Signaalapparaten B.V.
Singer Librascope
SOFREXAN
Sperry Gyroscope

SUBMARINE PERISCOPES
Barr & Stroud
D.T.C.N.
Dubigeon Normandie
SOFREXAN
Thomson C.S.F.

SUBMARINES
D.T.C.N.
Howaldtswerke-Deutsche Werft
Ingenieurkontor Lübeck
Netherlands United Shipbuilding Bureaux Ltd.
SOFREXAN
Split Shipyard
Rhine-Schelde-Verolme

SUBMARINES (CONVENTIONAL)
D.T.C.N.
Dubigeon Normandie
Ingenieurkontor Lübeck
Netherlands United Shipbuilding Bureaux Ltd.
Rhine-Schelde-Verolme
SOFREXAN

SUBMERSIBLES (WET)
Sperry Gyroscope
Split Shipyards

SUPERHEATERS
Blohm & Voss AG
Bremer Vulcan Schiffbau und Maschinenfabrik
D.T.C.N.
Yarrow (Shipbuilders) Ltd.

SUPPORT SERVICES
Fairey Marine Ltd.
Vosper Thornycroft Group, The

SURVEY EQUIPMENT
D.T.C.N.

SWITCHBOARDS
Blohm & Voss AG
Fr. Lürssen Werft
Plessey Company Ltd., The
Vosper Thornycroft Group, The
Whipp & Bourne Ltd.

SWITCHBOARDS AND SWITCHGEAR
Fr. Lürssen Werft
Vosper Thornycroft Group, The
Whipp & Bourne Ltd.

TACTICAL TRAINING SIMULATORS
Ferranti Ltd.
Hollandse Signaalapparaten B.V.
Marconi Radar Systems Ltd.
Van Der Heem Electronics N.V.

TANKERS
Batservice Verft A/S
Blohm & Voss AG
Bremer Vulcan Schiffbau und Maschinenfabrik
Fr. Lürssen Werft
Howaldtswerke-Deutsche Werft
Rhine-Schelde-Verolme
Split Shipyard
Yarrow (Shipbuilders) Ltd.

TANKERS (SMALL)
Bremer Vulcan Schiffbau und Maschinenfabrik
Dubigeon Normandie
Fr. Lürssen Werft
Rhine-Schelde-Verolme
Split Shipyard
Yarrow (Shipbuilders) Ltd.

TANKS, OIL AND WATER STORAGE
Bremer Vulcan Schiffbau und Maschinenfabrik
British Hovercraft Corporation
Howaldtswerk-Deutsche Werft
Split Shipyards

TECHNICAL PUBLICATIONS
D.T.C.N.
Vosper Thornycroft Group, The

TELECOMMUNICATIONS EQUIPMENT
C.I.T. Alcatel
D.T.C.N.
SOFREXAN
Thomson C.S.F.

TELEGRAPH SYSTEMS
Thomson C.S.F.

TELEMOTORS
D.T.C.N.
MacTaggart, Scott & Co. Ltd.

TENDERS
Blohm & Voss AG
Bremer Vulcan Schiffbau und Maschinenfabrik
Brooke Marine Ltd.
David Cheverton
Fr. Lürssen Werft
Netherlands United Shipbuilding Bureaux Ltd.
Yarrow (Shipbuilders) Ltd.
Vosper Thornycroft Group, The

TEST EQUIPMENT FOR FIRE CONTROL SYSTEMS
C.I.T. Alcatel
Hollandse-Signaalapparaten N.V.
Singer Librascope
Thomson C.S.F.

TEXTILE FIBRES
D.T.C.N.

TORPEDO CONTROL SYSTEMS
C.I.T. Alcatel
D.T.C.N.
Hollandse Signaalapparaten B.V.
Plessey Company Ltd.
SOFREXAN
Sperry Gyroscope
Thomson C.S.F.
USEA

TORPEDO CRAFT BUILDERS
Batservice Verft A/S
Brooke Marine Ltd.
Cammenga Jachtbouw B.V.
C.I.T. Alcatel
D.T.C.N.
Fairey Marine Ltd.
Fr. Lürssen Werft
Netherlands United Shipbuilding Bureaux Ltd.
Vosper Thornycroft Group, The
Yarrow (Shipbuilders) Ltd.

TORPEDO DEPTH AND ROLL RECORDERS
Barr & Stroud
D.T.C.N.

TORPEDO ORDER AND DEFLECTION CONTROL
C.I.T. Alcatel
D.T.C.N.

TORPEDO SIDE-LAUNCHERS
D.T.C.N.
SOFREXAN
Vosper Thornycroft Group, The

TORPEDOES AND TORPEDO TUBES
C.I.T. Alcatel
D.T.C.N.
Plessey Company Ltd.
SOFREXAN

TRAINING EQUIPMENT
C.I.T. Alcatel
D.T.C.N.
Ferranti Ltd.
Hollandse Signaalapparaten B.V.
Plessey Company Ltd.
SOFREXAN
USEA
Van Der Heem Electronics N.V.

TRAWLERS
Brooke Marine Ltd.
D.T.C.N.
Dubigeon Normandie
Yarrow (Shipbuilders) Ltd.

TUGS
Brooke Marine Ltd.
D.T.C.N.
Dubigeon Normandie
Yarrow (Shipbuilders) Ltd.

TURBINE GEARS
Bremer Vulcan Schiffbau und Maschinenfabrik
C.I.T. Alcatel
D.T.C.N.

TURBINES
Blohm & Voss AG
Bremer Vulcan Schiffbau und Maschinenfabrik
D.T.C.N.
Fiat
Yarrow (Shipbuilders) Ltd.

TURBINES, EXHAUST
Bremer Vulcan Schiffbau und Maschinenfabrik
D.T.C.N.

TURBINES, GAS MARINE
D.T.C.N.
FIAT
Yarrow (Shipbuilders) Ltd.

TURBINES, STEAM MARINE
Blohm & Voss AG
D.T.C.N.
Yarrow (Shipbuilders) Ltd.

UNDERWATER LIGHTS
SOFREXAN

UNDERWATER TELEVISION EQUIPMENT
Edo Corporation
SOFREXAN
Thomson C.S.F.

VALVES AND COCKS
Cockburns Ltd.
Split Shipyard

VALVES AND COCKS, HYDRAULICS
Cockburns Ltd.
MacTaggart, Scott & Co. Ltd.
Split Shipyard

VALVES, AUTOMATIC PLATE OR DISC
Cockburns Ltd.

VALVES, BUTTERFLY FLUID AND VENTILATION
D.T.C.N.
Cockburns Ltd.

V/STOL AIRCRAFT
Hawker Siddeley

VOLTAGE REGULATORS, AUTOMATIC
D.T.C.N.
Ferranti Ltd.
Korody-Colyer Corporation

WARSHIP REPAIRERS
AB Bofors
Bremer Vulcan Schiffbau und Maschinenfabrik
Brooke Marine Ltd.
D.T.C.N.
Fr. Lürssen Werft
Howaldtswerke-Deutsche Werft
Netherlands United Shipbuilding Bureaux Ltd.
Rhine-Schelde-Verolme
Split Shipyard
Vosper Thornycroft Group, The
Yarrow (Shipbuilders) Ltd.

WARSHIPS
Blohm & Voss AG
D.T.C.N.
Dubigeon Normandie
Fr. Lürssen Werft
Netherlands United Shipbuilding Bureaux Ltd.
Rhine-Schelde-Verolme
SOFREXAN
Split Shipyard
Vosper Thornycroft Group, The
Yarrow (Shipbuilders) Ltd.

WATER TUBE BOILERS
Bremer Vulcan Schiffbau und Maschinenfabrik
Blohm & Voss AG
D.T.C.N.
Rhine-Schelde-Verolme
Yarrow (Shipbuilders) Ltd.

WEAPON SYSTEMS
AB Bofors
Aerospatiale
D.T.C.N.
Fr. Lürssen Werft
Ferranti Ltd.
Hollandse Signaalapparaten B.V.
OTO Melara
Plessey Company Ltd.
Selenia
SOFREXAN
Sperry Gyrosope
Thomson C.S.F.
Vosper Thornycroft Group, The

WEAPON SYSTEMS (SONAR COMPONENTS)
C.I.T. Alcatel
D.T.C.N.
Edo Corporation
Plessey Company Ltd.
Sippican Oceanographic Systems
SOFREXAN
Thomson C.S.F.
Van Der Heem Electronics N.V.

WELDING, ARC, ARGON ARC OR GAS
D.T.C.N.
Fr. Lürssen Werft
Rhine-Schelde-Verolme
Yarrow (Shipbuilders) Ltd.

WINCHES
MacTaggart, Scott & Co. Ltd.

X-RAY WORK
Fr. Lürssen Werft
Split Shipyard

YACHTS (POWERED)
Cammenga Jachtbouw B.V.
Cantieri Baglietto
Cantieri Navali Italcraft
Dubigeon Normandie
Fairey Marine Ltd.
Fr. Lürssen Werft
Vosper Thornycroft Group, The
Yarrow (Shipbuilders) Ltd.

That's what the ancient Romans called the Mediterranean. They meant "Our Sea". The sea belonging to us all.

The sea we know and can sail on. Well aware of the dangers and relying on their rough-and-ready ships only they sailed these waters, their sea, hoping to reach some quiet landing-place.

That's how it was then.

Today every sea is "our sea" for CRM, beyond the Straits of Gibraltar too, of course.

And that's why no sea exists, remote or unknown, that doesn't become smooth to sail on with CRM engines, the engines that widened the world's frontiers once and for all...

That's how things are today.

And more so in the future.

MARE NOSTRUM

OCCHIOMAGICO 73

CRM 18D/S-2 ENGINE
OVERALL PISTON DISPLACEMENT: 57.25 cm^3
MAXIMUM RATING: 1,350 HP AT 2,075 R.P.M.
DRY WEIGHT (INCLUDING REVERSE GEAR): 2,075 KG

ENGINE RANGE: 9-CYLINDER W-TYPE, 12-CYLINDER V-TYPE, 18-CYLINDER W-TYPE.
RATINGS RANGING FROM 400 TO 1,350 HP OVERGEARS, REDUCTION GEARS, VEE-DRIVES.

CRM 20121 milano via manzoni 12 tel. 708326/708327 telegr. cremme

Harrier

The V/STOL Harrier has landed and taken off from a wider range of ships than any other fixed-wing aircraft. Here are just some of them.

The implications for maritime tactics are enormous – because Harrier puts combat jet power within reach of more

Carriers.

seaborne forces than ever before.

At sea, or on land, Harrier changes everything.

1 *Foch,* France. 27,300 tons.
2 *Guam,* U.S.A. 18,300 tons.
3 *Jeanne d'Arc,* France. 12,365 tons.
4 *Blake,* Great Britain. 12,100 tons.
5 *Dedalo,* Spain. 15,800 tons.
6 *25 de Mayo,* Argentina. 19,900 tons.
7 *Green Rover,* Great Britain. 11,520 tons.
8 *Andrea Doria,* Italy. 6,500 tons.

HAWKER SIDDELEY AVIATION

Kingston upon Thames, England
Hawker Siddeley Group supplies mechanical, electrical and aerospace equipment with world-wide sales and service.

Naval refits-modernisation and support services

Weapons electronics systems

The high cost of building a modern naval vessel places a heavy burden on defence budgets but for a Navy to maintain an adequate degree of preparedness it is necessary to ensure that its ships do not become operationally obsolescent.

Plessey Services is staffed by professionals who will discuss your operational and technical requirements and undertake the entire task of electronics and weapons modernisation, from initial survey through sea trials to handover and logistics support.

Support bases

To maintain naval forces at an adequate state of efficiency a comprehensive planned maintenance and logistic support service is needed.

Plessey Services will design and implement a complete base maintenance facility including buildings, workshops, equipment and supervisory staff for a training and logistic support programme until the customer's naval personnel are ready to take over.

The Plessey Company Limited, Addlestone, Surrey, England KT15 2PW.
Tel: Weybridge (0932) 47282. Telex: 262329.

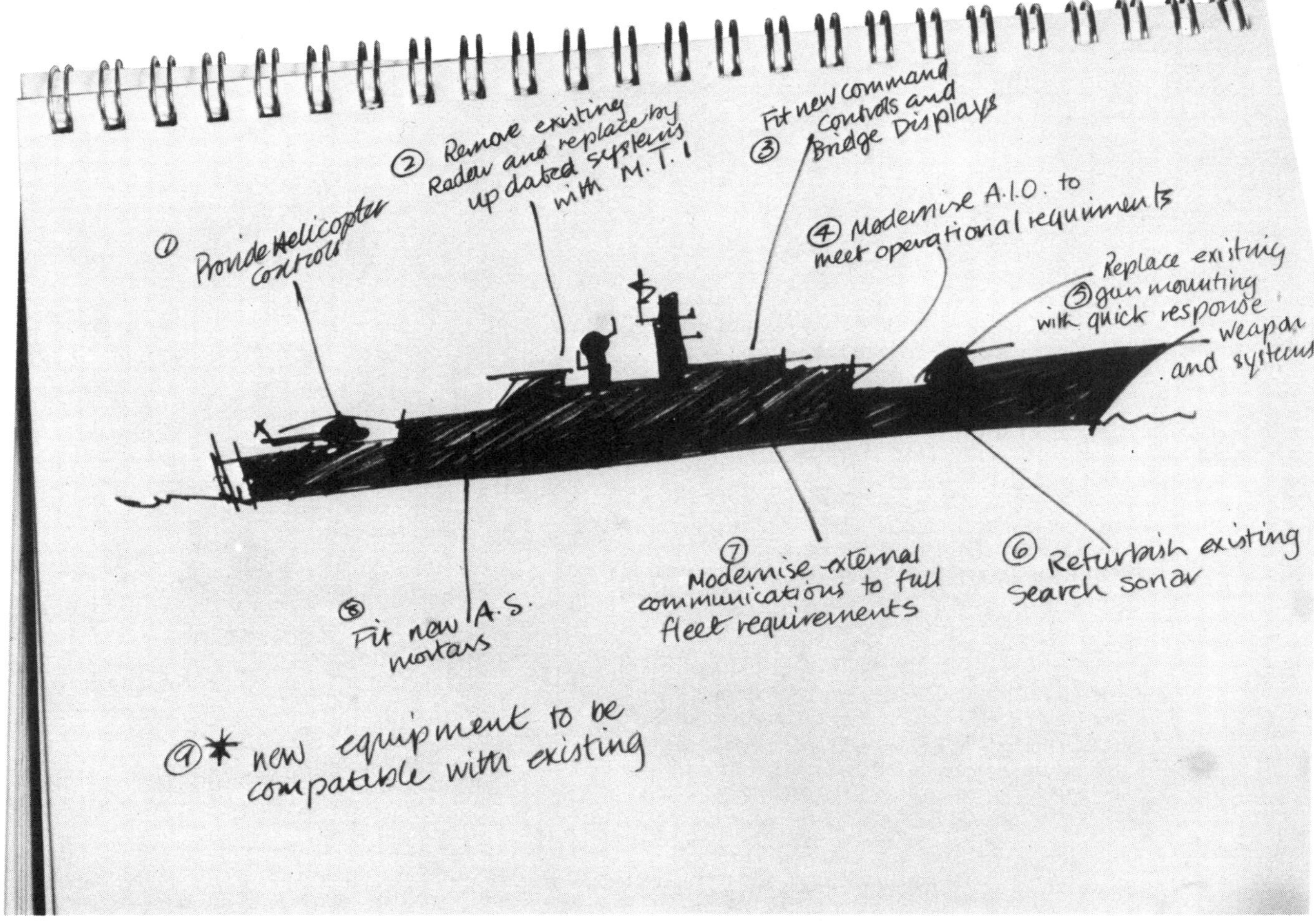

EXOCET MM 38 AM 39

MM 39 MM 40 EXOCET

FOR SEA-POWER

Naval forces today have at their disposal an incomparable weapon - EXOCET - the missile which evades all enemy defences.

Its autonomy and sea-skimming flight make it virtually invulnerable. The range, speed, accuracy and hitting power of EXOCET weapon systems provide tactical superiority to those navies which adopt them.

In production or under development are:

☐ MM 38 already operational in 9 navies and which is suitable for all types of surface vessels from patrol-boat to cruiser,

☐ AM 39 fired from helicopters and assault or naval patrol aircraft,

☐ MM 39 capable of being fitted in quadruple mounts in the smallest types of naval craft,

☐ MM 40 with a range of more than 35 nautical miles for over-the-horizon engagement of surface targets.

MM 38, 39 and 40 can also be installed on shore as fixed or mobile coastal batteries.

aerospatiale

DIVISION ENGINS TACTIQUES
2, rue Béranger - Châtillon 92320-FRANCE

AEROSPATIALE MISSILES Ltd.,
178, Piccadilly, London W1V OBA

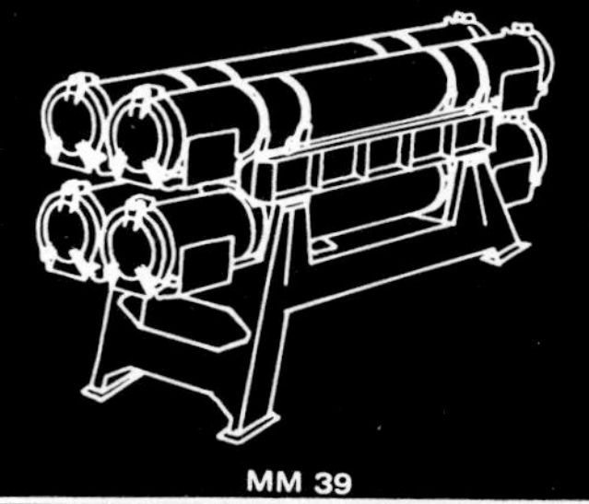

MM 39

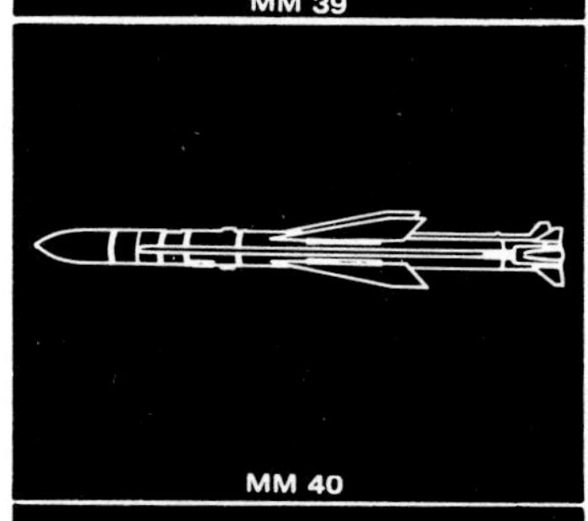

MM 40

Exocet - mobile coastal battery
MM38 – MM39 – MM40

HMS Royal Sovereign
HMS Amazon
HMS Leander
HMS Bristol
HMS Courageous
HMS Hermes
COURAGEOUS

What's in a name?

The Royal Navy sets a special value on names.

Royal Sovereign, Amazon, Leander, Bristol, Courageous, Hermes – they help to carry down its tradition from one generation to another. All the great old ships seen opposite have their present day namesakes, whose purpose and duties are the same, though their methods and equipment are very different.

Every one of them carries a Ferranti computer system.

The nuclear powered submarine Sovereign carries a Ferranti FM1600B system for tactical purposes.

The Royal Navy's new frigate Amazon carries two computer systems – CAAIS for operations room display and WSA4 for control of her gun and Seacat armament. Each is based on an FM1600B computer.

H.M.S. Leander, built in 1961, heads a highly successful class of ASW frigates. Fire control for the IKARA missile, as well as tactical and display facilities, are provided by the ship's Ferranti ADA Weapon System Mk 5.

The Type 82 guided missile ship Bristol has an ADAWS 2 system based on two Ferranti FM1600 computers for control of all her main weapons together with tactical display and data exchange facilities.

Courageous is today a nuclear powered Fleet submarine of the Churchill class. Units of this class are fitted with Ferranti FM1600B computer systems to assist in tactical data handling display and appreciation. The present Hermes, built in 1953, was converted to a helicopter carrier in 1970 and her Operations Room is now fitted with a Ferranti CAAIS system.

In their own field, Ferranti too, are a great name.

At the end of the last century they were one of the pioneers in electrical engineering and in the early nineteen-fifties they were responsible for the first commercially available British computer.

Today they are recognised as leaders in the application of digital systems for naval, airborne, military and civil uses.

Ferranti Limited, Digital Systems Division,
Western Road, Bracknell, Berkshire, RG12 1RA
Telephone: 0344 3232 Telex: 848117

DS 55 rb

Submarine Launched Expendable Bathythermograph

sippican
ssxbt

launched from the aft signal ejector of a moving, submerged submarine, transmits temperature data back to the launching ship over a fine wire. A temperature/depth profile of the water is displayed on a permanent recording aboard the submarine.

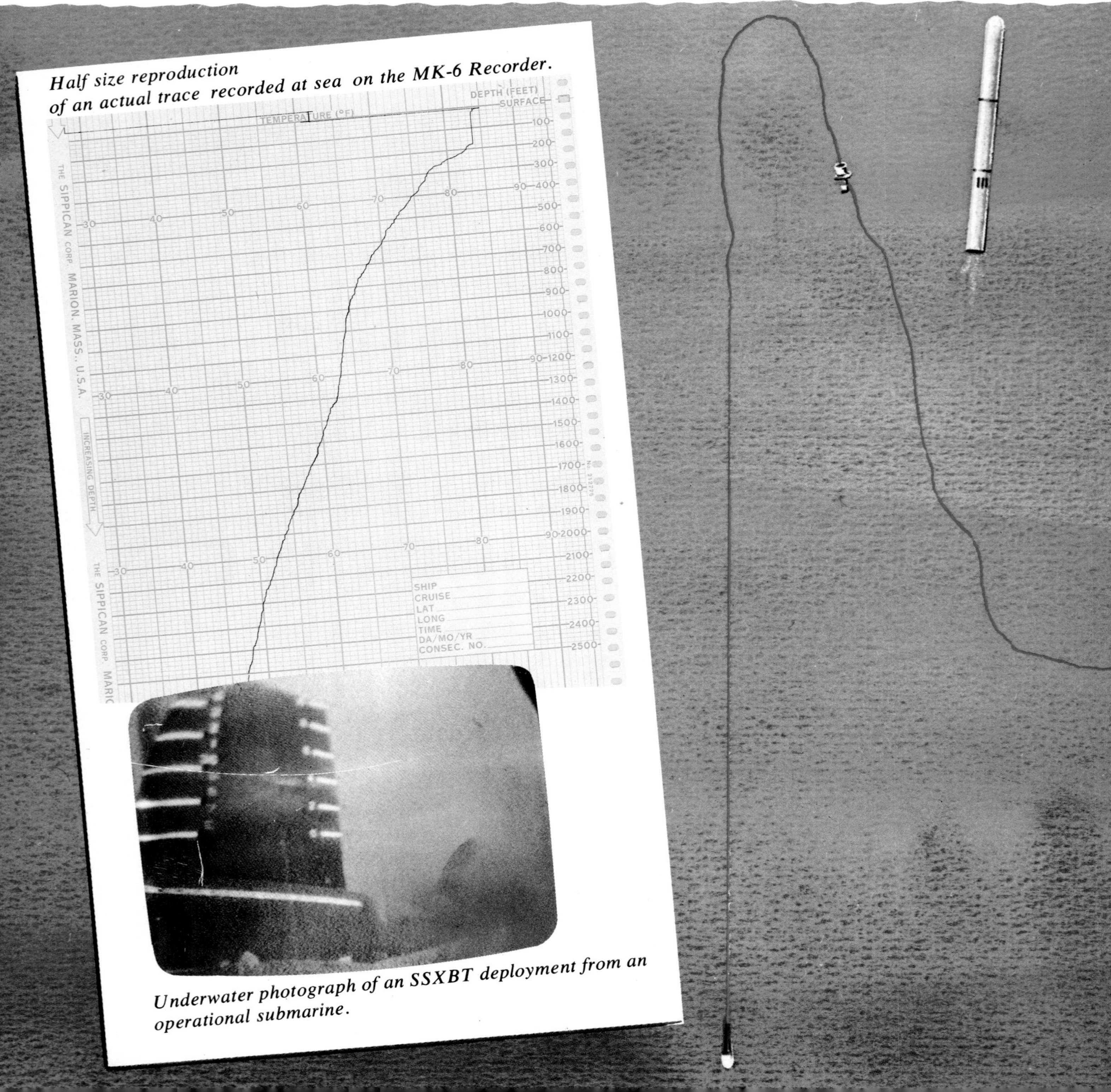

Half size reproduction of an actual trace recorded at sea on the MK-6 Recorder.

Underwater photograph of an SSXBT deployment from an operational submarine.

A NEW WORD IN MI

The MAFIUS series (Missile armed fas
chapter in the field c

MAFIUS 300

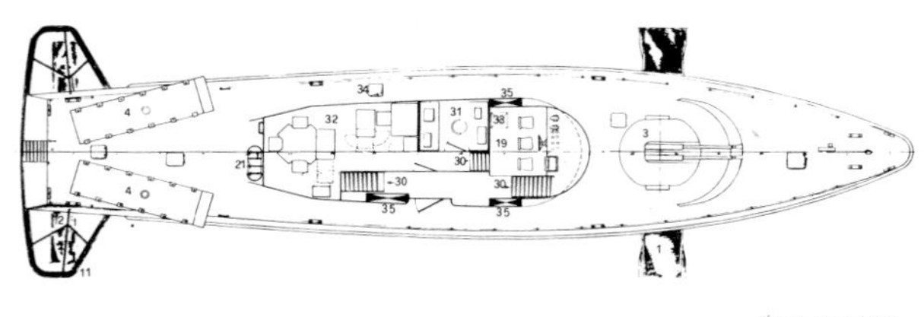

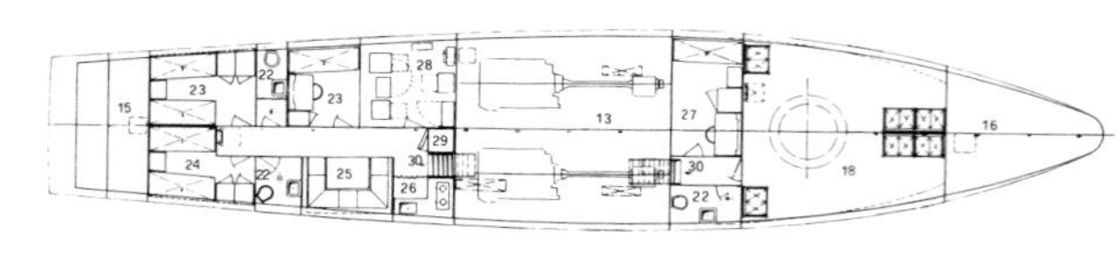

SIMPLE, RELIABLE, DIESEL PROPELLED
PERFORMANCE OF THE MOST SOPHIS

120 PASSENGER CARRYING H
IN 24 CO

CANTIERE NAVALTECNICA S.p.A. -Messina, Italy
With the Technical Expertise of L Rodriquez Shipyard
Via S. Raineri, 22 - Messina - Phone: PBX 44801 - Telex 98030 Roc

SSILE HYDROFOILS

Italian unsinkable ship) opens a new
military light forces

MAFIUS 600

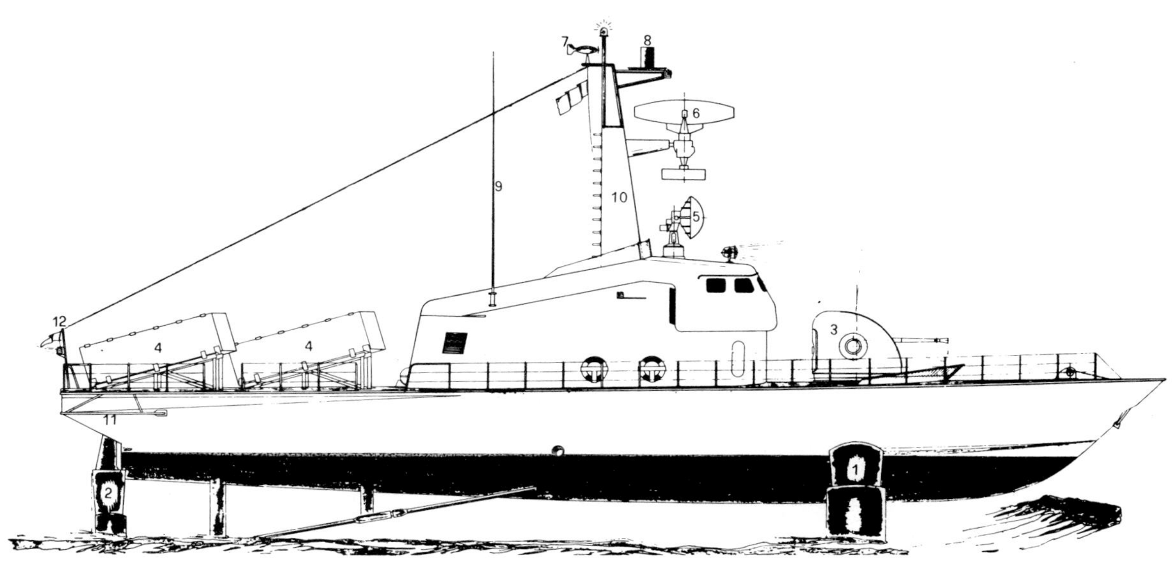

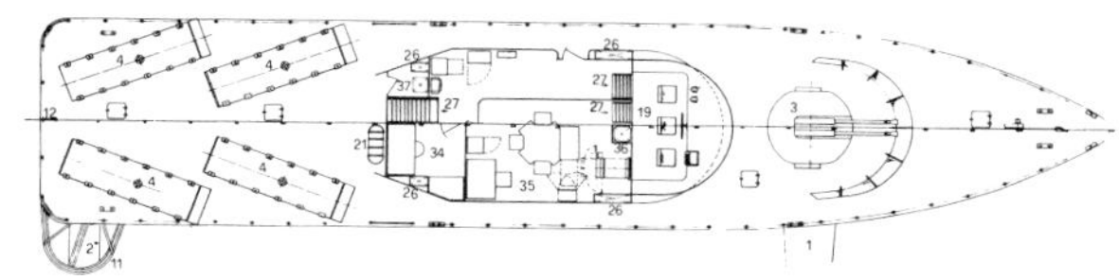

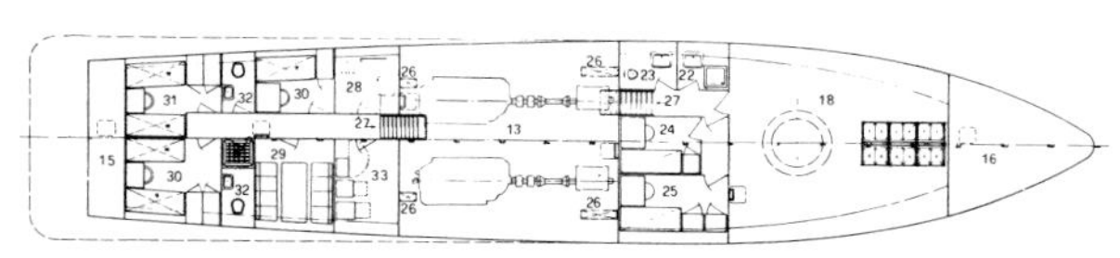

NSINKABLE HYDROFOILS WITH THE
CATED AND EXPENSIVE FAST CRAFT

DROFOILS BUILT AND SOLD
TRIES

kez **Cables: Navaltecnica**

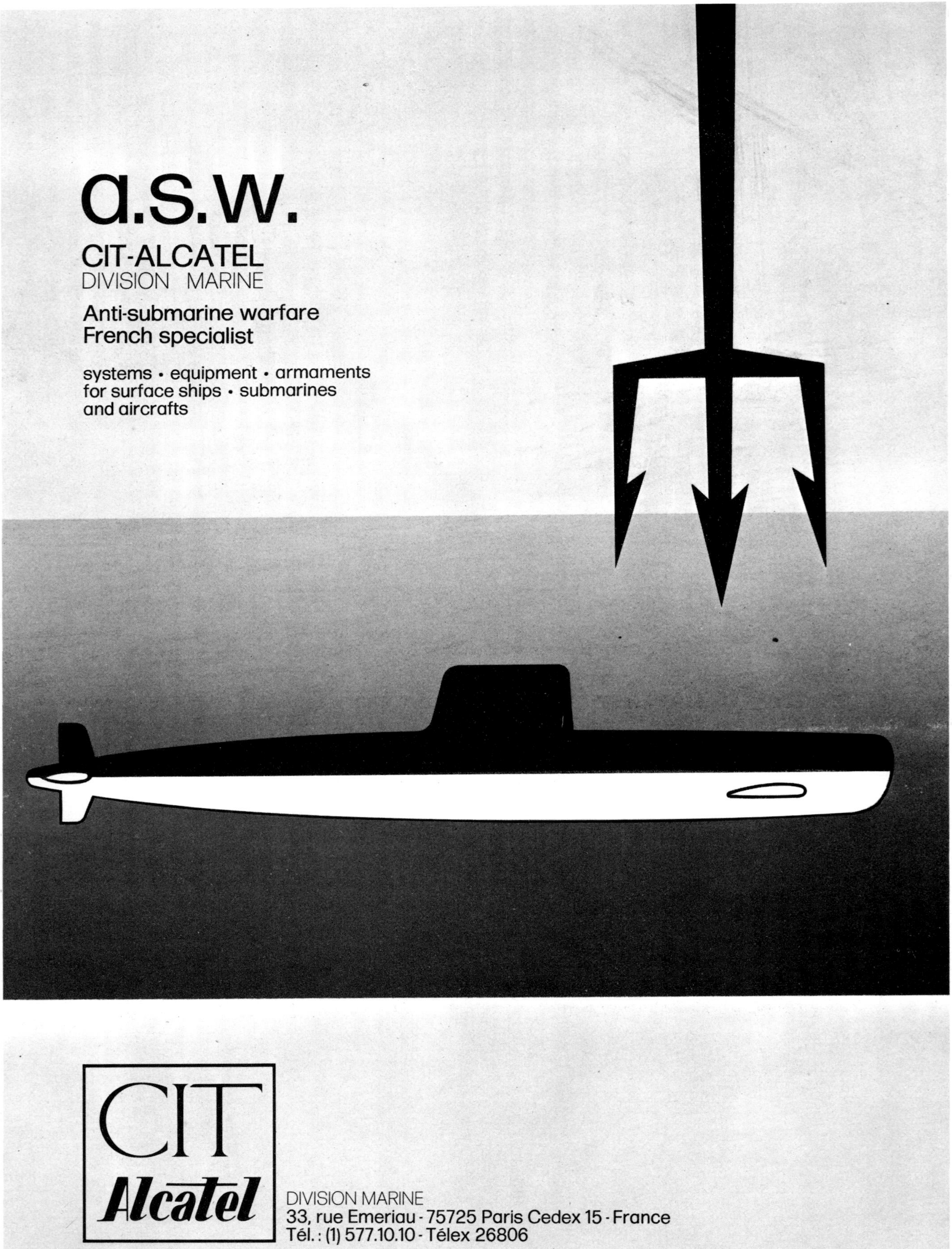

SHIPBOARD
AIRCONDITIONING
AERIMPIANTI
AERIMPIANTI
THE HIGHEST STANDARD IN
EQUIPMENTS - DESIGN -
ERECTION
TECHNICAL ASSISTANCE IN THE
SHIPYARD AND DURING
NAVIGATION
Address:
20124 Milano – Italy ■ Via F. Filzi, 25 ■ Tel. (02) 653051
Telex: 33211 AERIMP ■ 61593 AERIMPRO ■ 77123 AERIMPNA
Milan Rome Naples

Submarine "1076 type"
SAURO class

This type has been designed in accordance with the latest requirements of the evolution of underwater fighting means and their use.
Special stress has been put on those features and performances that, also in the near future, will undoubtedly represent the most essential factors for efficient undersea combat, mainly in SSK and attack tasks.

Main characteristics

Length overall	63.85 m
Beam	6.83 m
Height overall (masts in)	12.38 m
Light displacement	1250 tons
Surface displacement	1450 tons
Surface mean draught	5.70 m
Submerged displacement	1630 tons

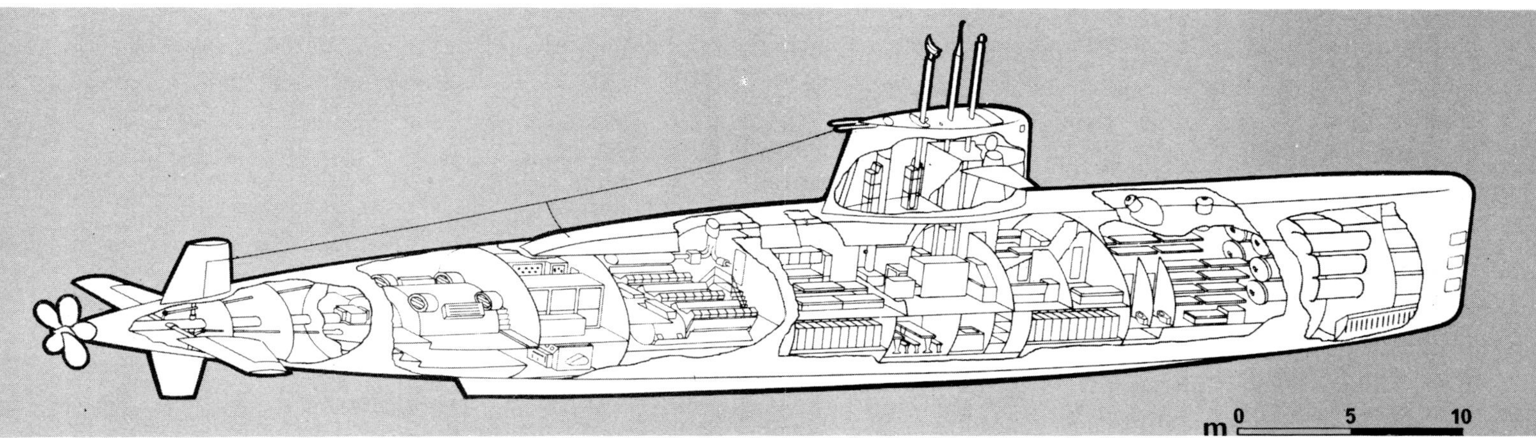

Submarine "1077 type"
500 - ton class

This is the latest Italcantieri design. It has been developed to exploit to the utmost the operational possibilities of the 500-ton class submarines, simplifying as far as possible handling and service problems whilst keeping the cost comparatively low.

Main characteristics

Length overall	47.47 m
Beam	4.77 m
Height overall (masts in)	8.67 m
Light displacement	465 tons
Surface displacement	550 tons
Surface mean draught	4.00 m
Submerged displacement	610 tons

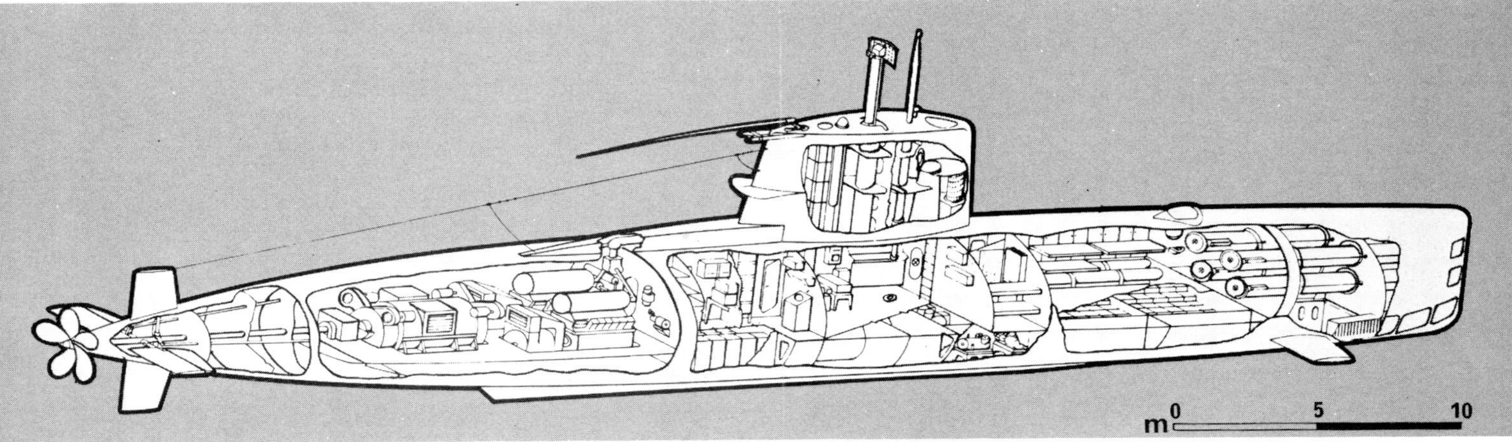

Some devices for submarines designed and manufactured by

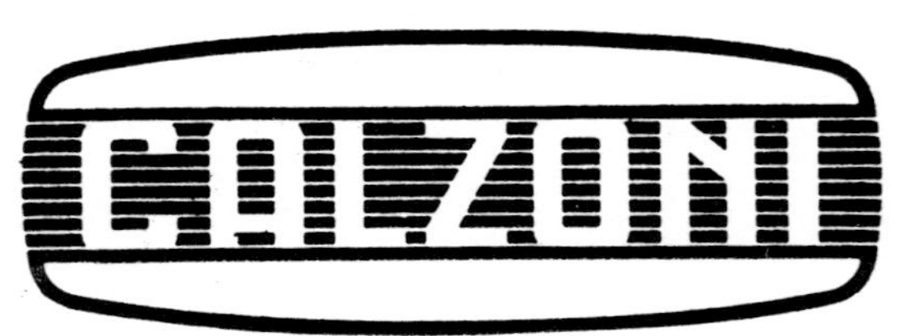

MAXIMUM SILENCE

Very silent hydraulic pump, variable delivery, provided with built-in power regulator.

NO PROBLEM CAUSED BY GAS EXHAUST

Gas exhaust valve hermatically tight, provided with hot fumes protected gaskets.

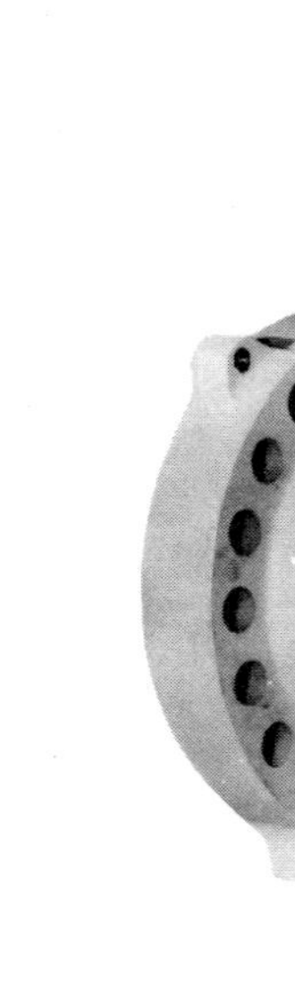

MAXIMUM SAFETY UNDER SHOCK

Hull valve provided with double shut off in a single body, with oil remote control and manual local control. Qualified by the Italian Navy for a very high shock factor against underwater explosion.

GREATER SPACE AVAILABLE ON BOARD

Radar antenna hoisting device, completely contained inside the sail (it does not pass through the control room).
ECM and UHF antennae hoisting devices, analogous to the preceeding one.

Patented Devices

Simulation at three levels.

Ferranti are probably the most experienced people in the world when it comes to designing and manufacturing custom built simulator systems for naval training.

Our Military Systems Division has been making training simulators since 1962 and has therefore had years of insight into the problems of training naval operators and command team personnel in the use of sophisticated equipment.

Our simulators cover naval action at three levels — in helicopters, surface ships and submarines — and are being used not only by the Royal Navy but in several other countries.

Besides training simulators, the Ferranti Military Systems Division produces store and forward message switching systems, command and control systems, police/fire control systems, muzzle velocity measurement equipment, defence displays and large screen displays.

Contact A. M. Bell,
Military Systems Division Sales,
Ferranti Limited,
Wythenshawe, Manchester M22 5LA,
Telephone: 061-437 5291 Telex: 669045

FERRANTI

MSD 10 rb

TRITON radar antenna surveillance,
radar of VEGA system.

VEGA

Surveillance and Weapon Control System for Surface Fighting Ships.

MISSIONS

- □ Surface and air surveillance
- □ Display and exploitation of ECM data
- □ Designation of surface and air targets
- □ Control of Weapons:
  - all-calibre guns (against surface, air or shore targets)
  - surface-to-surface missiles such as EXOCET, OTOMAT and HARPOON
  - torpedoes
  - surface-to-air missiles (SEA-CAT, SEA-SPARROW, CROTALE)

DESIGN

- □ Modularity allowing to select the configuration best fit for the ship's mission and armament
- □ Effective antijamming protection
- □ Perfect adaptation to modern operational requirements
- □ Ease of use
- □ High reliability and maintainability

THOMSON-CSF

DIVISION RADARS DE SURFACE
1, RUE DES MATHURINS / B.P. 10
92222 BAGNEUX / FRANCE / TEL. (1) 657.13.65

THE SUBMARINES

BUILT BY
SHIPYARD • SPLIT •
SPLIT - YUGOSLAVIA

NAVY
54
630
NAYAIR
USN
POLAR STAR
ELLSWORTH TRANS-ANTARCTIC FLIGHT
NR-12269
Allan Mardon

AN OLD TRADITION FOR MODERN WEAPONS

35mm OERLIKON

NAVAL TWIN MOUNTING

— Provides the most effective defence against missiles and high performance aircraft

— Installation entirely above deck

CHARACTERISTICS

• Rate of fire	1,100 r.p.m.
• Muzzle velocity	1,175 m/sec
• Total Weight with 336 rounds	5,700 Kg.

OERLIKON ITALIANA
Via Sensellini 14, Milano - ITALY
Tel. 6450575 - 76 - 77
Telex 37259 OERLIKON

For over three decades, Librascope has helped to pioneer technological advancements in all aspects of Naval weapon systems. Our first product was an aircraft weight and balance computer for use in aircraft operation. From this beginning in mechanical linkage computers, Librascope worked with the Navy to develop electro-mechanical analog computers for Naval antiaircraft and antisubmarine weapon control systems. The alliance between Librascope and the Navy has paid off in progress. Today, virtually every ASW weapon control system installed aboard surface ships and submarines of the U. S. Navy was designed and manufactured by Librascope.

To keep pace with the rapidly

Good ideas...

OFFICIAL U.S. NAVY PHOTO

advancing sophistication of submarine weapon systems, Librascope designs and manufactures control systems like this Analyzer Console Mk78. This highly interactive computer-controlled display is modular in design and sets new standards in reliability. And its flexibility permits it to accommodate the latest in Naval advancements in new

weapons and sensors. At Librascope, we're working to advance today's technology to shape more sophisticated and reliable Naval combat systems for tomorrow.

SINGER
AEROSPACE & MARINE SYSTEMS
LIBRASCOPE DIVISION
833 Sonora Avenue, Glendale, California 91201

have a way of growing on you.

OFFICIAL U.S. NAVY PHOTO

TWIN NAVAL MOUTING
40 mm. L/70 "COMPACT"
AUTOMATIC FEEDING DEVICES
FOR 40 mm. L/70 NAVAL
MOUNTINGS
MULTIPURPOSE
ROCKET LAUNCHER
OF "SCLAR" SYSTEM
LONG RANGE
ANTI-TANK
WEAPON SYSTEM
"SPARVIERO"
AUTOMATIC FEEDING DEVICES FOR
40 mm. L/70 FIELD GUNS
SHORT RANGE ANTI-TANK
WEAPON SYSTEM "FOLGORE"
SATURATION
WEAPON SYSTEM
"S.A.R.C."
BREDA
BREDA MECCANICA BRESCIANA
VIA LUNGA, 2 / 25100 BRESCIA / ITALY
TELEX: 30056 BREDARMI

Heavy Lift Ro/Ro Ship M.V. STARMAN loading two 33m. patrol craft for delivery to the Royal New Zealand Navy. All three ships designed and built by Brooke Marine.

RECENTLY DELIVERED

One of a number of 33m. Fast Patrol Craft recently delivered and now under construction for the Federal Military Government of the Republic of Nigeria.

H.M.S. FAWN one of four survey craft for the Ministry of Defence (Navy).

We predict that you'll need this sound ray path analyser for Sonar operations.

The SPI-03 is efficient, reliable and, above all, versatile. Use it to predict the optimum mode for fixed transducer operation and VDS transducer depth for surface ships: to predict optimum listening and escape depths for submarines: to predict optimum transducer depths for helicopters and effective operating areas for sonobuoys. As a trainer, use it to teach sonar operators in acoustic ray path relationship.

CONVERGENCE ZONE

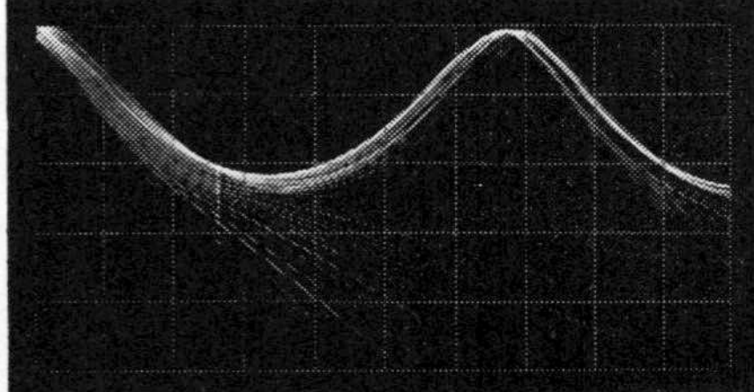

Bottom reflections off

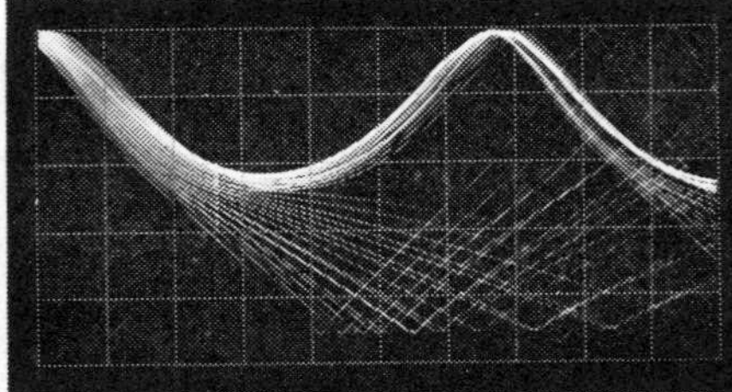

Bottom reflections on

PREDICTION FOR VDS ADJUSTMENT

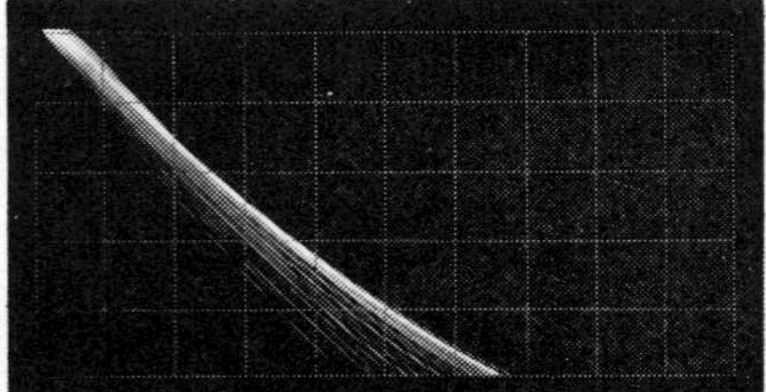

Hull mounted sonar

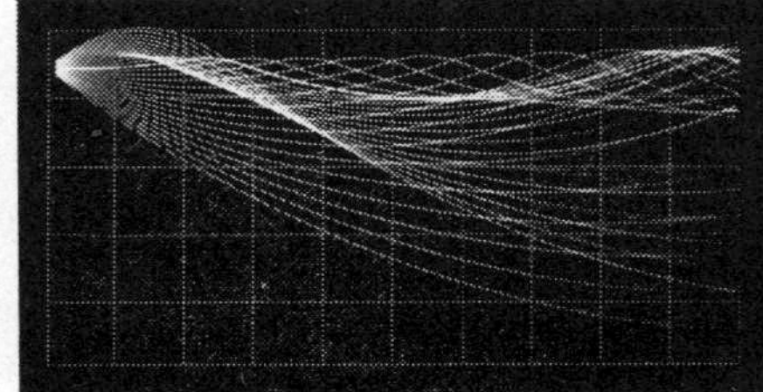

Variable depth sonar, same conditions

SOUND CHANNELS

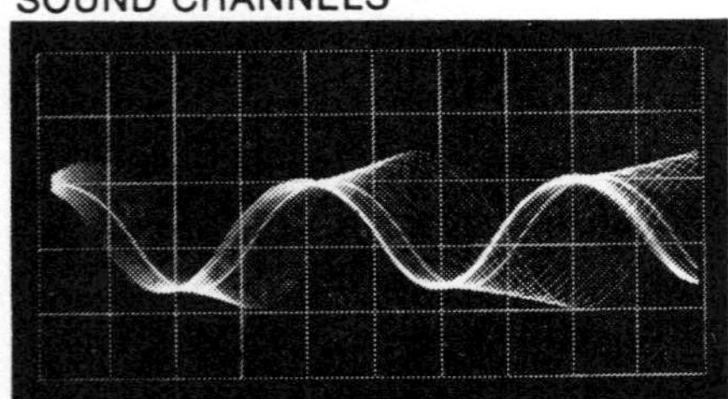

Deep sound channel

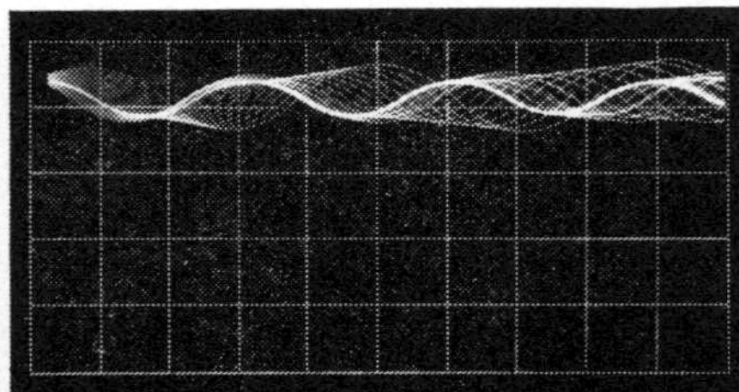

Shallow sound channel

It features:

7 in x 3½ in sound ray path CRT display
5 adjustable water layers and constant gradient in the sixth or bottom layer
maximum calculation time 74ms.
adjustable beam widths from 5° - 40°
5-position test switch
easy alignment and maintenance
compact construction
all solid state.

Program:

- Sound ray path analysers
- Sonar
- Shipborne simulators
- Shorebased training systems

sonar systems

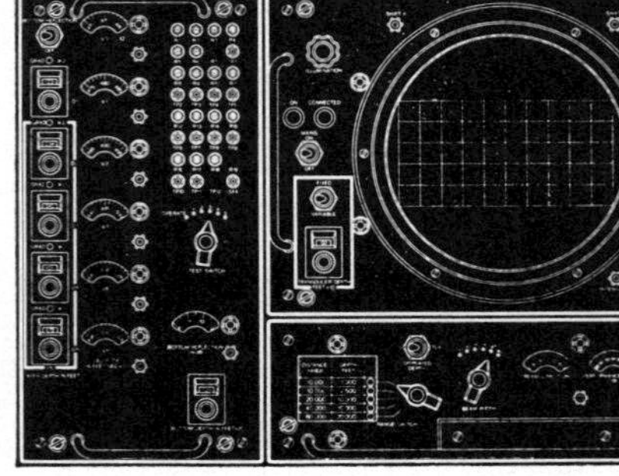

VAN DER HEEM ELECTRONICS B.V.
P.O. BOX 1060, THE HAGUE,
THE NETHERLANDS

H2

- Navy small and medium caliber automatic rapid fire guns. Remote control systems for naval armament. Anti-ship missiles. Studies of land and naval munitions.
- Handling and launching equipment for naval anti-ship and anti-aircraft medium and long range missiles. Army missiles handling and transport equipments.
- Mono-propellant and bi-propellant auxiliary propulsion systems for attitude and orbital control of artificial satellites.
- Tanks production. Track floating personnel carrier vehicles production, and special armed versions. Armament of self-propelled howitzers.
- Army medium caliber artillery. Automatic loading devices for field medium caliber guns and tanks.

OTO MELARA

OTO MELARA S.p.A I-19100 LA SPEZIA-ITALY TELEX 27368(OTO)-TEL.504041

OERLIKON/OTO 35 mm.
Naval Twin Mounting.

76/62 OTO COMPACT Anti-Ship and Anti-Aircraft Mounting.

127/54 OTO COMPACT Anti-Ship and Anti-Aircraft Mounting.

OTOMAT Anti-Ship Missile System.

Studio Grafico Restani - 116925037411.

WHIPP and BOURNE

2,000 Amp 'IFA'
Loose Circuit Breaker

2,000 Amp A.C.
Breaker Tilted

the BIG name in switchgear

When it comes to switchgear our name stands out above all others. We may not be the largest company but our reputation for reliability is second to none.

Whipp & Bourne High Fault Level Heavy Current 415 Volt AIR CIRCUIT BREAKERS are designed for use in Industry, Power Stations, Marine, Chemical, Steel Works and Traction application.

With a breaking capacity up to 57MVA and a current rating up to 4,000 amperes they can be supplied as loose circuit breakers or as complete switchboards to comply with relevant B.S. specifications.

Whipp & Bourne switchgear is thoroughly checked right through from first design to final installation to give you switchgear you can rely on.

Write for
technical literature:
Whipp & Bourne (1975) Ltd.
Castleton, Rochdale,
Lancashire, England.
Telephone: Rochdale
32051 (10 lines)
Telex 63442
(Whipborn, Casltn.)

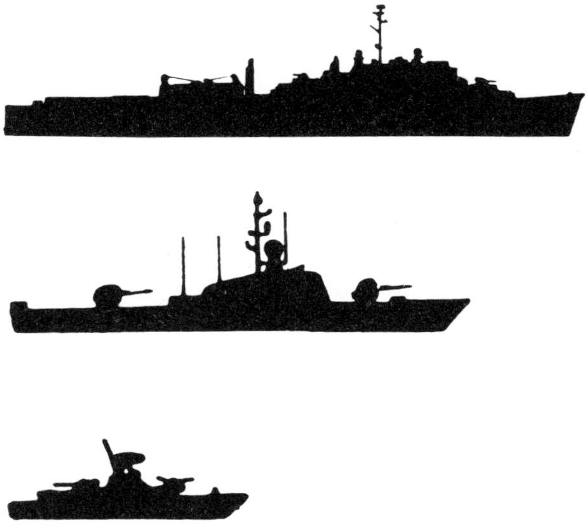

SELENIA
ELECTRONIC WARFARE

ESM & ECM require:
Technical skill and operational experience
We have got them working in this area since 1962
Knowledge of existing and foreseeable threats
We design and produce sophisticated radars incorporating the threat technologies of tomorrow
Full integration with command and control systems
We are system integration experts for optimal operational effectiveness
Selenia electronic warfare production line includes the RQN and TQN series of advanced radar and IR detection and warning receivers, as well as active jammers and associated peripherals

they boast their radars cannot be blinded or deceived. we are sure they can and we know how.

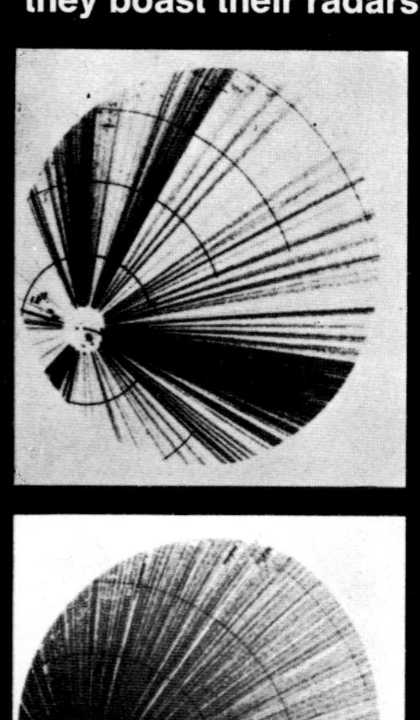

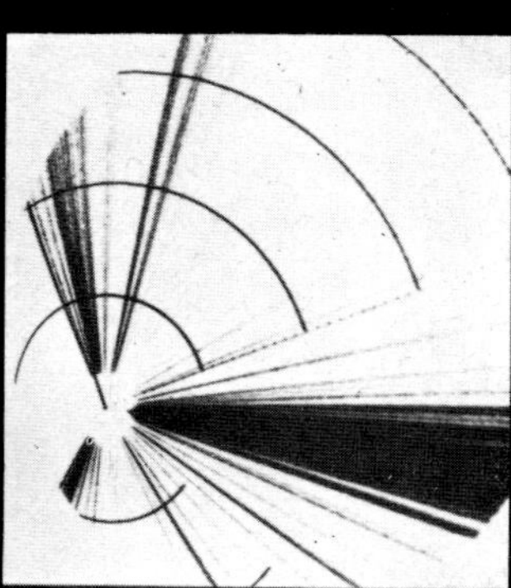

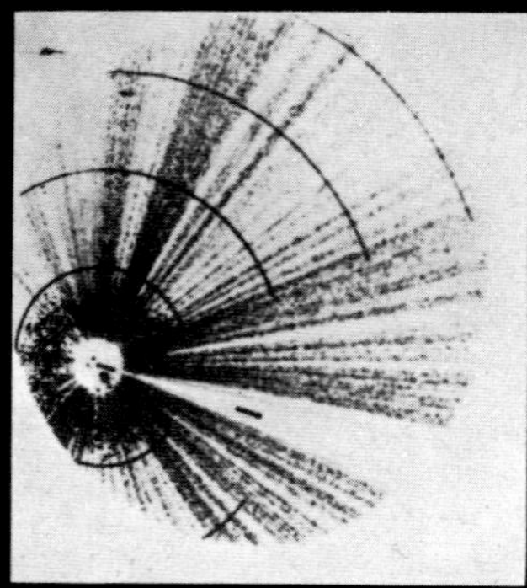
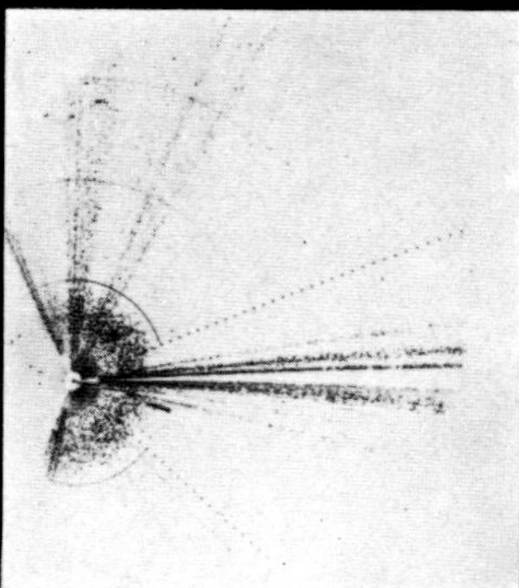

Now-small ship displays get mini computers to speed tactical data
New Plessey A10/CIC systems for command and control.
Faster decision-making is aided by this entirely new concept from Plessey Radar; naval autonomous displays with individual minicomputers. These processors, with their firmware programs, enable the tactical picture to be compiled rapidly, then distributed and presented in the action information system. Integration of sensors and weapons is achieved without the need for a large central computer complex. And the firmware removes all on-board program handling problems, whilst retaining the ability to evolve new tactics and procedures.
Contact us at the address below for further information.
DISPLACEMENT CORRECTION
BUQUE
UNIDAD
UNIDAD
PLESSEY RADAR
The Plessey Company Limited,
Addlestone, Weybridge, Surrey, England.
Tel: Weybridge 47282. Telex: 262329.
603 P024

HMS SHEFFIELD — MoD 1974

JANE'S FIGHTING SHIPS

FOUNDED IN 1897 BY FRED T. JANE

EDITED BY
CAPTAIN JOHN E. MOORE RN, FRGS

1975-76

I.S.B.N. 0-531 03251 5
L. of C. Cat. No. 75-15172

JANE'S YEARBOOKS

FRANKLIN WATTS INC.
NEW YORK

Paulton House, 8 Shepherdess Walk, London, N1 7LW

First Published in the United Kingdom 1975 by Jane's Yearbooks
First American Publication 1975 by Franklin Watts Inc.

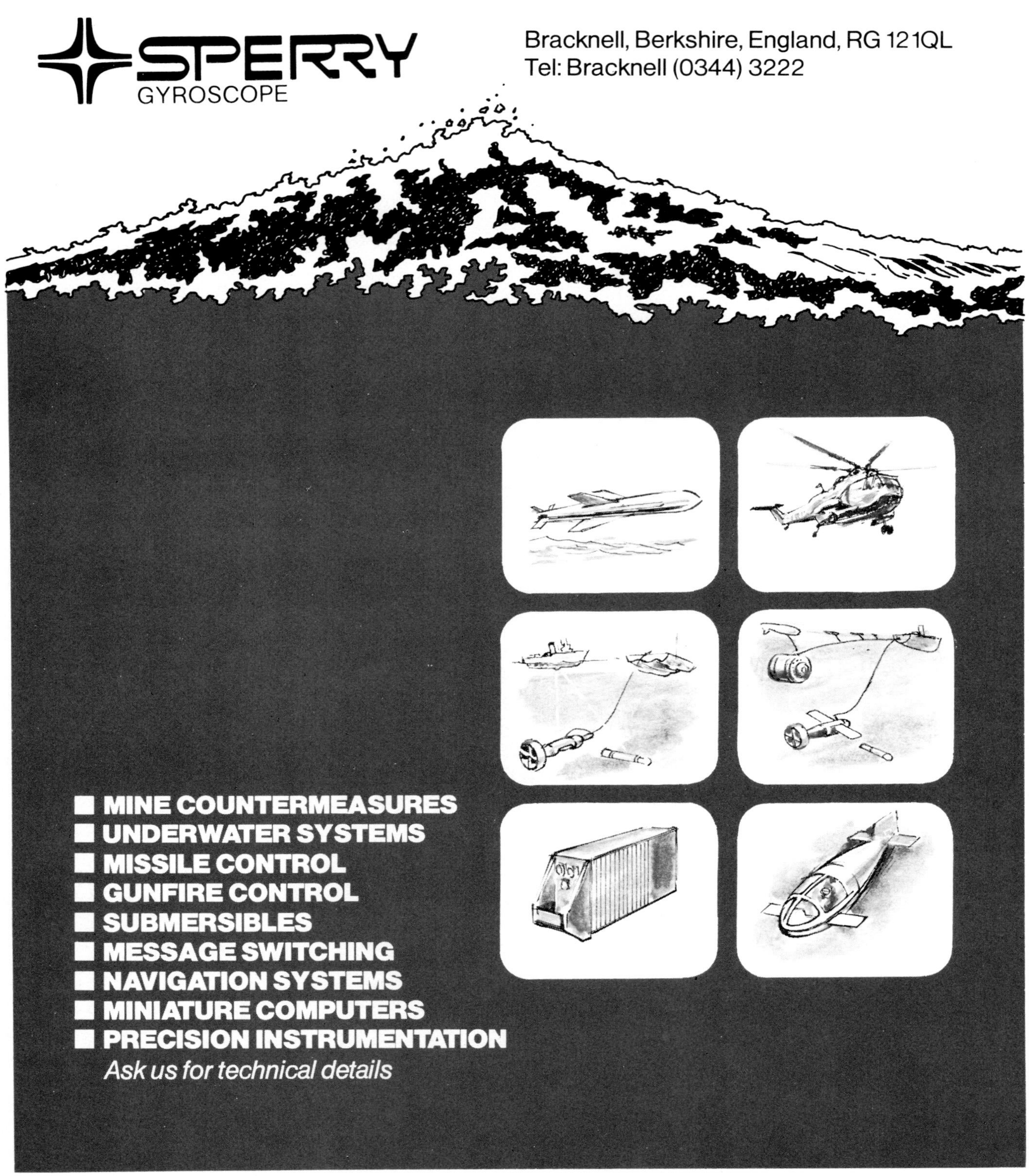
SPERRY
GYROSCOPE
■ MINE COUNTERMEASURES
■ UNDERWATER SYSTEMS
■ MISSILE CONTROL
■ GUNFIRE CONTROL
■ SUBMERSIBLES
■ MESSAGE SWITCHING
■ NAVIGATION SYSTEMS
■ MINIATURE COMPUTERS
■ PRECISION INSTRUMENTATION
Ask us for technical details

JANE'S FIGHTING SHIPS 1975-76

EDITED BY

CAPTAIN JOHN E. MOORE

The sections on United States of America, Philippines, South Korea, South Vietnam, and Taiwan were edited and compiled by:

NORMAN POLMAR

CONTENTS

FOREWORD

Amongst the hundreds of letters and reviews resulting from last year's edition there were a number critical of facts and format which have been most useful in the preparation of this book. Others, though, were critical of more abstract things, the approach and attitude taken in the previous Foreword. These ranged from out-and-out objections to war-mongering, through criticisms of the "political flavour" to complaints of "lack of objectivity" towards the Soviet cause. It is worthwhile to reflect on these statements because they incorporate a whole body of misapprehension.

In JANE'S FIGHTING SHIPS of 1905-06 the founder of this annual made a policy statement which has been a guide for all subsequent editors—"Sympathy with one side or the other is totally outside the scope of this book". This was referring to the Russo-Japanese war but the principle is as true today as it was seventy years ago. The aim of this book is to present a factual statement of the state of the world's navies which will be of assistance to all those concerned in any way with maritime affairs. Unfortunately, too many of these users are insufficiently versed in the many problems involved in naval operations and, too often, the compilation of a list of numbers is considered adequate for argument or debate. This approach totally fails to appreciate the true nature of sea-power which has been defined as "That strength in naval ships, associated aircraft and training which enables a country to promote the political and trading interests of itself and its allies in peacetime and their supremacy over the enemy in war." Like all definitions this can be argued about, but the basic elements are there—ships, aircraft, training, political and trading interests—and these are sufficient for a brief discussion of the background to the world's fleets, which is so necessary if the reasoning behind the formation of the major naval forces is to be understood.

The complaint of "war-mongering" ignores the historical fact that sea-power, of which fighting ships are the prime integral part, has been a major factor in maintaining peace for a very large proportion of the last 160 years. The enunciation of the Monroe Doctrine in 1823 warned external powers to keep out of the affairs of the American continents and the fact that it was, with only one major exception, honoured by those powers was due in very large part to the backing of British sea-power. The almost total suppression of piracy and slaving was due to the same cause, and the first renewed threat to world peace sprang from the German challenge to that force. The political motives of Kaiser Wilhelm required the defeat of the Royal Navy, and to this end huge expenditures were made on ships designed for this single purpose. It is here that the necessity for understanding the politics which lie behind the creation of navies becomes manifest. The complaint of "political flavour" ignores this vital fact—fleets are created as instruments of policy, whether that be a desire for world-domination, a requirement to protect trade against external interference or warlike moves, or a determination to protect one's own coasts against smugglers and illegal immigrants.

It is, therefore, very necessary to approach the question of policies, of nations' motives, with total objectivity and to make the differentiation between the creation of sea-power for the promotion of trading or political ends. Throughout this book each country has a notation of the size of its merchant navy extracted from Lloyd's annual statistical tables. This does not provide a true indication of the reliance of that country on trade, because some, such as Liberia with over 55 million tons, Panama with over 11 million tons and Cyprus with 3 million tons, are inflated by the addition of "flag of convenience" ships. Nor does the total stress the enormous reliance of some countries on seaborne trade. The USA, with a steadily rising overseas trade which now tops the $80 billion mark, relies heavily on foreign shipping because she ranks only fifth in merchant ship carrying capacity after Japan, the United Kingdom, Norway and Greece. At the same time the fact that the USSR is only marginally behind the USA in carrying capacity (deadweight tons) does not mean that the Soviets are equally dependent on foreign trade for survival. With national self-sufficiency in all but a few of the major raw materials, this fleet of ships is probably primarily intended as a means of earning foreign exchange. Thus there is once again the danger of reaching false conclusions from consideration of only the numbers of ships involved. It is those countries which are in the greatest need of foreign trade for their survival that have a requirement for the larger navies to ensure unhampered passage on the sea routes of the world. Such protection requires certain clearly defined types of ships and this requirement must be an equation combining range, sea-keeping and fighting ability as well as cost. High costs reduce numbers and in the trade-protection affair we have one of those occasions when numbers must be a primary consideration because of geographical separation. In 1939 Great Britain entered a major war with a legal allowance, agreed to and supported by her politicians, of 81 destroyers. The result of this absurdly meagre total meant not only that the convoys reaching her ports were inadequately protected but also that the strain on ships and their companies seriously reduced their efficiency. The first major Canadian troop convoy which sailed from Halifax to the United Kingdom was, except for the last few hundred miles, provided with one battleship as escort. Today the Royal Navy at 67 light cruisers, destroyers and frigates is well below the 81 of 1939 and faces a problem far more complex than that of thirty-six years ago.

The USSR today possesses a growing fleet of nuclear and conventional submarines, far more potent than the 57 patrol submarines which Germany could deploy in 1939. Are these intended as protectors of the Soviet merchant fleet which would not be required in the event of hostilities? If so they are extremely expensive vessels for the job. Now that the nuclear strike task has been assumed by the Polaris/Poseidon/Triton submarine fleet of the USA, France and Great Britain it can be argued that the Russian force is intended for the anti-SSBN role, but the numbers concerned must be a classic case of "over-kill". Although the detection of SSBNs is still a highly problematic task a commander can deploy only a certain number of submarines into a particular area of sea and the available Soviet numbers far exceed those needed to hunt a maximum of fifty SSBNs as well as the aircraft-carriers with a nuclear strike capability. Their total must, then, surely allow for a fairly high proportion tasked with anti-ship (either naval or mercantile) missions. This is an objective assessment based largely upon the fact that submarines of whatever class or type have little place in the simpler aspects of political presence. Their capabilities are not understood by less-educated peoples and they must be classified in the higher "threat" category. Submarines at today's prices are not generally provided for mercantile defence and must be placed in the upper bracket of political pressure—as a threat to mercantile shipping lanes.

We have now moved beyond the plain protection of mercantile interests into the realms of the use of navies as instruments of political power. Certain governments of Queen Victoria's era were prone to the use of "gunboat diplomacy"—a contagious disease which transmitted itself to the Germans, the citizens of the USA and other powers. Today it is still as potent a weapon as it was in the 19th Century although normally used with rather more delicacy than by our forefathers. The appearance of a grey ship which clearly possesses the capability to exert strong pressure on any opposition is as inhibiting to uprisings as it was a hundred years ago. But the ships of today are enormously more powerful than their predecessors, and it is this point which must be examined if we are to understand the world naval balance. The cruise missile has altered the naval equation beyond recognition. A small power possessed of fast attack craft with missiles now occupies a position where it can deny sea areas to the ships of far larger navies. The passage of straits and narrow waters is today most necessary for fleets which are intended for intervention or

support—their movements could be totally inhibited by high-speed, missile-armed craft bent on delaying or deterring their progress. Difficult targets themselves, these craft are possessed of a power of destruction hitherto unbelievable. No major naval power can believe itself invulnerable in the face of such a threat.

So we find a strange imbalance amongst the world's navies. The major nations may consider their power, their ability to deploy considerable forces to areas where they wish to exert pressure, as pre-eminent, but the number of localities where such a move could be unopposed is decreasing. The comparative cheapness and simplicity of the counter is making it available to many countries hitherto considered as non-starters in any naval race.

Yet there remain many areas where this ability for counter-offence remains non-existent and these are, frequently, where the major powers are at variance. If we are to accept the writings of Lenin concerning world-domination as current Soviet doctrine and if the various Doctrines of Truman, Eisenhower and Nixon are to be taken at face value then there must exist the possibility of conflict. Added to this danger must be the current attitude of so many minor political elements, the greed and self-seeking of so many leaders, the intolerance of many ruling parties and the almost total rejection by a large number of groups of the principle of "Reverence for Life." The whole adds up to a highly volatile situation in which many centres of conflict may be added to the hundred or so which now plague the globe. Intervention by air may be an immediate short-term remedy but this is made problematical by difficulties of ranges, over-flying rights and fuelling stops. Sea-power is the only sure and self-contained element which can be deployed by the politicians into an area of strife or incipient trouble.

The balance of power at sea is therefore of vital importance not only to the governments directing the major fleets but also to all those who would suffer if the mismanagement of affairs were to result in hostilities. In considering this vital item in the international equation it cannot be too strongly stressed that the habit of allocating "First Place" to any particular navy, of counting numbers, of comparing like with unlike, of adopting an "I'm King of the Castle" approach is as unrewarding and misleading as it is mischievous. The Royal Navy of 1939 had a majestic preponderance over that of Nazi Germany but nearly lost the war to the latter's submarines. Quality, training, experience and, in a world which appears to hate the term, tradition are frequently of more importance than numbers. The Germans had a submarine force in 1939 which had all these advantages, which was opposed by inadequate numbers of escorts and very nearly brought off a dazzling success. All aspects must be considered before a final balance is struck and this is frequently wrong. Firm predictions can never be made—a quirk of weather, a minor error in navigation can well tip the balance.

In considering this balance it is sensible to begin with the two "super-power" navies—the USN and the Soviet fleet. To the question "Which is Number One?" there is no answer and to show this in its clearest light it is best to compare their strength and capabilities. Admiral Gorshkov is clearly reasonably satisfied with the progress of the Soviet navy. He sees it as a striking force with a world-wide mission in support of his country's policies. In contrast to this situation the following statement by Admiral Zumwalt, CNO of the USN until July 1974, is of interest: "In 1970, when I first became CNO, it was my judgement that we had just slightly better than an even chance . . . . . . of winning a sea-control war at that time with the Soviets . . . . . . In the years since 1970 our chances for success have diminished." The decline in numbers must have influenced this comment—no matter how good a ship, it can be in only one place at a time. In 1975 less than 500 ships (including fleet oilers and ocean tugs) are in the list of the USN, compared with 508 at this time last year, 976 at the peak of the Vietnam war, about 900 in 1964 and some 500 in 1939.

Aircraft-carriers are the main force of the USN surface-fleet today. The total of fourteen in commission with another in reserve outnumbers the whole of the rest of the world's navies and, in addition, these ships possess a far greater potential. The two nuclear-propelled carriers *Nimitz* and *Enterprise* are unique, providing almost unlimited cruising range and a much augmented aircraft strength. There is no way in which these ships can be compared with the far smaller Soviet carriers of the "Kuril" class of which the first, *Kiev*, is expected in commission later in 1975. Of some 35,000 tons their air-wing is unlikely to consist of more than helicopters and VTOL aircraft, valuable in an intervention situation only if operating in a friendly or neutral air environment. In support of them are still the eight-year-old helicopter cruisers of the "Moskva" class comparable only to the Sea-Control Ships of the USN which were last year deleted from the American programme by a decision of Congress. There is certainly a place in the US Fleet for such a vessel, although it may well have to be a larger and faster class, such as the British "Invincible", and provided with a larger helicopter complement.

Other major surface ships present a marked contrast between the design-thinking of the two largest navies. In 1975, as well as commissioning *Nimitz*, the USN will complete *Spruance* (DD963), *Tarawa* (the first new assault ship LHA1) and *Pegasus* (hydrofoil missile craft PHM 1) and will be carrying out trials of equipment for the guided missile frigates of the "Oliver Hazard Perry" class. In comparison, the Soviet Navy, in addition to *Kiev*, will complete additional "Kara" and "Kresta II" class cruisers, "Krivak" class destroyers and "Grisha" and "Nanuchka" class corvettes. New "Sonya" class minesweepers and "Turya" class hydrofoils are also in the building yard while much is being done to advance the construction of air-cushion vehicles and fleet-support ships.

In the submarine world there appears to be no abatement of the Soviet building programme. The run of "Delta" and "Delta II" submarines could mean a dozen of these huge craft in commission by the end of the year, capable of launching their 4,200 mile SSN-8 missiles to any part of the USA, and a large area of China, without leaving the safety of the Barents Sea. Well beyond the detection limits of either sea-borne or bottom-moored surveillance systems, these submarines have introduced a new factor into nuclear deterrence at least seven years before the first of the US "Trident" class (at $800 million by today's costs) is due for completion. Whether smaller Ballistic Missile Submarines will be designed for the USN is still a matter for discussion, as is the replacement programme for the Fleet Submarines (SSNs). The first of the new "Los Angeles" class (SSN 688), a huge vessel of some 7,000 tons, is another 1975 commissioning.

The remainder of the Soviet programme is much as before with extra "Charlie" and "Victor" submarines being joined by the first of the new "Uniform.' class, possibly an enlarged "Victor" although still smaller than "Los Angeles".

For those with a passion for numbers and in order to avoid misunderstanding and misquotation the following table sets out a comparison of the major ships of the two navies, ignoring the very substantial amphibious forces of the USN and more than 150 missile-armed corvettes and fast attack craft of the USSR. The figures give the active ships, with ships in reserve or building in brackets.

	USN	*Soviet Navy*
Attack-Carriers	14 (+4)	0
A/S Carriers	(4)	3 (+1)
Cruisers	27 (+12)	33 (+3)
Destroyers	105 (+31)	106 (+2)
Frigates	65 (+10)	109
Ballistic Missile Submarines—Nuclear (SSBN)	41 (+3)	49 (+15)
Ballistic Missile Submarines—Diesel (SSB)	0	23
Cruise Missile Submarines—Nuclear (SSGN)	0	40 (+2)
Cruise Missile Submarines—Diesel (SSG)	0	28
Nuclear-propelled Fleet Submarines (SSN)	64 (+25)	31 (+2)
Diesel Submarines (SS)	12 (+3)	140 (+77)

An examination of what this table does not show may help in understanding the dangers of using numbers only as a reference base. It does not show that:

(a) Some of the Soviet building figures are tentative forecasts.

(b) Four of the US attack carriers will be nuclear propelled.

(c) Twenty of the Soviet cruisers and ten of her destroyers are armed with surface-to-surface missiles which will not enter fleet service in the USN until 1976.

(d) The smaller number of US Frigates are much larger and more valuable vessels than the 109 Soviet ships.

(e) The short ballistic missile range of the Soviet SSBs makes them more vulnerable to A/S measures.

(f) A large number of the Soviet SS are in reserve and becoming due for deletion.

(g) The US SSNs are, on the whole, quieter than the Soviet boats, although the latter are improving in this respect.

Those are some of the material considerations. What is also important is the planned future construction. The USN naval staff estimates that a total of 600 active ships will be required to meet the tasks of the 1980s, needing a building programme of 34 per year. The proposed Fiscal Year 1976 budget allows for 23, part of a proposed Department of Defence Estimate 15 per cent below the pre-Vietnam War level in real money, which also has its hardware vote reduced by rising costs. While expenditure on manpower, which accounts for more than half the defence budget, is rising steadily, inflation may well double the price of a ship in four years. Compared with these problems in Washington the Soviet high command is not afflicted with inflationary problems of the same magnitude. With a similar manpower total of about half-a-million she has a much smaller bill to meet, with over 70 per cent of her number being comparatively low-paid conscripts, as opposed to the all-volunteer force of the USN where pay has to be in competition with civilian rates. For these, amongst other reasons, the USSR has spent 50 per cent more than the USA on naval shipbuilding in the last ten years and is currently expending one third more than the USA for this purpose.

The value of a fleet cannot be measured only by its order-of-battle, and a comparison between the two superpower navies is valueless without consideration of the men and women who man them. The fully voluntary USN is receiving a high quality of officers and enlisted personnel. First term re-enlistments are running at a record level, a particularly important element in manning highly complex ships. While this situation may be due in part to unemployment problems in the USA it does ensure that the fleet is efficiently and adequately manned by highly professional ships' companies, backed by recent combat experience, long periods at sea and a fighting tradition of great quality. Sea-time is certainly being reduced due to the fuel situation but there can be little doubt of the ability of the USN.

The Soviet fleet must remain something of an enigma in this direction. The officers receive a high-level technical training which, by Western standards, is somewhat confined. However, there remains a need for technical ability in a navy which has a deficiency in senior ratings and an enormous training problem for the juniors. With an intake of some 50-60,000 eighteen-year-old conscripts each spring and autumn, men who will, if drafted to sea, serve a three-year period, it would be extraordinary if a considerable weight of responsibility were not thrown on their seniors. Soviet equipment is tough and, presumably, reasonably "sailor-proof", but little is seen of actual firings to show the efficiency of weapons. Propulsion machinery appears to give good service and standards of ship-handling and manoeuvring have improved over the years. In some cases, though, there is still a "could do better" tag. Their submarines probably claim the cream of both officers and ratings and this, plus the fact that the captains of the larger boats are senior to those in similar Western appointments, has resulted in a marked improvement in their handling over the last fifteen years.

The recent Russian naval exercise Okean 1975 has shown the world how far, in fact, the Soviet navy has advanced in the fifteen years since the fleet began its imposing programme of home-designed ships. Operations involving over 220 ships and submarines were conducted by three main groups, including a convoy serial, in the North Atlantic, a cruiser group in the Western Mediterranean, "in-house" squadrons in the Black Sea towards the Turkish Straits area, a force in the Arabian Sea and four groups in the Western Pacific. Support by naval strike and reconnaissance aircraft took place in the North Atlantic and Pacific from bases in the USSR, in the Central Atlantic by Bear aircraft based in Cuba and Guinea and in the Indian Ocean by planes from Somalia and the USSR. With Admiral Gorshkov and Marshal Grechko embarked for a period this was a sign to both the Western World and the Politburo that here was a major, self-contained navy with excellent communications and friendly havens in foreign countries.

The future of the two rival navies may be as different as their current composition. In the monolithic dictatorship of the USSR, with the people having no say in their country's policies, it would need an almost cataclysmic change as the ageing leaders are displaced for there to be any alteration in programmes. On the other hand the people of the USA are now faced with international variations which must affect the whole of their military strategy. The Communist victories in South Vietnam, Laos and Cambodia, doubt about bases in Thailand and the Philippines, and major alterations actual or possible in the make-up of NATO require new plans and fresh initiatives. Coupled with a domestic situation of some fragility and the very vocal, and sometimes downright dishonest, efforts of a number of influential people who see their mission in life as the emasculation of America's defences, this all adds up to a problem which will need an informed and objective approach for its successful solution.

The remainder of the world's navies can best be considered in the areas in which they operate, the only two which have any major overseas commitments being those of France and the United Kingdom. The first of these is moving steadily towards a position at the head of the Western European fleets. Two new construction projects in this edition illustrate the imaginative approach which is achieving this status.

The nuclear-propelled helicopter carrier, PH 75, due for trials in 1979, is of great interest. With a tonnage of 18,400 (full load) she has been designed to carry 25 Lynx or 10 Super Frelon helicopters with the embarkation of VTOL aircraft as a possibility. As well as the main nuclear propelled machinery she will have emergency diesels but it is in her internal arrangements that she shows a departure from more usual designs. Realising the tremendous value of a ship of this size in times of natural disaster, the constructors have allowed for three main hospital wards, an infectious diseases ward, an X-ray ward and an intensive-care unit as well as providing spaces which can be turned into accommodation for 1,500 passengers. All this has been achieved without diminishing the fighting qualities of the ship, an example which might well be followed by other navies in their re-equipment programmes.

The French submarine service now has six SSBNs built or building, a sensible number to ensure that mishaps or damage do not disrupt the patrol pattern. These are boats which follow similar patterns to those in other navies—the startling difference comes in the details of the first French SSN, SNA 72. In this case, as the sizes of this type are increasing in other fleets, the proposed tonnage is 2,500 which, for a single screw boat with possibly four torpedo tubes and twenty reloads and a speed of 25 knots, will be a remarkable achievement.

The surface ships of the French Navy are, in many cases, receiving missiles and this includes a new class, the "Trident" fast attack craft. The 1,170 ton A69 and A70 frigates are now entering service, fourteen in the original order and probably a larger number in the future. These will provide the general purpose backing for a fleet which will eventually include twenty-four of the "Georges Leygues" class 4,100-ton missile- and helicopter-armed destroyers.

The deployment of the French navy is of considerable interest. The plan to move both the aircraft carriers to the Mediterranean and the decision to have eventually one

squadron of SSNs in the Mediterranean and one in the Atlantic will reinforce this as a two-ocean navy. With a permanent squadron in the Indian Ocean and requests for base facilities at Mauritius it is clear that the French intend to discharge their defence responsibilities as a major world power.

The approach taken by the neighbouring government of Great Britain is different. Harassed by the ever-growing problems of inflation, the increasing disruption of labour relations and production, the expenditure of vast sums on the nationalisation of industry, and the pressure for unilateral disarmament from within its own party, it has been forced into major reductions in defence spending. The main bulk of these were contained in the March 1975 Defence Review, with a further and unheralded chop in the Budget which followed soon after. The effects on the Royal Navy have been far-reaching. With its one remaining aircraft-carrier due for disposal in the near future the helicopter-carriers of the Amphibious Forces have taken a knock. One is for disposal in the next year, the second is to have a primary role in the A/S sphere. A number of other ships and submarines are to be disposed of early and cuts have been made in the building programmes. Allied with a reduction in the number of Nimrod A/S aircraft this will result in a diminution of the navy's capability to deal with a submarine threat.

This reduction in A/S and amphibious capacity prompts a number of questions which are of general application. The primary aim of the NATO navies is deterrence, both in the major strategical sphere and in the equally important one of preventing piratical acts and harassment at sea which could result in an increase of tension leading eventually to the open conflict which all sane men and women seek to avoid. The current problem is the existence of an ever-growing Soviet navy which has outrun the legitimate requirements of national defence and has no logical merchant-defence role in time of war. Until the adherents of unilateral disarmament can persuade the Soviets that they should reduce their massive armaments to the level of necessity, the NATO nations must abide by the lesson of history—unnecessarily large forces are intended for aggressive action.

If deterrence at sea is to be successful new approaches must be made to overcome present problems. In the anti-submarine war the emphasis on active sonar presents a valuable target for the submarine. The size of the latter is generally increasing, making it more difficult to handle at periscope depth. As a result greater reliance has to be placed on acoustic detection, and here, from the submarine's standpoint, the ever more powerful active sonars in the surface ships play a valuable part. Total reliance on passive operations could, in the long run, be defeated by total silencing and so some active capability must be retained, but this success is still well in the future. In the underwater affair it must also be remembered that the increasing size of nuclear boats renders them less and less capable of operating within the Continental Shelf—100 fathoms, 200 metres, however you measure it. Here there is surely an argument for the retention of the diesel-propelled patrol submarine, the only system which today can be carried in a small hull.

The need for embarked aircraft, both fixed-wing and rotary, is proved in exercise after exercise. The continuation of the A/S cruiser programme in the Royal Navy is one method of achieving this, particularly since the decision to provide a force of twenty-five naval Harrier aircraft was at last announced on 15 May 1975. Tankers and supply-ships provide the necessary deck-area for such a task and if amphibious forces were provided with high-speed transports built to modern merchant navy specifications these too would provide additional platforms.

In the surface-ship categories of destroyers and frigates there is a need for very long range plus the ability to move at high speed when required. Diesel propulsion provides the first and gas-turbines the second—there appears to be no valid reason why these two methods should not be combined. A 2,500-ton ship of reasonable length, scantlings and block coefficient should be capable of 37 knots on 70,000 hp—not beyond the range of modern gas-turbine capabilities. The value of such a ship in defence of a force being trailed could be considerable.

The French emphasis on the A69 and A70 avisos brings the next query. What is to be the general purpose ship of the future?—the ship for the day-to-day tasks. This has been the Holy Grail sought by naval planners for many years, a design combining good sea-going qualities, adequate sensors and communications without undue complexity, a gun and a helicopter. Once again the joint diesel/gas-turbine propulsion could provide speed, acceleration and long range, while reductions in man-power, missiles and costly equipment would balance the expenses.

This is not the type of ship chosen by the Royal Navy for the North Sea patrols necessitated by the isolation of oil-rigs and possible future fishery protection problems. This gap is to be filled by a class of advanced trawler-design with 16 knots and a helicopter pad. Many ask if this is sufficient and urge more advanced ships (which would be a great deal more costly) without considering that the protection of off-shore oil is primarily a matter of command and control in order to ensure the correct employment of all resources. But it is strange that these new ships cannot be designed to carry a light helicopter such as is borne on a number of similar civilian vessels. Speed of reaction and long-range reconnaissance would both be greatly enhanced by this comparatively inexpensive addition.

In sum the Royal Navy is by no means on its beam-ends, but even with the present high morale and professional efficiency of those manning the fleet it would be desperately stretched in the event of a crisis. For the tasks which would result from a two-nation confrontation the Holy Grail could well be the answer. If the matter were more widespread and NATO became involved it would be incumbent upon the British to provide naval support in proportion to their reliance upon the sea. "Look to your moat" may have become a catch-phrase but it is far more realistic than complex juggling with percentages of GNP and bitter comments about other partners.

The remaining Atlantic members of European NATO are busily employed in building programmes which, in the North, are mainly concentrated on fast attack craft armed with missiles. In addition Norway and Federal Germany are well-stocked with small submarines, suitable for inshore waters. Both Belgium and the Netherlands have produced frigate programmes which will be of considerable assistance in policing the shallow waters in their vicinity, although the latter is aiming at two ASW groups assigned to CINEASTLANT by the 1980s.

In the Mediterranean Spain has been smitten by financial problems but, after imposing reductions, is still left with a building programme of a helicopter carrier, thirteen (or possibly fifteen) frigates, two submarines and twelve large patrol craft. Problems too for Italy, where a larger building programme is again blocked by financial stringency. Her neighbour Yugoslavia is forging ahead with new submarines and new missile craft. Further south, Greece, having opted out of the military affairs of NATO and cancelled the agreement for home-porting USN ships in her waters, is continuing to build up her Light Forces, a much needed supplement for surveillance and operations in the Aegean.

In the Black Sea a not unexpected reinforcement for the Romanian navy has come in the form of Chinese-designed "Shanghai" fast attack craft and "Hu Chwan" hydrofoils. These are presumed to be locally built and a further increase in numbers would not be any surprise. This new departure must be of interest to Turkey whose current construction is centred on missile craft and submarines.

Light Forces are the theme, too, in Syria with a strengthening of her "Osa" and "Komar" forces, while Israel is increasing the building rate of the "Dabur" class as well as that of the excellent "Reshef" class. These latter proved themselves both magnificent sea-boats and thoroughly dependable craft when they made the passage from Haifa to Eilat, on the Gulf of Aquaba, via the Mediterranean and Cape of Good Hope. There are few vessels of their size which could have accomplished this passage with such efficiency.

Light forces are on order for both Libya and Morocco which, combined with those of Egypt, complete a formidable

array of home-based navies around the Mediterranean in addition to the forces of the USN and Soviet Navy.

The greatest change of balance since last year is to be noticed in the Indian Ocean. With South Africa, aware of the inadvisability of trusting other countries contracts, preparing to build her own frigates at Durban, India showing a continued impartiality in adding ships of both Western and Russian design to her fleet, and Pakistan taking Western and Chinese ships on her list, these areas seemed to be the main focus of attention. The presence of the Soviet squadron in the Arabian Sea and the establishment of a Russian base at Berbera lent further interest. Today, however, the focus of naval power may well be shifting to the Persian Gulf. Here the general mood is probably epitomised by the accord recently reached between those long-term antagonists, Iran and Iraq, and their stated mutual desire to keep other powers away from their maritime borders. In each edition the number of Gulf countries listed increases—now it includes Iraq, Kuwait, Saudi-Arabia, Bahrain, Qatar, Abu Dhabi, Dubai, Ras Al Khaima, Oman and, with the largest programme of all, Iran. Small some of these forces may be, but so, too, in the past were those of Saudi-Arabia and Iran. The wealth is there and, apparently, the determination. This has received the strongest practical demonstration from the Shah with his order of six "Spruance" class destroyers and four PF frigates from the USA, twelve fast attack missile craft from France and a £450 million order for submarines which, had it not been for government dilatoriness and prevarication, would now have been placed in Great Britain. The Saudis, meanwhile, are reported to be negotiating the purchase of twenty-six ships from America. The message is clear enough—with their own growing number of tankers, new docks such as the 300,000-ton construction in Bahrain, new oil installations and a standard of living rising at an unprecedented rate, the rulers of the Gulf States intend to rule their own sea areas.

In the Far East, the missile craft of Singapore and Malaysia guard the northern entrance from the West, while the Indonesian navy, doing all in its power to modernise its order-of-battle, guards the southern straits. What the outcome of the victories of the autonomous and independent Communists in Cambodia, Vietnam and Laos will be it is far too early to suggest in any depth. What does seem fairly clear is that it is most unlikely that these countries will automatically afford staging posts for the Soviet fleet.

To the North, Chinese policies appear to be reflected in their fleet. Last year a building programme of large destroyers and new frigates was assumed to be an indication of a plan to move outwards, to follow up Chinese forays into Africa and the Arabian Peninsula. This year there is clear evidence of a considerable reduction in the building rate for these ships. Allowing for a normal lead time, their designs were probably drawn up during the period when Lin Pao was Minister of Defence and Mao Tsetung's nominated successor. The reason that his death in 1971 was welcomed in China was that he was credited with personal and imperialist ambitions. If this is true his programme for the fleet might well have been intended for overseas adventures and with his departure the need no longer existed. The fact that the submarine building schedule has been stepped up and the reinforcement of the largest fleet of fast attack craft in the world has been sustained goes some distance towards supporting the Chinese claim that theirs is a defensive navy.

China's neighbours in the Korean peninsula present a troubled picture. The navy of North Korea as given in this edition is of a much greater size than previously reported—extra submarines, more attack craft, of which the majority are now locally built, and various amphibious and support forces now make up an impressive fleet. That of South Korea is also no mean navy with seven destroyers and three frigates leading the list. At a time when internal dissension in the South is allied with continual minor conflicts on the border with the North, and the situation uncertain when US troops are withdrawn, the state of these two navies might well be of considerable importance.

The Japanese Maritime Self Defence Force continues to expand, though at a rate reduced by the impact of inflation. The second of the very useful "Haruna" class was completed in November and the third is still in the "projected" list. On 4,700 tons they carry three A/S helicopters and an Asroc, as well as two 5 inch guns and six torpedoe tubes. In combination with the "Tachikaze" class armed with Standard RIM 60A missiles as well as guns, Asroc and A/S tubes these ships will form the nucleus of a valuable force.

In the Antipodes of the Western Pacific the Royal Australian Navy has suffered severe cuts in its planned new construction programme. With the cancellation of the whole DDL programme a decision has been made by the government to order two PF frigates from the USA, with a proviso that further proposals would be needed later for additional destroyers of a type yet to be determined. With the "Darings" coming nearer to their twenty years and the four more elderly members of the "River" class more than halfway through their lives this is a decision which cannot long be delayed. The present strength of five destroyers and six frigates allows little flexibility in the event of more than one crisis area around the vast Australian coast and certainly insufficient to allow for any further deployments. New Zealand, too, has little reserve to call upon, and unless some future increase in forces takes place, must be content with a minimal mercantile-protection force and a capacity for harbour defence of her major ports, all of which are vulnerable to covert minelaying operations.

The Eastern Pacific, apart from providing the bases for an important proportion of the USN, contains the second Canadian base at Esquimalt. The Maritime Force based here is part of a navy which has considerable commitments to NATO in the Atlantic and, with a comparatively small force of 4 DDHs, 16 frigates and 3 submarines, would be hard-pressed should there be any pressure applied in the Pacific.

The various South American navies have all been making steady progress in re-equipment. While a number retain elderly ex-US destroyers, frigates and submarines there has been a notable reinforcement. New submarines have been ordered by or delivered to Ecuador, Peru, Chile, Argentina, Brazil and Venezuela, two British Type 42 destroyers for Argentina, six "Niteroi" class from Vosper Thornycroft for Brazil, two British "Leander" class for Chile, four Italian "modified Lupo" class for Peru as well as a number of light forces for Venezuela and other countries. All these will presumably have a home-defence role but one looks in vain for any sign of a major increase in those most necessary adjuncts for such a task—the long range maritime patrol aircraft. Argentina and Brazil both have one aircraft-carrier but have apparently ignored the fact that their huge coastlines provide ample scope for the deployment of these very valuable aeroplanes. It is reported that Brazil has given some thought to this reinforcement but, apparently, so far without results.

The last geographical area to be looked at is the Caribbean where a whole batch of small coastguard services are coming into operation. To the West the major navy is that of Mexico whose ability to sustain patrols off her own coast is being enhanced by the acquisition of twenty-one "Azteca" class patrol craft built in Britain, with a possible follow-up order to come. In central position is the Cuban navy which, although not recently reinforced, has a powerful force of twenty-three Soviet-built missile craft and a considerable number of corvettes and torpedo craft from the same source. Although the USA is now making suggestions for the relaxation of the long-standing embargo on trade with the island, it is unlikely that the visits by the Soviet Navy and the use of its facilities by Bear aircraft of the Soviet Naval Air Force will therefore cease. They may even increase, an indication of the strategic importance of Cuba in the Western Hemisphere.

This may seem a lengthy foreword but when dealing with over 120 navies and more than 15,000 ships, and at the same time seeking to explain the relevance of sea-power in the daily lives of the world's inhabitants, brevity is difficult to achieve. What of the future? There seems little likelihood of a major change in the pattern over the next twelve months, although the increasing number of submarines and fast attack craft with missiles in the smaller navies will undoubtedly have an impact on naval thought. So too

Able bodied valve

Cockburns butterfly valves are well proved at sea. Reliable, efficient, hard working.

The famous MSJ series of resilient lined wafer-type valves are to be found hard at work in ships all over the world, paying their way by reducing laid-up and maintenance time.

Equally at home on sea going or shipside duty, handling gas, liquids or free flowing solids Cockburns valves faithfully and efficiently work under the most demanding conditions.

The MSJ general purpose wafer type butterfly valve gives a sealed shut-off under pressures of up to 200 psig (with a temperature of 212°F) and under vacuum conditions. Designed for control of media in pipelines between 50mm and 895mm (larger and special sizes are made to order).

For a fast off-the-shelf service, Cockburns have introduced the 210 series of Resilient Seated Wafer butterfly valves—in a range of 50mm to 250mm.

For full advice on applications of butterfly valves call in a Cockburns' professional.

The most reliable butterfly valve in the world.

Cockburns Butterfly Valves

Cockburns Limited, Cardonald, Glasgow G52 2EB
Telephone: 041-883 6193 Telex: 77-471

*A member of the Lake & Elliot **Fluid Control** Division.*

For details of Cockburns range of butterfly valves complete and post this coupon.

Name ....
Position ....
Company ....
Address ....
....
Tel. No. ....
Application JF1

will the problem of the world's oil supplies. No more has been heard of the use of liquefied coal but some method of economising on fuel consumption will have to be found. Research into the use of hydro-jets instead of the traditional screw propeller might yield dividends, further investigation of the fuel cell may produce economical results.

The improvement of hull form and the employment of catamaran types could assist in higher speeds for similar power and the embarkation of more helicopters on an equivalent displacement. All these things are possible and only with imaginative research will the navies of the world be able to maintain the strength required for their traditional roles. The possibility of conflict remains ever present while political systems remain in opposition. Sea-power has the ability to restrain or localise such outbreaks.

John E. Moore

ACKNOWLEDGEMENTS

This, my third edition, has been greatly assisted by the comments and facts sent to me by hundreds of correspondents and to all of them I offer my unstinted thanks. As usual it is extremely difficult to single out a small number without missing others whose contributions have been of very great value. But the following have once again provided me with so much support in both facts and photographs that it would be churlish not to mention them separately: Contre Amiral M. J. Adam CVO, CBE, Dr. Giorgio Arra, Herr Siegfried Breyer, Commander A. Fraccaroli, Lieutenant-Commander A. Hague VRD, Mr. G. K. Jacobs, Captain F. de Blocq van Kuffeler, M. Henri le Masson, Mr. S. L. Morison, Mr. J. S. Rowe, Mr. C. W. E. Richardson, Lieutenant Toshio Tamura, Senor J. Taibo, Mr. R. F. Winfield.

The Ministries of the majority of countries approached have responded in a most helpful manner and I am most grateful to them and to their attachés in London for all their help.

To everybody who is prepared to help may I make one plea? Information, no matter how valuable and important, is of little use if it arrives too late for inclusion. If the majority of data and photographs reach me by late November it is possible to meet the publisher's very tight deadlines. This year delays in major inputs have seriously prejudiced the publication date and such problems, involving alterations to galleys and proofs, cause additional expenses at a time when book-production is becoming more and more costly.

The editorial team has been unchanged, with my wife's encouragement and research being, as ever, of the greatest value while Mrs. Jean Parsons has done her best to ensure that correspondence is dealt with as swiftly as possible. It is not her fault if answers have been delayed, the responsibility is all mine.

The publishers have maintained a benign but firm hold on the book's production and their Production Manager, Ken Harris, has achieved much to my advantage. Mrs. Barbara Hessler and the team of girls at Paulton House have done great things in interpretation of my copy, and corrections and last-minute miracles have been wrought by the men of Netherwood Dalton and Co. Ltd., the printers. Finally, my thanks to Jane's editorial team who assisted greatly in the preparation of this years' edition.

The sections on South Korea, the Philippines, Taiwan, the United States and South Vietnam have, for the eighth consecutive year, been the responsibility of Mr. Norman Polmar. For this I am most grateful and for the American background which he provided for the Foreword.

To the editors of the other naval annuals I give my thanks for the part they have played; *Almanacco Navale* edited by Dr. Giorgio Giorgerini and Signor Augusto Nani, *Flottentaschenbuch* edited by Herr Gerhard Albrecht, *Flottes de Combat* edited by M. J. Labayle-Couhat and M. Henri le Masson and *Marinkalender* edited by Captain Allan Kull.

Mr. Norman Polmar, the editor and compiler of the United States sections is particularly in debt to the following individuals for assistance in the preparation of this edition: Vice-Admiral William D. Houser, Captain C. R. Smith, and Captain Gerald H. Barkalow of the Office of the Deputy Chief of Naval Operations (Air Warfare); Captain Don Walsh, Deputy Director of Naval Laboratories; Lieutenant Commander Wes Boer II, Mr. Robert Carlisle, and Miss Anna Urban of the Office of Navy Information; Mr. Richard C. Bassett and Mrs. Eleanor Prentiss of the Naval Sea Systems Command; Mr. H. A. Taylor of the Bureau of Naval Personnel; Captain Adrian Lonsdale and Miss Elizabeth Segedi of the Public Information Division, US Coast Guard; Mr. Raymond Wilcove of the National Oceanic and Atmospheric Administration; Mr. Larry C. Manning and Mr. Russ Egnor of the Military Sealift Command; Commander Ronald Black and Lieutenant Richard Merki of the Information Directorate of the Department of Defense; and especially to Messrs Samuel L. Morison, A. D. Baker III, Stefan Terzibaschitsch, and Giorgio Arra.

Contributions for the United States, South Korean, Philippine and Taiwan sections should be addressed to:

Mr. Norman Polmar,
400 Skyline Center,
5205 Leesburg Pike,
Falls Church, Virginia
22041, USA.

Contributions for the next edition, which is already in preparation, should be sent as soon as possible to:

Captain J. E. Moore, RN,
Editor, Jane's Fighting Ships
Elmhurst,
Rickney,
Hailsham,
Sussex BN27 1SF,
England.

CLASSIFICATION

In an effort to standardise the type designations in the various navies, despite somewhat idiosyncratic listing in some fleets, a regular formula has been used wherever possible in the majority of sections. This has caused some queries and comments, therefore a list is given below.

TYPE DESIGNATIONS

Aircraft Carriers

Attack Carriers (Large)	Over 50,000 tons (all US ships)
Attack Carriers (Medium and Light)	*Essex*, *Ark Royal*, 2 French *et al*
Helicopter Carriers/ Cruisers	*Kiev* and *Moskva*

Major Surface Ships

A/S Cruisers	"Invincible" class
Cruisers	Pre 1960 cruisers, including missile conversions
Light Cruisers	Above 5,000 tons
Destroyers	3,000 tons and over, plus original conventional destroyers
Frigates	1,100 to 3,000 tons
Corvettes	500 to 1,100 tons

Light Forces

Fast Attack Craft	FAC (Missile)
25 and above 25 knots	FAC (Gun)
	FAC (Torpedo)
	FAC (Patrol)

Patrol Craft	Large Patrol Craft (100 to 500 tons)
Below 25 knots	Coastal Patrol Craft (below 100 tons)

Submarines

Strategic Missile	(Nuclear propelled and conventionally propelled)
Fleet Submarines	(Nuclear propelled)
Patrol Submarines	(Conventionally propelled)

Amphibious Forces

Command Ships
Assault Ships
Landing Ships
Landing Craft
Transports

Mine Warfare Forces

Mine Layers
MCM Support Ships
Mine Sweepers (Ocean)
Mine Hunters
Mine Sweepers (Coastal)
Mine Sweepers (Inshore)
Mine Sweeping Boats

Surveying Vessels

Surveying Ships
Coastal Surveying Craft
Inshore Surveying Craft

SUMMARY OF MAJOR NAVAL PROGRAMMES

ABU DHABI
There have been additions of 6 140-ton Vosper Thornycroft large patrol craft and 5 Fairey Marine "Spear" class.

ALBANIA
Thirty "Hu Chwan" class hydrofoils are in service.

ARGENTINA
The first Type 42 destroyer will be completed by Vickers in 1975. Two new Type 209 submarines, *Sata* and *San Luis*, have been commissioned, and two German Type 148 fast attack missile craft, mounting Gabriel, are being built. Two "Combattante 11" fast attack gun craft have been commissioned. A new survey ship *Comodoro Rivadavia*, has been commissioned and two more are being built.

AUSTRALIA
An order has been placed in the USA for two Patrol Frigates. Three DDGs are to be modernised, and more destroyers may be ordered later. The Papua New Guinea Defence Force was founded, and has a fleet of five patrol boats and two LCHs.

BANGLADESH
Two large patrol craft have been received from India.

BELGIUM
Four "E-71" class frigates have been laid down.

BRAZIL
Three more "Niteroi" class destroyers have been launched, and the second "Oberon" class submarine, the *Tonelero*, has been completed. There have also been additions of two new MSC and two new river patrol ships.

BRUNEI
Three new "Perwira" class (71-feet) patrol craft have been completed.

CANADA
Four frigates and one submarine were paid off for subsequent disposal.

CHILE
The two "Leander" class frigates arrived in home waters.

CHINA
The building programme for both "Luta" class DDGs and "Kiangtung" frigates has been reduced. Meanwhile the building rate of "Romeo" class submarines has been increased to six a year. The construction programme of fast attack missile craft is being continued, while some of the older craft of Light Forces have been paid off.

COLOMBIA
Two Type 209 submarines will be completed in 1975.

CUBA
Three additional "Osa" class vessels are in service.

DENMARK
The completion of a new frigate is expected in September, 1975.

ECUADOR
Two Type 209 submarines have been ordered, (see addenda), there are also plans for three fast attack missile craft.

EGYPT
The appearance of rocket launchers in "P6" class and smaller craft should be noted, as well as the emergence of swimmer delivery vehicles.

FINLAND
Four "Osa" class fast attack missiles craft have been ordered from the USSR, and a class of six MSIs with GRP hulls has been completed.

FRANCE
Particulars have been released of the new PH 75 nuclear-propelled helicopter-carrier, and the first "Georges Leygues" class destroyer has been laid down. The second and third "Tourville" class has undergone trials and two destroyers, two frigates and one submarine have been deleted. The fourth SSBN started trials in January, 1975, and the first Type A69 frigate is due for trials in October, 1975. January 1976 is the date for the first SSN to be laid down, the tonnage will be 2,500. The trials of the first "Agosta" class submarine took place on 9th November, 1974. The first of the "Trident" class fast attack missile craft will begin trials on 1st October, 1975. The replenishment tanker, *La Charente*, has been converted for service as an Indian Ocean flagship.

GERMANY (FDR)
Ten fast attack hydrofoil craft (missile), Type 162, were ordered from Boeing of Seattle in April, 1974, and the first trials of the Type 143 took place in February, 1975.

GREECE
Four new "Combattante III" class, and two 32-metre patrol craft have been ordered in France.

INDIA
New "Foxtrot" class submarines, "Petya" class frigates and "Polnocny" class LCTs have been delivered, "Leander" class and Indian-designed patrol craft have also been constructed.

INDONESIA
Two more "Claud Jones" class frigates have been transferred from the USA, and at least seven "Whisky" class submarines and a considerable number of surface ships have been disposed of.

IRAN
There are important plans for expansion here, with orders for six "Spruance" class destroyers and four "PF" frigates to the USA and twelve "La Combattante II" fast attack missile craft from France. There is also some interest in the building of submarines.

IRAQ
The fleet of "Osa" class has been increased to six.

ISRAEL
The building rate of the "Reshef" class fast attack craft (six are being built) and the "Dabur" class patrol craft has been increased. An LSD and LSM have also been acquired.

ITALY
Four "Lupo" class frigates, two "Sauro" class submarines and additional hydrofoils have been ordered, and a new survey ship and supply ship launched.

JAPAN
Although the new construction programme has suffered from inflation, building of new DDGs, DDNs, submarines, LSTs, fast attack craft and minesweepers continues.

KENYA
Three new Brooke Marine patrol craft are under construction.

KOREA, NORTH
Additional information on the strength of their fleet includes "Romeo" class submarines, "Najin" class corvettes and a greatly increased force of fast attack craft.

KUWAIT
Navy has two additional patrol craft.

LEBANON
Three patrol craft have been ordered from West Germany.

LIBYA
There are reports of an order for ten "La Combattante II" fast attack missile craft.

MEXICO
The first of an order for 21 130-ton patrol craft, built in Britain, has been completed, a follow-up order has been reported.

MOROCCO
It has been reported that orders, placed or planned, for four corvettes, twenty large patrol craft and three LSLs have been given to France.

NETHERLANDS
It is hoped that four ASW groups will be provided in the future, three with DLG support, and the two Eastlant groups, each with a fast support ship, therefore new construction is being concentrated on the eight "Kortenaer" class frigates and the second support ship.

NEW ZEALAND
Four new "Lake" class large patrol craft were in commission in 1975.

NIGERIA
Two large patrol craft and a survey ship have been ordered from Brooke Marine, UK.

NORWAY
New construction of Type 210 submarines (with FDR) and the "Improved Storm" class fast attack missile craft is in the planning stage.
OMAN
Two ex-Netherlands MSCs have been acquired, four Brooke Marine large patrol craft and one Logistic Support ship have been ordered. and two "Loadmasters" and a "Spear" patrolcraft have been delivered.
PAKISTAN
Refit details are awaited for the ex-British frigates *Tenby* and *Scarborough*.
PERU
Four Italian "Modified Lupo" class have been ordered, and the first of two Type 209 submarines has been delivered and the second launched.
POLAND
Two "Skory" class have been paid off, and new "Ropucha" class LSTs are under construction.
PORTUGAL
The last of the "Joao Coutinho" class frigates has been completed.
QATAR
Six Vosper-Thornycroft large patrol craft are completing and seven Fairey "Spear" class coastal patrol craft have been delivered.
RAS AL KHAIMA
Five patrol craft have been delivered.
ROMANIA
Ten "Shanghai" class fast attack craft, one "Hu Chwan" class and a river patrol craft, all locally built, have been delivered.
ST. KITTS
One Fairey "Spear" has been delivered.
SAUDI ARABIA
There have been reports of twenty-six ships being ordered from the USA.
SIERRA LEONE
One "Spear" and two "Huntresses" have been delivered.
SINGAPORE
All six "TNC 48" fast attack missile craft are in commission.
SOUTH AFRICA
Six frigates, possibly with Gabriel missiles, are to be built at Durban.
SPAIN
Financial problems have caused the new construction programme to be cut to one helicopter-carrier, five frigates (5), eight or ten smaller frigates, two submarines (1), twelve large patrol craft (12), two oceanographic ships (2) and two coastal survey ships. (Figures in brackets show current construction).
SWEDEN
New construction of five submarines, one minelayer, sixteen fast attack missile craft, one icebreaker, new minehunters and LCVs. Two corvettes are also planned.
SYRIA
The "Osa" class strength has been increased to six.
TAIWAN
Two ex-US "Allen M. Sumner" class destroyers have been transferred.
THAILAND
There have been reports of an order for three fast attack missile craft.
TURKEY
Two ex-US "Guppy" class submarines have been acquired and the building of two Type 209 submarines and four fast attack missile craft is being continued.
UNITED KINGDOM
The *Invincible* and her class are to be continued. *Sheffield* has been completed, five more of her class are being built, and two more are to be ordered. The *Amazon* has been commissioned, and three more of her class will be commissioned in 1975, four more are being built. One Type 22 "Weapon" class has been laid down, and one more is to be ordered in 1975. The SSNs *Swiftsure* and *Sovereign* have been commissioned, three are being built, and one more will be ordered during 1975. The first new MCM vessel, *Brecon,* has been ordered, and the survey ship *Herald* and two fleet tankers have been commissioned. Five patrol ships have been ordered for North Sea duties, and the first of a new patrol craft, *Kingfisher,* is to be completed in 1975, three more will follow. Finally, two fleet replenishment ships are being built.
UNITED STATES OF AMERICA
Five lead ships for various new classes will be completed in 1975, they are, *Nimitz* (CVAN 68), *Spruance* (DD 963), *Los Angeles* (SSN 688), *Tarawa* (LHA 1), and *Pegasus* (PHM 1). The Sea Control Ship project has been cancelled by Congress.
UNION OF SOVIET SOCIALIST REPUBLICS
Kiev, the first Soviet aircraft-carrier, is expected to commission in 1975. Additional ships of the "Kara", "Kresta II" and "Krivak" classes are being built. The first of the new "Uniform" class submarines has appeared, and is thought to be possibly an enlarged version of the "Victor" class. The new "Sonya" class MSC and new "Turya" class hydrofoils have also appeared. It should be noted that the sections on river patrol craft, survey and research ships and tugs have been expanded considerably.
VENEZUELA
Two Type 209 submarines and all six Vosper Thornycroft 37-metre fast attack craft are expected to be completed during 1975.
VIETNAM
It is possible that a large proportion of the South Vietnamese fleet will be absorbed into that of North Vietnam.
YUGOSLAVIA
There have been reports of a submarine and fast attack craft building programme.
ZANZIBAR
The last of four 75 ft "Keith Nelson" patrol craft has been delivered.
N.B. The naval aircraft and missile sections have been tabulated for ease of reference and comparison of data.

IDENTIFICATION SILHOUETTES

Scale shown against each type or class as appropriate

BATTLESHIP

Scale: 177 Feet to 1 Inch

IOWA CLASS (USA)

AIRCRAFT CARRIERS

Scale: 138 Feet to 1 Inch

COLOSSUS CLASS (ARGENTINA, BRAZIL)

NB Minas Gerais different island

Scale :140 Feet to 1 Inch

MAJESTIC CLASS (AUSTRALIA, INDIA)

Scale: 173 Feet to 1 Inch

CLEMENCEAU CLASS (FRANCE)

Scale: 147 Feet to 1 Inch

BULWARK CLASS (UK)

AIRCRAFT CARRIERS

Scale: 169 Feet to 1 Inch ARK ROYAL (UK)

Scale: 154 Feet to 1 Inch HERMES (UK)

Scale: 225 Feet to 1 Inch ENTERPRISE CLASS (USA)

Scale: 179 Feet to 1 Inch ESSEX AND HANCOCK CLASS (USA)

AIRCRAFT CARRIERS

Scale: 207 Feet to 1 Inch

FORRESTAL CLASS (USA)

Scale: 118 Feet to 1 Inch

IWO JIMA CLASS (USA)

Scale: 212 Feet to 1 Inch

KITTY HAWK (USA)

Scale: 195 Feet to 1 Inch

MIDWAY CLASS (USA)

SUBMARINES

LONG RANGE BALLISTIC MISSILE SUBMARINES

Scale: 122 Feet to 1 Inch

REDOUTABLE CLASS (FRANCE)

RESOLUTION CLASS (UK)

ETHAN ALLEN CLASS (USA)

LAFAYETTE CLASS (USA)

GEORGE WASHINGTON CLASS (USA)

YANKEE CLASS (USSR)

HOTEL CLASS (USSR)

GOLF CLASS (USSR, CHINA)

SUBMARINES

Scale: 80 Feet to 1 Inch

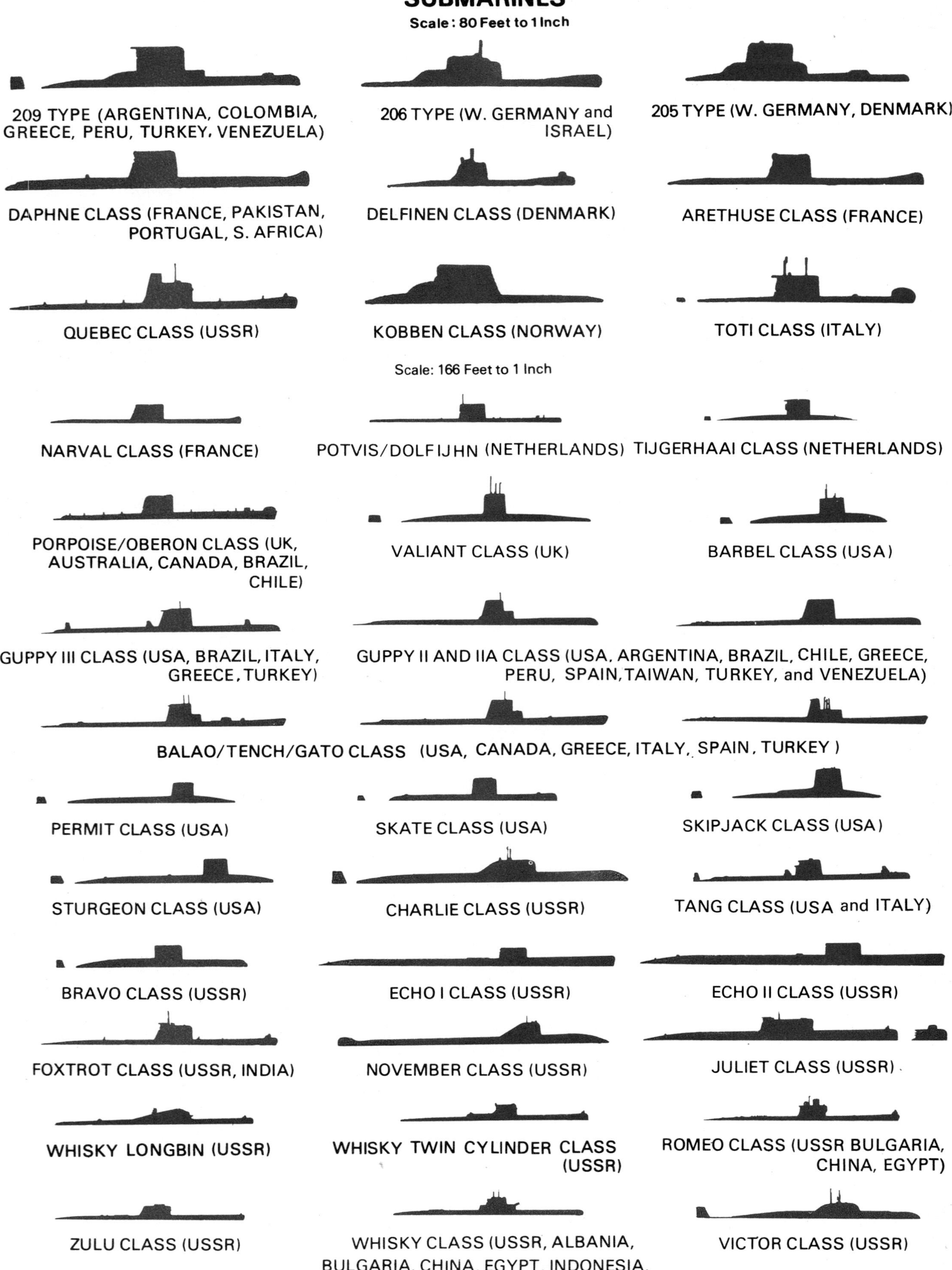

CRUISERS

Scale: 266 Feet to 1 Inch

CRUISERS

Scale: 160 Feet to 1 Inch

TRUXTON (USA)

CALIFORNIA CLASS (USA)

COUNTY CLASS (UK)

BRISTOL (UK)

DESTROYERS

Scale: 161 Feet to 1 Inch

IROQUOIS CLASS (CANADA)

ACONIT (FRANCE)

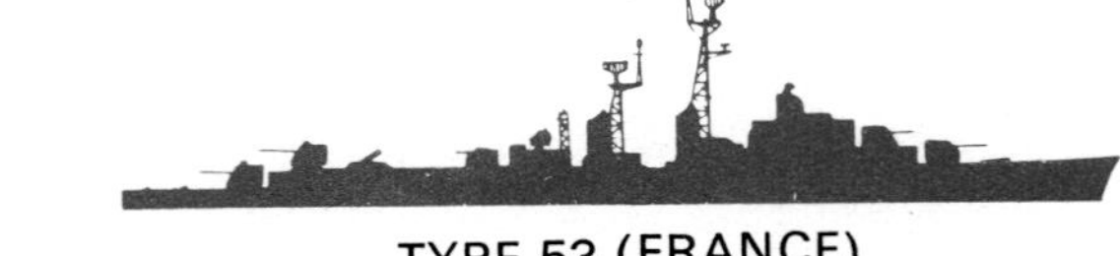
TYPE 53 (FRANCE)

TYPE 47 (ASW) (FRANCE)

TYPE 47 (DDG))FRANCE)

SUFFREN CLASS (FRANCE)

TOURVILLE CLASS (FRANCE)

HAMBURG CLASS (W. GERMANY)

LÜTJENS CLASS (W. GERMANY)

AUDACE CLASS (ITALY)

IMPAVIDO CLASS (ITALY)

FLETCHER CLASS (USA)

DESTROYERS

Scale: 160 Feet to 1 Inch

ALLEN M. SUMNER CLASS (USA, ARGENTINA, GREECE, IRAN, SPAIN, TAIWAN)

ADAMS CLASS (USA— AUSTRALIA Similar)

SHEFFIELD CLASS (UK AND ARGENTINA)

FORREST SHERMAN CLASS (CONVERTED) (USA)

FORREST SHERMAN CLASS (USA)

GEARING CLASS (USA, GREECE, TAIWAN AND TURKEY)

GEARING CLASS (FRAM 2)(USA, GREECE, TAIWAN AND TURKEY)

MITSCHER CLASS (USA)

SPRUANCE CLASS (USA)

KANIN CLASS (USSR)

KASHIN CLASS (USSR)

KILDIN CLASS (USSR)

KOTLIN CLASS (USSR) (WITH HELICOPTER PLATFORM)

KOTLIN CLASS (USSR)

SAM KOTLIN (USSR)

SKORY CLASS (USSR, EGYPT, INDONESIA, POLAND)

KRIVAK CLASS (USSR)

KRUPNY CLASS (USSR)

TALLIN CLASS (USSR)

FRIESLAND/HOLLAND CLASS (NETHERLANDS)

DESTROYERS

Scale: 161 Feet to 1 Inch

IMPETUOSO CLASS (ITALY)

BELKNAP CLASS (USA)

COONTZ CLASS (USA)

LEAHY CLASS (USA)

FRIGATES

Scale: 161 Feet to 1 Inch

PEDER SKRAM CLASS (DENMARK)

HVIDBJÖRNEN CLASS (DENMARK)

COMMANDANT RIVIÈRE CLASS (FRANCE)

LE CORSE CLASS (FRANCE)

KÖLN CLASS (W. GERMANY)

ALPINO CLASS (ITALY)

LE NORMAND CLASS (FRANCE)

BERGAMINI CLASS (ITALY)

CENTAURO CLASS (ITALY)

VAN SPEIJK CLASS (NETHERLANDS)

OSLO CLASS (NORWAY)

DE SILVA CLASS (PORTUGAL)

ESCOBAR (PORTUGAL)

AMAZON CLASS (UK)

BLACKWOOD CLASS (UK)

LEANDER CLASS (UK)

LEOPARD CLASS (UK)

ROTHESAY (UK)

SALISBURY CLASS (UK)

TRIBAL CLASS (UK)

WHITBY CLASS (UK)

FRIGATES

Scale: 160 Feet to 1 Inch

ANNAPOLIS CLASS (CANADA)

MACKENZIE CLASS (CANADA)

ST. LAURENT CLASS (CANADA)

RESTIGOUCHE CLASS (CANADA)

Scale: 125 Feet to 1 Inch

A69 (FRANCE)

KOLA CLASS (USSR)

RIGA CLASS (USSR, BULGARIA, CHINA, FINLAND, E. GERMANY, INDONESIA)

BROOKE CLASS (USA)

KNOX CLASS (USA)

GARCIA CLASS (USA)

MIRKA CLASS (USSR)

CORVETTES

Scale: 110 Feet to 1 Inch

ALBATROS/TRITON CLASS (DENMARK, ITALY)

THETIS CLASS (W. GERMANY)

CRISTOFARO CLASS (ITALY)

WOLF CLASS (NETHERLANDS)

COUTINHO CLASS (PORTUGAL)

POTI CLASS (USSR)

PETYA CLASS (USSR)

Scale: 125 Feet to 1 Inch

GRISHA CLASS (USSR)

NANUCHKA CLASS (USSR)

SOI CLASS (USSR)

AMPHIBIOUS FORCES

Scale: 170 Feet to 1 Inch

OURAGAN CLASS (FRANCE)

JEANNE D'ARC (FRANCE)

FEARLESS CLASS (UK)

AUSTIN CLASS (USA)

NEWPORT CLASS (USA)

THOMASTON CLASS (USA)

Scale: 117 Feet to 1 Inch

SIR LANCELOT CLASS (UK)

Scale: 148 Feet to 1 Inch

RALEIGH CLASS (USA)

Scale: 157 Feet to 1 Inch

ALLIGATOR CLASS (USSR)

POLNOCNY CLASS (USSR, POLAND, INDIA, EGYPT, S.YEMEN)

MP8 CLASS (USSR)

LIGHT FORCES

Scale: 58 Feet to 1 Inch

JAGUAR CLASS (W. GERMANY)

TYPE 143 (W GERMANY)

TYPE 148 (W GERMANY)

STORM CLASS (NORWAY)

TJELD CLASS (NORWAY, GREECE)

KOMAR CLASS (USSR)

OSA 1 & 2 CLASS (USSR)

SHERSHEN CLASS (USSR, EGYPT, E. GERMANY, YUGOSLAVIA)

P. CLASS (P6, 8 and 10 — ALGERIA, USSR, CHINA, CUBA, EGYPT, E. GERMANY, GUINEA, INDONESIA, IRAQ, NIGERIA, POLAND, SOMALIA, N. VIETNAM)

Scale: 125 Feet to 1 Inch

STENKA CLASS (USSR)

MINE WARFARE FORCES

Scale: 111 Feet to 1 Inch

FALSTER CLASS (DENMARK)

GOR CLASS (NORWAY)

ABDIEL (UK)

MINE WARFARE FORCES

Scale: 97 Feet to 1 Inch

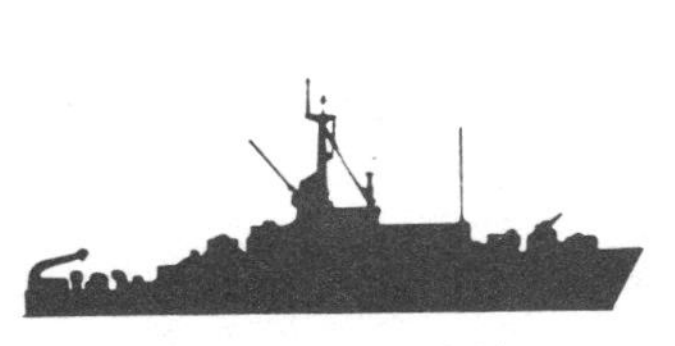

CIRCE (FRANCE)

KRAKE (E.GERMANY)

KONDOR (E.GERMANY)

LINDAU CLASS (W. GERMANY)

SCHUTZE CLASS (W. GERMANY, BRAZIL)

KASADA (JAPAN)

DOKKUM WILDERVANK (NETHERLANDS, ETHIOPIA)

KROGULEC (POLAND)

ALMANZORA (SPAIN)

TON (UK, ARGENTINA, AUSTRALIA, GHANA, INDIA, MALAYSIA, S.AFRICA)

AGILE (USA, BELGIUM, FRANCE, ITALY, NETHERLANDS, PORTUGAL, SPAIN, URUGUAY)

AUK (USA, S.KOREA, NORWAY, PERU, TAIWAN, PHILLIPINES, URUGUAY)

BLUEBIRD (USA, BELGIUM, DENMARK, FRANCE, GREECE, IRAN, INDONESIA, ITALY, KOREA, JAPAN, NETHERLANDS, NORWAY, PAKISTAN, PORTUGAL, PHILLIPINES, TAIWAN, SPAIN, THAILAND, TURKEY, S. VIETNAM)

NATYA CLASS (USSR)

SASHA CLASS (USSR)

T-43 CLASS (USSR, ALBANIA, CHINA, EGYPT, INDONESIA, POLAND, SYRIA)

T-58 CLASS (USSR, INDIA)

T301 CLASS (USSR)

VANYA CLASS (USSR, BULGARIA)

YURKA CLASS (USSR)

SUPPORT SHIPS

Scale: 156 Feet to 1 Inch

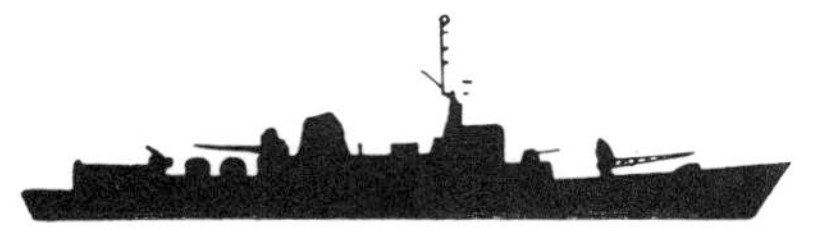

ZINNIA (BELGIUM)

GODETIA (BELGIUM)

RHEIN CLASS (W. GERMANY)

PRESERVER CLASS (CANADA)

DON CLASS (USSR)

LAMA CLASS (USSR)

UGRA CLASS (USSR, INDIA)

ENGADINE (UK)

Scale: 85 Feet to 1 Inch

ENDURANCE (UK)

Scale: 152 Feet to 1 Inch

BORIS CHILIKIN CLASS (USSR)

Scale: 206 Feet to 1 Inch

DEUTSCHLAND (W. GERMANY)

Scale: 160 Feet to 1 Inch

SAN GIORGIO (ITALY)

Scale: 200 Feet to 1 Inch

TRIUMPH (UK)

ABU DHABI

Administration

Sea Wing Commander:
Commander G. A. St. G. Poole

Personnel

(a) 1975: 150 officers and men
(b) Voluntary service

The Naval Force of Abu Dhabi was formed in March 1968. The Force's function is to patrol territorial waters and oil installations in the UAE Marine Areas.

LIGHT FORCES

6 VOSPER THORNYCROFT TYPE (LARGE PATROL CRAFT)

AL ADAID +5

Displacement, tons	110 standard; 140 full load
Dimensions, ft (*m*)	110 oa × 21 × 5·5 (*33·5 × 6·4 × 1·7*)
Guns	2—40 mm
Main engines	2 Paxman Valenta diesels = 29 knots
Range, miles	1 500 at 14 knots
Complement	27

Of this class of round bilge steel hull craft launchings took place on 8 Apr 1974, and 6 May 1974. Others were laid down in early 1974, the last being ordered in May.

BANI YAS P 563 **KAWKAB** P 561 **THOABAN** P 562

Displacement, tons	32
Dimensions, ft (*m*)	57 × 16·5 × 4·5 (*17·4 × 5·1 × 1·4*)
Guns	2—20 mm (single)
Main engines	2 Caterpillar diesels. 750 bhp = 19 knots
Range, miles	300 at 10 knots
Complement	11 (2 officers, 9 men)

Built by Keith Nelson & Co. Ltd. Bembridge, Isle of Wight. Of glass fibre hull construction. Launch dates—*Bani Yas* July 1969, *Kawkab* and *Thoaban* Jan 1969.

BANI YAS *1974, Abu Dhabi Naval Force*

5 FAIREY MARINE "SPEAR" CLASS (COASTAL PATROL CRAFT)

Dimensions, ft (*m*)	29·8 × 9·2 × 2·6 (*9·1 × 2·8 × ·8*)
Guns	2—7·62 mm MGs
Main engines	2 Perkins diesels of 290 hp = 25 knots
Complement	3

Order placed in Feb 1974 . Craft delivered between July 1974 and Jan 1975.

"SPEAR" CLASS 1974 Faireys.

6 "DHAFEER" CLASS (COASTAL PATROL CRAFT)

DHAFEER	P 401	**HAZZA**	P 403
DURGHAM	P 404	**MURAYJIB**	P 406
GHADUNFAR	P 402	**TIMSAH**	P 405

Displacement, tons	10
Dimensions, ft (*m*)	41 × 12 × 3·5 (*12·5 × 3·7 × 1·1*)
Guns	1 × 7·62 MG, 2 light MG
Main engines	2 Cummins diesels; 370 bhp = 19 knots
Range, miles	150 at 12 knots
Complement	6 (1 officer, 5 men)

All built by Keith Nelson & Co. Ltd, Bembridge, Isle of Wight. Of glass fibre hull construction. Launch dates *Murayjib* Feb 1970, *Durgham* and *Timsah* Sept 1968, *Ghadunfar* and *Hazza* May 1968, *Dhafeer* Feb 1968.

HAZZA *1974, Abu Dhabi Naval Force*

ALBANIA

Strength of the Fleet

Corvettes	4	Minesweepers—Ocean	2	Tankers	4
Submarines	4	Minesweepers—Inshore	6	Small Auxiliaries	20
Fast Attack Craft (Torpedo)	42	MSB	10		

Bases

Durazzo (Durresi) and Valona (Vlora)

Personnel

(a) 1975: Total 3 000 including 300 coastal frontier guards.
(b) Ratings on 3 years military service.

Mercantile Marine

Lloyd's Register of Shipping: 20 vessels of 57 368 tons gross

CORVETTES

4 Ex-USSR "KRONSTADT" CLASS

Displacement, tons	310 standard; 380 full load
Dimensions, ft (*m*)	170·6 × 21·5 × 9·0 (*52·0 × 6·5 × 2·7*)
Guns	1—3·5 in (*85 mm*); 2—37 mm AA (single); 6—12·7 AA MG (3 vertical twin)
A/S weapons	2 depth charge projectors; 2 DC rails
Main engines	3 Diesels; 3 shafts; 3 300 bhp = 24 knots
Range, miles	1 500 at 12 knots
Complement	65

Equipped for minelaying: 2 rails; about 40 mines. Four were transferred from the USSR in 1958. Albania sent two for A/S updating in 1960 and two others in 1961.

RADAR. Surface search—Ball Gun. Navigation—Neptun. IFF—High Pole.

"KRONSTADT" Class Ex-USSR

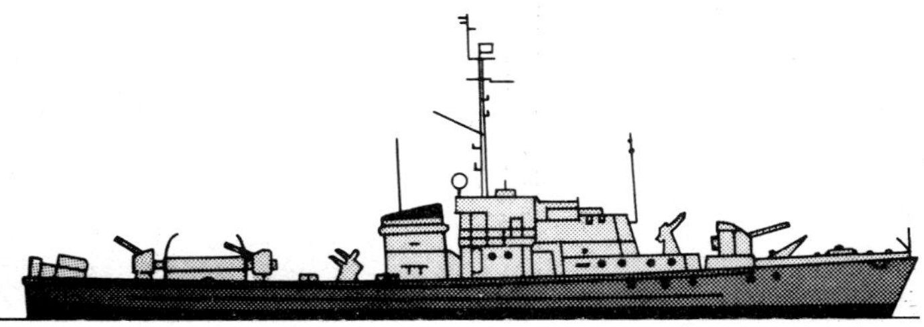

"KRONSTADT" Class

SUBMARINES

4 Ex-USSR "WHISKY" CLASS

Displacement, tons	1 030 surface; 1 180 dived
Dimensions, ft (*m*)	240·0 × 22·0 × 15·0 (*73·2 × 6·7 × 4·6*)
Tubes	6—21 in (4 bow, 2 stern); 18 torpedoes or 40 mines
Main machinery	Diesels; 4 000 bhp; 2 shafts = 17 knots surface Electric motors; 2 500 hp = 15 knots dived
Range, miles	13 000 at 8 knots surfaced
Complement	60

Three of the four "W" class submarines are operational and one is now used as a stationary training hulk. All are based at Vlora. Two were transferred from the USSR in 1960, and two others were reportedly seized from the USSR in mid-1961 upon the withdrawal of Soviet ships from their Albanian base.

RADAR. Snoop Plate.

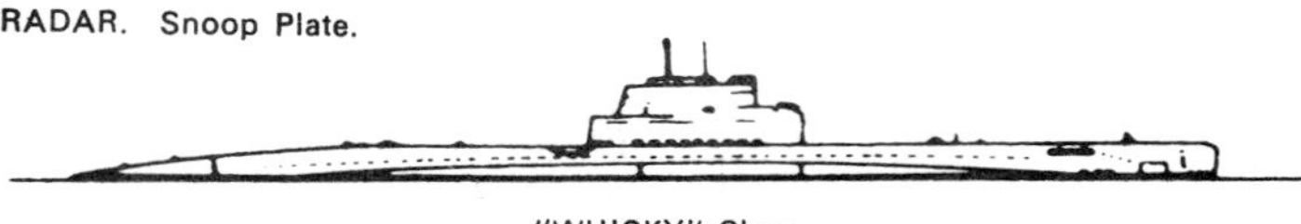

"WHISKY" Class

LIGHT FORCES

12 USSR "P-4" CLASS (F.A.C. TORPEDO)

Displacement, tons	25
Dimensions, feet	62·3 × 11·5 × 5·6 (*19·0 × 3·5 × 1·7 metres*)
Guns	2 or 4—12·7 mm AA MG (see notes)
Tubes	2—18 in (*450 mm*)
Main engines	2 Diesels; 2 Shafts; 2200bhp = 50 knots

Six were transferred from the USSR in 1956 (with radar and 2—12·7 mm MG) and six from China, three in April 1965 and three in Sep 1965, without radar and 4—12·7 mm MG (2 twin). Radar now fitted.

"P-4" Class Ex-USSR

30 Ex-CHINESE "HU CHWAN" CLASS (F.A.C. TORPEDO)

Displacement, tons	45
Dimensions, ft (*m*)	71 × 14·5 × 3·1 (*21·8 × 4·5 × 0·9*)
Guns	2—14·5 mm (twin vertical)
Torpedo tubes	2—21 inch
Main engines	2 M50 Diesels; 2 shafts; 2 200 hp = 55 knots

Built in Shanghai and transferred as follows: 6 in 1968, 15 in 1969, 2 in 1970 and 7 in 1971.

RADAR. Skinhead.

HU CHWAN *China, 1972*

MINE WARFARE FORCES

2 Ex-USSR "T 43" CLASS (MINESWEEPERS, OCEAN)

Displacement, tons	500 standard; 610 full load
Dimensions, ft (*m*)	190·2 × 28·2 × 6·9 (*58·0 × 8·6 × 2·1*)
Guns	4—37 mm AA (2 twin); 4—25 mm AA
Main engines	2 Diesels; 2 shafts; 2 000 bhp = 17 knots
Range, miles	1 600 at 10 knots
Complement	40

"T 43" class fleet minesweepers acquired from the USSR. Transferred in Aug 1960.

"T 43" Class Ex-USSR

Mine Warfare Forces —*continued*

10 Ex-SOVIET "PO 2" CLASS (MSB)

Displacement, tons	40 to 45 standard; 45 to 50 full load
Dimensions, ft (*m*)	82·0 × 16·7 × 5·6 (*25 × 5·1 × 1·7*)
Guns	2—25 mm or 2—13 mm
Main engines	Diesels = 30 knots

There are reports of some 10 "PO 2" class in service and possibly 3 ex-Italian MS 501. The "PO 2" class, though primarily minesweeping boats, are also general utility craft. They were transferred as follows: 4 in 1957, 3 in 1958-59, 3 in 1960.

6 Ex-USSR "T 301" CLASS (MINESWEEPERS—INSHORE)

Displacement, tons	150 standard; 180 full load
Dimensions, ft (*m*)	128·0 × 18·0 × 4·9 (*39·0 × 5·5 × 1·5*)
Guns	2—37 mm AA; 2—25 mm AA
Main engines	2 diesels; 2 shafts; 1 440 bhp = 17 knots
Range, miles	2 200 at 10 knots
Complement	25

Transferred from USSR—two in 1957, two in 1959 and two in 1960.

"T 301" Class Ex-USSR

DEGAUSSING SHIP

1 Ex-USSR "SEKSTAN" CLASS

Dimensions, ft (*m*)	134·0 × 40·0 × 14·0 max (*40·9 × 12·2 × 4·3*)
Main engines	Diesels; 400 bhp = 11 knots
Complement	35

Built in Finland in 1956. Transferred from the USSR in 1960.

OILERS

2 Ex-USSR "KHOBI" CLASS

Displacement, tons	800
Measurement, tons	1 600 deadweight; 1 500 oil
Dimensions, ft (*m*)	220·0 × 33·0 × 15·0 (*67·1 × 10·1 × 4·6*)
Main engines	2 diesels; 1 600 bhp = 12 knots

Launched in 1956. Transferred from the USSR in Sep 1958 and Feb 1959. In addition to the above there are reported to be a number of small auxiliaries.

RADAR. Neptun.

1 Ex-USSR "TOPLIVO 1" CLASS

Displacement, tons 280

Transferred from the USSR in March 1960. Similar to "Khobi" class in appearance though smaller.

1 Ex-USSR "TOPLIVO 3" CLASS

Displacement, tons 275

Transferred from the USSR in 1960. Funnel aft.

TENDERS

There are reported to be a dozen or so harbour and port tenders including YPs, a water carrier and torpedo recovery vessel of the Soviet "Poluchat 1" class. The "Atrek" class submarine tender transferred from USSR in 1961 as a depot ship was converted into a merchant ship.

TUGS

Several small tugs are employed in local duties or harbour service.

ALGERIA

Strength of the Fleet

Fast Attack Craft (Missile)	9	Minesweepers—Ocean	2
Fast Attack Craft (Patrol)	6	Training Ship	1
Fast Attack Craft (Torpedo)	12		

Personnel

(a) 1975: Total 3 500 (250 officers and cadets and 3 250 men)
(b) Voluntary service

Bases

Algiers, Annaba, Mers el Kebir

Mercantile Marine

Lloyd's Register of Shipping: 75 vessels of 239 815 tons gross

LIGHT FORCES

3 Ex-SOVIET "OSA" CLASS (FAST ATTACK CRAFT—MISSILE)

Displacement, tons	165 standard; 200 full load
Dimensions, ft (*m*)	128·7 × 25·1 × 5·9 (*39·3 × 7·7 × 1·8*)
Missiles	4 SSN 2A (Styx)
Guns	4—30 mm (2 twin)
Main engines	3 diesels; 13 000 hp = 32 knots
Range, miles	800 at 25 knots
Complement	25

One boat was delivered by USSR on 7 Oct 1967. Two others have been reported since.

"OSA 1" Class

12 Ex-SOVIET "P6" CLASS (FAST ATTACK CRAFT—TORPEDO)

Displacement, tons	66 standard; 75 full load
Dimensions, ft (*m*)	84·2 × 20·0 × 6·0 (*25·7 × 6·1 × 1·8*)
Tubes	2—21 inch plus mines or depth charges
Guns	4—25 mm (twin)
Main engines	4 Diesels, 4 shafts, 4 800 hp = 43 knots
Range, miles	450 at 30 knots
Complement	25

Six were acquired from the USSR in 1964. Two more boats reported to be in reserve were received from Egypt in 1963.

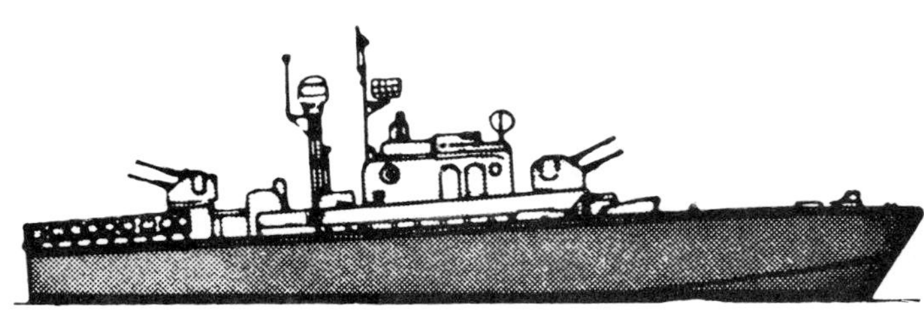

"P 6." Class

6 Ex-SOVIET "KOMAR" CLASS

(FAST ATTACK CRAFT—MISSILE)

Displacement, tons	70 standard; 80 full load
Dimensions, ft (*m*)	83·7 × 19·8 × 5·0 (*25·5 × 6·0 × 1·5*)
Missiles	2 SSN 2A (Styx)
Guns	2—25 mm (twin)
Main engines	4 diesels, 4 shafts, 4 800 hp = 40 knots
Range, miles	400 at 30 knots

Acquired in 1967 from USSR.

6 Ex-SOVIET "SO I" CLASS

(FAST ATTACK CRAFT—PATROL)

Displacement, tons	215 light; 250 normal
Dimensions, ft (*m*)	138·6 × 20·0 × 9·2 (*42·3 × 6·1 × 2·8*)
Guns	4—25 mm (2 twin mounts)
A/S weapons	4—5 barrelled rocket launchers
Main engines	3 diesels; 6 000 bhp = 29 knots
Complement	30
Range, miles	1 100 at 13 knots

Delivered by USSR on 7 and 8 Oct 1967, first two, and the other four since 1968.

"SO I" Class

MINE WARFARE FORCES

2 Ex-SOVIET "T 43" CLASS (MINESWEEPERS, OCEAN)

Displacement, tons	500 standard; 610 full load
Dimensions, ft (*m*)	190·2 × 28·2 × 6·9 (*58·0 × 8·6 × 2·1*)
Guns	4—37 mm (twin); 4—25 mm (twin)
Main engines	2 Diesels; 2 shafts; 2 000 hp = 17 knots
Range, miles	1 600 at 10 knots
Complement	40

"T 43" Class

TRAINING SHIP

SIDI FRADJ (ex- *Darfour*)

Displacement, tons	215 standard; 270 full load
Dimensions, feet	136 oa × 24·5 × 6
Guns	1—3 in; 2—20 mm AA
Main engines	Diesels; 1 000 bhp = 13 knots

Two ex-US BYMS type coastal minesweepers were presented to Algeria by Egypt to form the nucleus of the new Algerian Navy. Both *Darfour* (ex-BYMS 2041) and *Tor* (ex-BYMS 2175) arrived in Algiers on 4 Nov 1962, being handed over on 6 Nov and renamed *Sidi Fradj* and *Djebel Aures*, respectively, but the latter was wrecked off Algiers in Apr 1963 and *Sidi Fradj* has been used as a training ship since 1965. Now considered obsolescent.

ARGENTINA

Naval Board

Commander of the Navy and Chief of Naval Operations:
Rear Admiral E. E. Massera

Chief of Naval Staff:
Rear Admiral A. Lambruschini

Diplomatic Representation

Naval Attaché in London and The Hague and Head of the Argentine Naval Mission in Europe:
Rear Admiral R. G. Franke

Naval Attaché in Washington:
Rear Admiral D. R. H. De La Riva

Naval Attaché in Paris:
Captain J. C. Malugani

Personnel

(a) 1975: 32 900 (2 890 officers, 18 010 petty officers and ratings and 12 000 conscripts)
Marine Corps: 5 000 officers and men
(b) Volunteers plus 14 months national service

Naval Bases

Puerto Belgrano, Mar del Plata, Ushuaia

Darsena Note (B.A.) Rio Santiago

Deletions and Transfers

Attack Carrier (medium)

1971 *Independencia*

Cruiser

1973 *La Argentina*

Destroyers

1971 *Buenos Aires, Misiones, San Luis*
1973 *Entre Rios, San Juan, Santa Cruz*

Frigates

1973 *Juan B Azopardo, Piedrabuena, Azopardo*

Minesweeper Support Ship

1971 *Corrientes*

Submarines

1972 *Santa Fe* (ex-*Lamprey*) *Santiago del Estero* (ex-*Macabi*), scrapped for spares

Amphibious Forces

1971 *BDI 15, BDM 1*
1973 *BDI 1, EDVP 4, 5, 6, 11, 20, 22, 27,*

Survey Ships

1970 *Commodoro Augusto Lasserre*
1973 *Ushuia* sunk in collision, *Capitan Canepa*

Transport

1973 *Bahia Thetis*

Oilers

1971 *Punta Rasa, Punta Lara*

Salvage Ship

1974 *Guardiamarina Zicari*

Tugs

1971 *Querendi*
1974 *Mataco*

Prefectura Nacional Maritima

PNM is responsible for coastguard and rescue duties. It also administers the Merchant Navy School at Buenos Aires.

Strength of the Fleet

Type	*Active*	*Building*
Attack Carrier (Medium)	1	—
Cruisers	2	—
Destroyers	8	2
Corvettes	11	—
Patrol Submarine	4	—
Landing Ships (Tank)	5	—
Landing Craft (Tank)	1	—
Minor Landing Craft	19	—
Fast Attack Craft (Missile)	—	2
Fast Attack Craft (Gun)	2	—
Fast Attack Craft (Torpedo)	2	—
Large Patrol Craft	5	—
Minesweepers (Coastal)	4	—
Minehunters	2	—
Survey Ships	5	2
Survey Launches	2	—
Transports	3	—
Oiler (Underway Replenishment)	1	—
Oilers (Fleet Support)	2	—
Icebreaker	1	—
Training Ship	1	—
Tugs	15	—

Mercantile Marine

Lloyd's Register of Shipping:
366 vessels of 1 408 129 tons gross

AIRCRAFT CARRIER

1 Ex-BRITISH "COLOSSUS" CLASS

Name	No.	Builders	Laid down	Launched	Completed
VEINTICINCO DE MAYO (ex-*HNMS Karel Doorman*, ex-*HMS Venerable*)	V 2	Cammell Laird & Co Ltd Birkenhead	3 Dec 1942	30 Dec 1943	17 Jan 1945

Displacement, tons	15 892 standard; 19 896 full load
Length, feet (*metres*)	630 (*192·0*) pp 693·2 (*211·3*) oa
Beam, feet (*metres*)	80 (*24·4*)
Draught, feet (*metres*)	25 (*7·6*)
Width, feet (*metres*)	121·3 (*37·0*) overall
Hangar:	
Length, feet (*metres*)	455 (*138·7*)
Width, feet (*metres*)	52 (*15·8*)
Height, feet (*metres*)	17·5 (*5·3*)
Aircraft	Capacity 21; operates with variable complement of S-2A Trackers, A-4Q Skyhawks and S-61D Sea King ASW helicopters
Guns, AA	10—40 mm
Main engines	Parsons geared turbines; 40 000 shp; 2 shafts
Boilers	4 three-drum; working pressure 400 psi (*28·1 kg/cm²*); Superheat 700°F (*371°C*)
Speed, knots	24·25
Oil fuel, tons	3 200
Range, miles	12 000 at 14 knots, 6 200 at 23 knots
Complement	1 500

GENERAL
Purchased from Great Britain on 1 Apr 1948 and commissioned in the Royal Netherlands Navy on 28 May 1948. Damaged by boiler fire on 29 Apr 1968. Sold to Argentina on 15 Oct 1968 and refitted at Rotterdam by N. V. Dok en Werf Mij Wilton Fijenoord. Commissioned in the Argentine Navy on 12 Mar 1969. Completed refit on 22 Aug 1969 and sailed for Argentina on 1 Sep 1969. With modified island superstructure and bridge, lattice tripod radar mast, and tall raked funnel, she differs considerably from her former appearance and from her original sister ships in the British, Australian, Brazilian, French and Indian navies.

ENGINEERING. The turbine sets and boilers are arranged *en echelon*, the two propelling-machinery spaces having two boilers and one set of turbines in each space, on the unit system. She was reboilered in 1965-1966 with boilers removed from HMS *Leviathan*. During refit for Argentina in 1968-1969 she received new turbines, also from HMS *Leviathan*.

MODERNISATION: Fitted with Ferranti CAAIS with Plessey Super-CAAIS displays.

RADAR
Search: Two Philips LWO series early warning radars with associated height finders of VI series for air interception.
Tactical: DA Series tactical and navigation radar.

RECONSTRUCTION. Underwent extensive refit modernisation in 1955-1958 including angled flight deck and steam catapult, rebuilt island, mirror sight landing system, and new anti-aircraft battery of ten 40 mm guns, at the Wilton-Fijenoord Shipyard, at a cost of 25 million guilders. Conversion completed in July 1958.

DRAWING. Starboard elevation and plan. Redrawn in 1971. Scale: 105 feet = 1 inch

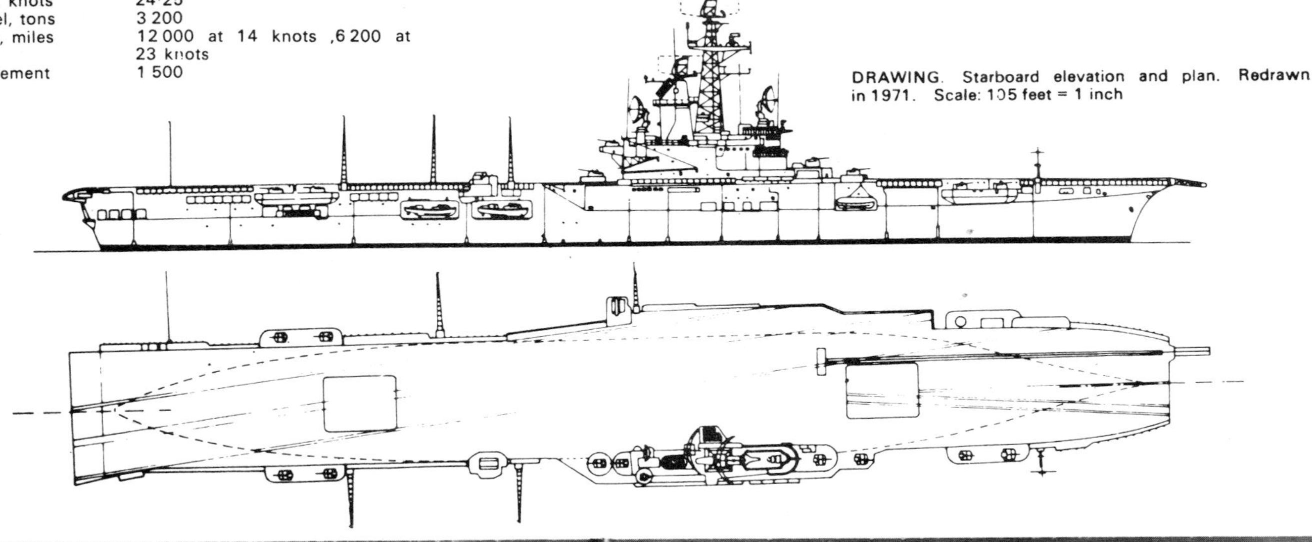

25 DE MAYO *1974, Argentine Navy*

CRUISERS

2 Ex-US "BROOKLYN" CLASS

Name	No.	Builders	Laid down	Launched	Completed
GENERAL BELGRANO (ex *17 de Octubre*, ex-*Phoenix*, CL 46)	C 4	New York S.B. Corp Camden	15 Apr 1935	12 Mar 1938	18 Mar 1939
NUEVE DE JULIO (ex-*Boise* CL 47)	C 5	Newport News S.B. & D.D. Co	1 Apr 1935	3 Dec 1936	1 Feb 1939

Displacement, tons	*Gen. Belgrano:* 10 800 standard; 12 650 normal; 13 645 full load *Nueve de Julio:* 10 500 standard 12 300 normal; 13 645 full load
Length, feet (*metres*)	608·3 (*185·4*) oa
Beam, feet (*metres*)	69 (*21·0*)
Draught, feet (*metres*)	24 (*7·3*)
Aircraft	2 helicopters
Missiles, AA	2 quadruple "Sea Cat" launchers (*General Belgrano* only)
Guns	15—6 in (*153 mm*) 47 cal; 8—5 in (*127 mm*) 25 cal (*Gen. Belgrano*) (6 only in *Nueve de Julio*) 20—40 mm; (*Gen. Belgrano*); 28—40 mm (*Nueve de Julio*) 4—47 mm (saluting)
Armour	Belt 4 in—1½ in (*100—38 mm*) Decks 3 in+2 in (*76+51 mm*) Turrets 5 in—3 in (*127—76 mm*) Conning Tower 8 in (*203 mm*)
Main engines	Parsons geared turbines; 100 000 shp; 4 shafts
Boilers	8 Babcock & Wilcox Express type
Speed, knots	32·5 (when new)
Range, miles	7 600 at 15 knots
Oil fuel, tons	2 200
Complement	1 200

GENERAL BELGRANO — *1973, Argentine Navy*

GENERAL
Former cruisers of the United States Navy "Brooklyn" class. Superstructure was reduced, bulges added, beam increased, and mainmast derricks and catapults removed. Purchased from the United States in 1951 at a cost of $7 800 000 representing 20 per cent of their original cost plus the expense of reconditioning them. Both were transferred to the Argentine Navy on 12 Apr 1951. *General Belgrano* was commissioned under the name *17 de Octubre* at Philadelphia on 17 Oct 1951. *9 de Julio* was commissioned into the Argentine Navy at Philadelphia on 11 Mar 1952. *9 de Julio* refers to 9 July 1816, when the Argentine provinces signed the Declaration of Independence. *17 de Octubre* was renamed *General Belgrano* in 1956 following the overthrow of President Peron the year before.

RADAR
Search: LWO and DA Series (Signaal).

HANGAR. The hangar in the hull right aft accommodates two helicopters together with engine spares and duplicate parts, though 4 aircraft was the original complement.

DRAWING: Starboard elevation and plan. Re-drawn in 1971. Scale 120 feet = 1 inch. "Sea-cats" abreast bridge in *General Belgrano* only

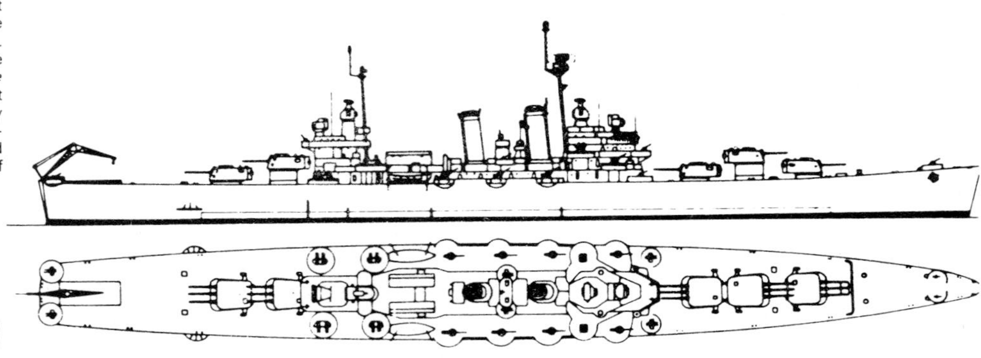

DESTROYERS

2 BRITISH TYPE 42

Name	No.	Builders	Laid down	Launched	Commissioning
HERCULES	D 01	Vickers, Barrow in-Furness	16 June 1971	24 Oct 1972	mid 1975
SANTISSIMA TRINIDAD	D 02	AFNE, Rio Santiago	11 Oct 1971	Mar 1974	1976

Displacement, tons	3 500 full load
Length, feet (*metres*)	392·0 (*119·5*) wl; 410·0 (*125·0*) oa
Beam, feet (*metres*)	47·0 (*14·3*)
Draught, feet (*metres*)	22·0 (*6·7*)
Missile launchers	2 "Sea Dart" (1 twin)
Aircraft	1 Lynx helicopter
Guns	1—4·5 in automatic; 2—20 mm Oerlikon
Main engines	Rolls Royce Olympus gas turbines for full power; Rolls Royce Tyne gas turbines for cruising; 2 shafts; 50 000 shp
Speed, knots	30 designed
Range, miles	4 000 at 18 knots
Complement	300

These two destroyers are of the British Type 42. On 18 May 1970 the signing of a contract between the Argentine Government and Vickers Ltd Barrow-in-Furness was announced. This provided for the construction of these two ships, one to be built at Barrow-in-Furness and the second at Rio Santiago with British assistance and overseeing.

HERCULES (TYPE 42)

Destroyers—*continued*

5 Ex-US "FLETCHER" CLASS

Name	No.	Builders	Laid down	Launched	Commissioning
BROWN (ex-USS *Heermann*, DD 532)	D 20	Bethlehem Steel Co, San Francisco	8 May 1942	5 Dec 1942	6 July 1943
ESPORA (ex-USS *Dortch*, DD 670)	D 21	Federal S.B. & D.D. Co, Port Newark	2 Mar 1943	20 June 1943	7 Aug 1943
ROSALES (ex-USS *Stembel*, DD 644)	D 22	Bath Iron Works Corporation, Bath, Maine	21 Dec 1942	8 May 1943	16 July 1943
DOMECQ GARCIA (ex-USS *Braine*, DD 630)	D 23	Bath Iron Works Corp.	12 Oct 1942	7 Mar 1943	11 May 1943
ALMIRANTE STORNI (ex-USS *Cowell*, DD 547)	D 24	Bethlehem Co, San Pedro	7 Sep 1942	18 Mar 1943	23 Aug 1943

Displacement, tons: 2 100 standard; 3 050 full load
Length, feet (*metres*): 376·5 (*114·8*) oa
Beam, feet (*metres*): 39·5 (*12·0*)
Draught, feet (*metres*): 12·2 (*3·7*) mean; 18 (*5·5*) max
Guns, surface: 4—5 in (*127 mm*) 38 cal.
Guns, AA: 6—3 in (*76 mm*) 50 cal.
Torpedo tubes: 5—21 in (*533 mm*) quintupled; 6—Mk 32 (Triples)
A/S depth charges: 2 fixed Hedgehogs; 1 DC rack
A/S torpedo racks: 2 side-launching
Main engines: 2 sets GE or AC geared turbines 60 000 shp; 2 shafts
Boilers: 4 Babcock & Wilcox
Speed, knots: 35
Range, miles: 6 000 at 15 knots
Oil fuel, tons: 650
Complement: 300

GENERAL
First three transferred to the Argentine Navy on 1 Aug 1961. *Espora* is of the later "Fletcher" class. Last pair transferred 17 Aug 1971. *Brown* is division leader. USS *Knapp* (D 653) is also reported transferred as source of spare parts.

RADAR. Search: L Band SPS 6. Tactical: C Band SPS 10. Fire Control: X Band, antenna on Director.

ESPORA *1974, Argentine Navy*

ex-Fletcher

ALMIRANTE STORNI 1972, *Argentine Navy*

2 Ex-US "ALLEN M. SUMNER" CLASS

Name	No.	Builders	Launched	Commissioning
BOUCHARD (ex-USS *Borie* DD 704)	D 26	Federal SB & DD Co.	4 July 1944	21 Sep 1944
SEGUI (ex-USS *Hank* DD 702)	D 25	Federal SB & DD Co.	21 May 1944	28 Aug 1944

Displacement, tons: 2 200 standard; 3 320 full load
Length, feet (*metres*): 376·5 (*114·8*) oa
Beam, feet (*metres*): 40·9 (*12·5*)
Draught, feet (*metres*): 19 (*5·8*)
Guns: 6—5 in (*127 mm*) 38 cal; DP (twin) 4—3 in (*Hank* only)
A/S Weapons: 2 Triple torpedo tubes (Mk 32); 2 ahead-firing Hedgehogs; Facilities for small helicopter
Main engines: 2 geared turbines; 60 000 shp; 2 shafts
Boilers: 4
Speed, knots: 34
Range, miles: 3 865 at 11 knots; 990 at 31 knots
Complement: *Bouchard* 291; *Segui* 331

Transferred to Argentina 1 July 1972. *Bouchard* has been modernised with VDS, helicopter facilities and hangar. Third unit, ex-USS *Mansfield* DD 728, transferred June 1974 for spares.

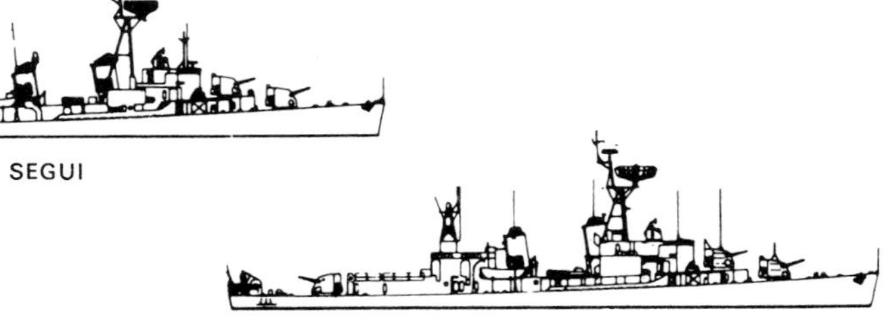

SEGUI

BOUCHARD

RADAR (*Bouchard*). SPS 10, SPS 40 and GFCS Mk 25.

SONAR (*Bouchard*). SQA 10A, SQS 30.

1 FRAM II "GEARING" CLASS

Name	No.	Builders	Laid down	Commissioning
PY (ex-USS *Perkins* DD 877)	D 27	Consolidated Steel Corpn.	7 Dec 1944	5 Apr 1945

Displacement, tons: 2 425 standard; approx 3 500 full load
Length, feet (*metres*): 390·5 (*119·0*)
Beam, feet (*metres*): 40·9 (*12·4*)
Draught, feet (*metres*): 19·0 (*5·8*)
Guns: 6—5 inch (*127 mm*), 38 cal. DP (twins)
A/S weapons: 2 Fixed Hedgehogs; 2 triple torpedo tubes (Mk 32) Facilities for small helicopter
Main engines: 2 geared Westinghouse turbines
Boilers: 4 Babcock & Wilcox
Speed, knots: 31·5
Range, miles: 6 150 at 11 knots; 1 475 at 30 knots
Complement: 275

Transferred by sale 15 Jan 1973.

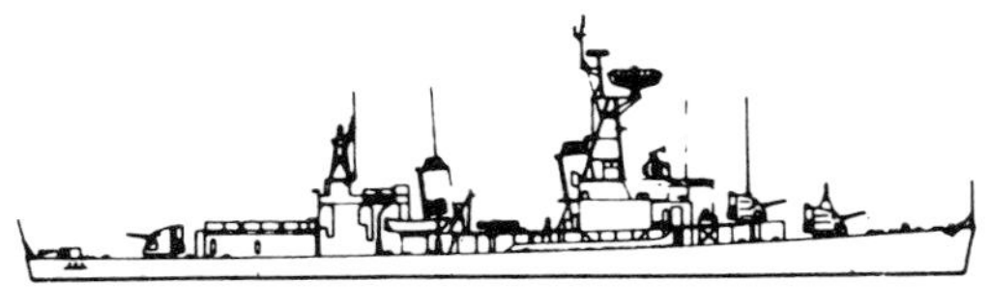

PY

RADAR. SPS 10, SPS 40 and GFCS Mk 25.

SONAR. SQS 23.

CORVETTES

2 "KING" CLASS

Name	No	Builders	Laid down	Launched	Completed
KING	P 21	Astillero Nav. Rio Santiago	Dec 1938	Dec 1943	28 July 1946
MURATURE	P 20	Astillero Nav. Rio Santiago	June 1938	July 1945	18 Nov 1946

Displacement, tons	913 standard; 1 000 normal; 1 032 full load
Length, feet (*metres*)	252·7 (*77·0*)
Beam, feet (*metres*)	29 (*8·8*)
Draught, feet (*metres*)	7·5 (*2·3*)
Guns, surface	3—4·1 (*105 mm*)
Guns, AA	4—40 mm Bofors; 2—MG
A/S	4—DCT
Main engines	2—Werkspoor 4-stroke diesels; 2 500 bhp; 2 shafts
Speed, knots	18
Oil fuel (tons)	90
Range, miles	6 000 at 12 knots
Complement	130

MURATURE *1974, Argentine Navy*

KING, MURATURE

GENERAL
Named after Captain John King, an Irish follower of Admiral Brown, who distinguished himself in the war with Brazil, 1826-28; and Captain Murature, who performed conspicuous service against the Paraguayans at the Battle of Cuevas on Aug 6 1865. Used for cadet training.

2 Ex-US ATF TYPE

Name	No.	Builder	Launched	Completed
COMMANDANTE GENERAL IRIGOYEN (ex-USS *Caliuilla* ATF 152)	A 1	Charleston SB and DD Co	2 Nov 1944	10 Mar 1945
COMANDANTE GENERAL ZAPIOLA (ex-USS *Arpaho* ATF 68)	A 2	Charleston SB & DD Co.	22 June 1942	20 Jan 1943

Displacement, tons	1 235 standard; 1 675 full load
Dimensions, ft (*m*)	195 wl; 205 oa × 38·2 × 15·3 (*62·5 × 11·6 × 4·7*)
Guns	4—40 mm AA (2 twin); 2—20 mm
Main engines	4 sets diesels with electric drive; 3 000 bhp = 16 knots
Complement	85

Former US fleet ocean tugs of the "Cherokee" class. Fitted with powerful pumps and other salvage equipment. Transferred to Argentina at San Diego, California, in 1961. Classified as tugs until 1966 when they were re-rated as patrol vessels.

6 Ex-US ATA TYPE

Name	No.	Builders	Completed
ALFEREZ SOBRAL (ex-USS *Catawba, ATA* 210)	A 9	Levingstone SB Co, Orange	1947
CHIRIGUANO (ex- US *ATA* 227)	A 7	,,	1947
COMODORO SOMELLERA (ex- USS *Salish ATA* 187)	A 10	,,	1947
DIAGUITA (ex-US *ATA* 124)	A 5	,,	1947
SANAVIRON (ex-US *ATA* 228)	A 8	,,	1947
YAMANA (ex-US *ATA* 126)	A 6	,,	1947

Displacement, tons	689 standard; 800 full load
Dimensions, ft (*m*)	134·5 wl; 143 oa × 34 × 12 (*43·4 × 10·4 × 3·6*)
Guns	1—40 mm; 2—20 mm AA
Main engines	Diesel-electric; 1 500 bhp = 12·5 knots
Oil fuel (tons)	154
Range, miles	16 500 at 8 knots
Complement	49

Former US auxiliary ocean tugs. *Diaguita* and *Yamana* are fitted as rescue ships. A 5, A 6, A 7 and A 8 bear names of South American Indian tribes. Classified as ocean salvage tugs until 1966 when they were re-rated as patrol vessels. A 9 and A 10 were transferred on 10 Feb 1972. A 10 operated by Coast Guard.

YAMANA *1969, Argentine Navy*

Name	No.	Builder	Launched	Completed
SPIRO	GC 12	Rio Santiago	7 June 1937	1938

Displacement, tons	560 normal; 650 full load
Dimensions, feet	197 oa × 24 × 11·5
Guns	4—40 mm
Main engines	2 MAN Diesels; 2 000 bhp = 13 knots
Range, miles	3 000 at 10 knots
Complement	77

SPIRO *1969, Argentine Navy*

GENERAL
Former minesweeper of the "Bouchard" class, now operated by the Prefectura Naval Argentina. Sister ships *Bouchard, Py* and *Seaver* were transferred to the Paraguayan Navy. This class, originally of 9, were the first warships built in Argentine yards.

SUBMARINES

2 TYPE 209 NEW CONSTRUCTION

SALTA S 31 **SAN LUIS** S 32

Displacement, tons	980 surface; 1 230 dived
Length, feet (*metres*)	183·4 (*55·9*)
Beam, feet (*metres*)	20·5 (*6·25*)
Draught, feet (*metres*)	17·9 (*5·4*)
Torpedo tubes	8—21 in; bow tubes (with reloads)
Main machinery	Diesel electric; MTU Diesels, 4 generators; 1 shaft; 5 000 hp
Speed, knots	22 dived, 10 surfaced
Complement	32

Built in sections by Howaldswerke Deutsche Werft AG, Kiel from the IK 68 design of Ingenieurkontor, Lübeck. Sections were shipped to Argentina for assembly at Tandanor, Buenos Aires. *Salta* launched 21 Nov 1972 and *San Luis* May 2 1973. Both commissioned in 1974.

SALTA *1973, Argentine Navy*

2 "GUPPY (IA and II)" CLASS

SANTA FE (ex-USS *Catfish* SS 339) S 21
SANTIAGO DEL ESTERO (ex-USS *Chivo* SS 341) S 22

Displacement, tons	1 870 surface; 2 420 (*Santa Fe*); 2 540 (*Santiago*) dived
Length, feet (*metres*)	307·5 (*93·8*) oa
Beam, feet (*metres*)	27·2 (*8·3*)
Draught, feet (*metres*)	18·0 (*5·5*) (*Santa Fe*); 17·0 (*5·2*) (*Santiago*)
Torpedo tubes	10—21 in (*533 mm*); 6 fwd, 4 aft
Main machinery	3 diesels; 4 800 shp; 2 electric motors; 5 400 shp; 2 shafts
Speed, knots	18 surfaced; 15 dived
Range, miles	12 000 at 10 knots
Oil fuel, tons	300
Complement	82-84

GENERAL
Both of the "Balao" class built by Electric Boat Co being launched on 19 Nov 1944 and 14 Jan 1945 and commissioned on 19 Mar 1945 and 28 April 1945, respectively. *Catfish* was modified under the Guppy II programme (1948-50) and *Chivo* under the Guppy 1A programme (1951). Both transferred to Argentina at Mare Island on 7 Jan 1971.

SANTA FE *1972, Argentine Navy*

AMPHIBIOUS FORCES

1 Ex-US LANDING SHIP (TANK)

CANDIDO DE LASALA Q 43 (ex-USS *Gunston Hall, LSD* 5)

Displacement, tons	5 480 standard; 9 375 full load
Dimensions, feet	457·8 oa × 72·2 × 18·0
Guns	12—40 mm AA
Main engines	2 Skinner Unaflow; 2 shafts; 7 400 shp = 15·4 knots
Boilers	2 Two drum
Range, miles	8 000 at 15 knots
Complement	Accommodation for 326 (17 officers and 309 men)

GENERAL
Built by Moor Dry Dock Co, Oakland, Calif. Laid down on 28 Dec 1942, launched on 1 May 1943 and completed on 10 Nov 1943. Arcticized in 1948/9. Transferred from the US Navy on 1 May 1970. Carries 14 LCA and has helicopter facilities.

CANDIDO DE LASALA *1973, Argentine Navy*

3 Ex-US LST TYPE

CABO SAN GONZALO Q 44 (ex-US *LST* 872)
CABO SAN ISIDRO Q 46 (ex-US *LST* 919)
CABO SAN PIO Q 50 (ex-US *LST* 1044)

Displacement, tons	2 366 beaching; 4 080 full load
Dimensions, feet	316 wl; 328 oa × 50 × 14
Main engines	2 diesels; 2 shafts; 1 800 bhp = 11 knots
Oil fuel, tons	700
Range, miles	9 500 at 9 knots
Complement	80

GENERAL
Built by Puget Sound Bridge and Dredging Co, Seattle, USA. Launched in 1944. Transferred 1946-47. All ships have two rudders.

MEDIUM LANDING SHIPS

Of the former United States landing ships, (medium) BDM 2 (ex-USN *LSM* 86) was converted into a minelayer support vessel in 1968.

1 LANDING SHIP (TANK)

CABO SAN ANTONIO Q 42

Displacement, tons	4 300 light; 8 000 full load
Dimensions, feet	445 oa × 62 × 16·5
Guns	6—3 in (3 twin)
Main engines	Diesels; 2 shafts; 13 700 bhp = 16 knots
Complement	124

Built at the AFNE Rio Santiago. Designed to carry a helicopter and two landing craft. Launched 1968, completed 1973. Commissioned 1974.
Modified US "Suffolk County" Class.
RADAR. Plessey AWS-1.

CABO SAN ANTONIO *1974, Argentine Navy*

1 Ex-US LCT TYPE

BDI Q 56 (ex-USS *LCIL* 583)

Displacement, tons	230 light; 387 full load
Dimensions, feet	153 wl; 159 oa × 23·2 × 5
Guns	2—20 mm AA
Main engines	8 sets diesels; 3 200 bhp = 14 knots. Two reversible propellers
Oil fuel, tons	110
Range, miles	6 000 at 12 knots
Complement	30

Used for training.

19 MINOR LANDING CRAFT

LCM 1 **LCM 2** **LCM 3** **LCM 4**

It was stated in Jan 1971 that four LCMs built in the USA had been incorporated in the Fleet.

EDVP 1, 3, 7, 8, 9, 10, 12, 13, 17, 19, 21, 24, 28, 29, 30

Displacement, tons	12
Dimensions, feet	39·5 × 10·5 × 5·5
Main engines	Diesel, 9 knots

Ex USN LCVPs. Transferred 1946.

LIGHT FORCES

2 GERMAN TYPE 148 (FAST ATTACK CRAFT—MISSILE)

Displacement, tons	234 standard; 265 full load
Dimensions, ft (*m*)	154·2 × 23·0 × 5·9 (*47 × 7 × 2*)
Missiles	Triple launcher for Gabriel missiles
Guns	1—76 mm; 1—40 mm
Torpedoes	2—21 in (or 8 mines)
Main engines	4 Diesels = 38 knots
Range, miles	600 at 30 knots
Complement	30

Building in Argentina.

GERMAN TYPE 148 — *1974, Federal German Navy*

2 COMBATTANTE II TYPE (FAST ATTACK CRAFT—GUN)

INTREPIDA ELPR 1 **INDOMITA** ELPR 2

Displacement, tons	240
Dimensions, ft (*m*)	164 × 24 (*50 × 7·3*)
Guns	1—3 in (*76 mm*) Otomelara AA, 2—40 mm AA
Torpedo tubes	Designed for 2—21 inch
Main engines	Diesels; 4 shafts; speed 40 knots
Complement	35

These two fast patrol vessels were ordered in 1970 and were built by Lürssen, Bremen. Of Combattante II type. *Intrepida* launched 12 Dec 1973 and *Indomita* May 1974. Both commissioned in 1974.

1 LARGE PATROL CRAFT

SURUBI P 55

Displacement, tons	100
Guns	2—20 mm
Speed, knots	20

Completed 1951 by Ast. Nav. del Estero.

3 "LYNCH" CLASS (LARGE PATROL CRAFT)

EREZCANO GC 23 **LYNCH** GC 21 **TOLL** GC 22

Displacement, tons	100 normal; 117 full load
Dimensions, feet	90 × 19 × 6
Gun	1—20 mm
Main engines	2 Maybach Diesels; 2 700 bhp = 22 knots
Complement	16

GENERAL
Patrol craft operated by the Prefectura Naval Argentina.

LYNCH — *1969, Argentine Navy*

1 LARGE PATROL CRAFT

GC 31
Dimensions generally similar to US 63 ft AVR class but of slightly different silhouette.

GC 31 — *1971*

2 EX-US "HIGGINS CLASS" (FAC—TORPEDO)

ALAKUSH P 82 **TOWORA** P 84

Displacement, tons	45
Dimensions, feet	78·7 × 9·8 × 4·6
Guns	2—40 mm; 4—MG
Torpedo launchers	4—21 inch
Rocket launchers	2 sextuple sets
Main engines	3 Packard; 4 050 hp = 45 knots
Range, miles	1 000 at 20 knots
Complement	12

The last of a class of nine. Given names in 1972.

Note. In addition the following are listed as operated by PNM: *Delfin* of 1 000 tons and 15 knots, *Robalo, Mandubi, Adhara, Albatross, Dorado*, LT 1 and 8, PAV 1, 2 and 3, PAM 1, 2 and 3, V 2 and 6, GN 1, 4, 38 and 42, PF 17, P 2, 5, 13, 22, 26, 39 and 41.

MINE WARFARE FORCES

6 Ex-BRITISH "TON" CLASS

(MINESWEEPERS—COASTAL and MINEHUNTERS)

CHACO (ex-HMS *Rennington*)	M 5
CHUBUT (ex-HMS *Santon*)	M 3
FORMOSA (ex-HMS *Ilmington*)	M 6
NEUQUEN (ex-HMS *Hickleton*)	M 1
RIO NEGRO (ex-HMS *Tarlton*)	M 2
TIERRA DEL FUEGO (ex-HMS *Bevington*)	M 4

CHACO (HUNTER) — *1972, Argentine Navy*

Displacement, tons	360 standard; 425 full load
Dimensions, ft (*m*)	140 pp; 153 oa × 28·8 × 8·2 (*46·3 × 8·8 × 2·5*)
Guns	1—40 mm AA
Main engines	2 Diesels; 2 shafts; 3 000 bhp = 15 knots
Oil fuel, tons	45
Range, miles	2 300 at 13 knots; 3 000 at 8 knots
Complement	Minsweepers 27; Minehunters 36

Former British coastal minesweepers of the "Ton" class. Of composite wooden and non-magnetic metal construction. Purchased in 1967. In 1968 *Chaco* and *Formosa* were converted into minehunters in HM Dockyard, Portsmouth, and the other four were refitted and modernised as minesweepers by the Vosper Thornycroft Group with Vosper activated fin stabiliser equipment.

NEUQUEN (SWEEPER) — *1974, Argentine Navy*

SURVEY SHIPS

COMODORO RIVADAVIA

Displacement, tons	655
Dimensions, ft (*m*)	167 × 28·9 × 8·5 (*50·9* × *8·8* × *2·6*)
Main engines	2 Werkspoor Diesels = 12 knots
Complement	30

Building by Mestrina, Tigre, Argentina. Laid down 17 July 1971, launched 2 Dec. 1972,. Commissioned late 1974. Rated as "Buque Hidrografico Auxiliar".

1 NEW CONSTRUCTION SURVEY SHIP

Displacement, tons	1 960 standard

Laid down in 1974 at Alianza, Avellaneda.

1 NEW CONSTRUCTION OCEANOGRAPHIC SHIP

Displacement, tons	2 100 standard
Dimensions, ft (*m*)	249 × 43·4 × 14·9 (*75·9* × *13·2* × *4·5*)
Engine	1 Diesel; 2 600 hp = 12 knots

Laid down at Astarsa, San Fernando in 1974.

ISLAS ORCADAS (ex-USS *Eltanin*, T-AGOR 8)

Displacement, tons	2 036 light; 4 942 full load
Dimensions, ft (*m*)	262·2 oa × 51·5 × 18·7 (80 × 15·7 × 5·7)
Main engines	Diesel electric; 3 200 bhp; 2 shafts = 12 knots
Complement	12 officers, 36 men, 38 scientists

Built by Avondale Marine Ways, New Orleans, delivered 2 Aug 1957. Converted for Antarctic Research 1961. Operated in conjunction by Argentine Navy, US National Science Foundation and Argentine National Directorate of the Antarctic.

2 Ex-US TUG TYPE

GOYENA (ex-USS *Dry Tortuga*) Q 17
THOMPSON (ex-USS *Sombrero Key*) A 4

Displacement, tons	1 863 full load
Dimensions, ft (*m*)	191·3 × 37 × 18 (*58·3* × *11·3* × *5·5*)
Guns	2—40 mm Bofors (twin); 2—20 mm (single)
Main engines	2 Enterprise Diesels; 2 250 bhp = 12 knots
Oil fuel, tons	532
Complement	60

Built by Pendleton Shipyard Co, New Orleans. Launched in 1943 and leased to Argentina in 1965. Temporarily used as survey ships.

THOMPSON *1973, Argentine Navy*

1 AUXILIARY SAILING SHIP

EL AUSTRAL (ex-US *Atlantis*) Q 7

Displacement, tons	571
Dimensions, feet	110 pp 141 oa × 27 × 20
Main engines	Diesel; 400 bhp
Oil fuel, tons	22
Complement	19

GENERAL
Built by Burmeister & Wain, Copenhagen. Launched and completed in 1931. Incorporated into the Argentine Navy on 30 April ,1966. Acquired from USA. Officially rated as *Buque Oceanagrafico*.

Survey Ships—*continued*

CORMORAN

Coastal survey launch of 102 tons with complement of 19, built in 1963. Speed 13 knots.

PETREL

Coastal survey launch of 50 tons with complement of 9, built in 1965.

TRANSPORTS

BAHIA AGUIRRE B 2 **BAHIA BUEN SUCESO** B 6

Displacement, tons	3 100 standard; 5 000 full load
Dimensions, ft (*m*)	334·7 × 47 × 13·8 (*95·1* × *14·3* × *7·9*)
Main engines	2 sets Nordberg diesels; 2 shafts; 3 750 bhp = 16 knots
Oil fuel, tons	442 (B 6); 355 (B 2)
Complement	100

GENERAL
Built by Canadian Vickers, Halifax, Nova Scotia. *Bahia Buen Suceso* was completed in June 1950.

BAHIA BUEN SUCESO *1974, Argentine Navy*

SAN JULIAN (ex-*FS* 281) B 7

Displacement, tons	930
Dimensions, feet	176 × 32·5 × 11
Main engines	2 sets diesels; 2 shafts; 1 000 bhp = 10 knots
Oil fuel tons	75
Complement	40

GENERAL
Ex-US Army small cargo carrier. Built by Wheeler Shipbuilding Corpn. Launched in 1944. In May 1960 it was planned to convert this ship into a salvage vessel—a plan that was dropped in 1961.

TANKERS

PUNTA DELGADA (ex-*Sugarland*, ex-*Nanticoke*, *AOG 66*) B 16 (FLEET SUPPORT)

Displacement, tons	5 930 standard; 6 090 full load
Dimensions, feet	325 × 48·2 × 20
Main engines	Westinghouse diesel; 1 shaft; 1 400 bhp = 11·5 knots
Oil fuel tons	150
Range, miles	9 000 at 11 knots
Complement	72

GENERAL
Named after geographical location. USMS type T1-M-BT1. Built by St. John's River SB Corp, Jacksonville, Fla. Launched on 7 Apr 1945.

PUNTA ALTA B 12 (FLEET SUPPORT)

Displacement, tons	1 600 standard; 1 900 full load
Measurement, tons	800 deadweight
Dimensions, feet	210 × 33·8 × 12·5
Main engines	Diesel; 1 shaft; 1 850 bhp = 8 knots
Oil fuel, tons	146

GENERAL
Built at Puerto Belgrano. Launched in 1937. Named after a headland.

Tankers—*continued*

PUNTA MEDANOS B 18 (UNDERWAY REPLENISHMENT)

Displacement, tons	14 352 standard; 16 331 full load
Measurement, tons	8 250 deadweight,
Dimensions, feet	470 pp; 502 oa × 62 × 28·5
Main engines	Double reduction geared turbines. 2 shafts; 9 500 shp = 18 knots (over 19 knots attained on trials)
Boilers	2 Babcock & Wilcox two-drum integral furnace water-tube
Oil fuel, tons	1 500
Range, miles	13 700 at 15 knots
Complement	99

GENERAL
Built by Swan, Hunter & Wigham Richardson Ltd, Wallsend-on-Tyne. Launched on 20 Feb 1950. Completed on 10 Oct 1950. Available as a training vessel. She was, when completed, the finest equipped and fastest of her type afloat. Boilers built under licence by the Wallsend Slipway & Engineering Company. Steam conditions of 400 lb per sq in pressure and 750 deg F.

PUNTA MEDANOS *1973, Argentine Navy*

TRAINING SHIP

LIBERTAD Q 2

Displacement, tons	3 025 standard; 3 765 full load
Dimensions, feet	262 wl; 301 oa × 47 × 21·8
Guns	1—3 in; 4—40 mm AA; 4—47 mm saluting
Main engines	2 Sulzer diesels; 2 400 bhp = 13·5 knots
Complement	370 (crew) plus 150 cadets

GENERAL
Built in the state owned shipyards at Rio Santiago. Launched on 20 June 1956. She is the largest sail training ship in the world and set up the fastest crossing of the N. Atlantic under sail in 1966 a record which still stands.

ICEBREAKER

GENERAL SAN MARTIN Q 4

Displacement, tons	4 854 standard; 5 301 full load
Measurement, tons	1 600 deadweight
Dimensions, feet	279 × 61 × 21
Guns	1—4 in; 2—40 mm AA Bofors
Aircraft	1 reconnaissance aircraft and 1 helicopter
Main engines	4 diesel-electric; 2 shafts; 7 100 hp = 16 knots
Range, miles	35 000 at 10 knots
Oil fuel, tons	1 100
Complement	160

GENERAL
Built by Seebeck Yard of Weser AG. Launched on 24 June 1954. Completed in Oct 1954. Fitted for research. New second radar mast fitted on after end of the hanger in late 1972.

GENERAL SAN MARTIN (2nd radar mast now fitted) *1970, Argentine Navy*

TUGS

GUAYCURU R 33 **QUILMES** R 32

Displacement, tons	368 full load
Dimensions, feet	107·2 × 24·4 × 12·5
Main engines	Skinner Unaflow engines; 645 ihp = 9 knots
Boilers	Cylindrical
Oil fuel, tons	52
Range, miles	2 200 at 7 knots
Complement	14

GENERAL
"Quilmes" class tugs built at Rio Santiago Naval Yard. Laid down on 23 Aug and 15 Mar 1956 respectively, launched on 27 Dec 1959 and 8 July 1957 and completed on 29 July and 30 Mar 1960.

PEHUENCHE R 29 **TONOCOTE** R 30

Displacement, tons	330
Dimensions, feet	105 × 24·7 × 12·5
Main engines	Triple expansion; 600 ihp = 11 knots
Boiler	2
Oil fuel, tons	36
Range, miles	1 200 at 9 knots
Complement	13

GENERAL
Both built in Rio Santiago Naval Yard. Commissioned for service in 1954.

TOBA R 4

Displacement, tons	600
Measurement, tons	339 gross
Dimensions, feet	130·5 pp; 137 wl; 139 oa × 28·5 × 11.5
Main engines	Triple expansion; 2 shafts; 1 200 ihp = 12 knots
Boilers	2
Oil fuel, tons	95
Range, miles	3 900 at 10 knots
Complement	34

GENERAL
Built by Hawthorn Leslie, Ltd, Hebburn-on-Tyne. Launched on 23 Dec 1927 and completed in Mar 1928.

HUARPE R 12

Displacement, tons	370
Dimensions, feet	107 × 27·2 × 12
Main engines	Triple expansion; 800 ihp
Boilers	1 cylindrical (Howaldt Werke)
Oil fuel, tons	58
Complement	13

GENERAL
Built by Howaldt Werke in 1927. Entered service in the Argentine Navy in 1942.

CALCHAQUI	R 6 (ex-US 445)	**CHULUPI**	R 10 (ex-US 426)
CAPAYAN	R 16 (ex-US 443)	**MOCOVI**	R 5 (ex-US 441)
CHAQUILLAN	R 18 (ex-US 444)	**MORCOYAN**	R 19 (ex-US 448)

Displacement, tons	70
Dimensions, feet	67 × 14 × 13
Main engines	Diesel; 310 bhp = 10 knots
Oil fuel, tons	8·7
Complement	5

Built in USA and allocated the above pennant numbers in 1969.

Two harbour tugs built by Vicente Forte entered service in 1974.

FLOATING DOCKS

Number	*Dimensions, ft*	*Capacity, tons*
Y 1 (ex-ARD 23)	150 × 27 × 17·1	3 500
2	91·5 × 18·3 × 12·5	1 000
ASD 40	65·8 × 14 × 13·7	750
—	65·8 × 14 × 13·7	750

First three are at Darsena Norte, Buenos Aires and the fourth at Puerto Belgrano.

MISCELLANEOUS

Four auxiliaries, *E 6*, *Fortuna*, *Itati* and *Juana* listed.
The ex-training ship *Presidente Sarmiento* is retained at Buenos Aires as a museum ship.

AUSTRALIA

Administration

Minister for Defence (and Navy):
Hon. Mr. L. H. Barnard, MP

Chairman of the Chiefs of Staff:
Admiral Sir Victor Smith, KBE, CB, DSC

Naval Authorities

Chief of Naval Staff:
Vice-Admiral H. D. Stevenson, CBE

Chief of Naval Personnel:
Rear-Admiral G. J. Willis

Chief of Naval Technical Services:
Rear-Admiral M. P. Reed

Chief of Supply and Works:
Rear-Admiral A. G. McFarlane

Deputy Chief of the Naval Staff:
Rear-Admiral G. V. Gladstone, DSC *

Special Deputy (Navy Office):
Mr. F. J. Green

Senior Appointments

Flag Officer Commanding Australian Fleet:
Rear-Admiral D. C. Wells, CBE

Flag Officer Commanding East Australian Area:
Rear-Admiral W. J. Dovers, CBE, DSC

Naval Procurement and Modernisation

In April 1974 the Australian Government decided to acquire two United States Patrol Frigates rather than proceed with the proposed DDL project, (see Jane's 1974). At the same time it was stated that further proposals will later be necessary for the acquisition of additional destroyers of a type to be determined.
3 Destroyers (DDG's *Hobart, Perth and Brisbane*) being modernised (see class notes). Older frigates to have extended refits.
10 Sea King helicopters (in lieu of 20) at a cost of $A43 million. Delivery of majority expected in the first half of 1975. A Sea King flight simulator costing $A2·5 million is scheduled to be operational by March 1976.

Naval Bases

FOCEA.—Sydney and Jervis Bay
NOC Queensland.—Brisbane and Cairns
NOC Northern Territory.—Darwin
NOC W. Australia.—Cockburn Sound (completing 1978)

Naval Shipyards

Building at Williamstown (Melbourne) and Cockatoo Island (Sydney). Refits at Garden Island (Sydney).

Diplomatic Representation

Australian Naval Representative in London:
Commodore A. A. Willis, OBE

Naval Attaché in Washington:
Commodore R. Percy

Naval Attaché in Tokyo:
Captain P. M. Rees

Naval Attaché in Jakarta:
Captain M. A. McK. Clarke

Navy Estimates

$A
1971-72: 270 244 000 *
1972-73: 293 094 000 *
1973-74: 319 994 000 *
1974-75: 375 014 000 *
*includes United States Credits

Personnel

1 January 1972: 17 000 officers and sailors
1 January 1973: 17 128 officers and sailors
1 January 1974: 16 743 officers and sailors
1 January 1975: 16 200 officers and sailors
(Includes 246 Papua Defence Force)

Fleet Air Arm

Squadron	*Aircraft*
HT 723	Iroquois and Bell 206B-1 helos
VC 724	A4G and TA4G Skyhawks, Macchi Trainers (Training, FRU and Trials)
HT 725	Wessex 31B helos (training and FRU)
VF 805	A4G Skyhawks (Front line fighter/strike)
VS 816	S2E Trackers (Front line A/S)
HS 817	Wessex 31B helos (Front line A/S)
VC 851	S2E Trackers, HS 748 (Training, communications and FRU)

Papua-New Guinea Defence Force

The RAN base in the Admiralty Islands, HMAS *Tarangau*, was decommissioned 14.11.74 and handed over to the PNG Defence Force. It is now the PNGDF Patrol Boat Base Lombrum. Five RAN "Attack"-class patrol boats, *Aitape, Ladava, Lae, Madang* and *Samarai*, plus two LCH's *Buna* and *Salamau* have been re-commissioned as PNG Ships and are fully or partially manned by PNG personnel. The ships will remain units of the RAN until Independence in PNG, or transfer of defence power if this is earlier.

Prefix to Ships' Names

HMAS. Her Majesty's Australian Ship
PNGS. Papua New Guinea Ship

Strength of the Fleet

Type	*Active*	*Building*
Attack Carrier (Medium)	1	—
Destroyers	5 (3DDG)	—
Frigates (PF)	—	2
Frigates	6	—
Patrol Submarines	4	2
MCM Vessels	3	—
Large Patrol Craft	17	—
Survey Ships	4	1
Fleet Support Ships	2	—
Landing Craft (Heavy)	8	—
Training Ship	1	—
Others	11	—

Mercantile Marine

Lloyd's Register of Shipping:
394 vessels of 1 168 367 tons gross

Disposals

ex-Carrier

Sydney For disposal 20.7.73

Destroyers

Arunta sank in tow to breaker 13.2.69
Tobruk left Sydney for Taiwan 10.4.72
Anzac Disposal 11.8.74

Frigates

Barcoo left Sydney for Taiwan 17.3.72
Culgoa left Sydney for Taiwan 17.3.72
Quickmatch left Sydney for Japan 10.4.72
Quiberon left Sydney for Japan 6.7.72
Gascoyne left Sydney for Taiwan 6.7.72
Queenborough Sales List 1974

MCM Vessels

Hawk Sales List 1974
Gull Sales List 1974

Miscellaneous

SDBs 1321, 1324, 1325 1972
Karakara (Hulk) scuttled 30.1.73
Paluma Sold 1974
Otter Sales List 1974

Large Patrol Craft

Archer and *Bandolier* to Indonesia 21.10.74 and 16.11.73
Arrow Sunk Darwin (Hurricane Tracy) 25.12.74

PENNANT LIST

Aircraft Carrier

Melbourne	21

Submarines

Oxley	57
Otway	59
Onslow	60
Ovens	70

Destroyers

Perth	38
Hobart	39
Brisbane	41
Vendetta	08
Vampire	11

Frigates

Yarra	45
Parramatta	46
Stuart	48
Derwent	49
Swan	50
Torrens	53

Training Ship

Duchess	154

Minehunters

Snipe	1102
Curlew	1121

Minesweepers (Coastal)

Ibis (O)	1183

Survey Ships

Moresby	73
Diamantina	266
Flinders	312
Kimbla	314

Support Ships

Supply	195
Stalwart	215

Landing Craft

Brunei	127
Labuan	128
Tarakan	129
Wewak	130
Salamaua (P)	
Buna (P)	
Betano	
Balikpapan	

Reserve Training Ships

Banks	244
Bass	247

Patrol Boats

Advance	83
Assail	89
Attack	90
Barbette	97
Barricade	98
Bayonet	101
Aitape (P)	84
Ladava (P)	92
Lae (P)	93
Madang (P)	94
Samarai (P)	85
Aware	91
Ardent	87
Bombard	99
Buccaneer	100
Adroit	82
Acute	81

Notes
O=Operational Reserve
P=Papua-New Guinea Defence Force

AIRCRAFT CARRIER

Name	*No.*	*Builders*	*Laid down*	*Launched*	*Commissioned*
MELBOURNE (ex-*Majestic*)	21	Vickers-Armstrong, Barrow-in-Furness	15 Apr 1943	28 Feb 1945	28 Oct 1955

1 MODIFIED "MAJESTIC" CLASS

Displacement, tons	16 000 standard; 19 966 full load
Length, feet (*metres*)	650·0 (*198·1*)wl; 701·5 (*213·8*)oa
Beam, feet (*metres*)	80·2 (*24·5*) hull
Draught, feet (*metres*)	25·5 (*7·8*)
Width, feet (*metres*)	80·0 (*24·4*) flight deck 126·0 (*38·4*) oa including 6 deg angled deck and mirrors
Hangar, feet (*metres*)	444×52×17·5 (*135·3×15·8×5·3*)
Aircraft	8 Sky Hawk jet fighters; 6 Tracker aircraft; 10 Westland Wessex A/S helicopters (see *Aircraft* notes)
Guns, AA	12—40 mm (4 twin, 4 single) Bofors
Boilers	4 Admiralty 3-drum type
Main engines	Parsons single reduction geared turbines; 2 shafts; 42 000 shp
Speed, knots	24; sea speed 23 max
Range, miles	12 000 at 14 knots; 6 200 at 23 knots
Complement	1 335 (includes 347 Carrier Air Group personnel); 1 070 (75 officers and 995 sailors) as Flagship

MELBOURNE — *1973, Royal Australian Navy*

GENERAL

At the end of the Second World War, when she was still incomplete, work on this ship was brought to a standstill pending a decision as to future naval requirements. When full-scale work was resumed during 1949-55, and after her design had been re-cast several times, she underwent reconstruction and modernisation in Great Britain, including the fitting of the angled deck, steam catapult and mirror deck landing sights, and was transferred to the RAN on completion. She was commissioned and renamed at Barrow-in-Furness on 28 Oct 1955, sailed from Portsmouth on 5 Mar 1956, and arrived at Fremantle, Australia, on 23 April 1956. She became flagship of the Royal Australian Navy at Sydney on 14 May 1956. She cost £A8 309 000.

AIRCRAFT. The aircraft complement formerly comprised 8 Sea Venom jet fighters, 17 Gannet turbo-prop anti-submarine aircraft, and 2 Sycamore helicopters, later 4 Sea Venom, 6 Gannet and 10 Wessex A/S helicopters. Fourteen S2E Tracker anti-submarine aircraft and ten A4G Skyhawk fighter/bombers were purchased in 1966 in the USA (in service 1967) at a cost of $A46 000 000. Another 10 A4G Skyhawk (including 2 TA4G Trainers) were delivered during 1971. *Melbourne* now carries Skyhawks, Trackers and Wessex.

MODERNISATION. *Melbourne* completed her extended refit during 1969 at a cost of over $A8 750 000 to enable her to operate with S2E Tracker and A4G Skyhawk aircraft, and to improve habitability. In 1971 the catapult was rebuilt and a bridle-catcher fitted, and the flight deck was strengthened. Under refit from November 1972 to July 1973.

RADAR. Search: Philips LWO series early warning and associated height finders for aircraft direction. Tactical: Type 293 Target Indication and surface warning. E.W.: Electronic intelligence and warfare equipment also fitted. Carrier controlled approach Radar. (Dome on island.)

MELBOURNE — *1974, John Mortimer*

DRAWING. Starboard elevation and plan as converted with the angled deck. Scale: 120 feet = 1 inch.

MELBOURNE — *1974*

DESTROYERS

3 "PERTH" CLASS (DLGs)

Name	No.	Builders	Laid down	Launched	Commissioned
BRISBANE	41	Defoe Shipbuilding Co, Bay City, Mich.	15 Feb 1965	5 May 1966	16 Dec 1967
HOBART	39	Defoe Shipbuilding Co, Bay City, Mich.	26 Oct 1962	9 Jan 1964	18 Dec 1965
PERTH	38	Defoe Shipbuilding Co, Bay City, Mich.	21 Sep 1962	26 Sep 1963	17 July 1965

Displacement, tons	3 370 standard; 4 618 full load
Length, feet (*metres*)	431·0 (*131·4*)wl; 437·0 (*132·2*)oa
Beam, feet (*metres*)	47·1 (*14·3*)
Draught, feet (*metres*)	20·1 (*6·1*)
Missile launchers	1 single for "Tartar" (see Modernisation note)
A/S weapons	2 single launchers for long range "Ikara" system
Guns	2—5 in (*127 mm*) 54 cal, dp, single-mount, rapid fire
Torpedo tubes	6 (2 triple) for A/S torpedoes
Boilers	4 Foster Wheeler "D" type, 1 200 psi; 950°F
Main engines	2 GE double reduction turbines, 2 shafts; 70 000 shp
Speed, knots	35
Range, miles	6 000 at 14 knots 1 600 at 30 knots
Complement	333 (21 officers, 312 sailors)

"PERTH" Class

1974

GENERAL
On 6 Jan 1962, in Washington, US defence representatives and Australian military officials (on behalf of the Royal Australian Navy) and executives of the Defoe Shipbuilding Company, of Bay City, Michigan, signed a $A25 726 700 contract for the construction of two guided-missile destroyers (shipbuilding cost only). On 22 Jan 1963 it was announced by the Navy Minister in Canberra, Australia, that a third guided-missile destroyer was to be built in USA for Australia. The first of their kind for the Australian Navy, they constitute the 1st Destroyer Squadron, RAN. All three ships have been in action off Vietnam where they served with the US 7th fleet.

COST. Original estimate $A12 800 000 to $A14 000 000 each (with missiles and electronics $A40 000 000 each). The total cost of *Perth* was reported to be $A50 000 000.

DESIGN. Generally similar to the US "Charles F. Adams" class, but they differ by the addition of a broad deckhouse between the funnels enclosing the Ikara anti-submarine torpedo-carrying missile system, and the mounting of a single-arm launcher, instead of a twin, for the Tartar surface-to-air guided missiles. They have a new hull design with aluminium superstructures. The most recent habitability improvements have been incorporated into their construction, including air-conditioning of all living spaces.

MODERNISATION. *Perth* sailed from Sydney on 31.7.74 for the Long Beach Naval Shipyard to be modernised. The work will include the installation of a Naval Combat Data System, updating of the Tartar missile fire control system, replacing 5-inch gun mounts and modernising radars. The Australian Government has announced that *Hobart* and *Brisbane* would be given similar modernisations in Australia. This is a reversal of the previous Government's policy to have all modernisation completed in the United States. *Hobart's* gun mounts were modernised in the U.S. in 1972. *Brisbane's* gun mounts will be stripped and re-installed in Australia, with the gun mount re-engineering being done in the U.S.

PERTH *1971, Royal Australian Navy*

BRISBANE *1974, John Mortimer*

Destroyers—*continued*

3 "DARING" CLASS (DD)

Displacement, tons	2 800 standard; 3 600 full load
Length, feet (*metres*)	366 (*111·3*)pp; 388·5 (*118·4*)oa
Beam, feet (*metres*)	43 (*13·1*)
Draught, feet (*metres*)	12·8 (*3·9*)
Guns, surface	6—4·5 in (*115 mm*) in 3 twin turrets, two forward and one aft
Guns, AA	6—40 mm (2—40 mm in *Duchess*)
A/S weapons	1 3-barrelled DC mortar (see Design notes)
Boilers	2 Foster Wheeler; 650 psi; 850°F
Main engines	English Electric geared turbines; 2 shafts; 54 000 shp
Speed, knots	30·5
Range, miles	3 700 at 20 knots; 3 000 at 20 knots (*Duchess*)
Oil fuel, tons	584
Complement	320 (14 officers, 306 sailors)

Name	*No.*	*Builders*	*Begun*	*Launched*	*Completed*
VAMPIRE	11	Cockatoo Island Dockyard, Sydney	1 July 1952	27 Oct 1956	23 June 1959
VENDETTA	08	HMA Naval Dockyard, Williamstown	4 July 1949	3 May 1954	26 Nov 1958
DUCHESS	154	John I. Thornycroft & Co, Southampton	2 July 1948	9 Apr 1951	23 Oct 1952

GENERAL
The above particulars refer to *Vampire* and *Vendetta*, which constitute the 2nd Destroyer Squadron, RAN. *Vampire* and *Vendetta* are the largest destroyers ever built in Australia. They were ordered in 1946. Their sister ship, *Voyager*, the prototype of the class, collided with the aircraft carrier *Melbourne* and sank off the southern coast of New South Wales on the night of 10 Feb 1964. She was replaced by the British destroyer *Duchess*, lent to Australia by the United Kingdom for four years on 8 May 1964, later extended to 1971 and purchased by RAN in 1972.
Four large destroyers of this type were originally projected, to have been named after the Royal Australian Navy's famous "Scrap Iron Flotilla" of destroyers during the Second World War, but *Waterhen* was cancelled in 1954.

DESIGN. *Vampire* and *Vendetta* were of similar design, (including all welded construction) to that of the "Daring" class, built in Great Britain, but were modified to suit Australian conditions and have "Limbo" instead of "Squid" anti-submarine mortars. The superstructure is of light alloy, instead of steel, to reduce weight.

MODERNISATION. *Vampire* completed in Dec 1971. *Vendetta* completed May 1973. The $A20 million programme for both ships included new Mk 22 fire-control systems, new LW02 air-warning and navigation radars, new action-information centre, modernised communications, fitting modernised turrets, improved habitability, the fitting of an enclosed bridge and new funnels. The work was carried out by Williamstown Dockyard. These alterations afford an interesting comparison with the Peruvian "Darings" (ex-*Decoy* and *Diana*) with their eight Exocet SSMs and rebuilt forefunnel and radar.

RADAR. Philips LW02 early warning, (not *Duchess*).

Note. *Duchess* has been converted for training purposes, including the removal of X-turret and Squid to make way for new upper-deck classrooms. She retains her forward battery radar (Type 293 and X-band fire control) and sonar (in maintenance). Completed August 1974.

VAMPIRE, VENDETTA — *1974*

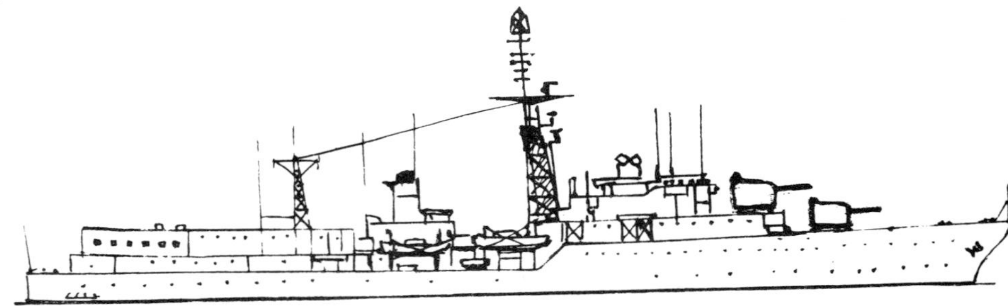

DUCHESS — *1974*

DUCHESS — *1974, Royal Australian Navy*

VAMPIRE — *1974, John Mortimer*

FRIGATES

6 "RIVER" CLASS

Name	*No.*	*Builders*	*Laid down*	*Launched*	*Commissioned*
YARRA	45	Williamstown Naval Dockyard, Melbourne	9 Apr 1957	30 Sep 1958	27 July 1961
PARRAMATTA	46	Cockatoo Island Dockyard, Sydney	3 Jan 1957	31 Jan 1959	4 July 1961
STUART	48	Cockatoo Island Dockyard, Sydney	20 Mar 1959	8 Apr 1961	28 June 1963
DERWENT	49	Williamstown Naval Dockyard, Melbourne	16 June 1958	17 Apr 1961	30 Apr 1964
SWAN	50	Williamstown Naval Dockyard, Melbourne	18 Aug 1965	16 Dec 1967	20 Jan 1970
TORRENS	53	Cockatoo Island Dockyard, Sydney	18 Aug 1965	28 Sep 1968	19 Jan 1971

Displacement, tons	2 100 standard; 2 700 full load
Length, feet (*metres*)	360·0 (*109·7*) pp; 370·0 (*112·8*) oa
Beam, feet (*metres*)	41·0 (*12·5*)
Draught, feet (*metres*)	17·3 (*5·3*)
Missile launchers	1 quadruple for "Seacat"
A/S weapons	1 launcher for "Ikara" long range system 1 "Limbo" 3-barrelled DC mortar
Guns, dual purpose	2—4·5 in (*115 mm*)
Boilers	2 Babcock & Wilcox; 550 psi; 850°F
Main engines	2 double reduction geared turbines; 2 shafts; 30 000 shp
Speed, knots	30
Range, miles	4 500 at 12 knots
Complement	247 (13 officers, 234 sailors) in *Swan* and *Torrens*; 250 (13 officers, 237 sailors) in other four ships

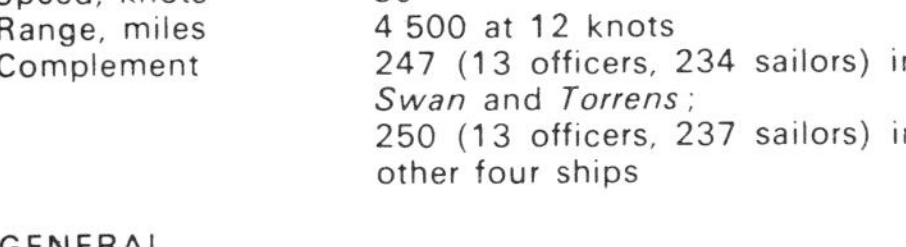

PARRAMATTA 1973, *John Mortimer*

GENERAL
The design of the first four is basically similar to that of British "Type 12", the last pair to that of the "Leander" frigates. All are modified by the Royal Australian Navy to incorporate improvements in equipment and habitability. *Stuart* was the first ship fitted with the "Ikara" anti-submarine guided missile; trial ship for the system. *Derwent* was the first RAN ship to be fitted with "Seacat". The variable depth sonar has been removed from *Derwent* and *Stuart*. Note difference in silhouette between *Swan* and *Torrens* and the earlier ships of the class, the former pair having a straight-run upper deck.

MODERNISATION. Some, at least, of this class will shortly be modernised. This will include improved accommodation consequent on a reduction in crew, new fire control systems, an improved Ikara system and, possibly, the fitting of Mulloka, a new and improved Australian sonar.

RADAR. Search: All ships fitted with Philips LWO series of L Band early warning radars. Type 293 combined air and surface warning, except *Swan* and *Torrens* which have Philips/HSA X Band radar. Fire Control: MRS 3 or HSA systems, X Band radar.

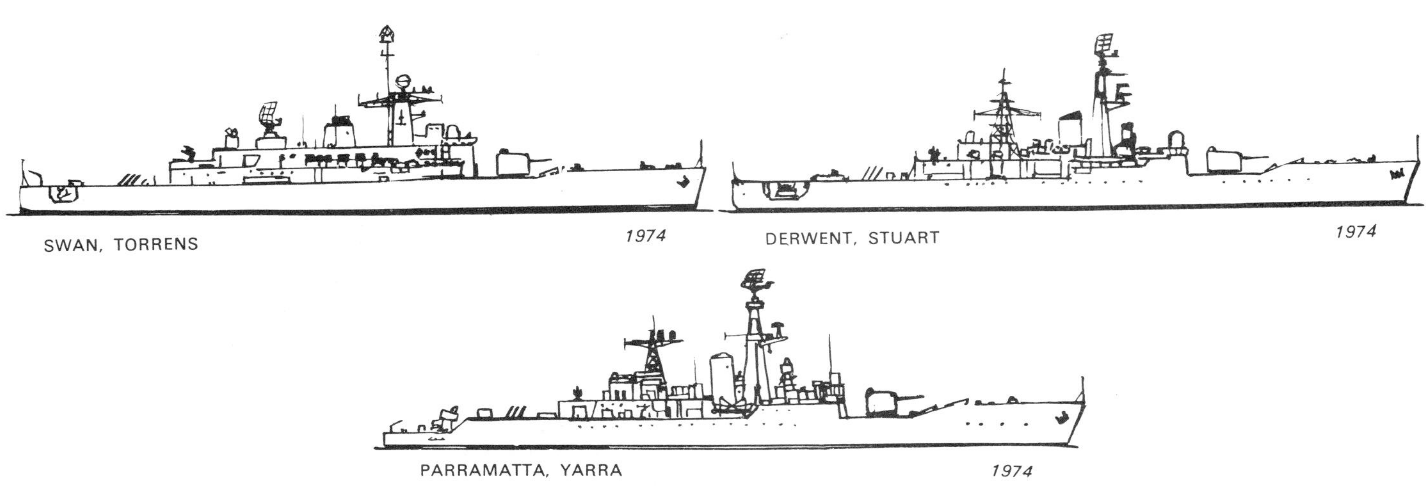

SWAN, TORRENS 1974

DERWENT, STUART 1974

PARRAMATTA, YARRA 1974

TORRENS 1974, *John Mortimer*

SUBMARINES

4 + 2 "OXLEY" CLASS (BRITISH "OBERON" CLASS)

Name	No.	Builders	Laid down	Launched	Commissioned
ONSLOW	60	Scotts' Shipbuilding & Eng Co Ltd, Greenock	4 Dec 1967	3 Dec 1968	22 Dec 1969
OTWAY	59	Scotts' Shipbuilding & Eng Co Ltd, Greenock	29 June 1965	29 Nov 1966	23 Apr 1968
OVENS	70	Scotts' Shipbuilding & Eng Co Ltd, Greenock	17 June 1966	4 Dec 1967	18 Apr 1969
OXLEY	57	Scotts' Shipbuilding & Eng Co Ltd, Greenock	2 July 1964	24 Sep 1965	18 Apr 1967
ORION	61	Scotts' Shipbuilding & Eng Co Ltd, Greenock	6 Oct 1972	16 Sep 1974	Due 1975
OTAMA		Scotts' Shipbuilding & Eng Co Ltd, Greenock	25 May 1973	Due 1975	Due 1976

Displacement, tons	1 610 standard; 2 196 surface; 2 417 submerged
Length, feet (*metres*)	241 (*73·5*) pp; 295·5 (*90·1*) oa
Beam, feet (*metres*)	26·5 (*8·1*)
Draught, feet (*metres*)	18 (*5·5*)
Torpedo tubes	8—21 in (*533 mm*) (6 bow, 2 stern)
Main machinery	2 Admiralty Standard Range diesels. 3 600 bhp; 2 shafts; 2 electric motors, 6 000 shp; Electric drive
Speed, knots	16 surface; 18 dived
Oil fuel, tons	300
Range, miles	12 000 at 10 knots
Complement	62 (7 officers, 55 sailors)

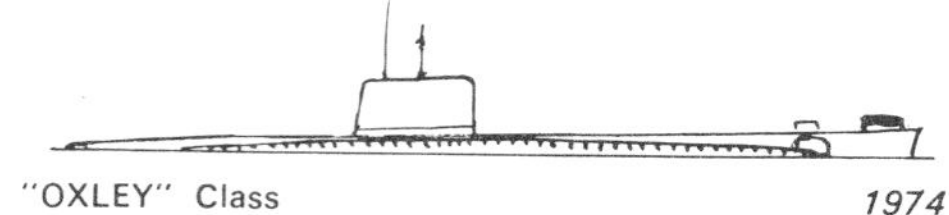
"OXLEY" Class *1974*

GENERAL
It was announced by the Minister for the Navy on 22 Jan 1963 that four submarines of the "Oberon" class were to be built in British shipyards under Admiralty supervision at an overall cost of £A5 000 000 each. These were to constitute the 1st Submarine Squadron RAN based at HMAS Platypus, Neutral Bay, Sydney. Subsequently two more were ordered in October 1971 for delivery in 1975-76

NAMES. *Oxley* and *Otway* are named after two earlier RAN submarines, completed in 1927. *Otama* is the Queensland aboriginal word for Dolphin, *Onslow* is a town in Western Australia, *Ovens* was an early explorer and *Orion* is named after the constellation.

R.N. SQUADRON. The last unit of the Fourth Submarine Squadron of the Royal Navy, *Trump*, was withdrawn from Balmoral, Sydney in Jan 1969.
Odin arrived in Australian waters in Dec 1972 for a three year attachment to the RAN.

OTWAY AND SYDNEY OPERA HOUSE *1974, John Mortimer*

OXLEY *1974, John Mortimer*

MINE WARFARE SHIPS

3 "TON" CLASS (MODIFIED)

CURLEW (ex-HMS *Chediston*, ex-*Montrose*) 1121 **SNIPE** (ex-HMS *Alcaston*) 1102
IBIS (ex-HMS *Singleton*) 1183

Displacement, tons	375 standard; 445 full load
Dimensions, feet	140 pp; 152 oa × 28·8 × 8·2
Guns	*Ibis* 2—40 mm, *Curlew* and *Snipe* 1—40 mm
Main engines	Napier Deltic diesels; 2 shafts; 3 000 bhp = 16 knots
Range, miles	2 300 at 13 knots; 3 000 at 8 knots
Complement	*Ibis* 34 (4 officers; 30 sailors), *Curlew* and *Snipe* 38 (3 officers, 35 sailors)

"Ton" class coastal minesweepers. Purchased from the United Kingdom in 1961, and modified in British Dockyards to suit Australian conditions. Turned over to the Royal Australian Navy, commissioned and re-named on 21 Aug, 7 Sept and 11 Sept, respectively. Mirlees diesels were replaced by Napier Deltic, and ships air-conditioned and fitted with stabilisers. Sailed from Portsmouth to Australia on 1 Oct 1962. Constitute the 1st Mine Countermeasures Squadron. *Curlew* and *Snipe* have been converted into minehunters.

SNIPE *1974, John Mortimer*

PATROL BOATS

17 "ATTACK" CLASS

Australia

ACUTE	81	**ARDENT**	87	**AWARE**	91	**BAYONET**	101
ADROIT	82	**ASSAIL**	89	**BARBETTE**	97	**BOMBARD**	99
ADVANCE	83	**ATTACK**	90	**BARRICADE**	98	**BUCCANEER**	100

New Guinea

AITAPE 84 **LADAVA** 92 **LAE** 93 **MADANG** 94 **SAMARAI** 85

Displacement, tons	146 full load
Dimensions, feet	107·5 oa × 20 × 7·3
Guns	1—40 mm; 2 medium MG (no guns in *Aware* and *Madang*)
Main engines	Paxman 16 YJCM Diesels 3 500 hp; 2 shafts = 21·24 knots
Complement	19 (3 officers, 16 sailors). PNG boats: 2 officers, 14 sailors

Five patrol boats for the formation of the Papua-New Guinea Defence Force and fifteen for general duties were built. Steel construction. Builders: Evans Deakin & Co. Pty Ltd, Brisbane, and Walkers Ltd, Maryborough. Ordered in Nov 1965. First vessel was originally scheduled for delivery in Aug 1966, but was not launched until Mar 1967. Cost $A800 000 each.

TRANSFERS. *Bandolier* transferred to Indonesia after refit 16 Nov 1973. *Archer* transferred 21 Oct 1974.

DARWIN HURRICANE. On 25 Dec 1974 *Arrow* and *Attack* were lost during Hurricane Tracy at Darwin. The latter was subsequently salved for repair.

SILHOUETTE OF "ATTACK" CLASS after modification

BAYONET *1973, Royal Australian Navy*

OCEANOGRAPHIC AND SURVEY SHIPS

1 NEW CONSTRUCTION

COOK 291

Displacement, tons	1 910 standard; 2 650 full load
Length, feet (*metres*)	317·5 (*91·2*)
Beam, feet (*metres*)	44·0 (*13·4*)
Draught, feet (*metres*)	15·1 (*4·6*)
Main engines	Diesels; 2 shafts; 3 400 bhp
Speed, knots	17
Oil fuel, tons	640
Range, miles	11 000 at 14 knots
Complement	150 including 13 scientists

GENERAL
Intended to replace HMAS *Diamantina*. She will have dual hydrographic and oceanographic roles. The after part of the ship will contain research equipment and facilities. Accommodation for 13 scientists. Design work in hand.

COOK *1972, Official, revised artists impression*

Name	*No.*	*Builders*	*Laid down*	*Launched*	*Commissioned*
MORESBY	573	State Dockyard, Newcastle NSW	June 1961	7 Sep 1963	6 Mar 1964

Displacement, tons	1 714 standard; 2 351 full load
Length, feet (*metres*)	284·5 (*86·7*) pp; 314·0 (*95·7*) oa
Beam, feet (*metres*)	42·0 (*12·8*)
Draught, feet (*metres*)	15·0 (*4·6*)
Guns	2—40 mm Bofors AA (single)
Aircraft	1 Westland Scout Helicopter
Main engines	Diesel-electric; 3 diesels; 3 990 bhp; 2 electric motors; 2 shafts; 5 000 shp = 19 knots
Complement	146 (13 officers, 133 sailors)

GENERAL
The Royal Australian Navy's first specifically designed survey ship. Built at a cost of £A2 000 000 ($A4 000 000).

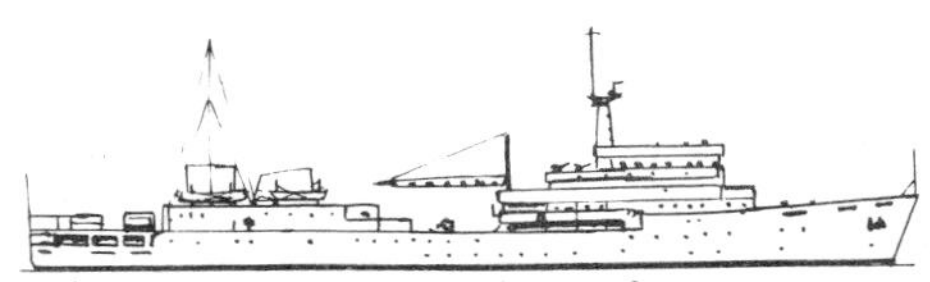

MORESBY *1974*

MORESBY *1973, Royal Australian Navy*

Survey Ships—*continued*

Name	*No.*	*Builders*	*Laid down*	*Launched*	*Completed*
DIAMANTINA	266 (ex-F 377)	Walkers Ltd, Maryborough, Queensland	12 Apr 1943	6 Apr 1944	27 Apr 1945

Displacement, tons	1 340 standard; 2 127 full load
Length, feet (*metres*)	283 (*86·3*) pp; 301·3 (*91·8*) oa
Beam, feet (*metres*)	36·7 (*11·2*)
Draught, feet (*metres*)	12·5 (*3·8*)
Gun	1—40 mm
Boilers	2 Admiralty 3-drum
Main engines	Triple expansion 5 500 ihp; 2 shafts
Speed, knots	19·5
Range, miles	7 700 at 12 knots
Complement	125 (6 officers, 119 sailors)

GENERAL
Frigate converted in 1959-60 for survey and completed conversion for oceanographic research in June 1969. The conversion included the provision of special laboratories. Sister ship *Lachlan* was sold to the Royal New Zealand Navy.

ARMAMENT. The two 4-inch guns and two "Squid" A/S mortars in "B" position were removed. The forward 4-inch gun was in "A" position with the 40 mm gun superimposed.

DIAMANTINA *1974*

Name	*No.*	*Builders*	*Laid down*	*Launched*	*Commissioned*
FLINDERS	312	HMA Dockyard Williamstown	11 June 1971	29 July 1972	27 Apr 1973

Displacement, tons	750
Dimensions, feet	161 × 33 × 12
Main engines	2 Paxman Ventura Diesels, total hp 1 680
Speed, knots	13·5
Range, miles	5 000 at 9 knots
Complement	38 (4 officers, 34 men)

Similar in design to *Atyimba* built for the Philippines, she replaced *Paluma* in April 1973, the latter having been running steadily since her conversion from stores tender in 1959. *Flinders* is based at Cairns, with her primary responsibility in the Barrier Reef area.

FLINDERS *1973, Royal Australian Navy*

KIMBLA A 314

Displacement, tons	762 standard; 1 021 full load
Dimensions, feet	150 pp; 179 oa × 32 × 12
Main engines	Triple expansion; 1 shaft; 350 ihp
Speed, knots	9·5
Complement	40 (4 officers, 36 men)

Built as a boom defence vessel by Walkers Ltd, Maryborough. Laid down 4 Nov 1953, launched 23 Mar 1955, completed 26 Mar 1956. Converted to trials vessel in 1959. Guns were removed (1—40 mm; 2—20 mm).

SUPPORT SHIPS

Note. On 22 August 1973, the Australian Government decided, amongst other things, that the construction of the third ship of this type, the 600 ft *Protector* should not go on. Examination of cheaper alternatives is in hand.

STALWART 215

Displacement, tons	10 000 standard; 15 500 full load
Length, feet (*metres*)	515·5 (*157·1*) oa
Beam, feet (*metres*)	67·5 (*20·6*)
Draught, feet (*metres*)	29·5 (*9·0*)
Missiles	Provision for Seacat
Guns, AA	4—40 mm (2 twin)
Main engines	2 Scott-Sulzer 6-cyl turbo-diesels 2 shafts; 14 400 bhp
Speed, knots	20
Complement	396 (23 officers and 373 sailors)

GENERAL
Largest naval vessel designed and built in Australia. Built at Cockatoo Island Dockyard by Vickers (Australia) Pty Ltd, Sydney. Ordered on 11 Sep 1963. Laid down in June 1964 and launched on 7 Oct 1966. Commissioned 9 Feb 1968. Designed to maintain destroyers and frigates, and advanced weapons systems, including guided missiles. She has a helicopter flight deck and is defensively armed. High standard of habitability. Formerly rated as Escort Maintenance Ship. Redesignated Destroyer Tender in 1968. Cost officially estimated at just under $A15 000 000.

STALWART *1974, John Mortimer*

STALWART *1974*

SUPPLY (ex-*Tide Austral*) 195

Displacement, tons	15 000 standard; 25 941 full load
Measurement, tons	17 600 deadweight; 11 200 gross
Dimensions, feet	550 pp; 583 oa × 71 × 32
Guns	6—40 mm AA (2 twin, 2 single)
Main engines	Double reduction geared turbines; 15 000 shp = 17·25 knots
Complement	13 officers, 187 sailors

Built for Australia by Harland & Wolff, Ltd, Belfast. Launched 1 Sep 1954, completed March 1955. British "Tide" Class. Lent to Great Britain until 1 Sep 1962, when *Tide Austral* was re-named HMAS *Supply* and commissioned in the Royal Australian Navy at Portsmouth 15 Aug 1962. Sailed for Australia 1 Oct 1962.

SUPPLY *1974, John Mortimer*

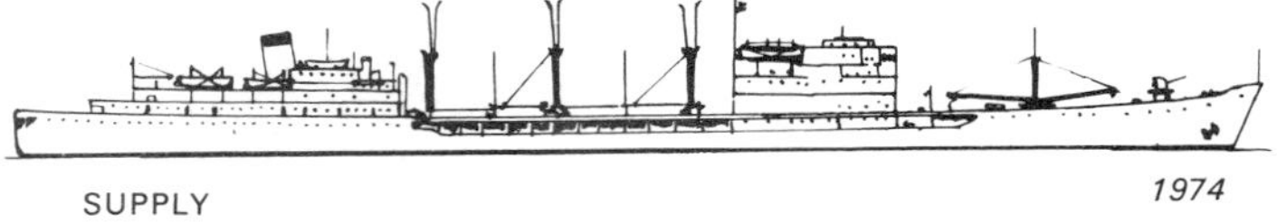

SUPPLY *1974*

AMPHIBIOUS FORCES

8 LANDING CRAFT (HEAVY) (LCH)

BALIKPAPAN	126	**WEWAK**	130 (10.8.73)
BRUNEI	127 (5.1.73)	**SALAMAUA**	131
LABUAN	128 (9.3.73)	**BUNA**	132
TARAKAN	129 (15.6.73)	**BETANO**	133

Displacement, tons	310 light; 503 full load
Dimensions, ft (*m*)	146 × 33 × 6·5 (*44·5 × 10·1 × 1·9*)
Guns	2 0·5 in MG
Main engines	2 GM Diesels. Twin screw = 10 knots
Complement	13 (2 officers, 11 sailors)

Originally this class was ordered for the Army with whom *Balikpapan* remained until mid-1974. All now transferred to RAN. Known commissioning dates in brackets.

PNG. *Buna* and *Salamaua* transferred to Papua-New Guinea Defence Force.

BUNA *1974, John Mortimer*

DIVING TENDERS

PORPOISE (ex-*Neasham*) Y 280 **SEAL** (ex-*Popham*) Y 298

Displacement, tons	120 standard; 159 full load
Dimensions, feet	100 pp × 22 × 5·8
Main engines	2 Paxman diesels; 1 100 bhp = 14 knots
Range, miles	2 000 at 9 knots; 1 500 at 12 knots
Complement	7 (can accommodate 14 divers)

Transferred from the Royal Navy in 1966-67, these ex-inshore Minesweepers were converted to Diving Tenders and attached to the Diving School at Sydney.

PORPOISE (ignore lamp-post on quarterdeck) *1974, John Mortimer*

GENERAL PURPOSE VESSELS

BANKS (16 Feb 1960) **BASS** (25 May 1960)

Displacement, tons	207 standard; 255 and 260 full load respectively
Dimensions, feet	90 pp; 101 oa × 22 × 8
Main engines	Diesels; speed = 10 knots
Complement	14 (2 officers, 12 sailors)

"Explorer" class. Of all steel construction. *Banks* was fitted for fishery surveillance and *Bass* for surveying, but both were used for other duties, including reserve training. Both built by Walkers, Maryborough. Completion dates in brackets.

TORPEDO RECOVERY VESSELS

TRV 253, 254, 255

Displacement, tons	91·6
Dimensions, feet	88·5 × 20·9 × 4·5
Main engines	3 GM Diesels; 890 = 13 knots
Complement	9 (1 officer, 8 men)

All built at Williamstown—completed between Jan 1970 and Apr 1971.

TRV 254 *1973, Royal Australian Navy*

TUGS

501 502 503 504

Displacement, tons	47·5
Dimensions, feet	50 × 15 ×
Main engines	2 GM Diesels; 340 bhp = 8—9 knots
Complement	3

First pair built by Stannard Bros. Sydney in 1969 and second pair by Perrin Engineering Brisbane in 1972.

AUSTRIA

Diplomatic Representation

Defence Attaché in London:
Brigadier General H. Wingelbauer

A Danube River patrol is run by the Austrian School of Military Engineering.

NIEDERÖSTERREICH

Displacement, tons	75
Dimensions, ft (*m*)	96·8 × 17·8 × 3·6 (*29·4 × 5·4 × 1·1*)
Guns	1—20 mm SPz Mk 66 Oerlikon in a turret; 1—12·7 mm MG; 1—Mk 42 MG; 2—8·4 cm PAR 66 "Carl Gustav" AT rifles
Main engines	2 V 16 Diesels; 1 600 hp = 22 knots
Complement	9

Built by Korneuberg Werft AG. Fully welded.

NIEDERÖSTERREICH *1973, Heeres Film*

River Patrol Class—*continued*

OBERST BRECHT A 601

Displacement, tons	10
Dimensions, ft (*m*)	40·3 × 8·2 × 2·5 (*12·3 × 2·5 × 0·75*)
Gun	1—12·7 mm MG
Main engines	2 Diesels; 107 hp = 10 knots
Complement	5

Built by Korneugburg Werft AG. Welded.

3 Ex-US "M3" PATROL CRAFT

Even smaller riverine craft.

OBERST BRECHT *1974, Heeres Film*

BAHAMAS

Mercantile Marine

Lloyd's Register of Shipping:
129 vessels of 153 202 tons gross

PATROL CRAFT

4 60 ft GRP TYPE

ACKLINS **ANDROS** **GLENTHIRA** **SAN SALVADOR**

Displacement, tons	30 standard approx
Dimensions, feet	62·0 oa × 15·8 × 4·6
Guns	1 MG forward; 2 LMG on bridge
Main engines	2 Caterpillar diesels = 20 knots
Complement	11

"60 ft" Keith Nelson patrol craft built by Vosper Thornycroft in glass reinforced plastic, delivered in 1970 as the first four units of the Bahamas Police Marine Division. With air-conditioned living spaces, these craft are designed for patrol amongst the many islands of the Bahamas Group. The foredeck is specially strengthened for a 20 mm MG with light MGs in sockets either side of the bridge.

ANDROS *1972, Vosper Thornycroft*

BAHRAIN

Mercantile Marine

Lloyd's Register of Shipping:
16 vessels of 5 140 tons

Note. Two coastal patrol craft of $4\frac{1}{4}$ tons and 28 knots armed with 2 MG ordered from Fairey (Marine) Ltd. in September 1974.

2 PATROL CRAFT

HOWRA **JIDA**

Displacement, tons	15
Dimensions, feet	45·5 × 12 × 3
Main engines	2 Diesels; 1 080 bhp = 23 knots

BANGLADESH

Administration

Chief of Staff:
Commodore M. Hossain Khan

Strength:	4 Armed River Steamers 2 Large Patrol Craft
Personnel:	700—1 000
Bases:	Chittagong (H. R. Khan) Dacca (Haji Mohsin) Khulna (Mir)

Prefix to Ships' Names

BNS

Mercantile Marine

Lloyd's Register of Shipping:
98 vessels of 115 682 tons gross

The Bangladesh Navy was the last of the three services to be formed, Commander Nurul Huq being appointed Chief of Staff at the end of March 1972. Commodore Khan took over in Nov 1973 when Nurul Huq became Chairman of the BIWT. The first armed river steamer was commissioned by General Osmani on 12 June 1972 as P101. Two more, P102 and 103, were commissioned in late July being followed by P104. In December 1974 Sheikh Mujibur Rahman stated that this Navy "will be developed into a formidable sea power". Four Soviet "Vanya" class coastal minesweepers were operating in Bangladesh waters until 1974. The activities of the Soviet Navy in this area suggest that, if adequate credit is not available in Western countries, the Bangladesh navy may be based on Russian ships.

It is reported that two Pakistani ships sunk in the Indo-Pakistan war—*Jessore* at Chittagong and one other at Chalna—have been salved and may be incorporated in the Navy.

4 ARMED RIVER STEAMERS

PADMA P 101 **NOAKHALI** P 102
— P 103 — P 104

Displacement, tons	25 tons (approx)
Dimensions, feet	55 × 14 × 5
Gun	1—37 mm
Complement	20

Built at Naryangang the first being commissioned on 12 June 1972.

2 LARGE PATROL CRAFT

The 150-ton ships *Ajay* and *Akshay* transferred from India in 1974.

BARBADOS

Mercantile Marine

Lloyd's Register of Shipping:
30 vessels of 3 897 tons gross

Coastguard

This was formed early in 1973

1 20 Metre "GUARDIAN" CLASS (COASTAL PATROL CRAFT)

GEORGE FERGUSON CG 601

Displacement, tons	60
Dimensions, ft (*m*)	65·6 × 17·4 × 4·3 (*20 × 5·3 × 1·3*)
Guns	2—·76 mm MG
Main engines	2 GM diesels; 1 300 hp = 24 knots
Range, miles	650 cruising
Complement	11

GRP hull by Halmatic Ltd; fitting out by Aquarius Ltd Christchurch, England. Air conditioned and designed for coastguard/SAR duties. Launched 16 Oct 1974 for delivery in December.

3 12 Metre "GUARDIAN" CLASS (COASTAL PATROL CRAFT)

COMMANDER MARSHALL CG 402 **TT LEWIS** CG 403 — CG 404

Displacement, tons	11
Dimensions, ft (*m*)	41 × 12·1 × 3·3 (*12·5 × 3·7 × 1*)
Gun	1—·76 mm MG
Main engines	2 Caterpillar Diesels; 580 hp = 24 knots
Complement	4

12 Metre "GUARDIAN" Class *1974, Aquarius Ltd.*

Same general notes as for 20 metre "Guardian" above. CG 402 delivered Dec 1973, 403 Feb 1974, 404 launched 16 Oct 1974.

BELGIUM

Naval Board

Chief of Naval Staff:
Rear Admiral J. P. L. van Dyck

Diplomatic Representation

Naval, Military and Air Attaché in London:
Colonel (BEM) Jules Kaisin

Naval, Military and Air Attaché in Washington:
Brigadier-General de Wilde

Naval, Military and Naval Attaché in Paris:
Colonel (BEM) Hugo Rel

Personnel

(a) 1972: 330 officers and 4 085 men
1973: 330 officers and 4 150 men
1974: 330 officers and 4 125 men
(b) 12 months Military Service

Strength of the Fleet

Type	*Active*	*Building/Planned*
Frigates	—	4
Minesweepers (Ocean)	7	—
Minesweepers (Coastal)	9	—
Minesweepers (Inshore)	14	—
Support Ships	2	—
River Patrol Boats	6	—
Research Ships	2	—
Auxiliary and Service Craft	13	—

Mercantile Marine

Lloyd's Register of Shipping:
251 vessels of 1 214 707 tons gross

Naval Aviation

3 Alouette III Helicopters
2 Sikorsky S58 Helicopters

Base

Ostend

FRIGATES

4 "E-71" CLASS

Name	*Pennant No.*	*Builders*	*Laying down*	*Delivery*
WIELINGEN	F 910	Boelwerf, Temse	5 Mar 1974	1 Dec 1976
WESTDIEP	F 911	Cockerill, Hoboken	2 Sep 1974	1 June 1977
WANDERLAAR	F 912	Boelwerf, Temse	1 Mar 1975	1 Dec 1977
WESTHINDER	F 913	Cockerill, Hoboken	1 Sep 1975	1 June 1978

Displacement, tons	1 500 standard, 2 340 full load
Length, feet (*metres*)	347·7 (*106*)
Beam, feet (*metres*)	39·4 (*12*)
Draught, feet (*metres*)	17·2 (*5·3*)
Guns	1—3·9 in (*100 mm*) Twin 40 mm or 1—57 mm aft
Missiles	1 NATO Sea Sparrow SAM, with 8 tubes; 4 Exocet SSM
Torpedo Launchers	2 L-5 Torpedo Launchers
A/S Rocket Launchers	1—6 × 375 mm LR Bofors
Rocket Launchers	2—8-barrelled Corvus dual-purpose ECM/flare launchers
Main engines	CODOG—1 Rolls Royce Olympus TM3 gas turbine; 28 000 bhp; 2 Cockerill CO-240 diesels 6 000 bhp. Twin vp propellers
Speed, knots	28 (15 on 1 diesel, 20 on 2 diesels)
Range, miles	3 000 at 18 knots; 5 000 at 14 knots; 4 000 on diesels
Complement	14 officers, 146 men

GENERAL
This compact, well-armed class of frigate is the first class fully designed and constructed by the Belgian Navy. All to be fitted with hull-mounted sonar and fin stabilisers

ELECTRONICS. Fully integrated and automated weapons command and control system of HSA (SEWACO 4). ESM and ECM capability.

TYPE E 71 FRIGATE — *1973, Belgian Navy*

MISSILES (SAM). Sea Sparrow RIM 7H-2 manufactured under licence by Selenia.

RADAR. Air and surface warning and target indication radar with Control System (HSA). Navigation radar by Raytheon.

MINE WARFARE FORCES

(MINESWEEPERS (OCEAN) and MINEHUNTER)

7 U.S. MSO (Ex-AM) TYPE 498

Name	*Pennant No.*	*Builders*	*Laid down*	*Launched*	*Completed*	*Transferred*
A.F. DUFOUR (ex-*Lagen*, M 950, ex-*MSO* 498)	M 903	Bellingham Shipyard Inc. Wash	1954	13 Aug 1954	27 Sep 1955	15 Apr 1966
ARTEVELDE (ex-*MSO* 503, ex-*AM* 503)	M 907	Tacoma Boatbuilding Co. Tacoma, Wash	1953	19 June 1954	15 Dec 1955	15 Dec 1955
BREYDEL (ex-*MSO* 504, ex-*AM* 504)	M 906	Tacoma Boatbuilding Co. Tacoma, Wash	1954	25 Mar 1955	15 Feb 1956	15 Feb 1956
DE BROUWER (ex-*Namsen*, M 951, ex-*MSO* 499)	M 904	Bellingham Shipyard Inc. Wash	1954	15 Oct 1954	1 Nov 1955	15 Apr 1966
F. BOVESSE (ex-*MSO* 516, ex-*AM* 516)	M 909	Tampa Shipbuilding Co Inc, Tampa, Fla	1954	2 Aug 1956	25 Jan 1957	25 Jan 1957
G. TRUFFAUT (ex-*MSO* 515, ex-*AM* 515)	M 908	Tampa Shipbuilding Co Inc, Tampa, Fla	1955	11 Nov 1955	12 Oct 1956	12 Oct 1956
VAN HAVERBEKE (ex-*MSO* 522)	M 902	Petersen Builders Inc, Sturgeon Bay, Wisc	1959	29 Oct 1959	7 Nov 1960	9 Dec 1960

Displacement, tons	720 standard; 780 full load
Length, feet (*metres*)	165·0 (*50·3*) wl; 172·5 (*52·6*) oa
Beam, feet (*metres*)	35·0 (*10·7*)
Draught, feet (*metres*)	11·0 (*3·4*)
Gun	1—40 mm
Main engines	2 GM diesels; 2 shafts; 1 600 bhp
Speed, knots	14
Range, miles	2 400 at 12 knots; 3 000 at 20 knots
Oil fuel, tons	50
Complement	72 (5 officers, 67 men)

Wooden hulls and non-magnetic structure. Capable of sweeping mines of all types. Diesels of non-magnetic stainless steel alloy. Controllable pitch propellers.

Artevelde was converted to Diving Vessel in 1972. *De Brouwer* and *Dufour* were modernised and converted to Minehunters/Sweepers in 1973 and 1974 respectively.

BREYDEL — *12 1974. C. and S. Taylor.*

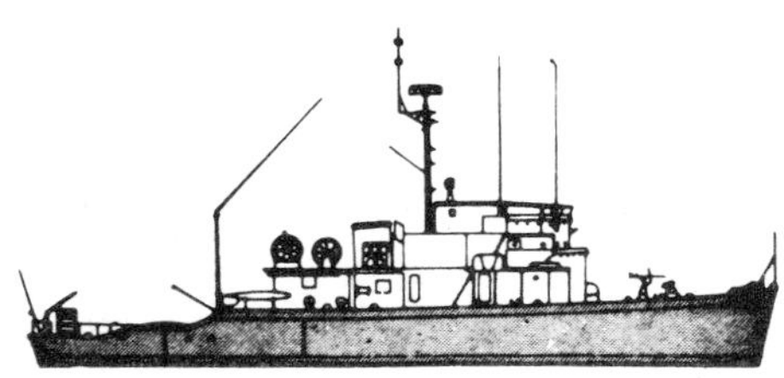

DUFOUR

MINE WARFARE FORCES

9 U.S. MSC (ex-AMS) TYPE 60 (MINESWEEPERS—COASTAL)

M 929 HEIST
M 931 KNOKKE
M 933 KOKSIJDE
M 932 NIEUWPOORT
M 930 ROCHEFORT
M 927 SPA
M 928 STAVELOT
M 934 VERVIERS (ex-*MSC* 259)
M 935 VEURNE (ex-*MSC* 260)

Displacement, tons	330 light; 390 full load
Dimensions, ft (*m*)	139 pp; 144 oa × 27·9 × 7·5 (8 max) (*42·4; 44·0 × 8·5 × 2·3 (2·6 max)*)
Gun	1—40 mm
Main engines	2 GM Diesels; 2 shafts; 880 bhp = 13·5 knots max
Oil fuel, tons	28
Range, miles	3 000 at economical speed (10·5 knots)
Complement	39

Coastal minesweepers with wooden hulls and constructed throughout of materials with the lowest possible magnetic signature. M 934 and 935 were built in USA, under MDAP, and M 926-933 of same type were built in Belgium with machinery and equipment from USA. M 934 (ex-MSC 259) transferred 19 June 1956, M 935 (ex-MSC 260) was transferred on 7 Sep 1956. M 926 to 933 were all laid down in 1953-54 and launched and completed in 1954-55. *Verviers* and *Veurne* converted to minehunters with Voith-Schneider propellers.

RECLASSIFICATION. *Mechelen*, M 926, former coastal minesweeper of this class, was re-rated as a research ship and re-numbered A 962 in 1968 (see next page).

NIEUWPOORT — *1973, Giorgio Arra*

14 "HERSTAL" CLASS (MINESWEEPERS—INSHORE)

M 485 ANDENNE (ex-MSI 97) May 1958
M 484 DINANT (ex-*MSI* 96) 5 Apr 1958
M 471 HASSELT March 1958
M 478 HERSTAL (ex-*MSI* 90) 6 Aug 1956
M 479 HUY (ex-*MSI* 91) 17 Nov 1956
M 472 KORTRYK May 1957
M 473 LOKEREN 18 May 1957
M 476 MERKSEM 5 Apr 1958
M 477 OUDENAERDE May 1958
M 483 OUGREE (ex-*MSI* 95) 16 Nov 1957
M 480 SERAING (ex-*MSI* 92) Mar 1957
M 475 TONGEREN 16 Nov 1957
M 474 TURNHOUT 7 Sep 1957
M 482 VISÉ (ex-*MSI* 94) 7 Sep 1957

Displacement, tons	160 light; 190 full load
Dimensions, ft (*m*)	106·7 pp; 113·2 oa × 22·3 × 6 (*32·5; 34·5 × 6·9 × 1·8*)
Guns	2—·5 AA (Twin)
Main engines	2 diesels; 2 shafts; 1 260 bhp = 15 knots
Oil fuel tons	18
Range, miles	2 300 at 10 knots
Complement	17

MSI type. Modified AMI "100-foot" class. All built in Belgium. The first MSI *Herstal* was launched at the Mercantile Marine Yard, Kruibeke on 6 Aug 1956 and completed in June 1957. A second MSI was launched in 1956 and six more pairs in 1957-58 (see launch dates above).

The first group of eight (M 478 to 485) was a United States "off shore order", the remaining eight (M 470 to 477) being financed under the Belgian Navy Estimates.

OUDENAERDE — *5/1974, C. and S. Taylor*

SUPPORT SHIPS

ZINNIA A 961

Displacement, tons	1 705 light; 2 685 full load
Length, feet (*metres*)	299·2 (*91·2*) pp; 309 (*94·2*) wl; 326·4 (*99·5*) oa
Beam, feet (*metres*)	49·9 (*14·0*)
Draught, feet (*metres*)	11·8 (*3·6*)
Guns	3—40 mm AA (single)
Aircraft	1 helicopter
Main engines	2 Cockerill V 12 RT 240 CO diesels; 5 000 bhp; 1 shaft
Speed, knots	20
Oil fuel, tons	500
Range, miles	14 000 at 12·5 knots
Complement	125

Laid down at Hoboken by J. Cockerill on 8 Nov 1966. Launched on 6 May 1967. Completed on 12 Sep 1967. Controllable pitch propeller. Design includes a platform and a retractable hangar for one light liaison-helicopter. Rated as Command and Logistic Support Ship.

ZINNIA — *1973 Belgian Navy*

Support Ships—*continued*

GODETIA A 960

Displacement, tons	1 700 light; 2 500 full load
Dimensions, ft (*m*)	289 wl; 301 oa × 46 × 11·5 (*88·0; 91·8* × 14 × *3·5*)
Guns	2—40 mm (twin)
Aircraft	Provision for light helicopter
Main engines	4 ACEC—MAN diesels; 2 shafts; 5 400 bhp = 19 knots
Oil fuel, tons	294
Range, miles	8 700 at 12·5 knots
Complement	100 plus 35 spare billets

Built at Temse by J. Boel and Sons. Laid down on 15 Feb 1965, launched on 7 Dec 1965 and completed on 2 June 1966. Controllable pitch propellers. Provided with a platform which can take a light liaison-helicopter.

GODETIA *1972, Belgian Navy*

RIVER PATROL BOATS

LEIE **LIBERATION** **MEUSE** **SAMBRE** **SCHELDE** **SEMOIS**

Displacement, tons	25 light; 27·5 full load
Dimensions, ft (*m*)	75·5 pp; 82 oa × 12·5 × 3 (*23·0*; 25·*0* × 3·8 × *0·9*)
	Liberation 85·5 × 13·1 × 3·2 (*26·0* × *4·0* × *1·0*)
Guns	2—13 mm MG
Main engines	2 diesels; 2 shafts; 440 bhp = 19 knots
Complement	7

Built at the Theodor Shipyards of Regensburg, Germany, in 1953, except *Liberation* in 1954.

MEUSE *1974, Belgian Navy*

RESEARCH SHIPS

ZENOBE GRAMME A 958

Displacement, tons	149
Dimensions, ft (*m*)	92 × 22·5 × 7; (*28·2* × *6·8* × *2·1*)
Main engines	1 MWM diesel; 1 shaft; 200 bhp = 10 knots
Complement	14

Auxiliary sail ketch. Built by J. Boel in Temse, Belgium, in 1961. Designed for scientific research.

Research Ships—*continued*

MECHELEN A 962 (ex-M 926)

Displacement, tons	330 light; 390 full load
Dimensions, ft (*m*)	139 pp; 144 oa × 27·9 × 7·5 (*42·4*; *44·0* × *8·5* × *2·3*)
Main engines	2 GM diesels; 2 shafts; 880 bhp = 13·5 knots
Oil fuel, tons	28
Range, miles	3 000 at economical speed (10·5 knots)
Complement	39

Former coastal minesweeper built in 1954. Re-rated as a research ship in 1968.

MECHELEN *1974, Neptunus, Ostend*

TUGS

VALCKE A 950

Displacement, tons	110
Dimensions, ft (*m*)	78·8 pp; 95 oa × 21 × 5·5 (*24·0*; *29·0* × *6·4* × *1·7*)
Main engines	1 diesel; 1 shaft; 600 bhp = 12 knots
Complement	14

Built in Haarlem, Netherlands in 1951.

There are also two port tugs, *Bij* and *Krekel*, displacement 71 tons, length 57·8 feet 2 Voith-Schneider propellers, 400 hp; three harbour tugs, *Hommel* and *Wasp*, displacement 22 tons, length 43 feet, with 300 bhp diesels and Voith-Schneider propellers, built in Germany in 1953, and *Mier*, displacement 17·5 tons, length 41 feet, with 90 bhp diesels and Voith-Schneider propellers, built in Belgium in 1962.

AUXILIARY CRAFT

HARBOUR CRAFT. There are three barges, namely *FN 4*, *FN 5* and *FN 6*, displacement 300 tons, length, 105 feet, built in the Netherlands; the ammunition ship *Ekster*, displacement 140 tons, length 118 feet; built in Belgium in 1953; two diving cutters, ZM 3 and ZM 4, displacement 8 tons, length 33 feet, built in Belgium in 1953; and the harbour transport cutter *Spin*, displacement 32 tons, length 47·8 feet, with 250 bhp diesels = 8 knots and Voith-Schneider propeller, built in the Netherlands in 1958.

BOLIVIA

Senior Appointment

Rear Admiral Javier Pinto Telleria

Personnel

(a) 1975: 1 500 officers and men
(b) 12 months selective military service

Prefix to Ships Names

FNB

A small navy used for patrolling Lake Titicaca.

1 TRANSPORT

CORONEL ABAROA M 08

16 PATROL CRAFT

Of various sizes.

BRAZIL

Naval Board

Chief of Naval Staff:
Admiral J de Carvalho Jordão
Chief of Naval Material:
Admiral A de Negreiros Jannuzzi
Chief of Naval Personnel:
Admiral G de Azevedo Henniug

Diplomatic Representation

Naval and Defence Attaché in Athens:
Captain Julio Cesar Perdigao Coelho

Naval and Defence Attaché in Buenos Aires:
Captain Milton Ribeiro de Carvalho

Naval and Defence Attaché in Lima:
Captain Nayrthon Amazonas Coelho

Naval and Defence Attaché in Lisbon and Madrid:
Captain Henrique Rubem Costa Veloso

Naval Attaché in London:
Captain Wilson Mourão Dos Santos

Naval Attaché in Paris:
Captain Odyr Marques Buarque de Gusmão

Naval and Defence Attaché in Santiago:
Captain Paulo Henschell Martins

Naval and Defence Attaché in Tokyo:
Captain Delcio Raymundo de Moura Bentes·

Naval Attaché in Washington:
Rear Admiral Roman Gomes Leite Labarthe

Personnel

(a)

1971: 40 600 (3 800 officers and 36 800 men) including marines

1972: 42 125 (3 264 officers and 38 861 men) including marines and auxiliary corps.

1973: 44 339 (3 591 officers and 40 746 men) including marines and auxiliary corps.

1974: 49 600 (3 887 officers and 45 713 men) including marines and auxiliary corps.

1975: 43 100 (3 800 officers and 39 300 men) including marines and auxiliary corps.

(b) 1 years National service

Strength of the Fleet

Type	*Active*	*Building*
Attack Carrier (medium)	1	—
Cruiser	1	—
Destroyers	15	6
Frigates	3	—
Corvettes	10	—
Submarines (Patrol)	8	2
Landing Ships	2	—
Monitor and Gunboats	9	—
River Patrol Ships	5	—
Minesweepers (Coastal)	8	2
Survey Ships	6	—
Survey Launches	11	—
S/M Rescue Ships	1	—
Repair Ship	1	—
Oilers	2 (1 small)	—
Transports	4	—
Tugs	3	—
Floating Docks	3	—

Disposals

Cruiser

1973 *Barroso*

Destroyers

1973 *Amazonas, Mariz, E. Barros, Piaui, Santa Catarina*

Frigates

1973 *Baependi, Bracui*

Submarines

1972 *Rio Grande do Sul* (ex-*Sandlance*) for alongside training. *Bahia* (ex-*Plaice*)

Light Forces

1971 *Piraju, Piranha*
1972 *Paraguaçu*
1973 *Pirague*

Tankers

1970. *Raza* and *Rijo*

Prefix to Ship Names

These vary, indicating the type of ship e.g N Ae L = Aircraft Carrier; CL = Light Cruiser; CT = Destroyer; F = Frigate.

Proposed New Construction

1 Helicopter Carrier
3 A-A Frigates
4 Coastal Patrol Craft
1 Replenishment Oiler
4 LVC
4 LCVP
10 LCM
1 Survey Ship
3 Tugs

Naval Bases

Rio de Janeiro (main base with 3 dry docks and 1 floating dock);
Aratu (Bahia) (major naval yard with 1 dry dock and 1 floating dock);
Belém (naval base and repair yard with 1 dry dock);
Recife (naval base and repair yard);
Natal (small naval base and repair yard with 1 floating dock);
Florianapolis (small naval base);
Lodario (river base of *Mato Grosso* flotilla)

Maritime Aviation

A Fleet Air Arm was formed on 26 January 1965.

A (Air Force)
12 Grumman S-2A Trackers (to be replaced by S-2E)
B (Navy)
6 Sikorsky SH-3D
4 Sikorsky SH-34J (SH-1)
5 Westland Whirlwind Srs. 3 (UH-5)
3 Westland Wasp HAS-1 (UH-2)
18 Bell 206B Jetrangers
12 Westland Lynx WG 13 to be provided for "Niteroi" class
C (Air Force)
10 Lockheed P2-E Neptunes (to be replaced by Brazilian EMB-111)
12 Grumman HU-16A Albatross (SAR)
3 Lockheed RC-130E Hercules (SAR/PR)
8 Convair PBY-5A Catalinas (Transport)
20 North American T-6 (naval liaison)

Mercantile Marine

Lloyd's Register of Shipping:
471 vessels of 2 428 972 tons gross

ATTACK CARRIER (MEDIUM)

1 Ex-BRITISH TYPE
("COLOSSUS" CLASS)

	Pennant No.	*Builders*	*Laid down*	*Launched*	*Completed*	*Reconstructed*
MINAS GERAIS (ex-HMS *Vengeance*)	A 11	Swan, Hunter & Wigham Richardson, Ltd, Wallsend on Tyne	16 Nov 1942	23 Feb 1944	15 Jan 1945	Verolme Dock, Rotterdam, 1957-60

Displacement, tons	15 890 standard; 17 500 normal; 19 890 full load (see *Displacement* note)
Length, feet (*metres*)	630 (*192·0*) pp; 695 (*211·8*) oa
Beam, feet (*metres*)	80 (*24·4*)
Draught, feet (*metres*)	21·5 (*6·6*) mean; 24·5 (*7·5*) max
Flight deck,	
Length, feet (*metres*)	690 (*210·3*)
Width, feet (*metres*)	121 (*37·0*) oa as reconstructed
Height, feet (*metres*)	39 (*11·9*) above water line
Catapults	1 steam
Aircraft	20 aircraft including 7 S2A, 4 Sea Kings
Guns, AA	10—40 mm (2 quadruple, 1 twin)
Guns, saluting	2—47 mm
Boilers	4 Admiralty 3-drum type; Working pressure 400 psi (*28 kg/cm²*); max superheat 700°F (371°C)
Main engines	Parsons geared turbines; 2 shafts; 40 000 shp
Speed, knots	24; 25·3 on trials after reconstruction
Range, miles	12 000 at 14 knots; 6 200 at 23 knots
Oil fuel, tons	3 200
Complement	1 000 (1 300 with air group)

MINAS GERAIS — *1971, Brazilian Navy*

GENERAL AND CONVERSION
Served in the British Navy from 1945 onwards. Fitted out in late 1948 to early 1949 for experimental cruise to the Arctic. Lent to the Royal Australian Navy early in 1953, returned to the Royal Navy in Aug 1955. Purchased by the Brazilian Government on 14 Dec 1956. Reconstructed at Verolme Dock, Rotterdam from summer 1957 to Dec 1960. The conversion and overhaul included the installation of the angled deck, steam catapult, mirror sight deck landing system, armament fire control and radar equipment. The ship was purchased for $9 000 000 and the reconstruction cost $27 000 000. Commissioned in the Brazilian Navy at Rotterdam on 6 Dec 1960. Left Rotterdam for Rio de Janeiro on 13 Jan 1961. Used primarily for anti-submarine aircraft and helicopters.

ENGINEERING. The two units each have one set of turbines and two boilers installed side by side. Maximum speed at 120 rpm. Steam capacity was increased when the boilers were retubed during reconstruction in 1957-60.
ELECTRICAL. During reconstruction an alternating current system was installed with a total of 2 500 kW supplied by four turbo-generators and one diesel generator.

Aircraft Carrier —*continued*

HANGAR. Dimensions: length, 445 feet; width, 52 feet; clear depth, 17·5 feet. Aircraft lifts: 45 feet by 34 feet. During reconstruction in 1957-60 new lifts replaced the original units.

RADAR. Air Surveillance SPS 12; Surface Search SPS 4; FD SPS 8B; Air Control SPS 8A; Fire Control SPG 34; Navigation MP 1402.

OPERATIONAL. Single track catapult for launching, and arrester wires for recovering, 30 000 lb aircraft at 60 knots. Catapult accelerator gear port side forward.

DISPLACEMENT. Before reconstruction: 13 190 tons standard; 18 010 tons full load.

DRAWING. Starboard elevation and plan. Re-drawn in 1971. Scale: 107 feet = 1 inch

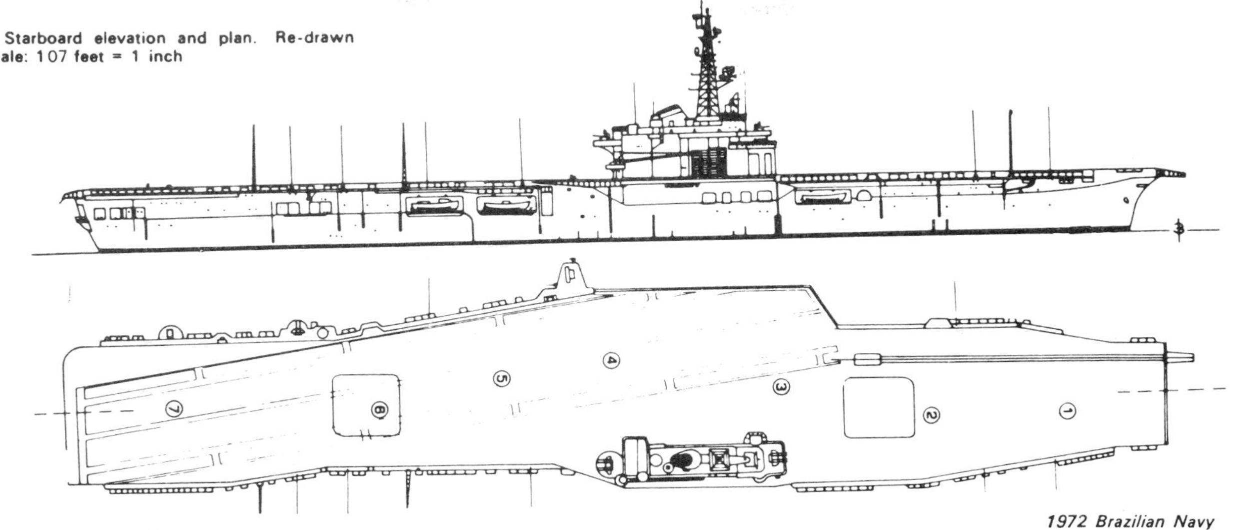

MINAS GERAIS

1972 Brazilian Navy

CRUISER

Name	*Pennant No.*	*Builders*	*Laid down*	*Launched*	*Completed*
TAMANDARÉ (ex-USS *St. Louis CL* 49)	C 12	Newport News S. B. & DD. Co.	10 Dec 1936	15 Apr 1938	10 Dec 1939

Displacement, tons	10 000 standard; 13 500 full load
Length, feet (*metres*)	608·5 (*185·5*) oa
Beam, feet (*metres*)	69 (*21·0*)
Draught, feet (*metres*)	24 (*7·3*) max
Aircraft	1 Helicopter (see *Hangar notes*)
Guns	15—6 in (*153 mm*) 47 cal (5 triple) 8—5 in (*127 mm*) 38 cal (4 twin) 28—40 mm, 8—20 mm
Armour, inches (*mm*)	Belt 5 in—1½ in (*127 mm—38 mm*); Decks 3 in—2 in (*76 mm—51 mm*); Turrets 5 in—3 in (*127 mm—76 mm*); C.T. 8 in (*203 mm*)
Boilers	8 Babcock & Wilcox Express
Main engines	Parson's geared turbines; 100 000 shp; 4 shafts
Speed, knots	32·5
Range, miles	14 500 at 15 knots
Oil fuel, tons	2 100
Complement	975

TAMANDARÉ

1972, Brazilian Navy

GENERAL
"St. Louis" class. Transferred from USA on 29 Jan 1951.

HANGAR. The hangar in the hull right aft could originally accommodate 6 aircraft if necessary together with engine spares and duplicate parts, though 4 aircraft was the normal capacity.

RADAR. SPS 12 search and SPS 10 tactical radar.

DRAWING. Starboard elevation and plan: Re-drawn in 1971. Scale: 121 feet = 1 inch.

DESTROYERS

6 "NITEROI" CLASS

VOSPER THORNYCROFT MARK 10

Name	*Pennant No.*	*Builder*	*Laid down*	*Launch*	*Completion*
CONSTITUIÇÃO	F 44	Vosper Thornycroft Ltd.	13 Mar 1974	1976	1978-79
DEFENSORA	F 41	Vosper Thornycroft Ltd.	14 Dec 1972	27 Mar 1975	1977-78
INDEPENDENCIA	F 42	Arsenal de Marinho, Rio de Janeiro	11 June 1972	2 Sept 1974	1976-77
LIBERAL	F 45	Vosper Thornycroft Ltd.	Nov 1974	1976	1979-80
NITEROI	F 40	Vosper Thornycroft Ltd.	8 June 1972	8 Feb 1974	1976
UNIÃO	F 43	Arsenal de Marinho, Rio de Janeiro	11 June 1972	14 March 1975	1976-77

Displacement, tons	3 200 standard; 3 800 full load
Length, feet (*metres*)	400 (*121·9*) wl; 424 (*129·2*) oa
Beam, feet (*metres*)	44·2 (*13·5*)
Draught, feet (*metres*)	18·2 (*5·5*)
Aircraft	One WG 13 Lynx helicopter
Missile launchers	2 twin Exocet MM 38 surface-to-surface in General Purpose version; 2 triple Seacat; Ikara in Anti-Submarine version
Guns	2—4·5 inch Mark 8 in General Purpose version 1—4·5 inch Mark 8 in Anti-Submarine version; 2—40 mm
A/S weapons	One Bofors 375 mm twin tube A/S rocket launcher; Two triple Mark 32 torpedo tubes; 1 DC rail
Main engines	CODOG system; 2 Rolls Royce Olympus gas turbines = 56 000 bhp; 4 MTU diesels, = 18 000 shp
Speed, knots	30 on gas turbines; 22 on diesels
Range, miles	5 300 at 17 knots (2 diesels); 4 200 at 19 knots (4 diesels); 1 300 at 28 knots (gas turbine)
Endurance	45 days stores 60 days provisions
Complement	200 officers and ratings

GENERAL
A very interesting design of handsome appearance. The moulded depth is 28½ feet (*8·8 metres*). Exceptionally economical in personnel, amounting to a fifty per cent reduction of manpower in relation to previous warships of this size and complexity. Require 80 fewer men than the British Type 42 of approximately similar characteristics.

CLASS. F 40, 41, 44 and 45 are of the A/S configuration. F 42 and 43 are General Purpose design.

CONTRACT. A contract, announced on 29 Sep 1970, valued at about £100 000 000, was signed between the Brazilian Government and Vosper Thornycroft Ltd, Portsmouth, England for the design and building of these six Vosper Thornycroft Mark 10 frigates comparable with the British Type 42 guided missile destroyers being built for the Royal Navy.

CONSTRUCTION. Four of the ships are being built at Vosper Thornycroft's Woolston, Southampton shipyard and two by the Naval Dockyard in Brazil with materials, equipment and lead-yard services supplied by Vosper Thornycroft.

ELECTRONICS. CAAIS. Equipment by Ferranti (FM1600B computers) ECM by Decca.

SONAR. 1 EDO 610E medium range. 1 EDO 700E VDS (A/S ships).

RADAR. 1 Plessey AWS-2 Air Warning with Mk 10 IFF. 1 Signaal ZWO-6 Surface Warning and navigation. 2 Selenia RTN-10X Weapon control and tracking. 1 Ikara Tracker radar (A/S ships).

NAMES. The name *Niteroi* was previously borne by the Brazilian Submarine chaser *Joao Pessoa Niteroi* built at Rio in 1943. The names of the six ships as originally allocated in 1971 were: *Campista, Constituição, Defensora, Imperatriz, Isabel* and *Niteroi*.

"NITEROI" Class

NITEROI — *1971, Vosper Thornycroft Group and Brazilian Navy*

3 "AMAZONAS" CLASS

Name	*No*	*Laid down*	*Launched*	*Completed*
ACRE	D 10	28 Dec 40	30 May 45	10 Dec 51
ARAGUAIA	D 14	20 July 40	24 Nov 43	3 Sep 49
ARAGUARI	D 15	28 Dec 40	14 July 46	23 June 51

Displacement, tons	1 450 standard; 2 180 full load
Length, feet (*metres*)	323·0 (*98·5*) oa
Beam, feet (*metres*)	35·0 (*10·7*)
Draught, feet (*metres*)	10·5 (*3·2*)
Guns, surface	3—5 in (*127 mm*) 38 cal
Guns, AA	4—40 mm (2 twin); 2—20 mm
A/S weapons	4 DCT
Torpedo tubes	6—21 in (*533 mm*), two triple
Boilers	3 three-drum type
Main engines	Parsons geared turbines; 2 shafts; 34 000 shp
Speed, knots	35·5 designed; 34 sea
Range, miles	6 000 at 15 knots
Oil fuel, tons	450
Complement	190

"AMAZONAS" Class

ARAGUARI — 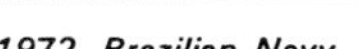 *1972, Brazilian Navy*

All built by Ilha das Cobras, Rio de Janeiro, to British design. Named after rivers. Refitted with tripod mast.

RADAR. Search: SPS 4. Tactical: SPS 10.

Destroyers—*continued*

7 Ex-US "FLETCHER" CLASS

Name	Pennant No.	Builders	Laid down	Launched	Completed
PARA (ex-USS *Guest*, DD 472)	D 27	Boston Navy Yard	27 Sep 1941	20 Feb 1942	15 Dec 1942
PARAIBA (ex-USS *Bennett*, DD 473)	D 28	Boston Navy Yard	10 Dec 1941	16 Apr 1942	9 Feb 1943
PARANA (ex-USS *Cushing*, DD 797)	D 29	Bethlehem Steel Co (Staten Island)	3 May 1943	30 Sep 1943	17 Jan 1944
PERNAMBUCO (ex-USS *Hailey*, DD 556)	D 30	Seattle-Tacoma S.B. Corpn, (Seattle)	1 Apr 1942	9 Mar 1943	30 Sep 1943
MARANHAO (ex-USS *Shields*, DD 596)	D 33	Puget Sound Navy Yard	10 Aug 1943	25 Sep 1944	8 Feb 1945
PIAUI (ex-USS *Lewis Hancock*, DD 675)					
SANTA CATARINA (ex-USS *Irwin*, DD 794)					

Displacement, tons	2 050 standard; 3 050 full load
Length, feet (*metres*)	376·5 (*114·8*) oa
Beam, feet (*metres*)	39·3 (*12·0*)
Draught, feet (*metres*)	18 (*5·5*) max
Missiles	1 quadruple Seacat (*Maranhao* only)
Guns, dual purpose	5—5 in (*127 mm*) 38 cal; except *Pernambuco*: 4—5 in
Guns, AA	10—40 mm (2 quadruple and 1 twin) except *Pernambuco* 6—3 in (*76 mm*) 50 cal (3 twin) and *Para*: 6—40 mm (3 twin
Torpedo tubes	5—21 in (*533 mm*)
A/S weapons	2 Hedgehogs; 1 DC rack; 2 side launching torpedo racks 2 Triple Mk 32 torpedo launchers (*Maranhao* only)
Boilers	4 Babcock & Wilcox
Main engines	2 GE geared turbines; 2 shafts; 60 000 shp
Speed, knots	35
Range, miles	5 000 at 15 knots; 1 260 at 30 knots
Oil fuel, tons	650
Complement	260

GENERAL
Para was transferred on loan 5 June 1959; *Paraiba* on loan 15 Dec 1959 and subsequently by sale 1 Aug 1973. *Parana* on loan 20 July 1961 and subsequently by sale 8 Jan 1973; *Pernambuco* on loan 20 July 1961 and *Maranhao* by sale 1 July 1972. *Piaui* (ex-*Lewis Hancock* DD 675) was transferred on loan 2 Aug 1967 whilst *Santa Catarina* (ex-*Irwin* DD 794) was transferred on loan 10 May 1968, and both by sale 11 April 1973.

RADAR. Search: SPS 6. Tactical: SPS 10. Fire Control: X Band.

PERNAMBUCO — *1974, Brazilian Navy*

PIAUI (five 5-inch guns) (similar to *Paraná*) — *1972, Brazilian Navy*

PERNAMBUCO

"PARA" Class

1 Ex-US "ALLEN M. SUMNER" and 4 "FRAM II" CLASS

Name	Pennant No.	Builder	Launched	Commissioned
ALAGOAS (ex-USS *Buck* DD 761)	D 35	Bethelhem (San Francisco)	11 Mar 1945	28 June 1946
ESPIRITO SANTO (ex-USS *Lowry* DD 770)	D 38	Bethlehem (San Pedro)	6 Feb 1944	23 July 1944
RIO GRANDE DO NORTE (ex-USS *Strong* DD 758)	D 37	Bethlehem (San Francisco)	23 Apr 1944	8 Mar 1945
SERGIPE (ex-USS *James C. Owens* DD 776)	D 36	Bethlehem (San Pedro)	1 Oct 1944	17 Feb 1945
MATO GROSSO (ex-USS *Compton*, DD 705)	D 34	Federal S.B. & D.D. Co.	17 Sep 1944	4 Nov 1944

Displacement, tons	2 200 standard; 3 320 full load
Length, feet (*metres*)	376·5 (*114·8*) oa
Beam, feet (*metres*)	40·9 (*12·4*)
Draught, feet (*metres*)	19 (*5·8*)
Guns	6—5 in (*127 mm*) 38 cal DP (twins)
A/S weapons	2 triple torpedo launchers; 2 ahead-firing Hedgehogs; facilities for small helicopter (Fram II). Depth charges (*Matto Grosso*)
Main engines	2 geared turbines; 60 000 shp; 2 shafts
Boilers	4
Speed, knots	34
Range, miles	4 600 at 15 knots, 1 260 at 30 knots
Complement	274

GENERAL
Transferred to Brazil as follows: D 34 27 Sept 1972, D 35 and 36 16 July 1973, D 38 29 Oct 1973, D 37 31 Oct 1972, the last four being FRAM II conversions, D 34 being of the original "Sumner" class.

GUNNERY. 3 inch guns in D 34 removed before transfer.

RADAR. SPS 6 and 10 (*Matto Grosso*).

SONAR. SQS 31 (*Matto Grosso*).

MATO GROSSO — *1974, Brazilian Navy*

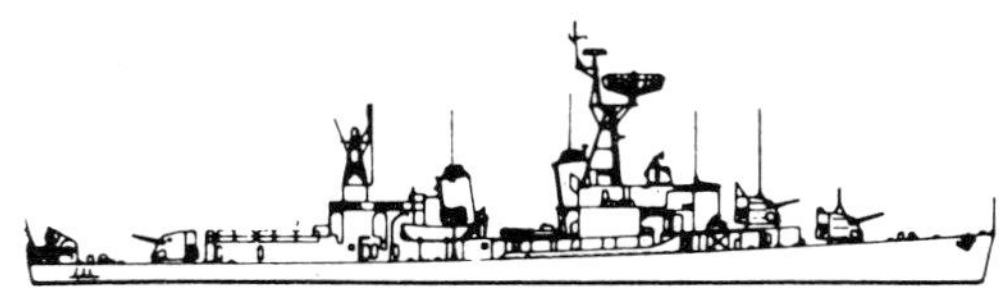
"ALLEN M. SUMNER" (FRAM II) Class

Destroyers—*continued*

2 + 4 Ex-US "GEARING" (FRAM I) CLASS

Name	Pennant No.	Builder	Launched	Completed
MARCILIO DIAS (ex-USS *Henry W. Tucker* DD 875)	D 25	Consolidated Steel	8 Nov 1944	12 Mar 1945
MARIZ E. BARROS (ex-USS *Brinkley Bass* DD 887)	D 26	Consolidated Steel	26 May 1945	1 Oct 1945
FRONTIN	D 23			
GREENHALGH	D 24			
INHAUMA	D 21			
JACEGUAY	D 22			

Displacement, tons	2 425 standard; 3 500 full load
Length, feet (*metres*)	390·5 (*119·0*)
Beam, feet (*metres*)	40·9 (*12·4*)
Draught, feet (*metres*)	19 (*5·8*)
Guns	4—5 inch (*127 mm*) 38 cal DP (twin)
A/S weapons	1 Asroc 8-tube launcher; 2 triple Mk 32 torpedo launchers; facilities for small helicopter
Main engines	2 GE geared turbines; 60 000 shp; 2 shafts
Boilers	4 Babcock & Wilcox
Speed, knots	34
Range, miles	5 800 at 15 knots
Complement	274 (14 officers, 260 men)

GENERAL
Enlarged "A. M. Sumner" class—14 feet longer. Fitted with VDS. First pair transferred 3 Dec 1973, the remainder to be acquired in the future.

RADAR. SPS-10 and SPS 40.

SONAR. SQS-23.

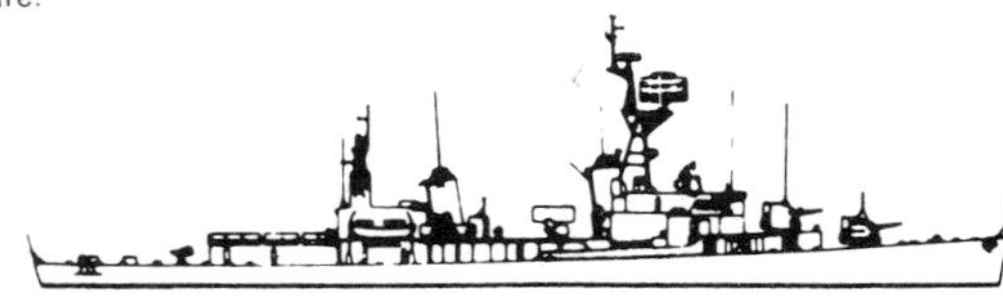

"GEARING" (FRAM I) Class

FRIGATES

3 ex-US DE TYPE "BERTIOGA" CLASS

Name	Pennant No.	Laid down	Launched	Completed
BAURU (ex-USS *McAnn*, DE 179)	U 28 (ex-D 18)	17 May 1943	22 Aug 1943	11 Oct 1943
BENEVENTE (ex-USS *Christopher*, DE 100)	U 30 (ex-D 20)	7 Dec 1942	June 1943	23 Oct 1943
BOCAINA (ex-USS *Marts*, DE 174)	U 32 (ex-D 22)	26 Apr 1943	8 Aug 1943	3 Sep 1943

Displacement, tons	1 240 standard; 1 900 full load
Length, feet (*metres*)	306 (*93·3*) oa
Beam, feet (*metres*)	36·7 (*11·2*)
Draught, feet (*metres*)	12 (*3·7*)
Guns	3—3 in (*76 mm*); 2—40 mm (twin); 4—20 mm (single)
Main engines	4 GM diesels; 2 electric motors; diesel-electric drive; 2 shafts; 6 000 bhp
Speed, knots	21
Range, miles	11 500 at 11 knots
Oil fuel, tons	300
Complement	200

GENERAL
Former US "Bostwick" class destroyer escorts, transferred in 1944. Built by Federal, Port Newark. Formerly designated CTE (Destroyer Escorts) but reclassified as *Avisos Oceanicos* in 1965.

"BERTIOGA" class

CORVETTES

10 "IMPERIAL MARINHEIRO" CLASS

ANGOSTURA	V 20	**FORTE DE COIMBRA**	V 18	**IPIRANGA**	V 17
BAIANA	V 21	**IGUATEMI**	V 16	**MEARIM**	V 22
CABOCLA	V 19	**IMPERIAL MARINHEIRO**	V 15	**PURUS**	V 23
				SOLIMOES	V 24

Displacement, tons	911 standard
Dimensions, feet	184 × 30·5 × 11·7
Guns	1—3 in 50 cal; 4—20 mm AA
Main engines	2 Sulzer diesels; 2 160 bhp = 16 knots
Oil fuel, tons	135
Complement	60

SOLIMOES — *1972, Brazilian Navy*

"IMPERIAL MARINHEIRO" Class

All built in the Netherlands, launched in 1954-55, and incorporated into the Brazilian Navy in 1955. Actually fleet tugs. Equipped for fire fighting.

SUBMARINES

3 NEW CONSTRUCTION BRITISH "OBERON" CLASS

HUMAITA S 20 — **TONELERO** S 21 — **RIACHUELO** S 22

Displacement, tons	1 610 standard estimated; 2 060 full buoyancy surface; 2 200 normal surface; 2 420 submerged, official figure
Length, feet (*metres*)	295·5 (*90·1*) overall
Beam, feet (*metres*)	26·5 (*8·1*)
Draught, feet (*metres*)	18·0 (*5·5*)
Tubes	8—21 in (*533 mm*), 6 bow and 2 stern for homing torpedoes
Main machinery	2 Admiralty Standard Range 1 16-cyl diesels; 3 680 bhp; 2 electric motors; 6 000 shp; 2 shafts; electric drive
Speed, knots	15 on surface max; 17·5 submerged designed
Complement	70 (6 officers and 64 men)

HUMAITA — *1973, Vickers Ltd*

GENERAL
In 1969 it was announced that two submarines of the British "Oberon" class were ordered from Vickers, Barrow. The third boat was ordered in 1972. *Humaita* was laid down 3 Nov 1970, launched 5 Oct 1971 and completed 18 June 1973. *Tonelero* was laid down 18 Nov 1971, launched 22 Nov 1972 and completed in 1974. *Riachuelo* was laid down 26 May 1973. Diesels by Vickers Shipbuilding Group. Electric Motors by AEI-English Electric. Sonar, modern navigational aids and provision for modern fire control system developed by Vickers.

Submarines—*continued*

2 Ex-US "GUPPY III" TYPE

AMAZONAS (ex-USS *Greenfish,* SS 351) S16
GOIAZ (ex-USS *Trumpetfish,* SS 425) S15

Displacement, tons	1 975 standard; 2 450 dived
Length, feet (*metres*)	326·5 (*99·4*)
Beam, feet (*metres*)	27 (*8·2*)
Draught, feet (*metres*)	17 (*5·2*)
Torpedo tubes	10—21 in; 6 bow 4 stern
Main machinery	4 Diesels; 6 400 hp; 2 electric motors; 5 400 hp; 2 shafts
Speed, knots	20 surface, 15 dived
Complement	85

Converted in 1960-62. *Greenfish* built by Electric Boat Co, completed 7 June 1946. *Trumpetfish* built by Cramp Shipbuilding Co, completed on 29 Jan 1946. S 15 transferred by sale 15 Oct 1973 and S 16 by sale 19 Dec 1973.

SONAR. BQR-2 array, BQG-4 (PUFFS) fire control sonar (fins on casing).

AMAZONAS 1969, USN

5 Ex-US "GUPPY II" TYPE

BAHIA (ex-USS *Sea Leopard* SS 483) S 12
CEARA (ex-USS *Amberjack* SS 522) S 14
GUANABARA (ex-USS *Dogfish* SS 350) S10
RIO DE JANEIRO (ex-USS *Odax* SS 484, ex- *Guanabara*) S 13
RIO GRANDE DO SUL (ex-USS *Grampus* SS 523) S 11

Displacement, tons	1 870 standard; 2 420 dived
Length, feet (*metres*)	307·5 (*93·8*) oa
Beam, feet (*metres*)	27·2 (*8·3*)
Draught, feet (*metres*)	18 (*5·5*)
Torpedo tubes	10—21 in (6 bow, 4 stern)
Main engines	3 diesels, 4 800 shp; 2 motors; 5 400 shp; 2 shafts
Speed, knots	18 surfaced; 15 dived
Range, miles	12 000 at 10 knots (surfaced)
Complement	82

GENERAL
Dogfish built by Electric Boat Co. Commissioned 29 April 1946. *Odax* and *Sea Leopard* built by Portsmouth Navy Yard, commissioned 11 July 1945 and 11 June 1945 respectively. *Grampus* and *Amberjack* built in Boston Navy Yard and commissioned 26 Oct 1949 and 4 March 1946 respectively. Transferred 13 May 1972 (*Rio Grande do Sul*), 8 July 1972 (*Rio de Janeiro*), 28 July 1972 (*Guanabara*), 27 Mar 1973 (*Bahia*), 17 Oct 1973 (*Ceara*). All by sale.

RIO GRANDE DO SUL 1972, Brazilian Navy

AMPHIBIOUS FORCES

1 TANK LANDING SHIP

DUQUE DE CAXIAS G 26 (ex-USS *Grant County* LST 1174)

Displacement, tons	3 828 light; 7 804 full load
Dimensions, ft (*m*)	445 oa × 62 × 16·9 (*135·7* × *18·9* × *5·2*)
Guns	2—3 in 50 cal (twins)
Main engines	Diesels; 13 700 shp; 2 shafts; CP propellers = 17·2 knots
Complement	175 (11 officers, 164 men)
Troops	App. 575

Built by Avondale, New Orleans. Launched 12 Oct 1956 and transferred 15 Jan 1973. On lease.

28 LCVP

Built in Japan 1959-60.

7 EDVP

Fitted with Saab-Skania Diesels of 153 hp and with glass-fibre hulls. Built in Brazil in 1971-73.

1 TANK LANDING SHIP (LST 511-1152 Series)

GARCIA D'AVILA G 28 (ex-USS *Outagamie County* LST 1073)

Displacement, tons	1 653 standard; 2 366 beaching; 4 080 full load
Dimensions, feet	316 wl; 328 oa × 50 × 14
Guns	8—40 mm AA (2 twin, 4 single)
Main engines	GM diesels; 2 shafts; 1 700 bhp = 11·6 knots
Complement	119
Troops	147
Completed	7 Apr 1945

Transferred on loan to Brazil by USN 21 May 1971, purchased 1 Dec 1973.

GARCIA D'AVILA 1973, Brazilian Navy

LIGHT FORCES

1 THORNYCROFT TYPE (RIVER MONITOR)

PARNAIBA U 17 (ex-P 2)

Displacement, tons	620 standard; 720 full load
Dimensions, feet	180·5 oa × 33·3 × 5·1
Guns	1—3 in, 50 cal; 2—47 mm; 2—40 mm AA; 6—20 mm AA
Armour	3 in side and partial deck protection
Main engines	2 Thornycroft triple expansion; 2 shafts; 1 300 ihp = 12 knots
Boilers	2 three drum type, working pressure 250 psi
Oil fuel, tons	70
Range, miles	1 350 at 10 knots
Complement	90

Built at Rio de Janeiro. Laid down on 11 June 1936. Launched on 2 Sep 1937 and completed in Nov 1937. In Mato Grosso Flotilla. Rearmed with the above guns in 1960.

PARNAIBA *1971, Brazilian Navy*

2 "PEDRO TEIXEIRA" CLASS (RIVER PATROL SHIPS)

PEDRO TEIXEIRA P 20
RAPOSO TAVARES P 21

Displacement, tons	700 standard
Dimensions, feet	203·4 × 30·7 × 6·3
Guns	1—40 mm AA 2—81 mm mortars 6—·50 cal MG
Main engines	4 diesels; 2 shafts = 16 knots

Both built in Arsenal de Marinha, Rio de Janeiro. Helicopter platform and fitted. *Teixeira* launched 14 Oct 1970. Both commissioned 17 Dec 1973. Carry one LCVP.

3 "RORAIMA" CLASS (RIVER PATROL SHIPS)

AMAPA P 32 **RORAIMA** P 30 **RONDONIA** P 31

Displacement, tons	340 standard; 365 full load
Dimensions, feet	147·6 × 27·7 × 4·2
Guns	1—40 mm; 2—81 mm mortars; 6—·50 cal MGs
Main engines	Diesels; 2 shafts = 14·5 knots

Built by Maclaren, Niteroi. *Roraima* commissioned Mar 1974. *Rondônia* launched 10 Jan 1973, *Amapa* 9 Mar 1973, both completed in 1974.

6 "PIRATINI" CLASS (LARGE PATROL CRAFT)

PAMPEIRO (ex-USN PGM 118) P 12
PARATI (ex-USN PGM 119) P 13
PENEDO (ex-USN PGM 120) P 14
PIRAJA (ex-USN PGM 110) P 11
PIRATINI (ex-USN PGM 109) P 10
POTI (ex-USN PGM 121) P 15

Displacement, tons	105 standard;
Dimensions, feet	95 × 19 × 6
Guns	3—·50 cal MG; 1—81 mm mortar
Main engines	4 diesels; 1 100 bhp = 17 knots
Range, miles	1 700 at 12 knots
Complement	15 officers and men

Six coastal gunboats of the "Piratini" class were built in the Arsenal de Marinha do Rio de Janeiro under offshore agreement. *Piratini* entered service in Nov 1970 and the remainder between Mar and Oct 1971.

POTI *1972, Brazilian Navy*

4 RIVER PATROL CRAFT

Built in 1968. Of about 30 tons and 45 feet in length. Capable of 17 knots and with a range of 1 400 miles at 10 knots. Operate on the Upper Amazon.

Light Forces—*continued*

6 "ANCHOVA" CLASS (RIVER PATROL CRAFT)

ACARA R 57 **ANCHOVA** R 54 **ARUANA** R 59
AGULHA R 58 **ARENQUE** R 55 **ATUM** R 56

Displacement, tons	11
Dimensions, ft (*m*)	42·6 × 12·5 × 3·9) (*13 × 3·8 × 1·2*)
Main engines	2 Diesels; 280 hp = 25 knots
Range, miles	400 at 20 knots
Complement	3 plus 12 passengers

Built in Brazil in 1965-67.

MINE WARFARE FORCES

6 "ARATU" CLASS (MINESWEEPERS—COASTAL)

ABROLHOS M 19 **ANHATOMIRIM** M 16 **ARATU** M 15
ALBARDÃO M 20 **ARACATUBA** M 18 **ATALAIA** M 17

Displacement, tons	230 standard; 280 full load
Dimensions, feet	154·9 × 23·6 × 6·9
Gun	1—40 mm AA
Main engines	4 Maybach diesels; 2 shafts; 4 500 bhp = 24 knots
Range, miles	710 at 20 knots
Complement	39

Builders: Abeking & Rasmussen, Lemwerder. Wooden hulled. First four ordered in Apr 1969 and another pair in Sept 1973. *Aratu* and *Anhatomirim* entered service on 5 May 1971 and 30 November 1971 respectively, the second pair 13 Dec 1972. *Albardão* was launched 24 May 1974 and *Abrolhos* on 21 July 1974—both completed Dec 1974.

ARATU *1972, Brazilian Navy*

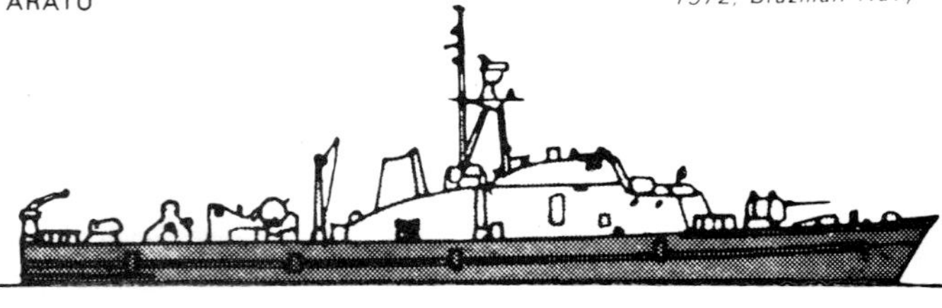

"ARATU" Class

4 "JAVARI CLASS" (MINESWEEPERS—COASTAL)

JAVARI (ex-USS *Cardinal*) M 11 **JUTAI** (ex-USS *Egret*) M 12
JURUA (ex-USS *Jackdaw*) M 13 **JURUENA** (ex-USS *Grackle*) M 14

Displacement, tons	270 standard; 350 full load
Dimensions, feet	136 × 24·5 × 8
Guns	4—20 mm in two twin mountings
A/S weapons	2 DCT
Main engines	2 GM diesels; 2 shafts; 1 000 bhp = 15 knots
Oil fuel, tons	16
Range, miles	2 300 at 8·5 knots
Complement	50

GENERAL
Of wooden construction, launched in 1942-43. Originally known in USA as Auxiliary Motor minesweepers (AMS). *Javari* and *Jutai* were transferred to Brazil by USA at Charleston Naval Shipyard on 15 Aug 1960 as the nucleus of a Brazilian mine force, and renamed after Brazilian rivers. *Juruá* was transferred in Jan 1963, and *Juruena* in Apr 1963. Used for patrol and escort duties.

JURUENA *1972, Brazilian Navy*

SURVEY SHIPS

Note. *Alvaro Alberto* (AGOR) ordered 1973.

2 FRIGATE TYPE

Name	*Pennant No.*	*Laid down*	*Launched*	*Completed*
CANOPUS	H 22	13 Dec 1956	20 Nov 1957	15 Mar 1958
SIRIUS	H 21	13 Dec 1956	30 July 1957	1 Jan 1958

Displacement, tons	1 463 standard; 1 800 full load
Dimensions, feet	236·2 pp; 246 wl; 255·7 oa × 39·3 × 12.2
Guns	1—3 in AA; 4—20 mm MG
Main engines	2 Sulzer diesels; 2 shafts; 2 700 bhp = 15·75 knots
Range, miles	12 000 at cruising speed of 11 knots
Complement	102

GENERAL
Built by Ishikawajima Heavy Industries Co. Ltd., Tokyo, Japan. Helicopter platform aft. Special surveying apparatus, echo sounders, Raydist equipment, sounding machines installed, and helicopter, landing craft (LCVP), jeep, and survey launches carried. All living and working spaces are air-conditioned. Controllable pitch propellers.

SIRIUS — *1970, Brazilian Navy*

3 COASTAL TYPE

Name	*Pennant No.*	*Laid down*	*Launched*	*Commissioned*
ARGUS	H 31	12 Dec 1955	6 Dec 1957	29 Jan 1959
ORION	H 32	12 Dec 1955	5 Feb 1958	11 June 1959
TAURUS	H 33	12 Dec 1955	7 Jan 1958	23 Apr 1959

Displacement, tons	250 standard; 300 full load
Dimensions, feet	138 pp; 147·7 oa × 20 × 6·6
Guns	2—20 mm AA
Main engines	2 diesels coupled to two shafts; 1 200 bhp = 15 knots
Oil fuel, tons	35
Range, miles	1 200 at 15 knots

All built by Arsenal da Marinha, Rio de Janeiro.

TAURUS — *1972, Brazilian Navy*

GRAÇA ARANHA H 34 (LIGHT AND BUOY TENDER)

Displacement, tons	1 250
Dimensions, ft (*m*)	247·6 × 42·6 × 12·1 (*75·5 × 13 × 3·7*)
Aircraft	1 Helicopter
Main engine	1 Diesel; 2 000 hp = 13 knots

Built in Brazil—laid down in 1971 and completed 1973.

Survey Ships—*continued*

ALMIRANTE SALDANHA U 10 (ex-NE 1)

Displacement, tons	3 325 standard; 3 825 full load
Dimensions, feet	262 pp; 307·2 oa × 52 × 18·2
Main engines	Diesel; 1 400 bhp = 11 knots
Range, miles	12 000 at 10 knots
Complement	356

Former training ship with a total sail area of 25 990 sq ft and armed with four 4-in guns one 3-in AA gun and four 3-pounders. Built by Vickers Armstrongs Ltd Barrow. Launched on 19 Dec 1933. Cost £314 500. Instructional minelaying gear was included in equipment. The single 21-in torpedo tube was removed. Re-classified as an Oceanographic Ship (NOc) Aug 1959, and completly remodelled by 1964. A photograph as sailing ship appears in the 1952-53 to 1959-60 editions.

ALMIRANTE SALDANHA — *1972, Brazilian Navy*

SURVEY LAUNCHES

CAMOCIM H 16
CARAVELAS H 17
ITACURUSSA H 15
RIO BRANCO H 12
PARAIBANO H 11

Displacement, tons	32 standard; 50 full load
Dimensions, feet	52·5 × 15·1 × 4·3
Main engines	1 diesel; 165 bhp = 11 knots
Range, miles	600 at 11 knots

FAROLEIRO SANTANA H 28
FAROLEIRO NASCIMENTO H 30
CASTELHANOS H 24
FAROLEIRO AREAS H 27
MESTRE JOÃO DOS SANTOS H 13

Buoy Tenders. Taken over 1973.

SUBMARINE RESCUE SHIP

GASTÃO MOUTINHO (ex-USS *Skylark* ASR 20) K 10

Displacement, tons	1 235 standard; 1 740 full load
Dimensions, feet	205 oa × 38·5 × 15·3
Main engines	Diesel electric; 1 shaft; 3 000 bhp = 14 knots
Complement	85

Built by Charleston SB & DD Co, and converted to present form in 1957. Fitted with special pumps, compressors and submarine rescue chamber. Fitted for oxy-helium diving. Transferred 30 June 1973.

REPAIR SHIP

BELMONTE (ex-USS *Helios*, ARB 12, ex-*LST* 1127) G 24

Displacement, tons	1 625 light; 2 030 standard; 4 100 full load
Dimensions, feet	316 wl; 328 oa × 50 × 11
Guns	8—40 mm AA
Main engines	GM diesels; 2 shafts; 1 800 bhp = 11·6 knots
Oil fuel, tons	1 000
Range, miles	6 000 at 9 knots

GENERAL
Former United States battle damage repair ship. Built by Maryland DD Co, Baltimore Md. Laid down on 23 Nov 1944. Launched on 14 Feb 1945. Completed on 26 Feb 1945. Loaned to Brazil by USA in Jan 1962 under MAP.

TANKERS

MARAJÓ G 27

Measurement, tons	10 500 deadweight
Dimensions, feet	440·7 × 63·3 × 24
Main engines	Diesel; one shaft = 13·6 knots
Capacity, *cu metres*	14 200
Complement	80
Range, miles	9 200 at 13 knots

Laid down on 13 Dec 1966 and launched on 31 Jan 1968. Built by Ishikawajima Do Brasil-Estaleisos SA. Completed on 22 Oct 1968.

MARAJO *1972, Brazilian Navy*

POTENGI G 17

Displacement, tons	600
Dimensions, feet	175·5 pp; 178·8 oa × 24·5 × 6
Main engines	Diesels, 2 shafts; 550 bhp = 10 knots
Oil, tons	450
Complement	19

Built at the Papendrecht yard in the Netherlands. Launched on 16 Mar 1938. Employed in the Mato Grosso Flotilla on river service.

MARTIN DE OLIVEIRA R 11

Of 588 tons. Taken over 1973.

ANITA GARIBALDI

TRANSPORTS

4 "PEREIRA" CLASS

Name	Pennant No.	Laid down	Launched	Completed
ARY PARREIRAS	G 21	13 Dec 1955	24 Aug 1956	29 Dec 1956
BARROSO PEREIRA	G 16	13 Dec 1953	10 Aug 1954	1 Dec 1954
CUSTÓDIO DE MELLO	U 26	13 Dec 1953	10 June 1954	30 Dec 1954
SOARES DUTRA	G 22	13 Dec 1955	13 Dec 1956	23 Mar 1957

Displacement, tons	4 800 standard; 7 300 full load
Measurement, tons	4 200 deadweight; 4 879 gross (Panama)
Dimensions, feet	362 pp; 391·8 oa × 52·5 × 20·5 max
Guns	4—3 in (U 26); 2—3 in (others); 2/4—20 mm
Main engines	Ishikawajima double reduction geared turbines; 2 shafts; 4 800 shp = 17·67 knots (sea speed 15 knots)
Boilers	2 Ishikawajima two drum water tube type, oil fuel
Complement	127 (Troop capacity 497)

GENERAL
All built in Japan by Ishikawajima Heavy Industries Co, Ltd, Tokyo. Transports and cargo vessels. Flush deckers with forecastle and long poop. Elevator type helicopter landing platform aft. Troop carrying capacity for 497, with commensurate medical, hospital and dental facilities. Working and living quarters are mechanically ventilated with partial air conditioning. Refrigerated cargo space 15 500 cubic feet. Can carry 4 000 tons of cargo. *Barroso Pereira* and *Custódio de Mello* were incorporated into the Brazilian Navy on 22 Mar 1955 and 8 Feb 1955 respectively. Formerly armed with eight 40 mm AA guns. *Custódio de Mello* has been classified as a training ship since July 1961.

SOARES DUTRA *1972, Brazilian Navy*

Transports— *continued*

PARAGUASSU (ex-*Guarapunava*) G 15 (RIVER TRANSPORT)

Of 285 tons. Acquired in 1971. Capable of 12 knots, with a range of 2 500 miles at 10 knots. Command ship of the Mato Grosso flotilla.

TUGS

TRIDENTE R 22 (ex-*ATA 235*)
TRITÃO R 21 (ex-*ATA 234*)
TRIUNFO R 23 (ex-*ATA 236*)

Displacement, tons	534 standard; 835 full load
Dimensions, feet	133·7 wl; 143 oa × 33 × 13·2
Guns	2—20 mm AA
Main engines	GM diesel-electric; 1 500 hp = 13 knots

GENERAL
All built by Gulfport Boiler & Welding Works, Inc, Port Arthur, Texas, and launched in 1954. Ex-US *ATRs*.

LAURINDO PITTA R 14

Of 514 tons. Built by Vickers 1910. Reconstructed 1969.

WANDENKOLK R 20

Of 350 tons. Built in UK 1910.

ANTONIO JOÃO R 26

Of 80 tons. Mato Grosso flotilla.

AUDAZ	R 31	**LAMEGO**	R 34
CENTAURO	R 32	**PASSO DE PATRIA**	R 35
GUARANI	R 33	**VOLUNTARIO**	R 36

Of 130 tons. Built by Holland Nautic Yard, Haarlem 1953.

ISLAS DE NORONHA

Of 200 tons. Built 1972.

MISCELLANEOUS

Stores Transports. *Tenente Fabio, Tenente Raul*

Of 55 tons built in 1969.

Munitions Transports. *San Francisco dos Santos* (1964). *Ubirajara dos Santos* (1968), *Operario Luis Leal* (1968).

Torpedo Transports. *Miguel dos Santos, Aprendiz Ledio, Conceicão.*

Water Boats. *Paulo Afonso, Itapura.*

Tenders. *Faroleiro Wanderley, Tenente Possolo, Tenente Lahmeyer, Maria Quiteria. Marisco, Tenente Claudio, Alme Brasil, Dr Gondim, Guaira, Iguacu, Rio Pardo, Rio Negro.*

FLOATING DOCKS

3 FLOATING DOCKS

CIDADE DE NATAL (ex-AFDL 39)

Displacement, tons	7 600
Length, feet (*metres*)	390·3 (119)
Beam, feet (*metres*)	86·9 (26·5)
Capacity, tons	2 800

Concrete floating dock loaned to Brazil by USN ,10 Nov. 1966.

ALMIRANTE JERONIMO GONÇALVES (ex-AFDL 4)

Displacement, tons	3 000
Length, feet (*metres*)	200 (*61*)
Beam, feet (*metres*)	44 (*13·4*)
Capacity, tons	1 000

Steel floating dock acquired by Brazil from USN, 10 Nov 1966.

AFONSO PENA (ex-*ARD* 14, ex-*Ceara*) G 25

Displacement, tons	5 200
Dimensions, feet	402·0 × 81·0

Formerly the United States auxiliary repair dry dock *ARD* 14. Transferred from the US Navy to the Brazilian Navy and first allocated the name *Ceara* in 1963.

BRUNEI

Askar Melayu Diraja Brunei (Royal Brunei Malay Regiment) Flotilla:
Commanding Officer: Commander J. G. S. Widdicombe RN

Personnel

(a) 1975: 240 (17 officers and 223 ratings)
(b) Voluntary

Prefix to Ship's Names

KDB

LIGHT FORCES

P 01 (FAST ATTACK CRAFT MISSILE)

PALAWAN

Displacement, tons	95 standard; 114 full load
Dimensions, feet	90·0 pp; 96·0 wl; 99·0 oa × 25·2 × 7·0
Missiles	8—SS 12 on 2 launchers
Guns	1—40 mm; 1—20 mm Hispano Suiza
Main engines	3 Bristol Siddeley Proteus gas turbines; 3 shafts; 12 750 bhp = 57 knots max; 2 diesels for cruising and manoeuvring
Range, miles	450 at full speed; 2 300 at 10 knots
Complement	20

PALAWAN *1974, Royal Brunei Malay Regiment*

Ordered from Vosper Ltd, Portsmouth, England, on 10 Dec 1965. Launched on 5 Dec 1966. Completed 19 Oct 1967. Constructed of resin bonded timber with aluminium alloy superstructure. Missile launchers fitted in May 1972.

3 "PERWIRA" CLASS (COASTAL PATROL CRAFT)

PERWIRA P 14 **PEMBURU P 15** **PENYARANG P 16**

Displacement, tons	30
Dimensions, feet	71 × 16 × 5
Guns	2—20 mm Hispano Suiza; 2—7·62 MG
Main engines	2 MTU Diesels; 2 250 bhp total
Speed, knots	32
Range, miles	600 at 22 knots; 1 000 miles cruising
Complement	12

PERWIRA *1974, Royal Brunei Malay Regiment*

Perwira ordered from Vosper-Thornycroft, Singapore and launched 9 May 1974. Completed 9 Sept 1974. Other two ordered June 1974 for completion Apr 1975

3 "MASNA" CLASS (COASTAL PATROL CRAFT)

MASNA P 11 **NORAIN P 13** **SALEHA P 12**

Displacement, tons	25
Dimensions, feet	62·0 × 16·0 × 4·5
Guns	2—20 mm Hispano-Suiza; 2 MG
Main engines	2 GM diesels; 1 250 bhp = 26 knots
Range, miles	600 at 23 knots
Complement	8

NORAIN *1974, Royal Brunei Malay Regiment*

These boats were built specially for the Flotilla by Vosper Thornycroft (Private) Ltd. Singapore. Fitted with Decca 202 radar. *Norain*, last of the three, completed August 1972. Named after Brunei princesses.

3 PATROL CRAFT (RIVERINE)

BENDAHARA P 21 **KEMAINDERA P 23** **MAHARAJALELA P 22**

Displacement, tons	10
Dimensions, feet	47·0 × 12·0 × 3.0
Guns	2 MG (2 twin MG 42, 7·62 cal in conversion)
Main engines	2 GM diesels; 334 bhp = 20 knots
Range, miles	200
Complement	6

Fitted with Decca 202 radar.

CONVERSION. *Kemaindera* was converted in July 1974 for riverine duties. Other pair will be similarly converted during 1975.

MAHARAJALELA *1974, Royal Brunei Malay Regiment*

BULGARIA

Naval Board

Commander-in-Chief, Navy:
Vice-Admiral VG Yanakiev

Diplomatic Representation

Naval, Military and Air Attaché in London:
Lt. Colonel Dimitar Toskov

Strength of the Fleet

Type	*Active*	*Building*
Frigates	2	—
Corvettes	2	—
Patrol Submarines	4	—
FAC (Missile)	2	—
FAC (Patrol)	6	—
FAC (Torpedo)	12	—
Minesweepers (Ocean)	2	—
Minesweepers (Coastal)	4	—
Minesweepers (Inshore)	2	—
Minesweeping Boats	24	—
Landing Craft	20	—
Auxiliaries	several	—

Personnel

(a) 1975: 9 000 officers and ratings
(b) 3 years national service

Mercantile Marine

Lloyd's Register of Shipping:
106 vessels of 610 982 tons gross

FRIGATES

2 "RIGA" CLASS

DRUZKI **SMELI**

Displacement, tons	1 200 standard; 1 600 full load
Length, feet (*metres*)	298·8 (*91·0*) oa
Beam, feet (*metres*)	33·7 (*10·2*)
Draught, feet (*metres*)	11·0 (*3·4*)
Guns	3—3·9 in (*100 mm*); 4—37 mm
A/S Weapons	2 16 barrelled rocket launchers; 4 DCT
Tubes	3—21 in (*533 mm*)
Main engines	Geared turbines; 2 shafts; 25 000 shp
Speed, knots	28
Range, miles	2 500 at 15 knots
Complement	150

Transferred from USSR in 1957-8.

RADAR. Search—Slim Net; Navigation—Neptun; IFF— High Pole A; FC—Wasphead/Sunvisor A.

"RIGA" Class

CORVETTES

2 "KRONSTADT" CLASS

Displacement, tons	310 standard; 380 full load
Dimensions, ft (*m*)	170·6 × 21·5 × 9·0 (*52·0 × 6·5 × 2·7*)
Guns	1—3·5 in; 2—37 mm AA; 4—25 mm AA
A/S weapons	Depth charge throwers
Main engines	3 Diesels; 3 shafts; 3 300 hp = 24 knots
Oil fuel, tons	20
Range, miles	1 500 at 12 knots
Complement	65

Transferred from USSR in 1957. Pot Drum Radar.

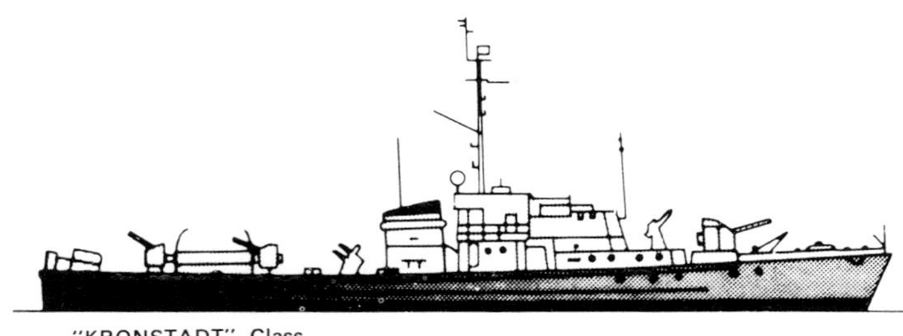

"KRONSTADT" Class

SUBMARINES (PATROL)

2 Ex-USSR "ROMEO" CLASS

Displacement, tons	1 100 surfaced; 1 600 dived
Dimensions, ft (*m*)	246 × 24 × 14·5 (*75 × 7·3 × 5·8*)
Torpedo tubes	6—21 in bow tubes
Main machinery	2 Diesels; 4 000 hp; 2 main motors; 4 000 hp
Speed, knots	17 surfaced, 14 dived
Complement	65

Transferred in 1972. Snoop Plate radar.

"ROMEO" Class

2 Ex-USSR "WHISKY" CLASS

POBEDA **SLAVA**

Displacement, tons	1 030 surface; 1 180 submerged
Dimensions, ft (*m*)	240 × 22 × 15 (*73·2 × 6·7 × 4·6*)
Torpedo tubes	6—21 in (*533 mm*), 4 bow, 2 stern
Main machinery	2 Diesels 4 000 hp; 2 Main Motors 2 500 hp
Speed, knots	17 surfaced; 15 dived
Range, miles	13 000 at 8 knots (surface)
Complement	60

Transferred from the USSR in 1958. Snoop Plate radar

"WHISKY" Class

LIGHT FORCES

3 "OSA I" CLASS (FAST ATTACK CRAFT—MISSILE)

Displacement, tons	165 standard; 200 full load
Dimensions, ft (*m*)	128·7 × 25·1 × 5·9 (*39·3 × 7·7 × 1·8*)
Missile launcher	4 in two pairs abreast for "SSN-2" system
Guns	4—30 mm (2 twin, 1 forward, 1 aft)
Main engines	3 diesels; 13.000 bhp = 32 knots
Range, miles	800 at 25 knots
Complement	25

Reported to have been transferred from the USSR in 1970-71.

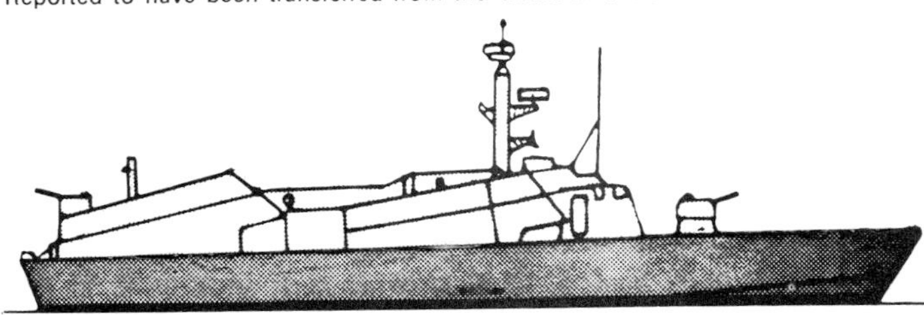

"OSA 1" Class

6 "SO I" CLASS (FAST ATTACK CRAFT—PATROL)

Pennants 41-46

Displacement, tons	215 light; 250 full load
Dimensions, ft (*m*)	138·6 × 20·0 × 9·2 (*42·3 × 6·1 × 2·8*)
Guns	4—25 mm (2 twin)
A/S weapons	4 five-barrelled ahead throwing MBU launchers
Main engines	3 diesels; 6 000 bhp = 29 knots
Range, miles	1 100 at 13 knots
Complement	30

Steel hulled patrol vessels transferred from USSR in 1963.

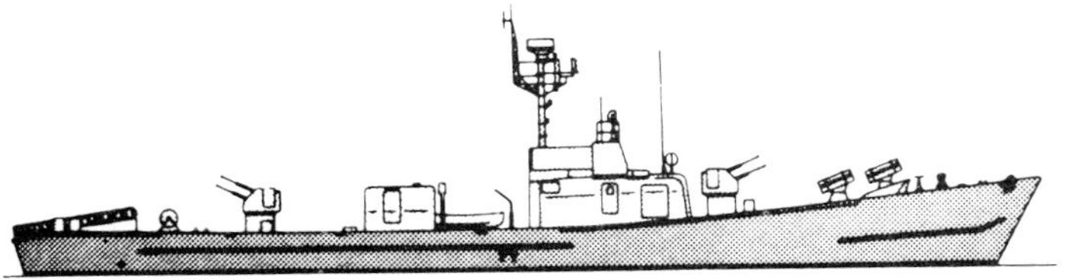

"SO 1" Class

4 "SHERSHEN" CLASS (FAST ATTACK CRAFT—TORPEDO)

Displacement, tons	150 standard; 160 full load
Dimensions, ft (*m*)	115·5 × 23·1 × 5·0 (*35·2 × 7·1 × 1·5*)
Guns	4—30 mm AA (2 twin)
Tubes	4—21 in (single)
A/S armament	12 DCs
Main engines	3 Diesels; 3 shafts; 13 000 bhp = 41 knots
Complement	16

Transferred in 1971. Pot Drum and Drum Tilt Radar. High Pole A IFF.

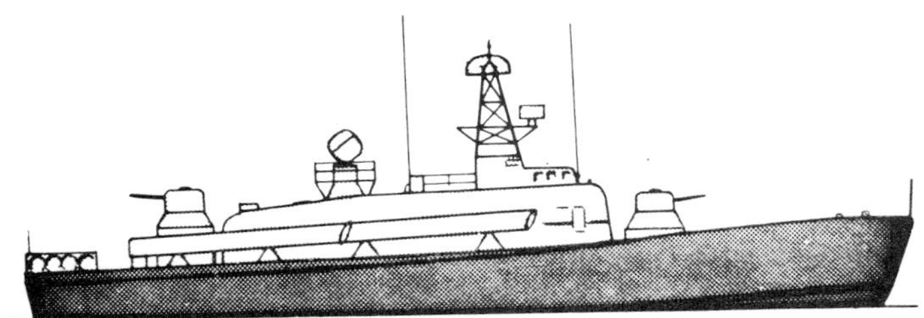

"SHERSHEN" Class

8 "P 4" CLASS (FAST ATTACK CRAFT—TORPEDO)

Displacement, tons	25 full load
Dimensions, ft (*m*)	62·7 × 11·6 × 5·6 (*25·5 × 6·0 × 1·8*)
Guns	2—25 mm AA
Torpedo tubes	2—18 in
Main engines	2 diesels; 2 shafts; 2 200 bhp = 50 knots

Transferred from the USSR in 1956.

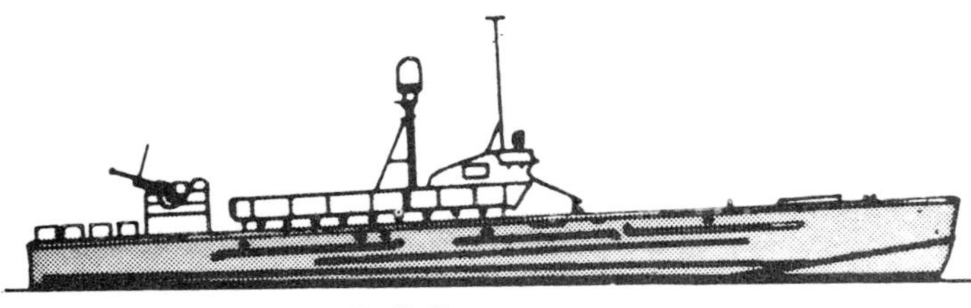

"P 4" Class

MINE WARFARE FORCES

2 "T 43" CLASS (MINESWEEPERS—OCEAN)

Displacement, tons	500 standard; 610 full load
Dimensions, ft (*m*)	190·2 × 28·2 × 6·9 (*58·0 × 8·6 × 2·1*)
Guns	4—37 mm (twin); 2—25 mm (twin)
Main engines	2 Diesels; 2 shafts; 2 000 hp
Speed, knots	17
Range, miles	1 600 at 10 knots
Complement	40

Three were transferred from USSR in 1953—One scrapped for spares.

4 "VANYA" CLASS (MINESWEEPERS—COASTAL)

36, 37, 38, 39

Displacement, tons	250 standard; 275 full load
Dimensions, ft (*m*)	130·7 × 24 × 6·9 (*39·9 × 7·3 × 2·1*)
Guns	2—30 mm (twin)
Main engines	2 Diesels; 2 200 bhp
Speed, knots	18
Complement	30

Transferred from USSR in 1971-72.

2 "T 301" CLASS (MINESWEEPERS—INSHORE)

Displacement, tons	150 standard; 180 full load
Dimensions, ft (*m*)	128 × 18 × 4·9 (*39 × 5·5 × 1·5*)
Guns	2—37 mm AA; 2—MG
Main engines	2 diesels; 2 shafts; 1 440 hp = 17 knots
Range, miles	2 200 at 10 knots

Four were transferred from the USSR in 1955. These have probably reached the end of their seagoing lives. Two recently deleted.

24 "PO 2" CLASS (MSB)

Former Soviet craft. 12 were reported to have been acquired in 1950 and 12 in 1956 for general purpose duties.

LANDING CRAFT

10 "VYDRA" CLASS

Displacement, tons	300 standard; 500 full load
Dimensions, ft (*m*)	157·4 × 24·6 × 7·2 (*48 × 7·5 × 2·2*)
Main engines	2 diesels; 2 shafts; 400 bhp = 10 knots

Transferred from the USSR in 1970.

"VYDRA" Class *1971*

10 MFP TYPE

Dimensions, ft (*m*)	164·0 oa × 20·0 × 6·6 (*50 × 6·1× 2·0*)
Gun	1—37 mm AA or none

Built in Bulgaria in 1954. Based on a German Second World War MFP design.

AUXILIARIES

A number of auxiliaries, harbour oilers and tugs have been reported.

BURMA

Administration

Vice-Chief of Staff, Defence Services (Navy):
Commodore Thaung Tin

Diplomatic Representation

Naval, Military and Air Attaché in London:
Lieutenant-Colonel Soe Myint

Naval, Military and Air Attaché in Washington:
Colonel Tin Htut

Strength of the Fleet

Type	*Active*	*Building*
Frigates	2	—
Corvettes	4	—
Fast Attack Craft	5	—
River Patrol Craft	35	—
Gunboats	36	—
Survey Vessels	2	—
Auxiliaries	11	—

Personnel

(a) 1975: 7 000 including 800 marines
(b) 2 years national service

Mercantile Marine

Lloyd's Register of Shipping:
40 vessels of 54 877 tons gross

FRIGATES

1 Ex-BRITISH "RIVER" CLASS

Name	*Builders*	*Laid down*	*Launched*	*Completed*
MAYU (ex-HMS *Fal*)	Smiths Dock Co Ltd, South Bank-on-Tees, Middlesbrough, England	20 May 1942	9 Nov 1942	2 July 1943

Displacement, tons	1 460 standard; 2 170 full load
Length, feet (*metres*)	283 (*86·3*) pp; 301·3 (*91·8*) oa
Beam, feet (*metres*)	36·7 (*11·3*)
Draught, feet (*metres*)	12 (*3·7*)
Guns, dual purpose	1—4 in (*102 mm*)
Guns, AA	4—40 mm
Boilers	2—three drum type
Main engines	Triple expansion 5 500 ihp; 2 shafts
Speed, knots	19
Range, miles	4 200 at 12 knots
Oil fuel, tons	440
Complement	140

"River" class frigate. Acquired from Great Britain and renamed in March 1948.

RADAR. British Type 974.

MAYU *Burmese Navy*

1 Ex-BRITISH "ALGERINE" CLASS

Name	*Builders*	*Laid down*	*Launched*	*Completed*
YAN MYO AUNG (ex-HMS *Mariner*, ex-*Kincardine*)	Port Arthur Shipyards, Canada	26 Aug 1943	9 May 1944	23 May 1945

Displacement, tons	1 040 standard; 1 335 full load
Length, feet (*metres*)	225 (*68·6*) pp; 235 (*71·6*) oa
Beam, feet (*metres*)	35·5 (*19·8*)
Draught, feet (*metres*)	11·5 (*3·5*)
Guns, surface	1—4 in (*102 mm*)
Guns, AA	4—40 mm
Boilers	2 three-drum type
Main engines	Triple expansion 2 000 shp; 2 shafts
Speed, knots	16·5
Range, miles	4 000 at 12 knots
Complement	140

Former ocean minesweeper in the British Navy, used as escort vessel. Handed over to Burma in London and renamed *Yan Myo Aung*, on 18 Apr 1958. Fitted for minelaying and can carry 16 mines, eight on each side.

RADAR. Decca Type 202.

SONAR. British Type 144

YAN MYO AUNG *1964, Burmese Navy*

CORVETTES

1 Ex-US PCE TYPE

YAN TAING AUNG, PCE 41 (ex-USS *Farmington*, PCE 894)

Displacement, tons	640 standard; 903 full load
Dimensions, ft (*m*)	180 wl; 184 oa × 33 × 9·5 (*56 × 10·1 × 2·9*)
Guns	1—3 in, 50 cal dp; 2—40 mm AA (1 twin); 8—20 mm AA (4 twin)
A/S weapons	1 hedgehog; 2 DCT; 2 DC tracks
Main engines	GM diesels; 2 shafts; 1 800 bhp = 15 knots

Former US Patrol ship (escort). Built by Willamette Iron & Steel Corp, Portland, Oregon. Laid down on 7 Dec 1942, launched on 15 May 1943 and completed 10 Aug 1943. Transferred on 18 June 1965.

1 Ex-US MSF TYPE

YAN GYI AUNG, PCE 42 (ex-USS *Craddock*, MSF 356)

Displacement, tons	650 standard; 945 full load
Dimensions, ft (*m*)	180 wl; 184·5 oa × 33 × 9·8 (*56 × 10·1 × 2·8*)
Guns	1—3 in 50 cal single forward; 4—40 mm (2 twin); 4—20 mm (2 twin)
A/S weapons	1 US Hedgehog; 2 DCT; 2 DC Racks
Main engines	Diesels; 2 shafts; 1 710 shp = 14·8 knots
Range, miles	4 300 at 10 knots

Former US steel hulled fleet minesweeper of the "Admirable" class. Built by Willamette Iron & Steel Corp, Portland, Oregon. Laid down on 10 Nov 1943 and launched on 22 July 1944. Transferred at San Diego on 31 Mar 1967.

2 BURMESE-BUILT TYPE

NAGAKYAY **NAWARAT**

Displacement, tons	400 standard; 450 full load
Dimensions, ft (*m*)	163 × 26·8 × 5·8 (*49·7 × 8·2 × 1·8*)
Guns	2—25 pdr QF; 2—40 mm AA
Main engines	2 Paxman-Ricardo turbo-charged diesels; 2 shafts; 1 160 bhp = 12 knots
Complement	43

Built at the Government Dockyard, Dawbon, Rangoon, Burma, *Nagakyay* was completed on 3 Dec 1960 and *Nawarat* on 26 Apr 1960.

NAGAKYAY *1962, Burmese Navy*

LIGHT FORCES

5 SAUNDERS ROE FAST ATTACK CRAFT

T 201 (ex-*PTS 101*) **T 203** (ex-*PTS 103*) **T 205** (ex-*PTS 105*)
T 202 (ex-*PTS 102*) **T 204** (ex-*PTS 104*)

Displacement, tons	50 standard; 64 full load
Dimensions, ft (*m*)	67 pp; 71·5 oa × 19·5 × 6 max (*21·8 × 5·9 × 1·8*)
Guns	As MGB: 1—4·5 in; 1—40 mm AA; As MTB: 2—20 mm AA
Tubes	As MTB: 4—21 in
Main engines	2 Napier Deltic diesels; 5 000 shp = 42 knots
Complement	20

T 202 *1966, Burmese Navy,*

Built by Saunders Roe (Anglesey) Ltd, England. Convertible craft of aluminium construction, with riveted skin and aluminium alloy framework. Auxiliary power is provided by diesels. The Saunders-Roe slow-speed electric drive was fitted to facilitate manoeuvring in the confined inland waters where the craft may be required to operate. Armament and layout of the vessels were similar to the British fast patrol boats of the "Dark" Class. The cost including engines, equipment, and spares of the five boats was over £1 800 000. T 201 was launched 24 Mar 1956. All were completed in 1956-57.

RADAR. British Type 974.

10 BURMESE-BUILT RIVER PATROL CRAFT

Small craft, 50 feet long, built in Burma in 1951-52.

25 YUGOSLAV-BUILT RIVER PATROL CRAFT

Small craft, 52 feet long, acquired from Yugoslavia in the mid 1960s.

GUN BOATS

4 Ex-BRITISH LCG (M) TYPE

INDAW **INLAY** **INMA** **INYA**

Displacement, tons	381
Dimensions, ft (*m*)	154 oa × 22·5 × 7·8 (*47·1 × 6·8 × 2·4*)
Guns	2—25 pdr; 2—2 pdr
Main engines	Paxman Ricardo diesels; 2 shafts; 1 000 bhp = 13 knots
Complement	39

Former British landing craft, gun (medium) *LCG* (M). Employed as gunboats.

RADAR. British Type 974.

INMA *Burmese Navy*

2 IMPROVED YUGOSLAV TYPE GUNBOATS

Y 311 **Y 312**

Guns. 2—40 mm (single); 4—20 mm (single).

Dimensions approximately as Y-type Built in Burma 1969.

Gunboats—*cont.*

10 YUGOSLAVIAN-BUILT "Y" TYPE GUNBOATS

Y 301 Y 302 Y 303 Y 304 Y 305 Y 306 Y 307 Y 308 Y 309 Y 310

Displacement, tons	120
Dimensions, ft (*m*)	100 pp; 104·8 oa × 24 × 3 (*32 × 7·3 × 0·9*)
Guns	2—40 mm AA; 1—2 pdr
Main engines	2 Mercedes-Benz diesels; 2 shafts; 1 000 bhp = 13 knots
Complement	29

All ten of these boats were completed in 1958 at the "Uljanik" Shipyard, Pula, in Yugoslavia. For detailed building dates see 1966-67 and earlier editions.

Y 310 *1964, Burmese Navy*

8 GUNBOATS (ex-TRANSPORTS)

SABAN **SEINDA** **SETYAHAT** **SHWETHIDA**
SAGU **SETKAYA** **SHWEPAZUN** **SINMIN**

Displacement, tons	98
Dimensions, ft (*m*)	94·5 × 22 × 4·5 (*28·8 × 6·7 × 1·4*)
Guns	1—40 mm; 3—20 mm
Main engines	Crossley ERL—6 diesel; 160 bhp = 12 knots
Complement	32

SHWEPAZUN *1971, Burmese Navy*

6 US-BUILT PGM TYPE GUNBOATS

PGM 401 **PGM 402** **PGM 403** **PGM 404** **PGM 405** **PGM 406**

Displacement, tons	100
Dimensions, ft (*m*)	95 × 19 × 5 (*29 × 5·8 × 1·5*)
Guns	2—40 mm (single); 2—0·5 Browning MG
Main engines	4 GM diesels; 2 shafts; 1 000 bhp = 16 knots
Complement	17

Built by the Marinette Marine Corporation, USA. Ex-US PGM 43-46, 51 and 52 respectively. Machinery comprises 2-stroke, 6-cylinder, tandem geared twin diesel propulsion unit—1 LH and 1 RH; 500 bhp per unit.

RADAR. Raytheon 1 500 in PGM 405-6; EDO 320 in PGM 401-4.

PGM 401 *1962, Burmese Navy*

Gunboats—*cont.*

6 Ex-UNITED STATES CGC TYPE GUNBOATS

MGB 101 MGB 102 MGB 104 MGB 105 MGB 106 MGB 110

Displacement, tons	49 standard; 66 full load
Dimensions, ft (*m*)	78 pp; 83 oa × 16 × 5·5 (*25·3 × 4·9 × 1·7*)
Guns	1—40 mm AA; 1—20 mm AA
Main engines	4 GM diesels; 2 shafts; 800 bhp = 11 knots
Complement	16

Ex-USCG 83-ft type cutters with new hulls built in Burma. Completed in 1960. For detailed building dates see 1966-67 and earlier editions. Machinery comprises 2-stroke, 6 cylinder, tandem geared, twin diesel propulsion units—1 LH and 1 RH drive; 400 bhp per unit. Three of this class are reported to have been sunk.

MGB 102 *1962, Burmese Navy*

SURVEY VESSELS

THU TAY THI

Ocean Survey ship, 204 feet overall and 1 100 tons displacement, acquired from Yugoslavia in the mid-1960s. Complement 99.

YAY BO (UBHL 807)

Coastal survey vessel, possibly Dutch built with complement of 25 and a displacement of 108 tons.

SUPPORT SHIP

YAN LON AUNG

Light forces support ship of 520 tons, acquired from Japan in 1967.

TRANSPORTS

PYIDAWAYE

Measurement tons	2 217·31 gross
Dimensions, ft (*m*)	270 × 47 × 15 (*82·3 × 14·3 × 4·6*)
Main engines	Fleming & Ferguson triple expansion 2 000 ihp
Boilers	2 Scotch (return type)
Range, miles	2 000
Complement	88

Former passenger ship. In service since 1962. Bears the Burmese naval ensign.

PYIDAWAYE *1964, Burmese Navy*

2 Ex-US LCU TYPE

AIYAR LULIN (ex-USS *LCU 1626*) 603 + 1

Displacement, tons	200 light; 342 full load
Dimensions, ft (*m*)	135·2 oa × 29 × 5·5 (*41·2 × 8·8 × 1·7*)
Main engines	Diesels; 2 shafts; 1 000 bhp = 11 knots

US type utility landing craft 603 completed in Rangoon 1966. Transferred under MAP in 1967. Used as transports.

8 Ex-US LCM 3 TYPE

LCM 701 LCM 702 LCM 703 LCM 704 LCM 705 LCM 706 LCM 707 LCM 708

Displacement, tons	28
Dimensions, ft (*m*)	56 × 14 × 4 (*17·0 × 4·3 × 1·2*)
Guns	2—20 mm single
Main engines	2 Gray Marine diesels; 225 bhp = 9 knots

US-built LCM type landing craft. Used as local transports for stores and personnel.

CAMEROON

Personnel
1975: 300 officers and men

Base
Douala

Mercantile Marine
Lloyd's Register of Shipping:
18 vessels of 3 199 tons gross

LIGHT FORCES

1 LARGE PATROL CRAFT

Displacement, tons	250 full load
Dimensions, ft (*m*)	157·5 × 23·3 × 7·5 (*48 × 7·1 × 2·3*)
Guns	2—40 mm
Main engines	2 AGO Diesels; 4 000 hp = 20 knots
Range, miles	2 000 at 16 knots

Ordered from Soc. Français Construction Naval in Sep 1974 for delivery in 1976. Similar to "Bizerte" class in Tunisia.

2 COASTAL PATROL CRAFT

VIGILANT (ex-*VC 6*, P 756) **AUDACIEUX** (ex-*VC 8*, P 758)

Displacement, tons	75 standard; 82 full load
Dimensions, ft (*m*)	104·2 × 15·5 × 5·5 (*31·8 × 4·7 × 1·7*)
Guns	2—20 mm AA
Main engines	Mercedes-Benz diesels; 2 shafts; 2 700 bhp = 28 knots
Range, miles	1 500 at 15 knots
Complement	15

Former French seaward defence motor launches of the VC type. Built by Constructions Mécaniques de Normandie, Cherbourg. Completed in 1957-58 *Vigilant* was officially handed over from France to the Republic of Cameroon on 7 Mar 1964.

ALFRED MOTTO

Displacement, tons	80 approx.
Dimensions, ft (*m*)	110 × 16 (*33·6 × 4·9*)

ALFRED MOTTO *1973, Y. Bertrand*

BRIGADIER M'BONGA TOUNDA

Displacement, tons	20 full load
Dimensions, ft (*m*)	60 × 13·5 × 4 (*18·3 × 4·1 × 1·2*)
Guns	1—12·7 mm MG
Main engines	Caterpillar Diesel; 2 shafts; 540 bhp = 21 knots
Complement	8

Built by Ch Navals de L'Esterel in 1967. Customs duties.

VALEUREUX

Displacement, tons	45 full load
Dimensions, ft (*m*)	78·1 × 16·3 × 5·1 (*23·8 × 5·0 × 1·6*)
Guns	2—20 mm AA
Main engines	2 Diesels; 2 shafts; 960 hp = 25 knots
Complement	9

Built by Ch Navals de L'Esterel in 1970.

3 LCVP

SOUELLABA INDÉPENDANCE REUNIFICATION

Built by Ateliers et Chantiers de l'Afrique Equatoriale, near Libreville, Gabon. Of 11 tons and 10 knots.

2 LCM

Built by Carena, Abidjan, Ivory Coast.

MISCELLANEOUS

Tornade and *Ouragan*.—Built in 1966. *St. Sylvestre*.—Built in 1967.
Four small outboard craft.
Mungo operated by Transport Ministry. *Dr. Jamot* operated by Health Ministry.

CANADA

Ministerial

Minister of National Defence:
The Hon. James Richardson MP

Senior Naval Appointments

Chief of Maritime Operations:
Rear-Admiral A. L. Collier, DSC, CD

Commander, Maritime Command:
Vice-Admiral D. S. Boyle, CD

Commander, Maritime Forces, Pacific:
Rear-Admiral R. J. Pickford, CD

Diplomatic Representation

Senior Liaison Officer (Maritime) London:
Captain (N) J. W. Mason, CD

Canadian Forces Attaché and Maritime Liaision Officer, Washington:
Commodore M. A. Martin, CD

Canadian Forces Attaché (Naval) Moscow:
Commander H. R. Waddell, CD

Navy Estimates

1971-72: $348 000 000
1972-73: $363 000 000
1973-74: $394 300 000
1975-76: $472 268 000

Personnel

(a) 1971: 16 906 (2 379 officers, 14 527 men and women)
1972: 15 223 (2 590 officers, 12 633 men and women)
1973: 16 003 (1 985 officers, 14 018 men and women)
1974: 14 000 (2 000 officers, 1 2000 men and women)
(b) Voluntary Service

Establishment

The Royal Canadian Navy was officially established on 4 May 1910, when Royal Assent was given to the Naval Service Act. On 1 April 1968 the Canadian Forces Reorganisation Act unified the three branches of the Canadian Forces and the title "Royal Canadian Navy" was dropped.

Strength of the Fleet

Type	*Active*	*Building*
Destroyers (DDH)	4	—
Frigates (some with helicopters)	16	—
Patrol Submarines	3	—
Replenishment Ships	3	—
Small Oilers	2	—
Patrol Escorts (Small)	7	—
Research Ships	3	—
Diving Support Ships and Tenders	2	—
Gate Vessels	5	—
Tugs (Large)	7	—
Tugs (Small)	12	5
Police Patrol Vessels	31	—
Hydrofoil	1	—

Air Arm

In an integrated force there is no specific Fleet Air Arm, but two squadrons of Sea King helicopters provide for ships' needs.

Bases

Halifax and Esquimalt

Disposals

Attack Carrier (medium)
1970 *Bonaventure* paid off 1 April, towed to Taiwan for scrap, leaving Halifax 27 October

Destroyers

1971 *Algonquin* left Victoria BC for Taiwan 21 April
Crescent left Victoria BC for Taiwan 21 May

Frigates

1973 *St. Laurent, Columbia, St. Croix, Chaudiere*
1974 *Granby*

Maintenance Ships

1972 *Cape Breton* and *Cape Scott* decommissioned.

Research Vessels

1972 *Fort Frances*

Transfers

Patrol Escorts (Small)

1973 *Fort Steele* from RCMP to DND

Gate Vessels

1974 *Porte Dauphine* from MOT to DND

Mercantile Marine

Lloyd's Register of Shipping:
1 231 vessels of 2 459 998 tons gross

PENNANT NUMBERS

Destroyers

Iroquois	280
Huron	281
Athabaskan	282
Algonquin	283

Frigates

*St. Laurent	205
Saguenay	206
Skeena	207
Ottawa	229
Margaree	230
Fraser	233
Assiniboine	234
*Chaudiere	235
Gatineau	236
*St. Croix	256
Restigouche	257
Kootenay	258
Terra Nova	259
*Columbia	260
Mackenzie	261
Saskatchewan	262
Yukon	263
Qu'Appelle	264
Annapolis	265
Nipigon	266

Submarines

Ojibwa	72
Onondaga	73
Okanagan	74
*Rainbow	75

Replenishment Ships

Provider	AOR 508
Protecteur	AOR 509
Preserver	AOR 510
Dundalk	AOC 501
Dundurn	AOC 502

Research Vessels

Sackville	AGOR 113
Bluethroat	AGOR 114
Endeavour	AGOR 171
Quest	AGOR 172
Kapuskasing	AGOR 173
Laymore	AGOR 516

Patrol Escort (PFL)

Fort Steele	140
Fundy	159
Chignecto	160
Thunder	161
Cowichan	162
Miramichi	163
Chaleur	164

Gate Vessels

Porte St. Jean	180
Porte St. Louis	183
Porte de la Reine	184
Porte Quebec	185
Porte Dauphine	186

Tugs

Heatherton	ATA 527
Riverton	ATA 528
Clifton	ATA 529
St. Anthony	ATA 531
St. Charles	ATA 533
Glenside	YTB 500
Glenbrook	YTB 501
Glenevis	YTB 502
Glendyne	YTB 503
Glenlivet II	YTB 504
Eastwood	YMT 550
Greenwood	YMT 551
Mannville	YTS 577
Adamsville	YTS 582
Beamsville	YTS 583
Queensville	YTS 586
Plainsville	YTS 587
Youville	YTS 588
Loganville	YTS 589
Lawrenceville	YTS 590
Parkesville	YTS 591
Listerville	YTS 592
Merrickville	YTS 593
Marysville	YTS 594

*Declared surplus 1974.

DESTROYERS (DDH)

4 "TRIBAL" CLASS (DDH)

Displacement, tons	4 200 full load
Length, feet (*metres*)	398 (*121·3*) pp 426 (*129·8*) oa
Beam, feet (*metres*)	50 (*15·2*)
Draught, feet (*metres*)	14·5 (*4·4*)
Aircraft	2 "Sea King" CHSS-2 A/S helicopters
Missiles	(see note)
Gun	1—5 in (*127 mm*) 54 cal single Oto-Melara
A/S	1 Mk 10 "Limbo"
Torpedo tubes	2 triple Mk 32 for A/S homing torpedoes
Main engines	Gas turbines; 2 Pratt & Whitney FT4A2 50 000 shp + 2 Pratt & Whitney FT12AH3 7 400 shp for cruising; 2 shafts
Speed, knots	29 +
Range, miles	4 500 at 20 knots
Complement	245 (20 officers, 225 men) (plus air unit, 12 officers + 33 men)

Name	*No.*	*Builders*	*Laid down*	*Launched*	*Completion*
ALGONQUIN	283	Davie SB Co, Lauzon	1 Sep 1969	23 Apr 1971	30 Sept 1973
ATHABASKAN	282	Davie SB Co, Lauzon	1 June 1969	27 Nov 1970	30 Nov 1972
HURON	281	Marine Industries Ltd, Sorel	15 Jan 1969	3 Apr 1971	16 Dec 1972
IROQUOIS	280	Marine Industries Ltd, Sorel	15 Jan 1969	28 Nov 1970	29 July 1972

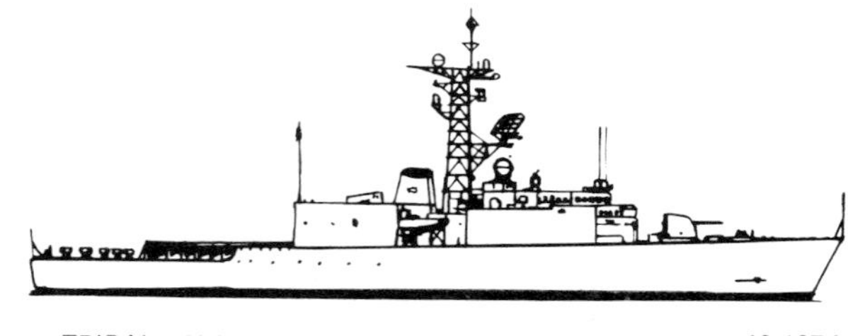

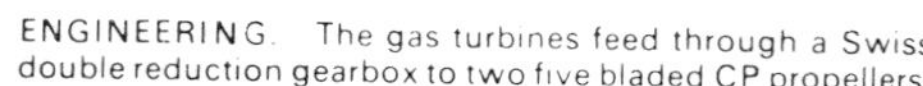

TRIBAL" CLASS *12/1974*

GENERAL
These ships have the same hull design, dimensions and basic characteristics as the large general purpose frigates cancelled at the end of 1963 (see particulars and illustration in the 1963-64 edition). Designed as anti-submarine ships, they are fitted with variable depth and hull sonar, landing deck equipped with double hauldown and Beartrap, flume type anti-rolling tanks to stabilise the ships at low speed, pre-wetting system to counter radio-active fallout, enclosed citadel, and bridge control of machinery.

ENGINEERING. The gas turbines feed through a Swiss double reduction gearbox to two five bladed CP propellers.

ELECTRONICS. Mk 22 Weapon System Control by Hollandse Signaal.

MISSILES. Launch system (GMLS) by Raytheon for Mk III Sea Sparrow missiles. Two quadruple launchers in forward end of the superstructure.

RADAR. SPQ 2D Surface warning and Navigation; SPS 501 (SPS 12) long range warning; M 22 fire control.
SONAR. SQS 505 Hull mounted in 14 ft dome; VDS. 18 ft towed body aft; SQS 501 Bottomed target classification.

TORPEDOES. The Mk 32 tubes are to be used with Mk 46 torpedoes.

IROQUOIS *1973, Canadian Forces*

ATHABASKAN *1974, John G. Callis*

FRIGATES

2 "ANNAPOLIS" CLASS

Displacement, tons	2 400 standard; 3 000 full load
Length, feet (*metres*)	371·0 (*113·1*) oa
Beam, feet (*metres*)	42·0 (*12·8*)
Draught, feet (*metres*)	14·4 (*4·4*)
Aircraft	1 CHSS-2 "Sea King" helicopter
Guns	2—3 in (*76 mm*) 50 cal (1 twin)
A/S weapons	1 Mk 10 "Limbo" in after well
Boilers	2 water tube
Main engines	Geared turbines; 2 shafts: 30 000 shp
Speed, knots	28, 30 trials
Range, miles	4 750 at 14 knots
Complement	210 (11 officers, 199 ratings)

These two ships represented the logical development of the original "St. Laurent" class, through the "Restigouche" and "Mackenzie" designs. Due to the erection of a helicopter hangar and flight deck, and Variable Depth Sonar only one "Limbo" mounting could be installed. Also the 50 cal 3 inch mounting had to be moved forward to replace the 70 cal mounting in the original design.

Name	*No.*	*Builders*	*Work started*	*Launched*	*Completed*
ANNAPOLIS	265	Halifax Shipyards Ltd, Halifax	July 1960	27 Apr 1963	19 Dec 1964
NIPIGON	266	Marine Industries Ltd, Sorel	Apr 1960	10 Dec 1961	30 May 1964

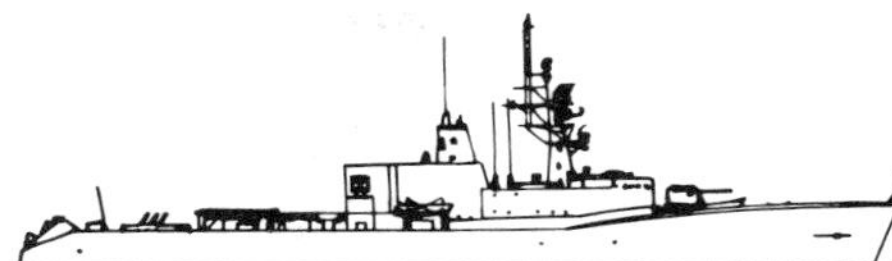

ANNAPOLIS, NIPIGON

CLASSIFICATION. Officially classified as DDH.

CONSTRUCTION. As these are largely prefabricated no firm laying down date is officially given. Work on hull units started under cover long before components were laid on the slip.

RADAR. Search: SPS 12. Tactical: SPS 10. Fire Control: X Band.

ANNAPOLIS — *6/1974 J. L. M van der Burg*

4 "MACKENZIE" CLASS

Displacement, tons	2 380 standard; 2 880 full load
Length, feet (*metres*)	366·0 (*111·5*) oa
Beam, feet (*metres*)	42·0 (*12·8*)
Draught, feet (*metres*)	13·5 (*4·1*)
Guns, AA	4—3 in (*76 mm*) 2 twin (70 cal fwd, 50 cal aft)
A/S weapons	2 Mk 10 "Limbo" in well aft
Main engines	Geared turbines; 2 shafts; 30 000 shp
Boilers	2 water tube
Speed, knots	28
Range, miles	4 750 at 14 knots
Complement	210 (11 officers, 199 ratings)

Name	*No.*	*Builders*	*Laid down*	*Launched*	*Completed*
MACKENZIE	261	Canadian Vickers Ltd, Montreal	15 Dec 1958	25 May 1961	6 Oct 1962
QU'APPELLE	264	Davie Shipbuilding & Repairing	14 Jan 1960	2 May 1962	14 Sep 1963
***SASKATCHEWAN**	262	Victoria Machinery (and Yarrow)	16 July 1959	1 Feb 1961	16 Feb 1963
YUKON	263	Burrard DD & Shipbuilding	25 Oct 1959	27 July 1961	25 May 1963

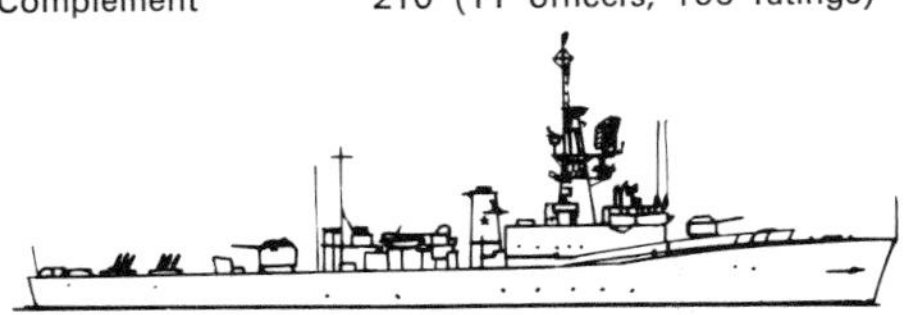

"MACKENZIE" Class — *12/1974*

CLASSIFICATION. Officially classified as DDE.

RADAR. Search: SPS 12. Tactical: SPS 10. Fire Control: X Band.

**Saskatchewan* was launched by Victoria Machinery Depot Co Ltd, but completed by Yarrow's Ltd.

YUKON — *5/1974, John G. Callis*

3 "RESTIGOUCHE" CLASS

Displacement, tons	2 370 standard; 2 880 full load
Length, feet (*metres*)	366·0 (*111·5*) oa
Beam, feet (*metres*)	42·0 (*12·8*)
Draught, feet (*metres*)	13·5 (*4·1*)
Guns, AA	4—3 in (*76 mm*) 2 twin
A/S weapons	2 Mk 10 "Limbo" in well aft
Main engines	Geared turbines; 2 shafts; 30 000 shp
Boilers	2 water tube
Speed, knots	28
Range, miles	4 750 at 14 knots
Complement	248 (12 officers, 236 ratings)

Name	*No*	*Builder*	*Laid down*	*Launched*	*Completed*
CHAUDIERE	235	Halifax Shipyards Ltd	30 July 1953	13 Nov 1957	14 Nov 1959
COLUMBIA	260	Burrard DD and Shipbuilding	11 June 1953	1 Nov 1956	7 Nov 1959
ST. CROIX	256	Marine Industries Ltd, Sorel	15 Oct 1954	17 Nov 1957	4 Oct 1958

CHAUDIERE

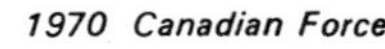

1970 Canadian Forces

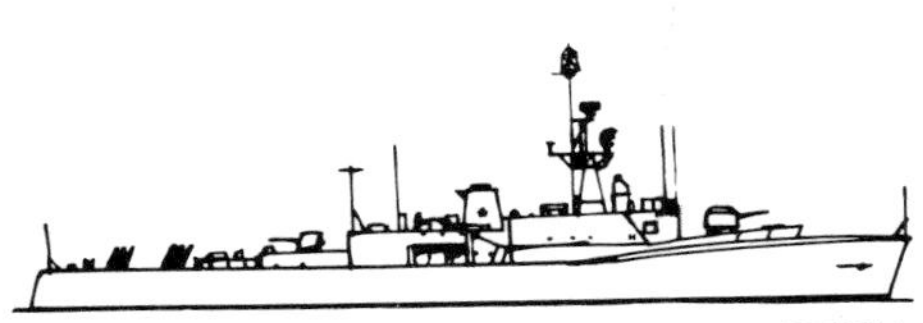

"RESTIGOUCHE" Class — *12/1974*

GENERAL
All three declared surplus and paid off in 1974.

CLASSIFICATION Officially classified as DDE.

RADAR. Search: SPS 12. Tactical: SPS 10. Fire Control: X Band.

Frigates—*continued*

4 "IMPROVED RESTIGOUCHE"

Name	No.	Builder	Laid down	Launched	Completed
GATINEAU	236	Davie Shipbuilding & Repairing	30 Apr 1953	3 June 1957	17 Feb 1959
KOOTENAY	258	Burrard DD & Shipbuilding	21 Aug 1952	15 June 1954	7 Mar 1959
RESTIGOUCHE	257	Canadian Vickers, Montreal	15 July 1953	22 Nov 1954	7 June 1958
TERRA NOVA	259	Victoria Machinery Depot Co	14 Nov 1952	21 June 1955	6 June 1959

Displacement, tons	2 390 standard; 2 900 full load
Length, feet (*metres*)	371·0 (*113·1*)
Beam, feet (*metres*)	42·0 (*12·8*)
Draught, feet (*metres*)	14·1 (*4·3*)
Guns, AA	2—3 in (*76 mm*) 70 cal forward
A/S weapons	ASROC aft and 1 Mk 10 "Limbo" in after well
Main engines	Geared turbines; 2 shafts; 30 000 shp
Boilers	2 water tube
Speed, knots	28 plus
Range, miles	4 750 at 14 knots
Complement	214 (13 officers, 201 ratings)

CLASSIFICATION. Officially classified as DDE.

CONVERSION. These four ships were refitted with ASROC aft and lattice foremast. Work included removing the after 3 inch 50 cal twin gun mounting and one "Limbo" A/S Mk 10 triple mortar, to make way for ASROC and Variable Depth Sonar. Dates of refits, *Terra Nova* was completed on 18 Oct 1968; *Gatineau* completed in 1972 and *Kootenay* and *Restigouche* in 1973. Refit also included improvements to communications fit.

RADAR. Search: SPS 12. Tactical: SPS 10. Fire Control: X Band.

GATINEAU 1972, *Canadian Forces*

GATINEAU

RESTIGOUCHE

7 "ST. LAURENT" CLASS

Name	No.	Builders	Laid down	Launched	Completed
ST. LAURENT	DDE 205	Canadian Vickers, Ltd, Montreal	22 Nov 1950	20 Nov 1951	29 Oct 1955
SAGUENAY	DDE 206	Halifax Shipyards, Ltd, Halifax	4 Apr 1951	30 July 1953	15 Dec 1956
SKEENA	DDE 207	Burrard Dry Dock & Shipbuilding	1 June 1951	19 Aug 1952	30 Mar 1957
OTTAWA	DDE 229	Canadian Vickers, Ltd, Montreal	8 June 1951	29 Apr 1953	10 Nov 1956
MARGAREE	DDE 230	Halifax Shipyards Ltd, Halifax	12 Sep 1951	29 Mar 1956	5 Oct 1957
***FRASER**	DDE 233	Yarrows Ltd, Esquimalt, B.C.	11 Dec 1951	19 Feb 1953	28 June 1957
ASSINIBOINE	DDE 234	Marine Industries Ltd, Sorel, Q	19 May 1952	12 Feb 1954	16 Aug 1956

Displacement, tons	2 260 standard; 2 858 full load
Length, feet (*metres*)	366·0 (*111·5*) oa
Beam, feet (*metres*)	42·0 (*12·8*)
Draught, feet (*metres*)	13·2 (*4·0*)
Aircraft	1 CHSS-2 "Sea King" helicopter
Guns	2—3 in (*76 mm*) 50 cal (1 twin)
A/S weapons	1 Mk 10 "Limbo" in after well
Main engines	English Electric geared turbines; 2 shafts; 30 000 shp
Boilers	2 water tube
Speed, knots	28·5
Range, miles	4 570 at 12 knots
Complement	208 (11 officers, 197 ratings) (plus air unit of 7 officers and 13 men)

"ST. LAURENT" Class (except *Fraser*) 12/1974

GENERAL
The first major warships to be designed in Canada. In design, much assistance was received from the Royal Navy (propelling machinery of British design) and the US Navy. *St Laurent* declared surplus in 1974.

**Fraser* was launched by Burrard Dry Dock & Shipbuilding but completed by Yarrows Ltd.

FRASER 12/1974

CLASSIFICATION. Officially classified as DDH.

GUNNERY. Original armament was 4—3 inch, 50 cal AA (2 twin), 2—40 mm AA (single), and 2 "Limbo" mortars.

RADAR. Search: SPS 12. Tactical: SPS 10.

RECONSTRUCTION. All have helicopter platforms and VDS. Twin funnels were fitted to permit forward extension of the helicopter hangar.

Gunhouses are of fibreglass. In providing helicopter platforms and hangars it was possible to retain only one three barrelled "Limbo" mortar and only one twin 3-inch gun mounting. Dates of recommissioning after conversion: *Assiniboine* 28 June 1963, *St Laurent* 4 Oct 1963, *Ottawa* 21 Oct 1964, *Saguenay* 14 May 1965, *Skeena* 15 Aug 1965, *Margaree* 15 Oct 1965, *Fraser* 31 Aug 1966.

SKEENA 1971, *Wright & Logan*

SUBMARINES

3 "OJIBWA" (BRITISH OBERON) CLASS (PATROL SUBMARINES)

Name	No.	Builders	Laid down	Launched	Commissioned
OJIBWA (ex-*Onyx*)	72	HM Dockyard, Chatham	27 Sep 1962	29 Feb 1964	23 Sep 1965
OKANAGAN	74	HM Dockyard, Chatham	25 Mar 1965	17 Sep 1966	22 June 1968
ONONDAGA	73	HM Dockyard, Chatham	18 June 1964	25 Sep 1965	22 June 1967

Displacement, tons	2 060 full buoyancy surface; 2 200 normal surface; 2 420 dived
Length, feet (*metres*)	241 (*73·5*) pp; 294·2 (*90·0*) oa
Beam, feet (*metres*)	26·5 (*8·1*)
Draught, feet (*metres*)	18 (*5·5*)
Torpedo tubes	8—21 in (*533 mm*), 6 bow and 2 stern
Main machinery	2 Admiralty Standard Range diesels; 3 680 bhp; 2 shafts; 2 electric motors; 6 000 hp
Speed, knots	12 on surface; 17 dived
Complement	65 (7 officers, 58 ratings)

GENERAL
On 11 April 1962 the Minister of National Defence announced that Canada was to buy three "Oberon" class submarines in UK. The first of these patrol submarines was obtained by the Canadian Government from the Royal Navy construction programme. She was laid down as *Onyx* but launched as *Ojibwa*. The other two were specific Canadian orders. There were some design changes to meet specific new needs including installation of RCN communications equipment and increase of air-conditioning capacity to meet the wide extremes of climate encountered in Canadian operating areas.

ELECTRONICS. The equipment includes sonar with fore casing mounted array and X band surveillance radar installations.

NOMENCLATURE. The name *Ojibwa* is that of a tribe of North American Indians now widely dispersed in Canada and the USA and one of the largest remnants of aboriginal population. *Okanagan* and *Onondaga* are also Canadian Indian tribes.

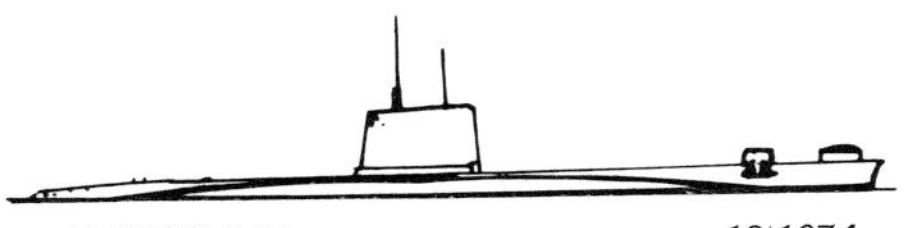
"OJIBWA" Class 12/1974

OKANAGAN 1969 *Canadian Maritime Command*

OKANAGAN 6/1973, *Wright and Logan*

1 Ex-US "TENCH" CLASS (PATROL SUBMARINE)

RAINBOW SS 75 (ex-USS *Argonaut* SS 475)

Displacement, tons	1 800 surface; 2 500 dived
Length, feet (*metres*)	311·2 (*95·0*)
Beam, feet (*metres*)	27·2 (*8·2*)
Draught, feet (*metres*)	17·1 (*5·2*)
Torpedo tubes	10—21 in (*533 mm*) 6 fwd, 4 aft
Main machinery	6 500 hp diesels; 4 610 hp motors
Speed, knots	20 on surface; 10 dived
Range, miles	12 000 at 10 knots surfaced
Complement	82 (8 officers, 74 men)

RAINBOW *1970, Canadian Maritime Command*

GENERAL
Built by Navy Yard, Portsmouth, New Hampshire. Laid down on 28 June 1944, launched on 1 Oct 1944 and completed on 15 Jan 1945. Purchased in Dec 1968 as a replacement for *Grilse*. Commissioned on 2 Dec 1968. Withdrawn from service Dec 31 1974. Disposal action to be decided.

RAINBOW

REPLENISHMENT SHIPS

Name	No.	Builders	Laid down	Launched	Completed
PRESERVER	AOR 510	Saint John Dry Dock Co Ltd, N.B.	17 Oct 1967	29 May 1969	30 July 1970
PROTECTEUR	AOR 509	Saint John Dry Dock Co Ltd, N.B.	17 Oct 1967	18 July 1968	30 Aug 1969

Displacement, tons	9 000 light; 22 100 full load
Measurement, tons	22 100 gross; 13 250 deadweight
Length, feet (*metres*)	546 (*168·4*) oa
Beam, feet (*metres*)	76 (23·2)
Draught, feet (*metres*)	30 (*9.1*)
Guns	2—3 in (*76 mm*)
A/S launcher	1 Sea Sparrow to be fitted
Aircraft	3 CHSS-2 "Sea King" helicopters
Boilers	2 forced draught water tube
Main engines	Geared turbine; 21 000 shp; 1 shaft
Range, miles	4 100 at 20, 7 500 at 11·5 knots
Complement	227 (15 officers, 212 ratings)

GENERAL
Contract price $47 500 000 for both ships. In design they are an improvement on that of the prototype *Provider*. They could carry spare anti-submarine helciopters, military vehicles and bulk equipment for sealift purposes. 14 122 tons fuel, 1 048 tons dry cargo. tion.

PROTECTEUR *9/1974, Reiner Nerlich*

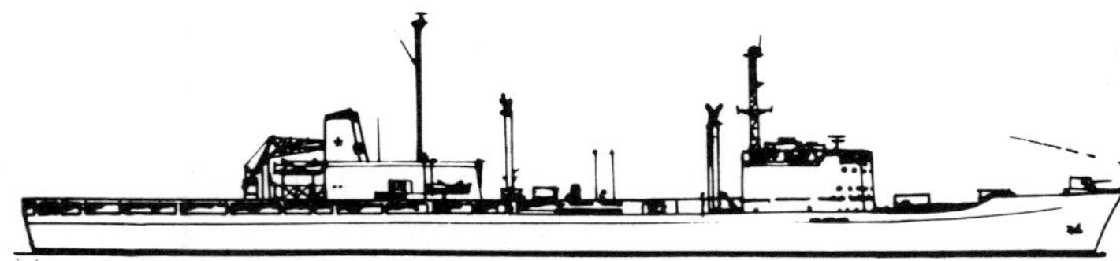
PROTECTEUR, PRESERVER *12/1974*

PROVIDER *12/1974*

Name	No.	Builder	Laid down	Launched	Completed
PROVIDER	AOR 508	Davie Shipbuilding Ltd, Lauzon	1 May 1961	5 July 1962	28 Sep 1963

Displacement, tons	7 300 light; 22 000 full load
Measurement, tons	20 000 gross; 14 700 deadweight
Length, feet (*metres*)	523 (*159·4*) pp; 555 (*169·2*) oa
Beam, feet (*metres*)	76 (*23·2*)
Draught, feet (*metres*)	32 (*9·8*)
Aircraft	3 CHSS-2 "Sea King" helicopters
Boilers	2 water tube
Main engines	Double reduction geared turbine; 21 000 shp; 1 shaft
Speed, knots	20
Range, miles	3 600 at 20 knots
Oil fuel, tons	1 200
Complement	166 (15 officers, 151 ratings)

PROVIDER *1971, Canadian Forces*

GENERAL
Preliminary construction work was begun in September 1960. Cost $15 700 000.

The helicopter flight deck is aft with the hangar at the same level and immediately below the funnel. The flight deck can receive the largest and heaviest helicopters. A total of 20 electro-hydraulic winches are fitted on dec for ship-to-ship movements of cargo and supplies. a well as shore-to-ship requirements when alongside.

2 "DUN" CLASS OILERS

DUNDALK AOC 501

DUNDURN AOC 502

Displacement, tons	950
Dimensions, feet	178·8 × 32·2 × 13
Main engines	Diesel; 700 bhp = 10 knots

Small tankers, classed as fleet auxiliaries.

DUNDURN *1969, Mr G·R Hooper (Master)*

MAINTENANCE SHIPS

2 "CAPE" CLASS

Name	No.	Builders	Laid down	Launched	Completed
CAPE BRETON	100	Burrard Dry Dock Co, Vancouver, BC	5 July 1944	7 Oct 1944	25 Apr 1945
CAPE SCOTT	101	Burrard Dry Dock Co, Vancouver, BC	8 June 1944	27 Sep 1944	20 Mar 1945

Displacement, tons	8 580 standard; 10 000 full load
Dimensions, feet	441·5 × 57 × 20 mean at standard displacement

GENERAL
Alongside Base Ships for FMU'S on each coast. They are decommissioned and no further operational role is planned. These ships, with a number of sisters, were originally built in Canada for the R.N.

CAPE SCOTT *1971, Canadian Forces*

RESEARCH VESSELS

BLUETHROAT AGOR 114

Displacement, tons	785 standard; 870 full load
Dimensions, feet	150·7 pp; 157 oa × 33 × 10
Main engines	Diesel; 2 shafts; 1 200 bhp = 13 knots

Authorised under 1951 Programme. Built by Geo. T. Davie & Sons Ltd, Lauzon. Laid down on 31 Oct 1952. Launched on 15 Sep 1955. Completed on 28 Nov 1955 as mine and Loop Layer. In 1957 she was rated Controlled Minelayer, NPC 114. Redesignated as Cable Layer (ALC) in 1959, and as Research Vessel (AGOR) and GP craft in 1964.

SACKVILLE AGOR 113

Displacement, tons	1 085 standard; 1 350 full load
Dimensions, feet	190 pp; 205 oa × 33 × 14·5
Main engines	Triple expansion; 2 750 ihp = 16 knots
Boilers	2 SE

Built by St. John Dry Dock Co, NB. Launched on 15 May 1941. Completed on 30 Dec 1941. Ex-"Flower" class corvette converted to loop layer. Employed by Naval Research Laboratories for oceanographic work. Designated AN 113—rated cable layer in 1959 (ALC), Redesignated as research vessel 1964.

KAPUSKASING AGOR 173

Displacement, tons	1 040 standard; 1 335 full load
Dimensions, feet	225 oa × 35 × 11
Main engines	Triple expansion; 2 shafts; 2 000 ihp = 16·5 knots
Boilers	2, of 3-drum type

Built by Port Arthur SB Co, Ontario. Completed 23 July 1943. Former "Algerine" class minesweeper—all this class was redesignated coastal escort (FSE) in 1953. Refitted as survey ship (AGH) in 1959—redesignated AGOR 1964.

QUEST AGOR 172

Displacement, tons	2 130
Dimensions, feet	235 oa × 42 × 15·5
Aircraft	Light helicopter
Main engines	Diesel electric; 2 shafts; 2 950 shp = 16 knots max; Bow thruster propeller
Range, miles	10 000 at 12 knots
Complement	55

Built by Burrard Dry Dock Co, Vancouver for the Naval Research Establishment of the Defence Research Board for acoustic, hydrographic and general oceanographic work. Capable of operating in heavy ice in the company of an icebreaker. Construction began in 1967. Launched on 9 July 1968. Completed on 21 Aug 1969. Based at Halifax.

QUEST — *1972, Canadian Maritime Command*

ENDEAVOUR AGOR 171

Displacement, tons	1 560
Dimensions, feet	215 wl; 236 oa × 38·5 × 13
Aircraft	1 light helicopter
Main engines	Diesel electric; 2 shafts; 2 960 shp = 16 knots
Range, miles	10 000 at 12 knots
Complement	10 officers, 13 scientists, 25 ratings (plus helicopter pilot and engineer)

A naval research ship designed primarily for anti-submarine research. Flight deck 48 by 31 feet. Stiffened for operating in ice-covered areas. Built by Yarrows Ltd, Esquimalt, BC. Accepted for service on 9 Mar 1965. She is able to turn in 2·5 times her own length. Her crow's-nest is fitted with engine and steering controls for navigation in ice. A bulbous bow reduces pitch and she has anti-roll tanks. Two 9-ton Austin-Weston telescopic cranes are fitted. There are two oceanographical winches each holding 5 000 fathoms of wire, two bathythermograph winches and a deep-sea anchoring and coring winch. She has acoustic insulation in her machinery spaces.

ENDEAVOUR — *1970, Canadian Maritime Command*

LAYMORE AGOR 516 (ex-AKS 516)

Measurement, tons	560 gross, 262 net
Dimensions, feet	176·5 × 32 × 8
Main engines	GM diesels; 1 000 bhp = 10·8 knots

Former coastal supply vessel, rated as fleet auxiliary and designated AKS. Converted to research vessel 2 Aug 1965 to Mar 1966 and reclassified AGOR.

TRAINING SHIPS

6 "BAY" CLASS Ex-CMS (PFL)

Name	No	Builder	Completed
CHALEUR	164	Marine Industries	12 Sep 1957
CHIGNECTO	160	George T. Davie Ltd	1 Aug 1957
COWICHAN	162	Yarrows	19 Dec 1957
FUNDY	159	Davie Shipbuilding	27 Nov 1956
MIRAMICHI	163	Victoria Machinery	28 Oct 1957
THUNDER	161	Port Arthur	3 Oct 1957

Displacement, tons	390 standard; 464 full load
Dimensions, feet	140·0 pp; 152·0 oa × 28·0 × 7·0
Main engines	2 GM V-12 diesels; 2 shafts; 2 400 bhp = 16 knots
Oil fuel, tons	52
Range, miles	3 290 at 12 knots
Complement	18+ (2 officers, 16 ratings, + trainees)

Extensively built of aluminium, including frames and decks. There were originally 14 vessels of this class. Named after Canadian straits and bays. Designation changed from AMC to MCB in 1954. They were redesignated as Patrol Escorts (small) (PFL) in 1972 being used as training ships.

FUNDY — *1972, Canadian Maritime Command*

1 "FORT" CLASS PATROL ESCORT (PFL)

FORT STEELE 140

Displacement, tons	85
Dimensions, feet	110 wl; 118 oa × 21 × 7
Main engines	2 Paxman Ventura 12 YJCM diesels; 2 shafts; Camewa cp propellers; 2 800 bhp = 18 knots
Complement	16

Built by Canadian SB and Eng Co. Completed Nov 1958. Steel hull. Twin rudders Acquired by DND in 1973 from RCMP—acts as Reserve Training ship based on Halifax.

5 "PORTE" CLASS (GATE VESSELS)

Name	No.	Builders	Laid down	Launched	Completed
PORTE DE LA REINE	184	Victoria Machinery	4 Mar51	28 Dec 51	19 Sep 52
PORTE QUEBEC	185	Burrard Dry Dock	15 Feb 51	28 Aug 51	7 Oct 52
PORTE ST. JEAN	180	Geo. T. Davie	16 May50	21 Nov 50	4 June52
PORTE ST. LOUIS	183	Geo. T. Davie	21 Mar 51	22 July 52	28 Aug 52
PORTE DAUPHINE	186	Ferguson Ind.	21 Apr 51	22 Aug 52	12 Dec 52

Displacement, tons	429 full load
Dimensions, feet	125·5 × 26·3 × 13
Main engines	Diesel; A/C Electric; 1 shaft; 600 bhp = 11 knots
Complement	3 officers, 20 ratings

Of trawler design. Multi-purpose vessels used for operating gates in A/S booms, fleet auxiliaries, anti-submarine netlayers for entrances to defended harbours. Can be fitted for minesweeping. Designation changed from YNG to YMG in 1954. All used during summer for training Reserves. *Porte Dauphine* was reacquired from MOT in 1974 and employed in Reserve Training in Great Lakes area.

DIVING TENDERS and TRVs

Displacement, tons	110
Dimensions, feet	80 × 20 × 4·8
Main engines	GM diesels; 228 bhp = 10·75 knots

YMT 11 was completed in Jan 1962 and YMT 12 on 7 Aug 1963, both by Ferguson Industries Ltd, Picton, Nova Scotia. They can dive four men at a time to a depth of 250 feet and are fitted with a recompression chamber.
There are small diving tenders YMT 6, YMT 8, YMT 9 and YMT 10, 70 tons, 75 × 18·5 × 8·5 feet, 2 diesels 165 bhp. YMT 1 (46 ft) was transferred to the Naval Research Establishment as a yard craft. YMT 2 and YMT 7 are 46 ft wooden hulled single screw vessels. Two new diving tenders, YSD 1 and YSD 2, entered service in 1965.
Also torpedo recovery vessels *Nimpkish*, YMR 120, and *Songhee*, YMR 1. The yacht *Oriole*, QW 3, used for officer cadet training has been in commission since 1953.

7 "VILLE" CLASS (OLD)

ADAMSVILLE	YTS 582	**PLAINSVILLE**	YTS 587
BEAMSVILLE	YTS 583	**QUEENSVILLE**	YTS 586
LOGANVILLE	YTS 589	**YOUVILLE**	YTS 588
MANNVILLE	YTS 577		

Dimensions, feet	40 × 10·5 × 4·8
Main engines	Diesel; 1 shaft; 150 bhp

Small harbour tugs now used for Reserve training.

1 ANTI-SUBMARINE HYDROFOIL (FHE)

BRAS D'OR FHE 400

Displacement, tons	180
Dimensions, feet	150·8 × 21·5 × 15 (hull depth); 23 (hull borne); × 7·5 (60 knots) draught on foils) Foil base 90
Main engines	Pratt & Whitney FT4A-2 gas turbine on foils; 22 000 shp = 50-60 knots; Davey Paxman Diesel when hull borne; 2 000 shp = 12-15 knots

Pratt and Whitney ST 6A gas-turbine for hull-borne boost and foil-borne auxiliary power—390 shp.
A prototype craft designed by De Havilland Aircraft (Canada). After very successful trials she was laid up ashore at Halifax in 1971 for 5 years.

R.C.M.P PATROL VESSELS

1 "BIRD" CLASS

VICTORIA MP 31

Displacement, tons	66 full load
Dimensions, feet	92 × 17 × 5·3
Main engines	2 diesels; 1 200 bhp = 14 knots
Complement	20

Victoria was built for the RCMP by Yarrows Ltd Victoria. Completed in Dec 1965. She was a steel copy of the wooden "Bird" class inshore patrol vessels built for the Navy.

2 75 ft "DETACHMENT" CLASS

STAND OFF **NICHOLSON**

Displacement, tons	55
Dimensions, feet	75 oa × 17 × 6·5
Main engines	2 diesels; 1 400 bhp = 16 knots
Complement	5

Both of wood construction. Both built by Smith and Rhuland Shipyard of Lunenburg, NS and completed in 1967 and 1968 respectively. Intended for service on the Atlantic coast.

11 65 ft "DETACHMENT" CLASS

ACADIAN **ADVERSUS** **BURIN** **CAPTOR** **DETECTOR** **GANGES** **INTERCEPTOR** **NANAIMO** **TAHSIS** **TOFINO** **WESTVIEW**

Displacement, tons	48
Dimensions, feet	65 × 15 × 4
Main engines	1 Cummins diesel; 1 shaft; 410 bhp = 12 knots

Coastal patrol police boats for service on the east and west coasts.

1 TURBOJET TYPE

SIDNEY

Displacement, tons	27
Dimensions, feet	55 × 14 × 4
Main engines	2 General Motors turbojet engines; 600 bhp = 16 knots

This turbojet craft with one other (*Little Bow II*) were built as an experiment and no additions are contemplated.

1 52 ft PATROL VESSEL

RIVETT-CARNAC

Displacement, tons	14·5
Dimensions, feet	52 × 14·75 × 3
Main engines	2 Cummins 903 (320 hp each), twin shafts = 20 knots

RIVETT-CARNAC *1974, RCMP*

6 "DETACHMENT" CLASS (GREAT LAKES)

CARNDUFF II **CHILCOOT II** **CUTKNIFE II** **MOOSOMIN II** **SHAUNAVON II** **TAGISH II**

Dimensions, feet	50 × 15 × 3
Main engines	2 diesel, 600 bhp = over 17 knots

A class of small fast patrol craft built for service on the Great Lakes.

There are also *Advance, Athabasca, Beaver, Fort Erie, Fort Francis II, Kenora III, Sorel* and *Valleyfield*, 26 to 36 feet in length with gasoline engines, speeds up to 27 knots. Six are on the Great Lakes and four on the West Coast. In addition, there are also the following, *Battleford, Dauphine, Moose Jaw, Bruce, Reliance, Manyberries, McClellan* and *Harvison*.

TUGS

2 "SAINT" CLASS

Name	*No.*	*Laid down*	*Launched*	*Completed*
SAINT ANTHONY	ATA 531	15 July 1954	2 Nov 1955	22 Feb 1957
SAINT CHARLES	ATA 533	28 Apr 1954	10 July 1956	7 June 1957

Displacement, tons	840 full load
Dimensions, feet	151·5 × 33 × 17
Main engines	Diesel; 1 shaft; 1 920 bhp = 14 knots

Ocean tugs. Authorised under the 1951 Programme. Both built by the St. John Dry Dock Co. Originally class of three.

3 "NORTON" CLASS

CLIFTON ATA 529 **HEATHERTON** ATA 527 **RIVERTON** ATA 528

Displacement, tons	462
Dimensions, feet	104 pp, 111 2 oa × 28 × 11
Main engines	Dominion Sulzer diesel, 1 000 bhp = 11 knots
Complement	17

Large harbour tugs. *Clifton* was launched on 31 July 1944.

5 "GLEN" CLASS

GLENBROOK YTB 501
GLENDYNE YTB 503
GLENEVIS YTB 502
GLENLIVET II YTB 504
GLENSIDE YTB 500

Dimensions, feet	80 × 20·7 × 7·2
Main engines	Diesel; 300 bhp = 9 knots

Big harbour tugs.

5 "VILLE" CLASS (NEW)

LAWRENCEVILLE YTS 590
LISTERVILLE YTS 592
MARYSVILLE YTS 594
MERRICKVILLE YTS 593
PARKESVILLE YTS 591

Dimensions, feet	64 × 15·5 × 9
Main engines	Diesel; 1 shaft; 365 bhp = 9·8 knots

Small harbour tugs employed at Esquimalt and Halifax. Built by Vito Steel & Barge Co, BC (590, 591), Georgetown S'yd. PEI (592-4). All completed 1974.

2 "WOOD" CLASS

EASTWOOD YMT 550 **GREENWOOD** YMT 551

Dimensions, feet	60 oa × 16 × 5 (aft full load)
Main engines	250 hp = 10 knots

Medium harbour tugs. Used as A/S Target Towing Vessels. Launched 1944. Other medium harbour tugs are:

FT1, FT2. Employed as fire tugs, Hull numbers YMT 556 and 557 respectively. Sister fire tug FT3; YMT 558, was taken out of service on 31 Mar 1964 and transferred to Dept of Public Works, St. John's Newfoundland.

CANADIAN COAST GUARD

Administration

Minister of Transport:
Hon Jean Marchand MP, PC

Deputy Minister of Transport:
Mr. O. G. Stoner, BA

Administrator, Marine Transportation Administration:
Mr. R. Illing

Director (Canadian Coast Guard):
Captain W. J. H. Stuart

Establishment

In January 1962 all ships owned and operated by the Federal Department of Transport with the exception of pilotage and canal craft, were amalgamated into the Canadian Coast Guard, a civilian service.

Ships

The Canadian Coast Guard comprises 146 ships and craft of all types (including 63 barges). They operate in Canadian waters from the Great Lakes to the northernmost reaches of the Arctic Archipelago.

There are heavy icebreakers, icebreaking ships for tending buoys and lighthouses, marine survey craft, weather-oceanographic ships, and many specialised vessels for tasks such as search and rescue, cable lifting and repair, marine research and shallow-draft operations in areas such as the Mackenzie River system and some parts of the Arctic.

The Ship Building and Heavy Equipment Branch of the Department of Defence Productions arranges for the design, construction and repair of Coast Guard ships and also provides this service for a number of other Canadian Government departments.

Principal bases for the ships are the department's 11 District offices, located at—St. John's, Newfoundland; Dartmouth, N.S.; Saint John, N.B.; Charlottetown, P.E.I.; Quebec and Sorel, Que.; Prescott and Parry Sound, Ont.; Victoria and Prince Rupert, B.C.; and at Hay River, on Great Slave Lake.

Flag

The Canadian Coast Guard has its own distinctive jack, a red maple leaf on a white ground at the hoist and two gold dolphins on a blue ground at the fly.

Canadian Coast Guard vessels have white funnels with a red band at the top and the red maple leaf against the white.

Missions

The Canadian Coast Guard carries out the following missions:

1. Icebreaking and Escort. Icebreaking is carried out in the Gulf of St. Lawrence and River St. Lawrence and the Great Lakes in winter to assist shipping and for flood control, and in Arctic waters in summer.
2. Icebreaker-Aids to Navigation Tenders. Installation, supply and maintenance of fixed and floating aids-to-navigation in Canadian waters.
3. Organise and provide icebreaker support and some cargo vessels for the annual Northern sealift which supplies bases and settlements in the Canadian Arctic and Hudson Bay.
4. Provide and operate special patrol cutters and lifeboats for marine search and rescue.
5. Provide and operate survey and sounding vessels for the St. Lawrence River Ship Channel.
6. Provide and operate weatherships for Ocean Station "Papa" in the Pacific.
7. Provide and operate vessel for the repairing of undersea cables.
8. Provide and operate vessel for Marine Traffic Control on the St. Lawrence river.
9. Operate a small fleet of aircraft primarily for aids to navigation, ice reconnaissance, and pollution control work.

Fleet Strength

Heavy Icebreakers	5
Medium Icebreaker	1
Medium Icebreaking aid to navigation vessels	7
Light Icebreaking aid to navigation vessels	7
Ice strengthened aid to navigation vessels	4
Aid-to-navigation tenders	16
Northern supply vessels	3
Search and Rescue—Offshore patrol cutters	2
Great Lakes patrol cutters	3
Shore-based hovercraft	1
Shore-based lifeboats	10
Shore-based launches	6
R Class cutters	5
St. Lawrence light icebreaking survey and sounding vessel	1
St. Lawrence ship channel survey and sounding vessels	5
Weather ships for ocean station Papa in the Pacific	2
Cable repair ship	1
St. Lawrence River marine traffic control vessel	1
Training vessels	2
Experimental hovercraft	1
Total	83

Aircraft

Fixed wing	1
Helicopters	31

WEATHER SHIPS

Name	*Laid down*	*Launched*	*Completed*
QUADRA	Feb 1965	4 July 1966	Mar 1967
VANCOUVER	Mar 1964	29 June 1965	4 July 1966

Displacement, tons	5 600 full load
Dimensions, feet	361·2 pp; 404·2 oa × 50 × 17·5
Aircraft	1 helicopter
Main engines	Turbo-electric; 2 shafts; 7 500 shp = 18 knots
Boilers	2 automatic Babcock & Wilcox D type
Range, miles	10 400 at 14 knots
Complement	96

Turbo-electric twin screw weather and oceanographic vessels for Pacific Ocean service. Both built by Burrard Drydock Limited, North Vancouver, B.C. They have bow water jet reaction system to assist steering at slow speeds. Flume stabilisation systems are fitted. They are turbo-electric powered, with oil-fired boilers to provide the quiet operation needed for vessels housing much scientific equipment. Their complement includes 15 technical officers such as meteorologists, oceanographers and electronics technicians.

VANCOUVER — *1970, Canadian Coast Guard*

Name	*Laid down*	*Launched*	*Completed*
JOHN CABOT	May 1963	15 April 1964	July 1965

Displacement, tons	6 375 full load
Dimensions, feet	313·3 × 60 × 21·5
Aircraft	1 helicopter
Main engines	Diesel-electric ;2 shafts; 9 000 shp = 15 knots
Range, miles	10 000 at 12 knots
Complement	85 officers and men

Combination cable repair ship and icebreaker. Built by Canadian Vickers Limited, Montreal. Designed to repair and lay cable over the bow only. For use in East Coast and Arctic waters. Bow water jet reaction manoeuvring system, heeling tanks and Flume stabilisation system. Three circular storage holds handle a total of 400 miles of submarine cable. Personnel include technicians and helicopter pilots.

JOHN CABOT — *1970, Canadian Coast Guard*

NORTHERN SUPPLY VESSELS

2 FORMER TANK LANDING CRAFT (LCT 8s)

EIDER **SKUA**

Measurement, tons 1 083 to 1 104 gross
Dimensions, feet 231·2 oa × 38 × 7
Main engines Diesel; 1 000 shp = 9 knots

Converted LCT (8)s, acquired from Great Britain in 1957-61. Built by Harland & Wolff, Belfast (*Skua*) and Sir Wm. Arrol & Co Ltd, Glasgow (*Eider*). Both completed in 1946.

SKUA *Canadian Coast Guard*

FORMER TANK LANDING CRAFT (LCT 4)

MINK

Displacement, tons 586 full load
Dimensions, feet 187·2 × 33·8 × 4
Main engines Diesel; 920 shp = 8 knots

Converted LCT (4) acquired from Great Britain in 1958. Completed in 1944. Formerly officially rated as Steel Landing Craft for Northern Service, now re-rated as Aids to Navigation Tender, in reserve.

MINK *1963, Canadian Coast Guard*

ICEBREAKERS

LOUIS S. ST. LAURENT

Displacement, tons 13 800 full load
Dimensions, feet 366·5 oa × 80 × 31
Aircraft 2 helicopters
Main engines Turbo-electric; 3 shafts; 24 000 shp = 17·75 knots
Range, miles 16 000 miles at 13 knots cruising speed
Complement Total accommodation for 216

This new icebreaker for service in the Arctic and the Gulf of St. Lawrence was built at Canadian Vickers Limited, Montreal. She is larger than any of the former Coast Guard icebreakers. This triple screw ship with a steam turbo-electric propulsion system is the world's most powerful non-nuclear powered icebreaker. She has a helicopter hangar below the flight deck, with an elevator to raise the two helicopters to the deck when required. She was launched on 3 Dec 1966 and completed in Oct 1969. She is officially rated as a heavy icebreaker.

LOUIS S. ST. LAURENT *1971, Canadian Coast Guard*

Icebreakers—*continued*

NORMAN MCLEOD ROGERS

Displacement, tons 6 320 full load
Dimensions, feet 295 oa × 62·5 × 20
Aircraft 1 helicopter
Landing craft 2
Main engines 4 diesels and 2 gas turbines powering 2 electric motors; 2 shafts; 12 000 shp = 15 knots
Complement 55

A new type of icebreaker for use in the Gulf of St. Lawrence and East Coast waters, Built at the yard of Canadian Vickers Limited, Montreal. This is the world's first application of gas turbine/electric propulsion in an icebreaker. Completed in Oct 1969, Officially rated as a heavy Icebreaker.

NORMAN MCLEOD ROGERS *1970, Canadian Coast Guard*

JOHN A. MACDONALD

Displacement, tons 9 160 full load
Measurement, tons 6 186 gross
Dimensions, feet 315 × 70 × 28
Aircraft 2 Helicopters
Main engines Diesel-electric; 15 000 shp = 15·5 knots

Completed by Davie Shipbuilding Limited, Lauzon Port Quebec, in Sep 1960. Officially rated as a heavy icebreaker.

JOHN A. MACDONALD *1971, Canadian Coast Guard*

MONTCALM **WOLFE**

Displacement, tons 3 005 full load
Measurement, tons 2 022 gross
Dimensions, feet 220 × 48 × 16
Aircraft 1 Helicopter
Main engines Steam reciprocating; 4 000 ihp = 13 knots

Wolfe was built by Canadian Vickers Limited, Montreal, and completed in Nov 1959, *Montcalm* was built by Davie Shipbuilding Ltd, Lauzon, and completed in June 1957. Officially rated as Medium Icebreaking Aids to Navigation Vessels.

MONTCALM *1972, Canadian Coast Guard*

Icebreakers—*continued*

CAMSELL

Displacement, tons	3 072 full load
Measurement, tons	2 020 gross
Dimensions, feet	223·5 × 48 × 16
Main engines	Diesel-electric; 4 250 shp = 13 knots

Completed by Burrard Dry Dock Company Limited, Vancouver, BC in Oct 1959. Officially rated as Medium Icebreaking Aids to Navigation Vessel.

CAMSELL *1972, Canadian Coast Guard*

SIR HUMPHREY GILBERT

Displacement, tons	3 000 full load
Measurement, tons	1 930 gross
Dimensions, feet	220 × 48 × 16·3
Main engines	Diesel-electric; 4 250 shp = 13 knots

Completed by Davie Shipbuilding Limited, Lauzon, Port Quebec, in June 1959. Officially rated as Medium Icebreaking Aids to Navigation Vessel.

SIR HUMPHREY GILBERT *1970, Canadian Coast Guard*

LABRADOR

Displacement, tons	6 490 full load
Measurement, tons	3 823 gross
Dimensions, feet	269·0 pp; 290·0 oa × 63·5 × 29·0
Aircraft	Provision for 2 helicopters
Main engines	Diesel-electric; 10 000 shp = 16 knots

Built by Marine Industries Limited, Sorel, Quebec. Ordered in Feb 1949, laid down on 18 Nov 1949, launched on 14 Dec 1951 and completed for the Royal Canadian Navy on 8 July 1954, but transferred to the Department of Transport in Feb 1958. Officially rated as a Heavy Icebreaker. She was the first naval vessel to traverse the North West passage and circumnavigate North America, when she was Canada's largest and most modern icebreaker.

LABRADOR *1970, Canadian Coast Guard*

d'IBERVILLE

Displacement, tons	9 930 full load
Measurement, tons	5 678 gross
Dimensions, feet	310 × 66·5 × 30·2
Main engines	Steam reciprocating; 10 800 ihp = 15 knots

Completed by Davie Shipbuilding Limited Lauzon, Port Quebec, in May 1953. Officially rated as a Heavy Icebreaker.

ERNEST LAPOINTE

Displacement, tons	1 675 full load
Measurement, tons	1 179 gross
Dimensions, feet	184 × 36 × 15·5
Main engines	Steam reciprocating; 2 000 ihp = 13 knots

Completed by Davie Shipbuilding Limited, Lauzon, Port Quebec in Feb 1941. Officially rated as St. Lawrence Ship Channel Icebreaking Survey and Sounding Vessel.

N. B. McLEAN

Displacement, tons	5 034 full load
Measurement, tons	3 254 gross
Dimensions, feet	277 × 60·5 × 24·0
Main engines	Steam reciprocating; 6 500 ihp = 13 knots

Completed by Halifax Shipyards Limited, Halifax, NS, in 1930. Officially rated as Medium Icebreaker.

GRIFFON

Displacement, tons	3 096
Dimensions, feet	234 × 49 × 15·5
Main engines	Diesel; 4 000 bhp; 13·5 knots

Completed in Dec 1970 by Davie Shipbuilding Ltd, Lauzon, Quebec. Officially rated as a Medium Icebreaking Aid to Navigation Vessel.

J. E. BERNIER

Displacement, tons	3 096
Dimensions, feet	231 × 49 × 16
Aircraft	1 helicopter
Main engines	Diesel Electric; 4 250 bhp = 13·5 knots (trial speed)

Built by Davie Shipbuilding Co, Ltd, Lauzon, Quebec; completed in Aug 1967. Officially rated as Medium Icebreaking Aid to Navigation Vessel.

SIMCOE

Displacement, tons	1 300 full load
Dimensions, feet	179·5 × 38 × 12
Main engines	Diesel-electric; 2 000 shp = 12 knots

Completed by Canadian Vickers in 1962. Officially rated as Ice Strengthened Aid to Navigation Vessel.

SIMON FRASER TUPPER

Displacement, tons	1 876 full load
Measurements, tons	1 357 gross
Dimensions, feet	204·5 × 42 × 14
Main engines	Diesel-electric; 2 900 shp = 13·5 knots

Simon Fraser was completed by Burrard Dry Dock Company Limited, N. Vancouver in Feb 1960 and *Tupper* by Marine Industries Limited, Sorel Quebec in Dec 1959. Both officially rated as Light Icebreaking Aid to Navigation Vessels.

THOMAS CARLETON

Displacement, tons	1 532 full load
Dimensions, feet	180 × 42 × 13
Main engines	Diesel; 2 000 bhp = 12 knots

Built by Saint John Dry Dock Limited Saint John, NB. Completed in 1960. Officially rated as a light Icebreaking Aid to Navigation Vessel.

ALEXANDER HENRY

Displacement, tons	2 497 full load
Measurements, tons	1 647 gross
Dimensions, feet	210 × 43·5 × 16
Main engines	Diesel; 3 550 bhp = 13 knots

Built by Port Arthur Shipbuilding Limited, Port Arthur. Completed in July 1959. Officially rated as a Medium Icebreaking Aid to Navigation Vessel.

EDWARD CORNWALLIS

Displacement, tons	3 700 full load
Measurement, tons	1 965 gross
Dimensions, feet	259 × 43·5 × 18
Main engines	Steam reciprocating; 2 800 ihp = 13·5 knots

Built by Canadian Vickers Limited, Montreal. Completed in Dec 1949. In reserve Officially rated as a Light Icebreaking Aid to Navigation Vessel.

EDWARD CORNWALLIS *1971, Canadian Coast Guard*

WALTER E. FOSTER

Displacement, tons	2 715 full load
Measurement, tons	1 672 gross
Dimensions, feet	229·2 × 42·5 × 16
Main engines	Steam reciprocating; 2 000 ihp = 12·5 knots

Built by Canadian Vickers, Limited, Montreal. Completed in Dec 1954. Officially rated as a Light Icebreaking Aid to Navigation Vessel.

SIR WILLIAM ALEXANDER

Displacement, tons	3 555 full load
Measurements, tons	2 153 gross.
Dimensions, feet	227·5 × 45 × 17·5
Main engines	Diesel electric; 4 250 shp = 15 knots

Built by Halifax Shipyards, Limited, Halifax. Completed in June 1959. Equipped with Flume Stabilisation System. Officially rated as a Medium Icebreaking Aid to Navigation Vessel.

DEPOT SHIP

NARWHAL

Measurement, tons 2 064 gross
Dimensions, feet 251·5 × 42·0 × 12·0
Main engines Diesel; 2 000 bhp
Range, miles 9 200 cruising
Complement 32

Built by Canadian Vickers, Montreal. Completed in July 1963. Officially rated as Sealift Stevedore Depot Vessel.

NARWHAL *1970, Canadian Coast Guard*

SEARCH AND RESCUE CUTTERS

ALERT

Displacement, tons 2 025
Dimensions, feet 234·3 × 39·9 × 15·1
Aircraft 1 helicopter
Main engines Diesel Electric; 7 716 hp = 18·75 knots
Range, miles 6 000

Completed by Davie Shipbuilding Ltd Lauzon Dec 1969. Officially rated as offshore Patrol Cutter.

ALERT *1971, Canadian Coast Guard*

DARING (ex-*Wood*, ex-MP 17)

Displacement, tons 600 standard
Dimensions, feet 178 oa × 29 × 9·8
Main engines 2 Fairbanks-Morse diesels; 2 shafts; 2 660 bhp = 16 knots

Corvette type. Built by Geo. T. Davie and Sons Ltd Lauzon, Quebec. Completed in July 1958. Used for patrol on the east coast of Canada, this ship is built of steel, strengthened against ice, with aluminium superstructure. Transferred from the Royal Canadian Mounted Police Marine Division to the Ministry of Transport in 1971, and renamed *Daring*.

DARING (as *Wood*) *1966, Director of Marine Services*

RACER RALLY RAPID READY RELAY RIDER

Measurement, tons 153 gross
Dimensions, feet 95·2 × 20 × 6·5
Main engines Diesel; 2 400 bhp = 20 knots designed

Built by Yarrows Ltd, Esquimalt, BC; Davie Shipbuilding Ltd, Lauzon, PQ; Ferguson Industries, Picton, NS; Burrard Dry Dock, Vancouver; and Kingston Shipyard, respectively. All completed in 1963. *Rider*, completed for the Dept of Fisheries, was taken over by the Coast Guard in Mar 1969. *Relay* rerated as St. Lawrence River Marine Traffic Control Vessel.

SPINDRIFT SPRAY SPUME

Measurement, tons 57 gross
Dimensions, feet 70 × 16·8 × 4·7
Main engines 2 diesels; 1 050 bhp = 19 knots

Built by Cliff Richardson Boats Ltd. Meaford, Ont; J. J. Taylor & Sons, Ltd, Toronto; and Grew Ltd, Penetanguishene, Ont, respectively. Completed in 1963-64 for service on Great Lakes Patrol.

SPINDRIFT *1966, Canadian Coast Guard, Official*

AIDS TO NAVIGATION VESSELS

BARTLETT PROVO WALLIS

Displacement, tons 1 620
Dimensions, feet 189·3 × 42·5 × 12·5
Main engines Diesel; 1 760 bhp = 12 knots

In service since 1970. Classed as Ice Strengthened Aid to Navigation Vessels.

MONTMORENCY

Displacement, tons 1 006 full load
Measurement, tons 750 gross
Dimensions, feet 163 × 34 × 11
Main engines Diesel; 1 200 bhp

Built by Davie Shipbuilding Limited, Lauzon, Port Quebec. Completed in Aug 1957. Officially rated as an Ice Strengthened Aid to Navigation Vessel.

MONTMAGNY

Displacement, tons 565 full load
Dimensions, feet 148·0 × 29·0 × 8·0
Main engines Diesels; 1 000 bhp

Built by Russel Bros. Owen Sound, Ont. Completed in May 1963. Officially rated as Aid to Navigation Tender.

MONTMAGNY *1970, Canadian Coast Guard*

VERENDRYE

Displacement, tons 400 full load
Dimensions, feet 125·0 × 26·0 × 7·0
Main engines Diesels; 760 bhp

Built by Geo. T. Davie & Sons Ltd, Lauzon. Completed in Oct 1959. Officially rate as Aid to Navigation Tender.

ALEXANDER MACKENZIE SIR JAMES DOUGLAS

Displacement, tons 720 full load
Dimensions, feet 150·0 × 30·0 × 10·3
Main engines Diesels; 1 000 bhp

Built by Burrard Dry Dock Vancouver and completed 1950 and Nov 1956 respectivel Officially rated as Aid to Navigation Tenders.

SURVEY AND SOUNDING VESSELS

BEAUPORT

Displacement, tons 767 full load
Dimensions, feet 167·5 × 24·0 × 9·0
Main engines Diesels; 1 280 bhp

Completed in 1960.

DETECTOR

Displacement, tons 584 full load
Dimensions feet 140·0 × 35·0 × 10·0
Main engines Steam reciprocating

NICOLET

Displacement, tons 935 full load
Dimensions, feet 166·5 × 35·0 × 9·6
Main engines Diesels; 1 350 bhp

VILLE MARIE

Displacement, tons 493 full load
Dimensions, feet 134·0 × 28·0 × 9·5
Main engines Diesel electric; 1 000 hp

Completed in 1960.

There are also two smaller vessels *Glenada* and *Jean Bourdon* for the St. Lawrence Ship Channel.

SHORE - BASED CRAFT

DUMIT ECKALOO MISKANAW TEMBAH NAHIDIK

Assist navigation in Mackenzie River operations. Small tug/buoy tender type.

For search and rescue and patrol duties: Ten lifeboats (CG 101-109 and 114), six launches (*Mallard*, *Moorhen*, CG 110-113) and one Hovercraft (CG 021). An additional Hovercraft, *Voyageur* of 50 tons and 50 knots acquired Mar 1974.

CHILE

Naval Board

Commander-in-Chief of the Navy:
Admiral José Toribio Merino Castro

Chief of the Naval Staff:
Rear-Admiral Carlos A. LeMay Délano

Personnel

(a) 1975: 22 000 (1,300 officers, 18 500 ratings, 2 200 marines)

(b) 1 year national service

Disposals

Frigates

1973 *Riquelme*

Submarines

1972 *Thomson*

Landing Craft

1971 *Bolados* (LCU 95)

Maritime Air

(B) 4 Bell 206 A JetRangers
2 Bell 47
(C) 4 Lockheed SP-2 Neptunes (Air force)
5 Grumman HU-16B Albatros (Air force)
3 Convair PBY-6A Catalina (SAR)
5 Douglas C 47
5 Beech D 18S/C-45
1 Piper PA-31-310 Navajo
6 Beech T-34B Mentor

Diplomatic Representation

Naval Attaché in Brasilia:
Captain Sergio Fuanzalida Vigar

Naval Attaché in Buenos Aires and Montevideo:
Commander Hernan Rivero Calderon

Naval Attaché in London, Paris, The Hague and Stockholm:
Rear Admiral R. Lopez Silva

Naval Attaché in Madrid:
Commander Ary Acuna Figueroa

Naval Attaché in Quito:
Captain Carlos Barra von Kretschmann

Naval Attaché in Tokyo:
Commander Francisco Ghilsofo Araya

Naval Attaché in Washington:
Rear Admiral Jorge Paredes Wetzer

Naval Attaché in Lima:
Captain Jorge Grez Casarino

Strength of the Fleet

Type	*Active*	*Building*
Cruisers	3	—
Destroyers	6	—
Frigates	5	—
Patrol Submarines	1	2
Landing Ships (Tank)	2	—
Repair Ships (ex-LST)	2	—
Landing Ships (M)	2	—
Landing Craft (U)	2	—
Fast Attack Craft (T)	4	—
Large Patrol Craft	6	—
Coastal Patrol Craft	1	—
Survey Ship	1	—
Sail Training Ship	1	—
Transports	4	—
Tankers	3	—
Floating Docks	2	—
Tugs	6	—

Naval Bases

Talcahuano. Main Naval Base, Schools, major repair yard, (2 dry docks, 2 floating docks) 2 floating cranes.
Valparaiso. Naval Base, Schools, major repair yard.
Puerto Montt. Small naval base.
Punta Arenas. Small naval base. Repair yard with slipway.
Puerto Williams. Small naval base.

Mercantile Marine

Lloyd's Register of Shipping:
135 vessels of 364 364 tons gross

Pennant List

Cruisers

02 O'Higgins
03 Prat
04 Latorre

Destroyers/Frigates

06 Condell
07 Lynch
14 Blanco Encalada
15 Cochrane
16 Zenteno
17 Pordales
18 A. Riveros
19 A. Williams
26 Serrano
27 Orella
28 Riquelme
29 Uribe

Submarines

20 Thomson
21 Simpson
22 O'Brien
23 Hyatt

Light Forces

37 Papudo
60 Lientur
62 Lautaro
63 Aldea
75 Fuentealba
76 Cabo Odger
79 Contramaestro Ortiz
80 Guacolda
81 Fresia
82 Quidora
83 Tegualda

Survey Ship

64 Yelcho

Training Ship

43 Esmeralda

Amphibious Forces

88 C. Hemmerdinger
89 C. Araya
90 Elicura
91 Aguila
92 Morel
93 Tellez
94 Orompello
96 Diaz
97 C. Toro

Transports

45 Piloto Pardo
47 Aquiles
110 Meteoro
111 Cirujano Videla

Tankers

52 Al Jorge Montt
53 Araucano
54 Beagle

Tugs

63 S. Aldea
73 Colocolo
104 Ancud
105 Monreal
120 Reyes
127 Caupolican
128 Cortez

CRUISERS

	No.	Builders	Laid down	Launched	Completed
LATORRE (ex-*Göta Lejon*)	04	Eriksberg Mekaniska Verkstad, Göteborg	27 Sep 1943	17 Nov 1945	15 Dec 1947

Displacement, tons	8 200 standard; 9 200 full load
Length, feet (*metres*)	590·5 (*180·0*) wl; 597 (*182·0*) oa
Beam, feet (*metres*)	54 (*16·5*)
Draught, feet (*metres*)	21·5 (*6·6*)
Guns, surface	7—6 in (*150 mm*) 53 cal.
Guns, AA	4—57 mm; 11—40 mm
Tubes	6—21 inch
Armour	3 in—5 in (*75—125 mm*)
Main engines	2 sets De Laval geared turbines; 100 000 shp; 2 shafts
Boilers	4 Swedish 4-drum type
Speed, knots	33 designed
Complement	610

Scale 1 inch = 118 ft.

GENERAL
Radar control arrangements were installed for 6-inch guns. Fitted for minelaying with a capacity of 120 mines. Reconstructed in 1951-52, modernised in 1958, with new radar, 57 mm guns etc.

GUNNERY. The 6 inch guns are high angle automatic anti-aircraft weapons with an elevation of 70 degrees.

RADAR. Search: LWO 3, Type 227. Tactical: Type 293. Fire Control: X band.

TRANSFER. Purchased by Chile from Sweden July 1971.

LATORRE *1973, Chilean Navy*

2 "PRAT" CLASS

Name	*No.*	*Builders*	*Laid down*	*Launched*	*Commissioned*
O'HIGGINS (ex-USS *Brooklyn*, CL 40)	02	New York Navy Yard	12 Mar 1935	30 Nov 1936	18 July 1938
PRAT (ex-USS *Nashville*, CL 43)	03	New York S.B. Corp.	24 Jan 1935	2 Oct 1937	25 Nov 1938

Displacement, tons	
O'Higgins	9 700 standard; 13 000 full load
Prat	10 000 standard; 13 500 full load
Length, feet (*metres*)	608·3 (*185·4*) oa
Beam, feet (*metres*)	69 (*21·0*)
Draught, feet (*metres*)	24 (*7·3*)
Aircraft	1 Bell helicopter
Guns, surface	15—6 in (*153 mm*) 47 cal (5 triple); 8—5 in (*127 mm*) 25 cal (single)
Guns, AA	28—40 mm; 24—20 mm
Armour, inches (*mm*)	Belt 4 in—1½ in (*102—38*); Decks 3 in+2 in (*76+51*); Turrets 5 in—3 in (*127—76*); C.T. 8 in (*203*)
Boilers	8 Babcock & Wilcox Express type
Main engines	Parsons geared turbines 100 000 shp; 4 shafts
Speed, knots	32·5
Range, miles	14 500 at 15 knots
Oil fuel (tons)	2 100
Complement	888 to 975 (peace)

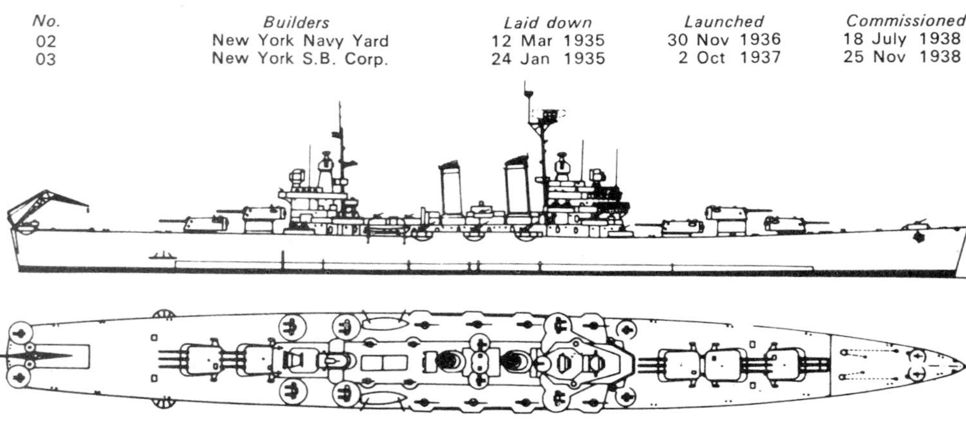

Former "light" cruisers of the US "Brooklyn" Class. Purchased from the United States in 1951 at a price representing 10 per cent of their original cost ($37 000 000) plus the expense of reconditioning them.

HANGER. The hanger in the hull right aft could accommodate 6 aircraft if necessary together with engine spares and duplicate parts, though 4 aircraft was the normal capacity. Above the hanger two catapults were mounted as far outboard as possible, and a revolving crane was placed at the stern extremity overhanging the aircraft hatch.

RADAR
Search: SPS 12. Tactical: SPS 10.

DRAWING. Starboard elevation and plan. Drawn in 1971. Scale: 121 feet = 1 inch

PRAT *1971. Chilean Navy.*

SUBMARINES

2 BRITISH "OBERON" CLASS

Name	No.	Builder	Laid down	Launched	Completion
O'BRIEN	22	Scotts Greenock	17 Jan 1971	21 Dec 1972	Mid-1974
HYATT	23	Scotts Greenock	10 Jan 1972	26 Sep 1973	Late 1974

Displacement, tons	1 610 standard; 2 030 surface; 2 410 submerged
Length, feet (*metres*)	241·0 (*73·5*) pp; 295·2 (*90·0*) oa
Beam, feet (*metres*)	26·5 (*8·1*)
Draught, feet (*metres*)	18·1 (*5·5*)
Torpedo tubes	8—21 in (*533 mm*)
Main machinery	2 diesels 3 680 bhp; 2 electric motors 6 000 shp; 2 shafts, electric drive
Speed, knots	12 surface, 17 submerged

Ordered from Scott's Shipbuilding & Engineering Co, Ltd, Greenock, late 1969

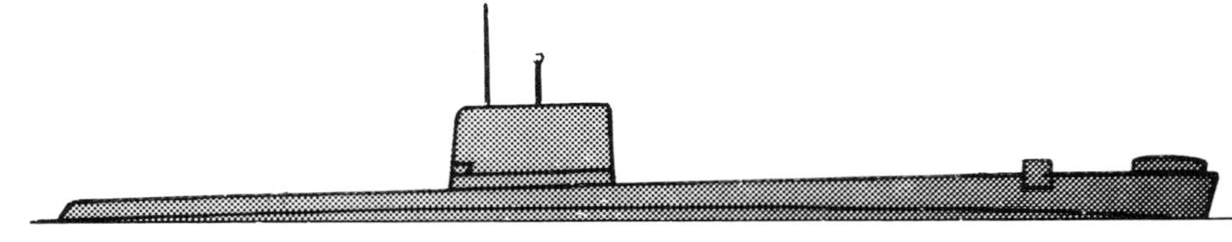

OBERON *Class*

1 Ex-US "BALAO" CLASS

SIMPSON (ex-USS *Spot*, SS 413) 21

Displacement, tons	1 526 standard; 1 816 surface; 2 425 submerged
Length, feet (*metres*)	311·6 (*95·0*)
Beam, feet (*metres*)	27·0 (*8·2*)
Draught, feet (*metres*)	17·0 (*5·2*)
Torpedo tubes	10—21 in (*533 mm*), 6 bow; 4 stern
Main machinery	6 500 hp GM 2-stroke diesels; 4 610 hp electric motors
Speed, knots	20 on surface, 10 submerged
Complement	80

Built at Mare Island Navy Yard. *Simpson*, launched on 20 May 1944 and completed on 3 Aug 1944, was transferred end of 1961. Streamlined fleet type. *Thomson*, of same class, was paid off for spares in September 1972.

SIMPSON *1972, Chilean Navy*

AMPHIBIOUS FORCES

2 ex-US LANDING SHIPS (LST)

COMANDANTE ARAYA (ex-USS *Nye County*, LST 1067) 89
COMANDANTE HEMMERDINGER (ex-USS *New London County*, LST 1066) 88

Displacement, tons	1 653 standard; 4 080 full load
Dimensions, feet	328 × 50 × 14
Main engines	GM Diesels; 1 700 shp; 2 shafts = 11·6 knots
Complement	approx. 40

Transferred 29 Aug 1973.

ASPIRANTE MOREL (ex-USS *Aloto, LSM 444*) 92

Displacement, tons	743 standard; 1 095 full load
Dimensions, feet	196·5 wl; 203·5 oa × 34·5 × 7·3
Main engines	Diesel; 2 shafts; 2 800 bhp = 12 knots
Oil fuel (tons)	60
Range, miles	2 500 at 9 knots
Complement	60

Former United States medium landing ship launched in 1945. *Aspirante Morel* (ex-*Aloto*) was leased to Chile on 2 Sep 1960 at Pearl Harbour to replace the older LSM of the same name.

MOREL *1972, Chilean Navy*

GRUMETE DIAZ (ex-LCU 1396) 96 **GRUMETE TELLEZ** (ex-LCU 1458) 93

Displacement, tons	143 to 160 light; 309 to 329 full load
Dimensions, feet	105 wl; 119 oa × 32·7 × 5 max
Main engines	Diesel; 3 shafts; 675 bhp = 10 knots
Oil fuel (tons)	11
Range, miles	700 at 7 knots
Complement	12

Former United States tank landing craft of the LCT (6) type. Launched in 1944. Transferred in 1960.

ELICURA 90 **OROMPELLO** 94

Displacement, tons	290 light; 750 full load
Dimensions, feet	138 wl; 145 oa × 34 × 12·8
Main engines	Diesels; 2 shafts; 900 bhp = 10·5 knots
Oil fuel (tons)	77
Range, miles	2 900 at 9 knots
Complement	20

Orompello wqs built for the Chilean Government by Dade Drydock Corporation, Miami, Florida, and transferred on 15 Sep 1964. *Elicura* was built at Talcahuano, launched on 21 April 1967, and handed over on 10 Dec 1968.

OROMPELLO *1971, Chilean Navy*

REPAIR SHIPS

AGUILA ex-ARV 135 (ex-USS *Aventinus*, ARVE 3, ex-LST 1092) 91
COMANDANTE TORO (ex-USS LST 277) 97
TORO LST 97 (ex-USS LST 277)

Displacement, tons	1 625 light; 4 100 full load
Dimensions, feet	316 wl; 328 oa × 50 × 11·2
Guns	8—40 mm AA
Main engines	GM diesels; 2 shafts; 1 800 bhp = 11·6 knots

Aguila was United States aircraft repair ship (Engine). Built by American Bridge Co. Ambridge, Pa. Laid down on 8 Jan 1945, launched on 24 Mar 1945, and completed on 19 May 1945. Transferred to the Chilean Navy by USA in 1963 under the Military Aid Program. Also used as a destroyer tender and submarine repair ship. *Toro* transferred 2 Feb 1973.

LIGHT FORCES

FRESIA 81 **GUACOLDA** 80 **QUIDORA** 82 **TEGUALDA** 83

(FAST ATTACK CRAFT—TORPEDO)

Displacement, tons	134
Dimensions, feet	118·1 × 18·4 × 7·2
Guns	2—40 mm AA
Tubes	4—21 in
Main engines	Diesels; 2 shafts; 4 800 bhp = 32 knots
Range, miles	1 500 at 15 knots
Complement	20

Built in Spain at Cadiz to German Lürssen design. *Fresia* and *Guacolda* were delivered on 9 Dec 1965 and 30 July 1965, respectively, *Quidora* and *Tegualda* in 1966.

FRESIA *1971, Chilean Navy*

ALDEA (ex-US *ATF* 98, *Arikara*) 63 (LARGE PATROL CRAFT)

Displacement, tons	1 235 standard; 1 675 full load
Dimensions, feet	195·0 wl; 205·0 oa × 38·5 × 15·5
Guns	1—3 in 50 cal AA
Main engines	Diesel Electric; 1 shaft; 3 000 bhp = 15 knots
Complement	85

Former USN fleet ocean tug, launched on 22 June 1943. Transferred on 7 Jan 1971

ALDEA *1972, Chilean Navy*

PAPUDO 37 (LARGE PATROL CRAFT)

Displacement, tons	450
Dimensions, feet	173·0 × 23·0 × 12·0
Guns	1—40 mm; 4—20 mm
A S weapons	1 Hedgehog; 4 "K" DCT; 1 DC rack
Complement	69 (4 officers, 65 men)

Built in Asmar, Talcahuano, Chile. Completed 27 Nov 1971.

PAPUDO *1972, Chilean Navy*

	Pennant No.	*Launched*
LAUTARO (ex-USS *ATA 122*)	62	27 Nov 1942
LIENTUR (ex-USS *ATA 177*)	60	5 June 1944

(LARGE PATROL CRAFT)

Displacement, tons	534 standard; 835 full load
Dimensions, feet	134·5 wl; 143 oa × 33 × 13·2
Guns	1—3 in AA; 2—20 mm AA
Main engines	GM diesel-electric; 1 500 shp = 12·5 knots
Oil fuel, tons	187
Complement	33

Former United States Navy auxiliary ocean tugs of the ATA type ("Maricopa" class), originally ocean rescue tugs (ATRs), transferred to the Chilean Navy and reclassified as patrol vessels. Built by Levingstone Shipbuilding Co, Orange, Texas, USA.

LAUTARO *1969, Chilean Navy*

MARINERO FUENTEALBAS 75 **CABO ODGER** 76 (LARGE PATROL CRAFT)

Displacement, tons	215
Dimensions, feet	80 × 21 × 9
Guns	1—20 mm AA
Main engines	One Cummins diesel 340 hp = 9 knots
Range, miles	2 600 at 9 knots
Complement	19

Both these vessels were built in Chile by Astilleros Y Maeslronzas De La Armada (ASMAR); *Fuentealbas* was completed in 22 July 1966 and *Odger* 21 April 1967.

FUENTEALBAS *1972, Chilean Navy*

CONTRAMAESTRO ORTIZ 79 (COASTAL PATROL CRAFT)

Displacement, tons	33
Length, ft (*m*)	59·4 (*18·1*)
Guns	2—20 mm
Speed, knots	15

SURVEY SHIP

YELCHO (ex-USS *Tekesta*, ATF 93) 64

Displacement, tons	1 235 standard; 1 675 full load
Dimensions, feet	195 wl; 205 oa × 38·5 × 15·3
Guns	2—40 mm AA
Main engines	4 diesels/Diesel electric; 1 shaft; 3 000 bhp = 16 knots
Complement	85

Former United States fleet ocean tug of the ATF type ("Apache" class) fitted with powerful pumps and other salvage equipment. *Yelcho* was built by Commercial Iron Works, Portland, Oregon, laid down on 7 Sep 1942, launched on 20 Mar 1943, completed on 16 Aug 1943, and loaned to Chile by the USA on 15 May 1960, having since been employed as Antarctic research ship and surveying vessel.

YELCHO *1972, Chilean Navy*

TRAINING SHIP

ESMERALDA (ex-*Don Juan de Austria*) 43

Displacement, tons	3 040 standard; 3 673 full load
Dimensions, feet	308·8 oa; 260 pp × 43 × 23
Guns	2—57 mm
Sail area	Total 26 910 sq feet
Main engines	1 Fiat Auxiliary diesel; 1 shaft; 1 400 bhp = 11 knots
Range, miles	8 000 at 8 knots
Complement	271 plus 80 cadets

ESMERALDA *1971, A. & J. Pavia*

Four-masted schooner completed in 1952. Built in Spain by the Echevarrieta Yard, Cadiz, and originally intended for the Spanish Navy. Transferred to Chile on 12 May 1953. Near sister ship of *Juan Sebastian de Elcano* in the Spanish Navy. Similar to the Brazilian training ship *Almirante Saldanha* before her major reconstruction. Replaced transport *Presidente Pinto* as training ship.

TRANSPORTS

AQUILES (ex-Danish *Tjaldur*) 47

Displacement, tons	2 660 registered; 1 462 net; 1 395 dw
Dimensions, feet	288 × 44 × 17
Main engines	1 Slow Burmeister and Wain Diesel; 3 600 bhp = 16 knots
Range, miles	5 500 at 16 knots
Complement	60 crew plus 447 troops

Ex-Danish MV *Tjaldur* built in 1953 by Aalborg Verft, Denmark, bought by Chile in 1967.

AQUILES *1968, Chilean Navy*

PILOTO PARDO 45

Displacement, tons	1 250 light; 2 000 standard; 3 000 full load
Dimensions, feet	269 × 39 × 15
Aircraft	1 helicopter
Guns	1—101·6/50; 2—20 mm
Main engines	2 diesel-electric; 2 000 hp = 14 knots
Complement	44 (plus 24 passengers)
Range, miles	6 000 at 10 knots

Built by Haarlemsche Scheepsbouw Mij, Haarlem, Netherlands. Antarctic patrol ship, transport and research vessel with reinforced hull to navigate in ice. Officially listed as transport. Delivered in 1959.

PILOTO PARDO *1969, Chilean Navy*

METEORO 110

Displacement, tons	205
Main engines	Diesel = 8 knots

Transport for 220 Troops built by ASMAR Talcahuano.

CIRUJANO VIDELA 111

Displacement, tons	140
Dimensions, ft (*m*)	101·7 × 21·3 × 6·6 (*31 × 6·5 × 2*)
Main engines	Diesel; 700 hp = 14 knots

Hospital and dental facilities are fitted in this Transport built by ASMAR Talcahuano.

TANKERS

BEAGLE AOG 54 (ex-AOG 8 USS *Genesee*)

Displacement, tons	4 240 standard
Dimensions, feet	310 × 48·7 × 16
Guns	2—3 inch 50 cal; 4—20 mm
Range, miles	6 670 at 10 knots

Transferred on loan 5 July 1972.

BEAGLE *1972, Chilean Navy*

Tankers—*continued*

ARAUCANO 53

Displacement, tons	17 300
Measurement, tons	18 030 deadweight
Dimensions, feet	497·6 × 74·9 × 28·8
Guns	4—40 mm
Main engines	B and W diesels; 10 800 bhp = 15·5 knots (17 on trials)
Range, miles	12 000 at 15·5 knots

Naval tanker built by Burmeister & Wain, Copenhagen, Denmark. Launched on 21 June 1967.

ARAUCANO *1972, U.S. Navy*

ALMIRANTE JORGE MONTT 52

Displacement, tons	9 000 standard; 17 500 full load
Measurement, tons	11 800 gross; 17 750 deadweight
Dimensions, feet	548 × 67·5 × 30
Main engines	Rateau Bretagne geared turbine; 1 shaft; 6 300 shp = 14 knots
Boilers	2 Babcock & Wilcox
Range, miles	16 500 at 14 knots

Naval supply tanker. Built by Ateliers et Chantiers de la Seine Maritime, Le Trait, France. Laid down in 1954. Launched on 14 Jan 1956. Completed in Mar 1956.

ALMIRANTE JORGE MONTT *1969, Chilean Navy*

FLOATING DOCK

2 ex-US ARD

MUTILLA (ex-US *ARD 32*) 132 — (ex-US *ARD 25*)

Displacement, tons	5 200
Capacity, tons	3 000
Dimensions, feet	492 × 84 × 5·7 to 33·2 feet

Mutilla leased to Chile 15 May 1960. *ARD 25* transferred 20 Aug 1973.

2 Floating Cranes of 30 and 180 tons lift are at Talcahuano.

TUGS

COLOCOLO 73

Displacement, tons	790
Dimensions, feet	126·5 × 27·0 × 12·0 mean
Main engines	Triple expansion; 1 050 shp = 11 knots
Oil fuel, tons	155

Built by Bow, McLachlan & Co, Paisley. Formerly classed as coastguard vessel. Rebuilt in 1962-63. Of four sister ships *Janequeo* was withdrawn from service in 1958, *Sobenes* in 1965, *Galvarino* in 1968 and *Cabrales* in 1971.

ANCUD 104 **CORTEZ** 128 **REYES** 120
CAUPOLICAN 127 **MONREAL** 105

Fortuna (YT 123) and *Galvez* (YT 102) were withdrawn from service in 1965, *Moctezuma* (YT 108) in 1968 and *Ugarte* (YT 107) in 1971. *Yagan* (YT 126) was lost in 1964 while assisting a merchant ship during a storm.

MISCELLANEOUS

Notes (a) *Huascar*, completed 1865, previously Peruvian, now a museum ship at Talcahuano.
(b) Two new ships, *Castor* and *Sabenes*, now listed.

CHINA

Administration

Minister of National Defence:
Yeh Chien-ying

Chief of Staff of the Armed Forces:
Teng Hsiao-ping

Commander-in-Chief of the Navy:
Hsiao Ching Kuang

Diplomatic Representation

Defence and Naval Attaché in London:
Shih Hsin-jen

Personnel

(a) 1975: 170 000 officers and men, including 25 000 naval air force and 28 000 marines

(b) 4 years National service

Bases

North Sea Fleet: Tsingtao, Lu Shun
East Sea Fleet: Shanghai, Chusan
South Sea Fleet: Huan Pu, Chan Chiang
(The fleet is split with the main emphasis on the North Sea Fleet).

Mercantile Marine

Lloyd's Register of Shipping:
360 vessels of 1 870 567 tons gross

Strength of the Fleet

Type	*Active*	*Building (Estimated)*
Destroyers (DDG)	43	
Frigates	14 (7 with missiles)	1 ?
Corvettes	32	4
Fleet Submarines	1	?
Missile-Firing Submarines	1	—
Patrol Submarines	56	6
Fast Attack Craft (Missile)	100	15
Fast Attack Craft (Gun)	440	20 ?
Fast Attack Craft (Torpedo)	215	—
Minesweepers (Ocean)	16	—
Minesweepers (Coastal)	10	2 ?
Landing Ships LST	15	—
LSM's	16	4 ?
LSIL's	15	—
LCT's	15	—
LCM's	450	—
Survey & Research Ships	8	—
Range Instrumentation Ships	4	?
Supply Ships	8 (+ ?12)	—
Oilers (small)	8	—
Boom Defence Vessels	6	—
Escorts (old)	13	—
Coast Defence Vessels (Old)	6	—
River Defence Vessels (Old)	13	—
Repair Ship	1	—
Misc. Small Craft	375	—

The Chinese Navy

Despite setbacks under the Manchus, the Chinese have possessed a navy in some force since 200BC. In addition they have had the will and capability to use their fleet, as their expeditions to the Persian Gulf and Africa in the 15th Century bear witness. So today's navy has a tradition older than any other except the Greek and Italian and a modern, rapidly expanding force capable of operations abroad. In the following pages the Chinese Navy is shown in two parts—the new fleet of Hsiao Ching Kuang and the antique remnants of the Nationalist navy. While studying these it must be remembered that not only is there a steady building programme of all classes in the modernised Chinese Yards but also the Chinese have an advanced nuclear and missile capability. This combination will make the Chinese navy, already twice as strong in manpower as the Royal Navy, an important element in the future balance of power East of Suez.
In the last year there has been evidence of delays in all the new building programmes except Light Forces. Whether this is due to problems of weapon production, faults discovered in new construction ships or a straight political decision is not known. It is of interest that these delays appear to date from 1972, shortly after the flight and death of Lin Piao, the Defence Minister under whom the programmes were presumably generated. This may be coincidence but the plain fact is that the main emphasis today is on defensive units rather than the long-range projection forces whose design must have started in the mid or early 1960s.

Chinese Naval Air Force

With 20 000 officers and men and over 450 aircraft, this is a considerable land-based naval air force. Equipped with about 400 MIG 17 and 19 (and possibly MIG 21) fighter aircraft and SA2-SAM, with 100 IL 28 Torpedo bombers, Tu-2 bombers, Madge flying boats, Hound M14 helicopters and transport and communication aircraft this is primarily a defensive force. Chinese ingenuity should find little difficulty in getting a proportion of these aircraft afloat, particularly in view of the increasing tempo of their shipbuilding programme.

DESTROYERS

3 + 4 "LUTA" CLASS (DDG)

Displacement, tons	3 250 standard; 3 750 full load
Dimensions, ft (*m*) (approx)	450 × 45 × 15 (*137·3 × 13·7 × 4·6*)
Missile launchers	2 Twin SSN-2 type
Guns	4—130 mm (2 twins) 8—57 mm 8—25 mm
A/S weapons	2—A/S rocket launchers
Main engines	Geared turbines
Speed	32+
Range, miles (estimated)	4 000 at 15 knots
Complement (approx)	300

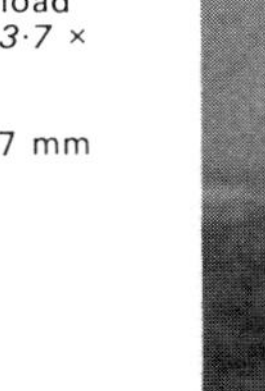

GENERAL
Most of the above figures are approximate, designed to show the anticipated capability of this new class, which is being built in Luta yard, Dairen (and other yards).

COMPLETION. 1 in 1971, 2 in 1972. None has been completed since 1972 although four are under construction.

RADAR. Air search, Slim Net., Cross Slot: Fire Control, Guns, Wasphead; Missiles: Square Tie: Navigation: Neptun.

"LUTA" Class — *1972 Chinese*

"LUTA" Class — *1973*

FRIGATES

1 + 1(?) "KIANGTUNG" CLASS

Displacement, tons 1 500—2 000 tons standard
Dimensions, ft (*m*) 350 × 40 approx (*106 × 12*)
Missile launchers 1 or 2 Twin SAM
Guns 2 or 4 twin 3·9 inch (*100 mm*)

The first unit reported as laid down in 1971 for launch in 1973. There have apparently been no additions to this class—further evidence of the delays in new construction.

4 Ex-SOVIET "GORDY" CLASS

ANSHAN **CHI LIN**
CHANG CHUN **FU CHUN**

Displacement, tons 1 657 standard; 2 040 full load
Length, feet (*metres*) 357·7 (*109·0*) pp; 370 (*112·8*) oa
Beam, feet (*metres*) 33·5 (*10·2*)
Draught, feet (*metres*) 13 (*4·0*)
Missile launchers 1 twin SSN—2
Guns 4—5·1 in (*130 mm*); 8—37 mm
A/S 8 DCT
Main engines Tosi geared turbines 48 000 shp; 2 shafts
Boilers 3-drum type
Speed, knots 36
Oil fuel (tons) 540
Range, miles 800 at 36 knots; 2 600 at 19 knots
Complement 250

CHANG CHUN (before conversion) *Hajime Fukaya*

GENERAL
Gordy Type 7 of Odero-Terni-Orlando design. All launched in 1936-41. Fitted for minelaying. Two transferred in Dec 1954 and two in July 1955.

CONVERSION. All converted between 1971 and 1974. The alterations consist of the replacement of the torpedo tubes by a twin SSN-2 launcher and the fitting of twin 37 mm mounts in place of the original singles.

RADAR. Air Search: Cross Bird. Fire Control: Square Tie. Navigation: Neptun. IFF: Skipole.

5 "KIANGNAN" CLASS

Displacement, tons 1 000 standard; 1 350 full load
Length, feet (*metres*) 298 (*90·8*)
Beam, feet (*metres*) 33·5 (*10·2*)
Draught, feet (*metres*) 11 (*3·4*)
Guns, dual purpose 3—3·9 in (*100 mm*) 56 cal, 1 fwd, 2 aft; 6 or 8—37 mm (twin); 4 or 8—25 mm (twin)
A/S weapons Depth charges
Main engines Diesels; 9 000 shp
Speed, knots 30
Complement 175

"KIANGNAN" Class *1973*

GENERAL
Built at Canton and Shanghai between 1965 and 1969. The Chinese Navy embarked on a new building programme in 1965 of which this class was the first.

RADAR. Fire Control: Sun Visor.

4 "RIGA" CLASS

CH'ENG TU **KUEI YANG**
KUEI LIN **K'UN MING**

Displacement, tons 1 200 standard; 1 600 full load
Length, feet (*metres*) 298·8 (*91*) oa
Beam, feet (*metres*) 33·7 (*10·2*)
Draught, feet (*metres*) 10 (*3·0*)
Missile launchers 1 twin SSN—2
Guns 3—3·9 in (*100 mm*) (single) 4—37 mm
A/S 4 DC projectors
Mines 50 capacity, fitted with rails
Main engines Geared turbines 25 000 shp; 2 shafts
Boilers 2
Speed, knots 28
Oil fuel (tons) 300
Range, miles 2 500 at 15 knots
Complement 150

GENERAL
First of the class, launched on 28 Apr 1956 at Hutang Shipyard, Shanghai, had light tripod mast, but was later converted with heavier mast and larger bridge as in the other three. Second vessel was launched on 26 Sep 1956. Third vessel was built at Shanghai and the fourth in 1957. Similar to the Soviet "Riga" class destroyer escorts. Two were redesigned with modified superstructure.
CONVERSION. Two started conversion in 1971 for the replacement of the torpedo tubes by a twin SSN-2 launcher. All now converted.

RADAR. Surface warning: Slim Net. Fire Control: Sun Visor for Guns, Square Tie for missiles; Navigation; Neptun.

"RIGA" Class (before conversion) *1971*

CORVETTES

20 "KRONSTADT" CLASS

Nos. 251 252 253 261 262 263 264 265 266 286 + 10

Displacement, tons 310 standard; 380 full load
Dimensions, ft (*m*) 170·6 × 21·5 × 9 (*52 × 6·5 × 2·7*)
Guns 1—3·5 in; 2—37 mm AA; 6—12·7 mm AA
A/S weapons 2 Rocket launchers; 2 DC racks
Mines 2 rails for 8-10 mines
Main engines Diesels; 2 shafts; 3 300 shp; speed 24 knots
Range, miles 1 500 at 12 knots
Complement 65

Six built in 1950-53 were received from USSR in 1956-57. Remainder were built at Shanghai and Canton, with 12 completed in 1956. The last was assembled by 1957.

RADAR. Ball Gun, Skinhead.

"KRONSTADT" class firing Rocket Launchers *1972*

12 "HAINAN" CLASS

Displacement, tons 500 standard
Dimensions, ft (*m*) 200 × 25 × 9 (*61 × 7·6 × 2·7*)
Guns 2—3 in (fore and aft) (first pair); 4—57 mm (twins) (remainder); 4—25 mm (twins)
Main engines Diesels; 3 300 shp (estimated)
Speed, knots About 25

Chinese built. Low freeboard. The 25 mm guns are abaft the bridge. Programme started 1963-64 and continues. Skinhead Radar.

SUBMARINES

Note. In 1973 the visit to West Germany from Peking of a party led by Professor Chang Wei highlighted Chinese interest in nuclear propulsion for ships. It also suggests that the Chinese may be meeting design problems as such visits are rare events. However, reports suggest the construction of at least one nuclear submarine. This combined with the known Chinese capability to build liquid-fuelled rockets of the MRBM, IRBM and ICBM types and the completion of a solid-propellant factory, suggests that the forecast of a Chinese ballistic-missile nuclear submarine within the 1970s may not be out of the question.

1 "HAN" CLASS

This is the first report of a possible Chinese nuclear submarine. With an Albacore hull it was probably laid down in 1971-72. Its construction may have been delayed if the problems mentioned in the note above have been encountered.

2 "MING" CLASS

Displacement, tons	Possibly about 1 500 tons standard
Length, feet	Possibly about 250 feet
Armament	Possibly 6—21 in tubes
Main machinery	Probably diesels and main motors

First believed to have been laid down in 1971-72 which would give an operational date around late 1974 or 1975.

1 "GOLF" CLASS

(BALLISTIC MISSILE TYPE)

Displacement, tons	2 350 surface; 2 800 dived
Length, feet (*metres*)	320·0 (*97·5*)
Beam, feet (*metres*)	25·1 (*7·6*)
Draught, feet (*metres*)	22·0 (*6·7*)
Missile launchers	3 vertical tubes
Torpedo tubes	10—21 in (*533 mm*) bow
Main machinery	3 diesels, total 6 000 hp; 3 shafts 3 electric motors, total 6 000 hp
Speed, knots	20 surface; 17 dived
Range, miles	22 700 surface cruising
Complement	86 (12 officers, 74 men)

Ballistic missile submarine similar to the Soviet "G" class. Built at Dairen in 1964. The missile tubes are fitted in the conning tower. It is not known whether this boat has been fitted with missiles, although it is possible and well within Chinese technical capability (see note above concerning SLBM's)

"GOLF" Class 1972

30 SOVIET "ROMEO" CLASS

(PATROL TYPE)

Displacement, tons	1 100 surface; 1 600 dived
Length, feet (*metres*)	246·0 (*75·0*)
Beam, feet (*metres*)	24 (*7·3*)
Draught, feet (*metres*)	14·5 (*4·4*)
Torpedo tubes	6—21 in (bow) 18 torpedoes
Main machinery	2 Diesels, total 4 000 hp; 2 Electric motors, total 4 000 hp; 2 shafts
Speed, knots	17 surface; 14 dived
Complement	65

The Chinese are now building their own Soviet designed "Romeo" class submarines possibly at a rate of 6 a year.

"ROMEO" Class 1972

21 SOVIET "WHISKY" CLASS

(PATROL TYPE)

Displacement, tons	1 030 surface; 1 180 dived
Length, feet (*metres*)	240 (*73·2*)
Beam, feet (*metres*)	22 (*6·7*)
Draught, feet (*metres*)	15 (*4·6*)
Torpedo tubes	6—21 in (*533 mm*); 4 bow 2 stern (20 torpedoes or 40 mines)
Main machinery	Diesel-electric; 2 shafts; 4 000 bhp diesels; 2 500 hp electric motors
Speed, knots	17 surface; 15 dived
Range, miles	13 000 at 8 knots surfaced
Complement	60

Medium size streamlined, long range submarines similar to the "Whisky" class built in the USSR. Equipped with snort. Assembled from Soviet components in Chinese yards between 1956 and 1964.

"WHISKY" Class 1972

2 Ex-SOVIET "S-1" CLASS

(PATROL TYPE)

Displacement, tons	840 surface; 1 050 submerged
Length, feet (*metres*)	256 (*78·0*)
Beam, feet (*metres*)	21 (*6·4*)
Draught, feet (*metres*)	13 (*4·0*)
Torpedo tubes	6—21 in (*533 mm*)
Main machinery	4 200 hp diesels; 2 200 hp electric motors
Speed, knots	19 surface; 8·5 submerged
Range, miles	9 800 at 9 knots
Oil fuel, tons	105
Complement	50

Launched in 1939. Transferred from the USSR in 1955.

1 Ex-SOVIET "M-V" CLASS

(COASTAL PATROL TYPE)

Displacement, tons	350 surface; 420 submerged
Length, feet (*metres*)	167·3 (*51·0*)
Beam, feet (*metres*)	16·0 (*4·9*)
Draught, feet (*metres*)	12·1 (*3·7*)
Guns, AA	1—45 mm 1 MG
Torpedo tubes	2—21 in (*533 mm*)
Main machinery	1 000 hp diesels; 800 hp electric motors
Speed, knots	13 surface; 10 submerged
Range, miles	4 000 at 8·5 knots
Oil fuel, tons	21
Complement	24

Designed for coastal operations, latterly used for training and instruction but nearing the end of its life. Four were transferred from the USSR in 1954-55.

LIGHT FORCES

50 SOVIET "OSA" and CHINESE "HOLA" CLASS

(FAST ATTACK CRAFT—MISSILE)

Displacement, tons	165 standard; 200 full load
Dimensions, ft (*m*)	128·7 × 25·1 × 5·9 (*39·3 × 7·7 × 1·8*)
Missiles, surface	4 SSN-2 system launchers in two pairs abreast aft
Guns	4—30 mm (2 twin, 1 forward and 1 aft)
Main engines	3 Diesels; 13 000 bhp = 32 knots
Range, miles	800 at 25 knots
Complement	25

It was reported in Jan 1965 that one "Osa" class guided missile patrol boat had joined the Navy from the USSR. Four more were acquired in 1966-67, and two in 1968. A building programme of 10 boats in China a year is assumed. The first boat of the "Hola" class, a Chinese variant of the "Osa", has now joined the fleet. The chief difference is the fitting of a radome aft.

RADAR. Square Tie and Drum Tilt in "Osas".

"OSA" Class *1972*

50 SOVIET "KOMAR" and CHINESE "HOKU" CLASS

(FAST ATTACK CRAFT—MISSILE)

Displacement, tons	70 standard; 80 full load
Dimensions, ft (*m*)	83·7 oa × 19·8 × 5 (*25·5 × 6 × 1·8*)
Missiles, surface	2 "Styx" type launchers
Guns	2—25 mm AA (1 twin forward)
Main engines	Diesels; 2 shafts; 4 800 bhp = 40 knots

One "Komar" class guided missile boat was reported as joining the fleet in 1965. Two more were delivered in 1967 and seven in 1968 to 1971. A building programme of 10 a year is assumed. The first boat of the "Hoku" class, a Chinese variant of the "Komar", has now joined the fleet. The chief difference is the siting of the launchers clear of the bridge and further inboard, eliminating sponsons. A hydrofoil variant has also been reported.

"KOMAR" Class *1972*

25 "SHANGHAI" CLASS TYPE I (FAST ATTACK CRAFT—GUN)

Displacement, tons	100 full load
Dimensions, feet	115 × 18 × 5·5
Guns	1—57 mm (forward); 2—37 mm (twin, aft)
Torpedo tubes	Twin 18 in
A/S armament	8 DCs
Mines	Minerails can be fitted
Main engines	4 diesels; 4 800 bhp = 28 knots
Complement	25

The prototype of these boats appeared in 1959. Main difference from successors is lack of midships guns. Skinhead Radar.

310 "SHANGHAI" CLASS TYPES II, III and IV

(FAST ATTACK CRAFT—GUN)

Displacement, tons	120 standard; 155 full load
Dimensions, ft (*m*)	128 × 18 × 5·6 (*39 × 5·5 × 1·7*)
Guns	Type II: 1—57 mm (forward); 2—37 mm (twin, aft); 2—25 mm (twin, abaft bridge) Types III and IV; 4—37 mm (twins, forward and aft); 2—25 mm (twin abaft bridge) *Note.* In some boats a twin 75 mm recoilless rifle is mounted forward
Torpedo tubes	Some earlier boats had twin 18 in tubes mounted abaft the bridge
A/S armament	8 DCs
Mines	Min rails can be fitted but probably for no more than 10 mines
Main engines	4 Diesels; 4 800 bhp = 30 knots
Complement	25

GENERAL
Construction continues at Shanghai and other yards.

APPEARANCE. The three types vary slightly in the outline of their bridges.

RADAR. Skinhead.

TRANSFERS. 4 to Albania, 7 to North Korea, 12 to Pakistan, 12 to Romania, 5 to Sri Lanka in 1972, 2 to Sierra Leone in 1973, 6 to Tanzania in 1970-71, 4 to North Vietnam in May 1966.

"SHANGHAI III and IV Class" (with 75 mm forward)

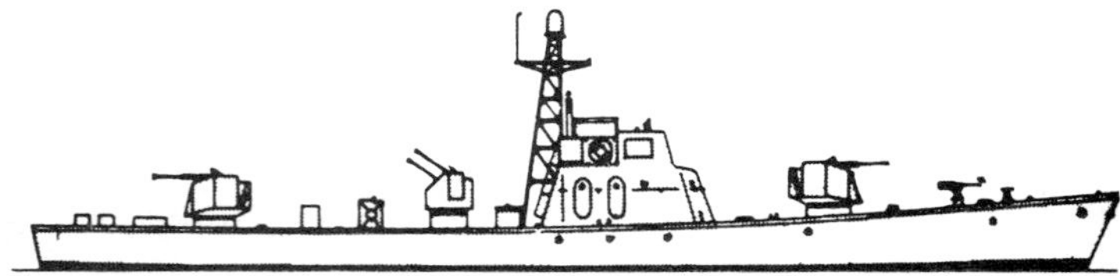

"SHANGHAI IV" Class *1970*

50 "SWATOW" CLASS (FAST ATTACK CRAFT—GUN)

Displacement, tons	80 full load
Dimensions, ft (*m*)	83·5 × 19 × 6·5 (*25·5 × 5·8 × 2*)
Guns	4—37 mm, in twin mountings; 2—12·7 mm (some boats mount a twin 75 mm recoilless rifle forward)
A/S weapons	8 DC
Main engines	4 diesels; 4 800 bhp = 42 knots
Range, miles	500 at 30 knots; 750 at 15 knots
Complement	17

"P 6" type motor torpedo boat hulls with torpedo tubes removed. In 1958 "P-6" hulls were converted to "Swatow" class motor gunboats at Dairen, Canton, and Shanghai.

TRANSFERS. 50 to North Vietnam.

70 "HU CHWAN" CLASS (FAST ATTACK CRAFT—TORPEDO)

Displacement, tons	45
Dimensions, feet	70 × 16·5 × 3·1
Torpedo tubes	2—21 inch
Guns	4—12·7 mm (2 twins)
Main engines	Possibly 2 M50 12 Cylinder Diesels; 2 shafts; 2 200 hp = 55 knots (calm conditions)
Range, miles	500 cruising

Hydrofoil torpedo boats, designed and built by China, in the Hutang yard, Shanghai having been under construction since 1956. At least 25 motor torpedo boats of the hydrofoil type were reported to be in the South China Fleet in 1968. Of all-metal construction with a bridge well forward and a low super-structure extending aft. The guns are mounted one pair on the main deck and one on the superstructure. Forward pair of foils can apparently be withdrawn into recesses in the hull.

TRANSFERS. 30 to Albania, 4 to Pakistan, 1 to Romania.

HU CHWAN

Light Forces—*continued*

65 "P4" CLASS (FAST ATTACK CRAFT—TORPEDO)

Displacement, tons	25
Dimensions, ft (*m*)	62·7 × 11·6 × 5·6 (*19·1 × 3·5 × 1·7*)
Guns	2—25 mm
Torpedo tubes	2—18 in
Main engines	2 Diesels; 2 200 bhp; 2 shafts = 50 knots

This class has aluminium hulls. Numbers decreasing.

"P 4" Class

80 "P6" CLASS (FAST ATTACK CRAFT — TORPEDO)

Displacement, tons	66 standard; 75 full load
Dimensions, ft (*m*)	84 × 20 × 6 (*25·7 × 6·1 × 1·8*)
Guns	4—25 mm
Torpedo tubes	2—21 in (or mines or DCs)
Main engines	Diesels 5 000 bhp = 43 knots
Range, miles	450 at 30 knots
Complement	25

This class has wooden hulls. Some were constructed in Chinese yards. All built since 1966.

RADAR. Pothead or Skinhead.

TRANSFERS. 6 to North Vietnam in 1967. 2 to Guinea in 1973.

"P 6" Class

50 "WHAMPOA" CLASS (FAST ATTACK CRAFT—GUN)

Displacement, tons	40 standard
Length feet (*metres*)	80 (approx) (*24·4*)
Guns	1—37 mm (forward); 2—25 mm (twin, aft)
Main engines	2 Diesels = 25 knots
Complement	20

Entered service late 1950s, now probably decreasing in numbers.

5 "SHANTUNG" CLASS (FAST ATTACK CRAFT—GUN)

Displacement, tons	75-85
Dimensions, ft (*m*)	80 × 16 × 6 (*24·4 × 4·9 × 1·8*)
Guns	4—37 mm (twins)
Speed, knots	40

Numbers decreasing.

MINE WARFARE FORCES

16 SOVIET "T 43" CLASS (MINESWEEPERS—OCEAN)

Displacement, tons	500 standard; 610 full load
Dimensions, ft (*m*)	190·2 × 28·2 × 6·9 (*58·0 × 2·6 × 6·1*)
Guns	4—37, mm AA (2 twin); 4—25 mm (2 twin)
Main engines	2 diesels; 2 shafts; 2 000 bhp = 17 knots
Range, miles	1 600 at 10 knots
Complement	40

Two were acquired from USSR in 1954-55. Eighteen more were built in Chinese shipyards, the first two in 1956. The construction of "T 43" class fleet minesweepers was stopped at Wuchang, but continued at Canton. 4 converted for surveying.

RADAR. Skinhead or Ballgun.

"T 43" class *1972*

Note. There are also some 60 auxiliary minesweepers of various types including trawlers.

AMPHIBIOUS WARFARE FORCES

(see also under "OLD NAVY")

3-4 "YU LING" CLASS (LSM)

250 ft—1 500 ton LSMs building in China since 1971.

In addition a total of 450 LCMs is reported.

SUBMARINE SUPPORT SHIP

TA CHIH

Displacement, tons	5-6 000
Dimensions, ft (*m*)	350 × 50 × 20 (*106·8 × 15·3 × 6·1*)
Guns	4—37 mm (twins); 4—25 mm (twins)

Reported in 1973.

SURVEY AND RESEARCH SHIPS

(see also under "OLD NAVY")

1 "FAN HUNG" CLASS

TUNG FAN HUNG (AGOR)

Completed in 1965, possibly at Shanghai. Similar to Soviet 3 000-ton "Zubov" class.

4 SOVIET "T-43" CLASS

For details see under Mine Warfare Forces. Converted from Minesweepers for use as Survey Ships.

RANGE INSTRUMENTATION SHIPS (AGM)

4 CHINESE BUILT

HSIANG YANG HUNG WU

Completed Canton 1971-72.

HSIANG YANG HUNG SAN +2 others, maybe more

These ships, of varying tonnage but all of an ocean-going size, operate in conjunction with the Academy of Science.

SUPPLY SHIPS

(see also under "OLD NAVY")

2 "GALATZ" CLASS (AK)

From Romania.

HAI YUN 318 **HAI CHIU** 600

Ex-commercial cargo ships, 330 feet long.

1 "AN TUNG" CLASS

Chinese built AK.

2-3 "TAN LIN" CLASS

1 500 ton AKLs.

There may be another 12 merchant ships operating under naval control.

OILERS

3 (?) "LU CHOU" CLASS

The existence of these ships, reported as 2 500 tons, has not been confirmed.

3 "LEI CHOU" CLASS

LEI CHOU **FOU CHOU** + 1 (?)

Ships of 1 000-1 500 tons, the number in the class not yet being confirmed.

2 ex-US "MATTAWEE" CLASS

Originally petrol tankers.

2 ex-USSR "TM" CLASS

ICEBREAKERS

2 "HAI PING" CLASS

101 —

3 000 ton ships built for commercial use in 1970. Two others may be in service.

"THE OLD NAVY"

ESCORTS

Note. It is reported that the majority of these escorts are, in fact, not only still in commission but have been refitted and rearmed.

Class	*Total*	*Names*	*Nos.*	*Displacement tons standard*	*Speed (knots)*	*Guns*	*Date (launched)*	*Range, miles*	*Complement*
Ex-Japanese "Ukuru"	1	**HUI AN** (ex-*Shisaka*)	218	940	19·5	3—3·9 in 4—37 mm	1943	5 000 at 16 knots	—
Ex-Japanese "Etorofu"	1	**CHANG PAI** (ex-*Oki*)		870	19·5	3—3·9 in 3—37 mm	1942	8 000 at 16 knots	—
Ex-Japanese "Uji"	1	**NAN CHANG** (ex-*Uji*)		950	20	2—5·1 in 5—37 mm	1940	3 460 at 14 knots	—
Ex-Japanese "C"	1	**SHEN YANG**		745	16·5	2—5·1 in 6—37 mm	1945	6 500 at 14 knots	150
Ex-Japanese "D"	5	**TUNG AN** **CHANG SHA** **CHI NAN** **HSI AN** **WU CHANG**	215 216 217 219 220	740	17·5	2—3 in or 5—37 mm	1944 1945	4 500 at 14 knots	150
Ex-Canadian "Castle"	1	**KUANG CHOU** (ex-*Bowmanville*)		1 100	16·5	2—5·1 in 10—37 mm	1944	5 400 at 9·5 knots	120
Ex-British "Flower"	2	**KAI FENG** (ex-*Clover*)	211						
		LIN I (ex-*Heliotrope*)	213	1 020	16	2—3·9 in	1941	—	—
Ex-Australian "Bathurst"		**LOYANG** (ex-*Bendigo*)		815	15	2—3·9 in 4—37 mm	1941	4 300 at 10 knots	100

HUI AN *1974*

NAN CHANG showing replacement 5.1 gun *1973 Chinese*

MINE WARFARE FORCES

4 Ex-US YMS TYPE (MINESWEEPERS—COASTAL)

Ex-**YMS 346** Ex-**YMS 367** Ex-**YMS 393** Ex-**YMS 2017**

Displacement, tons	270 standard; 350 full load
Dimensions, feet	136 × 24·5 × 6
Guns	1—3 in; 2—20 mm; 2 DCT
Main engines	2 GM Diesels; 1 000 bhp = 13 knots

Built of wood in USA in 1942-43, and transferred to the Chinese Navy in 1948. Some are fitted as gunboats. Ex-YMS 339 was deleted from the list in 1963.

Two have one funnel, two have two.

2 Ex-JAPANESE AMS TYPE (MINESWEEPERS—COASTAL)

Ex-**No. 4** **No. 201** (ex-No. 14)

Displacement, tons	222
Dimensions, feet	97·1 oa × 19·3 × 7·3
Guns	1—3·1 in; 4—25 mm (No. 201. 1—40 mm; 1—25 mm; 2—13 mm; 3—7·7 mm)
Main engines	1 Diesel; 300 bhp = 9·5 knots
Range, miles	1 700 at 9·5 knots

Ex-Japanese auxiliary minesweepers. Trawler type No. 201, completed in 1943, was delivered to China at Tsingtau on 3 Oct 1947, and taken over by the Chinese Republic.

SURVEY SHIPS

1 Ex-JAPANESE "KAIBOKAN" CLASS

Displacement, tons	740
Speed, knots	17·5

Believed built in 1945.

Ex-**CHUNG NING** (ex-Japanese *Takebu Maru*)

Displacement, tons	200 standard
Dimensions, feet	115 × 16 × 6
Main engines	Speed; 10 knots

Former Japanese. Employed for hydrographic and general purpose duties.

Ex-**FUTING**

Displacement, tons	160 standard
Dimensions, feet	90 × 20 × 8
Main engines	Speed; 11 knots

AMPHIBIOUS FORCES

15 Ex-US LST TYPE

CHANG PAI SHAN
CHING KANG SHAN
CHUNG (ex-USS *LST* 355)
Ex-**CHUNG 101** (ex-USS *LST* 804)
Ex-**CHUNG 102**
Ex-**CHUNG 107** (ex-USS *LST* 1027)
Ex-**CHUNG 110**
Ex-**CHUNG 111** (ex-USS *LST* 805)
Ex-**CHUNG 116** (ex-USS *LST* 406)
Ex-**CHUNG 122** (ex-*Ch'ing Ling*)
Ex-**CHUNG 125**
I MENG SHAN (ex-*Chung* 106, ex-USS *LST* 589)
TA PIEH SHAN
TAI HSING SHAN
SZU CH'ING SHAN

Displacement, tons	1 653 standard; 4 080 full load
Dimensions, feet	316 wl; 328 oa × 50 × 14
Main engines	Diesel; 2 shafts; 1 700 bhp = 11 knots

There were reported to be 20 ex-US LSTs in naval service, but several are out of commission. Two transferred to N. Vietnam. Eleven other ex-US LSTs were in the merchant service.

US LST *1968, USN*

13 Ex-US LSM TYPE

Ex-**CHUAN SHIH SHUI**
Ex-**HUA 201** (ex-USS *LSM* 112)
Ex-**HUA 202** (ex-USS *LSM* 248)
Ex-**HUA 204** (ex-USS *LSM* 430)
Ex-**HUA 205** (ex-USS *LSM* 336)
Ex-**HUA 207** (ex-USS *LSM* 282)
Ex-**HUA 208** (ex-USS *LSM* 42)
Ex-**HUA 209** (ex-USS *LSM* 153)
Ex-**HUA 211**
Ex-**HUA 212**
Ex-**HUAI HO** (ex-Chinese *Wan Fu*)
Ex-**HUANG HO** (ex-Chinese *Mei Sheng* ex-USS *LSM* 433)
Ex-**YUN HO** (ex-Chinese *Wang Chung*)

Displacement, tons	743 beaching; 1 095 full load
Dimensions, feet	196·5 wl × 203·5 oa × 34·5 × 8·8
Guns	4—37 mm (twins)
Main engines	Diesel; 2 shafts; 2 800 = 12 knots

Built in USA in 1944-45. Some were converted for minelaying. Armament varies. Up to ten of these may be transferred temporarily to commercial operations.

15 Ex-US LSIL TYPE

MIN 301
MIN 303
MIN 306
MIN 311
MIN 312
MIN 313
MIN 319
MIN 321

Displacement, tons	230 light; 387 full load
Dimensions, feet	159 × 23·7 × 5·7
Guns	4—20 or 25 mm
Main engines	Diesel; 2 shafts; 1 320 bhp = 14 knots

Built in USA in 1943-54. Reported to be fitted with rocket launchers. Some are fitted as minesweepers. Armament varies.

15-20 Ex-US or BRITISH LCU (ex-LCT) TYPE

Displacement, tons	160 light; 320 full load
Dimensions, feet	105 wl; 119 oa × 33 × 5
Main engines	Diesel; 3 shafts; 475 bhp = 10 knots
Oil fuel (tons)	80

Former United States Navy Tank Landing Craft later reclassified as Utility Landing Craft. There are reported to be ten utility landing craft comprising two of the ex-British LCT (3) class and eight of the ex-US LCT (5) and LCT (6) class.

REPAIR SHIP

TAKU SHAN (ex-*Hsing An*, ex-USS *Achilles*, *ARL* 41, ex-*LST* 455)

Displacement, tons	1 625 light; 4 100 full load
Dimensions, feet	316 wl; 328 oa × 50 × 11
Guns	1—3 in; 8—40 mm AA
Main engines	Diesel-electric; 2 shafts; 1 800 bhp = 11 knots

Launched on 17 Oct 1942. Burned and grounded in 1949, salvaged and refitted.

BOOM DEFENCE VESSELS

1 Ex-BRITISH "BAR" CLASS

Ex-Japanese No. 101 (ex-HMS *Barlight*)

Displacement, tons	750 standard; 1 000 full load
Dimensions, feet	150 pp; 173·8 oa × 32·2 × 9·5
Guns	1—3 in dp; 6 MG
Main engines	Triple expansion; 850 ihp = 11·75 knots
Boilers	2 single-ended

Boom defence vessel of British "Bar" Class. Built by Lobnitz & Co Ltd, Renfrew. Launched on 10 Sep 1938. Captured by Japanese in 1941. Acquired by China in 1945.

5 Ex-US "TREE" CLASS

Displacement, tons	560 standard; 805 full load
Dimensions, feet	146 wl; 163 oa × 30·5 × 11·8
Gun	1—3 in AA
Main engines	Diesel-electric; 800 bhp = 13 knots

Former United States netlayers of the "Tree" class taken over by the Peoples Republic.

TRAINING SHIP

CH'ANG CHAING

Ex-coast defence vessel of 464 tons built in 1929, converted for training.

SUPPLY SHIPS

5-8 Ex-US ARMY FS 330 TYPE

Ex-US Army FS 146 (ex-*Clover*)
Ex-US Army FS 155 (ex-*Violet*)
Ex-**TA CHEN** (ex-US)
Ex-US Army FS——
Ex-US Army FS——

Displacement, tons	1 000 standard
Dimensions, feet	175 oa × 32 × 10
Main engines	GM diesels; 1 000 bhp = 12 knots

Built in USA in 1944-54. Two are reported to be employed as motor torpedo boat tenders.

TUGS

7 "GROMOVOY" CLASS (SALVAGE TUG)

1 Ex-USSR "ROSLAVL" CLASS (SALVAGE TUG)

2 Ex-US 149' ATA

2 Ex-US 143' ATA

5 Ex-US ARMY 75' YTL

SERVICE CRAFT

There are also reported to be 125 armed motor junks, 100 armed motor launches and 150 service craft and miscellaneous boats.

COLOMBIA

Administration

Fleet Commander:
Vice Admiral Jaime Barrera Larrarte

Chief of Naval Operations:
Vice Admiral Alfonso Diaz Osorio

Chief of Naval Staff:
Rear Admiral Héctor Calderón Salagar

Diplomatic Representative

Naval Attaché in Washington:
Captain Rafael Grau Arano

Personnel

(a) 1975: 700 officers and 6 500 men and 1 000 marines
(b) 1 year's national service

Strength of the Fleet

Type	*Active*	*Building*
Destroyers	5	—
Frigates	4	—
Submarines	2 (70 tons)	2
Coastal Patrol Craft	25	—
Survey Vessels	4	—
Transports	6	—
Oilers	3	—
Training Ship	1	—
Tugs	13	—
Floating Docks	2	—
Floating Workshop	1	—

Disposals

Destroyers

1974 *Antioquia*

Frigates

1973 *Almirante Padilla*
1974 *Almirante Brion*

Light Forces

1974 *Gen. Rafael Reyes, Alberto Restrepo, Independiente, Palace, Tormentosa, Triunfante, Valerosa, Voladora*

Survey Ships

1974 *Bocas de Ceniza*

Transports

1974 *Bell Salter*

Tankers

1970 *Tumaco, Barran Cabermeja*
1974 *Covenas, Mamonal, Sancho Jimeno*

Prefix to Ships' Names

Ships names are prefaced by the letters "ARC" (Armada Republica de Colombia)

Mercantile Marine

Lloyd's Register of Shipping:
54 vessels of 211 083 tons gross

DESTROYERS

2 MODIFIED "HALLAND" CLASS

Name	*No.*	*Builders*	*Laid down*	*Launched*	*Completed*
SIETE DE AGOSTO	06	Götaverken, Göteberg	Nov 1955	19 June 1956	31 Oct 1958
VEINTE DE JULIO	05	Kockums Mek Verkstads A/B, Malmo	Oct 1955	26 June 1956	15 June 1958

Displacement, tons	2 650 standard; 3 300 full load
Length, feet (*metres*)	380·5 (*116·0*)pp; 397·2 (*121·1*)oa
Beam, feet (*metres*)	40·7 (*12·4*)
Draught, feet (*metres*)	15·4 (*4·7*)
Guns	6—4·7 in (*120 mm*) (3 twin turrets); 4—40 mm (single)
Torpedo tubes	4—21 in (*533 mm*)
A/S weapons	1 quadruple DC rocket launcher
Main engines	De Laval double reduction geared turbines; 2 shafts; 55 000 shp
Speed, knots	30 nominal, 16 economical
Boilers	2 Penhöet, Motala Verkstad; 568 psi; 840°F
Range, miles	445 at full power
Oil fuel, tons	524
Complement	260 (20 officers, 240 men)

GENERAL
Modified Swedish "Halland" Class ordered in 1954. The hull and machinery are similar to the Swedish class but they have different armament (six 4·7 inch instead of four, no 57 mm guns, four 40 mm guns instead of six, and four torpedo tubes instead of eight) and different accommodation arrangements. They have an anti-submarine rocket projector, more radar and communication equipment, and air-conditioned living spaces, having been designed for the tropics.

ENGINEERING. Although the designed speed was 35 knots, it is officially stated that the maximum sustained speed does not exceed 25 knots.

RADAR. Search: HSA LWO 3—SGR 114. Tactical: HSA DA 02—SGR 105. Fire Control: X Band, probably HSA M 20 series.

7 DE AGOSTO — *1971, Colombian Navy*

20 DE JULIO — *1970, Colombian Navy*

2 Ex-US "ALLEN M. SUMNER" CLASS

	No	*Builder*	*Launched*	*Commissioned*
CALDAS (ex-USS *Willard Keith,* DD 775)	D 02	Bethlehem (San Pedro)	29 Aug 1944	27 Dec 1944
SANTANDER (ex-USS *Waldron* DD 699)	D 03	Federal SB Co	26 Mar 1944	8 June 1944

Displacement, tons	2 200 standard; 3 320 full load
Length, feet (*metres*)	376 (*114·8*) oa
Beam, feet (*metres*)	40·9 (12·4)
Draught, feet (*metres*)	19 (*5·8*)
Guns	6—5 in (twins); 4—3 in (twins) (*Caldas* only)
A/S Weapons	2 Fixed Hedgehogs; 2 triple torpedo tubes (Mk 32) Facilities for small helicopter (*Santander* only)
Main engines	2 geared turbines; 2 shafts; 60 000 shp
Boilers	4
Speed, knots	34
Range, miles	2 400 at 25 knots; 4 800 at 15 knots
Complement	274

Caldas transferred 1 July 1972 by sale, *Santander,* by sale on 30 Oct 1973.

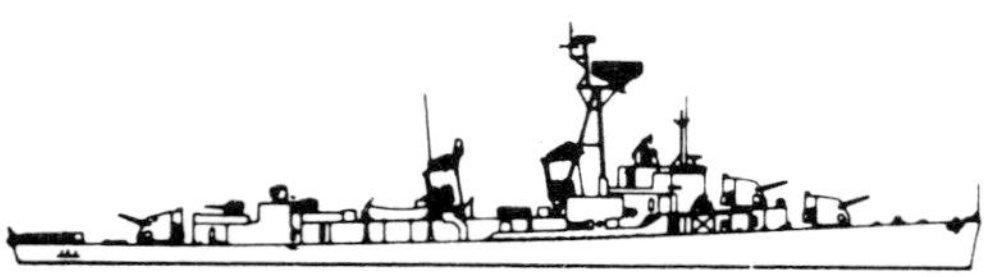

"ALLEN M. SUMNER" Class

CALDAS — *1974*

FRIGATES

3 Ex-US APD's

ALMIRANTE TONO (ex-USS *Bassett APD* 73, ex-*DE* 672) DT 04
CORDOBA (ex-USS *Ruchamkin LPR* 89 ex-*APD* 89, ex-*DE* 228) DT 15

GENERAL
Almirante Tono was built by Consolidated Steel Co, Orange, Tex, laid down on 28 Nov 1943, launched on 15 Jan 1944, completed on 23 Feb 1945 and transferred at Boston, Mass, on 6 Sep 1968. *Cordoba* was built by Philadelphia Navy Yard, laid down on 14 Feb 1944, launched on 15 June 1944 and transferred on 24 Nov 1969.

CORDOBA *1974*

1 Ex-US "DEALEY" CLASS

BOYACA DE 16 (ex-USS *Hartley* DE 1029)

Displacement, tons	1 450 standard; 1 914 full load
Dimensions, feet	314·5 oa × 36·8 × 13·6
Guns	2—3 in; 50 cal
A/S Weapons	2 triple torpedo tubes
Main engines	1 De Laval geared turbine; 20 000 shp; 1 shaft
Boilers	2 Foster Wheeler
Speed, knots	25
Complement	165

Built by New York SB Corpn. Commissioned 26 June 1957. Transferred 8 July 1972, by sale.

BOYACA *1974*

SUBMARINES

2 TYPE 209 PATROL SUBMARINES

Displacement, tons	1 000 surface; 1 290 dived
Length, feet (*metres*)	183·4 (*55·9*)
Beam, feet (*metres*)	20·5 (*6·25*)
Torpedo tubes	8—21 in bow with reloads
Main machinery	Diesel electric; 1 shaft; 5 000 hp
Speed, knots	22 dived

Building by Howaldtswerke, Kiel. Ordered in 1971. Delivery July and Sept. 1975.

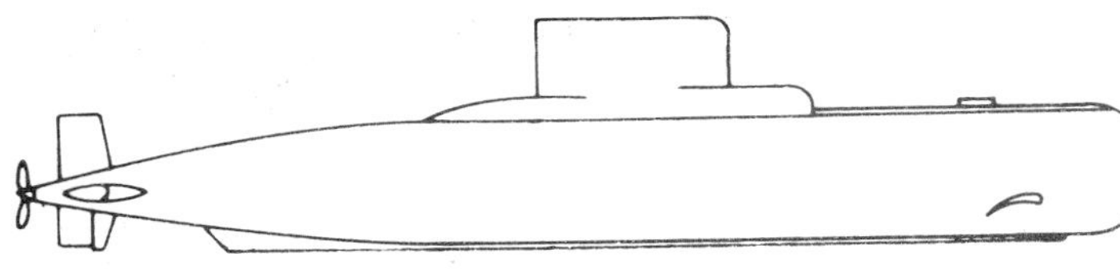

2 MIDGET SUBMARINES

These boats, purchased from Italy and of about 70 tons were delivered in July-August 1972 for assembly in Cartagena.

LIGHT FORCES

GENERAL VASQUES COBO AN 02

Displacement, tons	146
Dimensions, feet	118 pp; 124·7 oa × 23 × 5
Gun	1—40 mm
Main engines	2 Maybach diesels; 2 400 bhp = 18 knots

Built by Lürssen Werft, Vegesack. Launched on 27 Sep 1955.

CARLOS ALBAN **NITO RESTREPO**
JORGE SOTO DEL CORVAL

Displacement, tons	100
Main engines	2 Diesels = 19 knots

First of class entered service in 1971.

CARLOS ALBAN *1971, Colombian Navy*

CARLOS E. RESTREPO AN 206 **PEDRO GUAL** AN 204
ESTEBAN JARAMILLO AN 205

Displacement, tons	85
Dimensions, feet	107·8 pp × 18 × 6
Gun	1—20 mm
Main engines	2 Maybach diesels; 2 450 bhp = 26 knots

Built by Werft Gebr. Schurenstedt KG Bardenfleth in 1964.

PEDRO GUAL *1965, Colombian Navy*

OLAYA HERRERA AN 203

Displacement, tons	40
Dimensions, feet	68·8 pp × 12·8 × 3·5
Gun	1—·50 mm Browning AA
Main engines	2 Merbens diesels; 570 bhp = 20 knots

Built by Astilleros Magdalena Barranquilla, in 1960.

ESPARTANA GC 100

Displacement, tons	50
Dimensions, feet	90 wl; 96 oa × 13·5 × 4
Gun	1—20 mm AA
Main engines	2 diesels; 300 bhp = 13·5 knots

Launched on 22 June 1950 at Cartagena Naval Dockyard.

CAPITAN R. D. BINNEY GC 101

Displacement, tons	23
Dimensions, feet	67 × 10·7 × 3·5
Main engines	Diesels; 115 bhp = 13 knots

Built at Cartagena in 1947. Buoy and lighthouse inspection boat. Named after first head of Colombian Naval Academy, Lt-Commander Ralph Douglas Binney, RN.

CARLOS GALINDO LR 128 (1954)
HUMBERTO CORTES LR 126 (26 Nov 1952)
JUAN LUCIO LR 122 (2 May 1953)

Displacement, tons	35
Dimensions, feet	76·8 pp; 81·8 oa × 12 × 2·8
Guns	1—20 mm AA; 4 MG
Main engines	2 GM diesels; 260 bhp = 13 knots
Complement	13

Built at Cartagena. Launch dates above. Originally class of four.

ALFONSO VARGAS LR 123 (3 July 1952)
FRITZ HAGALE LR 124 (19 July 1952)

Displacement, tons	33
Dimensions, feet	72 pp; 76 oa × 12 × 2·8
Guns	1—20 mm AA; 4 GM
Main engines	2 GM diesels 280 bhp = 13 knots
Complement	10

Built at Cartagena naval base. Designed for operations on rivers. Named after naval officers. Launch dates above.

DILIGENTE LR 138 **VENGADORA** LR 139

Launched at the Naval Base, Cartagena, in 1952-54. Originally a class of eight.

Light Forces—*continued*

3 "ARAUCA" CLASS GUNBOATS

ARAUCA CF 37 **LETICIA** CF 36 **RIOHACHA** CF 35

Displacement, tons	184 full load
Dimensions, feet	163·5 oa × 23·5 × 2·8
Gun	2—3 in, dp, 50 cal; 4—20 mm
Main engines	2 Caterpillar diesels; 916 bhp = 14 knots
Range, miles	1 890 at 14 knots
Complement	43 (*Leticia* 39 and 6 orderlies)

Built by Union Industrial de Barranquilla (Unial) Colombia. Launched in 1955. Completed in 1956. *Leticia* has been equipped as a hospital ship with 6 beds.

RIOHACHA *1966, Colombian Navy*

1 "BARRANQUILLA" CLASS GUNBOAT

CARTAGENA CF 33

Displacement, tons	142
Dimensions, feet	130 pp; 137·8 oa × 23·5 × 2·8
Guns	2—3 in, 1—20 mm AA; 4 MG
Main engines	2 Gardner semi-diesels; 2 shafts working in tunnels; 600 hp = 15·5 knots
Oil fuel (tons)	24
Complement	39

Built by Yarrow & Co. Ltd, Scotstoun, Glasgow, and launched on 22 Mar 1930. Sister ship *Santa Marta*, CF 32, was withdrawn from service in Dec 1962, and *Barranquilla* in 1970.

CARTAGENA *1971, Colombian Navy*

SURVEY VESSELS

SAN ANDRES (ex-USS *Rockville*, PCER 851) BO 151

Displacement, tons	674 standard; 858 full load
Dimensions, feet	180·0 wl; 184·5 oa × 33·6 × 7·0
Main engines	2 diesels; 2 shafts; 1 800 bhp = 15 knots
Complement	60

Former US patrol rescue escort vessel built by Pullman Standard Car Mfg Co, Chicago, laid down on 18 Oct 1943, launched on 22 Feb 1944, completed on 15 May 1944, acquired on 5 June 1969 for conversion to a surveying vessel.

GORGONA FB 161

Displacement, tons	560
Dimensions, feet	135 × 29·5 × 9·3
Main engines	2 Nohab diesels; 910 bhp = 13 knots

Built by Lidingoverken, Sweden. Launched in May 1954. Formerly classified as a tender.

GORGONA *1971, Colombian Navy*

Survey Vessels—*continued*

QUINDIO (ex-US Y 443) BO 153

Displacement, tons	380 light; 600 full load
Dimensions, feet	131 × 29·8 × 9
Main engines	2 diesels, 300 hp = 10 knots
Complement	17

Launched in 1943. Originally small cargo ship.

TRANSPORTS

CIUDAD DE QUIBDO TM 43

Displacement, tons	633
Dimensions, feet	165 × 23·5 × 9
Main engines	1 Main diesel; 1 shaft; 390 bhp = 11 knots
Oil fuel (tons)	32
Complement	12

Built by Gebr. Sander Delfzijl, in the Netherlands.

CIUDAD DE QUIBDO *1971, Colombian Navy*

HERNANDO GUTIERREZ TF 52 **MARIO SERPA** TF 51 **SOCORRO** (ex-*Alberto Gomez*) BD 33

Displacement, tons	70
Dimensions, feet	82 × 18 × 2·8
Main engines	2 GM diesels; 260 bhp = 9 knots
Oil fuel (tons)	4
Range, miles	650 at 9 knots
Complement	12 (berths for 48 troops and medical staff)

River transports. Launched at Cartagena in 1954, 1953 and 1955 respectively. Named after Army Officers. *Socorro* was converted in July 1967 into a floating surgery. *Hernando Gutierrez* and *Mario Serpa* were also converted into dispensary ships in 1970.

TRAINING SHIP

GLORIA

Displacement, tons	1 300
Dimensions, feet	212 × 34·8 × 21·7
Main engines	Auxiliary diesel; 500 bhp = 10·5 knots

Sail training ship. Built at Bilbao in 1968. Barque rigged. Hull is entirely welded. Sail area: 1 675 sq yards (*1,400 sq. metres*).

GLORIA *1971, Colombian Navy*

TUGS

PEDRO DE HEREDIA (ex-USS *Choctaw*, ATF 70) RM 72

Displacement, tons	1 235 standard; 1 764 full load
Dimensions, feet	195 wl; 205 oa × 38·5 × 15·5
Main engines	4 diesels, electrical drive; 3 000 bhp = 16·5 knots

Former United States ocean tug of the "Apache" class. Launched on 18 Oct 1942.

PEDRO DE HEREDIA *1971, Colombian Navy*

BAHIA HONDA (ex-USS *Umpqua* ATA 209) RM 74
BAHIA UTRIA (ex-USS *Kalmia* ATA 184) RM 75

Displacement, tons	534 standard; 858 full load
Dimensions, feet	133·9 wl; 143·0 oa × 33·9 × 8·0
Gun	1—3 in dp
Main engines	2 GM diesel-electric; 1 shaft; 1 500 bhp = 13 knots
Complement	45

RM 75 launched 29 Aug 1944 RM 74 launched 2 Feb 1945
Transferred from the United States Navy on 1 July 1971 on lease.

TENIENTE SORZANO RM 73

Displacement, tons	54
Dimensions, feet	60 pp; 65·7 oa × 17·5 × 9
Main engines	6-cylinder diesel; 240 bhp

ANDAGOYA RM 71

Displacement, tons	100
Main engines	Caterpillar diesel; 80 bhp = 8 knots

Launched in 1928. Re-engined in 1955.

ABADIA MENDEZ

Displacement, tons	39
Dimensions, feet	52·5 × 11 × 4
Main engines	Caterpillar diesel; 80 bhp = 8 knots

Built in Germany in 1924. Harbour tug. There are also the harbour tug, *La Colombiana* and the river tug *Joves Fiallo*, RR 90.

CANDIDO LEGUIZAMO
CAPITAN ALVARO RUIZ
CAPITAN CASTRO
CAPITAN RIGOBERTO GIRALDO
CAPITAN VLADIMAR VALEK
JOVES EIALLO
TENIENTE LUIS BERNAL

Displacement, tons	50
Dimensions, feet	63 × 14 × 2·5
Main engines	2 GM diesels; 260 bhp = 9 knots

TENIENTE MIGUEL SILVA RM 89

Dimensions, feet	73·3 × 17·5 × 3
Main engines	2 diesels; 260 bhp = 9 knots

River tug. Built by Union Industrial (Unial) of Barranquilla.

FLOATING DOCK

MAYOR ARIAS

Displacement, tons	700
Capacity, tons	165
Length, feet	140

CONGO

The Republic of Congo, which became independent on 15 Aug 1960, formed a naval service, but the patrol vessel *Reine N'Galifowou* (ex-French P 754) which was transferred 16 Nov, 1962 was returned to France on 18 Feb 1965 and then re-transferred to Senegal as *Siné Saloum*.

Personnel

(a) 1975: 200 officers and men
(b) Voluntary service

Mercantile Marine

Lloyd's Register of Shipping: 6 vessels of 1 534 tons gross

14 ex-CHINESE (COASTAL PATROL CRAFT)

Of ten tons, the first four being delivered from China in late 1970.

9 KRUPP TYPE (COASTAL PATROL CRAFT)

Small craft, primarily intended for river patrols. Built by Krupps, W. Germany.

COSTA RICA

Personnel

(a) 1975: 50 officers and men
(b) Voluntary

Mercantile Marine

Lloyd's Register of Shipping:
13 vessels of 5 603 tons gross

3 COASTAL PATROL CRAFT

401, 402, 403

Displacement, tons	10
Dimensions, feet	41 × 10 × 2·3
Gun	1 MG

Built in early 1950's. Of the pre-war US Coastguard 40 type.

CUBA

Senior Appointment

Commander in Chief:
Commodore Aldo Santamaria

Personnel

(a) 1975: 6 000 (380 officers, 220 subordinate officers and 5 400 men)
(b) 3 years national service

Standard of Efficiency

The US embargo on exports to Cuba has been running for over a decade. As a result all ex-USN ships in the Cuban Navy must be suffering from lack of spares, though some may have been stripped to provide for others. Cuba has the highest estimated defence expenditure in Central America and the Caribbean at about £120 million, a fair proportion of this being on Soviet aid. The navy is the smallest of the three services but, with an adequate budget and Soviet assistance in training, must be assessed as having a reasonable level of tactical and material efficiency.

Naval Establishments

Naval Academy:
At Mariel, for officers and cadets

Naval school:
At Morro Castle, for petty officers and men

Naval Bases:
Mariel, Cienfuegos and Cabanas

Naval Airforce

A helicopter force of 15 Mi-4 (Hound) from USSR is in existence.

Frigates

The three ex-US frigates of the PF type—*Antonio Maceo, Jose Marti, Maximo Gomez*—which were completed in 1944 and acquired in 1947 are still in existence as harbour hulks but have no operational value.

Mercantile Marine

Lloyd's Register of Shipping:
259 vessels of 409 064 tons gross

Disposals

Cruiser (so-called)

1972 *Cuba*

Corvettes

1973 *Sibony*

Light Forces

1973 *Donotivo, Matanzas*

CORVETTES

12 Ex-USSR "SO I" CLASS

Displacement, tons	215 standard; 250 full load
Dimensions, ft (*m*)	138·6 × 20 × 9·2 (*42·3 × 6·1 × 2·8*)
Guns	4—25 mm (2 twin)
A/S weapons	4 five-barrelled rocket launchers
Main engines	3 diesels; 6 000 bhp = 29 knots
Range, miles	1 100 at 13 knots
Complement	30

Six were transferred from the USSR by Sep 1964, and six more in 1967.

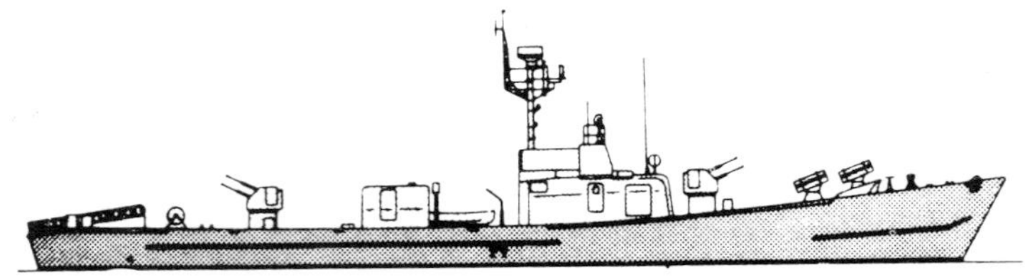

"SO I" Class

6 Ex-USSR "KRONSTADT" CLASS

Displacement, tons	310 standard; 380 full load
Dimensions, ft (*m*)	170·6 × 21·3 × 9 (*52·0 × 6·5 × 2·7*)
Guns	1—3·5 in; 2—37 mm AA; 4—25 mm AA
A/S weapons	1 DC thrower
Mines	6 on two racks at the stern
Main engines	3 diesels; 3 shafts; 3 030 hp = 24 knots
Range, miles	1 500 at 12 knots
Complement	65

Transferred from the USSR in 1962.

RADAR. Surface; Skinhead or Ballgun. Navigation; Don IFF; High Pole A.

"KRONSTADT" Class

1 Ex-US PCE TYPE ESCORT PATROL VESSEL

CARIBE (ex-USS PCE 872) PE 201

Displacement, tons	640 standard; 903 full load
Dimensions, feet	180 wl 184·5 oa × 33 × 9·5
Guns	1—3 in dp; 3—40 mm AA; 4—20 mm AA
A/S weapons	Hedgehog; DCT and racks
Main engines	12 cylinder diesels; 2 shafts; 1 800 bhp = 14 knots
Complement	99

Built in USA. Completed 1943-44. Refitted at Key West 1956.

CARIBE *Cuban Navy*

LIGHT FORCES

5 Ex-USSR "OSA" CLASS (FAST ATTACK CRAFT—MISSILE)

Displacement, tons	165 standard; 200 full load
Dimensions, ft (*m*)	128·7 × 25·1 × 5·9 (*39·3 × 7·7 × 1·8*)
Missiles	4 SSN-2 launchers in two pairs
Guns	4—30 mm (2 twin, 1 forward, 1 aft)
Main engines	3 diesels; 13 000 bhp = 32 knots
Range, miles	800 at 25 knots
Complement	25

Two boats of this class were transferred to Cuba from the USSR in January 1972 and three in 1973. With the obvious rundown of the ex-USN ships in the Cuban Navy and the determination of the Cuban Government to maintain an Independent Naval presence in the Caribbean, these could be the forerunners of further reinforcements. With the "Komar" class units there are now twenty-three hulls mounting 56 of the proven and effective "Styx" missiles in a highly sensitive area.

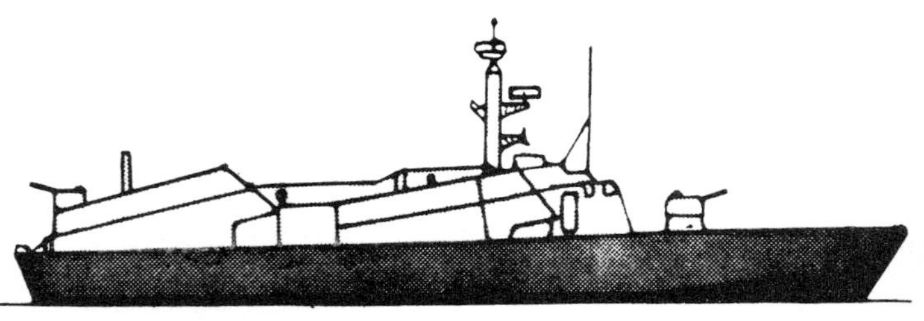

"OSA" Class

Light Forces—*continued*

18 Ex-USSR "KOMAR" CLASS (FAST ATTACK CRAFT—MISSILE)

Displacement, tons 70 standard; 80 full load
Dimensions, ft (*m*) 83·7 × 19·8 × 5·0 (*25·5 × 6·0 × 1·8*)
Missiles 2 SSN-2 launchers
Guns 2—25 mm AA
Main engines 4 diesels; 4 shafts; 4 800 bhp = 40 knots
Range, miles 400 at 30 knots

First twelve transferred in 1962. Last pair arrived in Dec 1966.

'KOMAR" Class *1970 USN*

12 Ex-USSR "P 6" CLASS (FAST ATTACK CRAFT—TORPEDO)

Displacement, tons 66 standard; 75 full load
Dimensions, ft (*m*) 84·2 × 20 × 6 (*25·7 × 6·1 × 1·8*)
Guns 4—25 mm AA (two twin)
Tubes 2—21 in (two single)
Main engines 4 diesels; 4 shafts; 4 800 hp = 43 knots
Range, miles 450 at 30 knots
Complement 25

Transferred in 1962. Pothead or Skinhead Radar. Can carry mines or depth charges in place of torpedo tubes.

"P 6" Class

12 Ex-USSR "P 4" CLASS (FAST ATTACK CRAFT—TORPEDO)

Displacement, tons 25
Dimensions, ft (*m*) 62·7 × 11·6 × 5·6 (*19·1 × 3·5 × 1·7*)
Guns 2—25 mm AA
Tubes 2—18 in
Main engines 2 diesels; 2 200 bhp; 2 shafts = 50 knots

Transferred from the USSR in 1962-64.

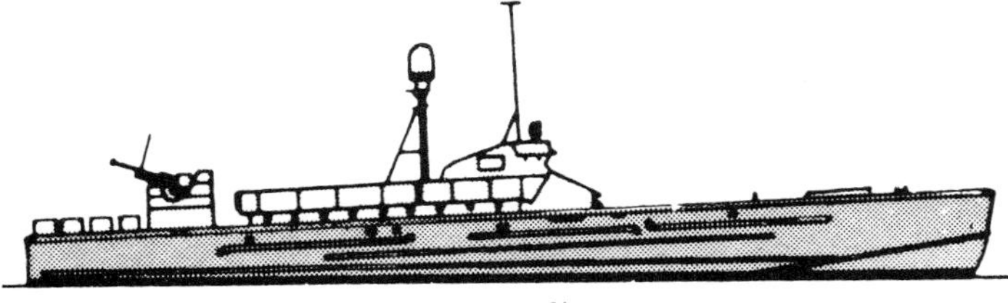

"P 4" Class

HABANA (ex-*SC* 1291) GC 107 **ORIENTE** (ex-*SC* 1000) GC 104
LAS VILLAS (ex-*SC* 1290) GC 106 **PINAR DEL RIO** (ex-*SC* 1301) GC 108

Displacement, tons 95
Dimensions, feet (*m*) 107·5 wl; 111 oa × 17 × 6·6 (*33·7 × 5·7 × 2*)
Guns 2—20 mm AA
Main engines 2 GM diesels; 2 shafts; 1 000 bhp = 15 knots
Complement 25

Built in the United States by Dingle Boat Works (*Oriente*), W. A. Robinson, Inc. Ipswich, Mass. (*Havana* and *Las Villas*), and Perkins & Vaughn Inc, Wickford, RI (*Pinar del Rio*) in 1942/43.

HABANA *Cuban Navy*

LEONCIO PRADO GC 101

Displacement, tons 80
Dimensions, feet 110 × 17·7 × 6·2
Gun 1—20 mm AA
Main engines 2 8-cycle, 2 stroke diesels; 1 000 bhp = 15 knots
Oil fuel 2 232 gallons

Built at Havana. Launched in 1946. Of wooden hulled construction.

LEONCIO PRADO *1966, Cuban Navy*

GC 11 (ex-USCGC 83351) **GC 13** (ex-USCGC 83385)
GC 14 (ex-USCGC 83395)

Displacement, tons 45
Dimensions, ft (*m*) 83 × 16 × 4·5 (*25·3 × 4·9 × 1·4*)
Gun 1—20 mm AA
Main engines 2 Sterling Viking petrol motors; 1 200 hp = 18 knots
Complement 12

Built in USA. Ex-Coast Guard Cutters. Launched in 1942-43. Of wooden hulled construction. Received from US Navy in March 1943.

GC 32 (ex-USCGC 56191) **GC 33** (ex-USCGC 56190)
GC 34 (ex-USCGC 56192)

Displacement, tons 45
Dimensions, ft (*m*) 83 × 16 × 4·5 (*25·3 × 4·9 × 1·4*)
Gun 1—20 mm
Main engines 2 Superior diesels; 460 bhp = 12 knots
Complement 12

Built in USA. Ex-Coast Guard cutters. Launched in 1942-43.

R 41 (ex-*PT* 715) **R 42** (ex-*PT* 716)

Displacement, tons 35
Dimensions, feet 71 × 19·2 × 5
Guns 2 MG
Main engines 2 Packard gas engines; 3 shafts; 3 600 bhp = 35 knots

Former US motor torpedo boats of the PT type. Built in the USA by Annapolis Yacht Yard Inc, Annapolis, Md. Launched on 9 July 1945 (R 41) and 17 July 1945 (R 42). Sunk during a hurricane on 5 Oct 1948, but were salvaged and put into service as sea-air rescue craft.

SV 7 **SV 8** **SV 9** **SV 10** **SV 12** **SV 14**

Dimensions, feet Length 40
Gun 1—50 cal MG
Main engines 2 GM diesels; speed 25 knots

Later boats of the SV type assigned to naval stations for coastal patrol. Equipped with radar.

SV 1 **SV 2** **SV 3** **SV 4** **SV 5** **SV 6**

Displacement, tons 6·15
Dimensions, feet 32 × 10 × 2·8
Main engines 2 Chrysler Crown, 230 bhp = 18 knots

Auxiliary patrol boats for port patrol, launched in 1953.

ENRIQUE COLLAZO (ex-*Joaquin Godoy*)

Displacement, tons 815
Dimensions, ft (*m*) 211 × 24 × 9 (*64 × 10·5 × 2·8*)
Main engines Triple expansion; 2 shafts; 672 ihp = 8 knots

Built at Paisley, Scotland. Launched in 1906. Acquired in 1950 from Cuban mercantile marine. Lighthouse tender.

BERTHA SF 10

Displacement, tons 98
Dimensions, ft (*m*) 104 × 19 × 11 (*31·5 × 5·8 × 3·4*)
Main engines 2 Gray Marine diesels; 450 bhp = 10 knots

Launched in 1944. Lighthouse tender.

Light Forces—*continued*

10 DE OCTUBRE (ex-*ATR* 4) RS 210

Displacement, tons	852 standard; 1 315 full load
Dimensions, ft (*m*)	155 wl; 165·5 oa × 33·3 × 16 (*47·3; 50·4 × 10·2 × 4·9*)
Main engines	Triple expansion; 1 600 ihp = 12 knots
Boilers	2 Babcock & Wilcox D-type; oil burning

Former US ocean rescue tug. Built in the USA. Launched in 1943. Largely of wooden construction. Purchased in 1948.

GRANMA A 11

Yacht which landed in Cuba on 2 Dec 1956 with Dr Fidel Castro and the men who began the liberation war. Historic vessel incorporated into the Navy as an auxiliary.

A1 **A2** **A3**

Displacement, tons	60
Dimensions, feet	74 × 15 × 5
Gun	1 MG
Main engines	2 diesels

CYPRUS

LIGHT FORCES

Mercantile Marine

Lloyd's Register of Shipping:
722 vessels of 3 394 880 tons gross

6 "P 4" CLASS

Displacement, tons	25
Dimensions, ft (*m*)	62·7 × 11·6 × 6·5 (*19·1 × 3·5 × 1·7*)
Guns	2—25 mm
Tubes	2—18 in
Main engines	2 diesels; 2 200 bhp; 2 shafts = 50 knots

Four of these were transferred by USSR in Oct 1964 and two in Feb 1965. Also reported that two extra engines have been supplied since that time.

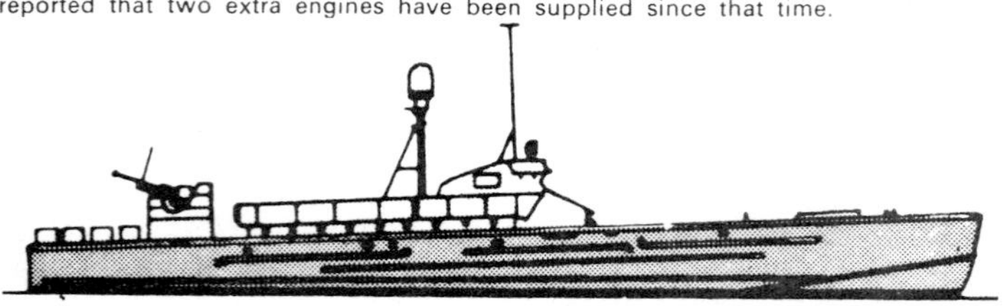

"P 4" Class

2 Ex-GERMAN "R" TYPE

Displacement, tons	125
Dimensions, feet	124 × 19 × 4·5
Guns	1—40 mm; 1—20 mm
Main engines	2 MAN diesels; 1 800 bhp = 20 knots

Originally three of this class were taken up from mercantile use and re-armed. One was destroyed by Turkish air attack on 8 Aug 1964 at Xeros. It was reported that there are 10 small craft of about 50 tons, armed with one or two 20 mm guns.

"R" Type *1972, Dr. Giorgio Arra*

DENMARK

Administration

Commander-in-Chief:
Vice-Admiral S. Thostrup, RDN

Diplomatic Representation

Defence Attaché, London:
Colonel H. H. Prince Georg of Denmark, KCVO

Assistant Defence Attaché, London:
Commander I. E. Eriksen, MVO, RDN

Defence Attaché, Washington:
Colonel P. S. Sørensen

Personnel

(a) 1975: 5 800 officers and men
(Reserves of 3 100 Maritime Home Guard)
(b) 9 months National service

Prefix to Ships Names

Names prefixed by HDMS

Naval Bases

Copenhagen, Korsør, Frederikshaven, Grønnedal (Greenland)

Strength of the Fleet

Type	*Active*	*Building*
Frigates	6	1
Corvettes	3	—
Submarines (Patrol)	6	—
Fast Attack Craft (Missile)	—	10
Fast Attack Craft (Torpedo)	10	—
Large Patrol Craft	24	—
Coastal Patrol Craft	16	—
Minelayers	5	—
Minesweepers (Coastal)	8	—
Depot Ship	1	—
Oilers (Small)	2	—
Icebreakers	3	—
Royal Yacht	1	—

Navy Estimates

1970-71: 441 800 000 Kr.
1971-72: 478 500 000 Kr.
1972-73: 520 400 000 Kr.
1973-74: 583 600 000 Kr.
1974-75: 638 500 000 Kr.

Farvands Direktoratet

This Directorate of Waters (under the MOD) now controls the Pilot Service, Lighthouse Service, and Lifeboat service.

Disposals

Corvette

1974 *Diana*

Fast Attack Craft

1974 6 Flyvefisken Class

Large Patrol Craft

1972 *Alholm*

Mine Warfare Forces

1974 2 Lougen Class Minelayers
4 VIG Class Inshore Minesweepers

Tenders

1970 *Hollaenderdybet, Kongedybet*

Icebreaker

1972 *Lillebjørn*

Mercantile Marine

Lloyd's Register of Shipping:
1 349 vessels of 4 460 219 tons gross

FRIGATES

2 "PEDER SKRAM" CLASS

Displacement, tons	2 030 standard; 2 720 full load
Length, feet (*metres*)	354·3 (108) pp; 396·5 (*112·6*) oa
Beam, feet (*metres*)	39·5 (*12*)
Draught, feet (*metres*)	11·8 (*3·6*)
Guns,	4—5 in (*127 mm*) 38 cal; 4—40 mm
A/S weapons	DC
Main engines	CODOG; 2 shafts:— 2 GM 16-567 D diesels; 4 800 hp; 2 Pratt & Whitney PWA GG 4A-3 gas turbines; 44 000 hp total output
Speed, knots	30 18 economical
Complement	112

Name	*No.*	*Builders*	*Laid down*	*Launched*	*Completed*
HERLUF TROLLE	F 353	Helsingörs J. & M.	18 Dec 1964	8 Sep 1965	16 Apr 1967
PEDER SKRAM	F 352	Helsingors J. & M.	25 Sep 1964	20 May 1965	30 June 1966

PEDER SKRAM *1974, Royal Danish Navy*

GENERAL
Fast frigates of Danish design built at Helsingör. They were to have been armed, additionally to guns, with three 21 inch torpedo tubes and the "Terne" anti-submarine weapon. There is space on the quarter deck for installation of Sea Sparrow in 1974-75.

RADAR. Search: Two S Band air and surface search. Tactical: X Band. Fire Control: Three X Band and Contraves.

Frigates—*continued*

4 "HVIDBJØRNEN" CLASS

Name	No.	Builders	Laid down	Launched	Completed
FYLLA	F 351	Aalborg Værft	27 June 1962	18 Dec 1962	10 July 1963
HVIDBJØRNEN	F 348	Aarhus Flydedok	4 June 1961	23 Nov 1961	15 Dec 1962
INGOLF	F 350	Svendborg Værft	5 Dec 1961	27 July 1961	27 July 1963
VÆDDEREN	F 349	Aalborg Værft	30 Oct 1961	6 Apr 1962	19 Mar 1963

Displacement, tons 1 345 standard; 1 650 full load
Length, feet (*metres*) 219·8 (*67·0*) pp; 238·2 (*72·6*) oa
Beam, feet (*metres*) 38·0 (*11·6*)
Draught, feet (*metres*) 16 (*4·9*)
Aircraft 1 Alouette III helicopter
Gun, 1—3 in (*76 mm*)
Main engines 4 GM 16—567C diesels; 6 400 bhp; 1 shaft
Speed, knots 18
Range, miles 6 000 at 13 knots
Complement 75

GENERAL
Ordered in 1960-61. Of frigate type for fishery protection and surveying duties in the North Sea, Faroe Islands and Greenland waters. They are equipped with a helicopter platform aft.

RADAR. Search: S Band combined air and surface Navigation: X Band.

INGOLF *1974, Royal Danish Navy*

1 MODIFIED "HVIDBJØRNEN" CLASS

BESKYTTEREN F 340

Length, feet (*metres*) 244 (*74·4*) oa
Beam, feet (*metres*) 39 (*11·8*)
Draught, feet (*metres*) 15 (*4·5*)
Aircraft 1 Alouette III helicopter
Gun, 1—3 in (*76 mm*)
Main engines 4 B.W. Alpha diesels; 7 440 bhp; 1 shaft
Speed, knots 18
Complement 60

Laid down in 1970 for completion Oct 1975.

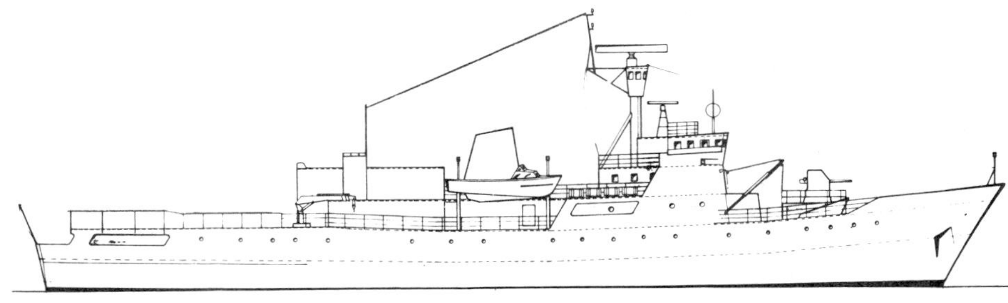
BESKYTTEREN *1975, Royal Danish Navy*

CORVETTES

3 "TRITON" CLASS

Name	No.	Builders	Launched	Transferred
BELLONA	F 344	Naval Meccanicia, Castellammare	9 Jan 1955	31 Jan 1957
FLORA	F 346	Cantiere del Tirreno, Riva, Trigoso	25 June 1955	28 Aug 1956
TRITON	F 347	Cantiere Navali di Taranto	12 Sep 1954	10 Aug 1955

Displacement, tons 760 standard; 873 full load
Length, feet (*metres*) 242·8 (*74·0*) pp; 250·3 (*76·3*) oa
Beam, feet (*metres*) 31·5 (*9·6*)
Draught, feet (*metres*) 9 (*2·7*)
Guns, 2—3 in (*76 mm*); 1—40 mm
A/S 2 Hedgehogs; 4 DCT
Main engines 2 Ansaldo Fiat 409T diesels 4 400 bhp; 2 shafts
Speed, knots 20
Range, miles 3 000 at 18 knots
Complement 110

GENERAL
These were built in Italy for the Danish Navy under the United States "offshore" account. Sisters of the Italian "Albatros" class. *Diana* deleted 1974.

RADAR. Search: Plessey AWS 1. Navigation: S Band.

CLASSIFICATION. Officially classified as corvettes in 1954, but have "F" pennant numbers.

FLORA *1974, Royal Danish Navy*

SUBMARINES

2 "NARHVALEN" CLASS

Name	No.	Laid down	Launched	Completed
NARHVALEN	S 320	16 Feb 1965	10 Sep 1968	27 Feb 1970
NORDKAPEREN	S 321	20 Jan 1966	18 Dec 1969	22 Dec 1970

Displacement, tons 370 surface; 450 dived
Length, feet (*metres*) 144·4 (*44·3*)
Beam, feet (*metres*) 15 (*4·6*)
Draught, feet (*metres*) 12·5 (*3·8*)
Torpedo tubes 8—21 in (*533 mm*) bow,
Main machinery 2 MB Diesels; 1 500 bhp surface; 2 electric motors; 1 500 bhp dived
Speed, knots 12 surface; 17 dived
Complement 22

These coastal submarines are similar to the German Improved Type 205 and were built under licence at the Royal Dockyard, Copenhagen with modifications for Danish needs. They are fitted with snort and radar.

NAHRVALEN *1974, Royal Danish Navy*

4 "DELFINEN" CLASS

Name	No.	Laid down	Launched	Completed
DELFINEN	S 326	1 July 1954	4 May 1956	16 Sep 1958
SPÆKHUGGEREN	S 327	1 Dec 1954	20 Feb 1957	27 June 1959
SPRINGEREN	S 329	3 Jan 1961	26 Apr 1963	22 Oct 1964
TUMLEREN	S 328	22 May 1956	22 May 1958	15 Jan 1960

Displacement, tons 550 standard; 595 surface; 643 submerged
Length, feet (*metres*) 117·2 (*54·0*)
Beam, feet (*metres*) 15·4 (*4·7*)
Draught, feet (*metres*) 13·1 (*4·0*)
Torpedo tubes 4—21 in (*533 mm*)
Main machinery 2 Burmeister & Wain diesels; 1 200 bhp surface; electric motors; 1 200 hp submerged
Speed, knots 15 surface and submerged
Range, miles 4 000 at 8 knots
Complement 33

Built in the Royal Dockyard, Copenhagen. Equipped with snort and radar.

SPRINGEREN *1974, Royal Danish Navy*

LIGHT FORCES

2 "AGDLEQ-k1" CLASS (LARGE PATROL CRAFT)

AGDLEQ Y 386 **AGPA** Y 387

Displacement, tons 300
Dimensions, ft (*m*) 101·7 × 25·3 × 10·9 (*31 × 7·7 × 3·3*)
Guns 2—20 mm (twin)
Speed, knots 12

Built by Svendborg Vaerft. Completed *Agdleq*, 12 Mar 1974; *Agpa* 14 May 1974. Designed for service off Greenland.

AGDLEQ *1974, Royal Danish Navy*

10 "WILLEMOES-k1" CLASS (FAST ATTACK CRAFT—MISSILE)

P 540–549

Displacement, tons 220
Dimensions, feet 151 × 24 × 8
Guided weapons To be installed
Guns 1—76 mm Oto Melara or 1—57 mm L 70 Bofors
Torpedo tubes 4—21 in
Main engines CODAG arrangement of 3 Rolls Royce Proteus gas turbines plus diesels for cruising on wing shafts
Speed, knots 40 max approx

First four ordered in 1971 to complete in 1975-76. Further four now building. Lürssen Werft design. Basically similar to "Combattante II" class. Controllable pitch propellers. All building at Frederikshavn Vaerft and Flydedok.

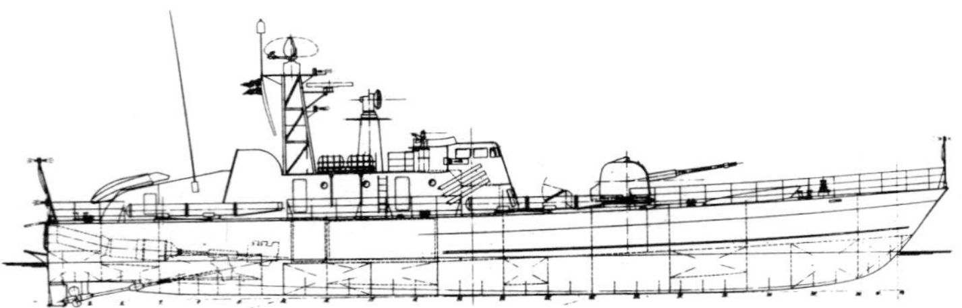

"WILLEMOES" Class *1975, Royal Danish Navy*

4 "FALKEN" CLASS (FAST ATTACK CRAFT—TORPEDO)

Name	*Pennant No.*	*Laid down*	*Launched*	*Completed*
FALKEN	P 506	1 Nov 1960	19 Dec 1961	4 Oct 1962
GLENTEN	P 507	3 Jan 1961	15 Mar 1962	15 Dec 1962
GRIBBEN	P 508	15 May 1961	18 July 1962	26 Apr 1963
HØGEN	P 509	1 Sep 1961	4 Oct 1962	6 June 1963

Displacement, tons 119
Dimensions, feet 118 × 17·8 × 6
Guns 1—40 mm AA; 1—20 mm AA
Tubes 2—41 in (side)
Main engines 3 diesels; 3 shafts; 9 000 bhp = 40 knots
Complement 23

Ordered under US offshore procurement in the Military Aid Programme All built at the Royal Dockyard, Copenhagen.

HØGEN *1974, Royal Danish Navy*

6 "SØLØVEN" CLASS (FAST ATTACK CRAFT—TORPEDO)

Name	*Pennant No.*	*Laid down*	*Launched*	*Completed*
SØLØVEN	P 510	27 Aug 1962	19 Apr 1963	June 1964 *
SØRIDDEREN	P 511	4 Oct 1962	22 Aug 1963	June 1964 *
SØBJORNEN	P 512	9 July 1963	19 Aug 1964	Sep 1965
SØHESTEN	P 513	5 Sep 1963	31 Mar 1965	June 1966
SØHUNDEN	P 514	18 Aug 1964	12 Jan 1966	Dec 1966
SØULVEN	P 515	30 Mar 1965	27 Apr 1966	Mar 1967

Displacement, tons 95 standard; 114 full load
Dimensions, feet 90 pp; 96 wl; 99 oa × 25·5 × 7
Guns 2—40 mm Bofors AA
Tubes 4—21 in (side)
Main engines 3 Bristol Siddeley Proteus gas turbines; 3 shafts; 12 750 bhp = 54 knots
GM diesels on wing shafts for cruising = 10 knots
Range, miles 400 at 46 knots
Complement 29

The design is a combination of the "Brave" class hull form and "Ferocity" type construction. *Søløven* ("Sea Lion") and *Søridderen* ("Sea Knight") were built by Vosper Limited, Portsmouth, England (*delivered to the Royal Danish Navy on 12 and 10 Feb 1965, respectively); and the remaining four under licence by the Royal Dockyard, Copenhagen.

SØHUNDEN *1974, Royal Danish Navy*

9 "BARSØ" CLASS (LARGE PATROL CRAFT)

BARSØ Y 300 **SAMSØ** Y 303 **FARØ** Y 306
DREJØ Y 301 **THURØ** Y 304 **LAESØ** Y 307
ROMSØ Y 302 **VEJRØ** Y 305 **ROMØ** Y 308

Displacement, tons 155
Dimensions, feet 83·7 × 19·7 × 9·8
Speed 11 knots

Rated as patrol cutters. First six launched and completed in 1969. Remainder in 1972-73.

DREJØ *1974, Royal Danish Navy*

2 "MAAGEN" CLASS (LARGE PATROL CRAFT)

MAAGEN (Y 384) **MALLEMUKKEN** Y 385

Displacement, tons 190
Dimensions, feet 88·5 × 21·7 × 9·5
Gun 1—40 mm AA
Main engines 385 hp; 1 shaft; speed 11 knots

Of steel construction. Built at Helsingør, laid down 15 Jan 1960, launched 1960.

1 "TEJSTEN" CLASS (LARGE PATROL CRAFT)

TEJSTEN Y 383

Displacement, tons 130
Dimensions, feet 82 × 20·7 × 9·4
Gun 1—37 mm
Main engines Alfa Diesel; 180 bhp = 9 knots

Of wooden construction. Built by Holbaek Skibsbyggeri. Launched 1951. For service in Greenland waters.

Light Forces—*continued*

9 "DAPHNE" CLASS (LARGE PATROL CRAFT)

Name	*Pennant No.*	*Laid down*	*Launched*	*Completed*
DAPHNE	P 530	1 Apr 1960	10 Nov 1960	19 Dec 1961
DRYADEN	P 531	1 July 1960	1 Mar 1961	4 Apr 1962
HAVFRUEN	P 533	15 Mar 1961	4 Oct 1961	20 Dec 1962
HAVMANDEN	P 532	15 Nov 1960	16 May 1961	30 Aug 1962
NAJADEN	P 534	20 Sep 1961	20 June 1962	26 Apr 1963
NEPTUN	P 536	1 Sep 1962	29 May 1963	18 Dec 1963
NYMFEN	P 535	1 Apr 1962	1 Nov 1962	4 Oct 1963
RAN	P 537	1 Dec 1962	10 July 1963	15 May 1964
ROTA	P 538	19 July 1963	25 Nov 1963	20 Jan 1965

Displacement, tons 170
Dimensions, feet 121·3 × 20 × 6·5
Gun 1—40 mm AA
A/S weapons 2—51 mm rocket launchers, depth charges
Main engines Diesels; 2 shafts; 2 600 bhp = 20 knots (plus 1 cruising engine; 100 bhp)
Complement 23

All built at the Royal Dockyard, Copenhagen. 4 built under US offshore programme.

NEPTUN *1974, Royal Danish Navy*

1 "FYRHOLM" CLASS (COASTAL PATROL CRAFT)

LINDHOLM Y 374 (ex-*MSK* 6)

Displacement, tons 68
Dimensions, feet 65·7 × 16·8 × 7·5
Main engines Diesel; 120 bhp = 9 knots

Built by Sydhavns Vaerft. Launched in 1945.

1 "ALHOLM" CLASS (COASTAL PATROL CRAFT)

ERTHOLM Y 371 (ex-*MSK* 3)

Displacement, tons 70
Dimensions, feet 69 × 17 × 9
Gun 1—20 mm AA
Main engines Diesel; 120 bhp = 10 knots

Built by Frederikssund Vaerft. Launched in 1945.

5 "Y" TYPE

Y 338 **Y 339** **Y 343** **Y 354** **Y 359**

Miscellaneous patrol cutters (ex-fishing vessels) all built in 1944-45. Y 342 and Y 347 were removed from the list in 1971.

7 "FÆNØ" CLASS (COASTAL PATROL CRAFT)

ASKØ MHV 81 (ex-Y 386, ex-M 560, ex-MS 2)
BAAGØ MHV 84 (ex-Y 387, ex-M 561, ex-MS 3)
ENØ MHV 82 (ex-Y 388, ex-M 562, ex-MS 5)
FÆNØ MHV 69 (ex-M 563, ex-MS 6)
HJORTØ MHV 85 (ex-Y 389, ex-M 564, ex-MS 7)
LYØ MHV 86 (ex-Y 390, ex-M 565, ex-MS 8)
MANØ MHV 83 (ex-Y 391, ex-M 566, ex-MS 9)

Displacement, tons 74
Dimensions, feet 78·8 × 21 × 5
Guns 1—20 mm
Main engines Diesel; 1 shaft; 350 bhp = 11 knots

Of wooden construction. All launched in 1941. Former inshore minesweepers. Used by the Maritime Home Guard.

FÆNO *1974, Royal Danish Navy*

3 MHV TYPE

MHV 60 **MHV 71** **MHV 72**

Displacement, tons 76
Gun 1—20 mm AA
Main engines 200 bhp = 10 knots

Built in 1958. Patrol boats and training craft for the Naval Home Guard. Of the fishing cutter type. Formerly designated DMH, but allocated MHV numbers in 1969. In addition there are some 20 small vessels of the trawler and other types.

MHV 71 *1974, Royal Danish Navy*

MINE WARFARE FORCES

4 "FALSTER" CLASS MINELAYERS

Name	*No.*	*Builders*	*Laid down*	*Launched*	*Completed*
FALSTER	N 80	Nakskov Skibsvaerft	12 Apr 1962	19 Sep 1962	7 Nov 1963
FYEN	N 81	Frederikshavn Værft	12 Apr 1962	3 Oct 1962	18 Sep 1963
MØEN	N 82	Frederikshavn Værft	4 Oct 1962	6 Mar 1963	29 Apr 1964
SJÆLLAND	N 83	Nakskov Skibsværft	17 Jan 1963	14 June 1963	7 July 1964

Displacement, tons 1 900 full load
Length, feet (*metres*) 238 (*72·5*) pp; 252·6 (*77·0*) oa
Beam, feet (*metres*) 41 (*12·5*)
Draught, feet (*metres*) 10 (*3·0*)
Missiles Being fitted with Seasparrow
Guns, dual purpose 4—3 in (*76 mm*), 2 twin mountings
Mines 400
Main engines 2 GM—567D 3 diesels; 4 800 shp 2 shafts
Speed, knots 17
Complement 120

GENERAL
Minelayers of a novel Scandinavian-NATO design. Ordered in 1960-61. All are named after Danish islands. The steel hull is flush-decked with a raking stem, a full stern and a prominent knuckle forward. The super structure has a block outline surmounted by a squat streamlined funnel, two light lattice masts, high angle director control towers fore and aft and whip aerials. The hull has been specially strengthened for ice navigation.

RADAR. Search: C Band low coverage. Navigation: S and X Band.

SJÆLLAND *1972 Royal Danish Navy*

Minewarfare Forces—*continued*

1 "LANGELAND" CLASS

(COASTAL MINELAYER)

Displacement, tons	310 standard; 332 full load
Dimensions, feet	133·5 oa; 128·2 pp × 23·7 × 7·2
Guns	2—40 mm; 2—20 mm Madsen
Main engines	Diesel; 2 shafts; 385 bhp = 11·6 knots
Complement	37

Built at the Royal Dockyard, Copenhagen. Laid down in 1950. Launched on 17 May 1950. Completed in 1951.

LANGELAND — *1973, Royal Danish Navy*

8 "SUND" CLASS (MINESWEEPERS—COASTAL)

AARØSUND (ex-*AMS* 127) M 571 **GULDBORGSUND** (ex-*MSC* 257) M 575
ALSSUND (ex-*AMS* 128) M 572 **OMØSUND** (ex-*MSC* 221) M 576
EGERNSUND (ex-*AMS* 129) M 573 **ULVSUND** (ex-*MSC* 263) M 577
GRØNSUND (ex-*MSC* 256) M 574 **VILSUND** (ex-*MSC* 264) M 578

Displacement, tons	350 standard; 376 full load
Dimensions, feet	138 pp; 144 oa × 27 × 8·5
Guns	2—20 mm
Main engines	Diesels; 2 shafts; 1 200 bhp = 13 knots
Range, miles	2 500 at 10 knots
Complement	35

MSC (ex-AMS) 60 class NATO coastal minesweepers all built in USA. Completed in 1954-56. *Aarøsund* was transferred on 24 Jan 1955, *Alssund* on 5 Apr 1955, *Egernsund* on 3 Aug 1955, *Grønsund* on 21 Sep 1956, *Guldborgsund* on 11 Nov 1956, *Omøsund* on 20 June 1956, *Ulvsund* on 20 Sep 1956 and *Vilsund* on 15 Nov 1956. *Guldborgsund* has been fitted with a charthouse between bridge and funnel and is employed on surveying duties.

GULDBORGSUND — *1973, Royal Danish Navy*

SLEIPNER

A 200 ton torpedo recovery/transporter.

DEPOT SHIP

HENRIK GERNER (ex-M/S *Hammershus*) A 542

Displacement, tons	2 200 standard
Dimensions, feet	252·7 × 40 × 18·3
Main engines	Burmeister & Wain diesel; speed = 15 knots
Complement	230

Former Danish passenger ship. Built in 1936. Transferred to the Royal Danish Navy on 8 Jan 1964, refitted at the Royal Dockyard, Copenhagen, and commissioned as a depot ship for submarines.

HENRIK GERNER — *1971, Royal Danish Navy*

TANKERS

RIMFAXE (ex-US *YO* 226) A 568 **SKINFAXE** (ex-US *YO* 229) A 569

Displacement, tons	422 light; 1 390 full load
Dimensions, feet	174 oa × 32 × 13·2
Main engines	1 GM diesel; 560 bhp = 10 knots
Complement	23

Transferred to the Royal Danish Navy from the USA on 2 Aug 1962.

RIMFAXE — *1971, Royal Danish Navy*

ICEBREAKERS

Note. Icebreakers are controlled by the Ministry of Trade and Shipping, but are maintained by RDN at Frederikshavn in summer.

ELBJØRN

Displacement, tons	893 standard; 1 400 full load
Dimensions, feet	156·5 × 40·3 × 14·5
Main engines	Diesels; electric drive; 3 600 bhp = 12 knots

Built in 1953. Recently used by RDN for surveying in summer.

DANBJØRN **ISBJØRN**

Displacement, tons	3 685
Dimensions, feet	252 × 56 × 20
Main engines	Diesels; Electric drive; 11 880 bhp = 14 knots
Complement	34

Built in 1965.

DANBJØRN — *1970, Royal Danish Navy*

STOREBJØRN

Displacement, tons	2 540
Dimensions, feet	197 × 49·2 × 19

Built in 1931.

ROYAL YACHT

DANNEBROG A 540

Displacement, tons	1 130
Dimensions, feet	246 oa × 34 × 11·2
Guns	2—37 mm
Main engines	2 sets Burmeister & Wain 8 cylinder; 2 cycle diesels. 1 800 bhp = 14 knots
Complement	57

Built at the Royal Dockyard, Copenhagen. Launched on 10 Oct 1931.

DANNEBROG — *1971, Royal Danish Navy*

DOMINICAN REPUBLIC

Administration

Under Secretary for the Navy:
Commodore Francisco A. Amiama Castillo

Chief of Naval Staff:
Commodore Manuel A. Logroño Contin

Vice-Chief of Naval Staff:
Captain Francisco A. Marte Victoria

Personnel

(a) 1975: 3 810 officers and men
(b) Selective military Service

Strength of the Fleet

Type	*Active*	*Projected*
Frigates	3	—
Corvettes	2	5(?)
Large Patrol Craft	5	—
Coastal Patrol Craft	7	—
LSM	1	—
LCU	2	—
Minesweepers (Ocean)	2	—
Survey Vessels	2 (1 launch)	—
Oilers (Small)	2	—
Tugs (Large)	4	—
Tugs (Harbour)	8	—

Naval Bases

Las Calderas, San Pedro de Macoris

Disposals

Destroyers

1972 *Duarte*

Corvettes

1972 *Gerardo Jansen, Juan Bautista Cambiaso, Juan Bautista Maggiola*

Mercantile Marine

Lloyd's Register of Shipping:
20 vessels of 11 963 tons gross

FRIGATES

2 Ex-US "TACOMA" CLASS

Name	*Pennant No.*	*Builders*	*Laid down*	*Launched*	*Completed*
CAP. GENERAL PEDRO SANTANA (ex-*Presidente Peynado*, ex-USS *Knoxville*, PF 64)	453 (ex-F 104)	Kaiser S.Y. Richmond, Cal.	14 Nov 1943	20 Jan 1944	27 May 1944
GREGORIO LUPERON (ex-*Presidente Troncoso*, ex-USS *Pueblo*, PF 13)	452 (ex-F 103)	Leatham D. Smith S.B. Co, Wis.	15 Apr 1943	10 July 1943	29 Apr 1944

Displacement, tons	1 430 standard; 2 415 full load
Length, feet (*metres*)	298·0 (*90·8*) wl; 304·0 (*92·7*) oa
Beam, feet (*metres*)	37·5 (*11·4*)
Draught, feet (*metres*)	12·0 (*3·7*); 13·7 (*4·2*)
Guns	3—3 in (*76 mm*) single; 4—40 mm (2 twin); 6—20 mm; 4—0·5 in (*12·7 mm*) MG (2 twin)
Main engines	Triple expansion; 2 shafts; 5 500 ihp
Speed, knots	19
Boilers	2 of three-drum type
Oil fuel, tons	760
Range, miles	9 500 at 12 knots
Complement	140

Formerly United States patrol frigates, PF of the "Tacoma" class similar to the contempory British frigates of the "River" class. Transferred from the US Navy to the Dominican Republic Navy in 1949. Renamed in 1962.

GREGORIO LUPERON *1972, Dominican Navy*

1 Ex-CANADIAN "RIVER" CLASS

MELLA (ex-*Presidente Trujillo*, ex-HMS *Carlplace*) 451

Displacement, tons	1 400 standard; 2 125 full load
Length, feet (*metres*)	301·5 (*91·9*)
Beam, feet (*metres*)	36·7 (*11·2*)
Draught, feet (*metres*)	12·0 (*3·7*) mean
Guns	1—4 in; 2—47 mm; 1—40 mm; 4—20 mm (2 twin)
Main engines	Triple expansion; 2 shafts; 5 500 ihp
Speed, knots	20
Boilers	2 of three-drum type
Oil fuel, tons	645
Range, miles	4 200 at 12 knots
Complement	195 (15 officers, 130 ratings, 50 midshipmen)

MELLA *1972, Dominican Navy*

Built by Davies SB & Repairing Co, Lauzon, Canada. Launched on 6 July 1944. Completed on 13 Dec 1944. Transferred to the Dominican Navy in 1946. Modified for use as Presidential Yacht with extra accommodation and deck-houses built up aft. Pennant number as a frigate was F 101, but as the Presidential Yacht it was no longer worn. Now carries pennant number 451 as training ship. Renamed *Mella* in 1962. Used for training midshipmen.

CORVETTES

2 Ex-CANADIAN "FLOWER" CLASS

Name	*Pennant No.*	*Builders*	*Launched*	*Completed*
CRISTOBAL COLON (ex-HMCS *Lachute*)	401 (ex-C 101)	Morton Ltd, Quebec City, P.Q.	9 June 1944	24 Oct 1944
JUAN ALEJANDRO ACOSTA (ex-HMCS *Louisburg*)	402 (ex-C 102)	Morton Ltd, Quebec City, P.Q.	13 July 1943	13 Dec 1943

Displacement, tons	1 060 standard; 1 350 full load
Length, feet (*metres*)	193·0 (*58·8*) pp; 208·0 (*63·4*) oa
Beam, feet (*metres*)	33·0 (*10·0*)
Draught, feet (*metres*)	13·3 (*4·0*) mean
Guns,	1—4 in (*102 mm*); *C. Colon:* 2—40 mm (twin); 6—20 mm; 4—0·5 in MG (2 twin); *J. A. Acosta*: 1—40 mm; 6—20 mm; 2—0·5 in MG
Main engines	Triple expansion; 2 750 ihp
Speed, knots	16
Boilers	2 of three-drum type
Oil fuel, tons	282
Range, miles	2 900 at 15 knots
Complement	53

Built in Canadian shipyards under the emergency construction programme during the Second World War. Transferred to the Dominican Navy in 1947. Pennant numbers were changed in 1968.

JUAN ALEJANDRO ACOSTA *1972, Dominican Navy*

LIGHT FORCES

3 Ex-USCG WPC TYPE (LARGE PATROL CRAFT)

INDEPENDENCIA (ex-USCGC *Icarus*) 204 (ex-P 105)
LIBERTAD (ex-*Rafael Atoa*, ex-USCGC *Thetis*) 205 (ex-P 106)
RESTAURACION (ex-USCGC *Galathea*) 203 (ex-P 104)

Displacement, tons	337 standard
Dimensions, feet	165·0 × 25·2 × 9·5
Guns	1—3 in; 1—40 mm AA; 1—20 mm AA
Main engines	2 Diesels; 1 280 bhp = 15 knots
Range, miles	1 300 at 15 knots
Complement	49 (5 officers, 44 men)

Ex-US Coastguard Cutters. *Independencia* was completed by Bath Iron Works in 1932, and *Restauracion* by John H. Machis & Co, Camden, NJ, in 1933.

RESTAURACION *1972, Dominican Navy*

1 US PGM TYPE (LARGE PATROL CRAFT)

BETELGEUSE (ex-US *PGM* 77) GC 102

Displacement, tons	145·5
Dimensions, feet	101·5 × 21·0 × 5·0
Guns	1—40 mm; 4—20 mm AA (2 twin); 2—0·5 in 50 cal MG
Main engines	4 diesels; 2 shafts; 2 200 bhp = 21 knots
Range, miles	1 500 at 10 knots
Complement	20

Built in the USA and transferred to the Dominican Republic under the Military Aid Programme. Completed in 1966 by Peterson Builders. Transferred on 14 Jan 1966.

BETELGEUSE *1972, Dominican Navy*

2 "ATLANTIDA" CLASS (COASTAL PATROL CRAFT)

PUERTO HEMOSA LA 7 **ATLANTIDA** LA 8

4 "BELLATRIX" CLASS (COASTAL PATROL CRAFT)

BELLATRIX GC 106 **CAPELLA** GC 108 **PROCYON** GC 103
+ 1

Displacement, tons	60
Dimensions, feet	85 × 18 × 5
Guns	3—·5 mg
Main engines	2 GM Diesels; 500 bhp = 18·7 knots

Built by Sewart Seacraft Inc. at Berwick, Louisiana. Transferred to the Dominican Navy by USA, *Bellatrix* on 18 Aug 1967, *Procyon* on 1 May 1967 and *Capella* on 15 Oct 1968. Fourth of class delivered May 1972.

BELLATRIX *1970, Dominican Navy*

Light Forces—*continued*

CAPITAN ALSINA GC 105 (ex-RL 101) (LARGE PATROL CRAFT)

Displacement, tons	100 standard
Dimensions, feet	92·0 wl; 104·8 oa × 19·2 × 5·8
Guns	2—20 mm AA
Main engines	2 GM diesels; 2 shafts; 1 000 hp = 17 knots
Complement	20

Of wooden construction. Launched in 1944. Named as above in 1957.

CAPITAN ALSINA

RIGEL GC 101 (ex-US AVR) (COASTAL PATROL CRAFT)

Displacement, tons	27 standard; 32·2 full load
Dimensions, feet	63·0 × 15·5 × 5·0
Guns	2—50 cal MG
Main engines	General Motors V8—71 diesels = 18·5 knots
Complement	9

Originally built in 1953. Reconditioned by NAUSTA, Keywest, USA.

MAYMYON (COASTAL PATROL CRAFT)

Displacement, tons	21
Dimensions, feet	43·3 × 7·2 × 3·3
Main engines	2 petrol engines; 500 hp = 14 knots

Built in 1946. Probably employed on surveying duties.

MINESWEEPERS (OCEAN)

2 Ex-US MSF TYPE

SEPARACION (ex-USS *Skirmish*, MSF 303) BM 454
TORTUGERO (ex-USS *Signet*, MSF 302) BM 455

Displacement, tons	650 standard; 900 full load
Dimensions, feet	180·0 wl; 184·5 oa × 33·0 × 14·5
Guns	1—3 in; 2—40 mm AA; 6—20 mm AA
Main engines	2 diesels; 2 shafts; 1 710 bhp = 14 knots
Range, miles	5 600 at 9 knots
Complement	90 (8 officers, 82 men)

Former US fleet minesweepers of the "Admirable" class. Completed in 1943. Purchased on 13 Jan 1965.

SEPARACION *1972, Dominican Navy*

AMPHIBIOUS FORCES

1 Ex-US LSM

SIRIO (ex-USS *LSM* 483) 301 (ex-BA 104)

Displacement, tons	734 standard; 1 100 full load
Dimensions, feet	196 wl; 203·5 oa × 34 × 10
Main engines	2 General Motors diesels; 2 shafts; 1 800 bhp = 14 knots
Oil fuel, tons	164
Complement	30

Ex-United States *LSM* (Medium Landing Ship). Built by Brown Shipbuilding Co, Houston, Texas. Laid down on 17 Feb 1945, launched on 10 Mar 1945 and completed on 13 April 1945. Transferred to the Dominican Navy in 1960. Refitted in Dominican Republic in 1970.

SIRIO *1968, Dominican Navy*

2 LCUs

ENRIQUILLO (ex-*17 de Julio*) 303 (ex-LA 3) **SAMANA** 302 (ex-LA 2)

Displacement, tons	150 standard; 310 full load
Dimensions, feet	105 wl; 119·5 oa × 36 × 3
Gun	1 50 cal
Main engines	3 General Motors diesels; 441 bhp = 8 knots
Oil fuel, tons	80
Complement	17

Both built by Astilleros Navales Dominicanos in 1957-58. The new *Samana*, LA 2, replaced the *Samana* LA 2 lost in bad weather. *Enriquillo* (ex-17 *de Julio*) was launched on 24 Oct 1957. Renamed in 1962.

SAMANA *1972, Dominican Navy*

SURVEY VESSELS

CAPOTILLO (ex-*Camillia*) (ex-FB 101) 1

Displacement, tons	337
Dimensions, feet	117 × 24 × 7·8
Main engines	2 Diesels; 880 bhp = 10 knots
Complement	29

Built in the United States in 1911. Acquired from the United States Coast Guard in 1949. Underwent a major refit in Dominican Republic in 1970.

CAONABO LA 5

Displacement, tons	12
Dimensions, feet	53 × 9 × 4
Main engines	2 motors; 500 hp = 14 knots
Complement	6

Acquired for the Hydrographic Service of the Navy in 1960.

CAONABO *1971*

TANKERS

2 Ex-US YO TYPE

CAPITAN W ARVELO BT 4 (ex-USS *YO 215*) **CAPITAN BEOTEGUI** BT 5 (ex-US *YO 213*)

Displacement, tons	370 light; 1 400 full load
Dimensions, feet	174·0 × 32·0 × 13·0
Gun	1—20 mm
Main engines	1 Fairbanks-Morse diesel; 525 bhp = 8 knots max
Capacity	6 570 barrels
Complement	27

Former United States self-propelled fuel oil barges. Both built by Ira S. Bushey & Sons, Inc, Brooklyn, New York in 1943-45. Loaned by the USA in Mar 1964.

TUGS

1 Ex-US "APACHE" CLASS

MACORIX RM 21 (ex-USS *Kiowa* ATF 72)

Displacement, tons	1 235 standard; 1 675 full load
Dimensions, feet	195 wl; 205 oa × 38·5 × 15·5
Gun	1—3 in 50 cal LA
Main engines	Diesel-electric; 1 shaft; 3 000 bhp = 15 knots
Complement	85

Built in USA—launched 5 Nov 1942. Carries additional salvage equipment. Transferred 16 Oct 1972.

MACORIX *1970, USN*

1 Ex-US "MARICOPA" CLASS

CAOMABO RM 18 (ex-USS *Sagamore* ATA 208)

Displacement, tons	534 standard; 835 full load
Dimensions, feet	143 oa × 33·9 × 13
Gun	1—3 in 50 cal
Main engines	2 GM diesel-electric; 1 shaft; 1 500 bhp = 13 knots

Completed 1944. Transferred 1 Feb 1972.

2 "HERCULES" CLASS

HERCULES RP 12 (ex-R 2) **GUACANAGARIX** RP 13 (ex-R 5)

Displacement, tons	200 (approx)
Dimensions, feet	70·0 × 15·6 × 9·0
Main engines	1 Caterpillar motor; 500 hp; 1 225 rpm
Complement	8 to 11

Small tugs of coastal type built by Astilleros Navalis Dominicos in 1960.

BOHECHIO RP 16 **CALDERAS** RP 19 **CONSUELO** RP 18 **MAGUANA** RP 14 (ex-R 10) **ISABELA** RP 20 (ex-R 1) **HAINA** RP 17 **SANTANA** RP 15 (ex-R 7)

+1 Ex-US YTL

Small tugs for harbour and coastal use. Not all of uniform type and dimensions.

ECUADOR

Administration

Minister of Defence:
General Victor Aulestia

Commander-in-Chief of the Navy:
Rear Admiral Reinaldo Vallejo Vivas

Diplomatic Representation

Naval Attaché in London:
Rear Admiral G. Jarrin

Naval Attaché in Washington:
Commander M. Valviviezo

Strength of the Fleet

Type	*Active*	*Building*
Frigates	3	—
Corvettes	2	—
Fast Attack Craft (Patrol)	3	3
Large Patrol Craft	2	—
Coastal Patrol Craft	6	—
LSM's	2	—
Survey Ship	1	—
Tugs	3	—
Supply Ship (Small)	1	—
Auxiliary Dock	1	—
Miscellaneous	3	—

New Construction

The Ecuadorian Navy, after considering the purchase of two "Whitby" class frigates from UK is now investigating new construction frigates.

Disposals

Frigates
1972 *Guayas*

Prefix to Ships' Names

The names of Ecuadorian naval vessels are prefaced by "BAE"

Establishments

The Naval Academy is in Salinas

Naval Bases

Guayaquil (main Naval base), San Lorenzo and Galapagos Island (small base)

Naval Air

1 Cessna 177 and 1 Cessna 320 work with the Navy.

Personnel

(a) 1975: Total 3 800 (300 officers and 3 500 men)
(b) Two years selective National Service

Mercantile Marine

Lloyd's Register of Shipping:
38 vessels of 128 473 tons gross

FRIGATES

1 Ex-US APD TYPE

25 DE JULIO D 1 (ex-E 12)
(ex-*Enright*, APD 66, ex-DE 216)

Displacement, tons	1 400 standard; 2 130 full load
Dimensions, feet	306·0 oa × 37·0 × 12·6
Guns	1—5 in 38 cal; 4—40 mm
A/S weapons	DC racks
Boilers	2 "D" Express
Main engines	GE geared tubines with electric drive; 2 shafts; 12 000 shp = 23 knots
Range, miles	2 000 at 23 knots
Complement	204

Former US high speed transport (modified destroyer escort). Built by the Navy Yard, Philadelphia, Pa. Laid down on 22 Feb 1943, launched on 29 May 1943 and completed on 21 Sep 1943. Transferred to Ecuador on 14 July 1967 under MAP. Could carry 162 troops.

25 DE JULIO (Now D 1) *1968, Ecuadorian Navy*

2 Ex-BRITISH "HUNT" CLASS (TYPE 1)

Name	*Pennant No.*	*Builders*	*Laid down*	*Launched*	*Completed*
PRESIDENTE ALFARO (ex-HMS *Quantock*)	D 2 (ex-D 01)	Scotts' S.B. & Eng Co Ltd, Greenock	26 July 1939	22 Apr 1940	6 Feb 1941
PRESIDENTE VELASCO IBARRA (ex-HMS *Meynell*)	D 3 (ex-D 02)	Swan Hunter & Wigham Richardson, Wallsend	10 Aug 1939	7 June 1940	30 Dec 1940

Displacement, tons	1 000 standard; 1 490 full load
Length, feet (*metres*)	272·3 (*83·0*) pp; 280 (*85·4*) oa
Beam, feet (*metres*)	29 (*8·8*)
Draught, feet (*metres*)	14 (*4·3*)
Guns	4—4 in (*102 mm*); 2—40 mm (twin); 2—20 mm
A/S weapons	DC throwers, DC racks
Boilers	2 Admiralty 3-drum
Main engines	Parsons geared turbines (by Wallsend Slipway in *Presidente Velasco Ibarra*) 19 000 shp; 2 shafts
Speed, knots	23
Range, miles	2 000 at 12 knots; 800 at 25 knots
Oil fuel, tons	280
Complement	146

PRESIDENTE ALFARO *1970, Ecuadorian Navy*

"Hunt" class, Type 1, purchased by Ecuador from Great Britain on 18 Oct 1954, and refitted by J. Samuel White & Co. Ltd. Cowes, Isle of Wight. *Quantock* was taken over by the Ecuadorian Navy in Portsmouth Dockyard on 16 Aug 1955, when she was renamed *Presidente Alfaro*. Sister ship *Meynell* was transferred to the Ecuadorian Navy and renamed *Presidente Velasco Ibarra* in Aug 1955.

CORVETTES

2 Ex-US PCE TYPE

ESMERALDAS (ex-E 22, ex-E 03)
(ex-USS *Eunice*, PCE 846) P 22
MANIBA (ex-E 23, ex-E 02)
(ex-USS *Pascagoula*, PCE 874) P 23

Displacement, tons	640 standard; 903 full load
Dimensions, feet	180 wl; 184·5 oa × 33 × 9·5
Guns	1—3 in dual purpose; 6—40 mm AA
A/S weapons	4 DCT; 2 DC Racks
Main engines	GM diesels; 2 shafts; 1 800 bhp = 15·4 knots
Range, miles	4 300 at 10 knots
Complement	100 officers and men

Former United States patrol vessels (180 ft Escorts) completed on 4 Mar 1944 and 31 Dec 1943 respectively and transferred from the US Navy to the Ecuadorian Navy on 29 Nov amd 5 Dec 1960.

MANABI *1974*

LIGHT FORCES

3 + 3 "MANTA" CLASS (FAST ATTACK CRAFT—PATROL)

MANTA LT 91 **TENA** LT 93 **TULCAN** LT 92

Displacement, tons	119 standard; 134 full load
Dimensions, feet (*m*)	119·4 × 19·1 × 6·0 (*36 × 5·8 × 1·7*)
Guns	1—20 mm; 1—81 mm rocket launcher
Torpedo tubes	2—21 inch
Machinery	Diesels; 3 shafts; 9 000 bhp = 35 knots
Range, miles	700 at 30 knots; 1 500 at 15 knots
Complement	19

Built by Lürssen Werft, Bremen 1970-71. 3 further boats of this class, possibly armed with Exocet MM 38, are planned.

MANTA *1972, Ecuadorian Navy*

2 Ex-US PGM TYPE (LARGE PATROL CRAFT)

GUAYAQUIL (ex-US *PGM* 76) LC 62 (ex-LC 72)
QUITO (ex-US *PGM* 75) LC 61 (ex-LC 71)

Displacement, tons	130 standard; 147 full load
Dimensions, ft (*m*)	101 oa × 21 × 6 (*30·8 × 6·4 × 1·9*)
Guns	1—40 mm; 2—20 mm
Main engines	4 diesels; 2 shafts; 2 200 bhp = 21 knots
Range, miles	1 500 at cruising speed
Complement	15

US built. Transferred to the Ecuadorian Navy under MAP on 30 Nov 1965.

GUAYAQUIL *1967, Ecuadorian Navy*

6 ML TYPE (COASTAL PATROL CRAFT)

LSP 1 **LSP 2** **LSP 3** **LSP 4** **LSP 5** **LSP 6**

Displacement, tons	45 standard; 64 full load
Dimensions, ft (*m*)	76·8 × 13·5 × 6·3 (*23·4 × 4·6 × 1·8*)
Guns	Light MG
Main engines	Bohn & Kähler diesel; 2 shafts; 1 200 bhp = 22 knots
Range, miles	550 at 16 knots
Complement	9

Built by Hermann Havighorst, Bremen-Blumenthal. Ordered in 1954. First two were delivered in Aug 1954 and the remainder in 1955. Pennant Nos. LP 81 to LP 86.

LSP 6 *1963, Ecuadorian Navy*

AMPHIBIOUS SHIPS

JAMBELI (ex-USS *LSM* 539) T 31 **TARQUI** (ex-USS *LSM* 555) T 32

Displacement, tons	743 beaching; 1 095 full load
Dimensions, ft (*m*)	196·5 wl; 203·0 oa × 34·0 × 7·9 (*61·9 × 10·3 × 2·4*)
Guns	2—40 mm
Range, miles	2 500 at 12 knots
Main engines	Diesels; 2 shafts; 2 800 bhp = 12·5 knots

Former US Landing Ships. Medium. *Jambeli* was laid down by Brown S.B. Co, Houston, on 10 May 1945. *Tarqui* was laid down by the Navy Yard, Charleston, SC on 3 Mar 1945 and launched on 22 Mar 1945. Purchased from USA in 1958 and transferred to the Ecuadorian Navy at Green Cove Springs, Florida in Nov 1958.

JAMBELI *1967, Ecuadorian Navy*

SURVEY SHIP

ORION (ex-USS *Mulberry*, AN 27) 101

Displacement, tons	560 standard; 805 full load
Dimensions, feet	146 wl; 163 oa × 30·5 × 11·8
Gun	1—3 in
Main engines	Diesel-electric; 800 bhp = 13 knots
Complement	35

Former United States netlayer. Built by Commercial Iron Works, Portland, Oregon. Launched on 26 Mar 1941. Loaned by US under MAP. Transferred to Ecuador in Nov 1965.

TUGS

CAYAMBE (ex-*Los Rios*, ex-USS *Cusabo, ATF* 155) R 101 (ex-R 51, ex-R 01)

Displacement, tons	1 235 standard; 1 675 full load
Dimensions, feet	195 wl; 205 oa × 38·5 × 15·5
Guns	1—3 in; 4—40 mm; 2—20 mm
Main engines	4 diesels with electric drive; 3 000 bhp = 16·5 knots
Complement	85

Former US "Apache" class fleet ocean tug. Launched on 26 Feb 1945. Fitted with powerful pumps and other salvage equipment. Transferred to Ecuador by lease on 2 Nov 1960 and renamed *Los Rios*. Again renamed *Cayambe* in 1966.

CAYAMBE *1970, Ecuadorian Navy*

SANGAY (ex-*Loja*) R 102 (ex-R 52)

Displacement, tons	295 light; 390 full load
Dimensions, feet	107 × 26 × 14
Main engines	Fairbanks Morse diesel; speed = 12 knots

Built in 1952. Acquired by the Ecuadorian Navy in 1964. Renamed in 1966.

COTOPAXI (ex-*R. T. Ellis*) R 103 (ex-R 53)

Displacement, tons	150
Dimensions, feet	82 × 21 × 8
Main engines	Diesel; 1 shaft; 650 bhp = 9 knots

Former US tug. Built by Equitable Building Co, Incorp. Purchased from the United States in 1947.

MISCELLANEOUS

CALICUCHIMA (ex-US *FS* 525) T 34 (ex-T 42) (SUPPLY SHIP).

Displacement, tons	650 light; 950 full load
Dimensions, feet	176 × 32 × 14
Main engines	Diesels; 2 shafts; 500 bhp = 11 knots

Former United States small cargo ship of the Army FS type. Leased to Ecuador on 8 Apr 1963 and purchased in April 1969. Provides service to the Galapagos Islands.

2 Ex-USN YP

ISLA DE LA PLATA UT 111 **ISLA DE PUNA** UT 112

Transferred 1962. Coastguard utility boats.

PUTU MAYO BT 62 (ex-USN YR 34)

Repair barge leased July 1962.

ATAHUALPA (ex-US *YW* 131) T 33 (ex-T 41, ex-A 01) (WATER BOAT)

Displacement, tons	415 light; 1 235 full load
Dimensions, feet	174·0 × 32·0 × 15·0
Main engines	GM diesels; 750 bhp = 11·5 knots

Built by Leatham D. Smith SB Co, Sturgeon Bay in 1945. Transferred from USA in Mar 1963. Acquired by the Ecuadorian Navy on 2 May 1963.

AMAZONAS (ex-US *ARD* 17) (AUXILIARY DOCK)

Measurement, tons	3 500 lifting capacity
Dimensions, feet	491·7 oa × 81·0 oa × 32·9

Former United States auxiliary floating dock. Built in 1943-44. Transferred on loan on 7 Jan 1961. Suitable for docking destroyers and landing ships. Dry dock companion craft YFND 20 was leased on 2 Nov 1961.

Note. 1 40 ft CGB transferred by USA 1971.

EGYPT

Administration

Commander Naval Forces:
Vice-Admiral Fuad Zikry

Diplomatic Representation

Defence Attaché in London:
Brigadier-General A. Mohamed Ali

Personnel

(a) 1975: 15 000 officers and men, including the Coast Guard
(b) 3 years National Service

Strength of the Fleet

Type	*Active*	*Building*
Destroyers	5	—
Frigates	3	—
Corvettes	12	—
Submarines (patrol)	12	—
Fast Attack Craft (Missile)	12	—
Fast Attack Craft (Torpedo)	36	—
Coastal Patrol Craft	?	—
LCTs	3	—
LCU's	14	—
Minesweepers (Ocean)	10	—
Minesweepers (Inshore)	2	—
Training Ships	2	—
Tugs	4	—

Bases

Alexandria, Port Said, Mersa Matru, Port Tewfik and Berenice (Ras Banas) on the Red Sea.

Coastal Defences

The Samlet missiles employed for Coastal Defence are Naval-manned.

Mercantile Marine

Lloyd's Register of Shipping:
134 vessels of 248 591 tons gross

DESTROYERS

4 Ex-USSR "SKORY" CLASS

AL NASSER **DAMIETTE**
AL ZAFFER **SUEZ**

Displacement, tons	2 600 standard; 3 500 full load
Length, feet (*metres*)	395·2 (*120·5*)
Beam, feet (*metres*)	38·7 (*11·8*)
Draught, feet (*metres*)	15·1 (*4·6*)
Guns,	4—5·1 in (*130 mm*) 50 cal. 2—3·4 in (*88 mm*); 8—37 mm (unmodified); 4—57 mm (quad); 4—37 mm (twins) (modified)
A/S weapons	4 DCT (unmodified) 2—12 barrelled MBU 2500A (Modified)
Torpedo tubes	10—21 in (*533 mm*) in two mounts (unmodified); 1 mounting with 5 tubes (modified)
Mines	80 can be carried
Boilers	3
Main engines	Geared turbines; 2 shafts; 60 000 shp
Speed, knots	35
Range, miles	4 000 at 15 knots
Complement	260

SKORY *1966*

Former "Skory" class destroyers of the Soviet Navy. Launched in 1951. *Al Nasser* and *Al Zaffer* were delivered to the Egyptian Navy on 11 June 1956 at Alexandria. Two more were delivered at Alexandria in Jan 1962. In April 1967 one pair was exchanged for ships with modified secondary and A/S armament.

RADAR. Search: Probably S Band. Tactical: Probably C Band. Fire Control: Hawkscreech.

1 Ex-BRITISH "Z" CLASS

EL FATEH (ex-HMS *Zenith*)

Name	*Builders*	*Laid down*	*Launched*	*Completed*
EL FATEH (ex-HMS *Zenith*)	Wm. Denny & Bros Dumbarton	19 May 1942	5 June 1944	22 Dec 1944

Displacement, tons	1 730 standard; 2 575 full load
Length, feet (*metres*)	350 (*106·8*) wl; 362·8 (*110·6*) oa
Beam, feet (*metres*)	35·7 (*10·9*)
Draught, feet (*metres*)	17·1 (*5·2*)
Guns,	4—4·5 in (*115 mm*) 6—40 mm
A/S weapons	4 DCT
Boilers	2 Admiralty 3-drum
Main engines	Parsons geared turbines; 2 shafts; 40 000 shp
Speed, knots	31
Radius, miles	2 800 at 20 knots
Oil fuel, tons	580
Complement	250

GENERAL
Purchased from Great Britain in 1955. Before being taken over by Egypt, *El Fateh* was refitted by John I. Thornycroft & Co Ltd, Woolston, Southampton in July 1956, subsequently modernised by J. S. White & Co Ltd, Cowes completing July 1964.

RADAR. Search: Type 960 Metric wavelength. Tactical: Type 293. S Band. Fire Control: X Band.

EL FATEH

FRIGATES

1 EX-BRITISH "BLACK SWAN" CLASS

Name	*No.*	*Builders*	*Laid down*	*Launched*	*Completed*
TARIK (ex-*Malek Farouq*, ex-HMS *Whimbrel*)	42	Yarrow & Co Ltd, Glasgow	31 Oct 1941	25 Aug 1942	13 Jan 1943

Displacement, tons	1 490 standard; 1 925 full load
Length, feet (*metres*)	283 (*86·3*) pp; 299·5 (*91·3*) oa
Beam, feet (*metres*)	38·5 (*11·7*)
Draught, feet (*metres*)	14·0 (*4·3*)
Guns,	6—4 in (*102 mm*) 4—40 mm; 2—20 mm
A/S weapons	4 DCT
Boilers	2 three-drum type
Main engines	Geared turbines; 2 shafts; 4 300 shp
Speed, knots	19·75
Range, miles	4 500 at 12 knots
Oil fuel, tons	370
Complement	180

Transferred from Great Britain in Nov 1949.

TARIK

Frigates—*continued*

1 Ex-BRITISH "RIVER" CLASS

Name	*No*	*Builders*	*Laid down*	*Launched*	*Completed*
RASHID (ex-HMS *Spey*)	43	Smith's Dock Co Ltd.	18 July 1941	10 Dec 1941	19 May 1942

Displacement, tons	1 490 standard; 2 216 full load
Length, feet (*metres*)	283 (*86·3*) pp; 301·5 (*91·9*) oa
Beam, feet (*metres*)	36·7 (*11·2*)
Draught, feet (*metres*)	14·1 (*4·3*)
Guns,	1—4 in (*102 mm*) 2—40 mm; 6—20 mm
A/S weapons	4 DCT
Boilers	2 Admiralty 3-drum type
Main engines	Triple expansion; 2 shafts; 5 500 ihp
Speed, knots	18
Range, miles	7 700 at 12 knots
Oil fuel, tons	640
Complement	180

RASHID *1968*

1 Ex-BRITISH "HUNT" CLASS

Name	*No.*	*Builders*	*Laid down*	*Launched*	*Completed*
PORT SAID (ex-*Mohamed Ali*, ex-*Ibrahim el Awal*, ex-HMS *Cottesmore*)	11	Yarrow & Co. Ltd, Scotstoun, Glasgow	12 Dec 1939	5 Sep 1940	29 Dec 1940

Displacement, tons	1 000 standard; 1 490 full load
Length, feet (*metres*)	273 (*83·2*) wl; 280 (*85·3*) oa
Beam, feet (*metres*)	29 (*8·8*)
Draught, feet (*metres*)	15·1 (*4·3*) max
Guns,	4—4 in (*103 mm*) 2—37 mm; 2—50 cal (twin)
A/S weapons	2 DCT
Boilers	2 three-drum type
Main engines	Parsons geared turbines; 2 shafts; 19 000 shp
Speed, knots	25
Range, miles	2 000 at 12 knots
Oil fuel, tons	280
Complement	146

Transferred from the British Navy to the Egyptian Navy in July 1950: Sailed for Egypt in April 1951, after a nine months refit by J. Samuel White & Co Ltd, Cowes.

PORT SAID (ex-*Mohamed Ali*)

SUBMARINES

6 Ex-USSR "ROMEO" CLASS

Displacement, tons	1 100 surface; 1 600 dived
Length, feet (*metres*)	246·0 (*75·0*)
Beam, feet (*metres*)	24·0 (*7·3*)
Draught, feet (*metres*)	14·5 (*4·4*)
Torpedo tubes	6—21 in (*533 mm*) bow
Main machinery	2 Diesels; 4 000 bhp 2 Electric motors; 4 000 hp
Speed, knots	17 surface; 14 dived
Complement	65

One "Romeo" was transferred to Egypt in Feb 1966. Two more replaced "Whiskys" in May 1966 and another pair was delivered later that year. The sixth boat joined in 1969.

"ROMEO" Class *1968, Skyfotos*

6 Ex-USSR "WHISKY" CLASS

Displacement, tons	1 030 surface; 1 180 dived
Length, feet (*metres*)	240 (*73·2*) oa
Beam, feet (*metres*)	22 (*6·7*)
Draught, feet (*metres*)	15 (*4·6*)
Torpedo tubes	6—21 in (*533 mm*); 4 bow, 2 stern
Main machinery	2 diesels; 4 000 bhp; 2 electric motors; 2 500 hp
Speed, knots	17 surface; 15 dived
Range, miles	13 000 at 8 knots surfaced
Complement	60

The first four "Whisky" class were transferred from the Soviet Navy to the Egyptian Navy in June 1957. Three more arrived at Alexandria on 24 Jan 1958. Another was transferred to Egypt at Alexandria in Jan 1962. Two were replaced by "Romeos" in Feb 1966.
Two "Whisky" class sailed from Alexandria to Leningrad in late 1971 under escort, being replaced the following year.

"ROMEO" Class

"WHISKY" Class

CORVETTES

12 Ex-USSR "SO I" CLASS

Displacement, tons	215 light; 250 full load
Dimensions, ft (*m*)	138·6 × 20 × 9·2 (*42·3 × 6·1 × 2·8*)
Guns	4—25 mm (2 twin mountings)
A/S weapons	4 five-barrelled ahead throwing rocket launchers
Main engines	3 diesel; 6 000 bhp = 29 knots
Range, miles	1 100 at 13 knots
Complement	30

Former Soviet submarine chasers. Eight reported to have been transferred by the USSR to Egypt in 1962 to 1967 and four others later.

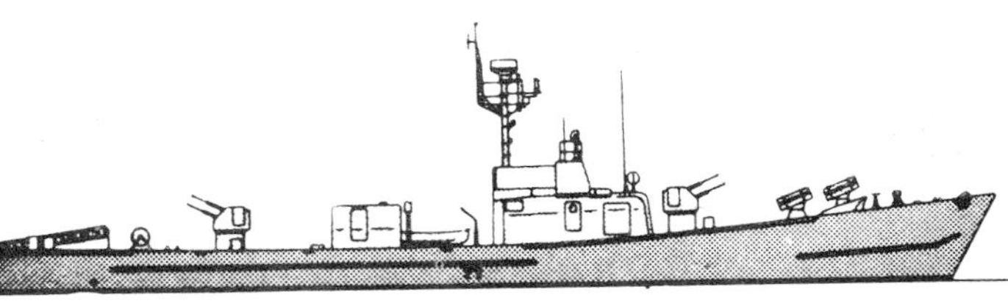

"SO I" Class

LIGHT FORCES

8 Ex-USSR "OSA" CLASS (FAST ATTACK CRAFT—MISSILE)

Displacement, tons	165 standard; 200 full load
Dimensions, ft (*m*)	128·7 × 25·1 × 5·9 (*39·3 × 7·7 × 1·8*)
Missiles	4 launchers in two pairs abreast for SSN 2 system
Guns	4—30 mm (2 twin, 1 forward, 1 aft)
Main engines	3 diesels; 13 000 bhp = 32 knots
Complement	25

Reported to have been delivered to Egypt by the Soviet Navy in 1966. Four reported sunk during the Israeli War October 1973.

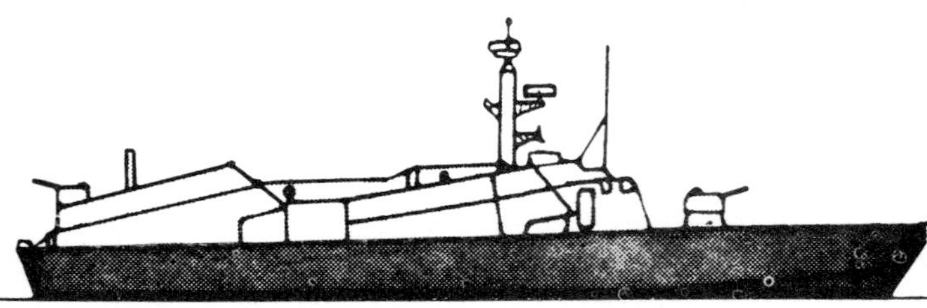

"OSA" Class

4 Ex-USSR "KOMAR" CLASS (FAST ATTACK CRAFT—MISSILE)

Displacement, tons	70 standard; 80 full load
Dimensions, ft (*m*)	83·6 × 19·8 × 5·0 (*25·5 × 6 × 1·8*)
Missiles	2 launchers for SSN-2 system
Guns	2—25 mm
Main engines	4 diesels; 4 shafts; 4 800 hp = 40 knots
Range, miles	400 at 30 knots

Former Soviet missile boats transferred from the USSR in 1962 to 1967. One of this type was sunk by Israeli jets on 16 May 1970. Two reported sunk in Israeli War October 1973.

"KOMAR" Class *1966, Col. Bjorn Borg*

6 Ex-USSR "SHERSHEN" CLASS (FAST ATTACK CRAFT—TORPEDO)

Displacement, tons	150 standard; 160 full load
Dimensions, ft (*m*)	115·5 × 23 × 5 (*35·2 × 7·1 × 1·5*)
Guns	4—30 mm AA (2 twin)
Torpedo tubes	4—21 in (single)
A/S weapons	12 DC
Main engines	3 diesels; 3 shafts; 13 000 hp = 41 knots
Complement	16

One delivered from USSR in Feb 1967, two more in Oct 1967, and three since.

"SHERSHEN" Class

24 Ex-USSR "P 6" CLASS (FAST ATTACK CRAFT—TORPEDO)

Displacement, tons	66 standard; 75 full load
Dimensions, ft (*m*)	84·2 × 20 × 6 (*25·7 × 6·1 × 1·8*)
Guns	2 or 4—25 mm
Tubes	2—21 in
Main engines	4 diesels; 4 shafts; 4 800 hp = 43 knots
Range, miles	450 at 30 knots
Complement	25

The first twelve boats arrived at Alexandria on 19 Apr 1956, 6 more in 1960. Two were destroyed by British naval aircraft on 4 Nov 1956, two were sunk by the Israeli destroyer *Elath* off Sinai on 12 July 1967, two by Israeli MTBs off Sinai coast on 11 July 1967, two by Israeli air attacks in 1969, and two in the Red Sea on 22 Jan 1970.

"P 6" Class with 6 barrelled rocket launcher *10/1974*

6 Ex-YUGOSLAVIAN TYPE (FAST ATTACK CRAFT—TORPEDO)

Displacement, tons	55 standard; 60 full load
Dimensions, ft (*m*)	69 pp; 78 oa × 21·3 × 7·8 (*23·8 oa × 6·5 × 2·4*)
Gun	1—40 mm
Tubes	2
Main engines	3 Packard motors; 3 shafts; 5 000 bhp = 36 knots
Complement	14

Purchased from Yugoslavia in 1956. Similar to the boats of the US "Higgins" class.

BERTRAM TYPE (COASTAL PATROL CRAFT)

An unknown number of this type, approximately 8 tons, now in service.

"BERTRAM" Type *10/1974*

Note. Two Egyptian built patrol boats of 110 tons (Nisr 1 and 2) reported launched May 1963.

AMPHIBIOUS FORCES

2 Ex-USSR "POLNOCNY" CLASS
(LCT)

Displacement, tons	780 standard; 1 000 full load
Dimensions, ft (*m*)	246 × 29·5 × 9·8 (*75 × 9 × 3*)
Guns	2—30 mm (twin)
A/S weapons	2—18 barrelled MBUs
Main engines	2 diesels; 5 000 bhp = 18 knots

Can carry 6 tanks. Transferred early 1970's.

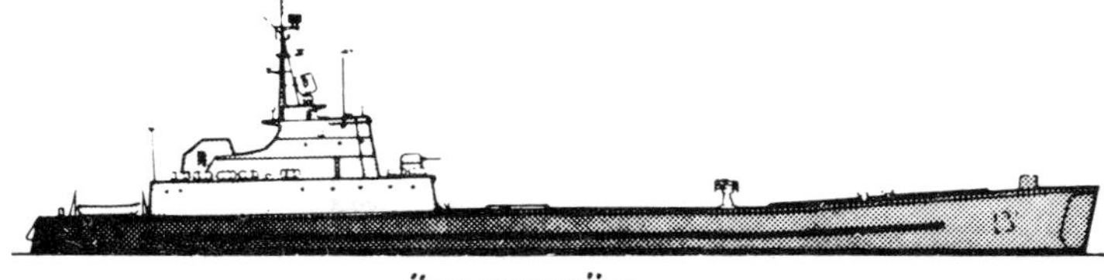

"POLNOCNY" Class

10 Ex-USSR "VYDRA" CLASS (LCU)

Displacement, tons	300 standard; 500 full load
Dimensions, feet	157·4 × 24·6 × 7·2
Main engines	2 diesels; 2 shafts; 400 bhp = 15 knots

Can carry and land up to 250 tons of military equipment and stores

4 Ex-USSR "SMB 1" CLASS (LCU)

Displacement, tons	200 standard; 420 full load
Dimensions, feet	157·5 × 21·3 × 5·6
Main engines	2 diesels; 2 shafts; 400 hp speed = 11 knots

Several utility landing craft of the MP-SMB 1, delivered to the Egyptian Navy in 1965. Predecessors of the "Vydra" type. Can carry 150 tons of military equipment. (The tank landing ship *Aka* (ex-LST 178) was sunk as a block-ship near Lake Timsah in the Suez canal on 1 Nov 1956). The LCM type was deleted in 1971.

MINEWARFARE FORCES

6 Ex-USSR "T 43" CLASS (MINESWEEPERS—OCEAN)

ASSIUT **BAHAIRA** **CHARKIEH** **DAKHALIA** **GHARBIA** **SINAI**

Displacement, tons	500 standard; 610 full load
Dimensions, feet	190·2 × 28·2 × 6·9 (*58·0 × 8·6 × 2·1*)
Gun	4—37 mm; 4—25 mm
Main engines	2 diesels; 2 shafts; 2 000 hp = 17 knots
Range, miles	1 600 at 10 knots
Complement	40

Three were transferred from the Soviet Navy and delivered to Egypt 1956-59, and three since 1970. *Miniya* was sunk by Israeli air attack in the Gulf of Suez on 6 Feb 1970 but was later replaced.

"T 43" Class

4 Ex-USSR "YURKA" CLASS (MINESWEEPERS—OCEAN)

ASWAN **GIZA** **SOHAG** **QENA**

Displacement, tons	500 standard; 550 full load
Dimensions, ft (*m*)	172 × 31 × 8·9 × (*52·5 × 9·5 × 2·7*)
Guns	4—30 mm AA (2 twin)
Main engines	2 diesels; 4 000 bhp = 18 knots

Steel-hulled minesweepers transferred from USSR 1970-71.

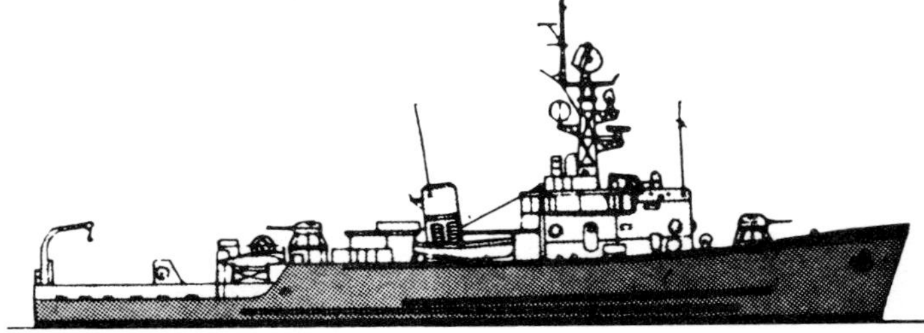

"YURKA" Class *USSR*

2 Ex-USSR "T 301" CLASS (MINESWEEPERS—INSHORE)

Displacement, tons	130 standard; 180 full load
Dimensions, ft (*m*)	124·6 × 19·7 × 4·9 (*39 × 5·5 × 1·5*)
Guns	2—37 mm; 2—MG
Main engines	2 Diesels; 2 shafts; 1 440 hp = 17 knots
Range, miles	2 200 at 10 knots
Complement	30

Reported to have been transferred by the USSR to Egypt in 1962; a third ship may have been transferred later.

MISCELLANEOUS

4 Ex-USSR "OKHTENSKY" CLASS TUGS

A number of Soviet fleet tugs were reported transferred to the Egyptian Navy in 1966

SWIMMER DELIVERY VEHICLES

There is a strong underwater team in the Egyptian navy who use, amongst other equipment, the 2-man SDVs shown here. Range could be 4 hours at 3-4 knots.

SDV *10/1974*

2 TRAINING SHIPS

El Horria (ex-*Mahroussa*) of 4 560 tons, built by Sanuda, Poplar in 1865 and once the Egyptian Royal Yacht has been completely refitted and is used as a training ship.

Intishat, a smaller training ship.

EL SALVADOR

Personnel
(a) 1975: 130 officers and men
(b) Voluntary Service

Mercantile Marine

Lloyd's Register of Shipping: 2 vessels of 291 tons gross

PATROL BOATS

GC 1 (ex-*Fle-Ja-Lis*) **GC 2** (ex-*Nohaba*)

Displacement, tons	46
Dimensions, feet	72 oa × 16 × 5·5
Gun	1—20 mm
Main engines	2 diesels; 2 shafts; speed = 12 knots
Complement	16

Former British HDML type. Purchased from commercial sources in 1959.

GC 3 **GC 4**

Displacement, tons	14

USCG 40 ft type built in 1950.

GC 5

Displacement, tons	33
Dimensions, ft (*m*)	65 × 16·3 × 5·0 (*19·8 × 4·9 × 1·5*)
Guns	3 MG
Main engines	GM Diesels; 1 600 hp = 25 knots

Built by Sewart, USA in 1967. Transferred Sept 1967.

ETHIOPIA

Administration

All command arrangements under review.

Commander-in-Chief —

Chief of Staff: —

Naval Officer in Charge, "Haile Selassie I" Naval Base, Massawa:
Captain P. W. Stewart, RN(Retd)

Naval Establishments

"Haile Selassie I" Massawa: Naval Base and College, established in 1956.
Embaticalla: Marine Commando Training School.
Assab: Naval Base, expanding to include a ship repair facility.

Personnel

(a) 1975: 1 380 officers and men
(b) Voluntary Service

Mercantile Marine

Lloyd's Register of Shipping: 23 vessels of 25 034 tons gross

MINESWEEPERS (COASTAL)

1 Ex-NETHERLANDS "WILDERVANK" CLASS

MS 41 (ex-*Elst*, M 829)

Displacement, tons	373 standard; 417 full load
Dimensions, feet	149·8 oa × 28·0 × 7·5
Guns	2—40 mm AA
Main engines	2 diesels; 2 shafts; 2 500 bhp = 14 knots
Oil fuel, tons	25 tons
Range, miles	2 500 at 10 knots
Complement	38

Western Union type minesweeper of the "Wildervank" class built in the Netherlands in 1954-56. Purchased by Ethiopia and transferred from the Royal Netherlands Navy in 1971.

MISSILES. It has been reported that MS 41 has been fitted for launching SS-12 missiles.

MS 41 *1972*

TRAINING SHIP

ETHIOPIA (ex-USS *Orca*, AVP 49) A 01

Displacement, tons	1 766 standard; 2 800 full load
Dimensions, feet	300 wl; 310·8 oa × 41 × 13·5
Guns	1—5 in 38 cal; 5—40 mm AA
Main engines	2—sets diesels; 2 shafts; 6 080 bhp = 18·2 knots
Complement	215

Former United States seaplane tender. Built by Lake Washington Shipyard, Houghton Wash. Laid down 13 July 1942, launched on 4 Oct 1942 and completed on 23 Jan, 1944. Transferred from the US Navy in Jan 1962.

ETHIOPIA *1972, Imperial Ethiopian Navy*

LIGHT FORCES

5 PGM TYPE (LARGE PATROL CRAFT)

PC 11 (ex-USCG *WVP* 95304) **PC 13** (ex-USN *PGM* 53)
PC 12 (ex-USCG *WVP* 95310) **PC 14** (ex-USN *PGM* 54)
PC 15 (ex-USN *PGM* 58)

Displacement, tons	145·5 full load
Dimensions, feet	101·5 × 21 × 5
Guns	1—40 mm AA; 1—50 cal MG
Main engines	4 diesels; 2 shafts; 2 200 bhp = 21 knots
Range, miles	1 500 at cruising speed
Complement	20

PC 12 *1970, Imperial Ethiopian Navy*

4 "CAROLINE" CLASS (COASTAL PATROL CRAFT)

CAROLINE GB 22
JACQUELINE GB 24
JOHN GB 21
PATRICK GB 23

Length, feet	40
Guns	2—·50 calibre machine guns
Speed, knots	20 approx
Complement	7

Built by Seward Seacraft Inc, Berwick, La. *Caroline* and *John* were delivered in 1966, *Jacqueline* and *Patrick* in 1967. Their complement is 3 officers and 4 ratings or 2 officers and 5 ratings.

JOHN *1970, Imperial Ethiopian Navy*

LANDING CRAFT

There are 4 of the US LCM type.

LC 34 *1972, Imperial Ethiopian Navy*

FINLAND

Administration

Commander-in-Chief Finnish Navy:
Rear-Admiral S. O. Wikberg

Diplomatic Representation

Naval Attaché in London:
Captain Erik Wihtol

Naval Attaché in Washington:
Colonel T. O. Lehti

Naval Attaché in Moscow:
Colonel E. Pallasvirta

Naval Attaché in Paris:
Lieutenant-Colonel Erkki Palmujoki

Personnel

(a) 1972: 2 000 (150 officers and 1 850 ratings)
1973: 2 500 (200 officers and 2 300 ratings)
1974: 2 500 (200 officers and 2 300 ratings)
1975: 2 500 (200 officers and 2 300 ratings)
(b) 8-11 months National Service

Strength of the Fleet

Type	*Active*	*Building*
Frigates	2	—
Corvettes	2	—
Fast Attack Craft (Missile)	1	—
Fast Attack Craft (Gun)	15	—
Large Patrol Craft	4	—
Transports (LCUs)	11	—
Tugs	6	—
Cable Ship	1	—
Icebreakers	8	2
Coastguard Vessels	14	—

Disposals

COASTGUARD VESSELS

1970 VMV 11, 13, 19 and 20
1971 Aura

Treaty Limitations

The Finnish Navy is limited by the treaty of Paris 1947 to 10 000 tons of ships and 4 500 personnel. Submarines and motor torpedo boats are prohibited.

Hydrographic Department

This office and the Survey Ships come under the Ministry of Trade and Industry.

Coast Guard

All Coast Guard Vessels come under the Ministry of the Interior.

Icebreakers

All these ships work for the Board of Navigation.

Mercantile Marine

Lloyd's Register of Shipping:
362 vessels of 1 507 582 tons gross

FRIGATES

2 "UUSIMAA" CLASS

HÄMEENMAA **UUSIMAA**

Displacement, tons	1 200 standard; 1 600 full load
Length, feet (*metres*)	298·8 (*91*)
Beam, feet (*metres*)	33·7 (*10·2*)
Draught, feet (*metres*)	11 (*3·4*)
Guns	3—3·9 in (*100 mm*) dp single; 2—40 mm; 2—30 mm (twin) (in bow)
A/S weapons	1 Hedgehog; 4 DC projectors
Torpedo tubes	3—21 in (*533 mm*)
Mines	50 (capacity)
Main engines	Geared turbines; 2 shafts; 25 000 shp
Speed, knots	28
Boilers	2
Range, miles	2 500 at 15 knots
Complement	150

Former Soviet frigates of the "Riga" class. Purchased from the USSR and transferred to the Finnish Navy on 28 Apr 1964 and 12 May 1964, respectively. Armament modified in 1971.

UUSIMAA *1974, Finnish Navy—SA Kuva*

RADAR. Search: Slimnet. Fire Control: Wasphead, Sun Visor A. Navigation: Neptun. IFF: High Pole A.

MATTI KURKI (ex-HMS *Porlock Bay*, ex-*Loch Seaforth*, ex-*Loch Muick*)

Displacement, tons	1 580 standard; 2 420 full load
Length, feet (*metres*)	286·0 (*87·2*) pp; 307·5 (*93·7*) oa
Beam, feet (*metres*)	38·5 (*11·7*)
Draught, feet (*metres*)	15·2 (*4·6*)
Guns	4—4 in (*102 mm*); 2 twin; 6—40 mm AA (2 twin, 2 single)
Main engines	Triple expansion; 2 shafts; 5 500 ihp
Speed, knots	18
Boilers	2 Admiralty 3-drum
Range, miles	9 500 at 12 knots
Oil fuel, tons	724
Complement	160

Former British frigate of the "Bay" class. Built by Charles Hill & Sons, Bristol. Laid down on 22 Nov 1944, launched on 14 June 1945 and completed on 8 Mar 1946. Transferred in Mar 1962. Employed as a training ship (*Koululaiva*).

RADAR. Search and Tactical. Type 293.

MATTI KURKI *1972, Wright & Logan*

CORVETTES

2 "TURUNMAA" CLASS

KARJALA **TURUNMAA**

Displacement, tons	660 standard; 770 full load
Dimensions, ft (*m*)	243·1 × 25·6 × 7·9 (*74·1 × 7·8 × 2·4*)
Guns	1—4·7 in (*120 mm*) automatic dp forward; 2—40 mm AA; 2—30 mm AA (1 twin) aft
A/S weapons	Depth charge projectors
Main engines	CODOG (combined diesel or gas turbine). 3 Mercedes-Benz diesels; 3 990 bhp; 1 Rolls Royce Olympus gas turbine; 22 000 hp = 35 knots
Complement	70

Ordered on 23 Feb 1965 from Wärtsilä, Helsinki. Flus decked. Rocket flare guide rails on sides of 4·7 in turret. Fitted with Vosper Thornycroft fin stabilisers equipment. *Karjala* was launched on 16 Aug 1967 and completed on 21 Oct 1968. *Turunmaa* was launched on 11 July 1967 and completed on 29 Aug 1968.

RADAR. Search and Tactical: X Band. (HSA).

KARJALA *1971, Finnish Navy*

LIGHT FORCES

4 ex-USSR "OSA" CLASS (FAST ATTACK CRAFT—MISSILE)

Displacement, tons	165 standard; 200 full load
Dimensions, ft (*m*)	128·7 × 25·1 × 5·9 (*39·3 × 7·7 × 1·8*)
Missiles	4—SSN-2 system launchers
Guns	4—30 mm (twin)
Main engines	3 Diesels; 13 000 hp
Speed, knots	32
Range, miles	800 at 25 knots
Complement	25

Ordered from USSR for delivery 1974-75.

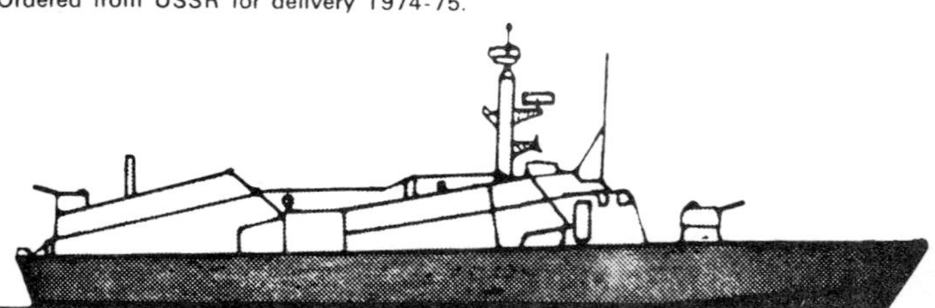

"OSA" Class

ISKU (FAST ATTACK CRAFT—MISSILE)

Displacement, tons	115
Dimensions, ft (*m*)	86·5 × 28·6 × 6·6 (*26 × 8·7 × 2*)
Missiles launchers	4 SSN-2 system launchers
Guns	2—30 mm (1 twin)
Main engines	4 diesels; 4 800 bhp = 25 knots

Guided missile craft of novel design completed for the Finnish Navy in 1970. Built at the Reposaaren Konepaja. The construction combines a missile boat armament on a landing craft hull. The missile launchers are of similar type to Soviet SSN-2 system.

ISKU *1972, Finnish Navy*

13 "NUOLI" CLASS (FAST ATTACK CRAFT—GUN)

NUOLI 1-13

Displacement, tons	45 standard; 64 full load
Dimensions, ft (*m*)	72·2 × 21·7 × 5·0 (*22 × 6·6 × 1·5*)
Guns	1—40 mm; 1—20 mm
A/S weapons	DCs
Main engines	3 diesels; 2 700 bhp = 40 knots
Complement	15

Designed and built by Laivateollisuus, Turku. First four were launched in 1961, five more in 1962 and two more in 1963. Fitted with X Band radar.

NUOLI 13 *1968, Finnish Navy*

TURSAS (LARGE PATROL CRAFT)

Displacement, tons	400
Dimensions, ft (*m*)	131·2 × 23·5 × 14 (*40 × 7·2 × 4·3*)
Main engines	Diesel; 620 bhp = 12 knots

Built by Crichton-Vulkan, Turku. Launched in 1933. Belongs to the Coast Guard.

TURSAS *1968, Finnish Navy*

2 "VASAMA" CLASS (FAST ATTACK CRAFT—GUN)

VASAMA 1 **VASAMA 2**

Displacement, tons	50 standard; 70 full load
Dimensions, ft (*m*)	67·0 pp; 71·5 oa × 19·5 × 6·0 (*21·8 oa × 5·9 × 1·8*)
Guns	2—40 mm
Main engines	2 Napier Deltic diesels; 5 000 bhp = 42 knots
Complement	20

British "Dark" type built by Saunders Roe (Anglesey) Ltd, Beaumaris, in 1955-57.

VASAMA 2 *1970, Finnish Navy*

VALPAS (LARGE PATROL CRAFT)

Displacement, tons	540
Dimensions, ft (*m*)	159·1 × 27·9 × 12·5 (*48·5 × 8·5 × 3·8*)
Main engines	Diesel; 1 800 bhp = 15 knots

Completed in 1971. Coastguard vessel built by Laivateollisuus, Turku.

VALPAS *1974, Finnish Navy*

SILMÄ (LARGE PATROL CRAFT)

Displacement, tons	500
Dimensions, ft (*m*)	160·8 × 27·2 × 11·8 (*49 × 8·3 × 3·6*)
Main engines	1 800 bhp = 15 knots

Coast Guard vessel built by Laivateollisuus, Turku, in 1962-63.

SILMÄ *1964, Finnish Navy*

UISKO (LARGE PATROL CRAFT)

Displacement, tons	400
Dimensions, ft (*m*)	141 × 24 × 12·8 (*43 × 7·3 × 3·9*)
Main engines	1 800 bhp = 15 knots

Coast Guard vessel built by Valmet, Helsinki. Launched in 1958. Completed in 1959.

UISKO *Finnish Navy*

Light Forces—*continued*

VIIMA

Displacement, tons	135
Dimensions, ft (*m*)	118·1 × 21·7 × 7·5 (*36 × 6·6 × 2·3*)
Gun	1—20 mm AA
Main engines	3 diesels; 4 050 hbp = 24 knots

Coast Guard patrol boat built by Laivateollisuus, Turku, Finland in 1964.

VIIMA *1974, Finnish Navy*

8 "KOSKELO" CLASS

KAAKKURI **KOSKELO** **TELKKA** **KURKI**
KIILSA **KUOVI** **KUIKKA** **TAVI**

Displacement, tons	75 standard; 97 full load
Dimensions, ft (*m*)	95·1 × 16·4 × 4·9 (*29 × 5 × 1·5*)
Guns	2—20 mm
Main engines	2 Mercedes-Benz diesels; 2 shafts; 1 000 bhp = 16 knots
Complement	8

Built of steel and strengthened against ice, *Koskelo* and *Kuikka* were completed in 1956. Remaining six were completed in 1958-60. Some have been modified—more powerful engines and new bridge arrangement.

KIILSA (new bridge) *1974, Finnish Navy*

5 "R" CLASS

RAISIO (No. 4) **RÖYTTA** (No. 5) **RUISSALO** (No. 3)

Displacement, tons	110 standard; 130 full load
Dimensions, ft (*m*)	108·3 × 18·0 × 5·9 (*33 × 5·5 × 1·8*)
Guns	1—40 mm; 1—20 mm
A/S weapons	1 Squid mortar
Main engines	2 Mercedes-Benz diesels; 2 500 bhp = 17 knots

Built by Laivateollisuus, Turku, in 1959.

RUISSALO *1969, Finnish Navy*

RIHTNIEMI (No. 1) **RYMÄTTYLÄ** (No. 2)

Displacement, tons	90 standard; 110 full load
Dimensions, ft (*m*)	101·7 × 18·7 × 5·9 (*31 × 5·6 × 1·8*)
Guns	1—40 mm; 1—20 mm
Main engines	2 Mercedes-Benz diesels; 1 400 bhp = 15 knots

Built by Rauma-Repola Shipyard. Ordered in July 1955, launched in 1956 and delivered on 20 May 1957. Controllable pitch propellers.

RIHTNIEMI *1968, Finnish Navy*

MINE WARFARE SHIPS

KEIHÄSSALMI

Displacement, tons	360
Dimensions, ft (*m*)	168 × 23 × 6 (*52 × 7 × 1·9*)
Guns	4—30 mm (twins); 2—20 mm
Mines	Up to 100 capacity
Main engines	2 Wärtsilä diesels; 2 shafts; 2 000 bhp = 15 knots
Complement	60

Of improved "Ruotsinsalmi" Class, built at Valmet, Helsinki under contract dated June 1955. Launched on 16 Mar 1957. Armament modified in 1972. X Band Search and Tactical radar.

KEIHÄSSALMI *1974, Finnish Navy*

RUOTSINSALMI

Displacement, tons	310
Dimensions, ft (*m*)	150 × 23 × 5 (*45 × 7 × 1·5*)
Guns	2—40 mm AA; 2—20 mm AA
Mines	Up to 100 capacity
Main engines	2 MAN diesels; 2 shafts; 1 200 bhp = 15 knots
Complement	60

RUOTSINSALMI *1969, Finnish Navy*

6 "KUHA" CLASS GRP TYPE

(MINESWEEPERS—INSHORE)

KUHA 21-26

Displacement, tons	c. 90
Dimensions, ft (*m*)	84 × 23 (*25·6 × 7*)
Guns	1/2—20 mm
Main engines	2 Diesels; 600 shp
Complement	15

Built by Laivateollisuus, Turku 1974-75. *Kuha 21* completed 28 June 1974. Hulls are of Glass Reinforced Plastic (GRP).

KUHA 22 *1974, Finnish Navy—SA Kuva*

MISCELLANEOUS

KORSHOLM (HQ SHIP)

Displacement, tons	650
Dimensions, ft (*m*)	160·8 × 27·9 × 10·8 (*49 × 8·5 × 3·3*)
Speed, knots	10·5

Converted merchant ship of the small passenger and cargo type. Built in 1931.

6 "KALA" CLASS

KALA 1-6

Displacement, tons	60
Dimensions, ft (*m*)	81·8 × 26·2 × 6 (*24·9 × 8 × 1·8*)
Main engines	2 diesels; 360 bhp = 9 knots

Launched in 1956. Completed in 1959. Of LCU (utility landing craft) type.

KALA 2 — *7/1974, Dittmair*

5 "KAVE" CLASS (SMALL TRANSPORTS)

KAVE 1-4 and 6

Displacement, tons	30
Dimensions, ft (*m*)	75·8 × 16·4 × 5·9 (*23·1 × 5 × 1·8*)
Gun	1—20 mm
Main engines	2 Diesels; 370 hp = 9 knots

LCU type. Built 1956-60

KAVE 4 — *1961, Finnish Navy*

3 "PANSIO" CLASS (TUG TYPE)

PANSIO (1947) **PORKKALA** (1940) **PUKKIO** (1939)

Displacement, tons	162 standard
Dimensions, ft (*m*)	92·0 × 21·5 × 9·0 (*28·1 × 6·6 × 2·7*)
Guns	1—40 mm AA; 1—20 mm AA
Main engines	Diesels; 300 bhp = 9 knots

Built by Valmet, Turku. Launch dates above. Vessels of the tug type used as transports, minesweeping tenders, minelayers and patrol vessels. Can carry 20 mines.

3 "PIRTTISAARI" CLASS TUGS

PIRTTISAARI (ex-*DR* 7) **PYHTÄA** (ex-*DR* 2) **PURHA** (ex-*DR* 10)

Displacement, tons	106
Dimensions, ft (*m*)	69 × 20 × 8·5 (*21 × 6·1 × 2·6*)
Gun	1—20 mm
Main engines	1 diesel; 400 bhp = 9 knots

Former US Army Tugs. Launched in 1943-44. General purpose vessels used as minesweepers, minelayers, patrol vessels, tenders, tugs or personnel transports. *DR 2* and *DR 7*, were adapted as the Coast Artillery transports *Pyhtää* and *Pirttisaari* in 1958 and 1959, respectively.

PIRTTISAARI — ***1970, Finnish Navy.***

PUTSAARI (CABLE SHIP)

Displacement, tons	430
Dimensions, ft (*m*)	147·6 × 38·5 × 9·8 (*44·8 × 11·7 × 3*)
Main engines	Diesel; 450 bhp = 10 knots

Built by Rauma Repola, Rauma. Launched in Dec 1965.

ICEBREAKERS

2 NEW CONSTRUCTION

URHO + 1

Displacement, tons	7 800
Dimensions, ft (*m*)	337·8 × 77·1 × 24·6 (*103 × 23·5 × 7·5*)
Aircraft	1 helicopter
Main engines	Diesel-electric; 5 diesels 20 000 bhp = 17 knots
Complement	57

Construction considerably larger than the "Tarmo" class which was ordered on 11 Dec 1970. Completed in January 1975. The second was ordered on 14 April 1971 for completion in Jan 1976. Fitted with two screws aft, taking 60% of available power and one forward, taking the remainder. Both from the Wärtsilä company.

3 "TARMO" CLASS

TARMO **VARMA** **APU**

Displacement, tons	4 890
Dimensions, ft (*m*)	281·0 × 71·0 × 21·0 (*85·7 × 21·7 × 6·4*)
Aircraft	1 helicopter
Main engines	Wärtsila-Sulzer diesels; electric drive; 4 shafts (2 screws forward 2 screws aft); 12 000 bhp = 17 knots

Built by Wärtsila, Helsinki. *Tarmo* was completed in 1963, *Varma* in 1968 (launched 29 Mar) and *Apu* on 25 Nov 1970.

TARMO — *1968, Finnish Navy*

3 "KARHU" CLASS

KARHU **MURTAJA** **SAMPO**

Displacement, tons	3 540
Dimensions, ft (*m*)	243·2 × 57 × 20 (*74·2 × 17·4 × 6·1*)
Main engines	Diesel-electric; 4 shafts; 7 500 bhp = 16 knots

Built by Wärtsilä, Helsinki. *Karhu* was launched on 22 Oct 1957, and completed at the end of 1958. *Murtaja* was launched on 23 Sep 1958. *Sampo* was completed in 1960.

VOIMA

Displacement, tons	4 415
Dimensions, ft (*m*)	274 oa × 63·7 × 20·3 (*83·6 × 19·4 × 6.2*)
Main engines	Diesels with electric drive; 4 shafts; 14 000 bhp = 16·5 knots
Oil fuel (tons)	740

Built by Wartsila, Helsinki. Launched and completed in 1953. Built for deep-sea work. Two propellers forward and aft.

SISU

Displacement, tons	2 075
Dimensions, ft (*m*)	210·2 oa × 46·5 × 16·8 (*64·1 × 14·2 × 5·1*)
Guns	2—3·9 in AA
Main engines	2 sets Atlas Polar Diesels with electric drive; 2 shafts and a bow propeller; 4 000 hp = 16 knots
Complement	100

Built by Wärtsilä, Helsinki. Launched on 24 Sep 1938.

There is also the West German owned, Finnish manned, icebreaker *Hansa*, of the "Sampo" class, completed on 25 Nov 1966, which operates off Germany in winter and off Finland at other times.

COASTGUARD VESSELS

NV 1-10

10 ton craft of 20 knots built 1956-59.

VMV 11, 13, 19, 20

35 ton craft with a 20 mm gun—first pair built 1935, second pair in 1943.

FRANCE

Administration

Conseil Supérieur de la Marine:
Amiraux Joire Noulens and Iehle

Vice-Amiraux d'Escadre Bourdais, Daille, Guillou, Sanguinetti le Franc and Caillot.

C in C Atlantic Theatre (CECLANT) and Préfet Maritime de la Deuxième Région (PREMAR DEUX):
Vice-Amiral d'Escadre Daille

Préfet Maritime de la Première Région (PREMAR UN):
Vice-Amiral Frédéric Moreau

C in C Mediterranean Theatre (CECMED) and Préfet Maritime de la Troisième Région (PREMAR TROIS):
Vice-Amiral d'Escadre Bourdais

C in C French Naval Forces, Polynesia:
Vice-Amiral Tardy

Diplomatic Representation

Naval Attaché in London (& Defence Attaché):
Contre-Amiral François Flohic

Naval Attaché in Washington:
Contre-Amiral Chaline

Naval Attaché in Moscow:
Capitaine de Vaisseau Cahuac

Naval Attaché in Ottawa:
Capitaine de Frégate Sauvage

Personnel

(a) 1970: 69 300 (4 880 officers 64 420 ratings)
1971: 68 586 (4 732 officers, 63 854 ratings)
1972: 68 308 (4 604 officers, 63 704 ratings)
1973: 67 600 (4 400 officers, 63 200 ratings)
1974: 67 700 (4 500 officers, 63 200 ratings)
1975: 68 000 (4 550 officers, 63 450 ratings)
(personnel to be increased by 5 000 under the 15-year re-equipment plan)

(b) National Service 12 months

Bases

Cherbourg, Brest, Lorient, Toulon.

Mercantile Marine

Lloyd's Register of Shipping:
1 341 vessels of 8 834 519 tons gross

Strength of the Fleet

Type	*Active*	*Building or Projected*
Attack Carriers (Medium)	2	1 (Nuclear powered)
Cruisers	2	—
Destroyers	20	3
Frigates	25	14 (+ ? Type A 70)
Submarines (Strat Missile)	4 1 (Diesel powered)	2
Submarines (Fleet)	—	1
Submarines (Patrol)	19	3
Corvettes	22	—
Fast Attack Craft (Missile)	1	30
Large Patrol Craft	6	—
LPD	2	—
LST	5	—
LCT	13	—
LCM	14	—
Minesweepers (Ocean)	13	—
Minesweepers (Coastal)	39	—
Minehunters	5	—
Surveying Ships	7	—
Coastal Survey Ships	4	—
Inshore Survey Craft	2	—
Tankers (UR)	5	2
Tankers (Support)	4	—
Maintenance Ships	3	—
Depot Ships	5	—
Repair Ships (ex-LCT)	5	—
Trials Ships	3	—
Boom Defence Vessels	15	—
Torpedo Recovery Vessels	2	—
Victualling Supply Ship	1	—
Store Ship	1	—
Light Transports	2	—
Small Transports	14	—
Tenders	10	—
Tugs	111	—
Miscellaneous	14	—

Submarine Service

Now known as Force Océanique Stratégique (FOST) with HQ at Houilles near Paris. SSBN (*SNLE*) force based at Ile Longue Brest with a training base at Roche-Douvres and VLFW/T station at Rosay. Patrol submarines are based at Lorient and Toulon. Plans for nuclear fleet submarines are included in the 15 year plan.

15-Year Re-equipment Plan

This programme provides for the following fleet by 1985:
2 Aircraft Carriers
2 Helicopter carriers
30 Frigates or corvettes
35 Avisos
6 SSBN
20 Patrol Submarines (or Fleet)
30 Patrol craft
MHC and MSC as necessary
5 Replenishment Oilers
Logistic Support and Maintenance Ships
2 Assault Ships
Landing Ships and craft
Transports
50 LRMP aircraft
Carrier borne aircraft
Helicopters

1971-75 New Construction Plan

1 Helicopter Carrier (PH 75)
3 Guided Missile Destroyers ("Corvettes") "C 70" Type
3 Guided Missile Destroyers ("Corvettes") "C 67" Type
14 Escorts (officially rated as *Avisos*) "A 69" Type
3 Nuclear Powered Ballistic Missile Submarines
4 Patrol Submarines
4 Patrol Boats (for overseas service)
1 Fleet Support & Repair Ship (major conversion)
1 Fleet Replenishment Ship
2 Medium Landing Ships (Transports)

Disposals

Helicopter Carrier

1974 *Arromanches*

Cruiser

1973 *De Grasse*

Destroyer

1971 *Surcouf* Forward section sank after collision—after section used for spares
1974 *Chevalier Paul, Cassard*

Frigate

1971 *Gustave Zédé* (Command Ship)
1974 *Le Bordelais, Le Corse*

Submarines

1970 *Eurydice*, Lost
1972 *Sirène* sank at Lorient (subsequently salved) and
1974 deleted

MCM Vessels

1974 *Begonia*, and *Glaieul* deleted; *Aries* (To Morocco)

Amphibious Forces

1974 LCT 9099 deleted; LCT 9095 (to Senegal)

Survey Ship

1973 *La Coquille*

Service Forces

1972 *Lac Chambon, Lac Tchad*
1973 *Médoc*
1974 *Oasis*

Trials Ship

1973 *Arago*

BDV

1972 *Tarantule*
1974 *Scorpion, Locuste*

Miscellaneous

1970 6 Water Boats
1974 M691 (ex-SC 525), FNRS 3

PENNANT NUMBERS

R Aircraft and Helicopter Carriers

97 Jeanne d'Arc
98 Clemenceau
99 Foch

S Submarines

610 Le Foudroyant
611 Le Redoutable
612 Le Terrible
613 L'Indomptable
614 Le Tonnant
631 Narval
632 Marsouin
633 Dauphin
634 Requin
635 Aréthuse
636 Argonaute
637 Espadon
638 Morse
639 Amazone
640 Ariane
641 Daphné
642 Diane
643 Doris
645 Flore
646 Galatée
648 Junon
649 Venus
650 Psyche
651 Sirène
655 Gymnote

C Cruiser

611 Colbert

D Missile Leaders and Destroyers

602 Suffren
603 Duquesne
610 Tourville
611 Duguay-Trouin
612 De Grasse
622 Kersaint
624 Bouvet
625 Dupetit Thouars
627 Maillé Brézé
628 Vauquelin
629 D'Estrées
630 Du Chayla
631 Casablanca
632 Guépratte
633 Duperré
634 La Bourdonnais
635 Forbin
636 Tartu
637 Jauréguiberry
638 La Galissonniere
640 Georges Leygues
641 Dupleix
642 Montcalm

F Frigates, Escorts and Corvettes

703 Aconit
725 Victor Schoelcher
726 Commandant Bory
727 Amiral Charner
728 Doudart de La Grée
729 Balny
733 Commandant Rivière
740 Commandant Bourdais
748 Protet
749 Enseigne Henry
762 Le Brestois
763 Le Boulonnais
765 Le Normand
766 Le Picard
767 Le Gascon
768 Le Lorrain
769 Le Bourguignon
770 Le Champenois
771 Le Savoyard
772 Le Breton
773 Le Basque
774 L'Agenais
775 Le Béarnais
776 L'Alsacien
777 Le Provençal
778 Le Vendéen
781 D'Estienne d'Orves
782 Amyot d'Inville
783 Drogou
784 Detroyat
785 Jean Moulin
786 Quartier-Maître Anquetil
787 Commandant de Pimodan
788 Seconde-Maître Le Bihan
789 Lieutenant-de-Vaisseau le Henaff
790 Lieutenant-de-Vaisseau Lavallée
791 Commandant l'Herminier
792 Premier-Maître l'Her
793 Commandant Blaison
794 Enseigne-de-Vaisseau Jacoubet

M Coastal and Inshore Minesweepers

609 Narvik
610 Ouistreham
612 Alençon
613 Bernèval
615 Cantho
616 Dompaire
617 Garigliano
618 Mytho
619 Vinh-long
620 Berlaimont
622 Autun
623 Baccarat
624 Colmar
632 Pervenche
633 Pivoine
635 Rèsèda
638 Acacia
639 Acanthe
640 Marjolaine
668 Azalée
670 Bleuet
671 Camélia
672 Chrysantheme
674 Cyclamen
675 Eglantine
677 Giroflée
679 Glycine
680 Jacinthe
681 Laurier
682 Lilas
684 Lobelia
685 Magnolia
687 Mimosa
688 Muguet
691 ex-SC 525
703 Antares
704 Algol
707 Véga
712 Cybèle
713 Calliope
714 Clio
715 Circe
716 Ceres
737 Capricorne
740 Cassiopée
741 Eridan
743 Sagittaire
747 Bételgeuse
749 Phénix
750 Bellatrix
755 Capella
756 Céphée
757 Verseau
758 Aries
759 Lyre
765 Mercure

P Patrol Vessels, Coastal Escorts

630 L'Intrépide
635 L'Ardent
637 L'Etourdi
638 L'Effronté
639 Le Frondeur
640 Le Fringant
644 L'Adroit
645 L'Alerte
646 L'Attentif
647 L'Enjoué
648 Le Hardi
650 Arcturus
651 La Malouine
652 La Lorientaise
653 La Dunkerquoise
654 La Bayonnaise
655 La Dieppoise
656 Altair
657 La Paimpolaise
658 Croix du Sud
659 Canopus
660 Etoile Polaire
661 Jasmin
662 Petunia
670 Trident
671 Glaive
672 Epée
673 Pertuisane
674 Rapière
675 Sabre
730 La Combattante
784 Geranium
787 Jonquille
788 Violette

L Landing Ships

9003 Argens
9004 Bidassoa
9007 Trieux
9008 Dives
9009 Blavet
9021 Ouragan
9022 Orage
9030 Champlain
9031 Francis Garnier
9061 LCT
9070 LCT
9071 LCT
9072 LCT
9073 LCT
9074 LCT
9081 Workshop
9082 Workshop
9083 Workshop
9084 Workshop
9091 LCT
9092 LCT
9093 LCT
9094 LCT
9096 LCT

(CTM LCMs 1-14)

A Auxiliaries and Support Ships

603 Henry Poincaré
608 Moselle
610 Ile d'Oléron
614 Falleron
615 Loire
617 Garonne
618 Rance
619 Aber Wrach
620 Jules Verne
621 Rhin
622 Rhône
625 Papenoo
626 La Charente
627 La Seine
628 La Sâone
629 La Durance
630 Lac Tonlé Sap
632 Punaruu
637 Maurienne
638 Sahel
640 Origny
643 Aunis
644 Berry
646 Triton
648 Archimède
649 Etoile
650 La Belle Poule
652 Mutin
653 La Grande Hermine
660 Hippopotame
661 Infatigable
665 Goliath
666 Eléphant
667 Hercule
668 Rhinocéros
669 Tenace
671 Le Fort
672 Utile
673 Lutteur
674 Centaure
675 Isère
682 Alidade
683 Octant
684 Coolie
685 Robuste
686 Actif
687 Laborieux
688 Valeureux
692 Travailleur
694 Efficace
695 Acharne
698 Petrel
699 Pelican
701 Ajonc
702 Girelle
706 Courageux
710 Myosotis
711 Gardénia
714 Tourmaline
716 Oiseau des Iles
722 Poseidon
723 Liseron
718 Pachyderme
719 Bélier
724 Belouga
727 Araignée
730 Libellule
731 Tianée
733 Saintonge
735 Hibiscus
736 Dahlia
737 Tulipe
738 Capucine
739 Oeillet
740 Hortensia
741 Armoise
742 Paquerette
748 Cataracte
753 La Découverte
755 Commandant Robert Giraud
756 Espérance
757 D'Entrecasteaux
758 La Recherche
759 Marcel Le Bihan
760 Cigale
761 Criquet
762 Fourmi
763 Grillon
764 Scarabée
766 Estafette
777 Luciole
780 L'Astrolabe
781 Boussole
789 Archéonaute
794 Corail (ex-Marc Joly)

Y

601 Acajou
602 Aigrette
604 Ariel
607 Balsa
608 Bambu
611 Bengali
612 Bouleau
613 Faune
616 Canari
617 Mouette
618 Cascade
620 Chataigner
621 Mésange
623 Charme
624 Chène
628 Colibri
629 Cormier
630 Bonite
631 Courlis
632 Cygne
633 Delange
634 Rouget
635 Equeurdibille
636 Martinet
637 Fauvette
640 Fontaine
641 Forméne
644 Fréne
645 Gave
646 Geyser
647 Giens
648 Goeland
649 Grive
651 Hanneton
652 Haut Barr
653 Heron
654 Hétre
655 Hévéat
657 Hirondelle
658 Ibis
659 Jonque
661 Korrigan
662 Dryade
663 Latanier
664 Lutin
666 Manguier
667 Tupa
668 Méléze
669 Merisier
670 Merle
671 Morgane
673 Moineau
675 Martin Pêcheur
678 Moule
680 Muréne
682 Okoume
683 Ondée
684 Oued
685 Oursin
686 Palétuvier
687 Passereau
688 Peuplier
689 Pin
690 Pingouin
691 Pinson
694 Pivert
695 Platane
696 Alphée
698 Calmar
699 Poulpé
702 Rascasse
704 Rossignol
706 Chimère
708 Saule
709 Sycomore
710 Sylphe
711 Farfadet
712 Tréberou
717 Ébene
718 Erable
719 Olivier
720 Santal
721 Alouette
722 Vauneau
723 Engoulevent
724 Surcelle
725 Marabout
726 Toucan
727 Macreuse
728 Grand Duc
729 Eider
730 Ara
731 Persistante
735 Merlin
736 Mélusine
738 Marronier
739 Noyer
740 Papayer
741 Elfe
743 Palangrin
745 Aiguiére
746 Embrun
747 Loriot
748 Gelinotte
749 La Prudente
750 La Persévérante
751 La Fidèle
760 PB
761 PB

NAVAL AIR ARM

NAVAL AIR ARM

Squadron Number	Base	Aircraft	Task
	Embarked Squadrons		
4F	Lann Bihoue	BR1050 "Alize"	Patrol & A/S
6F	Nimes Garons	BR1050 "Alize"	Patrol & A/S
11F	Landivisiau	ETD IVM	Fighter Bomber
12F	Landivisiau	F8E "Crusader"	Interceptors
14F	Landivisiau	F8E "Crusader"	Interceptors
16F	Landivisiau	ETD IV P	Reconnaissance
17F	Hyeres	ETD IV M	Fighter Bomber
31F	St. Mandrier	HSS 1	A/S
32F	Lanveoc Poulmic	Super-Frelon	A/S
33F	St. Mandrier	HSS 1	Assault
J. d'Arc	J. d'Arc or St. Mandries	HSS 1	Training
SRL	Landivisiau	MS 760 Paris	Support
	Support Squadrons		
2S	Lann Bihoue	Navajo, Nord 262	Support 1st & 2nd Region
3S	Hyeres	Navajo, Nord 262	Support 3rd Region
10S	St. Raphael	Nord 2504, BR1050 Navajo MS 733	Trials CEPA
20S	St. Raphael	AL 11, AL 111 AL 111 ASM HSSI Super Frelon	Trials CEPA
22S	Lanveoc Poulmic	AL 11, AL 111 AL 111 VSV	Support 2nd Region SAR
23S	St. Mandrier	AL11 AL111	Support 3rd Region SAR
SSD	Dugny	C 54, Nord 262 Navajo	Support

Squadron Number	Base	Aircraft	Task
	Maritime Patrol Squadrons		
21F	Nimes Garons	BR 1150 "Atlantic"	MP
22F	Nimes Garons	BR 1150 "Atlantic"	MP
23F	Lann Bihoue	BR 1150 "Atlantic"	MP
24F	Lann Bihoue	BR 1150 "Atlantic"	MP
25F	Lann Bihoue	Neptune P2H	MP
	Training Squadrons		
55S	Aspretto	Nord 262, SNB 5	Twin-engine conversion
56S	Nimes Garons	C 47	Flying School
59S	Hyeres	ET IV, BR 1050 CM 175 "Zephyr"	Fighter School
SVS	Lanveoc Poulmic	MS 733	Naval School Recreational
Esalat Dax	Dax	AL 11	Helicopter School
	Overseas Detachments		
New Caledonia	Tontouta	C 54, C 47	Support and Liaison
Malagasy	Diego Suarez	C 47	Support and Liaison
	CEP Formations		
Sectal Pac.	Hao	AL 111	Support
27S	Hao	Super-Frelon	Support
12S	Papeete	Neptune P2H	MP

AIRCRAFT CARRIERS

1 PH 75
(NUCLEAR PROPELLED HELICOPTER CARRIER)

Displacement, tons	16 400 trials; 18 400 full load
Length, feet (*metres*)	682·2 oa (*208*)
Length, feet (*metres*)	662·6 flight deck (*202*)
Beam, feet (*metres*)	86·6 wl (*26·4*)
Beam, feet (*metres*)	157·4 flight deck (*48*)
Aircraft	25 WG 13 Lynx or 10 Super Frelon or 15 Puma helicopters
Missiles	2 Crotale SAM systems; 4 SAM systems with a sea-skimming capability for anti-missile defence are eventually to replace the guns
Guns	8—40 mm Breda-Bofors (4 twins)
Main engines	1—CAS 230 reactor to two turbines; 65 000 ihp; two emergency AGO diesels
Speed, knots	28
Range, miles	Unlimited on reactor; 3 000 at 10 knots (diesels)
Endurance	Stores for 45 days; 30 days for passengers
Complement	890 plus 1 500 passengers

GENERAL
Coming at a time of financial stringency this is a bold design showing the French Navy's appreciation of the great and universal value of helicopters in both peace and war. While her wartime role in a force composed of both A/S and A/A ships is clear she has been designed with an intervention role in mind as well. For peacetime duties in the event of natural disasters her large passenger and hospital capacity will be of immense value. Construction by DCAN, Brest with a programme allowing for trials in 1979 and service in 1980.

ACCOMMODATION. A crew of 840 plus 50 staff and Ground Intervention Staff is provided for. Passenger accommodation is available for 1 000, with more austere conditions on portable bunks for an extra 500 in the garage (forward of the hangar).

AIRCRAFT. Although designed primarily for helicopter operations the possibility of VTOL operations was also taken into account.

ELECTRICAL SUPPLY. A total of 9 400 kW from two turbines each driving a pair of 1 500 kW alternators and four diesel alternators of 850 kW each.

FLIGHT DECK. The flight deck, 662 feet long, is 157 feet wide at its maximum and 102 feet at the island. Four spots are provided for Super Frelon helicopters and eight for Lynx or Puma.

HANGAR. One hangar, 275 × 69 × 21 feet, is provided with two lateral lifts to starboard at the rear of the island. Storage for 1 000 cubic metres of TR5 fuel in tanks is available. One fixed crane and one mobile crane are provided.

HOSPITAL. 3 main wards, 1 X-ray ward, 1 intensive-care ward, 1 infectious diseases ward, 2 dental surgeries and a laboratory.

MAIN ENGINES. The CAS 230 reactor of 230 megawatts is being constructed under the supervision of l'Etablissement, des Constructions et Armes Navales d'Indret.

OPERATIONS ROOMS. Normal operations Room, ASW centre and Communication Offices are supplemented by an Operations Centre with facilities for Ground Intervention Forces and Air Intervention Forces. These include a Warfare Coordinating Centre, an Air Intervention Command Centre and a Helicopter Command Station.

RADAR. 1 DRBV 26 long range air search set; 1 DRBV 51C combined search set; 2 Decca systems; 2 DRBC 32 for missile guidance.

REPLENISHMENT. 1 250 tons of fuel is carried for replenishment of Escorts.

SONAR. 1 DUBA 25.

R75

H. Simoni

PH 75 — *1974, French Navy*

Aircraft Carriers—*continued*

2 "CLEMENCEAU" CLASS

Name	*No.*	*Builders*	*Laid down*	*Launched*	*Completed*
CLEMENCEAU	R 98	Brest	Nov 1955	21 Dec 1957	22 Nov 1961
FOCH	R 99	Chantier de L'Atlantique	Feb 1957	28 July 1960	15 July 1963

Displacement, tons	27 307 normal; 32 780 full load
Length, feet (*metres*)	780·8 (*238·0*)pp; 869·4 (*265·0*)oa
Beam, feet (*metres*)	104·1 (*31·7*) hull (with bulges)
Width, feet (*metres*)	168·0 (*51·2*) oa
Draught feet (*metres*)	24·6 (*7·5*) 28·2 (*8·6*) screws
Aircraft	Capacity 40, including jet aircraft. Each carries 3 Flights—1 of *Etendard IV*, 1 of *Crusader*, 1 of Breguet *Alizé*
Catapults	2 Mitchell-Brown steam, Mk BS 5
Armour	Flight deck, island superstructure and bridges, hull (over machinery spaces and magazines)
Guns	8—3·9 in (*100 mm*) AA automatic in single turrets
Main engines	2 sets Parsons geared turbines; 2 shafts; 126 000 shp
Speed, knots	32
Boilers	6; steam pressure 640 psi (*45 kg/cm²*), superheat 842°F (450°C)
Range, miles	7 500 at 18 knots; 4 800 at 24 knots; 3 500 at full power
Oil fuel, tons	3 720
Complement	2 239 (179 officers, 2 060 men)

CLEMENCEAU *1974 French Navy*

GENERAL. First aircraft carriers designed as such and built from the keel to be completed in France. Authorised in 1953 and 1955, respectively. *Clemenceau* ordered from Brest Dockyard on 28 May 1954 and begun in Nov 1955. *Foch* begun at Chantiers de l'Atlantique a St. Nazaire, Penhoet-Loire, in a special dry dock (contract provided for the construction of the hull and propelling machinery) and completed by Brest Dockyard.

ELECTRONICS. Comprehensive DF and ECM equipment. Both fitted wtih SENIT 4 Tactical data automation system.

FLIGHT DECK. Angled deck incorporated, two lifts, measuring 52·5 × 36 feet, one on the starboard deck edge, two steam catapults for aircraft up to 11 tons, and two deck landing aids. The flight deck measures 543 × 96·8 feet and is angled at 8 degrees.

Flight deck letters: F = *Foch*, U = *Clemenceau*.

HANGAR. Dimensions of the hangar are 590·6 × 78·7 × 23·0 feet.

RADAR. One DRBV 20C; One DRBV 23B; Two DRBI 10; One DRBV 50; One DRBC 31.

SONAR. One SQS 505

GUNNERY. Originally to have been armed with 24—2·25 inch guns in twin mountings, but the armament was revised to 12—3·9 inch (*100 mm*) in 1956 and to 8—3·9 inch (*100 mm*) in 1958. Rate of fire 60 rounds per minute.

BULGES. *Foch* was completed with bulges. These having proved successful, *Clemenceau* was modified similarly on first refit, increasing her beam by 6 feet.

DRAWING. Starboard elevation and plan. Scale: 118 feet = 1 inch

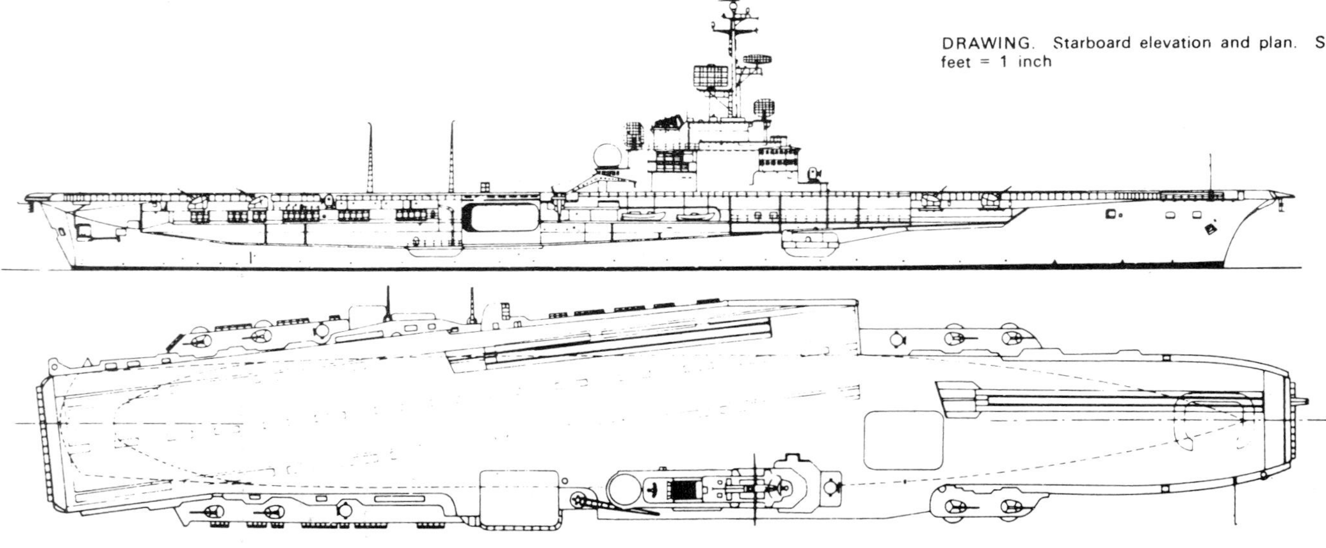

FOCH *7/1974 Wright and Logan*

CRUISERS

Name	*No.*	*Builders*	*Ordered*	*Laid down*	*Launched*	*Completed*
JEANNE D'ARC (ex-*La Résolue*)	R 97	Brest Dockyard	8 Mar 1957	7 July 1960	30 Sep 1961	1 July 1963 (trials) 30 June 1964 (service)

Displacement, tons	10 000 standard; 12 365 full load
Length, feet (*metres*)	564·2 (*172*) pp; 597·1 (*182·0*) oa
Beam, feet (*metres*)	78·7 (*24·0*) hull
Draught, feet (*metres*)	24·0 (*7·3*) max
Flight deck	203·4 × 68·9 (*62·0* × *21·0*)
Aircraft	Heavy A/S helicopters (4 in peacetime as training ship; 8 in wartime)
Missiles	4-MM38 Exocet (in 1975)
Guns	4—3·9 in (*100* mm) AA single
Main engines	Rateau-Bretagne geared turbines; 2 shafts; 40 000 shp
Speed, knots	26·5
Boilers	4; working pressure 640 psi (*45 kg/cm²*); 842°F (*450°C*)
Range miles	6 000 at 15 knots
Oil fuel, tons	1 360
Complement	906 (44 officers, 670 ratings and 192 cadets)

GENERAL
Authorised under the 1957 estimates. Used for training officer cadets in peacetime in place of the old training cruiser *Jeanne d'Arc* (which was decommissioned on 28 July 1964 and sold for scrap in Dec 1965 at Brest). In wartime, after rapid modification, she would be used as a commando ship, helicopter carrier or troop transport with commando equipment and a battalion of 700 men. The lift has a capacity of 12 tons. The ship is almost entirely air-conditioned.

MODIFICATIONS. Between first steaming trials and completion for operational service the ship was modified with a taller funnel to clear the superstructure and obviate the smoke and exhaust gases swirling on to the bridges.

ELECTRONICS. The ship is almost as well equipped with electronic apparatus as the aircraft carrier *Clemenceau*.

RADAR. One DRBV 22D; one DRBV 50; one DRBN 32; one DRBI 10.

SONAR. One SQS 503.

NAMES. The name *La Résolue* was only a temporary one until the decommissioning of the training cruiser *Jeanne d'Arc* which was relieved by *La Résolue* in 1964 when the latter ship took the name *Jeanne d'Arc*, on 16 July.

JEANNE D'ARC *1972, W. A. Fuller, Esq.*

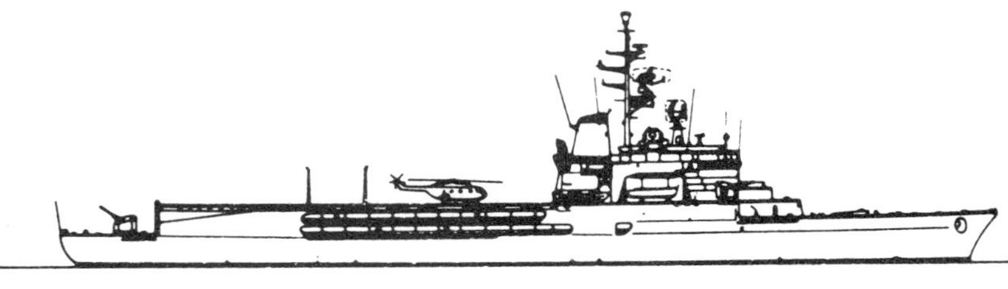

JEANNE D'ARC

JEANNE D'ARC *1966, French Navy*

Cruisers—*continued*

Name	*Pennant No.*	*Builders*	*Laid down*	*Launched*	*Completed*	*Commissioned*
COLBERT	C 611	Brest Dockyard	Dec 1953	24 Mar 1956 (floated out of dry dock)	1958 (trials end of 1957)	5 May 1959

Displacement, tons	8 500 standard; 11 300 full load
Length, feet (*metres*)	593·2 (*180·8*)
Beam, feet (*metres*)	64·6 (*19·7*)
Draught, feet (*metres*)	25·2 (*7·7*) screws
Missile launchers	1 twin "Masurca" surface-to-air aft 4-MM38 Exocet to be fitted
Guns	2—3·9 in (*100 mm*) single automatic; 12—57 mm in 6 twin mountings, 3 on each side
Armour	50—80 mm belt and 50 mm deck
Main engines	2 sets CEM-Parsons geared turbines; 2 shafts; 86 000 shp
Speed, knots	32
Boilers	4 Indret multitubular; 640 psi (*45 kg/cm²*); 842°F (450°C)
Range, miles	4 000 at 25 knots
Oil fuel, tons	1 492
Complement	796 (69 officers, 727 men) as Flagship after reconstruction

Provision was made in the original design for her to be fitted with guided missiles. She was equipped as command ship and for radar control of air strikes.

ELECTRONICS. Senit data automation system; Radar intercept equipment; wireless intercept equipment; two Knebworth Corvus dual-purpose launchers for CHAFF.

RECONSTRUCTION. Between April 1970 and October 1972 she underwent a complete reconstruction and rearmament. The gunnery systems were altered to those given above, the "Masurca" surface-to-air missile system was fitted and helicopter facilities were installed on the quarter-deck. Reductions in the original armament schedule saved 80 mil francs from the original refit cost of 350 mil francs.

MISSILES. *Colbert* carries 48 Masurca missiles. Mk 2 mod 3 semi-active radar homing version.

RADAR. One Decca RM416 (navigation); one DRBV 50 (surveillance); one DRBV 23C (air surveillance); one DRBV 20 (warning); two DRBR 51 (f.c.); one DRBR 32c; two DRBC 31; one DRBI 10D (height-finder).

GUNNERY. Prior to Apr 1970 the armament comprised sixteen 5 inch (*127 mm*) dual purpose guns in eight twin mountings, and twenty 57 mm Bofors anti-aircraft guns in ten twin mountings.

SONAR. Hull mounted set.

COLBERT *1973, French Navy*

COLBERT *1973, French Navy*

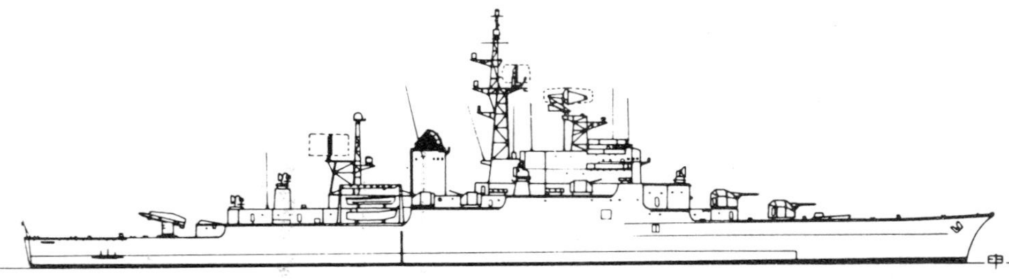

COLBERT *1973, French Navy*

DESTROYERS

3 "GEORGES LEYGUES" CLASS (C70 TYPE)

GEORGES LEYGUES	D 640
DUPLEIX	D 641
MONTCALM	D 642

Displacement, tons: 3 800 standard; 4 100 full load
Dimensions, ft (*m*): 455·9 oa × 45·9 (*139 × 14*)
Aircraft: 2 WG 13 "Lynx" helicopters with Mk 44 or 46 torpedoes
Missile launchers: 4 MM 38 Exocet; 1 Crotale
Guns: 1—3·9 in (*100 mm*); 2—20 mm
Torpedoes: 10 tubes in 2 mountings for Mk L5
Main engines: CODOG; 2 Rolls Royce Olympus gas turbines; 2 SEMT-Pielstick diesels; 2 shafts VP screws
Speed, knots: 29·75 (19·5 on diesels)
Complement: 252 (19 officers 233 ratings)
Range, miles: 9 000 at 18 knots on diesels

A new C 70 type of so-called "corvette". Three are included in the new construction programme. *Georges Leygues* laid down Sep 1974 for trials in 1977 and service in 1978. *Dupleix* to be laid down in 1975 for trials in 1978 and *Montcalm* to be laid down in 1975 for trials 1979.
A total of 24 is planned for completion by 1985, eighteen being an A/S version like *G. Leygues* and six in an A/A version.

ELECTRONICS. SENIT.

HELICOPTER. The Lynx, as well as its A/S role, can have an anti-surface role when armed with 4 AS 12 missiles.

MISSILES. A/A version to carry Standard SM2 system.

RADAR. 1—DRBV 26; 1—DRBV 51C; 1—DRBV 32E.

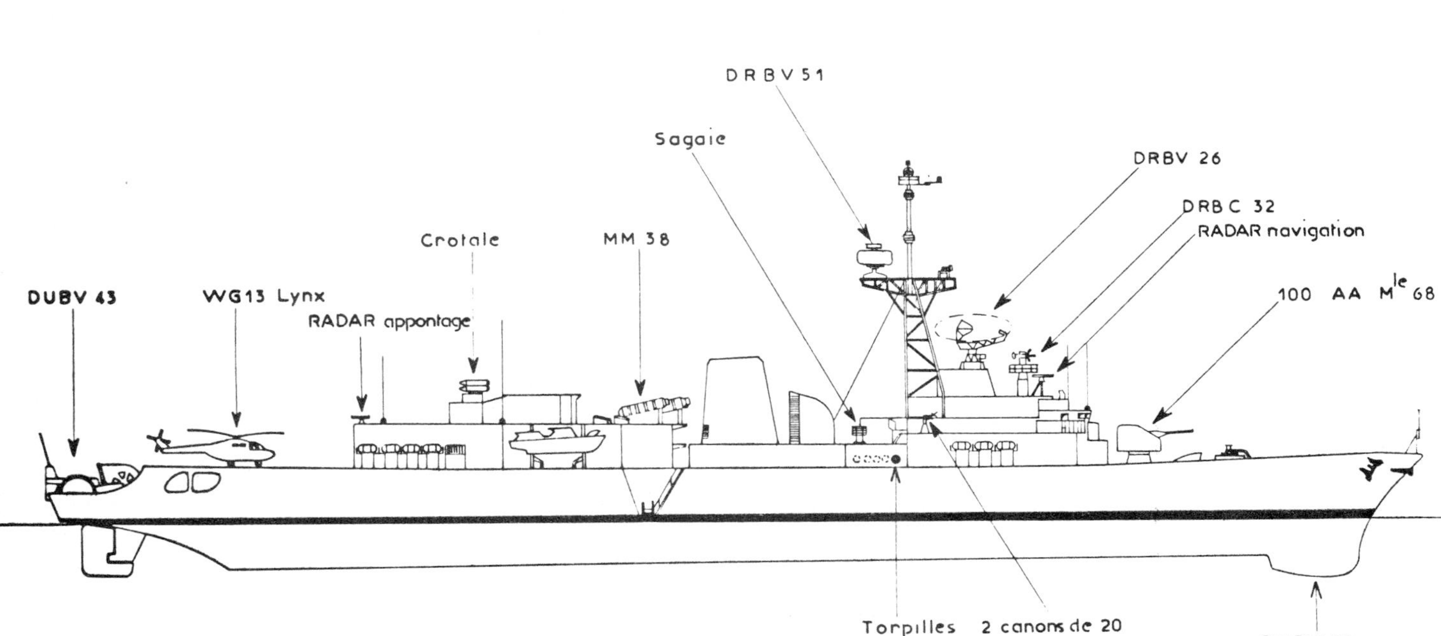

"GEORGES LEYGUES" Class

1974 French Navy

Destroyers— *continued*

2 "SUFFREN" CLASS

Name	*No.*	*Builders*	*Laid down*	*Launched*	*Trials*	*Operational*
DUQUESNE	D 603	Brest Dockyard	Nov 1964	12 Feb 1966	July 1968	Apr 1970
SUFFREN	D 602	Lorient Dockyard	Dec 1962	15 May 1965	Dec 1965	July 1967

Displacement, tons	5 090 standard; 6 090 full load
Length, feet (*metres*)	517·1 (*157·6*) oa
Beam, feet (*metres*)	50·9 (*15·5*)
Draught, feet (*metres*)	20·0 (*6·1*)
Missile launchers	Twin "Masurca" surface-air
Guns	2—3·9 in (*100 mm*) automatic, single AA 2—30 mm (automatic, single) AA
A/S weapons	"Malafon" rocket/homing torpedo single launcher 13 missiles carried
Torpedo tubes	4 (2 each side) for A/S homing torpedoes
Main engines	Double reduction geared turbines; 2 shafts; 72 500 shp
Speed, knots	34
Boilers	4 automatic; working pressure 640 psi (*45 kg/cm²*); superheat 842°F (450°C)
Range, miles	5 000 at 18 knots; 2 400 at 29 knots
Complement	426 (38 officers, 388 men)

GENERAL
Ordered under the 1960 Programme. The structure provides best possible resistance to atomic blast. Equipped with gyro controlled stabilisers. Air-conditioning of accommodation and operational areas.

ELECTRONICS. *Senit I* action data automatic system.

MISSILES. Carry 48 *Masurca* missiles, a mix of Mk 2 Mod 2 beam riders and Mk 2 Mod 3 semi-active homers.

RADAR. One DRBN 32 search and navigation set; one DRBI 23 L band stacked-beam three dimensional air surveillance and target designator in radome; one DRBV 50 surface surveillance radar; two DRBR 51 Masurca fire control; one DRBC 32A fire control for forward guns

SONAR. One DUBV 23 hull-mounted set and a DUBV 43 VDS.

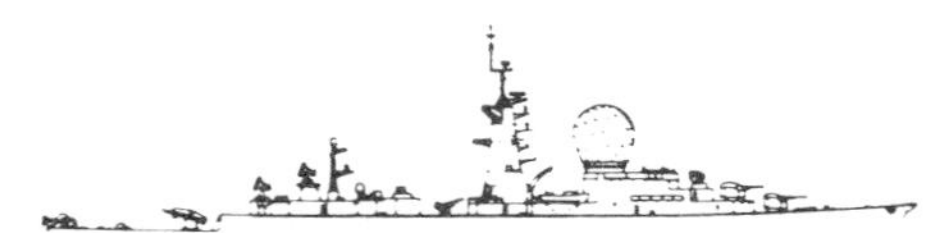

DUQUESNE *1973 French Navy*

DUQUESNE *1973, French Navy*

SUFFREN *6/1974, Wright and Logan*

Destroyers—*continued*

3 "TOURVILLE" CLASS (F67 TYPE ex-C-67A)

Name	No.	Builders	Laid down	Launched	Trials
TOURVILLE	D 610	Lorient	Mar 1970	13 May 1972	Nov 1972
DUGAY-TROUIN	D 611	Lorient	Jan 1971	1 June 1973	1974
DE GRASSE	D 612	Lorient	1972	30 Nov 1974	1975

Displacement, tons	4 580 standard; 5 745 full load
Length, feet (*metres*)	510·3 (*152·8*) oa
Beam, feet (*metres*)	50·2 (*15·3*)
Draught, feet (*metres*)	18·7 (*5·7*)
Aircraft	2 WG 13 Lynx ASW helicopters
Missile launchers	6 "MM 38" ("Exocet") 1—Crotale SAM (*De Grasse*)
Guns	3—3·9 in (*100 mm*) AA (2 in *De Grasse*)
A/S Weapons	"Malafon" rocket/homing torpedo (13 missiles)
Torpedoes	2 mountings for Mk L5
Main engines	Rateau geared turbines; 2 shafts; 54 400 shp
Speed, knots	31
Boilers	4 automatic
Range, miles	5 000 at 18 knots
Complement	303 (25 officers, 278 men)

Developed from the "Aconit" design. Originally rated as "corvettes" but reclassified as "frigates" on 8 July 1971 and given "D" pennant numbers like destroyers.

RADAR. One DRBV 26; one DRBV 51; one DRBC 32D; two Decca Type 1226; Senit.

SONARS. 1 DUBV 23 hull-mounted; one DUBV 43 VDS.

TOURVILLE — 3/1974, French Navy

TOURVILLE — 1974, ECP, Armées de France

1 TYPE 56

Name	Pennant No.	Builders	Laid down	Launched	Completed
LA GALISSONNIÈRE	D 638	Lorient Naval Dockyard	Nov 1958	12 Mar 1960	July 1962

Displacement, tons	2 750 standard; 3 740 full load;
Length, feet (*metres*)	435·7 (*132·8*) oa
Beam, feet (*metres*)	41·7 (*12·7*)
Draught, feet (*metres*)	15·4 (*4·7*) aft; 18·0 (*5·5*) screws
Aircraft	1 A/S helicopter
A/S weapons	"Malafon" rocket/homing torpedoes, 1 launcher
Guns	2—3·9 in (*100 mm*) AA automatic, single
Torpedo tubes	6—21·7 in (*550 mm*) ASM, 2 triple for Mks K2 and L3
Main engines	2 sets geared turbines; 2 shafts; 63 000 shp (72 000 on trials, light)
Boilers	4 A & C de B Indret; 500 psi (*35 kg/cm²*); 617°F (*380°C*)
Speed, knots	34 (32 full load)
Range, miles	5 000 at 18 knots
Oil fuel, tons	725
Complement	333 (20 officers, 313 men)

GENERAL
Designed as a flotilla leader. Same characteristics as regards hull and machinery as T 47 and T 53 types, but different armament. She has a hangar and a platform for landing a helicopter. When first commissioned she was used as an experimental ship for new sonars and anti-submarine weapons.

ARMAMENT. First French combatant ship to be armed with Malafon. This is the reason for the two 3·9 in (*100 mm*) guns instead of the 3 or 4 previously planned. France's first operational guided missile ship.

ELECTRONICS. Tacan beacon and full DF and ECM fit.

LA GALISSONIÈRE — 1974, Wright and Logan

RADAR. One DRBN 32; one DRBV 50 search/navigation set; one DRBV 22 L-band search set; one DRBC 32A X band fire-control.

SONAR. One hull-mounted DUBV 23; one DUBV 43 VDS.

Destroyers—*continued*

1 TYPE 47 (MODIFIED)

Name	Pennant No.	Builder	Laid down	Launched	Completed
DUPERRÉ	D 633	Lorient	Nov 1954	23 June 1956	8 Oct 1957

Displacement, tons: 2 800 standard; 3 900 full load
Length, feet (*metres*): 435·7 (*132·8*) oa
Beam, feet (*metres*): 41·7 (*12·7*)
Draught, feet (*metres*): 15·4 (*4·7*) aft; 18·0 (*5·5*) screws
Aircraft: 1 WG 13 Lynx helicopter
Missiles: 4 MM 38 Exocet
Gun: 1—3·9 in (*100 mm*)
Torpedo tubes: 1 mounting for Mk L5
Main engines: 2 sets geared turbines; 2 shafts; 63 000 shp (72 000 on trials; light)
Boilers: 4 A & C de B Indret; 500 psi (*35 kg/cm²*); 617°F (*380°C*)
Speed, knots: 34 (32 full load)
Range, miles: 5 000 at 18 knots
Oil fuel, tons: 725
Complement: 255 (16 officers, 239 men)

GENERAL
After serving as trial ship from 1967-71 she was converted at Brest to her present state in 1972-73.

RADAR. One DRBV 22A; one DRBV 51; one DRBC 32E; two Decca, one nav, and one for helicopter control.

SONAR. DUBV 23 hull-mounted; DUBV 43 VDS.

DUPERRÉ *1974, French Navy*

4 TYPE 47 (DDG)

Name	Pennant No.	Builder	Laid down	Launched	Completed
KERSAINT	D 622	Lorient	June 1951	3 Oct 1953	20 Mar 1956
BOUVET	D 624	Lorient	Nov 1951	3 Oct 1953	13 May 1956
DUPETIT THOUARS	D 625	Brest	Mar 1952	4 Mar 1954	15 Sep 1956
DU CHAYLA	D 630	Brest	July 1953	27 Nov 1954	4 June 1957

Displacement, tons: 2 750 standard; 3 740 full load
Length, feet (*metres*): 421·3 (*128·4*)
Beam, feet (*metres*): 41·7 (*12·7*)
Draught, feet (*metres*): 17·7 (*5·4*)
Missiles: Single Mk 13 Tartar launcher (40 missiles—SMI or SMIA)
Guns: 6—57 mm AA (twins)
Torpedoes: 2 triple mountings (*550 mm*) for Mk K2 and L3
A/S weapons: 375 mm Mk 54 projector
Main engines: 2 geared turbines; 63 000 shp; 2 shafts
Speed, knots: 34 (32 fully laden)
Range, miles: 5 000 at 18 knots
Oil fuel, tons: 800
Complement: 278 (17 officers, 261 men)

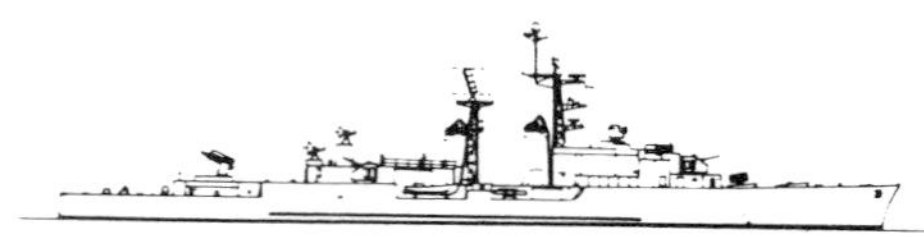

TYPE 47 (DDG)

RADAR. One DRBV 20 (search); one SPS 39A or B; one DRBV 31 (navigation); two SPG 51 B (tartar control); one DRBC 31; Senit.

SONARS. One DUBA 1; one DUBV 24.

DU CHAYLA *7/1973, Wright and Logan*

Destroyers—*continued*

4 TYPE 53

Name	*Pennant No.*	*Builder*	*Laid down*	*Launched*	*Completed*
LA BOURDONNAIS	D 634	Brest	Aug 1954	15 Oct 1955	Mar 1958
FORBIN	D 635	Brest	Aug 1954	15 Oct 1955	1 Feb 1958
TARTU	D 636	At. Chantiers de Bretagne	Nov 1954	2 Dec 1955	5 Feb 1958
JAURÉGUIBERRY	D 637	Gironde	Sept 1954	5 Nov 1955	July 1958

Displacement, tons	2 750 standard; 3 740 full load
Length, feet (*metres*)	421·3 (*128·4*)
Beam, feet (*metres*)	41·7 (*12·7*)
Draught, feet (*metres*)	17·7 (*5·4*)
Guns	6—5 in (*127 mm*) (twins); (*Forbin* 4—5 in); 6—57 mm (twin); 2—20 mm
Torpedoes	2 triple mountings (*550 mm*) for Mk K2 and L3
A/S weapons	375 mm Mk 54 projector
Main engines	2 geared turbines; 63 000 shp; 2 shafts
Speed, knots	34 (32 fully laden)
Range, miles	5 000 at 18 knots
Oil fuel, tons	800
Complement	274 (14 officers, 260 men)

Type 53

GENERAL
Air-direction ships—*Forbin* has helicopter platform aft in place of Y mount.

Forbin acts as a training ship for L'École d'Application des Enseignes de Vaisseau, being part of the *Jeanne d'Arc* group.

RADAR. One DRBV 22A (air search); one DRBI 10A; one DRBV 31; Tacan; Senit.
SONAR. One DUBA 1; one DUBV 24.

FORBIN (with helo platform) *1973, French Navy*

LA BOURDONNAIS *1973, Dr. Giorgio Arra*

Destroyers—*continued*

5 TYPE 47 (ASW)

Displacement, tons	2 750 standard; 3 900 full load
Length, feet (*metres*)	434·6 (*132·5*)
Beam, feet (*metres*)	41·7 (*12·7*)
Draught, feet (*metres*)	14·4 (*4·4*)
Guns	2—3·9 in (*100 mm*) (singles); 2—20 mm
A/S weapons	1 Malafon; 1 375 mm Mk 54 projector
Torpedo tubes	Two triple mountings (*550 mm*) for Mk K2 and L3
Main engines	2 geared turbines; 63 000 shp; 2 shafts
Speed, knots	34 (32 fully laden)
Range, miles	5 000 at 18 knots
Oil fuel, tons	800
Complement	320 (21 officers, 299 men)

RADAR. One DRBV 22A; one DRBV 50; one DRBN 32; two DRBC 23A; Senit.

SONARS. One DUBV 23 hull mounted; one DUBV 43 VDS.

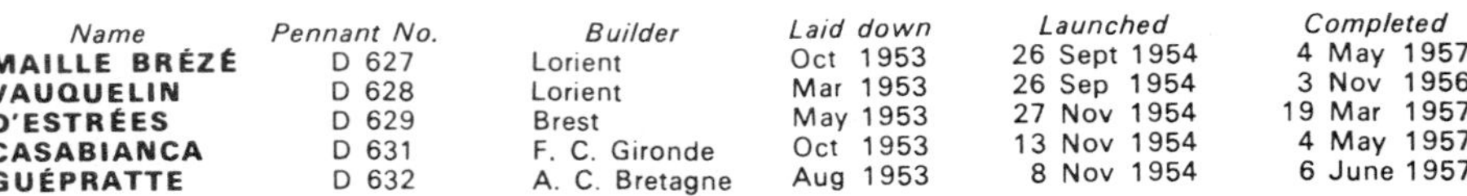

Name	*Pennant No.*	*Builder*	*Laid down*	*Launched*	*Completed*
MAILLE BRÉZÉ	D 627	Lorient	Oct 1953	26 Sept 1954	4 May 1957
VAUQUELIN	D 628	Lorient	Mar 1953	26 Sep 1954	3 Nov 1956
D'ESTRÉES	D 629	Brest	May 1953	27 Nov 1954	19 Mar 1957
CASABIANCA	D 631	F. C. Gironde	Oct 1953	13 Nov 1954	4 May 1957
GUÉPRATTE	D 632	A. C. Bretagne	Aug 1953	8 Nov 1954	6 June 1957

TYPE 47 (ASW)

GUÉPRATTE *1973, French Navy*

MAILLE BRÉZÉ *1973 French Navy*

1 "ACONIT" CLASS

ACONIT F 703

Displacement, tons	3 500 standard; 3 800 full load
Length, feet (*metres*)	416·7 (*127·0*) oa
Beam, feet (*metres*)	44·0 (*13·4*)
Draught, feet (*metres*)	18·9 (*5·8*) screws
Missiles, A/S	"Malafon" rocket/homing torpedo MM 38 Exocet to be fitted
Guns	2—3·9 in (*100 mm*) AA
A/S weapons	1 quadruple 12 in (*305 mm*) mortar
Torpedoes	2 launchers for Mk L5
Main engines	Rateau geared turbine; 1 shaft; 28 650 shp
Boilers	2 automatic
Speed, knots	27
Range, miles	5 000 at 18 knots
Complement	215 (15 officers, 200 men)

Rated as "Corvette". Laid down at Lorient in Jan 1966 and launched on 7 Mar 1970, commissioned 15 May 1971 for service in 1972.

RADAR. One DRBV 13 (S-band surveillance); one DRBC 32B (X-band fire control); one DRBN 32 (search/navigation set); one DRBV 32A; Senit.

SONAR. One hull-mounted DUBV 23; one VDS type DUBV 43.

ACONIT *1974, Wright and Logan*

ACONIT *French Navy*

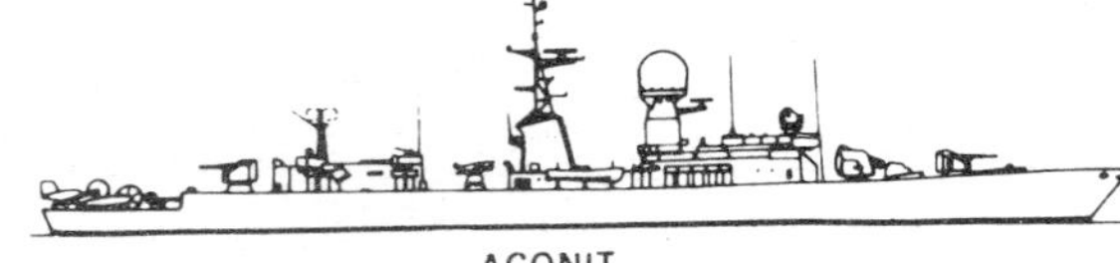

ACONIT

FRIGATES

9 "COMMANDANT RIVIÈRE" CLASS

Displacement, tons	1 750 standard; 2 250 full load (*Balny* 1 650 standard; 1 950 full load)
Length, feet (*metres*)	321·5 (*98·0*) pp; 338 (*103*) oa
Beam, feet (*metres*)	37·8 (*11·5*)
Draught, feet (*metres*)	12·5 (*3·8*) mean; 14·1 (*4·3*) max
Aircraft	1 light helicopter can land aft
Missiles	See note
Guns	3—3·9 in (*100 mm*) automatic, singles (*Balny, Henry* and *Bourdais* 2 only); 2—30 mm
A/S	1—12 in (*305 mm*) quadruple mortar
Torpedo tubes	6—21 in (*533 mm*) (triple) for Mk K2 and L3
Main engines	4 SEMT-Pielstick diesels; 16 000 bhp; 2 shafts; (except *Balny:* CODAG; 2 diesels (16 cyl); one TG Turboméca M38; 1 shaft; VP screw).
Speed, knots	25 max (26·6 trials)
Range, miles	4 500 at 15 knots (*Balny* 8 000 at 12 knots)
Complement	215 (15 officers, 200 men)

GENERAL
All built by Lorient Dockyard. Fitted for operations under widely differing conditions. Capable of accepting a light helicopter aft. Can carry a force of up to 80 soldiers in an emergency, as well as two 30 ft LCAs. *Balny's* trials continued for several years. *Commandant Bourdais, Victor Schoelcher, Amiral Charner* and *Enseigne Henry* had helicopter platforms rigged in place of X Gun in 1973-74. *Commandant Bory* had experimental machinery replaced by conventional diesels in 1973. *Victor Schoelcher* acts as training ship, with an additional deck-house aft. *Com, Belo* class of Portugal is similar.

Name	No.	Launched	Completed
AMIRAL CHARNER	F 727	Mar 1960	Dec 1962
BALNY	F 729	Mar 1962	Feb 1971
COMMANDANT BORY	F 726	Oct 1958	Mar 1964
COMMANDANT BOURDAIS	F 740	Apr 1961	Mar 1963
COMMANDANT RIVIÈRE	F 733	Oct 1958	Dec 1962
DOUDART DE LA GRÉE	F 728	Apr 1961	Mar 1963
ENSEIGNE HENRY	F 749	Dec 1963	Jan 1965
PROTET	F 748	Dec 1962	May 1964
VICTOR SCHOELCHER	F 725	Oct 1958	Dec 1962

BALNY (before fitting of Exocet) *1974, French Navy*

MISSILES. All of this class except *Victor Schoelcher* are to be fitted with 4—MM 38 Exocet in place of X gun or the helicopter deck where fitted. *Bory* is currently being fitted, to be followed by *De La Grée*.

RADAR. Search: DRBV 22A. Tactical: S Band. Fire Control: X Band DRBC 32A. One DRBV 50; one DRBN 32.

SONAR. One DUBA 3; one SQS 17.

14 "LE NORMAND" CLASS

(E52 TYPE)

Displacement, tons	1 250 standard; 1 702 full load
Length, feet (*metres*)	311·7 (*95·0*) pp; 325·8 (*99·8*) oa
Beam, feet (*metres*)	33·8 (*10·3*)
Draught, feet (*metres*)	11·2 (*3·4*) aft; 13·5 (*4·1*) screws
Guns,	6—2·25 in (*57 mm*) in twin mountings (4 only in F 771, 772 773); 2—20 mm
A/S	Sextuple Bofors ASM (*lance-roquettes*) mortar forward (*except* F 776, 777, 778 with 1—12 in (*305 mm*) quadruple mortar) 2 DC mortars; 1 DC rack
Torpedo tubes	12 ASM (4 triple mountings aft) for Mk K2 and L3
Boilers	2 Indret; pressure 500 psi (*35·2 kg/cm²*); superheat 725°F (385°C)
Main engines	Parsons or Rateau geared turbines 20 000 shp
Speed, knots	27
Range, miles	4 500 at 15 knots
Oil fuel, tons	310
Complement	205 (13 officers, 192 men)

GENERAL
The E 52 type have similar characteristics to the E 50 type as regards hull and machinery but are easily distinguished in that they have the ASM tubes aft and the heavy hedgehog or ASM howitzer forward while the E 50 type have the ASM torpedo tubes forward. *L'Agenais, L'Alsacien, Le Basque, Le Béarnais, Le Breton, Le Provencal* and *Le Vendéen* have a different arrangement of bridges. *L'Alsacien, Le Provencal* and *Le Vendéen* are of the E 52B type and have the Strombos-Velensi modified funnel cap.

RADAR. Search: DRBV 22A. Fire Control: One DRBV 32; one DRBC 31.

SONAR. One DUBV 24; one DUBA 1 (except 771, 772, 773, one DUBV 1 and one DUBA 1).

Name	No.	Builders	Laid down	Launched	Completed
L'AGENAIS	F 774	Lorient	Aug 1955	23 June 1956	14 May 1958
L'ALSACIEN	F 776	Lorient	July 1956	26 Jan 1957	27 Aug 1960
LE BASQUE	F 773	Lorient	Dec 1954	25 Feb 1956	18 Oct 1957
LE BÉARNAIS	F 775	Lorient	Dec 1955	23 June 1956	18 Oct 1958
LE BRETON	F 772	Lorient	June 1954	2 Apr 1955	20 Aug 1957
LE BOURGUIGNON	F 769	Penhoet	Jan 1954	28 Jan 1956	11 July 1957
LE CHAMPENOIS	F 770	A. C. Loire	May 1954	12 Mar 1955	1 June 1957
LE GASCON	F 767	A. C. Loire	Feb 1954	23 Oct 1954	29 Mar 1957
LE LORRAIN	F 768	F. Ch de la Medit	July 1953	13 Feb 1954	3 Nov 1956
LE NORMAND	F 765	F. Ch. de la Medit	July 1953	13 Feb 1954	3 Nov 1956
LE PICARD	F 766	A. C. Loire	Nov 1953	31 May 1954	20 Sep 1956
LE PROVENCAL	F 777	Lorient	Feb 1957	5 Oct 1957	6 Nov 1959
LE SAVOYARD	F 771	F. Ch. de la Medit	Nov 1953	7 May 1955	14 June 1956
LE VENDÉEN	F 778	F. Ch. de la Medit	Mar 1957	27 July 1957	1 Oct 1960

L'ALSACIEN, LE PROVENCAL, LE VENDÉEN

"LE NORMAND" Class

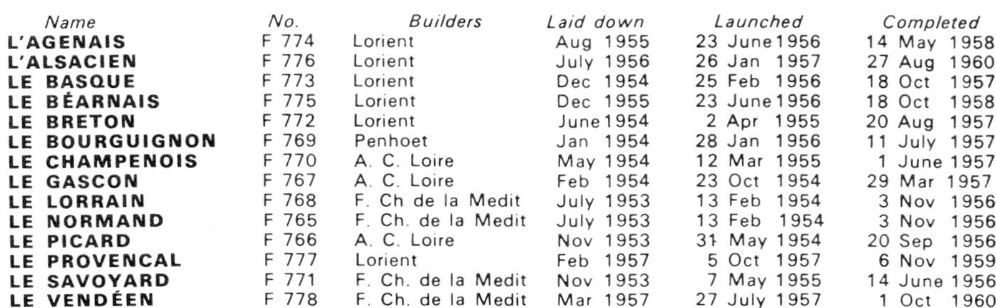
LE VENDÉEN *1972, Dr. Giorgio Arra*

LE BEARNAIS *1972, Dr. Giorgio Arra*

Frigates—*continued*

2 E50 TYPE

Name	No.	Builders	Laid down	Launched	Completed
LE BOULONNAIS	F 763	A. C. Loire	Mar 1952	12 May 1953	5 Aug 1955
LE BRESTOIS	F 762	Lorient Navy Yard	Nov 1951	16 Aug 1952	19 Jan 1956

Displacement, tons: 1 250 standard; 1 528 for trials; 1 702 full load
Length, feet (*metres*): 311·7 (*95·0*) pp; 327·3 (*99·8*) oa
Beam, feet (*metres*): 33·8 (*10·3*)
Draught, feet (*metres*): 13·5 (*4·1*) screws
Guns, AA: 6—2·25 in (*57 mm*) (twins); 2—20 mm
A/S weapons: 1—375 mm Mk 54 rocket launcher;
Torpedo tubes: 12 tubes (four triple mounts forward) for Mk K2 and L3
Main engines: 2 Rateau A & C de B geared turbines; 20 000 shp; 2 shafts
Speed, knots: 27 (29 on trials); economical speed 14
Range, miles: 4 500 at 15 knots
Oil fuel, tons: 292
Complement: 205 (13 officers, 192 men)

GENERAL
Le Brestois has similar mast arrangement to that in *Le Provencal.*

GUNNERY. *Le Brestois* had a single 3·9 in (*100 mm*) automatic AA gun mounted in place of the after twin 57 mm mounting for experimental purposes and after her refit, completed in 1963, she retained this mounting.

RADAR. Search: DRBV 20; one DRBN 32; one DRBC 31.

SONAR. One DUBV 1; one DUBA 1.

E 50 Type

LE BRESTOIS — *1972, Dr, Giorgio Arra*

14 NEW CONSTRUCTION TYPE A69

Name	No.	Laid down	Launched	Service
D'ESTIENNE D'ORVES	F 781	Aug 1972	1 June 1973	Oct 1975
AMYOT D'INVILLE	F 782	Sep 1973	30 Nov 1974	July 1976
DROGOU	F 783	Oct 1973	30 Nov 1974	July 1976
DETROYAT	F 784	1974	1975	July 1977
JEAN MOULIN	F 785	15 Jan 1974	1 Feb 1976	Jan 1977
QUARTIER-MAITRE ANQUETIL	F 786	1 Aug 1975	15 Aug 1976	June 1977
COMMANDANT DE PIMODAN	F 787	1 Sep 1975	15 Aug 1976	Dec 1977
SECOND-MAITRE LE BIHAN	F 788	15 Feb 1976	Mar 1977	Dec 1977
LIEUTENANT-DE-VAISSEAU LE HÉNAFF	F 789	15 Mar 1976	Mar 1977	Jan 1978
LIEUTENANT-DE-VAISSEAU LAVALLÉE	F 790	1 Sep 1976	Sep 1977	July 1978
COMMANDANT L'HERMINIÈR	F 791	1 Oct 1976	Sep 1977	Aug 1978
PREMIER-MAITRE L'HER	F 792	15 Mar 1977	Apr 1978	Feb 1979
COMMANDANT BLAISON	F 793	15 Apr 1977	Apr 1978	Feb 1979
ENSEIGNE-DE-VAISSEAU JACOUBET	F 794	Oct 1977	Oct 1978	Aug 1979

Displacement, tons: 950 standard; 1 170 full load
Length, feet (*metres*): 262·5 (*80·0*) oa
Beam, feet (*metres*): 33·8 (*10·3*)
Draught, feet (*metres*): 9·8 (*3·0*)
Missiles: See Note.
Guns: 1—3·9 in (*100 mm*) AA; 2—20 mm AA
A/S weapons: 1—375 mm Mk 54 Rocket launcher
Torpedoes: 4 fixed tubes for Mk L3 and L5
Main engines: 2 SEMT Pielstick PC2V diesels; 2 shafts; controllable pitch propellers; 11 000 bhp
Speed, knots: 24
Range, miles: 4 500 at 15 knots
Complement: 62 (4 officers, 58 men)

GENERAL
Primarily intended for coastal A/S operations—officially classified as "Avisos". Also available for overseas patrols and can carry a detachment of 2 officers and 29 men. *D'Estienne D'orves* commissioned for trials 26 Oct 1974. All building at Lorient

MISSILES. 2—MM 38 Exocet will probably be fitted.

RADAR. One Decca type 202 navigation set; one DRBV 51 stabilised surveillance and target designator; One DRBC 32E fire control; one DRBN 32.

SONAR. One hull mounted sonar DUBA 25.

A 69 TYPE (A70 similar hull)

D'ESTIENNE D'ORVES after launching — *1973, French Navy*

NEW CONSTRUCTION TYPE A70

Very similar to the type A 69, ships of this type are planned for building in the near future with Lorient acting as the lead yard. The details and remarks listed for Type A 69 apply also to Type A 70—in addition the latter will mount two MM 38 Exocet launchers with associated radar.

SUBMARINES

5+1 NUCLEAR POWERED BALLISTIC MISSILE TYPE (SNLE)

Name	No.	Builders	Laid down	Launched	Trials	Operational
LE REDOUTABLE	S 611	Cherbourg Naval Dockyard	30 Mar 1964	29 Mar 1967	July 1969	1 Dec 1970
LE TERRIBLE	S 612	Cherbourg Naval Dockyard	24 June 1967	12 Dec 1969	1971	1 Jan 1973
LE FOUDROYANT	S 610	Cherbourg Naval Dockyard	1969	4 Dec 1971	May 1973	6 June 1974
L'INDOMPTABLE	S 613	Cherbourg Naval Dockyard	1971	17 Sep 1974	11 Jan 1975	Oct 1976
LE TONNANT	S 614 (Q 259)	Cherbourg Naval Dockyard	1973	1975	—	July 1978
—	— (Q 260)	Cherbourg Naval Dockyard	—	—	—	1982

Displacement, tons	7 500 surface; 9 000 dived
Length, feet (*metres*)	420 (*128·0*)
Beam, feet (*metres*)	34·8 (*10·6*)
Draught, feet (*metres*)	32·8 (*10·0*)
Missile launchers	16 tubes amidships for ICBM's;
Torpedo tubes	4—21·7 inch (18 torpedoes)
Nuclear reactor	1 pressurised water-cooled
Main machinery	2 turbo-alternators; 1 electric motor; 15 000 hp; 1 shaft
Auxiliary propulsion	1 diesel (5 000 miles fuel)
Speed, knots	20 on surface; 25 dived
Complement	Two alternating crews each of 135 (15 officers, 120 men)
Diving Depth	Over 700 ft

GENERAL
Le Redoutable was the first French nuclear powered, ballistic missile armed submarine and the prototype of the *"Force de dissuasion"* of six such vessels which the Navy plans to have in the early 1980s. The decision to build a fourth unit of this class was announced on 7 Dec 1967 the fifth in Feb 1972 and the sixth on 30 Apr 1974.

MISSILES. First boats armed with MSBS M-1 of 18 tons launch weight. *Le Foudroyant* is armed with MSBS M-2 of 19·9 tons with a 1 300 n. mile range carrying a 500 KT head. *Le Redoutable* will be fitted with M-2 at her first refit. *L'Indomptable* will receive the M-20 system with 1 500 n. mile range missiles carrying a megaton reinforced head. All of this class will later receive the M-4 system with a range reportedly in the 3 000 mile bracket and carrying MIRV warheads.

LE REDOUTABLE *1972, French Navy*

RADAR. *Le Redoutable* is equipped with Calypso X Band radar for navigation and attack. Has passive ECM and DF systems.

REACTOR. The reactor is a natural-water-cooled type running on enriched uranium, feeding twin turbines and two turbo-alternators.

LE REDOUTABLE, LE TERRIBLE, LE FOUDROYANT *1973, French Navy*

1 EXPERIMENTAL MISSILE TYPE

Name	No.	Builders	Laid down	Launched	Completed
GYMNOTE	S 655	Cherbourg Naval Dockyard	17 Mar 1963	17 Mar 1964	17 Oct 1966

Displacement, tons	3 000 surface; 3 250 dived
Length, feet (*metres*)	275·6 (*84·0*)
Beam, feet (*metres*)	34·7 (*10·6*)
Draught, feet (*metres*)	25 (*7·6*)
Missile launchers	4 tubes for MSBS
Main machinery	4 sets 620 kW diesel electric; 2 electric motors; 2 shafts; 2 600 hp
Speed, knots	11 surface; 10 dived
Complement	78 (8 officers, 70 men)

An experimental submarine for testing ballistic missiles for the first French nuclear powered deterrent submarines, and for use as an underwater laboratory to prove equipment and arms for nuclear powered submarines.

HULL. *Gymnote* was the hull laid down in 1958 as the nuclear powered submarine Q 244 which was cancelled in 1959. The hull was still available when a trials vessel for the French "Polaris" type missiles was required and was completed as *Gymnote*.

GYMNOTE *1970, French Navy*

Submarines—*continued*

1 NEW CONSTRUCTION FLEET SUBMARINE

SNA 72

It was announced in 1973 that a nuclear-propelled fleet submarine would be included in the 1974 Programme. She will be laid down in January 1976.
The tonnage proposed is 2 500, a remarkable figure indicating an unexpected advance in the design of smaller reactors. The general layout and appearance, armament and equipment will be similar to that of the "Agosta" class.
She will have a single reactor and one screw, giving a speed of 25 knots. Studies of the machinery are in progress at Cadarache.

Two squadrons of these submarines are forecast, one to be stationed at Brest and the other at Toulon from 1982.

1 + 3 "AGOSTA" CLASS

Displacement, tons	1 200 standard; 1 470 surface; 1 790 dived
Length, feet (*metres*)	221·7 (*67·9*)
Beam, feet (*metres*)	22·3 (*6·8*)
Draught, feet (*metres*)	17·7 (*5·2*)
Tubes	4—21·4 in (*550 mm*) 20 reload torpedoes
Main machinery	Diesel-electric; 2 SEMT Peilstick diesels 3 600 hp; 1 main motor 4 600 hp; 1 cruising motor; 1 shaft
Speed, knots	12 surfaced; 20 submerged
Range, miles	9 000 at 9 knots (snorting); 350 at 3·5 knots (dived)
Endurance	45 days
Complement	50 (7 officers, 43 men)

Name	*No.*	*Builder*	*Laid down*	*Launched*	*Operational*
AGOSTA	S 620	Cherbourg	7 Feb 1972	19 Oct 1974	1976 (Trials 9 Nov 1974)
BÉVÉZIERS	S 621	Cherbourg	17 May 1973	1975	1976
LA PRAYA	S 622	Cherbourg	1974	1975	1976
OUESSANT	S 623	Cherbourg	1974	1976	1977

GENERAL
New type of patrol submarines of high performance, the building of which was announced in 1970 under the third five-year new construction plan 1971-75.

RADAR. Possibly X Band Calypso Th D 1030 or 1031 for search/navigation.

SONAR. DUUA 2 active sonar with transducers forward and aft; DSUV passive sonar with 36 hydrophones; passive ranging; intercept set.

TORPEDO TUBES. A new design allowing for Torpedo discharge at all speeds and down to full diving depth. Rapid reloading fitted.

FOREIGN ORDERS. Two to be built at Cartagena for Spanish Navy.

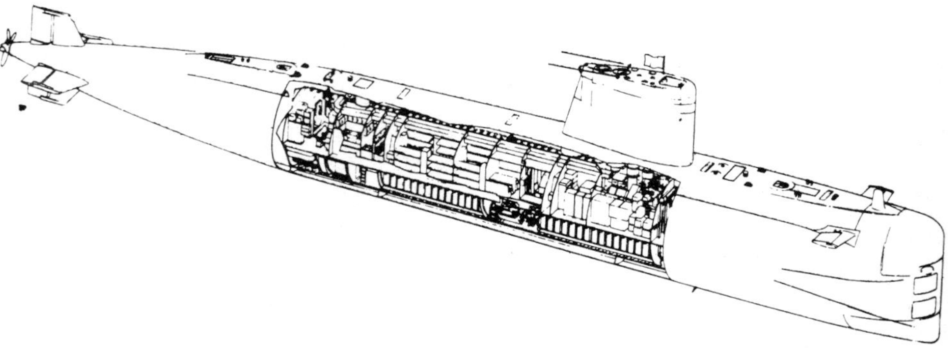

BEVEZIERS *1973, Cols Bleus*

8 "DAPHNE" CLASS

Displacement, tons	869 surface; 1 043 dived
Length, feet (*metres*)	189·6 (*57·8*)
Beam, feet (*metres*)	22·3 (*6·8*)
Draught, feet (*metres*)	15·1 (*4·6*)
Torpedo tubes	12—21·7 in (*550 mm*) 8 bow 4 stern
Main machinery	SEMT-Pielstick diesel-electric 1 300 bhp surface; 1 600 hp motors dived; 2 shafts
Range, miles	2 700 at 12·5 knots (surfaced); 4 500 at 5 knots (snorting); 3 000 at 7 knots (snorting)
Speed, knots	13·5 surface; 16 dived
Complement	45 (6 officers, 39 men)

Name	*No.*	*Builder*	*Laid down*	*Launched*	*Completed*
DAPHNÉ	S 641	Dubigeon	Mar 1958	20 June 1959	1 June 1964
DIANE	S 642	Dubigeon	July 1958	4 Oct 1960	20 June 1964
DORIS	S 643	Cherbourg	Sep 1958	14 May 1960	26 Aug 1964
FLORE	S 645	Cherbourg	Sep 1958	21 Dec 1960	21 May 1964
GALATÉE	S 646	Cherbourg	Sep 1958	22 Sep 1961	25 July 1964
JUNON	S 648	Cherbourg	July 1961	11 May 1964	25 Feb 1966
VENUS	S 649	Cherbourg	Aug 1961	24 Sep 1964	1 Jan 1966
PSYCHÉ	S 650	Brest	May 1961	28 June 1967	July 1969

GENERAL
Improved "Arethuse" class with diving depth about 1 000 ft (*300 metres*).

DELETION. *Sirene* sank at Lorient in 1972, was subsequently salved and later scrapped.

MODERNISATION. In hand from 1971 to improve sonar and armament—completed in *Galatée, Diane, Doris*. *Flore* in hand.

RADAR. X Band Calypso II for search/navigation.

SONAR. DUUA 2 active sonar with transducers forward and aft; passive ranging; intercept set.

FOREIGN ORDERS. South Africa (3), Pakistan (3), Portugal (4), Spain (building in Spain) (4).

DAPHNÉ *1974, Wright and Logan*

DAPHNÉ *1973, Dr, Giorgio Arra*

Submarines—*continued*

4 "ARÉTHUSE" CLASS

Name	No.	Programme	Builders	Laid down	Launched	Completed
AMAZONE	S 639	1954	Cherbourg	Dec 1955	3 Apr 1958	1 July 1959
ARÉTHUSE	S 635	1953	Cherbourg	Mar 1955	9 Nov 1957	23 Oct 1958
ARGONAUTE	S 636	1953	Cherbourg	Mar 1955	29 June 1957	11 Feb 1959
ARIANE	S 640	1954	Cherbourg	Dec 1955	12 Sep 1958	16 Mar 1960

Displacement, tons	400 standard; 543 surface; 669 submerged
Length, feet (*metres*)	162·7 (*49·6*)
Beam, feet (*metres*)	19 (*5·8*)
Draught, feet (*metres*)	13·1 (*4·0*)
Torpedo tubes	4—21·7 in (*550 mm*) bow, 4
Main machinery	12-cyl. SEMT-Pielstick diesel-electric; 1 060 bhp surface; 1 300 hp motors dived; 1 shaft
Speed, knots	12·5 surface; 16 dived
Complement	40 (6 officers, 34 men)

GENERAL
An excellent class of small submarines with a minimum number of ballast tanks and a diving depth of about 600 feet.

ARÉTHUSE — *1974, Wright and Logan*

6 "NARVAL" CLASS

Name	No.	Programme	Builders	Laid down	Launched	Completed
NARVAL	S 631	1949	Cherbourg	June 1951	11 Dec 1954	1 Dec 1957
MARSOUIN	S 632	1949	Cherbourg	Sept 1951	21 May 1955	1 Oct 1957
DAUPHIN	S 633	1950	Cherbourg	May 1952	17 Sep 1955	1 Aug 1958
REQUIN	S 634	1950	Cherbourg	June 1952	3 Dec 1955	1 Aug 1958
ESPADON	S 637	1954	Normand	Dec 1955	15 Sep 1958	2 Apr 1960
MORSE	S 638	1954	Seine Maritime	Feb 1956	10 Dec 1958	2 May 1960

Displacement, tons	1 320 standard; 1 635 surface; 1 910 dived
Length, feet (*metres*)	257·2 (*77·6*)
Beam, feet (*metres*)	25·6 (*7·8*)
Draught, feet (*metres*)	18·5 (*5·4*)
Torpedo tubes	6—21·7 in (*550 mm*) bow; 14 reload torpedoes; capable of minelaying
Main machinery	Diesel electric, three 12-cyl SEMT-Pielstick diesels; two 2 400 hp electric motors; 2 shafts
Speed, knots	15 surface; 18 dived
Range, miles	15 000 at 8 knots (snorting)
Endurance	45 days
Complement	63 (7 officers, 56 men)

NARVAL — *1974, French Navy*

GENERAL
Improved versions based on the German XXI type. *Dauphine, Marsouin, Narval* and *Requin* were built in seven prefabricated parts each of 10 metres in length.

RECONSTRUCTION. During a five-year reconstruction programme, announced in 1965 and completed by the end of 1970, these submarines, *Requin* in Spring 1967 and *Espadon* and *Morse* in succession at Lorient followed by the other three, were given a new diesel electric power plant as well as new weapon and detection equipment.

ENGINEERING. New main propelling machinery installed on reconstruction during 1965 to 1970 includes diesel-electric drive on the surface with SEMT-Pielstick diesels. The original main machinery was Schneider 4 000 bhp 7 cyl. 2 str. diesels for surface propulsion and 5 000 hp electric motors submerged.

SONAR. DUUA 1.

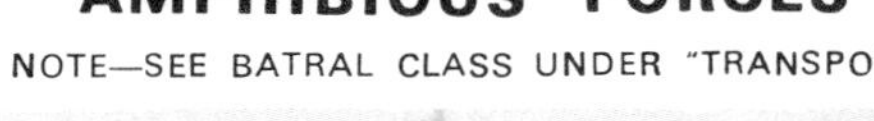

AMPHIBIOUS FORCES

NOTE—SEE BATRAL CLASS UNDER "TRANSPORTS"

2 LANDING SHIPS (DOCK) (TCD)

OURAGAN L 9021 **ORAGE** L 9022

Displacement, tons	5 800 light; 8 500 full load; 15 000 when fully immersed
Length, feet (*metres*)	488·9 (*149·0*)
Beam, feet (*metres*)	70·5 (*21·5*)
Draught, feet (*metres*)	16·1 (*4·9*); 28·5 (*8·7*) max
Guns	2—4·7 in (*120 mm*) mortars; 6—30 mm
Main engines	2 diesels; 2 shafts; 8 640 bhp
Speed, knots	17
Range, miles	4 000 at 15 knots
Complement	239 (16 officers, 223 men)

OURAGAN — *1970, Contre Amiral M. Adam*

Built at Brest Dockyard. *Ouragan* was laid down in June 1962, launched on 9 Nov 1963, completed for trials in 1964, and commissioned in Jan 1965. *Orage* was laid down in June 1966, launched on 22 Apr 1967 and completed in Mar 1968. Bridge is on the starboard side. Fitted with a platform for four heavy helicopters. Able to carry EDICs loaded with eleven light tanks each, or 18 loaded LCMs, also 1 500 tons of material and equipment handled by two 35 ton cranes. *Orage* is allocated to the Pacific Nuclear Experimental Centre. Can carry 350 troops normally or 470 for short periods.

SONAR. One SQS-17 in *Ouragan*.

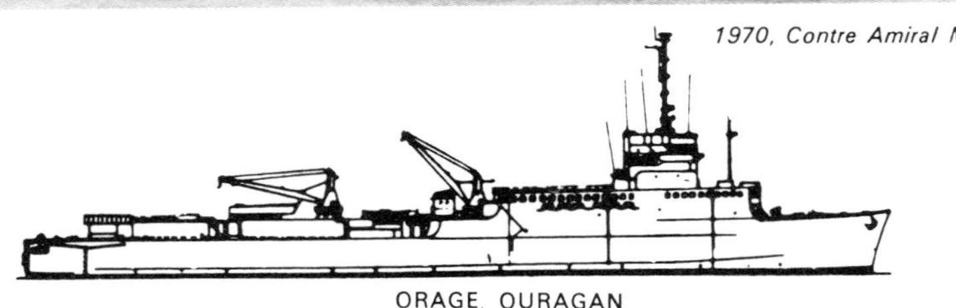

ORAGE, OURAGAN

ORAGE — *1969, French Navy*

Amphibious Forces—*continued*

5 LANDING SHIPS (TANK)

ARGENS L 9003 **BIDASSOA** L 9004 **BLAVET** L 9009 **DIVES** L 9008 **TRIEUX** L9007

Displacement, tons	1 400 standard; 1 765 normal; 4 225 full load
Dimensions, ft (*m*)	328 oa × 50 × 14 (*102·1 × 15·5 × 3·2*)
Guns	2—40 mm AA; 4—20 mm AA (*Argens, Trieux*) 1—4·7 in mortar; 3—40 mm AA (*Bidassoa, Blavet, Dives*)
Main engines	SEMT-Pielstick diesels; 2 shafts; 2 000 bhp = 11 knots
Range, miles	18 500 at 10 knots
Complement	85 (6 officers and 79 men.) Plus 170 troops (normal)

Built by Chantiers Seine Maritime (*Bidassoa, Dives*) and Chantiers de Bretagne, Nantes (others). Launched on 7 Apr 1959, 30 Dec 1960, 15 Jan 1960, 29 June 1960 and 6 Dec 1958, respectively. All commissioned in 1960-61. Can carry: 4 LCVP's, 1 800 tons of freight, 335 (up to 807 if required) troops (329 in bunks, 552 in hammocks). *Blavet* and *Trieux* are fitted as light helicopter carriers with a hanger before the bridge and can carry two Alouette III.

ARGENS *1971, Dr. Giorgio Arra*

10 LANDING CRAFT (TANK) (EDIC)

L 9091 (7 Jan 1958) **L 9092** (2 Dec 1958) **L 9093** (17 Apr 1958) **L 9094** (24 July 1958) **L 9096** (11 Oct 1958) **L 9070** (30 Mar 1967) **L 9071** (4 Nov 1967) **L 9072** (1968) **L 9073** (1968) **L 9074** (22 July 1969)

Displacement, tons	250 standard; 670 full load
Dimensions, ft (*m*)	193·5 × 39·2 × 4·5 (*59 × 12 × 1·3*)
Guns	2—20 mm AA
Main engines	MGO diesels; 2 shafts; 1 000 bhp = 8 knots
Range, miles	1 800 at 8 knots
Complement	16 (1 officer, and 15 men)

Seven were built by C. N. Franco Belges, two by Toulon Dockyard, two by La Perrière. Launch dates above. Can carry 11 lorries or 5 Light Fighting Vehicles.
TRANSFER. L 9095 transferred to Senegal 1 July 1974 as *La Faleme*.

EDIC L 9092 *1973, Dr, Giorgio Arra*

ISSOLE L 9097 (LCT)

Displacement, tons	600 full load
Dimensions, feet	160·8 × 32 × 7·2
Main engines	2 diesels; 1 000 bhp = 12 knots

Built at Toulon in 1957-58. Coaster with bow doors and ramp.

ISSOLE *1969, Godfrey H. Walker*

LCT 9061 (ex-HMS *Buttress*, LCT(8) 4099)

Displacement, tons	657 standard; 1 000 full load
Dimensions, ft (*m*)	231·2 × 39 × 5·9 (*70·5 × 11·9 × 1·8*)
Guns	2—20 mm; 1—120mm mortar
Main engines	4 Paxman diesels; 2 shafts; 1 840 bhp = 9 knots
Complement	29 (2 officers, 27 men)

Former British landing craft bought in July 1965.

14 LCM's

CTM 1 to 14

Displacement, tons	56 standard; 150 full load
Dimensions, ft (*m*)	92·8 × 21 × 3·9 (*28·3 × 6·4 × 1·2*)
Main engines	Hispano diesels; 2 shafts; 225 hp = 9·5 knots
Complement	6

Can carry up to 90 tons in coastal or protected waters.

CORVETTES

"LE FOUGUEUX" CLASS

L'ADROIT (5 Oct 1957) P 644
L'ALERTE (5 Oct 1957) P 645
L'ATTENTIF (5 Oct 1957) P 646
L'ARDENT (17 July 1958) P 635
L'EFFRONTÉ (27 Jan 1959) P 638
L'ENJOUÉ (5 Oct 1957) P 647
L'ÉTOURDI (5 Feb 1958) P 637
LE FRINGANT (6 Feb 1959) P 640
LE FRONDEUR (26 Feb 1959) P 639
LE HARDI (17 Sep 1958) P 648
L'INTRÉPIDE (12 Dec 1958) P 630

Displacement, tons	325 standard; 400 full load
Dimensions, ft (*m*)	170 pp × 23 × 6·5 (*53 × 7·3 × 3·1*)
Guns	2—40 mm Bofors AA; 2—20 mm AA (P 641—3 only)
A/S weapons	1 hedgehog; 4 DC mortars; 2 DC racks; (P 641—3 only); 1—120 mm A/S mortar; 2 DC mortars; 2 DC racks (rest)
Tubes	*L'Intrepide* has a tube mounted on the stern
Main engines	4 SEMT-Pielstick diesel engines coupled 2 by 2; 3 240 bhp = 18·6 knots (22 knots on trial)
Range, miles	3 000 at 12 knots; 2 000 at 15 knots
Complement	63 (4 officers, 59 men)

Five were built under the 1955 and six under the 1956 estimates. These have a different armament, and modified bridge. Original 3 of this class of 14 deleted 1974.

SONAR. One DUBA 2 (P 641—3); one QCU2. (remainder)

SIMILAR CLASSES. Four "Boavista" class (Portugal) and one in Yugoslavia.

L'ATTENTIF *11/1973, Wright and Logan*

6 "LA DUNKERQUOISE" CLASS

LA DUNKERQUOISE (ex-*Fundy*) P 653
LA MALOUINE (ex-*Cowlcham*) P 651
LA BAYONNAISE (ex-*Chignecto*) P 654
LA PAIMPOLAISE (ex-*Thunder*) P 657
LA DIEPPOISE (ex-*Chaleur*) P 655
LA LORIENTAISE (ex-*Miarmachi*) P 652

Displacement, tons	370 full load; 470 standard;
Dimensions, ft (*m*)	140 pp; 152 oa × 28 × 8·7 (*50 × 9·2 × 2·8*)
Gun	1—40 mm
Main engines	General Motors diesels; 2 shafts; 2 500 bhp = 15 knots max
Oil fuel, tons	52
Range, miles	4 500 at 11 knots
Complement	43 (4 officers, 39 men)

La Bayonnaise (launched 12 May 1952), *La Malouine* (launched 12 Nov 1951) and *La Paimpolaise* (launched 17 July 1953) were transferred to the French flag at Halifax on 1 Apr 1954, *Dunkerquoise* (launched 17 July 1953) on 30 Apr 1954, and *La Dieppoise* (launched 21 June 1952) and *La Lorientaise* (launched in 1953) on 10 Oct 1954. All similar to the "Bay" class in the Royal Canadian Navy. All transferred from minesweeping to overseas patrol operations 1973. They have been air conditioned.

LA DIEPPOISE *1971, French Navy*

5 "SIRIUS" CLASS

ALTAIR P 656
ARCTURUS P 650
CROIX DU SUD P 658
CANOPUS P 659
ÉTOILE POLAIRE P 660

All of "Sirius" class minesweepers (see Minewarfare Section for details) transferred for coastal patrol operations 1973.

LIGHT FORCES

Note. Orders placed by (a) Iran for twelve "Combattante II" class (6 in June 1974 and 6 in Nov 1974). (b) Greece for four "Combattante III" in Oct 1974.

LA COMBATTANTE P 730 (FAST ATTACK CRAFT—MISSILE)

Displacement, tons	180 standard; 202 full load
Dimensions, ft (*m*)	147·8 × 24·2 × 6·5 (*45 × 7·4 × 2·5*)
Gun	1—30 mm AA
Launchers	1 quadruple for SS 11; 1 for 14 flares
Main engines	2 SEMT-Pielstick diesels; 2 shafts; controllable pitch propellers; 3 200 bhp = 23 knots
Range, miles	2 000 at 12 knots
Complement	25 (3 officers, 22 men)

Authorised under the 1960 Programme. Built by Constructions Mécaniques de Normandie. Laid down in April 1962, launched on 20 June 1963, and completed on 1 Mar 1964. Of wooden and plastic laminated non-magnetic construction. Was fitted for trials of the MM 38 missile system (Exocet).

LA COMBATTANTE *1972, Dr. Giorgio Arra*

6 + 24 "TRIDENT" CLASS (FAST ATTACK CRAFT—MISSILE)

TRIDENT	P 670	**PERTUISANE**	P 673
GLAIVE	P 671	**RAPIÉRE**	P 674
EPÉE	P 672	**SABRE**	P 675

Displacement, tons	125 standard; 147·5 full load
Dimensions, ft (*m*)	121·4 × 18 × 5·2 (*40·4 × 5·9 × 1·6*)
Missiles	6—SS 12
Gun	1—30 mm
Main engines	2 Ago diesels; 4 000 hp = 25 knots
Range, miles	1 500 at 15 knots
Complement	19 (2 officers and 17 men)

Trident laid down 1973. Builders—Auroux, Arcachon for 670 and 671. CMN Cherbourg for second pair. These are lead boats for a class of 30 in the "Blue Plan". of which 16 are to be adapted for overseas service. Trials for *Trident* due to start 1 Oct 1975, for *Glaive* and *Epée* on 1 Feb 1976 and *Pertuisane* on 1 May 1976.

1 FAIRMILE ML TYPE (LARGE PATROL CRAFT)

OISEAU DES ILES A 716

Displacement, tons	140 full load
Dimensions, feet	111·5 × 18·4 × 4·3 (*34 × 5·6 × 1·3*)
Speed, knots	11·5

Former Fairmile motor launch was allocated to the Navy for training frogmen.

Y 760 (ex-P 9786) **Y 761** (ex-P 9785)

Displacement, tons	45
Dimensions, feet	79·3 × 14·8 × 4·2
Guns	8—0·5 MG (four twin mountings)
Main engines	2 Daimler-Benz diesels; 2 shafts; 1 000 bhp = 18 knots

Built by Burmeister-Bremen and Bodenwerft-Kressbronn. Completed in 1954.

5 Ex-BRITISH "HAM" CLASS (LARGE PATROL CRAFT)

GÉRANIUM (ex-*Tibenham* (ex-M 784) P 784
JONQUILLE (ex-*Sulham*) (ex-M 787) P 787
VIOLETTE (ex-*Mersham*) (ex-M 773) P 788
JASMIN (ex-M 776) P 661
PETUNIA (ex-M 789) P 662

Displacement, tons	140 standard; 170 full load
Dimensions, ft (*m*)	100 pp; 106·5 oa × 21·2 × 5·5 (*32·4 × 6·5 × 1·7*)
Gun	1—20 mm Oerlikon AA forward
Main engines	2 Paxman diesels; 550 bhp = 14 knots
Oil fuel, tons	15
Complement	12 (2 officers, 10 men)

Former British inshore minesweepers of the "Ham" class transferred to France under the US "off-shore" procurement programme in 1955. Now used as patrol craft, the first three by Gendarmerie Maritime.

MINE WARFARE FORCES

5 "CIRCE" CLASS (MINEHUNTERS)

CYBÈLE	M 712	**CALLIOPE**	M 713	**CLIO**	M 714
CIRCE	M 715	**CERES**	M 716		

Displacement, tons	460 standard; 495 normal; 510 full load
Dimensions, ft (*m*)	152·6 × 29·2 × 8·0 (*46·5 × 8·9 × 2·5*)
Gun	1—20 mm
Main engines	Diesels; single axial screw; 1 800 bhp = 15 knots
Range, miles	3 000 at 12 knots
Complement	50 (5 officers, 45 men)

Ordered in 1968. Built by Constructions Mécaniques de Normandie, Cherbourg. *Circe* launched 15 Dec 1970, in service 18 May 1972; *Clio* launched 10 June 1971, in service 18 May 1972; *Calliope* launched 21 Nov 1971, in service 28 Sept 1972; *Cybèle* launched Jan 1972, in service 28 Sept 1972; *Ceres* launched 10 Aug 1972 in service 8 Mar 1973.

MINEHUNTING. All ships are fitted with DUBM 20 minehunting sonar. The 9 foot long PAP is propelled by two electric motors at 6 knots. Fitted with a television camera, this machine detects the mine and lays its 100 kgm charge nearby. This is then detonated by an ultra-sonic signal.

MINESWEEPING. These ships carry no normal minesweeping equipment.

CERES *1972, French Navy*

13 Ex-US MSO "BERNEVAL" CLASS

(MINESWEEPERS—OCEAN and MINEHUNTERS)

NARVIK (ex-*AM* 512)	M 609	**MYTHO** (ex-*AM* 475)	M 618
OUISTREHAM (ex-*AM* 513)	M 610	**VINH LONG** (ex-*AM* 477)	M 619
ALENCON (ex-*AM* 453)	M 612	**BERLAIMONT** (ex-*AM* 500)	M 620
BERNEVAL (ex-*AM* 450)	M 613	**AUTUN** (ex-*AM* 502)	M 622
CANTHO (ex-*AM* 476)	M 615	**BACCARAT** (ex-*AM* 505)	M 623
DOMPAIRE (ex-*AM* 454)	M 616	**COLMAR** (ex-*AM* 514)	M 624
GARIGLIANO (ex-*AM* 452)	M 617		

Displacement, tons	700 standard; 780 full load
Dimensions, ft (*m*)	165 wl; 171 oa × 35 × 10·3 (*50·3 × 10·7 × 3·2*)
Gun	1—40 mm AA
Main engines	2 GM diesels; 2 shafts; 1 600 bhp = 13·5 knots
Range, miles	3 000 at 10 knots
Complement	56 (4 officers, 52 men)

The USA transferred to France eight new AMs in 1953, and four in 1954. Three more transferred in 1956. *Bir Hacheim* M 614 (ex-*AM* 451) was returned to the US Navy at Brest on 4 Sept 1970 and transferred to Uruguayan navy, being renamed *Maldonado*.

APPEARANCE. *Autun, Baccarat, Berlaimont, Colmar, Narvik* and *Ouistreham* have a taller funnel.

MINEHUNTERS. *Garigliano, Mytho, Cantho, Vinh Long* and *Dompaire* are to be converted for minehunting between 1975 and 1977.

GARIGLIANO (short funnel—before conversion) *1974, French Navy*

Mine Warfare Forces—*continued*

16 "SIRIUS" CLASS (MINESWEEPERS—COASTAL)

ALGOL (15 Apr 1953)	M 704	**DÉNÉBOLA** (12 July 1956)	M 751
ANTARES (21 Jan 1954)	M 703	**ÉRIDAN** (18 May 1954)	M 741
BELLATRIX (21 July 1955)	M 750	**LYRE** (3 May 1956)	M 759
BETELGEUSE (12 July 1954)	M 747	**PHÉNIX** (23 May 1955)	M 749
CAPELLA (6 Sep 1955)	M 755	**PÉGASE** (21 June 1955)	M 710
CAPRICORNE (8 Aug 1956)	M 737	**SAGITTAIRE** (12 Jan 1955)	M 743
CASSIOPÉE (16 Nov 1953)	M 740	**VEGA** (14 Jan 1953)	M 707
CÉPHÉE (3 Jan 1956)	M 756	**VERSEAU** (26 Apr 1956)	M 757

Displacement, tons	365 standard; 424 full load
Dimensions, feet	140 pp; 152 oa × 28 × 8·2
Guns	1—40 mm Bofors, 1—20 mm Oerlikon (several have 2—20 mm)
Main engines	SIGMA free piston generators and Alsthom or Rateau-Bretagne gas turbines or SEMT-Pielstick 16-cyl fast diesels; 2 shafts; 2 000 bhp = 15 knots (11·5 knots when sweeping)
Oil fuel, tons	48
Range, miles	3 000 at 15 knots
Complement	38

Of wooden and aluminium alloy construction. Launch dates above. Of same general characteristics as the British "Ton" class, but of different hull construction. Propelled by Alsthom or Rateau gas turbines with SIGMA free piston generators, except *Bételgeuse, Capella, Céphée, Lyre, Phénix* and *Verseau*, which have SEMT-Pielstick light diesels. 16 vessels were built under the "off-shore" programme.

TRANSFERS. D 25, D 26 and D 27 were allocated to Yugoslavia. *Fomalhaut, Orion, Pollux* and *Procyon* were returned to the USN in 1970, *Achernar* and *Centaure* in 1971. *Aries* (M 758) loaned to Morocco for four years Nov 1974.

CASSIOPÉE (40 mm gun) — *7/1974, Wright and Logan*

22 Ex-US "ACACIA" CLASS (MINESWEEPERS—COASTAL)

PERVENCHE (ex-*AMS* 141)	M 632	**CYCLAMEN** (ex-*AMS* 119)	M 674
PIVOINE (ex-*AMS* 125)	M 633	**EGLANTINE** (ex-*AMS* 117)	M 675
RÉSÉDA (ex-*AMS* 126)	M 635	**GIROFLÉE** (ex-*AMS* 85)	M 677
ACACIA (ex-*AMS* 69)	M 638	**GLYCINE** (ex-*AMS* 118)	M 679
ACANTHE (ex-*AMS* 70)	M 639	**JACINTHE** (ex-*AMS* 115)	M 680
MARJOLAINE (ex-*Aconit*, ex-*AMS* 66)	M 640	**LAURIER** (ex-*AMS* 86)	M 681
		LILAS (ex-*AMS* 93)	M 682
AZALÉE (ex-*AMS* 67)	M 668	**LISERON** (ex-*AMS* 98)	M 683
BLEUÉT (ex-*AMS* 116)	M 670	**LOBÉLIA** (ex-*AMS* 96)	M 684
CAMÉLIA (ex-*AMS* 68)	M 671	**MAGNOLIA** (ex-*AMS* 87)	M 685
CHRYSANTHÈME (ex-*AMS* 113)	M 672	**MIMOSA** (ex-*AMS* 99)	M 687
		MUGUET (ex-*AMS* 97)	M 688

Displacement, tons	320 standard; 370 full load
Dimensions, ft (*m*)	136·2 pp; 141 oa × 26 × 8·3 (*43 × 8 × 2·6*)
Guns	2—20 mm AA
Main engines	2 GM diesels; 2 shafts; 1 200 bhp = 13 knots (8 sweeping)
Oil fuel, tons	40
Range, miles	2 500 at 10 knots
Complement	38 (3 officers, 35 men)

GENERAL
The USA agreed in Sep 1952 to allocate to France in 1953, 36 new AMS (later re-designated MSC) under the Mutual Defence Assistance Programme, but only 30 were finally transferred to France in 1953.

ALTERATIONS. *Ajonc* (ex-M 667) A 701, *Liseron* (ex-AMS 98) M 683 are diving-school tenders and *Gardénia* (ex-M 676) A 711 is a clearance-diving training ship.

TRANSFERS. Three were returned to the USA after delivery to Saigon for Indo-China, and two of these were allocated to Japan (AMS 95 and 144). Three were not delivered, two having been allocated to Spain (139 and 143) and one to Taiwan (140). *Marguerite* (ex-*AMS* 94) was returned to the USN at Toulon in Nov 1969 and transferred to the Uruguayan Navy, renamed *Rio Negro*. *Pavot* (ex-*MSC* 124) and *Renocule* (ex-*MSC* 142) were returned to the USN on 24 March 1970 and transferred to the Turkish Navy. *Coquelicot* (ex-M 673) to Tunisia 1973.

LILAS — *1973, Dr. Giorgio Arra*

Minewarfare Forces—*continued*

1 SPECIAL TYPE (DBI) (MINESWEEPER—COASTAL)

MERCURE M 765

Displacement, tons	333 light; 365 normal; 400 full load
Dimensions, ft (*m*)	137·8 pp; 145·5 oa × 27 × 8·5 (*44·4 × 8·3 × 4*)
Guns	2—20 mm AA
Main engines	2 Mercedes-Benz diesels; 2 shafts; Kamewa variable pitch propellers; 4 000 bhp = 15 knots
Oil fuel, tons	48
Range, miles	3 000 at 15 knots
Complement	48

Ordered in France from Mécaniques de Normandie under the "off-shore" programme. Laid down in Jan 1955. Launched on 21 Dec 1957. Completed in Dec 1958.
FOREIGN SALES
Six built for W. Germany.

MERCURE — *1968, French Navy*

SURVEY SHIPS

MARARA

Dimensions, ft (*m*)	141·1 × 29·2 × 14·1
Main engines	2 Baudouin diesels; 1 200 bhp; 1 cp screw
Speed, knots	12·2
Complement	18 + 10 scientists

Delivered 3 Aug 1973 for operations in Tahiti area.

D'ENTRECASTEAUX A 757

Displacement, tons	2 400 full load
Dimensions, ft (*m*)	295·2 × 42·7 × 12·8 (*89 × 13 × 3.9*)
Main engines	2 diesel-electric; 1 000 kW; 2 controllable pitch propellers; Speed:15 knots
Auxiliary engines	2 Schottel trainable and retractable
Range, miles	10 000 at 12 knots
Complement	81 (9 officers, 72 men)

This ship was specially designed for oceanographic surveys and built at Brest. Completed 10 Oct 1970. Accommodation for 38 scientists. Hangar for Alouette II helicopter.

D'ENTRECASTEAUX — *1972, T, A, Jedrlinic*

ESPÉRANCE (ex-*Jacques Coeur*) A 756
ESTAFETTE (ex-*Jacques Cartier*) A 766

Displacement, tons	956 standard; 1 360 full load
Dimensions, ft (*m*)	196·1 × 32·2 × 14·8 (*63·5 × 9·8 × 5·9*)
Main engines	MAN diesels; 1 850 bhp = 15 knots
Range, miles	7 500 at 13 knots
Complement	29 (5 officers, 24 men)

Former trawlers built in 1962 at Gdynia and purchased in 1968-69. Adapted as survey ships commissioning in 1969 and 1972.

APPEARANCE. *Espérance* has a normal foremast in place of the crane in *Estafette*.

ESTAFETTE — *1973, French Navy*

Survey Ships—*continued*

LA RECHERCHE (ex-*Guyane*) A 758

Displacement, tons	810 standard; 910 full load
Dimensions, ft (*m*)	221·5 oa × 34·2 × 13 (*67·5 × 10·4 × 4·5*)
Main engines	1 Werkspoor diesel; 1 535 bhp = 13·5 knots
Range, miles	3 100 at 10 knots
Complement	23 (2 officers, 21 men) (plus 43 surveyors)

Former passenger motor vessel built by Chantiers Zeigler at Dunkirk. Launched on 17 Sep 1951. Purchased in 1960 and converted by Cherbourg Dockyard into a surveying ship. Commissioned into the French Navy in Mar 1961 and her name changed from *Guyane* to *La Recherche*. To improve stability she was fitted with bulges. Now comes under the Colonial ministry.

LA RECHERCHE *1970, French Navy*

1 "BERNEVAL" CLASS

ORIGNY A 640

Displacement, tons	700 standard; 795 full load
Dimensions, ft (*m*)	171 × 35 × 10·5 (*52·2 × 10·7 × 3·2*)
Gun	1—40 mm
Main engines	2 GM diesels; 2 shafts; 1 600 bhp = 13·5 knots
Range, miles	3 000 at 10 knots
Complement	52

Launched Feb 1955 as a Minesweeper—Ocean of "Berneval" class. Converted for Oceanographic research 1961-62.

ORIGNY *1974, Wright and Logan*

LA DÉCOUVERTE (ex-*Amalthée*, ex-*Plantagenet*, ex-*Barwood*) A 753

Displacement, tons	750 standard; 927 full load
Dimensions, ft (*m*)	159·7 × 30·7 × 13 (*49 × 9·3 × 4·8*)
Main engines	Triple expansion; 720 ihp = 9·5 knots
Boilers	Cylindrical
Range, miles	2 900 at 9 knots
Complement	33 plus 25 surveyors

Formerly the British boom defence vessel HMS *Plantagenet* (ex-*Barwood*) built by Lobnitz & Co Ltd, Renfrew and launched on 23 Feb 1939. She became the commercial oil research ship *Amalthée* under the French flag in 1960. She was purchased for the French Navy in 1969 and converted as a survey ship.

Survey Ships—*continued*

LA DÉCOUVERTE *1970, courtesy Admiral M. Adam*

L'ASTROLABE A 780 **BOUSSOLE** A 781

Displacement, tons	330 standard; 440 full load
Dimensions, ft (*m*)	137·8 × 27 × 8·2 (*42·7 × 8·5 × 2·9*)
Guns	1—40 mm AA; 2 MG
Main engines	2 Baudouin DV.8 diesels; 1 shaft; variable pitch propeller; 800 bhp = 13 knots max
Range, miles	4 000 at 12 knots
Complement	34 (3 officers, 31 men)

Authorised under the 1961 Programme. Specially designed for surveys in tropical waters. Built by Chantiers de la Seine Maritime. Le Trait. Laid down in 1962, launched on 27 May and 11 Apr 1963 respectively, and commissioned in 1964.

L'ASTROLABE *1972, French Navy*

ALIDADE (ex-*Evelyne Marie*) A 682 **OCTANT** (ex-*Michel Marie*) A 683

Displacement, tons	128 standard; 133 full load
Dimensions, ft (*m*)	78 × 20 × 10·5 (*24 × 6·1 × 3·2*)
Main engines	2 diesels; 1 shaft; variable pitch; 200 bhp = 9 knots
Complement	13
Range, miles	2 000 at 7 knots

Two small fishing trawlers purchased by the Navy and converted into survey craft by the Constructions Mécaniques de Normandie at Cherbourg as tenders to *La Recherche*. Wooden hull and steel upperworks. *Alidada* completed conversion on 15 Nov 1962 and *Octant* on 20 Dec 1962. Commissioned in 1963.

OCTANT *1973, Dr, Giorgio Arra*

CORAIL (ex-*Marc Joly*) A 794 (INSHORE SURVEY CRAFT)

Operating in New Caledonia from 1974.

SERVICE FORCES

1 + 2 NEW CONSTRUCTION

(UNDERWAY REPLENISHMENT TANKERS)

LA DURANCE A 629 **+ 2**

Displacement, tons	17 450 standard; 17 800 full load
Dimensions, ft (*m*)	515·9 × 69·5 × 28·5 (*157·3 × 21·2 × 8·7*)
Aircraft	1 WG 13 Lynx helicopter
Guns	2—40 mm
Main engines	2 diesels SEMT-Pielstick 16 PC 2·5V; 20 000 hp = 19 knots
Range, miles	9 000 at 15 knots
Complement	150 (45 passengers)

GENERAL
Building at Brest—laid down 1973 for completion in late 1975. Beam fuelling both sides as well as astern. Helicopter hangar. Classed as P.R.E. (Pétrolier Ravitailleur d'Escadre).

CAPACITY. To carry a total of 10 000 tonnes (7 500 FFO, 1 500 Dieso, 500 TR5, 130 Distilled Water, 170 Victuals, 150 munitions, 50 naval stores).

LA CHARENTE (ex-*Beaufort*) A 626
(UNDERWAY REPLENISHMENT TANKER and COMMAND SHIP)

Displacement, tons	7 440 light; 26 000 full load
Dimensions, ft (*m*)	587·2 × 72 × 30·3 (*179 × 21·9 × 9·3*)
Guns	4—40 mm
Main engines	1 General Electric geared turbine; 1 screw = 17·5 knots
Boilers	2
Complement	70 (6 officers, 64 men)

Former Norwegian tanker built by Haldnes Mek. Verksted Tönsberg in 1957. Purchased by the French Navy in May 1964. Now converted for service as flagship of the Flag Officer commanding Indian Ocean forces. Fitted with helicopter platform and hangar and carries LCVP.

LA CHARENTE (after conversion) *1974, French Navy*

ISÈRE (ex-*La Mayenne*, ex-*Caltex Strasbourg*) A 675
(UNDERWAY REPLENISHMENT TANKER)

Displacement, tons	7 440 standard; 26 700 full load
Dimensions, ft (*m*)	559 × 71·2 × 30·3 (*170·4 × 21·7 × 9·3*)
Main engines	1 single geared Parsons turbine; 8 260 shp = 16 knots
Boilers	2
Complement	112 (6 officers, 106 men)

Built by Seine Maritime. Launched on 22 June 1959. Former French tanker. Purchased in 1965. Fitted for beam fuelling as well as stern rig.

ISÈRE *1974, Wright and Logan*

Service Forces—*continued*

LA SAONE A 628 **LA SEINE** A 627

(UNDERWAY REPLENISHMENT TANKERS)

Displacement, tons	8 550 light; 24 200 full load
Dimensions, ft (*m*)	525 × 72·5 × 33 (*160 × 22·1 × 10*)
Main engines	Parsons geared turbines; 2 shafts; 15 800 shp = 18 knots
Boilers	3 Penhoet
Complement	200

Ordered as fleet tankers. Completed as merchant tankers in 1948. Returned to the French Navy from charter company in Sep 1953. *La Seine* was fitted as a fleet replenishment ship in 1961, *La Saône* in 1962. They carry 11 500 tons of fuel, 275 tons of food and wine tanks holding 82 000 litres. Fitted with automatic tensioning.

LA SEINE *1971, French Navy*

FLEET SUPPORT SHIPS

LAC TONLÉ SAP A 630
(SUPPORT TANKER)

Displacement, tons	800 light; 2 700 full load
Dimensions, ft (*m*)	235 × 37 × 15·8 (*71·7 × 11·3 × 4·8*)
Guns	3—20 mm AA
Main engines	2 Fairbanks-Morse diesels; 1 150 bhp = 11 knots
Range, miles	6 300 at 11 knots
Complement	37 (2 officers, 35 men)

Ex-US Oil Barge acquired in 1945.

LAC TONLÉ SAP *1973, French Navy*

PAPENOO (ex-Norwegian *Bow Queen*) A 625
PUNARUU (ex-Norwegian *Bow Cecil*) A 632 (SUPPORT TANKERS)

Displacement, tons	1 195 standard; 2 927 full load
Dimensions, ft (*m*)	272·2 × 45·6 × 18·0) (*83 × 13·9 × 5·5*)
Main engines	2 Diesels; 1 vp screw; 2 050 hp = 12 knots (bow screw in addition)

Two small oilers added to the navy in late 1969.

ABER-WRACH (ex-*CA* 1) A 619 (SUPPORT TANKER)

Displacement, tons	1 220 standard; 3 500 full load
Dimensions, ft (*m*)	284 oa × 40 × 15·8 (*86·6 × 12·2 × 4·8*)
Gun	1—40 mm AA
Main engines	1 diesel; vp propeller; 3 000 bhp = 12 knots

Built at Cherbourg. Authorised in 1956. Ordered in 1959. Laid down in 1961. The after part with engine room was launched on 24 Apr 1963. The fore part was built on the vacated slip, launched and welded to the after part. Complete hull floated up on 21 Nov 1963. Commissioned in 1966.

ABER WRACH *1970, French Navy*

AUNIS (ex-*Regina Pacis*) A 643 (STORE SHIP)

Displacement, tons	2 900 full load
Dimensions, ft (*m*)	284·5 × 38 × 15 (*86·5 × 11·6 × 4·6*)
Main engines	MAN diesels geared to 1 shaft; 2 400 bhp = 12 knots
Range, miles	4 500 at 12 knots

Built by Roland Werft, Bremen. Launched on 3 July 1956. Purchased in Nov 1966 from Seatto, Ambrosino & Pugliese and converted in Toulon 1972-73. Employed as trials ship in Operation Cormoran.

Fleet Support Ships—*continued*

SAHEL A 638

Displacement, tons	630 light; 1 450 full load
Measurement, tons	650 deadweight
Dimensions, ft (*m*)	176·2 × 29·5 × 14·5 (*53·7 × 9 × 4·5*)
Guns	2—20 mm AA
Main engines	2 diesels; 1 400 bhp = 12 knots

Completed in Aug 1951 by Chantiers Naval de Caen. Fuel carrier.

SAHEL *1972, Dr. Giorgio Arra*

5 "RHIN" CLASS (DEPOT SHIPS)

Name	*No.*	*Laid down*	*Launched*	*Completed*
GARONNE	A 617	Nov 1963	8 Aug 1964	1 Sep 1965
LOIRE	A 615	July 1965	1 Oct 1966	10 Oct 1967
RANCE	A 618	Aug 1964	15 May 1965	5 Feb 1966
RHIN	A 621	May 1961	17 Mar 1962	1 Mar 1964
RHÔNE	A 622	Feb 1962	8 Dec 1962	1 Dec 1964

Displacement, tons	2 075 standard; 2 445 full load (*Rhin, Rance* and *Rhône*) 2 320 standard (*Garonne and Loire*).
Dimensions feet	302·0 pp 331·5 oa × 43·0 × 12·1
Guns	3—40 mm AA (except *Garonne*)
Aircraft	1/3 Alouette helicopter (except *Garonne* and *Loire*)
Landing craft	2 (LCP)
Main engines	2 SEMT-Pielstick diesels; 1 shaft; 3 300 bhp = 16·5 knots
Range, miles	13 000 at 13 knots
Complement	*Rhine* and *Rhône* 71 (5 officers, 66 men) and about 100 technicians; *Rance* 150 (10 officers, 140 men) and about 118 extras; *Garonne* 221 (10 officers, 211 men); *Loire* 175 (13 officers, 162 men)

Designed for supporting various classes of ships. Have a 5 ton crane, carry two LCP (S) and have a helicopter platform (except *Garonne*). *Rhin and Rhône* have a hangar and carry an Alouette helicopter. *Rance* carries three in her hangar and *Loire* has only the helicopter platform. *Garonne* is designed as a Repair Workshop, *Loire* for minesweeper support. *Rance* for laboratory and radiological services, *Rhin* for electronic maintenence and *Rhône* for submarine support. *Loire* and *Rhône* are currently operating in support of North Atlantic fishery patrols.

RADAR. 1 DRBV 50 (in *Rhin* and *Rhône*)

RHIN (LOIRE similar) *1972, Dr. Giorgio Arra*

RHONE *1972, Dr. Giorgio Arra*

RANCE *1969, French Navy*

GARONNE *French Navy*

Fleet Support Ships—*continued*

MAURIENNE (ex-M/S *Brazza*) A 637 (MAINTENANCE SHIPS)
MOSELLE (ex-*Foucauld*) A 608

Displacement, tons	8 200 standard; 8 700 full load
Dimensions, ft (*m*)	480 oa × 62 × 22·3 (*146·3 × 18·9 × 6·9*)
Main engines	2 Doxford diesels; 2 shafts; 8 800 bhp = 15 knots
Complement	177 (7 officers, 170 men)

Former motor passenger ships of the *Chargeurs Réunis* (West Africa Coast Service). Built by Swan, Hunter & Wigham Richardson Ltd, Wallsend-on-Tyne. Launched on 14 Oct and 17 July 1947. Completed in 1948. *Maurienne* was purchased in Nov 1964, converted at Brest in 1965 and admitted to active service on 8 Mar 1966; helicopter landing platform aft. *Moselle* was converted in 1967 (no platform). Used as Base Ships in Pacific Trial Centre.

MOSELLE *1972, Dr. Giorgio Arra*

JULES VERNE (ex- *Achéron*) A 620 (MAINTENANCE and REPAIR SHIP)

Displacement, tons	8 800 full load
Dimensions, ft (*m*)	482·2 × 70·5 × 21·3 (*147 × 21·5 × 6·5*)
Aircraft	2 Helicopters
Main engines	2 diesels SEMT-Pielstick; 1 shaft; 21 500 hp = 18 knots
Range, miles	9 500 at 18 knots
Complement	323 (20 officers, 303 men)

Ordered in 1961 budget, originally as an Armament Supply Ship. Role and design changed—now rated as Engineering and Electrical Maintenance Ship. Launched 30 May 1970.

1 REPAIR SHIP (Ex-BRITISH LCT)

Displacement, tons	200 standard; 500 full load
Dimensions, ft (*m*)	187·3 × 38·9 × 4·5 (*57·1 × 11·8 × 1·3*)
Main engines	2 Paxman Diesels; 1 000 hp = 8 knots

Purchased from UK in 1964—used as Mechanical Workshop.

4 REPAIR SHIPS (Ex-LCT)

L 9081 **L 9082** **L 9083** **L 9084**

Displacement, tons	310 standard; 685 full load
Dimensions, ft (*m*)	193·5 × 39 × 5 (*59 × 11·9 × 1·6*)
Main engines	2 Diesels MGO; 1 000 bhp = 8 knots
Range, miles	1 800 at 8 knots

Built in 1964-65 by Ch. N. Franco-Belge. Repair facilities grafted onto LCT hulls. First pair are fitted with mechanical workshops, 9083 with electronic workshops and 9084 is primarily an electrical stores ship.

EDIC 9082 *1972, Dr. Giorgio Arra*

BERRY (ex-M/S *Médoc*) A 644 (VICTUALLING STORES SHIP)

Displacement, tons	1 148 standard; 2 700 full load
Dimensions, ft (*m*)	284·5 oa × 38 × 15 (*86·7 × 11·6 × 4·6*)
Main engines	2 MWM diesels coupled on one shaft; 2 400 bhp = 15 knots

Built by Roland Werft, Bremen. Launched on 10 May 1958. Purchased in Oct 1964 and refitted in 1964-66.

BERRY *1969, French Navy*

TRIALS RESEARCH SHIPS

HENRI POINCARÉ (ex-*Maina Marasso*) A 603

Displacement, tons	24 000 full load
Dimensions, ft (*m*)	565·0 pp; 590·6 oa × 72·8 × 28·9 (*180 × 22·2 × 9·4*)
Guns	2—20 mm
Main engines	1 Parsons geared turbine; 1 shaft; 10 000 shp = 15 knots
Boilers	2 Foster Wheeler high pressure water tube
Range, miles	11 800 at 13·5 knots
Complement	305 (21 officers, 9 civilians, 275 men)

Built by Cantieri Riuniti de Adriaticos, Monfalcone. Launched in Oct 1960. Former Italian tanker. Purchased in Sep 1964. Converted in Brest dockyard from 1 Oct 1964 to Mar 1968. To work with the experimental guided missile station in the Landes (SW France). Named after the mathematician and scientist.

AIRCRAFT. Can land heavy helicopters and has space for two large or five light helicopters in her hangar.

OPERATIONS. She is primarily a missile-range-ship and to enable her to plot the trajectory etc of missiles fired from land or sea she is equipped with three tracking radars, a telemetry station, transit nav-aid, cinetheodolite, infra-red tracking as well as an up-to-date fit of hull-mounted sonar, meteorological and oceanographic equipment.

RADAR. In addition to tracking radars, one DRBV 22D.

HENRI POINCARÉ *1969, French Navy*

ILE d'OLÉRON (ex-*Munchen*, ex-*Mur*) A 610

Displacement, tons	5 500 standard; 6 500 full load
Dimensions, ft (*m*)	350·0 pp; 377·5 × 50·0 × 21·3(*106·7 pp; 115·2 oa × 15·2 × 6·5*)
Main engines	MAN 6-cylinder diesels; 1 shaft; 3 500 bhp
Speed, knots	14·5
Oil fuel, tons	340
Range, miles	7 200 at 12 knots
Complement	195 (15 officers, 180 men)

Launched in Germany in 1939. Taken as a war prize. Formerly rated as a transport. Converted to experimental guided missile ship in 1957-58 by Chantiers de Provence and l'Arsenal de Toulon. Commissioned early in 1959. Equipped with stabilisers.

EXPERIMENTAL. When converted was designed for experiments with two launchers for ship to air missiles, the medium range "Masurca" and the long range "Masalca", and one launcher for ship to shore missiles, the "Malaface". Latterly fitted with one launcher for target planes. Now fitted for trials on MM 38 ("Exocet").

RADAR. One DRDV 22C, one DRBV 50, one DRBI 10. The missile system tracking radar operates in C band.

ILE D'OLERON

ILE d'OLÉRON *1974, Wright and Logan*

Trials Research Ships—*continued*

TRITON A 646

Displacement, tons	1 410 standard; 1 510 full load
Dimensions, ft (*m*)	242·7 × 38·9 × 12 (*74 × 11·8 × 3·7*)
Main engines	2 MGO V Diesels driving a Voith Schneider screw aft; 2 electric motors driving a Voith Schneider forward
Speed, knots	13
Range, miles	4 000 at 13 knots
Complement	62 (4 officers, 41 men + 5 officers and 12 men for diving)

GENERAL
Under sea recovery and trials ship to replace *Elie Monnier*. Equipped with a helicopter platform. Launched at Lorient on 7 Mar 1970 and in service 1972. Support ship for the 2-man submarine *Griffon*.

OPERATIONS. Operated by G.E.R.S. (Groupe d'Etude et de Recherches Sousmarins) for trials of submarines and deep-sea diving equipment. Underwater TV, decompression chamber and laboratories are fitted. Available as submarine rescue ship.

RADAR. Navigational

SONAR. Special equipment for deep operations.

SUBMARINE. The 16 ton *Griffon* can dive to 2 000 feet and be used for deep recovery operations.

TRITON *1972, French Navy*

1 DEEP SUBMERGENCE VEHICLE

ARCHIMÉDE A 648

Built in Toulon. 68·9 feet long with displacement 65 tons. Diving depth 36 000 feet (*11 000 metres*). *Marcel le Bihan* acts as tender. FNRS 3 deleted 1974.

ARCHIMÉDE *1974, Wright and Logan*

1 ARCHAEOLOGICAL RESEARCH CRAFT

ARCHÉONAUTE A 789

Built by Auroux, Arcachon August 1967. 120 tons full load and 96 feet long (*29·3 metres*). For underwater archaeological research carries a complement of 2 officers, 4 men, 3 archaeologists and 6 divers.

1 RADIOLOGICAL RESEARCH CRAFT

PALANGRIN Y 743

Acquired 1969. Of 44 tons with single diesel.

BOOM AND MOORING VESSELS

LA FIDÈLE Y 751 **LA PERSÉVÉRANTE** Y 750 **LA PRUDENTE** Y 749

Displacement, tons	446 standard; 626 full load
Dimensions, ft (*m*)	142·8 × 32·8 × 9·2 (*43·5 × 10 × 2·8*)
Main engines	2 Baudouin diesels; Diesel-electric; 1 shaft; 620 bhp = 10 knots
Range, miles	4 000 at 10 knots
Complement	30 (1 officer, 29 men)

Net layers and tenders built by Atel. Ch. La Manche, Dieppe, (*La Fidèle* and *La Prudente*) and Atel. Ch. La Rochelle (*La Persévérante*). Launched on 26 Aug 1968 (*La Fidèle*), 14 May 1968 (*La Persévérante*) and 13 May 1968 (*La Prudente*). 25 ton lift.

LA PERSÉVÉRANTE — *1973, Commander Aldo Fraccaroli*

TIANÉE A 731

Displacement, tons	842 standard; 905 full load
Dimensions, ft (*m*)	178·1 × 34·8 (*54·3 × 10·6*)
Main engines	Diesel-electric; 2 diesels; 1 shaft = 12 knots
Range, miles	5 200 at 12 knots
Complement	37 (1 officer, 36 men)

Built at Brest. Launched 17 Nov 1973. For service in the Pacific. Fitted with lateral screws in bow tunnel.

TIANÉE — *1974, French Navy*

CIGALE (ex-*AN* 98) A 760
CRIQUET (ex-*AN* 96) A 761
FOURMI (ex-*AN* 97) A 762
GRILLON (ex-*AN* 95) A 763
SCARABÉE (ex-*AN* 94) A 764

Displacement, tons	770 standard; 850 full load
Dimensions, ft (*m*)	151·9 oa × 33·5 × 10·5 (*46·3 × 10·2 × 3·2*)
Guns	1—40 mm Bofors AA; 4—20 mm AA
Main engines	2, 4-stroke diesels, electric drive, 1 shaft; 1 600 bhp = 12 knots
Range, miles	5 200 at 12 knots
Complement	45

US off-shore order. Sister ship G 6 was allocated to Spain. *Cerberus* transferred to Netherlands and subsequently to Turkey as AG 6. *Criquet* was launched on 3 June 1954, *Cigale* on 23 Sep 1954, *Fourmi* on 6 July 1954, *Grillon* on 18 Feb 1954 and *Scarabée* on 21 Nov 1953.

FOURMI — *1974, Wright and Logan*

3 Ex-US AN TYPE NETLAYERS

ARAIGNÉE (ex-*Hackberry*, ex-*Maple*) A 727
LIBELLULE (ex-*Rosewood*) A 730
LUCIOLE (ex-*Sandalwood*) A 777

Displacement, tons	560 standard; 850 full load
Dimensions, ft (*m*)	146·0 wl; 163·0 oa × 30·5 × 11·7 (*50 × 9·3 × 4·8*)
Guns	1—3 in AA; some MG
Main engines	2 GM diesels; diesel-electric; 1 shaft; 1 300 bhp = 13 knots
Range, miles	7 200 at 12 knots
Complement	39 (2 officers, 37 men)

Launched on 6 Mar 1941, 1 Apr 1941, 6 Mar 1941 respectively. *Luciole* was purchased in 1967, *Libellule* in 1969.

LUCIOLE — *1974, Wright and Logan*

MARCEL LE BIHAN (ex-*Greif*) A 759

Displacement, tons	800 standard; 1 250 full load
Dimensions, ft (*m*)	236·2 × 34·8 × 10·5 max (*72 × 10·6 × 3·2*)
Guns	4—20 mm AA (twins)
Main engines	2 GM diesels; 2 shafts; 4 400 bhp = 13 knots
Range, miles	2 500 at 13 knots
Complement	53 (3 officers, 50 men), accommodation for 22 extra hands

Former German aircraft tender. Built by Lubecker Fleudewerke. Launched in 1936. Completed in 1937. Transferred by USA in Feb 1948. 4·1 in gun and 2—40 mm removed. Tender for DSV *Archimède*.

MARCEL LE BIHAN — *1974. Wright and Logan*

COMMANDANT ROBERT GIRAUD (ex- *Immelmann*) A 755 (ex-F 755)

Displacement, tons	1 142 standard; 1 220 full load
Length, feet (metres)	239·0 (*72·9*) pp; 256·0 (*78·0*) oa
Beam, feet (*metres*)	36·0 (*11·0*)
Draught, ft (*metres*)	12·0 (*3·7*)
Main engines	4 MAN diesels; 2 shafts; 5 720 bhp
Range, miles	9 000 at 10 knots
Oil fuel, tons	236
Complement	39

Ex-German aircraft tender. Built by Norderwerft, Hamburg. Launched in Dec 1941. Transferred by Great Britain in Aug 1946, with *Paul Goffeny*. The diesels are coupled two by two with hydraulic transmission on two shafts. Crane lift 18 tons.

COMMANDANT ROBERT GIRAUD — *1972. Dr. Giorgio Arra*

PERSISTANTE Y 731

Displacement, tons	350
Main engines	500 hp = 8 knots

TORPEDO RECOVERY VESSELS

PÉLICAN (ex-*Kerfany*) A 699

Displacement, tons	362 standard; 425 full load
Dimensions, ft (*m*)	121·4 × 28·0 × 13·1 (*37 × 8·6 × 4*)
Tubes	One
Main engines	Diesel; 1 shaft; 650 bhp = 11 knots
Complement	19

Built in USA in 1951. Purchased in 1965 and converted from tunny fisher into torpedo recovery craft in 1966.

PÉLICAN *1972, Dr. Giorgio Arra*

PÉTREL (ex-*Cap Lopez*) A 698

Displacement, tons	227 standard; 318 full load
Dimensions, ft (*m*)	98·4 × 25·6 × 11·5 (*30 × 7·8 × 3·5*)
Main engines	2 Baudouin diesels; 1 vp screw; 600 bhp = 10 knots
Complement	19

Built in Daubigeon 1960. Purchased 1965 and converted from tunny fisher to torpedo recovery craft.

TRANSPORTS

2 "BATRAL" TYPE (LIGHT TRANSPORTS)

CHAMPLAIN L 9030 **FRANCIS GARNIER** L 9031

Displacement, tons	750 standard; 1 250 full load
Dimensions, ft (*m*)	262·4 × 42·6 × 7·5 (*80 × 13 × 2·3*)
Guns	2—40 mm; 2—81 mm Mortars
Main engines	2 Diesels; 2 shafts; 1 800 hp = 16
Range, miles	3 500 at 13 knots
Complement	37

Fitted with bow doors, and stowage for vehicles above and below decks. Helicopter landing platform. Can carry a company of 5 officers and 133 men with 12 vehicles. Built at Brest, launched 17 Nov 1973 for completion 1974.

CHAMPLAIN *1974, DCAN Brest*

SMALL TRANSPORTS

(SMALL TRANSPORTS)

ALPHÉE Y 696
ARIEL Y 604
DRYADE Y 662
ELFE Y 741
FAUNE Y 613
KORRIGAN Y 661
MORGANE Y 671

Displacement, tons	195 standard; 225 full load
Dimensions, ft (*m*)	132·8 × 24·5 × 10·8 (*40·5 × 7·5 × 3·3*)
Main engines	2 diesels; 2 shafts; 1 640 bhp = 15 knots
Complement	9

Ariel was launched on 27 Apr 1964. *Korrigan* on 6 Mar 1964, *Alphée* on 10 June 1969. *Elfe* on 14 Apr 1970, *Faune* on 8 Sept 1971 *Dryade* in 1973, *Morgane* in May 1973. All built by S. F. de CN. except Y671 by A. du Mourillon. Can carry 400 passengers.

ALPHÉE *1972, courtesy Admiral M. Adam*

SYLPHE Y 710

Displacement, tons	171 standard; 189 full load
Dimensions, ft (*m*)	126·5 × 22·7 × 8·2 (*38·5 × 6·9 × 2·5*)
Main engines	MGO diesel; 1 shaft; 425 bhp = 12 knots
Complement	9

Small transport for personnel, built by Chantiers Franco-Belge in 1959-60.

SAINTONGE (ex-*Santa Maria*) A 733

Measurements, ton	300 standard; 990 full weight
Dimensions, ft (*m*)	177× 28 × 10·5 (*54 × 8·5 × 3·2*)
Main engines	1 diesel; 1 shaft; 760 bhp = 10 knots
Complement	15

Built by Chantiers Duchesne et Bossière, Le Havre, for a Norwegian owner under the name of *Sven Germa*. Launched on 12 July 1956. Purchased in Apr 1965 from the firm of H. Beal & Co, Fort de France for the Pacific Nuclear Experimental Centre.

FALLERON (ex-German *Welle*) A 614

Displacement, tons	200 standard; 429 full load
Dimensions, ft (*m*)	128·0 × 22·0 × 7·8 (*39 × 6·7 × 2·3*)
Main engines	1 Sulzer diesel; 280 bhp = 8 knots
Range, miles	1 600 at 8 knots
Complement	11

MÉLUSINE Y 736 **MERLIN** Y 735

Displacement, tons	170
Dimensions, ft (*m*)	103·3 × 23·2 × 7·9 (*31·5 × 7·1 × 2·4*)
Main engines	MGO diesels; 2 shafts; 960 bhp = 11 knots

Small transports for 400 personnel built in 1966 by Chantiers Navals Franco-Belges at Chalon sur Saône. Both laid down in Dec 1966 and accepted on 1 June 1968. Their home port is Toulon.

TRÉBÉRON (ex-B 254) Y 712

Displacement, tons	120 standard; 140 full load
Dimensions, ft (*m*)	82·0 × 19·7 × 9·5 (*25 × 6 × 2·9*)
Main engines	Diesel; 1 shaft; 120 bhp = 8·5 knots

Former German danlayer used as small personnel transport for local port service.

LUTIN (ex-*Georges Clemenceau*) Y 664

Displacement, tons	68
Main engines	400 hp = 10 knots

Purchased in 1965. Ex-vedette. Detection school, Toulon.

DIVING TENDERS

Note. Ex-minesweepers *Ajonc* A 701 and *Gardénia* A 711 of "Acacia" class and *Myosotis* A 710 of "Ham" class operate as Diving Tenders.

ARMOISE (ex-M 772)	A 741	**HORTENSIA** (ex-M 783)	A 740
CAPUCINE (ex-M 782)	A 738	**OEILLET** (ex M 774)	A 739
DAHLIA (ex-M 786)	A 736	**PAQUERETTE** (ex-M 775)	A 742
HIBISCUS (ex-M 785)	A 735	**TULIPE** (ex-M 771)	A 737

Ex-MSI's of "HAM" class. See under Minewarfare Forces for details.

BELOUGA A 724 (ex-*Côte d'Argent*)

Displacement, tons	225 standard; 270 full load
Dimensions, ft (*m*)	85·3 × 22·6 × 9·8 (*26 × 6·9 × 3*)
Main engines	1 Baudouin DV 8 diesel; 400 bhp = 9·5 knots
Complement	11 (1 officer, 10 men)

Tunny fisher built 1958. purchased in 1966 for conversion into a diving tender. Used for training groups of up to 16 clearance divers.

Diving Tenders—*continued*

BELOUGA *9/1973, Wright and Logan*

SSBN TENDER. A 1 200-ton service lighter of 1 000 hp for nuclear fuel elements of SSBNs was launched on 26 Oct 1967 for delivery in May 1968.

SAIL TRAINING SHIPS

CHIMERE Y 706 **FARFADET** Y 711

Auxiliary sail training ships built at Bayonne in 1971. Tenders to the Naval School.

LA BELLE-POULE A 650 **L'ÉTOILE** A 649

Displacement tons	227
Dimensions, ft (*m*)	128 oa × 23·7 × 11·8 (*32·3* × *7* × *3·2*)
Main engines	Sulzer diesels; 120 bhp = 6 knots

Auxiliary sail vessels. Built by Chantiers de Normandie (Fécamp) in 1932. Accommodation for 3 officers, 30 cadets, 5 petty officers, 12 men. Attached to Navy School.

LA GRANDE HERMINE (ex-*Ménestral*) A 653

Ex sailing fishing boat built in 1936. Purchased in 1963 in replacement for *Dolphin* (ex-*Simone Marcelle*) as the School of Manoeuvre Training ship. Length 46 feet.

MUTIN A 652

A small 57 ton coastal tender built in 1927. Auxiliary diesel and sails. Attached to the Navigation School.

TUGS

ACHARNÉ A 695 **TENACE** A 669 **EFFICACE** A 694 **CENTAURE** A 674

Displacement, tons	1 080 light; 1 454 full load
Dimensions, ft (*m*)	167·3 oa × 37·8 (*51* × *11·5*)
Main engines	2 diesels; Kort engines 4 600 hp = 15 knots
Range, miles	9 500 at 15 knots
Complement	42

New oceangoing tugs. *Tenace* built by Joelkers, Hamburg, *Centaure* built at La Pallice 1972-74. *Acharne* launched 13 Feb 1974 and delivered 5 July 1974. *Efficace* launched 30 Mar 1974. Both the latter built at Chantiers de Perriere, Lorient.

TENACE *1973, Reiner Nerlich*

Tugs—*continued*

2 NEW CONSTRUCTION

Dimensions, ft (*m*)	92·7 × 25 × 13 (*28·3* × *7·6* × *4*)
Main engines	1 MGO diesel; 1 000 hp = 11 knots

Built at Lorient. Delivery, one at Toulon Jan 1974, one at Brest May 1974.

ACTIF	A 686	**HERCULE**	A 667	**ROBUSTE**	A 685
COURAGEUX	A 706	**LABORIEUX**	A 687	**TRAVAILLEUR**	A 692
LE FORT	A 671	**LUTTEUR**	A 673	**VALEUREUX**	A 688
				UTILE	A 672

Displacement, tons	230
Dimensions, feet	92 × 26 × 13
Main engines	1 MGO diesel; 1 050 bhp = 11 knots
Range, miles	2 400 miles
Complement	15

Courageux, *Hercule*, *Robuste* and *Valeureux* were completed in 1960 and the other four in 1962-63 at Le Havre, and F. Ch.de la Méditerranée for service at Cherbourg (*Lutteur*). Toulon (*Actif*, *Robuste* and *Travailleur*) and Brest (*Hercule*, *Laborieux* and *Valeureux*).

HIPPOPOTAME (ex-*Utrecht*) A 660 **RHINOCEROS** A 668

Displacement tons	640
Main engines	Diesel-electric; 1 850 shp = 12 knots

A 660 built as USN ATA of "Maricopa" class. Former Netherlands Ocean tug. Built in 1943. Purchased by the French Navy in Jan 1964 to be used at the Experimental Base in the Pacific.

BÉLIER A 719 **PACHYDERME** A 718

Displacement, tons	900 standard; 1 185 and 1 115 full load respectively
Main engines	2 000 ihp = 12 knots
Oil fuel (tons)	180
Range, miles	3 000

PACHYDERME *1971, Commander Aldo Fraccaroli*

INFATIGABLE (ex- *Polangen*) A 661

Displacement, tons	715
Main engines	1 300 ihp = 11 knots

ÉLÉPHANT (ex-*Bar*) A 666

Displacement, tons	810 standard; 1 180 full load
Main engines	2 000 ihp = 12 knots

COOLIE A 684

Displacement, tons	300
Main engines	1 000 hp

GOLIATH A 665

Displacement, tons	380
Main engines	900 hp

88 HARBOUR TUGS

Y 601 *Acajou*, Y 602 *Aigrette*, Y 607 *Balsa*, Y 608 *Bambu*, Y 611 *Bengali*, Y 612 *Bouleau*, Y 616 *Canari*, Y 617 *Mouelte*, Y 618 *Cascade*, Y 620 *Chataigner*, Y 621 *Mésange*, Y 623 *Charme*, Y 624 *Chène*, Y 628 *Colibri*, Y 629 *Cormier*, Y 630 *Bonite*, Y 631 *Courlis*, Y 632 *Cygne*, Y 633 *Délange*, Y 634 *Rouget*, Y 635 *Equeurdiville*, Y 636 *Martinet*, Y 637 *Fauvelte*, Y 640 *Fontaine*, Y 641 *Forméne*, Y 644 *Fréne*, Y 645 *Gave*, Y 646 *Geyser*, Y 647 *Giens*, Y 648 *Goeland*, Y 649 *Grive*, Y 651 *Hanneton*, Y 652 *Haut-Barr*, Y 653 *Heron*, Y 654 *Hétre*, Y 655 *Hévéat*, Y 657 *Hirondelle*, Y 658 *Ibis*, Y 659 *Jonque*, Y 663 *Latanier*, Y 666 *Manguier*, Y 667 *Tupa*, Y 668 *Méléze*, Y669 *Merisier*, Y 670 *Merle*, Y 673 *Moineau*, Y 675 *Martin Pécheur*, Y 678 *Moule*, Y 680 *Muréne*, Y 682 *Okoume*, Y 683 *Ondée*, Y 684 *Oued*, Y 685 *Oursin*, Y 686 *Palétuvier*, Y 687 *Passereau*, Y 688 *Peuplier*, Y 689 *Pin*, Y 690 *Pingouin*, Y 691 *Pinson*, Y 694 *Pivert*, Y 695 *Platane*, Y 698 *Calmar*, Y 699 *Poulpé*, Y 702 *Rascasse*, Y 704 *Rossignol*, Y 708 *Saule*, Y 709 *Sycomore*, Y 717 *Ébène*, Y 718 *Erable*, Y 719 *Olivier*, Y 720 *Santal*, Y 721 *Alouette*, Y 722 *Vauneau*, Y 723 *Engoulevent*, Y 724 *Sarcelle*, Y 725 *Marabout*, Y 726 *Toucan*, Y 727 *Macreuse*, Y 728 *Grand Duc*, Y 729 *Eider*, Y 730 *Ara*, Y 738 *Marronier*, Y 739 *Noyer*, Y 740 *Papayer*, Y 745 *Aiguiere*, Y 746 *Embrun*, Y 747 *Loriot*, Y 748 *Gelinotte*.

MISCELLANEOUS

CATARACTE A 748

Small water carrier of 330 tons and 10 knots.

GERMANY (Federal Republic)

Bundesmarine Administration

Chief of Naval Staff, Federal German Navy:
Vice-Admiral Heinz Kühnle

Commander-in-Chief of the Fleet:
Vice Admiral Paul Hartwig

Diplomatic Representation

Naval Attaché in London
Rear Admiral Dr. W. Schünemann

Naval Attaché in Washington:
Captain Jürgen Steindorff

Naval Attaché in Paris:
Captain Werner Köve

Personnel

(a) 1970: 39,000 (3 900 officers, 35 100 men)
1971: 35 000 (3 200 officers, 31 800 men)
1972: 35 900 (4 500 officers, 31 400 men)
1973: 36 000 (4 550 officers, 31 450 men)
1974: 36 000 (4 550 officers, 31 450 men)
1975: 35 900 (4 717 officers, 31 183 men)
(Includes Naval Air Arm)
(b) 15 months National Service

Future Development

Interest is being shown by the Naval Staff in various and varied projects.
(a) Development of more powerful ship-to-ship missiles.
(b) Development of SAM's and ASM's.
(c) Construction of 230 ton hydrofoils of US *Tucumcari* type.
(d) New frigates of 2 500 tons with guided weapons to replace "Hamburg," "Fletcher" and "Köln" Classes—12 planned.

Strength of the Fleet

Type	*Active*	*Building (Projected)*
Destroyers	11	—
Frigates	6	(10)
Corvettes	6	—
Submarines—Patrol	24	—
Fast Attack Craft (Missile)	20	10
Fast Attack Craft (Torpedo)	20	—
LCUs	22	—
LCMs	28	—
Minesweepers—Coastal	40	—
Minesweepers—Inshore	18	—
Depot Ships	13	—
Repair Ships	3 (1 small)	—
Replenishment Tankers (Small)	6	—
Support Tankers	5	—
Supply Ships	9	—
Ammunition Transports	2	—
Mine Transports	2	—
Training Ship	1	—
Sail Training Ships	2	—
Misc. Tenders	5	—
Rescue Launches	7	—
Tugs—Ocean	16	—
Tugs—Harbour	9	—
*Icebreakers	3	—
*Coastguard Craft	8+	—
*Survey Ships	6	—
*Fishery Protection Ships	7	—
*Experimental Ships	10	—

*Non-naval

Naval Air Arm

6 000 men total
2 LRPM squadrons (15 Breguet Atlantic)
4 Fighter bomber squadrons (60 F104G)
1 Helicopter squadron (re-equipping with 22 Sea King Mk 41 for SAR.
Liaison aircraft (20 DO28)

Mercantile Marine

Lloyd's Register of Shipping:
2 088 vessels of 7 980 453 tons gross

Hydrographic Service

This service is under the direction of the Ministry of Transport, is civilian manned with HQ at Hamburg. Survey ships are listed at the end of the section.

Disposals

Destroyers
1972 Z1

Frigates
1972 *Scharnhorst* and *Gneisenau*

Submarines
1974 5 Type 205

Fast Attack Craft (Torpedo)
1972 *Marder, Weihe, Pinguin*
1973 *Fuchs, Häher, Jaguar, Kranich, Leopard, Luchs, Panther, Reiher*
1974 *Storch, Dommel, Elster, Alk, Pelikan*

Coastal Patrol Craft
1974 TM 1, KW 2, KW 8, FW 2, FW 3

Minelayers
1972 *Bochum, Bottrop* Transferred to Turkey.

Minesweepers Coastal
1973 5 "Vegesack" class, 8 "Schütze" class

Supply Ships
1972 *Angeln* Transferred to Turkey
1974 *Schwazwald*

DESTROYERS

3 MODIFIED "ADAMS" CLASS DDG

Name	*No.*	*Builders*	*Laid down*	*Launched*	*Completion*
LUTJENS	D 185 (USN-DDG 28)	Bath Iron Works Corp	1 Mar 1966	11 Aug 1967	12 Mar 1969
MOLDERS	D 186 (USN-DDG 29)	Bath Iron Works Corp	12 Apr 1966	13 Apr 1968	12 Sep 1969
ROMMEL	D 187 (USN-DDG 30)	Bath Iron Works Corp	22 Aug 1967	1 Feb 1969	24 Apr 1970

Displacement, tons	3 370 standard; 4 500 full load
Length, feet (*metres*)	431 (*131·4*) wl; 440 (*134·1*) oa
Beam, feet (*metres*)	47 (*14·3*)
Draught, feet (*metres*)	20 (*6·1*)
Missile launchers	1 "Tartar" single
Guns, dual purpose	2—5 in (*127 mm*) single
A/S launchers	"Asroc"; 2 triple torpedo; 1 DCT
Boilers	4 Combustion Engineering; 1 200 psi (*84·4 kg/cm²*)
Main engines	Geared steam turbines 70 000 shp; 2 shafts
Oil fuel, tons	900
Range, miles	4 500 at 20 knots
Speed, knots	35
Complement	340 (21 officers, 319 men)

LÜTJENS *1974, Federal German Navy*

GENERAL
Destroyers basically of the "Charles F. Adams" type; but modified to suit Federal German requirements and practice and presenting a different silhouette. 1965 contract. Cost $43 754 000. Due for modernisation from Autumn 1974, starting with *Rommel.*

RADAR. SPS 52 three dimensional air search and target designator with aerial on after funnel. SPS 40 air surveillance with aerial on mainmast. Two SPG 51 Tartar fire control aerials abaft after funnel. One SPS 10 surface warning set. One GFCS 68 for gun armament. Tacan beacon. Satir 1 ADA system (believed similar to Senit 2).

SONAR. Probably SQS 23.

"LÜTJENS" Class

Destroyers—*continued*

4 "HAMBURG" CLASS

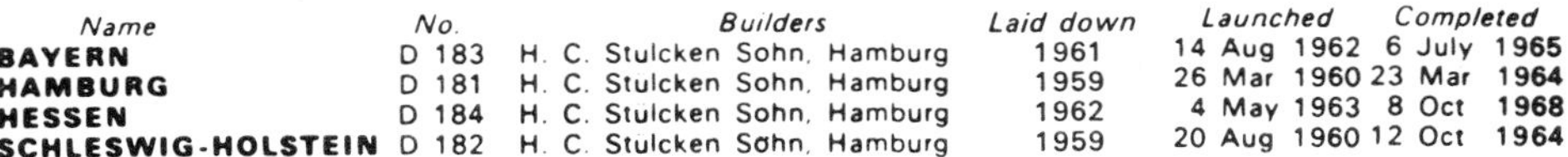

Name	*No.*	*Builders*	*Laid down*	*Launched*	*Completed*
BAYERN	D 183	H. C. Stulcken Sohn, Hamburg	1961	14 Aug 1962	6 July **1965**
HAMBURG	D 181	H. C. Stulcken Sohn, Hamburg	1959	26 Mar 1960	23 Mar **1964**
HESSEN	D 184	H. C. Stulcken Sohn, Hamburg	1962	4 May 1963	8 Oct **1968**
SCHLESWIG-HOLSTEIN	D 182	H. C. Stulcken Sohn, Hamburg	1959	20 Aug 1960	12 Oct **1964**

Displacement, tons	3 400 standard; 4 400 full load
Length, feet (*metres*)	420 (*128*) wl; 439·7 (*134·0*) oa
Beam, feet (*metres*)	44 (*13·4*)
Draught, feet (*metres*)	17 (*5·2*)
Guns, dual purpose	4—3·9 in (*100 mm*) single
Guns, AA	8—40 mm, 4 twin
A/S weapons	2 Bofors 4-barrel DC Mortars; 1 DCT
Torpedo tubes	5—21 in (*533 mm*), 3 bow and 2 stern; 2—12 in for AS torpedoes
Boilers	4 Wahodag; 910 psi (*64 kg/cm²*), 860°F (460°C)
Main engines	2 Wahodag dr geared turbines; 68 000 shp; 2 shafts
Speed, knots	35·8 max; 18 economical sea
Range, miles	6 000 at 13 knots; 920 at 35 knots
Complement	280 (17 officers, 263 men)

GENERAL
All named after countries of the German Federal Republic. Capable of minelaying.

ELECTRONICS. FCS for Bofors A/S launcher, Torpedoes and DC from Hollandse. ECM fitted.

RADAR. All Radar by Hollandse Signaalapparaten. One air warning LW 02/3. One DAO 2 target designator. One nav/surface warning set. Two M45 100 mm fire control sets. Two M45 40 mm fire control sets.

HESSEN *1973, Wright & Logan*

"HAMBURG" Class

BAYERN *1971, Wright & Logan*

HESSEN *2/1974, Reiner Nerlich*

Destroyers—*continued*

4 Ex-US "FLETCHER" CLASS

Name	No.	Builders	Laid down	Launched	Completed	German commissioned
Z 2 (ex-USS *Ringgold, DD* 500)	D 171	Federal SB & DD Co, Port Newark	25 June 1942	11 Nov 1942	24 Dec 1942	14 July **1959**
Z 3 (ex-USS *Wadsworth, DD* 516)	D 172	Bath Iron Works Corporation, Maine	18 Aug 1942	10 Jan 1943	16 Mar 1943	6 Oct **1959**
Z 4 (ex-USS *Claxton, DD* 571)	D 178	Consolidated Steel Corporation, Orange	25 June 1941	1 Apr 1942	8 Dec 1942	15 Dec **1959**
Z 5 (ex-USS *Dyson, DD* 572)	D 179	Consolidated Steel Corporation, Orange	25 June 1941	15 Apr 1942	30 Dec 1942	23 Feb **1960**

Displacement, tons: 2 100 standard; 2 750 full load
Length, feet (*metres*): 368·4 (*112·3*) wl; 376·5 (*114·8*) oa
Beam, feet (*metres*): 39·5 (*12*)
Draught, feet (*metres*): 18 (*5·5*) max
Guns, dual purpose: 4—5 in (*127 mm*) 38 cal.
Guns, AA: 6—3 in (*76 mm*) 50 cal., 3 twin mountings
A/S: 2 hedgehogs; 1 DC rack
Torpedo tubes: 5—21 in (*533 mm*), quintuple bank; 2 ASW tubes
Boilers: 4 Babcock & Wilcox; 569 psi (*40 kg/cm²*); 851°F (*455°C*)
Main engines: 2 sets GE geared turbines 60 000 shp; 2 shafts
Speed, knots: 35 max; 17 economical sea speed
Range, miles: 6 000 at 15 knots
Oil fuel, tons: 540
Complement: 250

GENERAL
Former US "Fletcher" class destroyers. Their loan from the United States for five years was extended. First ship arrived at Bremerhaven on 14 Apr 1958. *Ringgold* was transferred by the USA at Charleston, S.C. on 14 July 1969. Capable of minelaying.

RADAR. Search: SPS 6. Tactical: SPS 10. Fire Control: GFCS 56 and 68.

"Z 1" Class

Z 3 — *1973, Dr, Giorgio Arra*

FRIGATES

6 "KOLN" CLASS

Name	No.	Builders	Launched	Completed
AUGSBURG	F 222	H. C. Stülcken Sohn, Hamburg	15 Aug 1959	7 Apr 1962
BRAUNSCHWEIG	F 225	H. C. Stülcken Sohn, Hamburg	3 Feb 1962	16 June 1964
EMDEN	F 221	H. C. Stülcken Sohn, Hamburg	21 Mar 1959	24 Oct 1961
KARLSRUHE	F 223	H. C. Stülcken Sohn, Hamburg	24 Oct 1959	15 Dec 1962
KÖLN	F 220	H. C. Stülcken Sohn, Hamburg	6 Dec 1958	15 Apr 1961
LUBECK	F 224	H. C. Stülcken Sohn, Hamburg	23 July 1960	6 July 1963

Displacement, tons: 2 100 standard; 2 550 full load
Length, feet (*metres*): 360·9 (*110*)
Beam, feet (*metres*): 36·1 (*11·0*)
Draught, feet (*metres*): 11·2 (*3·4*)
Guns, dual purpose: 2—3·9 in (*100 mm*)
Guns, AA: 6—40 mm; 2 twin and 2 single
A/S: 2 Bofors 4-barrel DC mortars (rocket launchers)
Torpedo tubes: 2 for ASW torpedoes
Main engines: Combined diesel and gas turbine plant: 4 MAN 16-cyl. diesels, total 12 000 bhp; 2 Brown-Boveri gas turbines, 24 000 bhp; total 36 000 shp; 2 shafts
Speed, knots: 32 max; 23 economical sea speed;
Range, miles: 920 at full power
Oil fuel, tons: 333
Complement: 210

GENERAL
Ordered in Mar 1957. All ships of this class are named after towns of West Germany. Capable of minelaying.

ELECTRONICS. Hollandse FCS for Bofors A/S launchers M9 torpedo fire control.

ENGINEERING. Each of the two shafts is driven by two diesels coupled and geared to one BBC gas turbine. Controllable pitch propellers. A speed of 32 knots is reported to have been attained on full power trials.

RADAR. All by Hollandse. One DA 02 target designator. One nav/surface warning set. Two M45 100 mm fire control sets. Two M45 40 mm fire control sets.

BRAUNSCHWEIG — *6/1974, Reiner Nerlich*

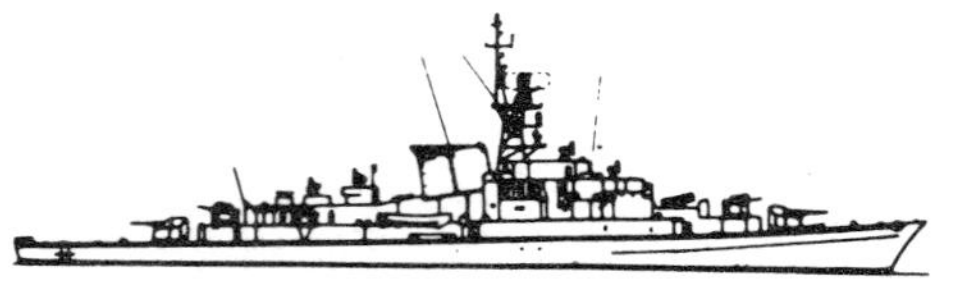

"KÖLN" Class

CORVETTES

HANS BÜRKNER A 1449

Displacement, tons	982 standard; 1 100 full load
Dimensions, feet	265·2 oa × 30·8 × 10
Guns	2—40 mm AA (twin mounting)
A/S weapons	1 DC mortar (four-barrelled) 2 DC racks
Main engines	4 MAN diesels; 2 shafts; 13 600 shp = 25 knots
Complement	50

Built by Atlaswerke, Bremen. Launched on 16 July 1961. Completed on 18 May 1963. Named after designer of German pre-First World War battleships.

HANS BÜRKNER (old Pt number) *1970*

5 "THETIS" CLASS

HERMES P 6053
NAJADE P 6054
THESEUS P 6056
TRITON P 6055
THETIS P 6052

Displacement, tons	564 standard; 680 full load
Dimensions, feet	229·7 × 27 × 7·5
Guns	2—40 mm AA (twin mounting) (To be replaced by 1—3 in Oto Melara)
A/S weapons	Bofors DC mortar (*Hermes* 2 tubes)
Main engines	2 MAN diesels; 2 shafts; 6 800 bhp = 24 knots
Complement	48

Built by Roland Werft, Bremen-Hemelingen. S ne have computer house before bridge. *Thetis* commissioned on 1 July 1961, *Hermes* on 16 Dec 1961, *Najada* on 12 May 1962, *Triton* on 10 Nov 1962, *Theseus* on 15 Aug 1963. Combined nav/surface warning radar. HSA M9 series torpedo control.

THESEUS (blockbridge type—old Pt number) *1970*

NAJADE (forebridge type) *1970, Skyfotos*

SUBMARINES

18 NEW CONSTRUCTION TYPE 206

U 13 S 192
U 14 S 193
U 15 S 194
U 16 S 195
U 17 S 196
U 18 S 197
U 19 S 198
U 20 S 199
U 21 S 170
U 22 S 171
U 23 S 172
U 24 S 173
U 25 S 174
U 26 S 175
U 27 S 176
U 28 S 177
U 29 S 178
U 30 S 179

Displacement, tons	500 nominal, 600 submerged
Length, feet (*metres*)	147·6 (*45·0*)
Beam, feet (*metres*)	15·4 (*4·7*)
Torpedo tubes	8 bow
Main machinery	Diesel-electric; 1 shaft; 1 800 hp
Speed, knots	17 max submerged
Complement	22

Authorised on 7 June 1969 from Howaldtswerke Deutsche Werft (8) and Reinstahl Nordseewerke (10).

U 13, U 14, U 15, U 16, U 17, U 18, and U 19, were completed in 1973. Launch dates of remainder as follows: U 20, 16 Jan 1973—U 21, 9 Mar 1973—U 22, 27 Mar 1973—U 23, 22 May 1974—U 24 24 June 1973—U 25, 23 May 1973—U 26, 20 Nov 1973—U 27, 21 Aug 1973—U 28, 22 Jan 1974—U 29, 5 Sep 1973—U 30, 26 Mar 1974.

U 13 and U 14 *4/1973, Reiner Nerlich*

6 TYPE 205

U 1 (21 Oct 1961) S 180
U 2 (25 Jan 1962) S 181
U 9 (20 Oct 1966) S 188
U 10 (20 July 1967) S 189
U 11 (9 Feb 1968) S 190
U 12 (10 Sep 1968) S 191

Displacement, tons	370 surface; 450 submerged
Length, feet (*metres*)	142·7 (*43·5*) oa
Beam, feet (*metres*)	15·1 (*4·6*)
Draught, feet (*metres*)	13·5 (*4·3*)
Torpedo tubes	8 in bow
Main machinery	2 MB diesels; total 1 200 bhp 2 electric motors, total 1 700 bhp; single screw
Speed, knots	10 on surface; 17 submerged
Complement	21

GENERAL
All built by Howaldtswerke, Kiel in floating docks. Original launch dates above. Fitted with schnorkel. First submarines designed and built by Germany since the end of the Second World War. U 4-12 were built to a heavier and improved design. U 1 and U 2 were modified accordingly and refloated on 17 Feb 1967 and 15 July 1966 respectively. U 1 was reconstructed late 1963 to 4 Mar 1965. (See original appearance in the 1962-63 and 1963-64 editions). U9-12 have hulls of different steel alloys of non-magnetic properties. U 11 entered service on 21 June 1968. U 12 was completed on 14 Jan 1969. U 3 of this class lent to Norway on 10 July 1962 and temporarily named *Kobben* (S 310), was returned to Germany in 1964 and decommissioned on 15 Sep 1967 for disposal.

U I *1973, Howaldtswerke, Kiel*

RADAR. French Thomson-CSF Calypso, nav/attack set. Passive DF.

TORPEDO EQUIPMENT. The boats are trimmed by the stern to load through the bow caps. Also fitted for minelaying. Fire control by Hollandse Sig. Mk 8.

Submarines—*continued*

1 CONVERTED TYPE XXI

WILHELM BAUER (ex-U 2540) Y 880

Displacement, tons	1 620 surface; 1 820 submerged
Length, feet (*metres*)	252·7 (*77·0*) pp
Beam, feet (*metres*)	21·7 (*6·6*)
Draught, feet (*metres*)	20·3 (*6·2*)
Torpedo tubes	4—21 in (*533 mm*) in bow
Main machinery	Diesel-electric drive 2 diesels total 4 200 bhp 2 electric motors total 5 000 hp
Speed, knots	15·5 surface; 17·5 submerged

Launched in 1944 by Blohm & Voss, Hamburg. Sunk on 3 May 1945. Raised in 1957. Rebuilt in 1958-59 at Howaldtswerke, Kiel. Commissioned on 1 Sep 1960. Used for experiments on submarine equipment. Conning tower was modified.

WILHELM BAUER *1973, Howaldtswerke, Kiel*

LIGHT FORCES

10 NEW CONSTRUCTION TYPE 162

(FAST ATTACK CRAFT—MISSILE)
S 61—70

Displacement, tons	202 standard; 228 full load
Dimensions, ft (*m*)	131·9 × 29·2 × 6·2 (*40·2 × 8·9 × 1·9*)
Missiles	4 launchers for Exocet MM 38
Gun	1—76 mm; 2—20 mm
Main engines	Gas turbines, 26 200 bhp; 2—MTU diesels; 1 340 bhp
Speed, knots	50 on turbines; 12 on diesels
Complement	21

Planned for future construction.

10 TYPE 143

(FAST ATTACK CRAFT—MISSILE)

S 61	P 6111	**S 64**	P 6114	**S 67**	P 6117	**S 69**	P 6119
S 62	P 6112	**S 65**	P 6115	**S 68**	P 6118	**S 70**	P 6120
S 63	P 6113	**S 66**	P 6116				

Displacement, tons	295 nominal; 378 full load
Dimensions, ft (*m*)	200·0 × 24·6 × 8·5 (*57 × 7·8 × 2·4*)
Missiles	4 launchers for "Exocet" MM 38
Guns	2—76 mm AA (Italian Oto Melara)
Torpedoes	2—21 in wire guided aft
Main engines	4 MTU diesels; 4 shafts = 38 knots
Range, miles	1 300 at 30 knots 16 000 hp
Complement	40

GENERAL
Ordered in 1972. To be completed from 1974 to 1976 to replace ten torpedo boats of the "Jaguar" class. Final funds allocated 13 July 1972. First laid down late 1972. Builders; S 61-64, 66, 68 and 70 at Lürssen and S 65, 67 and 69 at Kröger, Rendsburg.

GENERAL
Ordered in 1972, for completion from 1974 to 1976 to replace ten boats of the "Jaguar" class. Final funds allocated 13 July 1972. First laid down 1973. Builders; S 61-64, 66, 68 and 70 at Lürssen and S 65, 67 and 69 at Kröger, Rendsburg.

ELECTRONICS.
Believed that data automation system AGIS is being fitted to permit use of Type 143 as control ship for concerted operation of Type 148 boats.

RADAR.
All by Hollandse Signaal. WM 27 in radome for Exocet, gun and torpedo control.

MODEL TYPE 143 *1974, Federal German Navy*

20 TYPE 148

(FAST ATTACK CRAFT—MISSILE)

S 41	P 6141	**S 42**	P 6142	**S 43**	P 6143	**S 44**	P 6144
S 45	P 6145	**S 46**	P 6146	**S 47**	P 6147	**S 48**	P 6148
S 49	P 6149	**S 50**	P 6150	**S 51**	P 6151	**S 52**	P 6152
S 53	P 6153	**S 54**	P 6154	**S 55**	P 6155	**S 56**	P 6156
S 57	P 6157	**S 58**	P 6158	**S 59**	P 6159	**S 60**	P 6160

Displacement, tons	234 standard; 265 full load
Dimensions, ft (*m*)	154·2 × 23·0 × 5·9 (*47 × 7 × 2*)
Missiles	4 launchers for "Exocet" MM 38
Guns	1—76 mm AA (Oto Melara); 1—40 mm AA (Bofors)
Main engines	4 MTU diesels; 4 shafts; 14 400 bhp = 38·5 knots
Oil fuel, tons	39
Range, miles	600 at 30 knots
Complement	30 (4 officers, 26 men)

GENERAL
Ordered in Oct 1970. To be completed from 1973 onwards to replace the "Jaguar" class. All to be operational by end 1975. Builders: Constructions Mecaniques de Normandy, Cherbourg. Eight hulls contracted to Lürssen but all are to fit-out in France.

Launch and completion dates:

	Launched	*Completion*
S 41	27 Mar 1972	30 Oct 1972
S 42	12 Dec 1972	8 Jan 1973
S 43	7 Mar 1973	9 Apr 1973
S 44	5 May 1973	14 June 1973
S 45	3 July 1973	21 Aug 1973
S 46	9 Apr 1973	17 Oct 1973
S 47	20 Sep 1973	15 Nov 1973
S 48	1973	9 Jan 1974
S 49	1973	26 Feb 1974
S 50	1973	27 Mar 1974
S 51	1973	12 June 1974
S 52	1973	17 July 1974
S 53	1974	24 Sep 1974

S 54 laid down 1974.
S 55-60 planned

RADAR. X-Band nav radar. Triton C-band air and surface search and target designator with IFF aerial POLLUX X-band tracking radar. Thomson-CSF VEGA-POLLUX PCET control system and radar for control of EXOCET, torpedoes and guns. Less sophisticated than type 143.

S 41 *1974, Federal German Navy*

Light Forces—*continued*

10 "ZOBEL" CLASS

(TYPE 142 FAST ATTACK CRAFT—TORPEDO)

DACHS	P 6094	**HERMELIN**	P 6095	**OZELOT**	P 6101
FRETTCHEN	P 6100	**HYÄNE**	P 6099	**PUMA**	P 6097
GEPARD	P 6098	**NERZ**	P 6096	**WIESEL**	P 6093
				ZOBEL	P 6092

Displacement, tons	225 full load
Dimensions, ft (*m*)	139·4 × 23·4 × 7·9 (*42·5* × *7·2* × *2·4*)
Guns	2—40 mm AA Bofors L 70 (single)
Tubes	2—21 in for Seal wire-guided torpedoes
Main engines	4 Mercedes-Benz 20 cyl diesels; 4 shafts; 12 000 bhp = 40·5 knots
Complement	39

Originally units of the "Jaguar" class, but, after conversion, known as the "Zobel" class. Two M 20 series Radars in radome for control of guns and torpedoes. Three built by Kröger, Rendsburg and seven by Lürssen, Vegesack.

FRETTCHEN *1974, Federal German Navy—Marineamt*

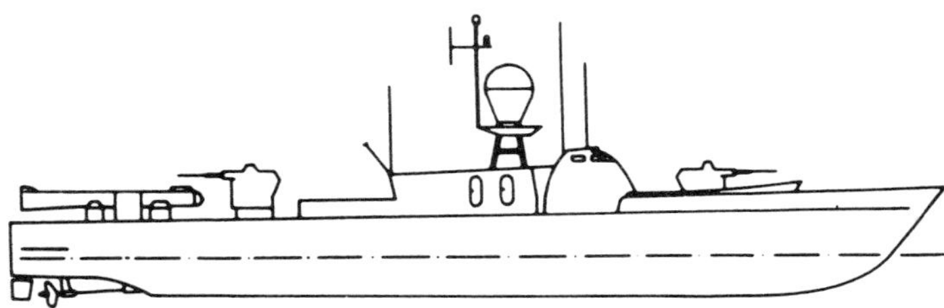

14 "JAGUAR" CLASS

(TYPE 140 141 FAST ATTACK CRAFT—TORPEDO)

ALBATROS *	P 6069	**GREIF** *	P 6071	**PELIKAN**	P 6086
ALK	P 6084	**HABICHT** *	P 6075	**SEEADLER** *	P 6068
BUSSARD *	P 6074	**ILTIS**	P 6058	**SPERBER** *	P 6076
DOMMEL	P 6091	**KONDOR** *	P 6070	**STORCH**	P 6085
ELSTER	P 6088	**KORMORAN** *	P 6077	**TIGER**	P 6063
FALKE *	P 6072	**LÖWE**	P 6065	**WOLF**	P 6062
GEIER *	P 6073				

Displacement, tons	160 standard; 190 full load
Dimensions, ft (*m*)	139·4 × 23·4 × 7·9 (*42·5* × *7·2* × *2·4*)
Guns	2—40 mm AA Bofors L 70 (single)
Tubes	4—21 in (2 torpedo tubes can be removed for 4 mines)
Main engines	Mercedes-Benz 20 cyl or Maybach 16 cyl diesels; 4 shafts; 12 000 bhp = 42 knots
Complement	39

32 boats were built by Lürssen, Vegesack in 1957-62 and eight by Kröger, Rendsburg in 1958-64. Of composite construction, with steel frames, mahogany diagonal carvel hulls, alloy bulkheads and superstructure. Units marked * are type 141 with Maybach diesels. Remainder are Type 140 with Mercedes-Benz diesels. Ten were converted into Type 142, see above. All to be paid off on replacement by Types 143 and 148. Some may be available for foreign sale *Löwe*, *Tiger* and *Wolf* paid off until May 1975.

ILTIS *6/1974, Reiner Nerlich*

AMPHIBIOUS FORCES

28 LCM TYPE

LCM 1-28

Displacement, tons	116 standard; 140 full load
Dimensions, ft (*m*)	77·1 × 21·4 × — (*23·5* × *6·5* × —)
Main engines	1 320 hp = 10 knots

Similar to US LCM 8 Type. Built 1965-67.

22 LCU TYPE

BARBE	L 790	**FELCHEN**	L 793	**LACHS**	L 762	**SALM**	L 799
BRASSE	L 789	**FLUNDER**	L 760	**MAKRELE**	L 796	**SCHLEI**	L 765
BUTT	L 788	**FORELLE**	L 794	**MURANE**	L 797	**STÖR**	L 766
DELPHIN	L 791	**INGER**	L 795	**PLOTZE**	L 763	**TÜMMLER**	L 767
DORSCH	L 792	**KARPFEN**	L 761	**RENKE**	L 798	**WELS**	L 768
				ROCHEN	L 764	**ZANDER**	L 769

Displacement, tons	200 light; 403 full load
Dimensions, ft (*m*)	136·5 × 28·9 × 6·9 (*41·6* × *8·8* × *2·1*)
Guns	1 or 2—20 mm AA
Main engines	GM diesels; 2 shafts; 1 380 bhp = 12 knots
Complement	17

Similar to the United States LCU (Landing Craft Utility) type. Provided with bow and stern ramp. Built by Howaldt, Hamburg, 1964-67. To carry 160 tons load. *Inge* employed for seamanship training.

MURÄNE (2—20 mm guns) *8/1974, Reiner Nerlich*

MINE WARFARE FORCES

Note. A new class of Minehunters, Type 342 is planned.

18 "LINDAU" CLASS (MINESWEEPERS—COASTAL and MINEHUNTERS)

CUXHAVEN	M 1078	**KONSTANZ**	M 1081	**TÜBINGEN**	M 1074
DÜREN	M 1079	**LINDAU**	M 1072	**ULM**	M 1083
FLENSBURG	M 1084	**MARBURG**	M 1080	**VÖLKLINGEN**	M 1087
FULDA	M 1068	**MINDEN**	M 1085	**WEILHEIM**	M 1077
GÖTTINGEN	M 1070	**PADERBORN**	M 1076	**WETZLAR**	M 1075
KOBLENZ	M 1071	**SCHLESWIG**	M 1073	**WOLFSBURG**	M 1082

Displacement, tons	370 standard; 420 full load
Dimensions, ft (*m*)	137·8 pp; 147·7 oa × 27·2 × 8·5 (*49·7 × 8·3 × 2·5*)
Guns	1—40 mm; 2—20 mm
Main engines	Maybach diesels; 2 shafts; 4 000 bhp = 16·5 knots
Range, miles	850 at 16·5 knots
Complement	46

Lindau, first German built vessel for the Federal German Navy since the Second World War, launched on 16 Feb 1957. Basically of NATO WU type but modified for German requirements. Built by Burmester, Bremen-Berg. Seventeen were built in German yards in 1958-60. The hull is of wooden construction, laminated with plastic glue. The engines are of non-magnetic materials. The first six, *Göttingen, Koblenz, Lindau, Schleswig, Tubingen* and *Wetzlar*, were modified with lower bridges in 1958-59. *Schleswig* was lengthened by 6·8 feet in 1960—all others in 1960-64. *Fulda* and *Flensburg* were converted into minehunters in 1968-69 as part of a total of twelve ships to be so converted.

FLENSBURG *7/1974, Reiner Nerlich*

22 "SCHÜTZE" CLASS (MINESWEEPERS—COASTAL (FAST))

ATAIR	M 1067	**NEPTUN**	M 1093	**SKORPION**	M 1060
CASTOR	M 1051	**PERSEUS**	M 1090	**SPICA**	M 1059
DENEB	M 1064	**POLLUX**	M 1054	**STIER**	Y 849
FISCHE	M 1096	**PLUTO**	M 1092	**WAAGE**	M 1063
GEMMA	M 1097	**REGULUS**	M 1057	**WEGA**	M 1089
HERKULES	M 1095	**RIGEL**	M 1056	**WIDDER**	M 1094
JUPITER	M 1065	**SCHÜTZE**	M 1062		
MARS	M 1058	**SIRIUS**	M 1055		

Displacement, tons	204 standard; 230 full load
Dimensions, ft (*m*)	124·7 × 27·2 × 6·6 (*43·8 × 8·2 × 2*)
Gun	1—40 mm AA
Main engines	Diesels = 14 knots
Range, miles	2 000 at 13 knots
Complement	24

30 originally built between 1959 and 1964.

Castor, Fische, Gemma, Mars, Pollux, Regulus, Rigel, Schütze, Sirius, Skorpion, Spica, Steinbock, Stier, Waage, and *Wega* were built by Abeking & Rasmussen, Lemwerder; *Deneb, Jupiter, Pluto*, and *Widder* by Schürenstedt, Bardenfl; *Atair, Herkules, Neptun*, and *Perseus* by Schlichting, Travemünde. The design is a development of the "R" boats of the Second World War. All this class are named after stars. *Stier*, former hull number M 1061, carries no weapons, but has a decompression chamber, being clearance diving vessel.
Formerly classified as inshore minesweepers, but re-rated as fast minesweepers in 1966.

WIDDER *2/1974 Reiner Nerlich*

STIER (decompression chamber) *1972*

10 "FRAUENLOB" CLASS (MINESWEEPERS—INSHORE)

ACHERON	M 2667	**FRAUENLOB**	M 2658	**MEDUSA**	M 2661
ATLANTIS	M 2666	**GEFION**	M 2660	**MINERVA**	M 2663
DIANA	M 2664	**LORELEY**	M 2665	**NAUTILUS**	M 2659
				UNDINE	M 2662

Displacement, tons	230 standard; 280 full load
Dimensions, ft (*m*)	154·5 oa × 22·3 × 7·2 (*47·2 × 7·2 × 2·1*)
Gun	1—40 mm AA (except *Stier*)
Main engines	Maybach diesels; 2 shafts; Escher-Wyss propellers; 3 600 bhp = 24·5 knots
Complement	39

Built by Kröger Werft, Rendsberg. Launched in 1965-67. Completed in 1965-68. Originally designed coastguard boats with "W" pennant numbers. Rated as inshore minesweepers in 1968 with the "M" hull numbers.

FRAUENLOB *1973, Stefan Terzibaschitsch*

HOLNIS Y 836 (ex-M 2651) (MINESWEEPER—INSHORE)

Displacement, tons	180
Dimensions, feet	116·8 × 24·3 × 6·9
Guns	1—20 mm AA
Main engines	2 Mercedes-Benz diesels; 2 shafts; 2 000 bhp = 14·5 knots
Complement	21

Now serving for test and evaluation purposes. *Holnis* was launched on 22 May 1965 and completed in 1966 by Abeking & Rasmussen, Lemwerde, as the prototype of a new design of *Binnenminensuchboote* projected as a class of 20 such vessels but she is the only unit of this type, the other 19 boats having been cancelled. Hull number changed from M 2651 to Y 836 in 1970.

HOLNIS ***1972***

Mine Warfare Forces—*continued*

2 "NIOBE" CLASS (MINESWEEPERS—INSHORE)

HANSA Y 806 **NIOBE** Y 1643

Displacement, tons	150 standard; 180 full load
Dimensions, ft (*m*)	115·2 × 21·3 × 5·6 (*35·1 × 6·5 × 1·7*)
Gun	1—40 mm
Mines	Laying capability
Main engines	*Hansa:* 1 Mercedes-Benz diesel; 1 shaft; 950 bhp = 14 knots *Niobe:* 2 Mercedes-Benz diesels; 2 shafts; 1 900 bhp = 16 knots
Range, miles	1 100 at max spd
Complement	*Hansa:* 19; *Niobe* 22

Built by Kröger Werft, Rendsburg. Completed in 1958. *Hansa* serves as support ship for clearance divers. *Niobe* serves for test and evaluation purposes.

HANSA *1970, Stefan Terzibaschitsch*

8 "ARIADNE" CLASS (MINESWEEPERS—INSHORE)

AMAZONE	(27 Feb 1963)	M 2656	**HERTHA**	(18 Feb 1961)	M 2653
ARIADNE	(23 Apr 1960)	M 2650	**NIXE**	(3 Dec 1962)	M 2655
FREYA	(25 June 1966)	M 2651	**NYMPHE**	(20 Nov 1962)	M 2654
GAZELLE	(14 Aug 1963)	M 2657	**VINETA**	(17 Sep 1960)	M 2652

Displacement, tons	184 standard; 210 full load
Dimensions, ft (*m*)	124·3 × 27·2 × 6·6 (*37·9 × 8·3 × 2*)
Gun	1—40 mm
Mines	Laying capability
Main engines	2 Mercedes-Benz diesels; 2 shafts; 2 000 bhp = 14 knots
Range, miles	740 at 14 knots
Complement	23

Launch dates above. All completed by Kröger Werft, Rendsburg, in 1960-63. All named after former cruisers, 1897-1900. Formerly classified as patrol boats but re-rated as inshore minesweepers in 1966, and given new M hull numbers in Jan 1968, Y hull numbers in 1970, and M numbers once more in 1974.

HERTHA *8/1974, Reiner Nerlich*

SERVICE FORCES

12 "RHEIN" CLASS (DEPOT SHIPS)

DONAU	A 69	**LECH**	A 56	**RHEIN**	A 58
ELBE	A 61	**MAIN**	A 63	**SAAR**	A 65
ISAR	A 54	**MOSEL**	A 67	**WERRA**	A 68
LAHN	A 55	**NECKAR**	A 66	**WESER**	A 62

Displacement, tons	2 370 standard; 2 540 full load except *Lahn* and *Lech* 2 460 standard; 2 680 full load
Length, feet (*metres*)	304·5 (*92·8*) wl; 323·5 (*99*) oa
Beam, feet (*metres*)	38·8 (*11·8*)
Draught, feet (*metres*)	11·2 (*3·4*); 12·2 (*3·7*) in *Lahn* and *Lech*
Guns	2—3·9 in (*100 mm*); none in *Lahn, Lech*; 4—40 mm
Main engines	6 Maybach or Daimler diesels; Diesel-electric drive in *Isar, Lahn, Lech, Mosel, Saar* 11 400 bhp; 2 shafts
Speed, knots	20·5, 15 economical
Range, miles	1 625 at 15 knots
Oil fuel, tons	334
Complement	110 (accommodation for 200) 198 (*Lahn* and *Lech*)

RHEIN *1974, Federal German Navy—Marineamt*

GENERAL
Elbe, Mosel, Rhein, and *Ruhr* were built by Schliekerwerft, Hamburg, *Isar* by Blohm & Voss, Hamburg, *Weser* by Elsflether Werft, *Neckar* by Lürssen, Bremen-Vegesack, *Saar* by Norderwerft, Hamburg, *Donau* by Schlichting, Travemunde, *Lahn* and *Lech* by Flender, Lübeck, *Main, Werra* by Lindenau, Kiel-Friedrichsort. All completed in 1961-64. Rated as Depot Ships for minesweepers (*Isar, Mosel, Saar*), submarines (*Lahn, Lech*), Type 206 submarines (*Rhein*), and motor torpedo boats (others) but these ships with their 3·9 in (*100 mm*) guns could obviously be used in lieu of frigates.

RADAR. All by Hollandse. Search: HSA DA 02. Fire Control: Two HSA M 45 for 100 mm and 40 mm.

STATUS. Five of these comparatively new ships, namely *Donau, Isar, Lahn, Lech* and *Weser*, were placed in reserve by July 1968. This was part of the economy programme announced by the Federal German Navy in Sep 1967.

"RHEIN" Class

2 Ex-US LST (REPAIR SHIPS)

ODIN	(ex-USS *Diomedes. ARB* 11, ex-*LST* 1119)	A 512
WOTAN	(ex-USS *Ulysses, ARB* 9, ex-*LST* 967)	A 513

Displacement, tons	1 625 light; 3 455 full load
Dimensions, ft (*m*)	328 oa × 50 × 9·2 (*100 × 15·2 × 2·8*)
Guns	4—20 mm AA
Main engines	2 GM diesels, 2 shafts; 1 800 bhp = 11·6 knots
Oil fuel, tons	600
Range, miles	2 000 at 9 knots
Complement	187

Repair Ships. Transferred under MAP in June 1961. *Odin* commissioned in Jan 1966 and *Wotan* on 2 Dec 1965.

WOTAN *1970*

MEMMERT Y 805

The small repair ship *Memmert* Y 805 (ex-USN 106, ex-*India*, ex-BP 34), 165 tons and 8 knots, rated as torpedo repair ship, salvage vessel with a derrick.

Service Forces—*cont.*

FRANKENLAND (ex-*Münsterland*, ex-*Powell*) A 1439 (ex-Y 827) (REPLENISHMENT TANKER)

Displacement, tons 11 708 standard; 16 060 full load
Dimensions, ft (*m*) 521·8 × 70·2 × 37·5 (*167 × 21·4 × 9·1*)
Main engines Diesels; 5 800 bhp = 13·5 knots

Built by Lithgows, Glasgow. Launched in 1950. Commissioned on 29 Apr 1959.

FRANKENLAND *1972*

2 "EMSLAND" CLASS (REPLENISHMENT TANKERS)

EMSLAND (ex-*Antonio Zotti*) A 1440 (ex-Y 828)
MÜNSTERLAND (ex-*Angela Germona*) A 1441 (ex-Y 829)

Measurement, tons 6 200 gross (*Emsland*); 6 191 (*Münsterland*)
Dimensions, ft (*m*) 461 × 54·2 × 25·8 (*141 × 16·5 × 7·8*)
Main engines Diesels; CRDA; 4 800 bhp (*Emsland*); Fiat 5 500 bhp (*Münsterland*) = 12·5 knots

Built by CRDA Monfalcone, and Ansaldo, Genoa, respectively. Both launched in 1943. Completed in 1947 and 1946 respectively. Purchased in 1960 from Italian owners. Converted in 1960-61 by Schliekerwerft, Hamburg, and Howaldtswerke, Hamburg, respectively. Commissioned 7 Nov 1961 and 16 Oct 1961. Civilian crew.

MÜNSTERLAND *1973, Dr. Giorgio Arra*

2 "BODENSEE" CLASS (REPLENISHMENT TANKERS)

BODENSEE (ex-*Unkas*) A 1406 (ex-A 54) **WITTENSEE** (ex-*Sioux*) A 1407

Measurement, tons 1 238 deadweight; 985 gross
Dimensions, ft (*m*) 208·3 × 32·5 × 15 (*61·2 × 9·8 × 4·3*)
Main engines Diesels; 1 050—1 250 bhp = 12 knots
Complement 21

Built by P. Lindenau, Kiel-Friedrichsort. Launched on 19 Nov 1955 and on 23 Sep 1958, respectively. Commissioned on 26 Mar 1959. Details above for *Bodensee—Wittensee* slightly larger.

WITTENSEE *10/1974, Reiner Nerlich*

EIFEL (ex-*Friedrich Jung*) A 1429 (REPLENISHMENT TANKER)

Displacement, tons 4 720
Dimensions, ft (*m*) 334 × 47·2 × 23·3 (*102 × 14·4 × 7·1*)
Main engines 3 360 hp = 13 knots

Built by Norderwerft, Hamburg. Launched on 29 Mar 1958. Purchased in 1953 for service in the Bundesmarine. Commissioned on 27 May 1963.

EIFEL *1970*

4 "WALCHENSEE" CLASS (SUPPORT TANKERS)

AMMERSEE A 1425 **WALCHENSEE** A 1424
TEGERNSEE A 1426 **WESTENSEE** A 1427

Displacement, tons 2 174
Dimensions, ft (*m*) 233 × 36·7 × 13·5 (*74·2 × 11·2 × 4·1*)
Main engines Diesels; 2 shafts; 1 400 bhp = 12·6 knots

Built by Lindenau, Friedrichsort. Launched on 22 Sep 1966, 22 Oct 1966, 10 July 1965 and 25 Feb 1966 and commissioned on 2 Mar 1967 23 Mar 1967, 29 June 1966 and 6 Oct 1967 respectively.

WESTENSEE *1971*

8 "LÜNEBURG" CLASS (SUPPLY SHIPS)

COBURG A 1412 **LÜNEBURG** A 1411 **OFFENBURG** A 1417
FREIBURG A 1413 **MEERSBURG** A 1418 **SAARBURG** A 1415
GLÜCKSBURG A 1414 **NIENBURG** A 1416

Displacement, tons 3 254
Dimensions, ft (*m*) 341·2 × 43·3 × 13·8 (*104 × 13·2 × 4·2*)
Guns 4—40 mm AA
Main engines 2 Maybach diesels; 2 shafts; 5 600 bhp = 17 knots
Complement 103

Lüneberg, Coburg, Glücksburg, Meersburg and *Nienburg* were built by Flensburger Schiffbau and Vulkan, Bremen, others by Blohm & Voss, Hamburg. Commissioned on 9 July, 27 May, 9 July, 9 July, 25 June, 1 Aug, 27 May and 30 July, respectively, 1968.

COBURG *8/1974, Reiner Nerlich*

HARZ (ex-*Claere Jung*) A 1428 (SUPPORT TANKER)

Measurement, tons 3 696 deadweight
Dimensions, ft (*m*) 303·2 × 43·5 × 21·7 (*92·4 × 13·2 × 6·6*)
Main engines 2 520 hp = 12 knots

Built in 1953 by Norderwerft, Hamburg. Purchased in 1963 for service as an oiler in the Bundesmarine. Commissioned on 27 May 1963.

HARZ *1970*

Service Forces—*continued*

1 "ANGELN" CLASS (SUPPLY SHIP)

DITHMARSCHEN (ex-*Hébé*) A 1409

Measurement, tons	2 350 deadweight
Dimensions, ft (*m*)	296·9 × 43·6 × 20·3 (*90·5 × 13·3 × 4·5*)
Main engines	Pielstick diesels; 1 shaft; 3 000 bhp = 16 knots
Complement	57

Built by Ateliers et Chantiers de Bretagne, Nantes. Purchased from shipowners S. N. Caennaise, Caen. Launched on 7 May 1955 and commissioned on 19 Dec 1959.

DITHMARSCHEN *1972, Wright & Logan*

6 "FW" CLASS (WATER BOATS)

FW 1 Y 864 **FW 2** Y 865 **FW 3** Y 866 **FW 4** Y 867 **FW 5** Y 868 **FW 6** Y 869

Measurement, tons	350 deadweight
Dimensions, ft (*m*)	144·4 × 25·6 × 8·2 (*44·1 × 7·8 × 2·5*)
Main engines	MWM diesel, 230 bhp = 9·5 knots

Built in pairs by Schiffbarges, Unterweser, Bremerhaven—H. Rancke, Hamburg—Jadewerft, Wilhelmshaven, in 1963-64.

2 "WESTERWALD" CLASS (AMMUNITION TRANSPORTS)

ODENWALD A 1436 **WESTERWALD** A 1435

Displacement, tons	3 460
Dimensions, ft (*m*)	347·8 × 46 × 12·2 (*106 × 14 × 3·7*)
Guns	4—40 mm
Main engines	Diesels; 5 600 bhp = 17 knots
Complement	60

Built by Lübecker Masch in 1966-67. *Odenwald* was launched on 5 May 1966 and commissioned on 23 Mar 1967 and *Westerwald* was launched on 25 Feb 1966 and commissioned on 1 Feb 1967.

2 "SACHSENWALD" CLASS (MINE TRANSPORTS)

SACHSENWALD A 1437 **STEIGERWALD** A 1438

Displacement, tons	3 850 full load
Dimensions, ft (*m*)	363·5 × 45·6 × 11·2 (*111 × 13·9 × 3·4*)
Guns	4—40 mm (two twin mountings)
Mines	Laying capacity
Main engines	2 diesels; 2 shafts; 5 600 hp = 17 knots
Range, miles	3 500
Complement	65

Built by Blohm & Voss, Hamburg as mine transports. Laid down on 1 Aug 1966 and 9 May 1966. Launched on 10 Dec 1966 and 10 Mar 1967. Both commissioned on 20 Aug 1969. Have mine ports in the stern and can be used as minelayers.

SACHSENWALD *1970*

1 "DEUTSCHLAND" CLASS (TRAINING SHIP)

Name	*No.*	*Builders*	*Laid down*	*Launched*	*Completed*
DEUTSCHLAND	A 59	Nobiskrug, Rendsburg	1959	5 Nov 1960	25 May 1963

Displacement, tons	4 880 normal; 5 400 full load
Length, feet (*metres*)	452·8 (*138·0*) pp; 475·8 (*145·0*) oa
Beam, feet (*metres*)	52·5 (*16·0*)
Draught, feet (*metres*)	15·7 (*4·8*)
A/S weapons	2 Bofors 4-barrel rocket launchers
Guns	4—3·9 in (*100 mm*) single; 6—40 mm; 2 twin and 2 single
Torpedo tubes	4 for A/S; 2 for surface
Mines	Laying capability
Boilers	2 Wahodag; 768 psi (*54 km/cm²*); 870°F (*465°C*)
Main engines	6 680 bhp diesels (2 Daimler-Benz and 2 Maybach); 2 shafts; 8 000 shp double reduction MAN geared turbines; 1 shaft
Speed, knots	22 max (3 shafts); 17 (2 shafts); 14 economical (1 shaft)
Range, miles	1 700 at 17 knots
Oil fuel, tons	230 furnace; 410 diesel
Complement	554 (33 officers, 271 men, 250 cadets)

DEUTSCHLAND *1974, Federal German Navy*

GENERAL

First West German naval ship to exceed the post-war limit of 3 000 tons. Designed with armament and machinery of different types for training purposes. The name originally planned for this ship was *Berlin*. Ordered in 1956. Carried out her first machinery sea trials on 15 Jan 1963.

RADAR. All by Hollandse. Search: HSA LW 02/3. Tactical: HSA DA 02. One nav/surface warning radar. Fire Control: HSA 2 M45 100 mm and 40 mm fire control. HSA fire control for Bofors A/S launcher, torpedoes and DC.

Service Forces—*continued*

GORCH FOCK A 60 (SAIL TRAINING SHIP)

Displacement, tons 1 760 standard; 1 870 full load
Dimensions, ft (*m*) 257 oa × 39·2 × 15·8 (*81·3 × 12 × 4·8*)
Main engines Auxiliary MAN diesel; 880 bhp = 11 knots
Sail area, sq ft 21 141
Range, miles 1 990
Complement 206 (10 officers, 56 ratings, 140 cadets)

Sail training ship of the improved "Horst Wessel" type. Barque rig. Launched by Blohm & Voss, Hamburg, on 23 Aug 1958 and commissioned on 17 Dec 1958.

NORDWIND Y 834 (SAIL TRAINING SHIP)

Displacement, tons 110
Dimensions, ft (*m*) 78·8 × 22 × 9 (*24 × 6·4 × 2·5*)
Main engines Diesel; 150 bhp = 8 knots. (Sail area 2 037·5 sq ft)

Ketch (KFK).

There are over 70 other sailing vessels of various types serving for sail training and recreational purposes. *Achat, Alarich, Amsel, Argonaut, Borasco, Brigant, Dankwart, Diamont, Dietrich, Drossel Dompfaff, Fafnir, Fink, Flibustier, Freibeuter, Gernot, Geiserich, Geuse, Giselher, Gödicke, Gunnar, Gunter, Hadubrand, Hagen, Hartnaut Hildebrand, Horand, Hunding, Jaspis, Kaper, Klipper, Korsar, Kuchkuch, Lerche, Likendeeler, Magellan, Michel, Mime, Meise, Mistral, Monsun, Nachtigall, Ortwin, Ostwind, Pampero, Pirol, Ruediger, Samum, Saphir, Schirocco, Seeteufel, Siegfried, Siegmund, Siegura Smaragd, Star, Stieglitz, Stortebecker, Taifun, Teja, Topas, Tornadon, Totila Vitalienbrüder, Volker, Walter, Wate Westwind, Wiking, Wittigo, Zeisig.*

LAUNCHES

FL 5 Y 857 (ex-W 11) **FL 7** Y 859 (ex-W 13) **FL 8** Y 860 (ex-W 14)

Displacement, tons 45 standard; 60 full load
Dimensions, ft (*m*) 93·5 oa × 15·5 × 4·0 (*28·9 × 4·9 × 1·5*)
Main engines 2 Mercedes-Benz diesels; 2 000 bhp = 25 knots
Complement 14

Built in 1951-53. Employed on SAR duties.

FL 6 (now deleted—remainder similar) *1968*

FL 9 Y 861 (ex-D 2763) **FL 10** Y 862 (ex-D 2765) **FL 11** Y 863 (ex-D 2766)

Displacement, tons 70
Dimensions, ft (*m*) 95·2 × 15·6 × 4·2 (*29 × 5 × 1·3*)
Main engines Maybach diesels; 2 shafts; 3 200 bhp = 30 knots
Range, miles 600 at 25 knots

Built by Kröger, Rendsburg. Completing in 1955. Employed on SAR duties.

FL 10 *1972*

13 TRVs

TF 1-6 (Y 851-856) **TF 101-104** (Y 883-886) **TF 106-108** (Y 872-874)

All of approximately 30-40 tons and built—TF 1-6 and 106-108 in 1966, the remainder a deal older.

COASTAL PATROL CRAFT

KW 15 Y 827
KW 16 Y 830
KW 17 Y 845
KW 18 Y 832
KW 19 Y 833
KW 20 Y 846

Same particulars as FL 5 (Rescue Launches)

KW 3. Of 112 tons and 8 knots built in 1943.

TUGS

BALTRUM A 1454
JUIST A 1456
LANGEOOG A 1453
NORDERNEY A 1455
SPIEKEROOG A 1452
WANGEROOGE A 1451

Displacement, tons 854 standard; 1 024 full load
Dimensions, ft (*m*) 170·6 × 39·4 × 12·8 (*52·0 × 12·1 × 3·9*)
Gun 1—40 mm
Main engines Diesel-electric; 2 shafts; 2 400 hp = 14 knots
Range, miles 5 000 at 10 knots
Complement 24-35

Built by Schichau, Bremerhaven. *Wangerooge*, prototype, salvage tug, was launched on 4 July 1966 and commissioned on 9 Apr 1968, *Langeoog* and *Spiekeroog* on 14 Aug 1968, *Baltrum* on 8 Oct 1968.

FEHMARN A 1458 **HELGOLAND** A 1457

Displacement, tons 1 310 standard; 1 643 full load
Dimensions, ft (*m*) 223·1 × 41·7 × 14·4 (*68·0 × 12·7 × 4·4*)
Guns 2—40 mm
Main engines Diesel-electric; 4 MWM diesels; 2 shafts; 3 800 hp = 17 knots
Range, miles 6 000 at 10 knots
Complement 36-45

Salvage tugs. Built by Unterweser, Bremerhaven. Launched on 25 Nov 1965 and 8 Apr 1965 and commissioned on 1 Feb 1967 and 8 Mar 1966. Carry firefighting equipment.

FEHMARN *1974, Federal German Navy—Marineamt*

AMRUM Y 822 **FÖHR** Y 821 **NEUWERK** Y 823 **SYLT** Y 820

Displacement, tons 266 standard
Dimensions, ft (*m*) 100·7 oa × 25·2 (*30·6 × 7·5*)
Main engines 1 Deutz diesel 800 bhp = 12 knots
Complement 10

Built by Schichau, Bremerhaven. Launched in 1961. All completed in 1962-63.

PELLWORM Y 801

Displacement, tons 437 standard; 500 full load
Dimensions, feet (*m*) 38·7 × 8·5 × 3·6
Main engines 1—MWM-DM Diesel; 1 shaft; 800 hp = 12 knots
Range, miles 2 900 at 8 knots

Built by Schichau, Königsberg, 1939.

ELLERBEK Y 1682 **HEPPENS** Y 1681 **NEUENDE** Y 1680

Displacement, tons 122
Dimensions, ft (*m*) 87·2 × 24·3 × 8·5 (*26·6 × 7·4 × 2·6*)
Main engines 1 MWM diesel; 1 shaft; 800 hp
Speed, knots 12
Complement 6

Harbour tugs by Schichau, Bremerhaven in 1971.

HARBOUR TYPE. There are also nine small harbour tugs all completed in 1958-60:— *Blauort* Y 803, *Knechtsand* Y 814, *Langeness* Y 819, *Lütje Horn* Y 812, *Mellum* Y 813, *Nordstrand* Y 817, *Scharhörn* Y 815 *Trischen* Y 818 and *Vogelsand* Y 816.

ICEBREAKERS

HANSE

Displacement, tons 3 700
Dimensions, feet 243·2 × 57 × 20
Main engines Diesel-electric; 4 shafts; 7 500 bhp = 16 knots

Built by Wärtsilä Oy, Helsinki, Finland. Laid down on 12 Jan 1965. Launched on 17 Oct 1966. Completed on 25 Nov 1966. Commissioned on 13 Dec 1966. Although owned by West Germany she sails under the Finnish flag, manned by a Finnish crew. Only when the winter is so severe that icebreakers are needed in the southern Baltic will she be transferred under the German flag and command. She is of improved "Karhu" class. She does not belong to the Bundesmarine.

EISBAR A 1402 **EISVOGEL** A 1401

Displacement, tons 560 standard
Dimensions, ft (*m*) 125·3 × 31·2 × 15·1 (*38·2 × 9·5 × 4·6*)
Gun 1—40 mm
Main engines 2 Maybach diesels; 2 shafts; 2 000 bhp = 14 knots

Built by J. G. Hitzler, Lauenburg. Launched on 9 June and 28 Apr 1960, and commissioned on 1 Nov and 11 Mar 1961, respectively.

AUXILIARY SHIPS

EIDER (ex-*Catherine*, ex-*Dochet*) Y 1663 (ex-A 50) (MC TRAINING SHIP)

Displacement, tons	480 standard; 750 full load
Dimensions, ft (*m*)	164·0 pp; 177·2 oa × 27·5 × 14.0 (*53·9 × 8·4 × 4*)
Guns	1—40 mm; 1—20 mm
Main engines	Triple expansion; 1 shaft; 750 ihp = 12 knots
Range, miles	3 700
Oil fuel, tons	130
Complement	45

Former British "Isles" type minesweeping trawler. Built in Canada by Davie & Sons, Lauzon, in 1942. Employed as a mine clearance training vessel. She has been civilian manned since 1 Jan 1968.

OSTE (ex-USN 101, *Puddefjord*) A 52 (RADAR TRIALS SHIP)

Measurement, tons	567 gross
Dimensions, ft (*m*)	160 × 29·7 × 17 (*48·8 × 9 × 5·2*)
Main engines	1 Akers diesel; 1 shaft; 1 600 bhp = 12 knots

Built in 1943 at Akers Mekaniske Vaerkstad. Oslo. Taken over from the US Navy, Converted in 1968.

OSTE (as radar testing ship) *1970, Stefan Terzibaschitsch*

ALSTER (ex-*Mellum*) A 50 **OKER** (ex-*Hoheweg*) A 53

Measurement, tons	1 187
Dimensions, ft (*m*)	237·8 × 34·4 × 16·1 (*72·5 × 10·5 × 4·9*)
Main engines	Diesel-electric; 1 screw = 15 knots
Complement	30

Built by Unterweser, Bremen in 1971-72.

EMS (ex-USN 104, ex-*Harle*) Y 1662 (ex-A 53) (DIVING TENDER)

Measurement, tons	660 gross
Dimensions, ft (*m*)	185·7 oa × 29 × 15·5 (*56·6 × 8·8 × 4·7*)
Guns	4—20 mm
Main engines	Sulzer diesels; 1 000 bhp = 12 knots
Range, miles	2 400 at 12 knots

Built in 1941 by Kremer & Sohn, Elmshorn.

EMS *1972*

WALTHER VON LEDEBUR Y 841

Displacement, tons	725
Dimensions, ft (*m*)	219·8 × 34·8 × 8·9 (*63 × 10·6 × 2·7*)
Main engines	Maybach diesels; 2 shafts; 5 000 bhp = 19 knots
Complement	11 + 10

Wooden hulled vessel. Built by Burmester, Bremen-Berg. Launched on 30 June 1966.

WALTHER VON LEDEBUR *1971*

Auxiliary Ships—*continued*

5 Ex-COASTAL MINESWEEPERS

ADOLF BESTELMEYER (ex-*BYMS* 2213) Y 881
H. C. OERSTED (ex-*Vinstra*, ex-*NYMS* 247) Y 877
HERMAN VON HELMOLTZ Y 878
RUDOLF DIESEL (ex-*BYMS* 2279) Y 889
OT 2 Y 847

Displacement, tons	270 standard; 350 full load
Dimensions, feet	136 × 24·5 × 8
Main engines	2 diesels; 2 shafts; 1 000 bhp = 15 knots

Of US YMS type. Built in 1943. *Adolf Bestelmeyer* and *Rudolf Diesel* are used for gunnery purposes. *H. C. Oersted* was acquired from the Royal Norwegian Navy. *Herman von Helmholtz*, commissioned on 18 Dec 1962, is used as a degaussing ship.

PLANET A 1450 of 1943 tons and 13·5 knots. Built in 1967.

WILHELM PULLWER Y 838, **SP I** Y 837 of 160 tons and 12·5 knots. Built in 1966.

HEINZ ROGGENKAMP Y 871. Of 785 tons and 12 knots. Built in 1952.

FRIEDRICH VOGE Y 888. Of 179 tons.

KARL KOLLS Y 887. Of 189 tons.

OTTO MEYCKE. Diving Trials.

EF 3 Y 840 of 100 tons and 13·4 knots, ex-FPB built in 1943.

TB 1 Y 1678 of 70 tons and 14 knots. Diving boat built in 1972.

LP 1, 2 and **3**. Battery workshop craft of 180 tons built in 1963-73

FORDE Y 1641 **JADE** Y 1642

Tank cleaning vessels. Of 600 tons, completed in 1967.

KNURRHAHN Y 811 of 261 tons.
ARCONA (ex-*Royal Prince*) Y 809

Both accommodation ships

BARBARA Y 844, lifting ship of 3 500 tons.

GRIEP Y 876, **HIEV** Y 875, Floating cranes.

SURVEY SHIPS

PASSAU
The last of 6 "Vegesack" class minesweepers of 380 tons and 15 knots currently under conversion for oceanographic research.

The following ships operate for the Deutsches Hydrographisches Institut, under the Ministry of Transport.

METEOR (Research Ship) 3 085 tons, launched 1964, Complement 55
KOMET (Survey and Research) 1 595 tons, launched 1969, Complement 42
GAUSS (Survey and Research) 1 074 tons, launched 1949, Complement 40
SÜDEROOG (Survey Ship) 211 tons, launched 1956, Complement 16
ATAIR (Survey and Wrecks) 148 tons, launched 1962, Complement 13
WEGA (Survey and Wrecks) 148 tons, launched 1962, Complement 12

COASTGUARD VESSELS

(BUNDESGRENZSCHUTZ—SEE)

Note. This paramilitary force consists of about 1 000 men who operate the craft below as well as helicopters.

8 LARGE PATROL CRAFT

ALSFELD	BG 16	**ESCHWEGE**	BG 15
BAD BRAMSTEDT	BG 12	**NEUSTADT**	BG 11
BAYREUTH	BG 17	**ROSENHEIM**	BG 18
DUDERSTADT	BG 14	**UELTZEN**	BG 13

Displacement, tons	203
Length, feet (*metres*)	127·1 (*38·5*)
Guns	2—40 mm
Main engines	3 Diesels; 4 500 hp = 30 knots

All built between 1969 and late 1970—BG 13 by Schlichting, Travemünde, the remainder by Lürssen, Vegesack. Form two flotillas BG 11-14 the 1st and BG 15-18 the 2nd. A third flotilla of smaller craft has been formed.

ROSENHEIM *8/1974 Dittmair*

FISHERY PROTECTION SHIPS

Operated by Ministry of Agriculture and Fisheries.

ANTON DOHRN of 1 950 tons and 15 knots
FRITHJOF of 2 150 tons and 15 knots.
MEERKATZE of 1 000 tons and 12 knots.
NORDENHAM of 975 tons and 16 knots.
POSEIDON of 935 tons and 12 knots.
ROTHERSAND of 1 000 tons. Built in 1974.
UTHÖRN of 110 tons and 9 knots
WALTHER HERTWIG of 2 500 tons and 15 knots.

GERMANY (Democratic Republic)

Administration

Commander-in-Chief, Volksmarine:
Vice Admiral Willi Ehm

Chief of Naval Staff:
Rear Admiral Gustav Hesse

Personnel

(a) 1973: 1 700 officers and 15 200 men (including GBK)
1974: 1 750 officers and 15 300 men (including GBK)
1975: 1 800 officers and 15 500 men (including GBK)

(b) 18 months National Service

Strength of the Fleet

Type	*Active*	*Building*
Frigates	2	—
Corvettes	18	—
Fast Attack Craft—Missile	12	—
Fast Attack Craft—Torpedo	55	—
Fast Attack Craft—Patrol	4 (GBK)	—
Coastal Patrol Craft	18	—
Landing Ships and Craft	18	—
Minesweepers—Ocean	3	—
Minesweepers—Coastal	52	3
Intelligence Ships	3	—
Survey Ships	7	—
Supply Ships	4	—
Support Tankers	3	—
Buoy Tenders	10	—
Ice Breakers	3	—
Tugs	13	—
Tenders	4	—
Training Ships and Craft	10	—
Cable Layer	1	—
Torpedo Recovery Vessels	2	—

GRENZBRIGADE KUSTE (GBK)

The seaborne branch of the Frontier Guards, this is a force of about 3 000 men. Their various craft are difficult to disentangle from those of the Navy, many being taken from that list. Where possible mention of this is made in the notes.

Naval Air

1 Squadron with 8 Mi-4 helicopters

Mercantile Marine

Lloyd's Register of Shipping:
431 vessels of 1 223 859 tons gross

FRIGATES

2 Ex-SOVIET "RIGA" CLASS

ERNEST THÄLMANN 141 **KARL MARX** 142

Displacement, tons	1 200 standard; 1 600 full load
Dimensions, feet	298·8 × 33·7 × 11
Guns	3—3·9 in single; 4—37 mm AA twin
Tubes	3—21 in
A/S weapons	4 depth charge projectors; 2 rocket launchers
Main engines	Geared turbines; 2 shafts; 25 000 shp = 28 knots
Oil fuel, tons	300
Range, miles	2 500 at 15 knots
Complement	150

Designed to carry 50 mines. Sister ships *Friedrich Engels* 124 and *Karl Liebnecht* 123 were scrapped in 1971. A fifth ship of this type was burnt out at the end of 1959 and became a total wreck. Two of these hulks are beached at Warnemünde.

KARL MARX *1965, Werner Kähling*

CORVETTES

4 USSR "SO-I" CLASS

421 **422** **423** **424**

Displacement, tons	215 standard; 250 full load
Dimensions, ft (*m*)	138 × 20 × 9·2 (*42·3 × 6·1 × 2·8*)
Guns	4—25 mm AA (2 twin mounts)
A/S weapons	4 MBU 1 800 5 barrelled launchers; 2 DCT
Main engines	3 diesels; 6 000 bhp = 29 knots
Range, miles	1 100 at 13 knots
Complement	30

Fitted with mine rails. These vessels belonged to the coast guard (GBK) but have now been returned to the navy.

G22 *1970, Niels Gartig*

Corvettes—*continued*

14 "HAI" CLASS

BAD DOBERAN
BÜTZOW
GREVESMÜHLEN
GADEBUSCH
LÜBZ
LUDWIGSLUST
PARCHIM
PERLEBERG
RIBNITZ-DAMGARTEN
STERNBERG
TETEROW
WISMAR + 2

Displacement, tons	300 standard; 370 full load
Dimensions, feet	174 pp; 187 oa × 19 × 10
Guns	4—30 mm (2 twin)
A/S weapons	2 MBU 1 800 5 barrelled launchers
Main engines	2 gas turbines; diesels; 8 000 bhp = 25 knots
Complement	45

Built at Peenewerft, Wolgast. The prototype vessel was completed in 1963. All were in service by the end of 1969, and the programme is now completed. Pennant numbers are; 411-414, 431-434, 451-454, V 81 and 1 unknown.

HAI No. 411 *1971, S. Breyer*

LIGHT FORCES

12 Ex-SOVIET "OSA" CLASS (FAST ATTACK CRAFT—MISSILE)

ARVID HARNACK
AUGUST LÜTTGENS
FRITZ GAST
HEINRICH DORRENBACH
JOSEF SCHARES
KARL MESEBERG
MAX REICHPIETSCH
OTTO TOST
PAUL EISENSCHNEIDER
PAUL WIECZOREK
RICHARD SORGE
RUDOLF EGELHOFER

Displacement, tons	165 standard; 200 full load
Dimensions, feet	128·7 × 25·1 × 5·9
Missile launchers	4 mountings in 2 pairs abreast aft for "Styx"; SSN-2A
Guns	4—30 mm (2 twin, 1 forward, 1 aft)
Main engines	3 diesels; 13 000 hp = 32 knots

Pennant numbers: 711-714, 731-734, 751-754.

"OSA" Class *1965, Reinecke*

Light Forces—*continued*

15 Ex-SOVIET "SHERSHEN" CLASS

(FAST ATTACK CRAFT—TORPEDO)

ADAM KUCKHOFF
ARTHUR BECKER
BERNHARD BÄSTLEIN
BRUNO KÜHN
EDGAR ANDRÉ
ERNST SCHNELLER
FIETE SCHULZE
FRITZ HECKERT
HANS COPPI
RUDOLF BREITSCHEID
WILLI BANSCH
+4

Displacement, tons	150 standard; 160 full load
Dimensions, ft (*m*)	115·5 × 23·1 × 5 (*35·2 × 7·1 × 1·5*)
Guns	4—30 mm (2 twin)
A/S weapons	12 DC
Tubes	4—21 in (single)
Main engines	3 Diesels; 13 000 bhp; 3 shafts = 41 knots
Complement	16

Acquired from the USSR. Four were delivered in 1968-69, the first instalment of a flotilla. They do not differ from the Soviet boats of the class. Pennant numbers **811-5, 831-5, 851-5**

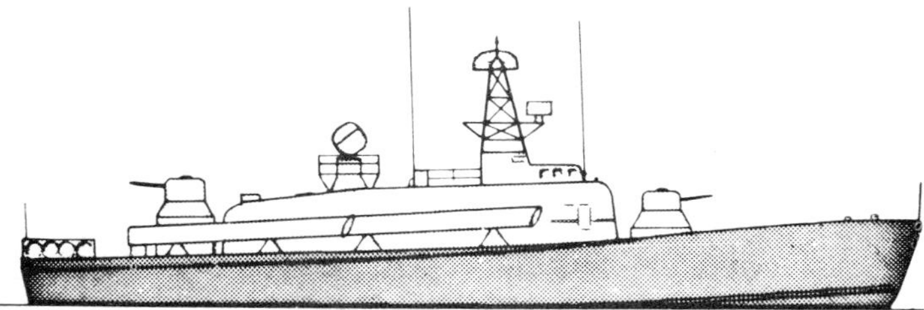

"SHERSHEN" Class

40 "ILTIS" CLASS (FAST ATTACK CRAFT—TORPEDO)

Displacement, tons	20
Dimensions, ft (*m*)	55·8 × 10·5 × 2·5 (*17 × 3·2 × ·8*)
Tubes	2—21 in (torpedoes fired over stern). Some have three tubes (Type 3) Mines can be carried in place of torpedo tubes
Main engines	Diesels; 3 000 bhp = 30 knots

No guns. Numbered in a 900 series. Several different types of this class exist, varying in hull material and silhouette, eg Type 1 are flush-decked and Type 2 have a raised forecastle. With the torpedo tubes removed these boats are used to land frogmen and raiding parties. Displacement and dimensions given are for Type 2. Others vary slightly. Built by Mitteldeutschland, starting in 1962. Pennant numbers in 970, 980, 990 series.

No. 912 — *1971, S. Breyer*

4 Ex-SOVIET "P6" CLASS (FAST ATTACK CRAFT—PATROL)

Displacement, tons	66 standard; 75 full load
Dimensions, ft (*m*)	84·2 × 20 × 6 (*25·7 × 6·1 × 1·8*)
Guns	4—25 mm (2 twin mountings)
Main engines	4 diesels; 4 800 bhp; 4 shafts = 43 knots max
Range, miles	450 at 30 knots
Complement	25

Acquired in 1957-60 from the USSR. Originally there were 27. Wooden hull. Most of this class has been scrapped or converted. Four have had their tubes removed and been transferred to the GBK with pennant Nos G81-84. Pot Head radar.

"P 6" Class No. 864 (Tubes now removed) — *1970, Niels Gartig*

Light Forces—*continued*

18 "KB 123" CLASS (COASTAL PATROL CRAFT)

Displacement, tons	about 25
Dimensions, ft (*m*)	64 × 16·4 × —) (*20 × 5 × —*)

This class (total uncertain) was introduced in 1971 for operations on rivers and inland waterways by the GBK. It appears to be fast and unarmed, though small arms are certainly carried.

"KB 123" Class — *1972*

AMPHIBIOUS FORCES

6 "ROBBE" CLASS (LST)

EBERSWALDE
ELSENHÜTTENSTADT
GRIMMEN
HOYERSWERDA
LÜBBEN
SCHWEDT

Displacement, tons	600 standard; 800 full load
Dimensions, feet	196·8 × 32·8 × 6·6
Guns	2—57 mm AA (1 twin); 4—25 mm AA (2 twin)
Main engines	Diesels = 12 knots

Amphibious vessels of a type midway between the landing ship and landing craft categories. Launched in 1962-64.

"ROBBE" Class — *1971, S. Breyer*

12 "LABO" CLASS (LCT)

GERHARD PRENZLER
HEINZ WILKOWSKI
ROLF PETERS
+9

Displacement, tons	150 standard; 200 full load
Dimensions, feet	131·2 × 27·9 × 5·9
Guns	4—25 mm AA (2 twin)
Main engines	Diesels = 10 knots

Landing craft of a lighter type. Built by Peenewerft, Wolgast. Launched in 1961-63.

"LABO" Class — *1969, S. Breyer*

MINE WARFARE FORCES

3 "KRAKE" CLASS (MINESWEEPERS—OCEAN)

BERLIN **POTSDAM** **ROSTOCK**

Displacement, tons	650 standard
Dimensions, ft (*m*)	229·7 × 26·5 × 12·2 (*70* × *8·1* × *3·7*)
Guns	1—3·4 in; 10—25 mm AA paired vertically
A/S weapons	4 DCT
Mines	Can carry 30
Main engines	Diesels; 2 shafts; 3 400 bhp = 18 knots
Complement	90

Built in 1956-58 at Peenewerft, Wolgast. Of the original ten, four completed in 1958, were originally for Poland. Appearance is different compared with the first type, the squat wide funnel being close to the bridge with lattice mast and radar. Fitted for minelaying. On 1 Mar 1961 they were given the names of the capitals of districts etc. of East Germany. Pennant numbers are S11-13. All used for training.

"KRAKE" Class *1970, Niels Gartig*

52 "KONDOR I" and "II" CLASS (MINESWEEPERS—COASTAL)

AHRENSHOOP	**GREIFSWALD**	**STRASBURG**
ANKLAM	**KLÜTZ**	**TANGERHÜTTE**
BERGEN	**KUHLUNGSBORN**	**TEMPLIN**
BITTERFELD	**KYRITZ**	**UCKERMUNDE**
BERNAU	**NEURUPPIN**	**VITTE**
DEMMIN	**NEUSTRELITZ**	**WARNEMUNDE**
DESSAU	**PASEWALK**	**WEISSWASSER**
GENTHIN	**PREROW**	**WOLGAST**
GRAAL-MÜRITZ	**ROBEL**	**ZERBST**
	ROSSLAU	**ZINGST** + **23**

Displacement, tons	245 standard; 280 full load
Dimensions, ft (*m*)	154·2 × 23·0 × 6·6 (*47* × *7* × 2) (*Kondor II* plus 2 metres)
Guns	2—25 mm or 2—30 mm (Kondor I); 6—25 mm (twins) (Kondor II)
Main engines	2 diesels; 2 shafts; 4 000 bhp = 21 knots

GENERAL

A new class of medium fast minesweepers and patrol vessels built at Peenewerft. Five units were operational in 1970 and 15 by the end of 1971. They replace the small minesweepers of the "Schwalbe" class. Type II has additional length and extra MG s. First appeared in 1971. Production continues.

PENNANT NUMBERS

These have been changed with some frequency. At present the following is as near as can be offered:

Type I (Total 22) Prototype-V31. S24-26. Attached to GBK;-G11-16. G21-26 G41-46. Conversion for torpedo recovery-B73 and B74. Conversion to AGIs Meteor and Komet.

Type II (Total 30) Prototype-V32. Active minesweepers 311-316, 321-327, 331-336 341-347. S21-23.

"KONDOR II" Class *1973, S. Breyer*

INTELLIGENCE SHIPS

2 "KONDOR I" CLASS

METEOR **KOMET**

Displacement, tons	245 standard; 280 full load
Dimensions, ft (*m*)	154·2 × 23·0 × 6·6 (*47* × *7* × *2*)
Guns	2—30 mm
Main engines	2 diesels; 2 shafts; 4 000 bhp
Speed, knots	21

Conversions from standard Coastal Minesweepers.

HYDROGRAPH

Displacement, tons	500
Dimensions ft (*m*)	167 × 28·8 × — (*50·9* × *8·7* × —)
Main engines	Diesel; 540 hp = 11 knots

Built in 1960 by Volkswerft, Stralsund.

SURVEY SHIPS

KARL F. GAUS

Built in 1952-55. Of 200 tons and 9·5 knots. Seiner type.

ARKONA **DASSER ORT** **STUBBEN KAMMER**

Built in 1956. Of 55 tons and 10 knots.

PROFESSOR KRÜMMEL

Built in 1954. Of 135 tons and 10 knots. Similar to "KFK" Class. Civilian Research Ship.

JORDAN

Of 100 tons and 9 knots.

FLAGGTIEF

Built in 1953. Of 50 tons and 8 knots.

SERVICE FORCES

1 "BASKUNCHAK" CLASS (SUPPLY SHIP)

USEDOM

Displacement, tons	2 500
Dimensions, ft (*m*)	227 × 29 × 12·3 (*70* × *8·9* × *3·8*)
Speed, knots	13

Tanker converted to act as supply ship.

USEDOM *1973, S. Breyer*

3 TYPE 600 (SUPPORT TANKERS)

HIDDENSEE **POEL** **RIEMS**

Displacement, tons	600 DWT
Dimensions, feet	195 oa × 29·5 × 12·5
Main engines	2 diesels; 2 800 bhp = 14 knots
Complement	26

Built at Peenewerft, Wolgast, in 1960-61.

RIEMS *1971, S. Breyer*

5 "KUMO" CLASS

RUDEN **E 18** **RUGEN** V 71 **E 44** **VILM**

Displacement, tons	400
Dimensions, ft (*m*)	118 × 24 × 8·9 (*36 × 7·3 × 2·7*)
Speed, knots	10

Built in mid-1950's. *Rugen* is a torpedo Trials Ship, *Vilm* a tanker and the other three employed as Supply Ships.

1 Ex-SOVIET "KAMENKA" CLASS BUOY LAYER)

BUK

Displacement, tons	1 000 standard
Dimensions, ft (*m*)	180·5 × 31·2 × 11·5 (*55 × 9·5 × 3·4*)
Main engines	Diesels = 16 knots

DORNBUSCH

Cable layer of 700 tons with bow rollers.

2 "KONDOR I" CLASS (TRVs)

B 73 **B 74**

Details under Minewarfare Forces. Converted for Torpedo Recovery.

FREESENDORF

Built in 1963. Buoy-layer.

LUMME

Small diving tender. Tug type.

2 "TAUCHER" CLASS

Small Diving Tenders of 200 tons.

8 BUOY TENDERS

BREITLING **GOLWITZ** **LANDTIEFF** **RAMZOW**
ESPER ORT **GRASS ORT** **PALMER ORT** **ROSEN ORT**

Displacement, tons	158
Dimensions, feet	97 × 20·3 × 6·2
Main engines	1 diesel; 580 hp = 11·5 knots

Delivery 1970-72.

10 TRAINING SHIPS

Sailing vessels and old minesweepers attached to the Naval Academy.

ICEBREAKERS

STEPHAN JANSEN

Of 2 500 tons and 13 knots built in 1965. Of Soviet "Nikitch" class. Civilian manned.

EISBAR **EISVOGEL**

Of 550 tons and 12 knots built in 1957. Civilian Manned.

TUGS

1 "700" CLASS

A 14

Of 800 tons and 12 knots.

WISMAR

Of 700 tons and 14 knots. Possibly civilian manned.

11 HARBOUR TUGS

Of varying Classes.

Note. Gesellschaft für Sport und Technik (GST) (Association for Sport and Technical Science) controls fifteen training ships—*Ernst Thälman*, a retired "Habicht I" Class minesweeper; *Ernst Schneller*, "Tummler" class; *Partisan*, and *Pionier* of 80 tons; *Freundschaft* of 200 tons; *F. L. Jahn* of 100 tons; and the sail training ships *Wilhelm Pieck*, *Seid Bereil*, *Jonny Scheer*, *Max Reichpietsch II* and *Knechtsand II*.

GHANA

Administration

Commander of the Navy: Commodore P. F. Quaye

Personnel

(a) 1975: 1 300 (150 officers, 1 150 ratings)
(b) Voluntary Service

Naval Base

Tema, near Accra

Deletions

1973 3 ex-USSR "Poluchat I" Class Patrol Craft

Mercantile Marine

Lloyd's Register of Shipping: 77 vessels of 173 018 tons gross

CORVETTES

2 "KROMANTSE" CLASS

KROMANTSE F 17 **KETA** F 18

Displacement, tons	380 light; 440 standard; 500 full load
Dimensions, feet	162 wl; 177 oa × 28·5 × 13
Guns	1—4 in; 1—40 mm AA (see notes)
A/S weapons	1 Squid triple-barrelled depth charge mortar
Main engines	2 Bristol Siddeley Maybach diesels; 2 shafts; 390 rpm; 7 100 bhp = 20 knots
Oil fuel, tons	60
Range, miles	2 000 at 16 knots; 2 900 at 14 knots
Complement	54 (6 + 3 officers, 45 ratings)

Anti-submarine vessels of a novel type designed by Vosper Ltd, Portsmouth, a joint venture with Vickers-Armstrong's Ltd, one ship being built by each company. Comprehensively fitted with sonar, air and surface warning radar. Vosper roll damping fins, and air conditioning throughout excepting machinery spaces. Generators 360 kW. The electrical power supply is 440 volts, 60 cycles ac. A very interesting patrol vessel design, an example of what can be achieved on a comparatively small platform to produce an inexpensive and quickly built anti-submarine vessel. *Kromantse* was launched by Vosper Ltd at the Camber Shipyard, Portsmouth, on 5 Sep 1963, and commissioned on 27 July 1964. *Keta* was launched at Newcastle on 18 Jan 1965, and commissioned on 18 May 1965.

RADAR. Search. Plessey AWS 1.

KROMANTSE

MINESWEEPER FORCES

1 Ex-BRITISH "TON" CLASS (MINESWEEPER—COASTAL)

EJURA (ex-*Aldington*) M 16

Displacement, tons	360 standard; 425 full load
Dimensions, feet	140 pp; 153 oa × 28·8 × 8·2
Guns	1—40 mm AA forward; 2—20 mm AA aft
Main engines	Deltic diesels; 2 shafts; 3 000 bhp = 15 knots
Oil fuel, tons	45
Range	2 300 at 13 knots
Complement	27

Lent to Ghana by Britain in 1964.

Minesweepers—*continued*

EJURA *1971, Ghana Navy*

2 Ex-BRITISH "HAM" CLASS (MINESWEEPERS—INSHORE)

AFADZATO (ex-*Ottringham*) M 12 **YOGAGA** (ex-*Malham*) M 11

Displacement, tons	120 standard; 159 full load
Dimensions, feet	100 pp; 107·5 oa × 22 × 5·8
Gun	1—15 mm AA
Main engines	2 Paxman diesels; 1 100 = 14 knots
Oil fuel, tons	15
Range, miles	2 000 at 9 knots
Complement	22

Malham commissioned on 2 Oct 1959, and *Ottringham* commissioned on 30 Oct 1959, sailed for Ghana on 31 Oct 1959, and were transferred from the Royal Navy to the Ghana Navy at Takoradi at the end of Nov 1959 and renamed after hills in Ghana. Fitted with funnel.

YOGAGA *1966, Ghana Navy*

LIGHT FORCES

2 "FORD" CLASS (LARGE PATROL CRAFT)

ELMINA P 13 **KOMENDA** P 14

Displacement, tons	120 standard; 142 full load
Dimensions, feet	110 wl; 117·5 oa × 20 × 7
Gun	1—40 mm, 60 cal Bofors AA
A/S weapons	Depth charge throwers
Main engines	2 Davey Paxman diesels; 2 shafts; 1 000 bhp = 18 knots.
Complement	19

KOMENDA *1969, Ghana Navy*

ASUANTSI (ex-*MRC* 1122)

Displacement, tons	657
Dimensions, feet	225 pp; 231·3 oa × 39 × 3·3 forward, 5 aft
Main engines	4 Paxman, 1 840 bhp = 9 knots cruising

Acquired from Britain in 1965 and arrived in Ghana waters in July 1965. Used as a base workshop at Tema Naval Base. Is kept operational, and does a fair amount of seatime in general training and exercise tasks.

GREECE

Administration

Chief, Hellenic Navy:
Vice-Admiral Egolfopoulos

Deputy Chief:
Rear-Admiral S. Kapsalis

Commander of the Fleet:
Vice-Admiral S. Konofaos

Diplomatic Representation

Naval Attaché in London:
Captain K. Paizis-Paradelis

Naval Attaché in Washington:
Captain O. Kapetos

Naval Attaché in Cairo:
Captain P. Vossos

Naval Attaché in Bonn:
Captain T. Alicampiotis

Naval Attaché in Ankara:
Captain G. Tsakonas

Strength of the Fleet

Type	*Active*	*Building*
Destroyers	11	—
Frigates	4	—
Corvettes	5	—
Patrol Submarines	7	—
Fast Attack Craft—Missile	4	4
Fast Attack Craft—Torpedo	12	—
Large Patrol Craft	5	—
Landing Ships	14	—
LCU's	8	—
Minelayers—Coastal	2	—
Minesweeper—Coastal	15	—
Survey Vessels	5	—
Support Tankers	2	—
Harbour Tankers	6	—
Salvage Ship	1	—
Repair Ship	1	—
Lighthouse Tenders	2	—
Tugs	12	—
Netlayer	1	—
Water Boats	5	—

Prefix to Ship's Names

H.S. (Hellenic Ship)

Disposals

Destroyers

1972 *Doxa, Niki* (Gleaves class)

Submarine

1972 *Poseidon*

Patrol Craft

1971 *Antiploiarkhos Laskos, Ploiarchos Meletopoulos*

Minesweepers—Coastal

1972 *Kichu*
1973 *Afroessa, Kalymnos, Karteria, Kerkyra, Papalos, Zakynthos*

Survey Vessel

1973 *A. Idhi*

Minesweeper Depot Ship

1973 *Hermes*

Tugs

1972 *Aegeus*

Water Boat

1972 Kaliroe

Personnel

(a) 1975: 17 600 (1 900 officers and 15 700 ratings)
(b) 2 years National Service

Naval Bases

Salamis and Crete

Merchantile Marine

Lloyd's Register of Shipping:
2 651 vessels of 21 759 449 tons gross

DESTROYERS

1 Ex-US "GEARING FRAM II" CLASS
3 Ex-US "GEARING FRAM I" CLASS

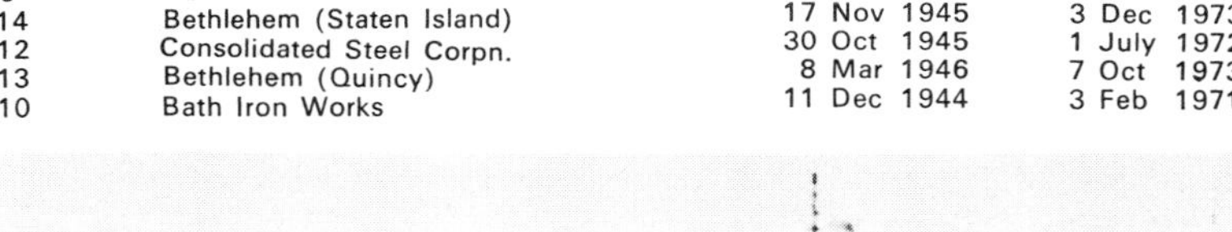

Name	*No*	*Builder*	*Commissioned*	*Transferred*
SACHTOURIS (ex-USS *Arnold J Isbell*, DD 869)	214	Bethlehem (Staten Island)	17 Nov 1945	3 Dec 1973
KANARIS (ex-USS *Stickell*, DD 888)	212	Consolidated Steel Corpn.	30 Oct 1945	1 July 1972
KONTOURIOTIS (ex-USS *Rupertus*, DD 851)	213	Bethlehem (Quincy)	8 Mar 1946	7 Oct 1973
THEMISTOCLES (ex-USS *Frank Knox*, DD 742)	210	Bath Iron Works	11 Dec 1944	3 Feb 1971

Displacement, tons	2 425 standard; 3 500 full load
Length, feet (*metres*)	390·5 (*119·0*) oa
Beam, feet (*metres*)	40·9 (*12·4*)
Draught, feet (*metres*)	19·0 (*5·8*)
Guns	6—5 in (*127 mm*) 38 cal dp (twin) (210 only); 4—5 in (twin) in Fram I's
A/S weapons	2 fixed Hedgehogs, (210 only); 1 ASROC 8-barrelled launcher and facilities for small helicopter in Fram I's
Torpedo tubes	2 triple (Mk 32)
Main engines	2 Westinghouse geared turbines; 2 shafts; 60 000 shp
Boilers	4 Babcock & Wilcox
Speed, knots	34
Range, miles	4 800 at 15 knots
Complement	269 (16 officers, 253 men)

Themistocles was a Fram II Radar Picket conversion, *Kanaris* was a Fram I Radar Picket conversion and the other pair Fram I DD conversions.

THEMISTOCLES (FRAM II) *1972, Helenic Navy*

KANARIS (FRAM I) *1973, Helenic Navy*

Destroyers—*continued*

1 Ex-US "ALLEN M. SUMNER" CLASS

Name	No.	Builder	Commissioned	Transferred
MIAOULIS (ex-USS *Ingram*, DD 694)	211	Federal SB & DD Co	10 Mar 1944	July 1971

Displacement, tons	2 200 standard; 3 320 full load
Length, feet (*metres*)	376·5 (*114·8*) oa
Beam, feet (*metres*)	40·9 (*12·4*)
Draught, feet (*metres*)	19·0 (*5·8*)
Guns	6—5 in (*127 mm*) 38 cal dp
A/S weapons	2 triple torpedo launchers, Mk 32; 2 ahead throwing hedgehogs
Main engines	2 geared turbines; 2 shafts; 60 000 shp
Boilers	4
Speed, knots	34
Range, miles	4 600 at 15 knots
Complement	269 (16 officers, 94 POs, 159 men)

Former fleet destroyer of the "Allen M. Sumner" class which had been modernised under the FRAM II programme.

MIAOULIS *1973, Hellenic Navy*

6 Ex-US "FLETCHER" CLASS

Name	No.	Builder	Laid down	Launched	Completed
ASPIS (ex-USS *Conner, DD* 582)	D 06	Boston Navy Yard	16 Apr 1942	18 July 1942	8 June 1943
LONCHI (ex-USS *Hall, DD* 583)	D 56	Boston Navy Yard	16 Apr 1942	18 July 1942	6 July 1943
NAVARINON (ex-USS *Brown, DD* 546)	D 63	Bethlehem (S. Pedro)	27 June 1942	22 Feb 1943	10 July 1943
SFENDONI (ex-USS *Aulick, DD* 569)	D 85	Consolidated Steel Corp, Texas	14 May 1941	2 Mar 1942	27 Oct 1942
THYELLA (ex-USS *Bradford, DD* 545)	D 28	Bethlehem (S. Pedro)	28 Apr 1942	12 Dec 1942	12 June 1943
VELOS (ex-USS *Charette, DD* 581)	D 16	Boston Navy Yard	20 Feb 1941	3 June 1942	18 May 1943

Displacement, tons	2 100 standard; 3 050 full load
Length, feet (*metres*)	376·5 (*114·7*) oa
Beam, feet (*metres*)	39·5 (*12·0*)
Draught, feet (*metres*)	18 (*5·5*) max
Guns, dual purpose	4—5 in (*127 mm*) 38 cal. in *Aspis, Lonchi, Sfendoni* and *Velos*, 5 in *Navarinon* and *Thyella*
Guns, AA	6—3 in (*76 mm*), 3 twin, in *Aspis, Lonchi, Sfendoni* and *Velos*. 10—40 mm (2 quadruple, 1 twin) in *Navarinon* and *Thyella*
A/S weapons	Hedgehogs; DC's
Torpedo tubes	5—21 in (*533 mm*), quintuple bank, in *Aspis, Lonchi, Sfendoni* and *Velos*, none in *Navarinon* and *Thyella*
Torpedo racks	Side-launching for A/S torpedoes
Boilers	4 Babcock & Wilcox; 615 psi (*43·3 kg/cm²*) 800°F (*427°C*)
Main engines	2 sets GE geared turbines; 2 shafts; 60 000 shp
Speed, knots	35 designed, 30 to 32 max
Range, miles	6 000 at 15 knots; 1 260 to 1 285 at 30 to 32 knots
Oil fuel, tons	506
Complement	250

Transferred from USA, *Aspis, Lonchi* and *Velos* at Long Beach ,Cal, on 15 Sep 1959, 9 Feb 1960 and 15 June 1959, respectively, *Sfendoni* at Philadelphia on 21 Aug 1959, *Navarinon* and *Thyella* at Seattle, Wash, on 27 Sep 1962.

RADAR. Search: SPS 6, SPS 10. Fire Control: GFC 56 and 63 systems.

SFENDONI *1974, Hellenic Navy*

"FLETCHER" Class (4 guns)

FRIGATES

4 Ex-US "BOSTWICK" DE TYPE

Name	No.	Builders	Laid down	Launched	Completed
AETOS (ex-USS *Slater*, DE 766)	D 01	Tampa SB Co.	9 Mar 1943	13 Feb 1944	1 May 1944
IERAX (ex-USS *Elbert*, DE 768)	D 31	Tampa SB Co	1 Apr 1943	23 May 1944	12 July 1944
LEON (ex-USS *Eldridge*, DE 173)	D 54	Federal SB & DD Co	22 Feb 1943	25 June 1943	27 Aug 1943
PANTHIR (ex-USS *Garfield Thomas*, DE 193)	D 67	Federal SB & DD Co	23 Sep 1943	12 Dec 1943	24 Jan 1944

Displacement, tons	1 240 standard; 1 900 full load
Length, feet (*metres*)	306 (*93·3*) oa
Beam, feet (*metres*)	36·7 (*11·2*)
Draught, feet (*metres*)	14 (*4·3*)
Guns,	3—3 in (*76 mm*) 50 cal. 6—40 *mm*, 3 twin 14—20 *mm*, 7 twin
A/S weapons	Hedgehog; 8 DCT; 1 DC rack
Torpedo racks	Side launching for A/S torpedoes
Main engines	4 sets GM diesel-electric 6 000 bhp; 2 shafts
Speed, knots	19·25
Range, miles	9 000 at 12 knots
Oil fuel (tons)	316
Complement	220 (war)

Former US destroyer escorts of the "Bostwick" class. *Aetos* and *Ierax* were transferred on 15 Mar 1951 and *Leon* and *Panthir* on 15 Jan 1951. Their 3—21 inch torpedo tubes in a triple mount were removed.

LEON *1972, Hellenic Navy,*

CORVETTES

5 Ex-BRITISH "ALGERINE" TYPE

Name	No.	Builders	Launched
ARMATOLOS (ex-HMS *Aries*)	M 12	Toronto Shipyard	19 Sep 1942
MAHITIS (ex-HMS *Postillion*)	M 58	Redfern Construction Co	14 Nov 1942
NAVMACHOS (ex-HMS *Lightfoot*)	M 64	Redfern Construction Co	31 Aug 1942
POLEMISTIS (ex-HMS *Gozo*)	M 74	Redfern Construction Co	18 Mar 1943
PYRPOLITIS (ex-HMS *Arcturus*)	M 76	Redfern Construction Co	27 Jan 1943

Displacement, tons	1 030 standard, 1 325 full load
Length, feet (*metres*)	225 (*68·6*) oa
Beam, feet (*metres*)	35·5 (*10·8*)
Draught, feet (*metres*)	11·5 (*3·5*) max
Guns, dual purpose	2—3 in (*76 mm*) US Mark 21 (1 in *Pirpolitis*, none in *Mahitis*)
Guns, AA	4—20 mm (US), 2MG
A/S weapons	2 to 4 DCT
Main engines	2 triple expansion; 2 shafts 2 700 ihp = 16 knots
Boilers	2 Yarrow, 250 psi (*17·6 kg cm²*)
Oil fuel, tons	235
Range, miles	5 000 at 10 knots; 2 270 at 14·5 knots
Complement	85

Former British ocean minesweepers of the "Algerine" class. Acquired from the Executive Committee of Surplus Allied Material. Latterly employed as Corvettes. The armament of *Mahitis* was removed when she became a training ship. *Armatolos* and *Navmachos* were used as auxiliaries and others as personnel transports.

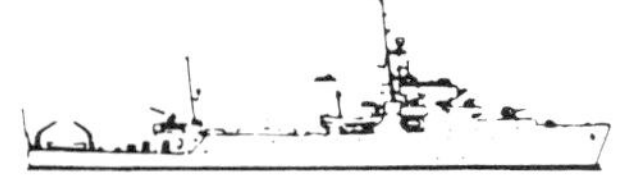

ex-"ALGERINE" Class

POLEMISTIS *1974, Hellenic Navy*

SUBMARINES

4 TYPE 209 "GLAVKOS" CLASS

GLAVKOS S 110
NEREUS S 111
PROTEUS S 113
TRITON S 112

Displacement, tons	990 surfaced; 1 290 dived
Length, feet (*metres*)	177·1 (*54·0*)
Beam, feet (*metres*)	20·3 (*6·2*)
Torpedo tubes	8—21 in (with reloads) bow
Main machinery	Diesel-electric; 4 MTU; Siemens diesel-generators; 1 Siemens electric motor; 1 shaft
Speed	10 surfaced; 22 dived
Range	50 days
Complement	31

Designed by Ingenieurkontor, Lübeck for construction by Howaldtswerke, Kiel and sale by Ferrostaal Essen all acting as a consortium.
A single-hull design with two ballast tanks and forward and after trim tanks. Fitted with snort and remote machinery control. The single screw is slow revving. Very high capacity batteries with GRP lead-acid cells and battery cooling—by Wilh. Hagen and VARTA. Active and passive sonar, sonar detection, equipment, sound ranging and underwater telephone. Fitted with two periscopes, radar and Omega receiver. Fore-planes retract.
Glavkos launched Sep 1970, completed Sep 1971, *Nereus* in Sep 1971 and Feb 1972, *Triton* in 1971 and Sep 1972, *Proteus* in 1971 and 1973.

GLAVKOS *1973, Hellenic Navy*

TRITON *1973, Hellenic Navy*

1 Ex-US "BALAO" CLASS

Name	No.	Builder	Completed	Transferred
TRIAINA (ex-USS *Scabbard Fish* SS 397)	S 86	Portsmouth Navy Yard	29 Apr 1944	26 Feb 1965

Displacement, tons	1 816 surface; 2 425 submerged
Length, feet (*metres*)	311·5 (*94·9*) oa
Beam, feet (*metres*)	27·0 (*8·2*)
Draught, feet (*metres*)	17·0 (*5·2*)
Torpedo tubes	10—21 in (*533 mm*), 6 bow, 4 stern
Main machinery	6 500 bhp diesels (surface) 4 610 hp motors (submerged)
Speed, knots	20 on surface, 10 submerged
Range, miles	12 000 at 10 knots (surface)
Complement	85

Originally one of the wartime "Balao" class later having a streamlined fin fitted.

TRIAINA *1974, Hellenic Navy*

Submarines—continued

1 Ex-US "GUPPY IIA" CLASS

Name	No.	Builder	Completed	Transferred
PAPANIKOLIS (ex-USS *Hardhead* SS 365)	S 114	Manitowoc SB Co.	Apr 1944	26 July 1972

Displacement, tons	1 840 standard; 2 445 dived
Length, feet (*metres*)	306 (*93·2*)
Beam, feet (*metres*)	27 (*8·3*)
Draught, feet (*metres*)	17 (*5·2*)
Torpedo tubes	10—21 inch; 6 bow, 4 stern
Main engines	3 Diesels; 4 800 shp/2 Motors, 5 400 shp; 2 shafts
Speed	17 surface; 15 dived
Range, miles	12 000 at 10 knots (surface)
Complement	84

PAPANIKOLIS *1973, Hellenic Navy*

1 Ex-US "GUPPY III" CLASS

Name	No.	Builder	Completed	Transferred
KATSONIS (ex-USS *Remora* SS 487)	S 115	Portsmouth Navy Yard	3 Jan 1946	29 Oct 1973

Displacement, tons	1 975 standard; 2 450 dived
Dimensions, ft (*m*)	326 × 27 × 17 (*99·4 × 8·2 × 5·2*)
Torpedo tubes	10—21 in; 6 bow 4 stern
Main machinery	4 Diesels; 6 400 hp;—2 electric motors; 5 400 shp; 2 shafts
Speed, knots	20 surface; 15 dived
Range, miles	12 000 at 10 knots (surfaced)
Complement	85

Originally of the wartime "Tench" class, subsequently converted under the Guppy II programme and, in 1961-62 to Guppy III. Amongst other modifications this involved the fitting of BQG-4 Sonar (Puffs) for dived fire-control, in addition to the BQR-2 array sonar.

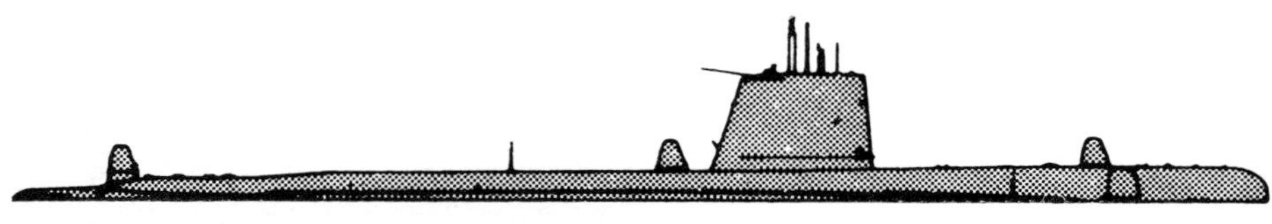

GUPPY III

LIGHT FORCES

4 "LA COMBATTANTE III" CLASS

(FAST ATTACK CRAFT—MISSILE)

Displacement, tons	332 standard
Dimensions, feet	55·5 × 7·4 × 4·2
Missiles	4 MM 38 Exocet surface-to-surface
Guns	2—76 mm; 4—30 mm (2 twin)
Torpedo tubes	2—21 inch aft for wire-guided torpedoes
Main engines	4 Diesels; 15 000 bhp = 32·5 knots
Complement	38

Ordered in September 1974 from Constructions Mécaniques de Normandie, Cherbourg.

4 "LA COMBATTANTE II" CLASS

(FAST ATTACK CRAFT—MISSILE)

CALYPSO P 54 **EVNIKI** P 55 **KYMOTHOI** P 53 **NAVSITHOI** P 56

Displacement, tons	234 standard; 255 full load
Dimensions, feet	154·2 × 23·3 × 8·2
Missiles	4 MM 38 Exocet surface-to-surface
Guns	4—35 mm AA (2 twin)
Torpedo tubes	2 aft for wire-guided torpedoes
Main engines	4 diesels; 4 shafts; 12 000 bhp = 36·5 knots
Oil fuel, tons	39 bunkerage
Range, miles	850 at 25 knots
Complement	40 (4 officers, and 36 men)

Ordered in 1969 from Constructions Mécaniques de Normandie Cherbourg. Fitted with Thomson CSF Triton radar and Plessey IFF Mk 10.
Calypso launched 26 Apr 1971, completed Apr 1972. *Euniki* launched 8 Sept 1971, completed June 1972. *Kymothoi* launched 26 Jan 1971, completed Dec 1971. *Navsithoi* launched 20 Dec 1971 completed July 1972.

5 "SILBERMÖWE" CLASS (FAST ATTACK CRAFT—TORPEDO)

DOLPHIN (ex-*Sturmmöwe*) P 15
DRAKON (ex-*Silbermöwe*) P 16
FOINIX (ex-*Eismöwe*) P 27
POLIKOS (ex-*Raubmöwe*) P 17
POLIDEFKIS (ex-*Wildschwan*) P 18

Displacement, tons	119 standard; 155 full load
Dimensions, feet	116·1 × 16·7 × 5·9
Torpedo tubes	2—21 in
Guns	1—40 mm AA; 2—20 mm AA (1 twin)
Main engines	3 diesels; 3 shafts; 9 000 bhp = 38 knots

Old S-Boote taken over from Germany 17 Dec 1968. Built by Lurssen, Vegesack, 1951-56.

5 "TJELD" CLASS (FAST ATTACK CRAFT—TORPEDO)

ANDROMEDA P 21 **KASTOR** P 23 **KYKNOS** P 24 **PIGASSOS** P 25 **TOXOTIS** P 26

Displacement, tons	69 standard; 76 full load
Dimensions, feet	75 pp; 80·4 oa × 24·6 × 6·9
Torpedo tubes	4—21 In
Guns	2—40 mm AA
Main engines	2 Napier Deltic T 18-37 K diesels; 3 100 bhp = 43 knots
Complement	22

Andromeda and *Imionos* were taken over in Feb 1967 from Mandal, Norway. *Kastor* and *Kykonos*, and the third pair, *Pigassos* and *Toxotis*, were delivered in succession in 1967.

NAVSITHOI *1973, Hellenic Navy*

ANDROMEDA *1974, Hellenic Navy*

Light Forces—*continued*

1 VOSPER "BRAVE" CLASS (FAST ATTACK CRAFT—TORPEDO)

ASTRAPI P 20 (ex-*Strahl* P 6194)

Displacement, tons	95 standard; 110 full load
Dimensions, feet	96 (full); 99 oa × 25 × 7
Torpedo chutes	4—21 in side launching
Guns	2—40 mm AA
Main engines	3 Bristol Siddeley Marine Proteus gas turbines; 3 shafts; 12 750 bhp = 55·5 knots

Built by Vosper, Portsmouth. Launched on 10 Jan 1962. Commissioned in Federal German Navy on 21 Nov 1962. Transferred to Royal Hellenic Navy in Apr 1967. Refitted by Vosper in 1968. Of similar design to British "Brave" class.

ASTRAPI *1972, Hellenic Navy*

1 VOSPER "FEROCITY" CLASS (FAST ATTACK CRAFT—TORPEDO)

AIOLOS P 19 (ex-*Pfeil* P 6193)

Displacement, tons	75 standard; 80 full load
Dimensions, feet	92 wl; 95 oa × 23·9 × 6·5
Torpedo chutes	4—21 in side launching
Guns	2—40 mm AA
Main engines	2 Bristol Siddeley Marine Proteus gas turbines; 2 shafts; 8 500 bhp = 50 knots

Built by Vosper, Portsmouth. Launched on 26 Oct 1961. Commissioned in German Navy on 27 June 1962. Transferred to Royal Hellenic Navy in Apr 1967. Refitted by Vosper in 1968. Based on design of Vosper prototype *Ferocity*.

AIOLOS *1972, Hellenic Navy*

3 PGM TYPE (LARGE PATROL CRAFT)

ANTIPLOIARKHOS PEZOPOULOS (ex-*PGM* 21, ex-*PC* 1552)	P 70
PLOTARKHIS ARSLANOGLOU (ex-*PGM* 25, ex-*PC* 1556)	P 14
PLOTARKHIS CHADZIKONSTANDIS (ex-*PGM* 29, ex-*PC* 1565)	P 96

Displacement, tons	335 standard; 439 full load
Dimensions, feet	170 wl; 174·7 oa × 23 × 10·8
Guns	1—3 in; 6—20 mm
A/S weapons	Hedgehog; side launching torpedo racks; depth charges
Main engines	2 GM diesels; 2 shafts; 3 600 bhp = 19 knots

All launched in 1943-44. Acquired from USA in Aug 1947. The two 40 mm AA guns were removed and a hedgehog was installed in 1963.

ANTIPLOIARKHOS PEZOPOULOS *1973, Hellenic Navy*

Light Forces—*continued*

2 LSSL TYPE (LARGE PATROL CRAFT)

PLOTARKHIS MARIDAKIS (ex-USS *LSSL* 65) L 94 (ex-P 94)
PLOTARKHIS VLACHAVAS (ex-USS *LSSL* 35) L 95 (ex-P 95)

Displacement, tons	257 standard; 395 full load
Dimensions, feet	157·0 × 23·2 × 5·7
Guns	1—3 in; 4—40 mm AA (2 twin); 4—20 mm
Main engines	Diesels; 2 shafts; 1 600 bhp = 14·4 knots

Built by Albina Engine & Machinery Works Inc. Portland, Oreg, and Commercial Iron Works, Portland, and launched on 14 Nov and 17 Sep 1944, respectively. *Plotarkhis Vlachavas* was transferred from USA on 12 Aug 1957 and *Plotarkhis Maridakis* in June 1958. Given L instead of P pennant numbers in 1971

AMPHIBIOUS FORCES

1 Ex-US LSD

NAFKRATOUSSA (ex-USS *Fort Mandan, LSD* 21) L 153

Displacement, tons	4 790 light; 9 375 full load
Dimensions, feet	457·8 oa × 72·2 × 18
Guns	8—40 mm AA
Main engines	Geared turbines; 2 shafts; 7 000 shp = 15·4 knots
Boilers	2

Built at Boston Navy Yard. Laid down on 2 Jan 1945. Launched on 22 May 1945 Completed on 31 Oct 1945. This dock landing ship taken over from USA in 1971 replacing the previous *Nafkratoussa* (ex-*Hyperion*, ex-*LSD* 9) out of service in 1971 as Headquarters ship of Captain, Landing Forces.

NAFKRATOUSSA *1973, Hellenic Navy*

8 Ex-US LSTs

KRITI (ex-USS *Page County, LST* 1076)	L 171
IKARIA (ex-USS *Potter County, LST* 1086)	L 154
LESBOS (ex-USS *Boone County, LST* 389)	L 172
RODOS (ex-USS *Bowman County, LST* 391)	L 157
SYROS (ex-USS *LST* 325)	L 144
CHIOS (ex *LST* 35)	L 195
LIMNOS (ex *LST* 36)	L 158
SAMOS (ex *LST* 33)	L 179

Displacement, tons	1 653 standard; 2 366 beaching; 4 080 full load
Dimensions, ft (*m*)	328 × 50 × 14 (*100* × *15·3* × *2·9*)
Guns	8—40 mm; 6—20 mm (*Rodos* 10—40 mm)
Main engines	2 GM diesels; 2 shafts; 1 700 bhp = 11·6 knots
Range, miles	9 500 at 9 knots
Complement	93 (8 officers, 85 men)

Former United States tank landing ships. Cargo capacity 2 100 tons. *Ikaria, Lesbos* and *Rodos* were transferred to the Royal Hellenic Navy on 9 Aug 1960. *Syros* was transferred on 29 May 1964 at Portsmouth, Virginia, under MAP. *Kriti* was transferred in Mar 1971. Last three under lease-lend in 1943.

LIMNOS *1972, Hellenic Navy*

Amphibious Forces—*continued*

5 Ex-US LSM's

IPOPLIARKHIS KRISTALIDIS (ex-USS *LSM* 541) L 165
IPOPLIARKHOS DANIOLOS (ex-USS *LSM* 227) L 163
IPOPLIARKHOS GRIGOROPOULOS (ex-USS *LSM* 45) L 161
IPOPLIARKHOS ROUSSEN (ex-USS *LSM* 399) L 164
IPOPLIARKHOS TOURNAS (ex-USS *LSM* 102) L 162

Displacement, tons	743 beaching; 1 095 full load
Dimensions, feet	196·5 wl; 203·5 oa × 34·2 × 8·3
Guns	2—40 mm AA; 8—20 mm AA
Main engines	Diesel direct drive; 2 shafts; 3 600 bhp = 13 knots

Former US Medium Landing Ships. *LSM* 541 and *LSM* 557 were handed over to Greece at Salamis on 30 Oct 1958 and *LSM* 45, *LSM* 102, *LSM* 227 and *LSM* 399 at Portsmouth, Virginia on 3 Nov 1958. All were renamed after naval heroes killed during World War 2.

IPOPLIARKHIS KRISTALIDIS *1974, Hellenic Navy*

8 Ex-US LCUs

LCU 763 (*Kithnos*)
LCU 677 (*Sifnos*)
LCU 827 (*Sciathos*)
LCU 852 (*Skopelos*)
LCU 971 (*Kimolos*)
LCU 1229 (*Kea*)
LCU 1379 (*Karpathos*)
LCU 1382 (*Kassos*)

Displacement, tons	143 standard; 309 full load
Dimensions, feet	105 wl; 119 oa × 32·7 × 5
Guns	2—20 mm
Main engines	Diesel; 3 shafts; 440 bhp = 8 knots
Complement	13

Former US Utility Landing Craft of the *LCU* (ex-*LST* (6)) type. *Sciathos* and *Scopelos* were acquired in 1959. *Kea, Kithnos* (original No. 149) and *Sifnos* were transferred from USA in 1961, and *Karpathos* (original No. 146) *Kassos* and *Kimolos* in 1962. These LCUs are referred to by their hull numbers and not by name. There are also 13 LCMs and 34 LCVPs all transferred from USA.

LCU 763 *1971, Hellenic Navy*

MINE WARFARE FORCES

2 COASTAL MINELAYERS

AKTION (ex-*LSM* 301, ex-MMC 6) N 04
AMVRAKIA (ex-*LSM* 303, ex-MMC 7) N 05

Displacement, tons	720 standard; 1 100 full load
Dimensions, feet	203·5 oa × 34·5 × 8·3
Guns	8—40 mm dp (4 twin); 6—20 mm AA (single)
Mines	Capacity 100 to 130
Main engines	2 diesels; 2 shafts; 3 600 bhp = 12·5 knots
Range, miles	3 000 at 12 knots
Complement	65

Former US Medium Landing Ships. Both built at Charleston Naval Shipyard. *Aktion* was launched on 1 Jan 1945 and *Amvrakia* on 14 Nov 1944. Converted in the USA into all purpose seagoing minelayers for the Royal Hellenic Navy. Underwent extensive rebuilding from the deck up. Twin rudders. Transferred on 1 Dec 1953.

AMVRAKIA *1974, Hellenic Navy*

10 Ex-US "BLUEBIRD" CLASS (MINESWEEPERS—COASTAL)

AEDON (ex-*MSC* 310) M 248
AIGLI (ex-*MSC* 299) M 246
ARGO (ex-*MSC* 317) M 213
AVRA (ex-*MSC* 318) M 214
ALKYON (ex-*MSC* 319) M 211
DAFNI (ex-*MSC* 307) M 247
DORIS (ex-*MSC* 298) M 245
KICHLI (ex-*MSC* 308) M 241
PLEIAS (ex-*MSC* 314) M 240
KISSA (ex-*MSC* 309) M 242

Displacement, tons	320 standard; 370 full load
Dimensions, feet	138 pp; 144 oa × 28 × 8·2
Guns	2—20 mm AA (twin)
Main engines	2 GM diesels; 2 shafts; 880 bhp = 13 knots
Complement	39

Built in USA for Greece. *Aedon, Aigli, Dafni, Doris, Kichli* and *Kissa*, were completed and transferred in 1964-65, *Argo* and *Avra* in 1968, *Alkyon* and *Pleias* in 1969-70. Built of wood and non-magnetic materials.

AVRA *1974, Hellenic Navy*

5 ex.-US MSC TYPE 60

ANTIOPI (ex-Belgian *Herve, M* 921, ex-USS *MSC* 153) M 205
ATALANTI (ex-Belgian *St. Truiden, M* 919 ex-USS *MSC* 169) M 202
NIOVI (ex-Belgian *Laroche, M* 924. ex-USS *MSC* 171) M 254
FAEDRA (ex-Belgian *Malmedy, M* 922, ex-USS *MSC* 154) M 206
THALIA (ex-Belgian *Blankenberge, M* 923, ex-USS *MSC* 170) M 210

Displacement, tons	330 standard; 402 full load
Dimensions, feet	145·0 oa × 27·9 × 8·0 feet
Guns	2—20 mm Oerlikon (1 twin)
Main engines	2 GM diesels; 2 shafts; 900 bhp = 14 knots
Complement	38 officers and men

Former Belgian vessels taken over on 29 July 1969 (*Herve* and *St. Truiden*) and 26 Sep 1969 (*Laroche, Malmedy* and *Blankenberge*).

NIOVI *1971, Michael D. J. Lennon*

SURVEY VESSELS

ATALANTI

Of 383 tons, launched in 1954 with a complement of 35.

VEGAS (ex-*BYMS* 2078) A 478

Of 350 tons and with a complement of 33.
Former coastal minesweeper of the wooden hulled BYMS type.

ANEMOS A 469 (ex-German *KFK KW7*)

Displaces 112 tons, was launched in 1944 and has a complement of 16. Added to the Navy List in 1969.

HEPHESTOS (ex-USS *Josiah Willard Gibbs*, T-AGOR 1, ex-USS *San Carlos*, AVP 51) A 413

Displacement, tons	1 750 standard; 2 800 full load
Dimensions, feet	300·0 wl; 310·8 oa × 41·2 × 13·5
Main engines	2 Fairbanks-Morse diesels. 2 shafts; 6 080 bhp = 18 knots
Range, miles	10 000 at 14 knots
Endurance	30 days
Complement	82 (8 officers and 74 men)

Former US seaplane tender converted for oceanographic research. Built by Lake Washington Shipyard, Houghton, Wash. Laid down on 7 Sep 1942, launched on 20 Dec 1942 and completed on 21 Mar 1944. Transferred to the Hellenic Navy on 7 Dec 1971.

HEPHESTOS *1974, Hellenic Navy*

1 SURVEYING LAUNCH

Of 25 tons, launched in 1940. Complement 9.

SERVICE FORCES

2 SUPPORT TANKERS

ARETHOUSA (ex-USS *Natchaug, AOG* 54) A 377
ARIADNI (ex-USS *Tombigbee, AOG* 11) A 414

Displacement, tons	1 850 light; 4 335 full load
Measurement, tons	2 575 deadweight; cargo capacity 2 040
Dimensions, feet	292 wl; 310·8 oa × 48·5 × 15·7 max
Guns	4—3 in dp; 50 cal
Main engines	GM diesels; 2 shafts; 3 300 bhp = 14 knots
Complement	43 (6 officers, 37 men)

Former US petrol carriers. A 377 built by Cargill Inc, Savage, Minn. Laid down on 15 Aug 1944. Launched on 16 Dec 1944. Transferred from the USA to Greece under the Mutual Defense Assistance Program at Pearl Harbour, Hawaii in July 1959.
A 414 transferred 7 July 1972.

ARETHOUSA *1972, Hellenic Navy*

Service Forces—*cont.*

ZEUS (ex-YOG 98) A 372 (PETROL CARRIER)

Dimensions, feet 165 × 35 × 10

Former US yard petrol carrier. Launched in 1944. Capacity 900 tons.

SIRIOS (ex-*Poseidon*, ex-*Empire Faun*) A 345 (HARBOUR TANKER)

Formerly on loan from Great Britain, but purchased outright in 1962. This ship was renamed *Sirios* when the name *Poseidon* was given to the submarine *Lapon* acquired from the USA in 1958. Capacity 850 tons.

VIVIES A 471 (HARBOUR TANKER)

Originally a water carrier. Capacity 687 tons.

PROMETHEUS A 374 (HARBOUR TANKER)

Launched in 1959. Capacity 520 tons.

KRONOS (ex-*Islay*, ex-*Dresden*) A 373 (HARBOUR TANKER)

Displacement, tons 311 Capacity 110 tons

ORION (ex-US tanker Y 126) A 376 (HARBOUR TANKER)

Formerly small United States yard tanker. Capacity 700 tons.

ORION *1969, Hellenic Navy*

SOTIR (ex-*Salventure*) A 384 (SALVAGE SHIP)

Displacement, tons	1 440 standard; 1 700 full load
Measurement, tons	1 112 gross
Dimensions, feet	216 oa × 37·8 × 13
Main engines	Triple expansion; 2 shafts; 1 500 ihp = 12 knots
Oil fuel, tons	310
Complement	60

Former British Royal Fleet Auxiliary ocean salvage vessel of the "Salv" class. On loan from Great Britain. Equipped with a decompression chamber.

SOTIR *1972, Dr Giorgio Arra*

Service Forces—*continued*

SAKIPIS (ex-*KNM Ellida*, ex-USS *ARB* 13, ex-USS *LST* 50) A 329 (REPAIR SHIP)

Displacement, tons	3 800 standard; 5 000 full load
Dimensions, feet	316 wl; 328 oa × 50 × 11
Guns	12—40 mm AA; 12—20 mm AA
Main engines	GM diesels; 2 shafts; 1 800 bhp = 10 knots
Complement	200

Former US tank landing ship. Built by Dravo Corporation, Pittsburgh. Laid down on 29 Aug 1943, launched on 16 Oct 1943, completed on 27 Nov 1943. Converted to a repair ship in 1952 by Puget Sound Bridge & Dry Dock Co. Taken over by the Royal Norwegian Navy at Seattle on 14 Nov 1952. Returned to the US Navy on 1 July 1960. Transferred to Greece on 16 Sep 1960 at Bergen Norway.

SAKIPIS *1972, Hellenic Navy*

THETIS (ex-USS *AN* 103) A 307 (NETLAYER)

Displacement, tons	680 standard; 805 full load
Dimensions, feet	146 wl; 169·5 oa × 33·5 × 11·8
Guns	1—40 mm AA; 4—20 mm AA
Main engines	MAN diesels; 1 shaft; 1 400 bhp = 12 knots
Complement	48

Built by Krúger, Rendsburg as a US offshore order. Launched in 1959. Taken over by the Royal Hellenic Navy on 9 Apr 1960.

THETIS *1971, Hellenic Navy*

SKYROS A 485

Displacement tons	350

Acts as Lighthouse Tender.

ST LYKOUDIS (ex-*Chania*, ex-HMS *Nasturtium*) A 481

Displacement, tons	1 020 standard; 1 280 full load
Dimensions, feet	190 pp; 205 oa × 33 × 14·5
Main engines	Triple expansion; 2 750 ihp = 14 knots
Boilers	2 SE
Oil fuel, tons	230

Former corvette of the British "Flower" class. Launched in 1940. Sold to Greece as a merchant ship in 1948. Now acts as Lighthouse Tender.

ST. LYKOUDIS *1969, Hellenic Navy*

12 TUGS

ACCHILEUS (ex-*Confident*)
AIAS
ANTAIOS (ex-*Busy*)
ATLAS (ex-*F* 5)
ATROMITOS A 410
CIGAS
MINOTAVROS (ex-*Theseus*, ex-*ST* 539)
PERSEUS (ex-*ST 772*)
ROMALEOS
TITAN
SAMSON (ex-*F* 16
— (ex-*YTM* 767)

5 WATER BOATS

ILIKI **KASTORIA** **STYMFALIA** **TRICHONIS** **VOLVI**

Capacity: *Iliki* and *Stymfalia* 120 tons, *Trihonis* 300 tons, *Volvi* 350 tons, *Kastoria* 520 tons.

GABON

Personnel

(a) 1975: 100 officers and men
(b) Volunteers

Mercantile Marine

Lloyd's Register of Shipping: 13 vessels of 32 159 tons gross

Bases

Libreville, Port Gentil

PATROL BOATS

PRESIDENT ALBERT BERNARD BONGO

Displacement, tons	80
Dimensions, ft (*m*)	104 × 19 × 5 (*32 × 5·8 × 1·5*)
Guns	2—20 mm
Main engines	2 MTU diesels; 2 700 hp = 30 knots
Range, miles	1 500 at 15 knots
Complement	17 (3 officers, 14 ratings)

Built by Chantiers Navals de l'Esterel. Delivered March 1972. Fitted with radar and echo sounder.

PRESIDENT ALBERT BERNARD BONGO *1972, Chantiers Navals de L'Esterel*

PRESIDENT LEON M'BA GCO 1

Displacement, tons	85 standard
Dimensions, ft (*m*)	92 × 20·5 × 5 (*28 × 6·3 × 1·5*)
Guns	1—75 mm; 1—12·7 mm MG
Main engines	Diesel = 12·5 knots
Complement	16

Built in Gabon, launched on 16 Jan 1968

BOUET-WILLAUMEZ (ex-HDML 1021).

Displacement, tons	40
Dimensions, ft (*m*)	70·8 × 15·3 × 5·9 (*21·6 × 4·7 × 1·8*)
Guns	2—20 mm AA
Main engines	2 Diesels; 300 hp = 12·5 knots
Complement	8

Launched in 1943. Transferred in 1961 by France and still, apparently, going strong.

NOTE. Plans exist for a 60 ft Patrol Boat and four LCVP s.

GRENADA

Note. Grenada was granted self-government, in association with Great Britain (who was responsible for her defence) on 3 March 1967. Full self-government was achieved in February 1973.

Mercantile Marine

Lloyd's Register of Shipping: 2 vessels of 226 tons gross

PATROL BOAT

Displacement, tons	15
Dimensions, ft (*m*)	40 × 12 × 2 (*12·2 × 3·7 × ·6*)
Guns	3 MG
Main engines	2 Diesels; 370 hp = 22 knots

Delivered by Brooke Marine, Lowestoft early in 1972.

GUATEMALA

On 5 Jan 1959 Guatemala announced the establishment of a navy for coastguard work. Subsequently the navy was assigned missions of search and rescue and the support of amphibious operations. The commissioning of a Marine Elevator (Synchrolift) at Santo Tomás on 23 June 1973 (230 ton lift) has greatly improved this navy's repair facilities.

Personnel

(a) 1975: 400 (50 officers and 350 men, including 10 officers and 200 men of the Marines)
(b) 2 years National Service

Bases

Santo Tomás de Castillas (Atlantic); Sipacate (Pacific)

Mercantile Marine

Lloyd's Register of Shipping: 6 vessels of 8 222 tons gross

2 COASTAL PATROL CRAFT

UTATLAN P 851 **USORIO SARAVIA** P 852

Displacement, tons	42
Dimensions, ft (*m*)	85 × 18·7 × 3 (*25·9 × 5·7 × ·9*)
Guns	2 MG
Main engines	2 GM Diesels; 2 200 bhp = 23 knots
Range, miles	400 at 12 knots
Complement	12 (2 officers, 10 ratings)

Built by Sewart, Florida to "Commercial Cruiser" design. *Utatlan* transferred May 1967; *Saravia* 1972.

UTATLAN *1973, Guatamalian Navy*

3 65ft COASTAL PATROL CRAFT

TECUNUMAN P 651 **KAIBILBALAM** P 652 **AZUMANCHE** P 653

Displacement, tons	32
Dimensions,ft (*m*)	64·5 × 17 × 3 (*19·7 × 5·2 × ·9*)
Guns	2 MG
Main engines	2 GM Diesels = 25 knots
Complement	10 (2 officers, 8 ratings)

Built by Halter (US). Delivered 1972.

2 63ft COASTAL CRAFT (ex-SAR CRAFT)

CABRAKAN P 631 **HUNAHPU** P 632

Displacement, tons	32
Dimensions, ft (*m*)	63·3 × 15·4 × 3 (*19·3 × 4·7 × 0·9*)
Guns	2 MG
Main engines	2 GM Diesels 8V71 = 25 knots
Complement	10 (2 officers, 8 men)

2 Ex-USCG UTILITY BOATS MK IV

TIKAL P 401 **XIMICHE** P 402

Of 40 ft. Transferred Aug 1963.

2 28ft COASTAL PATROL CRAFT

XUCUXUY P 281 **CAMALOTE** P 282

triker Utility Patrol Craft modified for one GM 6-53 Diesel. 28 ft, 6½ tons with 1 MG.

1 Ex-US LCM 6 MK VI

CHINALTENANGO 561

6 LCUs

Transferred in late 1960s.

1 Ex-US REPAIR BARGE

ex-US YR 40. Transferred in 1952.

1 TUG

Note. Three other names listed—*Escuintla*, *Mazatenango*, *Retalhuleu*—in addition to two yachts—*Mendieta* and one other.

GUINEA

Personnel

1975: 350 officers and men

Mercantile Marine

Lloyd's Register of Shipping: 9 vessels of 15 538 tons gross

LIGHT FORCES

4 Ex-USSR "P 6" CLASS (FAST ATTACK CRAFT—TORPEDO)

Displacement, tons	66 standard; 75 full load
Dimensions, ft (*m*)	84·2 × 20·0 × 6·0 (*25·7 × 6·1 × 1·8*)
Guns	4—25 mm AA
Tubes	2—21 in (or mines or depth charges)
Main engines	4 Diesels; 4 shafts; 4 800 bhp = 43 knots
Range, miles	450 at 30 knots
Complement	25

It seems unlikely that the torpedo armament is operational.

2 Ex-USSR "POLUCHAT I" CLASS (COASTAL PATROL CRAFT)

P 215 **P 425**

Displacement, tons	86 standard; 91 full load
Dimensions, ft (*m*)	98·0 pp × 15·0 × 4·8 (*29·9 × 4·6 × 1·5*)
Guns	2—14·5 mm AA (1 twin)
Main engines	2 diesels; 2 shafts; 1 200 bhp = 18 knots
Oil fuel, tons	9·25
Range, miles	460 at 17 knots
Complement	16 (2 officers, 14 ratings)

2 Ex-USSR "MO VI" CLASS (COASTAL PATROL CRAFT)

Displacement, tons	64 standard; 73 full load
Dimensions, ft (*m*)	83·6 × 19·7 × 4·0 (*25·5 × 6 × 1·2*)
Guns	4—25 mm (twin)
A/S weapons	DC mortars and racks
Main engines	4 Diesels; 4 shafts; 4 800 hp = 40 knots

Transferred 1972-73. Radar—Pot Head.

LANDING CRAFT

2 SMALL UTILITY TYPE

Recent visits by considerable numbers of Soviet ships may have increased these numbers.

GUYANA

Mercantile Marine

Lloyd's Register of Shipping: 53 vessels of 15 689 tons gross

PATROL LAUNCHES

JAGUAR **MARGAY** **OCELOT**

Displacement, tons	10
Dimensions, ft (*m*)	40 × 12 × 3·5 (*12·2 × 3·7 × 1·1*)
Guns	7·62 mm general purpose machine guns
Main engines	2 Cummins diesels; 370 hp = 19 knots
Range, miles	150 at 12 knots
Complement	6

They have glass fibre hulls with aluminium superstructures. Completed 29 Apr 1971 (*Jaguar*) 21 May 1971 (*Margay*), 22 June 1971 (*Ocelot*).

JAGUAR *1971, C. and S. Taylor*

HAITI

Personnel

(a) 1975: Total 300 (40 officers and 260 men)
(b) Voluntary service

COAST GUARD VESSELS

JEAN JACQUES DESSALINES (ex-USS *Tonawanda, AN 89*) GC 10

Displacement, tons	650 standard; 785 full load
Dimensions, feet	168·5 × 33 × 10·8
Guns	1—76 mm; 3—20 mm
Main engines	Busch-Sulzer diesel-electric; 1 500 shp = 12 knots

Former United States Navy netlayer of the "Cohoes" class. Built by Leatham D. Smith S.B. Co. Launched on 14 Nov 1944. Loaned to Haiti in 1960.

AMIRAL KILLICK (ex-USCG *Black Rock, WAGL* 367) GC 7

Displacement, tons	160
Length, feet	114

Former buoy tender purchased from the US Coast Guard in 1955, commissioned in Jan 1956.

LA CRETE A PIERROT (ex-USCG 95315) GC 8 **VERTIÈRES** GC 9

Displacement, tons	100
Dimensions, feet	95 × 19 × 5
Gun	1—40 mm AA
Main engines	4 diesels; 2 shafts; 2 200 bhp = 21 knots
Range, miles	1 500
Complement	15

Former US Coast Guard steel cutters. Built at US Coast Guard Yard, Curtiss Bay, Maryland. *La Crête a Pierrot* was acquired on 26 Feb 1956. *Vertières* was transferred to Haiti at Norfolk, Virginia in Oct 1956 and commissioned in Dec 1956.

16 AOUT 1946 (ex-*SC* 453) GC 2

Displacement, tons	110 standard; 138 full load
Dimensions, feet	110·5 × 18·8 × 6·5
Guns	2—40 mm; 2—20 mm
Main engines	Diesels; 2 shafts; 1 000 = 15 knots

Of the SC type acquired during 1947 from the US Navy. Launched in 1943. Laid up in reserve.

SAVANNAH GC 1

Displacement, tons	47
Dimensions, feet	56 × 16 × 4·2
Main engines	Diesels; 2 shafts; 200 bhp = 9 knots
Complement	12

Ex-USCG cutter 563200, built by Wheeler Shipyard, Brooklyn, USA, in 1944 and acquired in 1944.

ARTIBONITE (ex-US *LCT*) GC 5

Displacement, tons	134 standard; 285 full load
Dimensions, feet	120·3 oa × 32 × 4·2
Main engines	3 diesels; 675 bhp = 8 knots
Range, miles	700 at 7 knots
Complement	12

Former US tank landing craft. Salvaged by Haitian Coast Guard after grounding and converted. Laid up in reserve having been damaged by grounding in Mar 1956.

SANS SOUCI (ex-*Captain James Taylor*)

Displacement, tons	161
Main engines	2 diesels; 2 shafts; 300 bhp = 10 knots

Employed, when required, as the Presidential Yacht.

HONDURAS

Coast Guard

There are three small coastguard cutters.

Mercantile Marine

Lloyd's Register of Shipping: 56 vessels of 69 561 tons gross

HONDURAS, BRITISH

2 PATROL CRAFT

BELIZE PBM 01 **BELMOPAN** PBM 02

Displacement, tons	15
Dimensions, feet	40 × 12 × 2
Guns	3 MG
Main engines	2 Diesels; 370 hp = 22 knots

Built by Brooke Marine, Lowestoft.

HONG KONG

Mercantile Marine

Lloyd's Register of Shipping: 93 vessels of 269 945 tons gross

All the following craft are operated by the Marine District of the Royal Hong Kong Police Force.

Personnel

(a) 1975: 52 officers, 300 NCOs, 876 constables

7 78ft VOSPER THORNYCROFT PATROL CRAFT

Nos. 50-56

Displacement, tons	82
Dimensions, feet	78·5 oa × 17·2 × 5·6
Gun	1—·50 cal MG
Main engines	Two Cummins diesels; 1 500 hp = 20·7 knots
Range, miles	4 000 at 20 knots
Complement	16

Steel hulled craft built by Vosper Thornycroft Private Ltd, Singapore. Delivered May 1972 to May 1973 to the Royal Hong Kong Police. Can carry an extra Platoon. Cost $HK 1 873 800.

POLICE LAUNCH No. 51 — *1974, RHKP*

1 78ft PATROL CRAFT

No. 4

Slightly smaller than the above with 3 diesels, a speed of 15·5 knots and a range of 600 miles at that speed.

2 COMMAND VESSELS

No 1 **No 2**

Displacement, tons	222·5
Dimensions, feet	111·3 × 24 × 10·5
Main engines	2 Diesels of 337 bhp = 11·8 knots
Range, miles	5 200 at 11·8 knots
Complement	25

Built at Taikoo 1965. Can carry two platoons in addition to complement. Cost $HK 1 778 550.

POLICE LAUNCH No. 2 — *1974, RHKP*

9 70ft PATROL CRAFT

Nos. 26-34

Displacement, tons	52
Dimensions, feet	70 × 17 × 5·2
Main engines	2 Diesels of 215 bhp = 10 knots
Range, miles	1 600 at 10 knots
Complement	11

1 65ft PATROL CRAFT

No. 6

Slightly smaller than Nos. 26-34 with single diesel and 48 tons. Complement 12. Range 1 400 miles at 9 knots.

10 45ft PATROL CRAFT

Nos. 5, 8-16

Displacement, tons	27·7
Dimensions, feet	45 × 15 × 7
Main engines	1 Diesel; 144 bhp = 9 knots
Range, miles	1 700 at 8 knots
Complement	5

Built in Australia—1944.

3 40ft PATROL CRAFT

Nos. 20-22

Displacement, tons	17
Dimensions, feet	40·3 × 11·6 × 2
Main engines	2 Diesels of 370 bhp = 24 knots
Range, miles	380 at 24 knots
Complement	4

Built in Choy Lee in 1971.

POLICE LAUNCH No. 22 — *1974, RHKP*

1 58ft LOGISTIC CRAFT

No. 3

Of 37 tons and 16 knots with a range of 240 miles at 15 knots. Complement 8. Built by Thornycroft Singapore in 1958.

POLICE LAUNCH No. 3 — *1974, RHKP*

1 42ft LOGISTIC CRAFT

No. 24

Of 15 tons and 11 knots with a range of 60 miles at 11 knots. Built by Thornycroft Singapore in 1959.

11 22ft LAUNCHES

Nos. 35-45

Of 4·8 tons and 20 knots with a range of 160 miles at full speed. Built in Choy Lee in 1970.

HUNGARY

Diplomatic Representation

Military and Air Attaché London: Lieut Colonel Károly Mészáros

Personnel

(a) 1974: 500 officers and men
(b) 2 years national service

Mercantile Marine

Lloyd's Register of Shipping: 17 vessels of 49 150 tons gross

The Navy was dissolved by 1969 but a maritime wing of the Army is still very active on the Danube.

10 100 ton PATROL CRAFT

No. 542 — *1972, Hungarian River Guard*

5 LCUs

ICELAND

Duties

The Coast Guard Service (Landhelgisgaezlan) deals with fishery protection, salvage, rescue, hydrographic research, surveying and lighthouse duties.

Strength of the Coast Guard

7 Patrol Vessels; colour: dark grey
1 Patrol Aircraft and helicopter

Personnel

1975: 120 officers and men

Mercantile Marine

Lloyd's Register of Shipping:
35 vessels of 148 695 tons gross

COAST GUARD PATROL VESSELS

ÆGIR TYR

Displacement, tons	1 150
Dimensions, feet	204 × 33 × 13
Gun	1—57 mm
Main engines	2 diesels; 2 shafts; 8 000 bhp = 19 knots
Complement	22

Aegir was the first new construction patrol vessel for the Icelandic Coast Guard Service for about eight years. Projected in Feb 1965. Built by Aalborg Vaerft, Denmark. Laid down in May 1967. Completed in 1968. *Tyr*, basically similar to *Aegir*, but of a slightly improved design with higher speed was launched by Aarhus Flyedock AS, Aalborg, Denmark in October 1974 for delivery in 1975.

ÆGIR *1969, Icelandic Coast Guard Service*

THOR

Displacement, tons	920
Dimensions, feet	183·3 pp; 206 oa × 31·2 × 13
Guns	2—57 mm
Main engines	2 diesels; 3 200 bhp = 17 knots
Complement	22

Built at Aalborg, Denmark. Launched in 1951. Completed and commissioned in late 1951. Rated as coastal inspection and salvage vessel. Fitted with helicopter platform during refit in 1972.

THOR *1969, Icelandic Coast Guard Service*

ODINN

Measurement, tons	1 000
Dimensions, feet	187 pp × 33 × 13
Gun	1—57 mm
Main engines	2 diesels; 2 shafts; 5 000 bhp = 18 knots
Complement	22

Designed as a coast guard vessel. Built at Aalborg Vaerft AS, Denmark. Laid down in Jan 1959. Launched in Sep 1959. Completed in Jan 1960. Refitted with a new tripod mast in 1972.

ODINN *1967, Icelandic Coast Guard Service*

ARVAKUR

Displacement, tons	716
Dimensions, feet	106 × 33 × 13
Gun	1 MG
Main engine	1 diesel; 1 000 bhp = 12 knots
Complement	12

Built as a lighthouse tender in the Netherlands in 1962. Acquired by Iceland for duty in the Coast Guard Service in 1969.

ARVAKUR *1969, Icelandic Coast Guard Service*

ALBERT

Measurement, tons	200 gross
Dimensions, feet	Length: 111·2
Gun	1—47 mm
Main engine	1 Nohab diesel; 650 bhp = 12·5 knots
Complement	15

Launched in 1956. Completed and commissioned for service in Apr 1957. Refitted in 1972.

HARBAKUR

Displacement, tons	941
Main engines	Diesel

Launched 8 Feb 1974 by Astilleros Luzuriaga, (Pasajes) Spain.

NOTE. Two 20 knot whale-catchers were requisitioned in 1972 and returned to their owners in 1973.

INDIA

Administration

Chief of the Naval Staff:
Admiral S. N. Kohli

Flag Officer C in C, Western Naval Command:
Vice-Admiral J. Cursetji

Flag Officer Commanding Western Fleet:
Rear-Admiral N. P. Datta

Flag Officer C in C. Eastern Naval Command:
Vice-Admiral K. L. Kulkarni

Flag Officer Commanding Eastern Fleet:
Rear-Admiral R. K. S. Ghandi

Flag Officer, Southern Naval Area:
Rear-Admiral R. L. Pereira

Diplomatic Representation

Naval Attaché in Bonn
Captain L. Ramdas

Naval Adviser, Dacca:
Captain R. B. Mukherjee

Naval Attaché in Djakarta:
Captain R. Vir

Naval Adviser in London:
Commodore C. L. Sachdeva

Naval Attaché in Moscow:
Commodore G. K. Nadkar

Defence Attaché in Washington:
Brigadier Srendra Singh MC

Personnel

(a) 1975: 30 000 officers and ratings (including Naval Air Arm)
(b) Voluntary service

Strength of the Fleet

Type	*Active*	*Building*
Attack Carrier (Medium)	1	—
Cruisers	2	—
Destroyers	3	—
Frigates	23	4
Patrol Submarines	8	—
Fast Attack Craft—Missile	8	—
Large Patrol Craft	1	—
Coastal Patrol Craft	14	—
Landing Ships	1	—
Landing Craft	3	—
Minesweepers—Coastal	4	—
Minesweepers—Inshore	4	—
Survey Ships	4	—
Submarine Tenders	1	—
Submarine Rescue Ships	1	—
Replenishment Tanker	1	—
Support Tankers	3	—
Harbour Tankers	2	—
Repair Ship	1	—
Ocean Tug	1	—

Prefix to Ships Names

IS (Indian Ship)

Naval Air Arm

Squadron No.	*Aircraft*	*Role*
300	Seahawk FGA6	Strike
310	Alize 1050	ASW
321	Alouette III	SAR
330	Sea Kings	ASW
331	Alouette III	ASW
550	Alize, Alouette	Training
561	HTZ16, Devon Hughes 300, Alouette III	Training

Naval Bases and Establishments

Bombay (C in C Western Fleet, barracks and main Dockyard);
Vishakapatnam (C in C Eastern Command, submarine base, dockyard and barracks);
Cochin (FO Southern Area Naval Air Station, barracks and professional schools);
Lonavala and Jamnagar (professional schools);
Calcutta, Goa, and Port Blair (small bases only.)

Mercantile Marine

Lloyd's Register of Shipping:
451 vessels of 3 484 751 tons gross

AIRCRAFT CARRIER (*Attack Medium*)

Name	*No.*	*Builders*	*Engineers*	*Laid down*	*Launched*	*Completed*
VIKRANT (ex-HMS *Hercules*)	R 11	Vickers-Armstrong Ltd, Tyne	Parsons Marine Steam Turbine Co	14 Oct 1943	22 Sep 1945	4 Mar 1961

1 Ex-BRITISH "MAJESTIC" CLASS

Displacement, tons	16 000 standard; 19 500 full load
Length, feet (*metres*)	630 (*192·0*) pp; 700 (*213·4*) oa
Beam, feet (*metres*)	80 (*24·4*) hull
Width, feet (*metres*)	128 (*39·0*)
Draught, feet (*metres*)	24 (*7·3*)
Aircraft	21 capacity
Guns,	15—40 mm; 4 twin, 7 single
Boilers	4 Admiralty 3-drum; 400 psi; 700°F
Main engines	Parsons single reduction geared turbines; 40 000 shp; 2 shafts
Speed, knots	24·5 designed
Complement	1 343, designed accommodation

Acquired from Great Britain in Jan 1957 after having been suspended in May 1946 when structurally almost complete and 75% fitted out. Taken in hand by Harland & Wolff Ltd, Belfast, in Apr 1957 for completion in 1961 Commissioned on 4 Mar 1961 and renamed *Vikrant*.

AIRCRAFT. Still equipped with Seahawks although re-equipment is planned. Harrier trials in mid-1972 showed promise, but subsequently the IN is understood to have preferred Soviet Yakovlev VTOL aircraft due to problems in purchasing the Harrier.

ENGINEERING. Engines and boilers are arranged *en echelon*, one set of turbines and two boilers being installed side by side in each of the two propelling machinery spaces, on the unit system, so that the starboard propeller shaft is longer than the port.

FLIGHT DECK. The aircraft including strike and anti-submarine aircraft, operate from an angled deck with steam catapult, landing sights and two electrically operated lifts.

HABITABILITY. Partially air-conditioned and insulated for tropical service, the ship's sides being sprayed with asbestos cement instead of being lagged. Separate messes and dining halls.

RADAR. Search: Type 960, Type 277. Tactical: Type 293. Miscellaneous: Type 963 Carrier Controlled Approach.

DRAWING. Scale: 115 feet = 1 inch

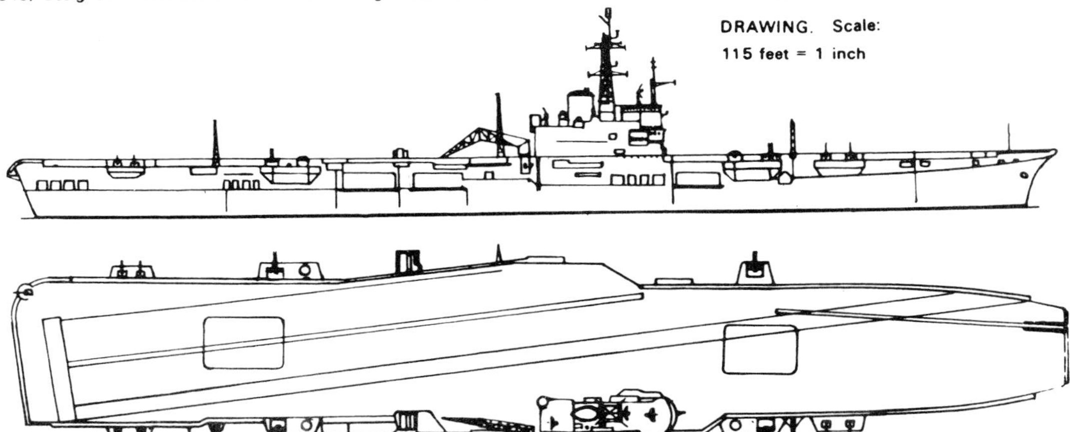

VIKRANT — 1971, John G Collis

CRUISERS

Name	*No.*	*Builders*	*Engineers*	*Laid down*	*Launched*	*Completed*
MYSORE (ex- HMS *Nigeria*)	C 60	Vickers-Armstrongs, Ltd, Tyne	Parsons	8 Feb 1938	18 July 1939	23 Sep 1940

Displacement, tons	8 700 standard; 11 040 full load
Length, feet (*metres*)	538·0 (*164·0*)pp; 549·0 (*167·3*)wl 555·5 (*169·3*) oa
Beam, feet (*metres*)	62·0 (*18·9*)
Draught, feet (*metres*)	21·0 (*6·4*)
Guns	9—6 in (*152 mm*), 3 triple; 8—4 in (*102 mm*) LP, 4 twin; 12—40 mm AA; 5 twin, 2 single
Armour	Side 4½ in—3 in (*114—76 mm*); Deck 2 in (*51 mm*); Conning tower 4 in (102 *mm*); Turrets 2 in (*51 mm*)
Main engines	Parsons geared turbines; 4 shafts; 72 500 shp
Speed, knots	31·5
Boilers	4 Admiralty 3-drum type
Complement	800

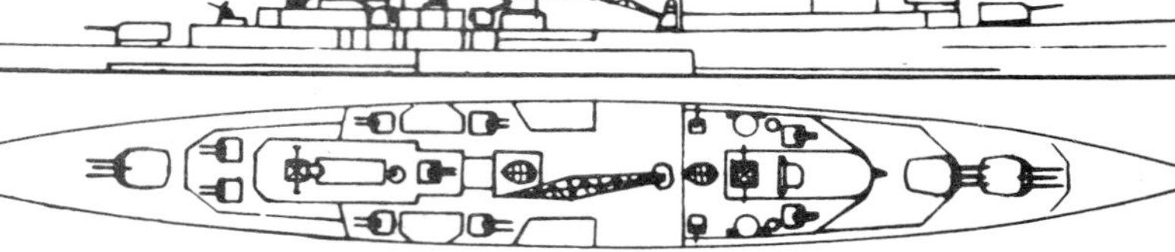

GENERAL

Formerly a "Colony" class cruiser in the Royal Navy. Purchased from Great Britain on 8 Apr 1954 for £300 000. Extensively refitted and reconstructed by Cammell Laird & Co Ltd, Birkenhead, before commissioning. Formally handed over to the Indian Navy at Birkenhead and renamed *Mysore* on 29 Aug 1957. Involved in two serious collisions, the second in late 1972 with *Beas*, resulting in two months of repairs.

RADAR. Search: Type 960, Type 277. Tactical: Type 293. Fire Control: X Band.

RECONSTRUCTION. Ship formerly had tripod masts. During reconstruction the triple 6 inch turret in "X" position and the 6—21 inch torpedo tubes (tripled) were removed, the bridge was modified, two lattice masts were stepped, all electrical equipment was replaced and the engine room and other parts of the ship were refitted.

DRAWING. Starboard elevation and plan. Drawn in 1971. Scale: 125 feet = 1 inch

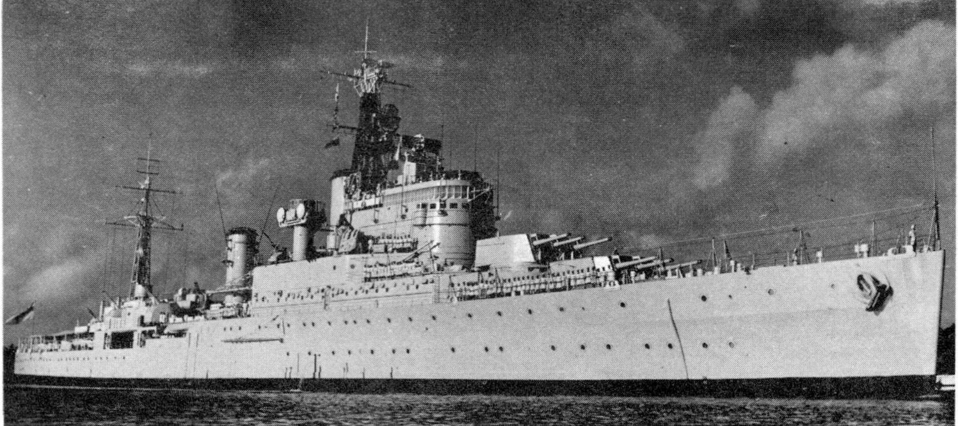

MYSORE *1971, Roland Rodwell*

Name	*No.*	*Builders*	*Laid down*	*Launched*	*Completed*
DELHI (ex HMS *Achilles*)	C 74	Cammell Laird & Co Ltd, Birkenhead	11 June 1931	1 Sep 1932	5 Oct 1933

Displacement, tons	7 114 standard; 9 740 full load
Length, feet (*metres*)	522·0 (*159·1*)pp; 544·5 (*166·0*)oa
Beam, feet (*metres*)	55·2 (*16·8*)
Draught, feet (*metres*)	20·0 (*6·1*)
Guns	6—6 in (*152 mm*); 8—4 in (*102 mm*) AA; 14—40 mm AA; 4—3 pdr saluting
Armour	4 in-2 in side; 1 in gunhouses; 1 in bridge; 2 in deck
Main engines	Parsons geared turbines; 4 shafts 72 000 shp
Speed, knots	32
Boilers	4 Admiralty 3-drum type
Oil fuel, tons	1 800
Complement	800

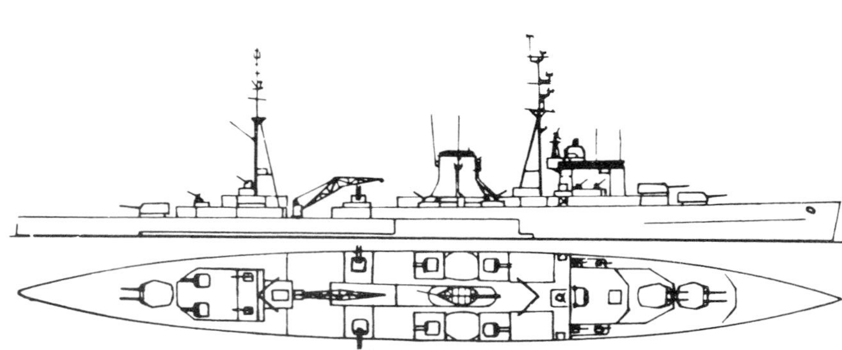

Formerly a "Leander" class light cruiser in the Royal Navy. Purchased from Great Britain and delivered on 5 July 1948. Refitted in 1955. Now used for training.

DRAWING. Starboard elevation and plan. Drawn in 1971. Scale: 122 feet = 1 inch

RADAR. Search: Type 960, Type 277. Tactical: Type 293. Fire Control: Early design.

HISTORICAL. As HMS *Achilles*, then lent to the Royal New Zealand Navy, this ship, with HMS *Ajax* and HMS *Exeter*, defeated the German battleship *Admiral Graf Spee* in the Battle of the River Plate on 13 Dec 1939.

TORPEDO TUBES. In 1958 the original eight 21 inch torpedo tubes, in two quadruple banks, were removed, and the forecastle deck plating was consequently extended aft to the twin 40 mm AA gun mounting abreast the boat stowage.

DELHI

DESTROYERS

3 Ex-BRITISH "R" CLASS

Name	No.	Builders	Laid down	Launched	Completed	Transferred
RANA (ex-HMS *Raider*)	D 115	Cammell Laird & Co Ltd Birkenhead	16 Apr 1941	1 Apr 1942	16 Nov 1942	9 Sep 1949
RAJPUT (ex-HMS *Rotherham*)	D 209	John Brown & Co Ltd. Clydebank	10 Apr 1941	21 Mar 1942	27 Aug 1942	29 July 1949
RANJIT (ex-HMS *Redoubt*)	D 141	John Brown & Co Ltd. Clydebank	19 June 1941	2 May 1942	1 Oct 1942	4 July 1949

Displacement, tons	1 725 standard; 2 424 full load
Length, feet (*metres*)	339·5 (*103·5*)wl; 362·0 (*110·3*)oa
Beam, feet (*metres*)	35·7 (*10·9*)
Draught, feet (*metres*)	17·1 (*5·2*)
Guns	4—4·7 in (*120 mm*); 4—40 mm AA
A/S weapons	4 DCT
Torpedo tubes	8—21 in (2 quadruple) in *Rana*
Main engines	Parsons geared turbines; 2 shafts 40 000 shp
Speed, knots	32
Boilers	2 Admiralty 3-drum type
Oil fuel, tons	490
Range, miles	2 500 at 20 knots
Complement	240

First British destroyers with officers accommodation forward instead of aft. Refitted and modernised before transfer. Arrived in Indian waters in Jan 1950. Constitute 11th Destroyer Squadron of which *Rajput* is Leader. *Rana* now in reserve.

RADAR. Search: Type 293. Fire Control: Early design.

RAJPUT

FRIGATES

6 "LEANDER" CLASS

DUNAGIRI **UDAYGIRI**
HIMGIRI F 234 **NILGIRI** F 233 + **2**

Displacement, tons	2 450 standard; 2 800 full load
Length, feet (*metres*)	360 (*109·7*) wl; 372 (*113·4*) oa
Beam, feet (*metres*)	43 (*13·1*)
Draught, feet (*metres*)	18 (*5·5*)
Aircraft	1 Wasp helicopter
Missiles, AA	2 "Seacat" quadruple launchers
Guns	2—4·5 in (*115 mm*) 1 twin 2—40 mm
A/S weapons	1 "Limbo" 3 barrelled DC mortar
Boilers	2
Main engines	2 geared turbines; 30 000 shp
Speed, knots	30
Oil fuel, tons	460
Range, miles	4 500 at 12 knots
Complement	263

First major warships built in Indian yards. Of similar design to later (broad beam) "Leander" class general purpose frigates in the Royal Navy. All ordered from Mazagon Docks Ltd, Bombay. *Nilgiri* was laid down in Oct 1966, launched on 23 Oct 1968 and was commissioned on 3 June 1972. *Himgiri* was launched on 6 May 1970. Commissioned in 1974. The third ship was laid down on 14 Sep 1970. Two further ships of the class are projected to complete at yearly intervals, but it is reported that these may be replaced by the two French A69 Aviso's.

"LEANDER" Class

11 "PETYA" CLASS

AMIN	P 69	**KADMATT**	P 78
ANDAMAN	P 74	**KAMORTA**	P 77
ANDROTH	P 69	**KATCHAL**	P 81
ANJADIP	P 73	**KAVARATTI**	P 80
ARNALA	P 68	**KILTAN**	P 79
AMINDIYI	—		

Displacement, tons	950 standard; 1 150 full load
Length, feet (*metres*)	250·0 (*76·2*) wl; 270 (*82·3*) oa
Beam, feet (*metres*)	29·9 (*9·1*)
Draught, feet (*metres*)	10·5 (*3·2*)
Guns	4—3 in (*76 mm*) dp, 2 twin
A/S weapons	4 MBU 2 500; 16 barrelled rocket launchers
Torpedo tubes	5—16 in ("K" Series); 3—21 in ("A" Series)
Main engines	2 gas turbines; 30 000 hp; 2 diesels; 2 shafts; 6 000 hp
Speed, knots	34

Transferred to the Indian Navy since 1969. *Andaman* delivered Mar 1974, *Amin* delivered mid 1974. *Amindiyi* late 1974.

RADAR. "K" series, Head Net A. "A" series, Slim Net.

"PETYA" Class

Ex-Soviet

"PETYA" Class

Frigates—continued

2 "WHITBY" CLASS

Name	No	Builders	Launched	Completed
TALWAR	F 140	Cammell Laird & Co Ltd, Birkenhead	18 July 1958	1960
TRISHUL (*Leader*)	F 143	Harland & Wolff Ltd, Belfast	18 June 1959	1960

Displacement, tons	2 144 standard; 2 545 full load (*Talwar*), 2 557 (*Trishul*)
Length, feet (*metres*)	360 (*109·7*) pp 369·8 (*112·7*) oa
Beam, feet (*metres*)	41 (*12·5*)
Draught, feet (*metres*)	17·8 (*5·4*)
Guns, surface	2—4·5 in (*115 mm*)
Guns, AA	4—40 mm (1 twin before "Limbos", 2 singles abaft funnel)
A/S weapons	2 "Limbo" 3-barrelled DC mortars
Boilers	2 Babcock & Wilcox
Main engines	2 sets geared turbines; 30 000 shp; 2 shafts
Speed, knots	30
Oil fuel, tons	400
Range, miles	4 500 at 12 knots
Complement	231 (11 officers, 220 men)

TALWAR, TRISHUL

TALWAR *A. & J. Pavia*

GENERAL
Built in Great Britain and generally similar to the British frigates of the "Whitby" class, but slightly modified to suit Indian conditions.

RADAR. Tactical: Type 293. Fire Control: X Band.

3 "LEOPARD" CLASS

Name	No.	Builders	Launched	Completed
BEAS	F 137	Vickers-Armstrongs Ltd, Newcastle-on-Tyne	9 Oct 1958	24 May 1960
BETWA	F 139	Vickers-Armstrongs Ltd, Newcastle-on-Tyne	15 Sep 1959	8 Dec 1960
BRAHMAPUTRA (ex-*Panther*)	F 31	John Brown & Co Ltd, Clydebank	15 Mar 1957	28 Mar 1958

Displacement, tons	2 251 standard; 2 515 full load
Length, feet (*metres*)	320·0 (*97·5*) pp; 330·0 (*100·6*) wl; 339·8 (*103·6*) oa
Beam, feet (*metres*)	40·0 (*12·2*)
Draught, feet (*metres*)	16·0 (*4·9*)
Guns	4—4·5 in (*114 mm*), 2 twin; 4—40 mm AA
A/S weapons	1 Squid 3-barrelled DC mortar
Main engines	Admiralty standard range diesels 2 shafts; 12 380 bhp
Speed, knots	25
Range, miles	7 500 at 16 knots
Complement	210

BRAHMAPUTRA *1971, Indian Navy.*

BEAS, BETWA, BRAHMAPUTRA

Brahmaputra, originally ordered as *Panther* for the Royal Navy on 28 June 1951, was the first major warship to be built in Great Britain for the Indian Navy since India became independent. All three ships are generally similar to the British frigates of the "Leopard" class, but modified to suit Indian conditions.

RADAR. Search: Type 960. Tactical: Type 293. Fire Control: X Band forward and aft.

2 "BLACKWOOD" CLASS

Name	No	Builders	Launched	Completed
KIRPAN	F 144	Alex Stephen & Sons Ltd, Govan, Glasgow	19 Aug 1958	July 1959
KUTHAR	F 146	J. Samuel White & Co Ltd, Cowes, Isle of Wight	14 Oct 1958	1959

Displacement, tons	1 180 standard; 1 456 full load
Length, feet (*metres*)	300 (*91·4*) pp; 310 (*94·5*) oa
Beam, feet (*metres*)	33 (*10·0*)
Draught, feet (*metres*)	15·5 (*4·7*)
Guns, AA	3—40 mm (single)
A/S weapons	2 "Limbo" 3-barrelled DC mortars
Boilers	Babcock & Wilcox
Main engines	1 set geared turbines; 15 000 shp; 1 shaft
Speed, knots	27·8
Range, miles	4 000 at 12 knots
Oil fuel, tons	300
Complement	150

KIRPAN, KUTHAR

Built in Great Britain, and generally similar to the British frigates of the "Blackwood" class, but slightly modified to suit Indian requirements. *Khukri* of this class was sunk in the Pakistan war on 9 Dec 1971.

RADAR. Fitted with S band air and surface surveillance radar.

3 "HUNT" CLASS TYPE II

Name	No.	Builders	Laid down	Launched	Completed
GANGA (ex-HMS *Chiddingfold*)	D 94	Scott's Shipbuilding & Engineering Co Ltd., Greenock	1 Mar 1940	10 Mar 1941	16 Oct 1941
GODAVARI (ex-HMS *Bedale*, ex-*Slazak*, ex-*Bedale*)	D 92	R. & W. Hawthorn, Leslie & Co Ltd, Hebburn	29 May 1940	5 Sep 1941	18 June 1944
GOMATI (ex-HMS *Lamerton*)	D 93	Swan, Hunter & Wigham Richardson Ltd, Wallsend	10 Apr 1939	14 Dec 1940	16 Aug 1944

Displacement, tons	1 050 standard; 1 610 full load
Length, feet (*metres*)	264·2 (*80·5*) pp; 280·0 (*85·3*) oa
Beam, feet (*metres*)	31·5 (*9·6*)
Draught feet (*metres*)	14·0 (*4·3*)
Guns	6—4 in (*102 mm*) dp; 4—20 mm
Main engines	Parsons geared turbines; 2 shafts; 19 000 shp
Speed, knots	25
Boilers	2 Admiralty 3-drum
Oil fuel, tons	280
Range, miles	3 700 at 14 knots
Complement	150

GANGA, GODAVARI, GOMATI

Former "Hunt" class, Type II frigates F 131, F 126 and F 88, respectively, (ex-Escort Destroyers). Transferred from Great Britain in Apr/May 1953. Lent to the Indian Navy for three years, subject to extension by agreement.

Officially rated as destroyers with D pennant Nos. Constitute the 22nd Destroyer Squadron of which *Godavari* is leader. Now used for training.

Frigates—*continued*

2 "KISTNA" CLASS

Name	*No*	*Builders*	*Laid down*	*Launched*	*Completed*
KAVERI	F 110	Yarrow & Co Ltd Scotstoun Glasgow	28 Oct 1942	15 June 1943	21 Oct 1943
KISTNA	F 46	Yarrow & Co Ltd Scotstoun Glasgow	14 July 1942	22 Apr 1943	23 Aug 1943

Displacement, tons 1 470 standard; 1 925 full load
Length, feet (*metres*) 283·0 (*86·3*) pp; 295·5 (*90·1*) wl; 299·5 (*91·3*) oa
Beam, feet (*metres*) 38·5 (*11·7*)
Draught, feet (*metres*) 11·2 (*3·4*)
Guns 4—4 in (*102 mm*); 4—40 mm AA
A/S weapons 2 DCT
Main engines Parsons geared turbines; 2 shafts; 4 300 shp
Speed, knots 19
Boilers 2 three-drum type
Range, miles 4 500 at 12 knots
Oil fuel, tons 370
Complement 210

Former sloops of the British "Black Swan" class built for India and modified to suit Indian conditions. *Cauvery* was renamed *Kaveri* in 1968.

RADAR. Fitted with S band air and surface surveillance radar and ranging radar for the gunfire control system.

1 "RIVER" CLASS

TIR F 256 (ex-HMS *Bann*)

Displacement, tons 1 463 standard; 1 934 full load
Length, feet (*metres*) 283·0 (*86·3*) pp; 303 (*92·4*) oa
Beam, feet (*metres*) 37·6 (*11·2*)
Draught, feet (*metres*) 14·5 (*4·4*)
Guns 1—4 in (*102 mm*); 1—40 mm; 2—20 mm
Main engines Triple expansion; 2 shafts; 5 500 ihp
Speed, knots 18
Boilers 2 Admiralty 3-drum type
Range, miles 4 200 at 12 knots
Oil fuel, tons 385
Complement 120

Former "River" class frigate in the Royal Navy. Built by Charles Hill & Sons Ltd, Bristol. Laid down on 18 June 1942, launched on 29 Dec 1942, completed on 7 May 1942 and transferred on 3 Dec 1945. Converted to a Midshipman's Training Frigate by Bombay Dockyard in 1948. Originally the sister ship of *Investigator*, see under Survey Ships.

SUBMARINES

8 Ex-SOVIET "FOXTROT" CLASS

KALVARI	S 121	**VELA**	S 140
KANDERI	S 122	**VAGIR**	S 141
KARANJ	S 123	**VAGLI**	S 142
KURSURA	S 124	**VAGSHEER**	S 143

Displacement, tons 2 000 surface; 2 300 dived
Length, feet (*metres*) 296·8 (*90·5*)
Beam, feet (*metres*) 42·1 (*7·3*)
Draught, feet (*metres*) 19·0 (*5·8*)
Tubes 10—21 in (20 torpedoes carried)
Main machinery 3 diesels; 3 shafts; 6 000 bhp; 3 electric motors; 6 000 hp
Speed, knots 20 surface; 15 dived
Complement 70

Kalvari arrived in India on 16 July 1968, *Kanderi* in Jan 1969. *Karanj* in Oct 1970 and *Kursura* in Dec 1970. *Vela* Nov 1973, *Vagir* Dec 1973, *Vagli* Sept 1974, *Vagsheer* May 1975.

ADDITIONS. There are reports, so far unconfirmed, that a further pair may be transferred later.

KANDERI — *1971, Dr. Louis Th. Berge*

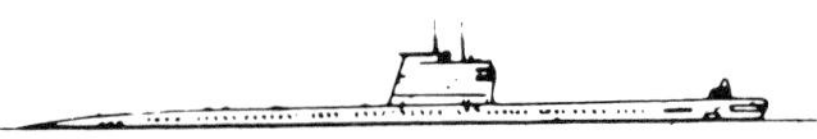

"FOXTROT" Class

Note: India is still discussing plans to build her own submarines though no details have been released.

LIGHT FORCES

NOTE. The first of a new class of Large Patrol Craft, believed to be slightly larger edition of *Abhay*, is under construction at Garden Reach, Calcutta.

8 Ex-SOVIET "OSA" CLASS (FAST ATTACK CRAFT—MISSILE)

NASHAK	P 684	**VEER**	P 686
NIPAT	P 691	**VIDYUT**	P 694
NIRBHIK	P 685	**VIJETA**	P 693
NIRGHAT	P 690	**VINASH**	P 692

Displacement, tons 165 standard; 200 full load
Dimensions, feet 128·7 × 25·1 × 5·9
Guns 4—30 mm (2 twin)
Main engines 3 diesels; 3 shafts; 13 000 bhp = 32 knots
Missile launchers 4 in two pairs for SSN 2A (Styx)

Some of these craft took part in a night attack with Styx off Karachi on 4-5 Dec 1971. They sank the PNS *Khaibar*, damaged *Badr* and a CMS as well as one Panamanian m/s without damage to themselves.

RADAR. Square Tie. IFF—Ski Pole.

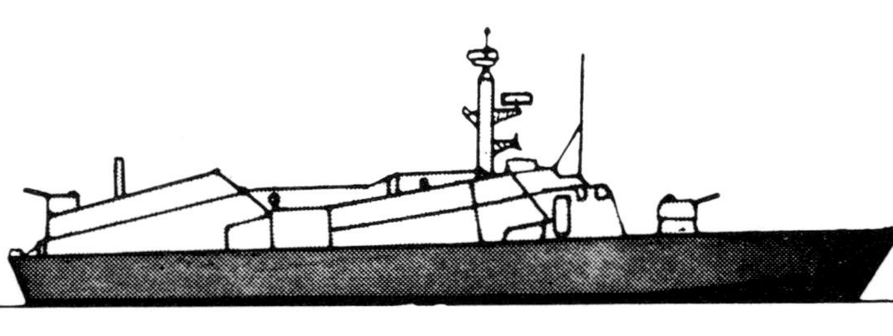

"OSA" Class

5 Ex-USSR "POLUCHAT" CLASS (COASTAL PATROL CRAFT)

PAMBAN P 247 **PANVEL** P 246 **PURI** P 248
PANAJI P 249 **PULICAT** P 250

Displacement, tons 86 standard; 91 full load
Dimensions, feet 98 × 15 × 4·8
Guns 2—14·5 mm (twin)
Main engines 2 Diesels; 2 shafts; 1 200 bhp = 18 knots
Range, miles 460 at 17 knots
Complement 16

Six originally supplied—one transferred to Bangladesh but returned

1 "ABHAY" CLASS (LARGE PATROL CRAFT)

ABHAY P3135

Displacement, tons 120 standard; 151 full load (*Ajay* 146)
Dimensions, feet 110 pp; 117·2 oa × 20 × 5
Gun 1—40 mm AA
Main engines 2 diesels; speed = 18 knots

Generally similar to the "Ford" class in the Royal Navy. Built by Hoogly Docking and Engineering Company Ltd, Calcutta and commissioned on 13 Nov 1961. *Ajay* and *Akshay* transferred to Bangladesh 1974, *Amar* to Mauritius April 1974.

1 "SHARADA" CLASS (COASTAL PATROL CRAFT)

SHARADA SPB 3133

Displacement, tons 86
Dimensions, feet 103·2 length
Guns Small arms
Main engines Diesels

Built in Yugoslavia. Commissioned on 5 Dec 1959.

4 "SAVITRI" CLASS (COASTAL PATROL CRAFT)

SAVITRI SPB 3128 **SHARAYU** SPB 3129 **SUBHADRA** SPB 3130 **SUVARNA** SPB 3131

Displacement, tons 63
Dimensions, feet 85·3 pp; 90·2 oa × 20 × 5
Guns Small Arms
Main engines 2 diesels; 2 shafts; 1 900 bhp = 21 knots

Built in Italy. Commissioned on 6 Feb 1958, 28 Oct 1957, 20 Aug 1957 and 28 Aug 1957, respectively. Constitute the 322nd SDB Squadron. *Sharayu* is Leader.

4 HDML TYPE (COASTAL PATROL CRAFT)

SPC 3110 (ex-*HDML* 1110) **SPC 3117** (ex-*HDML* 1117)
SPC 3112 (ex-*HDML* 1112) **SPC 3118** (ex-*HDML* 1118)

Displacement, tons 48 standard; 54 full load
Dimensions, feet 72 oa × 16 × 4·7
Guns 2—20 mm AA
Main engines Diesel; 2 shafts; 320 bhp = 12 knots
Complement 14

Former British Harbour Defence Motor Launches. These boats constitute the 321st Sea/Land Patrol Craft Squadron.

AMPHIBIOUS FORCES

3 Ex-SOVIET "POLNOCNY" CLASS

GHARIAL L 3032
GULDAR L 3033
GHORPAD L 3034

Displacement, tons	780 standard; 1 000 full load
Dimensions, ft (*m*)	246 × 29·5 × 9·8 (*75 × 9 × 3*)
Guns	2—30 mm
A/S weapons	2 18 barrelled MBU
Main engines	2 diesels; 5 000 bhp = 18 knots

First pair transferred from USSR in 1966 and *Ghorpad* in 1975.

"POLNOCNY" Class

MAGAR (ex-HMS *Avenger*, LST (3) 3011)

Displacement, tons	2 256 light; 4 980 full load
Dimensions, feet	347·5 oa × 55·2 × 11·2
Guns	2—40 mm AA; 6—20 mm AA; (2 twin, 2 single)
Main engines	Triple expansion; 2 shafts; 5 500 ihp = 13 knots

Former British tank landing ship of the LST (3) type transferred in 1949. There is also LCT 4294 (ex-1294), yard craft of 200 tons, 187·2 × 38·8 × 3·5 feet, speed 9·5 knots.

MAGAR — *1964, A. & J. Pavia*

MINE WARFARE FORCES

4 Ex-BRITISH "TON" CLASS (MINESWEEPERS—COASTAL)

CANNANORE (ex-*Whitton*) M 1191
KUDDALORE (ex-*Wennington*) M 1190
KAKINADA (ex-*Durweston*) M 1201
KARWAR (ex-*Overton*) Leader M 1197

Displacement, tons	360 standard; 425 full load
Dimensions, feet	140·0 pp; 153·0 oa × 28·8 × 8·2
Guns	2—20 mm AA
Main engines	Napier Deltic diesels; 2 shafts; 1 250 bhp = 15 knots
Oil fuel, tons	45
Range, miles	3 000 at 8 knots
Complement	40

"Ton" class coastal minesweepers of wooden construction built for the Royal Navy, but transferred from Great Britain to the Indian Navy in 1956. *Cannanore* was built by Fleetlands Shipyard, Ltd Gosport and launched 30 Jan 1956, *Karwar* was built by Camper & Nicholson, Ltd, Gosport, and launched 30 Jan 1956. *Kuddalore*, built by J. S. Doig Ltd, Grimsby, and *Kakinada*, built by Dorset Yacht Co Ltd, Hamworthy were taken over in Aug 1956, and sailed for India in Nov-Dec 1956. Named after minor ports in India. Constitute the 18th Mine Counter Measures Squadron, together with the inshore minesweepers.

4 Ex-BRITISH "HAM" CLASS (IMS)

BASSEIN (ex-*Littleham*) M 2707
BHATKAL M 89
BIMLIPITAN (ex-*Hildersham*) M 2705
BULSAR M 90

Displacement, tons	120 standard; 170 full load
Dimensions, feet	98·0 pp; 107·0 oa × 22·0 × 6·7
Gun	1—20 mm AA
Main engines	2 Paxman diesels; 550 bhp = 14 knots (9 knots sweeping)
Oil fuel, tons	15
Complement	16

"Ham" class inshore minesweepers of wooden construction two of which were built for the Royal Navy but transferred from Great Britain to the Indian Navy in 1955. *Bassein* was built by Brooke Marine Ltd, Oulton Broad, Lowestoft, and launched on 4 May 1954; *Bimlipitan* was built by Vosper Ltd, Portsmouth, and launched on 5 Feb 1954. Two further units were built at Magazon Dockyard Bombay. *Bhaktal* was launched in Apr 1967, and *Bulsar* on 17 May 1969.

Barq (ex-*MMS* 132), *MMS* 130 and *MMS* 154, former British motor minesweepers of the "105 ft" type of wooden construction, transferred from Great Britain, are employed as yard craft. *MMS* 1632 and *MMS* 1654 are yard craft in Bombay.

KARWAR — 1971, *Wright & Logan*

BASSEIN — *1971, A. & J. Pavia*

SURVEY SHIPS

DARSHAK

Displacement, tons	2 790
Length, feet (*metres*)	319 (*97·2*) oa
Beam, feet (*metres*)	49 (*14·9*)
Draught, feet (*metres*)	28·8 (*8·8*)
Main engines	2 diesel-electric units, 3 000 bhp
Speed, knots	16
Complement	150

DARSHAK

DARSHAK — *1967*

First ship built by Hindustan Shipyard, Vishakapatnam for the Navy. Launched on 2 Nov 1959 and commissioned on 28 Dec 1964. Provision was made to operate a helicopter. The ship is all welded.

Survey Ships—*continued*

1 "RIVER" CLASS (Ex-FRIGATE)

INVESTIGATOR F 243 (ex-*Khukri*, ex-HMS *Trent*)

Displacement, tons	1 460 standard; 1 930 full load
Length, feet (*metres*)	283 (*86·3*) pp; 303 (*92·4*) oa
Beam, feet (*metres*)	36·7 (*11·2*)
Draught, feet (*metres*)	14 (*4·3*)
Boilers	2 Admiralty 3-drum
Main engines	Triple expansion 5 500 shp; 2 shafts
Speed, knots	18
Range, miles	5 000 at 10 knots
Oil fuel, tons	400
Complement	172

INVESTIGATOR

INVESTIGATOR *1965, Indian Navy*

Former "River" class frigate in the Royal Navy. Built by Charles Hill & Sons Ltd, Bristol. Laid down on 31 Jan 1942, launched on 10 Oct 1942, completed on 15 Feb 1943, and transferred in April 1946. Converted to a survey ship and renamed *Investigator* in 1951. Originally the sister ship of the training frigate *Tir*.

2 "SUTLEJ" CLASS

(Ex-FRIGATES Ex-SLOOPS)

JUMNA F 11 **SUTLEJ** F 95

Displacement, tons	1 300 standard; 1 750 full load
Length, feet (*metres*)	276 (*84·1*) wl; 292·5 (*89·2*) oa
Beam, feet (*metres*)	37·5 (*11·4*)
Draught, feet (*metres*)	11·5 (*3·5*)
Boilers	2 Admiralty 3-drum
Main engines	Parsons geared turbines 3 600 shp; 2 shafts
Speed, knots	18
Range, miles	5 600 at 12 knots
Oil fuel, tons	370
Complement	150

JUMNA

JUMNA *1971, Indian Navy*

Former frigates employed as survey ships since 1957 and 1955 respectively. Both ships are generally similar to the former British frigates of the "Egret" class. *Jumna* and *Sutlej* together with *Kaveri* and *Kistna* (see previous page) formerly constituted the 12th Frigate Squadron.

CONSTRUCTION. Both built by Wm. Denny & Bros Ltd, Dumbarton. *Jumna* was laid down on 20 Feb 1940, launched on 16 Nov 1940 and completed on 13 May 1941. *Sutlej* was laid down on 4 Jan 1940, launched on 10 Oct 1940 and completed on 23 Apr 1941.

SERVICE FORCES

AMBA A 14 (SUBMARINE TENDER)

Displacement, tons	6 000 light; 9 000 full load
Dimensions, feet	370 pp; 420 oa × 65 × 20
Guns	4—3 in (*76 mm*) (Twins)
Main engines	Diesels; 2 shafts; 7 000 bhp = 17 knots

Modified "Ugra" type acquired from the USSR in 1968. Provision for helicopter.

RADAR. Slim Net.

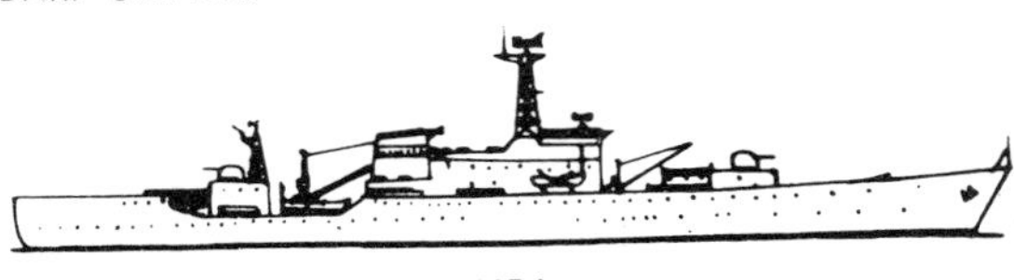

AMBA

NISTAR (SUBMARINE RESCUE SHIP)

Displacement, tons	790 standard; 900 full load
Dimensions, feet	220·0 × 29·5 × 7·9
Main engines	2 diesels; 2 shafts; 5 000 bhp = 18 knots

Converted from a fleet minesweeper of the Soviet "T 58" type to a submarine rescue ship and transferred from USSR late-1971.

DHARINI A 306 (ex-*Hermine*) (REPAIR SHIP)

Displacement, tons	1,530 (oil capacity 1 000)
Dimensions, feet	202 × 30·7 × 13
Main engines	Triple expansion; 809 ihp = 9 knots
Oil fuel, tons	621

Cargo ship converted to a tender. Commissioned in May 1960.

DHARINI *1964, Indian Navy*

DEEPAK A 1750 (REPLENISHMENT TANKER)

On charter to Indian Navy from Mogul Lines. Fleet replenishment tanker. Fitted with a helicopter landing platform aft, but no hangar.

SHAKTI A 136 (SUPPORT TANKER)

Displacement, tons	3 500
Dimensions, feet	323 × 44 × 20
Main engines	Diesel; speed = 13 knots

Rated as Fleet Replenishment Group Tanker. Acquired from Italy in Nov 1953.

HOOGHLY (SUPPORT TANKER)

Formerly *"Baqir"* of Gulf Shipping Corp. Ltd. Acquired in 1972.

DESH DEEP (SUPPORT TANKER)

Ex-merchant tanker taken over in 1972.

CHILKA **SAMBHAR** (HARBOUR TANKERS)

Displacemrnt. tons	1 530 (oil capacity 1 000)
Dimensions, feet	202 × 30·7 × 13
Main engines	Triple expansion; 809 ihp = 9 knots

Chilka built by Blythwood Shipbuilding Co, Scotstoun. *Sambhar* by A. & J. Inglis, Ltd, Glasgow, launched 1942. Both acquired in 1948. Engined by David Rowan & Co. Two steam dynamos, two steam pumps, ballast pump. Rated as yard craft.

HATHI (TUG—OCEAN)

Displacement, tons	668
Dimensions, feet	147·5 × 23·7 × 15
Main engines	Triple expansion; speed = 13 knots

Built by the Taikoo Dock & Engineering Company, Hong Kong. Launched in 1932.

INDONESIA

Administration

Commander-in-Chief of the Navy and Chief of the Naval Staff:
Admiral R. Subono

Deputy Chief of the Naval Staff Operations:
Rear-Admiral Wulujo Sugito

Inspector General of the Navy:
Commodore M. Wibowo

Chief for Naval Material:
Rear Admiral Sudiono

Chief for Naval Personnel:
Commodore R. Saheran

Commander of Navy Marine Corps:
Major General Moch, Anwar

Commander-in-Chief Indonesian Fleet:
Rear-Admiral Rudy Purwana

Diplomatic Representation

Naval Attaché in Bangkok:
Colonel Barata

Naval Attaché in Cairo:
Colonel Isnjoto

Naval Attaché in Canberra:
Colonel Sigir Sudarjadi

Naval Attaché in Delhi:
Colonel Sudarsono

Naval Attaché and Naval Attaché for Air in London:
Lt. Colonel Abu

Naval Attaché in Moscow:
Commodore R. Suhardjo

Naval Attaché in Tokyo:
Commodore Wardiman

Naval Attaché and Naval Attaché for Air in Washington:
Colonel Kko. Santose

Personnel

(a) 1975: 39 000 including 5 000 Marine Commando Corps and Naval Air Arm
(b) Selective National Service

Strength of the Fleet

Note. This is a formidable total of ships but the number truly operational is probably a fairly small proportion of that total.

Type	*Active*	*Building*
Frigates	12	—
Corvettes	16	—
Patrol Submarines	3	—
Fast Attack Craft—Missile	12	—
Fast Attack Craft—Torpedo	19	—
Large Patrol Craft	32	—
Coastal Patrol Craft	2	—
LST s	8	—
LCT s	6	—
Minesweepers—Ocean	6	—
Minesweepers—Coastal	11	—
Survey Ships	4	—
Submarine Tenders	3	—
Destroyer Depot Ship	1	—
Repair Ship	1	—
Support Tankers	8	—
Harbour Tankers	3	—
Cable Ship	1	—
Tugs	4	—
Auxiliary Patrol Craft	16	—
Training Ship	1	—

Ex-Soviet Ships

Indonesia obtained 104 ships from the USSR. Of these half have now been deleted and all will have gone by end 1976.

Future Plans

It is planned, over the next 20 years, to provide a Navy of some 25 000 seamen and 5 000 marines to man a Fleet including 4 fast A/S Frigates, some Submarines, Light Forces of Fast Attack Craft — Missile and —Torpedo Minelayers, Minesweepers, a fast HQ ship and a fast Supply Ship. Enquiries for frigate construction have already been made in Europe and tenders for four ships have been submitted by Germany, UK and Netherlands. Patrol craft will be built in Indonesia.

Naval Air Arm

6—C 47 and 3 Alouette III helicopters.

Disposals

Cruiser

1972 *Irian*

Destroyers

1973 *Brawidjaja, Sandjaja, Sultan Babarudin*

Frigates

1973 *Lambung Mangkurat, Slamet Rijadi*

Corvettes

1974 *Palu, Tenggiri*

Submarines

1974 *Alugoro, Hendradjala, Nagarangsang, Tjandrasa, Tjundmani, Trisula, Widjajadanu* (all "Whisky" class)

Amphibious Forces

1974 3 ex-Yugoslav LCTs

Minewarfare Forces

1974 4 ex-Dutch CMS, 5 "R" Class

Light Forces

1970 *310, 314, 315, 316* (Kraljevica), *Dorang, Lajang, Rubara*
1974 2 "Jaguar" class, 25 HDMLs, 10 Motor Launches

Survey Ships

1972 *Hidral*

Auxiliaries

1974 2 Transports, 1 Salvage Vessel, 1 Tug, 37 Patrol Craft

Mercantile Marine

Lloyd's Register of Shipping:
616 vessels of 762 278 tons gross

FRIGATES

4 Ex-US "CLAUD JONES" CLASS

Name	*No.*	*Builder*	*Laid down*	*Completed*	*Transferred*
SAMADIKUN (ex-USS *John R Perry* DE 1034)	D 1	Avondale Marine Ways	1 Oct 1957	5 May 1959	20 Feb 1973
MARTADINATA (ex-USS *Charles Berry* DE 1035)	D 2	Avondale Marine Ways	29 Oct 1958	25 Nov 1959	31 Jan 1974
NGURAH RAI (ex-*McMorris* DE 1036)	D 3	Avondale Marine Ways	5 Nov 1958	4 Mar 1960	16 Dec 1974
MONGINSIDI (ex-*Claud Jones* DE 1033)	D 4	Avondale Marine Ways	1 June 1957	10 Feb 1959	1975

Displacement, tons: 1 450 standard; 1 750 full load
Length, feet (*metres*): 310 (*95*) oa
Beam, feet (*metres*): 37 (*11·3*)
Draught, feet (*metres*): 18 (*5·5*)
Guns: 1—3 in 50 cal
A/S weapons: 2 triple Torpedo Tubes (Mk 32)
Main engines: 4 diesels; 9 200 hp; 1 shaft
Speed, knots: 22
Complement: 175

Samadikun acts as fleet flagship.

RADAR. SPS 6 and 10.

SONAR. SQS 29.

MARTADINATA (as *Charles Berry*) *USN*

4 Ex-USSR "RIGA" CLASS

JOS SUDARSO 351
KAKIALI 359
NGURAH RAI 353
NUKU 360

Displacement, tons: 1 200 standard; 1 600 full load
Length, feet (*metres*): 298·8 (*91*)
Beam, feet (*metres*): 33·7 (*10·2*)
Draught, feet (*metres*): 11 (*3·4*)
Guns, dual purpose: 3—3·9 in (*100 mm*) single mounts
Guns, AA: 4—37 mm
A/S weapons: 4 DC projectors
Torpedo tubes: 3—21 in (*533 mm*)
Mines: Fitted with mine rails
Boilers: 2
Main engines: Geared steam turbines; 2 shafts, 25 000 shp
Speed, knots: 28
Range, miles: 2 500 at 15 knots
Complement: 150

Transferred in 1964.

"RIGA" Class *Sergei Romanov*

RADAR. Slim Net search and warning; fire control Sun Visor A with Wasp Head director; navigation Neptun; IFF, High Pole A.

Frigates—*continued*

2 "SURAPATI" CLASS

SURAPATI 251 **IMAN BONDJOL** 250

Name	No.	Builders	Laid down	Launched	Completed
IMAN BONDJOL	250	Ansaldo, Leghorn	8 Jan 1956	5 May 1956	19 May 1958
SURAPATI	251	Ansaldo, Leghorn	8 Jan 1956	5 May 1956	28 May 1958

Displacement, tons	1 150 standard; 1 500 full load
Dimensions, ft (*m*)	325 × 36 × 8·5 (*99 × 11 × 2·6*)
Guns	4—4 in (*102 mm*) (twins) 6—30 mm (twins) 6—20 mm (twins)
A/S weapons	2 hedgehogs; 4 DCT
Torpedo tubes	3—21 in (*533 mm*)
Boilers	2 Foster Wheeler
Main engines	2 sets Parsons geared turbines, 2 shafts; 24 000 shp
Speed, knots	32
Range, miles	2 800 at 22 knots
Oil fuel, tons	350
Complement	200

Both completed in May 1958 by Ansaldo, Genoa. Near sisters of the "Almirante Clemente" class of Venezuela.

IMAN BONDJOL *Dr Ing Luigi Accorsi*

2 "PATTIMURA" CLASS

	Launched	Completed
PATTIMURA 252	1 July 1956	28 Jan 1958
SULTAN HASANUDIN 253	24 Mar 1957	8 Mar 1958

Displacement, tons	950 standard; 1 200 full load
Length, feet (*metres*)	246 (*75·0*) pp; 270·2 (*82·4*) oa
Beam, feet (*metres*)	34 (*10·4*)
Draught, feet (*metres*)	9 (*2·7*)
Guns, AA	2—3 in (*76 mm*) 40 cal. 2—30 mm 70 cal twin
A/S weapons	2 hedgehogs; 4 DCT
Main engines	3 Ansaldo-Fiat diesels; 3 shafts; 6 900 bhp
Speed, knots	22
Range, miles	2 400 at 18 knots
Oil fuel, tons	100
Complement	110

Both laid down on 8 Jan 1956 by Ansaldo, Leghorn. Similar to Italian "Albatros" class.

PATTIMURA *Dr Ing Luigi Accorsi*

CORVETTES

13 Ex-USSR "KRONSTADT" CLASS

BARAKUDA 817
KAKAP 816
KATULA 811
LANDJURU
LAPAI
LUMBA LUMBA
MADIDIHANG
MOMARE
PANDRONG 814
SURA 815
TOHOK 829
TONGKOL
TJUTJUT

Displacement, tons	310 standard; 380 full load
Dimensions, ft (*m*)	170·6 × 21·5 × 9 (*52·0 × 6·5 × 2·7*)
Guns	1—3·5 in; 2—37 mm AA; 4—25 mm AA
A/S weapons	Depth charge projectors
Mines	2 mine rails for 10 mines
Main engines	3 Diesels; 3 shafts; 3 300 bhp = 24 knots
Oil fuel, tons	20
Range, miles	1 500 at 12 knots
Complement	65

"KRONSTADT" Class

Built in 1951-54. Transferred to the Indonesian Navy on 30 Dec 1958.

RADAR. Ball Gun or Don 2; IFF, High Pole A

3 Ex-US PC TYPE

HIW (ex-USS *Malvern, PC* 580) 318
TJAKALANG (ex-USS *Pierre, PC* 1141) 313
TORANI (ex-USS *Manville, PC* 581) 317

Displacement, tons	280 standard; 450 full load
Dimensions, feet	170 wl; 173·7 oa × 23 × 10·8
Guns	1—3 in; 1—40 mm AA; 2—20 mm AA; 4 DCT
Main engines	2 GM diesels; 2 shafts; 2 880 bhp = 20 knots
Oil fuel, tons	60
Range, miles	5 000 at 10 knots
Complement	54 (4 officers, 50 men)

Built in 1942-43. *Pierre* transferred from the US Navy at Pearl Harbour, Hawaii in Oct 1958 and *Malvern* and *Manville* in Mar 1960.

PC TYPE *1966, Indonesian Navy*

SUBMARINES

3 Ex-USSR "WHISKY" CLASS

BRAMASTRA 412
NAGABANDA 403
PASOPATI 410

Displacement, tons	1 030 surface; 1 180 submerged
Length, feet (*metres*)	240 (*73·2*)
Beam feet (*metres*)	22 (*6·7*)
Draught, feet (*metres*)	15 (*4·6*)
Torpedo tubes	6—21 in (*533 mm*) 4 forward, 2 aft; 18 torpedoes carried
Mines	40 in lieu of torpedoes
Main machinery	4 000 bhp diesels; 2 500 hp electric motors, diesel-electric drive; 2 shafts
Speed, knots	17 on surface; 15 dived
Range, miles	13 000 at 8 knots surfaced
Complement	60

"WHISKY" Class

The four Soviet submarines of the "W" class, which arrived in Indonesia on 28 June 1962, brought the total number of this class transferred to Indonesia to 14 units, but it was reported that only six would be maintained operational, while six would be kept in reserve and two used for spare parts. Now reduced to three operational boats of which two are being refitted and receiving new batteries.

LIGHT FORCES

12 Ex-USSR "KOMAR" CLASS

(FAST ATTACK CRAFT—MISSILE)

GUAWIDJAJA **HARDADALI** **KALAMISANI** **KALANADA** **KATJABOLA** **KELAPLINTAH** **PULANGGENI** **NAGAPASA** **SUROTAMA** **SARPAMINA** **SARPAWASESA** **TRITUSTA**

Displacement, tons	70 standard; 80 full load
Dimensions, ft (*m*)	83·7 × 19·8 × 5 (*25·5 × 6·0 × 1·8*)
Guns	2—35 mm AA (1 twin)
Guided weapons	2 launchers for SSN2A (Styx)
Main engines	4 diesels; 4 800 hp = 40 knots
Range, miles	400 at 30 knots

Six were transferred to Indonesia in 1961-63, four more in Sep 1964 and two in 1965.

5 GERMAN-BUILT "JAGUAR" CLASS

(FAST ATTACK CRAFT—TORPEDO)

ANOA 602 **BIRUANG** 603 **HARIMAU** 604 **MATJAN KUMBANG** 605 **SERIGALA** 607

Displacement, tons	160 standard; 190 full load
Dimensions, feet	131 pp; 138 oa × 22 × 7·5
Guns	2—40 mm AA (single)
Torpedo tubes	4—21 in
Main engines	4 Daimler-Benz diesels; 4 shafts; 12 000 bhp = 42 knots
Complement	39

Built by Lürssen, Bremen-Vegesack in 1959-60. The first four boats had wooden hulls.

HARIMAU *Indonesia*

14 Ex-USSR "P6" CLASS (FAST ATTACK CRAFT—TORPEDO)

ANGIN BADAI **ANGIN BOHOROK** **ANGIN BRUBU** **ANGIN GENDING** **ANGIN GRENGGONG** **ANGIN KUMBANG** **ANGIN PASAT** **ANGIN PRAHARA** **ANGIN PUJUH** **ANGIN RIBUT** **ANGIN TAUFAN** **ANGIN TONGGI** **ANGIN WAMANDAIS** **ANGIN WAMBRAU**

Displacement, tons	66 standard; 75 full load
Dimensions, ft (*m*)	84·2 × 20 × 6 (*25·7 × 6·1 × 1·8*)
Guns	4—25 mm AA (2 twin)
Tubes	2—21 in (single)
Main engines	4 Diesels; 4 800 bhp; 4 shafts = 43 knots
Range, miles	450 at 30 knots
Complement	25

A total of 14 were reported delivered since 1961, eight in 1961, and six in 1962. Fitted with *Skinhead* target detection radar.

ANGIN KUMBANG *1968, Indonesian Navy*

18 Ex-USSR "BK" CLASS (LARGE PATROL CRAFT)

Displacement, tons	120
Dimensions, feet	124·7 × 19 × 4·6
Guns	1—85 mm; 4—25 mm AA
Main engines	Diesels; speed 20 knots

First of class transferred from the USSR to Indonesia in 1962.

3 Ex-USN PGM TYPE (LARGE PATROL CRAFT)

SILUNGKANG (ex-*PGM 55*) 572
WAITATIRE (ex-*PGM 56*) 571
KALAKUANG (ex-*PGM 57*) 570

Displacement, tons	122 full load
Dimensions, feet	100 × 21 × 8·5
Guns	2—20 mm AA 2 MG
Main engines	2 diesels, 2 shafts = 17 knots
Transferred 1965.	

Used as Amphibious Control Craft.

2 Ex-AUSTRALIAN "ATTACK" CLASS

(LARGE PATROL CRAFT)

SUBARO (ex-*Bandolier*) — (ex-*Archer*)

Displacement, tons	146 full load
Dimensions, feet	107·5 × 20 × 7·3
Guns	1—40 mm; 2 medium MG s
Main engines	2 Paxman diesels; 2 shafts = 21 knots
Complement	19 (3 officers 16 men)

Transferred from RAN after refit—*Bandolier* 16 Nov 1973, *Archer* in 1974. It is reported, though not confirmed, that another six may be transferred.

6 Ex-YUGOSLAVIAN "KRALJEVICA" CLASS

(LARGE PATROL CRAFT)

BUBARA **DORANG** **KRAPU** **LAJANG** **LEMADANG** **TODAK**

Displacement, tons	190 standard; 245 full load
Dimensions, feet	134·5 × 20·8 × 7
Guns	1—3 in; 1—40 mm AA; 6—20 mm AA
A/S weapons	DC
Main engines	2 MAN diesels; 2 shafts; 3 300 bhp = 20 knots
Oil fuel, tons	15
Range, miles	1 500 at 12 knots
Complement	54

Former Yugoslavian craft of the "Kraljevica" class. Purchased and transferred on 27th Dec 1958.

DORANG *1968, Indonesian Navy*

3 "MAWAR" CLASS (LARGE PATROL CRAFT)

KALAHITAM **KELABANG** **KOMPAS**

Displacement, tons	147
Guns	40 mm AA
Main engines	2 diesels; speed 21 knots

Indonesian built.

KALAHITAM *1968, Indonesian Navy*

2 FAIREY MARINE "SPEAR" CLASS

(COASTAL PATROL CRAFT)

Dimensions, ft (*m*)	29·8 × 9·2 × 2·6 (*9·1 × 2·8 × ·8*)
Main engines	Twin 180 hp diesels
Speed, knots	30
Range, miles	200 at 26 knots

Purchased in 1973-74

AMPHIBIOUS VESSELS

7 Ex-US LCT TYPE

TANDJUNG NUSANIVE	(ex-USS *Lawrence City* LST 889)	887
TELUK BAJUR	(ex-USS *LST 616*)	502
TELUK KAU	(ex-USS *LST 652*)	504
TELUK SALEH	(ex-USS *Clarke County LST* 601)	510
TELUK MANADO	(ex-USS *LST 657*)	505
TELUK BONE	(ex-USS *Iredell County LST 839*)	511
TELUK LANGSA	(ex-USS *LST 1128*)	501

Displacement, tons	1 653 standard; 4 080 full load
Dimensions, feet	316 wl; 328 oa × 50 × 14
Guns	7—40 mm AA; 2—20 mm AA
Main engines	GM diesels; 2 shafts; 1 700 bhp = 11·6 knots
Oil fuel tons	600
Range, miles	7 200 at 10 knots
Cargo capacity	2 100 tons
Complement	119 (accommodation for 266)

TRANSFERS:
505 in Mar 1960, 887 in Dec 1960, 502, 510 and 511 in June 1961, 504 and 501 in July 1970.

3 Ex-US LC1 TYPE

AMAHAI (ex-*Tropenvogel, LCI* 467) 864 **MARICH** (ex-*Zeemeeuw*) 866 **PIRU** (ex-*Zeearend, LCI* 420) 868

Displacement, tons	250 standard; 381 full load
Dimensions, feet	158 × 23 × 7
Guns	1—37 mm; 2 Vickers MG
Main engines	GM diesels; 1 800 bhp = 15 knots
Complement	60

Former US infantry landing craft. Turned over from Netherlands East Indies Government on formation of Indonesian Navy in 1950. Sister ship *Baruna* (ex-*Ijsvogel* LCI 948) and *Namlea* (ex-*Stormvogel* LCI 588) were rerated as pilot ship and light ship in 1961.

1 JAPANESE TYPE

TELUK AMBOINA LST 869

Displacement, tons	2 200 standard; 4 800 full load
Dimensions, feet	327 × 50 × 15
Guns	2—85 mm; 4—40 mm
Main engines	MAN diesels; 2 shafts; 3 000 bhp = 13·1 knots
Oil fuel, tons	1 200
Range, miles	4 000 at 13·1 knots
Complement	88 (accommodation for 300)

Built in Japan. Launched on 17 Mar 1961 and transferred in June 1961.

2 Ex-"LCVT" TYPE

DORE **AMURANG**

Displacement, tons	182 standard; 275 full load
Dimensions, feet	125·7 × 32·8 × 5·9
Main engines	Diesels; 210 hp = 8 knots
Complement	17

1 Ex-USSR LCT TYPE

TELUK PARIGI

Displacement, tons	600 standard; 800 full load
Dimensions, feet	246·0 × 39·3 × 9·8
Main engines	Diesels; 2 shafts; 2 200 hp = 10 knots

MINE WARFARE FORCES

6 Ex-USSR "T43" CLASS (MINESWEEPERS—OCEAN)

PULAU RANI **PULAU RADJA** **PULAU RATENO** **PULAU RONDO** **PULAU ROON** **PULAU RORBAS**

Displacement, tons	500 standard; 610 full load
Dimensions, ft (*m*)	190·2 × 28·2 × 6·9 (*58 × 8·6 × 2·1*)
Guns	4—37 mm AA; 4—25 mm AA
Main engines	2 diesels; 2 shafts; 2 000 bhp = 17 knots
Range, miles	1 600 at 10 knots
Complement	40

Transferred to Indonesia by the USSR, four in 1962 and two in 1964
Pulau Rondo is in reserve.

6 Ex-US "BLUEBIRD" CLASS (MINESWEEPERS—COASTAL)

PULAU ALOR (ex-*Meadowlark*)	717
PULAU ANJER (ex-*Limpkin*)	719
PULAU ANTANG (ex-*Frigate Bird*)	721
PULAU ARU (ex-*Falcon*)	722
PULAU ARUAN (ex-*Jacana*)	718
PULAU IMPALASA (ex-*Humming Bird*)	720

Displacement, tons	320 light; 370 full load
Dimensions, feet	138·0 pp; 144·0 oa × 28·0 × 8·2
Guns	2—20 mm AA (1 twin)
Main engines	Packard diesels; 2 shafts; 1 200 bhp = 12·5 knots
Complement	39

Transferred from the USN in 1971; *Falcon* (24 June), *Frigate Bird* (11 Aug), *Humming Bird* (12 July), *Jacana* (12 July), *Limpkin* (24 June), *Meadowlark* (11 Aug). All have wooden hulls with low magnetic signature.

5 "R" CLASS (MINESWEEPERS—COASTAL)

PULAU RAU **PULAU RENGAT** **PULAU RINDJA** **PULAU RUPAT** **PULAU RUSA**

Displacement, tons	139·4 standard
Dimensions, feet	129 × 18·7 × 5
Guns	1—40 mm AA; 2—20 mm AA
Main engines	2 MAN diesels; 12 cyl; 2 800 bhp = 24·6 knots
Complement	26

Built by Abeking & Rasmussen Jacht-und Bootswerft, Lemwerder in 1954-57. Originally a class of ten. These boats have a framework of light metal covered with wood.

"R" Class *Indonesian Navy*

SURVEY SHIPS

BURUDJULASAD 1006

Displacement, tons	2 150 full load
Dimensions, feet	269·5 × 37·4 × 11·5
Machinery	4 MAN diesels; 2 shafts; 6 850 bhp = 19·1 knots
Complement	113

Burudjulasad was launched in 1966; her equipment includes laboratories for oceanic and meteorological research, a cartographic room, and a helicopter.

BURDIAMHAL

Displacement, tons	1 500 full load
Dimensions, feet	211·7 oa; 192 pp × 33·2 × 10
Main engines	2 Werkspoor diesels; 1 160 bhp = 10 knots
Complement	90

Built by Scheepserf De Waal, Zaltbommel. Launched on 6 Sep 1952. Completed on 6 July 1953.

JALANIDHI

Displacement, tons	985
Complement	58

Launched in 1962.

ARIES (ex-*Samudera*)

Measurement, tons	200 gross
Dimensions, feet	125·2 × 21·5 × 9·8
Main engines	Werkspoor diesel engines; 450 bhp

Built by Ferus Smit, Foxol. Launched on 28 May 1952. Completed on 28 Aug 1952. Same type as "Bango" class motor patrol vessels. Equipped as a laboratory ship, used for deep sea exploration in Indonesian waters. Another survey ship, *Dewa Kembar*, was laid up in reserve in Feb 1972.

SERVICE FORCES

MULTATULI 476 (SUBMARINE TENDER)

Displacement, tons	3 220
Dimensions, feet	338 pp; 365·3 oa × 52·5 × 23
Guns	1—85 mm; 4—40 mm (single mountings)
Main engines	B & W diesel; 5 500 bhp = 18·5 knots
Oil fuel, tons	1 400
Range, miles	6 000 at 16 knots cruising speed
Complement	134

Built in Japan by Ishikawajima-Harima Heavy Industries Co. Ltd. as a submarine tender. Launched on 15 May 1961. Delivered to Indonesia Aug 1961. Flush decker. Capacity for replenishment at sea (fuel oil, fresh water, provisions, ammunition, naval stores and personnel). Medical and hospital facilities. Equipment for supplying compressed air, electric power and distilled water to submarines. Air-conditioning and mechanical ventilation arrangements for all living and working quarters.

1 Ex-USSR "ATREK" CLASS (SUBMARINE TENDER)

THAMRIN

Displacement, tons	3 500 standard; 6 700 full load
Measurement, tons	3 258 gross
Dimensions, feet	336 × 49 × 20
Main engines	Steam expansion and exhaust turbine; 2 450 ihp = 13 knots
Boilers	2
Range, miles	3 500 at 13 knots

Built in 1955-57 and converted to naval use from a mercantile freighter. Arrived in Indonesia on 28 June 1962.

1 Ex-USSR "DON" CLASS (SUBMARINE TENDER)

RATULANGI

Displacement, tons	6 700 standard; 9 000 full load
Dimensions, feet	458·9 × 57·7 × 22·3
Guns	4—3·9 in; 8—57 mm AA
Main engines	Diesels; 14 000 bhp = 21 knots approx
Complement	300

A submarine support ship, escort vessel and maintenance tender transferred from the USSR to Indonesia in 1962, arriving in Indonesia in July. Fitted with SLIM NET search and warning radar and with fire control radar.

RATULANGI *1968, Indonesian Navy*

DJAJA WIDJAJA (ex-USS *Askari* 9109, ex-*ARL* 30, ex-*LST* 1131) 9017 (REPAIR SHIP)

Displacement, tons	1 625 light; 4 100 full load
Dimensions, feet	316·0 wl; 328·0 oa × 50·0 × 11·0
Guns	8—40 mm AA (2 quadruple)
Main engines	General Motors diesels; 2 shafts; 1 800 bhp = 11·6 knots
Complement	280

Of wartime construction this ship was in reserve from 1956-66. She was recommissioned and reached Vietnam in 1967 to support River Assault Flotilla One. She was used by the USN and Vietnamese Navy working up the Mekong in support of the Cambodian operations in May 1970. Transferred on lease to Indonesia at Guam on 31 Aug 1971.

DUMAI (ex-USS *Tidewater*) AD 31 (DESTROYER DEPOT SHIP)

Displacement, tons	8 165 standard; 16 635 full load
Dimensions, feet	465 wl; 492 oa × 69·5 × 27·2
Guns	1—5 in; 38 cal dp
Main engines	Geared turbines; 1 shaft; 8 500 shp = 18·4 knots
Boilers	2 Babcock & Wilcox
Complement	778

Transferred Feb 1971 as destroyer depot ship. Also used to maintain off-shore drilling rigs.

2 Ex-USSR TYPE (SUPPORT TANKERS)

BUNJU 904 **SAMBU** 903

Displacement, tons	2 170 standard; 6 170 full load
Dimensions, feet	350·5 × 49·2 × 20·2
Guns	2—20 mm
Main engines	Polar diesel; 1 shaft; 2 650 bhp = 10 knots
Oil fuel, tons	390
Cargo capacity	4 739 tons
Complement	71

Transferred to the Indonesian Navy on 19 June 1959. Both laid up in 1969.

TJEPU (ex-*Scandus*, ex-*Nordhem*) 901 (SUPPORT TANKER)

Displacement, tons	1 372
Measurement, tons	1 042 gross
Dimensions, feet	226·5 × 34 × 14·2
Main engines	Polar diesel; 1 shaft; 850 bhp = 11 knots

Built in Sweden in 1949. Acquired in 1951. Laid up in 1969.

5 Ex-USSR "UDA" CLASS (SUPPORT TANKERS)

BALIKPAPAN **PANGKALAN BRANDAN** **WONOKROMO** +2

Displacement, tons	5 500 standard; 7 200 full load
Dimensions, feet	400·3 × 51·8 × 20·3
Main engines	Diesels; 2 shafts; 8 000 bhp = 17 knots

TARAKAN **BULA** (HARBOUR TANKERS)

Displacement, tons	1 340 full load
Dimensions, feet	352·0 × 37·7 × 14·8
Main engines	Diesels; 1 shaft; 1 500 bhp = 13 knots

PAKAN BARU (HARBOUR TANKER)

Displacement, tons	1 500 full load
Dimensions, feet	63 × 11·5 × 4·5
Main engines	Diesels; 2 shafts; 800 bhp = 11 knots

CABLE SHIP

BIDUK

Displacement, tons	1 250 standard
Dimensions, feet	213·2 oa × 39·5 × 11·5
Main engines	1 Triple expansion engine; 1 600 ihp = 12 knots
Complement	66

Cable Layer, Lighthouse Tender, and multi-purpose naval auxiliary. Built by J. & K. Smit, Kinderijk. Launched on 30 Oct 1951. Completed on 30 July 1952.

TUGS

RAKATA (ex-USS *Menominee*, *ATF* 73) 928

Displacement, tons	1 235 standard; 1 675 full load
Dimensions, feet	195 wl; 205 oa × 38·5 × 15·5
Guns	1—3 in; 4—40 mm AA; 2—20 mm
Main engines	4 diesels with electric drive; 3 000 bhp = 16·5 knots
Complement	85

Former American fleet ocean tug of the "Apache" class. Launched on 14 Feb 1942. Transferred from the United States Navy to the Indonesian Navy at San Diego in Mar 1961.

LAMPO BATANG 934 **TAMBORA** 935

Displacement, tons	250
Dimensions, feet	92·3 oa; 86·7 pp × 23·2 × 11·3
Main engines	2 diesels; 1 200 bhp = 11 knots
Oil fuel, tons	18
Range, miles	1 000 at 11 knots
Complement	43

Ocean tug. Built in Japan. Launched in April 1961. Delivered in Nov 1961.

BROMO 936

Displacement, tons	150
Dimensions, feet	71·7 wl; 79 oa × 21·7 × 9·7
Main engines	MAN diesel; 2 shafts; 600 bhp = 10·5 knots
Oil fuel, tons	9
Range, miles	690 at 10·5 knots
Complement	15

Harbour tugs. Built in Japan. Launched in June 1961. Delivered in Aug 1961.

AUXILIARY PATROL CRAFT

10 DKN TYPE

DKN 901-910

Displacement, tons	140
Dimensions, feet	128 × 19 × 5·2
Guns	4—20 mm AA
Main engines	Maybach diesels; 2 shafts; 3 000 bhp = 24·5 knots

Patrol craft and police boats. 901, 902 and 904 were built by Lürssen, Vegesack, 903 and 905 by Abeking & Rasmussen Lemwerder.

6 "PAT" CLASS

PAT 01 **PAT 02** **PAT 03** **PAT 04** **PAT 05** **PAT 06**

Dimensions, feet	91·9 pp; 100 oa × 17 × 6
Main engines	2 Caterpillar diesels; 340 bhp

TRAINING SHIP

DEWARUTJI

Displacement, tons	810 standard; 1 500 full load
Dimensions, feet	191·2 oa; 136·2 pp × 31·2 × 13·9
Main engines	MAN diesels; 600 bhp = 10·5 knots
Complement	110 (32 + 78 midshipmen)

Built in Germany by H. C. Stülcken & Sohn, Hamburg. Launched on 24 Jan 1953. Completed on 9 July 1953. Barquentine of iron construction. Sail area, 1 305 sq yds (*1 091 sq metres*). Speed with sails 12·8 knots.

IRAN

Administration

Commander-in-Chief Imperial Iranian Navy:
Vice Admiral R. A. Attaie

Diplomatic Representation

Naval Attaché in London:
Commander F. Fiuzi

Naval Attaché in Washington:
Captain Movaghari

Personnel

(a) 1975: 13 000 officers and men
(b) 2 years National Service

Note. A Naval Infantry Division is being formed.

Strength of the Fleet

Type	*Active*	*Building/ (Planned)*
Destroyers	3	6
Frigates	4	(4)
Corvettes	4	—
Large Patrol Craft	7	(?12)
Coastal Patrol Craft	9	—
Hovercraft	12	2
Landing Craft	2	—
Minesweepers—Coastal	4	—
Minesweepers—Inshore	2	—
Supply Ships	—	2
Repair Ships	2	—
Harbour Tanker	1	—
Water Boat	1	—
Tug	1	—
Yachts	2	—
Floating Docks	2	—
Fast Attack Craft (Missile)	—	6

New Construction

Interest is being shown by Iranian authorities in the building of both frigates and submarines. No details or orders have yet been released
There are other reports of interest in an "Invincible" class command-cruiser.

Bases

Persian Gulf: Bandar Abbas (MHQ)
Khorramshar (Light Forces)
Kharg Island
Indian Ocean: Chah Bar (under construction)
Caspian Sea: Bandar—Pahlavi (Training)

Mercantile Marine

Lloyd's Register of Shipping:
115 vessels of 291 928 tons

Naval Air

Helicopters—4 AB 205-A, 14 AB 206-A, 6 AB-212, 10 SH-3D
Maritime Patrol a/c—6 P-3 Orions on order (first delivered late 1974)

DESTROYERS

0 + 6 US "SPRUANCE" CLASS

Displacement, tons	7 800 full load
Dimensions, ft (*m*)	563·3 oa × 55 × 29 (*171·1 × 17·6 × 8·8*)
Missiles	Sea-Sparrow multiple launcher
Guns	2—5 in Mk 45, 54 cal DP (single)
A/S weapons	1 helicopter; 1 Asroc; 2 triple Mk 32 torpedo tubes
Main engines	4 gas turbines; 80 000 shp; 2 shafts
Speed, knots	30+
Complement	250

Ordered from Litton Industries, USA, in 1974, first to be delivered in 1978.

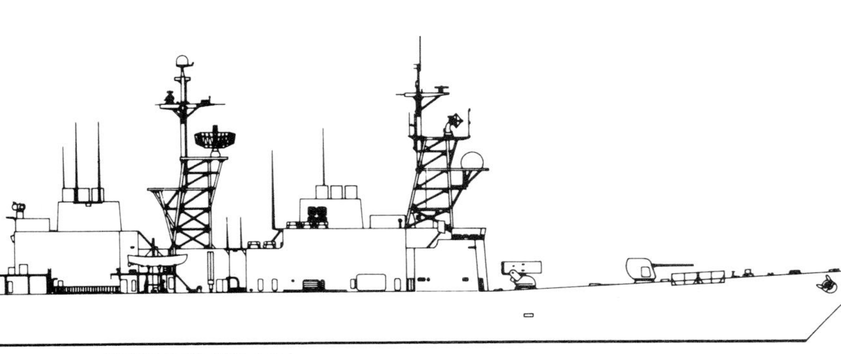

SPRUANCE (DD 963)

1 Ex-BRITISH "BATTLE" CLASS

Name	*No*	*Builders*	*Laid down*	*Launched*	*Completed*
ARTEMIZ (ex-HMS *Sluys*, D 60)	D 5	Cammell Laird & Co Ltd, Birkenhead	24 Nov 1943	28 Feb 1945	30 Sep 1946

Displacement, tons	2 325 standard; 3 360 full load
Length, feet (*metres*)	355·0 (*108·2*) pp; 379·0 (*115·5*) oa
Beam, feet (*metres*)	40·5 (*12·3*)
Draught, feet (*metres*)	17·5 (*5·2*)
Guns	4—4·5 in (*115 mm*) 2 twin forward; 8—40 mm Bofors AA
Missile launchers	1 quadruple "Seacat" AA aft
A/S weapons	1 "Squid" 3-barrelled DC mortar
Main engines	Parsons geared turbines; 2 shafts; 50 000 shp
Speed, knots	35·5
Boilers	2 Admiralty 3-drum type
Oil fuel, tons	680
Range, miles	3 000 at 20 knots
Complement	270

Transferred to Iran at Southampton on 26 Jan 1967, and handed over to the Imperial Iranian Navy after a 3-year modernisation refit by the Vosper Thornycroft Group.

MISSILES. Standard missiles to be fitted in 1975.

RADAR. Search: Plessey AWS 1. Air surveillance with on-mounted IFF; Contraves Sea-Hunter fire control; Decca RDL 1 radar intercept; Racal DF equipment.

ARTEMIZ *1971*

ARTEMIZ

Destroyers—*continued*

2 EX-US "ALLEN M. SUMNER" CLASS

Name	No.	Builders	Launched	Commissioned
BABR (ex-USS *Zellars*, DD 777)	D 7	Todd Pacific Shipyards	19 July 1944	25 Oct 1944
PALANG (ex-USS *Stormes*, DD 780)	D 9	Todd Pacific Shipyards	4 Nov 1944	27 Jan 1945

Displacement, tons	2 200 standard; 3 320 full load
Length, feet (*metres*)	376·5 (*114·8*) oa
Beam, feet (*metres*)	40·9 (*12·4*)
Draught, feet (*metres*)	19 (*5·8*)
Missiles	4 Standard launchers with 7 reloads each
Aircraft	1 A/S helicopter
Guns	4—5 inch (*127 mm*) 38 calibre dual-purpose (twin)
ASW weapons	2 fixed Hedgehogs; depth charges 2 triple torpedo launchers (Mk 32)
Main engines	2 geared turbines; 60 000 shp; 2 shafts
Boilers	4
Speed, knots	34
Complement	274 (14 officers, 260 ratings) (designed wartime 345)

Two "FRAM II" conversion destroyers of the "Allen M Sumner" class nominally transferred to Iran from the USN in March 1971 for delivery in 1972.
USS *Gainard* (DD 706) was taken over in Mar 1971, but, being beyond repair, was used for spares and training; being replaced by USS *Stormes* (DD 780).

CONVERSION. Both ships received a full refit as well as conversion at Philadelphia NSY before sailing for Iran. This included a much-improved air-conditioning layout, the removal of B gun-mount with its magazine, altered accommodation, the fitting of a Canadian telescopic hangar, the siting of the four Standard missile launches beside the new torpedo stowage between the funnels and the rigging of VDS.

RADAR. SPS 10 search; SPS 37 air-surveillance with on-mounted IFF; Gun fire control system Mk 56 with radar on director.

SONAR. SQS 23 or SQS 29; VDS.

SPARES. Ex-US *Kenneth D. Bailey* (DD 713) purchased 13 Jan 1975 for spares.

BABR and PALANG (after conversion) *1975*

BABR (as ZELLARS before conversion) *United States Navy*

FRIGATES

Note. It is reported that four PF 109 frigates were ordered from USA in late 1974.

4 "SAAM" CLASS

Name	No.	Builders	Laid down	Launched	Completed
FARAMAZ	DE 18	Vosper Thornycroft, Woolston	25 July 1968	30 July 1969	28 Feb 1972
ROSTAM	DE 16	Vickers, Newcastle & Barrow	10 Dec 1967	4 Mar 1969	June 1972
SAAM	DE 12	Vosper Thornycroft, Woolston	22 May 1967	25 July 1968	20 May 1971
ZAAL	DE 14	Vickers, Barrow	3 Mar 1968	4 Mar 1969	1 Mar 1971

Displacement, tons	1 110 standard; 1 290 full load
Length, feet (*metres*)	310·0 (*94·4*) oa
Beam, feet (*metres*)	34·0 (*10·4*)
Draught, feet (*metres*)	11·2 (*3·4*)
Missile launchers	1 quintuple "Seakiller" surface-to-surface; 1 triple "Seacat" surface-to-air
Guns	1—4·5 in (*115 mm*) Mk 8 (Mk 5 in *Saam, Zaal*) 2—35 mm Oerlikon (1 twin) AA
A/S weapons	1 "Limbo" 3-barrelled DC mortar
Main engines	2 Rolls-Royce "Olympus" gas turbines; 2 Paxman diesels; 2 shafts; 46 000 + 3 800 shp
Speed, knots	40
Complement	125 (accommodation for 146)

GENERAL
It was announced on 25 Aug 1966 that Vosper Ltd, Portsmouth had received an order for four vessels for the Iranian Navy. Air-conditioned throughout. Fitted with Vosper stabilisers. *Rostam* was towed to Barrow for completion.

RADAR. Plessey AWS 1 air surveillance with on-mounted IFF. Two Contraves Seahunter systems for control of 35 mm, Seakillers and Seacats. Decca RDL 1 passive DF equipment.

FARAMAZ *1972, C. & S. Taylor*

CORVETTES

4 US PF TYPE

Name	No.	Builders	Laid down	Launched	Completed
BAYANDOR	F 25 (ex-USS *PF* 103)	Levingstone Shipbuilding Co, Orange, Texas	20 Aug 1962	7 July 1963	18 May 1964
KAHNAMUIE	F 28 (ex-USS *PF* 106)	Levingstone Shipbuilding Co, Orange, Texas	12 June 1967	4 Apr 1968	13 Feb 1969
MILANIAN	F 27 (ex-USS *PF* 105)	Levingstone Shipbuilding Co, Orange, Texas	1 May 1967	4 Jan 1968	13 Feb 1969
NAGHDI	F 26 (ex-USS *PF* 104)	Levingstone Shipbuilding Co, Orange, Texas	12 Sep 1962	10 Oct 1963	22 July 1964

Displacement, tons	900 standard; 1 135 full load
Length, feet (*metres*)	275·0 (*83·8*) oa
Beam, feet (*metres*)	33·0 (*10·0*)
Draught, feet (*metres*)	10·2 (*3·1*)
Guns	2—3 in (*76 mm*); 2—40 mm AA
A/S weapons	1 Hedgehog, 4 DCT
Main engines	F-M diesels; 2 shafts; 6 000 bhp
Speed, knots	20 max
Complement	140

"BAYANDOR" Class

KAHNAMUIE *1972, Imperial Iranian Navy*

Built as two pairs, five years apart. Transferred from the USA to Iran under the Mutual Assistance Programme in 1964 (*Bayandor* and *Naghdi*) and 1969 (*Kahnamuie* and *Milanian*).

RADAR. SPS 12 search and navigation.

LIGHT FORCES

0 + 12 "LA COMBATTANTE II (MODIFIED)" CLASS

(FAST ATTACK CRAFT—MISSILE)

Displacement, tons	234 standard; 265 full load
Dimensions, ft (*m*)	154·2 × 23·3 × 8·2 (*47 × 7·1 × 2·5*)
Missiles	4—MM 38 "Exocet" surface-to-surface
Guns	1—76 mm; 1—40 mm
Main engines	4 MTU diesels; 4 shafts; 12 000 bhp = 36 knots
Range, miles	600 at 30 knots
Complement	30

Ordered from Construction de Mécanique, Normandie—first 6 in Feb 1974, second 6 in Aug 1974. Believed to be similar to West German Type 148.

3 IMPROVED PGM TYPE (LARGE PATROL CRAFT)

BATTRAAM (ex-US PGM 112) PGM 66
NAHID (ex-US PGM 122) PGM 67
PARVIN (ex-US PGM 103) PGM 65

Displacement, tons	105 standard; 146 full load
Dimensions, feet	100 × 22 × 10
Guns	1—40 mm; 2—20 mm, 2—50 cal MG
Main engines	8 MG diesels; 2 000 bhp = 15 knots

Motor gunboats of an enlarged design, compared with the "Kayvan" class below. Built in USA by Tacoma Boatbuilding Co of Tacoma and Petersen Builders Inc of Sturgeon Bay, Wisconsin, and transferred to Iran under MAP in 1967-70.

Note: In February 1974 Iran concluded an agreement with France for the construction of 6 La Combattante II Class Fast Attack Craft armed with Exocet missiles.

PARVIN 1971

AT LEAST 6 40ft TYPE (COASTAL PATROL CRAFT)

MAHNAVI-HAMRAZ **MAHNAVI-VAHEDI** **MORVARID**
MAHNAVI-TAHERI **MARDJAN** **SADAF**

Displacement, tons	10 standard
Dimensions, feet	40·0 × 11·0 × 3·7
Guns	Light MG
Main engines	2 General Motors diesels = 30 knots

Small launches for port duties of Sewart (USA) standard 40 ft type. Pennant numbers 5001 and above. Some serve in the Caspian Sea.

3 US COASTGUARD "CAPE" CLASS

(LARGE PATROL CRAFT)

KAYVAN **MAHAN** 64 **TIRAN**

Displacement, tons	85 standard; 107 full load
Dimensions, feet	90 pp; 95 oa × 20·2 × 6·8
Gun	1—40 mm
A/S weapons	8-barrelled 7·2 in projector, 8—300 lb depth charges
Main engines	4 Cummins diesels; 2 shafts; 2 200 bhp = 20 knots
Range, miles	1 500 cruising
Complement	15

Kayvan, built in USA in 1955, was delivered to Iran on 14 Jan 1956. *Tiran* was built by the US Coast Guard at Curtis Bay, Maryland, and transferred to Iran in 1957. *Mahan* and *Mehran* were delivered to Iran in 1959.

MAHAN *1969, Imperial Iranian Navy*

3 PATROL BOATS (COASTAL PATROL CRAFT)

GOHAR **SHAHPAR** **No. 3**

Displacement, tons	70
Dimensions, feet	75·2 × 16·5 × 6
Main engines	2 diesels; 1 100 hp; 2 shafts = 27 knots

Built by Abeking and Rasmussen. *Gohar* launched 22 Jan 1970, *Shahpar* on 19 Mar 1970.

Light Forces—*continued*

6 "WELLINGTON" (BH.7) CLASS (HOVERCRAFT)

101 **102** **103** **104** **105** **106**

Displacement, tons	50 max weight, 33 empty
Dimensions, feet	76 × 45 × 42 (height inflated)
Missiles	SSMs in last four
Guns	2 Browning MG
Main engines	1 Proteus 15 M/541 gas turbine = 60 knots
Oil fuel, tons	10

First pair are BH 7 Mk 4 (delivered Nov 70 and Mar 71) and the next four are Mk 5 craft (two in mid 1974, one in late 1974, and one in early 1975). Mk 5 craft fitted for, but not with, surface-to-surface missiles.

101 *1971*

8 "WINCHESTER" (SR.N6) CLASS (HOVERCRAFT)

01 **02** **03** **04** **05** **06** **07** **08**

Displacement, tons	10 normal gross weight (basic weight 14 200 lbs; disposable load 8 200 lbs)
Dimensions, feet	48·4 × 25·3 × 15·9 (height)
Main engines	1 Gnome Model 1050 gas turbine = 58 knots 1 Peters diesel as auxiliary power unit.

The Imperial Iranian Navy has the world's largest fully operational hovercraft squadron, which is used for coastal defence and logistic duties.

03 *1971*

LANDING CRAFT

QUESM (ex-USS *LCU* 1431) LCU 47

Displacement, tons	160 light; 320 full load
Dimensions, feet	119 × 32 × 5·7
Guns	2—20 mm AA
Main engines	Diesels; 675 bhp = 10 knots
Complement	14

LCU 1431 was transferred to Iran by US in 1964 under the Military Aid Programme.

QUESM *1971*

MINE WARFARE FORCES

3 MSC TYPE (MINESWEEPERS—COASTAL)

KARKAS (ex-USS *MSC* 292) 34
SHAHROKH (ex-USS *MSC* 276) 31 **SIMORGH** (ex-USS *MSC* 291) 33

Displacement, tons	320 light; 378 full load
Dimensions, feet	138 pp; 145·8 oa × 28 × 8·3
Gun	1—20 mm
Main engines	2 GM diesels; 2 shafts; 890 bhp = 12·8 knots
Oil fuel, tons	27
Range, miles	2 400 at 11 knots
Complement	40 (4 officers, 2 midshipmen, 34 men)

Built by Bellingham Shipyards Co (*Shahrokh*), Petersen Builders Inc. (*Karkas*) and Tacoma Boatbuilding Co, (*Simorgh*). Of wooden construction. Launched in 1958-61 and transferred from US to Iran under MAP in 1959-62. *Shahrokh* now in the Caspian Sea. *Shahbaz* deleted 1974.

SHAHROKH *1971, John G. Callis*

2 US MSI TYPE (MINESWEEPERS—INSHORE)

HARISCHI (ex-*Kahnamuie*) 301 (ex-*MSI* 14) **RIAZI** 302 (ex-*MSI* 13)

Displacement, tons	180 standard; 235 full load
Dimensions, feet	111 × 23 × 6
Guns	MG
Main engines	diesels; 650 bhp = 13 knots
Oil fuel, tons	20
Range, miles	1 000 at 9 knots
Complement	23 (5 officers, 18 men)

Built in USA by Tacoma Boatbuilding Co and delivered to Iran under MAP. Laid down on 22 June 1962 and 1 Feb 1963, and transferred at Seattle, Washington, on 3 Sep 1964 and 15 Oct 1964, respectively. In Aug 1967 *Kahnamuie* was renamed *Harischi* as the name was required for one of the new US PFs, see above.

RIAZI ***1971***

SERVICE FORCES

Note. I UK "OL" Class Tanker ordered from Swan Hunter Oct 1974.

2 LANDING SHIPS (LOGISTIC)

HENGAM **LARAK**

Displacement, tons	2 500
Length, feet	300
Aircraft	1 helicopter
Guns	4—40 mm (single)
Main engines	Diesels; 2 shafts; 5 600 bhp
Speed, knots	16

Similar in many respects to British *'Sir Lancelot'* but smaller with bridge amidships. Ordered 1972 from Yarrow, Clyde. *Hengam* laid down late 1972, launched 24 Sep 1973, completed 12 Aug 1974; *Larak* laid down 1973, launched 7 May 1974, completed 12 Nov 1974.

3 FLEET SUPPLY SHIPS

BANDAR ABBAS A 42 **BOOSHEHR** A 43 +1

Measurement, tons	3 250 deadweight
Dimensions, ft (*m*)	354·2 × 54·4 × 14·8 (*108 × 16·6 × 4·5*)
Aircraft	1 helicopter
Main engines	2 MAN Diesels; 2 shafts; 6 000 bhp
Speed, knots	16
Complement	60

Combined tankers and store-ships carrying victualling, armament and general stores. Built by C. Lühring Yard, Brake, W Germany. *Bandar Abbas* launched 11 Aug 1973 and completed Apr 1974. *Booshehr* launched 23 Mar 1974 and completed Nov 1974.

BANDAR ABBAS *8/1974, Wright and Logan*

Service Forces—*continued*

1 Ex-US AR TYPE (REPAIR SHIP)

CHAHBAHAR (ex-USS *Amphion*) A 41

Displacement, tons	7 826 standard; 14 490 full load
Dimensions, feet	456·0 wl; 492·0 oa × 70·0 × 27·5
Guns	2—3 in 50 cal AA
Main engines	Westinghouse turbines; 1 shaft; 8 500 shp = 16·5 knots
Boilers	2 Foster-Wheeler
Complement	Accommodation for 921.

Built by Tampa Shipbuilding Co. Launched on 15 May 1945. Commissioned on 30 Jan 1946. Transferred to IIN on 1 Oct 1971. Based at Bandar Abbas.

CHAHBAHAR *1972, Imperial Iranian Navy*

HORMUZ (ex-*YO* 247) 43 (HARBOUR TANKER)

Displacement, tons	1 250 standard; 1 700 full load
Dimensions, feet	171·2 wl; 178·3 oa × 32·2 × 14
Main engines	1 Ansaldo Q 370, 4 cycle diesel
Oil fuel, tons	25

Hormuz was built by Cantiere Castellamare di Stabia. Own oil fuel: 25 tons. Cargo oil capacity: 5 000 to 6 000 barrels.

HORMUZ *1970, Imperial Iranian Navy*

LENGEN (ex-USS *YW* 88) 46 (WATER BOAT)

Displacement, tons	1 250 standard
Dimensions, feet	178 × 32 × 14
Main engines	Diesels; speed = 10 knots

Transferred to Iran by US in 1964. Similar to oiler *Hormuz* (above).

BAHMANSHIR 45 (TUG)

Harbour tug (ex-US Army ST 1002), 150 tons, transferred in 1962.

2 HARBOUR TUGS

— (ex- **FDR** *Karl*) — (ex-**FDR** *Ise*)

Sister ships of 134 tons taken over from W. Germany 17 June 1974. Both built 1962-63.

Ex-ISE and KARL *4/1974 Reiner Nerlich*

FLOATING DOCKS

Ex-US *Windsor* and ARD 12 transferred 1971. Both of steel construction with a 3 000 ton lift.

IMPERIAL YACHTS

KISH

Displacement, tons	178
Dimensions, feet	122 × 25 × 7
Main engines	2 sets by Motor und Turbinen Union Friedrichshafen GMBH MAN-Maybach-Mercedes-Benz; 2 920 hp

A smaller and more modern Imperial Yacht built by Yacht und Bootswerft, Burmester, Germany. Commissioned in 1970. In the Persian Gulf.

KISH *1971*

Imperial Yachts—*continued*

SHAHSAVAR

Displacement, tons	530
Dimensions, feet	176 × 25·3 × 10·5
Main engines	2 sets diesels; 1 300 bhp

Built by N. V. Boele's Scheepwerven, Bolnes, Netherlands. Engined by Gebr Stork of Hengelo. Launched in 1936. In the Caspian Sea.

SHAHSAVAR *1971, Imperial Iranian Navy*

IRAQ

Administration

Commander-in-Chief:
Rear-Admiral Abd Al Diri

Chief of Staff:
Commander Samad Sat Al Mufti

Personnel

(a) 1975: 2 000 officers and men
(b) 2 years National Service

Mercantile Marine

Lloyd's Register of Shipping: 49 vessels of 229 603 tons gross

SOVIET-IRAQI TREATY

Under this treaty, signed in April 1972, the Soviet fleet will have access to the Iraqi base of Umm Qasr. In return Soviet assistance will be given to strengthen Iraq's defences. From the naval aspect, taking into account the small number of personnel, this is most likely to be confined to Light Forces.

CORVETTES

3 Ex-USSR "SO I" CLASS

Displacement, tons	215 light; 250 full load
Dimensions, feet	138·6 × 20 × 9·2
Guns	4—25 mm AA
A/S weapons	4 five-barrelled ahead-throwing rocket launchers.
Main engines	3 diesels; 6 000 bhp = 29 knots
Complement	30

Delivered by the USSR to Iraq in 1962.

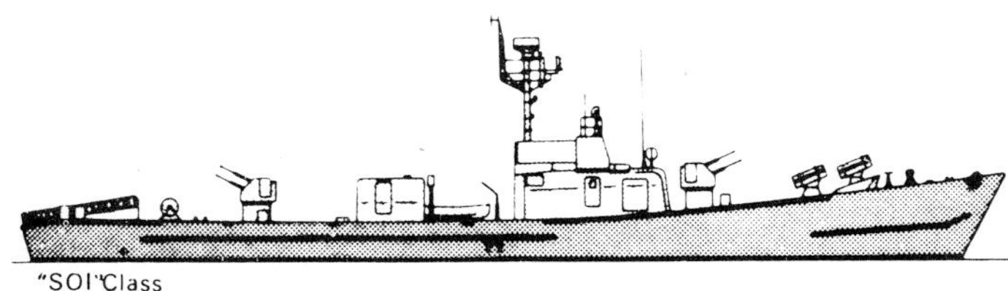

"SOI" Class

LIGHT FORCES

6 Ex-USSR "OSA" CLASS (FAST ATTACK CRAFT—MISSILE)

Displacement, tons	165 standard; 200 full load
Dimensions, ft (*m*)	128·7 × 25·1 × 5·9 (*39·3 × 7·7 × 1·8*)
Missiles	4 launchers for SS-N-2 (Styx)
Guns	4—30 mm (twin)
Main engines	3 Diesels; 13 000 hp = 32 knots
Range, miles	800 at 25 knots
Complement	25

This increase in the Iraqi navy must make a major impact on naval affairs in the Persian Gulf. Other navies have shown the effectiveness of the Styx missiles, even in comparatively untrained hands, against unalerted forces. It will be a surprise if this Soviet incursion does not accelerate the build up of high-effectiveness forces in this area

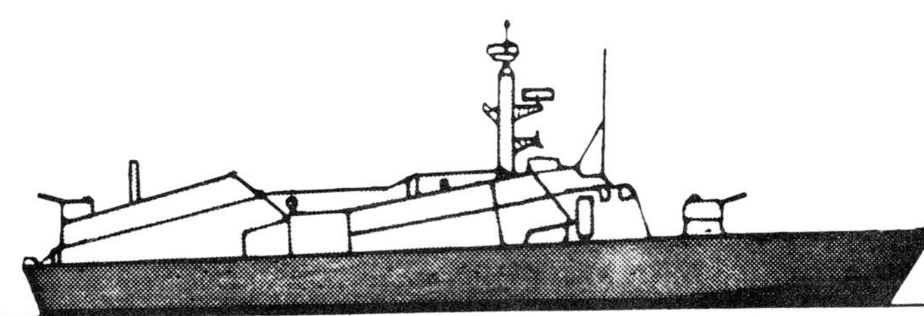

"OSA" *Class*

12 Ex-USSR "P 6" CLASS

Displacement, tons	66 standard; 75 full load
Dimensions, feet	84·2 × 20 × 6
Guns	4—25 mm
Tubes	2—21 in
Main engines	Diesels; 4 800 bhp = 45 knots
Complement	25

Transferred from the USSR. Two were received in 1959, four in Nov 1960, and six in Jan 1961. Some remain non-operational.

"P 6" Class

No. 1 **No. 2** **No. 3** **No. 4**

Displacement, tons	67
Dimensions, feet	100 × 17 × 3 mean
Guns	1—3·7 in howitzer; 2—3 in mortars; 4 MG
Main engines	2 Thornycroft diesels; 2 shafts; 280 bhp = 12 knots

Protected by bullet-proof plating. All built by John I. Thornycroft & Co Ltd, Woolston Southampton. All launched, completed and delivered in 1937.

No. 1 *John I. Thornycroft & Co. Ltd*

2 Ex-USSR "POLUCHAT" CLASS (LARGE PATROL CRAFT)

Displacement, tons	100 standard
Dimensions, feet	98·4 × 19·0 × 5·9
Guns	2—25 mm

Transferred by USSR in late 1960s.

4 COASTAL PATROL CRAFT

Reported as ex-USSR "Nyriat" Class used as diving craft.

8 THORNYCROFT 36 ft TYPE

Length, feet	36
Main engines	1 diesel; 125 bhp

Patrol boats built by John I. Thornycroft & Co for the Iraqi Ports Administration.

4 THORNYCROFT 21 ft TYPE

Length, feet	21
Main engines	1 diesel; 40 bhp

Pilot despatch launches built by John I. Thornycroft & Co for the Iraqi Ports

TUG

ALARM (ex-*St. Ewe*)

Displacement, tons	570 standard; 820 full load
Dimensions, feet	135 × 30 × 14·5
Main engines	Triple expansion; 1 shaft; 1 200 ihp = 12 knots
Boilers	2 oil-fired

Former British Rescue type tug of the "Saint" class. Built by Murdock & Murray. Launched in 1919.

LIGHTHOUSE TENDER

(ex-*Sans Peur*, ex-*Restless*)

Displacement, tons	1 025
Dimensions, feet	186 × 29·5 × 14·5
Main engines	Triple expansion; 2 shafts; 850 ihp = 13 knots
Boilers	1 oil-fired

Former Royal Yacht. Designed by G. L. Watson Ltd. Built by John Brown & Co Ltd. Clydebank. Launched in 1923.

PRESIDENTIAL YACHT

AL THAWRA (ex-*Malike Aliye*)

Displacement, tons	746
Main engines	Diesels; 2 shafts; 1 800 shp = 14 knots

Royal Yacht before assassination of King Faisal II in 1958, after which she was renamed *Al Thawra* (*The Revolution*) instead of *Malike Aliye* (*Queen Aliyah*).

AL THAWRA *1966, Aldo Fraccaroli*

IRELAND (REPUBLIC OF)

Administration

Minister for Defence: Mr. P. Donegan, TD

Commanding Officer and Director Naval Service: Captain P. Kavanagh, NS

The Irish Naval Service is administered from Naval Headquarters, Department of Defence, Dublin, by the Commanding Officer and Director Naval Service. The naval base and dockyard are on Haulbowline island in Cork Harbour.

Personnel

1975: Approximately 500 officers and men

Disposals

Cliona (ex-HMS *Bellwort*) and *Macha* (ex-HMS *Borage*), both built by George Brown, & Co (Marine) Ltd, Greenock, were sold for breaking up in 1970-71. *Maev* (ex-HMS *Oxlip*) deleted 1972. Tender *Wyndham* sold in 1968 and *General McHardy* in 1971.

Mercantile Marine

Lloyd's Register of Shipping:
88 vessels of 208 700 tons gross

FISHERY PROTECTION VESSEL

1 + 1 "DEIRDRE" CLASS

DEIRDRE FP 20

+ 1

Displacement, tons	972
Dimensions, ft (*m*)	184·3 pp × 34·1 × 14·4 (*56·2 × 10·4 × 4·4*)
Guns	1—40 mm Bofors
Main engines	2 British Polar diesels coupled to 1 shaft; 4 200 bhp = 18 knots
Oil fuel	170 bunker capacity
Range, miles	10 000 at 12 knots
Complement	42

Designed as an all weather ship. Built by Verolme, Cork. Controllable pitch propeller stabilisers and sonar. The first vessel ever built for the Naval Service in the Republic of Ireland. Launched on 29 Dec 1971. Completed May 1972. A second vessel of this class is in the planning stage.

DEIRDRE *1974, Irish Naval Service*

COASTAL MINESWEEPERS

3 Ex-BRITISH "TON" CLASS

BANBA (ex-HMS *Alverton*, M 1104) CM 11
FÖLA (ex-HMS *Blaxton*, M 1132) CM 12
GRÁINNE (ex-HMS *Oulston*, M 1129) CM 10

Displacement, tons	360 standard; 425 full load
Dimensions, feet	140·0 pp; 153·0 oa × 28·8 × 8·2
Guns	1—40 mm AA; 2—20 mm AA
Main engines	2 diesels; 2 shafts; 3 000 bhp = 15 knots
Oil fuel, tons	45
Range, miles	2 300 at 13 knots
Complement	30 average

Former British "Ton'. class coastal minesweepers. Built in 1954-59. Double mahogany hulls and otherwise constructed of aluminium alloy and other materials with the lowest possible magnetic signature. Purchased from Great Britain in 1971. See fuller particulars of the numerous "Ton" class in the United Kingdom section on later page. Acquired for fishery protection duties as replacements for the old corvettes. Arrived in Irish waters in spring 1971. Conversions included covered bridges in all three ships.

FOLA *1972, Irish Naval Service*

JOHN ADAMS

Measurement, tons	94 gross
Dimensions, feet	85 × 18·5 × 7
Main engines	Diesel; 125 bhp = 8 knots

Built by Richard Dunston, Ltd, Thorne, Doncaster, Yorks. Launched in 1934.

ISRAEL

Administration

Commander in Chief of the Israeli Navy:
Rear Admiral Benjamin Telem

Diplomatic Representation

Naval, Military and Air Attaché in London and Paris:
Commodore H. Kimchy

Defence and Naval Attaché in Rome:
Captain R. Ashkenazi

Personnel

(a) 1975: 4 500 (350 officers and 4 150 men, including a Naval Commando of whom 1 000 are conscripts)
(b) 3 years National Service for Jews and Druses.
Note (An additional 5 000 Reserves available on mobilisation).

Strength of the Fleet

Type	*Active*	*Building*
Patrol Submarines	2	3
Fast Attack Craft (Missile)	18	6
Large Patrol Craft	2	—
Coastal Patrol Craft	43	—
"Firefish"	1	?
LSD	1	—
LSM	3	—
LCTs	7	—
LCMs	3	—
Transports	2	—
Training Ship	1	—

Prefix to Ships' Names

INS (Israeli Naval Ship)

Bases

Haifa, Ashdod, Sharm-el-Sheikh
A repair base is being built at Eilat where a synchro-lift is being installed.

Mercantile Marine

Lloyd's Register of Shipping:
76 vessels of 611 300 tons gross

SUBMARINES

3 IKL/VICKERS TYPE 206

Displacement, tons	420 surfaced; 600 dived
Dimensions, ft (*m*)	146·7 × 15·4 × 12 (*45·0 × 4·7 × 3·7*)
Torpedo tubes	8—21 in bow
Main machinery	Diesels; 2 000 hp; Electric motor; 1 800 hp; 1 shaft; diesel-electric
Speed, knots	11 surfaced; 17 dived
Complement	22

A contract was signed for the building of these boats by Vickers in April 1972. They will, presumably, be operational from 1976 onwards.

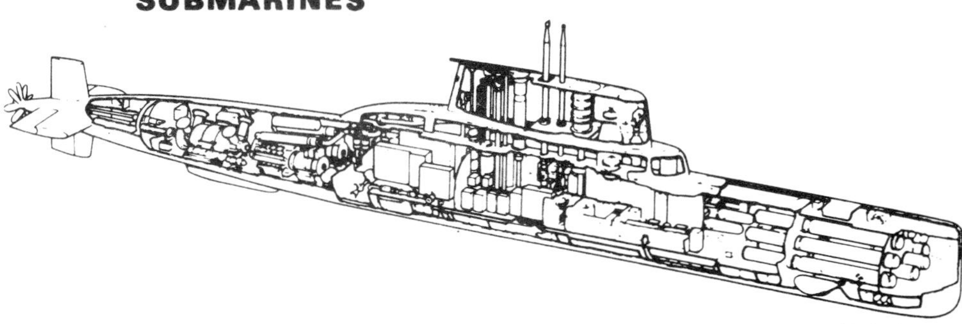

Cutaway impression of the Vickers/IKL 500-ton oceangoing submarine *1972, Vickers Limited*

2 Ex-BRITISH "T" CLASS

(PATROL SUBMARINES)

Displacement, tons	*Dolphin:* 1 310 standard; 1 535 surface; 1 740 submerged; *Leviathan:* 1 280 standard; 1 505 surface; 1 700 submerged
Length, feet (*metres*)	*Dolphin:* 293·5 (*89·5*) oa; *Leviathan:* 285·5 (*87·0*) oa
Beam, feet (*metres*)	26·5 (*8·1*)
Draught, feet (*metres*)	14·8 (*4·5*)
Torpedo tubes	6—21 in (*533 mm*) 4 bow, 2 stern
Main machinery	Diesels; 2 500 bhp (surface); Electric Motors: 2 900 hp (submerged)
Speed, knots	15·25 on surface; 15 to 18 submerged
Complement	*Dolphin:* 65; *Leviathan:* 69

Name	*No.*	*Builders*	*Laid down*	*Launched*	*Completed*
LEVIATHAN (ex-HMS *Turpin*)	75	HM Dockyard, Chatham	24 May 1943	5 Aug 1944	18 Dec 1944
DOLPHIN (ex-HMS *Truncheon*)	77	HM Dockyard, Devonport	5 Nov 1942	22 Feb 1944	25 May 1945

LEVIATHAN *1972, Israeli Navy*

Both aged "T" class who were lengthened and modernised during conversion (*Leviathan* plus 12 feet *Dolphin* plus 20 feet). Handed over after extensive refit. *Leviathan* on 19 May 1967, *Dolphin* on 9 Jan 1968.

LOSS. Original sister ship *Dakar* (ex-HMS *Totem*), handed over to Israel on 10 Nov 1967, was lost in the Eastern Mediterranean on 25 Jan 1968.

LIGHT FORCES

6 + 6 "SAAR IV" CLASS

(FAST ATTACK CRAFT—MISSILE)

RESHEF	**ROMAH**	+2
KESHET	**KIDON**	+6

Displacement, tons	415 standard
Dimensions, ft (*m*)	190·6 × 25 × 8 (*58 × 7·8 × 2·4*)
Missile launchers	7 Gabriel
Guns	2—76 mm Oto Melara. 2 MGs
A/S weapons	4 DC
Engines	4 Maybach diesels; 2,670 hp each; 2 screws
Speed, knots	32
Range, miles	approx 1 500 at 30 knots
Complement	45

Built in Haifa Shipyard, Israel, these steel-hulled boats carry Israeli-made missiles and electronics.

Reshef was launched on 19 Feb 1973, entering service April 1973; *Keshet* launched 2 Aug 1973, entering service Oct 1973; *Romah* commissioned early 1974 and *Kidon* Sept 1974. The last pair commissioned early 1975.
This very interesting class has an extremely long range at cruising speed, at least one pair having made the passage from Israel to the Red Sea via the Strait of Gibraltar and Cape of Good Hope, relying entirely on refuelling at sea. This is a great tribute not only to their endurance but also to their sea-keeping qualities.
The first pair was successfully engaged in the Arab-Israeli War, Oct 1973. It is presumed that the whole class will eventually be equipped with the new 22 mile range Gabriel missiles.
An expansion of the building slips at Haifa Dockyard will allow the more rapid construction of the next six boats ordered in January 1975.

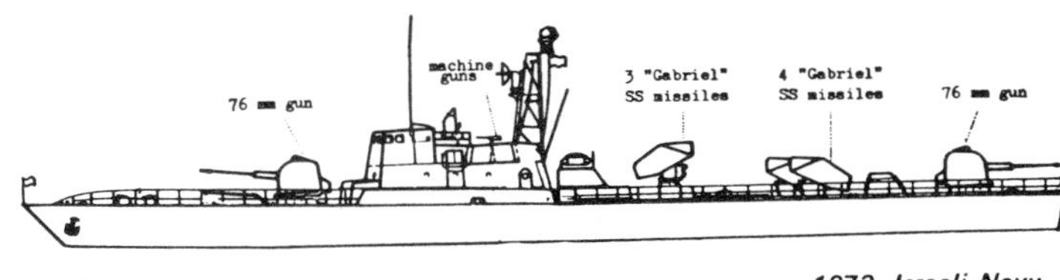

RESHEF *1973, Israeli Navy*

"SAAR IV" Class *1974*

Light Forces—*continued*

12 "SAAR" CLASS (FAST ATTACK CRAFT—MISSILE)

***ACCO**	***HAIFA**	**HETZ**	***MIZNAK**
***EILAT**	**HANIT**	***MISGAV**	**SAAR**
GAASH	**HEREV**	***MIVTACH**	**SOUFA**

*Group A

Displacement, tons	220 standard; 250 full load
Dimensions, feet	147·6 oa × 23·0 × 5·9 (8·2) max
Missile launchers	Gabriel surface to surface (see notes)
Guns, AA	40 mm or 76 mm (see notes)
Tubes	2 side launchers for 21 in torpedoes (surface or A/S)
Main engines	4 Maybach diesels; 13 500 bhp 4 shafts = 40+ knots
Oil fuel, tons	30
Range, miles	2 500 at 15 knots; 1 600 at 20 knots; 1 000 at 30 knots
Complement	35 to 40

Built by Ch de Normandie, Cherbourg, from designs by Lürssen Werft of Bremen. Political problems caused their building in France instead of Germany—a political embargo kept the last five in France until their journey to Israel began on Christmas Eve 1969. Two batches were built, the first six (Group A—*Acco, Eilat, Haifa, Misgav, Mivtach, Miznak*) being fitted originally with three 40 mm AA guns and ordered in 1965. The second six (*Gaash, Hanit, Herev, Hetz, Saar, Soufa*) were ordered in 1966 and fitted with 76 mm Oto Melara AA guns. Five of these ships were delivered to Israel and two (*Acco* and *Saar*) made the journey on completion of local trials after the 1969 French arms embargo. The last five arrived off Haifa in January 1970 after a much-publicised passage which proved the remarkable endurance of this class.
The first batch was fitted for sonar but this was omitted from the 76 mm gun fitted group. Since their arrival in Israel provision of Gabriel surface to surface missiles has progressed. The first group can mount an armament varying from one 40 mm gun and eight Gabriel missiles (two single fixed mounts forward and two triple trainable mounts amidships) to three 40 mm guns and two twin 21 inch torpedo launchers. The second group can mount the two triple Gabriel launchers amidships as well as the 76 mm Oto Melara gun forward.
The Gabriel missile system is controlled by radar and optical sights and launches a low-altitude missile with a 150 lb HE head to a range of 12·5 miles in the first configuration and 22 miles in the later versions.

"SAAR" Class with 76 mm and five Gabriel missiles *1973*

"SAAR" Class with three 40 mm and Torpedo Tubes *1974*

HANIT with one 40 mm and six Gabriel missiles *1971, Israeli Navy*

"SAAR" Class with 40 mm guns and Torpedo Tubes *1974*

2 "YAR" CLASS (LARGE PATROL CRAFT)

YARDEN 42 **YARKON** 44

Displacement, tons	96 standard, 109 full load
Dimensions, feet	100 × 20 × 6
Guns,	2—20 mm AA
Main engines	Diesels, 2 shafts; speed 22 knots
Complement	16

Both built by Yacht & Bootswerft, Burmester Bremen-Burg, Germany. *Yarkon* was launched on 25 July 1956 and *Yarden* in 1957.

YARDEN *Israeli Navy*

4 "KEDMA" CLASS (COASTAL PATROL CRAFT)

KEDMA 46 **NEGBA** 52 **YAMA** 48 **ZAFONA** 60

Displacement, tons	32
Dimensions, feet	67·0 × 15·0 × 4·8
Guns	2—20 mm
Main engines	2 diesels; 2 shafts; 1 540 bhp = 25 knots
Complement	10

Built in Japan during 1968. Handy boats of the small seaward defence type. Used for coastguard and police work in peace time.

KEDMA *1970, Israeli Navy*

Light Forces—*continued*

10+ "DABUR" CLASS (COASTAL PATROL CRAFT)

Displacement, tons	35 full load
Dimensions, ft (*m*)	64·9 × 19 × 2·6 (*19·8 × 5·8 × 0·8*)
Guns	2 Twin ·5 MGs on bridge wings; 2—20 mm
A/S weapons	DC launchers
Main engines	2 geared diesels; 960 shp; 2 shafts = 25 knots
Complement	6

Built to the general design of the US "Swift" class but with 16·5 feet greater length and 4 ft greater beam. There are several variations in their armament. Deployed in the Mediterranean and Red Seas. Good rough weather performance.

DABUR *1972, Dr. Giorgio Arra*

12 "BERTRAM" TYPE (COASTAL PATROL CRAFT)

Displacement, tons	7·5
Length, feet	30·2 oa
Gun	1—0·5 MG
Main engines	Diesels; speed = 24 knots
Complement	5

Joined the fleet in 1971. Commercial cruisers bought from Bertrams, USA. Armed and equipped in Israel.

BERTRAM PATROL CRAFT *Israeli Navy*

14+ US-BUILT (COASTAL PATROL CRAFT)

Commercial Cruisers bought from Swift Ships Inc, USA. Armed with 1—20 mm and 2 twin ·5 MG.

3 ex-US "PBR" TYPE (COASTAL PATROL CRAFT)

Dimensions, feet	32 × 11 × 2·6
Guns	3—50 cal MG; 1 grenade launcher
Main engines	2 geared diesels; waterjets = 25 knots
Complement	5

Purchased 1974.

FIREFISH MODEL III

Displacement, tons	6
Dimensions, feet	28 × 7·5
Main engines	2 Mercruiser V-8; 430 hp
Speed, knots	52
Range, miles	250 cruising; 150 max speed

Under construction by Sandaire, San Diego. Glass fibre craft, can carry five men. Capable of being radio-controlled for attack missions or minesweeping under ship or aircraft control.

FIREFISH Model III *1972, Courtesy Sandaire*

AMPHIBIOUS FORCES

1 ex-US "CASA GRANDE" CLASS

— (ex-*Casa Grande* LSD 13)

Displacement, tons	4 790 standard; 9 375 full load
Dimensions, feet	475·4 oa × 76·2 × 18
Guns	12—40 mm
Main engines	Geared turbines; 2 shafts; 7 000 shp = 15·4 knots
Complement	265

Built by Newport News SB & DD Co. Commissioned 5 June 1944. Purchased 1975 for use as dock for "Saar IV" and "Saar" Class Fast Attack Craft.

3 ex-US LSM TYPE

Displacement, tons	1 095 full load
Dimensions, feet	203·5 oa × 34·5 × 7·3
Guns	2—40 mm; 4—20 mm
Main engines	Diesels; 2 800 bhp; 2 shafts = 12·5 knots
Complement	70

Purchased in 1972 from commercial sources.

BEIT SHAFEI (LCT)

Dimensions, feet	225·0 × 38·9 × 5·0
Capacity	16 tanks
Speed, knots	12·5

3 "ASH" CLASS (LCT)

ASHDOD 61 **ASHKELON** 63 **ACHZIV** 65

Displacement, tons	400 standard; 730 full load
Dimensions, feet	180·5 pp; 205·5 oa × 32·8 × 5·8
Guns	2—20 mm AA
Main engines	3 MWM diesels; 3 shafts; 1 900 bhp = 10·5 knots
Oil fuel, tons	37
Complement	20

These three landing craft were completed during 1966-67 by Israel Shipyards, Haifa.

ASHDOD *Israeli Navy*

3 LC TYPE (LCT)

ETZION GUEBER 51 **SHIKOMONA** 53 **LC 55**

Displacement, tons	182 standard; 230 full load
Dimensions, feet	120·0 × 23·2 × 4·7 (*Etzion Geuber* of only 90 ft length)
Guns, AA	2—20 mm
Main engines	2 diesels; 2 shafts; 1 280 bhp = 10 knots
Complement	12

Built by Israeli shipyards, Haifa.

SHIKOMONA *Israeli Navy*

3 LCM TYPE

Displacement, tons	22 tons standard; 60 full load
Dimensions, feet	50 × 14 × 3·2
Main engines	2 diesels; 450 bhp = 11 knots

Former United States vessels of the LCM (Landing Craft Mechanised) type.

TRANSPORTS

1 "BAT SHEVA" CLASS

BAT SHEVA

Displacement, tons	900
Dimensions, feet	311·7 × 36·7 × 26·9
Guns	4—20 mm
Main engines	diesels; speed = 10 knots
Complement	26

BAT SHEVA *1971, Israeli Navy*

1 "BAT YAM" TYPE

BAT YAM

A small armed merchant ship used as a transport.

Note. Training ship '*Nogah*' converted from 500 ton coaster.

ITALY

Administration

Chief of Naval Staff:
Ammiraglio di Squadra Girolamo Fantoni

Commander, Allied Naval Forces, Southern Europe (Naples):
Ammiraglio di Squadra Giovanni Ciccolo

Commander-in-Chief Dipartimento Alto Tirreno:
Ammiraglio di Squadra Giuseppe Oriana

Commander-in-Chief Dipartimento Adriatico:
Ammiraglio di Squadra Filippo Ferrari-Aggradi

Commander-in-Chief Dipartimento dello Jonio e Canale d'Otranto:
Ammiraglio di Squadra Luigi Tomasuolo

Commander-in-Chief of Fleet (and Comedcent):
Ammiraglio de Squadra Aldo Baldini

Commander 1st Naval Division:
Contrammiraglio Angelo Monassi

Commander 2nd Naval Division:
Contrammiraglio Luigi de Ferrante

Commander 3rd Naval Division:
Contrammiraglio Carlo Falcone

Commander 4th Naval Division:
Contrammiraglio Vitaliano Rauber

Director General Navy Personnel:
Ammiraglio de Divisione Lorenzo Dutto

Diplomatic Representation

Naval Attaché in London:
Captain F. Mottolese

Naval Attaché in Washington:
Commander Carlo A. Vandini

Naval Attaché in Moscow:
Captain Ubaldo Garagnani

Naval Attaché in Paris:
Captain P. Della Croce di Dojola

Personnel

(a) 1975: 42 350 (including Naval Air Arm and an expanding Force of Marines)
(b) 2 years National Service

Strength of the Fleet

Type	*Active*	*Building*
Cruisers	3	—
Destroyers	9	—
Frigates	11	4
Corvettes	12	—
Submarines, Patrol	10	2
Hydrofoil—Missile	1	3
Fast Attack Craft—Torpedo	8	—
Fast Attack Craft (Convertible)	4	—
LSTs	2	—
LCTs	2	—
Minesweepers—Ocean	4	—
Minesweepers—Coastal	33	—
Minesweepers—Inshore	10	—
Survey Vessels	2	1
Replenishment Tanker	1	—
Transports	2	1
Fleet Support Ship	1	—
Coastal Transports	9	—
Transports (LCM)	22	—
Transports (LCVP)	36	—
Sail Training Ships	4	—
Netlayers	2	—
Lighthouse Tenders	4	—
Salvage Ship	1	—
Repair Craft	7	—
Water Carriers	16	—
Tugs—Large	26	—
Tugs—Small	30	—

Naval Air Arm

3 LRMP Squadrons. 18 Breguet Atlantics.

Helicopters. 24 SH-3D, 30 AB-204B Bell 47, HU-16A.

Deletions

Cruiser
1971 *Giuseppe Garibaldi*

Destroyers
1971 *San Marco, Artigliere*

Corvettes
1970-72 12 "Ape" Class

Submarines
1972 *Pietro Calvi*
1973 *Leonardo da Vinci, Enrico Tazzoli*
1974 *Morosini*

Minesweepers (Coastal)
1966-67 17 ships of "Azalea" and "Anemone" classes
1974 *Rovere, Acacia, Betulla, Ciliegio*

Minesweepers (Inshore)
1974 *Arsella, Attinia, Calamaro, Conchiglia, Dromia, Ostrica, Paguro, Seppia, Tellina, Totano*

Amphibious Forces
1974 *Anteo*, MTM 9903, 9904, 9906, 9921. MTP 9701, 9702, 9704-6, 9709, 9712, 9717, 9718, 9721, 9722, 9724, 9731

Light Forces
1974 MS 472 (ex 813)

Miscellaneous

1974 *Aviere* (experimental ship), *Po, Flegetonte, Isonzo, Sesia, Metauro, Arno, Leno* and *Sprugola* (water carriers). 24 tugs

Bases

Main—La Spezia, Taranto.
Secondary—Brindisi, Augusta, Messina, La Maddalena, Cagliari, Napali, Venezia

Mercantile Marine

Lloyd's Register of Shipping:
1 710 vessels of 9 322 015 tons gross

PENNANT NUMBERS

Cruisers

550 Vittorio Veneto
553 Doria
554 Duilio

Destroyers

550 Ardito
551 Audace
555 Geniere
558 Impetuoso
559 Indomito
561 Fante
562 San Giorgio
570 Impavido
571 Intrepido

Frigates

551 Canopo
553 Castore
554 Centauro
555 Cigno
580 Alpino
581 Carabiniere
590 Aldebaran
593 Bergamini
594 Fasan
595 Margottini
596 Rizzo

Corvettes

540 De Cristofaro
541 Grosso
542 Aquila
543 Albatros
544 Alcione
545 Airone
546 Visintini
549 Bombarda
550 Todaro
567 Ape
569 Chimera
579 Sfinge
597 Vedetta

Submarines

501 Longobardo
502 Gazzana Priaroggia
505 Bagnolini
506 Toti
507 Cappellini
512 Torricelli
513 Dandolo
514 Mocenigo
515 Piomarta
516 Romei

Light Forces

420 Sparviero
490 Folgore
491 Lampo
492 Baleno
493 Freccia
484 Saetta

Minesweepers

5430 Salmone
5431 Storione
5432 Sgombro
5433 Squalo
5450 Aragosta
5452 Astice
5457 Gambero
5458 Granchio
5459 Mitilo
5462 Pinna
5463 Polipo
5464 Porpora
5465 Riccio
5466 Scampo
5501 Abete
5504 Castagno
5505 Cedro
5507 Faggio
5508 Frassino
5509 Gelso
5510 Larice
5511 Noce
5512 Olmo
5513 Ontano
5514 Pino
5515 Pioppo
5516 Platano
5517 Quercia
5519 Mandorlo
5521 Bambù
5522 Ebano
5523 Mango
5524 Mogano
5525 Palma
5527 Sandalo
5531 Agave
5532 Alloro
5533 Edera
5534 Gaggia
5535 Gelsomino
5536 Giaggiolo
5537 Glicine
5538 Loto
5540 Timo
5541 Trifolgio
5542 Vischio

Amphibious Forces

9870 Etna
9871 Bafile
9881 Quarto
9890 Grado
9891 Caorle

Service Forces

5301 Cavezzale
5303 Amm. Magnaghi
5304 Alicudi
5305 Filicudi
5306 Mirto
5307 Pioppo
5309 Rampino
5310 Proteo
5311 Palinuro
5312 Vespucci
5313 Stella Polare
5316 Corsaro II
5319 Ciclope
5320 Colosso
5321 Forte
5322 Gagliardo
5323 Robusto
5324 Ustica
5325 Titano
5326 S. Giusto
5327 Stromboli
5331-5338 MOC 1021-1208
5341-5352 MTC 1001-1102
5354 Piave
5355 Tevere
5356 Basento
5357 Bradano
5358 Brenta
5359 Bormida
5361-5363 MTF
5366 Volturno
5368 Sterope
5369 Adige
5374 Mincio
5376 Tanaro
5377 Ticino
5378 Porto d'Ischia
5379 Riva Trigoso
5381 Caprera
5382 Pantelleria
5385 Favignana
5386 Porto Pisano
5387 Porto Recanati
5390 Porto Vecchio
5391 Salvore
5392 Tino
5394 Vigoroso
5396 Pianosa
5397 Levanzo

CRUISERS

1 HELICOPTER CRUISER

Name	No.	Builders	Laid down	Launched	Completed
VITTORIO VENETO	C 550	Navalmeccanica Castellammare di Stabia	10 June 1965	5 Feb 1967	30 Apr 1969

Displacement, tons	7 500 standard; 8 850 full load
Length, feet (*metres*)	589 (*179·6*) oa
Beam, feet (*metres*)	63·6 (*19·4*)
Draught, feet (*metres*)	19·7 (*6*)
Aircraft	9 A/B 240B ASW helicopters
Missiles, AA	1 "Terrier"/"Asroc" twin launcher forward
Guns,	8—3 in (*76 mm*) 62 cal.
Torpedo tubes	2 triple for A/S torpedoes
Boilers	4 Foster-Wheeler; 711 psi (*50 kg/cm²*); 842°F (*450°C*)
Main engines	2 Tosi double reduction geared turbines; 73 000 shp; 2 shafts
Speed, knots	32
Range, miles	6 000 at 20 knots
Oil fuel, tons	1 200
Complement	560 (60 officers, 500 men)

VITTORIO VENETO — *1971, Commander Aldo Fraccaroli*

GENERAL
Developed from the "Doria" class but with much larger helicopter squadron and improved facilities for anti-submarine operations. Projected under the 1959-60 New Construction Programme, but her design was recast several times. She was commissioned for service on 12 July 1969. Flagship of C-in-C Fleet.

RADAR. SPS 48 3-dimensional air search and target designator on fore funnel. SPS 40 long range search set on after funnel. One SMA/SPQ-2 combined search and navigation set-X band. 2 SPG-55A fire control groups forward for Terrier. 4 Orion fire-control sets for guns.

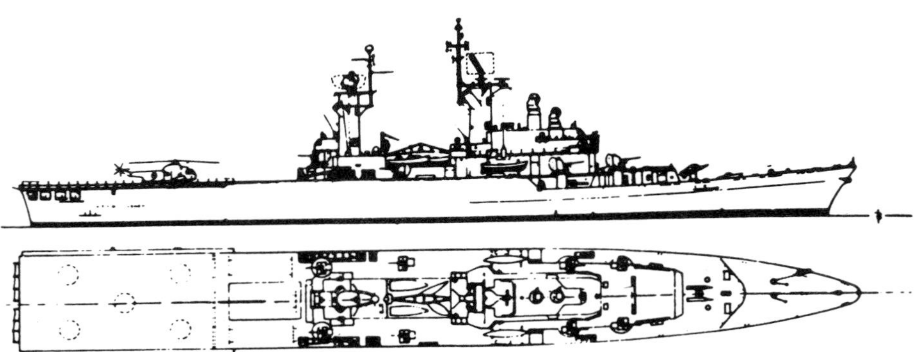

DRAWING. Scale 125 feet = 1 inch (1 : 1 500)

VITTORIO VENETO — *1971, Commander Aldo Fraccaroli*

2 "ANDREA DORIA" CLASS

Name	*No.*	*Builders*	*Laid down*	*Launched*	*Completed*
ANDREA DORIA	553	Cantieri del Tirreno, Riva Trigoso	11 May 1958	27 Feb 1963	23 Feb 1964
CAIO DUILIO	554	Navalmeccanica Castellammare di Stabia	16 May 1958	22 Dec 1962	30 Nov 1964

Displacement, tons	5 000 standard; 6 500 full load
Length, feet (*metres*)	489·8 (*149·3*) oa
Beam, feet (*metres*)	56·4 (*17·2*)
Draught, feet (*metres*)	16·4 (*5·0*)
Aircraft	4 A/B 204B ASW helicopters
Missiles,	1 "Terrier" twin launcher forward
Guns	8—3 in (*76 mm*) 62 cal.
Torpedo tubes	2 triple for 12 in (*305 mm*) A/S torpedoes
Main engines	2 double reduction geared turbines 60 000 shp; 2 shafts
Boilers	4 Foster-Wheeler; 711 psi (*50 kg/cm²*); 842°F (*450°C*)
Speed, knots	31 (*31·6* on trials)
Range, miles	6 000 at 20 knots
Oil fuel, tons	1 100
Complement	485 (45 officers, 440 men)

Escort cruisers of novel design and generous beam with a good helicopter capacity in relation to their size. *Enrico Dandolo* was the name originally allocated to *Andrea Doria*.

ANDREA DORIA *1973, Dr Giorgio Arra*

GUNNERY. The anti-aircraft battery includes eight 3-inch fully automatic guns of a new pattern, disposed in single turrets, four on each side amidships abreast the funnels and the bridge.

HELICOPTER PLATFORM. Helicopters operate from a platform aft measuring 98·5 feet by 52·5 feet (*30* by *16 metres*). The Harrier, designed and built by Hawker Siddeley, demonstrated its capabilities of operating from shipborne platforms when it completed a two-day demonstration with a vertical landing on the comparatively small helicopter flight deck of the *Andrea Doria*.

ROLL DAMPING. Both ships have Gyrofin-Salmoiraghi stabilisers.

RADAR. SPS 39 three dimensional air surveillance and target designator on main mast. SPS-40 search set forward. Nav-radar. Two SPG-55 control groups for Terrier. Four Orion fire control radars for guns. ELSAG NA-9 gun fire control system. ECM and DF. Tacan beacon.

ANDREA DORIA

CAIO DUILIO *1974, Commander Aldo Fraccaroli*

DESTROYERS *(DDG)*

2 "AUDACE" CLASS (DDG)

Name	*No.*	*Builders*	*Laid Down*	*Launched*	*Completed*
ARDITO	D 550	Navalmeccanica Castellamare	19 July 1968	27 Nov 1971	5 Dec 1973
AUDACE	D 551	Cantieri del Tirreno, Riva Trigoso	27 April 1968	2 Oct 1971	16 Nov 1972

Displacement, tons	3 600 standard; 4 400 full load
Length, feet (*metres*)	446·4 (*136·6*)
Beam, feet (*metres*)	47·1 (*14·5*)
Draught, feet (*metres*)	15 (*4·6*)
Aircraft	2 A/S helicopters (AB204B)
Missile launchers	1 RIM-66A Standard
Guns,	2—5 in (*127 mm*) 54 cal single 4—3 in (*76 mm*) 62 cal
Torpedo tubes	6 A/S (two tripled) 4 fixed tubes
Main engines	2 geared turbines; 73 000 shp; 2 shafts
Boilers	4 Foster Wheeler type
Speed, knots	33
Complement	380 (30 officers, 350 men)

GENERAL
It was announced in Apr 1966 that two new guided missile destroyers would be built. They are basically similar to, but an improvement in design on that of the "Impavido" class.

AIRCRAFT. Originally planned to carry two AB 204 AS helicopters carrying two A/S torpedoes. These may be replaced by two Sea King SH3Ds.

ELECTRONICS. Fitted with SCLAR control and launch units for 105 mm rockets which can be fitted with chaff dispensers, flares or HE heads having a range of 7 miles.

RADAR. SPS-52 three dimensional air surveillance on after funnel; two SPG 51 tracking and missile guidance; three Orion RTN 10X for Argo NA 10 fire control system; SPS 12 nav radar; Elsag NA 10 fire control system.

TORPEDO TUBES. The two triple Mk 32 launchers for Mk 44 torpedoes are on either beam amidships. The four fixed torpedo tubes (Canguro System) for A/S or anti ship torpedoes are built into the transom, a pair being fitted high on either quarter.

AUDACE — *1974 Commander Aldo Fraccaroli*

AUDACE — *1973 Dr Giorgio Arra*

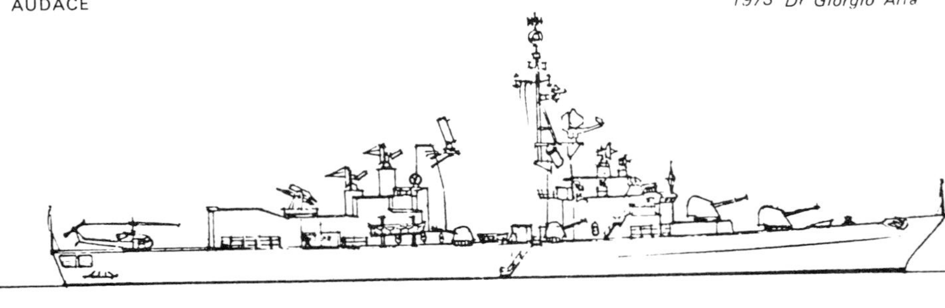
"AUDACE" Class

ARDITO — *1974, Commander Aldo Fraccaroli*

Destroyers—*continued*

2 "IMPAVIDO" CLASS (DDG)

Name	No.	Builders	Laid down	Launched	Completed
IMPAVIDO	D 570	Cantieri del Tirreno, Riva Trigoso	10 June 1957	25 May 1962	16 Nov 1963
INTREPIDO	D 571	Ansaldo, Leghorn	16 May 1959	21 Oct 1962	30 Oct 1964

Displacement, tons	3 201 standard; 3 851 full load
Length, feet (*metres*)	429·5 (*131·3*)
Beam, feet (*metres*)	44·7 (*13·6*)
Draught, feet (*metres*)	14·8 (*4·5*)
Aircraft	1 AB 204 AS helicopter
Missiles	1 "Tartar" launcher, aft
Guns	2—5 in (*127 mm*) 38 cal. forward 4—3 in (*76 mm*) 62 cal.
Torpedo tubes	2 triple for A/S torpedoes
Boilers	4 Foster Wheeler; 711 psi (*50 kg/cm²*); 842°F (*450°C*)
Main engines	2 double reduction geared turbine 70 000 shp; 2 shafts
Speed, knots	34
Range, miles	3 300 at 20 knots; 2 900 at 25 knots
Oil fuel, tons	650
Complement	325 (15 officers, 310 men)

GENERAL
Built under the 1956-57 and 1958-59 programmes respectively. Both ships have stabilisers.

ENGINEERING. On first full power trials *Impavido*, at light displacement, reached 34·5 knots (33 knots at normal load).

RADAR. Search: SPS 12 and SPS 39 (3-D.)
Fire Control: SPG 51 for "Tartar", X Band for guns.

IMPAVIDO — 1974, *Dr Giorgio Arra*

INTREPIDO — 1974, *Italian Navy*

Name	No.	Builders	Laid down	Launched	Completed
SAN GIORGIO (ex-*Pompeo Magno*)	D 562	Cantieri N. Riuniti Ancona	23 Sep 1939	28 Aug 1941	24 June 1943

Displacement, tons	3 950 standard; 4 350 full load
Length, feet (*metres*)	455·2 (*138·8*)wl; 466·5 (*142·3*)oa
Beam, feet (*metres*)	47·2 (*14·4*)
Draught, feet (*metres*)	21·0 (*4·5*)
Guns	4—5 in (*127 mm*) 38 cal; 3—3 in (*76 mm*) 62 cal
A/S weapons	1 three-barrelled mortar; 2 triple torpedo tubes
Main engines	2 Tosi Metrovick gas turbines; 15 000 hp; and 4 Fiat diesels; 16 600 bhp; 2 shafts
Speed, knots	20 (diesels), 28 (diesel and gas)
Range, miles	4 800 at 20 knots
Oil fuel, tons	500 (diesel oil)
Complement	295 (15 officers, 280 men) plus 130 cadets

Converted into fleet destroyer in 1951 by Cantieri del Tirreno, Genova, being completed 1 July 1955. Underwent complete re-construction at the Naval Dockyard, La Spezia, in 1963-65. The modernisation included her adaptation as a Training Ship for 130 cadets of the Accademia Navale. Changes were made in the armament and new machinery was fitted, gas turbines and diesels replacing steam turbines and boilers.

RADAR. Search: SPS 6. Fire control: 4 X Band Navset.

SAN GIORGIO — 1972, *Dr Giorgio Arra*.

SAN GIORGIO

Destroyers—*continued*

2 "IMPETUOSO" CLASS

Name	*No.*	*Builders*	*Ordered*	*Laid down*	*Launched*	*Completed*
IMPETUOSO	D 558	Cantieri del Tirreno, Riva Trigoso	Nov 1950	7 May 1952	16 Sep 1956	25 Jan 1958
INDOMITO	D 559	Ansaldo, Leghorn (formerly OTO)	Nov 1950	24 Apr 1952	7 Aug 1955	23 Feb 1958

Displacement, tons	2 755 standard; 3 800 full load
Length, feet (*metres*)	405 (*123·4*) pp; 418·7 (*127·6*) oa
Beam, feet (*metres*)	43·5 (*13·3*)
Draught, feet (*metres*)	17·5 (*4·5*)
Guns	**4—5 in (*127 mm*) 38 cal. 16—40 mm, 56 cal.**
A/S weapons	1 three-barrelled mortar; 4 DCT; 1 DC rack
Tubes	**6 (2 triple) for A/S torpedoes**
Main engines	**2 double reduction geared turbines; 2 shafts; 65 000 shp**
Boilers	4 Foster-Wheeler; 711 psi (*50 kg/cm²*) working pressure; 842°F (*450°C*) superheat temperature
Speed, knots	34 (see *Engineering* notes)
Range, miles	3 400 at 20 knots
Oil fuel, tons	650
Complement	315 (15 officers, 300 men)

Italy's first destroyers built since Second World War Armament if and when converted: 1 single "Tartar" launcher 2—5 in, 4—3 in guns

ENGINEERING. On their initial sea trials these ships attained a speed of 35 knots at full load.

IMPETUOSO — *1973, Dr Giorgio Arra*

IMPETUOSO, INDOMITO

INDOMITO — *5/1974, Commander Aldo Fraccaroli*

2 Ex-US "FLETCHER" CLASS

Name	*No.*	*Builders*	*Laid down*	*Launched*	*Completed*
FANTE (ex-USS *Walker*, DD 517)	D 561	Bath Iron Works Corpn	31 Aug 1942	31 Jan 1943	2 Apr 1943
GENIERE (ex-USS *Pritchett*, DD 561)	D 555	Seattle-Tacoma SB Corpn	20 July 1942	31 July 1943	15 Jan 1944

Displacement, tons	2 080 standard; 2 940 full load
Length, feet (*metres*)	376·5 (*114·3*) oa
Beam, feet (*metres*)	39·5 (*12·0*)
Draught, feet (*metres*)	18 (*5·5*)
Guns,	2—5 inch, 38 cal (4 in *Geniere*) 4—3 inch, 50 cal (6 in *Geniere*) in twin mountings
A/S weapons	1 DC rack, 2 side-launching torpedo racks, 2 fixed Hedgehogs
Main engines	GE geared turbines; 2 shafts; 60 000 shp
Boilers	4 Babcock & Wilcox
Speed, knots	35 designed (32 sea)
Oil, fuel tons	650
Range, miles	6 000 at 15 knots
Complement	250 (10 officers, 240 men)

GENERAL
Walker was transferred from the United States Navy and commissioned as *Fante* on 2 July 1969. *Pritchett* was transferred at San Diego on 10 Jan 1970 and renamed *Geniere*. She left San Francisco Navy Yard for Italy and arrived Taranto on 31 Oct 1970.

RADAR. Search: SPS 6 and SPS 10. Fire Control: US Mk 57 forward.

TORPEDO TUBES. The five 21-inch torpedo tubes (originally ten, in two quintuple banks) were removed.

GENIERE — *1972, Commander Aldo Fraccaroli*

FRIGATES

4 "LUPO" CLASS

Name	No.	Builder	Laid down	Launched	Completion
LUPO	—	Riva Trigoso	11 Oct 1974	Mar 1976	Dec 1976
2	—	Riva Trigoso	Sep 1975	Dec 1976	Nov 1977
3	—	Riva Trigoso	Apr 1976	June 1977	Apr 1978
4	—	Riva Trigoso	Feb 1977	Apr 1978	Feb 1979

Displacement, tons 2 208 standard; 2 500 full load
Dimensions, ft (*m*) 347·7 × 39·4 × 12·1) (*106 × 12 × 3·7*)
Aircraft 1 or 2 helicopters
Missiles Ota-Melara surface-to-surface; Sea-Sparrow; 4—4·1 in rocket launchers
Guns 1—5 in (127/54) Ota Melara; 4—40 mm 70 cal Breda
Torpedo tubes 6—for Mk 32 A/S torpedoes (triples)
Main engines CODOG—2 Fiat LM 2 500 gas turbines; 50 000 hp; 2 A-230-20-M Grandi Matore, Trieste diesels, 7 800 hp; 2 shafts
Speed, knots 34 on turbines; 22 on diesels
Complement 185 (16 officers, 169 ratings)

Similar class being built for Peru. First of class named after the most famous Italian torpedo-boat of 2nd World War.

RADAR. Air Search; Selenia. Surface search, SPQ-2F (SMA)

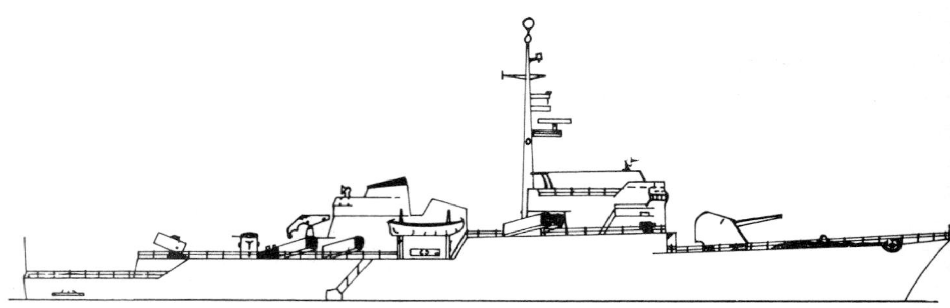

"LUPO" CLASS

2 "ALPINO" CLASS

Name	No.	Builders	Laid down	Launched	Completed
ALPINO (ex-*Circe*)	F 580	Cantiere Navali del Tirreno, Riva Trigoso	27 Feb 1963	10 June 1967	14 Jan 1968
CARABINIERE (ex-*Climene*)	F 581	Cantiere Navali del Tirreno, Riva Trigoso	9 Jan 1965	30 Sep 1967	28 Apr 1968

Displacement, tons 2 700 full load
Length, feet (*metres*) 349·0 (*106·4*) pp; 352·0 (*107·3*) wl; 371·7 (*113·3*) oa
Beam, feet (*metres*) 43·6 (*13·3*)
Draught, feet (*metres*) 12·7 (*3·9*)
Aircraft 2 A/B 204B ASW helicopters
Guns 6—3 in (*76 mm*) dp 62 cal single
A/S weapons 1 single depth charge mortar
Tubes 6 (2 triple) 12 in (*305 mm*) for A/S torpedoes
Main engines 4 Tosi diesels = 16 800 hp; 2 Tosi Metrovick gas turbines = 15 000 hp; 2 shafts; 31 800 hp
Speed, knots 22 (diesel), 29 (diesel and gas)
Range, miles 4 200 at 18 knots
Oil fuel, tons 275
Complement 253 (20 officers, 233 men)

CARABINIERE *1974, Wright and Logan*

Circe and *Climene* were provided for under the 1959-60 programme. The original "Circe" class project was modified in 1962, in respect of both macninery and armament. The originally allocated names *Circe* and *Climene* were changed to *Alpino* and *Carabiniere*, respectively in June 1965. The new design is an improved version of that of the "Centauro" class combined with that of the "Bergamini" class. They have similar basic characteristics but increased engine power.

RADAR. Search: SPS 12. SMA/SPQ-2 combined air/surface search/nav radar-X band. MM/SPR-A radar intercept. 3 Orion fire-control radars in ELSAG Argo "O" fire control system.

SONAR. Possibly SQS-4, SQS-30, SQS-36 with ELSAG fire control system DLB-1.

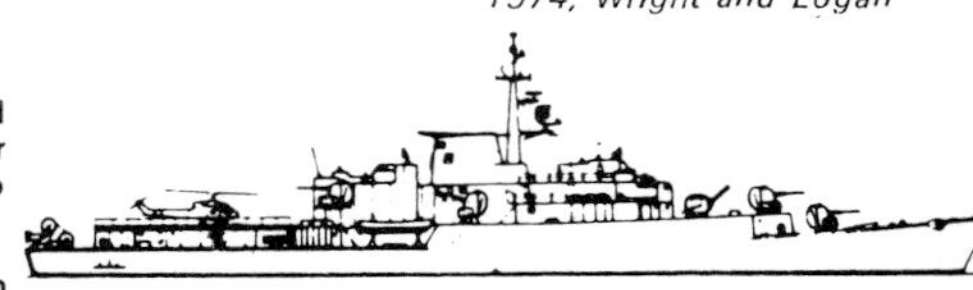

ALPINO CARABINIERE

4 "BERGAMINI" CLASS

Name	No.	Builders	Laid down	Launched	Completed
CARLO BERGAMINI	F 593	San Marco, CRDA Trieste	19 May 1957	16 June 1960	23 June 1962
CARLO MARGOTTINI	F 595	Navalmeccanica, Castellammare	26 May 1957	12 June 1960	5 May 1962
LUIGI RIZZO	F 596	Navalmeccanica, Castellammare	26 May 1957	6 Mar 1957	15 Dec 1961
VIRGINIO FASAN	F 594	Navalmeccanica, Castellammare	6 Mar 1960	9 Oct 1960	10 Oct 1962

Displacement, tons 1 650 full load
Length, feet (*metres*) 311·7 (*95·0*) oa
Beam, feet (*metres*) 37·4 (*11·4*)
Draught, feet (*metres*) 10·5 (*3·2*)
Aircraft 1 A/B-204B helicopter
Guns 2—3 in (*76 mm*) dp 62 cal single
A/S weapons 1 single depth charge mortar
Tubes 6 (2 triple) 12 in (*305 mm*) for A/S torpedoes
Main engines 4 diesels (Fiat in *Fasan* and *Margottini*, Tosi in others); 2 shafts; 15 000 bhp
Speed, knots 24·5
Range, miles 4 000 at 18 knots
Complement 158 (19 officers, 139 men)

BERGAMINI *5/1974, Commander Aldo Fraccaroli*

ANTI-SUBMARINE. The single-barrelled automatic depth charge mortars have a range of 1 000 yards. Rate of fire is 15 DC per minute. The 12-inch torpedoes have a life of six minutes at 30 knots. ELSAG DLB-1 fire control system.

MODIFICATION. The anti-submarine capability was augmented in *Carlo Margottini* in 1968, *Virginio Fasan* in 1969, *Carlo Bergamini* in 1970 and *Luigi Rizzo* in 1971 by the allocation of an AB-204 A/S helicopter for the operation of which the enlargement of the flight deck was necessary together with the removal of the 3-inch gun aft.

RADAR. Search: SPS 12. Fire Control: X Band. Single ARGO NA2 fire control system and radar. MM/ SPR-A radar intercept. Nav-Surface warning.

ROLL DAMPING. Two Denny-Brown stabilisers reduce inclination in heavy seas from 20 to 5 degrees.

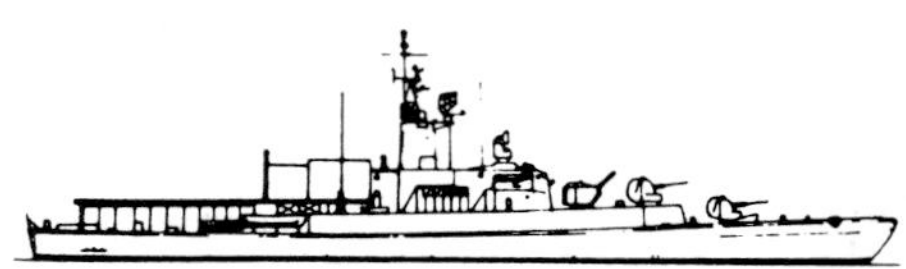

"BERGAMINI" Class

Frigates—*continued*

4 "CENTAURO" CLASS

Name	*No.*	*Builders*	*Laid down*	*Launched*	*Completed*
CANOPO	F 551 (ex-D 570)	Cantieri Navali di Taranto	15 May 1952	20 Feb 1955	1 Apr 1958
CASTORE	F 553 (ex-D 573)	Cantieri Navali di Taranto	14 Mar 1955	8 July 1956	14 July 1957
CENTAURO	F 554 (ex-D 571)	Ansaldo Leghorn	31 May 1952	4 Apr 1954	5 May 1957
CIGNO	F 555 (ex-D 572)	Cantieri Navali di Taranto	10 Feb 1954	20 Mar 1955	7 Mar 1957

Displacement, tons — 1 807 standard; 2 250 full load
Length, feet (*metres*) — 308·4 (*94*) pp; 338·4 (*103·1*) oa
Beam, feet (*metres*) — 39·5 (*12*)
Draught, feet (*metres*) — 12·6 (*3·8*)
Guns, — 3—3 in (*76 mm*) 62 cal single
A/S weapons — 1 three-barrelled depth charge mortar
Tubes — 6 (2 triple) 12 in (*305 mm*) for A/S torpedoes
Main engines — 2 double reduction geared turbines 2 shafts; 22 000 shp
Speed, knots — 25
Boilers — 2 Foster Wheeler; 626 psi (*44* kg/cm^2) working pressure; 842°F (*450°C*) superheat temperature
Oil fuel, tons — 400
Range, miles — 3 660 at 20 knots
Complement — 225 (16 officers, 209 men)

CANOPO — *1974, Commander Aldo Fraccaroli*

Built to Italian plans and specifications under the US off-shore programme.

CONVERSION. Carried out as follows: *Castore*—1966-67, *Canopo*—1968-69, *Centauro*—1970-71, *Cigno*—1972-73. This provided the new 3 in (*76 mm*) armament.

RADAR. Search: SPS 6. Fire Control: X Band. SMA/SPQ-2 combined surface and air search-navigation—X band. MM/SPR-A intercept.

SONAR. SQS-11.

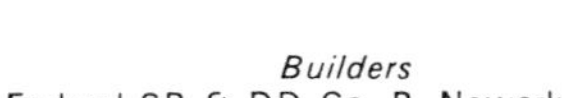

"CENTAURO" Class as converted

ALDEBARAN

Name	*No.*	*Builders*	*Laid down*	*Launched*	*Completed*
ALDEBARAN (ex-USS *Thornhill, DE* 195)	F 590	Federal SB & DD Co. P. Newark	7 Oct 1943	30 Dec 1943	1 Feb 1944

Displacement, tons — 1 900 full load
Length, feet (*metres*) — 306 (*93·3*) oa
Beam, feet (*metres*) — 36·7 (*11·2*)
Draught, feet (*metres*) — 14 (*4·3*)
Guns — 3—3 in (*76 mm*) 50 cal. 6—40 mm; 18—20 mm
A/S weapons — 1 Hedgehog; 8 DCT; 2 DC racks
Main engines — GM diesel-electric; 2 shafts; 6 000 hp
Speed, knots — 21
Range, miles — 11 500 at 11 knots
Oil fuel, tons — 300
Complement — 113 (10 officers, 103 men)

Ex-US destroyer escort of the "Bostwick" class. Transferred on 10 Jan 1951. In 1956 a pentapod foremast was stepped in place of the former polemast.

RADAR. Search: SPS 6. Fire Control: X Band.

ALDEBARAN — *1973, Italian Navy*

4 "ALBATROS" CLASS

Name	*No.*	*Builders*	*Launched*	*Completed*
AIRONE	F 545	Navalmeccanica Castellammare di Stabia	21 Nov 1954	29 Dec 1955
ALBATROS	F 543	Navalmeccanica Castellammare di Stabia	18 July 1954	1 June 1955
ALCIONE	F 544	Navalmeccanica Castellammare di Stabia	19 Sep 1954	23 Oct 1955
AQUILA	F 542	Breda Marghera, Mestre, Venezia	31 July 1954	2 Oct 1956

Displacement, tons — 800 standard; 950 full load
Length, feet (*metres*) — 250·3 (*76·3*) oa
Beam, feet (*metres*) — 31·5 (*9·6*)
Draught, feet (*metres*) — 9·2 (*2·8*)
Guns, — 4—40 mm 70 cal. Bofors (see *Gunnery*)
A/S weapons — 2 Hedgehogs Mk II; 2 DCT; 1 DC rack;
Tubes — 2 triple A/S
Main engines — 2 Fiat diesels; 2 shafts; 5 200 bhp
Speed, knots — 19
Range, miles — 3 000 at 18 knots
Oil fuel, tons — 100
Complement — 109

ALBATROS — *1974, Dr Giorgio Arra*

Eight ships of this class were built in Italy under US offshore MDAP orders. 3 for Italy, 4 for Denmark and 1 for the Netherlands. *Aquila*, laid down on 25 July 1953, which was ceded to the Italian Navy on 18 Oct 1961 at Den Helder.

GUNNERY. The two 3-inch guns originally mounted, one forward and one aft, were temporarily replaced by two 40 mm guns in 1963. The ultimate armament will include two 3-inch guns of the OTO Melara model.

RADAR. SMA/SPQ-2 X band combined air and surface navigation set. ELSAG NA-2 fire control.

"ALBATROS" Class

CORVETTES

4 "DE CRISTOFARO" CLASS

Name	*No.*	*Builders*	*Laid down*	*Launched*	*Completed*
LICIO VISINTINI	F 546	CRDA Monfalcone	30 Sep 1963	30 May 1965	25 Aug 1966
PIETRO DE CRISTOFARO	F 540	Cantiere Navali de Tirreho, Riva Tregoso	30 Apr 1963	29 May 1965	19 Dec 1965
SALVATORE TODARO	F 550	Cantiere Ansaldo, Leghorn	21 Oct 1962	24 Oct 1964	25 Apr 1966
UMBERTO GROSSO	F 541	Cantiere Ansaldo, Leghorn	21 Oct 1962	12 Dec 1964	25 Apr 1966

Displacement, tons 850 standard; 1 020 full load
Length, feet (*metres*) 246 (*75·0*) pp; 263·2 (*80·2*) oa
Beam, feet (*metres*) 33·7 (*10·3*)
Draught, feet (*metres*) 9 (*2·7*)
Guns, 2—3 in (*76 mm*), 62 cal, single
A/S weapons 1 single-barrelled DC mortar
Tubes 2 triple for A/S torpedoes
Main engines 2 diesels = 8 400 bhp; 2 shafts
Speed, knots 23·5
Range, miles 4 000 at 18 knots
Oil fuel, tons 100
Complement 131 (8 officers, 123 men)

LICIO VISINTINI *1972, Italian Navy*

The design is an improved version of the "Albatros" class.

RADAR. Air and surface surveillance radar with antenna mounted at top of foremast. Gunfire control system has director mounted aft, above compass platform, with X band tracker radar.

SONAR. SQS-36. ELSAG DLB-1 fire control system.

"DE CRISTOFARO" Class.

3 "APE" CLASS

BOMBARDA F 549 **SFINGE** F 579
CHIMERA F 569

Displacement, tons 670 standard; 771 full load
Length, feet (*metres*) 192.8 (*58·8*) wl; 212·6 (*64·8*) oa
Beam, feet (*metres*) 28·5 (*8·7*)
Draught, feet (*metres*) 8·9 (*2·7*)
Guns, 4—40 mm 56 cal in *Chimera* and *Sfinge*; 2—40 mm 56 cal and 2—20 mm 70 cal in *Bombarda*
A/S weapons 1 Hedgehog Mk 10
Main engines 2 Fiat diesels; 2 shafts; 3 500 bhp
Speed, knots 15
Range, miles 2 450 at 15 knots
Oil fuel, tons 64
Complement 56 (6 officers, 50 men)

Completed in 1942 (*chemera*), 1943 (*Sfinge*), 1951 (*Bombarda*). Originally fitted for minesweeping. Modified with navigating bridge. *Ape* is now support ship (*nave appoggio*) for frogmen and commandos.

RADAR. Search: SPS 6 in *Sfinge*.

CHIMERA *1973, Dr Giorgio Arra*

VEDETTA (ex-*Belay Deress*, ex-USS *PC* 1616) F 597

Displacement, tons 325 standard; 450 full load
Dimensions, feet 170 pp; 174 oa × 23 × 10
Guns 2—40 mm 56 cal Bofors AA; 2—20 mm AA
Main engines 4 diesels; 2 shafts; 3 240 bhp = 19 knots
A/S weapons 1 Hedgehog; 4 DCT; 2 DC racks
Range, miles 3 000 at 12 knots
Complement 60 (6 officers, 54 men)

She was sold to Italy, being transferred on 3 Feb 1959. Air-conditioning equipment is installed. Refitted in La Spezia Navy Yard in 1959. Employed as a Fishery Protection Vessel.

VEDETTA *1969, Italian Navy*

SUBMARINES

2 "SAURO" CLASS

NAZARIO SAURO +1

Displacement, tons	1 300 surface; 1 450 dived
Length, feet (*metres*)	210 (*64*)
Beam, feet (*metres*)	22·5 (*6·8*)
Draught, feet (*metres*)	15 (*4·5*)
Torpedo tubes	6—21 in (bow)
Main machinery	2 Diesels; 2 electric motors; 1 shaft
Speed, knots	11 surfaced; 19 dived
Complement	45

Two of this class were originally ordered in 1967 but were cancelled in the following year. Reinstated in the building programme in 1972. To be fitted with Selenia passive and active Sonars, search/navigation radar and ECM.

4 "TOTI" CLASS

Name	No.	Builders	Laid down	Launched	Completed
ATTILIO BAGNOLINI	S 505	CRDA Monfalcone	15 Apr 1965	26 Aug 1967	16 June 1968
ENRICO DANDOLO	S 513	CRDA Monfalcone	10 Mar 1967	16 Dec 1967	25 Sep 1968
LAZZARO MOCENIGO	S 514	CRDA Monfalcone	12 June 1967	20 Apr 1968	11 Jan 1969
ENRICO TOTI	S 506	CRDA Monfalcone	15 Apr 1965	12 Mar 1967	22 Jan 1968

Displacement, tons	460 standard; 524 surface; 582 submerged
Length, feet (*metres*)	151·5 (*46·2*)
Beam, feet (*metres*)	15·4 (*4·7*)
Draught, feet (*metres*)	13·1 (*4·0*)
Torpedo tubes	4—21 in
Main machinery	2 Fiat MB 820 N/I diesels, 1 electric motor, Diesel-electric drive; 2 200 hp; 1 shaft
Speed, knots	14 on surface; 15 dived
Range, miles	3 000 at 5 knots (surfaced)
Complement	31 (6 officers, 25 men)

Italy's first indigenously-built submarines since the Second World War. The design was recast several times.

ELECTRONICS. WT, HF, UHF and VLF equipment. Computer based fire control.

RADAR. Search/nav set. IFF, ECM.

SONAR. Passive set in stem. Active set in bow dome. Passive range finding. Ray path analyzer.

TOTI — *1974, Italian Navy*

2 Ex-US GUPPY III TYPE

Name	No.	Builders	Laid down	Launched	Completed	Transferred
PRIMO LONGOBARDO (ex-USS *Pickerel* SS 524)	501	Portsmouth Navy Yard	15 June 1945	17 Jan 1946	10 Jan 1948	18 Aug 1972
GIANFRANCO GAZZANA PRIAROGGIA (ex-USS *Volador* SS 490)	502	Boston Navy Yard	8 Feb 1944	15 Dec 1944	4 Apr 1949	18 Aug 1972

Displacement, tons	1975 standard; 2 450 dived
Length, feet (*metres*)	326·5 (*99·4*) oa
Beam, feet (*metres*)	27 (*8·2*)
Draught, feet (*metres*)	17 (*5·2*)
Torpedo tubes	10—21 in; 6 bow, 4 stern
Main machinery	4 diesels; 6 400 bhp—2 electric motors; 5 400 shp; 2 shafts
Speed, knots	20 surface; 15 dived
Range, miles	12 000 at 10 knots (surfaced)
Oil fuel, tons	300
Complement	85 (10 officers, 75 men)

Arrived in Taranto 19 Oct 1972.

GIANFRANCO GAZZANA PRIAROGGIA — *1973, Dr Giorgio Arra*

2 Ex-US "BALAO" CLASS

Name	No.	Builders	Launched	Completed	Transferred
ALFREDO CAPPELLINI (ex-USS *Capitaine, SS* 336)	S 507	Electric Boat Div. General Dynamics Corpn	1 Oct 1944	26 Jan 1945	5 Mar 1966
EVANGELISTA TORRICELLI (ex-USS *Lizardfish, SS* 373)	S 512	Manitowoc SB Co. Manitowoc, Wisconsin	16 July 1944	30 Dec 1944	9 Jan 1960
FRANCESCO MOROSINI (ex-USS *Besugo, SS* 321)	S 508	Electric Boat Div. General Dynamics Corpn	27 Feb 1944	19 June 1944	31 Mar 1966

Displacement, tons	1 600 standard; 1 855 surface; 2 455 submerged
Length, feet (*metres*)	311·5 (*95·0*)
Beam, feet (*metres*)	27 (*8·2*)
Draught, feet (*metres*)	17 (*5·2*)
Torpedo tubes	10—21 in (*533 mm*) 6 bow and 4 stern
Main machinery	4 GM 16/278 diesels, 6 000 hp; 4 electric motors; 2 750 hp
Speed, knots	18 on surface; 10 submerged
Range, miles	14 000 at 10 knots
Oil fuel, tons	300
Complement	85 (10 officers, 75 men)

Lizardfish was originally to have been renamed *Luigi Torelli.*

CAPPELLINI — *1974, Dr Giorgio Arra*

2 Ex-US "TANG" CLASS

Name	No	Builder	Laid down	Launched	Completed	Transferred
ROMEO ROMEI (ex-USS *Harder* SS 568)	516	Electric Boat Co. Groton	30 June 1950	14 June 1951	31 Mar 1952	20 Feb 1974
LIVIO PIOMARTA (ex-USS *Trigger* SS 564)	515	Electric Boat Co. Groton	24 Feb 1949	3 Dec 1951	19 Aug 1952	10 July 1973

Displacement, tons	2 100 surface; 2 700 dived
Length, feet (*metres*)	287 (*87·4*)
Beam, feet (*metres*)	27·3 (*8·3*)
Draught, feet (*metres*)	19 (*6·2*)
Torpedo tubes	8—21 in, 6 bow, 2 stern
Main machinery	3 Diesels 4 500 shp; 2 electric motors 5 600 hp
Speed, knots	20 surface; 18 dived
Complement	83 (8 officers, 75 men)

Livio Piomarta arrived at Taranto in Apr 1974. *Romeo Romei* expected in April 1975. Both refitted in Philadelphia Navy Yard.

LIVIO PIOMARTA — *1973, Italian Navy*

LIGHT FORCES

1 + 3 "SPARVIERO" CLASS (HYDROFOIL—MISSILE)

SPARVIERO P 420 + 3

Displacement, tons	62·5
Dimensions, feet	75 × 36·5 × 14·4 (length and beam foils extended, draught hullborne)
Missile launchers	2 fixed for "Otomat" ship-to-ship missiles
Guns	1 Oto Melara 76 mm automatic anti-aircraft
Main engines	Rolls Royce "Proteus" gas turbine driving waterjet pump; 4 500 bhp; diesel and retractable propeller unit for hullborne propulsion
Range, miles	400 at 45 knots; 1 200 at 8 knots
Speed, knots	50 max, 42 cruising (sea state 4)
Complement	21 (6 officers, 15 men)

Completed for trials 9 May 1973 by Oto Melara, La Spezia. Missiles made by Oto Melara Matra. Fitted with Elsag NA-10 Mod 1 fire control system with Orion RTN-10X radar. Delivered to the Navy as class prototype on 15 July 1974. Three more hydrofoils planned.

SPARVIERO *1974, Italian Navy*

2 "FRECCIA" CLASS (FAST ATTACK CRAFT—CONVERTIBLE)

FRECCIA (ex-*MC* 590) P 493 **SAETTA** (ex-*MC* 591) P 494

Displacement, tons	188 standard; 205 full load
Dimensions, feet	150 × 23·8 × 5·5
Guns	*As Gunboat*: 3—40 mm, 70 cal or 2—40 mm, 70 cal *As Fast Minelayer*: 1—40 mm AA with 8 mines *As Torpedo Boat*: 1—40 mm, 70 cal
Tubes	*As Torpedo Boat*: 2—21 in
Main engines	2 diesels; 7 600 bhp; 1 Bristol Siddeley Proteus gas turbine, 4 250 shp; Total hp 11 850 = 40 knots
Complement	31 (8 officers, 23 men)

Freccia was laid down by Cantiere del Tirreno, Riva Trigoso on 30 Apr 1963, launched on 9 Jan 1965 and commissioned on 6 July 1965. *Saetta* was laid down by CRDA, Monfalcone on 11 June 1963, launched on 11 Apr 1965, and completed in 1966. Can be converted in 24 hours to gunboat, torpedo boat, fast minelayer, or missile boat. Fitted with S band navigation and tactical radar. The gunfire control system has a director with X band tracker radar. *Saetta* has been armed with Sea Killer Mk I system with 5 round trainable launcher, Contraves fire control, including target-tracking radar, with TV camera mounted on top. It is planned to fit *Freccia* with Otomat, Selina radar, and Ecograph sonar in the near future.

SAETTA experimentally armed with 5 short range missiles *1970, Italian Navy*

FRECCIA *1974, Italian Navy*

2 "LAMPO" CLASS (FAST ATTACK CRAFT—CONVERTIBLE)

BALENO (ex-*MC* 492) P 492 **LAMPO** (ex-*MC* 491) P 491

Displacement, tons	170 standard; 196 full load
Dimensions, feet	131·5 × 21 × 5
Guns	*As Gunboat*: 3—40 mm, 70 cal or 2—40 mm, 70 cal *As Torpedo Boat*: 1—40 mm, 70 cal
Tubes	*As Torpedo Boat*: 2—21 in
Main engines	2 Fiat diesels, 1 Metrovick gas turbine; 3 shafts; total 11 700 hp = 39 knots
Complement	33 (5 officers, 28 men)

Convertible gunboats, improved versions of the *Folgore* prototype. Both built by Arsenale MM Taranto. *Lampo* was laid down on 4 Jan 1958, launched on 22 Nov 1960 and commissioned in July 1963. *Baleno* was laid-down on the same slip on 22 Nov 1960, launched on 10 May 1964 and commissioned on 16 July 1965. She has been converted to an improved design.

BALENO *1972, Dr. Giorgio Arra*

FOLGORE (ex-*MC* 490) P 490 (FAST ATTACK CRAFT—TORPEDO)

Displacement, tons	160 standard; 190 full load
Dimensions, feet	129·5 × 19·7 × 5
Guns	2—40 mm AA
Tubes	2—21 in
Main engines	4 diesels; 4 shafts; 10 000 bhp = 38 knots (accelerating from 20 knots to full speed very rapidly)
Complement	39 (9 officers, 30 men)

Authorised in Nov 1950, launched on 21 Jan 1954 from CRDA Monfalcone Yard, and commissioned on 21 July 1955. Two rudders.

FOLGORE *1972, Dr. Giorgio Arra*

MS 441 (ex-841) **MS 443** (ex-843) **MS 452** (ex-852) **MS 453** (ex-853)

(FAST ATTACK CRAFT—TORPEDO)

Displacement tons	64 full load
Dimensions, feet	78 × 20 × 6
Guns	1—40 mm, 56 cal; 2 or 3—20 mm, 70 cal
Torpedoes	2—17·7 in (no tubes)
Main engines	3 petrol motors; 3 shafts; 4 500 bhp = 34 knots
Range, miles	1 000 at 20 knots
Complement	24 (3 officers, 21 men)

MS 453 *1974, Italian Navy*

MS 441 converted into a fast transport for commandos and frogmen. Former US PT boats of "Higgins" class. Refitted in Italy in 1949-53. New radar installed. MS 442 (ex-842). MS 451 (ex-851), transferred to Customs in 1966.

Light Forces—*continued*

MS 473 (ex-813) **MS 474** (ex-614) **MS 481** (ex-615)

(FAST ATTACK CRAFT—TORPEDO)

Displacement, tons	72 full load
Dimensions, feet	92 × 15 × 5
Guns	1 or 2—40 mm, 56 cal
Torpedoes	2—17·7 in
Main engines	Petrol motors; 3 shafts; 3 450 bhp = 27 knots
Range, miles	600 at 16 knots
Complement	24 (3 officers, 21 men)

Built in 1942-43 at CRDA Monfalcone yard; converted as MV (motovedette) with no tubes under the Peace Treaty. Reconverted in 1951-53. MS 473 was refitted as convertible boat in 1960 and MS 474 and MS 481 in 1961. Originally class of four.

The British MTBs *Dark Avenger, Dark Biter, Dark Hunter* and *Dark Invader* were taken over in 1967 for the Guardia di Finanza (Customs House Guard).

MS 481 and 473 *1974, Italian Navy*

AMPHIBIOUS FORCES

2 Ex-US "COUNTY" CLASS (LSTs)

GRADO (ex-USS *De Soto County*, LST 1171) L 9890
CAORLE (ex-USS *York County*, LST 1175) L 9891

Displacement, tons	4 164 light; 8 000 full load
Dimensions, ft (*m*)	444 × 62 × 16·5 (*133·4 × 18·9 × 5*)
Guns	6—3 inch (*76 mm*)
Main engines	Diesels; 1 440 shp; 2 shafts; (CP propellers) = 17·5 knots
Complement	165 (10 officers, 155 men)
Troops	Approx 575

Both completed 1957 and transferred 17 July 1972.

STROMBOLI (TRANSPORT AND SUPPORT SHIP)

Displacement, tons	3 556 light; 8 706 full load
Dimensions, ft (*m*)	423·1 oa × 59 × 21·3 (*120 oa × 18 × 6·5*)
Guns	1—76 mm/62 OTO; 2—40 mm
Main engines	2 Fiat diesel C 428 SS; 4 800 hp; 1 shaft; 4-bladed LIPS propeller
Complement	115 (9 officers, 106 men)

Laid down by Cantieri del Tirreno e Riuniti, Riva Trigoso on 1 Oct 1973. Launch early 1975.

GRADO *1974, Dr Giorgio Arra*

1 AV TYPE (TRANSPORT)

ANDREA BAFILE (ex-USS *St. George*, AV 16, ex-A 5314) L 9871

Displacement, tons	8 510 standard; 14 000 full load
Dimensions, ft (*m*)	492 oa × 69·5 × 26 (*163 × 23 × 8·5*)
Aircraft	1 or 2 helicopters
Guns	2—5 in 38 cal
Main engines	Allis-Chalmers geared turbines; 1 shaft; 8 500 shp = 17 knots
Boilers	2 Foster-Wheeler
Range, miles	13 400 at 13 knots
Complement	58 (10 officers, 48 men)

Former USN seaplane carrier, launched on 14 Feb 1944. Purchased and commissioned in the Italian Navy on 17 May 1969 and modified. Troop transport and command ship. Serves as a depot ship for "Special Forces" (frogmen etc.).

ANDREA BAFILE *1974, Italian Nav*

1 AKA TYPE (TRANSPORT)

ETNA (ex-USS *Whitley, AKA* 91, ex-A 5328) L 9870

Displacement, tons	7 430 light; 14 200 full load
Measurement, tons	5 145 gross; 7 700 deadweight
Dimensions, ft (*m*)	435·0 wl; 459·2 oa × 63·0 × 26·3 max (*140 × 19·2 × 7·8*)
Guns	4—40 mm
Main engines	GE geared turbines; 1 shaft; 6 000 shp = 15 knots
Boilers	2 Combustion Engineering
Range, miles	18 900 at 12 knots

Former US Navy attack cargo ship of the "Andromeda" class. Built by Moore DD Co, Oakland, California. Launched on 22 June 1944. Completed on 21 Sep 1944. C2—S—B 1 type. Transferred to Italy in Feb 1962.

ETNA *1974, Dr Giorgio Arra*

QUARTO L 9881 (LCT)

Displacement, tons	764 standard; 980 full load
Dimensions, feet	226·4 × 31·3 × 6
Guns	4—40 mm AA (2 twin)
Main engines	3 diesels; 2 300 bhp = 13 knots
Range, miles	1 300 at 13 knots

Quarto was laid down on 19 Mar 1966 at Taranto Naval Shipyard and launched on 18 Mar 1967. The design is intermediate between that of LSM and LCT.

QUARTO, *1971, Commander Aldo Fraccaroli*

MINE WARFARE FORCES

4 "SALMONE" CLASS (Ex-US MSO TYPE) (MINESWEEPERS—OCEAN)

SALMONE (ex-*MSO* 507)	M 5430	**SQUALO** (ex-*MSO* 518)	M 5433
SGOMBRO (ex-*MSO* 517)	M 5432	**STORIONE** (ex-*MSO* 506)	M 5431

Displacement, tons	665 standard; 750 full load
Dimensions, feet	165 wl; 173 oa × 35 × 13·6 (*52·7 × 10·7 × 4*)
Gun	1—40 mm 56 cal AA
Main engines	2 diesels; 2 shafts; 1 600 bhp = 14 knots
Oil fuel, tons	46
Range, miles	3 000 at 10 knots
Complement	51 (7 officers, 44 men)

Former US "Agile" class. Wooden hulls and non-magnetic diesels of stainless steel alloy. Controllable pitch propellers. *Storione*, launched on 13 Nov 1954, was built by Martinolich SB Company, San Diego and transferred on 23 Feb, 1956. *Salmone*, launched on 19 Feb 1955 was built by Martinolich SB Co, and transferred at San Diego, on 17 June 1956. *Sgombro* and *Squalo* were delivered in June 1957.

SGOMBRO *1972, Commander Aldo Fraccaroli*

15 "ABETE" CLASS (MINESWEEPERS—COASTAL)

ABETE	M 5501	**GELSO**	M 5509	**ONTANO**	M 5513
CASTAGNO	M 5504	**LARICE**	M 5510	**PINO**	M 5514
CEDRO	M 5505	**MANDORLO**	M 5519	**PIOPPO**	A 5307
FAGGIO	M 5507	**NOCE**	M 5511	**PLATANO**	M 5516
FRASSINO	M 5508	**OLMO**	M 5512	**QUERCIA**	M 5517

Displacement, tons	378 standard; 405 full load (*Mandorlo* 360)
Dimensions, feet	138 pp; 144 oa × 26·5 × 8·5
Guns	2—20 mm, 70 cal AA
Main engines	2 diesels; 2 shafts; 1 200 bhp = 13·5 knots
Oil fuel, tons	25
Range, miles	2 500 at 10 knots
Complement	38 (5 officers, 33 men)

Wooden hulled *Dragomine Costieri* constructed throughout of anti-magnetic materials All transferred by the US in 1953-54. *Pioppo* used for surveying. Originally class of 18.

ONTANO *1972, Dr. Giorgio Arra*

18 "AGAVE" CLASS (MINESWEEPERS—COASTAL)

BAMBÙ	*M 5521	**AGAVE**	M 5531	**GLICINE**	M 5537
EBANO	*M 5522	**ALLORO**	M 5532	**LOTO**	M 5538
MANGO	*M 5523	**EDERA**	M 5533	**MIRTO**	A 5306
MOGANO	*M 5524	**GAGGIA**	M 5534	**TIMO**	M 5540
PALMA	*M 5525	**GELSOMINO**	M 5535	**TRIFOGLIO**	M 5541
SANDALO	*M 5527	**GIAGGIOLO**	M 5536	**VISCHIO**	M 5542

Displacement, tons	375 standard; 405 full load
Dimensions, ft (*m*)	144 oa × 25·6 × 8·5 (*43 × 8 × 2·6*)
Guns	2—20 mm 70 cal AA
Main engines	2 diesels; 2 shafts; 1 200 bhp = 13·5 knots
Oil fuel, tons	25
Range, miles	2 500 at 10 knots
Complement	38 (5 officers, 33 men)

Non-magnetic minesweepers of composite wooden and alloy construction similar to those transferred from the US but built in Italian yards. First six were built by CRDA, Monfalcone, and launched in 1956. *Mirto* used for surveying. Originally class of nineteen.

TRIFOGLIO *1972 Dr. Giorgio Arra*

10 "ARAGOSTA" CLASS (MINESWEEPERS—INSHORE)

ARAGOSTA	M 5450	**GRANCHIO**	M 5458	**POLIPO**	M 5463
ASTICE	M 5452	**MITILO**	M 5459	**PORPORA**	M 5464
GAMBERO	M 5457	**PINNA**	M 5462	**RICCIO**	M 5465
				SCAMPO	M 5466

Displacement, tons	188 full load
Dimensions, ft (*m*)	106 × 21 × 6 (*32·5 × 6·4 × 1·8*)
Main engines	2 diesels; 1 000 bhp = 14 knots
Oil fuel, tons	15
Range, miles	2 000 at 9 knots
Complement	16 (4 officers, 12 men)

Similar to the British "Ham" class. All constructed in Italian yards to the order of NATO in 1955-57. All names of small sea creatures. Designed armament of one 20 mm gun not mounted. Originally class of twenty.

POLIPO *1971, Italian Navy*

SURVEY VESSEL

AMMIRAGLIO MAGNAGHI A 5303

Displacement, tons	1 700
Dimensions, ft (*m*)	271·3 × 44·9 × 11·5 (*82·7 × 13·7 × 3·5*)
Aircraft	1—AB 204 helicopter
Gun	1—40 mm
Main engines	2 Fiat diesels = 3 000 hp; 1 shaft; Auxiliary electric motor— 240 hp = 4 knots
Speed, knots	17
Range, miles	6 000 at 12 knots (1 diesel); 4 200 at 17 knots (2 diesels)
Complement	145 (15 officers, 15 scientists, 115 men)

Building by Cantieri Navali di Tirreno é Riuniti. Ordered under 1972 programme. Laid down 13 June 1973. Launched 11 Oct 1974 for completion 1975. Equipped with flight-deck and hangar.

AMMIRAGLIO MAGNAGHI (launching) *10/1974, Commander Aldo Fraccaroli*

MIRTO A 5306 **PIOPPO** A 5307

Mirto of the "Agave" class and *Pioppo* of the "Abete" class (see Minewarefare section for details) have been converted for surveying duties.

MIRTO *1973, Dr Giorgio Arra*

SERVICE FORCES

1 Ex-US "T2" TYPE (REPLENISHMENT TANKER)

STEROPE (ex-*Enrico Insom*) A 5368

Displacement, tons	5 350 light; 21 800 full load
Dimensions, ft (*m*)	523·5 oa × 68 × 30·8 (*159·5 × 20·7 × 9*)
Main engines	Turbo-electric; 6 000 shp = 15 knots
Boilers	2 Babcock & Wilcox
Complement	115 (11 officers, 104 men)

Former United States built oiler of the T 2 type acquired by the Italian Navy in 1959 and refitted at La Spezia Navy Yard in April 1959.

STEROPE *5/1974, Commander Aldo Fraccaroli*

1 AVP TYPE (SUPPORT SHIP)

PIETRO CAVEZZALE (ex-USS *Oyster Bay, AVP* 28, ex-*AGP* 6) A 5301

Displacement, tons	1 766 standard; 2 800 full load
Dimensions, ft (*m*)	300 wl; 311·8 oa × 41 × 13·5 (*95 × 12·5 × 3·7*)
Guns	1—76 mm; 2—40 mm, 56 cal AA
Main engines	2 sets diesels; 2 shafts; 6 080 bhp = 16 knots
Oil fuel, tons	400
Range, miles	10 000 at 11 knots
Complement	143 (12 officers, 131 men)

Former United States seaplane tender (previously motor torpedo boat tender) of the "Barnegat" class, built at Lake Washington Shipyard and launched on 7 Sep 1942. Transferred to the Italian Navy on 23 Oct 1957 and renamed.

PIETRO CAVEZZALE *1971, Commander Aldo Fraccaroli*

9 Ex-GERMAN MFP TYPE (COASTAL TRANSPORTS)

MTC 1001 **MTC 1004** **MTC 1005** **MTC 1006** **MTC 1007** **MTC 1008** **MTC 1009** **MTC 1010** **MTC 1102**

Displacement, tons	240 standard
Dimensions, feet	164 × 21·3 × 5·7
Guns	2 or 3—20 or 37 mm
Main engines	2 or 3 diesels; 500 bhp = 10 knots
Complement	19 (1 officer, 18 men)

Moto-Trasporti Costieri, MTC 1001 to 1010 are Italian MZ (*Motozattere*). MTC 1102 and 1103 are ex-German built in Italy. MTC 1002 was removed from the effective list in 1964, MTC 1101 and MTC 1104 in 1970, and MTC 1103 in 1971.

MTC 1006 *1974, Italian Navy*

22 Ex-US LCM TYPE

MTM 9901 **MTM 9902** **MTM 9905** **MTM 9908** **MTM 9909** **MTM 9911** **MTM 9912** **MTM 9913** **MTM 9914** **MTM 9915** **MTM 9916** **MTM 9917** **MTM 9918** **MTM 9919** **MTM 9920** **MTM 9922** **MTM 9923** **MTM 9924** **MTM 9925** **MTM 9926** **MTM 9927** **MTM 9928**

Displacement, tons	20 standard
Dimensions, feet	49·5 × 14·8 × 4·2
Guns	2—20 mm AA
Main engines	Diesels; speed 10 knots

Rated as *Moto-Trasporti Medi*. Former US landing craft of the LCM type.

37 Ex-US LCVP TYPE

MTP 9703 **MTP 9707** **MTP 9708** **MTP 9710** **MTP 9711** **MTP 9713** **MTP 9714** **MTP 9715** **MTP 9719** **MTP 9720** **MTP 9723** **MTP 9726** **MTP 9727** **MTP 9728** **MTP 9729** **MTP 9730** **MTP 9732** **MTP 9733** **MTP 9734** **MTP 9735** **MTP 9736** **MTP 9737** **MTP 9738** **MTP 9739** **MTP 9740** **MTP 9741** **MTP 9742** **MTP 9743** **MTP 9744** **MTP 9745** **MTP 9748** **MTP 9749** **MTP 9750** **MTP 9751** **MTP 9752** **MTP 9753** **MTP 9754**

Displacement, tons	8 to 10 standard
Dimensions, feet	36·5 × 10·8 × 3
Guns	2 MG
Main engines	Diesels; Speed: 10 knots

Rated as *Moto-Trasporti Piccoli*. MTP 9703 to 9723 are former US landing craft of the LCVP type. MTP 9726 of 10 tons displacement and similar characteristics is of Italian construction.

TRAINING SHIPS

AMERIGO VESPUCCI A 5312

Displacement, tons	3 543 standard; 4 146 full load
Dimensions feet (*m*)	229·5 pp; 270 oa hull; 330 oa bowsprit × 51 × 22 (*82·4 × 15·5 × 7*)
Guns	4—3 in, 50 cal; 1—20 mm
Main engines	Two Fiat diesels with electric drive to 2 Marelli motors, 1 shaft; 2 000 hp = 10 knots
Sail area	22 604 square feet
Endurance	5 450 miles at 6·5 knots
Complement	67 (7 officers, 60 men)

Built at Castellammare. Launched on 22 March 1930 and completed in 1931. Hull, masts and yards are of steel. Extensively refitted at La Spezia Naval Dockyard in 1964.

AMERIGO VESPUCCI *1974, Wright and Logan*

PALINURO (ex-*Commandant Louis Richard*) A 5311.

Displacement, tons	1 042 standard; 1 450 full load
Measurement, tons	858 gross
Dimensions, ft (*m*)	204 pp; 226·3 oa × 32 × 18·7 (*59 × 10 × 4·8*)
Main engines	1 diesel; 1 shaft; 450 bhp = 7·5 knots
Endurance, miles	5 390 at 7·5 knots
Sail area, square feet	1 152

Barquentine, ex-French, launched in 1920. Purchased in 1950. Rebuilt and commissioned in Italian Navy on 16 July 1955.

PALINURO *1968, Italian Navy*

CORSARO II A 5316

Measurement, tons	47
Dimensions, feet	6·9 × 15·4 × 9·8
Sail area, square feet	2 200
Complement	13 (7 officers, 6 men)

Special yacht for sail training and oceanic navigation. RORC class. Built by Costaguta Yard, Voltri, in 1959-60.

STELLA POLARE A 5313

Measurement, tons	41
Dimensions, ft (*m*)	68·6 × 15·4 × 9·5 (*20·9 × 4·7 × 2·9*)
Auxiliary engines	1 Mercedes-Benz diesel, 96 bhp
Sail area	2 117 square feet
Complement	14 (8 officers, 6 men)

Yawl rigged built by Sangermani, Chiavari in 1964-65 as a sail training vessel for the Italian Navy.

NETLAYERS

2 "ALICUDI" CLASS

ALICUDI (ex-USS AN 99) A 5304
FILICUDI (ex-USS AN 100) A 5305

Displacement, tons	680 standard; 834 full load
Dimensions, ft (*m*)	151·8 pp; 165·3 oa × 33·5 × 10·5 (*46·3 × 10·2 × 3·2*)
Guns	1—40 mm, 70 cal AA; 4—20 mm, 70 cal AA
Main engines	Diesel-electric: 1 200; hp = 12 knots
Complement	51 (5 officers, 46 men)

Built to the order of NATO. Laid down on 22 Apr 1954 and 19 July 1954, respectively, by Ansaldo, Leghorn, launched on 11 July 1954 and 26 Sep 1954.

FILICUDI *1972, Dr. Giorgio Arra*

LIGHTHOUSE TENDERS

RAMPINO A 5309

Displacement, tons	350 standard; 645 full load
Dimensions, feet	158·8 × 24·2 × 13
Main engines	Triple expansion = 7 knots
Complement	40 (3 officers, 37 men)

Buoy tender. Of netlayer type. Built at Osaka.

3 Ex-BRITISH LCT(3) TYPE

MTF 1301 **MTF 1302** **MTF 1303**

Displacement, tons	296 light; 700 full load
Dimensions, feet	192 × 31 × 7
Guns	1—40 mm, 56 cal AA; 2—20 mm, 70 cal AA
Main engines	Diesel; 1 shaft; speed = 8 knots
Complement	23 (3 officers, 20 men)

Converted landing craft of the British LCT (3) type. Lighthouse motor transports.

MTF 1301 *1968, Italian Navy*

SALVAGE SHIP

PROTEO (ex-*Perseo*) A 5310

Displacement, tons	1 865 standard; 2 147 full load
Dimensions, feet	220·5 pp; 248 oa × 38 × 21
Main engines	2 diesels; 4 800 bhp; single shaft = 16 knots
Range, miles	7 500 at 13 knots
Complement	130 (10 officers, 120 men)

Laid down at Cantieri Navali Riuniti, Ancona, in 1943. Suspended in 1944. Seized by Germans and transferred to Trieste. Construction re-started at Cantieri Navali Riuniti, Ancona, in 1949. Formerly mounted one 3·9 inch AA gun and two 20 mm.

PROTEO *1969, Italian Navy*

REPAIR CRAFT

MOC 1201 **MOC 1202** **MOC 1203** **MOC 1204** **MOC 1205** **MOC 1207** **MOC 1208**

Displacement, tons	350 standard; 640 full load
Dimensions, feet	192 × 31 × 7
Guns	2—40 mm; 2—20 mm (2 ships have 2—40 mm and 1 ship has 3—20 mm)
Main engines	Diesel = 8 knots
Complement	24 (3 officers, 21 men)

Former British LCT (3) type landing craft converted to repair craft. MOC 1207 and 1208 are ammunition transports.

MOC 1201 *1973, Dr Giorgio Arra*

WATER CARRIERS

PIAVE A 5354 **TEVERE** A 5355

4 973 tons full load—built 1971-73. Complement 55 (7 officers, 48 men).

PIAVE *1974, Commander Aldo Fraccaroli*

BASENTO A 5356 **BRADANO** A 5357 **BRENTA** A 5358

1 914 tons. Built by Inma di La Spezia. Laid down in 1969-70 and launched and completed in 1970-72. Complement 24 (3 officers, 21 men).

ADIGE (ex-*YW* 92) A 5369 **TANARO** (ex-*YW* 99) A 5376
TICINO (ex-*YW* 79) A 5377

Ex-US Army YW type. 1 470 tons full load. Complement 35 (4 officers, 31 men).

VOLTURNO A 5366

Complement 67 (7 officers, 60 men).

MINCIO A 5374

645 tons. Launched in 1929. Complement 19 (1 officer, 18 men).

BORMIDA A 5359

Complement 11 (1 officer, 10 men).

TIMAVO
645 tons. Built by COMI, Venezia, 1926.

FRIGIDO (ex-*Fukuiu Maru*)
398 tons Launched in 1912.

OFANTO
250 tons. Built 1913-14.

LENO **SIMETO** **SPRUGOLA** **STURA**
Small water carriers of 270, 167, 212 and 126 tons displacement, respectively.

SIMETO **STURA**

Small water carriers of 167 and 126 tons displacement, respectively.

TUGS

PORTO D'ISCHIA A 5378 **RIVA TRIGOSO** A 5379

Displacement, tons	296 full load
Dimensions, feet	83·7 × 23·3 × 10·8
Main engines	Diesel; 1 shaft; 850 bhp × 12·1 knots

Both launched in Sep 1969. Controllable pitch propeller.

AUSONIA **PANARIA**

Displacement, tons 240

Both launched in 1948. Coastal tugs for general utility duties.

CICLOPE A 5319

Displacement, tons	1 200
Dimensions, feet	157·5 × 32·5 × 13
Main engines	Triple expansion; 1 shaft; 1 000 ihp = 8 knots

Launched in 1944.

MISENO **MONTE CRISTO**

Displacement, tons 285

Former United States Navy harbour tugs.

ERCOLE A 5388 (1971) **GAGLIARDO** A 5322 (1938)
ROBUSTO A 5323 (1939) **VIGOROSO** A 5394 (1971)

Displacement, tons	389 standard; 506 full load
Main engines	1 000 ihp = 8 knots

PASSERO Y 439 (1934) **RIZZUTO** Y 473 (1956) **CICERO** Y 433 (1956)

Principally employed as ferry tugs.

SAN GIUSTO

Displacement, tons	486 standard
Main engines	900 hp = 12 knots

CAPRERA	A 5381 (1972)	**PORTO RECANATI**	A 5387 (1937)
LEVANZO	A 5397 (1973)	**PORTO VECCHIO**	A 5390 (1942)
PANTELLERIA	A 5382 (1972)	**SALVORE**	A 5391 (1927)
PIANOSA	A 5396 (1914)	**TINO**	A 5392 (1930)
PORTO PISANO	A 5386 (1937)		

Displacement, tons	226 to 270
Dimensions, feet	88·8 × 22 × 10
Main engines	600 ihp = 9 knots

Principally employed as harbour tugs.

COLOSSO (ex-*LT* 214) A 5320 **FORTE** (ex-*LT* 159) A 5321

Displacement, tons	525 standard; 835 full load
Dimensions, feet	142·8 × 32·8 × 11
Main engines	2 diesel-electric; 690 hp = 11 knots

Ex-US Army.

FAVIGNANA A 5385 (1973) **USTICA** A 5324 (1973)

Displacement, tons	270 standard
Dimensions, feet	114·8 × 29·5 × 13
Main engines	1 200 hp

VENTIMIGLIA

Displacement, tons	230 standard
Dimensions, feet	108·2 × 23 × 7·2
Main engines	550 hp = 10 knots

ABBAZIA	Y 411 (1968)	**MESCO**	Y 435 (1933)
ALBENGA	Y 412 (1973)	**NISIDA**	Y 437 (1943)
ARZACHENA	Y 414 (1931)	**PIOMBINO**	Y 440 (1969)
ASINARA	Y 415 (1936)	**POZZI**	Y 422 (1912)
BOEO	Y 417 (1943)	**SAN BENEDETTO**	Y 446 (1941)
CARBONARA	Y 419 (1936)	**SPERONE**	Y 454 (1965)
CHIOGGIA	Y 421 (1919)	**TAVOLARA**	Y 455 (1955)
CORDEVOLE	Y 423 (1915)	**No 78**	Y 469 (1965)
LAMPEDUSA	Y 416 (1972)	**No 96**	Y 474 (1962)
LINARO	Y 430 (1913)	**USTICA**	Y 478 (1973)

Small tugs for harbour duties.

RP 101 Y 403 (1972) **RP 103** Y 406 (1974) **RP 105** Y 408 (1974)
RP 102 Y 404 (1972) **RP 104** Y 407 (1974) **RP 106** Y 410 (1974)
RP 107 Y 413 (1974)

Displacement, tons	36 standard
Dimensions, feet	61·6 × 14·6 × 5·9
Main engines	1 diesel; 500 hp

Built by Cantiere Navale Visintini-Donado (Rovigo).

IVORY COAST

Bases

Use made of ports at Avidjan, Sassandra, Tabou and San Pedro

Personnel

1975: 140 officers and men

Mercantile Marine

Lloyd's Register of Shipping: 46 vessels of 121 276 tons gross

PATROL BOATS

1 FRANCO-BELGE TYPE

VIGILANT

Displacement, tons	240 normal
Dimensions, feet	149·3 pp; 155·8 oa × 23·6 × 8·2
Guns	2—40 mm AA
Missiles	8 SS12
Main engines	2 diesels; 2 shafts; 2 400 bhp = 18·5 knots
Range, miles	2 000 at 15 knots
Complement	25 (3 officers and 22 men)

Built by Franco-Belge. Laid down in Feb 1967. Launched on 23 May 1967. Completed in 1968. Sister ship to *Malaika* of Madagascan Navy.

1 Ex-FRENCH VC TYPE

PERSEVERANCE (ex-*VC* 9, *P* 759)

Displacement, tons	75 standard; 82 full load
Dimensions, feet	104·5 × 15·5 × 5·5
Guns	2—20 mm AA
Main engines	2 Mercedes-Benz diesels; 2 shafts; 2 700 bhp = 28 knots
Oil fuel, tons	10
Range, miles	1 100 at 16·5 knots; 800 at 21 knots
Complement	15

Former French seaward defence motor launch. Built by Constructions Mécaniques de Normandie, Cherbourg. Completed in 1958. Transferred from France to Ivory Coast 26 April 1963

PERSEVERANCE *1964, Ivory Coast Armed Forces*

4 RIVER PATROL CRAFT

Of varying sizes from 24-34 feet. Used for river and lake patrols

LOKODJO

Displacement, tons	450

Now used as a training and supply ship. Built in West Germany in 1953 and purchased in 1970. Trawler type.

LANDING CRAFT

2 LCVP

Displacement, tons	7
Guns	2 MG
Main engines	Mercedes diesels
Speed	9 knots

Built in Abidjan in 1970.

JAMAICA

Defence Force Coast Guard

Jamaica, which became independent within the Commonwealth, on 6 Aug 1962, formed the Coast Guard as the Maritime Arm of the Defence Force. This is based at HMJS Cagway, Port Royal.
The Jamaican Government signed an agreement with the USA for the transfer of a small number of coastguard vessels for the new navy.
Great Britain lent several RN petty officers for technical assistance. The British Mission included a technical team to survey sites for the establishment of local naval bases.

Administration

Officer Commanding Jamaican Defence Force Coast Guard:
Captain J. E Farnol D.S.C., RN.(Retd)

Personnel

1975: 12 officers, 70 Petty officers and ratings (*Coast Guard Reserve:* 8 officers 27 men)

Mercantile Marine

Lloyd's Register of shipping: 5 vessels of 6 740 tons gross

PATROL BOATS

DISCOVERY BAY P 4 **HOLLAND BAY** P 5 **MANATEE BAY** P 6

Displacement, tons	60
Dimensions, feet	85 × 18·8 × 5·9
Guns	3—·50 cal Browning
Main engines	3 GM 12 V71 TI diesels; 3 shafts; 2 000 shp = 26·5 knots
Oil fuel, tons	13
Range, miles	1 000 at 20 knots
Complement	10

Built by Teledyne Sewart Seacraft Inc, Berwick, La, USA. All aluminium construction. *Discovery Bay*, the prototype was launched in Aug 1966 and commissioned on 3 Nov 1966. *Holland Bay*, commissioned 4 Apr 1967, and *Manatee Bay*, commissioned 9 Aug 1967, were supplied under the US Military Assistance Programme. All three boats were extensively refitted and modified in 1972-73 by the builders with GM 12V 71 Turbo-injected engines to give greater range, speed and operational flexibility.

DISCOVERY BAY *1973, Jamaica C G*

NEW CONSTRUCTION

Dimensions, feet	105 × 19 × 7
Guns	2—20 mm; 3—·50 cal MG; 1—81 mm mortar
Main engines	2 Maybach MB 16V 538 TB90; 6 000 shp = 32 knots
Complement	15

Designed by Teledyne Sewart Inc, Berwick, La USA. First boat delivered in 1974. Boats will have accommodation for 24 soldiers and may be used as mobile hospitals in an emergency.

AVR TYPE
The former 3 ex-US AVR type patrol boats have been disposed of.

JORDAN

Coastal Guard

It was officially stated in 1969 that Jordan had no naval force known as such, but the Jordan Coastal Guard, sometimes called the Jordan Sea Force, took orders direct from the Director of Operations at General Headquarters. There is no longer a flotilla in the Dead Sea.

Base

Aqaba

Personnel

1975: 250 officers and men

Mercantile Marine

Lloyd's Register of Shipping: 1 vessel of 200 tons gross

2 "BERTRAM" TYPE (COASTAL PATROL CRAFT)

Standard conversions of the cruiser type. Glass fibre hulls.

2 "POLSON" TYPE (COASTAL PATROL CRAFT)

Small patrol craft with aluminium hulls.

4 PATROL CRAFT

Small wooden-hulled patrol craft.

JAPAN

Naval Board

Chief of the Maritime Staff. Defence Agency:
Admiral Hiroichi Samejima

Commander-in-Chief, Self-Defence Fleet:
Vice-Admiral Teiji Nakamura

Chief Administration Division Maritime Staff Office:
Rear Admiral Yasunori Yonemura

Diplomatic Representation

Defence (Naval) Attaché in London:
Captain Hideo Sato

Defence (Naval) Attaché in Washington:
Captain Tameo Oki

Naval Attaché in Moscow:
Captain Tsyneo Fujikawa

Defence Attaché in Paris:
Colonel Ryuzo Yabunaka

Five Year Defence Plan

The Fourth 5-year defence programme (1972-76) announced 9 October 1972 provides for the building of the following:

2 Haruna class DDH of 5 200 tons
1 SAM DDG of 3 900 tons
1 SSM DDG of 3 600 tons
3 DDs of 2 500 tons
3 Frigates of 1 450 tons
3 Frigates of 1 500 tons
3 Isoshio class submarines of 1 800 tons
2 Submarines of 2 200 tons
19 Minesweepers
3 Missile Boats of 160 tons
3 Torpedo Boats of 100 tons
2 LSTs of 1 500 tons
3 LSTs of 2 000 tons
1 Supply Ship of 5 000 tons
1 Submarine Tender of 2 700 tons
1 Oceanographic Research Ship of 2 000 tons
3 Patrol Boats
Plus miscellaneous craft

At the end of this programme the fleet should consist of 170 modern ships totalling 214 000 tons.

New Construction Programme

1973 1 Destroyer, 1 Frigate, 1 S/M, 2 MSC, 2 MSB, 1 PT, 1 LST
1974 1 DDK, 3 MSC, 1 LST
1975 1 DDH, 1 DDK, 1 S/M, 3 MSC, 1 LST, 1 AOE

Strength of the Fleet

Type	*Active*	*Building*	*Projected*
Destroyers	29	3	2
Frigates	16	4	—
Corvettes	20	—	—
Submarines—Patrol	15	2	1
Fast Attack Craft—Torpedo	4	1	1
Patrol Craft—Coastal	10	—	—
LSTs	3	3	1
Minelayers	2	—	—
M/S Support Ships	2	—	—
Minesweepers—Coastal	31	5	3
MSBs	6	—	—
Training Ships	1	—	—
S/M Rescue Vessels	2	—	—
Support Tanker	1	—	1
Icebreaker	1	—	—
Tugs	7 (6 small)	—	—
Auxiliaries	8	—	—

Personnel

1975: 46 000 (8 000 officers, 33 000 men, 5 000 civil)

Names

The practice of painting the ships' names on the broadsides of the hulls was discontinued in 1970.

Bases

Naval—Yokosuka, Kure, Sasebo, Maizuru, Oominato
Naval Air—Atsugi, Hachinohe, Iwakuni, Kanoya, Komatsu-jima, Okinawa, Ozuki, Oominato, Oomura, Shimofusa, Tateyama, Tokushima.

Fleet Air Arm

14 Air ASW Sqns. P2-J, P2V-7, PS-1, S2F-1, HSS-2
4 Air Training Sqns, P2-J, P2V-7, YS-11, B-65, KM-2, Mentor, Bell-47, OH-6 HSS-2.
1 Transport Sqn. YS-11.
1 MCM Sqn.

Deletions and Transfers

Destroyers

1974 *Ariake, Yugure*

Frigates

1970 *Kiri, Keyaki, Nire, Sugi, Shii* to US
1972 *Kaya, Bura, Kashi, Moni, Tochi, Ume, Maki, Kusu, Matsu, Nata, Sakura* (All ex-US PFs). *Wakaba.*

Submarines

1971 *Kuroshio* to US

Light Forces

1972 PT 2, 3, 4 and 9. *Kosoku* 1, 22-28, 30
1973 PT 7 and 8, *Kosoku* 3
1974 *Kosoku* 4 and 5
1975 PT 10

LST

1972 *Hayatomo*
1975 *Shimokita*

LSM

1973 3001

Maritime Safety Agency (Coast Guard)

9 Large Patrol Vessels
41 Medium Patrol Vessels
37 Small Patrol Vessels
3 Fire Fighting Craft
42 Patrol Craft
6 Surveying Vessels
5 Tenders
1 Underwater Research Vessel
150 Coastal Patrol Craft
33 Harbour Patrol Craft

Mercantile Marine

Lloyd's Register of Shipping:
9 469 vessels of 36 785 094 tons gross

List of Pennant Numbers

Destroyers

DD
101 Harukaze
102 Yukikaze
103 Ayanami
104 Isonami
105 Uranami
106 Shikinami
107 Murasame
108 Yuudachi
109 Harusame
110 Takanami
111 Oonami
112 Makinami
113 Yamagumo
114 Makigumo
115 Asagumo
116 Minegumo
117 Natsugumo
118 Murakumo
119 Aokumo
120 Akigumo
141 Haruna
142 Hiei
161 Akizuki
162 Teruzuki
163 Amatsukaze
164 Takatsuki
165 Kikuzuki
166 Mochizuki
167 Nagatsuki
168 Tachikaze

Frigates

DE
201 Akebono
202 Ikazuchi
203 Inazuma
211 Isuzu
212 Mogami
213 Kitakami
214 Ooi
215 Chikugo
216 Ayase
217 Mikuma
218 Tokachi
219 Iwase
220 Chitose
221 Niyodo
222 Teshio
223 Yoshino
224 Kumano
262 Asahi
263 Hatsuhi

Corvettes

PC
301 Kari
302 Kiji
303 Taka
304 Washi
305 Kamome
306 Tsubame
307 Misago
308 Hayabusa
309 Umitaka
310 Ootaka
311 Mizutori
312 Yamadori
313 Ootori
314 Kasasagi
315 Hatsukari
316 Umidori
317 Wakataka
318 Kumataka
319 Shiratori
320 Hiyodori

Submarines—Patrol

SS
511 Oyashio
521 Hayashic
522 Wakashio
523 Natsushio
524 Huyushio
561 Ooshio
562 Asashio
563 Harushio
564 Michishio
565 Arashio
566 Uzushio
567 Makishio
568 Isoshio
569 Narushio
570 Kuroshio
571 Takashio

Minesweepers—Coastal

MSC
610 Tatara
611 Tsukumi
612 Mikura
613 Shikine
614 Hirado
616 Hotaka
617 Karato
618 Hario
619 Mutsure
620 Chiburi
621 Ootsu
622 Kudako
623 Rishiri
624 Rebun
625 Amami
626 Urume
627 Minase
628 Ibuki
629 Katsura
630 Takami
631 Iou
632 Miyake
633 Utone
634 Awaji
635 Toushi
636 Teuri
637 Murotsu
638 Tashiro
639 Miyato
640 Takane
641 Muzuki
642 Yokose
643 Sakate

Minesweeper Tenders

MST
462 Hayase
473 Koozu

Mine Layers

MMC 951 Sooya
AMC 491 Erimo

Landing Ships

LST
4003 Shiretoko
4101 Atsumi
4102 Motobu
4151 Miura
4152 Ozika

Submarine Rescue Ships

ASR
401 Chihaya
402 Fushimi

Tanker

AO 411 Hamana

Training Ship

TV 3501 Katori

Training Support Ship

ATS 4201 Azuma

Cable Layer

ARC 481 Tsugaru

Icebreaker

AGB 5001 Fuji

Surveying Ship

AGS
5101 Akashi
01 Kasado
02 Habushi

DESTROYERS

2 NEW CONSTRUCTION DDG

TACHIKAZE DD 168 — **DD 169**

Displacement, tons	3 850
Dimensions, feet	443 × 47 × 15
Missiles	Standard RIM 60A SAM
Guns	2—5 in (singles)
A/S weapons	ASROC and 2 triple A/S torpedo tubes
Main engines	2 turbines; 60 000 hp
Speed	32 knots

Building by Mitsubishi, Nagasaki. *Tachikaze* laid down 19 June 1973. To be fitted with VDS. Completion Mar 1976. Second to complete in 1977.

TACHIKAZE *1975, Japanese Maritime Self-Defence Force*

2 +1 "HARUNA" CLASS

Name	No.	Builders	Laid down	Launched	Completion
HARUNA	141	Mitsubishi (Nagasaki)	19 Mar 1970	1 Feb 1972	22 Feb 1973
HIEI	142	Ishikawajima (Tokyo)	8 Mar 1972	13 Aug 1973	27 Nov 1974
—	143	—	—		1977(?)

Displacement, tons	4 700
Length, feet (*metres*)	502·0 (*153·0*)
Beam, feet (*metres*)	57·4 (*17·5*)
Draught, feet (*metres*)	16·7 (*5·1*)
Aircraft	3 anti-submarine helicopters
A/S weapons	Asroc multiple launcher
Guns	2—5 in (*127 mm*) single, rapid fire
Torpedo tubes	6—21 in (*533 mm*) 2 triple
Main engines	70 000 shp
Speed, knots	32
Range, miles	7 000 at 20 knots
Complement	364

Ordered under the third five-year defence programme (from 1967-71). The third of class projected under the 1974 programme.

HARUNA (DDH Helocarrier)

HARUNA *1973, Japanese Maritime Self-Defence Force*

4 ''TAKATSUKI'' CLASS

Name	No.	Builders	Laid down	Launched	Completed
KIKUZUKI	DD 165	Mitsubishi Jyuko Co, Nagasaki	15 Mar 1966	25 Mar 1967	27 Mar 1968
MOCHIZUKI	DD 166	Ishikawajima Jyuko Co, Tokyo	25 Nov 1966	15 Mar 1968	25 Mar 1969
NAGATSUKI	DD 167	Mitsubishi Jyuko Co, Nagasaki	2 Mar 1968	19 Mar 1969	12 Feb 1970
TAKATSUKI	DD 164	Ishikawajima Jyuko Com Tokyo	8 Oct 1964	7 Jan 1966	15 Mar 1967

Displacement, tons	3 050
Length, feet (*metres*)	446·2 (*136·0*) oa
Beam, feet (*metres*)	44·0 (*13·4*)
Draught, feet (*metres*)	14·5 (*4·4*)
Aircraft	2 Dash helicopters
A/S weapons	Octuple Asroc; 1 four barrelled rocket launcher
Guns	2—5 in (*127 mm*) 54 cal. single
Torpedo launchers	2 triple for A/S homing torpedoes
Boilers	2 Mitsubishi CE
Main engines	2 Mitsubishi WH geared turbines 60 000 shp; 2 shafts
Speed, knots	32
Range, miles	7 000 at 20 knots
Complement	270

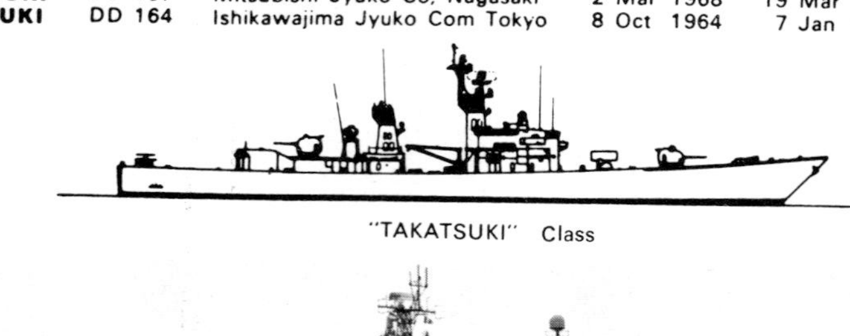

"TAKATSUKI" Class

Anti-submarine type. *Takatsuki* (High Moon) was provided under the 1963 programme. Equipped with drone anti-submarine helicopters and hangar.

RADAR. Search: Metric wavelength. Tactical; Probably C Band. Fire Control: GFCS 56 with X Band.

KIKUZUKI *1971, S Woodrifle*

Destroyers—*continued*

5 + 1 "YAMAGUMO" CLASS

Name	No.	Builders	Laid down	Launched	Completion
AKIGUMO	DD 120	Sumitomo Uraga	7 July 1972	23 Oct 1973	24 July 1974
AOKUMO	DD 119	Sumitomo Uraga	2 Oct 1970	30 Mar 1972	25 Nov 1972
ASAGUMO	DD 115	Maizuru	24 June 1965	25 Nov 1966	29 Aug 1967
MAKIGUMO	DD 114	Uraga Yokosuka	10 June 1964	26 July 1965	19 Mar 1966
YAMAGUMO	DD 113	Mitsui, Tamano	23 Mar 1964	27 Feb 1965	29 Jan 1966
—	DD 121	—	—	—	? 1977

Displacement, tons 2 150
Length, feet (*metres*) 377 (*115*)
Beam, feet (*metres*) 38 7 (*11·8*)
Draught, feet (*metres*) 13·1 (*4*)
Guns 4—3 in; 50 cal (2 twin)
A/S weapons 1 Asroc; 1 four barrelled rocket launcher
Torpedo tubes 2 triple mountings for A/S torpedoes
Main engines 6 Diesels; 26 500 bhp; 2 shafts
Speed, knots 27
Range, miles 7 000 at 20 knots
Complement 210

RADAR. Search; Metric.Tactical; C Band-Fire Control; GFCS 56 with X Band.

SONAR. *Yamagumo, Akigumo* and *Makigumo* fitted with VDS.

"YAMAGUMO" Class

AOKUMO *8/1974, Wright and Logan*

3 "MINEGUMO" CLASS

Name	No.	Builders	Laid down	Launched	Completed
MINEGUMO	DD 116	Mitsui, Tamano	14 Mar 1967	16 Dec 1967	21 Aug 1968
MURAKUMO	DD 118	Maizuru	19 Oct 1968	15 Nov 1969	21 Aug 1970
NATSUGUMO	DD 117	Uraga, Yokosuka	26 June 1967	25 July 1968	25 Apr 1969

All details as for "Yamagumo" class except:

Aircraft 2 Dash helicopter in place of ASROC

Note difference in silhouettes between this and the "Yamagumo" class.

"MINEGUMO" Class

NATSUGUMO *1972, Japanese Maritime Self-Defence Force*

1 "AMATSUKAZE" CLASS (DDG)

AMATSUKAZE DD 163

Displacement, tons 3 050 standard; 4 000 full load
Length, feet (*metres*) 429·8 (*131·0*)
Beam, feet (*metres*) 44 (*13·4*)
Draught, feet (*metres*) 13·8 (*4·2*)
Aircraft Can operate Helicopter
Missile launchers 1 single "Tartar" (US)
Guns 4—3 in (*76 mm*) 50 cal, 2 twin
A/S weapons ASROC; 2 Hedgehogs
Torpedo mountings 1 each side for A/S short torpedoes
Main engines 2 Ishikawajima GE geared turbines 2 shafts; 60 000 shp
Speed, knots 33
Boilers 2 Ishikawajima Foster Wheeler
Oil fuel, tons 900
Range, miles 7 000 at 18 knots
Complement 290

Ordered under the 1960 programme. Built by Mitsubishi, Nagasaki. Laid down on 29 Nov 1962, launched on 5 Oct 1963 and completed on 15 Feb 1965.

RADAR. Search: SPS 37 and SPS 39 3 D.
Fire Control: SPS 51 for "Tartar", X Band for guns.

AMATSUKAZE

AMATSUKAZE *1969, Japanese Maritime Self-Defence Force*

Destroyers—*continued*

2 "AKIZUKI" CLASS

Name	No.	Builders	Laid down	Launched	Completed
AKIZUKI	DD 161	Mitsubishi Zosen Co, Nagasaki	31 July 1958	26 June 1959	13 Feb 1960
TERUZUKI	DD 162	Shin Mitsubishi Jyuko Co, Kobe	15 Aug 1958	24 June 1959	29 Feb 1960

Displacement, tons	2 350 standard; 2 890 full load
Length, feet (*metres*)	387·2 (*118·0*) oa
Beam, feet (*metres*)	39·4 (*12·0*)
Draught, feet (*metres*)	13·1 (*4·0*)
Guns	3—5 in (*127 mm*) 54 cal. single 4—3 in (*76 mm*) 50 cal., 2 twin
Torpedo tubes	4—21 in (*533 mm*) quadrupled
A/S	1—US model Mk 108 rocket launcher; 2 hedgehogs; 2 Y-mortars; 2 DCT
Boilers	2 Mitsubishi CE type
Main engines	2 geared turbines:— *Akizuki:* Mitsubishi Escher-Weiss *Teruzuki:* Westinghouse 45 000 shp, 2 shafts
Speed, knots	32
Complement	330

Destroyers of unusual design with long forecastle hull. Built in Japan under the 1957 Military Aid Programme.

RADAR. Search: SPS 6. Tactical: SPS 10. Fire Control: X Band.

AKIZUKI, TERUZUKI

TERUZUKI — *1974, Japanese Maritime Self-defence Force*

3 "MURASAME" CLASS

Name	No.	Builders	Laid down	Launched	Completed
HARUSAME	DD 109	Urage Dock Co, Yokosuka	17 June 1958	18 June 1959	15 Dec 1959
MURASAME	DD 107	Mitsubishi Zosen Co, Nagasaki	17 Dec 1957	31 July 1958	28 Feb 1959
YUDACHI	DD 108	Ishakawajima Jyuko Co, Tokyo	16 Dec 1957	29 July 1958	25 Mar 1959

Displacement, tons	1 800 standard; 2 500 full load
Length, feet (*metres*)	354·3 (*108·0*) oa
Beam, feet (*metres*)	36 (*11·0*)
Draught, feet (*metres*)	12·2 (*3·7*)
Guns	3—5 in (*127 mm*) 54 cal 4—3 in (*76 mm*) 50 cal, 2 twin
A/S	8 torpedoes; 1 Hedgehog; 1 DC rack; 1 Y-gun
Boilers	2 (see *Engineering* notes)
Main engines	2 sets geared turbines 30 000 shp; 2 shafts
Speed, knots	30
Range, miles	6 000 at 18 knots
Complement	250

Murasame and *Yudachi* were built under the 1956 Programme, *Harusame* 1957 Programme.

ENGINEERING. *Murasame* has Mitsubishi Jyuko turbines and Mitsubishi CE boilers; and the other two have Ishikawajima Harima Jyuko turbines and Ishikawajima FW-D boilers.

RADAR. Search: SPS 6. Tactical: SPS 10. Fire Control: X Band.

"MURASAME" Class

MURASAME — *1972, Japanese Maritime Self-Defence Force*

7 "AYANAMI" CLASS

Name	No.	Builders	Laid down	Launched	Completed
AYANAMI	DD 103	Mitsubishi Zosen Co, Nagasaki	20 Nov 1956	1 June 1957	12 Feb 1958
ISONAMI	DD 104	Shin Mitsubishi Jyuko Co, Kobe	14 Dec 1956	30 Sep 1957	14 Mar 1958
MAKINAMI	DD 112	Iino Jyuko Co, Maizuru	20 Mar 1959	25 Apr 1960	30 Oct 1960
ONAMI	DD 111	Ishikawajima Jyuko Co, Tokyo	20 Mar 1959	13 Feb 1960	29 Aug 1960
SHIKINAMI	DD 106	Mitsui Zosen Co, Tamano	24 Dec 1956	25 Sep 1957	15 Mar 1958
TAKANAMI	DD 110	Mitsui Zosen Co, Tamano	8 Nov 1958	8 Aug 1959	30 Jan 1960
URANAMI	DD 105	Kawasaki Jyuko Co, Tokyo	1 Feb 1957	29 Aug 1957	27 Feb 1958

Displacement, tons	1 700 standard; 2 500 full load
Length, feet (*metres*)	357·6 (*109·0*) oa
Beam, feet (*metres*)	35·1 (*10·7*)
Draught, feet (*metres*)	12 (*3·7*)
Guns	6—3 in (*76 mm*) 50 cal (3 twin)
A/S weapons	2 US Model Mk 15 Hedgehogs; 2 Y-guns; 2 DC racks
Torpedo tubes	4—21 in (533 *mm*) quadruple
Torpedo launchers	4 fixed, for A/S homing torpedoes
Main engines	2 Mitsubishi Escher-Weiss geared turbines; 2 shafts; 35 000 shp
Speed, knots	32
Boilers	2 (see *Engineering*)
Range, miles	6 000 at 18 knots
Complement	230

ANTI-SUBMARINE. Trainable Hedgehogs forward of the bridge. Originally all ships fitted with A/S torpedo launchers on quarter-deck but in *Shikinami* (1972) *Isonami* (1971) *Uranami* (1970) and *Ayanami* (1969) these were removed and two triple A/S torpedo tubes were fitted.

ENGINEERING. Types of boilers installed are as follows: Mitsubishi CE in *Ayanami, Isonami* and *Uranami*; Hitachi, Babcock & Wilcox in *Onami, Shikinami* and *Takanami*; Kawasaki Jyuko BD in *Makinami*.

RADAR. Search: SPS 12 Tactical: SPS 10. Fire Control: X Band.

"AYANAMI" Class

MAKINAMI — *1972, Japanese Maritime Self-Defence Force*

Destroyers—*continued*

2 "HARUKAZE" CLASS

Name	No.	Builders	Laid down	Launched	Completed
HARUKAZE	DD 101	Mitsubishi Zosen Co, Nagasaki	15 Dec 1954	20 Sep 1955	26 Apr 1956
YUKIKAZE	DD 102	Shin Mitsubishi Jyuko Co, Kobe	17 Dec 1954	20 Aug 1955	31 July 1956

Displacement, tons: 1 700 standard; 2 340 full load
Length, feet (*metres*): 347·8 (*106·0*)wl; 358·5(*190·3*) oa
Beam, feet (*metres*): 34·5 (*10·5*)
Draught, feet (*metres*): 12·0 (*3·7*)
Guns: 3—5 in (*127 mm*) 38 cal dp; 8—40 mm (2 quadruple) AA
A/S weapons: Tubes for short homing torpedoes; 2 Hedgehogs; 1 DC rack; 4 K-guns
Main engines: 2 sets geared turbines; *Harukaze:* 2 Mitsubishi Escher Weiss; *Yukikaze:* 2 Westinghouse; 2 shafts; 30 000 shp
Speed, knots: 30
Boilers: *Harukaze:* 2 Hitachi-Babcock; *Yukikaze:* 2 Combustion Engineering
Range, miles: 6 000 at 18 knots
Oil fuel, tons: 557
Complement: 240

HARUKAZE, YUKIKAZE

HARUKAZE — *1972, Japanese Maritime Self-Defence Force*

YUKIKAZE — *1972, Toshio Tamura*

Authorised under the 1953 programme. First destroyer hulled vessels built in Japan after the Second World War. Electric welding was extensively used in hull construction; development of weldable high tension steel in main hull and light alloy in superstructure were also novel.
Nearly all the armament was supplied from the USA under the MSA clause.

ANTI-SUBMARINE. Armament was modified in Mar. 1969 when homing torpedo tubes were mounted and depth charge equipment correspondingly reduced.

RADAR. Search: L Band. Tactical: SPS 10. Fire Controls: X Band.

FRIGATES

9 + 2 "CHIKUGO" CLASS

Name	No.	Builder	Laid down	Launched	Completion
AYASE	DE 216	Shikawajima Harima Co	5 Dec 1969	16 Sep 1970	20 May 1971
CHIKUGO	DE 215	Mitsui Zoosen	9 Dec 1968	13 Jan 1970	31 July 1970
CHITOSE	DE 220	Hitachi, Maizuru	7 Oct 1971	25 Jan 1973	31 Aug 1973
IWASE	DE 219	Mitsui Zoosen	6 Aug 1971	29 June 1972	12 Dec 1972
MIKUMA	DE 217	Mitsui Zoosen	17 Mar 1970	16 Feb 1971	26 Aug 1971
NIYODO	DE 221	Mitsui Zoosen	20 Sep 1972	28 Aug 1973	8 Feb 1974
TOKACHI	DE 218	Mitsui Zoosen	11 Dec 1970	25 Nov 1971	17 May 1972
TESHIO	DE 222	Hitachi, Maizuru	11 July 1973	29 May 1974	10 Jan 1975
YOSHINO	DE 223	Mitsui, Tamano	28 Sep 1973	22 Aug 1974	Feb 1975
KUMANO	DE 224	Hitachi, Maizuru	29 May 1974	Mar 1975	Feb 1976
—	DE 225		—	—	1977 (?)

Displacement, tons: 1 470 standard; 1 750 full load
Length, feet (*metres*): 305·5 (*93·0*) oa
Beam, feet (*metres*): 35·5 (*10·8*)
Draught, feet (*metres*): 11·5 (*3·5*)
Guns: 2—3 in (*76 mm*) 50 cal, (1 twin); 2—40 mm (1 twin)
A/S weapons: Octuple ASROC
Torpedo launchers: 2 triple 12·7 in (*324 mm*)
Main engines: 4 Mitsui B & W diesels; 2 shafts; 16 000 shp
Speed, knots: 25
Complement: 165

RADAR. Search: L Band. Tactical: SPS 10. Fire Control: X Band.

SONAR. Fitted with VDS.

"CHIKUGO" Class

MIKUMA — *1972, Toshio Tamura*

4 "ISUZU" CLASS

Name	No.	Builders	Laid down	Launched	Completed
ISUZU	DE 211	Mitsui Zosen Co, Tamano	16 Apr 1960	17 Jan 1961	29 July 1961
KITAKAMI	DE 213	Ishikawajima-Harima Co, Tokyo	7 June 1962	21 June 1963	27 Feb 1964
MOGAMI	DE 212	Mitsubishi Zosen Co, Nagasaki	4 Aug 1960	7 Mar 1961	28 Oct 1961
OOI	DE 214	Maizuru (former Iino) Co, Maizuru	10 June 1962	15 June 1963	22 Jan 1964

Displacement, tons: 1 490 standard; 1 700 full load
Length, feet (*metres*): 308·5 (*94·0*) oa
Beam, feet (*metres*): 34·2 (*10·4*)
Draught, feet (*metres*): 11·5 (*3·5*)
Guns: 4—3 in (*76 mm*) 50 cal, 2 twin
A/S weapons: 1 4-barrelled rocket launcher;
Torpedo tubes: 4—21 in (*533 mm*) quadrupled
Torpedo launchers: 2 triple for A/S homing torpedoes
Main engines: 4 diesels, Mitsui in *Ooi, Isuzu,* Mitsubishi in *Kitakami, Mogami,* 16 000 hp; 2 shafts
Speed, knots: 25
Complement: 180

ISUZU, MOGAMI

KITAKAMI, OOI

MOGAMI — *1974, Japanese Maritime Self-Defence Force*

CLASS VARIATION. The second pair of this type, *Kitakami* and *Ooi*, have a number of improvements in armament and equipment and are of slightly different dimensions.

RADAR. Search: SPS 6. Tactical: SPS 10.

Frigates—*continued*

2 "IKAZUCHI" CLASS

Name	*No.*	*Builders*	*Laid down*	*Launched*	*Completed*
IKAZUCHI	DE 202	Kawasaki Jyuko Co, Kobe	18 Dec 1954	6 Sep 1955	29 May 1956
INAZUMA	DE 203	Mitsui Zosen Co, Tamano	15 Dec 1954	4 Aug 1955	5 Mar 1956

Displacement, tons	1 070 standard; 1 300 full load
Length, feet (*metres*)	287 (*87·5*) wl; 288·7 (*88·0*) oa
Beam, feet (*metres*)	28·5 (*8·7*)
Draught, feet (*metres*)	10·2 (*3·1*)
Guns	2—3 in (*76 mm*) 50 cal. dp; 2—40 mm AA
A/S weapons	1 Hedgehog; 8 K-guns; 2 DC racks
Main engines	12 000 hp diesels; Mitsubishi in *Ikazuchi:* Mitsui B & W in *Inazuma:* 2 shafts
Range, miles	5 500 at 15 knots
Speed, knots	25
Complement	160

RADAR. Search: SPS 6. Tactical: SPS 10. Fire Control: X Band.

INAZUMA *1974, Japanese Maritime Self-Defence Force*

IKAZUCHI, INAZUMA

1 "AKEBONO" CLASS

Name	*No.*	*Builders*	*Laid down*	*Launched*	*Completed*
AKEBONO	DE 201	Ishikawajima Jyuko, Co, Tokyo.	10 Dec 1954	15 Oct 1955	20 Mar 1956

Displacement, tons	1 060 standard; 1 350 full load
Length, feet (*metres*)	295 (*90·0*) oa
Beam, feet (*metres*)	28·5 (*8·7*)
Draught, feet (*metres*)	11 (*3·4*)
Guns, AA	2—3 in (*76 mm*) 50 cal; 1—40 mm
A/S weapons	4 K-guns; 1 Hedgehog; 1 DC rack
Main engines	Ishikawajima geared turbines; 2 shafts; 18 000 shp
Speed, knots	28
Boilers	2 Ishikawajima-Foster Wheeler
Range, miles	4 000 at 16 knots
Complement	190

RADAR. Search: SPS 6. Tactical: SPS 10. Fire Control: X Band.

AKEBONO *1972, Japanese Maritime Self-Defence Force*

AKEBONO

2 "ASAHI" CLASS

Name	*No.*	*Builders*	*Laid down*	*Launched*	*Completed*
ASAHI (ex-USS *Amick, DE* 168)	DE 262	Federal Port, Newark	30 Nov 1942	27 May 1943	26 July 1943
HATSUHI (ex-USS *Atherton, DE* 169)	DE 263	Federal Port, Newark	14 Jan 1943	27 May 1943	29 Aug 1943

Displacement, tons	1 250 standard; 1 900 full load
Length, feet (*metres*)	306 (*93·3*) oa
Beam, feet (*metres*)	36·1 (*11·0*)
Draught, feet (*metres*)	12 (*3·7*)
Guns	3—3 in (*76 mm*) 50 cal, dp
A/S weapons	8 K-guns; 1 DCT
Main engines	GM diesels; electric drive; 2 shafts; 6 000 hp
Range, miles	11 500 at 11 knots 5 500 at 18 knots
Speed, knots	20
Complement	220

ASAHI, HATSUHI

Former US "Bostwick" class destroyer escorts. Taken over from the US Navy on 14 June 1955.

ASAHI *1972, Toshio Tamura*

CORVETTES

8 "MIZUTORI" CLASS (PC)

Name	No.	Builders	Laid down	Launched	Completed
HATSUKARI	315	Sasebo Shipyard	25 Jan 1960	24 June 1960	15 Nov 1960
HIYODORI	320	Sasebo Shipyard	26 Feb 1965	25 Sep 1965	28 Feb 1966
KASASAGI	314	Fujinagata, Osaka	18 Dec 1959	31 May 1960	31 Oct 1960
MIZUTORI	311	Kawasaki, Kobe	13 Mar 1959	22 Sep 1959	27 Feb 1960
OTORI	313	Kure Shipyard	16 Dec 1959	27 May 1960	13 Oct 1960
SHIRATORI	319	Sasebo Shipyard	29 Feb 1964	8 Oct 1964	26 Feb 1965
UMIDORI	316	Sasebo Shipyard	15 Feb 1962	15 Oct 1962	30 Mar 1963
YAMADORI	312	Fujinagata, Osaka	14 Mar 1959	22 Oct 1959	15 Mar 1960

Displacement, tons	420 to 440 standard
Dimensions, feet	197·0 × 23·3 × 7·5
Guns	2—40 mm (1 twin)
A/S weapons	1 hedgehog; 1 DC rack; 6 homing torpedo launchers (Triple)
Main engines	2 MAN diesels; 2 shafts; 3 800 bhp = 20 knots
Complement	80
Range, miles	2 000 at 12 knots

OTORI *1972, Toshio Tamura*

1 "HAYABUSA" CLASS (PC)

HAYABUSA 308

Displacement, tons	360 standard
Dimensions, feet	190·2 × 25·7 × 7
Guns	2—40 mm (1 twin)
A/S weapons	1 hedgehog; 2 Y Guns; 2 DC racks
Main engines	2 diesels; 4 000 bhp; 2 shafts = 20 knots
Complement	75

Built under the 1954 fiscal year programme by Mitsubishi Shipbuilding & Engineering Co Ltd, Nagasaki. Laid down on 23 May 1956. Launched on 20 Nov 1956. Completed on 10 June 1957. A gas turbine was installed in Mar 1962 and removed in 1969.

HAYABUSA *1974, Japanese Maritime Self-Defence Force*

4 'UMITAKA" CLASS (PC)

Name	No.	Builders	Laid down	Launched	Completed
ŌTAKA	310	Kure Shipyard	18 Mar 1959	3 Sep 1959	14 Jan 1960
UMITAKA	309	Kawasaki, Kobe	13 Mar 1959	25 July 1959	30 Nov 1959
KUMATAKA	318	Fujinagata, Osaka	20 Mar 1963	21 Oct 1963	25 Mar 1964
WAKATAKA	317	Kure Shipyard	5 Mar 1962	13 Nov 1962	30 Mar 1963

Displacement, tons	440 to 460 standard
Dimensions,feet	197·0 × 23·3 × 8·0)
Guns	2—40 mm (1 twin)
A/S weapons	1 Hedgehog, 1 DC rack; 2 triple A/S torpedo launchers
Main engines	2 B & W diesels; 2 shafts; 4 000 bhp = 20 knots
Complement	80

OTAKA *1967, Hajime Fukaya*

KUMATAKA *1972, Japanese Maritime Self-Defence Force*

7 "KARI" and "KAMOME" CLASS (PC)

Name	No.	Builders	Laid down	Launched	Completed
KAMOME	305	Uraga	27 Jan 1956	3 Sep 1956	14 Jan 1957
KARI	301	Fujimagata, Osaka	18 Jan 1956	26 Sep 1956	8 Feb 1957
KIJI	302	Iino, Maizuru	14 Dec 1955	11 Sep 1956	29 Jan 1957
MISAGO	307	Uraga	27 Jan 1956	1 Nov 1956	11 Feb 1957
TAKA	303	Fujimagata, Osaka	18 Jan 1956	17 Nov 1956	11 Mar 1957
TSUBAME	306	Kure Shipyard	15 Mar 1956	10 Oct 1956	31 Jan 1957
WASHI	304	Iino, Maizuru	14 Dec 1955	12 Nov 1956	20 Mar 1957

Displacement, tons	330 standard; (*Kari, Kiji, Taka, Washi,* 310)
Dimensions, feet	173·3 oa × 21·8 × 6·8
Guns	2—40 mm (1 twin)
A/S weapons	1 Hedgehog; 2-Y guns; 2 DC racks
Main engines	2 diesels (*Kari, Kiji, Taka,* and *Washi* Kawasaki-MAN; others Mitsui-Burmeister & Wain). 2 shafts; 4 000 bhp = 20 knots
Oil fuel (tons)	21·5
Range, miles	2 000 at 12 knots
Complement	70

Authorised under the 1954 programme. At the time they were an entirely new type of fast patrol vessels, reminiscent of the United States PC type but modified and improved in many ways. *Kari* class (301-304). *Kamome* class (305-307).

MISAGO *1970, Japanese Maritime Self Defence Force*

SUBMARINES

5 + 2 "UZUSHIO" CLASS

Name	No.	Builders	Laid down	Launched	Completion
UZUSHIO	SS 566	Kawasaki	25 Sep 1968	11 Mar 1970	21 Jan 1971
MAKISHIO	SS 567	Mitsubishi	21 June 1969	27 Jan 1971	2 Feb 1972
ISOSHIO	SS 568	Kawasaki	9 July 1970	18 Mar 1972	25 Nov 1972
NARUSHIO	SS 569	Mitsubishi	8 May 1971	22 Nov 1972	28 Sep 1973
KUROSHIO	SS 570	Kawasaki	5 July 1972	22 Feb 1974	27 Nov 1974
TAKASHIO	SS 571	Mitsubishi	6 July 1973	July 1974	Feb 1976
—			—	—	1976

Displacement, tons	1 850 standard
Length, feet (*metres*)	236·2 (*72·0*)
Beam, feet (*metres*)	32·5 (*9·9*)
Draught, feet (*metres*)	24·6 (*7·5*)
Torpedo tubes	6—21 in (*533 mm*); bow
Main machinery	2 diesels; 3 400 bhp; 1 shaft; 1 electric motor; 7 200 hp
Speed, knots	12 on surface; 20 submerged
Complement	80

Of double-hull construction and "tear-drop" form.

NARUSHIO *1973, Japanese Maritime Self-Defence Force*

5 "OOSHIO" CLASS

Name	No.	Builders	Laid down	Launched	Completed
ARASHIO	SS 565	Mitsubishi Jyuko, Kobe	5 July 1967	24 Oct 1968	25 July 1969
ASASHIO	SS 562	Kawasaki Jyuko Co, Kobe	5 Oct 1964	27 Nov 1965	13 Oct 1966
HARUSHIO	SS 563	Mitsubishi Jyuko Co, Kobe	12 Oct 1965	25 Feb 1967	1 Dec 1967
MICHISHIO	SS 564	Kawasaki Jyuko, Kobe	26 July 1966	5 Dec 1967	29 Aug 1968
OOSHIO	SS 561	Mitsubishi Jyuko Co, Kobe	29 June 1963	30 Apr 1964	31 Mar 1965

Displacement, tons	1 650 standard; *Ooshio* 1 600
Length, feet (*metres*)	288·7 (*88·0*)
Beam, feet (*metres*)	26·9 (*8·2*)
Draught, feet (*metres*)	16·2 (*4·9*). *Ooshio* 15·4 (*4·7*)
Torpedo tubes	8—21 in (*533 mm*); 6 bow 2 stern
Main machinery	2 diesels; 2 900 bhp; 2 shafts; 2 electric motors; 6 300 hp
Speed, knots	14 on surface; 18 submerged
Complement	80

Double-hulled boats. This class is the first ever built in Japanese yards with a deep-diving capability. A bigger design to obtain improved seaworthiness, a larger torpedo capacity and more comprehensive sonar and electronic devices. *Ooshio* was built under the 1961 programme, *Asashio* 1963. Cost $5 600 000.

MICHISHIO *1972, Japanese Maritime Self-Defence Force*

4 "HAYASHIO" and "NATSUSHIO" CLASS

Name	No.	Builders	Laid down	Launched	Completed
FUYUSHIO	SS 524	Kawasaki Jyuko Co, Kobe	6 Dec 1961	14 Dec 1962	17 Sep 1963
HAYASHIO	SS 521	Shin Mitsubishi Jyuko Co, Kobe	6 June 1960	31 July 1961	30 June 1962
NATSUSHIO	SS 523	Shin Mitsubishi Jyuko Co, Kobe	5 Dec 1961	18 Sep 1962	29 June 1963
WAKASHIO	SS 522	Kawasaki Jyuko Co, Kobe	7 June 1960	28 Aug 1961	17 Aug 1962

Displacement, tons	750 standard (SS 521, 522); 790 standard (SS 523, 524)
Length, feet (*metres*)	193·6 (*59·0*) oa (SS 521, 522); 200·1 (*61·0*) oa (SS 523, 524)
Beam, feet (*metres*)	21·3 (*6·5*)
Draught, feet (*metres*)	13·5 (*4·1*)
Torpedo tubes	3—21 in (*533 mm*); bow
Main machinery	2 diesels, total 900 hp; 2 shafts 2 electric motors, total 2 300 hp
Speed, knots	11 on surface; 15 submerged
Complement	40

Medium submarines of improved type, with more efficient sonar devices, giving them slightly increased displacement. Very handy and successful boats, with a large safety factor, complete air-conditioning and good habitability.

Hayashio class	SS 521; 522
Natsushio class	SS 523; 524

NATSUSHIO *1973, Japanese Maritime Self-Defence Force*

1 "OYASHIO" CLASS

OYASHIO SS 511

Displacement, tons	1 100 surface; 1 420 submerged
Length, feet (*metres*)	258·5 (*78·8*)
Beam, feet (*metres*)	23 (*7·0*)
Draught, feet (*metres*)	15·2 (*4·6*)
Torpedo tubes	4—21 in (*533 mm*); 10 torpedoes
Main machinery	2 diesels, total 2 700 hp 2 electric motors, total 5 900 hp
Speed, knots	13 on surface; 19 submerged
Range, miles	5 000 at 10 knots
Complement	65

OYASHIO *1972, Japanese Maritime Self-Defence Force*

Ordered under the 1956 Programme. Built by Kawasaki Jyuko Co Kobe. Laid down on 25 Dec 1957, launched on 25 May 1959 and completed on 30 June 1960. The first submarine built in a Japanese shipyard after the Second World War, *Oyashio* is the name of a Tidal stream in the Pacific off Honshu. First estimated to cost £2 718 000, but this figure was exceeded. Of double-hull construction.

LIGHT FORCES

PT 11 PT 12 PT 13 PT 14 PT 15 (FAST ATTACK CRAFT—TORPEDO)

Displacement, tons	100
Dimensions, feet	116·4 × 30·2 × 3·9
Guns	2—40 mm AA
Tubes	4—21 inch
Main engines	2 Mitsubishi diesels; 2 IHI gas turbines; 3 shafts; 11 000 hp (PT 11; 10 500 hp) = 40 knots

Built by Mitsubishi, Shimonoseki. PT 11 laid down 17 Mar 1970, completed 27 Mar 1971. PT 12 laid down 22 April 1971, completed 28 Mar 1972. PT 13 laid down 28 Mar 1972, completed 16 Dec 1972. PT 14 laid down 23 Mar 1973, completed 15 Feb 1974. PT 15 launched Jan 1975. One more projected.

PT 13 *1972, Ships of the World*

PB 19, 20, 21, 22, 23, 24, 25, 26, 27 (PATROL CRAFT—COASTAL)

Displacement, tons	18
Dimensions, feet	55·8 × 14·1 × 2·7
Gun	1—20 mm
Main engines	2 diesels; 760 hp = 20 knots
Complement	6

19-22 completed 31 Mar 1971; 23-24, 31 Mar 1972; 25-27, 29 Mar 1973. All built by Ishikawajima Yokohama. GRP hulls.

KOSOKU 6 ASH 06

Displacement, tons	40
Dimensions, feet	75·9 × 18·2 × 3·3
Main engines	3 Diesels; 2 800 bhp = 30 knots

Of aluminium construction. Laid down on 28 June 1966 at Mitsubishi Shimonoseki under the 1965 Programme. Launched 22 Nov 1966. Completed 20 Mar 1967.

KOSOKU 6 *1974, Japanese Maritime Self-Defence Force*

AMPHIBIOUS SHIPS

3 "MIURA" CLASS (LST)

MIURA 4151 **OZIKA** 4152 — 4153

Displacement, tons	2 000
Dimensions, ft (*m*)	321·4 × 45·9 × 9·8 (*98 × 14 × 3*)
Guns	2—3 in (twin); 2—40 mm (twin)
Main engines	4 400 hp = 14 knots

Fitted with bow doors. *Miura* laid down 26 Nov 1973, launched 13 Aug 1974, completion Jan 1975. *Ozika* laid down 10 June 1974 at Ihi for completion Mar 1976.

MIURA *1974, Japanese Maritime Self-Defence Force*

1 "OOSUMI" CLASS (LST)

SHIRETOKO (ex-USS *Nansemond County*, LST 1064) 4003

Displacement, tons	1 650 standard; 4 080 full load
Dimensions, feet	316·0 wl; 328·0 oa × 50·0 × 14·0
Guns	4—40 mm single; 2—40 mm twin; 12—20 mm AA single
Main engines	GM diesels; 2 shafts; 1 700 bhp = 11 knots
Complement	100

Shiretoko due for disposal 1976. Built by Bethlehem Steel Co, Hingham, Mass. in 1954-55. Commissioned in the Japanese MSDF on 1 Apr 1961.

2 "ATSUMI" CLASS (LST)

ATSUMI 4101 **MOTOBU** 4102

Displacement, tons	1 480
Dimensions, ft (*m*)	291·9 × 42·6 × 8·5 (*89 × 13 × 2·7*)
Guns	4—40 mm (twins)
Main engines	2 diesels; 4 400 hp = 13 knots
Complement	95

Atsumi completed 27 Nov 1972 at Sasebo Jyuko Co, Sasebo. *Motobu* laid down at Sasebo 23 April 1973, launched 3 Aug 1973. Completion 21 Dec 1973.

MOTOBU *1974, Japanese Maritime Self-Defence Force*

MINE WARFARE FORCES

1 "SOOYA" CLASS MINELAYER

SOOYA 951

Displacement, tons	2 150 standard; 3 050 full load
Length, feet (*metres*)	324·8 (*99·0*)
Beam, feet (*metres*)	49·5 (*15·0*)
Draught, feet (*metres*)	13·9 (*4·2*)
Guns	2—3 in (*76 mm*) 50 cal. (1 twin); 2—20 mm
Torpedo tubes	6 anti-submarine type (2 triple)
Main engines	4 diesels; 4 000 bhp; 2 shafts
Speed, knots	18
Complement	185

Laid down by Hitachi Zosen, Maizuru on 9 July 1970, launched 31 Mar 1971 and completed 30 Sept 1971. With twin rails can carry 200 buoyant mines. Has helicopter platform aft and acts at times as command ship for MCM forces.

SOOYA *1974, Japanese Maritime Self-Defence Force*

ERIMO 491 (MINELAYER)

Displacement, tons	630 standard
Dimensions, feet	210 × 26 × 8
Guns	2—40 mm AA; 2—20 mm AA
A/S weapons	1 Hedgehog; 2 K-guns; 2 DC racks
Main engines	Diesel; 2 shafts; 2 500 bhp = 18 knots
Complement	80

Authorised under 1953 fiscal programme. Built by Uraga Dock Co. Laid down on 10 Dec 1954. Launched on 12 July 1955. Completed on 28 Dec 1955.

ERIMO *1970, Japanese Maritime Self-Defence Force*

HAYASE 462 (MINESWEEPER SUPPORT SHIP)

Displacement, tons	2 000 standard
Length, feet (*metres*)	324·8 (*99·0*)
Beam, feet (*metres*)	42·7 (*13·0*)
Draught, feet (*metres*)	12·5 (*3·8*)
Guns	2—3 in (*76 mm*) 50 cal. (1 twin); 2—20 mm
Torpedo tubes	6 anti-submarine type (2 triple)
Main engines	2 diesels; 4 000 bhp; 2 shafts
Speed, knots	18
Complement	185

Laid down by Ishikawajima Haruna 16 Sep 1970, launched 21 June 1971, completed 6 Nov 1971. Has helicopter platform aft.

HAYASE *1972, Japanese Maritime Self Defence Force*

19 "KASADO" CLASS (MINESWEEPERS—COASTAL)

Name	*No.*	*Laid down*	*Launched*	*Completed*
AMAMI	MSC 625	1 Mar 1966	31 Oct 1966	6 Mar 1967
CHIBURI	MSC 620	27 Mar 1963	29 Nov 1963	25 Mar 1964
HARIO	MSC 618	19 Mar 1962	10 Dec 1962	23 Mar 1963
HIRADO	MSC 614	14 Mar 1960	3 Oct 1960	17 Dec 1960
HOTAKA	MSC 616	22 Mar 1961	23 Oct 1961	24 Feb 1962
IBUKI	MSC 628	27 Feb 1967	2 Dec 1967	27 Feb 1968
KARATO	MSC 617	15 Mar 1962	11 Dec 1962	23 Mar 1963
KATSURA	MSC 629	10 Feb 1967	18 Sep 1967	15 Feb 1968
KUDAKO	MSC 622	17 Feb 1964	20 Nov 1964	24 Mar 1965
MIKURA	MSC 612	30 Mar 1959	14 Mar 1960	27 May 1960
MINASE	MSC 627	1 Feb 1966	10 Jan 1967	25 Mar 1967
MUTSURE	MSC 619	28 Mar 1963	16 Dec 1963	24 Mar 1964
OOTSU	MSC 621	7 Mar 1964	5 Nov 1964	24 Feb 1965
REBUN	MSC 624	27 Mar 1965	7 Dec 1965	24 Mar 1966
RISHIRI	MSC 623	9 Mar 1964	22 Nov 1965	5 Mar 1966
SHIKINE	MSC 613	12 Jan 1960	22 July 1960	15 Nov 1960
TATARA	MSC 610	30 Mar 1959	14 Jan 1960	26 Mar 1960
TSUKUMI	MSC 611	24 Mar 1959	12 Jan 1960	27 Apr 1960
URUME	MSC 626	1 Feb 1966	12 Nov 1966	30 Jan 1967

Displacement, tons	330 standard (380 later ships)
Dimensions, feet	150·9 × 28 × 7·5; 171·6 × 28·9 × 7·9 later ships
Gun	1—20 mm AA
Main engines	2 diesels; 2 shafts; 1 200 bhp, 1 440 later ships = 14 knots

Hull is of wooden construction. Otherwise built of non-magnetic metarials. Built by Hitachi, Kanagawa Works, and Nippon Steel Tube Co, Tsurumi.

SHIKINE *1972, Toshio Tamura*

Minewarfare Forces—*continued*

14 + 3 "TAKAMI" CLASS (MINESWEEPERS—COASTAL)

Name	*No.*	*Laid down*	*Launched*	*Completed*
AWAJI	MSC 634	20 Apr 1970	11 Dec 1970	29 Mar 1971
IOU	MSC 631	21 Sep 1968	12 Aug 1969	22 Jan 1970
MIYAKE	MSC 632	14 Aug 1969	3 June 1970	19 Nov 1970
MIYATO	MSC 639	22 Apr 1972	3 Apr 1973	24 Aug 1973
MUROTSU	MSC 637	16 Apr 1971	16 Dec 1971	3 Mar 1972
TAKAMI	MSC 630	25 Sep 1968	15 July 1969	15 Dec 1969
TASHIRO	MSC 638	26 May 1972	2 Apr 1973	30 July 1973
TEURI	MSC 636	12 Apr 1971	19 Oct 1971	10 Mar 1972
TOUSHI	MSC 635	14 May 1970	12 Dec 1970	18 Mar 1971
UTONE	MSC 633	6 Aug 1969	6 Apr 1970	3 Sep 1970
TAKANE	MSC 640	26 Apr 1973	8 Mar 1974	28 Aug 1974
MUZUKI	MSC 641	7 June 1973	5 Apr 1974	28 Aug 1974
YOKOSE	MSC 642	2 July 1974	July 1975	Dec 1975
SAKATE	MSC 643	6 Aug 1974	Sep 1975	Mar 1976
—	MSC —	—	—	—
—	MSC —	—	—	-
—	MSC —	—	—	-

Of similar dimensions to "Kasado" class but of slightly different construction and with a displacement of 380 tons. Same builders as "Kasado" class.

TAKAMI *1972, Japanese Maritime Self-Defence Force*

1 "KOOZU" CLASS

Similar to "Kasado" class but has had minesweeping gear removed and was fitted as MCM Command Ship in June 1972.

3 "YASHIMA" CLASS

TOSHIMA (ex-USS *MSC* 258) YAS 61
TSUSHIMA (ex-USS *MSC*, ex-*AMS* 255) YAS 60
YASHIMA (ex-USS *AMS* 144) YAS 46

Displacement, tons	335 standard; 375 full load
Dimensions, feet	138 pp; 144 oa × 26·5 × 8·3
Gun	1—20 mm AA
Main engines	2 GM diesels; 880 bhp = 13 knots
Range, miles	2 500 at 10 knots

Former US auxiliary minesweepers *Hashima* and *Yashima* now used as accommodation ships. *Tsushima* and *Toshima* now act as auxiliaries.

6 "NANA-GO" CLASS (MSBs)

07 08 09 10 11 12

Displacement, tons	40 (53 for 07-12)
Dimensions, feet	62·3 oa × 16 × 4 (07-12 73·8 × 17·7 × 3·3)
Main engines	2 diesels; 2 shafts; 320 bhp = 10 knots (07-12 480 hp = 11 knots)
Complement	10

07 laid down 26 May 1972 and completed 30 Mar 1973. No. 08 laid down 3 Aug 1972 and completed 27 Mar 1973. No. 09 laid down 5 July 1973, completed 28 Mar 1974. No. 10 laid down 7 June 1973, completed 29 Mar 1974. No. 11 laid down 2 July 1974 and No. 12 launched Jan-Feb 1975.

MSB 07 *1974, Japanese Maritime Self-Defence Force*

SERVICE FORCES

AZUMA 4201 (TRAINING SHIP)

Displacement, tons	1 950 standard; 2 500 full load
Length, feet (*metres*)	323·4 (*98·6*)
Beam, feet (*metres*)	42·7 (*13·0*)
Draught, feet (*metres*)	12·5 (*3·8*)
Aircraft	1 helicopter
Gun	1—3 in (*76 mm*) 50 cal.
A/S weapons	2 triple torpedo launchers
Main engines	2 diesels; 2 shafts; 4 000 bhp
Speed, knots	18
Complement	185

Built by Maizuru Jyuko Co, Maizuru as a training support ship. Laid down on 15 July 1968, launched on 14 Apr 1969 and completed 26 Nov 1969. Has helicopter hangar amidships. Acts as drone carrier.

AZUMA *1974, Japanese Maritime Self-Defence Force*

KATORI 3501 (TRAINING SHIP)

Displacement, tons	3 350 standard; 4 000 full load
Length, feet (*metres*)	422·4 (*128·0*)
Beam, feet (*metres*)	49·5 (*15·0*)
Draught, feet (*metres*)	14·6 (*4·3*)
Aircraft	1 helicopter
Guns	4—3 in (*76 mm*) 50 cal
A/S weapons	1 four barrelled rocket launcher
Torpedo launchers	6 (2 triple mounts) for homing torpedoes
Main engines	geared turbines; 2 shafts; 20 000 shp
Range, miles	7 000 at 18 knots
Speed, knots	25
Complement	460 including trainees

Built by Ishikawajima Harima, Tokyo. Laid down 8 Dec 1967, launched on 19 Nov 1968 and completed on 10 Sep 1969. Provided with a landing deck aft for a helicopter and amidships hangar.

RADAR. Search: SPS 12. Tactical: SPS 10.

KATORI

KATORI *1974, Japanese Maritime Self-Defence Force*

Service Forces—*continued*

FUSIMI ASR 402 (SUBMARINE RESCUE)

Displacement, tons	1 430 standard
Dimensions, feet	249·5 × 41 × 12
Main engines	2 diesels; 1 shaft; 3 000 bhp = 16 knots
Complement	100

Built by Sumnitomo SB & Machinery Co, laid down on 5 Nov 1968, launched 10 Sep 1969, completed 10 Feb 1970. Has a rescue chamber and two decompression chambers.

FUSIMI *1972, Japanese Maritime Self-Defence Force*

CHIHAYA ASR 401 (SUBMARINE RESCUE)

Displacement, tons	1 340 standard
Dimensions, feet	239·5 × 39·3 × 12·7
Main engines	Diesels; 2 700 bhp = 15 knots
Complement	90

Authorised under the 1959 programme. The first vessel of her kind to be built in Japan. Laid down on 15 Mar 1960. Launched by Mitsubishi Nippon Heavy Industries Co, Yokohama on 4 Oct 1960. Completed on 15 Mar 1961 Has rescue chamber, 2 decompression chambers, four-point mooring equipment and a 12 ton derrick.

CHIHAYA *1972, Japanese Maritime Self-Defence Force*

SHOBO 41 (SALVAGE VESSEL)

Displacement, tons	45
Dimensions, feet	75 × 18 × 3·3
Main engines	4 diesels; 3 shafts; Speed = 19 knots

Built by Azumo Zosen, Yokosuka. Completed 28 Feb 1964.

TSUGARU ARC 481 (CABLE LAYER)

Displacement, tons	2 150 standard
Dimensions, feet	337·8 × 40·7 × 16
Guns	2—20 mm AA
Main engines	2 Diesels; 2 shafts; 3 200 bhp = 13 knots
Complement	100

Dual purpose cable layer and coastal minelayer. Built under the 1953 programme by Yokohama Shipyard & Engine Works, Mitsubishi Nippon-Heavy Industries Ltd. Laid down on 18 Dec 1954. Launched on 19 July 1955. Completed on 15 Dec 1955. Converted to cable-layer 10 July 1969-30 April 1970 by Nippon Steel Tube Co.

TSUGARU *1972, Toshio Tamura*

HAMANA (SUPPORT TANKER)

Displacement, tons	2 900 light; 7 550 full load
Dimensions, feet	420 × 51·5 × 20·5
Guns	2—40 mm AA
Main engines	Diesel; 5 000 bhp = 16 knots

Built by Uraga Dock Co under the 1960 programme. Laid down on 17 Apr 1961 launched on 24 Oct 1961, and completed on 10 Mar 1962. Named after the lake.

SURVEYING SHIPS

1 "AKASHI" CLASS (AGS)

AKASHI 5101

Displacement, tons	1 420
Dimensions, ft (*m*)	244·2 × 42·2 × 14·2 (*74·0 × 13·0 × 4·3*)
Main engines	2 diesels, 2 shafts; 3 200 bhp
Speed knots,	16
Complement	65

AKASHI *1974, Japanese Maritime Self-Defence Force*

2 "KASADO" CLASS

KASADO 01 **HABUSHI** 02

Displacement tons,	340
Dimensions, feet	150·9 × 28·4 × 7·5
Main engines	2 diesels; 2 shafts; 1 200 bhp = 14 knots

MISCELLANEOUS

5 "500 TON" CLASS

Name	*Laid down*	*Launched*	*Completed*
YAS 101	10 Oct 1967	18 Jan 1968	30 Mar 1968
YAS 102	25 Sep 1968	20 Dec 1968	31 Mar 1969
YAS 103	2 Apr 1971	24 May 1971	30 Sep 1971
YAS 104	4 Feb 1972	15 June 1972	13 Sep 1972
YAS 105	20 Feb 1973	16 July 1973	19 Sep 1973

Displacement, tons	500
Dimensions, feet	171·6 × 33·0 × 8·3
Main engines	2 diesels; 2 shafts; 1 600 bhp = 14 knots

Training support and rescue.

TSUSHIMA YAS 60
TOSHIMA YAS 61
SHISAKA (ex-MSC 605) YAS 62
KOSHIKI (ex-MSC 615) YAS 63

Details as for "Kasado" Class.

ICEBREAKER

FUJI 5001

Displacement, tons	5 250 standard; 7 760 normal, 8 566 full load
Dimensions, feet	328 × 72·2 × 29
Aircraft	3 helicopters
Main engines	4 diesel-electric; 2 shafts; 12 000 shp = 16 knots
Range, miles	5 000 at 15 knots
Complement	200 plus 35 scientists and observers

Antarctic Support Ship. Built by Tsurumi Shipyard, Yokohama, Nippon Kokan Kabushiki Kaisha. Laid down on 28 Aug 1964, launched on 18 Mar 1965, delivered on 15 July 1965. Hangar and flight deck aft. Named after the mountain.

FUJI *1968, Japanese Maritime Self-Defence Force*

MARITIME SAFETY AGENCY

Commandant: Hisayoshi Terai

Established in May 1948

Personnel 1975: 11 203

LARGE PATROL VESSELS

2 "IZU" CLASS

IZU PL 31 **MIURA** PL 32

Displacement, tons	2 080 normal
Dimensions, feet	295·3 wl × 38 × 12·8
Main engines	diesel; 2 shafts; 10 400 bhp = 21·6 knots
Range, miles	14 500 at 12·7 knots; 5 000 at 21 knots
Complement	72

Izu was laid down in Aug 1966, launched in Jan 1967 and completed in July 1967. *Miura*, built by Maizuru Jukogyo Lts, was laid down in May 1968, launched in Oct 1968 and completed in Mar 1969. Employed in long range rescue and patrol and weather observation duties. Equipped with weather observation radar, various types of marine instruments. Ice proof hull for winter work.

MIURA *1970, Japanese Maritime Safety Agency*

4 "ERIMO" CLASS

DAIO PL 15 **ERIMO** PL 13 **SATSUMA** PL 14
MUROTO PL 16

Displacement, tons	1 009 normal (1 206 *Daio*)
Dimensions, feet	239·5 wl × 30·2 × 9·9 (31·5 × 10·7 *Daio*)
Guns	1—3 in 50 cal; 1—20 mm AA (1—40 mm; 1—20 mm *Daio*)
Main engines	Diesels; 2 shafts; 4 800 bhp = 19·78 knots (7 000 bhp = 20 knots, *Daio*)
Range, miles	5 000 at 17 knots

First pair built by Hitachi Zosen Co Ltd. *Erimo* was laid down on 29 Mar 1965, launched on 14 Aug 1965 and completed on 30 Nov 1965. Her structure is strengthened against ice. Employed as a patrol vessel off northern Japan. *Satsuma*, completed on 30 July 1966, is assigned to guard and rescue south of Japan. *Daio* built by Hitachi Maizuru—laid down 18 Oct 1972, launched 19 June 1973, completed 28 Sep 1973 (cp propellers). *Murato* built by Naikai Zosen Co Ltd. Laid down 15 Mar 1974, launched 5 Aug 1974, completed 30 Nov 1974.

DAIO *1973, Japanese Maritime Safety Agency*

KOJIMA PL 21

Displacement, tons	1 100
Dimensions, feet	228·3 × 33·8 × 10·5
Guns	1—3 in; 1—40 mm AA; 1—20 mm AA
Main engines	Diesels; 2 600 hp = 17 knots
Range, miles	6 000 at 13 knots
Complement	17 officers, 42 men, 47 cadets

Maritime Safety Agency training ship. Completed on 21 May 1964 at Kure Zosen.

KOJIMA *1965, Japanese Maritime Safety Agency*

2 "NOJIMA" CLASS

NOJIMA PL 11 **OJIKA** PL 12

Displacement, tons	950 standard; 980 normal; 1 100 full load
Dimensions, feet	208·8 pp; 226·5 oa × 30·2 × 10·5
Main engines	2 sets diesels; 3 000 bhp = 17·5 knots
Complement	51

Nojima was built by Uraga Dock Co Ltd. Laid down on 27 Oct 1961, launched on 12 Feb 1962, and completed on 30 Apr 1962. *Ojika* was completed on 10 June 1963. Both employed as patrol vessels and weather ships.

OJIKA *1972, Japanese Maritime Safety Agency*

SOYA PL 107

Displacement, tons	4 364 normal; 4 818 full load
Dimensions, feet	259·2 wl × 51·9 (*including bulge*) × 18·9
Aircraft	4 helicopters (see *notes*)
Main engines	2 sets diesels; 4 800 bhp = 12·5 knots on trials
Range, miles	10 000 at 12 knots
Complement	96

Assigned to guard and rescue service as a patrol vessel.

SOYA *1970, Japanese Maritime Safety Agency*

MEDIUM PATROL VESSELS

2 "BIHORO" CLASS

BIHORO PM 73 **KUMA** PM 74

Displacement, tons	636 standard; 677 full load
Dimensions, feet	208 × 25·6 × 14·1
Gun	1—20 mm
Main engines	Diesels; 2 shafts; 3 000 hp = 18 knots
Range, miles	3 200 at 18 knots
Complement	34

Bihoro built by Tohoku Zosen Co Ltd. *Kuma* built by Usuki Tekko Co Ltd. Completed 28 Feb 1974.

KUMA *1974, Japanese Maritime Safety Agency*

3 "MIYAKE" CLASS

AWAJI PM 71 **MIYAKE** PM 70 **YAEYAMA** PM 72

Displacement, tons	530 standard; 574 full load
Dimensions, feet	190·4 oa × 24·2 × 8·2
Gun	1—20 mm
Main engines	Diesels; 2 shafts; 3 200 hp = 17·8 knots
Range, miles	3 580 at 16 knots
Complement	40

Miyake and *Awaji* completed on 25 Jan 1973, *Yaeyama* 20 Dec 1972. Of similar hull design to "Kunashiri" class. CP propellers.

MIYAKE *1973, Japanese Maritime Safety Agency*

4 "KUNASHIRI" CLASS

KAMISHIMA PM 68
MINABE PM 66
KUNASHIRI PM 65
SAROBETSO PM 67

Displacement, tons	498 normal
Dimensions, feet	190·4 oa × 24·2 × 7·9
Gun	1—20 mm AA
Main engines	2 sets diesels; 2 600 bhp = 17·6 knots
Range, miles	3 000 at 16·9 knots
Complement	40

Kunashiri was built by Maizuru Jukogyo Ltd. Laid down in Oct 1968, launched in Dec 1968 and completed in Mar 1969. *Minabe*, laid down in Oct 1969, and completed in Mar 1970.

KUNASHIRI *1970, Japanese Maritime Safety Agency*

5 "CHIFURI" CLASS

CHIFURI PM 18 **KOZU** PM 20 **SHIKINE** PM 21
DAITO PM 22 **KUROKAMI** PM 19

Displacement, tons	465 standard· 483 normal
Dimensions, feet	169 pp; 177 wl × 25·2 × 8·5
Guns	1—3 in 50 cal; 1—20 mm AA
Main engines	2 sets diesels; 1 300 bhp = 15·8 knots
Range, miles	3 000 at 12 knots

DAITO *1970, Japanese Maritime Safety Agency*

14 "REBUN" CLASS

AMAKUSA	PM 09	**HIRADO**	PM 17	**NOTO**	PM 13
GENKAI	PM 07	**IKI**	PM 05	**OKI**	PM 06
HACHIJO	PM 08	**KOSHIKI**	PM 16	**OKUSHIRI**	PM 10
HEKURA	PM 14	**KUSAKAKI**	PM 11	**REBUN**	PM 04
		MIKURA	PM 15	**RISHIRI**	PM 12

Displacement, tons	450 standard; 488 trials; 495 normal
Dimensions, feet	155·2 pp; 164 wl; 170 oa × 26·5 × 8·5
Guns	1—3 in 50 cal; 1—20 mm AA
Main engines	2 sets diesels; 1 300 bhp = 15 knots
Range, miles	3 000 at 12 knots

A development of the original "Awaji" class medium patrol vessel design. All completed in 1951.

HIRADO *1972, Japanese Maritime Safety Agency*

5 "MATSUURA" CLASS

AMAMI PM 62 **MATSUURA** PM 60 **SENDAI** PM 61
KARATSU PM 64 **NATORI** PM 63

Displacement, tons	420 standard; 425 normal
Dimensions, feet	163·3 pp; 181·5 oa × 23 × 7·5
Gun	1—20 mm AA
Main engines	2 sets diesels; 1 400 bhp = 16·5 knots (*Matsuura, Sendai*); 1 800 bhp = 16·8 knots (*Amami, Natori*); 2 600 bhp (*Karatsu*)
Range, miles	3 500 at 12 knots
Complement	37

Matsuura and *Sendai* were built by Osaka Shipbuilding Co Ltd. *Matsuura* was laid down on 16 Oct 1960, launched on 24 Dec 1960 and completed on 18 Mar 1961. *Sendai* was laid down on 23 Aug 1961, launched on 18 Jan 1962 and completed on 21 Apr 1962. *Amami* completed on 29 Mar 1965, *Natori*, completed in 1966, and *Karatsu*, delivered to MSA on 31 Mar 1967, were built by Hitachi Zosen Co Ltd.

MATSUURA *1970, Japanese Maritime Safety Agency*

7 "YAHAGI" CLASS

CHITOSE	PM 56	**SORACHI**	PM 57	**YAHAGI**	PM 54
HORONAI	PM 59	**SUMIDA**	PM 55	**YUBARI**	PM 58
OKINAWA	PM 69				

Displacement, tons	333·15 standard; 375·7 normal
Dimensions, feet	147·3 pp; 157·2 wl × 24 × 7·4
Gun	1—40 mm AA
Main engines	2 sets diesels; 1 400 bhp = 15·5 knots
Range, miles	3 500 at 12 knots
Complement	37

All built by Niigata Engineering Co Ltd, *Yahagi* was laid down on 9 Dec 1955, launched on 19 May 1956 and completed on 31 July 1956. *Sumida* was completed on 30 June 1957. *Chitose* was laid down on 20 Sep 1957, launched on 24 Feb 1958 and completed on 30 Apr 1958. *Sorachi* was completed in Mar 1959, *Yubari* on 15 Mar 1960 *Horonai* on 4 Feb 1961.

SORACHI *1972, Japanese Maritime Safety Agency*

Medium Patrol Vessels—*continued*

2 "TOKACHI" CLASS

TATSUTA PM 52 — **TOKACHI** PM 51

Displacement, tons	336 standard; 381 normal (*Tokachi*) 324 standard; 369 normal (*Tatsuta*)
Dimensions, feet	157·5 pp; 164 wl; 170 oa × 21·9 × 11·2
Gun	1—40 mm AA
Main engines	2 sets of 4 cycle single acting diesels 1 500 bhp = 16 knots (*Tokachi*) 1 400 bhp = 15 knots (*Tatsuta*)
Range, miles	3 800 at 12 knots
Complement	37

Tokachi was built by Harima Dockyard, Kure. Laid down on 14 Nov 1953, launched on 8 May 1954 and completed on 31 July 1954. *Tatsuta* was completed on 10 Sep 1954.

TOKACHI — *1972, Japanese Maritime Safety Agency*

SMALL PATROL VESSELS

TESHIO PM 53

Displacement, tons	421·5 normal
Dimensions, feet	149·4 pp; 159 wl × 23 × 8·2
Gun	1—40 mm AA
Main engines	2 sets diesels; 1 400 bhp = 15·71 knots
Range, miles	3 800 at 12 knots
Complement	37

Built by Uraga Dock Co Ltd. Laid down on 15 Sep 1954, launched on 12 Jan 1955, completed on 19 Mar 1955.

3 "NAGARA" CLASS

KITAKAMI PS 20 — **NAGARA** PS 18 — **TONE** PS 19

Displacement, tons	260
Dimensions, feet	131·2 × 23 × 7·2
Gun	1—40 mm AA
Main engines	2 diesels; 2 shafts; 800 bhp = 13·5 knots
Range, miles	2 000 at 12 knots
Complement	35

Improved versions of the "Fuji" class. All launched and completed in 1952.

NAGARA — *1970 Japanese Maritime Safety Agency*

16 "FUJI" CLASS

ABUKUMA	PS 10	**KIKUCHI**	PS 08	**NOSHIRO**	PS 13
CHIKUGO	PS 16	**KISO**	PS 14	**OYODO**	PS 07
FUJI	PS 02	**KUMANO**	PS 17	**SAGAMI**	PS 05
ISHIKARI	PS 06	**KUZURYU**	PS 09	**SHINANO**	PS 15
ISUZU	PS 04	**MOGAMI**	PS 11	**TENRYU**	PS 03
				TOSHINO	PS 12

Displacement, tons	258 standard; 275 normal
Dimensions, feet	122 pp; 126·3 wl; 132·2 oa × 23 × 7·5
Gun	1—40 mm AA
Main engines	2 sets diesels; 800 bhp = 13·6 knots
Range, miles	2 000 at 12 knots
Complement	35

Built in the early 1950's.

MOGAMI — *1970, Japanese Maritime Safety Agency*

Small Patrol Vessels—*continued*

14 "HIDAKA" CLASS

ASHITAKA	PS 43	**IBUKI**	PS 45	**ROKKO**	PS 35
AKIYOSHI	PS 37	**KAMUI**	PS 41	**TAKANAWA**	PS 36
HIDAKA	PS 32	**KUNIMI**	PS 38	**TAKATSUKI**	PS 39
HIYAMA	PS 33	**KURAMA**	PS 44	**TOUMI**	PS 46
		NOBARU	PS 49	**TSURUGI**	PS 34

Displacement, tons	166·2 to 164·4 standard; 169·4 normal
Dimensions, feet	100 pp; 111 oa × 20·8 × 5·5
Main engines	1 set diesels; 1 shaft; 690 to 700 bhp = 13·5 knots
Range, miles	1 200 at 12 knots

Hidaka was built by Azuma Shipbuilding Co. Laid down on 4 Oct 1961, launched on 2 Mar 1962 and completed on 23 Apr 1962. Both *Hiyama* and *Tsurugi* were completed in Mar 1963 by Hitachi Shipbuilding Co. *Kunimi* was built under the 1964 fiscal year programme by Hayashikane Shipbuilding & Engineering Co, Shimoneseki, laid down on 15 Nov 1964, launched on 19 Dec 1964 and completed on 15 Feb 1965. Three more local patrol ships were completed in 1965, two in 1966, two in 1967 and two in 1968.

ASHITAKA — *1972, Japanese Maritime Safety Agency*

TSUKUBA PS 31

Displacement, tons	65
Dimensions, feet	80·5 × 21·5 × 3·7
Main engines	2 Niigata diesels; 1 800 bhp = 18·4 knots trials
Range, miles	230 at 15 knots

Built by Hitachi Zosen, Kanagawa and completed on 30 May 1962.

ASAMA PS 47 — **BIZAN** PS 42 — **SHIRAMINE** PS 48

Displacement, tons	40 normal; *Shiramine* 48 normal
Dimensions, feet	80·5 × 18·3 × 2·8
Guns	1 MG aft
Main engines	2 Mitsubishi diesels; 1 140 bhp = 21·6 knots; *Shiramine*, 2 Benz diesels; 2 200 bhp = 25 knots
Range, miles	400 at 18 knots; *Shiramine* 250 at 25 knots

Bizan and *Asama* were built by Shimonoseki Shipyard & Engine Works, Mitsubishi Heavy Industries Ltd. Completed in Mar 1966 and in Feb 1969 respectively. *Shiramine* was built by the same shipyard and completed in Dec 1969. Of light metal construction.

SHIRAMINE — *1972, Japanese Maritime Safety Agency*

SPECIAL RESCUE TYPE

AKAGI PS 40

Displacement, tons	42
Dimensions, feet	78·8 oa × 17·8 × 3·2
Main engines	2 Mercedes Benz diesels; 2 200 bhp = 28 knots
Range, miles	350 at 21 knots

Completed by Hitachi Zosen Kanagawa in 1965.

PATROL CRAFT

2 "HATSUNAMI" CLASS

SUZUNAMI PC 08 — **HAYANAMI** PC 10

6 "MAKIGUMO" CLASS

HATAGUMO	PC 31	**YAEGUMO**	PC 33	**NATSUGUMO**	PC 35
MAKIGUMO	PC 32	**ASAGUMO**	PC 34	**TATSUGUMO**	PC 36

Patrol craft—*continued*

3 "HANAYUKI" CLASS

HANAYUKI PC 37 **MINEYUKI** PC 38 **ISOYUKI** PC 39

Displacement, tons	42 to 46 normal
Dimensions, feet	69 oa × 17·2 × 3·2 (Makigumo Class) 72 oa × 17·6 × 3·2 (Hanayuki Class)
Main engines	2 diesels; 700 bhp = 13·9 knots (*Hatsunami*) 2 diesels; 1 400 bhp = 20·5 knots (*Makigumo*) 3 diesels; 1 500 bhp = 20·7 knots (*Hanayuki*) 2 diesels; 1 800 bhp = 21·3 knots (*Isoyuki*)

Isoyuki was completed in Feb 1960, *Hanayuki* and *Mineyuki* in Mar 1959, *Asagumo Natsugumo* and *Tatsugumo* in Apr 1955 and the others before 1954. Of light wooden hulls.

2 "AKIZUKI" CLASS

AKIZUKI PC 64 **SHINONOME** PC 65

Displacement, tons	74
Dimensions, feet	85·3 oa × 20·7 × 9·8
Main engines	3 Mitsubishi diesels; 3 000 bhp = 22·1 knots
Range, miles	220 at 22 knots
Complement	10

Built by Mitsubishi Heavy Industries Co Ltd. Completed 28 Feb 1974.

AKIZUKI *1974, Japanese Maritime Safety Agency*

14 "MATSUYUKI" CLASS

MATSUYUKI	PC 40	**SHIMAYUKI**	PC 41	**TAMAYUKI**	PC 42
HAMAYUKI	PC 43	**YAMAYUKI**	PC 44	**KOMAYUKI**	PC 45
UMIGIRI	PC 46	**ASAGIRI**	PC 47	**HAMAGIRI**	PC 48
SAGIRI	PC 49	**SETOGIRI**	PC 50	**HAYAGIRI**	PC 51
HAMANAMI	PC 52	**MATSUNAMI**	PC 53		

Displacement, tons	39 for 40, 40 for 41-43, 41 for 44-45, 42 for 46-47 and 49-51 51 for 48, 60 for 52
Dimensions, feet	69 oa × 16·6 × 3·2
Gun	1—13 mm
Main engines	2 Mercedes Benz diesels; 2 200 bhp = 26·3 knots; PC 48 1 140 bhp = 14·6 knots; PC 52 = 21.8 knots; PC 53 = 20·8
Range, miles	About 300 miles at near maximum speed
Complement	10

Since 1964 two or three craft of this type have been built per year by Hitachi Kanagawa Dockyard; PC's 40-47 and 49-51 were built of light alloy frames with wooden hulls. PC's 48 and 52 were built of steel; PC 53 was built completely of light alloy.

16 "SHIKINAMI" CLASS

HARUZUKI	PC 61	**MOCHIZUKI**	PC 60	**TAMANAMI**	PC 67
ISENAMI	PC 57	**MUTSUKI**	PC 59	**TOMONAMI**	PC 55
KIYONAMI	PC 69	**OKINAMI**	PC 70	**URANAMI**	PC 66
KIYOZUKI	PC 62	**SHIKINAMI**	PC 54	**URAZUKI**	PC 63
MINEFUMO	PC 68	**TAKANAMI**	PC 58	**WAKAGUMO**	PC 71
				WAKANAMI	PC 56

Displacement, tons	44
Dimensions, feet	69 oa × 17·4 × 3·2
Main engines	2 Mercedes Benz Diesels, 2 200 bhp = 26·5 knots
Range, miles	280 miles at near maximum speed
Complement	10

Since 1971 four or five craft of this type have been built per year by Hitachi Kanagawa Dockyard and Mitsubishi Shimonoseki Factory. They were built completely of light alloy.

KIYONAMI *1973, Japanese Maritime Safety Agency*

149 15 METRE MOTOR LAUNCH TYPE

CL 04, 05, 09, 12, 14-16, 18-140, 301-319

Displacement, tons	20·2 full load
Dimensions, feet	49·2 × 13·5 × 3·1
Main engines	Diesels; 2 shafts; 520 bhp = 19 knots
Range, miles	160 at 15 knots

For coastal patrol and rescue duties. Since 1971 about 20 of this class, built of high tensile steel, have been delivered each year.

MUROKAZE—CL 127 *1973, Japanese Maritime Safety Agency*

18 HARBOUR PATROL CRAFT

CS 57, 58, 100, 105, 107, 108, 115-126

SURVEYING VESSELS

SHOYO HL 01

Displacement, tons	2 000
Dimensions, feet	262·4 × 40·3 × 13·8
Main engines	2 Fuji V-12; 4 800 hp; 1 shaft = 17·4 knots
Complement	73

Built by Hitachi Zosen, Maizuru. Completed March 1972. Fully equipped for all types of hydrographic and oceanographic work.

SHOYO *1973, Japanese Maritime Safety Agency*

TENYO HM 05

Displacement, tons	181
Dimensions, feet	95 × 19·2 × 9·2
Main engines	Diesels; 230 bhp = 10 knots
Range, miles	3 160 at 10 knots

HEIYO HM 04

Displacement, tons	69
Dimensions, feet	73·5 × 14·5 × 8
Main engines	Diesel; 150 bhp = 9 knots
Range, miles	670 at 9 knots

Completed by Shimuzu Dockyard of Nippon Kokan Kabushiki Kaisha in Mar 1955. There are 21 other smaller vessels of HS type ranging from 5 to 8 tons displacement.

MEIYO HL 03

Displacement, tons	486 normal
Measurements, tons	360 gross
Dimensions, feet	133 wl; 146 oa × 26·5 × 9·5
Main engines	1 set diesel; 700 bhp = 12 knots
Range, miles	5 000 at 11 knots
Complement	40

Built by Nagoya Shipbuilding & Engineering Co, Nagoya. Laid down on 14 Sep 1962, launched 22 Dec 1962 and completed 15 Mar 1963. Controllable pitch propeller.

MEIYO *1971, Maritime Safety Agency*

Survey Vessels—*continued*

TAKUYO HL 02

Displacement, tons: 880 standard; 930 normal
Dimensions, feet: 185 pp; 192·8 wl × 31·2 × 10·7
Main engines: 2 sets diesels; 1 300 bhp = 14 knots
Range, miles: 8 000 at 12 knots

Built for the Maritime Safety Agency, by Niigata Engineering Co Ltd. Laid down on 19 May 1956, launched on 19 Dec 1956, and completed in March 1957.

TAKUYO *1971, Japanese Maritime Safety Agency*

KAIYO HM 06

Displacement, tons: 378 normal
Dimensions, feet: 132·5 wl; 146 oa × ×26·5 × 7·8
Main engines: 1 set diesels; 450 bhp = 12 knots
Range, miles: 6 100 at 11 knots

Built by Nagoya Shipbuilding & Engineering Co, Nagoya. Completed on 14 Mar 1964. Rated as Medium Surveying Vessel. Controllable pitch propeller.

KAIYO *1972, Japanese Maritime Safety Agency*

TENDERS

MYOJO LM 11

Displacements, tons: 318 normal
Dimensions, feet: 78·8 pp; 87·1 oa × 39·4 × 8·8
Main engines: 2 sets diesels; 600 bhp = 11·1 knots
Range, miles: 3 679 at 10 knots

Completed in Mar 1974 to replace an identical ship of the same name, completed in 1967, which was lost in collision April 1972. Catamaran type buoy tender, propelled by controllable pitch propeller, this ship is employed in maintenance and position adjustment service to floating aids to navigation.
There are also 8 LM s for the same maintenance service, 87 LS s and 18 HS s. Eight LS class tenders were scrapped and eight replacements built, and one was purchased.

WAKAKUSA LL 01

Displacement, tons: 1 815
Dimensions, feet: 204 × 32·2 × 19·1
Main engines: 1 850 hp

Built by Hitachi Inoshima Dockyard in Mar 1946. Purchased from Osaka Shosen Kaisha in Jan 1956. Rated as Navigation Aid Vessel (Lighthouse Supply Ship).

WAKAKUSA *1971, Maritime Safety Agency*

GINGA LL 12 | **HOKUTO** LL 11 | **KAIO** LL 13

Displacements, tons: 500
Dimensions, feet: 128·7 × 31·2 × 13·9
Main engines: 2 diesels; 420 bhp = 11·26 knots
Range, miles: 2 800 at 10 knots

The above three are not sister ships. The above particulars refer to *Ginga* which was built by Osaka Shipbuilding Co Ltd. Laid down on 11 Nov 1953, launched on 6 May 1954 and completed on 30 June 1954. Equipped with 15 ton derrick for laying buoys. Rated as Navigation Aid Vessels (Buoy Tenders).

Tenders—*continued*

GINGA *1971, Maritime Safety Agency*

There are also 9 LMs (LM 101 to LM 109) and 15 navigation and buoy tenders for miscellaneous service.

UNDERWATER RESEARCH VESSEL

SHINKAI HU 06

Displacement, tons: 91
Dimensions, feet: 54·2 oa × 21·6 × 13
Main engines: 1 set electric motor; 11 kW
Range, hours: 4·6 at 2·3 knots
Complement: 4

Laid down in Sep 1967, launched in Mar 1968 and completed in March 1969 by Kawasaki Heavy Industries Ltd. An underwater vehicle designed for making researches of biological and underground resources of the continental shelves. With a main propeller and two auxilary ones installed on each side of the hull, this ship can dive 2 000 feet and stay on the sea bed for sampling, observing and photographing.

SHINKAI *1970, Japanese Maritime Safety Agency*

FIRE FIGHTING CRAFT

3 "HIRYU" CLASS

HIRYU FL 01 | **NANRYU** FL 03 | **SHORYU** FL 02

Displacement, tons: 251 normal
Dimensions, feet: 90·2 oa × 34·1 × 7·2
Main engines: 2 sets diesels; 2 200 bhp = 13·5 knots
Range, miles: 395 at 13·4 knots
Complements: 14

Hiryu, a catamaran type fire boat, was built by Nippon Kokan Kabushiki Kaisha, Asano Dockyard. Laid down in Oct 1968, launched in Feb 1969 and completed in Mar 1969. Designed and built for fire fighting services to large tankers. *Shoryu* was completed in Mar 1970, and *Nanryu*, in Mar 1971, both at the same Asano Dockyard.

HIRYU *1970, Japanese Maritime Safety Agency*

NUNOBIKI FM 01

Displacement, tons: 87
Dimensions, feet: 75·4 oa × 19·7 × 14·1
Main engines: 1 Mercedes-Benz diesel plus 2 Nissan diesels; 11 00 bhp + 500 bhp = 14 knots
Range, miles: 180 at 14 knots
Complement: 12

Completed by Yokohama Yacht Co Ltd in 1974.

SALVAGE CRAFT

FS 01 to **FS 07** (7 boats) for fire-fighting service, rescue and salvage duties.

UTILITY LAUNCHES

There are 14 local and miscellaneous boats of various sizes and employment.

KENYA

Establishment

The Kenya Navy, which is based in Mombasa, was inaugurated on 12 Dec 1964, the first anniversary of Kenya's independence.

Administration

Commander, Kenya Navy: Lieut. Col. J. C. J. Kimaro

Personnel

(a) 1974: 300 officers and men
(b) Volunteers

Mercantile Marine

Lloyd's Register of Shipping: 21 vessels of 21 829 tons gross

Prefix to Ships' Names

KNS (Kenyan Naval Ship)

LIGHT FORCES

4 BROOKE MARINE 37·5 metre TYPE

(LARGE PATROL CRAFT)

MAMBA P 3100 + **3**

Displacement, tons	125 standard; 160 full load
Dimensions, ft (*m*)	123 × 22·5 × 5·2 (*37·5 × 6·9 × 1·6*)
Guns	2—40 mm Bofors
Main engines	2—16 cylinder Rustons diesels; 4 000 hp = 25 knots
Range, miles	3 300 at 13 knots
Complement	25 (3 officers, 22 men)

Built by Brooke Marine Lowestoft. Laid down 17 Feb 1972, handed over 7 Feb 1974. *Mamba* means crocodile. A further three craft of this class were ordered 10 May 1973. They are slightly smaller (145 tons full load and 107 ft oa) and fitted with Ruston-Paxman Valenta diesels giving an additional ·5 knot. The complement is 21. All three currently under construction.

MAMBA 1974

3 VOSPER TYPE (LARGE PATROL CRAFT)

CHUI P 3112 **NDOVU** P 3117 **SIMBA** P 3110

Displacement, tons	96 standard; 109 full load
Dimensions, feet	95 wl; 103 oa × 19·8 × 5·8
Guns	2—40 mm Bofors AA
Main engines	2 Paxman Ventura diesels; 2 800 bhp = 24 knots
Range, miles	1 000 at economical speed; 1 500 at 16 knots
Complement	23 (3 officers and 20 ratings)

The first ships specially built for the Kenya Navy. Designed and built by Vosper Ltd, Portsmouth. Ordered on 28 Oct 1964. *Simba* was launched on 9 Sep 1965 and completed on 23 May 1966, *Chui* was handed over on 7 July 1966 and *Ndovu* was handed over on 27 July 1966. All three left Portsmouth on 22 Aug 1966 and arrived at their base in Mombasa on 4 Oct 1966. Air-conditioned. Fitted with modern radar communications equipment and roll damping fins. *Chui* means Leopard, *Ndovu* means Elephant. *Simba* means Lion.

SIMBA *1973, Kenyan Navy*

KHMER REPUBLIC

The Marine Royale Khmer was established on 1 March 1954 and became Marine Nationale Khmer on 9 October 1970.

Chief of Staff of Marine Nationale Khmer (MNK): Commodore Vong Sarendy

Personnel

(a) 1975: 11 000 officers and men including Marine Corps (4 000 officers and men)

(b) 18 months National Service

War Losses

As it is impossible to keep track of the frequent casualties which are occurring on the river approaches to Phnom Penh no attempt has been made to delete such losses from the totals given here.

Mercantile Marine

Lloyd's Register of Shipping: 3 vessels of 2 090 tons gross

CORVETTES

2 Ex-US PC TYPE

E 311 (ex-*Flamberge, P 631*, ex-*PC 1086*) **E 312** (ex-*L'Inconstant, P 636*, ex-*PC 1171*)

Displacement, tons	325 standard; 400 full load
Dimensions, feet	170 wl; 173·7 oa × 23 × 6·5
Guns	1—3 in dp; 1—40 mm AA, 4—20 mm AA
Main engines	2 GM diesels, 2 shafts; 3 600 bhp = 18 knots
Oil fuel, tons	62
Range, miles	2 300 at 18 knots; 6 000 at 10 knots
Complement	63

Former US submarine chasers of the PC type. Transferred from the US Navy to the French Navy in 1951 and served in Indo-China and again transferred to the Marine Nationale Khmer in 1955-56. Built of steel.

E 312

2 EX-US LSIL TYPE

P 111 (ex-*LSIL 9039*, ex-*LSIL 875*)

Displacement, tons	230 standard; 387 full load
Dimensions, feet	169 × 23·7 × 5·7
Guns	1—3 in; 1—40 mm AA; 2—20 mm AA
Main engines	2 GM diesels; 2 shafts; 1 000 bhp = 15 knots
Oil fuel (tons)	100
Range, miles	8 000 at 12 knots
Complement	58

Former US infantry landing ship of the LSIL type. Transferred from the US Navy to the French Navy, on 2 Mar 1951 and stationed in Indo-China; and again transferred to the MNK in 1957.

Ex-US LSIL *1971*

P 112 (ex-*Medecin Capitaine Le Gall*, ex-US LSIL)

Displacement, tons	230 standard; 350 full load
Dimensions, feet	160 × 23 × 6
Guns	1—3 in; 5—20 mm AA
Main engines	2 GM diesels; 2 shafts; 1 800 bhp = 15 knots
Oil fuel	120 tons
Range, miles	8 000 at 12 knots
Complement	40

Transferred 1955.

LIGHT FORCES

2 Ex-YUGOSLAV "101" CLASS (FAST ATTACK CRAFT—TORPEDO)

VR 1 **VR 2**

Displacement, tons	55 standard; 60 full load
Dimensions, feet	69 pp; 78 oa × 21·3 × 7·8
Guns	1—40 mm AA; 4—12·7 mm MG
Tubes	2—21 in
Main engines	3 Packard petrol motors; 5 000 bhp = 36 knots
Complement	14

Torpedo boats presented by Yugoslavia in 1965 and numbered by the MNK. Similar to US "Higgins" class.

"101" CLASS *Yugoslavian Navy*

20 Ex-US "SWIFT" CLASS (COASTAL PATROL CRAFT)

Displacement, tons	22·5
Dimensions, feet	50 × 13 × 3·5
Guns	1—81 mm mortar; 3—50 cal MG
Main engines	2 diesels; 960 hp; 2 shafts = 28 knots
Complement	6

Transferred in 1972 73

2 Ex-US AVR TYPE (COASTAL PATROL CRAFT)

VR 3 **VR 4**

Displacement, tons	30
Dimensions, feet	63 × 13 × 4·6
Guns	4—12·7 mm MG
Main engines	GM Diesel 500 bhp = 15 knots
Complement	12

65 Ex-US PBR MARK I and II (RIVER PATROL CRAFT)

Displacement, tons	8
Dimensions, feet	32 × 11 × 2·6
Guns	3—·50 cal MG; 1 grenade launcher
Main engines	2 geared diesels; water jets = 25 knots
Complement	5

Transferred 1973-74.

PBR Mk II Type *United States Navy*

3 Ex-CHINESE CPB TYPE (COASTAL PATROL CRAFT)

VP 1 **VP 2** **VP 3**

Displacement, tons	7·7 standard; 9·7 full load
Dimensions, feet	42 × 9 × 3·9
Guns	2—12·7 mm MG
Main engines	Diesel, 300 bhp = 20 knots
Complement	10

Coastal patrol boats transferred from the People's Republic of China in Jan 1968.

Light Forces—*continued*

1 Ex-HDML TYPE (COASTAL PATROL CRAFT)

VP 212 (*ex-VP 748*, ex-*HDML 1223*)

Displacement, tons	46 standard; 54 full load
Dimensions, feet	72 oa × 16 × 5·5
Guns	2—20 mm AA; 4—7·5 mm MG
Main engines	2 diesels; 2 shafts; 300 bhp = 10 knots
Complement	8

Former British harbour defence motor launch of the HDML type. Transferred from the British Navy to the French Navy in 1950 and again transferred from the French Navy to the MNK in 1956.

AMPHIBIOUS VESSELS

4 Ex-US LCU TYPE

SKILAK (ex-US YFU 73) T 920
T 919 (ex-US YFU 68, ex-LCU 1385)
T 918 (ex-US YFU 56, ex-LCU 646)
T 917 (ex-US YFU, ex-LCU 1577)

Displacement, tons	320 full load
Dimensions, feet	119 oa × 32·7 × 5
Guns	2—20 mm
Main engines	Diesels; 675 bhp; 3 shafts = 10 knots
Complement	13

Landing craft transferred as follows; 917 Oct 1969, 918 and 919 Nov 1972, 920 Nov 1973.

US LCU Type *1970, Defoe Shipbuilding*

1 EDIC TYPE

T 916 (ex-*EDIC 606*)

Displacement, tons	292 standard; 650 full load
Dimensions, feet	193·5 × 39·2 × 4·5
Guns	1—81 mm mortar; 2—12·7 mm MG
Main engines	2 MGO diesels; 2 shafts; 1 000 bhp = 10 knots
Complement	16 (1 officer, 15 men)

Completed and transferred from the French Government in Aug 1969.

2 Ex-US LCU TYPE

T 914 (ex-USS *LCU 783*) **T 915** (ex-USS *LCU 1421*)

Displacement, tons	180 standard, 360 full load
Dimensions, feet	115 wl; 119 oa × 34 × 6
Guns	2—20 mm AA
Main engines	3 diesels; 3 shafts; 675 bhp = 8 knots
Complement	12

Former US utility landing craft of the LCU type. LCU 783 and LCU 1421 were transferred on 31 May 1962. T 919 (ex-USS *LCU* 1577) was sunk by a mine on 5 May 1970. Former LCT(6)s 9085 (ex-622) and 9091 (ex-720) were deleted from the list in 1969, with ex-LCU 9073 (ex-USS *LCU* 1420).

T 913 *1969, Marine Nat. Khmere*

TUG

PINGOUIE R 911 (ex-USS *YTL* 556)

KOREA (North)

Administration

Commander of the Navy: Rear Admiral Yu Chang Kwon

Personnel

(a) 1975: 18 000 officers and men
(b) National Service; 3-4 years

Strength of the Fleet

Type	*Active*	*Building*
Submarines—Patrol	8	—
Corvettes	22	1
Fast Attack Craft—Missile	18	—
Fast Attack Craft—Torpedo	136	—
Fast Attack Craft—Gun	51	—
Large Patrol Craft	2	—
Coastal Patrol Craft	70	—
LCUs	20/30	—
Trawlers etc.	5/10	

Bases

Ch'ongjin, Haeju, Nampo, Najin, Munchon, Wonson, Pipa-got, Cha-ho, Mayang Do, Sagon-ni.

Mercantile Marine

Lloyd's Register of Shipping: 13 vessels of 60 347 tons gross

SUBMARINES

4 Ex-CHINESE "ROMEO" CLASS (PATROL TYPE)

Displacement, tons	1 100 surfaced; 1 600 dived
Dimensions, ft (*m*)	246 × 24 × 14·5 (*75 × 7·3 × 4·4*)
Tubes	6—21 in (bow); 18 torpedoes
Main machinery	2 diesels—4 000 bhp; 2 electric motors—4 000 hp; 2 shafts
Speed, knots	17 surfaced; 14 dived
Complement	65

Two transferred from China 1973 and two in 1974.
Stationed on West coast (Yellow Sea).

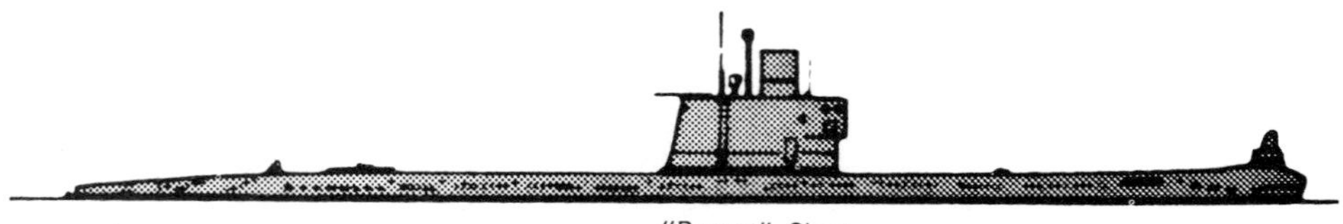

"Romeo" Class

4 Ex-USSR "WHISKY" CLASS (PATROL TYPE)

Displacement, tons	1 030 surface; 1180 submerged
Dimensions, ft (*m*)	240 × 22 × 15 (*73·2 × 6·7 × 4·6*)
Tubes	6—21 in (4 bow, 2 stern); 18 torpedoes carried normally (or up to 40 mines)
Main Machinery	2 diesels; 4 000 bhp; 2 Electric motors: 2 500 hp; 2 shafts
Range, miles	13 000 at 8 knots
Speed, knots	17 surfaced; 15 dived
Complement	60

Stationed on East Coast (Sea of Japan).

"WHISKY" Class

CORVETTES

15 Ex-USSR "SO 1" CLASS

Displacement, tons	215 light; 250 normal
Dimensions, ft (*m*)	138·6 × 20·9 × 9·2 (*42·3 × 6·1 × 2·8*)
Guns	4—25 mm (2 twin)
A/S weapons	4 five barrelled launchers
Main engines	3 diesels; 6 000 bhp = 29 knots
Range, miles	1 100 at 13 knots
Complement	30

6 transferred by USSR in 1957-58. Remainder built in North Korea.

"SO 1" Class *1972*

3 "SARIWAN" CLASS

Displacement, tons	600-650
Dimensions, feet	203·5 × 24 × 7·8
Guns	1—3·9 in (*100 mm*) 56 cal DP; 4—37 mm (twin); 4—25 mm (twin vertical)
A/S weapons	2/4 DC Racks
Mines	30
Main engines	2 diesels; 3 000 bhp; 2 shafts
Speed, knots	21 (estimated)
Complement	65-70

The predecessors of the "Najin" class built in North Korea in the mid 1960s.

RADAR. Skinhead, surface search; Ski Pole or Yard Rake. IFF,

3 "NAJIN" CLASS

Displacement, tons	900
Dimensions, feet	230 × 26 × 9
Guns	1—3·9 in (*100 mm*), 56 cal DP; 4—57 mm (twin); 4—25 mm AA (twin vertical)
A/S weapons	4 DC racks
Mines	30 (estimated)
Main engines	2 diesels; 5 000 bhp; 2 shafts
Speed, knots	25 (estimated)
Complement	90 (estimated)

Enlarged edition of ex-Soviet "Tral" class built in North Korea. Laid down 1971-72 for completion 1973.

RADAR. Skinhead, surface search; possible Ski Pole, IFF.

1 or 2 Ex-USSR "TRAL" CLASS

Displacement, tons	475
Dimensions, ft (*m*)	203·5 × 23·8 × 7·8 (*62 × 7·2 × 2·4*)
Guns	1—3·9 in (*100 mm*) 56 cal DP; 3—37 mm (singles); 4—12·7 mm MG
A/S weapons	2 DC racks
Mines	30
Main engines	2 diesels; 2 800 hp; 2 shafts
Speed, knots	18
Complement	55

An elderly class of Fleet Minesweepers of which some 4-5 were transferred by USSR in mid 1950s. Used for escort purposes.

RADAR. Skinhead, surface search; Yard Rake, IFF.

LIGHT FORCES

8 Ex-USSR "OSA" CLASS (FAST ATTACK CRAFT—MISSILE)

Displacement, tons	165 standard, 200 full load
Dimensions, ft (*m*)	128·7 × 25·1 × 5·9 (*39·3 × 7·7 × 1·8*)
Missile launchers	4 in two pairs abreast for *Styx* missiles
Guns	4—30 mm (1 twin forward, and aft)
Main engines	3 diesels; 13 000 bhp = 32 knots
Range, miles	800 at 25
Complement	25

The combination of the "Osa" flotilla and the "Komar" units (below), both armed with the very potent 23 mile range "Styx" missiles, provides a powerful striking force on the South Korean border and within 250 miles of Japan.

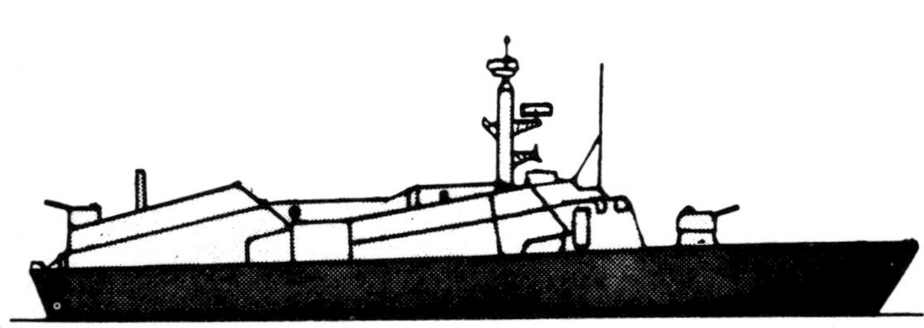

"OSA" Class

10 Ex-USSR "KOMAR" CLASS

(FAST ATTACK CRAFT—MISSILE)

Displacement, tons	70 standard; 80 full load
Dimensions, ft (*m*)	83·7 × 19·8 × 5·0 (*25·5 × 6·0 × 1·8*)
Missile launchers	2 for "Styx" missiles
Guns	2—25 mm AA (1 twin forward)
Main engines	4 diesels; 4 shafts; 4 800 bhp = 40 knots
Range, miles	400 at 30 knots

See note under "Osa" class above.

15 Ex-CHINESE "SHANGHAI II" CLASS

(FAST ATTACK CRAFT—GUN)

Displacement, tons	120 standard; 155 full load
Dimensions, ft (*m*)	128 × 18 × 5·6 (*39 × 5·5 × 1·7*)
Guns	4—37 mm (twin); 4—25 mm (abaft bridge); 2—3 in (*75 mm*) recoilless rifles (bow)
Main engines	4 diesels; 4 800 bhp = 30 knots
A/S weapons	8 DC
Mines	Rails can be fitted for 10 mines
Range, miles	800 at 17 knots
Complement	25

Acquired from China since 1967. Skinhead radar.

"SHANGHAI II" Class

Light Forces—*continued*

8 Ex-CHINESE "SWATOW" CLASS

(FAST ATTACK CRAFT—GUN)

Displacement, tons	80
Dimensions, ft (*m*)	83·5 × 19 × 6·5 (*25·5 × 5·8 × 2*)
Guns	4—37 mm; 2—12·7 mm
A/S weapons	8 DC
Main engines	4 diesels; 4 800 bhp = 42 knots
Range, miles	500 at 30 knots
Complement	17

Transferred from China in 1968.

4 "CHODO" CLASS (FAST ATTACK CRAFT—GUN)

Displacement, tons	130 (estimated)
Dimensions, feet	140 × 19 × 8·5
Guns	1—3 in (*76 mm*) 50 cal (forward); 3—37 mm (single); 4—25 mm (twin, vertical)
Main engines	Diesels; 2 shafts; 6 000 bhp
Speed, knots	24 (estimated)
Complement	40 (estimated)

Built in North Korea in mid 1960s.

RADAR. Skin Head Search.

4 "K-48" CLASS (FAST ATTACK CRAFT—GUN)

Displacement, tons	110 (estimated)
Dimensions, feet	125 × 18 × 5
Guns	1—3 in (*76 mm*) 50 cal (forward); 3—37 mm (single); 4—25 mm (twin, vertical); 4/6—14·5 MG (twin)
Main engines	Diesels; 4-5 000 bhp; 2 shafts
Speed, knots	24 (estimated)

Probably built in North Korea in late 1950s.

RADAR. Skin Head Search.

20 Ex-USSR "MO IV" CLASS (FAST ATTACK CRAFT—GUN)

Displacement, tons	56
Guns	1—37 mm; 1/2—14·5 mm MG
Main engines	Diesels; 2 600 hp = 25 knots

Transferred in 1950s.

4 Ex-USSR "SHERSHEN" CLASS

(FAST ATTACK CRAFT—TORPEDO)

Displacement, tons	150 standard; 160 full load
Dimensions, ft (*m*)	115·5 × 23 × 5 (*35·2 × 7·1 × 1·5*)
Guns	4—30 mm (2 twin)
Torpedo tubes	4—21 in (single)
A/S weapons	12 DC
Main engines	3 diesels; 3 shafts; 13 000 bhp = 41 knots
Complement	16

Transferred in 1973-74.

"SHERSHEN" Class

Light Forces—*continued*

45 Ex-USSR "P 6" CLASS (FAST ATTACK CRAFT—TORPEDO)

Displacement, tons	66 standard; 75 full load
Dimensions, ft (*m*)	84·2 × 20 × 6 (*25·7 × 6·1 × 1·8*)
Guns	4—25 mm
Torpedo tubes	2—21 in (or mines or DC)
Main engines	4 Diesels; 4 800 hp; 4 shafts = 43 knots
Range, miles	450 at 30 knots

There is a growing number of these craft in N. Korea with local building programme in hand. About fifteen of this class have a different armament including 2—37 mm (single) and 4—25 mm (twin, vertical).

RADAR. Pothead or Skinhead.

"P 6" Class

12 Ex-USSR "P 4" CLASS (FAST ATTACK CRAFT—TORPEDO)

Displacement, tons	25
Dimensions, ft (*m*)	62·7 × 11·6 × 5·6 (*19·1 × 3·5 × 1·7*)
Guns	2—MG
Tubes	2—18 in
Main engines	2 diesels; 2 200 bhp = 50 knots

Built in 1951-57. Aluminium hulls. Some locally built.

"P 4" Class *1971*

15 "IWON" CLASS (FAST ATTACK CRAFT—TORPEDO)

Displacement, tons	40
Dimensions, feet	63 × 12 × 5
Guns	4—25 mm (twin, vertical)
Tubes	2—21 in

Built in North Korea in late 1950s. Similar to older Soviet "P 2" class.

RADAR. Skinhead.

Light Forces—*continued*

"CHAHO" CLASS (FAST ATTACK CRAFT—TORPEDO)

Reported as building in North Korea.

6 "AN JU" CLASS (FAST ATTACK CRAFT—TORPEDO)

Displacement, tons	35
Dimensions, feet	65 × 12 × 6
Guns	2—25 mm (twin, vertical)
Tubes	2—21 in

Built in North Korea in 1960s.

60 "SIN HUNG" and "KOSONG" CLASSES (FAST ATTACK CRAFT—TORPEDO)

Displacement, tons	35
Dimensions, feet	60 × 11 × 5·5
Guns	2—14·5 mm (twin)
Tubes	2—18 in or 2—21 in

Built in North Korea mid 1950s to 1970. Frequently operated on South Korean border. All resemble the Soviet "D-3" class of 25 years ago.

1 or 2 Ex-USSR "ARTILLERIST" CLASS (LARGE PATROL CRAFT)

Displacement, tons	240
Dimensions, ft (*m*)	160·8 × 19 × 6·5 (*49 × 5·8 × 2*)
Guns	1—3·9 in (*100 mm*); 2—37 mm (singles); 4/6—25 mm (twin, vertical)
Main engines	2 diesels; 3 300 bhp; 2 shafts
Speed, knots	25
Complement	30

Transferred in mid 1950s.

10 Ex-USSR "KM 4" CLASS (COASTAL PATROL CRAFT)

Displacement, tons	10
Dimensions, ft (*m*)	46 × 10·5 × 3 (*14 × 3·2 × ·9*)
Guns	1—36 mm; 1—14·5 mm MG
Main engines	Petrol; 146 shp; 2 shafts
Complement	10

20 LIGHT GUNBOATS

Believed to be for inshore patrols. Locally built.

AMPHIBIOUS FORCES

20/30 LCM now in service with others building in North Korea. Used on South Korean border.

SERVICE FORCES

5/10 Large Trawlers and small cargo vessels used as store ships. Some of the trawlers operate on South Korean border where three have been sunk in the last four years.

KOREA (REPUBLIC OF)

Administration

Chief of Naval Operations:
Rear Admiral Kyu-Sup Kim

Vice Chief of Naval Operations:
Vice-Admiral Yun-Kyong Oh

Commander-in-Chief of Fleet:
Rear-Admiral Chong-Yon Hwang

Personnel

Approx 20 000 in Navy and approx 20 000 in Marine Corps.

Strength of the Fleet

7	Destroyers
3	Frigates
6	Escort Transports
11	Patrol Vessels (over 100 ft)
30+	Patrol Boats
13	Minesweepers
8	Tank Landing Ships
12	Medium Landing Ships
1	Survey Ship
13	Auxiliary Ships

Diplomatic Representation

Naval Attaché in London:
Colonel Yull-Sec Dong (Air Force)

Naval Attaché in Paris:
Colonel Ock-Sup Yoon (Army)

Naval Attaché in Washington:
Captain Choong Hah Choi (Navy)

Mercantile Marine

Lloyd's Register of Shipping:
650 vessels of 1 225 679 tons gross

DESTROYERS

2 Ex-US "GEARING" CLASS

Name	*No.*	*Launched*	*US Comm*	*Transferred*
CHUNG BUK (ex-USS *Chevalier*, DD 805)	DD 95	29 Oct 1944	9 Jan 1945	5 July 1972
JEONG BUK (ex-USS *Everett F. Larson*, DD 830)	DD 96	28 Jan 1945	6 Apr 1945	30 Oct 1972

Displacement, tons	2 425 standard; approx 3 500 full load
Length, feet (*metres*)	383 (*116·7*) wl; 390·5 (*119·0*) oa
Beam, feet (*metres*)	40·9 (*12·4*)
Draught, feet (*metres*)	19 (*5·8*)
Guns	6—5 inch (*127 mm*) 38 cal DP (twin)
A/S weapons	6—12·75 inch (*324 mm*) torpedo tubes (Mk 32 triple); 2 fixed hedgehogs (Mk 11)
Main engines	2 geared turbines (General Electric); 60 000 shp; 2 shafts
Boilers	4 (Babcock & Wilcox)
Speed, knots	34
Complement	approx 275

Former US "Gearing" class destroyers. Both ships built by Bath Iron Works Corp, Bath, Maine.
These ships were converted to radar picket destroyers (DDR) in 1949; subsequently modernised under the US Navy's Fleet Rehabilitation and Modernisation (FRAM II) programme. Fitted with small helicopter hangar and flight deck. Anti-ship torpedo tubes and secondary gun armament have been removed.

ELECTRONICS. These ships have SPS-40 and SPS-10 search radar antennas on the tripod mast; SQS-29 series hull mounted sonar.

JEONG BUK *1973*

2 Ex-US "ALLEN M. SUMNER" CLASS

Name	*No.*	*Launched*	*US Comm.*	*Transferred*
DAE GU (ex-*USS Wallace L Lind*, DD 703)	DD 97	14 June 1944	8 Sep 1944	3 Dec 1973
IN CHEON (ex-*USS De Haven*, DD 727)	DD 98	9 Jan 1944	31 Mar 1944	4 Dec 1973

Displacement, tons	2 200 standard; 3 320 full load
Length, feet (*metres*)	376·5 (*114·8*) oa
Beam, feet (*metres*)	40·9 (*12·4*)
Draught, feet (*metres*)	19 (*5·8*)
Guns	6—5 inch (*127 mm*) 38 calibre DP (twin)
A/S weapons	6—12·75 inch (*324 mm*) torpedo tubes (Mk 32 triple); 2 fixed hedgehogs (Mk 11)
Main engines	2 geared turbines (General Electric); 60 000 shp; 2 shafts
Boilers	4 (Babcock & Wilcox)
Speed, knots	34
Complement	approx 275

Former US "Allen M. Sumner" class destroyers; built by Bath Iron Works Corp, Bath Maine, and Federal SB & DD Co, Kearny, New Jersey, respectively.
Both ships were modernised under the US Navy's Fleet Rehabilitation and Modernisation (FRAM II) programme. Fitted with small helicopter deck and hangar. Anti-ship torpedo tubes and secondary gun armament have been removed.

ELECTRONICS. *Dae Gu* fitted with SPS-40 and SPS-10 search radar antennas; *In Cheon* has SPS-37 and SPS-10 antennas. Fitted with SQS-29 series hull-mounted sonar and SQA-10 variable depth sonar (VDS) on stern).

PHOTOGRAPHS. The ex-"Gearing" class destroyers can be distinguished from the ex-"Sumner" class by the wider spacing of the funnels in the former ships. The basic configuration and equipment are the same in both classes.

DAE GU (as USS *Wallace L Lind*) *1967, United States Navy*

Destroyers—*continued*

3 Ex-US "FLETCHER" CLASS

Name	No.	Launched	US Comm.	Transferred
CHUNG MU (ex-USS *Erben*, DD 631)	DD 91	21 Mar 1943	28 May 1943	1 May 1963
SEOUL (ex-USS *Halsey Powell*, DD 686)	DD 92	30 June 1943	25 Oct 1943	27 Apr 1968
PUSAN (ex-USS *Hickox*, DD 673)	DD 93	4 July 1943	10 Sep 1943	15 Nov 1968

Displacement, tons	2 050 standard; 3 050 full load
Length, feet (*metres*)	360 (*110·3*) wl; 376·5 (*114·8*) oa
Beam, feet (*metres*)	39·6 (*12·0*)
Draught, feet (*metres*)	18 (*5·5*)
Guns	5—5 inch (*127 mm*) 38 calibre DP (single) 10—40 mm AA (2 quad, 1 twin) except *Seoul* (none)
A/S weapons	6—12·75 inch (*324 mm*) torpedo tubes (Mk 32 triple); 2 hedgehogs (Mk 10/11); depth charges
Main engines	Geared turbines (General Electric); 60 000 shp; 2 shafts
Boilers	4 (Babcock & Wilcox)
Speed, knots	35
Complement	approx 250

Former US "Fletcher" class destroyers. *Chung Mu* built by Bath Iron Works, Bath, Maine; *Seoul* built by Bethlehem Steel, Staten Island, New York; *Pusan* built by Federal Shipbuilding, Kearny, New Jersey.
Tripod masts have been fitted to support larger radar antennas; the two 21 inch quintuple torpedo tube mounts originally fitted have been removed as have the 20 mm light anti-aircraft guns.

ELECTRONICS. SPS-10 and SPS-6 search radar antennas are fitted.

SEOUL — *1968, United States Navy*

FRIGATES

1 Ex-US "RUDDEROW" CLASS

Name	No.	Launched	US Comm.	Transferred
CHUNG NAM (ex-USS *Holt*, DE 706)	DE 73	15 Feb 1944	9 June 1944	19 June 1963

Displacement, tons	1 450 standard; 1 890 full load
Length, feet (*metres*)	300 (*91·5*) wl; 306 (*83·2*) oa
Beam, feet (*metres*)	37 (*11·3*)
Draught, feet (*metres*)	14 (*4·3*)
Guns	2—5 inch (*127 mm*) 38 cal DP 4—40 mm AA (twin)
A/S weapons	6—12·75 inch (*324 mm*) torpedo tubes (Mk 32 triple) 1 hedgehog; depth charges
Main engines	Turbo-electric drive (General Electric geared turbines); 12 000 shp; 2 shafts
Boilers	2 (Combustion Engineering)
Speed, knots	24
Complement	approx 210

Former US destroyer escort of the TEV design. Built by Defoe Shipbuilding, Bay City, Michigan. Triple 21 inch torpedo tube mount originally fitted was removed shortly after completion.

ELECTRONICS. SPS-5 and SPS-6 search radars are fitted.

CHUNG NAM — *1971, Korean Navy*

2 Ex-US "BOSTWICK" CLASS

Name	No.	Launched	US Comm.	Transferred
KYONG KI (ex-USS *Muir*, DE 770)	DE 71	4 June 1944	30 Aug 1944	2 Feb 1956
KANG WON (ex-USS *Sutton*, DE 771)	DE 72	6 Aug 1944	22 Dec 1944	2 Feb 1956

Displacement, tons	1 265 standard; 1 700 full load
Length, feet (*metres*)	300 (*91·5*) wl; 306 (*93·3*) oa
Beam, feet (*metres*)	36·6 (*11·2*)
Draught, feet (*metres*)	14 (*4·3*)
Guns	3—3 inch (*76 mm*) 50 cal AA 6—40 mm AA (twin) 4—20 mm AA (single)
A/S weapons	6—12·75 inch (*324 mm*) torpedo tubes (Mk 32 triple); 1 hedgehog; depth charges
Main engines	Diesel-electric (4 General Motors diesels); 6 000 bhp; 2 shafts
Speed, knots	21
Complement	approx 210

Former US destroyer escorts of DET design. Built by Tampa Shipbuilding, Tampa, Florida. Triple 21 inch torpedo tube mount originally fitted was removed Shortly after completion. Refitted at Pearl Harbour, Hawaii, in 1964, being provided with tripod masts to support improved radar antennas; also fitted with more modern sonar and anti-submarine weapons.

ELECTRONICS. Fitted with SPS-6 and SPS-5 search radars.

KYONG KI — *Korean Navy*

Ex-US "TACOMA" CLASS

None of these ships remain in active service with the Korean Navy.

Former US "Tacoma" class patrol frigate, similar in desgn to the British "River" class. Built by Kaiser Co, Richmond, California, as Maritime Commission type S2-S2-AQ1.
Apnok (PF 62, ex-USS *Rockford*, PF 48), transferred to South Korea in 1950, was damaged in a collision on 21 May 1952; returned to US Navy and sunk as target in 1953. *Du Man* (PF 61, ex-USS *Muskogee*, PF 49)
Nak Tong (PF 65, ex-USS *Hoquiam*, PF 5), *Tae Tong* (PF 63 ex-USS *Tacoma*, PF 3), and *Im Chin* (PF 66, ex-USS *Sausalito*, PF 4, transferred to South Korea in 1950-1952. scrapped in 1972-1973 except *Tae Tong* retained as dockside training ship and museum.
Ex-USS *Pasco* (PF 6) and *Gloucester* (PF 22) were towed from storage in Japan to Korea for spare parts cannibalisation.
See 1972-1973 and previous editions for characteristics and photographs.

ESCORT TRANSPORTS

6 Ex-US APD TYPE

Name	No.	Launched	US Comm.	Transferred
KYONG NAM (ex-USS *Cavallaro*, APD 128)	APD 81	15 June 1944	13 Mar 1945	Oct 1959
AH SAN (ex-USS *Harry L. Corl*, APD 108)	APD 82	1 Mar 1944	5 June 1945	June 1966
UNG PO (ex-*Julius A. Raven*, APD 110)	APD 83	3 Mar 1944	28 June 1945	June 1966
KYONG PUK (ex-USS *Kephart*, APD 61)	APD 85	6 Sep 1943	7 Jan 1944	Aug 1967
JONNAM (ex-USS *Hayter*, APD 80)	APD 86	11 Nov 1943	16 Mar 1944	Aug 1967
CHR JU (ex-*William M. Hobby*, APD 95)	APD 87	11 Feb 1944	4 Apr 1945	Aug 1967

Displacement, tons 1 400 standard; 2 130 full load
Length, feet (*metres*) 300 (*91·4*) wl; 306 (*93·3*) oa
Beam, feet (*metres*) 37 (*11·3*)
Draught, feet (*metres*) 12·6 (*3·2*)
Guns 1—5 inch (*127 mm*) 38 cal. DP; 6—40 mm AA (twin)
A/S weapons depth charges
Main engines Turbo-electric (General Electric turbines); 12 000 shp; 2 shafts
Boilers 2 (Foster Wheeler "D" Express)
Speed, knots 23·6
Complement approx 200
Troop capacity approx 160

All begun as destroyers escorts (DE), but converted during construction or after completion to high-speed transports (APD). APD 81 built by Defoe Shipbuilding Co, Bay City, Michigan; APD 82 and APD 83 by Bethlehem Shipbuilding Co. Hingham, Massachusetts; APD 85-87 by Charleston Navy Yard, South Carolina.
In Korean service four latter ships originally rated as gunboats (PG); changed in 1972 to APD. All are fitted to carry approximately 160 troops.

PHOTOGRAPHS. Note davits aft of funnel for carrying four LCVP-type landing craft or other small boats. Two different configurations: ex-APD 37 class with high bridge and lattice mast supporting 10-ton capacity boom; ex-APD 87 class with low bridge and tripod mast supporting 10-ton capacity boom.
One twin 40 mm gun mount is forward of bridge; two others aft, on either side of boom.

KYONG NAM

PATROL VESSELS

3 MULTI-MISSION PATROL SHIPS (PSMM)

Displacement, tons approx 250 full load
Dimensions, feet 165 oa × 24
Missile launchers 4 launchers for Standard surface-to-surface missile (planned)
Guns 1—3 inch (*76 mm*) 50 cal AA (forward); 1—40 mm AA (aft) pending installation of Standard SSN
Main engines 6 gas turbines (Avco Lycoming TF35); 2 shafts = 40+ knots

Two ships of this type have been constructed by the Tacoma Boatbuilding Co of Tacoma, Washington; launched in January 1975 and February 1975, respectively. A third unit is reported under construction in the Republic of Korea. Although the same length as the US "Asheville" class, the PSMM is a new design with (in the Korean configuration) all-gas turbine propulsion. Standard SSMs are planned for this class and probably will be fitted in the *Paek Ky*.

1 Ex-US "ASHEVILLE" CLASS

PAEK KU (ex-USS *Benicia*, PG 96) PGM 11 20 Dec 1969

Displacement, tons 225 standard; 245 full load
Dimensions, feet 164·5 oa × 23·8 × 9·5
Guns 1—3 inch (*76 mm*) 50 cal AA (forward); 1—40 mm AA (aft); 4—·50 cal MG (twin)
Main engines CODAG: 2 diesels (Cummins); 1 450 bhp; 2 shafts = 16 knots; 1 gas turbine (General Electric); 13 300 shp; 2 shafts = 40+ knots
Complement approx 25

Former US "Ashville" class patrol gunboat. Built by Tacoma Boatbuilding Co, Tacoma, Washington; launch date above; commissioned in US Navy on 25 Apr 1970; transferred to ROK Navy on 15 Oct 1971 and arrived in Korea in January 1972. See United States section for design, engineering, and gunnery notes. No anti-submarine sensors or weapons are fitted.

MISSILES. During 1971, while in US Navy service, this ship was fitted experimentally with one launcher for the standard surface-to-surface missile. The box-like container/launcher held two missiles. See 1971-1972 edition for additional photo of *Benicia* in missile configuration (page 706).

3 Ex-US "AUK" CLASS MSF TYPE

SHIN SONG (ex-USS *Ptarmigan*, MSF 376)	PCE 1001	15 July 1944
SUNCHON (ex-USS *Speed*, MSF 116)	PCE 1002	18 Apr 1942
KOJE (ex-USS *Dextrous*, MSF 341)	PCE 1003	17 Jan 1943

Displacement, tons 890 standard; 1 250 full load
Dimensions, feet 215 wl; 221·2 oa × 32·2 × 10·8
Guns 2—3 inch (*76 mm*) 50 cal AA (single); 4—40 mm AA (twin), 4—20 mm AA (twin)
A/S weapons 3—12·75 inch (*324 mm*) torpedo tubes (Mk 32 triple); 1 hedgehog; depth charges
Main engines Diesel-electric (General Motors diesels); 3 532 bhp; 2 shafts = 18 knots
Complement approx 110

"AUK" CLASS—*continued*

Former US Navy minesweepers (originally designated AM). Built by Savannah Machine & Foundry Co, Savannah, Georgia; American SB Co, Lorain, Ohio; and Gulf SB Corp., Madisonville, Texas, respectively. Launch dates above; PCE 1001 commissioned in US Navy on 15 Jan 1944, PCE 1002 on 15 Oct 1942, and PCE 1003 on 8 Sep 1943; PCE 1001 transferred to ROK Navy in July 1963, PCE 1002 in Nov 1967, and PCE 1003 in Dec 1967.
The minesweeping gear was removed prior to transfer and a second 3 inch gun fitted aft; additional anti-submarine weapons also fitted. See 1973-1974 edition for broadside views.

SHIN SONG

7 Ex-US 185-ft PCE TYPE

RO RYANG (ex-USS PCEC 882)	PCEC 51	3 Dec 1943
MYONG RYANG (ex-USS PCEC 896)	PCEC 52	22 May 1943
HAN SAN (ex-USS PCEC 873)	PCEC 53	5 May 1943
OK PO (ex-USS PCEC 898)	PCEC 55	3 Aug 1943
PYOK PA (ex-USS *Dania*, PCE 870)	PCE 57	27 Feb 1943
RYUL PO (ex-USS *Somerset*, PCE 892)	PCE 58	1 May 1943
SA CHON (ex-USS *Batesburg*, PCE 903)	PCE 59	6 Sep 1943

Displacement, tons 640 standard; 950 full load
Dimensions, feet 180 wl; 184·5 oa × 33 × 9·5
Guns 1—3 inch (*76 mm*) 50 cal AA; 6—40 mm AA (twin) except *Ko Jin* only 4—40 mm; 4 or 8—20 mm AA (single or twin)
A/S weapons 1 hedgehog (except *Ko Jin*); depth charges
Main engines Diesels (General Motors); 2 000 bhp; 2 shafts = 15 knots
Complement approx 100

Former US Navy patrol craft. Launch dates above. Four units had been modified in US service as "control" ships (PCEC) for operation with landing craft, being fitted with additional communications equipment in an enlarged bridge area.
Ro Ryang and *Myong Ryang* transferred to South Korea in Feb 1955; *Han San* and *Ok Po* in Sep 1955; *Pyok Pa*, *Ryul Po*, and *Sa Chon* in Dec 1961.
Tang Po (PCE 56, ex-USS *Maria*, PCE 842) was sunk by North Korean coastal guns on 19 Jan 1967, *Ko Jin* (PCE 50, ex-USS *Report*, MSF 289) scrapped in 1973.

Patrol Vessels—*continued*

OK PO 1969

Ex-US 173-ft PC TYPE

All former US PC type submarines chaser transferred to South Korea have been scrapped or discarded. *O Tae San* PC 707 (ex-USS *Winnemuca*, PC 1145), *Kum Chong San* PC 708 (ex-USS *Grosse Point*, PC 1546), *Sol Ak* PC 709 (ex-USS *Chadron*, PC 564) scrapped in 1973. See 1974-1975 and previous editions for characteristics and earlier PC disposals.

Ex-US 136-ft PCS TYPE

The former US wood-hulled PCS type submarine chasers loaned to South Korea in 1952 have been returned to US custody and discarded: *Hwa Song* PCS 201 (ex-USS PCS 1426), *Kum Song* PCS 202 (ex-USS PCS 1445), *Mok Song* PCS 203 (ex-USS PCS 1446), and *Su Song* PCS 205 (ex-USS PCS 1448).

8 Ex-US COAST GUARD 95-ft TYPE

PB 3 (ex-USCGC *Cape Rosier*, WPB 95333)
PB 5 (ex-USCGC *Cape Sable*, WPB 95334)
PB 6 (ex-USCGC *Cape Providence*, WPB 95335)
PB 8 (ex-USCGC *Cape Porpoise*, WPB 95327)
PB 9 (ex-USCGC *Cape Falcon*, WPB 95330)
PB 10 (ex-USCGC *Cape Trinity*, WPB 95331)
PB 11 (ex-USCGC *Cape Darby*, WPB 95323)
PB 12 (ex-USCGC *Cape Kiwanda*, WPB 95329)

Displacement, tons	98 full load
Dimensions, feet	95 oa × 19 × 6
Guns	1—50 cal MG/1—81 mm mortar; several ·30 cal MG
Main engines	4 diesels (General Motors); 2 200 bhp; 2 shafts = 20 knots
Complement	13

Former US Coast Guard steel-hulled patrol craft. Built in 1958-1959. Nine units transferred to South Korea in Sep 1968. PB 7 (ex-USCGC *Cape Florida*, WPB 95325) stricken after grounding in May 1971.
Combination machinegun/mortar mount is forward; single light machineguns are aft. See US Coast Guard listings for additional details.

PB 5

PB 11

1 COASTAL PATROL AND INTERDICTION CRAFT

Displacement, tons	approx 70 full load
Dimensions, feet	99·1 oa × 18 × 6
Guns	2—30 mm (twin)
Main engines	3 gas turbines (Avco Lycoming TF 35); 5 400 hp; 3 shafts = 40+ knots maximum; 2 diesels (300 bhp) with outboard drive for low-speed cruising.

The prototype Coastal Patrol and Interdiction Craft (CPIC) sponsored by the US Navy was constructed by Tacoma Boatbuilding Co, Tacoma, Washington; after completion in mid-1973 the craft was to undergo trials for the US Navy and then transfer to South Korea.
The CPIC was designed to intercept infiltration attempts into South Korea and other nations with long and vulnerable coastlines. Plans for additional craft for US and foreign use are under study. See United States section for CPIC illustration. Twin 30 mm rapid-fire gun mount planned for these craft reportedly is encountering development problems.

Reportedly, at least two addition units of this type will be constructed for South Korea.

2 100-ft PATROL TYPE

PK 10 **PK 11**

Displacement, tons	120
Dimensions, feet	100 oa
Guns	1—40 mm AA; 1—20 mm AA
Main engines	Diesels (Mercedes Benz); 10 200 bhp; 3 shafts = 35 knots

Two patrol craft reported built in Korea in 1971-1972.

10+ 72-ft PATROL TYPE

Displacement, tons	30
Dimensions, feet	72 oa × 11·5 × 3·6
Guns	2—20 mm AA (single)
Main engines	Diesels; 1 600 bhp; 2 shafts

At least 10 and possibly as many as 20 patrol craft of this type are being built in Korea, with the first units completed in 1973. Believed to be designated in the PB series.

9 65-ft SEWART TYPE

FB 1 **FB 3** **FB 6** **FB 8** **FB 10**
FB 2 **FB 5** **FB 7** **FB 9**

Displacement, tons	33 full load
Dimensions, feet	65 oa × 16
Guns	2—20 mm (single)
Main engines	3 diesels (General Motors); 1 590 bhp; 3 shafts = 25 knots
Complement	5

These craft were built in the United States by Sewart. The design is adapted from a commercial 65-foot craft. Referred to as "Toksuuri" No. 1 through 10 by the South Koreans (with the No. 4 being considered unlucky and not assigned). Transferred to South Korea in August 1967.

FB 10 on marine railway

4 US 40-ft SEWART TYPE

SB 1 **SB 2** **SB 3** **SB 5**

Displacement, tons	9·25 full load
Dimensions, feet	40 oa × 12 × 3
Guns	1—·50 cal MG; 2—·30 cal MG
Main engines	2 diesels (General Motors); 500 bhp; 2 shafts = 31 knots
Complement	7

These are aluminium-hulled craft built in the United States by Sewart. Transferred to South Korea in 1964. No. 4 not assigned.

MOTOR TORPEDO BOATS

Ol Pa Mi (ex-USS PT 812) stricken in 1969; *Kal Mae Ki* (ex-USS PT 616) stricken [illegible] Latter craft returned to United States for use as a memorial.

MINESWEEPERS

8 Ex-US MSC TYPE

KUM SAN (ex-US MSC 284) MSC 522
KO HUNG (ex-US MSC 285) MSC 523
KUM KOK (ex-US MSC 286) MSC 525
NAM YANG (ex-US MSC 295) MSC 526
NA DONG (ex-US MSC 296) MSC 527
SAM CHOK (ex-US MSC 316) MSC 528
YONG DONG (ex-US MSC 320) MSC 529 (under construction)
OK CHEON (ex-US MSC 321) MSC 530 (under construction)

Displacement, tons	320 light; 370 full load
Dimensions, feet	144 oa × 28 × 8·2
Guns	2—20 mm AA
Main engines	2 diesels; 1 200 bhp; 2 shafts = 14 knots
Complement	approx 40

"Bluebird" class coastal minesweepers built by the United States specifically for transfer under the Military Aid Programme. Wood hulled with non-magnetic metal fittings.
Kum San transferred to South Korea in June 1959, *Ko Hung* in Sep 1959, *Kum Kok* in Nov 1959, *Nam Yang* in Sep 1963, *Ha Dong* in Nov 1963, and *Sam Chok* in July 1968.
Two additional units MSC 230 and MSC 321 under construction at Peterson Builders, Sturgeon Bay, Wisconsin, both launched in 1974 and scheduled for delivery in 1975.

KUM KOK

4 Ex-US YMS TYPE

KWANG CHU (ex-USS YMS 413) MSC 503
KUM HWA (ex-USS *Curlew*, MSCO 8, ex-AMS 8, ex-YMS 218) MSC 519
KIM PO (ex-USS *Kite*, MSCO 22, ex-AMS 22, ex-YMS 375) MSC 520
KO CHANG (ex-USS *Mockingbird*, MSCO 27, ex-AMS 27, YMS 419) MSC 521

Displacement, tons	270 standard; 350 full load
Dimensions, feet	136 oa × 24·5 × 8
Guns	1—40 mm AA; 2—20 mm AA
Main engines	diesels; 1 000 bhp = 15 knots
Complement	approx 50

Former US Navy auxiliary motor minesweepers built 1941-1942. Wood hulled. *Kum Hwa*, *Kim Po*, and *Ko Chang* transferred to South Korea in Jan 1956.
See 1974-1975 and previous editions for disposals of other ex-US YMS type minesweepers transferred to South Korea.

KO CHANG — *Korean Navy*

MSB 1 (ex-US MSB 2)

Displacement, tons	30 light; 39 full load
Dimensions, feet	57·2 oa × 15·3 × 4
Guns	machineguns
Main engines	2 geared diesels (Packard); 600 bhp; 2 shafts = 12 knots

Former US Navy Minesweeping boat transferred on 1 Dec 1961. Wood hulled.

LANDING SHIPS

8 Ex-US LST TYPE

UN PONG	(ex-USS LST 1010)	LST 807	29 Mar 1944
DUK BONG	(ex-USS LST 227)	LST 808	21 Sep 1943
BI BONG	(ex-USS LST 218)	LST 809	20 July 1943
KAE BONG	(ex-USS *Berkshire County*, LST 288)	LST 810	7 Nov 1943
WEE BONG	(ex-USS *Johnson County*, LST 849)	LST 812	30 Dec 1944
SU YONG	(ex-USS *Kane County*, LST 853)	LST 813	17 Nov 1944
BUK HAN	(ex-USS *Lynn County*, LST 900)	LST 815	9 Dec 1944
HWA SAN	(ex-USS *Pender County*, LST 1080)	LST 816	2 May 1945

Displacement, tons	1 653 standard; 2 366 beaching; 4 080 full load
Dimensions, feet	316 wl; 328 oa × 50 × 14
Guns	10 or 8—40 mm AA
Main engines	diesels; 1 700 bhp; 2 shafts = 11·6 knots
Complement	approx 110

Ex-US LST Type—*continued*

Former US Navy tank landing ships. Cargo capacity 2 100 tons. Launch dates above. *Un Bong* transferred to South Korea in Feb 1955, *Duk Bong* in Mar 1955, *Bi Bong* in May 1955, *Kae Bong* in Mar 1956, *Wee Bong* in Jan 1959, *Su Yong* and *Buk Han* in Dec 1958, and *Hwa San* in Oct 1958.
LSTs previously operated by South Korea and stricken were: ex-USS LST 120, ex-USS LST 213, *Dan Yang* ex-USS LST 343, ex-USS LST 378, ex-USS LST 380, *Ryong Pi* LST 806 ex-USS LST 388, *An Tong* LST 803 ex-USS LST 491 sunk in 1952, ex-USS LST 536, ex-USS LST 594, *Chon Po* LST 805 ex-USS LST 595, ex-USS LST 624 *Ryong Hwa* LST 801 ex-USS LST 659, *Lyung Wha* ex-USS LST 805.

HWA SAN

1 Ex-US LSMR TYPE

SI HUNG (ex-USS *St Joseph River*, LSMR 527) LSMR 311

Displacement, tons	944 standard; 1 084 full load
Dimensions, feet	204·5 wl; 206·2 oa × 34·5 × 10
Guns	1—5 inch (*127 mm*) 38 cal DP; 2—40 mm AA; 4—20 mm AA
Rocket launchers	8 twin rapid-fire launchers for 5 inch rockets
Main engines	2 diesels (General Motors); 2 800 bhp; 2 shafts = 12·6 knots
Complement	approx 140

Former US Navy landing ship completed as a rocket-firing ship to support amphibious landing operations. Transferred to South Korea on 15 Sep 1960. Configuration differs from conventional LSM type with "island" bridge structure and 5 inch gun aft; no bow doors.

SI HUNG — *1967, Korean Navy*

11 Ex-US LSM TYPE

TAE CHO (ex-USS LSM 546) LSM 601
TYO TO (ex-USS LSM 268) LSM 602
KA TOK (ex-USS LSM 462) LSM 605
KO MUN (ex-USS LSM 30) LSM 606
PIAN (ex-USS LSM 96) LSM 607
PUNG TO (ex-USS LSM 54) LSML 608
WOL MI (ex-USS LSM 57) LSM 609
KI RIN (ex-USS LSM 19) LSM 610
NUNG RA (ex-USS LSM 84) LSM 611
SIN MI (ex-USS LSM 316) LSM 612
UL RUNG (ex-USS LSM 17) LSM 613

Displacement, tons	743 beaching; 1 095 full load
Dimensions, feet	196·5 wl; 203·5 oa × 34·6 × 8·5
Guns	2—40 mm AA (twin); several 20 mm AA
Main engines	2 diesels (direct drive; Fairbanks Morse except *Tyo To* General Motors); 2 800 bhp; 2 shafts = 12·5 knots
Complement	approx 60

Former US Navy medium landing ships. Built 1944-1945. LSM 601, 602, and 605 transferred to South Korea in 1955; others in 1956. *Sin Mi* served in Indonesia as French L 9014 and *Ul Rung* as French L 9017 during 1954-1955; returned to United States in Oct 1955 and retransferred to South Korea in autumn 1956.
Pung To serves as mine force flagship fitted with mine-laying rails and designated LSML. Arrangement of 20 mm guns differs; some ships have two single mounts adjacent to forward 40 mm mount on forecastle; other 20 mm guns along sides of cargo well.
Tok To LSM 603 (ex-USS LSM 419) scrapped in 1963.
Po Song Man LSSL 109 (ex-USS LSSL 54), *Yung Hung Man* LSSL 107 (ex-USS LSSL 77), *Yong Il Man* LSSL 110 (ex-USS LSSL 84), and *Kang Hwa Man* LSSL 108 (ex-USS LSSL 91) have been scrapped.

TYO TO — *1969*

Landing Ships—*continued*

1 Ex-US LCU TYPE

LCU 1 (ex-USS LCU 531)

Displacement, tons	309 full load
Dimensions, feet	105 wl; 119·1 oa × 32·66 × 5
Main engines	diesels (Gray Marine); 675 bhp; 3 shafts = 10 knots

Former US Navy utility landing craft. Built in 1943 as LCT(6) 531. Transferred to South Korea in Dec 1960. No name assigned.

AUXILIARY SHIPS

1 REPAIR SHIP: Ex-US ARL TYPE

TUK SU (ex-USS *Minotaur*, ARL 15, ex-LST 645) ARL 1

Displacement, tons	2 366 standard; 4 100 full load
Dimensions, feet	316 wl; 328 oa × 50 × 11·2
Guns	8—40 mm AA, 12—20 mm AA
Main engines	diesels (General Motors); 1 800 bhp; 2 shafts = 11·6 knots
Complement	approx 250

Former US Navy landing craft repair ship. Converted during construction from an LST. Launched on 20 Sep 1944 and commissioned in US Navy on 30 Sep 1944. Transferred to South Korea in Oct 1955.

TUK SU

6 SUPPLY SHIPS: Ex-US FREIGHT SUPPLY TYPE

IN CHON	(ex-US Army FS 198)	AKL 902
CHIN NAM PO	(ex-US Army FS 356)	AKL 905
MOK PO	(ex-USCGC *Trillium*, WAK 170, ex-US Army FS 397)	AKL 907
KUN SAN	(ex-USS *Sharps*, AKL 10, ex-AG 139, ex-US Army FS 385)	AKL 908
MA SAN	(ex-USS AKL 35, ex-US Army FS 383)	AKL 909
UL SAN	(ex-USS *Brule*, AKL 28, ex-US Army FS 370)	AKL 910

Displacement, tons	approx 700
Dimensions, feet	176·5 oa × 32·8 × 10
Guns	2—20 mm AA (single) in most ships
Main engines	diesel; 1 000 bhp; 1 shaft = 10 knots
Complement	approx 20

Originally US Army freight and supply ships built in World War II for coastal operation. *In Chon* built by Higgins Industries, *Chin Nam Po* by J. K. Welding, *Ul San* by Sturgeon Bay, others by Ingalls (Dectaur, Alabama).

Many subsequently served in US Navy and Military Sea Transportation Service (now Military Sealift Command). Details and configurations differ. *Chin Nam Po* placed in reserve in 1971.

In Chon and *Chin Nam Po* transferred to South Korea in 1951; *Mok Po, Kin San*, and *Ma San* in 1956; *Ul San* on 1 Nov 1971.

Pusan AKL 901 (ex-US Army FS 162), *Wonsan* AKL 903 (ex-US Army FS 254), *Song Chin* AKL 906 (ex-US Army FS 285) scrapped in 1958.

MA SAN 1957

1 OILER NORWEGIAN TYPE:

CHUN JI (ex-*Birk*) AO 2

Displacement, tons	1 400 standard, 4 160 full load
Dimensions, feet	297·5 oa × 44·5 × 18·2
Guns	1—40 mm AA, several 20 mm AA
Main engines	2 diesels; 1 800 bhp; 1 shaft = 12 knots
Complement	approx 70

Former Norwegian tankers built by A/S Berken Mek Verks, Bergen, Norway, in 1951. Transferred to South Korea in Sep 1953. Sister ship *Pujon* AO 3 (ex-*Hassel*) ran aground and was lost on 24 May 1971.

CHUN JI 1969

1 OILER: Ex-US 235-ft YO TYPE

HWA CHON (ex-*Paek Yeon* AO 5, ex-USS *Derrick* YO 59) AO 5

Displacement, tons	890 standard; 2 700 full load
Dimensions, feet	236 oa × 39·9 × 15
Guns	several 20 mm AA
Main engines	diesel (Fairbanks Morse); 1 150 bhp; 1 shaft = 10·5 knots
Complement	approx 45

Former US Navy self-propelled fuel barge. Transferred to South Korea on 14 Oct 1955. Capacity 10 000 barrels petroleum. Reportedly, the ship has been laid up in reserve.

HWA CHON 1969

2 OILERS: Ex-US 174-ft YO TYPE

KU YONG (ex-USS YO 118) YO 1 (ex-USS YO 179) YO 6

Displacement, tons	1 400 full load
Dimensions, feet	174 oa × 32
Guns	several 20 mm AA
Main engines	diesel (Union); 500 bhp; 1 shaft = 7 knots
Complement	approx 35

Former US Navy self-propelled fuel barges. Transferred to South Korea on 3 Dec 1946 and 13 Sep 1971, respectively. Cargo capacity 6 570 barrels.

2 AUXILIARY TUGS: Ex-US ATA TYPE

YONG MUN	(ex-USS *Keosanqua*, ATA 198)	ATA 2	17 Jan 1945
DO BONG	(ex-USS *Pinola*, ATA 206)	ATA (S) 3	14 Dec 1944

Displacement, tons	538 standard; 835 full load
Dimensions, feet	133·66 wl; 143 oa × 33·8
Guns	1—3 inch (*76 mm*) 50 cal AA; 4—20 mm AA
Main engines	diesel (General Motors); 1 500 bhp; 1 shaft = 13 knots
Complement	approx 45

Former US Navy auxiliary ocean tugs. Built by Levingston SB Co, Orange, Texas, and Gulfport Boiler & Welding Works, Port Arthur, Texas, respectively; launch dates above. Both transferred to South Korea in February 1962. *Do Bong* modified for salvage work.

The South Korean Navy also operates nine small harbour tugs (designated YTL). These are one ex-US Navy craft (YTL 550) and five ex-US Army craft.

SERVICE CRAFT

The South Korean Navy operates approximately 35 small service craft in addition to the YO-type oilers listed above and the harbour tugs noted above. These craft include open lighters, floating cranes, diving tenders, dredges, ferries, non-self-propelled fuel barges, pontoon barges, and sludge removal barges. Most are former US Navy craft.

HYDROGRAPHIC SERVICE

The following craft are operated by the Korean Hydrographic Service and are not rated as Navy. All are engaged in surveying operations.

1 Ex-US ATA TYPE

TAN YUNG (ex-USS *Tillamook*, ATA 192) 15 Nov 1944

Characteristics similar to the two ex-US ocean tugs listed previously. Launch date above. Transferred to South Korea on 25 July 1971 for use as surveying ship.

2 Ex-BELGIAN MSI TYPE

SURO 5 (ex-Belgian *Temse*) **SURO 6** (ex-Belgian *Tournai*, ex-US MSI 93)

Displacement, tons	160 light; 190 full load
Dimensions, feet	113·2 oa × 22·3 × 6
Main engines	Diesels; 1 260 bhp; 2 shafts = 15 knots

Former Belgian inshore minesweepers. Built in Belgium, the *Tournai* being financed by United States. Launched on 6 Aug 1956 and 18 May 1957, respectively. Transferred to South Korea in March 1970

1 Ex-US YMS TYPE

SURO 3 (ex-USC & GS *Hodgson*)

Displacement, tons	289 full load
Dimensions, feet	136 oa × 24·5 × 9·25
Main engines	2 diesels; 1 000 bhp; 2 shafts = 15 knots

YMS type transferred to South Korea from US Coast & Geodetic Survey in 1968.

COAST GUARD

The Korean Coast Guard operates about 25 small ships and craft including several tugs and small rescue craft.

KUWAIT

Personnel

1975: 200 (Coastguard) Administered by Ministry of the Interior

Mercantile Marine

Lloyd's Register of Shipping: 162 vessels of 681 692 tons gross

LIGHT FORCES

10 78 ft TYPE (COASTAL PATROL CRAFT)

AL SALEMI	**AMAN**	**MASHHOOR**	**MURSHED**
AL SHURTI	**INTISAR**	**MAYMOON**	**WATHAH**
AL MUBARAKI	**MARZOOK**		

Displacement, tons	40
Dimensions, feet	78 oa × 15·5 × 4·5 mean
Guns	1 MG
Main engines	2 Rolls Royce 8-cylinder 90° V form marine diesels; 1 340 shp at 1 800 rpm, 1 116 shp at 1 700 rpm = 20 knots
Range, miles	700 at 15 knots
Complement	12 (5 officers, 7 men)

Two were built by Thornycroft before the merger and eight by Vosper-Thornycroft afterwards. *Al Salemi* and *Al Mubaraki* were shipped to Kuwait on 8 Sep 1966. Hulls are of welded steel construction, with superstructures of aluminium alloy. Twin hydraulically operated rudders, Decca type D 202 radar. The later boats are slightly different in appearance with modified superstructure and no funnel, see photograph of *Intisar*.

INTISAR *1972, Vosper Thornycroft*

2 56 ft TYPE (COASTAL PATROL CRAFT)

DASTOOR **KASAR**

Displacement, tons	25
Length, feet	56
Main engines	2 MTU MB6 V.331 diesels; 1 350 hp = 26 knots
Guns	1—20 mm, 2 MG
Range, miles	320 at 20 knots
Complement	8 (2 officers, 6 men)

Ordered from Vosper Thornycroft, Private Ltd, Singapore September 1973. Both laid down 31 Oct 1973. Completion June 1974.

Vosper Thornycroft 56 ft Type *1973, Vosper Thornycroft*

1 VOSPER THORNYCROFT 17m TYPE

A 42 ft craft with a speed of 21 knots and mounting two 20 mm guns.

VOSPER THORNYCROFT 17 m Type *1974, Vosper Thornycroft*

7 50 ft TYPE (COASTAL PATROL CRAFT)

Built by the Singapore Yard of Thornycroft (Malaysia) Limited, now the Tanjong Rhu, Singapore, Yard of Vosper Thornycroft Private Ltd. Known as 50-foot patrol craft. Completed in 1962.

8 35 ft TYPE (COASTAL PATROL CRAFT)

Built by Vosper Thornycroft Private Ltd, Singapore. Of double-skinned teak construction with twin turbo-charged Perkins diesels they are capable of 24 knots. Ordered July 1972. All delivered by May 1973.

LANDING CRAFT

WAHEED **FAREED** +1

Two 88-ft landing craft built for the Ministry of the Interior, Kuwait by Vosper Thornycroft Private Ltd, Singapore. Ordered 1970 and handed over May 1971. Used for storing parties working on Kuwait's off-shore islands. A third ordered from the same yard in Oct 1974.

LAOS

Administration

Commander, Royal Lao Navy and Chief of Naval Staff: Colonel Prince Sinthanavong Kindavong

Personnel

1975: 550 officers and men

RIVER PATROL CRAFT

7 LCM (6) Type	28 tons	4 in commission, 3 in reserve
6 Cabin Type	21 tons	2 in commission, 4 in reserve
2 Chris Craft Type	15 tons	2 in commission
12 11 metre Type	10 tons	5 in commission, 7 in reserve
8 8 metre Type	6 tons	8 in reserve
7 Cargo Transport	50 tons	1 in commission, 6 in reserve

The above craft are formed into four squadrons, although at least half of them must be considered non-operational.

LEBANON

Diplomatic Representation

Naval Military and Air Attaché in London: Colonel F. El Hussami

Personnel

1975: 250 officers and men

Mercantile Marine

Lloyd's Register of Shipping: 88 vessels of 120 130 tons gross

LIGHT FORCES

Note. Three patrol craft ordered in West Germany 9 January 1974.

TARABLOUS 31 (LARGE PATROL CRAFT)

Displacement, tons	105 standard
Dimensions, feet	124·7 × 18 × 5·8
Guns	2—40 mm
Main engines	2 Mercedes-Benz diesels, 2 shafts; 2 700 bhp = 27 knots
Range, miles	1 500
Complement	19 (3 officers, 16 men)

Tarablous was built by Ch. Navals de l'Estérel. Laid down in June 1958. Launched in June 1959. Completed in 1959.

TARABLOUS *1968, Lebanese Navy*

DJOUNIEH 41 (LARGE PATROL CRAFT)

Displacement, tons	82 standard; 130 full load
Dimensions, feet	112 × 18 × 7·5
Guns	1—20 mm; 2—12·7 mm MG
Main engines	2 GM diesels; 2 shafts = 16 knots
Complement	16

Ex-Fairmile "B" motor launch of the Royal Navy built in 1940-41.

DJOUNIEH *1970, Lebanese Navy*

3 "BYBLOS" CLASS (COASTAL PATROL CRAFT)

BYBLOS 11 **SIDON** 12 **BEYROUTH** (ex-*TIR*) 13

Displacement, tons	28 standard
Dimensions, feet	66 × 13·5 × 4
Guns	1—20 mm AA, 2 MG
Main engines	General Motors diesels, 2 shafts, 530 bhp = 18·5 knots

French built ML type craft. Built by Ch. Navals de l'Estérel. Launched in 1954-55

LANDING CRAFT

SOUR (ex-LCU 1474)

Displacement, tons	180 standard; 360 full load
Dimensions, feet	115 × 34 × 6
Guns	2—20 mm AA
Main engines	3 diesels; 3 shafts; 675 bhp = 10 knots

Former United States utility landing craft built in 1957, transferred in Nov 1958.

LIBERIA

Personnel

1975: about 150 officers and men

Mercantile Marine

Lloyd's Register of Shipping: 2 332 vessels of 55 321 641 tons gross

MOTOR GUNBOAT

ALERT (ex-USN *PGM* 102) 102

Displacement, tons	100
Dimensions, feet	95 oa × 19 × 5
Gun	1—40 mm AA
Main engines	4 diesels; 2 shafts; 2 200 bhp = 21 knots
Complement	15

PGM 102 (US number) was built in the United States for transfer under the Military Aid Programme in 1967.

PRESIDENTIAL YACHT

LIBERIAN (ex-*Virginia*)

Measurement, tons	692·27 gross; 341·6 net
Dimensions, feet	173 wl; 209 oa × 29·7 × 13·1

Motor yacht of 742 tons (yacht measurement) built in 1930 by William Beardmore & Co Ltd, Dalmuir. Purchased by Liberia for use as the Presidential Yacht in 1957. Extensively refitted by Cammell Laird & Co Ltd, Birkenhead, at the end of 1962.

PATROL BOATS

ML 4001 **ML 4002**

Displacement, tons	11·5
Dimensions, feet	40·5 oa × 11·5 × 3·5
Guns	2 MG
Main engines	2 GM diesels; 2 shafts; 380 bhp = 23 knots max

Coastguard cutters built at the United States Coast Guard Yard, Curtis Bay, Maryland, presented by the USA and transferred during 1957.

ML 4002 *Dr Giorgio Arra*

LANDING CRAFT

Landing craft reported to be used for transport and general utility purposes.

LIBYA

Establishment

The Libyan Navy was established in Nov 1962 when a British Naval Mission was formed and first recruits were trained at HMS *St. Angelo*, Malta. Cadets were also trained at the Britannia Royal Naval College, Dartmouth, and technical ratings at HMS *Sultan*, Gosport, and HMS *Collingwood*, Fareham, England.

Administration

Senior Officer, Libyan Navy: Captain A. Shaksuki

Personnel

(a) 1975: Total 2 000 officers and ratings, including Coast Guard
(b) Voluntary service

Mining Capability

Although none of the listed Libyan ships is credited with a mining capability the fact that, in June 1973, two minefields were laid off Tripoli harbour, some eight miles out, suggests that a stock of mines is available.

Strength of the Fleet
(no new construction in hand)

Type	*Active*
Frigate	1
LSD	1
Corvette	1
Fast Attack Craft—Missile	3
Large Patrol craft	10
Coastal Patrol Craft	1
MRC	1

Mercantile Marine

Lloyd's Register of Shipping: 25 vessels of 160 180 tons gross

Deletions

Inshore Minesweepers
1973 *Brak* and *Zuara* disposed of.

FRIGATE

1 VOSPER THORNYCROFT MARK 7

DAT ASSAWARI F 01

Displacement, tons	1 325 standard; 1 625 full load
Length, feet (*metres*)	310·0 (*94·5*) pp 330·0 (*100·6*) oa
Beam, feet (*metres*)	36·0 (*11·0*)
Draught, feet (*metres*)	11·2 (*3·4*)
A/S weapons	1 Mortar Mark 10
Missile launchers	6 (2 triple) Seacat close range ship-to-air
Guns	1—4·5 in ;2—40 mm (twin); 2—35 mm (twin)
Main engines	CODOG arrangement; 2 shafts; with Kamewa cp propellers; 2 Rolls Royce gas turbines; 23 200 shp = 37·5 knots; 2 Paxman diesels; 3 500 bhp = 17 knots economical cruising speed
Range, miles	5 700 at 17 knots

DAT ASSAWARI *1973, John G. Callis*

Mark 7 Frigate ordered from Vosper Thornycroft on 6 Feb 1968. Generally similar in design to the two Iranian Mark Vs built by this firm, but larger and with different armament. Laid down 27 Sep 1968, was launched without ceremony in Sep 1969 and completed 1 Feb 1973. After trials she carried out work-up at Portland, England, reaching Tripoli autumn 1973.

RADAR. AWS-1 air surveillance set; fire control radar and RDL-1 radar direction finder.

LOGISTIC SUPPORT SHIP

1 DOCK TYPE

ZELTIN

Displacement, tons	2 200 standard; 2 470 full load
Length, feet (*metres*)	300·0 (*91·4*) wl; 324·0 (*98·8*) oa
Beam, feet (*metres*)	48·0 (*14·6*)
Draught, feet (*metres*)	10·2 (*3·1*); 19·0 (*5·8*) aft when flooded
Dock:	
Length, feet (*metres*)	135·0 (*41·1*)
Width, feet (*metres*)	40·0 (*12·2*)
Guns	2—40 mm AA
Main engines	2 Paxman 16 cyl diesels; 3 500 bhp; 2 shafts
Speed, knots	15
Range, miles	3 000 at 14 knots
Complement	As Senior Officer Ship: 101 (15 officers and 86 ratings)

ZELTIN *1969*

The ship provides full logistic support, including mobile docking maintenance and repair facilities for the Libyan fleet. Craft up to 120 ft can be docked. Used as tender for Light Forces.

The Vosper-Thornycroft Group received the order for this ship in Jan 1967 for delivery in late 1968. She was designed and built at the Group's Woolston Shipyard. Launched on 29 Feb 1968. Commissioned (with *Sirte* and *Susa*) on 23 Jan 1969.

Fitted with accommodation for a flag officer or a senior officer and staff. Operational and administrative base of the squadron. Workshops with a total area of approx 4 500 sq ft are situated amidships with ready access to the dock, and there is a 3-ton travelling gantry fitted with outriggers to cover ships berthed alongside up to 200 feet long.

CORVETTE

TOBRUK

Displacement, tons	440 standard; 500 full load
Dimensions, feet	162 wl; 177 oa × 28·5 × 13
Guns	1—4 in; 4—40 mm AA (single)
Main engines	2 Paxman Ventura 16 YJCM diesels; 2 shafts; 3 800 bhp = 18 knots
Range, miles	2 900 at 14 knots
Complement	63 (5 officers and 58 ratings)

Designed and built by Vosper Limited, Portsmouth, in association with Vickers Limited. Launched on 29 July 1965, completed on 30 Mar 1966, commissioned for service at Portsmouth on 20 Apr 1966, and arrived in Tripoli on 15 June 1966. Fitted with surface warning radar, Vosper roll damping fins and air-conditioning. A suite of State apartments is included in the accommodation.

TOBRUK *1971, A. & J. Pavia*

LIGHT FORCES

Note. It has been reported that 10 "Combattante II" class Fast Attack Craft (Missile) have been ordered in France. Confirmation awaited.

3 "SUSA" CLASS (FAST ATTACK CRAFT—MISSILE)

SEBHA (ex-*Sokna*) **SIRTE** **SUSA**

Displacement, tons	95 standard; 114 full load
Dimensions, feet	90·0 pp; 96·0 wl; 100·0 oa × 25·5 × 7·0
Missiles	8—SS 12
Guns	2—40 mm AA (single)
Main engines	3 Bristol Siddeley "Proteus" gas turbines; 3 shafts; 12 750 bhp = 54 knots
Complement	20

The order for these three fast patrol boats from Vosper Limited, Portsmouth, England, was announced on 12 Oct 1966. They are generally similar to the "Soloven" class designed and built by Vosper for the Royal Danish Navy. Built at the Vosper-Thornycroft Group's Portchester shipyard. Fitted with air-conditioning and modern radar and radio equipment. *Susa* was launched on 31 Aug 1967, *Sirte* on 10 Jan 1968 and *Sokna* (renamed *Sebha*) on 29 Feb 1968. First operational vessels in the world to be armed with Nord-Aviation SS 12(M) guided weapons with sighting turret installation and other equipment developed jointly by Vosper and Nord. These weapons, of which eight can be fired by each boat without reloading, have a destructive power equivalent to a six-inch shell.

SEBHA *1969, Wright & Logan*

1 THORNYCROFT TYPE (COASTAL PATROL CRAFT)

Dimensions, feet	78 × 15 × 4·5
Gun	1 MG
Main engines	3 Rolls-Royce diesels; 3 shafts; 945 bhp = 22·5 knots
Range, miles	400 at 15 knots

Built by John I. Thornycroft, Singapore in 1962. Two similar but smaller boats transferred to Malta in 1974.

Light Forces—*continued*

4 "GARIAN" CLASS (LARGE PATROL CRAFT)

KHAWLAN **MERAWA** **SABRATHA** **ZLEITEN** (ex-*Garian*)

Displacement, tons	120 standard; 159 full load
Dimensions, feet	100 pp; 106 oa × 21·2 × 5·5
Gun	1—20 mm
Main engines	2 Paxman diesels; 1 100 bhp = 14 knots
Range, miles	1 500 at 12 knots
Complement	15 to 22

Built by Brooke Marine, Lowestoft. Launched on 21 Apr, 29 May, 25 Oct and 30 Sep 1969, respectively, and completed on 30 Aug 1969 (*Garian* and *Khawlan*) and early 1970 (other two).

KHAWLAN *1970, Brooke Marine*

6 THORNYCROFT TYPE (LARGE PATROL CRAFT)

AKRAMA **BENINA** **HOMS**
AR RAKIB **FARWA** **MISURATA**

Displacement, tons	100
Dimensions, feet	100 × 21 × 5·5
Gun	1—20 mm
Main engines	3 Rolls-Royce DV8TLM Diesels; 1 740 bhp = 18 knots
Range, miles	1 800 at 14 knots

Welded steel construction. *Ar Rakib* and *Farwa* completed 4 May 1967 by John I. Thornycroft, Woolston; *Benina* and *Misurata*, 29 Aug 1968 and last pair in early 1969, all by Vosper-Thornycroft. Slight difference in silhouette between first pair and the remainder.

FARWA *1969, Thornycroft*

MAINTENANCE REPAIR CRAFT

(ex-*MRC* 1013, ex-LCT)

Displacement, tons	657 standard; 900 approx full load
Dimensions, feet	225·0 pp, 231·3 oa × 39·0 × 3·3 forward, 5·0 aft
Main engines	4 Paxman diesels; 2 shafts; 1 840 bhp = 9 knots cruising

Built in 1944-45. Purchased from Great Britain on 5 Sep 1966. Depot ship for minesweepers.

MALAWI

Three small patrol-boats are deployed on Lake Nyasa; the first was bought in 1968.

MALAYSIA

SEE ALSO SABAH

Ministerial

Minister of Defence:
Hon. Tun Haji Abdul Razak bin Hussain

Administration

Chief of the Naval Staff:
Rear-Admiral Dato K. Thanabalasingam, DPMJ, JMN, SMJ

Commander Naval Forces West Malaysia:
Commander Mohd Sidek Bin Shabudin

Commander Naval Forces East Malaysia:
Captain P. K. Nettur

Diplomatic Representation

Services Adviser in London:
Colonel M. Shah Bin Yahaya

Strength of the Fleet

Type	*Active*	*Building*
Frigates	2	—
Fast Attack Craft—Missile	8	—
Fast Attack Craft	—	6
Large Patrol Craft	24	—
Minesweepers—Coastal	6	—
Diving Tender	1	—
Survey Vessel	1	—
Support Ship	1	—
Police Launches	24	—

Personnel

(a) 1975: 4 900 (430 officers and 4 470 ratings)
(b) Voluntary service

Prefix to Ships' Names

The names of Malaysian warships are prefixed by KD, (Kapal Diraja) meaning Royal Ship

Mercantile Marine

Lloyd's Register of Shipping:
122 vessels of 337 511 tons gross

FRIGATES

1 YARROW TYPE

RAHMAT (ex-*Hang Jebat*) F 24

Displacement, tons	1 250 standard; 1 600 full load
Length, feet (*metres*)	300·0 (*91·44*)pp; 308 (*93·9*) oa
Beam, feet (*metres*)	34·1 (*10·4*)
Draught, feet (*metres*)	14·8 (*4·5*)
Aircraft	1 helicopter
Missile launchers	1 quadruple Seacat surface-to-air
Guns,	1—4·5 in (*114 mm*) 2—40 mm 1 Limbo three-barrelled mortar
Main engines	1 Bristol Siddeley Olympus gas turbine; 19 500 shp; Crossley Pielstick diesel; 3 850 bhp; 2 shafts
Speed, knots	26 boosted by gas turbine; 16 on diesel alone
Range, miles	6 000 at 16 knots 1 000 at 26 knots
Complement	140

General purpose frigate of new design developed by Yarrow. Fully automatic with saving in complement. Delivered mid-1971.

RAHMAT *1972, Wright & Logan*

Ordered from Yarrow & Co Ltd, Scotstoun, on 11 Feb 1966. Launched on 18 Dec 1967. Delivered 13 Sep 1972.

RADAR. Air Surveillance: HSA LW 02. Fire control; M 20 with radar in spherical radome for guns; M 44 for Seacat.

1 Ex-BRITISH "LOCH" CLASS

HANG TUAH (ex-HMS *Loch Insh*) F 433

Displacement, tons	1 575 standard; 2 400 full load
Length, feet (*metres*)	297·2 (*90·6*) wl; 307·0 (*93·6*) oa
Beam, feet (*metres*)	38·5 (*11·7*)
Draught, feet (*metres*)	14·8 (*4·5*)
Guns,	6—40 mm
Boilers	2 Admiralty 3-drum
Main engines	2 triple expansion; 5 500 ihp; 2 shafts
Speed, knots	19·5 designed
Range, miles	6 400 at 10 knots
Complement	140

HANG TUAH *1972, Royal Malaysian Navy*

Built by Henry Robb Ltd, Leith. Laid down on 17 Nov 1943, launched on 10 May 1944 and completed on 20 Oct 1944. On transfer, refitted (in Portsmouth Dockyard) with helicopter deck, air-conditioning, modern radar and extra accommodation. Re-commissioned on 12 Oct 1964. Sailed on 12 Nov 1964. Converted into a training ship in Apr 1971, the two 4-inch guns and the two "Squid" mortars having been removed. *Hang Tuah* was the name of a Malay Admiral of the 15th century.

RADAR. Search: Type 227.

LIGHT FORCES

4 "PERDANA" CLASS
(FAST ATTACK CRAFT—MISSILE)

PERDANA	**SERANG**
GANAS	**GANYANG**

Displacement, tons	234 standard; 265 full load
Dimensions, ft (*m*)	154·2 × 23·1 × 12·8 (*47·0 × 7·0 × 3·9*)
Missile launchers	2 MM38 (Exocet) surface-to-surface
Guns	1—57 mm Bofors; 1—40 mm 70 cal Bofors
Main engines	4 MTU diesels; 4 shafts; 14 000 bhp = 36·5 knots
Range, miles	800 at 25 knots

GANAS *4/1973, Wright & Logan*

First pair built by Constructions Mécaniques de Normandie, *Perdana* launched 31 May 1972 completed December 1972 and *Ganas* launched 26 Oct 1972 for completion 28 Feb 1973. Second pair built by Société Francaise de Constructions Navales (ex-Franco-Belge), *Serang* launched 22 Dec 1971, completed 31 Jan 1973 and *Ganyang* launched 16 March 1972, completed 20 March 1973. All of basic "La Combattante II" design. Left Cherbourg for Malaysia 2 May 1973.

Light Forces—*continued*

4 "PERKASA" CLASS (FAST ATTACK CRAFT—MISSILE)

GEMPITA P 152 **HANDALAN** P 151 **PENDEKAR** P 153 **PERKASA** P 150

Displacement, tons	95 standard; 114 full load
Dimensions, feet	90 pp; 96 wl; 99 oa × 25·5 × 7
Guns	1—40 mm AA; 1—20 mm AA
Missiles	8—SS 12(M) in 2 quadruple launchers
Main engines	3 Rolls Royce Proteus gas turbines; 3 shafts; 12 750 bhp = 54 knots GM diesels on wing shafts for cruising = 10 knots

The design is a combination of the "Brave" class hull form and "Ferocity" type construction. Ordered from Vosper Limited, Portsmouth, England, on 22 Oct 1964. Generally similar to the motor torpedo boats built by Vosper for the Royal Danish Navy. They can also operate in the gunboat role or a minelaying role. *Perkasa* (Valiant) was launched on 26 Oct 1965, *Handalan* (Reliant) on 18 Jan 1966, *Gempita* (Thunderer) on 6 Apr 1966 and *Pendekar* (Champion) on 24 June 1966. The hull is entirely of glued laminated wooden construction, with upperworks of aluminium alloy. Equipment includes Rover gas turbine generating sets, full air-conditioning, Decca radar, and comprehensive navigation and communications system. The craft were shipped to Malaysia in mid-1967. They were re-armed with eight SS.12 missiles in place of four 21-inch torpedoes in 1971.

GEMPITA (Firing SS 12 missile) *1972, Royal Malaysian Navy*

6 "KEDAH" CLASS (LARGE PATROL CRAFT)

SRI KEDAH P 3138 **SRI PAHANG** P 3141 **SRI SELANGOR** P 3139
SRI KELANTAN P 3142 **SRI PERAK** P 3140 **SRI TRENGGANU** P 3143

4 "SABAH" CLASS (LARGE PATROL CRAFT)

SRI MELAKA P 3147 **SRI SABAH** P 3144
SRI NEGRI SEMBILAN P 3146 **SRI SARAWAK** P 3145

14 "KRIS" CLASS (LARGE PATROL CRAFT)

BADEK P 37, **BELEDAU** P 44, **KELEWANG** P 45, **KERAMBIT** P 43, **KRIS** P 34, **LEMBING** P 40, **PANAH** P 42, **RENCHONG** P 38, **RENTAKA** P 46, **SERAMPANG** P 41, **SRI JOHOR** P 49, **SRI PERLIS** P 47, **SUNDANG** P 36, **TOMBAK** P 39

Displacement, tons	96 standard; 109 full load
Dimensions, feet	95 wl; 103 oa × 19·8 × 5·5
Guns	2—40 mm; 70 cal AA
Main engines	2 Bristol Siddeley/Maybach MD 655/18 diesels; 3 500 bhp = 27 knots
Range, miles	1 400 (*Sabah* class 1 660) at 14 knots
Complement	22 (3 officers, 19 ratings)

All 24 craft were built by Vosper Limited, Portsmouth. The first six boats, constituting the "Kedah" class were ordered in 1961 for delivery in 1963. The four boats of the "Sabah" class were ordered in 1963 for delivery in 1964. The remaining 14 boats of the "Kris" class were ordered in 1965 for delivery between 1966 and 1968. All are of prefabricated steel construction and are fitted with Decca radar, air-conditioning and Vosper roll damping equipment. The differences between the three classes are minor, the later ones having improved radar, communications, evaporators and engines of Maybach, as opposed to Bristol Siddeley construction. *Sri Johor*, the last of the 14 boats of the "Kris" class, was launched on 22 June 1967.

BADEK ("Kris" Class) *1972, Royal Malaysian Navy*

MINE WARFARE FORCES

6 Ex-BRITISH "TON" CLASS (MINESWEEPERS—COASTAL)

BRINCHANG (ex-*Thankerton*) M 1172 **LEDANG** (ex-*Hexton*) M 1143
JERAI (ex-*Dilston*) M 1168 **MAHAMIRU** (ex-*Darlaston*) M 1127
KINABALU (ex-*Essington*) M 1134 **TAHAN** (ex-*Lullington*) M 1163

Displacement, tons	360 standard; 425 full load
Dimensions, feet	140 pp; 152 oa × 28·8 × 8·2
Guns	1—40 mm AA forward; 2—20 mm AA aft
Main engines	Diesels; 2 shafts; 2 500 bhp = 15 knots
Oil fuel, tons	45
Range, miles	2 300 at 13 knots
Complement	39

Mahamiru transferred from the Royal Navy on 24 May 1960. *Ledang*, refitted at Chatham Dockyard before transfer, commissioned for Malaysia in Oct 1963. *Jerai* and *Kinabalu*, refitted in Great Britain, arrived in Malaysia summer 1964. *Brinchang* and *Tahan*, refitted in Singapore, transferred to Malaysian Navy in May and Apr 1966, respectively. All six underwent a 9-month refit by Vosper-Thornycroft, Singapore during 1972-73 which will extend their availability by some years.

MAHAMIRU *1972, Royal Malaysian Navy*

DIVING TENDER

DUYONG

Displacement, tons	120 standard; 140 full load
Dimensions, feet	99·5 wl; 110·0 oa × 21·0 × 5·8
Gun	1—20 mm
Main engines	2 Cummins diesels, 1 900 rpm; 500 bhp = 10 knots
Complement	23

Built by Kall Teck (Pte) Ltd, Singapore. Launched on 18 Aug 1970. Commissioned on 5 Jan 1971.

DUYONG *1973*

Royal Malaysian Police

18 PX CLASS

Mahkota, Temenggong, Hulubalang, Maharajasetia, Maharajalela, Pahlawan, Bentara, Perwira, Pertanda, Shahbandar, Sangsetia, Laksamana, Pekan, Kelang, Kuala Kangsar, Arau, Sri Gumantong, Sri Labuan, (Numbered PX 1-18).

Displacement, tons	85
Dimensions, feet	87·5 oa × 19 × 4·8
Guns	2—20 mm
Main engines	2 Mercedes Benz diesels; 2 shafts; 2 700 hp = 25 knots
Range, miles	700 at 15 knots
Complement	15

6 IMPROVED PX CLASS

Alor Star, Kota Bahru, Kuala Trengganu, Johore Bahru, Sri Menanti, Kuching (Numbered PX 19-24).

Displacement, tons	92
Dimensions, feet	91 oa
Guns	2—20 mm
Main engines	2 diesels; 2 460 hp = 25 knots
Range, miles	750 at 15 knots
Complement	18

All 24 boats built by Vosper Thornycroft Private, Singapore, PX class between 1963 and 1970, Improved PX class 1972-73. *Sri Gumantong* and *Sri Labuan* operated by Sabah Government, remainder by Royal Malaysian Police.

SRI MENANTI *1972, Yam Photos, Singapore*

3 PATROL CRAFT

— PX 25 **SRI KUDAT** PX 26 **SRI TAWAU** PX 27

Of 62·5 tons and 25 knots with 1—20 mm. Completed mid-1973. Three more on order.

Malaysia—*continued*

SURVEY VESSEL

1 Ex-BRITISH "TON" CLASS

PERANTAU (ex-HMS *Myrmidon* ex-HMS *Edderton*) A 151

Displacement, tons	360 standard; 420 full load
Dimensions, feet	153 oa × 28·8 × 8·5
Main engines	Diesels; 2 shafts; 3 000 bhp = 15 knots
Range, miles	2 300 at 13 knots
Complement	35

A former coastal minesweeper of the "Ton" type, converted by the Royal Navy into a survey ship, renamed *Myrmidon* in Apr 1964, and commissioned for service on 20 July 1964. Paid off in 1968 and purchased by Malaysia in 1969. Service in Malaysian waters since 1970.

REPLACEMENT. A contract was placed in early 1975 for a replacement new-design survey ship to be built in Malaysia with assistance from Lürssen, Vegesack.

PERANTAU *1972, Royal Malaysian Navy*

SUPPORT SHIP

SRI LANGKAWI (ex-USS *Hunterdon County* LST 838, AGP 838) A 1500

Displacement, tons	1 653 standard; 2 366 beaching; 4 080 full load
Dimensions, feet	316·0 wl; 328·0 oa × 50·0 × 14·0
Guns	8—40 mm (2 twin, 4 single)
Main engines	GM diesels; 2 shafts; 1 700 bhp = 11·6 knots
Complement	138 (11 officers, 127 ratings)

An LST of the 511-1152 series built in 1945. Transferred from the US Navy and commissioned in the Royal Malaysian Navy on 1 July 1971.

SRI LANGKAWI *1972, Royal Malaysian Navy*

MALAGASY

Personnel

1975: 300 officers and men (including Marine Coy)

Mercantile Marine

Lloyd's Register of Shipping: 50 vessels of 53 409 tons gross

PATROL VESSELS

MALAIKA

Displacement, tons	235 light
Dimensions, feet	149·3 pp; 155·8 oa × 23·6 × 8·2
Guns	2—40 mm AA
Main engines	2 MGO diesels; 2 shafts; 2 400 bhp = 18·5 knots
Range, miles	4 000 at 18 knots
Complement	25

Ordered by the French Navy to be built by Chantiers Navals Franco-Belges for delivery to Madagascar. Laid down in Nov 1966, launched on 22 Mar 1967 and completed in Dec 1967.

FANANTENANA (ex-*Richelieu*)

Displacement, tons	1 040 standard; 1 200 full load
Dimensions, feet	183·7 pp; 206·4 oa × 30 × 14·8
Guns	2—40 mm AA
Main engines	2 Deutz diesels; 1 shaft; 1 060 + 500 bhp = 12 knots

Trawler purchased and converted in 1966-67 to Coast Guard and training ship. 691 tons gross. Built in 1959 by A. G. Weser, Bremen, Germany.

JASMINE (ex-*D* 385, ex-*D* 211, ex-*YMS* 31)

Displacement, tons	280 standard; 325 full load
Dimensions, feet	134·5 × 24·5 × 12
Main engines	2 diesels; 2 shafts; 1 000 bhp = 12 knots
Oil fuel, tons	22

Former coastal minesweeper of the YMS type launched on 10 Apr 1942 and acquired by France in 1954. Acquired by Madagascar on 19 Aug 1965 as a light tender. Same type originally as *Tanamasoandro* (ex-*Marjolaine*, ex-*D* 337, ex-*YMS* 69) which was discarded on delivery of *Malaika* (ex-*P* 758, *VC* 8) and returned to the French Navy in 1967.

5 PATROL BOATS

Displacement, tons	46
Gun	1—40 mm
Main engines	2 diesels = 22 knots

Used by the Maritime Police. Built by Küstenwache in 1962.

1 "BATRAM" CLASS

DIEGO SUAREZ (TRANSPORT)

Displacement, tons	810
Dimensions, ft (*m*)	208·9 × 41 × 6·2 (*63·7* × *12·5* × *1·9*)
Guns	1—3 in; 2—20 mm; 1—81 mm mortar
Main engines	2 diesels = 13 knots
Complement	27
Troops	120 with Transport

Building at Diego Suarez for completion in 1975. Smaller version of French "Batral"

MALI

Personnel

1975: 50 officers and men

Patrol Craft

A small river patrol service with 3 craft

MALTA

A coastal patrol force of small craft was formed in 1973. It is manned by the Maltese Regiment and primarily employed as a coastguard.

Mercantile Marine

Lloyd's Register of Shipping: 26 vessels of 38 011 tons gross

2 Ex-US "SWIFT" CLASS

Displacement, tons	22·5
Dimensions, feet	50 × 13 × 3·5
Guns	3 MG
Main engines	2 Diesels = 28 knots
Complement	6

Transferred Feb 1971.

3 Ex-GERMAN CUSTOMS LAUNCHES

2 Ex-LIBYAN CUSTOMS LAUNCHES

Built by Thornycroft in 1962—the first was transferred on 16 Jan 1974.

MAURITANIA

Personnel

(a) 1975: 200 officers and men
(b) Voluntary service

Mercantile Marine

Lloyd's Register of Shipping: 4 vessels of 1 681 tons gross

PATROL BOATS

DAR EL BARKA **TICHITT**

Displacement, tons	75 standard; 82 full load
Dimensions, feet	105 × 18·9 × 5·5
Guns	1—20 mm AA 1 MG
Main engines	2 Mercedes Maybach diesels; 2 shafts; 2 700 bhp = 28 knots
Range, miles	1 500 at 15 knots
Complement	19

Built by Ch. Navales de L'Estérel, in service June and April 1969 respectively.

IM RAQ NI **SLOUGHI**

Displacement, tons	20
Dimensions, feet	59 × 13·5 × 3·8
Gun	1—12·7 mm
Main engines	2 GM diesels; 512 bhp = 21 knots
Range, miles	860 at 12 knots

Built by Ch. Navales de L'Estérel in 1965 and 1968, respectively.

MEXICO

Administration

Secretary of the Navy:
Admiral C. G. Demn. Luis M. Bravo Carrera

Under-Secretary of the Navy:
Rear-Admiral Ing. M. N. Ricardo Chazaro Lara

Commander-in-Chief of the Navy:
Vice-Admiral C. G. Demn. Humberto Uribe Escandon

Chief of the Naval Staff:
Rear-Admiral C. G. Demn. Miguel A. Gomez Ortega

Director of Services:
Rear-Admiral C. G. Demn. Mario Artigas Fernandez

Diplomatic Representation

Naval Attaché in London:
Rear-Admiral C. Lopez Sotelo

Naval Attaché in Washington:
Vice-Admiral Miguel Manzarraga

Personnel

(a) 1975: Total 11 000 officers and men (including Naval Air Force and Marines)
(b) Voluntary Service

Naval Air Force

5 PBY Catalinas
4 Bell 47G Helicopters
1 Bell 47J Helicopter
4 Alouette III helicopters.

Strength of the Fleet

Type	*Active*	*Building*
Destroyers	2	—
Frigates	10	—
Minesweepers (Ocean) (some as escorts)	34	—
Fishery protection vessels	—	21
Oceanographic Ship	1	—
Survey Ships	1	—
Coastal Patrol Craft	10	—
LST's (1 repair ship)	3	—
Tankers-Harbour	2	—
Tugs	5	—
Floating Cranes	6	—

Mercantile Marine

Lloyd's Register of Shipping:
261 vessels of 514 544 tons gross

DESTROYERS

2 Ex-US "FLETCHER" CLASS

Name	*No.*	*Builders*	*Laid down*	*Launched*	*Completed*
CUAUTHEMOC (ex-*Harrison* DD 573)	F 1	Consolidated Steel	25 July 41	7 May 42	25 Jan 43
CUITLAHUAC (ex-*John Rodgers* DD 574)	F 2	Consolidated Steel	25 July 41	7 May 42	9 Feb 43

Displacement, tons: 2 100 standard; 3 050 full load
Length, feet (*metres*): 376·5 (*114·7*) oa
Beam, feet (*metres*): 39·5 (*12·0*)
Draught, feet (*metres*): 18·0 (*5·5*)
Guns (*original*): 5—5 in (*127 mm*); 14—40 mm
Torpedo tubes: 5—21 in (*533 mm*) quintupled
A/S weapons: 8 DCT, 2 Hedgehogs
Main engines: 2 geared turbines; 2 shafts; 60 000 shp
Boilers: 4
Speed, knots: 34
Oil fuel, tons: 650
Range, miles: 5 000 at 15 knots
Complement: 250

Former US destroyers of the original "Fletcher" class. Transferred to the Mexican Navy in Aug 1970.

CUAUTHEMOC — *1972, Mexican Navy*

FRIGATES

1 Ex-US "EDSALL" CLASS

Name	*No.*	*Builders*	*Launched*	*Completed*	*Transferred*
MANUEL AZUETA (ex-USS *Hurst* DE 205)	TA 06	Brown SB Co, Houston	14 Apr 1943	30 Aug 1943	1 Oct 1973

Displacement, tons: 1 200 standard; 1 850 full load
Dimensions, ft (*m*): 306 × 36·6 × 11 (*93·3 × 11·3 × 3·4*)
Guns: 3—3 in (*76 mm*), 50 cal AA
AS weapons: 2 Hedgehogs; DC racks
Main engines: 4 diesels; 6 000 shp; 2 shafts
Speed, knots: 21
Complement: 149

Transferred to Mexico 1 Oct 1973.

"EDSALL" Class — *USN*

1 "DURANGO" CLASS

Name	*No.*	*Builders*	*Launched*	*Completed*
DURANGO	B—1 (ex-128)	Union Naval de Levante, Valencia	28 June 1935	1936

Displacement, tons: 1 600 standard; 2 000 full load
Length, feet (*metres*): 256·5 (*78·2*) oa
Beam, feet (*metres*): 36·6 (*11·2*)
Draught, feet (*metres*): 10·5 (*3·1*)
Guns: 2—4 in (*102 mm*); 2—2·24 in (*57 mm*); 4—20 mm
Main engines: 2 Enterprise DMR-38 diesels electric drive; 2 shafts; 5 000 bhp
Speed, knots: 18 max, 12 sea (cruising)
Range, miles: 3 000 at 12 knots
Oil fuel, tons: 140
Complement: 149 (24 officer and 125 men)

Originally designed primarily as an armed transport with accommodation for 20 officers and 450 men. The two Yarrow boilers and Parsons geared turbines of 6 500 shp installed when first built were replaced with two 2 500 bhp diesels in 1967 when the ship was re-rigged with remodelled funnel. Carries a lighter armament than the "Guanajuato" class (see next page) which besides troop carrying and transport capacity are equivalent to frigates in many ways. *Durango* replaced *Zaragoza* as training ship in Mar 1964.

DURANGO — *1972, Mexican Navy*

Frigates—*continued*

5 Ex-US "APD" TYPE

		No.	Builders	Laid down	Launched	Completed
CHIHUAHUA	(ex-USS *Rednour*, APD 102, ex-DE 592)	B 8	Bethlehem SB Co, Hingham	9 Jan 1944	1 Mar 1944	15 Mar 1945
COAHUILA	(ex-USS *Barber*, LPR, ex-APD 57, ex-*DE* 161)	B 2	Norfolk Navy Yard, Norfolk, Va	27 Apr 1943	20 May 1943	10 Oct 1943
PAPALOAPAN	(ex-USS *Earhart*, APD 113, ex-*DE* 603)	B 4 (ex-H 4)	Bethlehem SB Co, Hingham	20 Mar 1945	12 May 1945	26 July 1945
TEHUANTEPEC	(ex-USS *Joseph M. Auman*, APD 117, ex-DE 674)	B 5 (ex-H 5)	Consolidated Steel Corp, Orange	8 Nov 1943	5 Feb 1944	25 Apr 1945
USUMACINTA	(ex-USS *Don O. Woods*, APD 118, ex-DE 721)	B 6 (ex-H 6)	Consolidated Steel Corp, Orange	1 Dec 1943	19 Feb 1944	28 May 1945

Displacement, tons	1 400 standard; 2 130 full load
Length, feet (*metres*)	300·0 (*91·5*) wl; 306·0 (*93·3*) oa
Beam, feet (*metres*)	37·0 (*11·3*)
Draught, feet (*metres*)	12·7 (*3·9*)
Guns	1—5 in (*127 mm*) 38 cal. dp; 6—40 mm AA (3 twin)
Main engines	GE turbo-electric; 2 shafts; 12 000 shp
Speed, knots	23·6 full; 13 economical sea
Boilers	2 Foster Wheeler "D" with superheater; 475 psi (*33·4 kg/cm²*) 750°F (*399°C*)
Range, miles	5 000 at 15 knots
Oil fuel, tons	350
Complement	204 plus 162 troops

B 4-6 were purchased by Mexico in December 1963 and B 2 and 8 on 17 Feb 1969. The first four replaced the four ex-US "Tacoma" type frigates bearing the same names, which were deleted in June and Aug 1964. *California* (ex-US *Belet* APD 109) stranded and lost 16 Jan 1972 on Bahia Peninsula.

PAPALOAPAN 1972, *Mexican Navy*

3 "GUANAJUATO" CLASS

Name	No.	Builders	Launched
GUANAJUATO	C-7	Sociedad Espanol de Construction Naval, Ferrol	29 May 1934
POTOSI	C-9	Sociedad Espanol de Construction Naval, Motagorda, Cadiz	24 Aug 1934
QUERETARO	C-8	Sociedad Espanol de Construction Naval, Ferrol	29 June 1934

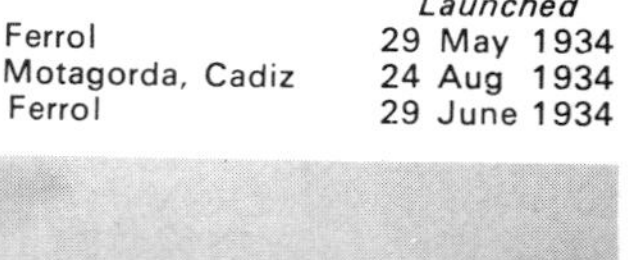

Displacement, tons	1 300 standard: 1 950; full load
Length, feet (*metres*)	264·0 (*80·5*)
Beam, feet (*metres*)	37·8 (*11·5*)
Draught, feet (*metres*)	11·5 (*3·5*)
Guns	3—4 in (*102 mm*) single; 4—20 mm, single
Main engines	2 Enterprise DMR-38 diesels; 2 shafts; 5 000 bhp
Speed, knots	14
Oil fuel, tons	140
Complement	140 (20 officers and 120 men)

Officially classified as gunboats (*canoneros*), but can be used as transports with berths for 120 troops. The Parsons geared turbines (2 shafts; 5 000 shp=19 knots,) and Yarrow boilers installed when originally built in 1934 were replaced with two diesels each of 2 500 bhp; *Querétaro* in 1958, *Potosi* in 1961, and *Guanajuato* in 1964.

GUANAJUATO 1970, *Wright & Logan*

CORVETTES

19 Ex-US "AUK" CLASS

Name	No.
FRANCISCO ZARCO (ex-*Threat*, MSF 124)	IG 13
GUILLERMO PRIETO (ex-*Symbol*, MSF 123)	IG 02
HERMENEGILDO GALEANA (ex-*Sage*, MSF 111)	IG 19
IGNACIO ALTAMIRANO (ex-*Sway*, MSF 120)	IG 12
IGNACIO L. VALLARTA (ex-*Velocity*, MSF 128)	IG 14
IGNACIO DE LA LLAVE (ex-*Spear*, MSF 322)	IG 08
JESUS G. ORTEGA (ex-*Chief*, MSF 315)	IG 15
JUAN ALDARMA (ex-*Pilot*, MSF 104)	IG 18
JUAN N. ALVARES (ex-*Ardent*, MSF 340)	IG 09
LEANDRO VALLE (ex-*Pioneer*, MSF 105)	IG 01
MANUAL G. ZAMORA (ex-*Scoter*, MSF 381)	IG 16
MANUAL DOBLADO (ex-*Defense*, MSF 317)	IG 05
MARIANO ESCOBEDO (ex-*Champion*, MSF 314)	IG 03
MARIANO MATAMOROS (ex-*Herald*, MSF 101)	IG 17
MELCHOR OCAMPO (ex-*Roselle*, MSF 379)	IG 10
PONCIANO ARRIAGA (ex-*Competent*, MSF 316)	IG 04
SANTOS DEGOLLADO (ex-*Gladiator*, MSF 319)	IG 07
SEBASTIAN L. DE TEJADA (ex-*Devastator*, MSF 318)	IG 06
VALENTIN G. FARIAS (ex-*Starling*, MSF 64)	IG 11

JUAN ALDARMA (ex Pilot) USN

Displacement, tons	890 standard; 1 250 full load
Dimensions, feet	215 wl; 221·2 oa × 32·2 × 10·8
Guns	1—3 in 50 cal; 2 or 4—40 mm
Main engines	Diesel electric; 2 shafts; 3 500 bhp = 18 knots
Complement	9 officers and 96 ratings

Transferred—6 in Feb 1973, 4 in Apr 1973, 9 in Sep 1973. Employed on patrol duties—*Matamoros* as survey ship.

MINESWEEPERS

17 Ex-US "ADMIRABLE" CLASS

Name	*No.*	*Ex-US Name & No.*		*Name*	*No.*	*Ex-US Name & No.*	
DM-01	ID-1	*Jubilant*	255	**DM-13**	IE-3	*Knave*	256
DM-02	ID-2	*Hilarity*	241	**DM-14**	IE-4	*Rebel*	284
DM-03	ID-3	*Execute*	232	**DM-15**	IE-5	*Crag*	214
DM-04	ID-4	*Specter*	306	**DM-16**	IE-6	*Dour*	223
DM-05	ID-5	*Scuffle*	298	**DM-17**	IE-7	*Diploma*	221
DM-06	ID-6	*Eager*	224	**DM-18**	IE-8	*Invade*	254
DM-10	ID-0	*Instill*	252	**DM-19**	IE-9	*Intrigue*	253
DM-11	ID-11	*Device*	220	**DM-20**	IE-0	*Harlequin*	365
DM-12	IE-2	*Ransom*	283				

Displacement, tons	650 standard; 945 full load
Dimensions, feet	180 wl; 184·5 oa × 33 × 10
Guns	1—3 in, 50 cal dp; 2—40 mm AA; 4—6 20 mm
Main engines	2 diesels; 2 shafts; 1 710 bhp = 15 knots
Range, miles	4 300 at 10 knots
Complement	104

Former US steel-hulled "180-ft" fleet minesweepers of the "Admirable" class. MSF, ex-AM type. All completed in 1943-44. Of the twenty vessels transferred at Orange, Texas, on 2 Oct 1962 ten were designated *dragaminas* for minesweeping duties, with D pennant numbers, and ten *escoltas* for escort and general purpose duties with E pennant numbers. (5 previous members of this class deleted and to be used for spare parts), ex-*Specter* (DM 04) acquired Feb 1973.

DM 17 1970, *Mexican Navy*

LIGHT FORCES

21 "AZTECA" CLASS (LARGE PATROL CRAFT)

ANDRES QUINTANA ROOS	P 01	**MANUEL CRECENCIO REJON**	P 07
MATIAS DE CORDOVA	P 02	**ANTONIO DE LA FUENTE**	P 08
MIGUEL RAMOS ARIZPE	P 03	**LEON GUZMAN**	P 09
JOSE MARIA IZAZAGU	P 04	**IGNACIO RAMIREZ**	P 10
JUAN BAUTISTA MORALES	P 05	**IGNACIO MARISCAL**	P 11
IGNACIO LOPEZ RAYON	P 06		P 12-21

Displacement, tons	130
Dimensions, ft (*m*)	111·8 × 28·1 × 6·8 (*34·1 × 8·6 × 2·0*)
Guns	1—40 mm; 1—20 mm
Main engines	2—12 cyl. Paxman Ventura diesels = approx 20 knots

Ordered by Mexico, for Fishery Protection duties, on 27 Mar 1973 from Associated British Tool, Machine Tool Makers Ltd. By Ailsa Shipbuilding Co (11), J. Lamont & Co Ltd. (5), and Scott & Sons, Bowling (5) for completion 1974-75.

P 01 launched 26 Mar 1974, completed 1 Nov 1974. **P 03** launched 6 June 1974, **P 05** 5 Sept 1974, **P 06** 5 Sept 1974, **P 07** 26 Nov 1974, **P 08** 26 Nov 1974, **P 10** 17 Feb 1975, **P 11** 17 Feb 1975—all by Ailsa Shipbuilding Co, Troon. **P 02** launched 22 May 1974, **P 04** launched 20 Aug 1974, **P 09** launched 10 Feb 1975—all by Scott and Sons (Bowling) Ltd.

HM Queen Elizabeth II went to sea in *Andres Quintana Roos* during her visit to Mexico in Mar 1975—an intention to place further orders for this class was announced shortly afterwards.

ANDRES QUINTANA ROOS *1975, Robert Christey*

2 "AZUETA" CLASS (COASTAL PATROL CRAFT)

AZUETA G9 **VILLAPANDO** G6

Displacement, tons	80 standard, 85 full load
Dimensions, feet	85·3 × 16·4 × 7·0
Guns	2—13·2 mm AA (1 twin)
Main engines	Superior diesels; 600 bhp = 12 knots

Of all steel construction. Built at Astilleros de Tampico in 1959 and 1960 respectively.

3 "POLIMAR" CLASS (COASTAL PATROL CRAFT)

POLIMAR 1 G1 **POLIMAR 2** G2 **POLIMAR 3** G3

Displacement, tons	37 standard; 57 full load
Dimensions, feet	60·1 × 15·1 × 4·0
Main engines	2 diesels; 456 bhp = 16 knots

Of steel construction. *Polimar 1* was built by Astilleros de Tampico in 1961 and entered service on I Oct 1962. *Polimar 2* and *Polimar 3* were built at Icacas Shipyard, Guerrero and entered service in 1966.

POLIMAR III *1972, Mexican Navy*

5 RIVER TYPE (RIVER PATROL CRAFT)

AM 4 **AM 5** **AM 6** **AM 7** **AM 8**

Displacement, tons	35
Main engines	Diesel; speed = 10 knots

Of steel construction. Built in Tampico and Veracruz. Entered service from 1960 to 1962.

TRANSPORT

ZACATECAS B 2

Displacement, tons	780 standard
Dimensions, feet	158 × 27·2 × 9
Guns	1—40 mm AA; 2—20 mm AA (single)
Main engines	1 MAN diesel; 560 hp = 10 knots
Complement	50 (13 officers and 37 men)

Built at Ulua Shipyard, Veracruz. Launched in 1959. Cargo ship type. The hull is of welded steel construction.

SURVEY SHIP

Note. Matamoros of "Auk" class (see previous page) also employed on surveying duties.

SOTAVENTO 1A

Displacement, tons	300 standard; 400 full load
Dimensions, feet	165·5 × 28 × 10
Main engines	Diesels; 1 800 bhp = 17 knots
Complement	30

Built by Higgins, New Orleans. Launched in 1947. Handsome, streamlined, with truncated funnel air-conditioned and equipped with radar. Formerly the Presidential Yacht, but officially reclassified as *Buque Hidrografico* in 1966.

SOTAVENTO *1967 Mexican Navy*

2 Ex-US LST (511-1152 Series)

RIO PANUCO (ex-USS *Park County* LST 1077) IA 01
MANZANILLO (ex-USS *Clearwater County* LST 602) IA 02

Displacement, tons	1 653 standard; 2 366 beaching; 4 080 full load
Dimensions, feet	316 wl; 328 oa × 50 × 14
Guns	6—40 mm (1 twin; 4 singles)
Main engines	GM diesels; 2 shafts; 1 700 bhp = 11·6 knots
Range, miles	6 000 at 11 knots
Complement	130
Troop capacity	147

Transferred to Mexico on 20 Sep 1971 and 25 May 1972 respectively. Both employed as rescue ships.

1 Ex-US ARV (ex-LST REPAIR SHIP)

VICENTE GUERRERO (ex-USS *Megara* ARV A6)

Displacement, tons	1 625 light; 4 100 full load
Dimensions, feet	328 oa × 50 × 14
Guns	8—40 mm
Main engines	2 GM diesels; 2 shafts; 1 800 bhp = 11·6 knots
Complement	250

Ex-aircraft repair ship sold to Mexico 1 Oct 1973.

HARBOUR TANKERS

2 Ex-US YOG TYPE

AGUASCALIENTES (ex-YOG 6) A 5 **TLAXCALA** (ex-YO 107) A 6

Displacement, tons	440 light; 1 480 to 1 800 full load
Dimensions, feet	174·5 oa × 33·0 × 11·8 max
Main engines	Union diesel direct; 500 bhp = 8 knots
Capacity	6 570 barrels
Complement	26 (5 officers and 21 ratings)

Former US self-propelled fuel oil barges. Built by Geo. H. Mathis Co Ltd, Camden, N.J. and Geo. Lawley & Son, Neponset, Mass, respectively, in 1943. Purchased in 1964. Entered service in Nov 1964.

TUGS

R-1 (ex-*Farallon*) A 11
R-2 (ex-*Montauk*) A 12
R-3 (ex-*Point Vicente*) A 13
R-5 (ex-*Burnt Island*) A 15

Acquired by the Mexican Navy in 1968.

7 FLOATING CRANES

Ex-US YDs 156, 157, 179, 180, 183, 194 and 203, transferred Sep 1964 to July 1971.

Ex-US YPD 43 leased Aug 1968.

TRAINING SHIP

Spanish merchant ship *Monte Anaga* purchased in late 1973 for conversion into a training ship. Of 6 813 tons and built in 1959.

MONTSERRAT

This small Crown Colony in the Leeward Islands purchased a single Brooke Marine 12 m Patrol Craft in 1971. This craft of 15 tons is powered by two 370 hp diesels, is capable of 22 knots and armed with 3 machine-guns.

MOROCCO

Diplomatic Representation

Defence Attaché in London:
Colonel Benomar Sbay

Personnel

(a) 1975: 2 000 officers and ratings (including 500 Marines)
(b) 18 months National Service

New Contruction Programme 1973-77

4—PR 72 Corvettes
20—32 metre Coastal Patrol Craft
3—"Batral" Type Landing Ships Logistics

Mercantile Marine

Lloyd's Register of Shipping: 43 vessels of 52 564 tons gross

FRIGATE

Name	*Builders*	*Laid down*	*Launched*	*Completed*
AL MAOUNA (ex-*La Surprise*, ex-HMS *Torridge*) 31 (ex-033)	Blyth Dry Dock & Ship Building Co	17 Oct 1942	16 Aug 1943	6 Apr 1944

Displacement, tons: 1 450 standard; 2 150 full load
Length, feet (*metres*): 283·0 (*86·3*) pp; 301·3 (*91·8*) oa
Beam, feet (*metres*): 36·5 (*11·1*)
Draught, feet *metres*): 12·5 (*3·8*)
Aircraft: 1 helicopter
Guns: 2—4·1 in (*105 mm*); 3—40 mm; 2—20 mm
A/S weapons: 1 "Hedgehog"; 4 DCT; 2 DC racks
Main engines: Triple expansion; 2 shafts; 5 500 ihp
Boilers: 2 Admiralty 3-drum
Speed, knots: 18
Oil fuel, tons: 645
Range, miles: 14 400 at 12 knots
Complement: 123 (10 officers, 113 men)

Former British "River" class frigate purchased by France in 1944. Sold to Morocco in June 1964 and converted as flagship and Royal yacht by Chantiers Dubigeon at Brest. A helicopter landing deck and extra accommodation were provided aft. SPS 6 search radar. Accepted on 5 March 1965.

CORVETTES

2 + 2 PR 72 TYPE

Displacement, tons: 370 standard; 440 full load
Dimensions, ft (*m*): 188·8 × 25 × 8·2 (*57·5 × 7·6 × 2·5*)
Guns: 1—76 mm Oto-Melara 1—40 mm L70 Bofors
Main engines: 4 diesels; 11 040 hp = 28 knots
Range, miles: 2 500 at 16 knots
Complement: 37

Ordered June 1973 from Soc. Francaise de Construction Navale. This type can be fitted with Exocet—as the Vega control system will be installed this would be a simple operation. Two more planned.

MINE WARFARE SHIPS

TAWFIG (ex-*Aries* M 758) (MINESWEEPER—COASTAL)

Displacement, tons: 365 standard; 424 full load
Dimensions, feet: 152 oa × 28 × 8·2
Guns: 1—40 mm; 1—20 mm
Main engines: 2 diesels; 2 shafts; 2 000 bhp = 15 knots
Range, miles: 3 000 at 15 knots
Complement: 38

Launched 31 Mar 1956 of the French "Sirius" class. Transferred on loan by France on 28 Nov 1974 for 4 years.

LIGHT FORCES

AL BACHIR 22 (ex-12) (LARGE PATROL CRAFT)

Displacement, tons: 125 light; 154 full load
Dimensions, feet: 124·7 pp; 133·2 oa × 20·8 × 4·7
Guns: 2—40, mm AA and MG
Main engines: 2 SEMT-Pielstick diesels; 2 shafts; 3 600 bhp = 25 knots
Oil fuel, tons: 21
Range, miles: 4 000 at 15 knots
Complement: 23

Ordered in 1964 from Constructions Mécaniques de Normandie, Cherbourg. Launched 25 Feb 1967, delivered 30 Mar 1967.

AL BACHIR — *1967, Royal Moroccan Navy*

ES SABIQ (ex-*P* 762, *VC* 12) 11 (LARGE PATROL CRAFT)

Displacement, tons: 60 standard; 82 full load
Dimensions, feet: 104·5 × 15·5 × 5·5
Guns: 2—20 mm AA
Main engines: Mercedes-Benz diesels; 2 shafts; 2 700 bhp = 28 knots
Range, miles: 3 000 at 15 knots
Complement: 17

Former French seaward defence motor launch of the VC type. Built by Chantiers Navals d'Estérel. Launched on 13 Aug 1957. Completed in 1958. Transferred from the French Navy to the Moroccan Navy on 15 Nov 1960 and renamed *Es Sabiq*.

6 + 14 P 92 TYPE (COASTAL PATROL CRAFT)

The first six of this 32 metre type of patrol craft were ordered from Construction de Mécanique, Normandie in Feb 1974. Fourteen more planned.

2 + 1 BATRAL TYPE

Displacement, tons: 750 standard; 1 250 full load
Dimensions, ft (*m*): 262·4 × 42·6 × 7·5 (*80 × 13 × 2·3*)
Guns: 2—40 mm; 2—81 mm mortars
Main engines: 2 Diesels; 2 shafts; 1 800 hp = 16 knots
Range, miles: 3 500 at 13 knots
Complement: 37

Fitted with helicopter landing platform and with vehicle-stowage above and below decks. Can carry an extra 140 men and twelve vehicles. Two ordered from Dubigeon in 1974. One more planned.

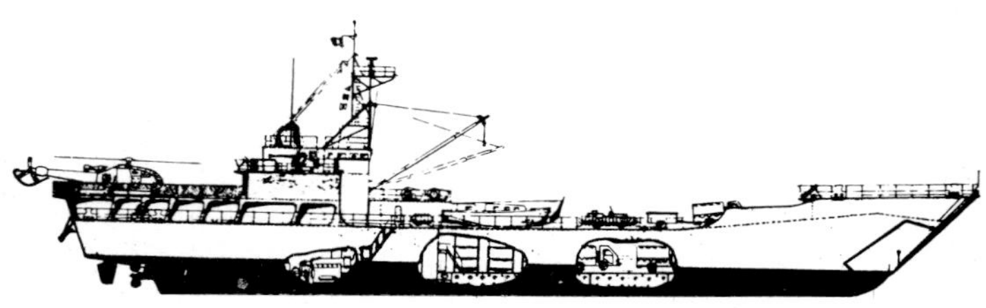

BATRAL TYPE — *1974 French Navy*

LIEUTENANT MALGHAGH 21

Displacement, tons: 292 standard, 642 full load
Dimensions, feet: 193 6 × 39 2 × 4 3
Guns: 2—20 mm AA
Main engines: MGO diesels; 2 shafts; 1 000 bhp = 8 knots
Complement: 16 (1 officer, 15 men)

Ordered early in 1963 from Chantiers Navals Franco-Belges and completed in 1964. Similar to the French landing craft of the EDIC type built at the same yard.

There are also the yacht *Essaoira*, 60 tons, from Italy in 1967, used as a training vessel for watchkeepers; and twelve customs boats, four of 40 tons, 82 feet, diesels 940 bhp = 23 knots, and eight 42·7 feet; all built in 1963. The *Murene*, Coast Guard Cutter, has also been reported.

NETHERLANDS

Administration

Minister of Defence:
Ir. H. Vredeling

State Secretary of Defence (Personnel):
C. L. J. van Lent

State Secretary of Defence (Equipment):
A. Stemerdink

Chief of the Defence Staff:
Lt-Gen. A. J. W. Wijting

Chairman Joint Services Material Board:
Vice-Admiral J. C. H. van den Bergh

Chief of the Naval Staff:
Vice-Admiral E. Roest

Vice Chief of the Naval Staff:
Rear-Admiral F. Paldermans

Flag Officer Naval Personnel:
Vice-Admiral F. H. Heckman

Flag Officer Naval Material:
Rear-Admiral J. L. Langenberg

Command

Admiral Netherlands Home Command:
Vice-Admiral B. Veldkamp

Commander Netherlands Task Group:
Rear-Admiral J. W. H. Wevers

Flag Officer Naval Air:
Rear Admiral R. J. Idzerda

Commandant General Royal Netherlands Marine Corps:
Major-General A. C. Lamers

Flag Officer Netherlands Antilles:
Commodore W. G. Landzaat

Diplomatic Representation

Naval Attaché in London:
Captain J. B. Genet

Naval Attaché in Washington and NLR SACLANT:
Rear-Admiral H. van Mastrigt

Naval Attaché in Paris:
Captain A. J. M. Stoffels

Naval Attaché in Bonn:
Captain J. P. L. de Rouw

Strength of the Fleet

	1974/5	*1977*	*1983*
CLG de Zeven Provincien	1	—	—
DLG Tromp class	—	2	2
Standard SAM frigate	—	—	1
Stand. ASW frigate Kortenaer class	—	2	8
Van Speyck cl. frigate	6	6	6
DD Holland class	2	1	—
DD Friesland class	8	8	—
Support ships Poolster class	1	2	2
SS Zwaardvis + improved Zwaardvis classes	2	2	4
SS Dolfijn and Potvis class	4	4	2
Onversaagd cl. auxiliaries	5	5	5
Minehunters Dokkum class	4	4	4
Sweepers Dokkum class	11	11	7
Dokkum cl. diving ships	3	3	2
Other CMS	9	—	—
CMI van Straelen class	16	16	16
New MCM ships	—	—	4
Survey ships	2	3	3

Future New Construction Programme

8 Frigates (ASW)
1 Fast Combat Support Ship
1 Oceanographic Ship
6 Lynx Helicopters

Planned Strength in 1980s

2 ASW Groups each of 6 ASW frigates, 1 DLG, 1 Support Ship (helicopters in all ships) to operate in *Eastlant* Area
1 ASW Group of 6 ASW frigates and 1 DLG to operate in Channel Approaches
1 ASW Group of 4 frigates to operate in Channel Command
6 Patrol Submarines
24 LRMP Aircraft in 3 squadrons (1 training)
2 MCM Groups of 12 ships each operating off Dutch ports.
1 MCM Group of 7 ships for Channel command
2 R. Neth. Marine Commando Groups and 1 Cold Weather Reinforced Company

Naval Air Force

Personnel: 2 000

3 MR Squadrons with 8 Atlantics, 15 Neptunes and 18 S-2N
12 Wasps and 7 AB-204B helicopters (new MR aircraft by late 70s—Lynx replacements by Mid 70s)

Bases

Main Base; Den Helder.
Minor bases; Flushing and Curacao.
Fleet Air Arm; NAS Valkenburgh (main), NAS De Kooy (helicopters).
R. Neth. Marines; Rotterdam.
Training Bases; Amsterdam and Hilversum.

Personnel

(a) 1 January 1975: 18 100 officers and ratings (including the Navy Air Service, Royal Netherlands Marine Corps and about 360 officers and women of the (W.R.Nl.NS)
(b) 18-21 months National Service

Disposals and Transfers

Cruiser

Oct 1972 *De Ruyter* to Peru as *Almirante Grau*

Destroyers

1973 *Gelderland* for harbour training
1974 *Noord Brabant* (after collision 9/1/74)
To disposal

Submarines

Nov 1970 *Zeeleuw* (ex-*Hawkbill*) } returned to US
Nov 1971 *Walrus* (ex-*Icefish*) } and scrapped

Minesweepers

1972 *Onvermoeid, Bolsward, Breukelen, Bruinisse* returned to USN
1973 *Grijpskerk* for harbour training
1974 *Wildervank, Meppel, Goes, Brummen, Brouwershaven* to disposal
Axel, Aalsmeer to Oman

Survey Ships

1972 *Luymes* to disposal
1973 *Snellius* as accommodation ship

Storeships

1972 *Woendi*
1973 *Pelikaan*

Netlayer

Sept 1970 *Cerberus* returned to US for transfer to Turkey

Mercantile Marine

Lloyd's Register of Shipping:
1 452 vessels of 4 972 244 tons gross

LIST OF PENNANT NUMBERS

Submarines

S 804 Potvis
S 805 Tonijn
S 806 Zwaardvis
S 807 Tijgerhaai
S 808 Dolfijn
S 809 Zeehond

Cruiser

C 802 De Zeven Provincien

Destroyers

F 801 Tromp
F 806 De Ruyter
D 808 Holland
D 809 Zeeland
D 810 Noord Brabant
D 812 Friesland
D 813 Groningen
D 814 Limburg
D 815 Overijssel
D 816 Drenthe
D 817 Utrecht
D 818 Rotterdam
D 918 Amsterdam

Frigates

F 802 Van Speijk
F 803 Van Galen
F 804 Tjerk Hiddes
F 805 Van Nes
F 814 Isaac Sweers
F 815 Evertsen

Corvettes

F 817 Wolf
F 818 Fret
F 819 Hermelijn
F 820 Vos
F 821 Panter
F 822 Jaguar

MCM Command/Support and Escort Ships

A 854 Onversaagd
A 855 Onbevreesd
A 856 Mercuur
A 858 Onvervaard
A 859 Onverdroten

Mine Hunters:

M 801 Dokkum
M 818 Drunen
M 828 Staphorst
M 842 Veere

Coastal Minesweepers

M 802 Hoogezand
M 809 Naaldwijk
M 810 Abcoude
M 812 Drachten
M 813 Ommen
M 815 Giethoorn
M 817 Venlo
M 823 Naarden
M 827 Hoogeveen
M 830 Sittard
M 841 Gemert
M 845 Beemster
M 847 Bedum
M 848 Beilen
M 849 Borculo
M 850 Borne
M 853 Blaricum
M 854 Brielle
M 855 Breskens
M 857 Boxtel

Inshore Minesweepers:

M 868 Alblas
M 869 Bussemaker
M 870 Lacomblé
M 871 Van Hamel
M 872 Van Straelen
M 873 Van Moppes
M 874 Chömpff
M 875 Van Well-Groeneveld
M 876 Schuiling
M 877 Van Versendaal
M 878 Van Der Wel
M 879 Van 't Hoff
M 880 Mahu
M 881 Staverman
M 882 Houtepen
M 883 Zomer

Diving Vessels:

M 806 Roermond
M 807 Waalwijk
M 820 Woerden
M 822 Leersum
M 844 Rhenen

Patrol Vessels:

P 802 Balder
P 803 Bulgia
P 804 Freijer
P 805 Hadda
P 806 Hefring

Auxiliary Ships

A 835 Poolster
A 847 Argus
A 848 Triton
A 849 Nautilus
A 850 Hydra
A 870 Wamandai
A 871 Wambrau
A 872 Westgat
A 873 Wielingen
A 903 Zeefakkel
A 904 Buyskes
A 905 Blommendal
A 912 Dreg 4
A 923 Zuiderkruis
A 932 Van Bochove

CRUISER

DE ZEVEN PROVINCIEN

Name	No.	Builders	Laid down	Launched	Completed
(ex-*De Ruyter*, ex-*Eendracht*, ex-*Kijkduin*)	C 802	Rotterdam Drydock Co	19 May 1939	22 Aug 1950	17 Dec 1953

Displacement, tons	9 529 standard; 11 850 full load
Length, feet (*metres*)	590·5 (*180·0*) pp; 614·5 (*190·3*) oa
Beam, feet (*metres*)	56·7 (*17·3*)
Draught, feet (*metres*)	22·0 (*6·7*) max
Missile launchers	1 twin Terrier aft
Guns	4—6 in (*152 mm*) in twin turrets; 6—57 mm in twin turrets; 4—40 mm AA
Main engines	2 De Schelde-Parsons geared turbines; 85 000 shp; 2 shafts
Speed, knots	32
Boilers	4 Werkspoor-Yarrow
Complement	940

DE ZEVEN PROVINCIEN *1972, Royal Netherlands Navy*

Scale 125 feet = 1 inch. (1 : 1 500)

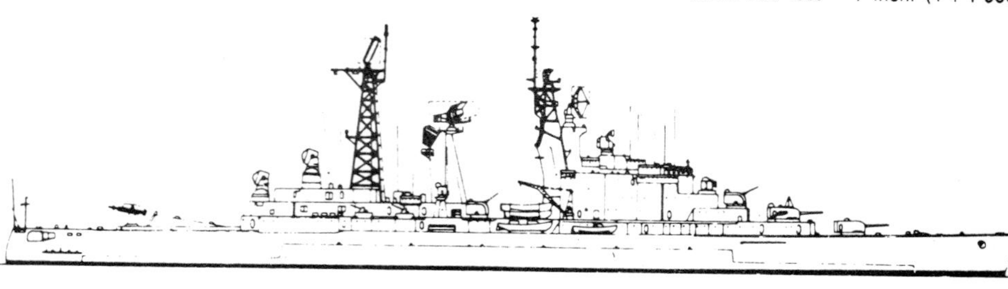

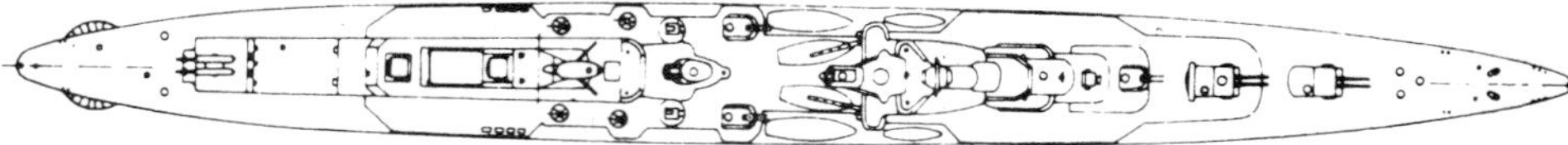

Machinery by K. M. de Schelde. Construction resumed in 1946. For disposal mid-1977.

RADAR. Search: LW 01, SPS 39 3-D, SGR 104 Height Finder. Tactical: DA 02. Fire Control: HSA M 20 series for larger guns. 2 SPG 55 for "Terrier". 2 M 45 for 40 mm guns.

MISSILE CONVERSION. *De Zeven Provincien* was converted in 1962-64 by Rotterdamsche Droogdok Mij, Rotterdam with "Terrier" installation by NV Dok en Werf Mij Wilton-Fijenoord Schiedam. She was again refitted and modernised in 1971-72.

GUNNERY. Main armament has 60 degrees elevation. All guns are fully automatic and radar controlled. The 6 inch guns have a rate of fire of 15 rounds per minute.

DESTROYERS

2 "TROMP" CLASS (DLG)

Name	No.	Builders	Laid down	Launched	Completion
DE RUYTER	F 806	Koninklijke Maatschappij De Schelde, Flushing	22 Dec 1971	4 June 1973	1975
TROMP	F 801	Koninklijke Maatschappij De Schelde, Flushing	4 Sep 1971	Early 1973	1976

Displacement, tons	4 300 standard; 5 400 full load
Length, feet (*metres*)	429·5 (*130·9*) pp; 454·1 (*138·4*) oa
Beam, feet (*metres*)	48·6 (*14·8*)
Draught, feet (*metres*)	15·1 (*4·6*)
Guns	2—4·7 in (twin turret)
Missile launchers	1 "Tartar" aft; Seasparrow Point defence missile system
Aircraft	1 Lynx helicopter armed with homing torpedoes
Main engines	2 Olympus gas turbines; 50 000 hp; 2 Tyne cruising gas turbines, 8 000 hp
Speed, knots	30
Complement	306

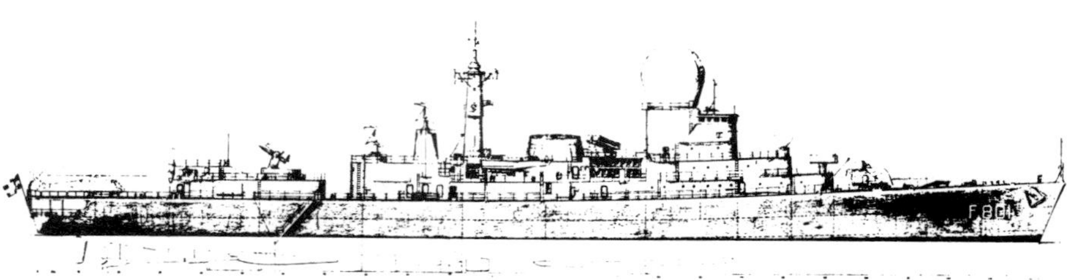

"TROMP" Class *1974, Royal Netherlands Navy*

GENERAL
First design allowance was voted for in 1967 estimates. Ordered (announced on 27 July 1970) for laying down in 1971 and completion in 1975. Hangar and helicopter spot landing platform aft. Fitted as flagships.
Tromp started trials mid-March 1975 for commissioning about September 1975. *De Ruyter* to follow six months later.

ENGINEERING. Each ship carries 4-1 000 KW Diesel generators by Ruston Paxman, England.

GUNNERY. Turrets from *Gelderland* with considerable modifications.

MISSILES. In Autumn 1974 it was announced that these ships would subsequently be fitted with Harpoon.

RADAR. HSA 3D search and target designator in main radome; WM 25 fire control with co-mounted search and tracker in smaller radome for Seasparrow and 4·7 in; 2 SPG-51 for Tartar; Sewaco 1 automated A.I.O.

"TROMP" Class

Destroyers—*continued*

8 "FRIESLAND" CLASS

Name	No.	Builders	Laid down	Launched	Completed
FRIESLAND	D 812	Nederlandse Dok en Scheepsbouw Mij, Amsterdam	17 Dec 1951	21 Feb 1953	22 Mar 1956
GRONINGEN	D 813	Nederlandse Dok en Scheepsbouw, Mij, Amsterdam	21 Feb 1952	9 Jan 1954	12 Sep 1956
LIMBURG	D 814	Koninklijke Maatschappij De Schelde, Flushing	28 Nov 1953	5 Sep 1955	31 Oct 1956
OVERIJSSEL	D 815	Dok-en-Werfmaatschappij Wilton-Fijenoord	15 Oct 1953	8 Aug 1955	4 Oct 1957
DRENTHE	D 816	Nederlandse Dok en Scheepsbouw Mij, Amsterdam	9 Jan 1954	26 Mar 1955	1 Aug 1957
UTRECHT	D 817	Koninklijke Maatschappij De Schelde, Flushing	15 Feb 1954	2 June 1956	1 Oct 1957
ROTTERDAM	D 818	Rotterdamse Droogdok Mij, Rotterdam	7 Jan 1954	26 Jan 1956	28 Feb 1957
AMSTERDAM	D 819	Nederlandse Dok en Scheepsbouw Mij, Amsterdam	26 Mar 1955	25 Aug 1956	10 Aug 1958

Displacement, tons	2 497 standard; 3 070 full load
Length, feet (*metres*)	370 (*112·8*) pp; 380·5 (*116·0*) oa
Beam, feet (*metres*)	38·5 (*11·7*)
Draught, feet (*metres*)	17 (*5·2*)
Guns,	4—4·7 in (*120 mm*) twin turrets 4—40 mm
A/S weapons	2 four-barrelled depth charge mortars Bofors rocket launchers
Boilers	4 Babcock
Main engines	2 Werkspoor geared turbines, 60 000 shp; 2 shafts
Speed, knots	36
Complement	284

GENERAL
These ships have side armour as well as deck protection. "Bofors" type anti-submarine rocket throwers. Twin rudders. Propellers 370 rpm. Named after provinces of the Netherlands, and the two principal cities. To be replaced by "Kortenaer" class of frigates.

RADAR. Search: LW 03. Tactical: DA 05. Fire Control HSA M 45 for 4·7 in. HSA fire control for 40 mm and A/S rockets.

GUNNERY. The 4·7 inch guns are fully automatic with a rate of fire of 50 rounds per minute. All guns are radar controlled. Originally six 40 mm guns were mounted.

TORPEDO TUBES. *Utrecht* was equipped with eight 21 inch A/S torpedo tubes (single, four on each side) in 1960 and *Overijssel* in 1961, and the others were to have been, but the project was dropped and tubes already fitted were removed.

"FRIESLAND" Class

FRIESLAND

1971, Royal Netherlands Navy

2 "HOLLAND" CLASS

Name	No.	Builders	Laid down	Launched	Completed
HOLLAND	D 808	Rotterdamse Droogdok Mij, Rotterdam	21 Apr 1950	11 Apr 1953	31 Dec 1954
ZEELAND	D 809	Koninklijke Maatschappji De Schelde, Flushing	12 Jan 1951	27 June 1953	1 Mar 1955

Displacement, tons	2 215 standard; 2 765 full load
Length, feet (*metres*)	360·5 (*109·9*) pp; 371·1 (*113·1*) oa
Beam, feet (*metres*)	37·5 (*11·4*)
Draught, feet (*metres*)	16·8 (*5·1*)
Guns	4—4·7 in (*120 mm*); 1—40 mm
A/S weapons	2 four-barrelled DC mortars, Bofors rocket launchers
Main engines	Werkspoor Parsons geared turbines; 2 shafts; 45 000 shp
Speed, knots	32
Boilers	4 Babcock
Complement	247

GENERAL
The two ships of this class are equipped with engines of the pre-war "Callenburgh" class design. (The four "Callenburgh" class destroyers were being built in 1940. *Isaac Sweers* was towed to England and completed there. *Tjerk Hiddes* was completed by the Germans as ZH 1. The other two, *Callenburgh* and *Van Almonde*, were too severely damaged for further use and were scrapped, the engines being installed in the "Holland" class).

SISTERSHIPS *Gelderland* now a harbour-training hulk in Amsterdam. *Noord Brabant* too severely damaged in collision 9 Jan 1974 for repair.
To be replaced by "Kortenaer" class.

RADAR. Search: LW 03. Tactical: DA 02. Fire Control: HSA M 45 for 4·7 in. HSA fire control for A/S rocket launcher.

GUNNERY. The 4·7 inch guns are fully automatic with a rate of fire of 50 rounds per minute. All guns are radar controlled.

"**HOLLAND**" Class

HOLLAND

1973, Royal Netherlands Navy

FRIGATES

4 + 4 "KORTENAER" CLASS

Name	Builders	Laid down	Commissioning
KORTENAER	Koninklijke Maatschappij "De Schelde", Flushing	8 Apr 1975	Autumn 1978
CALLENBURGH		July 1975	Autumn 1979
VAN KINGBERGEN		Sep 1975	Summer 1980
BANCKERT		1975	Spring 1981
+ 4			

Displacement, tons	3 500
Dimensions, ft (*m*)	419·8 × 47·2 × — (*128* × *14·4* × —)
Aircraft	1 Lynx helicopter
Missiles	Harpoon surface-to-surface; NATO Seasparrow PDMS
Gun	1—76 mm Oto Melara
Torpedo tubes	Two triple mountings for Mk 46 A/S torpedoes
Main engines	2 Rolls Royce Olympus gas turbines = 50 000 shp; 2 Rolls Royce Tyne gas turbines = 8000 shp; 2 variable pitch propellers
Speed, knots	30
Range, miles	4 000 on Tyne cruising turbines
Complement	185

"KORTENAER" Class — *1974, Royal Netherlands Navy*

GENERAL
First four of class ordered 31 Aug 1974, second four 28 Nov 1974. *Kortenaer* to be ready for trials 1 Apr 1978. Present intention is to order four more in 1977 including one ship fitted with surface-to-air missiles, and more to follow later. These ships are to replace the "Holland" and "Friesland" classes. Cost at 1974 prices £37 m.

COMPLEMENT. Reduced to 185 by adaption of large amount of automation.
RADAR. Hollandse Signaal for radar and fire-control.

SONAR. SQS 505.

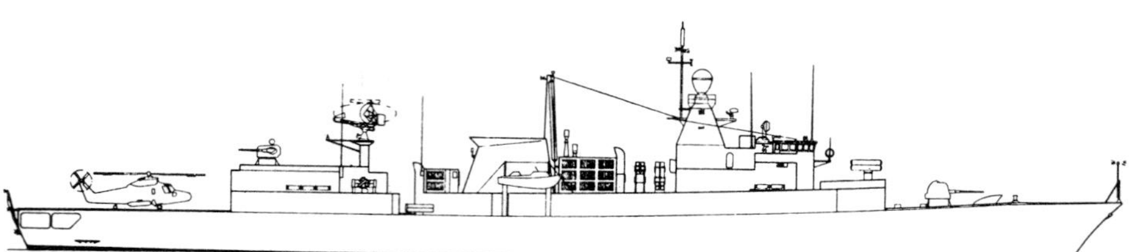

"KORTENAER" Class — *1973, Royal Netherlands Navy*

6 "VAN SPEIJK" CLASS

Name	No.	Builders	Laid down	Launched	Completed
TJERK HIDDES	F 804	Nederlandse Dok en Scheepsbouw Mij, Amsterdam	1 June 1964	17 Dec 1965	16 Aug 1967
VAN GALEN	F 803	Koninklijke Maatschappij De Schelde, Flushing	25 July 1963	19 June 1965	1 Mar 1967
VAN NES	F 805	Koninklijke Maatschappij De Schelde, Flushing	25 July 1963	26 Mar 1966	9 Aug 1967
VAN SPEIJK	F 802	Nederlandse Dok en Scheepsbouw Mij, Amsterdam	1 Oct 1963	5 Mar 1965	14 Feb 1967
EVERTSEN	F 815	Koninklijke Maatschappij De Schelde, Flushing	6 July 1965	18 June 1966	21 Dec 1967
ISAAC SWEERS	F 814	Nederlandse Dok en Scheepsbouw Mij, Amsterdam	5 May 1965	10 Mar 1967	15 May 1968

Displacement, tons	2 200 standard; 2 850 full load
Dimensions, feet	360 wl, 372 oa × 41 × 18
Guns	2—4·5 in (twin turret)
Missile launchers	2 quadruple Seacat anti-aircraft
A/S weapons	1 Limbo three-barrelled depth charge mortar
Aircraft	1 lightweight helicopter armed with homing torpedoes
Boilers	2 Babcock & Wilcox
Main engines	2 double reduction geared turbines; 2 shafts; 30 000 shp
Speed, knots	30
Complement	254

"VAN SPEIJK" Class

GENERAL. Four ships were ordered in Oct 1962 and two later. Have ECM and VDS. Ships of this class will undergo mid-life conversion from 1976 to 1980, consisting of the replacement of the turret by a Harpoon mounting, considerable improvement of the Seacat system, electronic equipment and accommodation.

DESIGN. Although in general these ships are based on the design of the British Improved Type 12 ("Leander" class), there are a number of modifications to suit the requirements of the Royal Netherlands Navy. As far as possible equipment of Netherlands manufacture was installed. This resulted in a number of changes in the ship's superstructure compared with the British "Leander" class. To avoid delay these ships were in some cases fitted with equipment already available, instead of going through long development stages.

RADAR. LW 02 air surveillance on mainmast; DA 05 target indicator on foremast; surface-warning/nav set on foremast; 1-M45 for 4·5 in guns; 2-M44 for Seacat.

EVERTSEN — *8/1973, Wright & Logan*

CORVETTES

6 "WOLF" CLASS

Name	No.	Builders	Laid down	Launched	Completed
FRET (ex-*PCE* 1604)	F 818	General Shipbuilding and Engineering Works, Boston	18 Dec 1952	30 July 1953	4 May 1954
HERMELIJN (ex-*PCE* 1605)	F 819	General Shipbuilding and Engineering Works, Boston	2 Mar 1953	6 Mar 1954	5 Aug 1954
JAGUAR (ex-*PCE* 1609)	F 822	Avondale Marine Ways, Inc. New Orleans, Louisiana	10 Dec 1952	20 Mar 1954	11 June 1954
PANTER (ex-*PCE* 1608)	F 821	Avondale Marine Ways, Inc, New Orleans, Louisiana	1 Dec 1952	30 Jan 1954	11 June 1954
VOS (ex-*PCE* 1606)	F 820	General Shipbuilding and Engineering Works, Boston	3 Aug 1952	1 May 1954	2 Dec 1954
WOLF (ex-*PCE* 1607)	F 817	Avondale Marine Ways, Inc, New Orleans, Louisiana	15 Nov 1952	2 Jan 1954	26 Mar 1954

Displacement, tons: 808 standard; 975 full load
Length, feet (*metres*): 180 (*54·9*) pp; 184·5 (*56·2*) oa
Beam, feet (*metres*): 33 (*10·0*)
Draught, feet (*metres*): 14·5 (*4·4*)
Guns: 1—3 in (*76 mm*); 6—40 mm (*Jaguar, Panter:* 4—40 mm); 8—20 mm
A/S: 1 Hedgehog; 2 DCT (*Jaguar, Panter:* 4); 2 DC racks
Main engines: 2 GM diesels; 1 600 bhp; 2 shafts
Range, miles: 4 300 at 10 knots
Speed, knots: 15
Complement: 96

20 mm guns not fitted in peacetime.

PANTER — *1972, Wright & Logan*

5 "BALDER" CLASS

Name	No.	Laid down	Launched	Completed
BALDER	P 802	12 Sep 1953	24 Feb 1954	6 Aug 1954
BULGIA	P 803	10 Oct 1953	24 Apr 1954	9 Aug 1954
FREYR	P 804	24 Feb 1954	21 July 1954	1 Dec 1954
HADDA	P 805	24 Apr 1954	2 Oct 1954	3 Feb 1955
HEFRING	P 806	21 July 1954	1 Dec 1954	23 Mar 1955

Displacement, tons: 149 standard; 225 full load
Dimensions, feet: 114·9 pp; 119·1 oa × 20·2 × 5·9
Guns: 1—40 mm; 3—20 mm
A/S weapons: 2 DGT, Mousetrap
Main engines: Diesels; 2 shafts; 1 050 shp = 15·5 knots
Range, miles: 1 000 at 13 knots
Complement: 27

Built in the Netherlands by Rijkswerf Willemsoord on US account. US submarine chaser type, SC Nos 1627-1631.

HEFRING — *1971, Royal Netherlands Navy*

SUBMARINES

Note. A sum was set aside in the 1975 Estimates to start design work on an "Improved Zwaardvis" class to be ordered in 1979.

2 "ZWAARDVIS" CLASS

Name	No.	Builders	Laid down	Launched	Completed
TIJGERHAAI	S 807	Rotterdamse Droogdok Mij, Rotterdam	14 July 1966	25 May 1971	20 Oct 1972
ZWAARDVIS	S 806	Rotterdamse Droogdok Mij, Rotterdam	14 July 1966	2 July 1970	18 Aug 1972

Displacement, tons: 2 350 surface; 2 640 submerged
Length, feet (*metres*): 213·3 (*65·0*)
Beam, feet (*metres*): 27·5 (*8·4*)
Draught, feet (*metres*): 23·3 (*7·1*)
Torpedo tubes: 6—21 in (*533 mm*)
Main machinery: Diesel-electric; 3 diesel generators; 1 shaft
Speed, knots: 13 on surface; 20 submerged
Complement: 67

In the 1964 Navy Estimates a first instalment was approved for the construction of two conventionally powered submarines of tear-drop design. HSA M8 Fire Control.

ZWAARDVIS — *1972, Royal Netherlands Navy*

Submarines—*continued*

2 "POTVIS" CLASS
2 "DOLFIJN" CLASS

Name	No.	Builders	Laid down	Launched	Completed
POTVIS	S 804	Wilton-Fijenoord, Schiedam	17 Sep 1962	12 Jan 1965	2 Nov 1965
TONIJN	S 805	Wilton-Fijenoord, Schiedam	27 Nov 1962	14 June 1965	24 Feb 1966
DOLFIJN	S 808	Rotterdamse Droogdok Mij, Rotterdam	30 Dec 1954	20 May 1959	16 Dec 1960
ZEEHOND	S 809	Rotterdamse Droogdok Mij, Rotterdam	30 Dec 1954	20 Feb 1960	16 Mar 1961

Displacement, tons	1 140 standard; 1 494 surface 1 826 submerged
Length, feet (*metres*)	260·9 (*79·5*)
Beam, feet (*metres*)	25·8 (*7·8*)
Draught, feet (*metres*)	15·8 (*4·8*)
Torpedo tubes	8—21 in (*533 mm*)
Main machinery	2 MAN diesels; total 3 100 bhp Electric motors, 4 200 hp; 2 shafts
Speed, knots	14·5 on surface; 17 submerged
Complement	64

These submarines are of a triple-hull design, giving a diving depth 980 feet (*300 metres*). *Potvis* and *Tonijn*, originally voted for in 1949 with the other pair, but suspended for some years, had several modifications compared with *Dolfijn* and *Zeehond* and were officially considered to be a separate class; but modernisation of both classes has been completed, and all four boats are now almost identical. HSA M8 Fire Control.

CONSTRUCTION. The hull consists of three cylinders arranged in a triangular shape. The upper cylinder accommodates the crew, navigational equipment and armament. The lower two cylinders house the propulsion machinery comprising diesel engines, batteries and electric motors, as well as store-rooms.

TONIJN *1973, Royal Netherlands Navy*

MINE WARFARE FORCES

5 "ONVERSAAGD" CLASS (MCM SUPPORT SHIPS and ESCORTS)

Name	No.	Laid down	Completed
ONVERSAAGD (ex-AM 480)	A 854 (ex-M 884)	1952	27 May 1954
ONBEVREESD (ex-AM 481)	A 855 (ex-M 885)	1952	21 Sep 1954
ONVERVAARD (ex-AM 482)	A 858 (ex-M 888)	1952	31 Mar 1955
ONVERDROTEN (ex-AM 485)	A 859 (ex-M 889)	1952	22 Nov 1954
MERCUUR (ex-*Onverschrokken*, ex-AM 483)	A 856 (ex-M 886)	1952	22 July 1954

Displacement, tons	735 standard; 790 full load
Dimensions, feet	165·0 pp; 172·0 oa × 36·0 × 10·6
Gun	1—40 mm
A/S weapons	2 DC
Main engines	Diesels; 1 600 bhp = 15·5 knots
Oil fuel, tons	46
Range, miles	2 400 at 12 knots
Complement	70

Built in USA for the Netherlands, *Onversaagd, Onbevreesd* and *Onvervaard* by Astoria Marine Construction Co and the remaining two by Peterson Builders, Wisconsin. Of wooden and non-magnetic construction. Originally designed as Minesweepers—Ocean—reclassified in 1966 and in 1972. *Onbevreesd, Onverdroten* and *Onvervaard* are MCM Command/Support Ships. *Mercuur* (ex-*Onverschrokken*) was converted into a Torpedo Trials Ship in 1972. *Onversaagd* has been converted for temporary duty as survey ship until the new construction Oceanographic Ship is delivered in 1975.

ONVERVAARD (Escort type) *1972, Royal Netherlands Navy*

18 "DOKKUM" CLASS (CMS and MINEHUNTERS)

ABCOUDE	M 810	**HOOGEZAND**	M 802	**ROERMOND**	M 806 D
DOKKUM	M 801 H	**HOOGEVEEN**	M 827	**SITTARD**	M 830
DRACHTEN	M 812	**NAALDWIJK**	M 809	**STAPHORST**	M 828 H
DRUNEN	M 818 H	**NAARDEN**	M 823	**VEERE**	M 842 H
GEMERT	M 841	**OMMEN**	M 813	**VENLO**	M 817
GIETHOORN	M 815	**RHENEN**	M 844 D	**WOERDEN**	M 820 D

(see "WILDERVANK" class for details)

2 "WILDERVANK" CLASS (ex-MSC—DIVING VESSELS)

LEERSUM M 822 D **WAALWIJK** M 807 D

Displacement, tons	373 standard; 417 full load
Dimensions, feet	149·8 oa × 28 × 6·5
Guns	2—40 mm
Main engines	2 diesels; Fyenoord MAN or Werkspoor; 2 500 bhp = 16 knots
Range, miles	2 500 at 10 knots
Complement	38

Of 32 Western Union type coastal minesweepers built in the Netherlands, 18 were under offshore procurement as the "Dokkum" class, with MAN engines, and 14 on Netherlands account as the "Wildervank" class, with Werkspoor diesels. All launched in 1954-56 and completed in 1955-56.
Of the "Dokkum" class four have been converted to minehunters (H), (1968-73) and three to diving vessels (D) (1962-68). The remaining eleven minesweepers of this class are subject to a fleet rehabilitation and modernisation programme between 1973 and 1977.
Of the "Wildervank" class the remaining two ships were converted as diving vessels (1962-68), whilst one was transferred to Ethiopia in 1972, two to Oman in 1974, one (*Grypskerk*) stationed at Amsterdam as alongside training ship. Eight have been scrapped.

DOKKUM (Hunter) *1971, Royal Netherlands Navy*

GEMERT (sweeper) *1973, C. and S. Taylor*

Minewarfare Forces—*continued*

9 "BEEMSTER" CLASS (MINESWEEPERS—COASTAL)

BEEMSTER (ex-*AMS* 105)	M 845	**BLARICUM** (ex-*AMS* 112)	M 853
BEDUM (ex-*Beerta* ex-*AMS* 106)	M 847	**BRIELLE** (ex-*AMS* 167)	M 854
BEILEN (ex-*AMS* 110)	M 848	**BRESKENS** (ex-*AMS* 148)	M 855
BORCULO (ex-*AMS* 107)	M 849	**BOXTEL** (ex-*AMS* 149)	M 857
BORNE (ex-*AMS* 108)	M 850		

Displacement, tons	330 standard; 384 full load
Dimensions, feet	138 pp; 144·7 oa × 27·9 × 7·5
Guns	2—20 mm AA
Main engines	2 diesels; 880 bhp = 13·6 knots
Range, miles	2 500 at 10 knots
Complement	37

All completed and transferred from USA in 1953-54. Of non-magnetic construction. Named after small towns in the Netherlands. Five have been returned to USA and remainder will be returned during period 1973-77 as "Dokkum" class conversions complete.

BORCULO *1973, Royal Netherlands Navy*

16 "VAN STRAELEN" CLASS (MINESWEEPERS—INSHORE)

ALBLAS	M 868	**MAHU**	M 880	**VAN MOPPES**	M 873
BUSSEMAKER	M 869	**SCHUILING**	M 876	**VAN STRAELEN**	M 872
CHÖMPFF	M 874	**STAVERMAN**	M 881	**VAN VERSENDAAL**	M 877
HOUTEPEN	M 882	**VAN DER WEL**	M 878	**VAN WELL GROENVELD**	M 875
LACOMBLÉ	M 870	**VAN HAMEL**	M 871		
		VAN 'T HOFF	M 879	**ZOMER**	M 883

Displacement, tons	151 light; 169 full load
Dimensions, feet	90 pp; 99·3 oa × 18·2 × 5·2
Gun	1—20 mm AA
Main engines	Werkspoor diesels; 2 shafts; 1 100 bhp = 13 knots
Complement	14

Built, 6 by Werf de Noord at Albasserdam; 5 by N.V. de Arnhemse Scheepsbouw Maatschappij at Arnhem; and 5 by Amsterdamsche Scheepswerft G. de Vries Lentsch Jr at Amsterdam. Eight were built under the offshore procurement programme, with MDAP funds, and the remaining eight were paid for by Netherlands. All ordered in mid-1957. Built of non-magnetic materials. *Alblas*, the first, was laid down at Werf de Noord N.V. at Albasserdam on 26 Feb 1958, launched on 29 June 1959, started trials on 15 Jan 1960 and completed on 12 Mar 1960. All the others were laid down in 1958-61, launched in 1958-61 and commissioned in 1960-62.

VAN WELL GROENVELD *1972, Wright & Logan*

AMPHIBIOUS FORCES

L 9521 **L 9526**

Displacement, tons	20
Dimensions, feet	50 × 11·8 × 5·8
Main engines	2 Kromhout diesels; 75 bhp = 8 knots
Complement	3

Now officially rated as LCA Type,

L 9510	**L 9512**	**L 9514**	**L 9517**	**L 9520**
L 9511	**L 9513**	**L 9515**	**L 9518**	**L 9522**

Displacement, tons	13·6
Dimensions, feet	46·2 × 11·5 × 6
Main engines	Rolls Royce diesel; Schottel propeller; 200 bhp = 12 knots
Complement	3

Landing craft made of plastic (polyester), all commissioned in 1962-63, except L 9520 in 1964.

SURVEY SHIPS

1 NEW CONSTRUCTION HYDROGRAPHIC/OCEANOGRAPHIC SHIP

TYDEMAN

Displacement, tons	2 950
Dimensions, ft (*m*)	295 × 47·2 × 15·7 (*90 × 14·4 × 4·8*)
Main engines	Diesel-electric
Speed, knots	15
Complement	64 plus 15 scientists

Ordered in Oct 1974 from Scheepswierfen Machine Fabriek in "De Merwed" for completion in late 1976. Cost £6·7 m. Will be able to operate down to 7 000 m. To be fitted with eight laboratories. Supplied with two bow propellers.

This ship is to replace *Luymes*. Until she is completed the converted Minesweeper—Ocean *Onversaagd* will serve in her place.

TYDEMAN *1974, Royal Netherlands Navy*

2 "BUYSKES" CLASS

BLOMMENDAL A 905 **BUYSKES** A 904

Displacement, tons	967 standard; 1 033 full load
Dimensions, ft (*m*)	196·6 oa × 36·4 × 12 (*60 × 11·1 × 3·7*)
Main engines	Diesel electric; 2 100 hp (3 × 700) = 13·5 knots
Complement	43

Built by Boele's Scheepswerven en Machinefabriek BV. Bolne to replace the survey ships *Snellius* and *Zeefakkel*. Both designed primarily for hydrographic work but have also limited oceanographic and meteorological capability. They will operate mainly in the North Sea. A data logging system is installed as part of the automatic handling of hydrographic data. They carry two 22 ft survey launches capable of 15 knots and two work-boats normally used for sweeping. Both ships can operate two floats, each housing an echo-sounding transducer, one streaming on each beam. This will enable the running of three simultaneous sounding lines 100 m. apart. *Buyskes* commissioned on 9 Mar 1973 and *Blommendal* on 22 May 1973.

BLOMMENDAL *1973, Royal Netherlands Navy*

DREG IV A 920

Displacement, tons	46 standard; 48 full load
Dimensions, feet	65·7 × 15·1 × 4·9
Main engines	120 hp = 9·5 knots
Complement	10

SERVICE FORCES

2 "POOLSTER" CLASS (FAST COMBAT SUPPORT SHIPS)

POOLSTER A 835 **ZUIDERKRUIS**

Displacement, tons	16 800 full load; 16 900 (*Zuiderkruis*)
Measurement, tons	10 000 deadweight
Dimensions, feet	515 pp; 556 oa × 66·7 × 27 (*Zuiderkruis* 561 oa)
Guns	2—40 mm AA
Aircraft	Capacity: 5 helicopters (official complement 3 SH-34 J)
Main engines	22 500 shp turbines = 21 knots; 2 Werkspoor 16TM410 diesels of 21 000 hp = 21 knots in *Zuiderkruis*
Complement	200

Fast fleet replenishment ships. *Poolster* built by Rotterdam se Droogdok Mij. Laid down on 18 Sep 1962. Launched on 16 Oct 1963. Trials mid-1964. Commissioned on 10 Sep 1964. Helicopter deck aft. Funnel heightened by 4·5 m. *Zuiderkruis* built by Verolme ship yards Alblasserdam. Ordered Oct 1972. Laid down 16 July 1973, launched 15 Oct 1974 for completion mid-1975.

POOLSTER (note modified funnel) *1972, Wright & Logan*

TRAINING SHIPS

ZEEFAKKEL A 903

Displacement, tons	355 standard; 384 full load
Dimensions, ft (*m*)	149 oa × 24·7 × 6·9 (*45·4 × 7·6 × 2·1*)
Guns	1—3 in AA; 1—40 mm AA
Main engines	2 Smit/MAN 8 cyl diesels; 2 shafts; 640 bhp = 12 knots
Complement	29

Built by J. & K. Smit, Kinderdijk. Laid down Sept 1949, launched 21 July 1950 and completed 22 May 1951. Former surveying vessel. Now used as local Training ship at Den Helder.

URANIA (ex-*Tromp*) Y 8050

Displacement, tons	38
Dimensions, feet	72 × 16·3 × 10
Main engines	Diesel; 65 hp
Complement	15

Schooner used for training in seamanship. Commissioned on 23 Apr 1938.

Note. Gelderland (ex-destroyer) and *Grypskerk* (ex-minesweeper) are used at Amsterdam as harbour training and accommodation ships for the Technical Training establishment. *Soemba* (ex-sloop) used at Den Oever as harbour training and accommodation ship for divers and underwater-swimmers.

TUGS

WESTGAT A 872 **WIELINGEN** A 873

Displacement, tons	185
Dimensions, feet	90·6 × 22·7 × 7·7
Guns	2—20 mm AA
Main engines	Bolnes diesel; 720 bhp = 12 knots

Built by Rijkswerf, Willemsoord. Launched on 22 Aug 1967 and 6 Jan 1968 and completed on 10 Jan 1968 and 4 Apr 1968, respectively. Equipped with salvage pumps and fire fighting equipment. Stationed at Den Helder.

WAMANDAI A 870 (ex-Y 8035)

Displacement, tons	159 standard; 185 full load
Dimensions, feet	89·2 × 21·3 × 7·5
Guns	2—20 mm AA
Main engines	Diesel; 500 bhp = 11 knots

Built by Rijkswerf, Willemsoord, Den Helder. Launched on 28 May 1960. Equipped with salvage pumps and fire fighting equipment. In the Netherlands Antilles since 1964.

Tugs—*continued*

WAMBRAU A 871

Displacement, tons	154 standard; 184 full load
Dimensions, feet	86·5 oa × 20·7 × 7·5
Guns	2—20 mm AA
Main engines	Werkspoor diesel and Kort nozzle; 500 bhp = 10·8 knots

Built by Rijkswerf Willemsoord. Launched on 27 Aug 1956. Completed on 8 Jan 1957. Equipped with salvage pumps and fire fighting equipment. Stationed at Den Helder.

BERKEL Y 8037 **DINTEL** Y 8038 **DOMMEL** Y 8039 **IJSSEL** Y 8040

Displacement, tons	139 standard; 163 full load
Dimensions, feet	82 oa × 20·5 × 7·3
Main engines	Werkspoor diesel and Kort nozzle; 500 bhp

Harbour tugs built by H. H. Bodewes, Millingen. Specially designed for use at Den Helder. Completed in 1956-57.
There are also five small harbour tugs — Y 8014, Y 8016, Y 8017, Y 8022, Y 8028.

ACCOMMODATION SHIPS

(See note under Training Ships)

Cornelis Drebbel is the name of the new "Boatel"—775 tons, length 206·7 feet, beam 38·7 feet, draught 3·6 feet, complement 200, cost 3m guilders. Ordered in 1969 from Scheepswerft Voorwaarts at Hoogezand, launched on 19 Nov 1970 and completed in 1971. Serves as accommodation vessel for crews of ships refitting at private yards in the Rotterdam area. *Snellius* (ex-survey ship) is used for accommodation for R. Neth. N. personnel at the RN Submarine Base, Faslane.

TENDER

VAN BOCHOVE A 923

Displacement, tons	150
Dimensions, feet	97·2 × 18·2 × 6
Main engines	Kromhout diesel; Schottel propeller; 140 bhp = 8 knots
Complement	8

Torpedo trials vessel. Built by Zaanlandse Scheepsbouw Mij, Zaandam. Ordered Oct 1961. Launched on 20 July 1962 and completed in Aug 1962.

NEW ZEALAND

Defence Headquarters Naval Staff

Chief of Naval Staff:
Rear-Admiral E. C. Thorne, CBE

Deputy Chief of Naval Staff:
Commodore R. H. L. Humby

The three New Zealand Service Boards were formally abolished in 1971 as part of the Defence Headquarters reorganisation. The former three Service Headquarters and Defence Office have been reorganised into functional branches and offices.
On 1 June 1970 the command and control of the three New Zealand Services was vested in the Chief of Defence Staff who exercises this authority through the three Service Chiefs of Staff.

Diplomatic Representation

Head of New Zealand Defence Liaison Staff, London and Senior Naval Liason Officer:
Commodore M. J. McDowell

Deputy Head of New Zealand Defence Staff, Washington and Naval Attaché:
Captain K. M. Saul

Personnel

(a) January 1973: 2 966 officers and ratings
January 1974: 2 730 officers and ratings
January 1975: 2 690 officers and ratings
(b) Voluntary

Strength of the Fleet

Type	*Active*	*Building*
Frigates	4	—
Corvettes	2	—
Patrol Craft	11	4
Survey Ship	1	—
Research Vessel	1	—
Tenders	2	—

Base

Auckland (Philomel)

Mercantile Marine

Lloyd's Register of Shipping:
113 vessels of 163 399 tons gross

Disposals

Cruiser

Dec 1971 *Black Prince*

Frigate

April 1971 *Blackpool* returned to Royal Navy

Miscellaneous

June 1971 *Endeavour* (ex-USS *Namakagon*) returned to USN for transfer to Taiwan. (now *Lung Chuan*)

FRIGATES

2 "LEANDER" CLASS

Name	*No*	*Builders*	*Laid down*	*Launched*	*Completed*
CANTERBURY	F 421	Yarrow Ltd, Clyde	12 Apr 1969	6 May 1970	22 Oct 197
WAIKATO	F 55	Harland & Wolff Ltd, Belfast	10 Jan 1964	18 Feb 1965	19 Sep 196

Displacement, tons	2 450 standard; 2 860 full load *Waikato*: 2 470 standard; 2990 full load *Canterbury*
Length, feet (*metres*)	360·0 (*109·7*) pp; 372·0 (*113·4*) oa *Waikato*; 370·0 (*112·8*) pp *Canterbury*
Beam, feet (*metres*)	41·0 (*12·5*) *Waikato*; 43·0 (*13·1*) *Canterbury*
Draught, feet (*metres*)	18 (*5·5*)
Aircraft	1 Wasp helicopter armed with homing torpedo
Missile launchers	1 quadruple "Seacat"
Guns	2—4·5 in (*155 mm*) in twin turret; 2—20 mm AA
A/S weapons	1 Limbo 3-barrelled DC mortar *Waikato*; 2—TF Mk 32 Mod 5 torpedo tubes *Canterbury*
Main engines	2 sets d.r. geared turbines; 2 shafts; 30 000 shp
Speed, knots	30 *Waikato*; 28 *Canterbury*
Boilers	2 Babcock & Wilcox
Complement	248 (14 officers, 234 ratings) *Waikato*; 243 (14 officers 229 ratings) *Canterbury*

Waikato, ordered on 14 June 1963. Commissioned on 16 Sep 1966, trials in the United Kingdom until spring 1967, arrived in New Zealand waters in May 1967. *Canterbury* was ordered in Aug 1968, arrived in New Zealand in Aug 1972.

RADAR. Search: Type 965. Tactical 993. Fire Control MRS 3 System and X Band.

Frigates—*continued*

2 "ROTHESAY" CLASS TYPE 12

Name	No.	Builders	Launched	Completed
OTAGO (ex-*Hastings*)	F 111	John I. Thornycroft & Co, Ltd, Woolston, Southampton	11 Dec 1958	22 June 1960
TARANAKI	F 148	J. Samuel White & Co, Ltd, Cowes, Isle of Wight	19 Aug 1959	28 Mar 1961

Displacement, tons	2 144 standard; 2 557 full load
Length, feet (*metres*)	360·0 (*109·7*) pp; 370·0 (*112·8*) oa
Beam, feet (*metres*)	41·0 (*12·5*)
Draught, feet (*metres*)	17·3 (*5·3*)
Missile launchers	1 quadruple "Seacat"
Guns	2—4·5 in (*115 mm*) in twin turret, 2—40 mm (*Taranaki* only)
A/S weapons	2 Limbo 3-barrelled DC mortars
Main engines	2 sets d.r. geared turbines; 2 shafts; 30 000 shp
Speed, knots	30
Boilers	2 Babcock & Wilcox
Complement	240 (13 officers; 227 ratings)

Anti-submarine frigates. *Taranaki* was ordered direct (announced by J. Samuel White & Co on 22 Feb 1957). For *Otago* New Zealand took over the contract (officially stated on 26 Feb 1957) for *Hastings* originally ordered from John I. Thornycroft & Co in Feb 1956 for the Royal Navy. Both vessels are generally similar to those in the Royal Navy, but were modified to suit New Zealand conditions. *Otago* has had enclosed foremast since 1967 refit; *Taranaki* was similarly fitted during 1969.

RADAR. Search Type 993 and Type 277. Fire Control X Band.

TUBES. The original twelve 21 in (*533 mm*) A/S torpedo tubes (8 single and 2 twin) were removed.

TARANAKI — *1971, Royal New Zealand Navy*

CORVETTES

2 "BATHURST" CLASS

Name	No	Builders	Laid down	Launched	Completed
INVERELL	M 233	Mort's Dock, Sydney	7 Dec 1941	2 May 1942	2 May 1943
KIAMA	M 353	Evans Deakins, Brisbane	2 Nov 1942	3 July 1943	26 Jan 1944

Displacement, tons	790 standard; 1 025 full load
Length, feet (*metres*)	162·0 (*49·4*) pp; 186·0 (*56·7*) oa
Beam, feet (*metres*)	31·0 (*9·4*)
Draught, feet (*metres*)	9·5 (*2·9*)
Guns	2—40 mm AA
Main engines	Triple expansion; 2 shafts; 1 800 ihp
Speed, knots	15
Boilers	2 Admiralty 3-drum small tube
Complement	71

Originally four vessels of this class were given to New Zealand by Australia in 1952, *Echuca* and *Stawell* being deleted in 1968.

Kiama was recommissioned on 15 Mar 1966 for training and fishery protection duties, her 4-inch gun being replaced by a 40 mm AA gun, and a deckhouse being built aft.

Inverell was recommissioned on 15 Aug 1965 as a training ship for new entry ratings, replacing the frigate *Rotoiti*. Her sweeping gear was removed and her deckhouse extended further aft. 4-inch gun replaced by 40 mm.

KIAMA — *1972, Royal New Zealand Navy*

SURVEY SHIPS

LACHLAN F 364

Displacement, tons	1 420 standard; 2 220 full load
Length, feet (*metres*)	301·2 (*91·8*)
Beam, feet (*metres*)	36·7 (*11·2*)
Draught, feet (*metres*)	16·0 (*4·9*)
Main engines	Triple expansion; 2 shafts; 5 500 ihp
Speed, knots	20
Boilers	2 Admiralty 3-drum type
Complement	143

Former Australian "River" class frigate. Built by Mort's Dock, Sydney, NSW, launched on 25 Mar 1944, transferred on loan from RAN in 1948 and purchased outright in 1962. Paid off at Auckland Feb 1975 for alongside service. To be replaced at sea by *Monowai*

LACHLAN — *1972, Royal New Zealand Navy*

MONOWAI (ex-*Moana Roa*)

Measurement, tons	2 893 gross; 1 318 net
Dimensions, feet	296·5 oa × 36 × 17
Main engines	2 7-cyl Sulzer diesels; 3 080 hp = 13·5 knots
Oil fuel, tons	300
Complement	120 approx

Previously employed on the Cook Is. Service. Taken over 1975—put out to tender in early 1975 for conversion which will include an up-rating of the engines and fitting of cp propellers and a bow thruster. Due for service late 1976.

Note. 2 HDMLs employed as surveying craft. See next page.

PATROL CRAFT

4 "LAKE" CLASS

HAWEA P 3571
PUKAKI P 3568
ROTOITI P 3569
TAUPO P 3570

Displacement, tons	105 standard; 138 full load
Dimensions, ft (*m*)	107·7 oa × 20 × 11·8 (*32·8 × 6·1 × 3·6*)
Guns	3—·5 in MG (Twin forward, single aft); 2—7·62 mm MGs
Main engines	2 Paxman 12YJCM Diesels; 3 000 hp = 21 knots
Complement	3 officers, 16 ratings

Built by Brooke Marine, Lowestoft, England. The first to complete, *Pukaki*, was finished on 20 July 1974. She and *Rotoiti* were shipped to New Zealand in Nov 1974. All four operational by May 1975.

PUKAKI *1974*

"LAKE" Class *1973, Brooke Marine*

11 HDML TYPE

HAKU P 3565 (ex-*Wakefield* ex-Q 1197)
KAHAWAI P3553 (ex-*Tamaki*)
KOURA P 3564 (ex-*Toroa* ex-Q 1350)
KUPARU P 3563 (ex-*Pegasus* ex-Q 1349)
MAKO P3551 (ex-Q 1183)
MANGA P3567 (ex-Q 1185)
PAEA P3552 (ex-Q 1184)
PARORE P3562 (ex-Q 1190 ex *Olphert*)
TAKAPU P3556 (ex-Q 1188)
TAMURE P3555 (ex-*Ngapona* ex-Q 1193)
TARAPUNGA (P 3566 ex-Q 1387)

Displacement, tons	46 standard; 54 full load
Dimensions, feet	72 × 16 × 5·5
Guns	Armament temporarily removed
Main engines	Diesel; 2 shafts; 320 bhp = 12 knots
Complement	9

Patrol Craft—*continued*

Originally known as Harbour Defence Motor Launches. All built in various yards in the United States and Canada and shipped to New Zealand. *Parore* beached in March 1974 after flooding from burst water pipe.

Takapu and *Tarapunga* are commissioned as surveying MLs. All others have been converted with lattice masts surmounted by a radar serial, *Mako*, *Paea*, *Kahawai* and *Haku* are employed on Fishery Protection duties, others are attached to RNZNVR Divisions. *Maroro* was disposed of in 1972. From 1974 onwards some of these will be phased-out as they are replaced by the "Lake" class.

HAKU *1973, Royal New Zealand Navy*

RESEARCH VESSEL

TUI A 2 (ex-USS *Charles H. Davis*, T-AGOR 5)

Displacement, tons	1 200 standard; 1 380 full load
Dimensions, feet	208·9 × 37·4 × 15·3
Main engines	Diesel-electric; 1 shaft; 10 000 hp = 12 knots
Complement	8 officers, 16 ratings, 15 scientists

Oceanographic research ship built by Christy Corp, Sturgeon Bay, Wis. Laid down on 15 June 1961, launched on 30 June 1962 and completed on 25 Jan 1963. On loan from US since 28 July 1970 for 5 years. Commissioned in the Royal New Zealand Navy on 11 Sep 1970. Bow propeller 175 hp.

TUI *1971, Royal New Zealand Navy*

TENDERS

ARATAKI **MANAWANUI**

Dimensions, feet	Length: 75
Main engines	Diesel

Steel tugs. *Arataki* is used as a dockyard tug and *Manawanui* as a diving tender.

NICARAGUA

Mercantile Marine

Lloyd's Register of Shipping: 11 vessels of 21 845 tons gross

Personnel

1975: 200 officers and men

PATROL CRAFT

1 SEWART TYPE

Displacement, tons	60
Dimensions, ft (*m*)	85 × 18·8 × 5·9 (*25·9 × 5·6 × 1·8*)
Guns	3—50 cal MG
Main engines	3 GM diesels; 3 shafts; 2 000 shp = 26·5 knots
Range, miles	1 000 at 20 knots
Complement	10

Delivered July 1972.

RIO CRUTA

Dimensions, feet	Length: 85
Gun	1—20 mm automatic cannon in bow
Main engines	Diesels; speed = 9 knots maximum
Complement	11

A wooden *guardacosta* of the Marine Section of the Guardia Nacional of Nicaragua.

Another *guardacosta* without name or number is a diesel launch of approx 26 ft with a 20 mm gun, a designed speed of 25 knots and a crew of 5 or 6. Also reported were six wooden patrol boats, four 90 ft and two about 80 ft, and a former patrol boat, 75 ft, wooden, built in 1925, used for training.

NIGERIA

Administration

Chief of the Naval Staff:
Rear-Admiral Nelson Bossman Soroh

Chief of Staff:
Commander Edwin Kentebe

Diplomatic Representation

Naval Attaché (Assistant Defence Adviser) in London:
Lieutenant Commander Emanuel Omotehinwa

Strength of the Fleet

Type	*Active*	*Building*
Frigate	1	—
Corvettes	2	—
Fast Attack Craft—Gun		
Large Patrol Craft	6	2
Coastal Patrol Craft	8	—
Landing Craft	1	—
Survey Ships	2	1
Fishery Protection Ships	2	—
Tug	1	—

Personnel

(a) 1975: 260 officers and 2 600 ratings
(b) Voluntary Service

Mercantile Marine

Lloyd's Register of Shipping:
78 vessels of 121 301 tons gross

FRIGATE

Name	*No.*	*Builders*	*Laid down*	*Launched*	*Completed*
NIGERIA	F 87	Wilton, Fijenoord NV	9 Apr 1964	12 Apr 1965	16 Sep 1965

Displacement, tons	1 724 standard; 2 000 full load
Length, feet (*metres*)	341·2(*104·0*) pp; 360·2(*109·8*) oa
Beam, feet (*metres*)	37·0 (*11·3*)
Draught, feet (*metres*)	11·5 (*3·5*)
Guns	2—4 in (*102 mm*) dp (1 twin); 5—40 mm AA single
A/S weapons	1—triple-barrelled DC mortar
Main engines	4 MAN Diesels; 2 shafts; 16 000 bhp
Speed, knots	26
Range, miles	3 500 at 15 knots
Complement	216

Anti-aircraft and anti-submarine frigate built in the Netherlands by Wilton, Fijenoord. Cost £3 500 000. Commissioned in Sep 1965. Helicopter platform laid on aft. Refitted at Birkenhead, 1973.

NIGERIA — *1970, Nigerian Navy*

CORVETTES

2 Mk 3 VOSPER THORNYCROFT TYPE

DORINA F81 **OTOBO** F 82

Displacement, tons	500 standard; 650 full load
Dimensions, feet	202 oa × 31 × 11·33 (over props)
Guns	2—4 in (1 twin); 2—40 mm Bofors (single) 2—20 mm cannons
Main engines	2 MAN diesels; = 23 knots max
Range, miles	3 500 at 14 knots
Complement	66 (7 officers and 59 ratings)

Ordered on 28 Mar 1968. *Dorina* laid down 26 Jan 1970, launched 16 Sep 1970, completed June 1972. *Otobo* laid down 28 Sep 1970, launched 25 May 1971, completed November 1972. Known as the "Hippopotamus" class as each name means "hippopotamus" in one of the principal Nigerian languages Plessey AWS-1 air search radar; HSA M 20 fire control. Decca TM 626 navigation radar. Plessey M 26 Sonar.

OTOBO — *1972, Wright and Logan*

LIGHT FORCES

2+2 BROOKE-MARINE TYPE (LARGE PATROL CRAFT)

HADEJIA P 168 **MAKURDI** P 167

Displacement, tons	115 standard; 143 full load
Dimensions, feet	107 × 20 × 11·5
Guns	2—40 mm; 2 Rocket flare launchers
Main engines	2 Ruston Paxman YJCM diesels; 3 000 bhp; 2 shafts = 20·5 knots
Complement	21

Built by Brooke Marine, Lowestoft, England. Ordered in 1971. Completed 14 Aug 1974. Two more ordered 30 Oct 1974.

MAKURDI 1974

6 "FORD" CLASS

BENIN (ex-HMS *Hinksford*)
BONNY (ex-HMS *Difford*) P 3111
ENUGU P 3137
KADUNA (ex-HMS *Axford*) P 03
SAPELE (ex-HMS *Dubford*) P 3119
IBADAN II (ex-HMS *Bryansford*)

Displacement, tons	120 standard; 160 full load
Dimensions, feet	110 pp; 117·2 oa × 20 × 5
Guns	1—40 mm Bofors AA; 2—20 mm Oerlikon
A/S weapons	DC rails and DC
Main engines	Davey Paxman diesels; Foden engine on centre shaft; 1 100 bhp = 18 knots max; 15 knots sea speed
Complement	26

Enugu was the first warship built for the Nigerian Navy. Ordered from Camper and Nicholson's Gosport, in 1960. Completed on 14 Dec 1961. Sailed from Portsmouth for Nigeria on 10 Apr 1962. Fitted with Vosper roll damping fins. *Benin, Ibadan* and *Kaduna* were purchased from Great Britain on 1 July 1966 and transferred at Devonport on 9 Sep 1966. *Ibadan* was seized by the Eastern Region prior to its declaration of independence as the Republic of Biafra on 30 May 1967 and renamed *Vigilance* but was sunk at Port Harcourt on 10 Sep 1967 by Nigerian Navy, salved but later scrapped at Lagos. *Dubford* and *Gifford* were purchased from Great Britain during 1967-68 and *Bryansford* in 1968-69.

KADUNA 1970, *Nigerian Navy*

3 Ex-SOVIET "P 6" CLASS (FAST ATTACK CRAFT—GUN)

EKPEN **EKUN** **ELOLE**

Displacement, tons	66 standard; 75 full load
Dimensions, ft (*m*)	84·2 × 20 × 6 (*25·7 × 6·1 × 1·8*)
Guns	4—25 mm (2 twin)
A/S weapons	2 DCT; 2 DC racks
Main engines	4 12 cyl diesels; 4 800 bhp = 43 knots
Complement	25
Range, miles	450 at 30 knots

Soviet built fast patrol boats of the small submarine chaser type purchased from the USSR in 1967. Torpedo tubes removed. POT HEAD search/navigation radar.

EKPEN 1969, *Nigerian Navy*

8 VOSPER-THORNYCROFT TYPE (COASTAL PATROL CRAFT)

Displacement, tons	15
Dimensions, feet	34 oa × 10 × 2·8
Guns	1 machine gun
Main engines	2 Diesels; 290 hp = 19 knots
Complement	6

Ordered for Nigerian Police March 1971, completed 1971-72. GRP hulls.

Light Forces—*continued*

2 FISHERY PATROL CRAFT

YOLA P 166 **ARGUNGU** P 165

Displacement, tons	90
Dimensions, ft (*m*)	95·1 × 18·0 × 5·2 (*29 × 5·5 × 1·6*)
Main engines	2 Paxman Diesels; 2 200 hp; 2 shafts = 20 knots
Complement	25

Completed Aug 1973 by Abeking and Rasmussen, Lemwerder.

ARGUNGU 10/1974, *Wright & Logan*

SURVEY SHIPS

1 NEW CONSTRUCTION

Displacement, tons	800 standard; 1 100 full load
Dimensions, ft (*m*)	189 × 37·5 × 12 (*57·8 × 11·4 × 3·7*)
Main engines	4 Diesels; 2 shafts; 3 000 bhp = 16 knots
Range, miles	4 500 at 12 knots
Complement	38

Ordered from Brooke Marine, Lowestoft in late 1973 for delivery in 1976.

PATHFINDER P 06

Measurement, tons	544 gross
Dimensions, feet	154·2 × 27 × 11
Gun	1—40 mm AA
Main engines	2 triple expansion; 200 ihp = 8 knots

Built by J. Samuel White & Co Ltd, Cowes, Isle of Wight. Launched on 23 Oct 1953 and completed in 1954.

PENELOPE P 11

Measurement, tons	79 gross
Dimensions, feet	79·5 × 7·8 × 4·5
Main engines	2 Gardner diesels; speed 10 knots

Built by Aldous Successors, Brightlingsea in 1958. Used for local survey duties.

TUGS

RIBADU

Displacement, tons	147
Dimensions, ft (*m*)	93·5 × 23·6 × 12·1 (*28·5 × 7·2 × 3·7*)
Main engines	Diesel; 800 shp = 12 knots

Completed 19 May 1973 by Oelkers, Hamburg. Fitted for firefighting and salvage work.

LANDING CRAFT

LOKOJA (ex-*LCT* (4) 1213)

Displacement, tons	350 standard; 586 full load
Dimensions, feet	187·5 × 38·8 × 4·5
Guns	2—20 mm AA
Main engines	2 Paxman diesels; 920 bhp = 10 knots

Purchased from Great Britain in 1959. Allocated the name *Lokoja* in 1961. Underwent a major refit in 1966-67, including complete replating of the bottom.

NORWAY

Ministerial

Minister of Defence:
Mr. Aasland

Administration

Inspector General:
Rear-Admiral O. P. Aakenes

Commander Coastal Fleet:
Commodore Rolf Henningsen

Commander Naval Logistics Services:
Rear-Admiral N. A. Owren

Diplomatic Representation

Assistant Defence Attaché (Naval) in London:
Commander J. C. Bøgh-Tobiassen

Defence Attaché in Washington (for USA and Canada):
Rear-Admiral Magne Braadland, CVO

Defence Attaché in Moscow:
Lt. Colonel A. V. W. Lenheim

Personnel

1973: 8 500 officers and ratings
1974: 8 400 officers and ratings
1975: 8 400 officers and ratings

(All above figures include the Coast Artillery)

Future New Construction

Submarines: A development project is in hand between the Norwegian and FDR Navies for a 750 ton Type 210 to replace Type 205 (FDR) and 207 (Norwegian) in 1980s.
Light Forces: An improved "Snögg" class of 14 boats is planned for early construction. They will be armed with Penguin missiles.

Prefix to Ships' Names

The prefix KNM is used before ships' names.

Naval Bases

Haakonsvern, Ramsund, Orlogsstasjon, Ramfjordnes

Strength of the Fleet

Type	*Active*
Frigates	5
Corvettes	2
Submarines—Coastal	15
Fast Attack Craft—Missile	26
Fast Attack Craft—Torpedo	20
Minelayers	5
Minesweeper—Coastal	10
LCTs	7
LCU	1
Depot Ship	1
Royal Yacht	1
Fishery Protection Ships (not under naval command)	6

FRIGATES

5 "OSLO" CLASS

Displacement, tons	1 450 standard; 1,745 full load
Length, feet (*metres*)	308 (*93·9*) pp; 317 (*96·6*) oa
Beam, feet (*metres*)	36·7 (*11·2*)
Draught, feet (*metres*)	17·4 (*5·3*)
Missile launchers	"Penguin", Nato Seasparrow in some
Guns	4—3 in (*76 mm*) 2 twin mounts
A/S weapons	"Terne" system
Torpedo launchers	2
Boilers	2 Babcock & Wilcox
Main engines	1 set De Laval Ljungstron double reduction geared turbines; 1 shaft; 20 000 shp
Speed, knots	25
Complement	151 (11 officers, 140 ratings)

Name	*No.*	*Builders*	*Laid down*	*Launched*	*Completed*
BERGEN	F 301	Marinens Hovedverft, Horten	1964	23 Aug 1965	15 June 1967
NARVIK	F 304	Marinens Hovedverft, Horten	1964	8 Jan 1965	30 Nov 1966
OSLO	F 300	Marinens Hovedverft, Horten	1963	17 Jan 1964	29 Jan 1966
STAVANGER	F 303	Marinens Hovedverft, Horten	1965	4 Feb 1966	1 Dec 1967
TRONDHEIM	F 302	Marinens Hovedverft, Horten	1963	4 Sep 1964	2 June 1966

"OSLO" Class

BERGEN *1971, Royal Norwegian Navy*

Built under the five-year naval construction programme approved by the Norwegian "Storting" (Parliament) late in 1960. Although all the ships of this class were constructed in the Norwegian Naval Dockyard, half the cost was borne by Norway and the other half by the United States. The design of these ships is based on that of the "Dealey" class destroyer escorts in the United States Navy, but modified to suit Norwegian requirements.

ENGINEERING The main turbines and auxiliary machinery were all built by De Laval Ljungstrom, Sweden at the company's works in Stockholm-Nacka.

RADAR. Search: DRBV 22. Tactical and Fire Control: HSA M 24 system.

MISSILES. All fitted with Terne and Penguin. Seasparrow being retrofitted—all to be completed in 1976.

NARVIK *6/1974, J. L. M. van der Burg*

CORVETTES

2 "SLEIPNER" CLASS

ÆGER F 311 **SLEIPNER** F 310

Displacement, tons	600 standard; 780 full load
Dimensions, feet	227·8 oa × 26·2
Guns	1—3 in; 1—40 mm
A/S weapons	"Terne" ASW system
Main engines	4 Maybach diesels; 2 shafts; 9 000 bhp = over 20 knots
Complement	62

Under the five-year programme only two instead of the originally planned five new patrol vessels were built. *Sleipner* was launched on 9 Nov 1963 at the Nylands Verksted shipyard, Oslo, and completed on 29 Apr 1956. *Aeger*, originally to have been named *Balder*, was launched on 24 Sep 1965, and completed on 31 Mar 1967. Temporarily employed as training ships until new construction is available.

SLEIPNER *1972, Royal Norwegian Navy*

SUBMARINES

15 TYPE 207

Name	*No.*	*Launched*	*Completed*
KAURA	S 315	16 Oct 1964	5 Feb 1965
KINN	S 316	30 Nov 1963	8 Apr 1964
KOBBEN	S 318	25 Apr 1964	17 Aug 1964
KUNNA	S 319	16 July 1964	1 Oct 1964
KYA	S 317	20 Feb 1964	15 June 1964
SKLINNA	S 305	21 Jan 1966	27 May 1966
SKOLPEN	S 306	24 Mar 1966	17 Aug 1966
STADT	S 307	10 June 1966	15 Nov 1966
STORD	S 308	2 Sep 1966	9 Feb 1967
SVENNER	S 309	27 Jan 1967	1 July 1967
ULA	S 300	19 Dec 1964	7 May 1965
UTHAUG	S 304	8 Oct 1965	16 Feb 1966
UTSIRA	S 301	11 Mar 1965	1 July 1965
UTSTEIN	S 302	19 May 1965	9 Sep 1965
UTVAER	S 303	30 June 1965	1 Dec 1965

Displacement, tons	370 standard; 435 submerged
Length, feet (*metres*)	149 (*45·2*)
Beam, feet (*metres*)	15 (*4·6*)
Draught, feet (*metres*)	14 (*4·3*)
Tubes	8—21 in (*533 mm*) bow
Main machinery	2 MB 820 Maybach-Mercedes-Benz diesels; 1 200 bhp; electric drive; 1 200 hp; 1 shaft
Speed, knots	10 surface; 17 dived
Complement	18 (5 officers, 13 men)

GENERAL
It was announced in July 1959 that the USA and Norway would share equally the cost of these submarines. All were built by Rheinstahl-Nordseewerke in Emden, West Germany. These are a development of IKL Type 205 (West German U4-U8) with increased diving depth. *Svenner* has a second periscope for COs training operations.

NAMES. *Kobben* was the name of the first submarine in the Royal Norwegian Navy. Commissioned on 28 Nov 1909.

KINN *1970, Royal Norwegian Navy*

SVENNER (with second periscope) *1972, Royal Norwegian Navy*

LIGHT FORCES

(N.B Armament varies in all classes as Penguin SSM is installed)

6 "SNÖGG" CLASS (FAST ATTACK CRAFT—MISSILE)

KJAPP P 985 **RAPP** P 981 **SNAR** P 982
KVIKK P 984 **RASK** P 983 **SNOGG** (ex-Lyr) P 980

Displacement, tons	100 standard; 125 full load
Dimensions, feet	120·0 × 20·5 × 5·0
Missile launchers	4 "Penguin" SSM; range 20 km plus
Gun	1—40 mm
Tubes	4—21 in
Main engines	2 Maybach diesels; 2 shafts; 7 200 bhp = 32 knots
Complement	18

These steel hulled torpedo boats of a new design ordered from Batservice Werft, A/S, Mandal, Norway, started coming into service in 1970. Hulls are similar to those of the "Storm" class gunboats. Armed with missiles in addition to gun and tubes.

RAPP *1973, Royal Norwegian Navy*

Light Forces—*continued*

20 "STORM" CLASS (FAST ATTACK CRAFT—MISSILE)

ARG	P 968	**DJERV**	P 966	**ODD**	P 975	**STEIL**	P 969
BLINK	P 961	**GLIMT**	P 962	**PIL**	P 976	**STORM**	P 960
BRANN	P 970	**GNIST**	P 979	**ROKK**	P 978	**TRAUST**	P 973
BRASK	P 977	**HVASS**	P 972	**SKJOLD**	P 963	**TROSS**	P 971
BROTT	P 974	**KJEKK**	P 965	**SKUDD**	P 967	**TRYGG**	P 964

Displacement, tons	100 standard; 125 full load
Dimensions, feet	120·0 × 20·5 × 5·0
Missile launchers	6 "Penguin" SSM; range 20 km plus
Guns	1—3 in; 1—40 mm
A/S weapons	DC throwers
Main engines	2 Maybach diesels; 2 shafts; 7 200 bhp = 32 knots

The first of 20 (instead of the 23 originally planned) gunboats of a new design built under the five-year programme was *Storm*, launched on 8 Feb 1963, and completed on 31 May 1963, but this prototype was eventually scrapped and replaced by a new series construction boat as the last of the class. The first of the production boats was *Blink*, launched on 28 June 1965 and completed on 18 Dec 1965. The first was armed with "Penguin" surface-to-surface guided missile launchers in 1970, in addition to originally designed armament.

TRAUST with 6 Penguins fitted *1971, A/S Kongsberg Vapenfabrikk*

20 "TJELD" CLASS (FAST ATTACK CRAFT—TORPEDO)

DELFIN	P 386	**HAI**	P 381	**LAKS**	P 384	**SKARV**	P 344
ERLE	P 390	**HAUK**	P 349	**LOM**	P 347	**SKREI**	P 380
FALK	P 350	**HVAL**	P 383	**LYR**	P 387	**STEGG**	P 348
GEIR	P 389	**JO**	P 346	**RAVN**	P 357	**TEIST**	P 345
GRIBB	P 388	**KNURR**	P 385	**SEL**	P 382	**TJELD**	P 343

Displacement, tons	70 standard; 82 full load
Dimensions, feet	75·5 pp; 80·3 oa × 24·5 × 6·8 max
Guns	1—40 mm AA; 1—20 mm AA
Tubes	4—21 in
Main engines	2 Napier Deltic Turboblown diesels; 2 shafts; 6 200 bhp = 45 knots
Range, miles	450 at 40 knots; 600 at 25 knots
Complement	18

SKARV *1973, Royal Norwegian Navy*

MINE WARFARE FORCES

Note. It is reported that an MSI of 130 tons and glass reinforced plastic hull has been ordered from Sweden.

BORGEN N 51 (CONTROLLED MINELAYER)

Displacement, tons	282 standard
Dimensions, feet	94·5 pp; 102·5 oa × 26·2 × 11
Main engines	2 GM diesels; 2 Voith-Schneider propellers; 330 bhp=9 knots

BORGEN *1972, Royal Norwegian Navy*

Minewarfare Forces—*continued*

4 ex-US "AUK" CLASS (MINELAYERS—COASTAL)

BRAGE (ex-USS *Triumph*, MMC 3)	N 49
GOR (ex-USS *Strive*, MMC 1)	N 48
TYR (ex-USS *Sustain*, MMC 2)	N 47
ULLER (ex-USS *Seer*, MMC 5)	N 50

Displacement, tons	890 standard; 1 250 full load
Dimensions, feet	215 wl; 221·2 oa × 32·2 × 16
Guns	1—3 in, 50 cal; 4—20 mm AA (2 twin) (*Brage, Gor, Tyr*) 1—3 in, 50 cal; 1—40 mm AA (*Uller*)
A/S weapons	2 Hedgehogs; 3 DCT (*Brage, Gor, Tyr*) "Terne" ASW system; 1 DCT (*Uller*)
Mines	Laying capability
Main engines	GM diesels; electric drive; 2 shafts; 2 070 bhp = 16 knots
Complement	83

Former US Coastal Minelayers (MMC) converted from "Auk" class MSOs. *Gor, Tyr* and *Uller* were built by American Shipbuilding Co in 1942 and *Brage* by Associated Shipbuilders in 1944. *Gor* and *Tyr* converted 1959 and *Brage* 1960 into coastal minelayers at Charleston Naval Shipyard, but *Uller* was converted in Norway. All transferred 1959-1960.

BRAGE *1972, Royal Norwegian Navy*

BRAGE, GOR, TYR, ULLER

10 "SAUDA" CLASS (MINESWEEPERS—COASTAL)

ALTA (ex-*Arlon* M 915, ex-*MSC* 104)	M 314
GLOMMA (ex-*Bastogne* M 916, ex-*MSC* 151)	M 317
KVINA	M 332
OGNA	M 315
SAUDA (ex-USS *AMS* 102)	M 311
SIRA (ex-USS *MSC* 132)	M 312
TANA (ex-*Roeselaere* M 914, ex-*MSC* 103)	M 313
TISTA	M 331
UTLA	M 334
VOSSO	M 316

Displacement, tons	333 standard; 384 full load
Dimensions, feet	144 × 28 × 8·5 max
Guns	2—20 mm AA
Main engines	GM diesels; 880 bhp = 13·5 knots
Oil fuel, tons	25
Complement	38

Sauda, built by Hodgeson Bros, Gowdy & Stevens, East Boothbay, Maine, was completed on 25 Aug 1953 and *Sira* on 28 Nov 1955. Hull of wooden construction. Five coastal minesweepers were built in Norway with US engines. Completed on 5 Mar 1955 (*Ogna*), 16 Mar 1955 (*Vosso*), 27 Apr 1955 (*Tista*), 12 July 1955 (*Kvina*) and 15 Nov 1955 (*Utla*). *Kvina, Ogna* and *Utla* were built by Båtservice Ltd, Mandal, *Tista* by Forende Batbyggeriex, Risör, and *Vosso* by Skaaluren Skibsbyggeri, Rosendal. *Alta, Glomma* and *Tana* were taken over from the Royal Belgian Navy in May, Sep and Mar 1966, respectively, having been exchanged for two Norwegian ocean minesweepers of the US MSO type, *Lagen* (ex-*MSO* 498) and *Nansen* (ex-*MSO* 499).

TISTA *1973, Royal Norwegian Navy*

AMPHIBIOUS FORCES

2 "KVALSUND" CLASS (LCT)

KVALSUND A 31 **RAFTSUND** A 32

5 "REINØYSUND" CLASS (LCT)

BORGSUND A 37 **REINØYSUND** A 33 **ROTSUND** A 36
MAURSUND A 35 **SØRØYSUND** A 34

Displacement, tons	560
Dimensions, feet	167·3 × 33·5 × 5·9
Guns	2—20 mm
Speed, knots	11

Built by Mjellem and Karlsen, Bergen. First pair delivered in 1970 remainder in following two years.

REINØYSUND *1973, Royal Norwegian Navy*

1 Ex-US LCU

TJELDSUND (ex-US LCU 1478) A 30

Displacement, tons	180 light; 360 full load
Dimensions, feet	119 oa × 34 × 6
Guns	2—20 mm
Main engines	3 Diesels; 3 shafts; 6 758 bhp = 10 knots
Complement	14

Transferred from US on completion 1952.

FISHERY PROTECTION SHIPS

O/S NORNEN

Measurement, tons	930 gross
Dimensions feet	201·8 × 32·8 × 15·8
Gun	1—3 in (*76 mm*)
Main engines	4 diesels; 3 500 bhp = 17 knots
Complement	32

Built by Mjellem & Karlsen, Bergen, Norway. Launched and completed in 1963.

NORNEN *1970, Royal Norwegian Navy*

O/S FARM **O/S HEIMDAL**

Measurement, tons	600 gross
Dimensions, feet	177 × 26·2 × 16·5
Gun	1—3 in (*76 mm*)
Main engines	2 diesels; 2 700 bhp = 16 knots
Complement	29

Farm was built by Ankerlokken Verft and *Heimdal* by Bolsones Verft, Molde, in 1962.

Fishery Protection Ships—*continued*

O/S ANDENES **O/S NORDKAPP** **O/S SENJA**

Measurement, tons	500 gross
Dimensions, feet	186 × 31 × 16
Gun	1—3 in (*76 mm*)
Main engines	MAN diesel; 2 300 bhp = 16 knots
Complement	29

All three built in the Netherlands in 1957 as whalers. Acquired by Norway in 1965 and converted into Fishery Protection Ships.

NORDKAPP *1974, Royal Norwegian Navy, Foto FRO*

DEPOT SHIPS

1 Ex-CANADIAN FRIGATE TYPE

VALKYRIEN (ex-*Garm*, ex-*Toronto*) A 535 (ex-F 315)

Displacement, tons	1 570 standard; 2 240 full load
Dimensions, feet	301·3 × 36·5 × 16
Guns	2—4 in, 2—40 mm
Main engines	Triple expansion; 2 shafts; 5 500 ihp = 19 knots
Complement	104

Former Canadian modernised "River" class frigate. Built by Davie Shipbuilding Co, Lauzon, Port Quebec, Canada, completed 6 May 1944. Loaned to Norway on 10 Mar 1956 and finally converted as depot ship for Light Forces.

VALKYRIEN *1972, Royal Norwegian Navy*

DRAUG **SARPEN**

Small depot ships for frogmen and divers. Completed in 1972 by Nielsen of Harstad.

ROYAL YACHT

NORGE (ex-*Philante*) A 533

Measurement, tons	1 686 (*Thames yacht measurement*)
Dimensions, feet	250·2 pp; 263 oa × 28 × 15·2
Main engines	8-cyl diesels; 2 shafts; 3 000 bhp = 17 knots

Built by Camper & Nicholson's Ltd, Gosport, England to the order of the late Mr T. O. M. Sopwith as escort and store vessel for the yachts *Endeavour I* and *Endeavour II*. Launched on 17 Feb 1937. Served in the British Navy as an anti-submarine escort during the Second World War, after which she was purchased by the Norwegian people for King Haakon at a cost of nearly £250,000 and reconditioned as a Royal Yacht at Southampton. Can accommodate about 50 people in addition to crew.

NORGE *1971, Royal Norwegian Navy*

H. U. SVERDRUP

Displacement, tons	400
Measurement, tons	295 gross
Dimensions, feet	127·7 oa; 111·5 pp × 25 × 13
Main engines	Wichmann diesel; 600 bhp = 11·5 knots
Oil fuel, tons	65
Range, miles	5 000 at 10 knots cruising speed
Complement	10 crew; 9 scientists

Built by Orens Mekaniske Verkstad, Trondheim in 1960. Operates for Norwegian Defence Research Establishment.

OMAN, SULTANATE OF

Personnel

(a) 1975: 450 officers and men
(b) Voluntary service

Mercantile Marine

5 vessels of 3 149 tons gross

CORVETTES

AL SAID

Displacement, tons	900
Dimensions, feet	203·4 × 35·1 × 9·8
Guns	1—40 mm
Main engines	2 Paxman Ventura 12 cyl diesels; 2 shafts; 2 470 bhp
Complement	32 + 7 staff + 32 troops

Built by Brooke Marine, Lowestoft. Launched 7 Apr 1970 as a yacht for the Sultan of Muscat and Oman, she was converted for a dual purpose role with a gun on her forecastle as flagship of the navy. Completed in 1971.

AL SAID *Brooke Marine, 1971*

2 ex-NETHERLAND "WILDERVANK" CLASS

AL NASIRI (ex-*Aalsmeer* M 811) **AL SALIHI** (ex-*Axel* M 808)

Dislacement, tons	373 standard; 417 full load
Dimensions, feet	149·8 oa × 28 × 6·5
Guns	3—40 mm
Main engines	2 Werkspoor diesels; 2 500 bhp
Speed, knots	16
Range, miles	2 500 at 10 knots
Complement	38

Acquired in March 1974 for conversion for patrol function.

AL NASIRI (as *Aalsmeer*) *Royal Netherlands Navy*

LIGHT FORCES

3 BROOKE MARINE 37·5 metre TYPE

AL BUSHRA B2 **AL MANSUR** B1 **AL NEJAH** B3

Displacement, tons	135 standard; 153 full load
Dimensions, feet	123 oa × 22·5 × 5·5
Guns	2—40 mm
Main engines	2 Paxman Ventura diesels; 4 800 bhp = 29 knots
Range, miles	3 300 at 15 knots
Complement	25

Built by Brooke Marine, Lowestoft, England. Ordered 5 Jan 1971. *Al Bushra* completed 22 Jan 1973, *Al Mansur* 26 Mar 1973, *Al Nejah* 13 May 1973.
4 more (B 4-7) ordered from Brooke Marine 26 Apr 1974 tor completion in 1976.

AL BUSHRA *1974, Omani Dept. of Defence*

Light Forces—*continued*

1 FAIREY MARINE "SPEAR" (COASTAL PATROL CRAFT)

Dimensions, ft (*m*)	29·8 × 9·2 × 2·6 (*9·1 × 2·8 × ·8*)
Main engines	Twin 180 hp diesels = 30 knots
Range, miles	200 at 26 knots

"SPEAR" class *1975, Fairey Marine*

2 CHEVERTON "LOADMASTERS"

Measurement, tons	60 deadweight
Dimensions, feet	60 oa × 20 × 3·5
Main engines	2 × 120 hp = 8·5 knots

Delivered Jan 1975.

LOADMASTER *1975, Cheverton Workboats*

AUXILIARIES

AL SULTANA (LOGISTIC SUPPORT SHIP)

Measurement, tons	1 380 dw
Dimensions, feet	214·3; oa × 35 × 13·5
Main engines	Mirrlees Blackstore diesel; 1 150 bhp = 11 knots

Built by Conoship, Gröningen. Delivered Apr 1975.

DHOFAR (TRAINING SHIP)

Displacement, tons	1 500 full load
Dimensions, feet	219 oa × 34 × 13
Main engines	MAK diesel = 1 500 bhp = 10·5 knots
Complement	22

Ex-Logistic ship now used for new entry training.

DHOFAR *1974, Omani Dept. of Defence*

PAKISTAN

Administration

Chief of the Naval Staff:
Vice-Admiral Hasan Hafeez Ahmad TQA

Vice Chief of the Naval Staff:
Rear-Admiral Leslie Norman Mungavin SK

Commander Pakistan Fleet:
Commodore M. Shariff

Diplomatic Representation

Naval Attaché in London:
Captain T. K. Khan

Naval Attaché in Paris:
Captain I. F. Quadir

Naval Attaché in Teheran:
Captain S. D. Choudari

Naval Attaché in Washington:
Captain Syed Quamar Raza, SJ

Strength of the Fleet

Type	*Active*
Cruiser	1
Destroyers	4
Frigates	2
Submarines—Patrol	3

Type	*Active*
Submarines—40 tons	6
Fast Attack Craft—Gun	12
Fast Attack Craft—Torpedo	4
Large Patrol Craft	1
Minesweepers—Coastal	7
Tankers	2
Tugs—Ocean	2
Tugs—Harbour	2
Water-boat	1

Personnel

(a) 1975: 11 000 (950 officers; 10 050 ratings)
(b) Two years selective National Service

Mercantile Marine

Lloyd's Register of Shipping:
88 vessels of 494 065 tons gross

Naval Base and Dockyard

Karachi

Prefix to Ships' Names

PNS

CRUISER (*Cadet Training Ship*)

Name	*No.*	*Builders and Engineers*	*Laid down*	*Launched*	*Completed*
BABUR (ex-HMS *Diadem*)	84	R. & W. Hawthorn Leslie & Co Ltd, Hebburn-on-Tyne	15 Nov 1939	26 Aug 1942	6 Jan 1944

Displacement, tons	5 900 standard; 7 560 full load
Length, feet (*metres*)	485 (*147·9*) pp; 512 (*156·1*) oa
Beam, feet (metres)	52·0 (*15·8*)
Draught, feet (*metres*)	18·5 (*5·6*)
Guns, surface	8—5·25 in (*133 mm*) 4 twin
Guns, AA	14—40 mm
Torpedo tubes	6—21 in (*533 mm*) 2 triple
Armour	3 in (*76 mm*) sides; 2 in (*51 mm*) decks and turrets
Range, miles	4 000 at 18 knots
Boilers	4 Admiralty 3-drum
Main engines	Parsons s.r. geared turbines; 4 shafts; 62 000 shp
Speed, knots	32
Oil fuel, tons	1 100
Complement	588

Former British Improved "Dido" class anti-aircraft light cruiser. Purchased on 29 Feb 1956. Refitted at HM Dockyard, Portsmouth and there transferred to Pakistan and renamed *Babur* on 5 July, 1957. Adapted as cadet training ship in 1961.

RADAR. Search: Type 960, Type 293. Fire Control: Early British design.

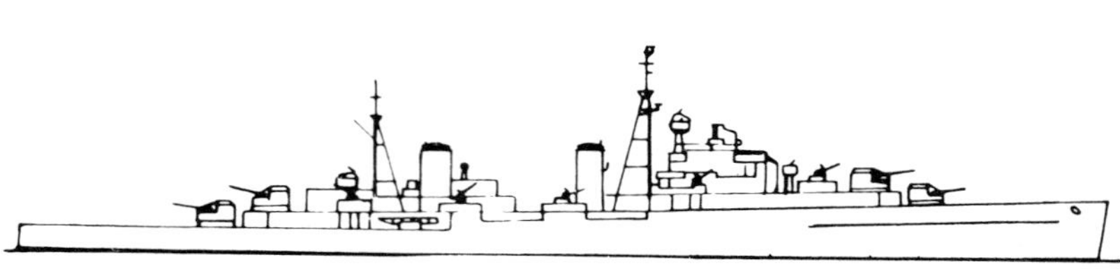

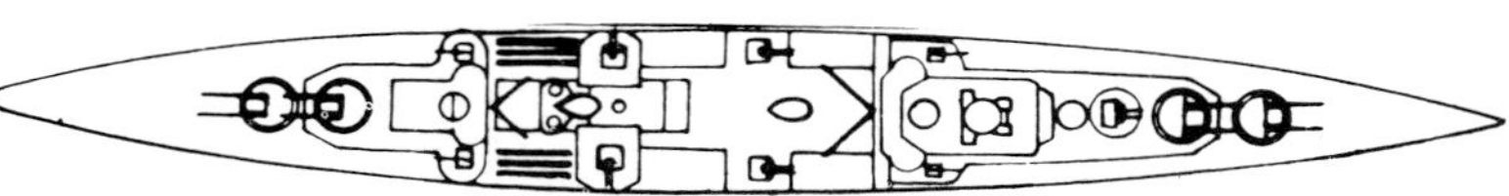

DRAWING. Starboard elevation and plan. Scale: 125 feet = 1 inch (1 : 1 500).

BABUR

1966 *Pakistan Navy*

DESTROYERS

1 Ex-BRITISH "BATTLE" CLASS

Name	No.	Builders	Laid down	Launched	Completed
BADR (ex-HMS *Gabbard*)	161 (ex-D 47)	Swan, Hunter & Wigham Richardson Ltd, Wallsend-on-Tyne	2 Feb 1944	16 Mar 1945	10 Dec 1946

Displacement, tons	2 325 standard; 3 361 full load
Length, feet (*metres*)	355·0(*108·2*) pp; 379·0(*115·5*) oa
Beam, feet (*metres*)	40·2 (*12·3*)
Draught, feet (*metres*)	17·0 (*5·2*)
Guns	4—4·5 in (*115 mm*); 10—40 mm AA
A/S weapons	"Squid" triple DC mortar
Torpedo tubes	8—21 in (*533 mm*) quadrupled
Main engines	Parsons geared turbines; 2 shafts; 50 000 shp
Speed, knots	35·75
Boilers	2 Admiralty 3-drum type
Range, miles	6 000 at 20 knots
Oil fuel, tons	680
Complement	270

Purchased from Britain on 29 Feb 1956. Modernised with US funds under MDAP. Refitted at Palmers Hebburn, Yarrow, transferred to Pakistan on 24 Jan 1957 and sailed from Portsmouth for Karachi on 17 Feb 1957.

LOSS
Sister ship *Khaibar* (ex-HMS *Cadiz*) No. 163 (ex-D 79) was sunk during the Indo-Pakistan War in Dec 1971.

RADAR. Search: Type 277, Type 293. Fire Control: X Band.

BADR — *1972, Pakistan Navy*

BADR,

1 Ex-BRITISH "CH" CLASS

SHAH JAHAN (ex-HMS *Charity*) 164 (ex-D 29)

Displacement, tons	1 710 standard; 2 545 full load
Length, feet (*metres*)	350·0(*106·7*) wl; 362·7(*110·5*) oa
Beam, feet (*metres*)	35·7 (*10·9*)
Draught, feet (*metres*)	17·0 (*5·2*)
Guns	3—4·5 in (*115 mm*); 6—40 mm AA
A/S weapons	2 "Squid" triple DC mortars
Torpedo tubes	4—21 in (*533 mm*) quadrupled
Main engines	Parsons geared turbines; 2 shafts; 40 000 shp
Speed, knots	36·75 designed; 31·25 sea
Boilers	2 Admiralty 3-drum type
Range, miles	5 600 at 20 knots
Complement	200

Built by John I. Thornycroft, Co Ltd, Woolston, laid down on 9 July 1943, launched on 30 Nov 1944 and completed on 19 Nov 1945. Purchased by USA and handed over to Pakistan on 16 Dec 1958, under MDAP, at yard of J. Samuel White & Co Ltd, Cowes, who refitted her.

RADAR. Search: Type 293. Fire Control: X Band.

SHAH JAHAN

Sister ship *Taimur* (ex-HMS *Chivalrous*) was returned to the Royal Navy and scrapped in 1960-61.

2 Ex-BRITISH "CR" CLASS

Name	No.	Builders	Laid down	Launched	Completed
ALAMGIR (ex-HMS *Creole*)	160 (ex-D 82)	J. Samuel White & Co Ltd, Cowes	3 Aug 1944	22 Nov 1945	14 Oct 1946
JAHANGIR (ex-HMS *Crispin*, ex-*Craccher*)	162 (ex-D 168)	J. Samuel White & Co Ltd, Cowes	1 Feb 1944	23 June 1945	10 July 1946

Displacement, tons	1 730 standard; 2 560 full load
Length, feet (*metres*)	350·0(*106·7*) wl; 362·8(*110·5*) oa
Beam, feet (*metres*)	35·7 (*10·9*)
Draught, feet (*metres*)	17·0 (*5·2*)
Guns	3—4·5 in (*115 mm*); 6—40 mm AA
A/S weapons	2 "Squid" triple DC mortars
Torpedo tubes	4—21 in (*533 mm*) quadrupled
Main engines	Parsons geared turbines; 2 shafts 40 000 shp
Speed, knots	36·75
Boilers	2 Admiralty 3-drum type
Range, miles	5 600 at 20 knots
Oil fuel, tons	580
Complement	200

Purchased by Pakistan in Feb 1956. Refitted and modernised in Great Britain by John I. Thornycroft & Co Ltd, Woolston, Southampton, in 1957-58 with US funds under MDAP. Turned over to the Pakistan Navy at Southampton in 1958 (*Crispin* on 18 Mar and *Creole* 20 June) and renamed.

GUNNERY. "B" gun replaced in 1956-57 and "X" gun was replaced by two "Squids".

RADAR. Search: Type 293. Fire Control: X Band.

ALAMGIR — *1973, Pakistan Navy*

JAHANGIR — *1972, Pakistan Navy*

ALAMGIR, JAHANGIR

FRIGATES

Note. Pakistan has now acquired the two "Whitby" class frigates *Tenby* and *Scarborough* from the Royal Navy. These are currently awaiting refit to take place when certain financial problems are resolved.

2 Ex-BRITISH TYPE 16

Name	*No.*	*Builders*	*Laid down*	*Launched*	*Completed*
TIPPU SULTAN (ex-HMS *Onslow*, ex-*Pakenham*)	260 (ex-F 249)	John Brown & Co Ltd, Clydebank	1 July 1940	31 Mar 1941	8 Oct 1941
TUGHRIL (ex-HMS *Onslaught*, ex-*Pathfinder*)	261 (ex-F 204)	Fairfield SB & Eng Co Ltd, Glasgow	14 Jan 1941	9 Oct 1941	19 June 1942

Displacement, tons	1 800 standard; 2 300 full load
Length, feet (*metres*)	328·7(*100·2*) pp; 345·0(*10·72*) oa
Beam, feet (*metres*)	35·0 (*10·7*)
Draught, feet (*metres*)	15·7 (*4·8*)
Guns	2—4 in (*102 mm*); 5—40 mm AA
A/S weapons	2 "Squid" triple DC mortars
Torpedo tubes	4—21 in (*533 mm*)
Main engines	Parsons geared turbines; 2 shafts; 40 000 shp
Speed, knots	34
Boilers	2 Admiralty 3-drum type
Complement	170

TUGHRIL — *1972, Pakistan Navy*

Originally three "O" class destroyers were acquired from Great Britain, *Tippu Sultan* being handed over on 30 Sep 1949; *Tariq* on 3 Nov 1949; and *Tughril* on 6 Mar 1951. An agreement was signed in London between Great Britain and USA for refit and conversion in the United Kingdom of *Tippu Sultan* and *Tughril* (announced 29 Apr 1957) with US funds. All three ships were scheduled for conversion into fast anti-submarine frigates. *Tippu Sultan* and *Tughril* were converted at Liverpool by Grayson Rolls & Clover Docks Ltd, Birkenhead, and C. & H. Crighton Ltd, respectively. *Tariq* was not converted. She was handed back to Great Britain at Portsmouth on 10 July 1959 and broken up at Sunderland, arriving there in Oct 1959.

Tughril employed on training duties.

RADAR. Equipped with Type 293 search radar.

TIPPU SULTAN, TUGHRIL

SUBMARINES

3 "HANGOR" CLASS (FRENCH "DAPHNE" CLASS)

Name	*Pennant No.*	*Builders*	*Laid Down*	*Launched*	*Completed*
HANGOR	S 131	Arsenal de Brest	1 Dec 1967	28 June 1969	12 Jan 1970
MANGRO	S 133	C. N. Ciotal (Le Trait)	8 July 1968	7 Feb 1970	8 Aug 1970
SHUSHUK	S 132	C. N. Ciotal (Le Trait)	1 Dec 1967	30 July 1969	12 Jan 1970

Displacement, tons	700 standard; 869 surface; 1 043 submerged
Length, feet (*metres*)	189·6 (*57·8*)
Beam, feet (*metres*)	22·3 (*6·8*)
Draught, feet (*metres*)	15·1 (*4·6*)
Torpedo tubes	12—21 in (*550 mm*) 8 bow, 4 stern (external)
Main engines	Diesel electric (SEMT-Pielstick); 1 300 bhp surface; electric motors 1 600 hp submerged; 2 shafts
Speed, knots	13 surface; 15·5 submerged
Complement	45

SHUSHUK — *1972*

These are the first submarines built for the Pakistan Navy. They are basically of the French "Daphne" class design, but slightly modified internally to suit Pakistan requirements and naval conditions. They are broadly similar to the submarines built in France for Portugal and South Africa and the submarines being constructed to the "Daphne" design in Spain.

It is reported that a fourth boat of this class was ordered in late 1973.

MANGRO — *1971, Admiral M. J. Adam*

6 "SX 404" CLASS

Displacement, tons	40
Dimensions, ft (*m*)	52·4 × 6·6 × — (*16 × 2 × —*)
Speed, knots	11 surfaced; 6·5 dived
Range, miles	1 200 surfaced; 60 dived
Complement	4

Purchased 1972-73 from Cosmos, Livorno. With a diving depth of 330 ft and capable of carrying 12 passengers these submarines are valuable craft for clandestine raids, reconnaissance and a multitude of shallow-water tasks. Only Colombia has submarines of a similar size.

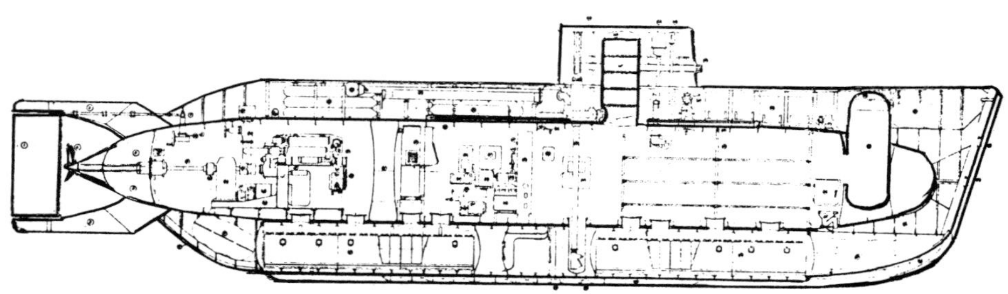
Drawing of "SX 404" Class — *1973*

LIGHT FORCES

12 Ex-Chinese "SHANGHAI II" CLASS

(FAST ATTACK CRAFT—GUN)

BAHAWAL PUR 140
BANNU 154
GILGET
KALAT 156
LAKARNA 157
LAHORE 142
MULTAN
PISHIN
QUETTA
SAHIWAL
SEHWON
SUKKUR 147

Displacement, tons	120 full load
Dimensions, feet	130 × 18 × 5·6
Guns	4—37 mm; 4—25 mm
Main engines	4 Diesels; 5 000 bhp = 30 knots
Complement	25

Reportedly transferred early 1972 (first eight) and remaining four in 1974. Three are reportedly armed with Styx type missiles.

PAKISTAN "SHANGHAI" Class

Light Forces—*continued*

4 Ex-Chinese "HU CHWAN" CLASS

(FAST ATTACK CRAFT—TORPEDO)

HDF 01, 02, 03, 04

Displacement, tons	45
Dimensions, ft (*m*)	70 × 16·5 × 3·1 (*21·4 × 5·0 × 0·9*)
Torpedo tubes	2—21 inch
Guns	4—12·7 mm (twins)
Main engines	2—12 cyl diesels; 2 shafts; 2 200 hp = 55 knots (calm)

Hydrofoil craft transferred by China in 1973.

PAKISTAN "HU CHWAN" Class

1 "TOWN" CLASS (LARGE PATROL CRAFT)

RAJSHAHI P 140

Displacement, tons	115 standard; 143 full load
Dimensions, feet	100 wl; 107 oa × 20 × 11
Guns	2—40 mm; 70 cal Bofors AA
Main engines	2 Maybach/Mercedes MD 655/18 diesels; 3 400 bhp (tropical) = 24 knots
Complement	19

The last survivor of a class of four built by Brooke Marine in 1965. Steel hull and aluminium superstructure.

RAJSHAHI *1973, Pakistan Navy*

MINE WARFARE FORCES

7 MSC TYPE (MINESWEEPERS—COASTAL)

MAHMOOD (ex-*MSC* 267) M 160
MOMIN (ex-*MSC* 293) M 161
MOSHAL (ex-*MSC* 294) M 167
MURABAK (ex-*MSC* 262) M 162
MUJAHID (ex-*MSC* 261) M 164
MUKHTAR (ex-*MSC* 274) M 165
MUNSIF (ex-*MSC* 273) M 166

Displacement tons	335 light; 375 full load
Dimensions, feet	138 pp; 144 oa × 27 × 8·5
Guns	2—20 mm
Main engines	GM diesels; 2 shafts; 880 bhp = 14 knots
Complement	39

Transferred to Pakistan by the US under MAP. *Mukhtar* and *Munsif* on 25 June 1959, *Muhafiz* on 25 Feb 1955, *Mujahid* in Nov 1956, *Mahmood*, M 160, in May 1957, *Murabak* in 1957, *Momin* in Aug 1962 and *Moshal* M 167, on 13 July 1963. *Muhafiz* M 163 sunk during Indo-Pakistan War Dec 1971.
M 161 and M 167 are of MSC 289 Type, remainder of MSC 60 type.

MUNSIF *1972, Pakistan Navy*

SURVEY SHIP

ZULFIQUAR (ex-*Dhanush*, ex-*Deveron*) 262 (ex-F 265)

Builders	Laid down	Launched	Completed
Smith's Dock Co Ltd, South Bank-on-Tees	16 Apr 1942	12 Oct 1942	2 Mar 1943

Displacement, tons	1 370 standard; 2 100 full load
Dimensions, ft (*m*)	301·5 oa × 36·7 × 12·5 (*91·9 × 11·2 × 3·8*)
Guns	1—4 in (*102 mm*); 2—40 mm AA
Main engines	Triple expansion; 5 500 ihp
Speed, knots	20
Boilers	2 Admiralty 3-drum type
Range, miles	6 000 at 12 knots
Complement	150

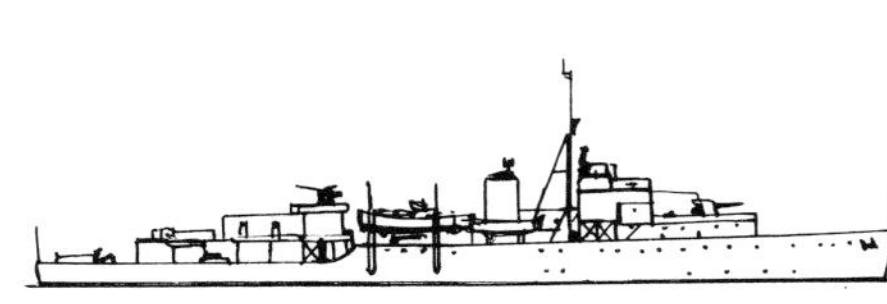

ZULFIQUAR

Former British frigate of the "River" class converted into a survey ship, additional charthouse aft. She has strengthened davits and carries survey motor boats. The after 4-inch gun was removed.

TANKERS

DACCA (ex-USNS *Mission Santa Cruz*, AO 132) A 41

Displacement, tons	5 730 light; 22 380 full load
Dimensions, feet	503 wl; 523·5 oa × 68 × 30·9
Main engines	Turbo-electric; 6 000 shp = 15 knots
Boilers	2 Babcock & Wilcox
Oil capacity	20 000 tons
Complement	160 (15 officers and 145 men)

Former US fleet tanker of the "T2-SE-A1" Type ("Mission" class). Transferred on loan to Pakistan under MDAP. Handed over from the US on 17 Jan 1963. Purchased 31 May 1974.

DACCA

ATTOCK (ex-USS YO 249) A 298

Displacement, tons	600 standard; 1 255 full load
Dimensions, feet	177·2 oa × 32 × 15
Main engines	Direct coupled diesel; speed 8·5 knots
Complement	26

A harbour oiler of 6 500 barrels capacity built in Trieste, Italy, in 1960 for the Pakistan Navy, under the Mutual Defence Assistance Programme of USA.

RESCUE SHIP

MADADGAR (ex-USS *Yuma*, *ATF* 94) A 42

Displacement, tons	1 235 standard; 1 675 full load
Dimensions, feet	195 wl; 205 oa × 38·5 × 15·3
Main engines	4 GM diesels; electric drive; 1 shaft; 3 000 bhp = 16·5 knots
Complement	85

Ocean-going salvage tug. Built by Commercial Iron Works, Portland, Oregon. Laid down on 13 Feb 1943. Launched on 17 July 1943. Completed on 31 Aug 1943. Transferred from the US Navy to the Pakistan Navy on 25 Mar 1959 under MDAP. Fitted with powerful pumps and other salvage equipment.

TUGS

RUSTOM

Dimensions, feet	105·0 × 30·0 × 11·0
Main engines	Crossley diesel; 1 000 bhp = 9·5 knots
Range, miles	3 000 at economic speed
Complement	21

General purpose tug for the Pakistan Navy originally ordered from Werf-Zeeland at Hansweert, Netherlands, in Aug 1952, but after the liquidation of this yard the order was transferred to Worst & Dutmer at Meppel. Launched on 29 Nov 1955.

BHOLU (ex-US YTL 755) **GAMA** (ex-US YTL 754)

Small harbour tugs built under an "off-shore" order by Costaguta-Voltz. Completed Sept 1958.

MISCELLANEOUS

ZUM ZUM YW 15 (WATER CARRIER)

Built in Italy under MDA programme.

PESHAWAR (ex-USN ARD 6) (FLOATING DOCK)

Transferred June 1961. 3 000 tons lift.

PANAMA

Mercantile Marine

Lloyd's Register of Shipping: 1 962 ships of 11 003 227 tons gross

2 VOSPER TYPE (LARGE PATROL CRAFT)

PANQUIACO GC 10 **LIGIA ELENA** GC 11

Displacement, tons	96 standard; 123 full load
Dimensions, feet	95·0 wl; 103·0 oa × 18·9 × 5·8
Guns	2—20 mm
Main engines	2 Paxman Ventura 12 cyl diesels; 2 800 bhp = 24 knots
Complement	23

Constructed with hull of welded mild steel and upperworks of welded or buck-bolted aluminium alloy. Vosper fin stabiliser equipment. *Panquiaco* was launched on 22 July 1970 and *Ligia Elena* on 25 Aug 1970 at Porchester, Portsmouth, England. Both completed March 1971.

2 US CG UTILITY TYPE (COASTAL PATROL CRAFT)

Displacement, tons	35
Dimensions, feet	69 × 14 × 5
Guns	1 MG
Main engines	400 hp = 13 knots
Complement	10

Transferred to Panama by the USA at the US Naval Station, Rodman, Canal Zone, in June 1962.

Note. Five additional small craft transferred by USA, three being Coastal Patrol Craft delivered 1965-66.

PARAGUAY

Strength of the Fleet

2 River Defence Vessels
3 Corvettes
1 Large Patrol Craft
8 Coastal Patrol Craft
2 Tugs
6 Service Craft

Personnel

1975: 1 900 officers and men including coastguard and marines.

Mercantile Marine

Lloyd's Register of Shipping:
26 vessels of 21 930 tons gross

RIVER DEFENCE VESSELS

2 "HUMAITA" CLASS

HUMAITA (ex-*Capitan Cabral*) C 2 **PARAGUAY** (ex-*Commodor Meza*) C 1

Displacement, tons	636 standard; 865 full load
Dimensions, feet	231 × 35 × 5·3
Guns	4—4·7 in; 3—3 in AA; 2—40 mm AA
Mines	6
Armour	·5 in side amidships; ·3 in deck; ·8 in CT
Main engines	Parsons geared turbines; 2 shafts; 3 800 shp = 17 knots
Boilers	2
Oil fuel, tons	150
Range, miles	3 400 at 16 knots
Complement	86

Rated as gunboats but also fitted for minelaying. The armour is of high tensile steel. Both built by Odero, Genoa, laid down in Apr 1929, launched in 1930, and completed in May 1931.

CORVETTES

3 "BOUCHARD" CLASS

CAPITAN MEZA (ex-*Parker*) **NANAVA** (ex-*Bouchard*)
TENIENTE FARINA (ex-*Py*)

Displacement, tons	450 standard; 620 normal; 650 full load
Dimensions, feet	164 pp; 197 oa × 24 × 8·5
Guns	4—40 mm Bofors AA; 2 MG
Main engines	2 sets MAN 2-cycle diesels; 2 000 bhp = 16 knots
Oil fuel tons	50
Range, miles	6 000 at 12 knots
Complement	70

Former Argentinian minesweepers of the "Bouchard" class. Built at Sanchez Shipyard, San Fernando, Rio Santiago Naval Yard, and Hansen & Puccini, San Fernando, respectively. Laid down in 1936, 1935 and 1937. Launched on 2 May 1937, 20 Mar 1936 and 18 Aug 1938. Can carry mines. Transferred from the Argentinian Navy to the Paraguayan Navy in Apr 1964 onward.

CAPITAN MEZA

LIGHT FORCES

CAPITAN CABRAL (ex-*Adolfo Riquelme*) A 1 (LARGE PATROL CRAFT)

Displacement, tons	180 standard; 206 full load
Dimensions, feet	98·5 pp; 107·2oa × 23·5 × 9·8
Guns	1—3 in Vickers; 2—37 mm Vickers; 4 MG
Main engines	Triple expansion; 1 shaft; 300 ihp = 9 knots
Complement	47

Former tug. Built by Werf-Conrad, Haarlem. Launched in 1907. Of wooden construction.

2 CG TYPE (COASTAL PATROL CRAFT)

P1 (ex-USCGC 20417) **P2** (ex-USCGC 20418)

Displacement, tons	16
Dimensions, feet	45·5 oa × 13·5 × 3·5
Guns	2—20 mm AA
Main engines	2 petrol motors; 2 shafts; 190 hp = 20 knots
Complement	10

Of wooden construction. Built in the United States in 1944. Acquired from the United States Coast Guard in 1944.

6 "701" CLASS (COASTAL PATROL CRAFT)

P 101 102 103 104 105 106

Patrol craft of 40 ft and 10 tons transferred by USA—2 in Dec 1967, 3 in Sept 1970 and 1 in Mar 1971.

TUG

YLT 559 A 4 (ex-US YTL 211) — (ex-US YTL 567)

Dimensions, feet	66·2 × 17 × 5
Main engines	Diesel; 300 bhp

Small harbour tugs transferred to Paraguay by the USA under the Military Aid Programme in March 1967. Built by Everett Pacific SB & DD Co, Wash. (YTL 211). YTL 567 loaned Apr 1974.

MISCELLANEOUS

Ex-US AFDL 26 (FLOATING DOCK)

Transferred March 1965, Lift 1 000 tons.

Ex-US YR 37 (FLOATING WORKSHOP)

Transferred March 1965.

TENIENTE O CARRERAS SAGUIER (DREDGER)

YFB 82 **YFB 86** (FERRIES)

Leased by USA in June 1970.

— (ex-Argentine *Corrientes*) (ex-LSM)

Of 1 095 full load with 4—40 mm guns and heliplatform. Acquired 1971.

PERU

Administration

Minister of Marine and Chief of Naval Operations:
Vice-Admiral Luis E. Vargas Caballero

Chief of Naval Staff:
Vice-Admiral Fernando Zapater Vantosse

Commander-in-Chief of the Fleet:
Rear-Admiral Oscar Cuadros

Diplomatic Representation

Naval Attaché in London and Paris:
Rear-Admiral Daniel Masias

Naval Attaché in Washington:
Vice-Admiral Jose Arce Larco

Personnel

(a) 1975: 8 000 (730 officers, 7 270 men)
(b) 2 years National Service

Strength of the Fleet

Type	*Active*	*Building*
Cruisers	3	—
Destroyers	4	—
Frigates	2	4
Corvettes	2	—
Submarines—Patrol	4	2
Large Patrol Craft	8	—
Coastal Patrol Craft	3	—
Lake Patrol Craft	11	—
River Gun Boats	5	—
Landing Ships	4	—
LCU's	3	—
LCA's	10	—
Transports	3	—
Tankers	6	—
Floating Docks	2	—
Survey Vessels	2	—
Tug	1	—
Water Boat	1	—

Prefix to Ships' Names

BAP (Baque Armada Peruana)

Bases

Callao—Main naval base; dockyard with ship-building capacity, 1 dry dock, 2 floating docks, 1 floating crane; naval academy; training schools.
Iquitos—River base for Amazon flotilla; small building yard, repair facilities.

Mercantile Marine

Lloyd's Register of Shipping:
675 vessels of 513 875 tons gross

Deletions

Frigates

1974 *Aguirre* (disposal)

Minewarfare Forces

1974 *Bondy, St. Martin* (ex-*YMS*) (disposal)

Transport

Sept 1972 *Callao*

CRUISERS

1 Ex-NETHERLANDS

Name	*No.*	*Builders*	*Laid down*	*Launched*	*Completed*
ALMIRANTE GRAU (*ex-de Ruyter*)	81	Wilton-Fijenoord Schiedam	5 Sep 1939	24 Dec 1944	18 Nov 1953

Displacement, tons	9 529 standard; 11 850 full load
Dimensions, ft (*m*)	590·5 pp; 614·5 oa × 56·7 × 22 (*180 pp; 190·3 oa × 17·3 × 6·7*)
Guns	8—6 in (twin turrets); 8—57 mm AA (twins); 8—40 mm AA
Main engines	2 De Schelde-Parsons geared turbines; 85 000 shp; 2 shafts
Boilers	4 Werkspoor-Yarrow
Speed, knots	32
Complement	926

Transferred by purchase 7 March 1973.

RADAR. Search: LWO 1; SPS 39 (3D); SGR 104, Heightfinder; Tactical: DA 02; Fire Control: HSA M20 for 6 in guns and M45 for secondary battery.

ALMIRANTE GRAU *1973, Peruvian Navy*

Cruisers—*continued*

2 Ex-BRITISH "CEYLON" CLASS

Name	*No.*	*Builders*	*Laid down*	*Launched*	*Completed*
CAPITAN QUIÑONES (ex-*Almirante Grau*, ex-HMS *Newfoundland*)	83	Swan, Hunter & Wigham Richardson, Ltd, Wallsend-on-Tyne	9 Nov 1939	19 Dec 1941	31 Dec 1942
CORONEL BOLOGNESI (ex-HMS *Ceylon*)	82	Alexander Stephen & Sons, Ltd, Govan, Glasgow	27 Apr 1939	30 July 1942	13 July 1943

Displacement, tons	*Capitan Quiñones:* **8 800 standard; 11 090 full load** *Col. Bolognesi:* **8 781 standard; 11 110 full load**
Length, feet (*metres*)	**538 (*164·0*) wl; 549 (*167·4*) wl; 555·5 (*169·3*) oa**
Beam, feet (*metres*)	**63·6 (*19·4*)**
Draught, feet (*metres*)	**16·5 (*5·0*) mean; 20·5 (*6·2*) max**
Guns, surface	**9—6 in (*152 mm*) three triple**
Guns, dual purpose	**8—4 in (4 twin)**
Guns, AA 12—40 mm	*Capitan Quiñones:* 18—40 mm *Col. Bolognesi*
Armour	**4 in (*102 mm*) sides and CT; 2 in (*51 mm*) turrets and deck**
Boilers	**4 Admiralty 3-drum; 400 psi (*28 kg/cm²*); 720°F (*382°C*)**
Main engines	**Parsons s.r. geared turbines 72 500 shp; 4 shafts**
Speed, knots	31·5
Range, miles	6 000 at 13 knots; 2 800 at full power
Oil fuel, tons	1 620
Complement	*Capitan Quiñones:* 743 *Col. Bolognesi:* 766

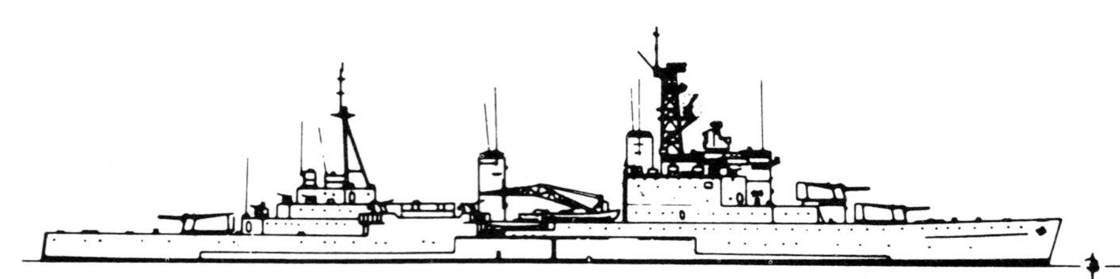

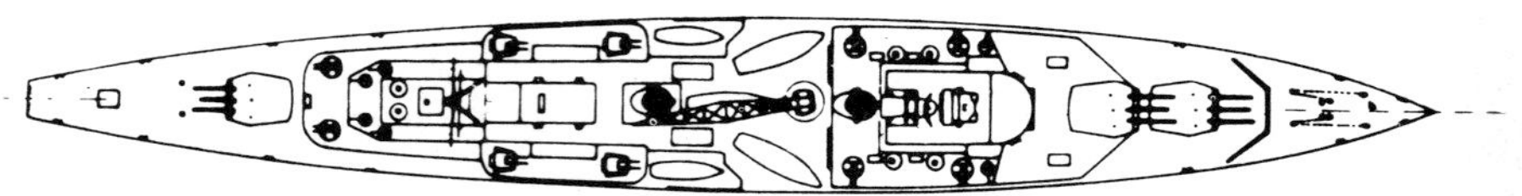

GENERAL
CL 83 was transferred as *Almirante Grau* in December 1959, being renamed *Capitán Quiñones* on 15 May 1973. CL 82 was transferred as *Coronel Bolognesi* on 9 Feb 1960.

RADAR. Search: Types 960, 277 and 293; Fire Control: S band surface, X band AA.

RECONSTRUCTION. CL 83 was reconstructed in 1951-53 at HM Dockyard, Devonport, with two lattice masts, new bridge and improved AA armament, her torpedo tubes being removed. CL 82 was similarly modified in 1955-56.

CAPITAN QUIÑONES (before pennant change) *1971, Peruvian Navy*

DESTROYERS

2 Ex-BRITISH "DARING" CLASS

Name	*No.*	*Builders*	*Laid down*	*Launched*	*Completed*
FERRÉ (ex-HMS *Decoy*)	74	Yarrow, Co Ltd, Scotstoun	22 Sep 1946	29 Mar 1949	28 Apr 1953
PALACIOS (ex-HMS *Diana*)	73	Yarrow, Co Ltd, Scotstoun	3 Apr 1947	8 May 1952	29 Mar 1954

FERRÉ *1973, C. & S. Taylor*

Displacement, tons	2 800 standard; 3 600 full load
Length, feet (*metres*)	366 (*111·7*) pp; 375 (*114·3*) wl; 390 (*118·9*) oa
Beam, feet (*metres*)	43 (*13·1*)
Draught, feet (*metres*)	18 (*5·5*) max
Missiles	8 MM 38 Exocet launchers abaft after funnel
Guns	6—4·5 in (*115 mm*); 2 twin fwd; 1 twin aft (Mk VI); 2—40 mm
A/S weapons	1 Squid 3 barrelled DC mortar
Torpedo tubes	5—21 in (*533 mm*)
Boilers	2 Foster Wheeler; Pressure 650 psi (*45·7 kg/cm²*); Superheat 850°F (454°C)
Main engines	English Electric dr geared turbines 2 shafts
Speed, knots	34·75
Range, miles	3 000 at 20 knots
Oil fuel, tons	580
Complement	297

Purchased by Peru in 1969 and refitted by Cammel Laird (Ship repairers) Ltd, Birkenhead, for further service.

REFIT. A second major refit was carried out in 1971-73. The main points after this refit are the reconstructed and enclosed foremast carrying Plessey AWS-1 radar and the Exocet launcher positions in place of the Close Range Blind Fire Director forward of X Turret.
Commissioned after refit—*Palacios* Feb 1973, *Ferré* April 1973.

RADAR. TSF fire control on fore-funnel; Plessey AWS-1

Destroyers—*continued*

2 Ex-US "FLETCHER" CLASS

Name	No.	Builders	Launched	Completed
GUISE (ex-USS *Isherwood, DD* 520)	72	Bethlehem Steel Co, Staten Island	24 Nov 1942	10 Apr 1943
VILLAR (ex-USS *Benham, DD* 796)	71	Bethlehem Steel Co, Staten Island	29 Aug 1943	20 Dec 1943

Displacement, tons: 2 120 standard; 2 715 normal; 3 050 full load
Length, feet (*metres*): 360·2 (*109·8*) pp; 370 (*112·8*) wl; 376·2 (*114·7*) oa
Beam, feet (*metres*): 39·7 (*12·1*)
Draught, feet (*metres*): 12·2 (*3·7*) mean; 18 (*5·5*) max
Guns: 4—5 in (*127 mm*) 38 cal (5—5 in *Guise*) 6—3 in (*76 mm*) 50 cal, 3 twin
A/S weapons: 2 fixed Hedgehogs; 1 DC rack
Torpedo tubes: 5—21 in (*533 mm*) quintupled
Torpedo racks: 2 side-launching for A/S torpedoes
Boilers: 4 Babcock & Wilcox: 600 psi (*42 kg/cm²*); 850°F (*455°C*)
Main engines: 2 GE impulse reaction geared turbines; 60 000 shp; 2 shafts
Speed, knots: 34
Range, miles: 5 000 at 15 knots; 900 at full power
Oil fuel, tons: 650
Complement: Allowance; 245 (15 officers and 230 men) Max accommodation: 275 (15 officers and 260 men)

GUISE, VILLAR

VILLAR — *1971, Peruvian Navy*

Former United States destroyers of the later "Fletcher" class (*Villar*) and "Fletcher" class (*Guise*).

RADAR. Search: SPS 6, SPS 10. Fire Control: GFCS 68 system forward, GFCS 56 system aft.

TRANSFER. Transferred from the United States Navy to the Peruvian Navy at Boston, Massachusetts, on 15 Dec 1960, and at San Diego, California, on 8 Oct 1961 respectively.

FRIGATES

4 ITALIAN "MODIFIED LUPO" CLASS

Displacement, tons: 2 208 standard; 2 500 full load
Dimensions, ft (*m*): 347·7 × 39·5 × 12 (*106* × *12* × 3·7)
Aircraft: 1 helicopter
Missiles: 2 Otomat twin-missile launchers; 1 Octuple Albatros (Seasparrow) launcher for Point Defence
Guns: 1—127 mm OTO Melara; 2—35 mm OTO-Oerlikon (twin)
Rocket launchers: 2—105 mm Breda ELSAG multi-purpose 20-barrelled launchers
Torpedo tubes: 6 tubes in triple mountings (port and starboard)
Main engines: CODOG with 2 GE Fiat LM 2500 gas turbines; 50 000 hp; 2 Fiat 20 cyl A 230 diesels; 7 800 hp
Speed: 35 knots

Two to be built by Cantiero Navale di Tireno e Riuniti (CNTR), the first being laid down on 8 Aug 1974. The second pair are to be built at Servicio Industrial de la Marina at Callao with technical assistance from CNTR. The design is similar to the "Lupo" class of Italy with a major modification in the inclusion of an A/S helicopter at the expense of four surface-to-surface missiles.

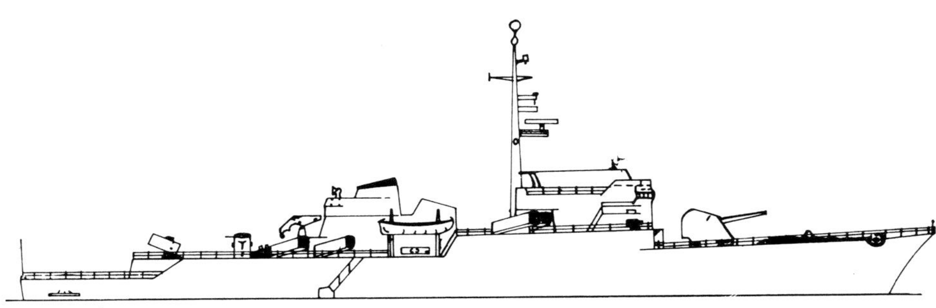
"LUPO" class before modification for Peru.

2 Ex-US "CANNON" CLASS

Name	No.	Launched	Completed
CASTILLA (ex-USS *Bangust, DE* 739)	61	6 June 1943	30 Oct 1943
RODRIQUEZ (ex-USS *Weaver, DE* 741)	63	20 June 1943	30 Nov 1943

Displacement, tons: 1 240 standard; 1 900 full load
Dimensions, ft (*m*): 306 oa × 36·9 × 14·1 (*93·3* × *11·2* × *4·3*)
Guns: 3—3 in (*76 mm*) 50 cal; 6—40 mm, 3 twin; 10—20 mm
A/S weapons: 1 Mk 10 ahead-throwing mortar; 8 K mortars; 2 DC racks aft
Main engines: 4 GM diesel-electric sets 60 000 hp; 2 shafts
Speed, knots: 21
Range, miles: 10 500 at 12 knots
Complement: Allowance: 172 (12 officers and 160 men); Max accommodation 212 (12 officers and 200 men)

Former United States destroyer escorts, DE, of the "Cannon" class. Both built by the Western Pipe & Steel Co, San Pedro, California, in 1943. Transferred to Peru on 26 Oct 1951, under the Mutual Defence Assistance Programme. Reconditioned and modernised at Green Cove Springs and Jacksonville, Flor. Actually arrived in Peru on 24 May 1952. Due for retirement. *Castilla* now used as a training ship and *Rodriquez* as submarine accommodation ship.

TORPEDO TUBES. The original three 21 inch torpedo tubes in a triple mounting were removed.

CASTILLA — *1970, Peruvian Navy*

CASTILLA, RODRIGUEZ

CORVETTES

2 Ex-US MSF TYPE

Name	No.	Laid down	Launched	Completed
DIEZ CANSECO (ex-USS *Shoveler, MSF* 382)	69	1 Apr 1944	10 Dec 1944	28 June 1945
GALVEZ (ex-USS *Ruddy, MSF* 380)	68	24 Feb 1944	29 Oct 1944	28 Apr 1945

Displacement, tons	890 standard; 1 250 full load
Dimensions, feet	215 wl; 221·2 oa × 32·2 × 11
Guns	1—3 in 50 cal dp; 2—40 mm AA
A/S weapons	1 Hedgehog
Main engines	Diesel electric; 2 shafts; 3 532 bhp = 18 knots
Range, miles	4 300 at 10 knots
Complement	100

DIEZ CANSECO, GALVEZ

GALVEZ — *1970, Peruvian Navy*

Former US "Auk" class fleet minesweepers, MSF. Both built by the Gulf Shipbuilding Corp. Activated at San Diego, California, and transferred to the Peruvian Navy under the Mutual Defence Assistance Programme on 1 Nov 1960. Sonar equipment was fitted so that they could be used as patrol vessels. The 3 inch gun director was removed. Both purchased by Peru in 1974.

SUBMARINES

2 TYPE 209

ISLAY S 45 **ARICA** S 46

Displacement, tons	990 surfaced; 1 290 dived
Length, feet (*metres*)	177·1 (*54·0*)
Beam, feet (*metres*)	20·3 (*6·2*)
Torpedo tubes	8—21 in (with reloads)
Main machinery	Diesel Electric; 4 MTU Siemens diesel-generators; 1 Siemens electric motor; 1 shaft
Speed, knots	10 surfaced; 22 dived
Range	50 days
Complement	31

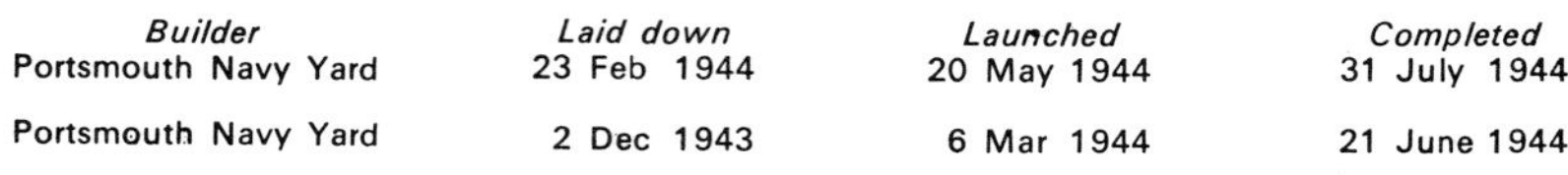

TYPE 209 — *1973, Howaldtswerke*

Designed by Ingenieurkontor, Lübeck for construction by Howaldtswerke, Kiel and sale by Ferrostaal Essen all acting as a consortium.
A single-hull design with two ballast tanks and forward and after trim tanks. Fitted with snort and remote machinery control. The single screw is slow revving, very high capacity batteries with GRP lead-acid cells and battery cooling—by Wilh. Hagen and VARTTA. Active and passive sonar, sonar detection equipment, sound ranging gear and underwater telephone. Fitted with two periscopes, radar and Omega receiver. Foreplanes retract.
Islay ran trials in June 1974 and has since been completed. *Arica* launched 17 Apr 1974.

2 ex-US "GUPPY 1A" CLASS

Name	No.	Builder	Laid down	Launched	Completed
LA PEDRERA (ex-*Pabellon de Pica*) (ex-USS *Sea Poacher* SS 406)	47	Portsmouth Navy Yard	23 Feb 1944	20 May 1944	31 July 1944
PACOCHA (ex-USS *Atule* SS 403)	48	Portsmouth Navy Yard	2 Dec 1943	6 Mar 1944	21 June 1944

Displacement, tons	1 870 standard; 2 440 dived
Dimensions, ft (*m*)	308 oa × 27 × 17 (*93·8* × *8·2* × *5·2*)
Torpedo tubes	10—21 in; 6 forward 4 aft
Main machinery	3 diesels; 4 800 hp—2 electric motors; 5 400 shp; 2 shafts
Speed, knots	18 surfaced; 15 dived
Complement	85

Modernised under the 1951 Guppy programme. Purchased by Peru—*La Pedrera* on 1 July 1974, *Pacocha* on 31 July 1974. The name of *La Pedrera* was changed a fortnight after purchase.

LA PEDRERA (as SEA POACHER) — *1966, Dr. Giorgio Arra*

4 "ABTAO" CLASS

Name	No.	Laid down	Launched	Completed
ABTAO (ex-*Tiburon*)	42	12 May 1952	27 Oct 1953	20 Feb 1954
ANGAMOS (ex-*Atun*)	43	27 Oct 1955	5 Feb 1957	1 July 1957
DOS DE MAYO (ex-*Lobo*)	41	12 May 1952	6 Feb 1954	14 June 1954
IQUIQUE (ex-*Merlin*)	44	27 Oct 1955	5 Feb 1957	1 Oct 1957

Displacement, tons	825 standard; 1 400 submerged
Length, feet (*metres*)	243 (*74·1*) oa
Beam, feet (*metres*)	22 (*6·7*)
Draught, feet (*metres*)	14 (*4·3*)
Guns, surface	1—5 in (*127 mm*) 25 cal (*Abtao* and *Dos de Mayo*)
Torpedo tubes	6—21 in (*533 mm*); 4 bow, 2 stern
Main machinery	2 GM 278A diesels; 2 400 bhp; Electric motors; 2 shafts
Speed, knots	16 on surface; 10 submerged
Range, miles	5 000 at 10 knots (surfaced)
Oil fuel, tons	45
Complement	40

All built by Electric Boat Division—General Dynamics Corporation, Groton, Connecticut. They are of modified US "Mackerel" class.

DOS DE MAYO — *1970, Peruvian Navy*

LIGHT FORCES

6 VOSPER TYPE (LARGE PATROL CRAFT)

DE LOS HEROS	23	**LARREA**	25	**SANTILLANA**	22
HERRERA	24	**SANCHEZ CARRION**	26	**VELARDE**	21

Displacement, tons	100 standard; 130 full load
Dimensions, feet	103·7 wl; 109·7 oa × 21 × 5·7
Guns	2—20 mm AA
Main engines	2 Napier Deltic 18 cyl, turbocharged diesels; 6 200 bhp = 30 knots
Range, miles	1 100 at 15 knots
Complement	25 (4 officers and 21 ratings)

Designed and built by Vosper Ltd, Portsmouth, England, for the Peruvian Navy. Of all-welded steel construction with aluminium upperworks. Designed for coastal patrol, air-sea-rescue, and fishery protection. Equipped with Vosper roll damping fins, Decca Type 707 true motion radar, comprehensive radio, up-to-date navigation aids, sonar, depth charges in racks aft, and air-conditioning. The first boat, *Velarde*, was launched on 10 July 1964, the last, *Sanchez Carrion*, on 18 Feb 1965. Can be armed as gunboat, torpedo boat (four side-launched torpedoes) or minelayer. A twin rocket projector can be fitted forward instead of gun.

SANCHEZ CARRION *1971, Peruvian Navy*

2 Ex-US PGM TYPE E (LARGE PATROL CRAFT)

RIO SAMA PC 11 (ex-USS *PGM* 78)
RIO CHIRA PC 12 (ex-USS *PGM* 111)

Displacement, tons	130 standard; 147 full load
Dimensions, feet	101 × 21 × 6
Guns	1—40 mm, 4—20 mm, 2—0·5 cal MG
Main engines	2 Diesels; 2 shafts; 1 800 hp = 18·5 knots
Range, miles	1 500 at 10 knots
Complement	15

PC 11 transferred in Sep 1966 from the United States under the Military Aid Programme. PC 12 transferred 30 June 1972.

RIO SAMA *1971, Peruvian Navy*

3 "RIO" CLASS (RIVER PATROL CRAFT)

RIO PIURA	04	**RIO TUMBES**	02	**RIO ZARUMILLA**	01

Displacement, tons	37 full load
Dimensions, feet	65·7 × 17 × 3·2
Guns	2—40 mm
Main engines	2 GM diesels; 2 shafts; 1 200 bhp = 18 knots

Built by Viareggio, Italy. Ordered in 1959, laid down on 15 July 1959, and entered service on 5 Sep 1960. *Rio el Salto*, 03, was deleted from the list in 1966.

2 "MARANON" CLASS (RIVER GUNBOATS)

MARAÑÓN	13	John I. Thornycroft & Co	23 Apr 1951	July 1951
UCAYALI	14	Ltd. Southampton. England	7 Mar 1951	June 1951

Displacement, tons	365 full load
Dimensions, feet	154·8 wl × 32 × 4 max
Guns	2—3 in 50 cal dp; 7—20 mm AA (2 twin, 3 single)
Main engines	British Polar M 441 diesels; 800 bhp = 12 knots
Range, miles	6 000 at 10 knots
Complement	40

Ordered early in 1950. Employed on police duties in Upper Amazon. Very shallow draught. Superstructure of aluminium alloy. Based at Iquitos.

Light Forces—*continued*

2 "LORETO" CLASS (RIVER GUNBOATS)

AMAZONAS 11 **LORETO** 12

Displacement, tons	250 standard
Dimensions, feet	145 × 22 × 4
Guns	1—3 in; 2—47 mm; 2—20 mm AA
Main engines	Diesel; 750 bhp = 15 knots
Range, miles	4 000 at 10 knots
Complement	35

Designed and built by the Electric Boat Co, Groton, Conn. Launched in 1934.

LORETO *1973, Peruvian Navy*

NAPO 301 (RIVER GUNBOAT)

Displacement, tons	98
Dimensions, feet	100 pp; 101·5 oa × 18 × 3
Main engines	Triple expansion; 250 ihp = 12 knots
Boilers	Yarrow
Complement	22

Built by Yarrow Co Ltd, Scotstoun, Glasgow. Launched in 1920. Built of steel. Converted from wood to oil fuel burning. In the Upper Amazon Flotilla. Converted to a Dispensary Vessel in 1968.

AMERICA 15 (RIVER GUNBOAT)

Displacement, tons	240
Dimensions, feet	133 × 19·5 × 4·5
Guns	2—3 pdr; 4—12·7 mm AA
Main engines	Triple expansion; 350 ihp = 14 knots
Complement	26

Built by Tranmere Bay Development Co Ltd, Birkenhead. Built of steel. Launched and completed in 1904. Converted from coal to oil fuel burning. In the Upper Amazon Flotilla. The river gunboat *Iquitos* was discarded in 1967 after 92 years service.

11 LAKE PATROL CRAFT

280-290

30 ft craft stationed on Lake Titicaca.

Patrol craft on Lake Titicaca *1973, Peruvian Navy*

AMPHIBIOUS FORCES

CHIMBOTE (ex-M/S *Rawhiti*, ex-USS *LST* 283) 34

Displacement, tons	1 625 standard; 4 050 full load
Dimensions, feet	316 wl; 328 oa × 50 × 14·1
Guns	1—3 in
Main engines	GM diesels; 2 shafts; 1 700 bhp = 10 knots
Oil fuel, tons	600 oil tanks; 1 100 ballast tanks
Range, miles	9 500 at 9 knots
Complement	Accommodation for 16 officers and 130 men

Former US tank landing ship of the 1-510 Series. Built by American Bridge Co, Ambridge, Pennsylvania. Laid down on 2 Aug 1943, launched on 10 Oct 1943 and completed on 18 Nov 1943. Sold to Peru by a British firm in 1951.

Amphibious Forces—*continued*

PAITA (ex-USS *Burnett County LST* 512) 35 (ex-*AT* 4)

Displacement, tons	1 653 standard; 4 080 full load
Dimensions, feet	316 wl; 328 oa × 50 × 14·5 max
Guns	6—40 mm AA; 6—20 mm AA
Main engines	GM diesels; 2 shafts; 1 700 bhp = 10 knots
Range, miles	9 500 at 9 knots
Complement	13 officers, 106 men

Former US tank landing ship of the 511-1152 Series. Built by Chicago Bridge & Iron Co, Seneca, Illinois. Laid down on 29 July 1943. Launched on 10 Dec 1943 and completed on 8 Jan 1944. Purchased by Peru in 1957.

PAITA — *1972, Peruvian Navy*

Name	*No.*	*Laid down*	*Launched*	*Completed*
ATICO	37	3 Mar 1945	22 Mar 1945	14 Sep 1945
LOMAS	36	13 Dec 1944	2 Jan 1945	23 Mar 1945

Displacement, tons	513 standard; 913 full load
Dimensions, feet	196·5 wl; 203·5 oa × 34·5 × 7
Guns	2—40 mm AA; 4—20 mm AA
Main engines	Diesels; 800 rpm; 2 shafts; 3 600 bhp = 12 knots
Range, miles	5 000 at 7 knots
Complement	Accommodation for 116 (10 officers and 106 men)

Former US medium landing ships of the LSM type. Both built by Charleston Navy Yard, Charleston, SC, USA. Purchased in 1959.

ATICO — *1972, Peruvian Navy*

3 Ex-US LCUs

PIRURA BT 4 (ex-US LCU 1161) **SALTO** BT 3 (ex-US LCU 855)
ZARUMILLA BT 1 (ex-US LCU 501)

Displacement, tons	160 light; 315 full load
Dimensions, feet	119 oa × 32·7 × 5
Guns	2—20 mm
Main engines	Gray Marine diesels; 3 shafts; 675 bhp = 10 knots
Complement	15

Sold to Peru Aug 1947.

10 LCAs

200-209

Employed on riverine operations.

SURVEY VESSELS

UNANUE

For details, see "Tug" Section.

CARDENAS

Of 19 tons, launched in 1950, with a complement of 4.

WATER CARRIER

MANTILLA (ex-US *YW* 122) 141

Displacement, tons	1 235 full load
Dimensions, feet	174 × 32
Gun	1 MG forward
Capacity gallons	200 000

Former US water barge. Built by Henry C. Grebe & Co Inc, Chicago, Ill. Lent to Peru in July 1963.

TRANSPORTS

INDEPENDENCIA (ex-USS *Bellatrix, AKA* 3, ex-*Raven, SKA* 20) 31 (ex-21)

Displacement, tons	6 194 light
Measurement, tons	Maritime Commission deadweight, 8 656
Guns	1—5 in 38 cal; 3—3 in 50 cal, 10—20 mm
Dimensions, feet	435 wl; 459 oa × 63 × 26·5
Main engines	1 Nordberg diesel; 1 shaft; 6 000 bhp = 16·5 knots

Former US attack cargo ship. Built by Tampa Shipbuilding Co, Tampa, Florida, in 1941. Transferred to Peru at Bremerton, Washington on 20 July 1963 under the Military Aid Programme. Training ship for the Peruvian Naval Academy.

Transports—*continued*

ILO 131 **RIMAC** 132

Displacement, tons	18 400 full load
Measurement, tons	13 000 deadweight
Dimensions, feet	507·7 × 67·3 × 27·2
Main engines	Diesels; Speed = 15·6 knots

The *Ilo* completed in Dec 1971 at Servicio Industrial de la Marina, Callao. Her sister ship *Rimac* was launched at the same yard on 12 Dec 1971.

ILO — *1972, Peruvian Navy*

TANKERS

3 "PARINAS" CLASS

Name	*No.*	*Launched*	*Completed*
PARINAS	155	2 May 1967	13 June 1968
PIMENTAL	156	30 Dec 1967	27 June 1969
+1		Building	

Displacement, tons	3 434 light; 13 600 full load
Measurement, tons	10 000 deadweight
Dimensions, feet	410·9 × 63·1 × 26
Main engines	Burmeister and Wain Type 750 diesel; 5 400 bhp = 14·5 knots

Built by the Servicio Industrial de la Marina in the Naval Arsenal at Callao. First two in service 1969.

2 "SECHURA" CLASS

LOBITOS 159 **ZORRITOS** 158

Displacement, tons	8 700 full load
Measurement, tons	4 300 gross; 6 000 deadweight
Dimensions, feet	360·0 wl; 385·0 oa × 52·0 × 21·2
Main engines	Burmeister & Wain diesels; 2 400 bhp = 12 knots (13·25 knots on trials)
Boilers	2 Scotch with Thornycroft oil burners for cargo tank cleaning

Both built by Servicio Industrial de la Marina, Callao. *Zorritos* launched 8 Oct 1958, *Lobitos* May 1965.

MOLLENDO (ex-*Amalienborg*) ATP 151

Displacement, tons	6 084 standard; 25 670 full load
Dimensions, feet	534·8 × 72·2 × 30
Main engines	674-VTFS-160 diesels; 7 500 bhp = 14·5 knots

This Japanese built tanker, completed Sep 1962, was acquired by Peru in Apr 1967.

TUGS

RIOS (ex-USS *Pinto ATF* 90) 123

Displacement, tons	1 235 standard; 1 675 full load
Measurement, tons	195 wl, 205 oa × 38·5 × 15·5
Main engines	4 GM diesel electric, 3 000 bhp = 16·5 knots

Former United States fleet ocean tug of the "Apache" class. Launched on 5 Jan 1943. Transferred to Peru in 1960 and delivered in Jan 1961. Fitted with powerful pumps and other salvage equipment.

UNANUE (ex-USS *Wateree, ATA* 174) 136

Displacement, tons	534 standard, 852 full load
Dimensions, feet	133·7 wl, 143 oa × 33·9 × 13·2
Main engines	GM diesel-electric, 1 500 bhp = 13 knots

Former United States auxiliary ocean tug of the "Maricopa" class. Built by Levingston SB Co, Orange, Texas. Laid down on 5 Oct 1943, launched on 18 Nov 1943 and completed on 20 July 1944. Purchased from the USA in Nov 1961 under MAP. Temporarily employed as a Survey Ship.

FLOATING DOCK

The former US auxiliary floating dry dock *ARD* 8 was transferred to Peru in Feb 1961; displacement 5 200 tons; length 492 feet; beam 84 feet; draught 5·7 to 33·2 feet. The former US floating dock *AFDL* 33 launched in Oct 1964 was transferred to Peru in July 1969; displacement 1 900 tons; length 288 feet; beam 64 feet; draught 8·2 to 31·5 feet.

PHILIPPINES

Administration

Flag Officer in Command, Philippine Navy:
Commodore Hilario M. Ruiz

Commander, Naval Operating Forces:
Captain Simeon M. Alejandro

Diplomatic Representation

Naval, Military, and Air Attaché in London:
Captain Jaime V. Francisco (Navy)

Naval Attaché in Washington, D C:
Captain Ramon P. Madrid (Navy)

Personnel

1 200 officers and 13 000 men including Coast Guard

Strength of the Fleet

1 Frigate	4 Minesweepers
15 Patrol Vessels	2 Command Ships
4 Hydrofoil Patrol Boats	11 Landing Ships
24 Patrol Boats	18 Auxiliary Ships

DESTROYERS

The Philippine Navy can be expected to begin operating ships of destroyer size during the 1970s in view of the increasing level of competence of the Philippine Navy and the reduction of US naval forces in the Western Pacific.

Ships

Most names are those of geographical locations and are prefixed by RPS (Republic of Philippines Ship).

Coast Guard

Established Oct 1967 as a specialised branch within the Navy.
Commandant: Commodore Ernesto R. Ogbinar

Mercantile Marine

Lloyd's Register of Shipping:
379 vessels of 766 478 tons

FRIGATES

1 Ex-US "BOSTWICK" CLASS

Name	*No.*	*Launched*	*US Comm.*	*Transferred*
DATU KALANTIAW (ex-USS *Booth*, DE 170)	PS 76	21 June 1943	21 July 1943	15 Dec 1967

Displacement, tons	1 220 standard; 1 620 full load
Length, feet (*metres*)	300 (*91·5*) wl; 306 (*93·2*) oa
Beam, feet (*metres*)	36·6 (*11·2*)
Draught, feet (*metres*)	14 (*4·3*)
Guns	3—3 inch (*76 mm*) 50 cal AA 6—40 mm AA (twin) 2—20 mm AA (single)
A/S weapons	1 hedgehog 6—12·75 inch (*324 mm*) torpedo tubes (Mk 32 triple); depth charges
Main engines	Diesel-electric drive (General Motors diesels); 6 000 bhp; 2 shafts
Speed, knots	21
Complement	Approx 165

Former US destroyer escort of the DET design. Built by Federal Shipbuilding & Dry Dock Co, Newark, New Jersey, and completed by the Norfolk Navy Yard. Triple 21 inch torpedo tube mount originally fitted has been removed. Equipped with SPS-5 and SPS-6 search radars and fitted with tripod mast.

DISPOSALS
Rajah Soliman D 66 (ex-USS *Bowers*, APD 40), which had been transferred to the Philippines in 1961, was sunk in a typhoon in the Philippines in June 1962; raised but stricken on 3 Dec 1964.

DATU KALANTIAW *Philippine Navy*

PATROL VESSELS

2 Ex-US "AUK" CLASS MSF TYPE

RIZAL (ex-USS *Murrelet*, MSF 372)	PS 69	29 Dec 1944
QUEZON (ex-USS *Vigilance*, MSF 324)	PS 70	5 Apr 1943

Displacement, tons	890 standard; 1 250 full load
Dimensions, feet	215 wl; 221·2 oa × 32·2 × 10·8
Guns	2—3 inch (*76 mm*) 50 cal AA (single); 4—40 mm AA (twin); 4—20 mm AA (twin)
A/S weapons	3—12·75 inch (*324 mm*) torpedo tubes (Mk 32 triple); 1 hedgehog; depth charges
Main engines	Diesel-electric (General Motors diesels); 3 532 bhp; 2 shafts = 18 knots
Complement	approx 100

Former US Navy minesweepers (originally designated AM). Built by Savannah Machine & Foundry Co, Savannah, Georgia, and Associated Shipbuilders, Seattle, Washington, respectively. Launch dates above. PS 69 commissioned in US Navy on 21 Aug 1945 and PS 70 on 28 Feb 1944; PS 69 transferred to the Philippines on 18 June 1965 and PS 70 on 19 Aug 1967.
Upon transfer the minesweeping gear was removed and a second 3 inch gun fitted aft; additional anti-submarine weapons also fitted.

RIZAL

5 Ex-US 185-ft PCE TYPE

CEBU (ex-USS PCE 881)	PS 28	10 Nov 1943
NEGROS OCCIDENTAL (ex-USS PCE 884)	PS 29	24 Feb 1944
LEYTE (ex-USS PCE 885)	PS 30	30 Apr 1945
PANGASINAN (ex-USS PCE 891)	PS 31	15 June 1944
ILOILO (ex-USS PCE 897)	PS 32	3 Aug 1943

Displacement, tons	640 standard; 850 full load
Dimensions, feet	180 wl; 184·5 oa × 34 × 9·5
Guns	1—3 inch (*76 mm*) 50 cal AA; 3 or 6—40 mm AA (single or twin); 4—20 mm AA (single)
A/S weapons	2—12·75 inch (*324 mm*) torpedo tubes (Mk 32 single); depth charges; hedgehog in some
Main engines	Diesels (General Motors); 2 000 bhp; 2 shafts = 15 knots
Complement	approx 100

Former US Navy patrol craft. PS 28, 29, and 30 built by Albina Engineering & Machine Works, Portland, Oregon; PS 31 and 32 built by Willamette Iron & Steel Corp, Portland, Oregon. Launch dates above; completed 1944-1945. All five units transferred to the Philippines in July 1948.
These ships can be easily distinguished from the larger ex-MSF type ships by the single funnel and farther aft location of the deck break in the ex-PCE.

CEBU *Philippine Navy*

Patrol Vessels—*continued*

4 Ex-US 173-ft PC TYPE

BATANGAS (ex-USS PC 1134)	PS 24	18 Jan 1943
NUEVA ECIJA (ex-USS PC 1241)	PS 25	24 Dec 1942
CAPIZ (ex-USS PC 1564)	PS 27	19 Apr 1944
NUEVA VISCAYA (ex-USAF *Altus*, ex-USS PC 568)	PS 80	25 Apr 1942

Displacement, tons	280 standard; 450 full load
Dimensions, feet	170 wl; 173·66 oa × 23 × 10·8
Guns	1—3 inch (*76 mm*) 50 cal AA; 1—40 mm AA; several—20 mm AA (single or twin)
A/S weapons	depth charges
Main engines	Diesels (General Motors); 2 880 bhp; 2 shafts = 20 knots
Complement	Approx 70

Former US Navy patrol craft. Launch dates above; completed 1942-1944. *Batangas* and *Capiz* transferred to the Philippines in July 1948; *Nueva Ecija* in Oct 1958; and *Nueva Viscaya* in Mar 1968. The *Nueva Viscaya* was stricken from the US Navy on 15 Mar 1963 and subsequently served with the US Air Force until transferred to the Philippines in March 1958.

Bohol PS 22 (ex-USS PC 1131) scrapped in 1969, *Camarines Sur* C 21 (ex-USS PC 1121) stricken in 1953, *Negros Oriental* C 26 (ex-USS PC 1563) sunk in typhoon at Guam in Nov 1962 (raised and stricken in 1963).

Tatlac PG 11 (ex-USS PCS 1399, ex-YMS 450) and *Laguna* PG 12 (ex-USS PCS 1403) scrapped in 1969.

CAPIZ *Philippine Navy*

4 100-ft PGM TYPE

AGUSAN	G 61	**ROMBLON**	G 63
CATANDUANES	G 62	**PALAWAN**	G 64

Displacement, tons	122 full load
Dimensions, feet	100·33 oa × 21·1 × 8·5
Guns	2—20 mm AA; 2—·50 cal MG
Main engines	Diesels (Mercedes Benz); 950 bhp; 2 shafts = 17 knots

Steel-hulled patrol gunboats built under US military assistance programme for the Philippines. Built by Tacoma Boatbuilding Co, Tacoma, Washington, and transferred to the Philippines upon completion, G 61 and 62 in Mar 1960, and G 63 and 64 in June 1960. Assigned US designations PGM 39-42 while under construction.
These craft are lengthened versions of the US Coast Guard 85-foot "Cape" class patrol boat design. *Catanduanes* is operated by the Philippine Coast Guard.

ROMBLON *1968, Philippine Navy*

110-ft PGM TYPE

Camarines PG 48, *Sulu* PG 49, *La Union* PG 50, *Antique* PG 51, *Mismamis Occidental* PG 53 reportedly were decommissioned in 1973-1974 and cannibalised for parts. See 1973-1974 edition for characteristics. Assigned US designations PGM 33-36 and 38 while under construction. *Masbate* PG 52 (built as PGM 37) sunk in 1965.

HYDROFOIL PATROL BOATS

CAMIGUIN Type on foils *1965*

Hydrofoil Patrol Boats—*continued*

2 ITALIAN DESIGN

CAMIGUIN HB 77 **SIQUIJOR** HB 76

Displacement, tons	36
Dimensions, feet	67·75 × 15·3 (24·1 overfoils) × 8·9 (3·8 foilborne)
Guns	1—20 mm AA
Main engines	Diesel (Mercedes Benz); 1 250 bhp; 2 shafts = 38 knots

Built by Cantiere Navale Leopoldo Rodriquez, Messina, Sicily. Laid down on 26 May and 28 Oct 1964. Completed in April 1965. For military and police patrol.

CAMIGUIN *Philippine Navy*

2 JAPANESE DESIGN

BALER HB 75 **BONTOC** HB 74

Displacement, tons	32 full load
Dimensions, feet	68·9 × 15·7 × 24·6 over foils
Guns	MG can be mounted fore and aft; normally unarmed
Main engines	Ikegai-Mercedes Benz diesel; 3 200 bhp = 37·8 knots (32 cruising). Also auxiliary engine
Complement	15 (3 officers, 12 ratings) in military role

Built by Hitachi Zosen, Kanagawa Japan. Completed in Dec 1966. For smuggling prevention. Also used as inter-island ferries.

BALER *Philippine Navy*

INSHORE PATROL CRAFT

De HAVILLAND TYPE

Additional small patrol boats of a De Havilland type are reported being constructed for the Philippine Navy in Australia.

6 65-ft SEWART TYPE

Displacement, tons	33 full load
Dimensions, feet	65 oa × 16
Guns	6 machineguns
Main engines	3 diesels (General Motors 12V71); 1 590 bhp; 3 shafts = 25 knots

These craft were ordered in the United States from Sewart in 1971. The design is adopted from a commercial 65-foot boat. Similar to the FB 1-10 operated by the South Korean Navy.

18 "SWIFT" TYPE

PCF 300 (ex-USN PCF 6633)	**PCF 309** (ex-USN PCF 684)
PCF 301 (ex-USN PCF 6634)	**PCF 310** (ex-USN PCF 685)
PCF 302 (ex-USN PCF 35)	**PCF 311** (ex-USN PCF 686)
PCF 303 (ex-USN PCF 36)	**PCF 312** (ex-USN PCF 687)
PCF 304 (ex-USN PCF 37)	**PCF 313** (ex-USN PCF 688)
PCF 305 (ex-USN PCF 38)	**PCF 314** (ex-USN PCF 6911)
PCF 306 (ex-USN PCF 681)	**PCF 315** (ex-USN PCF 6912)
PCF 307 (ex-USN PCF 682)	**PCF 316** (ex-USN PCF 6913)
PCF 308 (ex-USN PCF 683)	**PCF 317** (built 1970)

Displacement, tons	22·5 full load
Dimensions, feet	51·3 × 13·6
Guns	2—50 cal MG
Main engines	2 geared diesels (General Motors); 860 bhp; 2 shafts = 28 knots

Inshore patrol craft of the "Swift" type built in the United States. PCF 302-305 served in US Navy prior to transfer to the Philippines; others built for US military assistance programmes. PCF 300 and 301 transferred to Philippines in Mar 1966, PCF 302-305 in Aug 1966, PCF 306-313 in Feb 1968, PCF 314-316 in July 1970. PCF 317 is Philippine built (ferro concrete).

Inshore Patrol Craft—*Continued*

PCF 310 *1969, Philippine Navy*

PATROL MINESWEEPERS

2 Ex-US MSO TYPE

DAVAO DEL NORTE (ex-USS *Energy*, MSO 436)	PM 91	13 Feb 1953
DAVAO DEL SUR (ex-USS *Firm*, MSO 444)	PM 92	15 Apr 1953

Displacement, tons	665 light; 750 full load
Dimensions, feet	165 wl; 172 oa × 36 × 13·6
Guns	2—20 mm AA (twin)
Main engines	4 diesels (Packard); 2 280 bhp; 2 shafts (controllable-pitch propellers) = 15·5 knots
Complement	approx 70

Former US Navy ocean minesweepers of the "Agile" class. Built by J. M. Martinac Shipbuilding Corp, Tacoma, Washington; launch dates above. Commissioned in US Navy on 16 July 1954 and 12 Oct 1954, respectively. Wood-hulled with non-magnetic engines and fittings.
Both ships transferred to the Philippine Navy on 5 July 1972; designated PM for patrol-minesweepers.

DAVAO DEL NORTE (as USS *Energy*) *1968, US Navy*

2 Ex-US MSC TYPE

ZAMBALES (ex-USS MSC 218)	PM 55
ZAMBOANGA DEL NORTE (ex-USS MSC 219)	PM 56

Displacement, tons	320 light; 385 full load
Dimensions, feet	144 oa × 28 × 8·2
Guns	2—20 mm AA (twin)
Main engines	2 diesels; 880 bhp; 2 shafts = 12 knots
Complement	approx 40

"Bluebird" class coastal minesweepers built by the United States specifically for transfer under the military aid programme. Transferred on 7 Mar 1956 and 23 Apr 1956, respectively. Wood hulled with non-magnetic metal fittings.

ZAMBALES

COMMAND SHIPS

1 JAPANESE BUILT

THE PRESIDENT (ex-*Roxas*, ex-*Lapu-Lapu*) TP 777

Dimensions, feet	275 oa × 42·6 × 21
Guns	2—20 mm AA
Main engines	Diesels; 5 000 bhp; 2 shafts = 18 knots
Complement	approx 90

Built at Ishikawajima, Japan, as war reparation; launched in 1958 and completed in 1959. Used as presidential yacht and command ship.

Originally named *Lapu-Lapu* after the chief who killed Magellan; renamed *Roxas* on 9 Oct 1962 after the late Manuel Roxas, the first President of the Philippines Republic, and again renamed *The President* in 1967.

THE PRESIDENT *1968, Philippine Navy.*

1 Ex-US AM TYPE

MOUNT SAMAT (ex-*Pagasa*, ex-*Santa Maria* ex-*Pagasa*, ex-APO 21, ex-USS *Quest*, AM 281)	TK 21	16 Mar 1944

Displacement, tons	650 standard; 945 full load
Dimensions, feet	184·5 wl; 180 oa × 33 × 9·8
Main engines	Diesels (Cooper Bessemer); 1 710 bhp; 2 shafts = 14·8 knots
Complement	approx 60

Former US Navy minesweeper (AM). Built by Gulf Shipbuilding Corp. Launch date above; commissioned on 25 Oct 1944. Transferred to the Philippines in July 1948. Used as presidential yacht and command ship. A sister ship serves as a surveying ship in the Coast Guard as the *Samar*.

MOUNT SAMAT *1971*

LANDING SHIPS

9 Ex-US LST TYPE

BULACAN (ex-USS LST 843)	LT 38	29 Nov 1944
ALBAY (ex-USS LST 865)	LT 39	22 Nov 1944
MISAMIS ORIENTAL (ex-USS LST 875)	LT 40	29 Nov 1944
BATAAN (ex-USS *Caddo Parish*, LST 515)	LT 85	31 Dec 1943
CAGAYAN (ex-USS *Hickman County*, LST 825)	LT 86	11 Nov 1944
ILCOS NORTE (ex-USS *Madera County*, LST 905)	LT 87	30 Dec 1944
OCCIDENTAL MINDRO (ex-USNS T-LST 222)	LT 93	17 Aug 1943
SURIGAO DEL NORTE (ex-USNS T-LST 546)	LT 94	16 Feb 1944
SURIGAO DEL SUR (ex-USNS T-LST 488)	LT 95	5 Mar 1942

Displacement, tons	1 620 standard; 2 366 beaching; 4 080 full load
Dimensions, feet	316 wl; 328 oa × 50 × 14
Guns	7 or 8—40 mm AA (two twin, four single) in former USS ships; former USNS ships unarmed
Main engines	Diesels (General Motors); 1 700 bhp; 2 shafts = 11·6 knots
Complement	approx 60

Former US Navy tank landing ships. Cargo capacity 2 100 tons. Launch dates above. Three ships transferred in July 1948; three ships on 29 Nov 1969; and three ships on 15 July 1972.

Cutabato T 36 ex-USS LST 75 and *Pampanga* T 37 ex-USS LST 842 have been scrapped.

MISAMIS ORIENTAL *1968, Philippine Navy*

Landing Ships—*continued*

2 Ex-US LSM TYPE

ISABELA (ex-USS LSM 463) LP 41
ORIENTAL MINDORO (ex-USS LSM 320) LP 68

Displacement, tons	743 beaching; 1 095 full load
Dimensions, feet	196·5 wl; 203·5 oa × 34·6 × 8·5
Guns	2—40 mm AA (twin); several 20 mm AA
Main engines	Diesels (direct drive; General Motors except Fairbanks Morse in *Isabela*); 2 800 bhp; 2 shafts = 12·5 knots

Former US Navy medium landing ships. Built 1944-1945. Transferred to the Philippines in March 1961, and April 1962, respectively. *Batanes* LP 65 ex-USS LSM 236 ran aground in June 1971 and stricken in 1972.

BATANES—now stricken *1962, Courtesy Mr W. H. Davis*

2 REPAIR SHIPS: Ex-US ARL TYPES

KAMAGONG ex-*Aklan*, (ex-USS *Romulus*, ARL 22, ex-LST 926) AR 67
NARRA (ex-USS *Krishna*, ARL 38, ex-LST 1149) AR 88

Displacement, tons	2 366 standard; 4 100 full load
Dimensions, feet	316 wl; 328 oa × 50 × 11·2
Guns	8—40 mm AA (quad); several 20 mm AA
Main engines	Diesels (General Motors); 1 800 bhp; 2 shafts = 11·6 knots
Complement	approx 220

Former US Navy landing craft repair ships. Converted during construction from LSTs; launched on 15 Nov 1944 and 25 May 1945, respectively. Transferred to the Philippines in Nov 1961 and on 30 Oct 1971, respectively.

KAMAGONG *1968, Philippine Navy*

2 OILERS: Ex-US YO and YOG TYPE

LAKE MAUJAN (ex-USS YO 173) YO 43
LAKE BOHI (ex-USS YOG 73) YO 78

Displacement, tons	520 standard; 1 400 full load
Dimensions, feet	174 oa × 32 × 13·2
Guns	2—20 mm AA (single)
Main engines	Diesel; 560 bhp; 1 shaft = 8 knots

Former US Navy self-propelled fuel oil barges. Built in 1943-1944. Cargo capacity 6 570 barrels. *Lake Maujan* carries fuel oil and *Lake Bohi* carries gasoline and diesel fuel. *Lake Lanao* of same design (see photo). Transferred to the Philippines in July 1948 and July 1967, respectively.

1 WATER CARRIER: Ex-US YW TYPE

LAKE LANAO (ex-USS YW 125) YW 42

Displacement, tons	1 235 full load
Dimensions, feet	174 oa × 32 × 15
Guns	2—20 mm AA
Main engines	Diesel; 560 bhp; 1 shaft = 8 knots

Former US Navy self-propelled water barge. Cargo capacity 200 000 gallons fresh water. Transferred to the Philippines in July 1948.

1 TUG: Ex-US ATR TYPE

IFUGAO (ex-HMS *Emphatic*, ex-USS ATR 96) AQ 44

Displacement, tons	783 full load
Dimensions, feet	134·6 wl; 143 oa × 33·8 × 13·5
Guns	1—3 inch (*76 mm*) 50 cal AA; 2—20 mm AA
Main engines	Diesel; 1 500 bhp; 1 shaft = 13 knots

Rescue tug transferred to Royal Navy upon launching on 27 Jan 1944; subsequently returned to US Navy and retransferred to the Philippines in July 1948.

6 TUGS: Ex-US HARBOUR TYPE

MARANAO (ex-YTL 554)	YQ 221	**AETA** (ex-YTL 449)	YQ 224
IGOROT (ex-YTL 572)	YQ 222	**ILONGOT** ((ex-YTL 427)	YQ 225
TAGBANUA (ex-YTL 429)	YQ 223	**TASADAY** (ex-YTL 425)	YQ 226

Former US Navy 66-foot harbour tugs.

Auxiliary Ships—*continued*

1 CARGO SHIP: Ex-US C1-M-AV1 TYPE

MACTAN (ex-USCGC *Kukui*, WAK 186, ex-USS *Colquitt*, AK 174) TK 90

Displacement, tons	4 900 light; 5 636 full load
Dimensions, feet	320 wl; 338·5 oa × 50 × 18
Guns	Unarmed
Main engines	Diesel (Nordberg); 1 750 bhp; 1 shaft = 11·5 knots

Cargo-ship built by Froemming Brothers, Milwaukee, Wisconsin, launched on 21 Jan 1945 and commissioned in US Navy on 22 Sep 1945 and transferred to the Coast Guard two days later. Subsequently served as Coast Guard supply ship in Pacific until transferred to Philippines on 1 March 1972. Used to supply military posts and lighthouses in the Philippine archipelago.

1 TENDER: Ex-US COAST GUARD TENDER

KALINGA (ex-USCGC *Redbud*, WLB 398, ex-USNS *Redbud*, T-AKL 398) TK 89

Displacement, tons	935 standard
Dimensions, feet	180 oa × 37 × 13
Guns	Unarmed
Main engines	Diesel-electric; 1 200 bhp; 1 shaft = 13 knots

Originally US Coast Guard buoy tender (WAGL 398) built by Marine Iron & Shipbuilding Co, Duluth, Minnesota; launched on 11 Sep 1943. Transferred to US Navy on 25 Mar 1949 as AG 398; redesignated AKL 398 on 31 Mar 1949; transferred to Military Sea Transportation Service on 20 Feb 1952 (T-AKL 398); reacquired by Coast Guard on 20 Nov 1970 and transferred to Philippines on 1 Mar 1972.

3 TENDERS: Ex-US ARMY FS TYPE

BOJEADOE (ex-US Army FS 203) TK 46
LAUIS LEDGE (ex-US Army FS 185) TK 45
LIMASAWA (ex-USCGC *Nettle* WAK 169, ex-US Army FS 169) TK 79

Displacement, tons	470 standard; 811 full load
Dimensions, feet	180 oa × 23 × 10
Main engines	Diesels; 1 000 shp; 1 shaft = 11 knots

Former US Army freight and supply ships. Employed as tenders for buoys and light houses.

LAUIS LEDGE *1969, Philippine Navy*

1 TENDER: Ex-AUSTRALIAN TYPE

PEARL BANK (ex-US Army LO 4, ex-Australian MSL)

Displacement, tons	160 standard; 300 full load
Dimensions, feet	120 oa × 24·5 × 8
Main engines	Diesels (Fairbanks Morse); 240 bhp; 2 shafts = 7 knots

Originally an Australian motor stores lighter; subsequently transferred to the US Army and then to the Philippines. Employed as a lighthouse tender.

5 FLOATING DRY DOCKS

YD 200 (ex-AFDL 24) **YD 203** **YD 205** (ex-AFDL 44)
YD 201 **RD 204** (ex-AFDL 20)

Floating dry docks built in the United States; three are former US Navy units with YD 200 transferred in July 1948, RD 204 in October 1961, and YD 205 in September 1969; two other units built specifically for Philippine service were completed in May 1952 and August 1955, respectively.

COAST AND GEODETIC SERVICE

SAMAR (ex-USS *Project*, AM 278) M 33 20 Nov 1943

Former US Navy minesweeper, similar to the *Mount Samat*. Built by Gulf Shipbuilding Corp; launch dates above. Transferred to the Philippines in July 1948. Subsequently adapted for surveying and now operated by the Coast & Geodetic Service.

COAST GUARD

2 PATROL BOATS

ABRA FB 83 **BUKIDNON** FB 84

Displacement, tons	40 standard
Dimensions, feet	87·5 oa × 19 × 4·75
Guns	2—20 mm AA
Main engines	Diesels (Mercedes-Benz); 2 460 bhp; 2 shafts = approx 25 knots
Complement	15 (3 officers, 12 enlisted men)

One acquired from Singapore in late 1969. *Bukidnon* built at Cavite in 1970-1971. Wood hulls and aluminium superstructure.

The Coast Guard also has 14 40-foot utility boats, all transferred from the US Coast Guard except for the *CGC 127*, a 40-foot, 11-ton craft built in the Philippines with a ferro-concrete hull.

POLAND

Administration

Commander-in-Chief of the Polish Navy:
Vice-Admiral Ludwik Janczyszyn

Chief of the Naval Staff:
Rear-Admiral Henryk Pietraszkiewicz

Diplomatic Representation

Naval, Military and Air Attaché in London:
Colonel Henryk Krzeszowski

Naval, Military and Air Attaché in Washington:
Colonel Henryk Nowaczyk

Naval, Military and Air Attaché in Moscow:
Brigadier General Waclaw Jagas

Naval, Miliatry and Air Attaché in Paris:
Colonel Marian Bugaj

Personnel

(a) 1975: 25 000 (2 800 officers and 22 200 men)
(b) 3 years National Service

Strength of the Fleet

Type	*Active*
Destroyers	1 (2 static)
Submarines—Patrol	4
Fast Attack Craft—Missile	12
Fast Attack Craft—Torpedo	22
Large Patrol Craft	26
Coastal Patrol Craft	20
Minesweepers—Ocean	24
Minesweeping Boats	20
LSTs	1 +1
LCTs	23
Surveying Vessels	2
Training Ships	2
Tankers	6
TRV's	Several
Tugs	20
Icebreaker	1
TCV's	2

Prefix to Ships' Names

ORP, standing for *Okrety Polska Rzeczpospolita*

Naval Aviation

There is a Fleet Air Arm of about 50 fixed-wing aircraft (mainly MiG-17 and IL-28) and helicopters.

Mercantile Marine

Lloyd's Register of Shipping:
631 vessels of 2 072 531 tons gross

Deletions

Destroyer
1974 *Blyskawica* (museum ship in Gdynia in place of *Burza*)

Corvettes
1973 *Czuiny, Wytrwaly, Zawziety, Zrezczny, Zwinny, Zwrotny*
1974 *Grozny, Nieugiety* ("Kronstadt" class) disposals

Fast Attack Craft—Torpedo
1973 3 "P6" class
1974 6 "P6" class

DESTROYERS

1 Ex-SOVIET "SAM KOTLIN" CLASS

WARSZAWA 275

Displacement, tons	2 850 standard; 3 885 full load
Length, feet (*metres*)	415·0 (*126·5*) oa
Beam, feet (*metres*)	42·3 (*12·9*)
Draught, feet (*metres*)	16·1 (*4·9*)
Missile launchers	1 twin SAN-1 (Goa) aft for surface-to-air missiles
Guns	2—5·1 in dp (1 twin); 4—45 mm (quad); 4—30 mm (twin)
A/S weapons	2—16 barrelled MBU; 4 side launch DC projectors
Main engines	Geared turbines; 2 shafts; 72 000 shp
Oil fuel, tons	800
Range, miles	5 500 at 16 knots
Speed, knots	36
Complement	285

Transferred from the USSR to the Polish Navy in 1970.

WARSZAWA — *1973, Contre Amiral M. Adam*

RADAR. Air Search: Head Net C. Fire Control: Peel Group (SAN-1), Wasp Head/Sun Visor B (main armament), Egg Cup (45 mm), 2 Drum Tilt (30 mm); IFF: High Pole B.

2 Ex-SOVIET "SKORY" CLASS

GROM (ex-*Smetlivy*) 273 **WICHER** (ex-*Skory*) 274

Displacement, tons	2 600 standard; 3 500 full load
Length, feet (*metres*)	395·2 (*120·5*)
Beam, feet (*metres*)	38·9 (*11·8*)
Draught, feet (*metres*)	15·1 (*5·6*)
Guns,	4—5·1 in (*130 mm*), 2 twin mounts; 2—3·4 in (*85 mm*); 8—37 mm
A/S weapons	4 DCT
Torpedo tubes	10—21 in (*533 mm*) 2 quintuple
Mines	80 capacity
Boilers	4 high pressure
Main engines	Geared turbines; 2 shafts; 60 000 shp
Speed, knots	33
Range, miles	3 900 at 13 knots
Oil fuel, tons	700
Complement	260

Former Soviet destroyers of the first "Skory" type. *Wicher* was in fact the prototype of the class. To Poland on 15 Dec 1957 (*Grom*) and 28 June 1958 (*Wicher*).

STATUS. Both now moored as static AA batteries.

RADAR. Air Search: Cross Bird; Surface Search: High Sieve; Fire Control: Post Lamp; Navigation: Neptune; IFF: Ski Pole.

SUBMARINES

4 Ex-USSR "WHISKY" CLASS

BIELIK 295 **ORZEL** 292
KONDOR 294 **SOKOL** 293

Displacement, tons	1 030 surface; 1 180 dived
Length, feet (*metres*)	240 (*73·2*)
Beam, feet (*metres*)	22 (*6·7*)
Draught, feet (*metres*)	15 (*4·6*)
Torpedo tubes	6—21 in (*533 mm*), 4 bow, 2 stern; 18 torpedoes carried
Mines	40 mines in lieu of torpedoes
Main machinery	2 Diesels; 4 000 hp; 2 shafts; Electric motors; 2 500 hp
Speed, knots	17 on surface; 15 dived
Range, miles	13 000 at 8 knots (surfaced)
Complement	60

Built in the USSR and transferred to the Polish Navy.

RADAR. Snoop Plate.

SOKOL — ***1971, Polish Navy***

KONDOR — ***1972***

LIGHT FORCES

12 SOVIET "OSA" CLASS (FAST ATTACK CRAFT—MISSILE)

Displacement, tons	165 standard; 200 full load
Dimensions, ft (*m*)	128·7 × 25·1 × 5·9 (*39·3 × 7·7 × 1·8*)
Missiles	4 launchers for SSN-2A
Guns	4—30 mm (2 twin, 1 forward, 1 aft)
Main engines	3 diesels; 13 000 bhp = 32 knots
Range, miles	800 at 25 knots
Complement	25

All pennant numbers are in the low 100 series and are carried on side-boards on the bridge.

RADAR. Search: Square Tie and Strut Curve. Fire Control: Drum Tilt.

"Osa" class *1969*

12 "WISLA" CLASS (FAST ATTACK CRAFT—TORPEDO)

Displacement, tons	70 full load
Dimensions, ft (*m*)	82·0 × 18·0 × 6·0 (*25 × 5·5 × 1·8*)
A/S weapons	4 DC
Guns	2—30 mm AA Twin
Tubes	4—21 in (*533 mm*)
Main engines	Diesels; speed 30 knots

Polish built in a continuing programme. Pennant numbers in 490 series.

WISLA *1973*

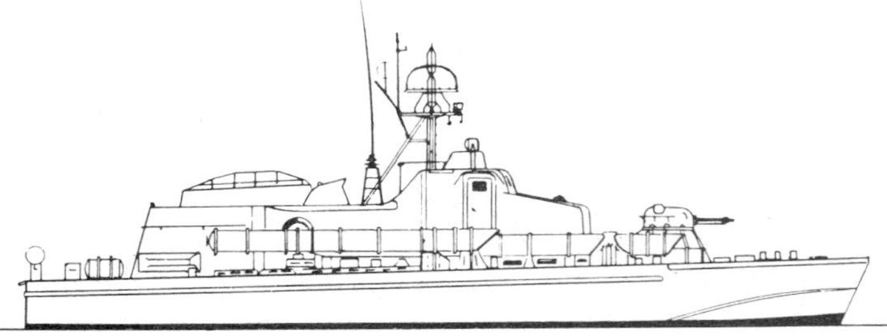
"WISLA" Class *1973, S, Breyer*

10 Ex-SOVIET "P 6" CLASS (FAST ATTACK CRAFT—TORPEDO)

410-419

Displacement, tons	66 standard; 75 full load
Dimensions, ft (*m*)	84·2 × 20 × 6 (*25·7 × 6·1 × 1·8*)
Guns	4—25 mm AA; 8 DC
Tubes	2—21 in
Main engines	4 diesels; 4 800 bhp = 45 knots
Complement	25

Acquired from the USSR in 1957-58. Torpedo tubes removed in some. SKIN HEAD surface search and navigation radar. At least two have been converted to target craft.

No. 410 ***1971, Polish Navy***

4 "OKSYWIE" CLASS (LARGE PATROL CRAFT)

301 302 303 304

Displacement, tons	170 standard
Dimensions, feet	134·5 × 19·0 × 6·9
Guns	4—37 mm (2 twin)
A/S weapons	DC throwers
Main engines	Diesels; speed = 20 knots

Improved versions of earlier patrol boats of the type. Depth charge racks fitted.

OKSYWIE *1972*

"OKSYWIE" Class *S. Breyer*

8 "MODIFIED OBLUZE" CLASS (LARGE PATROL CRAFT)

351 352 353 354 355 356 357 358

Displacement, tons	150
Dimensions, feet	137·8 × 19 × 6·6
Guns	2 or 4—30 mm
A/S weapons	DC throwers
Main engines	2 diesels = 20 knots

Slightly smaller than original "Obluze" class. Belong to WOP (Coastguard).

"OBLUZE" Class *1972, S. Breyer*

Light Forces—*continued*

5 "OBLUZE" CLASS (LARGE PATROL CRAFT)

321	322	323	324	325

Displacement, tons	170
Dimensions, feet	143·0 × 19·0 × 7·0
A/S weapons	DC throwers
Guns	4—30 mm AA (2 twins)

Built since 1965 at Oksywie Shipyard. Belong to WOP (coastguard).

OBLUZE (old number) *1969*

9 "GDANSK" CLASS (LARGE PATROL CRAFT)

311	313	315	317	319
312	314	316	318	

Displacement, tons	120
Dimensions, feet	124·7 × 19·2 × 5·0
Guns	2—37 mm AA
A/S weapons	DC rails
Main engines	Diesels; speed 20 knots

Built in 1960. Belong to WOP (coastguard).

GDANSK *1970*

"GDANSK" Class *S. Breyer*

20 "K8" CLASS (COASTAL PATROL CRAFT)

KP 118	KP 120	KP 122	KP 124	KP 126
KP 119	KP 121	KP 123	KP 125	+ 11

Displacement, tons	60
Guns	2 MG AA (in twin mounting)
Main engines	3 motors; speed 15 knots

Small patrol boats under the jurisdiction of the WOP (coastguard). Now obsolescent and due for replacement.

MINE WARFARE FORCES

12 "KROGULEC" CLASS (MINESWEEPERS—OCEAN)

ORLIK	613	KORMORAN	616		619		622
KROGULEC	614	CZAPLA	617	TUKAN	620		623
JASTRAB	615	ALABATROS	618		621		624

Displacement, tons	500
Dimensions, feet	190·3 × 24·6 × 8·2
Guns	6—25 mm AA
Main engines	Diesels, speed = 16 knots

Flushdecked minesweepers of a new type built at the Stocznia Yard from 1963 onwards. *Jastreb* and *Orlik* commissioned in 1964.

KROGULEC *1972, S. Breyer*

12 SOVIET "T 43" CLASS (MINESWEEPERS—OCEAN)

BIZON	605	DZIK	604	MORS	610	TUR	602
BOBR	606	FOKA	609	ROSOMAK	607	ZBIK	612
DELFIN	608	LOS	603	RYS	611	ZUBR	601

Displacement, tons	500 standard; 610 full load
Dimensions, feet	190·2 × 28·2 × 6·9
Guns	4—37 mm AA; 4—25 mm
Main engines	2 diesels; 2 shafts; 2 000 hp = 17 knots
Complement	40

Soviet "T43" class but built in Poland at Stocznia Gdynia in 1957-62.

DELFIN *1969, Polish Navy*

20 "K 8" CLASS (MSBs)

Displacement, tons	20 approx
Dimensions, feet	54·1 × 19·0 × 5·0

Minesweeping boats built in Poland. Pennant numbers run in 800 and 900 series.

AMPHIBIOUS FORCES

1 + 1 "ROPUCHA" CLASS (LST)

Reported to be of approximately the same characteristics as the Soviet "Alligator" class. Now building at Gdynia.

23 "POLNOCNY" CLASS (LCT)

801-811 **888-899**

Displacement tons	780 standard; 1 000 full load
Dimensions, feet	225 × 27·7 × 9·8
Armament	2—18 barrelled rocket projectors 1—30 mm
Main engines	2 diesels; 5 000 bhp = 18 knots

Polish built, in Gdansk, but same as the Soviet "Polnocny" class—can carry six tanks. Of various types including Polish variations.

POLNOCNY 806 1971

SURVEYING VESSELS

"MOMA CLASS"

KOPERNIK

Of 1 580 tons, launched in 1971.

BALTYK

Displacement, tons	1 200
Measurements, tons	658 gross; 450 deadweight
Dimensions, feet	194·3 oa; 175·3 pp × 29·5 × 14
Main engines	Steam; 1 000 hp = 11 knots

Trawler of B-10 type. Built in 1954 in Gdansk. Converted and structure altered.

BALTYK 1968

TRAINING SHIPS

GRYF (ex-*Zetempowiec*, ex-*Opplem*, ex-*Omsk*, ex-*Empire Contees*, ex-*Irene Oldendorf*)

Measurement, tons	1 959 gross
Dimensions, feet	282·2 × 44·2 × 18·8
Guns	2—3·9 in; 4—37 mm AA
Main engines	Steam, 1 200 hp = 10 knots

Former German "Hansa" class ship. Built by Burmeister & Wain. Launched in 1944. Taken over in 1947. Transferred to the Navy in 1949. The name was changed from *Zetempowiec* to *Gryf* in 1957. Used as a cadet training ship.

GRYF 1969

Training Ships—*continued*

ISKRA (ex-*Pigmy*, ex-*Iskra*, ex-*St Blanc*, ex-*Vlissingen*)

Displacement, tons	560
Dimensions, feet	128 × 25 × 10
Main engines	Diesels; 250 bhp = 7·5 knots
Complement	30, plus 40 cadets

A three masted schooner with auxiliary engines. Built by Muller, Foxhol, Holland. Launched in 1917. Cadet training ship.

ISKRA 1969

TANKERS

3 "MOSKIT" CLASS

Z 3 **Z 8** **Z 9**

Displacement, tons	approx 700
Guns	2—30 mm (Twin)

Z 5 **Z 6** **Z 7**

Lighters of 300 tons gross with diesels, converted into tankers for coastal service.

TORPEDO RECOVERY VESSELS

Some of a new class, including K 11, have been reported.

TUGS

Some 20 of various classes with H pennant numbers.

ICEBREAKER

PERKUN

Displacement, tons	800
Main engines	Diesel-electric, 2 shafts; 3 500 bhp = 12 knots

Icebreaker built in 1962 by P. K. Harris & Sons, Appledore, Devon, England. Not a naval vessel but can be employed with and for the Navy.

PERKUN 1972

DEGAUSSING VESSELS

URAN **URANIA**

Displacement, tons	254
Main engines	Speed = 8 knots

Degaussing vessel of the British MMS minesweeper 11 type, classed as auxiliaries. Being replaced by a more modern class of which SD 12 is a member.

PORTUGAL

Administration

Chief of Naval Staff:
Admiral J. B. Pinheiro de Azevedo

Diplomatic Representation

Naval Attaché in London:
Captain P. M. Cerujo

Naval Attaché in Washington:
Captain Jose L. Ferreira Lamas

Naval Attaché in Paris:
Commander Silvano J. Freitas-Braneo

Personnel

(a) 1975: 19 000 (1 800 officers and 17 200 men) including marines
(b) 4 years National Service

Strength of the Fleet

Type	Active	Building
Frigates	11	—
Corvettes	15	—
Submarines-Patrol	4	—
Large Patrol Craft	11	—
Coastal Patrol Craft	26	—
Minesweepers-Coastal	9	—
LCT	6	—
LCM	36	—
LCA	22	—
Survey Ships and Craft	7	—
Replenishment Tanker	1	—
Supply Ship	1	—
Sail Training Ship	1	—
Depot Ship	1	—
Fishery Protection Vessels	4	—
Ocean Tug	1	—
Harbour Tugs	2	—

Prefix to Ships' Names

NRP

Naval Bases

Main Base: Lisbon.
Dockyard: Arsenal do Alfeite.

Disposals

Frigates

1970 ***Francisco de Almeida, Pacheco Pereira***
1971 ***Alvares Cabral, Vasco da Gama***

Corvettes

1971 *Cacheu*
1973 *Porto Sante, Fogo Maio*

Minesweepers

1973 *Angra do Heroismo, Ponta Delgada, S. Pedro* (MSC), *Corvo, Pico, Graciosa, S. Jorge* (MSO)

Maritime Reconnaissance Aircraft

Whilst there are no aircraft belonging to the Navy, P2V Neptunes of the Portuguese Air Force are placed under naval operational control for specific maritime operations.

Mercantile Marine

Lloyd's Register of Shipping:
431 vessels of 1 243 128 tons gross

FRIGATES

4 "COMANDANTE JOÃO BELO" CLASS

Name	No.	Builders	Laid down	Launched	Completed
COMANDANTE HERMENEGILDO CAPELO	F 481	At et Ch de Nantes	13 May 1966	29 Nov 1966	26 Apr 1968
COMANDANTE JOÃO BELO	F 480	At et Ch de Nantes	6 Sep 1965	22 Mar 1966	1 July 1967
COMANDANTE ROBERTO IVENS	F 482	At et Ch de Nantes	13 Dec 1966	8 Aug 1967	23 Nov 1968
COMANDANTE SACADURA CABRAL	F 483	At et Ch de Nantes	18 Aug 1967	15 Mar 1968	25 July 1969

Displacement, tons	1 990 standard; 2 230 full load
Length, feet (*metres*)	321·5 (*98*) pp; 338 (*103·0*) oa
Beam, feet (*metres*)	37·7 (*11·5*)
Draught, feet (*metres*)	14·5 (*4·42*)
Guns	3—3·9 in (*100 mm*) AA single; 2—40 mm AA
A/S weapons	1—12 in quadruple mortar
Torpedo tubes	6—21·7 in (*550 mm*) ASM, 2 triple
Main engines	SEMT-Pielstick diesels; 2 shafts; 18 760 bhp
Speed, knots	25
Range, miles	4 500 at 15 knots; 2 300 at 25 knots
Complement	200 (14 officers, 186 men)

COMANDANTE ROBERTO IVENS *1970, Portuguese Navy*

CONSTRUCTION. The prefabricated construction of these frigates was begun on 1 Oct 1964 at the Ateliers et Chantiers de Nantes, France.

DESIGN. They are similar to the French "Commandant Riviére" class except for the 30 mm AA guns which were replaced by 40 mm AA guns.

RADAR. Search: DRBV 22. Tactical: Probably S Band. Fire Control: DRBC 32 radar director.

"COMANDANTE JOAO BELO" Class

COMANDANTE SACADURA CABRAL

1972, Portuguese Navy

Frigates—*continued*

3 "ALMIRANTE PEREIRA DA SILVA" CLASS

Name	*No.*	*Builders*	*Laid down*	*Launched*	*Completed*
ALMIRANTE GAGO COUTINHO	F 473 (ex-US DE 1042)	Estaleiros Navais Lisnave, Lisbon	2 Dec 1963	13 Aug 1965	29 Nov 1967
ALMIRANTE MAGALHÃES CORREA	F 474 (ex-US DE 1046)	Estaleiros Navais de Viana do Castelo	30 Aug 1965	26 Apr 1966	4 Nov 1968
ALMIRANTE PEREIRA DA SILVA	F 472 (ex-US DE 1039)	Estaleiros Navais Lisnave, Lisbon	14 June 1962	2 Dec 1963	20 Dec 1966

Displacement, tons	1 450 standard; 1 914 full load
Length, feet (*metres*)	314·6 (*95·9*)
Beam, feet (*metres*)	36·68 (*11·18*)
Draught, feet (*metres*)	14 (*4·3*) hull; 17·5 (*5·33*) max
Guns	4—3 in (*76 mm*) 50 cal. dp;
A/S weapons	2 Bofors 4-barrelled mortars 2 DC throwers
Torpedo tubes	6 (2 triple) for A/S torpedoes
Main engines	De Laval dr geared turbines; 1 shaft; 20 000 shp
Speed, knots	27 designed
Boilers	2 Foster Wheeler, 300 psi, 850°F
Range, miles	3 220 at 15 knots
Oil fuel, tons	400
Complement	166 (12 officers, 154 men)

CONSTRUCTION. The prefabrication of *Almirante Pereira da Silva* and *Almirante Gago Coutinho* was begun in 1961 at Lisnave (formerly Navalis Shipyard, Lisbon) and of *Almirante Magalhães Correa* in 1962.

ALMIRANTE GAGO COUTINHO *1973, Dr. Giorgio Arra*

ALMIRANTE PEREIRA DA SILVA *Class*

RADAR. Search: SPS 6. Tactical: X Band. Surface warning and navigation Air surveillance: S band. Extensive EW.

DESIGN. Similar to the United States destroyer escorts of the "Dealey" class, but modified to suit Portuguese requirements.

SONAR. Probably DUBV-43.

10 "JOÃO COUTINHO" CLASS

Name	*No.*	*Builders*	*Launched*	*Completed*
ANTONIO ENES	F 471	Empresa Nacional Bazan, Spain	16 Aug 1969	18 June 1971
AUGUSTO DE CASTILHO	F 484	Empresa Nacional Bazan, Spain	4 July 1969	14 Nov 1970
GENERAL PEREIRA D'ECA	F 477	Blohm and Voss A.G., Hamburg, Germany	26 July 1969	10 Oct 1970
HONORIO BARRETO	F 485	Empresa Nacional Bazan, Spain	11 Apr 1970	15 Apr 1971
JACINTO CANDIDO	F 476	Blohm and Voss A.G., Hamburg, Germany	16 June 1969	16 June 1970
JOÃO COUTINHO	F 475	Blohm and Voss A.G., Hamburg, Germany	2 May 1969	7 Mar 1970
JOÃO ROBY	F 487	Empresa Nacional Bazan, Spain	3 June 1973	June 1974
OLIVEIRA E CARMO	F 489	Empresa Nacional Bazan, Spain	Feb 1974	Feb 1975
AFONSO CERQUEIRA	F 488	Empresa Nacional Bazan, Spain	Oct 1973	Dec 1974
BAPTISTA DE ANDRADE	F 490	Empresa Nacional Bazan, Spain	Mar 1973	June 1974

Displacement, tons	1 203 standard; 1 380 full load
Length, feet (*metres*)	227·5 (*84·6*)
Beam, feet (*metres*)	33·8 (*10·3*)
Draught, feet (*metres*)	10·0 (*3·07*); 11·8 (*3·6*) deep
Guns	2—3 in (*76 mm*) dp; (1—3·9 in in last four) 2—40 mm
A/S weapons	1 Hedgehog; 2 DC throwers; 2 DC racks
Main engines	2 OEW 12 cyl. Pielstick diesels; 10 560 bhp
Speed, knots	24·4
Range, miles	5 900 at 18 knots
Complement	100 (9 officers, 91 men) plus 34 marine detachment

JOÃO COUTINHO *1971, Portuguese Navy*

RADAR. Equipped with SPS 10 search radar. S Band air surveillance and X-band surface warning and navigation. Plessey AWS-2 air search in last four.

"JOÃO COUTINHO" Class

Frigates—*continued*

PERO ESCOBAR F 335

Displacement, tons	1 270 standard; 1 390 full load
Length, feet (*metres*)	306·7 (*93·5*) wl; 321·5 (*98·0*) oa
Beam, feet (*metres*)	35·5 (*10·8*)
Draught, feet (*metres*)	10 (*3·0*); 12·2 (*3·7*) deep
Guns	2—40 mm; 2—20 mm
A/S weapons	2 "Squid" triple DC mortars
Torpedo tubes	6 (2 triple) for A/S torpedoes
Main engines	2 Ansaldo-Genova sr geared turbines; 2 shafts; 24 000 shp
Speed, knots	32·6
Boilers	2 Ansoldo-Foster Wheeler "D" 32 *kg/cm²*, 400°C
Complement	165 (10 officers, 155 men)

Built for the Portuguese Navy by Navalmeccanica, Castellammare di Stabia, Italy. Laid down on 9 Jan 1955. Launched on 25 Sep 1955. Completed on 30 June 1957.

PERO ESCOBAR *1973, Portuguese Navy*

RADAR. Search S Band air surveillance.
Fire Control: Elsag X Band.

MODERNISATION in 1970-71 included new guns, sonar and A/S torpedo tubes similar to those in the "Almirante Pereira da Silva" class. Armament before modernisation: 2 single 3 inch guns, 1 twin 40 mm AA, 2 twin 20 mm AA, 3—21 inch torpedo tubes.

PERO ESCOBAR

CORVETTES

3 PORTUGUESE BUILT "MAIO" CLASS

Name	*No.*	*Builders*	*Launched*	*Completed*
BOAVISTA	P 592	Est Nav do Mondego	10 July 1956	17 May 1957
BRAVA	P 590	EN de Viana do Castelo	2 May 1956	27 Dec 1956
SANTA LUZIA	P 594	Arsenal do Alfeite	17 Jan 1957	24 Oct 1958

Displacement, tons	366 standard; 400 full load
Dimensions, feet	170 pp; 173·8 oa × 23 × 10
Guns	2—40 mm; 2—20 mm
A/S weapons	1 Hedgehog, 4 DCT; 2 depth charge racks
Main engines	4 SEMT-Pielstick diesels (4-stroke, 14 cylinder V); 2 shafts; 3 500 bhp = 19 knots
Oil fuel, tons	45
Range, miles	4 500 at 18 knots
Complement	62 (5 officers, 57 men)

FOGO ("Maio" class similar) *1972, Portuguese Navy*

Built in Portugal under the US off-shore procurement programme in 1956-57. Class of five. Of all-welded construction.

1 FRENCH BUILT "MAIO" CLASS

Name	*No.*	*Builders*	*Launched*
S NICOLAU (ex-P 8)	P 589	Normand (Le Havre)	7 June 1955

Displacement, tons	366 standard; 400 full load
Dimensions, feet	170 pp; 173·7 oa × 23 × 10
Guns	2—40 mm; 2—20 mm
A/S weapons	1 Hedgehog; 4 DCT; 2 depth charge racks
Main engines	4 SEMT-Pielstick diesels; 2 shafts; 3 240 bhp = 18 knots
Range, miles	4 500 at 18 knots
Complement	62 (5 officers, 57 men)

S. NICOLAU *1973, Portuguese Navy*

Of PC design, but built in France as a US offshore procurement order under the Mutual Defense Assistance Program in 1954-55. Class of three. Fitted with two mine rails.

10 "CACINE" CLASS

CACINE	P 1140	**GEBA**	P 1145	**ROVUMA**	P 1143
CUNENE	P 1141	**LIMPOPO**	P 1160	**SAVE**	P 1161
CUANZA	P 1144	**MANDOVI**	P 1142	**ZAIRE**	P 1146
				ZAMBEZE	P 1147

Displacement, tons	292·5 standard; 310 full load
Dimensions, feet	144·0 oa × 25·2 × 7·1
Guns	2—40 mm AA; 1—32 barrelled rocket launcher 37 mm
Main engines	2 Maybach diesels; 2 000 bhp = 20 knots
Range, miles	4 400 at 12 knots
Complement	33 (3 officers, 30 men)

CACINE *1973, Portuguese Navy*

Cacine, Cunene Mandovi, Rovuma, Limpopo and *Save* were built in Arsenal do Alfeita, the other four in Estaleiros Navais do Mendogo in 1969-72.

SUBMARINES

4 "ALBACORA" CLASS (FRENCH "DAPHNE" CLASS)

Name	No.	Builders	Laid down	Launched	Completed
ALBACORA	S 163	Dubigeon-Normandie	6 Sep 1965	13 Oct 1966	1 Oct 1967
BARRACUDA	S 164	Dubigeon-Normandie	19 Oct 1965	24 Apr 1967	4 May 1968
CACHALOTE	S 165	Dubigeon-Normandie	27 Oct 1966	16 Feb 1968	25 Jan 1969
DELFIN	S 166	Dubigeon-Normandie	14 May 1967	23 Sep 1968	1 Oct 1969

Displacement, tons	700 standard; 869 surface; 1 043 submerged
Length, feet (*metres*)	189·6 (*57·8*)
Beam, feet (*metres*)	22·3 (*6·8*)
Draught, feet (*metres*)	15·1 (*4·6*)
Torpedo tubes	12—21·7 in (*550 mm*); 8 bow, 4 stern
Main machinery	SEMT-Pielstick diesels, 1 300 bhp Electric motors; 450 kW, 1 600 hp; 2 shafts
Speed, knots	13·2 on surface and 16 submerged
Range, miles	2 710 at 12·5 knots on surface; 2 130 at 10 knots snorting
Oil fuel, tons	90
Complement	50 (5 officers; 45 men)

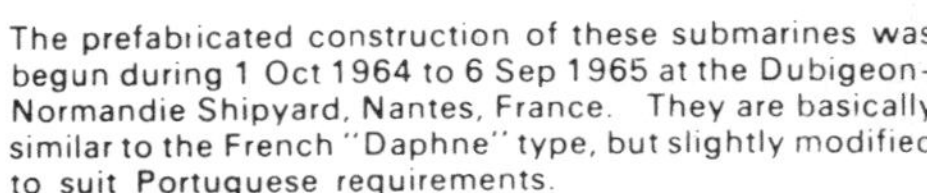
The prefabricated construction of these submarines was begun during 1 Oct 1964 to 6 Sep 1965 at the Dubigeon-Normandie Shipyard, Nantes, France. They are basically similar to the French "Daphne" type, but slightly modified to suit Portuguese requirements.

BARRACUDA — *1970, Captain Aluino Martins da Silva*

DELFIN — *1972, Portuguese Navy*

LIGHT FORCES

10 "ARGOS" CLASS (LARGE PATROL CRAFT)

ARGOS	P 372	**DRAGÃO**	P 374	**LIRA**	P 361
CASSIOPEIA	P 373	**ESCORPIÃO**	P 375	**ORION**	P 362
CENTAURO	P 1130	**HIDRA**	P 376	**PEGASO**	P 379
				SAGITARIO	P 1131

Displacement, tons	180 standard; 210 full load
Dimensions, feet	131·2 pp; 136·8 oa × 20·5 × 7
Guns	2—40 mm
Main engines	2 Maybach diesels; 1 200 bhp = 17 knots
Oil fuel, tons	16
Complement	24 (2 officers, 22 men)

Six built by Arsenal do Alfeite, Lisbon, and four by Estaleiros Navais de Viana do Castelo. All completed June 1963 to Sep 1965. Named after constellations.

DRAGÃO — *1973, Portuguese Navy*

SABRE P 1138 (RIVER PATROL CRAFT)

Displacement, tons	122 standard; 140 full load
Dimensions, feet (*metres*)	99·9 × 21·6 × 2·6 (27·7 × 6·6 × 0·8)
Guns	2—20 mm Oerlikon
Main engines	2 Daimler Benz Schottel; 244 hp = 10 knots
Complement	7 (1 officer, 6 men)

2 "DOM ALEIXO" CLASS (COASTAL PATROL CRAFT)

DOM ALEIXO P 1148 **DOM JEREMIAS** P 1149

Displacement, tons	62·6 standard; 67·7 full load
Dimensions, feet	82·1 oa × 17·0 × 5·2
Gun	1—20 mm
Main engines	2 Cummins diesels; 1 270 bhp = 16 knots
Complement	10 (2 officers, 8 men)

Dom Aleixo was commissioned on 7 Dec 1967 and *Dom Jeremias* on 22 Dec 1967.

DOM JEREMIAS — *1973, Portuguese Navy*

3 "ALVOR" CLASS (COASTAL PATROL CRAFT)

ALBUFEIRA P 1157 **ALJEZUR** P 1158 **ALVOR** P 1156

Displacement, tons	35·7 full load
Dimensions, feet	68 oa × 18 × 5·1
Gun	1—20 mm AA
Main engines	2 Cummins diesels; 235 bhp = 12·3 knots
Complement	7

They were all built at Arsenal do Alfeite and commissioned in 1967-86.

ALVOR — *1973, Portuguese Navy*

Light Forces—*continued*

11 "BELLATRIX" CLASS (COASTAL PATROL CRAFT)

ALDEBARAN	P 1152	**ESPIGA**	P 366	**PROCION**	P 1153
ALTAIR	P 377	**FOMALHAUT**	P 367	**RIGEL**	P 378
ARCTURUS	P 1151	**POLLUX**	P 368	**SIRIUS**	P 1154
BELLATRIX	P 363			**VEGA**	P 1155

Displacement, tons 23 light; 27·6 full load
Dimensions, feet 62·8 wl; 68·0 oa × 15·2 × 4·0
Gun 1—20 mm Oerlikon
Main engines 2 Cummins diesels; 450 bhp = 15 knots
Complement 7 (1 officer, 6 men)

The first batch was completed in 1961-62 in Germany by Beyerische Schiffbaugesellschaft and the last five (*Arcturus, Aldebaran* and *Procion,* commissioned on 17 May 1968, *Sirius* and *Vega*) were built in Arsenal do Alfeite, Lisbon.

ARCTURUS *1972, Portuguese Navy*

6 "JUPITER" CLASS (COASTAL PATROL CRAFT)

JUPITER	P 1132	**MERCURIO**	P 1135	**URANO**	P 1137
MARTE	P 1134	**SATURNO**	P 1136	**VENUS**	P 1133

Displacement, tons 32 standard; 43·5 full load
Dimensions, feet 69·0 oa × 16·5 × 4·3
Guns 2—20 mm (twin mount)
Main engines 2 Cummins diesels; 1 270 bhp = 20 knots
Complement 8 (1 officer, 7 men)

Built during 1964-65. All commissioned between 10 Mar 1965 and 12 Aug 1965.

JUPITER *Portuguese Navy*

CASTOR P 580 (COASTAL PATROL CRAFT)

Displacement, tons 22
Dimensions, feet 53·5 wl; 58 oa × 13·1 × 3·3
Gun 1—20 mm Oerlikon
Main engines 2 Cummins diesels; 500 bhp = 15 knots
Complement 7

Built at the Estalerios Navais do Mondego and commissioned on 3 Feb 1964.

ANTARES P 360 REGULUS P 369 (COASTAL PATROL CRAFT)

Displacement, tons 18
Dimensions, feet 56 oa; 51·5 wl × 15·2 × 4
Gun 1—20 mm Oerlikon
Main engines 2 Cummins diesels; 2 shafts; 460 bhp = 18·2 knots
Complement 7

Antares was built in 1959 by James Taylor (Shipbuilders) Ltd, Shoreham, Sussex, England. The hull is of Deborine resin glass fibre moulding. *Regulus* was built in Portugal by Navalis Shipyard, the hull being imported from England. Completed on 27 Jan 1962.

RIO MINHO P 370 (COASTAL PATROL CRAFT)

Displacement, tons 14
Dimensions, feet 49·2 × 10·5 × 2·3
Guns 2 light MG
Main engines 2 Alfa Romeo; 130 bhp = 9 knots
Complement 7

Built at Arsenal do Alfeite in 1955-57 for the River Minho on the Spanish border.

MINE WARFARE FORCES

4 "S. ROQUE" CLASS (MINESWEEPERS—COASTAL)

Name	*No*	*Launched*	*Completed*
LAGOA	M 403	15 Sep 1955	10 Aug 1956
RIBEIRA GRANDE	M 402	14 Oct 1955	8 Feb 1957
ROSARIO	M 404	29 Nov 1955	8 Feb 1956
S ROQUE	M 401	15 Sep 1955	6 June 1956

Displacement, tons 394·4 standard; 451·9 full load
Dimensions, feet 140·0 pp; 152·0 oa × 28·8 × 7·0
Guns 2—20 mm (twin mount)
Main engines 2 Mirrlees diesels; 2 shafts; 2 500 bhp = 15 knots
Complement 47 (4 officers, 43 men)

Similar to British "Ton" class coastal minesweepers, but built in Portugal. All laid down at CUF Shipyard, Lisbon, on 7 Sep 1954, under the OSP-MAP. *Lagoa* and *S Roque* were financed by USA and the other two by Portugal.
40 mm AA gun removed 1972.

LAGOA (Before change of armament) *1972, Portuguese Navy*

5 "PONTA DELGADA" CLASS (MINESWEEPERS—COASTAL)

HORTA	(ex-*AMS* 61)	M 406
LAJES	(ex-*AMS* 146)	M 411
SANTA CRUZ	(ex-*AMS* 92)	M 409
VELAS	(ex-*AMS* 145)	M 410
VILA DO PORTO	(ex-*AMS* 91)	M 408

Displacement, tons 338 standard; 370 full load
Dimensions, feet 138·0 pp; 144·0 oa × 27·0 × 8·0
Guns 2—20 mm (twin mount)
Main engines GM diesels; 900 bhp = 13 knots
Range, miles 1 800 at 13 knots
Complement 40 (4 officers, 36 men)

Of wooden and non-magnetic construction. Transferred by USA in 1954-55.

HORTA *1971, Portuguese Navy*

FISHERY PROTECTION VESSELS

4 "AZEVIA" CLASS

AZEVIA P595 **BICUDA** P596 **CORVINA** P 597 **DOURADA** P598

Displacement, tons 230 standard; 275 full load
Dimensions, feet 134·5 pp; 139·8 oa × 21·3 × 7·0
Guns 2—20 mm
Main engines 2 Sulzer 7-cyl 2-stroke diesels except first pair; 2 MAN 10-cyl 4-stroke diesels; 2 shafts; 2 400 bhp = 17 knots
Oil fuel, tons 25
Range, miles 2 250 at 12·8 knots; 1 080 at 17·3 knots
Complement 30 (2 officers, 28 men)

All launched in 1942

AZEVIA *1968, Portuguese Navy*

AMPHIBIOUS FORCES

2 "BOMBARDA" CLASS LGD (LCT)

ALABARDA LDG 202 | **BOMBARDA** LDG 201 (ex-105)

Displacement, tons	510 standard; 652 full load
Dimensions, feet	184·3 × 38·7 × 6·2
(*metres*)	(*56·2* × *11·8* × *1·9*)
Main engines	2 Maybach-Mercedes Benz diesels; 910 hp = 9·5 knots
Complement	20 (2 officers, 18 men)

BOMBARDA — *1972, Portuguese Navy*

4 "ALFANGE" CLASS LDG (LCT)

ALFANGE LDG 101
ARIETE LDG 102
CIMITARRA LDG 103
MONTANEE LDG 104

Displacement, tons	500
Dimensions, feet	Length: 187
Main engines	2 diesels; 1 000 bhp
Complement	20

Landing craft similar to the LCT (4) type built at the Estalerios Navias do Mondego and commissioned during 1965.

ALFANGE — *1968· Portuguese Navy*

17 LDM 400 CLASS (LCM)

LDM 401	LDM 404	LDM 407	LDM 410	LDM 413
LDM 402	LDM 405	LDM 408	LDM 411	LDM 414
LDM 403	LDM 406	LDM 409	LDM 412	LDM 415
				LDM 416
				LDM 417

Last of class commissioned 17 Aug 1973.

2 LDM 300 CLASS (LCM)

LDM 304 **LDM 309**

1 LDM 200 CLASS (LCM)

LDM 204

16 LDM 100 CLASS (LCM)

LDM 101	LDM 105	LDM 108	LDM 111	LDM 115
LDM 102	LDM 106	LDM 109	LDM 112	LDM 116
	LDM 107	LDM 110	LDM 113	LDM 117
			LDM 114	LDM 118

Displacement, tons	50 full load
Dimensions, feet	Length: 50
Main engines	2 diesels; 450 bhp

The above LCM type landing craft were commissioned in 1964 to 1966 setting up four classes in LDM 100, 200, 300 and 400 series as above. All built at the Estaleiros Navias do Mondego.

3 LDP 300 (Ex-LD) CLASS (LCA)

LDP 301 **LDP 302** **LDP 303**

16 LDP 200 CLASS (LCA)

LDP 201	LDP 203	LDP 206	LDP 209	LDP 212	LDP 215
	LDP 204	LDP 207	LDP 210	LDP 213	LDP 216
	LDP 205	LDP 208	LDP 211	LDP 214	LDP 217

Thirteen LDP 200 class were commissioned in 1965-67, four in Jan-Feb 1969.

3 LDP 100 (Ex-LD) CLASS (LCA)

LDP 105 **LDP 107** **LDP 108**

Displacement, tons	12 light; 18 full load
Dimensions, feet	Length: 46 oa
Main engines	2 diesels; 180 bhp

Built at the Estaleiros Navais do Mondego and commissioned on 22 Feb 1963 (LDP 105), 1964 (LDP 107, 108).

SURVEY SHIPS

AFONSO DE ALBUQUERQUE A 526
(ex-HMS *Dalrymple*, ex-*Luce Bay*,)

Displacement, tons	1 590 standard; 2 230 full load
Length, feet (*metres*)	286·0 (*87·2*) pp; 307·0 (*93·6*) oa
Beam, feet (*metres*)	38·5 (*11·7*)
Draught, feet (*metres*)	14·2 (*4·3*)
Main engines	4-cylinder triple expansion; 2 shafts; 5 500 ihp
Speed, knots	19·5
Boilers	2 Admiralty 3-drum type
Range, miles	7 055 at 9·1 knots
Complement	109 (9 officers, 100 men)

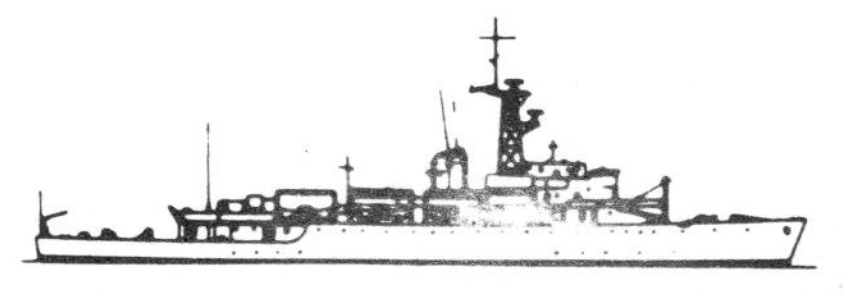

AFONSO DE ALBUQUERQUE

AFONSO DE ALBUQUERQUE — ***1970, Portuguese Navy***

Modified "Bay" class frigate. Built by Wm. Pickersgill & Sons Ltd, Sunderland, but completed at HM Dockyard Devonport. Laid down on 29 Apr 1944. Launched on 12 Apr 1945, completed on 10 Feb 1949. Equipped with radar and sonar. Purchased from Great Britain in Apr 1966. Main machinery by George Clark Ltd. Sunderland. Power at 220 volts DC from two 120 kw turbogenerators and two 150 kw diesel generators.

1 Ex-US "KELLAR" CLASS

ALMEIDA CARVALHO (ex-USNS *Kellar*, T-AGS 25)

Displacement, tons	1 200 standard; 1 400 full load
Dimensions, feet	191·5 wl; 109·0 oa × 39·0 × 15·0
Main engines	Diesel-electric; 1 shaft; 1 200 bp = 15 knots
Complement	30 (5 officers, 25 men)

Laid down on 20 Nov 1962, launched on 30 July 1964 and completed on 31 Jan 1969. On loan from the US Navy since 21 Jan 1972.

1 Ex-BRITISH "BANGOR" CLASS FLEET MINESWEEPER

ALMIRANTE LACERDA (ex-*Caraquet*) A 525

Displacement, tons	672 standard; 830 full load
Dimensions, feet	171·5 pp; 180·0 oa × 28·5 × 9·5
Guns	1—3 in; 2—20 mm AA
Main engines	Triple expansion; 2 shafts; 2 400 ihp = 16 knots
Boilers	2, of 3-drum small-tube type
Oil fuel, tons	160
Complement	49 (7 officers, 42 men)

Former British fleet minesweeper of the "Bangor" class, steam type. Built in Canada, launched on 2 June 1941, and purchased from Great Britain in 1946. Working off Mozambique.

Survey Ships—*continued*

1 "PEDRO NUNES" CLASS

PEDRO NUNES A 528

Displacement, tons	1 162 standard; 1 217 full load
Dimensions, feet	223·0 pp; 234·3 oa × 32·8 × 10·2
Guns	1—4·7 in, 50 cal; 4—20 mm (see Notes)
Main engines	2 sets MAN 8 cyl diesels; 2 400 bhp = 16·5 knots
Oil fuel, tons	110
Range, miles	6 400 at 13·4 knots
Complement	48 (7 officers, 41 men)

Built as a second class sloop at Lisbon Naval Yard. Laid down on 5 Nov 1931, launched on 17 Mar 1934 and completed on 11 Apr 1935. Converted into a survey ship in 1956, when the forward 4·7 inch gun was removed. Working off Guinea.

1 Ex-BRITISH "FLOWER" CLASS CORVETTE

CARVALHO ARAUJO (ex-M/V *Terje Ten*, ex-French *Commandant Drogou*, ex-HMS *Chrysanthemum*) A 524

Displacement, tons	1 020 standard; 1 340 full load
Dimensions, feet	190 pp; 205 oa × 33 × 16·5
Guns	1—3 inch; 4—20 mm
Main engines	Triple expansion; 2 750 ihp = 16 knots
Boilers	2 cylindrical
Oil fuel, tons	288
Complement	49 (7 officers, 42 men)

Former British "Flower" class corvette. Built by Harland & Wolff Ltd, Belfast. Laid down on 17 Feb 1940, launched on 11 Apr 1941, completed on 26 Jan 1942. Served in the French Navy during the Second World War. Sold out of the service after hostilities. Purchased by Portugal from the Hector Whaling Company, at Capetown, in Mar 1959, and equipped as a survey ship to replace the former *Carvalho Araujo* (ex-British "Flower" class minesweeping sloop *Jonquil* of World War I). Working off Angola and Sao Tomé.

CRUZEIRO DO SUL (ex-*Giroflée*)

Displacement, tons	100 standard
Dimensions, feet	93·2 × 17·8 × 8
Main engines	2 Gleenifer diesels; 320 bhp = 12 knots
Range, miles	2 000 at 10 knots (economical speed)
Complement	8 (1 officer, 7 men)

Launched 1935.

MIRA (ex-*Formalhaut*, ex-*Arrabida*)

Displacement, tons	30 standard
Dimensions, feet	62·9 × 15·2 × 4
Main engines	3 Perkins diesels; 300 bhp = 15 knots
Range, miles	650 at 8 knots (economical speed)
Complement	6 men

Launched 1961.

SERVICE FORCES

SAO GABRIEL A 5206 (REPLENISHMENT TANKER)

Displacement, tons	9 000 standard; 14 200 full load
Measurement, tons	9 854 gross; 9 000 deadweight
Dimensions, feet	452·8 pp 479·0; oa × 59·8 × 26·2
Main engines	1 Pametrada-geared turbine; 1 shaft; 9 500 shp= 17 knots
Boilers	2
Range, miles	6 000 at 15 knots
Complement	98 (10 officers, 88 men)

Built at Estaleiros de Viana do Castelo. Commissioned on 27 Mar 1963.

SAO GABRIEL — *1973, Portuguese Navy*

1 Ex-US ARC/LSM TYPE

S. RAFAEL (ex-*Medusa*, ex-USS *Portunus*, *ARC* 1 ex-*LSM* 275, ex-*LCT* (7) 1773) A 5214

Displacement, tons	743 standard; 1 220 full load
Dimensions, feet	196·5 pp; 221·1 oa × 34·5 × 10·5
Guns	2—40 mm; 2—20 mm
Main engines	GM direct drive diesel; 2 shafts; 2 800 bhp = 12 knots
Range, miles	5 240 at 10 knots
Complement	56 (6 officers, 50 men)

Former US medium landing ship, LSM type. Built by Federal Sbipbuilding and Drydock Co, Newark, New Jersey. Laid down on 1 Aug 1944, launched on 11 Sep 1944, and completed on 6 Oct 1944. Converted to a cable repairing or laying ship by the US Navy in 1952. Transferred to the Portuguese Navy under MAP in 1959. Delivered to Portugal on 16 Nov and commissioned on 18 Nov as a diving tender. Converted to a logistic ship in 1969 and guns mounted as above.

Service Forces—*continued*

SAM BRAS A 523 (FLEET SUPPLY SHIP)

Displacement, tons	5 766 standard; 6 374 full load
Dimensions, feet	333·1 pp; 356·8 oa × 47·3 × 16·5
Guns	1—3 in (*76 mm*); 2—40 mm; 2—20 mm
Main engines	B & W 2-stroke diesel; 1 shaft; 2,820 bhp = 12 knots
Oil fuel, tons	568
Range, miles	11 000 at 12 knots
Complement	100 (10 officers, 90 men)

Built at Arsenal do Alfeite. Laid down on 22 Feb 1941. Launched on 17 Mar 1942. Former fleet oiler converted to logistic ship and armed as above in Arsenal do Alfeite.

SAM BRAS — *1971, Portuguese Navy*

SAGRES (ex-*Guanabara*, ex-*Albert Leo Schlageter*) A 520 (TRAINING SHIP)

Displacement, tons	1 725 standard; 1 869 full load
Dimensions, feet	293·5 oa × 39·3 × 17·0
Main engines	2 MAN auxiliary diesels; 1 shaft; 750 bhp = 10 knots
Oil fuel, tons	52
Range, miles	3 500 at 6·5 knots
Complement	153 (10 officers, 143 men)

Former German sail training ship. Built by Blohm & Voss, Hamburg. Launched in June 1937 and completed on 1 Feb 1938. Sister of US Coast Guard training ship *Eagle* (ex-German *Horst Wessel*). Taken by USA as a reparation after the Second World War in 1945 and sold to Brazil in 1948. Purchased from Brazil and commissioned in the Portuguese Navy on 2 Feb 1972 at Rio de Janeiro and renamed *Sagres*. Sail area 20 793 sq ft. Height of main-mast 142 ft.

SAGRES — *1973, Portuguese Navy*

SANTO ANDRÉ (ex-*Sagres*, ex-*Flores*, ex-*Max*, ex-*Rickmer Rickmers*) A 5207 (DEPOT SHIP)

Displacement, tons	3 385 standard; 3 866 full load
Dimensions, feet	263·5 × 40·3 × 19·0
Guns	4—47 mm saluting
Main engines	2 Krupp diesels; 2 shafts; 700 bhp = 8 knots

Former German sailing vessel. Built at Bremerhaven. Launched in 1896. Captured during the First World War. Re-rigged as a barque and adapted as a naval training ship and renamed *Santo André* 31 Jan 1962. Replaced as seagoing training ship on 8 Feb 1962 by the *Sagres*.

BC 3 (ex-US YO 194) (HARBOUR TANKER)

Transferred April 1962.

TUGS

SCHULTZ XAVIER (OCEAN TUG)

Displacement, tons	900
Main engines	2 Diesels; 2 shafts; 2 400 hp = 14·5 knots
Range, miles	3 000 at 12·5 knots

A dual purpose ocean tug and buoy tender ordered late in 1968 from the Alfeite Naval Yard. Commissioned 14 July 1972.

2 HARBOUR TUGS

RB 1 (ex-ST 1994) **RB 2** (ex-ST 1996)

Transferred from US Navy—RB 1 Dec 1961, RB 2 Mar 1962.

QATAR

Now possesses an expanding Naval Force, generally described as "Coastguard". The geographical position of the state, dividing the Persian Gulf and covering Bahrein, gives this force added importance.

Mercantile Marine

Lloyd's Register of Shipping: 4 vessels of 928 tons gross

Personnel

(a) 300 officers and men
(b) Voluntary

6 VOSPER-THORNYCROFT 103ft TYPE

(LARGE PATROL CRAFT)

AL ADAID + 5

Displacement, tons	120
Dimensions, feet	103·7 pp; 109·7 oa × 21 × 5·5
Guns	2—20 mm
Main engines	2 Diesels; 4 000 hp = 27 knots
Complement	25

Ordered in 1972-73. All laid down between Sept 1973 and July 1974. First two launched 23 Apr 1974 and 25 June 1974. First completed 14 Dec 1974.

2 75ft (COASTAL PATROL CRAFT)

Length, feet	75
Guns	2—20 mm
Main engines	2 Diesels; 1 420 hp

Built by Whittingham and Mitchell, Chertsey 1969.

3 KEITH NELSON 45 ft TYPE

(COASTAL PATROL CRAFT)

Displacement, tons	15
Dimensions, feet	45 × 13·2 × 3·5
Guns	1—12·7 mm; 2—7·62 mm (singles)
Main engines	2 Diesels; 920 hp = 25 knots
Complement	6

7 FAIREY MARINE "SPEAR" CLASS

(COASTAL PATROL CRAFT)

Displacement, tons	4·3
Dimensions, ft (*m*)	29·8 × 9 × 2·8 (*9·1 × 2·8 × ·8*)
Guns	3—7·62 mm
Main engines	2 Diesels; 360 hp; 2 shafts = 30 knots
Complement	2

Ordered early 1974. Delivered 19 June 1974, 16 Sept 1974, 18 Sept 1974, 2 Nov 1974, Dec 1974, Jan 1975, Feb 1975.

RAS AL KHAIMAH

It is reported that up to five small patrol craft have been acquired recently.

ROMANIA

Commander in Chief of the Navy:
Rear Admiral Sebastian Ulmeanu

Diplomatic Representation

Naval Attaché in London:
Captain 1st Rank A. A. Dusa

Naval, Military and Air Attaché in Washington:
Colonel Nicolae Gheorghe Plesa

Strength of the Fleet

(No details of building programme available)

Type	*Active*
Corvettes	6
Fast Attack Craft (Missile)	6
Fast Attack Craft (Gun and Patrol)	10
Fast Attack Craft (Torpedo)	7
River Patrol Craft	1
Coastal Patrol Craft	10
Minesweepers Coastal	4
Minesweepers Inshore	12
MSBs	8
Training Ships	2
Tugs	2

(other unconfirmed vessels listed at end of section).

Personnel

(a) 1975: 8 000 officers and ratings
(b) 2 Years National Service

Mercantile Marine

Lloyd's Register of Shipping:
106 vessels of 610 982 tons gross

CORVETTES

3 Ex-USSR "POTI" CLASS

V 31 **V 32** **V 83**

Displacement, tons	550 standard; 650 full load
Dimensions, feet (*m*)	195·2 × 26·2 × 9·2 (*59·5 × 8 × 2·8*)
Guns	2—57 mm AA (1 twin mounting)
Tubes	4—16 in anti-submarine
A/S weapons	2—12 barrelled rocket launchers
Main engines	2 gas turbines; 2 diesels; 4 shafts; total 20 000 hp = 28 knots

Transferred from the USSR in 1970.

USSR "POTI" Class *1971*

Corvettes—*cont.*

3 Ex-USSR "KRONSTADT" CLASS

V-1 **V-2** **V-3**

Displacement, tons	310 standard; 380 full load
Dimensions, ft (*m*)	170·6 × 21·5 × 9 (*52 × 6·5 × 2·7*)
Guns	1—3·4 in dual purpose forward; 2—37 mm AA single aft; 4—25 mm in twin mounts
A/S weapons	2 DC throwers; 2 depth charge racks
Main engines	3 diesels; 3 shafts; 3 300 bhp = 24 knots
Range, miles	1 500 at 12 knots
Complement	65

Built in USSR in 1950.

"KRONSTADT" Class

LIGHT FORCES

10 ex-Chinese "SHANGHAI" CLASS

(FAST ATTACK CRAFT—GUN and PATROL)

VP 21-29 **VS 42**

Displacement, tons	120 standard; 155 full load
Dimensions, ft (*m*)	128 × 18 × 5·6 (*39 × 5·5 × 1·7*)
Guns	VP type: 1—57 mm; 2—30 mm (twin) VS type: 1—37 mm; 2—14·5 MG
A/S weapons	VS type: 2—5 barrelled MBU 1800
Main engines	4 diesels; 4 800 bhp = 30 knots
Complement	25

Two variants of the "Shanghai" class of which the VS type is a new departure. Presumed locally built 1973-74 in a continuing programme.

"SHANGHAI" Class—VS Type *8/1974*

5 Ex-USSR "OSA" CLASS (FAST ATTACK CRAFT—MISSILE)

PENNANTS 194 to 198

Displacement, tons	165 standard; 200 full load
Dimensions, feet (*m*)	128·7 × 25·1 × 5·9 (*39·3 × 7·7 × 1·8*)
Missile launchers	4 for SSN 2A
Guns, AA	4—30 mm (2 twin, 1 forward, 1 aft)
Main engines	3 diesels; 13 000 bhp = 32 knots
Range, miles	800 at 25 knots
Complement	25

Built since 1961.

1 ex-Chinese "HU CHWAN" CLASS

(FAST ATTACK CRAFT—TORPEDO)

VT 53

Displacement, tons	45
Dimensions, feet	70 × 16·5 × 3·1
Guns	4—14·5 mm (twins)
Torpedo tubes	2—21 in
Main engines	2 Diesels; 2 200 hp = 55 knots (foilborne in calm conditions)
Range miles	500 cruising

Hydrofoil of the same class as the Chinese which were started in 1956. Presumed locally built in 1973-74.

"HU CHWAN" Class *8/1974*

5 Ex-USSR "P 4" CLASS (FAST ATTACK CRAFT—TORPEDO)

PENNANTS 87 to 92.

Displacement, tons	25
Dimensions, feet	62·7 × 11·6 × 5·6
Guns	2 MG
Tubes	2—18 in
Main engines	2 diesels; 2 200 bhp = 50 knots

Built in 1955-56.

1 RIVER PATROL CRAFT

VB 76

Dimensions, feet	105 × 16 × 3
Guns	1—3·9 in; 1—37 mm; 2—14·5 mm; 2 Grenade Throwers
Complement	about 25

Built in Romania 1973-74.

RIVER PATROL CRAFT *8/1974*

10 "VG" CLASS (COASTAL PATROL CRAFT)

Displacement, tons	40
Dimensions, feet	52·5 × 14·4 × 4
Gun	1—20 mm
Main engines	2 Diesels; 600 hp = 18 knots
Complement	10

Steel-hulled craft built at Galata in 1954. Obsolescent.

MINE WARFARE FORCES

4 Ex-GERMAN "M 40" CLASS (MINESWEEPERS—COASTAL)

DESCATUSARIA DB 13 **DEMOCRATIA** DB 15
DESROBIREA DB 14 **DREPTATEA** DB 16

Displacements, ton	543 standard; 775 full load
Dimensions, feet	188 pp; 203·5 oa × 28 × 7·5
Guns	2—3·4 in; 2—37 mm (twin)
	3—20 mm (singles)
A/S weapons	2 DCT
Main engines	Triple expansion; 2 shafts; 2 400 ihp = 17 knots
Boilers	2 three-drum water tube
Range, miles	1 200 at 17 knots
Complement	80

German designed coal-burning minesweepers. Built in Romania from German materials 1943. Converted to oil in 1951.

DEMOCRATIA and DREPTATEA *1968*

12 Ex-USSR "T 301" CLASS (MINESWEEPERS—INSHORE)

Displacement, tons	130
Dimensions, feet	100 × 16 × 4·5
Guns	2—45 mm AA; 4—12·7 mm MG
Main engines	Diesel; 480 bhp = 10 knots
Complement	30

Former Soviet minesweepers transferred to Romania by the USSR in 1956-60 Probably half of these are non-operational.

8 Ex-POLISH "TR-40" CLASS (MSB's)

VD-241 VD-242 VD-243 VD-244 VD-245 VD-246 VD-247 VD-248

Displacement, tons	50 standard; 70 full load
Dimensions, feet	91·1 × 13·4 × 2·3
Guns	2—25 mm (twin)
Main engines	2 Diesels; 2 shafts; 600 hp = 16 knots
Complement	18

Eight "TR-40" Class minesweeping boats are employed on shallow water and river duties. These were originally a Polish class begun in 1955 but completed in Romania in late 1950's.

TUGS

2 Ex-USSR "ROSLAVL" CLASS

Displacement, tons	450
Dimensions, feet	135 × 29·3 × 11·8
Main engines	Diesels; 1 250 hp = 12·5 knots
Complement	28

Built in Galata shipyard 1953-54.

TRAINING SHIPS

MIRCEA

Displacement, tons	1 604
Dimensions, feet	239·5 oa; 267·3 (with bowsprit) × 39·3 × 16·5
Sail area	18 830 sq ft
Main engines	Auxiliary MAN 6-cylinder Diesel; 500 bhp = 9·5 knots
Complement	83 + 140 midshipmen for training

Built by Blohm & Voss, Hamburg. Laid down on 30 Apr 1938. Launched on 22 Sep 1938. Completed on 29 Mar 1939. Refitted at Hamburg in 1966.

MIRCEA *1970, Michael D. J. Lennon*

RASARITUL (ex-*Taifun*)

Measurement, tons	34 (*Thames* measurement)
Dimensions, feet	54·0 × 12·5 × 3·0
Main engines	2 petrol motors; 2 shafts

Built by J. Samuel White & Co Ltd, Cowes, Isle of Wight, England. Launched in 1938. Of wooden construction. Yacht used as sail training ship.

MISCELLANEOUS

Although details are not available the following have been reported — two survey craft, three tankers, ten transports and twelve landing craft.

SABAH

In addition to two PX-class 87 ft patrol boats on detachment from the Royal Malaysian Police the following have been provided direct to Sabah.

2 55 ft PATROL BOATS

SRI SEMPORNA **SRI BANGJI**

Displacement, tons	50
Dimensions, feet	55 × 15 × 30
Gun	1—MG
Main engines	Diesels; 1 200 hp = 20 knots
Range, miles	300 at 15 knots
Complement	11

Built by Chevertons, Isle of Wight.

2 91 ft PATROL BOATS

SRI GUMANTONG **SRI LABUAN**

Delivered in 1973.

1 YACHT

PUTRI SABAH

Displacement, tons	117
Dimensions, feet	91 × 19 × 5·5
Main engines	1 Diesel = 12 knots
Complement	22

ST. KITTS

Mercantile Marine

Lloyd's Register of Shipping: 1 vessel of 256 tons

1 FAIREY MARINE "SPEAR" CLASS

Displacement, tons	4·3
Dimensions, feet	29·8 × 9 × 2·8
Guns	2—7·62 mm
Main engines	2 Diesels; 360 hp = 30 knots
Complement	2

Ordered for the Police in June 1974—delivered 10 Sept 1974.

ST. LUCIA

Mercantile Marine

Lloyd's Register of Shipping: 2 vessels of 904 tons gross

1 BROOKE MARINE PATROL CRAFT

CHATOYER

Displacement, tons	15
Dimensions, feet	40 × 12 × 2
Guns	3 MG
Main engines	2 Diesels; 370 hp = 22 knots

ST. VINCENT

Mercantile Marine

Lloyd's Register of Shipping: 13 vessels of 4 808 tons gross

1 BROOKE MARINE PATROL CRAFT

HELEN

Details as *Chatoyer*, St Lucia.

SAUDI ARABIA

Diplomatic Representation

Defence Attaché in London:
Brigadier Abdullah Al-Saheal

Personnel

(a) 1975: 1 500 officers and men
(b) Voluntary Service

New Construction

There are reports of a considerable programme of new construction for Saudi Arabia by the USA. This is believed to consist of 26 ships in all, including 4 Minesweepers Coastal and 2 Large Tugs.

Mercantile Marine

Lloyd's Register of Shipping: 43 vessels of 61 275 tons gross

LIGHT FORCES

3 JAGUAR CLASS (FAST ATTACK CRAFT—TORPEDO)

RIFAQAT **SADAQAT** +1

Displacement, tons	160 standard; 190 full load
Dimensions, feet	138 oa × 23 × 5
Guns	2—40 mm
Torpedo tubes	4—21 in
Main engines	4 diesels; 12 000 bhp = 42 knots
Complement	33 (3 officers, 30 men)

Built in Germany and delivered in 1969.

RYADH (LARGE PATROL CRAFT)

Displacement, tons	100 standard
Dimensions, feet	95·0 × 19·0 × 6·0
Gun	1—40 mm AA
Main engines	4 diesels; 2 shafts; 2 200 bhp = 21 knots

Steel-hulled patrol boat of US CG design transferred to Saudi Arabia in 1960

2 Ex-US 40 ft UTILITY BOATS

Transferred late 1960's.

NOTE. All the following craft with the exception of ASR1 and 2 belong to the Saudi Coastguard.

20 45 ft PATROL BOATS

Built by Whittingham and Mitchell, Chertsey, England. Armed with one ·5 cal MG and powered with two 362 hp diesels.

10 23 ft HUNTRESS PATROL BOATS

Built by Fairey Marine, Hamble, England. Capable of 20 knots with a cruising range of 150 miles and a complement of four.

20 ft PATROL BOATS

Smaller editions of the 45 ft craft above. By the same builder.

8 SRN-6 HOVERCRAFT

Displacement, tons	10 normal (load 8 200 lbs)
Dimensions, feet	48·4 × 25·3 × 15·9 (height)
Main machinery	1 Gnome model 1050 gas turbine
Speed, knots	58

Acquired from British Hovercraft Corporation Ltd, between Feb and Dec 1970.

2 AIR SEA-RESCUE LAUNCHES

ASR 1 **ASR 2**

With two diesels of 1 230 hp and capable of 25 knots. Belong to Ministry of Transportation.

SENEGAL

Personnel

1975: approx 350 officers and men

Mercantile Marine

Lloyd's Register of Shipping: 48 vessels of 20 499 tons gross

LIGHT FORCES

2 "P 48" CLASS (LARGE PATROL CRAFT)

SAINT LOUIS **POPENGUINE**

Displacement, tons	235 standard
Dimensions, feet	149·3 pp; 155·8 oa × 23·6 × 8·2
Guns	2—40 mm AA
Main engines	2 MGO diesels; 2 shafts; 2 400 bhp = 18·5 knots
Range, miles	2 000 at 15 knots

Saint Louis ordered from Ch Navales Franco-Belges. Laid down on 20 Apr 1970, launched on 5 Aug 1970 and commissioned on 1 Mar 1971. *Popenguine* laid down in Dec 1973 by Soc. Francais de Constructions Navales, launched 22 Mar 1974 and completed 10 Aug 1974. Sisters to *Malaika* of Malagasy, *Vigilant* of Ivory Coast and *Bizerte* of Tunisian Navy.

"P 48" Class *1972*

1 Ex-US SC TYPE (LARGE PATROL CRAFT)

SÉNÉGAL (ex-*P* 700, ex-*CH* 62, ex-US *SC* 1344)

Displacement, tons	110 standard; 138 full load
Dimensions, feet	107·5 wl; 110·9 × 17 × 6·5
Guns	1—40 mm AA; 3—20 mm AA
Main engines	2 GM diesels; 2 shafts; 1 000 bhp = 13 knots
Complement	25

Former US submarine chaser transferred to France on 19 Nov 1943, and from France to Senegal on 12 July 1961. First ship of Senegalese naval force.

12 VOSPER 45 ft TYPE

Dimensions, feet	45 × 13·2 × 3·5
Guns	1—12·7 mm; 2—7·62 mm
Main engines	2 diesels; 920 hp = 25 knots
Complement	6

2 Ex-FRENCH VC TYPE

CASAMANCE (ex-*VC* 5, *P* 755)
SINE-SALOUM (ex-*Reine N'Galifourou*, ex-*VC* 4, *P* 754)

Displacement, tons	75 standard; 82 full load
Dimensions, feet	104·5 × 15·5 × 5·5
Guns	2—20 mm AA
Main engines	2 Mercedes-Benz diesels; 2 shafts; 2 700 bhp = 28 knots
Complement	15

Former French patrol craft (Vedettes de Surveillance Côtière). Built by the Constructions Mécaniques de Normandie, Cherbourg. Completed in 1958. *Casamance* was transferred from France to Senegal in 1963. *Sine-Saloum* was given to Senegal on 24 Aug 1965 after having been returned to France by the Congo in Feb 1965.

SINE-SALOUM *1967, Senegalese Navy*

1 FAIREY-MARINE "SPEAR" CLASS

Displacement, tons	4·3
Dimensions, feet	29·8 × 9 × 2·8
Guns	1—12·7 mm; 2—7·62 mm
Main engines	2 diesels; 360 hp = 30 knots
Complement	2

Completed 28 Feb 1974 for Senegal Customs.

2 FAIREY MARINE "HUNTRESS" CLASS

Dimensions, feet	23·2 × 8·8 × 2·8
Main engines	1 diesel; 180 hp; 29 knots
Complement	2

Completed Mar 1974 for Senegal Customs.

1 Ex-FRENCH EDIC

LA FALENCE (ex-9095) (LCT)

Displacement, tons	250 standard; 670 full load
Dimensions, ft (*m*)	193·5 × 39·2 × 4·5 (*59* × *12* × *1·3*)
Guns	2—20 mm
Main engines	2 MGO diesels; 2 shafts; 1 000 bhp = 8 knots
Complement	6

Launched 7 April 1958. Transferred 1 July 1974.

2 Ex-US LCM 6

DIOU LOULOU **DIOMBOS**

Transferred July 1968.

SIERRA LEONE

Personnel

(a) 1975: 150 officers and men
(b) Voluntary service

Mercantile Marine

Lloyd's Register of Shipping: 11 vessels of 5 045 tons gross

2 Ex-CHINESE "SHANGHAI II" CLASS

(FAST ATTACK CRAFT—GUN)

Displacement, tons	120 standard; 155 full load
Dimensions, feet	128 × 18 × 5·6
Guns	4—37 mm; 4—25 mm
A/S weapons	8 DC
Mines	Mine rails can be fitted
Main engines	4 Diesels; 4,800 hp = 30 knots
Complement	25

Transferred by China June 1973.

"SHANGHAI II" Class

SINGAPORE

Administration

Commander of the Republic of Singapore Navy: Lieutenant Colonel J. Aria

Personnel

(a) 1974: 1 100 officers and men
(b) 2-3 years National Service

Mercantile Marine

Lloyd's Register of Shipping: 511 vessels of 2 878 327 tons gross

Prefix to Ships' Names

RSS

LIGHT FORCES

6 VOSPER THORNYCROFT DESIGN

3 "TYPE A" (FAST ATTACK CRAFT—GUN)

INDEPENDENCE P 69 **FREEDOM** P 70 **JUSTICE** P 72

Displacement, tons	100 standard
Dimensions, feet	103·6 wl; 109·6 × 21·0 × 5·6
Guns	1—40 mm AA (forward); 1—20 mm AA aft
Main engines	2 Maybach diesels; 2 × 3 600 bhp = 32 knots (max)
Range, miles	1 100 at 15 knots
Complement	19 to 22

On 21 May 1968 the Vosper Thornycroft Group announced the receipt of an order for six of their 110-foot fast patrol boats for the Republic of Singapore. In design these vessels are of a hybrid type between that of the fast patrol craft built for the Malaysian Navy and those built for the Peruvian Navy. Two sub types, the first of each (*Independence* and *Sovereignty*) built in UK, the remainder in Singapore. Second type have more advanced armament. *Independence* was completed in 1970. *Freedom* and *Justice* in 1971.

INDEPENDENCE *1971, Vosper Thornycroft*

3 "TYPE B" (FAST ATTACK CRAFT—GUN)

SOVEREIGNTY P 71 **DARING** P 73 **DAUNTLESS** P 74

Displacement, tons	100 standard; 130 full load
Dimensions, feet	103·6 wl; 109·6 × 21·0 × 5·6
Guns	1—76 mm Bofors; 1—20 mm Oerlikon
Main engines	2 Maybach MD 872 diesels; 2 × 3 600 bhp = 32 knots
Range, miles	1 100 at 15 knots
Complement	19 (3 officers, 16 ratings)

Sovereignty was built by Vosper Thornycroft Ltd, Portsmouth, England. *Daring* and *Dauntless* built by Vosper Thornycroft Private Ltd (formerly Uniteers Yard) in Singapore. All completed 1971. Steel hulls of round bilge form with spray strake and spray deflecting knuckle extending for more than half the length. Aluminium alloy superstructure.

SOVEREIGNTY *1971, Vosper Thornycroft*

Light Forces—*continued*

6 LÜRSSEN VEGESACK "TNC 48" CLASS

(FAST ATTACK CRAFT—MISSILE)

SEA WOLF P 76 **SEA LION** P 77 **SEA TIGER** P 79 **SEA DRAGON** P 78 **SEA HAWK** P 80 **SEA SCORPION** P 81

Displacement, tons	230
Dimensions, ft (*m*)	158 × 23 × 7·5 (*48 × 7 × 2·3*)
Missiles	5 Gabriel
Guns	1—57 mm; 1—40 mm
Main engines	4 MTU diesels; 4 shafts; 14 400 hp = 34 knots
Complement	40

Designed by Lürssen Werft who built the first pair, *Sea Wolf* and *Sea Lion*, which arrived Autumn 1972. The remainder built by Singapore Shipbuilding and Engineering Co. All now in commission.

1 "FORD" CLASS (LARGE PATROL CRAFT)

PANGLIMA P 48

Displacement, tons	119 standard; 134 full load
Dimensions, feet	117·0 × 20·0 × 6·0
Gun	1—40 mm; 60 cal AA forward
Main engines	Paxman YHAXM supercharged B 12 diesels = 14 knots
Oil fuel, tons	15
Complement	15 officers and men

Built by United Engineers, Singapore. Laid down in 1954. Launched on 14 Jan 1956. Accepted by the Singapore Government in May 1956. Similar to the British seaward defence boats of the "Ford" class. Transferred to the Royal Malaysian Navy on the formation of Malaysia. Transferred to the Singapore Government (independent Republic of Singapore) in 1967.

PANGLIMA *1964*

4 VOSPER THORNYCROFT TYPE (COASTAL PATROL CRAFT)

PX 10 **PX 11** **PX 12** **PX 13**

Displacement, tons	40 standard
Length, feet	87·0
Guns	2—20 mm

Built by Vosper Thornycroft Group, Portsmouth, England for marine police duties. There is also the former Netherlands boat *Endeavor*, built in 1955.

AMPHIBIOUS FORCES

4 Ex-US LST TYPE

ENDURANCE A 81 (ex-USS *Holmes County*, LST 836)
(ex-USS *LST* 276)
(ex-USS *Chase County* LST 532)
(ex-USS *LST* 117)

Displacement, tons	1 653 light; 4 080 full load
Dimensions, feet	316·0 wl; 328·0 oa × 50·0 × 14·0
Guns	8—40 mm (4 twin)
Main engines	GM diesels; 2 shafts; 1 700 bhp = 11·6 knots
Complement	120

Endurance transferred from the United States Navy on 1 July 1971, remainder in 1973. There are also six small landing craft.

SOMALI REPUBLIC

Mercantile Marine

Lloyd's Register of Shipping: 276 vessels of 1916–2/3 tons gross

6 Ex-USSR "POWCHAT I" CLASS (LARGE PATROL CRAFT)

Displacement, tons	100 standard, 120 full load
Dimensions, feet	98·4 × 20·0 × 5·9
Guns	2—25 mm
Main engines	Diesels = 15 knots

Transferred in 1968.

4 Ex-USSR "P6" CLASS (FAST ATTACK CRAFT—TORPEDO)

Displacement, tons	66 standard 75 full load
Dimensions, feet	84·2 × 20·0 × 6·0
Guns	4—25 mm
Torpedo tubes	2—21 inch
Main engines	4 diesels; 4 shafts; 4 800 hp = 43 knots
Range, miles	450 at 30 knots
Complement	25

Transferred in 1967.

SOUTH AFRICA

Administration

Chief of South African Defence Force:
Admiral H. H. Biermann SSA, OBE

Chief of the Navy:
Vice-Admiral J. Johnson, SM, DSC

Chief of Naval Staff:
Rear-Admiral S. C. Biermann, SM

Diplomatic Representation

Armed Forces Attaché in London:
Maj Gen H. R. Meintjes, SM

Naval Attaché in London:
Captain D. F. Silberbauer

Defence Attaché in W. Germany:
Brigadier P. E. K. Bossman

Naval Attaché in Washington:
Commander R. L. Shelver

Naval Attaché in Paris:
Captain P. H. Wijnberg, SM

Strength of the Fleet

Type	*Active*	*Building (Planned)*
Destroyers	2	—
Frigates	7	—
Corvettes	—	(6)
Submarines Patrol	3	—
Large Patrol Craft	5	—
Minesweepers Coastal	10	—
Survey Ship	1	—
Fleet Replenishment Ship	1	—
BDV	1	—
TRV	1	—
Training Ships	2	—
Tugs	2	—
SAR Launches	4	—

Naval Base

HM Dockyard at Simonstown was transferred to the Republic of South Africa on 2 Apr 1957. The new submarine base at Simonstown, SAS *Drommedaris*, incorporating offices, accommodation and operations centre alongside a Synchrolift marine elevator, capable of docking all South African ships except the *Tafelberg*, was opened in July 1972.
A new Maritime Headquarters was opened in March 1973 at Silvermine on the Cape Peninsula.

Prefix to Ships' Names

SAS (Suid Afrikaanse Skip)

Personnel

(a) 1973: Total 4 665 (427 officers, 3 038 ratings and 1 200 National Service ratings)
1974: Total 4 204 (475 officers, 2 329 ratings and 1 400 National Service ratings)
1975: Total 4 250 (475 officers, 2 375 ratings and 1 400 National Service ratings)
(b) Voluntary plus 9-12 months National Service

Air Sea Rescue Base

The SAAF Maritime Group base at Langebaan was transferred to the South African Navy on 1 Nov 1969, becoming SAN Sea Rescue Base (SAS *Flamingo*). The ASR launches were given Naval Coastal Forces numbers to replace SAAF "R" numbers.

Mercantile Marine

Lloyd's Register of Shipping:
270 vessels of 535 322 tons gross

DESTROYERS

2 Ex-BRITISH "W" CLASS

Name	*No.*	*Builders*	*Laid down*	*Launched*	*Completed*
JAN VAN RIEBEECK (ex-HMS *Wessex*, ex-*Zenith*)	D 278	Fairfield SB & Eng Co Ltd, Govan, Glasgow	20 Oct 1942	2 Sep 1943	11 May 1944
SIMON VAN DER STEL (ex-HMS *Whelp*)	D 237	R. & W. Hawthorn Leslie & Co Ltd	1 May 1942	3 June 1943	25 Apr 1944

Displacement, tons	2 205 standard; 2 850 full load
Length, feet (*metres*)	339·5 (*103·6*)pp; 362·8 (*110·6*)oa
Beam, feet (*metres*)	35·7 (*10·9*)
Draught, feet (*metres*)	17·1 (*5·2*)
Aircraft	2 Westland "Wasp" helicopters
Guns	2—4 in (*102 mm*) 2 twin; 2—40 mm (single); 4—3 pdr. (saluting)
Torpedo tubes	4—21 in (quadruple)
Torpedo tubes, A/S	6 (2 triple)
A/S weapons	2 DCT; 2 DC racks
Boilers	2 Admiralty 3-drum type; 300 psi; 670°F
Main engines	2 Parsons sr geared turbines; 2 shafts; 40 000 shp
Speed, knots	36
Range, miles	3 260 at 14 knots; 1 000 at 30 knots
Oil fuel, tons	579 (95%)
Complement	192 (11 officers, 181 men)

Purchased from Great Britain, *Jan van Riebeeck* was transferred to South Africa on 29 Mar 1950, and *Simon van der Stel* early in 1952.

GUNNERY. The main armament formerly comprised four 4·7 inch guns.

MODERNISATION. *Simon van der Stel* was modernised in 1962-64 and *Jan van Riebeeck* in 1964-66.

RADAR. Search: Type 293. Fire Control: X Band (NSG NA 9 system)

JAN VAN RIEBEECK — 1973 *South African Navy*

JAN VAN RIEBEECK & SIMON VAN DER STEL

FRIGATES

6 NEW CONSTRUCTION

In February 1975 it was announced that 6 frigates, to be armed with Gabriel missiles, were to be built in Durban. It is understood that they will be similar to the Portuguese "João Coutinho" class, although no further details have been released.

3 "PRESIDENT" CLASS

Name	*No*	*Builders*	*Laid down*	*Launched*	*Completed*
PRESIDENT KRUGER	F 150	Yarrow & Co Scotstoun	6 Apr 1959	20 Oct 1960	1 Oct 1962
PRESIDENT PRETORIUS	F 145	Yarrow & Co Scotstoun	21 Nov 1960	28 Sep 1962	4 Mar 1964
PRESIDENT STEYN	F 147	Alex Stephen & Sons Govan	20 May 1960	23 Nov 1961	25 Apr 1963

Displacement, tons	2 250 standard; 2 800 full load
Dimensions, ft (*m*)	370 oa × 41·1 × 17·1 (*112·8 × 12·5 × 5·2*)
Aircraft	1 "Wasp" helicopter
Guns,	2—4·5 in (*115 mm*) 1 twin; 2—40 mm Bofors; 4—3 pdr. (saluting)
A/S weapons	1 "Limbo" 3-barrel DC mortar
Torpedo tubes	6 A/S tubes (2 triple)
Boilers	2 Babcock & Wilcox 550 psi; 850/F
Main engines	2 sets double reduction geared turbines; 2 shafts; 30 000 shp
Speed, knots	30
Range, miles	4 500 at 12 knots
Oil fuel, tons	430
Complement	203 (13 officers, 190 men)

Originally "Whitby" Type 12 frigates, *President Kruger* arrived in South Africa on 27 Mar 1963.

PRESIDENT KRUGER — *1973, South African Navy*

Frigates—*continued*

MODERNISATION. Refitted to carry a "Wasp" A/S helicopter, with hangar and landing deck. To accommodate this, one "Limbo" A/S mortar was removed and the two single 40 mm remounted on the hangar roof. *President Kruger* completed refit and recommissioned on 5 Aug 1969, *President Steyn* completed refit in 1971, when *President Pretorius* was taken in hand although delayed to take advantage gained from the previous conversions. The refits were carried out at S.A. Naval Dockyard, Simonstown and included replacement of the lattice foremast by a truncated pyramid tower. *Kruger* retained her original GDS5 director but will later be brought into line with the other pair. Small differences exist between all three ships.

RADAR. Thomson CSF Jupiter 23 cm surveillance; Type 293 air/surface warning; nav set. Elsag NA9C fire control (Kruger with original fire control radar) ECM and DF.

PRESIDENT KRUGER *1973*

PRESIDENT STEYN *1973, South African Navy*

1 FORMER BRITISH TYPE 15

VRYSTAAT (ex-HMS *Wrangler*) F 157

Displacement, tons	2 240 standard; 2 880 full load
Length, feet (*metres*)	339·5 (*103·5*) pp; 362·8 (*110·6*) oa
Beam, feet (*metres*)	35·7 (*10·9*)
Draught, feet (*metres*)	17·1 (*5·2*)
Guns,	2—4 in (*102 mm*) 1 twin 2—40 mm Bofors 4—3 pdr
A/S weapons	2 Limbo
Boilers	2 Admiralty 3-drum; 300 psi; 675°F
Main engines	Parsons single reduction geared turbines; 2 shafts; 40 000 shp
Speed, knots	36
Range, miles	3 200 at 14 knots 1 300 at full power
Oil fuel, tons	505
Complement	195 (13 officers, 182 men)

Built by Vickers-Armstrong, Barrow. Laid down on 23 Sep 1942, launched on 30 Dec 1943, completed on 14 June 1944. Fully converted into a Type 15 fast anti-submarine frigate from a fleet destroyer of the "W" class in 1951-52 by Harland & Wolf Ltd, Belfast. Refitted by the Mount Stewart Dry Dock Ltd, Cardiff, and taken over from the Royal Navy on 29 Nov 1956 as a unit of the South African Navy and renamed *Vrystaat*. Sailed for South Africa at the end of Jan 1957.

RADAR. Search: Type 277, Type 293. ECM and DF.

VRYSTAAT *1970, South African Navy*

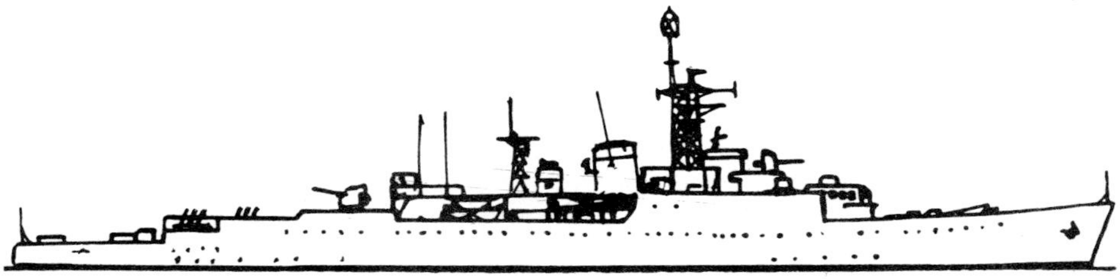

VRYSTAAT *1973*

2 FORMER BRITISH "LOCH" CLASS

Name	*No.*	*Builders*	*Laid down*	*Launched*	*Completed*
GOOD HOPE (ex-HMS *Loch Boisdale*)	F 432	Blyth Dry Docks & SB Co Ltd	8 Nov 1943	5 July 1944	1 Dec 1944
TRANSVAAL (ex-HMS *Loch Ard*)	F 602	Harland & Wolff, Ltd, Belfast	20 Jan 1944	2 Aug 1944	21 May 1945

Displacement, tons	1 610 standard; 2 450 full load
Length, feet (*metres*)	286 (*87·2*) pp; 307 (*93·6*) oa
Beam, feet (*metres*)	38·5 (*11·7*)
Draught, feet (*metres*)	15·1 (*4·6*)
Guns,	2—4 in (*102 mm*) 1 twin *Transvaal:* 6—40 mm Bofors *Good Hope:* 2—40 mm Bofors *Good Hope:* 4—3 pdr
A/S weapons	2 "Squid" triple DC mortars
Boilers	2 Admiralty 3-drum; 225 psi
Main engines	2 sets triple expansion; 2 shafts; 5 500 ihp
Speed, knots	19
Range, miles	9 500 at 12 knots
Oil fuel, tons	720
Complement	165 (10 officers, 155 men)

These two frigates, and a sister ship, *Natal*, were presented to South Africa by Great Britain in 1944-45.

CONSTRUCTION. *Transvaal* was completed by Lobnitz & Co Ltd, Renfrew.

MODIFICATION. When *Transvaal* was modernised she had her forecastle deck extended aft to provide extra accommodation (see photograph).

TRANSVAAL *1971, South African Navy*

CONVERSION. *Good Hope* was converted into a despatch vessel in 1955 as Administrative Flagship of the South African Navy. She has deckhouse superstructure for extra cabins, and reception platform above built on aft, and mainmast. Refitted in 1961. Sister ship *Natal* (survey ship) was sunk as a target on 19 Sept 1972.

RADAR. Equipment includes Type 277 search radar.

Frigates—*continued*

1 FORMER BRITISH "ALGERINE" CLASS

PIETERMARITZBURG (ex-HMS *Pelorus*) M 291

Displacement, tons	1 040 standard; 1 330 full load
Length, feet (*metres*)	212·5 (*64·8*) pp; 225 (*68·6*) oa
Beam, feet (*metres*)	35·5 (*10·8*)
Draught feet (*metres*)	11·5 (*3·5*)
Guns,	2—4 in (*102 mm*) 1 twin 2—40 mm Bofors
A/S weapons	4 DCT
Boilers	2 three-drum type; 250 psi
Main engines	2 sets triple expansion; 2 shafts; 2 400 ihp
Speed, knots	16
Range, miles	5 500 at 10 knots
Oil fuel, tons	270
Complement	115 (8 officers, 107 men)

Built as ocean minesweeper by Lobnitz & Co Ltd. Renfrew. Laid down on 8 Oct 1942, launched on 18 June 1943, completed on 7 Oct 1943. Purchased from Great Britain in 1947 Re-commissioned as midshipmen's training ship on 30 Aug 1962. Refitted in 1971.

PIETERMARITZBURG *1969, South African Navy*

SUBMARINES

3 FRENCH "DAPHNE" CLASS

Name	*No.*	*Builders*	*Laid down*	*Launched*	*Completed*
EMILY HOBHOUSE	S 98	Dubigeon—Normandie (Nantes-Chantenay)	18 Nov 1968	24 Oct 1969	25 Jan 1971
JOHANNA VAN DER MERWE	S 99	Dubigeon—Normandie (Nantes-Chantenay)	24 Apr 1969	21 July 1970	21 July 1971
MARIA VAN RIEBEECK	S 97	Dubigeon—Normandie (Nantes-Chantenay)	14 Mar 1968	18 Mar 1969	22 June 1970

Displacement, tons	850 surface; 1 040 submerged
Length, feet (*metres*)	190·3 (*58*)
Beam, feet (*metres*)	22·3 (*6·8*)
Draught, feet (*metres*)	15·4 (*4·7*)
Torpedo tubes	12—21·7 in (*550 mm*) (8 bow, 4 stern)
Main engines	SEMT-Pielstick diesel electric; 1 300 bhp surface, 1 600 hp submerged; 2 shafts
Speed, knots	16 surface and submerged
Range, miles	4 500 at 5 knots (snorting)
Complement	47 (6 officers, 41 men)

First submarines ordered for the South African Navy. They are of the French "Daphne" design, similar to those built in France for that country, Pakistan and Portugal and also built in Spain.

EMILY HOBHOUSE *1973, South African Navy*

LIGHT FORCES

5 BRITISH "FORD" CLASS (LARGE PATROL CRAFT)

GELDERLAND (ex-*Brayford*) P 3105
HAERLEM P 3126
NAUTILUS (ex-*Glassford*) P 3120
OOSTERLAND P 3127
REIJGER P 3125

Displacement, tons	120 standard; 160 full load
Dimensions, feet	110·0 wl; 117·2 oa × 20·0 × 4·5
Gun	1—40 mm AA
A/S weapons	2 DCT in *Haerlem*, *Oosterland* and *Rijger*
Main engines	2 Davey Paxman diesels; Foden engine on centre shaft; 1 100 bhp = 18 knots

Gelderland built by A. & J. Inglis Ltd, Glasgow, was purchased from Britain, and handed over to South Africa at Portsmouth on 30 Aug 1954. Second ship, *Nautilus* was purchased in 1955, *Reijger* was launched on 6 Feb 1958, *Haerlem* on 18 June 1958, *Oosterland* on 27 Jan 1959. All three of these later ships, built by Vosper Ltd. Portsmouth, are fitted with Vosper roll damping fins, *Haerlem* had a charthouse added aft as an inshore survey boat.

REIJGER *1971*

MINE WARFARE FORCES

10 BRITISH "TON" CLASS (MINESWEEPERS COASTAL)

DURBAN M 1499
EAST LONDON (ex-*Chilton*) M 1215
JOHANNESBURG (*Castleton*) M 1207
KAAPSTAD (ex-*Hazleton*) M 1142
KIMBERLEY (ex-*Stratton*) M 1210
MOSSELBAAI (ex-*Oakington*) M 1213
PORT ELIZABETH (*Dumbleton*) M 1212
PRETORIA (ex-*Dunkerton*) M 1144
WALVISBAAI (ex-*Packington*) M 1214
WINDHOEK M 1498

Displacement, tons	360 standard; 425 full load
Dimensions, feet	140·0 pp; 152·0 oa × 28·8 × 8·2
Guns	1—40 mm Bofors AA; 2—20 mm AA
Main engines	Mirrlees diesels in *Kaapstad* and *Pretoria*, 2 500 bhp; Deltic diesels in remainder; 3 000 bhp = 15 knots
Range, miles	2 300 at 13 knots

Kaapstad and *Pretoria*, open bridge and lattice mast, were purchased in 1955. *Windhoek*, frigate bridge and tripod mast, was launched by Thornycroft, Southampton, on 27 June 1957. *Durban*, covered bridge and tripod mast, was launched at Camper & Nicholson, Gosport, on 12 June 1957. *East London* and *Port Elizabeth*, transferred from the Royal Navy at Hythe on 27 Oct 1958, sailed for South Africa in Nov 1958. *Johannesburg*, *Kimberley* and *Mosselbaai* were delivered in 1959. *Walvisbaai* was launched by Harland & Wolff, Belfast on 10 Dec 1958 and delivered in 1959.

DURBAN *1971*

SURVEY SHIP

PROTEA

Displacement, tons	1 930 standard; 2 750 full load
Length, feet (*metres*)	235 (*71·6*); 260·1 (*79·3*)
Beam, feet (*metres*)	49·1 (*15·0*)
Draught, feet (*metres*)	15·1 (*4·6*)
Aircraft	1 helicopter
Main engines	4 Paxman/Ventura diesels geared to 1 shaft and controllable pitch propeller; 4 880 bhp
Speed, knots	16
Range, miles	12 000 at 11 knots
Oil fuel, tons	560
Complement	Total 123 (12 officers, 104 ratings plus 7 scientists)

An order was placed with Yarrow (Shipbuilders) Ltd, for a "Hecla" class survey ship on 7 Nov 1969. Equipped for hydrographic survey with limited facilities for the collection of oceanographical data and for this purpose fitted with special communications equipment, naval surveying gear, survey launches and facilities for helicopter operations. Hull strengthened for navigation in ice and fitted with a transverse bow thrust unit and passive roll stabilisation system. Laid down 20 July 1970. Launched 14 July 1971. Commissioned 23 May 1972.

PROTEA *1973, South African Navy*

FLEET REPLENISHMENT SHIP

TAFELBERG (ex-*Annam*) A 243

Measurement, tons	12 500 gross; 18 430 deadweight
Main engines	B & W diesels; 8 420 bhp = 15·5 knots
Complement	100 as naval vessel (40 as tanker)

Built by Nakskovs Skibsvaert as Danish East Asiatic Co tanker. Launched on 20 June 1958. Purchased by the Navy in 1965. Accommodation rehabilitated by Barens Shipbuilding & Engineering Co, Durban with extra accommodation, air conditioning, re-wiring for additional equipment, new upper RAS (replenishment at sea) deck to contain gantries, re-fuelling pipes. Remainder of conversion by Jowies, Brown & Hamer, Durban.

TAFELBERG *1973, South African Navy*

TAFELBERG *1973*

TORPEDO RECOVERY VESSEL

FLEUR P 3148

Displacement, tons	220 standard; 257 full load
Dimensions, feet	115·0 wl; 121·5 oa × 27·5 × 11·1
Main engines	2 Paxman Ventura diesels; 1 400 bhp

Built by Dorman Long (Africa) Ltd at Durban and completed on 28 Nov 1969. Commissioned 3 Dec 1969. Combined Torpedo Recovery Vessel and Diving Tender.

FLEUR *1973, South African Navy*

TRAINING VESSELS

HDML 1204

Displacement, tons	45 standard; 54 full load
Dimensions, feet	72·0 × 15·5 × 5·3
Main engines	2 Gardner 8-cylinder diesels; 300 bhp = 11 knots

Sole survivor of the class of twelve craft of the former British Admiralty type HDMLs (Harbour Defence Motor Launches) later designated Seaward Defence Motor Launches. Built in South Africa 1941-42. Guns removed. Attached to Military Academy, Saldanha, as Midshipmen's training vessle.

NAVIGATOR

Navigational Training Vessel. 75 tons displacement; 63 × 20 feet; 2 Foden diesels, 200 bhp = 9·5 knots. Based at Naval College, Gordon's Bay. Round bilge fishing boat wooden hull. Built by Fred Nicholls (Pty) Ltd, Durban in 1964.

BOOM DEFENCE VESSEL

SOMERSET (ex-HMS *Barcross*) P 285

Displacement, tons	750 standard; 960 full load
Dimensions, feet	150·0 pp; 182·0 oa × 32·2 × 11·5
Main engines	Triple expansion; 850 hp = 11 knots
Boilers	2 single ended
Oil fuel, tons	186

Originally two in the class.
Built by Blyth Dry Dock & SB Co Ltd. Laid down on 15 Apr 1941, launched on 21 Oct 1941, completed on 14 Apr 1942. Engined by Swan, Hunter & Wigham Richardson Ltd. Tyne.

NAVAL TUGS

DE NEYS **DE NOORDE**

Displacement, tons	180 and 170 respectively
Dimensions, feet	94·0 × 26·5 × 15·75 and 104·5 × 25·0 × 15·0
Main engines	2 Lister Blackstone diesels; 2 shafts; 608 bhp = 9 knots
Complement	10

Both built by Globe Engineering Works Ltd, Cape Town. Completed on 23 July 1969 and Dec 1961.

AIR SEA RESCUE LAUNCHES

P 1551 (ex-*R* 31) **P 1552** (ex-*R* 30) **P 1554** **P 1555**

Built by Fairey Marine and their associated firm of Groves and Cutteridge, Cowes. P 1554 and 1555: 26 tons, 64 × 16 × 5 feet, 2 diesels, 1 120 bhp = 28 kts. P 1551 and 1552: 87 tons, 96 × 19 × 4 feet, 2 diesels, 4 480 bhp = 30 kts (1962, 1961). There are also 2 ex-seaplane tenders, 41 ft, and 2 ex-marine tenders, 24 ft.

P1554 *1973, South African Navy*

SPAIN

Administration

Minister of the Navy:
Admiral Excmo Sr Don Gabriel Pita da Veiga

Chief of the Naval Staff:
Admiral Excmo Sr Don José Ramón González López

Vice Chief of the Naval Staff:
Vice-Admiral Excmo Sr Don Luis Arévalo Pelluz

Commander-in-Chief of the Fleet:
Vice-Admiral Excmo Sr Don Francisco J. de Elizalde

Captain General, Cantabrian Zone:
Admiral Excmo Sr Don Antonio González-Aller

Captain General, Straits Zone:
Admiral Excmo Sr Don Felipe Pita da Veiga

Captain General, Mediterranean Zone:
Admiral Excmo Sr Don José Yusty Pita

Commandant General, Marines:
Lieut-General Excmo Sr Don Francisco Martinez de Galinsoga

Diplomatic Representation

Naval Attaché in London:
Captain Don Jesus Diaz del Rio

Naval Attaché in Washington:
Captain Sr Don Adolfo Gregorio

Personnel

(a) 1975: Total 51 200 (4 550 officers, 33 000 ratings, 4 650 civil branch, 9 000 marines)
(b) 18 months National Service

Naval Air Service

12 Bell 47G
4 AB 204B
12 Sikorsky SH-3D
11 Hughes 369 HM
6 Bell AH-1G "Hueycobra"
4 Bell 212

NOTES:
(a) Harrier AV-8 aircraft ordered from US marines in 1973. Initial order of 8 with possible follow-up of 12 and an additional 4.
(b) It is reported that an additional 12 SH-3D and 12 AH-1G (Hueycobras) are to be ordered.

Strength of the Fleet

Type	*Active*	*Building*	*Proposed*
Helicopter Carrier	1	—	1
Cruiser	1 (Reserve)	—	—
Destroyers	13	—	—
Frigates	13	5	10
Corvettes	4	—	—
Submarines Patrol	8	2	2
Submarines Small	2	—	—
Fast Attack Craft—Torpedo	2	—	—
Large Patrol Craft	—	12	—
Coastal Patrol Craft	8	—	—
LSD	1	—	—
Attack Transports	2	—	—
LST	2	—	—
LSM	3	—	—
LCT	8	—	—
Minor Landing Craft	87	4	—
Minesweepers—Ocean	11	—	—
Minesweepers—Coastal	12	—	—
Survey Ships	7	—	—
Transport	1	—	—
Replenishment Tanker	1	—	—
Harbour Tankers	11	—	—
Training Ship	1	—	—
Auxiliary Patrol Craft	12	—	—
Tugs (Ocean, Coastal and Harbour)	27	—	—
Miscellaneous	56	—	—

New Construction

Because of financial considerations last year's programme has been cut to the following: 1 Helicopter carrier, 5 Frigates (PF), 8 smaller frigates (tentatively 10), 2 "Agosta" class submarines (tentatively 4), 6 400-ton Large Patrol Craft, 6 140-ton Large Patrol Craft, 2 Oceanographic ships, 2 coastal survey ships.

Of the above the following are under construction:
5 Frigates
1 Submarine
2 Oceanographic Ships
6 Large Patrol Craft (400 tons)
6 Large Patrol Craft (140 tons)

US Agreement

Under an Agreement of 6 Aug 1970 the USA agreed to supply 2 submarines, 5 destroyers, 4 MSOs, 3 LSTs, 1 AE and 1 AO. Of this list an LSD was substituted for the AE and the AO was in too poor condition for further service. All now transferred.

Bases

El Ferrol del Caudillo (Cantabrian Zone)
San Fernando, Cádiz (Straits Zone)
Cartagena (Mediterranean Zone)

Disposals

Destroyers

1970 *Am. Miranda*
1971 *Magallanes, Vasco Nunez de Balbao, Hernan Cortes*

Frigates

1971 *Mate*
1972 *Neptune, Eolo, Triton*
1973 *Osado*
1974 *Audaz, Furor, Rayo, Jupiter, Sarmiento de Gamboa*

Corvettes

1971 *Descubierta*
1973 *Diana*

Submarines

1971 D 2 (S 21), D 3 (S 22), G 7 (ex-U573 VII C) Midget submarines SA 41 (F 1), SA 42 (F 2)

Minesweepers

1971 *Lerez*
1972 *Bidasoa, Nervion, Segura, Tambre, Ter*

Amphibious Forces

1974 *LSM 3*

Light Forces

1970 *Arcila, Xanen*
1971 *Javier Quiroga*
1973 *Ciés*
1974 *V 2, V 12, V, 13 V 18, Candido Pérez, AR 10*

Survey Ships

1971 *Mataspina*
1975 Tofiño

Service Forces

1974 *PP 1, 3, 4. PB 5, 6, 17* (tankers)

Mercantile Marine

Lloyd's Register of Shipping:
2 520 vessels of 4 949 146 tons gross

LIST OF PENNANT NUMBERS

Helicopter Carrier PH
01 Dédalo

Cruiser C
21 Canarias

Destroyers D
21 Lepanto
22 Alm Ferrandiz
23 Alm Valdes
24 Galiano
25 Jorge Juan
41 Oquendo
42 Roger de Lauria
43 M. de la Ensenada
61 Churruca
62 Gravina
63 Mendez Nuñez
64 Langara
65 Blaz de Lezo

Frigates D and F
D 37 Temerario
38 Intrépido
39 Relámpago
51 Liniers
52 Alava
F 12 Vulcano
41 Vicente Yáñez Pinzon
42 Legazpi
71 Baleares
72 Andalucia
73 Cataluña
74 Asturias
75 Extremadura
81-5 New Construction
91-5 Proposed New Construction

Corvettes F

61 Atrevida
62 Princesa
64 Nautilus
65 Villa de Bilbao

Submarines S
32 Isaac Peral
33 N. Monturiol
34 Cosme Garcia
35 ex-Jallao
61 Delfin
62 Tonina
63 Marsopa
64 Narval
71-72 New Construction
SA 51-52 Tiburon class

Light Forces P
01 Lazaga
02 Alsedo
03 Cadarso
04 Villamil
05 Bonifaz
06 Recalde
11 Barceló
12 Laya
13 J. Quiroga
14 Ordóñez
15 Acevedo
16 C. Pérez
LT 30-31
LP 1-5
LAS 10, 20, 30
W 21 Pegaso
22 Procyon
32 Salvora
33 Centinela
34 Serviola
V 1, 4, 5, 6, 9, 10, 11, 17, 21

Amphibious Forces

TA 11 Aragon
TA 21 Castilla
TA 31 Galicia
L 11 Velasco
L 12 Martin Alvarez
L 13 C. de Venadito
LSM 1-2
K 1-8 BDK 1-8

Minewarfare Forces M
11 Guadiaro
12 Tinto
13 Eume
14 Almanzora
15 Navia
16 Guadalhorce
17 Eo
21 Nalón
22 Llobregat
23 Jucar
24 Ulla
25 Miño
26 Ebro
27 Turia
28 Duero
29 Sil
30 Tajo
31 Genil
32 Odiel
41 Guadalete
42 Guadalmedina
43 Guadalquivir
44 Guadiana

Survey Ships A
21 Castor
22 Pollux
23 Antares
24 Rigel
31 Malaspina
32 Tofiño
— Juan de la Cosa

Service Forces

A 41 Al Lobo
BP 11 Teide

HELICOPTER CARRIER

ALMIRANTE CARRERO

The design of this ship, planned as a replacement for *Dédalo*, was originally to be similar to that of the USN Sea Control Ship. Due to delays in obtaining Congressional approval for this latter programme the building of *Almirante Carrero* may also be set-back, although the design of such a ship by Spanish constructors is well within their capability. She is planned to be of 14 300 tons with air complement of Harriers and ASW helicopters and to be laid down by Bazán Factoria de Ferrol in 1976 for completion late 1978.

1 Ex-US CVL

Name	No	Builders	Laid down	Launched	Completed
DÉDALO (ex-USS *Cabot*, AVT 3, ex-CVL 28, ex-*Wilmington*, CL 79)	PH 01	New York Shipbuilding Corporation	16 Aug 1942	4 Apr 1943	24 July 1943

Displacement, tons	13 000 standard; 16 416 full load
Length, feet (*metres*)	600·0 (*182·8*)wl; 623·0(*189·9*) oa
Beam, feet (*metres*)	71·5 (*21·8*) hull
Width, feet (*metres*)	109·0 (*33·2*)
Draught, feet (*metres*)	26·0 (*7·9*)
Aircraft	20 helicopters (ASW/Sea Kings—Combat/Huey Cobras—Landings/specially embarked S55s or Bell 212s)
Guns	26—40 mm AA (2 quadruple, 9 twin)
Armour	2 to 5 in sides; 2 to 3 in deck
Main armour	GE geared turbines 4 shafts; 100 000 shp
Speed, knots	32
Boilers	4 Babcock & Wilcox
Range, miles	7 200 at 15 knots
Oil fuel, tons	1 800
Complement	1 112 (without Air Groups)

Completed as an aircraft carrier from the hull of a "Cleveland" class cruiser. Originally carried over 40 aircraft. Converted with strengthened flight and hangar decks, large port side catapult, revised magazine arrangements, new electronic gear, with stability corrected to offset the added top-weight. Hangar capacity altered to take 20 aircraft. Flight deck: 545 × 108 feet (*166·1 × 32·9 metres*).

Reactivated and modernised at Philadelphia Naval Shipyard, where she was transferred to Spain on 30 Aug 1967, on loan for five years. Purchased Dec 1973.

RADAR. SPS 6 and SPS 40 air search; SPS 10 tactical; SPS 8 heightfinder; four fire control radars; Tacan.

DEDALO — *1969 Spanish Navy*

CRUISER

Name	No.	Builders	Laid down	Launched	Completed
CANARIAS	C 21	Sociedad Española de Construcción Naval El Ferrol	15 Aug 1928	28 May 1931	1 Oct 1936

Displacement, tons	10 282 standard; 13 969 full load
Length, feet, (*metres*)	636·5 (*194·0*)
Beam, feet (*metres*)	64·0 (*19·5*)
Draught, feet (*metres*)	21·3 (*6·5*)
Guns	8—8 in (*203 mm*) 50 cal (4 twin); 8—4·7 in (*120 mm*) 45 cal. single; 4—1·5 in (*38 mm*) 80 cal (2 twin); 4—40 mm AA; 2—20 mm 70 cal AA
Armour	sides 1·5—2 in (*38—50 mm*); turrets and deck 1 in (*25 mm*); magazines 4 in (*100 mm*)
Main engines	Parsons geared turbines; 2 shafts; 92 000 shp
Speed, knots	28
Boilers	8 Yarrow type
Range, miles	8 000 at 15 knots
Oil fuel, tons	2 794
Complement	1 000 (40 officers, 960 men)

CANARIAS — *1970, Spanish Navy*

This ship was designed by the late Sir Philip Watts on the basic pattern of the contemporary British heavy cruisers of the later "County" classes. From initial completion until 1952 she had trunked funnels, but she emerged from refit in 1953 with two separate funnels, this being a reversion to the original design which had never been carried out.

RADAR. MLA-IB air search; Marconi surface warning; 2 Decca TM 626 navigation sets.

STATUS. Paid off into reserve at El Ferrol del Caudillo 2 Sept 1974. Future as yet undecided.

TORPEDO TUBES. The twelve 21 inch torpedo tubes in four triple mountings were removed in 1960.

GUNNERY. Elevation of the 8 inch guns is 70 degrees.

CLASS. Only sister ship *Baleares* was torpedoed and sunk on 6 Mar 1938 during the Spanish Civil War.

DESTROYERS

5 "D 60" CLASS

(Ex-US "GEARING" FRAM I CLASS)

Name	No.	Completed	Transferred
CHURRUCA (ex-USS *Eugene A. Greene* DD 711)	D 61	8 June 1945	31 Aug 1972
GRAVINA (ex-USS *Furse* DD 882)	D 62	10 July 1945	31 Aug 1972
MENDEZ NUÑEZ (ex-USS *O'Hare* DD 889)	D 63	29 Nov 1945	31 Oct 1973
LANGARA (ex-USS *Leary* DD 879)	D 64	7 May 1945	31 Oct 1973
BLAS DE LEZO (ex-USS *Noa* DD 841)	D 65	2 Nov 1945	31 Oct 1973

Displacement, tons	2 425 standard; 3 480 full load
Length, feet (*metres*)	390·5 (*119·0*) oa
Beam, feet (*metres*)	40·9 (*12·4*)
Draught, feet (*metres*)	19 (*5·8*)
Guns	4—5 in (*127 mm*) 38 cal DP twin
A/S weapons	1 Asroc launcher 2 Triple Mk 32 tubes Facilities for Hughes 369 HM helicopter
Main engines	2 geared turbines (GE or Westinghouse) 60 000 shp; 2 shafts
Boilers	4 Babcock and Wilcox
Speed, knots	34
Fuel, tons	650
Range, miles	4 800 at 15 knots (economical)
Complement	264 (17 officers, 247 ratings)

RADAR. D61 and 62—Air Search, SPS 40—remainder, SPS 37: Surface search, SPS 10; Fire control Mk 37.

REFITS. The first pair were refitted at El Ferrol on transfer. The remainder arrived at El Ferrol on July 23 1974 after refit in the USA.

SONAR. D 61 and 62—SQS 23 (hull mounted).

TRANSFERS. All finally purchased 1975.

CHURRUCA *1974, Spanish Navy*

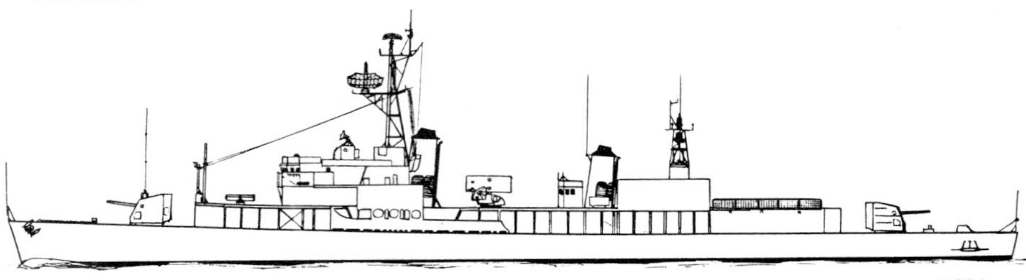
"D 60" Class (Churruca and Gravina) *1974*

2 "MODIFIED OQUENDO" CLASS

Name	No.	Laid down	Launched	Commissioned
MARQUÉS DE LA ENSENADA	D43	4 Sep 1951	15 July 1959	10 Sep 1970
ROGER DE LAURIA	D42	4 Sep 1951	12 Nov 1958	30 May 1969

Displacement, tons	3 370 standard; 3 785 full load
Length, feet (*metres*)	391·5 (*119·3*)
Beam, feet (*metres*)	42·7 (*13·0*)
Draught, feet (*metres*)	18·4 (*5·6*)
Aircraft	1 Hughes 369 HM ASW helo
Guns	6—5 in (*127 mm*) 38 cal (3 twin)
A/S weapons	2 triple Mk 32 tubes for Mk 44 A/S torpedoes
Torpedo, tubes	2—21 in (*533 mm*) fixed single Mk 25 tubes for Mk 37 torpedoes
Main engines	2 Rateau-Bretagne geared turbines; 2 shafts; 60 000 shp
Speed, knots	31
Boilers	3 three-drum type
Oil fuel, tons	673
Range, miles	4 500 at 15 knots
Complement	318 (20 officers, 298 men)

MARQUÉS DE LA ENSENADA, ROGER DE LAURIA

ROGER DE LAURIA *1970, Spanish Navy*

Ordered at Ferrol in 1948. Originally of the same design as *Oquendo*. Towed to Cartegena for reconstruction to a new design. *Roger de Lauria* was re-launched after being lengthened and widened on 29 Aug 1967 and *Marqués de la Ensenada* on 2 Mar 1968. Weapons and electronics identical to Gearing Fram II.

RADAR. Search: SPS 40. Tactical: SPS 10. Fire Control: One Mk 37 and one Mk 56.

SONAR. One hull mounted, probably SQS 29; one VDS, probably SQA 10.

1 "OQUENDO" CLASS

Name	No.	Laid down	Launched	Completed
OQUENDO	D 41	15 June 1951	5 Sep 1956	13 Sep 1960

Displacement, tons	2 582 standard; 3 005 full load
Length, feet (*metres*)	382 (*116·4*)
Beam, feet (*metres*)	36·5 (*11·1*)
Draught, feet (*metres*)	12·5 (*3·8*)
Guns	4—4·7 (*120 mm*) 50 cal (2 twin); 6—40 mm, 70 cal. single
A/S weapons	2 Hedgehogs
Torpedo tubes	2 Mk 4 with 3 Mk 32 homing torpedoes each
Main engines	2 Rateau-Bretagne geared turbines; 2 shafts; 60 000 shp
Speed, knots	32·4
Boilers	3 three-drum type
Oil fuel, tons	659
Range, miles	5 000 at 15 knots
Complement	250 (17 officers, 233 men)

Ordered at Ferrol in 1947. Initially completed on 13 Sep 1960. Completed modernisation on 22 April 1963.

CONSTRUCTION. Designed as a conventional destroyer but modified during construction. Seven 21-inch torpedo tubes and two depth charge throwers were replaced by different anti-submarine weapons.

RADAR. Search: British 293 type. Air Search; Marconi SNW 10. Nav; 1 set. Fire control; British type 275 on Mark 6 DCT and British Type 262 on CRBD.

OQUENDO *1974, Spanish Navy*

OQUENDO *1974*

Destroyers—*continued*

5 "D 20" CLASS

(Ex-US "FLETCHER" CLASS)

Name	No.	Builders	Laid down	Launched	Commissioned
ALCALA GALIANO (ex-USS *Jarvis, DD* 799)	D 24	Todd Pacific Shipyards	7 June 1943	14 Feb 1944	3 June 1944
ALMIRANTE FERRANDIZ (ex-USS *David W. Taylor, DD* 551)	D 22	Gulf SB Corpn, Chickasaw, Ala	12 June 1941	4 July 1942	18 Sep 1943
ALMIRANTE VALDES (ex-USS *Converse,* DD 509)	D 23	Bath Iron Works Corp, Maine	23 Feb 1942	30 Aug 1942	8 June 1943
JORGE JUAN (ex-USS *McGowan,* DD 678)	D 25	Federal SB & DD Co	20 Dec 1943	14 Nov 1943	20 Dec 1943
LEPANTO (ex-USS *Capps,* DD 550)	D 21	Gulf SB Corpn, Chickasaw, Ala	12 June 1941	31 May 1942	23 June 1943

Displacement, tons	2 080 standard; 2 750 normal; 3 050 full load
Length, feet (*metres*)	376·5 (*114·8*) oa
Beam, feet (*metres*)	39·5 (*12·0*)
Draught, feet (*metres*)	18·0 (*5·5*)
Guns	*D21, D22:* 5—5 in (*127 mm*) 38 cal; *Others:* 4—5 in (*127 mm*) single *D21, D22:* 6—40 mm, 60 cal, 3 twin; 6—20 mm, 70 cal, single *Others:* 6—3 in (*76 mm*) 50 cal, 3 twin
A/S weapons	2 Hedgehogs; 6 DCT in D21, D22, 4 in D23; 2 DC racks in D21, D22, 1 in others
Torpedo tubes	3—21 in (*533 mm*) in D 21, 22 and 23 only
Torpedo racks	2 side launching Mk 4 each with 3 Mk 32 A/S torpedoes
Main engines	Geared turbines; Westinghouse in D21, D22, GE in others; 2 shafts; 60 000 shp
Speed, knots	35
Boilers	4 Babcock & Wilcox
Range, miles	5 000 at 15 knots
Oil fuel, tons	650
Complement	290 (17 officers, 273 men)

JORGE JUAN (four 5 inch) *1972, Spanish Navy*

ALMIRANTE FERRANDIZ, LEPANTO, VALDES

ALCALA GALIANO, JORGE JUAN

Lepanto, and *Almirante Ferrandiz,* were reconditioned at San Francisco, Cal, and there turned over to the Spanish Navy on 15 May 1957, sailing for Spain on 1 July 1957. *Valdes* was transferred at Philadelphia on 1 July 1959, *Jorge Juan,* was transferred at Barcelona on 1 Dec 1960 and *Alcala Galiano,* at Philadelphia on 3 Nov 1960, both being of the later "Fletcher" class. Modernisation of A/S equipment is planned. All purchased from US on 1 Oct 1972.

RADAR. Search: SPS 6C. Tactical: SPS 10. Fire Control: D 23, 24 and 25—Mk 37 and Mk 56, 2 Mk 63 for 3 inch guns; D 21 and 22—Mk 37.

SONAR. One hull mounted set. SQS-29.

FRIGATES

5 "F 90" CLASS, NEW CONSTRUCTION

This is a projected class of PF frigates, planned to be built at El Ferrol. Reported as a fully-automated class with possibility of Westinghouse-Canada VDS and of Elettronica-San Giorgio ECM.

5 + 3 + 2 "F 80" CLASS

NEW CONSTRUCTION

Displacement, tons	1 200 standard; 1 400 full load
Dimensions, ft (*m*)	228 × 34 × 11·5 (*85 × 10·5 × 3·5*)
Missiles	1 Octuple Seasparrow mounting (16 reloads)
Guns	1—3 in (*76 mm*) 62 cal Oto Melara; 2—40 mm 70 cal (singles)
A/S Weapons	1—375 mm Bofors twin-barrelled rocket launcher
Torpedo tubes	6 (2 triple) Mk 32 for Mk 44 torpedoes
Main engines	2 MTU-Bazán diesels; 16 000 bhp
Speed, knots	27
Complement	approx 100

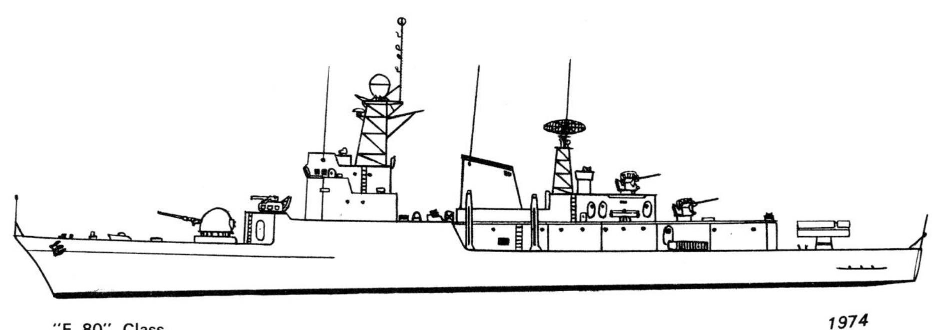

"F 80" Class *1974*

Similar to the Portuguese "João Coutinho" class being built by Bazán with modifications to the armament and main engines.

CLASS. Four were ordered from Bazán, Cartagena in 1973 and at least one more in 1974. Approval for three more received whilst two more are planned.

MISSILES. Selenia system (Albatros) for Seasparrow. This will be built partly in Spain.

RADAR. Search and fire control; 1 Hollandse Signaal M 22. Air Search; 1 Hollandse Signaal WO 4. Navigation; 1 set.

SONAR. Possibly Raytheon.

Frigates—*continued*

5 "BALEARES (F70)" CLASS

Displacement, tons	3 000 standard; 4 177 full load
Length, feet (*metres*)	415·0 (*126·5*) pp; 438·0 (*133·5*) oa
Beam, feet (*metres*)	46·9 (*14·3*)
Draught, feet (*metres*)	25·9 (*7·9*)
Missile launchers	1 single for Standard missiles
Guns	1—5 in (*127 mm*) 54 cal dp
A/S weapons	1 eight-tube ASROC launcher
Torpedo tubes	4 Mk 32 for Mk 44 torpedoes; 2 Mk 25 for Mk 37 torpedoes (stern)
Main engines	1 set geared turbines; 1 shaft; 35 000 shp
Boilers	2 high pressure V2M type; 1 200 psi (84·4 *kg/cm²*)
Speed, knots	28
Range	Over 4 000 miles at 20 knots
Complement	256 (15 officers, 241 men)

A/S System	8 Reloads carried for ASROC
Gunnery	600 5 inch rounds carried
Missile system	Mk 22 launcher with stowage for 16 missiles. Single director with two lines of fire against different targets

In June 1966 Spain and USA signed an agreement for the construction of five frigates by Empresa Nacional Bazán at El Ferrol with technical and material assistance by USA. Generally similar in appearance to the US escort ships of the "Knox" class but with modified weapons system and other characteristics to meet the requirements of the Spanish Navy. Equipped with weapons and electronic equipment furnished by USA.

RADAR. Search: SPS 52 (3D). Tactical: SPS 10. Fire Control: SPS 51 continuous wave for missiles; Mk 68 for guns with continuous wave injection for limited use with missiles.

TORPEDOES AND TUBES. All are fitted internally. Total of 41 torpedoes carried.

SONAR. SQS 23 bow mounted; SQS 35 VDS.

Name	No.	Laid down	Launched	Completion
ANDALUCIA	F 72	2 July 1969	30 Mar 1971	23 May 1974
ASTURIAS	F 74	30 Mar 1971	13 May 1972	May 1975
BALEARES	F 71	31 Oct 1968	20 Aug 1970	24 Sep 1973
CATALUÑA	F 73	20 Aug 1970	3 Nov 1971	Nov 1974
EXTREMADURA	F 75	3 Nov 1971	21 Nov 1972	Nov 1975

BALEARES — *1973, J. Talbo*

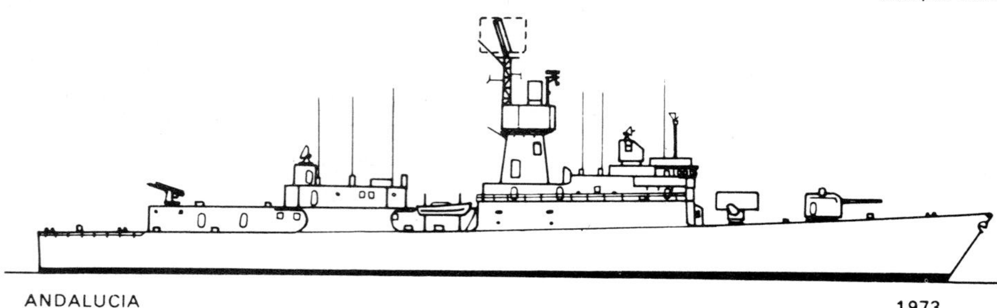
ANDALUCIA — 1973

3 "AUDAZ" CLASS

Displacement, tons	1 227 standard; 1 550 full load
Length, feet (*metres*)	295·2 (*90·0*) pp; 308·2 (*94·0*) oa
Beam, feet (*metres*)	30·5 (*9·3*)
Draught, feet (*metres*)	17·1 (*5·2*)
Guns	2—3 in (*76 mm*) 50 cal dp; 2—40 mm 70 cal AA
A/S weapons	2 Hedgehogs; 8 mortars; 2 DC racks
Torpedo tubes	2 side launching for Mk 32 A/S torpedoes (6 torpedoes)
Main engines	Rateau-Bretagne geared turbines; 2 shafts; 28 000 shp
Speed, knots	32
Boilers	2 La Seine 3-drum type
Range, miles	3 800 at 15 knots, 900 at 32 knots
Oil fuel, tons	290
Complement	199 (13 officers, 186 men)

Based on the French "Le Fier" design. All built at Ferrol. Allocated D Pennant numbers in 1961. *Meteoro* of this class employed as alongside training ship at El Ferrol.

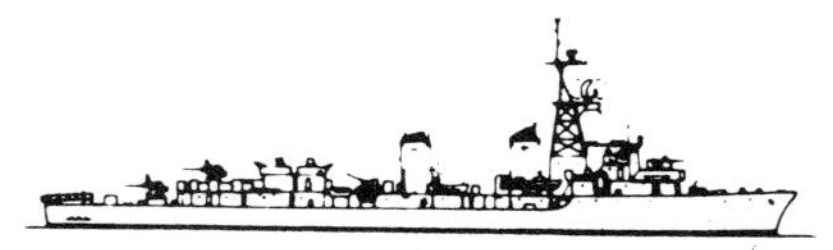
"AUDAZ" Class

Name	No.	Laid down	Launched	Completed
INTRÉPIDO	D 38	14 July 1945	15 Feb 1961	25 Mar 1965
RELÁMPAGO	D 39	14 July 1945	26 Sep 1961	7 July 1965
TEMERARIO	D 37	14 July 1945	29 Mar 1960	16 Mar 1964

INTRÉPIDO — *1969, Spanish Navy*

ENGINEERING. The boilers are in two compartments separated by the engine rooms.

RADAR. Surface search, SPS 5B; Air search, MLA-1B; Fire control, one Mk 63.

SONAR. One hull mounted set

2 "ALAVA" CLASS

Displacement, tons	1 842 standard; 2 287 full load
Length, feet (*metres*)	336·3 (*102·5*)
Beam, feet (*metres*)	31·5 (*9·6*)
Draught, feet (*metres*)	19·7 (*6·0*)
Guns	3—3 in (*76 mm*) 50 cal, Mk 22; 3—40 mm, 70 cal AA
A/S weapons	2 Hedgehogs; 8 DC mortars; 2 DC racks
Torpedo racks	2 side launching for Mk 32 torpedoes, 6 A/S torpedoes
Main engines	Parsons geared turbines; 2 shafts; 31 500 shp
Speed, knots	29
Boilers	4 Yarrow 3-drum type
Range, miles	4 100 at 15 knots
Oil fuel, tons	370
Complement	222 (15 officers, 207 men)

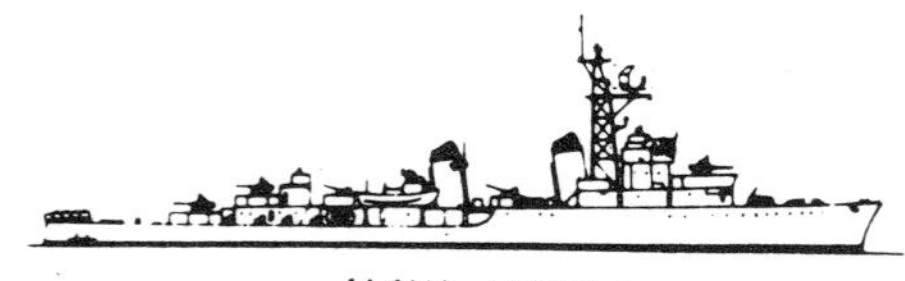
ALAVA, LINIERS

Name	No.	Builders	Laid down	Launched	Completed	Modernised
ALAVA	D 52 (ex-23)	Cartagena	21 Dec 1944	19 May 1947	21 Dec 1950	17 Jan 1962
LINIERS	D 51 (ex-21)	Cartagena	1 Jan 1945	1 May 1946	27 Jan 1951	18 Sep 1962

ALAVA — *1974, Spanish Navy*

Ordered in 1936, but construction was held up by the Civil War. After being resumed, was again suspended in 1940, but restarted at Empresa Nacional Bazan in 1944.

RADAR. Air search; MLA IB. One surface-search set. Fire Control: 2-Mk 63.

SONAR. One hull-mounted set, probably SQS-4

Frigates—*continued*

2 MODERNISED "PIZARRO" CLASS

Name	No.	Launched	Completed
LEGAZPI	F 42	8 Aug 1944	8 Aug 1951
VICENTE YAÑEZ PINZON	F 41	3 Aug 1944	5 Aug 1949

Displacement, tons	1 924 standard; 2 228 full load
Length, feet (*metres*)	279·0 (*85·0*) pp; 312·5 (*95·3*) oa
Beam, feet (*metres*)	39·5 (*12·0*)
Draught, feet (*metres*)	17·7 (*5·4*)
Guns	2—5 in (*127 mm*) 38 cal. 4—40 mm, 70 cal.
A/S weapons	2 Hedgehogs; 8 mortars; 2 racks
Torpedo racks	2 side launching for Mk 32 torpedoes
Main engines	2 sets Parsons geared turbines; 2 shafts; 6 000 shp
Speed, knots	18·5
Boilers	2 Yarrow type
Range, miles	3 000 at 15 knots
Oil fuel, tons	390
Complement	255 (16 officers 239 men)

LEGAZPI, VICENTE YANEZ PINZON

Built at Ferrol. Originally designed to carry 30 mines. Completed modernisation on 14 Jan and 25 Mar 1960 respectively.

RADAR. Surface search; SP 5B; Air search, MLA-1B; Fire Control: Mk 52.

VICENTE YAÑEZ PINZON — *1974, Spanish Navy*

1 "JUPITER" CLASS

Name	No.	Launched	Completed
VULCANO	F 12	12 Oct 1935	1937

Displacement, tons	2 103 standard; 2 360 full load
Length, feet (*metres*)	302·8 (*92·3*) pp; 328·1 (*100·0*) oa
Beam, feet (*metres*)	41·5 (*12·6*)
Draught, feet (*metres*)	11·5 (*3·5*)
Guns	4—3 in (*76 mm*) Mk 26, single; 4—40 mm, 70 cal AA
A/S weapons	2 Hedgehogs; 8 mortars; DC racks
Mines	238
Main engines	2 sets Parsons geared turbines; 2 shafts; 5 000 shp
Speed, knots	17·4
Boilers	2 Yarrow type
Range, miles	5 700 at 12 knots
Oil fuel, tons	340
Complement	255 (16 officers, 239 men)

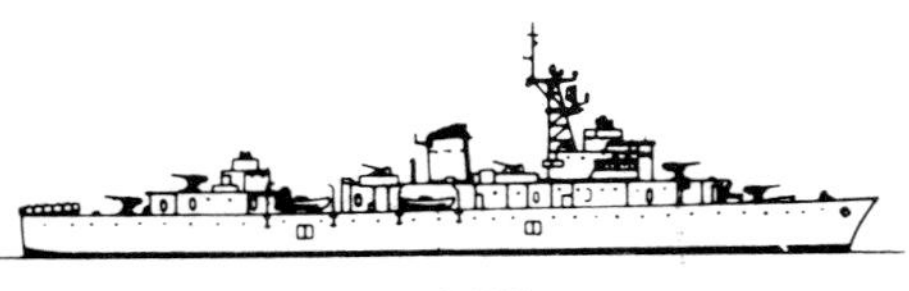

VULCANO

VULCANO — *1971, Spanish Navy*

Built by the Sociedad Española de Construccion Naval, El Ferrol. *Vulcano* completed modernisation on 28 Feb 1961. Allocated F pennant number in 1961.

RADAR. Air search, MLA-IB; Fire Control: MK 51.

4 "ATREVIDA - F 60" CLASS

Name	No.	Laid down	Launched	Completion of Modernization
ATREVIDA	F 61	26 June 1950	2 Dec 1952	14 June 1960
NAUTILUS	F 64	27 July 1953	23 Aug 1956	15 Dec 1959
PRINCESA	F 62	18 Mar 1953	31 Mar 1956	3 Oct 1959
VILLA DE BILBAO	F 65	18 Mar 1953	19 Feb 1958	2 July 1960

Displacement, tons	**1 031 standard; 1 135 full load**
Length, feet (*metres*)	**247·8 (*75·5*) oa**
Beam, feet (*metres*)	**33·5 (*10·2*)**
Draught, feet (*metres*)	**9·8 (*3·0*)**
Guns	**1—3 in (*76 mm*) 50 cal dp; 3—40 mm, 70 cal AA**
A/S weapons	**2 Hedgehogs; 8 mortars; 2 DC racks**
Mines	**20 can be carried**
Main engines	**Sulzer diesels; 2 shafts; 3 000 bhp**
Speed, knots	**18·5**
Range, miles	**8 000 at 10 knots**
Oil fuel, tons	**100**
Complement	**132 (9 officers. 123 men)**

Atrevida commissioned on 19 Aug 1954. All have been modernised since 1959. No funnel, the diesel exhaust being on the starboard side waterline. Allocated F pennant numbers in 1961.

RADAR. Modified SPS-5B combined air/surface search.

"ATREVIDA" Class

PRINCESA — *1974, Spanish Navy*

SUBMARINES

2 "S 70" CLASS

(FRENCH "AGOSTA" CLASS)

S 71 **S 72**

Displacement, tons	1 450 surfaced; 1 725 dived
Dimensions, ft (*m*)	221·7 × 22·3 × 17·7 (*67·6 × 6·8 × 5·4*)
Tubes	4—21·4 in (*550 mm*) (16 reloads)
Main machinery	Diesel-electric; 2 diesels; 3 600 hp; 1 main motor; 6 400 hp; 1 cruising motor; 1 shaft.
Speed, knots	12 surfaced; 20 dived
Range, miles	9 000 at 9 knots (snorting); 350 at 3·5 knots (dived)
Endurance	45 days
Complement	50

Ordered April 1974. To be built by Bazán Cartagena with some French advice. Two more may be ordered. First laid down mid-1975, and therefore, probably not operational until 1979.

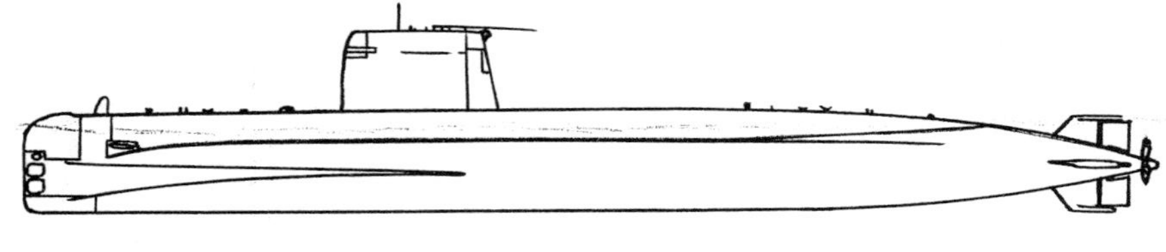

"S 70" Class *1974*

4 "S 60" CLASS

(FRENCH "DAPHNE" CLASS)

Name	*No.*	*Builders*	*Laid down*	*Launched*	*Commission*
DELFIN	S 61	E. N. Bazan, Cartegena	13 Aug 1968	25 Mar 1972	3 May 1973
TONINA	S 62	E. N. Bazan, Cartagena	1969	3 Oct 1972	10 July 1973
MARSOPA	S 63	E. N. Bazan, Cartagena	1971	15 Mar 1974	1975
NARVAL	S 64	E. N. Bazan, Cartagena	1971	14 Dec 1974	1975

Displacement, tons	870 surface; 1 040 submerged
Length, feet (*metres*)	189·6 (*57·8*)
Beam, feet (*metres*)	22·3 (*6·8*)
Draught, feet (*metres*)	15·1 (*4·6*)
Tubes	12—21·7 in (*550 mm*) (8 bow, 4 stern)
Main machinery	SEMT- Pielstick diesel-electric; 1 300 bhp surface; 1 600 hp submerged; 2 shafts

Basically similar to the French "Daphne" class and being built with extensive French assistance in the Cartagena Yard.

RADAR. Thompson CSF "Calypso II" plus ECM.

SONAR. Active, DUUA 1;
Passive with rangefinding DSUV.

DELFIN *1973, J. Taibo*

4 "S 30" CLASS

(Ex-US GUPPY IIA TYPE)

Name	*No.*	*Laid down*	*Launched*	*Completed*
ISAAC PERAL (ex-USS *Ronquil*, SS 396)	S 32	9 Sep 1943	27 June 1944	23 Apr 1944
NARCISO MONTURIOL (ex-USS *Picuda*, SS 382	S 33	15 Mar 1943	12 July 1943	16 Oct 1943
COSME GARCIA (ex-USS *Bang*. SS 385)	S 34	30 Apr 1943	30 Aug 1943	4 Dec 1943
(ex-USS *Jallao*)	S 35	29 Sep 1943	12 Mar 1944	8 July 1944

Displacement, tons	1 840 surface; 2 445 submerged
Length, feet (*metres*)	306·0 (*93·3*); ao
Beam, feet (*metres*)	27·0 (*8·2*)
Draught, feet (*metres*)	17·0 (*5·2*)
Torpedo tubes	10—21 in (*533 mm*), 6 bow, 4 stern
Main machinery	3 Fairbanks-Morse diesels; total 4 800 bhp; 2 shafts; 2 Elliot electric motors; 5 400 shp
Speed, knots	18 on surface; 15 submerged
Range, miles	12 000 at 10 knots
Complement	74

Built by Portsmouth Navy Yard, except *Jallao* (Manitowoc SB Co). Transferred to Spain on 1 July 1971 (*Ronquil*) 1 Oct 1972 (*Bang* and *Picuda*). 26 June 1974 (*Jallao*). All four finally purchased 18 Nov 1974.

APPEARANCE. S 33 and S 35 both have stepped section at forward end of fin.

NARCISO MONTURIOL *1974, Spanish Navy*

COSME GARCIA (PERAL similar) *1973, J. Taibo*

2 "TIBURON" CLASS

SA 51 **SA 52**

Displacement, tons	78 surface; 81 submerged
Length, feet (*metres*)	70·5 (*21·5*)
Beam, feet (*metres*)	9 (*2·7*)
Draught, feet (*metres*)	9 (*2·7*)
Torpedo tubes	2—21 in (*533 mm*)
Main engines	Pegaso diesels; 400 hp Electric motors; 400 hp
Speed, knots	10 on surface; 14·5 submerged
Range, miles	2 000 at 6 knots (surfaced) 150 at 7 knots (dived)
Complement	8

Launched in 1958, Originally rated as *Submarinos Experimentales*, but in 1963 designated Assault Submarines with "SA" numbers.

ENGINEERING. The diesels were built by ENASA (formerly Hispano-Suiza) Barcelona, 200 hp each at 2 000 rpm, with reduction gear on the single screw disposed in a nozzle in continuation of the conic after hull.

LIGHT FORCES

6 "LÀZAGA (P-OO)" CLASS

LAZAGA P 01 **CADARSO** P 03 **BONIFAZ** P 05
ALSEDO P 02 **VILLAMIL** P 04 **RECALDE** P 06

Displacement, tons	400 full load
Dimensions, ft (*m*)	190·2 × 24·9 × 8·5 (*58 × 7·6 × 2·6*)
Guns	1—3 in 62 cal Oto Melara; 1—40 mm 70 cal; 2—20 mm
A/S weapons	DC racks
Torpedo tubes	2 triple Mk 32 mountings
Main engines	2 MTU-Bazan diesels; 16 000 bhp
Speed, knots	29·5
Range, miles	4 200 at 17 knots
Complement	30

Ordered in 1972, primarily for Fishery Protection duties. Although all will be operated by the Navy half the cost is being borne by the Ministry of Commerce.
Lazaga was built by Lürssen Vegesack, being launched on 13 Oct 1974. She was steamed to Spain in April 1975 for equipping and arming, to commission late 1975. The other five are building at Bazán, La Carraca. *Alsedo* and *Cadarso* were launched on 8 Jan 1975, on which day *Villamil* and *Bonifaz* were laid down.

MISSILES. It is reported that provision has been made for fitting two surface-to-surface missiles.

RADAR. Surface search and Navigation-Hollandse Signaal M-20; ECM and IFF.

FIRE CONTROL. Optical director CSEE.

SONAR. One hull-mounted set.

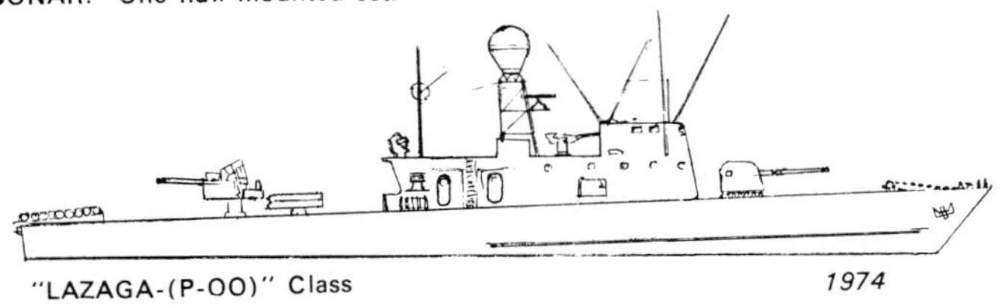

"LAZAGA-(P-OO)" Class 1974

6 "BARCELO (P 10)" CLASS (LARGE PATROL CRAFT)

BARCELO P 11 **ORDÓÑEZ** P 14
LAYA P 12 **ACEVEDO** P 15
JAVIER QUIROGA P 13 **CANDIDO PÉREZ** P 16

Displacement, tons	139
Guns	1—40 mm; 2—20 mm
Speed, knots	20 cruising; 40 max
Range, miles	1 200 at 20 knots

Ordered in late 1973, the prototype, *Barcelo*, to be built by Lürssen, Vegesack. Laid down 1974 for launch in Nov 1975. Remainder to be built by Bazán, La Carraca. All to be manned by the Navy although the cost is being borne by the Ministry of Commerce.

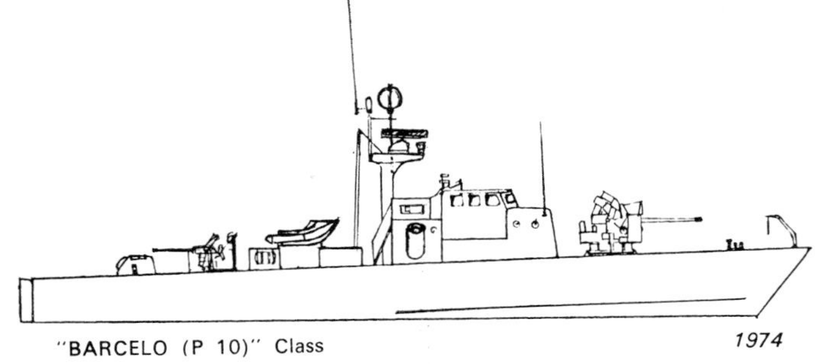

"BARCELO (P 10)" Class 1974

2 LÜRSSEN TYPE (FAST ATTACK CRAFT—TORPEDO)

LT 30 **LT 31**

Displacement, tons	100 standard; 116 full load
Dimensions, feet	114 × 16·8 × 5
Gun	1—20 mm AA
Tubes	2—21 in
Main engines	3 diesel; 3 shafts; 7 500 bhp = 41 knots
Oil fuel, tons	20
Range, miles	650 at 30 knots
Complement	26

Built at La Carraca, Cadiz, to the design of Lürssens of Bremen, LT 31 was commissioned on 21 July 1956. LT 32 of this class converted into target vessel for helicopters in Aug 1974, with sea-going capability at 12 knots.

LT 31 *1970, Spanish Navy*

5 "LP1" CLASS (COASTAL PATROL CRAFT)

LP 1 **LP 2** **LP 3** **LP 4** **LP 5**

Displacement, tons	25
Dimensions, feet	46 × 15·4 ×
Guns	2—7·62 mm

3 USCG 83ft TYPE (COASTAL PATROL CRAFT)

LAS 10 (ex-LAS 1) **LAS 20** (ex-LAS 2) **LAS 30** (ex-LAS 3)

Displacement, tons	49 standard; 63 full load
Dimensions, feet	78·0 pp; 83·3 oa × 16·1 × 6·6
Guns	1—20 mm AA; 2—7 mm (single)
A/S launchers	2 Mousetrap Mk 20 (4 rockets each)
Main engines	800 bhp = 15 knots
Complement	15

Of wooden hull construction. First units were built by E. N. Bazán, Cadiz in 1963-64.

LAS 30 *1974, Spanish Navy*

AGUILCHO (COASTAL PATROL CRAFT)

Displacement, tons	45
Dimensions, feet	85·5 oa × 16·7 × 4·3
Main engines	Diesels; 2 shafts; 2 750 bhp = 30 knots
Range, miles	750 at 30 knots

Launched 19 Feb 1973 for Coastguard duties. Transferred to Naval control 30 Nov 1974.

CENTINELA W 33 SERVIOLA W 34 (FISHERY PROTECTION VESSELS)

Displacement, tons	255 standard; 282 full load
Dimensions, feet	117·5 × 22·5 × 9·8
Guns	2—37 mm
Main engines	1 diesel; 430 bhp = 12 knots

Completed at Ferrol, in 1953. Given pennant numbers as above in 1972.

SERVIOLA *1974, Spanish Navy*

SALVORA W 32 (FISHERY PROTECTION VESSEL)

Displacement, tons	**180 standard; 275 full load**
Dimensions, feet	**107·0 × 20·5 × 9·0**
Guns	**1—20 mm MG**
Main engines	**1 Sulzer diesel; 400 bhp = 12 knots**
Complement	**24**

Purchased in Dec 1952.

RADAR. Decca RM 914.

3 PATROL VESSELS

RR 19 **RR 20** **R 29**

Displacement, tons	364 standard; 498 full load
Dimensions, feet	124·0 × 29·0 × 10·0
Guns	1—1·5 in, 85 cal or 1—47 mm; 1—20 mm AA
Main engines	Triple expansion; 1 shaft; 800 ihp = 11·5 knots
Boilers	1 cylindrical, 13 kg/cm
Fuel, tons	200 coal
Range, miles	620 at 10 knots

Former tugs. All launched in 1941-42. Some have navigation radar.

9 PATROL LAUNCHES

V 4	Displacement: 65 tons		Speed: 9 knots
V 5	Displacement: 4·5 tons		Speed: 5 knots
V 6	Displacement: 42 tons	Guns: 2—20 mm	Speed: 19·2 knots
V 9	Displacement: 15·6 tons		Speed: 9 knots
V 10	Displacement: 11·6 tons		Speed: 9·5 knots
V 11	Displacement: 11·6 tons		Speed: 9·5 knots
V 17	Displacement: 110·9 tons	Gun: 1—20 mm	Speed: 10·5 knots
V 21	Displacement: 16 tons		Speed: 17·6 knots

There is also **V 1**, yacht, ex-*Azor*. Coastal launches employed on surveillance and fishery protection duties. V 4 is named *Alcatraz*.

W 01 GAVIOTTA
Of 104·2 tons. Taken over by Navy on 26 Nov 1970 being a confiscated smuggling craft.

CABO FRADERA
Of 28 tons with 1—7·62 mm gun.

CUSTOMS SERVICE

There are, in addition to the above, a large number of customs launches of similar size operating off the Spanish coast.

AMPHIBIOUS FORCES

1 Ex-US "CASA GRANDE" CLASS (LSD)

GALICIA (ex-USS *San Marcos*, LSD 25) TA 31

Displacement, tons	4 790 standard; 9 375 full load
Dimensions, feet	475·4 oa × 76·2 × 18·0
Guns	12—40 mm, 60 cal AA (2 quadruple, 2 twin)
Main engines	Geared turbines; 2 shafts; 7 000 shp = 15·4 knots
Boilers	2
Range, miles	8 000 at 15 knots
Complement	265 (15 officers, 250 men)

Transferred to Spain on 1 July 1971. Fitted with helicopter platform. Can carry 3 LCUs or 18 LCMs. 1 347 tons of cargo or 100 2½ ton trucks or 27 M-48 tanks or 11 heavy helicopters. Accommodation for 137 troops (overnight) or 500 for short haul. Surface-search radar.

GALICIA (as *San Marcos*) *A. & J. Pavia*

1 Ex-US "HASKELL" CLASS (ATTACK TRANSPORT)

ARAGON (ex-USS *Noble*, APA 218) TA 11

Displacement, tons	6 720 light; 12 450 full load
Dimensions, feet	436·5 wl; 455 oa × 63·5 × 24
Guns	12—40 mm 60 cal (1 quad, 4 twin)
Main engines	Geared turbines; 8 500 shp = 17 knots
Boilers	2 Babcock & Wilcox
Range, miles	14 700 at 16 knots

Former US Attack Transport, transferred at San Francisco on 19 Dec 1964. Can carry 1 190 men and 680 tons cargo (or 11 2½ ton trucks and 49 ¾ ton trucks). 24 landing craft.
RADAR. Air search SPS 6; surface search.

ARAGON *1971, Michael D. J. Lennon*

1 Ex-US "ANDROMEDA" CLASS

CASTILLA (ex-USS *Achernar*, AKA 53) TA 21

Displacement, tons	7 430 light; 11 416 full load
Dimensions, feet	435 wl; 457·8 oa × 63 × 24
Guns	1—5 in 38 cal; 8—40 mm 60 cal (twins)
Main engines	2 GE geared turbines; 12 000 shp = 16 knots
Boilers	2 Foster-Wheeler

Former US Attack Cargo Ship transferred at New York on 2 Feb 1965, Can carry 98 men, 6 M-48 tanks, 36 2½ ton trucks and 267 Jeeps. 24 landing craft.

RADAR. Surface-search.

CASTILLA *1970, Spanish Navy*

2 Ex-BRITISH LCT (4)

BDK 1 K 1 **BDK 2** K 2

Displacement, tons	440 standard; 868 full load
Dimensions, ft m	185·3 × 38·7 × 6·2 (*56·5 × 11·8 × 1·9*)
Guns	2—20 mm (single)
Main engines	2 Paxman diesels; 2 shafts; 920 bhp = 10 knots
Range, miles	1 100 at 8 knots

Can carry 350 tons or 500 men.

3 Ex-US "TERREBONNE PARISH" CLASS (LST)

CONDE DE VENADITO (ex-USS *Tom Green County*, LST 1159) L 13
MARTIN ALVAREZ (ex-USS *Wexford County*, LST 1168) L 12
VELASCO (ex-USS *Terrebonne Parish*, LST 1156) L 11

Displacement, tons	2 590 standard; 5 800 full load
Dimensions, feet	384·0 oa × 55·0 × 17·0
Guns	6—3 in, 50 cal (3 twin, 2 forward, 1 aft)
Main engines	4 GM diesels; 2 shafts; 6 000 bhp = 15 knots
Range, miles	15 000 at 9 knots
Complement	116 (troops 395)

LST 1156 and 1168 transferred on 29 Oct 1971, LST 1159 on 5 Jan 1972. Can carry 395 men, 10 M-48 tanks or 17 LVTP. 4 landing craft.

SM 2 *1974, Spanish Navy.*

LSM 1 (ex-USS *LSM* 329) L 01
LSM 2 (ex-USS *LSM* 331) L 02

Displacement, tons	930 standard; 1 094 full load
Dimensions, feet	196·5 wl × 203·5 oa × 34·5 × 8·3
Guns	2—40 mm AA
Main engines	2 diesels; 2 shafts; 3 600 bhp = 12·5 knots

Medium landing ships transferred at Bremerton, Washington, on 25 Mar 1960. Can carry 49 men overnight or 400 for short haul. As transport can lift 306 tons of vehicles or 160 tons for landing.

LSM 2 *1974, Spanish Navy*

3 SPANISH BUILT LCT's

BDK 3 K 3 **BDK 4** K 4 **BDK 5** K 5

Displacement, tons	902 full load
Dimensions, ft (m)	186 × 38·4 × 6 (*56·6 × 11·6 × 1·7*)
Guns	2—20 mm singles
Main engines	2 M60 V8 AS diesels; 2 shafts; 1 000 hp = 8½ knots
Range, miles	1 000 at 7 knots
Complement	20 (1 officer, 19 men)

All commissioned 15 June 1959. Can carry 300 tons or 400 men.

BDK 5 *1971, Spanish Navy*

BDK 6 K 6 **BDK 7** K 7 **BDK 8** K 8 (LCTs)

Displacement, tons	315 standard; 665 full load
Dimensions, feet	193·5 × 39·0 × 5·0
Guns	1—20 mm AA; 2—12·7 mm AA MG
Main engines	2 diesels; 2 shafts; 1 040 bhp = 9·5 knots
Range, miles	1 500 at 9 knots

Landing craft of the French EDIC type built at La Carraca. Completed in Dec 1966.

4 (Possibly 6) NEW CONSTRUCTION (LCU)

This new class was ordered from three Spanish yards in 1974. Two are now complete but await engines from USA.

NOTE. Total of landing craft (including those attached to Aragón, Castilla, Galicia and LST's): 19 LCM, 38 LCVP, 14 LCP (L), 1 LCP (R), 16 LCU. All of US origin except 4 LCP (L) built at Cartagena.

MINE WARFARE FORCES

4 Ex-US "AGGRESSIVE" CLASS (MINESWEEPERS—OCEAN)

Name	No.	Ex-Name & No.		Launched	Completed
GUADALETE	M 41	*Dynamic*	MSO 432	17 Dec 1952	15 Dec 1953
GUADALMEDINA	M 42	*Pivot*	MSO 463	9 Jan 1954	12 July 1954
GUADALQUIVIR	M 43	*Persistant*	MSO 491	23 Apr 1955	3 Feb 1956
GUADIANA	M 44	*Vigor*	MSO 473	24 June 1953	8 Nov 1954

Displacement, tons	665 standard; 750 full load
Dimensions, feet	165·0 wl; 172·0 oa × 36·0 × 13·6
Guns	2—20 mm AA (Twin)
Main engines	4 Packard diesels; 2 shafts; controllable pitch propellers; 2 280 bhp = 15·5 knots
Range, miles	3 000 at 10 knots
Complement	71 (6 officers, 65 men)

The first three were transferred and commissioned on 1 July 1971. The fourth unit was delivered 4 April 1972. Surface search radar. VDS SQQ 14 with mine classification capability.

GUADALETE 1973, *J. Taibo*

12 "NALON" (M 20) CLASS (Ex-US AMS TYPE) (MINESWEEPERS—COASTAL)

DUERO (ex-*Spoonbill*, *MSC* 202)	M 28	**NALÓN** (ex-*AMS* 139)	M 21
EBRO (ex-*MSC* 269)	M 26	**ODIEL** (ex-*MSC* 288)	M 32
GENIL (ex-*MSC* 279)	M 31	**SIL** (ex-*Redwing*, *MSC* 200)	M 29
JUCAR (ex-*AMS* 220)	M 23	**TAJO** (ex-*MSC* 287)	M 30
LLOBREGAT (ex-*AMS* 143)	M 22	**TURIA** (ex-*AMS* 130)	M 27
MIÑO (ex-*AMS* 266)	M 25	**ULLA** (ex-*AMS* 265)	M 24

Displacement, tons	355 standard; 384 full load
Dimensions, feet	138·0 pp; 144·0 oa × 27·2 × 8·0
Guns	2—20 mm AA (1 twin)
A/S weapons	2 Mouse Trap Mk 20 rocket launchers
Main engines	2 diesels; 2 shafts; 900 bhp = 14 knots
Oil fuel, tons	30
Range, miles	2 700 at 10 knots
Complement	39

EBRO, Class B, small crane 1974, *Dr, Giorgio Arra*

Transferred from the USA, *Nalón* on 16 Feb 1954, *Llobregat* on 5 Nov 1954, *Turia* on 1 June 1955, *Jucar* on 22 June 1956, *Ulla* on 24 July 1956, *Miño* on 25 Oct 1956, *Sil* and *Duero* on 16 June 1959, *Ebro* on 19 Dec 1958, *Genil* on 11 Sep 1959, *Tajo* on 9 July 1959 and *Odiel* on 9 Oct 1959.

Two sub-types: (a) with derrick on mainmast: M 21, 22, 23, 24, 25, 27, 28, 29 (b) with no mainmast but crane abreast the funnel: M 26, 30, 31, 32. Tactical radar of various types. AN/UQS-1 sonar.

ULLA, Class A, with mainmast 1973, *Dr, Giorgio Arra*

7 "GUADIARO" CLASS (MINESWEEPERS—OCEAN AS PATROL VESSELS)

Name	No.	Builders	Launched	Completed	Modernised
ALMANZORA	M 14	Cartagena	27 July 1953	Nov 1954	20 May 1960
EO	M 17	Cadiz	22 Sep 1953	Mar 1955	22 Mar 1961
EUME	M 13	Cartagena	27 July 1953	Dec 1953	20 July 1960
GUADALHORCE	M 16	Cartagena	18 Feb 1953	Dec 1953	18 Feb 1960
GUADIARO	M 11	Cartagena	26 June 1950	Apr 1953	14 Dec 1959
NAVIA	M 15	Cadiz	28 July 1953	Mar 1955	22 Nov 1960
TINTO	M 12	Cartagena	26 June 1950	May 1953	28 July 1959

Displacement, tons	671 standard, 770 full load
Dimensions, feet	243·8 × 33·5 × 12·3
Guns	2—20 mm
Main engines	Triple expansion and exhaust turbines; 2 shafts; 2 400 hp = 13 knots after modernisation
Boilers	2 Yarrow
Oil fuel, tons	90
Range, miles	1 000 at 6 knots
Complement	79

Currently employed on patrol duties. Will be paid off when replaced by "Lazaga" class.

ALMANZORA 1971, *Cdr Aldo Fraccaroli*

SURVEY SHIPS

CASTOR A 21 **POLLUX** A 22 **ANTARES** A 23 **RIGEL** A 24

Displacement, tons	327 standard; 383 full load
Dimensions, feet	111 pp; 125·9 oa × 24·9 × 8·9
Main engines	1 Sulzer 4TD-36 diesel; 720 hp = 11·7 knots
Range, miles	3 620 at 8 knots
Complement	39 (A 23 and 24) 37 (A 21 and 22)

Built by E. N. Bazán, La Carraca. *Castor* completed on 10 Nov 1966, *Pollux* on 6 Dec 1966. *Antares* and *Rigel* ordered summer 1972, launched 1973 and commissioned 21 Nov 1974. *Antares* and *Rigel* fitted with Raydist, Omega and digital presentation of data.

CASTOR 1970, *Spanish Navy*

2 "MALASPINA" CLASS (OCEANOGRAPHIC SHIPS)

MALASPINA A 31 **TOFIÑO** A 32

Displacement, tons	820 standard; 1 090 full load
Dimensions, ft (*m*)	188·9 × 38·4 × 11·8 (*57·6* × *11·7* × *3·6*)
Guns	2—20 mm (single)
Main engines	2 diesels; 3 240 bhp; 2 VP propellers = 15 knots
Range, miles	4 000 at 12 knots; 3 140 at 14·5 knots.
Complement	63 (9 officers, 54 men)

Built by E. N. Bazán, La Carraca. *Malaspina* laid down early 1973, launched 15 Aug 1973. *Tofiño* launched 22 Dec 1973. Both commissioned early 1975. *Tofiño* named after her immediate predecessor.

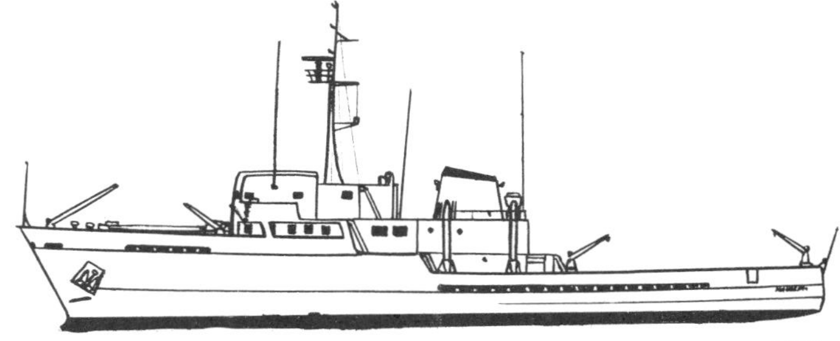

"MALASPINA" Class 1974

JUAN DE LA COSA (ex-*Artabro*)

Displacement, tons	770 standard; 1 100 full load
Dimensions, feet	188· × 35·5 × 8·8
Guns	2—20 mm
Main engines	B & W diesels; electric drive; 500 bhp = 9 knots
Complement	51

Launched by UNL, Valence in 1935 for scientific expedition to the Amazon. Taken over by the Navy in 1939.

SERVICE FORCES

ALMIRANTE LOBO (ex-*Torrelaguna*) A 41 (TRANSPORT)

Displacement, tons	5 662 standard; 8 038 full load
Dimensions, feet	362·5 × 48·2 × 25·7
Guns	1—1·5 in, 85 cal
Main engines	1 triple expansion; 2 000 ihp = 12 knots

Ex-cargo vessel. Built at Astilleros Echevarrieta, Cadiz. Commissioned 4 Oct 1954.

RADAR. Navigation; Decca 12

ALMIRANTE LOBO

TEIDE BP 11 (REPLENISHMENT TANKER)

Displacement, tons	**2 747 light; 8 030 full load**
Oil capacity, tons	**5 350**
Dimensions, feet	**385·5 × 48·5 × 20·3**
Guns	**1—4·1 in, not mounted, but provision for AA**
Main engines	**2 diesels; 3 360 bhp = 12 knots**

Ordered from Factoria de Bazán. Cartagena, in December 1952. Laid down on 11 Nov 1954. Launched on 20 June 1955. In service October 1956. Modernised in 1962 with refuelling at sea equipment.

RADAR. Navigation; Decca TM 707.

TEIDE *1968, Spanish Navy*

PP 1 (HARBOUR TANKER)

Displacement, tons	470
Dimensions, feet	138 pp; 147·5 oa × 25 × 9·5
Main engines	Deutz diesel; 220 bhp = 10 knots
Complement	12

Built at Santander and launched in 1939.

PP 5, PP 6 (HARBOUR TANKERS)

Follow on class of harbour tankers.

PB 1, 2, 3, 4, 20, 21, 22 (HARBOUR TANKERS)

Small harbour tankers with capacity between 100 and 300 tons. All built by Bazán between 1960 and 1965.

JUAN SEBASTIAN DE ELCANO (TRAINING SHIP)

Displacement, tons	3 420 standard; 3754 full load
Dimensions, feet	269·2 pp; 308·5 oa × 43 × 23
Guns	2—37 mm
Main engines	1 Sulzer diesel; 1 shaft; 1 500 bhp = 9·5 knots
Oil fuel, tons	230
Endurance, miles	10 000 at 9·5 knots
Complement	224 + 80 cadets

Four masted top sail schooner—sister of Chilean *Esmeralda*. Named after the first circumnavigator of the world (1519-26) who succeeded to the command of the expedition led by Magellanas after the latter's death. Built by Echevarrieta Yard, Cadiz. Launched on 5 Mar 1927. Completed in 1928.

RADAR. 2 Decca TM 626.

METEORO (SCHOOL SHIP)

Frigate of "Audaz" class used as alongside training ship at El Ferrol for Escuela de Maquinas.

AZOR (CHIEF OF STATE'S YACHT)

Displacement, tons	**442 standard; 486 full load**
Dimensions, feet	**153·0 × 25·2 × 12·5**
Main engines	**2 diesels; 1 200 bhp = 12 knots**
Range, miles	**4 000**

Built as the Caudillo's yacht by E. N. Bazan at El Ferrol. Launched on 9 June 1949. Commissioned on 20 July 1949. Underwent an extensive refit, her hull being cut to admit an extension in length.

RADAR. Decca TM 626.

CR 1 (ex-*G 6*) (BOOM DEFENCE VESSEL)

Displacement, tons	630 standard; 831 full load
Dimensions, feet	165·5 × 34 × 10·5
Guns	1—40 mm AA; 4—20 mm AA single
Main engines	2 diesels; electric drive; 1 shaft; 1 500 bhp = 12 knots
Range, miles	5 200 at 12 knots

Built by Penhoët, France, as a US off-shore order. Launched on 28 Sep 1954. Transferred from the US in 1955 under MDAP. Sister ship of French "Cigale" class.

PBP 1, 2 and 3

Gate Vessels.

PRA 1-8

Tugs for PBPs and PRs.

PR 1-5

Net laying barges.

6 OCEAN TUGS

RA 3 (ex-*Metinda III*)

Displacement, tons	762 standard; 1 080 full load
Dimensions, feet	137 × 33·1 × 15·5
Main engines	Triple expansion; 12 knots

RA 1 **RA 2**

Displacement, tons	757 standard; 1 039 full load
Dimensions, feet	184 × 33·5 × 12
Guns	2—20 mm (single)
Main engines	2 Sulzer diesels; 3 200 bhp = 15 knots

RADAR. Decca 12.

POSEIDON BS 1 **RA 4** **RA 5**

Displacement, tons	951 standard; 1 069 full load
Dimensions, feet	183·5 × 32·8 × 15·8
Main engines	2 Sulzer diesels; 3 200 bhp = 15 knots

All built at La Carraca, in 1963. RA 6 was renumbered BS 1 when she became a frogman support ship, known as *Poseidon*.

RADAR. Decca 707.

6 COASTAL TUGS

RR 50 **RR 51** **RR 52** **RR 53** **RR 54** **RR 55**

Displacement, tons	205 standard; 227 full load
Dimensions, feet	91·2 × 23 × 11
Main engines	Diesels; 1 shaft; 1 400 bhp (53 to 55), 800 bhp (50 to 52)

All built at Cartagena for naval service, first three in 1963, last three in 1967.

RADAR. Pilot 7 D 20 in RR 53, 54 and 55.

16 HARBOUR TUGS

RP 1-12

Of 65 tons and 200 bhp (Diesel). Commissioned 1965-67.

RP 18, RP 30

Of 160 tons and 300 ihp (coal-burning). Built in 1946 and 1952.

RP 38

Of 160 tons and 280 ihp (coal burning).

RP 40

Of 150 tons and 600 bhp (diesel). Commissioned 1961.

NOTE. 5 tug-launches of less than 50 tons:— LR 47, 51, 67, 68, 69.

WATER CARRIERS

A 1 **A 2** **A 6**

A 1 and A2 built in 1936, A 6 in 1949. Of 1 785 tons full load with 1 000 tons capacity. Ocean going.

A 7 **A 11**

2 ships built 1949-52. Of 610 tons full load with 350 tons capacity. A 9-11 completed in 1963 have radar Pilot 7 D 20. All oceangoing.

AB 1, 2, 3, 10, 17, 18

All of less than 400 tons. Harbour water boats with 200 tons or less capacity.

TORPEDO RECOVERY CRAFT

BTM 1-6

Built by Bazán 1961-63 of 100-300 tons. To carry torpedoes and mines and, in emergency, can act as minelayers.

L 51

Minewarfare training craft.

Torpedo tracking craft on range at Alcudia, Majorca.

LRT 3 and 4

TRVs built in 1956. Can carry 6 torpedoes. Have stern ramp and crane.

DIVING CRAFT

BZL 1, 3, 9 **NERIDA** (BZL 10)

Small self-propelled craft of less than 50 tons.

BL 10 and 13

Dumb barges for diving.

FLOATING CRANES

SANSÓN GRI (100 tons lift)
GR 3, 4 and 5 (30 tons lift)
GR 6, 7, 8, 9 and **10** (15 tons lift)

SRI LANKA

Administration

The Royal Ceylon Navy was formed on 9 Dec 1950 when the Navy Act was proclaimed. Now called the Sri Lanka Navy.

Commander of the Navy:
Commodore D. B. Goonesekera

Diplomatic Representation

Services Attaché in London:
Withdrawn from 1 November 1970

Personnel

(a) 1975: 2 300 (200 officers and 2 100 sailors)
(b) Voluntary Service

Naval Base

A Naval Base established at Trincomalee, which was a British base from 1795 until 1957.
Minor bases at Karainagar, Colombo, Welisara, Tangala and Kalpitiya.

Strength of the Fleet

1 Frigate
5 Fast Attack Craft—Gun
26 Coastal Patrol Craft
1 Tug

Deletions

1974 Short hydrofoil and 1 Thornycroft Patrol Craft (201)

Prefix to Ships' Names

SLNS

Defence Expenditure and Policy

Since the Indo-Pakistan war visits by US, British and Russian ships have taken place. It is reported that Defence spending has been doubled and that "20 small police and gunboats" have been acquired.

Mercantile Marine

Lloyd's Register of Shipping:
34 vessels of 54 099 tons gross

FRIGATE

Note: A new vessel, type unknown, is being provided by the Soviet Navy—presumably as a replacement for the aged *Gajabahu.*

1 Ex-CANADIAN "RIVER" CLASS

Name	*No.*	*Builders*	*Launched*
GAJABAHU (ex-*Misnak*, ex-HMCS *Hallowell*)	F 232	Canadian Vickers Ltd, Montreal	8 Aug 1944

Displacement, tons: 1 445 standard; 2 360 full load
Length, feet (*metres*): 283 (*86·3*) pp; 295·5 (*90·1*) wl; 310·5 (*91·9*) oa
Beam, feet (*metres*): 36·5 (*11·1*)
Draught, feet (*metres*): 13·8 (*4·2*)
Guns: 1—4 in (*102 mm*); 3—40 mm
Main engines: Triple expansion; 5 500 ihp; 2 shafts
Boilers: 2 three-drum type
Speed, knots: 20
Range, miles: 4 200 at 12 knots
Oil fuel, tons: 585
Complement: 160

GENERAL
Acquired from Canada by Israel in 1950 and sold by Israel to Ceylon in 1959. Guns above replaced 3—4·7 inch, 8—20 mm in 1965. Reportedly now non-operational.

GAJABAHU *1971, Royal Ceylon Navy*

LIGHT FORCES

"SOORAYA" CLASS

5 FAST ATTACK CRAFT (GUN)

BALAWATHA **SOORAYA**
DAKSAYA **WEERAYA**
RAMAKAMI

Displacement, tons: 120 full load
Dimensions, feet: 130 × 18 × 5·6
Guns: 4—37 mm (2 twin); 4—25 mm (2 twin abaft the bridge)
Main engines: 4 Diesels; 5 000 bhp = 30 knots
Complement: 25

GENERAL
All of the "Shanghai IV" class
The first pair was transferred by China in Feb 1972, the second pair in July 1972 and the last in December 1972. In monsoonal conditions off the coast of Sri Lanka these boats are lively and uncomfortable. Skinhead Radar.

SOORAYA *1974, Sri Lanka Navy*

20 THORNYCROFT TYPE (COASTAL PATROL CRAFT)

102-110, 201-211

Displacement, tons: 15
Dimensions, feet: 45·5 × 12 × 3
Main engines: 2 boats: Thornycroft K6SMI engines; 500 bhp = 25 knots; 7 boats: General Motors 6 71-Series; 560 bhp = 25 knots

GENERAL
Fast twin screw motor launches built by Thornycroft (Malaysia) Limited in Singapore The hulls are of hard chine type with double skin teak planking. Equipped with radar, radio, searchlight etc. Two ordered in 1965 and completed in 1966. Seven ordered in 1966 and completed in 1967. 12 more assembled in Sri Lanka and completed by Sep 1968.
They are based, as two squadrons, at Colombo and Karainagar.

PC 102 *1970, Royal Ceylon Navy*

2 COASTAL PATROL CRAFT

DIYAKAWA **KORAWAKKA**

Displacement, tons: 13
Dimensions, feet: 46 pp; 48 oa × 12 × 3
Main engines: 2 Foden FD.6 diesels; 240 bhp = 15 knots

Built in Italy in 1955.

SURVEY CRAFT

2 ITALIAN TYPE (COASTAL SURVEY CRAFT)

HANSAYA **LIHINIYA**

Displacement, tons: 36
Dimensions, feet: 63·5 pp; 66 oa × 14 × 4
Main engines: 3 General Motors diesels; 450 bhp = 16 knots

Built at Venice by the Korody Marine Corporation in 1956. Employed on Survey duties.

SERUWA **TARAWA**

Of similar characteristics to *Diyakawa* and *Korawakka* above.

TUG

ALIYA (ex-*Adept*, ex-*Empire Barbara*)

Displacement, tons: 503 full load
Dimensions, feet: 105 × 26·5 × 12·8
Main engines: Triple expansion; 850 ihp = 10 knots

Built by Cochrane & Sons Ltd., Selby, Yorks, England. Transferred from Great Britain Decommisioned in 1964 to be sold, but this intention was rescinded. She was recommissioned in 1966, and underwent major refit in 1967.

BOOM DEFENCE VESSEL. *Baron* was purchased from Great Britain by the Colombo Port Commission.

SWEDEN

Administration

Commander-in-Chief:
Vice-Admiral Bengt Lundvall

Chief of Naval Material Department:
Rear-Admiral Gunnar Grandin

Commander-in-Chief of Coastal Fleet:
Rear-Admiral Christer Kierkegaard

Chief of Naval Staff:
Major-General Bo Varenius (Coastal Artillery)

Chief of Staff Coastal Fleet (Acting):
Captain L. Jedeur-Palmgren

Diplomatic Representation

Naval Attaché in London:
Commodore N. U. Rydström

Naval Attaché in Washington:
Captain L. Forsman

Personnel

(a) 1975: 14 500 officers and men of Navy and Coast Artillery made up of 4 500 regulars, 2 500 Reservists and 7 500 National Servicemen. In addition 12 000 conscripts receive annual training.
(b) 9-18 months

Strength of the Fleet

Type	*Active*	*Building (Planned)*
Destroyers	8	—
Frigates	4	—
Submarines—Patrol	22	5
Corvettes—Light Forces	—	(2)
Fast Attack Craft—Missile	1	(16)
Fast Attack Craft—Torpedo	42	6
Large Patrol Craft	1	—
Coastal Patrol Craft	22	—
Minelayers	3	1
Minelayers—Coastal	9	(1)
Minelayers—Small	37	1
Minehunters	—	(6?)
Minesweepers—Coastal	18	—
Minesweepers-Inshore—	20	—
LCM s	9	—
LCU s	60	(25)
LCA s	54	—
Mine Transports	2	—
Survey Ships	5	—
Tankers—Support	1	—
Supply Ship	1	—
Command Ship	1	—
Tugs	8	—
Salvage Vessel	1	—
Sail Training Ships	2	—
Ice Breakers	6	1
TRV's	2	—
Tenders	4	—
Water Boats	1	—

Naval Air Arm

7 Alouette II helicopters
10 Jet Ranger helicopters
7 Kawasaki-Vertol 107 ((Hkp-4C)
3 Vertol 107 (Hkp-4B)

Bases

Stockholm, Karlskrona, Göteborg.
Minor base at Härnösand.

Composition of the Navy

In addition to seagoing personnel the Navy includes the Coastal Artillery, manning 20 mobile and 45 coastal batteries of both major guns and SSMs.

Disposals and Transfers

Cruiser

1971 *Göta Lejon* to Chile (*Latorre*)

Frigate

1974 *Karlskrona*

Light Forces

1973 *TV 101-106*

Depot Ship

1972 *Patricia*

Surveying Vessels

1972 *Johen Nordenankar, Petter Gedda*
1973 *Anden*

Miscellaneous

1973 *Gälnan* (water carrier)
1974 *Ymer* (Icebreaker)

Mercantile Marine

Lloyd's Register of Shipping:
785 vessels of 6 226 659 tons gross

DESTROYERS

4 "ÖSTERGÖTLAND" CLASS

Name	*No.*	*Builders*	*Laid down*	*Launched*	*Completed*
GÄSTRIKLAND	J 22	Götaverken, Göteborg	1 Oct 1955	6 June 1956	14 Jan 1959
HÄLSINGLAND	J 23	Kockums Mek Verkstads A/B	1 Oct 1955	14 Jan 1957	17 June 1959
ÖSTERGÖTLAND	J 20	Götaverken, Göteborg	1 Sep 1955	8 May 1956	3 Mar 1958
SÖDERMANLAND	J 21	Eriksberg Mekaniska Verkstad	1 June 1955	28 May 1956	27 June 1958

Displacement, tons	2 150 standard; 2 600 full load
Length, feet (*metres*)	367·5 (*112·0*) oa
Beam, feet (*metres*)	36·8 (*11·2*)
Draught, feet (*metres*)	12·0 (*3·7*)
Missile launchers	RB 08A (Mk 20) surface-to-surface; 1 quadruple "Seacat" (RB 07) surface-to-air
Guns	4—4·7 in (*120 mm*), 2 twin; 4—40 mm AA single
A/S weapons	Bofors triple barrelled mortar
Torpedo tubes	6—21 in (*533 mm*), 2 triple
Mines	60 can be carried
Main engines	De Laval turbines; 2 shafts; 40 000 shp
Speed, knots	35
Boilers	2 Babcock & Wilcox
Range, miles	2 200 at 20 knots
Oil fuel, tons	330
Complement	244 (18 officers, 226 men)

"ÖSTERGÖTLAND" Class

MODERNISATION. *Gästrikland* in 1965, *Södermanland* in 1967, *Hälsingland* in 1968, *Östergötland* in 1969.

RADAR. Thomson CSF Saturn S-band long-range search and target designator; HSA M 44 series for Seacat; M 45 series for guns.

HÄLSINGLAND *1972, Royal Swedish Navy*

Destroyers—*continued*

2 "HALLAND" CLASS

Name	No.	Builders	Laid down	Launched	Completed
HALLAND	J 18	Götaverken, Göteborg	1951	16 July 1952	8 June 1955
SMÅLAND	J 19	Eriksberg Mekaniska Verkstad, Göteborg	1951	23 Oct 1952	12 Jan 1956

Displacement, tons 2 800 standard; 3 400 full load
Length, feet (*metres*) 380·5 (*116·0*)wl; 397·2 (*121·0*)oa
Beam, feet (*metres*) 41·3 (*12·6*)
Draught, feet (*metres*) 14·8 (*4·5*)
Launcher 1 rocket launcher RB 08A (Mk 20)
Guns 4—4·7 in (*120 mm*) dp (2 twin) 2—57 mm AA; 6—40 mm AA
A/S weapons 2 four-barrelled mortars (Bofors)
Torpedo tubes 8—21 in (*533 mm*) 2 quadruple
Mines Can be fitted for minelaying
Main engines De Laval double reduction geared turbines; 2 shafts; 58 000 shp
Speed, knots 35
Boilers 2 Penhöet
Range, miles 3 000 at 20 knots
Oil fuel, tons 500
Complement 290 (18 officers, 272 men)

"HALLAND" Class

Both ordered in 1948. The first Swedish destroyers of post-war design and construction. Fully automatic gun turrets forward and aft, ahead throwing anti-submarine weapons of the Bofors type forward, and rocket launcher abaft the after funnel.

RADAR. Thomson CSF Saturn S-band long-range search and target designator on foremast; LW 02/03 air warning radar on main mast M 22 series with co-mounted search and tracking radars in radome. ECM.

HALLAND *1973, Wright and Logan*

2 "ÖLAND" CLASS

Name	No.	Builders	Laid down	Launched	Completed	Modernised
ÖLAND	J 16	Kockums Mek Verkstads A/B, Malmö	1943	15 Dec 1945	5 Dec 1947	1960, 1969
UPPLAND	J 17	Karlskrona Dockyard	1943	5 Nov 1946	31 Jan 1949	1963

Displacement, tons 2 000 standard; 2 400 full load
Length, feet (*metres*) 351 (*107·0*) pp; 367·5 (*112·0*) oa
Beam, feet (*metres*) 36·8 (*11·2*)
Draught, feet (*metres*) 11·2 (*3·4*)
Guns 4—4·7 in (*120 mm*) dp (2 twin); 6—40 mm AA single
A/S weapons 1 triple-barrelled DC mortar
Torpedo tubes 6—21 in (*533 mm*) 2 triple
Mines 60 capacity, fitted for laying
Main engines De Laval geared turbines; 2 shafts; 44 000 shp
Speed, knots 35
Boilers 2 Penhöet
Range, miles 2 500 at 20 knots
Oil fuel, tons 300
Complement 210

ÖLAND

Superstructure and machinery spaces lightly armoured.

GUNNERY. 4·7 inch guns semi-automatic with 80° elevation. 40 mm AA gun near jackstaff was removed in 1962, and eight 20 mm AA guns in 1964.

RADAR. Thomson CSF Saturn S-band long-range search and target-designator; Two M 45 series fire control radars for guns; navigation set.

RECONSTRUCTION. *Öland* was modernised with new bridge in 1960 and again in 1969; and *Uppland* with new bridge and helicopter platform in 1963.

ÖLAND ***1970, Royal Swedish Navy***

FRIGATES

4 "VISBY" CLASS

Name	No.	Builders	Launched	Completed
HÄLSINGBORG	F 13	Götaverken	23 Mar 43	30 Nov 43
KALMAR	F 14	Eriksberg	20 July 43	3 Feb 44
SUNDSVALL	F 12	Eriksberg	20 Oct 42	17 Sep 43
VISBY	F 11	Götaverken	16 Oct 42	10 Aug 43

Displacement, tons	1 150 standard; 1 320 full load
Length, feet (*metres*)	310·0 (*94·5*) wl; 321·5 (*98·0*) oa
Beam, feet (*metres*)	30 (*9·1*)
Draught, feet (*metres*)	12·5 (*3·8*)
Aircraft	1 helicopter pad (F 11 and F 12)
Guns	3—4·7 in (*120 mm*); 3—40 mm AA (2—57 mm only in F 11 and F 12)
A/S weapons	1 four-barrelled DC mortar
Torpedo tubes	5—21 in (*533 mm*) F 11 F 12
Main engines	De Laval geared turbines; 2 shafts; 36 000 shp
Speed, knots	39
Boilers	3 three-drum type
Range, miles	1 600 at 20 knots
Oil fuel, tons	150
Complement	140

SUNDSVALL *1972, Royal Swedish Navy*

All were originally fitted for minelaying. All four will be paid off for disposal in the near future.

RADAR. Thomson CSF Saturn S-band long-range search and target designator; M 24 fire control systems with co-mounted radars for search and tracking for guns.

"VISBY" Class

SUBMARINES

NEW CONSTRUCTION PATROL TYPE

5 "NÄCKEN" CLASS (A14)

NÄCKEN **NAJAD** **NEPTUN** +2

Displacement, tons	980 surfaced; 1 125 submerged
Length, feet (*metres*)	167·3 (*51·0*)
Beam, feet (*metres*)	20·0 (*6·1*)
Draught, feet (*metres*)	16·7 (*5·1*)
Torpedo tubes	4—21 in (*533 mm*) (8 reloads)
Main machinery	Diesels, electric motors; 1 shaft
Speed, knots	20 surface and submerged
Complement	25

Building at Karlskrona and Kockums, Malmö for completion in 1977-78.

SJÖBJÖRNEN *1971, Royal Swedish Navy*

5 "SJÖORMEN" CLASS (AIIB)

Name	Builders	Launched	Completed
SJÖORMEN	Kockums	25 Jan 67	31 July 67
SJÖLEJONER	Kockums	29 June 67	16 Dec 68
SJÖHUNDEN	Kockums	21 Mar 68	25 June 69
SJÖHÄSTEN	Karlskrona	6 Aug 68	15 Sep 69
SJÖBJÖRNEN	Karlskrona	9 Jan 68	28 Feb 69

Displacement, tons	11 25 standard; 1 400 submeged
Length, feet (*metres*)	167·3 (*51·0*)
Beam, feet (*metres*)	20·0 (*6·1*)
Draught, feet (*metres*)	16·7 (*5·1*)
Torpedo tubes	4—21 in (*533 mm*) 2 A/S tubes
Main machinery	Pielstick diesels; 1 large 5-bladed propeller; 1 900 bhp; electric motors
Speed, knots	15 surface; 20 submerged
Endurance	3 weeks
Complement	23

Albacore hull. Twin-decked. Diving depth 500 ft.

APPEARANCE. Distinctive letters painted on the conning tower Sor, *Sjöormen:* Sbj, *Sjöbjörnen*; Shä, *Sjöhästen:* Shu, *Sjöhünden*; Sle, *Sjölejoner.*

SJÖHUNDEN *1972, Royal Swedish Navy*

Submarines—*continued*

6 "DRAKEN" CLASS (A11)

Name	*Builders*	*Launched*	*Completed*
DELFINEN	Karlskrona	7 Mar 61	7 June 62
DRAKEN	Kockums	1 Apr 60	4 Apr 62
GRIPEN	Karlskrona	31 May 60	28 Apr 62
NORDKAPAREN	Kockums	8 Mar 61	4 Apr 62
SPRINGAREN	Kockums	31 Aug 61	7 Nov 62
VARGEN	Kockums	20 May 60	15 Nov 61

Displacement, tons	770 standard; 835 surface; 1 110 submerged
Length, feet (*metres*)	226·4 (*69·0*)
Beam, feet (*metres*)	16·7 (*5·1*)
Draught, feet (*metres*)	17·4 (*5·3*)
Torpedo tubes	4—21 in (*533 mm*) bow
Main machinery	Pielstick diesels; 1 700 bhp; electric motors
Speed, knots	17 surface; 20 submerged
Complement	36

APPEARANCE.
Distinctive letters painted on the conning tower are: Del, *Delfinen*; Dra, *Draken*; Gri, *Gripen*; Nor, *Nordkaparen* Spr, *Springaren*; Vgn, *Vargen*.

NORDKAPAREN *1971, Royal Swedish Navy*

6 "HAJEN" CLASS

Name	*Builders*	*Launched*	*Completed*
BÄVERN	Kockums	3 Feb 1958	29 May 1959
HÄJEN	Kockums	11 Dec 1954	28 Feb 1957
ILLERN	Kockums	15 Nov 1957	31 Aug 1959
SÄLEN	Kockums	3 Oct 1955	8 Apr 1957
UTTERN	Kockums	14 Nov 1958	15 Mar 1960
VALEN	Karlskrona	24 Apr 1955	4 Mar 1957

Displacement, tons	720 standard; 785 surface; 1 000 submerged
Length, feet (*metres*)	216·5 (*66·0*)
Beam, feet (*metres*)	16·7 (*5·1*)
Draught, feet (*metres*)	16·4 (*5·0*)
Torpedo tubes	4—21 in (*533 mm*) bow (8 torpedoes)
Main machinery	SEMT-Pielstick diesels; 1 700 bhp; Electric motors; electric drive on surface
Speed, knots	16 on surface; 17 submerged
Complement	44

Distinctive letters painted on the conning tower are: Bäv, *Bävern*; Hj, *Hajen*; In, *Illern*; Sa, *Sälen*; Utn, *Uttern*; Val, *Valen*.

HAJEN *1970, Royal Swedish Navy*

ILLERN *1972, Royal Swedish Navy*

5 "ABBORREN" CLASS

Name	*Builders*	*Launched*	*Reconstructed*
ABBORREN	Kockums	8 July 1943	1962
GÄDDAN	Kockums	23 Nov 1943	1963
LAXEN	Karlskrona	25 Apr 1944	1964
MAKRILLEN	Karlskrona	23 May 1944	1963
SIKEN	Kockums	18 Aug 1943	1964

Displacement, tons	420 standard; 430 surface; 460 submerged
Length, feet (*metres*)	164·0 (*50·0*)
Beam, feet (*metres*)	14·1 (*4·3*)
Draught, feet (*metres*)	12·5 (*3·8*)
Torpedo tubes	4—21 in (*533 mm*) 3 bow and 1 stern
Main machinery	2 MAN diesels, total 1 500 bhp; Electric motors, 750 hp
Speed, knots	14 on surface; 9 submerged
Complement	23

Distinctive letters painted on the conning tower are: Abb, *Abborren*; Gad, *Gäddan*; La, *Laxen*; Ma, *Makrillen*; Sik, *Siken*.

MAKRILLEN *1969, Royal Swedish Navy*

Note. A submarine-escape vehicle of French design was ordered from Kockums in mid-1974.

Displacement, tons	49
Dimensions, feet	44·3 × 14·1 × 9·5
Complement	5

With a diving depth of 1 500 ft it will be capable of operating and conducting rescues throughout the Baltic. Can lift up to 25 men at one time.

LAXEN *1972, Royal Swedish Navy*

LIGHT FORCES

2 PROJECTED MTB FLOTILLA LEADERS

K 1 **K 2**

Displacement, tons	700
Dimensions, feet	246·0 × 26·2 × 8·0
Guns	1—57 mm forward; 1—40 mm aft
A/S weapons	1 single barrelled depth charge mortar forward
Main engines	Gas turbines for power; diesels for cruising
Complement	70

A new type of corvette is planned to fill the need for ships to act as flotilla leaders for fast torpedo boats and missile gunboats and for escort duties to relieve old destroyers and frigates. It is reported they may turn out at 800 to 1 000 tons displacement.

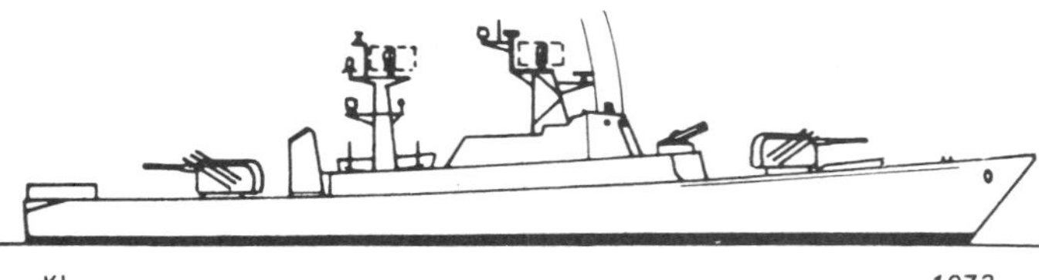

KI 1973

1+16 "JÄGAREN" CLASS (FAST ATTACK CRAFT—MISSILE)

JÄGAREN P 151 **P 152-167**

Displacement, tons	140
Dimensions, ft (*m*)	118 × 20·3 × 4·9 (*36 × 6·2 × 1·5*)
Missile launchers	4 improved Penguin surface-to-surface
Gun	1—57 mm Bofors
Torpedo tubes	Fitted for 4—21 inch (*533 mm*)
Main engines	2 MTU MB20V 672 TY90 diesels; 2 shafts; 7 000 bhp = 35 knots
Complement	20

Instead of the motor gunboats projected for several years a choice was made of fast attack craft similar to the Norwegian "Snögg" class armed with Penguin missiles. *Jägaren* was built in Norway, completed on 8 June 1972.
She then underwent extensive trials and, in late 1974, an order for a further sixteen was placed with Bergens Mekaniske Verksted, Norway. Guns and electronics are being provided from Sweden. Fitted for alternative minelaying capability aft.

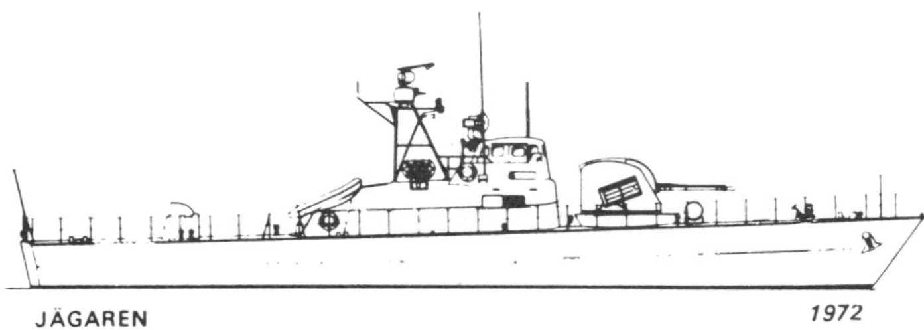

JÄGAREN 1972

12 "REPEAT SPICA" CLASS (FAST ATTACK CRAFT—TORPEDO)

HALMSTAD	T 140	**NYNÄSHAMN**	T 132	**VARBERG**	T 134
LULEÅ	T 139	**PITEÅ**	T 138	**VÄSTERÅS**	T 135
NORRKÖPING	T 131	**STRÖMSTAD**	T 141	**VÄSTERVIK**	T 136
NORRTÄLJE	T 133	**UMEÅ**	T 137	**YSTAD**	T 142

Displacement, tons	230 standard
Dimensions, ft (*m*)	134·5 × 23·3 × 5·2 (*41 × 7·1 × 1·6*)
Gun	1—57 mm Bofors L/70
Rocket launchers	8 for 57 mm flare rockets
Torpedo tubes	6—21 in (*533 mm*) for wire-guided torpedoes
Main engines	3 Rolls Royce Proteus gas turbines; 3 shafts; 12 900 bhp = 40·5 knots

Similar to the original "Spica" class from which they were developed. Building by Karlskronavarvet AB. Guided missiles are not included in the design to date. *Norrköping* launched 16 Nov 1972. Completed Feb 1973. Commissioned March 1973. *Norrtalje* launched 1973, *Nynäshamn* launched 21 Apr 1973.

RADAR. Philips Teleindustrie 9 LV 200-simultaneous air and surface search in X band with tracking in Ku band.

NORRKÖPING at launch *1972, Royal Swedish Navy*

6 "SPICA" CLASS (FAST ATTACK CRAFT—TORPEDO)

CAPELLA	T 123	**SIRIUS**	T 122	**VEGA**	T 125
CASTOR	T 124	**SPICA**	T 121	**VIRGO**	T 126

Displacement, tons	200 standard; 230 full load
Dimensions, ft (*m*)	134·5 × 23·3 × 5·2 (*41 × 7·1 × 1·6*)
Gun	1—57 mm Bofors AA
Torpedo tubes	6—21 in (*533 mm*) single, fixed
Rocket launchers	6—57 mm flare rockets; 4—10·3 mm flare rockets
Main engines	3 Bristol Siddeley Proteus 1 274 gas turbines; 3 shafts; 12 720 shp = 40 knots
Complement	28 (7 officers, 21 ratings)

The lead vessel, *Spica*, was completed in 1966 by Götaverken, Göteborg, and the other five completed in 1966 to 1968. *Sirius* and *Capella* were built by Götaverken and *Castor*, *Vega* and *Virgo* by Karlskronavervarvet. The 57 mm gun is in a power operated turret controlled by a radar equipped director.

RADAR. **M 22 fire control system with co-mounted radars in radome for guns and torpedoes.**

CAPELLA *1970, Royal Swedish Navy*

11 "PLEJAD" CLASS (FAST ATTACK CRAFT—TORPEDO)

ALDEBARAN	T 107	**ARCTURUS**	T 110	**POLARIS**	T 103
ALTAIR	T 108	**ARGO**	T 111	**POLLUX**	T 104
ANTARES	T 109	**ASTREA**	T 112	**REGULUS**	T 105
		PLEJAD	T 102	**RIGEL**	T 106

Displacement, tons	155 standard; 170 full load
Dimensions, ft (*m*)	147·6 × 19 × 5·2 (*45 × 5·8 × 1·6*)
Guns	2—40 mm Bofors AA with Rocket-Flare launchers
Tubes	6—21 in (*533 mm*)
Main engines	3 Mercedes-Benz diesels; 3 shafts; 9 000 bhp = 37·5 knots
Range, miles	600 at 30 knots
Complement	33

All built at Lurssen, Vegesack, launched between 1954 and 1959 and completed by 1960.

ARGO *1971, Royal Swedish Navy*

15 "T 42" CLASS (FAST ATTACK CRAFT—TORPEDO)

T 42	**T 45**	**T 48**	**T 51**	**T 54**
T 43	**T 46**	**T 49**	**T 52**	**T 55**
T 44	**T 47**	**T 50**	**T 53**	**T 56**

Displacement, tons	40 to 45 standard
Dimensions, ft (*m*)	75·5 × 19·4 × 4·6 (*23 × 5·9 × 1·4*)
Gun	1—40 mm Bofors AA with Rocket-Flare launchers
Tubes	2—21 in (*533 mm*)
Main engines	Petrol engines; speed = 45 knots

Built by Kockums Mekaniska Verkstads Aktiebolag, Malmo. All launched and completed between 1956 and 1959.

T 45 *1970, Royal Swedish Navy*

Light Forces—*continued*

4 "T 32" CLASS (FAST ATTACK CRAFT—TORPEDO)

T 38 **T 40**
T 39 **T 41**

Displacement, tons	40 standard
Dimensions, ft (*m*)	75·5 × 18·4 × 4·6 (*23 × 5·6 × 1·4*)
Guns	1—40 mm Bofors AA with Rocket-Flare launchers forward; 2 MG (twin)
Tubes	2—21 in
Main engines	Petrol engines; speed = 40 knots

Launched in 1950-52 and completed in 1951-53. Built by Kockums Mekaniska Verkstads Aktiebolag, Malmö. Of all welded steel construction. Originally class of ten.

T 34 (remainder similar) *1972, Royal Swedish Navy*

V 57 (LARGE PATROL CRAFT)

Displacement, tons	115 standard
Dimensions, ft (*m*)	98 × 17·3 × 7·5 (*30 × 5·3 × 2·3*)
Gun	1—20 mm
Main engines	Diesel; 500 bhp = 13·5 knots
Complement	12

Built at Stockholm. Launched in 1953. Fitted for minelaying. Coast Artillery.

17 COASTAL PATROL CRAFT

61-77

Displacement, tons	28 standard
Dimensions, ft (*m*)	69 × 15 × 5 (*21 × 4·6 × 1·5*)
Gun	1—20 mm
Main engines	Diesel; speed = 18 knots

These are attached to the Coast Artillery. "60" series launched in 1960-61 and "70' series in 1966-67.

5 COASTAL PATROL CRAFT

SVK 1 **SVK 2** **SVK 3** **SVK 4** **SVK 5**

Displacement, tons	19 standard
Dimensions, ft (*m*)	52·5 × 12·1 × 3·9 (*16 × 3·7 × 1·2*)
Gun	1—20 mm
Main engines	Diesels; 100 to 135 bhp = 10 knots

Patrol craft of the Sjövarnskarens (RNVR). All launched in 1944.

MINE WARFARE FORCES

1 + 2 NEW CONSTRUCTION (MINELAYERS)

ÄLVSBORG M 02 **VISBORG M 03** **M 04**

Displacement, tons	2 700
Length, feet (*metres*)	301·8 (*92*)
Beam, feet (*metres*)	48·2 (*14·7*)
Draught, feet (*metres*)	13·2 (*4·0*)
Aircraft	1 Helicopter
Guns	3—40 mm Bofors AA
Main engines	2 Nohab-Polar 12 cyl diesels; 1 shaft; 4 200 bhp
Speed, knots	15
Complement	95 (accommodation for 205 more)

ÄLVSBORG

The *Alvsbcrg* was ordered in 1968 from the Naval Dockyard in Karlskrona, launched on 11 Nov 1969, and completed on 10 Apr 1971. She replaced the submarine depot ship *Patricia* which was sold in 1972.

Visborg, laid down at Karlskrona in 1972 will succeed *Marieholm* as Command Ship for C-in-C Active Fleet. M 04 will succeed *Alvsnabben* as minelayer and training ship.

ALVSBORG *1972, Royal Swedish Navy*

ÄLVSNABBEN M 01 (MINELAYER)

Displacement, tons	4 250 standard
Length, feet (*metres*)	317·6 (*96·8*) wl; 334·7 (*102·0*) oa
Beam, feet (*metres*)	44·6 (*13·6*)
Draught, feet (*metres*)	16·4 (*5·0*)
Guns	2—6 in (*152 mm*); 2—57 mm Bofors; 2—40 mm AA; 4—37 mm saluting
Main engines	Diesels; 1 shaft; 3 000 bhp
Speed, knots	14
Complement	255 (63 cadets)

ÄLVSNABBEN

ÄLVSNABBEN *1969, Royal Swedish Navy*

Built on a mercantile hull by Eriksberg Mekaniska Verkstad Göteborg. Laid down on 31 Oct 1942, launched on 19 Jan 1943, completed on 8 May 1943. Employed as a training ship during 1953-58. Relieved the anti-aircraft cruiser *Gotland* as Cadet's Seagoing Training Ship in 1959. Re-armed in 1961. Formerly carried 4—6 inch, 8—40 mm AA, 6—20 mm AA.

RADAR. Thomson CSF Saturn S-band long-range search and target designator; M 45 fire control system for guns.

Mine warfare Forces—*continued*

Note. A new construction coastal minelayer MUL 20 projected.

MUL 11 (COASTAL MINELAYER)

Displacement, tons	200 full load
Dimensions, feet	98·8 × 23·7 × 11·8
Guns	2—20 mm AA
Main engines	2 Atlas diesels; 300 bhp = 10 knots

Launched in 1946.

MUL 11 *1971, Royal Swedish Navy*

8 COASTAL MINELAYERS

MUL 12 (1952) **MUL 13** (1952) **MUL 14** (1953) **MUL 15** (1953) **MUL 16** (1956) **MUL 17** (1956) **MUL 18** (1956) **MUL 19** (1956)

Displacement, tons	245 full load
Dimensions, feet	95·1 × 24·3 × 10·2 (*29 × 7·4 × 3·1*)
Gun	1—40 mm AA
Main engines	1 Nohab diesel-electric; 360 bhp = 10.5 knots

37+1 SMALL MINELAYERS

501 onwards

Ordered in 1969. Of 15 tons and 14 knots with Diesel engines.

6 (?) PROJECTED MINEHUNTERS

PROJECTED MINEHUNTER *Courtesy Captain Allan Kull*

6 "HANÖ" CLASS (MINESWEEPERS—COASTAL)

HANÖ M 51 **ORNÖ** M 55 **STURKÖ** M 54 **TÄRNÖ** M 52 **TJURKÖ** M 53 **UTÖ** M 56

Displacement, tons	270 standard
Dimensions, feet	131·2 × 23 × 8
Guns	2—40 mm AA
Main engines	Diesels; 2 shafts; 2 400 bhp = 14·5 knots

All of this class were built at Karlskrona and launched in 1953.

TÄRNÖ *1970, Royal Swedish Navy*

12 "ARKÖ" CLASS (MINESWEEPERS—COASTAL)

ARKÖ M 57 **ASPÖ** M 63 **BLIDÖ** M 68 **HASSLÖ** M 64 **IGGÖ** M 60 **KARLSÖ** M 59 **NÄMDÖ** M 67 **SKAFTÖ** M 62 **SPÅRÖ** M 58 **STYRSÖ** M 61 **VÅLLÖ** M 66 **VINÖ** M 65

Displacement, tons	285 standard; 300 full load
Dimensions, feet	131 *pp*; 144·5 *oa* × 23 × 8
Gun	1—40 mm AA
Main engines	Mercedes-Benz diesels; 2 shafts; 2 000 bhp = 14·5 knots

Of wooden construction. There is a small difference in the deck-line between M 57-59 and M60-68. *Arkö* was launched on 21 Jan 1957. *Arkö, Karlsö* and *Spårö* were completed in 1958, *Iggö* in 1961 *Aspö, Hasslö, Vinö, Skaftö* and *Styrsö* in 1962 *Vållö* 1963, *Bildö* and *Nämdö* in 1964.

3 "M 31" CLASS (MINESWEEPERS—INSHORE)

GÄSSTEN M 31 **NORSTEN** M 32 **VIKSTEN** M 33

Displacement, tons	120 standard; 135 full load
Dimensions, feet	75·5 *oa* × 21·7 × 6·5
Gun	1—40 mm AA
Main engines	Diesels = 11 knots

Ordered 1972. *Viksten* built of glass reinforced plastic as a forerunner to the new minehunters to be built at Karlskrona. *Gässten* launched July 1973. *Norsten* Oct 1973, *Viksten* April 1973. All completed 1972-74.

3 "M 47" CLASS (MINESWEEPERS—INSHORE)

GILLOGA M 47 **RÖDLÖGA** M 48 **SVARTLÖGA** M 49

Details same as "M 44" class. Built in 1964. Trawler type.

4 "M 44" CLASS (MINESWEEPERS—INSHORE)

BLACKAN M 44 **DÄMMAN** M 45 **GALTEN** M 46 **HISINGEN** M 43

Displacement, tons	140
Dimensions, ft (*m*)	72·2 × 21 × 11·2 (*22 × 6·4 × 3·4*)
Gun	1—40 mm
Main engines	2 Diesels = 9 knots

Built in 1960. Trawler Type.

2 "M 41" CLASS (MINESWEEPERS—INSHORE)

ORUST M 41 **TJÖRN** M 42

Displacement, tons	110
Dimensions, ft (*m*)	62·3 × 19·7 × 4·6 (*19 × 6 × 1·4*)
Gun	1—20 mm
Main engines	2 Diesels = 9 knots

Built in 1948. Trawler type.

SVARTLOGA *1970, Royal Swedish Navy*

8 "M 15" CLASS (MINESWEEPERS—INSHORE)

M 15 **M 16** **M 21** **M 22** **M 23** **M 24** **M 25** **M 26**

Displacement, tons	70 standard
Dimensions, ft (*m*)	85·3 × 16·5 × 4·5 (*26 × 5 × 1·4*)
Gun	1—20 mm
Main engines	Diesel; 600 bhp = 13 knots

All launched in 1941. M 17, M 18 and M 20 of this class were re-rated as tenders and renamed *Lommen, Spoven* and *Skuld* respectively: see later page.

M 26 *1972, Royal Swedish Navy*

2 MINE TRANSPORTS

FÄLLAREN A 236 **MINÖREN** A 237

Displacement, tons	165 standard
Dimensions, feet	105 × 20·3 × 7·2
Main engines	Speed = 9 knots

Launched in 1941 and 1940 respectively.

URD (ex-*Capella*) A 271 (EXPERIMENTAL CRAFT)

Built in 1929.

AMPHIBIOUS FORCES

3 LCM

BORE **GRIM** **HEIMDAL**

Displacement, tons	340 full load
Dimensions, feet (*m*)	118·1 × 27·9 × 8·5 (*36 × 8·5 × 2·6*)
Main engines	Diesels; 800 bhp = 12 knots

Launched in 1961 (*Grim*) and 1966. Attached to Coast Artillery.

BORE *1969, Royal Swedish Navy*

2 LCM

SKAGUL A 333 **SLEIPNER** A 335

Displacement, tons	335 standard
Dimensions, ft (*m*)	114·8 × 27·9 × 9·5 (*35 × 8·5 × 2·9*)
Main engines	Diesels; 640 bhp = 10 knots

Sleipner was launched in 1959 and completed in 1960. *Skagul* was launched and completed in 1960. Attached to Coast Artillery.

4 "ANE" CLASS (LCM)

ANE **BALDER** **LOKE** **RING**

Displacement, tons	135 standard
Dimensions, ft (*m*)	91·9 × 26·2 × 6·0 (*28 × 8 × 1·2*)
Gun	1—20 mm
Main engines	Speed = 8·5 knots

Built in 1943-45. Attached to Coast Artillery.

25 "256" CLASS (LCU)

Nos. 256-280

Probably similar to "201" class but not yet laid down.

14 "242" CLASS (LCU)

Nos. 242-255

Similar to the "201" class following with the same dimensions. Built in 1971-73.

41 "201" CLASS (LCU)

Nos. 201-204 **205-238** **239-241**

Displacement, tons	31
Dimensions, ft (*m*)	69 × 13·8 × 4·2 (*20 × 4·2 ×* 1·3)
Main engines	Diesels; 600 hp = 18 knots

Launched 1957-1960.

5 "L 51" CLASS (LCU)

L 51 **L 52** **L 53** **L 54** **L 55**

Displacement, tons	32 standard
Dimensions, ft (*m*)	50·8 × 16 × 3·2 (*14 × 4·8 × 1*)
Main engines	Diesel; 140 bhp = 8 knots

Launched in 1948.

54 LCAs

337-354 of 6 tons and 21 knots. Built 1970-73.
332-336 of 5·4 tons and 25 knots. Built in 1967.
331 of 6 tons and 20 knots. Built in 1965.
301-330 of 4 tons and 9·5 knots. Built in 1956-59.

SURVEY SHIPS

(Operated by Ministry of Transport)

ANDERS BURE (ex-*Rali*)

Displacement, tons	54
Dimensions, feet	82·0 × 19·4 × 6·9
Main engines	Diesels = 15 knots
Complement	11

Rali was built in 1968. She was purchased in 1971 and renamed.

Survey Ships—*continued*

RAN

Displacement, tons	285 standard
Dimensions, feet	98·4 × 23·0 × 8·5
Main engines	Diesels; 260 bhp = 9 knots
Complement	37

Ran was launched in 1945 and commissioned for service in 1946.

JOHAN MÅNSSON

Displacement, tons	977 standard; 1 030 full load
Dimensions, feet	183·7 × 36·1 × 11·5
Main engines	Diesels; 3 300 bhp = 15 knots
Complement	85

Launched on 14 Jan 1966. Her surveying launches are lowered and recovered over a stern ramp.

JOHAN MANSSON *1971, Royal Swedish Navy*

GUSTAF AF KLINT

Displacement, tons	750 standard
Dimensions, feet	170·6 × 28·5 × 15·4
Main engines	Diesels; 640 bhp = 10 knots
Complement	66

Launched in 1941. Reconstructed in 1963. She formerly displaced 650 tons with a length of 154 feet.

GUSTAV AV KLINT *1970, Royal Swedish Navy*

NILS STRÖMCRONA

Displacement, tons	140 standard
Dimensions, feet	88·6 × 17·0 × 8·2
Guns	None in peacetime
Main engines	Diesels; 300 bhp = 9 knots
Complement	14

Launched in 1894. and reconstructed in 1952.

LEDAREN

Of 360 tons built in 1926-27. An ex-Light Ship now used for coastal work with a crew of 20.

SERVICE FORCES

TANKERS

BRÄNNAREN A 228 (SUPPORT TANKER)

Displacement, tons	857
Speed, knots	11

Ex-German merchant tanker *Indio* purchased early 1972. Built 1965.

FREJA A 221 (SUPPLY SHIP)

Displacement, tons	415 standard; 450 full load
Dimensions, feet	160·8 × 27·9 × 12·1
Main engines	Diesels; 600 bhp = 11 knots

Built by Kroger, Rendsburg. Launched in 1953. Employed as a provision ship.

STAFF SHIPS

MARIEHOLM A 201 (COMMAND SHIP)

Displacement, tons	1 400 standard
Dimensions, feet	210 × 32·5 × 11·5
Aircraft	1 helicopter
Guns	2 MG (1—40 mm removed, see notes below)
Main engines	Steam reciprocating; 950 ihp = 12 knots

Former passenger ship. Completed in 1934. Converted during the Second World War to serve as a Base Communication Centre for the Commander-in-Chief of the Coastal Fleet. Recently used as a Staff Ship for the Commander-in-Chief in winter time, flying his flag. The ship had her mainmast removed and a helicopter platform installed aft in 1959 for employment as flagship of the Coastal Fleet. The 40 mm Bofors on the forecastle has been landed for the time being.

MARIEHOLM *1972, Royal Swedish Navy*

BELOS A 211 (SALVAGE VESSEL)

Displacement, tons	1 000 standard
Dimensions, feet	204·4 × 37·0 × 12·0
Aircraft	1 helicopter
Main engines	Diesels; 2 shafts; 1 200 bhp = 13 knots

Launched on 15 Nov 1961. Completed on 29 May 1963. Equipped with decompression chamber.

BELOS *1972, Wright & Logan*

2 SAIL TRAINING SHIPS

FALKEN S 02 **GLADAN** S 01

Displacement, tons	220 standard
Dimensions, feet	93 wl; 129·5 oa × 23·5 × 13·5
Main engines	Auxiliary diesel; 120 bhp

Sail training ships. Two masted schooners. Launched 1947 and 1946 respectively. Sail area 5 511 square feet. (512 square metres).

TENDERS

2 TRVs

PINGVINEN A 248

Displacement, tons	144
Dimensions, feet	109·2 × 20
Main engines	2 diesels; 1 100 hp = 13 knots

Ordered 1972 from Lundevarv-Oøverkstads AB, Kramfors for delivery in 1974. Torpedo recovery and rocket trials ship. Launched 6 Sep 1973.

PELIKANEN A 247

Displacement, tons	130 standard
Dimensions, feet	108·2 × 19·0 × 6·0
Main engines	Speed = 15 knots

Torpedo recovery and rocket trials vessel. Delivered on 26 Sep 1963.

5 TENDERS

SIGRUN A 256

Displacement, tons	250 standard
Dimensions, feet	105·0 × 22·3 × 11·8
Main engines	Diesels; 320 bhp = 11 knots

Launched in 1961.

Tenders—*cont.*

URD (ex-*Capella*) A 271

Displacement, tons	63 standard; 90 full load
Dimensions, feet	73·8 × 18·3 × 9·2
Main engines	Diesels; 200 bhp = 8 knots

Experimental vessel added to the official list in 1970. Launched in 1969.

LOMMEN (ex-*M* 17) A 231 **SKULD** (ex-*M* 20) A 371 **SPOVEN** (ex-*M* 18) A 232

Displacement, tons	70 standard
Dimensions, feet	85·3 × 16·5 × 4·5
Main engines	Diesel; 600 bhp = 13 knots

Former inshore minesweepers of the large motor launch type. All launched in 1941.

TUGS

ACHILLES A 251 **AJAX** A 252

Displacement, tons	450
Dimensions, feet	108·2 × 28·5 × 12
Main engines	Diesel, 1650 bhp = 12 knots

Achilles was launched in 1962 and *Ajax* in 1963. Both are icebreaking tugs.

AJAX *1970, Royal Swedish Navy*

HECTOR A 321 **HERMES** A 253 **HEROS** A 322

Displacement, tons	185 standard
Dimensions, feet	75·5 × 22·6 × 11·1
Main engines	Diesels; 630 bhp = 11 knots

Launched in 1953-57.

HERA A 324 **HERCULES** A 323

Displacement, tons	127 tons
Dimensions, feet	65·3 × 21·3 × 12·5
Main engines	Diesels; 615 bhp = 11·5 knots

HÄGERN (ex-*Torpedbargaren*) A246

Displacement, tons	50 standard
Dimensions, feet	88·6 × 16·4 × 4·9
Main engines	Diesels; 270 bhp = 10 knots

Hägern was launched in 1951.

WATER CARRIERS

2 WATER BOATS

FRYKEN A 217

Displacement, tons	307 standard
Dimensions, feet	105·0 × 18·7 × 8·9
Main engines	Diesels; 370 bhp = 10 knots

A naval construction water carrier. Launched in 1959 and completed in 1960.

UNDEN A 216

Displacement, tons	540 standard
Dimensions, feet	121·4 × 23·3 × 9·8 max
Main engines	Steam reciprocating; 225 ihp = 9 knots

Launched in 1946.

ICEBREAKERS

2 FINNISH "URHO" CLASS

ATLE **YMER**

Displacement, tons	7 800
Dimensions, ft (*m*)	337·8 × 77·1 × 24·6 (*103 × 23·5 × 7·5*)
Aircraft	1 helicopter
Main engines	5 Wärtsilä-Sulzer diesels; 4 Stromberg electric motors; 4 shafts (2 for'd, 2 aft); 20 000 hp = 17 knots
Complement	49 (with 15 extra berths)

Both ordered from Wärtsilä, Helsinki. *Atle* laid down 10 May 1973, launched 27 Nov 1973 and completed 21 Oct 1974. *Ymer* laid down 3 June 1974. Sister ships of Finnish "Urho" class.

ALE

Displacement, tons	1 488
Dimensions, ft (*m*)	150·9 × 42·6 × 16·4 (*46 × 13 × 5*)
Main engines	Diesels; 4 750 hp = 14 knots

Completed in 1973.

NJORD

Displacement, tons	5 150 standard; 5 686 full load
Dimensions, feet	260·8 pp; 283·8 oa × 69·6 × 20·3
Main engines	Wärtsilä diesel-electric; 4 shafts, 2 forward, 2 aft; 12 000 hp = 18 knots

Built by Wärtsilä, Finland. Launched on 20 Oct 1968 and completed in Dec 1969 Near sister ship of *Tor*.

NJORD *1971, Royal Swedish Navy*

TOR

Displacement, tons	4 980 standard; 5 290 full load
Dimensions, feet	254·3 pp; 277·2 oa × 69·5 × 20·3
Main engines	Wärtsilä-Sulzer diesel-electric; 4 shafts; 2 forward; 2 aft; 12 000 hp = 18 knots

Launched from Wärtsilä's Crichton-Vulcan yard, Turku, on 25 May 1963. Towed to Sandvikens Skeppsdocka, Helsingfors, for completion. Delivered on 31 Jan 1964. Larger but generally similar to *Oden*, and a near-sister to *Tarmo* built for Finland.

TOR *1972, Royal Swedish Navy*

THULE

Displacement, tons	2 200 standard; 2 280 full load
Dimensions, feet	187·0 wl; 204·2 oa × 52·8 × 19·4
Main engines	Diesel-electric; 3 shafts (1 for'd); 4 800 bhp = 14 knots
Complement	43

Launched at the Naval Dockyard, Karlskrona, in Oct 1951. Completed in 1953.

Icebreakers—*continued*

ODEN

Displacement, tons	4 950 standard; 5 220 full load
Dimensions, feet	255·9 pp; 273·5 oa × 63·7 × 22·7
Main engines	Diesel-electric; 4 shafts (2 for'd); 10 500 bhp = 16 knots
Oil fuel, tons	740
Complement	75

Similar to the Finnish *Voima* and 3 Soviet icebreakers. 4 screws, 2 forward, 2 aft. Built at Sandviken, Helsingfors. Launched on 16 Oct 1956. Completed in 1958

ODEN *1972, Royal Swedish Navy*

SUDAN

Establishment

The navy was established in 1962 to operate on the Red Sea coast and on the River Nile. The original training staff was from Yugoslavian Navy, but this staff left in 1972.

Diplomatic Representation

Naval, Military and Air Attaché in London:
Col. M. T. Khalil

Bases

Port Sudan for Red Sea operations with a separate riverine unit on the Nile.

Personnel

(a) 1975: 600 officers and men
(b) Voluntary service

Mercantile Marine

Lloyd's Register of Shipping: 14 vessels of 45 943 tons gross

2 Ex-YUGOSLAV "PBR 500" CLASS (LARGE PATROL CRAFT)

FASHER PBR 1 **KHARTOUM** PBR 2

Displacement, tons	190 standard; 245 full load
Dimensions, feet	134·5 × 20·7 × 7·0
Guns	2—40 mm AA; 2—20 mm AA
Main engines	Diesel; 2 shafts; 3 300 bhp = 20 knots
Range, miles	1 500 at 12 knots

Built in 1953-55. Transferred from the Yugoslavian Navy during 1969.

4 Ex-YUGOSLAV PBR TYPE (LARGE PATROL CRAFT)

GIHAD PB 1 **HORRIYA** PB 2 **ISTIQLAL** PB 3 **SHAAB** PB 4

Displacement, tons	100
Dimensions, feet	115 × 16·5 × 5·2
Guns	1—40 mm AA; 1—20 mm AA; 2—7·6 mm MG
Main engines	Mercedes-Benz diesels; 2 shafts; 1 800 bhp = 20 knots
Range, miles	1 400 at 12 knots
Complement	20 officers and men

Built by Mosor Shipyard, Trogir, Yugoslavia, in 1961-62. Of steel construction. First craft acquired by the newly established Sudanese Navy.

HORRIYA *Sudanese Navy*

Sudan—*continued*

6 PATROL CRAFT

Transferred by Yugoslavia in 1970.

2 LANDING CRAFT

SOBAT **DINDER**

Two ex-Yugoslavian landing craft of the DTK 221 type were taken over during 1969.

3 LCUs

Transferred by Yugoslavia 1970—of 40 tons.

FASHODA (ex-PN 17) (SUPPORT TANKER)

Displacement, tons	420 standard; 650 full load
Dimensions, feet	141·5 × 22·8 × 13·6
Main engines	300 bhp = 7 knots

Former Yugoslavian oiler rehabilitated and transferred to the Sudanese Navy in 1969.

TIENAGA (SURVEY SHIP)

A small vessel, converted into a hydrographic ship, acquired from Yugoslavia in 1969.

BARAKA (ex-PV 6) (WATER BOAT)

A small water carrier, transferred from Yugoslavia to the Sudanese Navy in 1969.

SWITZERLAND

Diplomatic Representation

Defence Attaché in London: Colonel H. W. Fischer

The Swiss Army operates ten Coastal Patrol Craft on the frontier lakes. These were originally built in 1942 against possible German operations and have been modernised. Fitted with machine guns and radar.

SWISS PATROL CRAFT *1966, Swiss Army*

SYRIA

Personnel

(a) 1975: 2 200 officers and men
(b) $2\frac{1}{2}$ years national service

Bases

Latakia, Baniyas

Mercantile Marine

Lloyd's Register of Shipping: 9 vessels of 2 643 tons gross

Note: Unconfirmed reports received that 2 ex-USSR "Vanya" class MSC were transferred in early 1973.

Syria—*continued*

6 Ex-USSR "OSA" CLASS (FAST ATTACK CRAFT—MISSILE)

Displacement, tons	165 standard; 200 full load
Dimensions, feet	128.7 × 25·1 × 5·9
Missile launchers	4, two pairs abreast, for SSN 2-A (Styx)
Guns	4—30 mm twins; 1 forward, 1 aft
Main engines	3 diesels; 13 000 bhp = 32 knots
Range, miles	800 at 25 knots
Complement	25

Original pair sunk in Oct 1973 war. Up to six replacements reported.

SYRIAN "OSA" Class *Dec, 1972*

6 Ex-USSR "KOMAR" CLASS (FAST ATTACK CRAFT—MISSILE)

Displacement, tons	70 standard; 80 full load
Dimensions, feet	83·7 × 19·8 × 5
Missile launchers	2 for SSN 2A (Styx)
Guns	2—25 mm AA
Main engines	4 diesels; 4 shafts; 4 800 bhp = 40 knots
Range, miles	400 at 30 knots

Transferred between 1963 and 1966. Three reported lost in Israeli war October 1973, but were replaced.

16 Ex-USSR "P 4 CLASS" (FAST ATTACK CRAFT—TORPEDO)

Displacement, tons	25 standard
Dimensions, feet	62·7 × 11·6 × 5·6
Tubes	2—18 in
Guns	2— MG (twin)
Main engines	2 diesels; 2 200 bhp 2 shafts = 50 knots

Five torpedo boats were transferred from the USSR at Latakia on 7 Feb 1957, and at least twelve subsequently. Only approximately ten of these can be considered operational. One reported lost in Israeli war October 1973.

3 Ex-FRENCH CH TYPE (LARGE PATROL CRAFT)

ABABEH IBN NEFEH **ABDULLAH IBN ARISSI** **TAREK IBN ZAYED**

Displacement, tons	107 standard; 131 full load
Dimensions, feet	116·5 pp; 121·8 oa × 17·5 × 6·5
Guns	1—3 in; 2—20 mm AA
A/S weapons	Depth charges
Main engines	MAN diesels, 2 shafts, 1 130 bhp = 16 knots
Oil fuel, tons	50
Range, miles	1 200 at 8 knots; 680 at 13 knots
Complement	28

All built in France and completed in 1940. Rebuilt in 1955-56 when the funnels were removed. These were transferred in 1962 to form the nucleus of the Syrian Navy. Two of these ships are probably non-operational.

1 Ex-USSR "T 43" CLASS (MINESWEEPER—OCEAN)

Displacement, tons	500 standard; 610 full load
Dimensions, feet	191·5 × 28·1 × 6·9
Guns	4—37 mm AA; 4—25 mm AA
Main engines	2 diesel motors; 2 shafts 2 000 hp = 17 knots
Range, miles	1 600 at 10 knots
Complement	40

Reported in 1962 to have transferred from the Soviet Navy to the Syrian Navy. One of this class was sunk in the Israeli War October 1973.

TAIWAN (REPUBLIC OF CHINA)

Administration

Commander-in-Chief of the Navy:
Admiral Soong Chang-chih

Deputy Commander-in-Chief:*
Vice-Admiral Chih Men-bing

Chief of Staff:
Vice-Admiral Chen Tung-hai

Commander, Fleet Command:
Vice-Admiral Li Pei-chou

*There has been only one Deputy C in C since Feb 1974.

Diplomatic Representation

Naval Attaché in Washington, D.C.:
Rear-Admiral Chiu Hua-ku

Personnel

7 100 officers and 28 000 enlisted in Navy;
3 000 officers and 26 000 enlisted in Marine Corps.

Strength of the Fleet

2 Submarines
18 Destroyers
13 Frigates
1 Frigate/Transport
3 Patrol Vessels
9 Torpedo Boats
14 Coastal Minesweepers
9 Mine Boats & Launches
1 Amphibious Flagship
28 Landing Ships
22 Utility Landing Craft
21 Auxiliary Ships
5 Floating Dry Docks

Mercantile Marine

Lloyd's Register of Shipping:
407 vessels of 1 416 833 tons gross

SUBMARINES

2 Ex-US GUPPY II TYPE

Name	No.	Launched	US Comm	Transferred
HAI SHIH (ex-USS *Cutlass*, SS 478)	SS 91	5 Nov 1944	17 Mar 1945	12 Apr 1973
HAI PAO (ex-USS *Tusk*, SS 426)	SS 92	8 July 1945	11 Apr 1946	18 Oct 1973

Displacement, tons: 1 870 standard; 2 420 submerged
Length, feet (*metres*): 307·5 (*93·6*) oa
Beam, feet (*metres*): 27·2 (*8·3*)
Draught, feet (*metres*): 18 (*5·5*)
Torpedo tubes: 10—21 inch (*533 mm*); 6 fwd; 4 aft
Main engines: 3 diesels (Fairbanks Morse); 4 800 bhp/ 2 electric motors (Elliott); 5 400 shp; 2 shafts
Speed, knots: 18 surface; 15 submerged
Complement: 81 (11 officers, 70 enlisted men)

Originally fleet-type submarines of the US Navy "Tench" class; extensively modernised under the GUPPY II programme. *Hai Shih* built by Portsmouth Navy Yard and *Hai Pao* by Federal SB & DD Co, Kearny, New Jersey. These submarines each have four 126-cell electric batteries; fitted with snorkel.

The Republic of China is the only nation in the Western Pacific to currently operate former US Navy submarines.

HAI SHIH — 1972, United States Navy

HAI SHIH — 1973, US Navy

DESTROYERS

5 Ex-US "GEARING" CLASS

Name	No.	Builder	Launched	US Comm	Transferred
DANG YANG (ex-USS *Lloyd Thomas*, DD 764)	DD 11	Bethlehem Steel (San Francisco)	5 Oct 1945	21 Mar 1947	12 Oct 1972
LIAO YANG (ex-USS *Hanson*, DD 832)	DD 12	Bath Iron Works Corp	11 Mar 1945	11 May 1945	18 Apr 1973
HAN YANG (ex-USS *Herbert J. Thomas*, DD 833)	DD 15	Bath Iron Works Corp	25 Mar 1945	29 May 1945	6 May 1974
LAO YANG (ex-USS *Shelton*, DD 790)	DD 20	Todd Pacific Shipyards	8 Mar 1946	21 June 1946	18 Apr 1973
CHIEN YANG (ex-USS *James E. Kyes*, DD 787)	DD 21	Todd Pacific Shipyards	4 Aug 1945	8 Feb 1946	18 Apr 1973

Displacement, tons: 2 425 standard; approx 3 500 full load
Length, feet (*metres*): 390·5 (*119·0*) oa
Beam, feet (*metres*): 40·9 (*12·4*)
Draught, feet (*metres*): 19 (*5·8*)
Guns: 4—5 inch (*127 mm*) 38 cal DP (twin)
several ·50 cal MG fitted in several ships
A/S weapons: 1 ASROC 8-tube launcher except in *Dang Yang* which has trainable Hedgehog (Mk 15)
6—12·75 inch (*324 mm*) torpedo tubes (Mk 32 triple)
Main engines: 2 geared turbines (General Electric); 60 000 shp; 2 shafts
Boilers: 4
Speed, knots: 34
Complement: approx 275

Former US Navy destroyers of the "Gearing" class. The *Dang Yang* was modified to a special anti-submarine configuration and reclassified as a "hunter-killer" destroyer (DDK) in 1949; changed to "escort" destroyer (DDE) in 1950; changed again to "straight" DD upon modernisation in 1962. These ships have been extensively modernised under the Fleet Rehabilitation and Modernisation programme, all to FRAM I standard except *Dang Yang* which was FRAM II (no ASROC). All have helicopter platform and hangar.

Armament listed above was at time of transfer. The *Lao Yang* has twin 5 inch gun mounts in "A" and "B" positions with A/S torpedo tubes alongside second funnel; other ships have the "A" and "Y" gun mounts with torpedo tubes in "B" position except *Dang Yang* has torpedo tubes between funnels.

In 1963-1964 the *Herbert J Thomas* was modified for protection against biological, chemical, and atomic attack; the ship could be fully "sealed" with enclosed lookout and control positions, special air-conditioning. Upon transfer to Taiwan China the *Herbert J Thomas* assumed name and pennant number of an ex-US "Benson" class destroyer in Taiwan service.

Three of the FRAM I ships were initially scheduled for transfer to Spain; however, they were declined by Spain and allocated to Taiwan China.

ELECTRONICS. At time of transfer three of these ships had SPS-37 and SPS-10 search radar antennas on their tripod mast; *Dang Yang* had older SPS-6 and SPS-10 antennas; *Chien Yang* had SPS-40 and SPS-10 (correction to previous edition). Fitted with SQS-23 sonar except *Dang Yang* with SQS-29 series.

Destroyers—*continued*

LIAO YANG (as USS *Hanson*) *1971, US Navy*

DANG YANG (as USS *Lloyd Thomas*) *1970, US Navy*

1 Ex-US "GEARING" CLASS RADAR PICKET

Name	*No.*	*Builder*	*Launched*	*US Comm*	*Transferred*
FU YANG (ex-USS *Ernest G. Small*, DD 838)	DD 7	Bath Iron Works Corp	14 June 1945	21 Aug 1945	19 Feb 1971

Displacement, tons	2 425 standard; approx 3 500 full load
Length, feet (*metres*)	390·5 (*119·0*) oa
Beam, feet (*metres*)	40·8 (*12·4*)
Draught, feet (*metres*)	19 (*5·8*)
Guns	6—5 inch (*127 mm*) 38 calibre DP (twin) 8—40 mm (twin) 4—·50 cal MG (single)
A/S weapons	6—12·75 inch (*324 mm*) torpedo tubes (Mk 32 triple); 2 fixed hedgehogs
Main engines	2 geared turbines; (General Electric); 60 000 shp; 2 shafts
Boilers	4 (Babcock & Wilcox)
Speed, knots	34
Complement	approx 275

Former US Navy radar picket destroyer of the "Gearing" class. Converted to a radar picket destroyer (DDR) during 1952 and subsequently modernised under the Fleet Rehabilitation and Modernisation (FRAM II) programme; redesignated as a "straight" destroyer (DD), but retained specialised electronic equipment. Not fitted with helicopter flight deck or hangar. 40 mm guns installed after transfer to Taiwan China.

ELECTRONICS. At time of transfer the *Fu Yang* had SPS-37 and SPS-10 search radars on forward tripod mast, and large TACAN (tactical aircraft navigation) "beehive" antenna on second tripod mast. Fitted SQS-29 series hull-mounted sonar and SQA-10 variable depth sonar.

FU YANG

8 Ex-US "ALLEN M. SUMNER" CLASS

Name	*No.*	*Builder*	*Launched*	*US Comm*	*Transferred*
HSIANG YANG (ex-USS *Brush*, DD 745)	DD 1	Bethlehem Steel (Staten Island)	28 Dec 1943	17 Apr 1944	Feb 1970
HENG YANG (ex-USS *Samuel N. Moore*, DD 747)	DD 2	Bethlehem Steel (Staten Island)	23 Feb 1944	24 June 1944	Feb 1970
HUA YANG (ex-USS *Bristol*, DD 857)	DD 3	Bethlehem Steel (San Pedro)	29 Oct 1944	17 Mar 1945	Feb 1970
YUEH YANG (ex-USS *Haynsworth*, DD 700)	DD 5	Federal SB & DD Co	15 Apr 1944	22 June 1944	May 1970
HUEI YANG (ex-USS *English*, DD 696)	DD 6	Federal SB & DD Co	27 Feb 1944	4 May 1944	Sep 1970
PO YANG (ex-USS *Maddox*, DD 731)	DD 10	Bath Iron Works Corp	19 Mar 1944	2 June 1944	July 1972
LO YANG (ex-USS *Taussig*, DD 746)	DD 14	Bethlehem Steel (Staten Island)	25 Jan 1944	20 May 1944	6 May 1974
NAN YANG (ex-USS *John W. Thomason*, DD 760)	DD 17	Bethlehem Steel (San Francisco)	30 Sep 1944	11 Oct 1945	6 May 1974

Displacement, tons	2 200 standard; 3 320 full load
Length, feet (*metres*)	376·5 (*114·8*) oa
Beam, feet (*metres*)	40·9 (*12·4*)
Draught, feet (*metres*)	19 (*5·8*)
Missile launchers	*Heng Yang* and others reported being fitted with Gabriel surface-to-surface missile
Guns	6—5 inch (*127 mm*) 38 calibre DP (twin) up to 6—3 inch (*76 mm*) 50 calibre AA (2 twin, 2 single) in most ships; others, including *Heng Yang* and *Yueh Yang*, have 8—40 mm (1 quad, 2 twin) several ·50 cal MG (single) in most ships
A/S weapons	6—12·75 inch (*324 mm*) torpedo tubes (Mk 32 triple); 2 fixed Hedgehogs; depth charges in some ships
Main engines	2 geared turbines (General Electric or Westinghouse); 60 000 shp; 2 shafts
Boilers	4 (Babcock & Wilcox)
Speed, knots	34
Complement	approx 275

YUEH YANG *1973*

"SUMNER" CLASS—*continued*

Former US Navy destroyers of the "Allen M. Sumner" class. These ships have not been modernised under the FRAM programmes, but retain their original configurations with removal of original torpedo tubes, and 40 mm and 20 mm AA guns, and installation of improved electronic equipment. Secondary gun battery now varies; during the 1950s most of these ships were rearmed with six 3 inch AA guns (two single alongside forward funnel and two twin amidships); number retained apparently varies from ship to ship, with some ships retaining original 40 mm guns. Tripod mast fitted.

Lo Yang and *Nan Yang* have names and numbers previously assigned to older ex-US destroyers.

ELECTRONICS. Most ships have SPS-6 and SPS-10 search radars on their tripod mast; *Po Yang* has SPS-40 and SPS-10 while *Nan Yang* has SPS-37 and SPS-10.

PHOTOGRAPHS. The *Fu Yang* can be distinguished from the other six-gun destroyers operated by Taiwan China by the former ship's additional space between funnels and the after tripod mast supporting large TACAN dome. The photographs of the *Heng Yang* and *Yueh Yang* show the 40 mm twin mounts, their directors, and stern depth charge racks.

HSIANG YANG *1971, United States Navy*

HENG YANG *courtesy "Ships of the World"*

Ex-US "BENSON" CLASS

Lo Yang DD 14 (ex-USS *Benson*, DD 421), **Han Yang** DD 15 (ex-USS *Hilary P Jones*, DD 427) stricken in 1975 wtih names and numbers assigned to later ships. See 1974-1975 and previous editions for characteristics and photographs.

4 Ex-US "FLETCHER" CLASS

Name	*No.*	*Launched*	*US Comm*	*Transferred*
KWEI YANG (ex-USS *Twining*, DD 540)	DD 8	11 July 1943	1 Dec 1943	Aug 1971
CHING YANG (ex-USS *Mullany*, DD 528)	DD 9	12 Oct 1942	23 Apr 1943	Oct 1971
AN YANG (ex-USS *Kimberly*, DD 521)	DD 18	4 Feb 1943	22 May 1943	June 1967
KUEN YANG (ex-USS *Yarnall*, DD 541)	DD 19	25 July 1943	30 Dec 1943	June 1968

Displacement, tons	2 100 standard; 3 050 full load
Length, feet (*metres*)	376·5 (*114·7*) oa
Beam, feet (*metres*)	35·9 (*11·9*)
Draught, feet (*metres*)	18 (*5·5*)
Guns	5—5 inch (*127 mm*) 38 calibre DP (single) except 4 guns in *Ching Yang*; 6—3 inch (*76 mm*) 50 calibre AA (twin) in *Kwei Yang* and *Ching Yang*; 6—40 mm AA (twin) in *An Yang* and *Kuen Yang*
A/S weapons	2 fixed hedgehogs; depth charges; 6—12·75 inch (*324 mm*) torpedo tubes (Mk 32 triple) in *Kwei Yang* and *Ching Yang*
Torpedo tubes	5—21 inch (*533 mm*) quintuple in *Kuen Yang*
Main engines	2 geared turbines (General Electric in *An Yang*, Allis Chalmers in *Kuen Yang*, Westinghouse in others); 60 000 shp; 2 shafts
Boilers	4 (Babcock & Wilcox)
Speed, knots	36
Complement	approx 250

Former US "Fletcher" class destroyers. Built by Bethlehem Steel Co, San Francisco, except *An Yang* by Bethlehem at Staten Island, New York. *An Yang* retains original pole mast; others have tripod mast. Only *Kuen Yang* retains anti-ship torpedo tubes installed between second funnel and third 5 inch gun mount. Reportedly, the ship has been fitted for minelaying.

KUEN YANG (with 21 inch torpedo tubes) *Toshio Tamura*

AN YANG *1971, Toshio Tamura*

1 TRAINING SHIP:

Ex-US "GLEAVES" CLASS

Name	*No*	*Launched*	*US Comm*	*Transferred*
HSIEN YANG (ex-*Hatakze*, ex-USS *Macomb*, DMS 23, ex-DD 458)	DD 1016	22 Sep 1941	26 Jan 1942	6 Aug 1970

Displacement, tons	1 700 standard; 2 575 full load
Length, feet (*metres*)	341 (*104·0*) wl; 348·33(*106·2*) oa
Beam, feet (*metres*)	36 (*11·0*)
Draught, feet (*metres*)	18 (*5·5*)
Guns	3—5 inch (*127 mm*) 38 calibre DP (single); several 40 mm AA; several 20 mm AA
A/S weapons	depth charges
Main engines	2 geared turbines (Westinghouse); 50 000 shp; 2 shafts
Boilers	4 (Babcock & Wilcox)
Speed, knots	34
Complement	250

The *Hsien Yang* is a former US destroyer of the "Gleaves" class; converted to a high speed minesweeper (DMS) in 1944 with removal of one (of five) 5 inch guns and torpedo tubes, and minesweeping gear fitted. Transferred to Japan on 19 Oct 1954 for service with the Maritime Self-Defence Force; subsequently transferred to Taiwan China on 6 Aug 1970. Decommissioned in 1974 for use as a dockside training ship, to be scrapped in 1975.

HSIEN YANG (ex-Hatazke) *1970, Toshio Tamura*

DISPOSALS

Nan Yang DD 17 (ex-USS *Plunkett*, DD 431) stricken in 1975 with name and number assigned to later ship; **Hsien Yang** DD 16 (ex-USS *Rodman*, DMS 21, DD 456) stricken in 1969 after running aground; name and number assigned to ex-USS *Macomb* (above).

FRIGATES

1 Ex-US "RUDDEROW" CLASS

Name	No.	Launched	US Comm	Transferred
TAI YUAN (ex-USS *Riley*, DE 579)	DE 27	29 Dec 1943	13 Mar 1944	10 July 1968

Displacement, tons: 1 450 standard; approx 2 000 full load
Length, feet (*metres*): 300 (*91·4*) wl; 306 (*93·3*) oa
Beam, feet (*metres*): 37 (*11·3*)
Draught, feet (*metres*): 14 (*4·3*)
Guns: 2—5 inch (*127 mm*) 38 calibre DP (single)
4—40 mm AA (twin)
4—20 mm AA (single)
A/S weapons: 6—12·75 inch (*324 mm*) torpedo tubes (Mk 32 triple)
1 hedgehog; depth charge
Main engines: Geared turbines (General Electric) with electric drive; 12 000 shp; 2 shafts
Boilers: 2 (Foster Wheeler)
Speed, knots: 24
Complement: approx 200

Former US Navy destroyer escort. Built by Bethlehem SB Co, Higham, Massachusetts. Refitted with tripod mast and platforms before bridge for 20 mm guns. (Hedgehog is on main deck, behind forward 5 inch mount). SFS-6 and SFS-10 search radars are installed.

TAI YUAN — *Iain G. B. Lovie*

1 Ex-US "BOSTWICK" CLASS

Name	No.	Launched	US Comm	Transferred
TAI HU (ex-USS *Bostwick*, DE 103)	DE 25	30 Aug 1943	1 Dec 1943	Nov 1948

Displacement, tons: 1 240 standard; 1 900 full load
Length, feet (*metres*): 300 (*91·4*) wl; 306 (*93·3*) oa
Beam, feet (*metres*): 36·6 (*11·2*)
Draught, feet (*metres*): 14 (*4·3*)
Guns: 2—5 inch (*127 mm*) 38 cal DP
8—40 mm AA (2 twin, 4 single)
4—20 mm AA (single)
A/S weapons: 6—12·75 inch (*324 mm*) torpedo tubes (Mk 32 triple); 1 hedgehog depth charges
Main engines: Diesel-electric (4 General Motors diesels); 6 000 bhp; 2 shafts
Speed, knots: 21
Complement: approx 200

Former US Navy destroyer escort; built by Dravo Corp, Wilmington, Delaware, but completed by Norfolk Navy Yard (Virginia). Reportedly the *Tai Hu* has been fitted for minelaying.

GUNNERY. The original main battery of three 3 inch 50 cal guns have been replaced by two 5 inch guns in open mounts.

TAI HU

DISPOSALS
Tai Ho DE 23 (es-USS *Thomas*, DE 102), **Tai Chong** DE 24 (ex-USS *Breeman*, DE 104), **Tai Chao** (ex-USS *Carter*, DE 112) scrapped 1972-1973.

DISPOSALS.
The frigate **Tai Kang** DE 21 (ex-USS *Wyffel*, DE 6) of the so-called "short-hull" type was scrapped in 1972 (see 1971-1972 and previous editions for description).

11 FRIGATES / 1 TRANSPORT — Ex-US APD TYPE

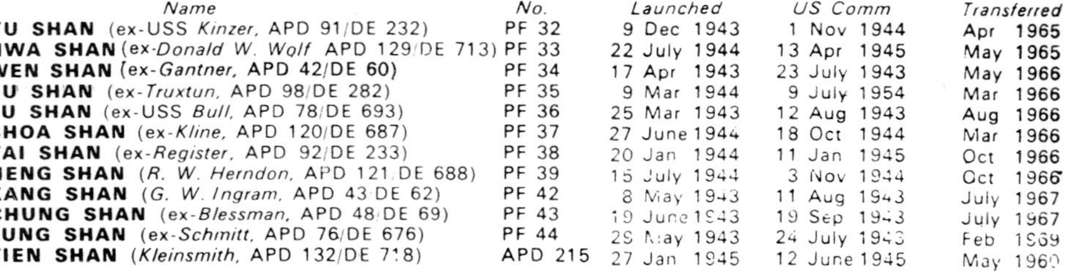

Name	No.	Launched	US Comm	Transferred
YU SHAN (ex-USS *Kinzer*, APD 91/DE 232)	PF 32	9 Dec 1943	1 Nov 1944	Apr 1965
HWA SHAN (ex-*Donald W. Wolf* APD 129/DE 713)	PF 33	22 July 1944	13 Apr 1945	May 1965
WEN SHAN (ex-*Gantner*, APD 42/DE 60)	PF 34	17 Apr 1943	23 July 1943	May 1966
FU SHAN (ex-*Truxtun*, APD 98/DE 282)	PF 35	9 Mar 1944	9 July 1954	Mar 1966
LU SHAN (ex-USS *Bull*, APD 78/DE 693)	PF 36	25 Mar 1943	12 Aug 1943	Aug 1966
SHOA SHAN (ex-*Kline*, APD 120/DE 687)	PF 37	27 June 1944	18 Oct 1944	Mar 1966
TAI SHAN (ex-*Register*, APD 92/DE 233)	PF 38	20 Jan 1944	11 Jan 1945	Oct 1966
HENG SHAN (*R. W. Herndon*, APD 121/DE 688)	PF 39	15 July 1944	3 Nov 1944	Oct 1966
KANG SHAN (*G. W. Ingram*, APD 43/DE 62)	PF 42	8 May 1943	11 Aug 1943	July 1967
CHUNG SHAN (ex-*Blessman*, APD 48/DE 69)	PF 43	19 June 1943	19 Sep 1943	July 1967
LUNG SHAN (ex-*Schmitt*, APD 76/DE 676)	PF 44	29 May 1943	24 July 1943	Feb 1969
TIEN SHAN (*Kleinsmith*, APD 132/DE 718)	APD 215	27 Jan 1945	12 June 1945	May 1960

Displacement, tons: 1 400 standard; 2 130 full load
Length, feet (*metres*): 300 (*91·4*) wl; 306 (*93·3*) oa
Beam, feet (*metres*): 37 (*11·3*)
Draught, feet (*metres*): 12·6 (*3·2*)
Guns: 2—5 inch (*127 mm*) 38 cal DP
6—40 mm AA (twin)
4—20 m AA (single) except *Hwa Shan* and possibly others have eight guns (twin mounts)
A/S weapons: 6—12·75 inch (*324 mm*) torpedo tubes (Mk 32 triple) except *Heng Shan* and possibly others have two hedgehogs depth charges
Main engines: Geared turbines (General Electric) with electric drive; 12 000 shp; 2 shafts
Boilers: 2 (Foster Wheeler)
Speed, knots: 23·6
Complement: approx 200

Former US Navy high speed transports (APD) employed as frigates. All designated PF except *Tien Shan* which is designated APD.

All begun as destroyer escorts (DE), but converted during construction or after completion to high speed transports carrying 160 troops, commandos, or frogmen, PF 32 and 35 built by Charleston Navy Yard, South Carolina; PF 33, 36, and APD 215 by Defoe SB Co, Bay City, Michigan; PF 34, 42, and 43 by Bethlehem SB Co, Higham, Massachusetts; PF 37, 39, and 44 by Bethlehem, Quincy, Mass.

LUNG SHAN — *1973*

Frigates—*continued*

Ex-US APD TYPE—*continued*

The ex-USS *Walter B Cobb* (APD 106/DE 596) transferred to Taiwan China in 1966 was lost at sea while under tow to Taiwan; replaced by ex-USS *Bull*.
Configurations differ: APD 37 class has high bridge; APD 87 class has low bridge. Radars and fire control equipment vary.
The *Heng Shan*, *Chung Shan*, and *Lung Shan* were decommissioned in 1974 and laid up in reserve. Others are active.

GUNNERY. All ships are now believed to have been refitted with a second 5 inch gun aft. One twin 40 mm gun mount is forward of bridge and two twin mounts are amid ships. Note after 5 inch mount and depth charge racks in photo of *Lung Shan*. Davits amidships can hold four LCVP-type landing craft.

FU SHAN — *Courtesy "Ships of the World"*

PATROL VESSELS

3 Ex-US MSF TYPE

WU SHENG	(ex-USS *Redstart*, MSF 378)	PCE 66	18 Oct 1944
CHU YUNG	(ex-USS *Waxwing*, MSF 389)	PCE 67	10 Mar 1945
MO LING	(ex-USS *Steady*, MSF 118)	PCE 70	6 June 1942

Displacement, tons	890 standard; 1 250 full load
Dimensions, feet	215 wl; 221·1 oa × 32·1 × 10·8
Guns	2—3 inch (*76 mm*) 50 cal AA (single); 4—40 mm AA (twin); 4—20 mm AA (twin)
A/S weapons	1 hedgehog; 3—12·75 inch (*324 mm*) torpedo tubes (Mk 32 triple); depth charges
Main engines	Diesel-electric (General Motors diesels); 3 530 bhp; 2 shafts = 18 knots
Complement	approx 80

Former US Navy minesweepers of the "Auk" class; originally designated AM. *Wu Sheng* built by Savannah Machine & Foundry Co, Georgia, others by American SB Co, Cleveland, Ohio, respectively; launch dates above. *Wu Sheng* transferred to Taiwan China in July 1965, *Chu Yung* in Nov 1965 and *Mo Ling* in Mar 1968.
Minesweeping equipment removed and second 3 inch gun fitted aft in Taiwan service. *Chein Men* FCE 45 (ex-USS *Toucan*, MSF 387) sunk by Communist Chinese warships south of Cuemcy Island on 6 Aug 1965.

MO LING

Ex-US 185-ft PCE TYPE

All former US Navy 185-foot patrol escorts have been stricken. **Wei Yuan** PCE 68 (ex-*Yung Hsiang*, PF 42, ex-USS PCE 869) decommissioned in 1972 and subsequently scrapped. See 1973-1974 and previous editions for characteristics and earlier disposals.

ExUS 185 ft-AM TYPE

All former US Navy 185-foot minesweepers of the "Admirable" class have been stricken, including one ship reclassified as a minelayer and two reclassified as auxiliaries: **Yung Feng** MMC 150 (ex-USS *Prime*, AM 279), **Yang Ming** AGS 562 (ex-*Yung Ting*, MSF 45, ex-USS *Lucid*, AM 259), **Yung Hsiu** ADG 152 (ex-MSF 48, ex-USS *Pinnacle*, AM 274) all decommissioned in 1972 and reported subsequently stricken. See 1973-1974 and previous editions for characteristics.

Ex-US 173-ft PC/PGM TYPE

All former US Navy 173-foot submarine chasers and motor gunboats have been stricken, with two units now operated by the Customs Service (listed on later page). See 1971-1972 and previous editions for characteristics and ship lists.

Ex-US 110-ft SC TYPE

All former US Navy wood-hull, 110-foot submarine chasers have been stricken. See 1971-1972 and previous editions for characteristics and ship lists.

Approx 10 PATROL BOATS (PB)

Displacement, tons	approx 30 tons
Guns	1—40 mm

Small patrol boats designated PB. Constructed in Taiwan with the first of an estimated ten units completed about 1971.

PB 1

TORPEDO BOATS

At least three additional torpedo boats are known to be in service; details were not available when this edition went to press.

2 79-ft TYPE

FUH KWO PT 515 **TIAN KWO** PT 516

Displacement, tons	46 light; 53 full load
Dimensions, feet	79 oa × 23·25 × 5·5
Guns	1—40 mm AA; 2—·50 cal MG (single)
Torpedo launchers	2
Main engines	3 gasoline engines; 3 shafts=39 knots max; 32 knots cruising
Complement	12

Built by Huckins Yacht Corp, Jacksonville, Florida. Transferred to Taiwan China on 1 Sep 1957.

Torpedo Boats—*continued*

2 71-ft TYPE

FAAN KONG PT 513 **SAO TANG** PT 514

Displacement, tons	39 light; 46 full load
Dimensions, feet	71 oa × 19 × 5
Guns	1—20 mm AA 4—·50 cal MG (twin)
Torpedo launchers	2 (?)
Main engines	3 gasoline engines; 3 shafts = 42 knots max; 32 knots cruising
Complement	12

Built by Annapolis Yacht Yard, Annapolis, Maryland. Transferred to Taiwan China on 19 Aug 1957 and 1 Nov 1957, respectively.

2 JAPANESE TYPE

FUH CHOW PT 511 **HSUEH CHIH** PT 512

Displacement, tons	33 light; 40 full load
Dimensions, feet	69 oa × 19·9
Guns	1—40 mm AA; 2—20 mm AA (twin)
Torpedo launchers	2—18 inch (*457 mm*)
Main engines	3 gasoline engines; 3 shafts = 40 knots max; 27 knots cruising
Complement	12

Built by Mitsubishi SB Co. Transferred to Taiwan China on 1 June 1957 and 6 Nov 1957, respectively. The 40 mm gun is not mounted in the adjacent photograph (can be fitted forward of bridge).

PT 511

Several small craft designated in the PT 600 series are used for frogman operations.

MINESWEEPERS

14 US MSC TYPE

YUNG PING	MSC 155 (ex-US MSC 140)
YUNG AN	MSC 156 (ex-US MSC 140)
YUNG NIEN	MSC 157 (ex-US MSC 277)
YUNG CHOU	MSC 158 (ex-US MSC 278)
YUNG HSIN	MSC 159 (ex-US MSC 302)
YUNG JU	MSC 160 (ex-US MSC 300)
YUNG LO	MSC 161 (ex-US MSC 306)
YUNG FU	MSC 162 (ex-*Diest*, ex-US MSC 77)
YUNG CHENG	MSC 165 (ex-*Maasieck*, ex-US MSC 78)
YUNG SHAN	MSC 164 (ex-*Lier*, ex-US MSC 63)
YUNG CHING	MSC 163 (ex-*Eekloo*, ex-US MSC 101)
YUNG LO	MSC 161 (ex-US MSC 306)
YUNG CHI	MSC 166 (ex-*Charleroi*, ex-US MSC 152)
YUNG SUI	MSC 168 (ex-*Diksmude*, ex-US MSC 65)

Displacement, tons	approx 380 full load
Dimensions, feet	144 oa × 28 × 8·5
Guns	2—20 mm AA (twin)
Main engines	Diesels (General Motors); 880 bhp; 2 shafts = 13·5 knots
Complement	40 to 50

Non-magnetic, wood-hulled minesweepers built in the United States specifically for transfer to allied navies. First seven units listed above transferred to Taiwan China upon completion: MSC 155 and 156 in June 1965, MSC 157 in Dec 1958, MSC 158 in July 1959, MSC 159 in Mar 1965, MSC 160 in Apr 1965, and MSC 161 in June 1966. The seven other units were transferred to Belgium upon completion in 1953-1955; retransferred to Taiwan China in Nov 1969.
All are of similar design; the ex-Belgium ships have a small boom aft on a pole mast. They carried a single 40 mm gun forward in Belgium service.

YUNG SHAN (pole mast aft)

Minesweepers—*continued*

YUNG CHOU (no pole mast aft)

MSB 12 (ex-US MSB 4)

Former US Army minesweeping boat; assigned hull number MSB 4 in US Navy and transferred to Taiwan China in Dec 1961.

MSML 1	**MSML 5**	**MSML 7**	**MSML 11**
MSML 3	**MSML 6**	**MSML 8**	**MSML 12**

Fifty-foot minesweeping launches built in the United States and transferred to Taiwan China in March 1961.

AMPHIBIOUS FLAGSHIPS

1 Ex-US LST TYPE

KAO HSIUNG (ex-*Chung Hai*, LST 219, ex-USS *Dukes County*, LST 735) AGC 1

Dimensions, feet	316 wl; 328 oa × 50 × 14
Guns	several 40 mm AA (twin)
Main engines	Diesel (General Motors); 1 700 bhp; 2 shafts = 11·6 knots

Former US Navy tank landing ship built by Dravo Corp, Neville Island, Pennsylvania; launched on 11 Mar 1944; commissioned on 26 Apr 1944. Transferred to Taiwan China in May 1957 for service as an LST. Converted to a flagship for amphibious operations and renamed and redesignated (AGC) in 1964. A second LST has not been converted to this role as previously reported.
Note lattice mast atop bridge structure, modified bridge levels, and antenna mountings on main deck.

KAO HSIUNG

LANDING SHIPS

1 Ex-US "ASHLAND" CLASS

TUNG HAI (ex-USS *White Marsh*, LSD 8) LSD 191

Displacement, tons	4 790 standard; 8 700 full load
Dimensions, feet	454 wl; 457·8 oa × 72 × 18
Guns	12—40 mm AA
Main engines	Skinner Unaflow; 7 400 ihp; 2 shafts = 15 knots
Boilers	2

Built by Moore Dry Dock Co, Launched on 19 July 1943. Designed to serve as parent ship for landing craft and coastal craft. Transferred from the US Navy to Taiwan on 17 Nov 1960.

TUNG HAI *Courtesy "Ships of the World"*

CHUNG HSING

Landing Craft—*continued*

1 Ex-US "CASA GRANDE" CLASS

Fort Marion LSD 22 of the "Casa Grande" class was stricken from the US Navy in 1974, reportedly for subsequent transfer to Taiwan China.

22 Ex-US LST TYPE

LST	*Name*	*Transferred*
201	**CHUNG HAI** (ex-USS LST 755)	Apr 1946
203	**CHUNG TING** (ex-USS LST 537)	Mar 1946
204	**CHUNG HSING** (ex-USS LST 557)	Mar 1946
205	**CHUNG CHIEN** (ex-USS LST 716)	June 1946
206	**CHUNG CHI** (ex-USS LST 1017)	Dec 1946
208	**CHUNG SHUN** (ex-USS LST 732)	Mar 1946
209	**CHUNG LIEN** (ex-USS LST 1050)	Jan 1947
210	**CHUNG YUNG** (ex-USS LST 574)	Mar 1959
216	**CHUNG KUANG** (ex-USS LST 503)	June 1960
217	**CHUNG SUO** (ex-USS *Bradley County*, LST 400)	Sep 1958
218	**CHUNG CHIE** (ex-USS *Berkley County*, LST 279)	June 1960
221	**CHUNG CHUAN** (ex-LST 1030)	Feb 1948
222	**CHUNG SHENG** (ex-LST 211, ex-USS LST 1033)	Dec 1947
223	**CHUNG FU** (ex-USS *Iron County*, LST 840)	July 1958
224	**CHUNG CHENG** (ex-USS *Lafayette County*, LST 859)	Aug 1958
225	**CHUNG CHIANG** (ex-USS *San Bernadino County*, LST 1110)	Aug 1958
226	**CHUNG CHIH** (ex-USS *Sagadahoc County*, LST 1091)	Oct 1958
227	**CHUNG MING** (ex-USS *Sweetwater County*, LST 1152)	Oct 1958
228	**CHUNG SHU** (ex-USS LST 520)	Sep 1958
229	**CHUNG WAN** (ex-USS LST 535)	Sep 1958
230	**CHUNG PANG** (ex-USS LST 578)	Sep 1958
231	**CHUNG YEH** (ex-USS *Sublette County*, LST 1144)	Sep 1961

Displacement, tons	1 653 standard; 4 080 full load
Dimensions, feet	316 wl; 328 oa × 50 × 14
Guns	varies; up to 10—40 mm AA (2 twin, 6 single) with some modernised ships rearmed with 2—3 inch AA (single) and 6—40 mm AA (twin) several 20 mm AA (twin or single)
Main engines	Diesel (General Motors); 1 700 bhp; 2 shafts = 11·6 knots
Complement	varies: 100 to 125 in most ships

Former US Navy tank landing ships constructed during World War II. Dates transferred to Taiwan China are listed above. These ships have been rebuilt in Taiwan.

LST 211 ex-USS LST 1033 changed to LST 222 on 13 Nov 1957. Other Taiwan pennant numbers in the LST series may have been assigned to more than one ship.

Several LSTs have been stricken: ex-USS LST 717 (no name assigned; acquired in 1946 and reported sunk in 1948); *Chung Cheng* LST 207 ex-USS LST 1075, *Chung Hsun* LST 208 ex-USS LST 993, *Chung Kung* LST 213 ex-USS LST 945, *Chung Yu* LST 215 ex-USS LST 330. One of these ships is believed to have been sunk by Communist Chinese torpedo boats off Quemoy Island on 25 Aug 1958.

CHUNG YUNG

4 Ex-US LSM TYPE

Name	*No.*	*Transferred*
MEI CHIN (ex-USS LSM 155)	LSM 341	May 1946
MEI SUNG (ex-USS LSM 431)	LSM 347	June 1946
MEI PING (ex-USS LSM 471)	LSM 353	Nov 1956
MEI LO (ex-USS LSM 362)	LSM 356	May 1962

Displacement, tons	1 095 full load
Dimensions, feet	196·5 wl; 203·5 oa × 34·5 × 7·3
Guns	2—40 mm AA (twin); 4 or 8—20 mm AA (4 single or 4 twin)
Main engines	Diesels; 2 800 bhp; 2 shafts = 12·5 knots
Complement	65 to 75

Former US Navy medium landing ships constructed during World War II. Originally numbered in the 200-series in Taiwan Chinese service, but changed in 300-series as above. Some numbers may have been assigned to more than one ship. These ships are being rebuilt in Taiwan.

MEI PING

Landing Craft—*continued*

Ex-US LCU TYPE—*continued*

22 Ex-US LCU TYPE

Name	*LCU*	*Name*	*LCU*
HO CHUN (ex-LCU 892)	481	**HO CHUN** (ex-LCU 1225)	494
HO CH'UNG (ex-LCU 1213)	482	**HO YUNG** (ex-LCU 1271)	495
HO CHUNG (ex-LCU 849)	484	**HO CHIEN** (ex-LCU 1278)	496
HO CHANG (ex-LCU 512)	485	**HO CHI** (ex-LCU 1212)	501
HO CHENG (ex-LCU 1145)	486	**HO HOEI** (ex-LCU 1218)	502
HO SHAN (ex-LCU 1596)	488	**HO YAO** (ex-LCU 1244)	503
HO CHUAN (ex-LCU 489)	489	**HO DENG** (ex-LCU 1367)	504
HO SENG (ex-LCU 1598)	490	**HO FENG** (ex-LCU 1397)	505
HO MENG (ex-LCU 1599)	491	**HO CHAO** (es-LCU 1429)	506
HO MOU (ex-LCU 1600)	492	**HO TENG** (ex-LCU 1452)	507
HO SHOU (ex-LCU 1601)	493	**HO CHIE** (ex-LCU 700)	SB 1

LCU 501 series:

Displacement, tons	158 light; 268 full load
Dimensions, feet	115·1 oa × 32 × 4·2
Guns	2—20 mm AA (single); some units also may have 2—·50 cal MG
Main engines	3 diesels; 675 bhp; 3 shafts = 10 knots
Complement	10 to 25 assigned

LCU 1466 series:

Displacment, tons	130 light; 280 full load
Dimensions, feet	115·1 oa × 34 × 4·1
Guns	3—20 mm AA (single); some units may also have 2—·50 cal MG
Main engines	3 diesels; 675 bhp; 3 shafts = 10 knots
Complement	15 to 25 assigned

The LCU 501 series formerly were built in the United States during World War II; initially designated LCT(6) series. LCU 1466 series built by Ishikawajima Heavy Industries Co, Tokyo, Japan, for transfer to Taiwan China; completed in 1955. All originally numbered in 200-series; subsequently changed to 400 and 500-series numbers.

LANDING SHIP INFANTRY AND SUPPORT SERIES

All former US Navy LSI(G), LSI(L), LSI(M), and LSS(L) ships transferred to Taiwan China have been stricken. See 1971-1972 and previous editions for ship lists and characteristics.

HO MOU (LCU 492 ex-LCU 292)

AUXILIARY SHIPS

1 REPAIR SHIP: Ex-US "LIBERTY" TYPE

PIEN TAI (ex-USS *Tutuila*, ARG 4)ARG 516

Displacement, tons	5 766 standard; 14 350 full load
Dimensions, feet	416 wl; 441·5 oa × 57 × 23
Guns	(current armament unknown)
Main engines	Triple expansion (General Machinery Corp), 2 500 ihp; 1 shaft = 12·5 knots
Boilers	2 (Babcock & Wilcox)

"Liberty" ship (EC2) built by Bethlehem Steel Co, Baltimore, Maryland; launched on 12 Sep 1943 and commissioned on 8 Apr 1944. Originally fitted to repair internal combustion engines, but capabilities subsequently expanded. Transferred from active US Fleet to Taiwan China on 21 Feb 1972.

PIEN TAI (ex-USS *Tutuila*)

Auxiliary Ships—*continued*

1 REPAIR SHIP: Ex-US C-3 TYPE

YU TAI (ex-USS *Cadmus*, AR 14) AR 521

Displacement, tons	7 826 standard; 14 490 full load
Dimensions, feet	456 wl; 492 oa × 70 × 27·5
Guns	1—5 inch (*127 mm*) 38 calibre DP
Main engines	Turbines (Westinghouse); 8 500 shp; 1 shaft = 16·5 knots
Boilers	2 (Foster Wheeler)

Former US Navy repair ship built by Tampa Shipbuilding Co, Tampa, Florida; launched on 5 Aug 1945; commissioned on 23 Apr 1946. Transferred to Taiwan China on 15 Jan 1973. A sister ship (ex-USS *Amphion*, AR 13) serves with the Iranian Navy.

1 TRANSPORT: Ex-US LST TYPE

WU TAI (ex-*Sung Shan*, ARL 236, ex-USS *Agenor*, ARL 3, ex-LST 490) AP 520

Displacement, tons	1 625 light; 4 100 full load
Dimensions, feet	316 wl; 328 oa × 50 × 11
Guns	8—40 mm (quad)
Main engines	Diesels (General Motors); 1 800 bhp; 2 shafts = 11·6 knots
Troops	600

Begun for the US Navy as an LST but completed as a repair ship for landing craft (ARL); built by Kaiser Co, Vancouver, Washington; launched on 3 Apr 1943; commissioned on 20 Aug 1943. Transferred to France in 1951 for service in Indochina; subsequently returned to United States and retransferred to Taiwan China on 15 Sep 1957.
Employed as a repair ship (ARL 336, subsequently ARL 236) until converted in 1973-1974 to troop transport.

WU TAI (as repair ship)

1 SURVEYING SHIP: Ex-US C1-M-AV1 TYPE

CHU HWA (ex-USNS *Sgt. George D. Keathley*, T-AGS 35, ex-T-APC 117) AGS 564

Displacement, tons	6 090 tons
Dimensions, feet	338·8 oa × 50·3 × 17·5
Guns	(current armament unknown)
Main engines	Diesel; 1 750 bhp; 1 shaft = 11·5 knots

Built in 1945 as merchant ship; subsequently acquired by US Army for use as transport, but assigned to Navy's Military Sea Transportation Service in 1950 and designated as coastal transport (T-APC 117). Refitted for oceanographic survey work in 1966-1967 and redesignated T-AGS 35. Transferred to Taiwan China on 29 Mar 1972.

1 SURVEYING SHIP: Ex-US AUXILIARY TUG

CHIU LIEN (ex-USS *Geronimo*, ATA 207) AGS 563

Displacement, tons	835
Dimensions, feet	143 oa × 33·9 × 13·2
Main engines	Diesel (General Motors); 1 500 bhp; 1 shaft = 13 knots

Former US Navy auxiliary tug. Built by Gulfport Boiler & Welding Works, Port Arthur, Texas; launched 4 Jan 1945 and commissioned 1 Mar 1945. Transferred to Taiwan China in Feb 1969 and converted to surveying ship. Currently employed as maritime college training ship; Navy manned.

The surveying ship *Lien Chang* AGSC 466 ex-USS LSIL 1017 was stricken in 1972.

CHIU LIEN

1 OILER: Ex-SOVIET MERCHANT TYPE

KUI CHI (ex-Soviet *Tuapse*) AOG 506 (ex-AOG 306)

Displacement, tons	18 100 full load
Dimensions, feet	489·75 × 62·8 oa × 25·4
Guns	AA weapons fitted
Main engines	Diesel; 5 520 bhp; 1 shaft = 14·5 knots
Cargo	11 000 tons fuel

Built by Burmeister & Wain, Copenhagen; completed in 1953 for Soviet merchant service. Seized by Taiwan China forces in Taiwan Straits in June 1954 and subsequently commissioned in naval service; commissioned 20 Oct 1955.

1 OILER: JAPANESE TYPE

WAN SHOU AOG 512

Displacement, tons	1 049 light; 4 150 full load
Dimensions, feet	283·8 oa × 54 × 18
Guns	2—40 mm AA (single); 2—20 mm AA
Main engines	Diesel; 2 100 bhp; 1 shaft = 13 knots
Complement	70
Cargo	73 600 gallons fuel; 62 000 gallons water

Built by Ujina Shipbuilding Co, Hiroshima, Japan for Taiwan China. Commissioned for naval service on 1 Nov 1969. Employed in resupply of offshore islands.

WAN SHOU

3 OILERS: Ex-US 310-ft AOG TYPE

CHANG PEI (ex-USS *Pecatonica* AOG 57)	AOG 507	17 Mar 1945
LUNG CHUAN (ex-HMNZS *Endeavour*, ex-USS *Namakagon*, AOG 53)	AOG 515	4 Nov 1944
HSIN LUNG (ex-USS *Elkhorn* AOG 7)	AOG 516	15 May 1943

Displacement, tons	1 850 light; 4 335 full load
Dimensions, feet	292 wl; 310·75 oa × 48·5 × 15·7
Main engines	Diesels (General Motors); 3 300 bhp; 2 shafts = 14 knots

Former US gasoline tankers of the "Patapsco" class. Built by Cargill, Inc, Savage, Minnesota; launch dates above. The *Chang Pei* was transferred to Taiwan China on 24 Apr 1961. The ex-USS *Namakagon* was transferred to New Zealand on 5 Oct 1962 for use as an Antarctic resupply ship; strengthened for polar operations and renamed *Endeavour*; returned to the US Navy on 29 July 1971 and retransferred to Taiwan China the same date. The *Hsin Lung* was transferred to Taiwan China on 1 July 1972.
The smaller (220·5 ft) *Yu Chuan* AOG 303 ex-USS *Wantanga* AOG 22 stricken in 1959 after running aground; *Hsin Kao* AOG 502 (ex-AOG 302), ex-USS *Towalgia* AOG 42 stricken in 1973.

CHANG PEI

[illegible] (as AOG 304)

Auxiliary Ships—*continued*

KUI CHI—see previous page

1 OILER: Ex-US YO TYPE

SZU MING (ex-US YO 198) AOG 504 (ex-AOG 304)

Displacement, tons	650 light; 1 595 full load
Dimensions, feet	174 oa × 32
Guns	*Szu Ming:* 1—40 mm AA; 5—20 mm AA (single)
Main engines	Diesel (Union); 560 bhp; 1 shaft = 10·5 knots
Complement	approx 65

Former US Navy self-propelled fuel oil barge, built by Manitowoc SB Co, Manitowoc, Wisconsin, in 1945. Transferred to Taiwan China in Dec 1949.

2 OILERS: JAPANESE TYPE

Two small oilers of Japanese construction are also reported to be in service.

DISPOSALS
Ho Lan AO 305, formerly the Polish *Praca* scrapped in 1964; *O Mei* AO 509 (ex-AO 309), formerly the USS *Maumee* AG 124 (ex-AO 2) scrapped in 1967; *Tai Yun* AOG 510 formerly the US YO 175 scrapped in 1972.

1 CARGO SHIP: Ex-US AKL TYPE

YUNG KANG (ex-USS *Mark*, AKL12 ex-AG 143, ex-US Army FS 214) AKL 514

Displacement, tons	approx 700
Dimensions, feet	176·5 oa × 32·8 × 10
Guns	(current armament unknown)
Main engines	Diesel; 1 000 bhp; 1 shaft = 10 knots

Built by Higgins in 1944 as a small cargo ship (freight amd supply) for the US Army. Transferred to US Navy on 30 Sep 1947; operated in Indochina area from 1963 until transferred to Taiwan China on 1 July 1971.

2 TUGS: Ex-US ATA TYPE

TA TUNG (ex-USS *Chickasaw*, ATF 83)	ATF 548	23 July 1942
(ex-USS *Apache*, ATF 67)	ATF 550	8 May 1942

Displacement, tons	1 235 standard; 1 675 full load
Dimensions, feet	195 wl; 205 oa × 38·5 × 15·5
Guns	1—3 inch (*76 mm*) 50 cal AA; several light AA
Main engines	Diesels electric drive; 3 000 bhp; 1 shaft = 15 knots

Former US Navy "Apache" class fleet tugs. Built by United Engineering Co, Alameda, California, and Charleston SB & DD Co, South Carolina, respectively; launch dates above. *Ta Tung* transferred to Taiwan China in January 1966; ex-USS *Apache* on 30 June 1974.

2 TUGS: Ex-US ATR TYPE

TA SUEH (ex-USS *Tonkawa*, ATA 176)	ATR 547	1 Mar 1944
TA TENG (ex-USS *Cahokia*, ATA 186)	ATR 549	18 Sep 1944

Displacement, tons	435 standard; 835 full load
Dimensions, feet	134·5 wl; 143 oa × 33·9 × 13
Guns	1—3 inch (*76 mm*) 50 cal AA; several light AA
Main engines	Diesel-electric (General Motors diesels); 1 500 bhp; 1 shaft = 13 knots

Former US Navy auxiliary ocean tugs. Built by Levingston SB Co, Orange, Texas; launch dates above. *Ta Sueh* transferred to Taiwan China in Apr 1966. *Ta Teng* assigned briefly to US Air Force in 1971; transferred to Taiwan China on 14 Apr 1973. A third tug of this type serves as a surveying ship.

11 TUGS: Ex-US HARBOUR TYPES

TA WU (ex-US Army LT 1)	ATA 542
TA MING (ex-US Army LT 220)	ATA 543
TA YU (ex-US Army LT 310)	ATA 545
TA CHING (ex-US Army LT 355)	ATA

Former US Army harbour tugs; first three ships transferred in 1949 originally numbered in 300-series.

Auxiliary Ships—*continued*

YTL 3 (ex-US Army ST 846)	**YTL 9** (ex-US Army ST 2004)
YTL 8 (ex-US Army ST 2002)	**YTL 10** (ex-US Army ST 2008)

Former US Army 76-foot harbour tugs.

YTL 11 (ex-USN YTL 454) **YTL 12** (ex-USN YTL 584) **YTL 13** (ex-USN YTL 585)

Former US Navy 66-foot harbour tugs.

5 Ex-US FLOATING DRY DOCKS

HAY TAN (ex-USN AFDL 36)	AFDL 1
KIM MEN (ex-USN AFDL 5)	AFDL 2
HAN JIH (ex-USN AFDL 34)	AFDL 3
FO WU 5 (ex-USN ARD 9)	ARD 5
FO WU 6 (ex-USS *Windsor*, ARD 22)	ARD 6

Former US Navy floating dry docks; see United States section for characteristics.

SERVICE CRAFT

Approximately 25 non-self-propelled service craft are in use; most are former US Navy service craft.

CUSTOMS SERVICE

Several small ships and small craft are in service with the Customs Service of Taiwan China, an agency of the Ministry of Finance. The larger ships include two former submarine chasers, listed below.

2 Ex-US PC TYPE

TUNG KIANG (ex-USS *Placerville*, PC 1087)	PC 119	21 Aug 1943
HSI KIANG (ex-USS *Susanville*, PC 1149)	PC 120	11 Jan 1944

Displacement, tons	450 full load
Dimensions, feet	173·66 oa × 23 × 10·8
Guns	1—3 inch (*76 mm*)) 50 cal AA; several lighter guns
Main engines	Diesels (General Motors); 2 880 bhp; 2 shafts = 20 knots

Former US Navy steel-hulled submarine chasers. Launch dates above. Originally transferred to Taiwan China for naval use; subsequently allocated to the Customs Service. Armament believed to have been retained.

TANZANIA

Mercantile Marine

Lloyd's Register of Shipping: 11 vessels of 18 218 tons gross

6 Ex-CHINESE "SHANGHAI" CLASS

(FAST ATTACK CRAFT—GUN)

Displacement, tons	100 full load
Dimensions, feet	120·0 × 18·0 × 6·0
Guns	4—37 mm (twin fore and aft)
Main engines	4 diesels; 4 800 bhp = 28 knots

Transferred by the Chinese People's Republic in 1970-71. A further pair may now be held.
There are reported to be four small patrol boats, two of 50 tons and two of 27 tons.

THAILAND

Administration

Commander-in-Chief of the Navy:
Admiral Sa-Ngad Chaloryoo Chanien Ruchibon

Deputy Commander-in-Chief:
Admiral Kamol Sitakalin

Chief of Staff (RTN):
Vice-Admiral Amorn Sirigaya

Commander-in-Chief, Fleet:
Admiral Ching Chullasukum

Diplomatic Representation

Naval Attaché in London:
Captain Sam-Arng Kresopon

Naval Attaché in Washington:
Captain Kasem Rakcharcon

Personnel

(a) 1975: *Navy,* 22 000 (2 000 officers and 18 000 ratings) including *Marine Corps:* 7000 (500 officers and 6 500 men)
(b) 2 years National Service

Strength of the Fleet

(No building programme known)

Type	*Active*
Frigates	7
Corvettes	14
Large Patrol Craft	14
Coastal Patrol Craft	16
Coastal Minelayers	6
MW Support Ship	1
MSB's	10
LST's	4
LSM's	3
LCG	1
LCI's	2
LCT's	6
LCM's	26
LCVP's	6
Survey Vessels	3
Support Tankers	2
Harbour Tankers	4
Water Boats	2
Tugs	4

Bases

Bangkok, Sattahip, Songkhla. A new base on the West coast has been reported.

New Construction

There is a reported interest in further new construction.

Disposals

Frigates

1973 *Bangpakong,*

Large Patrol Craft

1973 *SC 7*

Coastal Patrol Craft

1973 *CGC1* and *11, T 31, 33, 34* and *35*

Prefix to Ships' Names

HTMS.

Mercantile Marine

Lloyd's Register of Shipping:
80 vessels of 176 315 tons gross

FRIGATES

Name	*No.*	*Builders*	*Laid down*	*Launched*	*Completed*
MAKUT RAJAKUMARN	7	Yarrow & Co. Ltd. Scotstoun.	11 Jan 1970	18 Nov 1971	7 May 1973

Displacement, tons	1 780 standard; 1 900 full load
Length, feet (*metres*)	320·0 (*97·6*) oa
Beam, feet (*metres*)	36·0 (*11·0*)
Draught, feet (*metres*)	15·4 (*4·7*)
Missile launchers	1 quadruple Seacat
Guns	2—4·5 in Mk 8 (*114 mm*) (single) 2—40 mm 60 cal Bofors (single)
A/S weapons	1 triple barrelled Limbo mortar; 1 DC rack; 2 depth charge throwers
Main engines	1 Rolls-Royce Olympus gas Turbine; 23 125 shp; 1 Crossley-Pielstick 12 PC2V diesel; 6 000 bhp
Speed, knots	26, 18 on diesel
Range, miles	5 000 at 18 knots (diesel) 1 200 at 26 knots
Complement	140 (16 officers, 124 ratings)

An order was placed with Yarrow & Co Ltd, Scotstoun, Glasgow on 21 Aug 1969 for a general purpose frigate. A long range vessel of a new design developed by Yarrow resulting in a comparative low cost ship with an armament/displacement ratio superior to that of any comparable warship. The ship is largely automated with a consequent saving in complement, and has been most successful in service. Fitted as flagship.

ELECTRONICS. HSA CIC system. Racal DF.

RADAR. LW 04 air surveillance amidships; M 20 series fire control system with co-mounted search and tracking radars in radome for guns; M 44 aft for seacat. NAVIGATION. Decca type 626. IFF—UK Mod Mk 10. Missile control—H. Signaal WM 22 and VM 44.

SONAR. UK Mod Type 170 and Plessey Type MS 27.

MAKUT RAJAKUMARN *1973, W Ralston Ltd.*

TAPI 5 **KHIRIRAT** 6

Displacement, tons	900 standard; 1 135 full load
Length, feet (*metres*)	275 (*83·8*) oa
Beam, feet (*metres*)	33 (*10·0*)
Draught, feet (*metres*)	10 (*3·0*)
Guns	2—3 in (*76 mm*) 2—40 mm
A/S weapons	Torpedoes, DCs, Hedgehogs
Main engines	FM Diesels; 6 000 bhp
Speed, knots	20

Of similar design to the Iranian ships of the "Bayandor" class. *Tapi* was ordered from the American Shipbuilding Co, Toledo, Ohio on June 27 1969 laid down 1 Apr 1970, launched 17 Oct 1970 and completed 1 Nov 1971. *Khirirat* was ordered from Norfolk SB & DD Co on 25 June 1971, laid down 18 Feb 1972 and completed 10 August 1974.

MAKUT RAJAKUMARN *1973, Wright & Logan*

Frigates—*continued*

Name	*No.*	*Builders*	*Launched*	*Completed*
PIN KLAO (ex-USS *Hemminger DE* 746)	3 (ex-1)	Western Pipe & Steel Co	12 Sep 1943	30 May 1944

Displacement, tons	1 240 standard; 1 900 full load
Length, feet (*metres*)	306·0 (*93·3*) oa
Beam, feet (*metres*)	37·0 (*11·3*)
Draught, feet (*metres*)	14·1 (*4·3*)
Guns	3—3 in (*76 mm*) 50 cal 6—40 mm
A/S weapons	8 DCT
Torpedo tubes	6 (2 triple) for A/S torpedoes
Main engines	GM diesels with electric drive; 2 shafts; 6 000 bhp
Speed, knots	20
Range, miles	11 500 at 11 knots
Oil fuel, tons	300
Complement	220

Ex-US "Cannon" class. Transferred from US Navy to Royal Thai Navy at New York Navy Shipyard in July 1959 under MDAP. The 3—21 in torpedo tubes were removed and the 4—20 mm AA guns were replaced by 4—40 mm AA. The six A/S torpedo tubes were fitted in 1966. Finally purchased 1975.

PIN KLAO 1966, *Royal Thai Navy*

2 "PRASAE" CLASS

Name	*No.*	*Builders*	*Laid down*	*Launched*	*Completed*
PRASAE (ex-USS *Gallup, PF* 47)	2	Consolidated Steel Corpn, Los Angeles	18 Aug 1943	17 Sep 1943	29 Feb 1944
TAHCHIN (ex-USS *Glendale, PF* 36)	1	Consolidated Steel Corpn, Los Angeles	6 Apr 1943	28 May 1943	1 Oct 1943

Displacement, tons	1 430 standard; 2 100 full load
Length, feet (*metres*)	304·0 (*92·7*) oa
Beam, feet (*metres*)	37·5 (*11·4*)
Draught, feet (*metres*)	13·7 (*4·2*)
Guns	3—3 in (*76 mm*) 50 cal. 2—40 mm; 9—20 mm
A/S weapons	8 DCT
Main engines	Triple expansion; 2 shafts; 5 500 ihp
Speed, knots	19
Boilers	2 small water tube 3-drum type
Oil fuel, tons	685
Range, miles	7 800 at 12 knots
Complement	180

Former US patrol frigates of the "Tacoma" class. Delivered to the Royal Thai Navy on 29 Oct 1951. They were of similar design to the British frigates of the "River" class. *Prasea* partially non-operational after collision in Jan 1972.

PRASAE 1971

1 Ex-BRITISH "ALGERINE" CLASS

PHOSAMTON (ex-HMS *Minstrel*) MSF 1

Displacement, tons	1 040 standard; 1 335 full load
Length, feet (*metres*)	225·0 (*68·6*) oa
Beam, feet (*metres*)	35·5 (*10·8*)
Draught, feet (*metres*)	10·5 (*3·2*)
Guns	1—4 in (*102 mm*) 6—20 mm
A/S weapons	4 DCT
Main engines	Triple expansion; 2 shafts; 2 000 ihp
Speed, knots	16
Boilers	2 three-drum type
Oil fuel, tons	270
Range, miles	5 000 at 10 knots
Complement	103

Former British "Algerine" class ocean minesweeper capable of fleet sweeping and escort duties. Built by Redfern Construction Co. Laid down in 1943, launched on 5 Oct 1944, completed in 1945. Transferred in Apr 1947. The 20 mm guns were increased from 3 to 6, and the DCTs from 2 to 4 in 1966. Marginally operational—now used for training.

PHOSAMTON 1965 *Royal Thai Navy*

MAEKLONG No. 3

Displacement, tons	1 400 standard; 2 000 full load
Length, feet (*metres*)	269·0 (*82·0*)
Beam, feet (*metres*)	34·0 (*10·4*)
Draught, feet (*metres*)	10·5 (*3·2*)
Guns	4—4·7 in (*120 mm*) 3—40 mm; 3—20 mm
Main engines	Triple expansion; 2 shafts; 2 500 ihp
Speed, knots	14
Boilers	2 water tube
Oil fuel, tons	487
Range, miles	8 000 at 12 knots
Complement	155 as training ship

Built by Uraga Dock Co, Japan. Laid down in 1936, launched on 27 Nov 1936, completed in June 1937. Designed as dual-purpose sloop and torpedo boat. Employed as training ship. The 4—18 inch torpedo tubes were removed. Sister ship *Tachin*, heavily damaged on 1 June 1945, was scrapped.

MAEKLONG 1967, *Royal Thai Navy*

CORVETTES

7 "TRAD" CLASS

CHANDHABURI 16 Dec 1936 No. 22
CHUMPORN 18 Jan 1937 No. 31
PATTANI 16 Oct 1936 No. 13
PUKET 28 Sep 1935 No. 12
RAYONG 11 Jan 1937 No. 23
SURASDRA 28 Nov 1936 No. 21
TRAD 26 Oct 1935 No. 11

Displacement, tons	318 standard; 470 full load
Dimensions, feet	219 pp; 223 oa × 21 × 7
Guns	2—3 in AA; 1—40 mm AA; 2—20 mm AA; *Chumporn, Puket* and *Trad* 2—40 mm
Tubes	4—18 in (2 twin); *Chumporn, Puket* and *Trad* 2—18 in (twin)
Main engines	Parsons geared turbines; 2 shafts; 9 000 hp = 31 knots
Boilers	2 Yarrow
Oil fuel, tons	102
Range, miles	1 700 at 15 knots
Complement	70

Designed as torpedo boats, *Puket* and *Trad* were laid down on 8 Feb 1935 by Cantieri Riuniti dell' Adriatico, Monfalcone, for delivery by end of 1935. Launch dates above. Armament was supplied by Vickers-Armstrongs Ltd. First boat reached 32·34 knots on trials with 10 000 hp. All delivered by summer 1937. The 2 single 18 inch torpedo tubes and the 4—8 mm guns were removed.

TRAD

7 "LIULOM" CLASS (Ex US PC s)

LIULOM (ex-*PC* 1253) PC 7
LONGLOM (ex-*PC* 570) PC 8
PHALI (ex-*PC* 1185) PC 4
SARASIN (ex-*PC* 495) PC 1
SUKRIP (ex-*PC* 1218) PC 5
THAYANCHON (ex-*PC* 575) PC 2
TONGPLIU (ex-*PC* 616) PC 6

Displacement, tons	280 standard; 400 full load
Dimensions, feet	174 oa × 23·2 × 6
Guns	1—3 in AA; 1—40 mm AA; 5—20 mm AA
A/S weapons	2 ASW torpedo tubes (except *Sarasin*)
Main engines	Diesel, 2 shafts; 3 600 bhp = 19 knots
Oil fuel, tons	60
Range, miles	6 000 at 10 knots
Complement	62 to 71, *Sukeip* 69 (10 officers, 59 men)

Former US submarine chasers. Launched in 1941-43.

THAYANCHON *1969, Royal Thai Navy*

LIGHT FORCES

3 LÜRSSEN 45-METRE TYPE

(FAST ATTACK CRAFT—MISSILE)

It is reported that an order was placed in Singapore in June 1973 for three of these 230 ton craft (see Singapore section for full details). It is probable that Gabriel missiles will be mounted.

3 "KLONGYAI" CLASS (LARGE PATROL CRAFT)

KANTANG No. 7 **KLONGYAI** No. 5 **SATTAHIP** No. 8

Displacement, tons	110 standard; 135 full load
Dimensions, feet	131·5 × 15·5 × 4
Guns	1—3 in 1—20 mm
Tubes	2—18 in
Main engines	Geared turbines = 2 shafts; 1 000 shp = 19 knots
Boilers	2 water-tube
Range, miles	480 at 15 knots
Oil fuel, tons	18
Complement	31

Sattahip was built by the Royal Thai Naval Dockyard, Bangkok, laid down on 21 Nov 1956, launched on 28 Oct 1957 and completed in 1958. The other two were built by Ishikawajima Co, Japan, both launched on 26 Mar 1937 and completed on 21 June 1937.

Light Forces—*continued*

3 THAI DESIGN (PATROL CRAFT—COASTAL)

T 91 **T 92** **T 93**

Displacement, tons	87·5 standard
Dimensions, feet	104·3 × 17·5 × 5·5
Guns	1—40 mm AA; 1—20 mm AA
Main engines	Diesels; 1 600 bhp = 25 knots
Complement	21

Built by the Royal Thai Naval Dockyard, Bangkok, Completed 1971.

T 91 *1970, Royal Thai Navy*

10 LARGE PATROL CRAFT

T 11 (ex-US *PGM* 71)
T 12 (ex-US *PGM* 79)
T 13 (ex-US *PGM* 107)
T 14 (ex-US *PGM* 116)
T 15 (ex-US *PGM* 117)
T 16 (ex-US *PGM* 115)
T 17 (ex-US *PGM 113*)
T 18 (ex-US *PGM 114*)
T 19 (ex-US *PGM* 123)
T 110 (ex-US *PGM* 124)

Displacement, tons	130 standard; 147 full load
Dimensions, feet	99·0 wl; 101·0 oa × 21·0 × 6·0
Guns	1—40 mm AA; 4—20 mm AA; 2—·50 cal
Main engines	Diesels; 2 shafts; 1 800 bhp = 18·5 knots
Range, miles	1 500 at 10 knots
Complement	30

T 11 was built by Peterson Builders Inc, launched on 5 May 1965 and transferred to the Royal Thai Navy on 1 Feb 1966. T 13 was transferred 28 Aug 1967, T 14, T 15 on 18 Aug 1969 and 2 Oct 1969, T 16, T 17, and T 18 on 12 Feb 1970, T 19 on 25 Dec 1970 and T 110 in Oct 1970.

T 12 *1969, Royal Thai Navy*

1 Ex-US SC TYPE (LARGE PATROL CRAFT)

SC 8 (ex *SC*-32, ex-US *SC* 1633)

Displacement, tons	110 light; 125 full load
Dimensions, feet	111 × 17 × 6
Gun	1—40 mm; 3—20 mm
A/S weapons	Depth charges, Mousetrap
Main engines	High-speed diesel = 18 knots
Range, miles	2 000 at 10 knots

Former US wooden submarine chaser. Built by South Coast Co, Newport Reach, California, in 1954-55. Non-operational.

7 Ex-US "SWIFT" CLASS (COASTAL PATROL CRAFT)

T 21 **T 22** **T 23** **T 24** **T 25** **T 26** **T 27**

Displacement, tons	20 standard, 22 full load
Dimensions, feet	50 × 13
Guns	2—0·50 cal (1 twin)
Main engines	Diesels; 2 shafts; 480 bhp = 25 knots
Complement	5

"Swift" class patrol craft transferred from USN; T22 in Aug 1968, T23-25 in Feb 1970. T21 in May 1970, T26 in Mar 1970, T27 in Apr 1970.

3 Ex-US RPC TYPE (COASTAL PATROL CRAFT)

T 32 **T 35** **T 36**

Displacement, tons	10·4 standard; 13·05 full load
Dimensions, feet	35 × 10
Guns	2—0·50 cal (1 twin); 2—0·30 cal
Main engines	Diesels; 2 shafts; 225 bhp = 14 knots
Complement	7

Transferred Mar 1967.

There are reports that a patrol of Riverine Craft is maintained on the Upper Mekong although details are not available.

Light Forces—*continued*

5 COASTAL PATROL CRAFT

CGC 11 **CGC 13** **CGC 14** **CGC 15** **CGC 16**

Displacement, tons	95
Dimensions, feet	95 × 20·2 × 5
Guns	1—20 mm AA
A/S weapons	2 D.C. racks; 2 Mousetraps
Main engines	4 diesels; 2 shafts; 2 200 bhp = 21 knots
Range, miles	1 500 at 14 knots
Complement	15

US coastguard cutters transferred in 1954. Similar to those built for U.S.C.G. by US Coast Guard Yard, Curtis Bay, in 1953. Cost £475,000 each.

CGC 14 *Royal Thai Navy*

MINE WARFARE FORCES

2 "BANGRACHAN" CLASS (COASTAL MINELAYERS)

BANGRACHAN MMC 1 **NHONG SARHAI** MMC 2

Displacement, tons	368 standard; 408 full load
Dimensions, feet	160·8 × 25·9 × 7·2
Guns	2—3 in AA; 2—20 mm AA
Mines	142 capacity
Main engines	Burmeister & Wain diesels; 2 shafts; 540 bhp = 12 knots
Oil fuel, tons	18
Range, miles	2 700 at 10 knots
Complement	55

Launched by Cantiere dell'Adriatico, Monfalcone in 1936.

BANGRACHAN

4 US "BLUEBIRD" CLASS (MINESWEEPERS—COASTAL)

BANGKEO (ex-USS *MSC* 303) 6 **LADYA** (ex-USS *MSC* 297) 5
DONCHEDI (ex-USS *MSC* 313) 8 **TADINDENG** (ex-USS *MSC* 301) 7

Displacement, tons	330 standard; 362 full load
Dimensions, feet	145·3 oa × 27 × 8·5
Guns	2—20 mm AA
Main engines	4 GM diesels; 2 shafts; 1 000 bhp = 13 knots
Range, miles	2 500 at 10 knots
Complement	43 (7 officers, and 36 men)

Built by Peterson Builders Inc. Sturgeon Bay, Wisc, (*Ladya* and *Donchedi*), Tacoma Boat building Co, Tacoma, Wash. (*Tadindeng*) and Dorchester Shipbuilding Corp, Camden (*Bangkeo*) as new construction for Thailand. *Ladya* was delivered on 14 Dec 1963, *Bangkeo* on 9 July 1965, *Tadindeng* on 26 Aug 1965, and *Donchedi* on 17 Sep 1965.

BANGKEO *1971*

RANG KWIEN (ex-*Umihari Maru*) MCS 11 (MW SUPPORT SHIP)

Displacement, tons	586 standard
Dimensions, feet	162·3 × 31·2 × 13·0 max
Main engines	Triple expansion steam; Speed = 10 knots

Built in 1944 by Mitsubishi Co as a tug. Acquired by Royal Thai Navy on 6 Sep 1967.

RANG KWIEN *1969, Royal Thai Navy*

5 MSB

MSML 6-10

Thai built, 50 ft.

5 MSB

MSML 1-5

Thai built. 40 ft.

AMPHIBIOUS FORCES

4 Ex-US LST TYPE

ANGTHONG (ex-USS *LST* 294) LST 1
CHANG (ex-USS *Lincoln County LST* 898) LST 2
LANTA (ex-USS *Stone County LST* 1141) LST 4
PANGAN (ex-USS *Stark County LST* 1134) LST 3

Displacement, tons	1 625 standard; 4 080 full load
Dimensions, feet	316 wl; 328 oa × 50 × 14
Guns	6—40 mm; 4—20 mm
Main engines	GM diesels; 2 shafts; 1 700 bhp = 11knots
Range, miles	9 500 at 9 knots
Complement	80

Angthong is employed as training ship. *Chang*, transferred to Thailand in 1962, was built by Dravo Corp, laid down on 15 Oct 1944, launched on 25 Nov 1944 and completed on 29 Dec 1944. *Pangan* was transferred on 16 May 1966 and *Lanta* on 12 Mar 1970.

CHANG *1965, Royal Thai Navy*

3 Ex-US LSM TYPE

KRAM (ex-USS *LSM* 469) LSM 3 **KUT** (ex-USS *LSM* 338) LSM 1
PHAI (ex-USS *LSM* 333) LSM 2

Displacement, tons	743 standard; 1 095 full load
Dimensions, feet	196·5 wl; 203·5 oa × 34·5 × 8·3
Guns	2—40 mm AA
Main engines	Diesel direct drive; 2 shafts; 2 800 bhp = 12·5 knots
Range, miles	2 500 at 12 knots
Complement	55

Former United States landing ship of the LCM, later LSM (Medium Landing Ship), type. *Kram* was transferred to Thailand under MAP at Seattle, Wash, on 25 May 1962; she was built by Brown Shipbuilding Col, Houston, Tex, laid down on 27 Jan 1945, launched on 17 Feb 1945, and completed on 17 Mar 1945.

NAKA (ex-USS *LSSL* 102) LSSL 3 (LCG)

Displacement, tons	233 standard; 287 full load
Dimensions, feet	152 wl; 158 oa × 23 × 4·25
Guns	1—3 inch; 4—40 mm AA; 4—20 mm AA; 4—81 mm mortar
Main engines	Diesels; 2 shafts; 1 320 bhp = 15 knots
Range, miles	4 700 at 10 knots

Transferred in 1966. Acquired when Japan returned her to USA.

2 Ex-US LCI TYPE

PRAB (ex-*LCI M* 670) LCI 1 **SATAKUT** (ex-*LCI M* 739) LCI 2

Displacement, tons	230 standard; 387 full load
Dimensions, feet	157 × 23 × 6
Guns	2—20 mm AA
Main engines	Diesel; 2 shafts; 1 320 bhp = 14 knots
Complement	54

Former United States landing craft of the LCI (infantry Landing Craft) type. *Prab* non-operational

26 Ex-US LCM 6

14-16, 61-68, 71-78, 81-82, 85-87.

First 21 delivered 1969.

6 Ex-US LCVP

Amphibious Forces—*continued*

6 LCU Ex-US LCT (6) TYPE

ARDANG LCU 3 **MATAPHON** LCU 1 **RAWI** LCU 2
KOLUM LCU 5 **PHETRA** LCU 4 **TALIBONG** LCU 6

Displacement, tons 134 standard; 279 full load
Dimensions, feet 112 × 32 × 4
Guns 2—20 mm AA
Main engines Diesel; 3 shafts; 675 bhp = 10 knots
Complement 37

Former United States landing craft of the LCT (6) type. Employed as transport ferries.

LCAs

There is also a large but unknown number of Thai-built LCAs.

SURVEY SHIP

CHANDHARA AGS 11

Displacement, tons 870 standard; 996 full load
Dimensions, feet 229·2 oa × 34·5 × 10
Gun 1—20 mm AA
Main engines 2 diesels; 2 shafts; 1 000 bhp = 13·25 knots
Range, miles 10 000 (cruising)
Complement 72

Built by C. Melchers & Co, Bremen, Germany. Laid down on 27 Sep 1960. Launched on 17 Dec 1960. Can also be used as training ship and yacht.

CHANDHARA *1962, Royal Thai Navy*

2 OCEANOGRAPHIC CRAFT

Of 90 tons, with a crew of 8 launched in 1955

SUPPORT FORCES

CHULA AO 2 (SUPPORT TANKER)

Displacement, tons 2 395 standard
Dimensions, feet 328 × 43·2 × 25
Main engines Steam turbines

This tanker and *Matra* (see below) were acquired for naval oiling and supply duties.

CHULA *1969, Royal Thai Navy*

MATRA AO 3 (SUPPORT TANKER)
Displacement, tons 4 744
Dimensions, feet 328 × 45·2 × 20
Main engines Steam turbine

Employed as a freighting and fleet replenishment tanker and naval supply ship.

SAMED (HARBOUR TANKER)

Displacement, tons 360 standard; 485 full load
Dimensions, feet 120 × 20 × 10
Main engines Diesel; 500 bhp = 9 knots

Built by Royal Thai Naval Dockyard, Bangkok. Launched on 8 July 1966. Commissioned on 15 Dec 1970.

Support Forces—*continued*

SAMUI (ex-USS YOG 60) YO 4 (HARBOUR TANKER)

Displacement, tons 422 standard
Dimensions, feet 174·5 × 32 × 15
Main engines Diesel; 2 shafts; 600 bhp = 8 knots
Complement 29

Small tanker of the ex-YOG type. Employed as a fleet auxiliary attendant oiler.

PROET (HARBOUR TANKER)

Displacement, tons 360
Dimensions, feet 122·7 × 19·7 × 8·7
Main engines Diesels; 500 bhp = 9 knots

Built by the Royal Thai Naval Dockyard, Bangkok. Commissioned on 16 Jan 1970.

PRONG YO 5 (HARBOUR TANKER)

Displacement, tons 150 standard
Dimensions, feet 95 × 18 × 7·5
Main engines Diesel; 150 bhp = 10 knots
Complement 14

Launched in 1938. Employed as a small naval auxiliary servicing tanker.

SICHANG AKL 1 (TRANSPORT)

Displacement, tons 815 standard
Dimensions, feet 160 × 28 × 16
Main engines Diesel; 2 shafts; 550 bhp = 16 knots
Complement 30

Built by Harima Co, Japan. *Sichang* was launched on 10 Nov 1937. Completed in Jan 1938.

KLED KEO AF 7 (TRANSPORT)

Displacement, tons 382 standard; 450 full load
Dimensions, feet 154·9 × 25·4 × 14
Guns 3—20 mm
Main engines 1 diesel; 600 hp = 12 knots
Complement 54

Operates with patrol boat squadron.

CHUANG YW 8 (WATER BOAT)

Displacement, tons 305 standard; 485 full load
Dimensions, feet 98 × 18 × 7·2
Main engines GM diesel; 500 bhp = 11 knots
Complement 29

Built by the Royal Thai Naval Dockyard, Bangkok. Launched on 14 Jan 1965.

CHAN YW 6 (WATER BOAT)

Displacement, tons 355 standard
Dimensions, feet 139·5 × 24 × 10
Main engines Diesel; Speed = 6 knots

Probably non-operational.

4 TUGS

SAMAE SAN (ex-*Empire Vincent*) YTM 1

Displacement, tons 503 full load
Dimensions, feet 105·0 × 26·5 × 13·0
Main engines Triple expansion; 850 ihp = 10·5 knots
Complement 27

Built by Cochrane & Sons Ltd., Selby, Yorks, England.

KLUENG BADAN (ex-USN *YTL*) YTL 2 **RAD** (ex-USN *YTL*) YTL 1
MARN VICHAI (ex-USN *YTL*) YTL 3

Displacement, tons 63 standard (*Rad* 52 standard)
Dimensions, feet 64·7 × 16·5 × 6·0 (*Rad* 60·7 × 17·5 × 5·0)
Main engines Diesels; speed = 8 knots (*Rad* 6 knots)

Rad transferred 1955 from US, the other pair bought from Canada 1953.

TRINIDAD AND TOBAGO

COAST GUARD

Administration

Commanding Officer, T. & T. Coast Guard: Captain D. F. A. Bloom MOM, GM

Personnel

(a) 1975: 200 (25 officers, 175 ratings)
(b) Voluntary

Mercantile Marine

Lloyd's Register of Shipping: 31 vessels of 15 574 tons gross

PATROL CRAFT

2 LATER VOSPER TYPE

BUCCO REEF CG 4 — **CHAGUARAMUS** CG 3

Displacement, tons	100 standard; 125 full load
Dimensions, feet	95·0 wl; 103·0 × 19·8 × 5·8
Gun	1—20 mm Hispano Suiza
Main engines	2 Paxman Ventura diesels; 2 900 bhp = 24 knots
Oil fuel, tons	20
Range, miles	2 000 at 13 knots
Complement	19 (3 officers, 16 ratings)

Chaguaramus was laid down on 1 Feb 1971 and launched on 29 Mar 1971. Both commissioned at Portsmouth on 18 Mar 1972. Fitted with modern navigational equipment, air-conditioning and roll-damping.

CHAGUARAMUS — *1972, Wright & Logan*

2 VOSPER TYPE

COURLAND BAY CG 2 — **TRINITY** CG 1

Displacement, tons	96 standard; 123 full load
Dimensions, feet	95·0 wl; 102·6 oa × 19·7 × 5·5
Gun	1—40 mm Bofors
Main engines	2 Vee-form 12 cyl Paxman Ventura YJCM turbo-charged diesels; 2 910 bhp = 24·5 knots
Oil fuel, tons	18
Range, miles	1 800 at 13·5 knots
Complement	17 (3 officers, 14 ratings)

Designed and built by Vosper Limited, Portsmouth. Of steel construction with aluminium alloy superstructure. Up-to-date radar and navigational equipment is fitted, and the boats are air-conditioned throughout except the engine room. Vosper roll-damping equipment is fitted for improved sea-keeping and greater efficiency and comfort of the crews. Laid down Oct 1963. *Trinity* was launched on 14 Apr 1964. Both were commissioned at Portsmouth on 20 Feb 1965. *Trinity* is named after Trinity Hills, so named by Columbus on making his landfall in 1498, and *Courland Bay* after a bay in Tobago where a settlement was founded by the Duke of Courland in the 17th century.

COURLAND BAY — *1972, Trinidad & Tobago Coast Guard*

1 60 ft TYPE

SEA HAWK

Dimensions, feet	60 × 17·3 × 3·5
Gun	1 machine gun
Main engines	2 Rolls Royce diesels; 250 hp = 14·5 knots
Range, miles	400
Complement	6 (1 officer, 5 men)

Built by J. Taylor (Shipbuilders) Ltd, Shoreham-by-Sea. Extensively refitted in 1969; but taken out of service in Dec 1971 and placed in reserve.

1 45 ft TYPE

SEA SCOUT CG 5

Length, feet	45·0
Main engines	1 GM 671 diesel; speed = 12 knots

Built by J. Taylor (Shipbuilders) Ltd, Shoreham-by-Sea. Refitted in 1970 with a single GM 671 diesel in place of the former two Perkins diesels.

SEA SCOUT — *1972, Trinidad & Tobago Coast Guard*

4 INSHORE TYPE

CG 6 **CG 7** **CG 8** **CG 9**

Three Glastron glass fibre runabouts and one locally built (also of glass fibre), all capable of 27 knots, are used for inshore patrol work, mainly in the Gulf of Paria.

TONGA

On 10 Mar 1973 King Taufa 'ahau Tupou IV commissioned the first craft of Tonga's Maritime Force, a necessary service in a Kingdom of seven main groups of islands spread over 270 square miles.

Mercantile Marine

Lloyd's Register of Shipping: 9 vessels of 9 081 tons gross

NGAHAU KOULA P 101

Length, feet	40
Gun	1—·50 Browning MG
Main engines	2 Cummins V8 Diesels = 29 knots
Complement	5

Fitted with Decca Super 100 radar, DF and echo-sounder (Ferrograph). Manned by volunteers from the Royal Guard and Tongan Defence Force.

NGAHAU KOULA — *1973 Statham*

TOGO

Togo, which proclaimed independence on 27 April 1960 and has a port at Lomé operates one 130 ft patrol vessel, three 100 ft patrol vessels, and one 95 ft river gunboat. Personnel is 250 officers and men.

TUNISIA

Administration

Chief of Naval Staff: Capitaine de Fregate Jedidi Bechir

Personnel

(a) 1975: 2 100 officers and men
(b) 1 year National Service

Strength of the Fleet

Type	*Active*	*Building*
Frigate	1	—
Corvette	1	1
MSC	1	—
Large Patrol Craft	3	—
Coastal Patrol Craft	12	—
Tug	1	—

Mercantile Marine

Lloyd's Register of Shipping:
25 vessels of 28 561 tons gross

FRIGATE

1 Ex-US "SAVAGE" CLASS

PRÉSIDENT BOURGUIBA (ex-USS *Thomas J. Gary* DER 326) E 7

Displacement, tons	1 590 standard; 2 100 full load
Dimensions, ft (*m*)	306 oa × 36·6 × 14 (*93·3 × 11·1 × 4·3*)
Guns	2—3 in (*76 mm*) 50 cal; 2—20 mm
Torpedo tubes	2 triple Mk 32
A/S weapon	1 Hedgehog
Main engines	4 diesels; 6 000 bhp; 2 shafts = 19 knots
Range, miles	11 500 at 11 knots
Complement	169

Built by Consolidated Steel Corpn. Completed 27 Nov 1943. Converted to Radar Picket in 1958. Transferred 27 Oct 1973.

RADAR. SPS 28 and SPS 10.

PRÉSIDENT BOURGUIBA *1974, Tunisian Navy*

CORVETTE

1 FRENCH A-69 TYPE AVISO

Displacement, tons	950 standard; 1 260 full load
Dimensions, feet	262·5 oa × 33·8 × 9·8
Guns	1—3·9 in AA (100 mm); 1—40 mm; 4—20 mm
A/S weapons	1 sextuple Mk 64 rocket launcher (375 mm) 4 fixed torpedo launchers for homing torpedoes
Main engines	2 SEMT Pielstick PC2V Diesels; 2 shafts; c-p propellers; 1 100 shp = 24 knots
Range, miles	4 500 at 15 knots
Complement	62

Ordered from France in 1972. (See Coastal minesweeper below).

TYPE A69

1 Ex-FRENCH "FOUGEUX" CLASS

SAKIET SIDI YOUSSEF (ex-*UW 12*) P 303

Displacement, tons	325 standard; 440 full load
Dimensions, feet	170 pp × 23 × 6·5
Guns	1—40 mm; 2—20 mm
A/S weapons	1 hedgehog; 4 DCT; 2 DC racks
Main engines	4 Pielstick-SEMT diesels; 3 240 bhp = 18·7 knots
Range, miles	2 000 at 15 knots
Complement	4 officers, 59 men

Patrol vessel of the "Fougueux" class. Built in France by Dubigeon, Nantes, under US off-shore order. Purchased by Federal Germany in 1957 and served as A/S trials vessel. Transferred to Tunisia in Dec 1969.

SAKIET SIDI YOUSSEF *1974, Tunisian Navy*

COASTAL MINESWEEPER

1 Ex-US "ACACIA" CLASS

HANNIBAL (ex-*Coquelicot* ex-USN MSC 84)

Displacement, tons	320 standard; 372 full load
Dimensions, ft (*m*)	141 oa × 26 × 8·3 (*43 × 8 × 2·6*)
Guns	2—20 mm
Main engines	2 GM Diesels; 2 shafts; 1 200 bhp = 13 knots
Oil fuel, tons	40
Range, miles	2 500 at 10 knots
Complement	38

Built for France under MDAP in 1951-54 in USA. Transferred to France in 1953 and to Tunisia in 1973. On loan until such time as the A 69 Type Aviso is completed.

HANNIBAL *1974, Tunisian Navy*

LIGHT FORCES

3 "P 48" CLASS (LARGE PATROL CRAFT)

BIZERTE P 301 **HORRIA** (ex-*Liberté*) P 302 **MONASTIR** P 304

Displacement, tons	250
Dimensions, feet	157·5 × 23·3 × 7
Guns	2—40 mm AA
Main engines	2 diesels; 4 800 bhp = 20 knots
Range, miles	2 000 at 16 knots

Built by Ch Franco-Belges (Villeneuve, la Garenne). Ordered in 1968. *Bizerte* was launched on 20 Nov 1969 and completed 10 July 1970. *Horria* launched 12 Feb 1970 and completed Oct 1970. *Monastir* ordered from Soc. Francaise Constructions Navale in Aug 1973, laid down Jan 1974, launched 25 June 1974 and completed Feb 1975.

BIZERTE *1974, Tunisian Navy*

4 32-metre COASTAL PATROL CRAFT

EL JALA P 203
ISTIKLAL (ex-*VC* 11, *P* 761) P 201
JOUMHOURIA P 202
REMADA P 204

Displacement, tons	60 standard; 82 full load
Dimensions, ft (*m*)	104·5 × 15·5 × 5·6 (*31·5* × *5·8* × *1·7*)
Gun	1—20 mm
Main engines	2 Mercedes-Benz diesels; 2 shafts; 2 700 bhp = 28 knots
Range, miles	1 400 at 15 knots
Complement	17

Built by Ch Navale d'Esterel. *Istiklal* transferred Mar 1959; *El Jala* Feb 1963; *Remada* delivered July 1967; *Joumhouria* delivered Jan 1969.

ISTIKLAL *1971, Tunisian Navy*

8 25-metre COASTAL PATROL CRAFT

V 101 **V 102** **V 103** **V 104** **V 105** **V 106** **V 107** **V 108**

Displacement, tons	38
Dimensions, feet	83 × 15·6 × 4·1
Guns	1—20 mm
Main engines	2 twim GM diesels; 2 400 hp = 23 knots
Range, miles	900 at 16 knots
Complement	11

V 101-106 built by Ch Navale d'Esterel 1961-63. Two further craft of the same design (V 107 and V 108) but unarmed were supplied to the Fisheries Administration in 1971.

V 104 *1970, Tunisian Navy*

V 105 *1974, Tunisian Navy*

2 COASTAL PATROL CRAFT

JAOUEL EL BAHR T 1
SABBACK EL BAHR T 2

25 metre patrol craft built by Ch. Navale d'Esterel.

TUG

RAS ADAR (ex-*Zeeland*, ex-*Pan American*, ex-*Ocean Pride*, ex-HMS *Oriana*, *BAT 1*)

Displacement, tons	540 standard
Dimensions, ft (*m*)	144·4 × 33 × 13·5 (*43* × *10* × *4*)

Built by the Gulfport Boilerworks & Eng Co in 1942 and lend leased to the Royal Navy in that year as BAT 1 HMS *Oriana*, returned and sold in 1946 as *Ocean Pride*, then *Pan America* in 1947, then *Zeeland* in 1956.

TURKEY

Naval Command

Commander in Chief, Turkish Naval Forces:
Admiral Hilmi Firat

Fleet Commander:
Vice-Admiral Bülent Ulusu

Diplomatic Representation

Naval Attaché in London:
Captain Y. Özesen

Naval Attaché in Washington:
Captain Erhan Gürcan

Personnel

(a) 1975: 40 000 officers and ratings
(b) 20 months national service

Naval Bases

Headquarters: Ankara
Main Naval Base: Gölçük
Senior Flag Officers: Istanbul, Izmir
Other Flag Officers: Eregli, Bosphorus, Heybeli Ada (Training), Dardanelles, Iskenderun
Dockyards: Gölçük, Taskizak (Istanbul)

Strength of the Fleet

Type	*Active*	*Building*
Destroyers	12	—
Frigates	2	—
Corvettes	2	—
Submarines—Patrol	14	2
Fast Attack Craft—Missile	—	4
Fast Attack Craft—Torpedo	9	—
Large Patrol Craft	41	—
Coastal Patrol Craft	13	—
Minelayers—Large	3	—
Minelayers—Coastal	6	—
Minesweepers—Coastal	16	—
Minesweepers—Inshore	4	—
LST	2	—
LCT's	17	—
LCU's	16	—
LCM's	20	—
Support Tankers	8	—
Repair Ships	3	—
Transport	3	—
S/M Rescue Ships	2	—
BDV's	7	—
Gate Vessels	3	—
Tugs—Ocean	4	—
Tugs—Harbour	4	—
Floating Docks	7	—
Training Ship	1	—
Survey Vessels	6	—

Deletions

Destroyers

1973 *Gaziantep, Giresun*
1974 *Kocatepe* sunk in error by Turkish Air Force off Cyprus on 22 July. *Gelibolu* and *Gemlik*

Corvettes

1973 *Edremit, Eregli*
1974 *Cardak, Cesme, Edinicik*

Submarines

(Most replaced by submarines of same name).

1973 *Birinci Inönü, Canakkale, Cerbe, Ikinci Inönü, Pirireis*
1974 *Gür* (ex-*Chub*), *Sakarya* (ex *Boarfish*)

Fast Attack Craft

1973 *Dogan, Marti, AB 1-4, 6-7*

Naval Air Arm

3 AB-204B Helicopters
16 S2E ASW Aircraft

Mercantile Marine

Lloyd's Register of Shipping:
353 vessels of 756 807 tons gross

DESTROYERS

5 "TEPE" CLASS (Ex-US "GEARING" CLASS)

Name	*No.*	*Builders*	*Launched*	*Completed*
ADATEPE (ex-USS *Forrest Royal*, DD 872)	D 353	Bethlehem (Staten Is.)	17 Jan 1946	28 June 1946
GAYRET (ex-USS *Eversole* DD 789)	D 352	Todd Pacific Shipyard	8 Jan 1946	10 July 1946
M. FEVZI CAKMAK (ex-USS *Charles H. Roan* DD 853)	D 351	Bethlehem Steel Co, Quincy	15 May 1946	12 Sep 1946
TINAZTEPE (ex-USS *Keppler*, DD 765)	D 355	Bethlehem (San Francisco)	24 June 1945	23 May 1947
— (ex-USS *Norris*, DD 859)	—	Bethlehem (San Pedro)	25 Feb 1945	9 June 1945

Displacement, tons: 2 425 standard; 3 500 full load
Length, feet (*metres*): 390·5 (*119·0*) oa
Beam, feet (*metres*): 40·9 (*12·5*)
Draught, feet (*metres*): 19·0 (*5·8*)
Guns: 4—5 in (*127 mm*) 38 cal dual purpose (2 twin)
A/S weapons: Fram I; 1 Asroc 8-tube launcher; 2 triple torpedo tubes (Mk 32); Facilities for small helo
Fram II; 1 Trainable Hedgehog; 2 Triple torpedo tubes (Mk 32); 2 Fixed Torpedo tubes (Mk 28). Facilities for small Helo
Main engines: 2 geared turbines; 2 shafts; 60 000 shp
Boilers: 4 Babcock & Wilcox
Speed: 34 knots
Oil fuel, tons: 650
Range, miles: 4 800 at 15 knots, 2 400 at 25 knots
Complement: 275 (15 officers, 260 ratings)

ADATEPE — *1973, Dr. Giorgio Arra*

GENERAL
Adatepe, Gayret and *Cakmak* FRAM I conversions and ex-*Norris* and *Tinaztepe* FRAM II. They were transferred to Turkey on 27 Mar 1971 (*Adatepe*) 30 June 1972 (*Tinaztepe*) 11 July 1973 (*Gayret*) and 21 Sept 1973 (*Cakmak*), *Adatepe* and *Kocatepe* purchased 15 Feb 1973 and ex-*Norris* 7 July 1974.

REPLACEMENT. *Kocatepe* D 354 was sunk in error by the Turkish Air Force off Cyprus 22 July 1974. Ex-USS *Norris* had been purchased for spares on 7 July 1974 and is being re-activated to replace *Kocatepe*.

RADAR. Fram I: SPS 40 long range air search; SPS 10 surface search; gun fire control Mk 68 radar. Fram II; SPS 6 long range S band air surveillance; SPS 10 surface search; Mk 68 as above.

SONAR. Fram I SQS 23. Fram II SQS 29.

GEARING FRAM I

1 Ex-US "ROBERT H. SMITH" CLASS

Name	*No.*	*Builders*	*Launched*	*Completed*
MUAVENET (ex-USS *Gwin*, ex- DM 33, ex DD 772)	DM 357	Bethlehem, San Pedro	9 Apr 1944	30 Sep 1944

Displacement, tons: 2 250 standard; 3 375 full load
Dimensions, ft (*m*): 376·5 × 41 × 19 (*114·8* × *12·5* × *5·8*)
Guns: 6—5 in (*127 mm*) 38 cal (twins); 12—40 mm; 11—20 mm
Mines: 80
Boilers: 4 Babcock and Wilcox
Main engines: Geared turbines; 60 000 shp 2 shafts
Speed: 34
Range, miles: 4 600 at 15 knots
Complement: 274

Modified "Allen M. Sumner" class converted for minelaying. After modernisation at Philadelphia she was transferred on 22 Oct 1971.

RADAR. SPS 6 air search; Mk 68 radar director.

SONAR. SQS 29.

Destroyers—*continued*

"ALLEN M. SUMNER (FRAM II)" CLASS

Name	No.	Builders	Launched	Completed
ZAFER (ex-USS *Hugh, Purvis* ex-DD 709)	D 356	Federal SB and DD Co	17 Dec 1944	1 Mar 1945

Displacement, tons	2 200 standard; 3 320 full load
Length, feet (*metres*)	376·5 (*114·8*)
Beam, feet (*metres*)	40·9 (*12·5*)
Draught, feet (*metres*)	19·0 (*5·8*)
Guns	6—5 in 38 cal (twins)
A/S weapons	2 Triple torpedo launchers Mk 32; 2 Hedgehogs, 2 Mk 25 torpedo tubes
Machinery	2 geared turbines; 2 shafts; 60 000 shp
Boilers	4 Babcock & Wilcox
Speed	34 knots
Oil fuel, tons	650
Range, miles	4 600 at 15 knots
Complement	275 (15 officers, 260 ratings)

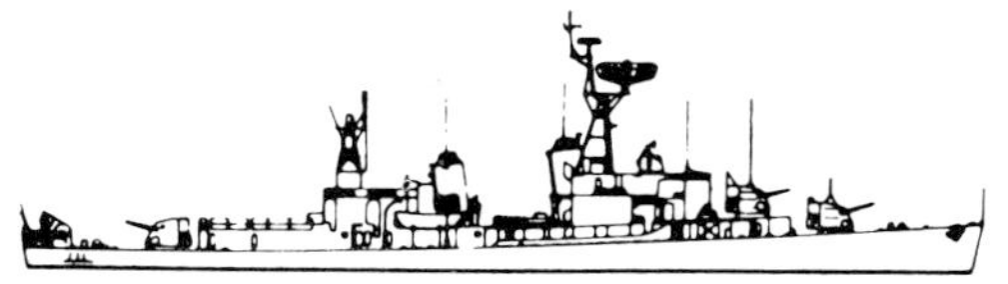

"Allen M. Sumner" Class FRAM II

GENERAL
Zafer is a standard FRAM II Sumner class purchased 15 Feb 1973.

RADAR. SPS 40 long range air search and SPS 10 surface search.

SONAR. SQS 29.

5 "I" CLASS (Ex-US "FLETCHER" CLASS)

Name	No.	Builders	Launched	Completed
ICEL (ex-USS *Preston,* DD 795)	D 344	Bethlehem Company, San Pedro	12 Dec 1943	20 Mar 1944
ISKENDERUN (ex-USS *Boyd,* DD 544)	D 343	Bethlehem Company, San Pedro	29 Oct 1942	8 May 1943
ISTANBUL (ex-USS *Clarence K. Bronson* DD 668)	D 340	Federal SB & DD Co, Newark	18 Apr 1943	11 June 1943
IZMIR (ex-USS *Van Valkenburgh* DD 656)	D 341	Gulf Shipbuilding Corp	19 Dec 1943	2 Aug 1944
IZMIT (ex-USS *Cogswell,* DD 651)	D 342	Bath Iron Works Corpn	5 June 1943	17 Aug 1943

Displacement, tons	2 050 standard; 3 000 full load
Length, feet (*metres*)	376·5 (*114·8*) oa
Beam, feet (*metres*)	39·5 (*12·1*)
Draught, feet (*metres*)	18·0 (*5·5*)
Guns	4—5 in (*127 mm*) 38 cal; 6—3 in (*76 mm*)
A/S weapons	2 Hedgehogs
Torpedo tubes	5—21 in (*533 mm*) quintupled
Main engines	GE geared turbines; 2 shafts; 60 000 shp
Speed, knots	34
Boilers	4 Babcock & Wilcox
Oil fuel, tons	650
Range, miles	5 000 at 15 knots
Complement	250

TRANSFERS. Transferred as follows *Istanbul* 14 Jan 1967, *Izmir* 28 Feb 1967, *Iskenderun* and *Ismit* on 1 Oct 1969, and *Icel* on 15 Nov 1969.

IZMIT — *1972, Turkish Navy*

RADAR. Search: SPS 6. Tactical: SPS 10. Fire Control: GFCS 68.

FRIGATES

2 "BERK" CLASS

BERK D 358 — **PEYK** D 359

Displacement, tons	1 450 standard; 1 950 full load
Length, feet (*metres*)	311·7 (*95·0*)
Beam, feet (*metres*)	38·7 (*11·8*)
Draught, feet (*metres*)	18·1 (*5·5*)
Guns	4—3 in (*76 mm*) 2 twin
Tubes	6—12·6 in (*320 mm*) 2 triple
Aircraft	1 helicopter
Main engines	4 Fiat diesels; 2 shafts; 24 000 bhp
Speed, knots	25

First major warships built in Turkey. The prototype, *Berk*, was laid down in the Gölcük naval yard on 9 Mar 1967, and *Peyk* on 18 Jan 1968. *Berk* was launched 25 June 1971 and completed 12 July 1972. *Peyk* was launched 7 June 1972 for completion in June 1974. Both are named after famous ships of the Ottoman Navy.

BERK — *1972, Turkish Navy*

CORVETTES

(Note—*Cardak*, *Cesme* and *Edinicik* transferred to Disposal List).

2 "ALANYA" CLASS

Name	*No.*	*Builders*	*Launched*
ALANYA (ex-*Broome*)	A 589 (ex-M 501)	Evans Deakin, Brisbane	6 Oct 1941
AYVALIK (ex- *Antalya*, ex-*Geraldton*)	A 588 (ex-M 500)	Poole & Steele, Sydney	16 Aug 1941

Displacement, tons	**790 standard; 1 025 full load**
Length, feet (*metres*)	**162·0 (*49·4*) pp; 186·0 (*56·7*) oa**
Beam, feet (*metres*)	**31·0 (*9·4*)**
Draught, feet (*metres*)	**8·5 (*2·6*)**
Guns, surface	**1—4 in (*102 mm*)**
Guns, AA	**1—40 mm; 4—20 mm**
A/S weapons	**2 DCT**
Main engines	**Triple expansion; 2 shafts; 1 800 ihp**
Speed, knots	**15**
Boilers	**2 water tube**
Oil fuel, tons	170
Range, miles	4 500 at 10 knots
Complement	85

Both Australian built "Bathurst" class fleet minesweepers, 1940-42. Served in the Royal Navy. Acquired from Great Britain in Aug 1946. Named after Turkish ports. Both are now Logistic Support Ships.

AYVALIK *1968*

SUBMARINES

2 TYPE 209 (HOWALDTSWERKE)

Displacement, tons	990 surfaced; 1 290 dived
Length, feet (*metres*)	183·7 (*56·0*)
Beam, feet (*metres*)	20·3 (*6·2*)
Torpedo tubes	8—21 inch (with reloads)
Main machinery	Diesel electric. 4 MTU Siemens diesel-generators; 1 Siemens electric motor; 1 shaft
Speed, knots	10 surfaced; 22 dived
Range	50 days
Complement	31

Designed by Ingenieurkontor, Lübeck for construction by Howaldtswerke, Kiel and sale by Ferrostaal Essen all acting as a consortium.

TYPE 209 *1973 Howaldtswerke*

A single-hull design with two ballast tanks and forward and after trim tanks. Fitted with snort and remote machinery control. The single screw is slow revving. Very high capacity batteries with GRP lead-acid cells and battery cooling—by Wilh. Hagen and VARTA. Active and passive sonar, sonar detection equipment, sound ranging gear and underwater telephone. Fitted with two periscopes, radar and Omega receiver. Fore-planes retract. Building at Kiel. First boat laid down 2 Aug 1972—completion probably late 1975.

2 Ex-US "GUPPY III" CLASS

Name	*No.*	*Builder*	*Launched*	*Completed*
CANAKKALE (ex-USS *Cobbler* SS 344)	S 341	Electric Boat Co.	1 Apr 1945	8 Aug 1945
IKINCI INONÜ (ex-USS *Corporal* SS 346)	S 333	Electric Boat Co.	10 June 1945	9 Nov 1945
— (ex-USS *Tiru* SS 416)	—	Mare Island Navy Yard	17 Apr 1944	1 Sep 1948
— (ex-USS *Clamagore* SS 343)	—	Electric Boat Co.	16 Mar 1944	21 Oct 1944

Displacement, tons	1 975 standard; 2 540 dived
Dimensions, ft (*m*)	326·5 × 27 × 17 (*99·4 × 8·2 × 5·2*)
Torpedo tubes	10—21 inch (*533 mm*) 6 bow, 4 stern
Main machinery	4 diesels; 6 400 shp; 2 electric motors 5 400 bhp; 2 shafts
Speed	20 surfaced; 15 dived
Complement	86

First pair transferred 21 Nov 1973. Ex-*Clamagore* purchased 12 June 1975, ex-*Tiru* on 1 July 1975.

CANAKKALE (as *Cobbler*) *1970, A. & J. Pavia*

7 "GUPPY IIA" CLASS

Name	*No.*	*Builders*	*Launched*	*Completed*	*Transferred*
BIRINCI INÖNÜ (ex-USS *Threadfin*, SS 410)	346	Portsmouth Navy Yard	26 June 1944	30 Aug 1944	15 Aug 1973
BURAKREIS (ex-USS *Seafox*, SS 402)	335	Portsmouth Navy Yard	28 Mar 1944	13 June 1944	25 June 1971
CERBE (ex-USS *Trutta*, SS 421)	340	Portsmouth Navy Yard	22 May 1944	16 Nov 1944	24 Aug 1972
MURATREIS (ex-USS *Razorback*, SS 394)	336	Portsmouth Navy Yard	27 Jan 1944	3 Apr 1944	17 Dec 1971
ORUÇREIS (ex-USS *Pomfret*, SS 391)	337	Portsmouth Navy Yard	27 Oct 1943	19 Feb 1944	3 May 1972
PREVEZE (ex-USS *Entemedor*, SS 340)	345	Electric Boat Co.	17 Dec 1944	6 Apr 1945	24 Aug 1972
ULUÇALIREIS (ex-USS *Thornback*, SS 418)	338	Portsmouth Navy Yard	7 July 1944	13 Oct 1944	24 Aug 1972

1 "GUPPY IA" CLASS

Name	*No.*	*Builders*	*Launched*	*Completed*	*Transferred*
DUMLUPINAR (ex-USS *Caiman*, SS 323)	339	Electric Boat Co.	30 Mar 1944	17 July 1944	24 Aug 1972

Displacement, tons	1 840 standard; 2 445 dived
Dimensions, ft (*m*)	306 × 27 × 17 (*93·2 × 8·2 × 5·2*)
Torpedo tubes	10—21 in (*533 mm*) 6 bow, 4 stern; 24 torpedoes carried
Main machinery	3 GM diesels; 4 800 hp; 2 electric motors; 5 400 hp
Speed, knots	17 surfaced; 15 dived
Range, miles	12 000 at 10 knots surfaced
Complement	85

The fact that the same names are used for replacement submarines as for their predecessors can be confusing. eg *"Cerbe"* was used for both ex-USS *Hammerhead* and now for ex-USS *Trutta*.

ORUCREIS (as *Pomfret*) *1972, Turkish Navy*

Submarines—*continued*

2 Ex-US MODIFIED FLEET TYPE (Ex-"BALAO" CLASS)

Name	*No.*	*Builders*	*Launched*	*Completed*	*Transferred*
HIZIRREIS (ex-USS *Mero*, SS 378)	344	Manitowoc SB Co.	17 Jan 1945	17 Aug 1945	20 Apr 1960
TURGUTREIS (ex-USS *Bergall*, SS 320)	342	Electric Boat Co.	16 Feb 1944	12 June 1944	17 Oct 1958

Displacement, tons	1 526 standard; 1 829 surface; 2 424 dived
Dimensions, ft (*m*)	311·8 × 27·2 × 13·8 (*95 × 8·3 × 4·2*)
Torpedo tubes	10—21 inch (*533 mm*); 6 bow, 4 stern; 24 torpedoes carried
Main machinery	4 GM diesels; 6 400 shp; 2 electric motors; 5 400 shp
Speed, knots	20 surfaced; 10 dived
Range, miles	12 000 at 10 knots
Complement	85

Streamlined boats of "Balao" class. Now becoming obsolescent. *Turgutreis* purchased 15 Aug 1973 probably for spare parts eventually.

5 HARBOUR TRAINING SUBMARINES

Ex-USS *Blueback* SS 326, *Bumper*, SS 333, *Guitarro* SS 363, *Hammerhead* SS 364, and *Mapiro* SS 376 have been taken over as non-operational harbour training boats and numbered Y 1241, Y 1240, Y 1243, Y 1242 and Y 1244 respectively.

LIGHT FORCES

4 FAST ATTACK CRAFT—MISSILE

These craft of 400 tons, one to be built by Lürssen Vegesack and three in Turkey at Taskizak Naval Yard were ordered on 3 Aug 1973.

2 Ex-US "ASHEVILLE" CLASS (LARGE PATROL CRAFT)

BORA (ex-USS *Surprise* PG97) P339
YILDIRIM (ex-USS *Defiance* PG 95) P 338

Displacement, tons	225 standard; 245 full load
Dimensions, feet	164·5 oa × 23·8 × *9·5*
Guns	1—3 in 50 cal; 1—40 mm; 4—50 cal MG
Main engines	CODAG; 2 Cummins Diesels; 1 450 hp = 16 knots; 1 GE gas turbine; 13 300 shp = 40 knots
Complement	25

These vessels belong to the largest Patrol Type built by the USN since World War II and the first of that Navy to have gas turbines. Built by Petersens, Wisconsin in 1969 for the USN and transferred to Turkey on 28th Feb 1973 and 11 June 1973 respectively.

YILDIRIM (as *Defiance*) *1970, US Navy*

6 "AKHISAR" CLASS (LARGE PATROL CRAFT)

AKHISAR (ex-*PC* 1641) P 114
DEMIRHISAR (ex-*PC* 1639) P 112
KOCHISAR (ex-*PC* 1643) P 116
SIVRIHISAR (ex-*PC* 1642) P 115
SULTANHISAR (ex-*PC* 1638) P 111
YARHISAR (ex-*PC* 1640) P 113

Displacement, tons	280 standard; 412 full load
Dimensions, feet	170 wl; 173·7 oa × 23 × 10·2
Guns	1—3 inch dp; 1—40 mm AA
A/S weapons	4 DCT
Main engines	2 FM Diesels; 2 shafts; 2 800 bhp = 19 knots
Range, miles	6 000 at 10 knots
Complement	65 (5 officers, and 60 men)

Similar to US 173 ft class submarine chasers. Built by Gunderson Bros. Engineering Co, Portland, Oregon, except *Kochisar* built in Gölcük Dockyard, Turkey. Transferred on 3 Dec 1964, 22 Apr 1965, 22 Apr 1965, 2 May 1964, 24 Sep 1964 and 22 Apr 1965 respectively.

YARHISAR *1972, Turkish Navy*

9 "KARTAL" CLASS (FAST ATTACK CRAFT—TORPEDO)

ALBATROS P 327 (ex-P 325)
ATMACA P 322 (ex-P 335)
DENIZKUSU P 321 (ex-P 336)
KARTAL P 324 (ex-P 333)
KASIRGA P 329 (ex-P 338)
MELTEM P 325 (ex-P 330)
PELIKAN P 326
SAHIN P 323 (ex-P 334)
SIMSEK P 328 (ex-P 332)

Displacement, tons	160 standard, 180 full load
Dimensions, feet	140·5 × 23·5 × 7·2
Guns	2—40 mm AA
Tubes	4—21 inch
Main engines	4 Maybach diesels, 4 shafts; 12 000 bhp = 42 knots

Of the German "Jaguar" type. Built by Lürssen, Vegesack, in 1966-67 (P 321, 322, 323, 324, 329,) others in 1968.

SIMSEK *1972, Turkish Navy*

10 LARGE PATROL CRAFT

AB 25 (P 1225)
AB 26 (P 1226)
AB 27 (P 1227)
AB 28 (P 1228)
AB 29 (P 1229)
AB 30 (P 1230)
AB 31 (P 1231)
AB 32 (P 1232)
AB 33 (P 1233)
AB 34 (P 1234)

Displacement, tons	170
Dimensions, feet	132 × 21 × 5·5
Guns	2—40 mm
Speed	22 knots

Built at Taskizak Naval Yard. First was launched on 9 Mar 1967. Six similar launches are operated by the Gendarmerie.

AB 28 *1970, Turkish Navy*

4 LARGE PATROL CRAFT

AB 21 (ex-PGM-104) P 1221
AB 22 (ex-PGM-105) P 1222
AB 23 (ex-PGM-106) P 1223
AB 24 (ex-PGM-108) P 1224

Displacement, tons	130 standard, 147 full load
Dimensions, feet	101 × 21 × 7
Guns	1—40 mm; 4—20 mm
Main engines	2 diesels; 2 shafts; 1 850 hp = 18·5 knots
Range, miles	1 500 at 10 knots
Complement	15

Patrol gunboat type supplied from the United States in Dec 1967 (first three) and Apr 1968.

AB 23 *1970, Turkish Navy*

Light Forces—*continued*

19 LARGE PATROL CRAFT

J 12-J 30

Displacement, tons	150
Dimensions, ft (*m*)	129·3 × 20·6 × 4·9 (*34·4 × 6·3 × 1·5*)
Guns	2—40 mm
Main engines	4 MB diesels; 2 shafts; 3 200 bhp = 22 knots

J 12-20 built in 1960-61 by Schweers, Bardenfleth. J 21 and 22 built at Gölcük Navy Yard. J 23 to 26 built at Taskizak in 1968 and J 27 and 28 at Taskizak in 1970.

J 21 — *1972, Dr. Giorgio Arra*

4 Ex-US COASTGUARD "83 ft" CLASS
(COASTAL PATROL CRAFT)

LS 9 P 1209
LS 11 P 1211
LS 10 P 1210
LS 12 P 1212

Displacement, tons	63 standard
Dimensions, feet	83·0 × 14·0 × 5·0
Gun	1—20 mm AA
A/S weapons	2 A/S Rocket launchers
Main engines	2 Cummins diesels; 1 100 bhp = 20 knots

Ex-US type, transferred on 25 June 1953.

9 COASTAL PATROL CRAFT

MTB 1 P 311
MTB 2 P 312
MTB 3 P 313
MTB 4 P 314
MTB 6 P 316
MTB 7 P 317
MTB 8 P 318
MTB 9 P 319
MTB 10 P 320

Displacement, tons	70 standard
Dimensions, feet	71·5 × 13·8 × 8·5
Main engines	Diesel; 2 000 bhp = 20 knots

All launched in 1942. General purpose craft. MTB 5 (315) was scrapped.

LS 9 — *1972, Turkish Navy*

MINE WARFARE FORCES

1 LARGE MINELAYER

NUSRET N 110 (ex-N 108)

Displacement, tons	1 880 standard
Length feet (*metres*)	246 (*75·0*) pp; 252·7 (*77·0*) oa
Beam, feet (*metres*)	41 (*12·6*)
Draught, feet (*metres*)	11 (*3·4*)
Guns,	4—3 in (*76 mm*), 2 twin mountings
Mines	400 capacity
Main engines	GM diesels; 4 800 hp; 2 shafts
Speed, knots	18
Complement	146

Minelayer of special Scandinavian-NATO design. Built at Frederikshaven Dockyard, Denmark. Laid down in 1962, launched in 1964, and completed in 1965. Commissioned on 16 Sep 1964 at Copenhagen. Similar to Danish "Falster" class.

RADAR. Search: RAN 7S. Fire Control: X Band Navigation Radar.

NUSRET — *1972, Turkish Navy*

NUSRET

2 Ex-US LST TYPE (MINELAYERS)

SANCAKTAR (ex-German *Bochum*, ex-USS *Rice County*) N 112
BAYRAKTAR (ex-German *Bottrop*, ex-USS *Saline County*) N 111

Displacement, tons	1 653 standard; 4 080 full load
Dimensions, feet	328 oa × 50 × 14
Guns	6—40 mm (2 twin, 2 single)
Main engines	2 GM Diesels; 2 shafts; 1 700 bhp = 11 knots
Range, miles	15 000 at 9 knots
Complement	125

Formerly USN LSTs, transferred to Germany in 1961 and thence to Turkey on 13 Dec 1972. Converted into minelayers 1973.

SANCAKTAR — *1973, Reiner Nerlich*

Mine warfare Forces—*continued*

5 LSM TYPE (COASTAL MINELAYERS)

MARMARIS (ex-*LSM* 481) N 103
MERIÇ (ex-*LSM* 490) N 102
MERSIN (ex-*LSM* 492) N 104
MORDOGAN (ex-*LSM* 484) N 101
MÜREFTE (ex-*LSM* 493) N 105

Displacement, tons	743 standard; 1 100 full load
Dimensions, feet	196·5 wl; 203·2 oa × 34·5 × 8·5
Guns	2—40 mm AA; 2—20 mm AA
Main engines	Diesels; 2 shafts; 2 880 bhp = 12 knots
Oil fuel, tons	60
Range, miles	2 500 at 12 knots
Complement	89

Ex-US Landing Ships Medium. All launched in 1945, converted into coastal minelayers by the US Navy in 1952 and taken over by the Turkish Navy (LSM 481, 484 and 490) and the Norwegian Navy (LSM 492 and 493) in Oct 1952 under MAP. LSM 492 (*Vale*) and LSM 493 (*Vidar*) were retransferred to the Turkish Navy on 1 Nov 1960 at Bergen, Norway.

MERSIN 1969

1 YMP TYPE (COASTAL MINELAYER)

MEHMETCIK (ex-US *YMP* 3) N 115

Displacement, tons	540 full load
Dimensions, feet	130 × 35 × 6
Main engines	Diesels; 2 shafts; 600 bhp = 10 knots
Complement	22

Former US motor mine planter. Built by Higgins Inc, New Orleans. Completed in 1958. Steel hulled. Transferred under MAP in 1958. For harbour defence.

MEHMETCIK

12 MSC TYPE (MINESWEEPERS—COASTAL)

SAMSUN (ex-USS *MSC* 268) M 510
SAPANCA (ex-USS *MSC* 312) M 517
SARIYER (ex-USS *MSC* 315) M 518
SAROS (ex-USS *MSC* 305) M 515
SEDDULBAHIR (ex-*MSC* 272) M 513
SELÇUK (ex-*AMS* 124) M 508
SEYHAN (ex-*AMS* 142) M 509
SEYMEN (ex-*AMS* 131) M 507
SIGACIK (ex-USS *MSC* 311) M 516
SILIFKE (ex-USS *MSC* 304) M 514
SINOP (ex-USS *MSC* 270) M 511
SURMENE (ex-USS *MSC* 271) M 512

Displacement, tons	320 standard; 370 full load
Dimensions, feet	138·0 pp; 144·0 oa × 28·0 × 9·0
Guns	2—20 mm AA
Main engines	2 diesels; 2 shafts; 1 200 bhp = 14 knots
Oil fuel, tons	25
Range, miles	2 500 at 10 knots
Complement	38 (4 officers, 34 men)

Transferred on 30 Sep 1958, 26 July 1965, 8 Sep 1967, 8 Nov 1965, 9 July 1959, 24 Mar 1970, 24 Mar 1970, 19 Nov 1970, 29 May 1965, 25 Oct 1965, 30 Jan 1959, 27 Mar 1959, respectively. *Selçuk* (ex-AMS 124) and *Seyhan* (ex-AMS 142) were transferred from France (via USA) on 24 Mar 1970 and *Seyman* from Belgium (via USA) on 19 Nov 1970.

SAMSUN 1969

4 MCB TYPE (MINESWEEPERS—COASTAL)

TIREBOLU (ex-HMCS *Comax*) M 532
TEKIRDAG (ex-HMCS *Ungave*) M 533
TERME (ex-HMCS *Trinity*), M 531
TRABZON (ex-HMCS *Gaspe*) M 530

Displacement, tons	390 standard; 412 full load
Dimensions, feet	140·0 pp; 152·0 oa × 20·8 × 7·0
Gun	1—40 mm
Main engines	Diesels; 2 shafts; 2 400 bhp = 16 knots
Oil fuel, tons	52
Range, miles	4 500 at 11 knots
Complement	44

Ex-Canadian MCBs. Sailed from Sydney, Nova Scotia, to Turkey on 19 May 1958

TIREBOLU *1970, Turkish Navy*

4 Ex-US MINESWEEPERS—INSHORE

FATSA (ex-*MSI* 17) M 502
FETHIYE (ex-*MSI* 16) M 501
FINIKE (ex-*MSI* 18) M 503
FOÇA (ex-*MSI* 15) M 500

Displacement, tons	180 standard; 235 full load
Dimensions, feet	111·9 × 23·5 × 7·9
Gun	1—50 cal
Main engines	4 diesels; 2 shafts; 960 bhp = 13 knots
Complement	30

Built in USA and transferred under MAP at Boston, Mass, Aug-Sep 1967. *Finike* was delivered by Peterson Builders Inc. on 8 Nov 1967.

FOCA *1970, Turkish Navy*

AMPHIBIOUS FORCES

2 Ex-US LST

ERTUGRUL (ex-USS *Windham County, LST 1170*) L 401
SEDAR (ex-USS *Westchester County, LST 1169*) L 402

Displacement, tons	2 590 light; 5 800 full load
Dimensions, feet	384 oa × 55 × 17
Guns	6—3 in 50 cal (twins)
Main engines	4 GM diesels; 2 shafts (cp propellers); 6 000 bhp = 15 knots
Complement	116
Troops	395

Transferred by US June 1973. (L 401) and 27 Aug 1974 (L 402)
Built by Christy Corpn in 1954.

5 Ex-US LCT s

C 101 and 103-106

Displacement, tons	500 light; 700 full load
Dimensions, feet	180·9 × 27·7 × 5·4
Guns	2—20 mm
Complement	15

Built in USA in 1942. Transferred 25 Sept 1967

12 TURKISH-BUILT LCTs

C 107-118

Displacement, tons	400 light; 600 full load
Dimensions, feet	180·9 × 36·8 × 4·8
Guns	2—20 mm
Speed, knots	10·5
Complement	15

Built in Turkey 1966-1973.

12 TURKISH-BUILT LCU s

C 205-216

Displacement, tons	320 light; 405 full load
Dimensions, feet	142 × 28 × 5·7
Guns	2—20 mm
Main engines	GM diesels; 2 shafts; 600 bhp = 10 knots

Built in Turkey 1965-66.

Amphibious Forces—*continued*

4 Ex-US LCU 501 SERIES

C201-204 (ex-US LCU 588, 608, 666 and 667)

Displacement, tons	160 light; 320 full load
Dimensions, feet	119 oa × 32·7 × 5
Guns	2—20 mm
Main engines	3 diesels; 675 bhp = 10 knots
Complement	13

Transferred from USA Oct-Dec 1966.

20 TURKISH-BUILT LCM8 TYPE

C 301-320

Displacement, tons	58 light; 113 full load
Dimensions, feet	72 × 20·5 × 4·8
Guns	2—12·7 mm
Main engines	GM diesels; 2 shafts; 660 bhp = 9·5 knots
Complement	9

Built in Turkey in 1965.

SURVEY SHIPS

CARSAMBA A 594 **CANDARLI** A 593

Displacement, tons	1 010 standard; 1 250 full load
Dimensions, ft (*m*)	221 oa × 32 × 10·8 (*67·4 × 9·8 × 3·3*)
Main engines	Diesel electric; 2 shafts; 3 500 bhp
Speed, knots	18
Complement	98 (8 officers, 90 ratings)

Ex-US "Auk" class minesweepers. Both launched in 1942, they are the survivors of a class of five transferred via UK in 1947.

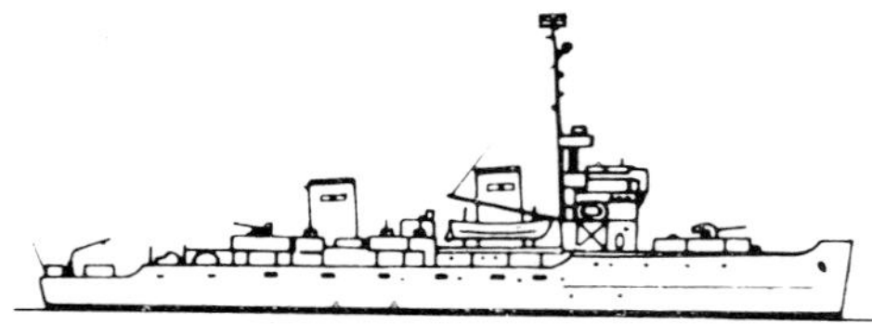

CANDARLI *Class*

MESAHA 1 and 2
Of 45 tons with a complement of 8—built in 1966.
MESAHA 3 and 4
Of 60 tons with a complement of 10—built in 1943.

SERVICE FORCES

ULABAT Y 1209 **VAN** Y 1208 (SUPPORT TANKERS)

Displacement, tons	1 200
Main engines	Designed for a speed of 14·5 knots

Two small tankers for the Turkish Navy built in the Gölcük Dockyard, Izmit, in 1968-70.

BINBASI SAADETTIN GÜRCAN A 573 (SUPPORT TANKER)

Displacement, tons	1 505 tandard; 4 460 full load
Dimensions, feet	299 × 39·4 × 18
Main engines	Diesels; 4 400 bhp

Built at Taskizak Naval Yard. Launched 1 July 1969.

ALBAY HAKKI BURAK A 572 (SUPPORT TANKER)

Displacement, tons	3 800 full load
Dimensions, feet	251·3 pp; 274·7 oa × 40·2 × 18
Main engines	2 GM diesels; electric drive; 4,400 bhp = 16 knots
Complement	88
Built in 1964.	

ALBAY HAKKI BURAK *1972, Turkish Navy*

GÖLÇUK (ex-A 573) Y 1207 (SUPPORT TANKER)

Displacement, tons	1 255
Measurement, feet	750 deadweight
Dimensions, feet	185 × 31·1 × 10
Main engines	B. & W. diesel; 700 bhp = 12·5 knots

Built by Gölcük Dockyard, Ismit. Launched on 4 Nov 1953.

Service Forces—*continued*

YUZBASI TOLUNAY A 571 (SUPPORT TANKER)

Displacement, tons	2 500 standard; 3 500 full load
Dimensions, feet	260 × 41 × 19·5
Main engines	Atlas Polar-diesels; 2 shafts; 1 920 bhp = 14 knots

Built at Taskizak by Haskoy Naval D.Y., Istanbul. Launched on 22 Aug 1950.

YUZBASI TOLUNAY *1972, Turkish Navy*

AKAR (ex-*Istanbul*, ex-*Adour*) A 570 (SUPPORT TANKER)

Displacement, tons	4 289 light; 13 200 full load
Dimensions, feet	433 × 52·7 × 27
Main engines	Parsons geared turbines; 5 200 shp = 15 knots
Range, miles	10 000 at 10 knots

AKAR (Old Pennant No. 580) *1970, Turkish Navy*

AKPINAR (ex-*Chiwaukum*) A 574 (SUPPORT TANKER)

Displacement, tons	700 light; 2 700 full load
Measurement, feet	1 453 deadweight
Dimensions, feet	212·5 wl; 220·5 oa × 37 × 12·8
Main engines	Diesel; 800 bhp = 10 knots

Formerly the United States oiler *AOG 26*. Built by East Coast S.Y. Inc., Bayonne. Laid down on 2 Apr 1944. Launched on 5 May 1944. Completed on 22 July 1944. Transferred to Turkey in 1949.

DONATAN (ex-USS *Anthedon, AS* 24) A 583 (REPAIR SHIP)

Displacement, tons	8 100 standard
Dimensions, feet	492 × 69·5 × 26·5
Main engines	Geared turbines; 1 shaft; 8 500 shp = 14·4 knots
Boilers	2

Former US submarine tender of the "Aegir" class transferred to Turkey on 7 Feb 1969.

DONATAN *1972, Turkish Navy*

2 Ex-US REPAIR SHIPS

BASARAN (ex-*Patroclus, ARL* 19, ex-*LST* 955) A 582
ONARAN (ex-*Alecto, AGP* 14, ex-*LST* 558) A 581

Displacement, tons	1 625 standard; 4 080 full load
Dimensions, feet	316 wl; 328 oa × 50 × 14
Guns	2—40 mm AA; 8—20 mm AA
Main engines	Diesel; 2 shafts; 1 700 bhp = 11 knots
Oil fuel, tons	1 000
Range, miles	9 000 at 9 knots
Complement	80

Former US repair ship and MTB tender, respectively, of the LST type. *Basaran* was launched on 22 Oct 1944 by Bethlehem Hingham Shipyard, *Onaran* on 14 Apr 1944 by Missouri Valley Bridge & Iron Co. Acquired from the USA in 1952 and 1947, respectively.

ONARAN *1973, Dr. Giorgio Arra*

Service Forces—*continued*

ÜLKÜ (ex-*Angeln*) A 586 (TRANSPORT)

Displacement, tons	3 088
Dimensions, feet	296·9 × 43·6 × 20·3
Main engines	Pielstick Diesel; 1 shaft; 3 000 bhp = 17 knots
Complement	57

Transferred by W. Germany. 22 March 1972.

DENIZALTI BARCI (ex-US APL 47) Y 1204 (TRANSPORTS)
— (ex-US APL 53) Y 1205

Transferred; Y 1204 on 1 Dec 1971 and Y 1205 on 6 Dec 1974.

KURTARAN (ex-*Bluebird*, ASR 19, ex-*Yurak* AT 165) A 584 (SUBMARINE RESCUE SHIP)

Displacement, tons	1 294 standard; 1 675 full load
Dimensions, feet	205·0 oa × 38·5 × 12·0
Guns	1—3 inch; 2—40 mm AA
Main engines	Diesel-electric; 3 000 bhp = 16 knots

Former salvage tug adapted as a submarine rescue vessel in 1947. Transferred from the US Navy on 15 Aug 1950.

KURTARAN 1971, A. & J. Pavia

AKIN (ex-*Greenlet ASR* 10) A 585 (SUBMARINE RESCUE SHIP)

Displacement, tons	1 770 standard; 2 321 full load
Dimensions, feet	251·3 × 42·2 × 14·7
Guns	1—40 mm; 2—20 mm (twin)
Main engines	Diesel-electric; 1 shaft; 3 000 bhp = 15 knots
Complement	85

Submarine rescue vessel, ex-USN "Chanticleer" class built by Moore SB & DD Co., Oakland in 1942. Transferred 12 June 1970 and purchased 15 Feb 1973.

ERKIN (ex-*Trabzon* ex-*Imperial*) A 591 (SUBMARINE SUPPORT)

Displacement, tons	10 900
Dimensions, feet	441 × 58·5 × 23
Guns	2—40 mm
Speed, knots	16
Complement	128

Built in 1938. Purchased in 1968 and placed on the Navy list in 1970.

AG 6 (ex-*Cerberus* A 895) P 306 (BOOM DEFENCE VESSEL)

Displacement, tons	780 standard; 902 full load
Dimensions, feet	165·0 × 33·0 × 10·0
Guns	1—3 in; 4—20 mm AA
Main engines	Diesel-electric; 1 shaft; 1 500 bhp = 12·8 knots

Netlayer built by Bethlehem Steel Co, Staten Island. Launched in May 1952 and completed on 10 Nov 1952. Transferred from USA to Netherlands in Dec 1952. Used first as a boom defence vessel and latterly as salvage and diving tender since 1961 but retained her netlaying capacity. Handed back to USN (formality) on 17 Sep 1970 but immediately turned over to the Turkish Navy.

AG 5 (*ex AN 104*) P 305 (BDV)

Displacement, tons	680 standard; 860 full load
Dimensions, feet	148·7 pp; 173·8 oa × 35·0 × 13·5
Guns	1—40 mm AA; 3—20 mm AA
Main engines	4 MAN diesels; 2 shafts; 1 450 bhp = 12 knots

Netlayer *AN 104* built in US off-shore programme by Kröger, Rendesburg for Turkey. Launched on 20 Oct 1960. Delivered on 35 Feb 1961.

AG 4 (ex-*Larch*, ex-*AN* 21) P 304 (BDV)

Displacement, tons	560 standard; 805 full load
Dimensions, feet	146·0 wl; 163·0 oa × 30·5 × 10·5
Guns	1—3 inch AA
Main engines	Diesel-electric; 800 bhp = 12 knots

Former US netlayer of the "Aloe" class. Built by American S.B. Co, Cleveland. Laid down in 1940. Launched on 2 July 1941. Completed in 1941. Acquired in 1947.

AG 4 1969

3 "BAR" CLASS (BDV's)

AG 1 (ex-*Barbarian*, 21 Oct 1937) P 301 **AG 2** (ex-*Barbette*, 15 Dec 1937) P 302
AG 3 (ex-*Barfair*, 21 May 1938) P 303

Displacement, tons	750 standard; 1 000 full load
Dimensions, feet	150·0 pp; 173·8 oa × 32·2 × 9·5
Gun	1—3 inch AA
Main engines	Triple expansion; 850 ihp = 11·5 knots
Boilers	2 SE

Former British boom defence vessels. First two were built by Blyth S.B. Co. and the third by J. Lewis & Sons. Launch dates above.

KALDIRAY P 309 (BDV)

Measurement, tons	732 gross
Main engines	Steam reciprocating; 500 ihp = 10 knots
Complement	97

Built in 1938. Former French vessel. Purchased in 1964.

KAPI I, II, III (Y 1201, 1202, 1203) (GATE VESSELS)

Displacement, tons	360
Dimensions, feet	102·7 × 34 × 4·7

These gate vessels were built by US for Turkey under MAP. Transferred Mar 1961.

TUGS

AKBAS Y 1118
KEPEZ Y 1119

Displacement, tons	971
Dimensions, feet	149 × 33·9 × 14
Speed, knots	12

GAZAL (ex USS *Sioux ATF* 75) A 587

Displacement, tons	1 235 standard; 1 675 full load
Dimensions, feet	205 oa × 38·5 × 16
Gun	1—3 inch
Main engines	Diesel electric; 3 000 bhp = 16 knots
Complement	85

Transferred 30 Oct 1972. Purchased 15 Aug 1973.

ÖNCU Y 1123 **ÖNDER** Y 1124

Displacement, tons	500
Speed	12 knots

The US harbour tugs ex-YTL 155, 751 were transferred under MAP.

KUVVET Y 1122

Displacement, tons	390
Dimensions, feet	107 × 26·5 × 12

KUDRET Y 1229

Displacement, tons	128
Dimensions, feet	65 × 19·6 × 9

FLOATING DOCKS

Y 1081
16 000 tons lift.
Y 1082
12 000 tons lift.
HAVUZ No. 2 (ex-US AFDL) Y 1083.
2 500 tons lift.
Y 1084
4 500 tons lift.
Y 1085
400 tons lift.
Y 1086
3 000 tons lift.

HAVUZ No. 3 (ex-US ARD 12) Y 1087. Transferred Nov 1971
3 500 tons lift.

MISCELLANEOUS

SARKÖY Y 1156 Small transport.

— Y 1163, *ERDER* Y 1164, *ECEABAT* Y 1165, — Y 1166

Hrabour ferries with minelaying capability.

TRAINING SHIP

SAVARONA

Displacement, tons	5 100
Length, feet (*metres*)	349·5 (*106·5*)wl; 408·5 (*124·5*)oa
Beam, feet (*metres*)	53 (*16·2*)
Draught, feet (*metres*)	20·5 (*6·2*)
Guns	4—3 in (*76 mm*) 2—40 mm; 2—20 mm
Main engines	6 geared turbines; 2 shafts; 10 750 shp
Speed, knots	18
Boilers	4 watertube; 400 psi
Oil fuel, tons	2 100
Range, miles	9 000 at 15 knots
Complement	132 + 81 midshipmen

Built by Blohm & Voss, Hamburg. Launched on 28 Feb 1931. Formerly probably the most sumptuously fitted yacht afloat. Equipment includes Sperry gyro-stabilisers. Converted into a training ship in 1952, the saloons and dining rooms being adapted as classrooms, workshops and libraries for midshipmen.

SAVARONA

UNITED KINGDOM

Admiralty Board

Secretary of State for Defence (Chairman):
The Right Honourable Mr. Roy Mason, MP
Minister of State: Ministry of Defence (Vice-Chairman) and Minister of State for Defence Procurement:
Mr William Rodgers, MP
Parliamentary Under-Secretary of State for Defence for the Royal Navy:
Mr Frank Judd, MP
Chief of the Naval Staff and First Sea Lord:
Admiral Sir Edward Ashmore, GCB, DSC
Chief of Naval Personnel and Second Sea Lord:
Admiral Sir David Williams, KCB
Controller of the Navy:
Admiral Sir Anthony Griffin, GCB
Chief of Fleet Support:
Vice-Admiral P. White, CBE
Vice-Chief of the Naval Staff:
Vice-Admiral R. D. Lygo
Chief Scientist (Royal Navy): Mr Basil Wilfred Lythall, CB, MA
Deputy Under Secretary of State (Navy): Mr Sydney Redman, CB
Second Permanent Under-Secretary for Administration: Mr J. M. Wilson, CBE
Second Permanent Uhder-Secterary for Equipment: Sir Martin Flett, KCB

Commanders-in-Chief

Commander in-Chief, Naval Home Command:
Admiral Sir Derek Empson, KCB
Commander-in-Chief, Fleet:
Admiral Sir Terence Lewin, KCB, MVO, DSC

Flag Officers

Flag Officer, 1st Flotilla:
Vice-Admiral H. C. Leach
Flag Officer, 2nd Flotilla:
Rear-Admiral J. D. E. Fieldhouse
Flag Officer, Submarines:
Vice-Admiral I. G. Raikes, CBE, DSC
Flag Officer Naval Air Command:
Vice-Admiral P. M. Austin
Flag Officer Carriers and Amphibious Ships:
Rear-Admiral J. H. F. Eberle
Flag Officer Scotland and Northern Ireland:
Vice-Admiral J. A. R. Troup, DSC and Bar
Flag Officer Medway:
Rear-Admiral S. F. Berthon
Flag Officer Plymouth:
Vice-Admiral A. G. Tait DSC
Flag Officer Sea Training:
Rear-Admiral J. R. S. Gerard-Pearse
Flag Officer Malta:
Rear Admiral O. N. A. Cecil
Flag Officer Gibraltar:
Rear-Admiral R. S. Sandford
Flag Officer Spithead:
Rear Admiral E. J. W. Flower

General Officers, Royal Marines

Commandant-General, Royal Marines:
Lieutenant General P. J. F. Whiteley, OBE
Chief of Staff to Commandant-General, Royal Marines:
Major General P. J. Ovens, OBE, MC
Major General Training Group, Royal Marines:
Major-General D. C. Alexander
Major-General Commando Forces Royal Marines:
Major-General E. G. D. Pounds

Diplomatic Representation

British Naval Attaché in Bonn:
Captain C. V. Howard, DSC

British Naval Attaché in Moscow:
Captain R. J. F. Turner, RN

British Naval Attaché in Paris:
Captain L. A. Bird, RN

British Naval Attaché in Rome:
Captain C. E. T. Baker, MBE

British Naval Attaché in Washington:
Rear-Admiral R. W. Halliday DSC

Personnel

(a) 1973: 84 000
1974: 81 000
1975: 77 100
(b) Voluntary Service

Mercantile Marine:

Lloyd's Register of Shipping: 3 628 vessels of 30 159 543 tons gross

Strength of the Fleet

Type	*Active*	*Building (Projected)*	*Reserve*
Aircraft Carrier	1	—	
A/S Cruisers	1	(?2)	
Helicopter Cruisers	2	—	
Light Cruisers	9	—	
Destroyers	1	5 (2)	
Frigates	60	9	4
Sonar Trials Ship	1	—	
SSBNs	4	—	
Submarines—Fleet	8	4	
Submarines—Patrol	20	—	
Commando Ships	2	—	
Assault Ships (LPD)	2	—	
LSL	6	2	
LST	1	—	
LCTs	5	—	
LCMs	15	—	
LCVPs	22	—	
LCPLs	3	—	
Fast Attack Craft—Patrol	1	—	
Large Patrol Craft	7	4	
Fast Training Boats	3	—	
MCM Support Ship	1	—	
Minehunters	16	(?)	
Minesweepers—Coastal	23	—	
Minesweepers—Inshore	6	—	
Maintenance Ships	3	—	
Submarine Depot Ships	2	—	
Survey Ships	4	—	
Coastal Survey Ships	4	—	
Inshore Survey Craft	5	—	
Ice Patrol Ship	1	—	
Royal Yacht	1	—	
Hovercraft	4	—	
Diving Support Ship	1	—	
Replenishment Tankers	8	—	
Freighting Tankers	4	—	
Bulk Tanker	1	—	
Small Fleet Tankers	6	—	
Helicopter Support Ship	1	—	
Stores Support Ships	4	—	
Fleet Replenishment Ships	4	2	
Store Carriers	3	—	
MSBVs	14	—	
Trials Ships	3	1	
TRVs	9	—	
Cable Ships	2	—	
Armament Carriers	6	—	
Water Carriers	16	—	
Ocean Tugs	14	—	
Harbour Tugs	83	—	
Tenders	54	—	
RNXS Craft	13	—	
MFVs	61	—	
DG Vessels	3	—	
TCVs	7	—	

Deletions

(Note following Disposal List)

Carriers (of all kinds)

1972 *Centaur* and *Albion*

Frigates

1970 *Loch Killisport, Loch Fada, Ulysses, Zest, Murray*
1971 *Urania, Relentless, Pellew, Wakeful, Alert, Grafton*
1972 *Verulam, Venus*
1974 *Tenby, Scarborough* to Pakistan

Destroyers

1970 *Aisne, Trafalgar, Camperdown*
1971 *Daring, Delight, Scorpion, Cambrian*
1972 *Crossbow, Defender, Saintes*
1974 *Agincourt* (1 Nov Milford Haven)

Submarines

1970 *Talent, Thermopylae, Anchorite, Astute*
1971 *Ambush, Alaric, Trump, Taciturn*
1972 *Artemis, Acheron, Alderney*
1975 *Andrew*

MCM Vessels

1970-71 *Dalswinton, Invermoriston, Maddiston, Puncheston, Quainton, Wilkieston*

Auxiliaries

1974 *Wave Chief, Derwentdale* (returned to owners), *Brown Ranger* (Tankers). *Barmond* (BDV), *Samson* (Tug to Chile), *Miner III*

Disposal List

The following ships not on the Active or Reserve list are held in the ports shown pending disposal by sale or scrap.

Aircraft Carrier

Eagle (Plymouth)

Cruiser

Lion (Rosyth)

Destroyers

Caprice (Plymouth)
Cavalier (Chatham)
Barrosa (Portsmouth)

Frigates

Blackpool (Portsmouth)
Blackwood (Portsmouth)
Grenville (Portsmouth)
Palliser (Portsmouth)
Puma (Chatham)
Rapid (Chatham)
Undaunted (Gibraltar-Target)

Minesweepers—Coastal

Ashton (Rosyth)
Belton (Rosyth)
Boulston (Portsmouth)
Dufton (Portsmouth)
Maddiston (Porstmouth)

Fast Attack Craft

Brave Borderer (Pembroke Dock)
Brave Swordsman (Pembroke Dock)
Dark Gladiator (Portsmouth)
Dark Hero (Portsmouth)

LSTs

Lofoten (Rosyth)
Messina (Plymouth)
Stalker (Rosyth)
Zeebrugge (Plymouth)

Survey Ship

Vidal (Chatham)

LIST OF PENNANT NUMBERS

*Disposal List

Aircraft Carriers

R	05	Eagle *
R	09	Ark Royal

Commando Carriers

R	08	Bulwark
R	12	Hermes

Submarines

S	01	Porpoise
S	02	Rorqual
S	03	Narwhal
S	04	Grampus
S	05	Finwhale
S	06	Cachalot
S	07	Sealion
S	08	Walrus
S	09	Oberon
S	10	Odin
S	11	Orpheus
S	12	Olympus
S	13	Osiris
S	14	Onslaught
S	15	Otter
S	16	Oracle
S	17	Ocelot
S	18	Otus
S	19	Opossum
S	20	Opportune
S	21	Onyx
S	22	Resolution
S	23	Repulse
S	26	Renown
S	27	Revenge
S	46	Churchill
S	48	Conqueror
S	50	Courageous
S	63	Andrew *
S	101	Dreadnought
S	102	Valiant
S	103	Warspite
S	104	Sceptre
S	108	Sovereign
S	109	Superb
S	111	Spartan
S	112	Severn
S	113	—
S	126	Swiftsure

Cruisers

C	20	Tiger
C	34	Lion *
C	99	Blake

Light Cruisers and Destroyers

D	01	Caprice *
D	02	Devonshire
D	06	Hampshire
D	12	Kent
D	16	London
D	18	Antrim
D	19	Glamorgan
D	20	Fife
D	21	Norfolk
D	23	Bristol
D	35	Diamond
D	43	Matapan
D	73	Cavalier *
D	80	Sheffield
D	86	Birmingham
D	87	Newcastle
D	88	Glasgow
D	108	Cardiff
D	118	Coventry

Frigates

F	10	Aurora
F	12	Achilles
F	14	Leopard
F	15	Euryalus
F	16	Diomede
F	18	Galatea
F	27	Lynx
F	28	Cleopatra
F	32	Salisbury
F	34	Puma *
F	36	Whitby
F	37	Jaguar
F	38	Arethusa
F	39	Naiad
F	40	Sirius
F	42	Phoebe
F	43	Torquay
F	45	Minerva
F	47	Danae
F	48	Dundas
F	52	Juno
F	53	Undaunted *
F	54	Hardy
F	56	Argonaut
F	57	Andromeda
F	58	Hermione
F	59	Chichester
F	60	Jupiter
F	61	Llandaff
F	69	Bacchante
F	70	Apollo
F	71	Scylla
F	72	Ariadne
F	73	Eastbourne
F	75	Charybdis
F	76	Mermaid
F	77	Blackpool
F	80	Duncan
F	83	Ulster
F	84	Exmouth
F	85	Keppel
F	94	Palliser *
F	97	Russell
F	99	Lincoln
F	101	Yarmouth
F	103	Lowestoft
F	104	Dido
F	106	Brighton
F	107	Rothesay
F	108	Londonderry
F	109	Leander
F	113	Falmouth
F	114	Ajax
F	115	Berwick
F	117	Ashanti
F	119	Eskimo
F	122	Gurkha
F	124	Zulu
F	125	Mohawk
F	126	Plymouth
F	127	Penelope
F	129	Rhyl
F	131	Nubian
F	133	Tartar
F	138	Rapid *
F	169	Amazon
F	170	Antelope
F	171	Active
F	172	Ambuscade
F	173	Arrow
F	174	Alacrity
F	175	Ardent
F	176	Avenger
F	197	Grenville *

Assault Ships

L	10	Fearless
L	11	Interpid

Logistic Landing Ships and LCTs

L	3004	Sir Bedivere
L	3005	Sir Galahad
L	3027	Sir Geraint
L	3029	Sir Lancelot
L	3036	Sir Percivale
L	3505	Sir Tristram
L	4002	Agheila
L	4041	Abbeville
L	4061	Audemer
L	4062	Aachen
L	4097	Andalnes

List of pennant numbers—*continued*

Helicopter Support Ship

K	08	Engadine

Minelayer

N	21	Abdiel

Support Ships & Auxiliaries

A	00	Britannia
A	70	Echo
A	71	Enterprise
A	72	Egeria
A	75	Tidespring
A	76	Tidepool
A	77	Pearleaf
A	78	Plumleaf
A	80	Orangeleaf
A	82	Cherryleaf
A	84	Reliant
A	85	Faithful
A	86	Forceful
A	87	Favourite
A	88	Agile
A	89	Advice
A	90	Accord
A	91	Griper
A	92	Grinder
A	93	Dexterous
A	94	Director
A	95	Typhoon
A	96	Tidereach
A	97	Tideflow
A	98	Tidesurge
A	108	Triumph
A	111	Cyclone
A	122	Olwen
A	123	Olna
A	124	Olmeda
A	127	Torrent
A	128	Torrid
A	133	Hecla
A	134	Rame Head
A	135	Nordenfelt
A	137	Hecate
A	144	Hydra
A	171	Endurance
A	176	Bullfinch
A	179	Whimbrel
A	185	Maidstone
A	187	Forth
A	191	Berry Head
A	200	Vidal *
A	219	Dewdale
A	220	Loyal Moderator
A	222	Spapool
A	224	Spabrook
A	231	Reclaim
A	232	Kingarth
A	241	Robert Middleton
A	257	Spaburn
A	259	St. Margarets
A	260	Spalake
A	261	Eddyfirth
A	264	Reward
A	268	Green Rover
A	269	Grey Rover
A	270	Blue Rover
A	271	Gold Rover
A	273	Black Rover
A	280	Resurgent
A	281	Kinbrace

Support Ships and Auxiliaries—*continued*

A	288	Sea Giant
A	289	Confiance
A	290	Confident
A	310	Invergorden
A	311	Ironbridge
A	312	Ixworth
A	329	Retainer
A	332	Caldy
A	333	Coll
A	334	Bern
A	336	Lundy
A	338	Skomer
A	339	Lyness
A	340	Graemsay
A	344	Stromness
A	345	Tarbatness
A	346	Switha
A	364	Whitehead
A	377	Maxim
A	378	Kinterbury
A	382	Loyal Factor
A	385	Fort Grange
A	386	Fort Austin
A	404	Bacchus
A	406	Hebe
A	480	Resource
A	482	Kinloss
A	486	Regent
A	507	Uplifter
A	510	Loyal Governor

Auxiliaries

Y	—	Watercourse
Y	—	Waterfowl
Y	17	Waterfall
Y	18	Watershed
Y	19	Waterspout
Y	20	Waterside
Y	21	Oilpress
Y	22	Oilstone
Y	23	Oilwell
Y	24	Oilfield
Y	25	Oilbird
Y	26	Oilman

Boom Defence Vessels

P	190	Laymoor
P	191	Layburn
P	192	Mandarin
P	193	Pintail
P	194	Garganey
P	195	Goldeneye
P	196	Goosander
P	197	Pochard
P	202	Barfoot
P	284	Moorsman

Light Forces

P	260	Kingfisher
P	261	Cygnet
P	262	Petrel
P	263	Sandpiper
P	271	Scimitar
P	274	Cutlass
P	275	Sabre
P	276	Tenacity
P	1007	Beachampton
P	1055	Monkton
P	1089	Wasperton
P	1093	Wolverton
P	1096	Yarnton
P	3104	Dee (Beckford)
P	3113	Droxford

Coastal Minesweepers

M	1103	Kilmorey (Alfriston)
M	1109	Killecrankie (Bickington)
M	1110	Bildeston
M	1113	Brereton
M	1114	Brinton
M	1115	Bronington
M	1124	St. David (Crichton)
M	1125	Cuxton
M	1130	Highburton
M	1133	Bossington
M	1136	Curzon (Fittleton)
M	1140	Gavinton
M	1141	Glasserton
M	1146	Venturer (Hodgeston)
M	1147	Hubberston
M	1151	Iveston
M	1153	Kedleston
M	1154	Kellington
M	1157	Kirkliston
M	1158	Laleston
M	1165	Maxton
M	1166	Nurton
M	1167	Clyde (Repton)
M	1173	Mersey (Pollington)
M	1180	Shavington
M	1181	Sheraton
M	1182	Shoulton
M	1187	Upton
M	1188	Walkerton
M	1194	Thames (Woolaston)
M	1195	Wotton
M	1198	Ashton *
M	1199	Belton *
M	1200	Soberton
M	1204	Montrose (Stubbington)
M	1205	Northumbria (Wiston)
M	1208	Lewiston
M	1209	Chawton
M	1216	Solent (Crofton)

Inshore Minesweepers

M	2002	Aveley
M	2010	Isis (Cradley)
M	2603	Arlingham
M	2611	Bottisham R
M	2614	Bucklesham TRV
M	2616	Chelsham R
M	2621	Dittisham
M	2622	Downham TRV
M	2626	Everingham TRV
M	2628	Flintham
M	2630	Fritham TRV
M	2635	Haversham TRV
M	2636	Lasham TRV
M	2716	Pagham RNXS
M	2717	Fordham DGV
M	2720	Waterwitch (Powderham)
M	2726	Shipham RNXS
M	2733	Thakeham RNXS
M	2735	Tongham RNXS
M	2737	Warmingham DGV
M	2780	Woodlark (Yaxham)
M	2781	Portisham RNXS
M	2783	Odiham RNXS
M	2784	Puttenham RNXS
M	2785	Birdham RNXS
M	2790	Thatcham DGV
M	2793	Thornham

DGV = *Degaussing Vessels*
PAS = *Port Auxiliary Service*
RNXS = *Royal Naval Auxiliary Service*
TRV = *Torpedo Recovery Vessels*
R = Reserve (ex-RAF)

AIRCRAFT CARRIER

Note. Eagle; see Disposal List.

Name	*Deck Letter*	*No.*	*Builders*	*Laid down*	*Launched*	*Completed*
ARK ROYAL (ex-*Irresistable*)	R	R 09	Cammell Laird, Birkenhead	3 May 1943	3 May 1950	25 Feb 1955

Displacement, tons	43 060 standard; 50 786 full load
Length, feet (*metres*)	720·0 (*219·5*) pp; 845·0 (*257·6*) oa
Beam, feet (*metres*)	112·8 (*34·4*) hull
Draught, feet (*metres*)	36·0 (*11·0*)
Width, feet (*metres*)	166·0 (*50·6*)
Catapults	2 improved steam
Aircraft	30 fixed wing + 6 helicopters
Missile launchers	Fitted for four quadruple "Seacat" (not fitted)
Armour	4·5 in belt; 4 in flight deck; 2·5 in hangar deck; 1·5 in hangar side
Main engines	Parsons single reduction geared turbines; 4 shafts; 152 000 shp
Speed, knots	31·5
Boilers	8 Admiralty 3-drum type; pressure 400 psi (*28·1 kg/cm²*); superheat 600°F (316°C)
Oil fuel, tons	5 500 capacity
Complement	260 officers (as Flagship) 2 380 ratings (with Air Staff)

ARK ROYAL 1972

GENERAL
First British aircraft carrier with steam catapults. Had first side lift in a British aircraft carrier, situated amidships on the port side and serving the upper hangar but in 1959 this was removed, the deck park provided by the angled deck having obviated its necessity, leaving her with two centre lifts. In 1961, the deck landing projector sight, "Hilo" long range guidance system, and more powerful steam catapults were installed. Ship, originally cost £21 428 000. Due for disposal in 1978/79.

MODERNISATION. A three-years "special refit" and modernisation costing £32 500 000, from Mar 1967 to Feb 1970, enables her to operate both Phantom and Buccaneer Mk 2 aircraft. A fully angled deck 8·5 degrees off the centre line was fitted, involving two large extensions to the flight deck, and the size of the island was increased. A new waist catapult with an increased launching speed allows her to operate aircraft at almost "nil" wind conditions. A new direct acting gear was installed to enable bigger aircraft to be landed on at greater speeds.

CORVUS. Eight barrelled launcher fitted. Has multi-purpose use including launching of illuminants and "Chaff".

RADAR. Search: Type 965 (2 sets), Type 993. Aircraft Direction: Type 982 and Type 983 height finder. Miscellaneous: Carrier controlled Approach Radar.

DRAWING. Starboard elevation and plan. 1974 scale: 96 feet = 1 inch

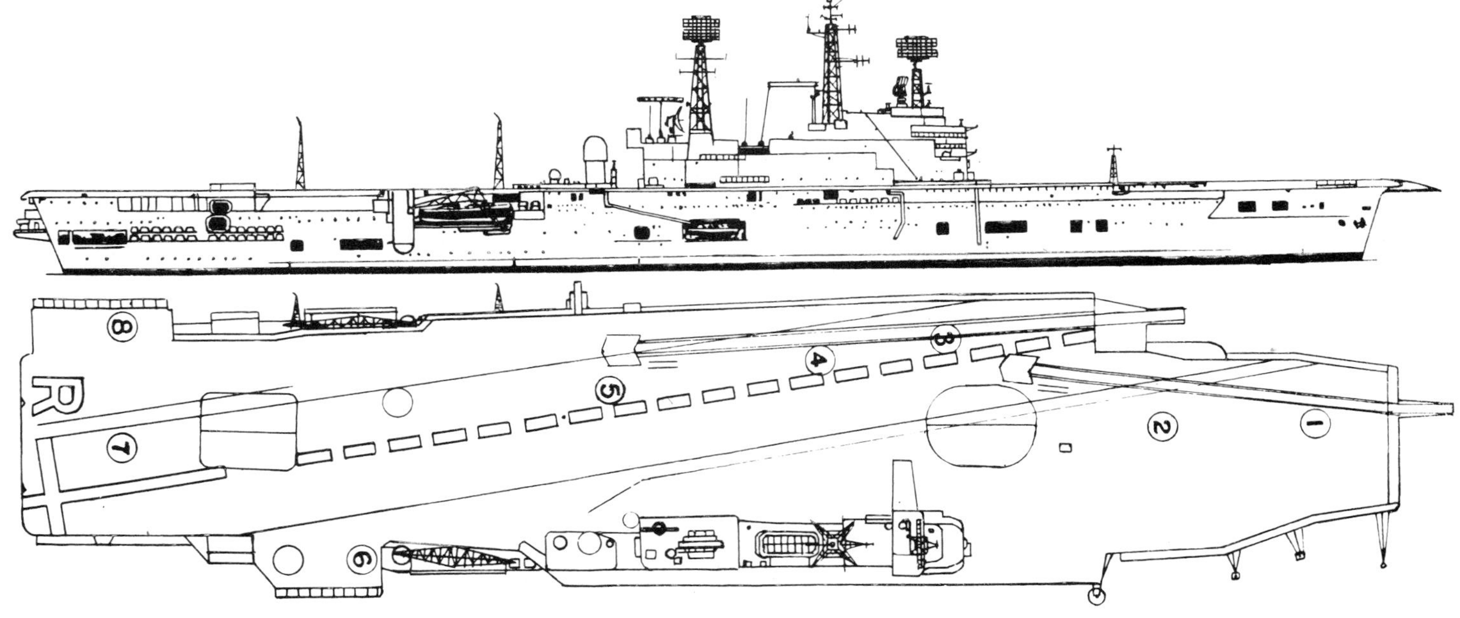

ARK ROYAL 1971

CRUISERS

1 + 2 ANTI-SUBMARINE CRUISERS

INVINCIBLE

Displacement, tons	19 000 to 20 000 estimated
Length, feet (*metres*)	650·0 (*198·1*) approx
Beam, feet (*metres*)	84·0 (*25·6*) approx
Flight Deck, ft (*m*)	100 (*30·5*)
Draught, feet (*metres*)	24·0 (*7·3*) approx
Aircraft	Total of 15: 9 Sea King helicopters (could carry 6 Harriers)
Missile launchers	2 twin "Sea Dart"
Main engines	4 "Olympus" gas turbines; 112 000 shp; "Tyne" gas turbines
Speed, knots	30
Complement	1 200 (including aircrew)

First-of-class order from Vickers 17 April 1973, if follow-up orders are made, completion could be—first in 1978-79, second in 1980 and third in 1981-82. *Invincible* laid down at Barrow 20 July 1973.

She will be capable of providing a landing deck and hangar for helicopters, together with facilities for the command and control of naval and maritime air forces. The ship will be configured for a through deck, i.e. flight deck area, and approach will be unobstructed by super-structure, providing a limited run for V/STOL aircraft. With an angled deck she will virtually be a novel type of light fleet aircraft carrier. She will have two column masts and two funnels with an island bridge super-structure on the starboard side. Open forecastle head.

RADAR. As presently planned—Type 965 long range surveillance radar with double AKE-1 array; Type 992 Q general purpose radar; two Type 909 fire control and target radars for Sea Dart.

INVINCIBLE *1973, Vickers Ltd.*

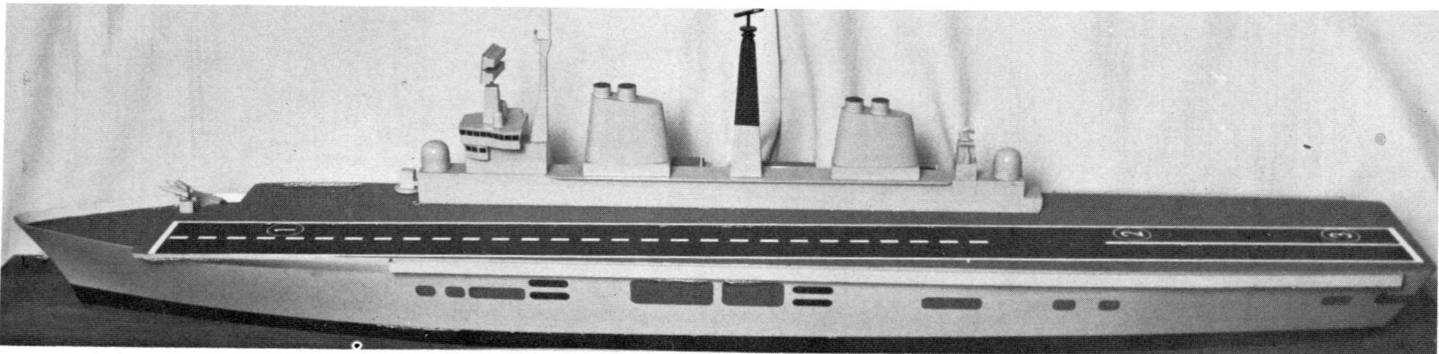

INVINCIBLE model *1973, MOD*

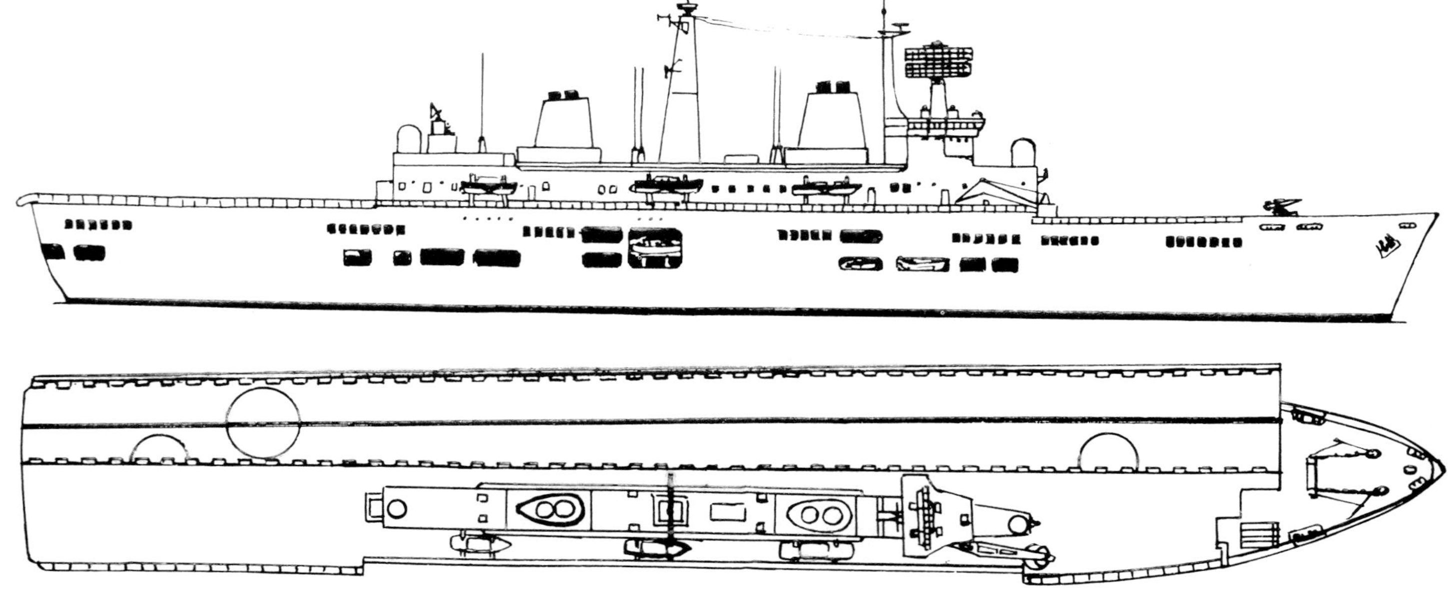

INVINCIBLE *1974*

Cruisers—*continued*

2 "TIGER" CLASS

Name	*No.*	*Builders and Engineers*	*Laid down*	*Launched*	*Completed*
BLAKE (ex-*Tiger*, ex-*Blake*)	C 99	Fairfield SB & Eng. Govan	17 Aug 42	20 Dec 45	8 Mar 61
TIGER (ex-*Bellerophon*)	C 20	John Brown, Clydebank	1 Oct 41	25 Oct 45	18 Mar 59

Displacement, tons: 9 500 standard; 12 080 full load
Length, feet (*metres*): 538·0 (*164·0*)pp; 550·0(*167·6*) wl 566·5 (*172·8*) oa
Beam, feet (*metres*): 64·0 (*19·5*)
Draught, feet (*metres*): 23·0 (*7·0*)
Aircraft: 4 Sea King helicopters
Missile launchers: 2 quadruple "Seacat"
Guns: 2—6 in (*152 mm*) 1 twin; 2—3 in (*76 mm*) (twin)
Armour: Belt 3·5 in—3·2 in (*89—83 mm*); deck 2 in (*51 mm*); turret 3 in—1 in (*76—25 mm*)
Main engines: 4 Parsons geared turbines; 4 shafts; 80 000 shp
Boilers: 4 Admiralty 3-drum type
Speed, knots: 31·5 max
Range, miles: 2 000 at 30 knots; 4 000 at 20 knots; 6 500 at 13 knots
Oil fuel, tons: 1 850
Complement: 85 officers, 800 ratings

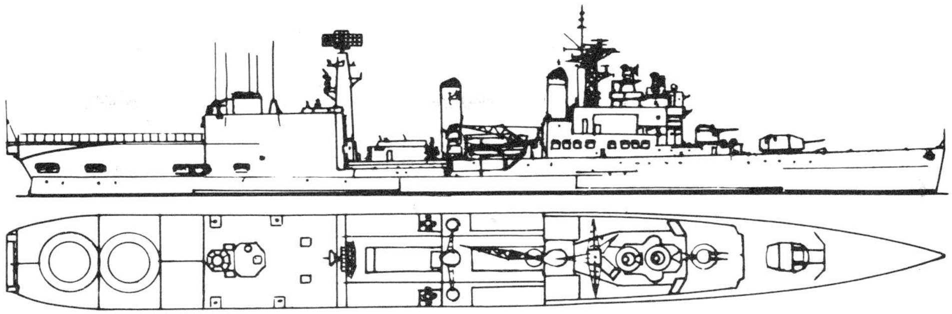

TIGER (Funnels higher than *Blake's*) 1974

Originally designed as orthodox cruisers. Work on the ships was stopped in July 1946, for eight years. The decision to complete them was announced on 15 Oct 1954. Delayed for resumption to a new design in 1955. *Tiger* cost £13 113 000 and *Blake* £14 940 000. Helicopter conversion cost £5 500 000 for *Blake* and the astonishing total of £13 250 000 for *Tiger*.

ELECTRICAL. 4 turbo-generators provide 4 000 kW ac, the first time this type of power used in British cruisers.

ENGINEERING. Main machinery is largely automatic and can be remotely controlled. Steam conditions 400 psi pressure and 640°F. Propellers 11 ft dia, 285 rpm.

CLASS. It was announced in Feb 1972 that the unconverted sister ship *Lion* had been approved for disposal by scrapping. There were originally to be eight ships of this class—*Hawke* and *Bellerophon* were additional names.

CONVERSION. *Blake* was converted to a command helicopter cruiser at HM Dockyard, Portsmouth from early 1965 until she recommissioned on 23 Apr 1969. *Tiger* was similarly converted during 1968 to 1972.

DRAWING. Starboard elevation and plan of *Tiger*. Redrawn in 1974.

GUNNERY. The 6 inch fully automatic guns of advanced design are equally effective in surface and anti-aircraft roles. Rate of fire is 20 rpm, more than twice that of any previous cruiser. The 3 inch guns are capable of 90 rpm.

RADAR. Search: Type 965 and Type 992.
Height/Finder: Type 277.
Fire control: 4 MRS 3 fire control directors.

TIGER 1973, Wright and Logan

BLAKE (SCOT-FITTED) 5/1974, C. and S. Taylor

LIGHT CRUISERS

1 TYPE 82

Name	*No.*	*Builders*	*Laid down*	*Launched*	*Commissioned*
BRISTOL	D 23	Swan Hunter & Tyne Shipbuilders Ltd	15 Nov 1967	30 June 1969	31 Mar 1973

Displacement, tons	5 650 standard 6 750 full load
Length, feet (*metres*)	490·0 (*149·4*)wl; 507·0 (*154·5*)oa
Beam, feet (*metres*)	55·0 (*16·8*)
Draught, feet (*metres*)	22·5 (*6·9*)
Aircraft	Landing platform for 1 "Wasp" helicopter
Missile launchers	1 twin "Seadart" GWS 30 launcher aft
A/S weapons	1 "Ikara" single launcher forward; 1 "Limbo" three-barrelled depth charge mortar (Mark 10) aft
Guns	1—4·5 in (*115 mm*) Mark 8 forward;
Main engines	COSAG arrangement (combined steam and gas turbines) 2 sets Standard Range geared steam turbines, 30 000 shp; 2 Bristol-Siddeley marine "Olympus" gas turbines, 44 600 shp; 2 shafts; Total 74 600 shp
Speed, knots	32
Boilers	2
Range, miles	Over 4 500 at 18 knots
Complement	433 (33 officers, 400 ratings)

GENERAL.
Three funnels, one amidships and two aft abreast the mainmast.

Designed around Seadart GWS 30 weapons system. Fully stabilised to present a steady weapon platform. The gas turbines provide emergency power and high speed boost. The machinery is remotely-controlled from a ship control centre. Automatic steering, obviating the need for a quartermaster. Many labour-saving items of equipment fitted to make the most efficient and economical use of manpower resulting in a smaller ship's company for tonnage than any previous warship. Fitted with Action Data Automation Weapon System. Started trials 10 April 1972. Remainder of class cancelled owing to high cost and cancellation of aircraft-carrier building programme for which they were intended as A/A escorts.

COST. £22 500 000 (£27 000 000 overall). GEC-Marconi equipment for radar, weapons and communications cost over £3 000 000.

COMMUNICATIONS. By GEC-Marconi to include SCOT satellite system compatible with both SKYNET and the US Defence satellites.

MISSILES. The Seadart ship missile system, developed to meet the air threat of the 1970's and 1980's, also has a reasonable anti-ship capability.
Ikara is a long-range anti-submarine weapon system, developed in Australia.

RADAR. Type 965 long range search radar with AKE double aerial outfit and IFF; Type 992 General-purpose radar; Type 909 fire control and target radar for Sea Dart.

BRISTOL *1973, Wright and Logan*

BRISTOL *5/1973, John G, Callis*

BRISTOL *4/1974, John G, Callis*

BRISTOL *1973, C. and S. Taxlor*

Light Cruisers—*continued*

8 "COUNTY" CLASS

Name	No.	Builders	Laid down	Launched	Completed
ANTRIM	D 18	Fairfield SB & Eng Co Ltd, Govan	20 Jan 66	19 Oct 67	14 July 70
DEVONSHIRE	D 02	Cammell Laird & Co Ltd, Birkenhead	9 Mar 59	10 June 60	15 Nov 62
FIFE	D 20	Fairfield SB & Eng Co Ltd, Govan	1 June 62	9 July 64	21 June 66
GLAMORGAN	D 19	Vickers-Armstrongs Ltd, Newcastle-on-Tyne	13 Sep 62	9 July 64	11 Oct 66
HAMPSHIRE	D 06	John Brown & Co (Clydebank) Ltd, Glasgow	26 Mar 59	16 Mar 61	15 Mar 63
KENT	D 12	Harland & Wolff Ltd, Belfast	1 Mar 60	27 Sep 61	15 Aug 63
LONDON	D 16	Swan, Hunter & Wigham Richardson, Wallsend	26 Feb 60	7 Dec 61	4 Nov 63
NORFOLK	D 21	Swan, Hunter & Wigham Richardson, Wallsend	15 Mar 66	16 Nov 67	7 Mar 70

Displacement, tons: 5 440 standard; 6 200 full load
Length, feet (*metres*): 505·0 (*153·9*) wl; 520·5 (*158·7*) oa
Beam, feet (*metres*): 54·0 (*16·5*)
Draught, feet (*metres*): 20·0 (*6·1*)
Aircraft: 1 "Wessex" helicopter
Missile launchers: Exocet in four ships (see *Missile* note) 1 twin "Seaslug" aft; 2 quadruple "Seacat" either side abreast hangar.
Guns: 4—4·5 in (*115 mm*), 2 twin turrets forward; 2—20 mm, single (2—4·5 only in ships with Exocet)
Boilers: 2 Babcock & Wilcox
Main engines: Combined steam and gas turbines. 2 sets geared steam turbines, 30 000 shp; 4 gas turbines, 30 000 shp. 2 shafts; Total 60 000 shp; (see *Engineering* notes)
Speed, knots: 32·5
Complement: 471 (33 officers and 438 men)

GENERAL
Fife, Glamorgan, Antrim and *Norfolk,* have the more powerful "Seaslug" II systems. All fitted with stabilisers and are fully air-conditioned.

APPEARANCE. *Kent* and *London* have mainmast stepped further aft than remainder. The last four of the class have distinctive tubular foremast and twin radar "bedstead".

ELECTRICAL. Two 1 000 kW turbo-alternators and three gas turbines alternators total 3 750 kW, at 440 V.a.c.

ENGINEERING. These are the first ships of their size to have COSAG (combined steam and gas turbine machinery). Boilers work at a pressure of 700 psi and a temperature of 950 deg F. The steam and gas turbines are geared to the same shaft. Each shaft set consists of a high pressure and low pressure steam turbine of 15 000 shp combined output plus two G.6 gas turbines each of 7 500 shp. The gas turbines are able to develop their full power from cold within a few minutes, enabling ships lying in harbour without steam to get under way instantly in emergency.

GUNNERY. The 4·5 inch guns are radar controlled fully automatic dual-purpose quick-firing. The 20 mm guns were added for picket duties in S.E. Asia, but have been retained for general close range duties.

MISSILES. Four Exocet fitted in *Norfolk, Antrim* and *Glamorgan* and to be fitted in *Fife* in place of B turret. No reloads carried. *Norfolk* Exocet trials on French missile range (Mediterranean) in April 1974.

RADAR. Type 992 search radar; Height Finder Type 278; Type 901 fire control and Target radar aft for Seaslug; MRS 3 forward, port and starboard for gunnery fire control; GWS 22 (for Seacat) in *Kent, Norfolk, Antrim, Fife* and *Glamorgan*—remainder have optical sighting; Type 965 with double AKE-2 aerial outfit in *Norfolk, Glamorgan, Antrim* and *Fife* while the remainder have single AKE-1; IFF.

NORFOLK with Exocet — *10/1973, John G, Callis*

HAMPSHIRE — *1974, Michael D, J, Lennon*

KENT — *10/1974, C, and S, Taylor*

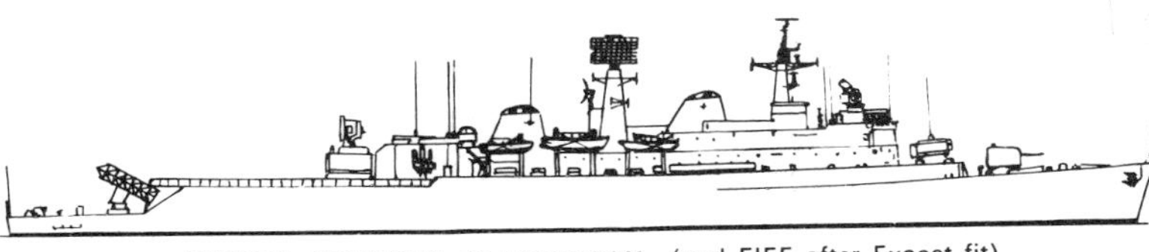
ANTRIM, NORFOLK, GLAMORGAN (and FIFE after Exocet fit)

KENT, LONDON

DEVONSHIRE, HAMPSHIRE

ANTRIM with Exocet — *10/1974, C, and S, Taylor*

DESTROYERS

1 + 5 + 2 "TYPE 42"

Name	No.	Builders	Ordered	Laid down	Launched	Commissioned
SHEFFIELD	D 80	Vickers Ltd Shipbuilding Group, Barrow	14 Nov 1968	15 Jan 1970	10 June 1971	28 Feb 1975
BIRMINGHAM	D 86	Cammell Laird & Co, Ltd, Birkenhead	21 May 1971	28 Mar 1972	30 July 1973	1976
COVENTRY	D 118	Cammell Laird & Co, Ltd, Birkenhead	21 May 1971	22 Mar 1972	21 June 1974	1976/77
CARDIFF	D 108	Vickers Ltd, Shipbuilding Group, Barrow	10 June 1971	3 Nov 1972	22 Feb 1974	1977
NEWCASTLE	D 87	Swan Hunter, Wallsend on Tyne	11 Nov 1971	21 Feb 1973	—	1977
GLASGOW	D 88	Swan Hunter, Wallsend on Tyne	11 Nov 1971	7 Mar 1974	—	1977

Displacement, tons	3 150 standard; 3 500 full load
Length, feet (*metres*)	392·0 (*119·5*)wl; 410·0 (*125·0*)oa
Beam, feet (*metres*)	48 (*14·6*)
Draught, feet (*metres*)	17 (*5·2*)
Aircraft	1 twin engined "Lynx" anti-submarine helicopter
Missile launchers	1 twin "Sea Dart" medium range surface-to-air (surface-to-surface capability) GWS 30 system
Guns	1—4·5 in automatic, Mark 8, 2—20 mm Oerlikon; 2 saluting
A/S weapons	Helicopter launched Mk 44 torpedoes (2 sets 12·75 in A/S tubes to be fitted at 1st refit)
Main engines	COGOG arrangement of Rolls Royce Olympus gas turbines for full power; and 2 Rolls Royce Tyne gas turbines for cruising; controllable pitch propellers for manoeuvring; 2 shafts; 50 000 shp
Speed, knots	30
Endurance	Over 4 000 miles at 18 knots
Complement	300 (20 officers and 280 ratings) (accommodation for 312)

GENERAL
This is a class of all gas-turbine ships fitted with four sets of stabilisers. The helicopter will carry the Skua (CK 834) air-to-surface weapon for use against lightly defended surface ship targets such as fast patrol boats. Advantages include ability to reach maximum speed with great rapidity, reduction in space and weight and 25 per cent reduction in technical manpower. To cost £23 000 000 per ship. All to be in service by 1978.

ELECTRONICS. Twin Scot Skynet satellite communication aerials; ADAWS 4 for coordination of action information.

ENGINEERING. Considerable automation has allowed a cut in engine-room staff required, a number of machinery spaces operating unmanned. Propellers by Stone Manganese (Type XX).

RADAR. Type 965 with AKE-2 and IFF; Type 992Q General-purpose radar; Type 1006 navigation radar; Two Type 909 Sea Dart fire control and target radars; ECM; D/F.

SHEFFIELD *1975*

SHEFFIELD *1974, K. E. Royall*

SHEFFIELD *1974, Vickers Ltd*

FRIGATES

4 + 4 "AMAZON" (TYPE 21) CLASS

Name	No.	Builders	Laid down	Launched	Commissioning
AMAZON	F 169	Vosper Thornycroft, Woolston	6 Nov 1969	26 Apr 1971	11 May 1974
ANTELOPE	F 170	Vosper Thornycroft, Woolston	23 Mar 1971	16 Mar 1972	Feb 1975 (trials)
ACTIVE	F 171	Vosper Thornycroft, Woolston	23 July 1971	23 Nov 1972	1975
AMBUSCADE	F 172	Yarrow & Co, Ltd, Glasgow	July 1971	18 Jan 1973	1975
ARROW	F 173	Yarrow & Co, Ltd, Glasgow	June 1972	5 Feb 1974	1975
ALACRITY	F 174	Yarrow & Co, Ltd, Glasgow	Feb 1973	18 Sep 1974	—
ARDENT	F 175	Yarrow & Co, Ltd, Glasgow	26 Feb 1974	9 May 1975	—
AVENGER	F 176	Yarrow & Co, Ltd, Glasgow	30 Oct 1974	—	—

Displacement, tons: 2 000 standard; 2 500 full load
Length, feet (*metres*): 360·0 (*109·7*)wl; 384·0(*117·0*)oa
Beam, feet (*metres*): 41·8 (*12·7*)
Draught, feet (*metres*): 12·3 (*3·7*)
Aircraft: 1 twin engined "Lynx" anti-submarine helicopter
Missile launchers: 1 quadruple "Seacat" surface-to-air (later ships will have "Seawolf") Exocet MM 38 (see Missile note)
Guns: 1—4·5 in Mark 8; 2—20 mm Oerlikon
A/S weapons: Helicopter launched torpedoes
Torpedo tubes: 6 (2 triple) (to be fitted)
Main engines: COGOG arrangement of 2 Rolls Royce "Olympus" gas turbines for speed; 2 Rolls Royce "Tyne" gas turbines for cruising; 2 shafts; 50 000 shp; controllable pitch propellers
Speed, knots: 34
Range, miles: 4 500 at 18 knots
Complement: 170 (11 officers, and 159 ratings)

The Navy awarded Vosper Thornycroft, Portsmouth and Southampton, a contract on 27 Feb 1968 for the design of a patrol frigate to be prepared in full collaboration with Yarrow Ltd, Scotstoun. This is the first custom built gas turbine frigate (designed and constructed as such from the keel up, as opposed to conversion) and the first warship designed by commercial firms for many years. All eight were planned for completion by end 1977 but the building of the last five at Yarrows has been delayed by lack of technical information from beyond the shipyard.

MISSILES. It is planned to fit Exocet MM 38 in the last four ships.

RADAR. Type 992 Q general-purpose search radar; Type 978 navigation radar; GWS 24 fire control fore and aft for Seacat; Orion RTN-10X WSA-4 fire control system for guns; Cossor Type 1010 IFF interrogator; Plessey PTR 461 IFF transponder; CAAIS.

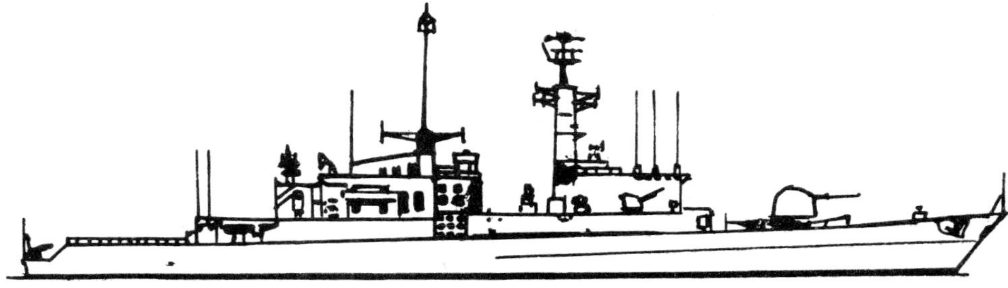
AMAZON

AMAZON — *1974, Michael D. J. Lennon*

AMAZON — *10/1974, C. and S. Taylor*

2 "WEAPON" CLASS (TYPE 22)

BROADSWORD +1

Displacement, tons: 3 500 standard; 3 860 full load
Dimensions, ft (*m*): 430 oa × 38·5 × 14 (*131·2* × *14·8* × *4·3*)
Aircraft: 2 "Lynx" helicopters
Missile launchers: 2 "Sea Wolf" surface-to-air systems; 2 twin Exocet surface-to-surface launchers
Main engines: COGOG arrangement of 2 Rolls Royce "Olympus" gas turbines and 2 Rolls Royce "Tyne" gas turbines driving 2 shafts = Total 56 000 hp
Speed, knots: 30 (18 on Tynes)
Complement: 250 (approx)

Designed as successors to the "Leander" class, the construction of which ceased with the completion of the scheduled programme of 26 ships. Order for first of class, *Broadsword*, to be built by Yarrows was placed on 26 Feb 1974. She was laid down on 7 Feb 1975. The name of the second ship has been reported as *Battleaxe*.

BROADSWORD model — *1974 MOD*

Frigates—*continued*

16 "LEANDER" CLASS

10 "BROAD-BEAMED LEANDER" CLASS

Displacement, tons	2 450 standard; 2 860 full load (Leanders) 2 500 standard; 2 962 full load (Broad-beamed)
Length, feet (*metres*)	360 (*109·7*) wl; 372 (*113·4*) oa
Beam, feet (*metres*)	41 (*12·5*) (Leanders) 43 (*13·1*) (Broad-beamed)
Draught, feet (*metres*)	18 (*5·5*)
Aircraft	1 Wasp helicopter
Missiles	Exocet in some and Seacat (see *Notes*)
Guns (see *Notes*)	2—4·5 in (*115 mm*) (twin) 2—40 mm (varies) 2—20 mm (Seacat ships)
A/S weapons	Ikara in some (see *Notes*) 1 "Limbo" 3 barrelled mortar
Main engines (see *Notes*)	2 double reduction geared turbines; 2 shafts; 30 000 shp
Boilers	2
Speed, knots	30
Oil fuel, tons	460
Complement	251 (Leanders) 263 (Broad-beamed)

Name	No.	Builders	Laid down	Launched	Completed
AJAX	F 114	Cammell Laird & Co. Ltd. Birkenhead	12 Oct 59	16 Aug 62	10 Dec 63
DIDO	F 104	Yarrow & Co Ltd, Scotstoun, Glasgow	2 Dec 59	22 Dec 61	18 Sep 63
LEANDER	F 109	Harland & Wolff Ltd, Belfast	10 Apr 59	28 June 61	27 Mar 63
PENELOPE	F 127	Vickers-Armstrong Ltd, Tyne	14 Mar 61	17 Aug 62	31 Oct 63
AURORA	F 10	John Brown & Co (Clydebank) Ltd	1 June 61	28 Nov 62	9 Apr 64
EURYALUS	F 15	Scotts Shipbuilding & Eng, Greenock	2 Nov 61	6 June 63	16 Sep 64
GALATEA	F 18	Swan, Hunter & Wigham Richardson, Tyne	29 Dec 61	23 May 63	25 Apr 64
ARETHUSA	F 38	J. Samuel White & Co Ltd, Cowes	7 Sep 62	5 Nov 63	24 Nov 65
NAIAD	F 39	Yarrow & Co Ltd, Scotstoun, Glasgow	30 Oct 62	4 Nov 63	15 Mar 65
CLEOPATRA	F 28	HM Dockyard, Devonport	19 June 63	25 Mar 64	4 Jan 66
SIRIUS	F 40	HM Dockyard, Portsmouth	9 Aug 63	22 Sep 64	15 June 66
MINERVA	F 45	Vickers-Armstrong Ltd, Tyne	25 July 63	19 Dec 64	14 May 66
PHOEBE	F 42	Alex Stephen & Sons Ltd, Glasgow	3 June 63	8 July 64	15 Apr 66
DANAE	F 47	HM Dockyard, Devonport	16 Dec 64	31 Oct 65	7 Sep 67
JUNO	F 52	John I. Thornycroft Ltd, Woolston	16 July 64	24 Nov 65	18 July 67
ARGONAUT	F 56	Hawthorn Leslie, Ltd, Hebburn-on-Tyne	27 Nov 64	8 Feb 66	17 Aug 67

"BROAD BEAMED LEANDER" CLASS

Name	No.	Builders	Laid down	Launched	Completed
ANDROMEDA	F 57	HM Dockyard, Portsmouth	25 May 66	24 May 67	2 Dec 68
JUPITER	F 60	Yarrow & Co Ltd, Scotstoun, Glasgow	3 Oct 66	4 Sep 67	9 Aug 69
HERMIONE	F 58	Alex Stephen & Sons Ltd, Glasgow	6 Dec 65	26 Apr 67	11 July 69
BACCHANTE	F 69	Vickers Ltd, High Walker, Newcastle	27 Oct 66	29 Feb 68	17 Oct 69
SCYLLA	F 71	HM Dockyard, Devonport	17 May 67	8 Aug 68	12 Feb 70
CHARYBDIS	F 75	Harland & Wolff Ltd, Belfast	27 Jan 67	28 Feb 68	2 June 69
ACHILLES	F 12	Yarrow & Co Ltd, Scotstoun	1 Dec 67	21 Nov 68	9 July 70
DIOMEDE	F 16	Yarrow & Co Ltd, Scotstoun	30 Jan 68	15 Apr 69	2 Apr 71
APOLLO	F 70	Yarrow & Co Ltd, Scotstoun	1 May 69	15 Oct 70	28 May 72
ARIADNE	F 72	Yarrow & Co Ltd, Scotstoun	1 Nov 69	10 Sep 71	10 Feb 73

GENERAL
This class, whose construction extended over ten years, was an improvement on the Type 12. As originally designed there were several significant improvements—a helicopter, VDS and long-range air warning radar being the most important. Recently a number of conversions have been put in hand (see *Notes* below).

ELECTRICAL. 440 volts, 60 cycle AC. 1 900 kw in earlier ships, 2 500 kw in later ones.

ENGINEERING. The first ten have Y-100 machinery, the remainder of the "Leanders" Y-136." Broad-beamed Leanders" have Y-160 machinery.

EXOCET. This is to be mounted forward in place of the 4·5 in turret in the following—*Cleopatra* (Oct 1975), *Phoebe* (started Aug 1974—completion 1976), *Sirius* (started Mar 1975), *Dido* (started July 1975), *Argonaut* (to start Nov 1975), *Minerva* (to start Dec 1975), *Juno* (to start May 1976), *Danae* (to start June 1976) and the ten Broad-beam ships.

GUNNERY. 4·5 in turret removed in Exocet and Ikara conversions and in *Penelope*. 40 mm are not fitted in unconverted ships mounting Seacat. Ikara conversions mount 2 twin 40 mm abaft the bridge. Two single 20 mm are mounted abaft the bridge in place of 40 mm in Seacat fitted ships.

IKARA. Already mounted in *Leander, Galatea* and *Ajax* in place of 4·5 in turret. To be fitted in *Naiad* (completion June 1975), *Aurora* and *Euryalus* (completion Dec 1975), *Arethusa* (completion June 1976) and *Penelope*.

RADAR. Search: Type 965 with single AKE aerial array and Type 993 combined surface and air warning. Fire Control: X band. MRS.3/GWS-22 fire control directors. DF equipment. In Ikara conversions and *Penelope* Type 965 aerial is removed to compensate for top-weight.

SEACAT. Single Seacat first fitted in *Naiad*, subsequently to replace 40 mm guns in all but Ikara conversions who have two Seacat mounts. *Penelope* currently has none.

SEAWOLF. An experimental outfit is mounted in *Penelope*, replacing the 4·5 in turret. She carries different radars and additional deckhouses, though no Seacat. Ikara will eventually replace Seawolf in this ship.

SONAR. VDS was originally fitted in all but *Diomede*. In some the VDS has been removed leaving the well—in others the well has been plated over to provide extra accommodation.

ANDROMEDA — *1974, Michael D. J. Lennon*

"Leander" class with 4·5 in guns and Seacat

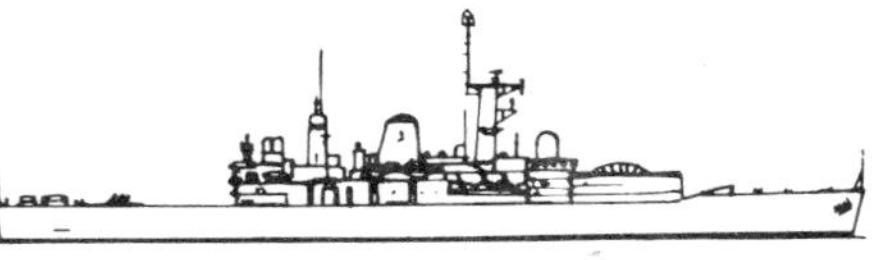
"Leander" class with Ikara

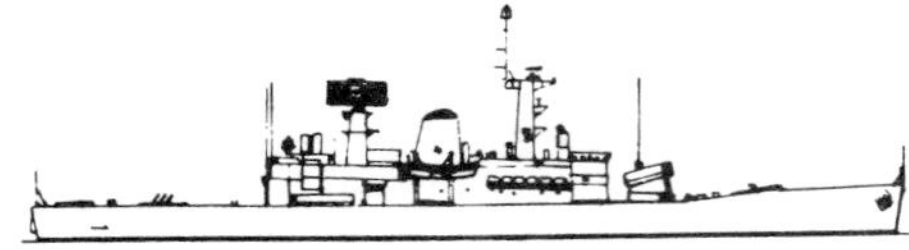
"Leander" class with Exocet

PENELOPE with Seawolf

Frigates—*continued*

AJAX with IKARA *8/1974, C. and S. Taylor*

HERMIONE *10/1974, C. and S. Taylor*

JUNO *8/1973, C. and S. Taylor*

Frigates—*continued*

9 "ROTHESAY" CLASS
MODIFIED TYPE 12

Displacement, tons	2 380 standard; 2 800 full load
Length, feet (*metres*)	360·0 (*109·7*)wl; 370·0 (*112·8*)oa
Beam, feet (*metres*)	41·0 (*12·5*)
Draught, feet (*metres*)	17·3 (*5·3*) max (props)
Aircraft	1 "Wasp" helicopter
Missile launchers	1 quadruple for "Seacat"
Guns	2—4·5 in (*115 mm*) dp (1 twin) 2—20 mm AA single
A/S weapons	1 Limbo 3-barrelled DC mortar
Main engines	2 double reduction geared turbines; 2 shafts; 30 000 shp
Speed, knots	30
Boilers	2 Babcock & Wilcox
Oil fuel, tons	400
Complement	235 (15 officers and 220 ratings)

Name	*No.*	*Builders*	*Laid down*	*Launched*	*Completed*
BERWICK	F 115	Harland & Wolff Ltd, Belfast	16 June 1958	15 Dec 1959	1 June 1961
BRIGHTON	F 106	Yarrow & Co Ltd, Scotstoun	23 July 1957	30 Oct 1959	28 Sep 1961
FALMOUTH	F 113	Swan Hunter, Wigham Richardson	23 Nov 1957	15 Dec 1959	25 July 1961
LONDONDERRY	F 108	J. Samuel White & Co Ltd, Cowes	15 Nov 1956	20 May 1958	22 July 1960
LOWESTOFT	F 103	Alex Stephen & Sons Ltd, Govan	9 June 1958	23 June 1960	18 Oct 1961
PLYMOUTH	F 126	HM Dockyard, Devonport	1 July 1958	20 July 1959	11 May 1961
RHYL	F 129	HM Dockyard, Portsmouth	29 Jan 1958	23 Apr 1959	31 Oct 1960
ROTHESAY	F 107	Yarrow & Co Ltd, Scotstoun	6 Nov 1956	9 Dec 1957	23 Apr 1960
YARMOUTH	F 101	John Brown & Co Ltd, Clydebank	29 Nov 1957	23 Mar 1959	26 Mar 1960

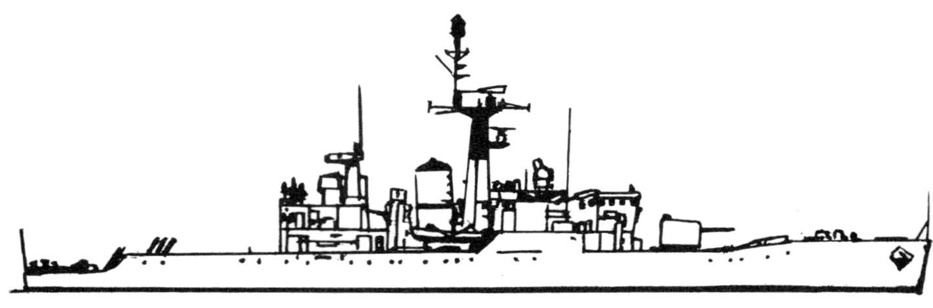

ROTHESAY Class

Provided under the 1954-55 programme. Originally basically similar to the "Whitby" class but with modifications in layout as a result of experience gained.

ELECTRICAL. Two turbo generators and two diesel generators in all ships. Total 1 140 kW. Alternating current, 440 volts, three phase, 60 cycles per second.

ENGINEERING. Two Admiralty Standard Range turbines each rated at 15 000 shp. Propeller revolutions 220 rpm. Steam conditions 550 psi (*38·7 kg/cm²*) pressure and 850° F (450°C) temperature at boilers.

MODERNISATION. The "Rothesay" class was reconstructed and modernised from 1966-72 during which time they were equipped to operate a Wessex Wasp helicopter armed with homing torpedoes. A flight deck and hangar were built on aft, necessitating the removal of one of her anti-submarine mortars. A "Seacat" replaced the 40 mm gun.

RADAR. Search: Some ships are fitted with Type 993 and others with Type 293. Fire Control: MRS.3. fire control: Type 978 air warning radar; optical Seacat director; DF.

YARMOUTH *1974, Michael D. J. Lennon*

FALMOUTH *5/1974, C. and S. Taylor*

LOWESTOFT *9/1974, C. and S. Taylor*

Frigates—*continued*

3 "WHITBY" CLASS (TYPE 12)

(see Disposal List for *Blackpool*)

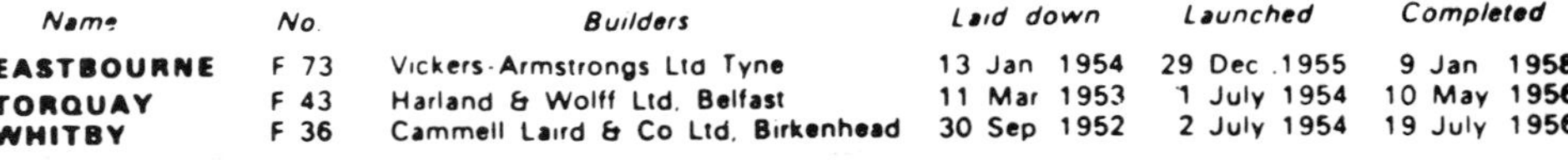

Name	No.	Builders	Laid down	Launched	Completed
EASTBOURNE	F 73	Vickers-Armstrongs Ltd Tyne	13 Jan 1954	29 Dec 1955	9 Jan 1958
TORQUAY	F 43	Harland & Wolff Ltd, Belfast	11 Mar 1953	1 July 1954	10 May 1956
WHITBY	F 36	Cammell Laird & Co Ltd, Birkenhead	30 Sep 1952	2 July 1954	19 July 1956

Displacement, tons	2 150 standard; 2 560 full load
Length, feet (*metres*)	360·0 (*109·7*)wl; 369·8 (*112·7*)oa
Beam, feet (*metres*)	41·0 (*12·5*)
Draught, feet (*metres*)	17 (*5·2*)
Guns	2—4·5 in (*115 mm*) 1 twin 2—40 mm Bofors (1 twin) (not in *Torquay*)
A/S weapons	2 Limbo 3-barrelled DC mortars (1 only in *Torquay*)
Boilers	2 Babcock & Wilcox Pressure 550 psi (*38·7 kg/cm²*) Temperature 850°F (454°C)
Main engines	2 sets d.r. geared turbines; 2 shafts; 30 430 shp
Speed, knots	31
Oil fuel (tons)	370
Complement	225 (12 officers and 213 ratings)

Ordered in 1951. Good sea-keeping qualities enable them to maintain their high speed in rough seas. Their twin-rudders improve manoeuvrability. They are all welded and were specially designed with the lightest possible structure.

CLASS. *Whitby* currently in reserve. *Torquay* used as Navigation/Direction training and trials ship at Portsmouth, having a large deck-house aft and carrying the first CAAIS (Computer Assisted Action Information System) to go to sea. *Eastbourne*, stripped of her gun and A/S armament, is based at Rosyth for engine-room trainees from HMS *Caledonia*. *Blackpool* now on the disposal list. *Tenby* and *Scarborough* sold to Pakistan in 1974. Now awaiting decision on extent of refit required.

ELECTRICAL. System is alternating current, 440 volts; three phase, 60 cycles per second. Two turbo alternators and two diesel alternators. Total 1 140 kilowatts.

ENGINEERING. Propelling machinery includes geared turbines of Y 100 design and high power. Double reduction gearing allows low propeller revolutions of 220 rpm at high power and the propeller efficiency is correspondingly high. This, with improvements in hull design, enables these frigates to achieve over 30 knots on only 75 per cent of the power required by older destroyers of comparable displacement.

RADAR. Search: Type 293 and Type 277 for surface search. Fire Control: Mk 6M DCT with Type 275.

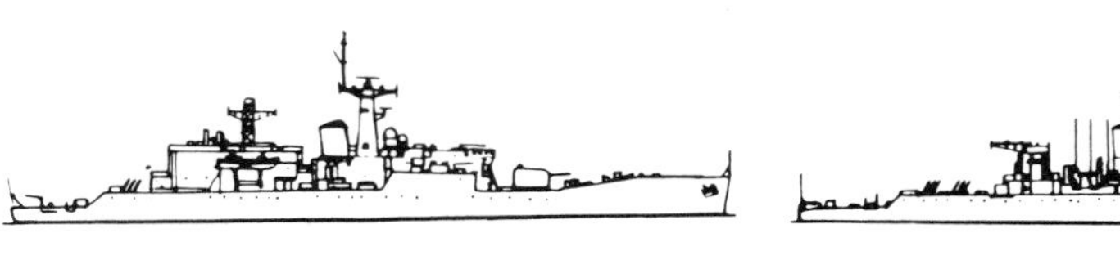

TORQUAY 1974

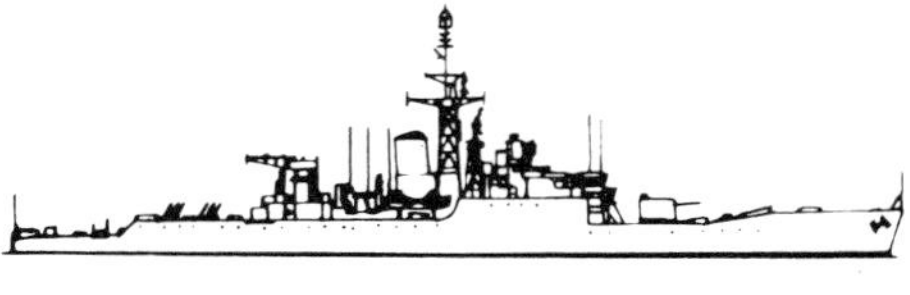

WHITBY 1974

WHITBY 9/1974, C. and S. Taylor

EASTBOURNE after removal of armament 1973, C. and S. Taylor

TORQUAY 5/1974, C. and S. Taylor

Frigates—*continued*

5 "BLACKWOOD" CLASS (TYPE 14)

Displacement, tons	1 180 standard; 1 456 full load
Length, feet (*metres*)	300 (*91·4*) wl; 310 (*94·5*) oa
Beam, feet (*metres*)	33·0 (*10·1*)
Draught, feet (*metres*)	15·5 (*4·7*)
Guns, AA	2—40 mm Bofors
A/S weapons	2 "Limbo" 3-barrelled DC mortars
Boilers	2 Babcock & Wilcox; Pressure 550 psi (*38·7 kg/cm²*); Temperature 850°F (454°C)
Main engines	1 set geared turbines; 1 shaft; 15 000 shp
Speed, knots	27·8
Range, miles	4 000 at 12 knots
Oil fuel, tons	275
Complement	140 (8 officers, and 132 ratings)

THREE ACTIVE SHIPS— (see Disposal List for *Blackwood* and *Palliser*)

Name	*No.*	*Builders*	*Laid down*	*Launched*	*Completed*
DUNDAS	F 48	J. Samuel White & Co. Ltd.	17 Oct 1952	25 Sep 1953	16 Mar 1956
HARDY	F 54	Yarrow & Co. Ltd.	4 Feb 1953	25 Nov 1953	15 Dec 1955
KEPPEL	F 85	Yarrow & Co. Ltd.	27 Mar 1953	31 Aug 1954	6 July 1956

TWO HARBOUR TRAINING SHIPS

RUSSELL	F 97	Swan Hunter & Wigham Richardson	11 Nov 1953	10 Dec 1954	7 Feb 1957
DUNCAN	F 80	John I. Thorncroft & Co. Ltd.	17 Dec 1953	30 May 1957	21 Oct 1958

Originally a class of twelve.

Of comparatively simple construction. Built in prefabricated sections. In 1958-59 their hulls were strengthened to withstand severe and prolonged sea and weather conditions on fishery protection in Icelandic waters.

CLASS. The first three are currently operational. *Duncan* is at Rosyth for harbour training and *Russell* at Portsmouth for similar duties with HMS *Sultan*.

ENGINEERING. All engined by their builders, except *Russell*, by Wallsend Slipway & Eng Co Ltd. Four-bladed, 12 ft diameter propeller, 220 rpm.

RADAR. Equipped with Type 978 search radar.

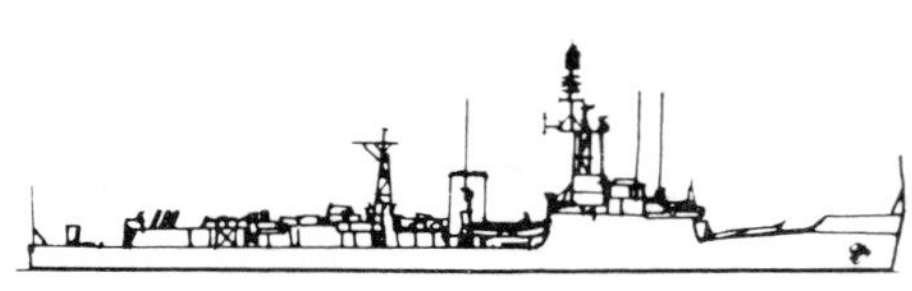

"Blackwood" Class *1974*

DUNDAS *1973, Wright and Logan*

1 TYPE 14 CONVERSION

Name	*No.*	*Builder*	*Laid down*	*Launched*	*Completed*
EXMOUTH	F 84	J. Samuel White & Co. Ltd	24 Mar 1954	16 Nov 1955	20 Dec 1957

Details of displacement, dimensions and armament as for "Blackwood" Class Type 14 above.

Main engines	1 Olympus Gas Turbine; 22 500 hp; 2 Proteus Gas Turbines; 6 500 hp; 1 shaft; controllable pitch propeller
Speed, knots	28

GENERAL
The conversion of *Exmouth* to gas-turbine propulsion was completed in Chatham Dockyard on 20 July 1968. She was the first all gas-turbine major warship in the Royal Navy.

ENGINEERING. She can be propelled on only one system at a time, either the Olympus or the pair of Proteus engines.

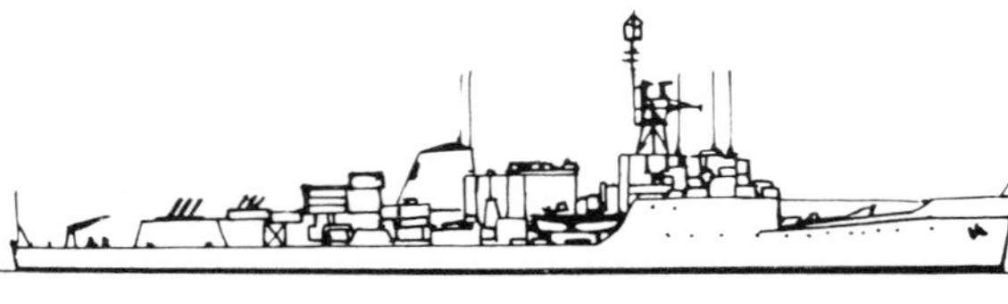

EXMOUTH *1974*

EXMOUTH *1973, C. and S. Taylor*

Frigates—*continued*

7 "TRIBAL" CLASS. TYPE 81

Name	No	Builders	Laid down	Launched	Completed
ASHANTI	F 117	Yarrow & Co Ltd Scotstoun	15 Jan 1958	9 Mar 1959	23 Nov 1961
ESKIMO	F 119	J Samuel White & Co Ltd Cowes	22 Oct 1958	20 Mar 1960	21 Feb 1963
GURKHA	F 122	J I Thornycroft & Co Ltd Woolston	3 Nov 1958	11 July 1960	13 Feb 1963
MOHAWK	F 125	Vickers-Armstrongs Ltd Barrow	23 Dec 1960	5 Apr 1962	29 Nov 1963
NUBIAN	F 131	HM Dockyard Portsmouth	7 Sep 1959	6 Sep 1960	9 Oct 1962
TARTAR	F 133	HM Dockyard Devonport	22 Oct 1959	19 Sep 1960	26 Feb 1962
ZULU	F 124	Alex Stephen & Sons Ltd Govan	13 Dec 1960	3 July 1962	17 Apr 1964

Displacement, tons	2 300 standard; 2 700 full load
Length, feet (*metres*)	350·0 (*106·7*)wl; 360·0 (*109·7*)oa
Beam, feet (*metres*)	42·3 (*12·9*)
Draught, feet (*metres*)	17·5 (*5·3*) max (props)
Aircraft	1 "Wasp" helicopter
Missile launchers	2 quadruple Seacats
Guns	2—4·5 in dp (singles) 2—20 mm
A/S weapons	1 "Limbo" 3-barrelled DC mortar
Main engines	Combined steam and gas turbine; Metrovick steam turbine; 12 500 shp. Metrovick gas turbine; 7 500 shp; 1 shaft; 20 000 shp
Speed, knots	28
Boilers	1 Babcock & Wilcox (plus 1 auxiliary boiler)
Oil fuel, tons	400
Complement	253 (13 officers and 240 ratings)

Ashanti, Eskimo and *Gurkha* were ordered under the 1955-56 estimates, *Nubian* and *Tartar* 1956-57, and *Mohawk* and *Zulu* 1957-58 designed as self-contained units for service in such areas as the Persian Gulf *Ashanti* cost £5 220 000.

CONSTRUCTION. All-welded prefabrication. Denny Brown stabilisers fitted to reduce rolling in heavy seas. Enclosed bridge and twin rudders.

ELECTRICAL. Generator capacity of 1 500 kW.

ENGINEERING. The gas turbine is used to boost the steam turbines for sustained bursts of high speed and also enables the ship lying in harbour without steam up to get under way instantly in emergency. The machinery is remotely controlled. The main boiler works at a pressure of 550 psi and a temperature of 850 deg F. Five-bladed propeller, 11·75 ft diameter, 280 rpm. The forward funnel serves the boiler, the after one the gas turbine.

GUNNERY. Optical Seacat directors fitted.

RADAR. Search: Type 965 with single AKEI with IFF. Air and surface warning; Type 293. Fire Control; MRS 3.

SONAR. *Ashanti* and *Gurkha* were fitted with variable depth sonar equipment in the counter well in 1970, see photographs.

GURKHA — *1973, C. and S. Taylor*

ASHANTI — *1974, Michael D. J. Lennon*

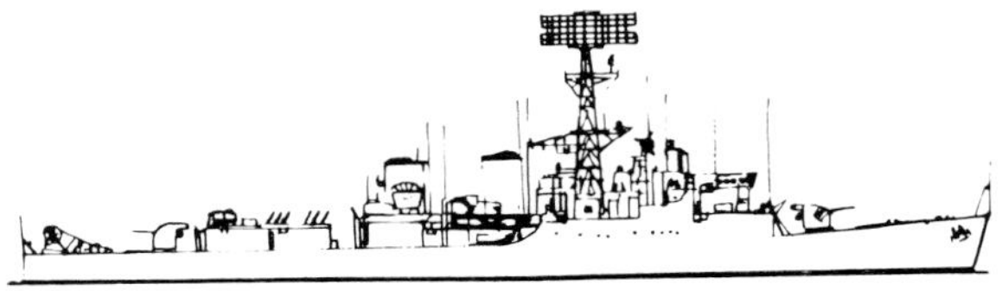

"TRIBAL" Class — *1974*

NUBIAN — *1973, C. and S. Taylor*

Frigates—*continued*

3 "LEOPARD" CLASS TYPE 41

(see Disposal List for *Puma*)

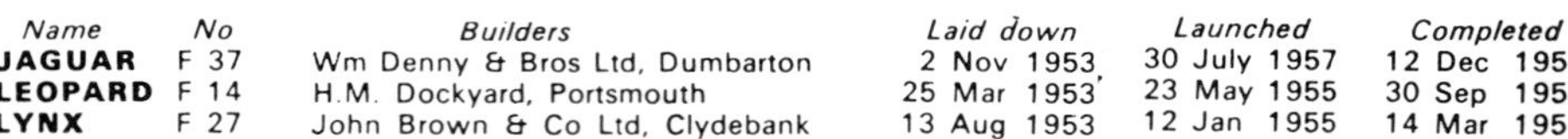

Name	*No*	*Builders*	*Laid down*	*Launched*	*Completed*
JAGUAR	F 37	Wm Denny & Bros Ltd, Dumbarton	2 Nov 1953	30 July 1957	12 Dec 1959
LEOPARD	F 14	H.M. Dockyard, Portsmouth	25 Mar 1953	23 May 1955	30 Sep 1958
LYNX	F 27	John Brown & Co Ltd, Clydebank	13 Aug 1953	12 Jan 1955	14 Mar 1957

Displacement, tons	2 300 standard; 2 520 full load
Length, feet (*metres*)	320 (*97·5*) pp; 330 (*100·6*) wl; 339·8 (*103·6*) oa
Beam, feet (*metres*)	40 (*12·2*)
Draught, feet (*metres*)	16 (*4·9*)
Guns,	4—4·5 in (*115 mm*), 2 twin turrets 1—40 mm
A/S weapons	1 Squid 3-barrelled DC mortar
Main engines	8 ASR 1 diesels in three engine rooms; 14 400 bhp; 2 shafts; 4 engines geared to each shaft
Speed, knots	24
Range, miles	2 300 at full power; 7 500 at 16 knots
Oil fuel (tons)	220
Complement	235 (15 officers, 220 ratings)

Designed primarily for anti-aircraft protection. All welded. *Jaguar* and *Lynx* were ordered on 28 June 1951. Fitted with stabilisers.

LEOPARD *1973, Wright and Logan*

ENGINEERING. The propelling machinery comprises Admiralty Standard Range 1 diesels coupled to the propeller shafting through hydraulic gear boxes. These diesels are of light weight, about 17 lb/shp. *Jaguar* is the only ship of this class to be fitted with controllable pitch propellers, 12 ft diameter 200 rpm. The fuel tanks have a compensating system, so that sea water replaces oil fuel as it is used.

RADAR. Search: Type 965 with single AKE 1 aerial and IFF and Type 993. Fire Control: Mk 6M X-band. Fire control director unit with Type 275. Type 975 nav radar. ECM and DF.

JAGUAR *1973, Wright and Logan*

RECONSTRUCTION. *Lynx* was extensively refitted in 1963 with new mainmast. *Leopard* was similarly refitted in Oct 1964-Feb 1966, followed by *Jaguar*.

TRANSFER. Another ship of this class, *Panther*, was transferred to India while building and renamed *Brahmaputra*.

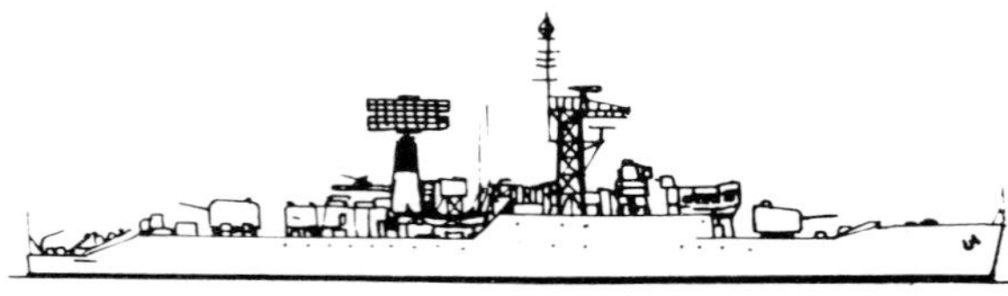

"LEOPARD" Class *1974*

LYNX *1973*

Frigates—*continued*

4 "SALISBURY" CLASS TYPE 61

Displacement, tons	2 170 standard; 2 408 full load
Length, feet (*metres*)	320·0 (*97·5*) pp; 330·0 (*100·6*) oa 339·8 (*103·6*) oa
Beam, feet (*metres*)	40·0 (*12·2*)
Draught, feet (*metres*)	15·5 (*4·7*)
Missile launchers	1 quadruple "Seacat" in *Lincoln* and *Salisbury* which also have 2 sextuple 3 in rocket launchers
Guns	2—4·5 in (*115 mm*) 4—40 mm (*Chichester*); 2—40 mm (*Llandaff*); 2—20 mm (all but *Llandaff*)
A/S weapons	1 Squid triple-barrelled DC mortar
Main engines	8 ASR 1 diesels in three engine rooms; 2 shafts; 14 400 bhp
Speed, knots	24
Range, miles	2 300 at full power; 7 500 at 16 knots
Oil fuel, tons	230
Complement	237 (14 officers and 223 ratings)

Name	No.	Builders	Laid down	Launched	Completed
CHICHESTER	F 59	Fairfield SB & Eng Co Ltd, Govan	25 Jan 1953	21 Apr 1955	16 May 1958
LINCOLN	F 99	Fairfield SB & Eng Co Ltd, Govan	20 May 1955	6 Apr 1959	7 July 1960
LLANDAFF	F 61	Hawthorn Leslie Ltd, Hebburn-on-Tyne	27 Aug 1953	30 Nov 1955	11 Apr 1958
SALISBURY	F 32	HM Dockyard, Devonport	23 Jan 1952	25 June 1953	27 Feb 1957

Designed primarily for the direction of carrier-borne and shore-based aircraft. Ordered on 28 June 1951 except *Salisbury*, the prototype ship. Construction was all welded and largely prefabricated. The construction of the three other ships *Exeter*, *Gloucester* and *Coventry* cancelled in the 1957 defence economies. Fitted with stabilisers (except *Lincoln*). Original lattice masts replaced by tower masts during 1960's.

ENGINEERING. Powered by Admiralty Standard Range 1 heavy oil engines coupled to the propeller shafts through hydraulic couplings and oil operated reverse and reduction gear boxes. *Llandaff* is the only Type 61 frigate to have a 500 kW gas-turbine alternator and three diesel generators *Lincoln* is fitted with controllable pitch propellers, rotating at 200 rpm, which are 12 feet in diameter, manufactured by Stone Marine & Engineering Co Ltd. The fuel tanks have a compensating system whereby sea water replaces oil fuel as it is consumed.

HONG KONG GUARDSHIP. In 1973 *Chichester* was re-equipped for service as permanent HK Guardship. This involved removal of Type 965, the top weight saved being used to mount extra 40 mm guns.

RADAR. Type 965 long-range surveillance with double AKE 2 with IFF (except in *Chichester*); Type 993 combined air and surface warning; Type 277 Q height finder; Type 982 high definition target indicator; Mk 6M fire control director with Type 275; GWS-22 radar director aft for Seacat (*Salisbury* and *Lincoln* only); Type 975 nav radar.

LINCOLN *1974, Wright and Logan*

CHICHESTER as Hong Kong guardship *1973*

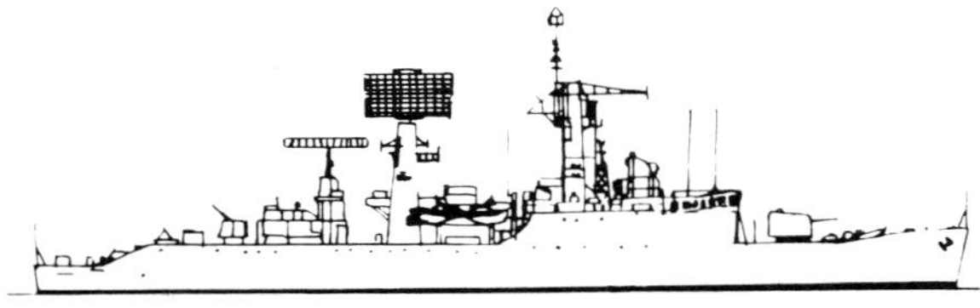
"SALISBURY" Class except *Chichester* *1974*

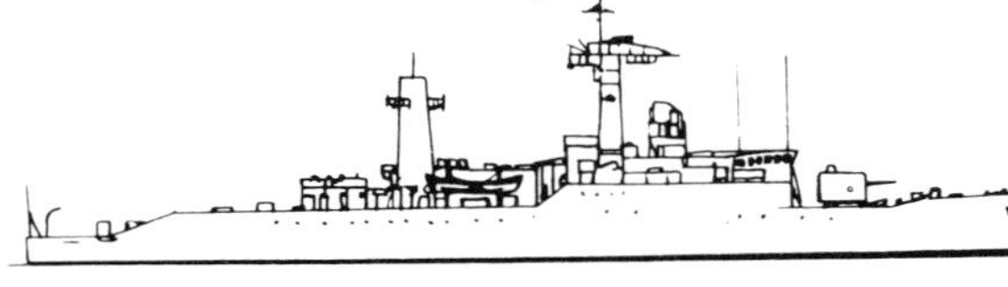
CHICHESTER *1974*

LLANDAFF *1973, C. and S. Taylor*

Frigates—*continued*

1 YARROW TYPE

Name	*No.*	*Builders*	*Launched*	*Completed*
MERMAID	F 76	Yarrow Shipbuilders & Co Ltd	29 Dec 1966	May 1973 (see *Notes*)

Displacement, tons	2 300 standard; 2 520 full load
Dimensions, ft	320 pp; 330 wl; 339·3 oa × 40 × 12
Guns	2—4 inch (twin). 4—40 mm
A/S weapons	1 Squid
Main engines	8 Diesels; 2 shafts; 2cp propellers
Oil fuel, tons	230
Range, miles	4 800 at 15 knots

Similar in hull and machinery to "Leopard" and "Salisbury" classes. Originally built for Ghana as a display ship for Nkrumah at a cost of £5 m. but put up for sale after his departure. She was launched without ceremony on 29 Dec 1966 and completed in 1968. She was transferred to Portsmouth dockyard in April 1972 being acquired by the Royal Navy. Refit started October 1972 at Chatham. Commissioned in Royal Navy 16 May 1973 and currently based at Singapore.

MERMAID 5/1974, C. and S. Taylor

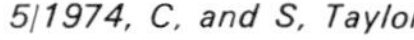

MERMAID 1975

MERMAID 1974, Michael D. J. Lennon

TYPE 15

For *Grenville* and *Undaunted* see Disposal List. With *Ulster*, acting as accommodation ship at Portsmouth, these are the sole survivors of the wartime "R", "T", "U", "V", "W" and "Z" classes of destroyers, launched in 1942-43. Of the 48 ships of these classes 33 were converted into Type 15 frigates and 7 ("T" Class) into Type 16 (limited conversion) frigates. A number have been transferred to other navies.

SONAR TRIALS SHIP

Name	*No.*	*Builders*	*Laid down*	*Launched*	*Completed*	*Converted*
MATAPAN	D 43	John Brown, Clydebank	11 Mar 1944	30 Apr 1945	5 Sep 1947	1971-1972

Displacement, tons	3 835 full load
Length, feet (*metres*)	388 (*118·3*) oa
Beam, feet (*metres*)	40·5 (*12·3*)
Draught, feet (*metres*)	27 (*8·2*)
Boilers	2 Admiralty 3-drum; 400 psi (*28·1 kg/cm²*); (650°F (*343°C*)
Main engines	Parsons geared turbines; 50 000 shp; 2 shafts
Speed, knots	31
Range, miles	1 300 at full power; 3 000 at 20 knots; 4 400 at 12 knots
Oil fuel, tons	680

MATAPAN 1973, C. and S. Taylor

A former standard "Battle Class" destroyer which went into reserve almost immediately after being completed. Attached to the Admiralty Underwater Weapons Establishment at Portland after conversion.

CONVERSION. Taken in hand at HM Dockyard, Portsmouth in Jan 1971 for conversion into a Sonar Trials Ship. The rebuilding involved a new clipper bow, different bridge, remodelled superstructure, extension of the forecastle deck aft all the way to the counter, thus converting her into a flushdecker, adding a second funnel, and a helicopter landing deck. Commissioned 2 Feb 1973 after a £2½m conversion.

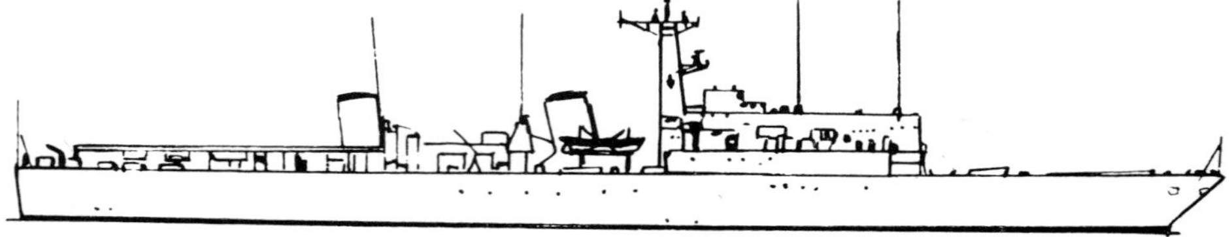

MATAPAN 1974

SUBMARINES

Nuclear Powered Ballistic Missile Submarines (SSBN)

4 "RESOLUTION" CLASS

Name	No.	Builders	Laid down	Launched	Completion
RENOWN	S 26	Cammell Laird & Co Ltd, Birkenhead	25 June 1964	25 Feb 1967	15 Nov 1968
REPULSE	S 23	Vickers-Armstrongs Ltd, Barrow-in-Furness	12 Mar 1965	4 Nov 1967	28 Sept 1968
RESOLUTION	S 22	Vickers-Armstrongs Ltd, Barrow-in-Furness	26 Feb 1964	15 Sep 1966	2 Oct 1967
REVENGE	S 27	Cammell Laird & Co Ltd, Birkenhead	19 May 1965	15 Mar 1968	4 Dec 1969

Displacement, tons	7 500 surface; 8 400 submerged
Length, feet (*metres*)	360 (*109·7*) pp; 425 (*129·5*) oa
Beam, feet (*metres*)	33 (*10·1*)
Draught, feet (*metres*)	30 (*9·1*)
Missiles, surface	16 tubes amidships for "Polaris" A—3 IRBM s, range 2 500 nautical miles
Torpedo tubes	6—21 in (*533 mm*) forward
Nuclear reactors	1 pressurised water cooled
Main machinery	Geared steam turbines; 1 shaft
Speed, knots	20 on surface; 25 submerged
Complement	141 (13 officers, 128 ratings); 2 crews (see *Personnel*)

In Feb 1963 it was officially stated that it was intended to order four or five 7 000 ton nuclear powered submarines, each to carry 16 "Polaris" missiles, and it was planned that the first would be on patrol in 1968. Their hulls and machinery would be of British design. As well as building two submarines Vickers-Armstrongs would give lead yard service to the builder of the other two. Four "Polaris" submarines were in fact ordered in May 1963. The plan to build a fifth Polaris submarine was cancelled on 15 Feb 1965. Britain's first SSBN *Resolution*, put to sea on 22 June 1967 and completed 6 weeks trial in the Firth of Clyde and Atlantic on 17 Aug 1967.

SONAR AND RADAR. Fitted with a large sonar array mounted in the chin position and an X band short range surveillance radar.

PERSONNEL. Each submarine, which has accommodation for 19 officers and 135 ratings, is manned on a two-crew basis, in order to get maximum operational time at sea.

COST. *Resolution*, £40 240 000; *Renown*, £39 950 000; *Repulse*, £37 500 000; *Revenge*, £38 600 000; completed ships excluding missiles.

RESOLUTION *1967*

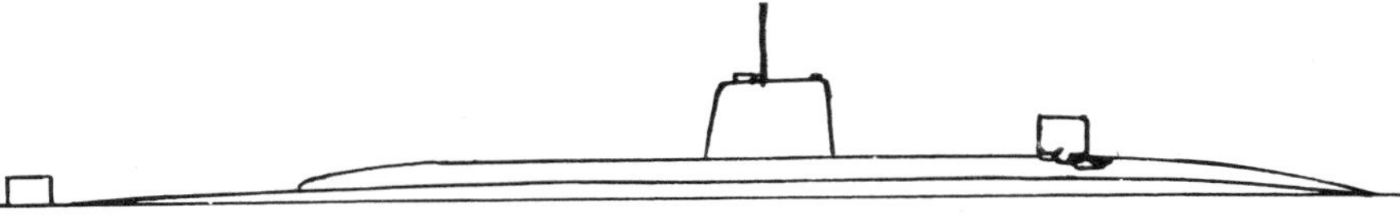

"RESOLUTION" Class *1975*

REVENGE *1971*

REPULSE ***1971***

Fleet Submarines

5 "VALIANT" CLASS

Name	No.	Builder	Ordered	Laid down	Launched	Commissioned
VALIANT	S 102	Vickers Ltd Shipbuilding Group, Barrow	31 Aug 1960	22 Jan 1962	3 Dec 1963	18 July 1966
WARSPITE	S 103	Vickers Ltd Shipbuilding Group, Barrow	12 Dec 1962	10 Dec 1963	25 Sep 1965	18 Apr 1967
CHURCHILL	S 46	Vickers Ltd Shipbuilding Group, Barrow	21 Oct 1965	30 June 1967	20 Dec 1968	15 July 1970
CONQUEROR	S 48	Cammell Laird & Co Ltd, Birkenhead	9 Aug 1966	5 Dec 1967	28 Aug 1969	9 Nov 1971
COURAGEOUS	S 50	Vickers Ltd Shipbuilding Group, Barrow	1 Mar 1967	15 May 1968	7 Mar 1970	16 Oct 1971

Displacement, tons	3 500 standard; 4 500 submerged
Length, feet (*metres*)	285 (*86·9*);
Beam, feet (*metres*)	33·2 (*10·1*)
Draught, feet (*metres*)	27 (*8·2*)
Torpedo tubes	6—21 in (*533 mm*) homing;
Nuclear reactor	1 pressurised water cooled
Main machinery	EE Geared steam turbines; 1 shaft
Speed, knots	30
Complement	103 (13 officers, 90 men)

It was announced on 31 Aug 1960 that the contract for a second nuclear powered submarine (*Valiant*) had been awarded to Vickers Ltd, the principal sub-contractors being Vickers-Armstrong (Engineers) Ltd, for the machinery and its installation, and Rolls Royce and Associates for the nuclear steam raising plant. The class, of which she is the first, is broadly of the same design as that of *Dreadnought*, but slightly larger. She was originally scheduled to be completed in Sep 1965, but work was held up by the "Polaris" programme.

SONAR AND RADAR. Fitted with a large sonar array mounted in the "chin" position around the bow. Also fitted with X band short range surveillance radar.

ENDURANCE. On 25 Apr 1967 *Valiant* completed the 12 000-mile homeward voyage from Singapore, the record submerged passage by a British submarine, after 28 days non-stop.

ENGINEERING. *Valiant's* reactor core was made in Great Britain, with machinery of British design and manufacture similar to the shore prototype installed in the Admiralty Reactor Test Establishment at Dounreay. The main steam turbines and condensers were designed and manufactured by the English Electric Company, Rugby, and the electrical propulsion machinery and control gear by Laurence, Scott & Electromotors Ltd.

Valiant Class

COURAGEOUS — *1974, Michael D. J. Lennon*

7 "SWIFTSURE" CLASS

Name	No.	Builder	Ordered	Laid down	Launched	Commissioned
SWIFTSURE	S 126	Vickers Ltd Shipbuilding Group, Barrow	3 Nov 1967	15 Apr 1969	7 Sep 1971	17 Apr 1973
SOVEREIGN	S 108	Vickers Ltd Shipbuilding Group, Barrow	16 May 1969	17 Sep 1970	17 Feb 1973	11 July 1974
SUPERB	S 109	Vickers Ltd Shipbuilding Group, Barrow	20 May 1970	16 Mar 1973	30 Nov 1974	—
SCEPTRE	S 104	Vickers Ltd Shipbuilding Group, Barrow	1 Nov 1971	25 Oct 1973	—	—
SPARTAN	S 111	Vickers Ltd Shipbuilding Group, Barrow	17 Feb 1973	1975	—	—
SEVERN	S 112	Vickers Ltd Shipbuilding Group, Barrow	1974	—	—	—
—	S 113	Vickers Ltd Shipbuilding Group, Barrow	1975	—	—	—

Displacement, tons	3 500 standard; 4 500 dived
Length, feet (*metres*)	272·0 (*82·9*)
Beam, feet (*metres*)	33·2 (*10·1*)
Draught, feet (*metres*)	27 (*8·2*)
Torpedo tubes	5—21 in
Nuclear reactor	1 pressurised water-cooled
Main machinery	English Electric geared steam turbines; 1 shaft
Speed, knots	30
Complement	97 (12 officers, 85 men)

In many respects similar to the "Valiant" and "Churchill" submarines these are slightly shorter with the fore-planes set further forward and with one less torpedo tube. It is noticeable that whilst *Churchill* took three years from the date of laying down to commissioning the average now is about four years—over a year longer than the time taken for the later boats of the "Sturgeon" class in the USN. This much shorter building period presumably results from a considerable and continuing programme.

ENGINEERING. Whilst the basic reactor design remains similar to previous types core-life has probably increased.

SONAR and RADAR. A "chin"-mounted sonar gives both passive and active performance. Fitted with X-band short range surveillance radar.

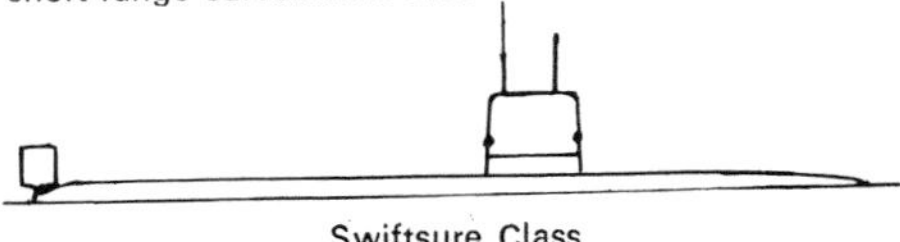

Swiftsure Class

SWIFTSURE — *1974 MOD*

Submarines—*continued*

1 "DREADNOUGHT" CLASS (FLEET SUBMARINE)

Name	*No.*	*Builders*	*Engineers*	*Laid down*	*Launched*	*Commissioned*
DREADNOUGHT	S 101	Vickers-Armstrongs, Barrow	Rolls-Royce and Westinghouse	12 June 1959	21 Oct 1960	17 Apr 1963

Displacement, tons	3 000 standard; 3 500 surface; 4 000 submerged
Length, feet (*metres*)	265·8 (*81·0*)
Beam, feet (*metres*)	32·2 (*9·8*)
Draught, feet (*metres*)	26 (*7·9*)
Torpedo tubes	6—21 in (*533 mm*) bow, all internal
Nuclear reactor	1 S5W pressurised water-cooled
Main machinery	Geared steam turbines; 1 shaft
Speed, knots	30
Complement	88 (11 officers, 77 men)

As originally planned *Dreadnought* was to have been fitted with a British designed and built nuclear reactor, but in 1958 an agreement was concluded with the United States Government for the purchase of a complete set of propulsion machinery of the type fitted in USS *Skipjack*. This agreement enabled the submarine to be launched far earlier. The supply of this machinery was made under a contract between the Westinghouse Electric Corporation and Rolls-Royce. The latter were also supplied with design and manufacturing details of the reactor and with safety information and set up a factory in this country to manufacture similar cores. *Dreadnought* has a hull of British design both as regards structural strength and hydrodynamic features, although the latter are based on the pioneering work of the US Navy in *Skipjack* and *Albacore*. From about amidships aft, the hull lines closely resemble *Skipjack* to accommodate the propulsion machinery. The forward end is wholly British in concept. In the Control Room and Attack Centre the instruments are fitted into consoles.
The improved water distilling plant for the first time provides unlimited fresh water for shower baths and for washing machines in the fully equipped laundry.
She is fitted with an inertial navigation system and with means of measuring her depth below ice and was the first British submarine to surface at the North Pole in 1970.

DREADNOUGHT *1974, Michael D. J. Lennon*

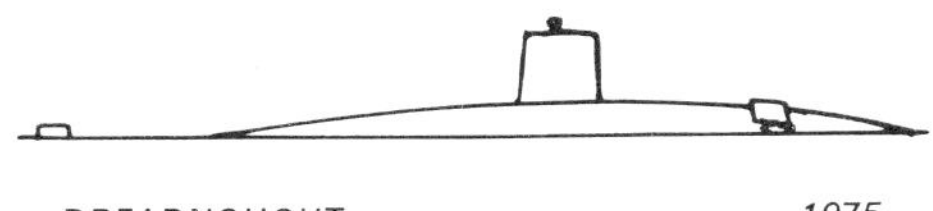

DREADNOUGHT 1975

SONAR AND RADAR. Fitted with a large sonar array mounted in the "chin" position around the bow. Also fitted with X band short range surveillance radar.

DREADNOUGHT *1971, C. and S. Taylor*

Submarines—*continued*
Patrol Submarines

Note. Andrew, the last of the "A" class, was paid off to the disposal list on 31 Dec 1974. She was the last of the 46 submarines of this class ordered during the war of which only 16 were finally completed.

13 "OBERON" CLASS
8 "PORPOISE" CLASS

Displacement, tons	1 610 standard; 2 030 surface; 2 410 submerged
Length, feet (*metres*)	241 (*73·5*) pp; 295·2 (*90·0*) oa
Beam, feet (*metres*)	26·5 (*8·1*)
Draught, feet (*metres*)	18 (*5·5*)
Torpedo tubes	8—21 in (*533 mm*) 6 bow 2 stern; 30 torpedoes carried
Main machinery	2 ASR 1, 16 VMS diesels; 3 680 bhp; 2 electric motors; 6 000 shp, 2 shafts;
Speed, knots	12 surface, 17 submerged
Complement	68 (6 officers, 62 men) 71 (6 officers, 65 men) in "Porpoise" class

CONSTRUCTION. For the first time in British submarines plastic was used in the superstructure construction of the Oberon class. Before and abaft the bridge the superstructure is mainly of glass fibre laminate in most units of this class. The superstructure of *Orpheus* is of light alloy aluminium.

RCN. The submarine of the Oberon class laid down on 27 Sep 1962 at HM Dockyard, Chatham, as *Onyx* for the Royal Navy was launched on 29 Feb 1964 as *Ojibwa* for the Royal Canadian Navy. She was replaced by another "Oberon" class submarine named *Onyx* for the Royal Navy built by Cammell Laird, Birkenhead.

SONAR AND RADAR. Fitted with sonar with bow dome; and X Band surveillance radar.

GUNNERY. "O" class submarines serving in the Far East carried an Oerlikon gun during Indonesian Confrontation.

MODIFICATION. *Oberon* has been modified with deeper casing to house equipment for the initial training of personnel for nuclear powered submarines. Others of of this class are currently undergoing modification.

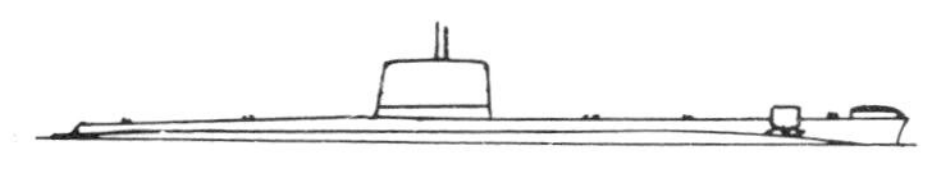

"Oberon" Class

"OBERON" CLASS

Name	*No*	*Builders*	*Laid down*	*Launched*	*Completed*
OBERON	S 09	H.M. Dockyard, Chatham	28 Nov 1957	18 July 1959	24 Feb 1961
OCELOT	S 17	H.M. Dockyard, Chatham	17 Nov 1960	5 May 1962	31 Jan 1964
ODIN	S 10	Cammell Laird & Co Ltd, Birkenhead	27 Apr 1959	4 Nov 1960	3 May 1962
OLYMPUS	S 12	Vickers-Armstrong Ltd, Barrow	4 Mar 1960	14 June 1961	7 July 1962
ONSLAUGHT	S 14	H.M. Dockyard, Chatham	8 Apr 1959	24 Sep 1960	14 Aug 1962
ONYX	S 21	Cammell Laird & Co Ltd, Birkenhead	16 Nov 1964	18 Aug 1966	20 Nov 1967
OPOSSUM	S 19	Cammell Laird & Co Ltd, Birkenhead	21 Dec 1961	23 May 1963	5 June 1964
OPPORTUNE	S 20	Scotts' S.B. & Eng Co Ltd, Greenock	26 Oct 1962	14 Feb 1964	29 Dec 1964
ORACLE	S 16	Cammell Laird & Co Ltd, Birkenhead	26 Apr 1960	26 Sep 1961	14 Feb 1963
ORPHEUS	S 11	Vickers-Armstrong Ltd, Barrow	16 Apr 1959	17 Nov 1959	25 Nov 1960
OSIRIS	S 13	Vickers-Armstrong Ltd, Barrow	26 Jan 1962	29 Nov 1962	11 Jan 1964
OTTER	S 15	Scotts' S.B. & Eng Co Ltd, Greenock	14 Jan 1960	15 May 1961	20 Aug 1962
OTUS	S 18	Scotts' S.B. & Eng Co Ltd, Greenock	31 May 1961	17 Oct 1962	5 Oct 1963

"PORPOISE" CLASS

Name	*No,*	*Builders*	*Laid down*	*Launched*	*Completed*
CACHALOT	S 06	Scotts' S.B. & Eng Co Ltd, Greenock	1 Aug 1955	11 Dec 1957	1 Sep 1959
FINWHALE	S 05	Cammell Laird & Co Ltd, Birkenhead	18 Sep 1956	21 July 1959	19 Aug 1960
GRAMPUS	S 04	Cammell Laird & Co Ltd, Birkenhead	16 Apr 1955	30 May 1957	19 Dec 1958
NARWHAL	S 03	Vickers-Armstrong Ltd, Barrow	15 Mar 1956	25 Oct 1957	4 May 1959
PORPOISE	S 01	Vickers-Armstrong Ltd, Barrow	15 June 1954	25 Apr 1956	17 Apr 1958
RORQUAL	S 02	Vickers-Armstrong Ltd, Barrow	15 Jan 1955	5 Dec 1956	24 Oct 1958
SEALION	S 07	Cammell Laird & Co Ltd, Birkenhead	5 June 1958	31 Dec 1959	25 July 1961
WALRUS	S 08	Scotts' S.B. & Eng Co Ltd, Greenock	12 Feb 1958	22 Sep 1959	10 Feb 1961

OBERON — *1974, Michael D. J. Lennon*

OBERON — *1974, Dr. Giorgio Arra*

WALRUS — *1973, John G. Callis*

AMPHIBIOUS WARFARE SHIPS

Name	*Deck Letter*	*No.*	*Builders*	*Laid down*	*Launched*	*Completed*
HERMES (ex-*Elephant*)	H	R 12	Vickers-Armstrongs, Barrow-in-Furness	21 June 1944	16 Feb 1953	18 Nov 1959

Displacement, tons	23 900 standard; 28 700 full load
Length, feet (*metres*)	650·0 (*198·1*) pp; 744·3 (*226·9*) oa
Beam, feet (*metres*)	90·0 (*27·4*) hull
Draught, feet (*metres*)	29·0 (*8·8*)
Width, feet (*metres*)	160·0 (*48·8*) overall
Aircraft	20 Wessex Sea King, and Sioux helicopters
Armour	Reinforced flight deck
Missiles	2 quadruple Seacat launchers either side abaft the after lift
Boilers	4 Admiralty 3-drum type
Main engines	Parsons geared turbines; 2 shafts; 76 000 shp
Speed, knots	28
Oil fuel, tons	3 880 furnace; 320 diesel;
Complement	980 plus Commando of 750. In emergency a second commando can be embarked

HERMES *1973, C. and S. Taylor*

Originally name ship of a class including *Albion*, *Bulwark* and *Centaur*, but design was modified to a more advanced type, incorporating new equipment and improved arrangements, including five post-war developments—angled deck, steam catapult, landing sight, 3-D radar, and deck edge-lift. Air-conditioned. Embarked air squadrons and joined the Fleet summer 1960. Long refit 1964 to 1966, costing £10 000 000.

CONVERSION. *Hermes* was taken in hand for conversion to a Commando Carrier on 1 Mar 1971, commissioning for this role on 17 Aug 1973. Fixed wing facilities such as catapults and arrester gear were removed. The whole performance cost over £25 million. She retains a STOL/VTOL capability.

FLIGHT DECK. Angled 6·5 deg off centre line of ship, the biggest angle that could be contrived in an aircraft carrier of the size. Strengthened to take Harrier aircraft.

RADAR. Type 984; Type 992Q; GWS-22 for Seacat; Tacan beacon.

ROLE. Primary role as Anti-Submarine Carrier (with Commando role retained) from 1976.

HERMES *1973, Wright and Logan*

HERMES *1974*

Amphibious Warfare Ships—*continued*

Name	Deck Letter	No.	Builders	Laid down	Launched	Completed	Converted
BULWARK	B	R 08	Harland & Wolff Ltd, Belfast	10 May 1945	22 June 1948	4 Nov 1954	1959-60

Displacement, tons	23 300 standard ; 27 705 full load
Length, feet (*metres*)	650 (*198·1*) pp ; 737·8 (*224·9*) oa
Beam, feet (*metres*)	90 (*27·4*) hull
Draught, feet (*metres*)	28 (*8·5*)
Width, feet (*metres*)	123·5 (*37·7*) overall
Aircraft	20 Wessex and Sioux helicopters
Landing craft	4 LCVP
Guns	8—40 mm (twins) Bofors Mk V
Boilers	4 Admiralty 3 drum
Main engines	Parsons geared turbines 76 000 shp ; 2 shafts
Speed, knots	28
Oil fuel, tons	3 880 furnace ; 320 diesel
Complement	980 plus 750 Royal Marine Commando and troops

GENERAL

Former fixed-wing aircraft carrier. Converted into commando ship in Portsmouth Dockyard, Jan 1959 to Jan 1960. A full strength commando is available, which the ship can quickly transport and land with equipment. Their helicopters can disembark the commando's vehicles. The ship has sufficient stores and fuel to support the commandos in operations ashore.

CONVERSION. Basically *Bulwark* was not changed during her initial conversion, although the fixed wing capability, arrester wires and catapults were removed. Alterations and modifications were made to render the ship suitable as an all-helicopter troop carrier with 16 Westland Whirlwind aircraft, replaced at a later date by the Wessex, and four landing craft (vehicle or personnel).

DISPOSAL. For disposal in 1976.

ENGINEERING. The three-bladed propellers in *Bulwark* were replaced by four-bladed propellers. Propeller diameter 15·5 feet. At 28 knots the propellers work at 230 rpm.

RADAR. Search: Type 293 ; Aircraft Direction: Type 982, Type 983.

BULWARK — *1973, C. and S. Taylor*

BULWARK — *1972, MOD (N)*

BULWARK with Harriers on deck — *1973, C. and S. Taylor*

DRAWING. Starboard elevation and plan. Drawn in 1972. Scale: 87 feet = 1 inch.

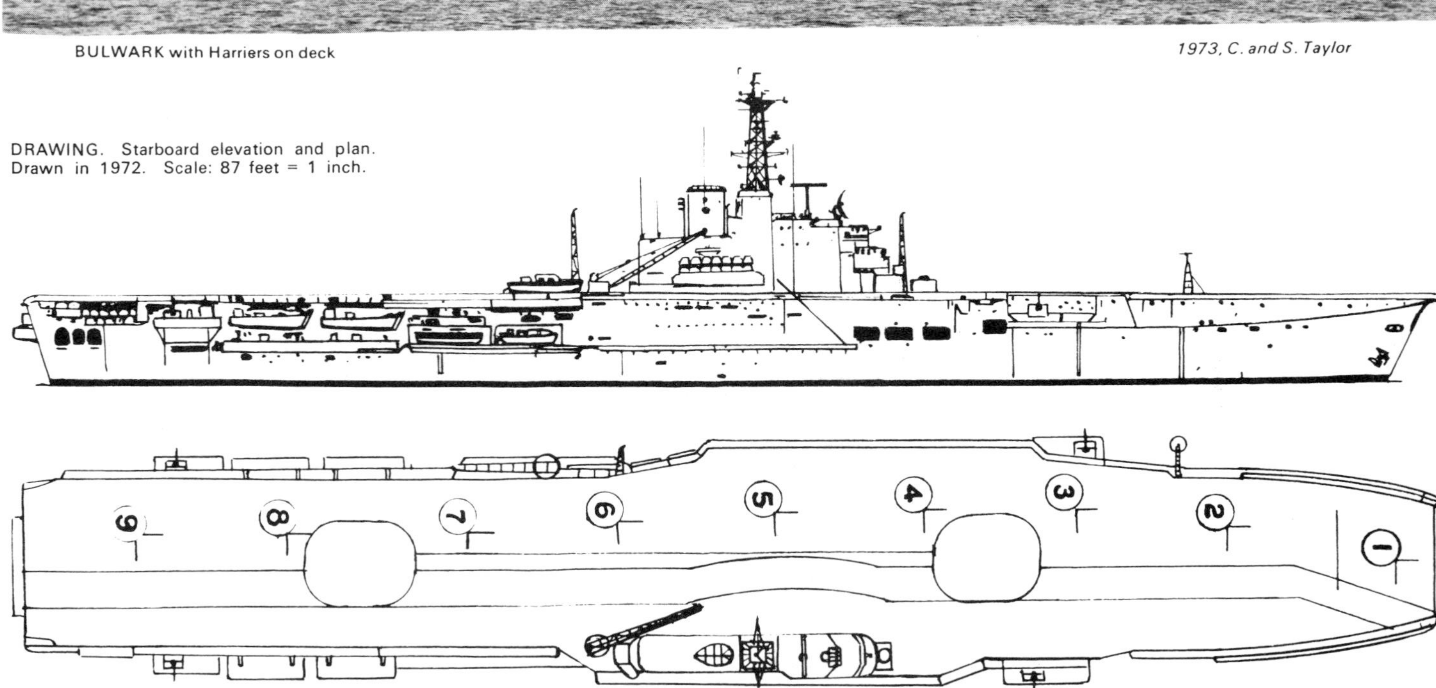

Amphibious Warfare Ships—*continued*

2 ASSAULT SHIPS (LPD)

Name	*No*	*Builders*	*Ordered*	*Laid down*	*Launched*	*Completed*
FEARLESS	L 10 (ex-L 3004)	Harland & Wolff Ltd Belfast	1 Dec 1961	25 July 1962	19 Dec 1963	25 Nov 1965
INTREPID	L 11 (ex L 3005)	John Brown & Co (Clydebank) Ltd	1 May 1962	19 Dec 1962	25 June 1964	11 Mar 1967

Displacement, tons	11 060 standard; 12 120 full load; 16 950 ballasted
Length, feet (*metres*)	500 (*152·4*) wl; 520 (*158·5*) oa
Beam, feet (*metres*)	80 (*24·4*)
Draught, feet (*metres*)	20·5 (*6·2*)
Draught, ballasted	32 (*9·8*) aft; 23 (*7·0*) fwd; 27·5 (*8·4*) mean
Landing craft	4 LCM(9) in dock; 4 LCVP at davits
Vehicles	*Specimen load*: 15 tanks, 7 three-ton and 20 quarter-ton trucks (20 three tonners on flight deck)
Aircraft	Flight deck facilities for 5 Wessex helicopters
Missiles, AA	4 "Seacat" systems
Guns, AA	2—40 mm Bofors
Boilers	2 Babcock & Wilcox
Main engines	2 EE turbines; 22 000 shp; 2 shafts
Speed, knots	21
Range, miles	5 000 at 20 knots
Complement	580 (see Troops note)

These assault ships, with commando carriers, replace the former ships of the Amphibious Warfare Squadron. They carry landing craft which are floated through the open stern by flooding compartments of the ship and lowering her in the water; are able to deploy tanks, vehicles and men; have seakeeping qualities much superior to those of tank landing ships, and greater speed and range. Capable of operating independently. Another valuable feature is a helicopter platform which is also the deckhead of the dock from which the landing craft are floated out. Officially estimated building cost: *Fearless* £11 250 000; *Intrepid* £10 300 000.

ELECTRICAL. Power at 440V 60 c/s 3-phase a.c. is supplied by four 1 000 kW AEI turbo-alternators.

ENGINEERING. The two funnels are staggered across the beam of the ship, indicating that the engines and boilers are arranged *en echelon*, two machinery spaces having one turbine and one boiler installed in each space. The turbines were manufactured by the English Electric Co Rugby, the gearing by David Brown & Co, Huddersfield. Boilers work at a pressure of 550 lbs per sq in and a temperature of 850 deg F. Two 5-bladed propellers, 12·5 feet diameter, 200 rpm in *Fearless*.

OPERATIONAL. Each ship is fitted out as a Naval Assault Group/Brigade Headquarters with an assault Operations Room from which naval and military personnel, can mount and control the progress of an assault operation.

RADAR. Fitted with type 993 air and surface warning radar.

SATELLITE SYSTEM. The Royal Navy fitted its first operational satellite communications system in *Intrepid* in 1969, the contract having been awarded to Plessey Radar—now removed.

TRAINING. *Fearless* used for the sea training of officers from the Britannia Royal Naval College, Dartmouth, When *Fearless* is refitting *Intrepid* will take over. Both retain full amphibious capabilities.

TROOPS. Each ship can carry 380 to 400 troops at ship's company standards, and an overload of 700 marines and military personnel can be accommodated for short periods.

FEARLESS — *1972*

INTREPID — *1974, Michael D. J. Lennon*

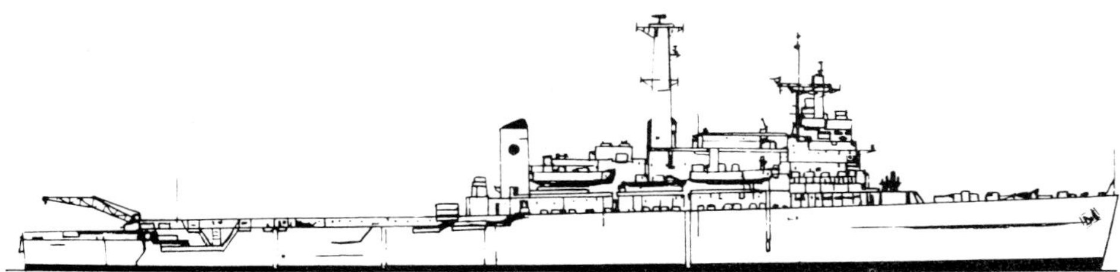

FEARLESS, INTREPID — *1974*

INTREPID flooded down — *1973, C. and S. Taylor*

Amphibious Warfare Ships—*continued*

6 LOGISTIC LANDING SHIPS

(RFA MANNED)

Name	No.	Builder	Laid down	Launched	Completed
SIR LANCELOT	L 3029	Fairfield	Mar 1962	June 1963	Jan 1964
SIR GALAHAD	L 3005	Alex Stephen	Feb 1965	19 Apr 1966	17 Dec 1966
SIR GERAINT	L 3027	Alex Stephen	June 1965	26 Jan 1967	12 July 1967
SIR BEDIVERE	L 3004	Hawthorn Leslie	Oct 1965	20 July 1966	18 May 1967
SIR PERCIVAL	L 3036	Hawthorn Leslie	Apr 1966	4 Oct 1967	23 Mar 1968
SIR TRISTRAM	L 3505	Hawthorn Leslie	Feb 1966	12 Dec 1966	14 Sep 1967

Displacement, tons	3 270 light; 5 674 full load (3 370 and 5 550 in *Sir Lancelot*)
Dimensions, feet	366·3 pp; 412·1 oa × 59·8 × 13·0
Aircraft	Can carry 20 Wessex helicopters
Guns	Fitted for 2—40 ......—not normally carried
Main engines	2 Mirrlees Diesels; 9 400 bhp; 2 shafts; (2 Denny/Sulzer diesels; 9 520 bhp in *Sir Lancelot*)
Speed, knots	17
Oil fuel, tons	815
Range, miles	8 000 at 15 knots
Complement	68 (18 officers, 50 ratings)
Military lift	340

GENERAL
Sir Lancelot was the prototype of this class which was originally built for the Army but transferred to RFA in Jan and Mar 1970. Fitted for bow and stern loading with drive-through facilities and deck-to-deck ramps. Facilities provided for on-board maintenance of vehicles and for laying out pontoon equipment.

AIRCRAFT. Helicopters can be operated from the well-deck and the after platform by day or night in the later ships. In *Sir Lancelot* well-deck operations are limited to fair weather-day conditions. If required to carry helicopters 11 can be stowed on the Tank Deck and 9 on the Vehicle Deck.

SIR GALAHAD *4/1974, John G. Callis*

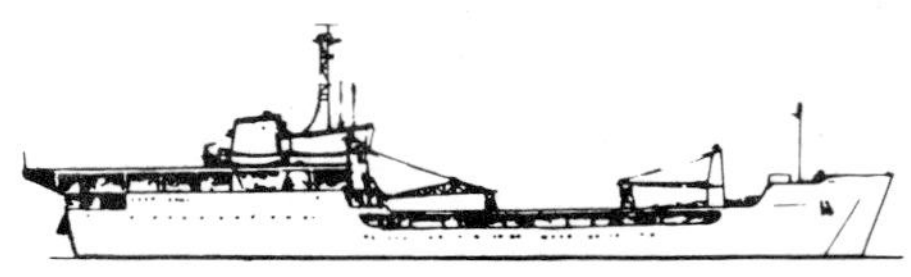
LSL *1973*

SIR TRISTRAM *1973, John G. Callis*

14 LCM (9) TYPE

LCM (9) 700, **LCM (9) 701**, **LCM (9) 702**, **LCM (9) 703**, **LCM (9) 704**, **LCM (9) 705**, **LCM (9) 706**, **LCM (9) 707**, **LCM (9) 708**, **LCM (9) 709**, **LCM (9) 710**, **LCM (9) 711**, **LCM (9) 3507**, **LCM (9) 3508**

Displacement, tons	75 light; 176 loaded
Dimensions, feet	77 pp; 85 oa × 21·5 × 5·5
Capacity	2 battle tanks or 100 tons of vehicles
Main engines	2 Paxman 6 cyl YHXAM diesels; 2 shafts; 624 bhp = 10 knots Screws enclosed in Kort nozzles to improve manoeuvrability

LCM (9) 3507 and LCM (9) 3508 were the first operational minor landing craft to be built since the Second World War. Ramped in the traditional manner forward, a completely enclosed radar-fitted wheelhouse is positioned aft. Upon completion they carried out familiarisation trials to perfect the new techniques required in launching and recovering LCMs from the flooded sterns of the parent assault ships. Four each of the 700 Series allocated to assault ships.

LCM (9) 709 (*HMS Intrepid*) *10/1974, C. and S. Taylor*

LCM (9) 3507 (RCT) *9/1974, C. and S. Taylor*

2 LOGISTIC LANDING SHIPS (RCT)

Ordered from Brooke Marine Ltd Lowestoft in October 1974 for the RCT. Details not yet available.

3 LCP (L) (3)

LCP (L) (3) 501, 503, 556

Displacement, tons	6·5 light; 10 loaded
Dimensions, feet	37 × 11 × 3·2
Main engines	225 bhp = 12 knots

NOTE. Five LCT (8)'s operated by the Royal Corps of Transport are listed under auxiliaries.

2 LCM (7)

7037 **7100**

Displacement, tons	28 light; 63 loaded
Dimensions, feet	60·2 × 16 × 3·7
Main engines	290 bhp = 9·8 knots

Employed as naval servicing boats and store carriers. Re-engined with Gray Marine diesels.

29 LCVP (1) (2) and (3)

LCVP (1) 102, 112, 118, 120, 123, 124, 127, 128, 133-136
LCVP (2) 142-149 **LCVP (3) 150-158**

Displacement, tons	8·5 light; 13·5 full load;
Dimensions, feet	41·5 (LCVP (2); 43 (LCVP (3)) × 10 × 2·5
Main engines	130 bhp = 8 knots; 2 Foden diesels, 200 bhp = 10 knots (LCVP (2))

LCVP (2)s carried by *Intrepid* and *Fearless* can carry 35 troops or 2 Land Rovers. Crew 4. LCA (2)s were redesignated LCVPs (Landing Craft Vehicle and Personnel) in 1966.
There were also a number of variations and prototypes of about the same length (43 feet).
Note. Raiding Landing Craft, including LCR 5507 and 5508, and Navigational Landing Craft, including LCN 604 (ex-LCR 5505).

Amphibious Warfare Ships—*continued*

5 LCT (8) TYPE (RCT)

AACHEN L 4062
ABBEVILLE L 4041
AGHEILA L 4002
ANDALNES L 4097
AUDEMER L 4061

Displacement, tons	657 light; 895 to 1 017 loaded
Dimensions, feet	225 pp; 231·2 oa × 39 × 3·2 forward; 5 aft Beaching draughts
Main engines	4 Paxman engines; 1 840 bhp 12·6 knots
Complement	33 to 37

All transferred to the Army's Royal Corps of Transport from the Royal Navy.

APPEARANCE. *Aachen* has twin funnels. *Audemer* has an enlarged bridge.

AACHEN *1973, Wright and Logan*

ANDALNES *1969 Skyfotos*

1 LST (3) (RFA)

EMPIRE GULL (ex-*Trouncer*) L 3513

Measurements, tons	4 257·9 gross
Dimensions, feet	347 × 54·1 × 12
Main engines	2 Triple Expansion; 2 shafts; 5 500 shp
Boilers	2 Water Tube
Oil fuel	950 tons
Complement	63 officers and men
Troop accommodation	8 officers, 72 ORs

Launched 9 July 1945.

EMPIRE GULL *9/1974, C. and S. Taylor*

HELICOPTER SUPPORT SHIP

ENGADINE K 08

Displacement, tons	8 000 to 9 000 full load
Measurement, tons	6 384 gross; 2 848 net
Dimensions, feet	424·0 oa × 58·4 × 22·1
Aircraft	4 Wessex and 2 Wasp or 2 Sea King helicopters
Main engines	1 Sulzer two stroke, 5 cyl turbo charged 5RD68 diesel; 5 500 bhp = 16 knots
Complement	RFA: 63 (15 officers, 48 men); RN: 14 (2 officers, 12 ratings) Accommodation for a further RN 113 (29 officers and 84 ratings)

Projected under the 1964-65 Navy Estimates. Built by Henry Robb Ltd, Leith. Ordered on 18 Aug 1964. Laid down on 9 Aug 1965. Officially named on 15 Sep 1966. Accepted into service on 15 Dec 1967. Largest ship then built by the company. Intended for the training of helicopter crews in deep water operations. Fitted with Denny Brown stabilisers to provide greater ship control during helicopter operations, the only RFA vessel so equipped.

ENGADINE *1972, Wright & Logan*

ENGADINE *1969*

MINE WARFARE FORCES

ABDIEL N 21

Displacement, tons	1 375 standard; 1 500 full load
Dimensions, feet	244·5 *pp*; 265 *oa* × 38·5 × 10
Mines	44 carried
Main engines	2 Paxman Ventura 16 cyl pressure charged diesels; 1 250 rpm; 2 690 bhp = 16 knots
Complement	77

Exercise minelayer ordered in June 1965 from John I. Thornycroft & Co Ltd, Woolston, Southampton. Laid down on 23 May 1966. Launched on 27 Jan 1967. Completed on 17 Oct 1967. Main machinery manufactured by Davey Paxman, Colchester. Main gearing supplied by Messrs Wisemans. Her function is to support mine countermeasure forces, maintain these forces when they are operating away from their shore bases, and lay exercise mines. Cost £1 500 000.

ABDIEL. *3/1974, C. and S. Taylor*

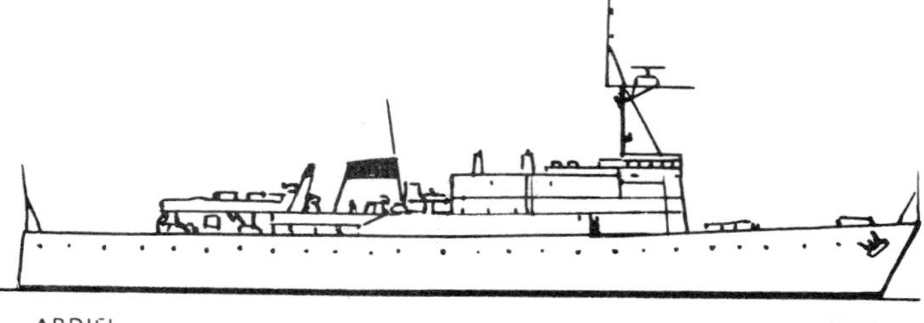

ABDIEL *1975*

NEW GRP MCM VESSELS
"BRECON" CLASS

A new class of MCM Vessels combining both hunting and sweeping capabilities is still in the design stage—a contract has been negotiated with Vosper-Thornycroft, the order for the first ship being placed in 1975. The cost of these ships is likely to be in the region of £4-5 million.

Artists Impression of new MCMV *1974, MOD (N)*

WILTON M 1116

Displacement, tons	450 standard
Dimensions, feet	153·0 *oa* × 28·8 × 8·5
Main engines	2 English Electric Deltic 18 diesels; 2 shafts; 3 000 bhp = 16 knots
Gun	1—40 mm Mark VII
Cost	£2 000 000
Complement	37 (5 officers and 32 ratings)

The world's first GRP warship. Contract signed on 11 Feb 1970. Laid down 16 Nov 1970. Launched on 18 Jan 1972 and commissioned 14 July 1973. Prototype built of glass reinforced plastic to the existing minehunter design by Vosper Thornycroft at Woolston. Similar to the "Ton" class and fitted with reconditioned machinery and equipment from the scrapped *Derriton*.

WILTON *3/1974, C. and S. Taylor*

Mine Warfare Forces —*continued*

37 "TON" CLASS

(see Disposal List)

15 MINEHUNTERS

BILDESTON	M 1110	**IVESTON**	M 1151
BOSSINGTON	M 1133	**KEDLESTON**	M 1153
BRERETON	M 1113	**KELLINGTON**	M 1154
BRINTON	M 1114	**KIRKLISTON**	M 1157
BRONINGTON	M 1115	**MAXTON**	M 1165
GAVINTON	M 1140	**NURTON**	M 1166
HUBBERSTON	M 1147	**SHERATON**	M 1181
		SHOULTON	M 1182

11 MINESWEEPERS—COASTAL

CHAWTON	M 1209	**SHAVINGTON**	M 1180
CUXTON	M 1125	**SOBERTON**	M 1200
GLASSERTON	M 1141	**UPTON**	M 1187
HIGHBURTON	M 1130	**WALKERTON**	M 1188
LALESTON	M 1158	**WOTTON**	M 1195
LEWISTON	M 1208		

11 MINESWEEPERS—COASTAL (RNR)

CLYDE (ex-*Repton*)	M 1167	**NORTHUMBRIA** (ex-*Wiston*)	M 1205
CURZON (ex-*Fittleton*)	M 1136	**ST DAVID** (ex-*Crichton*)	M 1124
KILLIECRANKIE (ex-*Bickington*)	M 1109	**SOLENT** (ex-*Crofton*)	M 1216
KILMOREY (ex-*Alfriston*)	M 1103	**THAMES** (ex-*Woolaston*)	M 1194
MERSEY (ex-*Pollington*)	M 1173	**VENTURER** (ex-*Hodgeston*)	M 1146
MONTROSE (ex-*Stubbington*)	M 1204		

Displacement, tons	360 standard; 425 full load
Dimensions, feet	140·0 pp; 153·0 oa × 28·8 × 8·2
Guns	Vary in different ships, some sweepers having no 40 mm, some 1—40 mm whilst hunters have 1 or 2—40 mm; 2—20 mm
Main engines	2 diesels; 2 shafts; 2 500 bhp (JVSS 12 Mirrlees), 3 000 bhp (18A-7A Deltic) = 15 knots; see *Engineering*
Oil fuel, tons	45
Range, miles	2 300 at 13 knots
Complement	29 (38 in minehunters, 5 officers and 33 ratings)

The survivors of a class of 118 built between 1953 and 1960, largely as a result of lessons from the Korean War. John I. Thornycroft & Co Ltd, Southampton were the lead yard for these ships which have double mahogany hull and incorporate a considerable amount of non-magnetic material. Fitted with Vospers stabilisers. The majority has now been fitted with nylon in place of copper sheathing.

APPEARANCE. Enclosed bridges in *Bidleston, Brereton, Brinton, Iveston, Kellington, Kirkliston, Lewiston, Solent, Thames, Bossington, Bronington, Chawton, Clyde, Gavinton, Hubberston, Kedleston, Maxton, Mersey, Montrose, Northumbria, Nurton Sheraton, Shoulton, Soberton, Walkerton*.

CONVERSIONS. *Beachampton, Monkton, Wasperton, Wolverton,* and *Yarnton* were converted into coastal patrol vessels late in 1971, (see Light Forces). *Laleston* was converted into diving trials ship in 1966-67. *Walkerton* used by Dartmouth RN College as Navigation Training Ship. *Shoulton* was the original minehunter conversion, fitted with pump-jet and bow thruster.

ENGINEERING. Earlier vessels had Mirrlees diesels, but later units had Napier Deltic lightweight diesels. *Highburton*, the first with Deltic diesels, was accepted on 21 Apr 1955. All minehunters have Deltics and active rudders. Generators for electrical power are in a separate engine room in Mirrlees, Deltic-conversions and minehunters. Deltic built minesweepers have a generator in the mainengine-room and two generators in the generator-room. Mirrlees still fitted in *Glasserton, Laleston, Cuxton* and *Clyde*. Three-bladed propellers, 6 ft diameter, 400 rpm. *Shoulton*, refitted 1965-67, has pump-jet propulsion.

FISHERY PROTECTION. Carried out by *Brereton, Brinton, Chawton, Highburton, Kedleston, Kellington, Shavington, Soberton, Upton Cuxton* refitting for Fishery Duties.

OSBOURNE SWEEP. *Glasserton* is fitted with derricks for Osbourne sweep. *Highburton* used in initial trials.

ROYAL NAVAL RESERVE. Eleven units were renamed and attached to Royal Naval Reserve Division Headquarters as follows (Division under *Name*):—

Thames	*Curzon*	*Solent*	*Venturer*	*St. David*	*Mersey*
London	Sussex	Solent	Severn	S. Wales	Mersey
Kilmorey	*Clyde*	*Montrose*	*Killiecrankie*	*Northumbria*	
Ulster	Clyde	Tay	Forth	Tyne	

TRANSFERS. Argentine (6 in 1968), Australia (6 in 1962), Ghana (1 in 1964), India (4 in 1956), Ireland (3 in 1971), Malaysia (7 in 1960-68), South Africa (10 in 1958-59).

BOSSINGTON, Minehunter — *1973, C. and S. Taylor*

LEWISTON, Minesweeper — *1973, Wright and Logan*

MERSEY, RNR Minesweeper — *1974, Michael D. J. Lennon*

4 "HAM" CLASS (MINESWEEPERS—INSHORE)

ARLINGHAM	M 2603
DITTISHAM	M 2621
FLINTHAM	M 2628
THORNHAM (ABERDEEN)	M 2793

Displacement, tons	120 standard; 159 full load
Dimensions, feet	2601 Series: 100 pp; 106·5 oa × 21·2 × 5·5
	2793 100 p; 107·5 oa × 22 × 5·8
Gun	1—20 mm Oerlikon AA forward
Main engines	2 Paxman diesels; 1 100 bhp = 14 knots
Oil fuel (tons)	15
Complement	15 (2 officers, 13 ratings)

The first inshore minesweeper, *Inglesham*, was launched by J Samuel White & Co Ltd, Cowes, on 23 Apr 1952. The 2601 series were of composite construction. In all 95 of this class were built.
Arlingham is permanent guardship at Gibraltar. *Thornham* attached to Aberdeen University RNU.

TRANSFERS. Australia (3 in 1966-68), France (15 in 1954-55) Ghana (2 in 1959), India (2 in 1955), Libya (2 in 1963), Malaysia (4 in 1958-59), South Yemen (3 in 1967). Ships subsequently returned are not listed.

DITTISHAM — *1973, John G. Callis*

2 "LEY" CLASS. M 2001 SERIES

AVELEY M 2002 — **ISIS** (ex-*Cradley*) M 2010

Displacement, tons	123 standard; 164 full load
Dimensions, feet	100 pp; 107 oa × 21·8 × 5·5
Guns	1—40 mm AA or 1—20 mm AA forward
Main engines	2 Paxman diesels; 700 bhp = 13 knots
Complement	15 (2 officers, 13 ratings)

The "Ley" class, originally of ten ships, differed from the "Ham" class. They were of composite (non-magnetic metal and wooden) construction, instead of all wooden construction. Their superstructure and other features also differed. They had no winch or sweeping gear, as they were minehunters, not sweepers. *Aveley* is attached to Plymouth. *Isis* was transferred to Southampton University RNU on 1 Apr 1974.

ISIS — *8/1974, C. and S. Taylor*

MAINTENANCE SHIPS

Name	No.	Builders	Laid down	Launched	Completed
TRIUMPH	A 108 (ex-*R* 16)	R & W Hawthorn Leslie, Hebburn	27 Jan 1943	2 Oct 1944	9 Apr 1946

Displacement, tons	13 500 standard; 17 500 full load
Length, feet (*metres*)	630·0 (*192·0*) pp; 650·0 (*198·1*) wl; 699·0 (*213·1*) oa
Beam, feet (*metres*)	80·0 (*24·4*)
Draught, feet (*metres*)	23·5 (*7·2*)
Width, feet (*metres*)	112·5 (*34·3*) overall
Aircraft	3 helicopters in flight deck hangar
Guns	4—40 mm AA; 3 saluting
Main engines	Parsons geared turbines; 2 shafts; 40 000 shp
Speed, knots	24·25
Boilers	4 Admiralty 3-drum type; Pressure 400 psi (*28·1 kg/cm²*); Temperature 700°F (*371°C*)
Range, miles	10 000 at 14 knots; 5 500 at full speed
Oil fuel, tons	3 000
Complement	500 (27 officers, 473 men) plus 285 (15 officers, 270 men) of maintenance staff

Originally an aircraft carrier of the "Colossus" class. Converted for present role at a cost of £10·2 mill. at Portsmouth between 1958 and 1965. Now in reserve at Chatham in preservation.

TRIUMPH — *9/1974, Dr. Giorgio Arra*

2 "HEAD" CLASS

Name	No.	Builders	Laid down	Launched	Completed
BERRY HEAD	A 191	North Vancouver Ship Repairs	15 June 1944	21 Oct 1944	30 May 1945
RAME HEAD	A 134	Burrard DD Co, Vancouver	12 July 1944	22 Nov 1944	18 Aug 1945

Displacement, tons	9 000 standard; 11 270 full load
Length, feet (*metres*)	416·0 (*126·8*) pp; 441·5 (*134·6*) oa
Beam, feet (*metres*)	57·5 (*17·5*)
Draught, feet (*metres*)	22·5 (*6·9*)
Guns, AA	11—40 mm
Boilers	2 Foster Wheeler
Main engines	Triple expansion; 2 500 ihp
Speed, knots	10 approx
Oil fuel, tons	1 600 capacity
Complement	425

Escort Maintenance Ships. In reserve in 1972. *Berry Head* was refitted in 1968-69 to relieve HMS *Triumph* in the Far East, but returned in 1970 and is now in reserve at Chatham. *Rame Head* accommodation ship at Londonderry.

SUBMARINE DEPOT SHIPS

Name	No.	Builders	Laid down	Launched	Completed	Reconstructed
FORTH	A 187	John Brown, Clydebank	30 June 1937	11 Aug 1938	14 May 1939	1962-1966
MAIDSTONE	A 185	John Brown, Clydebank	17 Aug 1936	21 Oct 1937	5 May 1938	1958-1962

Displacement, tons	10 000 standard; 13 000 full load
Length, feet (*metres*)	497·0 (*151·5*) pp; 531·0 (*161·8*) oa
Beam, feet (*metres*)	73·0 (*22·3*)
Draught, feet (*metres*)	21·2 (*6·5*)
Guns, AA	5—40 mm Bofors (see *Gunnery*)
Boilers	4 Admiralty 3-drum type
Main engines	Geared turbines (Brown Curtis in *Forth*; Parsons in *Maidstone*) 2 shafts; 7 000 shp
Speed, knots	16
Oil fuel, tons	2 300
Complement	695 (45 officers and 650 men) Accommodation for 1 159 (119 officers and 1 040 men) normal; over 1 500 max

Equipment includes foundry, coppersmith's, plumbers', carpenters'; heavy and light machine, electrical and torpedo repair shops and plant for charging submarine batteries. Designed for maintaining nine operational submarines, and supplying over 140 torpedoes and a similar number of mines. Repair facilities on board for all material in attached submarines, and extensive diving and salvage equipment. There are steam laundry, hospital, chapel, two canteens, bakery, barber shops, operating theatre and dental surgery.
In Oct 1969, *Maidstone* was restored and recommissioned as an accommodation ship for 2 000 troops and sent to Belfast.

As the Fleet Maintenance Base, Devonport and parent ship of the 2nd Submarine Squadron *Forth* is the depot ship of HMS *Defiance*.

FORTH — *1973, John G. Callis*

RECONSTRUCTION. *Maidstone* was extensively reconstructed in HM Dockyard, Portsmouth in 1958-62 as support ship for nuclear powered submarines with a lattice foremast and additional superstructure amidships. The conversion and modernisation included refitting as parent ship for the nuclear-powered submarine *Dreadnought*. *Forth* was similarly modernised and converted into a support ship for nuclear powered submarines in HM Dockyard Chatham, in 1962-66.

ROYAL YACHT

BRITANNIA A 00

Displacement, tons	3 990 light; 4 961 full load
Measurement, tons	5 769 gross
Dimensions, feet	360·0 pp; 380·0 wl; 412·2 oa × 55·0 × 17·0 max
Main engines	Single reduction geared turbines; 2 shafts; 12 000 shp = 21 knots
Boilers	2
Radius, miles	2 100 at 20 knots; 2 400 at 18 knots; 3 000 miles at 15 knots
Oil fuel, tons	330 (490 with auxiliary fuel tanks)
Complement	270

Designed as a medium sized naval hospital ship for use by Her Majesty The Queen in peacetime as the Royal Yacht. Built by John Brown & Co Ltd, Clydebank. Completed on 14 Jan 1954. Construction conformed to mercantile practice. Fitted with Denny-Brown single fin stabilisers to reduce roll in bad weather from 20 deg to 6 deg. Cost £2 098 000. To pass under the bridges of the St. Lawrence Seaway when she visited Canada, the top 20 feet of her mainmast and the radio aerial on her foremast were hinged in Nov 1958 so that they could be lowered as required.

BRITANNIA — *1973, Wright and Logan*

SURVEY SHIPS

3 "HECLA" CLASS

Name	No.	Builders	Laid down	Launched	Completed
HECATE	A 137	Yarrow & Co Ltd, Scotstoun	26 Oct 1964	31 Mar 1965	20 Dec 1965
HECLA	A 133	Yarrow & Co — Blythswood	6 May 1964	21 Dec 1964	9 Sep 1965
HYDRA	A 144	Yarrow & Co — Blythswood	14 May 1964	14 July 1965	5 May 1966

Displacement, tons	1 915 light; 2 733 full load
Measurement, tons	2 898 gross
Length, feet (*metres*)	235 (*71·6*) pp; 260·1 (*79·3*) oa
Beam, feet (*metres*)	49·1 (*15·0*)
Draught, feet (*metres*)	15·6 (*4·7*)
Aircraft	1 Wasp helicopter
Main engines	Diesel-electric drive; 1 shaft. 3 Paxman "Ventura" 12-cyl Vee turbocharged diesels; 3 840 bhp 1 electric motor; 2 000 shp
Speed, knots	14
Range, miles	20 000 at 9 knots
Oil fuel, tons	450
Complement	118 (14 officers, 104 ratings)
Accommodation	123 (19 officers, 104 ratings)

The first to be designed with a combined oceanographical and hydrographical role. Of merchant ship design and similar in many respects to the Royal Research ship *Discovery*, they have range and endurance to fit them for their specialised work. The hull is strengthened for navigation in ice, and a propeller built into a transverse tunnel in the bow for good manoeuvrability. The fore end of the superstructure incorporates a Landrover garage and the after end a helicopter hanger with adjacent flight deck. Equipped with chartroom, drawing office and photographic studio; two laboratories, dry and wet; electrical engineering and shipwright workshops, and large storerooms. Capable of operating independently of shore support for long periods. Air-conditioned throughout.

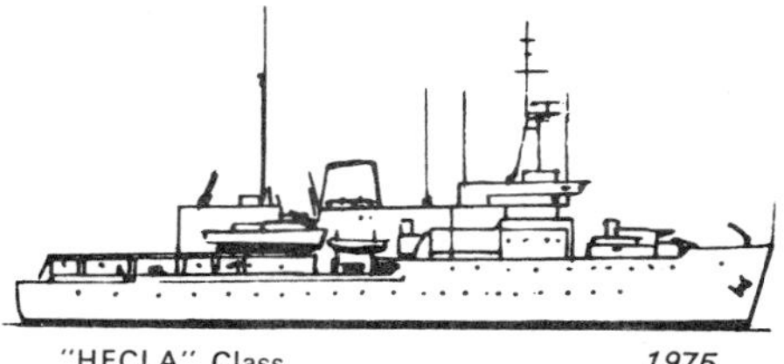

"HECLA" Class 1975

1 IMPROVED "HECLA" CLASS

HERALD

Displacement, tons	2 000 standard; 2 945 full load
Dimensions, ft (*m*)	260·1 oa × 49·1 × 15·6 (*79·3 × 15 × 4·7*)
Aircraft	1 Wasp helicopter
Main engines	Diesel-electric drive; 1 shaft
Speed, knots	14
Range, miles	12 000 at 11 knots
Complement	128

A later version of the "Hecla" class design. Ordered under the 1972-73 Supply (Ministry of Defence) Estimates. Built by Robb Caledon, Leith, with main machinery manufactured by GEC AEI Projects Ltd. Fitted with Hydroplot Satellite navigation system, computerised data logging, gravimeter, magnetometer, sonars, echo-sounders, coring and oceanographic winches and two surveying motor-boats. Fitted with passive stabilisation tank and bow thruster.

HECATE 1974, Michael D, J, Lennon

Laid down 9 Nov 1972. Launched by Mrs Mary Hall, wife of the Hydrographer, on 4 Oct 1973. Completed 31 Oct 1974.

COASTAL SURVEY SHIPS

4 "FAWN" CLASS

BEAGLE A 319 **BULLDOG** A 317 **FAWN** A 325 **FOX** A 320

Displacement, tons	800 standard 1 088 full load
Dimensions, feet	189 oa × 37·5 × 12
Main engines	4 Lister Blackstone ERS8M, 8 cyl. 4 str. diesels, coupled to 2 shafts, 2 000 bhp = 15 knots controllable pitch propellers
Range, miles	4 000 at 12 knots cruising
Complement	38 (4 officers, 34 ratings)

Designed for duty overseas, working in pairs. *Fawn* and *Fox* replaced the coastal minesweeper conversions. The first ship of the class launched was *Bulldog* on 12 July 1967 at Brooke Marine Ltd, Lowestoft, followed by *Beagle* on 7 Sep 1967, *Fox* on 6 Nov 1967 and *Fawn* on 29 Feb 1968. *Bulldog* was commissioned on 21 Mar 1968 and the others by the end of 1968. Built to commercial standards. Fitted with passive tank stabilizer to reduce rolling, most modern echo sounders, precision ranging radar, Decca "Hifix" system, automatic steering. Air-conditioned throughout. Carry 28·5 ft survey motor launch in davits.

BEAGLE 9/1974, Dr Giorgio Arra

FAWN 1974 Michael D. J. Lennon

INSHORE SURVEY CRAFT

3 "E" CLASS

ECHO A 70 **EGERIA** A 72 **ENTERPRISE** A 71

Displacement, tons	120 standard; 160 full load
Dimensions, feet	100·0 pp; 106·8 oa × 22·0 × 6·8
Main engines	2 Paxman diesels; 2 shafts; controllable pitch propellers; 700 bhp = 14 knots
Oil fuel, tons	15 capacity
Endurance, miles	1 600 at 10 knots
Complement	18 (2 officers, 16 ratings); accommodation for 22 (4 officers, 18 ratings)

Echo, the first Inshore Survey Craft, was built by J. Samuel White & Co Ltd, Cowes, launched on 1 May 1957, and commissioned on 12 Sep 1958. *Egeria* was built by Wm Weatherhead & Sons Ltd, Cockenzie, and *Enterprise* by M. W. Blackmore & Sons Ltd, Bideford. Equipped with two echo sounding machines, sonar, radar, wire sweep gear and echo sounding launch.

EGERIA 10/1974, C. and S. Taylo.

2 "HAM" CLASS

MODIFIED INSHORE MINESWEEPERS

WATERWITCH (ex-*Powderham*) M 2720 **WOODLARK** (ex-*Yaxham*) M 2780

Displacement, tons	120 standard; 160 full load
Dimensions, feet	107·5 oa × 22 × 5·5
Main engines	Diesels; 2 shafts; 1 100 bhp = 14 knots
Endurance, miles	1 500 at 12 knots
Complement	18 (2 officers, 16 ratings)

Former inshore minesweepers of the "Ham" class converted to replace the old survey motor launches *Meda* and *Medusa* for operation in inshore waters at home. *Waterwitch*, ex-M 2720, was seconded to Port Auxiliary Service in 1968.

WATERWITCH 1974, Michael D, J, Lennon

LIGHT FORCES

(see Disposal List for "Dark" and "Brave" Classes)

5 NEW CONSTRUCTION

The construction of five trawler-type patrol vessels of 16 knots designed particularly for oil-rig protection was announced 11 Feb 1975. To be fitted with helicopter pad.

4 NEW CONSTRUCTION (LARGE PATROL CRAFT)

CYGNET P 261
KINGFISHER P 260
PETREL P 262
SANDPIPER P 263

Length, feet	120
Main engines	Ruston diesels
Complement	24

Building by Dunston (Thorne) at Hessle. Of similar type to "Seal" class RAF rescue launches with improved sea-keeping qualities and fitted with stabilisers. To be used initially for coastal Fishery Protection duties. *Kingfisher* launched 20 Sep 1974.

1 VOSPER THORNYCROFT (FAST ATTACK CRAFT—PATROL)

TENACITY P 276

Displacement, tons	165 standard; 220 full load
Dimensions, feet	130·0 wl; 142·0 deck; 144·5 oa × 26·6 × 7·8
Guns	2 MGs
Main engines	3 Rolls Royce Proteus gas turbines; 3 shafts; 12 750 bhp = 40 knots max 2 Paxman Ventura 6 cyl diesels on wing shafts for cruising = 16 knots
Range, miles	2 500 at 15 knots
Complement	32 (4 officers, 28 ratings)

Built as a private venture by Vosper Thornycroft Limited. Launched on 18 Feb 1969 at Camber Shipyard, Portsmouth. Steel hull and aluminium alloy superstructure. Purchased by the Ministry of Defence (Navy) on 25 Jan 1972 for approximately £750 000 "as lying" and refitted with minor alterations and additions to meet naval requirements. To be used for exercises and fishery protection. Decca nav, radar. Commissioned 17 Feb 1973.

TENACITY *1974, Michael D. J. Lennon*

3 FAST TRAINING BOATS

CUTLASS P 274
SABRE P 275
SCIMITAR P 271

Displacement, tons	102 full load
Dimensions, feet	90·0 wl; 100·0 oa × 26·6 × 6·4
Main engines	2 Rolls Royce Proteus gas turbines = 40 knots (2 Foden diesels for cruising in CODAG arrangement)
Range, miles	425 at 35 knots; 1 500 at 11·5 knots
Complement	12 (2 officers, 10 ratings)

Hull of glued laminated wood construction. Design developed from that of "Brave" class fast patrol boats. Complete July—December 1970. All built by Vosper Thornycroft Group, Porchester Shipyard. Design permits fitting of third gas-turbines and a gun armament if required.

SCIMITAR *1972, John G. Callis*

5 MODIFIED "TON" CLASS

(FORMER COASTAL MINESWEEPERS)

BEACHAMPTON P 1007 (ex-M 1107)
MONKTON P 1055 (ex-M 1155)
WASPERTON P 1089 (ex-M 1189)
WOLVERTON P 1093 (ex-M 1193)
YARNTON P 1096 (ex-M 1196)

Displacement, tons	360 standard; 425 full load
Dimensions, feet	140·0 pp; 153·0 oa × 28·8 × 8·2
Guns	2—40 mm Bofors AA, single, 1 forward, 1 aft
Main engines	2 diesels; 2 shafts; 3 000 bhp = 15 knots
Oil fuel, tons	45 bunkerage
Range, miles	2 300 at 13 knots
Complement	30 (5 officers and 25 ratings, but varies)

Former coastal minesweepers of the "Ton" class, refitted as gunboats at the end of 1971, re-designated as coastal patrol vessels. Form 6th Patrol Squadron Hong Kong.

MONKTON *1974, Michael D. J. Lennon*

2 "FORD" CLASS (SDBs)

DEE (ex-*Beckford*) P 3104
DROXFORD P 3113

Displacement, tons	120 standard; 142 full load
Dimensions, feet	110·0 wl; 117·2 oa × 20·0 × 7·0 props
Guns	1—40 mm Bofors AA
A/S weapons	DC rails; large and small DC
Main engines	Davey Paxman diesels. Foden engine on centre shaft. 1 100 bhp = 18 knots max; 15 knots sea
Oil fuel, tons	23
Complement	19

Built in 1953-57. Last survivors of a class of 20. *Dee* attached to Liverpool University RNU (administered by RNR Mersey) and *Droxford* to Glasgow University RNU (administered by RNR Clyde).

DROXFORD *1972, Wright & Logan*

ICE PATROL SHIP

ENDURANCE (ex-*Anita Dan*) A 171

Displacement, tons	3 600
Measurement, tons	2 641 gross
Length, feet (*metres*)	300 (*91·44*) oa, 305 (*92·96*) including helicopter deck extension
Beam, feet (*metres*)	46 (*14·02*)
Draught, feet (*metres*)	16·5 (*5·03*); 18 (*5·5*)
Aircraft	2 Whirlwind Mk IX helicopters
Guns	2—20 mm
Main engines	B & W 550 VTBF diesels; 3 220 ihp; 1 shaft
Speed, knots	14·5
Range, miles	12 000 at 14·5 knots
Complement	119 (13 officers, 106 men, including a small Royal Marine detachment) plus 12 spare berths for scientists

Designed and built by Krögerwerft, Rendsburg completing in 1956. Purchased from J. Lauritzen Lines, Copenhagen (announced on 20 Feb 1967). Strengthened for operation in ice. Converted by Harland & Wolff, Belfast, into an ice patrol ship for southern waters to replace *Protector*, undertaking hydrographic and oceanographic surveys and acting as support ship and guard vessel.

ENDURANCE *1972, MOD (UK)*

An unusual feature for one of HM ships is her hull painted a vivid red for easy identification in the ice. Another feature is that the ship can be controlled from the crow's nest.

HOVERCRAFT

Note: The RN Hovercraft Trials Unit was established at Lee-on-the-Solent in 1974.

2 "WINCHESTER" (SRN60) TYPE

Displacement, tons	10 normal gross weight
Dimensions, feet	48·4 × 23·0 × 15·0 oa (height) × 4·0 (skirt)
Main engines	1 Rolls Royce Gnome gas turbine; 900 shp = 50 knots
Range	200 miles

Modified with radar and military communications equipment for its primary role of a fast amphibious communication craft to support Royal Marine units.

SRN6 *1971*

1 "WELLINGTON" (BHN7) TYPE

Displacement, tons	50 max weight; 33 light
Dimensions, feet	78·33 × 45·5 × 34·0 oa (height) × 5·5 (skirt)
Main engines	1 Rolls Royce Proteus gas turbine; 4 250 shp = 60 knots
Complement	14 plus trials crew

First "hover warship" costing about £700 000, delivered to the inter-Service Hovercraft Trials Unit at the Royal Naval Air Station, Lee-on-Solent, in Apr 1970. She could be used as a missile armed fast patrol craft or amphibious assault craft. Winter trials in Swedish waters in Feb 1972. Records established: longest open sea voyage, furthest north, and sustained speeds of over 55 knots in the Baltic.

1 SRN 5 TYPE

This small hovercraft is used for crew training.

DIVING SHIP

RECLAIM ((ex-*Salverdant*) A 231

Displacement, tons	1 200 standard; 1 800 full load
Dimensions, feet	200 pp; 217·8 oa × 38 × 15·5
Main engines	Triple expansion; 2 shafts; 1 500 ihp = 12 knots
Oil fuel, tons	310
Range, miles	3 000
Complement	100

Built by Wm. Simons & Co Ltd, Renfrew. Engined by Aitchison Blair Ltd. Laid down on 9 Apr 1946. Launched on 12 Mar 1948. Completed in Oct 1948. Construction based on the design of a "King Salvor" class naval ocean salvage vessel. First deep diving and submarine rescue vessel built as such for the Royal Navy. Fitted with sonar, radar, echo-sounding apparatus for detection of sunken wrecks, and equipped for submarine rescue work. Due for replacement.

RECLAIM *1972*

ROYAL FLEET AUXILIARY SERVICE

LARGE FLEET TANKERS

3 "OL" CLASS

OLMEDA (ex-*Oleander*) A 124
OLNA A 123
OLWEN (ex-*Olynthus*) A 122

Displacement, tons	10 890 light; 33 240 full load
Measurement, tons	22 350 deadweight; 18 600 gross
Dimensions, feet	611·1 pp; 648·0 oa × 84·0 × 34·0
Aircraft	2 Wessex helicopters (can carry 3)
Main engines	Pametrada double reduction geared turbines; 26 500 shp = 19 knots (21·2 on trials)
Boilers	2 Babcock & Wilcox, 750 lbs sq in, 950 deg F
Complement	87 (25 officers and 62 ratings)

Largest and fastest ships when they joined the Royal Fleet Auxiliary Service. *Olmeda* was launched on 19 Nov 1964 and completed on 18 Oct 1965 by Swan Hunter, Wallsend, with machinery by Wallsend Slipway & Eng Co Ltd, while *Olna* and *Olwen* were launched on 28 July 1965 and 10 July 1964 and completed on 1 Apr 1966 and 21 June 1965, respectively, by Hawthorn Leslie, Hebburn, engined by Hawthorn Leslie (Engineers) Ltd.

Designed for support of the Fleet, with handling gear for transferring fuels and stores by jackstay and derricks whilst steaming at speed A helicopter landing platform and hangar enable ships to collect stores by air. Specially strengthened for operations in ice. Accommodation of a high standard, fully air-conditioned. *Olna* has a transverse bow thrust unit for improved manoeuvrability in confined waters and a new design of replenishment at sea systems.

OLMEDA *1973, Wright and Logan*

OLWEN *1974, Wright and Logan*

2 LATER "TIDE" CLASS

TIDESPRING A 75
TIDEPOOL A 76

Displacement, tons	8 531 light; 25 931 full load
Measurement, tons	17 400 deadweight; 14 130 gross
Dimensions, feet	550·0 pp; 583·0 oa × 71·0 × 32·0
Main engines	Double reduction geared turbines; 15 000 shp = 17 knots
Boilers	2 Babcock & Wilcox
Complement	110 (30 officers and 80 ratings

Built by Hawthorn Leslie, Hebburn with machinery by Hawthorn Leslie (Engineers) Ltd. Highly specialised ships for fuelling (13 000 tons cargo fuel) and storing naval vessels at sea and capable of high performance under rigorous service conditions. Their all-round capability is enhanced by a helicopter platform and hangar. *Tidespring* was laid down on 24 July 1961, launched on 3 May 1962, and accepted on 18 Jan 1963. *Tidepool* was laid down on 4 Dec 1961 launched on 11 Dec 1962 and accepted on 28 June 1963.

TIDEPOOL *1971*

3 "TIDE" CLASS

TIDEFLOW (ex-*Tiderace*) A 97
TIDESURGE (ex-*Tiderange*) A 98
TIDEREACH A 96

Displacement, tons	9 040 light; 25 940 full load
Measurement, tons	16 900 deadweight; 13 700 gross
Dimensions, feet	550 pp, 583 oa × 71 × 32
Main engines	Double reduction geared turbines; 15 000 shp = 17 knots

Tidereach, launched by Swan Hunter & Wigham Richardson Ltd, Wallsend-on-Tyne, on 2 June 1954, and completed on 30 Aug 1955, was the first of the new Fleet Replenishment Tankers. The main machinery was manufactured by the Wallsend Slipway Co. Designed for the support of the Fleet and replenishment under way. *Tiderange* (renamed *Tidesurge* in 1958) was launched at I. L. Thompson & Sons Ltd, Sunderland, on 30 Aug 1954, the main machinery being manufactured by North Eastern Marine Engineering Co Ltd, Wallsend. A fourth ship, *Tide Austral*, built for Australia, was renamed *Supply* on 7 Sep 1962.

TIDEFLOW *1973, John Mortimer*

SUPPORT TANKERS

ORANGELEAF (ex-M.V. *Southern Satellite*) A 80

Measurement, tons	17 475 deadweight; 12 481 gross; 6 949 net
Dimensions, feet	525 pp; 556·5 oa × 71·7 × 30·5
Main engines	Doxford 6-cyl. diesel; 6 800 bhp = 15 knots
Oil fuel (tons)	1 610

Built by Furness Shipbuilding Co Ltd, Haverton Hill on Tees. Launched on 8 Feb 1955. Completed June 1955. From South Georgia Co Ltd, 25 May 1959. Astern and abeam fuelling.

ORANGELEAF *8/1974, C. and S. Taylor*

CHERRYLEAF (ex-*Overseas Adventurer*) A 82

Measurement, tons	18 560 deadweight; 12 402 gross, 7 338 net
Dimensions, feet	544 × 72·7 × 30·6
Machinery	6 cyl Doxford diesel; 6 800 bhp = 13 knots

Built by Sir James Laing & Sons Ltd in 1953. Transferred to RFA in March 1973

CHERRYLEAF *1973, John G. Callis*

PLUMLEAF A 78

Displacement, tons	24 920 full load
Measurement, tons	18 562 deadweight; 12 692 gross
Dimensions, feet	534 pp; 560 oa × 72 × 30
Main engines	N E Doxford 6-cyl diesels; 9 350 bhp = 15·5 knots

Built by Blyth DD & Eng Co Ltd Launched 29 Mar 1960. Completed July 1960. Astern and abeam fuelling.

PLUMLEAF *1972, Wright & Logan*

PEARLEAF A 77

Displacement, tons	24 900 full load
Measurement, tons	18 045 deadweight, 12 139 gross, 7 215 net
Dimensions, feet	535 pp, 568 oa × 71·7 × 30
Main engines	Rowan Doxford 6-cyl diesels; 8 800 bhp = 15·8 knots

Built by Scotstoun Yard of Blythswood Shipbuilding Co Ltd, for Jacobs and Partners Ltd, London. Launched on 15 Oct 1959 and completed in Jan 1960. Chartered by the Royal Navy on completion. Can carry three different grades of cargo. Astern and abeam fuelling.

PEARLEAF *1970, MOD (N)*

MOBILE RESERVE TANKER

DEWDALE (ex-M.V. *Edenfield*) A 219

Measurement, tons	21 542 net; 35 805 gross; 63 588 deadweight
Dimensions, feet	747·0 pp; 774·5 oa × 107·8 × 41·5
Main engines	B. & W. 9 cyl diesels; 1 shaft; 17 000 bhp = 15 knots
Complement	51

In July 1967 the Ministry of Defence chartered three large tankers for service East of Suez. After limited modifications the ships operated in the Indian Ocean area. But *Ennerdale* sank on 1 June 1970 after striking a submerged hazard in the Indian Ocean. *Dewdale* is the largest RFA tanker at present in service.

DEWDALE *1974, Michael D. J. Lennon*

SMALL FLEET TANKERS

5 "ROVER" CLASS

GREEN ROVER A 268 **GREY ROVER** A 269 **BLUE ROVER** A 270
GOLD ROVER A 271 **BLACK ROVER** A 273

Displacement, tons	11 522 full load
Measurement, tons	3 185 net; 7 060 deadweight; 7 510 gross
Dimensions, feet	461·0 oa × 63·0 × 24·0
Main engines	2 Ruston & Hornsby 16 cyl. uni-directional diesels; 1 shaft; controllable pitch propeller; 16 000 bhp = 19 knots (Pielstick diesels in last pair)
Complement	47 (16 officers and 31 men)

Small fleet tankers designed to replenish HM ships at sea with fuel, fresh water, limited dry cargo and refrigerated stores under all conditions while underway. *Blue Rover* is classified as "Fleet Replenishment Tanker". A helicopter landing platform is provided, served by a stores lift, to enable stores to be transferred at sea by helicopter. Built at Swan Hunter, Hebburn-on-Tyne, *Green Rover* was launched on 19 Dec 1968, *Grey Rover* on 17 Apr 1969, *Blue Rover* on 11 Nov 1969 and *Gold Rover* on 7 Mar 1973. *Black Rover* launched 30 Oct 1973 was completed (last of class) 23 Aug 1974. The cost of *Black Rover* was £7 mill. an increase of £4 mill. on the price of the original ships. Announced in early 1974 that the first three will be re-engined with Pielstick diesels at first refit.

BLACK ROVER *9/1974, Michael D. J. Lennon*

COASTAL TANKER

1 "EDDY" CLASS

EDDYFIRTH A 261

Displacement, tons	1 960 light; 4 160 full load
Measurement, tons	2 300 gross; 2 200 deadweight
Dimensions, feet	270 pp; 286 oa × 44 × 17·2
Main engines	1 set triple expansion; 1 shaft; 1 750 ihp = 12 knots
Boilers	2 oil burning cylindrical

Built bu Lobnitz & Co Ltd, Renfrew. Completed on 10 Feb 1954. Cargo capacity: 1 650 tons oil.

EDDYFIRTH *1973, C. and S. Taylor*

FLEET REPLENISHMENT SHIPS

2 NEW CONSTRUCTION "FORT" CLASS

FORT AUSTIN A 386 **FORT GRANGE** A 385

Dimensions, feet	603 × 79 × 25
Aircraft	1 Wessex helicopter
Main engines	Diesel; 23 300 hp single screw

Ordered from Scott-Lithgow in Nov 1971. To be fitted with a helicopter flight-deck and hangar, thus allowing not only for vertical replenishment but also a fuelling point for Force A/S helicopters. *Fort Grange* laid down 9 Nov 1973.

New Construction "Fort" Class *1972, MOD (N) Drawing*

REGENT A 486 **RESOURCE** A 480

Displacement, tons	19 000 full load
Measurements, tons	18 029 gross
Dimensions, feet	600·0 pp; 640·0 oa × 77·2 × 26·1
Aircraft	1 Wessex helicopter
Guns	Fitted for 2—40 mm Bofors (single) which are not carried in peacetime
Main engines	AEI steam turbines; 20 000 shp = 20 knots
Complement	119 R.F.A. officers and ratings; 52 Naval Dept industrial and non-industrial civil servants; 11 Royal Navy (1 officer and 10 ratings) for helicopter flying and maintenance

Ordered on 24 Jan 1963. Built by Scott's Shipbuilding & Engineering Co, Greenock, and Harland & Wolff, Belfast. They have lifts for armaments and stores, and helicopter platforms for transferring loads at sea. Designed from the outset as Fleet Replenishment Ships (previous ships had been converted merchant vessels). Air-conditioned. *Resource* was launched at Greenock on 11 Feb 1966, *Regent* at Belfast on 9 Mar 1966. Official title is Ammunition, Food, Explosives, Stores Ship (AFES).

RESOURCE *1973, John Mortimer*

RESURGENT (ex-*Changchow*) A 280 **RETAINER** (ex-*Chungking*) A 329

Displacement, tons	14 000 (approx)
Measurement, tons	*Resurgent* 9 511 gross; *Retainer* 9 301 gross
Dimensions, feet	451 pp; 477·2 oa × 62 × 29
Main engines	Doxford diesel; 1 shaft; 6 500 bhp = 15 knots
Oil fuel (tons)	925
Complement	107

Built by Scotts' Shipbuilding and Engineering Co Ltd, Greenock, and completed in 1951 and 1950, respectively. *Retainer* was purchased in 1952 and converted into a naval storeship during autumn 1954-April 1955 by Palmers Hebburn Co Ltd, where further conversion was carried out Mar-Aug 1957 to extend her facilities as a stores ship, including the fitting out of holds to carry naval stores, the installation of lifts for stores, the provision of extra cargo handling gear and new bridge wings. *Resurgent* was taken over on completion for employment as a fleet replenishment ship.

RESURGENT *9/1972, C, and S, Taylor*

STORES SUPPORT SHIP

LYNESS A 339 **STROMNESS** A 344 **TARBATNESS** A 345

Displacement, tons	16 500 laden
Measurements, tons	12 359 gross; 4 744 net; 7 782 deadweight
Dimensions, feet	490 pp; 524 oa × 72 × 25·5
Aircraft	Facilities for helicopters
Main engines	Wallsend-Sulzer 8-cyl RD.76 diesel; 11 520 bhp = 17 knots
Complement	105

Designed and built by Swan Hunter & Wigham Richardson Ltd, Wallsend-on-Tyne. Lifts and mobile appliances provided for handling stores internally, and a new replenishment at sea system and a helicopter landing platform for transferring loads at sea. A novel feature of the ships is the use of close circuit television to monitor the movement of stores. All air-conditioned. *Lyness* was completed on 22 Dec 1966, *Stromness* on 21 Mar 1967, and *Tarbatness* Sept 1967. *Lyness* is an Air-Stores Support Ship.

LYNESS *1972*

AIR STORES SUPPORT SHIP

(See Lyness above)

RELIANT (ex-*Somersby*) A 84

Displacement, tons	4 447 light as built; 13 737 full load
Measurement, tons	9 290 deadweight (summer), 8 460 gross
Dimensions, feet	440 pp; 468·8 oa × 61·5 × 26·2
Main engines	Doxford 6 cyl, diesel; 8 250 bhp = 18 knots
Complement	102

Built by Sir James Laing & Sons Ltd, Sunderland. Engined by Hawthorne Leslie. Completed in 1954. Converted for her new role at North Shields. Sailed from Chatham on 4 Nov 1958 for the Far East as the Royal Navy's first air/victualling stores issuing ship capable of replenishing aircraft carriers at sea. Has an endurance of 50 days steaming at 16 knots, and carries 40 000 different patterns of aircraft spares and general naval stores. As refitted she has a helicopter pad aft for stores transfer.

RELIANT *12/1974, C, and S, Taylor*

STORE CARRIERS

2 "BACCHUS" CLASS

BACCHUS A 404 **HEBE** A 406

Displacement, tons	2 740 light; 7 958 full load
Measurement, tons	4 823 gross; 2 441 net; 5 218 deadweight
Dimensions, feet	350 pp; 379 oa × 55 × 22
Main engines	Swan Hunter Sulzer diesel; 1 shaft; 5 500 bhp = 15 knots
Oil fuel, tons	720
Complement	57

Built by Henry Robb Ltd, Leith, for the British India Steam Navigation Co. Taken over by the Royal Navy on completion on long term "bare-boat" charter. *Bacchus* was completed in Sep 1962, *Hebe* in May 1962. Crew accommodation and engines aft as in tankers. In 1973 both purchased by P and O SN Co, remaining on charter to MOD (N).

BACCHUS *1972, C, and S, Taylor*

ROBERT MIDDLETON A 241 (COASTAL STORE CARRIER)

Displacement, tons	900 light; 1 900 full load
Measurement, tons	1 000 deadweight; 1 125 gross
Dimensions, feet	210 pp; 222·5 oa × 36 × 13·5
Main engines	Atlas Polar Diesel; 1 shaft; 960 bhp = 10·5 knots
Oil fuel, tons	60
Complement	17

Coastal store carrier. Built by Grangemouth Dockyard Co Ltd. Machinery by British Auxiliaries Ltd, Govan. Launched on 29 June 1938.

ROYAL MARITIME AUXILIARY SERVICE AND PORT AUXILIARY SERVICE

NOTE. To avoid over complication the ships and vessels of the Royal Naval Auxiliary Service and some of the Royal Corps of Transport are included here.

MOORING SALVAGE AND BOOM VESSELS

2 "WILD DUCK" CLASS

2 "IMPROVED WILD DUCK" CLASS

2 "LATER WILD DUCK" CLASS

RMAS
GARGANEY P 194
MANDARIN P 192
GOOSANDER P 196
POCHARD P 197

PAS
GOLDENEYE P 195
PINTAIL P 193

Displacement, tons	950; 1 125 (*Goosander* and *Pochard*)
Dimensions, feet	198·3 including horns (*Goosander* and *Pochard*) 190 including horns (*Garganey* and *Goldeneye*) 182 × 40 × 11·3 including horns (*Mandarin* and *Pintail*)
Main engines	1 Davey Paxman 16 cyl diesel; 1 shaft; controllable pitch propeller; 550 bhp = 10 knots
Range, miles	3 000 at 10 knots
Complement	24 (6 officers, 6 petty officers, 12 ratings) 32 (including salvage party) (*Goosander* and *Pochard*

Mandarin was the first of a new class of marine service vessels. Launched on 17 Sep 1963 and handed over on 5 Mar 1964. *Pintail* was launched on 3 Dec 1963. Both built by Cammell Laird & Co Ltd, Birkenhead. *Garganey* and *Goldeneye* were built in 1965-67 by Brooke Marine Ltd, Lowestoft. *Goosander* and *Pochard* of the later "Wild Duck" class were built by Robb Caledon Ltd and launched 12 Apr 1973 and 21 June 1973 respectively. Completion 10 Sep and 11 Dec 1973. Previously their three tasks were separately undertaken by specialist vessels. Capable of laying out and servicing the heaviest moorings used by the Fleet and also maintaining booms for harbour defence. Heavy lifting equipment enables a wide range of salvage operations to be performed, especially in harbour clearance work. The special heavy winches have an ability for tidal lifts over the apron of 200 tons.

GOLDENEYE — *9/1974, Dr. Giorgio Arra*

5 "KIN" CLASS (RMAS)

DISPENSER	(22 Apr 43)	**KINLOSS** A 482	(14 Apr 45) PAS
KINBRACE A 281	(17 Jan 45) PAS	**UPLIFTER** A 507	(29 Nov 43)
KINGARTH A 232	(22 May 44)		

Displacement, tons	950 standard; 1 050 full load
Measurement, tons	775 gross; 262 deadweight
Dimensions, feet	150·0 pp; 179·2 oa × 35·2 × 9·5 mean; 12·0
Main engines	1 British Polar Atlas M44M diesel; 630 bhp = 9 knots; *Dispenser:* Triple expansion; 1 shaft; 600 ihp = 9 knots
Boilers	1 return tube cylindrical (30 ton) in *Dispenser*
Complement	34

Originally classified as Coastal Salvage Vessels, but re-rated Mooring, Salvage and Boom Vessels in 1971. Launch dates above. Equipped with horns and heavy rollers. Can lift 200 tons deadweight over the bow. *Kinbrace, Kingarth, Kinloss* were built by A. Hall, Aberdeen, *Uplifter* by Smith's Dock Co Ltd. *Dispenser* was on charter to Liverpool & Glasgow Salvage Association, but returned in 1971. *Kinbrace, Kingarth* and *Uplifter* were refitted with diesel engines in 1966-67, and *Kinloss* in 1963-64.

KINBRACE — *1974, Michael D. J. Lennon*

LAYBURN P 191 (RMAS)   **LAYMOOR** P 190 (RN)

Displacement, tons	800 standard; 1 050 full load
Dimensions, feet	160 pp; 192·7 oa × 34·5 × 11·5
Main engines	Triple expansion; 1 shaft; 1 300 ihp = 10 knots
Boilers	2 Foster Wheeler "D" type; 200 psi
Complement	2 officers; 29 to 34 ratings

Both built by Wm. Simons & Co Ltd (Simons-Lobnitz Ltd). *Layburn*, which cost £565 000 was completed on 7 June 1960. *Laymoor* was accepted on 9 Dec 1959. Designed for naval or civilian manning. Lifting capacity is greater than that of predecessors; improvement in accommodation enables them to be operated in any climate.

LAYBURN — *1973, John G. Callis*

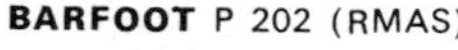

BARFOOT P 202 (RMAS)

Displacement, tons	750 standard, 1 000 full load
Dimensions, feet	150 pp; 173·8 oa; 182 over horns × 23·2 × 11·5
Main engines	Triple expansion; 850 ihp = 11 knots
Boilers	2 single ended (200 lbs per sq in)
Fuel, tons	214 coal
Radius, miles	3 000
Complement	32

Launched by John Lewis & Sons Ltd, Aberdeen on 25 Sep 1942.

Bow lift of 27 to 70 tons.

TRANSFERS. *Barbrake* and *Barcross* were transferred to South Africa, *Barbarian*, *Barbette* (first of this name in the class, launched on 15 Dec 1937) and *Barfair* to Turkey, *Baron* to Ceylon in 1958 (purchased by the Colombo Port Commission).

BARFOOT

COASTAL TANKERS

6 "OILPRESS" CLASS (PAS)

OILBIRD Y 25
OILFIELD Y 24
OILMAN Y 26
OILPRESS Y 21
OILSTONE Y 22
OILWELL Y 23

Displacement, tons	280 standard; 530 full load
Dimensions, feet	130·0 wl; 139·5 oa × 30·0 × 8·3
Main engines	1 Lister Blackstone ES6 diesel; 1 shaft; 405 shp at 900 rpm
Complement	11 (4 officers and 7 ratings)

Ordered on 10 May 1967 from Appledore Shipbuilders Ltd. Three are diesel oil carriers and three FFO carriers.

OILWELL *8/1974, John G, Callis*

TRIALS SHIPS

1 NEW CONSTRUCTION

Ordered from Scott-Lithgow November 1971. Laid down 19 Dec 1973. Similar to *Whitehead* below. Mirrlees-Blackstone diesel. Prime duty sonar propagation trials.

WHITEHEAD A 364 (RMAS)

Displacement, tons	3 040 full load
Dimensions, feet	291·0 wl; 319·0 oa × 48·0 × 17·0
Main engines	2 Paxman 12 YLCM diesels; 1 shaft; 3 400 bhp = 15·5 knots
Range, miles	4 000 at 12 knots
Complement	10 officers, 32 ratings, 15 trials and scientific staff

Designed to provide mobile preparation, firing and control facilities for weapons and research vehicles. Built by Scotts, Shipbuilding Co Ltd, Greenock. Launched on 5 May 1970. Named after Robert Whitehead, the torpedo development pioneer and engineer. Fitted with equipment for tracking weapons and targets and for analysing the results of trials.

WHITEHEAD *1972*

CRYSTAL RDV 01 (Dockyard Control)

Displacement, tons	3 040 deep
Dimensions, feet	410·0 wl; 413·5 × 56·0 × 5·5
Complement	60, including scientists

Unpowered floating platform for Sonar Research and Development. Built at H.M. Dockyard, Devonport. Ordered in Dec 1969. Begun in Mar 1970 for completion in Sep 1971. A harbour-based laboratory without propulsion machinery or steering which provides the Admiralty Underwater Weapons Establishment at Portland with a stable platform on which to carry out acoustic tests and other research projects.

CRYSTAL *1972*

Trials Ships—*continued*

ICEWHALE (PAS)

Displacement, tons	289 standard; 350 full load
Dimensions, feet	120 × 24 × 9
Main engines	Speed = 9 knots
Range, miles	4 000 at 12 knots
Complement	12 (Master, Mate and 10 ratings), 15 trials and scientific staff

Experimental Trials Vessel for the Underwater Weapons Establishment, Portland.

ICEWHALE *1968, John G. Callis*

2 "MINER" CLASS

BRITANNIC (PAS) **STEADY** (PAS)

Displacement, tons	300 standard; (355 full load)
Dimensions, feet	110·2 × 26·5 × 8·0
Main engines	Ruston & Hornsby diesels; 2 shafts; 360 bhp = 10 knots

Built by Philip & Son Ltd, Dartmouth, and engined by Ruston & Hornsby Ltd. Lincoln. *Miner V* was converted into a cable lighter and renamed *Britannic* in 1960 with PAS as store carrier. *Miner VII* was adapted as a stabilisation trials ship at Portsmouth and renamed *Steady* in 1960 with PAS.

BRITANNIC *1974, Michael D, J, Lennon*

TORPEDO RECOVERY VESSELS

TORRENT A 127 (PAS) **TORRID** A 128 (PAS)

Measurement, tons	550 gross
Dimensions, feet	151·0 × 31·5 × 11
Main engines	Paxman diesels, 700 bhp = 12 knots
Complement	19

Torrent was completed on 10 Sept 1971 and *Torrid* in Jan 1972 by Swan Hunter (Tyne). These ships have a stern well for torpedo recovery—can carry 22 torpedoes in hold and 10 on deck.

TORRID *7/1974, C, and S, Taylor*

THOMAS GRANT (PAS)

Displacement, tons	209 light; 461 full load
Measurement, tons	252 deadweight; 218 gross
Dimensions, feet	113·5 × 25·5 × 8·8
Main engines	2 diesels; Speed = 9 knots

Built as a local store carrier by Charles Hill & Sons Ltd, Bristol. Launched on 11 May 1953 and completed in July 1953. Converted into a torpedo recovery vessel in 1968.

THOMAS GRANT *Added 1969*

6 "HAM" CLASS (PAS)

BUCKLESHAM M 2614
DOWNHAM M 2622
EVERINGHAM M 2626
FRITHAM M 2630
HAVERSHAM M 2635
LASHAM M 2636

Details similar to other "Ham" class in Mine Warfare section but converted for TRV in 1964 onwards. Now fitted with stern well.

CABLE SHIPS (RMAS)

BULLFINCH (19 Aug 1940) A 176 **ST. MARGARETS** (13 Oct 1943) A 259

Displacement, tons	1 300 light; 2 500 full load
Measurement, tons	1 524 gross; 1 200 deadweight
Dimensions, feet	228·8 pp; 252 oa × 36·5 × 16·3
Main engines	Triple expansion; 2 shafts; 1 250 ihp = 12 knots

Both built by Swan, Hunter & Wigham Richardson Ltd. Launch dates above. Provision was made for mounting one 4 inch gun and four 20 mm AA guns but no armament is fitted.

BULLFINCH *1970*

EXPERIMENTAL SHIPS

WHIMBREL (ex-LCT) A 179

Displacement, tons	300
Dimensions, feet	187 × 29·5 × 5
Main engines	Diesels; 2 shafts

Employed for weapon research by Underwater Weapons Establishment, Portland.

WHIMBREL *1974, Michael D, J, Lennon*

TARGET SHIP

WAKEFUL (ex-*Dan*, ex-*Hercules*)

Displacement, tons	492
Dimensions, feet	145·8 oa × 35 × 15·5
Complement	18

Purchased from Sweden in 1974. Built as a tug and now operated as Submarine Target Ship in the Clyde.

ARMAMENT CARRIERS

KINTERBURY A 378 **THROSK**

Displacement, tons	1 490 standard; 1 770 full load
Measurement, tons	600 deadweight
Dimensions, feet	185 pp; 199·8 × 34·3 × 13
Main engines	Triple expansion; 1 shaft; 900 ihp = 11 knots
Coal, tons	154

Launched on 14 Nov 1942 and in 1943 and completed on 4 Mar 1943 and 22 Dec 1943, respectively. Both built by Philip & Son Ltd. Rated as naval armament carriers Converted in 1959 with hold stowage and a derrick for handling guided missiles.

KINTERBURY *1972, Wright & Logan*

BOWSTRING **CATAPULT** **FLINTLOCK** (PAS)

Of various displacements and data.

MAXIM A 377 (PAS)

Displacement, tons	604 to 663
Measurement, tons	340 deadweight
Dimensions, feet	144·5 × 25 × 8
Main engines	Reciprocating; 500 ihp = 9 knots
Complement	13

Built by Lobnitz & Co Ltd, Renfrew.

WATER CARRIERS

6 "WATER" CLASS (PAS)

WATERFALL Y 17 **WATERSHED** Y 18 **WATERSIDE** Y 20 **WATERSPOUT** Y 19 **WATERCOURSE** **WATERFOWL**

Measurement, tons	285 gross
Dimensions, feet	123 pp; 131·5 oa × 24·8 × 8
Main engines	1 Diesel; 1 shaft; 600 bhp = 11 knots
Complement	11

Built by Drypool Engineering & Drycock Co, Hull. Launched on 30 Mar 1966, 3 Aug 1966, 20 June 1967 and 29 Dec 1966, respectively and last pair in 1973. *Waterfowl* completed May 25 1974.

WATERFALL *1972, Wright & Logan*

4 "SPA" CLASS (PAS)

SPALAKE (10 Aug 1946) A 260 **SPAPOOL** (28 Feb 1946) A 222 **SPABROOK** (24 Aug 1944) A 224 **SPABURN** (5 Jan 1946) A 257

Displacement, tons	1 219 full load
Measurement, tons	630 deadweight; 672 to 719 gross
Dimensions, feet	160 pp; 172 oa × 30 × 12
Main engines	Triple expansion; 675 ihp = 9 knots
Coal, tons	90

Spalake and *Spapool* were built by Charles Hill & Sons Ltd, Bristol and *Spabrook* and *Spaburn* by Philip & Son Ltd, Dartmouth. *Spapool* in Mombasa.

SPAPOOL *1967, MOD (N)*

6 "FRESH" CLASS (PAS)

FRESHBURN **FRESHLAKE** **FRESHMERE** **FRESHPOND** **FRESHPOOL** **FRESHSPRING**

Displacement, tons	594
Dimensions, feet	126·2 × 25·5 × 10·8
Main engines	Triple expansion; 450 ihp = 9 knots

Freshspring was converted from coal to oil fuel, in 1961. *Freshpool* is in reserve.

FRESHPOOL *1966, courtesy Dr. Giorgio Arra*

TUGS

3 OCEAN TUGS (RMAS)

ROBUST (PAS) **ROLLICKER** **ROYSTERER**

Displacement, tons	1 630 full load
Dimensions, feet	162·0 pp; 179·7 oa × 38·5 × 18·0
Main engines	2 Mirrlees KMR 6 diesels (by Lister Blackstone Mirrlees Marine Ltd); 2 shafts; 4 500 bhp at 525 rpm = 15 knots
Range, miles	13 000 at 12 knots
Complement	31 (10 officers and 21 ratings) (and able to carry salvage party of 10 RN officers and ratings)

These are the biggest and most powerful ocean tugs ever built for the Royal Navy. Bollard pull—50 tons. Built by Charles D. Holmes at Beverley Shipyard, Hull. Designed principally for salvage and long range towage but can be used for general harbour duties, which *Robust* now undertakes. Cost well over £2 million apiece. Completion dates *Roysterer* 26 Apr 1972, *Rollicker* Feb 1973, *Robust* Mar 1974. *Robust* now at Gibraltar.

ROLLICKER *4/1974, John G. Callis*

TYPHOON A 95 (RMAS)

Displacement, tons	800 standard; 1 380 full load
Dimensions, feet	181·0 pp; 200·0 oa × 40·0 × 13·0
Main engines	2 turbocharged vee type 12-cyl diesels; 1 shaft; 2 750 bhp = over 16 knots

Built by Henry Robb & Co Ltd, Leith. Launched on 14 Oct 1958. Completed in 1960. Diesels manufactured by Vickers-Armstrong Ltd, Barrow-in-Furness. The machinery arrangement of two diesels geared to a single shaft was an innovation for naval ocean tugs in the RN. Controllable pitch propeller, 150 rpm. Fitted for fire fighting, salvage and ocean rescue, with a heavy mainmast and derrick attached. Bollard pull 32 tons.

TYPHOON *1973, Wright and Logan*

6 "CONFIANCE" CLASS (PAS)

ACCORD (17 Sept 1957) A 90
ADEPT
ADVICE (16 Oct 1958) A 89
AGILE (2 July 1958) A 88
CONFIANCE (15 Nov 1955) A 289
CONFIDENT (17 Jan 1956) A 290

Displacement, tons	760 full load
Dimensions, feet	140·0 pp; 154·8 oa × 35·0 × 11·0
Main engines	4 Paxman HAXM diesels; 2 shafts; 1 800 bhp = 13 knots
Complement	29 plus 13 salvage party

Confiance and *Confident* were built by A. & J. Inglis Ltd, Glasgow. Launch dates above. *Confiance* was completed on 27 Mar 1956. Fitted with 2·50 m diam Stone Kamewa controllable pitch propellers. *Accord, Advice* and *Agile*, formerly rated as dockyard tugs' were officially added to the "Confiance "class in 1971 as part of the Royal Maritime Auxiliary Service ocean towing force. *Adept* remains a dockyard tug. Fitted for 1—40 mm AA.

AGILE *1974, Wright and Logan*

2 "SAMSON" CLASS (PAS)

SEA GIANT (2 June 1954) A 288 **SUPERMAN** (23 Nov 1953)

Displacement, tons	1 200 full load
Measurement, tons	850 gross
Dimensions, feet	165 pp; 180 oa × 37 × 14
Main engines	Triple expansion; 2 shafts; 3 000 ihp = 15 knots

Built and engined by Alexander Hall & Co Ltd, Aberdeen. Launch dates above. *Samson* sold to Chile 1974.

SEA GIANT *1972, John G. Callis*

2 "BUSTLER" CLASS (RMAS)

CYCLONE (ex-*Growler*, 10 Sep 1942) A 111 **REWARD** (13 Oct 1944) A 264

Displacement, tons	1 118 light; 1 630 full load
Dimensions, feet	190·0 pp; 205·0 oa × 40·2 × 16·8
Main engines	2 Atlas Polar 8-cyl diesels; 1 shaft; 4 000 bhp = 16 knots
Oil fuel, tons	405
Range, miles	17 000
Complement	42

Built by Henry Robb Ltd, Leith. Last of class of four. *Reward* taken out of reserve in 1975 to take part in oil-rig patrols.

CYCLONE *1974, Wright and Logan*

4 FLEET SERVICING TUGS (PAS)

EMPIRE ACE **EMPIRE DEMON** **EMPIRE FRED**
EMPIRE ROSA

All slightly different.

Tugs—*continued*

16 HARBOUR TUGS (PAS)

DIVER
DRIVER
EMINENT
FIDGET
FOREMOST
FREEDOM
FRISKY
HANDMAID
IMPETUS
INTEGRITY
PROMPT
SECURITY
TAMPEON
TRUNNION
VAGRANT
WEASEL

A miscellany of steam and diesel tugs.

PROMPT — *8/1974, C, and S, Taylor*

7 "DIRECTOR" CLASS (PAS)

DEXTROUS A93
DIRECTOR A94
FAITHFUL A85
FORCEFUL A86
FAVOURITE A87
GRIPER A91
GRINDER A92

Displacement, tons	710 full load
Dimensions, feet	157·2 oa × 30 (60 over paddle boxes) × 10
Main engines	Paxman diesels and BTH motors; diesel electric; 2 shafts; 2 paddle wheels; 2 000 bhp = 13 knots
Complement	21

Modern paddlers. *Dextrous* at Gibraltar.

FORCEFUL — *1973, Wright and Logan*

20 "DOG" CLASS (PAS)

AIREDALE
ALSATIAN
BASSET
BEAGLE
BOXER
CAIRN
COLLIE
CORGI
DALMATIAN
DEERHOUND
ELKHOUND
HUSKY
LABRADOR
MASTIFF
POINTER
SALUKI
SEALYHAM
SETTER
SHEEPDOG
SPANIEL

Harbour berthing tugs. *Airedale* and *Sealyham* at Gibraltar.

SETTER — *11/1974, C, and S, Taylor,*

8 "GIRL" CLASS (PAS)

AGATHA
AGNES
ALICE
AUDREY
BARBARA
BETTY
BRENDA
BRIDGET

The first of a new class of harbour berthing tugs, later to be known for some reason, as "Water tractors".

AUDREY — *1972, C, and S, Taylor*

10 "IMPROVED GIRL" CLASS (PAS)

CELIA
CHARLOTTE
CHRISTINE
CLARE
DAISY
DAPHNE
DORIS
DOROTHY
EDITH
FELICITY

Edith at Gibraltar.

EDITH — *1974, Michael D, J, Lennon*

18 "SUPER GIRL" CLASS (PAS)

FIONA
GEORGINA
GWENDOLINE
HELEN
IRENE
ISABEL
JOAN
JOYCE
KATHLEEN
KITTY
LESLEY
LILIAN
LILAH
MAY
MARY
MYRTLE
NANCY
NORAH

All completed by August 1974.

GEORGINA — *1973, Wright and Logan*

FLEET TENDERS

7 "INSECT" CLASS (PAS)

BEE **CICALA** **COCKCHAFER** **CRICKET** **GNAT** **LADYBIRD** **SCARAB** (RMAS)

Displacement, tons	450 full load
Dimensions, feet	111·8 oa × 28 × 11
Main engines	Lister-Blackstone Diesels; 1 shaft; 660 bhp = 10·5 knots
Complement	10

All built by C. D. Holmes Ltd, Beverley, Yorks in 1970-73, first three as stores carriers, two as armament carriers and *Scarab*, as mooring vessel.

CICALA — *1971, Wright and Logan*

12 "ABERDOVEY" CLASS (PAS)

ABERDOVEY **ABINGER** **ALNESS** **ALNMOUTH** **APPLEBY** **ASHCOTT** **BEAULIEU** **BEDDGELERT** **BEMBRIDGE** **BIBURY** **BLAKENEY** **BRODICK**

Displacement, tons	117·5 full load
Dimensions, feet	79·8 oa × 18 × 5·5
Main engines	1 Lister-Blackstone Diesel; 1 shaft; 225 bhp = 10·5 knots
Complement	6

"A" names built by Isaac Pimblott & Sons, Northwich. "B" names by J. S. Doig, Grimsby 1963-71. Sixty fleet tenders are planned to replace the ageing MFV's. Multi-purpose for stores (25 tons), passengers (200 standing) plus a couple of torpedos *Ashcott* at Gibraltar.

APPLEBY — *1973, Wright and Logan*

5 DIVING TENDERS

ILCHESTER
INSTOW
INVERGORDON A 310
IRONBRIDGE A 311
IXWORTH A 312

Of similar characteristics to "Cartmel" class. Built by Gregson Ltd, Blyth. *Ixworth* completed September 1974, and all in that year.

30 "CARTMEL CLASS" (PAS)

CARTMEL **CAWSAND** **CLOVELLY** **CRICCIETH** **CRICKLADE** **CROMARTY** **DATCHET** **DENMEAD** **DORNOCH** **DUNSTER** **ELKSTONE** **ELSING** **EPWORTH** **ETTRICK** **FELSTEDC** (RMAS) **FINTRY** **FOTHERBY** **FROXFIELD** **FULBECK** **GLENCOVE** **GRASMERE** **HAMBLEDON** **HARLECH** **HEADCORN** **HEVER** **HOLMWOOD** A 1772 **HORNING** A 1773 **LAMLASH** **LECHLADE** **LLANDOVERY**

Displacement, tons	143 full load
Dimensions, feet	80 oa × 21 × 6·5
Main engines	1 Lister-Blackstone diesel; 1 shaft; 320 bhp = 10·5 knots
Complement	6

All fleet tenders as "*Aberdovey*" class except *Datchet*, diving tender with Gray diesels, 2 shafts, 450 bhp = 12 knots and *Felsted* with RMAS. Builders — first 4 "C"s and *Glencove* by Pimblott; *Cricklade*, *Denmead* and *Fulbeck* by C. D. Holmes, Beverley; *Cromarty*, *Dornoch*, *Fintry* and *Grasmere* by J. Lewis, Aberdeen; four "E"s by J. Cook Wivenhoe; *Datchet* by Vospers; remainder by R. Dunston, Thorne. *Elsing* and *Ettrick* at Gibraltar. All completed by August 1973.

FROXFIELD — *5/1973, Wright and Logan*

DATCHET as Diving Tender — *9/1974, Dr. Giorgio Arra*

5 "LOYAL" CLASS (RNXS)

LOYAL FACTOR A 382
LOYAL GOVERNOR A510
LOYAL MODERATOR A 220
LOYAL CHANCELLOR
LOYAL PROCTOR

Details as for "Cartmel" class. All employed by RNXS except for *Loyal Moderator* who is used for PAS training.

LOYAL MODERATOR — *5/1974, John G. Callis*

Fleet Tenders—*continued*

8 "HAM" CLASS (RNXS)

BIRDHAM	M 2785	**PUTTENHAM**	M 2784
ODIHAM	M 2783	**SHIPHAM**	M 2726
PAGHAM	M 2716	**THAKEHAM**	M 2733
PORTISHAM	M 2781	**TONGHAM**	M 2735

Details in Minewarfare Section.

61 MFV TYPES (PAS)

MFV 2, 7, 15, 63, 93, 96, 119, 139, 140, 175, 205, 256, 278, 289, Length: 61·5 feet
MFV 642, 658, 686, 715, 740, 767, 775, 816, 911, Length: 45 feet
MFV 1021, 1033, 1037, 1048, 1051, 1062, 1077, 1151, 1190, 1255 Length: 75 feet
MV 1527 Length: 90 feet

MFV 642 — *11/1973, Wright and Logan*

TANK CLEANING VESSELS

7 "ISLES" CLASS (PAS)

BERN	A 334	(2 May 1942)	**LUNDY**	A 366	(29 Aug 1942)
CALDY	A 332	(31 Aug 1943)	**SWITHA**	A 346	(3 Apr 1942)
COLL	A 333	(7 Apr 1942)	**SKOMER**	A 338	(17 June 1943)
GRAEMSAY	A 340	(3 Aug 1942)			

Dimensions, feet	150 pp; 164 oa × 27·5 × 14
Main engines	Triple expansion; 1 shaft; 850 ihp = 12 knots
Boilers	1 cylindrical
Coal, tons	183

Built by Ardrossan Dockyard (2) Cook, Welton and Gemmell (2), John Lewis and Sons (2), A. & J. Inglis Ltd (1). Launch dates above. Former minesweeping trawlers converted to tank cleaning vessels.

BERN — *5/1973, Wright and Logan*

DEGAUSSING VESSELS

3 "HAM" CLASS (PAS)

FORDHAM M 2717 **THATCHAM** M 2790 **WARMINGHAM** M 2737

Of the "Ham" class of Inshore Minesweepers. For details see Mine Warfare Section.

WARMINGHAM — *10/1974, C. and S. Taylor*

NUCLEAR DECONTAMINATION VESSELS

MAC 1012 **MAC 1013**

1012 launched at Chatham early in 1971. 1013 built at Devonport 1973. Length 180 feet, beam 30 feet. To be used in connection with the disposal of radio active waste from the Chatham nuclear powered submarine refitting complex.

SCOTTISH FISHERY PROTECTION VESSELS

2 "JURA" CLASS

JURA **WESTRA**

Measurement, tons	942 gross
Dimensions, feet	195·3 oa × 35 × 22·3
Main engines	2 British Polar SP112VS-F diesels of 4 200 bhp
Speed, knots	16

Jura, completed by Hall, Russell & Co Aberdeen in 1973 has been leased by the Ministry of Defence for oil-rig patrol. *Westra* was launched by the same firm on 6 Aug 1974. Three other craft are operated by Scottish Home Dept.

UNITED STATES OF AMERICA

Compiled and Edited by Norman Polmar

ADMINISTRATION

Secretary of the Navy:
J. William Middendorf, II

Under Secretary of the Navy:
David S. Potter

PRINCIPAL FLAG OFFICERS

Chief of Naval Operations:
Admiral James Holloway, III, USN

Vice Chief of Naval Operations:
Admiral Harold E. Shear, USN

Deputy Chief of Naval Operations (Manpower and Naval Reserve):
Vice-Admiral David H. Bagley, USN

Deputy Chief of Naval Operations (Submarine Warfare):
Vice-Admiral R. L. J. Long, USN

Deputy Chief of Naval Operations (Surface Warfare):
Vice-Admiral James H. Doyle, Jnr, USN

Deputy Chief of Naval Operations (Air Warfare):
Vice-Admiral William D. Houser, USN

Deputy Chief of Naval Operations (Logistics):
Vice-Admiral Edward W. Cooke USN

Deputy Chief of Naval Operations (Plans and Policy):
Vice-Admiral Joseph P. Moorer, USN

***Commander-in-Chief Atlantic and Commander-in-Chief Atlantic Fleet:*
Admiral Isaac C. Kidd, Jnr, USN

**Commander-in-Chief Pacific:*
Admiral Noel A. M. Gayler, USN

Commander-in-Chief Pacific Fleet:
Admiral Maurice F. Weisner, USN

Commander Second Fleet (Atlantic):
Vice-Admiral John G. Finneran, USN

Commander Third Fleet (Eastern Pacific):
Vice-Admiral William T. Rapp, USN

Commander Sixth Fleet (Mediterranean):
Vice-Admiral Frederick C. Turner

Commander Seventh Fleet (Western Pacific):
Vice-Admiral Thomas B. Hayward, USN

Commander Military Sealift Command:
Rear-Admiral Sam H. Moore, USN

Chief of Naval Education and Training:
Vice-Admiral James Wilson, USN

Chief of Naval Reserve:
Vice-Admiral Pierre N. Charbonnet, Jnr, USN

Oceanographer of the Navy:
Rear-Admiral Joseph E. Snyder, Jnr, USN

MARINE CORPS

Commandant of the Marine Corps:
General Louis H. Wilson, Jnr USMC

Chief of Staff:
Lieutenant General John N. McLaughlin, USMC

MATERIÉL

Chief of Naval Material:
Admiral F. H. Michaelis, USN

Commander Naval Air Systems Command:
Vice-Admiral Kent L. Lee, USN

Commander Naval Electronic Systems Command:
Rear-Admiral R. J. Schneider (ED), USN

Commander Naval Facilities Engineering Command:
Rear-Admiral Albert R. Marschall, (CEC), USN

Commander Naval Ordnance Systems Command:
Rear-Admiral Roger E. Spreen, USN

Commander Naval Sea Systems Command:
Vice-Admiral Robert C. Gooding, (ED), USN

Commander Naval Supply Systems Command:
Rear-Admiral Wallace R. Dowd, Jnr (SC), USN

NOTES: *Unified Command with the Commander-in-Chief directing all US Army, Navy, and Air Force activities in the area. Only naval officers serving as Unified Commanders-in-Chief are listed. **In addition to Unified Commander, also Supreme Allied Commander Atlantic (NATO position). In July 1974 the Naval Ordnance Systems Command and Naval Ship Systems Command were merged into the new Naval Sea Systems Command.

DIPLOMATIC

Defense Attaché and Naval Attaché in London:
Rear Admiral James C. Longino, USN

Naval Attaché and Naval Attaché for air in Moscow:
Captain Ronald J. Kurth, USN

Naval Attaché and Naval Attaché for Air in Paris:
Captain George N. La Rocque, USN

STRENGTH OF THE FLEET

The following table provides a tabulation of the ship strength of the United States Navy and an index to the ship listings within the United States section of this edition. Ship arrangement is based on function and employment; the official arrangement of ship types is contained in the "List of classifications of naval ships and service craft" which appears on a later page in this section. Numbers of ships listed in the table are estimated as of 1 July 1975, based on official and unofficial sources.

	Category-Type	*Active* a	*Building* b	*Reserve*
STRATEGIC MISSILE SUBMARINES				
SSBN	Ballistic Missile Submarines	41	3	—
SUBMARINES				
SSN	Attack Submarines (nuclear)	62	23	1
SSN	Research Submarines (nuclear)	2	—	1
SS	Attack Submarines (diesel)	9	—	—
SSG	Guided Missile Submarines (diesel)	—	—	1
LPSS SS	Transport Submarines (diesel)	1	—	1
AGSS	Research Submarines (diesel)	2	—	1
AIRCRAFT CARRIERS				
CVAN/CVN	Aircraft Carriers (nuclear)	1	3	—
CVA/CV	Aircraft Carriers	13	—	1
CVS	Anti-Submarine Carriers	—	—	4
CVT	Training Carriers	1	—	—
CRUISERS				
CGN	Guided Missile Cruisers (nuclear)	5	4	—
CG/CLG	Guided Missile Cruisers	22	—	3
CA	Heavy Cruisers	—	—	5
BATTLESHIPS				
BB	Battleships	—	—	4
DESTROYERS				
DDG	Guided Missile Destroyers	39	—	—
DD	Destroyers	66a	30	1
FRIGATES				
FFG	Guided Missile Frigates	6	4	—
FF	Frigates	58	—	—
AGFF	Frigate Research Ships	1	—	—
DER	Radar Picket Escorts	—	—	6
COMMAND AND COMMUNICATION SHIPS				
AGF	Miscellaneous Flagships	1	—	—
CC	National Command Ships	—	—	2
AGMR	Communication Relay Ships	—	—	2
AMPHIBIOUS WARFARE SHIPS				
LCC	Amphibious Command Ships	2	—	4
LHA	Amphibious Assault Ships	—	5	—
LPH	Amphibious Assault Ships	7	—	—
LKA	Amphibious Cargo Ships	6a	—	5
LPA	Amphibious Transports	2a	—	7
LPR	Amphibious Transports (small)	—	—	3
LPD	Amphibious Transports Dock	14	—	—
LSD	Dock Landing Ships	13	—	11
LST	Tank Landing Ships	20	—	14
PATROL SHIPS AND CRAFT				
PHM	Patrol Hydrofoil Missile Ships	—	6	—
PGH	Patrol Gunboats (hydrofoil)	1	—	—
PCH	Patrol Craft (hydrofoil)	1	—	—
PG	Patrol Gunboats/Missile Boats	12a	—	—
PTF	Fast Patrol Craft	17a	—	—
MINE WARFARE SHIPS				
MSO	Ocean Minesweepers	25a	—	12
UNDERWAY REPLENISHMENT SHIPS		49	1	14
FLEET SUPPORT SHIPS		77	3	23
SEALIFT SHIPS		42	—	95
EXPERIMENTAL, RESEARCH AND SURVEYING SHIPS		42	—	2

NOTES: (a) Includes ships undergoing overhaul and refuelling in the case of nuclear-powered ships; also includes 34 destroyers, 3 amphibious ships, 22 minesweepers, 17 fast patrol craft, and several patrol combatants assigned to the Naval Reserve Force and manned by composite reserve and active duty crews. (b) Generally includes ships authorised through the Fiscal Year 1975 new construction programme although actual construction may not have begun.

MERCANTILE MARINE

US Maritime Administration: 559 vessels of 9 289 000 tons gross (13 538 000 tons deadweight) active as of 1 Jan 1975. Approx 350 additional vessels are inactive, over 80 of which are scheduled to be scrapped.

Lloyd's Register of Shipping: 4 086 vessels of 14 429 076 tons gross

SHIPBUILDING AND CONVERSION PROGRAMMES

Tentative Five-Year Shipbuilding Programme (Fiscal Years 1976-1980)

7 Nuclear-Powered FBM Submarines (Trident)
12 Nuclear-Powered Attack Submarines (SSN 688 class)
2 Attack Aircraft Carriers (CVX/CVNX concepts)
7 VSTOL Support Ships (VSS concept)
6 Nuclear-Powered Strike Cruisers (CSGN concept)
1 Nuclear-Powered Guided Missile Cruiser (CGN 38 class)
52 Guided Missile Frigates (FFG 7 class, ex-PF 109)
2 Patrol Hydrofoil Missile Ships (PHM 1 class)
4 Mine Warfare/Surveillance Ships
3 Ammunition Ships (AE)
3 Combat Stores Ships (AFS)
11 Oilers (AO)
46 Other Auxiliary Ships (AD-AS-ATF)

Fiscal Year 1976 New Construction Programme

1 Nuclear-Powered FBM Submarine (Trident)
2 Nuclear-Powered Attack Submarines (SSN 688 class)
1 Nuclear-Powered Guided Missile Cruiser (CGN 38 class)
10 Guided Missile Frigates (FFG 7 class, ex-PF 109)
2 Patrol Hydrofoil Missile Ships (PHM 1 class)
2 Destroyer Tenders (AD)
2 Oilers (AO)
3 Fleet Tugs (ATF)

Fiscal Year 1975 New Construction Programme

2 Nuclear-Powered FBM Submarines (Trident)
3 Nuclear-Powered Attack Submarines (SSN 688 class)
1 Nuclear-Powered Missile Frigate (DLGN 38 class)
7 Destroyers (DD 963 class)
3 Patrol Frigates (PF)
4 Guided Missile Patrol Hydrofoils (PHM 1 class)
1 Destroyer Tender (AD)
1 Oiler (AO)
1 Fleet Tug (ATF)

Fiscal Year 1975 Conversion Programme

3 Nuclear-Powered FBM Submarines (SSBN) to Poseidon
1 Submarine Tender (AS) to Poseidon support capability

Fiscal Year 1974 New Construction Programme

1 Nuclear-Powered FBM Submarine (Trident)
5 Nuclear-Powered Attack Submarines (SSN 688 class)
1 Nuclear-Powered Aircraft Carrier (CVAN 68 Class)
7 Destroyers (DD 963 Class)

Fiscal Year 1974 Conversion Programme

5 Nuclear-Powered FBM Submarines (SSBN) to Poseidon
1 Nuclear-Powered GM Frigate (DLGN) to improve AAW capability
2 Guided Missile Frigates (DLG) to improve AAW capability

Fiscal Year 1973 New Construction Programme

6 Nuclear-Powered Attack Submarines (SSN 688 class)
7 Destroyers (DD 963 class)
1 Patrol Frigate (PF)
2 Guided Missile Patrol Hydrofoils (PHM)
1 Destroyer Tender (AD 37 class)
1 Submarine Tender (AS 36 class)
2 Salvage and Rescue Tugs (ATS 1 class)

Fiscal Year 1973 Conversion Programme

2 Guided Missile Frigates (DLG) to improve AAW capability
6 Nuclear-Powered FBM Submarines (SSBN) to Poseidon
1 Submarine Tender (AS) to Poseidon support capability

Fiscal Year 1972 New Construction Programme

5 Nuclear-Powered Attack Submarines (SSN 688 class)
1 Nuclear-Powered Guided Missile Frigate (DLGN 38 class)
7 Destroyers (DD 963 class)
1 Replenishment Oiler (AOR 1 class)
1 Submarine Tender (AS 36 class)
1 Salvage and Rescue Tug (ATS 1 class)

Fiscal Year 1972 Conversion Programme

2 Guided Missile Frigates (DLG) to improve AAW capability
6 Nuclear-Powered Fleet Ballistic Missile Submarines (SSBN) to Poseidon

SPECIAL NOTES

United States Navy Ships that are in active commission are indicated by an asterisk next to the particular ship's name. It should be noted that this marking for active ships applies ONLY to the United States Navy section of *Jane's Fighting Ships*.

The introductory passages in the United States section of this edition are based primarily on official United States Government statements and congressional hearings on the Fiscal Year 1976 Defence Budget. Any interpretation of these statements and hearings is solely the responsibility of the Compiler and Editor of the United States section, Mr. Norman Polmar.

PERSONNEL

	30 June 1974 (Actual)	30 June 1975 (Planned)	30 June 1976 (Planned)
Navy			
Officers	66 992	65 854	64 380
Enlisted	475 479	466 020	460 028
Marine Corps			
Officers	18 740	18 572	18 572
Enlisted	170 062	177 804	177 731

NAVAL AVIATION

US Naval Aviation currently consists of approx 7 500 aircraft flown by the Navy and Marine Corps. The principal naval aviation organisations are 14 carrier air wings, 24 maritime reconnaissance/patrol squadrons, and three Marine Aircraft Wings. In addition, the Naval Reserve and Marine Corps Reserve operate 7 fighter squadrons, 11 attack squadrons, and 12 patrol squadrons, plus various helicopter and transport units.

Fighters: approx 965 flown by 28 Navy carrier-based squadrons (F-14, F-8, F-4) and 12 Marine fighter squadrons (F-4). F-14 Tomcat procurement planned for 12 Navy squadrons and 4 Marine squadrons; F-8 Crusaders will be phased out with deactivation of carriers *Oriskany* (CVA 34) and *Hancock* (CVA 19). Seven reserve fighter squadrons fly F-4 and F-8 aircraft.
Attack Aircraft: approx 1 540 flown by 42 Navy carrier-based squadrons (A-7, A-6, A-4) and 13 Marine attack squadrons (AV-8A, A-6, A-4). Eleven reserve attack squadrons fly primarily A-4 aircraft.
(In addition to fighter and attack aircraft, carrier air wings have various combinations of E-1B Tracer or E-2A/C Hawkeye early warning aircraft, EA-6 Prowler or EKA-3B Skywarrior electronic warfare aircraft, RA-5C Vigilante or RF-8G Crusader reconnaissance aircraft, KA-6 Intruder tanker aircraft; Marine aircraft wings also have EA-6 electronic warfare, RF-4 reconnaissance, KC-130 cargo-tanker, spotting, and utility aircraft, in addition to several squadrons of helicopters).
Anti-Submarine Aircraft: approx 150 S-3 Vikings and S-2 Tracker fixed-wing ASW aircraft flown by 10 squadrons, with the latter aircraft being phased out; 12 squadrons, each with 10 Vikings, planned for carrier operations in the 1980s. Approx 100 SH-3 Sea Kings flown by 9 squadrons with 12 squadrons each with 8 Sea Kings, planned for the 1980s. Approx 100 SH-2D LAMPS helicopters flown by 3 squadrons for operation from cruisers, destroyers, and frigates. Naval reserve S-2 Tracker squadrons are being phased out.
Patrol Aircraft: approx 450 P-3 Orion aircraft flown by 24 active Navy patrol squadrons plus special mission squadrons and detachments flying EP-3, RP-3, and WP-3 Orion variants for reconnaissance, weather reporting, and research. Reserve Patrol squadrons fly P-3 Orions and P-2 Neptunes.
Training Aircraft: approx 1 430 assigned to 27 Navy training squadrons (which train Marine and Coast Guard fliers in addition to Navy personnel).
Helicopters: approx 1 000 of all types used by Navy and Marine Corps in addition to ASW helicopters.
Cargo, Transport, and Utility Aircraft: approx 760 of all types used by Navy and Marine Corps.

MAJOR SHIPYARDS

Naval Shipyards

Boston Naval Shipyard, Boston, Massachusetts; closed in 1973-1974
Charleston Naval Shipyard, Charleston, South Carolina
Hunters Point Naval Shipyard, San Francisco, California (formerly a division of the San Francisco Bay Naval Shipyard and before that the San Francisco Naval Shipyard) closed 1973-1974
Long Beach Naval Shipyard, Long Beach, California
Mare Island Naval Shipyard, Vallejo, California (formerly a division of the San Francisco Bay Naval Shipyard)
Norfolk Naval Shipyard, Portsmouth, Virginia
Pearl Harbour Shipyard, Pearl Harbour, Hawaii
Philadelphia Naval Shipyard, Philadelphia, Pennsylvania
Portsmouth Naval Shipyard, Portsmouth, New Hampshire (located in Kittery, Maine)
Puget Sound Naval Shipyard, Bremerton, Washington

(Note: None of the above shipyards is now engaged in new construction, but are used for the overhaul and conversion of warships and auxiliaries).

Commercial Shipyards

Avondale Shipyards, Inc, New Orleans, Louisiana
Bath Iron Works Corp, Bath, Maine
Bethlehem Steel Corp, Sparrows Point, Maryland
General Dynamics Corp, Electric Boat Division, Groton, Connecticut (formerly Electric Boat Company)
General Dynamics Corp, Quincy Shipbuilding Division, Quincy, Massachusetts (formerly Bethlehem Steel Corp Yard)
Ingalls Shipbuilding Corp (Litton Industries), East Bank Yard, Pascagoula, Mississippi
Ingalls Shipbuilding Corp (Litton Industries), West Bank Yard, Pascagoula, Mississippi
Lockheed Shipbuilding & Construction Co, Seattle, Washington
National Steel & Shipbuilding Co, San Diego, California
Newport News Shipbuilding & Dry Dock Co, Newport News, Virginia
Todd Shipyards Corp, San Pedro, California
Todd Shipyards Corp, Seattle, Washington

(Note: All of the above yards are engaged in naval and commercial shipbuilding, overhaul, or modernisation except for the General Dynamics/Electric Boat yard which is engaged only in submarine work).

CLASSIFICATION OF NAVAL SHIPS AND SERVICE CRAFT

The following is the official US Navy list of classifications of naval ships and service craft as promulgated by the Secretary of the Navy on 6, Jan 1975.
In actual usage, symbols preceded by the letter "E" indicate that the ship or craft is a prototype in an experimental or developmental status; the prefix "T" indicates that the ship is assigned to the Navy's Military Sealift Command and is civilian manned; and the prefix "F" indicates a ship being constructed by the United States for a foreign government.

COMBATANT SHIPS

(1) Warships

Aircraft Carriers:

Aircraft Carrier	CV
Attack Aircraft Carrier	CVA
Attack Aircraft Carrier (nuclear propulsion)	CVAN
Aircraft Carrier (nuclear propulsion)	CVN
ASW Aircraft Carrier	CVS

Surface Combatants:

Battleship	BE
Heavy Cruiser	CA
Guided Missile Cruiser	CG
Guided Missile Cruiser (nuclear propulsion)	CGN
Destroyer	DD
Guided Missile Destroyer	DDG
Frigate	FF
Guided Missile Frigate	FFG
Radar Picket Frigate	FFR

Patrol Combatants:

Patrol Combatant	PG
Patrol Combatant Missile (hydrofoil)	PHM
Patrol Escort	PCE

Command Ship	CC

Submarines:

Submarine	SS
Submarine (nuclear propulsion)	SSN
Fleet Ballistic Missile Submarine (nuclear propulsion)	SSBN
Guided Missile Submarine	SSG

(2) Amphibious Warfare Ships

Amphibious Command Ship	LCC
Inshore Fire Support Ship	LFR
Amphibious Assault Ship (general purpose)	LHA
Amphibious Cargo Ship	LKA
Amphibious Transport	LPA
Amphibious Transport Dock	LPD
Amphibious Assault Ship	LPH
Amphibious Transport (small)	LPR
Amphibious Transport Submarine	LPSS
Dock Landing Ship	LSD
Tank Landing Ship	LST

(3) Mine Warfare Ships

Mine Countermeasures Ship	MCS
Minesweeper, Coastal (non-magnetic)	MSC
Minesweeper, Ocean (non-magnetic)	MSO

COMBATANT CRAFT

(1) Patrol Craft

Coastal Patrol Boat	CPC
Coastal Patrol and Interdiction Craft	CPIC
Patrol Boat	PB
Patrol Craft (Fast)	PCF
Patrol Craft (hydrofoil)	PCH
Patrol Gunboat (hydrofoil)	PGH
Fast Patrol Craft	PTF

(2) Landing Craft

Amphibious Assault Landing Craft	AALC
Landing Craft, Mechanised	LCM
Landing Craft, Personnel, Large	LCPL
Landing Craft, Personnel, Ramped	LCPR
Landing Craft, Utility	LCU
Landing Craft, Vehicle, Personnel	LCVP
Amphibious Warping Tug	LWT

(3) Mine Countermeasures Craft

Minesweeping Boat	MSB
Minesweeper, Drone	MSD
Minesweeper, Inshore	MSI
Minesweeper, River	MSM
Minesweeper, Patrol	MSR

(4) Riverine Warfare Craft

Assault Support Patrol Boat	ASPB
Mini-Armoured Troop Carrier	ATC
River Patrol Boat	PBR
Shallow Water Attack Craft, Medium	SWAM
Shallow Water Attack Craft, Light	SWAL

(5) SEAL Support Craft

Landing Craft Swimmer Reconnaissance	LCSR
Light SEAL Support Craft	LSSC
Medium SEAL Support Craft	MSSC
Swimmer Delivery Vehicle	SDV

(6) Mobile Inshore Undersea Warfare (MIUW) Craft

MIUW Attack Craft	MAC

AUXILIARY SHIPS

Destroyer Tender	AD
Degaussing Ship	ADG
Ammunition Ship	AE
Store Ship	AF
Combat Store Ship	AFS
Miscellaneous	AG
Auxiliary Deep Submergence Support Ship	AGDS
Frigate Research Ship	AGFF
Hydrofoil Research Ship	AGEH
Environmental Research Ship	AGER
Miscellaneous Command Ship	AGF
Patrol Combatant Support Ship	AGHS
Missile Range Instrumentation Ship	AGM
Major Communications Relay Ship	AGMR
Oceanographic Research Ship	AGOR
Patrol Craft Tender	AGP
Surveying Ship	AGS
Auxiliary Submarine	AGSS
Hospital Ship	AH
Cargo Ship	AK
Light Cargo Ship	AKL
Vehicle Cargo Ship	AKR
Oiler	AO
Fast Combat Support Ship	AOE
Gasoline Tanker	AOG
Replenishment Oiler	AOR
Transport	AP
Self-propelled Barracks Ship	APB
Repair Ship	AR
Battle Damage Repair Ship	ARB
Cable Repairing Ship	ARC
Internal Combustion Engine Repair Ship	ARG
Landing Craft Repair Ship	ARL
Salvage Ship	ARS
Submarine Tender	AS
Submarine Rescue Ship	ASR
Auxiliary Ocean Tug	ATA
Fleet Ocean Tug	ATF
Salvage and Rescue Ship	ATS
Guided Missile Ship	AVM
Training Aircraft Carrier	CVT
Surface Effects Ship	SES

SERVICE CRAFT*

Large Auxiliary Floating Dry Dock	AFDB
Small Auxiliary Floating Dry Dock	AFDL
Medium Auxiliary Floating Dry Dock	AFDM
Barracks Craft (non-self-propelled)	APL
Auxiliary Dry Dock	ARD
Medium Auxiliary Repair Dry Dock	ARDM
Deep Submergence Rescue Vehicle	DSRV
Deep Submergence Vehicle	DSV
Unclassified Miscellaneous	IX
Submersible Research Vehicle (nuclear propulsion)	NR
Miscellaneous Auxiliary (self-propelled)	YAG
Open Lighter	YC
Car Float	YCF
Aircraft Transportation Lighter	YCV
Floating Crane	YD
Diving Tender	YDT
Covered Lighter (self-propelled)	YF
Ferryboat or Launch (self-propelled)	YFB
Yard Floating Dry Dock	YFD
Covered Lighter	YFN
Large Covered Lighter	YFNB
Dry Dock Companion Craft	YFND
Lighter (special purpose)	YFNX
Floating Power Barge	YFP
Refrigerated Covered Lighter (self-propelled)	YFR
Refrigerated Covered Lighter	YFRN
Covered Lighter (Range Tender) (self-propelled)	YFRT
Harbour Utility Craft (self-propelled)	YFU
Garbage Lighter (self-propelled)	YG
Garbage Lighter (non-self-propelled)	YGN
Salvage Lift Craft, Heavy	YHLC
Dredge (self-propelled)	YM
Salvage Lift Craft, Medium	YMLC
Gate Craft	YNG
Fuel Oil Barge (self-propelled)	YO
Gasoline Barge (self-propelled)	YOG
Gasoline Barge	YOGN
Fuel Oil Barge	YON
Oil Storage Barge	YOS
Patrol Craft (self-propelled)	YP
Floating Pile Driver	YPD
Floating Workshop	YR
Repair and Berthing Barge	YRB
Repair, Berthing and Messing Barge	YRBM
Floating Dry Dock Workshop (Hull)	YRDH
Floating Dry Dock Workshop (Machine)	YRDM
Radiology Repair Barge	YRR
Salvage Craft Tender	YRST
Seaplane Wrecking Derrick (self-propelled)	YSD
Sludge Removal Barge	YSR
Large Harbour Tug (self-propelled)	YTB
Small Harbour Tug (self-propelled)	YTL
Medium Harbour Tug (self-propelled)	YTM
Water Barge (self-propelled)	YW
Water Barge	YWN

*Self-propelled barges are indicated in parenthesis. The final letter "N" generally indicates non-self-propelled.

CLASSIFICATION OF MARITIME COMMISSION SHIP DESIGNS

Ships constructed under the jurisdiction of the US Maritime Commission by private shipyards are assigned Maritime Commission design classifications. These classifications consist of three groups of letters and numbers.
First group letter(s) indicate type of ship and number indicates size class. The letters of Maritime Commission ship classifications now on the US Navy List are:

Cargo	C
Emergency Cargo (Liberty)	EC
Passenger	P
Refrigerator	R
Special Purpose	S
Tanker	T
Victory Cargo	VC

Second group letter(s) indicate type of propulsion and number "2" indicates twin shaft ship and "4" quadruple shaft ship.

Motor (diesel)	M
Motor (diesel) Electric	ME
Steam (reciprocating or turbine)	S
Steam	SE

Third group of letters and numbers indicates the design of a particular type of ship, beginning with A1.

STRATEGIC MISSILE SUBMARINES

LAFAYETTE (SSBN 616)

GEORGE WASHINGTON (SSBN 598)

SUBMARINES

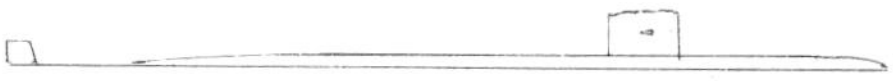

LOS ANGELES (SSN 688)

GLENARD P. LIPSCOMB (SSN 685)

NARWHAL (SSN 671)

STURGEON (SSN 637)

TULLIBEE (SSN 597)

PERMIT (SSN 594)

HALIBUT (SSN 587)

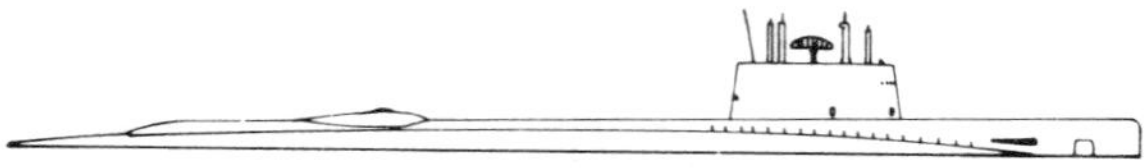

TRITON (SSN 586)

SKIPJACK (SSN 585)

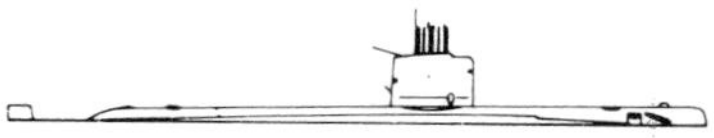

SWORDFISH (SSN 579)

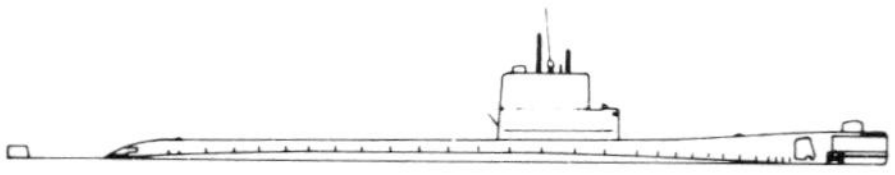

SEAWOLF (SSN 575)

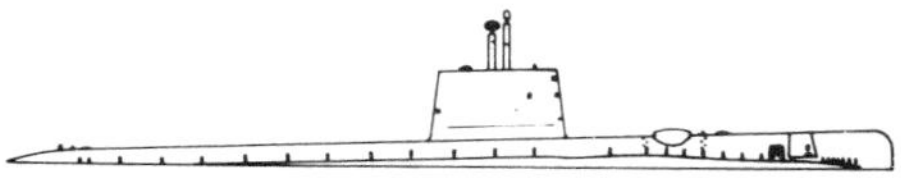

NAUTILUS (SSN 571)

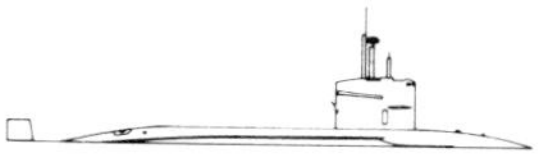

BARBEL (SS 580)

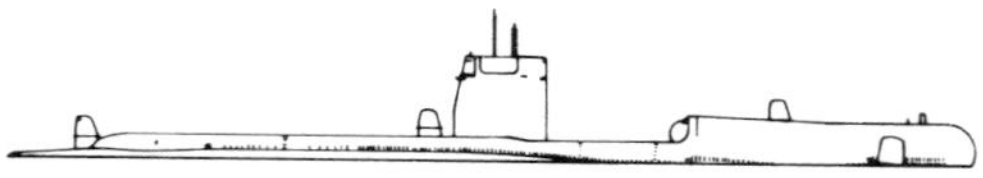

GRAYBACK (SS/LPSS 574)

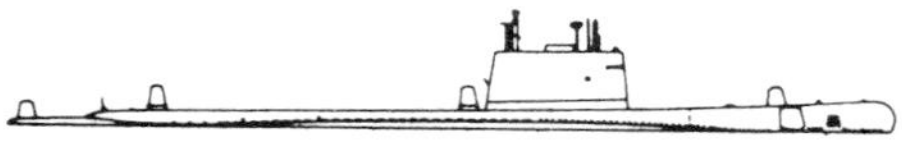

SAILFISH (SS 572)

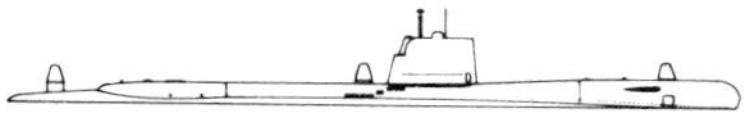

WAHOO (SS 565) Tang Class

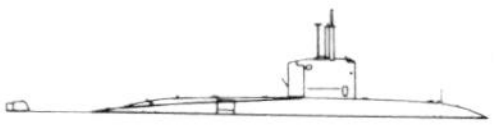

ALBACORE (AGSS 569)

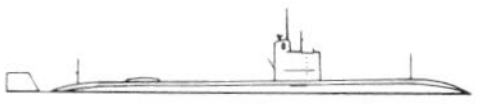

DOLPHIN (AGSS 555)

AIRCRAFT CARRIERS

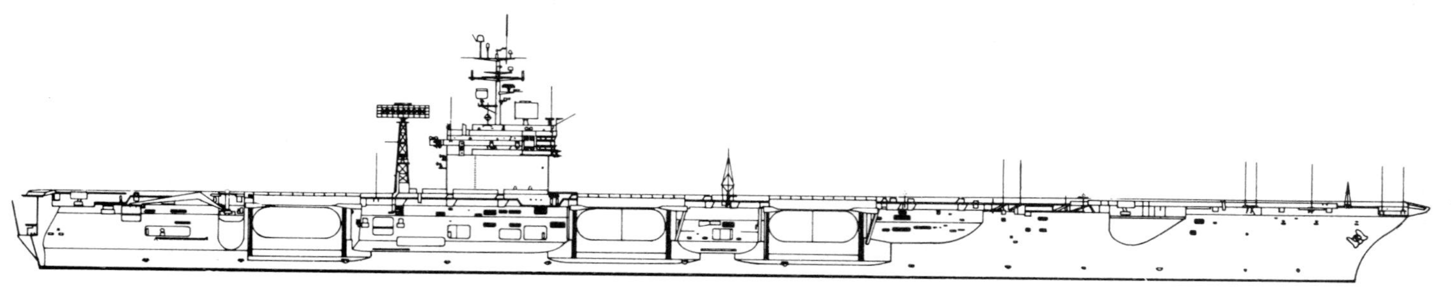

NIMITZ (CVAN 68)

Scale: 1 inch = 150 feet (1 : 1 800)

Drawings by A. D. Baker

Aircraft Carriers —*Continued*

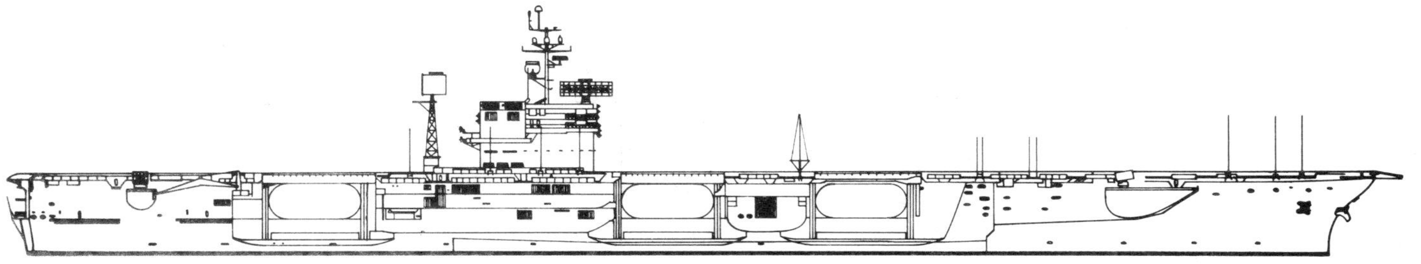

JOHN F. KENNEDY (CV 67)

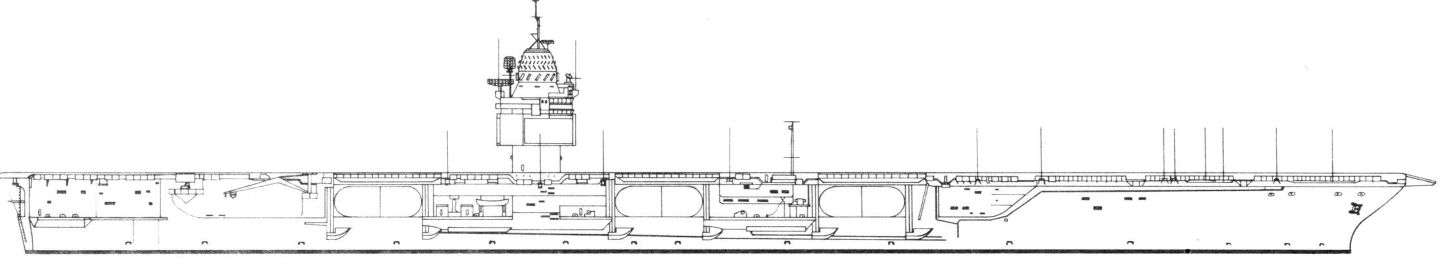

ENTERPRISE (CVAN 65)

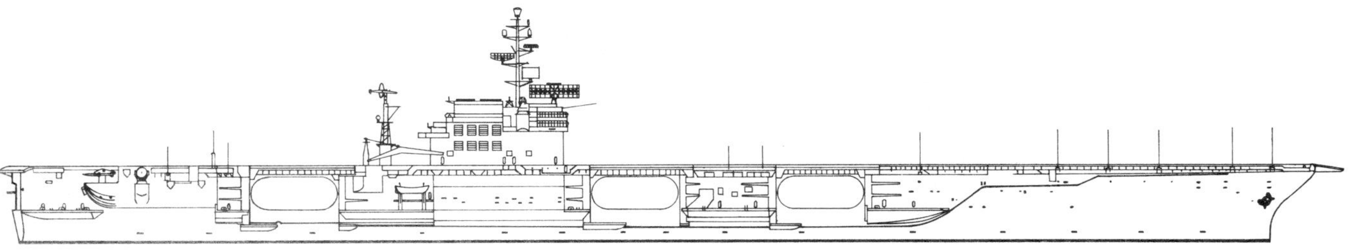

KITTY HAWK (CV 63)

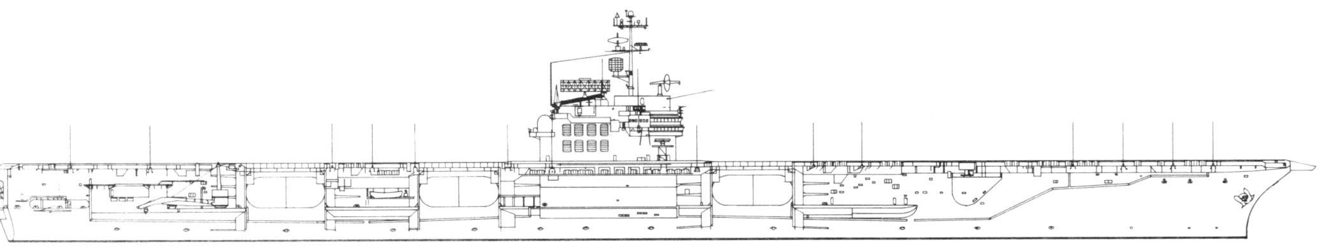

INDEPENDENCE (CV 62)

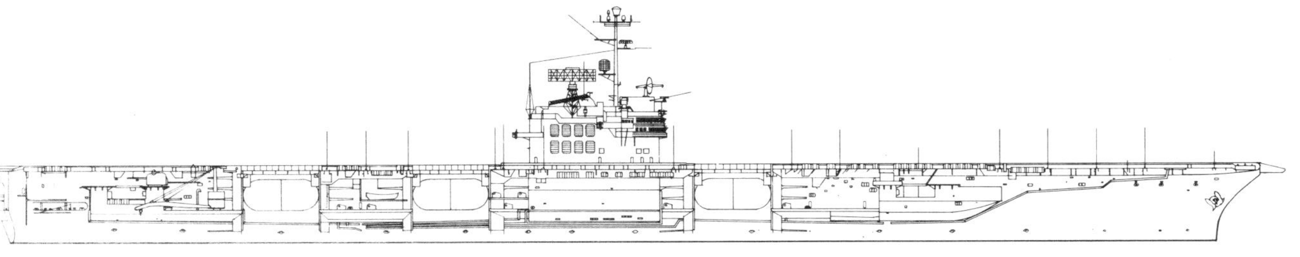

RANGER (CVA 61)

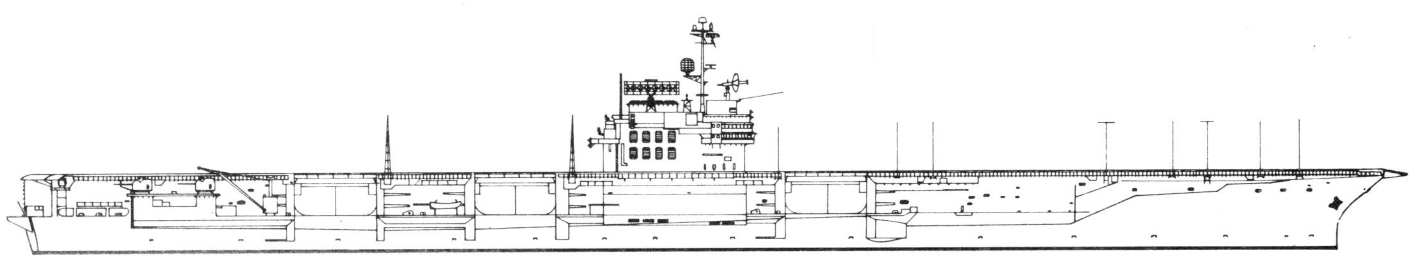

SARATOGA (CV 60) "Forrestal" Class

Scale: 1 inch = 150 feet (1 : 1 800)

Aircraft Carriers—*continued*

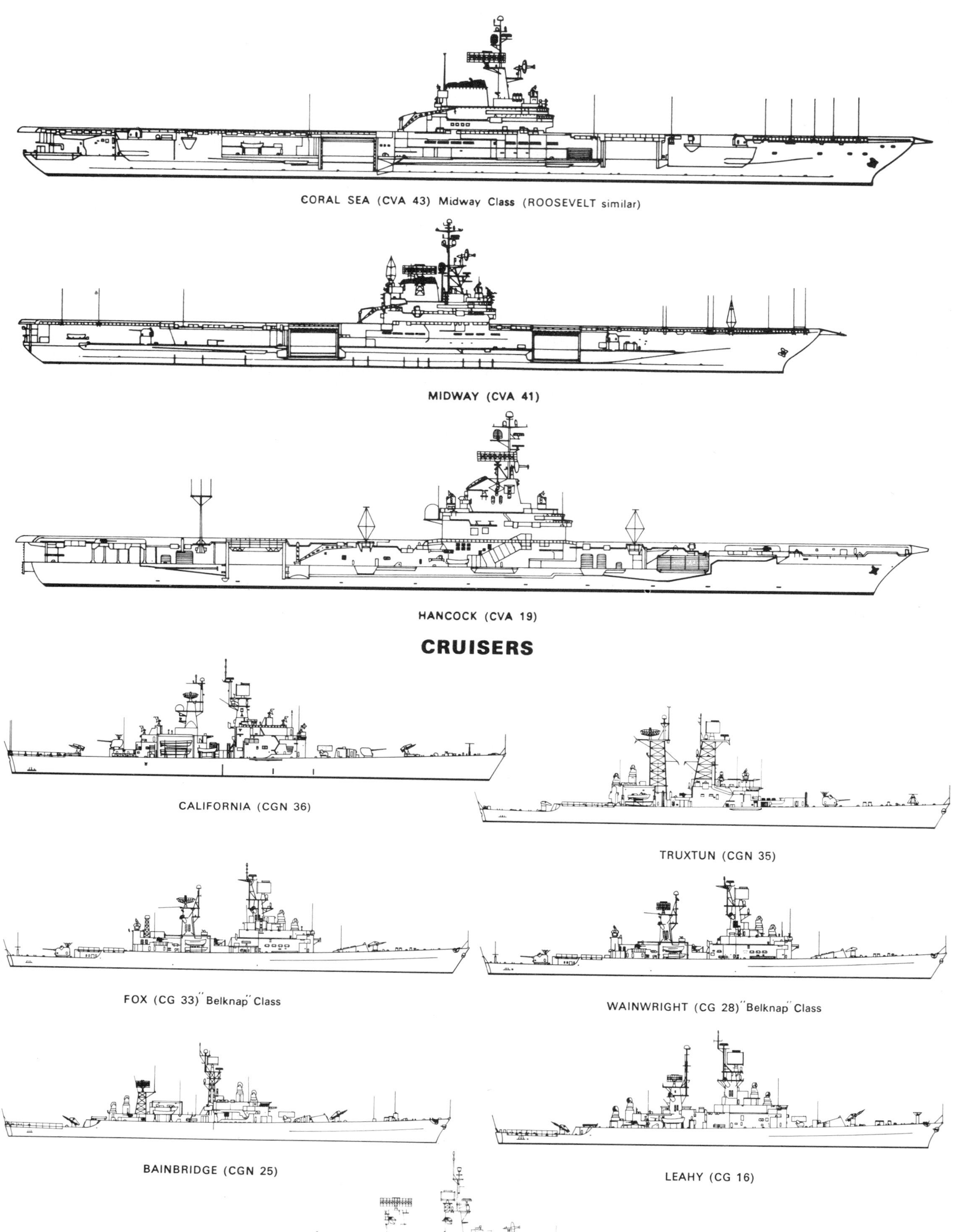

CORAL SEA (CVA 43) Midway Class (ROOSEVELT similar)

MIDWAY (CVA 41)

HANCOCK (CVA 19)

CRUISERS

CALIFORNIA (CGN 36)

TRUXTUN (CGN 35)

FOX (CG 33) "Belknap" Class

WAINWRIGHT (CG 28) "Belknap" Class

BAINBRIDGE (CGN 25)

LEAHY (CG 16)

CHICAGO (CG 11)

Cruisers—*continued*

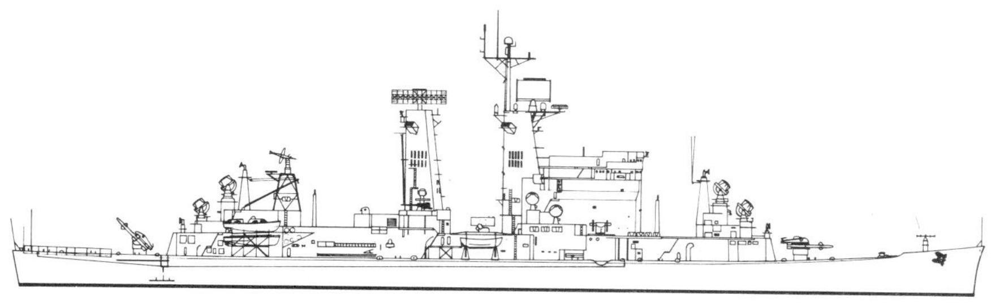

ALBANY (CG 10)

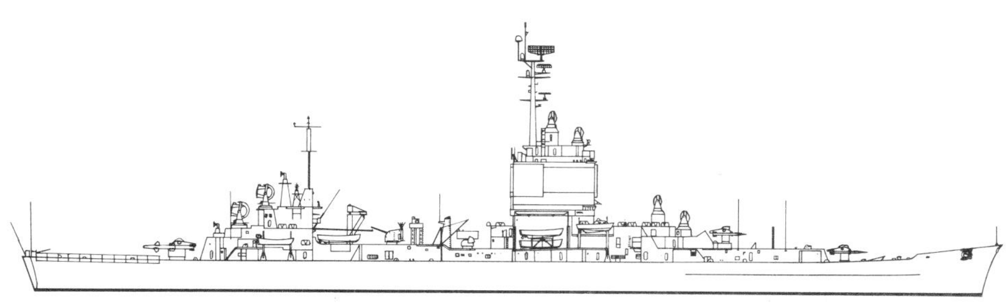

LONG BEACH (CGN 9)

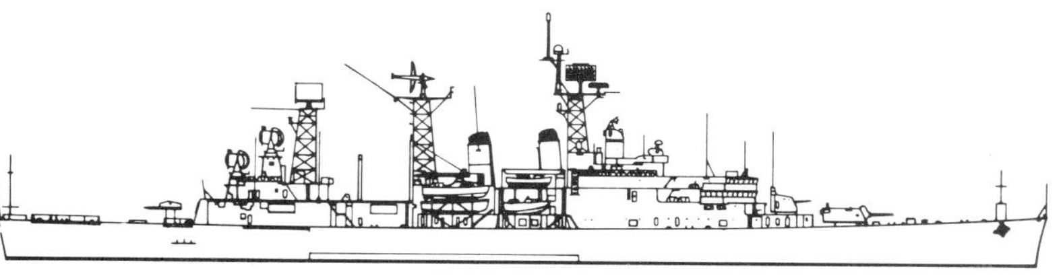

PROVIDENCE (CLG 6) Converted "Cleveland" Class (Terrier)

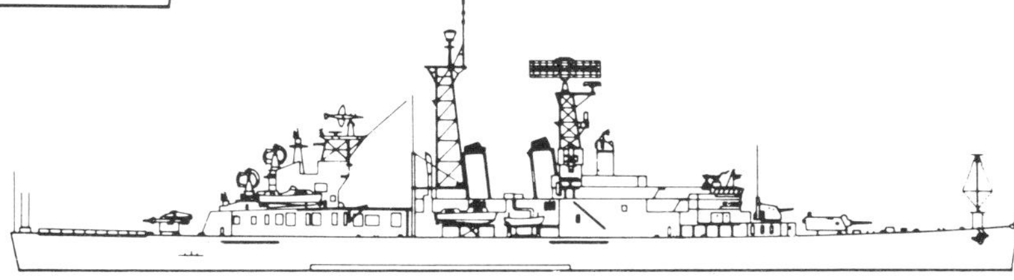

OKLAHOMA CITY (CG 5) Converted "Cleveland" Class (Talos)

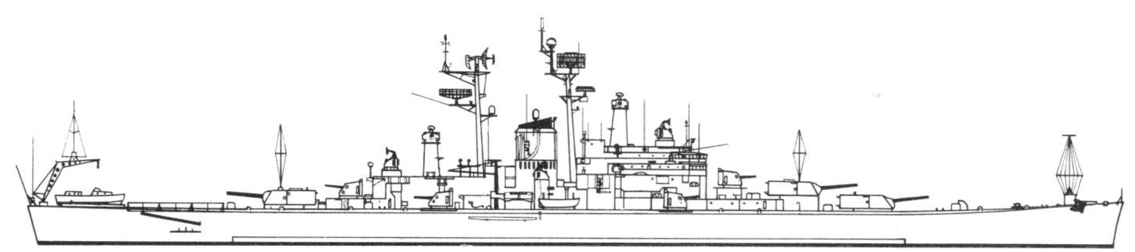

NEWPORT NEWS (CA 148) "Des Moines" Class

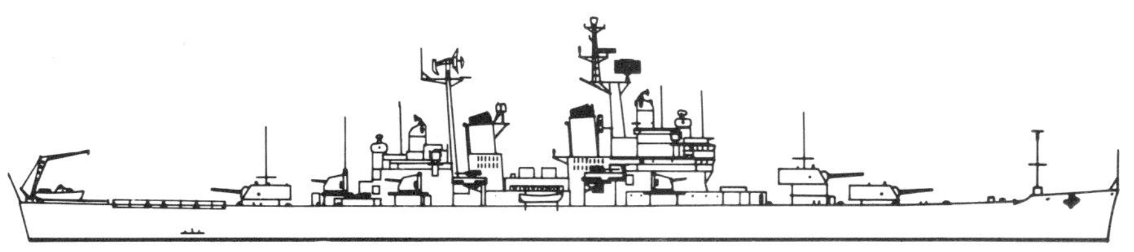

ST. PAUL (CA 73) "Baltimore" Class

DESTROYERS

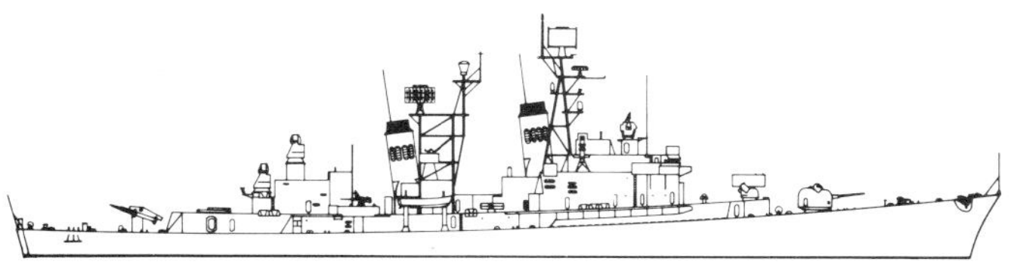

MAHAN (DDG 42) "Coontz" Class

FARRAGUT (DDG 37) "Coontz" Class

Destroyers—*continued*

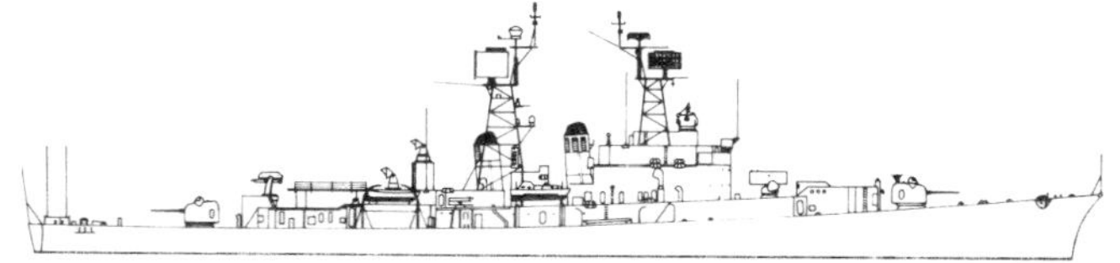

MITSCHER (DDG 35)

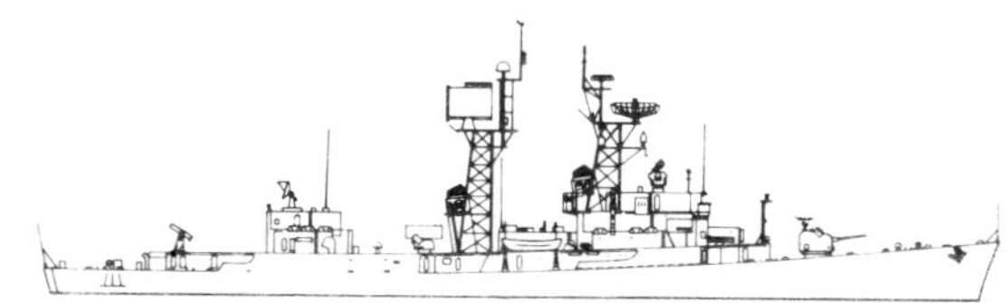

SOMERS (DDG 34) "Converted Forrest Sherman" Class

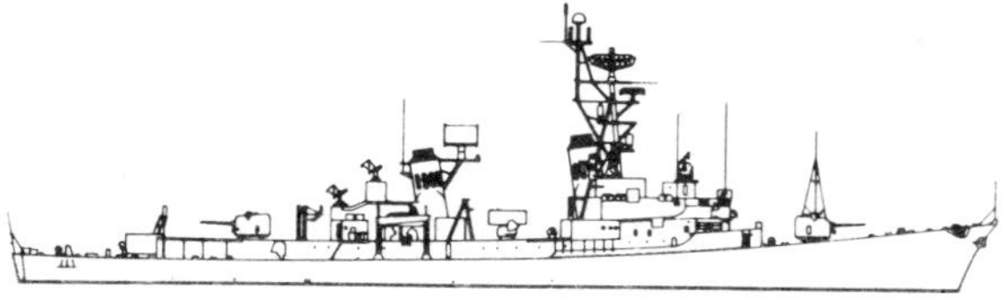

WADDELL (DDG 24) "Charles F. Adams" Class

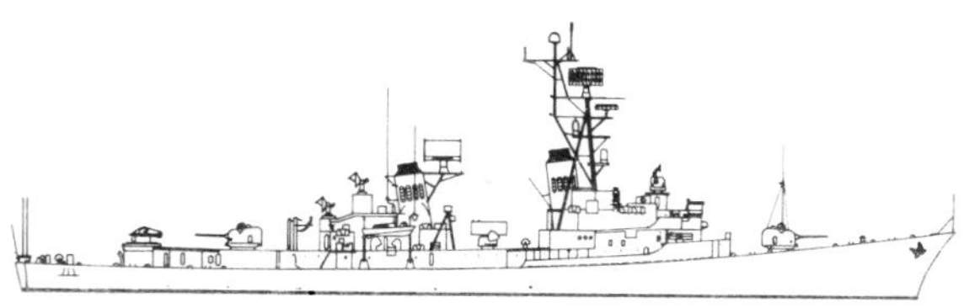

BARNEY (DDG 6) "Charles F. Adams" Class

MANLEY (DD 940) "Forrest Sherman" Class

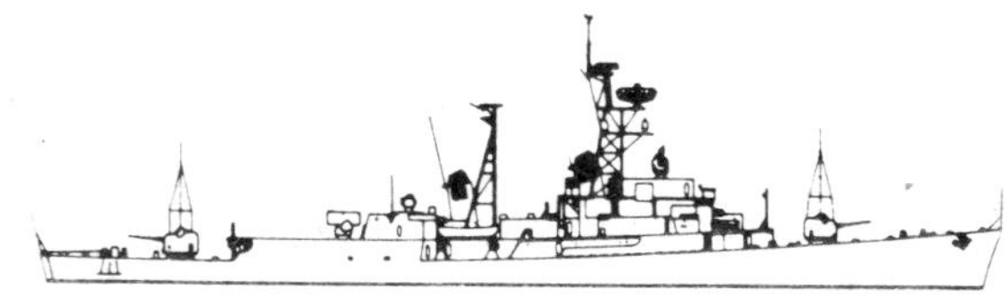

JONAS INGRAM (DD 938) "Forrest Sherman" Class (ASW)

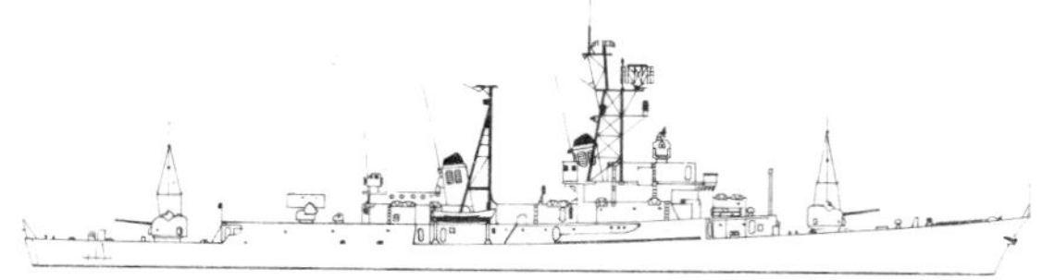

BARRY (DD 933) "Forrest Sherman" Class (ASW)

"Gearing" Class FRAM I (all guns forward)

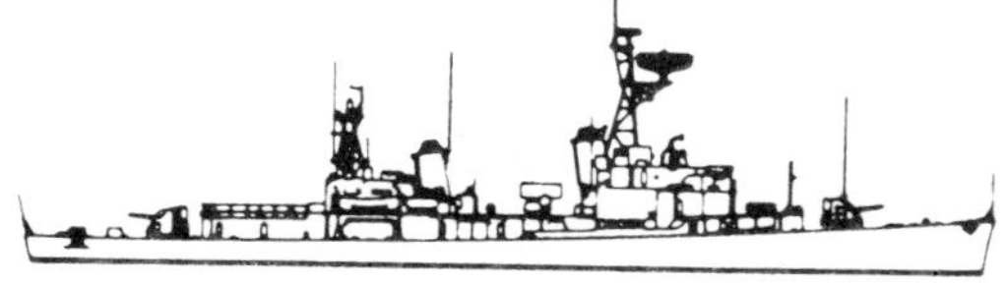

"Gearing" Class FRAM I (guns forward and aft)

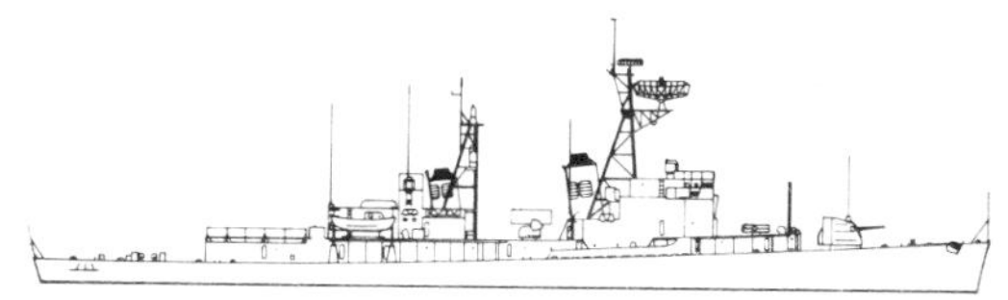

ROBERT A. OWENS (DD 827) "Carpenter" Class FRAM I

FRIGATES

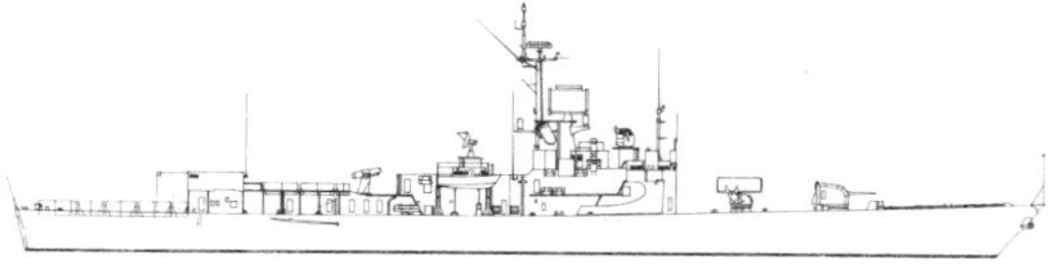

BROOKE (FFG 1)

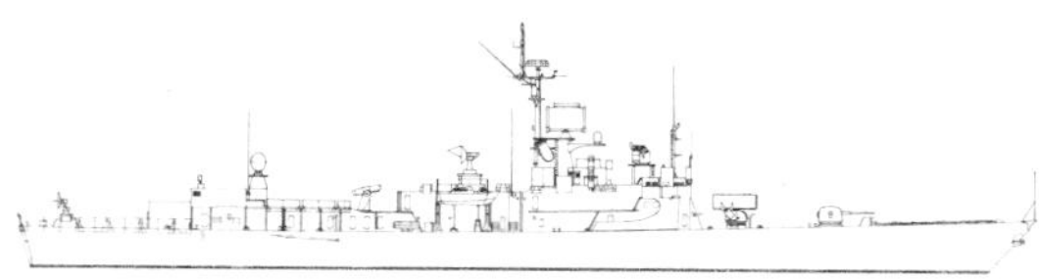

TALBOT (FFG 4)

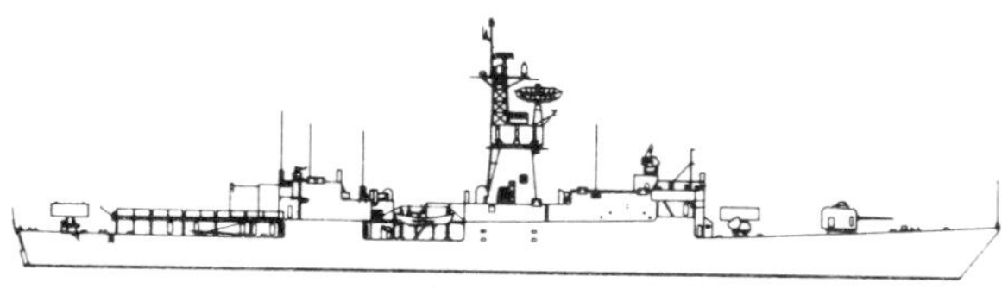

"Knox" Class (improved)

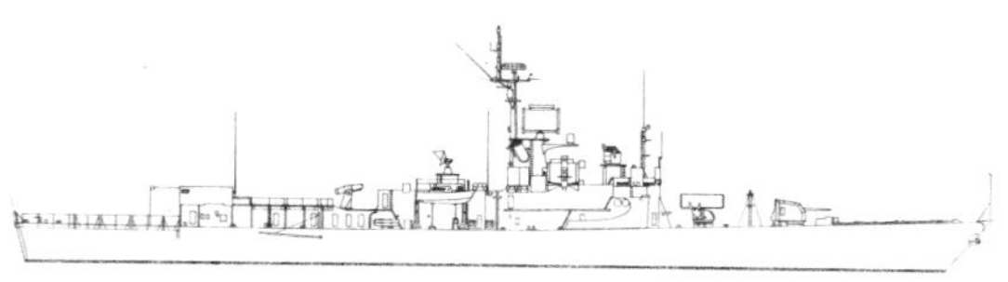

JULIUS A. FURER (FFG 6)

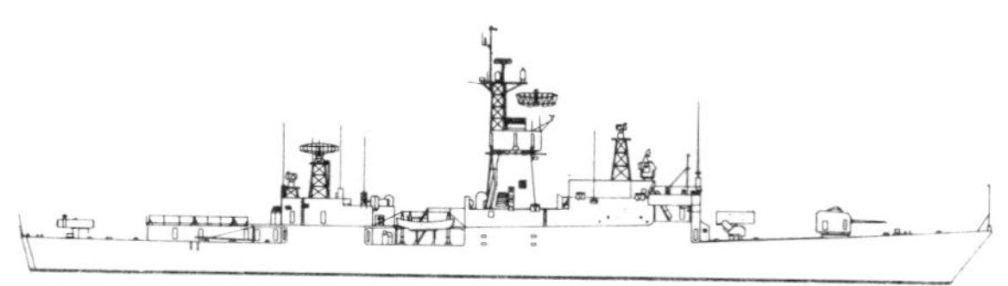

DOWNES (FF-1070) NATO Sea Sparrow

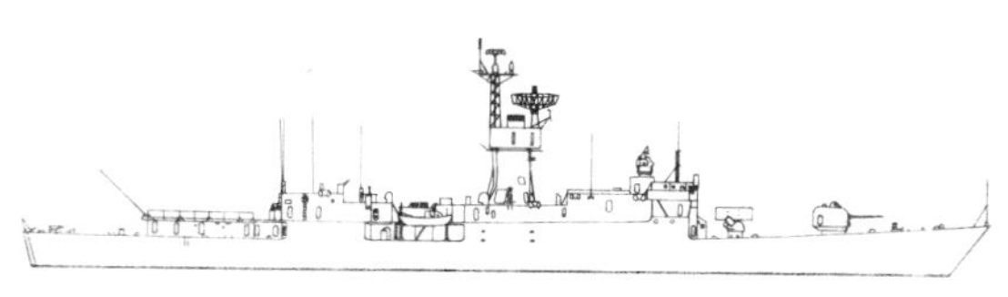

"KNOX" Class

Scale: 1 inch = 150 feet (1 : 1 800)

Frigates—*continued*

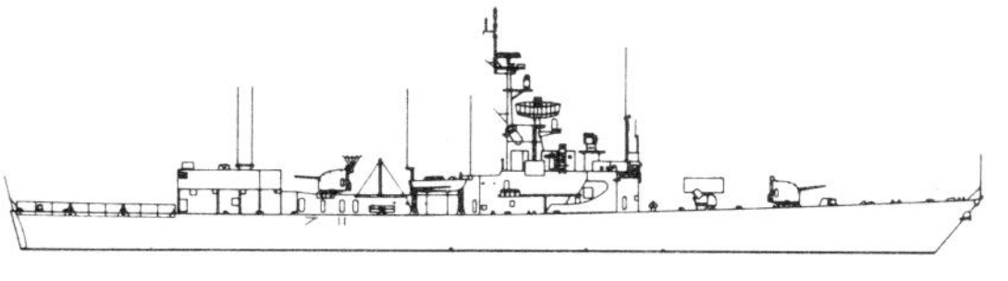

" Garcia " Class (LAMPS Modification)

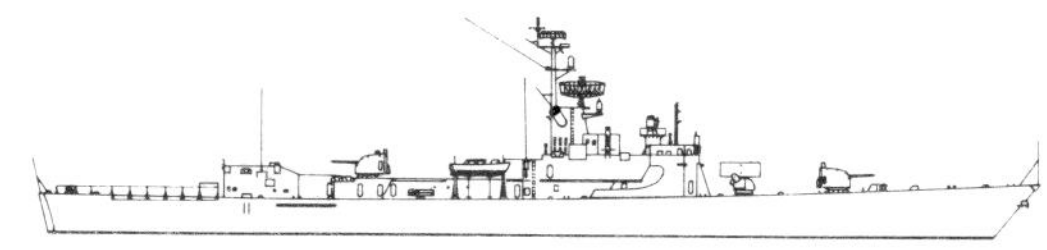

SAMPLE (FF 1048) " Garcia " Class

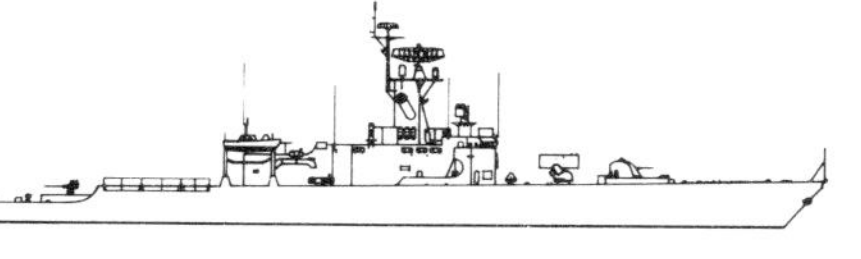

BRONSTEIN (FF 1037)

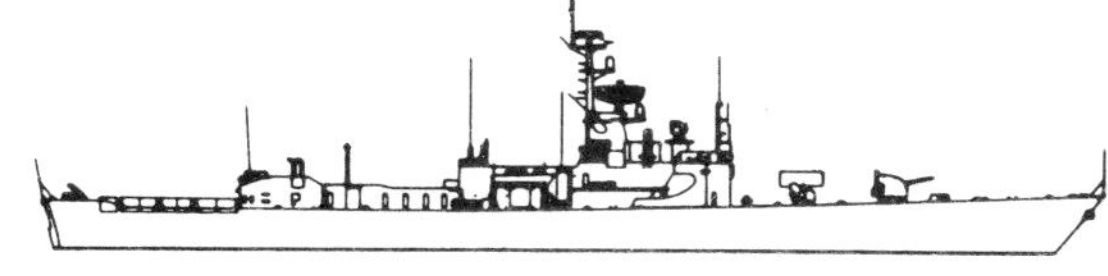

GLOVER (AGFF 1)

RADAR PICKET ESCORT

COMMAND SHIPS

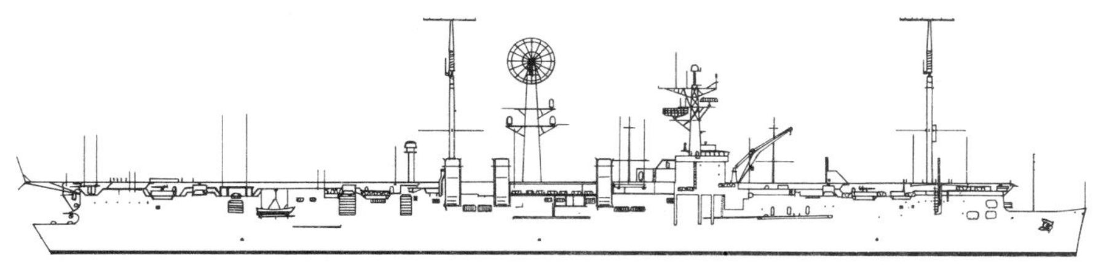

WRIGHT (CC 2)

AMPHIBIOUS WARFARE SHIPS

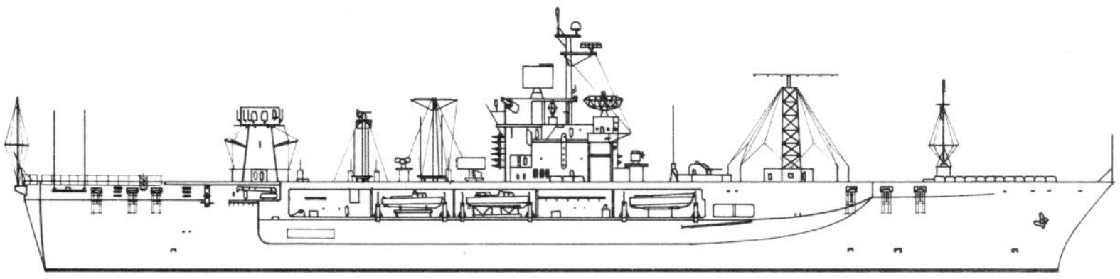

BLUE RIDGE (LCC 19)

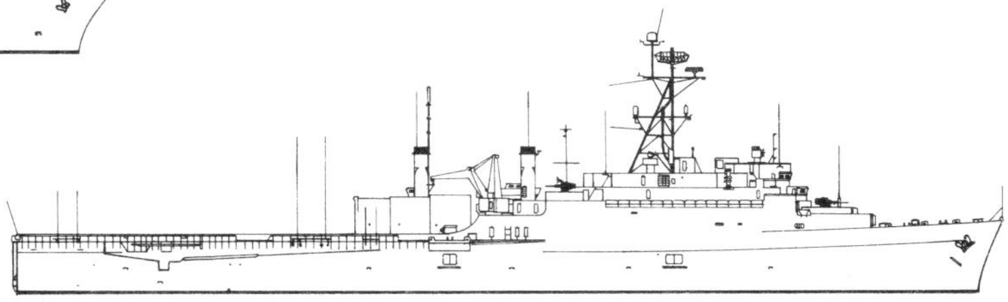

NASHVILLE (LPD 13)

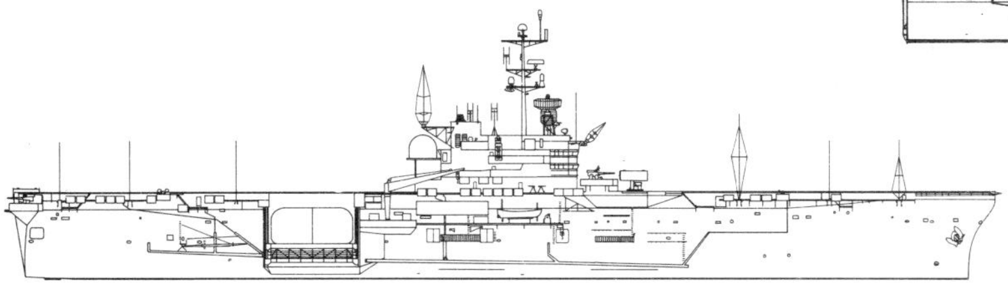

TRIPOLI (LPH 10)

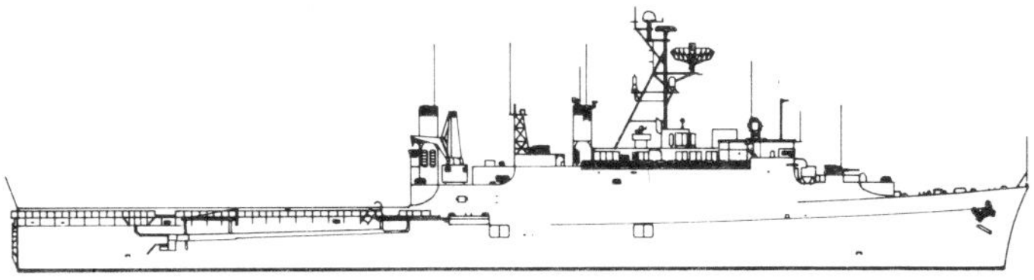

RALEIGH (LPD 1)

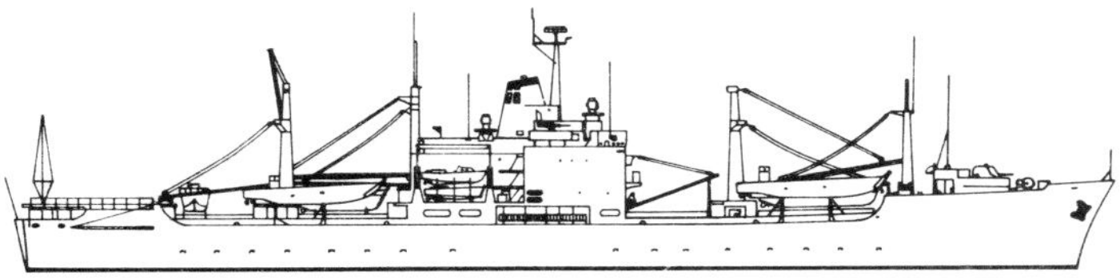

CHARLESTON (LKA 113)

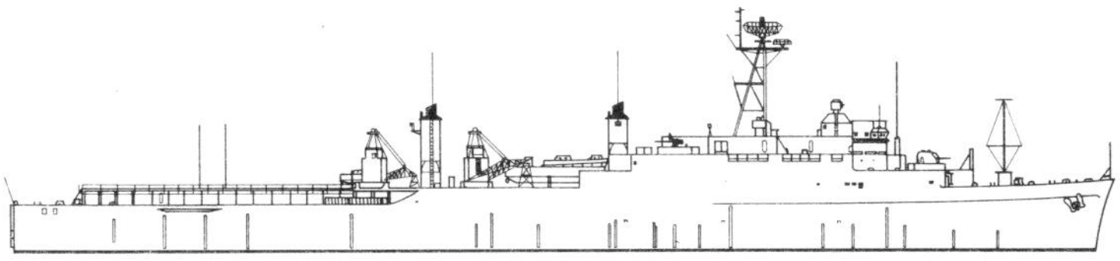

ANCHORAGE (LSD 36)

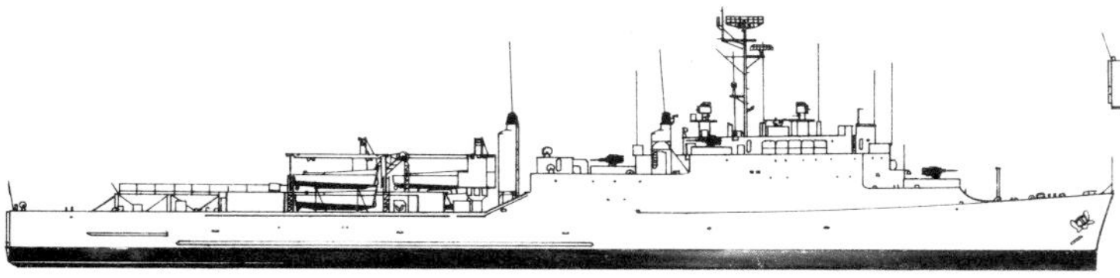

HERMITAGE (LSD 34) " Thomaston " Class

Scale: 1 inch = 150 feet (1 : 1 800)

Amphibious Warfare Ships—*continued*

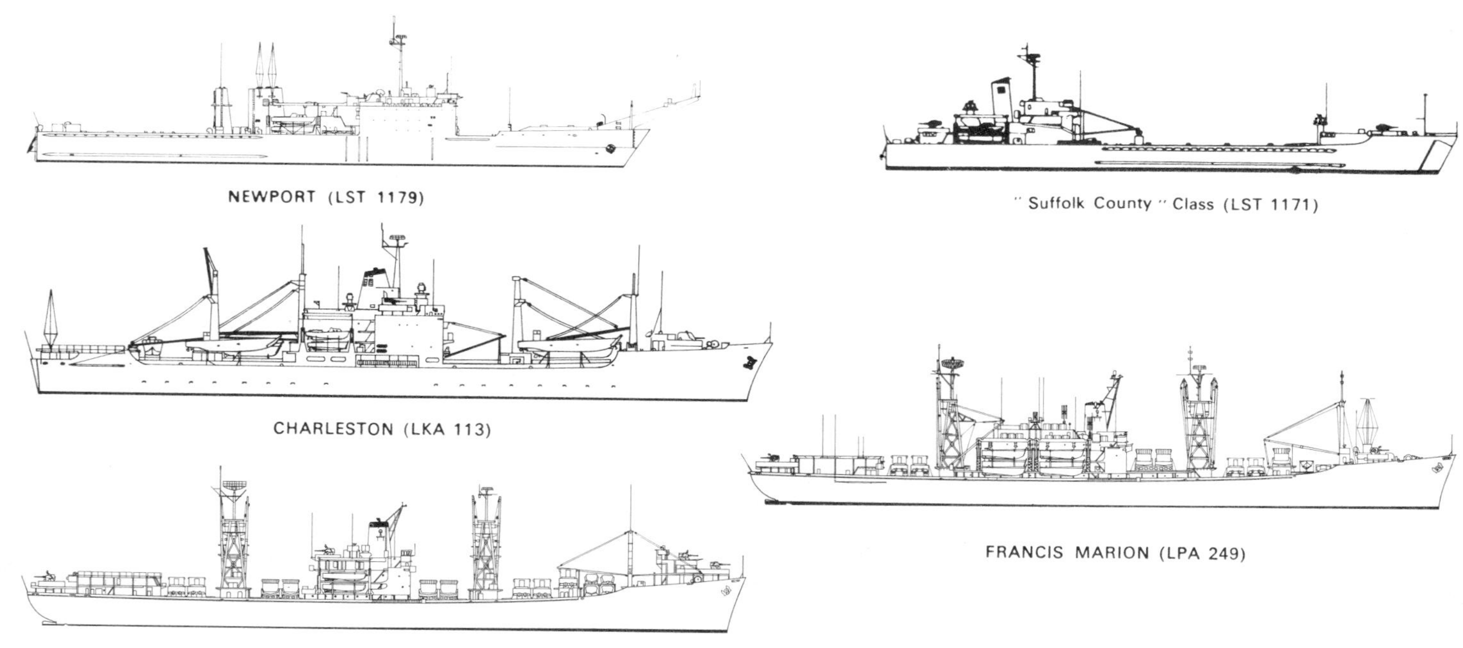

NEWPORT (LST 1179)

"Suffolk County" Class (LST 1171)

CHARLESTON (LKA 113)

FRANCIS MARION (LPA 249)

TULARE (LKA 112)

AUXILIARY SHIPS

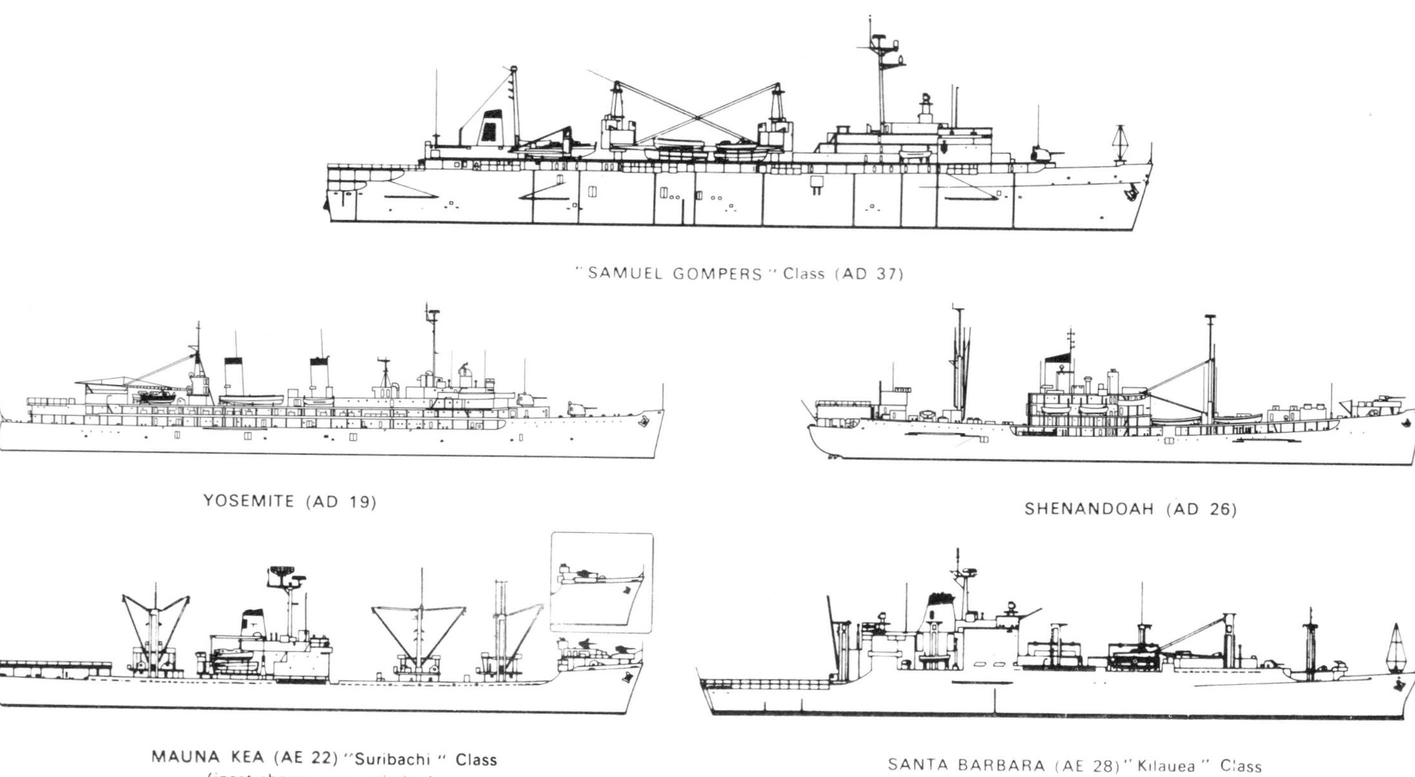

"SAMUEL GOMPERS" Class (AD 37)

YOSEMITE (AD 19)

SHENANDOAH (AD 26)

MAUNA KEA (AE 22) "Suribachi" Class
(inset shows gun variation)

SANTA BARBARA (AE 28) "Kilauea" Class

SAN JOSE (AFS 7) "Mars" Class

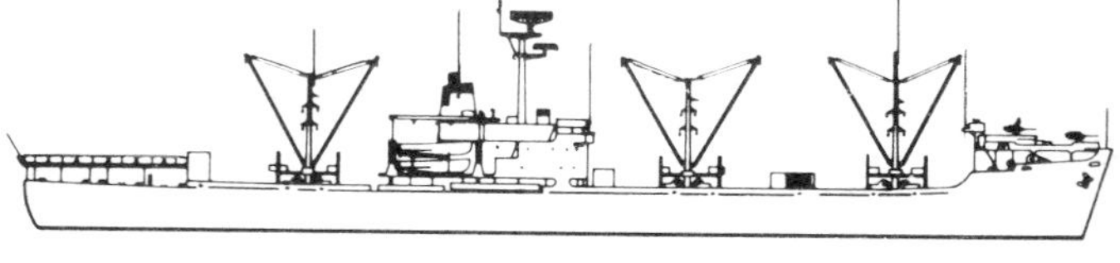

RIGEL (AF 58) R3-S-4A Type

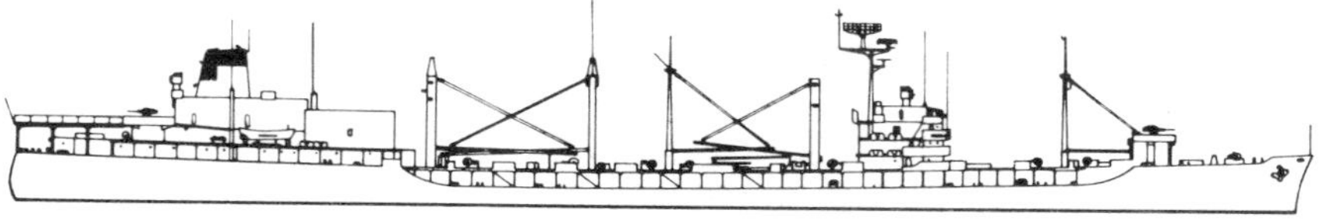

NEOSHO (AO 143)

Scale: 1 inch = 150 feet (1 : 1 800)

Auxiliary Ships—*continued*

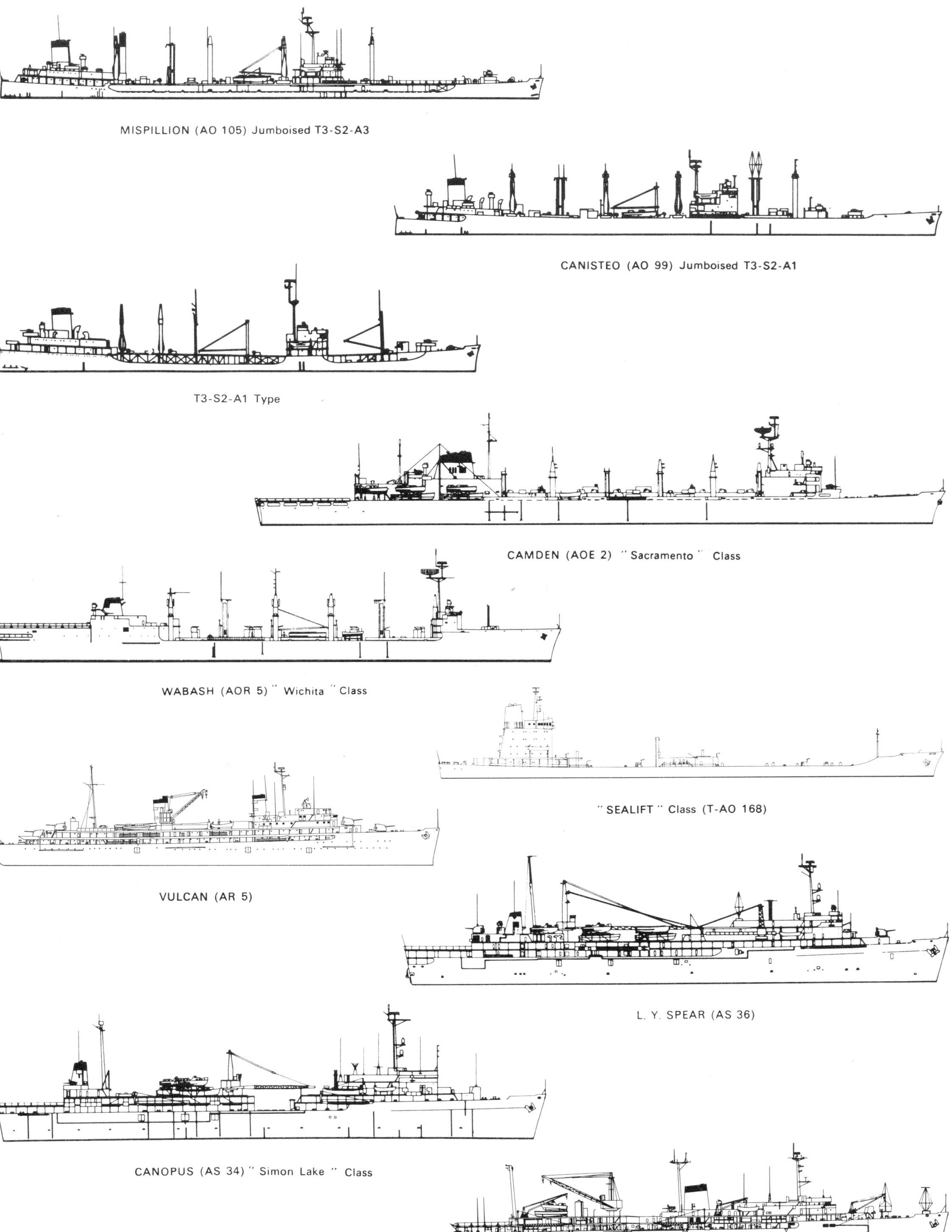

MISPILLION (AO 105) Jumboised T3-S2-A3

CANISTEO (AO 99) Jumboised T3-S2-A1

T3-S2-A1 Type

CAMDEN (AOE 2) "Sacramento" Class

WABASH (AOR 5) "Wichita" Class

"SEALIFT" Class (T-AO 168)

VULCAN (AR 5)

L. Y. SPEAR (AS 36)

CANOPUS (AS 34) "Simon Lake" Class

HUNLEY (AS 31)

Scale: 1 inch = 150 feet (1 : 1 800)

Auxiliary Ships—*continued*

HOWARD W. GILMORE (AS 16)

PIGEON (ASR 21)

EDENTON (ATS 1)

NORTON SOUND (AVM 1)

Scale: 1 inch = 150 feet (1 : 1 800)

PATROL SHIPS AND CRAFT

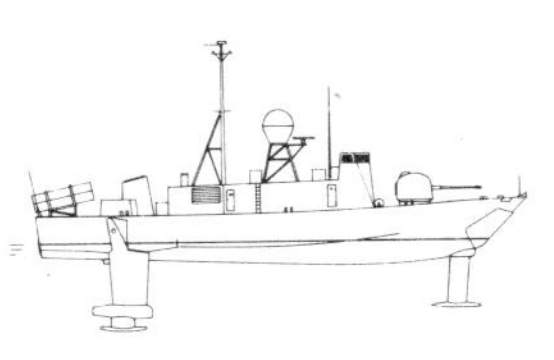

"PEGASUS" (PHM 1)

ANTELOPE (PG 86) "Asheville" Class

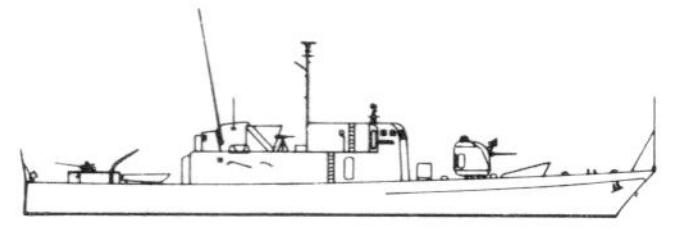

Asheville Class

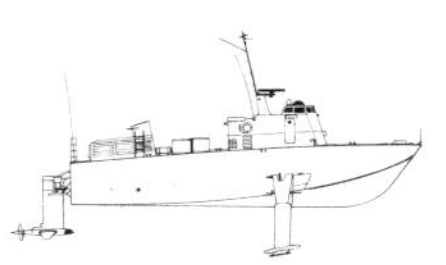

FLAGSTAFF (PGH 1)

Scale: 1 inch = 100 feet (1 : 1 200)

UNITED STATES SHIP HULL NUMBERS

(Type designations in order of arrangement within this volume; ships in numerical sequence)

Strategic Missile Submarines

SSBN—Fleet Ballistic Missile Submarines

"Geo. Washington" Class
598 George Washington
599 Patrick Henry
600 Theodore Roosevelt
601 Robert E. Lee
602 Abraham Lincoln

"Ethan Allen" Class
608 Ethan Allen
609 Sam Houston
610 Thomas A. Edison
611 John Marshall

"Lafayette" Class
616 Lafayette
617 Alexander Hamilton

"Ethan Allen" Class (Cont'd)
618 Thomas Jefferson

"Lafayette" Class (Cont'd)
619 Andrew Jackson
620 John Adams
622 James Monroe
623 Nathan Hale
624 Woodrow Wilson
624 Henry Clay
626 Daniel Webster
627 James Madison
628 Tecumseh
629 Daniel Boone
630 John C. Calhoun
631 Ulysses S. Grant
632 Von Steuben
633 Casimir Pulaski
634 Stonewall Jackson
635 Sam Rayburn
636 Nathanael Greene
640 Benjamin Franklin
641 Simon Bolivar
642 Kamehameha
643 George Bancroft
644 Lewis and Clark
645 James K. Polk
654 George C. Marshall
655 Henry L. Stimson
656 George Washington Carver
657 Francis Scott Key
658 Mariano G. Vallejo
659 Will Rogers

Submarines

SS SSN—Attack Submarines
AGSS—Auxiliary Submarines
LPSS—Amphibious Transport Submarines
SSG—Guided Missile Submarines

"Sealion" Type
315 Sealion LPSS

"Dolphin" Type
555 Dolphin AGSS

"Tang" Class
563 Tang AGSS
565 Wahoo
566 Trout
567 Gudgeon

"Albacore" Type
569 Albacore AGSS

"Nautilus" Type (SSN)
571 Nautilus

"Sailfish" Class
572 Sailfish
573 Salmon

"Grayback" Type
574 Grayback SS (LPSS)

"Seawolf" Type (SSN)
575 Seawolf

"Darter" Type
576 Darter

"Grayback" Type
577 Growler SSG

"Skate" Class (SSN)
578 Skate
579 Swordfish

"Barbel" Class
580 Barbel
581 Blueback
582 Bonefish

"Skate" Class (SSN) (Cont'd)
583 Sargo
584 Seadragon

"Skipjack" Class (SSN)
585 Skipjack

"Triton" Type (SSN)
586 Triton

"Halibut" Type (SSN)
587 Halibut

"Skipjack" Class (SSN) (Cont'd)
588 Scamp
590 Sculpin
591 Shark
592 Snook

"Permit" Class (SSN)
594 Permit
595 Plunger
596 Barb

"Tullibee" Type (SSN)
597 Tullibee

"Permit" Class (SSN) (Cont'd)
603 Pollack
604 Haddo
605 Jack
606 Tinosa
607 Dace
612 Guardfish
613 Flasher
614 Greenling
615 Gato
621 Haddock

"Sturgeon" Class (SSN)
637 Sturgeon
638 Whale
639 Tautog
646 Grayling
647 Pogy
648 Aspro
649 Sunfish
650 Pargo
651 Queenfish
652 Puffer
653 Ray
660 Sand Lance
661 Lapon
662 Gurnard
663 Hammerhead
664 Sea Devil
665 Guitarro
666 Hawkbill
667 Bergall
668 Spadefish
669 Seahorse

670 Finback
"Narwhal" Type (SSN)
671 Narwhal
"Sturgeon" Class (SSN) (Cont'd)
672 Pintado
673 Flying Fish
674 Trepang
675 Bluefish
676 Billfish
667 Drum
678 Archerfish
679 Silversides
680 William H. Bates
681 Batfish
682 Tunny
683 Parche
684 Cavalla

"Lipscomb" Type (SSN)
685 Glenard P. Lipscomb

"Sturgeon" Class (SSN) (Cont'd)
686 L. Mendel Rivers
687 Richard B. Russell

"Los Angeles" Class (SSN)
688 Los Angeles
689 Baton Rouge
690 Philadelphia
691 Memphis
692 Omaha
693 Cincinnati
694 Groton
695 Birmingham
696 New York City
697 Indianapolis
698 Bremerton
699 Jacksonville

Aircraft Carriers

CV CVA CVAN CVN—Attack Aircraft Carriers
CVS—ASW—Aircraft Carriers
CVT—Training Aircraft Carriers

"Hancock" Class
11 Intrepid CVS

Modernised "Essex" Class
12 Hornet CVS

"Hancock" class (Cont'd)
16 Lexington CVT
19 Hancock

Modernised "Essex" Class (Cont'd)
20 Bennington CVS

"Hancock" Class (Cont'd)
31 Bon Homme Richard
34 Oriskany
38 Shangri-La CVS
"Midway" Class
41 Midway
42 Franklin D. Roosevelt
43 Coral Sea

"Forrestal" Class
59 Forrestal
60 Saratoga
61 Ranger
62 Independance

"Kitty Hawk" Class
63 Kitty Hawk
64 Constellation

"Enterprise" Type (CVAN)
65 Enterprise

"Kitty Hawk" Class (Cont'd)
66 America
67 John F. Kennedy

"Nimitz" Class (CVN/CVAN)
68 Nimitz
69 Dwight D. Eisenhower
70 Carl Vinson

Cruisers

CLG—Guided Missile Light Cruisers
CG CGN—Guided Missile Cruisers
CA—Heavy Cruisers

Converted "Cleveland" Class
4 Little Rock
5 Oklahoma City
6 Province (CLG)
7 Springfi... (CLG)
"Long Beach" Type (CGN)
9 Long Beach

"Albany" Class
10 Albany
11 Chicago
12 Columbus

"Leahy" Class
16 Leahy
17 Harry E. Yarnell
18 Worden
19 Dale
20 Richmond K. Turner
21 Gridley
22 England
23 Halsey
24 Reeves

"Bainbridge" Type (CGN)
25 Bainbridge

"Belknap" Class
26 Bellknap
27 Josephus Daniels
28 Wainwright
29 Jouett
30 Horne
31 Sterett
32 William H. Standley
33 Fox
34 Biddle
"Truxtun" Type (CGN)
35 Truxtun

"California" Class (CGN)
36 California
37 South Carolina

"Virginia" Class (CGN)
38 Virginia
39 Texas
40 Mississippi
41 Arkansas
"Baltimore" Class
70 Canberra
73 St. Paul
"Salem" Class
134 Des Moines
"Baltimore" Class (Cont'd)
135 Los Angeles
"Salem" Class (Cont'd)
139 Salem
148 Newport News

BB—Battleships

"Iowa" Class
61 Iowa
62 New Jersey
63 Missouri
64 Wisconsin

Destroyers

DDG—Guided Missile Destroyers

"Chas F. Adams" Class
2 Charles F. Adams
3 John King
4 Lawrence
5 Claude V. Ricketts
6 Barney
7 Henry B. Wilson
8 Lynde McCormick
9 Towers
10 Sampson
11 Sellers
12 Robinson
13 Hoel
14 Buchanan
15 Berkeley
16 Joseph Strauss
17 Conyngham
18 Semmes
19 Tattnall
20 Goldsborough
21 Cochrane
22 Benjamin Stoddert
23 Richard E. Byrd
24 Waddell

Converted "Sherman" Class
31 Decatur
32 John Paul Jones
33 Parsons
34 Somers

Converted "Mitscher" Class
35 Mitscher
36 John S. McCain

"Coontz" Class
37 Farragut
38 Luce
39 MacDonough
40 Coontz
41 King
42 Mahan
43 Dahigren
44 William V. Pratt
45 Dewey
46 Preble

DD—Destroyers

"Fletcher" Class
566 Stoddard

"Gearing" Class
714 William R. Rush
715 William M. Wood
716 Wiltsie
717 Theo E. Chandler
718 Hammer
719 Epperson
743 Southerland
763 William C. Lawe
782 Rowan
783 Gurke
784 McKean
785 Henderson
786 Richard B. Anderson
788 Hollister
806 Highbee
817 Corry
818 New
819 Holder
820 Rich
821 Johnson
822 Robert H. McCard
824 Basilone
"Carpenter" Type
825 Carpenter
"Gearing" Class (Cont'd)
826 Agerholm

"Carpenter" Type (Cont'd)
827 Robert A. Owens

"Gearing" Class (Cont'd)
829 Myles C. Fox
835 Charles P. Cecil
836 George K. Mackenzie
837 Sarsfield
839 Power
840 Glennon
842 Fiske
844 Perry
845 Bausell
846 Ozbourn
847 Robert L. Wilson
849 Richard E. Kraus
850 Joseph P. Kennedy Jr.
852 Leonard F. Mason
858 Fred T. Berry
862 Vogelgesang
863 Steinaker
864 Harold J. Ellison
866 Cone
867 Stribling
868 Brownson
871 Damato
873 Hawkins
876 Rogers
877 Perkins
878 Vesole
880 Dyess
881 Bordelon
883 Newman K. Perry
885 John F. Craig
886 Orleck
888 Stickell
890 Meredith
"Forrest Sherman" Class
931 Forrest Sherman
933 Barry
937 George F. Davis
938 Jonas Ingram
940 Manley
941 Dupont
942 Bigelow
943 Blandy
944 Mullinnix
945 Hull
946 Edson
948 Morton
950 Richard S. Edwards
951 Turner Joy
"Spruance" Class
963 Spruance
964 Paul F. Foster
965 Kinkaid
966 Hewitt
967 Elliot
968 Arthur W. Radford
969 Peterson
970 Caron
971 David R. Ray
972 Oldendorf
973 John Young
974 Comte de Grasse

Frigates

FF—Frigates
FFG—Guided Missile Frigates
AGFF—Frigate Research Ships
DER—Radar Picket Escort Ships

"Brooke" Class (FFG)
1 Brooke
2 Ramsey
3 Schofield
4 Talbot
5 Richard L. Page
6 Julius A. Furer
2 Oliver Hazard Perry

"Bronstein" Class
1037 Bronstein
1038 McCloy

"Garcia" Class
1040 Garcia
1041 Bradley
1043 Edward McDonnell
1044 Brumby
1045 Davidson
1047 Voge
1048 Sample
1049 Koelsch
1050 Albert David
1051 O'Callahan

"Knox" Class
1052 Knox
1053 Roark
1054 Gray
1055 Hepburn
1056 Connole
1057 Rathburne
1058 Mayerkord
1059 W. S. Sims
1060 Lang
1061 Patterson
1062 Whipple
1063 Reasoner
1064 Lockwood
1065 Stein
1066 Marvin Shields
1067 Francis Hammond
1068 Vreeland
1069 Bagley
1070 Downes
1071 Badger
1072 Blakely
1073 Robert E. Peary
1074 Harold E. Holt
1075 Trippe
1076 Fanning
1077 Ouellet
1078 Joseph Hewes
1079 Bowen
1080 Paul
1081 Aylwin
1082 Elmer Montgomery
1083 Cook
1084 McCandless
1085 Donald B. Beary
1086 Brewton
1087 Kirk
1088 Barbey
1089 Jesse L. Brown
1090 Ainsworth
1091 Miller
1092 Thomas C. Hart
1093 Capodanno
1094 Pharris
1095 Truitt
1096 Valdez
1097 Moinester

"Glover" Type (AGFF)
1 Glover

Converted "Edsall" Class (DER)
324 Falgout
382 Ramsden
386 Savage
387 Vance
389 Durant
391 Chambers
400 Hissem

Command and Communication Ships

AGF—Miscellaneous Flagships

3 La Salle

CC—Command Ships

1 Northampton
2 Wright

AGMR—Major Communication Relay Ships

1 Annapolis
2 Arlington

Amphibious Warships

LCC—Amphibious Command Ships (ex-AGC)

"Mount McKinley" Class
7 Mount McKinley
12 Estes
16 Pocono
17 Taconic

"Blue Ridge" Class
19 Blue Ridge
20 Mount Whitney

LHA—Amphibious Assault Ships

1 Tarawa
2 Saipan
3 Belleau Wood
4 Nassau
5 Da Nang

LPH—Amphibious Assault Ships

"Iwo Jima" Class
2 Iwo Jima
3 Okinawa
7 Guadalcanal
9 Guam
10 Tripoli
11 New Orleans
12 Inchon

LKA—Amphibious Cargo Ships

"Andromeda" Class
54 Algol
57 Capricornus
61 Muliphen
88 Uvalde
93 Yancey
94 Winston
97 Merrick

"Rankin" Class
103 Rankin
104 Seminole
105 Skagit
106 Union
107 Vermilion
108 Washburn

"Tulare" Type
112 Tulare

"Charleston" Class
113 Charleston
114 Durham
115 Mobile
116 St. Louis
117 El Paso

LPA—Amphibious Transports

"Haskell" Class
194 Sandoval
199 Maggoffin
208 Talladega
213 Mountrail
215 Navarro
222 Pickaway
237 Bexar

"Paul Revere" Class
248 Paul Revere
249 Francis Marion

LPR—Amphibious Transports (Small)

55 Laning
127 Begor
132 Balduck

LPD—Amphibious Transport Docks

"Raleigh" Class
1 Raleigh
2 Vancouver

"Austin" Class
4 Austin
5 Ogden
6 Duluth
7 Cleveland
8 Dubuque
9 Denver
10 Juneau
11 Coronado
12 Shreveport
13 Nashville
14 Trenton
15 Ponce

LSD—Dock Landing Ships

"Casa Grande" Class
13 Casa Grande
14 Rushmore
15 Shadwell
16 Cabildo
17 Catamount
18 Colonial
19 Comstock
20 Donner
26 Tortuga
27 Whetstone

"Thomaston" Class
28 Thomaston
29 Plymouth Rock
30 Fort Snelling
31 Point Defiance
32 Speigel Grove
33 Alamo
34 Hermitage
35 Monticello

"Anchorage" Class
36 Anchorage
37 Portland
38 Pensacola
39 Mt. Vernon
40 Fort Fisher

LST—Tank Landing Ships

511-1152 series
722 Dodge County
762 Floyd County
819 Hampshire County
854 Kemper County
901 Litchfield County
980 Meeker County
1082 Pitkin County
1096 St. Clair County
1123 Sedgwick County

"Terrebonne Parish" Class
1157 Terrell County
1169 Whitfield County

"Suffolk County" Class
1173 Suffolk County
1177 Lorain County
1178 Wood County

"Newport" Class
1179 Newport
1180 Manitowac
1181 Sumter
1182 Fresno
1183 Peroria
1184 Frederick
1185 Schenectady
1186 Cayuga
1187 Tuscaloosa
1188 Saginaw
1189 San Bernadino
1190 Boulder
1191 Racine
1192 Spartanburg County
1193 Fairfax County
1194 Lamour County
1195 Barbour County
1196 Harlan County
1197 Barnstaple County
1198 Bristol County

Patrol Ships and Craft

PHM—Hydrofoil Missile Boats

1 Pegasus
2 Hercules

PGH—Hydrofoil Gunboats

1 Flagstaff

PCH—Hydrofoil Patrol Craft

1 High Point

PG—Patrol Gunboats

84 Asheville
85 Gallup
86 Antelope
86 Ready
88 Crockett
89 Marathon
90 Canon
92 Tacoma
93 Welch
94 Chehalis
98 Grand Rapids
101 Green Bay

Mine Warfare Ships

MSO—Ocean Minesweepers

"Agile" Class
421 Agile
427 Constant
428 Dash
429 Detector
430 Direct
431 Dominant
433 Engage
437 Enhance
438 Esteem
439 Excel
440 Exploit
441 Exultant
442 Fearless
443 Fidelity
446 Fortify
448 Illusive
449 Impervious
455 Implicit
456 Inflict
458 Lucid
459 Nimble
461 Observer
462 Pinnacle
464 Pluck
471 Skill
474 Vital
488 Conquest
489 Gallant
490 Leader
492 Pledge

494 Sturdy
495 Swerve
496 Venture

"Acme" Class
508 Acme
509 Adroit
510 Advance
511 Affray

AE—Ammunition Ships

"Lassen "Class
8 Mauna Loa

"Wrangell" Class
12 Wrangell
14 Firedrake

"Suribachi" Class
21 Suribachi
22 Mauna Kea
23 Nitro
24 Pyro
25 Haleakala

"Kilauea" Class
26 Kilauea
27 Butte
28 Santa Barbara
29 Mount Hood
32 Flint
33 Shasta
24 Mount Baker
35 Kiska

AF—Store Ships

C2-S-B1 Type
28 Hyades

R2-S-BV1 Type
49 Zelima
52 Arcturus
54 Pictor
55 Aludra

"Victory" Type
56 Denebola

R3-S-4A Type
58 Rigel
59 Vega
61 Procyon

AFS—Combat Store Ships

"Mars" Class
1 Mars
2 Sylvania
3 Niagara Falls
4 White Plains
5 Concord
6 San Diego
7 San Jose

AO—Oilers

T3-S2-A1 Type
25 Sabine

T2-A Type
36 Kennebec
43 Tappahannock

"Jumboised" T3-S2-A1 Type
51 Ashtabula

T3-S2-A1 Type (cont'd)
54 Chikaskia
56 Aucilla
57 Marias
62 Taluga
64 Tolovana
98 Caloosahatchee
99 Canisteo

"Jumboised" T3-S2-A3 Type
105 Mispillion
106 Navasota
107 Passumpsic
108 Pawcatuck
109 Waccamaw

"Neosho" Class
143 Neosho
144 Mississinewa
145 Hassayampa
146 Kawishiwi
147 Truckee
148 Ponchatoula

AOE—Fast Combat Support Ships

"Sacramento" Class
1 Sacramento
2 Camden
3 Seattle
4 Detroit

AOR—Replenishment Oilers

"Wichita" Class
1 Wichita
2 Milwaukee
3 Kansas City
4 Sabannah
5 Wabash
6 Kalamazoo
7 Roanoke

Fleet Support Ships

AD—Destroyer Tenders

"Dixie" Class
14 Dixie
15 Prairie

"Cascade" Type
16 Cascade

"Dixie" Type (cont'd)
17 Piedmont
18 Sierra
19 Yosemite

"Klondike" Class
24 Everglades
26 Shenandoah
29 Isle Royal
36 Bryce Canyon

"Gompers" Class
37 Samuel Gompers
38 Puget Sound

AGP—Gunboat Support Ship

1176 Graham County

AH—Hospital Ship

17 Sanctuary

APB—Self-Propelled Barracks Ships

37 Echols
39 Mercer
40 Nueces
47 Kingman

AR—Repair Ships

"Vulcan" Class
5 Vulcan
6 Ajax
7 Hector
8 Jason

"Delta "Class
9 Delta
12 Briareus

"Grand Canyon" Type
28 Grand Canyon

ARC—Cable Ships

"Neptune" Class
2 Neptune

Aeolus" Class
3 Aeolus
4 Thor

"Neptune" Class (cont'd)
6 Albert J. Myer

ARB—Battle Damage Repair Ships

5 Midas
7 Sarpedon

ARL—Landing Craft Repair Ships

8 Egeria
24 Sphinx
37 Indra

ARS—Salvage Ships

"Diver" Class
6 Escape
7 Grapple
8 Preserver
23 Deliver
24 Grasp
25 Safeguard
33 Clamp
34 Gear
38 Bolster
39 Conserver
40 Hoist
41 Opportune
42 Reclaimer
43 Recovery

AS—Submarine Tenders

"Fulton" Class
11 Fulton
12 Sperry
15 Bushnell
16 Howard W. Gilmore
17 Nereus
18 Orion
19 Proteus

"Hunley" Class
31 Hunley
32 Holland

"Simon Lake" Class
33 Simon Lake
34 Canopus

"L.Y. Spear" Class
36 L.Y. Spear
37 Dixon

ASR—Submarine Rescue Ships

"Chanticleer" Class
8 Coucal
9 Florikan
13 Kittiwake
14 Petrel
15 Sunbird
16 Tringa

"Pigeon" Class
21 Pigeon
22 Ortolan

ATA—Auxiliary Tugs

"Maricopa" Class
181 Accokeek
190 Samoset
193 Stallion
195 Tatnuck
213 Keywadin

ATF—Fleet Tugs

"Apache" Class
76 Ute
84 Cree
85 Lipan
86 Mataco
91 Seneca
92 Tawasa
96 Abnaki
100 Chowanoc
101 Cocopa
103 Hitchiti
105 Moctobi
106 Molala
110 Quapaw
113 Takelma
114 Tawakoni
149 Atakapa
156 Luiseno
157 Nipmuc
158 Mosospelea
159 Paiute
160 Papago
161 Salinan
162 Shakori

ATS—Salvage and Rescue Ships

"Edenton" Class
1 Edenton
2 Beaufort
3 Brunswick

ADVANCED SHIPBOARD SYSTEMS

ASROC (Anti-Submarine Rocket)
Anti-Submarine missile launched from surface ships with homing torpedo or nuclear depth charge as warhead. Launcher is Mk 10 or Mk 26 combination ASROC/surface-to-air missile launcher or Mk 16 eight-cell "pepper box". Installed in US Navy cruisers, destroyers, and frigates; Japanese, Italian, West German, and Canadian destroyer-type ships.
Weight of missile approximately 1 000 lbs; length 15 ft; diameter 1 ft; span of fins 2·5 ft; payload: Mk 44 or Mk 46 acoustic-homing torpedo or nuclear depth charge; range one to six miles.
Prime Contractors: Honeywell. Designation: RUR-5. Status: Operational.

AEGIS (formerly Advanced Surface Missile System)
Advanced surface-to-air missile system intended for use in planned strike cruisers (CSGN) scheduled for construction during the 1980s. To have a capability against high-performance aircraft and air-launched, anti-ship missiles. Launcher is Mk 26 with combined surface-to-air and ASW missile capability. Aegis will have an electronic scanning radar with fixed antennae, and will be capable of controlling friendly aircraft as well as detection. Additional components will include the UYK-7 computer (a component of the Naval Tactical Data System) and SPY-1 radar "illuminators" for missile guidance. Prime contractor: RCA. Status: Development (radars only; initially to use Standard missile). Being evaluated in *Norton Sound* (AVM 1).

BPDMS (Basic Point Defence Missile System)
Close-in air defence system employing the Sparrow AIM-7E or 7F series missile designated Sea Sparrow) and a modified ASROC-type "pepper box" launcher. Installed in aircraft carriers, ocean escorts, and amphibious ships. Status: Operational.

CAPTOR (Encapsulated Torpedo). Mk 46 torpedo inserted in mine casing. Prime contractor: Goodyear. Status: Operational.

CHAPARRAL Close-in Weapon System for defence against anti-ship missile and aircraft firing the Sidewinder AIM-9C missile. Adapted from Army MIM-72 Chaparral system.

CIWS (Close-in Weapon System) "Family" of advanced gun and missile systems to provide close-in or "point" defence for ships against anti-ship missiles and aircraft. Specific weapons being developed or evaluated under this programme include the Chaparral, Hybrid launcher, Pintle, Vulcan Air Defence, and Vulcan Phalanx described on this page as well as the OTO Melara 35 mm twin gun mount.

HYBRID Close-in Weapon System consisting of a launcher capable of firing different missiles against anti-ship missiles and aircraft, providing the opportunity of engaging a target at different ranges and aspects. Missiles being considered for the launcher include various Sidewinder and Sparrow modes, the Redeye (FIM-43) missile, and Hornet (AGM-64) missile.
Status: Development.

LAMPS (Light Airborne Multi-Purpose System)
Ship-launched helicopter intended for anti-submarine and missile-defence missions, with secondary roles of search-and-rescue and utility (e.g., parts and personnel transfer). For use aboard destroyer-type ships with hangars and certain amphibious warfare ships. Sensors include dipping sonar, magnetic airborne detection (MAD), and sonobuoys with digital relays to permit control and attack direction by launching ship. Radar provided to extend detection range vis-a-vis hostile surface missile ships. Weapons: 2 Mk 46 ASW torpedoes. Crew: pilot and 2 operators.
Status: 105 Kaman Seasprite helicopters being modified to SH-2D configuration as interim LAMPS. Deployed on cruisers, destroyers, and frigates.

NTDS (Naval Tactical Data System)
Combination of digital computers, displays, and transmission links to increase an individual ship commander's capability to assess tactical data and take action by integrating input from various sensors (e.g., radars) and providing display of tactical situation and the defence or offence options available. Data can be transmitted among NTDS-equipped ships. An automatic mode initiates action to respond to greatest threats in a tactical situation. Also can be linked to Airborne Tactical Data System (ATDS) in E-2 Hawkeye aircraft.
Fitted in all US Navy aircraft carriers, missile-armed cruisers, new amphibious command ships, and two frigates (*Voge* and *Koelsch*).
Status: Operational.

NATO Sea Sparrow Follow-on to BPDMS with a Target Acquisition System (TAS), powered director, smaller launcher, and control console combined with the Sea Sparrow missile. Planned for US amphibious and auxiliary ships.
Status: Under development; also a NATO co-operative programme with Belgium, Denmark, Italy, Netherlands and Norway. Being evaluated in *Downes* (DE 1070).

PINTLE Rapid-fire, close-in gun system similar to Vulcan/Phalanx weapon but firing 20 mm ammunition from a three-barrel light-weight "Gatling" gun.
Status: Development.

SINS (Ships' Inertial Navigation System) Navigation system providing exact navigation information without active input from terrestrial sources. Prime components are gyroscopes and accelerometers that relate movement of the ship in all directions, ship speed through water and over ocean floor, and true north to give a continuous report of the ship's position.
Status: Operational.

SUBROC (Submarine Rocket)
Anti-submarine missile launched from submarines with nuclear warhead. Launched from 21-inch torpedo tube. Carried in US Navy submarines of "Permit" and later classes with amidships torpedo tubes, BQQ-2 or BQQ-5 sonar and Mk 113 torpedo fire control systems. The missile is fired from the submerged submarine, rises up through the surface, travels through air towards the hostile submarine, and then re-enters the water to detonate.
Weight of missile approximately 4 000 lbs, length 21 ft; diameter 1·75 ft (maximum); estimated range 25 to 30 miles.
Prime contractor: Goodyear. Designation: UUM-44A. Status: Operational.

TASS (Towed Array Surveillance System) Ship-towed sonar array.

VULCAN/PHALANX
Rapid-fire, close-in gun system being developed to provide "last-ditch" defence against anti-ship missiles. Fires 20 mm ammunition from six-barrel "gatling" gun with "dynamic gun aiming" with fire control radar tracking projectiles and target(s). Theoretical rate of fire 3 000 rounds-per-minute. Initially planned for "Spruance" class destroyers, frigates, and some auxiliary ships; tentative programme calls for approx 360 units in 220 ships. Prime contractor: General Dynamics Corp, Pamona Division. Status: Development.

VULCAN/PHALANX on USS KING (DDG 41) *1974, US Navy*

VULCAN/PHALANX *1974, US Navy*

NAVAL MISSILES

Type(a)	System	Name	Launch Platform (tubes/launchers)	Range (n. miles)	Length (ft)	Weight (lbs)	Notes (b)
FBM	UGM-27B	Polaris A-2	"Lafayette" submarines (16)	1 500	31	30 000	thermo-nuclear; being replaced by Poseidon
FBM	UGM-27C	Polaris A-3	"Ethan Allen", "George Washington" submarines (16)	2 500	32	30,000	thermo-nuclear; MRV warhead
FBM	UGM-73A	Poseidon C-3	"Lafayette" submarines (16)	approx 2 500	34	65 000	thermo-nuclear; MIRV warhead
FBM	UGM-96A	Trident (I) C-4	Trident submarines (24)	approx 4 000	34		thermo-nuclear; MIRV warhead; under development
FBM	UGM	Trident (II) D-5	Trident submarines (24)	approx 6 000			proposed
SLCM	BGM-109		attack submarines	approx 1 500	18·25		nuclear; under development
SLCM	BGM-110		attack submarines	approx 1 500	18		nuclear; under development
SSM	RGM-66D/E	Standard-ARM	"Asheville" gunboats (4); some destroyers (ASROC launcher)	15	15	1 400	HE
SSM	RGM-84	Harpoon	surface ships	60	15	1 425	development; HE
SSM	RGM-84	Encapsulated Harpoon	attack submarines (torpedo tubes)	60	21		development; HE
SAM	RIM-2	Terrier	crusiers (1 or 2 twin); "Coontz" destroyers (1 twin); "Kitty Hawk", "America" carriers (2 twin)	20+	26·1	3 000	nuclear or HE
SAM	RIM-7	Sea Sparrow	surface ships	8	12	380	HE; Mk 25 or Mk 29 (NATO) multiple launcher; Basic Point Defence Missile System
SAM	RIM-8	Talos	"Albany", "Long Beach" cruisers (2 twin)	65+	31·2	7 000	nuclear or HE
SAM	RIM-24	Tartar	"Albany" cruisers (2 twin); "Chas. Adams" destroyers (1 twin or single); "Brooke" frigates (1 single); later cruisers	10+	15	1 425	HE
SAM	RIM-66	Standard-MR	Tartar replacement	20+	14	1 200	HE
SAM	RIM-67	Standard-ER	Terrier replacement	35+	26·2	2 900	HE
AAM	AIM-7	Sparrow III	F-4/F-8/F-14 fighters	9-16	12	500	
AAM	AIM-9C/D	Sidewinder-1B	F-4/F-8/F-14 fighters	8-15	9·5	185	
AAM	AIM-54	Phoenix	F-14 fighter (6)	60+	13	1 000	
AAM	AIM-95	Agile	fighters	2	7·8		development; close-in missile
ASM	AGM-12B	Bullpup-A	attack/patrol aircraft	7	10	571	
ASM	AGM-12C/D	Bullpup-B	attack/patrol aircraft	10	13·5	1 785	nuclear or HE
ASM	AGM-45	Shrike	attack/patrol aircraft	8-10	10	390	anti-radiation
ASM	AGM-53	Condor	attack/patrol aircraft	40-60	13·8	2 130	nuclear or HE
ASM	AGM-62	Walleye	attack/patrol aircraft	16	11·2	1 100	nuclear or HE; larger Walleye II has 35-mile range (2 400 lbs)
ASM	AGM-78	Standard ARM	attack/patrol aircraft	35	15		anti-radiation
ASM	AGM-83	Bulldog	attack/patrol aircraft	35			modified Bullpup
ASM	AGM-84	Harpoon	attack/patrol aircraft	60	12·6	1 115	development; HE
ASM	AGM-88	Harm	attack/patrol aircraft				development; anti-radiation; larger than Shrike
ASW	RUR-5	ASROC	cruisers, destroyers, frigates	1-6	15	1 000	nuclear depth charge, Mk 44, or Mk 46 torpedo; multiple launcher in most ships; Mk 26 launcher in later ships; 570 lbs with Mk 46
ASW	UUM-44	SUBROC	"Permit" and later attack submarines (torpedo tubes)	25-30	21	4 000	nuclear

(a) FBM=Fleet Ballistic Missile; SLCM=Submarine-Launched Cruise Missile= SSM= Surface-to-Surface Missile; SAM=Surface-to-Air Missile; AAM=Air-to-Air Missile; ASM=Air-ro-Surface Missile; ASW=Anti-Submarine Warfare.
(b) MRV=Multiple Re-entry Vehicle; MIRV=Multiple Independently-targeted Re-entry Vehicle.

TORPEDOES

Designation	Launch Platforms	Weight (pounds)	Length (feet)	Diameter (inches)	Propulsion	Guidance	Notes
Mk 37 Mod 2	**Submarines**	1 690	13·5	19	Electric	Wire	Anti-submarine
Mk 37 Mod 3	**Submarines**	1 400	11·3	19	Electric	Active-passive acoustic homing	Anti-submarine
Mk 44 Mod 1	Surface ships (Mk 32 tubes and ASROC); aircraft	433	8·5	12·75	Electric	Active acoustic homing	Anti-submarine
Mk 45 Mod 1 & Mod 2 (ASTOR)	**Submarines**	2 400	19·9	19	Electric	Wire	Anti-submarine; nuclear warhead; 10+ mile range
Mk 46 Mod 0	Surface ships (Mk 32 tubes and ASROC); aircraft	580	8·4	12·75	Solid-propellant	Active-passive acoustic homing	Anti-submarine; successor to Mk 44
Mk 46 Mod 1	Surface ships (Mk 32 tubes and ASROC); aircraft	512	8·4	12·75	Liquid mono-propellant	Active-passive acoustic homing	Anti-submarine; successor to Mk 44
Mk 48 Mod 1	**Submarines**	approx 3 600	19	21	Liquid mono-propellant	Wire/terminal acoustic homing	Anti-submarine and anti-shipping; larger warhead than Mod 0; in production by Gould Inc (formerly Clevite); range approx 25 miles
Mk 48 Mod 2	**Submarines**	approx 3 600	19	21	Liquid mono-propellant	Wire/terminal acoustic homing	Anti-submarine and anti-shipping; version of Mod 0; Westinghouse; effort terminated in favour of Mod 1; range approx 25 miles

STRATEGIC MISSILE SUBMARINES

The US Navy's 41 nuclear-propelled submarines armed with Polaris and Poseidon missiles are a primary component of the nation's strategic offensive forces. According to Secretary of Defense James R. Schlesinger, the Polaris-Poseidon submarines at sea are the least vulnerable element of US strategic forces and are likely to remain so as far ahead as can be seen at this time. In comparison with US land-based strategic bombers and land-based intercontinental missiles, the Submarine-Launched Ballistic Missile (SLBM) force contributes some 30 per cent of the estimated 2 150 launch vehicles (bombers and missiles) and, with completion of the Poseidon conversion programme, about 55 per cent of the 9 000 separate warheads or re-entry vehicles.
The Navy has begun a programme to construct ten Trident strategic missile submarines. These SLBM platforms, armed with a longer-range missile that the Polaris/Poseidon, will improve targeting options against the Soviet Union, increase submarine survivability against any Soviet "breakthrough" in anti-submarine warfare, and provide a replacement for the older Polaris submarine. However, the large size and comparatively conservative design of the Trident submarines have brought criticism from several quarters, including some proponents of moving an increasing portion of the US strategic deterrence to sea. Other problems associated with the Trident programme include the high construction costs (related to submarine size) and the limited nuclear submarine construction capability of US shipyards. These problems have led to a further slowdown in the planned construction schedule. Early planning by the Department of Defense proposed a three-submarine-per-year building rate; in 1974 the Department of Defense slowed this rate by proposing a two-per-year schedule, and in early 1975 this was revised again to an alternating 1-2-1-2-1-2-1 plan. This last schedule would commission the tenth Trident submarine about 1985, if schedules were met. At that time the ten oldest Polaris submarines would be 22 and 25 years old.
The available technical data on the Trident submarines is provided below. These submarines as well as some of the Poseidon submarines are to be fitted with the so-called Trident I (C-4) missile with an estimated range of 3 000 to 4 000 nautical miles and a multiple-warhead capability. The latter range would permit more than a four-fold increase in submarine operating areas while still targeting the Soviet Union.
Development of the 6 000-nautical mile Trident II (D-5) missile has been relegated to studies. The STRAT-X study of the late 1960s, which originally proposed the Trident programme, specifically called for the longer-range weapon. Subsequently, in February 1972 the Department of Defense accelerated the Trident programme because of high SLBM survivability and, employing Poseidon missile technology, divided the Trident effort into the Phase I and Phase II. This initial speed up helped dictate the conservative design of the Trident submarine and the reduced missile range.

SAM RAYBURN (SSBN 635) entering Holy Loch, Scotland. *1972, United States Navy*

NARWHAL PROGRAMME. The Fiscal Year 1975 budget requested funds to initiate design of a smaller and less costly SSBN than the Trident design (described below). Poseidon submarines could be rearmed with the Trident I missile to place that weapon at sea at a comparatively low cost, but the design and age of these submarines will make them comparatively vulnerable to advanced detection systems in the 1980s and 1990s. Consequently, additional SSBNs beyond the ten planned Trident submarines would have to be constructed to maintain a significant force of strategic missiles at sea as the older Polaris-Poseidon submarines are phased out. The characteristics of the new SSBN have not been determined, but the submarine would probably be only slightly larger than the "Lafayette" class ballistic missile submarines and would have a *Narwhal*-type nuclear reactor plant. According to official statements, the "Narwhal" SSBN would have about 16 missile tubes compared to the 24-tube Trident SSBN design.

STRATEGIC CRUISE MISSILE. The US Navy is studying the feasibility of a strategic cruise missile, a submarine-launched weapon with ram-jet propulsion that could deliver nuclear warheads at long range. A shorter range (*circa* 300-mile) version of the weapon with a conventional warhead could be employed as an over-the-horizon anti-ship weapon.
According to a 1972 statement by the Director Defense Research & Engineering: "Informal Navy studies with respect to the development of sea-based strategic cruise missiles have led us to the conclusion that such a missile could effectively diversify our strategic forces. Development of a strategic cruise missile system is within the state of the art and is technically feasible wtihout major new developments".
The strategic cruise missile would have a low-level, terrain following flight path over land, much like that of a manned bomber in contrast to the ballistic trajectory of a Polaris/Poseidon missile.

NOMENCLATURE. FBM submarines are named for "famous Americans", including South American and Hawaiian leaders as well as Europeans who aided the United States war for independence.

(10) FLEET BALLISTIC MISSILE SUBMARINES (SSBN): TRIDENT PROGRAMME

No	*Programme*	*Commission*
SSBN 726	Fiscal Year 1974 programme	1979
SSBN 727	Fiscal Year 1975 programme	
SSBN 728	Fiscal Year 1975 programme	
SSBN 729	Proposed FY 1976 programme	
SSBN 730	Planned FY 1977 programme	
SSBN 731	Planned FY 1977 programme	
SSBN 732	Planned FY 1978 programme	
SSBN 733	Planned FY 1979 programme	
SSBN 734	Planned FY 1979 programme	
SSBN 735	Planned FY 1980 programme	

Displacement, tons	approx to 12 000 surface; approx 15 000 submerged
Length, feet	560
Missiles	24 tubes for Trident I submarine-launched ballistic missile
Main engines	geared turbines; 1 shaft
Reactors	1 pressurised-water cooled S6G (General Electric)
Complement	150 (14 officers, 136 enlisted men)

These submarines will be the largest undersea craft yet constructed, being significantly larger than the Soviet "Delta" class missile submarines which are now the largest afloat. The lead submarine was contracted to the Electric Boat Division of the General Dynamics Corp (Groton, Connecticut) on 25 July 1974. The only other US shipyard currently capable of building submarines of this class is the Newport News SB & DD Co in Virginia. Both yards are also involved in construction of contracts for the SSBN 727 and SSBN 728 were awarded to Electric Boat on 28 Feb 1975 the "Los Angeles" class (SSN 688) attack submarines. The above characteristics are unofficial estimates based on statements of Navy officials before Congressional committees.

The principal characteristics of the Trident concept as proposed were: (1) long-range missile (circa 6 000 miles) to permit targeting the Soviet Union while the submarine cruises in remote areas, making effective ASW virtually impossible for the foreseeable future, (2) extremely quiet submarines, (3) a high at-sea to in-port ratio, (4) high systems reliability, (5) dedicated systems design to provide the most effective submarine, and (6) underwater launch capability. Modular construction techniques could greatly facilitate maintenance, overhaul, and subsequent modernisation.

DESIGN. The size of the Trident submarine is dictated primarily by the larger size missile required for 6 000-mile range and the larger reactor plant to drive the ship. The submarine will have 24 tubes in a vertical position penetrating the main submarine pressure hull. Early studies had indicated several advantages would accrue from advanced design concepts, such as housing the missiles in a horizontal position external to the main pressure hull. However, a conservative submarine design was adopted.

DESIGNATION. Initially the hull number SSBN 711 was planned for the first Trident submarine. However, on 21 Feb 1974 the designation SSBN 1 was assigned, confusing the Navy's submarine designation system which goes back to the USS *Holland* (SS 1), commissioned in 1900. Subsequently, the designation was again changed on 10 Apr 1974, with the "block" SSBN 726-735 being reserved for the Trident programme.

FISCAL. Construction of the lead Trident SSBN was funded at $781 000 000 in the Fiscal Year 1974 budget; SSBN 727 and SSBN 728 were funded at $604 000 000 per submarine ($281 000 000 in long-lead component Funding in FY 1974 and $927 000 000 requested in FY 1975). An additional $25 000 000 was requested in the "Supplemental" FY 1974 budget to "protect the option" for the SSBN 727 and SSBN 728.
The FY 1976 budget requests $290 000 000 to cover projected cost increases for SSBN 726-728, $560 000 000 to complete funding of the SSBN 729, and $43 000 000 in advance funding for SSBN 730-732.
These requests do not include funding for submarine component development and missile development. The FY 1976 budget requests $84 000 000 for submarine research, $733 000 000 for missile research, $237 000 000 for Trident I missile production start-up, and $195 000 000 for facility construction.

MISSILES. The Trident submarines will be armed initially with the Trident I missile, scheduled to become operational late in 1978. This missile is expected to have a range of 3 000 to 4 000 nautical miles, a range already exceeded by the SS-N-8 missile in the Soviet "Delta" class submarines. However, the US missile will have a MIRV warhead while at this writing no statements by US officials have indicated that the SS-N-8 has a multiple warhead (the SS-N-6 missile associate with the "Yankee" class submarine has been tested with a MRV warhead).
The Trident missile is expected to carry more than the 10 to 14 re-entry vehicles that the Poseidon can lift. In addition, the Mk 500 MaRV (Maneuvering Re-entry Vehicle) is under development for the purpose of demonstrating its compatability with the Trident I missile. This re-entry vehicle is intended to evade ABM interceptor missiles and is not terminally guided to increase its accuracy. The Mk 500 MaRV is expected to be less accurate than previous submarine-launched ballistic missile warheads, according to official statements.

Strategic Missile Submarines—*Continued*

31 FLEET BALLISTIC MISSILE SUBMARINES (FBM): "LAFAYETTE" CLASS

Name	*No.*	*Builder*	*Laid down*	*Launched*	*Commissioned*
***LAFAYETTE**	SSBN 616	General Dynamics (Electric Boat Div)	17 Jan 1961	8 May 1962	23 Apr 1963
***ALEXANDER HAMILTON**	SSBN 617	General Dynamics (Electric Boat Div)	26 June 1961	18 Aug 1962	27 June 1963
***ANDREW JACKSON**	SSBN 619	Mare Island Naval Shipyard	26 Apr 1961	15 Sep 1962	3 July 1963
***JOHN ADAMS**	SSBN 620	Portsmouth Naval Shipyard	19 May 1961	12 Jan 1963	12 May 1964
***JAMES MONROE**	SSBN 622	Newport News Shipbuilding & DD Co	31 July 1961	4 Aug 1962	7 Dec 1963
***NATHAN HALE**	SSBN 623	General Dynamics (Electric Boat Div)	2 Oct 1961	12 Jan 1963	23 Nov 1963
***WOODROW WILSON**	SSBN 624	Mare Island Naval Shipyard	13 Sep 1961	22 Feb 1963	27 Dec 1963
***HENRY CLAY**	SSBN 625	Newport News Shipbuilding & DD Co	23 Oct 1961	30 Nov 1962	20 Feb 1964
***DANIEL WEBSTER**	SSBN 626	General Dynamics (Electric Boat Div)	28 Dec 1961	27 Apr 1963	9 Apr 1964
***JAMES MADISON**	SSBN 627	Newport News Shipbuilding & DD Co	5 Mar 1962	15 Mar 1963	28 July 1964
***TECUMSEH**	SSBN 628	General Dynamics (Electric Boat Div)	1 June 1962	22 June 1963	29 May 1964
***DANIEL BOONE**	SSBN 629	Mare Island Naval Shipyard	6 Feb 1962	22 June 1963	23 Apr 1964
***JOHN C. CALHOUN**	SSBN 630	Newport News Shipbuilding & DD Co	4 June 1962	22 June 1963	15 Sep 1964
***ULYSSES S. GRANT**	SSBN 631	General Dynamics (Electric Boat Div)	18 Aug 1962	2 Nov 1963	17 July 1964
***VON STEUBEN**	SSBN 632	Newport News Shipbuilding & DD Co	4 Sep 1962	18 Oct 1963	30 Sep 1964
***CASIMIR PULASKI**	SSBN 633	General Dynamics (Electric Boat Div)	12 Jan 1963	1 Feb 1964	14 Aug 1964
***STONEWALL JACKSON**	SSBN 634	Mare Island Naval Shipyard	4 July 1962	30 Nov 1963	26 Aug 1964
***SAM RAYBURN**	SSBN 635	Newport News Shipbuilding & DD Co	3 Dec 1962	20 Dec 1963	2 Dec 1964
***NATHANAEL GREENE**	SSBN 636	Portsmouth Naval Shipyard	21 May 1962	12 May 1964	19 Dec 1964
***BENJAMIN FRANKLIN**	SSBN 640	General Dynamics (Electric Boat Div)	25 May 1963	5 Dec 1964	22 Oct 1965
***SIMON BOLIVAR**	SSBN 641	Newport News Shipbuilding & DD Co	17 Apr 1963	22 Aug 1964	29 Oct 1965
***KAMEHAMEHA**	SSBN 642	Mare Island Naval Shipyard	2 May 1963	16 Jan 1965	10 Dec 1965
***GEORGE BANCROFT**	SSBN 643	General Dynamics (Electric Boat Div)	24 Aug 1963	20 Mar 1965	22 Jan 1966
***LEWIS AND CLARK**	SSBN 644	Newport News Shipbuilding & DD Co	29 July 1963	21 Nov 1964	22 Dec 1965
***JAMES K. POLK**	SSBN 645	General Dynamics (Electric Boat Div)	23 Nov 1963	22 May 1965	16 Apr 1966
***GEORGE C. MARSHALL**	SSBN 654	Newport News Shipbuilding & DD Co	2 Mar 1964	21 May 1965	29 Apr 1966
***HENRY L. STIMSON**	SSBN 655	General Dynamics (Electric Boat Div)	4 Apr 1964	13 Nov 1965	20 Aug 1966
***GEORGE WASHINGTON CARVER**	SSBN 656	Newport News Shipbuilding & DD Co	24 Aug 1964	14 Aug 1965	15 June 1956
***FRANCIS SCOTT KEY**	SSBN 657	General Dynamics (Electric Boat Div)	5 Dec 1964	23 Apr 1966	3 Dec 1966
***MARIANO G. VALLEJO**	SSBN 658	Mare Island Naval Shipyard	7 July 1964	23 Oct 1965	16 Dec 1966
***WILL ROGERS**	SSBN 659	General Dynamics (Electric Boat Div)	20 Mar 1965	21 July 1966	1 Apr 1967

Displacement, tons	6 650 light surface; 7 320 standard surface; 8 250 submerged
Length, feet (*metres*)	425 (*129·5*) oa
Beam, feet (*metres*)	33 (*10·1*)
Draught, feet (*metres*)	31·5 (*9·6*)
Missile launchers	16 tubes for Polaris A-3 or Poseidon C-3 (see *Missile* notes)
Torpedo tubes	4—21 inch (*533 mm*) forward
Main engines	2 geared turbines 15 000 shp; 1 shaft
Nuclear reactor	1 pressurised-water cooled S5W (Westinghouse)
Speed, knots	20 surface; approx 30 submerged
Complement	145 (17 officers, 128 enlisted men)

These Fleet Ballistic Missile (FBM) submarines are the largest undersea craft to be completed in the West. The first four submarines (SSBN 616-620) of this class were authorised in the Fiscal Year 1961 shipbuilding programme with five additional submarines (SSBN 622-626) authorised in a supplemental FY 1961 programme; SSBN 627-636 (ten) in FY 1962, SSBN 640-645 (six) in FY 1963, and SSBN 654-659 (six) in FY 1964. Cost for the earlier ships of this class was approximately $109 500 000 per submarine.

CLASSIFICATION. The *Benjamin Franklin* and later submarines are officially considered a separate class; however, differences are minimal (eg, quieter machinery) and all 31 submarines are generally considered as a single class.

DESIGN. The *Daniel Webster* has diving planes mounted on bow in lieu of sail-mounted planes, the only "16-tube" FBM submarine of any navy with this configuration. (See photograph in 1974-1975 and previous editions).

ENGINEERING. The *Benjamin Franklin* and subsequent submarines of this class have been fitted with quieter machinery. All SSBNs have diesel-electric stand-by machinery, snorkels, and "outboard" auxiliary propeller for emergency use.
The nuclear cores inserted in refuelling these submarines during the late 1960s and early 1970s cost approximately $3 500 000 and provide energy for approximately 400 000 miles.

MISSILES. The first eight ships of this class were fitted with the Polaris A-2 missile (1 725 statute mile range) and the 23 later ships with the Polaris A-3 missile (2 880 statute mile range).
The SSBN 620 and SSBN 622-625 (5 ships) were rearmed with the Polaris A-3 missile during overhaul-refuellings from 1968 to 1970. Subsequently, all converted to carry the Poseidon C-3 missile.
The *James Madison* was the first submarine to undergo conversion to carry the Poseidon missile. She began conversion in February 1969 and was completed in June 1970. (See conversion table on following page.)
Poseidon conversion, overhaul, and reactor refuelling are conducted simultaneously. In addition to changes in missile tubes to accommodate larger Poseidon, the conversion provides replacement of Mk 84 fire control system with Mk 88 system. The Poseidon conversion programme was scheduled to complete in 1977.
Some of the options for the Trident missile programme include rearming submarines of this class with an advanced missile, providing a longer range capability than available with the Poseidon missile.

ULYSSES S. GRANT (SSBN 631) — *1969, United States Navy*

ULYSSES S. GRANT (SSBN 631) in floating dry dock — *1974, US Navy, PH1 Bob Woods*

Strategic Missile Submarines—*Continued*

THOMAS A. EDISON (SSBN 610), in rear, passing FRANCIS SCOTT KEY (SSBN 657) in Panama Canal *1973, United States Navy*

"LAFAYETTE" CLASS—*continued*

NAVIGATION. FBM submarines are equipped with an elaborate Ship's Inertial Navigation System (SINS), a system of gyroscopes and accelerometers which relates movement of the ship in all directions, true speed through the water and over the ocean floor, and true north to give a continuous report of the submarine's position. The system includes the capability of both optical and electronic checks. Navigation data produced by SINS can be provided to each missile's guidance package until the instant the missile is fired.
The Polaris-armed submarines have two Mk 2 Mod 3 SINS inertial navigation systems; as converted all Poseidon submarines have three Mk 2 Mod 4 SINS; all fitted with navigational satellite receivers.

OPERATIONAL. The *Andrew Jackson* launched the first Polaris A-3 missile from a submarine on 26 Oct 1963. The *Daniel Webster* was the first submarine to deploy with the A-3 missile, beginning her first patrol on 28 Sep 1964. The *Daniel Boone* was the first Polaris submarine to deploy to the Pacific, beginning her first patrol with the A-3 missile on 25 Dec 1964. The *James Madison* launched the first Poseidon C-3 missile from a submarine on 3 Aug 1970; the submarine began the first Poseidon deployment on 31 Mar 1971.

PERSONNEL. Each FBM submarine is assigned two alternating crews designated "Blue" and "Gold". Each crew mans the submarine during a 60-day patrol and partially assists during the intermediate 28-day refit alongside a Polaris tender. Beginning in January 1975 the submarines began making brief port visits mid-way through the 60-day patrol to break the monotony of the patrols. The "off-duty" crew is undergoing training or is on leave. All FBM submarines are fully air conditioned and the newer ships have elaborate crew study and recreation facilities.

POSEIDON CONVERSION SCHEDULE

No.	Programme	Conversion Yard	Start	Complete
SSBN 616	FY 1973	General Dynamics Corp (Electric Boat)	Oct 1972	Nov 1974
SSBN 617	FY 1973	Newport News SB & DD Co.	Jan 1973	Mar 1975
SSBN 619	FY 1973	General Dynamics Corp (Electric Boat)	Mar 1973	1975
SSBN 620	FY 1974	Portsmouth Naval Shipyard	Feb 1974	1975
SSBN 622	FY 1975		1975	
SSBN 623	FY 1973	Puget Sound Naval Shipyard	June 1973	1975
SSBN 624	FY 1974	Newport News SB & DD Co	Oct 1973	1975
SSBN 625	FY 1975	Newport News SB & DD Co	1975	
SSBN 626	FY 1975	General Dynamics Corp (Electric Boat)	1975	
SSBN 627	FY 1968	General Dynamics Corp (Electric Boat)	Feb 1969	June 1970
SSBN 628	FY 1970	Newport News SB & DD Co	Nov 1969	Feb 1971
SSBN 629	FY 1968	Newport News SB & DD Co	May 1969	Aug 1970
SSBN 630	FY 1969	Mare Island Naval Shipyard	Aug 1969	Feb 1971
SSBN 631	FY 1970	Puget Sound Naval Shipyard	Oct 1969	Dec 1970
SSBN 632	FY 1969	General Dynamics Corp (Electric Boat)	July 1969	Nov 1970
SSBN 633	FY 1970	General Dynamics Corp (Electric Boat)	Jan 1970	Apr 1971
SSBN 634	FY 1971	General Dynamics (Electric Boat)	July 1970	Oct 1971
SSBN 635	FY 1970	Portsmouth Naval Shipyard	Jan 1970	Sep 1971
SSBN 636	FY 1971	Newport News SB & DD Co	July 1970	Sep 1971
SSBN 640	FY 1971	General Dynamics Corp (Electric Boat)	Feb 1971	May 1972
SSBN 641	FY 1971	Newport News SB & DD Co	Feb 1971	May 1972
SSBN 642	FY 1972	General Dynamics Corp (Electric Boat)	July 1971	Oct 1972
SSBN 643	FY 1971	Portsmouth Naval Shipyard	Apr 1971	Aug 1972
SSBN 644	FY 1971	Puget Sound Naval Shipyard	Apr 1971	July 1972
SSBN 645	FY 1972	Newport News SB & DD Co	July 1971	Nov 1972
SSBN 654	FY 1972	Puget Sound Naval Shipyard	Sep 1971	Feb 1973
SSBN 655	FY 1972	Newport News SB & DD Co	Nov 1971	Mar 1973
SSBN 656	FY 1972	General Dynamics Corp (Electric Boat)	Nov 1971	Apr 1973
SSBN 657	FY 1972	Puget Sound Naval Shipyard	Feb 1972	Apr 1973
SSBN 658	FY 1973	Newport News SB & DD Co	Aug 1972	Dec 1973
SSBN 659	FY 1973	Portsmouth Naval Shipyard	Oct 1972	Feb 1974

PHOTOGRAPHS. Fleet ballistic missile submarines converted to Poseidon are virtually indistinguishable from pre-conversion appearance. FBM submarines rarely operate on the surface and photographs are difficult to obtain. On the previous page the *Ulysses S. Grant* is seen steaming out of Pearl Harbour, Hawaii, and in a floating dry dock in Holy Loch, Scotland. Note the landing craft and tug assisting the *Tecumseh* (below) at Arpa Harbour, Guam.

MARIANO C. VALLEJO (SSBN 658) *1974, United States Navy*

TECUMSEH (SSBN 628) approaching HUNLEY (AS 19) *United States Navy*

Strategic **Missile Submarines** —*continued*

5 FLEET BALLISTIC MISSILE SUBMARINES (SSBN): "ETHAN ALLEN" CLASS

Name	*No.*	*Builder*	*Laid down*	*Launched*	*Commissioned*
***ETHAN ALLEN**	SSBN 608	General Dynamics (Electric Boat Div, Groton)	14 Sep 1959	22 Nov 1960	8 Aug 1961
***SAM HOUSTON**	SSBN 609	Newport News Shipbuilding & DD Co	28 Dec 1959	2 Feb 1961	6 Mar 1962
***THOMAS A. EDISON**	SSBN 610	General Dynamics (Electric Boat Div, Groton)	15 Mar 1960	15 June 1961	10 Mar 1962
***JOHN MARSHALL**	SSBN 611	Newport News Shipbuilding & DD Co	4 Apr 1960	15 July 1961	21 May 1962
***THOMAS JEFFERSON**	SSBN 618	Newport News Shipbuilding & DD Co	3 Feb 1961	24 Feb 1962	4 Jan 1963

Displacement, tons	6 900 standard surface; 7 900 submerged
Length, feet (*metres*)	410·5 (*125·1*) oa
Beam, feet (*metres*)	33 (*10·1*)
Draught, feet (*metres*)	30 (*9·4*)
Missile launchers	16 tubes for Polaris A-3
Torpedo tubes	4—21 inch (*533 mm*) forward
Main engines	2 geared turbines (General Electric); 15 000 shp; 1 shaft
Nuclear reactor	1 pressurised-water cooled S5W (Westinghouse)
Speed, knots	20 surface; approx 30 submerged
Complement	140 (12 officers, 128 enlisted men)

These submarines were designed specifically for the FBM role and are larger and better arranged than the earlier "George Washington" class submarines. The first four ships of this class were authorised in the Fiscal Year 1959 programme; the *Thomas Jefferson* (which is out of numerical sequence) was in the FY 1961 programme. These submarines and the previous "George Washington" class will not be converted to carry the Poseidon missile because of material limitations and the age they would be after conversion. Also the "George Washington" class submarines are depth limited compared to the later FBM classes which, according to official statements, are based on the "Permit" SSN design.

DESIGN. These submarines and the subsequent "Lafayette" class are deep-diving submarines with a depth capability similar to the "Permit" class attack submarines; pressure hulls of HY-80 steel.

JOHN MARSHALL (SSBN 611) *1967, United States Navy*

MISSILES. These ships were initially armed with the Polaris A-2 missile (1 725 statute mile range). The *Ethan Allan* launched the first A-2 missile fired from a submarine on 23 Oct 1961. She was the first submarine to deploy with the A-2 missile, beginning her first patrol on 26 June 1962. The *Ethan Allan* fired a Polaris A-2 missile in the Christmas Island Pacific Test Area on 6 May 1962 in what was the first complete US test of a ballistic missile including detonation of the nuclear warhead. All five of these ships have been modified to fire the A-3 missile (2,880 statute mile range). They will not be fitted with the advanced Poseidon missile. Originally fitted with Mk 80 fire control system and compressed air missile ejectors; provided with Mk 84 fire control systems and gas-steam missile ejectors with A-3 missile.

NAVIGATION. Fitted with two Mk 2 Mod 3 Ship's Inertial Navigation Systems (SINS) and navigational satellite receiver.

PERSONNEL. Alternating "Blue" and "Gold" crews are assigned to these submarines as in "Lafayette" class submarines.

PHOTOGRAPHS. Note sail number is painted out in view of *Ethan Allen* underway off Rota, Spain.

ETHAN ALLEN (SSBN 608) *1971, United States Navy*

ETHAN ALLEN (SSBN 608) *1971, United States Navy*

Strategic Missile Submarines—*Continued*

5 FLEET BALLISTIC MISSILE SUBMARINES (SSBN): "GEORGE WASHINGTON" CLASS

Name	No.	Builder	Laid down	Launched	Commissioned
*GEORGE WASHINGTON	SSBN 598	General Dynamics (Electric Boat Div, Groton)	1 Nov 1957	9 June 1959	30 Dec 1959
*PATRICK HENRY	SSBN 599	General Dynamics (Electric Boat Div, Groton)	27 May 1958	22 Sep 1959	9 Apr 1960
*THEODORE ROOSEVELT	SSBN 600	Mare Island Naval Shipyard	20 May 1958	3 Oct 1959	13 Feb 1961
*ROBERT E. LEE	SSBN 601	Newport News Shipbuilding & DD Co	25 Aug 1958	18 Dec 1959	16 Sep 1960
*ABRAHAM LINCOLN	SSBN 602	Portsmouth Naval Shipyard	1 Nov 1958	14 May 1960	11 Mar 1961

Displacement, tons	5 900 standard surface; 6 700 submerged
Length, feet (*metres*)	381·7 (*115·8*) oa
Beam, feet (*metres*)	33 (*10·1*)
Draught, feet (*metres*)	29 (*8·8*)
Missile launchers	16 tubes for Polaris A-3
Torpedo tubes	6—21 inch (*533 mm*) forward
Main engines	2 geared turbines (General Electric); 15 000 shp; 1 shaft
Nuclear reactor	1 pressurised-water cooled S5W (Westinghouse)
Speed, knots	20 surface; approx 30 submerged
Complement	140 (12 officers, 128 enlisted men)

The *George Washington* was the West's first ship to be armed with ballistic missiles. A supplement to the Fiscal Year 1958 new construction programme signed on 11 Feb 1958 provided for the construction of the first three Fleet Ballistic Missile (FBM) submarines. The Navy had already ordered the just-begun attack submarine *Scorpion* (SSN 589) to be completed as a missile submarine on 31 Dec 1957, the hull was redesignated SSBN 598 and completed as the *George Washington*. The *Patrick Henry* similarly was re-ordered on the last day of 1957, her materials having originally been intended for the not-yet-started SSN 590. These submarines and three sister ships (two authorised in FY 1959) were built to a modified "Skipjack" class design with almost 130 feet being added to the original design to accommodate two rows of eight missile tubes, fore control and naivgation equipment, and auxiliary machinery.

ENGINEERING. The *George Washington* was the first FBM submarine to be overhauled and "refuelled". During her 4½ years of operation on her initial reactor core she carried out 15 submerged missile patrols and steamed more than 100 000 miles.

MISSILES. These ships were initially armed with the Polaris A-1 missile (1 380 statute mile range). The *George Washington* successfully fired two Polaris A-1 missiles while submerged off Cape Canaveral (Kennedy) on 20 July 1960 in the first underwater launching of a ballistic missile from a US submarine. She departed on her initial patrol on 15 Nov 1960 and remained submerged for 66 days, 10 hours. All five submarines of this class have been refitted to fire the improved Polaris A-3 missile (2 880 statute mile range). Missile refit and first reactor refuelling were accomplished simultaneously during overhaul. *George Washington* from 20 June 1964 to 2 Feb 1966, *Patrick Henry* from 4 Jan 1965 to 21 July 1966, *Theodore Roosevelt* from 28 July 1965 to 14 Jan 1967, *Robert E. Lee* from 23 Feb 1965 to 2 July 1966, and *Abraham Lincoln* from 25 Oct 1965 to 3 June 1967, four at Electric Boat yard in Groton, Connecticut, and *Robert E. Lee* at Mare Island Naval Shipyard (California). These submarines all have Mk 84 fire control systems and gas-steam missile ejectors (originally fitted with Mk 80 fire control systems and compressed air missile ejectors, changed during A-3 missile refit).
These submarines will not be modified to carry and launch the advanced Poseidon ballistic missile.

GEORGE WASHINGTON (SSBN 598) *United States Navy*

ABRAHAM LINCOLN (SSBN 602) *United States Navy*

NAVIGATION. Fitted with three Mk 2 Mod 4 Ship's Inertial Navigation Systems (SINS) and navigational satellite receiver.

PERSONNEL. Alternating "Blue" and "Gold" crews are assigned to these submarines as in "Lafayette" class submarines.

PHOTOGRAPHS. Note that "hump" of hull extension for housing missile tubes is more pronounced in these submarines than later classes. Note the bitts and capstans visible in view of *Abraham Lincoln* while mooring; as in SSNs, most hull projects are removable or retractable to provide a "clean" hull and reduce noise as submarine passes through water.

ROBERT E. LEE (SSBN 601) ***1966, United States Navy***

SUBMARINES

The US Navy's submarine forces consist of two principal categories: strategic missile submarines (SSBN), listed in the previous section, and attack submarines (SS and SSN).

The Navy's attack submarine force has apparently reached a 25-year nadir with some 75 nuclear and diesel attack, and special purpose submarines in commission on 1 January 1975. The number had dipped to a post-World War II low of 72 submarines in commission on the eve of the Korean War in mid-1950. US attack submarine construction during the next decade is expected to continue at the rate of 2½ submarines per year. This schedule will probably keep ahead of the retirement of older units; however, such a construction programme cannot attain the force level of about 90 nuclear attack submarines which the Department of Defense considers necessary for Navy mission requirements. Although the new nuclear attack submarines have many capabilities superior to their predecessors, the quality and quantity of the opposing Soviet surface and undersea units have improved considerably.

Construction of the 28 submarines that had been funded as of 1 January 1975 was being slowed by the late delivery of component equipment and problems in the hiring of shipyard workers. Further complicating the situation will be the start-up of the Trident missile submarine programme and the loss of the Litton/Ingalls yard at Pascagoula, Mississippi, which delivered its last nuclear submarine in 1974. This leaves only two shipyards in the United States building nuclear submarines. (No diesel-propelled submarines have been built in the United States since 1959).

There are no advanced nuclear attack submarine designs now planned by the US Navy beyond the "Los Angeles" class. A follow-on to the "Los Angeles" class can be expected to be developed by the late 1970s when about 40 of that design have been ordered. Early in 1975, Secretary of Defense Schlesinger stated that: "Looking to the longer term, we are examining the feasibility and desirability of building a new class of SSNs. We are particularly interested in a less costly SSN".

Current SSN construction is limited to the "Los Angeles" class, a large submarine intended in part to counter the high-speed submarines of the Soviet Navy. US nuclear submarines' classes had grown steadily in size since the "Skipjack" class of 1959 while retaining the same S5W reactor plant; accordingly, submarine performance has deteriorated. In contrast, Soviet attack submarine speeds appear to have steadily increased. Unofficial sources indicate that the lack of US progress in submarine reactor development required modification of a surface ship nuclear reactor plant for use in the "Los Angeles" class which, in turn, necessitated a larger submarine.

MISSIONS. Nuclear-powered attack submarines are primarily considered anti-submarine platforms because of their ability to operate covertly, especially in waters which are otherwise under the control of enemy surface and air forces where other US anti-submarine forces could not operate.

The US Navy is investigating the use of SSNs in other roles, including the open-ocean escorting of high-value surface ships such as aircraft carriers. Also, the increasing capabilities and oceanic operations of Soviet surface forces have caused renewed US Navy interest in the employment of the submarines in the antiship role, armed with torpedoes and anti-ship missiles.

ANTI-SHIP MISSILES. An encapsulated version of the Harpoon anti-ship missile is being developed for launching from submarines. The Harpoon, also capable of surface ship and aircraft launch, is a 15-foot weapon carrying a conventional high-explosive warhead. In the encapsulated version, the Harpoon is launched from a torpedo tube and travels to the surface where the protective capsule is discarded, the missile's fins extend, and the rocket engine ignites. The Harpoon has a range of about 60 nautical miles. Production will begin in 1975 with later submarines of the "Los Angeles" class to be armed with the weapon. Consideration is being given to retrofitting the missile in submarines of the "Permit" and "Sturgeon" classes as well as the early units of the "Los Angeles" class. The limited number of torpedo tubes in these submarines will restrict arming flexibility.

CONVENTIONAL SUBMARINES. The US Navy now operates only nine diesel-electric attack submarines. In addition, one diesel transport submarine and two diesel research submarines are in service.

NOMENCLATURE. US submarines generally have been named for fish and other marine life except that fleet ballistic missile submarines have been named for famous Americans. The tradition of naming "fleet" and "attack" submarines for fish was broken in 1971 when three submarines of the "Sturgeon" class and the one-of-a-kind SSN 685 were named for deceased members of the Congress. Previously US destroyer-type ships have honoured members of the Congress.

Later in 1971 the SSN 688, lead ship for a new class of attack submarines, was named *Los Angeles*, introducing "city" names to US submarines. This was the third name source applied to US submarines within a year, indicating the considerable confusion in ship nomenclature within the Navy.

(Of late, several types of auxiliary ships also have been named for cities, a name source traditionally applied to cruisers in the US Navy).

(26) NUCLEAR-POWERED ATTACK SUBMARINES (SSN): "LOS ANGELES" CLASS

Displacement, tons	6 900 submerged
Length, feet	360 oa
Beam, feet	33
Draught, feet	32
Torpedo tubes	4—21 inch (*533 mm*) amidships
A/S weapons	SUBROC and Mk 48 A/S torpedoes
Main engines	2 geared turbines; 1 shaft
Nuclear reactor	1 pressurised-water cooled
Speed, knots	30+ submerged
Complement	127 (12 officers, 115 enlisted men)

Name	*No.*	*Builder*	*Laid down*	*Launched*	*Commission*
LOS ANGELES	SSN 688	Newport News SB & DD Co	8 Jan 1972	6 Apr 1974	Nov 1975
BATON ROUGE	SSN 689	Newport News SB & DD Co	18 Nov 1972	26 Apr 1975	mid 1976
PHILADELPHIA	SSN 690	General Dynamics (Electric Boat)	12 Aug 1972	19 Oct 1974	Dec 1975
MEMHPIS	SSN 691	Newport News SB & DD Co	23 June 1973	Aug 1975	1977
OMAHA	SSN 692	General Dynamics (Electric Boat)	27 Jan 1973	June 1975	June 1976
CINCINNATI	SSN 693	Newport News SB & DD Co	6 Apr 1974	1976	1977
GROTON	SSN 694	General Dynamics (Electric Boat)	3 Aug 1973	Oct 1975	late 1976
BIRMINGHAM	SSN 695	Newport News SB & DD Co	26 Apr 1975	1976	1977
NEW YORK CITY	SSN 696	General Dynamics (Electric Boat)	15 Dec 1973	1976	1977
INDIANAPOLIS	SSN 697	General Dynamics (Electric Boat)	19 Oct 1974	1976	1977
BREMERTON	SSN 698	General Dynamics (Electric Boat)	14 Dec 1974	1976	1977
JACKSONVILLE	SSN 699	General Dynamics (Electric Boat)	Mar 1975	1976	1977
Six submarines	**SSN 700-705**	General Dynamics (Electric Boat)			1977-1979
Five submarines	**SSN 706-710**	General Dynamics (Electric Boat)			1979-1981
Three submarines	**SSN 711-713**	Fiscal Year 1975 programme			
Two submarines	**SSN 714-715**	Proposed FY 1976 programme			
Three Submarines	**SSN 716-718**	Planned FY 1977 programme			

These are "high-speed" attack submarines intended to counter the new Soviet classes of submarines that went to sea during the late 1960s and early 1970s.

The SSN 688-690 (3 ships) were authorised in the Fiscal Year 1970 new construction programme, SSN 691-694 (4 ships) in FY 1971, SSN 695-699 (5 ships) in FY 1972, SSN 700-705 (6 ships) in FY 1973, SSN 706-710 (5 ships) in FY 1974, SSN 711-713 (3 ships) in FY 1975, and SSN 714-715 (2 ships) proposed in the FY 1976 programme. Additional submarines are planned at the rate of five units every two years.

Detailed design of the SSN 688 class as well as construction of the lead submarine was contracted to the Newport News Shipbuilding & Dry Dock Company, Newport News, Virginia; the follow-on ships were awarded to Newport News and to the General Dynamics Electric Boat Division yard at Groton, Connecticut.

These ships are considerably behind schedule with the lead ship being completed 15 months late.

DESIGN. These submarines are considerably larger than the previous "Sturgeon" class. All construction features, including sail size, hull shape, propulsion plant design, machinery mounting technique, auxiliary machinery, etc, will be designed to provide the maximum degree of quietness possible. Their sound level is similar to the "Sturgeon" class when both submarines are travelling at comparable speeds.

ELECTRONICS. Electronic equipment in these submarines includes BQQ-5 (formerly BQS-13DNA) long-range detection sonar, BQS-15 close contact avoidance sonar, and BPS-15 surface search radar. A towed sonar array is fitted.

UYK-7 computer is installed to assist command and control functions; Mk 113 Mod 10 torpedo fire control system fitted.

ENGINEERING. Unofficial sources indicate that a modified surface ship nuclear reactor plant may be used in this class. The "smallest" surface ship reactor now available for submarine use is the D2G type used in the frigates *Bainbridge* and *Truxtun*; these reactors each produce approximately 30 000 shp. Reactor core life between "refuellings" is estimated at ten years.

PHILADELPHIA (SSN 690) *1974, General Dynamics, Electric Boat* ***Division***

FISCAL. The costs of these submarines have increased in every fiscal year programme; the estimated cost of the lead ship *Los Angeles* is $232 000 000; for the other FY 1970 submarines $153 700 000, for FY 1971 submarines $162 300 000, for FY 1972 submarines $177 600 000, for FY 1973 submarines $178 200 000, for FY 1974 submarines $183 400 000, and for FY 1975 submarines $272 500 000. These estimates are based on data available prior to completion of any of the submarines; later units probably will cost some $300 000 000 each.

Submarines—*continued*

1 NUCLEAR POWERED ATTACK SUBMARINE (SSN): "LIPSCOMB" TYPE

Name	*No.*	*Builder*	*Laid down*	*Launched*	*Commissioned*
***GLENARD P. LIPSCOMB**	SSN 685	General Dynamics	5 June 1971	4 Aug 1973	21 Dec 1974

Displacement, tons	5 800 standard ; 6 480 submerged
Length, feet	365 oa
Beam, feet	31·7
Torpedo tubes	4—21 inch (*533 mm*) amidships
A/S weapons	SUBROC and A/S torpedoes
Main engines	Turbine-electric drive (General Electric) ; 1 shaft
Nuclear reactor	1 pressurised-water cooled S5WA (Westinghouse)
Speed, knots	approx 25 submerged
Complement	120 (12 officers, 108 enlisted men)

The Turbine-Electric Drive Submarine (TEDS) was constructed to test "a combination of advanced silencing techniques" involving "a new kind of propulsion system, and new and quieter machinery of various kinds", according to the Department of Defense. The noise level produced by an operating submarine is an important factor in its ability to remain undetected by an opponent's passive listening devices and its own ability to detect the opponent. The TEDS project will permit an at-sea evaluation of improvements in ASW effectiveness due to noise reduction.

No class of turbine-electric nuclear submarines is planned at this time. Rather, quieting features developed in the SSN 685 which do not detract from speed will probably be incorporated in the SSN 688 design and subsequent SSN classes. (The TEDS design was several years ahead of the SSN 668 design).

Authorised in the Fiscal Year 1968 new construction programme; estimated construction cost was approximately $200 000 000.

Design of an advanced submarine specifically intended for quiet operation began with Navy studies which commenced in October 1964. Approval to construct the submarine was revoked on at least one occasion by the Department of Defense in an effort to combine several desired characteristics in a single submarine design. However, high speed and silent operation are apparently not compatible with available technolgy.

Final Department of Defense approval for construction of the turbine-electric drive submarine was announced on 25 Oct 1968. A contract was awarded to General Dynamics (Electric Boat Division) for construction of the SSN 685 on 16 Dec 1968.

ENGINEERING. Turbine-electric drive eliminates the noisy reduction gears of standard steam turbine power plants, the major source of noise in a nuclear-powered submarine. The turbine-electric power plant is larger and heavier than comparable steam turbine submarine machinery.

The *Tullibee* (SSN 597) was an earlier effort at noise reduction through a turbine-electric nuclear plant.

GLENARD P. LIPSCOMB (SSN 685) *1973, General Dynamics, Electric Boat Division*

1 NUCLEAR POWERED ATTACK SUBMARINE (SSN): "NARWHAL" TYPE

Name	*No*	*Builder*	*Laid down*	*Launched*	*Commissioned*
***NARWHAL**	SSN 671	General Dynamics (Electric Boat)	17 Jan 1966	9 Sep 1967	**12 July 1969**

Displacement, tons	4 450 standard ; 5 350 submerged
Length, feet (*metres*)	314 (*95·7*) oa
Beam, feet (*metres*)	38 (*11·5*)
Draught, feet (*metres*)	26 (*7·9*)
Torpedo tubes	4—21 inch (*533 mm*) amidships
A/S weapons	SUBROC and A/S torpedoes
Main engines	2 steam turbines ; approx 17 000 shp ; 1 shaft
Nuclear reactor	1 pressurised water-cooled S5G (General Electric)
Speed, knots	approx 20 surface ; approx 30 submerged
Complement	120 (12 officers, 108 enlisted men)

The *Narwhal* is a large attack submarine with an improved propulsion system. Authorised in the Fiscal Year 1964 new construction programme.

DESIGN. The *Narwhal* is similar to the "Sturgeon" class submarines in design.

ELECTRONICS. Fitted with BQQ-2 sonar system. See "Sturgeon" and "Permit" classes for general notes. Fitted with Mk 113 Mod 6 torpedo fire control system.

ENGINEERING. The *Narwhal* is fitted with the prototype sea-going S5G natural circulation reactor plant. According to Admiral H. G. Rickover the natural circulation reactor "offers promise of increased reactor plant reliability, simplicity, and noise reduction due to the elimination of the need for large reactor coolant pumps and associated electrical and control equipment by taking maximum advantage of natural convection to circulate the reactor coolant".

Natural circulation eliminates the requirement for primary coolant pumps, the second noisiest component of a pressurised-water propulsion system after the steam turbines.

The Atomic Energy Commission's Knolls Atomic Power Laboratory was given prime responsibility for development of the power plant. Construction of a land-based prototype plant began in May 1961 at the National Reactor Testing Station in Idaho. The reactor achieved initial criticality on 12 Sep 1965.

NARWHAL (SSN 671) *1969, General Dynamics, Electric Boat Division*

PHOTOGRAPHS. Note SAFETY track on submarine deck to permit men to move on the low-lying deck without railings; the small deck fins are for BQS-8 upward-looking sonar for under-ice operation.

Submarines—*continued*

37 NUCLEAR-POWERED ATTACK SUBMARINES (SSN): "STURGEON" CLASS

Displacement, tons	3 860 standard; 4 630 submerged
Length, feet (*metres*)	292·2 (*89·0*) oa
Beam, feet (*metres*)	31·7 (*9·5*)
Draught, feet (*metres*)	26 (*7·9*)
Torpedo tubes	4—21 inch (*533 mm*) amidships
A/S weapons	SUBROC and A/S torpedoes
Main engines	2 steam turbines; approx 15 000 shp; 1 shaft
Nuclear reactor	1 pressurised-water cooled S5W (Westinghouse)
Speed, knots	approx 20 surface; approx 30 submerged
Complement	120 (12 officers, 108 enlisted men)

The 37 "Sturgeon" class attack submarines comprise the largest US Navy group of nuclear-powered ships built to the same design (followed by the 31 "Lafayette" class ballistic missile submarines; the Soviet Navy has built 34 submarines of the same design in the "Yankee" class). These submarines are intended to seek out and destroy enemy submarines. They are similar in design to the previous "Permit" (ex-"Thresher") class but are slightly larger. SSN 637-639 (3 ships) were authorised in the Fiscal Year 1962 new construction programme. SSN 646-653 (8 ships) in FY 1963, SSN 660-664 (5 ships) in FY 1964, SSN 665-670 (6 ships) in FY 1965, SSN 672-677 (6 ships) in FY 1966, SSN 678-682 (5 ships) in FY 1967, SSN 683-684 (2 ships) in FY 1968, and SSN 686-687 (2 ships) in FY 1969.
Some of these ships required seven years for construction (keel laying to completion)

CONSTRUCTION. The *Pogy* was begun by the New York Shipbuilding Corp (Camden, New Jersey), but was towed to Ingalls Shipbuilding Corp for completion; contract with the New York Shipbuilding Corp was terminated on 5 June 1967; contract for completion awarded to Ingalls Shipbuilding Corp on 7 Dec 1967.
The *Guitarro* sank in 35 feet of water on 15 May 1969 while being fitted out at the San Francisco Bay Naval Shipyard. According to a congressional report, the sinking, caused by shipyard workers, was "wholly avoidable". Subsequently raised; damage estimated at $25 000 000 to repair damage due to interior flooding. Completion delayed more than two years.

DESIGN. These submarines are slightly larger than the previous "Permit" (ex-"Thresher") class and can be identified by their taller sail structure and the lower position of their diving planes on the sail (to improve control at periscope depth). Sail height is 20 feet, 6 inches above deck. Sail-mounted diving planes rotate to vertical for breaking through ice when surfacing in arctic regions.
These ships incorporate modifications of the submarine safety (SUBSAFE) programme established after the loss of the *Thresher*. These submarines probably are slightly slower than the previous "Permit" and "Skipjack" classes because of their increased size with the same propulsion system as in the earlier classes.

ELECTRONICS. These submarines are fitted with the advanced BQQ-2 sonar system. Principal components of the BQQ-2 include the BQS-6 active sonar, with transducers mounted in a 15-foot diameter sonar sphere, and BQR-7 passive sonar, with hydrophones in a conformal array on sides of forward hull. The active sonar sphere is fitted in the optimum bow position, requiring placement of torpedo tubes amidships. These submarines

Name	*No.*	*Builder*	*Laid down*	*Launched*	*Commissioned*
***STURGEON**	SSN 637	General Dynamics (Electric Boat)	10 Aug 1963	26 Feb 1966	3 Mar 1967
***WHALE**	SSN 638	General Dynamics (Quincy)	27 May 1964	14 Oct 1966	12 Oct 1968
***TAUTOG**	SSN 639	Ingalls Shipbuilding Corp	27 Jan 1964	15 Apr 1967	17 Aug 1968
***GRAYLING**	SSN 646	Portsmouth Naval Shipyard	12 May 1964	22 June 1967	11 Oct 1969
***POGY**	SSN 647	Ingalls Shipbuilding Corp	4 May 1964	3 June 1967	15 May 1971
***ASPRO**	SSN 648	Ingalls Shipbuilding Corp	23 Nov 1964	29 Nov 1967	20 Feb 1969
***SUNFISH**	SSN 649	General Dynamics (Quincy)	15 Jan 1965	14 Oct 1966	15 Mar 1969
***PARGO**	SSN 650	General Dynamics (Electric Boat)	3 June 1964	17 Sep 1966	5 Dec 1967
***QUEENFISH**	SSN 651	Newport News SB & DD Co	11 May 1965	25 Feb 1966	6 Dec 1966
***PUFFER**	SSN 652	Ingalls Shipbuilding Corp	8 Feb 1965	30 Mar 1968	9 Aug 1969
***RAY**	SSN 653	Newport News SB & DD Co	1 Apr 1965	21 June 1966	12 Apr 1967
***SAND LANCE**	SSN 660	Portsmouth Naval Shipyard	15 Jan 1965	11 Nov 1969	25 Sep 1971
***LAPON**	SSN 661	Newport News SB & DD Co	26 July 1965	16 Dec 1966	14 Dec 1967
***GURNARD**	SSN 662	San Francisco NSY (Mare Island)	22 Dec 1964	20 May 1967	6 Dec 1968
***HAMMERHEAD**	SSN 663	Newport News SB & DD Co	29 Nov 1965	14 Apr 1967	28 June 1968
***SEA DEVIL**	SSN 664	Newport News SB & DD Co	12 Apr 1966	5 Oct 1967	30 Jan 1969
***GUITARRO**	SSN 665	San Francisco NSY (Mare Island)	9 Dec 1965	27 July 1968	9 Sep 1972
***HAWKBILL**	SSN 666	San Francisco NSY (Mare Island)	12 Sep 1966	12 Apr 1969	4 Feb 1971
***BERGALL**	SSN 667	General Dynamics (Electric Boat)	16 Apr 1966	17 Feb 1968	13 June 1969
***SPADEFISH**	SSN 668	Newport News SB & DD Co	21 Dec 1966	15 May 1968	31 July 1969
***SEAHORSE**	SSN 669	General Dynamics (Electric Boat)	13 Aug 1966	15 June 1968	19 Sep 1969
***FINBACK**	SSN 670	Newport News SB & DD Co	26 June 1967	7 Dec 1968	4 Feb 1970
***PINTADO**	SSN 672	San Francisco NSY (Mare Island)	27 Oct 1967	16 Aug 1969	29 Apr 1971
***FLYING FISH**	SSN 673	General Dynamics (Electric Boat)	30 June 1967	17 May 1969	29 Apr 1970
***TREPANG**	SSN 674	General Dynamics (Electric Boat)	28 Oct 1967	27 Sep 1969	14 Aug 1970
***BLUEFISH**	SSN 675	General Dynamics (Electric Boat)	13 Mar 1968	10 Jan 1970	8 Jan 1971
***BILLFISH**	SSN 676	General Dynamics (Electric Boat)	20 Sep 1968	1 May 1970	11 Sep 1971
***DRUM**	SSN 677	San Francisco NSY (Mare Island)	20 Aug 1968	23 May 1970	15 Apr 1972
***ARCHERFISH**	SSN 678	General Dynamics (Electric Boat)	19 June 1969	16 Jan 1971	17 Dec 1971
***SILVERSIDES**	SSN 679	General Dynamics (Electric Boat)	13 Oct 1969	4 June 1971	5 May 1972
***WILLIAM H. BATES**	SSN 680	Ingalls Shipbuilding (Litton)	4 Aug 1969	11 Dec 1971	12 Apr 1973
***BATFISH**	SSN 681	General Dynamics(Electric Boat)	9 Feb 1970	9 Oct 1971	1 Sep 1972
***TUNNY**	SSN 682	Ingalls Shipbuilding (Litton)	22 May 1970	10 June 1972	26 Jan 1974
***PARCHE**	SSN 683	Ingalls Shipbuilding (Litton)	10 Dec 1970	13 Jan 1973	17 Aug 1974
***CAVALLA**	SSN 684	General Dynamics (Electric Boat)	4 June 1970	19 Feb 1972	9 Feb 1973
***L. MENDEL RIVERS**	SSN 686	Newport News SB & DD Co	26 June 1971	2 June 1973	1 Feb 1975
***RICHARD B. RUSSELL**	SSN 687	Newport News SB & DD Co	19 Oct 1971	12 Jan 1974	June 1975

ASPRO (SSN 648) *United States Navy*

NARWHAL (SSN 671)—see previous page *1969, General Dynamics, Electric Boat Division*

Submarines—*continued*

"STURGEON" CLASS—continued

also have BQS-8 and BQS-13 active passive sonars, transducers for the former are in two small domes aft of sail structure. BQS-8 sonar is intended primarily for Under-ice-navigation. Sonar suits of *Guitarro* and *Cavalla* are of improved designs. All will be refitted to BQQ-5 capability (vice BQQ-2) during regular overhauls. BPS-14 surface search radar fitted. These submarines have the Mk 113 torpedo fire control system (Mod 6 through SSN 677; Mod 8 in SSN 678-683; Mod 10 in later submarines).

MISSILES. Compatability tests were conducted during 1972-1973 with several submarines of this class and the encapsulated Harpoon anti-ship missile.

NOMENCLATURE. ***William H. Bates*** **ex-*****Redfish*****, renamed 25 June 1971 to honour deceased member of Congress.**

OPERATIONAL. **The *Whale*, *Pargo*, and older nuclear submarine *Sargo* conducted exercises in the Arctic ice pack during March-April 1969. The *Whale* surfaced at the geographic North Pole on April 6, the 60th anniversary of Rear Admiral Robert E. Peary reaching the North Pole. This was believed the first instance of single-screw US nuclear submarines surfacing in the Arctic ice.**

The *Hammerhead* and the older nuclear submarine *Skate* conducted exercises in the Arctic during November-December 1970, with the *Hammerhead* surfacing at the North Pole on 20 Nov 1970.

The *Trepang* operated in the Arctic with the *Skate* during the spring of 1971.

SUBMERSIBLES. **The *Hawkbill* has been modified to carry and support the Navy's Deep Submergence Rescue** Vehicles (DSRV). The *Hawkbill* can transport a 50-foot DSRV "piggyback" on her after deck and while submerged can launch and recover the DSRV. The DSRV also can "land" on the submarine's forward hatch as well as the after hatch to transfer personnel. See section on Deep Submergence Vehicles for additional DSRV details. The research submarine *Halibut* (SSN 587) also is fitted to carry the DSRV. The modifications do not affect the *Hawkbill's* combat capabilities.

PHOTOGRAPHS. These submarines have streamlined hulls with few deck projections to interrupt their clean lines; the two small fins on the main deck aft of the sail structure are BQS-8 sonar transducers and the darker "windows" on the sail structure (forward of diving planes) are BQS-8 hydrophones. Capstans and cleats are retractable.

The *Hawkbill* is shown carrying the submersible DSRV-1. The markings on the submarine's sail and around her forward hatch are luminescent to assist underwater "mating" operations.

L. MENDEL RIVERS (SSN 686) — *1974, Newport News SB & DD Co,*

ARCHERFISH (SSN 678) — *1971, General Dynamics, Electric Boat Division*

POGY (SSN 647) — *1973, United States Navy*

HAWKBILL (SSN 666) with DSRV-1 — *1971, United States Navy*

Submarines—*continued*

13 NUCLEAR-POWERED ATTACK SUBMARINES (SSN): "PERMIT" CLASS

Displacement, tons	3 750 standard, *Flasher, Greenling,* and *Gato* 3 800; 4 300 submerged except *Jack* 4 500 submerged, *Flasher, Greenling,* and *Gato* 4 600 submerged
Length, feet (*metres*)	278·5 (*84·9*) oa except *Jack* 296·7 (*89·5*), *Flasher, Greenling* and *Gato* 292·2 (*89·1*)
Beam, feet (*metres*)	31·7 (*9·6*)
Draught, feet (*metres*)	25·2 (*7·6*)
Torpedo tubes	4—21 inch (*533 mm*) amidships
A/S weapons	SUBROC and A/S torpedoes
Main engines	2 steam turbines, approx 15 000 shp; 1 shaft
Nuclear reactor	1 pressurised-water cooled S5W (Westinghouse)
Speed, knots	approx 20 surface; approx 30 submerged
Complement	120 (12 officers, 108 enlisted men)

Name	*No*	*Builder*	*Laid down*	*Launched*	*Commissioned*
***PERMIT**	SSN 594	Mare Island Naval Shipyard	16 July 1959	1 July 1961	29 May 1962
***PLUNGER**	SSN 595	Mare Island Naval Shipyard	2 Mar 1960	9 Dec 1961	21 Nov 1962
***BARB**	SSN 596	Ingalls Shipbuilding Corp	9 Nov 1959	12 Feb 1962	24 Aug 1963
***POLLACK**	SSN 603	New York Shipbuilding Corp	14 Mar 1960	17 Mar 1962	26 May 1964
***HADDO**	SSN 604	New York Shipbuilding Corp	9 Sep 1960	18 Aug 1962	16 Dec 1964
***JACK**	SSN 605	Portsmouth Naval Shipyard	16 Sep 1960	24 Apr 1963	31 Mar 1967
***TINOSA**	SSN 606	Portsmouth Naval Shipyard	24 Nov 1959	9 Dec 1961	17 Oct 1964
***DACE**	SSN 607	Ingalls Shipbuilding Corp	6 June 1960	18 Aug 1962	4 Apr 1964
***GUARDFISH**	SSN 612	New York Shipbuilding Corp	28 Feb 1961	15 May 1965	20 Dec 1966
***FLASHER**	SSN 613	General Dynamics (Electric Boat)	14 Apr 1961	22 June 1963	22 July 1966
***GREENLING**	SSN 614	General Dynamics (Electric Boat)	15 Aug 1961	4 Apr 1964	3 Nov 1967
***GATO**	SSN 615	Ingalls Shipbuilding Corp	15 Dec 1961	14 May 1964	25 Jan 1968
***HADDOCK**	SSN 621	Ingalls Shipbuilding Corp	24 Apr 1961	21 May 1966	22 Dec 1967

These submarines were the first of a series of advanced attack submarines intended to seek out and destroy enemy submarines. They have a greater depth capability than previous nuclear-powered submarines and are the first to combine the SUBROC anti-submarine missile capability with the advanced BQQ-2 sonar system. The lead ship of the class, the ill-fated *Thresher* (SSN 593), was authorised in the Fiscal Year 1957 new construction programme, the SSN 594-596 (3 ships) in FY 1958, SSN 603-607 (5 ships) in FY 1959, SSN 612-615 (4 ships) in FY 1960, and SSN 621 in FY 1961.

The *Thresher* (SSN 593) was lost off the coast of New England on 10 Apr 1963 while on post-overhaul trials. She went down with 129 men on board (108 crewmen plus four naval officers and 17 civilians on board for trials).

CLASS. These submarines were originally listed as belonging to the "Thresher" class; now referred to as the "Permit" class after loss of the *Thresher* in 1963.

CONSTRUCTION. *Greenling* and *Gato* were launched by the Electric Boat Division of the General Dynamics Corp (Groton, Connecticut); towed to Quincy Division (Massachusetts) for lengthening and completion.

DESIGN. The *Plunger, Barb, Pollack,* and *Dace* were ordered as guided missile submarines (SSGN) and were to each carry four Regulus II missiles. They were re-ordered as "Thresher" class attack submarines after the Regulus II programme was cancelled on 18 Dec 1958 (retaining numerical sequence in the submarine series). The *Jack* was built to a modified design to test a different power plant (see *Engineering* notes).

The *Flasher, Gato,* and *Greenling* were modified during construction; fitted with SUBSAFE features, heavier machinery, and larger sail structures.

These submarines have a modified "tear-drop" hull design. Their bows are devoted to sonar and their four torpedo tubes are amidships, angled out, two to port and two to starboard.

The sail structure height of these submarines is 13 feet, 9 inches to 15 feet above the deck, with later submarines of this class having a sail height of 20 feet.

ELECTRONICS. These submarines are fitted with the advanced BQQ-2 sonar system (first installed in the *Tullibee,* SSN 597). Principal components of the BQQ-2 include the BQS-6 active sonar, with transducers mounted in a 15-foot diameter sonar sphere, and BQR-7 passive sonar, with hydrophones in a conformal array along sides of forward hull. The active sonar sphere is fitted in the optimum bow position, requiring placement of torpedo tubes amidships. The advanced BQS-13DNA active/passive sonar will be fitted in these submarines as well as other equipment to provide them the BQQ-5 sonar system (vice BQQ-2) during regular overhauls.

These submarines have the Mk 113 Mod 6 torpedo fire control system.

ENGINEERING. The *Jack* is fitted with two propellers on essentially one shaft (actually a single shaft within a sleeve-like shaft) and a counter-rotating turbine without a reduction gear. Both innovations are designed to reduce operating noises. To accommodate the larger turbine the engine spaces were lengthened ten feet and the shaft structure was lengthened seven feet to mount the two propellers. The propellers are of different size and are smaller than in the other submarines of this class. Also eliminated in *Jack* was a clutch and secondary-propulsion electric motor.

The *Jack's* propulsion arrangement provides a ten per cent increase in power efficiency, but no increase in speed.

NOMENCLATURE. Names changed during construction: *Plunder ex-Pollack: Barb ex-Pollack: ex-Plunger: Pollack ex-Barb.*

PLUNGER (SSN 596) *United States Navy*

BARB (SSN 596) *1973, United States Navy*

TULLIBEE (SSN 597)—see following page *1968, United States Navy*

Submarines—*continued*

1 NUCLEAR-POWERED ATTACK SUBMARINE (SSN): "TULLIBEE" TYPE

Displacement, tons	2 317 standard; 2 640 submerged
Length, feet (*metres*)	273 (*83·2*) oa
Beam, feet (*metres*)	23·3 (*7·1*)
Draught, feet (*metres*)	21 (*6·4*)
Torpedo tubes	4—21 inch (*533 mm*) amidships
A/S weapons	A/S torpedoes
Main engines	Turbo-electric drive with steam turbine (Westinghouse); 2 500 shp; 1 shaft
Nuclear reactor	1 pressurised-water cooled S2C (Combustion Engineering)
Speed, knots	approx 15 surface; 15+ submerged)
Complement	87 (7 officers, 80 enlisted men)

Name	*No*	*Builder*	*Laid down*	*Launched*	*Commissioned*
•TULLIBEE	SSN 597	General Dynamics (Electric Boat)	26 May 1958	27 Apr 1960	9 Nov 1960

The *Tullibee* was designed specifically for anti-submarine operations and was the first US submarine with the optimum bow position devoted entirely to sonar. No additional submarines of this type were constructed because of the success of the larger, more-versatile "Permit" class. The *Tullibee* was authorised in the Fiscal Year 1958 new construction programme. She is no longer considered a "first line" submarine.

DESIGN. The *Tullibee* has a modified, elongated "tear-drop" hull design. Originally she was planned as a 1 000-ton craft, but reactor requirements and other considerations increased her size during design and construction.
The *Tullibee* has four amidships torpedo tubes angled out from the centreline, two to port and two to starboard. However, she is not fitted to fire the SUBROC anti-submarine missile. She cannot match the "Thresher" and later SSN classes in underwater speed or manoeuvrability.

ELECTRONICS. The *Tullibee* was the first submarine fitted with the integrated BQQ-2 sonar system (see "Permit" class listing for details). The fin-like sonar domes are PUFFs for BQG-4 passive fire control sonar; in the earlier photograph only two PUFF domes are installed (not to be confused with fin-like rudder); later photograph shows three PUFF domes with second dome (aft of sail structure) painted light colour.

PUFF is an acronym for Passive Underwater Fire-control Feasibility system. Fitted with Mk 112 Mod 1 torpedo fire control system.

TULLIBEE (SSN 597) *1960, United States Navy*

ENGINEERING. The *Tullibee* has a small nuclear power plant designed and developed by the Combustion Engineering Company.
The *Tullibee* propulsion system features turbo-electric drive rather than conventional steam turbines with reduction gears in an effort to reduce operating noises.

NAVIGATION. The *Tullibee* is fitted with Ships Inertial Navigation System (SINS).

5 NUCLEAR-POWERED ATTACK SUBMARINES (SSN): "SKIPJACK" CLASS

Displacement, tons	3 075 standard; 3 500 submerged
Length, feet (*metres*)	251·7 (*76·7*) oa
Beam, feet (*metres*)	31·5 (*9·6*)
Draught, feet (*metres*)	28 (*8·5*)
Torpedo tubes	6—21 inch (*533 mm*) forward
A/S weapons	A/S torpedoes
Main engines	2 steam turbines (Westinghouse in *Skipjack*; General Electric in others); approx 15 000 shp; 1 shaft
Nuclear reactor	1 pressurised-water cooled S5W (Westinghouse)
Speed, knots	approx 20 surface; 30+ submerged
Complement	112 (10 officers, 102 enlisted men)

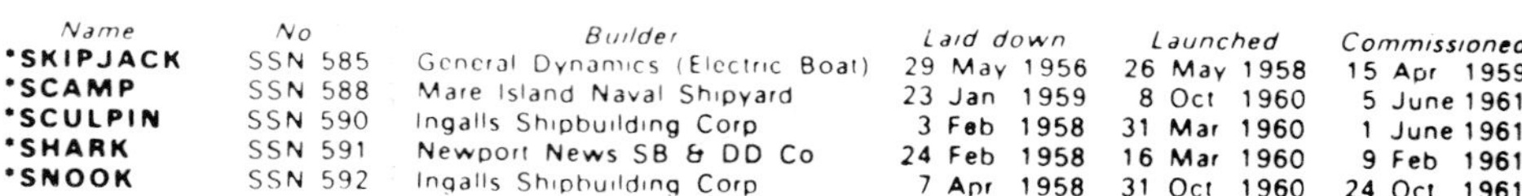

Name	*No*	*Builder*	*Laid down*	*Launched*	*Commissioned*
•SKIPJACK	SSN 585	General Dynamics (Electric Boat)	29 May 1956	26 May 1958	15 Apr 1959
•SCAMP	SSN 588	Mare Island Naval Shipyard	23 Jan 1959	8 Oct 1960	5 June 1961
•SCULPIN	SSN 590	Ingalls Shipbuilding Corp	3 Feb 1958	31 Mar 1960	1 June 1961
•SHARK	SSN 591	Newport News SB & DD Co	24 Feb 1958	16 Mar 1960	9 Feb 1961
•SNOOK	SSN 592	Ingalls Shipbuilding Corp	7 Apr 1958	31 Oct 1960	24 Oct 1961

The "Skipjack" class combines the high-speed endurance of nuclear propulsion with the high-speed "tear-drop" hull design tested in the conventionally powered submarine *Albacore* (AGSS 569) (See *Design* and *Engineering* notes). The *Skipjack* was authorised in the Fiscal Year 1956 new construction programme, the five other submarines of this class were authorised in FY 1957. Although they are now nearing their first decade of service, these submarines are still considered suitable for "first line" service. Officially described as fastest US nuclear submarines in service.
Each cost approximately $40 000 000.
The *Scorpion* (SSN 589) of this class was lost some 400 miles southwest of the Azores while en route from the Mediterranean to Norfolk, Virginia, in May 1968. She went down with 99 men on board.

CONSTRUCTION. The *Scorpion's* keel was laid down twice; the original keel laid down on 1 Nov 1957 was renumbered SSBN 598 and became the Polaris submarine *George Washington*; the second SSN 589 keel became the *Scorpion*. The *Scamp's* keel laying was delayed when material for her was diverted to the SSBN 599. This class introduced the Newport News Shipbuilding and Dry Dock Company and the Ingalls Shipbuilding Corporation to nuclear submarine construction. Newport News had not previously built any submarine since before World War I; Ingalls previously had built only one submarine, the *Blueback* (SS 581) launched in 1959.

SNOOK (SSN 592) *1964, United States Navy*

Submarines—*continued*

"SKIPJACK" CLASS—*continued*

DESIGN. The *Skipjack* was the first US nuclear submarine built to the "tear-drop" or modified spindle hull design for improved underwater performance. These submarines have a single propeller shaft (vice two in earlier nuclear submarines) and their diving planes are mounted on sail structures to improve underwater manoeuvrability. No after torpedo tubes are fitted because of their tapering sterns.

ELECTRONICS. Original sonar equipment was modified to provide improved anti-submarine capabilities. *Skipjack* fitted with Mk 101 Mod 20 torpedo fire control system; others with Mk 101 Mod 17.

ENGINEERING. The "Skipjack" class introduced the S5W fast attack submarine propulsion plant which has been employed in all subsequent US attack and ballistic missile submarines until the "Los Angeles" class (SSN 688) except the *Narwhal* (SSN 671) and *Glenard P. Lipscomb* (SSN 685). The plant was developed by the Bettis Atomic Power Laboratory.

PHOTOGRAPHS. Note streamlined shape and lack of topside projections; most equipment outside of the hull is either recessed or retractable. The *Sculpin* is shown at right during a rare high-speed surface run; her diving planes are mounted lower on the sail than later SSN classes

SCULPIN (SSN 590) *1967, United States Navy*

1 NUCLEAR-POWERED RESEARCH SUBMARINE (SSN): "HALIBUT" TYPE

Name	*No.*	*Builder*	*Laid down*	*Launched*	*Commissioned*
HALIBUT	SSN 587 (ex-SSGN 587)	Mare Island Naval Shipyard, Vallejo, Calif	11 Apr 1957	9 Jan 1959	4 Jan 1960

Displacement, tons	3 850 standard; 5 000 submerged
Length, feet (*metres*)	350 (*106·6*) oa
Beam, feet (*metres*)	29·5 (*8·9*)
Draught, feet (*metres*)	21·5 (*6·5*)
Torpedo tubes	6—21 inch (*533 mm*) 4 fwd; 2 aft
Main engines	2 steam turbines (Westinghouse); approx 6 000 shp; 2 shafts
Nuclear reactor	1 pressurised-water cooled S3W (Westinghouse)
Speed, knots	15·5 surface; 15+ submerged
Complement	120 (12 officers, 108 enlisted men)

The *Halibut* is believed to have been the first submarine designed and constructed specifically to fire guided missiles.
She was originally intended to have diesel-electric propulsion but on 27 Feb 1956 the Navy announced she would have nuclear propulsion. She was the US Navy's only nuclear powered *guided* missile submarine (SSGN) to be completed. Authorised in the Fiscal Year 1956 new construction programme and built for an estimated cost of $45 000 000.
The *Halibut* was reclassified as an attack submarine on 25 July 1965 after the Navy discarded the Regulus submarine-launched missile force. Her missile equipment was removed, she is no longer considered a first line" submarine and is employed in experimental work.
The submarine's large missile compartment makes her an excellent ship for underwater projects.
The Navy has stated that the *Halibut* and earlier *Seawolf* have been designated as "mother" submarines for the deep submergence research programmes. Reportedly the *Halibut* has been fitted with a ducted bow thruster to permit precise control and manoeuvering.
She can carry the 50-foot Deep Submergence Rescue Vehicle (DSRV) and other submersibles on her after deck; the submersibles can "take off" from and" land on" the *Halibut* while the larger craft is submerged.
The *Halibut* was being decommissioned during the latter half of 1975.

DESIGN. The *Halibut* was built with a large missile hangar faired into her bow. Her hull was intended primarily to provide a stable surface launching platform rather than for speed or manoeuvrability.

ENGINEERING. Fitted with same reactor propulsion plant as *Skate* and *Sargo*. Submerged speed of *Halibut* is less than "Skate" class because of larger hull volume and shape.

HALIBUT (SSN 587) *1970, United States Navy*

MISSILES. The *Halibut* was designed to carry two Regulus II surface-to-surface missiles. The Regulus II was a transonic missile which could carry a nuclear warhead and had a range of 1 000 miles. The Regulus II was cancelled before becoming operational and the *Halibut* operated from 1960 to 1964 carrying five Regulus I missiles, subsonic cruise missiles which could deliver a nuclear warhead on targets 500 miles from the launching ship or submarine.
During this period the US Navy operated a maximum of five Regulus "guided" (cruise) missile submarines, the *Halibut*, the post-war constructed *Grayback* (SSG 574 now LPSS 574) and *Growler* (SSG 577), and the World War II-built *Tunny* (SSG 282 subsequently LPSS 282) and *Barbero* (SSG 317). The *Grayback* and *Growler* each could carry four Regulus I missiles and the older submarines each carried two missiles.
As SSGN carried a complement of 11 officers and 108 enlisted men.

NAVIGATION. The *Halibut* is fitted with Ship's Inertial Navigation System (SINS).

PHOTOGRAPHS. Both views of the *Halibut* presented here show the submarine carrying a submersible simulator on deck. Note the "bulge" of missile hangar door forward of the sail structure.

HALIBUT (SSN 587) *1970, United States Navy*

Submarines—*continued*

1 NUCLEAR-POWERED ATTACK SUBMARINE (SSN): "TRITON" TYPE

Name	*No.*	*Builder*	*Laid down*	*Launched*	*Commissioned*
TRITON	SSN 586 (ex-SSRN 586)	General Dynamics Corp (Electric Boat), Groton, Conn	29 May 1956	19 Aug 1958	10 Nov 1959

Displacement, tons	5 940 standard; 7 780 submerged
Length, feet (*metres*)	447·5 (*136·3*) oa
Beam, feet (*metres*)	37 (*11·3*)
Draught, feet (*metres*)	24 (*7·3*)
Torpedo tubes	6—21 inch (*533 mm*) 4 fwd; 2 aft
Main engines	2 steam turbines (General Electric); approx 34 000 shp; 2 shafts
Nuclear reactors	2 pressurised-water cooled S4G (General Electric)
Speed, knots	27 surface; 20+ submerged
Complement as SSRN	172 (16 officers, 156 enlisted men)

The *Triton* was designed and constructed to serve as a radar picket submarine to operate in conjunction with surface carrier task forces. She is the longest submarine ever constructed and is exceeded in displacement only by the later Polaris missile submarines. Authorised in the Fiscal Year 1956 new construction programme and built for an estimated cost of $109 000 000.

The *Triton* circumnavigated the globe in 1960, remaining submerged except when her sail structure broke the surface to enable an ill sailor to be taken off near the Falkland Islands. The 41 500-mile cruise took 83 days and was made at an average speed of 18 knots.

The underwater giant was reclassified as an attack submarine (SSN) on 1 Mar 1961 as the Navy dropped the radar picket submarine programme. She is no longer considered a "first line" submarine and was decommissioned on 3 May 1969 to become the first US nuclear submarine to be relegated to the "mothball fleet". There had been proposals to operate the *Triton* as an underwater national command post afloat, but no funds were provided.

DESIGN. The *Triton* was designed to operate as a surface radar picket, submerging when in danger of enemy attack. She was fitted with an elaborate combat information centre and large radar antenna which retracted into the sail structure.

ENGINEERING. The *Triton* is the only US submarine with two nuclear reactors. The Atomic Energy Commission's Knolls Atomic Power Laboratory was given prime responsibility for development of the power plant. After 2½ years of operation, during which she steamed more than 110 000 miles, the *Triton* was overhauled and refuelled from July 1962 to March 1964.

TRITON (SSN 586) — *United States Navy*

4 NUCLEAR-POWERED ATTACK SUBMARINES (SSN): "SKATE" CLASS

Displacement, tons	2 570 standard; 2 861 submerged
Length, feet (*metres*)	267·7 (*81·5*) oa
Beam, feet (*metres*)	25 (*7·6*)
Draught, feet (*metres*)	21 (*6·4*)
Torpedo tubes	8—21 inch (*533 mm*) 6 forward; 2 aft (short)
Main engines	2 steam turbines (Westinghouse); approx 6 600 shp; 2 shafts
Nuclear reactor	1 pressurised-water cooled S3W (Westinghouse) in *Skate* and *Sargo*, 1 pressurised-water cooled S4W (Westinghouse) in *Swordfish* and *Seadragon*
Speed, knots	15·5 surface; 20+ submerged
Complement	108 (9 officers, 99 enlisted men)

Name	*No.*	*Builder*	*Laid down*	*Launched*	*Commissioned*
***SKATE**	SSN 578	General Dynamics (Electric Boat)	21 July 1955	16 May 1957	23 Dec 1957
***SWORDFISH**	SSN 579	Portsmouth Naval Shipyard	25 Jan 1956	27 Aug 1957	15 Sep 1958
***SARGO**	SSN 583	Mare Island Naval Shipyard	21 Feb 1956	10 Oct 1957	1 Oct 1958
***SEADRAGON**	SSN 584	Portsmouth Naval Shipyard	20 June 1956	16 Aug 1958	5 Dec 1959

The "Skate" class submarines were the first production model nuclear-powered submarines. They are similar in design to the *Nautilus* but smaller. The *Skate* and *Swordfish* were authorised in the Fiscal Year 1955 new construction programme and the *Sargo* and *Seadragon* in FY 1956.

The *Skate* was the first submarine to make a completely submerged transatlantic crossing; in 1958 she established a (then) record of 31 days submerged with a sealed atmosphere; on 11 Aug 1958 she passed under the North Pole during a polar cruise; and on 17 Mar 1959 she became the first submarine to surface at the North Pole. The *Sargo* undertook a polar cruise during January-February 1960 and surfaced at the North Pole on 9 Feb 1960. The *Seadragon* transited from the Atlantic to the Pacific via the Northwest Passage (Lancaster Sound, Barrow and McClure Straits) in August 1960. The *Skate* operating from New London, Connecticut and the *Seadragon*, based at Pearl Harbour rendezvoused under the North Pole on 2 Aug 1962 and then conducted anti-submarine exercises under the polar ice pack and surfaced together at the North Pole.

The *Skate* also operated in the Arctic Ocean during April-May 1969, conducting exercises under the Arctic ice pack with the later nuclear-powered attack submarines *Pargo* and *Whale*; and again during the spring of 1971 with the nuclear attack submarine *Trepang*.

DESIGN. The "Skate" design is similar to the *Nautilus-Seawolf* design with GUPPY hull, bow diving planes, and twin propellers.

ELECTRONICS. *Skate* and *Seadragon* fitted with Mk 101 Mod 19 torpedo fire control system; *Swordfish* and *Sargo* have Mk 101 Mod 15.

SEADRAGON (SSN 584) — *1965, United States Navy*

ENGINEERING. The reactors for this class were developed by the Atomic Energy Commission's Bettis Atomic Power Laboratory, the new propulsion system was similar to that of the *Nautilus* but considerably simplified with improved operation and maintenance. The propulsion plant developed under this programme had two arrangements, the S3W configuration in the *Skate*, *Sargo* and *Halibut* and the S4W configuration in the *Swordfish* and *Seadragon*. Both arrangements have proven satisfactory.

The *Skate* began her first overhaul and refuelling in January 1961 after steaming 120 862 miles on her initial reactor core during three years of operation. The *Swordfish* began her first overhaul and refuelling in early 1962 after more than three years of operation in which time she steamed 112 000 miles.

Submarines—*continued*

SWORDFISH (SSN 579)—see previous page *1970, United States Navy*

SKATE (SSN 578)—see previous page *United States Navy*

1 NUCLEAR-POWERED RESEARCH SUBMARINE (SSN): "SEAWOLF" TYPE

Name	*No.*	*Builder*	*Laid down*	*Launched*	*Commissioned*
*SEAWOLF	SSN 575	General Dynamics (Electric Boat)	15 Sep 1953	21 July 1955	30 Mar 1957

Displacement, tons	3 720 standard; 4 280 submerged
Length, feet (*metres*)	337·5 (*102·9*) oa
Beam, feet (*metres*)	27·7 (*8·4*)
Draught, feet (*metres*)	22 (*6·7*)
Torpedo tubes	6—21 inch (*533 mm*) forward
Main engines	2 steam turbines (General Electric), approx 15,000 shp; 2 shafts
Nuclear reactor	1 pressurised-water cooled S2Wa (Westinghouse)
Speed, knots	19 surface; 20+ submerged
Complement	120 (12 officers, 108 enlisted men)

The *Seawolf* was the world's second nuclear-propelled vehicle; she was constructed almost simultaneously with the *Nautilus* to test a competitive reactor design. Funds for the *Seawolf* were authorised in the Fiscal Year 1952 new construction programme.

The *Seawolf* established a submerged endurance record in 1958 when she remained submerged for 60 consecutive days, travelling a distance of 13 761 miles with a completely sealed atmosphere. She is no longer considered a "first line" submarine and has been engaged primarily in research work since 1969.

ELECTRONICS. Fitted with Mk 101 Mod 8 torpedo fire control system.

ENGINEERING. Initial work in the development of naval nuclear propulsion plants investigated a number of concepts, two of which were of sufficient interest to warrant full development: the pressurised water and liquid metal (sodium). The *Nautilus* was provided with a pressurised-water reactor plant and the *Seawolf* was fitted initially with a liquid-metal reactor.

Originally known as the Submarine Intermediate Reactor (SIR), the liquid metal-plant was developed by the Atomic Energy Commission's Knolls Atomic Power Laboratory.

The SIR Mark II/S2G reactor in the *Seawolf* achieved initial criticality on 25 June 1956. Steam leaks developed during the dockside testing. The plant was shut down and it was determined that the leaks were caused by sodium-potassium alloy which had entered the superheater steam piping. After repairs and testing the *Seawolf* began sea trials on 21 Jan 1957. The trials were run at reduced power and after two years of operation the *Seawolf* entered the Electric Boat yard for removal of her sodium-cooled plant and installation of a pressurised-water plant similar to that installed in the *Nautilus* (designated S2Wa). When the original *Seawolf* plant was shut down in December 1958 the submarine had steamed a total of 71 611 miles. She was recommissioned on 30 Sep 1960. The pressurised-water reactor was refuelled for the first between May 1965 and August 1967, having propelled the *Seawolf* for more than 161 000 miles on its initial fuel core.

SEAWOLF (SSN 575) *1974, William Whalen, Jr.*

PHOTOGRAPHS. Note luminescent markings on the *Seawolf's* sail to assist underwater "mating" of submersibles. The *Seawolf* is the only US nuclear submarine with a stepped sail structure.

Submarines—*continued*

SEAWOLF (SSN 575)—see previous page

1967, United States Navy

1 NUCLEAR POWERED ATTACK SUBMARINE (SSN): "NAUTILUS" TYPE

Displacement, tons	3 530 standard; 4 040 submerged
Length, feet (*metres*)	323·7 (*98·6*) oa
Beam, feet (*metres*)	27·6 (*8·4*)
Draught, feet (*metres*)	22 (*6·7*)
Torpedo tubes	6—21 inch (*533 mm*) forward
Main engines	2 steam turbines (Westinghouse), approx 15 000 shp; 2 shafts
Nuclear reactor	1 pressurised-water cooled S2W (Westinghouse)
Speed, knots	18 surface; 20+ submerged
Complement	120 (12 officers, 108 enlisted men)

Name	*No.*	*Builder*	*Laid down*	*Launched*	*Commissioned*
***NAUTILUS**	SSN 571	General Dynamics (Electric Boat)	14 June 1952	21 Jan 1954	30 Sep 1954

The *Nautilus* was the world's first nuclear-propelled vehicle. She predated the first Soviet nuclear-powered submarine by an estimated five years.

The Chief of Naval Operations initially established a requirement for a nuclear-propelled submarine in August 1949 and specified a "ready-for-sea" date of January 1955. The funds for construction of the *Nautilus* were authorised in the Fiscal Year 1952 budget. The *Nautilus* put to sea for the first time on 17 Jan 1955 and signalled the historic message: "Underway on nuclear power".

On her shakedown cruise in May 1955 the *Nautilus* steamed submerged from London, Connecticut, to San Juan, Puerto Rico, travelling more than 1 300 miles in 84 hours at an average speed of almost 16 knots; she later steamed submerged from Key West, Florida, to New London, a distance of 1 397 miles, at an average speed of more than 20 knots.

During 1958 the *Nautilus* undertook extensive operations under the Arctic ice pack and in August she made history's first polar transit from the Pacific to the Atlantic, steaming from Pearl Harbour to Portland, England. She passed under the geographic North Pole on 3 Aug 1958.

During 1972-74 the *Nautilus* underwent a 30-month overhaul and modification at the Electric Boat yard in Groton, Connecticut, where the submarine was built. Modified for submarine communications research.

DESIGN. The *Nautilus* and *Seawolf* have GUPPY-type hull configurations. The *Seawolf* has a stepped sail and a slight rise at the bow.

ELECTRONICS. Fitted with Mk 101 Mod 6 torpedo fire control system.

ENGINEERING. In January 1948 the Department of Defense requested the Atomic Energy Commission to undertake the design, development, and construction of a nuclear reactor for submarine propulsion. Initial research and conceptual design of the Submarine Thermal Reactor (STR) was undertaken by the Argonne National Laboratory. Subsequently the Atomic Energy Commission's Bettis Atomic Power Laboratory, operated by the Westinghouse Electric Corporation, undertook development of the first nuclear propulsion plant.

The *Nautilus* STR Mark II nuclear plant (redesignated S2W) was first operated on 20 Dec 1954 and first developed full power on 3 Jan 1955.

After more than two years of operation, during which she steamed 62 562 miles, the *Nautilus* began an overhaul which included refuelling in April 1957. She was again refuelled in 1959 after steaming 91 324 miles on her second fuel core, and again in 1964 after steaming approximately 150 000 miles on her third fuel core. (The prototype Mark I/S1W plant was refuelled in 1955, 1958, 1960, and 1967; it remains in operation as an experimental and training facility)

NAUTILUS (SSN 571)

1975, General Dynamics, Electric Boat Division

NAUTILUS (SSN 571)

United States Navy

Submarines—*continued*

3 ATTACK SUBMARINES (SS): "BARBEL" CLASS

Displacement, tons	2 145 surface; 2 895 submerged
Length, feet (*metres*)	219·5 (*66·8*) oa
Beam, feet (*metres*)	29 (*8·8*)
Draught, feet (*metres*)	28 (*8·5*)
Torpedo tubes	6—21 inch (*533 mm*) forward
Main engines	3 diesels 4 800 bhp (Fairbanks Morse); 2 electric motors (General Electric) 3 150 shp; 1 shaft
Speed, knots	15 on surface; 25 submerged
Complement	78 (8 officers, 70 men)

Name	*No.*	*Builder*	*Laid down*	*Launched*	*Commissioned*
*BARBEL	SS 580	Portsmouth Naval Shipyard	18 May 1956	19 July 1958	17 Jan 1959
*BLUEBACK	SS 581	Ingalls Shipbuilding Corporation	15 Apr 1957	16 May 1959	15 Oct 1959
*BONEFISH	SS 582	New York Shipbuilding Corp	3 June 1957	22 Nov 1958	9 July 1959

These submarines were the last non-nuclear combatant submarines built by the US Navy. All three were authorised in the Fiscal Year 1956 new construction programme.

CONSTRUCTION. The *Blueback* was the first submarine built by the Ingalls Shipbuilding Corp at Pascagoula, Mississippi, and the *Bonefish* was the first constructed at the New York Shipbuilding Corp yard in Camden, New Jersey. None of the three shipyards that built this class is now employed in submarine construction.

DESIGN. These submarines have the "tear drop" or modified spindle hull design which was tested in the experimental submarine *Albacore*. As built their diving planes were bow-mounted; subsequently relocated to the sail structure.
These submarines introduced a new concept in centralised arrangement of controls in an "attack centre" to increase efficiency; the concept has been adapted for all later US combat submarines.

ELECTRONICS. Fitted with Mk 101 Mod 20 torpedo fire control system.

PHOTOGRAPHS. Note forward position of diving planes on sail structure, bow configuration for maximum underwater performance, and clear decks that are void of projections.

BLUEBACK (SS 581) — *1967, United States Navy*

BONEFISH (SS 582) — *1969, United States Navy*

1 ATTACK SUBMARINE (SS): "DARTER" TYPE

Displacement, tons	1 720 surface; 2 388 submerged
Length, feet (*metres*)	268·6 (*81·9*) oa
Beam, feet (*metres*)	27·2 (*8·3*)
Draught, feet (*metres*)	19 (*5·8*)
Torpedo tubes	8—21 inch (*533 mm*) 6 fwd; 2 aft
Main engines	3 diesels (Fairbanks Morse); 4 500 bhp electric motors (Elliott); 2 shafts
Speed, knots	19·5 surface; 14 submerged
Complement	87 (8 officers, 79 men)

Name	*No.*	*Builder*	*Laid down*	*Launched*	*Commissioned*
*DARTER	SS 576	General Dynamics Corp (Electric Boat)	10 Nov 1954	28 May 1956	20 Oct 1956

Designed for high submerged speed with quiet machinery. Planned sister submarines *Growler* and *Grayback* were completed to missile-launching configuration.
Basic design of the *Darter* is similar to the "Tang" class described on a later page.
Authorised in Fiscal Year 1954 shipbuilding programme.

No additional submarines of this type were built because of shift to high-speed hull design and nuclear propulsion.

ELECTRONICS. Fitted with Mk 106 Mod 11 torpedo fire control system.

DARTER (SS 576) — *United States Navy*

Submarines—*continued*

1 GUIDED MISSILE SUBMARINE (SSG): "GROWLER" TYPE

Name	No	Builder	Laid down	Launched	Commissioned
GROWLER	SSG 577	Portsmouth Naval Shipyard	15 Feb 1955	5 Apr 1959	30 Apr 1958

Displacement, tons: 2 540 standard; 3 515 submerged
Length, feet (*metres*): 317·6 (*96·8*) oa
Beam, feet (*metres*): 27·2 (*8·2*)
Draught, feet (*metres*): 19 (*5·8*)
Torpedo tubes: 6—21 inch (*533 mm*) 4 fwd; 2 aft
Main engines: 3 diesels (Fairbanks Morse); 4 600 bhp/2 electric motors (Elliott); 5 600 shp; 2 shafts
Speed, knots: 20 surface; 17 submerged
Complement: 84 officers and enlisted men

The *Growler* was authorised in the Fiscal Year 1955 new construction programme; completed as a guided missile submarine to fire the Regulus surface-to-surface cruise missile (see *Halibut*, SSN 587, for *Missile* notes). When the Regulus submarine missile programme ended in 1964 the *Growler* and her near-sister submarine *Grayback* were withdrawn from service; the *Grayback* subsequently converted to an amphibious transport submarine (LPSS). The *Growler* was scheduled to undergo a similar conversion when the *Grayback* was completed, but the second conversion was deferred late in 1968 because of rising ship conversion costs.
The *Growler* is in reserve as an SSG.

DESIGN. The *Grayback* and *Growler* initially were designed as attack submarines similar to the *Darter*. Upon redesign as missile submarines they were cut in half on the building ways and were lengthened approximately 50 feet, two cylindrical hangars, each 11 feet high and 70 feet long, were superimposed on their bows, a missile launcher was installed between the hangars and sail structure, and elaborate navigation and fire control systems were fitted. The height of the sail structure on the *Growler* is approximately 30 feet above the deck; the *Grayback's* lower sail structure was increased during LPSS conversion.

PHOTOGRAPHS. The *Growler* is large, twin missile hangars faired into her bow are clearly visible; the Regulus missile launcher is between the hangars and soil structure. A side-by-side view of the *Grayback* and *Growle* appears in the 1974-1975 and previous editions.

GROWLER (SSG 577) — *1958, United States Navy*

2 ATTACK SUBMARINES (SS): "SAILFISH" CLASS

Name	No.	Builder	Laid down	Launched	Commissioned
*SAILFISH	SS 572 (ex-SSR 572)	Portsmouth Naval Shipyard	8 Dec 1953	7 Sep 1955	14 Apr 1956
*SALMON	SS 573 (ex-AGSS 573, ex-SSR 573)	Portsmouth Naval Shipyard	10 Mar 1954	25 Feb 1956	25 Aug 1956

Displacement, tons: 2 625 surface; 3 168 submerged
Length, feet (*metres*): 350·4 (*106·8*) oa
Beam, feet (*metres*): 28·4 (*8·8*)
Draught, feet (*metres*): 18 (*5·5*) max
Torpedo tubes: 6—21 inch (*533 mm*) forward
Main engines: 4 diesels (Fairbanks Morse); 6 000 bhp/2 electric motors (Elliott); 8 200 shp; 2 shafts
Speed, knots: 19·5 on surface; 14 submerged
Complement: 87 (8 officers, 79 enlisted men)

Largest non-nuclear submarines built by the US Navy since the *Narwhal* (SS 167) and *Nautilus* (SS 168) completed in 1930. The *Sailfish* and *Salmon* were built as radar picket submarines (SSR) with air search radar antennas on deck and elaborate air control centres. Authorised in Fiscal Year 1952 programme. Both submarines underwent FRAM II modernisation.
These are believed to be the largest non-nuclear submarines in service with any navy.

CLASSIFICATION. Reclassified from radar picket submarines (SSR) to SS on 1 Mar 1961; *Salmon* reclassified AGSS on 29 June 1968 to serve at test and evaluation submarine for Navy's Deep Submergence Rescue Vehicle (DSRV). However, the DSRV programme was delayed and the *Salmon* reverted to the SS designation on 30 June 1969.
All ten of the World War II-built submarines that had been converted to radar picket configurations have been stricken.
Radar picket submarines were to operate ahead of carrier task forces to provide early warning of air attack; upon coming under attack themselves they would submerge for safety. The Soviet Navy operates several modified "W" class submarines in the radar picket role. They are designated "canvas bag" by NATO.

ELECTRONICS. Fitted with BQG-4 passive fire control sonar (note three fin-like PUFF sonar domes). The fourth "fin" at stern is the upper rudder. See "Tang" class listing for details.
Fitted with Mk 106 Mod 21 torpedo fire control system.

PHOTOGRAPHS. Note size of PUFF fins in comparison to men in photograph of the *Salmon*.

SAILFISH (SS 572) — *1966, United States Navy*

SALMON (SS 573) — *United States Navy*

Submarines—*continued*

1 AMPHIBIOUS TRANSPORT SUBMARINE: "GRAYBACK" TYPE

		Builder	Laid down	Launched	Commissioned	LPSS Comm.
***GRAYBACK**	SS 574 (ex-LPSS 574, ex-SSG 574)	Mare Island Naval Shipyard	1 July 1954	2 July 1957	7 Mar 1958	9 May 1969

Displacement, tons	2 670 standard; 3 650 submerged
Length, feet (*metres*)	334 (*101·8*) oa
Beam, feet (*metres*)	30 (*9·0*)
Draught, feet (*metres*)	19 (*5·8*)
Torpedo tubes	8—21 inch (*533 mm*) 6 fwd; 2 aft
Main engines	3 diesels (Fairbanks Morse); 4 500 bhp/2 electric motors (Elliott); 5 600 shp; 2 shafts
Speed, knots	20 surface; 17 submerged
Complement	88 (10 officers, 78 enlisted men)
Troops	67 (7 officers, 60 enlisted men)

The *Grayback* has been fully converted to a transport submarine and is officially classified as an amphibious warfare ship. She was originally intended to be an attack submarine, being authorised in the Fiscal Year 1953 new construction programme, but redesigned in 1956 to provide a Regulus missile launching capability; completed as SSG 574 in 1958, similar in design to the *Growler* (SSG 577). See *Growler* listing for basic design notes.

CLASSIFICATION. The *Grayback* was reclassified as an attack submarine (SS) on 30 June 1975 although she retains her transport configuration and capabilities. The change apparently was made to meet attack submarine force level commitments.

CONVERSION. The *Grayback* began conversion to a transport submarine at the San Francisco Bay Naval Shipyard (Mare Island) in November 1967. The conversion was originally estimated at $15 200 000 but was actually about $30 000 000. She was reclassified from SSG to LPSS on 30 Aug 1968 (never officially designated APSS).
During conversion the *Grayback* was fitted to berth and mess 67 troops and carry their equipment including landing craft or swimmer delivery vehicles (SDV). Her torpedo tubes and hence attack capability are retained. As completed (SSG) the *Grayback* had an overall length of 322 ft 4 in; lengthened 12 ft during LPSS conversion. Conversion was authorised in Fiscal Year 1965 programme and completed in June 1969; delayed because of higher priorities being allocated to other submarine projects.

ELECTRONICS. Fitted with BQG-4 passive fire control sonar (note three fin-like PUFF sonar domes). See "Tang" class listing for details.

Fitted with Mk 106 Mod 12 torpedo fire control system.

PHOTOGRAPHS. Bow and stern views of the *Grayback* appear in the 1972-1973 edition.

GRAYBACK (SS 574) *1969, United States Navy*

3 ATTACK SUBMARINES (SS) / 1 RESEARCH SUBMARINE (AGSS) } "TANG" CLASS

Displacement, tons	2 100 surface; 2 700 submerged
Length, feet (*metres*)	287 (*87·4*) oa
Beam, feet (*metres*)	27·3 (*8·3*)
Draught, feet (*metres*)	19 (*6·2*)
Torpedo tubes	8—21 inch (*533 mm*) 6 fwd; 2 aft
Main engines	3 diesels (Fairbanks-Morse); 4 500 bhp/2 electric motors; 5 600 shp; 2 shafts
Speed, knots	16 surface; 16 submerged
Complement	87 (8 officers, 79 men)

Name	No.	Builder	Laid down	Launched	Commissioned
***TANG**	AGSS 563	Portsmouth Naval Shipyard	18 Apr 1949	19 June 1951	25 Oct 1951
***WAHOO**	SS 565	Portsmouth Naval Shipyard	24 Oct 1949	16 Oct 1951	30 May 1952
***TROUT**	SS 566	Electric Boat Co, Groton	1 Dec 1949	21 Aug 1951	27 June 1952
***GUDGEON**	SS 567	Portsmouth Naval Shipyard	20 May 1950	11 June 1952	21 Nov 1952

Six submarines of this class were constructed, incorporating improvements based on German World War II submarine developments. The *Tang* was authorised in the Fiscal Year 1947 new construction programme, *Wahoo* and *Trout* in FY 1948, and *Gudgeon* in FY 1949. The *Gudgeon* was the first US submarine to circumnavigate the world during Sep 1957-Feb 1958.
All remaining submarines of this class are active.

CLASSIFICATION. The *Tang* was reclassified as a research submarine (AGSS) on 30 June 1975 for use in acoustic research. She replaces the *Tigrone* (AGSS 419) which had served in that role for two decades.

ELECTRONICS. BQG-4 fire control sonar is fitted in these submarines; the small, fin-like structures are antenna domes for the sonar (referred to as PUFFS—an acronym for Passive Underwater Fire Control Feasibility Systsm).
Fitted with Mk 106 Mod 18 torpedo fire control system.

ENGINEERING. *Tang, Trout* and *Wahoo* were originally powered by a compact, radial type engine produced after five years of development work, comprising a 16-cylinder 2-cycle plant, mounted vertically with four rows of cylinders radially arranged. These new engines were half the weight and two-thirds the size of the engines previously available for submarines. They proved to be unsatisfactory and were replaced by machinery similar to that in *Gudgeon* which has Fairbanks-Morse high speed lightweight engines mounted horizontally. The electric motors are Elliott in *Tang*, General Electric in *Wahoo* and *Trout*, Westinghouse in *Gudgeon*.
Snorkel fitted as in all later US nuclear and conventionally propelled submarines.

GUDGEON (SS 567) *1970, United States Navy*

WAHOO (SS 565) *1968, United States Navy*

Submarines—*continued*

"TANG" CLASS—*continued*

RECONSTRUCTION. All six submarines of this class were built with an overall length of 269 ft 2 in. The units had their original diesel engines replaced during the late 1950's were cut in half and a 9 ft section inserted amidships. All six submarines were modernised during the 1960's with the installation of improved electronics equipment and other features; additional sections were added to give an overall length of 287 ft.

DISPOSALS AND TRANSFERS
Trigger (SS 564) transferred to Italy on 10 July 1973; **Harder** (SS 568) transferred to Italy on 15 Mar 1974.

"TANG" Class — *1974, William Whalen Jr*

1 RESEARCH SUBMARINE (AGSS): "ALBACORE" TYPE

Displacement, tons	1 500 surface; 1 850 submerged
Length, feet (*metres*)	210·5 (*63·6*) oa
Beam, feet (*metres*)	27·5 (*8·4*)
Draught, feet (*metres*)	18·5 (*5·6*)
Torpedo tubes	None
Main engines	2 diesels, radial pancake type (General Motors) electric motor (Westinghouse) 15 000 shp; 1 shaft
Speed, knots	25 on surface; 33 submerged
Complement	52 (5 officers, 47 men)

High speed experimental submarine. Conventionally powered submarine of radical design with new hull form which makes her faster and more manoeuvrable than any other conventional submarine. Officially described as a hydrodynamic test vehicle. Streamlined, whale shaped without the naval flat-topped deck. Conning tower resembles a fish's dorsal fin.

Name	*No.*	*Builder*	*Laid down*	*Launched*	*Commissioned*
ALBACORE	AGSS 569	Portsmouth Naval Shipyard	15 Mar 1952	1 Aug 1953	5 Dec 1953

The *Albacore* was decommissioned and placed in reserve on 1 Sep 1972.

EXPERIMENTAL. The *Albacore* has been extensively modified to test advanced submarine design and engineering concepts.
Phase I modifications were made from July 1954 to February 1955 to eliminate the many "bugs" inherent with completely new construction and equipment.
Phase II modifications from Dec 1955 to Mar 1956 during which conventional propeller-rudder-stern diving plane arrangement was modified; the new design provided for the propeller to be installed *aft* of the control surfaces. (At this time a small auxiliary rudder on the sail was removed)
A concave bow sonar dome was fitted for tests in 1960. Phase III modifications from Nov 1960 to Aug 1961 during which an entirely new stern was installed featuring the stern planes in an "X" configuration, a system of ten hydraulic operated dive brakes around the hull amidships, a dorsal rudder, and a new bow sonar dome. Phase IV modifications from Dec 1962 to Mar 1965 during which a silver-zinc battery was installed and counter-rotating stern propellers rotating around the same axis were fitted.
The *Albacore* conducted trials with towed sonar arrays from May to July 1966.
All modifications were made at the Portsmouth Naval Shipyard.

PHOTOGRAPH. Note stern rudder configuration; rounded hull without superstructure deck common to previous and contemporary submarines. Round electronic "ball" antenna on sail structure. Deck cleats and other equipment are recessed into hull.

ALBACORE (AGSS 569) — *United States Navy*

1 RESEARCH SUBMARINE (AGSS): "DOLPHIN" TYPE

Displacement, tons	800 standard; 930 full load
Length, feet	152
Beam, feet	19·3
Diameter, feet	18 (maximum)
Torpedo tubes	Removed
Main engines	Diesel/electric (2 Detroit 12V71 diesels), 1 500 hp; 1 shaft
Speed, knots	12+ submerged
Complement	24 (3 officers, 21 enlisted men) plus 4 to 7 scientists

Name	*No.*	*Builder*	*Laid down*	*Launched*	*Commissioned*
***DOLPHIN**	AGSS 555	Portsmouth Naval Shipyard	9 Nov 1962	8 June 1968	17 Aug 1968

The *Dolphin* is an auxiliary submarine specifically designed for deep-diving operations. Authorised in Fiscal Year 1961 new construction programme, but delayed because of changes in mission and equipment coupled with higher priorities being given to other submarine projects
The *Dolphin* is fitted for deep-ocean sonar and oceanographic research. She is highly automated and has three computer-operated systems, a safety system, hovering system, and one that is classified. The digital-computer submarine safety system monitors equipment and provides data on closed-circuit television screens; malfunctions in equipment or trends towards potentially dangerous situations set off an alarm and if they are not corrected within the prescribed time the system, unless overridden by an operator, automatically brings the submarine to the surface. There are several research stations for scientists in the *Dolphin* and she is fitted to take water samples down to her operating (test) depth. The single, experimental torpedo tube was removed in 1970.
Underwater endurance is limited (endurance and habitability were considered of secondary importance in design). On 24 Nov 1968 the *Dolphin* "descended to a depth greater than that recorded by any other operational submarine "according to official statements.

CLASSIFICATION. The *Dolphin's* number was taken from a block (551-562) authorised but cancelled late in World War II with no construction being assigned. (Submarines built in Norway and Denmark were assigned the hull numbers SS 553 and SS 554, respectively, for financial accounting purposes; hull numbers SS 551 and SS 552 in this series were assigned to the late hunter-killer submarines *Bass*, ex-SSK 2 and *Bonita* ex-SSK 3 respectively).

DESIGN. The *Dolphin* has a constant diameter cylindrical pressure hull approximately 15 feet in outer diameter closed at both ends with hemispherical heads. Pressure hull fabricated of HY-80 steel with aluminium and fibreglass used in secondary structures to reduce weight, a critical factor in retaining buoyancy at deep depths. No conventional diving planes are mounted, improved rudder design and other features provide manoeuvring control and hovering capability. Access is through a single hatch in the pressure hull (opening into sail structure).

ENGINEERING. Fitted with 330 cell silver zinc battery. Submerged endurance is approximately 24 hours with an at-sea endurance of 14 days.

STATUS. Completed in early 1969, approximately five years behind official schedule at time of keel laying. The *Dolphin* is in commission and has a commanding officer.

PHOTOGRAPHS. On the following page note the *Dolphin's* large sonar dome faired into the bow. Earlier configurations are shown in the 1974-1975 and previous editions.

Submarines—*continued*

DOLPHIN (AGSS 555) *United States Navy*

1 AMPHIBIOUS TRANSPORT SUBMARINE (LPSS): "SEALION" TYPE

Displacement, tons	2 145 surface; 2 500 submerged
Length, feet (*metres*)	311·5 (*95·0*)
Beam, feet (*metres*)	27 (*8·2*)
Draught, feet (*metres*)	17 (*5·2*)
Torpedo tubes	Removed
Guns	Removed
Main engines	2 diesels (General Motors), 2 305 bhp/4 electric motors (General Electric); 2 shafts
Speed, knots	13 surface; 10 submerged
Complement	74 (6 officers, 68 men)
Troops	160

Name	*No*	*Builder*	*Laid down*	*Launched*	*Commissioned*
SEALION	LPSS 315	Electric Boat Company, Groton	25 Feb 1943	31 Oct 1943	8 Mar 1944

Originally a "Balao" class submarine converted to underwater transport for carrying Marines, commandos or frogmen in covert operations where surface ships would be too vulnerable. The *Sealion* was to have been replaced by conversion of the *Growler* (SSG 577) to a transport submarine; however, conversion of *Growler* was cancelled.
The *Sealion* was decommissioned and placed in reserve in Feb 1970.

CLASSIFICATION. *Sealion* changed from SS to transport submarine (SSP) in March 1948; changed to auxiliary transport submarine (ASSP) in January 1950; changed to APSS in October 1956; changed again to amphibious transport submarine (LPSS) on 1 Jan 1969

CONVERSION. The *Sealion* was converted to a transport submarine at the San Francisco Naval Shipyard in 1948. All torpedo tubes and half of her diesel propulsion plant were removed to provide berthing for 160 troops; stowage provided for rubber rafts and other equipment in enlarged superstructure deck aft of conning tower.

ENGINEERING. Fitted with snorkel installation.

GUNNERY. The two 40 mm single guns shown on conning tower steps were removed prior to the *Sealion* being decommissioned.

STATUS. In 1960 the *Sealion* was assigned to operational reserve training duties; recommissioned late in 1961 with increase of US conventional warfare capabilities. See 1971-1972 edition for disposals of earlier transport submarines.

SEALION (LPSS 315) *1965, United States Navy*

PHOTOGRAPHS. Note SAFETY TRACK on deck, "bulge" AFT OF CONNING TOWER for raft stowage compartments, and propeller guards at stern.

"TIGRONE" TYPE

The research submarine *Tigrone* (AGSS 419) was stricken on 30 June 1975 after several delays in her demise. The former "Tench" class submarine had been employed for more than two decades in acoustic research. See 1974-1975 and previous editions for characteristics.

GUPPY SUBMARINES

All 52 submarines modernised to the GUPPY (Greater Underwater Propulsion Project) configurations have been stricken or transferred to other navies. The last GUPPY submarines to serve with the US Navy were the *Clamagore* (SS 343), transferred to Turkey on 12 June 1975, and *Tiru* (SS 416) transferred to Turkey in July 1975.
Additions to the comprehensive list of GUPPY disposals and transfers provided in the 1974-1975 edition include: *Blenny* (SS 324) transferred to Peru on 31 July 1974, and *Sea Poacher* (SS 406) transferred to Peru on 15 July 1974.

TRAINING SUBMARINES (SST)

All specifically designated target and training submarines have been stricken. See 1973-1974 and previous editions for characteristics.
The former "hunter-killer" type submarine **Barracuda** (SS-T3/SST 3/SSK 1) stricken on 1 Oct 1973.
The built-for-the-purpose training submarines **Mackerel** (SST 1/AGSS 570) and **Marlin** (SST 2) stricken on 31 Jan 1973.

MIDGET SUBMARINES

The US Navy's only "midget" submarine, the 50-foot long *X-1* was stricken on 16 Feb 1973; see 1972-1973 edition for characteristics.

DEEP SUBMERGENCE VEHICLES

The US Navy's Deep Submergence Vehicles (DSV) are listed in a separate section at the end of the United States Navy portion of this edition.

AIRCRAFT CARRIERS

Aircraft carriers remain a primary element of US political and military power, leading to the decision to initiate construction of a new series of aircraft carriers in Fiscal Year 1978. These ships will be required to permit a force level of 12 fully operational aircraft carriers in the mid-1980s and beyond. Secretary of Defense Schlesinger has stated that this number is "the minimum needed to support our strategy and peacetime commitments . . . we propose to retain in the force a 13th carrier without a dedicated air wing to provide greater flexibility for contingency deployments".

The US Navy operated 14 aircraft carriers into 1975. The two surviving "Hancock" class aircraft carriers were scheduled to be decommissioned by early 1976 at which time the long-delayed, nuclear-propelled carrier *Nimitz* would be completed although not fully operational.

This 13 carrier force would be retained into the mid-1980s, with the nuclear carriers *Dwight D. Eisenhower* and *Carl Vinson* subsequently replacing two "Midway" class carriers. The third ship of that older class would remain in limited commission, possibly operating Navy and Marine Corps reserve aircraft during contingency operations.

By the mid-1980s the oldest of the eight "Forrestal" class aircraft carriers will have been in service for 30 years and require replacement. Accordingly, the Navy plans to initiate construction of a new series of aircraft carriers (now designated CVNX for planning purposes). The lead ship will be requested in the FY 1977-1978 budgets and, assuming a six-year construction period, would be delivered about 1984-1985. Secretary Schlesinger has stated that follow-on ships would be built to replace the "Forrestal" class on a one-for-one basis at the rate of one CVNX every two years.

Specific characteristics of the CVNX have not yet been developed; however, it appears that the ship would be sized somewhere between the "Forrestal" and "Nimitz" classes. The Congress has passed a law requiring that all "combat vessels intended to operate in combat in aircraft carrier task groups (that is, aircraft carriers and the cruisers, frigates, and destroyers which accompany aircraft carriers)" be nuclear powered. Still, some analysis indicates that non-nuclear carriers could continue to be effective in a future force mix that includes the four nuclear carriers now built and under construction.

NIMITZ (CVAN 68) — *1975, United States Navy, PH3 D. E. Patton*

SEA CONTROL SHIPS

The Congress has refused to fund the so-called Sea Control Ships (SCS) that the Navy had planned to begin in the FY 1975 new construction programme. The Navy's proposed ship is discussed in detail in the 1974-1975 edition of *Jane's Fighting Ships*.

The Navy still requires a ship capable of operating a small number of VSTOL (Vertical/Short Take-offs and Landing) aircraft and helicopters for "sea control" missions in low-threat areas. Secretary Schlesinger has stated that: "Such a ship would provide greater flexibility for employment in a wider range of situations. Offensive options being examined include the operation of VSTOL strike aircraft and assault helicopters for an embarked Marine Corps unit". This notion implies multi-purpose ships, a concept demonstrated off North Vietnam and Suez when US Navy amphibious assault ships of the "Iwo Jima" class operated minesweeping helicopters.

VISTOL SUPPORT SHIPS

The current Navy design studies for a VSTOL carrier are labelled VSTOL Support Ship (VSS) and range from about 15 000 tons, or slightly larger than the previous SCS design, up to about 35 000 tons with one or more catapults and arresting gear. The larger designs would accommodate fixed-wing aircraft such as the S-3 Viking as well as VSTOL aircraft and helicopters.

The tentative five-year ship construction programme provides for construction of the lead VSTOL support ship under the FY 1977 budget and additional ships in subsequent years at the rate of two ships per year, apparently with a force level goal of eight ships.

NIMITZ (CVAN 68) — *1975, United States Navy, PH3 D. E. Patton*

TRAINING CARRIER. The "Hancock" class carrier *Lexington* (CVT 16) operates as a training carrier and is based at Pensacola, Florida. The ship has no aircraft maintenance or arming capabilities, and hence cannot be considered as a combat ship. In an emergency situation aircraft could be embarked to conduct anti-submarine or amphibious assault operations on a very restricted basis. The designation CVT is officially classified as an auxiliary ship.

AIR WINGS. Each large attack carrier normally operates an air wing of 85 to 95 aircraft; two fighter squadrons with 24 F-4 Phantoms or F-14 Tomcats as they become available, two or three light attack squadrons with 24 or 36 A-7 Corsairs, one medium attack squadron with 12 A-6 Intruders, and smaller squadrons or detachments with three RA-5C Vigilantes for reconnaissance, four EA-6B Prowlers for electronic warfare, four E-2C Hawkeyes or earlier aircraft for early warning, and four KA-6 Intruders for in-flight refuelling.

In the CV/CVN configuration the carrier trade off A-7 Corsairs and possibly RA-5C Vigilantes for a ten-plane squadron of S-2 Tracker or S-3 Viking anti-submarine aircraft, and eight SH-3 Sea King helicopters. The "Nimitz" class ships will accommodate all of the above simultaneously.

The "Hancock" class ships operate F-8 Crusader fighters, A-7 Corsair or A-4 Skyhawk attack planes, RF-8G Crusader photo-reconnaissance aircraft, and EKA-3B Skywarriors in the electronic warfare-tanker role.

Attack carriers generally have a C-1 Trader carrier on-board delivery (COD) cargo aircraft and utility helicopters assigned.

PHOTOGRAPHS. The accompanying photographs of the *Nimitz* show the super carrier on initial underway trials in February and March 1975. Note the conventional island configuration in comparison with the nuclear-propelled *Enterprise*. The *Nimitz* has a separate radar mast aft of the island, as in the previous "Kitty Hawk" class. A waterline view of the ship at launching in 1972 appears in the 1974-1975 edition.

Aircraft Carriers—*continued*

1 + 2 NUCLEAR-POWERED ATTACK AIRCRAFT CARRIERS (CVAN/CVN): "NIMITZ" CLASS

Name	No.	Builders	Laid down	Launched	Commission
NIMITZ	CVAN 68	Newport News	22 June 1968	13 May 1972	3 May 1975
DWIGHT D. EISENHOWER	CVAN 69	Newport News	14 Aug 1970	1975	mid 1977
CARL VINSON	CVN 70	Newport News	Nov 1975	Mar 1979	1981

Displacement, tons	91 400 full load
Length, feet (*metres*)	1 040 (*317·0*) wl; 1 092 (*332·0*) oa
Beam, feet (*metres*)	134 (*40·8*)
Draught, feet (*metres*)	37 (*11·3*)
Flight deck width, feet (*metres*)	252 (*76·8*)
Catapults	4 steam
Aircraft	approx 100
Missiles	3 Basic Point Defence Missile System (BPDMS) launchers with Sea Sparrow missiles (Mk 25)
Main engines	Geared steam turbines; 260 000 shp; 4 shafts
Nuclear reactors	2 pressurised-water cooled
Speed, knots	30+
Complement	3 300 plus approx 2 800 assigned to air wing for a total of 6 100 per ship

The lead ship for this class and the world's second nuclear-powered aircraft carrier was ordered 9½ years after the first such ship, the USS *Enterprise*. The *Nimitz* was authorised in the Fiscal Year 1967 new construction programme; the *Dwight D. Eisenhower* in the FY 1970 programme, and the *Carl Vinson* in the FY 1973-1974 programmes. All three ships are being constructed by the Newport News Shipbuilding & Dry Dock Co (Virginia), the only US shipyard now capable of constructing large, nuclear-propelled warships.

The completion of the first two ships has been delayed almost two years because of delays in the delivery and testing of nuclear plant components. The *Eisenhower* is contracted for delivery to the Navy 21 months after the *Nimitz*. The delays in these ships could further increase their costs. (See *Fiscal* notes).

DESIGNATION. The third ship of this class is designated an "aircraft carrier" (CV) because she will carry fighter, attack, and anti-submarine aircraft; the other ships will be modified to CV status after completion.

ELECTRONICS. These ships will have the Naval Tactical Data System (NTDS) and the following radars: SPS-10 surface search, SPS-43A two-dimensional air search, and SPS-48 three-dimensional air search, and SPN-42, SPN-43, and SPN-44 navigation equipment. These ships will not have sonar.

ENGINEERING. These carriers will each have only two nuclear reactors compared to the eight reactors required for the carrier *Enterprise*. The nuclear cores for the reactors in these ships are expected to provide sufficient energy for the ships to each steam for at least 13 years, an estimated 800 000 to 1 million miles between "refuelling". The two cores in one of these carriers will have the energy equivalent to 462 000 000 gallons (US) or 1 620 000 long tons of fuel oil.

FISCAL. The latest reported construction costs for these carriers are $683 900 000 for the *Nimitz*, $748 500 000 for the *Eisenhower*, and $1 194 800 000 for the *Vinson*. In addition, each ship will have "outfitting and post-delivery" costs. The FY 1976 budget requests for $268 000 000 funding of the "Nimitz" class. See previous editions for data on specific ships.

NOMENCLATURE. The *Nimitz* honours Fleet Admiral Chester W. Nimitz who was Commander-in-Chief Pacific Fleet and Commander-in-Chief Pacific Ocean Areas during World War II, and Chief of Naval Operations from December 1945 to December 1947.

The *Dwight D. Eisenhower* is believed the first major US surface warship to be named for an Army officer; General of the Army Eisenhower commanded Allied Forces in Western Europe in 1944-45, subsequently was first Supreme Allied Commander in NATO, and President of the United States from January 1953 to January 1961. The CVAN 69 was named *Eisenhower* on 21 Feb 1970; renamed *Dwight D. Eisenhower* on 25 May 1970, but Secretary of Defense Laird dedicated the ship as the "USS *Eisenhower*" at the keel laying on 15 Aug 1970.

The *Carl Vinson* is believed the first US naval ship to be named for a living person since the American Revolution when a small naval craft was named *Franklin* for American patriot Benjamin Franklin. Carl Vinson was a member of the House of Representatives from Georgia from 1914 to 1965; he served as Chairman of the House Naval Affairs Committee and later the House Armed Services Committee.

NIMITZ (CVAN 68) — *1975, United States Navy, PH3 D. E. Patton*

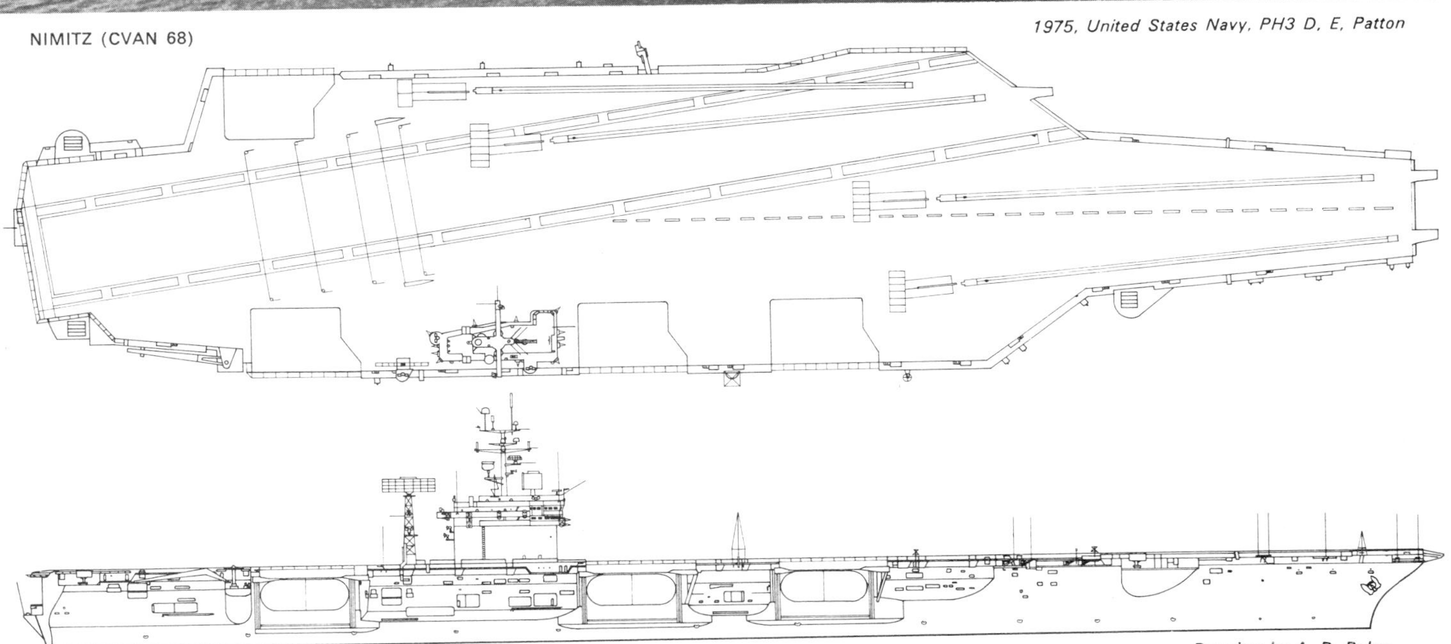

NIMITZ (CVAN 68) — *Drawing by A. D. Baker*

Aircraft Carriers—*Continued*

4 ATTACK AIRCRAFT CARRIERS (CVA/CV): "KITTY HAWK" CLASS

Name	*No.*	*Builder*	*Laid down*	*Launched*	*Commissioned*
***KITTY HAWK**	CV 63	New York Shipbuilding Corp, Camden, NJ	27 Dec 1956	21 May 1960	29 Apr 1961
***CONSTELLATION**	CVA 64	New York Naval Shipyard	14 Sep 1957	8 Oct 1960	27 Oct 1961
***AMERICA**	CVA 66	Newport News Shipbuilding & Dry Dock Co	9 Jan 1961	1 Feb 1964	23 Jan 1965
***JOHN F. KENNEDY**	CV 67	Newport News Shipbuilding & Dry Dock Co	22 Oct 1964	27 May 1967	7 Sep 1968

Displacement, tons	
Kitty Hawk	60 100 standard; 80 800 full load
Constellation	60 100 standard; 80 800 full load
America	60 300 standard; 80 800 full load
John F. Kennedy	61 000 standard; 87 000 full load
Length, feet (*metres*)	990 (*301·8*) wl
Kitty Hawk	1 062·5 (*323·9*) oa
Constellation	1 072·5 (*326·9*) oa
America J.F.K.	1047·5 (*319·3*) oa
Beam, feet (*metres*)	
Kitty Hawk, Constellation	129·5 (*38·5*)
America, J.F.K.	130 (*39·6*)
Draught, feet (*metres*)	35·9 (*10·9*)
Flight deck width, feet, (*metres*)	
J.F.K.	252 (*76·9*) maximum
Others	249 (*76·0*) maximum
Catapults	4 steam
Aircraft	approx 85 in *Kitty Hawk* and *Constellation*; approx 95 in *America* and *John F. Kennedy*
Missile launchers	2 twin Terrier surface-to-air launchers (Mk 10) in *Kitty Hawk, Constellation, America*; 3 Basic Point Defence Missile System (BPDMS) launchers (Mk 25) with Sea Sparrow missiles in *John F. Kennedy*
Main engines	4 geared turbines (Westinghouse) 280 000 shp; 4 shafts
Boilers	8—1 200 psi (*83·4 kg/cm²*) (Foster Wheeler)
Speed	35 knots
Complement	2 800 (150 officers, approx 2 645 enlisted men) plus approx 2 150 assigned to attack air wing for a total of 4 950 officers and enlisted men per ship

CONSTELLATION (CVA 64) — *1974, US Navy, PHCS Robert L. Lawson*

These ships were built to an improved "Forrestal" design and are easily recognised by their smaller island structure which is set farther aft than the superstructure in the four "Forrestal" class ships. Lift arrangements also differ (see design notes). The *Kitty Hawk* was authorised in Fiscal Year 1956 new construction programme, the *Constellation* in FY 1957, the *America* in FY 1961, and the *John F. Kennedy* in FY 1963. Completion of the *Constellation* was delayed because of a fire which ravaged her in the New York Naval Shipyard in December 1960. Construction of the *John F. Kennedy* was delayed because of debate over whether to provide her with conventional or nuclear propulsion.
Construction costs were $265 200 000 for *Kitty Hawk*, $264 500 000 for *Constellation*, $248 800 000 for *America*, and $277 000 000 for *John F. Kennedy*.

CLASSIFICATION. Officially known as the "Kitty Hawk" class; generally referred to as improved "Forrestals". The *John F. Kennedy* is officially a separate one-ship class.
These ships are being modified to operate as multi-purpose aircraft carriers, embarking anti-submarine aircraft as well as fighter/attack aircraft. *Kitty Hawk* redesignated CV 63 vice CVA 63 on 29 April 1973; *John F. Kennedy* redesignated CV 67 vice CVA 67 on 1 Dec 1974; others will follow in 1976.

KENNEDY (CV 67) — *1973, Giorgio Arra*

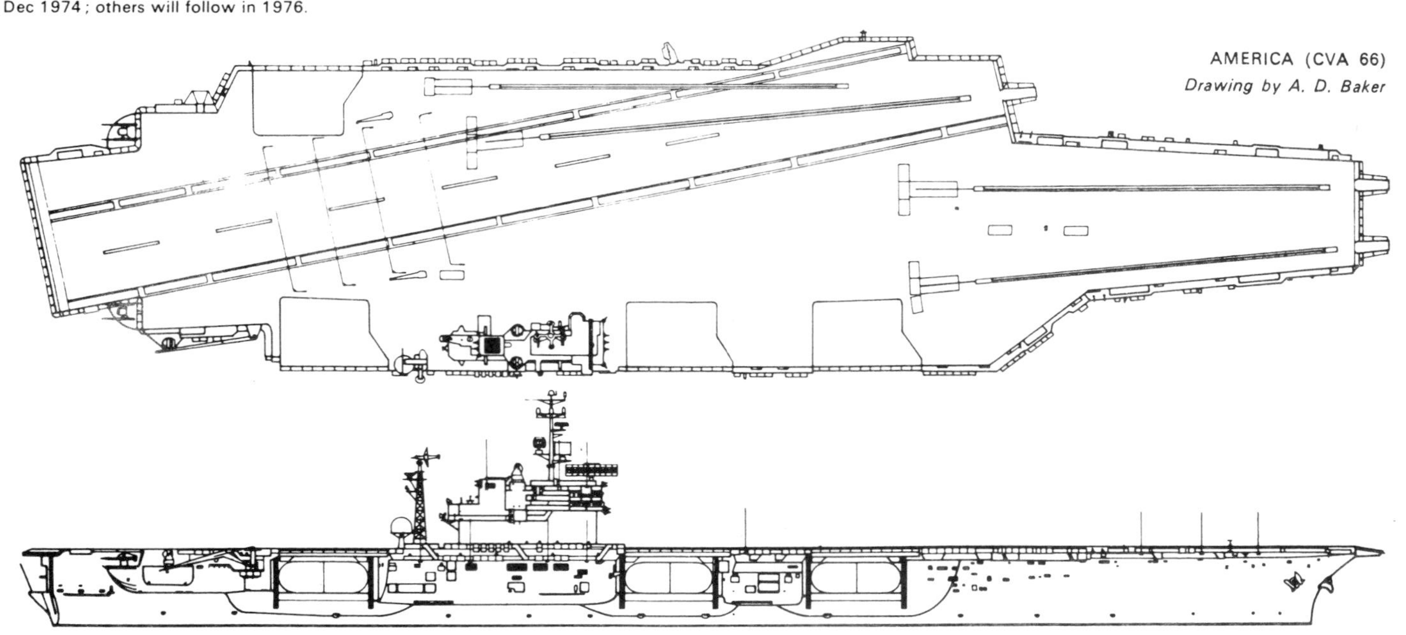

AMERICA (CVA 66)
Drawing by A. D. Baker

Aircraft Carriers—*continued*

"KITTY HAWK" CLASS—*continued*

DESIGN. These ships are officially considered to be of a different design than the "Forrestal" class. The island structure is smaller and set farther aft in the newer ships with two deck-edge lifts forward of the superstructure, a third lift aft of the structure, and the port-side left on the after quarter (compared with two lifts aft of the island and the port-side lift at the forward end of the angled deck in the earlier ships). This lift arrangement considerably improves flight deck operations. All four of these ships also have a small radar mast aft of the island structure. The *John F. Kennedy* and *America* have stern anchors because of their bow sonar domes.

ELECTRONICS. All four ships of this class have highly sophisticated electronic equipment including the Naval Tactical Data System (NTDS). The *America* and *John F. Kennedy* have bow-mounted SQS-23 sonar, the first US attack carriers with anti-submarine sonar (several ASW carriers have been fitted with sonar during modernisations).

All four ships have SPS-43 search radar antenna on island structure; three ships also have a three-dimensional SPS-52 search radar antenna on island and an SPS-30 search radar antenna on second mast while the *John F. Kennedy* has SPS-48 antenna on second mast; being fitted with SPS-58 radar to detect low-flying aircraft and missiles. All ships have TACAN navigation pods or "bee-hives".

MISSILES. The three Terrier-armed ships have a Mk 10 Mod 3 launcher on the starboard quarter and a Mod 4 launcher on the port quarter.
The *America* has updated Terrier launchers and guidance system that can accommodate Standard missiles; the *Constellation* and *Kitty Hawk* retain older Terrier HT systems which will be replaced by three NATO Sea Sparrow launchers (Mk 29).

Three Sea Sparrow BPDMS launchers were fitted in the *John F. Kennedy* early in 1969.

NOMENCLATURE. US aircraft carriers are generally named after battles and historic ships. However, the *Kitty Hawk* better honours the site where the Wright brothers made their historic flights than the converted aircraft ferry of that name which served in World War II. The *Constellation* remembers a frigate built in 1797 and a later ship still afloat at Baltimore, Maryland, although no longer in Navy commission. The name *America* was previously carried by a 74-gun ship of the line launched in 1782, and presented to France, by the racing schooner which gave her name to the America's Cup, and by the German liner *Amerika* which was taken over by the US Navy in World War I, renamed, and used as a troop transport. The *John F. Kennedy* remembers the martyred president who was assassinated in 1963.

PHOTOGRAPHS. Note the angled funnel and Sea Sparrow BPDMS launchers of the *John F. Kennedy*. These ships can be distinguished from the earlier "Forrestal" class carriers by the position of the island structure and the small radar mast aft of the island.

JOHN F. KENNEDY (CV 67) — *1973, United States Navy, PH1 D. D. Deverman*

AMERICA (CVA 66) — *1972, United States Navy*

CONSTELLATION (CVA 64) — *1974, United States Navy, PHCS Robert L. Lawson*

Aircraft Carriers—*continued*

1 NUCLEAR-POWERED ATTACK AIRCRAFT CARRIER (CVAN): "ENTERPRISE" TYPE

Name	*No.*	*Builder*	*Laid down*	*Launched*	*Commissioned*
***ENTERPRISE**	CVAN 65	Newport News Shipbuilding & Dry Dock Co	4 Feb 1958	24 Sep 1960	25 Nov 1961

Displacement, tons	75 700 standard; 89 600 full load
Length, feet (*metres*)	1 040 (*317·0*) wl; 1 123 (*341·3*) oa
Beam, feet (*metres*)	133 (*40·5*)
Draught, feet (*metres*)	35·8 (*10·8*)
Flight deck width, feet (*metres*)	257 (*78·3*) maximum
Catapults	4 Steam
Aircraft	approx 95
Missile launchers	2 Basic Point Defence Missile System (BPDMS) launchers (Mk 25) with Sea Sparrow missiles
Main engines	4 geared steam turbines (Westinghouse); approx 280 000 shp; 4 shafts
Nuclear reactors	8 pressurised-water cooled A2W (Westinghouse)
Speed, knots	35
Complement	3 100 (162 officers, approx 2 940 enlisted men) plus 2 400 assigned to attack air wing for a total of 5 500

The *Enterprise* was the largest warship ever built at the time of her construction and will be rivalled in size only by the nuclear-powered "Nimitz" class ships. The *Enterprise* was authorised in the Fiscal Year 1958 new construction programme. She was launched only 19 months after her keel was laid down.

The *Enterprise* was flagship of Task Force One during Operation Sea Orbit when the carrier, the nuclear-powered cruiser *Long Beach* (CGN 9), and the nuclear-powered frigate *Bainbridge* (DLGN 25) circumnavigated the world, in 1964, cruising more than 30 000 miles in 64 days (underway 57 days) without refuelling.

The cost of the *Enterprise* was $451 300 000.

The Fiscal Year 1960 budget provided $35 000 000 to prepare plans and place orders for components of a second nuclear-powered carrier, but the project was deferred.

ARMAMENT. The *Enterprise* was completed without any armament in an effort to hold down construction costs. Space for Terrier missile system was provided. Short-range Sea Sparrow BPDMS subsequently was installed in late 1967.

DESIGN. Built to a modified "Forrestal" Class design. The most distinctive feature is the island structure. Nuclear propulsion eliminated requirement for smoke stack and boiler air intakes, reducing size of superstructure, and reducing vulnerability to battle damage, radioactivity and biological agents. Rectangular fixed-array radar antennas ("billboards") are mounted on sides of island; electronic countermeasures (ECM) antennas ring cone-shaped upper levels of island structure. Fixed antennas have increased range and performance (see listing for cruiser *Long Beach*). The *Enterprise* has four deck-edge lifts, two forward of island and one aft on starboard side and one aft on port side (as in "Kitty Hawk" class).

ENTERPRISE (CVAN 65) — *1969, United States Navy*

ENTERPRISE (CVAN 65) — *1968, United States Navy*

ENTERPRISE (CVAN 65) — *Drawing by A. D. Baker*

Aircraft Carriers—*continued*

"ENTERPRISE" TYPE—*continued*

CLASSIFICATION. The *Enterprise* will refit as a multi-purpose carrier in 1975-1976; will change from CVAN 65 to CVN 65.

ELECTRONICS. Fitted with the Naval Tactical Data System (NTDS). In addition to SPS-32 and SPS-33 "billboard" radar systems, the *Enterprise* has SPS-10 and SPS-12 search radars and various navigation radar antennas atop her island structure; SPS-58 radar fitted to detect low-flying aircraft and missiles. TACAN navigation pod caps mast.

ENGINEERING. The *Enterprise* is the world's second nuclear-powered warship (the cruiser *Long Beach* was completed a few months earlier). Design of the first nuclear powered aircraft carrier began in 1950 and work continued until 1953 when the programme was deferred pending further work on the submarine reactor programme. The large ship reactor project was reinstated in 1954 on the basis of technological advancements made in the previous 14 months. The Atomic Energy Commission's Bettis Atomic Power Laboratory was given prime responsibility for developing the nuclear power plant.
The first of the eight reactors installed in the *Enterprise* achieved initial criticality on 2 Dec 1960, shortly after the carrier was launched. After three years of operation during which she steamed more than 207 000 miles, the *Enterprise* was overhauled and refuelled from November 1964 to July 1965. Her second set of cores provided about 300 000 miles steaming. The eight cores initially installed in the *Enterprise* cost $64 000 000; the second set cost about $20 000 000.
The *Enterprise* underwent an extensive overhaul from October 1969 to January 1971, which included installation of a new set of uranium cores in the ship's eight nuclear reactors. The overhaul and refuelling took place at the Newport News shipyard. Estimated cost of the overhaul was approximately $30 000 000, with $13 000 000 being for non-nuclear repairs and alterations, and $17 000 000 being associated with installation of the new nuclear cores (the latter amount being in addition to the $80 000 000 cost of the eight cores).
This third set of cores is expected to fuel the ship for 10 to 13 years, according to Adm H. G. Rickover.
In addition to virtually unlimited high-speed endurance nuclear propulsion for aircraft carriers provides additional space for aviation fuels and ordnance, elimination of stack gases and smoke which have corrosive effects on electronic antennas and aircraft, virtually unlimited electrical power, and the ability to quickly change speed without affecting the number of personnel on watch in the engineering spaces.
There are two reactors for each of the ship's four shafts. The eight reactors feed 32 heat exchangers. The *Enterprise* developed more horsepower during her propulsion trials than any other ship in history (officially "in excess of 200 000 shaft horsepower"; subsequently Navy officials stated that she can generate 280 000 hp).

NOMENCLATURE. Eight US Navy ships have carried the name *Enterprise*. The first was a British supply sloop captured in 1775 and armed for use on Lake Champlain. The seventh *Enterprise* (CV 6) was the most famous US carrier of World War II. She earned 20 battle stars. That "Big E" was sold in 1958 and scrapped.

PHOTOGRAPHS. The *Enterprise* can be distinguished from all other aircraft carriers by her "square" island structure with fixed "billboard" radar antennas topped by an antenna-studded dome (see *Design* notes). In the stern view on the previous page the ship's port-quarter Sea Sparrow launcher is at near full elevation.

ENTERPRISE (CVAN 65) *1971, United States Navy*

ENTERPRISE (CVAN 65) *1974, United States Navy*

Aircraft Carriers—*continued*

4 ATTACK AIRCRAFT CARRIERS (CVA/CV): "FORRESTAL" CLASS

Name	*No*	*Builder*	*Laid down*	*Launched*	*Commissioned*
*FORRESTAL	CVA 59	Newport News SB & DD Co	14 July 1952	11 Dec 1954	1 Oct 1955
*SARATOGA	CV 60	New York Naval Shipyard	16 Dec 1952	8 Oct 1955	14 Apr 1956
*RANGER	CVA 61	Newport News SB & DD Co	2 Aug 1954	29 Sep 1956	10 Aug 1957
*INDEPENDENCE	CV 62	New York Naval Shipyard	1 July 1955	6 June 1958	10 Jan 1959

Displacement, tons	
Forrestal	59 650 standard; 78 000 full load
Others	60 000 standard; 78 000 full load
Length, feet (*metres*)	990 (*301·8*) wl
Forrestal, Saratoga	
Ranger	1 039 (*316·7*) oa
Independence	1 046·5 (*319·0*) oa
Beam, feet (*metres*)	129·5 (*38·5*)
Draught, feet (*metres*)	37 (*11·3*)
Flight deck width, feet (*metres*)	
Ranger	260 (*79·2*) maximum
Others	252 (*76·8*) maximum
Catapults	4 Steam
Aircraft	approx 85
Guns	4—5 inch (*127 mm*) 54 cal DP (single) in *Ranger*
Missile launchers	2 Basic Point Defence Missile System (BPDMS) launchers (Mk 25) with Sea Sparrow missiles in all except *Ranger*
Main engines	4 geared turbines (Westinghouse) 4 shafts 260 000 shp in *Forrestal* 280 000 shp in others
Boilers	8—615 psi (*42·7 kg/cm²*) in *Forrestal*; 1 200 psi (*83·4 kg/cm²*) in others (all Babcock & Wilcox)
Speed, knots	
Forrestal	33
Others	35
Complement	2 790 (145 officers, approx 2 645 enlisted men) plus approx 2 150 assigned to attack air wing for a total of 4 940+ per ship

SARATOGA (CV 60) — *1971, Giorgio Arra*

The *Forrestal* was the world's first aircraft carrier designed and built after World War II. The *Forrestal* design drew heavily from the aircraft carrier *United States* (CVA 58) which was cancelled immediately after being laid down in April 1949. The *Forrestal* was authorised in the Fiscal Year 1952 new construction programme; the *Saratoga* followed in the FY 1953 programme, the *Ranger*, in the FY 1954 programme, and the *Independence* in the FY 1955 programme.

Construction costs were $188 900 000 for *Forrestal*, $213 900 000 for *Saratoga*, $173 300 000 for *Ranger*, and $225 300 000 for *Independence*.

CLASSIFICATION. The *Forrestal* and *Saratoga* were initially classified as Large Aircraft Carriers CVB 59 and 60, respectively; reclassified as Attack Aircraft Carriers (CVA) in October 1952 to reflect their purpose rather than size. The ill-fated *United States* was a "heavy" carrier (CVA).

The ships are being modified to operate as multi-purpose aircraft carriers, embarking anti-submarine aircraft as well as fighter/attack aircraft. *Saratoga* redesignated CV 60 vice CVA 60 on 30 June 1972; *Independence* to CV 62 on 28 Feb 1973; *Forrestal* and *Ranger* will be reclassified CV in 1975-1976.

DESIGN. The "Forrestal" Class ships were the first aircraft carriers designed and built specifically to operate jet-propelled aircraft. The *Forrestal* was redesigned early in construction to incorporate British-developed angled flight deck and steam catapults. These were the first US aircraft carriers built with an enclosed bow area to improve seaworthiness. Four large deck-edge lifts are fitted, one forward of island structure to starboard,

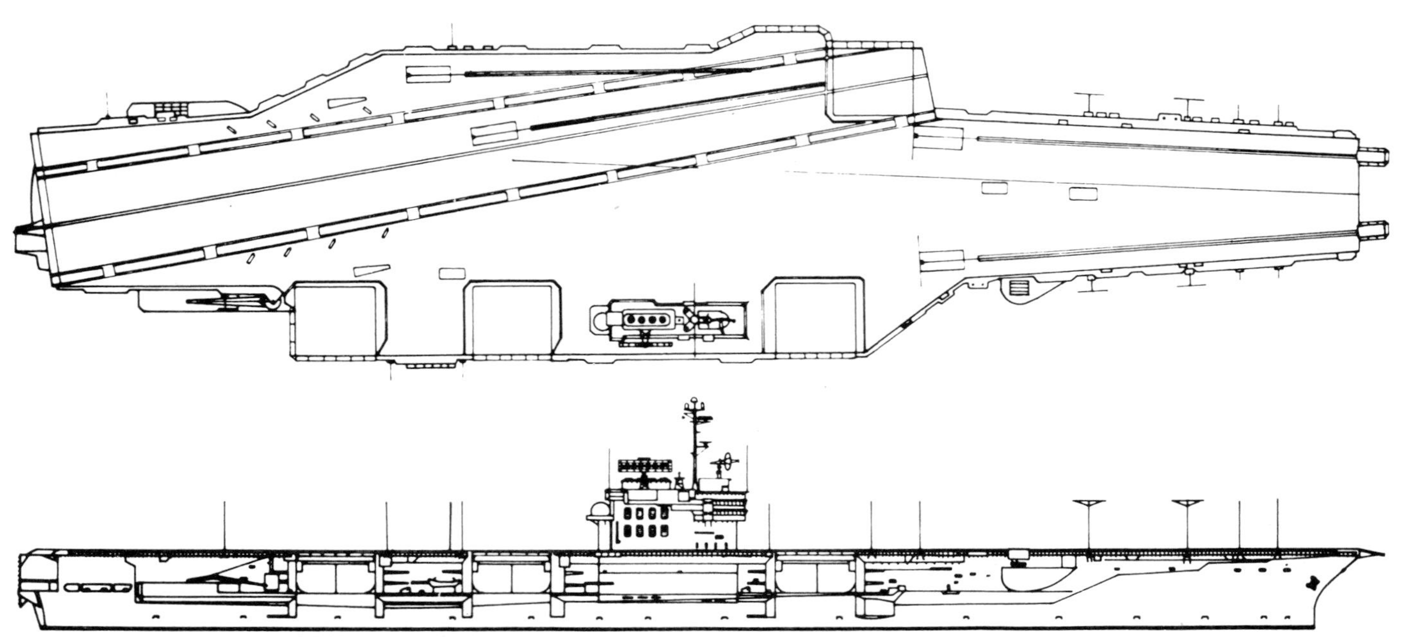

FORRESTAL (CVA 59) — *Drawing by A. D. Baker*

INDEPENDENCE (CV 62) with CH-46A Sea Knight overhead — *1973, United States Navy, PH2 Edwin L. Hawkins*

Aircraft Carriers—*continued*

"FORRESTAL" CLASS—*continued*

two aft of island structure to starboard and one at forward edge of angled flight deck to port. Other features include armoured flight deck and advanced underwater protection and internal compartmentation to reduce effects of conventional and nuclear attack. Mast configurations differ; the *Forrestal* originally had two masts, one of which was removed in 1967.

ELECTRONICS. The primary radars installed in these ships are SPS-43, SPS-30, and SPS-10 search radars, and SPN-10 navigation radar. Small TACAN navigation pods top the masts of these ships.

SPS-58 radar being installed to detect low-flying aircraft and missiles.

Naval Tactical Data System (NTDS) is installed in all four ships.

ENGINEERING. The *Saratoga* and later ships have an improved steam plant, increased machinery weight of the improved plant is more than compensated by increased performance and decreased fuel consumption.

GUNNERY. All four ships initially mounted 8—5 inch guns (Mk 42) in single mounts, two on each quarter. The forward sponsons carrying the guns interfered with ship operations in rough weather, tending to slow the ships down. The forward sponsons and guns were subsequently removed (except in *Ranger*), reducing armament to four guns per ship.

The after guns have been removed with installation of BPDMS launchers (see below).

MISSILES. The four after 5 inch guns were removed from the *Forrestal* late in 1967 and a single BPDMS launcher for Sea Sparrow missiles was installed forward on the starboard side. An additional launcher was provided aft on the port side in 1972. Two BPDMS launchers fitted in *Independence* in 1973 and two launchers in *Saratoga* in 1974. *Ranger* will receive three NATO Sea Sparrow launchers (Mk 29) in FY 1977.

NOMENCLATURE. The *Forrestal* honours James V. Forrestal, Secretary of the Navy from 1944 until he was appointed the first US Secretary of Defense in 1947, a post he held until shortly before his death in 1949. The *Saratoga* commemorates the battle at Saratoga, New York, in the American Revolution and five earlier US warships including a carrier of World War II fame (CV 3). The first USS *Ranger* was a sloop built in 1777 and a later ship of that name was the first US built-for-the-purpose carriers (CV 4). The first USS *Independence* was a sloop built in 1775 and a later ship of that name was a light carrier (CVL 22) that saw extensive combat in World War II.

RANGER (CVA 61) *1968, United States Navy*

FORRESTAL (CVA 59) *United States Navy, PH1 D. Withrow*

INDEPENDENCE (CV 62) *1973, United States Navy*

Aircraft Carriers—*continued*

3 ATTACK AIRCRAFT CARRIERS (CVA): "MIDWAY" CLASS

Name	*No.*	*Builder*	*Laid down*	*Launched*	*Commissioned*
***MIDWAY**	CVA 41	Newport News SB & DD Co	27 Oct 1943	20 Mar 1954	10 Sep 1945
***FRANKLIN D. ROOSEVELT**	CVA 42	New York Navy Yard	1 Dec 1943	29 Apr 1945	3 Nov 1945
***CORAL SEA**	CVA 43	Newport News SB & DD Co	10 July 1944	2 Apr 1946	1 Oct 1947

Displacement, tons	
Midway	51 000 standard
F. D. Roosevelt	51 000 standard
Coral Sea	52 500 standard
	all approx 64 000 full load
Length, feet (*metres*)	900 (*274·3*) wl; 979 (*298·4*) oa
Beam, feet (*metres*)	121 (*36·9*)
Draught, feet (*metres*)	35·3 (*10·8*)
Flight deck width, feet (*metres*)	238 (*72·5*) maximum
Catapults	2 steam except 3 in *Coral Sea*
Aircraft	approx 75
Guns	4—5 inch (*127 mm*) 54 cal DP in *F. D. Roosevelt*; three guns in *Midway* and *Coral Sea* (see *Gunnery* notes)
Main engines	4 geared turbines (Westinghouse in *Midway* and *Coral Sea*, General Electric in *F. D. Roosevelt*); 212 000 shp; 4 shafts
Boilers	12—165 psi (*42·7 kg cm²*) (Babcock & Wilcox)
Speed, knots	33
Complement	2 615 (140 officers, approx 2 475 enlisted men) except *Coral Sea* 2 710 (165 officers, approx 2 545 enlisted men) plus approx 1 800 assigned to attack air wing for a total of 4 400 to 4 500 per ship

MIDWAY (CVA 41) *1971, United States Navy*

FRANKLIN D. ROOSEVELT (CVA 43) *1973, United States Navy*

These carriers were the largest US warships constructed during World War II. Completed too late for service in that conflict, they were the backbone of US naval strength for the first decade of the Cold War. Beginning in 1949 they were modified to store, assemble, and load nuclear weapons, making them the world's first warships with a nuclear strike capability. (P2V-3C Neptunes and AJ-1 Savages were the first delivery aircraft.) All three ships operated in the Atlantic and Mediterranean during the Korean War, but subsequently they have operated in the Pacific. The entire class has been in active service (except for overhaul and modernisation) since the ships were completed.

The *Midway* was homeported at Yokosuka, Japan, in October 1973, the first US aircraft carrier to be based overseas.

One "Midway" class carrier will be decommissioned when the *Dwight D. Eisenhower* is completed and one when the *Vinson* is completed. The *Midway* will probably be retained in service into the 1980s to provide a 13 carrier force level.

Construction cost of *Midway* was $85 600 000, *F. D. Roosevelt* $85 700 000, and *Coral Sea* $87 600 000.

CLASSIFICATION. These ships were initially classified as Large Aircraft Carriers CVB 41-43, respectively, reclassified as Attack Aircraft Carriers (CVA) in October 1952.

DESIGN. These ships were built to the same design with a standard displacement of 45 000 tons, full load displacement of 60 100 tons, and an overall length of 968 feet. They have been extensively modified since completion (see notes below). These ships were the first US aircraft carriers with an armoured flight deck and the first US warships with a designed width too large to enable them to pass through the Panama Canal.

The unnamed CVB 44, 56 and 57 of this class were cancelled prior to the start of construction.

ELECTRONICS. Naval Tactical Data System (NTDS) in *Midway* and *Coral Sea*.

The principal radars installed on these ships are SPS-10, SPS-30, SPS-43, SPN-6, and SPN-10. *Midway* fitted with SPS-58 radar to detect low-flying aircraft and missiles. Note that *Coral Sea* retains large TACAN (Tactical Air Navigation) "bee hive" antenna atop mast compared to smaller antenna pods on *Midway* and *Franklin D. Roosevelt*.

GUNNERY. As built these ships mounted 18—5 inch guns (14 in *Coral Sea*), 84—40 mm guns, and 28—20 mm guns. Armament reduced periodically with 3 inch guns replacing lighter weapons. Minimal 5 inch armament remains. The 5 inch guns are 54 calibre Mk 39, essentially modified 5 inch/38 calibre with a longer barrel for greater range; not to be confused with rapid-fire 5 inch 54s of newer US warships.

MISSILES. The *Midway* is scheduled to be fitted with three Basic Point Defense Missile launchers (Mk 25) for the Sea Sparrow missile during Fiscal Year 1977.

MODERNISATION. All three "Midway" Class carriers have been extensively modernised. Their most extensive conversion "package" gave them angled flight decks, steam catapults, enclosed "hurricane" bows, new electronics, and new lift arrangement (*Franklin D. Roosevelt* from 1953 to 1956, *Midway* from 1954 to 1957, and *Coral Sea* from 1956 to 1960; all at Puget Sound Naval Shipyard). Lift arrangement was changed in *Franklin D. Roosevelt* and *Midway* to one centreline lift forward, one deck-edge lift aft of island on starboard side, and one deck-edge lift at forward end of angled deck on port side. The *Coral Sea* has an improved arrangement with one lift forward and one aft of island on starboard side and third lift outboard on port side aft. The *Midway* began another extensive modernisation at the San Francisco Bay Naval Shipyard in February 1966; she was recommissioned on 31 Jan 1970 and went to sea in March 1970.

Her modernisation included provisions for handling newer aircraft, new catapults, new lifts (arranged as in *Coral Sea*), and new electronics. A similar modernisation planned for the *Franklin D. Roosevelt*, to have begun in Fiscal Year 1970, has been cancelled because the *Midway* modernisation is taking longer and costing more than originally estimated (24 months and $88 000 000 was planned; actual work required approximately 52 months and $202 300 000). The *Franklin D. Roosevelt* completed an austere overhaul in June 1969 which enables her to operate the new A-6 Intruder and A-7 Corsair II attack aircraft; cost of overhaul was $46 000 000.

The *Midway* is now the most capable of the three ships (for example, her lifts can handle aircraft weights to 100 000 pounds compared to 74 000 pounds for the *Coral Sea* and *Franklin D. Roosevelt*).

PHOTOGRAPHS. The unusual flight deck configuration of the *Midway* can be easily compared with the *Franklin D. Roosevelt* in the above views. Note the *Midway's* port-quarter lift, an arrangement not found in the following "Forrestal" class but returned to in later US aircraft carrier designs. Aircraft visible on flight decks include saucer-topped E-2 Hawkeye early warning aircraft alongside the *Midway's* island and the earlier E-1B Tracer AEW aircraft in the same position on the F.D.R. When built these ships could accommodate 137 contemporary aircraft.

Aircraft Carriers—*continued*

FRANKLIN D. ROOSEVELT (CVA 42) *1972, Giorgio Arra*

MIDWAY (CVA 41) *1970, United States Navy*

CORAL SEA (CVA 43) *1971, United States Navy*

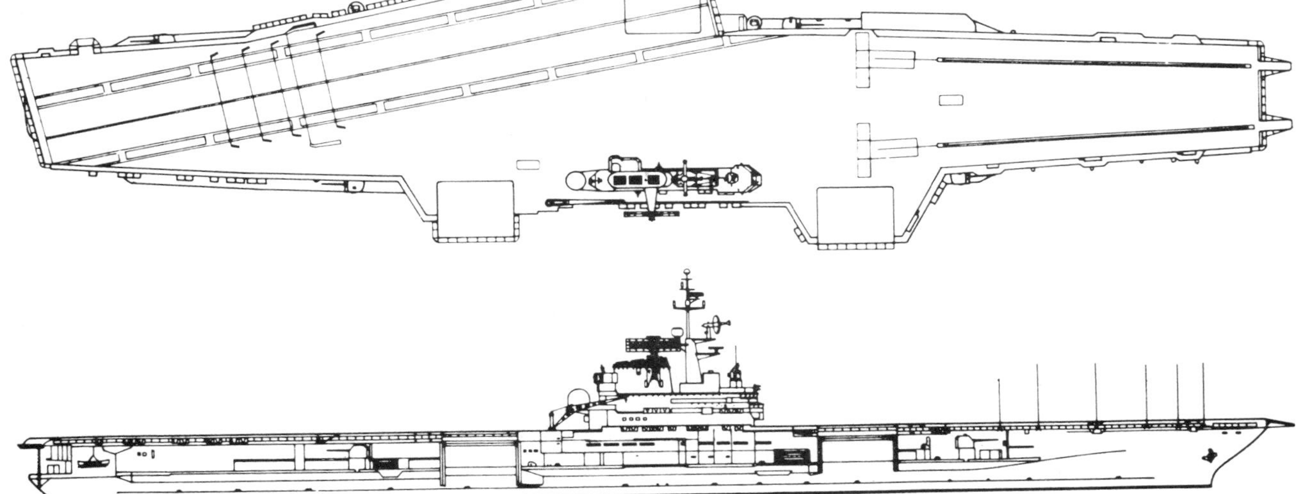
FRANKLIN D. ROOSEVELT (CVA 42) *Drawing by A. D. Baker*

Aircraft Carriers—*Continued*

3 ATTACK AIRCRAFT CARRIERS (CVA) 2 ASW AIRCRAFT CARRIERS (CVS) 1 TRAINING CARRIER (CVT) — "HANCOCK" CLASS

Name	*No.*	*Builder*	*Laid down*	*Launched*	*Commissioned*
INTREPID	CVS 11	Newport News Shipbuilding & Dry Dock Co	1 Dec 1941	26 Apr 1943	16 Aug 1943
***LEXINGTON**	CVT 16	Bethlehem Steel Co, Quincy, Mass	15 July 1941	26 Sep 1942	17 Feb 1943
***HANCOCK**	CVA 19	Bethlehem Steel Co, Quincy, Mass	26 Jan 1943	24 Jan 1944	15 Apr 1944
BON HOMME RICHARD	CVA 31	New York Navy Yard	1 Feb 1943	29 Apr 1944	26 Nov 1944
***ORISKANY**	CVA 34	New York Navy Yard	1 May 1944	13 Oct 1945	25 Sep 1950
SHANGRI-LA	CVS 38	Norfolk Navy Yard	15 Jan 1943	24 Feb 1944	15 Sep 1944

Displacement, tons: approx 32 800 standard, except *Oriskany* 33 250
CVA type: approx 44 700 full load
Others: approx 42 000 full load except *Lexington* 39 000
Length, feet (*metres*): 894·5 (*272·6*) oa except *Oriskany* 890 (*271·3*); 820 (*249·9*) wl
Beam, feet (*metres*): 103 (*30·8*) except *Oriskany* 106·5 (*32·5*)
Draught, feet (*metres*): 31 (*9·4*)
Flight deck width feet (*metres*): 192 (*58·5*) maximum except *Oriskany* 195 (*59·5*)
Catapults: 2 steam
Aircraft: 70 to 80 for CVA type; approx 45 for CVS type; none assigned to *Lexington*
Guns: 2—5 inch (*127 mm*) 38 cal dual-purpose (single) in *Hancock* and *Oriskany*; 4 guns in other ships except all removed from *Lexington*
Main engines: 4 geared turbines (Westinghouse) 150 000 shp; 4 shafts
Boilers: 8 (Babcock & Wilcox)
Speed, knots: 30+
Complement
CVA type: *Hancock* 1 985 (110 officers, 1 875 enlisted men); *Oriskany* 2 090 (110 officers, 1 980 enlisted men); plus approx 1 185 (135 officers, 1 050 enlisted men) in air wing for a total of approx 3,200 per ship
CVS type: 1 615 (115 officers, approx 1 500 enlisted men) plus approx 800 assigned to ASW air group for a total of 2 400 per ship
Lexington: 1 440 (75 officers, 1 365 enlisted men); no air unit assigned

HANCOCK (CVA 19) *United States Navy*

These ships originally were "Essex" class aircraft carriers; extensively modernised during 1950s, being provided with enclosed, hurricane-bow, angled flight deck, improved elevators, increased aviation fuel storage, and steam catapults (last feature permits operation of more advanced aircraft that can be flown from modernised "Essex" class). Construction of *Oriskany* suspended after World War II and she was completed in 1950 to a modified "Essex" design. See "Essex" class listing for additional notes.

Bon Homme Richard decommissioned on 2 July 1971, *Shangri-La* on 30 July 1971, and *Intrepid* on 30 March 1974. The *Intrepid* was the last "dedicated" anti-submarine carrier in service. All three ships are in reserve. The *Hancock* and *Oriskany* are expected to be decommissioned in January 1977 and March 1976 respectively.

CLASSIFICATION. All "Essex" class ships originally were designated as Aircraft Carriers (CV); reclassified as Attack Aircraft Carriers (CVA) in Oct 1952. *Intrepid* reclassified as ASW Support Aircraft Carrier (CVS) on 31 Mar 1962, *Lexington* on 1 Oct 1962, *Shangri-La* on 30 June 1969. The *Lexington* became the Navy's training aircraft carrier in the Gulf of Mexico on 29 Dec 1962; reclassified CVT on 1 Jan 1969.

LEXINGTON (CVT 16) *1972, US Navy, PH2 Gabriel Benzur*

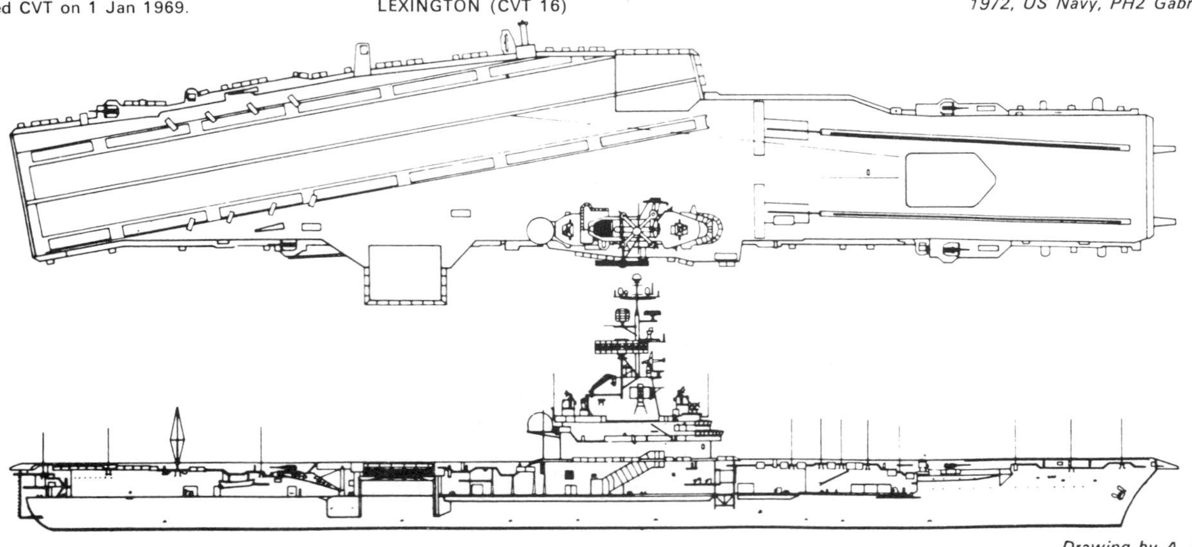
ORISKANY (CVA 34) *Drawing by A. D. Baker*

Aircraft Carriers—*Continued*

"HANCOCK" CLASS—*continued*

ELECTRONICS. The *Oriskany* and the frigates *King* (DLG 10) and *Mahan* (DLG 11) conducted the initial sea trials of the Naval Tactical Data System (NTDS) in 1961-1962.
The principal radars in these ships are SPS-43, SPS-30, and SPS-10 search radars, and SPN-10 navigation radar, except *Lexington* has SPS-43 SPS-12, SPS-10, and SPN-10 (the SPS-8 formerly mounted has been removed). TACAN aircraft navigation pods stop their masts.

MODERNISATION. These ships have been modernised under several programmes to increase their ability to operate more-advanced aircraft. The *Oriskany* was completed with some post-war ("jet age") features incorporated. The most prominent difference from their original configuration is angled flight deck and removal of twin 5-inch gun mounts from flight deck forward and aft of island structure. Three elevators fitted: "Pointed" centreline lift forward between catapults, deckedge lift on port side at leading edge of angled deck, and deckedge lift on starboard side aft of island structure.

Minimal gun battery retained (see description of original armament under "Essex" class listings). Remaining guns removed from *Lexington* in 1969; by 1975 the *Hancock* and *Oriskany* had only 2—5 inch guns fitted.

OPERATIONAL. The *Shangri-La* while designated as an anti-submarine carrier operated as a "limited attack carrier" off Vietnam during 1969-1970, carrying an air wing of A-4 Skyhawk and A-1 Skyraider attack planes, with the latter being phased out of the Navy during that period, and later F-8 Crusader fighters.
As of early 1975 the *Lexington* had recorded 340 000 arrested aircraft landings during her operational career (1943-1947, 1955-present).

NOMENCLATURE. All 24 "Essex" class carriers are named for early American ships or battles except for *Shangri-La*, which is named for the imaginary locale in James Hilton's novel which President Roosevelt told the press was the base for the Doolittle-Halsey raid against Japan in 1942. Several ships renamed during construction to carry on names of carriers lost in battle. The *Hancock* and *Ticonderoga* exchanged names during construction.

DISPOSALS
Nine "straight-deck" carriers of this class have been stricken: **Franklin** (AVT 8, ex-CVS 13) stricken on 1 Oct 1964; **Bunker Hill** (AVT 8, ex-CVS 17) stricken on 1 Nov 1966, but retained as moored electronic test ship at San Diego, California, until Nov 1972; **Tarawa** (AVT 12, ex-CVS 40) stricken on 1 June 1967; **Leyte** (AVT 10, ex-CVS 32) stricken on 1 June 1969; **Philippine Sea** (AVT 11, ex-CVS 47), **Lake Champlain** (CVS 39), and **Boxer** (LPH 4, ex-CVS 21) stricken on 1 Dec 1969; **Princeton** (LPH 5, es-CVS 37) stricken on 30 Jan 1970; **Valley Forge** (LPH 8, ex-CVS 45) stricken on 15 Jan 1970.
Of the "Essex" class ships modernised to an angled-deck configuration: **Wasp** (CVS 18) stricken on 1 July 1972; **Kearsarge** (CVS 33), **Antietam** (CVS 36) stricken on 1 May 1973; **Essex** (CVS 9), **Yorktown** (CVS 10), **Randolph** (CVS 15) stricken on 1 June 1973; **Ticonderoga** (CVS 14) stricken on 16 Nov 1973. The **Yorktown** is being retained as a memorial at Patriot's Point, South Carolina.

ORISKANY (CVA 34) — *1970, United States Navy*

HANCOCK (CVA 19) — *1971, United States Navy*

LEXINGTON (CVT 16) — *1972, United States Navy PH2 Gabriel Benzur*

Aircraft Carriers—*Continued*

2 ASW AIRCRAFT CARRIERS (CVS): MODERNISED "ESSEX" CLASS

Name	*No.*	*Builder*	*Laid down*	*Launched*	*Commissioned*
HORNET	CVS 12	Newport News Shipbuilding & Dry Dock Co	3 Aug 1942	29 Aug 1943	29 Nov 1943
BENNINGTON	CVS 20	New York Navy Yard	15 Dec 1942	26 Feb 1944	6 Aug 1944

Displacement, tons	approx 33 000 standard; approx 40 060 full load
Length, feet (*metres*)	820 (*249·9*) wl; 8900 (*271·3*) oa
Beam, feet (*metres*)	102 (*31*); 93 (*28·4*)
Draft, feet (*metres*)	31' (*9·4*)
Flight deck width feet (*metres*)	196 (*59·7*) maximum
Catapults	2 hydraulic
Aircraft	approx 45 (including 16 to 18 helicopters)
Guns	4—5 inch (*127 mm*) 38 cal dual-purpose (single)
Main engines	4 geared turbines (Westinghouse); 150 000 shp; 4 shafts
Boilers	8—600 psi (*41·7 kg/cm²*) (Babcock & Wilcox)
Speed, knots	30+
Complement	1 615 (115 officers, approx 1 500 enlisted men) plus approx 800 assigned to ASW air group for a total of 2 400 per ship

The two above ships and the previously listed "Hancock" class are the survivors of the 24 "Essex" class fleet carriers built during the World War II (with one ship, *Oriskany*, not completed until 1950). Both of the above ships were extensively modernised during the 1950s; however, they lack the steam catapults and other features of the "Hancock" class.

The late *Antietam* of this class was the world's first aircraft carrier to be fitted with an angled flight deck to increase efficiency and safety of high-performance aircraft operations aboard carriers.

The *Bennington* was decommissioned on 15 Jan 1970 and the *Hornet* on 26 June 1970; both ships are in reserve.

CLASSIFICATION. These ships originally were designated as Aircraft Carriers (CV); reclassified as Attack Carriers(CVA) in Oct 1952. Subsequently they became ASW Support Aircraft Carriers (CVS): *Hornet* on 27 June 1958, and *Bennington* on 30 June 1959.

DESIGN. All 24 "Essex" class ships were built to the same basic design except for the delayed *Oriskany*. Standard displacement as built was 27 100 tons, full load displacement was 36 380 tons, and overall length 888 or 972 feet. Two additional ships of this class were cancelled while under construction, the *Reprisal* (CV 35) and *Iwo Jima* (CV 46), and six others were cancelled prior to keel laying, the unnamed CV 50-55. See 1971-1972 and previous editions for notes on armament as originally completed and ship nomenclature.

ELECTRONICS. The primary radars in these ships were SPS-43, SPS-30, and SPS-10 search radars, and SPN-10 navigation radars; TACAN aircraft navigation pods top masts. Both ships have SQS-23 bow-mounted sonar.

MODERNISATION. These ships have been modernised under several programmes to increase their ability to operate advanced aircraft and to improve sea keeping. Also modernised to improve anti-submarine capabilities under the Fleet Rehabilitation and Modernisation (FRAM II) programme.

PHOTOGRAPHS. The *Bennington* is shown during an underway replenishment, fuelling from an oiler which also is fuelling a destroyer. Note *Bennington's* starboard deck-edge elevator is hinged upwards during replenishment. Both carriers have S-2 Tracker and E-1 Tracer aircraft, and SH-3 Sea King helicopters on their decks.

LIGHT AIRCRAFT CARRIERS (CVL)

All light aircraft carriers have been stricken from the Navy List, transferred or reclassified.

See 1973-1974 and previous editions for disposals of the nine ship "Independence" class light aircraft carriers (CVL 22-30).

The larger, built-for-the-purpose light carriers of the "Saipan" class have been converted to other roles: *Saipan* (AVT 6, ex-CVL 48) converted to major communications relay ship (AGMR 2) and *Wright* (AVT 7, ex-CVL 49) converted to command ship (CC 2).

BENNINGTON (CVS 20) — *1968, United States Navy*

HORNET (CVS 12) — *1968, United States Navy*

CRUISERS

The US Navy has reclassified its larger guided missile frigates (DLG/DLGN) as guided missile cruisers (CG/CGN), providing a classification more apropos of their size. Also, this provides a similarity in classification to the modern Soviet surface combatants which are designated as cruisers by Western navies although known to the Soviets as "large anti-submarine ships" (*Bolshoy Protivo Lodochny Korabi*) or "guided missile cruisers" (*Raketnyy Kreyseri*)

The reclassification of US guided missile frigates on 1 July, 1975, provides the Navy with 23 modern missile cruisers, of which five are nuclear powered, and four conversions of World War II-built ships. These cruisers are configured and employed primarily to provide air defence of aircraft carrier task forces except that two of the older ships are fleet flagships (see converted "Cleveland" class).

Four additional guided missile cruisers (nee frigates) of the "Virginia" class are under construction or fitting out, with a fifth unit proposed in the Fiscal Year 1976 new construction programme. When the last "Virginia" class cruiser is completed in 1980 the Navy will have ten nuclear-powered missile cruisers, a number sufficient to provide an "austere level" of anti-aircraft and anti-submarine protection for two nuclear-powered carriers. The construction of large surface combatants beyond the CGN 42 of the "Virginia" class proposed in the FY 1976 budget is uncertain. The design of a nuclear-powered strike cruiser is under "intense study", according to US defence officials.

STRIKE CRUISER (CSGN)

The proposed strike cruiser (designated CSGN for planning purposes) is being developed as a successor to the Navy's guided missile frigate/cruiser construction programme. According to Gen. George S. Brown, USAF, Chairman of the Joint Chiefs of Staff: "The CSGN will be able to assert sea control independently in all but the severest threat areas. CSGNs will combine with carriers operating in mutual support to carry out missions in the high threat areas".

The strike cruiser programme replaces the proposed Aegis destroyers (DG), 16 of which were tentatively planned for construction with completion scheduled for 1983-1987. The smaller gas-turbine propelled DG programme is discussed further in the Destroyer section of this edition. There was little specific information on the strike cruiser available into early 1975 and the data listed below is based on official statements, press reports, and the preliminary artist's sketch prepared by the Navy.

STRIKE CRUISER (CSG)

As originally envisioned, the strike cruiser was to have nuclear propulsion. However, during 1975 the concept of a non-nuclear (gas turbine) configuration was put forward as a lower-cost ship to supplement the CSGN. This ship would be based on the "Spruance" class (DD 963) design fitted with the Aegis air defence system and a limited number of advanced surface-to-surface missiles.

FIRE SUPPORT SHIPS

All US Navy ships carrying guns larger than 5 inch calibre are laid up in reserve except for the two cruiser flagships of the converted "Cleveland" class and the destroyer *Hull* (DD 945), which is fitted with an experimental, light-weight 8 inch gun. The total number of 6 inch gun barrels available in the two active cruisers is six, or one-half the main battery of a single Soviet "Sverdlov" class light cruiser.

No specific plans have been announced relative to fitting US destroyers or the proposed strike cruiser with the light-weight 8 inch gun. The Navy retains in reserve four "Iowa" class battleships and five heavy cruisers with main batteries aggregating 36—16 inch guns and 39—8 inch guns, respectively. Also in reserve are two additional converted "Cleveland" class cruiser-flagships with an aggregate of 6—6 inch guns.

NOMENCLATURE. US cruisers traditionally have been named for cities. However, after completion of the *Long Beach* (CGN 9) in 1961 city names were assigned to new-construction auxiliary ships (AOE/AOR/ATS), and additionally to attack submarines beginning with the "Los Angeles" class (SSN 688).

Twenty currently active cruisers formally classified as guided missile frigates (DLG/DLGN) retain their "destroyer-type" names, which remember Navy and Marine personnel, and Secretaries of the Navy. Further confusing cruiser nomenclature, beginning with the DLGN 36 (now CGN 36), guided missile frigates were named for states of the Union. The *California* honoured the home state of the then-incumbent president, Richard M. Nixon, and the *South Carolina* honoured the home state of L. Mendel Fivers, chairman of the House of Representatives Committee on Armed Services from 1965 until his death in 1971.

NUCLEAR-POWERED STRIKE CRUISERS (CSGN): PROPOSED

Displacement, tons	approx 14 000 full load
Length, feet	approx 600 overall
Aircraft	2 SH-3 Sea King or advanced LAMPS or VSTOL aircraft
Missile launchers	2 combination twin Tartar-D/ASROC launchers firing Standard MR surface-to-air missiles and Harpoon surface-to-surface missiles approx 6 tubes for long-range surface-to-surface missiles
Guns	2—20 mm Vulcan/Phalanx CIWS
A/S weapons	ASROC (see above); 2 triple torpedo tubes (Mk 32)
Main engines	2 geared turbines; 2 shafts
Reactors	2 pressurised-water cooled
Speed, knots	30+

These ships are planned as the successor to the nuclear-powered guided missile cruisers of the "California" and "Virginia" classes. Funding for long-lead time components could be requested as early as Fiscal Year 1977.

DESIGN. Indications are that the strike cruiser will have a conventional displacement hull configuration. Navy studies have indicated that the SWATH (Small Waterplane Area Twin Hull) configuration would be applicable to ships of this size. Although a SWATH ship of this size would be more feasible for non-nuclear propulsion and would be speed limited to about 30 knots, the twin-hulled ship could maintain high continuous speeds in rough seas and would have comparably more deck area for weapon systems and aircraft operations. SWATH differs from catamaran designs by having two torpedo-shaped hulls fully submerged with narrow supporting structures up to the main superstructure.

The artist's impression of the strike cruiser shown below has twin missile launchers forward and aft, long-range SSM launchers forward of the bridge structure, Aegis quadrant antennas on the forward and after superstructures, and Vulcan/Phalanx CIWS fitted on the after superstructure.

ELECTRONICS. The Aegis system planned for the strike cruiser is an advanced air defence electronics system intended to cope with future anti-ship missile and aircraft threats. See listing for the *Norton Sound* (AVM 1) under Experimental, Research, and Surveying ships for data.

FISCAL. Unofficial estimates for the strike cruiser predict a unit cost of approx $600 000 000 per ship built in the late 1970s or almost twice that of the last "Virginia" class cruiser.

MISSILES. The long-range SSM proposed for the strike cruiser would be an anti-ship weapon with a range of approx 300 nautical miles. The weapon would be developed from the BGM-109/BGM-110 strategic cruise missiles.

PHOTOGRAPHS. The line drawing presented on this page is based on the official Navy artist's concept reproduced below.

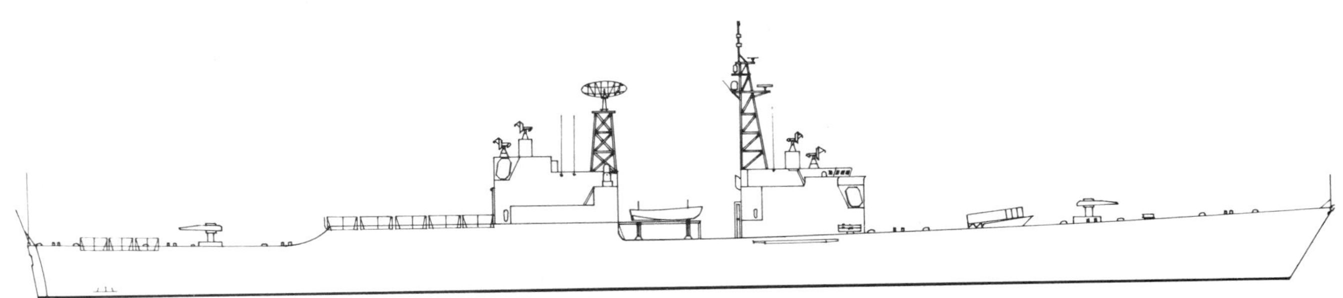

Drawing by A. D. Baker

NUCLEAR-POWERED STRIKE CRUISER (CSGN)

Cruisers—*continued*

(5) NUCLEAR-POWERED GUIDED MISSILE CRUISERS (CGN): "VIRGINIA" CLASS

Name	*No,*	*Builder*	*Laid down*	*Launched*	*Commission*
VIRGINIA	CGN 38 (ex-DLGN 38)	Newport News Shipbuilding & Dry Dock Co	19 Aug 1972	14 Dec 1974	mid-1976
TEXAS	CGN 39 (ex-DLGN 39)	Newport News Shipbuilding & Dry Dock Co	18 Aug 1973	Aug 1975	mid-1977
MISSISSIPPI	CGN 40 (ex-DLGN 40)	Newport News Shipbuilding & Dry Dock Co	22 Feb 1975	1976	late 1977
ARKANSAS	CGN 41	Fiscal Year 1975 programme			1979
	CGN 42	Proposed FY 1976 programme			

Displacement, tons	11 000 full load
Length, feet (*metres*)	585 (*177·3*) oa
Beam, feet (*metres*)	63 (*18·9*)
Draught, feet (*metres*)	29·5 (*9·0*)
Helicopters	2 (see *Helicopter* notes)
Missile launchers	2 combination twin Tartar-D/ASROC launchers firing Standard MR surface-to-air missile (Mk 26)
Guns	2—5 inch (*127 mm*) 54 calibre dual-purpose (Mk 45) (single)
A/S weapons	ASROC (*see above*) 2 triple torpedo tubes (Mk 32)
Main engines	2 geared turbines; 2 shafts
Reactors	2 pressurised-water cooled D2G (General Electric)
Speed, knots	30+
Complement	442 (27 officers, 415 enlisted men)

The *Virginia* was authorised in the Fiscal Year 1970 new construction programme, the *Texas* in FY 1971, the *Mississippi* in FY 1972, and the CGN 41 in FY 1975. The CGN 42 is proposed in the FY 1976 new construction programme.
Construction of this class has been delayed because of a shortage of skilled labour in the shipyard. Newport News SB & DD Co (Virginia) is the only shipyard in the United States now engaged in the construction of nuclear surface ships.
The first three ships of the class are more than one year behind their original construction schedules.

CLASSIFICATION. These ships were originally classified as guided missile frigates (DLGN); subsequently reclassified as guided missile cruisers (CGN) in July 1975.

DESIGN. The principal differences between the "Virginia" and "California" classes are the improved anti-air warfare capability, electronic warfare equipment, and anti-submarine fire control system. The deletion of the ASROC "pepper-box" Mk 16 launcher permitted the later ships to be ten feet shorter.

ELECTRONICS. These ships will have bow-mounted SQS-53A sonar (improved SQS-26 series); also to have Naval Tactical Data System (NTDS), SPS-48A three-dimensional radar, SPS-40B and SPS-55 radar antennas.

FISCAL. These ships have incurred major cost growth/escalation during their construction. Fiscal data on the earlier ships were in the 1974-1975 and earlier editions. The estimated cost of the CGN 41 is more than ($116 000 000 in FY 1970-1974P $152 000 000 in FY 1975). In addition, the FY 1976 budget requests $140 000 000 to cover cost increases in CGN 38-41. The CGN 42 is estimated to cost $368 000 000 ($257 000 000 proposed in FY 1976 and $111 000 000 in FY 1970-1975).

GUNNERY. These ships will have Mk 86 gunfire control directors.

HELICOPTERS. A hangar for helicopters is installed beneath the fantail flight-deck with a telescoping hatch cover and an electro-mechanical elevator provided to transport helicopters between the main deck and hangar. These are the first US post-World War II destroyer/cruiser ships with a hull hangar.

MISSILES. The initial design for this class provided for a single surface-to-air missile launcher; revised in 1969 to provide two Mk 26 launchers that will fire the Standard-Medium Range (MR) surface-to-air missile and the ASROC anti-submarine missile. "Mixed" Standard/ASROC magazines are planned for each launcher. The digital Mk 116 ASW fire control system will simplify weapon system interfaces compared to previous US missile-armed warships. Mk 74 missile control directors.

DRAWING. Chaff-rocket (CHAFROC) launchers are shown forward of bridge and aft of boat davits with triple anti-submarine torpedo tubes also aft of boat davits; "California" design on the following page has the torpedo tubes built into superstructure. Note enclosed radar towers, similar to "California" class.

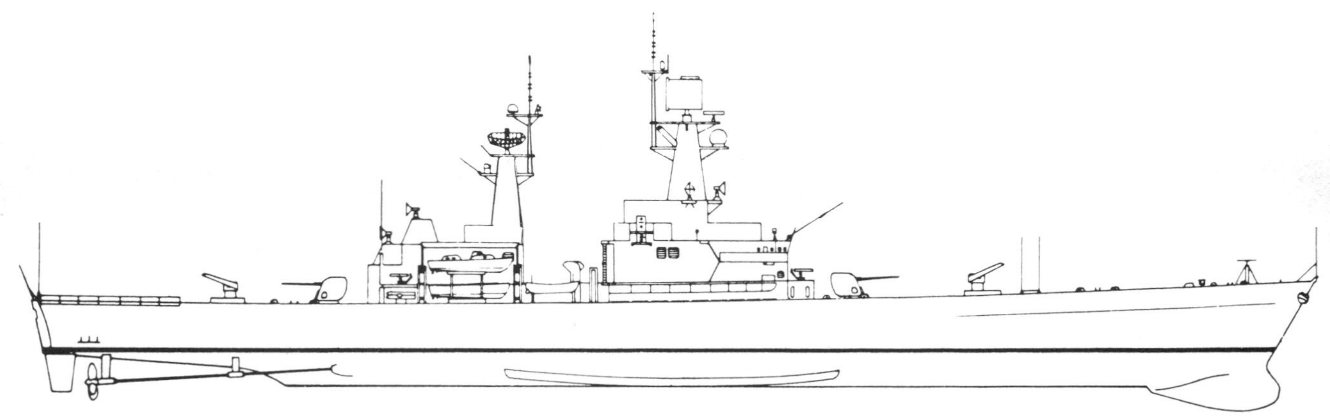

VIRGINIA (CGN 38) *Drawing by D. A. Baker*

SOUTH CAROLINA (CGN 37)—see following page *1974, Newport News SB & DD Co*

Cruisers—*continued*

2 NUCLEAR-POWERED GUIDED MISSILE CRUISERS (CGN): "CALIFORNIA" CLASS

Name	*No.*	*Builder*	*Laid down*	*Launched*	*Commissioned*
***CALIFORNIA**	CGN 36	Newport News Shipbuilding & Dry Dock Co	23 Jan 1970	22 Sep 1971	16 Feb 1974
***SOUTH CAROLINA**	CGN 37	Newport News Shipbuilding & Dry Dock Co	1 Dec 1970	1 July 1972	25 Jan 1975

Displacement tons	10 150 full load
Length, feet (*metres*)	596 (*181·7*) oa
Beam, feet (*metres*)	61 (*18·6*)
Draught, feet (*metres*)	31·5 (*9·6*)
Missile launchers	2 single Tartar-D surface-to-air launchers firing Standard MR (Mk 13 Mod 3)
Guns	2—5 inch (*127 mm*) 54 calibre dual-purpose (Mk 45) (single)
A/S weapons	4 torpedo tubes (Mk 32) 1 ASROC 8-tube launcher
Main engines	2 geared turbines; 2 shafts
Reactors	2 pressurised-water cooled D2G (General Electric)
Speed, knots	30+
Complement	540 (28 officers, 512 enlisted men)

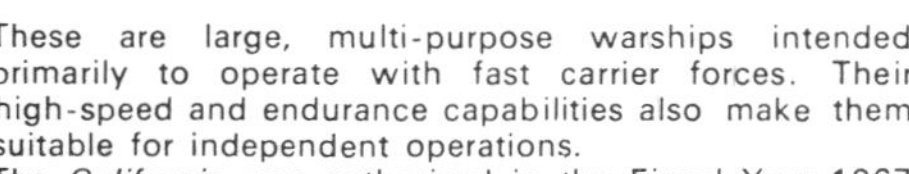

These are large, multi-purpose warships intended primarily to operate with fast carrier forces. Their high-speed and endurance capabilities also make them suitable for independent operations.
The *California* was authorised in the Fiscal Year 1967 new construction programme and the *South Carolina* in the FY 1968 programme. The construction of a third ship of this class (DLGN 38) was also authorised in FY 1968, but the rising costs of these ships and development of the DXGN/DLGN 38 design (now "Virginia" class) caused the third ship to be deferred.
The contract for both ships was awarded on 13 June 1968. Both ships are active.

CLASSIFICATION. These ships were originally classified as guided missile frigates (DLGN); subsequently reclassified as guided missile cruisers (CGN) in July 1975.

DESIGN. These ships have tall, enclosed towers supporting radar antennas in contrast to the open lattice masts of the previous nuclear frigates *Truxtun* and *Bainbridge*.

ELECTRONICS. Fitted with bow-mounted SQS-26CX sonar and the Naval Tactical Data System (NTDS). These ships have SPS-48 three-dimensional, SPS-10 and SPS-40 search radar antennas. Four SPG-51 missile directors are provided.

ENGINEERING. Estimated nuclear core life for these ships provide 700 000 miles "range"; estimated cost is $11 500 000 for the two initial nuclear cores.

FISCAL. Estimated cost is $200 000 000 for *California* and $180 000 000 for *South Carolina*. See 1971-1972 edition for funding history.

GUNNERY. Fitted with Mk 86 gunfire control system.

MISSILES. Reportedly, these ships carry some 80 surface-to-air missiles divided equally between a magazine beneath each launcher. The launchers will fire the Standard-MR missile.

PHOTOGRAPHS. The "California" class can be distinguished from the subsequent "Virginia" class cruisers by the ASROC launcher and "reload house" forward of the bridge and the after 5 inch gun being one level above the main deck in the earlier ships. Note the tower-like mast structures in both US classes; similar to the Soviet missile cruiser designs.

CALIFORNIA (CGN 36) *1973, Newport News SB & DD Co.*

SOUTH CAROLINA (CGN 37) *1974, United States Navy*

SOUTH CAROLINA (CGN 37) *1974, United States Navy*

Cruisers—*continued*

1 NUCLEAR-POWERED GUIDED MISSILE CRUISER (CGN): "TRUXTUN" TYPE

Name	*No.*	*Builder*	*Laid down*	*Launched*	*Commissioned*
***TRUXTUN**	CGN 35	New York Shipbuilding Corp (Camden, New Jersey)	17 June 1963	19 Dec 1964	27 May 1967

Displacement, tons	8 200 standard; 9 200 full load
Length, feet (*metres*)	64 (*117·9*) oa
Beam, feet (*metres*)	58 (*17·7*)
Draught, feet (*metres*)	31 (*9·4*)
Missile launchers	1 twin Terrier/ASROC launcher (Mk 10 Mod 7)
Guns	1—5 inch (*127 mm*) 54 calibre dual purpose 2—3 inch (*76 mm*) 50 calibre anti-aircraft (single)
A/S weapons	ASROC (see above) 4 fixed torpedo tubes (Mk 32) facilities for helicopter
Main engines	2 geared turbines; approx 60 000 shp; 2 shafts
Reactors	2 pressurised water-cooled D2G (General Electric)
Speed, knots	30+
Complement	approx 500 (35 officers, 456 enlisted men)

TRUXTUN (CGN 35) *1970, United States Navy*

The *Truxtun* was the US Navy's fourth nuclear powered surface warship. The Navy had requested seven oil-burning frigates in the Fiscal Year 1962 shipbuilding programme, the Congress authorised seven ships; but stipulated that one ship must be nuclear powered. Although the *Truxtun* design is adapted from the "Belknap" class design, the nuclear ship's gun-missile launcher arrangement is reversed from the non-nuclear ships. Construction cost was $138 667 000.

CLASSIFICATION. The *Truxtun* was originally classified as a guided missile frigate (DLGN); subsequently reclassified as a guided missile cruiser (CGN) in July 1975.

ELECTRONICS. The *Truxtun* has bow-mounted SQS-26 sonar and the Naval Tactical Data System (NTDS). Fitted with SPS-48 three-dimensional and SPS-10 search radars on forward mast and an SPS-40 search radar and TACAN (Tactical Aircraft Navigation) "pod" on after mast.

ENGINEERING. Power plant is identical to that of the frigate *Bainbridge*.

MISSILES. The twin missile launcher aft can fire both Terrier anti-aircraft missiles and ASROC anti-submarine rockets.

NOMENCLATURE. The *Truxtun* is the fifth ship to be named for Commodore Thomas Truxton (sic) who commanded the frigate *Constellation* (38 guns) in her successful encounter with the French frigate *L'Insurgente* (44) in 1799.

TORPEDOES. Fixed Mk 32 tubes are below 3-inch gun "tubs", built into superstructure. The two Mk 25 torpedo tubes built into her stern are not used.

PHOTOGRAPHS. The *Truxtun* can be readily identified by her squared lattice radar masts, empty "B" gun position and lack of funnel. Two chaff rocket (CHAFROC) launchers subsequently have been fitted in the "B" position.

TRUXTUN (CGN 35) *1970, United States Navy*

CALIFORNIA (DLGN 36)—see previous page *1973, Newport News SB & DD Co.*

Cruisers—*continued*

9 GUIDED MISSILE CRUISERS (CG): "LEAHY" CLASS

Displacement, tons	5 670 standard; 7 800 full load
Length, feet (*metres*)	533 (*162·5*) oa
Beam, feet (*metres*)	54·9 (*16·6*)
Draught, feet (*metres*)	24·5 (*7·4*)
Missile launchers	2 twin Terrier surface-ro-air launchers (Mk 10 Mod 5)
Guns	4—3 inch (*76 mm*) 50 cal anti-aircraft (twin)
A/S weapons	1 ASROC 8-tube launcher 2 triple torpedo tubes (Mk 32)
Main engines	2 geared turbines (see *Engineering* notes); 85 000 shp; 2 shafts
Boilers	4 (Babcock & Wilcox in CG 16-18, Foster Wheeler in CG 19-24)
Speed, knots	34
Complement	396 (31 officers, 365 enlisted men) including squadron staff

Name	*No.*	*Builder*	*Laid down*	*Launched*	*Commissioned*
***LEAHY**	CG 16	Bath Iron Works Corp.	3 Dec 1959	1 July 1961	4 Aug 1962
***HARRY E. YARNELL**	CG 17	Bath Iron Works Corp.	31 May 1960	9 Dec 1961	2 Feb 1963
***WORDEN**	CG 18	Bath Iron Works Corp.	19 Sep 1960	2 June 1962	3 Aug 1963
***DALE**	CG 19	New York SB Corp.	6 Sep 1960	28 July 1962	23 Nov 1963
***RICHMOND K. TURNER**	CG 20	New York SB Corp.	9 Jan 1961	6 Apr 1963	13 June 1964
***GRIDLEY**	CG 21	Puget Sound B & D Co.	15 July 1960	31 July 1961	25 May 1963
***ENGLAND**	CG 22	Todd Shipyards Corp.	4 Oct 1960	6 Mar 1962	7 Dec 1963
***HALSEY**	CG 23	San Francisco Naval Shipyard	26 Aug 1960	15 Jan 1962	20 July 1963
***REEVES**	CG 24	Puget Sound Naval Shipyard	1 July 1960	12 May 1962	16 May 1964

These ships are "double-end" missile cruisers especially designed to screen fast carrier task forces. They are limited in only having 3 inch guns in comparison with 5 inch or larger calibre guns in other US missile cruisers. This class was authorised as DLG 16-18 in the Fiscal Year 1958 new construction programme and DLG 19-24 in the FY 1959 programme.
All nine ships are active.

CLASSIFICATION. These ships were originally classified as guided missile frigates (DLG); reclassified as guided missile cruisers (CG) in July 1975.

DESIGN. These ships are distinctive in having twin missile launchers forward and aft with ASROC "pepper box" launcher between the forward missile launcher and bridge on main deck level. Masts and stacks are combined into "macks".
There is a helicopter landing area aft but only limited support facilities are provided; no hangar.

ELECTRONICS. These ships were fitted with the Naval Tactical Data System (NTDS) during AAW modernisation. SQS-23 bow mounted sonar installed. These ships have SPS-10 and SPS-48 search radars on forward mast (the latter replacing SPS-39 or SPS-52 in some ships) and an SPS-37 search radar on their after mast.
Halsey, *Worden*, *Richmond K, Turner*, and *Reeves* completed with only two SPG-55B missile directors; two additional directors were installed during AAW modernisation except for *Halsey*.

ENGINEERING. General Electric turbines in CG 16-18, De Laval turbines in CG 19-22, and Allis-Chalmers turbines in CG 23 and CG 24.

MISSILES. Reportedly, each ship carries 80 missiles divided between the two Terrier magazines.

MODERNISATION. These ships were modernised between 1967 and 1972 to improve their Anti-Air Warfare (AAW) capabilities. Superstructure enlarged to provide space for additional electronic equipment. including NTDS; improved TACAN fitted and improved guidance system for Terrier/Standard missiles installed, and larger ship's service turbo generators provided.
All ships modernised at Bath Iron Works except *Leahy* at Philadelphia Naval Shipyard.
Cost of *Leahy* modernisation was $36 100 000.

NOMENCLATURE. The *England* is the second US warship to honour a sailor killed at Pearl Harbor on 7 Dec 1941; the first *England* (DE 635) sank six Japanese submarines in just 12 days during May of 1944.

PHOTOGRAPHS. These ships can be distinguished from other non-nuclear missile cruisers by having twin surface-to-air missile launchers forward and aft, and from all other new missile cruisers by the absence of distinctive 5 inch gun mounts.

HARRY E. YARNELL (CG 17) — *1972, Giorgio Arra*

HARRY E. YARNELL (CG 17) — *1971, United States Navy*

ALBANY (CG 10)—see following page — *1972, Giorgio Arra*

Cruiser—*continued*

3 GUIDED MISSILE CRUISERS (CG): "ALBANY" CLASS

Name	*No*	*Builder*	*Laid down*	*Launched*	*Commissioned*	*CG Comm.*
• **ALBANY**	CG 10 (ex-CA 123)	Bethlehem Steel Co (Quincy)	6 Mar 1944	30 June 1945	15 June 1946	3 Nov 1962
• **CHICAGO**	CG 11 (ex-CA 136)	Philadelphia Navy Yard	28 July 1943	20 Aug 1944	1 Jan 1945	2 May 1964
COLUMBUS	CG 12 (ex-CA 74)	Bethlehem Steel Co (Quincy)	28 June 1943	30 Nov 1944	8 June 1945	1 Dec 1962

Displacement, tons	13 700 standard; 17 500 full load
Length, feet (*metres*)	664 (*202·4*) wl; 673 (*205·3*) oa
Beam, feet (*metres*)	70 (*21·6*)
Draught, feet (*metres*)	27 (*8·2*)
Missile launchers	2 twin Talos surface-to-air launchers 2 twin Tartar surface-to-air launchers
Guns	2—5 inch (*127 mm*) 38 calibre dual-purpose (see *Gunnery* notes)
A/S weapons	1 ASROC 8-tube launcher 2 triple torpedo tubes (Mk 32)
Helicopters	Utility helicopters carried
Main engines	4 geared turbines (General Electric); 120 000 shp; 4 shafts
Boilers	4 (Babcock & Wilcox)
Speed, knots	33
Complement	1 000 (60 officers, approx 940 enlisted men)

These ships were fully converted from heavy cruisers, the *Albany* having been a unit of the "Oregon City" class and the *Chicago* and *Columbus* of the "Baltimore" class. Although the two heavy cruiser classes differ in appearance (see Fire Support Ships), they have the same hull dimensions and machinery. These three missile ships now form a new, homogeneous class.
The cruiser *Fall River* (CA 131) was originally scheduled for missile conversion, but was replaced by the *Columbus*. Proposals to convert two additional heavy cruisers (CA 124 and CA 130) to missile ships (CG 13 and CG 14) were dropped, primarily because of high conversion costs and improved capabilities of newer missile-armed frigates.
The *Columbus* was decommissioned on 31 January 1975; other ships are active.

CONVERSION. During conversion to missile configuration these ships were stripped down to their main hulls with all cruiser armament and superstructure being removed. New superstructures make extensive use of aluminium to reduce weight and improve stability. Former masts and stacks were replaced by "macks" which support electronic antennas and have machinery exhausts vented from sides near top. The *Albany* was converted at the Boston Naval Shipyard between January 1959 and November 1962; the *Columbus* at Puget Sound Naval Shipyard from June 1959 to March 1963; and *Chicago* at San Francisco Naval Shipyard from July 1959 to September 1964.
Helicopter landing area on fantail, but no hangar or support facilities.

ELECTRONICS. These ships are fitted with SQS-23 sonar which is linked to the ASROC fire control system. The Naval Tactical Data System (NTDS) is fitted in the *Albany* and *Chicago*.
The radar arrangements differ slightly: the *Albany* has SPS-48 three-dimensional and SPS-10 search radars on her forward "mack", an SPS-43 radar on her second "mack", and an SPS-30 on the after platform (no SPS-30 atop bridge structure); the *Chicago* has SPS-30 forward and aft, SPS-52 and SPS-10 on her forward "mack", and an SPS-43 on her after "mack"; the *Columbus* has SPS-30 forward and aft, and an SPS-10 search radar on her forward "mack", and an SPS-43 on her after "mack".

GUNNERY. No guns were fitted when these ships were converted to missile cruisers. Two single open-mount 5 inch guns were fitted subsequently to provide minimal defence against low-flying, subsonic aircraft or torpedo boat attacks.
Two Mk 56 directors installed for gun control.

MISSILES. One twin Talos launcher is forward and one aft; a twin Tartar launcher is on each side of the main bridge structure. During conversion space was allocated amidships for installation of eight Polaris missile tubes, but the plan to install ballistic missiles in cruisers was cancelled in mid-1959. Reportedly 92 Talos and 80 Tartar missiles are carried.

MODERNISATION. The *Albany* underwent an extensive anti-air warfare modernisation at the Boston Naval Shipyard; "conversion" began in February 1967 and was completed in August 1969. She was formally recommissioned on 9 Nov 1968. The *Chicago* and *Columbus* will not have AAW modernisations.
The *Albany's* AAW conversion included installation of NTDS, a digital Talos fire-control system which provides faster and more-reliable operation, and improved SPS-48 and SPS-30 air search radars (the *Albany* also has an SPS-43 long-range and SPS-10 short-range search radars, and SPG-51C fire-control radar).

OPERATIONAL. During the US Navy aerial mining of North Vietnamese ports in May of 1972 the *Chicago* shot down a MiG aircraft at a range of 48 miles with a Talos missile.

ALBANY (CG 10) — *1970, Anthony & Joseph Pavia*

COLUMBUS (CG 12) — *1972, Giorgio Arra*

COLUMBUS (CG 12) — *1972, Giorgio Arra*

Cruisers—*continued*

1 NUCLEAR-POWERED GUIDED MISSILE CRUISER (CGN): "LONG BEACH" TYPE

Name	*No.*	*Builder*	*Laid down*	*Launched*	*Commissioned*
***LONG BEACH**	CGN 9 (ex-CGN 160, CLGN 160)	Bethlehem Steel Co. (Quincy, Massachusetts)	2 Dec 1957	14 July 1959	9 Sep 1961

Displacement, tons	14 200 standard; 17 350 full load
Length, feet (*metres*)	721·2 (*22·0*) oa
Beam, feet (*metres*)	73·2 (*22·3*)
Draught, feet (*metres*)	29 (*8·8*)
Missile launchers	1 twin Talos surface-to-air launcher (Mk 12 Mod 0) 2 twin Terrier surface-to-air launchers (Mk 10 Mod 1 and 2)
Guns	2—5 inch (*127 mm*) 38 calibre dual-purpose (see *Gunnery* notes)
A/S weapons	1 ASROC 8-tube launcher 2 triple torpedo tubes (Mk 32)
Helicopter	Utility helicopter carried
Main engines	2 geared turbines (General Electric); approx 80 000 shp; 2 shafts
Reactors	2 pressurised water cooled C1W (Westinghouse)
Speed, knots	approx 35
Complement	1 000 (60 officers, approx 950 enlisted men)

LONG BEACH (CGN 9) *1968, United States Navy*

The *Long Beach* was the first ship to be designed and constructed from the keel up as a cruiser for the United States since the end of World War II. She is the world's first nuclear-powered surface warship and the first warship to have a guided missile main battery. She was authorised in the Fiscal Year 1957 new construction programme. Estimated construction cost was $332 850 000. Construction was delayed because of shipyard strike.

CLASSIFICATION. The *Long Beach* was ordered as a guided missile light cruiser (CLGN 160) on 15 Oct 1956; reclassified as a guided missile cruiser (CGN 160) early in 1957 and renumbered (CGN 9) on 1 July 1957. Through 1975 all US guided missile cruisers were numbered in a single series: CAG 1-2, CLG 3-8, CGN 9, and CG 10-12.

DESIGN. The *Long Beach* was initially planned as a large destroyer or "frigate" of about 7 800 tons (standard displacement) to test the feasibility of a nuclear powered surface warship. Early in 1956 the decision was made to capitalise on the capabilities of nuclear propulsion and her displacement was increased to 11 000 tons and a second Terrier missile launcher was added to the design. A Talos missile launcher was also added to the design which, with other features, increased displacement to 14 000 tons by the time the contract was signed for her construction on 15 October 1956.

ELECTRONICS. The *Long Beach* has fixed-array ("billboard") radar which provides increased range over rotating antennas. Horizontal antennas on bridge superstructure are for SPS-32 bearing and range radar; vertical antennas are for SPS-33 target tracking radar. The SPS-33 uses an "S" band frequency and the SPS-32 is VHF; both frequency scan in elevation. Developed and produced by Hughes Aircraft, they are believed the first operational fixed-array radar systems in the Western world. Also installed in the nuclear-powered aircraft carrier *Enterprise* (CVAN 65).
SPS 12 and SPS-10 search radars are mounted on the forward mast.
The SPS-32/33 "Scanfar" radars and the associated computers were modified in 1970 to improve performance. She is equipped with Naval Tactical Data System (NTDS) and SQS-23 sonar.

ENGINEERING. The reactors are similar to those of the nuclear-powered aircraft carrier *Enterprise* (CVAN 65). The *Long Beach* first got underway on nuclear power on 5 July 1961. After four years of operation and having steamed more than 167 700 miles she underwent her first overhaul and refuelling at the Newport News Shipbuilding and Dry Dock Company from August 1965 to February 1966.

GUNNERY. Completed with an all-missile armament. Two single 5 inch mounts were fitted during 1962-1963 year period to provide defence against low-flying, subsonic aircraft and torpedo boats.

MISSILES. Initial plans provided for installation of the Regulus II surface-to-surface missile, a transonic missile which carried a nuclear warhead and had a 1 000-mile range. Upon cancellation of the Regulus II programme, provision was made for providing eight Polaris missile tubes, but they were never installed. Plans to provide Polaris were dropped early in 1961 in an effort to reduce construction costs.
The *Long Beach* has two Terrier twin missile launchers stepped forward and one Talos twin missile launcher aft. Reportedly, her magazines hold 120 Terrier missiles and 46 Talos missiles.

OPERATIONAL. Talos missiles fired from the *Long Beach* have downed Communist aircraft in what are believed to have been the first surface-to-air "kills" in combat with ship-launched missiles.
While operating in the Tonkin Gulf, the ship's Talos missiles shot down one supersonic MiG fighter on May 23, 1968, and a second MiG in June 1968; both aircraft were over North Vietnam at the time of their destruction.

LONG BEACH (CGN 9) ***1968, United States Navy***

Cruisers—*continued*

4 GUIDED MISSILE LIGHT CRUISERS (CLG): CONVERTED "CLEVELAND" CLASS

Name	No.	Builder	Laid down	Launched	Commissioned	CLG Comm.
***LITTLE ROCK**	CG 4 (ex-CLG 4, CL 92)	Cramp Shipbuilding (Philadelphia)	6 Mar 1943	27 Aug 1944	17 June 1945	3 June 1960
***OKLAHOMA CITY**	CG 5 (ex-CLG 5, CL 91)	Cramp Shipbuilding (Philadelphia)	8 Mar 1942	20 Feb 1944	22 Dec 1944	7 Sep 1960
PROVIDENCE	CLG 6 (ex-CL 82)	Bethlehem Steel Co. (Quincy)	27 July 1943	28 Dec 1944	15 May 1945	17 Sep 1959
SPRINGFIELD	CLG 7 (ex-CL 66)	Bethlehem Steel Co. (Quincy)	13 Feb 1943	9 Mar 1944	9 Sep 1944	2 July 1960

Displacement, tons	10 670 standard; 14 600 full load
Length, feet (*metres*)	600 (*182·9*) wl; 610 (*185·9*) oa
Beam, feet (*metres*)	66·3 (*20·2*)
Draught, feet (*metres*)	25 (*7·6*)
Missile launchers:	
CG 4, 5:	1 twin Talos surface-to-air launcher (Mk 7 Mod 0)
CLG 6, 7:	1 twin Terrier surface-to-air launcher (Mk 9 Mod 1)
Guns	3—6 inch (*152 mm*) 47 cal (triple) 2—5 inch (*127 mm*) 38 cal dual-purpose (twin)
Helicopters	utility helicopter carried
Main engines	4 geared turbines (General Electric); 100 000 shp; 4 shafts
Boilers	4 (Babcock & Wilcox)
Speed	31·6 knots
Complement	1 680 officers and enlisted men (including fleet staff)

PROVIDENCE (CLG 6) *United States Navy*

Originally a series of six ships converted from light cruisers of the "Cleveland" class; three ships converted to Terrier missile configuration aft and three ships to Talos missile, with two ships of each missile type configured to serve as fleet flagships.

The surviving ships are the *Little Rock* and *Oklahoma City* armed with the Talos missile, and the *Providence* and *Springfield* armed with the Terrier missile; all are fitted as fleet flagships.

The *Providence* was decommissioned on 31 Aug 1973 and the *Springfield* on 15 June 1974; both are in reserve. The *Little Rock* is active as flagship of the US Sixth Fleet in the Mediterranean (homeported in Gaeta, Italy) and the *Oklahoma City* as flagship of the US Seventh Fleet in the Western Pacific (homeported in Yokosuka, Japan).

CLASSIFICATION. Upon conversion to missile configuration these ships were reclassified as guided missile light cruisers (CLG). In July 1975 the two active ships were reclassified as guided missile cruisers (CG).

CONVERSION. All six of these ships had their two after 6 inch gun turrets replaced by a twin surface-to-air missile launcher, superstructure enlarged to support missile fire control equipment, lattice masts fitted to carry antennas, 5 inch battery reduced from original 12 guns and all 40 mm and 20 mm light anti-aircraft guns removed. The four ships fitted as fleet flagships additionally had their No. 2 turret of 6 inch guns removed and their forward superstructure enlarged to provide command and communications spaces.

The *Little Rock* began conversion at the New York Shipbuilding Corp (Camden, New Jersey) in January 1957 and was completed in June 1960; the *Oklahoma City* began conversion at the Bethlehem Steel shipyard in San Francisco in May 1957 and was completed in September 1960; the *Providence* began conversion at the Boston Naval Shipyard in June 1957 and was completed in September 1959; the *Springfield* began conversion at the Bethlehem Steel shipyard in Quincy, Massachusetts, in August 1957, but was moved to the Boston Naval Shipyard in March 1960 for completion in July 1960. There is a helicopter landing area on the fantail, but only limited support facilities are provided; no hangar.

ELECTRONICS. The Terrier-armed ships have SPS-43 and SPS-10 radars on their forward mast, an SPS-30 radar on the second mast, and an SPS-52 three-dimensional radar antenna on the third mast; the Talos-armed ships have SPS-43 and SPS-10 radars on their forward mast, an SPS-52 three dimensional radar on their after mast, and an SPS-30 on the after platform, except the *Little Rock* has no SPS-52.

These ships have no ASW sonar.

LITTLE ROCK (09-4) 1973 R RERHIER NERLICH

GUNNERY. As converted to missile-gun cruisers these ships each retained one Mk 37 and one Mk 39 gunfire control directors forward; some directors have been removed.

MISSILES. Reportedly, the cruisers armed with Terrier each carry 120 missiles and the ships armed with Talos each carry 46 missiles.

PHOTOGRAPHS. In the above photographs of the *Providence* and *Little Rock* the differences in mast and radar antenna configurations of the Terrier and Talos ships are clearly evident. Note that the *Little Rock* does not have an SPS-52 three dimensional radar antenna (empty platform on second mast) and retains the older, "bee-hive" TACAN antenna; a UH-2 Sea Sprite utility helicopter is on her stern.

DISPOSALS

Topeka (CLG 8, ex-CL 67) stricken on 1 Dec 1973; **Galveston** (CLG 3, ex-CL 93) stricken on 21 Dec 1973.

Cruisers—*continued*

SPRINGFIELD (CLG 7) *1973, United States Navy, PH2 H. E. Deffenbaugh*

OKLAHOMA CITY (CG 5) *1972, United States Navy*

DES MOINES (CA 134)—see following page *United States Navy*

Cruisers—*continued*

3 HEAVY CRUISERS (CA): "SALEM" CLASS

Displacement, tons	17 000 standard; 21 500 full load
Length, feet (*metres*)	700 (*213·4*) wl; 716·5 (*218·4*) oa
Beam, feet (*metres*)	76·3 (*23·3*)
Draught, feet (*metres*)	26 (*7·9*)
Guns	9—8 inch (*203 mm*) 55 cal (triple) except 6—8 inch guns in *Newport News* (see *Gunnery* notes)
	20—3 inch (*76 mm*) 50 cal AA (twin); removal from *Newport News*
Main engines	4 geared turbines (General Electric); 120 000 shp; 4 shafts
Boilers	4 (Babcock & Wilcox)
Speed, knots	33
Complement	approx 1 300 in *Newport News*

Names	*No.*	*Builder*	*Laid down*	*Launched*	*Commissioned*
DES MOINES	CA 134	Bethlehem Steel Co (Quincy)	28 May 1945	27 Sep 1946	17 Nov 1948
SALEM	CA 139	Bethlehem Steel Co (Quincy)	4 June 1945	25 Mar 1947	9 May 1949
NEWPORT NEWS	CA 148	Newport News SB & DD Co	1 Oct 1945	6 Mar 1947	29 Jan 1949

These ships were the largest and most powerful 8 inch gun cruisers ever built. Completed too late for World War II, they were employed primarily as flagships for the Sixth Fleet in the Mediterranean and the Second Fleet in the Atlantic. The *Salem* was decommissioned on 30 Jan 1959 and the *Des Moines* on 14 July 1961. The *Newport News* long served as flagship of the US Second Fleet in the Atlantic. Her decommissioning was delayed several times to retain the ship's "big guns" to support amphibious operations. Decommissioned in mid-1975, the last active all-gun cruiser of the US Navy.

AIRCRAFT. As completed the *Des Moines* had two stern catapults and carried four floatplanes; catapults removed.

DESIGN. These ships are an improved version of the previous "Oregon City" class. The newer cruisers have automatic main batteries, larger main turrets, taller fire control towers, and larger bridges. The *Des Moines* and *Newport News* are fully air-conditioned.
Additional ships of this class were cancelled: the *Dallas* (CA 140) and the unnamed CA 141-142, CA 149-153.

ELECTRONICS. The *Newport News* has an SPS-37 search radar antenna and TACAN on her forward mast, and SPS-8 and SPS-6 antennas on her after mast. (The small antenna on the forward mast is an SPS-10).

GUNNERY. These cruisers were the first ships to be armed with fully automatic 8 inch guns firing cased ammunition. The guns can be loaded at any elevation from —5 to +41 degrees; rate of fire is four times faster than earlier 8 inch guns. Mk XVI 8-inch guns in these ships; other heavy cruisers remaining on Navy List have Mk XV guns.
As built these ships mounted 12—5 inch guns, 24—3 inch guns (in twin mounts), and 12—20 mm guns (single mounts). The 20 mm guns were removed almost immediately and the 3 inch battery was reduced gradually as ships were overhauled. Last 3-inch guns removed from *Newport News* in 1973 (two twin mounts amidships). With full armament the designed wartime complement was 1 860.
The No. 2 main gun turret of the *Newport News* was severely damaged by an accidental explosion in October 1972; not repaired and centre gun subsequently removed. The turret is not operable (see photo).

MODERNISATION. The *Newport News* has been extensively modified to provide improved flagship facilities; note elaborate antennas on masts, forecastle, atop turrets, and on stern crane.

PHOTOGRAPHS. Note the built up amidships structure of the *Newport News*. As a fleet flagship the required additional working, communication, and accommodation spaces. Note absence of 3 inch guns in *Newport News* and two-gun main battery turret in "B" position.

NEWPORT NEWS (CA 148) *1973, Paul Stillwell*

SALEM (CA 139) *United States Navy*

SAINT PAUL (CA 73) *United States Navy*

Cruisers—*continued*

1 HEAVY CRUISER (CA): "BALTIMORE" CLASS

Name	*No.*	*Builder*	*Laid down*	*Launched*	*Commissioned*
SAINT PAUL	CA 73	Bethlehem Steel (Quincy, Mass)	3 Feb 1943	16 Sep 1944	17 Feb 1945

Displacement, tons	13 600 standard; 17 200 full load
Length, feet (*metres*)	664 (*204·4*) wl; 673·5 (*205·3*) oa
Beam, feet (*metres*)	70·9 (*21·6*)
Draught, feet (*metres*)	26 (*7·9*)
Guns	9—8 inch (*203 mm*) 55 cal (triple) 10—5 inch (*127 mm*) 38 cal DP (twin) 12—3 inch (*76 mm*) 50 cal AA (twin)
Main engines	4 geared turbines (General Electric); 120 000 shp; 4 shafts
Boilers	4 (Babcock & Wilcox)
Speed, knots	33
Complement	1 146 (61 officers, 1 085 enlisted men); designed wartime complement 1 969

SAINT PAUL (CA 73) — *1967, United States Navy*

The *Saint Paul* is the last all-gun cruiser of the "Baltimore" class. Fourteen of these ships were completed 1943-1945. This was the largest class of heavy (8-inch gun) cruisers built by any navy. Three missile ship conversions remain on the Navy List (see *Conversion* notes). The *Saint Paul* was the US Navy's last all-gun cruiser in commission except for the *Newport News*; the former ship was decommissioned in 1971 and placed in reserve.

AIRCRAFT. As completed the "Baltimore" class ships had two stern catapults and carried four floatplanes; catapults removed after World War II. Note helicopter on fantail in overhead view of *Saint Paul*.

CONVERSIONS. Two ships of this class were converted to partial missile configurations, the *Boston* (CA 69/CAG 1) and *Canberra* (CA 70/CAG 2); and two ships were converted to all-missile configurations, the *Columbus* (CA 74 now CG 12) and *Chicago* (CA 136 now CG 11). The *Canberra* and the two latter ships remain on the Navy List.

ELECTRONICS. The *Saint Paul's* principal radar antennas when decommissioned were an SPS-37 on the forward pylon mast and an SPS-8 on the after mast; a "bee-hive" TACAN (Tactical Air Navigation system to guide aircraft) was installed atop the forward mast.

GUNNERY. As built the "Baltimore" class cruisers were armed with nine 8 inch guns, 12—5 inch DP guns, 48—40 mm AA guns, and 23—20 mm AA guns. After World War II all 20 mm weapons were removed and the 40 mm guns were replaced by 20—3 inch AA guns (except in one ship). Subsequently the 5 inch twin mount forward of the bridge was removed from the *Saint Paul* and the number of 3 inch twin gun mounts was reduced.

Paul also lost the twin 5 inch mount forward of her bridge. Prior to being decommissioned the *Saint Paul* used rocket-assisted 8 inch projectiles during shore bombardment firing in the Vietnam conflict; reportedly, her guns attained a range of 34 miles (approx 60 000 yards), believed to be the longest distance ever fired by a naval gun. It can not be ascertained if this is the maximum range possible with the ship's guns that have been modified to fire the rocket-assisted projectiles that weigh some 113 pounds.

MODERNISATION. The *Saint Paul* was extensively modified to serve as flagship for the Seventh Fleet in the western Pacific; advanced communications equipment installed and amidships structure built up to provide more office space.

NOMENCLATURE. *Saint Paul* renamed during construction; ex-*Rochester*.

DISPOSALS
Macon (CA 132) stricken on 1 Nov 1969; **Baltimore** (CA 68) stricken on 15 Feb 1971; **Fall River** (CA 131) stricken on 19 Feb 1971; **Pittsburg** (CA 72) stricken on 1 July 1973; **Quincy** (CA 71), **Bremerton** (CA 130) stricken on 1 Oct 1973; **Helena** (CA 75), **Toledo** (CA 133), **Los Angeles** (CA 135) stricken on 1 Jan 1974.

1 HEAVY CRUISER (CA): "CANBERRA" TYPE (Ex-CAG)

Name	*No.*	*Builder*	*Laid down*	*Launched*	*Commissioned*	*CAG Comm.*
CANBERRA	CA 70 (ex-CAG 2)	Bethlehem Steel Co (Quincy, Mass.)	3 Sep 1941	19 Apr 1943	14 Oct 1943	15 June 1956

Displacement, tons	13 300 standard; 17 500 full load
Length, feet (*metres*)	664 (*222·3*) wl; 673·5 (*205·3*) oa
Beam, feet (*metres*)	70·9 (*21·6*)
Draught, feet (*metres*)	26 (*7·9*)
Missile launchers	2 twin Terrier surface-to-air launchers
Guns	6—8 inch (*203 mm*) 55 cal (triple) 10—5 inch (*127 mm*) 38 DP (twin) 8—3 inch (*76 mm*) 50 cal AA (twin)
Main engines	4 geared turbines (General Electric), 120 000 shp; 4 shafts
Boilers	4 (Babcock & Wilcox)
Speed, knots	33
Complement	1 273 (73 officers; 1 200 enlisted men)

The *Canberra* and her sister ship *Boston* (CA 69 ex-CAG 1) were the US Navy's first guided missile surface ships. They originally were heavy cruisers (CA) of the "Baltimore" class. The *Canberra* was converted 1952-1956 to a combination gun-missile configuration and reclassified CAG 2 on 4 Jan 1952. Subsequently reverted to original classification of CA 70 on 1 May 1968; as a CA the *Canberra* retained the Terrier missile systems.
Retention of 8 inch guns forward made the *Boston* and *Canberra* valuable in the fire support role during the Vietnam War.
The *Canberra* was decommissioned on 16 Feb 1970 and placed in reserve.

CONVERSION. The *Canberra* was converted to a missile configuration at the New York Shipbuilding Corp, Camden, New Jersey. Conversion included removal of after 8-inch gun turret (143 tons) and after twin 5-inch gun mount; all 40 mm and 20 mm guns replaced by six 3-inch twin mounts (subsequently reduced to four mounts). Original superstructure modified and twin funnels replaced by single large funnel as in "Oregon City" class. Forward pole mast replaced by lattice radar mast and radar platform fitted aft of pole mast. Missile systems include rotating magazine below decks, loading and check-out equipment, two large directors, and two launchers.

ELECTRONICS. The *Canberra* has an SPS-43 search radar antenna atop the pole mast and an SPS-30 antenna on the platform aft of the pole mast. The experimental radar atop the lattice mast has been removed (see photograph of *Boston* in the 1973-1974 and previous editions). TACAN antenna is mounted on the forward mast.

MISSILES. Reportedly, the *Canberra* carries 144 Terrier missiles in two rotating magazines. Each launcher can load and fire two missiles every 30 seconds; loading is completely automatic with the missiles sliding up onto the launchers when in the vertical positions.

NOMENCLATURE. The *Canberra* was originally named *Pittsburgh*; renamed while under construction to honour an Australian cruiser of that name which was sunk at the Battle of Savo Island with several US Navy ships in August 1942. She is the only US warship named for a foreign capital city.

DISPOSAL
Boston (CAG 1/CA 69) stricken on 1 Nov 1973.

CANBERRA (CA 70) — *1968 United States Navy*

DESTROYERS

The US Navy's destroyer force in mid-1975 was smaller than at any time previous to the post-World War II period. A score of former "destroyer type" ships (DLG/DLGN) have been reclassified as cruisers (CG/CGN), a change which reflects their size but not necessarily their primary role which is screening aircraft carriers.
The mid-1975 destroyer force consisted of 64 ships plus 10 former "frigates" and 34 ships manned partially by Naval Reserve personnel. These 108 ships compare with some 200 active destroyers in 1964, prior to the Vietnam War buildup (plus 13 reserve training ships).
The Navy is increasingly using frigates (formerly ocean escorts) for operations that previously required destroyers. Although the newer frigates have anti-submarine weapons and sensors similar to those of modern destroyers, they lack the guns, missiles, electronics, and 30-knot-plus speeds that are considered necessary for modern anti-air warfare and surface warfare operations.
When the last of the "Spruance" class ships are completed about 1979 the last of the World War II-built "Gearing" class destroyers will be discarded. At that time the Navy's destroyer force should number 83 ships: 30 "Spruance" class, 10 "Coontz" class (former DLG), 2 converted "Mitscher" class, 18 "Sherman" class (4 DDG and 14 DD), and 23 "Charles F. Adams" class. However, at that time some or all of the "Sherman" class ships are expected to be assigned to the Naval Reserve Force (NRF) and partially manned by reserve personnel.

DG PROGRAMME

The destroyer-type ship planned for construction in the 1980s and tentatively known as the DG has been dropped. These ships were to provide area anti-aircraft/anti-missile defence with the Aegis weapon system. The DG programme has apparently been deferred in favour of the larger strike cruiser design.
Tentative plans provided for ships with a full load displacement of 6 000 to 8 000 tons with gas turbine propulsion. The cost of follow-on ships would have a target goal of $125 000 000 each (in Fiscal Year 1973 dollars).

DXG PROGRAMME

These ships were a planned variation of the "DD 963" class all gun destroyers but with an improved anti aircraft capability afforded by a Tartar-D surface-to-air missile system.
Initial Department of Defence planning called for 28 ships of this design. However, construction of these ships was not proposed in the Fiscal Year 1971 shipbuilding programme as previously anticipated. In view of the increasing cost estimates of the non-missile "DD 963" class ships prior to the start of their construction, and probable new destroyer concepts, this class will apparently not be built. (The missile-armed DDG ships would of course have been more expensive than the "straight" DD ships).
The planned DDG/DXG programme provided for a ship similar in many respects to the "DD 963" class ships to reduce design and construction costs. The missile-armed design would be similar to the DD type, but somewhat larger.

FRIGATES

All guided missile frigates (DLG/DLGN) on the Navy List as of 1 July 1975 were reclassified as guided missile cruisers (CG/CGN) except for the ten ships of the "Coontz" class which were reclassified as guided missile destroyers (DDG).
Previously two all-gun frigates had been reclassified as guided missile destroyers upon conversion to a missile configuration: *Mitscher* DD 35 (ex DL 2, ex DD 927) and *John S' McCain* DDG 36 (ex-DL 3, ex-DD 928).
Three other all-gun frigates have been stricken: **Willis A. Lee** (DL 4) and **Wilkinson** (DL 5) of the "Mitscher" class stricken on 15 May 1972 and 1 May 1974, respectively; **Norfolk** (DL 1, ex-CLK 1), the only ship of that design, stricken on 1 Nov 1973.

NOMENCLATURE. Destroyer-type ships of the US Navy have traditionally been named for officers and enlisted personnel of the Navy and Marine Corps, Secretaries of the Navy, members of Congress who have influenced naval affairs, and inventors.

10 GUIDED MISSILE DESTROYERS (DD): "COONTZ" CLASS

Name	*No.*	*Builder*	*Laid down*	*Launched*	*Commissioned*
***FARRAGUT**	DDG 37 (ex-DLG 6)	Bethlehem Co. Quincy	3 June 1957	18 July 1958	10 Dec 1960
***LUCE**	DDG 38 (ex-DLG 7)	Bethlehem Co. Quincy	1 Oct 1957	11 Dec 1958	20 May 1961
***MACDONOUGH**	DDG 39 (ex-DLG 8)	Bethlehem Co. Quincy	15 Apr 1958	9 July 1959	4 Nov 1961
***COONTZ**	DDG 40 (ex-DLG 9)	Puget Sound Naval Shipyard	1 Mar 1957	6 Dec 1958	15 July 1960
***KING**	DDG 41 (ex-DLG 10)	Puget Sound Naval Shipyard	1 Mar 1957	6 Dec 1958	17 Nov 1960
***MAHAN**	DDG 42 (ex-DLG 11)	San Francisco Naval Shipyard	31 July 1957	7 Oct 1959	25 Aug 1960
***DAHLGREN**	DDG 43 (ex-DLG 12)	Philadelphia Naval Shipyard	1 Mar 1958	16 Mar 1960	8 Apr 1961
***WM V PRATT**	DDG 44 (ex-DLG 13)	Philadelphia Naval Shipyard	1 Mar 1958	16 Mar 1960	4 Nov 1961
***DEWEY**	DDG 45 (ex-DLG 14)	Bath Iron Works, Maine	10 Aug 1957	30 Nov 1958	7 Dec 1959
***PREBLE**	DDG 46 (ex-DLG 15)	Bath Iron Works, Maine	16 Dec 1957	23 May 1959	9 May 1960

Displacement, tons	4 700 standard; 5 800 full load
Length, feet (*metres*)	512·5 (*156·2*) oa
Beam, feet (*metres*)	52·5 (*15·9*)
Draught, feet (*metres*)	25 (*7·6*)
Missile launchers	1 twin Terrier surface-to-air launcher (Mk 10 Mod 0)
Guns	1—5 inch (*127 mm*) 54 cal dual purpose
A/S weapons	1 ASROC 8-tube launcher; 2 triple torpedo tubes (Mk 32)
Main engines	2 geared turbines; 85 000 shp; 2 shafts
Boilers	4 (Foster Wheeler in DLG 6-8; Babcock & Wilcox in DLG 9-15)
Speed, knots	34
Complement	377 (21 officers, 356 enlisted men)
Flag Staff	19 (7 officers, 12 enlisted men)

These destroyers (formerly designated frigates) are an improvement of the "Mitscher" class (DL/DDG). The DDG 37-42 were authorised in the Fiscal Year 1956 shipbuilding programme; DDG 43-46 in FY 1957 programme. Average cost per ship was $52 000 000. All are active.

CLASSIFICATION. The *Farragut*, *Luce* and *McDonough* were initially classified as frigates (DL 6-8, respectively); changed to guided missile frigate (DLG) 6-8 on 14 Nov 1956. The first ship ordered as a missile frigate was the *Coontz* which became the name ship for the class. All ten ships were classified as guided missile frigates (DLG 6-15) from completion until July 1975 when reclassified as guided missile destroyers (DDG 37-46).

DESIGN. These ships were the only US guided missile "frigates" with separate masts and funnels. They have aluminium superstructures to reduce weight and improve stability. Early designs for this class had a second 5 inch gun mount in the "B" position; design revised when ASROC "pepper box" launcher was developed.
Helicopter landing area on stern, but no hangar and limited support capability.

DEWEY (DDG 45 ex-DLG 14) — *1974, Stefan Terzibaschitsch*

ELECTRONICS. The *King* and *Mahan* along with the aircraft carrier *Oriskany* (CVA) 34 were the first ships fitted with the Naval Tactical Data System (NTDS), conducting operational evaluation of the equipment in 1961-1962.
As completed these ships had an SPS-10 and three-dimensional SPS-39 search radars on their forward mast, and an SPS-37 search radar and TACAN (Tactical Aircraft Navigation) "bee hive" antenna on second mast. Prior to AAW modernisation some ships had the SPS-39 replaced with the SPS-52 radar. During modernisation SPS-48 three-dimensional search radar fitted on the forward mast (except SPS-52 in *King* and *Pratt*), an improved TACAN "pod" fitted on the second mast, and NTDS installed. These ships have SQS-23 sonar.

ENGINEERING. De Laval turbines in DDG 37-39 and DDG 46; Allis-Chalmers turbines in DDG 40-45.

GUNNERY. These ships have a Mk 42 single 5 inch gun forward; along with the converted "Sherman" class DDGs they are the only US destroyers with one 5 inch gun. As built each ship of this class had 4—3 inch 50 cal AA guns in twin mounts amidships; removed during modernisation.
The *King* was fitted with the 20 mm Vulcan/Phalanx

WILLIAM V. PRATT (DDG 44 ex-DLG 13) — *1972, Giorgio Arra*

Destroyers—*continued*

"COONTZ" CLASS—*continued*

Close-In Weapon System (CIWS) for at-sea evaluation from August 1973 to March 1974. The rapid-fire, six-barrel cannon was fitted on the *King's* fantail.

MISSILES. The first five ships of this class were built with Terrier BW-1 beam-riding missile systems; five later ships built with Terrier BT-3 homing missile systems. See *Modernisation* notes for conversion of earlier ships to improved missile capability. Reportedly, each ship carries 40 missiles.

MODERNISATION. These ships were modernised between 1968 and 1975 to improve their Anti-Air Warfare (AAW) capabilities. Superstructure enlarged to provide space for additional electronic equipment, including NTDS (previously fitted in *King* and *Mahan*); improved TACAN installed, first five ships given improved guidance system for Terrier/Standard missiles (SPG-55 fire control radar), and larger ship's service turbo generators fitted. The *Farragut* also had improved ASROC reload capability provided (with additional structure forward of bridge) and second mast increased in height.
All ships modernised at Philadelphia Naval Shipyard, except *Mahan* at Bath Iron Works, Bath, Maine, and *King* at Boland Machine & Manufacturing Co, New Orleans, Louisiana.
Cost of modernisation was $39 000 000 per ship in FY 1970 conversion programme.

NOMENCLATURE. The *Luce* was to have been named *Dewey*; renamed in 1957.

PHOTOGRAPHS. On the previous page, the *William V. Pratt* is shown in the Mediterranean with SPS-52 radar on the forward mast and twin 3 inch gun mounts amidships; note the ASROC loading "house" forward of the *Farragut's* bridge (above). In the views of the *Dahlgren* and *Mitscher*, below, note the general similarities of arrangement of these former frigates. The most obvious differences are the large "reload house" between the forward 5 inch gun and ASROC launcher on the *Mitscher* and that ship's second 5 inch gun aft. Note that on both ships the triple Mk 32 torpedo tubes are one deck above the main deck, on the 01 level. The *Mistcher* has her 5 inch guns and ASROC launcher trained to port.

FARRAGUT (DDG 37, ex-DLG 6) *1970, United States Navy*

DAHLGREN (DDG 43, ex-DLG 12) *1973, United States Navy, PH 2 W. J. Dupuis*

MITSCHER (DDG 35) See following page *1973, Giorgio Arra*

Destroyers—*continued*

2 GUIDED MISSILE DESTROYERS (DDG): CONVERTED "MITSCHER" CLASS

Name	*No.*	*Builder*	*Laid down*	*Launched*	*DL Comm.*	*DDG Comm.*
•MITSCHER	DDG 35 (ex-DL 2, DD 927)	Bath Iron Works	3 Oct 1949	26 Jan 1952	15 May 1953	**29 June 1968**
•JOHN S. McCAIN	DDG 36 (ex-DL 3, DD 928)	Bath Iron Works	24 Oct 1949	12 July 1952	12 Oct 1953	**21 June 1969**

Displacement, tons	5 200 full load
Length, feet (*metres*)	493 (*150·3*) oa
Beam, feet (*metres*)	50 (*15·2*)
Draught, feet (*metres*)	21 (*6·7*)
Missile launchers	1 single Tartar surface-to-air launcher (Mk 13 Mod 2)
Guns	2—5 inch (*127 mm*) 54 calibre dual-purpose (single)
A/S weapons	1 ASROC 8-tube launcher 2 triple torpedo tubes (Mk 32)
Main engines	2 geared turbines (General Electric); 80 000 shp; 2 shafts
Boilers	4 (Combustion Engineering)
Speed, knots	33
Complement	377 (28 officers, 349 enlisted men)

These ships are former "Mitscher" class all-gun frigates which have been converted to a guided missile and improved ASW configuration.
Both ships are active.

CLASSIFICATION. These ships were originally classified as destroyers (DD); reclassified as destroyer leaders (DL) on 9 Feb 1951 while under construction. The DL symbol was changed to "frigate" on 1 Jan 1955. Both ships were changed to DDG on 15 Mar 1967 during Tartar missile conversion.

CONVERSION. Both ships were converted to DDG at the Philadelphia Naval Shipyard. The *Mitscher* began conversion in March 1966 and the *John S. McCain* in June 1966. Superstructure was modified with ASROC launcher installed forward of the bridge in "B" position; two heavy lattice masts fitted; triple Mk 32 torpedo tubes retained amidships; and single Tartar launcher installed aft (system weighs approximately 135 000 pounds).

ELECTRONICS. SQS-23 hull-mounted sonar installed; SPS-10 and SPS-37 search radar antennas on forward mast and SPS-48 three-dimensional search radar antenna on the after mast. The *John S, McCain* has a large "bee hive" TACAN (Tactical Air Navigation) antenna on the after mast; *Mitscher* has been refitted with a smaller TACAN dome (see photo on previous page).

GUNNERY. The original Mk 42 gun mounts have been replaced by modified Mk 42 mounts with local anti-aircraft control deleted (starboard "bubble" or "frog eye" on mount removed) port dome is for local surface fire control.

MISSILES. Tartar magazine capacity is reported to be 40 missiles.

PHOTOGRAPHS. The views of the *Mitscher* on the previous page and below show the Tartar missile launcher in the straight-up loading position. Note the cylindrical structure below the launcher which houses the rotating missile magazine.

JOHN S. McCAIN (DDG 36) *1969, United States Navy*

JOHN S. McCAIN (DDG 36) *1969, United States Navy*

MITSCHER (DDG 35) *1971, United States Navy*

Destroyers—*continued*

4 GUIDED MISSILE DESTROYERS (DDG): CONVERTED "FORREST SHERMAN" CLASS

Name	No.	Builder	Laid down	Launched	DD Comm.	DDG Comm
*DECATUR	DDG 31 (ex-DD 936)	Bethlehem Steel Co (Quincy)	13 Sep 1954	15 Dec 1955	7 Dec 1956	29 Apr 1967
*JOHN PAUL JONES	DDG 32 (ex-DD 932)	Bath Iron Works	18 Jan 1954	7 May 1955	5 Apr 1956	23 Sep 1967
*PARSONS	DDG 33 (ex-DD 949)	Ingalls Shipbuilding Corp	17 June 1957	19 Aug 1958	29 Oct 1959	3 Nov 1967
*SOMERS	DDG 34 (ex-DD 947)	Bath Iron Works	4 Mar 1957	30 May 1958	3 Apr 1959	10 Feb 1968

Displacement, tons	4 150 full load
Length, feet (*metres*)	
DDG 31-32	418·4 (*127·5*) oa
DDG 33-34	418 (*127·4*) oa
Beam, feet (*metres*)	
DDG 31-32	45·2 (*13·8*)
DDG 33-34	45 (*13·7*)
Draught, feet (*metres*)	20 (*6·1*)
Missile launchers	1 single Tartar surface-to-air launcher (Mk 13 Mod 1)
Guns	1—5 inch (*127 mm*) 54 calibre dual-purpose
A/S weapons	1 ASROC 8-tube launcher 2 triple torpedo tubes (Mk 32)
Main engines	2 geared turbines (Westinghouse in *John Paul Jones*; General Electric in others); 70 000 shp; 2 shafts
Boilers	4 (Foster Wheeler in *Decatur* and *Parsons*; Babcock & Wilcox in *John Paul Jones* and *Somers*)
Speed	33 knots
Complement	335 (22 officers, 313 enlisted men)

These four ships are former "Forrest Sherman" class destroyers that have been converted to a guided missile and improved ASW configuration. Plans for additional DDG conversions of this class were dropped (the *Turner Joy*, DD 951, was to have been the fifth missile ship of this type). The *Decatur* was reclassified as DDG 31 on 15 Sep 1966; the *John Paul Jones, Somers*, and *Parsons* became DDG on 15 Mar 1967. See "Forrest Sherman" class for additional notes.

CONVERSION. The *Decatur* began conversion to a DDG at the Boston Naval Shipyard on 15 June 1965, the *John Paul Jones* at the Philadelphia Naval Shipyard on 2 Dec 1965, the *Parsons* at the Long Beach (California) Naval Shipyard on 30 June 1965, and the *Somers* at the San Francisco Bay Naval Shipyard on 30 Mar 1966. During conversion all existing armament was removed except the forward 5 inch gun; two triple ASW torpedo tubes were installed forward of the bridge; two heavy lattice masts fitted; ASROC launcher mounted aft of second stack; single Tartar Mk 13 launcher installed aft (on 01 level; system weighs approximately 135 000 pounds).
Original DDG conversion plans provided for Drone Anti-Submarine Helicopter (DASH) facilities; however, ASROC was substituted in all four ships as DASH lost favour in the Navy.

ELECTRONICS. SQS-23 sonar installed. SPS-10 and SPS-37 search radars on forward mast except *Somers* has SPS-40 in lieu of SPS-37; all have SPS-48 three-dimensional search radar on after mast.

GUNNERY. The original Mk 42 forward gun mount has been replaced by a modified Mk 42 mount with the local anti-aircraft control deleted (starboard "bubble" or "frog-eye" on mount removed; port dome is for local surface fire control).

These ships and the "Coontz" class are the only US destroyers with one 5 inch gun.

MISSILES. Reportedly Tartar magazine capacity is 40 missiles.

NOMENCLATURE. The *John Paul Jones* honours the Scottish-born father of the American Navy who later served as a rear-admiral in the Russian Navy (1788).

DECATUR (DDG 31) — *1972, United States Navy.*

PARSONS (DDG 33) — *1968 United States Navy*

PARSONS (DDG 33) — *1972, United States Navy*

Destroyers—*continued*

23 GUIDED MISSILE DESTROYERS (DDG): "CHARLES F. ADAMS" CLASS

Displacement, tons: 3 370 standard; 4 500 full load
Length, feet (*metres*): 437 (*132·8*) oa
Beam, feet (*metres*): 47 (*14·3*)
Draught, feet (*metres*): 20 (*6·1*)
Missile launchers
DDG 2-14: 1 twin Tartar surface-to-air launcher (Mk 11 Mod 0)
DDG 15-24: 1 single Tartar surface-to-air launcher (Mk 13 Mod 0)
DDG 4 and 13: 1 multiple launcher for Chaparral (see *Missile* notes)
Guns: 2—5 inch (*127 mm*) 54 calibre DP (single)
A/S weapons: 1 ASROC 8-tube launcher; 2 triple torpedo tubes (Mk 32)
Main engines: 2 geared steam turbines (General Electric in DDG 2, 3, 7, 8, 10-13, 15-22; Westinghouse in DDG 4-6, 9, 14, 23, 24,); 70 000 shp; 2 shafts
Boilers: 4 (Babcock & Wilcox in DDG2, 3, 7, 8, 10-13, 20-22; Foster Wheeler in DDG 4-6, 9, 14; Combustion Engineering in DDG 15-19)
Speed, knots: 35
Complement: 354 (24 officers, 330 enlisted men).

Name	*No.*	*Builder*	*Laid down*	*Launched*	*Commissioned*
*CHARLES F. ADAMS	DDG 2	Bath Iron Works	16 June 1958	8 Sep 1959	10 Sep 1960
*JOHN KING	DDG 3	Bath Iron Works	25 Aug 1958	30 Jan 1960	4 Feb 1961
*LAWRENCE	DDG 4	New York Shipbuilding Corp	27 Oct 1958	27 Feb 1960	6 Jan 1962
*CLAUDE V. RICKETTS	DDG 5	New York Shipbuilding Corp	18 May 1959	4 June 1960	6 Jan 1962
*BARNEY	DDG 6	New York Shipbuilding Corp	18 May 1959	10 Dec 1960	11 Aug 1962
*HENRY B. WILSON	DDG 7	Defoe Shipbuilding Co	28 Feb 1958	23 Apr 1959	17 Dec 1960
*LYNDE McCORMICK	DDG 8	Defoe Shipbuilding Co	4 Apr 1958	9 Sep 1960	3 June 1961
*TOWERS	DDG 9	Todd Shipyards Inc, Seattle	1 Apr 1958	23 Apr 1959	6 June 1961
*SAMPSON	DDG 10	Bath Iron Works	2 Mar 1959	9 Sep 1960	24 June 1961
*SELLERS	DDG 11	Bath Iron Works	3 Aug 1959	9 Sep 1960	28 Oct 1961
*ROBISON	DDG 12	Defoe Shipbuilding Co	23 Apr 1959	27 Apr 1960	9 Dec 1961
*HOEL	DDG 13	Defoe Shipbuilding Co	1 June 1960	4 Aug 1960	16 June 1962
*BUCHANAN	DDG 14	Todd Shipyards Inc, Seattle	23 Apr 1959	11 May 1960	7 Feb 1962
*BERKELEY	DDG 15	New York Shipbuilding Corp	1 June 1960	29 July 1961	15 Dec 1962
*JOSEPH STRAUSS	DDG 16	New York Shipbuilding Corp	27 Dec 1960	9 Dec 1961	20 Apr 1963
*CONYNGHAM	DDG 17	New York Shipbuilding Corp	1 May 1961	19 May 1962	13 July 1963
*SEMMES	DDG 18	Avondale Marine Ways Inc	18 Aug 1960	20 May 1961	10 Dec 1962
*TATTNALL	DDG 19	Avondale Marine Ways Inc	14 Nov 1960	26 Aug 1961	13 Apr 1963
*GOLDSBOROUGH	DDG 20	Puget Sound B & DD Co	3 Jan 1961	15 Dec 1961	9 Nov 1963
*COCHRANE	DDG 21	Puget Sound B & DD Co	31 July 1961	18 July 1962	21 Mar 1964
*BENJAMIN STODDERT	DDG 22	Puget Sound B & DD Co	11 June 1962	8 Jan 1963	12 Sep 1964
*RICHARD E. BYRD	DDG 23	Todd Shipyards Inc, Seattle	12 Apr 1961	6 Feb 1962	7 Mar 1964
*WADDELL	DDG 24	Todd Shipyards Inc, Seattle	6 Feb 1962	26 Feb 1963	28 Aug 1964

These destroyers are considered excellent multi-purpose ships. The DDG 2-9 were authorised in the Fiscal Year 1957 new construction programme, DDG 10-14 in FY 1958, DDG 15-19 in FY 1959, DDG 20-22 in FY 1960, DDG 23 and DDG 24 in FY 1961. Three additional ships of this design have been built in US shipyards for Australia (DDG 25-27) and three for West Germany (DDG 28-30).

CLASSIFICATION. The first eight ships were initially assigned hull numbers in the standard DD series (DDG 952-959); renumbered while under construction. The DDG 1 was the *Gyatt* (ex-DD 712), which operated as a missile destroyer from 1956 to 1962; armed with a twin Terrier launcher.

DESIGN. These ships were built to an improved "Forrest Sherman" class design with aluminium superstructures and a high level of habitability including air conditioning in all living spaces. They do not have the second radar trellis mast nor secondary gun battery of the earlier class. DDG 20-24 have stem anchors because of sonar arrangements.
Several ships have been modified with an extension of the bridge structure on the starboard side on the 02 level, providing additional space for storage.

COCHRANE (DDG 21) — *1974, United States Navy, PH 3 D, J, Tyree*

ELECTRONICS. DDG 20-24 have bow-mounted SQS-23 sonar; earlier ships have SQS-23 sonar with hull domes.
DDG 2-14 have SPS-37 and SPS-10 search radars on tripod mast; DDG 15-24 have SPS-40 and SPS-10. All ships apparently being fitted with antenna associated with SPS-52 radar, but the ships retain SPS-39 system (three-dimensional search antenna on second stack); these ships were completed with SPS-39 radar antenna aft.
SPG-51 guided missile fire control radar is provided. The *Towers* is the first US Navy ship to be fitted with the Ship Anti-Missile Integrated Defence (SAMID) to counter the Soviet cruise missile threat (Styx, etc); this system integrates existing electronic equipment and weapons to reduce reaction time when under attack. Also fitted with chaff rockets (CHAFFROC).

GUNNERY. These ships have rapid-fire Mk 42 guns. The *Charles F. Adams* has modified mounts with local anti-aircraft controls deleted (starboard "bubble" or "frog-eye" on mounts removed; port dome is for local anti-surface control).

RICHARD E. BYRD (DDG 23) — *1973, Giorgio Arra*

MISSILES. The DDG 2-14 have a twin Mk 11 Tartar missile launcher while the DDG 15-24 have a single Mk 13 Tartar launcher. The Mk 11 launcher installation weighs 165 240 pounds while the Mk 13 weighs only 132 561 pounds. Reportedly, their magazine capacities are 42 and 40 missiles, respectively, and ships equipped with either launcher can load, direct, and fire about six missiles per minute. (The twin Mk 11 launcher is installed in the cruisers CG 10-12; the "Mitscher" and "Forrest Sherman" DDG conversions have a similar Mk 13 launcher which weighs approximately 135 000 pounds.)
Lawrence and *Hoel* fitted in 1972-1973 with multiple launcher for Chaparral (MIM-72A) and other point-defence missiles in addition to their Tartar launcher.
All are being fitted to fire the Standard surface-to-surface missile (launched from Mk 11 or Mk 13 launcher).

NOMENCLATURE. The DDG 5 was originally named *Biddle*; renamed *Claude V. Ricketts* on 28 July 1964 to honour the late Vice Chief of Naval Operations who had supported multi-national NATO manning of ballistic missile surface ships. (The name *Biddle* subsequently was assigned to the DLG 34.) The DDG 23 honours the famed polar explorer and naval aviator.

PHOTOGRAPHS. Note differance in radars on tripod mast and missile launchers on DDG 2-14 and DDG 15-24 series of this class.

Destroyers—*continued*

CLAUDE V. RICKETS (DDG 5)—"Charles F. Adams" Class *1973, Giorgio Arra*

SAMPSON (DDG 10)—"Charles F. Adams" Class *1973, Giorgio Arra*

MANLEY (DD 940)—"Forrest Sherman" Class *1973, Giorgio Arra*

SPRUANCE (DD 963)—"Spruance" Class *1975, Litton Industries*

Destroyers—*continued*

(30) DESTROYERS (DD): "SPRUANCE" CLASS

Name	*No.*	*Start Erection*	*Launch*	*Commission*
SPRUANCE	DD 963	17 Nov 1972	10 Nov 1973	Fall 1975
PAUL F. FOSTER	DD 964	6 Feb 1973	23 Feb 1974	Aug 1975
KINKAID	DD 965	19 Apr 1973	25 May 1974	Oct 1975
HEWITT	DD 966	23 July 1973	24 Aug 1974	Dec 1975
ELLIOTT	DD 967	15 Oct 1973	19 Dec 1974	1976
ARTHUR W. RADFORD	DD 968	14 Jan 1974	1 Mar 1975	1976
PETERSON	DD 969	29 Apr 1974	June 1975	1976
CARON	DD 970	1 July 1974	June 1975	1976
DAVID R. RAY	DD 971	23 Sep 1974	Aug 1975	1976
OLDENDORF	DD 972	27 Dec 1974	Oct 1975	1976
JOHN YOUNG	DD 973	17 Feb 1975	Dec 1975	1976
COMTE DE GRASSE	DD 974	4 Apr 1975	1975	1976
	DD 975	1975	1975	1976
7 ships	**DD 976-982**	1975	1976	1977
3 ships	**DD 983-985**	1976	1976	1977
7 ships	**DD 986-992**			1978

Displacement, tons	7 800 full load
Length, feet (*metres*)	529 (*161·2*) wl; 563·3 (*171·1*) oa
Beam, feet (*metres*)	55 (*17·6*)
Draft, feet (*metres*)	29 (*8·8*)
Guns	2—5 inch (*127 mm*) 54 calibre DP (Mk 45) (single)
Missile launchers	1 NATO Sea Sparrow multiple launcher (Mk 29) (planned)
A/S weapons	1 SH-3 Sea King or 2 SH-2D LAMPS helicopters 1 ASROC 8-tube launcher 2 triple torpedo tubes (Mk 32)
Main engines	4 gas turbines (General Electric); 80 000 shp; 2 shafts
Speed, knots	30+
Complement	approx 250 (18 officers, 232 enlisted men)

SPRUANCE (DD 963) *1974, Litton Industries*

These ships were intended as replacements for the large number of World War II-built destroyers that have undergone extensive modernisation (FRAM) to enable them to serve into the 1970s. According to official statements "The primary mission of these ships is anti-submarine warfare including operations as an integral part of attack carrier task forces. They also have the capability for shore bombardment and for surface warfare, and will have short range missiles for defense against airborne threats, including enemy missiles. Their effectiveness against submarines is expected to be far greater, particularly at high speeds, than that of current Navy ships due to ship silencing techniques and improved sea-keeping capabilities."

The Fiscal Year 1969 new construction programme proposed by the Department of Defense requested funding for the first five ships of this class, however; funds were denied by the Congress because of the design status. In the FY 1970 programme the Congress approved funds for five ships, but increasing costs forced the Department of Defense to construct only three ships under the FY 1970 programme (DD 963-965); six ships were authorised in the FY 1971 programme (DD 966-971); seven ships (DD 972-978) in the FY 1972 programme; and seven ships (DD 979-985) in the FY 1974 programme. The final seven ships were requested in the FY 1975 budget.

These ships have been the subject of severe criticism because of their large size and limited anti-air/anti-ship capabilities. They are believed to be the largest surface warships of contemporary design except for aircraft carriers which do not have a major surface-to-air missile system.

The Iranian Navy has ordered six additional ships of the "Spruance" class, which would be completed in the late 1970s. The Iranian ships will be armed with launchers for Standard surface-to-air and surface-to-surface missiles.

CONSTRUCTION. All ships of this class are being constructed by the Litton Ship Systems Division of Litton Industries in Pascagoula, Mississippi. The "production facility" is a new shipyard which launched its first ship (a commercial freighter) in 1971. Advanced production techniques including modular assembly of large ship components is featured. A contract for the development and production of the entire DD 963 class was awarded to Litton on 23 June 1970; that award also provided go-ahead for the first three ships.

CLASSIFICATION. During the early proposal stage these ships were designated as the DX project, the letter "X" signifying that the characteristics were not fully defined.

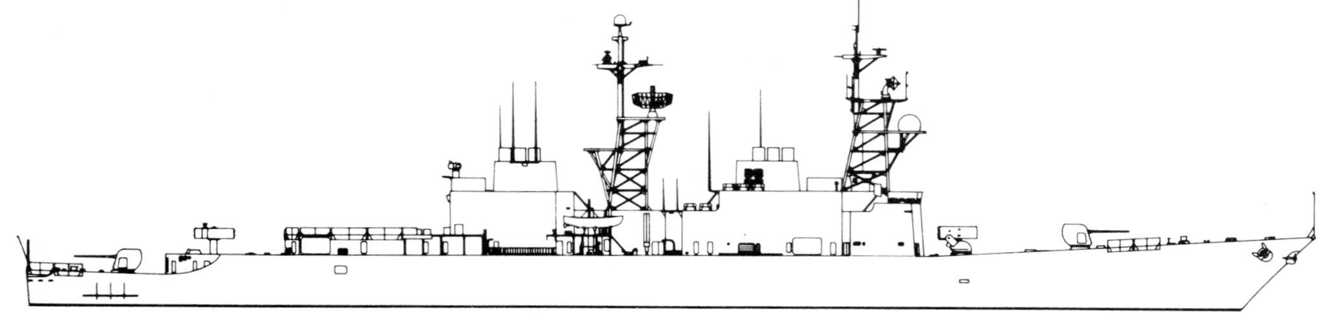

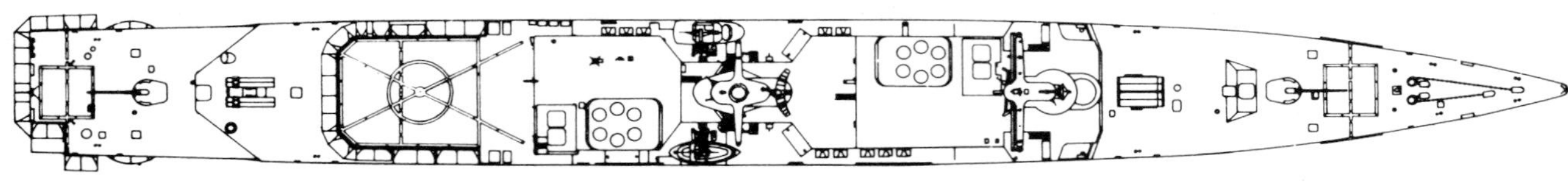

SPRUANCE (DD 963) *Drawing by A. D. Baker*

Destroyers—*continued*

"SPRUANCE" CLASS—*continued*

DESIGN. Extensive use of the modular concept is used to facilitate initial construction and bloc modernisation of the ships.
The ships will be highly automated, resulting in about 20 per cent reduction in personnel over a similar ship with conventional systems.

ELECTRONICS. These ships will have SQS-53 sonar and will be the first US warships with a completely digital command and control system, which will reduce complexity and speed up production. (Most existing systems have a mixture of digital and analogue components). To be fitted wtih SPS-40A and SPS-55 radar antennas and advanced electronic countermeasure (ECM) equipment. Provision in stern for installation of SQS-35 Independent Variable Depth Sonar (IVDS) but will not be fitted because of high performance of SQS-53 sonar (improvement of SQS-26).
Fire control system for guns is Mk 86.

ENGINEERING. These ships will be the first large US warships to employ gas turbine propulsion. Each ship will have four General Electric LM2500 marine gas turbine engines, a shaft-power version of the TF39 turbofan aircraft engine. The LM2500 is rated at approximately 20 000 horsepower. The gas turbine was selected because of comparatively low operating costs, smaller space requirements, rapid replacement capability, and cold-start capability (the engines can go from "cold iron" to full power in 12 minutes).
These ships will have controllable-pitch propellers because gas turbine engines cannot use a reversible shaft; to be fitted with advanced self-noise reduction features.
During normal operations these ships will "steam" on two engines, going to three and then four engines for higher speeds. Range is estimated at 6 000 miles at 20 knots.

FISCAL. The proposed FY 1973 defence budget requested $612 000 000 for the DD 979-985 (seven ships). Only $247 000 000 was approved in FY 1973 for long-lead time components. The FY 1974 budget provided $590 900 000 to complete funding of the ships.
The average cost per ship of this class is officially estimated at $85 000 000, but more likely will be in excess of $100 000 000 per ship. See 1971-1972 edition for additional fiscal data.

GUNNERY. These ships have the 5 inch 54 calibre, light-weight Mk 45 gun which has a limited rate-of-fire (approx 20 rounds-per-minute) but reduced manning requirements. An improved 5 inch 54 calibre Mk 65 gun is being considered for use in later ships of the class. Also, an 8 inch light-weight gun intended primarily for shore bombardment may be developed for installation in a few of these ships.
The 20 mm Vulcan/Phalanx rapid-fire Close-In Weapon System (CIWS) probably will be installed in these ships as a terminal defence against cruise missile attack.

HELICOPTERS. Full helicopter facilities are provided to accommodate the Light Airborne Multi-Purpose System (LAMPS), now the SH-2D helicopter. However, the ship can handle the larger SH-3 Sea King series.

NOMENCLATURE. The *Spruance* is named for Admiral Raymond A. Spruance, who had tactical command of the US carriers in the Battle of Midway (June 1942) and of the US fleet in the Battle of the Marianas (June 1944), two of the major engagements of the Pacific War. He also was considered one of the leading intellectuals of the US Navy.

PHOTOGRAPHS. An earlier artist's concept appears in the 1973-74 and previous edition. The stern configuration of later ships differ.
A broadside view of the *Spruance* being fitted out appears in the 1974-1975 edition.

SPRUANCE (DD 963) *1975, Litton Industries*

PAUL F. FOSTER (DD 964), SPRUANCE DD 963), HEWITT (DD 967) fitting out *1974, Litton Industries*

ELLIOTT (DD 967) *1974, Litton Industries*

Destroyers—*continued*

14 DESTROYERS (DD): "FORREST SHERMAN" CLASS

Name	No	Builder	Laid down	Launched	Commissioned
*FORREST SHERMAN	DD 931	Bath Iron Works	27 Oct 1953	5 Feb 1955	9 Nov 1955
*BIGELOW	DD 942	Bath Iron Works	6 July 1955	2 Feb 1957	8 Nov 1957
*MULLINNIX	DD 944	Bethlehem Steel Co (Quincy)	5 Apr 1956	18 Mar 1957	7 Mar 1958
*HULL	DD 945	Bath Iron Works	12 Sep 1956	10 Aug 1957	3 July 1958
*EDSON	DD 946	Bath Iron Works	3 Dec 1956	1 Jan 1958	7 Nov 1958
*TURNER JOY	DD 951	Puget Sound Bridge & DD	30 Sep 1957	5 May 1958	3 Aug 1959
ANTI-SUBMARINE MODIFIED					
*BARRY	DD 933	Bath Iron Works	15 Mar 1954	1 Oct 1955	31 Aug 1956
*DAVIS	DD 937	Bethlehem Steel Co (Quincy)	1 Feb 1955	28 Mar 1956	28 Feb 1957
*JONAS INGRAM	DD 938	Bethlehem Steel Co (Quincy)	15 June 1955	8 July 1956	19 July 1957
*MANLEY	DD 940	Bath Iron Works	10 Feb 1955	12 Apr 1956	1 Feb 1957
*DU PONT	DD 941	Bath Iron Works	11 May 1955	8 Sep 1956	1 July 1957
*BLANDY	DD 943	Bethlehem Steel Co (Quincy)	29 Dec 1955	19 Dec 1956	26 Nov 1957
*MORTON	DD 948	Ingalls Shipbuilding Corp	4 Mar 1957	23 May 1958	26 May 1959
*RICHARD S. EDWARDS	DD 950	Puget Sound Bridge & DD	20 Dec 1956	24 Sep 1957	5 Feb 1959

Displacement, tons	approx 2 800 standard approx 4 050 standard
Length, feet (*metres*)	
DD 931-944	418·4 (*127·5*) oa
except DD 953	425
DD 945-951	418 (*127·4*) oa
Beam, feet (*metres*)	
DD 931-944	45·2 (*13·8*)
DD 945-951	45 (*13·7*)
Draught, feet (*metres*)	20 (*6·1*)
Guns A/S Mod	2—5 in (*127 mm*) 54 calibre DP (single)
Others	3—5 in (*127 mm*) 54 calibre DP (single) except *Hull* (see *Gunnery* notes) 2—3 in (*76 mm*) 50 calibre AA (twin) in DD 931, 942, 944, 945, 946, 951
A/S weapons	2 triple torpedo tubes (Mk 32) 1 ASROC 8-tube launcher in A/S modified ships depth charges retained in *Mullinnix* and *Hull*
Main engines	2 geared turbines (Westinghouse in DD 931 and 933; General Electric in others); 70 000 shp; 2 shafts
Boilers	**4 (Babcock & Wilcox in DD 931 and 933, 940-942, 945, 946, 950, 951; Foster Wheeler in others)**
Speed	**33 knots**
Complement	292 (17 officers, 275 enlisted men) in unmodified ships; 304 in A/S Mod ships (17 officers, 287 enlisted men)

These ships were the first US destroyers of post-World War II design and construction. Four have been converted to a guided missile configuration and are listed separately. They were authorised in the Fiscal Year 1952-1956 new construction programmes. These ships each cost approximately $26 000 000.
All of these ships are active.

ARMAMENT. As built all 18 ships of this class had three single 5 inch guns, two twin 3 inch mounts, four fixed 21 inch ASW torpedo tubes (amidships); two ASW hedgehogs (forward of bridge), and depth charge racks.

BARRY (DD 933) *1972, United States Navy*

DESIGN. The entire superstructures of these ships are of aluminium to obtain maximum stability with minimum displacement. All living spaces are air conditioned. The *Decatur* and later ships have higher bows; the *Hull* and later ships have slightly different bow designs. The *Barry* had her sonar dome moved forward in 1959 and a stem anchor fitted.

ELECTRONICS. SQS-23 sonar installed with the *Barry* being the first US warship fitted with bow mounted sonar. Variable depth sonar installed on stern of A/S modified ships.
All of these ships have an SPS-10 search radar antenna and most also have SPS-40; a few retain older SPS-37 Several of the unmodified ships have elaborate electronic warfare electronic pods on the after mast.

GUNNERY. With original armament of one 5 inch mount forward and two 5 inch mounts aft, these were the first US warships with more firepower aft than forward. Note that *Barry* and later ships have their Mk 68 gunfire control director forward and Mk 56 director aft; positions reversed in earlier ships.
During 1974-1975 the *Hull* was experimentally fitted with an 8 inch gun forward to determine feasibility of installing a Major Calibre Light Weight Gun (MCLWG) in destroyer-type ship for shore bombardment. Forward 5 inch gun removed. See Addenda pages.

MODERNISATION. Eight ships of this class were extensively modified in 1967-1971 to improve their anti-submarine capabilities: *Barry, Davis, Du Pont* at the Boston Naval Shipyard; *Jonas Ingram, Manley, Blandy* at the Philadelphia Naval Shipyard; and *Morton, Richard S. Edwards* at the Long Beach (California) Naval Shipyard. During modernisation the anti-submarine torpedo tubes installed forward of bridge (on 01 level), deckhouse aft of second funnel extended to full width of ship, ASROC launcher installed in place of after gun mounts on 01 level, and variable depth sonar fitted at stern. Six ships of this class were not provided improved A/S capabilities because of increased costs.

FORREST SHERMAN (DD 931) *United States Navy*

Destroyers—*continued*

50 DESTROYERS (DD): MODERNISED "GEARING" CLASS (FRAM I)

Displacement, tons	2 425 standard; 3 480 to 3 520 full load
Length, feet (*metres*)	390·5 (*119·0*) oa
Beam, feet (*metres*)	40·9 (*12·4*)
Draught, feet (*metres*)	19 (*5·8*)
Guns	4—5 inch (*127 mm*) 38 calibre DP (twin)
A/S weapons	1 ASROC 8-tube launcher 2 triple torpedo tubes (Mk 32) facilities for small helicopter
Main engines	2 geared turbines (General Electric or Westinghouse); 60 000 shp 2 shafts
Boilers	4 (Babcock & Wilcox or combination Babcock & Wilcox and Foster-Wheeler)
Speed, knots	34
Complement	274 (14 officers, 260 enlisted men) 305 in Naval Reserve training ships (12 officers, 176 enlisted active duty; 5 officers, 112 enlisted reserve)

Name	No.	Builder	Launched	Commissioned
***WILLIAM R. RUSH** (NRF)	DD 714	Federal SB & DD Co	8 July 1945	21 Sep 1945
***WILLIAM M. WOOD**	DD 715	Federal SB & DD Co	29 July 1945	24 Nov 1945
***WILTSIE** (NRF)	DD 716	Federal SB & DD Co	31 Aug 1945	12 Jan 1946
***THEODORE E. CHANDLER** (NRF)	DD 717	Federal SB & DD Co	20 Oct 1945	22 Mar 1946
***HAMNER** (NRF)	DD 718	Federal SB & DD Co	24 Nov 1945	11 July 1946
***EPPERSON** (NRF)	DD 719	Federal SB & DD Co	22 Dec 1945	19 Mar 1949
***SOUTHERLAND** (NRF)	DD 743	Bath Iron Works Corp	5 Oct 1944	22 Dec 1944
***WILLIAM C. LAWE** (NRF)	DD 763	Bethlehem (San Francisco)	21 May 1945	18 Dec 1946
***ROWAN**	DD 782	Todd Pacific Shipyards	29 Dec 1944	31 Mar 1945
***GURKE**	DD 783	Todd Pacific Shipyards	15 Feb 1945	12 May 1945
***McKEAN** (NRF)	DD 784	Todd Pacific Shipyards	31 Mar 1945	9 June 1945
***HENDERSON** (NRF)	DD 785	Todd Pacific Shipyards	28 May 1945	4 Aug 1945
***RICHARD B. ANDERSON**	DD 786	Todd Pacific Shipyards	7 July 1945	26 Oct 1945
***HOLLISTER** (NRF)	DD 788	Todd Pacific Shipyards	9 Oct 1945	26 Mar 1946
***HIGBEE** (NRF)	DD 806	Bath Iron Works Corp	12 Nov 1944	27 Jan 1945
***CORRY** (NRF)	DD 817	Consolidated Steel Corp	28 July 1945	26 Feb 1946
***NEW**	DD 818	Consolidated Steel Corp	18 Aug 1945	5 Apr 1946
***HOLDER** (NRF)	DD 819	Consolidated Steel Corp	25 Aug 1945	18 May 1946
***RICH** (NRF)	DD 820	Consolidated Steel Corp	5 Oct 1945	4 July 1946
***JOHNSTON** (NRF)	DD 821	Consolidated Steel Corp	19 Oct 1945	10 Oct 1946
***ROBERT H. McCARD** (NRF)	DD 822	Consolidated Steel Corp	9 Nov 1945	26 Oct 1946
***BASILONE**	DD 824	Consolidated Steel Corp	21 Dec 1945	26 July 1949
***AGERHOLM**	DD 826	Bath Iron Works Corp	30 Mar 1946	20 June 1946
***MYLES C. FOX** (NRF)	DD 829	Bath Iron Works Corp	13 Jan 1945	20 Mar 1945
***CHARLES P. CECIL** (NRF)	DD 835	Bath Iron Works Corp	22 Apr 1945	29 June 1945
***GEORGE K. MacKENZIE**	DD 836	Bath Iron Works Corp	13 May 1945	13 July 1945
***SARSFIELD**	DD 837	Bath Iron Works Corp	27 May 1945	31 July 1945
***POWER** (NRF)	DD 839	Bath Iron Works Corp	30 June 1945	13 Sep 1945
***GLENNON**	DD 840	Bath Iron Works Corp	14 July 1945	4 Oct 1945
***FISKE** (NRF)	DD 842	Bath Iron Works Corp	8 Sep 1945	28 Nov 1945
***BAUSELL**	DD 845	Bath Iron Works Corp	19 Nov 1945	7 Feb 1947
***OZBOURN** (NRF)	DD 846	Bath Iron Works Corp	22 Dec 1945	5 Mar 1946
***RICHARD E. KRAUS** (ex-AG 151)	DD 849	Bath Iron Works Corp	2 Mar 1946	23 May 1946
***LEONARD F. MASON**	DD 852	Bethlehem (Quincy)	4 Jan 1946	28 June 1946
***VOGELGESANG** (NRF)	DD 862	Bethelehm (Staten Island)	15 Jan 1945	28 Apr 1945
***STEINAKER** (NRF)	DD 863	Bethlehem (Staten Island)	13 Feb 1945	26 May 1945
***HAROLD J. ELLISON** (NRF)	DD 864	Bethlehem (Staten Island)	14 Mar 1945	23 June 1945
***CONE** (NRF)	DD 866	Bethlehem (Staten Island)	10 May 1945	18 Aug 1945
***STRIBLING**	DD 867	Bethlehem (Staten Island)	8 June 1945	29 Sep 1945
***BROWNSON**	DD 868	Bethlehem (Staten Island)	15 Mar 1945	17 Nov 1945
***DAMATO** (NRF)	DD 871	Bethlehem (Staten Island)	21 Nov 1945	27 Apr 1946
***HAWKINS**	DD 873	Consolidated Steel Corp	7 Oct 1944	10 Feb 1945
***ROGERS** (NRF)	DD 876	Consolidated Steel Corp	20 Nov 1944	26 Mar 1945
***VESOLE**	DD 878	Consolidated Steel Corp	29 Dec 1944	23 Apr 1945
***DYESS** (NRF)	DD 880	Consolidated Steel Corp	26 Jan 1945	21 May 1945
***BORDELON**	DD 881	Consolidated Steel Corp	3 Mar 1945	5 June 1945
***NEWMAN K. PERRY** (NRF)	DD 883	Consolidated Steel Corp	17 Mar 1945	26 July 1945
***JOHN R. CRAIG** (NRF)	DD 885	Consolidated Steel Corp	14 Apr 1945	20 Aug 1945
***ORLECK** (NRF)	DD 886	Consolidated Steel Corp	12 May 1945	15 Sep 1945
***MEREDITH** (NRF)	DD 890	Consolidated Steel Corp	28 June 1945	31 Dec 1945

These ships are enlarged versions of the "Allen M. Sumner" class with an additional 14-foot section amidships for additional fuel tanks. All of the above listed ships have been extensively modernised under the FRAM I programme (see *Modernisation* notes). The *Richard E. Kraus* (ex-AG 151) and *Sarsfield* have been used for experimental work (EDD). (The former ship was designated AG 151 from 24 Aug 1949 to 11 Dec 1953).

The "Gearing" class initially covered hull numbers DD 710-721, 742, 743, 763-769, 782-791, 805-926. Forty-nine of these ships were cancelled in 1945 (DD 768, 796, 809-816, 854-856, and 891-926); four ships were never completed and were scrapped in the 1950s; *Castle* (DD 720), *Woodrow R. Thompson* (DD 721), *Lansdale* (DD 766), and *Seymour D. Owens* (DD 767).

Two similar ships completed to a modified design after World War II are listed separately as the "Carpenter" class.

All surviving ships of this class are active. Thirty-two ships are assigned to Naval Reserve training and are manned by composite active duty-reserve crews. These ships are noted as NRF (Naval Reserve Force).

ARMAMENT-DESIGN. As built these ships had a pole mast and carried an armament of six 5 inch guns (twin mounts), 12—40 mm AA guns (2 quad, 2 twin), 11—20 mm AA guns (single), and 10—21 inch torpedo tubes (quin). After World War II the after bank of tubes was replaced by an additional quad 40 mm mount. All 40 mm and 20 mm guns were replaced subsequently by six 3 inch guns (2 twin, 2 single) and a tripod mast was installed to support heavier radar antennas. The 3 inch guns and remaining torpedo tubes were removed during FRAM modernisation.

ELECTRONICS. These ships have SPS-10 and SPS-40 or SPS-37 search radars on their forward tripod mast; advanced electronic warfare equipment fitted to most ships with an enlarged electronic "stack" atop the helicopter hangar-ASROC magazine structure. Fitted with SQS-23 sonar. *Brownson* fitted with SQQ (modified SQS-23) and *Glennon* fitted with SQS-56 (modified SQS-23) for evaluation.

ENGINEERING. Range is 5 800 miles at 15 knots. During November 1974 the *Johnston* conducted experiments using liquified coal as fuel in one boiler (Project Seacoal).

HELICOPTERS. These ships no longer operate drone helicopters, but rely on ASROC and tube-launched torpedoes, for anti-submarine weapons. They had been fitted to operate the Drone Anti-Submarine Helicopter (DASH) during FRAM modernisation.

MODERNISATION. All of these ships have undergone extensive modernisation under the Fleet Rehabilitation and Modernisation (FRAM I) programme. They were stripped of all armament except two 5 inch mounts, new anti-submarine weapons were installed including facilities for operating ASW helicopters new electronic equipment was installed, machinery was overhauled, living and working spaces were rehabilitated. For budgeting reasons FRAM I work was officially considered a "conversion". Conversions undertaken between 1961 and 1965.

There are two basic FRAM I configurations: the DD 786, 826, and 890 have twin 5 inch mounts in "A" and "B" positions and Mk 32 torpedo launchers abaft second funnel; others have twin 5 inch mounts in "A" and "Y" positions and Mk 32 launchers on 01 level in "B" position.

PHOTOGRAPHS. Note special electronic installation on helicopter deck of the *Sarsfield*; a photograph taken the previous year without the installation appears in the 1974-1975 edition. The *Sarsfield* has an SPS-40 radar antenna on the tripod mast while the *Power* (above) has SPS-37.

POWER (DD 839) *1973, Giorgio Arra*

SARSFIELD (DD 837) *1974, Stefan Terzibaschitsch*

Destroyers—*continued*

"GEARING" CLASS FRAM I—*continued*

DISPOSALS AND TRANSFERS (since 1 Jan 1970) **Fechteler** (DD 870) stricken on 11 Sep 1970; **Samuel B. Roberts** (DD 823) stricken on 2 Nov 1970; **Forrest Royal** (DD 872) transferred to Turkey on 27 Mar 1971; **Stickell** (DD 888) transferred to Greece on 1 July 1972; **Eugene A. Greene** (DD 711), **Furse** (DD 882) transferred to Spain on 31 Aug 1972; **Warrington** (DD 843) stricken on 1 Oct 1972; **Shelton** (DD 790) transferred to Spain on 15 Mar 1973; **James E. Kyes** (DD 787), **Hanson** (DD 832) to Spain on 31 Mar 1973; **Gearing** (DD 710), **Dennis J. Buckley** (DD 808), **Perry** (DD 844), **Joseph P. Kennedy Jr.** (DD 850), **Floyd B. Parks** (DD 884) stricken on 2 July 1973; **Rupertus** (DD 851) transferred to Greece on 10 July 1973; **Eversole** (DD 789) transferred to Turkey on 11 July 1973; **Charles H. Roan** (DD 853) to Turkey on 21 Sep 1973; **Noa** (DD 841), **Leary** (DD 879), **O'Hare** (DD 889) transferred to Spain on 31 Oct 1973; **Henry W. Tucker** (DD 875), **Brinkley Bass** (DD 887) transferred to Brazil on 3 Dec 1973; **Arnold J. Isbell** (DD 869) transferred to Greece on 3 Dec 1973; **Herbert J. Thomas** (DD 833) stricken on 1 Apr 1974; **Robert L. Wilson** (DD 847) stricken on 30 Sep 1974; **Charles R. Ware** (DD 865) stricken on 12 Dec 1974.

Ex-ESCORT TYPE

Fred T. Berry (DD 858) stricken on 15 Sep 1970; **Harwood** (DD 861) transferred to Turkey on 17 Dec 1971; **Keppler** (DD 765) transferred to Turkey on 30 June 1972; **Lloyd Thomas** (DD 764) transferred to Taiwan China on 30 Oct 1972; **McCaffery** (DD 860) stricken on 30 Sep 1973; **Norris** (DD 859) stricken on 1 Feb 1974.

Ex-RADAR PICKET TYPE

Turner (DD 834) stricken on 26 Sep 1969; **Frank Knox** (DD 742) transferred to Greece on 23 Jan 1971; **Ernest G. Small** (DD 838) transferred to Taiwan China on 19 Feb 1971; **Chevalier** (DD 805) transferred to South Korea on 5 July 1972; **Everett F. Larson** (DD 830) to South Korea on 30 Oct 1972; **Perkins** (DD 877) transferred to Argentina on 15 Jan 1973; **Duncan** (DD 874) stricken on 1 Sep 1973; **Benner** (DD 807), **Kenneth D. Bailey** (DD 713), **Goodrich** (DD 831) stricken on 1 Feb 1974.

"GEARING" CLASS FRAM II

The 16 "Gearing" class destroyers modernised under the FRAM II programme have been stricken or transferred to foreign navies. See 1973-1974 and previous editions for characteristics and photographs.

HIGBEE (DD 806) *1974, United States Navy, PH3, J. A. Romesburg*

HENDERSON (DD 785) *1974, United States Navy, PH3 J. A. Romesburg*

DYESS (DD 880) *1972, Giorgio Arra*

ROBERT A. OWENS (DD 827)—see following page *1969, A. & J. Pavia*

Destroyers—*continued*

2 DESTROYERS (DD): "CARPENTER" TYPE (FRAM I)

Displacement, tons	2 425 standard; 3 410 full load
Length, feet (*metres*)	390·5 (*119·0*) oa
Beam, feet (*metres*)	40·9 (*12·4*)
Draught, feet (*metres*)	19 (*5·8*)
Guns	2—5 inch (*127 mm*) 38 calibre DP (twin)
A/S weapons	1 ASROC 8-tube launcher 2 triple torpedo tubes (Mk 32) facilities for small helicopter
Main engines	2 geared turbines (Westinghouse in *Carpenter*, General Electric in *Robert A. Owens*); 60 000 shp; 2 shafts
Boilers	4 (Babcock & Wilcox)
Speed, knots	34
Complement	305 (12 officers, 176 enlisted active duty; 5 officers, 112 enlisted reserve)

Name	*No*	*Builder*	*Launched*	*Commissioned*
***CARPENTER** (NRF)	DD 825	Consolidated Steel Corp	30 Dec 1945	15 Dec 1946
***ROBERT A. OWENS** (NRF)	DD 827	Bath Iron Works Corp	15 July 1946	5 Nov 1949

These ships were laid down as units of the "Gearing" class. Their construction was suspended after World War II until 1947 when they were towed to the Newport News Shipbuilding and Drydock Co for completion as "hunter-killer" destroyers (DDK). As specialised ASW ships they mounted 3 inch (76 mm) guns in place of 5 inch mounts and were armed with improved ahead-firing anti-submarine weapons (hedgehogs and Weapon Able/Alfa); special sonar equipment installed. The DDK and DDE classifications were merged in 1950 with both of these ships being designated DDE on 4 March 1950. Upon being modernised to the FRAM I configuration they were reclassified DD on 30 June 1962.

Both of these ships are assigned to Naval Reserve training; they are manned by composite active duty reserve crews.

ELECTRONICS. These ships have SPS-10 and SPS-40 search radars on their forward tripod mast and electronic warfare "pods" on a smaller tripod mast forward of their second funnel.

PHOTOGRAPHS. The *Carpenter* and *Robert A Owens* are distinguished as the only surviving war-built US destroyer with one 5 inch twin gun mount.

3 DESTROYERS (DD): "FLETCHER" CLASSES

Displacement, tons	2 050 standard; 3 050 full load
Length, feet (*metres*)	376·5 (*114·7*) oa
Beam, feet (*metres*)	39·5 (*11·9*)
Draught, feet (*metres*)	18 (*5·5*)
Guns	4—5 inch (*127 mm*) 38 calibre DP (single) except 5 guns in *Porterfield* 6—3 inch (*76 mm*) 50 calibre AA (twin) in *Picking*
A/S weapons	2 fixed hedgehogs 2 triple torpedo tubes (Mk 32) depth charges
Main engines	2 geared turbines (General Electric except Westinghouse in *Porterfield*); 60 000 shp; 2 shafts
Boilers	4 (Babcock & Wilcox)
Speed, knots	35
Complement	250 (14 officers, 236 enlisted men); designed wartime complement 329

Name	*No.*	*Builder*	*Launched*	*Commissioned*
STODDARD	DD 566	Seattle-Tacoma SB Corp	19 Nov 1943	15 Apr 1944
PORTERFIELD	DD 682	Bethlehem Steel Co (San Pedro)	13 June 1943	30 Oct 1943
PICKING	DD 685	Bethlehem Steel Co (Staten Island)	31 May 1943	21 Sep 1943

STODDARD (DD 566) *1966, United States Navy*

These ships are the survivors 119 "Fletcher" and 56 "repeat Fletcher" class destroyers completed between 1942 and 1945.
The above three ships are in reserve.

ARMAMENT-DESIGN. These ships marked reversion to flush-deck destroyers by the US Navy after several broken-deck designs built during the 1930s and early 1940s. This design was extremely successful. As built these ships mounted 5—5 inch guns, 6 to 10—40 mm guns (twin), and several 20 mm guns plus 10—21 inch torpedo tubes. After World War II most of these ships had their original pole mast replaced by a tripod mast and the five torpedo tubes between the funnels removed. All 20 mm guns were deleted and 41 ships had their No. 3 ("Q") 5 inch mount removed and the 40 mm guns replaced by 6—3 inch guns (twin). Subsequently some or all 3 inch guns were removed. Ships in commission during the 1960s had their remaining anti-ship torpedo tubes removed and were fitted with two triple tubes (Mk 32) for anti-submarine torpedoes.

ELECTRONICS. Fitted with SPS-6 and SPS-10 radar antennas.

TRANSFERS. Ships of these classes serve in the navies of Argentina, Brazil, Chile, Colombia, West Germany, Greece, Italy, Japan, South Korea, Mexico, Peru, Spain, Taiwan China and Turkey.

DISPOSALS AND TRANSFERS (since 1 Jan 1970)

ORIGINAL "FLETCHER" CLASS

Watts (DD 567) **La Vallette** (DD 448), stricken on 1 Feb 1974; **Terry** (DD 513) stricken on Apr 1974

Abbot (DD 629), **Daly** (DD 519), **Hazelwood** (DD 531), **James Miller** (DD 535), **Robinson** (DD 562), **Ross** (DD 653), **Rowe** (DD 564), **Sigourney** (DD 643), **Sigsbee** (DD 502), **Terry** (DD 513), **The Sullivans** (DD 537), **Wren** (DD 568) stricken on 1 Dec 1974.

LATER "FLETCHER" CLASS

Charles J. Badger (DD 657) stricken on 1 Feb 1974; **Bearss** (DD 654), **Caperton** (DD 650), **Cassin Young** (DD 793), **Cotten** (DD 669), **Dashiell** (DD 659), **Gatling** (DD 671), **Healy** (DD 672), **Hunt** (DD 674), **John Hood** (DD 655), **Kidd** (DD 661), **McNair** (DD 679), **Melvin** (DD 680), **Remey** (DD 688), **Stockham** (DD 683) stricken on 1 Dec 1974.

HENDERSON (DD 785)—GEARING CLASS *1974, United States Navy J. A. Romseburg*

"ALLEN M. SUMNER" CLASS

All surviving ships of the 70 destroyer "Allen M. Sumner" class have been stricken or transferred to other navies. Between 1943 and 1945, 58 destroyers and 12 minelayers were completed to this design. See 1974-1975 and earlier editions for characteristics.

Ships of this class serve in the navies of Argentina, Brazil, Chile, Colombia, Greece, Iran, South Korea, Taiwan, China, Turkey, and Venezuela.

DISPOSALS (since 1 Jan 1975)
Laffey (DD 724) stricken on 1 Mar 1975.

"BENSON" AND "GLEAVES" CLASSES

All destroyers of the "Benson" and "Gleaves" classes completed 1940-1943 have been stricken or transferred to other navies. See 1971-1972 and previous editions for characteristics. Several ships of these classes serve in the navies of Greece, Italy, Taiwan China, and Turkey.

FRIGATES

The US Navy has adopted the classification "frigate" for those ships designed primarily for open-ocean escort and patrol. Previously these ships were classified as "ocean escorts" (DE/DEG) by the US Navy with the type originally being known as "destroyer escort" when developed during World War II.
There are 65 frigates (FF/FFG/AGFF) in commission with another 56 planned for construction during the next few years. All ships now in commission have the large SQS-26 sonar, ASROC anti-submarine rockets, and a helicopter capability. However, only six have a surface-to-air missile capability for limited area defence. The planned 56 ships of the FFG 7 class will have the smaller SQS-56 sonar. The ASROC will be deleted but the ships will be able to operate two LAMPS (Light Airborne Multi-Purpose System) helicopters and will have a surface-to-air/surface-to-surface missile capability. The FFG 7 class ships will be more versatile than the previous "Knox" class frigates and several other navies have expressed interest in the newer design. The Royal Australian Navy has ordered two of the ships as replacements for ex-British "Daring" class destroyers.
The US Navy's frigates could be supplemented in the ocean escort role by the 12 "Hamilton" class high-endurance cutters operated by the Coast Guard. The Coast Guard ships are fitted with sonar and are armed with Mk 32 torpedo tubes (as well as a single 5-inch gun). They also have facilities for operating a large helicopter.

SURFACE EFFECT SHIPS. The planned 2 000-ton, ocean-going Surface Effect Ship (SES) has been redesignated as the Advanced Naval Vehicles programme and is listed separately, immediately following the Frigate section of this edition.

NOMENCLATURE. Frigates are generally named for deceased US Navy, Marine Corps, and Coast Guard personnel.

PHOTOGRAPHS. The "Brooke" class frigate *Talbot* is shown as refitted with the OTO Melara 76 mm/62 calibre (Mk 75) gun and electronic systems planned for the FFG 7 class. Note the ship's built up hangar structure to accommodate the LAMPS helicopter and stern opening for Mk 25 torpedo tubes.
The "Knox" class frigate *Downes* is shown with the NATO Sea Sparrow missile launcher (Mk 29) installed aft, the SPS-58 threat-detection radar (on lattice mast amidships), and two NATO Sea Sparrow directors (one on lattice mast atop the bridge structure and one mounted atop the hangar).
Both frigate classes were developed to operate in relatively low-threat areas, primarily against submarines. However, the Mk 22 missile launcher in the "Brooke" class and the Mk 13 launcher planned for the FFG 7 class provide a limited area defence and surface-to-surface missile capability.

TALBOT (FFG 4) *1974, United States Navy*

TALBOT (FFG 4) with advanced weapon and electronic systems *1974, United States Navy*

DOWNES (FF 1070) with NATO Sea Sparrow *1973, United States Navy*

Frigates—*continued*

(56) GUIDED MISSILE FRIGATES (FFG): "PERRY" CLASS

Name	No.	Builder	Laid down	Launch
OLIVER HAZARD PERRY	FFG 7	Bath Iron Works Corp	July 1975	May 1976
3 ships	FFG 8-11	Fiscal Year 1975 programme		
11 ships	FFG 12-21	Proposed FY 1976 programme		
10 ships	FFG 22-32	Planned FY 1977 programme		
31 ships	FFG	Planned FY 1978-1980 programmes		

Displacement, tons	3 500 full load
Length, feet	445 overall
Beam, feet	45
Draught, feet (*metres*)	24·5
Missile launchers	1 single launcher for Standard/Harpoon missiles (Mk 13 Mod 4)
Guns	1—76 mm 62 calibre dual-purpose (Mk 75) 1—20 mm Vulcan/Phalanx rapid-fire CIWS
A/S weapons	2 SH-2D LAMPS helicopters 2 triple torpedo tubes (Mk 32)
Main engines	2 gas turbines (General Electric); 40 000 shp; 1 shaft
Speed, knots	approx 28
Complement	176 (14 officers, 162 enlisted men)

GUIDED MISSILE FRIGATE FFG 7 — *United States Navy*

The Navy plans to construct a class of 56 ships of this type for the escort of amphibious forces, underway replenishment groups, and merchantile convoys. They are follow-on ships to the large numbers of ocean escorts (DE now FF) built in the 1960s and early 1970s, but with emphasis on anti-missile/anti-ship defences to complement the ocean escorts which emphasise anti-submarine capabilities (eg, large SQS-26 sonar and ASROC). These frigates will have a viable A/S role, employing a "medium" sonar and two helicopters, plus the ever present-Mk 32 torpedo tubes for close-in defence.
The lead ship was authorised in the Fiscal Year 1973 new construction programme, with the additional ships to be requested on the schedule listed above. The lead ship is being constructed by Bath Iron Works Corp, Bath, Maine, with the remaining ships to be broken into three contract groupings and probably allocated to one or two other yards in addition to Bath.
The Australian Navy has ordered two ships of this class from Bath Iron Works.

GUIDED MISSILE FRIGATE FFG 7 — *United States Navy*

CLASSIFICATION. These ships were originally classified as "patrol frigates" (PF) at a time when the term "frigate" was used in the US Navy to indicate highly capable ships of cruiser/destroyer leader size (DL/DLG/DLGN). Previously the US Navy used the term frigate for a series of World War II-built escort ships (PF 1-102) and later for coastal escorts built specifically for transfer to foreign navies (PF 103-108).
On 1 July 1975 the lead ship was reclassified as a guided missile frigate (FFG 7).

DESIGN. These ships are slightly longer but lighter than the preceding "Knox" class escort ships. There has been special emphasis on interior design for efficiency to reduce manning requirements and noise levels. The original single-hangar design (see drawing in 1973-1974 edition) has been changed to provide a larger hangar structure to house two SH-2D or follow on-LAMPS (Light Airborne Multi-Purpose System) helicopters.
The engineering plant, weapons, and sensors planned for the patrol frigate are based largely on equipment that is already in use in US and foreign ships. In addition, several systems are being evaluated at sea in the guided missile frigate *Talbot* (FFG 4).

ELECTRONICS. These ships will have the new SQS-56 hull-mounted sonar. This replaces the earlier planned SQS-23 PAIR.
The principal radars will be the SPS-49 for long-range search, SPS-55 for surface search and navigation, and a Separate Track and Illumination Radar (STIR), the last located between the second lattice mast and the 76 mm gun mount. A Mk 92 Mod 2 fire control system will be provided (Americanised version of the WM-28 system developed by N. V. Hollandse Signaalapparaten).

ENGINEERING. Each ship will be powered by two General Electric LM 2500 marine gas turbines. This is the same engine as is being used in the "Spruance" class destroyers and the PHM hydrofoil missile craft. Range is unofficially estimated at 4 500 miles at 20 knots.

FISCAL. The Navy requested reallocation of $51 600 000 of Fiscal Year 1972 funds on 30 July 1971 for initiation of this programme; however, the Congress did not act on this request. Approximately $12 000 000 was spent in FY 1971-1972 for studies and preliminary design. The FY 1973 new construction programme provided $193 000 000 to complete the design, fund "start-up" efforts for ship equipment, and fund the lead ship. The FY 1975 programme had requested ten ships, but Congress approved only three units at an estimated cost of $816 000 000. The FY 1976 programme requested $1 095 000 000 to fund ten additional ships and cover cost growth of previous FFGs. As of early 1975 the estimated unit cost for this class in a "large-quantity" buy was $122 000 000 per ship.

GUNNERY. The principal gun in this ship will be the single 76 mm OTO Melara with a 90-round-per-minute firing rate (designated Mk 75 in US service). The ship will also have a 20 mm Vulcan/Phalanx rapid-fire gun (shown at the after end of the superstructure). This is a Close-In Weapons System (CIWS) for use as a terminal defence against anti-ship missile attack.

MISSILES. The single-arm Tartar-type missile launcher will be capable of firing both Standard (MR) surface-to-air and Harpoon surface-to-surface missiles. "Mixed" missile magazines will be provided.

PHOTOGRAPHS. Note what in the above Navy artist concepts the *Perry* is designated PF 109, the ships original unofficial and misleading hull numbers.

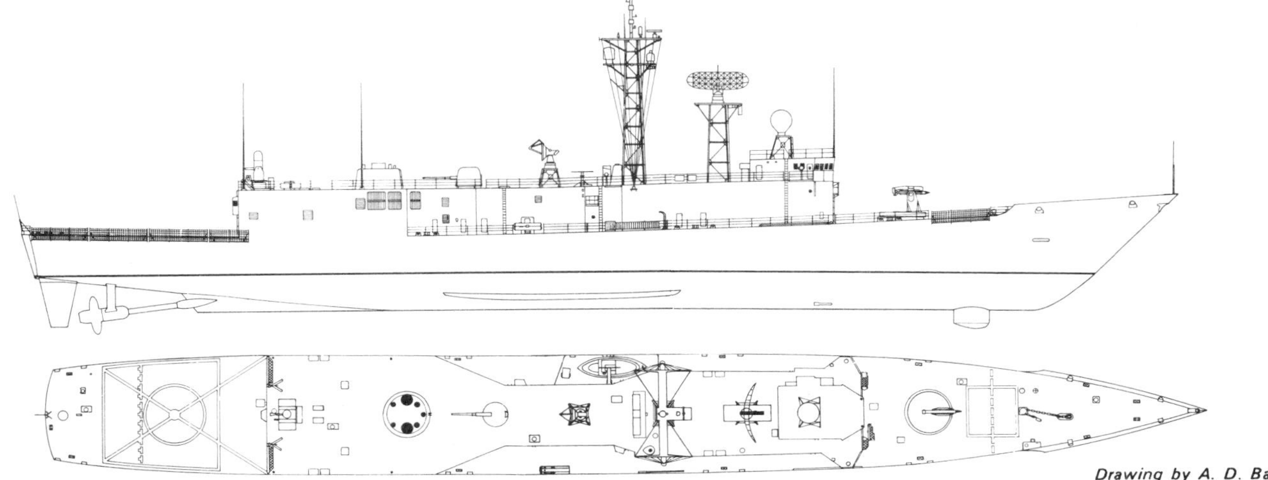
Drawing by A. D. Baker

Frigates—*continued*

6 GUIDED MISSILE FRIGATES (FFG): "BROOKE" CLASS

Displacement, tons	2 640 standard; 3 245 full load
Length, feet (*metres*)	414·5 (*126·3*) oa
Beam, feet (*metres*)	44·2 (*13·5*)
Draught, feet (*metres*)	24 (*7·3*)
Missile launchers	1 single Tartar surface-to-air launcher
Guns	1—5 inch (*127 mm*) 38 calibre DP (Mk 30 Mod 70) except 1—76 mm 62 calibre in *Talbot* (see notes)
A/S weapons	1 ASROC 8-tube launcher 2 triple torpedo tubes (Mk 32) 2 fixed torpedo tubes (stern) (Mk 25) 1 SH-2D LAMPS helicopter
Main engines	1 geared turbine (Westinghouse); 35 000 shp; 1 shaft
Boilers	2—1 200 psi (*83·4 kg/cm²*)
Speed, knots	27
Complement	241 (16 officers, 225 enlisted men)

Name	*No.*	*Builder*	*Laid down*	*Launched*	*Commissioned*
***BROOKE**	FFG 1	Lockheed SB & Construction Co	10 Dec 1962	19 July 1963	12 Mar 1966
***RAMSEY**	FFG 2	Lockheed SB & Construction Co	4 Feb 1963	15 Oct 1963	3 June 1967
***SCHOFIELD**	FFG 3	Lockheed SB & Construction Co.	15 Apr 1963	7 Dec 1963	20 Apr 1968
***TALBOT**	FFG 4	Bath Iron Works Corp	4 May 1964	6 Jan 1966	22 Apr 1967
***RICHARD L. PAGE**	FFG 5	Bath Iron Works Corp	4 Jan 1965	4 Apr 1966	5 Aug 1967
***JULIUS A. FURER**	FFG 6	Bath Iron Works Corp	12 July 1965	22 July 1966	11 Nov 1967

These ships are identical to the "Garcia" class escorts except for the Tartar missile system in lieu of a second 5 inch gun mount and different electronic equipment. Authorised as DEG 1-3 in the Fiscal Year 1962 new construction programme and DEG 4-6 in the FY 1963 programme. Plans for ten additional DEGs in FY 1964 and possibly three more DEGs in a later programme were dropped because of the $11 000 000 additional cost of a DEG over DE. See "Garcia" class for additional notes.

CLASSIFICATION. Built as DEG 1-6, respectively; reclassified as FFG 1-6 on 1 July 1975. The hull numbers DEG 7-11 were assigned to guided missile frigates built in Spain with US assistance ("Baleares" class).

ELECTRONICS. SQS-26AX bow mounted sonar installed. SPS-52 three-dimensional search radar is mounted on the "mack" (combination mast and stack) and SPS-10 search radar is installed on the mast. SPG-51C missile fire control radar is installed aft of the "mack". The advanced Mk 92 fire control system (Americanised version of the WM-28 radar and weapon control system) was installed in the *Talbot* in August 1974 for test and evaluation. The Mk 92 is scheduled for use in the FFG 7 class and the PHM missile boats.
The *Talbot* also is test ship for the SQS-56 sonar planned for the FFG 7 class.

GUNNERY. A single 76 mm/62 calibre OTO Melara rapid-fire gun (designated Mk 75 in US service) was installed in the *Talbot* in August 1974 for test and evaluation. The gun is scheduled for use in the FFG 7 class and the PHM missile boats.

HELICOPTERS. These ships were designed to operate Drone Anti-Submarine Helicopters (DASH), but the programme was cut back before helicopters were provided to these ships. These ships are being fitted to operate the Light Airborne Multi-Purpose System (LAMPS), now the SH-2D helicopter.

MISSILES. These ships have a single Tartar Mk 22 launching system which weighs 92 395 pounds. Reportedly, the system has a rate of fire similar to the larger Mk 11 and Mk 13 systems installed in guided missile destroyers, but the DEG system has a considerably smaller magazine capacity (16 missiles according to unofficial sources).
The DEGs have a single Mk 74 missile fire control system whereas the larger DDGs have two such systems, providing a considerably greater anti-air warfare capability. The DEG 4-6 have automatic ASROC loading system (note angled base of bridge structure aft of ASROC "pepper box" in these ships.)

SCHOFIELD (DEG 3) *1969, United States Navy*

BROOKE (DEG 1) *1969, United States Navy.*

RICHARD L. PAGE (DEG 5) *1973, Giorgio Arra*

Frigates—*continued*

46 FRIGATES (FF): "KNOX" CLASS

Name	No.	Builder	Laid down	Launched	Commissioned
*KNOX	FF 1052	Todd Shipyards (Seattle)	5 Oct 1965	19 Nov 1966	12 Apr 1969
*ROARK	FF 1053	Todd Shipyards (Seattle)	2 Feb 1966	24 Apr 1967	22 Nov 1969
*GRAY	FF 1054	Todd Shipyards (Seattle)	19 Nov 1966	3 Nov 1967	4 Apr 1970
*HEPBURN	FF 1055	Todd Shipyards (San Pedro)	1 June 1966	25 Mar 1967	3 July 1969
*CONNOLE	FF 1056	Avondale Shipyards	23 Mar 1967	20 July 1968	30 Aug 1969
*RATHBURNE	FF 1057	Lockheed SB & Constn Co	8 Jan 1968	2 May 1969	16 May 1970
*MEYERKORD	FF 1058	Todd Shipyards (San Pedro)	1 Sep 1966	15 July 1967	28 Nov 1969
*W. S. SIMS	FF 1059	Avondale Shipyards	10 Apr 1967	4 Jan 1969	3 Jan 1970
*LANG	FF 1060	Todd Shipyards (San Pedro)	25 Mar 1967	17 Feb 1968	28 Mar 1970
*PATTERSON	FF 1061	Avondale Shipyards	12 Oct 1967	3 May 1969	14 Mar 1970
*WHIPPLE	FF 1062	Todd Shipyards (Seattle)	24 Apr 1967	12 Apr 1968	22 Aug 1970
*REASONER	FF 1063	Lockheed SB & Constn Co	6 Jan 1969	1 Aug 1970	31 July 1971
*LOCKWOOD	FF 1064	Todd Shipyards (Seattle)	3 Nov 1967	5 Sep 1964	5 Dec 1970
*STEIN	FF 1065	Lockheed SB & Constn Co	1 June 1970	19 Dec 1970	8 Jan 1972
*MARVIN SHIELDS	FF 1066	Todd Shipyards (Seattle)	12 Apr 1968	23 Oct 1969	10 Apr 1971
*FRANCIS HAMMOND	FF 1067	Todd Shipyards (San Pedro)	15 July 1967	11 May 1968	25 July 1970
*VREELAND	FF 1068	Avondale Shipyards	20 Mar 1968	14 June 1969	13 June 1970
*BAGLEY	FF 1069	Lockheed SB & Constn Co	22 Sep 1970	24 Apr 1971	6 May 1972
*DOWNES	FF 1070	Todd Shipyards (Seattle)	5 Sep 1968	13 Dec 1969	28 Aug 1971
*BADGER	FF 1071	Todd Shipyards (Seattle)	17 Feb 1968	7 Dec 1968	1 Dec 1970
*BLAKELY	FF 1072	Avondale Shipyards	3 June 1968	23 Aug 1969	18 July 1970
*ROBERT E. PEARY	FF 1073	Lockheed SB & Constn Co	20 Dec 1970	23 June 1971	23 Sep 1972
*HAROLD E. HOLT	FF 1074	Todd Shipyards (San Pedro)	11 May 1968	3 May 1969	26 Mar 1971
*TRIPPE	FF 1075	Avondale Shipyards	29 July 1968	1 Nov 1969	19 Sep 1970
*FANNING	FF 1076	Todd Shipyards (San Pedro)	7 Dec 1968	24 Jan 1970	23 July 1971
*OUELLET	FF 1077	Avondale Shipyards	15 Jan 1969	17 Jan 1970	12 Dec 1970
*JOSEPH HEWES	FF 1078	Avondale Shipyards	15 May 1969	7 Mar 1970	27 Feb 1971
*BOWEN	FF 1079	Avondale Shipyards	11 July 1969	2 May 1970	22 May 1971
*PAUL	FF 1080	Avondale Shipyards	12 Sep 1969	20 June 1970	14 Aug 1971
*AYLWIN	FF 1081	Avondale Shipyards	13 Nov 1969	29 Aug 1970	18 Sep 1971
*ELMER MONTGOMERY	FF 1082	Avondale Shipyards	23 Jan 1970	21 Nov 1970	30 Oct 1971
*COOK	FF 1083	Avondale Shipyards	20 Mar 1970	23 Jan 1971	18 Dec 1971
*McCANDLESS	FF 1084	Avondale Shipyards	4 June 1970	20 Mar 1971	18 Mar 1972
*DONALD B. BEARY	FF 1085	Avondale Shipyards	24 July 1970	22 May 1971	22 July 1972
*BREWTON	FF 1086	Avondale Shipyards	2 Oct 1970	24 July 1971	8 July 1972
*KIRK	FF 1087	Avondale Shipyards	4 Dec 1970	25 Sep 1971	9 Sep 1972
*BARBEY	FF 1088	Avondale Shipyards	5 Feb 1971	4 Dec 1971	11 Nov 1972
*JESSE L. BROWN	FF 1089	Avondale Shipyards	8 Apr 1971	18 Mar 1972	17 Feb 1973
*AINSWORTH	FF 1090	Avondale Shipyards	11 June 1971	15 Apr 1972	31 Mar 1973
*MILLER	FF 1091	Avondale Shipyards	6 Aug 1971	3 June 1972	30 June 1973
*THOMAS S. HART	FF 1092	Avondale Shipyards	8 Oct 1971	12 Aug 1972	28 July 1973
*CAPODANNO	FF 1093	Avondale Shipyards	12 Oct 1971	21 Oct 1972	17 Nov 1973
*PHARRIS	FF 1094	Avondale Shipyards	11 Feb 1972	16 Dec 1972	26 Jan 1974
*TRUETT	FF 1095	Avondale Shipyards	27 Apr 1972	3 Feb 1973	1 June 1974
VALDEZ	FF 1096	Avondale Shipyards	30 June 1972	24 Mar 1973	27 July 1974
MOINESTER	FF 1097	Avondale Shipyards	25 Aug 1972	12 May 1973	2 Nov 1974

Displacement, tons	3 011 standard; 4 100 full load
Length, feet (*metres*)	438 (*133·5*) oa
Beam, feet (*metres*)	46·75 (*14·25*)
Draught, feet (*metres*)	24·75 (*7·55*)
Helicopters	1 SH-2D LAMPS being provided
Missile launchers	1 Sea Sparrow BPDMS multiple launcher in 30 ships (Mk 25) 1 NATO Sea Sparrow multiple launcher in *Downes* (Mk 29)
Guns	1—5 inch (*127 mm*) 54 calibre dual purpose 1—20 mm Vulcan Phalanx CIWS in *Lockwood*
A/S weapons	1 ASROC 8-tube launcher 4 fixed torpedo tubes (Mk 32)
Main engines	1 geared turbine (Westinghouse) 35 000 shp; 1 shaft
Boilers	2—1 200 psi (*83·4 kg/cm²*)
Speed, knots	27+
Complement	245 (17 officers, 228 enlisted men); increased to 283 (22 officers, 261 enlisted men) with BPDMS and LAMPS installation; as built 12 ships had accommodation for 2 staff officers

The 46 frigates of the "Knox" class comprise the largest group of destroyer or frigate type warships built to the same design in the West since World War II. These ships are similar to the previous "Garcia" and "Brooke" classes, but slightly larger because of the use of non-pressure-fired boilers.

Although now classified as frigates they were authorised as DE 1052-1061 (10 ships) in the Fiscal Year 1964 new construction programme, DE 1062-1077 (16 ships) in FY 1965, DE 1078-1087 (10 ships) in FY 1966, DE 1088-1097 (10 ships) in FY 1967, and DE 1098-1107 (10 ships) in FY 1968. However, construction of six ships (DE 1102-1107) was deferred in 1968 as US Navy emphasis shifted to the more versatile and faster DX DXG ships; three additional ships (DE 1099-1101) were deferred late in 1968 to finance cost overruns of FY 1968 nuclear-powered attack submarines and to comply with a Congressional mandate to reduce expenditures; the last ship of the FY 1968 programme (DE 1098) was deferred early in 1969.

The DEG 7-11 guided missile "frigates" constructed in Spain are similar to this design.

CLASSIFICATION. Originally classified as ocean escorts (DE); reclassified as frigates (FF) on 1 July 1975.

CONSTRUCTION. The ships built at Avondale Shipyards in Westwego, Louisiana, were assembled with a mass production technique of fabricating the hulls by using structural carbon steel tees split from wide-flange beams as longitudinal members. The hulls are built keel-up to permit downhand welding with the force of gravity allowing the molten weld to follow the contour of the hull and flow more easily between hull plates. Prefabricated, inverted hull modules first are assembled on a permanent platen, then lifted by hydraulic units and moved laterally into giant turning rings which rotate the hull into an upright position. Avondale, which also builds the "Hamilton" class cutters for the Coast Guard, side launches these ships.

DESIGN. These ships have a very large superstructure and a distinctive, cylindrical "mack" structure combining masts and engine exhaust stacks. A 4 000-pound lightweight anchor is fitted on the port side and an 8 000-pound anchor fits into the after section of the sonar dome.

ELECTRONICS. SQS-26CX bow-mounted sonar; installation of SQS-35 Independent Variable Depth Sonar (IVDS) on 3 ships began in 1971. The SQS-26CX is fitted in a tear-drop shake dome 20 feet wide weighing 26 tonnes.

These ships have SPS-40 and SPS-10 search radar antennas on their "mack" structure.

The *Downes* has SPS-58 threat detection radar with antenna on after lattice mast; the ship also has two directors fitted for the NATO Sea Sparrow (on forward lattice mast and helicopter hangar).

The *Barbey* has an experimental radar on the hangar structure.

ENGINEERING. DE 1101 was to have had gas turbine propulsion; construction of the ship was cancelled when decision was made to provide gas turbine propulsion in "Spruance" class (DD 963).

The *Patterson* is fitted with a Baldwin-Lima-Hamilton controllable-pitch propeller being evaluated for use in the "Spruance" class destroyers; her shafts are non-reversible. Another DE is being fitted to evaluate the Propulsion System Inc design controllable-pitch propeller.

FISCAL. These ships have cost considerably more than originally estimated. Official programme cost for the 46 ships as of January 1974 was $1·424 *billion* or an average of $30 959 000 per ship not including the LAMPS, Standard missile, VDS, or BPDMS installation.

LOCKWOOD (DE 1064) *1973, McDonnell Douglas*

GUNNERY. Gun armament for these ships consists of a single 5 inch/54 calibre Mk 42 mount forward with local anti-surface control (portside "bubble" or "frog-eye") but no local anti-aircraft control capability.

Lockwood fitted with 20 mm rapid-fire Close In Weapon System (CIWS) in 1972 for operational evaluation.

HELICOPTERS. These ships were designed to operate the now-discarded DASH unmanned helicopter. Beginning in 1972 they are being modified to accommodate the Light Airborne Multi-Purpose System, the SH-2D anti-submarine helicopter; hangar and flight deck are enlarged. Cost is approximately $1 000 000 per ship for LAMPS modification.

MISSILES. Sea Sparrow Basic Point Defence Missile System (BPDMS) launcher installed in 30 ships from 1971-1974 (DE 1052-1067, 1069, 1071-1083); also will be installed in DE 1068 during 1975.

Modified NATO Sea Sparrow installed in *Downes* for evaluation.

The remaining 14 ships of this class are scheduled to be fitted with the Chaparral short-range missile system which, like the BPDMS and NATO Sea Sparrow are anti-aircraft weapons.

In addition, some ships are being fitted with the Standard interim surface-to-surface missile which is fired from the ASROC launcher forward of the bridge.

Two of the eight "cells" in the launcher are modified to fire a single Standard. Cost is approximately $400 000 per ship for BPDMS and $750 000 for Standard missile modification.

The *Downes* and *Lockwood* have been used in at-sea firing tests and shipboard compatability for the Harpoon ship-to-ship missiles.

NOMENCLATURE. The lead ship of this class is named for naval historian Dudley W. Knox (the DD 742 was named for Frank Knox who was secretary of the Navy from 1940 to 1944). The *Harold E. Holt* honours the late Prime Minister of Australia, a firm supporter of U.S. policy in Southeast Asia during the Vietnam War. The *Jesse L. Brown* remembers the first US naval aviator of the Negro race; he was killed in action during the Korean War.

The DE 1073 originally was named *Conolly*; changed on 12 May 1971.

Frigates—*continued*

"KNOX" CLASS—cont

TORPEDOES. Improved ASROC-torpedo reloading capability as in some ships of previous "Garcia" class (note slanting face of bridge structure immediately behind ASROC "pepper box"). Four Mk 32 torpedo tubes are fixed in the amidships structure, two to a side angled out at 45 degrees. The arrangement provides improved loading capability over exposed triple Mk 32 torpedo tubes.

BARBEY (FF 1088) *1974, United States Navy*

Sea Sparrow BPDMS and SQS-35 sonar in FRANCIS HAMMOND (FF 1067)

SH-2D LAMPS helicopter in HAROLD E. HOLT (FF 1074) *1972, United States Navy*

DOWNES (FF 1070) with NATO Sea Sparrow *1972, United States Navy*

Frigates—*continued*

10 FRIGATES (FF): "GARCIA" CLASS

Displacement, tons	2 620 standard; 3 400 full load
Length, feet (*metres*)	414·5 (*126·3*) oa
Beam, feet (*metres*)	44·2 (*13·5*)
Draught, feet (*metres*)	24 (*7·3*)
Helicopters	1 SH-2D LAMPS helicopter
Guns	2—5 inch (*127 mm*) 38 calibre DP (single)
A/S weapons	1 ASROC 8-tube launcher 2 triple torpedo tubes (Mk 32)
Main engines	1 geared turbine (Westinghouse); 35 000 shp; 1 shaft
Boilers	2—1 200 psi (*83·4 kg/cm²*) (Foster Wheeler)
Speed, knots	27
Complement	247

Name	*No.*	*Builder*	*Laid down*	*Launched*	*Commissioned*
***GARCIA**	FF 1040	Bethlehem Steel (San Francisco)	16 Oct 1962	31 Oct 1963	21 Dec 1964
***BRADLEY**	FF 1041	Bethlehem Steel (San Francisco)	17 Jan 1963	26 Mar 1964	15 May 1965
***EDWARD McDONNELL**	FF 1043	Avondale Shipyards	1 Apr 1963	15 Feb 1964	15 Feb 1965
***BRUMBY**	FF 1044	Avondale Shipyards	1 Aug 1963	6 June 1964	5 Aug 1965
***DAVIDSON**	FF 1045	Avondale Shipyards	20 Sep 1963	2 Oct 1964	7 Dec 1965
***VOGE**	FF 1047	Defoe Shipbuilding Co	21 Nov 1963	4 Feb 1965	25 Nov 1966
***SAMPLE**	FF 1048	Lockheed SB & Construction Co	19 July 1963	28 Apr 1964	23 Mar 1968
***KOELSCH**	FF 1049	Defoe Shipbuilding Co	19 Feb 1964	8 June 1965	10 June 1967
***ALBERT DAVID**	FF 1050	Lockheed SB & Construction Co	29 Apr 1964	19 Dec 1964	19 Oct 1968
***O'CALLAHAN**	FF 1051	Defoe Shipbuilding Co	19 Feb 1964	20 Oct 1965	13 July 1968

These ships exceed many of the world's destroyers in size and ASW capability, but are designated as frigates by virtue of their single propeller shaft and limited speed. The FF 1040 and FF 1041 were authorised in the Fiscal Year 1961 new construction programme FF 1043-1045 in FY 1962, and FF 1047-1051 in FY 1963.
All ten ships are active.

CLASSIFICATION. Originally classified as ocean escorts (DE); reclassified as frigates (FF) on 1 July 1975. The hull numbers DE 1039, 1042, and 1046 were assigned to frigates built overseas for Portugal.

DESIGN. These ships are an enlargement of the previous "Bronstein" design. They have a flush deck, radically raked stem, stem anchor, and mast and stack combined into a "mack" structure. Anchors are mounted at stem and on portside, just forward of 5 inch gun. Fitted with gyrostabilising fins.

Hangar structure of this class modified during the early 1970s.

ELECTRONICS Bow-mounted SQS-26 AXR sonar in FF 1040-1045; SQS-26 BX sonar in FF 1046-1051. SPS-40 and SPS-10 search radar antennas on "mack". The *Voge* and *Koelsch* have been fitted with a specialised ASW Naval Tactical Data System (NTDS).

ENGINEERING. These ships have an advanced "pressure-fired steam generating plant" which generates 70 per cent more power than previous steam plants of the same size and weight. Each boiler has an integrated supercharger and associated control system which provides automatic regulation of fuel, air and water. The boilers can use JP-5 jet fuel or diesel oil which facilitates boiler maintenance and cleaning and ballasting empty fuel tanks with sea water. Finally, fewer engineering personnel are required to operate the plant.
A small auxiliary boiler is provided to supply steam when in port. Special noise-reduction features are provided.

HELICOPTERS. The Drone Anti-Submarine Helicopter (DASH) programme was cut back before these ships were provided with helicopters. Reportedly only the *Bradley* actually operated with DASH.
These ships are fitted to operate the Light Airborne Multi-Purpose System (LAMPS), now the SH-2D helicopter.

MISSILES. The *Bradley* was fitted with a Sea Sparrow Basic Point Defense Missile System (BPDMS) in 1967-1968; removed for installation in the carrier *Forrestal*. The BPDMS "pepperbox" was fitted between funnel and after 5 inch mount

TORPEDOES. Most of these ships were built with two Mk 25 torpedo tubes built into their transom for launching wire-guided ASW torpedoes However, they have been removed from the earlier ships and deleted in the later ships. The *Voge* and later ships have automatic ASROC reload system (note angled base of bridge structure behind ASROC "pepper box" in these ships).

EDWARD McDONNELL (FF 1043) with SH-2D LAMPS HELICOPTER *1973 United States Navy PHC Frederick Gotauco*

TRIPPE (FF 1075)—SEE Previous Page *1974 United States Navy PHC Frederick Gotauco*

Frigates—*continued*

GARCIA (FF 1040)—see previous page *1973, Giorgio Arra*

1 FRIGATE RESEARCH SHIP (AGFF): "GLOVER" TYPE

Displacement, tons	2 643 standard; 3 426 full load
Length, feet (*metres*)	414·5 (*126·3*) oa
Beam, feet (*metres*)	44·2 (*13·5*)
Draught, feet (*metres*)	14·5 (*4·3*)
Guns	1—5 inch (*127 mm*) 38 calibre DP
A/S weapons	1 ASROC 8-tube launcher; 2 triple torpedo tubes (Mk 32) facilities for small helicopter
Main engines	1 geared turbine (Westinghouse); 35 000 shp; 1 shaft
Boilers	2—1 200 psi (*83·4 kg/cm²*) (Foster Wheeler)
Speed, knots	27
Complement	236 plus 38 civilian technicians

Name	No.	Builder	Laid down	Launched	Commissioned
*GLOVER	AGFF 1 (ex-AGDE 1, AG 163)	Bath Iron Works	29 July 1963	17 Apr 1965	13 Nov 1965

The *Glover* was built to test an advanced hull design and propulsion system, much the same as the *Albacore* (AGSS 569) embodied advanced submarine design concepts. However, unlike the *Albacore* the *Glover* has a full combat capability.
The ship was originally authorised in the Fiscal Year 1960 new construction programme, but was postponed and re- introduced in the FY 1961 programme. Estimated construction cost was $29 330 000.

CLASSIFICATION. The *Glover* was originally classified as a miscellaneous auxiliary (AG 163); completed as an escort research ship (AGDE 1). Subsequently changed to frigate research ship on 1 July 1975.

DESIGN. The *Glover* has a massive bow sonar dome integral with her hull and extending well forward underwater.
No reload capability for ASROC because of space requirements for equipment and technical personnel.

ELECTRONICS. The *Glover* has bow-mounted SQS-26 AXR active sonar, hull-mounted SQR-13 Passive/Active Detection and Location (PADLOC) sonar, and SQS-35 Independent Variable Depth Sonar (IVDS) lowered from the stern.
SPS-40 and SPS-10 search radars are fitted on the "mack" structure.
The ship has a prototype tactical assignment console that integrates signals from the three sonars and radars to present combined and coordinated tactical situation presentations in the Combat Information Centre (CIC). Reportedly, the tactical assignment console increases the combat effectiveness of the ship to a considerable extent.

PHOTOGRAPH. Stern configuration differs from "Garcia" class escort ships. Covered door in stern for retractable variable depth sonar.

GLOVER (AGFF 1) *1969, United States Navy*

2 FRIGATES (FF): "BRONSTEIN" CLASS

Displacement, tons	2 360 standard; 2 650 full load
Length, feet (*metres*)	371·5 (*113·2*) oa
Beam, feet (*metres*)	40·5 (*12·3*)
Draught, feet (*metres*)	23 (*7·0*)
Guns	3—3 inch (*76 mm*) 50 calibre AA (twin forward, single aft)
A/S weapons	1 ASROC 8-tube launcher; 2 triple torpedo tubes (Mk 32) facilities for small helicopter
Main engines	1 geared turbine (De Lavel); 20 000 shp; 1 shaft
Boilers	2 (Foster Wheeler)
Speed, knots	26
Complement	220

Name	No.	Builder	Laid down	Launched	Commissioned
*BRONSTEIN	FF 1037	Avondale Shipyards	16 May 1961	31 Mar 1962	15 June 1963
*McCLOY	FF 1038	Avondale Shipyards	15 Sep 1961	9 June 1962	21 Oct 1963

These two ships may be considered the first of the "second generation" of post-World War II escort ships which are comparable in size and ASW capabilities to conventional destroyers. The *Bronstein* and *McCloy* have several features such as hull design, large sonar and ASW weapons that subsequently were incorporated into the mass-produced "Garcia", "Brooke", and "Knox" classes.
Both ships were built under the Fiscal Year 1960 new construction programme by Avondale Shipyards in Westwego, Louisiana.

CLASSIFICATION. These ships were originally classified as ocean escorts (DE); reclassified as frigates (FF) on 1 July 1975.

DESIGN. These ships have a sharply raked stem, stem anchor, and mast and stacks combined in a "mack" structure. Position of stem anchor and portside anchor (just forward of gun mount) necessitated by large bow sonar dome. Note the deckhouse adjacent to "mack" in photograph of *McCloy*.

ELECTRONICS. SQS-26 bow-mounted sonar installed. SPS-40 and SPS-10 search radars mounted on "mack".

McCLOY (FF 1038) *1971, United States Navy*

Frigates—*continued*

6 RADAR PICKET ESCORT SHIPS (DER): CONVERTED "EDSALL" CLASS

Displacement, tons	1 590 standard; 1 850 full load
Length, feet (*metres*)	306 (*93·3*) oa
Beam, feet (*metres*)	36·6 (*11·1*)
Draught, feet (*metres*)	14 (*4·3*)
Guns	2—3 inch (*76 mm*) 50 cal AA
A/S weapons	2 triple torpedo tubes (Mk 32) in most ships; 1 trainable hedgehog (Mk 15) depth charges
Main engines	4 diesels (Fairbanks Morse), 6 000 bhp; 2 shafts
Speed, knots	21
Complement	169 (19 officers, 150 enlisted men)

Name	*No.*	*Builder*	*Launched*	*Commissioned*
CHAMBERS	DER 391	Brown SB Co, Houston	17 Aug 1943	22 Nov 1943
FALGOUT	DER 324	Consolidated Steel Corpn	24 July 1943	15 Nov 1943
HISSEM	DER 400	Brown SB Co, Houston	26 Dec 1943	13 Jan 1944
RAMSDEN	DER 382	Brown SB Co, Houston	24 May 1943	19 Oct 1943
SAVAGE	DER 386	Brown SB Co, Houston	15 July 1943	29 Oct 1943
VANCE	DER 387	Brown SB Co, Houston	16 July 1943	1 Nov 1943

These ships are the survivors of 36 converted to a radar picket configuration between 1951 and 1958 for the seaward extension of the Distant Early Warning (DEW) line to detect Soviet bomber attacks against the United States.

Prior to DER conversion several of these ships served with the US Coast Guard from 1951 to 1954; they retained Navy names and were designated WDE with hull numbers upped by one hundred to avoid confusion with the Coast Guard numbering series. The DERs 324, 382, 386, 387 are the survivors of those which served as CG "cutters". After the DEW line naval components were disestablished in 1965 most DERs were laid up in reserve; several were used in the Vietnam War (1964-1972) as part of Operation Market Time to halt the Communist infiltration of men and arms into South Vietnam by sea.

All surviving ships of this class are in reserve, the last being the *Calcaterra* (DER 390), decommissioned in 1973.

ARMAMENT. Upon conversion to radar picket ships these ships were fitted with six 20 mm guns; subsequently removed. Forward 3 inch mount is generally enclosed; after mount is open or enclosed, depending upon availability.

Ships engaged in Operation Market Time additionally mounted several ·50 calibre machine guns.

CONVERSION. Conversion to radar picket escorts included removal of conventional torpedo tubes and 40 mm guns; installation of mess compartment on main deck and other habitability improvements; fitting of two tripod masts to support radar antennas and TACAN navigation "bee-hive" antenna; installation of SPS-8 height-finding radar antenna atop after deckhouse; combat information centre (CIC) expanded and improved; and aluminium superstructure installed. Note trainable hedgehog fitted in "B" position in place of second 3 inch mount. TACAN and SPS-8 removed from active ships when seaward radar picket barrier was ended in 1965. The DERs in service during the latter 1960s had SPS-28 and SPS-10 or SPS-8 radar antennas on their forward mast; and electronic warfare "pods" on after mast.

ENGINEERING. Maximum operational speed for remaining ships is about 19 knots.

PHOTOGRAPHS. The *Savage* is shown during the Vietnam War with the large TACAN antenna removed from the second tripod mast and the SPS-8 radar antenna removed from the afterdeckhouse. The *Vance* is shown with the original DER electronics.

DISPOSALS AND TRANSFERS (since 1 Jan 1970)
Camp (DER 251) transferred to South Vietnam on 13 Feb 1971; **Forster** (DER 334) transferred to South Vietnam on 25 Sep 1971. **Blair** (DER 317), **Sturtevant** (DER 239), **Joyce** (DER 317), **Strickland** (DER 313) stricken on 1 Dec 1972; **Calcaterra** (DER 390) stricken on 2 July 1973; **Kretchmer** (DER 329) stricken on 30 Sep 1973; **Thomas J. Gary** (DER 326) transferred to Tunisia on 22 Oct 1973; **Finch** (DER 328), **Lansing** (DER 388) stricken on 1 Feb 1974; **Durant** (DER 389) stricken on 1 Apr 1974; **Otterstetter** (DER 244), **Kirkpatrick** (DER 318), **Price** (DER 332), **Roy O. Hale** (DER 336), **Mills** (DER 383), **Rhodes** (DER 384) stricken on 1 Aug 1974.

SAVAGE (DER 386) *1968, United States Navy*

VANCE (DER 387) *1964, United States Navy*

CONV. "BUTLER" CLASS

The two former "John C. Butler" class escort ships whose construction was suspended after World War II and subsequently completed as radar picket escorts have been stricken: **Wagner** (DER 539), **Vandivier** (DER 540) on 1 Nov 1974. See 1974-1975 and previous editions for characteristics.

"CLAUD JONES" CLASS

The four "Claud Jones" class escort ships have been transferred to Indonesia: **John R. Perry** (DE 1034) on 20 Feb 1973; **Charles Berry** (DE 1035) on 31 Jan 1974; **Claud Jones** (DE 1033), **McMorris** (DE 1036) on 16 Dec 1974. See 1974-1975 and previous editions for full characteristics.

"DEALEY" AND "COURTNEY" CLASSES

All 13 ships of these near-similar classes have been stricken or transferred to other navies. These were the US Navy's first escort ships of post-World War II design. See 1973-1974 and previous editions for characteristics.

WORLD WAR II PROGRAMMES

All surviving escort ships of World War II construction have been stricken or transferred to other navies. Ships of the various DE classes serve in the navies of Brazil, France, Greece, Italy, Japan, South Korea, Peru, Philippines, Taiwan China, Thailand and Uruguay.

McCLOY (FF 1038)—see previous page *1972, United States Navy*

ADVANCED NAVAL VESSELS

The US Navy is pursuing the development of the surface effect ship (SES) for the surface combatant role. The programme has been designated as Advanced Naval Vessels instead of the previously used DSX designation. In addressing this programme, early in 1975, Secretary of Defence Schlesinger stated: "A year ago it was expected that the high technical risks of this programme would have been resolved to the point where we could proceed with the building of a 2 000-ton prototype in FY 1976. The programme has been progressing well, but there remain some problem areas to be resolved. Therefore, for this reason and due to the budgetary constraints on research and development funds, an additional year of testing of the two 100-ton crafts is the prudent course to follow to reduce the risk in this important new programme before requesting funds for a 2 000-ton prototype". (The two 100-ton SES test platforms are described under Experimental, Research and Surveying Ships in this edition).

The SES concept differs from the air cushion vehicle (ACV) by having rigid "sidewalls" that penetrate into the water, providing stability for high-speed operations and in rough water. Flexible "skirts" forward and aft trap the air bubble under the hull.

2 000-ton ADVANCED NAVAL VESSEL

Weight, tons	2 000 gross
Length, feet	approx 240
Beam, feet	approx 100
Helicopters	2 large (SH-3 Sea King type)
Missile launchers	Harpoon surface-to-surface launchers Sea Sparrow surface-to-air launchers
Main/lift engines	gas turbines
Speed, knots	80-100

The above characteristics are those of a 2 000-ton national combat-capable surface effect ship. Contracts have been awarded to the Bell Aerospace Division of Textron and to Rohr Industries to undertake the development and design of such a ship.

2 000-ton Advanced Naval Vessel Design — *Bell Aerospace*

$61 000 000 was provided in Fiscal Year 1974 for this programme and $46 000 000 in FY 1975; $38 000 000 is proposed for FY 1976 and $87 000 000 in FY 1977.

The two artist's concepts on this page show the Bell design for a 2 000-ton SES configured for combat operations.

2 000-ton Advanced Naval Vessel Design

Bell Aerospace

FALGOUT (DER 324) — *United States Navy*

CHAMBERS (DER 391) — *United States Navy*

BATTLESHIPS

4 BATTLESHIPS (BB): "IOWA" CLASS

Displacement, tons	45 000 standard; 59 000 full load
Length, feet (*metres*)	860 (*262·1*) wl; 887·2 (*270·4*) oa except *New Jersey* 887·6 (*270·5*)
Beam, feet (*metres*)	108·2 (*33·0*)
Draught, feet (*metres*)	38 (*11·6*)
Guns	9—16 inch (*406 mm*) 50 cal (triple); 20—5 inch (*127 mm*) 38 cal dual purpose (twin) several 40 mm guns in all except *New Jersey*
Main engines	4 geared turbines (General Electric in BB 61 and BB 63; Westinghouse in BB 62 and BB 64; 212 000 shp; 4 shafts
Boilers	8 (Babcock & Wilcox)
Speed, knots	33 (all have reached 35 knots in service)
Complement	designed complement varied, averaging 169 officers and 2 689 enlisted men in wartime; *New Jersey* was manned by 70 officers and 1 556 enlisted men (requirements reduced with removal of all light anti-aircraft weapons floatplanes, and reduced operational requirements) in 1968-1969.

Name	*No.*	*Builder*	*Laid down*	*Launched*	*Commissioned*
IOWA	BB 61	New York Navy Yard	27 June 1940	27 Aug 1942	22 Feb 1943
NEW JERSEY	BB 62	Philadelphia Navy Yard	16 Sep 1940	7 Dec 1942	23 May 1943
MISSOURI	BB 63	New York Navy Yard	6 Jan 1941	29 Jan 1944	11 June 1944
WISCONSIN	BB 64	Philadelphia Navy Yard	25 Jan 1941	7 Dec 1943	16 Apr 1944

NEW JERSEY (BB 63) *1969, United States Navy*

These ships were the largest battleships ever built except for the Japanese *Yamato* and *Musashi* (64 170 tons standard, 863 feet overall, 9—18·1 inch guns). All four "Iowa" class ships were in action in the Pacific during World War II, primarily screening fast carriers and bombarding amphibious invasion objectives. Three were mothballed after the war with the *Missouri* being retained in service as a training ship. All four ships again were in service during the Korean War (1950-1953) as shore-bombardment ships, all mothballed 1954-1958.
The *New Jersey* began reactivation in mid-1967 at a cost of approximately $21 000 000; recommissioned on 6 Apr 1968. The *Iowa* and *Wisconsin* remained in reserve at the Philadelphia Naval Shipyard where the *New Jersey* had been berthed and reactivated; and the mothballed *Missouri* at the Puget Sound Naval Shipyard, Bremerton, Washington.
The *New Jersey* was again decommissioned on 17 Dec 1969 and mothballed at Bremerton with the *Missouri*.
Two additional ships of this class were laid down, but never completed: *Illinois* (BB 65), laid down 15 Jan 1945, and *Kentucky* (BB 66), laid down 6 Dec 1944. The *Illinois* was 22 per cent complete when cancelled on 11 Aug 1945. The *Kentucky* was 69·2 per cent complete when construction was suspended late in the war; floated from its building dock on 20 Jan 1950. Conversion to a missile ship (BBG) was proposed but no work was undertaken and she was stricken on 9 June 1958 and broken up for scrap.
Approximate construction cost was $114 485 000 for *Missouri*; other ships cost slightly less.

AIRCRAFT. As built, each ship carried three floatplanes for scouting and gunfire spotting and had two quarterdeck catapults. Catapults removed and helicopters carried during the Korean War.

ARMOUR. These battleships are the most heavily armoured US warships ever constructed, being designed to survive ship-to-ship combat with enemy ships armed with 16 inch guns. The main armour belt consists of Class A steel armour 12·1 inches thick tapering vertically to 1·62 inches; a lower armour belt aft of Turret No. 3 to protect propeller shafts is 13·5 inches; turret faces are 17 inches; turret tops are 7·25 inches; turret backs are 12 inches; barbetts have a maximum of 11·6 inches of armour; second deck armour is 6 inches; and the three-level conning tower sides are 17·3 inches with an armoured roof 7·25 inches (the conning tower levels are pilot house navigation bridge and flag-signal bridge).

DESIGN. These ships carried heavier armament than previous US battleships and had increased protection and larger engines accounting for additional displacement and increased speed. Design includes clipper bow and long foredeck, with graceful sheer (see photograph).
All fitted as fleet flagships with additional accommodations and bridge level for admiral and staff.

ELECTRONICS. During 1968-1969 the *New Jersey* was fitted with SPS-10 and SPS-6 search radars.

GUNNERY. The Mk VII 16 inch guns in these ships fire projectiles weighing up to 2 700 pounds (*1 225 kg*) (armour piercing) a maximum distance of 23 miles (*39 km*). As built, these ships had 80—40 mm and 49 to 60 —20 mm anti-aircraft guns (except *Iowa*, only 19 quad 40 mm mounts); all 20 mm guns removed and a reduced number of 40 mm weapons remain on the mothballed ships.
During 1968-1969 the *New Jersey* was fitted with two Mk 34 fire control directors in addition to the two Mk 56 and four Mk 37 previously installed. Mk 48 shore bombardment computer installed when reactivated.

NOMENCLATURE. US battleships are generally named for states; the exception was the *Kearsarge*, BB 5 launched in 1899 (later *Crane Ship No. 1*, AB 1). Beginning in 1969 the Navy has named frigates (now cruisers) for states.

OPERATIONAL. The *New Jersey* made one deployment to the western Pacific during her third commission (1968-1969).
During the deployment she was on the "gun line" off South Vietnam for a total of 120 days with 47 days being the longest sustained period at sea.
While on the "gun line" the *New Jersey* fired 5 688 rounds of ammunition from her 16 inch main battery guns and a total of 6 200 rounds during the commission, the additional firings being for tests and training. While off Vietnam she also fired some 15 000 rounds from her 5 inch secondary battery guns.
(In comparison, during World War II the *New Jersey* fired 771 main battery rounds and during two deployments in the Korean War and midshipmen training cruises she fired 6 671 main battery rounds).

PHOTOGRAPHS. The photograph above shows the battleship *New Jersey* in action off the coast of South Vietnam in April 1969, firing some of the last rounds to be fired by a battleship. Additional photographs of "Iowa" class ships appear in the 1973-1974 and previous editions.

NEW JERSEY (BB 62) *1968, United States Navy*

COMMAND AND COMMUNICATION SHIPS

This category consists of the command and communication ships operated in support of national and joint US commands. These are different functions than fleet and amphibious command ships that support essentially Navy or Navy-Marine Corp activities.

The only joint command flagship now in commission is the *La Salle* which serves as flagship for the Commander. US Middle East Force who represents US military interests "East of Suez" to the Straits of Malacca. The Commander US Middle East Force is generally a Rear Admiral.

In reserve are two ships configured to serve as afloat command posts for the President or other national authorities and two communication relay ships. The command ships *Northampton* and *Wright* were designated as National Emergency Command Posts Afloat (NECPA) and operated off the Atlantic coast of the United States, prepared to receive the President or other national authorities.

The major communication relay ships *Arlington* and *Annapolis* were operated by the Navy to provide mobile communication facilities for Navy and other service commanders where shore-based communication facilities were inadequate or did not exist. While the command ships *Northampton* and *Wright* are floating command headquarters and their communication facilities are for transmitting and receiving large volumes of voice and teletype communications (as well as electronic data), the communication relay ships *Annapolis* and *Arlington* are equipped to relay large volumes of teletype communications. Further, the two radio relay ships do not have the command centres, theatres, data display facilities, message centres, and staff accommodations that are the keys to the command ships' capabilities.

LA SALLE (AGF 3) — *1972, US Navy, PH1 Claude V. Sneed*

1 MISCELLANEOUS FLAGSHIP (AGF): CONVERTED AMPHIBIOUS TRANSPORT DOCK

Name	*No.*	*Laid down*	*Launched*	*Commissioned*
***LA SALLE**	AGF 3 (ex-LPD 3)	2 Apr 1962	3 Aug 1963	22 Feb 1964

Displacement, tons	8 040 light; 13 900 full load
Length, feet (*metres*)	500 (*152·0*) wl; 521·8 (*158·4*) oa
Beam, feet (*metres*)	84 (*25·6*)
Draught, feet (*metres*)	21 (*6·4*)
Guns	8—3 inch (*76 mm*) 50 cal AA (*twin*)
Main engines	Steam turbines; 24 000 shp; 2 shafts
Boilers	2
Speed, knots	20 sustained; 23 maximum
Complement	387 (18 officers, 369 enlisted men)
Flag accommodations	59 (12 officers, 47 enlisted men)

The *La Salle* is a former amphibious transport dock (LPD) of the "Raleigh" class. Authorised in Fiscal Year 1961 new construction programme; built by New York Naval Shipyards. The *La Salle* served as an amphbiious ship from completion until 1972.

The *La Salle* serves as flagship for the US Commander Middle East Force, operating in the Persian Gulf, Arabian Sea, and Indian Ocean; the ship is based at Bahrain. She replaced the *Valcour* (AGF 1) in 1972.

CONVERSION. Converted in 1972 with elaborate command and communications facilities being installed; accommodations provided for admiral and staff; additional air-conditioning fitted; painted white to help retard heat of Persian Gulf area. Reclassified as a flagship and designated AGF 3 on 1 July 1972 (the designation AGF 2 not used because of ship's previous "3" hull number).

DISPOSAL

Valcour (AGF 1, ex-AVP 55) stricken in 1972. All other AVP-type ships stricken from Navy List (see 1971-1972 and previous editions for description and disposals).

LA SALLE (AGF 3) — *1972, United States Navy*

NORTHAMPTON (CC 1) — *United States Navy*

Command and Communication Ships—*continued*

1 COMMAND SHIP (CC): CONVERTED HEAVY CRUISER

Name	*No.*	*Builder*	*Laid down*	*Launched*	*Commissioned*
NORTHAMPTON	CC 1 (ex-CLC 1, ex-CA 125)	Bethlehem Steel Co (Quincy)	31 Aug 1944	27 Jan 1951	7 Mar 1953

Displacement, tons	14 700 standard; 17 200 full load
Length, feet (*metres*)	664 (*202·4*) wl; 676 (*206·0*) oa
Beam, feet (*metres*)	71 (*21·6*)
Draught, feet (*metres*)	29 (*8·8*)
Guns	1—5 in (*127 mm*) 54 cal dual-purpose (see *Gunnery* notes)
Helicopters	2 normally carried
Armour	Side 6 in (*152 mm*); Decks 3 in + 2 in (*76 + 51 mm*)
Main engines	4 geared turbines (General Electric); 120 000 shp; 4 shafts
Boilers	4 (Babcock & Wilcox)
Speed, knots	33
Complement	1 191 (68 officers, 1 123 enlisted men)
Flag accommodations	approx 450

The *Northampton* was begun as a heavy cruiser of the "Oregon City" class, numbered CA 125. She was cancelled on 11 Aug 1945 when 56·2 per cent complete. She was re-ordered as a command ship on 1 July 1948 and designated CLC 1 (Task Force Command Ship and later Tactical Command Ship). As CLC 1 she was configured for use primarily by fast carrier force commanders and fitted with an elaborate combat information centre (CIC), electronic equipment, and flag accommodations. She was largely employed as flagship for Commander Second Fleet in the Atlantic prior to her being made available for use by national authorities. Her designation was changed to CC (Command Ship) on 15 April 1961 and she was relieved as Second Fleet flagship on October 1961.

Decommissioned on 8 April 1970 and placed in reserve.

DESIGN. The *Northampton* is one deck higher than other US heavy cruisers to provide additional office and equipment space. Her foremast is the tallest unsupported mast afloat (125 feet). All living and working spaces are air-conditioned. Helicopter landing area aft, but no hangar.

ELECTRONICS. Advanced communications, electronic data processing equipment, and data displays are installed; tropospheric scatter and satellite relay communications facilities. As CLC 1 the *Northampton* carried what was believed the largest radar antenna afloat (see 1968-69 and earlier editions); designated SPS-2; removed in 1963. SPS-37 and SPS-8A search radar antennas on after tower.

GUNNERY. As built the *Northampton* mounted 4—5 inch and 8—3 inch weapons. The 5 inch guns were Mk 16 54 calibre weapons capable of firing up to 45 rounds per minute. (Similar weapons are installed in US destroyer-type ships built since World War II.) The original 3 inch 50 calibre guns in open twin mounts were replaced by twin 3 inch/70 calibre rapid-fire guns in closed mounts. The latter were removed in 1962 because of high maintenance requirements; removal of the guns and their ammunition hoists, *et cetera*, provided additional space for berthing, offices, and electronic equipment. When decommissioned she was armed with only one 5 inch gun in the "X" position.

OPERATIONAL. The *Northampton* served as flagship of the US Sixth Fleet in the Mediterranean in 1954-1955, and as flagship of the US Second Fleet in the Atlantic from 1955 to 1961.

PHOTOGRAPHS. Penultimate configuration shown on the previous page; forward 5 inch gun and gun director above bridge subsequently removed. See 1972-1973 edition for later photograph.

1 COMMAND SHIP (CC) / 1 MAJOR COMMUNICATIONS RELAY SHIP (AGMR): CONVERTED AIRCRAFT CARRIERS

Name	*No.*	*Builder*	*Laid down*	*Launched*	*CVL Comm*	*CC-AGMR Comm*
WRIGHT	CC 2 (ex-AVT 7, ex-CVL 49)	New York SB Corp	21 Aug 1944	1 Sep 1945	9 Feb 1947	11 May 1963
ARLINGTON (ex-*Saipan*)	AGMR 2 (ex-CC 3, ex-AVT 6, ex-CVL 48)	New York SB Corp	10 July 1944	8 July 1944	14 July 1945	27 Aug 1966

Displacement, tons	14 500 standard; 19 600 full load
Length, feet (*metres*)	664 (*202·4*) wl; 683·6 (*208·4*) oa
Beam, feet (*metres*)	76·8 (*23·6*)
Draught, feet (*metres*)	28 (*8·5*)
Flight deck width, feet (*metres*)	109 (*33·2*)
Guns	*Wright* 8—40 mm anti-aircraft (twin); *Arlington* 8—3 inch (*76 mm*) 50 calibre AA (twin)
Helicopters	5 or 6 carried by *Wright*
Main engines	4 geared turbines (General Electric); 120 000 shp; 4 shafts
Boilers	4 (Babcock & Wilcox)
Speed, knots	33
Complement	746 plus approx 1 000 on command or communications staff

These ships were built as the light aircraft carriers *Saipan* (CVL 48) and *Wright* (CVL 49). They served as experimental and training carriers for a decade before being mothballed in 1967. Both were reclassified as Auxiliary Aircraft Transports on 15 May 1959, being designated AVT 6 (*Saipan*) and AVT 7 (*Wright*). The *Wright* was converted to a command ship at the Puget Sound Naval Shipyard, 1962-1963; the *Saipan* was to have been similarly converted, but the requirement for an additional ship of this category was cancelled. The *Saipan* subsequently was converted to a major communications relay ship at the Alabama Drydock and Shipbuilding Company in 1953-1965, and renamed *Arlington*. See Conversion and Nomenclature notes. The *Arlington* was decommissioned on 14 Jan 1970 and placed in reserve; the *Wright* was similarly decommissioned on 22 May 1970 and placed in reserve.

CONVERSION. The *Wright* was converted to a command ship under the Fiscal Year 1962 authorisation at a cost of $25 000 000. Like the *Northampton*, she is fitted with elaborate communications, data processing, and display facilities for use by national authorities. The command spaces include presentation theatres similar to those at command posts ashore. The *Wright* has the most powerful transmitting antennas ever installed on a ship. They are mounted on plastic-glass masts to reduce interference with electronic transmissions. The tallest mast is 83 feet high and is designed to withstand 100-mph winds. She was reclassified from AVT 7 to CC 2 on 1 Sep 1962.

The *Saipan* was converted to a major communications relay ship at a cost of $26 886 424. She actually began conversion to a command ship (CC 3) and work was halted in February 1964. Work was resumed for her conversion to a communications ship later that year.

WRIGHT (CC 2) — *1968, United States Navy*

She is fitted with elaborate communications relay equipment for the support of major commands afloat or ashore. The *Saipan* was reclassified from AVT 6 to CC 3 on 1 Jan 1964, and to AGMR 2 on 3 Sep 1964; she was renamed *Arlington* in April 1965.

The flat unencumbered deck of an aircraft carrier-type ship facilitates antenna placement for optimum electromagnetic wave propagation. The new "Blue Ridge" class of amphibious command ships has a similar appearance.

NOMENCLATURE. The Navy's two communications ships are named for the naval radio stations at Arlington, Virginia, and Annapolis, Maryland.

PHOTOGRAPHS. Both ships have three starboard-side funnels (built as CVLs with four funnels); the *Wright* could be distinguished by the large antenna pylon on the starboard side of the flight deck abaft the island structure.

Command and Communication Ships—*continued*

ARLINGTON (AGMR 2)—see previous page *1967, United States Navy*

1 MAJOR COMMUNICATIONS RELAY SHIP (AGMR): CONVERTED ESCORT CARRIER

Name	*No.*	*Builder*	*Laid down*	*Launched*	*CVE Comm.*	*AGMR Comm.*
ANNAPOLIS	AGMR 1 (ex-AKV 39, ex-CVE 107)	Todd Shipyards (Tacoma)	29 Nov 1943	20 July 1944	5 Feb 1945	7 Mar 1964

Displacement, tons	11 473 standard; 22 500 full load
Length, feet (*metres*)	525 (*160·0*) wl; 563 (*171·6*) oa
Beam, feet (*metres*)	75 (*22·9*)
Draught, feet (*metres*)	30·6 (*9·3*)
Flight deck width, feet (*metres*)	106 (*32·5*)
Guns	8—3 inch (*76 mm*) 50 calibre AA (twin)
Main engines	2 turbines (Allis Chalmers); 16 000 shp; 2 shafts
Boilers	4 (Combustion Engineering)
Speed, knots	18
Complement	720 (54 officers, 666 enlisted men)

The *Annapolis* was built as the escort aircraft carrier *Gilbert Islands* (CVE 107). She was decommissioned on 21 May 1946 and placed in reserve; again active as a CVE from Sep 1951 to Jan 1955 when she was again decommissioned. While in reserve, on 7 May 1959 she was reclassified as a Cargo Ship and Aircraft Ferry (AKV 39). Converted into a communications ship by the New York Naval Shipyard, 1962-1964.
Decommissioned on 20 Dec 1969 and placed in reserve.

CONVERSION. During conversion the ship was fitted with elaborate communications relay equipment including approximately 30 transmitters providing frequency band coverage from low frequency to ultra-high frequency. The power outputs of the transmitters vary from 10 to 10 000 watts. Numerous radio receivers also were installed as were five large antenna towers. The ship was renamed *Annapolis* and reclassified AGMR 1 on 1 June 1963.
The former escort carrier, *Vella Gulf* (AKV 11, ex-CVHE 111, ex-CVE 111) was to have been converted to the AGMR 2; her conversion never began because of the availability of the larger carrier *Saipan* for use in this role.

DESIGN. The *Gilbert Islands* was one of 19 "Commencement Bay" class escort carriers built during the latter part of World War II. This ship is the last escort or "jeep" aircraft carrier on the Navy List.

ANNAPOLIS (AGMR 1) *1964, United States Navy*

PHOTOGRAPHS. Note enclosed "hurricane bow" installed during conversion to AGMR to improve rough-sea operation. She has a small helicopter landing area on the port side of the former flight deck.

ANNAPOLIS (AGMR 1) ***1966, United States Navy***

AMPHIBIOUS WARFARE SHIPS

The US Navy amphibious force in mid-1975 consisted of 64 ships with a lift capability of slightly more than one Marine division/aircraft wing team and supporting elements (approx 30 000 troops). The ships are divided about equally between the Atlantic and Pacific Fleets, and are organised into squadrons which can carry one reinforced battalion landing team, generally referred to as a Marine Amphibious Unit (MAU). Three of these ships are assigned to the Naval Reserve Force and are manned patrially by reservists.

One MAU is deployed afloat continuously in the Mediterranean and two MAUs in the Western Pacific. Another MAU is deployed intermittently in the Caribbean. At this time only two of the deployed MAUs (the one in the Mediterranean and one of those in the Western Pacific) have helicopters assigned because of the availability of only seven helicopter ships (LPH).

When the five large amphibious assault ships (LHA) are delivered there will be sufficient flight-deck ships to provide four forward-deployed MAUs with helicopters.

With the five LHAs the Navy will operate 66 active amphibious ships plus three NRF ships with a lift capability of 1-1/3 Marine division/aircraft wing teams. According to Secretary of Defence Schlesinger, after shifting some ships from one ocean to another, a division/wing-size amphibious landing could be undertaken in a major combat theatre, such as the northern or southern flank of NATO, and still maintain a limited assault capability elsewhere.

VSTOL OPERATIONS. The *Guadalcanal* (LPH 9) operated as an interim sea control ship from 1972 to 1974, during which period she operated AV-8A Harrier VSTOL (Vertical/Short Take-Off and Landing) aircraft in the light attack and intercept role, and SH-3 Sea King helicopters in the anti-submarine role. See 1974-1975 edition for additional data.

The *Guadalcanal* has continued to carry a small number of Marine-flown Harriers upon return to the LPH role. Increasing VSTOL aircraft operations from the LPH/LHA ships are expected.

MINESWEEPING OPERATIONS. Several LPHs were used to operate RH-53D Sea Stallion helicopters in the mine countermeasures role during the 1973 sweeping of North Vietnamese ports and the 1974 sweeping of the Suez Canal.

FIRE SUPPORT SHIPS. Gunfire support for US amphibious operations is now limited to the 5 inch guns of cruisers, destroyers, and frigates, and the 6·16 inch guns in the two cruiser-flagships of the converted "Cleveland" class. However, the employment of the latter ships for the commanders of numbered fleets makes their use close inshore to support amphibious landings unlikely. The Navy is conducting tests of a light-weight 8 inch gun installed in the destroyer *Hull* (DD 945). Several battleships and cruisers with heavy guns are retained in the reserve (mothball) fleet.

TRANSPORT SUBMARINES. The transport submarine *Grayback* (SS 574, ex-LPSS 574) is in active commission and the older transport submarine *Sealion* (LPSS 315) is in reserve. Both submarines are listed in the Submarine section of this edition.

2 AMPHIBIOUS COMMAND SHIPS (LCC): "BLUE RIDGE" CLASS

Displacement, tons	19 290 full load
Length, feet (*metres*)	620 (*188·5*) oa
Beam, feet (*metres*)	82 (*25·3*)
Main deck width, feet (*metres*)	108 (*33*)
Draught, feet (*metres*)	27 (*8·2*)
Missile launchers	2 Basic Point Defense Missile System (BPDMS) launchers for Sea Sparrow missile (Mk 25)
Guns	4—3 inch (*76 mm*) 50 cal AA (twin)
Helicopters	Utility helicopter can be carried
Main engines	1 geared turbine (General Electric); 22 000 shp; 1 shaft
Boilers	2 (Foster Wheeler)
Speed, knots	20
Complement	720 (40 officers, 680 enlisted men)
Flag accommodations	700 (200 officers, 500 enlisted men)

Name	*No*	*Builder*	*Laid down*	*Launched*	*Commissioned*
* **BLUE RIDGE**	LCC 19	Philadelphia Naval Shipyard	27 Feb 1967	4 Jan 1969	14 Nov 1970
* **MOUNT WHITNEY**	LCC 20	Newport News SB & DD Co	8 Jan 1969	8 Jan 1970	16 Jan 1971

BLUE RIDGE (LCC 19) — *1974, United States Navy*

These are large amphibious force command ships of post-World War II design. They can provide integrated command and control facilities for sea, air and land commanders in amphibious operations. The *Blue Ridge* was authorised in the Fiscal Year 1965 new construction programme, the *Mount Whitney* in FY 1966. An AGC 21 was planned for the FY 1970 programme but cancelled late in 1968. It was proposed that the last ship combine fleet as well as amphibious force command-control facilities. The phasing out of the converted "Cleveland" class (CG) fleet flagships has fostered discussion of the potential use of these ships in that role. Their capabilities are greater than would be required by a fleet commander. Both ships are active, *Blue Ridge* in the Pacific and *Mount Whitney* in the Atlantic.

CLASSIFICATION. Originally designated Amphibious Force Flagships (AGC); redesignated Amphibious Command Ships (LCC) on 1 Jan 1969.

DESIGN. General hull design and machinery arrangement are similar to the "Iwo Jima" class assault ships.

ELECTRONICS. Fitted with SPS-48 three-dimensional search radar, SPS-40 and SPS-10 search radars on "island" structure. After "tower" does not have large antenna sphere originally intended for these ships. (See model photo in 1970-1971 edition.) Tactical Aircraft Navigation (TACAN) pod tops mast.

These ships have three computer systems to support their Naval Tactical Data System (NTDS), Amphibious Command Information System (ACIS), and Naval Intelligence Processing System (NIPS).

GUNNERY. At one stage of design two additional twin 3 inch mounts were provided on forecastle; subsequently deleted from final designs. Antennas and their supports severely restrict firing arcs of guns.

MISSILES. Two BPDMS launchers installed on each ship during 1974 (on antenna deck, aft of superstructure).

NOMENCLATURE. Amphibious command ships generally have mountain names. The *Mount Whitney* is named for a 14 494-foot peak in California, the highest point in the conterminous 48 states; the *Mount McKinley* is named for a 20 320-foot peak in Alaska, the highest point in the United States.

PERSONNEL. The ships' complements includes one Marine officer and 12 enlisted men to maintain communications equipment.

PHOTOGRAPHS. The antennas adjacent to the helicopter landing area swing out during flight operations.

BLUE RIDGE (LCC 19) — *1974, United States Navy*

Amphibious Warfare Ships—*continued*

4 AMPHIBIOUS COMMAND SHIPS (LCC): "MOUNT McKINLEY" CLASS

Displacement, tons	7 510 light; 12 560 full load
Length, feet (*metres*)	435 (*132·2*)wl; 594·3 (*150·5*) oa
Beam, feet (*metres*)	63 (*19·2*)
Draught, feet (*metres*)	28·2 (*8·5*)
Guns	1—5 inch (*127 mm*) 38 cal DP 4—40 mm AA (twin)
Helicopters	Utility helicopter carried
Main engines	1 turbine (General Electric) 6 000 shp; 1 shaft
Boilers	2 (Babcock & Wilcox in AGC); Combustion Engineering in others
Speed, knots	16·4
Complement (ship)	517 (36 officers, 486 enlisted men)

Name	*No.*	*Builder*	*Launched*	*Commissioned*
MOUNT McKINLEY	LCC 7	North Carolina SB Co	27 Sep 1943	1 May 1944
ESTES	LCC 12	North Carolina SB Co	1 Nov 1943	9 Oct 1944
POCONO	LCC 16	North Carolina SB Co	25 Jan 1945	29 Dec 1945
TACONIC	LCC 17	North Carolina SB Co	10 Feb 1945	17 Jan 1946

Acquired by the Navy in 1943-1944 while under construction to Maritime Commission C2-S-AJ1 design. After 5 inch gun and two twin 40 mm mounts replaced by helicopter platform. The *Pocono* and *Taconic* have a single mast aft in lieu of after king post in earlier ships. All survivors transferred to Maritime Administration reserve (remain on Navy List). They were unable to provide the communication facilities or personnel accommodations required for modern amphibious operations.

CLASSIFICATION. Originally referred to as Auxiliary Combined Operations and Communications Headquarters Ships, but designated Amphibious Force Flagships (AGC); five surviving ships redesignated Amphibious Command Ships (LCC) on 1 Jan 1969.

ELECTRONICS. The *Mount McKinley* and *Estes* had an SPS-37 search radar antenna on the forward king post SPS-30 and SPS-10 antennas on the lattice mast atop the superstructure, and a TACAN antenna installed on the after king post; the *Pocono* and *Taconic* had a TACAN antenna on the forward king post, SPS-30 and SPS-10 antennas on the lattice mast atop the superstructure, and an SPS-37 antenna on the after pole mast.

DISPOSALS
Fourteen World War II amphibious force flagships have been stricken from the Navy List: **Appalachian** (AGC 1) on 1 Mar 1959; **Blue Ridge** (AGC 2), **Rocky Mount** (AGC 3) on 1 Jan 1960; **Ancon** (AGC 4) on 25 Feb 1946; **Catoctin** (AGC 5) on 1 Mar 1959; **Mount Olympus** (AGC 8) in 1961; **Wasatch** (AGC 9) on 1 Jan 1960; **Auburn** (AGC 10), **Panamint** (AGC 13) in late 1960; **Teton** (AGC 14), **Adirondack** (AGC 15) in 1961; **Biscayne** (AGC 18, ex-AVP 11) transferred to US Coast Guard on 19 July 1946. **Eldorado** (AGC/LCC 11) stricken on 16 Nov 1972.

ESTES (LCC 12) *1969, United States Navy*

The **Duane** (AGC 6) was retained by the Coast Guard. All except the **Ancon, Duane,** and **Biscayne** were converted C2 merchants hull. Several other Coast Guard cutters served as amphibious command ships with WAGC designations (see "Campbell" class).

The yacht **Williamsburg** (ex-*Aras*, ex-PG 56) was designated AGC 369 in 1945, served as presidential yacht until stricken in 1962 (converted to oceanographic research ship, renamed *Anton Bruun*).

BLUE Ridge (LCC 19) with UH-1 "Huey" helicopter on deck—see previous page *United States Navy*

MOUNT WHITNEY (LCC 20)—see previous page *1970, United States Navy*

Amphibious Warfare Ships—*continued*

5 AMPHIBIOUS ASSAULT SHIPS (LHA): "TARAWA" CLASS

Displacement, tons	39 300 full load
Length, feet (*metres*)	778 (*237·8*) wl; 820 (*250*) oa
Beam, feet (*metres*)	106 (*32·3*)
Draught, feet (*metres*)	27·5 (*8·5*)
Aircraft	approx 30 troop helicopters; possibly Harrier AV-8 V/STOL aircraft in place of some helicopters
Guns	3—5 inch (*127 mm*) 54 cal DP (Mk 45) (single) 6—20 mm AA (Mk 68) (single)
Missile launchers	2 Basic Point Defence Missile Systems (BPDMS) launchers firing Sea Sparrow missiles
Main engines	Geared turbines; 70 000 shp; 2 shafts
Boilers	2
Speed, knots	approx 22 sustained; approx 34 max
Complement	approx 800
Troops	1 825 (163 officers, 1 662 enlisted men)

Name	*No.*	*Erection of First Module*	*Launched*	*Commission*
TARAWA	LHA 1	15 Nov 1971	1 Dec 1973	mid 1975
SAIPAN	LHA 2	21 July 1972	18 July 1974	Sep 1975
BELLEAU WOOD	LHA 3	2 Mar 1973	June 1975	early 1976
NASSAU	LHA 4	13 Aug 1973	June 1976	Autumn 1976
DA NANG	LHA 5	Feb 1975	Dec 1976	late 1976

This is a new class of large amphibious warfare ships combining the characteristics of several previous designs including a full-length flight deck, a landing craft docking well, a large garage for trucks and armoured vehicles, and troop berthing for a reinforced battalion. The LHA 1 was authorised in the Fiscal Year 1969 new construction programme, the LHA 2 and LHA 3 in FY 1970 and LHA 4 and LHA 5 in FY 1971. The Navy announced on Jan 20, 1971 that four additional ships of this type previously planned would not be constructed. All ships of this class are under construction by Litton Industries at a new ship production facility known as "Ingalls West". The new yard, located at Pascagoula, Mississippi, was developed specifically for multi-ship construction of the same design.
Late in 1971 the Navy announced that the LHA design work was behind schedule. Subsequently the Secretary of Defence announced that the ships will be delivered 24-44 months beyond original completion date.

AIRCRAFT. The flight deck can operate 9 CH-53 Sea Stallion or 12 CH-46 Sea Knight helicopters; the hangar deck can accommodate 19 CH-53 Sea Stallion or 30 CH-46 Sea Knight helicopters. A mix of these and other helicopters normally will be embarked.

CONTRACT. These were the first ships to be procured by the US Navy with the acquisition processes known as Concept Formulation, Contract Definition, and Total Package Procurement. The proposals of Litton Systems Inc and two other shipbuilding firms were submitted in response to specific performance criteria related to the ships' mission. The firms submitted detailed designs and cost estimates for series production of not less than five ships of this type. This procurement process subsequently has been abandoned.

DESIGN. The LHA is intended to combine the features of an amphibious assault ship (LPH), amphibious cargo ship (LKA), and amphibious transport dock (LPD) into a single hull. Beneath the flight deck is a half-length hangar deck, the two being connected by an elevator amidships on the port side and a stern lift; beneath the after elevator is a floodable docking well measuring 268 feet in length and 78 feet in width which is capable of accommodating four LCU 1610 type landing craft.
Storage for 10 000 gallons (US) of vehicle petrol and 400 000 gallons (US) of JP-5 helicopter petrol.

ELECTRONICS. Radars planned for these ships are the SPS-52 three-dimensional search, and SPS-10 and SPS-40; advanced communications and helicopter navigation equipment provided. Each ship also will have an Integrated Tactical Amphibious Warfare Data System (ITAWDS) to provide computerised support in control of helicopters and aircraft, shipboard weapons and sensors, navigation, landing craft control, and electronic warfare. SPN-35 aircraft navigation radar fitted on after end of "island" structure.
Chaff Rocket (CHAFFROC) launchers fitted on superstructure.

ENGINEERING. A 900 hp bow thruster is provided for holding position while unloading landing craft.

FISCAL. In early 1974 the estimated total cost ot the government of the five LHAs was $1·145 *billion* or an average of $229 000 000 per ship. A cancellation fee of $109 700 000 was due to the shipyard for cancellation of LHA 6-9. See 1973-1974 and previous editions for additional funding information.

GUNNERY. These ships will be armed with three 5 inch/54 calibre Mk 45 light-weight, rapid-fire guns. Six 20 mm guns will be fitted for close-in defence (not Close-in Weapon System).

MEDICAL. These ships are to be fitted with extensive medical facilities including operating rooms, X-ray room, hospital ward, isolation ward, laboratories, pharmacy, dental operating room and medical store rooms.

AMPHIBIOUS ASSAULT SHIP — *Artist's concept by G. Meyer*

TARAWA (LHA 1) — *1973, Litton Industries*

Amphibious Warfare Ships—*continued*

"TARAWA" CLASS—*continued*

NOMENCLATURE. These ships are named for actions involving US Marines with four of the names having previously been carried by aircraft carriers. *Tarawa* (previously honoured by CV 40) and *Saipan* (CVL 48) were World War II landings in the Pacific; *Da Nang* was a battle of the Vietnam War; *Belleau Wood* (CVL 24) was a bitter World War I action in France; and *Nassau* (CVE 16) was a Marine landing during the American Revolution. The *Da Nang* was expected to be renamed after the capture of that city by Communist Forces in the spring of 1975.

PHOTOGRAPHS. The photographs of the *Tarawa* show the ship being floated in a floating "launch platform" at the time of christening ceremonies. Note the openings for the ship's elevators and docking well stern gate. The photograph at right, with the ship riding high in the water, reveals the ducted thruster near the bow just below the waterline.

TARAWA (LHA 1) — *1973, United States Navy*

Drawing by A, D, Baker

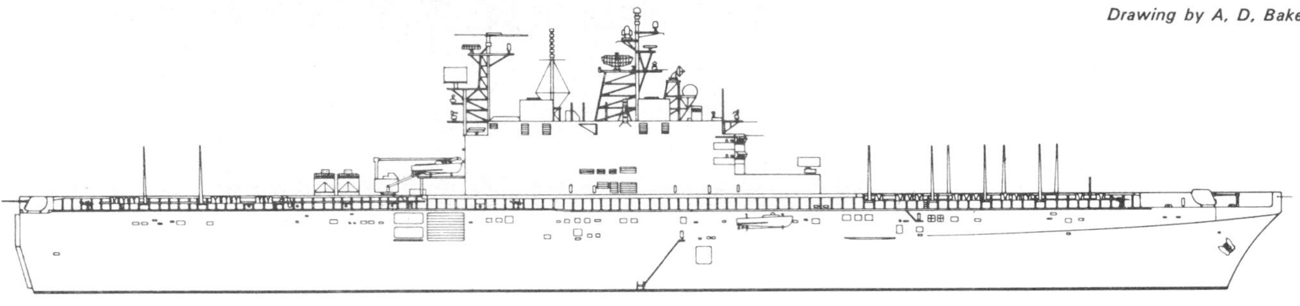

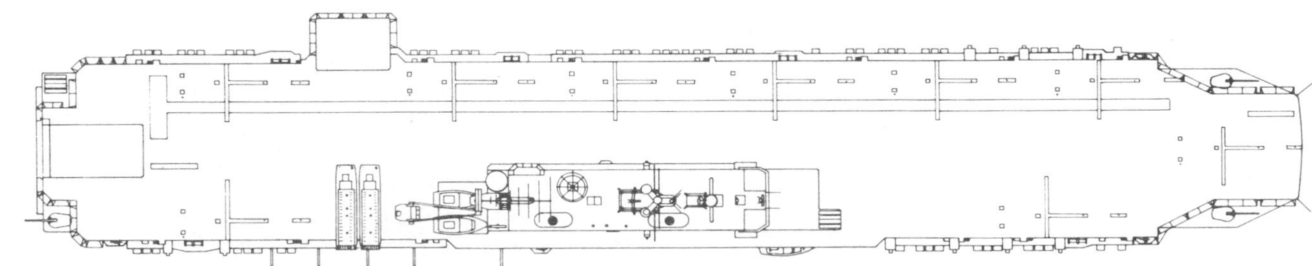

SAIPAN (LHA 2) — *1974, Litton Industries*

Amphibious Warfare Ships—*continued*

7 AMPHIBIOUS ASSAULT SHIPS (LPH): "IWO JIMA" CLASS

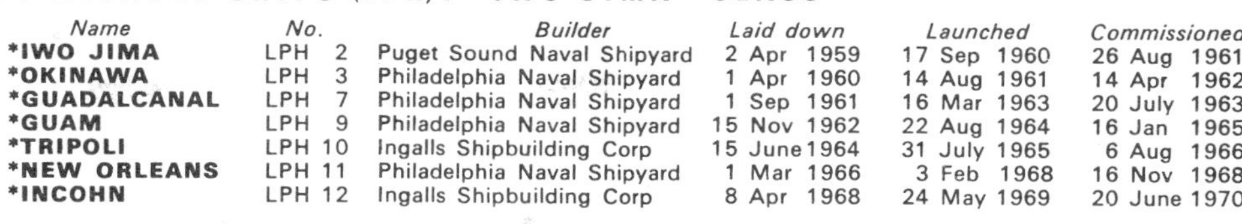

Name	*No.*	*Builder*	*Laid down*	*Launched*	*Commissioned*
***IWO JIMA**	LPH 2	Puget Sound Naval Shipyard	2 Apr 1959	17 Sep 1960	26 Aug 1961
***OKINAWA**	LPH 3	Philadelphia Naval Shipyard	1 Apr 1960	14 Aug 1961	14 Apr 1962
***GUADALCANAL**	LPH 7	Philadelphia Naval Shipyard	1 Sep 1961	16 Mar 1963	20 July 1963
***GUAM**	LPH 9	Philadelphia Naval Shipyard	15 Nov 1962	22 Aug 1964	16 Jan 1965
***TRIPOLI**	LPH 10	Ingalls Shipbuilding Corp	15 June 1964	31 July 1965	6 Aug 1966
***NEW ORLEANS**	LPH 11	Philadelphia Naval Shipyard	1 Mar 1966	3 Feb 1968	16 Nov 1968
***INCOHN**	LPH 12	Ingalls Shipbuilding Corp	8 Apr 1968	24 May 1969	20 June 1970

Displacement, tons 17 000 light; 18 300 full load
Length, feet (*metres*) 592 (*180·0*) oa
Beam, feet (*metres*) 84 (*25·6*)
Draught, feet (*metres*) 26 (*7·9*)
Flight deck width, feet (*metres*) 104 (*31·9*) *maximum*
Aircraft 20-24 medium (CH-46) helicopters
4 heavy (CH-53) helicopters
4 observation (HU-1) helicopters
6 Harrier AV-8 V/STOL aircraft in *Guam*
Guns 4—3 inch (*76 mm*) 50 cal AA (twin)
Missile launchers 2 Basic Point Defence Missile System (BPDMS) launchers firing Sea Sparrow missiles
Main engines 1 geared turbine; 23 000 shp; 1 shaft
Boilers 2—655 psi (Combustion Engineering or Babcock & Wilcox)
Speed, knots 20 (sustained)
Complement 528 (48 officers, 480 enlisted men)
Troops 2 090 (190 officers, 1 900 enlisted men)

The *Iwo Jima* was the world's first ship designed and constructed specifically to operate helicopters. These ships correspond to Commando Ships in the Royal Navy except that the US ships do not carry landing craft save for the *Inchon* which has davits aft for two LCVPs. Each LPH can carry a Marine battalion landing team, its guns, vehicles, and equipment, plus a reinforced squadron of transport helicopters and various support personnel. The *Iwo Jima* was authorised in the Fiscal Year 1958 new construction programme, the *Okinawa* in FY 1959, *Guadalcanal* in FY 1960, *Guam* in FY 1962, *Tripoli* in FY 1963, *New Orleans* in FY 1965, and *Inchon* in FY 1966. Estimated cost of the *Iwo Jima* is $40 000 000
The *Guam* was modified late in 1971 and began operations in January 1972 as an interim sea control ship. She operated Harrier AV-8 V/STOL aircraft and SH-3 Sea King A/S helicopters in convoy escort exercises; she reverted to the amphibious role in 1974. Several of these ships operated RH-53 minesweeping helicopters to clear North Vietnamese ports in 1973 and the Suez Canal in 1974.

AIRCRAFT. The flight decks of these ships provides for simultaneous take off or landing of seven CH-46 Sea Knight or four CH-53 Sea Stallion helicopters during normal operations. The hangar decks can accommodate 19 CH-46 Sea Knight or 11 CH-53 Sea Stallion helicopters, or various combinations of helicopters.
After reverting to the amphibious role the *Guam* continued to operate Harrier AV-8 V/STOL aircraft.

DESIGN. These ships resemble World War II-era escort carriers in size but have massive bridge structures, hull continued up to flight deck providing enclosed bows, and rounded flight decks. Each ship has two deck-edge lifts, one to port opposite the bridge and one to starboard aft of island. Full hangars are provided; no arresting wires or catapults. Two small elevators carry cargo from holds to flight deck. Storage provided for 6 500 gallons (US) of vehicle petrol and 405 000 gallons (US) of JP-5 helicopter petrol.

ELECTRONICS. These ships have SPS-40 and SPS-10 search radars, and SPN-10 navigation radar; TACAN pod tops mast; advanced electronic warfare equipment fitted.

GUNNERY. As built each ship had eight 3 inch guns in twin mounts, two forward of the island structure and two at stern "notched" into flight deck. Gun battery reduced by half with substitution of BPDMS launchers (see *Missile* notes).

MEDICAL. These ships are fitted with extensive medical facilities including operating room, X-ray room, hospital ward, isolation ward, laboratory, pharmacy, dental operating room, and medical store rooms.

MISSILES. All of these ships have been rearmed with two BPDMS launchers for the Sea Sparrow missile, one launcher forward of island structure and one on the port quarter. The *Okinawa* had one BPDMS launcher fitted in 1970 and the second in 1973; *Tripoli* and *Inchon* rearmed in 1972, *Iwo Jima* and *New Orleans* in 1973, *Guam* and *Guadalcanal* in 1974.

NOMENCLATURE. Amphibious assault ships are named for US Marine combat actions. *Iwo Jima, Okinawa, Guadalcanal,* and *Guam* were World War II campaigns. (The name *Iwo Jima* previously was assigned to the unfinished aircraft carrier CV 46). Marines fought Barbary pirates at Tripoli in 1801 and helped stop the British at New Orleans in 1814. There was also a naval battle at New Orleans during the American Civil War. *Inchon* was the near-perfect 1950 amphibious assault in Korea.

INCHON (LPH 12) *1973, United States Navy*

NEW ORLEANS (LPH 11) *1973, United States Navy, PH2 T. Ahlgrim*

TRIPOLI (LPH 10) *1973, United States Navy*

Amphibious Warfare Ships—*continued*

"IWO JIMA" CLASS—*continued*

PHOTOGRAPHS. The *Inchon* is shown after operation "End Sweep", the minesweeping of North Vietnamese ports. On her flight deck are a dozen large RH-53 minesweeping helicopters and a smaller CH-46 Sea Knight. The stern view of the *Tripoli*, also taken on her return to Subic Bay in the Philippines from "End Sweep", shows her with CH-46 Sea Knight helicopters and three small, UH-1 "Huey "helicopters (alongside island structure). Note the *Tripoli's* Sea Sparrow BPDMS launchers forward of the island and on the port quarter. The *Guam* is shown launching Harrier AV-8A aircraft operated by the US Marine Corps during her evaluation of the sea control ship concept. In the 1974-1975 edition.

DISPOSALS
The **Thetis Bay** (LPH 6, ex-CVHA 1, ex-CVE 90) was stricken on 1 Mar 1964. The **Block Island** (originally CVE 106) was reclassified LPH 1 on 22 Dec 1957 but conversion was cancelled and she reverted to CVE status on 17 Jan 1959; subsequently stricken (as AKV 38) and scrapped.

"ESSEX" CLASS

All three "Essex" class fast carriers employed as amphibious assault ships have been discarded: **Boxer** (LPH 4, ex-CVS 21) stricken on 1 Dec 1969, **Princeton** (LPH 5, ex-CVS 37) stricken on 30 Jan 1970, and **Valley Forge** (LPH 8, ex-CVS 45) stricken on 15 Jan 1970.

GUADALCANAL (LPH 7) *1973, Giorgio Arra*

5 AMPHIBIOUS CARGO SHIPS (LKA): "CHARLESTON" CLASS

Name	*No*	*Laid down*	*Launched*	*Commissioned*
***CHARLESTON**	LKA 113	5 Dec 1966	2 Dec 1967	14 Dec 1968
***DURHAM**	LKA 114	10 July 1967	29 Mar 1968	24 May 1969
***MOBILE**	LKA 115	15 Jan 1968	19 Oct 1968	29 Sep 1969
***ST. LOUIS**	LKA 116	3 Apr 1968	4 Jan 1969	22 Nov 1969
***EL PASO**	LKA 117	22 Oct 1968	17 May 1969	17 Jan 1970

Displacement, tons	20 700 full load
Dimensions, feet	575·5 oa × 82 × 25·5
Guns	8—3 inch (*76 mm*) 50 cal AA (twin)
Main engines	1 steam turbine; 22 000 shp; 1 shaft = 20+ knots
Boilers	2 (Combustion Engineering)
Complement	334 (24 officers, 310 enlisted men)
Troops	226 (15 officers, 211 enlisted men)

These ships are designed specifically for the attack cargo ship role; they carry 18 landing craft (LCM) and supplies for amphibious operations. Design includes two heavy-lift cranes with a 78·4-ton capacity, two 40-ton capacity booms, and eight 15-ton capacity booms; helicopter deck aft.
The LKA 113-116 were authorised in the Fiscal Year 1965 shipbuilding programme; LKA 117 in FY 1966 programme.

DURHAM (LKA 114) *1970, United States Navy*

CHARLESTON (LKA-113) with CH-46 SEA KING *1975 Georgio Arra*

CHARLESTON CLASS—continued

All built by Newport News Shipbuilding and Dry Dock Co, Virginia. Cost was approximately $21 000 000 per ship.

CLASSIFICATION. Originally designated Attack Cargo Ship (AKA). *Charleston* redesignated Amphibious Cargo Ship (LKA) on 14 Dec 1968; others to LKA on 1 Jan 1969.

ENGINEERING. These are among the first US Navy ships with a fully automated main propulsion plant; control of plant is from bridge or central machinery space console. This automation permitted a 45-man reduction in complement.

NOMENCLATURE. Amphibious cargo ships are named for counties.

MOBILE (LKA 115) *1971, United States Navy*

1 AMPHIBIOUS CARGO SHIP (LKA) "TULARE" TYPE

***TULARE** (ex-*Evergreen Mariner*) LKA 112

Displacement, tons	12 000 light; 16 800 full load
Dimensions, feet	564 oa × 76 × 26
Guns	12—3 inch (*76 mm*) 50 cal AA (twin)
Main engines	Steam turbine (De Laval); 22 000 shp; 1 shaft = 22 knots
Boilers	2 (Combustion Engineering)
Complement	437 (38 officers, 399 enlisted men)
Troops	319 (18 officers, 301 enlisted men)

Built by Bethlehem, San Francisco. Laid down on 16 Feb 1953, launched on 22 Dec 1953. Acquired by Navy during construction. Commissioned on 13 Jan 1956. C4-S-1 type. Has helicopter landing platform and booms capable of lifting 60-ton landing craft. Carries 9 LCM-6 and 11 LCVP landing craft as deck cargo. Designation changed from AKA 112 to LKA 112 on 1 Jan 1969.
The *Tulare* was assigned to the Naval Reserve Force on 1 July 1975 and is partially manned by reserve personnel.

CLASS. Thirty-five "Mariner" design C4-S-1 merchant ships built during the early 1950s; five acquired by Navy, three for conversion to amphibious ships (AKA-APA) and two for support of Polaris-Poseidon programme (designated AG).

Amphibious Warfare Ships—*continued*

TULARE (LKA 112) *1969, United States Navy*

5 AMPHIBIOUS CARGO SHIPS (LKA): "RANKIN" CLASS

Name	*No.*	*Launched*	*Commissioned*
RANKIN	LKA 103	22 Dec 1944	25 Feb 1945
SEMINOLE	LKA 104	28 Dec 1944	8 Mar 1945
UNION	LKA 106	23 Nov 1944	25 Apr 1945
VERMILION	LKA 107	12 Dec 1944	23 June 1945
WASHBURN	LKA 108	12 Dec 1944	17 May 1945

Displacement, tons	6 546 light; 14 160 full load
Dimensions, feet	459·2 oa × 63 × 26·3
Guns	1—5 inch (*127 mm*) 38 cal DP (removed from some ships); 8—40 mm AA (twin)
Main engines	Steam turbine (General Electric); 6 000 shp; 1 shaft = 16·5 knots
Boilers	2 (Combustion Engineering)
Complement	247
Troops	138

All built by North Carolina SB Co, Wilmington, North Carolina. Maritime Commission C2-S-AJ3 type. These ships carry 8 LCMs and 16 LCVPs as deck cargo. Ten 20 mm AA guns removed. Designation changed from AKA to LKA on 1 Jan 1969.
All of the above ships are in Maritime Administration reserve (remain on the Navy List).

RANKIN (LKA 103) 5 inch gun aft *United States Navy*

7 AMPHIBIOUS CARGO SHIPS (LKA): "ANDROMEDA" CLASS

Name	*No.*	*Launched*	*Commissioned*
THUBAN (ex-AK 68)	LKA 19	26 Apr 1943	10 June 1943
ALGOL (ex-*James Baines*)	LKA 54	17 Feb 1943	21 July 1944
CAPRICORNUS (ex-*Spitfire*)	LKA 57	14 Aug 1943	31 May 1944
MULIPHEN	LKA 61	26 Aug 1944	23 Oct 1944
YANCEY	LKA 93	8 July 1944	11 Oct 1944
WINSTON	LKA 94	30 Nov 1944	19 Jan 1945
MERRICK	LKA 97	28 Jan 1945	31 Mar 1945

Displacement, tons	7 430 light; 14 000 full load
Dimensions, feet	435 wl; 495·2 oa × 63 × 24
Guns	1—5 inch (*127 mm*) 38 cal (removed from some ships); 8—40 mm AA (twin) except *Thuban* 4—3 inch 50 cal AA in lieu of 40 mm
Main engines	Steam turbine (General Electric); 6 000 shp; 1 shaft = 16·5 knots
Boilers	2 (Foster Wheeler)
Complement	247
Troops	414

Algol, *Capricornus*, and *Yancey* built by Moore DD Co, Oakland, California; others by Federal SB & Co, DD Kearney, New Jersey. C2-S-B1 type. Can carry over 5 200 tons of cargo and 2 200 tons of tanks. *Wyandot*, AKA 92, assigned to the Navy's Military Sealift Command and manned by a civilian crew since 1963, was redesignated T-AK 283 on 1 Jan 1969. Designation of other ships remaining on Navy List changed from AKA to LKA on 1 Jan 1969.
All of the above ships are in Maritime Administration reserve (remain on the Navy List).

DISPOSALS (since 1 Jan 1970)
Arneb LKA 56 stricken on 13 Aug 1971.

MULIPHEN (LKA 61) *1968, United States Navy*

MULIPHEN (LKA 61) *1968, United States Navy*

2 AMPHIBIOUS TRANSPORTS (LPA): "PAUL REVERE" CLASS

Name	*No.*	*Launched*	*Commissioned*
***PAUL REVERE** (ex-*Diamond Mariner*)	LPA 248	13 Feb 1954	3 Sep 1958
***FRANCIS MARION** (ex-*Prairie Mariner*)	LPA 249	11 Apr 1953	6 July 1961

Displacement, tons	10 709 light; 16 838 full load
Dimensions, feet	563·5 oa × 76 × 27
Guns	8—3 inch (*76 mm*) 50 cal AA (twin)
Main engines	Steam turbine (General Electric); 22 000 shp; 1 shaft = 22 knots
Boiler	2 (Foster Wheeler)
Complement	414 (35 officers, 379 enlisted men)
Troops	1 657 (96 officers, 1 561 enlisted men)

Both ships built by New York Shipbuilding Corp, Camden, New Jersey. "Mariner" C4-S-1 merchant ships acquired for conversion to attack transports; *Paul Revere* converted by Todd Shipyard Corp, San Pedro, California, under the Fiscal Year 1957 conversion programme; *Francis Marion* converted by Bethlehem Steel Corp, Key Highway Yard, Baltimore, Maryland, under FY 1959 programme. Helicopter platform fitted aft; 7 LCM-6 and 16 LCVP landing craft carried as deck cargo. Fitted to serve as force flagships.
Designation of both ships changed from APA to LPA on 1 Jan 1969.
The *Paul Revere* was assigned to the Naval Reserve Force on 1 July 1975 and the *Francis Marion* on 1 Aug 1975; partially manned by reserve personnel.

PAUL REVERE (LPA 248) *1969, United States Navy*

FRANCIS MARION (LPA 249) *1970, United States Navy*

7 AMPHIBIOUS TRANSPORTS (LPA): "HASKELL" CLASS

Name	*No.*	*Launched*	*Commissioned*
SANDOVAL	LPA 194	11 Sep 1944	7 Oct 1944
MAGOFFIN	LPA 199	4 Oct 1944	25 Oct 1944
TALLADEGA	LPA 208	17 Aug 1944	31 Oct 1944
MOUNTRAIL	LPA 213	20 Sep 1944	16 Nov 1944
NAVARRO	LPA 215	3 Oct 1944	15 Nov 1944
PICKAWAY	LPA 222	5 Nov 1944	12 Dec 1944
BEXAR	LPA 237	25 July 1945	9 Oct 1945

Displacement, tons	6 720 light; 10 470 full load
Dimensions, feet	435·6 wl; 455 oa × 62 × 24
Guns	12—40 mm AA (1 quad, 4 twin); forward quad 40 mm mount removed from some ships
Main engines	Steam turbine; 8 500 shp; 1 shaft = 17·7 knots
Boilers	2 (Babcock & Wilcox)
Complement	536
Troops	1 560

Built by Permanente Metals Corp, Richmond, California, except *Sandoval* and *Magoffin* by Kaiser Co, Vancouver, Washington; *Bexar* by Oregon SB Corp, Portland, Oregon. VC2-S-AP5 "Victory" cargo ships. Original 5 inch gun removed; fitted to carry 2 LCM and 20 LCVP landing craft as deck cargo.
Designation changed from APA to LPA on 1 Jan 1969. All in Maritime Administration reserve (on Navy List). *Sherburne* APA 205 converted to missile range instrumentation ship; redesignated AGM 22.

DISPOSALS (since 1 Jan 1970)
Okanogan LPA 220 stricken on 1 June 1973.

Amphibious Warfare Ships—*continued*

"BAYFIELD" CLASS

All amphibious transports of the C3-S-A2 type have been stricken.
Cambria LPA 36 stricken on 14 Sep 1970; **Chilton** LPA 38 stricken on 1 July 1972; **Fremont** LPA 44, **Henrico** LPA 45 stricken on 1 June 1973.

SANDOVAL (LPA 194) *1969, United States Navy*

3 AMPHIBIOUS TRANSPORTS (SMALL) (LPR): CONVERTED DE TYPE

Name	No	Launched	Commissioned
LANING	LPR 55 ex-DE 159	4 July 1943	1 Aug 1943
BEGOR	LPR 127 ex-DE 711	25 May 1944	14 Mar 1945
BALDUCK	LPR 132 ex-DE 716	27 Oct 1944	7 May 1945

Displacement, tons	1 400 standard; 2 130 full load
Dimensions, feet	300 wl; 306 oa × 37 × 12·6
Guns	1—5 inch (*127 mm*) 38 cal DP; 4—40 mm AA (twin) in modernised ships; 8—40 mm AA (twin) in others
A/S weapons	2 triple torpedo tubes (Mk 32) in modernised ships; depth charges in others
Main engines	Geared turbines (General Electric) with electric drive; 12 000 shp; 2 shafts = 23·6 knots
Boilers	2 ("D" Express)
Complement	204 (designed wartime; 12 or 15 officers, 189 or 192 enlisted men, depending upon DE type)
Troops	162 (12 officers, 150 enlisted men)

These ships are former Destroyer Escorts (DE) converted or completed during World War II to transports for carrying commandoes, reconnaissance troops or frogmen. Fifty-six DEs were completed to this configuration and an additional 38 ships were converted after service as destroyer escorts.
Originally designated as High Speed Transports (APD); designation of 13 ships remaining on Navy List as of 1 Jan 1969 changed to Amphibious Transports (Small) (LPR). Converted from TE and TEV type destroyer escorts with troop quarters being provided, single 5 inch gun and six to eight 40 mm guns (twin) replacing previous armament, davits installed amidships for four LCVPs, and 10-ton capacity boom placed aft.

All surviving ships of this type in the US Navy are in reserve.

MODERNISATION. *Laning* and *Balduck* were modernised during the 1960s as part of the FRAM II programme. They have new bridge configurations, additional electronic equipment, tripod mast (in some ships place of forward pole mast), improved habitability, ASW torpedo launchers, and retain only two 40 mm twin mounts (aft).

TRANSFERS. Ships of this class serve in the navies of Chile, Colombia, Ecuador, South Korea, Mexico and Taiwan China.

DISPOSALS (since 1 Jan 1970)

Knudson LPR 101 stricken on 15 July 1972; **Hollis** LPR 86, **Kirwin** LPR 90, **Ringness** LPR 100, **Beverley W. Reid** LPR 119, **Diachenko** LPR 123, **Horace A. Bass** LPR 124, **Weiss** LPR 135 stricken on 15 Sep 1974.

BEVERLY W. REID (LPR 119)—now stricken *1968, United States Navy*

12 AMPHIBIOUS TRANSPORT DOCKS (LPD): "AUSTIN" CLASS

Name	*No.*	*Laid down*	*Launched*	*Commissioned*
***AUSTIN**	LPD 4	4 Feb 1963	27 June 1964	6 Feb **1965**
***OGDEN**	LPD 5	4 Feb 1963	27 June 1964	19 June **1965**
***DULUTH**	LPD 6	18 Dec 1963	14 Aug 1965	12 Apr **1966**
***CLEVELAND**	LPD 7	30 Nov 1964	7 May 1966	21 Apr **1967**
***DUBUQUE**	LPD 8	25 Jan 1965	6 Aug 1966	1 Sep **1967**
***DENVER**	LPD 9	7 Feb 1964	23 Jan 1965	26 Oct **1968**
***JUNEAU**	LPD 10	23 Jan 1965	12 Feb 1966	12 July **1969**
***CORONADO**	LPD 11	3 May 1965	30 July 1966	23 May 1970
***SHREVEPORT**	LPD 12	27 Dec 1965	22 Oct 1966	12 Dec 1970
***NASHVILLE**	LPD 13	14 Mar 1966	7 Oct 1967	14 Feb 1970
***TRENTON**	LPD 14	8 Aug 1966	3 Aug 1968	6 Mar 1971
***PONCE**	LPD 15	31 Oct 1966	20 May 1970	10 July 1971

Displacement, tons	10 000 light; 16 900 full load
Length, feet (*metres*)	570 (*173·3*) oa
Beam, feet (*metres*)	84 (*25·6*)
Draught, feet (*metres*)	23 (*7·0*)
Guns	8—3 inch (*76 mm*) 50 cal AA (twin)
Helicopters	up to 6 UH-34 or CH-46
Main engines	2 steam turbines (De Laval); 24 000 shp; 2 shafts = 20 knots sustained
Boilers	2 (Babcock & Wilcox)
Complement	490 (30 officers, 460 enlisted men)
Troops	930 in LPD 4-6 and LPD 14-16; 840 in LPD 7-13
Flag accommodation	Approx 90 in LPD 7-13

These ships are enlarged versions of the previous "Raleigh" class; most notes for the "Raleigh" class apply to these ships. All 12 of these ships are officially considered in a single class; earlier references to separate classes were based on contract awards to builders.
LPD 4-6 built by New York Naval Shipyard; LPD 7-8 built by Ingalls Shipbuilding Corp; LPD 9-15 built by Lockheed Shipbuilding & Construction Co, Seattle, Washington.
The LPD 4-6 were authorised in the Fiscal Year 1962 new construction programme, LPD 7-10 in FY 1963, LPD 11-13 in FY 1964, LPD 14 and LPD 15 in FY 1965, and LPD 16 in FY 1966. LPD 16 was deferred in favour of LHA programme; officially cancelled in Feb 1969. No additional ships of this type are planned in view of the LHA capabilities.
All ships of this class are active.

NOMENCLATURE. Amphibious transport docks are named for American cities that honour explorers and pioneers.

PHOTOGRAPHS. On the following page the *Cleveland* is shown with two CH-53 Sea Stallion helicopters on her deck; note telescoping hangar between funnels.

PONCE (LPD 15) *1973, Giorgio Arra*

SHREVEPORT (LPD 12) *1973, Giorgio Arra*

CLEVELAND (LPD 7)—"AUSTIN" class *1973, United States Navy, JOC Warren Grass*

RALEIGH (LPD 1)—"RALEIGH" class *1972, United States Navy, PH2 John Smith*

PORTLAND (LSD 37)—"ANCHORAGE" class *1972, Giorgio Arra*

HERMITAGE (LSD 34)—"THOMASTON" class *1971, Giorgio Arra*

Amphibious Warfare Ships—*continued*

AUSTIN (LPD) 4 *1973, Giorgio Arra*

PENSACOLA (LSD 38) *1971, General Dynamics Corp*

2 AMPHIBIOUS TRANSPORT DOCKS (LPD): "RALEIGH" CLASS

Name	*No.*	*Laid down*	*Launched*	*Commissioned*
•**RALEIGH**	LPD 1	23 June 1960	17 Mar 1962	8 Sep 1962
•**VANCOUVER**	LPD 2	19 Nov 1960	15 Sep 1962	11 May 1963

Displacement, tons	8 040 light; 13 900 full load
Length, feet (*metres*)	500 (*152·0*) wl; 521·8 (*158·4*) oa
Beam, feet (*metres*)	84 (*25·6*)
Draught, feet (*metres*)	21 (*6·4*)
Guns	8—3 inch (*76 mm*) 50 cal AA
Helicopters	up to 6 UH-34 or CH-46 (see *Helicopter* notes)
Main engines	2 steam turbines; (De Laval); 24 000 shp; 2 shafts = 20 knots sustained
Boilers	2 (Babcock & Wilcox)
Complement	490 (30 officers, 460 enlisted men)
Troops	930

The amphibious transport dock was developed from the dock landing ship (LSD) concept but provides more versatility. The LPD replaces the Amphibious Transport (LPA) and, in part, the Amphibious Cargo Ship (LKA) and dock landing ship. The LPD can carry a "balanced load" of assault troops and their equipment, has a docking well for landing craft, a helicopter deck, cargo holds and vehicle garages. The *Raleigh* was authorised in the Fiscal Year 1959 new construction programme, the *Vancouver* in FY 1960. Built by New York Naval Shipyard. Approximate construction cost was $29 000 000 per ship.
A third ship of this class, *La Salle* (LPD 3), was reclassified as a command ship (AGF 3) on 1 July 1972.

DESIGN. These ships resemble dock landing ships (LSD) but have fully enclosed docking well with the roof forming a permanent helicopter platform. The docking well is 168 feet long and 50 feet wide, less than half the length of wells in newer LSDs; the LPD design provides more space for vehicles, cargo and troops. Ramps allow vehicles to be driven between helicopter deck, parking area and docking well, side ports provide roll-on/roll off capability when docks are available. An overhead monorail in the docking well with six cranes facilitates loading landing craft.

HELICOPTERS. These ships are not normally assigned helicopters because they lack integral hangars and maintenance facilities. It is intended that helicopters from a nearby amphibious assault ship (LHA or LPH) would provide helicopters during an amphibious operation. Hangars have been fitted (see "Austin" class notes).

LANDING CRAFT. The docking well in these ships can hold one LCU and three LCM-6s or four LCM-8s or 20 LVTs (amphibious tractors). In addition, two LCM-6s or four LCPLs are carried on the boat deck which are lowered by crane.

5 DOCK LANDING SHIPS (LSD): "ANCHORAGE" CLASS

Name	*No.*	*Laid down*	*Launched*	*Commissioned*
•**ANCHORAGE**	LSD 36	13 Mar 1967	5 May 1968	15 Mar 1969
•**PORTLAND**	LSD 37	21 Sep 1967	20 Dec 1969	3 Oct 1970
•**PENSACOLA**	LSD 38	12 Mar 1969	11 July 1970	27 Mar 1971
•**MOUNT VERNON**	LSD 39	29 Jan 1970	17 Apr 1971	13 May 1972
•**FORT FISHER**	LSD 40	15 July 1970	22 Apr 1972	9 Dec 1972

Displacement, tons	8 600 light; 13 700 full load
Dimensions, feet	553·33 oa × 84 × 18·66
Guns	8—3 inch (*76 mm*) 50 cal AA (twin)
Main engines	steam turbines (De Laval); 24 000 shp; 2 shafts = 20 knots sustained
Boilers	2 (Foster Wheeler except Combustion Engineering in *Anchorage*)
Complement	397 (21 officers, 376 enlisted men)
Troops	376 (28 officers, 348 enlisted men)

Improved dock landing ships, slightly larger than previous class; designed to replace earlier LSDs which are unable to meet 20-knot amphibious lift requirement. Similar in appearance to earlier classes but with a tripod mast. Helicopter platform aft with docking well partially open; helicopter platform can be removed. Docking well approximately 430 × 50 feet can accommodate three LCU-type landing craft. Space on deck for one LCM, and davits for one LCPL and one LCVP. Two 50-ton capacity cranes.
LSD 36 was authorised in Fiscal Year 1965 shipbuilding programme; LSD 37-39 in FY 1966 programme; LSD 40 in FY 1967 programme. *Anchorage* built by Ingalls Shipbuilding; LSD 37-40 by General Dynamics (Quincy).
Estimated construction cost is $11 500 000 per ship.

NOMENCLATURE. Dock landing ships are named for historic sites in the United States except that the *Anchorage, Portland,* and *Pensacola* primarily honour cities.

PORTLAND (LSD 37) *1973, Giorgio Arra*

FORT FISHER (LSD 40) *1972, General Dynamics Corp.*

PORTLAND (LSD 37) *1973, Giorgio Arra*

8 DOCK LANDING SHIPS (LSD): "THOMASTON" CLASS

Name	*No*	*Launched*	*Commissioned*
•**THOMASTON**	LSD 28	9 Feb 1954	17 Sep 1954
•**PLYMOUTH ROCK**	LSD 29	7 May 1954	24 Jan 1955
•**FORT SNELLING**	LSD 30	16 July 1954	24 Jan 1955
•**POINT DEFIANCE**	LSD 31	28 Sep 1954	31 Mar 1955
•**SPIEGEL GROVE**	LSD 32	10 Nov 1955	8 June 1956
•**ALAMO**	LSD 33	20 Jan 1956	24 Aug 1956
•**HERMITAGE**	LSD 34	12 June 1956	17 Dec 1956
•**MONTICELLO**	LSD 35	10 Aug 1956	29 Mar 1957

Displacement, tons	6 880 light; 11 270 full load, *Alamo, Hermitage, Monticello, Spiegel Grove:* 12 150 full load
Dimensions, feet	510 oa × 84 × 19 max
Guns	12—3 inch (*76 mm*) 50 cal AA (twin)
Main engines	Steam turbines (General Electric); 24 000 shp; 2 shafts = 22·5 knots
Boilers	2 (Babcock & Wilcox)
Complement	400
Troops	340

Built by Ingalls Shipbuilding Corp, Pascagoula, Mississippi. Constructed to provide 20-knot LSD capability. Fitted with helicopter platform over docking well; two 5-ton capacity cranes; can carry 21 LCM(6) or 3 LCU and 6 LCM landing craft or approximately 50 LVTs (amphibious tractors) in docking well plus 30 LVTs on mezzanine and super decks (with helicopter landing area clear).
As built each ship had 16—3 inch AA guns; twin mount on each side wall (aft of boats davits) has been removed.
Note pole mast compared to tripod mast of subsequent "Anchorage" class for rapid identification; later class has enclosed 3 inch gun mounts forward of bridge.

Amphibious Warfare Ships—*continued*

FORT SNELLING (LSD 30)

PLYMOUTH ROCK (LSD 29) *1975, Giorgio Arra*

SPIEGEL GROVE (LSD 32) *1968, United States Navy*

10 DOCK LANDING SHIPS (LSD): "CASA GRANDE" CLASS

Name	*No*	*Launched*	*Commissioned*
CASA GRANDE	LSD 13	11 Apr 1944	5 June 1944
RUSHMORE	LSD 14	10 May 1944	3 July 1944
SHADWELL	LSD 15	24 May 1944	24 July 1944
CABILDO	LSD 16	28 Dec 1944	15 Mar 1945
CATAMOUNT	LSD 17	27 Jan 1945	9 Apr 1945
COLONIAL	LSD 18	28 Feb 1945	15 May 1945
COMSTOCK	LSD 19	28 Apr 1945	2 July 1945
DONNER	LSD 20	6 Apr 1945	31 July 1945
TORTUGA	LSD 26	21 Jan 1945	8 June 1945
WHETSTONE	LSD 27	18 July 1945	12 Feb 1946

Displacement, tons	4 790 standard; 9 375 full load
Dimensions, feet	475·4 oa × 76·2 × 18 max
Guns	8— or 12—40 mm AA (2 quad plus 2 twin in some ships)
Main engines	Geared turbines (Newport News except Westinghouse in *Fort Marion*); 2 shafts; 7 000 shp except 9 000 in *Fort Marion* = 15·4 knots
Boilers	2
Complement	265 (15 officers, 250 men)

"CASA GRANDE" CLASS—*continued*

LSD 13-19 built by Newport News SB & DD Co, Virginia; LSD 20, 26, 27 built by Boston Navy Yard; *Fort Snelling* LSD 23, and *Point Defiance* LSD 24 cancelled in 1945; former ship completed for merchant service, reacquired by Navy as cargo ship *Taurus*, T-AK 273, T-AKR 8 (stricken in 1968). LSD 9-12 of this class transferred to Britain in 1943-1944.
Docking well is 392 × 44 feet; can carry 3 LCUs or 18 LSMs or 32 LVTs (amphibious tractors) in docking well. All ships are fitted with helicopter platform.
Catamount, Colonial, Donner were modernised under the FRAM II programme in 1960-1962.
All surviving ships of this class are in Navy or Maritime Administration reserve (the latter ships remain on the Navy List). *Casa Grande* is under consideration for transfer to Israel.

TRANSFERS
Fort Mandan LSD 21 to Greece on 23 Jan 1971, **San Marcos** LSD 25 to Spain on 1 July 1971, **Fort Marion** LSD 22 stricken on 31 Oct 1974 for later transfer to Taiwan China.

DOCK LANDING SHIPS (LSD): "ASHLAND" CLASS

All ships of this class have been stricken or transferred to foreign navies; see 1972-1973 and previous editions for characteristics.

DONNER (LSD 20) *1968, United States Navy*

COMSTOCK (LSD 19) *1965, United States Navy*

PLYMOUTH ROCK (LSD 29) *1975, Giorgio Arra*

Amphibious Warfare Ships—*continued*

20 TANK LANDING SHIPS (LST): "NEWPORT" CLASS

Name	*No.*	*Laid down*	*Launched*	*Commissioned*
***NEWPORT**	LST 1179	1 Nov 1966	3 Feb 1968	7 June 1969
***MANITOWOC**	LST 1180	1 Feb 1967	4 June 1969	24 Jan 1970
***SUMTER**	LST 1181	14 Nov 1967	13 Dec 1969	20 June 1970
***FRESNO**	LST 1182	16 Dec 1967	28 Sep 1968	22 Nov 1969
***PEORIA**	LST 1183	22 Feb 1968	23 Nov 1968	21 Feb 1970
***FREDERICK**	LST 1184	13 Apr 1968	8 Mar 1969	11 Apr 1970
***SCHENECTADY**	LST 1185	2 Aug 1968	24 May 1969	13 June 1970
***CAYUGA**	LST 1186	28 Sep 1968	12 July 1969	8 Aug 1970
***TUSCALOOSA**	LST 1187	23 Nov 1968	6 Sep 1969	24 Oct 1970
***SAGINAW**	LST 1188	24 May 1969	7 Feb 1970	23 Jan 1971
***SAN BERNARDINO**	LST 1189	12 July 1969	28 Mar 1970	27 Mar 1971
***BOULDER**	LST 1190	6 Sep 1969	22 May 1970	30 Apr 1971
***RACINE**	LST 1191	13 Dec 1969	15 Aug 1970	9 July 1971
***SPARTANBURG COUNTY**	LST 1192	7 Feb 1970	11 Nov 1970	1 Sep 1971
***FAIRFAX COUNTY**	LST 1193	28 Mar 1970	19 Dec 1970	16 Oct 1971
***LA MOURE COUNTY**	LST 1194	22 May 1970	13 Feb 1971	18 Dec 1971
***BARBOUR COUNTY**	LST 1195	15 Aug 1970	15 May 1971	12 Feb 1972
***HARLAN COUNTY**	LST 1196	7 Nov 1970	24 July 1971	8 Apr 1972
***BARNSTABLE COUNTY**	LST 1197	19 Dec 1970	2 Oct 1971	27 May 1972
***BRISTOL COUNTY**	LST 1198	13 Feb 1971	4 Dec 1971	5 Aug 1972

Displacement, tons	8 342 full load
Dimensions, feet	522·3 hull oa × 69·5 × 17·5 (aft)
Guns	4—3 inch (*76 mm*) 50 cal AA (twin)
Main engines	6 diesels (Alco); 2 shafts, 16 000 hp = 20 knots (sustained)
Complement	223 (12 officers, 211 enlisted men)
Troops	386 (20 officers, 366 enlisted men)

These ships are of an entirely new design larger, and faster than previous tank landing ships. They operate with 20-knot amphibious squadrons to transport tanks, other heavy vehicles, engineer equipment, and supplies which cannot be readily landed by helicopters or landing craft.
The *Newport* was authorised in the Fiscal Year 1965 new construction programme. LST 1180-1187 (8 ships) in FY 1966, and LST 1188-1198 (11 ships) in FY 1967, LST 1179-1181 built by Philadelphia Naval Shipyard, LST 1182-1198 built by National Steel & Shipbuilding Co, San Diego, California. Seven additional ships of this type that were planned for the Fiscal Year 1971 new construction programme have been deferred.

All 20 ships of this class are active; they are the only LSTs remaining in US service. They are required to carry tanks, amphibious tractors, and other heavy equipment for amphibious landings.

DESIGN. These ships are the first LSTs to depart from the bow-door design developed by the British early in World War II. The hull form required to achieve 20 knots would not permit bow doors, thus these ships unload by a 112-foot ramp over their bow. The ramp is supported by twin derrick arms. A ramp just forward of the superstructure connects the lower tank deck with the main deck and a vehicle passage through the superstructure provides access to the parking area amidships. A stern gate to the tank deck permits unloading of amphibious tractors into the water, or unloading of other vehicles into an LCU or onto a pier. Vehicle stowage is rated at 500 tons and 19 000 square feet (5 000 sq ft more than previous LSTs). Length over derrick arms is 565 feet; full load draft is 11·5 feet forward and 17·5 feet aft.

NOMENCLATURE. LSTs are named for counties and parishes. In accord with the contemporary US Navy confusion over naming ships, some do not have county or parish suffix.

PHOTOGRAPHS. Note uneven, staggered funnels, bow opening when ramp is lowered, anchors on starboard side forward and at stern, funnel opening in superstructure, and helicopter spots marked aft of funnels. Twin 3 inch closed gun mounts are difficult to distinguish in clutter atop superstructure. *Sumter* is shown in Mediterranean carrying four pontoon barges lashed amidships; her stern gate is open for unloading amphibious tractors.

SUMTER (LST 1181) *1975, Giorgio Arra*

SUMTER (LST 1181) *1975, Giorgio Arra*

SPARTANBURG COUNTY (LST 1192) *1972, United States Navy*

SUMTER (LST 1181) with open stern gate and pontoon sections *1975, Giorgio Arra*

Amphibious Warfare Ships—*continued*

3 TANK LANDING SHIPS (LST): "SUFFOLK COUNTY" CLASS

Name	*No.*	*Builder*	*Launched*
SUFFOLK COUNTY	LST 1173	Boston Navy Yard	5 Sep 1956
LORAIN COUNTY	LST 1177	American SB Co, Lorrain, Ohio	22 June 1957
WOOD COUNTY	LST 1178	American SB Co, Lorrain, Ohio	14 Dec 1957

Displacement, tons: 4 164 light; 8 000 full load
Dimensions, feet: 445 *oa* × 62 × 16·5
Guns: 6—3 inch (*76 mm*) 50 cal AA (twin)
Main engines: Diesels; 14 400 bhp; 2 shafts; (controllable pitch propellers) = 17·5 knots
Complement: 184 (10 officers, 174 men)
Troops: approx 575

Originally a class of seven tank landing ships (LST 1171, 1173-1178 with LST 1172 not built). They were faster and had a greater troop capacity than earlier LSTs; considered the "ultimate" design attainable with the traditional LST bow-door configuration. *Suffolk County* commissioned on 15 Aug 1957, *Lorain County* on 3 Oct 1859, and *Wood County* on 5 Aug 1969.
The surviving ships were decommissioned in 1972 and are in reserve; they probably will be transferred to foreign navies or assigned to the Military Sealift Command for use as cargo ships.
The *Graham County* (LST 1176) has been converted to a gunboat support ship (AGP); see description under Fleet Support Ships.

DESIGN. High degree of habitability with all crew and troop living spaces air conditioned. Can carry 23 medium tanks or vehicles up to 75 tons on 288-foot-long (lower) tank deck. Davits for four LCVP-type landing craft. Liquid cargo capacity of 170 000 gallons (US) diesel or jet fuel plus 7 000 gallons (US) of petrol for embarked vehicles; some ships have reduced troop spaces and carry additional 250 000 gallons (US) of aviation petrol for pumping ashore or to other ships.

ENGINEERING. All built with six Nordburg diesels. *Suffolk County* refitted with six Fairbanks Morse diesels, electric couplings and reduction gears; *Lorain County* and *Wood County* refitted with six Cooper Bessemer diesels, electric couplings and reduction gears.

TRANSFERS
De Soto County LST 1171, **York County** LST 1175 transferred to Italy on 17 July 1972; **Grant County** LST 1174 transferred to Brazil on 15 Jan 1973.

PHOTOGRAPHS. The "Suffolk County" class LSTs are identified by their twin fire control towers forward.

WOOD COUNTY (LST 1178) — *1971, J. S. Kinross*

2 TANK LANDING SHIPS (LST): "TERREBONNE PARISH" CLASS

Name	*No.*	*Launched*	*Commissioned*
TERRELL COUNTY	LST 1157	6 Dec 1952	19 Mar 1953
WHITFIELD COUNTY	LST 1169	22 Aug 1953	14 Sep 1954

Displacement, tons: 2 580 light; 5 800 full load
Dimensions, feet: 384 *oa* × 55 × 17
Guns: 6—3 inch (*76 mm*) 50 cal AA (twin)
Main engines: 4 diesels (General Motors); 6 000 bhp 2 shafts (controllable pitch propellers) = 15 knots
Complement: 115
Troops: 395

Originally a class of 15 tank landing ships (LST 1156-1170). *Terrell County* built by Bath Iron Works Corp, Bath Maine; *Whitfield County* by Christy Corp.
Six ships were transferred from reserve to the Military Sealift Command in 1972 for use as cargo ships: *Tioga County* LST 1158, *Traverse County* LST 1160, *Wahkiakum County* LST 1162, *Waldo County* LST 1163, *Walworth County*, LST 1164 and *Washoe County* LST 1165. The ships listed above were to transfer to the Military Sealift Command during 1973 but transfer delayed and they were decommissioned. (See Sealift Ships).
In the photograph of the *Terrell County* two UH-1 "Huey" (Iroquois) helicopters are on the ship's deck during operations in Vietnam waters.

DISPOSALS AND TRANSFERS
Terrebonne Parish LST 1156, **Wexford County** LST 1168 transferred to Spain on 29 Oct 1971; **Tom Green County** LST 1159 transferred to Spain on 6 Jan 1972; **Windham County** LST 1170 transferred to Turkey on 1 June 1973; **Vernon County** LST 1161 transferred to Venezuela on 29 June 1973; **Washtenaw County** MSS 2, ex-LST 1166 stricken on 30 Aug 1973; **Westchester County** LST 1167 transferred to Turkey on 27 Aug 1974.

"TALBOT COUNTY" CLASS

Both ships of the "Talbot County" class have been stricken; see 1973-1974 and previous editions for characteristics and photographs.
Talbot County LST 1153 stricken on 1 June 1973; **Tallahatchie County** LST 1154 converted to aviation base ship (AVB 2)—stricken in 1970.

TERRELL COUNTY (LST 1157) — *1969, United States Navy*

9 TANK LANDING SHIPS (LST): 511-1152 SERIES

Name	*No.*	*Launched*	*Commissioned*
DODGE COUNTY	LST 722	21 Aug 1944	13 Sep 1944
FLOYD COUNTY	LST 762	1 Aug 1944	5 Sep 1944
HAMPSHIRE COUNTY	LST 819	21 Oct 1944	14 Nov 1944
KEMPER COUNTY	LST 854	20 Nov 1944	14 Dec 1944
LITCHFIELD COUNTY	LST 901	9 Dec 1944	11 Jan 1945
MEEKER COUNTY	LST 980	27 Jan 1944	26 Feb 1944
PITKIN COUNTY	LST 1082	26 Jan 1945	7 Feb 1954
ST. CLAIR COUNTY	LST 1096	10 Jan 1945	2 Feb 1945
SEDGWICK COUNTY	LST 1123	29 Jan 1945	19 Feb 1945

Displacement, tons: 1 653 standard; 2 080 full load
Dimensions, feet: 316 wl; 328 × *oa* × 50 × 14
Guns: 8—40 mm AA (2 twin and 4 single) in most ships
Main engines: Diesels (General Motors); 1 700 bhp; 2 shafts = 11·6 knots
Complement: 119
Troops: 147

The US Navy built 1 052 LSTs during World War II in two series: LST 1-510 and LST 511-1152; an even 100 ships were cancelled: LST 85-116, 142-156, 182-196, 232-236, 248-260, 296-300, 431-445. Forty-one were lost during the war. Hundreds of these ships have been transferred to foreign navies or converted to auxiliary configurations.
County or Parish names were assigned to 158 LSTs on the Navy List as of 1 July 1955; 36 Japanese-manned LSTs assigned to the Military Sea Transportation Service (MSTS) at that time were not named.
All of the surviving ships of this series are in reserve except for those operated by the Military Sealift Command (listed separately). The latter ships are used as cargo carriers and are no longer suitable for amphibious operations.

DESIGN. These ships are of the classical LST design developed early in World War II by the British; fitted with bow doors, tunnel-like tank deck with trucks, cargo, or landing craft carried on upper deck; small "island" structure aft with davits for two LCVP-type landing craft. Cargo capacity 2 100 tons. Fitted with tripod masts during postwar period.

TRANSFERS. Ships of this class serve in the navies of Brazil, Greece, Indonesia, Japan, South Korea, Malaysia, Mexico, Philippines, Singapore, Spain, Thailand, Taiwan China, Mainland China, and South Vietnam.

DISPOSALS AND TRANSFERS (Since 1 Jan 1970)
Jerome County LST 848 to South Vietnam on 1 Apr 1970; **Snohomish County** LST 1126 stricken on 1 July 1970; **Clarke County** LST 601, **Iredell County** LST 839 to Indonesia on 15 July 1970; **Luzerne County** LST 902, **Monmouth County** LST 1032 stricken on 12 Aug 1970; **Jennings County** LST 846 stricken on 25 Sep 1970; **Harnett County** LST/AGP 821 to South Vietnam on 12 Oct 1970; **Summit County** LST 1146 transferred to Maritime Administration reserve on 16 Mar 1970. **Page County** LST 1076 to Greece on 5 Mar 1971; **Holmes County** LST 836 to Singapore on 1 July 1971; **Outagamie County** LST 1073 to Brazil on 24 May 1971; **Garrett County** LST/AGP 786 to South Vietnam on 24 April 1971; **Hunterdon County** LST/AGP 838 to Malaysia on 1 July 1971; **Park County** LST 1077 to Mexico on 20 Sep 1971, **San Joaquin County** LST 1122 stricken on 1 May 1972, **Caroline County** LST 525, **Cheboygan County** LST 533, **Churchill County** LST 583, **Duval County** LST 758, **Middlesex County** LST 983, **Polk County** LST 1984, **Sumner County** LST 1148, **Sutter County** LST 1150 stricken on 15 Sep 1974.

LST 1-510 SERIES

All LSTs of this series have been stricken or transferred, the last unit on the Navy List being the **Blanco County** LST 344, stricken on 15 Sep 1974. Basic design and characteristics similar to LST 511-1152 series.

INSHORE FIRE SUPPORT SHIPS (LFR)

A l inshore fire support ships have been stricken; see 1973-1974 and previous editions for characteristics. The converted *Elk River* (ex-LSMR 501) survives as an ocean engineering range support ship (IX 501).

MEEKER COUNTY (LST 980) — *1967, United States Navy*

LANDING CRAFT

(1) AMPHIBIOUS ASSAULT LANDING CRAFT (AALC): AEROJET-GENERAL DESIGN (JEFF-A)

Weight, tons	85·8 empty; 166·4 gross
Dimensions, feet	96·2 oa × 48 × (height) 23
Main engines	4 gas turbines (Avco-Lycoming T40); 11 200 hp; 4 aircraft type propellers in rotating shrouds for propulsive thrust = approx 50 knots cruise
Lift engines	2 gas turbines (Avco-Lycoming T40); 5 600 hp; 8 horizontal fans (2 sets) for cushion lift
Complement	6

This is an Air Cushion Vehicle (ACV) landing craft being developed by the Aerojet-General Corp and being built by Todd Shipyards, Seattle, Washington, under Navy contract. Construction scheduled to be completed in February 1975 with one year of contractor testing before delivery to Navy in February 1976. (Construction shifted from Tacoma Boatbuilding Co after financial failure of that firm).
Above dimensions are for craft on air cushion; when at rest dimensions will be 97 × 44 × 19. Designed to carry 120 000 pound payload at a design speed of 50 knots (same as Jeff-B). Design features include aluminium construction, bow and stern ramps, cargo deck area of 2 100 square feet; two sound-insulated compartments each hold four persons; three engines housed in each side structure; two propellers in rotating shrouds provide horizontal propulsion and steering.
Performance parameters include four-hour endurance (200 n mile range), four foot obstacle clearance, and capability to maintain cruise speed in Sea State 2 with 25-knot headwind.
Scheduled for delivery late in 1976.

PROJECT. Aerojet-General and Bell Aerosystems were awarded contracts in January 1969 to design competitive assault landing craft employing ACV technology. Subsequently, awards were made to both companies in March 1971 to build and test one craft per company.
These are air cushion or bubble craft, supported above the land or water surface by a continuously generated cushion or bubble of air held by flexible "skirts" that surround the base of the vehicle. According to US Navy usage, they differ from surface effect ships (SES) which have rigid sidewalls that penetrate the water surface to help hold the cushion or bubble. Official designation of these craft is Amphibious Assault Landing Craft (AALC), with the Aerojet-General design being referred to as AALC—Jeff(A) and the Bell Aerosystems craft as AALC—Jeff(B)
The two SES constructed for the US Navy are listed with Experimental, Research, and Surveying Ships; also see listing for Patrol Ships and Craft in this edition for additional SES programme details.

AEROJET-GENERAL DESIGN (Model)

(1) AMPHIBIOUS ASSAULT LANDING CRAFT (AALC): BELL DESIGN (JEFF-B)

Weight, tons	162·5 gross
Dimensions, feet	86·75 oa × 47 × (height) 23·5
Main/lift engines	6 gas turbines (Avco-Lycoming T40); 16 800 hp; interconnected with 2 aircraft-type propellers in rotating shrouds for propulsive thrust and 4 horizontal fans for cushion lift = approx 50 knots cruise
Complement	6

ACV landing craft being built by Bell Aerosystems. Scheduled for completion in February 1975 with delivery to Navy in February 1976 after extensive builder's trials.
Above dimensions are for craft on air cushion; when at rest dimensions are 80 × 43 × 19.
Aluminium construction; bow and stern ramps; cargo area of 1 738 square feet; three engines housed in each side structure with raised pilot house on starboard side. Performance parameters similar to Jeff (A).
Distinguished form Aerojet-General craft by having only two shrouded propellers for thrust and steering.

BELL AEROSYSTEMS DESIGN (Model)

56 UTILITY LANDING CRAFT: LCU 1610 SERIES

LCU 1613	**LCU 1627**	**LCU 1641**	**LCU 1651**	**LCU 1661**	**LCU 1671**
LCU 1614	**LCU 1628**	**LCU 1644**	**LCU 1653**	**LCU 1662**	**LCU 1672**
LCU 1616	**LCU 1629**	**LCU 1645**	**LCU 1654**	**LCU 1663**	**LCU 1673**
LCU 1617	**LCU 1630**	**LCU 1646**	**LCU 1655**	**LCU 1664**	**LCU 1674**
LCU 1618	**LCU 1631**	**LCU 1647**	**LCU 1656**	**LCU 1665**	**LCU 1675**
LCU 1619	**LCU 1632**	**LCU 1648**	**LCU 1657**	**LCU 1666**	**LCU 1676**
LCU 1621	**LCU 1633**	**LCU 1649**	**LCU 1658**	**LCU 1667**	**LCU 1677**
LCU 1623	**LCU 1634**	**LCU 1650**	**LCU 1659**	**LCU 1668**	**LCU 1678**
LCU 1624	**LCU 1637**	**LCU 1651**	**LCU 1660**	**LCU 1669**	**LCU 1679**
				LCU 1670	**LCU 1680**

Displacement, tons	200 light; 375 full load
Dimensions, feet	134·9 oa × 29 × 6·1
Guns	2—50 cal machine guns
Main engines	Diesels (Detroit); 1 000 bhp; 2 shafts = 11 knots (see *Engineering* notes)
Complement	12 to 14 (enlisted men)

Improved landing craft, larger than previous series; can carry three M-103 or M-48 tanks (approx 64 tons and 48 tons respectively). Cargo capacity 170 tons.
LCU 1610-1612 built by Christy Corp, Sturgeon Bay, Wisconsin; LCU 1613-1619, 1623, 1624 built by Gunderson Bros Engineering Corp, Portland, Oregon; LCU 1620, 1621,1625,1626,1629,1630 built by Southern Shipbuilding Corp, Slidell, Louisiana; LCU 1622 built by Weaver Shipyards, Texas; LCU 1627, 1628, 1631-1636 built by General Ship and Engine Works (last six units completed in 1968). LCU 1638-1645 built by Marinette Marine Corp, Marinette, Wisconsin (completed 1969-1970); LCU 1646-1666 built by Defoe Shipbuilding Co, Bay City, Michigan (completed 1970-1791). The one-of-a-kind aluminium hull, 133·8 ft LCU 1637 built by Pacific Coast Engineering Co, Alameda, California; LCU 1667-1670 built by General Ship & Engine Works, East Boston, in 1973-1974; LCU 1671-1680 built by Marinett Marine Corp, 1974-1976.
LCU 1636, 1638, 1639, 1640 reclassified as YFB 88-91 in October 1969 LCU 1620 and 1625 to YFU 92 and 93 respectively, in April 1971; LCU 1611, 1615 1622 to YFU 97-99 in Feb 1972; LCU 1610,1612 to YFU 100 and 101 respectively, in Aug 1972

ENGINEERING. These landing craft have four 250 bhp diesel engines with Kort-nozzle propellers on twin shafts except for the LCU 1620, 1621, and 1925 which have two 500-bhp diesel engines on vertical shafts fitted with vertical-axis, cycloidal six-bladed propellers. The cycloidal propellers provide thrust in any horizontal direction alleviating the need for rudders. The LCU 1622 was to have been fitted with gas-turbine propulsion machinery, but this project was cancelled.
Endurance is 1 200 miles at eight knots.

TRANSFERS. LCU 1626 was transferred to Burma in 1967.

PHOTOGRAPHS. Note amidships, right-side "island" structure of LCU 1649; LCU 1625 differs with built up-structure aft. All except LCU 1621 and 1625 have stern ramps.

LCU 1649 — *1970, Defoe Shipbuilding*

24 UTILITY LANDING CRAFT: LCU 1466 SERIES

LCU 1466	**LCU 1472**	**LCU 1485**	**LCU 1490**	**LCU 1537**
LCU 1467	**LCU 1477**	**LCU 1486**	**LCU 1492**	**LCU 1539**
LCU 1468	**LCU 1482**	**LCU 1487**	**LCU 1525**	**LCU 1547**
LCU 1469	**LCU 1484**	**LCU 1488**	**LCU 1535**	**LCU 1548**
LCU 1470		**LCU 1489**	**LCU 1536**	**LCU 1559**

Displacement, tons	180 light; 360 full load
Dimensions, feet	115 wl; 119 oa × 34 × 6 max
Guns	2—20 mm
Main engines	3 diesels (Gray Marine); 675 bhp; 3 shafts = 18 knots
Complement	14

These are enlarged versions of the World War II-built LCTs; constructed during the early 1950s. LCU 1608 and 1609 have modified propulsion systems; LCU 1582 and later craft have Kort nozzle propellers. LCU 1496 reclassified as YFU 70 on 1 Mar 1966; LCU 1471 to YFU 88 in May 1968; LCU 1576, 1582 and 1608 to YFU 89-91, respectively, in June 1970; LCU 1488, 1491, and 1609 to YFU 94-96 on 1 June 1971; YFU 94 reverted to LCU 1488 on 1 Feb 1972.

CLASSIFICATION. The earlier craft of this series were initially designated as Utility Landing Ships (LSU); redesignated Utility Landing Craft (LCU) on 15 Apr 1952 and classified as sevice craft.

DISPOSALS, TRANSFERS AND LOSSES

LCU 1478 was transferred to Norway and **LCU 1479, 1480, 1501, 1502** were transferred to South Vietnam upon completion; **LCU 1504-1593** were built under US Navy contract for US Army; **LCU 1594-1607** were built in Japan for the Japanese and Nationalist Chinese navies; **LCU 1503** lost accidentally in Aug 1953; **LCU 1476, 1483, 1495, 1497, 1499** to Department of the Interior in 1960-1979; **LCU 1475** to South Vietnam in 1969; **LCU 1493 1494** to South Vietnam in 1970; **LCU 1500** sunk in Vietnam in Mar 1969; **LCU 1481, 1498** to South Vietnam in 1972; **LCU 1473** to Mexico in 1975.

Landing Craft—*continued*

LCU 1468 with mast lowered *United States Navy*

LCU 1488 *1965, United States Navy*

21 UTILITY LANDING CRAFT: LCU 501 SERIES

LCU 539	**LCU 660**	**LCU 768**	**LCU 1124**	**LCU 1430**
LCU 588	**LCU 666**	**LCU 803**	**LCU 1241**	**LCU 1451***
LCU 599	**LCU 667**	**LCU 871**	**LCU 1348**	**LCU 1462**
LCU 608	**LCU 674**	**LCU 893**	**LCU 1348**	
LCU 654	**LCU 742**	**LCU 1045**	**LCU 1387**	

Displacement, tons	143 160 light; 309 to 320 full load
Dimensions, feet	105 wl; 119 oa × 32·7 × 5 max
Guns	2—20 mm
Main engines	Diesels (Gray Marine); 675 bhp; 3 shafts = 10 knots
Complement	13 (enlisted men)

Formerly LCT(6) 501-1465 series; built in 1943-1944. Can carry four tanks or 200 tons of cargo. LCU 524, 529, 550, 562, 592, 600, 629, 664, 666, 668, 677, 686, 742, 764, 776, 788, 840, 869, 877, 960, 973, 974, 979, 980, 1056, 1082, 1086, 1124, 1136, 1156, 1159, 1162, 1195, 1224, 1236, 1250, 1283, 1286, 1363, 1376, 1378, 1384, 1386, 1398, 1411, and 1430 reclassified as YFU 1 through 46, respectively, on 18 May 1958; LCU 1040 reclassified YFB 82 on 18 May 1958; LCU 1446 reclassified YFU 53 in 1964; LCU 509, 637, 646, 709, 716, 776, 851, 916, 973, 989, 1126, 1165, 1203, 1232, 1385, and 1388 reclassified as YFU 54 through 69, respectively, on 1 Mar 1966; LCU 780 reclassified as YFU 87. YFU 9 reverted to LCU 666 on 1 Jan 1962; LCU 1459 converted to YLLC 4; LCU 1462 to YFU 102 on 1 Aug 1973 changes reflect employment as general cargo craft assigned to shore commands (see section on Service Craft).

CLASSIFICATION. Originally rated as Landing Craft, Tank (LCT(6)); redesignated Utility Landing Ships (LSU) in 1949 to reflect varied employment; designation changed to Utility Landing Craft (LCU) on 15 Apr 1952 and classified as service craft.

See 1970-1971 edition for war losses, disposals, and transfers prior to 1965.

MECHANISED LANDING CRAFT: LCM 8 TYPE

Displacement, tons	115 full load (steel) or 105 full load (aluminium)
Dimensions, feet	75·6 × 73·7 oa or 21 × 5·2
Main engines	2 diesels (Detroit or General Motors); 650 bhp; 2 shafts = 9 knots
Complement	5 (enlisted men)

Constructed of welded-steel and (later units) aluminium. Can carry one M-48 or M-60 tank (both approx 48 tons) or 60 tons cargo; range is 150 nautical miles at full load. Also operated in large numbers by the US Army.

LCM-8 carrying M-48 tank *1970, United States Navy*

MECHANISED LANDING CRAFT: LCM 6 TYPE

Displacement, tons	60 to 62 full load
Dimensions, feet	56·2 oa × 14 × 3·9
Main engines	2 diesels; 450 bhp; 2 shafts = 9 knots

Welded-steel construction. Cargo capacity is 34 tons or 80 troops.

LANDING CRAFT VEHICLE AND PERSONNEL (LCVP)

Displacement, tons	13·5 full load
Dimensions, feet	35·8 oa × 10·5 × 3·5
Main engines	diesel; 1 shaft; 325 bhp = 9 knots

Constructed of wood or fibreglass-reinforced plastic. Fitted with 30-calibre machine guns when in combat areas. Cargo capacity, 8 000 lbs; range, 110 nautical miles at full load.

LCVP from LST 1157 *1969, United States Navy*

2 WARPING TUGS (LWT); NEW CONSTRUCTION

LWT 1 **LWT 2**

Displacement, tons	61 (hoisting weight)
Dimensions, feet	85 oa × 22 × 6·75
Main engines	2 diesels (Harbourmaster); 420 bhp; 2 steerable shafts = 9 knots
Complement	6 (enlisted men)

These craft are employed in amphibious landings to handle pontoon causeways. The LWT 1 and 2 are prototypes of a new, all-aluminium design completed in 1970. A collapsable A-frame is fitted forward to facilitate handling causeway anchors and ship-to-shore fuel lines. They can be "side loaded" on the main deck of an LST 1179 class ship or carried in an LPD/LSD type ship.

The propulsion motors are similar to outboard motors, providing both steering and thrust, alleviating the need for rudders.

Built by Campbell Machine, San Diego, California.

LWT 2 *United States Navy*

WARPING TUGS (LWT)

Displacement, tons	approx 120
Dimensions, feet	92·9 oa × 23 × 6·5
Main engines	2 outboard propulsion units = 6·5 knots

These craft are fabricated from pontoon sections and are assembled by the major amphibious commands as required.

LWT 85 *United States Navy*

PATROL SHIPS AND CRAFT

The US Navy programme to construct a series of 30 hydrofoil missile "ships" is intended to provide small surface combatants to help counter Soviet surface naval forces. Now designated "patrol combatant missile (hydrofoil)," these PHMs would operate against enemy surface ships and small craft, and conduct surveillance, screening, and special operations in coastal and inland water areas, and narrow seas.
The construction schedule of the PHM programme has been slowed due to funding difficulties; however, as noted below, it is hoped that they will be overcome during the next year to permit completion of the 30-ship class by 1980. According to the US Secretary of Defence, West Germany is interested in purchasing PHMs for NATO Baltic and North Sea operations. Reportedly, an initial German procurement of ten PHMs is planned.
Beyond the PHM programme, the US Navy continues to operate several "Asheville" class gun and missile craft in both active and Naval Reserve Force status. Two earlier hydrofoil craft, the *High Point* (PCH 1) and *Flagstaff* (PGH 1), are operated in a test and evaluation status. During 1974-1975 both craft were evaluated by the US Coast Guard (subsequently returned to Navy control). Finally, several patrol and riverine warfare craft are operated by the Naval Reserve Force, and two new designs (CPIC and PB) are being developed for US and foreign use. US use of these craft will be minimal; rather they are intended to compete with contemporary small craft built overseas in the foreign sales market.

SURFACE EFFECT SHIPS. The US Navy's effort to develop a 2 000-ton, 80-knot ocean-going SES as the prototype for warships of this configuration has been redesignated as the Advanced Naval Vehicles programme. This programme is described immediately after the listing for Frigates in this edition. The two 100-ton SES constructed for research and development are listed in the section on Experimental, Research, and Surveying Ships.

HERCULES (PHM 2) *Drawing by John J. Olson*

1+29 PATROL COMBATANTS—MISSILE (HYDROFOILS)

Name	*No*	*Laid down*	*Launch*	*Commission*
PEGASUS	PHM 1	10 May 1973	9 Nov 1974	July 1975
HERCULES	PHM 2	30 May 1974	1975	1975-1976
Four	**PHM 3-6**	Fiscal Year 1975 programme		
Two	**PHM 7-8**	Proposed FY 1976 programme		
Nine	**PHM 9-17**	Planned FY 1977 programme		
Thirteen	**PHM 18-30**	Planned FY 1978-1979 programmes		

Displacement, tons	221 full load
Dimensions, ft (*m*)	foils extended: 131·2 (*40·0*) oa × 29 (*8·9*) hull × 23·2 (*7·1*) foils retracted: 147·5 (*45·0*) oa × 29 (*8·9*) hull × 9·5 (*2·9*)
Missile launchers	8 launchers (quad) for Harpoon surface-to-surface missile
Guns	1—76 mm 62 calibre AA (Mk 75)
Main engines	foil borne; 1 gas turbine (General Electric); 18 000 shp; waterjet propulsion = 40+ knots hull borne; 2 diesels (Mercedes-Benz); 1 600 bhp; 2 waterjet propulsion units = 12 knots
Complement	approx 21 (accommodations for 4 officers, 17 enlisted men)

The Navy plans to construct 30 "ships" of this design for "shadowing" Soviet naval forces in restricted sea areas, as well as surveillance, screening of amphibious forces, and special missions. The PHM 1 and PHM 2 are being built by the Boeing Company, Seattle, Washington.
The PHM is being developed in conjunction with other NATO navies in an effort to develop a basic design that would be universally acceptable with minor modifications. Germany and Italy have joined the PHM effort with financial support of the ship's development.

The PHM 1 and PHM 2 were authorised in the Fiscal Year 1973 programme. Original estimated cost of the two ships was $77 000 000; subsequent cost increases caused an indefinite postponement of the second ship in 1974 with an additional $11 000 000 to complete test and evaluation of the PHM 1. The FY 1975 programme provided $92 300 000 for the PHM 3-6 with another $85 000 000 in FY 1976 to complete the four units ($44 325 000 each); additional funding is requested for "tooling up" to support a potential production capability of 12 ships per year (for US and allied requirements).
It is anticipated that the *Pegasus* will be engaged in trails and evaluation for several months after commissioning.

CLASSIFICATION. The designation PHM originally was for Patrol Hydrofoil-Missile; reclassified Patrol Combatant Missile (Hydrofoil) in July 1975.

ELECTRONICS. Fitted with the Mk 92 Mod 1 fire control system (Americanised version of the WM-28 radar and weapons control system developed by N. V. Hollandse Signaalapparaten). The Mk 92 will be used in the FFG 7 class guided missile frigates.

The LM 2500 marine gas turbine is also used in the "Spruance" class (DD 963) destroyers and FFG 7 class guided missile frigates.

GUNNERY. Gun armament is a single 76 mm OTO Melara rapid-fire weapon (designated Mk 75 Mod 1 in US service). The same gun will also be used in the FFG 7. No secondary gun armament is planned in US units.

MISSILES. Each PHM will have two four-tube lightweight cannister launchers for the Harpoon surface-to-surface missile. No reloads will be carried. This is double the Harpoon armament originally planned.

NOMENCLATURE. PHMs will be named for mythological terms. The PHM 1 originally was named *Delphinus*: renamed *Pegasus* on 26 Apr 1974.

PEGASUS (PHM 1) *1974, US Navy, PH2 Paul S. Burns*

PEGASUS (PHM 1) *1974, US Navy, PH2 Paul S. Burns*

OPERATIONAL. It is planned that these ships will be "in commission" and have commanding officers vice being "in service" with officers-in-charge. Normally they will have an operational endurance of five days, after which they will require refuelling and resupply.

PHOTOGRAPHS. The *Pegasus* is shown on this page and the following at time of launching; note she was fitted with only four missile launchers on fantail at that time. Three photographs of the *Pegasus* under construction appeared in the 1974-1975 edition.

Patrol Ships and Craft—*continued*

PEGASUS (PHM 1) *1974, Boeing Company*

14 PATROL COMBATANTS: "ASHEVILLE" CLASS

Name	*No.*	*Builder*	*Commissioned*
***ASHEVILLE** (NRF)	PG 84	Tacoma Boatbuilding	6 Aug 1966
***GALLUP**	PG 85	Tacoma Boatbuilding	22 Oct 1966
***ANTELOPE**	PG 86	Tacoma Boatbuilding	4 Nov 1967
***READY**	PG 87	Tacoma Boatbuilding	6 Jan 1968
***CROCKETT** (NRF)	PG 88	Tacoma Boatbuilding	24 June 1967
***MARATHON** (NRF)	PG 89	Tacoma Boatbuilding	11 May 1968
***CANON**	PG 90	Tacoma Boatbuilding	26 July 1968
***TACOMA**	PG 92	Tacoma Boatbuilding	14 July 1969
***WELCH**	PG 93	Peterson Builders	8 Sep 1969
***CHEHALIS**	PG 94	Tacoma Boatbuilding	11 Aug 1969
***GRAND RAPIDS**	PG 98	Tacoma Boatbuilding	5 Sep 1970
***BEACON**	PG 99	Peterson Builders	21 Nov 1969
***DOUGLAS**	PG 100	Tacoma Boatbuilding	6 Feb 1971
***GREEN BAY**	PG 101	Peterson Builders	5 Dec 1969

Displacement, tons	225 standard; 245 full load
Dimensions, feet	164·5 oa × 23·8 × 9·5
Missile launchers	2 launchers for Standard surface-to-surface missile in *Antelope, Ready, Grand Rapids, Douglas*
Guns	1—3 in (*76 mm*) 50 cal (forward); 1—40 mm (aft); 4—50 cal MG (twin) except 40 mm gun removed from ships with Standard missile
Main engines	CODAG: 2 diesels (Cummins); 1 450 shp; 2 shafts = 16 knots 1 gas turbine (General Electric); 13 300 shp; 2 shafts = 40+ knots
Complement	24 to 27 (3 officers, 21 to 24 enlisted men)

Originally a class of 17 patrol gunboats (PG ex-PGM) designed to perform patrol, blockade, surveillance, and support missions. No anti-submarine capability. Requirement for these craft was based on the volatile Cuban situation in the early 1960s. They are the largest patrol-type craft built by the US Navy since World War II and the first US Navy ships with gas-turbine propulsion.

Built by Tacoma Boatbuilding Co of Tacoma, Washington, and Petersen Builders of Sturgeon Bay, Wisconsin. PG 84 and PG 85 authorised in Fiscal Year 1963 new construction programme; PG 86 and PG 87 in FY 1964; PG 88-90 in FY 1965; PG 92-101 in FY 1966. *Asheville* was laid down on 15 Apr 1964 and launched on 1 May 1965; later ships approximately 18 months from keel laying to completion. Cost per ship approximately $5 000 000.

Only three units assigned to Naval Reserve Force and manned by composite active-reserve crews; 11 units retained in active service with four missile-armed units based in Mediterranean. Furthur transfers to other Navies have been delayed.

CLASSIFICATION. These ships were originally classified as motor gunboats (PGM); reclassified as patrol boats (PG) with same hull numbers on 1 Apr 1967. This created a duplication of hull numbers used by the US Navy during World War II for designating ex-British "Arabis" or "Flower" class corvettes acquired under "reverse" lend lease in early 1942 and similar ships built in Canada with US funds (the Canadian-built ships serving in the US or Royal Navy); the first PG 101 was the Canadian-built *Asheville* the first of the US Navy's World War II "frigates" (subsequently redesignated PF 1).
PGM 1-32 were submarine chasers modified during World War II with additional guns; PGM 33-83, 91, 102-121 assigned to gunboats built since 1955 for transfer to foreign navies.
Classification of the 14 surviving PGs changed again in July 1975 to patrol combatants.

DESIGN. All-aluminium hull and aluminium-fibreglass superstructure. Because of the heat-transmitting qualities of the aluminium hull and the amount of waste heat produced by a gas turbine engine the ships are completely air conditioned.

ENGINEERING. These ships have a Combination Diesel and Gas Turbine (CODAG) propulsion system with twin diesel engines for cruising and a gas turbine for high-speed operations. The gas turbine is an LM1500 with the gas generator essentially the same as the J-79-8 aircraft engine (used in the F-4 Phantom and other aircraft). The transfer from diesel to gas turbine propulsion (or vica versa) can be accomplished while underway with no loss of speed. From full stop these ships can attain 40 knots in one minute; manoeuvrability is exellent due in part to controllable pitch-propellers. Speed and propeller pitch is controlled directly from the pilot house console. Either JP-5 or diesel fuel can be used for both the gas turbine and diesels.
Arrangement of gas turbine intake differs on later ships.

GUNNERY. The *Antelope* and *Ready* have the Mk 87 weapons control system for rapid acquisition and tracking of fast-moving targets; the system can also direct and fire appropriate weapons automatically. The Mk 87 can operate in a radar mode or with a stabilised optical sight on the weather decks. No further procurement of this advanced fire control system is planned in the Navy although it is being fitted to a number of foreign warships. (The Mk 87 is an American-produced copy of the Hollandse Signaalapparaten M22 weapons control system). Other ships have Mk 63 Mod 29 Gunfire Control System with SPG-50 fire control radar.
Mk 34 3 inch gun forward in closed mount and Mk 3 40 mm gun in open mount aft.

"ASHEVEILLE" CLASS—*continued*

MISSILES. The *Benica* (PG 96) was experimentally fitted with a single launcher aft for the Standard interim anti-ship missile in 1971; removed prior to transfer to South Korea later that year.
During the latter part of 1971 the *Antelope* and *Ready* were provided with two standard missile launchers. The box-like missile launchers are fitted at the stern (40 mm gun removed); a reload is provided in an adjacent magazine for each launcher; subsequently *Grand Rapids* and *Douglas* fitted with missiles.

NOMENCLATURE. Patrol gunboats are named for small American cities; however, the *Surprise* remembers several earlier US naval ships.

TRANSFERS
Benecia (PG 96) transferred to South Korea on 2 Oct 1971; **Surprise** (PG 97) transferred to Turkey on 28 Feb 1973. **Defiance** (PG 95) transferred to Turkey on 11 June 1973; **Beacon** (PG 99), **Green Bay** (PG 101) transferred to Greece in 1975.

PHOTOGRAPHS. Note Mk 87 antenna in *Antelope* and *Ready*. The first *Antelope* photograph shows s Standard missile raised to firing position on fantail. The gas turbine air intake is immediately aft of the bridge structure; the adjacent large funnel is the turbine exhaust with a smaller diesel exhaust stack on either side. A photograph of the *Antelope* firing a Standard missile appears in the 1974-1975 edition.

ANTELOPE (PG 86) *1972, General Dynamics*

READY (PG 87) *1973, Giorgio Arra*

ANTELOPE (PG 86) *1973, Giorgio Arra*

DOUGLAS (PG 100) *1971, Tacoma Boatbuilding*

Patrol Ships and Craft—*continued*

1 HYDROFOIL GUNBOAT (PGH): "FLAGSTAFF" TYPE

Name	No.	Laid down	Launched	In service
*FLAGSTAFF	PGH 1	15 July 1966	9 Jan 1968	July 1968

Displacement, tons	56·8 full load
Dimensions, feet	74·4 oa × 21·4 × 4·5 (hull borne) or 13·5 (foils down)
Guns	removed
Main engines	foil borne: 1 gas turbine (Rolls Royce); 3 620 hp; controllable pitch propeller = 40+ knots hull borne; 2 diesels (General Motors); 300 bhp water-jet propulsion = 8 knots
Complement	13 (1 officer, 12 enlisted men)

The *Flagstaff* was a competitive prototype evaluated with the *Tucumcari* (PGH 2). Built by Grumman Aircraft Corporation in Stuart, Florida. Construction cost was $3 600 000. The *Flagstaff* has conducted sea trials with a 152 mm howitzer (see *Gunnery* notes), foil-mounted sonars, and towed shapes representing variable depth sonar (VDS). From 1 November 1974 to 20 December 1974 the *Flagstaff* was evaluated by the Coast Guard to determine possible roles for this type of craft.

DESIGN. The *Flagstaff* has a conventional foil arrangement with 70 per cent of the craft's weight supported by the forward set of foils and 30 per cent of the weight supported by the stern foils. Steering is accomplished by movement of the stern strut about its vertical axis. Foil-borne operation is automatically controlled by a wave-height sensing system. The foils are fully retractable for hull-borne operations. Aluminium construction.

ENGINEERING. During foil-borne operations the propeller is driven by a geared transmission system contained in the tail strut and in the pod located at the strut-foil connection. During hull-borne operation two diessel engines drive a water-jet propulsion system. Water enters the pump inlets through openings in the hull and the thrust is exerted by water flow through nozzles in the transome. Steering in the hull-borne mode is by deflection vanes in the water stream. Rolls-Royce Tyne Mk 621 gas turbine engine.

GUNNERY. Originally armed with one 40 mm gun forward, four ·50 cal MG amidships, and an 81 mm mortar aft. Rearmed in 1971 with a 152 mm gun forward. The weapon was the same used on the Army's Sheridan armoured reconnaissance vehicle; low-velocity firing a fully combustible cartridge. After firing trials in 1971 the gun was removed. See 1974-1975 and previous editions for photographs showing guns installed.

FLAGSTAFF *United States Navy*

FLAGSTAFF (PGH 1) *1974, US Coast Guard*

FLAGSTAFF (PGH 1) *1974, US Coast Guard*

1 HYDROFOIL SUBMARINE CHASER (PCH): "HIGH POINT" TYPE

Name	No.	Laid down	Launched	In service
*HIGH POINT	PCH 1	27 Feb 1961	17 Aug 1962	3 Sep 1963

Displacement, tons	100 full load
Dimensions, feet	115 oa × 31 × 6 (hull borne) or 17 (foils down)
Guns	removed
A/S weapons	4 torpedo tubes (twin)
Main engines	foil borne; 2 gas turbines (Bristol Siddeley Marine Proteus); 6 200 shp; 2 paired counter-rotating propellers = 48 knots hull borne; diesel (Curtis Wright); 600 bhp; retractable outdrive with 1 propeller = 12 knots
Complement	13 (1 officer, 12 enlisted men)

Experimental hydrofoil submarine chaser. Authorised under Fiscal Year 1960 programme. Built jointly by Boeing Aircraft Corpn, Seattle, Washington, and J. M. Martinac, Tacoma, Washington, at Martinac's Tacoma Yard. Employed in experimental hydrofoil work. During March 1975 the *High Point* was evaluated by the Coast Guard.

DESIGN. The *High Point's* forward foil is supported by a single strut and the after foil by twin struts. Twin underwater nacelles at the junction of the vertical struts and main full housed contra-rotating, super-cavitating propellers for foil-borne propulsion. After foils modified in 1973 and nacelles repositioned to improve performance in heavy sea states. Also, forward foil strut made steerable to improve manoeuvrability. Note outboard propeller in raised position in the photographs. The twin "hump" cover the retracted hydrofoil struts.

GUNNERY. A single 40 mm gun was mounted forward in 1968; subsequently removed.

MISSILES. During 1973-1974 the *High Point* was employed as a test ship for the light-weight cannister launchers for the Harpoon surface-to-surface missile intended for the PHM.

LOSSES

The hydrofoil gunboat **Tucumcari** (PGH 2) ran aground on 16 Nov 1972 and wrecked; plans to restore the craft were dropped due to high costs and she was scrapped in October 1973.

HIGH POINT (PCH 1) firing Harpoon *1973, McDonnell Douglas*

HIGH POINT (PCH 1) firing Harpoon *1973, McDonnell Douglas*

HIGH POINT (PCH 1) on early trials *United States Navy*

Patrol Ships and Craft—*continued*

4 FAST PATROL BOATS (PTF): PTF 23 TYPE

• PTF 23 **• PTF 24** **• PTF 25** **• PTF 26**

Displacement, tons	105 full load
Dimensions, feet	94·66 oa × 23·2 × 7
Guns	1—81 mm mortar; 1—50 cal MG (mounted over mortar); 1—40 mm (aft); 2—20 mm (single)
Main engines	2 diesels (Napier Deltic); 6 200 bhp; 2 shafts = approx 40 knots
Complement	approx 20

PTF 23-26 built by Sewart Seacraft Division of Teledyne Inc of Berwick, Louisiana. First unit completed in 1967, others in 1968. Aluminium hulls. Commercial name is "Osprey".

All 17 PTFs are in service and are assigned to the Naval Reserve Force. 5 are based at San Diego, California; 5 at Norfolk, Virginia; 4 at New Orleans, Louisiana; and 3 on the Great Lakes.

PTF 23 TYPE *United States Navy*

6 FAST PATROL BOATS (PTF): PTF 17 TYPE

• PTF 17 **• PTF 18** **• PTF 19** **• PTF 20** **• PTF 21** **• PTF 22**

Displacement, tons	85 full load
Dimensions, feet	80·3 oa × 24·5 × 6·8
Guns (may vary)	1—81 mm mortar; 1—40 mm; 2—20 mm (single); 1—50 cal MG (mounted over mortar)
Main engines	2 diesels (Napier-Deltic); 6 200 bhp; 2 shafts = approx 45 knots
Complement	19 (3 officers, 16 enlisted men)

PTF 17-22 built by John Trumpy & Sons, Annapolis, Maryland; lead boat completed in late 1967, others 1968-1970. Based on "Nasty" design.
All six units are in service (PTF 21 and 22 were given "commissioned" status on 14 May 1969 but subsequently returned to "in service" on 23 Sep 1970).

PTF 17 Type *1972, Courtesy Ships of the World*

7 FAST PATROL BOATS (PTF): "NASTY" TYPE

• PTF 3 **• PTF 5** **• PTF 6** **• PTF 7** **• PTF 10** **• PTF 11** **• PTF 12**

Displacement, tons	85 full load
Dimensions, feet	80·3 oa × 24·5 × 6·8
Guns (may vary)	1—81 mm mortar; 1—40 mm; 2—20 mm (single); 1—50 cal MG (mounted over mortar)
Main engines	2 diesels (Napier-Deltic); 6 200 bhp; 2 shafts = 45 knots
Complement	19 (3 officers, 16 enlisted men)

PTF 3-16 of the "Nasty" type were built by Boatservice Ltd A/S of Mandal, Norway. Same design as the Norwegian Navy's "Tjeld" class torpedo boats. PTF 3 and PTF 4 delivered to USA in December 1962, PTF 5-8 in April 1964, and PTF 9-16 in September 1964. Hulls made of two layers of mahogany which sandwich a layer of fibreglass. British engines. Endurance is 450 miles at 41 knots or 600 miles at 25 knots.

DISPOSALS AND LOSSES
PTF 1 (ex-PT 810) and **PTF 2** (ex-PT 811) stricken from the Navy list on 1 Aug 1955 (sunk as targets). Sunk in Vietnam: **PTF 4** on Nov 4 1965, **PTF 8** on 16 June 1966, **PTF 9** on 7 Mar 1966, **PTF 14** on 22 Apr 1966, **PTF 15** on 22 Apr 1966, and **PTF 16** on 19 Aug 1966; **PTF 13** disposed of in 1972.

PTF 6 *1973, United States Navy*

1 COASTAL PATROL AND INTERDICTION CRAFT

Displacement, tons	71·25 full load
Dimensions, feet	99·2 oa × 18 × 6
Guns	2—30 mm MG (twin)
Main engines	3 gas turbines (Avco-Lycoming TF-25); 5 400 hp; water-jet propulsion = 45 knots; 2 auxiliary outboard drive diesels; 300 bhp
Complement	approx 15 (varies with armament)

The US Navy has developed the Coastal Patrol and Interdiction Craft (CPIC) for coastal/inshore operations, succeeding the PTF types. The CPIC is capable of operating in rougher water than the PTFs and is more adaptable for cold and hot weather operating areas.

The prototype CPIC was built by Tacoma Boatbuilding Co, Tacoma, Washington; completed in 1974. The prototype will be transferred to South Korea after trials and evaluation. Additional units are reported being built in South Korea. US Navy requirements for these craft are being studied.
Basic CPIC design provides for two 30 mm twin gun mounts, one forward and one amidships on 01 deck level aft of bridge. Other weapons may be carried as required for specific operations including possibly the Harpoon missile in light weight canister launcher.

CPIC on trials *1974, United States Navy*

5 PATROL BOATS (PB): NEW DESIGN

2 **PB** Mark I series
3 **PB** Mark III series

Displacement, tons	Mk I: 26·9 light; 36·3 full load Mk III: 31·5 light; 41·25 full load
Dimensions, feet	Mk I: 65 oa × 16 × 4·9 Mk III: 65 oa × 18 × 5·9
Guns	6—20 mm or ·50 cal MG (1 twin, 4 single)
Main engines	Diesel (Detroit); 1 635 bhp; 3 shafts = 26 knots

The PB series is being developed as replacements for the "Swift" type inshore patrol craft (PCF). Mk I built by Sewart Seacraft, Berwick, Louisiana; Mk III by Peterson Builders Sturgeon Bay, Wisconsin. Two Mark I prototypes completed in 1972 and delivered to the Navy in 1973 for evaluation; assigned to Naval Reserve Force. Additional units of the Mk III design are being constructed for the Philippine Navy. Procurement of the PB Mk III for the US Navy is under consideration. (The PB Mark II design was not built).

Basic weapons arrangement provides for a twin gun mounting above the pilot house and four single mountings on the main deck. The Mk III design has the pilot house offset to starboard to provide space on port side for installation of additional weapons (see drawing).

OPERATIONAL. These craft and the patrol and riverine craft listed on the following page are operated by the Naval Reserve Force.
Two Mk III units provided to Philippines (see Addenda).

PB Mk I on trials *1972, Sewart Seacraft*

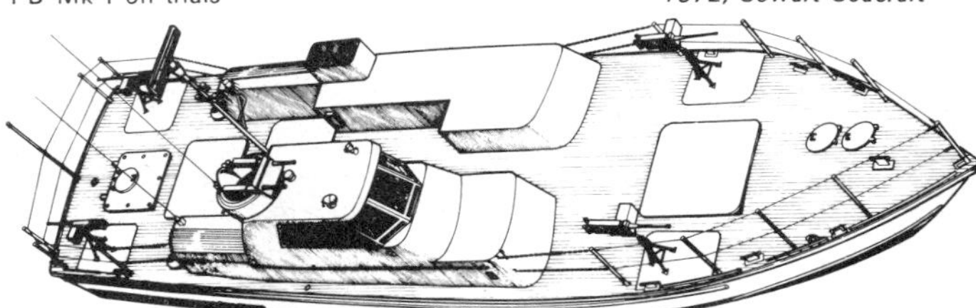

PB Mk III

Patrol Ships and Craft—*continued*

5 PATROL CRAFT (PCF): "SWIFT" TYPE

five **PCF** Mark I series

Displacement, tons	22·5 full load
Dimensions, feet	50·1 oa × 13 × 3·5
Guns	1—81 mm mortar, 3—50 cal MG (twin MG mount atop pilot house and single MG mounted over mortar)
Main engines	2 geared diesels (General Motors); 960 shp; 2 shafts = 28 knots
Complement	6 (1 officer, 5 enlisted men)

The "Swift" design is adapted from the all-metal crew boat which is used to support off-shore drilling rigs in the Gulf of Mexico. Approximately 125 built since 1965. Most transferred to South Vietnam (see below).
Designation changed from Fast Patrol Craft (PCF) to Inshore Patrol Craft on 14 Aug 1968.

TRANSFERS. PCF 33, 34, and 83-86 transferred to the Philippines in 1966. Additional PCFs of this type constructed specifically for transfer to Thailand, the Philippines, and South Korea; not assigned US hull numbers in the PCF series. 104 PCFs formerly manned by US Navy personnel transferred to South Vietnam in 1968-1970.

PCF MARK I TYPE *1969, United States Navy*

29 RIVER PATROL BOATS (PBR)

29 **PBR** Mk II series

Displacement, tons	8
Dimensions, feet	32 oa × 11 × 2·6
Guns	3—·50 cal MG (twin mount forward; single aft); 1—40 mm grenade launcher; 1—60 mm mortar in some boats
Main engines	2 geared diesels (General Motors); water jets = 25+ knots
Complement	4 or 5 (enlisted men)

Fibreglass hull river patrol boats. Approximately 500 built 1967-1973; most transferred to South Vietnam.

PBR Mk II Type *United States Navy*

2 ASSAULT SUPPORT PATROL BOATS (ASPB)

Displacement, tons	36·25 full load
Dimensions, feet	50 oa × 15·6 × 3·75
Guns (varies)	1 or 2—20 mm (with 2—·50 cal MG in boats with one 20 mm) 2—30 cal MG; 2—40 mm high-velocity grenade launchers
Main engines	2 diesels (General Motors); 2 shafts = 14 knots sustained
Complement	6 (enlisted)

The ASPB was designed specifically for riverine operations to escort other river craft, provide mine countermeasures during river operations, and interrupt enemy river traffic. Welded-steel hulls. Armament changed to above configuration in 1968; some boats have twin—50 cal MG "turret" forward in place of single 20 mm gun.
Note that open stern well is plated over in the ASPB pictured here (A-131-2); a view of an ASPB with 81 mm mortar/·50 cal MG aft appears in the 1968-1969 editions.

ASSAULT SUPPORT PATROL BOAT (ASPB) *1968, United States Navy*

14 "MINI" ARMOURED TROOP CARRIERS (ATC)

Dimensions feet	36 oa × 12·66 × 3·5
Main engines	2 diesels (General Motors); water-jet propulsion = 28 knots except one unit with gas turbines.
Complement	2
Troops	15 to 20

A small troop carrier for riverine and swimmer delivery operations; aluminium hull; ceramic armour. Draft is one foot when underway at high speed. The last of the Vietnam-era ATCs have been disposed of along with several hundred other riverine warfare craft.

"MINI" ARMOURED TROOP CARRIER (36-ft)

1 COMMAND AND CONTROL BOAT (CCB)

Displacement, tons	80 full load
Dimensions, feet	61 oa × 17·5 × 3·4
Guns	3—20 mm; 2—·30 cal MG; 2—40 mm high velocity-grenade launchers
Main engines	2 diesels (Detroit); 2 shafts = 8·5 knots max (6 knots sustained)
Complement	11

These craft serve as afloat command posts providing command and communications facilities for ground force and boat group commanders. Heavily armoured. Armament changed to above configuration in 1968. Converted from LCM-6 landing craft.

COMMAND CONTROL BOAT *United States Navy*

SUPPORT CRAFT

The US Navy operates several specialised craft in support of "frogmen" (combat swimmers) assigned to SEAL (Sea-Air-Land) teams, Underwater Demolition Teams (UDT), and Explosive Ordnance Disposal (EOD) teams. Most of the craft listed in previous editions have been discarded and the primary craft in service today is the 36-foot Medium SEAL Support Craft (MSSC). Several SEAL support craft are operated by the Naval Reserve Force. A new craft for this role will probably be developed in the near future.

MEDIUM SEAL SUPPORT CRAFT(MSSC) *United States Navy*

MINE WARFARE SHIPS

The US Navy's mine warfare forces have undergone substantial reductions during the past few years. The Navy currently operates only three ocean minesweepers (MSO) in active service with another 22 assigned to the Naval Reserve Force and partially manned by reserve personnel. The nine smaller coastal minesweepers (MSC) that had been assigned to the NRF have been phased out of service.
The reductions have been offset, in part, by the use of mine countermeasures helicopter. As of mid-1975 the Navy operated 21 RH-53D Sea Stallion helicopters in Mine Countermeasure Squadron 12. These helicopters tow hydrofoil sleds and other devices to detonate underwater mines. They were used extensively to clear North Vietnamese ports and inland waterways during Operation End Sweep in 1973 and to help clear the Suez Canal during Operation Nimbus Star in 1974. The RH-53 Sea Stallions can operate from amphibious ships, especially the LPH/LHA helicopter carriers, and are air-transportable in Air Force C-5A Galaxy long-range transports. These helicopters do not have a good airborne mine-hunting capability and are limited in their ability to clear mines. The Navy's proposed five-year shipbuilding programme includes a new series of mine countermeasure craft with one unit planned for funding in the Fiscal Year 1978 budget and three in FY 1980.
The US Navy maintains no surface ships with a minelaying capability. Rather, the Navy can plant mines by carrier-based attack aircraft (as was done in Vietnam), land-based maritime patrol aircraft, and attack submarines. Although the covert nature of submarine operations makes them preferable in certain minelaying situations, modern US attack submarines have only four torpedo tubes and a limited number of reload spaces, severely restricting their capacity for the tube-launched mines. The large B-52 Stratofortress bombers of the Strategic Air Command can also plant sea mines. The use of B-52s in the minelaying role presupposes the availability of the aircraft for this purpose, the proximity of suitable air bases, and no interference from hostile aircraft in the mining area.

PHOTOGRAPHS. At right a CH-53A Sea Stallion modified as an interim mine countermeasures helicopter lifts a Mk 106 minesweeping sled from the deck of the amphibious transport dock *Trenton* (LPD 14). During operation the Y-shape foils on the sled fold down for high-speed towing through the water.

ADVANCE (MSO 510) *1968, United States Navy*

OCEAN MINESWEEPER (MSO): "ABILITY" CLASS

The two surviving minesweepers of this class, **Alacrity** (MSO 520) and **Assurance** (MSO 521), have been allocated to sonar test programmes and redesignated as auxiliary ships AG 520 and AG 521, respectively. See listing under Experimental, Research, and Surveying Ships. **Ability** (MSO 519) of this class stricken on 1 Feb 1971.

4 OCEAN MINESWEEPERS (MSO): "ACME" CLASS

Name	No.	Launched	Commissioned
ACME	MSO 508	23 June 1955	27 Sep 1956
***ADROIT** (NRF)	MSO 509	20 Aug 1955	4 Mar 1957
ADVANCE	MSO 510	12 July 1957	16 June 1958
***AFFRAY** (NRF)	MSO 511	18 Dec 1956	8 Dec 1958

Displacement, tons	720 light; 780 full load
Dimensions, feet	173 oa × 35 × 10
Guns	1—20 mm AA or 1—40 mm AA; 2—·50 cal MG
Main engines	4 diesels (Packard), 2 800 bhp; 2 shafts = 14 knots
Complement	78 (8 officers, 70 enlisted men); 86 in NRF ships (3 officers, 36 enlisted active duty; 3 officers, 44 enlisted reserve)

This class is different from the "Agile" type but has similar basic particulars. All built by Frank L. Sample, Jnr, Inc, Boothbay Harbour, Maine. Plans to modernise these ships were cancelled (see notes under "Agile" class).
Two ships were decommissioned and placed in reserve late in 1970. *Adroit* and *Affray* are assigned to Naval Reserve training, manned partially by active and partially by reserve personnel (see notes under "Agile" class).

NOMENCLATURE. The ocean minesweepers are named for terms expressing action or aggressiveness.

PHOTOGRAPHS. Note 40 mm gun in *Affray* and 20 mm gun visible in *Advance*.

ADVANCE (MSO 510) *1968, United States Navy*

AFFRAY (MSO 511) *1969, United States Navy*

33 OCEAN MINESWEEPERS (MSO): "AGILE" CLASS

Name	No.	Launched	Commissioned
***CONSTANT** (NRF)	MSO 427	14 Feb 1952	8 Sep 1954
***DASH** (NRF)	MSO 428	20 Sep 1952	14 Aug 1953
***DETECTOR** (NRF)	MSO 429	5 Dec 1952	26 Jan 1954
***DIRECT** (NRF)	MSO 430	27 May 1953	9 July 1954
***DOMINANT** (NRF)	MSO 431	5 Nov 1953	8 Nov 1954
***ENGAGE** (NRF)	MSO 433	18 June 1953	29 June 1954
***ENHANCE** (NRF)	MSO 437	11 Oct 1952	16 Apr 1955
***ESTEEM** (NRF)	MSO 438	20 Dec 1952	10 Sep 1955
***EXCEL** (NRF)	MSO 439	25 Sep 1953	24 Feb 1955
***EXPLOIT** (NRF)	MSO 440	10 Apr 1953	31 Mar 1954
***EXULTANT** (NRF)	MSO 441	6 June 1953	22 June 1954
***FEARLESS** (NRF)	MSO 442	17 July 1953	22 Sep 1954
***FIDELITY**	MSO 443	21 Aug 1953	19 Jan 1955
***FORTIFY** (NRF)	MSO 446	14 Feb 1953	16 July 1954
***ILLUSIVE**	MSO 448	12 July 1952	14 Nov 1953
***IMPERVIOUS** (NRF)	MSO 449	29 Aug 1952	15 July 1954
***IMPLICIT** (NRF)	MSO 455	1 Aug 1953	10 Mar 1954
***INFLICT** (NRF)	MSO 456	6 Oct 1953	11 May 1954
LUCID	MSO 458	14 Nov 1953	4 May 1955
NIMBLE	MSO 459	6 Aug 1954	11 May 1955
OBSERVER	MSO 461	19 Oct 1954	31 Aug 1955
PINNACLE	MSO 462	3 Jan 1955	21 Oct 1955
***PLUCK** (NRF)	MSO 464	6 Feb 1954	11 Aug 1954
SKILL	MSO 471	23 Apr 1955	7 Nov 1955
VITAL	MSO 474	12 Aug 1953	9 June 1955
***CONQUEST** (NRF)	MSO 488	20 May 1954	20 July 1955
***GALLANT** (NRF)	MSO 489	4 June 1954	14 Sep 1955
***LEADER**	MSO 490	15 Sep 1954	16 Nov 1955
***PLEDGE** (NRF)	MSO 492	20 July 1955	20 Apr 1956
STURDY	MSO 494	28 Jan 1956	23 Oct 1957
SWERVE	MSO 495	1 Nov 1955	27 July 1957
VENTURE	MSO 496	27 Nov 1956	3 Feb 1958

Mine Warfare Ships—*continued*

"AGILE" CLASS—*continued*

Displacement, tons	665 light; 750 full load
Dimensions, feet	165 wl; 172 × 36 × 13·6
Guns	1—40 mm AA; 2—·50 cal MG (replaced by 2—20 mm AA in several ships); some modernised ships are unarmed
Main engines	4 diesels (Packard); 2 shafts; controllable pitch propellers; 2 280 bhp = 15·5 knots; *Dash, Detector, Direct* and *Dominant*, have 4 diesels (General Motors); 1 520 bhp (see *Modernisation* notes)
Complement	78 (8 officers, 70 enlisted men); 86 in NRF ships (3 officers, 36 enlisted active duty; 3 officers, 44 enlisted reserve)

These ships were built on the basis of mine warfare experience in the Korean War (1950-1953); they have wooden hulls and non-magnetic equipment. All of the above ships were built in private shipyards. Thirty-six ships of this class transferred to NATO navies upon completion.
Initially designated as minesweepers (AM); reclassified as ocean minesweepers (MSO) in Feb 1955. Originally fitted with UQS-1 mine detecting sonar.
Beginning in 1970 most of these ships have been decommissioned and placed in reserve or assigned to Naval Reserve training; see *Status* notes.

ENGINEERING. Diesel engines are fabricated of non-magnetic stainless steel alloy to help reduce possibility of detonating magnetic mines. Range is 2 400 miles at ten knots.

MODERNISATION. The 62 ocean minesweepers in commission during the mid-1960s were all to have been modernised; estimated cost and schedule per ship were $5 000 000 and ten months in shipyard. However, some of the early modernisations took as long as 26 months which, coupled with changes in mine countermeasures technique, led to cancellation of programme after 13 ships were modernised: MSO 433, 437, 438, 441-443, 445, 446, 448, 449, 456, 488, and 490.
The modernisation provided improvements in mine detection, engines, communications, and habitability: four Waukesha Motor Co diesel engines installed (plus two or three diesel generators for sweep gear), SQQ-14 sonar with mine classification as well as detection capability provided, twin 20 mm AA in some ships (replacing single 40 mm because of space requirements for sonar hoist mechanism), habitability improved, and advanced communications equipment fitted; bridge structure in modernised ships extended around mast and aft to funnel. Complement in active modernised ships is 6 officers and 70 enlisted men.
Some MSOs have received SQQ-14 sonar but not full modernisation.

OPERATIONAL. Only three of these ships remain in active Navy commission: *Fidelity, Illusive*, and *Leader*; 20 others are assigned to the Naval Reserve Force and are manned by mixed active duty and reserve crews; and 10 ships are laid up in reserve.

TRANSFERS. Ships of this class serve in the navies of Belgium, France, Italy, Netherlands, Norway, Peru, Philippines, Portugal, Spain, Taiwan China, Thailand, and Uruguay.

DISPOSALS AND TRANSFERS (since 1 Jan 1970)
Avenge MSO 423 stricken on 1 Feb 1970 (fire); **Sagacity** MSO 469 stricken on 1 Oct 1970 (grounding); **Notable** MSO 460, **Rival** MSO 468, **Salute** MSO 470, **Valor** MSO 472 stricken on 1 Feb 1971; **Vigor** MSO 473 transferred to Spain on 5 Apr 1972; **Conflict** MSO 426, **Guide** MSO 447 stricken on 9 June 1972; **Dynamic** MSO 432; **Pivot** MSO 463, **Persistent** MSO 491 to Spain on 1 Aug 1972; **Endurance** MSO 435, **Loyalty** MSO 457 stricken on 1 July 1972; **Energy** MSO 436, **Firm** MSO 444 transferred to the Philippines on 5 July 1972; **Force** MSO 445 sunk 24 April 1973 (fire); **Aggressive** MSO 422, **Embattle** MSO 434 transferred to Peru, **Bold** MSO 424, **Bulwark** MSO 425 transferred to Taiwan China, **Prime** MSO 466, **Reaper** MSO 467 transferred to Thailand, all 1974-1975.

LEADER (MSO 490) no gun — *1972, Harbor Boat Building Co*

EXCEL (MSO 439) no gun — *1971, United States Navy*

EXPLOIT (MSO 440) with 40 mm gun — *1969, United States Navy*

ENHANCE (MSO 437) no gun — *1971, Harbor Boat Building Co*

COASTAL MINESWEEPERS (MSC): "BLUEBIRD" CLASS

All surviving coastal minesweepers of the 144-foot "Bluebird" class were to have been stricken during 1975-1976. The nine ships active into 1975 were assigned to the Naval Reserve Force. See 1974-1975 and previous editions for characteristics and photographs.

TRANSFERS. Minesweepers of this class serve in the navies of Belgium, Denmark, France, Greece, Indonesia, Japan, South Korea, Netherlands, Norway, Pakistan, Philippines, Portugal, Spain, Taiwan China, Thailand, Tunisia, Turkey, and South Korea. (See 1971-1972 and previous editions for details of earlier transfers).

DISPOSALS AND TRANSFERS (since 1 Jan 1970)
Jacana MSC 193, **Meadow Lark** MSC 196 transferred to Indonesia on 7 Apr 1971; **Falcon** MSC 190, **Limpkin** MSC 195 to Indonesia on 24 June 1971; **Hummingbird** MSC 192 to Indonesia on 12 July 1971; **Frigate Bird** MSC 191 to Indonesia on 11 Aug 1971; **Kingbird** MSC 194 stricken on 1 July 1972 (collision); **Parrot** MSC 197 stricken in Aug 1972; **Widgeon** MSC 208 stricken on 2 July 1973; **Parrot** MSC 197 stricken on 22 Aug 1973 (employed as training ship for Navy League Sea Cadets in Washington, DC); **Comorant** MSC 122 stricken on 15 Mar 1974; **Bluebird** MSC 121 transferred to Thailand in 1975; **Peacock** MSC 198, **Phoebe** MSC 199, **Shrike** MSC 201, **Thrasher** MSC 203, **Thrush** MSC 204, **Vireo** MSC 205, **Warbler** MSC 206, **Whippoorwill** MSC 207, **Woodpecker** MSC 209 stricken in 1975-1976.
Albatross MSC 289 and **Gannet** MSC 290 of a modified design were stricken on 1 Apr 1970.

FLEET MINESWEEPERS (MSF): "AUK" AND "ADMIRABLE" CLASSES

The 29 surviving fleet minesweepers (MSF) of the "Auk" and "Admirable" classes were stricken by the US Navy on 1 July 1972. See 1972-1973 and previous editions for names, hull numbers, and characteristics. Subsequently, 21 of these ships were transferred to Mexico on 19 Sep 1972 and in Feb 1973, with 10 ships intended for active service and the remainder for parts cannibalisation.

TRANSFERS. Ships of the "Auk" class serve in the navies of South Korea, Mexico, Norway, Peru, Philippines, Taiwan China, and Uruguay; ships of the "Admirable" class serve in the navies of Burma, Dominican Republic, Mexico, Taiwan China, and South Vietnam.

Bittern MHC 43, a prototype coastal mine hunter built in 1955-1957, has been on loan to a commercial operator since July 1966; officially stricken by US Navy on 1 Feb 1972.

MINE COUNTERMEASURES SHIPS (MCS)

The large mine countermeasures ship **Ozark** MCS 2 (ex-LSV 2, ex-CM 7, ex-AP 107) stricken in 1974.
All other mine countermeasure ships, fleet minelayers (MMF), and fast minelayers (MMD) have been stricken or transferred to other navies. See 1973-1974 and previous editions for MCS characteristics and ship lists.

MINE COUNTERMEASURES CRAFT

ILLUSIVE (MSO 4488) alongside WESTCHESTER COUNTY (LST 1167) *1973, US Navy, JOC J.J. Gravat*

MSB towing sweep gear *United States Navy*

MINESWEEPING BOATS (MSB)

Displacement, tons	30 light; 39 full load except MSB 29, 80 full load
Dimensions, feet	57·2 × 15·5 × 4 except MSB 29, 82 × 19 × 5·5
Guns	several MG (Vietnam configuration)
Main engines	2 geared diesels (Packard); 2 shafts; 600 bhp = 12 knots
Complement	6 (enlisted)

Wooden-hull minesweepers intended to be carried to theatre of operations by large assault ships; however, they are too large to be easily handled by cranes and assigned to sweeping harbours. From 1966 to Sep 1970 they were used extensively in Vietnam for river operations.

Of 49 minesweeping boats of this type built only a few remain in active service all based at Charleston, South Carolina. (See 1971-1972 and previous editions for details of earlier disposals and additional data).
MSB 1-4 were ex-Army minesweepers built in 1946 (since discarded), MSB 5-54 (less MSB 24) were completed in 1952-1956. MSB 24 was not built. MSB 29 built to enlarged design by John Trumpy & Sons, Annapolis, Maryland in an effort to improve seakeeping ability.
Normally commanded by chief petty officer or petty officer first class.

GUNNERY. MSBs serving in South Vietnam were fitted with several machineguns and removable fibreglass armour. Note machineguns in tub amidships and on bow of MSB 17; shown below sweeping on the Long Tao river, in South Vietnam.

MSB 17 *1966, United States Navy*

1 INSHORE MINESWEEPER (MSI): "COVE" CLASS

***CAPE** MSI 2

Displacement, tons	120 light; 240 full load
Dimensions, feet	105 × 22 × 10
Main engines	2 GM diesels; 1 shaft; 650 bhp = 12 knots
Complement	21 (3 officers, 18 men)
Guns	removed

The *Cape* and a sister ship *Cove* (MSI 1) were prototype inshore minesweepers authorised under the Fiscal Year 1956 new construction programme. Both built at Bethlehem Shipyards Co, Bellingham, Washington. *Cape* laid down on 1 May 1957, launched on 5 Apr 1968, and placed in service on 27 Feb 1959.
The *Cape* is operated by the Naval Undersea Research Development Center, San Diego, California; neither in service nor in commission.
Cove MSI 1 transferred to Johns Hopkins Applied Physics Laboratory on 31 July 1970; technically she remains on the Navy List.
MSI 3-10 were built in the Netherlands for the Dutch Navy under US Military Assistance Programme. MSI 11 and MSI 12 built in Denmark under MAP. MSI 13 and MSI 14 built in United States for Iran. MSI 15-19 built in United States for Turkey.

CAPE MSI 2 *1968, United States Navy*

SPECIAL MINESWEEPERS (MSS)

The special minesweeper **MSS 1** (ex-SS *Harry L. Gluckman*) was stricken in 1974. See 1973-1974 and previous editions for characteristics and photographs.

MINESWEEPING LAUNCHES (MSL)

None of the 36-foot minesweeping launches remain in service. See 1973-1974 and previous editions for characteristics and photographs.

RIVERINE MINE COUNTERMEASURE CRAFT

None of the riverine minecountermeasure craft developed by the US Navy during the Vietnam War remain in service; they have been transferred to South Vietnam or scrapped, except for a few laid up in reserve. These craft were patrol minesweepers (MSR), modified ASPB patrol craft; river minesweepers (MSM), converted from LCM-6 landing craft; and small drone minesweepers (MSD). See 1972-1973 and previous editions for characteristics and photographs.

UNDERWAY REPLENISHMENT SHIPS

Underway replenishment (UNREP) ships provide fuel, munitions, provisions, spare parts, and other materiel to warships in forward areas.

In addition, most US Navy replenishment ships are fitted with helicopter platforms to permit helicopters to transfer supplies by vertical replenishment (VERTREP). Virtually all materiel except fuel oil can be transferred by helicopter, reducing, or if fuel oil is not required alleviating, the need for the replenishment ship and warship to steam in close company. Helicopters are carried specifically for this purpose by the newer ammunition ships (AE), the combat store ships (AFS), and the fast combat support ships (AOE). Carrier-based helicopters are sometimes employed in this role when an aircraft carrier is in the area.

Planned UNREP ship force levels provide a wartime capability to support deployed carrier and amphibious task groups in up to four or five locations simultaneously. This plan is based on the availability of some storage depots on foreign territory, and the use of Military Sealift Ships to carry fuels, munitions, and stores from the United States or overseas sources for transfer to UNREP ships in overseas areas.

During peacetime some 16 to 18 UNREP ships normally are deployed in the Mediterranean and western Pacific areas in support of the 6th and 7th Fleets, respectively. A few of these ships are homeported overseas.

Early in 1974 the Secretary of Defense announced plans for modernisation of the UNREP force, with two ammunition ships (AE), three combat stores ships (AFS), and ten fleet oilers (AO) planned for the Fiscal Year 1975-1979 new construction programmes.

Most UNREP ships are Navy manned and armed; however, beginning in 1972, an increasing number of these ships are being operated by the Military Sealift Command (MSC) with civilian crews. The latter ships are not armed and have T- designations.

8 AMMUNITION SHIPS (AE): "KILAUEA" CLASS

Name	No.	Laid down	Launched	Commissioned
*KILAUEA	AE 26	10 Mar 1966	9 Aug 1967	10 Aug 1968
*BUTTE	AE 27	21 July 1966	9 Aug 1967	29 Nov 1968
*SANTA BARBARA	AE 28	20 Dec 1966	23 Jan 1968	11 July 1970
*MOUNT HOOD	AE 29	8 May 1967	17 July 1968	1 May 1971
*FLINT	AE 32	4 Aug 1969	9 Nov 1970	20 Nov 1971
*SHASTA	AE 33	10 Nov 1969	3 Apr 1971	26 Feb 1972
*MOUNT BAKER	AE 34	10 May 1970	23 Oct 1971	22 July 1972
*KISKA	AE 35	4 Aug 1971	11 Mar 1972	16 Dec 1972

Displacement, tons	20 500 full load
Dimensions, feet	564 oa × 81 × 25·7
Guns	8—3 inch (*76 mm*) 50 cal AA (twin)
Helicopters	2 UH-46 Sea Knight cargo helicopters normally assigned
Main engines	Geared turbines (General Electric); 22 000 shp; 1 shaft = 20 knots
Boilers	3 (Foster Wheeler)
Complement	401 (28 officers, 373 enlisted men)

Ammunition ships of an advanced design. Fitted for rapid transfer of missiles and other munitions to ships alongside or with helicopters in vertical replenishment operations (VERTREP). Helicopter platform and hangar aft. AE 26 and 27 authorised in Fiscal Year 1965 new construction programme, AE 28 and 29 in FY 1966, AE 32 and 33 in FY 1967, and AE 34 and 35 in FY 1968. AE 26 and 27 built by General Dynamics Corp, Quincy, Massachusetts; AE 28 and 29 Bethlehem Steel Corp, Sparrows Point, Maryland; and AE 32-35 by Ingalls Shipbuilding Corp, Pascagoula, Mississippi.

The 3 inch guns are arranged in twin closed mounts forward and twin open mounts aft, atop superstructure, between funnel and after booms.

All of these ships are active.

KISKA (AE 35) *1972, Ingalls Shipbuilding*

BUTTE (AE 27) *1972, Giorgio Arra*

5 AMMUNITION SHIPS (AE): "SURIBACHI" CLASS

Name	No.	Laid down	Launched	Commissioned
*SURIBACHI	AE 21	31 Jan 1955	2 Nov 1955	17 Nov 1956
*MAUNA KEA	AE 22	16 May 1955	3 May 1956	30 Mar 1957
*NITRO	AE 23	20 May 1957	25 June 1958	1 May 1959
*PYRO	AE 24	21 Oct 1957	5 Nov 1958	24 July 1959
*HALEAKALA	AE 25	10 Mar 1958	17 Feb 1959	3 Nov 1959

Displacement, tons	7 470 light; 10 000 standard; 17 500 full load
Dimensions, feet	512 oa × 72 × 29
Guns	4—3 inch (*76 mm*) 50 cal AA (twin)
Main engines	Geared turbines (Bethlehem); 16 000 shp; 1 shaft = 20·6 knots
Boilers	2 (Combustion Engineering)
Complement	316 (18 officers, 298 enlisted men)

Ammunition ships designed specifically for underway replenishment. All built by Bethlehem Steel Corp, Sparrows Point Maryland. A sixth ship of this class to have been built under the FY 1959 programme was cancelled.

All ships modernised in 1960s, being fitted with high-speed transfer equipment, three holds configured for stowage of missiles up to and including the 33-foot Talos, and helicopter platform fitted aft (two after twin 3 inch gun mounts removed).

Arrangements of twin 3 inch gun mounts differ, some ships have them in tandem and and others side-by-side.

All of these ships are active.

NOMENCLATURE. Ammunition ships are named for volcanoes and explosives (eg *Nitro* for nitroglycerine and *Pyro* for pyrotechnic).

PYRO (AE 24) *1971, United States Navy*

HALEAKALA (AE 25) *1968, United States Navy*

FLINT (AE 32) *1971, Ingalls Shipbuiding*

Underway Replenishment Ships—*continued*

(2) AMMUNITION SHIPS (AE): NEW CONSTRUCTION

Two additional ammunition ships are scheduled for construction with authorisation during the Fiscal Year 1978-1980 period. These would bring the number of modern ammunition ships to 15 by the early 1980s.

2 AMMUNITION SHIPS (AE): "WRANGELL" CLASS

Name	No	Launched	Commissioned
WRANGELL (*ex-Midnight*)	AE 12	14 Apr 1944	28 May 1944
FIREDRAKE (*ex-Winged Racer*)	AE 14	12 May 1944	27 Dec 1944

Displacement, tons	6 350 light; 15 295 full load
Dimensions, feet	435 wl; 459·2 oa × 63 × 28·2
Guns	2 or 4—3 inch (*76 mm*) 50 cal AA (single)
Main engines	Geared turbine (General Electric); 6 000 shp; 1 shaft = 16·4 knots
Boilers	2 (Babcock & Wilcox or Combustion Engineering)
Complement	approx 265

C2 type cargo ships built by North Carolina Shipbuilding Co, Wilmington, NC. Officially the "Mount Hood" class, the *Mount Hood* AE 11 of this type being sunk in World War II. One 5 inch gun and four 40 mm AA guns removed; the *Firedrake* has a helicopter platform installed aft in place of two after 3 inch guns. Both ships are in reserve.

DISPOSALS
Diamond Head AE 19 stricken on 1 Mar 1973; **Paricutin** AE 18 stricken on 1 June 1973; **Great Sitkin** AE 17 stricken on 2 July 1973; **Vesuvius** AE 15, **Mount Katmai** AE 16 stricken on 14 Aug 1973.

WRANGELL (AE 12) *1968, United States Navy*

FIREDRAKE (AE 14) *1969, United States Navy*

1 AMMUNITION SHIP (AE): "LASSEN" CLASS

Name	No.	Launched	Commissioned
MAUNA LOA	AE 8	14 Apr 1943	27 Oct 1943

Displacement, tons	5 220 light; 14 225 full load
Dimensions, feet	435 wl; 459 oa × 63 × 26·5
Guns	2—3 inch (*76 mm*) 50 cal AA (single)
Main engines	Diesel (Nordberg); 6 000 bhp; 1 shaft = 15·3 knots
Complement	281

Built by the Tampa Shipbuilding Co, Tampa, Florida. Modified C2 type, converted by Navy. Original armament was one 5 inch gun, four 3 inch guns, and four 40 mm AA AA guns. *Mauna Loa* transferred to Maritime Administration reserve in 1960; re-acquired and returned to the Navy in Sep 1961 and recommissioned on 27 Nov 1961; fitted with helicopter platform aft. Decommissioned and placed in reserve in 1970.

MAUNA LOA (AE 8) *1965, United States Navy*

5 STORE SHIPS (AF): R2-S-BV1 TYPE

Name	No.	Launched	Commissioned
ZELIMA (*ex-Golden Rocket*)	AF 49	2 Mar 1945	27 July 1946
ARCTURUS (*ex-Golden Eagle*)	AF 52	15 Mar 1942	18 Nov 1961
PICTOR (*ex-Great Republic*)	AF 54	4 June 1942	13 Sep 1950
ALUDRA (*ex-Matchless*)	AF 55	14 Oct 1944	7 July 1952
PROCYON (*ex-Flying Scud*)	AF 61	1 July 1942	24 Nov 1961

Displacement, tons	6 914 light; 15 500 full load
Dimensions, feet	459·2 oa × 63 × 28
Guns	8—3 inch (*76 mm*) 50 cal AA (twin) in *Aludra*; most of others are unarmed
Main engines	Geared turbine; 6 000 shp; 1 shaft = 16 knots
Boilers	2

All built by Moore Dry Dock Co, Oakland, California. R2-S-BV1 type refrigerated cargo ships; similar to C2-S-B1 design but built as "reefers".
Arcturus is formerly USNS *Golden Eagle*, transferred from Military Sea Transportation Service to active Navy; renamed on 13 Sep 1961 and commissioned as USS on 18 Nov 1961 after modification for underway replenishment at the New York Naval Shipyard. These ships have been fitted with helicopter platforms.
All have been decommissioned and are in Navy or Maritime Administration reserve fleets; last active ship was *Arcturus*, decommissioned in 1973.

NOMENCLATURE. Store ships are named for stars and constellations.

DISPOSALS
Sirius AF 60 stricken in 1965, **Bellatrix** AF 62 stricken on 1 Oct 1968, **Alstede** AF 48 stricken on 31 Oct 1969.

PROCYON (AF 61) *1970, United States Navy*

ALUDRA (AF 55) *1967, United States Navy*

2 STORE SHIPS (AF): R3-S-4A TYPE

Name	No.	Launched	Commissioned
•**RIGEL**	AF 58	15 Mar 1955	2 Sep 1955
•**VEGA**	AF 59	26 Apr 1955	10 Nov 1955

Displacement, tons	7 950 light; 15 540 full load
Dimensions, feet	475 wl; 502 oa × 72 × 29 max
Guns	4—3 inch (*76 mm*) 50 cal AA (twin)
Main engines	Geared turbine (General Electric); 16 000 shp; 1 shaft = 20 knots
Boilers	2 (Combustion Engineering)
Complement	approx 350

Built by Ingalls Shipbuilding Co, Pascagoula. R3-S-4A type. Helicopter platform fitted (two after twin 3 inch mounts removed). Both of these ships are active.

RIGEL (AF 58) *1968 United States Navy*

Underway Replenishment Ships—*continued*

1 STORE SHIP (AF): "VICTORY" TYPE

Name	No.	Launched	Commissioned
*DENEBOLA (ex-*Hibbing Victory*)	T-AF 56	10 June 1944	20 Jan 1954

Displacement, tons	6 700 light; 12 130 full load
Dimensions, feet	455·2 × 62 × 28·5
Guns	removed
Main engines	Geared turbine (Westinghouse); 8 500 shp; 1 shaft = 18 knots
Boilers	2 (Combustion Engineering)
Complement	225

Built by Oregon Shipbuilding Co, Portland, Oregon. Originally VC2-S-AP3 "Victory" type. Acquired by the Navy on 1 May 1952 and converted to underway replenishment ship at New York Naval Shipyard.
Two after twin 3 inch gun mounts removed and helicopter platform fitted two forward 3 inch gun mounts removed with transfer to MSC.
The *Denebola* was assigned to the Military Sealift Command late in July 1975 and operated by a civilian crew (redesignated T-AF and disarmed).

DISPOSALS
Regulus AF 57 driven aground and wrecked by a typhoon in Hong Kong harbour on 18 Aug 1971; subsequently scrapped.

DENEBOLA (AF 56) *1971, United States Navy*

1 STORE SHIP (AF): C2-S-E1 TYPE

Name	No.	Launched	Commissioned
HYADES (ex-*Iberville*)	AF 28	12 June 1943	30 Sep 1943

Displacement, tons	6 313 light; 15 300 full load
Dimensions, feet	468·66 oa × 63 × 28
Guns	2—3 inch (*76 mm*) 50 cal AA (single)
Main engines	Geared turbine (General Electric); 6 000 shp; 1 shaft = 15·5 knots
Boilers	2 (Babcock & Wilcox)
Complement	252

Built by Gulf Shipbuilding Co, Chickensaw, Alabama. Original armament included one 5 inch gun. Helicopter deck fitted aft in place of two single 3 inch guns during 1962 Decommissioned and placed in reserve in 1969.

DISPOSALS
Graffias AF 29 stricken on 19 Dec 1969.

HYADES (AF 28) *Ing Augusti Nani*

7 + 3 COMBAT STORE SHIPS (AFS): "MARS" CLASS

Name	No.	Laid down	Launched	Commissioned
*MARS	AFS 1	5 May 1962	15 June 1963	21 Dec 1963
*SYLVANIA	AFS 2	18 Aug 1962	15 Aug 1963	11 July 1964
*NIAGARA FALLS	AFS 3	22 May 1965	26 Mar 1966	29 Apr 1967
*WHITE PLAINS	AFS 4	2 Oct 1965	23 July 1966	23 Nov 1968
*CONCORD	AFS 5	26 Mar 1966	17 Dec 1966	27 Nov 1968
*SAN DIEGO	AFS 6	11 Mar 1965	13 Apr 1968	24 May 1969
*SAN JOSE	AFS 7	8 Mar 1969	13 Dec 1969	23 Oct 1970

Displacement, tons	16 500 full load
Dimensions, feet	581 oa × 79 × 24
Guns	8—3 inch (76 mm) 50 cal AA (twin)
Helicopters	2 UH-46 Sea Knight helicopters normally assigned
Main engines	Steam turbines; 22 000 shp; 1 shaft = 20 knots
Boilers	3 (Babcock & Wilcox) (one spare)
Complement	430 (30 officers, 400 enlisted men)

All built by National Steel & Shipbuilding, San Diego, California. Of a new design with a completely new replenishment at sea system. "M" frames replace conventional king posts and booms, which are equipped with automatic tensioning devices to maintain transfer lines taut between the ship and the warships being replenished despite rolling and yawing. Computers provide up-to-the-minute data on stock status with data displayed by closed-circuit television. Five holds (one refrigerated). Cargo capacity 2 625 tons dry stores and 1 300 tons refrigerated stores (varies with specific loadings).
Automatic propulsion system with full controls on bridge. The large SPS-40 radar fitted in *Mars* and *Sylvania* have been removed; some ships have TACAN (tactical aircraft navigation radar).
Mars authorised in Fiscal Year 1961 shipbuilding programme, *Sylvania* in FY 1962, *Niagara Falls* in FY 1964, *White Plains* and *Concord* in FY 1965, *San Diego* in FY 1966, *San Jose* in FY 1967.
Three additional ships of this type are planned with authorisations to be requested in the Fiscal Year 1978-1980 period.

NOMENCLATURE. Combat store ships are named for American cities.

PHOTOGRAPHS. Note the improved, smaller TACAN in the later photograph of the *Sylvania*. The stern view shows the ship's squared-off hangar and large helicopter deck with a UH-46 Sea Knight helicopter used for vertical replenishment (VERTREP) operations.

SYLVANIA (AFS 2) *1973, Giorgio Arra*

SYLVANIA (AFS 2) *1973, Giorgio Arra*

Underway Replenishment Ships—*continued*

SYLVANIA (AFS 2) *1972, Giorgio Arra*

STORES ISSUE SHIPS (AKS)

The last stores issue ship on the Navy List, the **Altair** AKS 32 (ex-AK 257) stricken on 1 June 1973. See 1973-1974 and previous editions for characteristics.

(9) OILERS (AO): NEW CONSTRUCTION

	No,	
	AO 177	Proposed FY 1976 programme
	AO 178	Proposed FY 1976 programme
	AO 179	Planned FY 1977 programme
	AO 180	Planned FY 1977 programme
Five oilers	**AO 181-185**	Planned FY 1978-1980 programmes

Displacement, tons	27 500 full load
Dimensions, feet	586·5 oa × 88 × 33·5
Main engines	Geared turbines; 2 shafts = 20 knots
Boilers	2
Complement	approx 140

Nine oilers of this class are planned to provide the Navy with a total of 26 modern UNREP fuel ships (AO-AOE-AOR). The lead ship requested in the Fiscal Year 1975 new construction programme was not approved by the Congress. Cargo capacity approximately 120 000 barrels of liquid fuels. In the artist's concept, below, rapid-fire Vulcan-Phalanx 20-mm gun mounts are installed forward and aft; helicopter deck on fantail.

CLASSIFICATION. The hull numbers AO 168-176 are assigned to the "Sealift" class tankers; listed with Sealift Ships.

6 OILERS (AO): "NEOSHO" CLASS

Name	*No.*	*Launched*	*Commissioned*
***NEOSHO**	AO 143	10 Nov 1953	24 Sep 1954
***MISSISSINEWA**	AO 144	12 June 1954	18 Jan 1955
***HASSAYAMPA**	AO 145	12 Sep 1954	19 Apr 1955
***KAWISHIWI**	AO 146	11 Dec 1954	6 July 1955
***TRUCKEE**	AO 147	10 Mar 1955	23 Nov 1955
***PONCHATOULA**	AO 148	9 July 1955	12 Jan 1956

Displacement, tons	11 600 light; 38 000 to 40 000 full load
Dimensions, feet	640 wl; 655 oa × 86 × 35
Guns	8 or 12—3 inch (*76 mm*) 50 cal AA (twin)
Main engines	Geared turbines (General Electric); 28 000 shp; 2 shafts = 20 knots
Boilers	2 (Babcock & Wilcox)
Complement	approx 360 (30 officers and 330 enlisted men including staff)

Neosho built by Bethlehem Steel Co, Quincy, Massachusetts; others by New York Shipbuilding Corp, Camden, New Jersey. These are the largest "straight" oilers (AO) constructed for the Navy. Cargo capacity is approximately 180 000 barrels of liquid fuels.

TRUCKEE (AO 147) *1972, Giorgio Arra*

"NEOSHO" CLASS—*continued*

Original armament was two 5 inch DP guns and 12 3 inch AA guns; former removed in 1969. Two twin 3 inch gun mounts removed from *Neosho, Mississinewa*, and *Truckee* and helicopter platform installed. Those ships also have additional superstructure installed forward of after "island" structure. All fitted to carry a service force commander and staff (12 officers). All of these ships are active.

NOMENCLATURE. Oilers are named after American rivers with Indian names.

NEOSHO (AO 143) *1972, United States Navy*

5 OILERS (AO): "JUMBOISED" T3-S2-A3 TYPE

Name	*No,*	*Launched*	*Commissioned*
***MISPILLION**	T-AO 105	10 Aug 1945	29 Dec 1945
***NAVASOTA**	AO 106	30 Aug 1945	27 Feb 1946
***PASSUMPSIC**	T-AO 107	31 Oct 1945	1 Apr 1946
***PAWCATUCK**	AO 108	19 Feb 1945	10 May 1946
***WACCAMAW**	T-AO 109	30 Mar 1946	25 June 1946

Displacement, tons	11 000 light; 34 750 full load
Dimensions, feet	646 oa × 75 × 35·5
Guns	4—3 inch (*76 mm*) 50 cal AA (single) removed from T-AOs
Main engines	Geared turbines (Westinghouse); 13 500 shp; 2 shafts = 16 knots
Boilers	4 (Babcock & Wilcox)
Compliment	290 (16 officers, 274 men)

All built by Sun Shipbuilding & Dry Dock Co, Chester, Pennsylvania. Originally T3-S2-A-3 oilers; converted during mid-1960s under "jumbo" programme. Enlarged midsections added to increase cargo capacity to approximately 150 000 barrels. Helicopter platform fitted forward. All of these ships are active.
The *Mispillion* was assigned to the Military Sealift Command in 1974 and provided with a civilian crew (guns removed); subsequently the *Waccamaw* and *Passumpsic* assigned to MSC.
Note two funnels in *Passumpsic*.

PASSUMPIC (T-AO 1071) *1971, United States Navy*

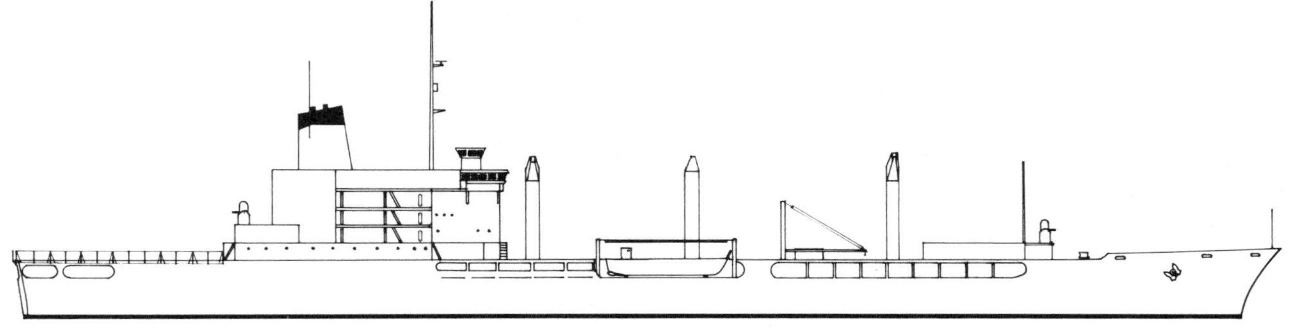

AO 177 TYPE *Drawing by A. D. Baker*

Underway Replenishment Ships—*continued*

3 OILERS (AO): "JUMBOISED" T3-S2-A1 TYPE

Name	*No.*	*Launched*	*Commissioned*
***ASHTABULA**	AO 51	22 May 1943	7 Aug 1943
***CALOOSAHATCHEE**	AO 98	2 June 1945	10 Oct 1945
***CANISTEO**	AO 99	6 July 1945	3 Dec 1945

Displacement, tons	34 750 full load
Dimensions, feet	644 oa × 75 × 31·5
Guns	4—3 inch (*76 mm*) 50 cal AA (single)
Main engines	Geared turbines; 13 500 shp; 2 shafts = 18 knots
Boilers	4 (Foster Wheeler)
Complement	300 (13 officers and 287 enlisted men)

All built by Bethlehem Steel Co, Sparrows Point, Maryland. Originally T3-S2-A1 oilers; converted during mid-1960s under "jumbo" programme. Enlarged midsections added to increase cargo capacity to approximately 143 000 barrels plus 175 tons of munitions and 100 tons refrigerated stores. No helicopter platform fitted.

ASHTABULA (AO 51) *1970, United States Navy*

PASSUMPSIC (T-AO 107) *1975, United States Navy*

KENNEBEC (AO 36) *1965, United States Navy*

TRUCKEE (AO 147) *1972, United States Navy*

CANISTEO (AO 99) *1973, Giorgio Arra*

Underway Replenishment Ships—*continued*

2 OILERS (AO): T2-A TYPE

Name	No.	Launched	Commissioned
KENNEBEC (ex-*Corsicana*)	AO 36	19 Apr 1941	4 Feb 1942
TAPPAHANNOCK (ex-*Jorkay*)	AO 43	18 Apr 1942	22 June 1942

Displacement, tons: 21 580 full load
Dimensions, feet: 501·4 oa × 68 × 30·75
Guns: 2 or 4—3 inch (*76 mm*) 50 cal AA (single)
Main engines: Geared turbine (Westinghouse); 12 000 shp = 16·7 knots
Boilers: 2 (Foster Wheeler in *Kennebec*, Babcock & Wilcox in *Tappahannock*)

Fleet oilers of World War II construction but smaller and less capable than the contemporary T-3 series. *Tappahannock* built by Sun Shipbuilding and Dry Dock Co. Chester, Pennsylvania; *Kennebec* by Bethlehem Steel Co, Sparrows Point, Maryland. Cargo capacity approximately 130 000 barrels.
Original armament for this class was one 5 inch DP gun, four 3 inch AA guns, and with 40 mm AA guns; subsequently reduced as above.
The *Tappahannock* is in Navy reserve; *Kennebec* is in Maritime Administration reserve fleet but remains on the Navy List.

DISPOSALS (since 1 Jan 1970)
Neches AO 47 stricken on 1 Oct 1970, **Mattaponi** AO 41 stricken on 15 Oct 1970, **Chukawan** AO 100 stricken on 1 July 1972, **Kankakee** AO 39 stricken on 1 June 1973.

MARIAS (T-AO 57) *1965, United States Navy*

OILERS (AO): T3-S-2A1 TYPE

Name	No.	Launched	Commissioned
SABINE (ex-*Esso Albany*)	AO 25	27 Apr 1940	25 Sep 1940
CHIKASKIA	AO 54	2 Oct 1943	10 Nov 1943
AUCILLA (ex-*Escanaba*)	AO 56	20 Nov 1943	22 Dec 1943
***MARIAS**	T-AO 57	21 Dec 1943	12 Feb 1944
***TALUGA**	T-AO 62	10 July 1944	25 Aug 1944
***TOLOVANA**	AO 64	6 Jan 1945	24 Feb 1945

Displacement, tons: 25 525 full load
Dimensions, feet: 553 oa × 75 × 31·5
Guns: 4—3 inch (*76 mm* 50 cal AA (single) in most ships; a few ships retain 5 inch guns of original armament (see notes); guns removed from T-AO ships
Main engines: Geared turbines; 13 500 shp; 2 shafts = 18 knots
Boilers: 4 (Foster Wheeler)
Complement: 274 (14 officers, 260 enlisted men)

Several ships of this type have been enlarged through the "jumbo" process and are listed separately on a previous page. The *Marias* and *Taluga* have been transferred to the Military Sealift Command for operation and have civilian crews; the other ship of this type in active service is Navy manned. All provide underway replenishment of Navy ships and are not point-to-point "tankers" (AO).
All built by Bethlehem Steel Co, Sparrows Point, Maryland. Original armament varied from 1 to 4—5 inch DP guns; up to 4—3 inch AA guns, and 8—40 mm AA guns.

Cargo capacity approximately 145 000 barrels.

DISPOSALS (since 1 Jan 1970)
Elokomin AO 55 stricken on 17 Mar 1970; **Chemung** AO 30 stricken on 18 Sep 1970; **Platte** AO 24 stricken on 25 Sep 1970; **Allagash** AO 97 stricken on 1 June 1973; **Nantahala** AO 60 stricken on 1 July 1973; **Cacapon** AO 52, **Manatee** AO 58, **Chipola** AO 63 stricken on 14 Aug 1973; **Caliente** AO 53 stricken on 1 Dec 1973; **Severn** AO 61 stricken on 1 July 1974; **Guadalupe** AO 32 stricken on 15 May 1975; **Tolovana** AO 64 stricken on 15 Apr 1975.

SEATTLE (AOE 3) *1973, Giorgio Arra*

SEATTLE (AOE 4) *1972, Giorgio Arra*

TALUGA (T-AO 62)—Navy manned and armed *1970, United States Navy*

Underway Replenishment Ships—*continued*

SEATTLE (AOE 3) *1972, Giorgio Arra*

4 FAST COMBAT SUPPORT SHIPS (AOE): "SACRAMENTO" CLASS

Name	No	Laid down	Launched	Commissioned
• **SACRAMENTO**	AOE 1	30 June 1961	14 Sep 1963	14 Mar 1964
• **CAMDEN**	AOE 2	17 Feb 1964	29 May 1965	1 Apr 1967
• **SEATTLE**	AOE 3	1 Oct 1965	2 Mar 1968	5 Apr 1969
• **DETROIT**	AOE 4	29 Nov 1966	21 June 1969	28 Mar 1970

Displacement, tons	19 200 light; 53 600 full load
Dimensions, feet	793 oa × 107 × 39·3
Guns	8—3 inch (*76 mm*) 50 cal AA (twin)
Helicopters	2 UH-46 Sea Knight helicopters normally assigned
Main engines	Geared turbines (General Electric); 100 000 shp; 2 shafts = 26 knots
Boilers	4 (Combustion Engineering)
Complement	600 (33 officers, 567 enlisted men)

These ships operate primarily with fast carrier task forces to provide rapid replenishment at sea of petroleum, munitions, provisions, and fleet freight. Fitted with helicopter platform, internal arrangements, and large hangar for vertical replenishment operations (VERTREP). Cargo capacity 177 000 barrels plus 2 150 tons munitions, 500 tons dry stores, 250 tons refrigerated stores (varies with specific loadings).

Built by Puget Sound Naval Shipyard except *Camden* by New York Shipbuilding Corp, Camden, New Jersey. *Sacramento* authorised in Fiscal Year 1961 new construction programme; *Camden* in FY 1963, *Seattle* in FY 1965, and *Detroit* in FY 1966. Construction of AOE 5 in FY 1968 was deferred and then cancelled in November 1969. No additional ships of this type are planned because of high cost, the availability of new-construction ammunition ships, and the great success of the smaller "Wichita" class replenishment oilers. Approximate cost of the *Camden* was $70 000 000.

ENGINEERING. *Sacramento* and *Camden* have machinery intended for the cancelled battleship *Kentucky* (BB 66).

NOMENCLATURE. Fast combat support ships are named for American cities. This name source was previously used for cruisers. It is now used for attack submarines, continuing the confusing of US Navy ship nomenclature.

PHOTOGRAPHS. These ships can be distinguished from the smaller "Wichita" class replenishment oilers by their larger superstructures and funnel, helicopter deck at higher level, and hangar structure aft of funnel.

GASOLINE TANKERS (AOG)

All of the small, gasoline tankers have been stricken or transferred to other navies. See 1974-1975 and previous editions for characteristics.

DISPOSALS AND TRANSFERS (since 1 Jan 1970)

Namakagon AOG 53 transferred to Taiwan China on 29 June 1971; **Elkhorn** AOG 7 transferred to Taiwan China on 1 July 1972; **Genesee** AOG 8 transferred to Chile on 1 July 1972; **Tombigbee** AOG 11 transferred to Greece on 7 July 1972; **Patabsco** AOG 1, **Kishwaukee** AOG 9 stricken on 1 Aug 1974; **Nespelen** AOG 55 stricken on 1 July 1975; **Noxubee** AOG 56 stricken in 1975; **Chewaucan** AOG 50 transferred to Columbia in 1975.

6 + 1 REPLENISHMENT OILERS (AOR): "WICHITA" CLASS

Name	No.	Laid down	Launched	Commissioned
***WICHITA**	AOR 1	18 June 1966	18 Mar 1968	7 June 1969
***MILWAUKEE**	AOR 2	29 Nov 1966	17 Jan 1969	1 Nov 1969
***KANSAS CITY**	AOR 3	20 Apr 1968	28 June 1969	6 June 1970
***SAVANNAH**	AOR 4	22 Jan 1969	25 Apr 1970	5 Dec 1970
***WABASH**	AOR 5	21 Jan 1970	6 Feb 1971	20 Nov 1971
***KALAMAZOO**	AOR 6	28 Oct 1970	11 Nov 1972	11 Aug 1973
ROANOKE	AOR 7	19 Jan 1974	late 1974	1975

Displacement, tons	38 100 full load
Dimensions, feet	659 oa × 96 × 33·3
Missile launchers	1 NATO Sea Sparrow multiple launcher (Mk 29) in *Roanoke*
Guns	4—3 inch (*76 mm*) 50 cal AA (twin) except *Roanoke*
Main engins	Geared turbines; 32 000 shp; 2 shafts = 20 knots (18 knots on 2 boilers)
Boilers	3 (Foster Wheeler)
Complement	345 (20 officers, 325 enlisted men)

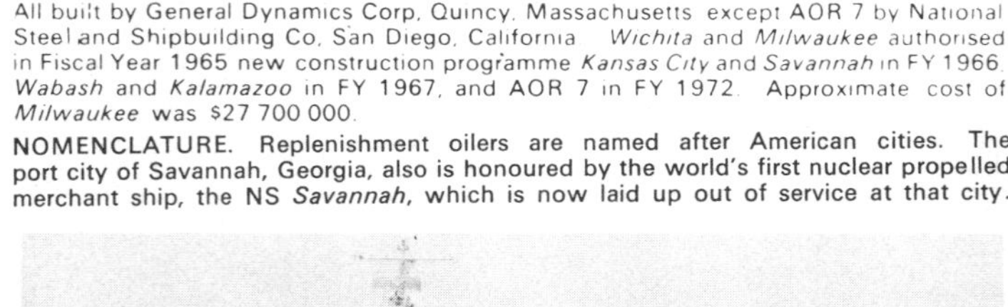

These ships provide rapid replenishment at sea of petroleum and munitions with a limited capacity for provision and fleet freight. Fitted with helicopter platform and internal arrangement for vertical replenishment operations (VERTREP), but no hangar. Cargo capacity 175 000 barrels plus 600 tons munitions, 425 tons dry stores, 150 tons refrigerated stores.

All built by General Dynamics Corp, Quincy, Massachusetts except AOR 7 by National Steel and Shipbuilding Co, San Diego, California. *Wichita* and *Milwaukee* authorised in Fiscal Year 1965 new construction programme *Kansas City* and *Savannah* in FY 1966. *Wabash* and *Kalamazoo* in FY 1967, and AOR 7 in FY 1972. Approximate cost of *Milwaukee* was $27 700 000.

NOMENCLATURE. Replenishment oilers are named after American cities. The port city of Savannah, Georgia, also is honoured by the world's first nuclear propelled merchant ship, the NS *Savannah*, which is now laid up out of service at that city.

MILWAUKEE (AOR 2) *1972, Giorgio Arra*

KALAMAZOO (AOR 6) *1973, United States Navy*

FLEET SUPPORT SHIPS

Fleet support ships provide primarily maintenance and related towing and salvage services at advanced bases and at ports in the United States. These ships normally do not provide fuel, munitions, or other supplies except when ships are alongside for maintenance. Two notable exceptions are the self-propelled barrack ships (APB), that serve as semi-autonomous advanced bases for small landing craft or riverine craft in advanced areas, and the dependant support ship (see hospital ship, AH) which was refitted to provide services for US civilian dependants in overseas areas.
Most fleet support ships operate from bases in the United States. The five Polaris/Poseidon submarine tenders (AS) are based at Holy Loch, Scotland; Rota, Spain; Charleston, South Carolina; and Apra harbour, Guam, with one ship generally in transit or overhaul. In addition, two support ships (AD/AR/AS type) generally are forward deployed in the Mediterranean and two in the western Pacific. Early in 1974 the Secretary of Defense announced plans for modernisation of the support ship forces, with five destroyer tenders (AD), two submarine tenders (AS), and ten fleet tugs (ATF) planned for the Fiscal Year 1975-1979 new construction programmes.
Fleet support ships are mainly Navy manned and armed; however, an increasing number are being operated by the Military Sealift Command (MSC) with civilian crews. The latter ships are not armed and have T- designations.

2 + 6 DESTROYER TENDERS (AD): "GOMPERS" CLASS

Name	No.	Laid down	Launched	Commissioned
***SAMUEL GOMPERS**	AD 37	9 July 1964	14 May 1966	1 July 1967
***PUGET SOUND**	AD 38	15 Feb 1965	16 Sep 1966	27 Apr 1968
	AD 40	Fiscal Year 1973 programme		1978
	AD 41	Fiscal Year 1975 programme		1978
	AD 42	Planned FY 1976 programme		1969
	AD 43	Planned FY 1977 programme		1980
	AD 44	Planned FY 1978 programme		1981
	AD 45	Planned FY 1979 programme		1982

Displacement, tons	22 260 full load
Dimensions, feet	643 oa × 85 × 22·5
Guns	1—5 inch (*127 mm*) 38 cal DP in *Samuel Gompers* and *Puget Sound*
Missile launchers	1 NATO Sea Sparrow system planned for AD 40 and later ships
Main engines	Steam turbines (De Laval); 20 000 shp; 1 shaft = 20 knots
Boilers	2 (Combustion Engineering)
Complement	1 806 (135 officers, 1 671 enlisted men)

These are the first US destroyer tenders of post-World War II design; capable of providing repair and supply services to new destroyer-type ships which have advanced missile, anti-submarine, and electronic systems. The tenders also have facilities for servicing nuclear power plants. Services can be provided simultaneously to six guided-missile destroyers moored alongside. Basic hull design similar to "L. Y. Spear" and "Simon Lake" submarine tenders. Provided with helicopter platform and hangar; two 7 000-pound capacity cranes.
Samuel Gompers authorised in Fiscal Year 1964 new construction programme and *Puget Sound* in FY 1965 programme. Both ships built by Puget Sound Naval Shipyard, Bremerton, Washington.
AD 39 of FY 1969 programme cancelled prior to start of construction to provide funds for overruns in other new ship programmes. AD 40 authorised in FY 1973 new construction programme; AD 41 in FY 1975 programme with four additional ships planned (AD 41 and later ships of a slightly modified design); estimated cost of AD 41 is $116 700 000.

NOMENCLATURE. Destroyer tenders generally are named for geographic areas; Samuel Gompers was an American labour leader.

SAMUEL GOMPERS (AD 37) *1968, United States Navy*

5 DESTROYER TENDERS (AD): "KLONDIKE" CLASS

Name	No.	Launched	Commissioned
EVERGLADES	AD 24	28 Jan 1945	25 May 1951
***SHENANDOAH**	AD 26	29 Mar 1945	13 Aug 1945
***YELLOWSTONE**	AD 27	12 Apr 1945	15 Jan 1946
ISLE ROYAL	AD 29	19 Sep 1945	9 June 1962
***BRYCE CANYON**	AD 36	7 Mar 1946	15 Sep 1950

Displacement, tons	8 165 standard; 16 635 to 16 900 full load
Dimensions, feet	465 wl; 492 oa × 69·5 × 27·2
Guns	1—5 inch (*127 mm*) 38 cal DP; removed from some ships including *Shenandoah*
Main engines	Steam turbines; 8 500 shp 1 shaft = 18·4 knots
Boilers	2 (Foster-Wheeler or Babcock & Wilcox)
Complement	778 to 918

These ships are of modified C-3 design completed as destroyer tenders. Officially considered two classes (see below). *Shenandoah, Yellowstone* built by Todd Shipyards, Los Angeles, Calif; *Bryce Canyon* by Charleston Navy Yard; *Everglades* by Los Angeles SB & DD Co; and *Isle Royal* by Todd Pacific Shipyards, Seattle, Wash. *Isle Royal* first commissioned on 26 Mar 1946 and placed in reserve before being completely outfitted; recommissioned for service on 9 June 1962 and commenced operations in January 1963.
Originally 14 ships of two similar designs, the "Klondike" class of AD 22-25 and "Shenandoah" class of AD 26-33, 35, and 36. *Great Lakes* (AD 30), *New England* (AD 32), *Canopus* (AD 33, ex-AS 27), *Arrow Head* (AD 35, ex-AV 19) cancelled before completion; *Klondike* (AD 22) reclassified AR 22; *Grand Canyon* (AD 28) reclassified AR 28.
Three ships remain in active service; others in reserve. *Yellowstone* was scheduled to be decommissioned early in 1975.

ARMAMENT. Original armament for "Klondike" class was 1—5 in gun, 4—3 in guns and 4—40 mm guns; for "Shenandoah" class was 2—5 in guns and 8—40 mm guns.

MODERNISATION. Most of these ships have been modernised under the FRAM II programme to service modernised destroyers fitted with ASROC, improved electronics, helicopters etc.

DISPOSALS AND TRANSFERS

Tidewater AD 31 transferred to Indonesia in Jan 1971 for use as tender to off-shore oil operations (Navy manned); **Frontier** AD 25 stricken on 1 Dec 1972; **Arcadia** AD 24 stricken on 1 July 1973.

ISLE ROYAL (AD 29) *1970, United States Navy*

PUGET SOUND (AD 38) *1972, United States Navy*

Fleet Support Ships—*continued*

SHENANDOAH (AD 26) *1973, US Navy, PH2 G. T. Leidy*

ISLE ROYAL (AD 29) *1970, United States Navy*

1 DESTROYER TENDER (AD): "CASCADE" TYPE

Name	*No.*	*Launched*	*Commissioned*
***CASCADE**	AD 16	7 June 1942	12 Mar 1943

Displacement, tons	9 800 standard; 16 600 full load
Dimensions, feet	492 oa × 69·5 × 27·2
Guns	1—5 inch (*127 mm*) 38 cal DP
Main engines	Steam turbines (General Electric); 8 500 shp 1 shaft = 18·4 knots
Boilers	2 (Foster-Wheeler)
Complement	857

Built by Western Pipe & Steel Co, San Francisco, C3-S1-N2 type. Modernised to service FRAM destroyers.
The *Cascade* was scheduled to be decommissioned in 1975.

CASCADE (AD 16) *1971, United States Navy*

PIEDMONT (AD 17) *1970, United States Navy*

5 DESTROYER TENDERS (AD): "DIXIE" CLASS

Name	*No.*	*Launched*	*Commissioned*
***DIXIE**	AD 14	27 May 1939	25 Apr 1940
***PRAIRIE**	AD 15	9 Dec 1939	5 Aug 1940
***PIEDMONT**	AD 17	7 Dec 1942	5 Jan 1944
***SIERRA**	AD 18	23 Feb 1943	20 Mar 1944
***YOSEMITE**	AD 19	16 May 1943	25 May 1944

Displacement, tons	9 450 standard; 17 176 full load
Dimensions, feet	520 wl; 530·5 oa × 73·3 × 25·5
Guns	1 or 2—5 inch (*127 mm*) 38 cal DP
Main engines	Steam turbines; 11 000 shp; 2 shafts = 19·6 knots
Boilers	4 (Babcock & Wilcox)
Complement	1 076 to 1 698 (total accommodation)

Dixie and *Prairie* built by New York Shipbuilding Corp, Camden, New Jersey; others by Tampa Shipbuilding Co, Florida. 2—5 inch guns (aft) and 8—40 mm guns removed. Parsons turbines in *Dixie* and *Prarie*, Allis Chalmers in others.
All five ships are active, amongst the oldest ships remaining in service with the US Navy.

MODERNISATION. All of these ships have been modernised under the FRAM II programme to service destroyers fitted with ASROC, improved electronics, helicopters, etc. Two or three 5 inch guns and eight 40 mm guns removed during modernisation.

YOSEMITE (AD 19) *1968, United States Navy*

YOSEMITE (AD 19) *1968 United States Navy*

DEGAUSSING SHIPS (ADG)

The Navy's four degaussing ships were to be stricken during 1975: **Lodestone** ADG 8, **Magnet** ADG 9, **Deperm** ADG 10, **Surfbird** AGD 383.

See 1974-1975 and previous editions for characteristics.

1 AUXILIARY DEEP SUBMERGENCE SUPPORT SHIP (AGDS): Ex-DOCK CARGO SHIP

Name	*No.*	*Launched*
***POINT LOMA** (ex-*Point Barrow*)	AGDS 2 (ex-AKD 1)	25 May 1957

Displacement, tons	9 415 standard; 14 094 full load
Dimensions, feet	475 wl; 492 oa × 78 × 22
Main engines	Steam turbines; 6 000 shp; 2 shafts = 18 knots
Boilers	2
Complement	160 (including scientific personnel and submersible operators)

A docking or "wet" well ship designed to carry cargo, vehicles, and landing craft (designated AKD). Built by Maryland Shipbuilding & Dry Dock Co, for the Military Sea Transportation Service (now Military Sealift Command); commissioned on 28 Feb 1958 and delivered to MSTS on 29 May 1958. Maritime Administration S2-ST-23A design; winterised for arctic service. Fitted with internal ramp and garage system.
Subsequently refitted with hangar over docking well and employed in transport of large booster rockets to Cape Kennedy Space Center. Primarily used to carry the second stage of the Saturn V moon rocket and Lunar Modules. Placed out of service in reserve on 1 Jan 1971 with reduction of US space programme.
Reactivated in mid-1972 for cargo work; transferred from Military Sealift Command to Navy on 28 Feb 1974 for modification to support deep submergence vehicles, especially the bathyscaph *Trieste II*. Placed in commission "special" on 8 Mar 1974 as the AGDS 2; renamed *Point Loma* for the location of the San Diego submarine base where Submarine Development Group 1 operates most of the Navy's submersibles. The *Point Loma* was scheduled to be placed in full commission in November 1974. Aviation gas capacity increased to approx 100 000 gallons (US) to support *Trieste II* which uses lighter-than-water avgas for flotation.

DESIGNATION. The designation AGDS was established on 3 Jan 1974; technically it is a service craft designation vice ship. The AGDS 1 was assigned briefly to the floating dry dock *White Sands* (ARD 20), the previous *Trieste II* support ship.

Fleet Support Ships—*continued*

POINT LOMA (AGDS 2 as T-AKD 1) *1970, United States Navy*

POINT LOMA (AGDS 2 as T-AKD 1) *1970, United States Navy*

1 GUNBOAT SUPPORT SHIP (AGP): CONVERTED LST

Name	No.	Launched	Commissioned
***GRAHAM COUNTY**	AGP 1176 (ex-LST 1176)	19 Sep 1957	17 Apr 1958

Displacement, tons	approx 8 000 full load
Dimensions, feet	445 oa × 62 × 16·5
Guns	6—3 inch (*76 mm*) 50 cal AA (twin)
Main engines	Diesels (Fairbanks-Morse); 9 600 bhp; 2 shafts (controllable-pitch-propellers) = 14·5 knots

Originally an LST of the "Suffolk" County class built by Newport News SB & DD Co, Newport News, Virginia. Converted in 1972 to support US patrol gunboats (PG) and hydrofoil gunboats (PHM) deployed to Mediterranean area. Redesignated gunboat support ship (AGP) on 1 Aug 1972. Fitted with repair shops and spare parts storage.

Four earlier LSTs modified to support riverine craft in Vietnam also were designated AGP (with LST hull numbers); see listing for Amphibious Warfare Ships in 1971-1972 and previous editions. AGP 1-20 were converted yachts, seaplane tenders, cargo ships, and LSTs employed during World War II to service motor torpedo boats.

GRAHAM COUNTY *Giorgio Arra*

1 DEPENDENT SUPPORT SHIP (AH): "HAVEN" CLASS

Name	No.	Launched	Commissioned
***SANCTUARY** (ex-*Marine Owl*)	AH 17	15 Aug 1944	20 June 1945

Displacement, tons	11 141 standard; 15 400 full load
Dimensions, feet	496 wl; 529 oa × 71·5 × 24
Main engines	Steam turbines (General Electric); 9 000 shp; 1 shaft = 18·33 knots
Boilers	2 (Babcock & Wilcox)
Complement	530 (70 officers, 460 enlisted)

The *Sanctuary* is the last of six hospital ships (AH) of the "Haven" class in active naval service. Built by Sun Shipbuilding & Dry Dock Co, Chester, Pennsylvania, on C4-S-B2 merchant hull. *Sanctuary* recommissioned from reserve in 1966 for service off Vietnam; decommissioned as a hospital ship on 15 Dec 1971 for modification to "dependent support ship" at Hunter's Point Naval Shipyard, San Francisco, California. Subsequently recommissioned on 18 Nov 1972.

As a dependent support ship the *Sanctuary* had special facilities for obstetrics, gynaecology, maternity, and nursery services fitted as a 74-bed hospital which can be expanded to 300 beds in 72 hours. She was the first US Navy ship with mixed male-female crew (although previously female nurses have been assigned to hospital ships and transports). The medical personnel consisted of 50 officers and approx 120 enlisted men including several female nurse officers; the ship's company consisted of 20 officers (including two women) and approx 330 enlisted (including 60 women). The ship was modified to support US dependents of ships homeported in Pireaus, Greece. However, she was not deployed to Greece but was decommissioned on 31 Mar 1974; laid up in Maritime Administration reserve.

Constellation (AH 15) of this class was chartered by a private group and operated under the name *Hope* as a floating hospital and medical school from 1961 to 1973; taken out of service at Philadelphia Naval Shipyard in 1974 and stripped of medical facilities.

DISPOSALS (since 1 Jan 1970)
Repose AH 16 stricken on 15 Mar 1974.

NET LAYING SHIPS

All US Navy net laying ships (ANL) have been discarded except for the *Naubuc* (ex-AN 84), in service as a salvage craft tender (designated YRST 4); see listing under Service Craft. *Naubuc* is a former "Cohoes" class net laying ship.

Cohoes (ANL 78, ex-AN 78) stricken on 30 June 1972. See 1972-1973 edition for characteristics and photograph.

All net laying ships of the "Tree" class have been stricken; last unit in US Navy service was *Butternut* (ex-ANL 9, ex-AN 9, ex-YN 4), lately employed in experimental work as YAG 60 until stricken on 1 July 1971.

SANCTUARY (AH 17) *1974, United States Navy*

4 SELF-PROPELLED BARRACKS SHIPS (APB)

Name	No.	Launched
ECHOLS	APB 37 (ex-APL 37)	30 July 1945
MERCER	APB 39 (ex-APL 39)	17 Nov 1944
NUECES	APB 40 (ex-APL 40)	6 May 1945
KINGMAN	APB 47 (ex-AKS 18, ex-LST 1113)	17 Apr 1945

Displacement, tons	2 189 light; 4 080 full load
Dimensions, feet	136 wl; 328 oa × 50 × 11
Guns	Vary (see notes)
Main engines	Diesels (General Motors); 1 600 to 1 800 bhp; 2 shafts = 12 (APB 41-50) or 10 knots (APB 35-40)
Complement	193 (13 officers, 180 enlisted men)
Troops	1 226 (26 officers, 1 200 enlisted men)

Self-propelled barracks ships (APB) that provide support and accommodations for small craft and riverine forces. All ex-LST type ships of the same basic characteristics. *Mercer* and *Nueces* recommissioned in 1968 for service in Vietnam; decommissioned in 1969-1971 as US riverine forces in South Vietnam were reduced.

These most useful ships supported the joint Army-Navy Mobile Riverine Force in the Mekong Delta region of South Vietnam (Navy River Assault Flotilla 1/Task Force 117/River Support Squadron 7). Complement of each ship in this role was 12 officers and 186 enlisted men, and 900 troops and boat crew personnel were carried. Recommissioned ships had an armament of 2—3 inch guns (single), 8—40 mm guns (two quad mounts), 8—·50 cal MG, and 10—·30 cal MG.

Each APB has troop berthing and messing facilities, evaporators which produce up to 40 000 gallons of fresh water per day, a 16-bed hospital, X-ray room, dental room, bacteriological laboratory, pharmacy, laundry, library, and tailor shop; living and most working spaces are air-conditioned. Most ships not activated for Vietnam have 40 mm AA guns (quad).

DISPOSALS (since 1 Jan 1970)
Vandenburgh APB 48 (ex-AKS 19, ex-LST 1114) stricken on 1 Apr 1972; **Benewah** APB 35 (ex-APL 35, changed to IX 311 on 26 Feb 1971) stricken on 1 Sep 1973; **Colleton** APB 36 (ex-APL 36), **Dorchester** APB 46 (ex-AKS 17, ex-LST 1112) stricken on 1 June 1973.

1 REPAIR SHIP (AR): Ex-DESTROYER TENDER

Name	No.	Launched	Commissioned
***GRAND CANYON**	AR 28 (ex-AD 28)	27 Apr 1945	5 Apr 1946

Displacement, tons	8 165 standard; 16 635 full load
Dimensions, feet	465 wl; 492 oa × 69·5 × 27·2
Guns	1—5 inch (*127 mm*) 38 cal DP
Main engines	steam turbines (Westinghouse); 8 500 shp; 1 shaft = 18·4 knots
Boilers	2 (Foster-Wheeler)

The *Grand Canyon* is a modified C-3 cargo ship completed as a destroyer tender and subsequently reclassified as a repair ship; redesignated AR 28 on 10 Mar 1971. Designed armament was 2—5 inch guns and 8—40 mm guns.

Built by Todd Shipyards Corp, Los Angeles, California. Modernised; fitted with helicopter platform and hangar aft. The *Grand Canyon* is active.

DISPOSALS
Klondike AR 22 (ex-AD 22) stricken on 15 Sep 1974.

NOMENCLATURE. Repair ships normally are named for mythological characters.

GRAND CANYON (AR 28) *1971, United States Navy*

Fleet Support Ships—*continued*

1 REPAIR SHIP (AR): Ex-DESTROYER TENDER

Name	No.	Commissioned
MARKAB (ex-*Mormacpenn*)	AR 23 (ex-AD 21, ex-AK 31)	15 June 1941

Displacement, tons	8 560 standard; 14 800 full load
Dimensions, feet	465 wl; 492·5 oa × 69·8 × 24·8
Guns	4—3 inch (*76 mm*) 50 cal AA (single)
Main engines	steam turbines (General Electric); 8 500 shp; 1 shaft = 18·4 knots
Boilers	2 (Foster-Wheeler)

Built by Ingalls SB Co, Pascagoula, Miss; launched on 21 Dec 1940. Former destroyer tender, reclassified as repair ship on 15 Apr 1960 and designation changed from AD to AR. One 5 inch gun and 4—40 mm guns were removed. The *Markab* was decommissioned on 19 Dec 1969 but remains in service in reserve as station ship at Mare Island, Calif.

MARKAB (AR 23) *United States Navy*

2 REPAIR SHIPS (AR): "DELTA" CLASS

Name	No.	Commissioned
DELTA (ex-*Hawaiian Packer*)	AR 9 (ex-AK 29)	16 June 1941
BRIAREUS (ex-*Hawaiian Planter*)	AR 12	16 Nov 1943

Displacement, tons	8 975 standard; 14 500 full load
Dimensions, feet	465·5 wl; 490·5 oa × 69·5 × 24·3
Guns	4—3 inch (*76 mm*) 50 cal AA (single)
Main engines	steam turbines (Newport News); 8 500 shp; 1 shaft = 17 knots knots
Boilers	2 (Foster-Wheeler and Babcock & Wilcox, respectively)
Complement	688 (29 officers, 559 enlisted men); 903 and 924, respectively, designed wartime

C-3 type built by Newport News SB & DD Co, Newport News, Va. Both launched in 1941 with *Briareus* serving as a merchant ship before being acquired by the Navy. The 5 inch and 4—40 mm guns removed. *Briareus* decommissioned in 1955 and placed in reserve; *Delta* decommissioned in 1970 remains in service in reserve as station ship at Bremerton, Wash.

DISPOSALS (since 1 Jan 1970)
Amphion AR 13 transferred to Iran on 1 Oct 1971; **Cadmus** AR 14 transferred to Taiwan China on 15 Jan 1973.

DELTA (AR 9) *1969, United States Navy*

4 REPAIR SHIPS (AR): "VULCAN" CLASS

Name	No.	Launched	Commissioned
***VULCAN**	AR 5	14 Dec 1940	16 June 1941
***AJAX**	AR 6	22 Aug 1942	30 Oct 1942
***HECTOR**	AR 7	11 Nov 1942	7 Feb 1944
***JASON**	AR 8	3 Apr 1943	19 June 1944

Displacement, tons	9 140 standard; 16 200 full load
Dimensions, feet	520 wl; 529·3 oa × 73·3 × 23·3
Guns	4—5 inch (*127 mm*) 38 cal DP (single)
Main engines	steam turbines; 11 000 shp; 2 shafts = 19·2 knots
Boilers	4 (Babcock & Wilcox 3-drum)
Complement	715 (23 officers, 692 enlisted men); 950 designed wartime

Vulcan was built by New York SB Corpn under the 1939 programme and the other three by Los Angeles SB & DD Corpn under the 1940 Programme. All carry a most elaborate equipment of machine tools to undertake repairs of every description. *Jason*, originally designated ARH 1 and rated as heavy hull repair ship, was reclassified AR 8 on 9 Sep 1957. 8—40 mm AA guns (twin) have been removed; the 4—5 inch guns were the standard main battery of large fleet support ships and oilers during World War II.

All of these ships are active.

AJAX (AR 6) *1970, United States Navy*

HECTOR (AR 7) *1971, United States Navy*

AJAX (AR 6) *1970, United States Navy*

NEW CONSTRUCTION CABLE SHIPS

The Navy plans to underwrite the financing of two new construction cable ships that would be long-term chartered to the Military Sealift Command. These ships could be operational by the late 1970s, when the four existing Navy cable ships are more than 30 years old. In addition to the cable ships listed here, the Military Sealift Command periodically charters the services of three commercial ships to support Navy requirements, the American-flag *Long Lines*, the Liberian-flag and German crewed *Neptun*, and the Canadian-owned and manned *John Cabot*. These are the only three commercial ships considered in part suitable for US defence needs.

2 CABLE SHIPS (ARC): "AEOLUS" CLASS

Name	No.	Commissioned
***AEOLUS** (ex-*Turandot*)	T-ARC 3 (ex-AKA 47)	18 June 1945
***THOR** (ex-*Vanadis*)	T-ARC 4 (ex-AKA 49)	9 July 1945

Displacement, tons	7 040 full load
Dimensions, feet	400 wl; 438 oa × 58·2 × 19·25
Guns	None
Main engines	Turbo-electric (Westinghouse); 6 000 shp; 2 shafts = 16·9 knots
Boilers	2 (Wickes)

Built as S4-SE2-BE1 attack cargo ships by Walsh-Kaiser Co, Providence, Rhode Island. Transferred to Maritime Administration and laid up in reserve from 1946 until reacquired by Navy for conversion to cable ships in 1955-1956. Converted to cable ships at the Key Highway Plant of Bethlehem Steel Corp, Baltimore, Maryland, being recommissioned on 14 May 1955 and 3 Jan 1956, respectively. Fitted with cable-laying bow sheaves, cable stowage tanks, cable repair facilities, and helicopter platform aft.

Both ships have been employed in hydrographic and cable operations. They were both Navy manned until 1973 when transferred to Military Sealift Command and provided with civilian crews. *Aeolus* laid up in reserve.

AEOLUS (T-ARC 3) *1970, United States Navy*

Fleet Support Ships—*continued*

THOR (T-ARC 4) *United States Navy*

AEOLUS (T-ARC 3) *United States Navy*

2 CABLE SHIPS (ARC): "NEPTUNE" CLASS

***NEPTUNE** (ex-*William H. G. Bullard*)	T-ARC 2
***ALBERT J. MEYER**	T-ARC 6

Displacement, tons 7 400 full load
Dimensions, feet 322 wl; 370 oa × 47 × 18
Guns removed
Main engines Reciprocating (Skinner); 4 800 ihp; 2 shafts = 14 knots
Boilers 2 (Combustion Engineering)

Built as S3-S2-BP1 type cable ships for Maritime Administration. Both ships built by Pusey & Jones Corp, Wilmington, Delaware, completed 1945-1946.
Neptune acquired by Navy from Maritime Administration in 1953 and sister ship *Albert J. Meyer* from US Army in 1966, latter ship for operation by Military Sea Transportation Service (now Military Sealift Command). They have been fitted with electric cable handling machinery (in place of steam equipment) and precision navigation equipment; helicopter platform in *Neptune*.
Both ships are operated by the Military Sealift Command with civilian crews; *Neptune* was Navy manned until 1973 when transferred to MSC.
The USNS *Neptune* (T-ARC 2) should not be confused with the commercial cable ship *Neptun* of the United States Undersea Cable Corp.

See 1971-1972 edition for disposals of other cable ships.

NEPTUNE (T-ARC 2) *United States Navy*

ALBERT J. MEYER (T-ARC 6) *United States Navy*

SPHINX (ARL 24) *1968, United States Navy*

5 REPAIR SHIPS (ARB-ARL): CONVERTED LST TYPE

Name	No.	Launched	Commissioned
MIDAS	ARB 5 (ex-LST 514)	24 Dec 1943	23 May 1944
SARPEDON	ARB 7 (ex-LST 596)	21 Aug 1944	20 Mar 1945
EGERIA	ARL 8 (ex-LST 136)	23 Nov 1943	18 Dec 1943
SPHINX	ARL 24 (ex-LST 963)	18 Nov 1944	12 Dec 1944
INDRA	ARL 37 (ex-LST 1147)	21 May 1945	28 May 1945

Displacement, tons 1 625 light; 4 100 full load
Dimensions, feet 316 wl; 328 oa × 50 × 11
Guns 8—40 mm AA (quad); several 20 mm AA in some ships
Main engines Diesels (General Motors); 1 800 bhp; 2 shafts = 11·6 knots
Complement 251 to 286

LST-type ships converted during construction to battle damage repair ships (ARB) and landing craft repair ships (ARL). All launched 1943-1945. Fitted with machine shops, material and parts storage, lifting gear, etc; the battle damage ships have 50-ton capacity booms and the landing craft ships have 50-ton (ARL 2 and 8) and 60-ton (ARL 24 and 37) capacities. The ARLs cater to small amphibious, minesweeping, and riverine craft. Most units have pole masts; note tripod mast in *Sphinx*, reactivated during Vietnam War. All surviving ships are in reserve.
Photographs of ARLs active in Vietnamese waters appear in the 1972-1973 and previous editions.

TRANSFERS. Former US Navy LSTs modified to fleet support ships (AGP-ARB-ARL-ARVE) are operated by the navies of Brazil, Chile, China, West Germany, Greece, Indonesia, Iran, South Korea, Malaysia, Philippines, Taiwan China, Turkey, Venezuela, and South Vietnam.

DISPOSALS AND TRANSFERS (since 1 June 1970)
Amycus ARL 2 (ex-LST 489) stricken on 1 June 1970; **Askari** ARL 30 (ex-LST 1131) transferred to Indonesia on 31 Aug 1971; **Satyr** ARL 23 (ex-LST 852) transferred to South Vietnam on 15 Oct 1971; **Krishna** ARL 38 (ex-LST 1148) transferred to the Philippines on 30 Oct 1971; **Atlas** ARL 7 (ex-LST 231), **Endymion** ARL 9 (ex-LST 513) stricken on 1 June 1972; **Zeus** ARB 4 (ex-LSR 132), **Telamon** ARB 8 (ex-LST 976), **Achelous** ARL 1 (ex-LST 10), **Fabius** ARVA 5 (ex-LST 1093), **Chloris** ARVE 4 (ex-LST 1094) stricken on 1 June 1973; **Megara** ARVA 6 (ex-LST 1095) transferred to Mexico on 1 Oct 1973.

"LIBERTY" TYPE

Tutuila ARG 4 transferred to Taiwan China on 21 Feb 1972.

14 SALVAGE SHIPS (ARS): "DIVER" CLASS

Name	No.	Launched	Commissioned
***ESCAPE**	ARS 6	22 Nov 1942	20 Nov 1943
***GRAPPLE**	ARS 7	31 Dec 1942	16 Dec 1943
***PRESERVER**	ARS 8	1 Apr 1943	11 Jan 1944
***DELIVER**	ARS 23	25 Sep 1943	18 July 1944
***GRASP**	ARS 24	31 July 1943	22 Aug 1944
***SAFEGUARD**	ARS 25	20 Nov 1943	31 Oct 1944
***CLAMP**	ARS 33	24 Oct 1942	23 Aug 1943
***GEAR**	ARS 34	24 Oct 1942	24 Sep 1943
***BOLSTER**	ARS 38	23 Dec 1944	1 May 1945
***CONSERVER**	ARS 39	27 Jan 1945	9 June 1945
***HOIST**	ARS 40	31 Mar 1945	21 July 1945
***OPPORTUNE**	ARS 41	31 Mar 1945	5 Oct 1945
***RECLAIMER**	ARS 42	25 June 1945	20 Dec 1945
***RECOVERY**	ARS 43	4 Aug 1945	15 May 1946

Displacement, tons 1 530 standard; 1 900 full load
Dimensions, feet 207 wl; 213·5 oa × 39 except later ships 43 × 13
Guns 1—40 mm AA (removed from some ships); 2—50 cal MG or 2—20 mm AA fitted in some ships
Main engines Diesel-electric (Cooper Bessemer); 3 000 shp; 2 shafts = 14·8 knots except 16 knots in later ships
Complement 85 (120 designed wartime)

These ships are fitted for salvage and towing; equipped with compressed air diving equipment. All built by Basalt Rock Co, Napa, California. Most have a single 40 mm gun fitted atop the superstructure forward of the funnel; replaced in several ships by smaller weapons on bridge wings. Early ships have 8-ton and 10-ton capacity booms; later ships have 10-ton and 20-ton booms.
ARS 38 and later ships are of a slightly different design, sometimes known as the "Bolster" class; however, generally considered to be the same class.
The *Gear* is operated by a commercial firm in support of Navy activities; two additional ships are on loan to private salvage firms, the *Cable* ARS 19 and *Curb* ARS 21, and support naval requirements as needed. The *Clamp* was stricken from the Navy List in 1963 but reacquired in 1973 and returned to service.

CONVERSIONS. *Chain* ARS 20 and *Snatch* ARS 27 converted to oceanographic research ships, designated AGOR 17 and AGOR 18, respectively.

NOMENCLATURE. Salvage ships are named for terms related to salvage activity.

PHOTOGRAPHS. Note the McCann submarine rescue chamber on the bow of the *Safeguard* (following page); these chambers normally are carried aboard submarine rescue ships.

DISPOSALS (since 1 Jan 1970)
Current ARS 22 stricken on 1 June 1973.

OPPORTUNE (ARS 41) *1973, Giorgio Arra*

Fleet Support Ships—*continued*

BOLSTER (ARS 38) *1973, US Navy, JQC Warren Grass*

SAFEGUARD (ARS 25) *1972, United States Navy*

SALVAGE LIFTING SHIPS (ARSD)

Gypsy ARSD 1 (ex-LSM 549), **Mender** ARSD 2 (ex-LSM 550) stricken on 1 June 1973. See 1973-1974 and previous editions for characteristics.

SALVAGE TENDERS (ARST)

Laysan Island ARST 1 (ex-LST 1098), **Palmyra** ARST 3 (ex-LST 1100) stricken on 1 June 1973. See 1973-1974 and previous editions for characteristics.

HELICOPTER REPAIR SHIP (ARVH)

Corpus Christi Bay T-ARVH 1 (ex-*Albermarle*, AV 5) stricken on 31 Dec 1974. See 1974-1975 and previous editions for characteristics.

2 + 4 SUBMARINE TENDERS (AS): "L. Y. SPEAR" CLASS

Name	*No.*	*Laid down*	*Launched*	*Commissioned*
***L. Y. SPEAR**	AS 36	5 May 1966	7 Sep 1967	28 Feb 1970
***DIXON**	AS 37	7 Sep 1967	20 June 1970	7 Aug 1971
	AS 39	Fiscal Year 1972 programme		1978
	AS 40	Fiscal Year 1973 programme		1978
	AS 41	Planned FY 1977 programme		
	AS 42	Planned		

Displacement, tons	13 000 standard; AS 36 and AS 37 23 350 full load; AS 39 and AS 40 24 000 full load
Dimensions, feet	643·8 oa × 85 × 28·5
Guns	2—5 inch (*127 mm*) 38 cal DP in *L. Y. Spear* and *Dixon*; 4—20 mm AA planned for AS 39 and AS 40
Missile launchers	NATO Sea Sparrow missile launcher planned for AS 39 and later ships
Main engines	steam turbines (General Electric); 20 000 shp; 1 shaft = 20 knots
Boilers	2 (Foster Wheeler)
Complement	AS 36 and 37 1 072 (42 officers, 1 030 enlisted men) AS 39 and 40 1 158 (50 officers, 1 108 enlisted men)
Flag accommodations	69 (25 officers, 44 enlisted men)

These ships are the first US submarine tenders designed specifically for servicing nuclear-propelled attack submarines with latter ships built to a modified design to support SSN-688 class submarines. (Four previous submarine tenders of post-World War II construction are configured to support ballistic missile submarines.) Basic hull design similar to "Samuel Gompers" class destroyer tenders. Provided with helicopter deck but no hangar. Each ship can simultaneously provide services to four submarines

"L. Y. SPEAR" CLASS—continued

moored alongside. AS 39 and later ships are especially configured to support SSN 688 class submarines.

L. Y. Spear authorised in Fiscal Year 1965 new construction programme and *Dixon* in FY 1966 programme. Both ships built by General Dynamics Corp, Quincy, Massachusetts.

AS 38 of FY 1969 programme cancelled prior to start of construction to provide funds for overruns in other new ship programmes.

AS 39 authorised in FY 1972 new construction programme and AS 40 in FY 1973 programme; both to be built by Lockheed Shipbuilding, Seattle, Washington. AS 41 planned for FY 1977 programme request with a sixth unit also planned.

NOMENCLATURE. Submarine tenders generally are named after pioneers in submarine development and mythological characters.

DIXON (AS 37) *1971, United States Navy*

2 SUBMARINE TENDERS (AS): "SIMON LAKE" CLASS

Name	*No*	*Laid down*	*Launched*	*Commissioned*
•**SIMON LAKE**	AS 33	7 Jan 1963	8 Feb 1964	7 Nov 1964
•**CANOPUS**	AS 34	2 Mar 1964	12 Feb 1965	4 Nov 1965

Displacement, tons	21 500 full load
Dimensions, feet	643·7 × 85 × 30
Guns	4—3 inch (*76 mm*) 50 cal AA (twin)
Main engines	steam turbines; 20 000 shp; 1 shaft = 18 knots
Boilers	2 (Combustion Engineering)
Complement	1 075 (55 officers, 1 020 men)

These ships are designed specifically to service fleet ballistic missile submarines (SSBN), with as many as three submarines alongside being supported simultaneously.

The *Simon Lake* was authorised in the Fiscal Year 1963 new construction programme and built by the Puget Sound Naval Shipyard, the *Canopus* was authorised in FY 1964 and built by Ignalls Shipbuilding Corp. AS 35 was authorised in FY 1965 programme, but her construction was deferred. The last ship would have permitted one tender to be assigned to each of five FBM submarine squadrons with a sixth ship available to rotate when another was in overhaul, however; only four SSBN squadrons were established.

Note cranes amidships, funnel location (flanked by gun mounts, and helicopter platform).

CANOPUS (AS 34) *1966, United States Navy*

L. Y. SPEAR (AS 36) *1970, United States Navy*

Fleet Support Ships—*continued*

2 SUBMARINE TENDERS (AS): "HUNLEY" CLASS

Name	No	Laid down	Launched	Commissioned
•HUNLEY	AS 31	28 Nov 1960	28 Sep 1961	16 June 1962
•HOLLAND	AS 32	5 Mar 1962	19 Jan 1963	7 Sep 1963

Displacement, tons: 10 500 standard; 18 300 full load
Dimensions, feet: 599 × 83 × 24
Guns: 4—3 inch (*76 mm*) 50 cal AA (twin)
Main engines: Diesel-electric (10 Fairbanks-Morse diesels); 15 000 bhp; 1 shaft = 19 knots
Complement: 1 081 (58 officers, 1 023 men) plus accommodation for 30 officers and 270 men from submarines

These ships are the first US submarine tenders of post-World War II construction; designed specifically to provide repairs and supply services to fleet ballistic missile submarines (SSBN). Provided with 52 separate workshops to provide complete support to nuclear plants, electronic and navigation systems, missiles, and other submarine systems. Helicopter platform fitted aft but no hangar. Both ships originally fitted with a 32-ton-capacity hammerhead crane (see 1972-1973 and previous editions for photographs); subsequently refitted with two amidships cranes as in "Simon Lake" class (see accompanying photographs).
Hunley authorised in Fiscal Year 1960 shipbuilding programme and built by Newport News Shipbuilding & Dry Dock Co, Virginia; *Holland* authorised in FY 1962 programme and built by Ingalls Shipbuilding Corp, Pascagoula, Mississippi. Former ship cost $24 359 800.

NOMENCLATURE. ***Holland* is named after John Philip Holland, an Irish emigrant to the United States, and submarine designer and builder. One of his submarines was accepted by the US Navy in 1900 and became Submarine Torpedo Boat No 1, named *Holland*, the first officially accepted US Navy submarine.**

CANOPUS (AS 34) servicing SSBN *1970, United States Navy*

HOLLAND (AS 32) *United States Navy*

7 SUBMARINE TENDERS (AS): "FULTON" CLASS

Name	No	Launched	Commissioned
•FULTON	AS 11	27 Dec 1940	12 Sep 1941
•SPERRY	AS 12	17 Dec 1941	1 May 1942
BUSHNELL	AS 15	14 Sep 1942	10 Apr 1943
•HOWARD W. GILMORE (*Neptune*)	AS 16	16 Sep 1943	24 May 1944
NEREUS	AS 17	12 Feb 1945	27 Oct 1945
•ORION	AS 18	14 Oct 1942	30 Sep 1943
•PROTEUS	AS 19	12 Nov 1942	31 Jan 1944

Displacement, tons: 9 734 standard; 18 000 full load except *Proteus:* 10 234 standard; 18 500 full load
Dimensions, feet: 530·5 except *Proteus* 574·5 oa × 73·3 × 25·5
Guns: 2—5 inch (*127 mm*) 38 cal DP except one gun in *Proteus*
Main engines: Diesel-electric (General Motors); 11 200 to 11 800 bhp; 2 shafts = 15·4 knots
Complement: 917 (34 officers, 883 enlisted men); except *Proteus* 1 121 (51 officers, 1 070 enlisted men)

These venerable ships are contemporaries of the similar-design "Dixie" class destroyer tenders. Four ships built by Mare Island Navy Yard, Vallejo, California; *Sperry, Orion,* and *Proteus* built by Moore Shipbuilding & Dry Dock Co, Oakland, California. As built they carried the then-standard large auxiliary armament of four 5 inch guns plus 8—40 mm AA guns (twin). The original 20-ton capacity cylinder cranes have been replaced in the *Howard W. Gilmore*.

CONVERSION. *Proteus* AS 19 was converted at the Charleston Naval Shipyard, under the Fiscal Year 1959 conversion programme, at a cost of $23 000 000 to service nuclear-powered fleet ballistic missile submarines (SSBN). Conversion was begun on 19 Jan 1959 and she was recommissioned on 8 July 1960. She was lengthened by adding a section amidships 44 feet in length, and the bare hull weight of this 6-deck high insertion was approximately 500 tons. Three 5 inch guns were removed and her upper decks extended aft to provide additional workshops. Storage tubes for Polaris missiles installed; bridge crane amidships loads and unloads missiles for alongside submarines.

MODERNISATION. *Bushnell, Fulton, Howard W. Gilmore, Nereus, Orion* and *Sperry* have undergone FRAM II modernisation to service nuclear powered attack submarines. Additional maintenance shops provided to service nuclear plant components and advanced electronic equipment and weapons. After two 5 inch guns and eight 40 mm guns (twin) removed.

NOMENCLATURE. *Howard W. Gilmore* remembers the commanding officer of a World War II submarine who, lying on the bridge wounded, ordered the boat to dive; he was posthumously awarded the Medal of Honour, the highest US military decoration.

DISPOSALS AND TRANSFERS
C-3 type: **Pelias** AS 14 stricken on 1 Aug 1971, **Griffin** AS 13 stricken on 1 Aug 1972.
C3-S-A2 type: **Anthendon** AS 24 and **Clytie** AS 26 stricken on 1 Sep 1961 (former ship subsequently transferred on 7 Sep 1969 from Maritime Administration reserve to Turkey). **Apollo** AS 25 stricken on 1 July 1963, **Aegir** AS 23 stricken on 25 Jan 1971.
Modified C-3 type: **Euryale** AS 22 stricken on 1 Dec 1971.

HOWARD W. GILMORE (AS 16) *1973, Giorgio Arra*

HOWARD W. GILMORE (AS 16) *1971, United States Navy*

HUNLEY (AS 31) *United States Navy*

Fleet Support Ships—*continued*

ORION (AS 18) *1973, United States Navy PHCS Boyd E. Spang*

2 SUBMARINE RESCUE SHIPS (ASR): "PIGEON" CLASS

Name	No.	Builder	Launched	Commissioned
***PIGEON**	ASR 21	Alabama DD & SB Co	13 Aug 1969	28 Apr 1973
***ORTOLAN**	ASR 22	Alabama DD & SB Co	10 Sep 1969	14 July 1973

Displacement, tons	4 200 full load
Dimensions, feet	251 oa × 86 (see *Design* notes) × 21·25
Guns	2—20 mm AA (single) 4—·50 cal MG
Main engines	4 diesels; 6 000 bhp; 2 shafts = 15 knots
Complement	115 (6 officers, 109 enlisted men)
Staff accommodation	14 (4 officers, 10 enlisted men)
Submersible operators	24 (4 officers, 20 enlisted men)

These are the world's first ships designed specifically for this role, all other ASR designs being adaptations of tug types. The ASR 21 class ships will serve as (1) surface support ships for the Deep Submergence Rescue Vehicles (DSRV), (2) rescue ships employing the existing McCann rescue chamber, (3) major deep-sea diving support ships, and (4) operational control ships for salvage operations.

The Navy had planned in the 1960s to replace the 10-ship ASR force with new construction ASRs. However, only two ships have been funded with procurement of others deferred.

ASR 21 authorised in Fiscal Year 1967 new construction programme and ASR 22 in FY 1968 programme. Both ships built by Alabama Dry Dock and Shipbuilding Co, Mobile, Alabama; they have been delayed more than two years by a shipyard strike and technical difficulties; additional delays encountered in special equipment installation.

DESIGN. These ships have twin, catamaran hulls, the first ocean-going catamaran ships to be built for the US Navy since Robert Fulton's steam gunboat *Demologus* of 1812. The design provides a large deck working area, facilities for raising and lowering submersibles and underwater equipment, and improved stability when operating equipment at great depths. Each of the twin hulls is 251 feet long and 26 feet wide. The well between the hulls is 34 feet across, giving the ASR a maximum beam of 86 feet. Fitted with helicopter platform.

DIVING. These ships have been fitted with the Mk II Deep Diving System to support conventional or saturation divers operating at depths to 850 feet. The system consists of two decompression chambers, two personnel transfer capsules to transport divers between the ship and ocean floor, and the associated controls, winches, cables, gas supplies *et cetera*. Submarine rescue ships are the US Navy's primary diving ships and the only ones fitted for helium-oxygen diving.

ELECTRONICS. Fitted with precision three-dimensional sonar system for tracking submersibles.

ENGINEERING. Space and weight are reserved for future installation of a ducted thruster in each bow to enable the ship to maintain precise position while stopped or at slow speeds. Range is 8 500 miles at 13 knots.

"PIGEON" CLASS—*continued*

GUNNERY. As built the *Pigeon* was armed with 2—3 inch AA guns in twin gun "tubs" forward of the bridge. She had two large mooring buoys ("spuds") forward of the bridge between the guns and two additional buoys aft, one on each stern. Subsequently the *Pigeon* was modified to the *Ortolan* configuration with four mooring buoys forward; 3 inch gun mounts removed. See 1974-1975 edition or photo of *Pigeon* with 3 inch guns.

NOMENCLATURE. Submarine rescue ships traditionally have carried bird names (the US Navy's first six ASRs were converted "Bird" class minesweepers).

OPERATIONAL. One ASR normally is deployed to the western Pacific and one in the Mediterranean with the others at US submarine bases in the continental United States and Hawaii.

SUBMERSIBLES. Each ASR is capable of transporting, servicing, lowering, and raising two Deep Submergence Rescue Vehicles (DSRV) (see section on Deep Submergence Vehicles).

"PENGUIN" CLASS

The three submarine rescue ships of the "Penguin" class, converted from fleet tugs (ATF), have been stricken; see 1973-1974 and previous editions for characteristics. **Bluebird** ASR 19 transferred to Turkey on 15 Aug 1950; **Penguin** ASR 12 stricken on 30 June 1970; **Skylark** ASR 20 transferred to Brazil on 30 June 1973

PIGEON (ASR 21) *1975, US Navy, PH2 Donald Westman*

ORTOLAN (ASR 22) *1973, United States Navy, Albert E. Flournoy*

Fleet Support Ships—*continued*

ORTOLAN (ASR 22) *1973, United States Navy*

6 SUBMARINE RESCUE SHIPS (ASR): "CHANTICLEER" CLASS

	ASR	Launched		ASR	Launched
***COUCAL**	8	29 May 1942	***PETREL**	14	26 Sep 1945
***FLORIKAN**	9	14 June 1942	***SUNBIRD**	15	3 Apr 1945
***KITTIWAKE**	13	10 July 1945	***TRINGA**	16	25 June 1945

Displacement, tons	1 653 standard; 2 290 full load
Dimensions, feet	240 wl; 251·5 oa × 42 × 14·9
Guns	2—20 mm AA (single) in some ships
Main engines	Diesel-electric (Alco in first 4 ships, GM in others); 3 000 bhp; 1 shaft = 14·9 knots
Complement	85 (102 designed wartime)

Large tug-type ships equipped with powerful pumps, heavy air compressors, and rescue chambers for submarine salvage and rescue operations. ASR 8-9 built by Moore SB & DD Co, Oakland, Calif, and ASR 13-16 by Savannah Machine & Foundry Co, Savannah, Ga. Fitted for helium-oxygen diving.
As built each ship was armed with 2—3 inch AA guns; removed 1957-1958. Some ships subsequently fitted with two 20 mm AA guns.

DISPOSALS AND TRANSFERS
Greenlet ASR 10 transferred to Turkey on 12 June 1970; **Chanticleer** ASR 7 stricken 1 June 1973.

PHOTOGRAPHS. In the first view of the *Florikan* note the 20 mm gun mount and two small mooring buoys abreast funnel and McCann submarine rescue chamber on fantail under boom; in the lower view the buoys are deployed. Note empty 3 inch gun tab forward of bridge.

FLORIKAN (ASR 9) *1970, United States Navy*

FLORIKAN (ASR 9) *1971, United States Navy*

PETREL (ASR 14) *United States Navy*

5 AUXILIARY TUGS (ATA): "MARICOPA" CLASS

	ATA	Launched		ATA	Launched
ACCOKEEK	181	27 July 1944	**TATNUCK**	195	14 Dec 1944
SAMOSET	190	26 Oct 1944	**STALLION**	193	24 Nov 1944
			KEYWADIN	213	9 Apr 1945

Displacement, tons	534 standard; 835 full load
Dimensions, feet	134·5 wl; 143 oa × 33·9 × 13
Guns	1—3 inch (*76 mm*) 50 cal AA or 4—20 mm AA (twin); all guns removed from some ships
Main engines	Diesel-electric (General Motors diesels); 1 500 bhp; 1 shaft = 13 knots
Complement	45 (5 officers, 40 enlisted men)

Steel-hulled tugs formerly designated as rescue tugs (ATR); renumbered in same series as larger fleet tugs (ATF) when designation changed to ATA in 1944. All above ships built by Livingston SB Corp, Orange, Texas, or Gulfport Boiler & Welding Works, Port Arthur, Texas. During 1948 they were assigned names that had been carried by discarded fleet and yard tugs.
All of the surviving ships were decommissioned in 1970-1971 and placed in reserve. Two ships of this class serve in the Coast Guard.

DISPOSALS AND TRANSFERS (since 1 Jan 1970)
Kalmia ATA 184, **Umpqua** ATA 209 transferred to Colombia on 1 July 1971; **Mahopac** ATA 196 transferred to Taiwan China on 1 July 1971; **Tillamook** ATA 192 transferred to South Korea on 25 July 1971; **Sagamore** ATA 208 transferred to Dominican Republic on 1 Feb 1972; **Salish** ATA 187, **Catawba** ATA 210 transferred to Argentina on 10 Feb 1972; **Cahokia** ATA 186 (loan to US Air Force in 1971) transferred to Taiwan China on 29 Mar 1972; **Koka** ATA 185 to US Department of Health, Education and Welfare on 3 Dec 1973; **Wandank** ATA 204 to US Department of Interior on 1 Aug 1973; **Penobscott** ATA 188 stricken on 28 Feb 1975.

ACCOKEEK (ATA 181) *1970, United States Navy*

FLEET TUGS (ATF): NEW DESIGN

One fleet tug	**T-ATF**	Fiscal Year 1975 programme
Three fleet tugs	**T-ATF**	Proposed FY 1976 programme
Six fleet tugs	**T-ATF**	Planned FY 1977-1967 programmes

Displacement, tons	2 000 full load
Dimensions, feet	208 oa × 42 × 15
Guns	2—20 mm AA; 2—·50 cal MG (space and weight provided)
Main engines	2 diesels; 4 500 bhp; 2 shafts (controllable-pitch propellers) = 15 knots
Complement	16 civilian plus 4 Navy communications personnel and 20 transient diving/salvage personnel

This is a new class of fleet tugs built to commercial standards; the ships will be operated by the Military Sealift Command and manned by civilian crews. Guns will not normally be installed. A 300 hp bow thruster will be provided: 10 ton capacity crane.
Estimated cost of the lead ship is $11 500 000 and an average of $15 000 000 for the FY 1976 ships.

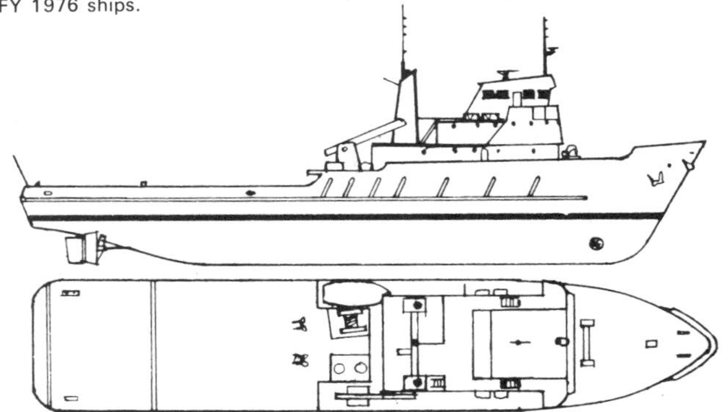

Fleet Support Ships—*continued*

22 FLEET TUGS (ATF): "APACHE" CLASS

	ATF	*Launched*		ATF	*Launched*
***UTE**	T-76	24 June 1942	***MOLALA**	106	23 Dec 1942
***CREE**	84	17 Aug 1942	***QUAPAW**	110	15 May 1943
***LIPAN**	T-85	17 Sep 1942	***TAKELMA**	113	18 Sep 1943
***MATACO**	86	14 Oct 1942	***TAWAKONI**	114	28 Oct 1943
SENECA	91	2 Feb 1943	***ATAKAPA**	T-149	11 July 1944
***TAWASA**	92	22 Feb 1943	***NIPMUC**	157	12 Apr 1945
***ABNAKI**	96	22 Apr 1943	***MOSOSPELEA**	T-158	7 Mar 1945
***CHOWANOC**	100	20 Aug 1943	***PAIUTE**	159	4 June 1945
***COCOPA**	101	5 Oct 1943	***PAPAGO**	160	21 June 1945
***HITCHITI**	103	29 Jan 1944	***SALINAN**	161	20 July 1945
***MOCTOBI**	105	25 Mar 1944	***SHAKORI**	162	9 Aug 1945

Displacement, tons	1 235 standard; 1 675 full load
Dimensions, feet	195 wl; 205 oa × 38·5 × 15·5 max
Guns	1—3 inch (*76 mm*) 50 cal AA; some ships have machine guns in "tubs" aft of bridge; guns removed from T-ATFs
Main engines	Diesel-electric drive; 3 000 bhp; 1 shaft = 15 knots
Complement	75 (5 officers, 70 enlisted men; 85 wartime)

Large ocean tugs fitted with powerful pumps and other salvage equipment. ATF 96 and later ships ("Abnaki" class) have smaller funnel. As built these ships mounted 2—40 mm guns in addition to 3 inch gun. All surviving ships built by Charleston SB & DD Co, or United Engineering Co, Alameda, Calif, except *Seneca* built by Cramp SB Co, Philadelphia, Pa, and *Tawasa* by Commercial Iron Works, Portland, Oreg.
Beginning in 1973 several fleet tugs have been assigned to the Military Sealift Command and provided with civilian crews these ships are designated T-ATF and are unarmed. ATF 85 and ATF 158 assigned to MSC in 1973; ATF 76, and ATF 149 to MSC in 1974; additional ATFs will follow.
Three ships of this class serve with the US Coast Guard. All remaining ATFs are active except the *Seneca* which is in Maritime Administration reserve (on Navy List).

NOMENCLATURE. US tugs of World War II construction and previous classes were named for Indian tribes and words.

DISPOSALS AND TRANSFERS (since 1 Jan 1970)
Utina ATF 163 transferred to Venezuela on 30 Sep 1971; **Arikara** ATF 98 transferred to Chile on 1 July 1972; **Kiowa** ATF 72 transferred to Dominican Republic on 16 Oct 1972; **Sioux** ATF 75 transferred to Turkey on 30 Oct 1972; **Apache** ATF 67 transferred to Taiwan China on 30 June 1974; **Pinto** ATF 90 transferred to Peru on 17 May 1974; **Luiscno** AFT 156 transferred to Argentina in 1975.

TAWASA (ATF 92)—large funnel *1973, US Navy, JOC Warren Grass*

CHOWANOC (ATF 100) *1973, US Navy, JOC Warren Grass*

COCOPA (ATF 101)—small funnel *1970, United States Navy*

3 SALVAGE AND RESCUE SHIPS (ATS): "EDENTON" CLASS

Name	*No.*	*Laid down*	*Launched*	*Commissioned*
***EDENTON**	ATS 1	1 Apr 1967	15 May 1968	23 Jan 1971
***BEAUFORT**	ATS 2	19 Feb 1968	20 Dec 1968	22 Jan 1972
***BRUNSWICK**	ATS 3	5 June 1968	14 Oct 1969	10 Dec 1972

Displacement, tons	3 117 full load
Dimensions, feet	282·66 oa × 50 × 15·1
Guns	2—20 mm AA; 4—·50 cal MG
Main engines	4 diesels (Paxman); 6 000 bhp; 2 shafts = 16 knots
Complement	102 (9 officers and 93 enlisted men)

These tugs are designed specifically for salvage operations and are capable of (1) ocean towing, (2) supporting diver operations to depths of 850 feet, (3) lifting submerged objects weighing as much as 600 000 pounds from a depth of 120 feet by static tidal lift or 30 000 pounds by dynamic lift, (4) fighting ship fires, and (5) performing general salvage operations.
The ATS 1 was authorised in the Fiscal Year 1966 shipbuilding programme; ATS 2 and ATS 3 in the FY 1967 programme. All three ships constructed by Brooke Marine, Lowestoft, England
ATF 4 was authorised in the FY 1972 new construction programme and ATS 5 in the FY 1973 programme, with several additional ships being planned. However, construction of these ships was deferred in 1973 with the smaller, new-design ATF being substituted in their place.
Designation changed from salvage tug (ATS) to salvage and rescue ship (ATS) on 16 Feb 1971.

DIVING. These ships can carry the air-transportable Mk 1 Deep Diving System to support four divers working in two-man shifts at depths to 850 feet. The system consists of a double-chamber decompression chamber a personnel transfer capsule to transport divers between the ships and ocean floor and the associated controls, winches, cables, gas supplies, *et cetera*. The ships organic diving capability is compressed air

ENGINEERING. Fitted with controllable-pitch propellers and tunnel bow thruster for precise manoeuvring.

NOMENCLATURE. These three ships are names for small American cities with namesakes in the United Kingdom.

BEAUFORT (ATS 2) *1974, US Navy, PH3. J. A. Romesburg*

EDENTON (ATS 1) *1971, United States Navy*

BEAUFORT (ATS 2) *1971, Brooke Marine*

SEALIFT SHIPS

Military Sealift Ships provide ocean transportation for all components of the Department of Defense. These ships are operated by the Navy's Military Sealift Command, renamed on 1 Aug 1970 from Military Sea Transportation Service (MSTS).

The cargo ships, tankers, troop transports and landing ships, listed below carry military cargo and personnel from port to port except that Military Sealift Command tankers do transfer petroleum to Navy oilers in overseas areas. In addition, the Military Sealift Command directs the chartering of merchantmen owned by shipping lines or private parties to carry government cargo.

The Commander, Deputy Commander, and Area Commanders (Atlantic, Pacific, and Far East) are flag officers of the Navy on active duty. All ships are civilian manned with most of their crews being Civil Service employees of the Navy. However, the tankers are operated under contract to commercial tanker lines and are manned by merchant seamen.

In addition to the ships listed in this section, the Military Sealift Command also operates a number of underway replenishment (UNREP) ships, fleet support ships, and Special Projects ships that support other defence related activities, mostly research, surveying and missile-range support ships (see Experimental, Research and Surveying Ships listing). Other Special Projects ships are the cable ships listed in the section on Fleet Support Ships.

A few Navy-manned logistic ships are included in this section although they are not under the control of the Military Sealift Command.

In addition to Navy-owned ships, the Military Sealift Command operates the roll-on/roll-off vehicle cargo ship *Admiral William M. Callaghan*

ARMAMENT. No ships of the Military Sealift Command are armed.

CLASSIFICATION. Military Sealift Command ships are assigned standard US Navy hull designations with the added designation prefix "T". Ships in this category are referred to as "USNS" (United States Naval Ship) vice "USS" (United States Ship) which is used for Navy-manned ships.

DISPOSALS

All store ships (AF) and medium landing ships (LSM light cargo ships (AKL), and transports (AP) operated by the Military Sealift Command in point-to-point operations have been stricken; see 1973-1974 and previous editions for characteristics.

All aircraft transports (AVT) and cargo and aircraft ferry ships (AKV) have been stricken from the Navy List. See 1971-1972 edition for characteristics of the last AKVs in service.

1 HEAVY LIFT SHIP (AK): "BROSTROM" TYPE

*** PVT. LEONARD C. BROSTROM** (ex-*Marine Eagle*) T-AK 255

Displacement, tons	13 865 deadweight
Dimensions, feet	520 oa × 71·5 × 33
Main engines	Geared turbine; 9 000 shp; 1 shaft = 15·8 knots
Boilers	2
Complement	57 (14 officers, 43 men)

The *Brostrom* is fitted with 150-ton capacity booms, providing the most powerful lift capability of any US ship. C4-S-B1 type built in 1943. Note the deckloaded tanks and trucks in the photograph of the *Brostrom*.

DISPOSALS

Marine Fiddler T-AK 267 transferred to Maritime Administration on 14 Sep 1973.

4 FBM CARGO SHIPS (AK): "VICTORY" TYPE

***NORWALK** (ex-*Norwalk Victory*)	T-AK 279
***FURMAN** (ex-*Furman Victory*)	T-AK 280
***VICTORIA** (ex-*Ethiopia Victory*)	T-AK 281
***MARSHFIELD** (ex-*Marshfield Victory*)	T-AK 282

Displacement, tons	6 700 light; *Betelgeuse* 15 580 full load; others 11 150 full load
Dimensions, feet	455·25 oa × 62 × 24
Guns	8—40 mm AA (twin) in *Betelgeuse*; others unarmed
Main engines	geared turbine; 8 500 shp; 1 shaft = 17 knots
Boilers	2
Complement	80 to 90 plus Navy detachment

Former merchant ships of the VC2-S-AP3 "Victory" type built during World War II. Extensively converted to supply supply tenders for Fleet Ballistic Missile (FBM) submarines. Fitted to carry torpedoes, spare parts, packaged petroleum products, bottled gas, black oil and diesel fuel, frozen and dry provisions, and general cargo as well as missiles. No. 3 hold converted to carry 16 Polaris missiles in vertical position; tankage provided for 355 000 gallons of diesel oil and 430 000 gallons of fuel oil (for submarine tenders). All subsequently modified to carry Poseidon missiles. All four ships are operated by the Military Sealift Command with civilian operating crews; small Navy detachment in each ship provides security and technical services.

Betelgeuse reactivated by the Navy in 1951 from Maritime Administration reserve fleet. Decommissioned in 1971 and placed in reserve.

Norwalk converted to FBM cargo ship by Boland Machine & Manufacturing Co, and accepted for service on 30 Dec 1963.

Furman converted by American Shipbuilding Co, and accepted in Oct 1964.

Victoria converted by Philadelphia Naval Shipyard, and accepted in Oct 1965.

Marshfield converted by Boland Machine & Manufacturing Co, and accepted in June 1970.

DISPOSALS

Betelgeuse AK 260 stricken on 1 Feb 1974.

MARSHFIELD (T-AK 282) *1970, United States Navy*

1 CARGO SHIP (AK): "BLAND" TYPE

***SCHUYLER OTIS BLAND** T-AK 277

Displacement, tons	15 910 full load
Dimensions, feet	478 × 66 × 30
Main engines	Geared turbine; 13 750 shp; 1 shaft; = 18·5 knots
Boilers	2

Acquired from the Maritime Administration by the Military Sea Transportation Service in July 1961. The only ship of the type (C3-S-DX1), built in 1961; prototype of the "Mariner" cargo ship design.

SCHUYLER OTIS BLAND (T-AK 277) *United States Navy*

1 CARGO SHIP (AK): "ELTANIN" TYPE

***MIRFAK** T-AK 271

Displacement, tons	2 036 light; 4 942 full load
Dimensions, feet	256·8 wl; 262·2 oa × 51·5 × 18·7
Main engines	Diesel-electric (ALCO diesels with Westinghouse electric motors); 3 200 bhp; 2 shafts = 13 knots

Built for MSTS by Avondale Marine Ways, New Orleans, La. Designed for Arctic operation with hull strengthened against ice. C1-M E2-13a type. Launched on 5 Aug 1957. Note icebreaking prow in photo.

CONVERSION. Two other ships of this class converted for oceanographic research: *Eltanin*, reclassified from T-AK 270 to T-AGOR 8 on 15 Nov 1962; *Mizar* T-AK 272 was reclassified T-AGOR 11 on 15 Apr 1964 (see Experimental, Research and Surveying Ships).

MIRFAK (T-AK 271) *United States Navy*

PVT LEONARD C. BROSTROM (T-AK 255) *United States Navy*

Sealift Ships—*continued*

5 CARGO SHIPS (AK): "VICTORY" TYPE

***GREENVILL VICTORY**	T-AK 237
***PVT. JOHN R. TOWLE** (ex-*Appleton Victory*)	T-AK 240
***SGT. ANDREW MILLER** (ex-*Radcliffe Victory*)	T-AK 242
***SGT. TRUMAN KIMBRO**	T-AK 254
***LIEUT. JAMES E. ROBINSON** (ex-T-AG 170, ex-T-AK 274, ex-AKV 3, ex *Czechoslovakia Victory*)	T-AK 274

Former merchant ships of the "Victory" type built during World War II. VC2-S-AP3 type capable of 17 knots except T-AK 254 is VC2 S AP2 type capable of 15 knots. Several other "Victory" cargo ships transferred to Navy after World War II have been converted to research (AG) and space/missile support ships (AGM). "Victory" type cargo ships initially configured as forward depot ships and as Fleet Ballistic Missile (FBM) cargo ships are listed separately.
These ships are unarmed and civilian manned by the Military Sealift Command.

RECLASSIFICATION. The former Military Sea Transportation Service aircraft cargo and ferry ships *Lieut. James E. Robinson* AKV 3 reclassified as cargo ship on 7 May 1959. *Kingsport Victory* T-AK 239, was renamed and reclassified *Kingsport* T-AG 164 in 1962 (see Experimental, Research and Surveying ships).
Lieut James E. Robinson T-AK 274, was to have been transferred to the Maritime Administration, but was modified for special project work and reclassified as T-AG 170 in 1963, and reverted to the original classification T-AK 274 on 1 July 1964.
Haiti Victory T-AK 238 and *Dalton Victory* T-AK 256 converted to satellite tracking and recovery ships, reclassified and renamed, *Longview* T-AGM 3 and *Sunnyvale* T-AGM 5, respectively.
Pvt. Joe E. Mann T-AK 253, ex-*Owensboro Victory*, was fitted out as a range instrumentation and telemetry ship for the Pacific Missile Range in Oct 1958 and renamed *Richfield* T-AGM 4.
The ship intended for designation AK 278 became the *Sea Lift*, T-LSV 9, subsequently changed to T-AKR 9.

DISPOSALS
Sgt. Archer T. Gammon T-AK 243 transferred to Maritime Administration in 1973 for scrapping; **Lieut Robert Craig** T-AK 252 stricken on 10 July 1973; **Lieut. George W. G. Boyce** T AK 251 stricken on 15 July 1973; **Pvt. Joseph F. Merrell** T-AK 275 stricken on 30 Jan 1974; **Sgt. Jack J. Pendleton** T-AK 276 stricken on 15 Feb 1974; **Pvt. Francis X. McGraw** T-AK 241 stricken on 15 May 1974; **Sgt. Morris E. Crain** T-AK 244 stricken on 1 Apr 1975.

GREENVILLE VICTORY (T-AK 237) *United States Navy*

PVT JOHN R. TOWLE (T-AK 240) in Antarctic *1961, US Navy*

1 CARGO SHIP (AK): Ex-AKA TYPE

***WYANDOT** T-AK 283 (ex-T-AKA 92)

Displacement, tons	7 430 light; 14 000 full load
Dimensions	435 wl; 459·2 oa × 63 × 24
Main engines	Geared turbines (General Electric); 6 000 shp; 1 shaft = 16·5 knots
Boilers	2 (Combustion Engineering)

Former attack cargo ship (AKA) of the "Andromeda" class; C2-S-B1 type. Built by Moore Dry Dock Co, Oakland, California; launched on 28 June 1944; commissioned on 30 Sep 1944 as AKA 92. Assigned to MSTS and manned by a civilian crew since 1963. Designation changed to T-AK 283 on 1 Jan 1969. Winterised for arctic service.

C1-M-AV1 TYPE

All surving small cargo ships of this type have been stricken: **Herkimer** T-AK 188, **Muskingum** T-AK 198 transferred to US Department of the Interior on 15 June 1973; **Short Splice** T-AK 249 stricken on 15 June 1973; **Col. William J. O'Brien** T-AK 246 stricken on 1 Sep 1973; **Fentress** T-AK 180, **Pvt. Frank J. Petrarca** T-AK 250 stricken on 15 Oct 1973. See 1973-1974 and previous editions for characteristics.

1 VEHICLE CARGO SHIP: "CALLAGHAN" TYPE

Name	*Builder*	*Launched*
***ADMIRAL WM. M. CALLAGHAN**	Sun SB & DD	17 Oct 1967

Displacement, tons	24 500 full load
Dimensions, feet	694 × 92 × 29
Main engines	2 gas turbines (General Electric LM 2500); 50 000 shp; 2 shafts = 26 knots
Complement	33

Roll-on/Roll-off vehicle cargo ship built specifically for long-term charter to Military Sealift Command. Internal parking decks and ramps for carrying some 750 vehicles on 167 537 sq ft of parking area; unloading via four side ramps and stern ramp, the *Callaghan* can off load and reload full vehicle capacity in 27 hours.

ADM WM. M. CALLAGHAN *United States Navy*

1 VEHICLE CARGO SHIP (AKR): "SEA LIFT" TYPE

***SEA LIFT** T-KAR 9 (ex-T-LSV 9)

Displacement, tons	11 130 light; 16 940 standard; 21 700 full load
Measurement, tons	15 750 gross; 12 100 deadweight
Dimensions, feet	540 oa × 83 × 29
Main engines	Geared steam turbines; 2 shafts; 19 400 shp = 20 knots
Boilers	2
Complement	62 plus 12 Passengers

Improved roll-on/roll-off vehicle cargo ship. Maritime Administration C4-ST-67a type. Built by the Puget Sound Bridge & Dry Dock Co, (now Lockheed Shipbuilding and Construction Co), Seattle, Wash, at a cost of $15 895 500. Authorised under the Fiscal Year 1963 programme. Laid down on 19 May 1964 and launched on 18 Apr 1965. Delivered to Navy on 25 Apr 1967 and to MSTS on 19 May 1967. Designed for point-to-point sea transportation of Department of Defense self-propelled, fully loaded, wheeled, tracked and amphibious vehicles and general cargo. Internal ramps, stern ramp and side openings provide for quick loading and unloading. Designation, changed from T-LSV to T-AKR on 1 Jan 1969.

SEA LIFT (T-AKR 9) *1965 Lockheed Shipbuilding*

SEA LIFT (T-AKR 9) *1966, Lockheed Shipbuilding*

Sealift Ships—*continued*

1 VEHICLE CARGO SHIP (AKR): "COMET" TYPE

***COMET** T-AKR 7 (ex-T-LSV 7, ex-T-AK 269)

Displacement, tons	7 605 light; 18 150 full load
Measurement, tons	12 750 gross; 6 500 deadweight
Dimensions, feet	465 pp; 499 oa × 78 × 28·8
Main engines	Geared turbines (General Electric); 2 shafts; 13 200 shp = 18 knots
Boilers	2 (Babcock & Wilcox)
Complement	73

Roll-on/roll-off vehicle carrier built for MSTS by Sun Shipbuilding & Dry Dock Co. C3-ST-14A type. Laid down on 15 May 1956. Launched on 31 July 1957. Completed on 27 Jan 1958. Has ramp system for loading and discharging. The hull is strengthened against ice. Can accommodate 700 vehicles in two after holds; the forward holds are for general cargo. Equipped with Denny-Brown Stabilisers. Reclassified from T-AK to T-LSV on 1 June 1963, and changed to T-AKR on 1 Jan 1969. LSV 1-6 were World War II-built amphibious ships; subsequently redesignated as mine warfare ships (MCS) and net cargo ship (AKN).

DISPOSALS

Taurus (T-AKR 8, ex-T-LSV 8, ex-AK 273, ex-LSD 23) deactivated in 1968 and subsequently scrapped; officially stricken on 22 June 1971 (almost two years after being sold for scrap).

Galilea AKN 6, ex-LSV 6, ex-AP 161 stricken from the Navy List on 1 Sep 1961 and transferred to Maritime Administration.

COMET (T-AKR 7) *United States Navy*

9 TANKERS: "SEALIFT" CLASS

Name	*No.*	*Builder*	*Launched*
***SEALIFT PACIFIC**	T-AO 168	Todd Shipyards	13 Oct 1973
***SEALIFT ARABIAN SEA**	T-AO 169	Todd Shipyards	26 Jan 1974
***SEALIFT CHINA SEA**	T-AO 170	Todd Shipyards	20 Apr 1974
***SEALIFT INDIAN OCEAN**	T-AO 171	Todd Shipyards	27 July 1974
***SEALIFT ATLANTIC**	T-AO 172	Bath Iron Works	26 Jan 1974
***SEALIFT MEDITERRANEAN**	T-AO 173	Bath Iron Works	9 Mar 1974
***SEALIFT CARIBBEAN**	T-AO 174	Bath Iron Works	8 June 1974
***SEALIFT ARCTIC**	T-AO 175	Bath Iron Works	31 Aug 1974
***SEALIFT ANTARCTIC**	T-AO 176	Bath Iron Works	26 Oct 1974

Dimensions, feet	587 oa × 84 × 34·4
Main engines	2 diesels; 14 000 bhp; 1 shaft = 16 knots
Complement	30 + 2 Maritime Academy cadets

Relatively small tankers built specifically for long term-charter by the Military Sealift Command. Four ships built by Todd Shipyards Corp, San Pedro, California; five by Bath Iron Works Corp, Bath, Maine. Operated for MSC by commercial firms with civilian crews. Delivered 1974-1975.

"SEALIFT" CLASS—continued

Fitted with bow thruster to assist docking; automated engine room. Approximately 25 000 tons deadweight; cargo capacity 220 000 barrels. Estimated cost $146 500 000 for the nine-ship class.

SEALIFT ARABIAN SEA (T-AO 169) *1974, Todd Shipyards*

1 TANKER (AO): "EXPLORER" TYPE

• AMERICAN EXPLORER T-AO 165

Displacement, tons	16 500 gross; 22 525 deadweight
Dimensions, feet	615 oa × 80 × 44·5
Main engines	Steam turbines; 22 000 shp; 1 shaft = 20 knots

T5-S-RM2a type. Laid down on 9 July 1957; launched on 11 Apr 1958. Built by Ingalls Shipbuilding Corporation, Pascagoula, for the Maritime Administration, but acquired by Military Sea Transportation Service. Cargo capacity 190 300 barrels. Operated for Military Sealift Command by commercial firm.

AMERICAN EXPLORER (T-AO 165) *United States Navy*

3 TANKERS (AO): "MAUMEE" CLASS

		Launched
***MAUMEE**	T-AO 149	16 Feb 1956
***SHOSHONE**	T-AO 151	17 Jan 1957
***YUKON**	T-AO 152	16 Mar 1956

Displacement, tons	25 000 deadweight
Measurement, tons	16 500 gross; 25 000 deadweight
Dimensions, feet	591 wl; 620 oa × 83·5 × 32
Main engines	Geared turbine; 20 460 shp; 1 shaft = 18 knots

Yukon laid down 16 May 1955 by Ingalls, Pascagoula, delivered May 1957. *Maumee* laid down 8 Mar 1955, delivered Dec 1956. *Shoshone* laid down 15 Aug 1955 by Sun Shipbuilding, Chester, delivered Apr 1957. T5-S-12A type. *Potomac* T-AO 150 sank at Morehead, North Carolina, after explosion on 26-27 Sep 1961, but was rebuilt in 1963-1964, renamed SS *Shenandoah* and chartered to MSTS. Cargo capacity 203 216 barrels.

Maumee provided with ice-strengthened bow during 1969-1970 modification at Norfolk SB & DD Co; employed in transporting petroleum products to Antarctica in support of US scientific endeavours.

These ships are operated for the Military Sealift Command by commercial firms.

SEALIFT PACIFIC (T-AO 168) *1974, United States Navy*

Sealift Ships—*continued*

SHOSHONE (T-AO 151) *United States Navy*

MISSION SANTA YNEZ (T-AO 134) *United States Navy*

5 TANKERS (AO): "MISSION" CLASS

Name	*No.*	*Launched*	*Commissioned*
***TALLULAH** (ex-*Valley Forge*)	T-AO 50	25 June 1942	5 Sep 1942
***MILLICOMA** (ex-*Conastoga*, ex-*King's Mountain*)	T-AO 73	21 Jan 1943	5 Mar 1943
***SAUGATUCK** (ex-*Newton*)	T-AO 75	7 Dec 1942	19 Feb 1943
***SCHUYLKILL** (ex-*Louisburg*)	T-AO 76	16 Feb 1943	9 Apr 1943
***MISSION SANTA YNEZ**	T-AO 134	19 Dec 1943	(see notes)

Displacement, tons	5 730 light; 22 380 full load
Dimensions, feet	503 wl; 523·5 oa × 68 × approx 30
Main engines	Turbo-electric drive; 6 000 shp (except *Mission Santa Ynez* 10 000 shp); 1 shaft = 15 knots (except *Mission Santa Ynez* 16 knots)
Boilers	2 (Babcock & Wilcox)

T2-SE-A1 tankers begun as merchant ships but acquired by Navy and completed as fleet oilers (AO) except the *Mission Santa Ynez* of T2-SE-A2 type delivered as merchant tanker on 13 March 1944 and subsequently acquired by Navy on 22 Oct 1947. During the post World War II period all of these ships were employed in the tanker role, carrying petroleum point-to-point.
All built by Sun Shipbuilding & Dry Dock Co, Chester, Pennsylvania, except *Mission Santa Ynez* built by Marine Ship Corp, Sausalito, California. Cargo capacity approximately 134 000 barrels.

DISPOSALS AND TRANSFERS (since 1 Jan 1970)
Mission San Rafael T-AO 130 stricken on 28 Apr 1970, **Mission Santa Cruz** T-AO 133 stricken on 15 Sep 1970, **Shawnee Trail** T-AO 142 stricken on 29 Feb 1972, **Chepachet** T-AO 78 stricken on 13 Mar 1972, **Mission Buenaventura** T-AO 111 stricken on 31 Mar 1972, **Cache** T-AO 67 stricken on 6 May 1972, **Cowanesque** T-AO 67 stricken on 1 June 1972, **Pioneer Valley** T-AO 140 stricken on 15 Aug 1972; **Mission Santa Clara** T-AO 132 transferred to Pakistan on 31 May 1974; **Pecos** T-AO 65 stricken on 1 Oct 1974; **Suamico** T-AO 49 stricken on 15 Nov 1974; **Cossatot** T-AO 77 stricken on 18 Nov 1974.

SCHUYLKILL (T-AO 76) *United States Navy*

TRANSPORTS (AP)

All US troop transports (AP) have been stricken or transferred; these ships differed from amphibious transports (LPA, formerly attack transports, APA) by being point-to-point carriers, operating between ports and not capable of unloading assault troops into landing craft.
The last transports on the Navy List were the three "Barrett" class ships; see 1973-1974 and previous editions for characteristics. **Geiger** T-AP 197 stricken on 27 Apr 1971 and transferred to Maritime Administration reserve; **Upshur** T-AP 198 stricken on 2 Apr 1973 and transferred to the State of Maine as a merchant training ship; **Barrett** T-AP 196 stricken on 2 July 1973 and transferred to Maritime Administration reserve fleet.

3 GASOLINE TANKERS (AOG): "PECONIC" CLASS

		Launched
***RINCON**	T-AOG 77	5 Jan 1945
***NODAWAY** (ex-*Belridge*)	T-AOG 78	15 May 1945
***PETALUMA** (ex-*Raccoon Bend*, ex-*Tavispan*)	T-AOG 79	9 Aug 1945

Displacement, tons	2 060 light; 6 000 full load
Dimensions, feet	325·2 oa × 48·2 × 19·1
Main engines	diesel; 1 400 bhp; 1 shaft = 10 knots

T1-M-BT2 gasoline tankers built by Todd Shipyards Corp, Houston, Texas, as merchant tankers. All acquired by Navy in 1950 and assigned to Military Sea Transportation Service and employed in point-to-point carrying of petroleum. Cargo capacity approximately 30 000 barrels.

DISPOSALS
T1-MET-24a type: **Chattahooche** T-AOG 82 stricken on 22 Feb 1972, **Alatna** T-AOG 81 permanently transferred to Maritime Administration reserve fleet on 8 Aug 1972; **Piscataqua** T-AOG 80 stricken on 1 Aug 1974.

RINCON (T-AOG 77) *United States Navy*

PETALUMA (T-AOG 79) *United States Navy*

14 CARGO SHIPS: LST TYPE

Sixteen LSTs configured for point-to-point cargo operations remain on the Navy List, all in Military Sealift Command reserve. They are expected to be stricken or transferred in the near future. See 1973-1974 and previous editions for ship characteristics. T-LSTs remaining on Navy/MSC List:
LST 47, 230, 278, 491, 579, 607, 613, 623, 629, 649, Daviess County T-LST 692, **Harris County** T-LST 822, **Orleans Parish** T-LST 1069 (ex-MCS 6), and **LST 1072.**
Six ships subsequently reactivated in 1975 for use in Western Pacific to support US resupply and evacuation efforts in Southeast Asia.

DISPOSALS
LST 600 stricken on 1 June 1969; **Chesterfield County,** T-LST 551 stricken on 1 June 1970; **Clearwater County** LST 602 (operated by US Air Force) transferred to Mexico on 25 May 1972; **LST 581, 626, Plumas County,** T-LST 1083 stricken on 1 June 1972; **LST 222, 488, 546** transferred to Philippines on 15 July 1972; **LST 277** transferred to Chile on 2 February 1973; **LST 117, 276, Chase County** T-LST 532 transferred to Singapore on 10 June 1973; **LST 456, 530, 572, 587, 590, 630, 643, 664** stricken on 15 June 1973; **New London County** T-LST 1066, **Nye County,** T-LST 1067 transferred to Chile on 29 Aug 1973; **LST 399, 550, 566, De Kalb County** T-LST 715, **LST 1088, Traverse County** T-LST 1160, **Wahkiakum County** T-LST 1162, **Waldo County** T-LST 1163, **Walworth County** T-LST 1164, **Washoe County** T-LST 1165 transferred to Maritime administration in 1973-1974. **LST 176** stricken on 1 Nov 1973.

EXPERIMENTAL, RESEARCH AND SURVEYING SHIPS

TEST AND EVALUATION SHIP (TES)

The Navy has developed the initial design for a Test and Evaluation Ship (TES) to provide a sea-going platform for the test and evaluation of future ship systems. The TES concept design sought to provide: (1) maximum flexibility in order to accept new systems with minimum modifications, (2) extensive use of modular concepts, (3) extensive use of quick-acting interface connections between the ship and test system, (4) a speed of 25 knots on two shafts plus a centreline shaft for testing prototype propulsion plants and propellers, and (5) power and other "hotel" services to meet projected requirements for the next 20 years.
Planning for future construction of a TES was halted early in 1975.

1 EXPERIMENTAL SURFACE EFFECT SHIP: AEROJET-GENERAL DESIGN

SES-100A

Weight, tons	100 gross
Dimensions, feet	81·9 oa × 41·9
Main/lift engines	4 gas turbines (Avco-Lycoming) 12 000 hp; three fans for lift and two water-jet propulsion systems = 80+ knots

Surface effects ship developed by Aerojet-General Corp, and built by Tacoma Boatbuilding Co, Tacoma, Washington, to test feasibility of large SES for naval missions. Christened in July 1971; underway in mid-1972 in competition with the Bell design described below. Aluminium construction with rigid sidewalls to hold cushion or bubble of air. Cargo capacity ten tons (instrumentation during evaluation); provision for crew of four and six observers. Fitted with four TF-35 gas turbine engines, marine version of the T55-L-11A developed for the CH-47C helicopter.

PROGRAMME. Two other types of ocean-going "air support" platforms are being developed for the US Navy at this time; air cushion vehicle (ACV) landing craft described in the section on Landing Craft and an armed SES design listed immediately after frigates in this edition.

SES-100A — *1972, Aerojet General*

1 EXPERIMENTAL SURFACE EFFECT SHIP: BELL AEROSYSTEMS DESIGN

SES-100B

Weight, tons	100 gross
Dimensions, feet	78 oa × 35
Main engines	3 gas turbines (Pratt & Whitney); 13 500 hp; 2 semi-submerged, super cavitating propellers = 80+ knots
Lift engines	3 gas turbines (United Aircraft of Canada); 1 500 hp; eight lift fans

Surface effects ship developed by Bell Aerospace Division of the Textron Corp; built Bell facility in Michoud, Louisiana. Christened on March 6, 1971; underway in Feb 1972 as competitive development platform for Navy.
Aluminium hull with rigid sidewalls to hold cushion or bubble of air. Cargo capacity ten tons (instrumentation during evaluation); provision for crew of four and six observers.
Fitted with three Pratt & Whitney FT-12 gas turbine engines and three United Aircraft of Canada ST-6J-70 gas turbine engines.
The SES-100B is credited with having set an SES speed record of more than 80 knots during trials in April 1974.

SES-100B — *1974, Bell Aerosystems*

SES-100B — *1974, Bell Aerosystems*

2 SONAR TEST SHIPS (AG): Ex-MINESWEEPERS

Name	*No.*	*Launched*	*Commissioned*
*ALACRITY	AG 520 (ex-MSO 520)	8 June 1957	2 Oct 1958
*ASSURANCE	AG 521 (ex-MSO 521)	31 Aug 1957	22 Nov 1958

Displacement, tons	810 light; 934 full load
Dimensions, feet	190 oa × 36 × 14·5
Guns	1—40 mm AA (as MSO)
Main engines	2 diesels (General Motors); 2 700 bhp; 2 shafts (controllable pitch propellers) = 15 knots

Former ocean minesweepers. Both built by Peterson Builders Inc., Sturgeon Bay, Wisconsin. Wood-hulled with non-magnetic engines and fittings. Both ships modified for sonar test activities and redesignated as miscellaneous auxiliaries (AG) on 1 June 1973 and 1 Mar 1973, respectively.

DISPOSALS
Ability MSO 519 stricken in 1 Feb 1971

ASSURANCE (AG 521) — *United States Navy*

1 HYDROGRAPHIC RESEARCH SHIP (AG)

***FLYER** (ex-*American Flyer*, ex-*Water Witch*) T-AG 178

Displacement, tons	7 360 light; 11 000 full load
Dimensions, feet	459·2 oa × 63 × 28
Main engines	Turbines; 6 000 shp; 1 shaft = 17 knots
Boilers	2
Complement	55 (14 officers, 41 men)

Acquired from Maritime Administration on 9 Feb 1965. C2-S-B1 type built in 1945. Operated by Military Sealift Command for Naval Electronic Systems Command, civilian manned.

Experimental, Research and Surveying Ships—*continued*

FLYER (T-AG 178) *United States Navy*

1 HYDROGRAPHIC RESEARCH SHIP (AG): "VICTORY" TYPE

•KINGSPORT (ex-*Kingsport Victory*) T-AG 164

Displacement, tons	7 190 light; 10 680 full load
Dimensions, feet	455 oa × 62 × 22
Main engines	Geared turbines; 8 500 shp; 1 shaft = 15·2 knots
Boilers	2
Complement	73 (13 officers, 42 men, 15 technicians)

VC2-S-AP3. Built in 1944 by the California Shipbuiding Corp, Los Angeles. Former cargo ship in the MSTS fleet. Name shortened, ship reclassified and converted in 1961-1962 by Willamette Iron & Steel Co, Portland, Oregon, into the world's first satellite communications ship, for Project Advent, involving the promotion of a terminal to meet the required military capability for high capacity, world-wide radio communications using high altitude hovering satellites, and the installation of ship-to-shore communications, facilities, additional electric power generating equipment, a helicopter landing platform, aerological facilities, and a 30-foot parabolic communication antenna housed in a 53-ft diameter plastic radome abaft the superstructure. Painted white for operations in the tropics. Project Advent Syncom satellite relay operations were completed in 1966, and *Kingsport* was reassigned to hydrographic research. Antenna sphere now removed.

Note antenna mast on helicopter platform in photograph; exhaust ducts fitted to funnel.

Operated by Military Sealift Command for Naval Electronic Systems Command; civilian manned.

KINGSPORT (T-AG 164) *United States Navy*

1 EXPERIMENTAL NAVIGATION SHIP (AG): "MARINER" TYPE

•COMPASS ISLAND (ex-*YAG* 56, ex-*Garden Mariner*) AG 153

Displacement, tons	16 076 full load
Dimensions, feet	529·5 wl; 563 oa × 76 × 29
Main engines	Geared turbines (General Electric); 19 250 shp; 1 shaft = 20 knots
Boilers	2

Originally a "Mariner" class merchant ship (C4-S-1a type); built by New York Shipbuilding Corp, Camden, New Jersey; launched on 24 Oct 1953 and acquired by the Navy on 29 Mar 1956.

Converted by New York Naval Shipyard; commissioned on 3 Dec 1956 for the development of the Fleet Ballistic Missile guidance and ship navigation systems. Her mission is to assist in the development and valuation of a navigation system independant of shore-based aids. Navy manned.

COMPASS ISLAND (AG 153) *United States Navy*

1 POSEIDON TEST SHIP (AG): "MARINER" TYPE

OBSERVATION ISLAND (ex-*YAG* 57, ex-*Empire State Mariner*) AG 154

Displacement, tons	17 600 full load
Dimensions, feet	529·5 wl; 563 oa × 76 × 29
Main engines	Geared turbines (General Electric); 19 250 shp; 1 shaft = 20 knots
Boilers	2
Complement	350

Built as a "Mariner" class merchant ship (C4-S-1a type) by the New York Shipbuilding Corp, Camden, New Jersey; launched on 15 Aug 1953; acquired by the Navy on 10 Sep 1956 for use as a Fleet Ballistic Missile (FBM) test ship. Converted at Norfolk Naval Shipyard; commissioned on 5 Dec 1958.

Fitted to test fire Polaris and later Poseidon missiles. Navy manned. Decommissioned on 25 Sep 1972 and placed in Maritime Administration reserve; remains on Navy List.

MISSILE TESTING. The ship is fitted with complete missile testing, servicing and firing systems. She fired the first ship-launched Polaris missile at sea on 27 Aug 1959. Refitted to fire the improved Poseidon missile in 1969 and launched the first Poseidon test missile fired afloat on 16 Dec 1969.

OBSERVATION ISLAND (AG 154) *1971, United States Navy*

1 HYDROFOIL RESEARCH SHIP (AGEH)

•PLAINVIEW AGEH 1

Displacement, tons	320 full load
Dimensions, feet	212 oa × 40·5 × 10 (hull borne) or 26 (with foils down)
A/S weapons	2 triple torpedo tubes (Mk 32)
Main engines	2 gas turbines (General Electric); 30 000 hp; 2 diesels; 1 200 = 50 knots
Complement	20 (6 officers, 14 men)

Aluminium hull experimental hydrofoil. Three retractable foils, 25 ft in height, each weighing 7 tons, fitted port and starboard and on stern, and used in waves up to 15 feet. Initial maximum speed of about 50 knots, with later modifications designed to raise the speed to 80 knots. Fitted with the largest titanium propellers made. The two 15 000 hp gas turbines are General Electric J-79 jet aircraft engines modified for marine use. Power plant and transmission designed to permit future investigation of various types of foils. Built by Lockheed Shipbuilding & Construction Co, Seattle, Washington. Laid down on 8 May 1964, launched on 28 June 1965, and placed in service on 1 May 1969. Delayed because of engineering difficulties. In service vice being in commission.

The photographs of the *Plainview* show the ship on foils and in displacement condition during experimental transfer of personnel from a CH-46A Sea Knight helicopter.

PLAINVIEW (AGEH 1) *1972, US Navy, PH2, E. E. Murphy*

PLAINVIEW (AGEH 2) *1972, US Navy, PH2, E. E. Murphy*

Experimental Research and Surveying Ships—*continued*

1 RANGE INSTRUMENTATION SHIP (AGM): Ex-"VICTORY" TYPE TRANSPORT

***RANGE SENTINEL** (ex-*Sherburne*) T-AGM 22 (ex-AFA 205)

Displacement, tons	11 860 full load
Dimensions, feet	455 oa × 62
Main engines	Turbine (Westinghouse); 8 500 hp; 1 shaft = 17·7 knots
Boilers	2 (Combustion Engineering)
Complement	95 (14 officers, 54 men, 27 technical personnel)

Former attack transport converted specifically to serve as a range instrumentation ship in support of the Poseidon Fleet Ballistic Missile (FBM) programme. Built by Permanente Metals Corp, Richmond, California; commissioned on 20 Sep 1944. VC2-S-AP5 type.
Stricken from the Navy List on 1 Oct 1958 and transferred to Maritime Administration reserve fleet; reacquired by the Navy on 22 Oct 1969 for AGM conversion.
Converted from Oct 1969 to Oct 1971; placed in service as T-AGM 22 on 14 Oct 1971.
Operated by Military Sealift Command and civilian manned.

RANGE SENTINEL (T-AGM 22) *1973, United States Navy*

2 RANGE INSTRUMENTATION SHIPS (AGM): "JUMBOISED" T2-SE-A2 TYPE

***VANGUARD** (ex-*Muscel Shoals*, ex-*Mission San Fernando*) T-AGM 19 (ex-T-AO 122)
***REDSTONE** (ex-*Johnstown*, ex-*Mission de Pala*) T-AGM 20 (ex-T-AO 114)

Displacement, tons	21 626 full load
Dimensions, feet	595 oa × 75 × 25
Main engines	Turbine-electric; 1 shaft; 10 000 shp = 16 knots
Boilers	2 (Babcock & Wilcox)
Complement	*Vanguard* 19 officers, 71 enlisted men, 108 technical personnel; *Redstone* 20 officers, 71 enlisted men, 120 technical personnel.

Former "Mission" class tankers converted in 1964-1966 to serve as mid-ocean communications and tracking ships in support of the Apollo manned lunar flights. Both built in 1944 by Marinship, Sausalito, California. T2-SE-A2 type.
Converted to range instrumentation ships by General Dynamics, Quincy Division, Massachusetts; each ship was cut in half and a 72-foot mid-section was inserted, increasing length, beam, and displacement; approximately 450 tons of electronic equipment installed for support of lunar flight operations, including communications and tracking systems; balloon hangar and platform fitted aft. Cost of converting the three ships was $90 000 000. Operated by Military Sealift Command for Air Force Eastern Test Range in Atlantic (*Vanguard*) and for NASA Goddard Space Flight Centre (*Redstone*). Civilian crews.
A third ship of this type has been stricken: **Mercury** (ex-*Flagstaff, Mission San Juan*) T-AGM 21 (ex-T-AO 126) transferred to Maritime Administration in 1969 and subsequently converted to merchant configuration.

VANGUARD (T-AGM 19) *1966, General Dynamics*

REDSTONE (T-AGM 20) *1970, United States Air Force*

2 RANGE INSTRUMENTATION SHIPS (AGM): C4-S-A1 TYPE

***GENERAL H. H. ARNOLD** (ex-USNS *General R E Callan*) T-AGM 9 (ex-T-AP 139)
***GENERAL HOYT S. VANDENBERG** (ex-USNS *General Harry Taylor*) T-AGM 10 (ex-T-AP 145)

Displacement, tons	16 600 full load
Dimensions, feet	552·9 oa × 71·5 × 26·3
Main engines	Geared turbines (Westinghouse); 9 000 shp; 1 shaft = 15 knots
Boilers	2 (Babcock & Wilcox)
Complement	205 (21 officers, 71 men, 113 technical personnel)

Former transports converted in 1962-1963 for monitoring Air Force missiles firing and satellite launches. Both ships built in 1944 by Kaiser Co. Richmond, California, as large troop transports. C4-S-A1 type. Upon conversion to Range Instrumentation Ships (RIS) they were placed in service in 1963 under Air Force operation, however assigned to MSTS for operation on 1 July 1964 (*Arnold*) and 13 July 1964 (*Vandenberg*).
Both ships are operated by Military Sealift Command for Air Force Eastern Test Range in Atlantic. Civilian manned.

GEN. HOYT S. VANDENBERG (T-AGM 10) *United States Navy*

1 RANGE INSTRUMENTATION SHIP (AGM): "VICTORY" TYPE

***WHEELING** (*Ex-Seton Hall Victory*) T-1AGM8.

Displacement, tons	10 680 full load
Dimensions, feet	455·3 oa × 62·2
Main engines	Geared turbines; 8 500 shp; 1 shaft = 17 knots
Boilers	2
Complement	107 (13 officers, 46 men, 48 technical personnel)

The *Wheeling* is the only survivor of a series of "Victory" type military, cargo and merchant ships converted to missile range instrumentation ships during the massive US space and military missile programmes of the 1960s.
Built in 1944 by Oregon SB Corp, Portland, Oregon. VC2-S-PA3 type. Assigned to Military Sea Transportation Service (later Military Sealift Command) on 28 May 1964; operated in support of Pacific Missile Range. Fitted with helicopter hangar and platform aft. Employed to test AWG-9 fire control system for use in the F-14 Tomcat fighter aircraft.

DISPOSALS
Richfield T-AGM 4, ex-T-AK 253; **Range Tracker** T-AGM 1, ex-T-AG 160, stricken on 28 Apr 1970; **Twin Falls** T-AGM II stricken on 28 Apr 1970 but reacquired by Navy for conversion to surveying ship (T-AGS 37); conversion subsequently cancelled and again stricken on 1 Sep 1972 and transferred to New York City for use as trade school facility; **Watertown** T-AGM 6 stricken on 16 Feb 1973; **Longview** T-AGM 3 ex-T-AK 238 stricken on 1 Nov 1974; **Huntsville** T-AGM 7 stricken on 8 Nov 1974; **Sunnyvale** T-AGM 5 ex-T-AK 256 stricken on 15 Dec 1974.

NOMENCLATURE. Range instrumentation ships have several name sources: "Range" names, as *Range Sentinel*; missile programmes, as *Vangurad*; and cities associated with space or missile programmes, as *Wheeling*. Two ships reactivated by the Air Force and briefly operated by that service carry the names of the Commanding General of the US Army Air Forces in World War II (Arnold) and the second Chief of Staff of the US Air Force (Vandenberg).

WHEELING (T-AGM 8) *United States Navy*

Experimental, Research and Surveying Ships—*continued*

2 UTILITY RESEARCH SHIPS (AGOR)

Name	*No.*	*Laid down*	*Launched*	*Delivered*
***GYRE**	AGOR 21	9 Oct 1972	25 May 1973	14 Nov 1973
***MOANA WAVE**	AGOR 22	10 Oct 1972	18 June 1973	16 Jan 1974

Displacement, tons	950 full load
Dimensions, feet	176 oa × 36 × 14·5
Main engines	2 turbo-charged diesels (Caterpillar); 1 700 bhp; 2 shafts (controllable pitch propellers) = 13 knots maximum; 12 knots cruising
Complement	21 (10 crew, 11 scientists)

Both ships built by Halter Marine Services Inc, New Orleans, Louisiana. They are based on a commercial ship design. Fitted with a 150 hp retractable propeller pod for low-speed or station keeping with main machinery shut down.
Open deck aft provides space for equipment vans to permit rapid change of mission capabilities. Each ship cost approximately $1 900 000.
The Navy plans to construct several of these small, utility oceanographic research ships to replace older and obsolescent ships now operated by civilian research and educational institutions in support of Navy programmes. The above ships are assigned to Texas A & M University and the University of Hawaii, respectively.

GYRE (AGOR 21) *1973, Halter Marine Services*

GYRE (AGOR 21) *1973, Halter Marine Services*

1 OCEANOGRAPHIC RESEARCH SHIP (AGOR): "HAYES" TYPE

***HAYES** (T-AGOR 16)

Displacement, tons	3 080 full load
Dimensions, feet	220 wl; 246·5 oa × 75 (see *Design* notes) × 18·8
Main engines	Geared diesels; 5 400 bhp; 2 shafts = 15 knots
Complement	74 (11 officers, 33 men, 30 scientists)

Authorised in Fiscal Year 1967 new construction programme. The T-AGOR 16 is one of two classes of modern US naval ships to have a catamaran hull, the other being the ASR 21 class submarine rescue ships. Built by Todd Shipyards, Seattle, Washington; completed in late 1971. Estimated cost is $15 900 000. Laid down 12 Nov 1969; launched 2 July 1970.
Operated by the Military Sealift Command for the Office of Naval Research under the technical control of the Oceanographer of the Navy; civilian crew.

DESIGN. Catamaran hull design provides large deck working area, centre well for operating equipment at great depths, and removes laboratory areas from main propulsion machinery. Each hull is 246·5 feet long and 24 feet wide (maximum). There are three 36-inch diameter instrument wells in addition to the main centre well.
The T-AGOR 16 differs in appearance from the ASR 21 class ships by the oceanographic ship having a small deck working space aft of the bridge structure and the absence of stern helicopter platform of the rescue ships.

ENGINEERING. Fitted with controllable pitch propellers. An auxiliary 165-shp diesel is fitted in each hull to provide "creeping" speed of 2 to 4 knots.
Separation of controllable pitch propellers by catamaran hull separation provides high degree of manoeuverability eliminating the need for bow thrusters.
Range is 6 000 miles at 13·5 knots.

NOMENCLATURE. Oceanographic research ships and surveying ships generally are named for naval oceanographers, hydrographers, and explorers. (Converted ships generally retain original names).
The AGOR 16 is named for Dr. Harvey C. Hayes of the Naval Research Laboratory, known as the "father of sonar in the US Navy".

TRANSFERS
Josiah Willard Gibbs T-AGOR 1 ex-AVP 51 transferred to Greece on 7 Dec 1971.

HAYES (T-AGOR 16) *1971, Todd Shipyards Corp*

HAYES (T-AGOR 16) *1971, Camera Craft*

HAYES (T-AGOR 16) *1971, US Navy, William Connick*

2 OCEANOGRAPHIC RESEARCH SHIPS (AGOR): "MELVILLE" CLASS

Name	*No.*	*Laid down*	*Launched*	*Delivered*
***MELVILLE**	AGOR 14	12 July 1967	10 July 1968	27 Aug 1969
***KNORR**	AGOR 15	9 Aug 1967	21 Aug 1968	14 Jan 1970

Displacement, tons	1 915 standard; 2 080 full load
Dimensions, feet	244·9 × 46·3 × 15
Main engines	Diesel 2 500 bhp; 2 cycloidal propellers = 12 knots
Complement	50 (9 officers, 16 men, 25 scientists)

Oceanographic research ships of an advanced design. AGOR 14 and AGOR 15 authorised in Fiscal Year 1966 new construction programme; AGOR 19 and AGOR 20 of this type in FY 1968 programme, but construction of the latter ships was cancelled. These ships are fitted with internal wells for lowering equipment; underwater lights and observation ports. Facilities for handling small research submersibles.
The *Melville* and *Knorr* built by Defoe Shipbuilding Co, Bay City, Michigan. *Melville* operated by Scripps Institution of Oceanography and *Knorr* by Woods Hole Oceano-

MELVILLE (AGOR 14) *1969, Defoe Shipbuilding*

Experimental, Research and Surveying Ships—*continued*

"MELVILLE" CLASS—continued

graphy Institution for the Office of Naval Research; under technical control of the Oceanographer of the Navy.

ENGINEERING. First US Navy ocean-going ships with cycloidal propellers permitting the ships to turn 360 degrees in their own length. One propeller is fitted at each end of the ship, providing movement in any direction and optimum station keeping without use of thrusters. They have experienced engineering difficulties.

7 OCEANOGRAPHIC RESEARCH SHIPS (AGOR): "CONRAD" CLASS

Name	*No.*	*Laid down*	*Launched*	*Delivered*
***ROBERT D. CONRAD**	AGOR 3	19 Jan 1961	26 May 1962	29 Nov 1962
***JAMES M. GILLISS**	T-AGOR 4	31 May 1961	19 May 1962	5 Nov 1962
***LYNCH**	T AGOR 7	7 Sep 1962	17 Mar 1964	22 Oct 1965
***THOMAS G. THOMPSON**	AGOR 9	12 Sep 1963	18 July 1964	4 Sep 1965
***THOMAS WASHINGTON**	AGOR 10	12 Sep 1963	1 Aug 1964	17 Sep 1965
***DE STEIGUER**	T-AGOR 12	12 Nov 1965	21 Mar 1966	28 Feb 1969
***BARTLETT**	T-AGOR 13	18 Nov 1965	24 May 1966	15 Apr 1969

Displacement, tons	varies; approx 1 200 standard; 1 380 full load
Dimensions, feet	191·5 wl; 208·9 oa × 37·4 × 15·3
Main engines	Diesel-electric (Caterpillar Tractor Co diesels); 10 000 bhp; 1 shaft = 13·5 knots
Complement	41 (9 officers, 17 men, 15 scientists except *De Steigeur* and *Bartlett*, 8 officers, 18 men)

This is the first class of ships designed and built by the US Navy for oceanographic research. Fitted with instrumentation and laboratories to measure the earth's gravity and magnetic fields, water temperature, sound transmission in water, and the geological profile of the ocean floor.

Special features include 10 ton capacity boom and winches for handling over-the-side equipment; bow thruster propulsion unit for precise manoeuvrability and station keeping; 620 hp gas turbine (housed in funnel structure) for providing "quiet" power when conducting operations in which use of main engines would generate too high a noise level (gas turbine also can drive the ship at 6·5 knots); endurance of 12 000 miles at 12 knots.

Robert D. Conrad built by Gibbs Corp, Jacksonville, Florida. Operated by Lamont Geological Observatory of Columbia University under technical control of the Oceanographer of the Navy.

James H. Gilliss built by Christy Corp, Sturgeon Bay, Wisconsin. Operated by the University of Miami (Florida) since 1970 in support of Navy programmes.

Lynch built by Marietta Manufacturing Co, Point Pleasant, West Virginia. Operated by Military Sealift Command under the technical control of the Oceanographer of the Navy. Civilian crew.

Thomas G. Thompson built by Marinette Marine Corp, Marinette, Wisconsin. Operated by University of Washington (state) under technical control of the Oceanographer of the Navy; civilian crew.

Thomas Washington built by Marinette Marine Corp, Marinette, Wisconsin. Operated by Scripps Institution of Oceanography (University of California) under technical control of the Oceanographer on the Navy; civilian crew.

De Steiguer and *Bartlett* built by Northwest Marine Iron Works, Portland, Oregon Operated by Military Sealift Command under the technical control of the Oceanographer of the Navy; civilian crew.

TRANSFERS

Charles H. Davis AGOR 5 of this type was transferred to New Zealand on 10 Aug 1970; **Sands** AGOR 6 was transferred to Brazil on 1 July 1974.

PHOTOGRAPHS. Note built-up structure amidships on *De Steiguer*; the *Thomas D. Thompson* has side structure built up amidships.

JAMES M. GILLISS (T-AGOR 4) *United States Navy*

THOMAS G. THOMPSON (AGOR 9) *United States Navy*

DE STEIGUER (T-AGOR 12) *United States Navy*

BARTLETT (T-AGOR 13) *United States Navy*

1 OCEANOGRAPHIC RESEARCH SHIP (AGOR): Ex-SALVAGE SHIP

Name	*No.*	*Launched*	*Commissioned*
***CHAIN**	AGOR 17 (ex-ARS 20)	3 June 1943	31 Mar 1944

Displacement, tons	2 100 full load
Dimensions, feet	207 wl; 213·5 oa × 39 × 15
Main engines	Diesel electric (4 Cooper Bessemer diesels); approx 3 000 bhp; 2 shafts = 14 knots
Complement	29 + 26 scientists

Converted from a salvage ship for oceanographic research. Built by Basalt Rock Co, Napa, California. Commission date as ARS. Converted to an oceanographic research ship by Savannah Machine & Foundry in 1958. The *Chain* is operated by the Woods Hole Oceanographic Institution for the Office of Naval Research under the technical control of the Oceanographer of the Navy. Civilian crew.

ENGINEERING. Fitted with an auxiliary 250 hp outboard propulsion unit for manoeuvering at low speeds (up to 4·5 knots).

DISPOSALS

Argo AGOR 18 (ex-*Snatch*, ARS 27) similarly converted; stricken on 1 May 1970.

1 OCEANOGRAPHIC RESEARCH SHIP (AGOR): Ex-CARGO SHIP

Name	*No.*	*Launched*	*Delivered*
MIZAR	T-AGOR 11 (ex-T-AK 272)	7 Oct 1957	22 Nov 1957

Displacement, tons	2 036 light; 4 942 full load
Dimensions, feet	256·8 wl; 262·2 oa × 51·5 × 22·8
Main engines	Diesel-electric (ALCO diesels, Westinghouse electric motors) 3 200 bhp; 2 shafts = 12 knots
Complement	56 (11 officers, 30 enlisted men, 15 scientists)

Built for Military Sea Transportation Service by Avondale Marine Ways, New Orleans, La. Designed for Arctic operation with hull strengthened against ice. C1-ME2-13a type. Delivered as cargo ship to MSTS (now Military Sealift Command) and subsequently converted to oceanographic research ship.

As research ship the *Mizar* is operated by the Military Sealift Command for Naval Research Laboratory, under technical control of the Oceanographer of the Navy; civilian crew.

CONVERSION. *Mizar* converted in 1962 into deep sea research ship. Equipped with centre well for lowering oceanographic equipment including towed sensor platforms, fitted with laboratories and elaborate photographic facilities, hydrophone system and computer for seafloor navigation and tracking towed vehicles. The *Mizar* had key roles in the searches for the US nuclear submarines *Thresher* and *Scorpion*; the French submarine *Eurydice*: and recovery of the H-bomb lost at sea off Palomares, Spain.

TRANSFERS

Eltanin T-AGOR 8 (ex-T-AK 270) transferred to Argentina on 19 Feb 1974.

MIZAR (T-AGOR 11) *United States Navy*

Experimental, Research and Surveying Ships—*continued*

OCEANOGRPAHIC RESEARCH CRAFT

The Navy also owns a number of smaller oceanographic research craft that are operated by various educational and research institutions in support of Navy programmes; under technical control of the Oceanographer of the Navy; no Navy hull numbers are assigned; all are 100 feet in length or smaller except for the *Lamb*, a converted 136-foot minesweeper (YMS/AMS type) operated by the Lamont Geophysical Laboratory.

1 SURVEYING SHIP (AGS): C1-M-AV1 TYPE

COASTAL CRUSADER T-AGS 36 (ex-T-AGM 16)

Dimensions, feet	338·8 oa × 50·3 × 12
Main engines	Diesel; 1 750 bhp; 1 shaft = 11·5 knots

Built in 1945 by Leatham D. Smith SB Co, Sturgeon Bay, Wisconsin. Acquired for conversion to a missile range tracking ship by US Air Force; transferred to Military Sea Transportation service as T-AGM 16 on 1 July 1964.
Reclassified as a surveying ship (T-AGS 36) on 1 Dec 1969 but taken out of service and placed in reserve prior to operation as an AGS; laid up in Maritime Administration reserve but remains on Navy List.

CONVERSION. The *Coastal Crusader* has been under consideration for conversion to a laser research ship. In that role she would provide a platform for fleet evaluation of high-energy lasers in the air defence role.

DISPOSALS
Sgt. George D. Keathley T-AGS 35 ex-T-APC 117 of this type transferred to Taiwan China on 29 Mar 1972.

COASTAL CRUSADER T-AGS 36 (as T-AGM 16) *United States Navy*

"S. P. LEE" CLASS

Both ships of this design, the first US Navy ships designed and constructed specifically for surveying operations, have been transferred from the Navy List: **Kellar** T-AGS 25 transferred to Portugal on 21 Jan 1972; **S. P. Lee** T-AG 192 (ex-T-AGS 31) transferred to the US Department of the Interior for geological survey on 27 Feb 1974.
See 1973-1974 and previous editions for characteristics.

2 SURVEYING SHIPS (AGS): "CHAUVENET" CLASS

Name	*No.*	*Laid Down*	*Launched*	*Delivered*
***CHAUVENET**	T-AGS 29	24 May 1967	13 May 1968	13 Nov 1970
***HARKNESS**	T-AGS 32	30 June 1967	12 June 1968	29 Jan 1971

Displacement, tons	4 200 full load
Dimensions feet,	393·2 oa × 54 × 16
Main engines	Diesel (Westinghouse); 3 600 bhp; 1 shaft = 15 knots
Complement	175 (13 officers, approx 150 men and technical personnel, 12 scientists)

A class of large research ships capable of extensive military hydrographic and oceanographic surveys, supporting coastal surveying craft, amphibious survey teams and helicopters. Fitted with helicoter hangar and platform.
Chauvenet authorised in Fiscal Year 1965 new construction programme; *Harkness* in FY 1966 programme. Both ships built by Upper Clyde Shipbuilders, Govan Division, Glasgow, Scotland.
These ships are operated by the Military Sealift Command for the Oceanographer of the Navy with Navy detachments on board. Civilian crews.

CHAUVENET (T-AGS 29) *1971, United States Navy*

HARKNESS (T-AGS 32) *United States Navy*

4 SURVEYING SHIPS (AGS): "BENT" CLASS

Name	*No.*	*Laid down*	*Launched*	*Delivered*
***SILAS BENT**	T-AGS 26	2 Mar 1964	16 May 1964	23 July 1965
***KANE**	T-AGS 27	19 Dec 1964	20 Nov 1965	19 May 1967
***WILKES**	T-AGS 33	18 July 1968	31 July 1969	28 June 1971
***WYMAN**	T-AGS 34	18 July 1968	30 Oct 1969	3 Nov 1971

Displacement, tons	1 935 standard; *Silas Bent* and *Kane* 2 558 full load; *Wilkes* 2 540 full load; *Wyman* 2 420 full load
Dimensions, feet	285·3 oa × 48 × 15·1
Main engines	Diesel-electric (Westinghouse diesels); 3 600 bhp; 1 shaft = 14 knots
Complement	77 to 79 (12 or 13 officers, 35 or 36 men, 30 scientists)

Designed specifically for surveying operations. Special features include seafloor mapping equipment; bow propulsion unit for precise manoeuvrability and station keeping. All four ships operated by Military Sealift Command for the Oceanographer of the Navy; civilian crews.
Silas Bent built by American SB Co, Lorain, Ohio; *Kane* built by Christy Corp, Sturgeon Bay, Wisconsin; *Wilkes* and *Wyman* built by Defoe SB Co, Bay City, Miehigan.

WILKES (T-AGS 33) *1971, United States Navy*

WYMAN (T-AGS 34) *1971, United States Navy*

SILAS BENT (T-AGS 26) *United States Navy*

Experimental, Research and Surveying Ships—*continued*

3 SURVEYING SHIPS (AGS): "VICTORY" TYPE

***BOWDITCH** (ex-SS *South Bend Victory*) T-AGS 21
***DUTTON** (ex-SS *Tuskegee Victory*) T-AGS 22
***MICHELSON** (ex-SS *Joliet Victory*) T-AGS 23

Displacement, tons	4 512 full load
Dimensions, feet	455·2 oa × 62·2 × 25
Main engines	Turbine; 8 500 shp; 1 shaft = 15 knots
Boilers	2
Complement	100 to 101 (13 or 14 officers, 47 men, approx 40 technical personnel)

VC2-S-AP3 type built in 1945, *Bowditch* and *Michelson* by Oregon Shipbuilding Co; *Dutton* by South Coast Co. Newport Beach, California. All converted to support the Fleet Ballistic Missile Programme, *Dutton* and *Michelson* at Philadelphia Naval Shipyard 8 Nov 1957 to 16 Nov 1958 and 1 Mar 1958 to 31 Dec 1968, respectively, and *Bowditch* at Charleston Naval Shipyard 10 Oct 1957 to 30 Sep 1958.
Designed to chart the ocean floor and to record magnetic fields and gravity.
Operated by Military Sealift Command for the Oceanographer of the Navy; civilian crews.

MICHELSON (T-AGS 23) *United States Navy*

DUTTON (T-AGS 22) *United States Navy*

1 GUIDED MISSILE SHIP (AVM): CONVERTED SEAPLANE TENDER

***NORTON SOUND** AVM 1 (ex-AV 11)

Displacement, tons	9 106 standard; 15 170 full load
Dimensions, feet	543·25 oa × 71·6 × 23·5
Missile launchers	1 twin Standard-MR surface-to-air launcher (Mk 26)
Machinery	Geared turbines (Allis-Chalmers); 12 000 shp; 2 shafts = 19 knots
Boilers	4 (Babcock & Wilcox)
Complement	approx 300

The *Norton Sound* is a seagoing laboratory and test centre for advanced weapon systems. Constructed as a seaplane tender of the "Currituck" class (AV 7); built by Los Angeles SB & DD Co, San Pedro, California; laid down 7 Sep 1942, launched 28 Nov 1943; commissioned 8 Jan 1945. In 1948 the *Norton Sound* was converted to a guided missile test ship, after operating briefly in the Pacific War and afterward as a seaplane tender. (See *Conversion* notes).
The *Norton Sound* has subsequently served as test ship for a number of research and weapon programmes, and is currently employed as a test platform for the Aegis advanced fleet defence system.

CLASSIFICATION. Changed from AV 11 to AVM 1 on 8 Aug 1951.

CONVERSION. The *Norton Sound* was initially fitted as a guided missile (test) ship in 1948 during a seven-month conversion at the Philadelphia Naval Shipyard; 30-ton capacity boom removed from fantail (similar boom retained on hangar structure); helicopter deck provided forward; provision for fuelling, checking out, monitoring, and firing rockets and missiles.
Converted from November 1962 to June 1964 at Maryland SB & DD Co, Baltimore, Maryland, to test ship for the Typhon advanced weapons control system (intended for a new class of nuclear-powered guided missile cruisers); Typhon system removed in July 1966.
Modified in 1974 to serve as test ship for the Aegis advanced fleet defence system. SPY-1 paired radar arrays to provide 180° coevrage (12 × 12 foot, six-sided "faces") installed atop forward superstructure; Mk 110 radar control system installed (including four UYK-7 computers to control phase steering of radars). The full Aegis system, as planned in warships, would have four radar "faces" to provide 360° coverage. Twin Srandard-MR (SM-2) fitted on stern.
Original armament consistsd of 4—5 inch guns (two single mounts forward and two single mounts atop hangar), and 20—40 mm AA guns (three quad, four twin). Forward guns removed to provide space or helicopter deck; all other original armament subsequently removed.

GUNNERY. Fitted in 1968 with light-weight 5 inch 54 calibre gun and associated Mk 86 gunfire control system for operational test and evaluation. See 1973-1974 edition for photograph showing gun installation.

MISSILES. Missiles and rockets test fired from the *Norton Sound* include the Aerobee, Loon (US version of the German V-1 "buzz bomb"), Lark, Regulus, Terrier, Tartar, and Sea Sparrow. During Project Argus in 1958 from a position south of the Faulkland Islands the *Norton Sound* launched three multi-stage missiles carrying low-yield nuclear warheads which were detonated approximately 300 miles above the earth. (The ship was also used to launch high-altitude balloons in Project Skyhook during 1949).

NOMENCLATURE. Seaplane tenders were named for bodies of water. Norton Sound is the largest Alaskan sound.

"NORTON SOUND" — *continued*

PHOTOGRAPHS. Note mast and TACAN pod atop large crane on hangar structure; lattice radar mast atop bridge structure and pole radar mast amidships. A starboard-view showing the Standard SAM launcher aft taken in 1973 appears in the 1974-1975 edition.

NORTON SOUND (AVM 1) *1974, United States Navy*

1 TEST RANGE SUPPORT SHIP (IX): CONVERTED LSMR

Name	*No.*	*Launched*	*Commissioned*
***ELK RIVER**	IX 501 (ex-LSMR 501)	21 Apr 1954	27 May 1945

Displacement, tons	1 100 full load
Dimensions, feet	225 oa × 50 × 9·2
Main engines	Diesels; 1 400 bhp; 2 shafts = 11 knots
Complement	25 + 20 technical personnel

The *Elk River* is a former rocket landing ship specifically converted to support Navy deep submergence activities on the San Clemente Island Range off the coast of Southern California. Built by Brown Shipbuilding Co, Houstan, Texas.
The ship is capable of supporting the following activities: (1) deep diving for man-in-the-sea programmes, (2) deep diving for salvage programmes, (3) submersible test and evaluation, (4) underwater equipment testing, and (5) deep mooring operations. Operated by combined Navy-civilian crew.

CONVERSION. The *Elk River* was withdrawn from the Reserve Fleet and converted to a range support ship in 1967-1968 at Avondale Shipyards Inc, Westwego, Louisiana, and the San Francisco Bay Naval Shipyard.
The basic LSMR hull was lengthened and eight-foot sponsons were added to either side to increase deck working space and stability; superstructure added forward. An open centre well was provided to facilitate lowering and raising equipment; also fitted with 65-ton-capacity gantry crane (on tracks) to handle submersibles and active positioning mooring system to hold ship in precise location without elaborate mooring and permit shifting within the moor. Five anchors including bow anchor.

DIVING. Fitted with prototype Mk 2 Deep Diving System (see "Pigeon" class submarine rescue ships).

ELK RIVER (IX 501) *1968, United States Navy*

ELK RIVER (IX 501) *1968, United States Navy*

Experimental, Research, and Surveying Ships—*continued*

1 TORPEDO TEST SHIP (IX)

***NEW BEDFORD** IX 308 (ex-AKL 17, ex-FS 289)

Displacement, tons	approx 700
Dimensions, feet	176·5 oa × 32·8 × 10
Main engines	Diesel; 1 000 bhp; 1 shaft = 10 knots

Small Army cargo ship (freight and supply) acquired by Navy on 1 Mar 1950 for cargo work and subsequently converted to support torpedo testing. Operated by Naval Torpedo Station, Keyport, Washington, since 1963. Other craft serving in this role are described in the section on Service Craft (YFRT type).

NEW BEDFORD (IX 308) *1973, United States Navy*

1 INSTRUMENTATION PLATFORM (IX)

***BRIER** IX 307 (ex-WLI 299)

Displacement, tons	178
Dimensions, feet	100 × 24 × 4·5
Machinery	Diesel with electric drive; 300 bhp; 2 shafts = 8·5 knots

Former Coast Guard buoy tender built in 1943; acquired by Navy on 10 Mar 1969 for use as instrument platform for explosive testing; redesignated IX 307 on 29 Aug 1970.

1 WEAPON TEST SHIP (IX)

***IX 306** (ex-FS 221)

Displacement, tons	906 full load
Dimensions, feet	179 oa × 33 × 10
Main engines	Diesel; 1 shaft = 12 knots

Former Army cargo ship (freight and supply) acquired by the Navy in January 1966 and subsequently converted to a weapon test ship, being placed in service late in 1969. Conducts research for the Naval Underwater Weapons Research and Engineering Station, Newport, Rhode Island; operates in Atlantic Underwater Test and Evaluation Centre (AUTEC) range in Caribbean. Manned by Navy and civilian RCA personnel. Note white hull with blue bow and torpedo tube opening on starboard side just aft of hull number.

IX 306 *1969, United States Navy*

DISPOSALS AND RECLASSIFICATIONS

Target ship **Atlanta** IX 304 (ex-CL 104), a converted light cruiser employed in explosive tests, was stricken from the Navy List on 1 Apr 1970 (sunk as target).

Mobile listening barge **MONOB I** IX 309 (ex-YW 87) reclassified as YAG 61 on 1 July 1970 (see Service Craft listing).

Hydrographic research ships **Rexburg** PCER 855 and **Marysville** PCER 857 stricken on 7 Mar 1970 and 15 July 1970, respectively.

Ex-aircraft carrier **Bunker Hill** AVT 9 (ex-CVS 17) stricken on 1 Nov 1966 served as a stationary electronic test ship from 1965 until late 1972. (See 1971-1972 edition for characteristics and photographs).

(The research ships *George Eastman* YAG 39 and *Granville S. Hall* YAG 40 are listed with service Craft; the experimental hydrofoil ships *Plainview* AGEH 1 and *High Point* PCH 1 are listed with Patrol Ships and Craft; the research escort ship *Glover* AGDE 1 is listed with Ocean Escorts).

MISCELLANEOUS

1 PRESIDENTIAL YACHT

***SEQUOIA** AG 23

Displacement, tons	approx 110
Dimensions, feet	99 wl; 104 oa × 18·2
Main engines	2 diesels; 450 bhp; 2 shafts = 11·5 knots
Complement	21 (1 officer, 20 enlisted men; accommodation for only 14 of crew)
Passengers	accommodation for 7 under normal conditions

SEQUOIA (AG 23) *United States Navy*

1 SAIL FRIGATE

***CONSTITUTION** IX 21 launched 21 Oct 1797

The oldest ship of the US Navy remaining on the Navy List. "In service" status as a relic at Boston. Periodically she is taken out into Boston Harbour and "turned around". The *Constitution* began an extensive, $4 200 000 overhaul in April 1973 at the Boston Naval Shipyard: completed in early 1975.

Characteristics and photograph appear in the 1970-1971 edition.

The sailing ship *Constellation* which survives under private ownership at Baltimore, Maryland, is apparently the last sailing man-of-war-built for the US Navy; she was constructed at the Norfolk (Virginia) Navy Yard in 1853-1854, built in part with material from the earlier frigate *Constellation* (launched 1797).

The self-propelled barracks ship **Benewah** (APB 35) was reclassified IX 311 on 1 Apr 1971; stricken on 1 Sep 1973.

The classification IX 310 has been assigned to a group of barges used at the Naval Underwater Sound Laboratory, Newport, Rhode Island.

The **Guardian** (ex-PT 809) transferred to Fleet Composite Support Squadron 6 at Little Creek, Virginia, in December 1974 for use as recovery boat for aerial targets and control boat surface target drone craft. Formerly employed as guard boat for presidential yacht. She is the last motor torpedo boat in US Navy service (built 1950).

YTB 787 and YTM 518 assisting MIDWAY (CVA 41) at Yokosuka, Japan *1973, US Navy*

SERVICE CRAFT

The US Navy operates several hundred service craft, primarily small craft that provide services to the Fleet in harbours and ports. Only the self-propelled craft are listed here. In addition, there are hundreds of non-self-propelled barge-like craft for carrying cargo, floating cranes, dredges, workshops, power barges, berthing barges, water and fuel barges, garbage scows, *et cetera*. In addition, a few "ships", and the nuclear-propelled research submersible NR-1 officially are designated as service craft. Only the Y- prefix ships and craft are listed in this section (the "Y" originally indicating yardcraft).

The specific type strengths are as of March 1975. Asterisks are used to indicate only those active service craft with names.

1 MOBILE LISTENING BARGE (YAG)

***MONOB I** YAG 61 (ex-IX 309, ex-YW 87)

Displacement, tons 1 390 full load
Dimensions, feet 174 oa × 33

The *Monob I* is a mobile listening barge converted from a self-propelled water barge. Built in 1943 and converted for acoustic research in 1969, being placed in service in May 1969. Conducts research for the Naval Ship Research and Development Centre; based at Port Everglades, Florida.
Designation changed from IX 301 to YAG 61 on 1 July 1970.

MONOB I *United States Navy*

1 RESEARCH SHIP (YAG): "LIBERTY" TYPE

GEORGE EASTMAN YAG 39

Displacement, tons 6 000 light; 11 600 full load
Dimensions, feet 422·7 oa × 57 × 34·7
Main engines Steam reciprocating; 2 500 ihp; 1 shaft = 11 knots
Boilers 2
Accommodation 169 (19 officers, 150 enlisted men)

EC2-S-C1 "Liberty" ship built by Permanente Metals Corp, Richmond, California; launched on 20 Apr 1943 and delivered as merchant ship on 5 May 1943. The ship was acquired by the Navy on 2 Apr 1953 for use as a nuclear effects research ship (designated YAG 39); not employed as minesweeping ship as were other "Liberty" type ships. The now-stricken *Granville S. Hall* was employed in a similar role.
As a research ship the *George Eastman* was fitted with instrumentation to detect nuclear fallout and radiation; ship controls enclosed in a specially protected compartment; also equipped for remote control for unmanned operation in contaminated areas. Also used in ship biological and chemical defence research. Now in reserve.

DISPOSALS
Granville S. Hall YAG 40 of the "Liberty" type was stricken in 1971.

The experimental minefield sweeper **YAG 37** (ex-*John L. Sullivan*) was scrapped in 1958, **YAG 36** (ex-*Floyd W. Spencer*) and **YAG 38** (ex-*Edward Kavanagh*) were stricken in 1960. The Fleet X-ray examination ship **Whidbey** AG 141, was stricken on 1 May 1959.
The former netlaying ship **Butternut** (ex-ANL 9, ex-AN 9, ex-YN 4) was reinstated on the Navy List as YAG 60 on 28 Oct 1969; after brief service in support of the Pacific Missile Range, she was taken out of service in late 1970 and stricken on 1 July 1971.

Sailing Yacht **Salude** YAG 87 stricken on 15 Apr 1974 (see 1973-1974 edition for characteristics).

GEORGE EASTMAN (YAG 39) *1966, United States Navy*

2 DIVING TENDERS (YDT)

Tenders used to support shallow-water diving operations. Three self-propelled diving tenders are on the Navy List: **Phoebus** YDT 14 ex-YF 294, and **Suitland** YDT 15 ex-YF 336. (Two non-self-propelled YDTs are in service).

2 COVERED LIGHTERS (YF)

Lighters used to transport material in harbours; self-propelled; four are on the Navy List, three of which are named: **Lynnhaven** (YF 328), **Keyport** (YF 885), and **Kodiak** (YF 886), the two former ones being active.

7 FERRYBOATS (YFB)

Ferryboats used to transport personnel and vehicles in large harbours; self-propelled; one is under construction and seven are on the Navy List, one of which is named: **Aquidneck** (YFB 14). The YFB 88-91 are the former LCU 1636, 1638-1640, all reclassified on 1 Sep 1969. All are active except the **Aquidneck** which is in reserve.

YFB 88 (ex-LCU 1636) *United States Navy*

YFB 87 *1970, United States Navy*

1 REFRIGERTATED COVERED LIGHTER (YFR)

Lighters used to store and transport food and other materials which require refrigeration. The YFR 888 remains on the Navy List in reserve.

YFR 890 *United States Navy*

6 COVERED LIGHTERS (RANGE TENDER) (YFRT)

Lighters used for miscellaneous purposes; YFRT 287, 411, 451, 520, and 523 active; YFRT 418 is in reserve. Note Mk 32 torpedo tubes on YFRT 520.
Range Recoverer YFRT 524 (ex-T-AGM 2, ex-T-AG 161, ex-US Army FS 278) stricken on 15 May 1974.

YFRT 520 *1969, United States Navy*

10 HARBOUR UTILITY CRAFT (YFU)

YFU 71	**YFU 74**	**YFU 76**	**YFU 79**	**YFU 81**
YFU 72	**YFU 75**	**YFU 77**	**YFU 80**	**YFU 82**

Dimensions, feet 125 oa × 36 × 7·5
Main engines diesels = 8 knots
Guns 2—50 cal MG

Militarised versions of a commercial lighter design. Used for off-loading large ships in harbours and ferrying cargo from one coastal port to another. Built by Pacific Coast Engineering Co. Alameda, California; completed 1967-1968. Can carry more than 300 tons cargo; considerable cruising range.

YFU 71-77 and YFU 80-82 loaned to US Army in 1970 for use in South Vietnam; returned to Navy control in 1973.

LOSSES AND TRANSFERS
YFU 78 sunk in Vietnam in March 1969; **YFU 73** transferred to Khmer Republic (Cambodia) on 15 Nov 1973.

Service Craft—*continued*

YFU 75 — *1968, United States Navy*

YFU 74 — *1969, United States Navy*

16 HARBOUR UTILITY CRAFT (YFU):

YFU 44 (ex-LCU 1398)	**YFU 67** (ex-LCU 1232)	**YFU 97** (ex-LCU 1611)
YFU 50 (ex-LCU 1486)	**YFU 83** (new; see notes)	**YFU 98** (ex-LCU 1615)
YFU 53 (ex-LCU 1446)	**YFU 89** (ex-LCU 1576)	**YFU 99** (ex-LSU 1622)
YFU 55 (ex-LCU 637)	**YFU 91** (ex-LCU 1608)	**YFU 100** (ex-LCU 1610)
YFU 57 (ex-LCU 709)	**YFU 93** (ex-LCU 1625)	**YFU 101** (ex-LCU 1612)
		YFU 102 (ex-LCU 1462)

Former utility landing craft employed primarily as harbour and coastal cargo craft (see section on Landing Craft for basic characteristics). The YFU 44 and YFU 53 have open centre wells for lowering research equipment into the water; both are assigned to the Naval Undersea Research and Development Centre in Long Beach, California.
YFU 83 built by Defoe Shipbuilding Co (same design as LCU 1646). Several YFUs were loaned to the US Army in 1970 for use in Vietnam after withdrawal of US Navy riverine and coastal forces.

CLASSIFICATIONS. YFU 1-70 and 84-102 all are former utility landing craft. Several reverted to LCU designations and three were modified for salvage work: YFU 2, 16, and 33 to YLLC 5, 2, and 3, respectively.

DISPOSALS AND TRANSFERS (since 1 Jan 1970)
YFU 5, 7, 20, 36, 37 stricken in 1970; **YFU** 8, 45, 47, 58, 50, 92 stricken in 1971; **YFU** 90 transferred to South Vietnam in 1971; **YFU** 25, 61, 87 stricken in 1972; **YFU** 56, 68 transferred to Khmer Republic (Cambodia) on 19 May 1972; **YFU** 88, 95 transferred to Spain on 28 June 1972; **YFU** 39, 59 stricken in 1973; **YFU** 4 stricken on 1 Oct 1974; **YFU** 24 stricken on 15 Oct 1974; **YFU** 96 stricken on 1 Dec 1974

YFU 83 — *1971, Defoe Shipbuilding*

27 FUEL BARGES (YO)

Small liquid fuel carriers intended to fuel ships where no pierside fuelling facilities are available; self-propelled; 27 are on the Navy List. Two are named: **Casing Heap** YO 47, **Crownbrock** YO 48.

YO 130 — *1970, United States Navy*

12 GASOLINE BARGES (YOG)

Similar to the fuel barges (YO), but carry gasoline and aviation fuels; self-propelled; 12 are on the Navy List. One is named: **Lieut. Thomas W. Fowler** YOG 107.

22 SEAMANSHIP TRAINING CRAFT (YP)

YP 587	**YP 591**	**YP 657**	**YP 660**	**YP 663**	**YP 666**	**YP 669**
YP 589	**YP 655**	**YP 658**	**YP 661**	**YP 664**	**YP 667**	**YP 670**
YP 590	**YP 656**	**YP 659**	**YP 662**	**YP 665**	**YP 668**	**YP 671**
						YP 672

YP 584 series:

Displacement, tons	50
Dimensions, feet	75 oa × 16 × 4·5
Main engines	2 diesels (Superior); 400 bhp; 2 shafts = 12 knots

YP 654 series:

Displacement, tons	69·5 full load
Dimensions, feet	80·4 oa × 18·75 × 5·3
Main engines	4 diesels (General Motors); 660 bhp; 2 shafts = 13·5 knots

These craft are used for instruction in seamanship and navigation at the Naval Academy, Annapolis, Maryland, and Naval Officer Candidate School, Newport, Rhode Island. Fitted with surface search radar, Fathometer, gyro compass, and UHF and MF radio; the YP 655 additionally fitted for instruction in oceanographic research.
YPs numbered below 654 are older craft of a once-numerous type employed for training and utility work. YP 654-663 built by Stephens Bros, Inc, Stockton, Calif. completed in 1958; YP 664 and 665 built by Elizabeth City Shipbuilders, Inc, Elizabeth City, North Carolina; YP 666 and 667 built by Stephens Bros; YP 668 built by Peterson Boatbuilding Co, Tacoma, Washington, completed in 1968; YP 669-672 built by Peterson completed in 1971-1972.
These craft are of wooden construction with aluminium deck houses.

YP 588 stricken on 1 Feb 1972; **YP 584, 585** stricken on 1 May 1974; **YP 587** stricken on 1 Oct 1974.

YP 654 type — ***United States Navy***

YP 669 — *1971, Peterson Builders*

11 SMALL HARBOUR TUGS (YTL)

Eleven of these craft are on the Navy List; unnamed. Six are active and five in reserve.

94 MEDIUM HARBOUR TUGS (YTM)

Numbered in YTM 128-779 series; several formerly designated YTB or are former US Army tugs. The YTM 659 fitted with triple Mk 32 torpedo tubes. Most have names. Seventy-seven are active and 17 in reserve.

MASCOUTAN (YTM 760) — *1971, United States Navy*

Service Craft—*continued*

81 LARGE HARBOUR TUGS (YTB)

Name	No.
EDENSHAW	YTB 752
MARIN	YTB 753
PONTIAC	YTB 756
OSHKOSH	YTB 757
PADUCAH	YTB 758
BOGALUSA	YTB 759
NATICK	YTB 760
OTTUMWA	YTB 761
TUSCUMBIA	YTB 762
MUSKEGON	YTB 763
MISHAWAKA	YTB 764
OKMULGEE	YTB 765
WAPOAKINETA	YTB 766
APALACHICOLA	YTB 767
ARCATA	YTB 768
CHESANING	YTB 769
DAHLONEGA	YTB 770
KEOKUK	YTB 771
NASHUA	YTB 774
WAUWATOSA	YTB 775
WEEHAWKEN	YTB 776
NOGALES	YTB 777
APOPKA	YTB 778
MANHATTAN	YTB 779
SAUGUS	YTB 780
NIANTIC	YTB 781
MANISTEE	YTB 782
REDWING	YTB 783
KALISPELL	YTB 784
WINNEMUCCA	YTB 785
TONKAWA	YTB 786
KITTANNING	YTB 787
WAPATO	YTB 788
TOMAHAWK	YTB 789
MENOMINEE	YTB 790
MARINETTE	YTB 791
ANTIGO	YTB 792
PIQUA	YTB 793
MANDAN	YTB 794
KETCHIKAN	YTB 795
SACO	YTB 796
TAMAQUA	YTB 797
OPELIKA	YTB 789
NATCHITOCHES	YTB 799
EFAULA	YTB 800
PALATKA	YTB 801
CHERAW	YTB 802
NANTICOKE	YTB 803
AHOSKIE	YTB 804
OCALA	YTB 805
TUSKEGEE	YTB 806
MASSAPEQUA	YTB 807
WENATCHEE	YTB 808
AGAWAN	YTB 809
ANOKA	YTB 810
HOUMA	YTB 811
ACCONAC	YTB 812
POUGHKEEPSIE	YTB 813
WAXAHATCHIE	YTB 814
NEODESHA	YTB 815
CAMPTI	YTB 816
HAYANNIS	YTB 817
MECOSTA	YTB 818
IUKA	YTB 819
WANAMASSA	YTB 820
TONTOGANY	YTB 821
PAWHUSKA	YTB 822
CANONCHET	YTB 823
SANTAQUIN	YTB 824
WATHENA	YTB 825
WASHTUCNA	YTB 826
CHETEK	YTB 827
CATAHECASSA	YTB 828
METACOM	YTB 829
PUSHMATHA	YTB 830
DEKANAWIDA	YTB 831
PETALESHARO	YTB 832
SHABONEE	YTB 833
NEWGAGON	YTB 834
SKENANDOA	YTB 835
POKAGON	YTB 836

Displacement, tons	350 full load
Dimensions, feet	109 oa × 30 × 13·8
Machinery	2 diesels; 2 000 bhp; 2 shafts
Complement	10 to 12 (enlisted)

Large harbour tugs ; 83 are in service or under construction. YTB 752 completed in 1959, YTB 753 in 1960, YTB 756-762 in 1961, YTB 763-766 in 1963, YTB 770 and YTB 771 in 1964, YTB 767-769, 776 in 1965, YTB 774, 775, 777-789 in 1966, YTB 790-793 in 1967, YTB 794 and 795 in 1968, YTB 796-803 in 1969, and YTB 804-815 completed in 1970-1972, YTB 816-827 completed 1972-1973, YTB 828-836 completed 1974-1975.
Navy tugs have Indian names.

PADUCAH (YTB 758) assisting JOHN F. KENNEDY (CVA 67) *US Navy*

TUSKEGEE (YTB 806) *1970, Peterson Builders*

17 WATER BARGES (YW)

Barges modified to carry water to ships in harbour; self-propelled; 17 of these craft are on the Navy List: 4 active and 13 in reserve.

RICHLAND (AFDM 8)—see following page *1969, Robert Fudge*

FLOATING DRY DOCKS

The US Navy operates a number of floating dry docks to supplement dry dock facilities at major naval activities, to support fleet ballistic missile submarines (SSBN) at advanced bases, and to provide repair capabilities in forward combat areas.
The larger floating dry docks are made sectional to facilitate movement overseas and to render them self docking. The ARD-type docks have the forward end of their docking well closed by a structure resembling the bow of a ship to facilitate towing. Berthing facilities, repair shops, and machinery are housed in sides of larger docks. None is self-propelled.
Eighteen floating dry docks are in Navy service (including two partial docks), 11 are out of service in reserve (including two partial docks), and 27 are on lease to commercial firms for private use. Several are on loan to other US services and foreign navies (including one partial dock). Asterisks indicate docks in active US service.

LARGE AUXILIARY FLOATING DRY DOCKS

Name-No.	Completed	Capacity	Construction	Notes
***AFDL 1**	1943	1 000 tons	Steel	Guantanamo Bay, Cuba
AFDL 2	1943	1 000 tons	Steel	Commercial lease
***AFDL 6**	1944	1 000 tons	Steel	Little Creek, Virginia
AFDL 7	1944	1 900 tons	Steel	Reserve
AFDL 8	1943	1 000 tons	Steel	Commercial lease
AFDL 9	1943	1 000 tons	Steel	Commercial lease
***AFDL 10**	1943	1 000 tons	Steel	Subic Bay, Philippines
AFDL 12	1943	1 000 tons	Steel	Reserve
AFDL 15	1943	1 000 tons	Steel	Commercial lease
AFDL 16	1943	1 000 tons	Steel	Commercial lease
AFDL 19	1944	1 000 tons	Steel	Commercial lease
***AFDL 21**	1944	1 000 tons	Steel	Guam, Marianas
***AFDL 23**	1944	1 900 tons	Steel	Danang, South Vietnam
AFDL 29	1943	1 000 tons	Steel	Commercial lease
AFDL 30	1944	1 000 tons	Steel	Commercial lease
AFDL 35	1944	2 800 tons	Concrete	Reserve
AFDL 37	1944	2 800 tons	Concrete	Commercial lease
AFDL 38	1944	2 800 tons	Concrete	Commercial lease
AFDL 40	1944	2 800 tons	Concrete	Commercial lease
AFDL 41	1944	2 800 tons	Concrete	Commercial lease
AFDL 43	1944	2 800 tons	Concrete	Commercial lease
AFDL 45	1944	2 800 tons	Concrete	Commercial lease
AFDL 47	1946	6 500 tons	Steel	Commercial lease
***AFDL 48**	1956	4 000 tons	Concrete	Long Beach Nav Shipyard

AUXILIARY REPAIR DRY DOCKS AND MEDIUM AUXILIARY REPAIR DRY DOCKS

Name-No.	Completed	Capacity	Construction	Notes
***ARD 5**	1942	3 000 tons	Steel	New London, Connecticut
***ARD 7**	1943	3 000 tons	Steel	New London, Connecticut
ARDM 3 (ex ARD 18)	1944	3 000 tons	Steel	Reserve
***OAK RIDGE** ARDM 1 (ex-ARD 19)	1944	3 000 tons	Steel	Rota, Spain
ARD 24	1944	3 000 tons	Steel	Reserve
***ALAMAGORDO** ARDM 2 (ex-ARD 26)	1944	3 000 tons	Steel	Charleston South Carolina
***ARD 30**	1944	3 000 tons	Steel	Pearl Harbour Nav Shipyard

YARD FLOATING DRY DOCKS

Name-No.	Completed	Capacity	Construction	Notes
YFD 7	1943	18 000 tons	Steel (3)	Commercial lease
YFD 8	1942	20 000 tons	Wood	Commercial lease
YFD 9	1942	16 000 tons	Wood	Commercial lease
YFD 23	1943	10 500 tons	Wood	Commercial lease
YFD 54	1943	5 000 tons	Wood	Commercial lease
YFD 68	1945	14 000 tons	Steel (3)	Commercial lease
YFD 69	1945	14 000 tons	Steel (3)	Commercial lease
YFD 70	1945	14 000 tons	Steel (3)	Commercial lease
***YFD 71**	1945	14 000 tons	Steel (3)	San Diego Naval Base
***YFD 83** (ex-AFDL 31)	1943	1 000 tons	Steel	US Coast Guard

LARGE AUXILIARY FLOATING DRY DOCKS

Name-No.	Completed	Capacity	Construction	Notes
***AFDB 1** (partial)	1943	40 000 tons	Steel (4)	Subic Bay, Philippines
AFDB 1 (partial)	——	60 000 tons	Steel (6)	Reserve
AFDB 2	1944	90 000 tons	Steel (10)	Reserve
AFDB 3	1944	81 000 tons	Steel (9)	Reserve
AFDB 4	1944	55 000 tons	Steel (7)	Reserve
AFDB 5	1944	55 000 tons	Steel (7)	Reserve
AFDB 6	1944	55 000 tons	Steel (7)	Reserve
AFDB 7 (partial)	1944	20 000 tons	Steel (2)	Reserve
***AFDB 7** (partial)	1945	10 000 tons	Steel (1)	US Army
***LOS ALAMOS** AFDB 7 (partial)	——	40 000 tons	Steel (4)	Holy Loch, Scotland

MEDIUM AUXILIARY FLOATING DRY DOCKS

Name-No.	Completed	Capacity	Construction	Notes
AFDM 1 (ex-YFD 3)	1942	15 000 tons	Steel (3)	Commercial lease
AFDM 2 (ex-YFD 4)	1942	15 000 tons	Steel (3)	Commercial lease
AFDM 3 (ex-YFD 6)	1943	18 000 tons	Steel (3)	Commercial lease
***AFDM 5** (ex-YFD 21)	1943	18 000 tons	Steel (3)	Subic Bay, Philippines
***AFDM 6** (ex-YFD 62)	1944	18 000 tons	Steel (3)	Subic Bay, Philippines
***AFDM 7** (ex-YFD 63)	1945	18 000 tons	Steel (3)	Davisville, Rhode Island
***RICHLAND** AFDM 8 (ex-YFD 64)	1944	18 000 tons	Steel (3)	Guam, Marianas
AFDM 9 (ex-YFD 65)	1945	18 000 tons	Steel (3)	Commercial lease
AFDM 10	1945	18 000 tons	Steel (3)	Commercial lease

Figures in parenthesis indicate the number of sections for sectional docks. Each section of the AFDB docks has a lifting capacity of about 10 000 tons. Four sections of the AFDB 7 form the floating dry dock *Los Alamos* at Holy Loch, Scotland, one section is used at Kwajalein atoll by the US Army in support of the Nike-X missile project and two sections are in reserve. (The AFDB sections each are 256 feet long, 80 feet in width, with wing walls 83 feet high; the wing walls, which contain compartments, fold down when the sections are towed).
The *White Sands* (ARD 20) was employed in support of the deep-diving bathyscaph *Trieste II* (see section on Deep Submergence Vehicles). Early in 1969 the *White Sands*, with *Trieste II* on board, was towed to the Azores to support investigation of the remains of the nuclear-powered submarine *Scorpion* (SSN 589). Reclassified as auxiliary deep submergence support vehicle (AGDS 1) on 1 Aug 1973; subsequently stricken.

TRANSFERS. The following floating dry docks are on foreign loan: ARD 23 to Argentina; AFDL 39, ARD 14 to Brazil; ARD 32 to Chile; ARD 28 to Columbia; ARD 13 to Ecuador; AFDL 11 to Khmer Republic (Cambodia); ARD 15, AFDL 28 to Mexico; ARD 6 to Pakistan; AFDL 26 to Paraguay; AFDL 33, ARD 8 to Peru; AFDL 20, AFDL 44 to Philippines; ARD 9, *Windsor* (ARD 22) to Taiwan China; ARD 13 to Venezuela; AFDL 22 to South Vietnam; ARD 12 to Turkey; *Arco* (ARD 29) to Iran; ARD 25 to to Chile; AFDL 25 to Khmer Republic (Cambodia); AFDL 24 to Philippines; ARD 11 to Mexico.

DISPOSALS
ARD 16 stricken on 1 Oct 1972; **ARD 27** stricken on 1 Apr 1973; **AFDL 35** stricken on 1 Aug 1973; **White Sands** AGDS 1 (ex-ARD 20) stricken on 1 Apr 1974; **ARD 31** stricken on 1 Apr 1974; **AFDL 42** stricken on 1 May 1974.

AFDL 21 under tow — *1965, United States Navy*

SSBN in OAK RIDGE (ARDM 1) — *1964, United States Navy*

SSBN in OAK RIDGE (ARDM 1) — *United States Navy*

DEEP SUBMERGENCE VEHICLES

The US Navy operates several deep submergence vehicles for scientific, military research, and operational military missions.
The US Navy acquired its first deep submergence vehicle with the purchase of the bathyscaph *Trieste* in 1958. The *Trieste* was designed and constructed by Professor Auguste Piccard, the noted Swiss physicist and aeronaut. The US Navy sponsored research dives in the Mediterranean Sea with the *Trieste* in 1957 after which the bathyscaph was purchased outright and brought to the United States.
The *Trieste* reached a record depth of 35 800 feet (*10 910 metres*) in the Challenger Deep off the Marianas on 23 Jan 1960, being piloted by Lieutenant Don Walsh, USN, and Jacques Piccard (son of Auguste). Rebuilt and designated *Trieste II*, the craft was subsequently used in the search for wreckage of the nuclear-powered submarine *Thresher* (SSN 593) was lost in 1963 and the *Scorpion* (SSN 589) lost in 1968.
After the loss of the *Thresher* the US Navy initiated an extensive deep submergence programme that led to construction of two Deep Submergence Rescue Vehicles (DSRV); however, other vehicles proposed in the recommended programme were not built because of a lack of interest, changing operational concepts, and funding limitations.
Several of these deep submergence vehicles and other craft and support ships are operated by Submarine Development Group One at San Diego, California. The Group is a major operational command that includes advanced diving equipment; divers trained in "saturation" techniques; the DSVs *Trieste II*, *Turtle*, *Sea Cliff*, DSRV-1, DSRV-2; the submarine *Dolphin* (AGSS 555); several submarine rescue ships.
The hull of the original *Trieste* and Krupp sphere are in the Navy Yard in Washington, D.C.

MIDGET SUBMARINES

The US Navy's only "Midget" submarine, the 50-foot long **X-1** was stricken on 16 Feb 1973. See 1972-1973 edition for characteristics and photographs.

NUCLEAR POWERED RESEARCH VEHICLE: PROPOSED

A second nuclear-powered submersible research vehicle has been proposed by Admiral H. G. Rickover, US Navy (Retired), Deputy Commander for Nuclear Propulsion, Naval Sea Systems Command. The craft would have a greater depth capability than the NR-1 (described below) and would employ a nuclear plant similar to that of the earlier craft. The vehicle would have a pressure hull of HY-130 steel.
Reportedly, Adm. Rickover began development of the so-called "NR-2" in 1971. Estimated construction time would be 2½ years; however, construction has not yet been approved. Unofficial estimates of construction costs range to more than $300 000 000.

1 NUCLEAR POWERED OCEAN ENGINEERING AND RESEARCH VEHICLE

Name	*Builder*	*Launched*
NR-1	General Dynamics (Electric Boat)	25 Jan 1969

Displacement, tons	400 submerged
Length, feet	136·4 *oa* × 12·4 × 14·6
Diameter, feet	12 maximum
Machinery	Electric motors, 2 propellers, four ducted thrusters
Reactor	1 pressurised-water cooled
Complement	7 (3 officers, 2 enlisted men, 2 scientists)

The NR-1 was built primarily to serve as a test platform for a small nuclear propulsion plant; however, the craft additionally provides an advanced deep submergence ocean engineering and research capability. Vice Admiral Rickover conceived and initiated the NR-1 in 1964-1965 (the craft was not proposed in a Navy research or shipbuilding budget).
Built by Electric Boat Division of General Dynamics Corp, Groton, Connecticut; laid down on 10 June 1967; launched on 25 Jan 1969; completed late in 1969. Commanded by an officer-in-charge vice commanding officer.

Describing the craft Admiral Rickover has stated: "The (NR-1) will be able to perform detailed studies and mapping of the ocean bottom, temperature, currents, and other oceanographic parameters for military, commercial, and scientific use. The development of a nuclear propulsion plant for an oceanographic research vehicle will result in greater independence from surface support ships and essentially unlimited endurance of propulsion and auxiliary power for detailed exploration of the ocean.
"The submarine (NR-1) will have viewing ports for visual observation of its surroundings and the ocean bottom. In addition, a remote grapple will be installed to permit collection of marine samples and other items. With its depth capability, the NR-1 is expected to be capable of exploring areas of the Continental Shelf, an area which appears to contain most accessible wealth in mineral and food resources in the seas. Such exploratory charting may also help the United States in establishing sovereignty over parts of the Continental Shelf".

CONSTRUCTION. Admiral Rickover originally planned to construct the NR-1 using "state of the art" equipment, with the cost of such a vehicle estimated to be $30 000 000 in March 1965. During detailed design of the NR-1 the Navy determined that improved equipment had to be developed and a larger hull than originally planned would be required. Consequently, in July 1967 the Navy obtained Congressional approval to proceed with construction of the NR-1 at an estimated cost of $58 000 300. The final estimated ship construction cost at time of launching was $67 500 000 plus $19 900 000 for oceanographic equipment and sensors, and $11 800 000 for research and development (mainly related to the nuclear propulsion plant), for a total estimated cost of $99 200 000.

DESIGN. The NR-1 is fitted with wheels beneath the hull to permit "bottom crawling". This will obviate the necessity of hovering while exploring the ocean floor. Submarine wheels, a concept proposed as early as the first decade of this century by submarine inventor Simon Lake, were tested in the small submarine *Mackerel* (SST 1).
The NR-1 is fitted with external lights, external television cameras, a remote-controlled manipulator, and various recovery devices. No periscopes, but fixed television mast. Credited with a 30 day endurance, but limited habitability makes missions of only a few days feasible. Reportedly, a surface "mother" ship is required to support the NR-1.

ENGINEERING. The NR-1 reactor plant was designed by the Atomic Energy Commission's Knolls Atomic Power Laboratory. She is propelled by two propellers driven by electric motors outside the pressure hull with power provided by a turbine generator within the pressure hull. Four ducted thrusters, two horizontal and two vertical, are provided for precise manoeuvring.

NR-1 — *1969, General Dynamics Electric Boat*

"NR-1"—continued

PHOTOGRAPHS. No photographs of the NR-1 have been released for publication since the craft's sea trials in 1969. Note fixed TV mast at after end of sail structure.

NR-1 — *1969 General Dynamics Electric Boat*

2 DEEP SUBMERGENCE RESCUE VEHICLES

No	*Builder*	*Launched*
DSRV-1	Lockheed Missiles and Space Co. (Sunnyvale, Calif)	24 Jan 1970
DSRV-2	Lockheed Missiles and Space Co. (Sunnyvale, Calif)	1 May 1971

Weight in air, tons	35
Length, feet	49·2 *oa*
Diameter, feet	8
Propulsion	Electric motors, propeller mounted in control shroud and four ducted thrusters
Speed, knots	5 (maximum)
Endurance	12 hours at 3 knots
Operating depth, feet	5 000
Complement	3 (pilot, co-pilot, rescue sphere operator) + 24 rescuees

The Deep Submergence Rescue Vehicle is intended to provide a quick-reaction, world-wide, all-weather capability for the rescue of survivors in a disabled submarine. The DSRV will be transportable by road, aircraft (in C-141 and C-5 jet cargo aircraft), surface ship (on ASR 21 class submarine rescue ships), and specially modified submarines (SSN type).
The operational effectiveness of the craft is limited severely by the lack of large numbers of ships and submarines that air transport and support the craft. They will be used for the foreseeable future for evaluation and research.
Upon notification that a submarine is disabled on the ocean floor the DSRV and its support equipment (all necessary check-out equipment and spare parts being housed in a mobile van) will be loaded in cargo aircraft and flown to a port near the disabled submarine. The DSRV and van will then be towed to a pier and loaded aboard a "mother" submarine, which had proceeded to the port upon notification that a submarine was disabled.
The mother submarine, with the DSRV attached to her main deck (aft of the sail structure), will then proceed to the disabled submarine and serve as an underwater base for the DSRV which will shuttle back and forth between the disabled submarine and the mother submarine. On each trip the DSRV will carry up to 24 survivors from the disabled submarine. The mother submarine will launch and recover the DSRV while submerged and, if necessary, while under ice. A total of six DSRVs were planned, but only two were funded.

COST. The estimated construction cost for the DSRV-1 is $41 000 000 and for the DSRV-2 $23 000 000. The development, construction, test, and support of both vehicles through Fiscal Year 1975 is now estimated at $220 000 000. This expenditure includes the design and construction of both vehicles, specific research and development associated with the rescue programme, surface support equipment, modifications to "mother" submarines, test and evaluation programmes, procurement of replacement and spare parts, and training of the DSRV operators and support personnel.

DESIGN. The DSRV outer hull is constructed of formed fibreglass. Within this outer hull are three interconnected spheres which form the main pressure capsule. Each sphere is 7·5 feet in diameter and is constructed of HY-140 steel. The forward sphere contains the vehicle's control equipment and is manned by the pilot and co-pilot, the centre and after spheres accommodate 24 passengers and a third crewman. Under the DSRVs centre sphere is a hemispherical protrusion or "skirt" which seals over the disabled submarine's hatch. During the mating operation the skirt is pumped dry to enable personnel to transfer between the DSRV and disabled or mother submarine.

ELECTRONICS. Elaborate search and navigational sonar, and closed-circuit television (supplemented by optical devices) are installed in the DSRV to determine the exact location of a disabled submarine within a given area and for pinpointing the submarine's escape hatches. Side-looking sonar will be fitted for search missions.

Deep Submergence Vehicles—*continued*

DEEP SUBMERGENCE RESCUE VEHICLES—*Continued*

ENGINEERING. Propulsion and control of the DSRV are achieved by a stern propeller in a movable control shroud and four ducted thrusters, two forward and two aft. These, plus a mercury trim system, permit the DSRV to manoeuvre and hover with great precision and to mate with submarines lying at angles up to 45 degrees from the horizontal. An elaborate Integrated Control and Display (ICAD) system employs computers to present sensor data to the pilots and transmit their commands to the vehicle's control and propulsion system.

OPERATIONAL. Upon notification that a submarine is disabled on the ocean floor the DSRV and its support equipment (all necessary check-out equipment and spare parts being housed in a mobile van) will be loaded in cargo aircraft and flown to a port near the disabled submarine. The DSRV and van will then be trucked to a pier and loaded aboard a "mother" submarine, which had proceeded to the port upon notification that a submarine was disabled.

PHOTOGRAPHS. An artist's concept of a DSRV "landing" on a submarine hatch appears in the 1971-1972 edition; a view of the DSRV-1 being assembled appears in the 1970-1971 edition.

DSRV-1 on HAWKBILL (SSN 666) *1971, United States Navy*

2 RESEARCH VEHICLES: MODIFIED "ALVIN" TYPE

Name	*No.*	*Launched*
SEA CLIFF (ex-*Autec I*)	DSV 4	11 Dec 1968
TURTLE (ex-*Autec II*)	DSV 3	11 Dec 1968

Weight, tons	21
Length, feet	25 oa
Beam, feet	8
Propulsion	Electric motors, trainable stern propeller; 2 rotating propeller pods
Speed, knots	2·5
Endurance	8 hours at 2 knots
Operating depth, feet	6 500
Complement	2 (pilot, observer)

Both submersibles built by Electric Boat Division of General Dynamic Corp, Groton Connecticut. Intended for deep submergence research and work tasks. Designated *Autec I* and *Autec II* during construction, but assigned above names in dual launching on 11 Dec 1968. Completed in 1969.
Designated DSV 4 and DSV 3, respectively, on 1 June 1971.

CONSTRUCTION. Three pressure spheres were fabricated for the *Alvin* submersible programme, one for installation in the *Alvin*, a spare, and one for testing. The second and third spheres subsequently were allocated to these later submersibles.

DESIGN. Twin-arm manipulator fitted to each submersible. Propulsion by stem propeller and two smaller, manoeuvering propeller "pods" on sides of vehicles; no thrusters.

SEA CLIFF *United States Navy*

ALVIN *1974*

1 RESEARCH VEHICLE: "ALVIN" TYPE

Name	*No.*
ALVIN	DSV 2

Weight, tons	16
Length, feet	22·5 oa
Beam, feet	8·5
Propulsion	Electric motors; trainable stern propeller; 2 rotating propeller pods
Speed, knots	2
Endurance	8 hours at 1 knot
Operating depth, feet	12 000
Complement	3 (1 pilot, 2 observers)

The *Alvin* was built by General Mills, Inc, Minneapolis, Minnesota, for operation by the Woods Hole Oceanographic Institution for the Office of Naval Research. Original configuration had an operating depth of 6 000 feet. Named for Allyn C. Vine of Woods Hole Oceanographic Institution.
The *Alvin* accidentally sank in 5 051 feet of water on 16 Oct 1968; subsequently raised in August 1969; refurbished from May 1971 to Oct 1972 in essentially original configuration; subsequently refitted with titanium pressure sphere to provide increased depth capability and again operational in November 1973. See 1968-1969 edition for photographs of original configuration.

1 BATHYSCAPH RESEARCH VEHICLE: "TRIESTE" TYPE

Name	*No.*
TRIESTE II	DSV 1 (ex-X-2)

Weight, tons	84
Displacement, tons	303 submerged
Length, feet	78·6
Beam, feet	15·3
Propulsion	Electric motors, 3 propellers aft, ducted thruster forward (see *Design* notes)
Speed, knots	2
Endurance	10-12 hours at 2 knots
Operating depth, feet	12 000 (see *Design* notes)
Complement	3 (2 operators, 1 observer)

The *Trieste II* is the extensively rebuilt *Trieste I* which the US Navy purchased in 1958 from professor Auguste Piccard. Several "modernisations" have resulted in the current vehicle being essentially a "new" craft, the third to be named *Trieste*. (The original *Trieste* was built at Castellammare, Italy; launched on 1 Aug 1953).
The vehicle is operated by Submarine Development Group One at San Diego, California, and is used primarily as a test bed for underwater equipment and to train deep submergence vehicle operators (hydronauts).
Designated as a "submersible craft" and assigned the designation X-2 on 1 Sep 1969; subsequently changed to DSV 1 on 1 June 1971.

DESIGN. The *Trieste II* is essentially a large float with a small pressure sphere attached to the underside. The float, which is filled with aviation petrol, provides buoyancy. Designed operating depth is 20 000 feet but dives have been limited to approximately 12 000 feet. (The record-setting Challenger Deep dive was made with a Krupp sphere which has a virtually unlimited depth capability).
The bathyscaph was essentially rebuilt for a second time at the Mare Island Naval Shipyard in Sep 1965-Aug 1966 with a modified float, pressure sphere, propulsion system, and mission equipment being fitted. In the broadside view the sphere is now largely hidden by protective supports to keep the sphere clear of the welldeck when the craft rests in a floating dry dock. (Compare with photographs of the earlier *Trieste II* configuration in the 1969-1970 edition).
Fitted with external television cameras and mechanical manipulator; computerised digital navigation system installed.

PHOTOGRAPHS. Note forward "Legs" to prevent pressure sphere from sinking into ocean floor when craft is resting on the bottom. Lights, manipulators, cameras, and other devices are mounted forward of the sphere, partially in view of sphere's viewpoint.

DISPOSALS

The 600-foot capability **Nemo** DSV 5 is on loan to the Southwest Research Institute, San Antonio, Texas.

TRIESTE II *1970, United States Navy*

COAST GUARD

Command

Chief of Staff: Rear Admiral Robert H. Scarborough
Commander, Atlantic Area: Vice Admiral William F. Rea, III
Commander, Pacific Area: Vice Admiral Joseph J. McClelland

Establishment

The United States Coast Guard was established by an Act of Congress approved Jan 28, 1915, which consolidated the Revenue Cutter Service (founded in 1790) and the Life Saving Service (founded in 1878). The act of establishment stated the Coast Guard "shall be a military service and branch of the armed forces of the United States at all times. The Coast Guard shall be a service in the Treasury Department except when operating as a service in the Navy".
The Congress further legislated that in time of national emergency or when the President so directs, the Coast Guard operates as a part of the Navy. The Coast Guard did operate as a part of the Navy during the First and Second World Wars.
The Lighthouse Service (founded in 1789) was transferred to the Coast Guard on July 1, 1939.
The Coast Guard was transferred to the newly established Department of Transportation on April 1, 1967.

Cutters

All Coast Guard vessels are referred to as "cutters". Cutter names are preceded by USCGC. Cutter serial numbers are prefixed with letter designations, the first letter being "W". The first two digits of serial numbers for cutters less than 100 feet in length indicate their approximate length over all. All Coast Guard cutters are active unless otherwise indicated.
Approximately 600 small rescue and utility craft also are in service.

Cutter Strengths

23 High Endurance Cutters
16 Medium Endurance Cutters
2 Oceanographic Cutters
76 Patrol Boats
9 Icebreakers
3 Training Cutters
35 Seagoing Buoy Tenders
67 Coastal-River-Inland Tenders
6 Oceangoing Tugs
29 Harbour Tugs
6 Lightships

Several of these cutters are laid up in reserve; see individual classes for status of specific cutters.

Personnel

July 1975: 4 403 officers, 1 298 warrant officers, 29 620 enlisted men.

Aviation

The Coast Guard operates a small air arm to support Coast Guard operations. Only the larger "Hamilton" class cutters and certain classes of icebreakers can support helicopters at sea.
As of 1 July 1975 the Coast Guard's aviation strength consisted of 49 fixed-wing aircraft and 126 helicopters:

1	EC-130	Hercules
20	HC-130	Hercules
26	HU-16	Albatross
1	VC-4A	Gulfstream I
1	VC-11A	Gulfstream II
38	HH-3F	Pelican
88	HH-52A	

Missions

The current missions of the Coast Guard are to (1) enforce or assist in the enforcement of applicable Federal laws upon the high seas and waters subject to the jurisdiction of the United States including environmental protection; (2) administer all Federal laws regarding safety of life and property on the high seas and on waters subject to the jurisdiction of the United States, except those laws specifically entrusted to other Federal agencies; (3) develop, establish, maintain, operate, and conduct aids to maritime navigation, ocean stations, icebreaking activities, oceanographic research, and rescue facilities; and (4) maintain a state of readiness to function as a specialised service in the Navy when so directed by the President.

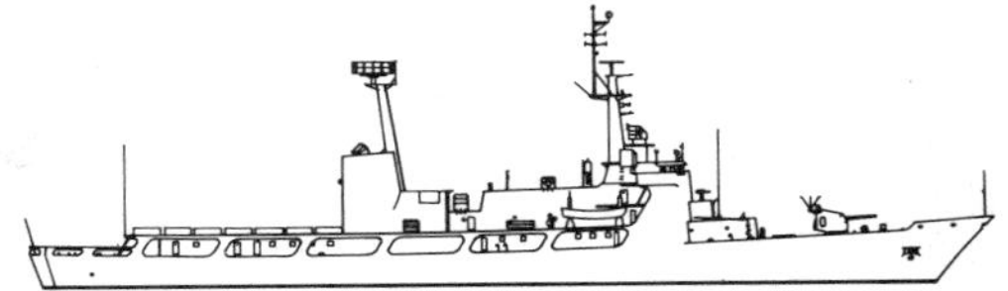

"HAMILTON" Class

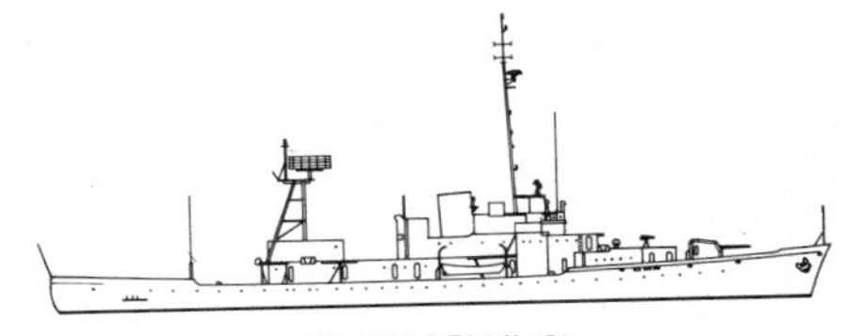

"CAMPBELL" Class

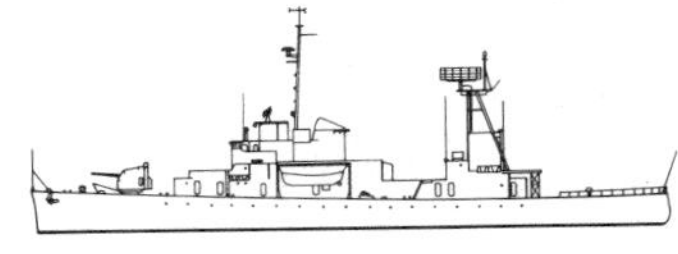

"OWASCO" Class

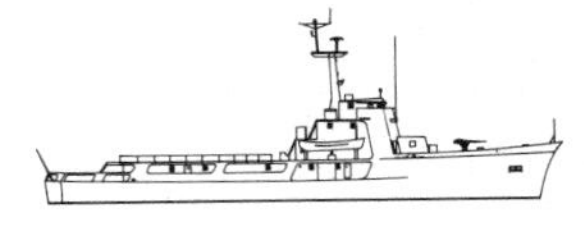

"RELIANCE" Class

"WIND" Class

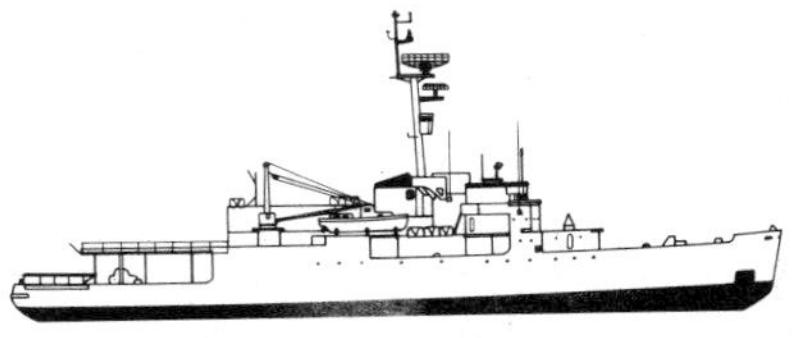

GLACIER

Scale: 1 inch = 150 feet (1 : 1 800)

Drawings by A. D. Baker

1972 US Coast Guard, SN Richard J. Geisman

VIGOROUS (WMEC 627) near iceberg in North Atlantic while on International Ice Patrol

HIGH ENDURANCE CUTTERS

12 HIGH ENDURANCE CUTTERS (WHEC): "HAMILTON" (378) CLASS

Displacement, tons	2 716 standard; 3 050 full load
Length, feet	350 wl; 378 oa
Beam, feet	42·8
Draught, feet	20
Guns	1—5 inch (*127 mm*) 38 cal DP (Mk 30)
A/S weapons	2 fixed hedgehogs (removed from some ships, see notes) 2 triple torpedo tubes (Mk 32)
Helicopters	1 HH-52 or HH-3 helicopter
Main engines	Combined Diesel and Gas turbine (CODAG): 2 diesels (Fairbanks-Morse) 7 000 hp; 2 gas turbines (Pratt & Whitney), 28 000 hp; aggregate 35 000 hp; 2 shafts
Speed	29
Complement	155 (15 officers, 140 enlisted men)

Name	*No*	*Laid down*	*Launched*	*Completed*
HAMILTON	WHEC 715	Jan 1965	18 Dec 1965	20 Feb 1967
DALLAS	WHEC 716	7 Feb 1966	1 Oct 1966	1 Oct 1967
MELLON	WHEC 717	25 July 1966	11 Feb 1967	22 Dec 1967
CHASE	WHEC 718	15 Oct 1966	20 May 1967	1 Mar 1968
BOUTWELL	WHEC 719	12 Dec 1966	17 June 1967	14 June 1968
SHERMAN	WHEC 720	13 Feb 1967	23 Sep 1967	23 Aug 1968
GALLANTIN	WHEC 721	17 Apr 1967	18 Nov 1967	20 Dec 1968
MORGENTHAU	WHEC 722	17 July 1967	10 Feb 1968	14 Feb 1969
RUSH	WHEC 723	23 Oct 1967	16 Nov 1968	3 July 1969
MUNRO	WHEC 724	18 Feb 1970	5 Dec 1970	10 Sep 1971
JARVIS	WHEC 725	9 Sep 1970	24 Apr 1971	30 Dec 1971
MIDGETT	WHEC 726	5 Apr 1971	4 Sep 1971	17 Mar 1972

These are large, attractive, multi-purpose cutters. All built by Avondale Shipyards, Inc, New Orleans, Louisiana. All these ships are in active service.

ANTI-SUBMARINE ARMAMENT. Hedgehog anti-submarine weapons are being removed from earlier ships during overhaul and Mk 309 fire control system for Mk 32 torpedo tubes are installed. Hedgehogs deleted in later ships. *Hamilton* was first to drop hedgehogs and receive Mk 309 during 1970 overhaul.

DESIGN. These ships have clipper bows, twin funnels enclosing a helicopter hangar, helicopter platform aft. All are fitted with oceanographic laboratories, elaborate communications equipment, and meteorological data gathering facilities. Superstructure is largely of aluminium construction. Bridge control of manoeuvring is by aircraft-type "joy stick" rather than wheel.

ELECTRONICS. Original SQS-36 sonar has been replaced by more-capable SQS-38. Fitted with SPS-29 and SPS-51 search radars.

ENGINEERING. The "Hamilton" are the largest US "military" ships with gas turbine propulsion pending completion of the Navy's "Spruance" class destroyers. The Pratt & Whitney gas turbines are FT-4A, marine variant of the J75 aircraft engine used in the Boeing 707 transport and F-105 fighter-bomber; the Fairbanks Morse diesels are 12 cylinder; variable pitch propellers fitted. Engine and propeller pitch consoles are located in wheel-house and at bridge wing stations as well as engine room control booth.
A retractable bow propulsion unit is provided for station keeping and precise manoeuvring (Unit is located directly below hedgehogs, immediately aft of sonar dome).
Range is 14 000 miles at 11 knots on diesels and 2 400 miles at 29 knots on gas turbines.

NOMENCLATURE. The first nine ships of this class were named for secretaries of the Treasury Department reflecting the Coast Guard being a part of that department from 1915 to 1967 when it was transferred to the newly formed Department of Transportation. Subsequent ships of this class honour Coast Guard heroes.
Later ships are referred to as "Hero" class.

BOUTWELL (WHEC 719) *1971, Giorgio Arra*

MIDGETT (WHEC) 726 with HH-3F and Hovercraft *1972, United States Coast Guard*

MELLON (WHEC 717), PONCHATOULA (AO 148), JARVIS (WHEC 725) *1972, United States Coast Guard*

High Endurance Cutters —*continued*

6 HIGH ENDURANCE CUTTERS (WHEC): "CAMPBELL" (327) CLASS

Name	No	Builder	Laid down	Launched	Completed
BIBB (ex-*George M Bibb*)	WHEC 31	Charleston Navy Yard	18 May 1935	14 Jan 1937	19 Mar 1937
CAMPBELL (ex-*George W. Campbell*)	WHEC 32	Philadelphia Navy Yard	1 May 1935	3 June 1936	22 Oct 1936
DUANE (ex-*William J Duane*)	WHEC 33	Philadelphia Navy Yard	1 May 1935	3 June 1936	16 Oct 1936
INGHAM (ex-*Samual D Ingham*)	WHEC 35	Philadelphia Navy Yard	1 May 1935	3 June 1936	6 Nov 1936
SPENCER (ex-*John C. Spencer*)	WHEC 36	New York Navy Yard	11 Sep 1935	6 Jan 1936	13 May 1937
TANEY (ex-*Roger B. Taney*)	WHEC 37	Philadelphia Navy Yard	1 May 1935	3 June 1936	19 Dec 1936

Displacement, tons	2 216 standard; 2 414 full load
Length, feet	308 wl; 327 oa
Beam, feet	41
Draught, feet	15
Guns	1—5 inch (*127 mm*) 38 cal DP (Mk 30)
A/S weapons	Removed
Main engines	Geared turbines (Westinghouse); 6 200 shp; 2 shafts
Boilers	2 (Babcock & Wilcox)
Speed, knots	19·8
Complement	143 (13 officers, 130 enlisted men)

Rated as 327-foot cutters. These were the Coast Guard's largest cutters until the *Hamilton* was completed in 1967.

The *Duane* served as an amphibious force flagship during the invasion of Southern France in August 1944 and was designated AGC 6 (Coast Guard manned); the other ships of this class, except the lost *Alexander Hamilton* (PG 34), similarly employed but retained Coast Guard number with WAGC prefix (amidships structure built up and one or two additional masts installed); all reverted to gunboat configuration after war (WPG designation).

All of these cutters remain in active service except the *Spencer*, decommissioned on 23 Jan 1974 and placed in reserve at the Coast Guard Yard, Curtis Bay, Maryland.

ANTI-SUBMARINE ARMAMENT. During the 1960s these ships each had an ASW armament of one ahead-firing fixed hedgehog and two Mk 32 triple torpedo launchers; subsequently removed from all ships.

DESIGNATION. These ships were desginated as high endurance cutters (WHEC) on 1 May 1966; previously WPG.

ENGINEERING. Range is 4 000 miles at 20 knots and 8 000 miles at 10·5 knots.

GUNNERY. As built these ships had two 5-inch 51 cal guns (single mounts forward) and several smaller guns; rearmed during World War II with an additional single 5 inch 51 cal gun installed aft plus two or three 3 inch 50 cal anti-aircraft guns, and several 20 mm anti-aircraft guns (depth charge racks installed); *Taney* was experimentally armed with four 5 inch 38 cal guns in single mounts. Armament of all ships after World War II reduced to one 5 inch 38 cal gun and two 40 mm guns.

NOMENCLATURE. Named for secretaries of the Department of Treasury; names shortened to surnames only in 1942.

PHOTOGRAPHS. In the above photograph the *Ingham* has a hedgehog forward of the bridge. The *Taney* has a WSR-S1 storm tracking radar dome mounted on her bridge. She operates on ocean weather station "Hotel", 200 miles northeast of Norfolk, Virginia.

INGHAM (WHEC 35) *1969, United States Coast Guard*

TANEY (WHEC 37) *1973, United States Coast Guard*

MUNRO (WHEC 724) *see previous page* *1971, United States Coast Guard*

High Endurance Cutters —*continued*

5 HIGH ENDURANCE CUTTERS: (WHEC): "OWASCO" (255) CLASS

Name	No.	Laid down	Launched	Completed
CHAUTAUQUA	WHEC 41	22 Dec 1943	14 May 1944	4 Aug 1945
WINONA	WHEC 65	8 Nov 1944	22 Apr 1945	15 Aug 1946
MINNETONKA (ex-*Sunapee*)	WHEC 67	26 Dec 1944	21 Nov 1945	20 Sep 1946
MENDOTA	WHEC 69	1 June 1943	29 Feb 1944	2 June 1946
PONTCHARTRAIN (ex-*Okeechobee*)	WHEC 70	1 July 1943	29 Apr 1944	28 July 1945

Displacement, tons	1 563 standard; 1 913 full load
Length, feet	254 oa
Beam, feet	43
Draught, feet	17
Guns	1—5 inch (*127 mm*) 38 cal DP (Mk 30) 2—81 mm mortars Several ·50 cal MG
A/S weapons	Removed
Main engines	Geared turbines (Westinghouse) with electric drive; 4 000 shp; 1 shaft
Boilers	2
Speed, knots	18·4
Complement	139 (13 officers, 126 enlisted men)

Rated as 255-foot cutters. All built by Western Pipe & Steel Company, San Pedro, California, except for the *Mendota* and *Pontchartrain*, built by Coast Guard yard, Curtis Bay, Maryland. These ships do not have a helicopter landing area.

The *Chautauqua*, *Mendota*, and *Pontchartrain* were decommissioned in 1973; *Winona* and *Minnetonka* were decommissioned in 1974; all laid up in reserve.

ANTI-SUBMARINE ARMAMENT. During the 1960s these ships each had an ASW armament of one ahead-firing fixed hedgehog and two Mk 32 triple torpedo launchers; subsequently removed from all ships.

DESIGNATION. These ships were originally designated as gunboats (WPG); changed to high endurance cutters (WHEC) on 1 May 1966.

ENGINEERING. Range is 12 000 miles at 10 knots.

GUNNERY. As built these ships each mounted four 5-inch guns (twin), four 40-mm anti-aircraft guns (twin), and four 20 mm anti-aircraft guns; subsequently reduced. (Original depth charge racks also removed).

MINNETONKA (WHEC 67) — *1975, United States Coast Guard*

DISPOSALS

Iroquois (WPG 43) was stricken in 1965; **Sebago** (WHEC 42) decommissioned in 1972 for disposal; **Owasco** (WHEC 39), **Winnebago** (WHEC 40), **Wachusett** (WHEC 44), **Escanaba** (WHEC 64), **Klamath** (WHEC 66), and **Androscoggin** (WHEC 68) decommissioned in 1973 for disposal.

MEDIUM ENDURANCE CUTTERS

15 MEDIUM ENDURANCE CUTTERS (WMEC) / 1 RESERVE TRAINING CUTTER (WTR) } "RELIANCE" (210) CLASS

Name	No.	Launched	Completed
RELIANCE	WTR 615	25 May 1963	20 June 1964
DILIGENCE	WMEC 616	20 July 1963	26 Aug 1964
VIGILANT	WMEC 617	24 Dec 1963	3 Oct 1964
ACTIVE	WMEC 618	31 July 1965	17 Sep 1966
CONFIDENCE	WMEC 619	8 May 1965	19 Feb 1966
RESOLUTE	WMEC 620	30 Apr 1966	8 Dec 1966
VALIANT	WMEC 621	14 Jan 1967	28 Oct 1967
COURAGEOUS	WMEC 622	18 Mar 1967	10 Apr 1968
STEADFAST	WMEC 623	24 June 1967	25 Sep 1968
DAUNTLESS	WMEC 624	21 Oct 1967	10 June 1968
VENTUROUS	WMEC 625	11 Nov 1967	16 Aug 1968
DEPENDABLE	WMEC 626	16 Mar 1968	22 Nov 1968
VIGOROUS	WMEC 627	4 May 1968	2 May 1969
DURABLE	WMEC 628	29 Apr 1967	8 Dec 1967
DECISIVE	WMEC 629	14 Dec 1967	23 Aug 1968
ALERT	WMEC 630	19 Oct 1968	4 Aug 1969

Displacement, tons	950 standard; 1 000 full load except WMEC 615-619 970 full load
Dimensions, feet	210·5 oa × 34 × 10·5
Guns	1—3 inch (*76 mm*) 50 calibre AA; 2—·50 cal MG
Helicopters	1 HH-52 helicopter embarked for missions
Main engines	2 turbo-charged diesels; 2 shafts; 5 000 hp = 18· knots; WMEC 615-619 also have 2 gas turbines (2 000 hp); no speed increase
Complement	61 (7 officers, 54 enlisted men)

Rated as 210-foot cutters. Designed for search and rescue duties. Design features include 360-degree visibility from wheelhouse; helicopter flight deck (no hangar); and engine exhaust vent at stern in place of conventional funnel. Capable of towing ships up to 10 000 tons. Air-conditioned throughout except engine room; high degree of habitability.

WMEC 615-617 built by Todd Shipyards; WMEC 618 built by Christy Corp; WMEC 619, 625, 628, 629 built by Coast Guard Yard, Curtis Bay, Baltimore, Maryland; WMEC 620-624, 626, 627, 630 by American Shipbuilding Co.

All of these cutters are active. The *Reliance* (ex-WMEC 615) was assigned as the Coast Guard's reserve training cutter in mid-1975, replacing the 311-foot *Casco* (WTR 379).

STEADFAST (WMEC 623) — *1971, United States Coast Guard*

HELICOPTERS. The *Alert* was the first US ship fitted with the Canadian-developed "Beartrap" helicopter hauldown system. An HH-52A helicopter conducted trials late in 1969, making 30 successful landings despite winds over 40 mph. No further procurement of this system has been funded.

DESIGNATION. These ships were originally designated as patrol craft (WPC); changed to WMEC on 1 May 1966

ENGINEERING. Fitted with controllable-pitch propellers. The first five ships have twin Solar, 2 000 hp gas turbines in addition to the diesels common to all ships of this class. Diesels are ALCO model 251-B.

Range is 6 100 miles at 13 knots for WMEC 615-619 and 6 100 miles at 14 knots for later ships.

Medium Endurance Cutters—*continued*

"ACTIVE" CLASS

All 33 of the steel patrol cutters of the 125-foot "Active" class have been stricken except the *Cuyahoga*, employed as a training ship and listed on a later page. The "Active" class boats were number WPC/WMEC 125-157; completed in 1926-1927.

TUG TYPE

Several tug-type cutters officially are listed as Medium Endurance Cutters. These ships are described on a later page under the heading Oceangoing Tugs.

AIR CUSHION VEHICLES

The three Coast Guard-operated Air Cushion Vehicles (ACV) have been discarded or lost: **Hover 02** lost operationally on Lake Michigan on 23 Nov 1971; **Hover 01** and **Hover 02** decommissioned and discarded in 1973.
All three operated by the US Navy from 1965 to 1969 as Patrol Air Cushion Vehicles (PACV). See 1973-1974 and previous editions for characteristics.

DAUNTLESS (WMEC 624) with HH-52A *United States Coast Guard*

PATROL BOATS

PATROL BOATS (WPB): 92ft CLASS

Displacement, tons: 76
Dimensions, feet: 92 oa × 20 × 6
Guns: 1—20 mm or 1—·50 cal MG (see notes)
Main engines: 2 diesels; approx 2 000 bhp; 2 shafts = 15-18 knots
Complement: 8 (1 officer, 7 enlisted men)

The Coast Guard plans to construct about 30 patrol boats of this type during the next few years, in part to replace the "A" series of the 95-foot WPBs described below. Three boats are proposed in the Fiscal Year 1977 budget. Final design is not firm with respect to armament and engines.

23 PATROL BOATS (WPB): 95ft CLASS

CAPE CARTER	95309	CAPE HORN	95322
CAPE CORAL	95301	CAPE JELLISON	95317
CAPE CORWIN	95326	CAPE KNOX	95312
CAPE CROSS	95321	CAPE MORGAN	95313
CAPE CURRENT	95307	CAPE NEWAGEN	95318
CAPE FAIRWEATHER	95314	CAPE ROMAIN	95319
CAPE FOX	95316	CAPE SHOALWATER	95324
CAPE GEORGE	95306	CAPE SMALL	95300
CAPE GULL	95304	CAPE STARR	95320
CAPE HEDGE	95311	CAPE WASH	95310
CAPE HENLOPEN	95328	CAPE YORK	95332

CG 95321—95335	CG 95312—95314, 95316—95320	CG 95300—95311
"C" Class (built 1958-59)	"B" Class (built 1955-56)	"A" Class (built 1953)

Displacement, tons: 106 (B); 105 (A); 98 (C)
Dimensions, feet: 95 oa × 19 × 6
Guns: 1—81 mm mortar and 2—50 cal MG or 2—50 cal MG
Main engines: 4 diesels; 2 200 bhp; 2 shafts = 20 knots
Complement: 14 (1 officer, 13 enlisted men)

Rated as 95 ft Cutters. Designed and built at Coast Guard Yard, Curtis Bay, Maryland for port security, search and rescue. Steel hulled, twin screws. "C" class boats, for search and rescue, have less electronics. *Cape Gull* is laid up in reserve; others are active.

ENGINEERING. Diesels are Cummings VT12-600M. Range is 2 600 miles for "A" class, 3 000 miles for "B" class, and 2 800 miles for "C" class, all at 9 knots.

TRANSFERS. Nine boats of this type were transferred to the South Korean Navy in 1968: *Cape Falcon* (95330), *Cape Providence* (95335), *Cape Rosier* (95333), *Cape Sable* (95334), *Cape Trinity* (95331), *Cape Darby* (95323), *Cape Florida* (95325), *Cape Kiwanda* (95329), and *Cape Porpoise* (95327).

DISPOSALS
Cape Higgon (95302), **Cape Upright** (95303), **Cape Hatteras** (95305) canibalised in 1974. (Previously planned transfer of these units cancelled).

CAPE CLASS (WPB) *1969, United States Coast Guard*

POINT CHARLES (WPB 82361) off Cape Kennedy *1972, US Coast Guard*

CAPE CROSS (WPB 95321) *1969, US Coast Guard*

CAPE KNOX (WPB 95312), POINT BARNES (WPB 82371) *1972, USCG*

Patrol Boats—*continued*

53 PATROL BOATS (WPB): 82ft CLASS

POINT ARENA	82346	**POINT LOBOS**	82366
POINT BAKER	82342	**POINT LOOKOUT**	82341
POINT BARROW	82348	**POINT MONROE**	82353
POINT BATAN	82340	**POINT NOWELL**	82363
POINT BENNETT	82351	**POINT RICHMOND**	82370
POINT BONITA	82347	**POINT ROBERTS**	82332
POINT BRIDGE	82338	**POINT SAL**	82352
POINT BROWN	82362	**POINT SPENCER**	82349
POINT CHARLES	82361	**POINT STEELE**	82359
POINT CHICO	82339	**POINT STUART**	82358
POINT COUNTESS	82335	**POINT SWIFT**	82312
POINT DIVIDE	82337	**POINT THATCHER**	82314
POINT ESTERO	82344	**POINT TURNER**	82365
POINT EVANS	82354	**POINT VERDE**	82311
POINT FRANCIS	82356	**POINT WARDE**	82368
POINT FRANKLIN	82350	**POINT WELLS**	82343
POINT GLASS	82336	**POINT WHITEHORN**	82364
POINT HANNON	82355	**POINT WINSLOW**	82360
POINT HERRON	82318	**POINT BARNES**	82371
POINT HEYER	82369	**POINT BROWER**	82372
POINT HIGHLAND	82333	**POINT CAMDEN**	82373
POINT HOPE	82302	**POINT CARREW**	82374
POINT HURON	82357	**POINT DORAN**	82375
POINT JUDITH	82345	**POINT HARRIS**	82376
POINT KNOLL	82367	**POINT HOBART**	82377
POINT LEDGE	82334	**POINT JACKSON**	82378
		POINT MARTIN	82379

CG 82332—82370
"C" class (built 1962-63 and 1965-67)

CG 82371—82379
"D" Class (built 1969-70)

Displacement, tons	64 standard; 67 full load
Dimensions, feet	78·1 wl; 83 oa × 17·2 × 5·8
Guns	C Class: 1—81 mm mortar and 1—·50 cal MG or 2—·50 cal MG with some boats unarmed D Class: 2—·50 cal MG
Main engines	2 diesels; 2 shafts; 1 600 bhp = 20 knots
Complement	8 (enlisted men)

Rated as 82 ft Cutters. Designed and built at Coast Guard Yard, for law enforcement, search and rescue. Steel hulls, unmanned engine room controlled from the bridge, power steering and air-conditioning. "C" class modifications (also 82318) include increase in bhp to 1 600 and speed to 20 knots. In 1965 26 of these craft were deployed with the Navy and transferred to duty in Vietnam (subsequently transferred to South Vietnamese Navy). As a result 17 replacement cutters were added to the construction programme plus nine already planned. Of the latter, *Point Arena, Point Barrow, Point Bonita, Point Franklin, Point Judith* and *Point Spencer* were built under the Fiscal Year 1965 Programme by Martinac SB, Tacoma, Wash, and 82351 to 82370 in the 1966 programme. Nine "D" class cutters built by Coast Guard Yard with first, *Point Barnes,* completed on 19 Dec 1969.

A few units in remote areas have an officer assigned (with seven enlisted men). Range is 1 500 miles at 9 knots.

NOMENCLATURE. CG 82301-82344 were assigned "Point" names in Jan 1964.

TRANSFERS. All 26 boats of this class that comprised Coast Guard Squadron One in Vietnam have been transferred to the South Vietnamese Navy: *Point League* (82304) *Point Garnet* (82310, *Point Clear* (82315), *Point Gammon* (82328), *Point Comfort,* (82317), *Point Ellis* (82330), *Point Slocum* (82313), *Point Hudson* (82322) transferred in 1969; *Point Arden* (82309), *Point Banks* (82 327), *Point Caution* (82301), *Point Cypress* (82326), *Point Dume* (82325), *Point Glover* (82307), *Point Grace* (82323), *Point Grey* (82324), *Point Jefferson* (82306), *Point Kennedy* (82320), *Point Lomas* (82321), *Point Mast* (82316), *Point Monroe* (82331), *Point Orient* (82319), *Point Partridge* (82305) *Point Welcome* (82329), *Point White* (82308) *Point Young* (82303) in 1970.

POINT CHARLES (WPB 82361) *1972, US Coast Guard*

ICEBREAKERS

2 ICEBREAKERS (WAGB): "POLAR" CLASS

Name	*No.*	*Laid down*	*Launched*	*Complete*
POLAR STAR	WAGB 10	15 May 1972	17 Nov 1973	June 1975
POLAR SEA	WAGB 11	27 Nov 1973	June 1975	June 1976

Displacement, tons	12 200 full load
Dimensions, feet	185 oa × 78 × 28
Main engines	Diesels supplemented by gas turbines; 3 shafts = 17 knots
Guns	unarmed
Helicopters	2 HH-52
Complement	155 plus 10 scientists

These ships are the first icebreakers built for US service since the *Glacier* constructed two decades earlier. The programme is intended to replace the World War II-built "Wind" class icebreakers. *Polar Star* authorised in the Fiscal Year 1971 budget of the Department of Transportation; *Polar Sea* in FY 1973 budget. No additional ships are planned for the near future.

Both ships built by Lockheed Shipbuilding Co, Seattle, Washington.

DESIGN. The "Polar" class icebreakers are the largest ships operated by the US Coast Guard. Their icebreaking capability—based on total horsepower available—is greater than any other icebreaker in service. However, the long-delayed Soviet "Arktika", rated as being "twice as powerful" as the *Lenin* by Soviet sources, will have a greater capability than the US ships.

These ships have a conventional icebreaker hull form with cutaway bow configuration and well rounded body sections to prevent being trapped in ice. Two 15-ton capacity cranes fitted aft; hangar and flight deck aft; extensive research laboratories provided for arctic and oceanographic research.

ENGINEERING. This new WAGB design provides for conventional diesel engines for normal cruising and gas turbines for maximum power situations. The diesel engines will drive generators producing AC power; the main propulsion DC motors will draw power through rectifiers permitting absolute flexibility in the delivery of power from alternate sources. The use of controllable-pitch propellers on three shafts will permit manoeuvering in heavy ice without the risk to propeller blades caused by stopping the shaft while going from ahead to astern.

The six Alco diesels provide a total of 18 000 bhp; the three Pratt and Whitney FT4A-12 gas turbines provide a total of 75 000 shp although maximum power output from the latter will be about 60 000 shp.

The Coast Guard had given consideration to the use of nuclear power for an icebreaker, however, at this time the gas turbine-diesel combination can achieve the desirable power requirements without the added cost and operating restrictions of a nuclear powerplant.

POLAR STAR *United States Coast Guard*

POLAR STAR at launching *1973, US Coast Guard*

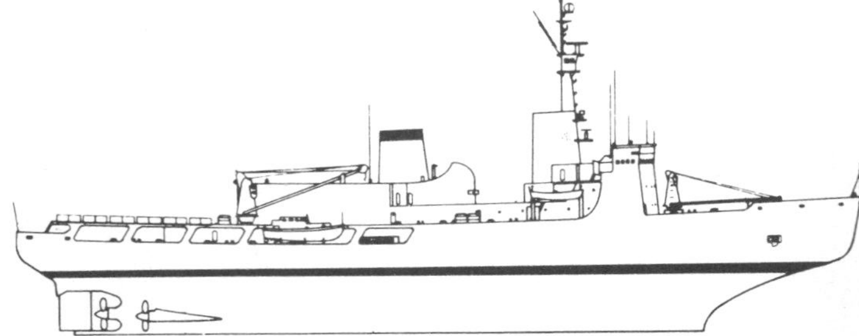

POLAR STAR *Drawing by A. D. Baker*

Icebreakers—*continued*

1 ICEBREAKER (WAGB): "GLACIER" TYPE

Name	No.	Launched	Commissioned
GLACIER	WAGB 4 (ex-AGB 4)	27 Aug 1954	27 May 1955

Displacement, tons	8 449 full load
Dimensions, feet	309·6 oa × 74 × 29
Guns	4—·50 cal MG
Helicopters	2 helicopters normally embarked
Main engines	Diesel-electric (10 Fairbanks-Morse diesels and 2 Westinghouse electric motors); 21 000 hp; 2 shafts = 17·6 knots
Complement	229 (14 officers, 215 enlisted men)

The largest icebreaker in US service prior to the "Polar" class; designed and built by Ingalls Shipbuilding Corp. Pascagoula, Mississippi; laid down on 3 Aug 1953. Transferred from Navy (AGB 4) to Coast Guard on 30 June 1966. During 1972 the *Glacier* and assigned helicopters were painted red to improve visibility in Arctic regions. All other icebreakers painted red during 1973.

ENGINEERING. When built the *Glacier* had the largest capacity single-armature DC motors ever built and installed in a ship. Range is 29 200 miles at 12 knots or 12 000 miles at 17·6 knots.

GUNNERY. As built the *Glacier* was armed with two 5 inch AA guns (twin), six 3 inch AA guns (twin), and four 20 mm AA guns; lighter weapons removed prior to transfer to Coast Guard; 5 inch guns removed in 1969.

GLACIER (WAGB 4) — *1972, US Coast Guard*

5 ICEBREAKERS (WAGB): "WIND" CLASS

Name	No.	Launched
STATEN ISLAND (ex-*Northwind*)	WAGB 278 (ex-AGB 5)	28 Dec 1942
WESTWIND	WAGB 281	31 Mar 1943
NORTHWIND	WAGB 282	25 Feb 1945
BURTON ISLAND	WAGB 283 (ex-AGB 1, ex-AG 88)	30 Apr 1946
EDISTO	WAGB 284 (ex-AGB 2, ex-AG 89)	29 May 1946

Displacement, tons	3 500 standard; 6 515 full load
Dimensions, feet	250 pp; 269 oa × 63·5 × 29
Helicopters	2 helicopters normally embarked
Guns	4—·50 cal MG (see *Gunnery* notes)
Main engines	Diesel-electric (4 or 6 diesels); 10 000 hp; 2 shafts = 16 knots
Complement	135

Originally seven ships in this class built by Western Pipe & Steel Co, San Pedro, California. Five ships were delivered to the US Coast Guard during World War II and two to the US Navy in 1946.

Three of the Coast Guard ships were transferred to the Soviet Navy in 1945: *Northwind* (first of name, WAGB 278) renamed *Severni Veter* and returned to US Navy in 1951 and commissioned as *Staten Island* (AGB 5); *Southwind* renamed *Kapitan Belusov* and returned to US Navy in 1950 and commissioned as *Atka* (AGB 3); *Westwind* renamed *Severni Polius* and returned to US Coast Guard in 1951 (carried US Navy designation AGB 6).

The four "Wind" class ships in the US Navy were transferred to the Coast Guard: *Edisto* on 20 Oct 1965, *Staten Island* on 1 Feb 1966, *Atka* on 20 Oct 1966 (renamed *Southwind* in January 1967), and *Burton Island* on 15 Dec 1966.

The *Westwind* operates on the Great Lakes. *Edisto* and *Staten Island* decommissioned on 15 Nov 1974 and laid up in reserve; the *Burton Island* was to be laid up early in 1976. Crews of *Northwind* and *Westwind* reduced from 181 to approx 135 during 1975.

ENGINEERING. These ships were built with a bow propeller shaft in addition to the two stern shafts; bow shaft removed from all units because it would continually break in hard storis ice. Main engines are Fairbanks Morse 38D81/8. Range is 38 000 miles at 10·5 knots or 16 000 miles at 16 knots.

Westwind re-engined with four *Enterprise* diesels in 1973-1974, and *Northwind* in 1974-1975; same bhp and speed. Note taller funnel in photograph of *Westwind* after engine change.

GUNNERY. As built the five Coast Guard ships each mounted four 5 inch guns (one twin mount forward and one twin mount aft on 01 level) and 12 40 mm anti-aircraft guns (quad); the two Navy Ships were completed with only forward twin 5 inch mount (as built a catapult and cranes were fitted immediately behind the funnel and one floatplane was carried). Armament reduced after war and helicopter platform eventually installed in all ships.

During the 1960s the *Northwind* carried two 5 inch guns (twin), and the three other ships each mounted one 5 inch gun; all armament removed in 1969-1970.

DISPOSALS

Eastwind WAGB 279 stricken in 1972; **Southwind** WAGB 280 (ex-AGB 3) stricken in 1974.

STATEN ISLAND (WAGB 278) — *1970, US Coast Guard*

WESTWIND (WAGB 281) — *1974, US Coast Guard*

NORTHWIND (WAGB 282) — *1969, US Coast Guard*

BURTON ISLAND (WAGB 283) — *US Coast Guard*

BURTON ISLAND (WAGB 283) — *1971, US Navy, PH2 J. J. Carmerrale*

Icebreakers—*continued*

1 ICEBREAKER (WAGB): "MACKINAW" TYPE

Name	No.	Launched	Commissioned
MACKINAW (ex-*Manitowac*)	WAGB 83	6 Mar 1944	20 Dec 1944

Displacement, tons	5 252
Dimensions, feet	290 oa × 74 × 19
Helicopters	1 helicopter
Main engines	Diesel; with electric drive; 3 shafts (1 forward, 2 aft); 10 000 bhp = 18·7 knots
Complement	127 (10 officers, 117 enlisted men)

Built by Toledo Shipbuilding Co, Ohio. Laid down on 20 Mar 1943. Completed in Jan 1945. Specially designed and constructed for service as icebreaker on the Great Lakes. Equipped with two 12-ton capacity cranes. Clear area for helicopter is provided on the quarter deck.
Range is 60 000 miles at 12 knots.

MACKINAW (WAGB 83) *United States Coast Guard*

1 ICEBREAKER (WMEC): "STORIS" TYPE

Name	No.
STORIS (ex-*Eskimo*)	WMEC 38 (ex-WAGB 38)

Displacement, tons	1 715 standard; 1 925 full load
Dimensions, feet	230 oa × 43 × 15
Guns	1—3 in, 50 cal; 2—·50 cal MG
Main engines	Diesel-electric; 1 shaft; 1 800 bhp = 14 knots
Complement	106 (10 officers, 96 enlisted men)

Built by Toledo Shipbuilding Co, Ohio. Laid down 14 July 1941; launched on 4 Apr 1942; completed on 30 Sep 1942. Ice patrol tender. Strengthened for ice navigation. Employed on Alaskan service for search, rescue and law enforcement.
Designation changed from WAG to WAGB on 1 May 1966; redesignated as medium endurance cutter (WMEC) on 1 July 1972.
Range is 22 000 miles at 8 knots or 12 000 miles at 14 knots.

STORIS (WMEC 38) *1968, US Coast Guard*

TRAINING CUTTERS

1 TRAINING CUTTER (IX): "ACTIVE" CLASS

CUYAHOGA WIX 157 (ex-WMEC 157, ex-WPC 157, ex-WAG 26)

Dimensions, feet	125 oa × 24 × 8
Guns	Removed
Main engines	Diesel; 2 shafts; 800 bhp = 13·2 knots
Complement	11 (1 officer, 10 enlisted men)

Built in 1926 as one of the 33 "Active" class steel patrol boats. The *Cuyahoga* is the only cutter of this type remaining on the Coast Guard list and probably the oldest US government-owned ship in active service. She is based at Yorktown, Virginia, for the training of officer candidates.

CUYAHOGA (WIX 157) *1966, United States Coast Guard*

1 TRAINING CUTTER (IX): "EAGLE" TYPE

EAGLE (ex-*Horst Wessel*) WIX 327

Displacement, tons	1 816 full load
Dimensions, feet	231 wl; 295·2 oa × 39·1 × 17
Sail area, sq ft	21 350
Height of masts, feet	fore and main 150·3; mizzen 132
Main engines	Auxiliary diesel (MAN); 728 bhp; 1 shaft = 10·5 knots (as high as 18 knots under full sail alone)
Endurance, miles	3 500 at 10 knots with diesel
Complement	280

Former German training ship for 200 naval cadets. Built by Blohm & Vos, Hamburg. Launched on 13 June 1936. Taken by the United States as part of reparations after the Second World War for employment in US Coast Guard Practice Squadron. Taken over at Bremerhaven in Jan 1946; arrived at home port, New London, Connecticut, in July 1946. She has made several cruises to European waters to train Coast Guard cadets.
Sister ship *Albert Leo Schlageter* was also taken by the United States in 1945 but was sold to Brazil in 1948 and re-sold to Portugal in 1962. Another ship of similar design, the *Gorch Foch*, transferred to the Soviet Union in 1946 and survives as the *Tovarisch*.

"CASCO" CLASS

The last of the former 311-foot Navy seaplane tenders, some of which served the Coast Guard from 1946 onward, was the *Unimak* WTR 379 (ex-WHEC 379, ex-AVP 31), decommissioned in mid-1975. She is expected to be transferred to South Vietnam and will probably be cannibalised to provide parts for other ships of this class serving in the Vietnamese Navy. See 1974-1975 edition for characteristics. Previous disposals of the "Casco" class are listed in the 1973-1974 and previous editions except the *Gresham* WAGW 387 (ex-WHEC 387, ex-AGP 9, ex-AVP 57) decommissioned on 1 May 1973 and transferred to the Maritime Administration for disposal. *Courier* WTR 410 (ex-WAGR 410, ex-AK 176) stricken in 1973; *Tanager* WTR 885 (ex-WTR 385, ex-MSF 385) stricken in 1972; *Lamar* WTR 889 (ex-PCE 889) stricken in 1971.

STORIS (WMEC 38) alongside the LAMUT, flagship of Soviet Bering Sea fishing fleet *1972, National Marine Fisheries Service*

Training Cutters—*continued*

EAGLE (WIX 327) *United States Coast Guard*

SEAGOING TENDERS

35 SEAGOING TENDERS (WLB) | 1 OCEANOGRAPHIC CUTTER (WAGO) | "BALSAM" CLASS

Name	No.	Launched	Name	No.	Launched
BALSAM *	WLB 62	1942	**BITTERSWEET**	WLB 389	1944
COWSLIP	WLB 277	1942	**BLACKHAW***	WLB 390	1944
GENTIAN	WLB 290	1942	**BLACKTHORN**	WLB 391	1944
LAUREL	WLB 291	1942	**BRAMBLE ***	WLB 392	1944
CLOVER	WLB 292	1942	**FIREBUSH**	WLB 393	1944
EVERGREEN	WAGO 295	1943	**HORNBEAM**	WLB 394	1944
SORREL *	WLB 296	1943	**IRIS**	WLB 395	1944
IRONWOOD	WLB 297	1944	**MALLOW**	WLB 396	1944
CITRUS *	WLB 300	1943	**MARIPOSA**	WLB 397	1944
CONIFER	WLB 301	1943	**SAGEBRUSH**	WLB 399	1944
MADRONA	WLB 302	1943	**SALVIA**	WLB 400	1944
TUPELO	WLB 303	1943	**SASSAFRAS**	WLB 401	1944
MESQUITE	WLB 305	1943	**SEDGE ***	WLB 402	1944
BUTTONWOOD	WLB 306	1943	**SPAR ***	WLB 403	1944
PLANETREE	WLB 307	1943	**SUNDEW ***	WLB 404	1944
PAPAW	WLB 308	1943	**SWEETBRIER**	WLB 405	1944
SWEETGUM	WLB 309	1943	**ACACIA**	WLB 406	1944
BASSWOOD	WLB 388	1944	**WOODRUSH**	WLB 407	1944

Displacement, tons	935 standard; 1 025 full load
Dimensions, feet	180 oa × 37 × 13
Guns	1—3 inch (*76 mm*) 50 calibre in *Citrus, Cowslip, Hornbeam,* and *Sorrel* (original armament); most others have ·50 calibre MG except *Sedge* has 2—20 mm guns; several ships are unarmed
Main engines	Diesel-electric; 1 000 bhp in tenders numbered WLB 62-303 series, except *Ironwood*; 1 shaft = 12.8 knots; others 1 200 bhp; 1 shaft = 15 knots
Complement	53 (6 officers, 47 enlisted men)

Seagoing buoy tenders. *Ironwood* built by Coast Guard yard at Curtis Bay, Baltimore, Maryland; others by Marine Iron & Shipbuilding Co, Duluth, Minnesota, or Zeneth Dredge, Co, Duluth Minnesota. Eight ships indicated by asterisks are strengthened for icebreaking. Three ships, *Cowslip, Bittersweet,* and *Hornbeam,* have controllable-pitch, bow-thrust propellers to assist in manoeuvering. All WLBs have 20-capacity booms. The *Evergreen* has been refitted as an oceanographic cutter (WAGO) and is painted white; several ships are laid up in reserve.

DISPOSALS AND TRANSFERS

Redbud WLB 298 (ex-US Navy T-AKL 398, ex-Coast Guard WAGL 398) transferred to Philippines on 1 Mar 1972; *Cactus* WLB 270, *Woodbine* WLB 289 stricken in 1972.

HORNBEAM (WLB 394) gun aft of funnel ***1969, US Coast Guard***

COASTAL TENDERS

EVERGREEN (WAGO 295) *1973, US Coast Guard*

5 COASTAL TENDERS (WLM): "RED" CLASS

Name	No.	Launched	Name	No.	Launched
RED WOOD	WLM 685	1964	**RED CEDAR**	WLM 688	1970
RED BEECH	WLM 688	1964	**RED OAK**	WLM 689	1971
RED BIRCH	WLM 687	1965			

Displacement, tons	471 standard; 512 full load
Dimensions, feet	157 oa × 33 × 6
Main engines	2 diesels; 2 shafts; 1 800 hp = 12·8 knots
Complement	31 (4 officers, 27 enlisted men)

All built by Coast Guard yard, Curtis Bay, Baltimore, Maryland. *Red Cedar* completed late in 1970 and *Red Oak* late in 1971.
Fitted with controllable-pitch propellers and bow thrusters; steel hulls strengthened for light icebreaking. Steering and engine controls on each bridge wing as well as in pilot house. Living spaces are air conditioned. Endurance is 3 000 miles at 11·6 knots. Fitted with 10-ton capacity boom.

RED BIRCH (WLM 687) *1968, US Coast Guard*

3 COASTAL TENDERS (WLM): "HOLLYHOCK" CLASS

FIR WLM 212 **HOLLYHOCK** WLM 220 **WALNUT** WLM 252

Displacement, tons	989
Dimensions, feet	175 × 34 × 12
Main engines	Diesel reduction, 2 shafts; 1 350 bhp = 12 knots
Complement	40 (5 officers, 35 enlisted men)

Launched in 1937 (*Hollyhock*) and 1939 (*Fir* and *Walnut*). *Walnut* was re-engined by Willamette Iron & Steel Co, Portland, Oregon, in 1958. Redesignated Coastal Tenders, WLM, instead of Buoy Tenders, WAGL on 1 Jan 1965. Fitted with 20-ton capacity boom.

1 COASTAL TENDER (WLM): "JUNIPER" TYPE

JUNIPER WLM 224

Displacement, tons	794
Dimensions, feet	177 × 33 × 9·2
Main engines	Diesel, with electric drive; 2 shafts; 900 bhp = 10·8 knots
Complement	38 (4 officers, 34 enlisted men)

Launched on 18 May 1940. Redesignated WLM vice WALG on 1 Jan 1965. Fitted with 20-ton capacity boom.

7 COASTAL TENDERS (WLM): "WHITE" CLASS

WHITE BUSH	WLM 542	**WHITE PINE**	WLM 547
WHITE HEATH	WLM 545	**WHITE SAGE**	WLM 544
WHITE HOLLY	WLM 543	**WHITE SUMAC**	WLM 540
WHITE LUPINE	WLM 546		

Displacement, tons	435 standard; 600 full load
Dimensions, feet	133 oa × 31 × 9
Main engines	Diesel: 2 shafts; 600 bhp = 9·8 knots
Complement	21 (1 officer, 20 enlisted men)

All launched in 1943. All seven ships are former US Navy YFs, adapted for the Coast Guard. The *White Alder* (WLM 541) was sunk in a collision on 7 Dec 1968. Fitted with 10-ton capacity boom.

INLAND TENDERS

JUNIPER (WLM 224) *1971, US Coast Guard, LT (jg) M. Robinson*

WHITE BUSH (WLM 542) *1969, US Coast Guard*

TERN WLI 80801

Displacement, tons	168 full load
Dimensions, feet	80 oa × 25 × 5
Main engines	Diesels; 2 shafts; 450 hp = 10 knots
Complement	7 (enlisted men)

The *Tern* is prototype for a new design of inland buoy tenders. A cutaway stern and gantry crane (the first installed in a Coast Guard tender) permit lifting buoys aboard from the stern. The crane moves on rails that extend forward to the deck house. Fitted with 125 hp bow thruster to improve manoeuvrability. Air conditioned. Built by Coast Guard yard at Curtis Bay, Baltimore, Maryland. Launched on 15 June 1968 and placed in service on 7 Feb 1969.

Narcissus WLI 238 decommissioned in 1971 and transferred to Guyana; *Zinnia* WLI 255 decommissioned in 1972 and transferred to US Air Force; *Maple* WLI 234 decommissioned in 1973 for disposal.

TAMARACK WLI 248

Displacement, tons	400 full load
Dimensions, feet	124 oa × 30 × 8
Main engines	Diesels; 1 shaft; 520 hp = 10 knots

Launched in 1934. Fitted with 10-ton capacity boom. Out of service.

COSMOS WLI 293 **BARBERRY** WLI 294 **RAMBLER** WLI 298 **BLUEBELL** WLI 313 **SMILAX** WLI 315 **PRIMROSE** WLI 316 **VERBENA** WLI 317

Displacement, tons	178 full load
Dimensions, feet	100 oa × 24 × 5
Main engines	Diesels; 2 shafts 600; hp = 10·5 knots except *Barberry* 11 knots
Complement	15 (1 officer, 14 enlisted men)

Cosmos launched in 1942, *Barberry* in 1943, *Bluebell* in 1945, others in 1944. The *Barberry* has controllable-pitch propellers. The *Barberry* and *Verbena* are fitted with pile drivers. *Barberry* decommissioned in 1970.

AZALEA WLI 641

Displacement, tons	200 full load
Dimensions, feet	100 oa × 24 × 5
Main engines	Diesels; 2 shafts; 440 hp = 9 knots
Complement	14 (1 officer, 13 enlisted men)

Launched in 1958. Fitted with pile driver.

BUCKTHORN WLI 642

Displacement, tons	200 full load
Dimensions, feet	100 oa × 24 × 4
Main engines	Diesels; 2 shafts; 600 hp = 7·3 knots
Complement	14 (1 officer, 13 enlisted men)

Launched in 1963.

CLEMATIS WLI 74286 **SHADBUSH** WLI 74287

Displacement, tons	93 full load
Dimensions, feet	74 oa × 19 × 4
Main engines	Diesels; 2 shafts; 330 hp = 8 knots
Complement	9 (enlisted men)

Launched in 1944.

BLUEBERRY WLI 65302

Displacement, tons	45 full load
Dimensions, feet	65 oa × 17 × 14
Main engines	Diesels; 2 shafts; 330 hp = 10·5 knots
Complement	5 (enlisted men)

Launched in 1942.

Inland Tenders—*continued*

BLACKBERRY WLI 65303 **CHOKEBERRY** WLI 65304 **LOGANBERRY** WLI 65305

Displacement, tons	68 full load
Dimensions, feet	65 oa × 17 × 4
Main engines	Diesels; 1 shaft; 220 hp = 9 knots
Complement	5 (enlisted men)

Launched in 1946.

BAYBERRY WLI 65400 **ELDERBERRY** WLI 65401

Displacement, tons	68 full load
Dimensions, feet	65 oa × 17 × 4
Main engines	Diesels; 2 shafts; 400 hp = 11·3 knots
Complement	5 (enlisted men)

Launched in 1954.

TERN (WLI 80801) *1969, United States Coast Guard*

BUCKTHORN (WLI 642) *1970, US Coast Guard*

CONSTRUCTION TENDERS

PAMLICO WLIC 800 **HUDSON** WLIC 801

Dimensions, feet	160 oa
Main engines	Diesels
Complement	13

New class under construction; scheduled to complete in late 1975 at the Coast Guard Yard, Curtis Bay, Maryland.

ANVIL WLIC 75301 **HAMMER** WLIC 75302 **SLEDGE** WLIC 75303 **MALLET** WLIC 75304 **VISE** WLIC 75305 **CLAMP** WLIC 75306 **WEDGE** WLIC 75307 **SPIKE** WLIC 75308 **HATCHET** WLIC 75309 **AXE** WLIC 75310

Displacement, tons	145 full load
Dimensions, feet	75 oa (WLIC 75306-75310 are 76 oa) × 22 × 4
Main engines	Diesels; 2 shafts; 600 hp = 10 knots
Complement	9 or 10 (1 officer in *Mallet*, *Sledge* and *Vise*; 9 enlisted men in all)

Launched 1962-1965

SPIKE (WLIC 75308) pushing barge *1971, US Coast Guard*

RIVER TENDERS

SUMAC WLR 311

Displacement, tons	*Sumac* 404 full load
Dimensions, feet	115 oa × 30 × 6
Main engines	Diesels; 3 shafts; 960 hp = 10·6 knots
Complement	23 (1 officer, 22 enlisted men)

Built in 1943. *Fern* WLR 304 stricken.

River Tenders—*continued*

DOGWOOD WLR 259 **FORSYTHIA** WLR 63 **SYCAMORE** WLR 268

Displacement, tons	230 full load, except *Forsythia* 280
Dimensions, feet	114 oa × 26 × 4
Main engines	Diesels; 2 shafts; 2 800 hp = 11 knots
Complement	21 (1 officer, 20 enlisted men)

Dogwood and *Sycamore* built in 1940; *Forsythia* in 1943.

FOXGLOVE WLR 285.

Displacement, tons	350 full load
Dimensions, feet	114 oa × 30 × 6
Main engines	Diesels; 3 shafts; 8 500 hp = 13·5 knots
Complement	21 (1 officer, 20 enlisted men)

Built in 1945.

Goldenrod WLR 213 and *Poplar* WLR241 decommissioned in 1973 and transferred to National Science Foundation.

LANTANA WLR 80310

Displacement, tons	235 full load
Dimensions, feet	80 oa × 30 × 6
Main engines	Diesels; 3 shafts; 10 000 hp = 10 knots
Complement	20 (1 officer, 19 enlisted men)

Built in 1943.

GASCONADE	WLR 75401	**CHEYENNE**	WLR 75405
MUSKINGUM	WLR 75402	**KICKAPOO**	WLR 75406
WYACONDA	WLR 75403	**KANAWHA**	WLR 75407
CHIPPEWA	WLR 75404	**PATOKA**	WLR 75408
		CHENA	WLR 75409

Displacement, tons	145 full load
Dimensions, feet	75 oa × 22 × 4
Main engines	Diesel; 2 shafts; 600 hp = 10·8 knots
Complement	12 (enlisted men)

Built 1964-1971.

OLEANDER WLR 73264

Displacement, tons	90 full load
Dimensions, feet	73 oa × 18 × 5
Main engines	Diesel; 2 shafts; 300 hp = 12 knots
Complement	10 (enlisted men)

Built in 1940.

OSAGE (WLR 65505) *US Coast Guard*

CHEYENNE (WLR 75405) with buoy barge *1971, VSCG*

River Tenders—*continued*

OUACHITA	WLR 65501	**SCIOTO**	WLR 65504
CIMARRON	WLR 65502	**OSAGE**	WLR 65505
OBION	WLR 65503	**SANGAMON**	WLR 65506

Displacement, tons	139 full load
Dimensions, feet	65·6 oa × 21 × 5
Main engines	Diesel; 2 shafts; 600 hp = 12·5 knots
Complement	10 (enlisted men)

Built in 1960-1962.

OCEANGOING TUGS

1 MEDIUM ENDURANCE CUTTER (WMEC) ARS TYPE
1 OCEANOGRAPHIC CUTTER (WAGO)

Name	*No.*	*Launched*	*Navy Comm.*
ACUSHNET (ex-USS *Shackle*)	WAGO 167 (ex-WAT 167, ARS 9)	1 Apr 1943	5 Feb 1944
YOCONA (ex-USS *Seize*)	WMEC 168 (ex-WAT 168, ARS 26)	8 Apr 1944	3 Nov 1944

Displacement, tons	1 557 standard; 1 745 full load
Dimensions, feet	213·5 oa × 39 × 15
Main engines	Diesels; 2 shafts; 3 000 hp = 15·5 knots
Complement	*Acushnet* 64 (7 officers, 57 enlisted men)
	Yocona 72 (7 officers, 65 enlisted men)

Large, steel-hulled tugs transferred from the Navy to the Coast Guard after World War II. Both by Basalt Rock Co, Napa, California. *Acushnet* modified for handling environmental data buoys and reclassified WAGO in 1969; *Yocona* reclassified as WMEC in 1969. Armament removed.

YOCONA (WMEC 168) *1970, United States Coast Guard*

3 MEDIUM ENDURANCE CUTTERS (WMEC): ATF TYPE

Name	*No.*	*Launched*	*Navy Comm.*
CHILULA	WMEC 153 (ex-WAT 153, ATF 153)	1 Dec 1944	5 Apr 1945
CHEROKEE	WMEC 165 (ex-WAT 165, ATF 66)	10 Nov 1939	26 Apr 1940
TAMAROA (ex-*Zuni*)	WMEC 166 (ex-WAT 166, ATF 95)	13 July 1943	9 Oct 1943

Displacement, tons	1 731 full load
Dimensions, feet	205 oa × 38·5 × 17
Guns	1—3 inch 50 calibre; 2—·50 cal MG
Main engines	Diesel electric (General Motors diesel); 1 shaft; 3 000 hp = 16·2 knots
Complement	72 (7 officers, 65 enlisted men)

Steel-hulled tugs transferred from the Navy to the Coast Guard after World War II; *Chilula* officially on loan since 9 July 1956 until stricken from the Navy List on 1 June 1969. Classification of all three ships changed to WMEC in 1969. *Chilula* built by Charleston Shipbuilding & Dry Dock Co, Charleston, South Carolina; *Cherokee* built by Bethlehem Steel Co, Staten Island, New York; *Tamaroa* built by Commercial Iron Works, Portland, Oregon.

DISPOSALS
Avoyel (WMEC 150, ex-WAT 150, ex-ATF 150) stricken in 1970.

TAMAROA (WMEC 166) *1970, United States Coast Guard*

Oceangoing Tugs—*continued*

2 MEDIUM ENDURANCE CUTTERS (WMEC): ATA TYPE

Name	*No.*	*Launched*	*Navy Comm.*
MODOC (ex-USS *Bagaduce*)	WMEC 194 (ex-WATA 194, ATA 194)	4 Dec 1944	14 Feb 1945
COMANCHE (ex-USS *Wampanoag*)	WMEC 202 (ex-WATA 202, ATA 202)	10 Oct 1944	8 Dec 1944

Displacement, tons 534 standard; 860 full load
Dimensions, feet 143 oa × 33·8 × 14
Armament 2—·50 cal MG
Main engines Diesel electric (General Motors diesel); 1 shaft; 1 500 hp = 13·5 knots
Complement 47 (5 officers, 42 enlisted men)

Steel-hulled tugs. The *Modoc* was stricken from the Navy List after World War II and transferred to Maritime Administration, transferred to Coast Guard on 15 Apr 1959. *Comanche* transferred on loan from Navy to Coast Guard from 25 Feb 1959 until stricken from Navy List on 1 June 1969. Both ships reclassified as WMEC in 1969. *Modoc* built by Levingston Shipbuilding Co, Orange, Texas; *Comanche* built by Gulfport Boiler & Welding Works, Port Arthur, Texas.

COMANCHE (WMEC 202) *1969, United States Coast Guard*

HARBOUR TUGS

NEW CONSTRUCTION

Displacement, tons 660 full load
Dimensions, feet 140 oa × 30 × 12·5
Main engines Diesel-electric; 2 500 bhp; 1 shaft
Complement 17 (3 officers, 14 enlisted men)

The Coast Guard is planning this new class of icebreaking harbour tugs to replace the ageing 110-foot harbour tugs. The initial units will operate on the Great Lakes. Three are planned for the Fiscal Year 1977 budget. The above data reflects preliminary designs.

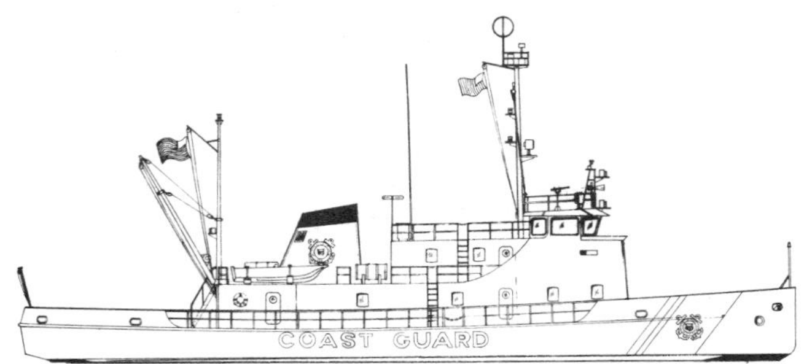

Harbour Tugs—*continued*

MANITOU	WYTM 60	**MOHICAN**	WYTM 73	**CHINOOK**	WYTM 96
KAW	WYTM 61	**ARUNDEL**	WYTM 90	**OJIBWA**	WYTM 97
APALACHEE	WYTM 71	**MAMONING**	WYTM 91	**SNOHOMISH**	WYTM 98
YANKTON	WYTM 72	**NAUGATUCK**	WYTM 92	**SAUK**	WYTM 99
		RARITAN	WYTM 93		

Displacement, tons 370 full load
Dimensions, feet 110 oa × 27 × 11
Main engines Diesel-electric; 1 shaft; 1 000 hp = 11·2 knots
Complement 20 (1 officer, 19 enlisted men)

Built in 1943 except WYTM 90-93 built in 1939.

MESSENGER WYTM 85009

Displacement, tons 230 full load
Dimensions, feet 85 oa × 23 × 9
Main engines Diesel; 1 shaft; 700 hp = 9·5 knots
Complement 10 (enlisted)

Built in 1944.

CAPSTAN	WYTL 65601	**CATENARY**	WYTL 65606	**LINE**	WYTL 65611
CHOCK	WYTL 65602	**BRIDLE**	WYTL 65607	**WIRE**	WYTL 65612
SWIVEL	WYTL 65603	**PENDANT**	WYTL 65608	**BITT**	WYTL 65613
TACKLE	WYTL 65604	**SHACKLE**	WYTL 65609	**BOLLARD**	WYTL 65614
TOWLINE	WYTL 65605	**HAWSER**	WYTL 65610	**CLEAT**	WYTL 65615

Displacement, tons 72 full load
Dimensions, feet 65 oa × 19 × 7
Main engines Diesel; 1 shaft; 400 hp = 9·8 knots except WYTL 65601-65606 10·5 knots
Complement 10 (enlisted men)

Built from 1961 to 1967.

LIGHTSHIPS

LIGHTSHIP COLUMBIA WLV 604 **LIGHTSHIP PORTLAND** WLV 612
LIGHTSHIP RELIEF WLV 605 **LIGHTSHIP RELIEF** WLV 613

Displacement, tons 617 full load, except WLV 612 and 613 are 607 full load
Dimensions, feet 128 oa × 30 × 11
Main engines Diesel; 550 bhp; 1 shaft = 10·7 knots, except WLV 612 and 613 = 11 knots

All launched 1950 except *Lightship Relief* (WLV 613) in 1952. *Lightship Columbia* assigned to Astoria, Oregon; *Lightship Relief* (605) to Seattle, Washington; *Lightship Portland* to Portland, Maine; and *Lightship Relief* (613) to Boston, Massachusetts.

LIGHTSHIP BOSTON WLV 189

Displacement, tons 600 full load
Dimensions, feet 128 oa × 30 × 11
Main engines Diesel; 600 bhp; 1 shaft = 9 knots

Launched in 1946. Assigned to Boston, Massachusetts.

LIGHTSHIP NANTUCKET WLV 534

Displacement, tons 1 100 full load
Dimensions, feet 149 oa × 32 × 16
Main engines Diesel; 900 bhp; 1 shaft = 9 knots

Launched in 1936. Assigned to Woods Hole, Massachusetts.

SUPPLY SHIPS (WAK)

All Coast Guard supply ships (WAK) have been stricken: *Kukui* WAK 186 ex-AK 174 transferred to Philippines on 1 Mar 1972; see "Balsam" class seagoing tenders for transfer of *Redbud* to Philippines.

YOCONA (WMEC 168) towing environmental data buoy *General Dynamics*

NATIONAL OCEANIC AND ATMOSPHERIC ADMINISTRATION

Command

Director, National Ocean Survey: Rear-Admiral Allen L. Powell

Associate Director, Office of Fleet Operations: Rear-Admiral Eugene A. Taylor

Director, Atlantic Marine Center: Rear-Admiral Alfred C. Holmes

Director, Pacific Marine Center: Rear-Admiral Herbert R. Lippold Jnr.

Missions

The National Ocean Survey operates the ships of the National Oceanic and Atmospheric Administration (NOAA), a federal agency created in 1970. During 1972-1973 the National Marine Fisheries Service (formerly the Bureau of Commercial Fisheries of the Department of Interior) was consolidated into the NOAA fleet which is operated by the National Ocean Survey. Approximately 15 small ships and craft 65 feet or longer are counted in the National Marine Fisheries Service. The former National Marine Fisheries vessels are not described because of the specialised, non-military nature of their work.

The National Ocean Survey prepares nautical and aeronautical charts; conducts geodetic, geophysical, oceanographic, and marine surveys; predicts tides and currents; tests, evaluates, and calibrates sensing systems for ocean use; and conducts the development and eventually will operate a national system of automated ocean buoys for obtaining environmental information.

The National Ocean Survey is a civilian agency that supports national civilian and military requirements. During time of war the ships and officers of NOAA can be expected to operate with the Navy, either as a separate service or integrated into the Navy.

Establishment

The "Survey of the Coast" was established by an act of Congress on Feb 10, 1807. Renamed US Coast Survey in 1834 and again renamed Coast and Geodetic Survey in 1878. The commissioned officer corps was established in 1917. The Coast and Geodetic Survey was made a component of the Environmental Science Services Administration on July 13, 1965, when that agency was established within the Department of Commerce. The Environmental Science Services Administration subsequently became the National Oceanic and Atmospheric Administration in October 1970 with the Coast and Geodetic Survey being renamed National Ocean Survey and its jurisdiction expanded to include the US Lake Survey, formerly a part of the US Army Corps of Engineers; the Coast Guard's national data buoy development project; and the Navy's National Oceanographic Instrumentation Centre.

Ships

National Ocean Survey ship designations are: OSS for Ocean Survey Ship, MSS for Medium Survey Ship, CSS for Coastal Survey Ship, and ASV for Auxiliary Survey Vessel. No National Ocean Survey Ships are armed. All ships are active in 1975.

Personnel

The National Ocean Survey which operates NOAA ships has approximately 225 commissioned officers and 2 250 officers and 2 250 civil service personnel. In addition, another 125 commissioned officers serve elsewhere in NOAA and several US Navy officers are assigned to NOAA.

Aviation

The National Ocean Survey's Coastal Mapping Division operates two aircraft for aerial photographic missions, a twin-engine de Havilland Canada Buffalo and a twin-engine North American Rockwell Aero Commander.

SURVEY SHIPS

1 OCEANOGRAPIC SURVEY SHIP (OSS): "RESEARCHER" TYPE

Name	*No.*	*Launched*	*Commissioned*
RESEARCHER	OSS 03	5 Oct 1968	8 Oct 1970

Displacement, tons	2 875 light
Dimensions, feet	278·25 oa × 51 × 16·25 (*84·7 m × 15·5 m × 4·9 m*)
Main engines	2 geared diesels ; 3 200 hp ; 2 shafts = 16 knots
Complement	11 officers, 55 crewmen
Scientists	13

The *Researcher* was designed specifically for deep ocean research; she is ice strengthened. Estimated cost $10 000 000. Fitted with 20-ton capacity crane, 5-ton capacity crane, four 2½-ton capacity cranes, and an A-frame with 10-ton lift capacity. Built by American Shipbuilding Co, Lorain, Ohio.

DESIGN. Fitted with computerised data acquisition system that automatically samples, processes, and records oceanographic, geophysical, hydrographic, and meteorological data. The 20-ton telescoping crane is designed to handle special sampling equipment and small submersible vehicles as well as small boats. S2-MT-MA74a type.

ENGINEERING. Controllable pitch propellers. A 450-horsepower, 360-degree retractable bow thruster provides sustained low speeds up to seven knots and permits precise positioning. Cruising speed is 14·5 knots with a range of 13000 nautical miles.

RESEARCHER (OSS 03) *National Ocean Survey*

2 OCEANOGRAPHIC SURVEY SHIPS (OSS): "OCEANOGRAPHER" CLASS

Name	*No.*	*Launched*	*Commissioned*
OCEANOGRAPHER	OSS 01	18 Apr 1964	13 July 1966
DISCOVERER	OSS 02	29 Oct 1964	29 Apr 1967

Displacement, tons	3 959 light
Dimensions, feet	303·3 oa × 52 × 18·5 (*92·4 m × 15·8 m × 5·6 m*)
Main engines	4 diesels with electric drive ; 5 000 bhp ; 2 shafts = 16+ knots
Complement	14 officers, 78 crewmen
Scientists	18

Ice strengthened construction. Fitted with a 5-ton capacity crane and a 3½-ton capacity crane. Built by Aerojet-General Corp, Jacksonville Shipyard, Jacksonville, Florida. *Discoverer* deactivated in 1973 and placed in reserve, but subsequently reactivated.

DESIGN. Fitted with computerised data acquisition system. Centre well 8 × 6 feet provides sheltered access to sea for SCUBA divers and for lowering research equipment. Six ports in submerged bow observation chamber. S2-MET-MA62a type.

ENGINEERING. A 400-horsepower, through-hull bow thruster provides precise manoeuvering. Not equipped for silent operation. Cruising speed is 16 knots with a range of 15 200 nautical miles.

OCEANOGRAPHER (OSS 01) *National Ocean Survey*

DISCOVERER (OSS 02) *National Ocean Survey*

Survey Ships—*continued*

DISCOVERER (OSS 02) see previous page *National Ocean Survey*

2 HYDROGRAPHIC SURVEY SHIPS (CSS): "PEIRCE" CLASS

Name	*No.*	*Launched*	*Commissioned*
PEIRCE	CSS 28	15 Oct 1962	6 May 1963
WHITING	CSS 29	20 Nov 1962	8 July 1963

Displacement, tons	760 light
Dimensions, feet	164 oa × 33 × 10·1 (*50·0 m × 10·0 m × 3·1 m*)
Main engines	2 diesels; 1 600 bhp; 2 shafts = 12·5+ knots
Complement	8 officers, 32 crewmen.

Designed for nearshore operations. Ice strengthened. Built by Marietta Manufacturing Co, Point Pleasant, West Virginia. SI-MT-59a type.

ENGINEERING. Controllable pitch-propellers. Cruising speed is 12·5 knots with a range of 4 500 nautical miles.

2 HYDROGRAPHIC SURVEY SHIPS (CSS): "McARTHUR" CLASS

Name	*No.*	*Launched*	*Commissioned*
McARTHUR	CSS 30	15 Nov 1965	15 Dec 1966
DAVIDSON	CSS 31	7 May 1966	10 Mar 1967

Displacement, tons	995 light
Dimensions, feet	175 oa × 38 × 11·5 (*53·0 m × 11·5 m × 3·5 m*)
Main engines	2 diesels; 1 600 bhp; 2 shafts = 13·5+ knots
Complement	8 officers, 32 crewmen

Designed for nearshore operations. Ice strengthened. Built by Norfolk SB & DD Co, Norfolk, Virginia. SI-MT-MA70a type.

ENGINEERING. Controllable-pitch propellers. Cruising speed is 13·5 knots with a range of 4 500 nautical miles.

McARTHUR (CSS 30) *National Ocean Survey*

1 HYDROGRAPHIC SURVEY SHIP (OSS): "SURVEYOR" TYPE

Name	*No.*	*Launched*	*Commissioned*
SURVEYOR	OSS 32	25 Apr 1959	30 Apr 1960

Displacement, tons	3 150 light
Dimensions, feet	292·3 oa × 46 × 18 (*88·8 m × 14·0 m × 5·5 m*)
Main engines	1 steam turbine (De Laval); 3 520 shp; 1 shaft = 15+ knots
Complement	14 officers, 106 crewmen
Scientists	9

Specially designed for marine charting and geophysical surveys. Fitted with helicopter platform aft. Ice strenghtened. Twin telescoping 2½-ton capacity cargo booms (forward) and 12½-ton capacity crane. Estimated cost $6 000 000 Built by National Steel & Co, San Diego, California. The *Surveyor* was deactivated in 1973 and placed in reserve, but subsequently reactivated.

DESIGN. Large bilge keel (18 inches × 70 feet) permits oceanographic observations to be performed up to Sea State 6. S2-S-RM28a type.

ENGINEERING. Retractable outboard motor mounted to stern for precision manoeuvering. Cruising speed is 15 knots with a range of 10 500 nautical miles.

DISPOSALS

Pathfinder OSS 30, ex-US Navy AGS 1 decommissioned in 1972 and stricken. See 1972-1973 edition for description and photograph.

SURVEYOR (OSS 32) *National Ocean Survey*

3 HYDROGRAPHIC SURVEY SHIPS (MSS): "FAIRWEATHER" CLASS

Name	*No.*	*Launched*	*Commissioned*
FAIRWEATHER	MSS 20	15 Mar 1967	2 Oct 1968
RAINIER	MSS 21	15 Mar 1967	2 Oct 1968
MT. MITCHELL	MSS 22	29 Nov 1966	23 Mar 1968

Displacement, tons	1 798 light
Dimensions, feet	231 oa × 42·07 × 13·9 (*70·2 m × 12·8 m × 4·2 m*)
Main engines	2 diesels; 2 400 bhp; 2 shafts = 13+ knots
Complement	12 officers, 64 crewmen
Scientists	2

Ice strengthened. Built by Aerojet-General Corp, Jacksonville Shipyard, Jacksonville, Fla. SI-MT-MA72a type.

ENGINEERING. Fitted with a 200-horsepower, through-bow thruster for precise manoeuvring. Controllable-pitch propellers. Cruising speed is 13 knots with a range of 9 000 nautical miles.

FAIRWEATHER (MSS 20) *National Ocean Survey*

RAINIER (MSS 21) *National Ocean Survey*

MT MITCHELL (MSS 22) *National Ocean Survey*

Survey Ships—*continued*

DAVIDSON (CSS 31) *National Ocean Survey*

WHITING (CSS 29) *National Ocean Survey*

PEIRCE (CSS 28) *National Ocean Survey*

COASTAL VESSELS

2 WIRE DRAG VESSELS (ASV); "RUDE" CLASS

Name	*No.*	*Launched*	*Commissioned*
RUDE	ASV 90	17 Aug 1966	29 Mar 1967
HECK	ASV 91	1 Nov 1966	29 Mar 1967

Displacement, tons	214 light
Dimensions, feet	90 oa × 22 × 7 (*27·4 m × 6·7 m × 2·1 m*)
Main engines	2 diesels ; 800 bhp ; 2 shafts = 11·5+ knots
Complement	2 officers, 8 crewmen

Designed to search out underwater navigational hazards along the coast using wire drags. Built by Jacobson Shipyard Inc, Oyster Bay, New York. SI-MT-MA71a type. A single commanding officer is assigned to both vessels; normally he rides one ship and the executive officer the other.

ENGINEERING. Propellers are guarded by shrouds similar to Kort nozzles. Auxiliary propulsion provides 50 horsepower to each propeller for dragging operations. Cruising speed is 11·5 knots with a range of 740 nautical miles (provisions carried for eight days.)

Coastal Vessels—*continued*

RUDE (ASV 90) *National Ocean Survey*

1 CURRENT SURVEY VESSEL (ASV); "FERREL" TYPE

Name	*No.*	*Launched*	*Commissioned*
FERREL	ASV 92	4 Apr 1968	4 June 1968

Displacement, tons	363 light
Dimensions, feet	133·25 × 32 × 7 (*40·5 m × 9·7 m × 2·1 m*)
Main engines	2 diesels ; 820 bhp ; 2 shafts = 10+ knots
Complement	3 officers, 13 crewmen

Specially designed to conduct nearshore and estuarine current surveys. Limited surface meteorological observations are also made. Buoy workshop provided in 450-square feet of enclosed deck area with buoy stowage on open after deck. Built by Zeigler Shipyard, Jennings, Louisiana. SI-MT-MA83a type.

ENGINEERING. Fitted with 100-horsepower, electric-driven bow thruster. Cruising speed is 10 knots (provisions for 15 days carried).

FERREL (ASV 92) *National Ocean Survey*

FERREL (ASV 92) *National Ocean Survey*

UNION OF SOVIET SOCIALIST REPUBLICS

Flag Officers Soviet Navy

Commander-in-Chief of the Soviet Navy and First Deputy Minister of Defence:	Admiral of the Fleet of the Soviet Union Sergei Georgiyevich Gorshkov
First Deputy Commander-in-Chief of the Soviet Navy:	Admiral of the Fleet N. I. Smirnov
Assistant Chief of the General Staff of the Armed Forces:	Admiral of the Fleet S. M. Lobov
Deputy Commander-in-Chief:	Admiral N. N. Amelko
Deputy Commander-in-Chief:	Engineer Admiral P. G. Kotov
Deputy Commander-in-Chief:	Engineer Vice-Admiral V. G. Novikov
Deputy Commander-in-Chief:	Admiral G. A. Bondarenko
Commander of Naval Aviation:	Colonel-General A. A. Mironenko
Chief of the Political Directorate:	Admiral V. M. Grishanov
Chief of Rear Services:	Vice-Admiral L. Y. Mizin
Chief of Naval Training Establishments:	Vice-Admiral I. M. Kuznetsov
Chief of Main Naval Staff:	Admiral of the Fleet N. D. Sergeyev
1st Deputy Chief of the Main Naval Staff:	Admiral V. N. Alekseyev
Chief of the Hydrographic Service:	Admiral A. I. Rassokho
Northern Fleet	
Commander-in-Chief:	Admiral of the Fleet G. M. Yegorov
1st Deputy Commander-in-Chief:	Vice-Admiral Ye. I. Volobuyev
Chief of Staff:	Vice-Admiral V. G. Kichev
In Command of the Political Department:	Vice-Admiral A. I. Sorokin
Pacific	
Commander-in-Chief:	Vice-Admiral V. P. Maslov
1st Deputy Commander-in-Chief:	—
Chief of Staff:	Vice-Admiral V. V. Sidorov
In Command of the Political Department:	Vice Admiral S. S. Bevz
Black Sea	
Commander-in-Chief:	Vice-Admiral N. I. Khovrin
1st Deputy Commander-in-Chief:	Vice-Admiral V. Samoylov
Chief of Staff:	Rear-Admiral V. Kh. Saakyan
In Command of the Political Department:	Vice-Admiral I. S. Rudnev
Baltic	
Commander-in-Chief:	Admiral V. V. Mikhailin
1st Deputy Commander-in-Chief:	Rear-Admiral Ya. M. Kudelkin
Chief of Staff:	Vice-Admiral A. Kosov
In Command of the Political Department:	Vice-Admiral N. I. Shablikov
Caspian Flotilla	
Commander-in-Chief:	Rear-Admiral L. D. Ryabtsev
In Command of the Political Department:	Rear-Admiral V. N. Sergeyev
Leningrad Naval Base	
Commanding Officer:	Vice-Admiral V. M. Leonenkov
In Command of the Political Department:	Rear-Admiral A. A. Plekhanov
Head of the Order of Lenin Naval Academy:	Admiral V. S. Sysoyev
Head of Frunze Naval College:	Vice-Admiral V. A. Khrenov

Diplomatic Representation

Naval Attaché London: Captain V. Z. Khuzhokov

Personnel

(a) 1975: Approximately 550 000 officers and ratings
(b) Voluntary service (approx 30%)—remainder 3 years National Service at sea and 2 if ashore

Mercantile Marine

Lloyd's Register of Shipping: 7 342 vessels of 18 175 918 tons gross

Main Naval Bases

North: Murmansk, Archangelsk, Polyarno, Severodvinsk (building).
Baltic: Leningrad (Kronstadt), Tallinn, Lepaia, Baltiisk.
Black Sea: Sevastopol, Tuapse, Poti, Nikolaev (building)
Pacific: Vladivostock, Nakhodka, Sovetskaia Gavan, Magadan, Petropavlovsk.

Deletions and Conversions

Whilst it is not possible to provide an accurate estimate of total deletions and conversions during the last year the following is a guide to those estimates used in this section.

Submarines
Echo I converted from SSGN to SSN
Decrease of 10 "Whisky" Class.

Destroyers
"Kashin" Class conversions with SSM
1 "Krupny" Class conversion to "Kanin" Class.
"Kildin" Class conversions continue.

Frigates
Possible conversions of "Kola" Class to auxiliaries.

Corvettes
Conversion of some "Grisha" Class to all-gun ships.
Deletion of 3 "Kronstadt" Class.

Fast Attack Craft
Deletion of 10 "Komar" Class.
Deletion of 20 "P6, 8 and 10" Classes.
Deletion of 5 "P4" Class.

Mine Warfare Forces
Deletion of 5 "T 301" Class.

Support Ships
2 "Tovda" Class deleted.

Pennant Numbers

The Soviet Navy has frequent changes of pennant numbers and so these are of little use in identifying individual ships. For that reason such a list has been omitted in this section.

Building Programme

The following is an abstract of the programme used in estimating force levels.

Aircraft Carriers
2 "Kuril" class building as start of continuing programme.

Submarines
Continuing programme for "Delta II", "Delta", "Charlie", "Victor", "Uniform" and "Tango" classes

Cruisers
Continuing programme for "Kara" and "Kresta II" classes

Destroyers
"Krivak" class continues

Corvettes
"Grisha" and "Nanuchka" class continue

Light Forces
New "Turya" class hydrofoil

Minewarfare Forces
New "Sonya" class (MSC). "Natya" class continues.

Amphibious Forces
New class of LCTs under construction

Air Cushion Vehicles
A large programme of unknown size

Support and Depot Ships
"Amur" and "Ugra" classes continuing
New "Amga" class

AGIs
One extra "Moma" class

Subsequent types and classes have been revised from new information, not necessarily as new construction.

SOVIET NAVAL STRENGTHS

Class	North	Baltic	Black Sea (incl. Caspian)	Pacific	Total
Submarines					
Delta II	1	—	—	—	1
Delta	6	—	—	—	5
Yankee	25	—	—	8	33
Hotel III	1	—	—	—	1
Hotel II	5	—	—	3	8
Papa	1	—	—	—	1
Charlie	12	—	—	—	12
Echo II	15	—	—	12	27
Echo I	1	—	—	—	1
Uniform	1	—	—	—	1
November	9	—	—	4	13
Victor	14	—	—	2	16
Golf I & II	14	—	—	8	22
Zulu V	1	—	—	—	1
Juliet	11	—	—	5	16
W Twin Cylinder W Long Bin	5	2	1	4	5 7
Alpha	1	—	—	—	1
Bravo	1	1	1	1	4
Tango	—	—	1	—	1
Foxtrot	31	14	—	11	56
Romeo	—	5	9	—	14
Quebec	—	11	11	—	22
Zulu IV	9	3	—	4	19
Whisky	10	40	22	28	100
Whisky Canvas Bag	1	—	—	2	3
Surface Ships					
Kuril	—	—	1+1	—	1+1
Kara	1	—	2	—	3
Moskva	—	—	2	—	2
Sverdlov	2	3	4	3	12
Chapaev	1	1	—	—	2
Kirov	—	1	1	—	2
Kresta II	3	2	1	—	6+2

Class	North	Baltic	Black Sea (incl. Caspian)	Pacific	Total
Kresta I	3	—	—	1	4
Kynda	—	—	2	2	4
Krivak	1	6	2	—	9
Kashin	3	3	8	5	19
Kanin	3	2	—	1	6
Krupny	—	—	—	1	1
SAM Kotlin	2	1	3	2	8
Kildin	—	2	2	—	4
Kotlin	3	3	4	8	18
Tallin	—	1	—	—	1
Skory	10	10	10	10	40
Nanuchka	3	5	4	—	12
Mirka I and II	4	4	8	4	20
Petya I and II	10	12	13	10	45
Kola	—	1	3	2	6
Riga	10	9	12	9	40
Ugra	5	3	—	2	10
Lama	2	—	1	2	5
Don	3	—	—	3	6
Grisha	4	6	5	2	17
Poti	25	25	5	15	70
Kronstadt	5	4	4	4	17
Purga	—	1	—	—	1
Amga	1	—	—	—	1
Alesha	1	1	—	—	2
W. Bauer	1	1	—	—	2
Amur	4	4	—	4	12
Oskol	3	3	1	3	10
Atrek	4	1	—	1	6
Dnepr	4	1	—	—	5
Tovda	—	1	—	—	1
Fleet Sweepers	40	61	40	50	191
					(16 Natya 45 Yurka 20 T 58 110 T 43)

Class	North	Baltic	Black Sea (incl. Caspian)	Pacific	Total
Coastal Sweepers	25	46	25	25	121
					(3 Sonya 3 Zhenya 70 Vanya 40 Sasha 5 T 301)
Inshore Sweepers	25	25	25	25	100
Pchela	—	10	15	—	25
Turya	—	6	6	—	12
Komar	—	5	10	—	15
Osa	25	35	25	35	120
					(65 Type I 55 Type II)
Stenka	10	24	4	7	45
SO 1	—	40	30	10	80
MO VI	—	15	—	—	15
FAC—Torpedo	15	60	15	40	130
					(45 Shershen 80 P6, 8, 10 5 P4)
River Patrol Craft	—	10	40	40	90
					(40 Schmel 30 BK III 20 BKL IV)
Alligator	2	4	3	3	12
Polnocny	12	15	18	15	60
Landing Craft	15	16	30	20	81
					(10 MP 10 5 MP 8 8 MP 6 15 MP 4 8 MP 2 35 Vydra)
Intelligence Ships (AGIs)	16	8	15	15	54

Overall Totals

Aircraft Carriers	2 building
Helicopter Cruisers	2
Submarines (SSBN)	49 + 15 building
Submarines (SSB)	23
Submarines (SSGN)	40
Submarines (SSG)	28
Submarines (SSN)	31
Submarines (SS)	217
Cruisers (CLG)	20 + 2 building
Cruisers (Gun)	13
Destroyers (DDG)	47
Destroyers (Gun)	59
Frigates	109
Corvettes (Missile)	26
Corvettes	170

Fast Attack Craft (Missile)	135
Fast Attack Craft (Patrol)	60
Fast Attack Craft (Hydrofoil)	37
Fast Attack Craft (Torpedo)	85
River Patrol Craft	90
Minesweepers—Ocean	191
Minesweepers—Coastal	121
Minesweepers—Inshore	100
LSTs	12
LCTs	60
LCUs	81
Depot and Repair Ships	61
Intelligence Collectors (AGI)	54
Survey Ships	97

Research Ships	32
Fishery Research Ships	192
Space Associated Ships	23
Fleet Replenishment Ships	4
Tankers	24
Harbour Tankers	18
Salvage Vessels	19
Rescue Ships	15
Training Ships	27
Lifting Ships	15
Icebreakers (Nuclear)	4
Icebreakers	38
Cable Ships	6
Large Tugs	120

SOVIET NAVAL AVIATION

The Soviet Navy operates 1 200 fixed-wing aircraft and helicopters in *Morskaya Aviatsiya*, the world's second largest naval air arm. The primary combat components are
(1) Long range and medium bombers employed in the maritime reconnaissance role
(2) Medium bombers mostly equipped with air-to-surface missiles in the anti-ship strike role.
(3) Land based patrol aircraft, amphibians and helicopters in the anti-submarine role.
The Soviet Navy flies no fixed-wing aircraft from ships, but several medium classes of destroyers and all modern missile armed cruisers, and the cruiser-helicopter ships *Moskva* and *Leningrad* can carry helicopters. The two helicopter ships are the largest built to date by any navy specifically for anti-submarine operations and are the first Soviet warships intended primarily for aviation activities.

Bombers. The Soviet naval air arm has about 55 heavy and 550 medium bombers in the anti-shipping, strike, tanker and reconnaissance roles. The main strike force comprises about 300 "Badger" equipped with "Kipper" and "Kelt" air-to-surface missiles. The reconnaissance aircraft are about 55 "Bear D" (long range recce); 55 "Badger" and a similar number of "Blinder A". The latter and some of the "Badger" have a bombing capability.

ASW Helicopters. Over 200 anti-submarine helicopters are believed to be in the naval air arm, mostly Ka-25 "Hormone" (a twin-turbine craft known as the "Harp" in the prototype stage) and some of the older Mi-4 "Hound" helicopters. The "Hormone" anti-submarine helicopters, armed with torpedoes or other ASW weapons operate from the large helicopter cruisers *Moskva* and *Leningrad* which can each operate some 15 to 20 helicopters, servicing them in a hangar below the flight deck. They have also been seen in the "Kara", "Kresta" I and "Kresta II" class cruisers which are the first Soviet ships of this type to be fitted with a helicopter hangar. In some of these ships the radar fitted helicopter may also have a reconnaissance role associated with the surface-to-surface missile system. The older MI-4 "Hound" and other "Hormone" helicopters are used in the ASW role from shore bases. Other types of helicopter are also used in the transport role ashore.

ASW Patrol Aircraft. The Soviet Union is the only nation other than Japan maintaining modern military flying boats, about 100 Be-12 "Mail" (turboprop) aircraft of this type being operational. The latter aircraft, an amphibian often photographed on runways, has an advanced anti-submarine capability evidenced by a radome extending forward, a Magnetic Anomaly Detector (MAD) boom extending aft and a weapons bay in the rear fuselage.
The "May", of which some 75 are in service, is a militarised version of the four-turboprop commercial air freighter (code name "Coot") in wide commercial service. The patrol/anti-submarine version has been lengthened and fitted with a MAD boom as well as other electronic equipment and a weapons capability similar to the US Navy's conversion of the Lockheed Electra into the P-3 "Orion" patrol aircraft.

Transports/Training Aircraft. There are also a few hundred transports, utility, and training fixed-wing aircraft and helicopters under Navy control.

*Aircraft names are NATO code names; "B" names indicate bombers, "H" names for helicopters, and "M" names for miscellaneous aircraft.

SOVIET NAVAL MISSILES

Surface-to-Surface

Type	System	Missile Code-Name	Launch Platform	No. of Tubes/ Launchers	Max speed	Max Range (n. miles)	Length (feet)	Notes
SSM (cruise)	SSN-1	Scrubber	1 "Krupny" destroyer	2	0·9	130	22·5	Subsonic and obsolescent. Limited use after 1975. Operational in 1958.
SSM (cruise)	SSN-2	Styx	15 "Komar" FAC 65 "Osa" I FAC	2 4	0·9	23	15	Two versions—A and B. Probably has an active radar homing capability. Operational in 1960.
SSM (cruise)	SSN-3	Shaddock	4 "Kynda" cruisers 4 "Kresta I" cruisers 16 "Juliet" submarines 27 "Echo II" submarines 7 "Whisky Long Bin" submarines 5 "Whisky Twin Cylinder" submarines	8 4 4 8 4 2	0·9-1·5	150-250	42	In some cases requires external guidance from aircraft. There is evidence that this missile may be pre-programmed for shorter ranges and have an active radar terminal homing capability. Operational in 1961-62.
Strat	SSN-4	Sark	11 "Golf I" submarines 1 "Zulu V" submarine	3 2	—	300	37·5	An obsolescent system now being phased-out with the submarines carrying it. Operational in 1958-60
Strat	SSN-5	Serb	11 "Golf II" submarines 8 "Hotel II" submarines	3 3	—	700	35	Development of SSN-4 system. Operational in 1963.
Strat	SSN-6	Sawfly	33 "Yankee" submarines	16	—	1 300	42	Dived launch. Operational in 1969.
SSM (dived cruise)	SSN-7		12 "Charlie" submarines	8	1·5	30	22	Dived launch. Operational in 1969-70.
Strat	SSN-8		6+14 "Delta" submarines 1 "Delta II" submarine	12 16 (?)	—	4 200	45 est	Dived launch. Operational in 1973.
SSM	SSN-9		12 "Nanuchka" missile corvettes	6	1·0+	150	30 est	Operational in 1968-69.
SSM	SS-N-10		3 "Kara" cruisers 8 "Kresta II" cruisers 9 "Krivak" destroyers	8 8 4	1·2	29	25 est	Operational in 1968.
SSM	SSN-11		55 "Osa II" FAC 4 Modified "Kildin" destroyers 1+ Modified "Kashin" destroyer	4 4 4	0·9	29	21	Probably modified Styx with folding wings. Low altitude capability.

Surface-to-Air

Type	System	Missile Code-Name	Launch Platform	No. of Tubes/ Launchers	Max speed	Slant Range	Length (feet)
SAM	SAN-1	Goa	8 SAM "Kotlin" destroyers	2 (1 twin)	2	17	
			6 "Kanin" destroyers	2 (1 twin)			
			19 "Kashin" destroyers	4 (2 twin)			
			4 "Kynda" cruisers	2 (1 twin)			
			4 "Kresta I" cruisers	4 (2 twin)			
SAM	SAN-2	Guideline	1 "Dzerzhinski" cruiser	2 (1 twin)		25	
SAM	SAN-3	Goblet	1+1 "Kuril" aircraft carriers	4 (2 twin)			
			2 "Moskva" cruisers	4 (2 twin)		20	
			8 "Kresta II" cruisers	4 (2 twin)			
SAM	SAN-4		3 "Kara" cruisers	4 (2 twin)			
			1+1 "Kuril" aircraft carriers	6 (3 twin)			
			2 "Sverdlov" conversion cruisers	2 (1 twin)		20	
			3 "Kara" cruisers	4 (2 twin)			
			9 "Krivak" destroyers	4 (2 twin)			
			12 "Nanuchka" missile corvettes	2 (1 twin)			
			14 "Grisha" corvettes	2 (1 twin)			
SAM	SAN-7	Grail	120 "Osa I and II" FAC 45 "Shershen" FAC	1	1·5	2	4·8

Air-to-Surface

Type	System	Missile Code-Name	Launch Platform	No. of Tubes/ Launchers	Max speed	Max Range (n. miles)	Notes
ASM	AS-1	Kennel	c50 "Badger B" bomber	2	0·9	55	Obsolete.
ASM	AS-2	Kipper	c150 "Badger C" bomber	1	1·0+	115	Obsolescent
ASM	AS-3	Kangaroo	c20 "Bear B" and "C" bomber	2	1·5+	400	
ASM	AS-4	Kitchen	? "Blinder B" bomber	1	2+	185	Inertial Guided.
ASM	AS-5	Kelt	c150 "Badger G"	2	0·9	120	Replacing AS-1 Active homer.
ASM	AS-6	—	c50 "Badger modified" bombers	2	2	300 ?	Possibly also to be used in "Backfire" Operational in 1970.

NOTE: Numbers of aircraft under AS-1 to AS-6 are approximate

SOVIET NAVAL RADARS

Code Name	Freq. Band	Function	Ship Application
Ball End	S	Surface warning	Kola
Ball Gun	S	Surface warning	Kronstadt and older Light Forces
Big Net	L	Long-range air warning	Kresta I, Kashin (some) Dzerzhinski
Boat Sail	S or L	Surveillance	Whisky Canvas Bag
Cross Bird	G	Early warning	Obsolescent older Destroyers
Dead Duck	C	IFF	General
Don-2	X	Navigation	
Drum Tilt	X	Short-range armament Control	General with 30 mm guns
Egg Cup	S	Fire Control	
Fan Song E	C	Control for SA-N-2	Dzerzhinski
Flat Spin	L or S	Air surveillance	Some destroyers
Hair Net	S	Search & Surveillance	Kildins, Kotlins and Frigates
Half Bow		Torpedo fire control	Older destroyers
Hawk Screech/ Owl Screech	C	Acquisition and fire control for main armament	Ships mounting 57—100 mm guns
Head Light	X and C	Missile control	Most modern major surface ships
Head Net A	S	Air surveillance	Kynda, Kashin, Krupny and other destroyers
Head Net B	S	Air surveillance	Krupny (some)
Head Net C	S	Air surveillance and Height Finder	Kiev, Moskva, Kara, Kresta I and II and SAM fitted destroyers
High Lune	S	Height finder	Dzerzhinski (with FanSong E)
High Pole	C	IFF	General
High Sieve	S	Surveillance	
Horn Spoon		Navigation	General
Knife Rest	I	Air warning	Sverdlov's and Kildin's
Long Bow		Torpedo fire control	Destroyers

Code Name	Freq. Band	Function	Ship Application
Low Sieve	S	Surface search	
Muff Cob	C or X	Fire control	Moskva, Kresta I & II, Ugra, Lama, Poti, T58, Polnocny, Light Forces
Neptune	X	Navigation	Light Forces
Owl Screech (see Hawk Screech)			
Peel Group	X	SA-N-1 fire control	Kresta I, Kashin, Kynda, SAM Kotlin, Kanin
Plinth Net		Surface search	Obsolete
Post Lamp	X	Fire Control	Older destroyers
Pot Drum	X	Surface search	Some Light Forces and Kronstadts
Pot Head	X	Surface search	Some Light Forces and Kronstadts
Round Top		Fire control system	Older destroyers
Scoop Pair	E	SS-N-3 guidance	Kresta I and Kynda
Ship Globe	E	Missile Tracking	Instrumentation ships
Skin Head	X	Surface search	Some Light Forces & Krupny
Slim Net	S	Surface search	Some destroyers and frigates
Snoop Plate	X	Surveillance	Submarines
Snoop Slab	X	Surveillance	Submarines
Snoop Tray	X	Surveillance	Submarines
Square Head	C	IFF interrogator	Osa, Kotlin and Skory
Square Tie	X	Surface search	Osa
Strut Curve	S	Medium range search	Poti, Support ships
Sun Visor B	X	Fire control	
Top Bow	X	Fire control	Some cruisers and destroyers
Top Sail	L	Air surveillance	Moskva, Kiev, Kara, Kresta II
Top Trough	S	Surface Search	Sverdlov's
Wasp Head		Fire control system	Older destroyers
Witch Five	C	IFF	Some cruisers and destroyers

AIRCRAFT CARRIERS

1+1 "KURIL" CLASS (AIRCRAFT CARRIERS)

KIEV **MINSK**

Displacement, tons	35 000-40 000
Length, feet (*metres*)	925 (*282*) oa; 880 (*268*) wl; 100 (*30·5*) (hull)
Beam, feet (*metres*)	200 (*61*) (overall, including flight deck and sponsons)
Aircraft (estimated)	25 fixed wing (? Freehand type) 25 Hormone A or modified Hind A helicopters
Missile launchers	2 twin SAN-3 for Goblet missiles 1 ASW twin launcher; possibly 3-4 SAN-4 launchers
Guns	28—57 mm (see note)
A/S weapons	2—12 barrelled MBU launchers forward
Speed, knots	At least 30

The *Kiev*, now fitting out at Nikolayev, and her sister building at the same yard, mark an impressive and logical advance by the Soviet Navy. The arrival of these ships has been heralded by Admiral Gorshkov's support for embarked tactical air as a necessity for navies employed in extending political influence far abroad, and by a softening of previous Soviet criticisms of this class of ship.

Kiev appears to be a carrier designed for VTOL aircraft and helicopter operations. There is at present no sign of steam catapults, arrester gear, mirror-landing-sights, and all the expensive gear required for fixed-wing operations. Nor is there yet any evidence of the existence of a fixed-wing aircraft suitable for carrier operations. On the other hand, the Freehand VTOL aircraft or its derivative, the Hormone A helicopter or a modification of the Army's Hind A helicopter could all be embarked. Two examples of the former, designed by Yakovlev, appeared at the 1967 Domodedovo air show, were clearly subsonic and mounted 16-round rocket packs under each wing in one aircraft. They were powered by twin Turbo-jet engines, had a wide fuselage to accommodate these and short delta wings of about 27 ft wing-span. The overall length of the aircraft was about 58 ft. Since 1967 further trials of what is apparently an improved version of Freehand have continued at Ramenskoye airfield near Moscow, culminating in sea trials from a specially fitted pad on the flight-deck of *Moskva*. These were primarily in the Black Sea—her subsequent deployment to the Mediterranean may have indicated stage two in these trials. The provision of a 550-600 ft angled flight deck in the *Kiev* would allow the VTOL aircraft an increase of up to 25% in their take-off weight.

A rough estimate of her hangar capacity suggests that *Kiev* could carry 25 of each type simultaneously. Her forward lift appears to be adequate to accommodate a Freehand type but until more detailed evidence is available this, with many other deductions, must remain conjectural. Her armament is of interest, her missiles being, if present estimates are correct, similar to those in *Moskva* with the addition of SAN 4 whilst she may carry a heavy armament of medium calibre guns. The missile systems SAN-3, using Goblet missiles with a slant range of some 20 miles, are possibly to balance the lack of embarked high-performance fighters and are of longer range than the BPDMS's with Sea Sparrow which are fitted in the latest U.S. carriers. The heavy gun armament is a complete break with the latter's armament—neither *Nimitz* nor *Enterprise* carry any guns. But provision of an increasingly heavy conventional gun-armament can be seen throughout the Soviet surface fleet and this class could be a prime example of this trend.

If *Kiev* turns out to have similar A/S weapons to *Moskva* (Twin A/S rocket launchers forward and a possible A/S weapon launcher) another radical change in carrier practice will have been seen. The A/S rocket launchers would presuppose a sonar fit of a hull mounted set and/or VDS, showing the Soviets have taken the submarine threat seriously. Success with such a system depends very largely on the speed and handling of that ship and the efficiency of the A/S helicopters which, presumably, would work with the weapon launcher.

With world-wide Soviet deployments a pair of ships is clearly insufficient, allowing for maintenance and any refitting required. The design of the carrier must have been on the drawing-board before *Moskva* was commissioned in 1967. Perhaps the decision to build more of the latter was delayed until after the extensive heavy-weather operations which *Moskva* and *Leningrad* carried out. It seems most likely that these were sufficiently successful to encourage the Soviet navy to proceed with the larger ships. A minimum of six would be not unlikely.

They will be a powerful addition to the political impact of the Soviet fleet in peacetime. With ships capable of operating VTOL strike aircraft and troop-lift helicopters their credibility in the intervention role would be increased, and their fleet would be that much more prepared for hostilities. Such ships roles could be changed merely by alterations in the number and type of aircraft enbarked. They are clearly not as enormously expensive as the US nuclear-powered carriers but will greatly enhance the manifest capability of the Soviet fleet to operate effectively world-wide in both peace and war.

GUNNERY. There is some doubt about the main battery. It may turn out to be a lesser number of 76 mm backed by some 57 mm.

RADAR. Top Sail and Headlight.

SONAR. Possibly hull-mounted and VDS.

SOVIET TYPE NAME. Protivo Lodochny Kreyser meaning Anti-submarine cruiser. This is an interesting designation for a ship of this size, suggesting a bias towards A/S in her future employment but more probably aimed at circumventing the restrictions on aircraft carriers in the Montreux Convention, regulating the use of the Turkish Straits.

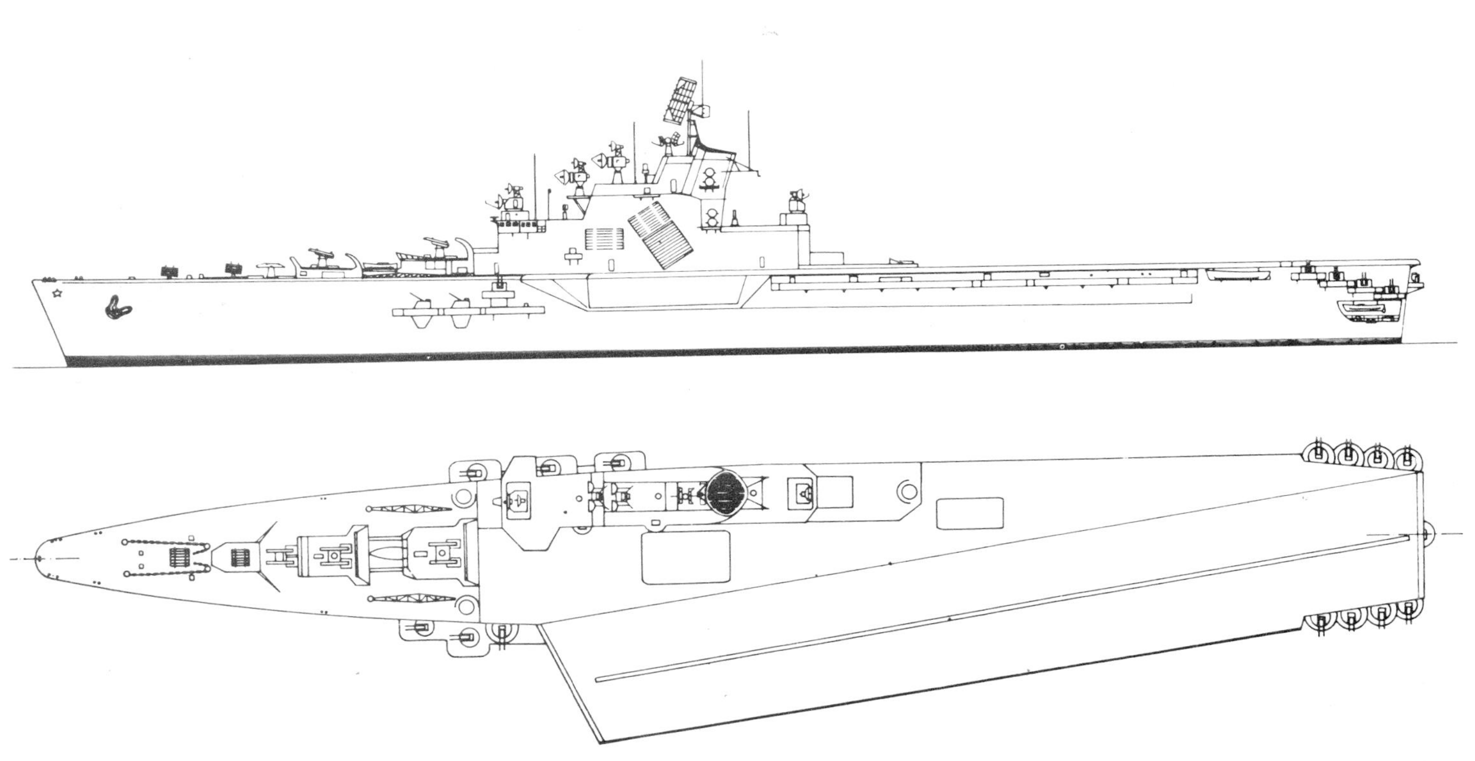

HELICOPTER CRUISERS

2 "MOSKVA" CLASS

LENINGRAD **MOSKVA**

Displacement, tons	15 000 standard; 18 000 full load
Length, feet (*metres*)	624·8 (*190·5*); 644·8 oa (*196·6*)
Flight deck, feet (*m*)	295·3 (*90·0*) aft of superstructure
Width, feet (*metres*)	115·0 (*35·0*)
Beam, feet (*metres*)	75·9 (*23*)
Draught, feet (*metres*)	24·9 (*7·6*)
Aircraft	18 Hormone A ASW helicopters
Missile launchers	2 surface-to-air "SAN-3" systems of twin launchers (180 reloads) and 1 twin launcher for anti-submarine missiles
Guns,	4—57 mm (2 twin mountings)
A/S weapons	2—12 tube MBUs on forecastle
Torpedo tubes	2 quintuple 21 inch
Main engines	Geared turbines; 2 shafts; 100 000 shp
Boilers	4 watertube
Speed, knots	30 max
Complement	800

GENERAL
Both built at Nikolayev, *Moskva* probably being laid down in 1962-3 as she carried out sea-trials in mid-1967. This class represented a radical change of thought in the Soviet fleet. The design must have been completed while the "*November*" class submarines were building and with her heavy A/S armament and efficient sensors (helicopters and VDS) suggests an awareness of the problem of dealing with nuclear submarines. Alongside what is apparently a primary A/S role these ships have a capability for A/A warning and self-defence as well as a command function. With a full fit of radar and ECM equipment they clearly represent good value for money. Both ships handle well in heavy weather and are capable of helicopter-operations under adverse conditions. Why only two were built is discussed earlier in the notes on the "*Kiev*" class aircraft carriers.

MODIFICATION. In early 1973 *Moskva* was seen with a landing pad on the after end of the flight deck, probably for flight tests of VTOL aircraft.

RADAR. Search: Top Sail 3-D and Head Net C 3-D. Fire control: Head Light (2). Muff Cob. Miscellaneous: Electronic warfare equipment.

SONAR. VDS and, probably, hull mounted set. In addition all helicopters have dunking-sonar.

SOVIET TYPE NAME. Protivo Lodochny Kreyser meaning Anti-Submarine Cruiser.

MOSKVA 1972

MOSKVA 1968, US Navy

Helicopter Cruisers—*continued*

MOSKVA with landing pad aft *1973*

MOSKVA *MOD. 1970*

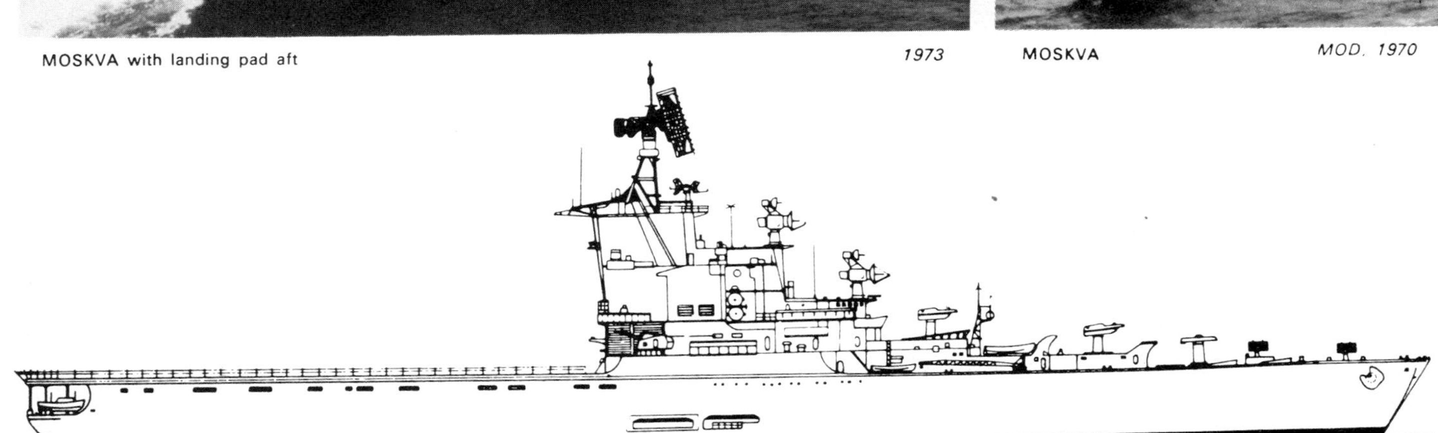

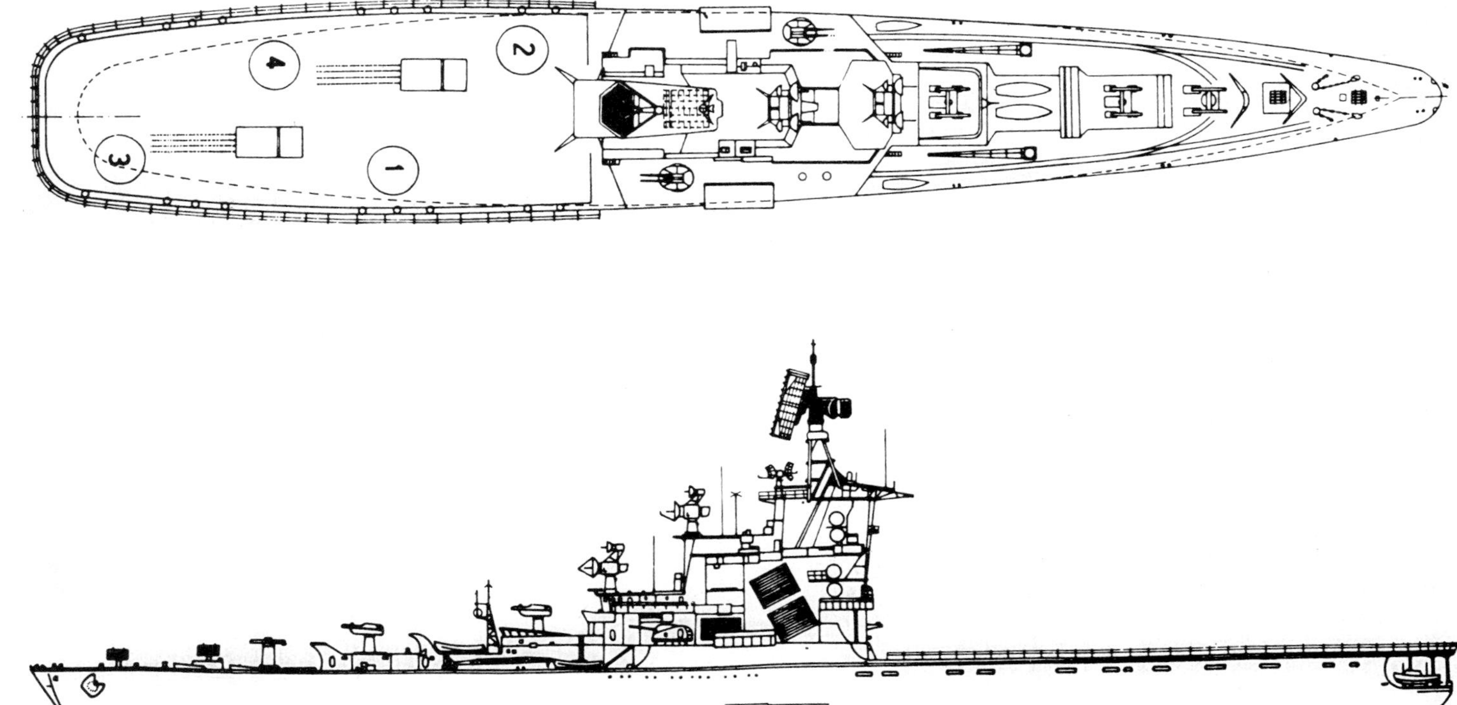

SUBMARINES

Ballistic Missile classes

1+1 "DELTA II" CLASS

(BALLISTIC MISSILE SUBMARINES SSBN's)

This submarine, announced in November 1973, is believed to carry more than the 12 launchers in the Delta class (possibly 16).

6 + 14 "DELTA" CLASS

(BALLISTIC MISSILE SUBMARINES SSBN's)

Displacement, tons	8 000 surfaced; 9 000 dived
Length, feet (*metres*)	426·5 (*130·0*)
Beam, feet (*metres*)	34·8 (*10·6*)
Draught, feet (*metres*)	32·8 (*10·0*)
Missile launchers	12 SSN-8 tubes
Torpedo tubes	8—21 in
Main machinery	Nuclear reactors; Steam turbines; 2 screws; 24 000 shp
Speed, knots	25
Complement	About 120

This reconstruction of the "Yankee" class SSBN s was announced at the end of 1972. The missile armament is twelve SSN-8 s with a range of 4 200 nautical miles. at present believed to carry single heads, rather than MRV s. As the SSN-6 has already been tested with MRV warheads, however, it is not unlikely that these missiles will, in due course be similarly armed. Otherwise the details of this class are similar to the "Yankee" class. The longer-range SSN-8 missiles are of greater length than the SSN-6s and, as this length can not be accommodated below the keel, they stand several feet proud of the after-casing. At the same time their presumed greater diameter and the need to compensate for the additional top-weight would seem to be the reasons for the reduction to twelve missiles in this class. The total "Delta" class building programme depends on the final outcome of the various Strategic Arms Limitation Talks (SALT). As this is unclear and dependent on so many external influences it is unwise to forecast any figure. A building rate of 6-8 SSBN s per year is well within Soviet capabilities.

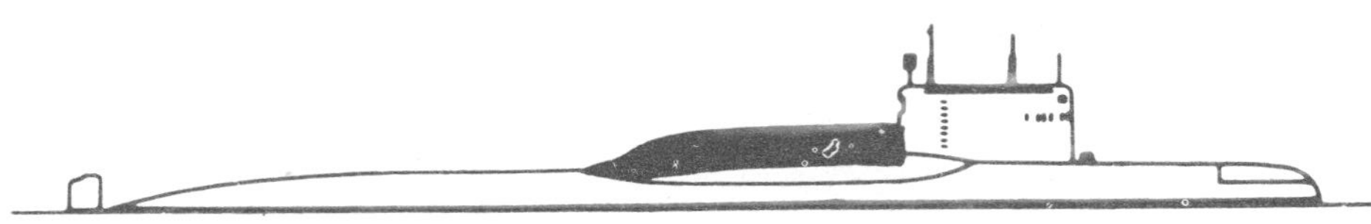

"Delta" Class

"Delta" Class 1973

Submarines— *continued*
Ballistic Missile classes

33 "YANKEE" CLASS

(BALLISTIC MISSILE SUBMARINES SSBN's)

Displacement, tons	8 000 surface; 9 000 submerged
Length, feet (*metres*)	426·5 (*130·0*)
Beam, feet (*metres*)	34·8 (*10·6*)
Draught, feet (*metres*)	32·8 (*10·0*)
Missile launchers	16 SSN-6 tubes
Torpedo tubes	8—21 in
Main-machinery	Nuclear reactors; steam turbines; 24 000 shp
Speed, knots	25
Complement	About 120

The first units of this class were reported in 1968. The vertical launching tubes are arranged in two rows of eight, and the missiles have a range of 1 300 nautical miles. These missiles have been tested with MRV warheads and these, presumably, will soon be operational.

At about the time that the USS *George Washington* was laid down (1 Nov 1957) as the world's first SSBN it is likely that the Soviet Navy embarked on its own major SSBN programme. With experience gained from the diesel-propelled "Golf" class and the nuclear-propelled "Hotel" class, both originally carrying three SS-N4 (350 mile) missiles in the fin, the "Yankee" design was completed mounting 16 SSN-6 missiles in the hull in two banks of 8. The first of the class was delivered late-1967 and the programme then accelerated from 4 boats in 1968 to 8 in 1971. The original deployment of this class was to the Eastern seaboard of the US giving a coverage at least as far as the Mississippi. Increase in numbers allowed a Pacific patrol to be established off California extending coverage at least as far as the Rockies. To provide greater coverage and more flexible operations a longer range missile system was needed and this is now at sea in the "Delta" class.

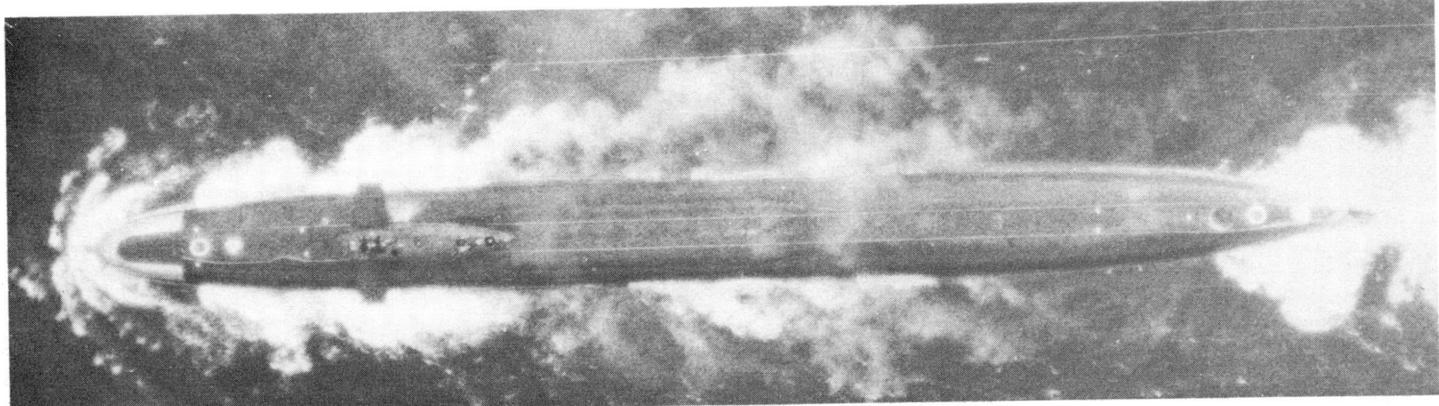

"Yankee" Class 1972

"Yankee" Class 1970

"Yankee" Class 1970 S. Breyer

Submarines—*continued*
Ballistic Missile classes

1 "HOTEL III" CLASS
8 "HOTEL II" CLASS
(BALLISTIC MISSILE SUBMARINES SSBNs)

Displacement, tons	3 700 surface; 4 100 submerged
Length, feet (*metres*)	377·2 (*115·2*)
Beam, feet (*metres*)	28·2 (*8·6*)
Draught, feet (*metres*)	25 (*7·6*)
Missile launchers	3 SSN-5 tubes
Torpedo tubes	6—21 in (bow); 4—16 in (aft) (anti-submarine)
Main machinery	Nuclear reactor, steam turbine; 22 500 shp
Speed, knots	20 (dived)
Complement	90

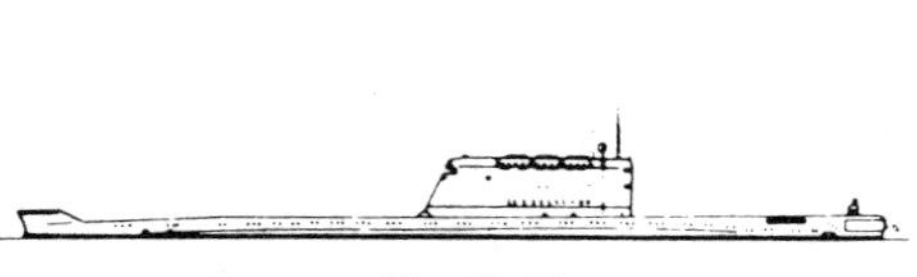

"Hotel" Class

"Hotel II" Class damaged in North Atlantic *Mar 1973*

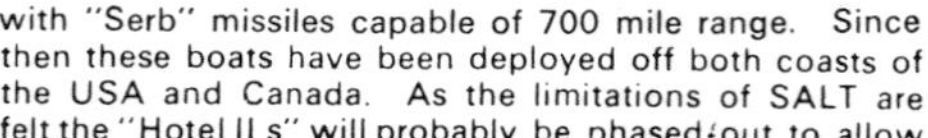

Long range submarines with three vertical ballistic missile tubes in the large fin. All this class were completed between 1958 and 1962. Originally fitted with SSN-4 system with Sark missiles (300 miles). Between 1963 and 1967 this system was replaced by the SSN-5 system with "Serb" missiles capable of 700 mile range. Since then these boats have been deployed off both coasts of the USA and Canada. As the limitations of SALT are felt the "Hotel II s" will probably be phased out to allow the maximum number of "Delta" class to be built.

The "Hotel III" was a single unit converted for the test firings of the SSN-8. The earlier boats of this class, which was of a similar hull and reactor design to the "Echo" class, will, by the late 1970 s, be reaching their twentieth year in service.

"Hotel II" Class *1972*

Submarines—*continued*

Ballistic Missile classes

22 "GOLF I and II" CLASS

(BALLISTIC MISSILE SUBMARINES SSB)

Displacement, tons	2 350 surface; 2 800 submerged
Length, feet (*metres*)	320·0 (*97·5*)
Beam, feet (*metres*)	25·1 (*7·6*)
Draught, feet (*metres*)	22·0 (*6·7*)
Missile launchers	3 SSN-4 (G 1); 3 SSN-5 (G II)
Torpedo tubes	10—21 in (6 bow 4 stern)
Main machinery	3 diesels; 3 shafts; 6 000 hp; Electric motors; 6 000 hp
Speed, knots	17·6 surface; 17 submerged
Range, miles	22 700 surface cruising
Complement	86 (12 officers, 74 men)

"Golf" *Class*

"Golf I" Class *1962, US Navy*

This type has a very large fin fitted with three vertically mounted tubes and hatches for launching ballistic missiles. Built at Komsomolsk and Severodvinsk. Building started in 1958 and finished in 1961-62. After the missile conversion of the "Hotel" class was completed in 1967 about half this class was converted to carry the SSN-5 system with 700 miles Serb missiles in place of the shorter range (300 mile) Sarks. One of this class has been built by China, although apparently lacking missiles.

"Golf I" Class (side opening hatches open) *1962, US Navy*

1 "ZULU V" CLASS

(Ex-BALLISTIC MISSILE SUBMARINE SSB)

Displacement, tons	2 100 surface; 2 600 submerged
Length, feet (*metres*)	259·3 (*90·0*)
Beam, feet (*metres*)	24·1 (*7·3*)
Draught, feet (*metres*)	19·0 (*5·8*)
Missile launchers	2 tubes for SSN-4 missiles
Torpedo tubes	10—21 in
Main machinery	3 diesels; 3 shafts; 10 000 bhp; 3 electric motors; 3 500 hp
Range, miles	13 000 surfaced cruising
Speed, knots	18 surface; 15 submerged
Complement	85

These were basically of "Z" class design but converted in 1955-57 to ballistic missile submarines with larger fins and two vertical tubes for launching Sark (300 mile) missiles on the surface. These were the first Soviet ballistic missile submarines. Of the six converted only one remains in the list. Three others have been converted for research duties as *Lira*, *Orion* and *Vega* whilst two more may have been converted back to patrol submarines.

"Zulu V" Class

"Zulu V" *Class* *1972*

Submarines—*continued*

Cruise Missile classes

1 "PAPA" CLASS
(CRUISE MISSILE SUBMARINES SSGN)

A new class of nuclear submarine, named "Papa".

12 "CHARLIE" CLASS (CRUISE MISSILE SUBMARINE SSGN)

Displacement, tons	4 300 surface; 5 100 submerged
Length, feet (*metres*)	295 (*90·0*)
Beam, feet (*metres*)	32·8 (*10·0*)
Draught, ft (*m*)	24·6 (*7·5*)
Missile launchers	8 tubes for SSN-7 missile system
Torpedo tubes	8—21 in
Main machinery	Nuclear reactor; steam turbines; 24 000 shp
Speed, knots	30 approx, submerged 20 surface
Complement	100

A class of cruise-missile submarine building at Gorky at a rate of about 3 per year. The first of class was delivered in 1968, representing a very significant advance in the cruise-missile submarine field. With a speed of at least 30 knots and mounting eight missile tubes for the SSN-7 system (30 miles range) which has a dived launch capability, this is a great advance on the "Echo" class. Having an improved hull and reactor design these boats must be assumed to have an organic control for their missile system and therefore pose a notable threat to any surface force. Their deployment to the Mediterranean, the area of the US 6th Fleet, suggests their probable employment. The only strange thing about them is their comparatively low building rate.

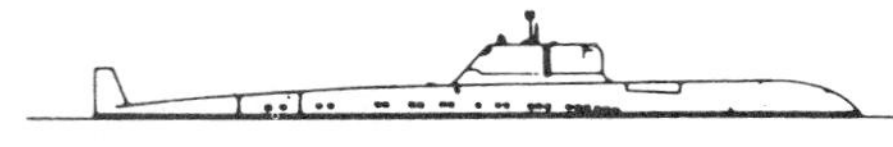

"CHARLIE" Class

"CHARLIE" Class 1974

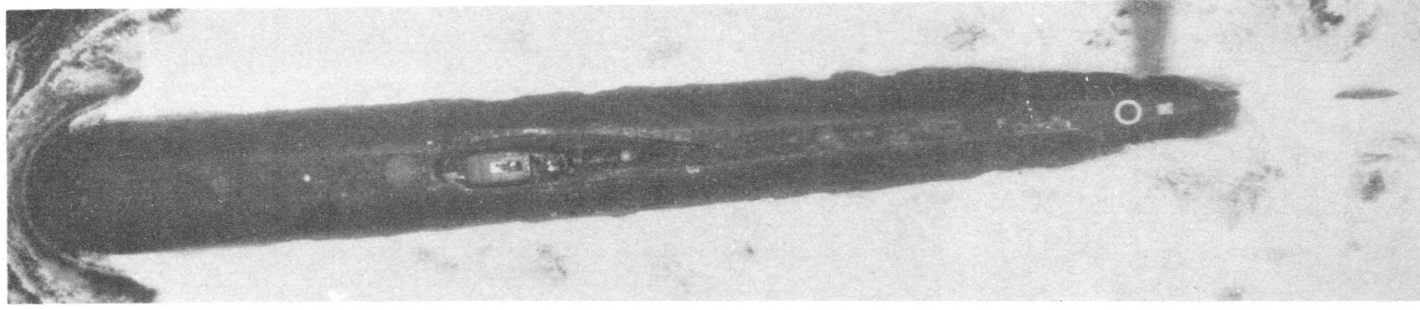

"CHARLIE" Class 1974

"CHARLIE" Class

Submarines—*continued*
Cruise Missile classes

27 "ECHO II" CLASS
(CRUISE MISSILE SUBMARINES SSGN)

Displacement, tons	5 000 surface; 5 600 submerged
Length, feet (*metres*)	387·4 (*118*)
Beam, feet (*metres*)	28·4 (*8·6*)
Draught, feet (*metres*)	25·9 (*7·9*)
Missile launchers	8 SSN-3 launching tubes
Torpedo tubes	6—21 in (bow); 4—16 in (aft)
Main machinery	Nuclear reactor; steam turbine; 22 500 shp
Speed, knots	20
Complement	100

"Echo II" *Class*

The "Echo II" was the natural development of the "Echo I". With a slightly lengthened hull, a fourth pair of launchers was installed and between 1963 and 1967 twenty-seven of this class were built. They are now deployed evenly between the Pacific and Northern fleets and still provide a useful group of boats for operations such as those of the mixed task force which was in the South China Sea in June 1972. As well as surface ships this included 3 "Echo II s" and an "Echo I".

"ECHO II" Class *1973*

(CRUISE MISSILE SUBMARINES SSG)
16 "JULIET" CLASS

Displacement, tons	2 200 surface; 2 500 submerged
Length, feet (*metres*)	280·5 (*85·5*)
Beam, feet (*metres*)	31·4 (*9·5*)
Draught, feet (*metres*)	20·0 (*6·1*)
Missile launchers	4 SSN-3 tubes; 2 before and 2 abaft the fin
Torpedo tubes	6—21 in (bow); 2 or 4—16 in (aft)
Main machinery	Diesels; 6 000 bhp; Electric motors; 6 000 hp
Speed, knots	16 surface; 16 submerged
Range, miles	15 000 surfaced cruising

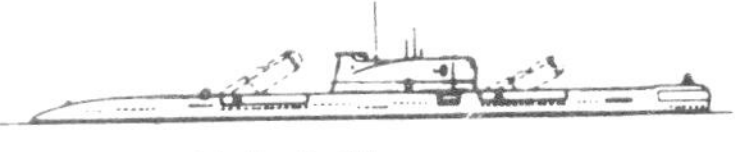

"Juliet" *Class*

Completed between 1962 and 1967. An unmistakable class with a high casing to house the 4 SS-N-3 launchers, one pair either end of the fin which appears to be comparatively low. This class was the logical continuation of the "Whisky" class conversions but was overtaken by the "Echo" class SSGN s. A number of this class has in the past been deployed to the Mediterranean.

"Juliet" Class *1973*

"Juliet" Class *1972, US Navy*

Submarines—*continued*
Cruise Missile classes

7 "WHISKY LONG-BIN" CLASS

(CRUISE MISSILE SUBMARINES SSG)

Displacement, tons	1 300 surface; 1 800 submerged
Length, feet (*metres*)	272·3 (*83·0*)
Beam, feet (*metres*)	19·8 (*6·0*)
Draught, feet (*metres*)	15·7 (*4·8*)
Missile launchers	4 SSN-3 tubes
Torpedo tubes	6—21 in (4 bow, 2 stern)
Main machinery	Diesels; 4 000 bhp; Electric motors; 2 500 hp
Speed, knots	17 surface; 15 submerged
Range, miles	13 000 surfaced, cruising

A more efficient modification of the "Whisky" class than the Twin-Cylinder with four SSN-3 launchers built into a remodelled fin on a hull lengthened by 26 feet. Converted between 1960-63—no organic guidance and therefore reliance must be made on aircraft or surface-ship cooperation. Must still be a very noisy boat when dived.

"Whisky" *Class* Long Bin

"Whisky Long-bin" Class *1970, Niels Gartig*

"Whisky Long-Bin" Class *1968, S. Breyer*

5 "WHISKY TWIN CYLINDER" CLASS

(CRUISE MISSILE SUBMARINES SSG)

Displacement, tons	1 100 surface; 1 600 submerged
Length, feet (*metres*)	247 (*75·3*)
Beam, feet (*metres*)	19 (*5·8*)
Draught, feet (*metres*)	15·1 (*4·6*)
Missile launchers	2 cylinders for SSN-3
Torpedo tubes	6—21 in (4 bow, 2 stern)
Main machinery	Diesels; 4 000 bhp; Electric motors; 2 500 hp
Speed, knots	17 surface; 15 submerged
Range, miles	13 000, surfaced, cruising

A 1958-60 modification of the conventional "Whisky" class designed to test out the SSN-3 system at sea. Probably never truly operational being a thoroughly messy conversion which must make a noise like a train if proceeding at any speed above dead slow when dived.

"Whisky" *Class* Twin Cylinder

The modification consisted of fitting a pair of launchers abaft the fin.

"Whisky" Twin Cylinder Class ***1970, Col Borg***

Submarines—*continued*

Fleet Submarine classes

1 "ALPHA" CLASS

(FLEET SUBMARINE SSN)

Displacement, tons 3 500 surfaced; 4 500 submerged

One unit only of this class was completed in 1970. Her form of propulsion is by no means certain nor is her purpose. It is, however, believed that this is a "one-off" nuclear boat.

16 "VICTOR" CLASS

(FLEET SUBMARINES SSN)

Dispalcement, tons	4 200 surface; 5 100 submerged
Length, feet (*metres*)	285·4 (*87·0*)
Beam, feet (*metres*)	32·8 (*10·0*)
Draught, feet (*metres*)	26·2 (*8·0*)
Torpedo tubes	8—21 in
Main machinery	Nuclear reactor; steam turbines; 24 000 shp
Speed, knots	26 surface; 30 plus submerged

Designed purely as a torpedo carrying submarine its much increased speed makes it a menace to all but the fastest ships. The first of class entered service in 1967-8 with a subsequent building rate of about two per year.

The majority is deployed with the Northern Fleet, although two have joined the Pacific Fleet.

1 "UNIFORM" CLASS

(FLEET SUBMARINE SSN)

Displacement, tons 4 500 surfaced; 6 000 submerged

One unit of a new class of nuclear-propelled submarines has been reported. This is believed to be an enlarged edition of the "Victor" class.

"VICTOR" Class *1974*

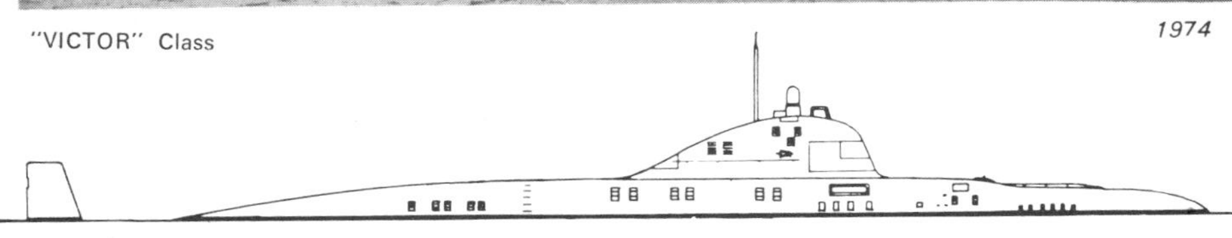

"Victor" Class

"Victor" Class *1974*

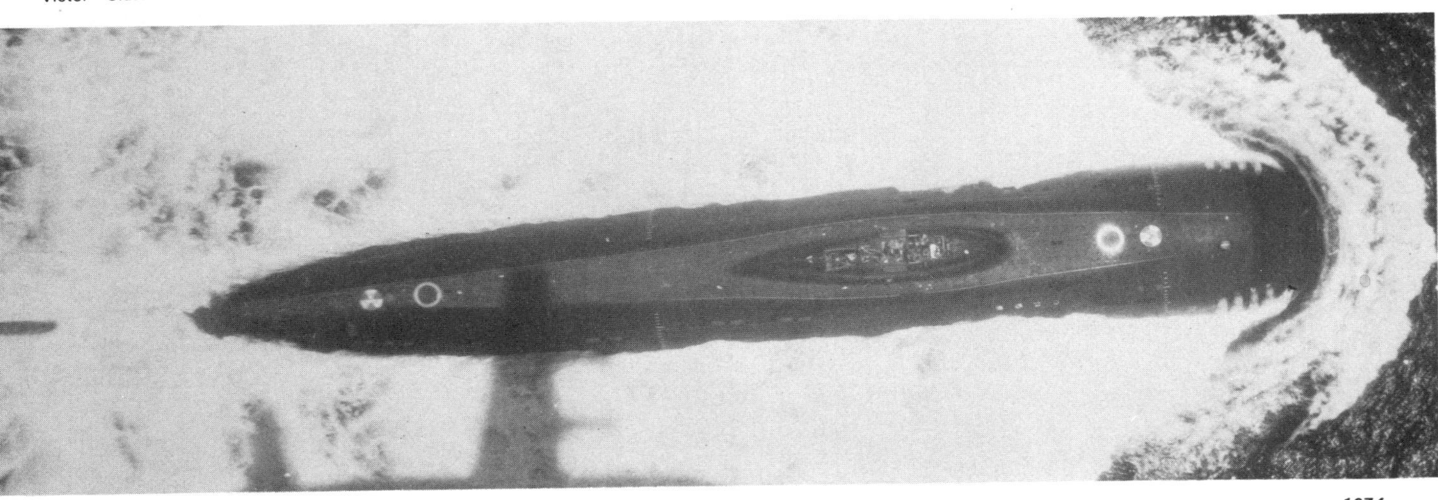

"Victor" Class *1974*

Submarines—*continued*

Fleet Submarine classes

13 "NOVEMBER" CLASS

(FLEET SUBMARINES SSN s)

Displacement, tons	3 500 surface; 4 000 submerged
Length, feet (*metres*)	360·9 (*110·0*)
Beam, feet (*metres*)	32·1 (*9·8*)
Draught, feet (*metres*)	24·3 (*7·4*)
Torpedo tubes	6—21 in (bow);
Main machinery	Nuclear reactor, steam turbines; 22 500 shp
Speed, knots	20 surface; 25 submerged
Complement	88

The first class of Soviet Fleet Submarines which entered service between 1958 and 1963. The hull form with the great number of free-flood holes in the casing suggests a noisy boat and it is surprising that greater efforts have not been made to supersede this class with the "Victors". In 1970 one of this class sank south-west of the United Kingdom.

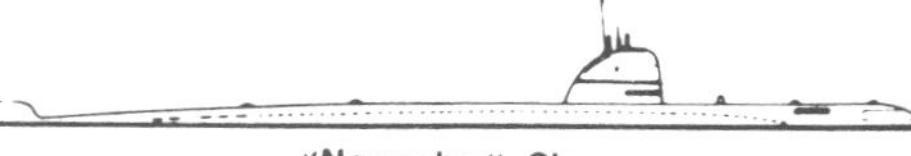
"November" Class

CLASS NAME. Reported as *Leninsky Komsomol*.

DIVING DEPTH. Reported as 1 650 feet (*500 metres*).

"November" Class foundering in Atlantic *April 1970*

"November" Class foundering in Atlantic *April 1970*

1 "ECHO I" CLASS

(FLEET SUBMARINES SSN)

Displacement, tons	4 600 surface; 5 000 submerged
Length, feet (*metres*)	380·9 (*116·0*)
Beam, feet (*metres*)	28·4 (8·6)
Draught, feet (*metres*)	25·9 (*7·9*)
Torpedo tubes	6—21 in (bow); 4—16 in (aft)
Main machinery	Nuclear reactor; steam turbine; 22 500 shp
Speed, knots	20
Complement	92 (12 officers; 80 men)

This class was completed in 1960-62. Originally mounted six SSN-3 launchers raised from the after casing. The hull of this class is very similar to the "Hotel"/"November" type and it is probably powered by similar nuclear plant. This class was started at about the same time as the "Juliet" diesel-driven SSGs, and may have been intended as a nuclear prototype using the same SSN-3 system. Only five "Echo 1s" were built, probably an adequate test for a new weapon system, being followed immediately by the "Echo IIs". In 1973-74 the last of the "Echo I" class was converted into a fleet submarine with the removal of the missile system.

"ECHO I" (Conversion) Class *1974*

Submarines—*continued*

Patrol Submarine classes

1 "TANGO" CLASS

(PATROL SUBMARINE SS)

Displacement, tons	1 900 surfaced; 2 500 submerged
Dimensions, feet	295 × 30 × 16
Complement	60

This class was first seen at the Sevastopol review in July 1973. Notable features are the rise in the fore-casing and a new shape for the snort exhaust. This class, following five years after the "Bravo", shows a continuing commitment to diesel-propelled boats which is of interest in view of the comparatively slow Fleet Submarine building programme. If the USSR wishes to maintain a preponderance in numbers as the more elderly patrol submarines are paid off this may be the class chosen for new construction. It would also provide a modern replacement for client nations' navies.

"Tango" Class

4 "BRAVO" CLASS

(PATROL SUBMARINES SS)

Displacement, tons	2 500 surface; 2 800 submerged
Length, feet (*metres*)	229·6 (*70*)
Beam, feet (*metres*)	24·8 (*7·5*)
Draught, feet (*metres*)	14·8 (*4·5*)
Torpedo tubes	6—21 in (?)
Main machinery	Diesel-Electric
Speed, knots	16 dived

"BRAVO" Class

The drawing is merely an indication of the general form which this class may be expected to have. The beam-to-length ratio is larger than normal in a diesel submarine which would account in part for the large displacement for a comparatively short hull.

First completed in 1968—built at Northern and Baltic yards. One attached to each of the main fleets, reinforcing the view that these are "padded targets" for torpedo and A/S firings.

"Foxtrot" Class 1972

56 "FOXTROT" CLASS

(PATROL SUBMARINES SS)

Displacement, tons	2 000 surface; 2 300 submerged
Length, feet (*metres*)	296·8 (*90·5*)
Beam, feet (*metres*)	24·1 (*7·3*)
Draught, feet (*metres*)	19·0 (*5·8*)
Torpedo tubes	10—21 in (6 bow, 4 stern) (20 torpedoes carried)
Main machinery	Diesels; 3 shafts; 6 000 bhp; 3 electric motors; 6 000 hp
Speed, knots	20 surface; 15 submerged
Complement	70
Range	20 000 miles surface cruising

Built between 1958 and 1967 at Sudomekh and Leningrad. A follow-on of the "Zulu" class with similar propulsion to the "Golf" class. A most successful class which has been deployed world-wide, forming the bulk of the Soviet submarine force in the Mediterranean. Four transferred to India in 1968-69 with a further four new construction following.

"Foxtrot" Class

"Foxtrot" Class *1971 USN*

"FOXTROT" Class *1973*

Submarines—*continued*

Patrol Submarine classes

19+3 "ZULU IV" CLASS

(PATROL SUBMARINES SS)

Displacement, tons	1 900 surface; 2 200 submerged
Length, feet (*metres*)	259·3 (*90·0*)
Beam, feet (*metres*)	23·9 (*7·3*)
Draught, feet (*metres*)	19·0 (*5·8*)
Torpedo tubes	10—21 in (6 bow, 4 stern); 24 torpedoes carried (or 40 mines)
Main machinery	Diesel-electric; 3 shafts 3 diesels; 10 000 bhp 3 electric motors; 3 500 hp
Speed, knots	18 surface; 15 submerged
Range, miles	20 000 surfaced, cruising
Complement	70

The first large post-war patrol submarines built by USSR. Completed from late 1951 to 1955. General appearance is streamlined with a complete row of free-flood holes along the casing. Eighteen were built by Sudomekh Shipyard, Leningrad, in 1952-55 and others at Severodvinsk. The general external similarity to the later German U-boats of WW II suggests that this was not an entirely indigenous design. All now appear to be of the "Zulu IV" type. This class, although the majority are probably still operational, is obsolescent and will soon be disposed of.

The "Zulu V" conversions of this class provided the first Soviet ballistic missile submarines with SSN-4 systems.

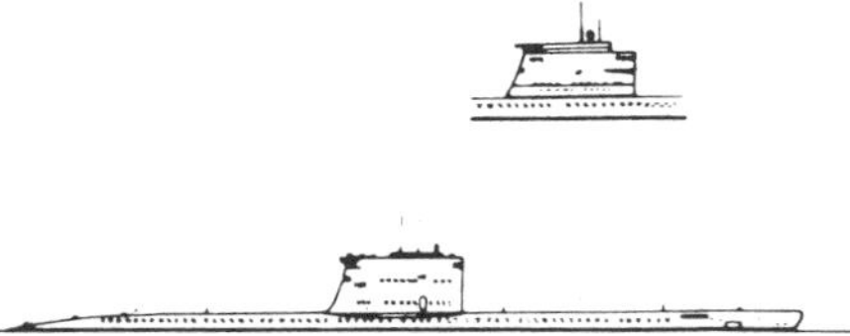

"Zulu IV" Class

"ZULU IV" Class 1974

12 "ROMEO" CLASS

(PATROL SUBMARINES SS)

"Romeo" Class

Displacement, tons	1 100 surface; 1 600 submerged
Length, feet (*metres*)	246·0 (*75·0*)
Beam, feet (*metres*)	24·0 (*7·3*)
Draught, feet (*metres*)	14·5 (*4·4*)
Torpedo tubes	6—21 in bow
Main machinery	Diesels; 4 000 bhp; Electric motors; 4 000 hp; 2 shafts
Speed, knots	17 surfaced; 14 submerged
Complement	65

These are an improved "W" class design with modernised conning tower, and sonar installation. All built in 1958 to 1961. This was presumably an interim class while the "November" class of Fleet Submarines was brought into service—an insurance against failure. Six of this class transferred to Egypt in 1966 and the Chinese are building a considerable force of the same class of submarines.

"ROMEO" Class 1974

Submarines—*continued*
Patrol Submarine classes

100 "WHISKY" CLASS

(PATROL SUBMARINES SS)

Displacement, tons	1 030 surface; 1 180 submerged
Length, feet (*metres*)	240·0 (*73·2*)
Beam, feet (*metres*)	22·0 (*6·7*)
Draught, feet (*metres*)	15·0 (*4·6*)
Torpedo tubes	6—21 in (4 bow, 2 stern); 18 torpedoes carried (or 40 mines)
Main machinery	Diesel-electric; 2 shafts Diesels; 4 000 bhp Electric motors; 2 500 hp
Speed, knots	17 surface; 15 submerged
Range, miles	13 000 at 8 knots (surfaced)
Complement	60

This was the first post-war Soviet design for a medium-range submarine. Like its larger contemporary the "Zulu", this class shows considerable German influence. About 240 of the "Whisky"s were built between 1951 and 1957 at yards throughout the USSR. Built in six types—I and IV had guns forward of the conning tower, II had guns both ends, whilst III and V have no guns. V is the most common variant whilst VA has a diver's exit hatch forward of the conning tower. Now being paid-off at possibly 15-20 per year. Up to 50% are probably now in reserve.

CONVERSIONS. Two of this class, named *Severyanka* and *Slavyanka*, were converted for oceanographic and fishery research.

FOREIGN TRANSFERS. Has been the most popular export model; currently in service in Albania (4) Bulgaria (2), China (21), Egypt (6), Indonesia (4), North Korea (4) and Poland (4).

"WHISKY V" Class *1974*

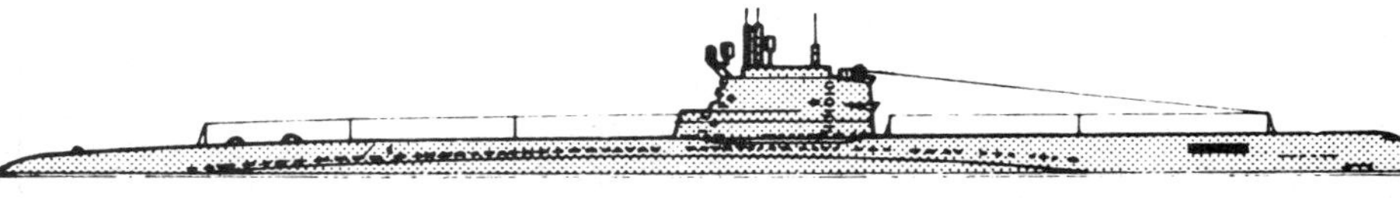

"Whisky V" Class

3 "WHISKY CANVAS BAG" CLASS

(RADAR PICKET SUBMARINES SSR)

Displacement, tons	1 100 surface; 1 200 submerged
Length, feet (*metres*)	240·0 (*73·2*)
Beam, feet (*metres*)	22·0 (*6·7*)
Draught, feet (*metres*)	15·0 (*4·6*)
Torpedo tubes	6—21 in (4 bow, 2 stern)
Main machinery	Diesels; 4 000 bhp Electric motors; 2 500 hp
Speed, knots	17 surface; 15 submerged
Range, miles	13 000 at 8 knots surfaced
Complement	65

Basically of same design as the "Whisky" class but with long-range Boat-Sail radar aerial mounted on the fin. The coy way in which this was covered prompted the title "Canvas Bag". Converted in 1959 to 1963.

"Whisky Canvas Bag" Class *1972, S. Breyer*

22 "QUEBEC" CLASS

(PATROL SUBMARINES SS)

Displacement, tons	650 surface; 740 submerged
Length, feet (*metres*)	185·0 (*56·4*)
Beam, feet (*metres*)	18·0 (*5·5*)
Draught, feet (*metres*)	13·2 (*4·0*)
Torpedo tubes	4—21 in bow
Main machinery	1 diesel; 3 shafts; 3 000 bhp 3 electric motors; 2 500 hp
Speed, knots	18 surface; 16 submerged
Oil fuel, tons	50
Range, miles	7 000 surface cruising
Complement	42

Short range, coastal submarines. Built from 1954 to 1957. Thirteen were constructed in 1955 by Sudomekh Shipyard, Leningrad. The earlier boats of this class were fitted wth what was possibly a closed-cycle propulsion, probably on the third shaft. This may however, have been a Walther HTP turbine but, whatever it was, it is believed to have been unsuccessful and subsequently removed. The majority of this class are now in reserve.

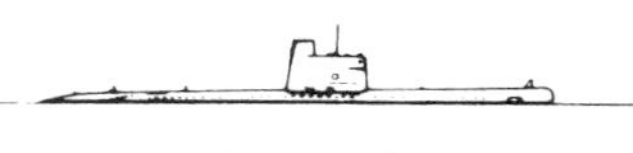

"Quebec" *Class*

"Quebec" Class *1965, S. Breyer*

CRUISERS

3 "KARA" CLASS (CLG)

NIKOLAYEV **OCHAKOV** +1

Displacement, tons	8 200 standard; 10 000 full load
Length, feet (*metres*)	570 (*173·8*)
Beam, feet (*metres*)	60 (*18·3*)
Draught, feet (*metres*)	20 (*6·2*)
Aircraft	1 Hormone A Helicopter (Hangar aft)
Missile Systems	8—SSN-10 (Two mounts abreast bridge) 4—SAN-4 (twins either side of mast) 4—SAN-3 (Twins for'd and aft)
Guns	4—76 mm (2 Twins abaft bridge) 4—30 mm (abreast funnel) (see *Gunnery* note)
A/S weapons	2—16 barrelled MBU launchers (forward) 2—6 barrelled MBU launchers aft
Torpedo tubes	10—21 in (2 quintuple mountings abaft funnel)
Main engines	Gas-turbine
Speed, knots	Approximately 34

GENERAL
Apart from the specialised "Moskva" class this is the first large cruiser to join the Soviet navy since the "Sverdlov"s. Built at Nikolayev, she was first seen in public when she entered the Mediterranean from the Black Sea on 2 March 1973. Clearly capable of prolonged operations overseas

ECM. A full outfit appears to be housed on the bridge and mast.

MISSILES. In addition to the "Kresta II" armament of eight tubes for the SS-N-10 (29 mile) surface-to-surface system and the pair of twin launchers for SA-N-3 system with Goblet missiles, "Kara" mounts the new SA-N-4 system in two silos, either side of the mast. The combination of such a number of systems presents a formidable capability, matched by no other ship.

GUNNERY. The sighting of both main and secondary armament on either beams in the waist follows the precedent of both "Kresta" classes, although the weight of the main armament is increased. The single mountings, classified above as 30 mm, appear to be some form of "Gatling" and are quite different from the usual twin 30 mm mountings.

RADAR. Topsail and Headnet C; Headlight for SA-N-3 system; Owl Screech for 76 mm guns; separate systems for SA-N-4; Drum Tilt for 30 mm guns.

SONAR AND A/S. VDS is mounted below the helicopter pad and is presumably complementary to a hull-mounted set or sets. The presence of the helicopter with dipping-sonar and an A/S weapon load adds to her long-range capability.

SOVIET TYPE NAME. Bolshoy Protivo Lodochny Korabl, meaning Large Anti-Submarine Ship.

NIKOLAYEV 1973

NIKOLAYEV

1973

"KARA" Class 1974

Cruisers—*continued*

ACCOMMODATION. Conditions below decks are presumably fairly spartan but certainly must have some form of air-conditioning. Magazine requirements from forward to aft will include:—

a) one amidships for forward MBUs
b) one amidships for forward SAN-3.
c) one on either beam for SSN-10 (if fitted).
d) one on either beam for 76 mm ammunition.
e) one on either beam for SAN-4.
f) one on either beam for 30 mm ammunition.
g) presumably one on either beam for reload torpedoes.
h) one amidships for after SAN-3.
i) one on either beam for after MBUs.

In addition there are space requirements for all the radar and ECM equipment and associated machines. All this will require a lot of room and produce a lot of heat in a comparatively small ship.

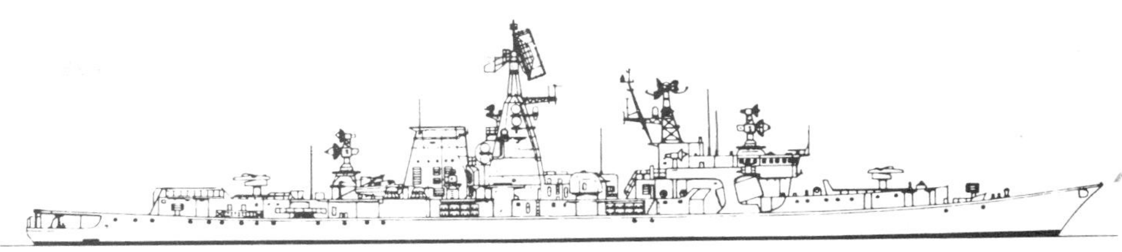

"KARA" CLASS *1974 S. Breyer*

NIKOLAYEV *1973, MOD (UK)*

NIKOLAYEV *1974*

Cruisers—*continued*

6 + 2 "KRESTA II" CLASS (CLG)

ADMIRAL ISAKOV
ADMIRAL MAKAROV
ADMIRAL NAKHIMOV
ADMIRAL OKTYABRSKY
KRONSTADT
MARSHAL VOROSHILOV

Displacement, tons	6 000 standard; 7 500 full load
Length, feet (*metres*)	519·9 (*158·5*)
Beam, feet (*metres*)	55·1 (*16·8*)
Draught, feet (*metres*)	19·7 (*6·0*)
Aircraft	1 Hormone A
Missile launchers	2 quadruple for SSN-10; 2 twin for SAN-3
A S weapons	2—12 barrelled MBU forward and 2—6 barrelled MBU aft
Torpedo tubes	10—21 in (two quintuple)
Guns	4—57 mm (2 twin) 8—30 mm (4 twin)
Main engines	Steam turbines; 2 shafts 100 000 shp
Boilers	4 watertube
Speed, knots	33
Range, miles	5 000 at 18 knots
Complement	500

GENERAL. The design was developed from that of the "Kresta I" class, but the layout is more sophisticated. The missile armament shows an advance on the "Kresta I" SAM armament and a complete change of practice in the fitting of the SS-N-10 system with 29 mile range missiles. This is a mach 1·2 missile and the fact that it has subsequently been fitted in the "Kara" and "Krivak" classes indicates a possible change in tactical thought. Built at Leningrad from 1968 onwards.

FLIGHT. A flight of two helicopters could be operated, although the normal would appear to be one on the apron aft with adjacent low hangar.

NEW CONSTRUCTION. Two building at Zhdanov Yard Leningrad (1975).

RADAR. The radar installation seems to be similar to that in the "Moskva" class with the same Top Sail 3 D and Head Net C 3D for search radar and the Head Light and Peel Group (2) fire control radar for surface to air missiles and "Drum Tilt" (2) for guns. Muff Cob also fitted.

SOVIET TYPE NAME. Bolshoy Protivo Lodochny Korabl, meaning Large Anti-Submarine Ship.

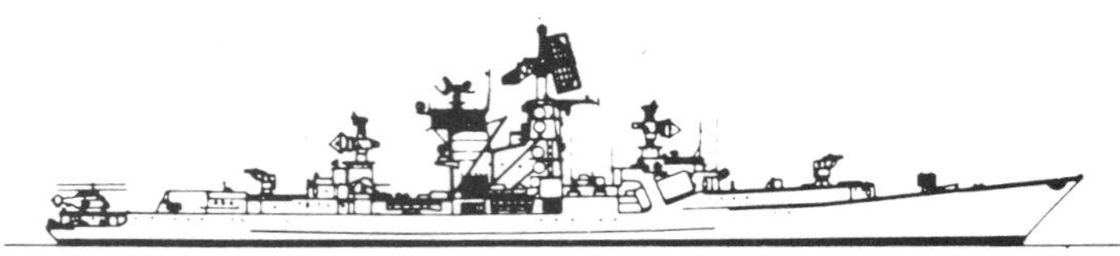

'KRESTA II'Class — *1969, S. Breyer*

MARSHAL VOROSHILOV — *1974*

ADMIRAL NAKHIMOV — *1974*

"KRESTA II"Class — *1971*

Cruisers—*continued*

4 "KRESTA I" CLASS (CLG)

VICE-ADMIRAL DROZD **SEVASTOPOL**
ADMIRAL ZOZULYA **VLADIVOSTOK**

Displacement, tons	5 140 standard; 6 500 full load
Length, feet (*metres*)	510 (*155·5*)
Beam, feet (*metres*)	55·1 (*16·8*)
Draught, feet (*metres*)	18·0 (*5·5*)
Aircraft	1 Hormone A helicopter with hangar aft
Missile launchers	2 twin SSN-3 for Shaddock (no reloads); 2 twin SAN-1 for Goa
A/S weapons	2—12 barrelled MBU (60 reloads) forward; 2—6 barrelled MBU aft
Torpedo tubes	10 (two quintuple) 21 in
Guns	4—57 mm (2 twin)
Main engines	Steam turbines; 2 shafts; 100 000 shp
Boilers	4 watertube
Speed, knots	34
Range, miles	4 500 at 18 knots
Complement	400

"KRESTA I" Class

GENERAL
Provided with a helicopter hangar and flight apron aft for the first time in a Soviet ship. This gives an enhanced A/S capability and could certainly provide carried-on-board target-location facilities for the 250 mile SS-N-3 system at a lower, possibly optimum, range. The "Kresta I" was therefore the first Soviet missile cruiser free to operate alone and distant from own aircraft.
Built at the Zhdanov Shipyard, Leningrad. The prototype ship was laid down in Sep 1964, launched in 1965 and carried out sea trials in the Baltic in Feb 1967. The second ship was launched in 1966 and the others in 1967-68.

RADAR. Four pods, or radomes, are fitted to the sides of the superstructure. These are similar to those fitted in the "Moskva" class helicopter missile cruisers and probably contain passive detection and active jamming equipment. Search: Head Net C 3D and Big Net. Fire Control: Scoop Pair for Shaddock system and Peel Group (2) for Goa system. Muff Cob.

SOVIET TYPE NAME. Bolshoy Protivo Lodochny Korabl, meaning Large Anti-Submarine Ship.

"KRESTA" I Class — *1971, US Navy*

"KRESTA I" Class — *1973, S. Breyer*

Cruisers—*continued*

4 "KYNDA" CLASS (CLG)

ADMIRAL FOKIN **GROZNY**
ADMIRAL GOLOVKO **VARYAG**

Displacement, tons	4 500 standard; 6 000 full load
Length, feet (*metres*)	465·8 (*142·0*)
Beam, feet (*metres*)	51·8 (*15·8*)
Draught, feet (*metres*)	17·4 (*5·3*)
Aircraft	Pad for helicopter on stern
Missile launchers	2 quadruple mounts, 1 fwd, 1 aft, for SSN-3 system (possible reloads) 1 twin mount on forecastle for SAN-1 system (30 reloads)
A/S weapons	2—12 barrelled MBUs on forecastle
Guns, AA	4—3 in (*76 mm*) 2 twin
Torpedo tubes	6—21 in (*533 mm*) 2 triple ASW amidships
Main engines	2 sets geared turbines; 2 shafts; 100 000 shp
Boilers	4 high pressure
Speed, knots	35
Complement	390

"KYNDA" Class

GENERAL
The first ship of this class was laid down in June 1960, launched in Apr 1961 at Zhdanov Shipyard, Leningrad, and completed in June 1962. The second ship was launched in Nov 1961 and fitted out in Aug 1962. The others were completed by 1965. Two enclosed towers, instead of masts, are stepped forward of each raked funnel. In this class there is no helicopter embarked, so guidance, for the SS-N-3 system would be more difficult than in later ships. She will therefore be constrained in her operations compared with the "Kresta I" with her own helicopter.

RADAR. This class showed at an early stage the Soviet ability to match radar availability to weapon capability. The duplicated aerials provide not only a capability for separate target engagement but also provide a reserve in the event of damage. Search: Head Net A. Fire Control: Scoop Pair (2) for "Shaddock" systems, Peel Group for "Goa" systems andOwl Screech for gun.

SOVIET TYPE NAME. Bolshoy Protivo Lodochny Korabl, meaning Large Anti-Submarine Ship.

ADMIRAL GOLOVKO 4/1974

"KYNDA" Class 11/1974, US Navy

"KYNDA" Class 1972

Cruisers—*continued*

1 "SVERDLOV" CLASS (CG)
2 "SVERDLOV" CLASS (CC)
9 "SVERDLOV" CLASS (CA)

ADMIRAL LAZAREV
ADMIRAL SENYAVIN
ADMIRAL USHAKOV
ALEKSANDR NEVSKI
ALEKSANDR SUVOROV
DMITRI POZHARSKI
DZERZHINSKI
MIKHAIL KUTUSOV
MURMANSK
OKTYABRSKAYA REVOLUTSIYA
SVERDLOV
ZHDANOV

Displacement, tons	15 450 standard; 19 200 full load
Length, feet (*metres*)	656·2 (*200·0*)pp; 689·0 (*210·0*)oa
Beam, feet (*metres*)	72·2 (*22·0*)
Draught, feet (*metres*)	24·5 (*7·5*)
Aircraft	Helicopter pad in *Zhdanov*. Pad and hangar in *Senyavin*
Armour	Belts 3·9—4·9 in (*100—125 mm*); fwd and aft 1·6—2 in (*40—50 mm*); turrets 4·9 in (*125 mm*); C.T. 5·9 in (*150 mm*); decks 1—2 in (*25—50 mm*) and 2—3 in (*50—75 mm*)
Missile launchers	Twin "SA-N-2" aft in *Dzerzhinski* 2 SAN-4 in *Zhdanov* and *Senyavin* (twin) (see conversions)
Guns	12—6 in (*152 mm*), (4 triple) (9—6 in in *Dzerzhinski* and *Zhdanov*—6—6 in in *Senyavin*) 12—3·9 in (*100 mm*), (6 twin) 16—37 mm (twin), 8—30 mm (twin)
Torpedo tubes	10—21 in (*533 mm*) 2 quintuple (see *Torpedoes*)
Mines	150 capacity—(except *Zhdanov* and *Senyavin*)
Boilers	6 watertube
Main engines	Geared turbines; 2 shafts; 130 000 shp
Speed, knots	34
Range, miles	8 700 at 18 knots
Oil fuel, tons	3 800
Complement	1 000 average

GENERAL

Of the 24 cruisers of this class originally projected, 20 keels were laid and 17 hulls were launched from 1951 onwards, but only 13 ships were completed by 1956. There were two slightly different types. *Sverdlov* and sisters had the 37 mm AA guns near the fore-funnel one deck higher than in later cruisers. All ships except *Zhdanov* and *Senyavin* are fitted for minelaying. Mine stowage is on the second deck. *Zhdanov* and *Senyavin* used as command ships with much increased communications capability. *Admiral Nakhimov* deleted in 1969.

CONVERSIONS. *Dzerzhinski* has been fitted with an SAN-2 launcher aft replacing X-Turret. In 1972 *Admiral Senyavin* returned to service with both X and Y turrets removed and replaced by a helicopter pad and a hangar surmounted by four 30 mm mountings and an SAN-4 mounting. At about the same time *Zhdanov* appeared on the scene with a different outfit. She has had only X-turret removed and replaced by a high deckhouse mounting an SAN-4 launcher.

NAMES. The ship first named *Molotovsk* was renamed *Oktyabrskaya Revolutsiya* in 1957.

TORPEDOES. *Oktyabrskaya Revolutsiya* and *Murmansk* no longer have tubes.

SOVIET TYPE NAME. Kreyser meaning Cruiser.

RADAR. Search: Head Net A, Strut Curve and some ships fitted with Big Net. (*Dzerzhinski* only.—Fire control: Peel Group and Drum Tilt. High Lune and Fan Song E for SA-N-2 system.
CC s only Big Net and Slim Net.

SVERDLOV 3/1974

ADMIRAL USHAKOV *1973, Commander Aldo Fraccorali*

DRAWING. Starboard elevation and plan of *Dzerzhinski*.
Scale: 145 feet = 1 inch

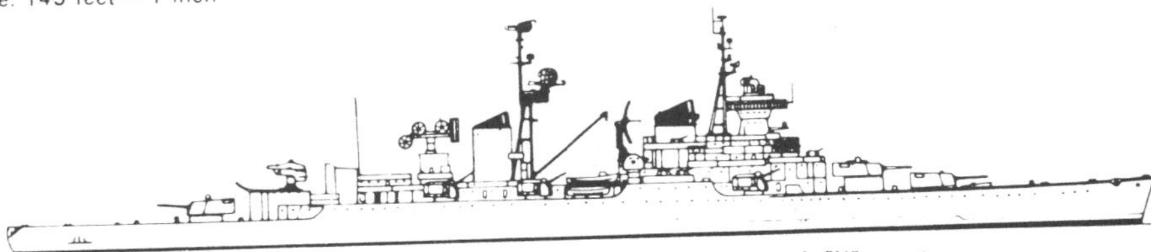

DZERZHINSKI. Twin missile launcher in place of "X" turret

"SVERDLOV" *Class*

Cruisers—*continued*

DZERZHINSKI with twin SA-N-2 launcher in place of "X" turret *1972*

ZHDANOV *1974*

ADMIRAL SENYAVIN *1973*

ADMIRAL SENYAVIN (after conversion showing hangar and SA-N-4) *1972*

Cruisers—*continued*

2 "CHAPAEV" CLASS (CA)

KOMSOMOLETS (ex-*Chkalov*) **ZHELEZNYAKOV**

Displacement, tons	11 300 standard; 15 000 full load
Length, feet (*metres*)	659·5 (*201·0*) wl; 665 (*202·8*)
Beam, feet (*metres*)	62 (*18·9*)
Draught, feet (*metres*)	24 (*7·3*)
Guns	12—6 in (*152 mm*) 57 cal, (4 triple) 8—3·9 in (*100 mm*) 70 cal, (4 twin) 24—37 mm (12 twin)
Mines	200 capacity; 425 ft rails
Boilers	6 watertube
Main engines	Geared turbines, with diesels for cruising speeds; 4 shafts 130 000 shp
Speed, knots	32
Range, miles	5 400 at 15 knots
Oil fuel, tons	2 500
Complement	900

Originally a class of six ships of which one was never completed—show signs of both Italian and German influence. Laid down in 1939-40. Launched during 1941-47. All work on these ships was stopped during the war, but was resumed in 1946-47. Completed in 1948-50 both in Leningrad. Catapults were removed from all ships of this type. Both remaining ships serve as training cruisers.

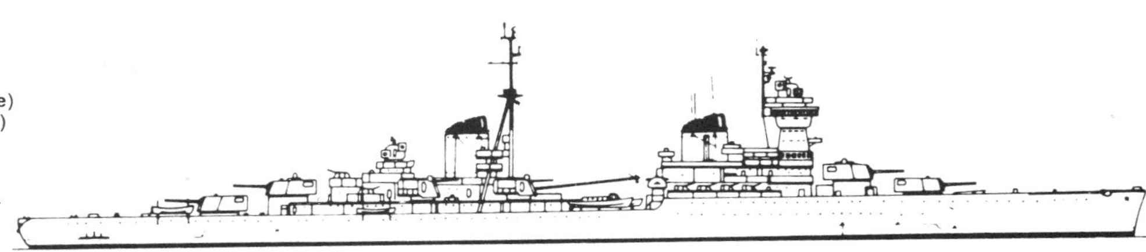

"CHAPAEV" CLASS

GUNNERY. Turret guns fitting allows independent elevation to 45 degrees.

RADAR. They have long range surveillance radars and gunfire control tracking radar. *Komsomolets* was fitted with modern radar in 1969-70. Surface—Low Sieve; Early warning—Slim Net and Knife Rest B; Fire control—Top Bow, Sun Visor B, Egg Cup; IFF— High Pole.

DRAWING. Starboard elevation. Scale: 125 feet = 1 inch (1 : 1 500).

SOVIET TYPE NAME. Kreyser meaning Cruiser.

ZHELENYAKOV — *1958, Antonov Rogov*

2 "KIROV" CLASS (CL)

Name	*Builders*	*Laid down*	*Launched*	*Completed*
KIROV	Putilov DY	1934	1 Dec 1936	26 Sep 1938
SLAVA (ex-*Molotov*)	Marti Yard, Nikolayev	1935	23 Feb 1939	1944

Displacement, tons	7 780 standard; 9 060 full load
Length, feet (*metres*)	613·5 (*178·0*) pp; 626·7 (*191·0*) oa
Beam, feet (*metres*)	58 (*18*)
Draught, feet (*metres*)	20 (*6·3*)
Armour	Side 3 in (*75 mm*); deck 2 in (*50 mm*); gunhouses 3·9 in (*100 mm*) CT 3 in (*75 mm*)
Guns	9—7·1 in (*180 mm*); 6—3·9 in (*100 mm*) 18—37 *mm* (*Kirov*); 12—37 mm (*Slava*)
Mines	180 capacity; 375 ft rails
Main engines	Geared turbines; with diesels for cruising; 2 shafts; 113 000 shp
Boilers	6 Yarrow
Speed, knots	34
Range, miles	4 000 at 15 knots
Oil fuel, tons	1 280
Complement	734 (training role)

Design and technical direction of construction by Ansaldo. The survivors of a class of six.

APPEARANCE. *Kirov* has very long forecastle, heavy tripod mast stepped abaft forebridge, *Slava* has high director tower on forebridge, light tripod foremast abaft bridge.

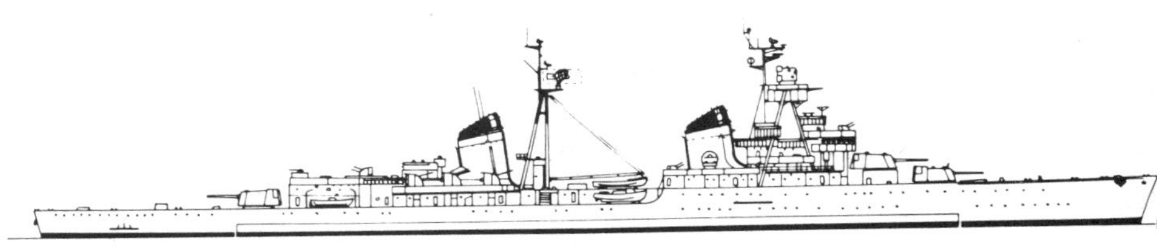

"KIROV" CLASS

CONVERSION. There is a report that one of this class has had her forecastle raised and is used in the Black Sea for missile and electronic trials.

RADAR. Search: Hair Net, Seagull, High Sieve. Fire Control: Top Bow, Sun Visor. IFF: High Pole A.

DRAWING. Starboard elevation of *Kirov*. Drawn in 1971. Scale: 125 feet = 1 inch (1 : 1 500).

SOVIET TYPE NAME. Kreyser, meaning Cruiser.

KIROV — *1970, Bertil Gard*

DESTROYERS

9 "KRIVAK" CLASS (DDG)

BDITELNY	**SILNY**
BODRY	**STOROZHEVOY**
DOBLESTNY	**SVIREPY**
DOSTOYNY	**+ 2**

Displacement, tons	3 500 standard; 4 200 full load
Length, feet (*metres*)	404·8 (*123·4*)
Beam, feet (*metres*)	45·9 (*14·0*)
Draught, feet (*metres*)	16·4 (*5·0*)
Missile launchers	4 for SSN-10 system, in "A" position; (quadruple); 2 for SAN-4 system (twins)
Guns	4—3 in (*76 mm*) dual purpose automatic (2 twin) in "X" and "Y" positions; 4—30 mm
A/S weapons	2 twelve-barrelled MBUs forward in "B" position
Torpedo tubes	8—21 in (*533 mm*) in two quadruple banks on either side amidships
Main engines	8 sets Gas turbines; 2 shafts; 112 000 shp
Speed, knots	38

"KRIVAK" Class

"KRIVAK" Class *1973, H. W. van Boeijen*

GENERAL
This handsome class, the first ship of which appeared in 1971, appears to be a most successful design incorporating surface and anti-air capability, a VDS with associated MBUs, two banks of tubes, all in a hull designed for both speed and sea-keeping. The use of gas-turbines gives the "Krivak" class a rapid acceleration and an availability which cannot be matched by steam driven ships. Building continues at about 2 per year.

MISSILES. The surface-to-surface missiles of the SS-N-10 system have a range of 29 miles, continuing the short-range trend of the "Kresta II" class and followed by the "Kara" class. The SA-N-4 SAMs are of a new design which is now mounted also in the "Kara", "Nanuchka" and "Grisha" classes. The launcher retracts into the mounting for stowage and protection, rising to fire and retracting to reload. The two mountings are forward of the bridge and abaft the funnel.

RADAR. Head Net C. Drum Tilt and Head Light.

SOVIET TYPE NAME. Bolshoy Protivo Lodochny Korabl, meaning Large Anti-Submarine Ship.

"KRIVAK" Class *1974*

"KRIVAK" Class *1974*

Destroyers—*continued*

19 "KASHIN" and "MODIFIED KASHIN" CLASS (DDG)

KOMSOMOLETS LATVY	**SLAVNY**
KOMSOMOLETS UKRAINY	**SMELY**
KRASNY-KAVKAZ	**SMETLIVY**
KRASNY-KRIM	**SMYSHLENY**
OBRAZTSOVY	**SOOBRAZITELNY**
ODARENNY	**SPOSOBNY**
OGNEVOY	**STEREGUSHCHY**
OTVAZHNY	**STROGNY**
PROVORNY	**STROYNY**
SKORY	

Displacement, tons	4 300 standard; 5 200 full load
Length, feet (*metres*)	470·9 (*143·3*) or 481 (*146·5*)
Beam, feet (*metres*)	52·5 (*15·9*)
Draught, feet (*metres*)	19 (*5·8*)
Missile launchers	4 (2 twin) SAN-1 mounted in "B" and "X" positions for surface-to-air missiles; 4 SSN-11 in mod-class
Guns	4—3 in (*76 mm*), 2 twin, in "A" and "Y" positions; 4—30 Gatlings in mod. class
A/S weapons	2—12 barrelled MBU forward; 2—6 barrelled MBU aft
Torpedo tubes	5—21 in (*533 mm*) quintuple, amidships for ASW torpedoes
Main engines	8 sets gas turbines; each 12 000 hp; 2 shafts; 96 000 shp
Speed, knots	35
Complement	350

GENERAL
The first class of warships in the world to rely entirely on gas-turbine propulsion giving them the quick getaway and acceleration necessary for modern tactics. These ships were delivered from 1962 onwards from the Zhdanov Yard, Leningrad and the Nosenko Yard, Nikolayev.

CONVERSION. As reported in the last two editions this class, although comparatively youthful, have been outdated by recent building. Lacking SSM, a modern SAM system and VDS they were in line for modernisation. This has now started—the conversion consists of a hull-lengthening by ten feet, the shipping of 4 SSN-11 SSM launchers, 4—30 mm Gatling guns, a VDS and MBU 4500 launchers.

LOSS. One of this class foundered in the Black Sea in September 1974, apparently as the result of an internal explosion followed by a fire which lasted for five hours. Nearly 300 of the ships company lost, making this the worst peacetime naval loss for many years.

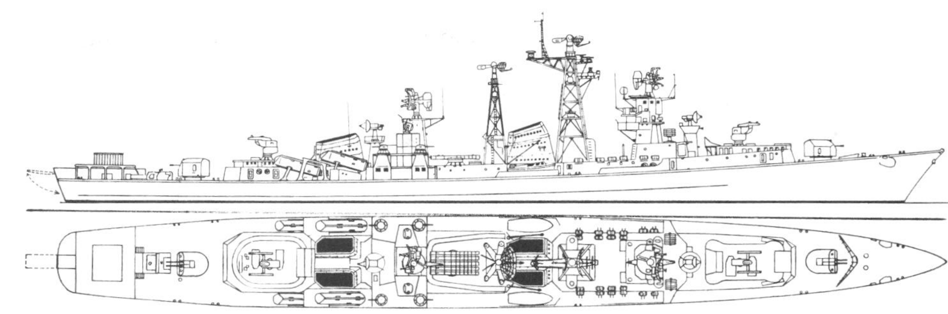

"MODIFIED KASHIN" Class — *1975, S. Breyer*

"MODIFIED KASHIN" Class — *1974, S. Breyer*

RADAR. Search: Head Net C and Big Net in some ships; Head Net A (2) in others. Fire control: Peel Group (2) for Goa system and Owl Screech (2) for guns.

SOVIET TYPE NAME. Bolshoy Protivo Lodochny Korabl, meaning Large Anti-Submarine Ship.

"KASHIN" Class — *1972, US Navy*

KRASNY-KAVKAZ — *7/1973, Wright and Logan*

Destroyers—*continued*

4 "KILDIN" CLASS (DDG)

BEDOVY **NEULOVIMY**
NEUDERSIMY **PROZORLIVY**

Displacement, tons	3 000 standard; 4 000 full load
Length, feet (*metres*)	414·9 (*126·5*)
Beam, feet (*metres*)	42·6 (*13·0*)
Draught, feet (*metres*)	16·1 (*4·9*)
Missile launchers	4 for SSN—II system
A/S Weapon	2—16 barrel MBU on forcastle
Guns	4—76 mm (twins aft); 16—57 mm (quads—2 forward, 2 between funnels)
Torpedo tubes	4—21 in (2 twin)
Main engines	Geared turbines; 2 shafts 72 000 shp
Boilers	4 high pressure
Speed, knots	36
Range, miles	5 500 at 16 knots
Complement	350 officers and men

Large destroyers with the "Kotlin" type hull, but re-designed as guided missile armed destroyers

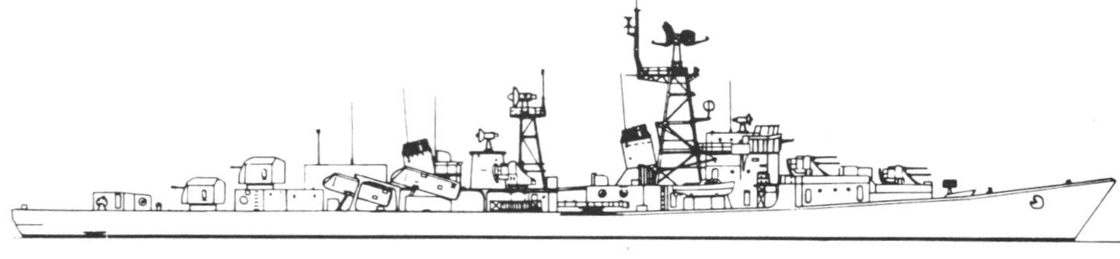

" KILDIN"Class after modernisation 1973 S. Breyer

CONVERSION. In 1972 *Neulovimy* was taken in hand for modification. This was completed in mid-1973 and consisted of the replacement of the SSN-1 on the quarterdeck by two super-imposed twin 76 mm turrets, the fitting of four SSN-11 launchers abreast the after funnel and the fitting of new radar. The substitution of the 29 mile SSN-11 system (a modified Styx) for the obsolescent SSN-1 system and the notable increase in gun armament illustrate two trends in Soviet thought. A second ship of the class has now completed this conversion.

RADAR. Search: Head Net A and Slim Net. Fire Control: New outfit at modernisation.

SOVIET TYPE NAME. Rated Bolshoy Protivo Lodochny Kerabl meaning Large Anti-Submarine Ship.

NEULOVIMY 1974

NEULOVIMY after modernisation 1973

NEULOVIMY after modernisation 1973, S. Brexer

Destroyers—*continued*

6 "KANIN" CLASS (DDG)

BOYKY	**GREMYASHCHYI**
DERZKY	**ZHGUCHY**
GNEVNY	**ZORKY**

Displacement, tons	3 700 standard; 4 600 full load
Length, feet (*metres*)	456·9 (*139·3*)
Beam, feet (*metres*)	48·2 (*14·7*)
Draught, feet (*metres*)	16·4 (*5·0*)
Aircraft	Helicopter pad
Missile launchers	1 twin SAN-1 mounted aft
A/S weapons	Three 12-barrelled MBU
Guns	8—57 mm (2 quadruple forward) 8—30 mm (twin) (by after funnel)
Torpedo tubes	10—21 in (*533 mm*) A/S (2 quintuple)
Main engines	2 sets geared steam turbines 2 shafts; 80 000 shp
Boilers	4 watertube
Oil fuel, tons	900
Speed, knots	34
Complement	350

GENERAL
All ships of this class have been converted from "Krupny"s at Zhdanov Yard, Leningrad from 1967 onwards, being given a SAM capability instead of the latter's SSM armament.

APPEARANCE. As compared with the "Krupny" class these ships have enlarged bridge, converted bow (probably for a new sonar) and larger helicopter platforms.

GUNNERY. The four twin 30 mm abaft the after funnel were a late addition to the armament.

RADAR. Search: Head Net C or Head Net A. Fire Control: Peel Group for "Goa", Hawk Screech for guns. Drum Tilt for additional 30 mm guns.

SOVIET TYPE NAME. Bolshoy Protivo Lodochny Korabl, meaning Large Anti-Submarine Ship.

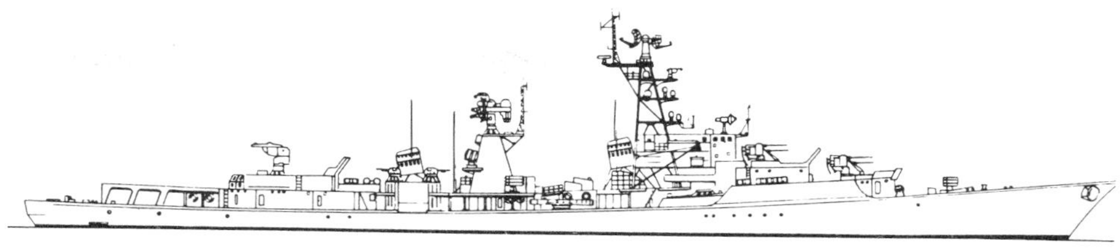

"KANIN" Class with additional 8—30 mm — 1973 S. Breyer

"KANIN" Class with additional 30 mm guns — 1973, S. Breyer

"KANIN" Class, Hull 2, — 1972

"KANIN" Class — 1972

Destroyers—*continued*

1 "KRUPNY" CLASS (DDG)

GORDY

Displacement, tons	3 650 standard; 4 650 full load
Length, feet (*metres*)	452 (*137·8*)
Beam, feet (*metres*))	48·2 (*14·7*)
Draught, feet (*metres*)	16·5 (*5·0*)
Missile launchers	2 mountings; 1 forward, 1 aft for SSN-1 system
Guns,	16—57 mm, (4 quadruple;
A/S weapons	2—16 barrelled MBUs
Torpedo launchers	6 (2 triple) for 21 in A/S torpedoes
Main engines	Geared steam turbines; 2 shafts 80 000 shp
Boilers	4 high pressure water tube
Speed, knots	34
Complement	360

This class was designed as flush-decked destroyers to carry surface-to-surface guided missiles. Helicopter spot landing apron on the stern. Initial construction started in 1958 at Leningrad. Four ships of this class were converted to carry surface-to-air missiles in 1967 to 1971 and are known as the "Kanin" class; two more subsequently converted.

RADAR. Search: Either Head Net C 3D or Head Net A. Fire Control: Hawk Screech (2) for guns, and, probably surface missiles. Skinhead.

SOVIET TYPE NAME. Rated as Raketny Korabl meaning Rocket Ship.

"KRUPNY" Class firing Scrubber missile — *1968*

"KRUPNY" Class

"KRUPNY" Class — *1969, MOD, UK*

"KRUPNY" Class — *1971, USN*

Destroyers—*continued*

8 "SAM KOTLIN" CLASS (DDG)

BRAVY	**SKROMNY**
NAKHODCHIVY	**SKRYTNY**
NASTOYCHIVY	**SOZNATELNY**
NESOKRUSHIMY	**VOZBUZHDENNY**

Displacement, tons	2 850 standard; 3 885 full load
Length, feet (*metres*)	414·9 (*126·5*)
Beam, feet (*metres*)	42·6 (*13·0*)
Draught, feet (*metres*)	16·1 (*4·9*)
Missile launchers	1 twin SAN-1 mounted aft
Guns	2—5·1 in (*110 mm*) dp (1 twin) 2 or 4—57 mm AA (1 twin or quadruple)
Torpedo tubes	1 quintuple 21in mounting
Guns	2—3.9 in (100 *mm*) dp (1 twin) 4—57 mm AA (1 quadruple) 4—30 mm in later ships
A/S weapons	6 side thrown DC projectors or 2—12 barrelled ASW rocket launchers
Main engines	Geared turbines; 2 shafts 72 000 shp
Boilers	4 high pressure
Speed, knots	36
Range, miles	5 500 at 16 knots
Complement	285

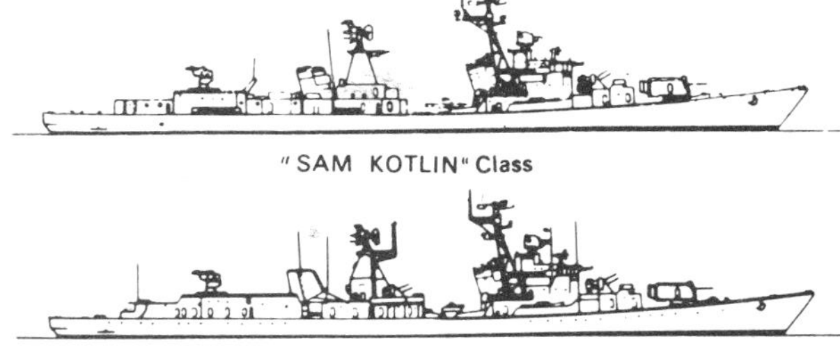

"SAM KOTLIN" Class

"SAM KOTLIN" Class (midship radar variant)

Converted "Kotlin" class destroyers with a surface-to-air missile launcher in place of the main twin turret aft and anti-aircraft guns reduced to one quadruple mounting.

The prototype conversion was completed about 1962 and the others since 1966. One ship transferred to Poland.

APPEARANCE. The prototype "Kotlin" SAM class has a different after funnel and different radar pedestal from those in the standard "Kotlin" SAM class.

RADAR. Search: Head Net C 3D or Head Net A. Fire Control: Peel Group for "Goa" system, Hawk Screech for guns. Drum Tilt for 30 mm in later ships.

SOVIET TYPE NAME. Rated as Esminets meaning Destroyer.

"SAM KOTLIN" Class — 1971, USN

Later "SAM KOTLIN" (with 2 extra Drum Tilt and 8—30 mm by after funnel) — 1973

"SAM KOTLIN" Class (with different design of midship radar pedestal and after funnel from the prototype). — 1971 MOD (UK)

Destroyers— *continued*

18 "KOTLIN" CLASS (DD)

BESSLEDNY	**SPOKOJNY**
BLAGORODNY	**SPRAVEDLIVY**
BLESTYASHCHY	**SVETLY**
BURLIVY	**VDOKHNOVENNY**
BYVALY	**VOZMUSHCHENNY**
NAPORISTY	**VYDERZHANNY**
PLAMENNY	**+ 2**
SPESHNY	

DALNEVOSTOCHNY KOMSOMOLETS
MOSKOVSKY KOMSOMOLETS

Displacement, tons	2 850 standard; 3 885 full load
Length, feet (*metres*)	414·9 (*126·5*)
Beam, feet (*metres*)	42·6 (*13·0*)
Draught, feet (*metres*)	16·1 (*4·9*) max
Guns	4—5·1 in (*130 mm*) dp (2 twin) 16—57 mm AA (4 quadruple) (8—30 mm in some)
A/S weapons	6 side thrown DC projectors or (2—16 barrelled MBUs in some)
Torpedo tubes	10—21 in (*533 mm*) (5 only in some)
Mines	80 capacity
Main engines	Geared turbines; 2 shafts; 72 000 shp
Boilers	4 high pressure
Speed, knots	36
Range, miles	5 500 at 16 knots
Complement	285

KOTLIN Class (with helicopter platform)

"KOTLIN" Class

GENERAL. Built in 1954-57. The last four hulls laid down were converted to "Kildins".

MODIFICATIONS. (a) Eight converted to "Sam Kotlins" plus one transferred to Poland. (b) *Svetly* and others provided with helicopter pad on stern. (c) Some had the after torpedo-tubes replaced by a deckhouse. (d) Some ships had two 16-barrelled MBUs fitted. (e) The latest addition in some ships is the fitting of eight 30 mm either side of the after-funnel.

RADAR. Search: Slim Net and Strut Curve. Fire Control: Hawk Screech (2). Hair Net. Square Head. Flat Spin in some.

SOVIET TYPE NAMES. Rated as Esminets meaning Destroyer.

"KOTLIN" Class with 5 torpedo tubes and additional 30 mm guns — *1973, USN*

"KOTLIN" Class — *1970, S. Breyer*

"KOTLIN" Class (helicopter platform aft) — *1969, MOD, (UK)*

Destroyers— *continued*

40 "SKORY" CLASS (DD)

SVOBODNY 1968

BDITELNY
BESNERVNY
BESSMENNY
BESSMERTNY
BEZUPRETCHNY
BEZUKORIZNENNY
OGNENNY
OSTERVENELY
OSTOROZNY
OSTROGLAZY
OTCHAYANNY
OTRETOVENNY
OTVETSTVENNY
OZHESTOCHENNY
OZHIVLENNY
SERDITY
SERIOZNY
SMELY
SMOTRYASHCHY
SMYSHLYONY
SOKRUSHITELNY
SOLIDNY
SOVERSHENNY
SPOSOBNY
STATNY
STEPENNY
STOJKY
STREMITELNY
SUROVY
SVOBODNY
VAZHNY
VDUMCHIVY
VERDUSHCHY
VERNY
VIDNY
VIKHREVOY
VNESAPNY
VNIMATELNY
VOLEVOY
VRAZUMITELNY

Displacement, tons	2 600 standard; 3 500 full load
Length, feet	395·2 (*120·5*)
Beam, feet (*metres*)	38.9 (*11·8*)
Draught, feet (*metres*)	15·1 (*4·6*)
Guns	4—5·1 in (*130 mm*), 2 twin 2—3·4 in (*86 mm*) 1 twin 8—37 mm (4 twin), (see *Modernisation Notes*)
A/S weapons	4 DCT
Torpedo tubes	10—21 in (*533 mm*) (see *Modernisation Note*)
Mines	80 can be carried
Main engines	Geared turbines; 2 shafts; 60 000 shp
Boilers	4 high pressure
Speed, knots	33
Range, miles	3 900 at 13 knots
Complement	260

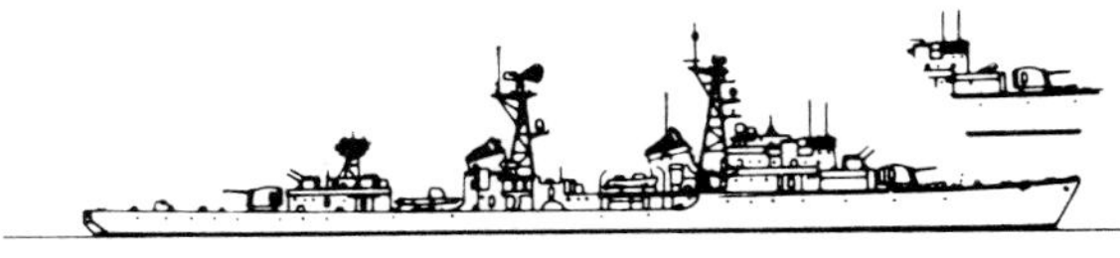

"SKORY" Modified Class

"SKORY" Original Class

There were to have been 85 destroyers of this class, but construction beyond 75 units was discontinued in favour of later types of destroyers, and the number has been further reduced to 40 by transfers to other countries, translations to other types and disposals at an increasing rate.

APPEARANCE. There were three differing types in this class, the anti-aircraft guns varying with twin and single mountings; and two types of foremast, one vertical with all scanners on top and the other with one scanner on top and one on a platform half way.

MODERNISATION. At least six ships, of the "Skory" class were modified from 1959 onwards including extensive alterations to anti-aircraft armament, electronic equipment and anti-submarine weapons. These now have five 57 mm single, five torpedo tubes and two 16-barrelled MBU.

RADAR. Search: Strut Curve and unknown S Band. Fire Control: Obsolescent X Band. Square Head.

RESERVE. Some 50% of this class now in reserve.

TRANSFERS. Of this class *Skory* and *Smeriivy* were transferred to the Polish Navy in 1957-58, two to the Egyptian Navy in 1956, four to the Indonesian Navy in 1959, and a further two (modernised) to Egypt in 1968.

SOVIET TYPE NAME. Rated as Esminets meaning Destroyer.

1 "TALLIN" CLASS (DD)

NEUSTRASHIMY

Displacement, tons	3 200 standard; 4 300 full load
Length, feet (*metres*)	440·0 (*134·0*) oa
Beam, feet (*metres*)	44·9 (*13·7*)
Draught, feet (*metres*)	16·1 (*4·9*)
Guns	4—5·1 in (*130 mm*) semi-automatic (2 twin) 16—57 mm (4 quadruple)
A/S weapons	2—16 barrelled MBUs and 2 DC launchers
Torpedo tubes	10—21 in (*533 mm*), 2 quintuple
Mines	70
Main engines	Geared turbines; 2 shafts; 80 000 shp
Boilers	4 water tube
Speed, knots	38
Range, miles	2 500 at 18 knots
Oil fuel, tons	850
Complement	340

Built in 1952-54.

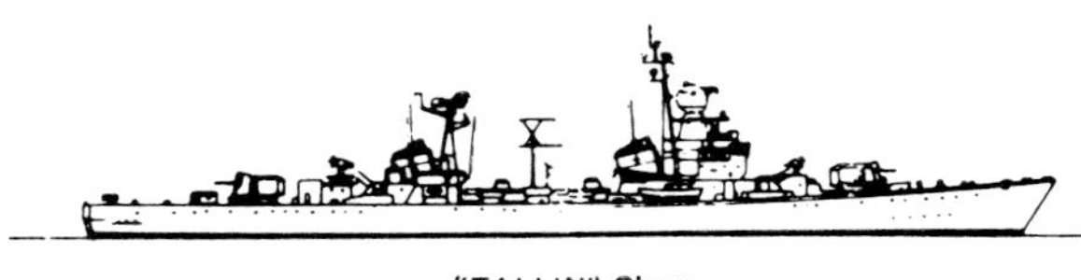

"TALLIN" Class

GUNNERY. The 5·1 inch (*130 mm*) guns in two twin turrets, including firing directors, are fully stabilised.

RADAR. Search: Slim Net and Strut Curve. Fire Control: Hawk Screech (2).

SOVIET TYPE NAME. Rated as Esminets meaning Destroyer.

NEUSTRASHIMY *Skyfotos*

FRIGATES

20 "MIRKA I AND II" CLASS

Displacement, tons	950 standard; 1 100 full load
Length, feet (*metres*)	269·9 (*82·3*)
Beam, feet (*metres*)	29·9 (*9·1*)
Draught, feet (*metres*)	9·8 (*3·0*)
Guns	4—3 in (*76 mm*) (2 twin) (I)
A/S weapons	4—12 barrel MBUs (2 forward, 2 aft) (1); 2—16 barrel MBUs (II)
Torpedo tubes	5—16 in anti-submarine (I) 10—16 in (II)
Main engines	2 diesels; total 6 000 hp; 2 gas-turbines, total 31 000 hp; 2 shafts
Speed, knots	33
Complement	100

"MIRKA II" Class (with two torpedo mountings)

This class of ships was built in 1964-69 as improved "Petya" class. The difference between the Mark I and II is that the latter have the after MBU rocket launchers removed and an additional quintuple 16-inch torpedo mounting fitted between the bridge and the mast. At least one mounts VDS aft.

SOVIET TYPE NAMES. Rated as Storozhevoy Korabl meaning Escort Ship.

"MIRKA" Class

RADAR. Search: Slim Net. Fire Control: Hawk Screech.

"MIRKA II" Class (with two torpedo mountings) 1972

20 "PETYA I" CLASS
25 "PETYA II" CLASS

Displacement, tons	950 standard; 1 150 full load
Length, feet (*metres*)	270 (*82·3*)
Beam, feet (*metres*)	29·9 (*9·1*)
Draught, feet (*metres*)	10·5 (*3·2*)
Guns	4—3 in (*76 mm*), (2 twin)
A/S weapons	4—16 barrelled MBUs (I) 2—12 barrelled MBUs (II)
Torpedo tubes	5—16 in (*406 mm*) (I) 10—16 in (*406 mm*) (II)
Main engines	2 diesels, total 6 000 hp; 2 gas-turbines; total 30 000 hp; 2 shafts
Speed, knots	30
Complement	100

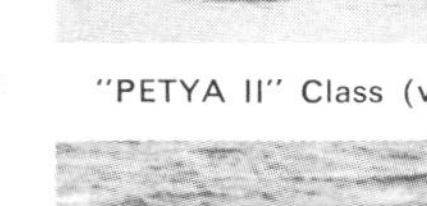

"PETYA" Class

Small freeboard with a low wide funnel. The first ship reported to have been built in 1960-61 at Kaliningrad. Construction continued until about 1964. Fitted with two mine rails. "Petya II's" sacrifice MBU's for extra tubes whilst some of both classes have lost the after 3 in turret to compensate for VDS.

RADAR. Search: Slim Net. Fire Control: Hawk Screech.

SOVIET TYPE NAME. Rated as Storozhevkoy Korabl meaning Escort Ship.

"PETYA II" Class (with VDS) *1973, S. Breyer*

"PETYA II" Class *1970, MOD (UK)*

"PETYA II" Class *10/1974, USN*

Frigates—*continued*

40 "RIGA" CLASS

BARSUK **BUJVOL** **BYK** **GEPARD** **GIENA** **KOBCHIK** **LEV** **LISA** **MEDVED** **PANTERA** **SAKAL** **TIGR** **TURMAN** **VOLK** +26

Displacement, tons	1 200 standard; 1 600 full load
Length, feet (*metres*)	298·8 (*91·0*)
Beam, feet (*metres*)	33·7 (10·2)
Draught, feet (*metres*)	11 (*3·4*)
Guns	3—3·9 in (*100 mm*) single 4—37 mm (2 twin); 4—30 mm (twin) in some
A/S weapons	2—16 barrelled MBUs (in some); 4 DC projectors
Torpedo tubes	3—21 in (*533 mm*) (2 (twin) in some)
Mines	50
Main engines	Geared turbines; 2 shafts; 25 000 shp
Boilers	2
Speed, knots	28
Range, miles	2 500 at 15 knots
Complement	150

Built from 1952 to 1959. Successors to the "Kola" class escorts, of which they are lighter and less heavily armed but improved versions. Fitted with mine rails.

ANTI-SUBMARINE. The two 16-barrelled MBU rocket launchers are mounted just before the bridge abreast "B" gun.

'RIGA" Class *1973, H. W. van Boeijen*

CONVERSIONS. A small number of this class has been converted. Some, designed for ECM operations, have a higher funnel, more complex electronics, no torpedo tubes but with MBU (A/S) launchers. Others have had the triple torpedo-tube mountings replaced by more modern twin mountings and have a twin 30 mm gun mounting on either side of the funnel.

RADAR. Search: Slim Net. Fire Control: Obsolescent type.

SOVIET TYPE NAME. Rated as Storozhevoy Korabl meaning Escort Ship.

"RIGA" Class

TRANSFERS. Bulgaria (2), China (4), East Germany (2), Finland (2), Indonesia (6).

"RIGA" Class *6/1974*

6 "KOLA" CLASS

DOBLESTNY **SOVIETSKY AZERBAIDJAN** **SOVIETSKY DAGESTAN** **SOVIETSKY TURKMENISTAN** **ZESKY** **ZIVUCHI**

Displacement, tons	1 500 standard; 1 900 full load
Length, feet (*metres*)	315·0 (*96·0*) oa
Beam, feet (*metres*)	35·4 (*10·8*)
Draught, feet (*metres*)	10·6 (*3·2*)
Guns,	4—3·9 (*100 mm*) single
A/S weapons	2 MBU-900, 4 DC racks, 4 DC rails
Torpedo tubes	3—21 in (*533 mm*)
Mines	30
Main engines	Geared turbines; 2 shafts; 30 000 shp
Boilers	2
Speed, knots	30
Range, miles	3 500 at 12 knots
Complement	190

Built in 1950-52. In design this class of flushdecked frigates appears to be a combination of the former German "Elbing" class destroyers, with a similar hull form, and of the earlier Soviet "Birds" class escorts. Three are stationed in the Caspian Sea, one is in reserve in the Baltic whilst two have been converted as auxiliaries.

GUNNERY. The four 3·9 inch guns were mounted as in the "Gordy" class destroyers.

RADAR. Ball Gun/Ball End, surface search; Cross Bird, air search; Wasp Head and Sun Visor, fire control; High Pole, IFF.

"KOLA" Class

SOVIET TYPE NAME. Rated as Storozhevoy Korabl meaning Escort Ship.

"KOLA" Class

CORVETTES

17 "GRISHA I" and "GRISHA II" CLASSES

Displacement, tons 750 full load
Dimensions, feet 234·8 × 32·8 × 9·2
Missile launchers SAN-4 surface-to-air (twin) ("Grisha I" class)
Guns 2—57 mm dual purpose (1 twin) (4 in "GRISHA II" class)
Torpedo tubes 4—16 anti-submarine
A/S weapons 2—12 barrelled MBUs
Main engines 2 gas-turbines; 2 diesels = 30 knots

Reported to have started series production in the late 1969-70 period. Five built by end of 1972, with a continuing programme of 4 a year. SAN-4 launcher mounted on the forecastle in "Grisha I" class. This is replaced by a second twin 57 mm in "Grisha II" Class.

SOVIET TYPE NAME. Rated as Maly Protivo Lodochny Korabl meaning Small Anti-Submarine Ship.

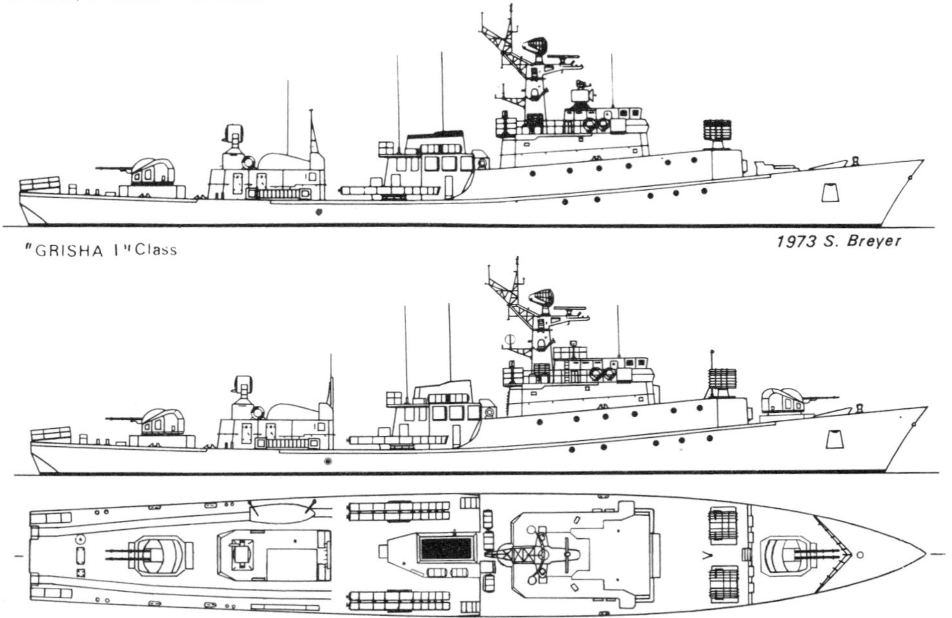
"GRISHA I" Class — *1973 S. Breyer*

"GRISHA II" Class — *1975. S, Breyer*

"GRISHA I" Class — *7/1974*

"GRISHA I" Class — *1972*

"GRISHA II" Class — *7/1974*

Corvettes—*continued*

70 "POTI" CLASS

Displacement, tons	550 standard; 650 full load
Dimensions, feet	195·2 × 26·2 × 9·2
Guns	2—57 mm AA (1 twin mounting)
Tubes	4—16 in anti-submarine
A/S weapons	2—12 barrelled MBUs
Main engines	2 gas turbines; 2 diesels; 4 shafts; total 20 000 hp = 28 knots

This class of ships was under series construction from 1961 to 1968. Strut Curve and Muff Cob Radars.

SOVIET TYPE NAME. Rated as Maly Protivo Lodochny Korabl meaning Small Anti-Submarine Ship.

"Poti" Class *1971*

"Poti" Class *1970, S. Breyer*

"POTI" Class

80 "SO I" CLASS

Displacement, tons	215 light; 250 normal
Dimensions, feet	138·6 × 20·0 × 9·2
Guns	4—25 mm AA (2 twin mountings) see notes
A/S weapons	4 five-barrelled MBUs
Main engines	3 diesels; 6 000 bhp = 29 knots
Range, miles	1 100 at 13 knots
Complement	30

Built since 1957. Steel hulled. Modernised boats of this class have only two 25 mm AA guns but also have four 16 in anti-submarine torpedo tubes. Being phased out of service.

SOVIET TYPE NAME. Rated as Maly Provito Lodochny Korabl meaning small Anti-Submarine ship.

"SO I" Class *1968*

"SO I" Class

17 "KRONSTADT" CLASS

Displacement, tons	310 standard; 380 full load
Dimensions, feet	170·6 × 21·5 × 9·0
Guns	1—3·5 in; 2—37 mm AA; 6 MGs (twins)
A/S weapons	Depth charge projectors (some have 2—5 barrelled MBUs)
Main engines	3 diesels; 3 shafts; 3 300 hp = 24 knots
Range, miles	1 500 at 12 knots
Complement	65

Built in 1948-56. Flush-decked with large squat funnel, slightly raked, and massive block bridge structure. Pot Head radar. Now being phased out of service due to age. About 20 ships were rebuilt as communications relay ships of the "Libau" class.

SOVIET TYPE NAME. Rated as Maly Protivo Lodochny Korabl meaning Small Anti-Submarine Ship.

TRANSFERS. Bulgaria (2), China (24), Cuba (18), Indonesia (14), Poland (8), Romania (3).

"KRONSTADT" Class

"Kronstadt" Class

"Kronstadt" Class *1970, courtesy, Godfrey H. Walker Esq.*

5 "T 43"/AGR CLASS

Displacement, tons	500 standard; 610 full load
Dimensions, feet	190·2 × 28·2 × 6·9
Guns	4—37 mm AA; 2—25 mm AA
Main engines	2 diesels; 2 shafts; 2 000 bhp = 17 knots
Range, miles	1 600 at 10 knots
Complement	60

Former fleet minesweepers of the "T 43" class converted into radar pickets with comprehensive electronic equipment. It is reported that there may be a dozen vessels of this type. A large Big Net -like radar is mounted on the mainmast.

"T43-AGR" Class *1973, S. Breyer*

Corvettes—*continued*

12 "NANUCHKA" CLASS

(MISSILE CORVETTE)

Displacement, tons	800 normal (approx)
Length, feet (*metres*)	196·8 (*60·0*)
Beam, feet (*metres*)	39·6 (*12·0*)
Draught, feet (*metres*)	9·9 (*3·0*)
Missile launchers	6 (2 triple) for SSN-9 surface-to-surface system SAN-4 surface-to-air system forward (twin)
Guns	2—57 mm AA (1 twin)
A/S weapons	1 or 2 MBUs
Main engines	Diesels
Speed, knots	32

A new class of diesel powered craft with SSM launchers as the main armament probably mainly intended for deployment in coastal waters. Reported to have a very high beam to length ratio making her a much steadier firing platform than the "*Osas*" and "*Komars*." Built from 1969 onwards. Has received many type designations including "Missile Cutter". Building continues at rate of about 3 a year at Leningrad.

RADAR. Search: Slim Net. Fire Control: Hawk Screech

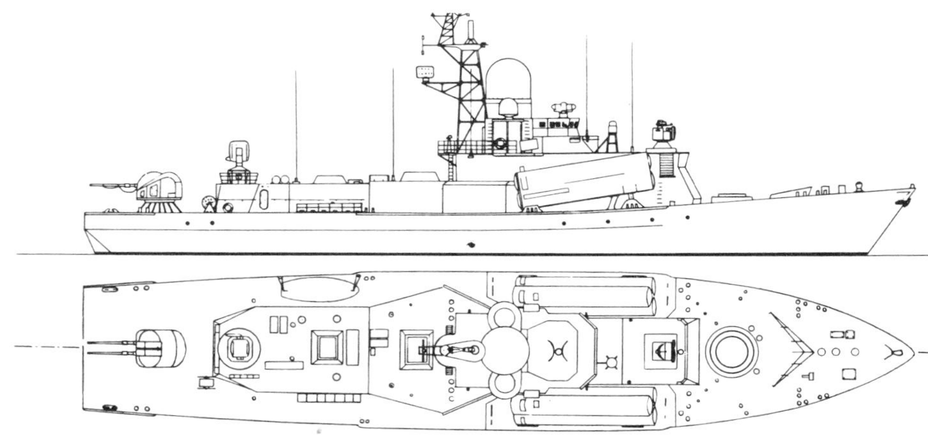

"NANUCHKA" Class fitting out — *1973*

"NANUCHKA" Class — *1974, S, Breyer*

"NANUCHKA" Class — *1974, S, Breyer*

LIGHT FORCES

120 "OSA I and II" CLASS (65 I and 55 II)

(FAST ATTACK CRAFT—MISSILE)

Displacement, tons	165 standard; 200 full load
Dimensions, feet	128·7 × 25·1 × 5·9
Missile launchers	4 in two pairs abreast for SSN-2A or SSN-11
Guns	4—30 mm; (2 twin, 1 forward, 1 aft)
Main engines	3 diesels; 13 000 bhp = 32 knots
Range, miles	800 at 25 knots
Complement	25

These boats, built since 1959, have a larger hull and four launchers in two pairs as compared with one pair in the "Komar" class. They have a surface-to-surface missile range of up to 23 miles. Later boats have cylindrical missile launchers, comprising the "Osa II" class.
This class was a revolution in naval shipbuilding. Although confined by their size and range to coastal operations the lethality and accuracy of the Styx missile have already been proved by the sinking of the Israeli destroyer *Eilat* on 21 Oct 1967 by an Egyptian "Komar". The operations of the Indian "Osa's" in the war with Pakistan in December 1971 were equally successful against merchant vessels by night. These operations surely represent a most important lesson in naval operations and, in light of this, the list of transfers should be noted.

TRANSFERS. Algeria (3), Bulgaria (3), China (17), Cuba (2), Egypt (12), East Germany (12), India (8), Iraq (5), Poland (12), Romania (5), Syria (5), Yugoslavia (10).

"Osa II" Class *1970, Godfrey H. Walker*

"Osa" I Class *1970*

"OSA I" (right) and "OSA II" Classes *1973, TASS*

15 "KOMAR" CLASS (FAST ATTACK CRAFT—MISSILE)

Displacement, tons	70 standard; 80 full load
Dimensions, feet	83·7 × 19·8 × 5·0
Missile launchers	2 for SSN-2A system
Guns	2—25 mm AA (1 twin forward)
Range, miles	400 at 30 knots
Main engines	4 diesels; 4 shafts; 4 800 bhp = 40 knots

A smaller type of boat converted from "P 6" class torpedo boats. Fitted with two surface-to-surface launchers aft in a hooded casing approximately 45 degrees to the deck line with a range of 23 miles. First units completed 1961. Being phased out of service.

TRANSFERS. Algeria (6), China (10), Cuba (18), Egypt (6), Indonesia (12), Korea (N) (6), Syria (3).

"Komar" Class

45 "STENKA" CLASS (FAST ATTACK CRAFT—PATROL)

Displacement, tons	170 standard; 210 full load
Dimensions, feet	130·7 × 25·1 × 6·0
Guns	4—30 mm AA (2 twin)
Torpedo tubes	4—16 in (*406 mm*) anti-submarine
A/S weapons	2 depth charge racks
Main engines	3 diesels; 10 000 bhp = 40 knots
Complement	25

Based on the hull design of the "Osa" class. Built from 1967-68 onwards.

RADAR. Search: Square Tie. Fire Control: Drum Tilt. Pot Drum.

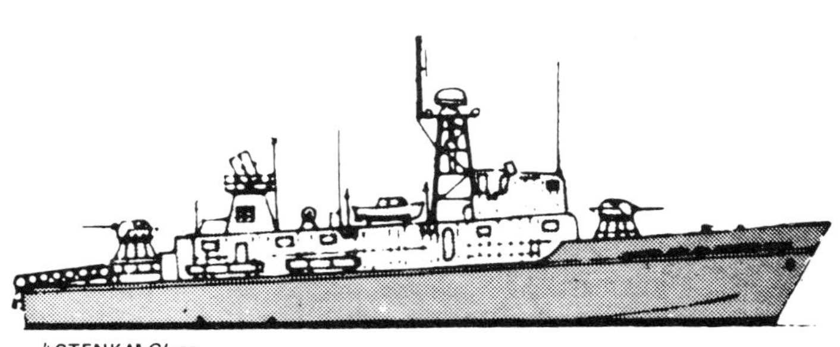

"STENKA" *Class*

"STENKA" Class *1974*

Light Forces—*continued*

12 "TURYA" CLASS (FAST ATTACK CRAFT—PATROL HYDROFOIL)

Displacement, tons	165
Dimensions, feet	123 × 27·9 × 5·9
Guns	2—57 mm (twin, aft); 2—25 mm (twin, f'd)
Torpdeo tubes	4—21 inch
Speed, knots	40

A new class of hydrofoils with a naval orientation rather than the earlier "Pchela" class. Entered service from 1973—in series production, possibly 3 per year.

RADAR. Pot Drum and Drum Tilt.

SONAR. A form of VDS is fitted on the transom. In view of this the apparent lack of A/S weapons is surprising. Could operate with shore-based helicopters.

"TURYA" Class *1974, S, Breyer*

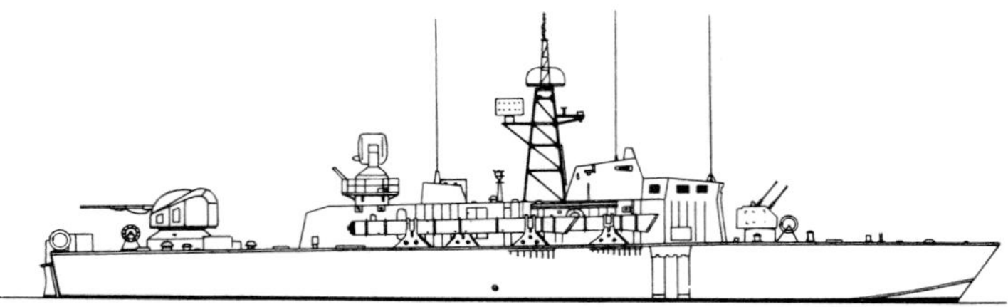

"TURYA" Class *1975, S, Breyer*

25 "PCHELA" CLASS

(FAST ATTACK CRAFT—TORPEDO HYDROFOIL)

Displacement, tons	70 standard; 80 full load
Dimensions, feet	82·0 × 19·7 × ?
Guns	4 MG (2 twin)
Main engines	2 diesels; 6 000 bhp = 50 knots

This class of hydrofoils, is reported to have been built since 1964-65. Also carry depth charges. Used for frontier guard duties by KGB.

"Pchela" Class *1970*

45 "SHERSHEN" CLASS (FAST ATTACK CRAFT—TORPEDO)

Displacement, tons	150 standard; 160 full load
Dimensions, feet	115·5 × 23·1 × 5·0
Guns	4—30 mm AA (2 twin)
Tubes	4—21 in (single)
A/S weapons	12 DC
Main engines	Diesels; 3 shafts; 13 000 bhp = 41 knots
Complement	16

RADAR. Pot Drum and Drum Tilt. High Pole IFF.

TRANSFERS. Bulgaria (4), East Germany (15), Egypt (6), Yugoslavia (13).

"Shershen" Class *1970, S. Breyer*

80 "P 6" "P 8" "P 10" CLASSES

(FAST ATTACK CRAFT—TORPEDO)

Displacement, tons	66 standard; 75 full load
Dimensions, feet	84·2 × 20·0 × 6·0
Guns	4—25 mm AA
Tubes	2—21 in (or mines, or depth charges)
Main engines	4 diesels; 4 shafts; 4 800 bhp = 43 knots. Gas-turbines in "P 8" and "P 10" classes
Range, miles	450 at 30 knots
Complement	25

The "P 6" class was of a standard medium sized type running into series production. Launched during 1951 to 1960. Known as "MO VI" class in the submarine chaser version. The later versions, known as the "P 8" and "P 10" classes, are powered with gas-turbines, and have different bridge and funnel, "P 8" boats have hydrofoils. This class is now being deleted because of old age.

TRANSFERS. Algeria (12), China (80, indigenous construction), Cuba (12), Egypt (24), East Germany (18), Guinea (4), Indonesia (14), Iraq (12), Nigeria (3), Poland (20), North Vietnam (6), Somalia (2).

"P 6" Class

" P 6" Class after modernisation *1972, S. Breyer*

"P 8" Class *1969, S. Breyer*

"P 10" Class *1968, S. Breyer*

Light Forces—*continued*

15 "MO VI" CLASS (FAST ATTACK CRAFT—PATROL)

Displacement, tons	64 standard; 73 full load
Dimensions, feet	83·6 × 19·7 × 4·0
Guns	4—25 mm AA (2 twin)
A/S weapons	2 depth charge mortars; 2 depth charge racks
Main engines	4 diesels; 4 shafts; 4 800 bhp = 40 knots

Built in 1956 to 1960. Based on the hull design of the "P-6"

"MO VI" Class *1972*

10 "P 4" CLASS (FAST ATTACK CRAFT—TORPEDO)

Displacement, tons	22
Dimensions, feet	62·7 × 11·6 × 5·6
Guns	2—15 mm MG (twin)
Tubes	2—18 in
Main engines	2 Diesels; 2 shafts; 2 200 bhp = 50 knots

Originally a numerically large class of boats with aluminium alloy hulls. Launched in 1951-58. The earlier units are being discarded.

TRANSFERS. Albania (12), Bulgaria (8), China (70), Cuba (12), Cyprus (6), North Korea (40), Romania (13), Somalia (4), Syria (17).

"P 4" Class

RIVER PATROL CRAFT

Attached to Black Sea and Pacific Fleets for operations on the Danube, Amur and Usuri Rivers, and to the Caspian Flotilla.

40 "SCHMEL" CLASS

Displacement, tons	120
Length, feet	92
Guns	1—76 mm; 2—25 mm (twin)
Speed, knots	20
Complement	15

Forward gun mounted in a tank-type turret. Some also mount a ten-barrelled rocket launcher amidships. Built between 1958 and 1966.

"SCHMEL" Class *1973, J, Rowe*

"SCHMEL" Class (with rocket launcher) *1972, TASS*

30 "BK 3" CLASS

Displacement, tons	120
Length, feet	95
Guns	1—76 mm; 4 MG (twin mounts)
Speed, knots	22
Complement	20

Not unlike the "Schmel" class but with an additional MG mounting at after end of the waist.

"BK 3" Class *1973, J, Meister*

20 "BKL 4" CLASS

Displacement, tons	60
Length, feet	55
Guns	2—20 mm; 6 MG
Speed, knots	28

PS 10

Displacement, tons	approx 250
Guns	2—20 mm
Speed, knots	15

Acts as Senior officers ship for the Danube squadron.

PS 10 *1973, J, Meister*

"PR" CLASS

Displacement, tons	90
Dimensions, feet	88 × 18 × 3
Guns	1—76 mm; 2—25 mm
Speed, knots	25

ROK 9

Of approximately 100 tons—probably acts as support ship to Danube squadron.

ROK 9 *1973, J, Meister*

MINE WARFARE FORCES

NOTE. The "Alesha" class (under Support and Depot Ships) probably has a primary minelaying role.

16 "NATYA" CLASS (MINESWEEPERS—OCEAN)

Displacement, tons	650
Dimensions, feet	200·1 × 34·1 × 7·2
Guns	4—30 mm AA (2 twin); 4—25 mm AA (2 twin)
A/S weapons	2 5-barrelled MBUs
Main engines	2 diesels; 5 000 bhp = 18 knots

A new class of fleet minesweepers first reported in 1971, evidently intended as successors to the "Yurka" class. Building rate of 3 a year.

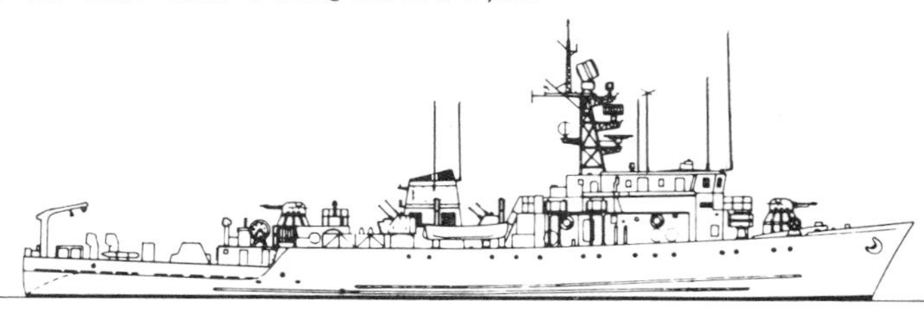

"NATYA" Class *1973, S. Breyer*

45 "YURKA" CLASS (MINESWEEPERS—OCEAN)

Displacement, tons	500 standard; 550 full load
Dimensions, feet	171·9 × 31 × 8·9
Guns	4—30 mm AA (2 twin)
Main engines	2 diesels; 4 000 bhp = 18 knots

A class of medium fleet minesweepers with steel hull. Built from 1963 to the late 1960s.
TRANSFER. 4 to Egypt.

"YURKA" Class *1974, S. Breyer*

20 "T 58" CLASS (MINESWEEPERS—OCEAN)

Displacement, tons	790 standard; 900 full load
Dimensions, feet	229·9 × 29·5 × 7·9
A/S weapons	2—5 barrelled MBUs
Guns	4—57 mm AA (2 twin)
Main engines	2 diesels; 2 shafts; 4 000 bhp = 18 knots

Built from 1957 to 1964. Of this class 14 were converted to submarine rescue ships with armament and sweeping gear removed, see later page ("Valdai" class).

"T 58" with Muff Cob fire control radar on bridge *1968*

110 "T 43" CLASS (MINESWEEPERS—OCEAN)

Displacement, tons	500 standard; 610 full load
Dimensions, feet	190·2 × 28·2 × 6·9
Guns	4—37 mm AA (2 twin); 4—25 mm AA (2 twin)
Main engines	2 diesels; 2 shafts; 2 000 bhp = 17 knots
Range, miles	1 600 at 10 knots
Complement	40

Built in 1948-57 in shipyards throughout the Soviet Union. A number of this class were converted into radar pickets. The remainder are gradually being replaced by newer types of fleet minesweepers.
TRANSFERS. Algeria (2), Albania (2), Bulgaria (2), China (20), Egypt (6), Indonesia (6), Poland (12), Syria (2).

"T 43" Class *1972*

3 "SONYA" CLASS

A new design of MSC of similar size to the "Zhenya" class. Now in series production.

3 "ZHENYA" CLASS (MINESWEEPERS—COASTAL)

Displacement, tons	320
Dimensions, feet	141 × 25 × 7
Guns	2—30 mm (twin)
Main engines	2 diesels = ? 18 knots

Reported to be a trial class for GRP hulls.

"ZHENYA" Class *1974, S. Breyer*

70 "VANYA" CLASS (MINESWEEPERS—COASTAL)

Displacement, tons	250 standard; 275 full load
Dimensions, feet	130·7 × 24 × 6·9
Guns	2—30 mm AA (1 twin)
Main engines	2 diesels; 2 200 bhp = 18 knots
Complement	30

A coastal class with wooden hulls of a type suitable for series production built from 1961 onwards. Basically similar to NATO type coastal minesweepers.

"Vanya" Class *1970, S. Breyer*

40 "SASHA" CLASS (MINESWEEPERS—COASTAL)

Displacement, tons	245 standard; 280 full load
Dimensions, feet	150·9 × 20·5 × 6·6
Guns	1—57mm dp; 4—25 mm AA (2 twin)
Main engines	2 diesels; 2 200 bhp = 18 knots
Complement	25

Basically similar to NATO coastal minesweepers, but of steel construction.

"Sasha" Class *1968, S. Breyer*

5 "T 301" CLASS (MINESWEEPERS—COASTAL)

Displacement, tons	150 standard; 180 full load
Dimensions, feet	128·0 × 18·0 × 4·9
Guns	2—37 mm AA; 4 MG (twin)
Main engines	2 diesels; 2 shafts; 1 440 bhp = 17 knots

Built from 1946 to 1956. Several were converted to survey craft, and many adapted for other purposes or used for port duty and auxiliary service. Now being withdrawn from service due to age.

"T 301" Class

"TR 40" CLASS (MINESWEEPERS—INSHORE)

Displacement, tons	40 standard; 60 full load
Dimensions, feet	55·8 × 11·5 × 4·0
Guns	2—25 mm (twin) 2 MG (twin)
Main engines	Diesels; speed 18 knots

"K 8" CLASS (MINESWEEPERS—INSHORE)

Displacement, tons	50 standard; 70 full load
Dimensions, feet	92·0 × 13·5 × 2·3
Guns	2 MG (twin)
Main engines	Diesels; 600 bhp = 14 knots

Auxiliary motor minesweeping boats of the inshore ("RT 40") and river ("K 8") types. A total of about 100 of both classes in service.

AMPHIBIOUS FORCES

12 "ALLIGATOR" CLASS (LST)

ALEKSANDR TORTSEV
DONETSKY SHAKHTER
KRASNAYA PRESNYA
KRYMSKY KOMSOMOLETS
PETR ILICHEV
TOMSKY KOMSOMOLETS
VORONEZHSKY KOMSOMOLETS
+5

Displacement, tons	4 100 standard; 5 800 full load
Dimensions, feet	374·0 × 50·9 × 12·1
Guns	2—57 mm AA
Main engines	Diesels; 8 000 bhp = 15 knots

Largest type of landing ship built in the USSR to date. First ship built in 1965-66 and commissioned in 1966. These ships have ramps on the bow and stern. Carrying capacity 1 700 tons. There are three variations of rig. In earlier type two or three cranes are carried—later types have only one crane. In the third type the bridge structure has been raised and the forward deck house has been considerably lengthened.

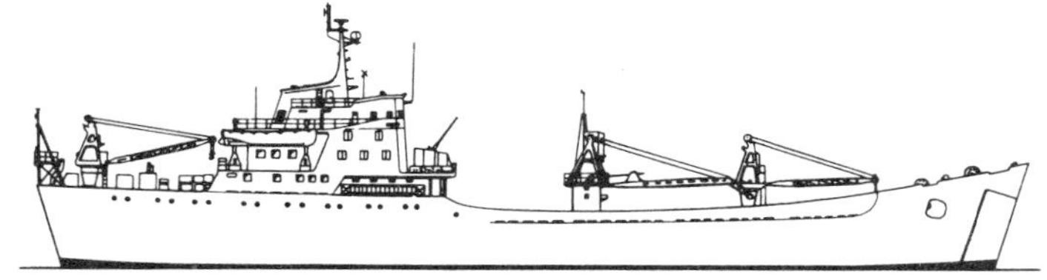

"ALLIGATOR I" Class — *1973 S. Breyer*

"ALLIGATOR" Class — *1972*

"ALLIGATOR II" Class — *1972, H W. Van Boeijen*

60 "POLNOCNY" CLASS (LCT)

(Note—A new class of LCTs, of which details are not available, has been reported).

Displacement, tons	780 standard; 1 000 full load (Type IX 1 300)
Dimensions, feet	246·0 × 29·5 × 9·8 (Type IX 285 × 27·7 × 9·8)
Guns	2—30 mm (twin) in all but earliest ships (see note)
A/S weapons	2—18 barrelled MBU
Main engines	2 diesels; 5 000 bhp = 18 knots

A type of amphibious vessel basically similar to the US medium landing ship, rocket (LSMR) type. Carrying capacity 350 tons. Can carry 6 tanks. Up to 9 types of this class have been built. In I to IV the mast and funnel are combined—in V onwards the mast is stepped on the bridge—in VI to VIII there is a redesign of the bow-form—IX is a completely new design of greater length with corresponding increase in tonnage and with 4—30 mm (2 twins). Muff Cob radar.

TRANSFERS. 3 to Egypt, 3 to India, 2 to S. Yemen.

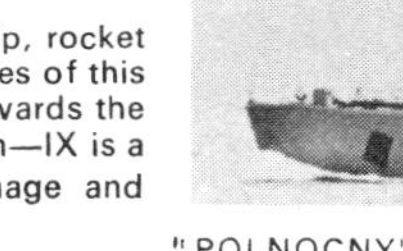

"POLNOCNY" Class with 2—30 mm AA before bridge and fire control radar on bridge

"POLNOCNY" Class—latest variant with higher funnel — *1974, S, Breyer*

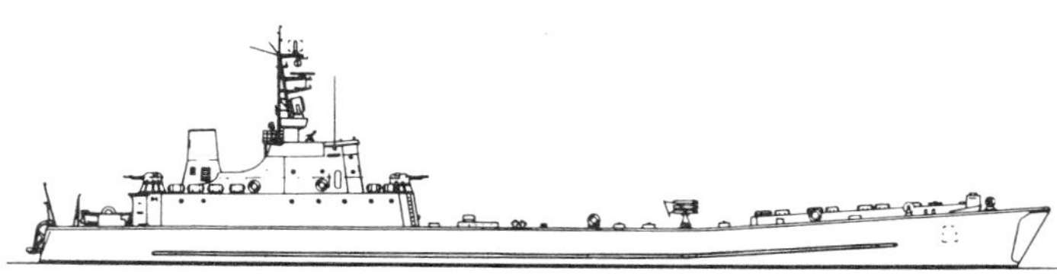

"POLNOCNY" Class with higher funnel — *1973, S. Breyer*

"POLNOCNY" Class — *1973*

Amphibious Forces —*continued*

35 "VYDRA" CLASS (LCU)

Displacement, tons	300 standard; 500 full load
Dimensions, feet	157·4 × 24·6 × 7·2
Main engines	2 diesels; 2 shafts; 400 hp = 15 knots

A new class of landing craft of the LCU type. Built from 1967-1969. No armament. Carrying capacity 250 tons.
TRANSFERS. 10 to Egypt.

"VYDRA" Class *1971*

8 "MP 2" CLASS (LCU)

Displacement, tons	750
Dimensions, feet	190 × 25 × 8·2
Guns	6—25 mm (twins)
Main engines	Diesels; 1 200 hp = 16 knots

Built 1956-60. Carrying capacity 200 tons.

15 "MP 4" CLASS (LCU)

Displacement, tons	800 full load
Dimensions, feet	183·7 × 26·2 × 8·9
Guns	4—25 mm (2 twin)
Main engines	Diesels; 2 shafts; 1 100 bhp = 12 knots

Built in 1956-58. Of the small freighter type in appearance. Two masts, one abaft the bridge and one in the waist. Gun mountings on poop and forecastle. Can carry 6 to 8 tanks. Several ships now serve as transports.

"MP 4" Class *1973, J. Rowe*

8 "MP 6" CLASS (LCU)

Displacement, tons	2 000
Dimensions, feet	246 × 40 × 10·5
Guns	4—45 mm (quad)
Main engines	Diesels; 2 400 hp = 14 knots

Ex-merchant ship hulls. Carrying capacity 500 tons. Built 1958-61.

5 "MP 8" CLASS (LCU)

Displacement, tons	800 standard; 1 200 full load
Dimensions, feet	239·5 × 34·8 × 15·1
Guns	4—57 mm (2 twin)
Main engines	Diesels; 4 000 bhp = 15 knots

Have a short and low quarter deck abaft the funnel. Can carry 6 tanks. Carrying capacity 400 tons. Built 1958-61.

"MP 8" Type *1970, S. Breyer*

10 "MP 10" CLASS (LCU)

Displacement, tons	200 standard; 420 full load
Dimensions, feet	157·5 × 21·3 × 6·5
Main engines	2 diesels; 2 shafts; 400 hp = 11 knots

A type of landing craft basically similar to the British LCT (4) type in silhouette and layout. Can carry 4 tanks. Loading capacity about 150 tons. Built 1959-66.

"MP 10" Class *1971*

"T 4" CLASS (LCM)

Main engines	3 diesels; 3 shafts; 3 300 bhp = 24 knots
Range, miles	1 500 at 12 knots

HYDROFOIL TYPE

A small landing craft of 92 ft length capable of carrying 2-3 tanks.

AIR CUSHION VEHICLES

(Numbers in service are not known. The following gives an indication of Soviet capability. Fuller details appear in *Jane's Surface Skimmers 1974-75*).

RESEARCH HOVERCRAFT

Operating weight,	15 tons
Dimensions, feet	70 × 30
Propulsion	2—350 hp aircraft radial engines;
Lift	1—350 hp aircraft radial with centrifugal fan
Speed, knots	50

In use in the Soviet Navy since 1967 for tests and evaluation.

Jane's Surface Skimmers

"SKATE" CLASS

Operating weight,	27 tons
Dimensions, feet	67·5 × 24
Propulsion	2—780 hp marine gas turbines (VP and reversible propellers)
Lift	1—780 hp marine gas turbine
Speed, knots	58
Range, miles	230 cruising

This is a naval version of a 50-seat passenger carrying craft, probably in use for the Naval Infantry.

A military derivitave of the "Skate" passenger ferry *Jane's Surface Skimmers*

ASSAULT CRAFT

Operating weight, tons	200 approx
Dimensions, feet	130 × 80 approx
Speed, knots	70 approx

Currently undergoing trials for Naval Infantry. Is the first large Soviet amphibious hovercraft. Similar to British SR.N4.

EKRANOPLAN CRAFT (WIG)

Dimensions, feet	400 × 125 (approx wing span)
Propulsion	Ten gas turbines (two to assist take-off then eight for cruising)
Speed, knots	300 approx

An experimental craft, a wing-in-ground-effect machine, with a carrying capacity of about 900 troops and with potential for a number of naval applications such as ASW, minesweeping or patrol. Claimed to be capable of operations in heavy weather as well as crossing marshes, ice and low obstacles.

EKRANOPLAN *Jane's Surface Skimmers*

SUPPORT AND DEPOT SHIPS

10 "UGRA" CLASS

(SUBMARINE DEPOT SHIP)

BORODINO
GANGUT
IVAN KOLYSHKIN
IVAN KUCHERENKO
TOBOL
VOLGA
+4

Displacement, tons	6 750 standard; 9 500 full load
Length, feet (*metres*)	463·8 (*141·4*)
Beam, feet (*metres*)	57·6 (*17·6*)
Aircraft	1 helicopter
Guns	8—57 mm (twin)
Range, miles	10 000 at 12 knots

Improved versions of the "Don" class. Built from 1961 onwards, all in Nikolayev. Equipped with workshops. Provided with a helicopter platform and, in later versions, a hangar. Carries a large derrick to handle torpedoes. Has mooring points in hull about 100 feet apart, and has baggage ports possibly for coastal craft and submarines. The last pair of this class mount a large superstructure from the mainmast to quarter-deck and are used for training.

RADAR. Search Slim Net. Fire Control: Hawk Screech (2). Strut Curve. Muff Cob.

TRANSFER. The ninth ship, *Amba*, which had four 76 mm guns, was transferred to India.

"UGRA" Class *Skyfotos*

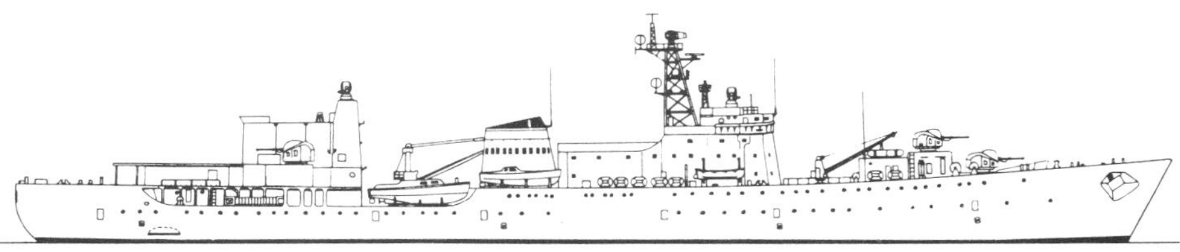

"UGRA" Class with raised helicopter platform and hangar *1973*

"UGRA" Class *1971, USN*

"UGRA" Class *1970, Niels Gartig*

"UGRA" Class *1972*

Support and Depot Ships—*continued*

6 "DON" CLASS (SUBMARINE SUPPORT)

DMITRI GALKIN	**MIKHAIL TUKAEVSKY**
FEDOR VIDYAEV	**NIKOLAY STOLBOV**
MAGOMED GADZHIEV	**VIKTOR KOTELNIKOV**

Displacement, tons	6 700 standard; 9 000 full load
Length, feet (*metres*)	458·9 (139·9)
Beam, feet (*metres*)	57·7 (*17·6*)
Draught, feet (*metres*)	22·3 (*6·8*)
Aircraft	Provision for helicopter in two ships
Guns	4—3·9 (*100 mm*) 8—57 mm (4 twin) (see *notes*)
Main engines	4 or 6 diesels; 14 000 bhp
Speed, knots	21
Complement	300

Support ships, all named after officers lost in WW II. Built in 1957 to 1962. Originally seven ships were built, all in Nikolaev. Quarters for about 450 submariners.

GUNNERY. In hull number III only 2—3·9 in. In IV no 3·9 in mounted. In some of class 8—25 mm (twin) are mounted.

RADAR. Search: Slim Net and probably Strut Curve. Fire Control: Hawk Screech (2).

TRANSFERS. 1 to Indonesia in 1962.

MAGOMED GADZHIEV 1970

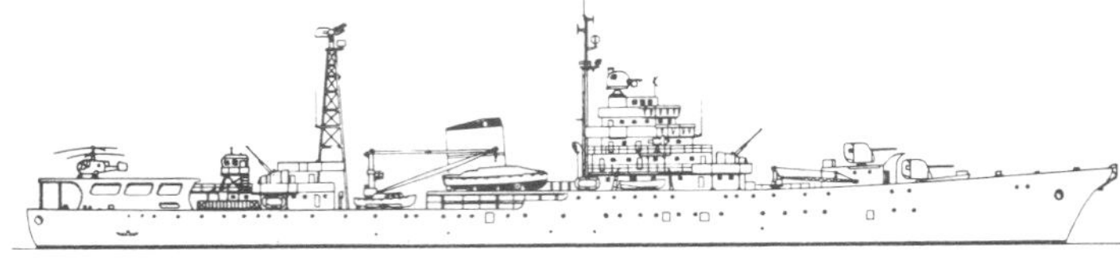

"DON" with helicopter platform S. Breyer

DMITRI GALKIN with new DF rig on mainmast 8/1974

1 "PURGA" CLASS

Displacement, tons	2 250 standard; 3 000 full load
Length, feet (*metres*)	324·8 (*99·0*)
Beam, feet (*metres*)	44·3 (*13·5*)
Draught, feet (*metres*)	17·1 (*5·2*)
Guns	4—3·9 in (*100 mm*) singles—2—25 mm
Mines	50 capacity
Main engines	Diesels
Speed, knots	18
Complement	250

Laid down in 1939 in Leningrad and completed in 1948. Sturdy oceangoing general purpose ship equipped as icebreaker, escort, training ship and tender. Fitted with directors similar to those in the "Riga" class frigates. Modernised in 1958-60.

"Purga" Class

Support and Depot Ships—*continued*

5 "LAMA" CLASS (MISSILE SUPPORT)

Displacement, tons	5 000 standard; 7 000 full load
Length, feet (*metres*)	370·0 (*112·8*) oa
Beam, feet (*metres*)	47·2 (*14·4*)
Draught, feet (*metres*)	19·0 (*5·8*)
Guns,	8—57 mm, 2 quadruple, 1 on the forecastle; 1 on the break of the quarter deck
Main engines	Diesels; 2 shafts; 5 000 shp
Speed, knots	15

The engines are sited aft to allow for a very large and high hangar or hold amidships for carrying missiles or weapons spares. This is about 12 feet high above the main deck. There are doors at the forward end with rails leading in and a raised turntable gantry or trâvelling cranes for transferring armaments to combatant ships.
There are mooring points along the hull for ships of low freeboard such as submarines to come alongside. The well deck is about 40 feet long, enough for a missile to fit horizontally before being lifted vertically for loading.

RADAR. Search: Slim Net and Strut Curve.
Fire Control: Hawk Screech, (2).

"Lama" Class *Skyfotos*

"LAMA" *Class* *S. Breyer*

1 "AMGA" CLASS

(MISSILE SUPPORT)

Displacement, tons	approx 5 500
Dimensions, ft (*m*)	361 × 56 × 19 (*110 × 17 × 5·8*)
Guns	4—30 mm (twins)
Main engines	Diesels = 18 knots

A single ship of similar size and duties to the "LAMA" class. May be distinguished from those ships by the break at the bridge, giving a lower freeboard than that of the "LAMAs". She is fitted with a large crane forward and is thus capable of handling much larger missiles than her predecessors. Probably, therefore, designed for servicing submarines, particularly those armed with SSN-8 missiles.

"AMGA" Class *1974, S, Breyer*

2 "ALESHA" CLASS (MINELAYERS)

075 **083**

Displacement, tons	3 600 standard; 4 300 full load
Dimensions, feet	337·9 × 47·6 × 15·7
Guns	4—57 mm AA (1 quadruple forward)
Mines	400
Main engines	4 diesels; 2 shafts; 8 000 bhp = 20 knots
Complement	150

In service since 1965. Fitted with four mine tracks to provide stern launchings. Also have a capability in general support role.

2 "WILHELM BAUER" CLASS (SUBMARINE TENDERS)

KUBAN (ex-*Waldemar Kophamel*) **PECHORA** (ex-*Otto Wünche*)

Displacement, tons	4 726 standard; 5 600 full load
Dimensions, feet	446·0 × 52·5 × 14·5
Main engines	4 MAN diesels; 2 shafts; 12 400 bhp = 20 knots

Former German. Launched in 1939. *Kuban* was salvaged in 1950-51 after being sunk in shallow water by bombing in WW II and was rehabilitated in 1951-57.

"ALESHA" Class *1972*

Support and Depot Ships—*continued*

12 "AMUR" CLASS (REPAIR SHIPS)

Displacement, tons	6 500 full load
Dimensions, feet	377·3 × 57·4 × 18·0
Main engines	Diesels; 2 shafts

A new class of general purpose depot ships built since 1969. Successors to the "Oskol" class. In series production at a rate of about 2 a year.

"AMUR" Class 1/1974

"AMUR" Class 1973

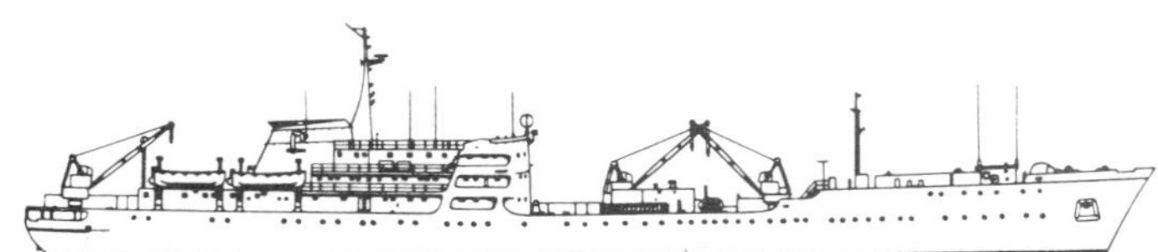

"AMUR" Class 1973 S. Breyer

10 "OSKOL" CLASS (REPAIR SHIPS)

Displacement, tons	2 500 standard; 3 000 full load
Dimensions, feet	295·2 × 39·4 × 14·8
Main engines	2 diesels; 2 shafts; speed = 16 knots

Three series: "Oskol I" class, well-decked hull, no armament; "Oskol II" Class, well-decked hull, armed with 2—57 mm guns (1 twin) and 4—25 mm guns (2 twin); "Oskol III" class, flush-decked hull. General purpose tenders and repair ships. Built from 1963 to 1970 in Poland.

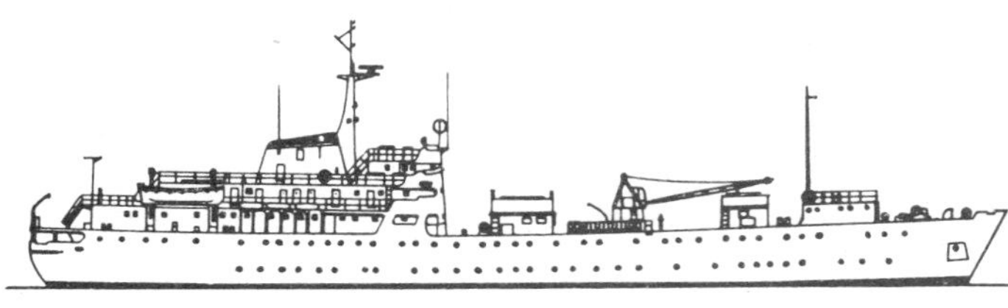

"OSKOL III" Class 1973, S. Breyer

6 "ATREK" CLASS (SUBMARINE SUPPORT)

ATREK AYAT BAKHMUT DVINA MURMATS OSIPOV

Displacement, tons	3 500 standard; 6 700 full load
Measurement, tons	3 258 gross
Dimensions, feet	336 × 49 × 20
Main engines	Expansion and exhaust turbines; 1 shaft; 2 450 hp = 13 knots
Boilers	2 water tube
Range, miles	3 500 at 13 knots

Built in 1956-58, and converted to naval use from "Kolomna" class freighters. There are six of these vessels employed as submarine tenders and replenishment ships. Some may have up to 6—37 mm (twins).

BAKHMUT 1974

5 "DNEPR" CLASS (SUBMARINE TENDERS)

Displacement, tons	4 500 standard; 5 250 full load
Dimensions, feet	370·7 × 54·1 × 14·4
Main engines	Diesels; 2 000 bhp = 12 knots

Bow lift repair ships for S/M support and maintenance. Built in 1957-66 and equipped with workshops and servicing facilities. The last two ships of this class form the "Dnepr II" Class.

"DNEPR II" Class 1974, S, Breyer

1 "TOVDA" CLASS (REPAIR SHIP)

TOVDA

Displacement, tons	3 000 standard; 4 000 full load
Dimensions, feet	282·1 × 39·4 × 16·0
Guns	6—57 mm AA (3 twin mountings)
Main engines	Triple expansion; 1 300 ihp = 11 knots

Polish built ex-tanker converted in 1958.

TOVDA 1959

54 INTELLIGENCE COLLECTORS (AGI'S)

6 "PRIMORYE" CLASS

PRIMORYE **KAVKAZ** **KRYM** **ZABAIKALYE** **ZAPOROZYE** **ZAKARPATYE**

Displacement, tons 5 000
Dimensions, feet 274 × 45 × 26·2

The most modern intelligence collectors in the world, apparently with built-in processing and possibly, analysis capability. Hull design is that of the "Majakowsky" class fish-factory ships.

"PRIMORYE"Class 1972

15 "OKEAN" CLASS

ALIDADA **AMPERMETR** **BAROGRAF** **BAROMETR** **DEFLEKTOR** **EKHOLOT** **GIDROFON** **KRENOMETR** **LINZA** **LOTLIN** **REDUKTOR** **REPITER** **TEODOLIT** **TRAVERZ** **ZOND**

Measurement, tons 680 gross
Dimensions, feet 178 × 30·6 × 15·9
Main engines Diesel; 1 shaft; 800 hp = 12 knots

Built in USSR 1965. Apparently identical to "Mayak" Class—both have the same variations in the superstructure with the port side closed in and the starboard side open.

REDUKTOR *1972, H. W. van Boeijen*

8 "LENTRA" CLASS

GS 34 **GS 36** **GS 41** **GS 43** **GS 46** **GS 47** **GS 55** **GS 59**

Displacement, tons 250
Measurement, tons 334 gross; 186 deadweight
Dimensions, feet 143 × 25 × 12·5
Main engines Diesel; 400 hp = 10·5 knots

All built in USSR 1957-63. Now have names in addition to numbers. Two known as *Neringa* and *Izvalta*.

"LENTRA" Class *1974, Michael D, J, Lennon*

8 "MAYAK" CLASS

ANEROID **GIRORULEVOY** **KHERSONES** **KURS** **KURSOGRAF** **LADOGA** **GS 239** **GS 242**

Measurement, tons 680 gross; 252 net
Dimensions, feet 178 × 30·6 × 15·9
Main engines Diesel = 13 knots

Built in USSR 1965. Apparently identical to "Okean" Class—see notes for that class.

"MAYAK" Class 1972

4 "MIRNY" CLASS

BAKAN **LOTSMAN** **VAL** **VERTIKAL**

Displacement, tons 850
Dimensions, feet 208 × 31·2 × 13·8
Main engines Diesel; 1 screw = 15 knots

"MINBY" Class AGI 1972

6 "MOMA" CLASS

ARKEPELAG **ILMEN** **JUPITER** **NAKHODKA** **PELORUS** **SELIGER**

Displacement, tons 1240 standard; 1800 full load
Dimensions, feet 219·8 × 32·8 × 13·2
Main engines Diesels = 16 knots

JUPITER *5/1974, Commander Aldo Fraccaroli*

Intelligence Collectors (AGIs)—*continued*

2 "PAMIR" CLASS

GIDROGRAF **PELENG**

Measurement, tons 2 000 gross
Dimensions, feet 256 oa × 42 × 13·5
Main engines 2—4 stroke Diesels; 2 shafts; 4 200 bhp = 17 knots

Built in Sweden 1959-60. Originally salvage tugs.

"PAMIR" Class *1970, S. Breyer*

2 "DNEPR" CLASS

IZMERITEL **PROTRAKTOR**

Measurement, tons 500 gross
Dimensions, feet 150 × 30 × 8
Main engines Diesel = 11 knots

1 "T 58" CLASS

GIDROLOG

Displacement, tons 900 full load
Dimensions, feet 229·9 × 29·5 × 7·9
Main engines 2 Diesels; 2 shafts; 4 000 bhp = 18 knots

Built in USSR 1962.

"T 58" Class

2 "ZUBOV" CLASS

G. SARYCHEV **K. LAPTEV**

Displacement, tons 3 021 full load
Dimensions, feet 295·2 × 42·7 × 15
Main engines Diesels; 2 shafts = 16·5 knots

Built in Poland 1975.

"ZUBOV" Class

SURVEY SHIPS

24 "MOMA" CLASS (+6 AGIs)

ALTAIR	**ASKOLD**	**KRILON**	**PELORUS**
ANADIR	**BEREZAN**	**KOLGUEV**	**RYBACHI**
ANDROMEDA	**CHELEKEN**	**LIMAN**	**SEVER**
ANTARES	**EKVATOR**	**MARS**	**TAYMYR**
ANTON KTYDA	**ELTON**	**MORSOVIEC**	**VEGA**
ARTIKA	**KILDIN**	**OKEAN**	**ZAPOLARA**

Displacement, tons 1 240 standard; 1 800 full load
Dimensions, feet 219·8 × 32·8 × 13·2
Main engines Diesels; speed 16 knots

Eight ships of this class were reported to have been built from 1967 to 1970 and the remainder since. Naval manned.

BEREZAN, *1974, Michael D. J. Lennon*

9 "KAMENKA" CLASS

10 "BIYA" CLASS

Displacement, tons 1 000 standard
Dimensions, feet 180·5 × 31·2 × 11·5
Main engines Diesels; speed 16 knots

The ships of these classes are not named but have a number with the prefix letters "GS". All reported to have been built since 1967-68. Naval manned.

4 "TELNOVSK" CLASS

AYTADOR **GROMOVA** **ULYA** **SVIYAGA**

Displacement, tons 1 200 standard
Measurement, tons 1 217 gross, 448 net
Dimensions, feet 229·6 × 32·8 × 13·1
Main engines Diesels; speed 10 knots

Formerly coastal freighters. Built in Bulgaria and Hungary. Refitted and modernised for naval supply and surveying duties. Naval manned.
Sister ship *Stvor* appears under Training Ships.

AYTADOR *1974, Michael D, J, Lennon*

IZUMRUD

Measurement, tons 3 862 gross; 465 net
Main engines Powered by diesel-electric machinery

A new type of research and survey ship built in 1970. Civilian manned.

IZUMRUD *1972, Michael D. J. Lennon*

Survey Ships—*continued*

16 "SAMARA" CLASS

AZIMUT **DEVIATOR** **GIDROLOG** **GIGROMETR** **GLOBUS** **GLUBOMER** **GORIZONT** **GRADUS** **KOMPAS** **PAMYAT MERKURYIA** **RUMB** **TROPIK** **ZENIT** **VAGACH** **VOSTOK** **YUG**

Displacement, tons	800 standard; 1 000 full load
Measurement, tons	1 276 gross; 1 000 net
Dimensions, feet	180·4 × 32·8 × 11·5
Main engines	Diesels; speed 16 knots

Built at Gdansk, Poland since 1962 for hydrographic surveying and research. Naval manned.

KOMPAS *1970, Michael D. J. Lennon*

GLOBUS *1972, Michael D. J. Lennon*

AZIMUT *1972, Michael D. J. Lennon*

AKADEMIK KOVALEVSKY   AKADEMIK VAVILOV

Measurement, tons	284 gross (*Vavilov* 255)
Dimensions, feet	126·8 × 23·7 × 11·5 (*Vavilov* 119·7 × 24·1 × 11·5)
Main engines	1 Diesel = 10 knots

Built in E. Germany in 1949.

AKADEMIK KOVALEVSKY *1974, Michael D, J, Lennon*

AKADEMIK ARKHANGELSKY

Measurement, tons	416 tons gross
Dimensions, feet	132·9 × 25 × 13
Main engines	1 Diesel = 10 knots

Built in USSR in 1963.

AKADEMIK ARKHANGELSKY *1974, Michael D. J. Lennon*

MGLA

Measurement, tons	299 gross
Dimensions, feet	129·5 × 24·3 × 11·8
Main engines	1 Diesel = 8·5 knots

MGLA *1974, Michael D. J. Lennon*

11 "DMITRI OVSTYN" CLASS

A. SMIRNOV **DMITRI LAPTEV** **DMITRI OVSTYN** **DMITRI STERLEGOV** **E. TOLL** **N. KOLOMEYTSEV** **N. YEVGENOV*** **S. KRAKOV*** **STEFAN MALYGIN** **VALERIAN ALBANOV** **V. SUKHOTSKY***

Displacement, tons	1 800 full load
Dimensions, feet	220 × 39 × 15
Main engines	Diesels; 2 000 bhp = 16 knots

Built by Turku, Finland. Launched 1970-72. Civilian manned. Employed largely on geological research and survey in the Arctic. Last three, marked *, completed Jan-Aug 1974.

Survey Ships—*continued*

MIKHAIL LOMONOSOV

Displacement, tons	5 960 normal
Measurement, tons	3 897 gross; 1 195 net
Dimensions, feet	336·0 × 47·2 × 14·0
Main engines	Triple expansion; 2 450 ihp = 13 knots

Built by Neptune, Rostock, in 1957 from the hull of a freighter of the "Kolomna" class. Operated not by the Navy but by the Academy of Science. Equipped with 16 laboratories. Carries a helicopter for survey. Civilian manned.

MIKHAIL LOMONOSOV — *1970, Michael D. J. Lennon*

9 "NIKOLAI ZUBOV" CLASS

A. CHIRIKOV
A. VILKITSKY
BORIS DAVIDOV
F. LITKE
NIKOLAI ZUBOV
S. CHELYUSKIN
SEJMEN DEZHNEV
T. BELLINSGAUSEN
V. GOLOVNIN

Displacement, tons	2 674 standard; 3 021 full load
Dimensions, feet	295·2 × 42·7 × 15
Main engines	2 diesels; speed = 16·7 knots
Complement	108 to 120, including 70 scientists

Oceanographic research ships built at Szczecin Shipyard, Poland in 1964. *Nikolai Zubov* visited London in 1965. Employed on survey in the Atlantic. Naval manned.

ANDREY VILKITSKY — *1973, Michael D, J, Lennon*

DOLINSK

Measurement, tons	10 826 deadweight; 5 419 gross, 2 946 net
Dimensions, feet	456·0 × 58·0 × 15·5
Main engines	2 diesels

Built at Abo in Finland in 1959. Converted for surveying. Naval manned.

DOLINSK — *1972, Michael D, J, Lennon*

ZARYA

Measurement, tons	71 net; 333 gross

Built in 1952 for geomagnetic survey work. Civilian manned.

ZARYA — *1972, Michael D, J, Lennon*

NEREY NOVATOR

Measurement, tons	369 gross
Dimensions, feet	118·1 × 24·7 × 11·5
Main engines	2 Diesels = 11 knots

Built in USSR in 1956 and 1955. Originally fleet tugs of the "G" class. Converted for research. Civilian manned.

NEREY — *1972, Michael D, J, Lennon*

PETRODVORETS (ex-*Bore II*)

Measurement, tons	1 965 gross; 985 net
Dimensions, feet	254·2 × 39·4 × 24·9
Main engines	Diesel = 13·5 knots

Built at Abo, Finland for Finnish owners in 1938. Sold to USSR in 1950 and renamed.

ZVEZDA

Measurement, tons	348 gross
Dimensions, feet	129 × 24·2 × 11·4
Main engines	Diesel = 10 knots

Built in East Germany in 1957. Carries winches in the chains on the quarters. Sister ships *Zarnitsa* and *Yug* are used for transporting crews to ships building outside the USSR.

ZVEZDA — *1974, Ian Brooke*

PALEH (ex-*Bratsk*)

Measurement, tons	2 285 gross; 987 net
Dimensions, feet	239·4 × 42·6 × 22
Main engines	1 Diesel; 1 shaft = 11 knots

Built in E. Germany in 1960 as fish-carrier of the "Evron" Class. Converted for surveying and renamed in 1966.

PALEH — *1972, Michael D, J, Lennon*

RESEARCH SHIPS

4 "MODIFIED AKADEMIK KURCHATOV" CLASS

ABKHASIA ADZHARIYA BASHKIRIYA MOLDAVYA

Of similar characteristics to the "A. Kurchatov" class but fitted with helicopter platform aft. Naval manned. Completed in 1973.

BASHKIRIYA 1/1974

7 "AKADEMIK KURCHATOV" CLASS

AKADEMIK KOROLEV
AKADEMIK KURCHATOV
AKADEMIK SHIRSHOV
AKADEMIK VERNADSKY
DMITRI MENDELEYEV
PROFESSOR ZUBOV
PROFESSOR VIZE

Displacement, tons	6 681 full load
Measurement, tons	1 387 net; 1 986 deadweight; 5 460 gross
Dimensions, feet	400·3 to 406·8 × 56·1 × 15·0
Main engines	2 Halberstadt 6-cylinder diesels; 2 shafts; 8 000 bhp = 18 to 20 knots

All built by Mathias Thesen Werft at Wismar, East Germany between 1965 and 1968. All have a hull of the same design as the "Mikhail Kalinin" class of merchant vessels. There are variations in mast and aerial rig. *Professor Vize* is similar to *A. Shirshov* whilst *A. Kurchatov, A. Vernadsky* and *D. Mendeleyev* are the same. Civilian manned.

AKADEMIK KURCHATOV 1973, Michael D. J. Lennon

AKADEMIK SHIRSHOV 1973, Michael D. J. Lennon

9 "PASSAT" CLASS

ERNST KRENKEL (ex-*Vikhr*)
GEORGI USHAKOV (ex-*Schkval*)
MUSSON
OKEAN
PASSAT
PRIBOI
PORIV
PRILIV
VOLNA

Research or weather ships built at Szczecin, Poland, since 1968.

PRILIV 1973, Michael D. J. Lennon

ERNST KRENKEL 1974, J. van der Woude

2 "LEBEDEV" CLASS

PETR LEBEDEV **SERGEI VAVILOV**

Measurement, tons	1 180 net; 3 561 gross
Main engines	Diesels

Research vessels with comprehensive equipment and accommodation. Both built in 1954.

PETR LEBEDEV 1970, Michael D. J. Lennon

SERGEI VAVILOV 1973, Michael D. J. Lennon

Research Ships—*continued*

3 "POLYUS" CLASS

BAIKAL **BALKHASH** **POLYUS**

Displacement, tons	6 900 standard
Dimensions, feet	365·8 × 47·2 × 20·7
Main engines	Diesel-electric; 3 400 hp = 14 knots

These ships of the "Polyus" class were built in East Germany in 1961-64. Oceanographic research ships.

POLYUS 1972

VLADIMIR OBRUCHEV

Measurement, tons	534 gross
Dimensions, feet	137·8 × 30·9 × 16·4
Main engines	2 Diesels = 11 knots

One of the "G" class tugs built in Romania in 1959 and subsequently converted for research duties.

VLADIMIR OBRUCHEV *1972, Michael D. J. Lennon*

VITYAZ (ex-*Mars*)

Displacement, tons	5 700 standard
Main engines	Diesels; 3 000 bhp = 14·5 knots
Range, miles	18 400 at 14 knots
Complement	137 officers and men including 73 scientists

Oceanographic research ship. Formerly a German freighter built at Bremen in 1939 Equipped with 13 laboratories.

VITYAZ *1972, Mr. Michael D. L. Jennon*

1 "MODIFIED DOBINYA NIKITICH" CLASS

VLADIMIR KAVRASKY

Displacement, tons	2 500 standard
Dimensions, feet	223·1 × 59·1 × 18·1
Main engines	3 shafts = 13·8 knots

One of a numerous class of icebreakers built at Leningrad in the early 1960s—converted for polar research in 1972.

1 "NEVELSKOY" CLASS

NEVELSKOY

Last of a class of three research ships.

3 "ORBELI" CLASS

AKADEMIK IOSIF ORBELI
PROFESSOR NIKOLAI BARABSKI
AKADEMIK S. VAVILOV

Built in Warnemünde 1969-71. Act as Supply Ships. Civilian manned.

AKADEMIK S. VAVILOV *1972, Michael D. J. Lennon*

FISHERY RESEARCH SHIPS

4 BMRT TYPE

AKADEMIK KNIPOVICH **AKADEMIK BERG**
PROFESSOR DERYUGIN **POSEIDON**

Measurement, tons	3 165 gross; 1 166 net
Dimensions, feet	277·8 × 46 × 32·9
Main engines	1 Diesel = 13 knots

Built as fishery research ships 1963-74.
Civilian manned.

POSEIDON *1972, Michael D. J. Lennon*

2 SOVIET "TRAWLER" TYPE

ISSLEDOVATEL **TAMANGO**

Measurement, tons	680 gross
Dimensions, feet	178 × 30·6 × 15·9
Main engines	1 Diesel = 12 knots

Apparently identical, except for aerials, to "Okean" and "Mayak" class AGIs. Have same different appearance of port and starboard sides of the superstructure, the former being closed in and the latter open.

TAMANGO *1973, Michael D. J. Lennon*

2 BMRT TYPE

Yu. M. SHOKALSKY **A. I. VOYEYVKOV**

Measurement, tons	3 200 gross
Dimensions, feet	278 × 46 × 33
Main engines	1 Diesel = 13 knots

Sister ships of BMRT type fish-factory ships with freezer plant removed. Survey ships registered at Vladivostok and operated in the Pacific. Completed in 1959 at Nikolayev,

2 ATLANTIK TYPE

GERAKL **PROFESSOR MESYATSYEV**

Measurement, tons	2 242 gross
Dimensions, feet	270 × 45 × 25
Main engines	2 8-cyl Karl Liebnecht diesels = 13 knots

Modified "Atlantik" Type stern-trawler fish-factory ships built at Stralsund, E. Germany in 1972.

GERAKL *1973, Michael D. J. Lennon*

3 EAST GERMAN TRAWLER TYPE

AYSBERG **OKEANOGRAF** **POLIARNIK**

Measurement, tons	265 gross
Dimensions, feet	126·3 × 23·6 × 11·5
Main engines	1 Diesel = 9·5 knots

Built in East Germany 1952-56. Civilian manned. Rigging of foremasts varies in different ships.

OKEANOGRAF *1973, Michael D. J. Lennon*

Note:
There are also at least 180 other ships and craft, mainly of smaller size, employed on Soviet fishery research.

SPACE ASSOCIATED SHIPS

Note. All civilian manned except "Baskunchak" class.

1 "GAGARIN" CLASS

KOSMONAUT YURI GAGARIN

Displacement, tons	45 000
Measurement, tons	32 291 gross; 5 247 net
Dimensions, feet	757·9; 773·3oa × 101·7 × 30·0
Main engines	2 geared steam turbines; 1 shaft; 19 000 shp = 17 knots max

Design based on the "Sofia" or "Akhtubu" (ex-"Hanoi") class steam tanker. Built at Leningrad in 1970, completed in 1971. Used for investigation into conditions in the upper atmosphere, and the control of space vehicles. She is the largest Soviet research vessel. Has bow and stern thrust units for ease of berthing. With all four aerials vertical and facing forward she experiences a loss in speed of 2 knots.

KOSMONAUT YURI GAGARIN *1972, Michael D. J. Lennon*

KOSMONAUT YURI GAGARIN *1972, Michael D. J. Lennon*

1 "KOMAROV" CLASS

KOSMONAUT VLADIMIR KOMAROV (ex-*Genichesk*)

Displacement, tons	17 500 full load
Measurement, tons	8 000 approximately
Dimensions, feet	510·8 × 75·5 × 29·5
Main engines	Diesels; 2 shafts; 24 000 bhp = 22 knots

She was launched in 1966 at Nikolaev as *Genichesk* and operated as a merchant ship in the Black Sea for about six months. Converted to her present role at Leningrad in 1967. The ship is named in honour of the Soviet astronaut who died when his space craft crashed in 1967.

KOSMONAUT VLADIMIR KOMAROV (with new forward aerial) *1974, J. van der Woude*

KOSMONAUT VLADIMIR KOMAROV *1972, Michael D. J. Lennon*

1 "KOROLEV" CLASS

AKADEMIK SERGEI KOROLEV

Displacement, tons	21 250
Measurement, tons	17 114 gross; 2 185 net
Dimensions, feet	597·1 × 82·0 × 30·0

Built at Nikolaev in 1970, completing in 1971. Equipped with the smaller type radome and two "saucers"

AKADEMIK SERGEI KOROLEV *1972, Michael D. J. Lennon*

AKADEMIK SERGEI KOROLEV *1972, Michael D. J. Lennon*

1 "BEZHITSA" CLASS

BEZHITSA

Measurement, tons	11 089 gross; 12 727 deadweight
Dimensions, feet	510·4 × 67·7 × 40·4
Main engine	Diesel = 17·5 knots

Former freighter of "Poltava" calss launched at Nikolaev in 1964, and subsequently completed as a research ship. The aerial horns were fitted in 1971. Directional aerials similar to those in *Dolinsk* and *Ristna* fitted on crane stowage forward of the bridge.

BEZHITSA *1972, Michael D. J. Lennon*

4 "SIBIR" CLASS

CHUKOTKA **SAKHALIN** **SIBIR** **SUCHAN**

Displacement, tons	4 000 standard; 5 000 full load
Measurement, tons	3 767 gross (*Chukotka* 3 800, *Suchan* 3 710)
Dimensions, feet	354 × 49·2 × 20
Guns	6—45 mm AA; 2 MG
Main engines	Triple expansion; 2 shafts; 3 300 ihp = 15 knots
Range, miles	3 300 at 12 knots

Converted bulk ore carriers employed as Missile Range Ships in the Pacific. *Sakhalin* and *Sibir* have three radomes forward and aft, and carry helicopters. *Suchan* is also equipped with a helicopter flight deck. Launched in 1957-59. Formerly freighters of the Polish "B 31" type. Rebuilt in 1958-59 as missile range ships in Leningrad.

Space Associated Ships—*continued*

7 "BASKUNCHAK" (ex-VOSTOK) CLASS

APSHERON (ex-*Tosnoles*)
BASKUNCHAK (ex-*Vostok 4*)
DAURIYA (ex-*Suzdal*)
DIKSON (ex-*Vagales*)
DONBASS (ex-*Kirishi*)
SEVAN (ex-*Vyborgles*)
TAMAN (ex-*Vostok 3*)

Measurement, tons	2 215 net; 6 450 deadweight; 4 896 gross
Dimensions, feet	400·3 × 55·1 × 14·0
Main engines	B & W 9-cylinder diesels; speed 15 knots

Standard timber carriers modified with helicopter flight decks. Built at Leningrad between 1963 and 1966. Entirely manned by naval personnel.

BASKUNCHAK *1970, Michael D. J. Lennon*

TAMAN *1972, Michael D, J, Lennon*

4 "MORZHOVETS" (ex-VOSTOK) CLASS

BOROVICHI (ex-*Svirles*) **KEGOSTROV** (ex-*Taimyr*) **MORZHOVETS** **NEVEL**

Former timber carriers but completely modified with a comprehensive array of tracking, direction finding and directional aerials. Additional laboratories built above the forward holds. Same measurements as the "Baskunchak" class, but tonnage increased to 5 277 gross and 967 net.

NEVEL *1972, Michael D, J, Lennon*

MORZHOVETS *1972, Michael D. J. Lennon*

3 "DSHANKOY" CLASS

CHAZHMA (ex-*Dangara*) **DSHANKOY** **CHUMIKAN** (ex-*Dolgeschtschelje*)

Displacement, tons	5 300 light; 14 065 full load
Dimensions, feet	457·7 × 59·0 × 25·9
Aircraft	1 helicopter;
Main engines	2—7 cyl diesels = 18 knots

Formerly bulk ore-carriers of the "Dzankoy" class (7 265 tons gross). Soviet Range Instrumentation Ships (SRIS). Active since 1963.

RISTNA

Measurement, tons	1 819 net; 4 200 deadweight; 3 724 gross
Dimensions, feet	347·8 × 47·9 × 14·0
Main engines	MAN 6-cylinder diesels; speed = 15 knots

Converted from a timber carrier. Built in East Germany at Rostok by Schiffswerft Neptun in 1963. Painted white. Fitted with directional aerials on top of bridge wings. Served as Missile Detection Ship.

RISTNA *1970, Michael D. J. Lennon*

COMMUNICATIONS RELAY SHIPS

20 "LIBAU" CLASS

Displacement, tons	310 standard; 380 full load
Dimensions, feet	170·6 × 21·5 × 9·0
Main engines	3 diesels; 2 shafts; 3 300 bhp = 24 knots
Range, miles	1 500 at 12 knots

CABLE SHIPS

NOTE. Four new 6 000 ton cable ships ordered from Wártsilá, two in 1972/73 and two on 16 July 1974. *Katyn*, first of class, launched 20 Mar 1974.

5 "KLASMA" CLASS

DONETZ **INGUL** **TSNA** **YANA** **ZEYA**

Displacement, tons	6 900
Measurement, tons	3 400 deadweight; 6 000 gross
Dimensions, feet	427·8 × 52·5 × 17
Main engines	5 Wärtsila Sulzer diesels; 4 950 shp = 14 knots
Complement	118

Ingul and *Yana* were built by Wärtsilä, Helsingforsvarvet, Finland, laid down on 10 Oct 1961 and 4 May 1962 and launched on 14 Apr 1962 and 1 Nov 1962 respectively. *Donetz* and *Tsna* were built at the Wärtsilä, Abovarvet, Abo. *Donetz* was launched on 17 Dec 1968 and completed 3 July 1969. *Tsna* was completed in summer 1968. *Zeya* was delivered on 20 Nov 1970. *Donetz*, *Tsna* and *Zeya* are of slightly modified design.

"KLASMA" Class *1974*

SERVICE FORCES

NOTES. (a) With the Soviet merchant fleet under State control any ships of the merchant service, including tankers, may be diverted to a fleet support role at any time. (b) Five 31 000 ton tankers (*Asheron, Grozny, Godermes, Makhachkaia* and *Mayrop*) currently building at Swan-Hunters for a Liberian firm could be used in Soviet naval operations.

3 "CHILIKIN" CLASS (FLEET REPLENISHMENT SHIPS)

BORIS CHILIKIN **DNESTR** **VLADIMIR KOLECHITSKY**

Displacement, tons	20 500 full load
Dimensions, feet	531·5 × 70·2 × 28·1 loaded
Guns	4—57 mm (2 twin)
Main engine	Diesel; 9 900 hp; 1 shaft = 16·5 knots

Based on the "Veliky Oktyabr" merchant ship tanker design *Chilikin* was built at Leningrad completing in 1971. This is the first Soviet Navy class of purpose built underway fleet replenishment ships for the supply of both liquids and solids, indicating a growing awareness of the need for afloat support for a widely dispersed fleet.

Carry 13 000 tons fuel oil, 400 tons ammunition, 400 tons spares and 400 tons victualling stores.

DNESTR 9/1974

BORIS CHILIKIN 1974, S, Breyer

1 "MANYCH" CLASS (FLEET REPLENISHMENT SHIP)

Displacement, tons	7 500
Guns	4—57 mm (2 twin) with Muff Cob radar

Completed 1972, probably in Finland. A smaller edition of the "*Boris Chilikin*" but showing the new interest in custom built replenishment ships. The high point on the single gantry is very similar to that on "*Chilikin's*" third gantry.

MANYCH 6/1974

MANYCH 2/1973

MANYCH 1973

1 "SOFIA" CLASS (REPLENISHMENT TANKER)

AKHTUBA (ex-*Khanoy*)

Displacement, tons	45 000 full load
Measurement, tons	62 000 deadweight, 32 840 gross, 16 383 net
Dimensions, feet	757·9 × 101·7 × 32·8

Built as the merchant tanker *Khanoy* in 1963 at Leningrad, she was taken over by the Navy in 1969 and renamed *Akhtuba*. The hull type was used in the construction of the space associated ship *Kosmonaut Yuri Gagarin*.

AKHTUBA 1972, Michael D. J. Lennon

3 "KAZBEK" CLASS (REPLENISHMENT TANKERS)

ALATYR **DESNA** **VOLKHOV**

Displacement, tons	16 250 full load
Measurement, tons	16 250 deadweight; 3 942 gross; 8 229 net
Dimensions, feet	447·4 × 63·0 × 23·0
Main engines	2 diesels driving single screw

Former "Leningrad" class merchant fleet tankers taken over by the Navy. Built at Leningrad and Nikolayev from 1951 to 1961. Seven others—*Karl Marx, Kazbek, Dzerzhinsk, Grodno, Cheboksary, Liepaya* and *Buguzuslan* have acted in support of naval operations. The original class numbered 64. Radar—Don 2.

"KAZBEK" Class 1973, Michael D. J. Lennon

6 "ALTAY" CLASS (SUPPORT TANKERS)

ALTAY **ELYENYA** **IZHORA** **KOLA** **TARKHANKUT** **YEGORLIK**

Displacement, tons	5 500 standard
Dimensions, feet	344·5 × 49·2 × 19·7
Main engines	Diesels, speed = 14 knots

Building from 1967 onwards. By early 1975 over 60 of this class had been completed for naval and mercantile use.

"ALTAY" Class 1973, Michael D, J, Lennon

6 "UDA" CLASS (SUPPORT TANKERS)

DUNAY **KOIDA** **LENA** **SHEKSNA** **TEREK** **VISHERA**

Displacement, tons	5 500 standard; 7 200 full load
Dimensions, feet	400·3 × 51·8 × 20·3
Main engines	Diesels; 2 shafts; 8 000 bhp = 17 knots

Koida has a beam fuelling rig on starboard side abaft bridge.

Built since 1961.

LENA 1/1975

Service Forces—*continued*

4 "PEVEK" CLASS (SUPPORT TANKERS)

IMAN **PEVEK** **OLEKMA** **ZOLOTOY ROG**

Displacement, tons	4 000 standard
Measurement, tons	4 500 deadweight
Dimensions, feet	344·5 × 47·9 × 20·0
Main engines	Diesels; 2 900 bhp = 14 knots

Part of a class of fifty merchant tankers built by Rauma-Repola, Finland between 1955 and 1966.

"PEVEK" Class — *1973, Michael D. J. Lennon*

4 "KONDA" CLASS (SUPPORT TANKERS)

KONDA **ROSSOSH** **SOYANNA** **YAKHROMA**

Displacement, tons	1 178 standard
Dimensions, feet	226·4 × 32·8 × 13·8
Main engines	1 100 bhp = 13 knots

15 "KHOBI" CLASS (HARBOUR TANKERS)

CHEREMSHAN	**KHOBI**	**ORSHA**	**SHELON**
INDIGA	**METAN**	**SEIMA**	**SOSVA**
+4	**LOVAT**	**SHACHA**	**TUNGUSKA**

Displacement, tons	800 light; 2 000 approx full load
Speed, knots	12 to 14

Built from 1957 to 1959.

3 "NERCHA" CLASS (HARBOUR TANKERS)

DORA **IRTYSH** **IRBIT**

SALVAGE VESSELS

1 "NEPA" CLASS

KARPATY

Displacement, tons	3 500 light; 5 000 standard
Dimensions, feet	410·1 × 52·5 × 16·4
Main engines	Diesels; 2 shafts

New type of submarine rescue and salvage ships similar to the "Prut" class but improved and enlarged and with a special high stern which extends out over the water for rescue manoeuvres. *Karpaty* completed 1969.

KARPATY — *1969*

10 "PRUT" CLASS

ALTAI **BRESHTAU** **ZHIGUILI** +7

Displacement, tons	2 120 standard; 3 500 full load
Dimensions, feet	296·0 × 36·1 × 13·1
Guns	2—25 mm
Main engines	Diesels; 4 200 bhp = 18 knots

Large rescue vessels. Built since 1960.

Salvage Vessels—*continued*

"PRUT" Class — *1970, S Breyer*

9 "SURA" CLASS

Displacement, tons	3 150 full load
Dimensions, feet	285·4 × 48·6 × 16·4
Main engines	Diesels; 1 770 bhp = 13·2 knots

Heavy lift ships built since 1965 in East Germany. Six built by 1972. Last, *Dioklas*, launched 21 Feb 1971.

"SURA" Class — *6/1974*

LIFTING VESSELS

15 "NEPTUN" CLASS

Displacement, tons	700 light; 1 230 standard
Dimensions, feet	170·6 × 36·1 × 12·5
Main engines	Oil fuelled, speed = 12 knots

Similar to Western boom defence vessels, or netlayers. Built in 1957-60 by Neptun Rostock. Have a crane of 75 tons lifting capacity on the bow. One of this class is now based at Murmansk for the Maritime Fleet. She is acting as a diving vessel for hydrogeologists and construction personnel.

"NEPTUN" Class

SUBMARINE RESCUE SHIPS

15 "VALDAY" CLASS (Ex-"T 58" CLASS)

Displacement, tons	725 standard; 850 full load
Dimensions, feet	222·1 × 29·9 × 7·5
Main engines	2 diesels; 2 shafts; 5 000 bhp = 20 knots

Basically of similar design to that of the "T 58" class larger fleet minesweepers, but the hulls were completed as emergency salvage vessels and submarine rescue ships at Leningrad. Equipped with diving bell, decompression chamber, lifting gear and emergency medical ward. It has been reported that there may be an extra six smaller rescue ships based on the "T 43" hull. One transferred to India (*Nistar*).

"VALDAY" Class — *1970, S. Breyer*

TRANSPORTS

2 "LAKE" CLASS

KAMCHATKA **MONGOL**

6 COASTAL TYPE

SHIM **OLGA** **USSURIJ** (ex *Okhotsk*)
OB **SHILKA** **VISHERA**

Olga and *Ishim* are Coast Guard transports. *Ob* is 1 194 ton diesel electric Antarctic support ship.

TORPEDO RECOVERY/PATROL BOATS

90 "POLUCHAT I" CLASS

Displacement, tons	100 standard
Dimensions, feet	98·4 × 19·7 × 5·9
Guns	2—25 mm (1 twin) or 2 MG (1 twin)

Employed as specialised or dual purpose torpedo recovery vessels and/or patrol boats. They have a stern slipway.

DISTILLATION SHIPS

10 "VODA" CLASS

Displacement, tons	2 100 standard
Dimensions, feet	267·3 × 37·7 × 14
Main engines	Diesels; speed = 12 knots

Water distillation ships built in 1956 onwards. No armament.

TRAINING SHIPS

STVOR

Displacement, tons	1 200 standard
Dimensions, feet	229·6 × 32·8 × 13·1
Main engines	Diesels = 10 knots

Built in Hungary in late 1950s as a survey ship of the "Telnovsk" class. Now converted as a naval training ship with additional accommodation immediately forward of the bridge.

STVOR 1972, *Michael D. J. Lennon*

NOTE. None of the following ships is in the Navy List but their products are largely intended for the Navy.

ANGARA (ex-*Hela*)

Displacement, tons	2 115 standard; 2 500 full load
Dimensions, feet	323 × 42·5 × 11
Guns	2—4·1 in; 1—37 mm AA; 2—20 mm AA
Main engines	4 MAN diesels; 2 shafts; 6 300 bhp = 18 knots
Range, miles	2 000 at 15 knots

Former yacht built by Stülcken, Hamburg. Launched in 1939. In the Black Sea.

3 "ZENIT" CLASS

GORIZONT **MERIDIAN** **ZENIT**

Measurements, tons	4 374 gross; 986 net
Length, feet	352·6
Beam, feet	47·2
Main engines	Two 8-cylinder diesels geared to one shaft

All were built in East Germany at Rostock by Schiffswerft Neptune in 1961-62. Mercantile Cadet Training but produces officers for the Navy.

MERIDIAN 1972, *Michael D. J. Lennon*

Training Ships—*continued*

2 "SEDOV" CLASS

KRUZENSTERN **SEDOV**

Measurement, tons	3 064 gross

Barques. Built in 1921. Employed as sail training ship for midshipmen, cadets and junior seamen.

KRUZENSTERN 1973, *Novosti*

1 Ex-GERMAN TYPE

TOVARISCH (ex-*Gorch Foch*)

Displacement, tons	1 350
Dimensions, feet	242·8 × 39·3 × 15
Sail area	19 350 sq ft
Guns	2—20 mm AA
Main engines	MAN diesel; 1 shaft; 520 bhp = 8 knots
Oil fuel, tons	25
Range, miles	3 500 at 8 knots
Complement	260

Barque. Ex-German training ship. Built by Blohm & Voss, Hamburg. Launched in 1933. Of mercantile attachment but produces personnel for the Navy. Sail area: 2 150 sq yds.

9 "PROFESSOR ANICHKOV" CLASS

PROFESSORS—ANICHKOV
KHLYUSTIN
KUDREVITCH
MINYAYEV
PAVLENKO
RYBALTOVSKI
SHCHYOGOLEV
UKHOV
YUSHCHEKO

Measurement, tons	5 993 gross; 1 512 net
Main engines	Diesels

Built at Szczecin, Poland between 1970-73. Used as training ships but can operate as store transports. *Professor Rybaltovski* has a series of square ports in place of the cutaway sections below the boat-deck.

PROFESSOR KHLYUSTIN 1972, *Michael D. J. Lennon*

10 SCHOONER TYPE

ENISEJ **PRAKTIKA** (ex-*Passat*) **TOBOL** **UCHEBA** (ex-*Mousson*) + 6

Displacement, tons	300 approximately (ships vary)

Three masts. In the Baltic. Sailing vessels for training cadets, boys and volunteers. There are about ten three-masted schooners of 300 tons with one square sail on the foremast of the same class as the *Praktika* and *Ucheba*, built in Finland.

There are also the engineering training ships *Professor Kudrevitch, Professor Shchyogolev, Professor Yushchenko* and *Professor Aruchkov*, all built in 1970-71.

ICEBREAKERS

NOTE. The majority of these ships are operated by V/O Sudoimport—only a small number being naval manned.

1 PROJECTED LARGE NUCLEAR POWERED

Main engines: Nuclear reactors; steam turbines; 80 000 hp

Reported as in the design stage in Oct 1974.

2 NUCLEAR POWERED

ARKTIKA **LEDOKOLY**

Displacement, tons	25 000 standard
Dimensions, feet	459 × 98·4 × 34
Aircraft	Helicopter with hangar
Main engines	2 nuclear reactors; steam turbines; 30 000 shp = 25 knots

Building yard—Leningrad. *Arktika* launched summer 1973, started trials on 30 Nov 1974. Fitted with new type of reactor, the development of which may have retarded these ships' completion.

ARKTIKA (Sketch) *1967*

1 NUCLEAR POWERED

LENIN

Displacement, tons	16 000
Dimensions, feet	440 × 90·5 × 25
Aircraft	2 helicopters
Main engines	3 pressurised water-cooled nuclear reactors. 4 steam turbines; 3 shafts (no shaft in bow); 44 000 shp = 18 knots max
Complement	230

The world's first nuclear powered surface ship to put to sea. Reported to have accommodation for 1 000 personnel.

CONSTRUCTION. Built at the Admiralty Yard, Leningrad. Launched on 5 Dec 1957. Completed and commissioned on 15 Sep 1959.

ENGINEERING. The original reactors, prototype submarine variety, were replaced during refit at Murmansk 1966-72. The new reactors presumably have a longer core-life than the 18 months of their predecessors. The turbines were manufactured by the Kirov plant in Leningrad. Three propellers aft, but no forward screw.

OPERATION. Can maintain a speed of 3-4 knots in 8 ft ice, giving a path of some 100 ft.

LENIN *1972*

3 "ERMAK" CLASS

ERMAK **ADMIRAL MAKAROV** +1

Displacement, tons	20 241
Dimensions, ft (*m*)	442·8 × 85·3 × 36·1 (*135 × 26 × 11*)
Aircraft	2 helicopters
Main engines	9 Wártsilá-Sulzer 12 cyl 12 ZH 40/48 diesels of 4 600 bhp each (total 41 400 hp) with Stromberg Ab generators feeding three Stromberg electric motors of total 36 000 shp; 3 shafts
Range, miles	40 000 at 15 knots
Speed, knots	19·5
Complement	115 plus 28 spare berths

The Soviet Union ordered three large and powerful icebreakers on 29 Apr 1970 from Wártsilá Shipyard, Helsinki, for delivery in 1974, 1975 and 1976. These are the largest diesel icebreakers in the world. Six Wártsilá auxiliary diesels, 7 200 bhp. Propelling and auxiliary machinery controlled electronically. These are the first vessels to be fitted with Wártsilá mixed-flow air-bubbling system to decrease friction between hull and ice. *Ermak* launched 7 Sep 1973 and completed 30 June 1974. *A. Makarov* laid down 10 Sept 1973 and launched 26 Apr 1974 for completion Feb 1975. Third unit laid down 9 July 1974 for launching March 1975—completion possibly Jan 1976.

ERMAK *1974, Wärtsila*

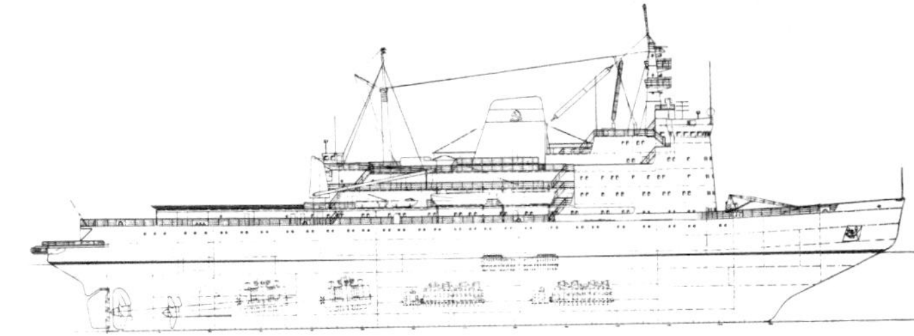

ERMAK *1974, Wärtsila*

5 "MOSKVA" CLASS

VLADIVOSTOCK **KIEV** **LENINGRAD** **MOSKVA** **MURMANSK**

Displacement, tons	12 840 standard; 15 360 full load
Dimensions, feet	368·8 wl; 400·7 oa × 80·3 × 34·5
Aircraft	2 helicopters
Main engines	8 Sulzer diesel-electric; 3 shafts; 22 000 shp = 18 knots
Oil fuel, tons	3 000
Range, miles	20 000
Complement	145

CONSTRUCTION. Built by Wärtsilä Shipyard, Helsinki. *Moskva* was launched on 10 Jan 1959 and completed in June 1960. *Leningrad* was laid down in Jan 1959. Launched on 24 Oct 1959, and completed in 1962. *Kiev* was completed in 1966. *Murmansk* was launched on 14 July 1967, and *Vladivostock* on 28 May 1968.

DESIGN. Designed to stay at sea for a year without returning to base. The concave embrasure in the ship's stern is a housing for the bow of a following vessel when additional power is required. There is a landing deck for helicopters and hangar space for two machines.

ENGINEERING. Eight generating units of 3 250 bhp each comprising eight main diesels of the Wärtsilä-Sulzer 9 MH 51 type which together have an output of 26.000 electric hp. Four separate machinery compartments. Two engine rooms, four propulsion units in each. Three propellers aft. No forward propeller. Centre propeller driven by electric motors of 11 000 hp and each of the side propellers by motors of 5 500 hp. Two Wärtsilä-Babcock & Wilcox boilers for heating and donkey work.

OPERATION. *Moskva* has four pumps which can move 480 metric tons of water from one side to the other in two minutes to rock the icebreaker and wrench her free of thick ice.

MOSKVA *1960, Wärtsilä*

Icebreakers—*continued*

3 SHALLOW-WATER TYPE NEW CONSTRUCTION

Dimensions, ft (*m*)	185·3 × 51·5 × 13·8 (*56·5 × 15·7 × 4·2*)
Main engines	Diesel-electric; 3 400 shp; 2 shafts; 2 rudders
Speed, knots	14

Contract signed with Wärtsilä, Helsinki on 22 Mar 1974 for the building of these three icebreakers for delivery in 1976. All to be fitted with Wärtsilä air-bubbler system.

Shallow water type — *1974, Wärtsila*

3 "KAPITAN" CLASS

Name	*Launched*	*Completed*
KAPITAN BELOUSOV	1954	1955
KAPITAN MELECHOV	19 Oct 1956	1957
KAPITAN VORONIN	1955	1956

Displacement, tons	4 375 to 4 415 standard; 5 350 full load
Dimensions, feet	265 wl; 273 oa × 63·7 × 23
Main engines	Diesel-electric; 6 Polar 8 cyl; 10 500 bhp = 14·9 knots
Oil fuel, tons	740
Complement	120

All built by Wärtsilä Shipyard, Helsinki. The ships have four screws, two forward under the forefoot and two aft.

KAPITAN BELOUSOV — *1970, Michael D. J. Lennon*

21 "DOBRINYA NIKITICH" CLASS

AFANASY NIKITIN
BURAN
DOBRINYA NIKITICH
EROFFREY KHABAROV
FEDOR LITKE
GEORGIJ SEDOV
ILYA MUROMETS
IVAN MOSKVITIN
IVAN KRUZENSHTERN
KHARITON LAPTEV
PERESVET
PETR PAKHTUSOV
PLUG
SADKO
SEMYON DEZHNEV
SEMEN CHELYUSHKIN
VASILY POYARKOV
VASILY PRONCHISHCHEV
VLADIMIR RUSANOV
YIRIY LISYANSKY
VYUGA

Displacement, tons	2 500 standard (average)
Measurements, tons	2 305 gross (ships vary)
Dimensions, feet	223·1 × 59·1 × 18·1
Main engines	3 shafts; speed = 13·8 knots

All built at Leningrad between 1961 and 1965. Divided between the Baltic, Black Sea and Far East.

YIRIY LISYANSKY — *1972, Michael D. J. Lennon*

2 "SIBIR" CLASS

Name	*Builders*	*Launched*	*Completed*
SIBIR (ex-*Yosif Stalin*)	Baltic Works, Leningrad	14 Aug 1937	1939
MIKOYAN (ex-*Otto Schmidt*)	Nikolayev	1938	1939

Displacement, tons	11 000
Measurement, tons	4 866 gross
Dimensions, feet	335·8 pp; 351 oa × 75·5 × 22
Aircraft	1 helicopter
Main engines	Triple expansion with diesel electric-propulsion for cruising; 3 shafts; 10 050 hp = 15·5 knots
Boilers	9
Fuel, tons	4 000 coal; and diesel oil
Complement	142

3 aircraft and 1 catapult were included in the design. Both in the White Sea.

MIKOYAN after refit — *1965, S. Breyer*

KRASSIN (ex-*Swiatogor*)

Displacement, tons	10 200
Main engines	13 500 hp = 15 knots
Complement	160

Built in 1917 by Armstrongs, Newcastle. Converted 1953-58, helicopter deck fitted.

ARMED ICEBREAKERS

2 "MODIFIED DOBRINYA NIKITCH" CLASS

IVAN SUSANIN +1

Of similar major characteristics to "D. Nikitch" class but lengthened by 80 feet and modified with new bridge structure, twin 76 mm forward, 2—30 mm Gatling guns aft and a helicopter platform.

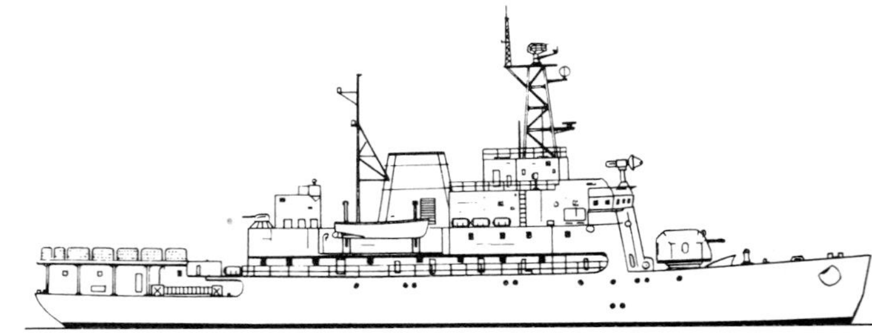

"MODIFIED DOBRINYA NIKITCH" Class — *1974, S. Breyer*

IVAN SUSANIN — *7/1974*

TUGS

2 "PAMIR" CLASS

AGATAN **ALDAN**

Measurement, tons	1 443 to 2 032 gross
Dimensions, feet	256 oa × 42 × 13·5
Main engines	Two 10 cyl 4 str diesels; 2 shafts; 4 200 bhp = 17 knots

Salvage tugs built at AB Gävie, Varv, Sweden, in 1959-60. Equipped with strong derricks, powerful pumps, air compressors, diving gear, fire fighting apparatus and electric generators.

50 "OKHTENSKY" CLASS

Displacement, tons	835
Dimensions, feet	134·5 wl; 143 oa × 34 × 15
Guns	1—3 in dp; 2—20 mm AA
Main engines	2 BM diesels; 2 electric motors. 2 shafts; 1 875 bhp = 14 knots
Oil fuel, tons	187
Complement	34

Oceangoing salvage and rescue tugs. Fitted with powerful pumps and other apparatus for salvage. Pennant numbers preceded by MB.

"OKHTENSKY" Class *1971, MOD*

50 SOVIET SALVAGE TUGS

Measurement, tons	828 gross
Dimensions, feet	171·5 × 37·7 × 19
Main engines	Diesel-electric = 14 knots

Built in late 1950s and early 1960s.

ATLANT—Soviet Salvage Tug *1972, Michael D. J. Lennon*

3 "SORUM" CLASS

Displacement, tons	approx 800
Length, feet	approx 160
Main engines	Diesels

A new class of ocean tugs first seen in 1973.

"SORUM" Class *11/1973*

FINNISH SALVAGE TUGS

Measurement, tons	1 070 gross
Dimensions, feet	201·2 × 39·2 × 18·1
Main engines	2 Diesels = 14 knots

Class of salvage and rescue tugs normally operated by Ministry of Fisheries with the fishing fleets. Built in Finland in late 1950s and early 1960s.

STREMITELNY—Finnish Salvage Tug *1972, Michael D. J. Lennon*

4 "OREL" CLASS

Displacement, tons	1 300
Main engines	Diesels = 11 knots

Ocean-going tugs built between 1955 and 1958. Now being superseded.

7 "KATUN" CLASS

Displacement, tons	950
Length, feet	210

Built in 1970-71.

15 "G" CLASS

Measurement, tons	534 gross
Dimensions, feet	156·5 × 32·2 × 16·4
Main engines	2 Diesels = 11 knots

Built in Romania in late 1950s. *Vladimir Obruchev* (see Research Ships) of same class.

GEROICHESKY—"G" Class *1972, Michael D. J. Lennon*

FINNISH "530 TON" CLASS

Measurement, tons	533 gross
Dimensions, feet	157·1 × 31·3 × 15·5
Main engines	Steam = 9·5 knots

Large class built in Finland in 1950s.

EAST GERMAN BERTHING TUGS

Measurement, tons	233 gross
Main engines	Diesels

Large class built in 1970 in East Germany.

EAST GERMAN HARBOUR TUGS

Measurement, tons	132 gross
Dimensions, feet	94·5 × 21.3 × 9·8
Main engines	1 Diesel = 10 knots

Very large class built in E. Germany on 1964.

There are a large number of other tugs available in commercial service which could be directed to naval use.

URUGUAY

Administration

Inspector General of the Navy:
Rear Admiral Pedro Torres Negreira

Diplomatic Representation

Naval Attache in Washington:
Captain Ademar Torres

Mercantile Marine

Lloyd's Register of Shipping:
37 vessels of 130 147 tons gross

Personnel

(a) 1975: Total: 3 000 officers and men
(b) Voluntary service

Base

Montevideo: Main naval base with a drydock and a slipway

Naval Air

B) 1 Sikorsky SH-34J
2 Bell 47G
C) 3 Grumman S-2A Tracker (ASW)
3 Beech SNB-5 (Training-Transport)
3 North American SNJ (Training)
1 Beech T-34 B Mentor (Training)
2 Piper PA-12 (Liaison)

Deletion

Large Patrol Craft

1974 *Salto*

FRIGATES

2 Ex-US "CANNON" CLASS

Name	*No.*	*Builders*	*Launched*	*Completed*
ARTIGAS (ex-USS *Bronstein DE* 189)	DE 2	Federal SB & DD Co, Pt. Newark	14 Nov 1943	13 Dec 1943
URUGUAY (ex-USS *Baron, DE* 166)	DE 1	Federal SB & DD Co, Pt. Newark	9 May 1943	5 July 1943

Displacement, tons: 1 240 standard; 1 900 full load
Length, feet (*metres*): 306·0 (*93·3*) oa
Beam, feet (*metres*): 37·0 (*11·3*)
Draught, feet (*metres*): 17·1 (*5·2*)
Guns: 3—3 in (*76 mm*) (single); 2—40 mm (see *Gunnery* notes)
A/S weapons: Hedgehog; 8 DCT; 1 DCR (see *Torpedo Tubes* note)
Main engines: Diesel-electric; 2 shafts; 6 000 bhp
Speed, knots: 19
Range, miles: 8 300 at 14 knots
Oil fuel, tons: 315 (95 per cent)
Complement: 160

Former United States destroyer escorts of the "Cannon" class, transferred to Uruguay in 1952.

APPEARANCE. Practically identical, but *Uruguay* can be distinguished by the absence of a mainmast, whereas *Artigas* has a diminutive pole mast aft.

GUNNERY. Formerly also mounted ten 20 mm anti-aircraft guns, but these have been removed.

RADAR. Equipped with SPS 6 search and tactical radar.

TORPEDO TUBES. The three 21-inch torpedo tubes in a triple mounting, originally carried, were suppressed.

ARTIGAS *1971*

MONTEVIDEO (ex-HMCS *Arnprior*, ex-HMS *Rising Castle*) PF 1

Displacement, tons: 1 010 standard; 1 600 full load
Length, feet (*metres*): 251·8 (*76·7*)
Beam, feet (*metres*): 36·7 (*11·2*)
Draught, feet (*metres*): 17·5 (*5·3*)
Guns: 1—3 in (*76 mm*) dp; 2—40 mm AA; 4—20 mm AA
A/S weapons: Hedgehog; 4 DCT; 1 DCR
Main engines: Triple expansion; 190 rpm; 2 750 ihp
Speed, knots: 17
Boilers: 2 water tube
Range, miles: 5 400 at 9·5 knots
Oil fuel, tons: 480 max
Complement: 90

Former successively British and Canadian "Castle" class corvette. Employed as a training ship.

MONTEVIDEO *1971*

1 Ex-US "DEALEY" CLASS

18 DE JULIO (ex-USS *Dealey*) DE 3

Displacement, tons: 1 450 standard; 1 900 full load
Length, feet (*metres*): 314·5 (*95·9*) oa
Beam, feet (*metres*): 36·8 (*11·2*)
Draught, feet (*metres*): 13·6 (*4·2*)
Guns: 4—3 in (*76 mm*)
A/S weapons: 2 triple torpedo tubes (Mk 32)
Main engines: 1 De Laval geared turbine; 20 000 shp; 1 shaft
Boilers: 2 Foster Wheeler
Speed, knots: 25
Complement: 165

Purchased 28 July 1972. *Dealey* was the first post-war US escort ship.

18 DE JULIO (as *Dealey*) *1968 USN*

CORVETTES

COMANDANTE PEDRO CAMPBELL MSF 1 (ex-USS *Chickadee*, MSF 59)

Displacement, tons	890 standard; 1 250 full load
Dimensions, feet	215 wl; 221·2 oa × 32·2 × 10·8
Guns	1—3 in, 50 cal dp; 2—40 mm AA
Main engines	Diesel electric; 2 shafts; 3 118 bhp = 18 knots
Complement	105

Former United States fleet minesweeper of the "Auk" class. Built by Defoe B. & M. Works. Launched on 20 July 1942. Transferred on loan and commissioned at San Diego, Calif. on 18 Aug 1966.

COMANDANTE PEDRO CAMPBELL *1971*

1 Ex-US MSO TYPE

MALDONADO (ex-*Bir Hakeim* M 614, ex-USS MSO 451)

Displacement, tons	700 standard; 795 full load
Dimensions, feet	165·0 wl; 171·0 oa × 35·0 × 10·3
Gun	1—40 mm AA
Main engines	2 GM diesels; 2 shafts; 1 600 bhp = 13·5 knots
Range, miles	3 000 at 10 knots
Complement	54

Former US ocean minesweeper transferred to France in Feb 1954. Returned to the US Navy and transferred to Uruguay on 9 April 1970.

LIGHT FORCES

(LARGE PATROL CRAFT)

PR 11 (COASTAL PATROL CRAFT)

Displacement, tons	70
Dimensions, feet	93·0 × 19·0 × 7·0
Speed, knots	25

Built by Lurssen in 1957.

PAYSANDU PR 12 (COASTAL PATROL CRAFT)

Displacement, tons	60
Dimensions, feet	83·0 × 18·0 × 6·0
Speed, knots	22

Built by Sewart, USA in 1968.

701 702 703 (COASTAL PATROL CRAFT)

43 ft craft transferred by USN in Feb 1970.

COASTAL MINESWEEPER

RIO NEGRO (ex-*Marguerite*, ex-USS MSC 94)

Displacement, tons	370 standard; 405 full load
Dimensions, feet	136·2 pp; 141·0 oa × 26·0 × 8·3
Guns	2—20 mm AA
Main engines	2 GM diesels; 2 shafts; 1 200 bhp = 13 knots
Oil fuel, tons	40
Range, miles	2 500 at 10 knots
Complement	38

Ex-US coastal minesweeper built for France under MDAP. Stricken from the French Navy in 1969 and returned to US ownership. She was transferred to Uruguay at Toulon on 10 Nov 1969.

SURVEY SHIP

CAPITAN MIRANDA CS 10

Displacement, tons	516 standard; 549 full load
Dimensions, feet	148 pp; 179 oa × 26 × 10·5
Main engines	1 MAN diesel; 500 bhp = 11 knots
Oil fuel, tons	37
Complement	49

Built by Sociedad Espanola de Construccion Naval, Matagorda, Cadiz. Launched in 1930.

CAPITAN MIRANDA *1971*

SALVAGE VESSEL

HURACAN (ex-USS Nahaut, *AN* 83)

Displacement, tons	560 standard; 760 full load
Dimensions, feet	146 wl; 163 oa × 30·5 × 11·8
Guns	4—20 mm single
Main engines	Diesel electric; 1 shaft; 1 000 bhp = 11·5 knots
Complement	48

Former US netlayer, purchased in April 1969 for salvage services.

RESCUE LAUNCH

AR 1

Displacement, tons	25 standard; 30 full load
Dimensions, feet	63·0 × 15·0 × 3·8
Guns	4 MG
Main engines	2 Hall-Scott Defender; 1 260 bhp = 33·5 knots
Range, miles	600 at 15 knots
Complement	8

British type rescue launch. Launched on 4 July 1944.

TANKERS

PRESIDENTE ORIBE AO 9

Measurement, tons	17 920 gross; 28 267 deadweight
Dimensions, feet	587·2 pp; 620 oa × 84·3 × 33
Main engines	1 Ishikawajima turbine; 12 500 shp = 16·75 knots
Boilers	2 Ishikawajima-Harima Foster Wheeler type
Range, miles	16 100 at 16 knots
Complement	76

Built by Ishikawajima-Harima Ltd, Japan. Delivered to the Uruguayan Navy on 22 Mar 1962.

PRESIDENTE ORIBE *1971*

PRESIDENTE RIVERA

Measurement, tons	19 350
Dimensions, feet	636·3 × 84 × 32
Main engines	15 300 bhp = 15 knots

Built in Spain, completed 1971.

VIGILANTE (ex-YTL 589)

of 350 tons.

TUG

GENERAL JOSE FELIX RIVAS (ex-USS *Oswegatchie* YTM 788)

Transferred March 1965.

VENEZUELA

Administration

Commander General of the Navy (Chief of Naval Operations):
Rear-Admiral Armando Perez Leefmans

Chief of Naval Staff:
Rear-Admiral Enrique Dominauez Garcia

Diplomatic Representation

Naval Attaché in London:
Captain C. A. Porras Rodrigo

Naval Attaché in Washington:
Rear Admiral Luis Ramirez Aranda

Personnel

(a) 1975: 7 500 officers and men including 4 000 of the Marine Corps
(b) 2 years National Service

Strength of the Fleet

Type	*Active*	*Building*
Destroyers	5	—
Frigates	6	—
Submarines, Patrol	3	2
Fast Attack Craft—Missile	3	3
Large Patrol Craft	10	—
Coastal Patrol Craft (manned by National Guard)	16	27
LST	1	—
LSM	4	—
Transport Landing Ship	1	—
Transports	3	—
Survey Ships and Craft	5	—
Ocean Tug	1	—
Harbour Tugs	9	—
Floating Dock	1	—

National Guard

The Fuerzas Armadas de Cooperacion, generally known as the National Guard, is a paramilitary organisation, 10 000 strong. It is concerned, amongst other things, with customs and internal security—the Maritime Wing operates the Coastal Patrol Craft listed under Light Forces, though these nominally belong to the Navy.

Mercantile Marine

Lloyd's Register of Shipping:
143 vessels of 480 230 tons gross

DESTROYERS

3 "ARAGUA" CLASS

Name	*No.*	*Builders*	*Laid down*	*Launched*	*Completed*
ARAGUA	D 31	Vickers Ltd, Barrow	29 June 1953	27 Jan 1955	14 Feb 1956
NUEVA ESPARTA	D 11	Vickers Ltd, Barrow	24 July 1951	19 Nov 1952	8 Dec 1953
ZULIA	D 21	Vickers Ltd, Barrow	24 July 1951	29 June 1953	15 Sep 1954

Displacement, tons	2 600 standard; 3 670 full load
Length, feet (*metres*)	384·0 (*117·0*)wl; 402·0 (*122·5*)oa
Beam, feet (*metres*)	43·0 (*13·1*)
Draught, feet (*metres*)	19·0 (*5·8*)
Missiles	2 quadruple "Seacat" in D 11
Guns	6—4·5 (*114 mm*), 3 twin 16—40 mm (8 twin) 4—40 mm (2 twin) in D 11 only
A/S weapons	2 Hedgehogs 2 DCT; 2 DC racks ("Squids" in D 11 and D 21)
Torpedo tubes	3—21 in (*533 mm*) triple (none in D 11)
Boilers	2 Yarrow
Main engines	Parsons geared turbines; 2 shafts; 50 000 shp
Speed, knots	34
Range, miles	5 000 at 10 knots
Complement	256 (20 officers, 236 men)

ARAGUA — *1969, Venezuelan Navy*

All built in Great Britain. *Nueva Esparta* and *Zulia* were ordered in 1950. Air conditioned. Two engine rooms and two boiler rooms served by a single uptake. The 4·5 inch guns are fully automatic. *Nueva Esparta* and *Zulia* refitted at Palmers Hebburn Works, Vickers in 1959, and at New York Navy Yard in 1960 to improve anti-submarine and anti-aircraft capabilities. *Aragua* refitted by Palmers Hebburn in 1964-65, *Nueva Esparta* at Cammell Laird in 1968-69 when "Seacat" launchers were fitted and some 40 mm and the torpedo tubes removed.

RADAR. Search: AWS 2 and (*Nueva Esparta*) SPS 6. Fire Control: X Band.

NUEVA ESPARTA — *1970, Venezuelan Navy*

1 Ex-US "ALLEN M. SUMNER FRAM II" CLASS

Name	*No.*	*Builders*	*Launched*	*Commissioned*
FALCON (ex-USS *Robert K. Huntington* DD 781)	D 21	Todd Pacific Shipyards	5 Dec 1944	3 Mar 1945

Displacement, tons	2 200 standard; 3 320 full load
Dimensions, ft (*m*)	376·5 × 40·9 × 19 (*114·8 × 12·4 × 5·8*)
Guns	6—5 in 38 cal DP (twins)
A/S weapons	2 Fixed Hedgehogs; 2 triple torpedo tubes (Mk 32); Facilities for small helicopter
Main engines	2 geared turbines; 60 000 shp; 2 shafts
Boilers	4
Speed, knots	34
Range, miles	4 600 at 15 knots
Complement	274

Purchased from USN 31 Oct 1973. Modernised under the FRAM II programme.

RADAR. SPS 40 and SPS 10.

SONAR. Hull mounted; SQS 29 series. VDS.

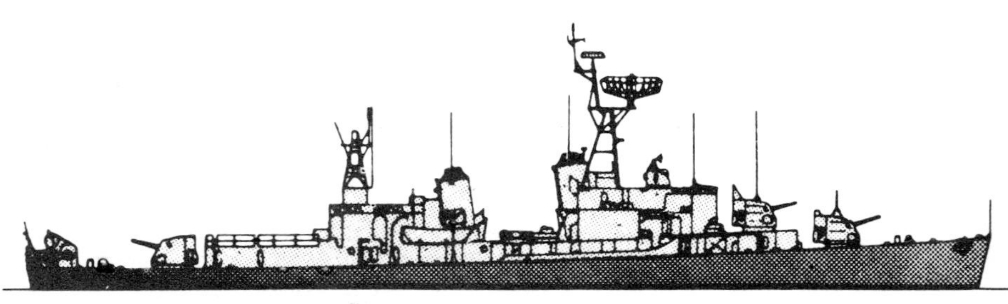
"ALLEN M. SUMNER FRAM II" Class

Destroyers—*continued*

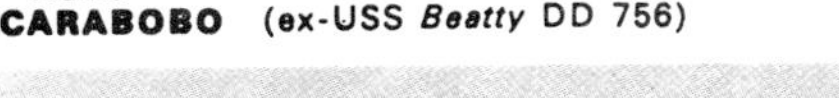

1 Ex-US "ALLEN M. SUMNER" CLASS

Name	*Builders*	*Launched*	*Commissioned*
CARABOBO (ex-USS *Beatty* DD 756)	Bethlehem, Staten Is.	30 Nov 1944	31 Mar 1945

Displacement, tons: 2 200 standard; 3 320 full load
Dimensions, ft (*m*): 376·5 × 40·9 × 19·0 (*114·8 × 12·4 × 5·8*)
Guns: 6—5 in dp (twins)
A/S weapons: 2 fixed Hedgehogs, DC's; 2 triple torpedo tubes (Mk 32)
Main engines: 2 geared turbines; 60 000 shp; 2 shafts
Boilers: 4
Speed, knots: 34
Range, miles: 4 600 at 15 knots
Complement: 274

Transferred from USN 14 July 1972.

CARABOBO (as *Beatty*) — *1965, Dr. Giorgio Arra*

FRIGATES

Note. It is reported that four 1 000 + ton frigates have been ordered from Tirreno e Riuniti (Riva Tregoso) with an option on a further four. Total order may be twelve.

6 "ALMIRANTE CLEMENTE" CLASS

Name	*No.*	*Laid down*	*Launched*	*Completed*
ALMIRANTE CLEMENTE	D 12	5 May 1954	12 Dec 1954	1956
ALMIRANTE JOSE GARCIA	D 33	12 Dec 1954	12 Oct 1956	1957
ALMIRANTE BRION	D 23	12 Dec 1954	4 Sep 1955	1957
GENERAL JOSÉ DE AUSTRIA	D 32	12 Dec 1954	15 July 1956	1957
GENERAL JOSÉ TRINIDAD MORAN	D 22	5 May 1954	12 Dec 1954	1956
GENERAL JUAN JOSÉ FLORES	D 13	5 May 1954	7 Feb 1955	1956

Displacement, tons: **1 300 standard; 1 500 full load**
Length, feet (*metres*): **325·11 (*99·1*) oa**
Beam, feet (*metres*): **35·5 (*10·8*)**
Draught, feet (*metres*): **12·2 (*3·7*)**
Guns: **4—4 in (*102 mm*) 2 twin; 4—40 mm; 8—20 mm (modified group 40 mm only)**
A/S weapons: 2 "Hegehogs", 4 DCT and 2 DC racks in original group; 1 A/S Mortar, 4 DCT and 2 DC racks in modified group
Torpedo tubes: **3—21 in (*533 mm*) triple (original group only)**
Boilers: **2 Foster Wheeler**
Main engines: **2 sets geared turbines; 2 shafts; 24 000 shp**
Speed, knots: 32
Range, miles: 3 500 at 15 knots
Oil, fuel tons: 350
Complement: 162 (12 officers, 150 men)

All built by Ansaldo, Leghorn. The first three were ordered in 1953. Three more were ordered in 1954. Aluminium alloys were widely employed in the building of all superstructure. All six ships are fitted with Denny-Brown fin stabilisers and air conditioned throughout the living and command spaces.

GUNNERY. The 4 inch anti-aircraft guns are fully automatic and radar controlled.

MODERNISATION. *Almirante José Garcia*, *Almirante Brion* and *General José de Austria* were refitted by Ansaldo, Leghorn, in 1962 to improve their anti-submarine and anti-aircraft capabilities: this group are known as "Modified Almirante Clemente" type. *Almirante Clemente* and *General José Trinidad Moran* were taken in hand for refit by Cammell Laird/Plessey group in April 1968. *Almirante Clemente* started her post-refit trials in Feb 1975 and *General Moran* is expected to run hers in May 1975.

RADAR. Search: MLA 1. Fire Control: X Band.

GENERAL JOSE TRINIDAD MORAN — *1972, Venezuelan Navy,*

GENERAL JOSE DE AUSTRIA (modified group) — ***1972, Venezuelan Navy***

SUBMARINES

2 HOWALDTSWERKE TYPE 209

Displacement, tons: 990 surfaced; 1 350 dived
Dimensions, ft (*m*): 177·1 × 20·3 × — (*54·0 × 6·2 × —*)
Torpedo tubes: 8—21 in (with reloads) bow
Main machinery: Diesel-electric; 4 MTU-Siemens diesel generators; 1 Siemens electric motor 5 000 hp; 1 shaft
Speed, knots: 10 surfaced; 22 dived
Range,: 50 days
Complement: 31

Type 209, IK81 designed by Ingenieurkontor Lübeck for construction by Howaldtswerke, Kiel and sale by Ferrostaal, Essen, all acting as a consortium.
A single-hull design with two main ballast tanks and forward and after trim tanks. Fitted with snort and remote machinery control. Slow revving single screw. Very high capacity batteries with GRP lead-acid cells and battery-cooling—by W. Hagen and VARTA. Active and passive sonar, sonar detection set, sound-ranging equipment and underwater telephone. Have two periscopes, radar and Omega receiver. Fore-planes retract. Ordered in 1971. Building in Germany for completion 1975.

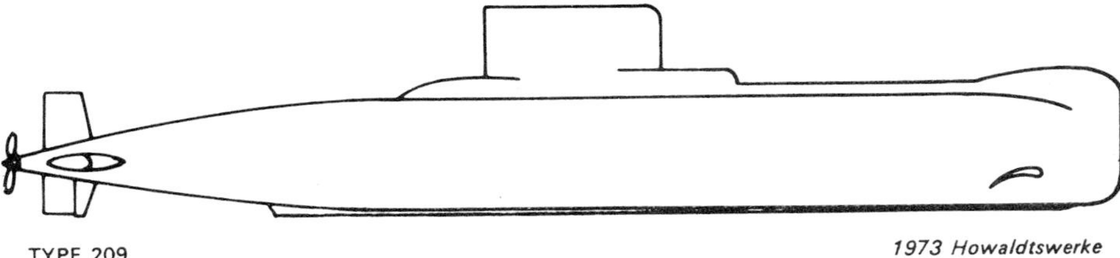

TYPE 209 — *1973 Howaldtswerke*

Submarines—*continued*

2 Ex-US "GUPPY II" CLASS

Name	No.	Builders	Launched	Commissioned
TIBURON (ex-USS *Cubera* SS 347)	S 12	Electric Boat Co, Groton	17 June 1945	19 Dec 1945
PICUDA (ex-USS *Grenadier* SS 525)	S 13	Boston Navy Yard	15 Dec 1944	10 Feb 1951

Displacement, tons	1 870 surface; 2 420 submerged
Length, feet (*metres*)	307·5 (*93·8*)
Beam, feet (*metres*)	27·0 (*8·2*)
Draught, feet (*metres*)	18·0 (*5·5*)
Torpedo tubes	10—21 in (*533 mm*), 6 bow, 4 stern
Main machinery	3 diesels; 4 800 shp; 2 electric motors; 5 400 shp; 2 shafts
Speed, knots	18 on surface; 15 submerged
Range, miles	12 000 at 10 knots
Oil fuel, tons	300
Complement	80

Transferred as follows—*Tiburon* 5 Jan 1972, *Picuda* 15 May 1973.

SPARES. USS *Blenny* (SS 324) was purchased for spares in early 1975.

PICUDA (as GRENADIER) *US Navy*

1 Ex-US "BALAO" CLASS

Name	No.	Builders	Launched	Commissioned
CARITE (ex-USS *Tilefish* SS 307)	S 11	Mare Island Navy Yard	25 Oct 1943	28 Dec 1943

Displacement, tons	1 450 standard; 2 400 dived
Dimensions, ft (*m*)	312 × 27·2 × 17·2 (*95·1* × *8·3* × *5·3*)
Torpedo tubes	10—21 in; 6 bow, 4 stern
Main machinery	4 diesels; 6 400 hp; 2 electric motors; 5 400 shp; 2 shafts
Range, miles	12 000 at 10 knots
Speed, knots	20 surface; 10 dived
Complement	85

Purchased from USN—Transfer 4 May 1960 after 4 month refit. Subsequently refitted with streamlined fin. Used for training.

CARITE *1969 Venezuelan Navy.*

LIGHT FORCES

Note. It is reported that 6 45-ton coastal patrol craft have been ordered in France.

6 VOSPER-THORNYCROFT 121 FT CLASS (FAST ATTACK CRAFT—MISSILE AND GUN)

CONSTITUTION	P 11	**LIBERTAD**	P 15
FEDERACION	P 14	**PATRIA**	P 13
INDEPENDENCIA	P 12	**VICTORIA**	P 16

Displacement, tons	150
Dimensions, ft (*m*)	121 oa × 23·3 × 5·6 (*36·9* × *7·6* × *1·7*)
Missiles	Second 3 to be armed with Otomat and 1—40 mm gun.
Guns	First 3 to be armed with Oto Melara 76 mm
Main engines	2 MTU diesels; 7 200 hp; 2 shafts
Speed, knots	27
Range, miles	1 350 at 16 knots
Complement	18

A £6m, order the first laid down in Jan 1973. A new design, fitted with Elsag fire-control system NA 10 mod 1 and Selenia radar.

Constitucion launched 1 June 1973, completed 16 Aug 1974; *Independencia* launched 24 July 1973, completed Oct 1974; *Patria* launched 27 Sep 1973, completed 9 Jan 1975; *Federacion* launched 26 Feb 1974; *Libertad* launched 5 Mar 1974; *Victoria* launched 3 Sep 1974.

CONSTITUCION (with 76 mm gun) *1974, Vosper-Thornycroft*

Light Forces—*continued*

10 Ex-US PC TYPE (LARGE PATROL CRAFT)

ALBATROS	(ex-USS PC 582)	P-04	***GAVIOTA**	(ex-USS PC 619)	P-10
ALCATRAZ	(ex-USS PC 565)	P-03	***PETREL**	(ex-USS PC 1176)	P-05
CALAMAR	(ex-USS PC 566)	P-02	***PULPO**	(ex-USS PC 465)	P-07
***CAMARON**	(ex-USS PC 483)	P-08	***MEJILLON**	(ex-USS PC 487)	P-01
CARACOL	(ex-USS PC 1077)	P-06	***TOGOGO**	(ex-USS PC 484)	P-09

(* in reserve)

Displacement, tons	280 standard; 430 full load
Dimensions, feet	170·0 wl; 173·7 oa × 23·0 × 10·8
Guns	1—3 in dp; 2—40 mm AA (1 twin); 2—20 mm AA
A/S weapons	Provision for 4 DCT
Main engines	2 Fairbanks-Morse diesels; 2 shafts; 2 800 bhp = 19 knots
Complement	65

Mejillon was refitted and overhauled by Diques y Astilleros Nacionalis, Venezuela, prior to commissioning in the Venezuelan Navy, and from 1962 onwards more ships of this type underwent similar preparation to join the fleet. Altogether twelve of these former United States PC's of the steel-hulled "173-ft" type were purchased from the USA in Oct 1960. *Camaron, Pulpo* and *Gaviota* were placed in reserve 1968-70.

ALBATROS *1972, Venezuelan Navy*

6 NEW CONSTRUCTION (COASTAL PATROL CRAFT)

Displacement, tons	45
Dimensions, feet (*m*)	88·6 × 16 × 4·9 (*27 × 4·9 × 1·5*)
Guns	1—20 mm; 1 MG
Main engines	2 diesels; 3 300 hp = 30 knots
Range, miles	1 500 at 15 knots
Complement	12

Built at Chantiers Navales d'Estrel. Manned by National Guard.

8 "RIO" CLASS (COASTAL PATROL CRAFT)

RIO APURE	**RIO CABRIALES**	**RIO GUARICO**	**RIO NEVERI**
RIO ARAUCA	**RIO CARONI**	**RIO NEGRO**	**RIO TUY**

Displacement, tons	38
Dimensions, feet	82 × 15 × 4
Main engines	2 MTU 12 V 493 diesels; 1 400 rpm; 1 350 bhp = 27 knots

All built by the Chantiers Navales de l'Esterel, Cannes, during 1954-56. Manned by National Guard

RIO NEGRO *1972, Venezuelan Navy*

GOLFO DE CARIACO (COASTAL PATROL CRAFT)

Displacement, tons	37
Dimensions, feet	65 × 18 × 9
Main engines	Diesels; speed = 19 knots
Complement	10

Manned by National Guard.

RIO SANTO DOMINGO (COASTAL PATROL CRAFT)

Displacement, tons	40
Dimensions, feet	70 × 15 × 6
Main engines	2 GM diesels; 1 250 bhp = 24 knots
Complement	10

Manned by National Guard.

21 NEW CONSTRUCTION (COASTAL PATROL CRAFT)

21 90 ft Coastal Patrol Craft are under construction. These were ordered from INMA, La Spezia in Mar 1973 and some are probably building in Venezuela.

AMPHIBIOUS FORCES

1 Ex-US "TERREBONNE PARISH" CLASS (LST)

AMAZONAS (ex-USS *Vernon County*, LST 1161) T 21

Displacement, tons	2 590 light; 5 800 full load
Dimensions, feet	384 × 55 × 17
Guns	6—3 in 50 cal (twins)
Main engines	4 GM diesels; 2 shafts; cp propeller; 6 000 bhp = 15 knots
Complement	116
Troops	395

Built by Ingalls Shipbuilding Corpn, 1952-53. Carries four LCVP landing craft. Transferred on loan 29 June 1973.

4 Ex-US LSM TYPE

LOS FRAILES T 15 (ex-USS *LSM* 544)	**LOS ROQUES** T 14 (ex-USS *LSM* 543)
LOS MONJES T 13 (ex-USS *LSM* 548)	**LOS TESTIGOS** T 16 (ex-USS *LSM* 545)

Displacement, tons	743 beaching; 1 095 full load
Dimensions, feet	196·5 wl; 203·5 oa × 34·5 × 8·3
Guns	1—40 mm AA; 4—20 mm AA
Main engines	Direct drive diesels; 2 shafts; 2 800 bhp = 12 knots
Range, miles	9 000 at 11 knots
Complement	59

All built by Brown Shipbuilding Co, Houston, Texas, in 1945. The former United States medium landing ships were sold to Venezuela under MAP in Aug 1958.

LOS MONJES *1970, Venezuelan Navy*

GUAYANA T 18 (ex-USS *Quirinus*, ARL 39, ex-LST 1151) (TRANSPORT)

Displacement, tons	1 625 light; 3 960 trials; 4 100 full load
Dimensions, feet	316 wl; 328 oa × 50 × 11·2
Guns	8—40 mm AA (two quadruple mountings)
Main engines	GM diesels; 2 shafts; 1 800 bhp = 11·6 knots
Complement	81 (11 officers 70 men)

Former US Navy landing craft repair ship. Built by Chicago Bridge and Iron Co, Seneca, Illinois. Laid down on 3 Mar 1945. Loaned to Venezuela in June 1962 and now used as a transport in the Venezuelan Navy.

GUAYANA *1970, Venezuelan Navy*

TRANSPORTS

PUNTA CABANA T 17

Small troop carrier of about 3 000 tons with a speed of 17 knots.

LAS AVES (ex-*Dos de Diciembre*) T 12

Displacement, tons	944
Dimensions, feet	234·2 × 33·5 × 10
Guns	4—20 mm (2 twin)
Main engines	2 diesels; 2 shafts; 1 600 bhp = 15 knots
Radius, miles	2 600 at 11 knots

Launched by Chantiers Dubigeon, Nantes-Chantenay, France in Sept 1954. Light transport for naval personnel. Renamed *Las Aves* in 1961.

LAS AVES *1970, Venezuelan Navy*

SURVEY SHIPS

3 "PUERTO" CLASS

PUERTO DE NUTRIAS (ex-USS *Tunxis*, AN 90)	H 02 *
PUERTO MIRANDA (ex-USS *Waxsaw*, AN 91)	H 03 *
PUERTO SANTO (ex-USS *Marietta*, AN 82)	H 01

(* in reserve)

Displacement, tons	650 standard; 785 full load
Dimensions, feet	146 wl; 168·5 oa × 33·9 × 10·2 max
Guns	1—20 mm AA
Main engines	Bush-Sulzer diesel-electric; 1 shaft; 1 500 bhp = 12 knots
Complement	46

Former US netlayers of the "Cohoes" class. *Puerto Santo* was built by Commercial Iron Works, Portland, Oregon. Laid down on 17 Feb 1945, launched on 27 Apr 1945. Loaned from USA in Jan 1961 under MAP and converted into hydrographic survey vessel and buoy tender by US Coast Guard Yard, Curtis Bay, Maryland, in Feb 1962. All ships originally carried one 3-inch 50 cal dp gun. *Puerto du Nutrias* and *Puerto Miranda*, built by Zenith Bridge Co, Duluth, Minn. launched in 1944, completed in 1945, were loaned to Venezuela in 1963 under MAP.

PUERTO SANTO *1970, Venezuelan Navy*

2 SURVEY LAUNCHES

GABRIELA P 119 **LELY** P 121

Displacement, tons	90
Dimensions, ft (*m*)	88·6 × 18·4 × 4·9 (*27 × 5·6 × 1·5*)
Main engines	2 diesels; 2 300 hp = 20 knots
Complement	16

Built by Abeking and Rasmussen, Lemwerder. *Lely* completed 7 Feb 1973 and *Gabriela* 5 Feb 1974.

TUGS

FELIPE LARRAZABAL (ex-USS *Utina*, ATF 163) R 21 (OCEAN TUG)

Displacement, tons	1 235 standard; 1 675 full load
Dimensions	205 oa × 38·5 × 15·5
Gun	1—3 in 50 cal AA
Main engines	Diesel-electric; 3 000 bhp; 1 shaft
Speed, knots	15
Complement	85

Transferred 3 Sept 1972. This is the third tug of this name. The first (ex-USS *Discoverer*) was deleted in 1962. The second (ex-USS *Tolowa*, ATF 116) was deleted in 1972 after damage when grounded.

FERNANDO GOMEZ (ex-USS *Dudley*, YTM 744) R 12 (HARBOUR TUG)

Displacement, tons	161
Dimensions, feet	80 × 19 × 8
Main engines	Clark diesel, 6-cyl, 315 rpm; 380 bhp= 15 knots
Complement	10

GENERAL JOSE FELIX RIBAS R 13 (ex-USS *Oswegatchie*, YTM 778, ex-YTB 515) (HARBOUR TUG)

Large harbour tug. Transferred on 4 June 1965 at San Diego, Calif.

2 Ex-US MEDIUM HARBOUR TUGS

FABIO GALLIPOLI (ex-*Wannalancet* YTM 385) R 14
DIANA III (ex-*Sassacus* YTM 193)

Leased to Venezuela in Aug 1965.

5 Ex-US SMALL HARBOUR TUGS

80 feet long, leased in Jan 1963.

FLOATING DOCK

DF 1 (ex-USS *ARD* 13)

The ex-USN ARD 13 of 3 000 tons and built of steel was transferred on loan to Venezuela in Feb 1962 as DF 1.

Ex-US YR 48 (Floating Workshop) transferred 1965.

VIETNAM (REPUBLIC OF)

SPECIAL NOTICE

Following the all-out assault by North Vietnamese forces, the government of South Vietnam surrendered on April 29, 1975. The status of various ships and craft of the South Vietnamese Navy at that time is unknown; most of the units that survived the intensive fighting of 1974-1975 are presumed to have been acquired by North Vietnamese forces. Several ships and small craft escaped from South Vietnamese waters prior to the surrender; see Addenda.

FRIGATES

7 Ex-US 311-ft COAST GUARD CUTTERS

Name	No.	Builder	Launched	US Navy Comm	Transferred
TRAN QUANG KHAI (ex-USCGC *Bering Strait*, WHEC 382 ex-AVP 34)	HQ 02	Lake Washington SY	15 Jan 1944	19 July 1944	1 Jan 1971
TRAN NHAT DUAT (ex-USCGC *Yakutat*, WHEC 380 ex-AVP 32)	HQ 03	Associated Shipbuilders	2 July 1942	31 Mar 1944	1 Jan 1971
TRAN BINH TRONG (ex-USCGC *Castle Rock*, WHEC 383, ex-AVP 35)	HQ 05	Lake Washington SY	11 Mar 1944	8 Oct 1944	21 Dec 1971
TRAN QUOC TOAN (ex-USCGC *Cook Inlet*, WHEC 384, ex-AVP 36)	HQ 06	Lake Washington SY	13 May 1944	5 Nov 1944	21 Dec 1971
THAM NGU LAO (ex-USCGC *Absecon*, WHEC 374, ex-AVP 23)	HQ 15	Lake Washington SY	8 Mar 1942	28 Jan 1943	15 July 1972
LY THOUNG KIET (ex-USCGC *Chincoteague*, WHEC 375, ex-AVP 24)	HQ 16	Lake Washington SY	15 Apr 1942	12 Apr 1943	21 June 1972
NGO KUYEN (ex-USCGC *McCulloch*, WHEC 386, ex-USS *Wachapreague*, AGP 8, AVP 56)	HQ 17	Lake Washington SY	10 July 1943	17 May 1944	21 June 1972

Displacement, tons	1 766 standard; 2 800 full load
Length, feet	300 wl; 310·75 oa
Beam, feet	41·1
Draught, feet	13·5
Guns	1—5 inch (*127 mm*) 38 cal DP 1 or 2—81 mm mortars in some ships; several MG
Main engines	Diesels (Fairbanks Morse); 6080 bhp; 2 shafts
Speed, knots	approx 18
Complement	approx 200

TRAN QUANG KHAI *1971, Vietnamese Navy*

Frigates—*continued*

Built as seaplane tenders of the "Barnegat" class for the US Navy; *Tran Nhat Duat* by Associated Shipbuilders, Seattle, Washington; others by Lake Washington Shipyard, Houghton, Washington.
All transferred to US Coast Guard in 1946-1948, initially on loan designated WAVP and then on permanent transfer except ex-*McCulloch* transferred outright from US Navy to Coast Guard; subsequently redesignated as high endurance cutters (WHEC). Transferred from US Coast Guard to South Vietnamese Navy in 1971-1972.
These ships are the largest combatants in the South Vietnamese Navy and the only ones to mount a 5 inch gun battery. All anti-submarine weapons are believed to have been removed prior to transfer.
The US Coast Guard training cutter *Unimak* (WTR 379, ex-WHEC 379, ex-US AVP 31) was expected to be transferred to South Vietnam in 1975 to provide parts for these ships.

PHOTOGRAPHS. These ships are distinguished from the former US Navy radar picket escorts of similar size by their pole masts forward, open side passages amidships, and radar antenna on second mast. Note combination ·50 cal MG/81 mm mortar forward of bridge in "B" position.

TRAN NHAT DUAT — *1971, Vietnamese Navy*

2 Ex-US DER TYPE

Name	No.	Launched	US Navy Comm.	Transferred
TRAN HUNG DAO (ex-USS *Camp*, DER 251)	HQ 01	16 Apr 1943	16 Sep 1943	6 Feb 1971
TRAN KHANH DU (ex-USS *Forster*, DER 334)	HQ 04	13 Nov 1943	25 Jan 1944	25 Sep 1971

Displacement, tons	1 590 standard; 1 850 full load
Length, feet	300 wl; 306 oa
Beam, feet	36·6
Draught, feet	14
Guns	2—3 inch (*76 mm*) 50 cal AA (single)
A/S weapons	6—12·75 inch (*324 mm*) torpedo tubes (Mk 32 triple) 1 trainable hedgehog (Mk 15) depth charge rack
Main engines	Diesel (Fairbank Morse); 6 000 bhp; 2 shafts
Speed, knots	21
Complement	approx 170

TRAN KHANH DU — *1971, Vietnamese Navy*

Former US Navy destroyer escorts, of the FMR design group. *Tran Hung Dao* built by Brown SB & Co, Houston, Texas; *Tran Khanh Du* built by Consolidated Steel Corp. Orange, Texas.
After World War II both ships were extensively converted to radar picket configuration to serve as seaward extension of US aircraft attack warning system; redesignated DER with original DE hull numbers. Large SPS-8 search radar and TACAN (tactical aircraft navigation) "pod" removed after radar picket barrier ended in 1965, but ships retained DER designation. Subsequently employed during 1960s in Indochina for coastal patrol and interdiction by US Navy (Operation MARKET TIME). Transferred to South Vietnamese Navy in 1971.
These ships are second in firepower in the South Vietanmese Navy only to the ex-US Coast Cuard cutters with respect to gun calibre; however, these ships each mount two guns (forward mount enclosed, after mount open).

ELECTRONICS. SPS-28 and SPS-10 search radars on forward tripod mast. Apparently most electronic warfare equipment was removed prior to transfer (compare after masts with "pods" in photographs of US ships of this class in the United States section).

THAN HUNG DAO — *Vietnamese Navy*

PATROL VESSELS

PATROL BOATS: US NEW CONSTRUCTION

The two 165-foot patrol boats reaverted in the US Navy's Fiscal Year 1975 new construction programme for transfer to South Vietnam were not approved by the US Congress.

3 Ex-US PCE TYPE

DONG DA II (ex-USS *Crestview, PCE* 895)	HQ 07	18 May 1943
NGOC HOI (ex-USS *Brattleboro, EPCER* 852)	HQ 12	1 Mar 1944
VAN KIEP II (ex-USS *Amherst, PCER* 853)	HQ 14	18 Mar 1944

Displacement, tons	640 standard; 903 full load
Dimensions, feet	180 wl; 184·5 oa × 33·1 × 9·5
Guns	1—3 inch (*76 mm*) 50 cal AA; 2—40 mm AA (single); 8—20 mm AA (twin)
A/S weapons	1 fixed hedgehog; depth charges
Main engines	Diesel (General Motors); 2 000 bhp; 2 shafts = 15 knots
Complement	approx 90

Former US Navy patrol vessels—escort (PCE), two of which were fitted as rescue ships (PCER) to pick up survivors of convoy sinkings. *Dong Da II* built by Willamette Iron & Steel Corp, Portland, Oregon; others by Pullman Standard Car Manufacturing Co, Chicago, Illinois; launch dates above. After World War II the *Ngoc Hoi* was employed as an experimental ship (designation given "E" prefix); others used for Naval Reserve training.
Dong Da II transferred to South Vietnam on 29 Nov 1961, *Ngoc Hoi* on 11 July 1966. and *Van Kiep II* in June 1970.
These ships are similar in design to the former minesweepers listed below.

NGOC HOI *1971, Vietnamese Navy*

CHI LANG II *1962, Vietnamese Navy*

4 Ex-US MSF TYPE

CHI LANG II (ex-USS *Gayety, MSF* 239)	HQ 08	19 Mar 1944
KY HOA (ex-USS *Sentry, MSF* 299)	HQ 09	15 Aug 1943
CHI LINH (ex-USS *Shelter, MSF* 301)	HQ 11	14 Nov 1943
HA HOI (ex-USS *Prowess,* IX 305, ex-MSF 280)	HQ 13	17 Feb 1944

Displacement, tons	650 standard; 945 full load
Dimensions, feet	180 wl; 184·5 oa × 33 × 9·75
Guns	1—3 inch (*76 mm*) 50 cal AA; 2—40 mm AA (single); up to 8—20 mm AA (twin)
A/S weapons	1 fixed hedgehog; depth charges
Main engines	Diesel (Cooper Bessemer); 1 710 bhp; 2 shafts = 14 knots
Complement	approx 80

Former US Navy minesweepers of the "Admirable" class (originally designated AM). Built by Winslow Marine Railway & SB Co, Winslow, Washington, except *Ha Hoi* built by Gulf SB Corp, Chicasaw, Alabama; launch dates above. *Ha Hoi* served as a Naval Reserve training ship from 1962 to 1971 (redesignated as an unclassified auxiliary IX 305 on 1 Mar 1966).
Chi Lang II transferred to South Vietnam in Apr 1962, *Ky Hoa* transferred in Aug 1962, *Chi Linh* transferred in Jan 1964, and *Ha Hoi* transferred on 4 June 1970. Minesweeping equipment has been removed and two depth charge racks fitted on fantail; employed in patrol and escort roles. All of these ships are believed to have two 20 mm twin mounts at after end of bridge and one or two 20 mm twin mounts on fantail.

LOSSES

Nhut Tao HQ 10 (ex-USS *Serene,* MSF 300) sunk by Chinese naval forces on 20 Jan 1974.

Patrol Vessels—*continued*

KY HOA

PATROL GUNBOATS

20 100-ft PGM TYPE

Name	*No*	*Transferred*
PHU DU	HQ 600 (PGM 64)	Feb 1963
TIEN MOI	HQ 601 (PGM 65)	Feb 1963
MINH HOA	HQ 602 (PGM 66)	Feb 1963
KIEN VANG	HQ 603 (PGM 67)	Feb 1963
KEO NGUA	HQ 604 (PGM 68)	Feb 1963
KIM QUI	HQ 605 (PGM 60)	May 1963
MAY RUT	HQ 606 (PGM 59)	May 1963
NAM DU	HQ 607 (PGM 61)	May 1963
HOA LU	HQ 608 (PGM 62)	July 1963
TO YEN	HQ 609 (PGM 63)	July 1963
DINH HAI	HQ 610 (PGM 69)	Feb 1964
TRUONG SA	HQ 611 (PGM 70)	Apr 1964
THAI BINH	HQ 612 (PGM 72)	Jan 1966
THI TU	HQ 613 (PGM 73)	Jan 1966
SONG TU	HQ 614 (PGM 74)	Jan 1966
TAT SA	HQ 615 (PGM 80)	Oct 1966
HOANG SA	HQ 616 (PGM 82)	Apr 1967
PHU QUI	HQ 617 (PGM 81)	Apr 1967
HON TROC	HQ 618 (PGM 83)	Apr 1967
THO CHAU	HQ 619 (PGM 91)	Apr 1967

Displacement, tons	117 full load
Dimensions, feet	100·33 oa × 21·1 × 6·9
Guns	1—40 mm AA; 2 or 4—20 mm AA (twin); 2—MG
Main engines	Diesel; 1 900 bhp; 2 shafts = 17 knots
Complement	approx 15

Welded-steel patrol gunboats built in the United States specifically for foreign transfer; assigned PGM numbers for contract purposes. Enlarged version of US Coast Guard 95-foot patrol boats with commercial-type machinery and electronic equipment. HQ 600-605 built by J. M. Martinac SB Corp, Tacoma, Washington; HQ 606-610 built by Marinette Marine Corp, Wisconsin.
All ships have a 20 mm twin mount on after end of deckhouse and some apparently have a second 20 mm mount aft; machineguns are atop deckhouse immediately behind low funnel and forward of 20 mm mount.

KIM QUI *1970, Vietnamese Navy*

DINH HAI *1967, United States Navy*

Ex-US PC TYPE

The **Van Don** HQ 6 (ex-USS *Anacortes,* PC 1569) was reported stricken in 1974. See 1974-1975 and previous editions for characteristics.

COASTAL MINESWEEPERS

The coastal minesweepers **Ham Tu II** HQ 114 (ex-US MSC 281) and **Chuong Duong II** (ex-US MSC 282) were reported stricken in 1974. See 1974-1975 and previous editions for characteristics.

PATROL BOATS

26 Ex-USCG 82-ft "POINT" CLASS

LE PHUOC DUI	HQ 700 (ex-*Point Garnet* 82310)
LE VAN NGA	HQ 701 (ex-*Point League* 82304)
HUYNH VAN CU	HQ 702 (ex-*Point Clear* 82315)
NGUYEN DAO	HQ 703 (ex-*Point Gammon* 82328)
DAO THUC	HQ 704 (ex-*Point Comfort* 82317)
LE NGOC THANH	HQ 705 (ex-*Point Ellis* 82330)
NGUYEN NGOC THACH	HQ 706 (ex-*Point Slocum* 82313)
DANG VAN HOANH	HQ 707 (ex-*Point Hudson* 82322)
LE DINH HUNG	HQ 708 (ex-*Point White* 82308)
THUONG TIEN	HQ 709 (ex-*Point Dume* 82325)
PHAM NGOC CHAU	HQ 710 (ex-*Point Arden* 82309)
DAO VAN DANG	HQ 711 (ex-*Point Glover* 82307)
LE DGOC AN	HQ 712 (ex-*Point Jefferson* 82306)
HUYNH VAN NGAN	HQ 713 (ex-*Point Kennedy* 82320)
TRAN LO	HQ 714 (ex-*Point Young* 82303)
BUI VIET THANH	HQ 715 (ex-*Point Patrige* 82305)
NGUYEN AN	HQ 716 (ex-*Point Caution* 82301)
NGUYEN HAN	HQ 717 (ex-*Point Welcome* 82329)
NGO VAN QUYEN	HQ 718 (ex-*Point Banks* 82327)
VAN DIEN	HQ 719 (ex-*Point Lomas* 82321)
HO DANG LA	HQ 720 (ex-*Point Grace* 82323)
DAM THOAI	HQ 721 (ex-*Point Mast* 82316)
HUYNH BO	HQ 722 (ex-*Point Grey* 82324)
NGUYEN KIM HUNG	HQ 723 (ex-*Point Orient* 82319)
HO DUY	HQ 724 (ex-*Point Cypress* 82326)
TROUNG BA	HQ 725 (ex-*Point Maromc* 82331)

Displacement, tons	64 standard ; 67 full load
Dimensions, feet	83 oa × 17·2 × 5·8
Guns	1—81 mm/.50 cal MG (combination) plus 2 to 4—·50 cal MG (single) or 1—20 mm
Main engines	2 diesels ; 1 200 bhp ; 2 shafts = 16·8 knots
Complement	8 to 10

Former US Coast Guard 82-ft patrol boats (designated WPB) ; actual length is 83 feet overall. All served in Vietnamese waters, manned by US personnel, comprising Coast Guard Squadron One. HQ 700-707 transferred to South Vietnamese Navy in 1969, HQ 708-HQ 725 in 1970.
Numerous units of this type are in service with the US Coast Guard.

POINT CLASS — *1970, Vietnamese Navy*

LANDING SHIPS

6 Ex-US LST TYPE

CAM RANH (ex-USS *Marion County, LST* 975)	HQ 500	6 Jan 1945
DA NANG (ex-USS *Maricopa County, LST* 938)	HQ 501	15 Aug 1944
THI NAI (ex-USS *Cayuga County, LST* 529)	HQ 502	17 Jan 1944
VUNG TAU (ex-USS *Cochino County, LST* 603)	HQ 503	14 Mar 1944
QUI NHON (ex-USS *Bullock County, LST* 509)	HQ 504	23 Nov 1943
HNA TRANG (ex-USS *Jerome County, LST* 848)	HQ 505	2 Jan 1943

Displacement, tons	2 366 beaching ; 4 080 full load
Dimensions, feet	316 wl ; 328 oa × 50 × 14
Guns	7 or 8—40 mm AA (1 or 2 twin ; 4 or 5 single) ; several 20 mm AA
Main engines	Diesel (General Motors) ; 1 700 bhp ; 2 shafts = 11 knots
Complement	110

Former US Navy tank landing ships ; launch dates above. HQ 500 and 501 built by Bethlehem Steel Co, Hingham, Massachusetts ; HQ 502 and 504 by Jeffersonville B & M Co Jeffersonville, Indiana ; HQ 503 by Chicago Bridge & Iron Co, Illinois ; HQ 505 by Kaiser Co, Richmond, California. HQ 500 and 502 have pole masts ; others have lattice tripod masts.

THI NAI — *Vietnamese Navy*

Landing Ships—*continued*

QUI NHON — *1971, Vietnamese Navy*

DA NANG — *1962, Vietnamese Navy*

7 Ex-US LSM TYPE

HAT GIANG (ex-LSM 9011, ex-USS LSM 335)	HQ 400	10 Nov 1944
HAN GIANG (ex-LSM 9012, ex-USS LSM 110)	HQ 401	28 Oct 1944
LAM GIANG (ex-USS LSM 226)	HQ 402	4 Sep 1944
NINH GIANG (ex-USS LSM 85)	HQ 403	15 Sep 1944
HUONG GIANG (ex-USS *Oceanside*, LSM 176)	HQ 404	12 Aug 1944
TIEN GIANG (ex-USS LSM 313)	HQ 405	24 May 1944
HAU GIANG (ex-USS LSM 276)	HQ 406	20 Sep 1944

Displacement, tons	743 beaching ; 1 095 full load
Dimensions, feet	196·5 wl ; 203·5 oa × 34·5 × 8·3
Guns	2—40 mm AA ; 4—20 mm AA
Main engines	Diesel ; 2 shafts ; 2 800 bhp = 12 knots
Complement	73

Former US Navy medium landing ships ; launch dates above.
Designed primarily to carry assault troops. First four transferred to French Navy for use in Indo-China, Jan 1954. *LSM* 9011, 9012 transferred to Vietnam Navy, Dec 1955. LSM 9014, 9017, 1098, returned to USA in 1955. *Oceanside LSM* 175 transferred at Los Angeles on 1 Aug 1961, LSM 313 in 1962, *Hau Giang* (ex-LSM 276) on 10 June 1965.
Hat Giang and *Han Giang* are hospital ships (LSM-H) ; refitted for treating casualties and assigned political warfare personnel (in addition to normal complement). All are armed.

LAM GIANG — *Vietnamese Navy*

HAT GIANG (LSM-H) — *Vietnamese Navy*

Landing Ships—*continued*

4 Ex-US LSSL TYPE

DOAN NGOC TANG (ex-USS LSSL 9)	HQ 228	17 Aug 1944
LULU PHU THO (ex-USS LSSL 101)	HQ 229	27 Jan 1945
NGUYEN NGOC LONG (ex-USS LSSL 96)	HQ 230	6 Jan 1945
NIGUYEN DUC BONG (ex-USS LSSL 129)	HQ 231	13 Dec 1944

Displacement, tons	227 standard; 383 full load
Dimensions, feet	158 × 23·7 × 5·7
Guns	1—3 inch; 4—40 mm AA; 4—20 mm AA; 4 MG
Main engines	Diesel; 2 shafts; 1 600 bhp = 14 knots
Complement	60

Former US Navy landing ships support; designed to provide close-in-fire support for amphibious assaults, but suitable for general gunfire missions. Launch dates above.

The *Doan Ngoc Tang* was transferred to France in 1951 (*Hallebarde* L. 9023); transferred to Japan 1956-1964; returned and transferred to South Vietnam in 1965. Three other ships served in Japanese Navy 1953 to 1964; retransferred to South Vietnam in 1965 and 1966.

Three ships of this type sunk; *Le Van Binh* HQ 227, ex-French *Javeline* L 9024, ex-USS LSSL 10 sunk in 1966; *Neuyen Van Tru* HQ 225, ex-French *Framee*, ex-USS LSSL 105 sunk in 1970; *Le Trong Dam* HQ 226, ex-French *Arquesbusei* L 9022, ex-USS LSSL 4 sunk in 1970.

NIGUYEN DUC BONG *Vietnamese Navy*

3 Ex-US LSIL TYPE

THIEN KICH (ex-French L 9038, ex-USS LSIL 872)	HQ 329	4 Oct 1944
LOI CONG (ex-French L 9034, ex-USS LSIL 699)	HQ 330	21 June 1944
TAM SET (ex-French L 9033, ex-USS LSIL 871)	HQ 331	3 Oct 1944

Displacement, tons	227 standard; 383 full load
Dimensions, feet	158 × 22·7 × 5·3
Guns	1—3 inch; 1—40 mm AA; 2—20 mm AA; 4 MG; and up to 4 army mortars (2—81 mm; 2—60 mm)
Main engines	Diesel; 2 shafts; 1 600 bhp = 14·4 knots
Complement	55

Former US Navy landing ships infantry; launch dates above. Designed to carry 200 troops. *Tam Set* originally transferred to France in 1951 and others in 1953 for use in Indochina; subsequently retransferred in 1956 to South Vietnam.
Two ships of this type sunk *Long Dao* HQ 327 ex-French L 9029, ex-USS LSIL 698, and *Thor Tien* HQ 328 ex-French L 9035, ex-USS LSIL 702, both in 1974.

THIEN KICH

Landing Ships—*continued*

LONG DAO—sunk in 1974 *1971, Vietnamese Navy*

LANDING CRAFT

17 Ex-US LCU TYPE

HQ 533 (ex-US LCU 1479)
HQ 534 (ex-US LCU 1480)
HQ 535 (ex-US LCU 1221)
HQ 537 (ex-US LCU 1501)
HQ 538 (ex-US LCU 1594)
HQ 539 (ex-US LCU 1502)
HQ 540 (ex-US LCU 1475)
HQ 542 (ex-US LCU 1494)
HQ 543 (ex-US LCU 1493)
HQ 544 (ex-US LCU 1485)
HQ 545 (ex-US LCU 1484)
HQ 546 (ex-US YFU 90, ex-LCU 1582)
HQ 547 (ex-US LCU 1481)
HQ 548 (ex-US LCU 1498)
HQ 560 (ex-US YLLC 1, LCU 1348)
HQ 561 (ex-US YLLC 5, YFU 2, LCU 529)
HQ 562 (ex-US YLLC 3, YFU 33, LCU 1195)

LCU 501 series

Displacement, tons	309 to 320 full load
Dimensions, feet	105 wl; 119 oa × 32·7 × 5
Main engines	Diesels (Gray Marine); 675 bhp; 3 shafts = 10 knots

LCU 1466 series

Displacement, tons	360 full load
Dimensions, feet	115 wl; 119 oa × 34 × 5·25
Main engines	Diesels (Gray Marine); 675 bhp; 3 shafts = 8 knots

Former US Navy utility landing craft; 501 series built during World War II with LCT (6) designation; 1466 series built during the early 1950s. Transferred to South Vietnam from 1954 to 1971, with some of the earlier craft serving briefly in French Navy in Indichina waters.
Three units (ex-YLLC) converted while in US Navy service for use as salvage lifting craft; fitted with 20-ton capacity "A" frame derrick, special anchors, diver's air compressors, welding equipment, and salvage pumps.
Most units armed with two 20 mm AA guns; armament varies with assignment.

HQ 538 *1971, Vietnamese Navy*

HQ 561 (ex YLLC 5) *United States Navy*

RIVERINE CRAFT

The US Navy has transferred approximately 700 armed small craft to South Vietnam since 1965 for use in riverine and coastal areas of Indochina. A few former French riverine craft also survive. The exact number of these craft now in service is not known. The following totals were the official South Vietnamese Navy listings for 1972. Some of these craft may not be operational because of maintenance limitations of the South Vietnamese Navy and many are believed to have been lost since the April-May 1972 invasion of South Vietnam by regular forces of the Democratic Republic of (North) Vietnam.
In addition to the armed craft grouped here under the category of Riverine Craft, there are numerous small landing craft which are armed.

107 Ex-US "SWIFT" TYPE

Displacement, tons	22·5 full load
Dimensions, feet	50 oa × 13 × 3·5
Guns	1—81 mm mortar/1—·50 cal mG combination Mount: 2—·50 cal MG (twin)
Main engines	2 geared diesels (General Motors); 960 bhp; 2 shafts = 28 knots
Complement	6

All-metal inshore patrol craft (PCF). Transferred to South Vietnam from 1968 to 1970. Numbered in HQ 3800-3887 and later series.

HQ 3825 — *1970, Vietnamese Navy*

293 Ex-US PBR TYPE

Displacement, tons	PBR I series: 7·5 PBR II series: 8
Dimensions, feet	PBR I series: 31 oa × 10·5 × 2·5 PBR II series: 32 oa × 11 × 2·6
Guns	3—·50 cal MG (twin mount forward; single gun aft)
Main engines	2 geared diesels; 440 bhp; water-jet propulsion = 25+ knots
Complement	4 or 5

River patrol boats (PBR) with fibreglass (plastic) hulls. Transferred to South Vietnam from 1968 to 1970. Numbered in HQ 7500-7749 nd 7800 series.

PBR TYPE — *1970, Vietnamese Navy*

PBR TYPE

27 Ex-US RPC TYPE

Displacement, tons	15·6
Dimensions, feet	35·75 oa × 10·3 × 3·6
Guns	varies: 2—·50 cal MG (twin); 3—·30 cal MG (twin mount aft and single gun at conning station); some units have additional twin ·30 cal mount in place of ·50 cal MH
Main engines	2 geared diesels; 2 shafts = 14 knots

River patrol craft (PRC); predecessor to PBR type. Welded-steel hulls. Few used by US Navy as minesweepers, but most of the 34 units built were transferred to South Vietnam upon completion in 1965; others in 1968-1969. Numbered HQ 7000-7028.

RPC TYPE — *1970, Vietnamese Navy*

84 Ex-US ASPB TYPE

Displacement, tons	36·25 full load
Dimensions, feet	50 oa × 15·6 × 3·75
Guns	varies: 1 or 2—20 mm (with 2—·50 cal MG in boats with one 20 mm); 2—·30 cal MG; 2—40 mm grenade launchers
Main engines	2 geared diesels; 2 shafts = 14 knots sustained
Complement	6

Assault support patrol boats (ASPB) with welded-steel hulls. Transferred to South Vietnam from 1969 to 1970. Numbered in HQ 5100 series. These craft operate in escort, river interdiction, and minesweeping roles.

ASPB TYPE — *1970, Vietnamese Navy*

42 Ex-US MONITORS

Displacement, tons	80 to 90 full load
Dimensions, feet	60·5 oa × 17·5 × 3·5
Guns	1—105 mm howitzer; 2—20 mm; 3—·30 cal MG; 2—40 mm grenade launchers
Main engines	2 geared diesels; 2 shaft = 9 knots
Complement	11

River monitors (MON). Transferred to South Vietnam in 1969-1970. Numbered in HQ 6500 series.

MONITOR — *1970, Vietnamese Navy*

Riverine Class—*continued*

22 Ex-US LCM MONITORS

Displacement, tons	75 full load
Dimensions, feet	60 oa × 17
Guns	varies: 1—81 mm mortar or 2 M10-8 flame throwers; 1—40 mm; 1—20 mm; 2—·50 cal MG; possibly 2 to 4—·30 cal MG
Main engines	2 geared diesels; 2 shafts = 8 knots
Complement	approx 10

Twenty-four LCM-6 landing craft converted to this configuration from 1964 to 1967. Predecessor to the "monitor" listed above. Transferred to South Vietnam from 1965 to 1970. Numbered in HQ 1800 series.

LCM MONITOR *1970, Vietnamese Navy*

100 Ex-US ATC TYPE

Displscement, tons	66 full load
Dimensions, feet	65·5 oa × 17·5 × 3·25
Guns	varies: 1 or 2—20 mm; 2—·50 cal MG; several ·30 cal MG; 2—40 mm grenade launchers
Main engines	2 geared diesels; 2 shafts = 8·5 knots (6 knots sustained)

Armoured troop carriers (ATC). Some fitted with steel helicopter platforms or evacuation of wounded. Transferred to South Vietnam in 1969. Numbered in HQ 1200 series. A few additional units of this design are fitted with extra fuel tanks and serve as refuellers.

ATC TYPE *1970, Vietnamese Navy*

9 Ex-US CCB TYPE

Displacement, tons	80 full load
Dimensions, feet	61 oa × 17·5 × 3·4
Guns	3—20 mm; 2—·30 cal MG; 2—40 mm grenade launchers
Main engines	2 geared diesels; 2 shafts = 8·5 knots maximum (6 knots sustained)
Complement	11

Command and control boats (CCB) to provide command and communication facilities for riverine commanders. Transferred to South Vietnam in 1969-1970. Numbered HQ 6100-6108.

4 Ex-US CSB TYPE

Dimensions, feet	56 oa × 18·75 × 6
Guns	4—·50 cal MG (twin)
Main engines	2 geared diesels; 2 shafts = 6 knots
Complement	6

Combat salvage boats (CSB) converted from LCM-6 landing craft; configured for river salvage and to support diving operations. Ten-ton capacity "A" frame forward.

Ex-FRENCH CRAFT

The Vietnamese Navy still lists 43 ex-French STCAN/FOM and 14 LCM Commandament as being in service. The latter are converted LCM-3 landing craft.

STCAN/FOM *Vietnamese Navy*

Riverine Class—*continued*

LCM-COMMANDAMENT *Vietnamese Navy*

MINESWEEPING LAUNCHES

The Vietnamese Navy lists 24 minesweeping launches; ten MLMS 50-foot type transferred in 1963 from US Navy (numbered HQ 150-155, 157-160; HQ 156 and 161 stricken in 1971); eight MSM 56-foot type transferred in 1970 (numbered HQ 1700-1707); six MSR 50-foot type transferred in 1970 (numbered HQ 1900-1905). Other riverine craft had a minesweeping capability (see minesweeping gear on stern of ATC at left).

MLMS *1971, Vietnamese Navy*

SUPPORT SHIPS

3 Ex-US MODIFIED LST TYPE

MY THO (ex-USS *Harnett County*, AGP 821, ex-LST 821)	HQ 800	27 Oct 1944
CAN THO (ex-USS *Garrett County*, AGP 786, ex-LST 786)	HQ 801	22 July 1944
VINH LONG (ex-USS *Satyr*, ARL 23, ex-LST 852)	HQ 802	13 Nov 1944

Displacement, tons	AGP type: 4 080 full load ARL type: 4 100 full load
Dimensions, feet	316 wl; 328 oa × 50 × 14
Guns	AGP type: 8—40 mm (2 twin, 4 single) ARL type: 8—40 mm AA (2 quad)
Main engines	Diesels (General Motors); 1 700 bhp except *Vinh Long* 1 800 bhp; 2 shafts = 11·6 knots

Former US Navy ships of LST design employed in support of coastal and riverine craft. Launch dates above. *Vinh Long* converted during construction to landing craft repair ship (ARL); others completed as standard LSTs but were modified in late 1960s to support US Navy small craft in Vietnamese waters; redesignated as patrol craft tenders (AGP) on 25 Sep 1970. The *Vinh Long* has more extensive repair facilities.

My Tho transferred to South Vietnam on 12 Oct 1970, *Can Tho* on 23 Apr 1971, and *Vinh Long* on 15 Oct 1971.

A photograph of the *Garrett County* supporting PBRs and UH-1B helicopters in Vietnamese waters appears in the 1970-1971 edition.

VINH LONG *Vietnamese Navy*

Support Ships—*continued*

MY THO *1971, Vietnamese Navy*

OILERS

6 Ex-US YOG TYPE

HQ 470 (ex-*L'Aulne*, ex-US YOG 80)
HQ 471 (ex-US *YOG* 33)
HQ 472 (ex-US *YOG* 67)
HQ 473 (ex-US *YOG* 71)
HQ 474 (ex-US *YOG* 131)
HQ 475 (ex-US *YOG* 56)

Displacement, tons	450 light; 1 253 full load
Dimensions, feet	174·0 × 32·0 × 10·9
Main engines	Diesels; 1 shaft = 10 knots
Cargo capacity	6 570 barrels

Former US Navy small gasoline tankers. HQ 470 transferred to South Vietnam in Jan 1951, HQ 471 in Aug 1963, HQ 472 in July 1967, HQ 473 in Mar 1970; HQ 474 in Apr 1971, and HQ 475 in June 1972. No Vietnamese names.

HQ 471 *Vietnamese Navy*

HQ 470 *1971, Vietnamese Navy*

WATER CARRIER

1 Ex-US YW TYPE

HQ 9118 (ex-US YW 152)
Former US Navy self propelled water carrier. Transferred to South Vietnam in 1956. No Vietnamese name assigned. HQ 9111 (ex-US YWN 151), HQ 9113 (ex-US YWN 153), and HQ 9018 (ex-US YWN 152) are non-self-propelled water carriers.

HARBOUR TUGS

8 Ex-US YTL TYPE

HQ 9500 (ex-US YTL 152)
HQ 9501 (ex-US YTL 245)
HQ 9503 (ex-US YTL 200)
HQ 9504 (ex-US YTL 206)
HQ 9508 (ex-US YTL 452)
HQ 9509 (ex-US YTL 456)
HQ 9510 (ex-US YTL 586)
HQ 9511 (ex-US YTL 457)

Former US Navy harbour tugs. HQ 9500 transferred to South Vietnam in 1955; HQ 9501, 9503, 9504 in 1956; others from 1968 to 1970.
HQ 9507 (ex-US YTL 423 scrapped in 1972).

Harbour Tugs—*continued*

TRAINING SHIPS

Hoa Giang HQ 451 (ex-*Dinh Ah*, ex-French *Ingenieur en Chef Griod*, ex-US Army FS 287, ex-*Governor Wright*) stricken in 1974. See 1974-1975 and previous editions for characteristics.

FLOATING DRY DOCK

HQ 9604 (ex-US AFDL 22)

Former US Navy floating dry dock. Steel hull with 1 000-ton lift capacity.

HQ 9604 with LSM

JUNK FORCE

There are approximately 250 motor-propelled junks in naval service. The breakdown as of January 1972 included 62 command junks, 31 Kien Giang junks, and 153 Yabuta junks. Some of the Yabuta junks are fabricated of ferrous cement. The Yabuta junk illustrated below has two ·50 cal MG; some also have a 60 mm mortar. Diesel propulsion permits them to overtake and search some of the thousands of coastal sailing craft in Indochina waters. The Vietnamese Navy has discarded the armed sailing junks previously employed in this role.

YABUTA JUNK *1971, Vietnamese Navy*

FERROUS CEMENT JUNK *Vietnamese Navy*

MISCELLANEOUS

Numerous craft are operated by the Vietnamese Navy in addition to those described above. However, details are not available.
The former US Coast Guard lightship WLV-523 was transferred to South Vietnam on 25 Sep 1971 for use as an offshore radar station to supplement 16 coastal radar stations on shore which are operated to detect seaborne infiltration effort; renamed *Da Bong* (304). The shore stations are manned by naval personnel.

VIETNAM (North)

Administration

Commander in Chief of the Navy: Rear Admiral Ta Xuan Thu

Strength of the Fleet

All figures approximate in this section

	Active		*Active*
Corvettes	3	Tenders	10
Fast Attack Craft—Missile	2	MSBs	4
Fast Attack Craft—Torpedo	12	LSMs	7
Fast Attack Craft—Gun	22	Landing Ships—various	17
Coastal Patrol Craft	30		

Personnel

1975: Total 4 000 officers and ratings

Mercantile Marine

Lloyd's Register of Shipping: 5 vessels of 5 002 tons

CORVETTES

3 USSR "SOI" CLASS

Displacement, tons	215 light; 250 normal
Dimensions, feet	138·6 × 20 × 9·2
Guns	4—25 mm (2 twin mountings)
A/S weapons	4—5 barrelled MBU; 2 DCT
Range, miles	1 100 at 13 knots
Main engines	3 diesels; 6 000 hp = 29 knots
Complement	30

Four submarine chasers of Soviet "SOI" type were originally transferred to North Vietnam, two in 1960-61 and two in 1964-65, but one was sunk by US Navy aircraft on 1 Feb 1966

SOI *Class*

LIGHT FORCES

2 Ex-USSR "KOMAR" CLASS (FAST ATTACK CRAFT—MISSILE)

Displacement, tons	70 standard; 80 full load
Dimensions, feet	83·7 × 19·8 × 5·0
Missiles	2—SSN-2 launchers
Guns	2—25 mm (twin-forward)
Main engines	4 Diesels; 4 shafts; 4 800 hp = 40 knots
Range, miles	400 at 30 knots

A sister ship was reported sunk on 19 Dec 1972.

6 USSR "P 6" CLASS (FAST ATTACK CRAFT—TORPEDO)

Displacement, tons	66 standard; 75 full load
Dimensions, feet	84·2 × 20 × 6
Guns	4—25 mm AA (2 twin)
Torpedo tubes	2—21 in (single)
Mines	4
Main engines	4 diesels; 4 800 bhp; 4 shafts = 43 knots
Range, miles	450 at 30 knots
Complement	25

Built in China and transferred in 1967. Some may have been lost in action.

P 6 *Class*

6 Ex-USSR "P 4" CLASS (FAST ATTACK CRAFT—TORPEDO)

Displacement, tons	25 standard
Dimensions, feet	62·7 × 11·6 × 5·6
Guns	2 MG (1 twin)
Torpedo tubes	2—18 in
Main engines	2 diesels; 2 200 bhp = 50 knots

Approximately a dozen aluminium hulled motor torpedo boats were transferred from the Soviet Union in 1961 and 1964, and some from China. A number have been lost in action.

Light Forces—*continued*

8 Ex-CHINESE "SHANGHAI" CLASS (FAST ATTACK CRAFT—GUN)

Displacement, tons	120 full load
Dimensions, ft (*m*)	128 × 18 × 5·5 (*39 × 5·5 × 1·7*)
Guns	4—37 mm (2 twin mountings); 4—25 mm (twins)
Main engines	4 diesels; 4 800 bhp = 30 knots
Complement	25

Four motor gunboats were received from the People's Republic of China (Communist) Navy in May 1966.

SHANGHAI II *1972, Aviation Fan*

14 Ex-CHINESE "SWATOW" CLASS (FAST ATTACK CRAFT—GUN)

Displacement, tons	80 full load
Dimensions, feet	83·5 × 19 × 6·5
Guns	4—37 mm; 2—20 mm
A/S weapons	8 depth charges
Main engines	4 diesels; 4 800 bhp = 40 knots
Range, miles	750 at 15 knots
Complement	17

Approximately 30 "Swatow" class motor gunboats built in China were transferred in 1958, and 20 were delivered in 1964 to replace those lost in action. Pennant numbers run in a 600 series. This class sustained heavy losses in action.

30 MOTOR LAUNCH TYPES (COASTAL PATROL CRAFT)

Some thirty motor launches were reported to have been incorporated into the North Vietnam Navy before May, 1966, but not all are still in service.

4 PATROL TYPE (MSB)

Four vessels for sweeping, patrol and general purpose duties have been reported delivered in recent years.

10 GENERAL UTILITY TYPES (TENDERS)

Tenders and launches commandeered from private and commercial sources to serve the fleet and naval establishments.

AMPHIBIOUS FORCES

7 US LSM TYPE

Displacement, tons	743 standard; 1 095 full load
Dimensions, feet	196·5 wl; 203·5 oa × 34·5 × 8·3
Guns	2—40 mm AA (1 twin mounting); 4—20 mm AA
Main engines	Diesels; 2 shafts; 2 800 bhp = 12 knots

One or two of these are reported to be out of operational service.

5 US LSSL TYPE

Displacement, tons	250 standard; 430 full load
Dimensions, feet	153·0 wl; 158·5 oa × 23·7 × 5·7
Guns	1—3 in; 4—40 mm AA; 4—20 mm AA
Main engines	Diesels; 2 shafts; 1 800 bhp = 14 knots
Range, miles	3 500 at 12 knots
Complement	71

There are also reported to be five of the LCI/LSIL type, one of the LCT(6) type, and six of the LCT (7) type.

AUXILIARY PATROL CRAFT

There is a substantial number of armed junks and similarly adapted craft.

VIRGIN ISLANDS

VIRGIN CLIPPER

Displacement, tons	15
Dimensions, feet	40 × 12 × 2
Guns	3 MG
Main engines	2 diesels; 370 hp = 22 knots

Standard Brooke Marine patrol craft.

YEMEN—NORTH (Arab Republic of)

Mercantile Marine

Lloyd's Register of Shipping: 3 vessels of 1 260 tons gross

Personnel

(a) 1975: 300 officers and men
(b) 3 years National Service

Base

Hodeida

5 Ex-USSR "P 4" CLASS (FAST ATTACK CRAFT—TORPEDO)

Displacement, tons	25
Dimensions, feet	62·7 × 11·6 × 5·6
Guns	2 MG
Torpedo tubes	2—18 in
Main engines	2 diesels; 2 shafts; 2 200 hp = 50 knots

Transferred by USSR in late 1960s.

NOTE. In addition a dozen smaller Patrol Craft and two small landing craft have been reported.

YEMEN—SOUTH (People's Democratic Republic of)

Mercantile Marine

Lloyd's Register of Shipping:
7 vessels of 2 180 tons gross

Personnel

(a) 1975: 250 officers and men
(b) Possibly 2 years National Service

CORVETTES

2 Ex-USSR "SO I" CLASS

Displacement, tons	215 standard; 250 full load
Dimensions, feet	138·6 × 20·0 × 9·2
Guns	4—25 mm
A/S weapons	4—5 barrelled MBUs
Main engines	3 diesels; 6 000 shp = 29 knots
Range, miles	1 100 at 13 knots
Complement	30

Transferred in late 1960's.

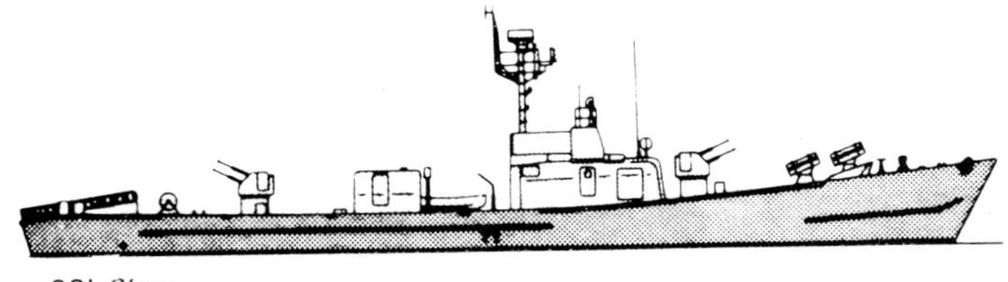

SOI *Class*

AMPHIBIOUS FORCES

2 Ex-USSR "POLNOCNY" CLASS

(LCT)

Displacement, tons	780 standard; 1 000 full load
Dimensions, ft (*m*)	246 × 29·5 × 9·8 (*75 × 9 × 3*)
Guns	2—30 mm (twin)
A/S weapons	2—18 barrelled MBUs
Main engines	2 diesels; 5 000 bhp = 18 knots

Can carry 6 tanks. Transferred early 1970's.

LCM's

Several smaller Soviet LCM's have also been transferred.

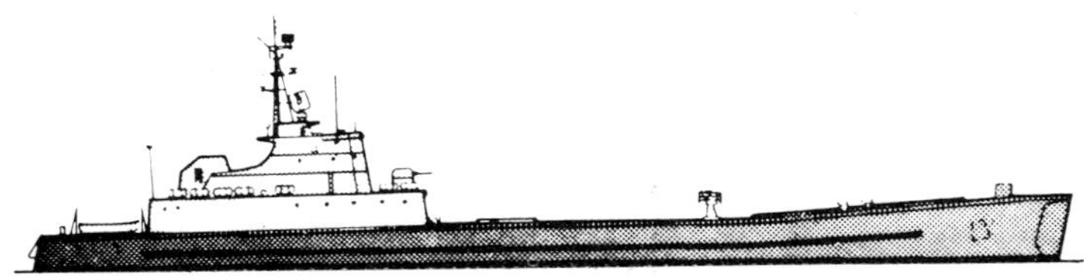

"POLNOCNY" Class

LIGHT FORCES

2 Ex-USSR "P 6" CLASS

Displacement, tons	66 standard; 75 full load
Dimensions, ft	84·2 × 20 × 6·0
Guns	4—25 mm (twins)
Tubes	2—21 in
Main engines	4 Diesels; 4 shafts; 4 800 bhp = 43 knots
Range, miles	450 at 30 knots
Complement	25

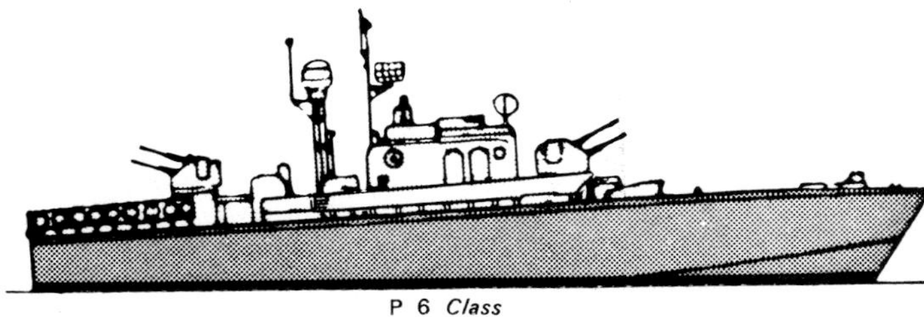

P 6 *Class*

INSHORE MINESWEEPERS

3 Ex-BRITISH "HAM" CLASS

AL SAQR (ex-*Bodenham*) **AL DAIRAK** (ex-*Blunham*)
AL GHAZALA (ex-*Elsenham*)

Displacement, tons	120 standard; 160 full load
Dimensions, feet	106·5 oa × 21·2 × 5·5
Gun	1—20 mm AA
Main engines	2 Paxman diesels; 1 100 bhp = 14 knots
Oil fuel, tons	15
Complement	15 officers and men

The British inshore minesweepers *Bodenham*, *Blunham* and *Elsenham* were transferred to the South Arabian Navy established by the Federal Government in 1967.

PATROL BOATS

15 COASTAL TYPE

Fifteen small diesel engined patrol boats were bought in the United Kingdom in 1970.

YUGOSLAVIA

Administration

Assistant Secretary of State for National Defence for the Navy:
Admiral Branko Mamula

Commander-in-Chief of the Fleet:
Vice-Admiral Ivo Purisic

Diplomatic Representation

Defence Attaché in London:
Colonel M. Sutlan

Naval, Military and Air Attaché in Washington:
Colonel Milan Mavric

Naval, Military and Air Attaché in Moscow:
Colonel S. Krivokapic

Personnel

(a) 1975: 27 000 (2 500 officers and 24 500 men)
(b) 18 months National Service

Strength of the Fleet

Type	*Active*	*Building*
Destroyer	1	—
Corvettes	3	—
Submarines—Patrol	5	?
Fast Attack Craft—Missile	10	4
Fast Attack Craft—Gun	20	—
Fast Attack Craft—Torpedo	14	—
Large Patrol Craft	26	—
Minesweepers—Coastal	4	—
Minesweepers—Inshore	10	—
River Minesweepers	14	—
LCT	30	—
Training Ships	2	—
Survey Ship	1	—
Despatch Vessels	2	—
Salvage Vessel	1	—
Tankers—Harbour	7	—
Transports	2	—
Tugs	20	—
Water Carriers	8	—
Yacht	1	—

Disposals

Destroyers

1971 *Kotor* (ex-*Kempenfelt*, ex-*Valentine*)
Pula (ex-*Wager*)

Frigates

1971 *Biokovo* (ex-*Aliseo*)
Triglav (ex-*Indomito*)

Submarines

1971 *Sava* (ex-*Nautilo*)

Bases

Dubrovnik, Kotor, Pula, Sibenik, Split, Zadar

Mercantile Marine

Lloyd's Register of Shipping:
398 vessels of 1 778 423 tons gross

DESTROYER

1 "SPLIT" CLASS

SPLIT (ex-*Spalato*,) R 11

Displacement, tons	2 400 standard; 3 000 full load
Length, feet (*metres*)	376·3 (*114·7*) pp; 393·7 (*120·0*) oa
Beam, feet (*metres*)	36·5 (*11·1*)
Draught, feet (*metres*)	12·3 (*3·8*)
Guns, surface	4—5 in (*127 mm*)
Guns, AA	12—40 mm
A/S weapons	2 "Squids", 6 DCT, 2 DC racks
Torpedo tubes	5—21 in (*533 mm*)
Mines	Capacity 40
Boilers	2 watertube type
Main engines	Geared turbines; 2 shafts; 50 000 shp
Speed, knots	31·5
Oil fuel, tons	590 capacity
Complement	240

Built by Brodogradiliste "3 Maj", Rijeka. The original ship was laid down in July 1939 by Chantieres de Loire, Nantes, in 1939 at Split Shipyard. Launched in 1940. Completed on 4 July 1958. Ready for operational service in 1959. The original design provided for an armament of 5—5·5 inch guns, 10—40 mm AA guns and 6—21·7 inch torpedo tubes (tripled), but the plans were subsequently modified.

SPLIT *Aldo Fraccaroli*

CORVETTES

2 "MORNAR" CLASS

MORNAR 551 **BORAC** 552

Displacement, tons	330 standard; 430 full load
Length, feet (*metres*)	170·0 (*51·8*) pp; 174·8 (*53·3*) oa
Beam, feet (*metres*)	23·0 (*7·0*)
Draught, feet (*metres*)	6·6 (*2·0*)
Guns,	2—3 in (single) 2—40 mm single; 2—20 mm single
A/S weapons	2 "Hedgehogs"; 2 DCT; 2 DC racks
Main engines	4 SEMT-Pielstick diesels; 2 shafts 3 240 bhp
Speed, knots	20
Range, miles	3 000 at 12 knots; 2 000 at 15 knots
Complement	60

Mornar was completed on 10 Sep 1959. Her design is an improved version of that of PBR 581. *Borac* was launched in 1965.

BORAC *Aldo Fraccaroli*

1 FOUGUEUX TYPE

UDARNIK (ex P 6) 581

Displacement, tons	325 standard; 400 full load
Dimensions, feet	170 pp × 23 × 6·5
Guns	2—40 mm AA; 2—20 mm AQ
A/S weapons	1 Hedgehog; 4 DCT; 2 DC racks
Main engines	4 Pielstick SEMT diesels; 3 240 bhp = 18·7 knots
Range, miles	3 000 at 12 knots; 2 000 at 15 knots
Complement	62

USA offshore procurement. Ordered in France. Built by F. C. Mediterranee (Graville). Launched on 1 June 1954. Transferred to Yugoslavia in 1956.

581 *1972, Yugoslavian Navy*

SUBMARINES

NOTE. There are reports from Yugoslavia of a submarine building programme but it is not known if this is for the Navy or for export.

3 "HEROJ" CLASS (PATROL SUBMARINES)

HEROJ 821 **JUNAK** 822 **USKOK** 823

Displacement, tons	1 068 submerged
Length, feet (*metres*)	210·0 (*64*)
Beam, feet (*metres*)	23·6 (*7·2*)
Draught, feet (*metres*)	16·4 (*5·0*)
Torpedo tubes	6—21 in (*533 mm*)
Main machinery	Diesels; electric motors; 2 400 hp
Speed, knots	16 on surface; 10 submerged
Complement	55

Heroj, the first submarine of this class, was built at the Uljanik Shipyard, Pula in 1968.

JUNAK *1972, S. and DE. Factory, Split*

JUNAK *1972, S. and DE. Factory, Split*

JUNAK *1972, S. and DE. Factory, Split*

2 "SUTJESKA" CLASS (PATROL SUBMARINES)

NERETVA 812 **SUTJESKA** 811

Displacement, tons	820 surfaced; 945 submerged
Length, feet (*metres*)	196·8 (*60·0*)
Beam, feet (*metres*)	22·3 (*6·8*)
Draught, feet (*metres*)	16·1 (*4·9*)
Torpedo tubes	6—21 in (*533 mm*)
Main machinery	Diesels; electric motors; 1 800 hp
Speed, knots	14 on surface; 9 submerged
Range, miles	4 800 at 8 knots
Complement	38

Sutjeska was launched on 28 Sep 1958 at Shipyard Factory, Split. The first submarine to be built in a Yugoslav yard. Commissioned on 16 Sep 1960.

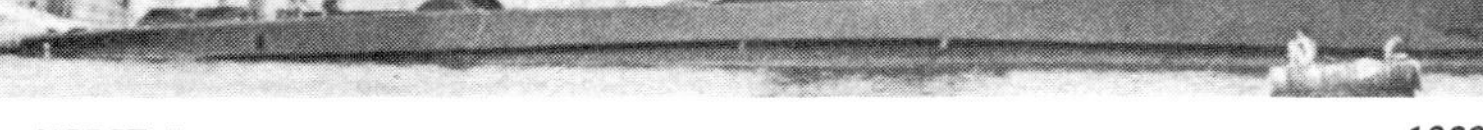

NERETVA *1969, Dr Giorgio Arra*

"MALA" CLASS (2 MAN SUBMARINES)

Dimensions, feet	25 × 6 approx
Main motors	1 electric motor; single screw
Complement	2

This class has been given trials by the Navy. It is a free-flood craft with the main motor, battery, navigation-pod and electronic equipment housed in separate watertight cylinders. Constructed of light aluminium it is fitted with fore- and after hydroplanes, the tail being a conventional cruciform with a single rudder abaft the screw. Large perspex windows give a good all-round view.

"MALA" Class *1973, S and DE Factory, Split*

LIGHT FORCES

4 NEW CONSTRUCTION (FAST ATTACK CRAFT—MISSILE)

Displacement, tons	200-250
Missiles	Reported as Exocet MM 38
Main engines	2 Rolls-Royce "Proteus" gas turbines; 8 500 shp = (?)35 knots; cruising diesels

Believed to be similar to the Swedish "Spica" class. Four reported building with more to follow.

10 USSR "OSA" CLASS (FAST ATTACK CRAFT—MISSILE)

301	**303**	**305**	**307**	**309**
302	**304**	**306**	**308**	**310**

Displacement, tons	165 standard; 200 full load
Dimensions, feet	128·7 × 25·1 × 5·9
Missile launchers	4 for SSN-2 system
Guns	4—30 mm (2 twin, 1 forward, 1 aft)
Main engines	3 diesels; 13 000 bhp = 32 knots
Range, miles	800 at 25 knots
Complement	25

Acquired between 1965 and 1969.

"OSA" Class — *1972, Yugoslavian Navy*

"OSA" Class — *1972*

14 USSR "SHERSHEN" CLASS (FAST ATTACK CRAFT—TORPEDO)

211	**213**	**215**	**217**	**219**	**221**	**223**
212	**214**	**216**	**218**	**220**	**222**	**224**

Displacement, tons	150 standard; 160 full load
Dimensions, feet	115·5 × 23·1 × 5·0
Torpedo tubes	4—21 in single
Guns	4—30 mm (2 twin)
A/S weapons	12 DC
Main engines	3 diesels; 3 shafts; 13 000 bhp = 41 knots
Complement	16

Acquired between 1965 and 1971, some from the USSR whilst the remainder were built in Yugoslavia.

"SHERSHEN" Class — *1972*

20 "101" CLASS (FAST ATTACK CRAFT—GUN)

Displacement, tons	55 standard; 60 full load
Dimensions, feet	69 pp; 78 oa × 21·3 × 7·8
Guns	1—40 mm AA; 4—12·7 mm MG
Tubes	2—18 in
Main engines	3 Packard motors; 3 shafts; 5 000 bhp = 36 knots
Complement	14

Of the same class as US "Higgins". Built in Yugoslavia 1951-60. Some have had their torpedo tubes removed. Can be used as FAC-gun when they mount 2—40 mm and either 2 twin 50 cal MG or 2—20 mm (singles). Two of this class were transferred to Ethiopia in 1960 and renamed *Barracuda* P 22 and *Shark* P 21.

Numbered between 102 and 201.

"101" Class — *Yugoslavian Navy*

10 TYPE 133 (LARGE PATROL CRAFT)

131	**133**	**135**	**137**	**139**
132	**134**	**136**	**138**	**140**

Displacement, tons	85 standard; 120 full load
Dimensions, feet	91·9 × 14·8 × 8·3
Guns	2—20 mm AA
Main engines	2 diesels; 900 bhp = 13 knots sea speed

Used for coastguard duties. Armament varies in individual boats. Built in Yugoslavia 1967-68.

Type 133 — *1968, Yugoslavian Navy*

16 "KRALJEVICA" CLASS (LARGE PATROL CRAFT)

501-512, 519-521 and 524.

Displacement, tons	195 standard; 250 full load
Dimensions, feet	134·5 × 20·7 × 7·2
Guns	1—3 in; 1—40 mm AA; 4—20 mm AA
A/S weapons	DCs plus Mousetrap in some
Main engines	Diesels; 2 shafts; 3 300 bhp = 20 knots

Built in 1952-58. Six transferred to Indonesia in 1959 and two to Sudan in 1969.

"KRALJEVICA" Class — *Yugoslavian Navy*

MINE WARFARE FORCES

4 "HRABRI" CLASS (MINESWEEPERS—COASTAL)

HRABRI M 151 (ex-*D* 25)
SLOBODNI M 153 (ex-*D* 27)
SMELI M 152 (ex-*D* 26)
SNAZNI M 161

Displacement, tons	365 standard; 424 full load
Dimensions, feet	140 ppa; 152 oa × 28 × 8·2
Guns	2—20 mm AA
Main engines	SIGMA free piston generators; 2 shafts; 2 000 bhp = 15 knots
Oil fuel, tons	48
Range, miles	3 000 at 10 knots
Complement	40

Hrabri, *Slobodni* and *Smeli* were built in France by A. Normand as US "off-shore" orders, launched on 27 Feb 1956, 26 May 1956, 26 June 1956, respectively, and allocated to the Yugoslav Navy at Cherbourg in Sep 1957. *Snazni* was built in Yugoslavia in 1960 with French assistance.

SLOBODNI *1966, Yugoslavian Navy*

6 "M 117" CLASS (MINESWEEPERS—INSHORE)

M 117 **M 118** **M 119** **M 121** **M 122** **M 123**

Displacement, tons	120 standard; 131 full load
Dimensions, feet	98·4 × 18 × 4·9
Guns	1—40 mm AA; 2—12·7 mm MG
Main engines	2 GM diesels; 1 000 bhp = 12 knots

A small type of inshore minesweeper built in Yugoslav shipyards between 1966 and 1968.

M 121 *1968, Yugoslavian Navy*

4 BRITISH "HAM" CLASS (MINESWEEPERS—INSHORE)

M 141 **M 142** **M 143** **M 144**

Displacement, tons	123 standard; 164 full load
Dimensions, feet	100 × 21·8 × 5·5
Gun	1—40 mm AA or 1—20 mm AA
Main engines	2 Paxman diesels; 1 100 bhp = 14 knots
Range, miles	2 000 at 9 knots
Complement	22

Built in Yugoslavia 1964-66 under the US Military Aid Programme. Of same design as British "Ham" class.

M 142 *1968, Yugoslavian Navy*

Mine Warfare Forces—*continued*

14 "M 301" CLASS (RIVER MINESWEEPERS)

M 301 **M 302** **M 303** **M 304** **M 305** **M 306** **M 307** **M 308** **M 309** **M 310** **M 311** **M 312** **M 313** **M 314**

Displacement, tons	38
Guns	1—20 mm
Main engines	Speed = 12 knots

All launched in 1951-53. Serve on the Danube.

AMPHIBIOUS FORCES

25 DTM 230 TYPE (LCT)

DTM 230 onwards

Displacement, tons	*circa* 220
Guns	4—20 mm AA

Capable of carrying at least two, possibly three of the heaviest tanks. Unlike other tank landing craft in that the lower part of the bow drops to form a ramp down which the tanks go ashore, underneath the prow, which is rigid. It is reported that probably some 25 of these craft are operational. Ex German.

DTM 230 *B. Hinchcliffe*

DTK 221 TYPE (LCT)

DTK 221

Displacement, tons	410
Dimensions, feet	144·3 × 19·7 × 7
Guns	1—20 mm AA, 2—12·7 mm
Main engines	Speed = 10 knots
Complement	15

DTK 221 *Yugoslavian Navy*

2 Ex-ITALIAN MZ TYPE (LCT)

D 206 (ex-*MZ* 713)
D 219 (ex-*MZ* 717)

Displacement, tons	225 and 239
Guns	1—20 mm AA; 2 MG AA
Main engines	Speed = 11 knots

Ex-Italian landing craft. Launched in 1942. Capable of carrying three tanks.

2 Ex-GERMAN TYPE (LCT)

D 203 **D 204**

Displacement, tons	220
Guns	1—3·4 in (88 mm); 2—20 mm AA
Main engines	Speed = 10 knots

Ex-German landing craft.

CATAMARAN TYPE (LCU)

Displacement, tons	*circa* 50

A smaller craft consisting of two pontoons some feet apart, secured to each other by cross-girders on which stand the bridge and cabins, etc. This vessel appears to be capable of carrying one medium tank, to be put ashore by two bridge members which can be seen quite clearly, folded back on the deck. Total number unknown.

Catamaran type *B. Hinchcliffe*

TRAINING SHIPS

1 "GALEB" CLASS

GALEB (ex-*Kuchuck*, ex-*Ramb III*) M 11

Displacement, tons	5 182 standard
Measurement, tons	3 667 gross
Length, feet (*metres*)	384·8 (*117·3*)
Beam, feet (*metres*)	51·2 (*15·6*)
Draught, feet (*metres*)	18·4 (*5·6*)
Main engines	2 diesels; 2 shafts; 7 200 bhp
Speed, knots	17

Ex-Italian. Built by Ansaldo, Genoa. Launched in 1938. Refloated and completed in 1952. Now training ship. Also Presidential Yacht. Former armament was four 3·5 inch, four 40 mm and 24—20 mm (six quadruple) guns. The guns were landed. Can act as minelayer.

GALEB *1972, Yugoslavian Navy*

JADRAN

Displacement, tons	720
Dimensions, feet	190 × 29·2 × 13·8
Sail area, sq ft	8 600
Main engines	1 Linke-Hofman Diesel; 375 hp = 8 knots

Topsail schooner. Launched in 1932. Accommodation for 150 Cadets. While in Italian hands she was named *Marco Polo*.

DESPATCH VESSELS

JADRANKA (ex-*Bjeli Orao*)

Displacement, tons	567 standard; 660 full load
Dimensions, feet	213·2 oa × 26·5 × 9·3
Guns	2—40 mm AA; 2 MG
Main engines	2 Sulzer diesels; 1 900 bhp = 18 knots

Built by C. R. dell Adriatico, San Marco, Trieste. Launched on 3 June 1939. Was used as Admiralty yacht and yacht of Marshall Tito. While in Italian hands was named *Alba*, for some days only, then *Zagaria*.

JADRANKA *1970, Yugoslavian Navy*

VIS Also reported in service.

SURVEY SHIP

A. MOHOROVIC PH 33

Displacement, tons	1 475 full load
Dimensions, feet	239·5 × 36·1 × 15·1
Main engines	2 diesels = 15 knots

Built in 1971 at the shipyard in Gdansk, Poland, and added to the Yugoslav Navy List in 1972.

A. MOHOROVICIC *1972, Yugoslavian Navy*

SALVAGE VESSEL

SPASILAC PS II

Displacement, tons	740
Dimensions, feet	174 × 26·2 × 13
Main engines	Triple expansion; 2 000 hp = 15 knots

Built by Howaldt, Kiel. Launched in 1929. Name means "Salvador". While in Italian hands she was called *Intangible*.

SPASILAC *1966, Yugoslavian Navy*

TANKERS

4 PN 13 TYPE (HARBOUR TANKERS)

PN 13 (ex-*Lovcen*) **PN 14** **PN 15** **PN 16**

Displacement, tons	695 standard
Main engines	Speed = 8·5 knots

PN 13 (ex-*Lovcen*) was launched in 1932. PN 17 was transferred to the Sudanese Navy in 1969.

PO 55 (HARBOUR TANKER)

Of 600 tons.

2 "KIT" CLASS (HARBOUR TANKER)

KIT **ULJESURA**

250 ton harbour tankers.

TRANSPORTS

2 PT 71 TYPE

PT 71 **PT 72**

Displacement, tons	310 standard; 428 full load
Dimensions, feet	141·5 × 22·2 × 16
Main engines	300 bhp = 7 knots

TUGS

LR II (ex-*Basiluzzo*)

Displacement, tons	108
Main engines	130 hp = 8 knots

Former Italian tug. Launched in 1915.

PR 51 (ex-*Porto Conte*)

Displacement, tons	226

Former Italian tug. Launched in 1936.

PR 52 (ex-*San Remo*)

Displacement, tons	170
Main engines	350 hp = 9 knots

Former Italian tug and multi-purpose vessel. Launched in 1937.

PR 54 (ex-*Ustrajni*)

Displacement, tons	160
Main engines	250 hp = 9 knots

Launched in 1917.

PR 55 (ex-*Snazi*)

Displacement, tons	100
Main engines	300 hp = 10 knots

Launched in 1917.

PR 58 (ex-*Molara*)

Displacement, tons	118
Main engines	250 hp = 8 knots

Former Italian tug. Launched in 1937.

There are also in service PP 1 (ex-*Marljivi*) of 130 tons, RRM 11, LR 67-74 new construction of 130 tons, BM 29, LD 21, LP 21 and RM 27—the last four being small mooring tugs—PR 28 and PR 37.

WATER CARRIERS

PV 6	**PV 11**	**PV 12**
PT 12	**PO 54**	+ 3

There are 8 water carriers of various types and of modern construction.

YACHT

ISTRANKA (ex-*Vila*, ex-*Dalmata*)

Displacement, tons	230
Dimensions, feet	40·4 × 5·1 × 2·1
Main engines	325 hp = 12 knots

Built in 1896

ZAIRE

Personnel

(a) 200 officers and men
(b) Voluntary service

Some of the following craft have been deployed on Lake Tanganyika since 1967.

ZAIRE (ex-*President Mobuto*, ex-*General Olsen*, ex-*Congo*)
(COASTAL PATROL CRAFT)

A 70 ton craft, the first in this naval force.

4 COASTAL PATROL CRAFT

Reported as transferred by China in late 1960's.

6 SEWART TYPE (COASTAL PATROL CRAFT)

Displacement, tons	33
Length, feet	65
Guns	6 MG
Main engines	2 GM diesels = 26 knots
Range, miles	1 000 at 18 knots

Purchased in USA in 1971.

1 COASTAL PATROL CRAFT

Of 18 tons, 25 knots and mounting 3 MG. Purchased in USA in 1968.

ZANZIBAR

Although part of the United Republic of Tanzania, Zanzibar retains a separate Executive and Legislature, the President of Zanzibar being First Vice-President of Tanzania.

4 VOSPER THORNYCROFT 75 FT TYPE

Displacement, tons	70
Dimensions, ft (*m*)	75 × 19·5 × 8 (*22·9 × 6·0 × 1·5*)
Guns	2—20 mm
Main engines	2 diesels; 1 840 hp
Speed, knots	24·5
Range, miles	800 at 20 knots
Complement	11

This is one of the first orders for the new Keith Nelson 75 ft craft. First pair delivered 6 July 1973, second pair 1974.

75 FT TYPE *1974, Vosper Thornycroft*

NAVAL AIRCRAFT

NAVAL AIRCRAFT

Notes: (a) For technical details see under country of origin A Carrier based B Helicopters C Land based

Country/ Manufacturer	Strength	Role	Class (See note)	Country of Origin	Max Speed	Service Ceiling	Range	Max Endurance	T/O Weight
ARGENTINA									
McDonnell Douglas Skyhawk (A-4Q)	15	Attack Bomber F/W	A	USA	(a)				
Grumman Tracker (S-2A)	6	Attack A/S, F/W	A	USA					
Grumman Albatross (HU-16B)	3	Amphibian, Search & Rescue, F/W	C	USA					
Aerospatiale Alouette III	4	Helicopter	B	France					
Sikorsky Sea King (S-61D-4)	4	Helicopter	B	USA					
Westland Lynx	2	Helicopter	C	UK					
Aermacchi MB 326GB	8	Trainer & F/W Light Attack	C	Italy					
Lockheed Neptune (P-2H)	6	Maritime F/W Patrol Bomber	C	USA					
AUSTRALIA									
McDonnell Douglas Skyhawk (A-4G)	16	Attack F/W	A	USA	(Plus 4 TA-4G trainers)				
Lockheed Orion (P-3B)	9	A/S Recce F/W	C	USA	(operated by Air Force)				
Lockheed Neptune (SP-2H)	10	A/S Recce F/W	C	USA	(operated by Air Force)				
Grumman Tracker (S-2E)	13	AS F/W	A	USA					
Bell Iroquois (UH-1D)	9	Helicopter	B	USA					
Westland Wessex AS.31B	25	Helicopter	B	UK					
Westland Sea King 50	10	Helicopter	B	UK					
BELGIUM									
Aerospatiale Alouette III	3	Coast Guard Helicopter	B	France					
Sikorsky S.58	3	Helicopter	B	USA					
BRAZIL									
Grumman Tracker (S-2A and CS2F-1)	12	A/S F/W	A	USA and Canada	(operated by Air Force) To be replaced by S-2Es (ten)				
Lockheed Neptune (P-2E)	10	Maritime F/W Patrol Bomber	C	USA	(operated by Air Force)				
Bell 47G-2 & 47 J	2	Helicopter	B	USA					
Fairchild Hiller FH-1100	4	Helicopter	B	USA					
Hughes 269/300	11	Helicopter	B	USA					
Sikorsky Sea King (SH-3D)	3	Helicopter	B	USA					
Sikorsky S.58	4	Helicopter	B	USA					
Westland Wasp	3	A/S Helicopter	B	UK					
Westland Whirlwind	5	Helicopter	B	UK					
Westland Lynx	9	A/S Helicopter	A	France UK	Carried on new destroyers and operated by the Air Force				
Bell Jetranger II	18	Helicopter	B	USA					
CANADA									
Sikorsky Sea King (CHSS-2)	37	Helicopter	B	USA					
Canadair Argus (CP-107)	13 Mk 1 20 Mk 2	F/W Maritime Reconnaissance	C	Canada	20,000 ft 274 knots	20,000 ft plus	5 124 n. miles at 194 knots		148 000 lb (*67,130 kg*)
Canadair CL-215		F/W Amphibian	C	Canada	157 knots (cruising)	—	1,220 n. miles		Land 43 500 lb (*19 731 kg*) Sea 37 700 lb (*17 000 kg*)
Grumman Tracker (CS2F-3)	40	F/W A/S	C	USA					
CHILE									
Bell Jetranger	4	Helicopter	B	USA					
Grumman Albatross (HU-16B)	5	Maritime F/W Amphibian	C	USA					
Beech C-45	5	F/W Transport	C	USA					
Douglas C-47	5	F/W Transport	C	USA					
Lockheed Neptune (SP-2E)	4	Maritime Recce F/W	C	USA					

Wing span Rotor diameter	Length	Height	Power Plant	Armament Capacity	Remarks
142 ft 3·5 in *(43·38 m)*	128 ft 9½ in *(39·25 m)*	36 ft 8·5 in *(11·19 m)*	4 × Wright R-3350 EA-1 turbo-compound radial piston engines 3 700 hp each	15,600 lb of weapons	In service with 4 Sqdns. (Nos. 404, 405, 407 and 415)
93 ft 10 in *(28·6 m)*	65 ft *(19·82 m)*	29 ft 6 in *(8·98 m)*	2 × 2 100 hp Pratt & Whitney R-2800 radial piston engines		Used by Spanish Air Force for search and rescue (Not by Canada)

Country/ Manufacturer	*Strength*	*Role*	*Class (See note)*	*Country of Origin*	*Max Speed*	*Service Ceiling*	*Range*	*Max Endurance*	*T/O Weight*
CHINA									
Ilyushin IL-28T	100	Torpedo Bomber	C	USSR (built in China)					
DENMARK									
Aerospatiale Alouette III	8	Helicopter	B	France	Flown from frigates				
FRANCE									
Breguet BR 1050 Alizé	50	A/S F/W	A	France	10 000 ft *(3 050 m)* 254 knots	26 250 ft *(8 000 m)*	Normal 1 350 n. miles	7 hrs 40 min	18 100 lb *(8 200 kg)*
Vought Crusader F-8E(FN)	36	F/W Interceptor	A	USA					
Dassault Etendard IV-M, IV-P	42	F/W Attack Recce	A	France	36 000 ft *(11 000 m)* Mach 1·02	49 000 ft *(15 000 m)*	at 510 mph with ext tanks 1 520 n. miles		22 650 lb *(10 275 kg)*
Aerospatiale Super Frelon SA321G	24	Heavy Assault and A/S Helicopter	B	France	at S/L 148 knots	10 325 ft *(3 150 m)*	at S/L 442 n. miles *(820 km)*		28 660 lb *(13 000 kg)*
Aerospatiale Alouette III	20	Gen-Purpose Helicopter	B	France	At S/L 113 knots	10 500 ft (3 200 *m*)	290 n. miles		4 840 lb *(2 200 kg)*
Breguet BR1150 Atlantic	38	Long Range F/W Maritime Patrol	C	France	High Altitude 355 knots	32 800 ft *(10 000 m)*	4 854 n. miles	At 169 knots 18 hours	95 900 lb *(43 500 kg)*
Aerospatiale N262	15	F/W Transport	C	France	208 knots	23 500 ft *(7 160 m)*	With max payload 525 n. miles		23 370 lb *(10 600 kg)*
Lockheed Neptune (P-2H)	23	F/W Maritime Patrol	C	USA					
FEDERAL REPUBLIC OF GERMANY									
Westland Sea King (SH-3D)	22	Helicopter	B	UK					
Breguet Atlantic (1150)	20	F/W Maritime Recce	C	France					
Dornier Skyservant 28 D-2	20	F/W Gen Duty	C	Germany	10 000 ft 175 knots	25 200 ft *(7 680 m)*	1 090 n. miles		8 470 lb *(3 842 kg)*
Lockheed Starfighter (F-104G)	120	F/W Fighter	C	USA (Built in Germany)					
INDIA									
Breguet Alize Br 1050	5	F/W A/S	A	France					
Armstrong Whitworth Sea Hawk	33	F/W Fighter Bomber	A	UK	Max cruise speed at S/L 512 knots				16 200 lb *(7 355 kg)*
Aerospatiale Alouette III	18	Helicopter	B	France					
Westland Sea King (SH-3D)	12	A/S Helicopter	B	UK					
INDONESIA									
Aerospatiale Alouette III	3	Helicopter	B	France					
Grumman Albatross (HU-16A)	5	F/W Maritime Patrol Amphibian	C	USA					
ITALY									
Agusta Sikorsky SH-3D	24	Helicopter	B	USA (built in Italy)					
Agusta-Bell 204B	30	A/S Helicopter	B	Italy	At S/L 104 knots	4 500 ft *(1 370 m)*	340 n. miles		9 500 lb *(4 310 kg)*
Breguet Br 1150 Atlantic	18	F/W Long Range Maritime	C	France	Operated by Air Force				
Grumman Tracker (S-2A/F)	30	F/W ASW	C	USA					
JAPAN									
Sikorsky Sea King (SH-3A)	40	A/S Helicopter	B	USA (built in Japan)					
Kawasaki KV 107 Boeing II-3	12?	Mine Countermeasures Helicopter	B	Japan USA					
Grumman Tracker (S-2A)	25	F/W A/S	C	USA					
Kawasaki P-2J	54	F/W A/S and Maritime Patrol Bomber	C	Japan	Max cruising 217 knots *(402 km/h)*	30 000 ft *(9 150 m)*	With max fuel 2 400 n. miles		Max 75 000 lb *(34 019 kg)*
Lockheed Neptune (P-2H)	50	F/W A/S and Maritime Patrol Bomber	C	USA					
Shin Meiwa P.S.I.	14	A/S F/W Flying Boat	C	Japan	Max level at 5 000 ft 295 knots	29 500 ft *(9 000 m)*	1 169 n. mile *(2 168 km)*	15 hrs	95 800 lb *(43 000 kg)*

Wing span Rotor diameter	Length	Height	Power Plant	Armament Capacity	Remarks
51 ft 2 in (*15·6 m*)	45 ft 6 in (*13·86 m*)	16 ft 5 in (*5·00 m*)	1 × 2,100 eshp Rolls-Royce Dart R.Da 21 turboprop	Depth charges, torpedoes, Rockets	
					These embarked on *Clemenceau* and *Foch* are fitted to carry 2 Matra R530 missiles each
31 ft 6 in (*9·60 m*)	47 ft 3 in (*14·40 m*)	14 ft 1 in (*4·30 m*)	1 × SNECMA Atar 8B turbojet	2 × 30 mm cannon, 3 000 lb rockets, bombs, Sidewinder missiles	
62 ft 0 in (*18·90 m*)	Inc tail rotor 65 ft 10¾ in (*20·08 m*)	21 ft 10¼ in (*6·66 m*)	3 × Turbomeca Turmo III E6 shaft turbine engines	Capacity 30 troops, 15 stretchers + 2 attendants or 11 023 lb (*5 000 kg*) payload	
36 ft × 1¾ in (*11·02 m*)	42 ft 1½ in (*12·84 m*)	9 ft 10 in (*3·00 m*)	1 × Turbomeca Artouste IIIB turboshaft engine	Missiles, torpedoes, 2 MAD equipment	
119 ft 1 in (*36·3 m*)	104 ft 2 in (*31·75 m*)	37 ft 2 in (*11·33 m*)	2 × R.R. Tyne R.Ty.20 Mk 21 turboprop engines	Bombs, depth charges, homing torpedoes, rockets or ASMs	
71 ft 10 in (*21·90 m*)	63 ft 3 in (*19·28 m*)	20 ft 4 in (*6·21 m*)	2 × 1 080 hp Turbomeca Bastan VIC turboprop engines	Seating for 29	Used by French Navy as light transports and aircrew trainer
51 ft 0¼ in (*15·55 m*)	37 ft 5¼ in (*11·41 m*)	12 ft 9½ in (*3·90 m*)	2 × 380 hp Lycoming IGSO-540-A1E piston engines	Seating for 12 or 13	
39 ft (*11·89 m*)	39 ft 8 in (*12·09 m*)	8 ft 8 in (*2·64 m*)	1 × R.R. Nene 103 turbojet	Cannon, bombs or rockets	Operational in carrier *Vikrant*
48 ft (*14·63 m*)	57 ft (*17·37 m*)		1 × Lycoming T53-IIA shaft turbine or 1 × Rolls Royce Bristol Gnome H1200 or General Electric T58-GE-3	2 × Mk 44 torpedoes (AB 204AS version) dipping sonar	
97 ft 8½ in (*29·78 m*)	95 ft 10¾ in (*29·23 m*)	29 ft 3½ in (*8·93 m*)	2 General Electric T64-IHI.10 turboprop engines and two pod mounted J3-IHI-7C turbojets	Classified; includes radar smoke detector and M.A.D.	
108 ft 8¾ in (*33·14 m*)	109 ft 11 in (*33·50 m*)	31 ft 10½ in (*9·72 m*)	4 Ishikawajima-built General Electric T64-IHI-10 turboprop engines each 3 060 ehp	Torpedoes, air-to-surface rockets, bombs, radar, MAD sonobuoys	23 ordered by JMSDF.

Country/ Manufacturer	Strength	Role	Class (See note)	Country of Origin	Max Speed	Service Ceiling	Range	Max Endurance	T/O Weight
MEXICO									
Aerospatiale Alouette III	4	Helicopter	B	France					
Bell 47-G	4	Helicopter	B	USA					
Bell 47-J	1	Helicopter	B	USA					
Catalina PBY-5	5	F/W	C	USA					
NETHERLANDS									
Agusta-Bell 204B A/S	7	Helicopter	B	Italy					
Westland Wasp HAS Mk 1	9	Helicopter	B	UK					
Breguet Br 1150 Atlantic	8	F/W A/S	C	France					
Lockheed Neptune (SP-2H)	15	F/W M.P.	C	USA					
NEW ZEALAND									
Westland Wasp HAS. Mk 1	3	A/S Helicopter	B	UK					
Lockheed Orion (P-3B)	5	M.P. F/W	C	USA	Operated by R.N.Z.A.F.				
NORWAY									
Westland Sea King (SH-3D)	10	ASR. Helicopter	B	USA, UK	Operated by Norwegian Air Force				
Lockheed Orion (P-3B)	5	M.P. F/W	C	USA	Operated by Norwegian Air Force				
PAKISTAN									
Westland Sea King (SH-3D)	6	A/S Helicopter	B	UK					
PERU									
Aerospatiale Alouette II SE 3130		Helicopter	B	France					
Bell 47G	8	Helicopter	B	USA					
Grumman Albatross (HU-16B)	4	MP F/W	C	USA	} Operated by Peruvian Air Force				
Lockheed Harpoon (PV-2)	4	MP F/W	C	USA					
POLAND									
Mil ("Hound") Mi-4	?	A/S Helicopter	B	USSR					
Ilyushin IL-28 ("Beagle")	10	F/W Recce & ECM	C	USSR					
PORTUGAL									
Lockheed Neptune (SP-2E)	8	LRMP F/W	C	USA	Operated by Portuguese Air Force				
SOUTH AFRICA									
Westland Wasp HAS Mk 1	6	A/S Helicopter	B	UK			Embarked in Destroyers *Jan Van Riebeeck* *Simon van der Stel*	Frigates *President Kruger* *President Pretorius* *President Steyn*	
Avro Shackleton MR.3	7	LRMP F/W	C	UK	Operated by S.A.A.F.				
SPAIN									
Agusta-Bell 212AS	4	A/S Helicopter	B	Italy					
Agusta-Bell 204BAS	4	Search & Rescue Helicopter	B	Italy					
Bell AH-1G Huey Cobra	20	Armed Helicopter	B	USA					
Sikorsky Sea King (SH-3D)	24	A/S Helicopter	B	USA					
Grumman Albatross (HU-16B)	11	F/W M.P.	C	USA	Operated by Spanish Air Force				
Hughes 500 M	12	A/S Helicopter	B	USA					
SWEDEN									
Agusta/Bell 206A Jetranger	10	Search and rescue Helicopter	B	USA					
Boeing Vertol 107-II	10	A/S & Gen Duty Helicopter	B	USA					
TURKEY									
Agusta-Bell 204B	3	A/S Helicopter	B	Italy					
Grumman Tracker (S-2E)	8	F/W A/S Attack	C	USA					

UNITED KINGDOM

Country/ Manufacturer	Strength	Role	Class (See note)	Country of Origin	Max Speed	Service Ceiling	Range	Max Endurance	T/O Weight
Hawker Siddeley Buccaneer S Mk 2	16	All weather Strike and Recce F/W	A	UK	at 200 ft Mach 0·85 approx		Tactical radius 1 000 n. miles	Strike range approx 2 000 n. miles	62 000 lb *(28 123 kg)*
Westland (Fairey) Gannet AEW Mk 3	12	AEW F/W	A	UK	220 knots approx		Approx 695 nm *(1 285 km)*	5-6 hours at 120 knots	
Hawker Siddeley Harrier (AV-8A)	(USMC 102)	V/STOL F/W Strike & Recce	A	UK	Over 640 knots	over 50 000 ft *(15 240 m)*	Nearly 3 000 n. miles basic		over 25 000 lb *(11 339 kg)*
McDonnell Douglas Phantom F.G.1 (F-4K)	16	Interceptor and Ground Attack F/W	A	USA	Mach 2+		Ferry Range 2 000 n. miles		
Westland Gazelle HT.2	30	Helicopter Trainer	B	UK France	At Sea Level 167 knots	16,400 ft *(5 000 m)*	At S/L with full fuel 361 n. miles		3 970 lb *(1 800 kg)*
Westland Lynx HAS.2	Approx 100	Helicopter Search and Strike	B	UK	180 knots		Mission radius 154 n. miles		9 500 lb *(4 309 kg)*
Westland Sea King HAS.1	56	Helicopter A/S	B	UK	Normal operating 114 knots	10 000 ft *(3 050 m)*	520 n. miles with normal fuel		20 500 lb *(9 300 kh)*
Westland Wasp HAS.1	80	G/P and A/S Helicopter	B	UK	At S/L 104 knots		approx 234 n. miles		5 600 lb *(2 495 kg)*
Westland Wessex HAS.1/3 & HU.5	150	A/S Assault and GP Helicopter	B	UK	At S/L 115 knots	(HAS.1) 14 000 ft *(4 300 m)*	Max fuel 10% reserve 415 n. miles		13 500 lb *(6 120 kg)*
Westland Whirlwind HAR.9	25	Rescue and GP Helicopter	B	UK	92 knots	Service 16 000 ft *(5 060 m)*	260 n. miles		8 000 lb *(3 630 kg)*
Hawker Siddeley Nimrod MR.1	46	Long Range Maritime Recce F/W	C	UK	500 knots		Ferry 4 500-5 000 n. miles		175 500 lb to 192 000 lb *(79 605-87 090 kg)*
Avro Shackleton MR.3		L R M Recce AEW F/W	C	UK	Level 152 knots *(282 km/h)*		2 515 n. miles		
Hawker Siddeley (Avro) Shackleton AEW.2	12	Airborne Early Warning	C	UK					

USA.

Country/ Manufacturer	Strength	Role	Class (See note)	Country of Origin	Max Speed	Service Ceiling	Range	Max Endurance	T/O Weight
Rockwell International Bronco OV-10A	114 built	Multi-purpose Counter Insurgency F/W	C	USA	At S/L W/O Weapons 244 knots		Ferry with aux. fuel 1 240 n.m.	With max weapon load 198 n. miles	14 466 lb *(6 536 kg)*
LTV A-7E Corsair II	950 built	Single-seat Attack Aircraft	A	USA	At S/L 562 knots		Ferry 2 800 n. miles		42 000 lb *(19 050 kg)*
LTV F-8H Crusader	Total all versions 200	Single-seat Fighter	A	USA	F-8 A.B.C. 868 knots + F-8D E. H. & J. nearly Mach 2			F8A 520 n. miles *(965 km)*	34 000 lb *(15 420 kg)*
Grumman C-2A Greyhound	25	COD Transport	A	USA	At 11 000 ft *(3 450 m)* 306 knots		At cruising speed and height 1 432 n. miles		54 830 lb *(24 870 kg)*
Grumman Hawkeye E-2B/C	90	F/W AEW	A	USA	325 knots	30 800 ft *(9 390 m)*	Ferry 1 394 n. miles		51 569 lb *(23 391 kg)*
Grumman A-6E Intruder	488 built	F/W Strike and Recce	A	USA	At S/L 563 knots	44 600 ft *(13 600 m)*	1 880 n. miles		60 400 lb *(27 400 kg)*
McDonnell Douglas F-4B Phantom II	Total built 1 189	F/W All Weather Fighter	A	USA	Mach 2·5	Combat 71 000 ft *(21 640 m)*	Ferry 1 997 n. miles	781 n. miles	54 600 lb *(24 765 kg)*
McDonnell Douglas A-4M Skyhawk	500	Attack Bomber F/W	A	USA	With 4 000 lb of bombs 560 knots		1 785 n. miles		24 500 lb *(11 113 kg)*
McDonnell Douglas EA-3B Skywarrior	100	F/W Electronic Countermeasure	A	USA	At 10 000 ft 530 knots	45 000 ft *(13 780 km)*	Normal 2 520 n. miles		73 000 lb *(33 112 kg)*
Grumman F-14A Tomcat	330	All Weather Fighter F/W	A	USA	Mach 2·34	Over 56 000 ft *(17 070 m)*			72 000 lb *(32 660 kg)*
Grumman E-1B Tracer	88 built	AEW F/W	A	USA	At S/L 230 knots			Endurance at 19 000 ft 156 knots 8 hrs	29 150 lb *(13 222 kg)*
Grumman S.2E Tracker	180	A/S Attack F/W	A	USA	At S/L 230 knots	21 000 ft *(6 400 m)*	Ferry 1 128 n. miles	Max endurance 9 hrs	29 150 lb *(13 222 kg)*
Lockheed S-3A Viking	180	F/W A/S	A	USA	440 knots	over 35 000 ft *(10 670 m)*	Ferry 3 000 n. miles+		42 500 lb *(19 277 kg)*
Rockwell International RA-5C Vigilante	100	F/W Tactical Recce	A	USA	Mach 2·1	64 000 ft *(19 500 m)*	2 600 n. miles		66 800 lb *(30 300 kg)*
Sikorsky S 58 Seabat Seahorse		A/S and GP Helicopter	B	USA	At S/L 107 knots	9 000 ft *(2 740 m)*	2 14 n. miles +10% reserve		14 000 lb *(6 350 kg)*

Wing span Rotor diameter	Length	Height	Power Plant	Armament Capacity	Remarks
44 ft (*13·41 m*)	63 ft 5 in (*19·33 m*)	16 ft 3 in (*4·95 m*)	Two RR RB 168-1A Spey Mk 101 turbofan engines	Bombs, rockets, air-to-surface missiles—camera. Max load 16 000 lb (*7 257 kg*)	
54 ft 6 in (*16·61 m*)	44 ft (*13·41 m*)	16 ft 10 in (*5·13 m*)	One Bristol Siddeley Double Mamba 102 turboprop 3 875 ehp	Electronics, early warning for long range ship and aircraft detection	
25 ft 3 in (*7·70 m*)	45 ft 6 in (*13·87 m*)	Approx 11 ft 3 in (*3·43 m*)	1 × RR Pegasus 103 vectored-thrust turbofan engine	Aden gun pods, bombs, rockets, flares, camera	In service with USMC. Total includes 8 TAV-8As
38 ft 5 in (*11·71 m*)	62 ft 11¾ in (*19·20 m*)		Two RR Spey Mk 201 turbojet engines with afterburners	Air-to-air missiles, Sparrow III missiles, bombs, rockets, etc.	
34 ft 5¾ in (*10·50 m*)	39 ft 3¼ in (*11·97 m*)	10 ft 2½ in (*3·15 m*)	One Turbomeca Astazou IIIA turboshaft engine		
42 ft (*12·80 m*)	49 ft 9 in (*15·16 m*)	12 ft 0 in (*3·66 m*)	Two RR BS 360.07.26 turboshaft engines	Two Mk 44 homing torpedoes or missiles	
62 ft 0 in (*18·90 m*)	72 ft 8 in (*22·15 m*)	16 ft 10 in (*5·13 m*)	Two RR Gnome H 1400 turboshaft engines	Dipping sonar type 195 system, radar, smoke floats, AD580 doppler navigation, torpedoes, depth charges, machine gun	
32 ft 3 in (*9·83 m*)	40 ft 4 in (*12·29 m*)	11 ft 8 in (*3·56 m*)	One RR Bristol Nimbus 503 turboshaft engine, derated to 710 shp	Two Mk 44 homing torpedoes or other stores	
56 ft 0 in (*17·07 m*)	65 ft 9 in (*20·03 m*)	16 ft 2 in (*4·93 m*)	1 × RR (Bristol) Gnome 112 and 1 Gnome 113 turboshaft engines, each 1,350 shp	Up to 13 troops or 7 stretchers A/S version (HAS.1) can carry weapons	
53 ft 0 in (*16·15 m*)	44 ft 2 in (*13·46 m*)	13 ft 2½ in (*4·03 m*)	1 × RR (Bristol) Gnome H 1000 turboshaft		
114 ft 10 in (*35·3 m*)	126 ft 9 in (*38·63 m*)	29 ft 8½ in (*9·08 m*)	4 RR RB168 Spey Mk 250 turbofan engines	Bombs, mines, depth charges, MAD, full range ASW detection equipment	Operated by RAF
119 ft 10 in (*36·52 m*)	87 ft 4 in (*26·52 m*)	23 ft 4 in (*7·11 m*)	4 RR Griffon 57A piston engines 2,455 hp each		Operated by SAAF
120 ft (*36·6 m*)	87 ft 4 in (*26·52 m*)	23 ft 4 in (*7·11 m*)	4 RR Griffon 67 piston engines, 2,450 hp each	Eerly warning electronics	Operated by RAF
40 ft 0 in (*12·19 m*)	41 ft 7 in (*12·67 m*)	15 ft 2 in (*4·62 m*)	2 × Garrett AiResearch T76-G-410/411 turboprops	4 × 0·30 in machine guns, anti-aircraft missiles, bombs, rockets, etc.	
38 ft 9 in (*11·80 m*)	46 ft 1½ in (*14·06 m*)	16 ft 0 in (*4·88 m*)	1 × Allison TF41-A-2 turbofan	Air-to-air, air-to-surface missiles, guns, rockets, bombs, drop tanks	Total includes A-7A/B/C
35 ft 8 in (*10·87 m*)	54 ft 6 in (*16·61 m*)	15 ft 9 in (*4·80 m*)	1 × Pratt & Whitney J57-P20 turbojet	Cannon, rockets, bombs, missiles	Also F-8J/K and RF-8G
80 ft 7 in (*24·56 m*)	56 ft 8 in (*17·27 m*)	15 ft 11 in (*4·85 m*)	2 × Allison T56-A-8A turboprops	10 000 lb freight	
80 ft 7 in (*24·56 m*)	57 ft 7 in (*17·55 m*)	18 ft 4 in (*5·59 m*)	2 × Allison T56-A-422 turboprops	Early warning and command electronics	Data for E-2C
53 ft 0 in (*16·15 m*)	54 ft 7 in (*16·64 m*)	16 ft 2 in (*4·93 m*)	2 × Pratt & Whitney J52-P-8A turbojets	Bombs, missiles and other stores	Total includes A-6A/B/C
38 ft 5 in (*11·70 m*)	58 ft 3 in (*17·76 m*)	16 ft 3 in (*4·96 m*)	2 × General Electric J79-GE-8 turbojets with after burners	Missiles, bombs, rockets	Also F-4J/N and 50 RF-4Bs
27 ft 6 in (*8·38 m*)	40 ft 3¼ in (*12·27 m*)	15 ft 0 in (*4·57 m*)	1 × Pratt & Whitney J52-P-408A turbojet	Cannon, bombs, rockets, missiles	Total includes A-4C/E/F/L
72 ft 6 in (*22·07 m*)	76 ft 4 in (*23·27 m*)	22 ft 8 in (*6·91 m*)	2 × Pratt & Whitney J57-P-10 turbojets	Bombs, torpedoes, cannon	Total includes tankers
Unswept 64 ft 1½ in 19·54 m)	61 ft 11·9 in (*18·89 m*)	16 ft 0 in (*4·88 m*)	2 × Pratt & Whitney TF30-P-412A turbofan with afterburners	Guns, missiles, bombs	
72 ft 7 in (*22·13 m*)	45 ft 4 in (13·82 *m*)	16 ft 10 in (*5·13 m*)	2 × Wright R.1820-82 piston engines	Early warning and command electronics	
72 ft 7 in (*22·13 m*)	43 ft 6 in (*13·26 m*)	16 ft 7 in (*5·06 m*)	2 × Wright R.1820-82WA piston engines	Depth charges, torpedoes, rockets sonobuoys	Total includes S-2 D/G
68 ft 8 in (*20·93 m*)	53 ft 4 in (*16·26 m*)	22 ft 9 in (*6·93 m*)	2 × General Electric TF34-GE-2 turbofan engines	Bombs, Depth bombs, rockets, missiles, mines, torpedoes, flares	
53 ft 0 in (*16·15 m*)	76 ft 7¼ in (*23·35 m*)	19 ft 5 in (*5·92 m*)	2 × General Electric J79-GE-10 turbojets	Variety of weapons inc. thermo nuclear bombs	
56 ft 0 in (*17·07 m*)	56 ft 8¼ in (*17·27 m*)	15 ft 11 in (*4·85 m*)	1 × Wright R.1820-84B/D piston engine	12 passengers	

Country/ Manufacturer	Strength	Role	Class (See note)	Country of Origin	Max Speed	Service Ceiling	Range	Max Endurance	T/O Weight
UNITED STATES—*continued*									
Bell AH-1J Seacobra	69	Close Support Helicopter	B	USA	180 knots	10 550 ft (*3 215 m*)	310 n. miles		10 000 lb (*4 535 kg*)
Sikorsky SH-3A/D/G Seaking	325	ASW and Transport Helicopter	B	USA	144 knots	14 700 ft (*4 480 m*)	542 n. miles 10% reserve		18 626 lb (*8 450 kg*)
Boeing Vertol UH-46D Sea Knight	450 built	Transport and Utility Helicopter	B	USA	144 knots	14 000 ft (*4 265 m*)	Approx 198 n. miles		Max 23 000 lb (*10 433 kg*)
Kaman SH-2D/F Seasprite	75	ASW Helicopter	B	USA	At S/L 143 knots	22 500 ft (*6 860 m*)	367 n. miles		12 500 lb (*5 670 kg*)
Sikorsky CH-53A/D Sea Stallion	275	Assault Transport Helicopter	B	USA	170 knots	21 000 ft (*6 400 m*)	223 n. miles approx.		42 000 lb (*19 050 kg*)
Bell UH-1E	190	Assault Support Helicopter	B	USA	140 knots	21 000 ft (*6 400 m*)	248 n. miles		9 500 lb (*4 309 kg*)
Hawker Siddeley AV-8A Harrier	102	V/STOL F/W Strike/Recce	A	UK					
Grumman EA-6A/B Prowler	104	ECM/ELINT F/W	A	USA	520 knots				58 500 lb (*26 535 kg*)
Gyrodyne QH-50C		Pilotless Weapon Carrier Helicopter	B	USA	80 knots	16 400 ft (*5 000 m*)	71 n. miles		2 285 lb (*1 036 kg*)
Grumman HU 16 Albatross		F/W GP Amphib	C	USA	At S/L 205 knots	21 500 ft (*6 550 m*)	2 475 n. miles		37 500 lb (*17 010 kg*)
Lockheed C130 Hercules	117	F/W LR Transport & Recce & Tanker	C	USA	333 knots	33 000 ft (*10 060 m*)	4 460 n. miles		155 000 lb (*70 310 kg*)
Lockheed SP-2H Neptune	50	LAMP F/W	C	USA	at 10 000 ft 350 knots	22 000 ft (*6 700 m*)	3 200 n. miles		79 895 lb (*36 240 kg*)
Lockheed P-3A/B/C and EP-3E Orion	400	A/S Recce F/W	C	USA	at 15 000 ft 411 knots	28 300 ft (*8 625 m*)		Mission radius 2 070 n. miles	142 000 lb (*64 410 kg*)
USSR									
Yakovlev Yak-36 VTOL Experimental ("Freehand" D)		V/STOL F/W	A	USSR	Approx 400 mph				
Mil Mi-4 ("Hound")		A/S Helicopter	B	USSR	113 knots	18 000 ft (*5 500 m*)	About 220 n. miles		17 200 lb (*7 800 kg*)
Kamov Ka-25 ("Hormone")		A/S and Strike Helicopter	B	USSR	119 knots	11 500 ft (*3 500 m*)	350 n. miles		16 100 lb (*7 300 kg*)
Tupolev ("Back Fire")		V/G F/W Bomber	C	USSR	Approx Mach 2·5		Approx 4 000 n. miles		272 000 lb (*123 350 kg*)
Tupolev Tu-16 ("Badger")		L. Range Bomber Maritime Recce	C	USSR	at 35 000 ft 510 knots	42 650 ft (*13 000 m*)	With max bomb load 2 605 n. miles		150 000 lb (*68 000 kg*)
Tupolev Tu-95 ("Bear")		L. Range Bomber Maritime Recce	C	USSR	Cruising at 32 000 ft 410 knots		With max load 6 775 n. miles		340 000 lb (*154 220 kg*)
Tupolev Tu-22 ("Blinder")		F/W Bomber	C	USSR	at 40 000 ft Mach 1·4	60 000 ft (*18 300 m*)	1 215 n. miles		185 000 lb (*83 900 kg*)
Beriev M-12 ("Mail")		A/S Recce Amphibian	C	USSR	329 knots	39 977 ft (*12 185 m*)	2 160 n. miles		65 035 lb (*29 500 kg*)
Ilyushin IL-38 ("May")		A/S Recce	C	USSR	365 knots	32 800 ft		Operating radius 1 500 n. miles	
VENEZUELA									
Bell 47G	4	Helicopter	B	USA					
URUGUAY									
Bell 47G-2	2	Helicopter	B	USA					
Grumman Tracker (S-2A)	3	A/S Patrol	C	USA					

Wing span *Rotor diameter*	*Length*	*Height*	*Power Plant*	*Armament Capacity*	*Remarks*
44 ft 0 in *(13·41 m)*	53 ft 4 in *(16·26 m)*	13 ft 8 in *(4·15 m)*	1 × 1,800 shp Pratt & Whitney T400-CP-400 turboshaft	Cannon and rockets	
62 ft 0 in *(18·90 m)*	72 ft 8 in *(22·15 m)*	16 ft 10 in *(5·13 m)*	2 General Electric T58-GE-10 turboshaft	Torpedoes, missiles. 840 lb of weapons	Data for SH-3D
51 ft 0 in *(15·54 m)*	Fuselage 44 ft 10 in *(13·66 m)*	16 ft 8½ in *(5·09 m)*	2 × GE-58-GE-10 turboshaft	Up to 10 000 lb load	Total includes CH-46s
44 ft 0 in *(13·41 m)*	Overall 52 ft 7 in *(16·03 m)*	15ft' 6 in *(4·72 m)*	2 × GE T58-GE-8F turboshaft	LAMPS equipt Details in JAWA	Data for SH-2D
72 ft 3 in *(22·02 m)*	88 ft 3 in *(26·90 m)*	24 ft 11 in *(7·60 m)*	2 × GE T64-GE-6 turboshaft engines	37 passengers or 24 stretchers with 4 attendants	Data for CH-53D
44 ft 0 in *(13·41 m)*	53 ft 0 in *(16·15 m)*	12 ft 7¼ in *(3·84 m)*	1 × Lycoming T53-L-11 shaft turbine	Machine guns, rockets, 8 passengers or 4 000 lb cargo	Total includes UH-1D/H/L
53 ft 0 in *(16·15 m)*	59 ft 5 in *(18·11 m)*		2 × Pratt & Whitney J52-P-8A Turbojets	Normally unarmed ECM equipment	Data for EA-6B
20 ft 0 in *(6·10 m)*			1 × Boeing T50-BO-8A shaft turbine	2 × Mk 44 homing torpedoes	Remote control drone
96 ft 8 in *(29·46 m)*	62 ft 10 in *(19·18 m)*		2 × Wright R.1820-76A radial piston engines	Torpedoes, depth charges or rockets	
132 ft 7 in *(40·41 m)*	97 ft 9 in *(29·78 m)*	38 ft 3 in *(11·66 m)*	4 × Allison T56-A-15 turboprop engines	Cargo up to 26 640 lb, 92 troops, 64 paras or 74 stretchers	Data for late-model transport
inc. tip tanks 103 ft 10 in *(31·65 m)*	91 ft 8 in *(27·94 m)*	29 ft 4 in *(8·94 m)*	2 × Wright R-3350-32W radial piston + 2 Westinghouse J34 turbojets	8 000 lb bombs, torpedoes, depth charges and rockets	
99 ft 8 in *(30·37 m)*	116 ft 10 in *(35·61 m)*	33 ft 8½ in *(10·29 m)*	4 × Allison T56-A-14 turboprops	Mines, depth bombs, torpedoes	Data for P-3C
27 ft 0 in *(8·25 m)*	57 ft 6 in *(17·50 m)*	14 ft 9 in *(4·50 m)*	2 turbojet engines	2 rocket packs	
68 ft 11 in *(21·0 m)*	55 ft 1 in *(16·3 m)*	17 ft *(5·18 m)*	1 ASh-82V 18 cylinder radial piston engine	Depth charges and small stores, search radar, undernose MAD sensors in towed Bird sonobuoys	
51 ft 8 in *(15·75 m)*	32 ft 0 in *(9·75 m)*	17 ft 7½ in *(5·37 m)*	2 × 900 shp Glushenkov GTD-3 turboshaft	A/S torpedoes, flares, small stores	
			Possibly 2 × Kuznetsov turbofans		
110 ft *(33·5 m)*	120 ft *(36·5 m)*	35 ft 6 in *(10·8 m)*	2 × Mikulin AM-3m turbojets	2 × 23 mm cannon in dorsal ventral and tail turrets	
159 ft *(48·5 m)*	155 ft 10 in *(47·5 m)*	28 ft 0 in *(13·50 m)*	4 × Kuznetsov NK-12 m turboprop	Bombs, missiles 2 to 6 × 23 mm cannon	
90 ft 10½ in *(27·70 m)*	132 ft 11½ in *(40·53 m)*	17 ft 0 in *(5·18 m)*	2 × turbojets with afterburners	A version free fall bombs B version missiles and ECM C version Recce.	
97 ft 6 in *(29·70 m)*	99 ft *(30·20 m)*	22 ft 11½ in *(7·00 m)*	2 × Ivchenko AI-20D turboprops	Torpedoes, depth charges, sonobuoys, MAD gear, nose radome	
122 ft 8½ in *(37·4 m)*	129 ft 10 in *(39·6 m)*		4 × Ivchenko AI-20 turboprops	A/S weapons, MAD gear, undernose radar	

NAVAL MISSILES

NAVAL MISSILES

(Further details can be found in the current edition of JANE'S WEAPON SYSTEMS)

Country/ Manufacturer	*Classification*	*Name*	*No.*	*Length ft*	*Launch Weight lbs.*	*Power plant*	*Guidance*	*Range n. miles*	*Mach Speed*	*Warhead*	*Remarks*
AUSTRALIA											
Dept of Supply	A/S	Ikara	—	11		Rocket	Radio/Radar	13	—	Torpedo	
FRANCE											
Aerospatiale	Strat	MSBS	M1	34·1	39 683	Solid fuel rocket 2 stage	Inertial	1 350	—	Nuclear	In "Le Reboutable" class SSBN
	Strat	MSBS	M2	35	44 000	as above	Inertial	1 620	—	Nuclear Thermonuclear by 1976	In production to replace M1
	Strat	MSMS	M4	—	—	as above	Inertial	2 000+	—	Thermonuclear with MRV	Production by late 1970s
CNIM	SSM	—	RP14	6·5	118	Solid fuel rocket	Nil	9	—	HE	22 rocket multiple launcher
Matra (with Oto Melara)	SSM	Otomat	—	15·8	1 543	Turbojet	Active homer	32	—	HE	Sea-skimmer for last 2 miles: can be ASM
Aerospatiale	SSM	Exocet	MM38	16·8	1 587	2 stage solid fuel rocket	Active homer	20	1+	200 lb HE	Sea-skimmer throughout flight
	SSM	—	SS11	3·9	66	2 stage solid fuel rocket	Wire-guided	1·6	330 knots	14 lb HE	Same characteristics as AS-11
	SSM	—	SS12	6·2	167	2 stage solid fuel rocket	Wire-guided	3·3	—	66 lb HE	Same characteristics as AS-12
Ecan Ruelle	SAM	Masurca	Mk 2	28·2	4 585	2 stage solid fuel rocket	Mod 2 Beam rider. Mod 3. semi active homer	22	2·5 (slant)	HE	Mounted in *Colbert, Suffren* and *Duquesne*
—	SAM	Hirondelle Super 530	—	—	—	—	—	—	—	—	Probably operational 1977. Four missile launchers.
—	SAM	Catulle	—	—	—	—	—	—	—	—	Development. Multi-barrelled rocket system firing salvoes of 40 mm shells
Matra	SAM	Crotale Navale	R440	9·5	36	Solid fuel rocket	Infra-red or command	5	2·3 (slant)	HE	Not yet in service
Matra-Hawker Siddeley	ASM	Martel	AS37/ AJ168	12 or 13·2	—	Solid fuel rocket	TV on HS version or passive radar homing	15 approx	—	HE	Also in service with RAF
Aerospatiale	ASM	—	AS20	8·5	319	2 stage solid fuel rocket	Radio command	4	—	HE	
	ASM	—	AS30	12·8	1 146	2 stage solid fuel rocket	Radio command	6·2	1·5	HE	
Matra	AAM	Magic	R550	8·6	200	Solid fuel rocket	Infra-red	6	—	HE	In service 1972
	AAM	—	R530	10·8	430	Solid fuel rocket	Infra-red or semi-active	9·5	2·7	HE	Proximity fused head
Latecoere	A/S	Malafon Mk 2	—	19·7	3 200	2 stage solid fuel rocket and booster	Radio	7	450 knots	Torpedo	Torpedo dropped by parachute 875 yards from target
GERMANY											
Messerschmitt-Bölkow-Blöhm	ASW	Kormoran	—	14·4	1 280	3 stage solid fuel rocket	Infra-red/ command	20	0·95	HE	Suitable for all fixed and rotary-wing aircraft
ISRAEL											
Israel Aircraft Industries	SSM	Gabriel I	—	11·0	882	—	Radar or optical with semi-active head	11 20 (Mk 2)	·9	330 lb HE (Mk 1)	Mounted in "Saar" and "Saar IV" classes. Now being exported, eg Singapore
ITALY											
Sistel	SSM	Sea Killer I (Nettuno)	—	12·3	370	1 stage solid fuel rocket	Beam ride/ radio-command or optical	5·4	1·9	77 lb HE	Operational for use in ships or helicopters. Five round launcher in ships
	SSM	Sea Killer II (Vulcano)	—	15·5	594	2 stage solid rocket motor	as above	13	1·9	155 lb HE	
	SSM	Sea Killer III	—	17·4	1 200	1 booster 2 sustainers	Active homer	24	1·9	330 lb HE	Under development
Otomat (with Matra)	SSM	Otomat (see "France")									
Sistel	SAM	Sea Indigo	—	11	266	1 stage solid fuel rocket	Radio command/ beam rider	5·5 (slant)	2·5	46 lb HE	Automatic reloading in ships over 500 tons
	ASM	Airtos	—	13	—	—	—	6	1·5	80 lb HE	All-weather system under development
NORWAY											
Kongsberg Vaapenfabrikk	SSM	Penguin	—	10	727	2 stage solid fuel rocket	Inertial/Passive homing	11	—	264 lb HE	Fitted in frigates and fast attack craft
	A/S	Terne Mk 8	—	6·4	298	2 stage solid fuel rocket	Nil	1·5	—	110 lb HE depth charge	Full salvo of six can be fired in 5 seconds. Reload time 40 seconds
SWEDEN											
Saab-Scania	SSM	—	RB 08A	18·8	2 675	Marboré turbo-jet	Radar homing	?100	0·85	HE	For ship and coast artillery use. Entered service 1967
UNITED KINGDOM											
—	Strat	Polaris A3 (see USA)	—	—	—	—	—	—	—	UK made 1 MT Thermonuclear	Carried in "Resolution" class
Hawker Siddeley	SAM/ SSM	Sea Dart	CF. 299	14·3	1 220	Solid fuel booster Ramjet sustainer	Radar guidance (Type 909) semi-active homing	20	—	HE	Fitted in *Bristol* and Type 42 destroyers
	SAM	Sea Slug Mk 1 and 2	—	20	—	4 solid fuel boosters, solid fuel sustainer	Beam-riding (Type 901)	24(Mk 1) (approx)	—	HE Proximity fuse	Surface-to-surface capability. Mk 2 has a longer range and better low-level capability
British Aircraft Corpn.	SAM	Sea Wolf	PX 430	6·5	About 200	Solid fuel rocket	Radio command with TV or radar tracking (Type 910)	—	—	HE	Entire system GWS 25. Lightweight versions for ships smaller than frigates are Seawolf Omega and Delta. Normally to be used from 6-barrelled launcher
Short Bros and Harland	SAM	Sea Cat	—	4·9	140	2 stage solid fuel rocket	Optical, Radar or TV	1·9	—	HE	Fitted in many systems GWS 20 (visual) GWS 22 and 24 (Radar). M4/3 (Radar), Signaal M40
	ASM	Sea Skua	CL 834	9·2	About 460	Solid fuel rocket	Radar/radio control Terminal homing	?5	—	?45 lb HE	Developed for use from helicopters

Country/ Manufacturer	Classifi- cation	Name	No.	Length ft.	Launch Weight lb.	Powerplant	Guidance	Range n. mile	Mach Speed	Warhead	Remarks
Hawker-Siddeley	AAM	Firestreak	—	10·5	300	Solid fuel rocket	Infra-red homing	4·3	2+	50 lb HE	Being replaced by Red Top (below)
	AAM	Red Top	—	10·8	320	Solid fuel rocket	Infra-red homing	6	3	68 lb HE	A much improved version of Firestreak
Short Bros and Harland	SAM	Slam (Blow pipe)	—	4·6	About 25	2 stage solid fuel rocket	Optical with radio guidance	—	—	HE	Privately developed as a weapon system by Vickers. Suitable for submarines or surface ships. No fitting programme as yet
USA Lockheed	Strat	Polaris A2, A3	UGM 27B and C	31	30 000(2) 35 000(3)	2 stage solid fuel rocket	Inertial	1 500(2) 2 500(3)	10 at burn-out	Thermonuclear	See USA section for fitting policy
	Strat	Poseidon	UGM 73A	34	60 000	2 stage solid fuel rocket	Inertial	2 500	—	Thermonuclear	As above. Double A3 payload MIRV warhead
	Strat	Trident I	—	—	—	3 stage solid fuel rocket	Inertial	3 750	—	Thermonuclear	MIRV. To replace Poseidon
	Strat	Trident II	—	—	—	3 stage solid fuel rocket	Inertial	6 000 approx.	—	Thermonuclear	MIRV. For fitting in "Trident" class SSBNs
McDonnell Douglas	SSM	Harpoon	RGM 84A	15	1 397	Solid fuel booster Turbojet sustainer	Pre-programmed Active radar homing	60	—	HE	For general surface-ship fitting. Submarine version under development
	ASM	Harpoon	AGM 84A	15	1 110	As above	As above	30+	—	HE	
	ASM	Condor	AGM 53A	5·5	2 100	1 solid fuel rocket	Radio control TV homing	45	—	HE (Possible nuclear)	For carrier-borne A/C particularly A6
Maxson	ASM	Bullpup	AGM 12B and C	11(B) 13·6(C)	571(B) 1 785(C)	1 liquid fuel rocket	Command	6(B) 9(C)	2	HE 250 lb(B) 1 000 lb(C)	Operational 1959
NASC/NWC	ASM	Shrike	AGM 45A	10	390	1 solid fuel rocket	Passive radar homing	7	2	HE	Production 1963
GDC-Pomona	ASM	Standard ARM	AGM 78A	14	1 300	1 solid fuel rocket	Radar homing	13	2	HE	Production 1968
Martin, Marietta	ASM	Walleye	AGM 62A	11·3	1 100	Nil	TV guided	—	—	HE	Details are for Walleye 1 Walleye 2 is much larger with 2 000 lb HE head. Glide-bombs
Raytheon	SAM	Seasparrow	RIM 7H	12	450	1 solid fuel rocket	Semi-active radar homing	12	—	HE	Can also be used as SSM
GDC-Pomona	SAM	Standard	RIM 66A	14	1 300	1 solid fuel rocket	Semi-active radar homing	10+	—	HE	To be used with AEGIS missile system
GDC-Pomona	SAM	Standard	RIM 67A	27	3 000	2 stage solid fuel rocket	Semi-active radar homing	30+	—	HE	SSM capability Terrier replacement
Bendix A/S	SAM	Talos	RIM 8F, G and H	31·3	7 000	Solid fuel booster ram-jet sustainer	Beam rider semi-active radar homing	65+	2·5	HE	SSM capability
GDC-Pomona	SAM	Tartar	RIM 24B	15	1 496	Dual-thrust solid fuel rocket	Semi-active radar homing	10+	2	HE	Ceiling 40 000 ft
GDC-Pomona	SAM	Terrier	RIM 2F	26·5	3 070	solid-fuel rocket	Semi-active radar homing	20+	2·5	HE	Ceiling 65 000 ft.
NWC-Hughes	AAM	Agile	—	—	—	—	—	—	—	HE	Planned replacement for Sidewinder
Hughes	AAM	Phoenix	AIM 54A	13	838	1 solid-fuel rocket	Radar homing	90	—	HE	In use in F14
Raytheon/NWC/ Philco Ford	AAM	Sidewinder	AIM 9G, J H and L	9·5	185	1 solid fuel rocket	Infra-red	2	2	HE	Ceiling 50 000 ft+ First AIM9B entered service 1962.
Raytheon	AAM	Sparrow	AIM 7E and F	12	450(E) 500(F)	1 solid fuel rocket	Semi-active radar homing	12(E) 24+(F)	3·5	HE	For carrier-borne aircraft
Honeywell	A/S	Asroc	15 RUR 5A		1 000	1 solid fuel rocket	Pre-programme	1—5	—	Mk 44 or 46 torpedo Nuclear D/C	Fired from 8-barrelled launcher
Goodyear	A/S or anti-surface-ship	Subroc	UUM 44A	22	4 000	1 solid fuel rocket	Pre-programme inertial	30	1+	Nuclear	Fired from normal 21 in torpedo tubes
USSR (NATO designations used—further details at head of USSR section)	Strat	Sark	SSN-4	37·5	—	?2 stage solid fuel rocket	Inertial	300	—	Nuclear	Operational 1958
	Strat	Serb	SSN-5	35	—	2 stage solid fuel rocket	Inertial	700	—	Nuclear	Operational 1963
	Strat	Sawfly	SSN-6	42	—	2 stage solid fuel rocket	Inertial	1 300	—	Nuclear (? MRV)	Operational 1967
	Strat	—	SSN-8	45 (est)	—	?	Inertial	4 200	—	Nuclear (MRV)	Operational 1973
	SSM	Scrubber	SSN-1	22·5	—	—	Radar Infra-red homing	130	0·9	—	Operational 1958
	SSM	Styx	SSN-2	15	—	2 stage solid fuel rocket	Active radar homing	23	0·9	HE	Operational 1960
	SSM	Shaddock	SSN-3	42	—	2 boosters Turbojet sustainer	Radar, mid-course guidance Radar or IR homing	150-250	1·5	—	Operational 1961-62
	SSM	—	SSN-7	22	—	—	—	30	1·5	—	Operational 1969-70
	SSM	—	SSN-9	30 (est)	—	—	Radar with mid-course guidance	150	1·0+	HE	Operational 1968-69
	SSM	—	SSN-10	25 (est)	—	—	Radar	29	1·2	—	Operational 1968
	SSM	—	SSN-11	21	—	? As in SSN-2	? Radar	29	0·9	—	Operational 1968
	SAM	Goa	SAN-1	19·3	—	2 stage solid fuel rocket	—	17	2	HE	Operational 1961
	SAM	Guideline	SAN-2	34·7	—	Solid booster liquid sustainer	Radar	25	3·5	HE (290 lb)	
	SAM	Goblet	SAN-3	20	—	2 stage solid fuel rocket	—	20	—	HE	
	SAM	—	SAN-4	—	—	—	—	20	—	—	
	ASM	Kennel	AS-1	27·9	—	1 Turbojet	? beam riding	55	0·9	—	Obsolete
	ASM	Kipper	AS-2	31	—	1 Turbojet	—	115	1·0+	—	Operational 1960
	ASM	Kangaroo	AS-3	49·2	—	1 Turbojet	—	400	1·5+	—	Operational 1961
	ASM	Kitchen	AS-4	37	—	1 stage liquid fuel rocket	? Inertial guidance	185	2+	—	Operational 1965
	ASM	Kelt	AS-5	30·8	—	1 stage liquid fuel rocket	Active radar homing	120	0·9	—	Operational 1968
	ASM	Kerry	AS-6	—	—	1 stage	—	? 300	3	—	Operational 1970-71

NAVAL STRENGTHS

NAVAL STRENGTHS

	Aircraft Carriers (L=light)	*Cruisers and Light Cruisers*	*Destroyers*	*Frigates*	*Corvettes*	*Ballistic Missile Sub-marines (N= Nuclear D= Diesel)*	*Cruise Missile Sub-marines (N= Nuclear D= Diesel)*	*Fleet Sub-marines*	*Patrol Sub-marines*	*FAC Missile*	*FAC Torpedo*	*FAC Gun*	*Patrol Craft*	*Mine-layers*
ARGENTINA	1 (L)	2	8 (2)		11				4	(2)	2	2	5	
AUSTRALIA	1 (L)		5	6 (2)					4 (2)				17	
BELGIUM				(4)									6	
BRAZIL	1 (L)	1	15 (6)	3	10				8 (2)				14	
BULGARIA				2	2				4	2	12		6	
BURMA				2	4						5		71	
CANADA			4	16					3				7	
CHILE		3	6	5					1 (2)		4		7	
CHINA			3 (2)	14 (1)	32 (4)	1		1	56 (6)	100 (15)	215	440 (20)	39	
COLOMBIA			5	4					2 (small) (2)				25	
CUBA					19					23	24		32	
DENMARK				6 (1)	3				6	(10)	10		40	5
DOMINICAN REP				3	2 (5)								12	
ECUADOR				3	2				(2)		3 (3)		8	
EGYPT			5	3	12				12	12	36			
FINLAND				2	2					1 (4)		15	18	2
FRANCE	2 (L) (1)	2	20 (3)	25 (14)	22	4 (2) (N)		(1)	19 (3)	1 (30)			6	
GERMANY (DEM)				2	18					12	55		22	
GERMANY (FED)			11	6 (10)	6				24	20 (10)	20			
GREECE			11	4	5				7	4 (4)	12		5	2
INDIA	1 (L)	2	3	23 (4)					8	8			15	
INDONESIA				12	16				3	12	19		34	
IRAN			3 (6)	4 (4)	4					(12)			16	
IRAQ					3					6	12	4	18	
ISRAEL									2 (3)	18 (6)			45	
ITALY		3	9	11 (4)	12				10 (2)		8	4		
JAPAN			29 (5)	16 (4)	20				15 (3)		4 (2)		10	2
KOREA (N)					23				8	18	136	51	72	
KOREA (S)			7	9									41	
MALAYSIA				2						8 (6)			24	
MEXICO			2	10									31	
NETHERLANDS		1	1 (1)	16 (6)	11				6				6	
NEW ZEALAND				4	2								15	
NORWAY				5	2				15	26	20			5
PAKISTAN		1	4	2 (2)					3+6		4	12	1	
PERU		3	4	2 (4)	2				4 (2)				27	
PHILLIPPINES				1	6							9	39	
POLAND			1						4	12	22		46	
PORTUGAL				11	15				4				37	
ROMANIA					6					6	7	10	11	
SOUTH AFRICA			2	7	(6)				3				5	
SPAIN	1 (L) (1)	0 (1)	13	13 (5)	4				8 (2)		2		8 (12)	
SWEDEN			8	4	(2)				22 (5)	1 (16)	42 (6)		23	49 (3)
TAIWAN			18	14					2		9		3	1
THAILAND				7	14								30	6
TURKEY			12	2	5				14 (2)	4	9		52	9
UNITED KINGDOM	1+2 (L)	12 (?2)	1 (5)	57 (10)		4		8 (3)	21				11 (4)	3
UNITED STATES	16 (2N) + 5+(2N)	27 (4) (+8 res)	107 (+3 res)	65 (4+6)		41 (N) (+1)	1 res (D)	65 (25+2)	12 (3)		17		12	
USSR	(2) (L)	35 (2)	106 (2)	109	196	49 (15) (N) 23 (D)	40 (N) 28 (D)	31	217	135	85		60+90	
VENEZUELA			5	6					3 (2)	2 (4)			28 (19)	
YUGOSLAVIA			1		3				5	10 (4)	44		25	

Ocean Mine-sweepers	*Coastal Mine-sweepers/ Mine-hunters*	*Inshore Mine-sweepers*	*Mine-sweeping Boats*	*Assault Ships*	*Landing Ships*	*Landing Craft*	*Depot Repair Main-tenance Ships*	*Survey Research Ships (Large and Small)*	*Supply Ships*	*Large Tankers*	*Small Tankers*	*Hydrofoils and ACVs*	*Misc-ellaneous*	
	4/2				5	20		7 (2)		1	2		20	ARGENTINA
	3					8		4 (1)	2				12	AUSTRALIA
7	9	14						2	2				15	BELGIUM
	8 (2)				2		2	17		1	1		9	BRAZIL
2	4	2	24			20								BULGARIA
								2					11	BURMA
							2	6	3		2	1	61	CANADA
					6	2	2	1		1	2		11	CHILE
16	10 (2)				46 (4)	465	1	12	20		8	70	380	CHINA
					1			4			3		21	COLOMBIA
														CUBA
	8						1				2		4	DENMARK
	2				1	2		2			2		12	DOMINICAN REP
					2			1	1				7	ECUADOR
10		2				17							6	EGYPT
						11							15 (2)	FINLAND
13	39/5	3		2	5	27	12	13	2	4 (2)	5		171	FRANCE
3	52 (3)	10				18		7	4		3		43	GERMANY (DEM)
	40	18				50	16	6	13		11		40	GERMANY (FED)
	15			1	14	8	2	5			8		20	GREECE
	4	4			1	3	3	4	1	1	5		1	INDIA
6	11				8	6	5	4			11		22	INDONESIA
	4	2				2	2		(2)		1	12 (2)	4	IRAN
													3	IRAQ
					4	10							3	ISRAEL
4	33	10			2	60	8	2 (1)	1	1	1	1 (3)	102	ITALY
	31 (8)	4	6		3 (4)	68	2				1 (1)		19	JAPAN
						30							10	KOREA (N)
	13				20			1	13					KOREA (S)
	6						1	1					24 (Police)	MALAYSIA
34	25				3			2			2		5	MEXICO
	24/4	16				12	2(1 bldg)	2 (1)	1 (1)				16	NETHERLANDS
	2							2					2	NEW ZEALAND
	10					8	1						7	NORWAY
	7							1			2		5	PAKISTAN
					4	13		2			6		4	PERU
4					11							4	20	PHILIPPINES
24			20		1 (1)	23		2			6		25	POLAND
	9					64	1	7	1	1			8	PORTUGAL
	4	12	8										6	ROMANIA
	10							1	1				10	SOUTH AFRICA
11	12			1	5	8+87	1 (2)	7		1	11		30	SPAIN
	18 (6)	20				123 (15)		5	1		1		26 (1)	SWEDEN
	14		9		28	22							21	TAIWAN
	4		10		7	41		3			6		6	THAILAND
	16	4			1	53	5	6			8		26	TURKEY
	23 (16)	6		2	7 (2)	21+33	6	4+9	8 (2)	19	6	4	303	UNITED KINGDOM
25 (12 res)				7 (5 bldg+4 res)	*53 (+48 res)	100	28 (+24 res)	42 (2)	77 (3+23)	50 (1+14)		3 (6 bldg)	84	UNITED STATES
191	121	100			12	60 +81	61	152	4	24	18	37+	250+ 54 AGIs	USSR
					6			5					14	VENEZUELA
	4	12	14 (river)			29		1			7		36	YUGOSLAVIA

* In addition there are 30 Cargo and Transport Ships (amphib), of which 22 are in reserve.

ADDENDA

ADDENDA

ABU DHABI

Vosper Thornycroft large patrol craft, *Al Wusal* completed 12 Dec 1974, remaining five now fitting out.

ANGUILA

Two Fairey Marine "Huntsman" class were acquired—one in 1974 and one in 1975.

ARGENTINA

Plans exist to build eight or more frigates.

BAHRAIN

One Fairey Marine "Tracker" class was acquired.

BRAZIL

The four frigates are planned to be AA versions of the Vosper-Thornycroft Mk 10.

CHINA

The total number of "Hu Chwan" class is reported as being 105. Two "Shih Jian" class AGOR have been completed.

Three "Shu Kuang" class AGOR were converted from "T 43" class.

DENMARK

New construction programme to 1982 includes: 6 corvettes, 6 submarines, 2 minelayers, 4 MCM vessels, 3 mine transports, 24 Fast Attack Craft.

DOMINICAN REPUBLIC

Plans exist to acquire five corvettes.

DUBAI

Two Fairey Marine "Spear" class were acquired—one in 1974 and one in 1975.

ECUADOR

Two Type 209 submarines were ordered from Howaldtswerke D.W.

FRANCE

Jeanne d'Arc is fitted with six, not four Exocet.

Le Boulonnais is in reserve at Brest.

GERMANY (FEDERAL REPUBLIC)

"Hamburg" class for conversion including two more ASW torpedo tubes.
Z 4 is to carry out trials of containerised Oto-Melara 3 in gun in 1975.
U 28 was completed 18 Dec 1974.
Type 162 fast attack craft are hydrofoils ordered from Boeing, Seattle.
Type 143 fast attack craft S 61 started trials Feb 1975.
Iltis paid off 31 Jan 1975.
"Lindau" class—ten ships are to be converted to Minehunters, starting with *Lindau* on 1 May 1975.

GREECE

Two 32-metre patrol craft were ordered in France in 1974.

INDIA

An extra "Petya" class, *Amindivi*, transferred (No. 11).
A third "Polnocny" class, *Ghorpad*, transferred Feb 1975.
Reports of French A69 or A70 building programme are unconfirmed.

IRAN

A submarine programme is planned. The location of the building-yard is still unknown due to delays by the British Government.

ITALY

New programme for 1975-1984

8 "Lupo" class (4 ordered)
2 "Sauro" class Submarines (ordered)
1 LPD
10 Minehunters
4 "Spada" class hydrofoils (1 ordered)
6 NATO hydrofoils
1 8 000 - ton supply ship
1 Survey ship
1 Salvage ship
2 Ocean tugs
10 Medium tugs
40 Helicopters

In addition the Maritime patrol aircraft are to be increased to 32 and a new helicopter carrier is to be built post 1982.

SHIH JIAN *1973*

JEANNE D'ARC *1975, French Navy*

STROMBOLI *2/1975, Dr Giorgio Arra*

Addenda—*continued*

JAPAN

Hiei DDH 142 was completed on 27 Nov 1974.
Tachikaze DDG 168 was launched on 17 Dec 1974.
Teshio DE 222 was completed on 10 Jan 1975.
Miura LST 4151 was completed on 10 Jan 1975.
Yoshino DE 223 was completed on 6 Feb 1975.
Kumano DE 224 was launched on 26 Feb 1975.
Kuroshio SS 570 was completed on 27 Nov 1974.
MSB 11 was launched on 17 Feb 1975, *MSB 12* was launched on 27 Jan 1975.
Cancellations in the building programme are as follows: 2 500 ton DDK; *Yuugumo*; *Nemuro* LST; 1 MSC; 1 PT craft; 1 support ship.

NETHERLANDS

Tromp began trials on 10 March 1975, to commission autumn 1975.
De Ruyter to start trials Jan 1976.
"Kortenaer" class—*Kortenaer* was laid down 8 Apr 1975, *Callenburgh* July 1975 and *van Kinsbergen* Sept 1975.
Tydeman was laid down in May 1975.
Zuiderkruis trials began on 25 April 1975, commissioned 20 June 1975.

TROMP on trials — *1975, Royal Netherlands Navy*

NEW ZEALAND

Taupo was launched on 25 July 1974, *Hawea* on 3 Sept 1974.

PERU

Islay SS 45 was completed on 4 Jan 1975.

PHILIPPINES

Two 65-foot Mark III series patrol boats built in USA transferred to Philippines on 24 Apr 1975; PCF 333 (built as US PB739) and PCF 334 (built as US PB7310).

QATAR

Vosper Thornycroft patrol boats; *Al' Adaid* was completed on 14 Dec 1974, No. 3 was launched on 20 Oct 1974 and No. 4 was launched on 10 Nov 1974.

SHAJAH

A Coastguard service was formed with the supply of two 50 ft patrol craft by Chevertons, Isle of Wight in 1974.

SPAIN

Malaspina commissioned 21 Feb 1975.
Juan de la Costa, 1 LCM, RP 30, RP 38 were deleted early 1975.

SOUTH KOREA

Kwang Chu MSC 503 decommissioned for disposal.

SOUTH VIETNAM

The following South Vietnamese ships are reported to have fled Vietnamese waters immediately after the surrender of Saigon on 29 April 1975, most of them heavily laden with refugees; their fate is unknown, but they probably will revert to US custody:

Tran Hung Dao	HQ 01
Tran Quang Khai	HQ 02
Tran Nhat Duat	HQ 03
Tran Binh Trong	HQ 05
Tran Quoc Toan	HQ 06
Dong Da II	HQ 07
Chi Lang II	HQ 08
Chi Linh	HQ 11
Ngoc Hoi	HQ 12
Van Kiep II	HQ 14
Ly Thoung Kiet	HQ 16
Ngo Kuyen	HQ 17
Doan Ngoc Tang	HQ 228
Lulu Phu Tho	HQ 229
Niguyen Duc Bong	HQ 231
Thien Kich	HQ 329
Han Giang	HQ 401
Huong Giang	HQ 404
HQ 470	
HQ 471	
Thi Nai	HQ 502
Phu Du	HQ 600
Hon Troc	HQ 618
Huynh Van Cu	HQ 702
My Tho	HQ 800
Can Tho	HQ 801
Vinh Long	HQ 802

The following ships are known to have been scuttled after reaching the open sea and transferring their cargo of refugees and their crews to US Navy ships: *Lam Giang* HQ 402, *HQ 474*, and *Keo Ngua* HQ 604. The frigate *Tran Khanh Du* HQ 04 was in a shipyard when Saigon surrendered and was captured by North Vietnamese troops.

TURKEY

Type 209 submarines; *Atilay* launched late 1974, *Saldiray* 1975.

UNITED KINGDOM

Antrim, *Glamorgan* and *Fife* completed Exocet conversion.
Two Type 42 were to be ordered in 1975.
Antelope started trials in Jan 1975. *Ambuscade* and *Arrow* to complete in 1975. *Ardent* was launched on 9 May 1975.
One Type 22 was to be ordered in 1975.
1 SSN was to be ordered in 1975.
Disposals: *Whitby* (1975), *Grampus* (1975), *Bulwark* (1976), *Hampshire* (1976), *Keppel* (1976), *Rorqual* (1976), *Berry Head* (1976).

URUGUAY

Plans are in hand for the purchase of one or two frigates/corvettes.
Type 209 submarines, *Congrio* and *Sabalo*
Patria completed on 9 Jan 1975.

YUGOSLAVIA

The new construction programme probably includes 600-ton corvettes and new submarines of 500 tons +.

Addenda—*continued*

USA

Strategic Missile Submarines

The Navy plans to backfit the Trident I (C-4) missile into "Lafayette" class Poseidon submarines commencing with one submarine in Fiscal Year 1979 followed by three submarines per year for a deployed level of ten submarines by the end of FY 1982. The proposed Trident II missile cannot be backfitted into existing Polaris/Poseidon submarines.

Attack Submarines

The "Los Angeles" (SSN 688) class plan as currently approved by the Department of Defence provides for 38 submarines in the Fiscal Year 1970-1980 shipbuilding programmes. Estimated average cost for later units is $293 700 000 per submarine.

Torpedoes

Development of an advanced lightweight torpedo (ALWT) was begun in Fiscal Year 1975 as a successor to the Mk-46 torpedo for use against projected submarine threats in the mid- to later 1980s.

HULL (DD 945) with 8 inch gun forward *1975, United States Navy*

HULL POINT (PCH 1) during Coast Guard evaluation *1975, United States Navy*

NIMITZ (CVAN 68) on sea trials *1975, Newport News SB & DD Co*

INDEXES

INDEX OF NAMED SHIPS

INDEX OF NAMED SHIPS

Abbreviations in brackets following the names of the ships indicate the country of origin

AbD	Abu Dhabi	F	France	L	Laos	Sin	Singapore
Al	Albania	G	Gabon	Leb	Lebanon	Som	Somalia
Alg	Algeria	Ger	Germany (Federal Republic)	Li	Liberia	S.A.	South Africa
A	Argentina	GE	Germany (Democratic Republic)	Lib	Libya	Sp	Spain
An	Anguila	Gh	Ghana	Ma	Malagasy	Sri	Sri Lanka
Aus	Australia	Gr	Greece	Ml	Malawi	StK.	St. Kitts
Au	Austria	Ga	Grenada	M	Malaysia	Su	Sudan
B	Bahamas	Gu	Guatemala	Mal	Malta	Sw	Sweden
Bah	Bahrain	Gui	Guinea	Mau	Mauritania	Sy	Syria
Ba	Bangla Desh	Guy	Guyana	Mex	Mexico	T.C.	Taiwan (Republic of China)
Bar	Barbados	H	Haiti	Mo	Montserrat	Tan	Tanzania
Bel	Belgium	Hon	Honduras	Mor	Morocco	Th	Thailand
Bo	Bolivia	HB	Honduras, British	N	Netherlands	To	Togo
Br	Brazil	HK	Hong Kong	N.Z.	New Zealand	Ton	Tonga
Bru	Brunei	Hun	Hungary	Nic	Nicaragua	T & T	Trinidad & Tobago
Bul	Bulgaria	Ice	Iceland	Nig	Nigeria	Tu	Tunisia
Bur	Burma	In	India	Nor	Norway	T	Turkey
Cam	Cameroon	Ind	Indonesia	O	Oman (Sultanate of)	U.K.	United Kingdom
Can	Canada	Ir	Iran	Pak	Pakistan	U.S.A.	United States of America
Chi	Chile	Ira	Iraq	Pan	Panama	Rus	Union of Soviet Socialist Republics
C	China (People's Republic)	Ire	Ireland (Republic of)	Par	Paraguay	U	Uganda
Col	Colombia	Is	Israel	P	Peru	Ur	Uruguay
Co	Congo	I	Italy	Ph	Philippines	Ven	Venezuela
C.R.	Costa Rica	I.C.	Ivory Coast	Po	Poland	V	Vietnam (Republic of)
Cu	Cuba	Jam	Jamaica	Por	Portugal	V.N.	Vietnam (North)
Cy	Cyprus	J	Japan	Q	Qatar	V.I.	Virgin Islands
D	Denmark	Jo	Jordan	R	Romania	Yem	Yemen
Dom	Dominican Republic	Ke	Kenya	S	Sabah	YS	Yemen (South)
Ec	Ecuador	Kh	Khmer Republic	St. L	St. Lucia	Y	Yugoslavia
Eg	Egypt	Kor	Korea (Republic of)	St. V	St. Vincent	Z	Zaire
ES	El Salvador	K.N.	Korea (North)	Sau	Saudi Arabia	Zan	Zanzibar
Et	Ethiopia	Ku	Kuwait	Sen	Senegal		
Fin	Finland			S.L.	Sierra Leone		

A. CHIRIKOV—ALEXANDER HENRY

Page

A

ALEXANDER MACKENZIE—BARBARA

BARBARA—CAPE SHOALWATER

CAPE SMALL—DALE

DALLAS—EVERGREEN

Page

E

EVERINGHAM—GRILLON

GRIM—IMAN

IMAN BONDJOL—KITTY

KITTY HAWK—LÖWE

LOWESTOFT—MURAYJIB

MÜREFTE—OURAGAN

OVENS—PROFESSOR KHLYUSTIN

PROFESSOR KRÜMMEL—SAGRES

SAGU—SOHAG

SÓHESTON—THORNHAM

THROSK—VIOLETTE

VIRGIN CLIPPER—ZWAARDVIS

INDEX OF CLASSES

INDEX OF CLASSES

ABBORREN—FEROCITY

FERREL—NERCHA

NEVELSKOY—UZUSHIO

VALDAY—ZWAARDVIS

Printed in England by Netherwood Dalton & Co. Ltd., Huddersfield